Oxford Dictionary of National Biography

Volume 23

Oxford Dictionary of National Biography

IN ASSOCIATION WITH

The British Academy

From the earliest times to the year 2000

Edited by
H. C. G. Matthew
and
Brian Harrison

Volume 23
Goss–Griffiths

OXFORD
UNIVERSITY PRESS

OXFORD

UNIVERSITY PRESS

Great Clarendon Street, Oxford OX2 6DP

Oxford University Press is a department of the University of Oxford.
It furthers the University's objective of excellence in research, scholarship,
and education by publishing worldwide in

Oxford New York

Auckland Bangkok Buenos Aires Cape Town
Chennai Dar es Salaam Delhi Hong Kong Istanbul Karachi
Kolkata Kuala Lumpur Madrid Melbourne Mexico City Mumbai Nairobi
São Paulo Shanghai Taipei Tokyo Toronto

Oxford is a registered trade mark of Oxford University Press
in the UK and in certain other countries

Published in the United States
by Oxford University Press Inc., New York

British Library Cataloguing in Publication Data
Data available

Library of Congress Cataloging in Publication Data
Data available: for details see volume 1, p. iv

ISBN 0-19-861373-3 (this volume)
ISBN 0-19-861411-X (set of sixty volumes)

Text captured by Alliance Phototypesetters, Pondicherry
Illustrations reproduced and archived by
Alliance Graphics Ltd, UK
Typeset in OUP Swift by Interactive Sciences Limited, Gloucester
Printed in Great Britain on acid-free paper by
Butler and Tanner Ltd,
Frome, Somerset

LIST OF ABBREVIATIONS

1 *General abbreviations*

AB	bachelor of arts
ABC	Australian Broadcasting Corporation
ABC TV	ABC Television
act.	active
A$	Australian dollar
AD	*anno domini*
AFC	Air Force Cross
AIDS	acquired immune deficiency syndrome
AK	Alaska
AL	Alabama
A level	advanced level [examination]
ALS	associate of the Linnean Society
AM	master of arts
AMICE	associate member of the Institution of Civil Engineers
ANZAC	Australian and New Zealand Army Corps
appx *pl.* appxs	appendix(es)
AR	Arkansas
ARA	associate of the Royal Academy
ARCA	associate of the Royal College of Art
ARCM	associate of the Royal College of Music
ARCO	associate of the Royal College of Organists
ARIBA	associate of the Royal Institute of British Architects
ARP	air-raid precautions
ARRC	associate of the Royal Red Cross
ARSA	associate of the Royal Scottish Academy
art.	article / item
ASC	Army Service Corps
Asch	Austrian Schilling
ASDIC	Antisubmarine Detection Investigation Committee
ATS	Auxiliary Territorial Service
ATV	Associated Television
Aug	August
AZ	Arizona
b.	born
BA	bachelor of arts
BA (Admin.)	bachelor of arts (administration)
BAFTA	British Academy of Film and Television Arts
BAO	bachelor of arts in obstetrics
bap.	baptized
BBC	British Broadcasting Corporation / Company
BC	before Christ
BCE	before the common (*or* Christian) era
BCE	bachelor of civil engineering
BCG	bacillus of Calmette and Guérin [inoculation against tuberculosis]
BCh	bachelor of surgery
BChir	bachelor of surgery
BCL	bachelor of civil law

BCnL	bachelor of canon law
BCom	bachelor of commerce
BD	bachelor of divinity
BEd	bachelor of education
BEng	bachelor of engineering
bk *pl.* bks	book(s)
BL	bachelor of law / letters / literature
BLitt	bachelor of letters
BM	bachelor of medicine
BMus	bachelor of music
BP	before present
BP	British Petroleum
Bros.	Brothers
BS	(1) bachelor of science; (2) bachelor of surgery; (3) British standard
BSc	bachelor of science
BSc (Econ.)	bachelor of science (economics)
BSc (Eng.)	bachelor of science (engineering)
bt	baronet
BTh	bachelor of theology
bur.	buried
C.	command [identifier for published parliamentary papers]
c.	*circa*
c.	*capitulum pl. capitula*: chapter(s)
CA	California
Cantab.	Cantabrigiensis
cap.	*capitulum pl. capitula*: chapter(s)
CB	companion of the Bath
CBE	commander of the Order of the British Empire
CBS	Columbia Broadcasting System
cc	cubic centimetres
C$	Canadian dollar
CD	compact disc
Cd	command [identifier for published parliamentary papers]
CE	Common (*or* Christian) Era
cent.	century
cf.	compare
CH	Companion of Honour
chap.	chapter
ChB	bachelor of surgery
CI	Imperial Order of the Crown of India
CIA	Central Intelligence Agency
CID	Criminal Investigation Department
CIE	companion of the Order of the Indian Empire
Cie	Compagnie
CLit	companion of literature
CM	master of surgery
cm	centimetre(s)

Cmd	command [identifier for published parliamentary papers]
CMG	companion of the Order of St Michael and St George
Cmnd	command [identifier for published parliamentary papers]
CO	Colorado
Co.	company
co.	county
col. *pl.* cols.	column(s)
Corp.	corporation
CSE	certificate of secondary education
CSI	companion of the Order of the Star of India
CT	Connecticut
CVO	commander of the Royal Victorian Order
cwt	hundredweight
$	(American) dollar
d.	(1) penny (pence); (2) died
DBE	dame commander of the Order of the British Empire
DCH	diploma in child health
DCh	doctor of surgery
DCL	doctor of civil law
DCnL	doctor of canon law
DCVO	dame commander of the Royal Victorian Order
DD	doctor of divinity
DE	Delaware
Dec	December
dem.	demolished
DEng	doctor of engineering
des.	destroyed
DFC	Distinguished Flying Cross
DipEd	diploma in education
DipPsych	diploma in psychiatry
diss.	dissertation
DL	deputy lieutenant
DLitt	doctor of letters
DLittCelt	doctor of Celtic letters
DM	(1) Deutschmark; (2) doctor of medicine; (3) doctor of musical arts
DMus	doctor of music
DNA	dioxyribonucleic acid
doc.	document
DOL	doctor of oriental learning
DPH	diploma in public health
DPhil	doctor of philosophy
DPM	diploma in psychological medicine
DSC	Distinguished Service Cross
DSc	doctor of science
DSc (Econ.)	doctor of science (economics)
DSc (Eng.)	doctor of science (engineering)
DSM	Distinguished Service Medal
DSO	companion of the Distinguished Service Order
DSocSc	doctor of social science
DTech	doctor of technology
DTh	doctor of theology
DTM	diploma in tropical medicine
DTMH	diploma in tropical medicine and hygiene
DU	doctor of the university
DUniv	doctor of the university
dwt	pennyweight
EC	European Community
ed. *pl.* eds.	edited / edited by / editor(s)
Edin.	Edinburgh

edn	edition
EEC	European Economic Community
EFTA	European Free Trade Association
EICS	East India Company Service
EMI	Electrical and Musical Industries (Ltd)
Eng.	English
enl.	enlarged
ENSA	Entertainments National Service Association
ep. *pl.* epp.	*epistola(e)*
ESP	extra-sensory perception
esp.	especially
esq.	esquire
est.	estimate / estimated
EU	European Union
ex	sold by (*lit.* out of)
excl.	excludes / excluding
exh.	exhibited
exh. cat.	exhibition catalogue
f. *pl.* ff.	following [pages]
FA	Football Association
FACP	fellow of the American College of Physicians
facs.	facsimile
FANY	First Aid Nursing Yeomanry
FBA	fellow of the British Academy
FBI	Federation of British Industries
FCS	fellow of the Chemical Society
Feb	February
FEng	fellow of the Fellowship of Engineering
FFCM	fellow of the Faculty of Community Medicine
FGS	fellow of the Geological Society
fig.	figure
FIMechE	fellow of the Institution of Mechanical Engineers
FL	Florida
fl.	*floruit*
FLS	fellow of the Linnean Society
FM	frequency modulation
fol. *pl.* fols.	folio(s)
Fr	French francs
Fr.	French
FRAeS	fellow of the Royal Aeronautical Society
FRAI	fellow of the Royal Anthropological Institute
FRAM	fellow of the Royal Academy of Music
FRAS	(1) fellow of the Royal Asiatic Society; (2) fellow of the Royal Astronomical Society
FRCM	fellow of the Royal College of Music
FRCO	fellow of the Royal College of Organists
FRCOG	fellow of the Royal College of Obstetricians and Gynaecologists
FRCP(C)	fellow of the Royal College of Physicians of Canada
FRCP (Edin.)	fellow of the Royal College of Physicians of Edinburgh
FRCP (Lond.)	fellow of the Royal College of Physicians of London
FRCPath	fellow of the Royal College of Pathologists
FRCPsych	fellow of the Royal College of Psychiatrists
FRCS	fellow of the Royal College of Surgeons
FRGS	fellow of the Royal Geographical Society
FRIBA	fellow of the Royal Institute of British Architects
FRICS	fellow of the Royal Institute of Chartered Surveyors
FRS	fellow of the Royal Society
FRSA	fellow of the Royal Society of Arts

FRSCM	fellow of the Royal School of Church Music	ISO	companion of the Imperial Service Order
FRSE	fellow of the Royal Society of Edinburgh	It.	Italian
FRSL	fellow of the Royal Society of Literature	ITA	Independent Television Authority
FSA	fellow of the Society of Antiquaries	ITV	Independent Television
ft	foot *pl.* feet	Jan	January
FTCL	fellow of Trinity College of Music, London	JP	justice of the peace
ft-lb per min.	foot-pounds per minute [unit of horsepower]	jun.	junior
FZS	fellow of the Zoological Society	KB	knight of the Order of the Bath
GA	Georgia	KBE	knight commander of the Order of the British Empire
GBE	knight or dame grand cross of the Order of the British Empire	KC	king's counsel
GCB	knight grand cross of the Order of the Bath	kcal	kilocalorie
GCE	general certificate of education	KCB	knight commander of the Order of the Bath
GCH	knight grand cross of the Royal Guelphic Order	KCH	knight commander of the Royal Guelphic Order
GCHQ	government communications headquarters	KCIE	knight commander of the Order of the Indian Empire
GCIE	knight grand commander of the Order of the Indian Empire	KCMG	knight commander of the Order of St Michael and St George
GCMG	knight or dame grand cross of the Order of St Michael and St George	KCSI	knight commander of the Order of the Star of India
GCSE	general certificate of secondary education	KCVO	knight commander of the Royal Victorian Order
GCSI	knight grand commander of the Order of the Star of India	keV	kilo-electron-volt
GCStJ	bailiff or dame grand cross of the order of St John of Jerusalem	KG	knight of the Order of the Garter
		KGB	[Soviet committee of state security]
GCVO	knight or dame grand cross of the Royal Victorian Order	KH	knight of the Royal Guelphic Order
		KLM	Koninklijke Luchtvaart Maatschappij (Royal Dutch Air Lines)
GEC	General Electric Company	km	kilometre(s)
Ger.	German	KP	knight of the Order of St Patrick
GI	government (*or* general) issue	KS	Kansas
GMT	Greenwich mean time	KT	knight of the Order of the Thistle
GP	general practitioner	kt	knight
GPU	[Soviet special police unit]	KY	Kentucky
GSO	general staff officer	£	pound(s) sterling
Heb.	Hebrew	£E	Egyptian pound
HEICS	Honourable East India Company Service	L	lira *pl.* lire
HI	Hawaii	l. *pl.* ll.	line(s)
HIV	human immunodeficiency virus	LA	Lousiana
HK$	Hong Kong dollar	LAA	light anti-aircraft
HM	his / her majesty('s)	LAH	licentiate of the Apothecaries' Hall, Dublin
HMAS	his / her majesty's Australian ship	Lat.	Latin
HMNZS	his / her majesty's New Zealand ship	lb	pound(s), unit of weight
HMS	his / her majesty's ship	LDS	licence in dental surgery
HMSO	His / Her Majesty's Stationery Office	*lit.*	literally
HMV	His Master's Voice	LittB	bachelor of letters
Hon.	Honourable	LittD	doctor of letters
hp	horsepower	LKQCPI	licentiate of the King and Queen's College of Physicians, Ireland
hr	hour(s)	LLA	lady literate in arts
HRH	his / her royal highness	LLB	bachelor of laws
HTV	Harlech Television	LLD	doctor of laws
IA	Iowa	LLM	master of laws
ibid.	*ibidem*: in the same place	LM	licentiate in midwifery
ICI	Imperial Chemical Industries (Ltd)	LP	long-playing record
ID	Idaho	LRAM	licentiate of the Royal Academy of Music
IL	Illinois	LRCP	licentiate of the Royal College of Physicians
illus.	illustration	LRCPS (Glasgow)	licentiate of the Royal College of Physicians and Surgeons of Glasgow
illustr.	illustrated	LRCS	licentiate of the Royal College of Surgeons
IN	Indiana	LSA	licentiate of the Society of Apothecaries
in.	inch(es)	LSD	lysergic acid diethylamide
Inc.	Incorporated	LVO	lieutenant of the Royal Victorian Order
incl.	includes / including	M. *pl.* MM.	Monsieur *pl.* Messieurs
IOU	I owe you	m	metre(s)
IQ	intelligence quotient		
Ir£	Irish pound		
IRA	Irish Republican Army		

m. *pl.* mm.	membrane(s)
MA	(1) Massachusetts; (2) master of arts
MAI	master of engineering
MB	bachelor of medicine
MBA	master of business administration
MBE	member of the Order of the British Empire
MC	Military Cross
MCC	Marylebone Cricket Club
MCh	master of surgery
MChir	master of surgery
MCom	master of commerce
MD	(1) doctor of medicine; (2) Maryland
MDMA	methylenedioxymethamphetamine
ME	Maine
MEd	master of education
MEng	master of engineering
MEP	member of the European parliament
MG	Morris Garages
MGM	Metro-Goldwyn-Mayer
Mgr	Monsignor
MI	(1) Michigan; (2) military intelligence
MI1c	[secret intelligence department]
MI5	[military intelligence department]
MI6	[secret intelligence department]
MI9	[secret escape service]
MICE	member of the Institution of Civil Engineers
MIEE	member of the Institution of Electrical Engineers
min.	minute(s)
Mk	mark
ML	(1) licentiate of medicine; (2) master of laws
MLitt	master of letters
Mlle	Mademoiselle
mm	millimetre(s)
Mme	Madame
MN	Minnesota
MO	Missouri
MOH	medical officer of health
MP	member of parliament
m.p.h.	miles per hour
MPhil	master of philosophy
MRCP	member of the Royal College of Physicians
MRCS	member of the Royal College of Surgeons
MRCVS	member of the Royal College of Veterinary Surgeons
MRIA	member of the Royal Irish Academy
MS	(1) master of science; (2) Mississippi
MS *pl.* MSS	manuscript(s)
MSc	master of science
MSc (Econ.)	master of science (economics)
MT	Montana
MusB	bachelor of music
MusBac	bachelor of music
MusD	doctor of music
MV	motor vessel
MVO	member of the Royal Victorian Order
n. *pl.* nn.	note(s)
NAAFI	Navy, Army, and Air Force Institutes
NASA	National Aeronautics and Space Administration
NATO	North Atlantic Treaty Organization
NBC	National Broadcasting Corporation
NC	North Carolina
NCO	non-commissioned officer
ND	North Dakota
n.d.	no date
NE	Nebraska
nem. con.	*nemine contradicente*: unanimously
new ser.	new series
NH	New Hampshire
NHS	National Health Service
NJ	New Jersey
NKVD	[Soviet people's commissariat for internal affairs]
NM	New Mexico
nm	nanometre(s)
no. *pl.* nos.	number(s)
Nov	November
n.p.	no place [of publication]
NS	new style
NV	Nevada
NY	New York
NZBS	New Zealand Broadcasting Service
OBE	officer of the Order of the British Empire
obit.	obituary
Oct	October
OCTU	officer cadets training unit
OECD	Organization for Economic Co-operation and Development
OEEC	Organization for European Economic Co-operation
OFM	order of Friars Minor [Franciscans]
OFMCap	Ordine Frati Minori Cappucini: member of the Capuchin order
OH	Ohio
OK	Oklahoma
O level	ordinary level [examination]
OM	Order of Merit
OP	order of Preachers [Dominicans]
op. *pl.* opp.	opus *pl.* opera
OPEC	Organization of Petroleum Exporting Countries
OR	Oregon
orig.	original
OS	old style
OSB	Order of St Benedict
OTC	Officers' Training Corps
OWS	Old Watercolour Society
Oxon.	Oxoniensis
p. *pl.* pp.	page(s)
PA	Pennsylvania
p.a.	per annum
para.	paragraph
PAYE	pay as you earn
pbk *pl.* pbks	paperback(s)
per.	[during the] period
PhD	doctor of philosophy
pl.	(1) plate(s); (2) plural
priv. coll.	private collection
pt *pl.* pts	part(s)
pubd	published
PVC	polyvinyl chloride
q. *pl.* qq.	(1) question(s); (2) quire(s)
QC	queen's counsel
R	rand
R.	Rex / Regina
r	recto
r.	reigned / ruled
RA	Royal Academy / Royal Academician

RAC	Royal Automobile Club		Skr	Swedish krona
RAF	Royal Air Force		Span.	Spanish
RAFVR	Royal Air Force Volunteer Reserve		SPCK	Society for Promoting Christian Knowledge
RAM	[member of the] Royal Academy of Music		SS	(1) Santissimi; (2) Schutzstaffel; (3) steam ship
RAMC	Royal Army Medical Corps		STB	bachelor of theology
RCA	Royal College of Art		STD	doctor of theology
RCNC	Royal Corps of Naval Constructors		STM	master of theology
RCOG	Royal College of Obstetricians and Gynaecologists		STP	doctor of theology
			supp.	supposedly
RDI	royal designer for industry		suppl. *pl.* suppls.	supplement(s)
RE	Royal Engineers		s.v.	*sub verbo / sub voce*: under the word / heading
repr. *pl.* reprs.	reprint(s) / reprinted		SY	steam yacht
repro.	reproduced		TA	Territorial Army
rev.	revised / revised by / reviser / revision		TASS	[Soviet news agency]
Revd	Reverend		TB	tuberculosis (*lit.* tubercle bacillus)
RHA	Royal Hibernian Academy		TD	(1) *teachtaí dála* (member of the Dáil); (2) territorial decoration
RI	(1) Rhode Island; (2) Royal Institute of Painters in Water-Colours		TN	Tennessee
RIBA	Royal Institute of British Architects		TNT	trinitrotoluene
RIN	Royal Indian Navy		trans.	translated / translated by / translation / translator
RM	Reichsmark		TT	tourist trophy
RMS	Royal Mail steamer		TUC	Trades Union Congress
RN	Royal Navy		TX	Texas
RNA	ribonucleic acid		U-boat	*Unterseeboot*: submarine
RNAS	Royal Naval Air Service		Ufa	Universum-Film AG
RNR	Royal Naval Reserve		UMIST	University of Manchester Institute of Science and Technology
RNVR	Royal Naval Volunteer Reserve			
RO	Record Office		UN	United Nations
r.p.m.	revolutions per minute		UNESCO	United Nations Educational, Scientific, and Cultural Organization
RRS	royal research ship			
Rs	rupees		UNICEF	United Nations International Children's Emergency Fund
RSA	(1) Royal Scottish Academician; (2) Royal Society of Arts			
			unpubd	unpublished
RSPCA	Royal Society for the Prevention of Cruelty to Animals		USS	United States ship
			UT	Utah
Rt Hon.	Right Honourable		*v*	verso
Rt Revd	Right Reverend		v.	versus
RUC	Royal Ulster Constabulary		VA	Virginia
Russ.	Russian		VAD	Voluntary Aid Detachment
RWS	Royal Watercolour Society		VC	Victoria Cross
S4C	Sianel Pedwar Cymru		VE-day	victory in Europe day
s.	shilling(s)		Ven.	Venerable
s.a.	*sub anno*: under the year		VJ-day	victory over Japan day
SABC	South African Broadcasting Corporation		vol. *pl.* vols.	volume(s)
SAS	Special Air Service		VT	Vermont
SC	South Carolina		WA	Washington [state]
ScD	doctor of science		WAAC	Women's Auxiliary Army Corps
S$	Singapore dollar		WAAF	Women's Auxiliary Air Force
SD	South Dakota		WEA	Workers' Educational Association
sec.	second(s)		WHO	World Health Organization
sel.	selected		WI	Wisconsin
sen.	senior		WRAF	Women's Royal Air Force
Sept	September		WRNS	Women's Royal Naval Service
ser.	series		WV	West Virginia
SHAPE	supreme headquarters allied powers, Europe		WVS	Women's Voluntary Service
SIDRO	Société Internationale d'Énergie Hydro-Électrique		WY	Wyoming
			¥	yen
sig. *pl.* sigs.	signature(s)		YMCA	Young Men's Christian Association
sing.	singular		YWCA	Young Women's Christian Association
SIS	Secret Intelligence Service			
SJ	Society of Jesus			

2 Institution abbreviations

All Souls Oxf.	All Souls College, Oxford
AM Oxf.	Ashmolean Museum, Oxford
Balliol Oxf.	Balliol College, Oxford
BBC WAC	BBC Written Archives Centre, Reading
Beds. & Luton ARS	Bedfordshire and Luton Archives and Record Service, Bedford
Berks. RO	Berkshire Record Office, Reading
BFI	British Film Institute, London
BFI NFTVA	British Film Institute, London, National Film and Television Archive
BGS	British Geological Survey, Keyworth, Nottingham
Birm. CA	Birmingham Central Library, Birmingham City Archives
Birm. CL	Birmingham Central Library
BL	British Library, London
BL NSA	British Library, London, National Sound Archive
BL OIOC	British Library, London, Oriental and India Office Collections
BLPES	London School of Economics and Political Science, British Library of Political and Economic Science
BM	British Museum, London
Bodl. Oxf.	Bodleian Library, Oxford
Bodl. RH	Bodleian Library of Commonwealth and African Studies at Rhodes House, Oxford
Borth. Inst.	Borthwick Institute of Historical Research, University of York
Boston PL	Boston Public Library, Massachusetts
Bristol RO	Bristol Record Office
Bucks. RLSS	Buckinghamshire Records and Local Studies Service, Aylesbury
CAC Cam.	Churchill College, Cambridge, Churchill Archives Centre
Cambs. AS	Cambridgeshire Archive Service
CCC Cam.	Corpus Christi College, Cambridge
CCC Oxf.	Corpus Christi College, Oxford
Ches. & Chester ALSS	Cheshire and Chester Archives and Local Studies Service
Christ Church Oxf.	Christ Church, Oxford
Christies	Christies, London
City Westm. AC	City of Westminster Archives Centre, London
CKS	Centre for Kentish Studies, Maidstone
CLRO	Corporation of London Records Office
Coll. Arms	College of Arms, London
Col. U.	Columbia University, New York
Cornwall RO	Cornwall Record Office, Truro
Courtauld Inst.	Courtauld Institute of Art, London
CUL	Cambridge University Library
Cumbria AS	Cumbria Archive Service
Derbys. RO	Derbyshire Record Office, Matlock
Devon RO	Devon Record Office, Exeter
Dorset RO	Dorset Record Office, Dorchester
Duke U.	Duke University, Durham, North Carolina
Duke U., Perkins L.	Duke University, Durham, North Carolina, William R. Perkins Library
Durham Cath. CL	Durham Cathedral, chapter library
Durham RO	Durham Record Office
DWL	Dr Williams's Library, London
Essex RO	Essex Record Office
E. Sussex RO	East Sussex Record Office, Lewes
Eton	Eton College, Berkshire
FM Cam.	Fitzwilliam Museum, Cambridge
Folger	Folger Shakespeare Library, Washington, DC
Garr. Club	Garrick Club, London
Girton Cam.	Girton College, Cambridge
GL	Guildhall Library, London
Glos. RO	Gloucestershire Record Office, Gloucester
Gon. & Caius Cam.	Gonville and Caius College, Cambridge
Gov. Art Coll.	Government Art Collection
GS Lond.	Geological Society of London
Hants. RO	Hampshire Record Office, Winchester
Harris Man. Oxf.	Harris Manchester College, Oxford
Harvard TC	Harvard Theatre Collection, Harvard University, Cambridge, Massachusetts, Nathan Marsh Pusey Library
Harvard U.	Harvard University, Cambridge, Massachusetts
Harvard U., Houghton L.	Harvard University, Cambridge, Massachusetts, Houghton Library
Herefs. RO	Herefordshire Record Office, Hereford
Herts. ALS	Hertfordshire Archives and Local Studies, Hertford
Hist. Soc. Penn.	Historical Society of Pennsylvania, Philadelphia
HLRO	House of Lords Record Office, London
Hult. Arch.	Hulton Archive, London and New York
Hunt. L.	Huntington Library, San Marino, California
ICL	Imperial College, London
Inst. CE	Institution of Civil Engineers, London
Inst. EE	Institution of Electrical Engineers, London
IWM	Imperial War Museum, London
IWM FVA	Imperial War Museum, London, Film and Video Archive
IWM SA	Imperial War Museum, London, Sound Archive
JRL	John Rylands University Library of Manchester
King's AC Cam.	King's College Archives Centre, Cambridge
King's Cam.	King's College, Cambridge
King's Lond.	King's College, London
King's Lond., Liddell Hart C.	King's College, London, Liddell Hart Centre for Military Archives
Lancs. RO	Lancashire Record Office, Preston
L. Cong.	Library of Congress, Washington, DC
Leics. RO	Leicestershire, Leicester, and Rutland Record Office, Leicester
Lincs. Arch.	Lincolnshire Archives, Lincoln
Linn. Soc.	Linnean Society of London
LMA	London Metropolitan Archives
LPL	Lambeth Palace, London
Lpool RO	Liverpool Record Office and Local Studies Service
LUL	London University Library
Magd. Cam.	Magdalene College, Cambridge
Magd. Oxf.	Magdalen College, Oxford
Man. City Gall.	Manchester City Galleries
Man. CL	Manchester Central Library
Mass. Hist. Soc.	Massachusetts Historical Society, Boston
Merton Oxf.	Merton College, Oxford
MHS Oxf.	Museum of the History of Science, Oxford
Mitchell L., Glas.	Mitchell Library, Glasgow
Mitchell L., NSW	State Library of New South Wales, Sydney, Mitchell Library
Morgan L.	Pierpont Morgan Library, New York
NA Canada	National Archives of Canada, Ottawa
NA Ire.	National Archives of Ireland, Dublin
NAM	National Army Museum, London
NA Scot.	National Archives of Scotland, Edinburgh
News Int. RO	News International Record Office, London
NG Ire.	National Gallery of Ireland, Dublin

NG Scot.	National Gallery of Scotland, Edinburgh
NHM	Natural History Museum, London
NL Aus.	National Library of Australia, Canberra
NL Ire.	National Library of Ireland, Dublin
NL NZ	National Library of New Zealand, Wellington
NL NZ, Turnbull L.	National Library of New Zealand, Wellington, Alexander Turnbull Library
NL Scot.	National Library of Scotland, Edinburgh
NL Wales	National Library of Wales, Aberystwyth
NMG Wales	National Museum and Gallery of Wales, Cardiff
NMM	National Maritime Museum, London
Norfolk RO	Norfolk Record Office, Norwich
Northants. RO	Northamptonshire Record Office, Northampton
Northumbd RO	Northumberland Record Office
Notts. Arch.	Nottinghamshire Archives, Nottingham
NPG	National Portrait Gallery, London
NRA	National Archives, London, Historical Manuscripts Commission, National Register of Archives
Nuffield Oxf.	Nuffield College, Oxford
N. Yorks. CRO	North Yorkshire County Record Office, Northallerton
NYPL	New York Public Library
Oxf. UA	Oxford University Archives
Oxf. U. Mus. NH	Oxford University Museum of Natural History
Oxon. RO	Oxfordshire Record Office, Oxford
Pembroke Cam.	Pembroke College, Cambridge
PRO	National Archives, London, Public Record Office
PRO NIre.	Public Record Office for Northern Ireland, Belfast
Pusey Oxf.	Pusey House, Oxford
RA	Royal Academy of Arts, London
Ransom HRC	Harry Ransom Humanities Research Center, University of Texas, Austin
RAS	Royal Astronomical Society, London
RBG Kew	Royal Botanic Gardens, Kew, London
RCP Lond.	Royal College of Physicians of London
RCS Eng.	Royal College of Surgeons of England, London
RGS	Royal Geographical Society, London
RIBA	Royal Institute of British Architects, London
RIBA BAL	Royal Institute of British Architects, London, British Architectural Library
Royal Arch.	Royal Archives, Windsor Castle, Berkshire [by gracious permission of her majesty the queen]
Royal Irish Acad.	Royal Irish Academy, Dublin
Royal Scot. Acad.	Royal Scottish Academy, Edinburgh
RS	Royal Society, London
RSA	Royal Society of Arts, London
RS Friends, Lond.	Religious Society of Friends, London
St Ant. Oxf.	St Antony's College, Oxford
St John Cam.	St John's College, Cambridge
S. Antiquaries, Lond.	Society of Antiquaries of London
Sci. Mus.	Science Museum, London
Scot. NPG	Scottish National Portrait Gallery, Edinburgh
Scott Polar RI	University of Cambridge, Scott Polar Research Institute
Sheff. Arch.	Sheffield Archives
Shrops. RRC	Shropshire Records and Research Centre, Shrewsbury
SOAS	School of Oriental and African Studies, London
Som. ARS	Somerset Archive and Record Service, Taunton
Staffs. RO	Staffordshire Record Office, Stafford

Suffolk RO	Suffolk Record Office
Surrey HC	Surrey History Centre, Woking
TCD	Trinity College, Dublin
Trinity Cam.	Trinity College, Cambridge
U. Aberdeen	University of Aberdeen
U. Birm.	University of Birmingham
U. Birm. L.	University of Birmingham Library
U. Cal.	University of California
U. Cam.	University of Cambridge
UCL	University College, London
U. Durham	University of Durham
U. Durham L.	University of Durham Library
U. Edin.	University of Edinburgh
U. Edin., New Coll.	University of Edinburgh, New College
U. Edin., New Coll. L.	University of Edinburgh, New College Library
U. Edin. L.	University of Edinburgh Library
U. Glas.	University of Glasgow
U. Glas. L.	University of Glasgow Library
U. Hull	University of Hull
U. Hull, Brynmor Jones L.	University of Hull, Brynmor Jones Library
U. Leeds	University of Leeds
U. Leeds, Brotherton L.	University of Leeds, Brotherton Library
U. Lond.	University of London
U. Lpool	University of Liverpool
U. Lpool L.	University of Liverpool Library
U. Mich.	University of Michigan, Ann Arbor
U. Mich., Clements L.	University of Michigan, Ann Arbor, William L. Clements Library
U. Newcastle	University of Newcastle upon Tyne
U. Newcastle, Robinson L.	University of Newcastle upon Tyne, Robinson Library
U. Nott.	University of Nottingham
U. Nott. L.	University of Nottingham Library
U. Oxf.	University of Oxford
U. Reading	University of Reading
U. Reading L.	University of Reading Library
U. St Andr.	University of St Andrews
U. St Andr. L.	University of St Andrews Library
U. Southampton	University of Southampton
U. Southampton L.	University of Southampton Library
U. Sussex	University of Sussex, Brighton
U. Texas	University of Texas, Austin
U. Wales	University of Wales
U. Warwick Mod. RC	University of Warwick, Coventry, Modern Records Centre
V&A	Victoria and Albert Museum, London
V&A NAL	Victoria and Albert Museum, London, National Art Library
Warks. CRO	Warwickshire County Record Office, Warwick
Wellcome L.	Wellcome Library for the History and Understanding of Medicine, London
Westm. DA	Westminster Diocesan Archives, London
Wilts. & Swindon RO	Wiltshire and Swindon Record Office, Trowbridge
Worcs. RO	Worcestershire Record Office, Worcester
W. Sussex RO	West Sussex Record Office, Chichester
W. Yorks. AS	West Yorkshire Archive Service
Yale U.	Yale University, New Haven, Connecticut
Yale U., Beinecke L.	Yale University, New Haven, Connecticut, Beinecke Rare Book and Manuscript Library
Yale U. CBA	Yale University, New Haven, Connecticut, Yale Center for British Art

3 Bibliographic abbreviations

Adams, *Drama* — W. D. Adams, *A dictionary of the drama*, 1: *A–G* (1904); 2: *H–Z* (1956) [vol. 2 microfilm only]

AFM — J O'Donovan, ed. and trans., *Annala rioghachta Eireann / Annals of the kingdom of Ireland by the four masters*, 7 vols. (1848–51); 2nd edn (1856); 3rd edn (1990)

Allibone, *Dict.* — S. A. Allibone, *A critical dictionary of English literature and British and American authors*, 3 vols. (1859–71); suppl. by J. F. Kirk, 2 vols. (1891)

ANB — J. A. Garraty and M. C. Carnes, eds., *American national biography*, 24 vols. (1999)

Anderson, *Scot. nat.* — W. Anderson, *The Scottish nation, or, The surnames, families, literature, honours, and biographical history of the people of Scotland*, 3 vols. (1859–63)

Ann. mon. — H. R. Luard, ed., *Annales monastici*, 5 vols., Rolls Series, 36 (1864–9)

Ann. Ulster — S. Mac Airt and G. Mac Niocaill, eds., *Annals of Ulster (to AD 1131)* (1983)

APC — *Acts of the privy council of England*, new ser., 46 vols. (1890–1964)

APS — *The acts of the parliaments of Scotland*, 12 vols. in 13 (1814–75)

Arber, *Regs. Stationers* — F. Arber, ed., *A transcript of the registers of the Company of Stationers of London, 1554–1640 AD*, 5 vols. (1875–94)

ArchR — *Architectural Review*

ASC — D. Whitelock, D. C. Douglas, and S. I. Tucker, ed. and trans., *The Anglo-Saxon Chronicle: a revised translation* (1961)

AS chart. — P. H. Sawyer, *Anglo-Saxon charters: an annotated list and bibliography*, Royal Historical Society Guides and Handbooks (1968)

AusDB — D. Pike and others, eds., *Australian dictionary of biography*, 16 vols. (1966–2002)

Baker, *Serjeants* — J. H. Baker, *The order of serjeants at law*, SeldS, suppl. ser., 5 (1984)

Bale, *Cat.* — J. Bale, *Scriptorum illustrium Maioris Brytannie, quam nunc Angliam et Scotiam vocant: catalogus*, 2 vols. in 1 (Basel, 1557–9); facs. edn (1971)

Bale, *Index* — J. Bale, *Index Britanniae scriptorum*, ed. R. L. Poole and M. Bateson (1902); facs. edn (1990)

BBCS — *Bulletin of the Board of Celtic Studies*

BDMBR — J. O. Baylen and N. J. Gossman, eds., *Biographical dictionary of modern British radicals*, 3 vols. in 4 (1979–88)

Bede, *Hist. eccl.* — *Bede's Ecclesiastical history of the English people*, ed. and trans. B. Colgrave and R. A. B. Mynors, OMT (1969); repr. (1991)

Bénézit, *Dict.* — E. Bénézit, *Dictionnaire critique et documentaire des peintres, sculpteurs, dessinateurs et graveurs*, 3 vols. (Paris, 1911–23); new edn, 8 vols. (1948–66), repr. (1966); 3rd edn, rev. and enl., 10 vols. (1976); 4th edn, 14 vols. (1999)

BIHR — *Bulletin of the Institute of Historical Research*

Birch, *Seals* — W. de Birch, *Catalogue of seals in the department of manuscripts in the British Museum*, 6 vols. (1887–1900)

Bishop Burnet's History — *Bishop Burnet's History of his own time*, ed. M. J. Routh, 2nd edn, 6 vols. (1833)

Blackwood — *Blackwood's [Edinburgh] Magazine*, 328 vols. (1817–1980)

Blain, Clements & Grundy, *Feminist comp.* — V. Blain, P. Clements, and I. Grundy, eds., *The feminist companion to literature in English* (1990)

BL cat. — *The British Library general catalogue of printed books* [in 360 vols. with suppls., also CD-ROM and online]

BMJ — *British Medical Journal*

Boase & Courtney, *Bibl. Corn.* — G. C. Boase and W. P. Courtney, *Bibliotheca Cornubiensis: a catalogue of the writings … of Cornishmen*, 3 vols. (1874–82)

Boase, *Mod. Eng. biog.* — F. Boase, *Modern English biography: containing many thousand concise memoirs of persons who have died since the year 1850*, 6 vols. (privately printed, Truro, 1892–1921); repr. (1965)

Boswell, *Life* — *Boswell's Life of Johnson: together with Journal of a tour to the Hebrides and Johnson's Diary of a journey into north Wales*, ed. G. B. Hill, enl. edn, rev. L. F. Powell, 6 vols. (1934–50); 2nd edn (1964); repr. (1971)

Brown & Stratton, *Brit. mus.* — J. D. Brown and S. S. Stratton, *British musical biography* (1897)

Bryan, *Painters* — M. Bryan, *A biographical and critical dictionary of painters and engravers*, 2 vols. (1816); new edn, ed. G. Stanley (1849); new edn, ed. R. E. Graves and W. Armstrong, 2 vols. (1886–9); [4th edn], ed. G. C. Williamson, 5 vols. (1903–5) [various reprs.]

Burke, *Gen. GB* — J. Burke, *A genealogical and heraldic history of the commoners of Great Britain and Ireland*, 4 vols. (1833–8); new edn as *A genealogical and heraldic dictionary of the landed gentry of Great Britain and Ireland*, 3 vols. (1843–9) [many later edns]

Burke, *Gen. Ire.* — J. B. Burke, *A genealogical and heraldic history of the landed gentry of Ireland* (1899); 2nd edn (1904); 3rd edn (1912); 4th edn (1958); 5th edn as *Burke's Irish family records* (1976)

Burke, *Peerage* — J. Burke, *A general [later edns A genealogical] and heraldic dictionary of the peerage and baronetage of the United Kingdom [later edns the British empire]* (1829–)

Burney, *Hist. mus.* — C. Burney, *A general history of music, from the earliest ages to the present period*, 4 vols. (1776–89)

Burtchaell & Sadleir, *Alum. Dubl.* — G. D. Burtchaell and T. U. Sadleir, *Alumni Dublinenses: a register of the students, graduates, and provosts of Trinity College* (1924); [2nd edn], with suppl., in 2 pts (1935)

Calamy rev. — A. G. Matthews, *Calamy revised* (1934); repr. (1988)

CCI — *Calendar of confirmations and inventories granted and given up in the several commissariots of Scotland* (1876–)

CClR — *Calendar of the close rolls preserved in the Public Record Office*, 47 vols. (1892–1963)

CDS — J. Bain, ed., *Calendar of documents relating to Scotland*, 4 vols., PRO (1881–8); suppl. vol. 5, ed. G. G. Simpson and J. D. Galbraith [1986]

CEPR letters — W. H. Bliss, C. Johnson, and J. Twemlow, eds., *Calendar of entries in the papal registers relating to Great Britain and Ireland: papal letters* (1893–)

CGPLA — *Calendars of the grants of probate and letters of administration [in 4 ser.: England & Wales, Northern Ireland, Ireland, and Éire]*

Chambers, *Scots.* — R. Chambers, ed., *A biographical dictionary of eminent Scotsmen*, 4 vols. (1832–5)

Chancery records — chancery records pubd by the PRO

Chancery records (RC) — chancery records pubd by the Record Commissions

CIPM	Calendar of inquisitions post mortem, [20 vols.], PRO (1904–); also Henry VII, 3 vols. (1898–1955)
Clarendon, Hist. rebellion	E. Hyde, earl of Clarendon, The history of the rebellion and civil wars in England, 6 vols. (1888); repr. (1958) and (1992)
Cobbett, Parl. hist.	W. Cobbett and J. Wright, eds., Cobbett's Parliamentary history of England, 36 vols. (1806–1820)
Colvin, Archs.	H. Colvin, A biographical dictionary of British architects, 1600–1840, 3rd edn (1995)
Cooper, Ath. Cantab.	C. H. Cooper and T. Cooper, Athenae Cantabrigienses, 3 vols. (1858–1913); repr. (1967)
CPR	Calendar of the patent rolls preserved in the Public Record Office (1891–)
Crockford	Crockford's Clerical Directory
CS	Camden Society
CSP	Calendar of state papers [in 11 ser.: domestic, Scotland, Scottish series, Ireland, colonial, Commonwealth, foreign, Spain [at Simancas], Rome, Milan, and Venice]
CYS	Canterbury and York Society
DAB	Dictionary of American biography, 21 vols. (1928–36), repr. in 11 vols. (1964); 10 suppls. (1944–96)
DBB	D. J. Jeremy, ed., Dictionary of business biography, 5 vols. (1984–6)
DCB	G. W. Brown and others, Dictionary of Canadian biography, [14 vols.] (1966–)
Debrett's Peerage	Debrett's Peerage (1803–) [sometimes Debrett's Illustrated peerage]
Desmond, Botanists	R. Desmond, Dictionary of British and Irish botanists and horticulturists (1977); rev. edn (1994)
Dir. Brit. archs.	A. Felstead, J. Franklin, and L. Pinfield, eds., Directory of British architects, 1834–1900 (1993); 2nd edn, ed. A. Brodie and others, 2 vols. (2001)
DLB	J. M. Bellamy and J. Saville, eds., Dictionary of labour biography, [10 vols.] (1972–)
DLitB	Dictionary of Literary Biography
DNB	Dictionary of national biography, 63 vols. (1885–1900), suppl., 3 vols. (1901); repr. in 22 vols. (1908–9); 10 further suppls. (1912–96); Missing persons (1993)
DNZB	W. H. Oliver and C. Orange, eds., The dictionary of New Zealand biography, 5 vols. (1990–2000)
DSAB	W. J. de Kock and others, eds., Dictionary of South African biography, 5 vols. (1968–87)
DSB	C. C. Gillispie and F. L. Holmes, eds., Dictionary of scientific biography, 16 vols. (1970–80); repr. in 8 vols. (1981); 2 vol. suppl. (1990)
DSBB	A. Slaven and S. Checkland, eds., Dictionary of Scottish business biography, 1860–1960, 2 vols. (1986–90)
DSCHT	N. M. de S. Cameron and others, eds., Dictionary of Scottish church history and theology (1993)
Dugdale, Monasticon	W. Dugdale, Monasticon Anglicanum, 3 vols. (1655–72); 2nd edn, 3 vols. (1661–82); new edn, ed. J. Caley, J. Ellis, and B. Bandinel, 6 vols. in 8 pts (1817–30); repr. (1846) and (1970)
DWB	J. E. Lloyd and others, eds., Dictionary of Welsh biography down to 1940 (1959) [Eng. trans. of Y bywgraffiadur Cymreig hyd 1940, 2nd edn (1954)]
EdinR	Edinburgh Review, or, Critical Journal
EETS	Early English Text Society
Emden, Cam.	A. B. Emden, A biographical register of the University of Cambridge to 1500 (1963)
Emden, Oxf.	A. B. Emden, A biographical register of the University of Oxford to AD 1500, 3 vols. (1957–9); also A biographical register of the University of Oxford, AD 1501 to 1540 (1974)
EngHR	English Historical Review
Engraved Brit. ports.	F. M. O'Donoghue and H. M. Hake, Catalogue of engraved British portraits preserved in the department of prints and drawings in the British Museum, 6 vols. (1908–25)
ER	The English Reports, 178 vols. (1900–32)
ESTC	English short title catalogue, 1475–1800 [CD-ROM and online]
Evelyn, Diary	The diary of John Evelyn, ed. E. S. De Beer, 6 vols. (1955); repr. (2000)
Farington, Diary	The diary of Joseph Farington, ed. K. Garlick and others, 17 vols. (1978–98)
Fasti Angl. (Hardy)	J. Le Neve, Fasti ecclesiae Anglicanae, ed. T. D. Hardy, 3 vols. (1854)
Fasti Angl., 1066–1300	[J. Le Neve], Fasti ecclesiae Anglicanae, 1066–1300, ed. D. E. Greenway and J. S. Barrow, [8 vols.] (1968–)
Fasti Angl., 1300–1541	[J. Le Neve], Fasti ecclesiae Anglicanae, 1300–1541, 12 vols. (1962–7)
Fasti Angl., 1541–1857	[J. Le Neve], Fasti ecclesiae Anglicanae, 1541–1857, ed. J. M. Horn, D. M. Smith, and D. S. Bailey, [9 vols.] (1969–)
Fasti Scot.	H. Scott, Fasti ecclesiae Scoticanae, 3 vols. in 6 (1871); new edn, [11 vols.] (1915–)
FO List	Foreign Office List
Fortescue, Brit. army	J. W. Fortescue, A history of the British army, 13 vols. (1899–1930)
Foss, Judges	E. Foss, The judges of England, 9 vols. (1848–64); repr. (1966)
Foster, Alum. Oxon.	J. Foster, ed., Alumni Oxonienses: the members of the University of Oxford, 1715–1886, 4 vols. (1887–8); later edn (1891); also Alumni Oxonienses … 1500–1714, 4 vols. (1891–2); 8 vol. repr. (1968) and (2000)
Fuller, Worthies	T. Fuller, The history of the worthies of England, 4 pts (1662); new edn, 2 vols., ed. J. Nichols (1811); new edn, 3 vols., ed. P. A. Nuttall (1840); repr. (1965)
GEC, Baronetage	G. E. Cokayne, Complete baronetage, 6 vols. (1900–09); repr. (1983) [microprint]
GEC, Peerage	G. E. C. [G. E. Cokayne], The complete peerage of England, Scotland, Ireland, Great Britain, and the United Kingdom, 8 vols. (1887–98); new edn, ed. V. Gibbs and others, 14 vols. in 15 (1910–98); microprint repr. (1982) and (1987)
Genest, Eng. stage	J. Genest, Some account of the English stage from the Restoration in 1660 to 1830, 10 vols. (1832); repr. [New York, 1965]
Gillow, Lit. biog. hist.	J. Gillow, A literary and biographical history or bibliographical dictionary of the English Catholics, from the breach with Rome, in 1534, to the present time, 5 vols. [1885–1902]; repr. (1961); repr. with preface by C. Gillow (1999)
Gir. Camb. opera	Giraldi Cambrensis opera, ed. J. S. Brewer, J. F. Dimock, and G. F. Warner, 8 vols., Rolls Series, 21 (1861–91)
GJ	Geographical Journal

Gladstone, *Diaries*	*The Gladstone diaries: with cabinet minutes and prime-ministerial correspondence*, ed. M. R. D. Foot and H. C. G. Matthew, 14 vols. (1968–94)
GM	*Gentleman's Magazine*
Graves, *Artists*	A. Graves, ed., *A dictionary of artists who have exhibited works in the principal London exhibitions of oil paintings from 1760 to 1880* (1884); new edn (1895); 3rd edn (1901); facs. edn (1969); repr. [1970], (1973), and (1984)
Graves, *Brit. Inst.*	A. Graves, *The British Institution, 1806–1867: a complete dictionary of contributors and their work from the foundation of the institution* (1875); facs. edn (1908); repr. (1969)
Graves, *RA exhibitors*	A. Graves, *The Royal Academy of Arts: a complete dictionary of contributors and their work from its foundation in 1769 to 1904*, 8 vols. (1905–6); repr. in 4 vols. (1970) and (1972)
Graves, *Soc. Artists*	A. Graves, *The Society of Artists of Great Britain, 1760–1791, the Free Society of Artists, 1761–1783: a complete dictionary* (1907); facs. edn (1969)
Greaves & Zaller, *BDBR*	R. L. Greaves and R. Zaller, eds., *Biographical dictionary of British radicals in the seventeenth century*, 3 vols. (1982–4)
Grove, *Dict. mus.*	G. Grove, ed., *A dictionary of music and musicians*, 5 vols. (1878–90); 2nd edn, ed. J. A. Fuller Maitland (1904–10); 3rd edn, ed. H. C. Colles (1927); 4th edn with suppl. (1940); 5th edn, ed. E. Blom, 9 vols. (1954); suppl. (1961) [see also *New Grove*]
Hall, *Dramatic ports.*	L. A. Hall, *Catalogue of dramatic portraits in the theatre collection of the Harvard College library*, 4 vols. (1930–34)
Hansard	*Hansard's parliamentary debates*, ser. 1–5 (1803–)
Highfill, Burnim & Langhans, *BDA*	P. H. Highfill, K. A. Burnim, and E. A. Langhans, *A biographical dictionary of actors, actresses, musicians, dancers, managers, and other stage personnel in London, 1660–1800*, 16 vols. (1973–93)
Hist. U. Oxf.	T. H. Aston, ed., *The history of the University of Oxford*, 8 vols. (1984–2000) [1: *The early Oxford schools*, ed. J. I. Catto (1984); 2: *Late medieval Oxford*, ed. J. I. Catto and R. Evans (1992); 3: *The collegiate university*, ed. J. McConica (1986); 4: *Seventeenth-century Oxford*, ed. N. Tyacke (1997); 5: *The eighteenth century*, ed. L. S. Sutherland and L. G. Mitchell (1986); 6–7: *Nineteenth-century Oxford*, ed. M. G. Brock and M. C. Curthoys (1997–2000); 8: *The twentieth century*, ed. B. Harrison (2000)]
HJ	*Historical Journal*
HMC	Historical Manuscripts Commission
Holdsworth, *Eng. law*	W. S. Holdsworth, *A history of English law*, ed. A. L. Goodhart and H. L. Hanbury, 17 vols. (1903–72)
HoP, *Commons*	*The history of parliament: the House of Commons* [*1386–1421*, ed. J. S. Roskell, L. Clark, and C. Rawcliffe, 4 vols. (1992); *1509–1558*, ed. S. T. Bindoff, 3 vols. (1982); *1558–1603*, ed. P. W. Hasler, 3 vols. (1981); *1660–1690*, ed. B. D. Henning, 3 vols. (1983); *1690–1715*, ed. D. W. Hayton, E. Cruickshanks, and S. Handley, 5 vols. (2002); *1715–1754*, ed. R. Sedgwick, 2 vols. (1970); *1754–1790*, ed. L. Namier and J. Brooke, 3 vols. (1964), repr. (1985); *1790–1820*, ed. R. G. Thorne, 5 vols. (1986); in draft (used with permission): *1422–1504*, *1604–1629*, *1640–1660*, and *1820–1832*]
IGI	*International Genealogical Index*, Church of Jesus Christ of the Latterday Saints
ILN	*Illustrated London News*
IMC	Irish Manuscripts Commission
Irving, *Scots.*	J. Irving, ed., *The book of Scotsmen eminent for achievements in arms and arts, church and state, law, legislation and literature, commerce, science, travel and philanthropy* (1881)
JCS	*Journal of the Chemical Society*
JHC	*Journals of the House of Commons*
JHL	*Journals of the House of Lords*
John of Worcester, *Chron.*	*The chronicle of John of Worcester*, ed. R. R. Darlington and P. McGurk, trans. J. Bray and P. McGurk, 3 vols., OMT (1995–) [vol. 1 forthcoming]
Keeler, *Long Parliament*	M. F. Keeler, *The Long Parliament, 1640–1641: a biographical study of its members* (1954)
Kelly, *Handbk*	*The upper ten thousand: an alphabetical list of all members of noble families*, 3 vols. (1875–7); continued as *Kelly's handbook of the upper ten thousand for 1878* [1879], 2 vols. (1878–9); continued as *Kelly's handbook to the titled, landed and official classes*, 94 vols. (1880–1973)
LondG	*London Gazette*
LP Henry VIII	J. S. Brewer, J. Gairdner, and R. H. Brodie, eds., *Letters and papers, foreign and domestic, of the reign of Henry VIII*, 23 vols. in 38 (1862–1932); repr. (1965)
Mallalieu, *Watercolour artists*	H. L. Mallalieu, *The dictionary of British watercolour artists up to 1820*, 3 vols. (1976–90); vol. 1, 2nd edn (1986)
Memoirs FRS	*Biographical Memoirs of Fellows of the Royal Society*
MGH	Monumenta Germaniae Historica
MT	*Musical Times*
Munk, *Roll*	W. Munk, *The roll of the Royal College of Physicians of London*, 2 vols. (1861); 2nd edn, 3 vols. (1878)
N&Q	*Notes and Queries*
New Grove	S. Sadie, ed., *The new Grove dictionary of music and musicians*, 20 vols. (1980); 2nd edn, 29 vols. (2001) [also online edn; see also Grove, *Dict. mus.*]
Nichols, *Illustrations*	J. Nichols and J. B. Nichols, *Illustrations of the literary history of the eighteenth century*, 8 vols. (1817–58)
Nichols, *Lit. anecdotes*	J. Nichols, *Literary anecdotes of the eighteenth century*, 9 vols. (1812–16); facs. edn (1966)
Obits. FRS	*Obituary Notices of Fellows of the Royal Society*
O'Byrne, *Naval biog. dict.*	W. R. O'Byrne, *A naval biographical dictionary* (1849); repr. (1990); [2nd edn], 2 vols. (1861)
OHS	Oxford Historical Society
Old Westminsters	*The record of Old Westminsters*, 1–2, ed. G. F. R. Barker and A. H. Stenning (1928); suppl. 1, ed. J. B. Whitmore and G. R. Y. Radcliffe [1938]; 3, ed. J. B. Whitmore, G. R. Y. Radcliffe, and D. C. Simpson (1963); suppl. 2, ed. F. E. Pagan (1978); 4, ed. F. E. Pagan and H. E. Pagan (1992)
OMT	Oxford Medieval Texts
Ordericus Vitalis, *Eccl. hist.*	*The ecclesiastical history of Orderic Vitalis*, ed. and trans. M. Chibnall, 6 vols., OMT (1969–80); repr. (1990)
Paris, *Chron.*	*Matthaei Parisiensis, monachi sancti Albani, chronica majora*, ed. H. R. Luard, Rolls Series, 7 vols. (1872–83)
Parl. papers	*Parliamentary papers* (1801–)
PBA	*Proceedings of the British Academy*

Pepys, *Diary*	*The diary of Samuel Pepys*, ed. R. Latham and W. Matthews, 11 vols. (1970–83); repr. (1995) and (2000)
Pevsner	N. Pevsner and others, Buildings of England series
PICE	*Proceedings of the Institution of Civil Engineers*
Pipe rolls	*The great roll of the pipe for* . . ., PRSoc. (1884–)
PRO	Public Record Office
PRS	*Proceedings of the Royal Society of London*
PRSoc.	Pipe Roll Society
PTRS	*Philosophical Transactions of the Royal Society*
QR	*Quarterly Review*
RC	Record Commissions
Redgrave, *Artists*	S. Redgrave, *A dictionary of artists of the English school* (1874); rev. edn (1878); repr. (1970)
Reg. Oxf.	C. W. Boase and A. Clark, eds., *Register of the University of Oxford*, 5 vols., OHS, 1, 10–12, 14 (1885–9)
Reg. PCS	J. H. Burton and others, eds., *The register of the privy council of Scotland*, 1st ser., 14 vols. (1877–98); 2nd ser., 8 vols. (1899–1908); 3rd ser., [16 vols.] (1908–70)
Reg. RAN	H. W. C. Davis and others, eds., *Regesta regum Anglo-Normannorum, 1066–1154*, 4 vols. (1913–69)
RIBA Journal	*Journal of the Royal Institute of British Architects* [later *RIBA Journal*]
RotP	J. Strachey, ed., *Rotuli parliamentorum ut et petitiones, et placita in parliamento*, 6 vols. (1767–77)
RotS	D. Macpherson, J. Caley, and W. Illingworth, eds., *Rotuli Scotiae in Turri Londinensi et in domo capitulari Westmonasteriensi asservati*, 2 vols., RC, 14 (1814–19)
RS	Record(s) Society
Rymer, *Foedera*	T. Rymer and R. Sanderson, eds., *Foedera, conventiones, literae et cuiuscunque generis acta publica inter reges Angliae et alios quosvis imperatores, reges, pontifices, principes, vel communitates*, 20 vols. (1704–35); 2nd edn, 20 vols. (1726–35); 3rd edn, 10 vols. (1739–45), facs. edn (1967); new edn, ed. A. Clarke, J. Caley, and F. Holbrooke, 4 vols., RC, 50 (1816–30)
Sainty, *Judges*	J. Sainty, ed., *The judges of England, 1272–1990*, SeldS, suppl. ser., 10 (1993)
Sainty, *King's counsel*	J. Sainty, ed., *A list of English law officers and king's counsel*, SeldS, suppl. ser., 7 (1987)
SCH	Studies in Church History
Scots peerage	J. B. Paul, ed. *The Scots peerage, founded on Wood's edition of Sir Robert Douglas's Peerage of Scotland, containing an historical and genealogical account of the nobility of that kingdom*, 9 vols. (1904–14)
SeldS	Selden Society
SHR	*Scottish Historical Review*
State trials	T. B. Howell and T. J. Howell, eds., *Cobbett's Complete collection of state trials*, 34 vols. (1809–28)
STC, 1475–1640	A. W. Pollard, G. R. Redgrave, and others, eds., *A short-title catalogue of . . . English books . . . 1475–1640* (1926); 2nd edn, ed. W. A. Jackson, F. S. Ferguson, and K. F. Pantzer, 3 vols. (1976–91) [see also Wing, *STC*]
STS	Scottish Text Society
SurtS	Surtees Society
Symeon of Durham, *Opera*	*Symeonis monachi opera omnia*, ed. T. Arnold, 2 vols., Rolls Series, 75 (1882–5); repr. (1965)
Tanner, *Bibl. Brit.-Hib.*	T. Tanner, *Bibliotheca Britannico-Hibernica*, ed. D. Wilkins (1748); repr. (1963)
Thieme & Becker, *Allgemeines Lexikon*	U. Thieme, F. Becker, and H. Vollmer, eds., *Allgemeines Lexikon der bildenden Künstler von der Antike bis zur Gegenwart*, 37 vols. (Leipzig, 1907–50); repr. (1961–5), (1983), and (1992)
Thurloe, *State papers*	*A collection of the state papers of John Thurloe*, ed. T. Birch, 7 vols. (1742)
TLS	*Times Literary Supplement*
Tout, *Admin. hist.*	T. F. Tout, *Chapters in the administrative history of mediaeval England: the wardrobe, the chamber, and the small seals*, 6 vols. (1920–33); repr. (1967)
TRHS	*Transactions of the Royal Historical Society*
VCH	H. A. Doubleday and others, eds., *The Victoria history of the counties of England*, [88 vols.] (1900–)
Venn, *Alum. Cant.*	J. Venn and J. A. Venn, *Alumni Cantabrigienses: a biographical list of all known students, graduates, and holders of office at the University of Cambridge, from the earliest times to 1900*, 10 vols. (1922–54); repr. in 2 vols. (1974–8)
Vertue, *Note books*	[G. Vertue], *Note books*, ed. K. Esdaile, earl of Ilchester, and H. M. Hake, 6 vols., Walpole Society, 18, 20, 22, 24, 26, 30 (1930–55)
VF	*Vanity Fair*
Walford, *County families*	E. Walford, *The county families of the United Kingdom, or, Royal manual of the titled and untitled aristocracy of Great Britain and Ireland* (1860)
Walker rev.	A. G. Matthews, *Walker revised: being a revision of John Walker's Sufferings of the clergy during the grand rebellion, 1642–60* (1948); repr. (1988)
Walpole, *Corr.*	*The Yale edition of Horace Walpole's correspondence*, ed. W. S. Lewis, 48 vols. (1937–83)
Ward, *Men of the reign*	T. H. Ward, ed., *Men of the reign: a biographical dictionary of eminent persons of British and colonial birth who have died during the reign of Queen Victoria* (1885); repr. (Graz, 1968)
Waterhouse, *18c painters*	E. Waterhouse, *The dictionary of 18th century painters in oils and crayons* (1981); repr. as *British 18th century painters in oils and crayons* (1991), vol. 2 of *Dictionary of British art*
Watt, *Bibl. Brit.*	R. Watt, *Bibliotheca Britannica, or, A general index to British and foreign literature*, 4 vols. (1824) [many reprs.]
Wellesley index	W. E. Houghton, ed., *The Wellesley index to Victorian periodicals, 1824–1900*, 5 vols. (1966–89); new edn (1999) [CD-ROM]
Wing, *STC*	D. Wing, ed., *Short-title catalogue of . . . English books . . . 1641–1700*, 3 vols. (1945–51); 2nd edn (1972–88); rev. and enl. edn, ed. J. J. Morrison, C. W. Nelson, and M. Seccombe, 4 vols. (1994–8) [see also *STC, 1475–1640*]
Wisden	*John Wisden's Cricketer's Almanack*
Wood, *Ath. Oxon.*	A. Wood, *Athenae Oxonienses . . . to which are added the Fasti*, 2 vols. (1691–2); 2nd edn (1721); new edn, 4 vols., ed. P. Bliss (1813–20); repr. (1967) and (1969)
Wood, *Vic. painters*	C. Wood, *Dictionary of Victorian painters* (1971); 2nd edn (1978); 3rd edn as *Victorian painters*, 2 vols. (1995), vol. 4 of *Dictionary of British art*
WW	*Who's who* (1849–)
WWBMP	M. Stenton and S. Lees, eds., *Who's who of British members of parliament*, 4 vols. (1976–81)
WWW	*Who was who* (1929–)

Goss, Alexander (1814–1872), Roman Catholic bishop of Liverpool, was born on 5 July 1814 in Ormskirk, Lancashire, the only son of John Goss and his wife, Elizabeth Moorcroft. Educated at St Cuthbert's College, Ushaw (1827–39), and at the English College, Rome, he was ordained priest in July 1841. His first major appointment was as vice-president of the new St Edward's College, Everton, Liverpool, in 1842, where he lived for the rest of his life. He was a shy person, able to speak his mind, as he said, only to 'plain, homely, Lancashire folks', but at 6 feet 3 inches tall he had a commanding public presence and was a forceful speaker and controversialist.

On 25 September 1853 Goss was consecrated bishop of Gerra, and appointed coadjutor to Dr George Brown, the first bishop of the new diocese of Liverpool. Their relationship was stormy, involving appeals to Rome, and Goss was very critical of Brown's lax administration, an attitude which did much to colour his aims when he succeeded him in January 1856. The keynote of Goss's episcopate was authority: to establish his own over his clergy and to define that of the new diocesan bishops in relation to both Westminster and Rome. He refused to recognize clerical claims to be consulted on matters of policy or appointments, established an efficient administration, and laid down detailed guidelines for the life of his priests. He joined battle with the Jesuits and Benedictines, insisting that as parish clergy they were under his jurisdiction, and he limited the right of gentry families to appoint their chaplains.

Goss was the unofficial leader of the bishops against both Cardinal Wiseman and Cardinal Manning, objecting to their interference in diocesan matters and stressing the independent rights and jurisdiction of each bishop. He distrusted Manning's intrigues at Rome and the ultramontane habit of looking to Rome for universal guidance. Wiseman thought he had an 'Anglican … unRoman spirit' while Manning regarded him as a 'radical anti-Romanist'. Both missed the point: Goss wanted to be allowed to administer his diocese as he thought best, with all the knowledge of the man on the ground. He had a low opinion of the abilities of Roman officials, and claimed that nothing had ever wounded his faith so much as their trickery. While he fully accepted the pope's primacy and his temporal power, he opposed the definition of infallibility in 1870 and would have voted against it had illness not prevented him from attending the First Vatican Council.

Goss was also concerned to kill any suggestion that Roman Catholics were alien or disloyal. He gloried in his Englishness, frequently telling his people, 'I am English, I am a real John Bull, indeed I am a Lancashire man'. 'In heart we are English', he claimed, 'in purpose we are loyal'. These sentiments did not endear him to the Irish majority of his flock, but he refused to treat them any differently from their English counterparts, hoping that they would integrate fully into English society. There was strong anti-Catholicism in Liverpool and he was frequently involved in local controversy. He fought for equality for Catholics in public institutions. His attitudes to social problems were those of a rather reactionary, paternalistic tory. Caution, perhaps, won out over originality, but his years as bishop saw a considerable increase in the number of churches (from 90 to 120), priests (from 137 to 202), and schools.

In line with the Counter-Reformation episcopal ideal Goss preached a strongly sacramental and individualistic piety and his personal life was one of asceticism, poverty, and unending devotion to duty. He still found time for scholarship, publishing *A Sacred History, Comprising the Leading Facts of the Old and New Testaments* (edited from a French original, 1856); *The Manchester Trials* (1864); and *The Chronicle of Man and the Sudreys* (2 vols., 1874). He was meticulous, persevering, and well-read—an ideal historical editor; he also collected materials for a projected history of northern Catholicism. He died of a stroke at St Edward's College on 3 October 1872, and was buried at Ford, Liverpool.   PETER DOYLE

Sources W. M. Brady, *The episcopal succession in England, Scotland, and Ireland, AD 1400 to 1875*, 3 (1877), 418–22; facs. edn (1971) · Gillow, *Lit. biog. hist.* · 'Consecration of the Right Rev. Doctor Goss at Liverpool', *The Tablet* (1 Oct 1853), 627–8 · *The Times* (4 Oct 1872) · *The Times* (10 Oct 1872) · *The Tablet* (12 Oct 1872), 467–71 · P. Doyle, 'Bishop Goss of Liverpool (1856–1872) and the importance of being English', *Religion and national identity*, ed. S. Mews, SCH, 18 (1982), 433–47 · P. Hughes, 'The bishops of the century', *The English Catholics, 1850–1950*, ed. G. A. Beck (1950), 186–222 · P. Doyle, 'Bishop Goss and the gentry', *North West Catholic History*, 12 (1985), 6–13 · P. Doyle, 'An episcopal historian', *North West Catholic History*, 15 (1988), 6–15 · *DNB* · parish register (baptism), St Anne's, Ormskirk, 12 July 1814
Archives Archive of the Archbishop of Liverpool, Liverpool curial offices · Archivio Vaticano, Vatican City, Propaganda Fide archives · Lancs. RO, corresp. and papers · Lancs. RO, Liverpool Roman Catholic diocesan archive · Ushaw College, Durham, corresp. and papers | Upholland College Library and Archive, Skelmersdale, Lancashire · Westm. DA, letters to Wiseman
Likenesses oils, Upholland College, Skelmersdale, Lancashire
Wealth at death under £4000: resworn probate, March 1873, *CGPLA Eng. & Wales* (1872)

Goss, Sir John (1800–1880), composer, was born at Fareham, Hampshire, on 27 December 1800, the son of Joseph Goss, organist at Fareham parish church. In 1808 he was sent to school in Ringwood, then in 1811 he became a chorister at the Chapel Royal under John Stafford Smith, and later lived with his uncle John Jeremiah Goss (1770–1817), a distinguished alto who sang at the Chapel Royal as well as St Paul's Cathedral and Westminster Abbey. When his voice broke he left the Chapel Royal school and became a pupil of the composer Thomas Attwood, under whom he studied Mozart's symphonies and in particular their scoring. In 1817 he was employed as an operatic chorus singer. His first published work was 'Negro Song' ('The loud wind roared') for three voices and small orchestra, composed and published in London, *c*.1819.

Around this time Goss began to compose vocal canons and the many glees which constitute his best-remembered secular music. These simple partsongs, usually for four unaccompanied voices, are characterized by imaginative harmonies and effective use of vocal textures. Among the best are 'There is beauty on the mountain' and 'Ossian's Hymn to the Sun', both published in

Sir John Goss (1800–1880), by unknown artist, *c*.1835

1826. In 1821 Goss became organist at Stockwell Chapel, Lambeth, and in the same year he married Lucy Emma Nerd (1800–1895). In 1824 he was appointed organist at St Luke's Church, Chelsea. As well as producing other compositions, notably solo songs, he continued with his output of glees, which were performed at London's most notable glee societies. His music received favourable reviews in periodicals such as *The Harmonicon*.

Two overtures, in F and E♭, date from around 1824, but were not performed or published until 1827. Both were well received, but Goss declined an invitation from the Philharmonic Society in 1833 to write a further instrumental work, perhaps because he recognized his own greater facility as a composer for voices. He did, however, compose incidental music to John Banim's play *The Serjeant's Wife*, performed at the English Opera House on 24 July 1827. In 1827 Goss became a professor of harmony at the Royal Academy of Music, a position he held until 1874. He was a distinguished and painstaking teacher, and a tasteful and virtuoso performer on the organ, creating marvellous effects on the then comparatively rudimentary instrument. He was one of the last great exponents in England of keyboard realization from a figured bass, and the first edition of his treatise *An Introduction to Harmony and Thorough-Bass* was published in 1833. In the same year he won the Gresham prize for his anthem 'Have mercy upon me, O God'. He edited and contributed to various publications, including the *Monthly Sacred Minstrel*.

In 1838, on Attwood's death, Goss was appointed organist of St Paul's Cathedral. There he attempted to combat slovenly music-making, undisciplined conduct, and frequent non-attendance by clergy and choir members, but his efforts did not receive the consistent support of the cathedral chapter. The reforms resulting from the Tractarian movement came too late to assist Goss, whose gentle and ineffectual manner was no match for the task confronting him. From 1843, together with James Turle, organist of Westminster Abbey, he brought out three volumes entitled *Cathedral Services, Ancient and Modern*. About 1843 he also published *Chants, Ancient and Modern*, in which first appeared his popular but artistically inappropriate adaptation as a psalm chant of the theme from the second movement of Beethoven's seventh symphony. He borrowed other themes from the music of 'eminent composers', adapting them for use with sacred words. He also brought much earlier music into regular use at St Paul's, introducing harmonized plainsong and music by Tallis and Merbecke.

Goss was one of the most important early Victorian church composers, his anthems and services being most notable for their flexibility of phrasing, attention to detail in word-setting, and sense of proportion and balance. His anthem 'Blessed is the man' (1842) was not well received by the St Paul's Cathedral choir, and he composed little in the next ten years apart from two exquisite miniature anthems, 'God so loved the world' and 'Let the wicked forsake his way' (both 1850). In 1852 his anthem 'If we believe that Jesus died', written for the funeral of the duke of Wellington, created a profound impression. In 1854 he produced the anthem 'Praise the Lord, o my soul' for the bicentenary festival of the sons of the clergy. In 1856, on William Knyvett's death, Goss was appointed composer to the Chapel Royal. This was the start of the period of his greatest productivity of services and anthems. Although his output was uneven in quality, it was versatile, including large-scale verse anthems as well as miniatures for full choir. Some of his anthems, including 'The Wilderness' (1861), 'O taste and see' (1863), and 'O saviour of the world' (1869), have held a modest but enduring place in the repertory of English church music. However, Goss is remembered more for his two most famous hymn tunes: that specially written for Henry Francis Lyte's words 'Praise my soul the King of Heaven' and first published in 1869, and the tune first published in 1871 and sung thereafter to the Christmas hymn 'See amid the winter's snow'.

In 1872 Goss's health began to fail. In February of that year his setting of the Te Deum and an anthem, 'The Lord is my strength', written for the public thanksgiving for the recovery of the prince of Wales, were performed. In the following month he was knighted, and resigned his duties at St Paul's, to be succeeded by his pupil John Stainer. In 1876, together with his former pupil Arthur Sullivan, he received the honorary degree of DMus at Cambridge University. Goss died at his home, 26 Lambert Road, Brixton Rise, on 10 May 1880, and was buried on 15 May in Kensal Green cemetery. In 1886 a memorial tablet was erected by his pupils and friends in the crypt of St Paul's Cathedral.

JUDITH BLEZZARD

Sources *DNB* · F. G. Edwards, *MT*, 42 (1901), 225–31, 375–83 · D. Gedge, 'John Goss, 1800–1880', *MT*, 121 (1980), 338–9, 461–3 · W. H. Husk and B. Carr, 'Goss, Sir John', *New Grove* · W. J. Gatens, *Victorian cathedral music in theory and practice* (1986) · L. Baillie and

R. Balchin, eds., *The catalogue of printed music in the British Library to 1980*, 62 vols. (1981–7), vol. 24 · E. H. Fellowes, *English cathedral music*, 5th edn, ed. J. A. Westrup (1969) · N. Temperley, *The music of the English parish church*, 1 (1979) · M. Frost, ed., *Historical companion to 'Hymns ancient and modern'* (1962) · B. Rainbow, *The choral revival in the Anglican church, 1839–1872* (1970) · J. Blezzard, *Borrowings in English church music* (1990) · A. Hutchings, *Church music in the nineteenth century* (1967)
Archives FM Cam., letters, mainly to George Cooper
Likenesses oils, *c.*1835, NPG [*see illus.*] · W. H. Thornycroft, bas-relief figure on tablet, St Paul's Cathedral, London · photograph, repro. in Edwards, *MT* · photograph, repro. in Gedge, *MT*
Wealth at death under £7000: probate, 3 June 1880, *CGPLA Eng. & Wales*

Gossage, Sir (Ernest) Leslie (1891–1949), air force officer, was born at Toxteth Park, Liverpool, on 3 February 1891, the eldest son of Lieutenant-Colonel Ernest Frederick Gossage, a soap manufacturer, and his wife, Emily Lewis Jackson. He was educated at Rugby School and Trinity College, Cambridge, where he graduated BA in 1912, and was then commissioned in the Royal Artillery. In 1914 he went to France with his battery and saw action at Mons, the Marne, and the Aisne and in the first battle of Ypres.

Gossage then responded to the call for volunteers to join the Royal Flying Corps and qualified for his wings in March 1915. He subsequently saw over three years' service with the corps in France, an unusually long period, during which he rose to flight commander (September 1915), squadron commander (June 1916), and finally wing commander (December 1917). While serving as commander of 56 squadron in 1916 he gained the MC for consistent good and zealous work both on patrol and during co-operation with the artillery in operations resulting in the capture of enemy positions. In 1917 he married Eileen Gladys, the daughter of Brigadier-General Edmund Donough John O'Brien, of Buxted, Sussex; the couple had two sons, one of whom was killed on active service. Two years later Gossage was awarded the DSO for distinguished services in operations, and he was mentioned in dispatches on four occasions.

In 1919 Gossage was permanently commissioned in the Royal Air Force as squadron leader. His clear and analytical brain predestined him for a career on the staff, and he went first to the directorate of fighter operations in the Air Ministry. After a short period at headquarters in Egypt he returned to the Air Ministry for duty in the department of the deputy chief of air staff. In 1921 he was appointed to command the School of Army Co-operation, and in 1925 he became a member of the directing staff of the Army Staff College, Camberley. In 1928 he became deputy director of staff duties at the Air Ministry, and in 1930 he carried out a tour as air attaché in Berlin. Here his kindly manner and ready sympathy stood him in good stead. A period as senior staff officer at headquarters, air defence of Great Britain, was followed by further posts abroad. In 1934 he was senior staff officer in Iraq, and in 1935 he was given command of British forces in Aden. His wide operational experience led him to deliver a series of lectures in 1937, at the University of London, on air power and its employment. These were subsequently published as a much-quoted textbook, *The Royal Air Force* (1937). In the same year he was appointed CB and CVO, and in 1941 he was advanced to the KCB.

From 1936 until spring 1940, with the rank of air vice-marshal, Gossage commanded the newly formed 11 fighter group. He brought the group to the keen fighting pitch which was so marked when it bore the brunt of the German attack during the battle of Britain. However, he left the group in February 1940 to become inspector-general of the RAF. Two months later he moved to the Air Council, where he was in charge of personnel; he was also created air marshal. In November he became air officer commanding of balloon command, an important position which he held until February 1944, when he was created chief commandant and director-general of the Air Training Corps (ATC). This new position had been created to strengthen the close association between the ATC and the RAF and provide favourable conditions for post-war development. It was a post in which Gossage's personal charm and organizational ability had full scope. In 1946 he retired, and his premature death, at his home, Abbotswood, Buxted, Sussex, on 8 July 1949, was a profound loss to his many friends. He was considered one of the most gifted staff officers of his time, and as an exponent of air policy and air fighting tactics he had few rivals.

P. B. JOUBERT, *rev.* RICHARD A. SMITH

Sources *The Times* (9 July 1949) · personal knowledge (1959) · RAF public relations department file, RAF Museum, Hendon · *WWW*
Archives FILM IWM FVA, actuality footage · IWM FVA, documentary footage
Likenesses W. Stoneman, photograph, 1937, NPG · H. Lamb, chalk drawing, 1942, IWM · H. Coster, photographs, NPG
Wealth at death £78,009 4s. 10d.: probate, 1 Oct 1949, *CGPLA Eng. & Wales*

Gossage, William (1799–1877), chemical manufacturer, was born on 12 May 1799 in Burgh-le-Marsh, Lincolnshire, the youngest of thirteen children of Thomas Gossage and his wife, Eleanor. He had little schooling, and went to work at the age of twelve, apprenticed to an uncle in a chemist and druggist business in Chesterfield. At once he showed a determined character, setting himself, for example, to master the French language. He took out his first patent at the age of twenty-four, after inventing a portable alarm to attach to watches and clocks. For a time he was assistant to the manager at a works at Ardwick Bridge owned by the Tennant Company of St Rollox. He set up on his own in Leamington, trading in medicinal salts, but in 1831 changed his activity to that of manufacturing salt and alkali in Stoke Prior in Worcestershire, a site valuable for its nearness to the Droitwich salt deposits, and to the new lines of transport communication provided by the Birmingham and Worcester Canal.

In 1836 Gossage demonstrated a solution to an outstanding environmental problem. The main method of alkali manufacture at the time was that of Nicolas Leblanc, which had the defect of pouring into the air large quantities of hydrogen chloride gas, an extremely noxious pollutant. In 1836 Gossage devised a method of absorbing the acid gas; a steady stream of water descending a tower (the

'Gossage tower') containing twigs, bracken, and bricks, came in contact with a steady stream of ascending gas, dissolving it and thus bringing the dangerous nuisance under a high degree of control. This power of control made it possible to enact the Alkali Works Act of 1863, the first statute to provide a quantitative measure of pollution control. Gossage's invention also provided the starting point for the process devised by Walter Weldon for making chlorine and bleaching powder, an invaluable aid to the textile industry.

For a time Gossage manufactured white lead in Birmingham (1841–4), and then adventured in copper smelting in Neath in south Wales (1844–8). Gossage moved to Widnes in 1850, and experimented with a method of extracting sulphur from copper ores, eventually concentrating on the manufacture of alkali. Sodium carbonate had been the main product of the alkali industry, but Gossage saw a need to develop sodium hydroxide (caustic soda) and pursued this. The suppression of the tax on soap in 1852 encouraged him to embark on soap manufacture. He set up his own works in 1855 and produced his first bar of mottled soap in 1857. This became famous under the brand name of Gossage. Outside business he made a significant contribution to the development of Widnes.

On 22 May 1824 Gossage married Mary Herbert of Leamington; they had a family of seven children. Two of the sons, Alfred and Frederick, continued to expand the family business after their father's death. Gossage died at Earlsleigh, Dunham Massey, Altrincham, Cheshire, on 9 April 1877. FRANK GREENAWAY, rev.

Sources J. Fenwick Allen, *Some founders of the chemical industry: men to be remembered* (1906) · D. W. F. Hardie, *A history of the chemical industry in Widnes* (1950) · D. W. F. Hardie, 'Chemical pioneers 15: William Gossage', *Chemical Age*, 79 (1958), 363 · P. N. Reed, 'William Gossage and the Widnes soap industry', *Journal of the North Western Society for Industrial Archaeology and History*, 3 (1982) · P. N. Reed, 'Gossage, William', *DBB* · d. cert. · *IGI*

Wealth at death under £160,000: probate, 2 May 1877, *CGPLA Eng. & Wales*

Sir Edmund William Gosse (1849–1928), by John Singer Sargent, 1886

Gosse, Sir Edmund William (1849–1928), writer, was born on 21 September 1849 at 13 Trafalgar Terrace, De Beauvoir Square, Hackney, Middlesex, the only child of Philip Henry *Gosse (1810–1888), zoologist, and his first wife, Emily *Gosse, née Bowes (1806–1857), writer of religious tracts. Edmund Gosse's childhood is described in his most important book, *Father and Son* (1907), subtitled 'a study of two temperaments'. In it Gosse suggests that most of his time until his mother's death was spent confined in a small dark London house, but almost as much was spent in Dorset, Devon, and Wales, where his father was gathering material for his books. Emily Gosse died of breast cancer in 1857 and father and son moved to Sandhurst, St Marychurch, near Torquay, where P. H. Gosse was to live for the rest of his life. In January 1867, patchily educated but already a passionate reader, seventeen-year-old Edmund Gosse left Devon to start work as a clerk in the library of the British Museum, a post secured for him with the help of his father's old friend Charles Kingsley.

The immense appeal of *Father and Son*, a book which was fundamentally to change Gosse's reputation, is that it shows in a most vivid form (full of the quiddity in which Gosse always delighted) the new generation freeing itself from the old, the son breaking away from the patterns and constraints of the father. P. H. Gosse FRS was a fundamentalist Christian who burnt with the need to protect Edmund from the world, the flesh, and the devil. His main concern, apart from his work, was his son's salvation. The conflict and struggle continued for years, with young Gosse attempting to define a Christianity he could practise without cutting himself off from the world. In 1873 he was still teaching in the Sunday school in Tottenham, where his father had found him lodgings with two devout elderly women. His work at the museum was tedious but it brought him into contact with some minor poets—Theo Marzials, Arthur O'Shaugnessy, and Richard Garnett—and within a few years, through his friendship with William Bell Scott and Ford Madox Brown, into a close relationship with the Pre-Raphaelites. Gosse was moving very slowly towards a position where he would say, as an elderly man, when asked what he believed in: 'Nothing supernatural, thank God!' (Benson, diary, 1905).

It was through Madox Brown that Gosse met Ellen Epps (1850–1929), always known as Nellie, who became his wife on 13 August 1875. She was one of the painter's pupils and her sister Laura was married to Lawrence Alma-Tadema. The Gosses' marriage was a good one and when apart they wrote to each other every day, with much of this correspondence surviving. Their first home was in Delamere Terrace, where they entertained regularly on Sunday afternoons, a practice they continued at Hanover Terrace,

Regent's Park, after their move in 1901. Osbert Sitwell's 'courteous revelation' in *Noble Essences* and the Beerbohm cartoon commemorating the 'birthday surprise' (Gosse confronted by his own bust) both enshrine the elderly man of letters surrounded by eminent admiring friends. Gosse's friendship with Hamo Thornycroft, the sculptor, was probably the most important in a life full of rewarding friendships. Friendship and art were the two things that mattered, and passionate friendship could even make books seem unimportant. Gosse's talk was famous. Sitwell wrote of his 'sense of the ludicrous', his 'gaiety and dash', his 'fighting spirit—a nature perhaps a little feline' (Sitwell, 46, 37). George Saintsbury said Gosse had 'a genius for knowing people' (Saintsbury). He also, according to another friend, Henry James, had 'a genius for inaccuracy' (*Henry James: Letters*, 3.338). This mattered as a critic and a biographer but his first ambition was to be a poet.

Gosse shared his first book—*Madrigals, Songs and Sonnets* (1870)—with his friend John Blaikie. Of the 140 copies printed, with Gosse's father's financial help, only 12 were actually sold. But the complimentary copies the young man circulated brought him several friends of importance, especially D. G. Rossetti and A. C. Swinburne, and Tennyson commented kindly on the poems when he met Gosse the following year. But Gosse was never to achieve the recognition he longed for as a leading poet of his period. When he was writing *King Erik (a Tragedy)* (1876), a verse play, Gosse said in an 1876 letter to Austin Dobson that 'rhymes flowed like the River of God'. It dealt with the journey of the Danish king to Jerusalem to expiate a sin. The dedication to the 1890 reissue of *On Viol and Flute* (1873) suggests that Gosse already realized his poetry would not survive.

Find room for this frail guest that comes—
This bunch of pale chrysanthemums.
An hour or two its blooms may give …

In 1901 Gosse wrote in a copy of *Firdausi in Exile* (1876): 'This is the volume of my verses which has most of the tension of real life in it.' Some of his best poems, such as 'The Wounded Gull' and 'The Wallpaper' (which Gosse left out of his *Collected Poems*, 1911), do suggest real life and feeling, but most are pale indeed, 'poetic' and 'literary', in the worst sense.

As a biographer Gosse remains very readable, particularly when writing partly from personal knowledge—as in his lives of his father, P. H. Gosse (1890), Coventry Patmore (1905), and Swinburne (1917). Although he initially had to exercise self-censorship in the case of Swinburne (making up for it later with a 'Confidential Paper' deposited in the British Museum), Gosse believed a biographer, though ideally sympathetic, should never be blind or indulgent. He recognized biography's role simply 'to satisfy curiosity', rather than to celebrate virtue (*Anglo-Saxon Review*, 26 Feb 1901). Gosse's two-volume life of John Donne (1899) and his brief lives of Thomas Gray, Sir Walter Raleigh, William Congreve, and Henrik Ibsen have long been superseded and are sometimes inaccurate, but made a considerable impact in their time.

Apart from *Father and Son*, Gosse's most enduring writing is found in his collections of essays. Most appeared first in American or English magazines and from 1919 in the *Sunday Times*, for which Gosse was chief book reviewer until his death in 1928. A collection, *Portraits from Life* (1991), brings together some of the best of Gosse's studies of his friends, including portraits of Robert Louis Stevenson, Robert Browning, Swinburne, and Henry James and an account of a visit in 1912 to Thomas Hardy, whom Gosse admired equally as novelist, poet, and friend.

Gosse's first critical book, *Studies in the Literature of Northern Europe* (1879), dealt with a subject which few of his reviewers knew anything about, and it established him as an impressive critic. His knowledge of the Scandinavian languages led to his early discovery and championship of Ibsen. Gosse had by then moved from the British Museum to the Board of Trade. His colleagues included the poet Austin Dobson, and his situation was now very different. He had a comfortable room to himself and there were many days when, as Arthur Waugh put it, 'the official translator was free of official translating and found time for talk and confidences before he settled down to write an article for the *Saturday Review* or the *St James's Gazette*' (Waugh, 191).

Gosse's reputation as a writer and speaker was such that in 1884 his friend W. D. Howells secured him an invitation to give the prestigious Lowell lectures in Boston, Massachusetts. Since 1881 Gosse had been the *Century Magazine*'s first London agent and his American connections were always important to him. At the first lecture all 850 seats were filled and 150 were turned away. Admittedly the seats were free, but it still seems an extraordinary audience for a lecture entitled 'Poetry at the death of Shakespeare'. Gosse had given the same lecture in Cambridge two months earlier, the first of his Clark lectures. His supporters for that appointment (which he felt would give him the longed-for academic respectability—and an honorary MA) included Matthew Arnold, Robert Browning, and Alfred, Lord Tennyson.

But it was these lectures, published by Cambridge University Press in 1885 as *From Shakespeare to Pope*, which gave rise to the most painful episode of Gosse's career—a 'beastly business' as Henry James called it (*Henry James: Letters*, 3.137). 'The scandal of the year' (*Critic*, 20 Nov 1886) dogged Gosse for the rest of his life. Gosse was ferociously attacked by his one-time friend John Churton Collins, a fanatic and pedant who was able to point out a number of glaring errors in his work. Collins was championing academic standards at a time when the study of English literature had yet to establish itself in the ancient universities, and while his attack was justified, Cambridge and literary London on the whole remained loyal to Gosse. With his social cleverness, his charm, his excellent talk, Gosse had somehow, for all his unorthodox background, succeeded in becoming part of the establishment.

Gosse became one of the most prolific and powerful writers of his time. In 1904 he was appointed librarian of the House of Lords, a position that suited him admirably, for he had long enjoyed the company of the aristocracy.

Edward Marsh felt that there had been nothing so suitable since the accession of Queen Victoria, but the noble Lords' weaknesses and foibles amused Gosse far more than their splendours impressed him. His closest friend, now and until the end of his life, was Lord Haldane. It was while Asquith was prime minister that Gosse was at the height of his influence. Asquith sought his advice on such things as the appointment to the new Cambridge English chair, on the new lord chamberlain, whether George Meredith should be buried in Westminster Abbey, whether Yeats should have a civil-list pension, and who in 1913 should be the new poet laureate. Gosse sat on countless committees, among them those of the Royal Society of Literature, the Royal Literary Fund, the Nobel prize English committee, the London Library, and the Anglo-French Society.

France was important to Gosse. On his seventieth birthday a French newspaper called him 'un grand ami de la France et grand ami de la littérature française'. He championed André Gide, seeing *La porte étroite* as a Gallic counterpart to *Father and Son*; they both owed to literature their liberation from the constraints of Calvinism. Gosse was made a commandeur of the Légion d'honneur and in 1925 received an honorary doctorate from the Sorbonne (in front of more than three thousand people), one of six honorary degrees he was awarded over the years.

In *The Criterion* in September 1927 T. S. Eliot's 'Sir Edmund Gosse on French poetry' concluded that Sir Edmund was 'completely out of touch with modern poetry'. Gosse was then seventy-eight and it was a measure of his unusual staying power that Eliot should have expected him still to be in touch. Certainly Gosse had little time for Eliot or Pound, but he admired Yeats, praised Robert Graves, and did a great deal to encourage Siegfried Sassoon.

Public criticism of Gosse was rare towards the end of his life, though both Virginia Woolf and Evelyn Waugh were muttering against him in their diaries. Gosse died on 16 May 1928, after an operation, in a nursing home at 50 Weymouth Street, London. He was survived by his three children: Emily Teresa (Tessa); Philip Henry George *Gosse (1879–1959), naturalist and physician; and (Laura) Sylvia *Gosse (1881–1968), artist [*see under* Sickert, Walter, pupils]. In the years that followed his death there have been regular suggestions that Gosse, far from being the pillar of the establishment Bloomsbury abhorred, had in fact been involved in the Wise forgeries and had been a secret homosexual. Neither suggestion was true. T. S. Eliot wrote in *The Criterion* in July 1931: 'The place that Sir Edmund Gosse filled in the literary and social life of London is one that no one can ever fill again, because it is, so to speak, an office that has been abolished.' But it now seems not only that Gosse held that office well but that he performed functions that still need to be performed by those who care about literature. ANN THWAITE

Sources A. Thwaite, *Edmund Gosse: a literary landscape, 1849–1928* (1984) • E. Charteris, *The life and letters of Sir Edmund Gosse* (1931) • P. Mattheisen, 'Edmund Gosse: a literary record', PhD diss., Rutgers University, New Brunswick, 1959 • M. Millgate and P. Mattheisen, *Transatlantic dialogue: selected American correspondence*

of Edmund Gosse (1980) • A. C. Benson, diary, Magd. Cam. • O. Sitwell, *Noble essences: a book of characters* (1950) • G. Saintsbury, *London Mercury*, 18 (1928) • A. Waugh, *One man's road* (1931) • *Henry James: letters*, ed. L. Edel, 3: *1883–1895* (1980) • D. L. Wertheimer, 'Philip Henry Gosse: science and revelation in the crucible', PhD diss., University of Toronto, 1977

Archives BL, corresp. • Bodl. Oxf., corresp. • CUL, corresp. and MSS • Duke U., Perkins L., corresp. and MSS • Harvard U., Houghton L., corresp. and MSS • HLRO, diary • Hunt. L., letters and literary MSS • NL Scot., travel journal • Ransom HRC, corresp. and MSS • Rutgers University, New Brunswick, Archibald S. Alexander Library, corresp. • U. Leeds, Brotherton L., corresp. and MSS • University of Rochester, New York, Rush Rhees Library, corresp. and papers • W. Yorks. AS, Leeds, MSS | BL, letters to William Archer, Add. MS 45291 • BL, corresp. with Sir Sydney Cockerell, Add. MS 52717 • BL, corresp. with Macmillans, Add. MS 55012 • BL, letters to T. Watts-Dunton, Ashley MS 822 • Bodl. Oxf., letters to Robert Bridges; letters to C. H. Daniel; corresp. with Gilbert Murray • Herts. ALS, letters to Lady Desborough • HLRO, corresp. with John St Loe Strachey • Hove Central Library, Sussex, letters to Lord and Lady Wolseley • LUL, corresp. with Austin Dobson • NL Scot., corresp.; corresp. with Sir Graham Balfour; corresp. with Lord Haldane • priv. coll., letters to Sir Norman Moore • Royal Literary Fund, London, letters as sponsor to Royal Literary Fund • Royal Society of Literature, letters to the Royal Society of Literature • Rutgers University, New Brunswick, letters to Siegfried Sassoon • TCD, corresp. with Edward Dowden • U. Leeds, Brotherton L., letters to Austin Dobson; letters to A. C. Swinburne; corresp. with Sir Hamo Thornycroft, etc.; letters to Theodore Watts-Dunton

Likenesses J. S. Sargent, oils, 1886, NPG [*see illus.*] • J. S. Sargent, oils, 1886, U. Leeds, Brotherton L. • B. Stone, two photographs, 1904, NPG • S. Gosse, etching, 1911, V&A • W. G. John, bronze bust, 1920, Palace of Westminster, London • W. Rothenstein, pencil drawing, 1928, NPG • M. Beerbohm, political caricatures, Savile Club, London • M. Beerbohm, political caricatures, Harvard TC • M. Beerbohm, political caricatures, U. Texas • M. Beerbohm, political caricatures, AM Oxf. • W. Bellows, photograph (with Thomas Hardy), NPG • D. Low, pencil caricature, NPG • J. Russell & Sons, cabinet photograph, NPG • J. Russell & Sons, photograph, NPG • W. Stoneman, photograph, NPG

Wealth at death £26,255 16s. 10d.: probate, 24 July 1928, *CGPLA Eng. & Wales*

Gosse [*née* Bowes], **Emily** (1806–1857), writer of religious tracts, was born on 10 November 1806 in London. Her father, William Bowes (1771–1850), son of a Boston merchant who was later banished as a loyalist, had been brought to England as a child in 1776. Described variously as 'gentleman' and 'independent', he held a lieutenant's commission in the South Devon militia (1798–1804). Her mother, Hannah (1768–1851), was the daughter of the Revd John Troutbeck of Cumberland, who had spent his middle years in Massachusetts. Her brothers, Edmund Elford and Arthur, were born in Wales in 1808 and 1813 respectively. Emily's childhood was spent in Merioneth and Exmouth, Devon. From 1819 to 1824 she lived mainly in London. She served as governess in the families of the Revd John Hawkins in Berkshire (1824–38) and the late Revd Sir Christopher John Musgrave in Hove (1838–41).

On returning to her parents' home in Clapton, London, Emily Bowes joined the Brethren assembly at Hackney where, two years later, the naturalist Philip Henry *Gosse (1810–1888) arrived. They married on 22 November 1848 at Brook Street Chapel, Tottenham. Their only child, Edmund William *Gosse, was born on 21 September 1849.

In Berkshire, Emily wrote many religious poems, and in London wrote her major work, *Abraham and his Children* (1855), which offers guidance on parental duties illustrated by biblical, mainly Old Testament, characters. More popular were her many articles in religious periodicals and more than sixty evangelistic tracts, which were printed in very large quantities. She herself was an ardent distributor of tracts. Emily died on 10 February 1857, at 58 Huntingdon Street, Islington, from breast cancer, and was buried in Abney Park cemetery, Stoke Newington.

Many of Edmund Gosse's references to his mother in his *Life of Philip Henry Gosse*, *Father and Son*, and his memoir of her in the *Dictionary of National Biography* are inaccurate, conflicting with her diary and correspondence: the date of his mother's death, for instance, differs from that given by her husband on her death certificate.

ROBERT BOYD and HAROLD H. ROWDON

Sources R. B. Freeman and D. Wertheimer, *Philip Henry Gosse: a bibliography* (1980) · P. H. Gosse, *A memorial of the last days on earth of Emily Gosse* (1857) · A. Shipton, *Tell Jesus* (1863) · d. cert.
Archives CUL, MSS

Gosse, Philip Henry (1810–1888), zoologist and religious writer, was born on 6 April 1810 at the High Street, Worcester, the second of four children of Thomas Gosse (1765–1844) a mezzotint engraver and itinerant painter of miniature portraits, and Hannah Best (1780–1860), who before her marriage had been a domestic servant. His childhood was spent in Poole, Dorset, where at an early age he demonstrated a marked enthusiasm for natural history which was encouraged by his aunt Susan Gosse (1750–1829), who was herself a gifted naturalist. After attending local schools, including Blandford grammar school in 1823–4, he began work as a junior clerk. In June 1827 he was indentured with the firm Slade, Elson & Co. of Carbonear, Newfoundland. There he developed further his interest in natural history. In 1832 he returned to England and during the voyage underwent a religious experience that was to determine the course of the rest of his life. On his return to Carbonear he joined the Methodist Society and became friends with an emigrant couple from Liverpool, Mr and Mrs Jaques, who had an important influence on the development of his religious views.

At this time Gosse also decided to professionalize his interest in natural history and to this end he began a careful documentation of the entomology of Newfoundland. The result was his 'Entomologia Terrae Novae', which although still unpublished is today of scientific importance as a valuable historical record of the distribution of the insects in Newfoundland.

On 21 June 1835 Gosse left Carbonear together with the Jaqueses to settle in Lower Canada, where they planned to set up an agricultural co-operative. Their plans, however, were doomed to failure for none of them had any farming experience and the land was poor. The farm of 110 acres which they purchased jointly for £100 was situated near the village of Waterville, 1 mile north of Compton in the county of Sherbrooke in the Eastern townships. They

Philip Henry Gosse (1810–1888), by Maull & Polyblank, 1855

quickly discovered that they had made a mistake in moving to Lower Canada, yet despite the considerable hardships incurred Gosse was able to maintain his optimism. Indeed, the outdoor life served to stimulate his passion for natural history, and he became known locally as 'that crazy Englishman who goes about collecting bugs' (Fyles, *Canadian Entomologist*, 17). During the long winter months he wrote up his scientific observations, which he submitted to the Literary and Historical Society of Quebec, and he supplemented his income by teaching in the Compton village school.

In March 1838 Gosse sold his part of the farm and left for the United States where he hoped to secure a teaching position. He visited the Academy of Natural Sciences in Philadelphia where he met the palaeontologist T. A. Conrad, who suggested that he should go to Alabama where there was a shortage of schoolmasters; accordingly, on 18 April 1838, Gosse departed aboard the schooner *White Oak* for Mobile. On his arrival in Alabama he secured a position in a small school in the village of Mount Pleasant, just north of Clairborne, but his stay there was unhappy, largely on account of the widespread abuse of slaves; he was particularly disturbed by the attitude of the local Methodist community in their strong defence of slavery. The upshot was that he decided to return to England, and on 6 January 1839 he left Mobile.

On his arrival in England, Gosse applied to the Methodist church to train as a full-time evangelist but was turned down on account of his age. He moved to London where he obtained dismal lodgings in Drury Lane and, desperate for money, trudged the streets selling his paintings. For a time things looked very bleak but towards the end of 1839 his fortunes changed when he took over a small day school in Hackney and a manuscript he had written of his Canadian experiences was accepted by the publisher Van Voorst. The book was published the following year with the title *The Canadian Naturalist: a Series of Conversations on the Natural History of Lower Canada*. It received widespread praise and although it was written in an archaic format it none the less demonstrated a freshness of style. It is important today as it reveals that Gosse had a practical grasp of the importance of conservation, far ahead of his time.

In October 1844 Gosse left London aboard the *Caroline* for Jamaica, where he intended to work as a professional collector for the dealer Hugh Cuming. In all he spent eighteen months on the island, this being the most productive and happy period of his life. He lived at Bluefields, near Savanna la Mar, then the centre of Moravian missionary activity, and to help him he engaged a young West Indian, Samuel Campbell (1827–1892), with whom he formed a successful collecting partnership. At this time he also collaborated with the naturalist Richard Hill (1795–1872) of Spanish Town.

Gosse left Jamaica on 26 June 1846 and on his return to London set about writing up his work. The result was the trilogy *The Birds of Jamaica* (1847), *Illustrations to the Birds of Jamaica* (1848–9), and *A Naturalist's Sojourn in Jamaica* (1851). The latter is considered to be his finest work. It is written in a congenial style and firmly established his reputation both as a naturalist and a writer. Today, Gosse is still remembered in Jamaica where he is referred to as the 'father of Jamaican ornithology' and there is a bird club named after him.

In 1843 Gosse was introduced by William Berger to a small group of Christians known as the Brethren who met weekly in his house in Hackney. It was at one of these meetings that he met Emily Bowes (1806–1857) [*see* Gosse, Emily], an established writer of evangelical tracts, whom he married on 22 November 1848. She had a profound influence on the development of his religious views. Their marriage proved extremely happy and on 21 September 1849 she gave birth to their only child, Edmund William *Gosse.

During the following years Gosse produced a succession of highly successful books on natural history, but the considerable overwork this entailed led to a breakdown in his health and he was advised to leave London for the country. Early in 1852 he settled in Torquay, then later in that year he moved to Ilfracombe. It was here he wrote *A Naturalist's Rambles on the Devonshire Coast*, published in 1853, which brought before the public the science of marine biology, and was partly responsible for the sea-shore craze of the mid-Victorian period. (As the famous, eccentric, and deeply religious Devon naturalist, he is the model for Theophilus Hopkins in Peter Carey's prize-winning novel *Oscar and Lucinda*, 1988.) In May 1853 he helped establish the first public aquarium in Regent's Park and later that year constructed one of the first domestic glass aquariums. The following year he published *The Aquarium* which triggered a second craze to sweep through Victorian society.

Much of Gosse's success was due to the fact that he was essentially a field naturalist who was able to impart to his readers something of the thrill of studying living animals at first hand rather than the dead disjointed ones of the museum shelf. In addition to this he was a skilled scientific draughtsman who was able to illustrate his books himself. Indeed the chromolithographic plates in *The Aquarium* and *Actinologia Britannica* (1860) were prepared from his own watercolours and were a major advance in natural history book illustration intended for the mass market.

In 1856 Gosse was elected FRS, and was now the leading popularizer of natural history in the country. However, in April tragedy struck when Emily Gosse discovered she had breast cancer. After much deliberation and prayer they opted for treatment by the American physician Jesse Weldon Fell (1819–1890); he claimed to have discovered a non-surgical cure for this disease, but it proved disastrous, and on 10 February 1857 Emily died after much suffering. Gosse wrote of the episode in a small monograph entitled *A Memorial of the Last Days on Earth of Emily Gosse*, a curious work originally intended for private circulation, which reveals much of Gosse's character and is today of considerable interest to the medical historian. At some time in 1857 Gosse became alarmed by the extent to which many scientists were taking the developmental theory, yet he could not deny the scientific evidence which indicated that the earth was far older than had been previously believed. His precipitate action was to publish, *Omphalos: an Attempt to Untie the Geological Knot*, which he hoped would reconcile geology with the biblical account of creation and so halt the decline into apostasy. In it he proposed the universal law of prochronism, and argued that the earth had been created with fossils already in the rocks, giving it a false appearance of age, just as Adam would have had a navel, indicating an apparent past (*omphalos* is the Greek for navel) although it had never been attached to an umbilical cord. Although *Omphalos* was widely reviewed, it was none the less universally condemned by both Christians and evolutionists alike. Gosse, however, stood firm and in 1866 issued a supplement entitled *Geology and God: which?*, in which he reaffirmed the prochronism hypothesis and replied to one of the main objections, namely that his theory implied God to be *Deus quidam deceptor*. Then in 1872 he again publicly defended *Omphalos* and wrote: 'Many have sneered at it (an easy process!) but I have not yet met with a single adversary who accepting my postulates have convicted me of non-sequitur' (*English Mechanic and World of Science*, 24 May 1872, 255). He claimed he had been greatly misunderstood, which is probably true (for it is clear he had never intended to defend a narrowly literalist interpretation of Genesis), but the damage had been done and his reputation had been ruined. To add to this *Omphalos* was a huge financial loss, but he bore this stoically and with good humour, for on 8 May 1869 he instructed his publisher Van Voorst to remainder the book and wrote: 'will you please arrange it: they will probably offer you as an old fox more than one whom they consider a Goose' ('Correspondence book of P. H. Gosse', privately held).

On 23 September 1857 Gosse moved to Sandhurst, St Marychurch, on the outskirts of Torquay. Soon afterwards he established an independent chapel in Fore Street, where for almost three decades he ministered to a congregation of about a hundred. On 18 December 1860 he married at the Zion Chapel, Frome, a Quaker spinster, Eliza Brightwen (1813–1900). She was a kind, tolerant woman who shared his interest in natural history as well as having considerable skills as a watercolourist. In 1864 she received a substantial inheritance and this gave Gosse the financial security he had previously lacked.

In addition to his scientific writing Gosse wrote widely on religious matters, his publications ranging from evangelical tracts to a history of the Jewish people. He was particularly interested by biblical prophecy and on this subject he published several fascinating monographs including *The Revelation* (1866). For relaxation he grew orchids and in his latter years took up astronomy and landscape painting. Although often misunderstood Gosse was a man of great goodness of heart who, beneath an austere outward appearance, had genuine warmth and sensitivity. He had a good sense of humour and to his generosity there was a practical dimension. Throughout his life he had an optimistic outlook: 'Hope has always been strong in me', he recalled (P. H. Gosse, CUL, Add. MS 7017, 212). He had good health and was physically strong. In March 1888 he suffered a heart attack; although he recovered, from then on his health gradually declined and he died at his home on 23 August that year. He was buried in the Torquay cemetery.   L. R. CROFT

Sources P. H. Gosse, 'Anecdotes and reminiscences of my life', 1868–88, CUL, Add. MSS 7016–7017 · E. Gosse, *The life of Philip Henry Gosse* (1890) · R. B. Freeman and D. Wertheimer, *Philip Henry Gosse: a bibliography* (1980) · D. L. Wertheimer, 'Philip Henry Gosse: science and revelation in the crucible', PhD diss., University of Toronto, 1977 · A. Thwaite, *Edmund Gosse: a literary landscape, 1849–1928* (1984) · P. Stageman, *A bibliography of the first editions of Philip Henry Gosse* (1955) · T. W. Fyles, 'A visit to the Canadian haunts of the late Philip Henry Gosse', *Annual Report of the Entomological Society of Ontario*, 23 (1892), 22–9 · R. Boyd, 'Philip Henry Gosse, 1810–1888', *Christian Brethren Research Fellowship Broadsheet* (March–April 1969), 4–5 · F. Gosse, 'Philip Henry Gosse, FRS', *The Gosses: an Anglo-Australian family* (1981), 42–62 · T. W. Fyles, *Canadian Entomologist*, 21 (1889), 17–19 · L. R. Croft, 'Edmund Gosse and the "new and fantastic cure" for breast cancer', *Medical History*, 38 (1994), 143–59 · A. Thwaite, *Glimpses of the wonderful: the life of Philip Henry Gosse, 1810–1888* (2002) · L. R. Croft, *Gosse: the life of Philip Henry Gosse* (2000)

Archives Canadian Museum of Nature, Ottawa · CUL, corresp. and papers · Horniman Museum and Library, London, corresp. and drawings · National Library of Jamaica, Kingston · NHM, notebooks · NRA, priv. coll., biblical and general notes · U. Edin. L., letters · U. Leeds, Brotherton L., corresp. and papers · University of Toronto Library, Thomas Fisher Rare Book Library, sketchbook · W. Yorks. AS, Leeds, papers | Bodl. Oxf., letters to Robert McLachlan · Horniman Museum and Library, London, letters to A. C. Haddon · Oxf. U. Mus. NH, letters to J. O. Westwood

Likenesses T. Gosse, watercolour, 1821, BL · W. Gosse, two oil paintings, 1827–35, CUL · W. Gosse, miniature, 1839, NPG · Maull & Polyblank, photograph, 1855, NPG [see illus.] · photograph, 1857, NPG · photograph, 1860, BM · J. E. Mayall, daguerreotype, BL

Wealth at death £16,196 8s. 1d.: probate, 12 Oct 1888, *CGPLA Eng. & Wales*

Gosse, Philip Henry George (1879–1959), general practitioner and writer on natural history, was born at 29 Delamere Terrace, Paddington, London, on 13 August 1879, the only son and second of three children of Sir Edmund William *Gosse (1849–1928), writer, and his wife, Ellen (Nellie; 1850–1929), painter, daughter of George Napoleon Epps; Ellen Gosse's sister was married to Sir Lawrence Alma-Tadema. Sylvia *Gosse [see under Sickert, Walter, pupils (act. 1890–1939)] was his sister. Educated at Haileybury College (1892–4), Gosse subsequently studied agriculture at Wellingore Hall, Lincolnshire (1894–6). His chief early interest, inherited from his grandfather, Philip Henry *Gosse (1810–1888), was natural history; this led to a trip to Newfoundland in 1895. In 1896 he was appointed naturalist to the Fitzgerald expedition to the Andes, and on his return he contributed 'Notes on the natural history of the Aconcagua valley' to E. A. Fitzgerald's *The Highest Andes* (1899).

Despite Gosse's passionate interest in natural history, his father insisted that he should have a recognized profession, and the choice eventually fell upon medicine. From 1899 he studied at St Bartholomew's Hospital, and qualified as MRCS and LRCP (1907); he attained the degree of MD (Durham) about 1910. After six months as a house surgeon at Essex County Hospital, Colchester, he set up as a country doctor in the New Forest, his amusing recollections of which appeared in *St Bartholomew's Hospital Journal* (1933–5).

Gosse's career was interrupted by the outbreak of war in 1914, in which he served as a captain in the Royal Army Medical Corps. In France until autumn 1917, he was then transferred to India until the armistice. His wartime recollections, *Memoirs of a Camp-Follower*, were published in 1934, and were later reissued as *A Naturalist Goes to War* (1942).

After 1918 Gosse worked as a medical referee for the Ministry of Pensions, and later at the Radium Institute, eventually becoming its medical superintendent. He retired from medicine in 1930 and became a full-time writer, producing three biographies, a history of St Helena (1938), and a *History of Piracy* (1932); this earned him an international reputation, and was translated into French, Spanish, and Dutch. Yet Gosse's most enjoyable works are his elegantly written and witty books of recollections, which include *Go to the Country* (1935), *Traveller's Rest* (1937), and *An Apple a Day* (1948).

Gosse was an entertaining companion; his somewhat mordant manner hid an essentially kind personality, and he was especially fond of young company. His humour was sometimes expressed in schoolboyish practical jokes, but he possessed also a quicksilver wit, as illustrated by his remark to Lady (Margaret) Keynes (née Darwin), who told him she had been bitten by an ape at Gibraltar: 'He was having revenge on the Darwins.'

Gosse's friends invariably forgave him for his wayward humour. He possessed a genius for friendship which is reflected in the many literary people who knew, liked, and respected him, from his cousin, Alec Waugh, and Vyvyan Holland, to Siegfried Sassoon (a distant relative) and the Sitwells. He was for many years Brother Buccaneer to the literary dining club, the Sette of Odd Volumes, where his repartee was much appreciated. From 1941 until 1959 he was a fellow commoner of Trinity College, Cambridge.

Gosse was married three times. On 14 July 1908 he married Gertrude Agnes Gosse Hay (b. 1872/3), an Australian cousin, the daughter of Alexander Hay, colonist and politician. They were divorced and on 28 November 1930 he married Irene Ruth Marden (b. 1897/8), a widow, daughter of Oliver Hawkshaw, gentleman of independent means. After another divorce he married, on 2 February 1943, Anna Gordon Keown (1896/7–1957), poet and novelist. She was the daughter of Robert Keown, a London wool merchant. There was a daughter by each of the first two marriages. Gosse died of food poisoning in Brookfields Hospital, Cambridge, on 3 October 1959, and was cremated at Cambridge crematorium four days later.

RAYMOND LISTER

Sources personal knowledge (2004) · R. Lister, *With my own wings* (1994) · private information (2004) [J. Gosse, daughter; T. Keown; M. Barber, granddaughter] · R. Lister, *A bibliographical check-list of works by Philip Gosse* (1952) · b. cert. · m. certs. · d. cert. · *CGPLA Eng. & Wales* (1960)
Archives CUL, MSS Add. 7019–7035, 7607 · NMM, papers relating to pirates | FM Cam., Raymond Lister archive, letters · Royal Society of Literature, London, letters to the Royal Society of Literature · U. Leeds, Brotherton L., corresp. · U. Reading, letters to Bodley Head Ltd
Likenesses S. Gosse, etching, priv. coll. · photographs, priv. coll.
Wealth at death £46,725 19s. 0d.: probate, 11 Feb 1960, *CGPLA Eng. & Wales*

Gosse, (Laura) Sylvia (1881–1968). *See under* Sickert, Walter, pupils (*act.* 1890–1939).

Gosselin, Sir Martin Le Marchant Hadsley (1847–1905), diplomatist, was born at Walfield, near Hertford, on 2 November 1847. He was grandson of Admiral Thomas Le Marchant *Gosselin and eldest son of Martin Hadsley Gosselin of Ware Priory and Blakesware, Hertfordshire, and his wife, Frances Orris, eldest daughter of Admiral Sir John Marshall of Gillingham House, Kent. Educated at Eton College and at Christ Church, Oxford, he entered the diplomatic service in 1868, and after working in the Foreign Office was appointed attaché at Lisbon in 1869. He was transferred in 1872 to Berlin, where he remained until promoted to be second secretary at St Petersburg in 1874. During the Congress of Berlin in 1878 he was attached to the special mission of the British plenipotentiaries Lord Beaconsfield and Lord Salisbury. In that year he was converted to Roman Catholicism. He was transferred from St Petersburg to Rome in 1879, returned to St Petersburg in the following year, and went to Berlin in 1882.

On 10 August 1880 Gosselin married Katherine Frances (d. 19 April 1924), second daughter of Robert Tolver Gerard, first Baron Gerard (1808–1887), and his wife, Harriet. They had one son and three daughters.

In 1885 Gosselin was promoted to be secretary of legation and was appointed to Brussels, where he served until 1892. In November 1887 he was appointed secretary to the

duke of Norfolk's special mission to Pope Leo XIII on the latter's jubilee. In 1889 and 1890 he and Alfred Bateman of the Board of Trade served as joint British delegates in the conferences held at Brussels to arrange for the mutual publication of customs tariffs, and in July of the latter year he signed the convention for the establishment of an international bureau for that purpose. He was also employed as one of the secretaries to the international conference for the suppression of the African slave trade, which sat at Brussels in 1889 and the following year and resulted in the General Act of 2 July 1890. In recognition of his services he was in 1890 made CB. Later in that year he was one of the British delegates at the conference held by representatives of Great Britain, Germany, and Italy to discuss and fix the duties to be imposed on imports in the conventional basin of the Congo, and he signed the agreement that was negotiated in December 1890. He was promoted in April 1892 to be secretary of embassy at Madrid, was transferred to Berlin in the following year, and to Paris in 1896; at the latter post he received the titular rank of minister-plenipotentiary. In 1897 he was selected to discuss with French commissioners the question of coolie emigration from British India to Réunion, and in that and the following year he served as one of the British members of the Anglo-French commission for the delimitation of the possessions and spheres of influence of the two countries to the east and west of the Niger River. The arrangement arrived at by the commission was embodied in a convention signed at Paris on 14 June 1898, and provided a solution to questions that had gravely threatened the good relations between the two countries. At the close of these negotiations Gosselin was created KCMG. From July 1898 to August 1902 he held the home appointment of assistant under-secretary of state for foreign affairs, and was then sent to Lisbon as British envoy, a post that he held until his death at Busaco, Portugal, on 26 February 1905 as the result of a car accident. The relations of Great Britain with Portugal during Gosselin's residence were uneventful, but Edward VII's sense of his services was marked by his preferment as KCVO in 1903 and as GCVO in 1904. Gosselin was a competent diplomatist of the second rank, a man of fair judgement, good temper, and charm of manner.

T. H. SANDERSON, *rev.* H. C. G. MATTHEW

Sources *The Times* (27 Feb 1905) · *FO List* (1906) · O. Browning, *Memoirs* (1911) · *CGPLA Eng. & Wales* (1905) · Burke, *Gen. GB*
Archives Herts. ALS, corresp. and papers | BL, letters to Sir Edward Walter Hamilton, Add. MSS 48622–48627 · Bodl. Oxf., corresp. with Lord Kimberley · King's AC Cam., letters to Oscar Browning
Wealth at death £33,908 7s. 1d.: probate, 8 June 1905, *CGPLA Eng. & Wales*

Gosselin, Thomas Le Marchant (1765–1857), naval officer, was born at St Peter Port, Guernsey, on 7 May 1765, the second son of Colonel Joshua Gosselin (1739–1813), of the North regiment of militia, of St Peter Port, and his wife, Martha, daughter of Thomas Le Marchant of Guernsey. He entered the navy in 1778 on the *Actaeon*, with Captain Boteler, whom he followed to the *Ardent*, and was captured with her off Plymouth by the combined fleets of

France and Spain on 16 August 1779. Having been appointed to the *Barfleur*, flagship of Sir Samuel (afterwards Lord) Hood, in October 1780, he was present in all the major actions in North America and the West Indies, notably the battle of the Saintes off Dominica on 12 April 1782. He was promoted lieutenant in 1787.

On 23 April 1793, while serving with Commodore Cornwallis in the *Crown*, on the East India station, Gosselin was promoted to command the brig *Dispatch*. He was moved into the sloop *Kingfisher* in March 1794, and in her was present at Lord Howe's victory in the north Atlantic on 1 June, and assisted in the capture of a small French convoy off Belleisle. In July 1794 he was posted into the *Brunswick*. He was appointed to the *Diamond* (38 guns) in 1795, and later moved to the *Syren* (32 guns), which he commanded during the operations on the coast of France under Sir Richard John Strachan. In March 1798 he went in charge of a convoy to Jamaica, and in August 1799 he assisted in the capture of Surinam. During the summer of 1804 he commanded the *Ville de Paris* (110 guns), as flag captain to Admiral Cornwallis, and in 1805, in the frigate *Latona*, he commanded the inshore squadron off Brest. In February 1806 he was appointed to the *Audacious* (74 guns), a ship in the squadron under Sir Richard Strachan, and afterwards, in 1807, one of the Channel Fleet. In 1808, with Sir Harry Burrard and his staff on board, he convoyed a large force of troops to the River Tagus in the Peninsula; and in January 1809 he covered the embarkation of the army at Corunna, a service for which he received the thanks of both houses of parliament. On 18 March 1809 he married Sarah, daughter of Jeremiah Rayment Hadsley of Ware Priory, Hertfordshire. They had children. He had no further service afloat, but he became rear-admiral on 4 June 1814, vice-admiral on 27 May 1825, and admiral on 23 November 1841. Gosselin died at his residence in Jersey on 27 November 1857, and was buried at Bengeo church, Hertfordshire.

Gosselin was a professional officer of real ability whose career came to a premature end; whether this was because of ill health or his marriage to an heiress remains uncertain. J. K. LAUGHTON, *rev.* ANDREW LAMBERT

Sources O'Byrne, *Naval biog. dict.* · W. L. Clowes, *The Royal Navy: a history from the earliest times to the present*, 7 vols. (1897–1903), vols. 4–5 · Boase, *Mod. Eng. biog.* · *GM*, 3rd ser., 3 (1857), 732
Archives NMM, logs and papers

Gosset, Isaac (1713–1799), frame maker and wax modeller, was born in St Helier, Jersey, on 2 May 1713, the sixth and posthumous son of Jean Gosset and his wife, Suzanne d'Allain. His parents had married in St Helier on 11 July 1696, his mother having earlier abjured Roman Catholicism in the parish church. Jean Gosset was a manufacturer of woollens and was said to be the designer of the jersey. The Gosset and d'Allain families had left their villages in the Bayeux area of Normandy as protestant refugees and settled in Jersey. Isaac Gosset spent his boyhood in his mother's parish of Grouville. He left Jersey to serve an apprenticeship in the Soho workshop of his uncle **Matthew Gosset** (1683–1744), a sculptor and wax modeller who had arrived in England direct from France and

became naturalized during the reign of Queen Anne. Matthew Gosset married Jeanne Ester le Touzay in 1700 and they had one child, Angelique-Elizabeth, who was born on 10 May 1709. He had a statuary yard at St Anne's, Westminster, and here in 1714 took on as his apprentice 'Rodney, son of Joseph Stone' (Gunnis, 176). He was elected a member of the Spalding Society in 1728 and was later one of the Band of Pensioners of George II. Following his death in 1744 he was buried in St Marylebone, where his monument bore 'specimens of his work' (ibid., 176).

With his elder brother Jacob Gosset (1701–1788), Isaac began in the Gosset workshop with the craft of frame-carving, for which he continued to accept commissions in later life if the work was prestigious and profitable (Gosset frames were supplied to William Hogarth and Thomas Gainsborough, and the latter painted Isaac's portrait). His reputation rests, however, on the wax cameo portraits he produced chiefly for the adornment of gentlemen's cabinets. He was noted for his rapid execution of remarkable and exquisite likenesses of his sitters in profile. For these he used an undisclosed wax composition in a tint of old ivory, the secret recipe for which is said to have perished with his only son, the Revd Isaac *Gosset (1745–1812), the bibliographer. He contributed to the first artists' exhibition in 1760 and was a member of the Incorporated Society of Artists, contributing twenty-four portraits to their exhibitions between 1760 and 1788. Matthew Gosset was also a wax modeller, though his pieces were of a lesser quality than those of his nephew. As the works of both are often unsigned and contemporary references indicate only 'Mr Gosset' or 'Gosset' as the artist of individual items, confusion has arisen over the attribution of some. The wax portrait of Benjamin Hoadley, bishop of Winchester (formerly in the collection of Horace Walpole), for example, has been attributed to both Matthew and Isaac Gosset. Wax portraits of twelve Roman emperors, and twelve Roman and Greek heads in one frame, recently described as the work of Isaac, were, during the time they were in the possession of the Revd Isaac Gosset, attributed to Matthew, together with an exquisite portrait in an oval frame of John Vincent Anthony Ganganelli, Pope Clement XIV. *The Calydonian Boar Hunt*, *Perseus with the Medusa's Head*, *The Wars of the Titans Against the Gods*, and *Ganymede in the Palace of Jupiter* (all formerly in the possession of Major Arthur Gosset), which are likely to have been based on the celebrated bronze reliefs by Guglielmo della Porta of subjects from Ovid's *Metamorphoses*, have been attributed to Matthew.

Signed works by Isaac Gosset that were formerly in the possession of various members of the Gosset family include *David Garrick* (a beautiful bust under a glass case); a Madonna; a bust, said to be of Sir Joshua Reynolds; a portrait of his own son; and various portraits of royalty, among which are *George II*, *George III*, and *Queen Charlotte*. In the Royal Collection are portraits of Frederick, prince of Wales, and his consort, Augusta; George III; Frederick, duke of York; Princess Augusta Sophia; the prince regent; and a circular medallion said to be of the duke of Sussex.

Gosset also worked for Josiah Wedgwood and modelled for him likenesses of royalty.

In 1761 Isaac Gosset married Françoise Buisset, who was the sister-in-law of his brother Gideon. They had six children, of whom only two appear to have survived, the eldest son, Isaac, and the youngest daughter, Ann, who married John Creuze, high sheriff for Surrey, in 1788. Isaac Gosset died in Kensington on 28 November 1799, aged eighty-six, and was buried in the family vault in Old Marylebone burial-ground. His obituary in the *Gentleman's Magazine* described him as 'one of those ingenious men rarely to be met with, who are at the same time equally amiable and inoffensive' (1799, p. 1088). There is a collection of his wax portraits at Stourhead, Wiltshire (National Trust); others are in the Schreiber Collection in the Victoria and Albert Museum, London, and in the National Portrait Gallery.

MATTHEW CRASKE and LESLEY CRASKE

Sources DNB · E. J. Pyke, *Dictionary of wax modellers* (1973) · T. Murdoch, 'Courtiers and classics: the Gosset family', *Country Life*, 177 (9 May 1985), 1282–3 · M. H. Gosset, 'A family of modellers in wax', *Proceedings of the Huguenot Society*, 3 (1888–91), 540–68, esp. 547 · T. Murdoch, 'Gosset, Isaac', *The dictionary of art*, ed. J. Turner (1996) · H. E. Coutanche, 'The Dallain family', *Channel Islands Family History Journal*, 28 (1985) · R. Gunnis, *Dictionary of British sculptors, 1660–1851* (1953); new edn (1968)
Likenesses T. Gainsborough, oils (Isaac Gosset)

Gosset, Isaac (1745–1812), book collector, was one of only two of the five children of Isaac *Gosset (1713–1799), a modeller of portraits in wax, and his wife, Françoise, to survive infancy. He was born at his father's house opposite the French Huguenot chapel in Berwick Street, Soho, London, on 13 October 1745. He received his first education at Dr John Conder's academy at Mile End, where, under the respected classical tutor Dr John Walker, he quickly mastered the rudiments of Greek, Latin, Hebrew, and Arabic. On 25 February 1764 he matriculated from Exeter College, Oxford, and was placed under George Stinton, later prebendary of Peterborough. At Oxford, Gosset's abilities as a biblical scholar were recognized, and his vivacity and communicativeness gained him many friends. He graduated BA on 10 October 1767 and MA on 27 June 1770. On 18 June 1772 he was elected to the Royal Society. He went out grand compounder for the degrees in divinity on 7 November 1782.

Gosset was a small man, sickly and deformed, and his resemblance to Alexander Pope was remarked on by the poet's friend the earl of Marchmont. Despite his short stature, which forced him to stand in the pulpit on two hassocks, he was a noted preacher at the Trinity Chapel in Conduit Street and elsewhere, and was much in demand for charity sermons. His politics were marked by a hatred of William Pitt and the income tax. On 9 January 1782 he married Catherine (c.1747–1831), daughter of Haydock Hill, a prosperous timber merchant of Newman Street, Marylebone. Mrs Gosset is said to have fallen in love with her husband because of his preaching. The couple had a daughter and three sons, one of whom died in infancy. The eldest son, Isaac Gosset (1782–1855), was vicar of New Windsor and chaplain to the royal household at Windsor

Castle under four sovereigns. The youngest son, Thomas Stephen Gosset (1791–1847), was a fellow of Trinity College, Cambridge, and vicar of Old Windsor.

Even before the bibliomania which began around the time of the Askew sale of 1775, Gosset was a familiar figure in the salerooms of the London book auctioneers. From his customary seat beside the rostrum he kept up a sort of running commentary on the lots as they were put up, his constant use of the phrase 'a pretty copy' causing amusement. While his opinion on bibliographical matters was deferred to, his high spirits in the rooms exposed him to ridicule, and he was taunted by Michael Lort because of his impatience. Offended by a caricature produced for the printseller Alexander Beugo about 1800, Gosset considered abandoning auctions altogether, but instead exchanged his tricorn hat for a more fashionable one, and the caricature was altered accordingly. Many stories are told of his bibliomania, the most celebrated being how, during the sale of Cardinal Maffeo Pinelli's library in 1789, he recovered from a serious illness when a single volume of Cardinal Ximenes' own copy of the Complutensian polyglot Bible on vellum was brought to his bedside. He features in the scabrous *Chalcographimania* (1814) as 'dirty snarling G—ss—t' (p. 57), and in Thomas James Mathias's *The Pursuits of Literature* as 'milk-white Gosset', 'an ingenious, learned, sensible, and chearful man' (quarto edn, 1812, 261).

Towards the end of his life Gosset moved from his residence at Kensington to Newman Street, where he died in his sleep on 16 December 1812. He was buried on 23 December 1812 in the family vault in the Old Marylebone cemetery, on the south side of Paddington Street. Gosset, who lived frugally, had inherited a considerable sum from his father, and by augmenting this with his wife's dowry and by dealing in stocks he was able to make generous provision for his family. Stephen Weston, who was godfather to one of his sons, composed a light-hearted poem on his death entitled 'The tears of the booksellers', which appeared in the *Gentleman's Magazine* (1st ser., 83/1, February 1813, 160), as well as a Latin tribute to him for the fourth edition of William Bowyer's *Critical Conjectures on the New Testament* (1812). Although Gosset's only publications consist of contributions to the third (1782) and fourth editions of Bowyer's book, many of his notes for an edition of the New Testament survive in manuscript in the Bodleian Library (Auct. S.8.9).

Gosset's unostentatious library, strong in grammars, classics, and theology, was sold by Leigh and Sotheby in 5740 lots over twenty-three days between 7 June and 2 July 1813, making a total of £3141 7s. 6d. The classical lots were keenly contested, the principal purchaser being Richard Heber, whom Gosset had regarded as his pupil in book collecting. Many items were acquired by the Bodleian, and others found their way into the collections of Edmund Henry Barker, James Bindley, William Van Mildert, and Martin Joseph Routh. The collection included a long run of sale catalogues, several of which were bought by Thomas Frognall Dibdin. Gosset was for a time Dibdin's neighbour at Kensington, and allowed him to make use of his library when writing the second edition of the *Introduction to the Classics* (1804). He had previously assisted Edward Harwood in the composition of the fourth edition of his *View of the Classics* (1790). Dibdin, whose portrayal of Gosset as Lepidus in the second edition of *Bibliomania* (1811) met with his subject's approval, describes him in his *Reminiscences* (1836) as 'one of the first bibliographers in the country' (Dibdin, *Reminiscences*, 205).

MARC VAULBERT DE CHANTILLY

Sources PRO, IR 26/546, fols. 156v–157v; IR 27/141, fol. 22v; RG 4/4548, fol. 21v · will, PRO, PROB 11/1539, fols. 216v–217r · Metropolitan City Archives, P89/MRY1/169, P89/MRY1/316 · *GM*, 1st ser., 82/1 (1812), 596–7, 669–670 · *GM*, 2nd ser., 28 (1847), 549 · *GM*, 2nd ser., 43 (1855), 435–6 · T. F. Dibdin, *Bibliomania, or, Book madness: a bibliographical romance*, 2nd edn, [2 vols.] (1811), 160–62 · T. F. Dibdin, *The bibliographical decameron*, 3 vols. (1817), 5–8, 78 · T. F. Dibdin, *Reminiscences of a literary life*, 2 vols. (1836), 205, 746–7 · *Kirby's wonderful … museum*, 6 vols. (1803–20), vol. 5, pp. 382–9 · *A catalogue of the library of the Rev. Isaac Gosset* [1813] [annotated copy, BL, SC Sotherby 81] · *N&Q*, 2nd ser., 8 (1859), 364 · W. Clarke, *Repertorium bibliographicum* (1819), 455–7 · Bodl. Oxf., MSS Gosset, Auct. S.8.9 · *Chalcographimania* (1814), 36–7, 57–8 · J. T. Smith, *A book for a rainy day* (1845), 94 · M. H. Gosset, 'A family of modellers in wax', *Proceedings of the Huguenot Society*, 3 (1888–91), 540–68 · Foster, *Alum. Oxon., 1715–1886*, 2.543 · T. H. Horne, *Introduction to the study of bibliography* (1814), 651–3 · *A catalogue of all graduates … in the University of Oxford, between … 1659 and … 1850* (1851), 267 · J. Foster, *The royal lineage of our noble and gentle families*, 3 vols. (1887–91), vol. 2, pp. 790–91 · *Classical Journal*, 16 (Dec 1813), 471–82 · Nichols, *Lit. anecdotes*, 8.150 · F. G. Stephens and M. D. George, eds., *Catalogue of political and personal satires preserved … in the British Museum*, 8 (1947), 45 · E. J. Pyke, 'Some notes on Isaac Gosset, the elder', *Proceedings of the Huguenot Society*, 21 (1965–70), 274 · A. N. L. Munby, *Essays and papers*, ed. N. Barber (1977), 7–9 · T. Murdoch, ed., *The quiet conquest: the Huguenots, 1685–1985* (1985), 214–18 [exhibition catalogue, Museum of London, 15 May – 31 Oct 1985] · *DNB*

Likenesses A. Beugo?, two caricatures, pubd c.1800, repro. in Munby, *Essays and papers* · S. Springsguth, line engraving, 1813, BM, NPG; repro. in *Kirby's Wonderful…museum* · J. Beugo, etching, BM · R. Cooper, stipple (after wax model by W. Behnes), BM, NPG · I. Gosset the elder, wax model, V&A · etching, BM, NPG

Wealth at death left £50,000 to his sons and £20,000 to his daughter: *Kirby's wonderful … museum*; PRO, death duty records, IR 26/546, fols. 156v–157v; IR 27/141, fol. 22v

Gosset, Matthew (1683–1744). *See under* Gosset, Isaac (1713–1799).

Gosset, Montague (1792–1854), surgeon, was born on 1 July 1792, the second son of Daniel Gosset, magistrate, at the family home, Langhedge Hall, Tanner's End, Edmonton, Middlesex. Educated at a school conducted by a clergyman in Broxbourne, Hertfordshire, Gosset wished to adopt a learned profession. However, his father decided that he should join the navy and in November 1806, aged fourteen, he joined HMS *Curlew*, commanded by Captain Thomas Young. In July 1807 he transferred to HMS *Guerrier*, and subsequently to HMS *Snake*, sloop of war, in which he narrowly escaped being shipwrecked. After serving for nearly three years, he was invalided home from the West Indies with a broken leg and shattered health. After recovering he left the navy to study surgery.

Apprenticed to Mr Stocker, apothecary to Guy's Hospital, in 1809, Gosset obtained membership of the Royal College of Surgeons in May 1814. A distinguished student at Guy's Hospital, he became a favoured pupil of Sir Astley Cooper, who recommended him to the marquess of Bute, then suffering from an eye complaint. In 1815 Gosset accompanied the marquess to Scotland for two years, after which he returned to Guy's Hospital for further studies until 1819. Gosset then commenced practice as a consulting surgeon in Great George Street, Westminster. He moved to the City of London in 1830, where he practised for thirty-four years, first in George Street and lastly in Broad Street Buildings.

In order to see disease on a large scale Gosset built up an extensive practice among the poor, often issuing 90 to 100 prescriptions in a morning. He performed all the major surgical procedures frequently; for example, one week he operated on three patients with bladder stones. Gosset was among the first to describe, in 1827, a peculiar accident to the elbow joint, namely the isolated dislocation of the ulna backwards and inwards. The case is mentioned in Sir Astley Cooper's *Treatise on the Dislocations and Fractures of the Joints* (1842, 451–2). In 1829 Gosset communicated to the London Medical Society the only case of renal artery aneurism then detected (*The Lancet*, 1829–30, 1.387–9), the preparation of which was deposited in the museum of Guy's Hospital; the diagnosis was subjected to acrimonious criticism by Dr W. F. Blicke, which ended in an apology to Gosset (*The Lancet*, 1829–30, 1.647). In 1834 Gosset drew attention to the successful use of silver-gilt wire in a case of vesico-vaginal fistula of eleven years' standing, on which Sir Astley Cooper had previously operated (*The Lancet*, 1834–5, 1.345–6). In 1835 he published a description of an improved tonsil ligature carrier, which facilitated the excision of enlarged tonsils (*The Lancet*, 1834–5, 1.648–50). In 1844 he described the application of nitric acid for the destruction of naevi, after twenty years' experience. He also reported an unusual case of cheek-bone fracture which reduced spontaneously (Cooper, 347–8).

Gosset was made one of the original 300 fellows of the Royal College of Surgeons of England in 1843. However, though warmly supported by many fellows and the whole medical press, he was never elected to its council, apparently for lack of attachment to a public hospital. Upon rejection he issued a strong protest to the profession. Following a post-mortem wound in 1851, he was extremely ill from erysipelas and lost the sight of his left eye. He died from a pulmonary infection, after a week's illness, at Broad Street Buildings on 21 October 1854, and was buried in the family vault at All Saints' Church, Edmonton. He had married early, and eight children survived him.

GORDON GOODWIN, rev. JOHN KIRKUP

Sources *GM*, 2nd ser., 42 (1854), 633–5 · V. G. Plarr, *Plarr's Lives of the fellows of the Royal College of Surgeons of England*, rev. D'A. Power, 1 (1930), 456–7 · A. Cooper, *Treatise on the dislocations and fractures of the joints*, ed. B. B. Cooper (1842), 347–8, 451–2

Gosset, William Sealy [*pseud.* Student] (**1876–1937**), chemist and statistician, was born on 13 June 1876 at 6 St Martin's Hill, St Martin, Canterbury, the eldest son of five children of Frederic Gosset, a lieutenant in the Royal Engineers then residing at the infantry barracks in Canterbury, and Agnes Sealy, daughter of Edward Didal. The

Gossets were an old Huguenot family who left France at the revocation of the edict of Nantes in 1685.

Gosset was a scholar at Winchester College in 1889–95 and won a scholarship to New College, Oxford. He obtained a first in the mathematical moderations in 1897 and left in 1899 with a first-class degree in chemistry. In October 1899 he became a brewer with Arthur Guinness, Son & Co., Ltd, manufacturers of stout at the St James's Gate Brewery in Dublin. (He was bound by his appointment not to publish in his own name, and this led to his subsequent adoption of the pseudonym Student.) Gosset's appointment at Guinness coincided with its introduction of scientific methods for brewing stout. The firm had large farming interests, especially in growing barley for beer, which led to Gosset's involvement with agricultural experiments and subsequently with laboratory tests. Guinness had by then not only begun to appoint men with first-class science degrees from Oxford and Cambridge, but it had also adopted a policy of sending staff away for specialized study.

Gosset became involved with agricultural experiments some time in 1905 when his advice was sought by the Guinness maltster Edwin S. Beaven, who carried out manurial experiments on eight varieties of barley in twenty small plots of wire cages at a nursery near Warminster in Wiltshire. The aim of these 'chessboard' experiments (so called from the arrangement of the plots) was to increase the yield of the grain, of which Guinness was a very large consumer. His pioneering work with Beaven played a prominent part in the efforts of the Irish department of agriculture and its cereal station at Ballindcurra to improve the Irish barley crop: this work led to Gosset's use of statistical methods to estimate the probable effect of experimental error. Gosset wrote his first statistical paper in 1904, on the application of the 'law of error' to the work in the brewery. The principal tools available to him were Airy's theory of errors of observations, and Merriman's method of least squares, though he found that there were no statistical tests that were suitable for his agricultural plots of barley (for his work at Guinness) because the sample sizes were quite often very small.

The Oxford chemist Vernon Harcourt introduced Gosset to the statistician Karl Pearson, whom Gosset visited at East Ilsey in Berkshire in July 1905. Six months later, on 16 January 1906, Gosset married Marjory Surtees Phillpotts (b. 1879/80) at the church of St James in Tunbridge Wells. They had one son and two daughters. The Gossets moved to London in September 1906 so that Gosset could attend Pearson's lectures and tutorials. They stayed in Wimbledon for two terms and left in the spring of 1907. Gosset kept in regular contact with Pearson until 1935. While many of the statistical problems in Pearson's biometric laboratory at University College, London, dealt with large samples, Gosset showed that the results of many agricultural and some chemical experiments produced small samples, and he was therefore concerned that these problems were outside the range of statistical enquiry.

On his return to Dublin, Gosset was put in charge of the experimental barley-growing project, which involved some statistical work. At Guinness he began to investigate the connection between laboratory analysis of various temperatures of malts and the length of time the resulting beer remained potable as measured by acidity. Using the statistical methods he learned in Pearson's biometric school, Gosset was able to deploy the same procedure in various conditions and to test for significant differences between them (as Pearson incorporated probability distributions in his methods). Moreover, he could accomplish all of this by himself without having to engage in the time-consuming procedure of comparing the results obtained by others to establish the degree of error. Gosset's best-known work was his investigation of the probable error of the mean which he published in *Biometrika* in 1908 under the name Student. This called for the distribution of the variance in normal samples (which Gosset found by calculating moments) and used one of Pearson's theoretical curves (from the Pearsonian family of curves) to produce tables from which could be computed the probability that the population mean would lie within certain numbers of standard deviations of the sample mean. This process of making full allowance for a statistical test for uncertainty regarding the standard deviation due to small numbers (by using ratios instead of absolute numbers) has sometimes been termed 'studentizing'. The significance of this paper was that an experimental scientist, who of necessity usually had only small samples from field or laboratory, had been so exercised about the precision of his estimates that he explored the actual distribution of the standard deviation and calculated a function of data that made accurate allowance for the errors of estimation. This became one of the first statistical tests for quality control in industry.

From 1912 to 1913 the Warminster chessboard experiment was extended to barley plots in Cambridge and in Cork. Beaven had been growing the barley for several years without learning much about its performance because he lacked the methods to analyse the results: he wanted to find the statistical difference between the yields of the various plots in the chessboard. Gosset found a single combined estimate of errors from all possible sets of difference between all eight varieties of barley; he devised a statistical method (known as Student's t-test) to test the significance of the differences of the barley in the various plots. He found the probability distribution of his t-test by using Pearson's Type III curve (taken from the family of theoretical curves that Pearson had constructed for data that did not conform with the normal distribution). Gosset's statistical work influenced that of R. A. Fisher, whom he met for the first time at Rothamsted in September 1922. Fisher extended and further developed Student's t-test when he devised his 'analysis of variance' for his classic design of experiments at Rothamsted.

Gosset was rejected by the armed forces when war broke out in 1914 because he was too short-sighted to serve, but he helped Pearson with the calculations involved in estimating the torsional strain in the blades of aeroplane propellers. He published some twenty-two statistical papers which were reissued by *Biometrika* in 1943 as

Student's Collected Papers (edited by Egon Pearson and John Wishart). Gosset was a Christian but was otherwise reticent about his religious views. He was a keen fruit grower and specialized in pears. He was also a good carpenter and built a number of boats. He enjoyed walking, cycling, fishing, skating, and skiing, and especially enjoyed the operas of Gilbert and Sullivan. In 1935 he left Dublin to take up his appointment as head brewer at the new Guinness brewery at Park Royal in north-west London. Gosset died after a heart attack, on 16 October 1937, at St Joseph's Nursing Home, Beaconsfield, Buckinghamshire. His wife survived him.   M. EILEEN MAGNELLO

Sources E. S. Pearson, *'Student': a statistical biography of William Sealy Gosset*, ed. R. L. Plackett and G. A. Barnard (1990) · L. McMullen and E. S. Pearson, 'William Sealy Gosset, 1876–1937', *Biometrika*, 30 (1939), 205–50 · J. F. Box, *R. A. Fisher: the life of a scientist* (1978) · J. F. Box, 'William Sealy Gosset', *American Statistician*, 35 (1981), 61–6 · R. A. Fisher, 'William Sealy Gosset', *Annals of Eugenics*, 9 (1939), 1–9 · J. F. Box, 'William Sealy Gosset', *Statistical Science*, 2 (1987), 45–52 · [W. S. Gosset], *Student's collected papers*, ed. E. S. Pearson and J. Wishart (1943) · E. S. Pearson, 'Mr W. S. Gosset "Student"', *Nature*, 140 (1937), 838 · C. Mollan, W. Davis, and B. Finucane, eds., *More people and places in Irish science and technology* (1990) · b. cert. · m. cert. · d. cert. · *CGPLA Eng. & Wales* (1938)
Archives UCL, Pearson MSS
Likenesses portrait, repro. in McMullen and Pearson, 'William Sealy Gossett' · portrait, repro. in Fisher, 'William Sealy Gossett'
Wealth at death £1553 19s. 11d.: probate, 10 June 1938, *CGPLA Eng. & Wales*

Gossip, Arthur John (1873–1954), Church of Scotland minister, was born on 20 January 1873 at Hillhead, Glasgow, the son of Robert Gossip, a newspaper editor, and his wife, Margaret Grieve Mundell, daughter of David Mundell of Inverlaul, Loch Broom. Gossip was educated at George Watson's College, Edinburgh, after which he attended Edinburgh University, graduating MA in 1898. He prepared for the ministry of the Free Church of Scotland at New College, Edinburgh, and was licensed in that church in 1898, serving first as assistant in the Morningside church, Edinburgh, 1898–9, before serving a succession of pastoral calls. The first was to St Columba's Church, Liverpool, where he was ordained on 3 November 1899. In December 1901 he moved to the West United Free Church, Forfar. From September 1910 he was minister of St Matthew's United Free Church, Glasgow. Following service as a chaplain at the front in Belgium and France during the First World War, 1917–18, he served at the Beechgrove church, Aberdeen, from 1921. In 1928 he was appointed by the general assembly of the United Free Church to be professor of Christian ethics and practical training in the divinity school of the United Free Church (known after 1929 as Trinity College). He taught at Glasgow University until his retirement in 1945, his position having become a university chair in 1939. Gossip married Janina (Nina) Henderson Carslaw (d. 1927), daughter of W. H. Carslaw of Helensburgh, on 4 January 1900; they had three sons and two daughters.

Gossip's publications included *From the Edge of the Crowd* (1924) and *Experience Worketh Hope* (1944), both of which, along with *The Hero in thy Soul*, were dedicated to his wife. Other works included *In Christ's Stead* (1925), *The Galilean*

Accent (1926), and *In the Secret Place of the most High* (1947). He also wrote the exposition of the gospel of St John in *The Interpreter's Bible Commentary* (1952) and the appreciation prefaced to W. M. Macgregor, *The Making of a Preacher: being the Warrack Lectures, 1942–1943* (1946). Gossip was himself the Warrack lecturer in 1925 and the McNeil-Frazer lecturer, 1932–5. He received the honorary degrees of DD from Edinburgh (1929) and LLD from Glasgow (1946).

While Gossip invested the greater portion of his life in an academic setting, as John Mauchline, the principal of his college, wrote of him, 'he remained in many ways a preacher'. It is indeed as a preacher, and not as a scholar, that he is best remembered. Ironically, though he wrote several popular books of sermons he is remembered chiefly for one sermon that emerged from his darkest hour. 'But when life tumbles in, what then?' was the first sermon he preached after the sudden death in 1927 of his wife while he was minister of Beechgrove. When, in 1928, he included this sermon in his anthology *The Hero in thy Soul*, he wrote, 'I have not had the heart to work over it; and it is set down as it was delivered' (A. J. Gossip, *The Hero in thy Soul*, vii). The sermon remains a memorable affirmation of Christian faith in the face of grief. After his retirement in 1945 Gossip lived at Inverton, Kingussie, Inverness-shire. He died in Glasgow on 26 May 1954.
MICHAEL JINKINS

Sources J. A. Lamb, ed., *The fasti of the United Free Church of Scotland, 1900–1929* (1956) · *Fasti Scot.*, new edn, vol. 9 · *WWW, 1951–60* · *Beechgrove church, Aberdeen: a record of fifty years, 1900–1950*, Beechgrove church [1950] · C. E. Fant and W. M. Pinson, *20 centuries of great preaching*, 8 (1971), 222 · J. Mauchline, 'The late Prof. A. J. Gossip', *Expository Times*, 65 (1953–4), 300–02
Likenesses photograph, Beechgrove church, Aberdeen; repro. in Fant and Pinson, *20 centuries of great preaching*
Wealth at death £16,115 15s. 9d.: confirmation, 16 July 1954, *CCI*

Gosson, Henry (*fl.* 1601–1630). *See under* Gosson, Stephen (*bap.* 1554, *d.* 1625).

Gosson, Stephen (*bap.* **1554**, *d.* **1625**), anti-theatrical polemicist and Church of England clergyman, was baptized as the eldest son and second child of Cornelius Gosson and Agnes Oxenbridge on 17 April 1554 in the church of St George the Martyr, Canterbury, Kent. His father was a joiner who emigrated from the Low Countries; a leading craftsman of the city, he was later asked to fashion a huge wooden cross to be placed in the town centre to honour Elizabeth I when she made her first visit as queen to Canterbury. Gosson's mother was the daughter of a grocer, Thomas Oxenbridge (or Oxynbregge), who earned his freedom in Canterbury in 1519. The family resided over Cornelius's shop in the parish of St George, a crowded part of the city that housed about eighty families along the south-east side of the cathedral close. Stephen entered the cathedral school as a scholar at the age of fourteen, where he was taught by John Gresshop, an MA from Christ Church, Oxford. Archbishop Matthew Parker, then the head of the school, provided the scholarship for Gosson to proceed to Corpus Christi College, Oxford.

At eighteen Gosson went up to Oxford, two years after

John Lyly, another Canterbury boy, entered Magdalen College there. Gosson went as a sizar—one of two financed by Parker for boys from Kent, and this probably determined his college and date of entry, though there was little competition for such positions. Corpus was known as 'the fountain head of pure Canterbury doctrine', and several of Gosson's schoolmates, including Richard Hooker and Henry Parry, were later important figures in the Elizabethan church. Gosson also learned the euphuistic style from lectures by John Rainoldes, just as George Pettie and Lyly did. But limited financial resources seem to have hampered him: although he requested graduation and was granted application on 31 October and 17 December 1576 and was admitted to the BA degree provided he could determine the following Lent, he never signed the matriculation book and never made his final disputation. Later in *Playes Confuted* he would complain that he was 'pulled from the University before I was ripe' (sig. G7v) and in his dedicatory letter he confesses a keen sense of inferiority to scholars from Oxford, Cambridge, and the inns of court. Gosson then apparently went to London, where he wrote four extant didactic and commissioned dedicatory poems. He also tried his hand at plays, although none is extant: in *The Schoole of Abuse* he refers to *Catalins Conspiracies*, designed to teach good government and show the evils of tyranny, and in *Playes Confuted* he talks of another moral play, *Praise of Parting*. But he also mentions there *The Comedy of Captain Mario*, 'a cast of Italian devices', and Thomas Lodge refers to a fourth play with 'Muscovian strangers' and '*Scythian* monsters' and 'one *Eurus* brought upon one stage in ships made of Sheepskins'. None succeeded.

By 1579 Gosson began a euphuistic romance, *The Ephemerides of Phialo*, but he interrupted this in September to write, fairly rapidly, a euphuistic attack on the misuse of art, *The Schoole of Abuse* (1579). Here he argues that poetry, music, and plays should present models of virtuous action, and that bad art subjects men's and women's reason to passions. In a pamphlet interlocking epideictic, forensic, and deliberative forms of argument, he urges the lord mayor to refuse all letters patent to players and urges women to remain at home. In a now famous description of the Southwark playhouses, he talks of petty crime and prostitution, but that passage closely imitates Ovid and should not be taken as wholly contemporary. Nevertheless, Gosson's most telling point—that the judgement of art necessarily relies on an understanding of human nature—would become the key issue of dramatic criticism until the Restoration. The fact that Gosson attacked plays aroused instant responses. The most famous is the partially extant work of Thomas Lodge published without title-page in 1579, causing Gosson to reply in *An Apology of 'The Schoole of Abuse'* appended to *The Ephemerides* (October 1579). There Gosson combines moral argument with personal experience and claims the final test of the efficacy of drama is in the results of performances. By the age of twenty-four, then, Gosson had become famous to some— and notorious to others (including Sidney, whose *Defence of*

Poesie cited Gosson's specific arguments in his refutation, and who may have been annoyed by Gosson's dedication of *The Schoole* to him). Gosson, meantime, retired to the country as a tutor and began working on an unfinished Latin treatise that is no longer extant.

In late 1580 Gosson received a copy of Lodge's rebuttal and spent another fourteen months reading Plato, patristic commentary, and Vives's work on Augustine, and mastering a new Attic style for more decisive argumentation. The result was *Playes Confuted in Five Actions* (1582). Concentrating solely on drama, Gosson defines plays by the four Aristotelian causes in *Physics*, 194-5: efficient (the cause of plays is the devil); material (actors must necessarily counterfeit); formal (dramatic conventions violate nature); and final (plays cause the overflow of powerful affections). To these, in analogy to the five actions of a play, he adds a fifth cause of unification, showing that all four causes reinforce one another. Along the way he becomes the first Elizabethan anti-theatrical polemicist to cite the sanction against cross-dressing in Deuteronomy. Thus where *The Schoole* had argued that playgoers falter by imitating performers, *Playes Confuted* argues that both playgoers and players are transformed—not actions but dispositions of the soul are corrupted. *Playes Confuted* was sold by **Thomas Gosson** (*fl.* 1577-1598), a London bookseller in St Paul's Churchyard and later in Cheapside, who was admitted to the Stationers' Company on 4 February 1577, and who may have been Stephen's younger brother, although there is no documentary evidence to support this. Thomas's son, **Henry Gosson** (*fl.* 1601-1630), succeeded to the business and was admitted to the Stationers' Company on 3 August 1601. Henry's earliest publication entered on the Stationers' register was *A Recantacon of a Browniste* (1 July 1606). During the early sixteenth century he had a shop on London Bridge and was busy producing broadsides until 1630.

Meanwhile, Stephen's increasing pious rigidity seems to have taken a strange turn: the next extant record is his registration in the Pilgrim Book of the English College at Rome on 15 April 1584, a Jesuit training ground for Catholics and converts meant to carry the Roman mission back to England. Two months later Gosson resigned, dispensed by Cardinal Severinus and departing for reasons of bad eyesight. The only satisfactory explanation is that Gosson was acting as an agent for Walsingham, and this seems borne out by the rest of Gosson's career. He returned to England and at thirty was appointed lecturer at St Martin Ludgate, a few hundred yards from St Paul's Cathedral. In 1585 he was made lecturer at St Dunstan and All Saints, Stepney, a far wealthier parish just east of London, where the parson, Humphrey Cole, was a former classmate of Gosson's at Corpus Christi. In October 1586 Gosson was appointed vicar of St Alban's Church, Sandridge, Hertfordshire, at the extraordinary salary of £80. While St Dunstan was clearly protestant, it was surely not puritan: extant records show Gosson was loyal to the Book of Common Prayer, wore a surplice, used the sign of the cross at baptism, and conducted the service at a proper font in the front of the church—easy assumptions that he was a puritan have no foundation in fact. He left St Alban's in December 1591 to become parson at Great Wigborough, Essex, at the bestowal of the queen, about 7 miles from Colchester. In 1596 he was called to Paul's Cross to preach; the sermon, *The Trumpet of War*, was published in 1598. This sermon may have led to his final appointment: on 8 April 1600 he was inducted as rector of St Botolph without Bishopsgate, London, one of England's wealthiest church livings, serving the Moorfields to the north and east of the city. Here he pursued his parishioners tirelessly for unpaid tithes, and conducted correspondence with the retired actor Edward Alleyn, founder of Dulwich College, with whom he set up a charity for three poor brethren of St Botolph.

Gosson married Elizabeth Acton (1554/5–1615) of London on 25 April 1587, at St Dunstan; they had two sons and a daughter. Elizabeth died on 2 December 1615 at the age of sixty and was buried in the choir of old St Botolph. Their daughter, Elizabeth, who married Paul Bassano, died little more than a year later, on 23 March 1617. Nothing more is known of Gosson's sons, which suggests that they may have predeceased him. Gosson carried on alone, dying on 13 February 1625 in his parish. Four days later he was buried at his request in the chancel of St Botolph, near to his wife and daughter, and at night, to save costs. He was survived by a sister, a niece, and a cousin, as well as by his brother William, by then a gentleman and drummajor to James I. He left each of them bequests, the largest to William, but he also remembered his curate, his maidservant, his parish clerk, and the poor of each parish in which he had served. ARTHUR F. KINNEY

Sources A. F. Kinney, *Markets of bawdrie: the dramatic criticism of Stephen Gosson* (1974) · W. Ringler, *Stephen Gosson: a biographical and critical study* (1942) · A. F. Kinney, 'Stephen Gosson's art of argumentation in *The schoole of abuse*', *Studies in English Literature, 1500–1900*, 7/1 (1967), 41–54 · T. Lodge, *A defence of poetry, music, and stageplays*, ed. D. Laing (1853) · L. Levine, *Men in women's clothing: antitheatricality and effeminization, 1579–1642* (1994) · S. S. Hilliard, 'Stephen Gosson and the Elizabethan distrust of the effects of drama', *English Literary Renaissance*, 9 (1979), 225–39 · S. P. Zitner, 'Gosson, Ovid, and the Elizabethan audience', *Shakespeare Quarterly*, 9 (1958), 206–8 · J. Barish, *The antitheatrical prejudice* (1981) · E. N. S. Thompson, *The controversy between the puritans and the stage* (1903) · R. Fraser, *The war against poetry* (1970) · E. H. Miller, *The professional writer in Elizabethan England* (1959) · DNB

Gosson, Thomas (*fl.* 1577–1598). *See under* Gosson, Stephen (*bap.* 1554, *d.* 1625).

Gostelow [Gorstelow], **Walter** (*bap.* 1604, *d.* 1662?), royalist prophet, was born at Prescott House, Prescote, near Cropredy, Oxfordshire, and baptized at St Mary's Church, Cropredy, on 26 April 1604, the third son and fifth of ten children of Richard Gorstelow (*c.*1568–1621), yeoman and gentleman of Prescote, and his wife, Anne (*d.* 1612). On 27 May 1613 his father married Katherine Hawes, wealthy widow of a prosperous London haberdasher. Richard Gorstelow also prospered, appointing a manger to handle the day-to-day operation of his farm while he developed his personal and business interests. He acted as a bailiff for Sir William Cope, high sheriff for Oxfordshire, and probably served as an under-sheriff for the same county from 1618. His will shows that he was well acquainted with a wide circle of influential friends, among whom he included Lord Danvers and Sir George Shirley, and Sir Thomas Chamberlain, for whom he acted as attorney.

It is unclear whether Walter Gostelow received any formal education. His father and paternal uncles were all taught at Williamscote School, near Cropredy, but the registers for subsequent years are incomplete. Three of his brothers studied at Oxford University; two, Thomas and William, graduated and became vicars of Farnborough and Maxtoke, Warwickshire, while the third, Richard, took no degree, but appears to have been the principal beneficiary of his father's estate. By his own account Walter was apprenticed in London by 1620. On the occasion of his daughter Anne's baptism (27 November 1629), he described himself as a milliner; a contemporary suggested that Gostelow once served in that capacity for Charles I. On 27 November 1628 Gostelow married Anne Ashe of Yorkshire at St Mary Woolnoth, Lombard Street, London. They had five children including Richard and Anne. Gostelow lived in a variety of London parishes before settling in 'Broadstreet, near the Church, over agin st Gresham Colledge' in the parish of St Peter-le-Poer, where he lived with his family from about 1634 to about 1658 (Gostelow, 143).

Between 1655 and 1658 Gostelow wrote two books, an unpublished manuscript, and a series of letters in which he endeavoured to portray himself as a prophet specially commissioned by God to interpret and proclaim his divine will and intention to all men. To this end his writings—many of which abound with fantastic accounts of alleged dreams, visions, and voices, and of assignations with the likes of Lord Broghill, Robert Boyle, Sir Gilbert Pickering, Oliver Cromwell, Charles Stuart, and the earl of Cork (for whom a relative of Gostelow's was a secretary), all in the course of travels in England, Ireland, and on the continent—purport to show how God was unhappy with the people for forsaking the church, true religion, and the Lord's anointed ruler on earth, 'Charls Stuart'. According to Gostelow, Charles was the 'son of man', foretold in biblical prophecies, who was destined to 'come in' and assume his rightful place on the throne. Moreover, Cromwell, whom God had chosen to be 'highly instrumental for the bringing of great and strange things to pass', was to invite Charles to return, and so be united with the king as his lieutenant (Gostelow, A7v–8r). For the timing of these miraculous events Gostelow put his faith in a variety of eschatological signs, all of which failed to materialize. Notably, however, like many of his contemporaries (including Cromwell) he believed that the readmission and conversion of the Jews would act as a prelude to a new millennium. In his first book *Charles Stuart and Oliver Cromwell United*, he wrote an open epistle to the rabbi Menasseh ben Israel, praising greatly his book *The Hope of Israel*, and the idea that the lost tribes of Israel would soon be gathered, although according to his own predilections he stressed that the Jews should look to Charles as their most likely means of readmission.

While original in neither their conception nor explication Gostelow's highly personalized accounts of his experiences are none the less interesting for the light that they throw on the ideas and aspirations of a small but vocal band of royalists during the interregnum. Like his fellow prophet Arise Evans—with whom he not only shared a vision of Charles Stuart's restoration, but also spent some time while attempting to lobby Cromwell in 1654—Gostelow was openly supportive of those who were, or might be, in a position to further the royalist cause, and equally critical of its detractors. That he was acutely aware of the political and propagandist value of his writings there can be no doubt. While some of his alleged exploits possess an air of plausibility, the measured style with which he presented those experiences, and the lack of any independent corroboration, severely undermines the veracity of his more incredible claims. Noticeably he also failed to excite any significant reaction, either adverse or otherwise, until the publication of his final book *The Coming of God in Mercy, in Vengeance*, for which its printer, Peter Lillicrap, was committed to the Tower.

After he signed his final book on 9 April 1658, the fate of Gostelow is uncertain. According to 'Ra. [Ralph?] Bathurst', after the death of Cromwell, Gostelow:

> finding that his prophecyes in this booke could not now come to passe; but that he should be counted for a deluded phantastic person, avoyed all company and discourse about any of these matters which had before so strongly possessd him, and with which he so vehemently endeavoured to possesse the world; and shortly after, for shame & grief dyed, at Prescot. (Gostelo, MS note, Thomason Tracts copy, E. 1612 (3), E8r)

However, there is no evidence of this. His brother Richard continued to live at Prescote until shortly before 22 April 1660, when he was buried at St Mary's Church, Cropredy, but Gostelow may have returned to London: administration of the estate of Walter Gostelow of London was granted in June 1662.   IAN L. O'NEILL

Sources W. Gostelow, *Charles Stuart and Oliver Cromwell united* (1655) • W. Gostelo, *The coming of God in mercy, in vengeance* (1658) • *VCH Oxfordshire* • *Reg. Oxf.*, 2/1–4 • P. Lillicrap, 'The humble petition of Peter Lillicrap printer', PRO, SP 29/77, 37 • T. Loveday, 'The registers of Williamscote School', *Cake and Cockhorse*, 2/3 (Jan 1963) • Foster, *Alum. Oxon.* • PRO, PROB 12/39, 18v • parish register, Cropredy, St Mary, 26 April 1604, Oxon. RO [baptism] • will of Richard Gorstelow, PRO, PROB 11/137, sig. 50
Archives Queen's College, Oxford, 'God's power and fyer from heaven purginge the earth', MS 449, 76

Gostlin, John (1565/6–1626), physician, was born in Norwich, the son of Robert Gostlin, sheriff of that city in 1570. He was a member of a trading family which had sent many members to Cambridge University. After being at the cathedral grammar school in Norwich for six years he was admitted, aged sixteen, at Gonville Hall on 22 November 1582 as a scholar. He graduated BA in 1587 and then MA from the re-founded Gonville and Caius College in 1590.

He was elected to a fellowship about Easter 1592, which he retained until he became master. Gostlin held many college offices in the 1590s, and so presumably had some contact with William Harvey, then an undergraduate at Gonville and Caius. Gostlin received the MD in 1602, being incorporated DM at Oxford on 14 July 1612.

It is clear that Gostlin forged a close friendship with Thomas Legge, master of Gonville Hall, and then Gonville and Caius College, from 1573 until his death in 1607. The Latin inscription on Legge's tomb reads 'Love joined them living, and so may the same earth link them in their tombs; O Legge, you still have Gostlin's heart with you'. Gostlin himself would later request in his own will that he be 'buryed as neare my worthy friend and patron Doctor Legge as may be' (Venn, *Annals*, 328). By the time of Legge's death Gostlin was forty, well regarded as an anatomist and Latinist, and was Legge's own choice to succeed him. The fellows concurred and immediately elected Gostlin on 12 July 1607, but they met with powerful opposition from the chancellor, the earl of Salisbury. Salisbury objected that a faction had rushed the election while many fellows were absent. Gostlin was then chosen by a larger quorum of fellows, but Salisbury again invalidated the election. The chancellor's accusations of procedural impropriety merely masked religious anxiety and court intrigue. Gonville and Caius under Legge had long been suspected of harbouring papists, and Gostlin's reputation at court suffered owing to suspicions of popery. The court instead supported the well-connected William Branthwaite, a protestant divine employed by James I in the project to translate the Bible. In defiance of the fellows Salisbury appointed Branthwaite on 14 December 1607. Gostlin then retired to Exeter, where he practised physic. Evidence indicates that he rarely visited Cambridge during the next decade. He made an exception in March 1615 when he was summoned to act as respondent in the medical disputations before the visiting James I. In addition to medicine Gostlin dabbled in politics and was returned as MP for Barnstaple in 1614.

On 14 February 1619 Branthwaite, by then vice-chancellor, died of consumption. While he lay dying a royal letter arrived reminding the fellows that the new master must be 'sound and untainted in religion' (Venn, *Biographical history*, 3.75). Once again the fellows immediately met, and chose Gostlin. A second royal letter was brought soon after, recommending Sir Thomas Wilson, keeper of the state records, but the fellows renewed their choice, and it was acceded to, largely thanks to the support of George Montaigne, bishop of Lincoln, who petitioned the court on behalf of Gostlin's Anglicanism. Gostlin became vice-chancellor in 1625. In 1623 Gostlin had been appointed regius professor of physic, to which he was recommended by Isaac Barrow as 'the best man of his profession in the university' (*CSP dom.*, 1623, 605, 619). He held these three posts until his death on 21 October 1626. There is an account of his death in Mead's letters (Harleian MS 390). His will is dated 9 October 1626 and was proved on 6 December 1626. It survives along with an account of his life in the Gonville and Caius *Annals*. His regius professorship inaugural address and several lectures are preserved in Caius College Library. Gostlin was buried in the college chapel on 16 November 1626, where a monument was erected to his memory. He was a generous benefactor to Gonville and Caius and St Catharine's colleges, founding scholarships at the former and leaving The Bull inn to the latter, a deed which the Society of Caius is said to have toasted annually (Fowler and Fowler, 118).

JOHN VENN, *rev.* KEVIN P. SIENA

Sources *CSP dom.*, *1607*; *1619*; *1623* · J. Venn and others, eds., *Biographical history of Gonville and Caius College*, 3: *Biographies of the successive masters* (1901), 74–85 · J. Caius, *The annals of Gonville and Caius College*, ed. J. Venn (1904), 214–16, 287–8, 307–8, 325–30 · J. Venn, *Caius College* (1923), 96–8, 104–11 · H. D. Rolleston, *The Cambridge medical school: a biographical history* (1932), 140–43 · C. N. L. Brooke, *A history of Gonville and Caius College* (1985), 79–80, 104–10, 114–16 · Fuller, *Worthies* (1811), 2.154–5 · C. H. Cooper, *Annals of Cambridge*, 2–3 (1843–5) · L. Fowler and H. Fowler, eds., *Cambridge commemorated: an anthology of university life* (1984) · BL, Harley MS 390 · R. Willis, *The architectural history of the University of Cambridge, and of the colleges of Cambridge and Eton*, ed. J. W. Clark, 1 (1886), 76–8, 96 · Venn, *Alum. Cant.* · private information (2004)

Archives Gon. & Caius Cam., medical disputations, MSS 432–433 | BL, Baker MSS, letter of thanks to James I, vi.183, B.189 · BL, Baker MSS, speeches, iv.243, A.281.xi.352 · CUL, Baker MSS, diary, xxviii.340–42

Likenesses oils, 1621, Gon. & Caius Cam.; repro. in Brooke, *History of Gonville and Caius College* · oils, St Catharine's College, Cambridge

Wealth at death wealthy: left two inns to Gonville and Caius College, Cambridge, and St Catharine's College, Cambridge, and founded scholarships for scholars from Norwich: will, Caius, *Annals*, 328–9

Gostlin, John (1632/3–1705), educational benefactor and physician, was baptized at Dickleburgh, Norfolk, on 29 January 1633. He was the son of John Gostlin (1604/5–c.1641), formerly fellow of Gonville and Caius College, Cambridge, and great-nephew of another John *Gostlin, formerly master of the same college—as is stated on his tomb in the college chapel. Gostlin was educated at Diss and Moulton in Norfolk. He was admitted to Caius on 6 July 1647. He failed to win a fellowship when the puritan William Dell was master of Caius during the Commonwealth, but moved to Peterhouse in 1653 and became for a time a fellow there; he graduated BA in 1651, MA in 1654, and MD in 1661. In 1661 he successfully petitioned Charles II—as a loyal supporter of his father, as he claimed—for a fellowship of Caius by royal mandate; and he remained a resident fellow of Caius until his death in Cambridge on 1 February 1705 at the age of seventy-two. He was buried two days later in the college chapel.

It is probable that Gostlin maintained a successful medical practice in and around Cambridge. The 'Exiit' books of the college show that he was rarely absent from the college for more than a few days at a time; and the 'Gesta', the minutes of the governing body, show him regular, though not constant, in attending college meetings. He composed a continuation of the college annals from 1660 to 1679 (Gonville and Caius College, MS 616/548). Gostlin was clearly a central figure in the college through most of the mastership of a more eminent physician, Robert Brady:

he was bursar (1661–5), steward (1667–70), and was made president (at that time, deputy to the master) by Brady in 1679, and remained so until his death. In December 1704 he gave £500 to the college to supplement scholarships endowed by his great-uncle; and he left the advowson of Hethersett, Norfolk, to the master of the college to present one of the fellows to it. He is a shadowy figure, but a fine, if simple, tomb in the college chapel records that he was 'very skilled in a happy method of curing' the sick, as well as his twenty-five years as president and his benefactions. He had evidently been a central and much respected figure in the college community.

C. N. L. BROOKE

Sources J. Venn and others, eds., *Biographical history of Gonville and Caius College*, 1: 1349–1713 (1897) · J. Venn and others, eds., *Biographical history of Gonville and Caius College*, 3: *Biographies of the successive masters* (1901), 168 and facing 168 (2)—Gostlin's tomb · *DNB* · gesta, 1669–1716, Gon. & Caius Cam., GOV/03/01/04 · exiit books, 1618–78, 1678–1747, Gon. & Caius Cam. · J. Gostlin, annals of the college, 1660–79, Gon. & Caius Cam., MS 616/548 [sometimes called his 'Historiola'] · C. Hall, 'College officers: the bursars, stewards and registraries of Gonville and Caius College', *The Caian* (1989–90), 114–26 · parish register (baptism), 29 Jan 1633, Dickleburgh, Norfolk · tomb, Gon. & Caius Cam.

Gostling, John (1649/50–1733), singer and Church of England clergyman, was born at East Malling, Kent, the son of Isaac Gostling (d. 1669), a chandler, and educated at the King's School, Rochester. In 1668, aged eighteen, he was admitted as sizar to St John's College, Cambridge; he was granted his BA degree in 1672–3 and ordained at Ely on 30 May 1675. He soon became a minor canon at Canterbury Cathedral and vicar of Littlebourne, posts which he retained until his death. He was later also rector of other Kent parishes. On 27 February 1675 he married his first wife, Elizabeth Turner (b. c.1653), and they were the parents of six children baptized at Canterbury between 1677 and 1684. Elizabeth died some time after the birth of her last child, Mary, in 1684. Gostling later married Dorothy Wyborne; their son William *Gostling was baptized at Canterbury on 30 January 1696.

In February 1679, described as 'a Base from Canterbury, master of Arts' (Ashbee and Harley, 1.38), Gostling was admitted as a gentleman of the Chapel Royal. He joined the choir of St Paul's Cathedral, was appointed minor canon there in 1683, and was made subdean in January 1690. Henry Purcell became organist at the Chapel Royal in 1682 and from that time the virtuoso bass parts in his anthems were almost certainly written for Gostling, whom John Evelyn called 'that stupendious Base' (Evelyn, 4.404). Sir John Hawkins, a friend of Gostling's son William, writes that 'King Charles II. could sing the tenor part of an easy song; he would oftentimes sing with Mr. Gostling; the duke of York accompanying them on the guitar'. Hawkins describes how Gostling, after being with the king and duke on the royal yacht in a violent storm, selected the texts for Purcell's anthem 'They that go down to the sea in ships', the bass part of which is such that 'hardly any person but himself was then, or has since been able to sing it' (Hawkins, 4.360). Charles II is reported to have said, 'You may talk as much as you please of your Nightingales, but I have one Gostling that excels them all'

(*GM*, 148), and to have presented Gostling with a silver egg filled with guineas, saying he had heard eggs were good for the voice. Gostling became a member of the royal private music under James II; William III gave him a prebend's place in Lincoln Cathedral and he was sworn chaplain-in-ordinary to the king on 20 December 1689. Hawkins tells of an occasion when Mary II sent for Gostling and the soprano Arabella Hunt to sing music by Purcell accompanied by the composer. Gostling was an industrious, if erratic, music copyist and his manuscripts are valuable sources for the church music of the period. The most important is the Gostling manuscript, now at Austin, Texas, which contains sixty-four anthems in full score, including seventeen by Purcell. In 1727 Gostling was too frail to travel to London and was sworn in under the new king at Canterbury, where he died on 17 July 1733. He was buried in the cathedral cloisters on 21 July.

OLIVE BALDWIN and THELMA WILSON

Sources A. Ashbee, ed., *Records of English court music*, 1 (1986); 2 (1987); 5 (1991); 8 (1995) · A. Ashbee and D. Lasocki, eds., *A biographical dictionary of English court musicians, 1485–1714*, 2 vols. (1998) · Venn, *Alum. Cant.*, 1/2 · J. Hawkins, *A general history of the science and practice of music*, 4 (1776) · *GM*, 1st ser., 47 (1777), 147–8, 210 · A. Ashbee and J. Harley, eds., *The cheque books of the Chapel Royal*, 2 vols. (2000) · Evelyn, *Diary*, vol. 4 · J. Gostling, ed., *The Gostling manuscript* (facs. edn, 1977) [incl. introduction by F. B. Zimmerman] · W. Shaw, *The Bing–Gostling part-books at York Minster* (1986)

Gostling, Mildred May (1873–1962). *See under* Mills, William Hobson (1873–1959).

Gostling, William (*bap.* 1696, *d.* 1777), antiquary and topographer, was baptized in Canterbury Cathedral on 30 January 1696, the seventh and last child of John *Gostling (*d.* 1733), Church of England clergyman and singer, but the only child of his second wife, Dorothy Wyborne. He was educated as a king's scholar at the King's School, Canterbury (1706–11), and then entered St John's College, Cambridge, matriculating in 1712. He graduated BA in 1716 and MA in 1719. He married, on 3 October 1717 at Canterbury Cathedral, Hester Thomas (1695/6–1760), and they had nine children between 1719 and 1736, of whom two sons and a daughter survived them. After university, all his life was passed in or near Canterbury, and he served in the diocese as curate or parish priest from his ordination on 5 March 1721. He was instituted to the rectory of Brook, near Wye, Kent, on 23 September 1722. He held a minor canonry at Canterbury from 1727 until his death. His father died on 17 July 1733, and thereby vacated the vicarage of Littlebourne, a few miles from the cathedral city, to which Gostling succeeded on 31 December, vacating the benefice of Brook. The living of Littlebourne was surrendered in 1753, on his being appointed to the vicarage of Stone in Oxney.

Thoroughly versed in the history of Canterbury, Gostling guided visitors around the city, and when confined by poor health for many years to his home, for he could not use his legs and his hands were much affected by gout, he wrote the well-regarded *A Walk In and About the City of Canterbury*. During the writing of this guide friends corrected his descriptions by personal observation. It was published

William Gostling (*bap.* 1696, *d.* 1777), by Conrad Martin Metz

in 1774 and ran to six editions, the last being in 1825. He also contributed articles to the *Philosophical Transactions* (1743 and 1744) and to the *Gentleman's Magazine* (1756 and 1776) on various subjects, as well as composing verse, notably a versified version of Ebenezer Forrest's account of a trip made by Hogarth and some friends over five days into Kent in May 1732, which version was printed in a limited edition of twenty copies in 1781 by John Nichols, who also included some of Gostling's verses in his *Select Collection of Poems* (1781–2). Gostling's house in Canterbury was filled with his inventions and collections, and was visited by travellers, who were escorted through it by his daughter Hester (1719–1798). Because of both his great knowledge of musical history and his fine collection of printed and manuscript music, part of which he had inherited from his father, he was consulted by the composer William Boyce in search of materials for his *Cathedral Music* and by Sir John Hawkins in 1772–3 for his *General History of the Science and Practice of Music*. Letitia-Matilda Hawkins, Sir John's daughter, in her *Anecdotes* described Gostling as being 'a wonderful mechanical genius', and recalled his 'model for a machine to cleanse one of the harbours on the Kentish coast' and an invention which 'opened his kitchen-windows, upper and lower sashes, all at once; and … in opposite directions'. She also described him as seemingly 'to live in continual banter and perpetual joke' (Hawkins, 246–7, 250).

Gostling died on 9 March 1777 at his house in Mint Yard, Canterbury, and was buried in the cloisters of Canterbury Cathedral on 15 March. He left his daughter Hester in difficult circumstances. The second edition of his *Walk* was in the same year made a subscription edition for her benefit; in it is a grateful preface by Hester. Sir John Hawkins prepared the catalogue of Gostling's music collection, which included an almost complete set of Purcell's dramatic compositions in manuscript, for auction on 26–27 May 1777 by Messrs Langford of London. His collection of Greek, Saxon, and English coins and medals was also disposed of by Langford in the following month, on 17 June. Gostling's books were sold by William Flackton of Canterbury in 1778.   R. J. Goulden

Sources R. Hovenden, ed., *The register booke of christenings, marriages, and burialls within the precinct of the cathedrall and metropoliticall church of Christe of Canterburie*, Harleian Society, register section, 2 (1878) · J. S. Sidebotham, *Memorials of the King's School, Canterbury* (1865), 58 · Venn, *Alum. Cant.* · E. Hasted, *The history and topographical survey of the county of Kent*, 3 (1790), 189, 542, 657 · Nichols, *Lit. anecdotes*, 3.677; 9.339–50, 747, 816 · J. M. Cowper, ed., *The memorial inscriptions of the cathedral church of Canterbury* (1897), 281–2 · *GM*, 1st ser., 47 (1777), 147–8 · L.-M. Hawkins, *Anecdotes, biographical sketches, and memoirs* (1822), 245–62 · B. H. Davis, *The Boyce-Hawkins 'Monumental inscription to the memory of Mr. Gostling'* (1973) · P. Collinson, P. N. Ramsay, and M. Sparks, eds., *A history of Canterbury Cathedral* (1995), 229, 239 · C. Mitchell, ed., *Hogarth's peregrination* (1952) · *DNB*
Archives BL, motets by Carissimi and Steffani transcribed by him, Add. MS 31477 | Herts. ALS, letters to second Earl Cowper
Likenesses R. B. Godfrey, line engraving (after C. M. Metz), BM, NPG; repro. in W. Gostling, *A walk in and about the city of Canterbury*, 2nd edn (1777) · C. M. Metz, engraving (after his earlier work), BM, NPG [*see illus.*]
Wealth at death income died with Gostling; possessions auctioned or sold 1777 and 1778; subscription made for daughter Hester 1777: Hester Gostling's preface on her circumstances, subscription edition of Gostling's *A walk*, 1777 · sales catalogues for music and coins extant: Davis, *Boyce-Hawkins 'Monumental inscription'*

Gostwick, Sir John (*b.* before **1490**, *d.* **1545**), administrator, was born at Willington, Bedfordshire, the eldest son of John Gostwick. His mother was a member of the Leventhorpe family. Nothing is known of Gostwick's own wife, Joan, whom he married some time before 1524, when their only son, William, was born.

After passing his youth at Potton in Bedfordshire, Gostwick was in London by 1514, where he soon joined the household of Cardinal Wolsey. His administrative career began in July 1523 with his appointment as auditor of the duchy of York; by 1527 he was also comptroller of the cardinal's household. Wolsey rewarded his 'old and trusty servant' with favourable leases, and facilitated Gostwick's purchase of Willington Manor from the duke of Norfolk in June 1529, confirmed by a private act of 1536 (28 Hen. VIII c. 47). In 1530 he was admitted to Gray's Inn.

Following Wolsey's fall Gostwick swiftly entered the service of his former colleague in the cardinal's household, Thomas Cromwell, who employed him as his personal treasurer. He was kept busy making payments and collecting debts, acting on his master's direct orders. When in November 1534 perpetual royal taxes were imposed upon the English clergy (first fruits and tenths), Cromwell determined to retain direct control over this lucrative new revenue. Accordingly he arranged the appointment of Gostwick as 'treasurer and receiver-

general of first fruits and tenths' on 7 May 1535. In addition to routine administrative duties, Gostwick occasionally attended upon foreign ambassadors (despite confessing to limited language skills), and he accompanied the chief mourner at the funeral of Katherine of Aragon (February 1536). In October 1536 Gostwick oversaw delivery of money and ordnance to the royal army sent north to crush the Pilgrimage of Grace.

Despite their close association, Gostwick did not share Cromwell's sympathy for evangelical reform; among reformers the treasurer was reputed a 'stark pharisee' (*LP Henry VIII*, 12, pt 1, no. 577). As a Bedfordshire MP in 1539 he accused Archbishop Cranmer of preaching heresy in his diocese. Incensed at this public attack upon his primate, Henry VIII denounced Gostwick as a 'varlett' and threatened him with severe punishment (Nichols, 254); a chastened Gostwick apologized and begged Cranmer to intercede with the king.

Religious turmoil threatened Gostwick's career once again the following year, when a council coup sent Cromwell to the Tower of London. Having relied upon his master's word as his warrant and accounting to Cromwell alone, Gostwick lacked proper discharge for the considerable sums that he had handled. He acted promptly, however, to commend himself to the king, and his appointment in January 1541 as treasurer of the newly erected court of first fruits and tenths regularized his position and limited disruption to clerical tax administration.

Knighted in 1540, Gostwick was honoured in October 1541 when the king lodged at Willington (earlier controversy now forgotten), and the following month he was pricked as sheriff of Bedfordshire and Buckinghamshire. From the late 1530s Gostwick steadily enlarged his Bedfordshire estates, acquiring a number of manors around Willington. A widower by May 1543 when he drew up his will, Gostwick was again selected as an MP for Bedfordshire in December 1544, but died on 15 April 1545, before parliament met. He was buried at Willington, in the church that he had rebuilt several years earlier. Gostwick's son, William, died without issue in December 1544, and Willington passed to his brother William and his heirs.   P. R. N. Carter

Sources H. P. R. Finberg, 'The Gostwicks of Willington', *The Gostwicks of Willington, and other studies*, Bedfordshire Historical RS, 36 (1956), 48–138 · G. R. Elton, *The Tudor revolution in government* (1953) · P. R. N. Carter, 'Royal taxation of the English parish clergy, 1535–58', PhD diss., U. Cam., 1994 · *LP Henry VIII* · J. G. Nichols, ed., *Narratives of the days of the Reformation*, CS, old ser., 77 (1859) · PRO, PROB 11/30, fol. 222r–222v · A. Luders and others, eds., *Statutes of the realm*, 11 vols. in 12, RC (1810–28), vol. 3 · *Bedfordshire, and the county of Huntingdon and Peterborough*, Pevsner (1968) · Y. Nicholls, ed., *Court of augmentations accounts for Bedfordshire*, 2 vols., Bedfordshire Historical RS, 63–4 (1984–5) · HoP, *Commons, 1509–58* · A. G. Dickens, 'Estate and household management in Bedfordshire, c.1540', *The Gostwicks of Willington, and other studies*, Bedfordshire Historical RS, 36 (1956), 38–45
Archives Folger | PRO, state papers, Henry VIII, SP1

Gosynhyll, Edwarde (*fl. c.***1542**), poet, acknowledged his authorship of *The Prayse of All Women called Mulierum Pean* (*c.*1542; 2nd edn, *c.*1560) in its last four stanzas, via three acrostics and a direct claim ('Say Edwarde Gosynhyll toke the labour … Call hym thyne authour'). The book appeared as part of a contentious literary debate on the nature of women, in reply to the anonymous *Schole House of Women* (1541, wrongly dated 1561), the period's most notorious misogynist satire, which draws on a wide variety of sources to catalogue female capriciousness, in crudely vigorous rhyme royal.

The narrator of *Mulierum pean*, a dream-poem also in rhyme royal, presents Venus's defence of womankind from classical, biblical, and practical example, including a 'tribute to mother love' that has been considered 'the most realistic, tender, and extensive' of the period (Utley, 293). The relation between the two poems is complicated by the 'remarkable circumstance of [their] simultaneous allusions … to each other' (Corser, *Collectanea*, 7.31). The *Schole House* asserts that:

> A foole of late contrived a book,
> And all in praise of the femynie
> … *Pehan* he calleth it

while Gosynhyll's narrator is petitioned by a group of women aggrieved 'by a boke, that lately is past … The scole of women', and urged to 'Sende forth … The *Pean* thou wrote'. This passage includes the detail that the precedent work 'by reporte, by the[e] was fyrst framed', but critical opinion is divided as to whether Gosynhyll indeed wrote both works as an exercise in rhetorical ingenuity. W. C. Hazlitt's suspicion that the *Schole House*'s author (and therefore possibly Gosynhyll himself) was Scottish remains tentative.

The pamphlet controversy—politically enlivened by the question of Queen Elizabeth's succession—enlisted many subsequent contributions, among them *A Dyalogue Defensyve for Women agaynst Malycyous Detractoures* (1542), long thought Robert Vaughan's, but from acrostic evidence probably by Robert Burdet, which stages a verse debate between two birds, and *The Defence of Women* (1560) by Edward More, in pedestrian fourteeners. Robert Wyer and John Kynge, the respective publishers of these works, had both published editions of the *Schole House* (*c*.1542 and 1560). Kynge also printed *A Dialogue betwene the Comen Secretary and Jelowsy* (*c*.1560), prompting its improbable ascription by Collier to Gosynhyll. Hazlitt's conjecture that Gosynhyll had died by 1560 (the *Schole House*'s reference to the answering 'foole' therefore a posthumous addition) was based on an incomplete knowledge of the texts.

NICK DE SOMOGYI

Sources F. L. Utley, *The crooked rib: an analytical index to the argument about women in English and Scots literature to the end of the year 1568* (1944) · T. Corser, *Collectanea Anglo-poetica, or, A … catalogue of a … collection of early English poetry*, 7, Chetham Society, 101 (1877) · B. White, 'Three rare books about women', *Huntington Library Bulletin*, 2 (1931), 165–72 · H. Stein, 'Six tracts about women: a volume in the British Museum', *The Library*, 4th ser., 15 (1934–5), 38–48 · S. H. Jackson, 'A sixteenth century poem: *A dialogue betwene the comen secretary and jelowsy*', *Archiv für das Studium der neueren Sprachen und Literaturen*, 215 (1978), 311–17 · W. C. Hazlitt, ed., *Remains of the early popular poetry of England*, 4 vols. (1864–6) · T. Warton, *The history of English poetry*, rev. edn, ed. R. Price, 4 vols. (1824)

Gotch, John Alfred (1852–1942), architect, was born on 28 September 1852 at Kettering, Northamptonshire, the third son of Thomas Henry Gotch (*b*. 1804) and his wife, Mary Anne, daughter of John Gale. He married Annie (*d*. 1924), daughter of John Maddock Perry, lace manufacturer, of Nottingham in 1886. They had one son, who was killed in action in 1916, and one daughter.

For more than 150 years the Gotch family was intimately associated with Kettering. Gotch's great-grandfather Thomas Gotch was the first to open a factory for the manufacture of boots and shoes, about 1786, an industry which in time became the town's staple trade.

Gotch went to Kettering grammar school and later studied at the University of Zürich and at King's College, London. In 1871 he was articled to Robert Winter Johnson, architect and surveyor, of Melton Mowbray, Leicestershire, for three years. This was followed by a period of three years in the office of J. M. Taylor in Manchester, after which Gotch travelled in Belgium. On his return he worked in the office of Joseph Gale before commencing independent practice in Kettering and London in 1878. On the death of Johnson about 1884, his practice at Kettering was taken over by Gotch and Charles Saunders who were subsequently joined by Ralph Surridge. The partnership endured for fifty-five years.

The Northamptonshire buildings for which the partnership was responsible included Corby House, Clopton Manor House (gutted by fire and rebuilt in a neo-Jacobean style, 1907), the neo-Stuart Thornby Grange (1911), Quenby Hall, The Gables (Peterborough), the Irthlingborough Viaduct over the Nene valley, the Alfred East Art Gallery, and the grammar school at Kettering (1913; now the Kettering municipal offices). They built a number of branch buildings for the Midland Bank and the firm was associated with Sir Edwin Lutyens in building the firm's head office in Poultry, London. They also designed secondary and elementary schools at Kettering and in Northamptonshire and Bedfordshire, as well as many war memorials in Kettering and elsewhere. In 1882 Gotch became surveyor to the Kettering urban district council.

Gotch was not only a successful practising architect, but also a prominent architectural historian. Among his publications the most notable include *The Buildings of Sir Thomas Tresham* (1883), *Kirby Hall* and *Haddon Hall* (both 1889), *Architecture of the Renaissance in England* (2 vols., 1891), *Early Renaissance Architecture in England* (1901), *The Growth of the English House* (1909), *The Original Drawings for the Palace at Whitehall* (1912), *The English Home from Charles I to George IV* (1918), *Old English Houses* (1925), *Inigo Jones* (1928), *The Old Halls and Manor-Houses of Northamptonshire* (1936), *Squires' Homes and other Old Buildings of Northamptonshire* (1939), together with a vast number of papers and lectures on related subjects.

All Gotch's writings bear the imprint of his character, which was one of extreme simplicity and solidity. His direct, almost blunt, speech, was tempered by a keen though quiet sense of humour, a courteous manner, and a natural dignity. His knowledge of and admiration for the work of the periods to which he devoted his life were so deeply engrained that he had no sympathy with modern trends in design. He made no attempt to understand them and was content to go on working in the past styles which he admired. He was happier restoring old buildings than in designing new ones, although to the latter he gave the best of his knowledge and skill. He loved the building crafts of earlier ages and attempted to reproduce some of these in his designs. In 1886–7 he was president of the Architectural Association, and for nearly forty years he was a member of the council of the Royal Institute of British Architects of which, in 1923–5, he was the first architect from outside London to serve as president. He received the honorary degree of MA from the University of Oxford in 1924 and in 1934 he edited the institute's centenary history: *The Growth and Work of the Royal Institute of British Architects, 1834–1934*. He was a member for some years of the Royal Fine Arts Commission, an honorary corresponding member of the American Institute of Architects, and he was the first president of the Northamptonshire Association of Architects.

For many years Gotch was a leading citizen of Northamptonshire. He was a member of the county council, served as chairman of the Kettering bench as early as 1893, was chairman of the Northamptonshire quarter sessions, of the records committee, and of the Kettering Liberal Association. He was president of Northamptonshire Men in London and in 1938 he was elected the first charter mayor of the borough of Kettering after its incorporation. His portrait as president of the Royal Institute of British Architects was painted by his brother Thomas Cooper Gotch (1854–1931) and hangs in the institute buildings, 66 Portland Place, London.

Gotch died at his home, Weekley Rise, Weekley, near Kettering, on 17 January 1942.

IAN MACALISTER, rev. JOHN ELLIOTT

Sources *The Builder*, 162 (1942), 78 · *RIBA Journal*, 49 (1941–2), 37, 66–7 · *Architect and Building News* (30 Jan 1942), 92 · *Architects' Journal* (22 Jan 1942), 69 · *Architects' Journal* (29 Jan 1942), 86 · *Architects' Journal* (5 Feb 1942), 107–8 · *Dir. Brit. archs.* · *Northamptonshire*, Pevsner (1961) · *CGPLA Eng. & Wales* (1942)
Archives Northants. RO, corresp., papers, and MSS · RIBA, sketchbooks and topographical drawings · RIBA BAL, MS of *Early Renaissance architecture in England* and misc. corresp.
Likenesses T. C. Gotch, oils, RIBA · photograph, RIBA · portrait, repro. in *Building News* (21 March 1890) · portrait, repro. in *The Builder* · portrait, repro. in *Architect and Building News* · portrait, repro. in *Architects' Journal* (29 Jan 1942)
Wealth at death £56,180 1s. 9d.: probate, 18 July 1942, *CGPLA Eng. & Wales*

Goter [Gother], **John** (*d.* 1704), Roman Catholic priest and religious writer, was born in Southampton, his parents reputedly 'rigid presbyterians'. He was educated 'in a well-populated town at the foot of the pulpit', being 'indoctrinated with all the prejudices against the Church of Rome which a tender mind full of zeal was capable of receiving' (Norman, 306–7). His dissatisfaction with this teaching led to his conversion about 1667, whereupon a Catholic relative, reputedly Thomas *Tylden (1622–1688), the controversialist, arranged his voyage to Lisbon, where he entered the English College on 10 January 1668. He took his oath on 9 January 1672, became a lecturer in philosophy on 10 April 1677, and prefect of studies on 11 November 1678.

Goter was sent to England on 18 October 1681 as a missionary. His first work, published under the pseudonym Lovell, was *A Papist Misrepresented and Represented, or, A Two-Fold Character of Popery* (1685), which made good use of his protestant antecedents, as in defining the papist misrepresented he was able to write: 'I have quoted no authors, but have described him exactly according to the apprehension I had of a papist framed by me when I was a protestant' (*DNB*). This work went through five editions in 1685 and elicited replies from eminent Anglican divines such as Edward Stillingfleet. In turn, Goter responded with *Reflections upon the 'Answer to the Papist Misrepresented and Represented'* (1686). This drew replies from William Sherlock and Abednego Seller, to which Goter responded with *Papists protesting against protestant-popery; in answer to a discourse intitled, 'A papist not misrepresented'* (1686). Other protestant controversialists were drawn into this pamphlet warfare, such as William Clagett and Nicholas Stratford. Goter may have penned as many as thirteen pamphlets during 1685–8, being perceived as by far the most eloquent Catholic apologist. Indeed John Dryden commended Goter as the only man 'besides himself' (*DNB*) who knew how to write the English language.

Goter established and built Lime Street Chapel in 1686 with the assistance of Father Andrew Giffard and the royal physician, John Betts, both of whom hailed from Hampshire, and Chris Tootal and James Dimmock, two midland priests. However, after six months the premises were appropriated for a Jesuit college. Shortly before the revolution of 1688 Goter accepted the post of chaplain to George Holman of Warkworth, Northamptonshire, who had recently married Lady Anastasia Howard, daughter of the Catholic peer William Howard, Viscount Stafford, who had been executed for treason in 1680. His new parish covered an extensive area and his charges included Richard Challoner, the son of Holman's housekeeper, whom he received into the church, and who subsequently became vicar apostolic of London.

Goter left England in order to return to Lisbon, 'to compose some unhappy differences' at Lisbon 'and to put that house upon a better footing for the future' (Norman, 309), possibly by means of succeeding the aged rector of the college, Matthias Watkinson. Four days after setting sail from Falmouth he died at sea on board the Genoese ship *San Caetano* on 13 October 1704 NS. Rather than be buried at sea his body was taken to Lisbon and interred on 28 October under the altar of St Thomas of Canterbury in the chapel in Lisbon College. His will made a few years previously left £5 and a diamond ring to a niece, Anne Goter, and £5 to Lady Anastasia Holman. The remainder of his estate was left to Miles Philipson of the Inner Temple, whom he named as his executor.

At Warkworth, Goter had 'concealed himself entirely from the world' (Dodd, 3.482–4), and produced works of a more spiritual nature compared to his earlier polemical offerings. These were published after his death. The most effective work was written at the end of the seventeenth century, *Instructions and Devotions for Hearing Mass* (1705), which was followed by *Instructions for Confession, Communion and Confirmation*. In these works Goter set out to provide the laity with simple instructions and prayers, eschewing controversy and adopting an undenominational tone. In 1718 the Revd William Crathorne collected and edited Goter's spiritual works, which ran to sixteen volumes and included many more 'Instructions'. With among others *Instructions for the Afflicted and Sick, Instructions for the Whole Year, Instructions for Masters, Traders, Labourers, Servants, Apprentices, Youths etc.*, and *A Practical Catechism, Divided into Fifty-Two Lessons, for each Sunday in the Year*, the Catholic laity acquired a comprehensive spiritual guide. Goter's work thus played an influential role in shaping the peculiarly English Catholic piety of the eighteenth century. STUART HANDLEY

Sources M. Norman, 'John Gother and the English way of spirituality', *Recusant History*, 11 (1972), 306–19 • M. Sharratt, ed., *Lisbon College register, 1628–1813*, Catholic RS, 72 (1991), 66–7 • Gillow, *Lit. biog. hist.*, 2.540–46 • PRO, PROB 11/479, sig. 253 • V. Guazzelli, 'John Gother: priest', *The Clergy Review*, new ser., 26 (1946), 583–90 • C. Dodd [H. Tootell], *The church history of England, from the year 1500, to the year 1688*, 3 (1742), 482–4 • C. Butler, *Historical memoirs of the English, Irish, and Scottish Catholics since the Reformation*, 3rd edn, 4 (1822), 425–6 • D. Brockway, 'Some new editions from the reign of James II', *The Papers of the Bibliographical Society of America*, 55 (1961), 118–30 • E. Petre, *Notices of the English colleges and convents established on the continent after the dissolution*, ed. F. C. Husenbeth (1849) • J. Bossy, *The English Catholic community, 1570–1850* (1975) • J. C. H. Aveling, *The handle and the axe* (1976)

Gotherson [née Scott; other married name Hogben], **Dorothea** (bap. 1611), Quaker preacher and writer, was baptized on 22 September 1611 at Godmersham, Kent, the youngest of five children of Thomas *Scott (c.1566–1635), later MP for Canterbury, and his second wife, Mary Knatchbull (d. 1616). According to her biographer, G. D. Scull, the Scotts could trace a lineage through the Scotts of Scot's Hall back to Edward I; Dorothea's great-grandfather was Thomas Wyatt the rebel. Although concerned about sin and mortality Dorothea remained aloof from any denomination during her early years. About 1635 she married Daniel Gotherson (d. 1666), later a major in Cromwell's army, and inherited her father's estate at Egerton, Kent, which returned nearly £500 annually. Together they had five daughters and a son, Daniel.

Some time during the 1650s the Gothersons joined the Society of Friends. In particular Dorothea was drawn by their unity and devotion; in 1661 she reflected on life after her convincement: 'then began I to be led by the Spirit of God out of darkness into his marvellous light' (Scull, 8). She ministered to Friends in Kent where Thomas Lovelace was among her auditors: in a later deposition he noted that 'this Mrs. Gotherson had long been a great Quaker, and she had a particular congregation … which went under her maiden name of "Scott's congregation", where he has heard her himself preach' (Scull, 6).

In 1661 Dorothea dedicated her Quaker tract, *To All that are Unregenerated, a Call to Repentence*, to the recently restored Charles II 'whom the Lord I believe hath set upon England's throne … that [he] mightst rule in righteousness' and to whom she probably presented a copy. The work recognized Charles's divine authority and hoped he would not 'think it below him to read that which many think above me to write, in respect to my sex' (Scull, 79). She exhorted him to 'rule and reign' in righteousness and pleaded with 'all people of England' to 'turn to the Lord' (Scull, 81, 88). A work written by her husband, *An Alarm to All Priests* (1660), may well have been co-written by Dorothea.

It was at Whitehall in the early 1660s that the Gothersons encountered the adventurer John *Scott, who claimed to be a descendant of the same Scott family as Dorothea. She believed him 'because some of Anchestors pictures were very like him' (Bodl. Oxf., MS Rawl. A.175, fol. 147r). Scott soon gained the confidence of both Dorothea and Daniel, convincing them that he had lived among the natives of Long Island from whom he had purchased large tracts of land. By 1663 Daniel had mortgaged the Egerton estate to pay Scott £2000 for land and houses on Long Island, and had entrusted the couple's son to Scott's care. When Daniel died about 1 September 1666 his will of the previous month left his Long Island holdings to family and friends, but Dorothea soon learned that neither Daniel nor Scott ever owned the Long Island land. In a petition to the king, probably written in 1668, she explained that she had been defrauded by Scott and that he had apparently 'exposed' her son 'to work for bread'; she asked that her case be referred to Francis Lovelace, the governor of New York (Scull, 11). For the next several years she sought legal redress, citing her illustrious ancestry in her appeals at court. Scott was never brought to justice, but in 1679 his activities both in the colonies and on the continent brought him to the attention of Samuel Pepys, who collected a number of depositions against Scott, including that from Dorothea.

In 1670 Dorothea married Joseph Hogben of Kent, of whom very little is known. In 1680 she sold the Egerton estate to Sir James Rushout, and in the autumn she and her children sailed for an estate at Oyster Bay in Long Island which her first husband had bought in August 1633. Little is known of her life thereafter, though her daughter, also named Dorothea, married John Davis, a Quaker, shortly after they arrived, and moved to Salem county, New Jersey, about 1705. STEVEN C. HARPER

Sources G. D. Scull, *Dorothea Scott, also Gotherson and Hogben* (1882); rev. edn (1883) • 'Dictionary of Quaker biography', RS Friends, Lond. [card index] • *CSP col.*, 5.607–8 • Pepys papers, Bodl. Oxf., MS Rawl. A.175, vol. 6, esp. fols. 112–48 • Bodl. Oxf., MS Rawl. A.194, fols. 125v–126r

Gott, Benjamin (1762–1840), cloth merchant and manufacturer, was born on 24 June 1762 at Woodhall, Calverley, near Leeds, the fifth of the six children of John Gott (1720–1793), an engineer and surveyor of bridges for the West Riding of Yorkshire, and his second wife, Susanna Jackson of Bradford. He was educated at Bingley grammar school and then, in 1780, apprenticed with the Leeds merchant house of Wormald and Fountaine. His father paid the large premium of £400 for his four-year period of training. It was money well spent. Running one of the top half-dozen firms of cloth merchants in the town, Wormald and Fountaine (related by marriage) were prominent members of the Leeds élite, both men having served office as mayor in the late 1770s. On new year's day 1785, straight out of his apprenticeship, Gott became a junior partner in the firm; his father raised £3660, admitting his son to a one-eleventh share of its capital and profits. Barely had the ink dried on the deed than John Wormald died, leaving three teenage sons for whom a share in the management of the firm had been explicitly reserved. Half a dozen years later Joseph Fountaine was dead, with an only daughter eager to withdraw her large interest from the business. Gott, not yet thirty, had become senior partner in one of the West Riding's principal merchant houses.

The second half of the 1780s and the early 1790s (in sharp contrast to the years 1775–83) were prosperous ones for the Yorkshire cloth industry. And in terms of technology they were momentous. Although the lead in the mechanization of its traditional processes in textile manufacture was given by the cotton industry, there were three innovations in the making of wool textiles in the West Riding during these years: spinning by the jenny; scribbling (preliminary carding) and carding by a machine adapted from Arkwright's water frame; and, not before 1792, the introduction of Boulton and Watt's rotary steam engine in Leeds. Gott, young, immensely talented, with a decade's training in a first-rate firm behind him, and, equally importantly, with its capital resources—if he could communicate his vision to his young Wormald partners—at his command, made the boldest of entrepreneurial leaps in 1792. He built the first large-scale factory in the West Riding woollen industry on a green-field site, Bean Ing, to the west of the smart Georgian squares and terraces of Leeds. Previously, merchants had not manufactured their own cloth, but bought it in the cloth halls or to order from some of the county's thousands of independent clothiers. Gott constructed a large factory (its buildings and machinery were insured for £10,000 to £12,000 when it was destroyed by fire in 1799), powered by a big 40 hp Boulton and Watt engine. In production eighteen months later, the factory housed the entire gamut of machinery necessary to produce and finish cloth.

By no means all of Gott's machinery was steam driven: the jennies, looms, and finishing tools definitely were not. In many ways the factory was a half-way house between the old domestic system of production and the large scale, power-driven factories of the 1820s and 1830s. Certainly, Gott continued to buy cloth in the halls (indeed he remained principally a great export merchant, selling three times more cloth than he made himself), and at Armley, one of the two other water-driven mills he later acquired, he continued to provide scribbling and fulling services for the district's independent clothiers. Nevertheless, the scale of his enterprise was exceptional. Park Mills at Bean Ing employed 761 workers in 1813; six years later, on 31 July 1819 (a difficult year for the cloth industry), the total work force, there and at Gott's other two mills and

warehouse, was 1019. In the late 1790s and 1800s his enterprise, together with that of a handful of other merchants running mills on a smaller scale, unnerved the entire cloth industry, creating the impression that the merchants would become factory owners, thereby squeezing out of existence the small, independent clothiers. The progress to a complete factory system, thoroughly examined in the famous *Report on the State of the Woollen Manufacture of England* (1806), in fact took more than half a century to complete.

Gott steered the great firm for more than thirty years before two of his sons, John (1791–1867) and William (1797–1863), took over in the mid-1820s, when the factory was twice extended and power-driven spinning mules and cloth-finishing machinery were installed. Although few accounts have survived among the Gott papers, it was clearly a most profitable venture—the return on Gott's great entrepreneurial vision. And in his early experiments with steam in the dyeing processes he was a bold innovator. The family's entry in the 1937 edition of Burke's *Landed Gentry* described him simply as 'one of the founders of the modern woollen industry in Yorkshire'. Yet in many ways Gott was not in the Arkwright mould of *nouveau riche* factory masters.

On 30 November 1790 Gott married Elizabeth (1768–1857), the daughter of William and Elizabeth Rhodes of Badsworth, with whom he had four sons and six daughters. A cultured woman, a regular churchgoer, and a socialite, she proved to be the ideal wife for the Conservative, Anglican Gott. A friend described her as 'a woman of infinite charm … possessed of great dignity and good looks' (Gott MS 194). At first Gott did the things expected of a leading member of the tory merchant élite in Leeds: he was mayor in 1799 and captain commandant of the Leeds Volunteers. In 1803 he acquired Armley House, a pleasant villa on the edge of Leeds, as a rural retreat for his large family. Seven years later he commissioned the leading landscape architect Humphrey Repton to design its 76 acre park, most unusually incorporating distant views of his factory and Leeds into the plans. And in 1822 Sir Robert Smirke was engaged to remodel Armley House in the Greek-revival style as a fitting home for his growing art collection.

The Gotts led a cultured life in Leeds. He was prominent in the affairs of the Northern Society for the Encouragement of the Fine Arts in 1809, lending Dutch and Italian pictures from his collection for its exhibitions, and generously patronizing a clutch of contemporary artists practising in the West Riding—Charles Schwanfelder, J. H. Rhodes, and J. C. Ibbetson. He was instrumental in securing commissions in Leeds for Francis Chantrey (Gott owned busts of James Watt and John Rennie by him) and John Flaxman, and he and Mrs Gott sat to Sir Thomas Lawrence for two fine portraits in 1826. Above all he patronized his second cousin, the sculptor Joseph Gott (1785–1860), from whom he commissioned between 1826 and 1840 'work for the Gott family … striking both in its quantity and diversity: monuments, portrait busts, medallions and figures, groups of children and children with animals, ancient and modern mythology and pugilism' (Friedman and Stevens, 16). Gott was the first president of the Leeds Philosophical and Literary Society (established 1818) and a founding member of the Leeds Mechanics' Institute (1824).

Life was not all profits and paintings. At times Gott was dogged by controversy. About 1800 he was involved in a protracted and bitter dispute with the master cloth dressers about the introduction of finishing machinery and apprenticeships. In 1824 he was prosecuted for smoke nuisance: the emissions from his and neighbouring mills, driven down the Aire valley by the prevailing westerlies, had effectively ruined the Georgian Parks development for its middle-class inhabitants. He was chairman of the Leeds and Selby Railway Company (1830), an early rail venture established, amid conflict, to provide an alternative route to Hull to that afforded by the long-founded, immensely profitable Aire and Calder Navigation Company.

Gott died at Armley House on 14 February 1840 and was buried at Armley Chapel. Joseph Gott erected a monument (removed to St Bartholomew's Church, Armley, in 1890) archly described by Sir Nikolaus Pevsner as a 'comfortable semi-reclining figure on a mattress rolled up at the top. He is wearing a dressing gown' (*Yorkshire: the West Riding*, 1959, 323). Gott was survived by two of his four sons (Benjamin had died in Athens in 1817 while collecting classical marbles, his brother Henry in Paris in 1825), who ran the firm until 1867, when it ceased cloth production.

R. G. WILSON

Sources U. Leeds, Brotherton L., Gott MSS · W. B. Crump, ed., *The Leeds woollen industry, 1780–1820* (1931) · T. Fawcett, *The rise of provincial art: artists, patrons and institutions outside London, 1800–1830* (1974) · T. Friedman and T. Stevens, *Joseph Gott, 1786–1860: sculptor* (1972) [exhibition catalogue, Leeds City Art Gallery and Walker Art Gallery, Liverpool] · R. J. Morris, *Class, sect, and party: the making of the British middle class, Leeds, 1820–1850* (1990) · Burke, *Gen. GB* · R. G. Wilson, *Gentlemen merchants: the merchant community in Leeds, 1700–1830* (1971) · D. T. Jenkins, *The West Riding wool textile industry, 1770–1835: a study of fixed capital formation* (1975) · H. Heaton, 'Benjamin Gott and the industrial revolution', *Economic History Review*, 3 (1931–2) · S. Daniels, 'Landscaping for a manufacturer: Humphrey Repton's commission for Benjamin Gott at Armley in 1809–10', *Journal of Historical Geography*, 7 (1981), 379–96 · P. Hudson, *The genesis of industrial capital: a study of the West Riding wool textile industry, c.1750–1850* (1986) · will, PRO, PROB 11/1927, sig. 333

Archives U. Leeds, Brotherton L.

Likenesses T. Lawrence, oils, 1826, Leeds City Art Gallery · J. Gott, monumental marble effigy, 1842, St Bartholomew's Church, Armley, Leeds

Gott, John (1830–1906), bishop of Truro, was born on 25 December 1830 at Denison Hall, Leeds, the third son and seventh child of William Gott (1797–1863) and Margaret (1795–1844), daughter of William Ewart of Mossley Hill, Liverpool. He was a grandson of Benjamin Gott of Armley House, the great Leeds textile manufacturer. After attending Winchester College from 1844 he read for his BA at Brasenose College, Oxford (1849–53). After a year of foreign travel and another spent at Wells Theological College, he was ordained deacon in 1857 and priest the next

John Gott (1830–1906), by Samuel Alexander Walker, pubd 1889

year. The following eight years he passed as a curate in Great Yarmouth, first in St Nicholas's and then in St Andrew's parish. On 10 June 1858 he married Harriet Mary Maitland (1835–1906), his first cousin and the daughter of W. Whitaker Maitland of Loughton Hall, Essex. They had one son and three daughters.

In 1866 Gott returned to his home town with the perpetual curacy of Bramley, where (despite complaints) he introduced surplices, candles, and an eastward position for the eucharist. In 1873 he succeeded J. R. Woodford in the semi-episcopal state of vicar of Leeds, complete with BD, DD, and a rural deanship. His tenure was busy but fairly peaceable, except for the opposition aroused by an allegedly Tractarian appointment to Headingley in 1881. Gott continued Woodford's interest in education. He was a prime mover in the foundation of Leeds Clergy School (1875) and the Leeds Church Day School Association (1885), and in the development of the Yorkshire College towards university status from 1877. He also pursued his predecessor's campaign of new church-building, extending the seating available in Leeds from 27,000 to 48,000. However, he considered as even more important the provision of less formal mission rooms, along the lines of the 'wherrymen's mission' with which he had been involved at Yarmouth. When Gott wrote *The Parish Priest of the Town* (1887), it was mainly with the problems of a great industrial city in mind.

The position of dean of Worcester, which Gott held

from 1886 to 1891, was intended to be less taxing. However, there being an industrial city still to hand in the diocese, he was unable to keep away from it, even if his constant theme was that it required detachment from Worcester—'we must do something for Birmingham', he repeated constantly (Worlledge, in Gott, 27). Election as bishop of Truro on 3 August 1891 took Gott to a very different position, one which his predecessor, G. H. Wilkinson, had found too much for him. Gott did preside over the long-awaited completion of Truro Cathedral in 1903, but lived mainly not at the bishop's residence there, Lis Escop, but at Trenython on St Austell Bay. He founded another clergy school—as at Leeds, this was to be a graduate establishment, to avoid 'a low and frivolous type of ordinand' (1892, Benson, MS 111, fol. 229). But he was never as at home as when in Yorkshire, where he returned when he could. *The Truth* (25 July 1906) claimed he was 'not a brilliant success' as bishop, being too 'high' for his diocese.

Gott was interested in the Anglican monastic movement and even more so in retreats for secular clergy. That he admitted to saying prayers for the dead in such a retreat would only have confirmed evangelical fears. He did not dislike clerical celibacy; his 'main issue' left with Rome was Mariolatry (*Letters*, 160–61, 176, 180). His politics were solidly Conservative, though he was remotely connected (through his mother) to W. E. Gladstone, with whom he maintained a friendly correspondence: writing to him in 1880, he expressed the wish 'to stave off for a time, if we cannot prevent, the day when the Church must side wholly with one political party against the other' (BL, Add. MS 46048, fol. 176). But, though he might 'revere and greatly like the man Gladstone', he found it increasingly baffling 'why so devoted a man should be so often and gravely wrong' (*Letters*, 230). Despite his Anglo-Catholicism (a label he accepted) and Conservatism, however, Gott advised against open ritualistic excesses; and his experience at Yarmouth, Leeds, and Truro led him to stress the need to woo dissenters.

In his last years, Gott increasingly justified the nickname Dr Forgot or Clean Forgot—a splendid episcopal garden party went to waste due to a failure to dispatch any invitations. His heart attack in October 1905 necessitated the appointment of a suffragan bishop of St Germans. The death of Gott's wife on 19 April 1906 was a final blow, and he suffered a fatal attack in his study at Trenython on 21 July 1906. He was buried four days later at nearby Tywardreath.   JULIAN LOCK

Sources [A. J. Worlledge], *Letters of Bishop Gott, arranged by members of his family, with a biographical sketch by A. J. Worlledge* (1918?) · *Church Times* (27 July 1906) · *The Record* (27 July 1906) · *Truth* (25 July 1906) · *Annual Register* (1906) · *ILN* (28 July 1906) · B. Donaldson, *The bishopric of Truro: the first twenty-five years, 1877–1902* (1902) · H. M. Brown, *A century for Cornwall: the diocese of Truro, 1877–1977* (1976) · N. Yates, *Leeds and the Oxford Movement*, Thoresby Society, 55 (1975) · C. G. Lang, ed., *Church and town for fifty years* (1891), 29–38 · E. D. Steele, 'Imperialism and Leeds politics, c.1850–1914', *A history of modern Leeds*, ed. D. Fraser (1980), 327–52 · BL, Gladstone MSS, Add. MSS 44478, 46048–46050 · LPL, Benson MSS · Burke, *Gen. GB* · Walford, *County families* · Crockford · *WWW* · *Men and women of the time* (1899)

Archives LPL, speeches and corresp. · U. Leeds, Brotherton L., corresp. with bibliographers | BL, letters to W. E. Gladstone, Add. MSS 44478, 46048–46050 · LPL, corresp. with Edward Benson · LPL, letters to Lady Burdett-Coutts · LPL, Tait MSS · LPL, F. Temple MSS · LPL, letters to J. A. L. Riley, MS 2344

Likenesses photograph, 1873–86, repro. in *Letters of Bishop Gott* · S. A. Walker, photograph, pubd 1889, NPG [*see illus.*] · photograph, c.1894, NPG · W. W. Ouless, portrait, 1899, repro. in *Letters of Bishop Gott*, frontispiece · portrait, 1903, Leeds Clergy School · J. Beagle & Co., postcard, in or before 1904 (after photograph), LPL · bronze tablet and statue, c.1906, Truro Cathedral · Elliott & Fry, photograph, repro. in *ILN*, 129 (1906), 120 · R. T. & Co., wood-engraving, NPG; repro. in *ILN* (13 June 1891) · Whitlock, photograph, repro. in *Worcester Herald* (4 April 1891) · bronze medallion, Leeds Clergy School · photographs, LPL

Wealth at death £82,611 8s. 6d.: probate, 12 Oct 1906, *CGPLA Eng. & Wales*

Gott, John William (1866–1922), freethought propagandist, was born at Cowling, Yorkshire, on 17 January 1866, the son of John Gott (b. 1841/2), farm labourer, and his wife, Mary, *née* Peel (b. 1842/3), house servant, both of Cowling. Little is known of his childhood. By 1891 he was a self-employed tailor and draper in Bradford where, through aggressive advertising in freethought and socialist periodicals, he built a successful mail-order business, employing as local agents men whose participation in unpopular movements had resulted in their dismissal from regular work. On 3 January that year he married Ada Dyson (1869–1912), weaver. There was one child of the marriage, Alice (b. 1893).

Gott had joined the National Secular Society under the presidency of George William Foote in 1887, and in March 1891 he became secretary of the revived Bradford branch of the society. In May 1894 he was business manager of the *Truth Seeker*, a local penny monthly freethought periodical. By 1900 he was editor, publisher, and proprietor of what was now a strongly anti-Christian paper that appeared intermittently until at least 1915. The attempt to revive secularism in Bradford in the 1890s was unsuccessful as new organizations were succeeded by others equally short-lived. Gott was central to most of them as secretary or treasurer. In 1903 he was summonsed five times and convicted once for selling freethought and other radical literature on a Sunday on Woodhouse Moor, Leeds, contrary to local by-laws, and was charged with blasphemy for a cartoon reprinted in the *Truth Seeker* for October, but the stipendiary magistrate dismissed this case on a technicality. This was the beginning of a propagandist war of attrition by a group of militant freethinkers which was to lead during the next few years to several blasphemy prosecutions. Gott's role was primarily as publisher, through his Freethought Socialist League, an organization formed about 1909 to combat the Liberal tendencies of G. W. Foote's secularism and the Christian tendencies of Keir Hardie's socialism. In 1911 he was prosecuted for blasphemy for publishing a pamphlet of crude anti-Christian questions entitled *Rib Ticklers, or, Questions for Parsons*, and was sentenced to four months in Armley gaol, Leeds. On 16 February 1912 his wife, Ada, suffered a stroke and died. The home secretary immediately ordered his release, but the circumstances of Ada's death added a personal edge to Gott's campaign.

In 1913 Gott was funding an anti-Christian lecture campaign, in November 1916 he was sentenced to two weeks' hard labour at Birkenhead police court for selling a profane book, and in July 1917 he was sentenced at the Birmingham assizes to six weeks' hard labour for blasphemous libel, again in the *Rib Ticklers*. On this occasion, the unsuccessful defence was led by Norman Birkett. In July 1918 Gott appeared before the Westminster police court charged under the Defence of the Realm Act with exhibiting a poster, for which he was fined £25 or two months' imprisonment, and in 1921 he was sentenced at the Birmingham assizes to six months' hard labour for blasphemous libel for publishing and sending through the post an obscene book, *How to Prevent Pregnancy*, and also again the *Rib Ticklers*. Shortly after release he was summoned before West Ham police court on a charge of obstruction, later changed to blasphemy, for selling the *Rib Ticklers* and similar publications. The case was heard at the Old Bailey in December 1921 where, after a retrial, he was found guilty and received nine months with hard labour. An appeal in January 1922 confirmed the sentence. This was the last time that anyone in Britain was imprisoned for blasphemy. Gott emerged in broken health and died at Victoria Hospital, Blackpool, of cancer of the pancreas, stomach, and liver, on 4 November 1922, survived by his daughter, Alice. He was buried on 8 November 1922 in Bradford.

Gott was a provocative agitator, yet he aroused considerable support among MPs, academics, and writers for a liberalization of the law in England and Wales, leading to unsuccessful campaigns to abolish the blasphemy laws. The works for which he was imprisoned seemed harmless a century later. EDWARD ROYLE

Sources *Truth Seeker* (Aug 1903), 6–7 · *The Freethinker* (4–25 Dec 1921) · *The Freethinker* (1 Jan–5 Feb 1922) · *The Freethinker* (11 June 1922) · *National Reformer* (4 Sept 1892), 153 · *National Reformer* (4 June 1893), 368 · 'Gott, J. W.', *Labour Annual* (1900), 152 · E. A. Pack, *A 'blasphemer' on 'blasphemy': the latest Leeds police fiasco* [n.d., 1903?] · E. A. Pack, *The trial and imprisonment of J. W. Gott for blasphemy* [1912] · T. A. Jackson, *God and Gott!* [1917] · *The Freethinker* (5–19 Nov 1922) · E. Royle, *Radicals, secularists and republicans: popular freethought in Britain, 1866–1915* (1980) · D. Nash, *Blasphemy in modern Britain, 1789 to the present* (1999) · b. cert. · m. cert. · d. cert.

Likenesses line drawing (in Armley gaol), repro. in Nash, *Blasphemy in modern Britain* · line drawing (in Armley gaol), repro. in Jackson, *God and Gott!* · photograph, repro. in *Truth Seeker*, 1/6 (Oct 1894), 1 · photograph, repro. in *Labour Annual*

Gott, Joseph (1785–1860), sculptor, was born probably in London and was baptized on 11 December 1785 at St Martin-in-the-Fields, London, the son of John Gott and his wife, Elizabeth, *née* Yarwood. He was apprenticed in London to the sculptor John Flaxman between 1798 and 1802 and entered the Royal Academy Schools in March 1805, where he gained a silver medal the following year. Nothing is recorded about his life from 1809 until 1819, when *Jacob Wrestling with the Angel* won the Royal Academy gold medal. In 1819 or 1820 he married Lydia, whose maiden name is unknown; they had one son and three daughters.

He began exhibiting at the Royal Academy in 1820, showing in that year *The Dying Spartacus* (Sir John Soane's Museum, London), his earliest surviving work, and thereafter regularly until 1848.

In 1822 Gott was sent to Rome on a pension from the painter Sir Thomas Lawrence, who described him in a letter of introduction to Antonio Canova as possessing 'blameless Integrity & Worth' and 'Talent if not Genius' (Bassano del Grappa, Museo Civico, Canova archives, V.550/3601). During 1822–4 Gott made hundreds of terracotta and plaster maquettes (a fine example is *Venus Dissuading Adonis from the Chase*, Leeds Museums and Galleries), from which he drew inspiration for the next two decades; many were transferred into white Italian marble, his preferred finished material. At first his career prospered through commissions from English visitors to Rome. In 1823 William, sixth duke of Devonshire, ordered *A Greyhound with her Two Puppies* (Chatsworth, Derbyshire), the first of a series of sensitively carved animal groups for which Gott became famous. His first Roman works were exhibited at the Royal Academy in 1826, when he was linked with the sculptor John Gibson as 'getting for themselves and for their country a high reputation' (Uwins, 351). To attract new clients Gott made several visits to England, the first in 1827. Over the next ten years Benjamin Gott, a relative and the leading Yorkshire woollen manufacturer, and other family members, commissioned some thirty-eight sculptures, including church monuments, ideal figures, children with animals, and various portrait types. Other patrons in the north of England included W. E. Gladstone, George Banks of Leeds, and many aristocrats. In 1828 Gott took a studio at via Babuino 155 in Rome, which he kept for the rest of his life. In that year the painter J. M. W. Turner wrote from Rome that sculpture 'carries away all the patronage … Gott's Studio is full' (Finberg, 308). This marked the beginning of his international reputation and period of greatest activity. Among many outstanding works are *Metobus and Camilla* (1830, Leeds Museums and Galleries), the monument to William Ewart (1832, St James's cemetery chapel, Liverpool), and *Ino Teaching Bacchus to Dance* (priv. coll.).

In 1838 Gott's Leeds commissions came to an end, there was little work in Rome owing to an epidemic of cholera, from which two of his daughters died, and his wife lost her memory. (She died in 1850.) His own powers now began to fail. *A Dancing Nymph* shown at the Royal Academy in 1845 was criticized for its 'excessive poverty of modelling' (*Art Union*, 195). Although he ceased producing sculpture, *Ceres* was shown at the Great Exhibition of 1851 and *Ruth Gleaning* at the Paris Universal Exhibition in 1855. Joseph Gott died in Rome on 8 January 1860 and was buried in the protestant cemetery there. He was one of the leading neo-classical sculptors, a skilled modeller and carver celebrated for the realism of his work. (His sitters are often portrayed in modern dress.) His prolific output and repertory of subjects were unequalled in the history of British sculpture. Examples of his work are in the collections of the Leeds Museums and Galleries, York City Art

Gallery, Castle Museum, Nottingham, and Victoria and Albert Museum and Sir John Soane's Museum, London, and at Chatsworth, Derbyshire.   TERRY FRIEDMAN

Sources T. Friedman and T. Stevens, *Joseph Gott, 1786–1860: sculptor* (1972) [exhibition catalogue, Leeds City Art Gallery and Walker Art Gallery, Liverpool] • A. J. Finberg, *The life of J. M. W. Turner* (1939), 308 • *Art Union*, 7 (1845), 195 • S. Uwins, *A memoir of Thomas Uwins*, 2 vols. (1858), 351 • P. Curtis and T. Friedman, eds., *Leeds sculpture collections: illustrated concise catalogue* (1996) • *IGI* • S. C. Hutchison, 'The Royal Academy Schools, 1768–1830', *Walpole Society*, 38 (1960–62), 123–91, esp. 162 • Museo Civico, Bassano del Grappa, Italy, Canova archives, MS V.550/3601
Archives priv. coll., Joseph Gott letters in collections of Charles Gott, Mr and Mrs John Gott, and Signora Giuseppina Sgambati (m 1972) • U. Leeds, family MSS | Museo Civico, Bassano del Grappa, Italy, Canova archives, letters, Lawrence MSS • RA, corresp. with Thomas Lawrence
Likenesses F. Lais, photograph, priv. coll.

Gott, William Henry Ewart (1897–1942), army officer, born at Scarborough on 13 August 1897, was the elder son of William Henry Gott (1852–1929), of Armley House, Leeds (which he sold in 1927), honorary lieutenant-colonel of the 4th battalion, West Yorkshire regiment, and his wife, Anne Rosamond (Rosa), third daughter of the Revd William Collins of Kirkman Bank, Knaresborough. A direct ancestor, Benjamin Gott (1762–1840), mayor of Leeds (1799), of Armley House, was one of the founders of the modern Yorkshire woollen industry; his son William (1797–1863) married Margaret, sister of William *Ewart (1798–1869), the Liberal politician. Other kinsmen of Gott were John *Gott (1830–1906), vicar of Leeds and later bishop of Truro, and A. J. *Ewart (1872–1937).

Gott was educated at Harrow School (1911–14) and the Royal Military College, Sandhurst (1914–15). In 1915 he was commissioned second lieutenant in the King's Royal Rifle Corps, and was soon nicknamed Strafer, after the German execration 'Gott strafe England'. He served with the 2nd battalion in France, where he was wounded at Nieuport in July 1917; later he received the MC. While awaiting evacuation at the field dressing-station he was captured by the enemy; he remained a prisoner until the end of the war despite several attempts at escape, once reaching the Dutch frontier. After the war he was promoted captain (1921) and much of his service was in India, but he was adjutant of the 13th London regiment, Territorial Army, from 1925 to 1928, which he found very congenial. He entered the Staff College, Camberley, in 1930 and graduated in 1931. On 30 June 1934 Gott married Pamela Frances Mary, younger daughter of Brigadier-General Walpole Swinton Kays, of the King's Royal Rifle Corps. They had two daughters but Gott never saw the younger. He was also promoted major in 1934, and held various staff appointments in India from 1934 to 1938, and after a brief period as second-in-command of the 2nd battalion, King's Royal Rifle Corps, in 1938 he was promoted lieutenant-colonel and appointed to command the 1st battalion, which had just arrived in Egypt from Burma.

Gott told his officers that the battalion must prepare for war, and energetically supervised its transformation into a motorized infantry battalion, as part of the newly formed armoured division in Egypt. He learnt, and trained his men to know, the desert well, a knowledge which proved invaluable when war came. After his promotion to brigadier in 1940 Gott became general staff officer, grade 1, of the 7th armoured division, and just before Italy entered the war (June 1940) he was made commander of the support group, comprising the artillery and the rifle (motor) battalions of the armoured division. In war conditions in the western desert, the support group seldom functioned as envisaged, and usually Gott had tanks and armoured cars under his command as well as infantry and artillery. He conducted a skilful withdrawal before Graziani's advance in September 1940, inflicting considerable damage on the Italians, with negligible casualties to his own force of 3000, the sole guard on the frontier; and he played an important part in O'Connor's victorious campaign which began with the battle of Sidi Barrani in December 1940, and resulted, though the British were heavily outnumbered, in the virtual destruction of the Italian armies in Libya in the spring of 1941. The decision to help Greece, however, ended the advance, and the 7th armoured division was withdrawn to Cairo for refitting.

The arrival in Libya of the German Afrika Korps under Rommel, and the subsequent defeat of the British holding forces, brought Gott back to the desert. With a small force he kept the Egyptian frontier in the summer of 1941, while the Australians in Tobruk held back sufficient Germans to prevent a large-scale invasion of Egypt. When the Eighth Army was formed Gott commanded the 7th armoured division, the left wing in the resumed offensive of the autumn of 1941. He was promoted lieutenant-general in 1942, and in February he took command of the 13th corps. Despite a stubborn defence, the Eighth Army was defeated in the battle of Gazala (May–June 1942) and after the fall of Tobruk Gott's corps took part in the retreat to the Alamein position. During the desert campaigns Gott received the DSO and bar (1941) and was appointed CBE (1941) and CB (1942).

In July 1942 Churchill decided on a personal visit to reorganize the British command in the Middle East. He considered Gott fully suited to command the Eighth Army. To make certain, however, that Gott was still physically fit despite his long, hard desert service, Churchill contrived a 'first and last meeting' with him on 5 August. Reassured, he next day recommended Gott's appointment. Nevertheless Viscount Montgomery later claimed in his memoirs that Gott should not have been appointed, was 'completely worn out and needed a rest' (Montgomery, 94), and himself knew it and said so privately. Gott was sent back to the delta on leave before taking over. Before he left Gott completed the broad plan of defence against the next German attack, discerning the importance of the Alam Halfa Ridge which a month later proved to be the essential barrier to the last offensive effort of the Germans in the western desert. The slow transport aircraft in which Gott was travelling to Cairo on 7 August 1942 was shot down by a German fighter, and Gott was killed; Lieutenant-General B. L. Montgomery replaced him.

Gott was a man of 6 feet 2 inches, with searching blue eyes, early silvered hair, and the appearance, some said, of a bishop. He had a marked, but unsought, capacity of gaining troops' confidence and, before Alamein, that 'Strafer has a plan' seemed sufficient. More than any British commander he stood out as a desert leader between Graziani's advance and the retreat to Alamein. He had exceptional breadth and patience in his judgement, uninfluenced by reverses or local opinion, and a serenity which held knowledge and humility. He was modest and reserved, with an individual sense of humour, and essentially peace-loving (although he could be ruthless when necessary). He knew the desert well. 'To him who knows it', he said, 'it can be a fortress: to him who does not, it can be a death trap.' He earned devotion because men believed that unlike others, he 'knew his stuff'. In 1943 a memorial tablet was unveiled in the Anglican cathedral in Cairo.

GYLES ISHAM, rev. ROGER T. STEARN

Sources The Times (11 Aug 1942) · The Times (14 Aug 1942) · W. S. Churchill, The Second World War, 4 (1951) · King's Royal Rifle Corps Chronicle (1942) · A. Clifford, Three against Rommel (1943) · priv. coll. · personal knowledge (1959) · WWW · Burke, Gen. GB (1937) · J. W. Moir, ed., The Harrow School register, 1885–1949, 5th edn (1951) · B. L. Montgomery, The memoirs of field-marshal the Viscount Montgomery of Alamein (1958) · J. Gooch, ed., Decisive campaigns of the Second World War (1990) · CGPLA Eng. & Wales (1942)
Archives FILM IWM FVA, actuality footage | SOUND IWM SA, oral history interview
Likenesses P. Phillips, oils, Royal Green Jackets Museum, Peninsula Barracks, Winchester
Wealth at death £79,803 17s. 5d.: probate, 26 Oct 1942, CGPLA Eng. & Wales

Gottmann, (Iona) Jean (1915–1994), geographer, the only child of prosperous Jewish parents, Elie Gottmann and Sonia-Fanny Ettinger, was born in Kharkov, Ukraine, Russia, on 10 October 1915. His parents were killed in the revolutionary year of 1917. His uncle, Michel Berchin, escaped with him to Paris, where he was raised by his uncle and aunt among an extended family. They were part of the vigorous, artistic, and intellectual emigré community which included Marc Chagall. Gottmann studied first at the Lycée Montaigne at Paris and then at the Lycée St Louis. He entered the Sorbonne and from 1932 he was particularly influenced by Albert Demangeon, E. F. Gautier, and André Siegfried. Gottmann's diplôme d'études supérieures (1934) and his licencié ès lettres (1937) were both taken in the customary French combination of 'histoire et géographie'. His research, however, was on contemporary issues: the Russian five-year plans; Soviet development in Turkestan, Uzbekistan, and Siberia; and irrigation and Jewish settlement in Palestine (the subjects of his first publications beginning in 1933, largely in Annales de Géographie).

The Nazi occupation of France deprived Gottmann of his research assistantship in human geography at the Sorbonne, a post which he held from 1937 to 1940. In 1942 he escaped over the Pyrenees, made his way to Portugal, and escaped to the United States, where he arrived on the day of the Japanese attack on Pearl Harbor. His first post in the USA was at the Institute for Advanced Studies at Princeton

University, after which he was lecturer and then associate professor in geography at Johns Hopkins University between 1943 and 1948. He became a regular member of the Institute for Advanced Studies at Princeton and spent a good deal of his time there, especially between 1949 and 1965.

Gottmann's energies were not confined to the university. He was a member of De Gaulle's Free French organization. He was given political missions and returned to Paris in early 1945 to serve on the staff of the minister of national economy. He held political office as chargé de mission au cabinet of Pierre Mendès France and later of René Pleven, and was involved in planning the post-war reconstruction of France. He spent 1946 and 1947 in New York at the United Nations secretariat, where he was director of studies and research, servicing the Economic and Social Council. In 1948 he returned to Paris where he worked as chargé de recherches at the Centre Nationale de Recherches Sociaux until 1956. His cis- and transatlantic career resumed with the research directorship of the Twentieth Century Fund at New York (1956–61), during which he produced the manuscript for Megalopolis: the Urbanized Northeastern Seaboard of the United States (1961). Gottmann's concept of the urban area centred on New York but stretching from Boston to Washington, DC, as a single, integrated, and dynamic region, has become part of the vernacular. His health was never good and at the United Nations building in 1952, he suffered a fall which broke his neck. For the rest of his life he hobbled with the aid of a walking stick and showed fortitude in pursuing an unremitting international itinerary. In New York he met and married his devoted American wife, Bernice Adelson, in 1957. They had no children.

Gottmann's professorship at the École des Hautes Études, which he held from 1960 until 1984, overlapped at the beginning with his New York post and at the end with his professorship and headship of department at the school of geography, University of Oxford, which he held from 1968 until his retirement in 1983. Gottmann's work was embraced by the Greek planner Doxiades, of whose World Society for Ekistics, Gottmann was president from 1971 to 1973. Through the society's annual Delos symposium, Gottmann made many influential international contacts and received regular invitations to Japan.

Gottmann was a prolific scholar in a range of geographical fields (particularly regional and political geography) but is best known for Megalopolis. He was laden with honours: FBA, chevalier of the Légion d'honneur, Victoria medal of the Royal Geographical Society, grand prix of the Société de Géographie, Paris, Charles Daly medal of the American Geographical Society, numerous honorary doctorates, and the honorary citizenship of Yokohama. Johnston remarks that, for an academic of such distinction, he had curiously little impact on the British geographical world (Johnston, 190). The concept of Megalopolis captured the popular and scholarly imagination at the time, but in geographical circles Gottmann is now more revered than read. He was a cosmopolitan but an outsider in each of the countries in which he held his major positions. He had great charm, but was at the same time distant: austere, bent, dark-suited, the red thread of the Légion d'honneur in his lapel, and with a strong French accent. He had a major impact on Oxford geography through revitalizing the graduate school. He had success with several of his appointments of departmental demonstrators. These were the personal gift of the head of department. His first, Andrew Goudie, succeeded him as professor. John Patten, his second, became minister of education in John Major's Conservative government and was subsequently made a peer. He died at his home, 19 Belsyre Court, Woodstock Road, Oxford, on 28 February 1994 and was buried in Cutteslowe cemetery, Banbury Road. His wife survived him.

CERI PEACH

Sources R. J. Johnston, 'Jean Gottmann: French regional and political geographer *extraordinaire*', *Progress in Human Geography*, 20/2 (1996), 183–93 · J. Patten, ed., *The expanding city: essays in honour of Professor Jean Gottmann* (1983) · M. J. Wise, 'Professor Jean Gottmann FBA, 1915–1994', *GJ*, 160 (1994), 245–6 · *The Independent* (5 March 1994) · *Daily Telegraph* (6 April 1994) · *The Times* (2 March 1994) · *New York Times* (2 March 1994) · J. Gottmann, 'A note on the background and interests of Jean Gottmann', typescript, 1980, priv. coll. · *WW* (1993) · *Oxford University Calendar* (1990) · personal knowledge (2004) · private information (2004) [S. O'Clarey]
Likenesses photograph, 1961, repro. in J. Gottmann, *Megalopolis: the urbanized northeastern seaboard of the United States* (1961), inside jacket · Gillman and Soames, group portrait, photograph, 1983 (*School of Geography staff*) · H. Rosotti, photograph, 1983, repro. in Patten, ed., *Expanding city*, frontispiece
Wealth at death £13,328: administration with will, 26 June 1995, *CGPLA Eng. & Wales*

Goudge, Elizabeth de Beauchamp (1900–1984), author, was born on 24 April 1900, at Wells, Somerset, the only child of the Revd Henry Leighton Goudge DD (1866–1939), at that time vice-principal of Wells Theological College, and his wife, Ida de Beauchamp Collenette (*d.* 1951), daughter of Adolphus Collenette, of Guernsey in the Channel Islands. Elizabeth Goudge grew up in Wells and Ely and was educated at Grassendale School, Southbourne, Hampshire (1914–18), and at the art school at Reading College. When her family moved to Oxford in 1923 on her father's appointment as regius professor of divinity, Elizabeth Goudge worked as a handicraft teacher. But in her spare time she began to write seriously, composing plays and poems before finding her métier as a novelist.

Elizabeth Goudge's first novel, *Island Magic* (1934), was inspired by her childhood holidays with her grandparents in Guernsey, and won immediate acclaim in Britain and America. A succession of novels and short stories followed, including *A City of Bells* (1936), which depicted the Wells of her childhood, and *Towers in the Mist* (1938), a novel of sixteenth-century Oxford, both based on cathedral cities in which her father had exercised his teaching ministry.

On her father's death in 1939 Elizabeth Goudge moved with her mother to a small bungalow at Marldon in south Devon. Deeply committed to nursing her ailing mother, she nevertheless managed to complete *Green Dolphin Country* (1944). This romantic novel achieved spectacular success. It was awarded a Metro-Goldwyn Mayer film prize of

$130,000 and was subsequently made into the film *Green Dolphin Street* in 1947. Set in the Channel Islands and New Zealand of the nineteenth century, it proved Elizabeth Goudge to be a born story-teller with a special facility for describing the country places and people she loved.

With *The Heart of the Family* (1953) Elizabeth Goudge completed the *Eliots of Damerosehay* trilogy which she had started with *The Bird in the Tree* (1940) and *The Herb of Grace* (1948). The three novels won the author a host of new readers, charmed by her portrayal of family life centred on a great country house. Like so much of her work they reflect Goudge's love of familiar places. Damerosehay was situated near Lymington on land known to the author from her schooldays and from later residence in her father's vacation bungalow at Barton-on-Sea, Hampshire.

Apart from anthologies and short stories, Elizabeth Goudge wrote sixteen novels and six children's books. Although her children's books, a mix of fantasy and reality, have been criticized for sickly-sweet sentimentality, the best of them have the timeless appeal of Victorian fiction. *The Little White Horse*, her own favourite among her books, won the Carnegie medal in 1947. Latterly she wrote more non-fiction works, including a life of Christ for younger readers, *God so Loved the World* (1951), and a life of St Francis of Assisi, *My God and my All* (1959).

Elizabeth Goudge was fragile in appearance and health (she suffered a nervous breakdown in the 1930s), and although she inherited her parents' good looks, she never married. After her mother died in 1951, Elizabeth Goudge moved to Oxfordshire. In 1952 she settled in a seventeenth-century cottage at Peppard Common near Henley-on-Thames. She loved the unhurried country life and never moved house again, happy in the companionship of a friend, Jessie Monroe, and a succession of much loved dogs. She once told an interviewer, 'There are not many excitements in my books. I have had too sheltered a life to know much about wickedness … I prefer writing about children and dogs and ordinary men and women in surroundings of natural beauty. My work also appeals to the old and the young and to those who are ill. The sick tell me my books help them forget their aches and pains' (Leasor). To her delight, she received grateful letters from men and women whose faith and confidence had been restored by her novels. These letters meant much more to Elizabeth Goudge than fame or the financial rewards of being a best-selling author.

Among Elizabeth Goudge's later novels, *The Scent of Water* (1963) gave rise to a huge correspondence revealing the exceptional rapport established between the author and her readers. The characters she created reflected the inherent charity and strong Anglican faith of their author who possessed the ability to convey her belief in the love of God to many unknown readers. Her autobiography *The Joy of the Snow* (1974) reveals the strength of this Christian conviction.

In choosing to write of things that were lovely and of good report, Elizabeth Goudge followed Jane Austen's advice 'to let other pens dwell on guilt and misery'. She was elected FRSL in 1945. Elizabeth Goudge died on 1 April 1984 at her home, Rose Cottage, Dog Lane, Peppard Common, near Henley-on-Thames, Oxfordshire.

JOHN ATTENBOROUGH, rev. VICTORIA MILLAR

Sources J. Leasor, *Author by profession* (1952), 142–56 · *The Times* (3 April 1984), 16 · J. Todd, ed., *British women writers: a critical reference guide* (1989) · T. Chevalier, ed., *Twentieth century children's writers* (1989) · E. Goudge, *The joy of the snow* (1974); pbk edn (1991) · private information (1990) · personal knowledge (1990) · 'Reconsidering Elizabeth Goudge', *Bookbird*, 34 (1996), 25 · *CGPLA Eng. & Wales* (1984)
Archives Oxon. RO, corresp. with Madeau Stewart
Wealth at death £308,802: probate, 27 July 1984, *CGPLA Eng. & Wales*

Goudy, Alexander Porter (1809–1858), minister of the Presbyterian Church in Ireland and religious controversialist, was the son of Andrew Goudy, Presbyterian minister of Ballywalter, co. Down, from 1802 to 1818, and Matilda, daughter of the Revd James Porter of Greyabbey (who was executed in 1798 for supposed complicity with the United Irishmen). He was born near Ballywalter in February 1809, and, after attending school at the Royal Belfast Academical Institution, entered its collegiate department in November 1823. He distinguished himself in several of the classes, and gained some reputation in the college debating society, where his chief rival was Thomas O'Hagan, afterwards lord chancellor of Ireland. He was licensed by the presbytery of Bangor on 29 December 1830, and ordained as assistant and successor to the Revd James Sinclair of Glastry, co. Down, on 20 September 1831. On 20 March 1833 he was installed in Strabane, where he continued as minister until his death.

In 1839 Goudy became involved in a notable controversy on the merits of episcopacy. The Revd Archibald Boyd, then curate in Derry Cathedral, subsequently dean of Exeter, had issued *Sermons on the Church* in 1838, in which he attacked Presbyterianism. In 1839 four ministers of the synod of Ulster, of whom Goudy was one, published a reply entitled *Presbyterianism defended, and the arguments of modern advocates of prelacy examined and refuted*. Boyd having replied in a book entitled *Episcopacy, Ordination, Lay Eldership, and Liturgies, in Five Letters*, the four ministers published *The Plea of Presbytery*, which soon became a standard work on the subject. This Boyd reviewed in *Misrepresentation Refuted*, which called forth *Mene tekel* from the four ministers. The last work in the controversy was by Boyd, entitled *Episcopacy and Presbytery*. Goudy's part in this battle of the books was impressive.

Shortly after, Goudy was embroiled in the agitation caused by a decision of the House of Lords (elicited by an appeal from the Irish courts), which affirmed the invalidity of a marriage celebrated by a Presbyterian minister, where one of the parties was an Episcopalian. The agitation was ended by the passing of the Marriages (Ireland) Act (7 & 8 Vict. c. 81), which legalizes all such marriages. In April 1846 Goudy married Isabella (1824–1906), daughter of John Kinross of Ayr; they had several children, including Henry *Goudy, professor of law and jurist. From this time Goudy was one of the leading debaters in his church, and could meet Dr Henry Cooke on equal terms. He was

one of the most prominent Presbyterians of his era being a Liberal in politics but a conservative in theology. In 1851 he received the degree of DD from Jefferson College in Canonsburg, Pennsylvania. In 1857 he became moderator of the general assembly. He died unexpectedly in Dublin on 14 December 1858 and was buried on 18 December in the old parish graveyard, Strabane. His wife survived him.

THOMAS HAMILTON, rev. DAVID HUDDLESTON

Sources T. Croskery and T. Witherow, *Life of the Rev. A. P. Goudy, D.D.* (1887) · W. T. Latimer, *A history of the Irish Presbyterians*, 2nd edn (1902) · *Northern Whig* (18 Dec 1858) · *CGPLA Ire.* (1859)
Likenesses woodcut, repro. in Croskery and Witherow, *Life of the Rev. A. P. Goudy*
Wealth at death under £1500: administration, 26 Jan 1859, *CGPLA Ire.*

Goudy, Henry (1848–1921), jurist, was born on 16 September 1848 at Strabane, co. Tyrone, the eldest son of the Revd Alexander Porter *Goudy DD (1809–1858), an Irish Presbyterian clergyman, and Isabella Kinross (1824–1906), daughter of an Ayr merchant. After his father's death his mother returned to Ayr. Between 1864 and 1867 Goudy studied at the University of Glasgow. He matriculated as a law student in Edinburgh in 1868, and graduated MA in 1870 and LLB in 1871. Goudy then spent a year studying law at the University of Königsberg, before his admission as an advocate on 22 November 1872.

The Scots bar was currently confident and buoyant, devoted to energetic intellectual endeavour, stimulated by the revival of legal education in the universities after 1860 and by contacts with German legal science. Shortly after his admission, Goudy demonstrated a talent for scholarship by writing an article for the *Journal of Jurisprudence* on the controversial topic of the liability of railway companies, focusing on a new German statute. With William C. Smith he published *Local Government* in 1880, a memorandum intended to facilitate discussion of reform. This was followed in 1886 by Goudy's *Law of Bankruptcy*. A vitally important work, which reached a fourth edition in 1914, it was for long the authoritative text in Scots law in this field, and was not entirely superseded in some respects even at the end of the century. Goudy was the first editor of the *Juridical Review*, to which he contributed throughout his life.

A Liberal, Goudy held a minor public office in Gladstone's governments in the 1880s. He was a candidate for the chair of Scots law in the University of Edinburgh in 1888, when the Conservative John Rankine was appointed. In 1889 he succeeded his own teacher, James Muirhead, as professor of civil law at Edinburgh. The main duty of the holder of this chair was to teach Roman law. If Goudy's publications had hitherto indicated an interest in Scots law, his training in Edinburgh and Königsberg had prepared him for this office. Possessed of a 'striking face and tall, commanding figure', Goudy was, according to James F. Whyte, 'a born teacher' who 'never missed an opportunity of helping his students' (Whyte, 163). He published a number of articles on Roman law in the *Juridical*

Review, and in 1899 he produced a second edition of Muirhead's *Historical Introduction to the Law of Rome*, the plagiarism of which by Hannis Taylor he exposed in a notable article in the *Juridical Review* in 1908.

In 1893 Goudy was called to the regius chair of civil law in the University of Oxford, in succession to his fellow Ulsterman James Bryce, who had advised Gladstone on the appointment. Here he helped to develop the embryonic law school. His inaugural lecture, 'Fate of Roman law north and south of the Tweed', published as a pamphlet in 1894, was a slight piece. In 1910 he published the interesting, if scarcely profound, *Trichotomy in Roman Law*, a German translation of which appeared in 1914, by E. Ehrlich. Goudy himself translated as *Law in Daily Life* (1904) a work of R. von Jhering, which set out a series of examination questions on legal issues arising out of everyday experience. If Goudy stressed the importance of historical knowledge in understanding the law, he had a strong interest in law reform; he argued in favour of codification to the Edinburgh Merchant Company in 1893 and was still addressing the Society of Public Teachers of Law on its benefits in 1919. In 1908 he had been one of the founders and first president of the society (and served again in 1918–19). Goudy also had a strong interest in international law and in 1915 was one of the founders and first vice-president of the Grotius Society.

Goudy was awarded the degrees of DCL from Oxford in 1894 and LLD from Edinburgh; in 1917 he was elected as an honorary bencher of Gray's Inn. Though troubled by ill health all his life, he did not retire from the regius chair until 1917. All Souls then continued him in his fellowship, and the university appointed him professor emeritus. He had long had a house in West Malvern. On 3 March 1921 he died, unmarried, at 7 Lansdown Crescent, Bath, and was buried in Bath.   JOHN W. CAIRNS

Sources J. Mackintosh, 'Henry Goudy', *Juridical Review*, 34 (1922), 53–7 · J. F. Whyte, 'Henry Goudy: an appreciation', *Juridical Review*, 33 (1921), 161–3 · F. de Zulueta and E. A. Whittuck, 'Henry Goudy', *Transactions of the Grotius Society*, 7 (1922), 22–9 · *WWW* · F. H. Lawson, *The Oxford law school, 1850–1965* (1968) · *Alphabetical list of graduates of the University of Edinburgh from 1859 to 1888*, University of Edinburgh (1889), 41 · T. Croskery and T. Witherow, *Life of the Rev. A. P. Goudy, D.D.* (1887) · matriculation album, U. Glas., Archives and Business Records Centre · matriculation albums, U. Edin. L., special collections division, university archives · A. L. Turner, *History of the University of Edinburgh, 1883–1933* (1933) · *Scots Law Times: Notes* (8 July 1893), 113–14 · F. J. Grant, ed., *The Faculty of Advocates in Scotland, 1532–1943*, Scottish RS, 145 (1944) · S. P. Walker, *The Faculty of Advocates, 1800–1986* (1987)
Archives Bodl. Oxf. | All Souls Oxf., letters to Sir William Anson
Likenesses photograph, *c.*1893, repro. in *Scots Law Times: Notes*
Wealth at death £15,833 18s. 6d.: probate, 22 June 1921, *CGPLA Eng. & Wales*

Gougaud, Louis Désiré Joseph Marie (1877–1941). *See under* Farnborough scholars (*act.* 1896–1945).

Gouge, Robert (1629/30–1705), clergyman and ejected minister, was born the son of Robert Gouge at Chelmsford, and after education at the grammar school there under Daniel Peake was admitted as a sizar in June 1647, aged seventeen, to Christ's College, Cambridge, where his tutor was the Platonist Henry More. Calamy suggests that his patron through university was one of the Mildmays who were *de jure* lords FitzWalter: if so, it would have been Sir Henry Mildmay (*c.*1585–1654) of Moulsham and Woodham Walter. After university Gouge took the mastership of the grammar school with the preachership of Maldon, which makes it seem more likely that his patron through university and beyond was that Sir Henry's better-known cousin and namesake, Sir Henry Mildmay the regicide (*d.* 1664), who was MP for the town.

Gouge remained at Maldon until in 1652 he was offered the rectory of St Helen's, Ipswich. His patron now was the influential puritan Robert Duncon (1594–1670), three times bailiff of Ipswich and brother of the political writer Samuel Duncon; Gouge's ailing and godly predecessor Robert Stansby died the following year. At St Helen's he was supported in part with £40 a year from the rents of the manor of Winston, near Debenham. Duncon and Gouge jointly signed a letter of sympathy to Thomas Taylor's independent congregation meeting at the shire house in Bury St Edmunds in March 1656, and Samuel Petto of South Elmham later described him as 'a very gracious man' (*DNB*). Gouge was not prepared to conform to the Act of Uniformity of 1662 and he was ejected from his living, which passed to the crown and was given to Cave Beck.

Gouge and his wife, Katherine, remained in Ipswich for about ten years, then moved with their sons Robert and Thomas to Coggeshall in Essex. Here after a short interregnum he succeeded John Sams (who died in December 1672) as pastor of a congregationalist church gathered in a licensed house, living in a house at the upper end of Stoneham Street. Two years later he hired a barn in East Street belonging to Isaac Hubbard, a deacon of the congregation, and converted it into the meeting-house where he ministered for the rest of his life. *The Faith of Dying Jacob*, several sermons which he preached on Hubbard's death, was published in 1688. In the Common Fund's review of dissenting ministers (largely compiled in 1690) it was reported that Gouge had some estate of his own and received a subscription of £40 per annum from his congregation. In November 1691 the fund discontinued an annual allowance of £5 formerly made to Gouge by the congregationalist minister Matthew Barker, as he had £50 per annum and his own estate to live on. In September 1696 Gouge received £5 from the Congregational Fund Board.

Gouge must have been affected by the death of his more eminent son, Thomas *Gouge, in 1700, and Calamy explains that 'a decay of his intellectuals through age, gave him his quietus' (Calamy, 645). On his death, at home in Stoneham Street in October 1705, his wife, his son Robert, and his granddaughter Sarah shared an inheritance of seven properties in Coggeshall. Gouge was buried at Coggeshall on 16 October 1705. The following year Edward Bentley took charge of the congregation.

J. M. BLATCHLY

Sources E. Calamy, ed., *An abridgement of Mr. Baxter's history of his life and times, with an account of the ministers, &c., who were ejected after the Restauration of King Charles II*, 2nd edn, 2 vols. (1713) · *Calamy rev.*, 229 · will, Essex RO, D/ACR 12/69 · B. Dale, *The annals of Coggeshall*

(1863) · *DNB* · A. Gordon, ed., *Freedom after ejection: a review (1690–1692) of presbyterian and congregational nonconformity in England and Wales* (1917), 39, 273 · Venn, *Alum. Cant.*

Archives U. Leeds, Brotherton L., notes on his sermons in diaries of Joseph Bufton

Wealth at death seven properties at Coggeshall: will, Essex RO, D/ACR 12/69

Gouge, Thomas (1605–1681), clergyman and ejected minister, was born on 19 September 1605 at Stratford-le-Bow, Middlesex, the eldest son of William *Gouge (1575–1653), minister, and his wife, Elizabeth Calton, or Caulton (1586/7–1625), the orphan daughter of a mercer. After studying at Eton College, Gouge was admitted to King's College, Cambridge, on 16 August 1625; he graduated BA in 1629 and proceeded MA in 1633. Shortly after he was appointed a fellow of King's on 16 August 1628, he left Cambridge to become curate and lecturer at St Anne Blackfriars, where his father was rector, and in 1632 he accepted an appointment at Sion College. Tragedy struck the family when the body of his murdered brother was found in the Thames on 22 June 1637. On 14 November 1637 Gouge was admitted as perpetual curate of Teddington, Middlesex, on 6 October 1638, vicar of St Sepulchre, Holborn, London, and on 16 May 1640, rector of Coulsdon, Surrey, which he held until his brother-in-law, Richard Roberts, was installed on 27 October 1641. In 1639 he married Anne (1615/16–1671), daughter of Sir Robert Darcy. They had six daughters and seven sons, including William (1642/3–1706), Thomas (*b.* 1644/5), and Edward, the last of whom emigrated to Boston, Massachusetts. Five of their children died young.

Gouge endorsed *A Testimony to the Truth* (14 December 1647), affirming presbyterian polity and the solemn league and covenant, and *A Vindication of the Ministers of the Gospel* (January 1649), dissociating the presbyterians' actions in the 1640s from the regicide. In 1654 he became an assistant to the London commission for the approbation of preachers. After his father's death he completed the final chapter of the latter's commentary on Hebrews (1655), for which he had been the amanuensis. In December 1660 he completed *Christian Directions* (1661), a guide to prayer, Bible reading, sabbath observance, and conduct, including arguments against gambling, bear-baiting, cock-fighting, the theatre, and dangerous sports such as football. His intent was to provide a free copy to every family in his parish, partly as thanks for their regular maintenance (as vicar he received a third of the tithes) and their care of the indigent, including free instruction in reading for their children. Leading by example he distributed alms weekly, provided hemp and flax for the able-bodied unemployed to spin, and sold their products for them. The importance of charity was the subject of his sermon, 'After what manner must wee give alms?', published by Samuel Annesley in *The Morning-Exercise at Cripple-Gate* (1661).

In September 1661 Sir Edward Broughton, keeper of the Gatehouse, included Gouge on a list of nineteen preachers who were reputedly seducing the people. On 1 April 1662 Gouge and his supporters at St Sepulchre annulled

I Rily Pinxit   R. White sculp.

The Reverend Mr Thomas Gouge.

Thomas Gouge (1605–1681), by Robert White, pubd 1682 (after John Riley)

the election of William Rogers as churchwarden, believing he would demand use of the Book of Common Prayer and placement of the communion table at the church's east end. Rogers and his allies persuaded Bishop Gilbert Sheldon to void the election of candidates supported by Gouge, but the latter refused to publish the judgment, prompting Rogers to mount a successful appeal to the privy council. Later that year Gouge was ejected from his living. According to Richard Baxter, an old university licence enabled Gouge to preach occasionally, though he was eventually excommunicated for such activity in Wales. He may have been in trouble in 1663, for the anonymous publisher of *Joshua's Resolution* (1663), which stressed the duty of believers to meet for worship despite persecution, issued it in an unfinished state, noting that the author had been called to another '*service*'. One of the most moderate nonconformists, Gouge was prepared to take the oath in the Five-Mile Act (1665) until Thomas Manton dissuaded him.

Although Gouge lost much in the great fire he assisted victims, serving as treasurer and visitor for a relief fund established by the draper Henry Ashurst. In 1668 he published *A Word to Sinners, and a Word to Saints*, hoping to awaken the consciences of the ungodly and persuade the regenerate to perform their duties. His standards were high: 'Every duty must be done, or as good you did none' (p. 64). According to the episcopal returns of 1669 he ministered to a congregation of 200 that worshipped near St Sepulchre, and the following year he published *The Young Man's Guide*, a primer on behaviour and spiritual duties intended primarily for apprentices, though with sections advising governors and masters of families. The importance he (like his father) attached to practical handbooks is also manifest in *The Christian Householder* (1663), a guide for parents and masters, and *The Principles of Christian Religion* (1672), a catechism based in part on the Westminster shorter catechism. In addition to expanded editions of his catechism in 1675 and 1679, he published a short summary entitled *The Heads of the Foregoing Catechism* (1679), a dozen copies of which sold for 6*d*., to facilitate widespread distribution. He was licensed to preach as a presbyterian at Snow Hill, London, in 1672, and two years later he published *The Surest & Safest Way of Thriving* (1674), in which he employed church fathers, contemporary examples, and such divines as Jeremy Taylor, Henry Hammond, and Thomas Jacomb to stress the importance of charity, averring that liberality was the best way to increase personal wealth. Published in 1676, the second edition included commendatory epistles by Baxter, Manton, John Owen, and William Bates.

Influenced by Joseph Alleine, Gouge began evangelizing work in Wales in 1672. Cited for preaching without authorization by Francis Davies, bishop of Llandaff, he displayed his old university licence, but when he failed to respond to a subsequent citation to appear he was excommunicated. He yielded to Davies, and later received permission to preach in Wales. By 1675, 2225 children were learning to read, write, and cast accounts in eighty-seven new charity schools in Wales, with all of the counties represented except Merioneth. He visited the schools once or twice a year, assisting them with monetary contributions. His most significant work was founding the Welsh Trust in 1674 in conjunction with Stephen Hughes and Charles Edwards. As part of its work he raised funds among affluent gentry and merchants in London and Wales to support the distribution of pious books in Welsh translation by such authors as Baxter, Arthur Dent, Lewis Bayly, and Gouge himself, often without charge. As he collected money for a Welsh edition of the Bible, he sought the support of Humphrey Lloyd, bishop of Bangor, in August 1676, but the latter complained to Archbishop Sheldon that Gouge had been sent by 'Leading sectaries' to lure the gentry into disaffection toward the government and the liturgy of the established church (Bodl. Oxf., MS Tanner 40, fols. 16–17). In fact, such gentry as Sir Edward Harley, Sir Trevor Williams, and Sir Edward Mansell supported the trust, as did the Anglican divines John Tillotson, Edward Stillingfleet, and Edward Fowler. So, too, did the wealthy London Socinian merchant Thomas Firmin. Gouge raised nearly £2000, which paid for 8000 copies of the Welsh Bible (1677), 1000 of which were distributed to the poor gratis, and the remainder sold for a modest 4*s*. 2*d*.

each. A subsequent edition followed in 1689, by which time Gouge was dead, but his contribution to the revival of Welsh-language evangelization was substantial.

When he was not travelling in Wales, Gouge catechized children at Christ's Hospital, London. With Baxter and nineteen other ministers he endorsed the 1675 edition of John Faldo's *Quakerism No Christianity*, which had been attacked by William Penn. Reflecting the widespread concern sparked by allegations of the Popish Plot, in October 1679 he completed *God's Call to England* (1680), in which he denounced Catholics as 'empty Pretenders to Christianity' and 'the bloudy Off-spring of devouring *Cannibals*', and asserted that their 'inhumane Massacres' could not be equalled by 'the most barbarous Inhabitants of the world' (pp. 98–9). After complaining of a heart problem for a fortnight, he died in his sleep on 29 October 1681 and was buried in his father's vault at St Anne Blackfriars. Tillotson preached his funeral sermon on 4 November. For his charitable work, which Baxter called the 'true Episcopacy of a silenced Minister' (*Reliquiae Baxterianae*, 190), he won the acclaim of Manton, Owen, and Benjamin Whichcote as well as Baxter.   RICHARD L. GREAVES

Sources CSP dom., 1637, 237; 1660–61, 95; 1661–2, 357 · *The works of the late reverend and pious Mr. Thomas Gouge* (1815) · Calamy rev. · Venn, *Alum. Cant.* · *Calendar of the correspondence of Richard Baxter*, ed. N. H. Keeble and G. F. Nuttall, 2 vols. (1991) · *Reliquiae Baxterianae, or, Mr Richard Baxter's narrative of the most memorable passages of his life and times*, ed. M. Sylvester, 1 vol. in 3 pts (1696), pt 3, pp. 17–18, 190 · Bodl. Oxf., MS Tanner 40, fols. 16–17 · PRO, SP29/41/56 · G. L. Turner, ed., *Original records of early nonconformity under persecution and indulgence*, 3 vols. (1911–14), vol. 2, p. 970; vol. 3, p. 89 · I. Green, *The Christian's ABC: catechisms and catechising in England, c.1530–1740* (1996) · W. Wilson, *The history and antiquities of the dissenting churches and meeting houses in London, Westminster and Southwark*, 4 vols. (1808–14), vol. 3, p. 555 · DNB

Archives Bodl. Oxf., Tanner MSS

Likenesses M. Vandergucht, line engraving, NPG · R. White, line engraving (after J. Riley), BM, NPG; repro. in J. Tillotson, *A sermon preached at the funeral of T. Gouge* (1682) [*see illus.*]

Gouge, Thomas (*c*.1665–1700), Independent minister, was born in Ipswich, the younger son of Robert *Gouge (1629/30–1705), ejected minister of St Helen's, Ipswich, and later minister at Coggeshall, Essex, and his wife, Katherine. He received his early education and religious instruction from his father at home before going on to complete his ministerial training in the Netherlands, but he does not appear to have attended either the University of Leiden or Utrecht. By the age of twenty-two he was the pastor of the English church in Amsterdam. When Edmund Calamy met him there in 1688 Gouge was closely involved with the astrologer John Partridge in attempting to calculate the exact date that the city of Rome would be destroyed by fire.

Gouge returned to England in either 1688 or 1689 and was chosen pastor of the Independent congregation at Three Cranes, Fruiterers' Alley, Thames Street, London. Here he proved to be a popular and useful minister and gained a reputation as an eloquent preacher. According to Isaac Watts, Gouge was one of the three greatest preachers of his younger time, the other two being John Howe and Joseph Stennett. In 1694 he was appointed a Merchants' lecturer at Pinners' Hall in succession to Daniel Williams. There he preached with 'great popularity to a crowded audience' (Wilson, 2.70). He was also one of the original members of the Congregational Fund board when it was established in 1695.

However, in the later part of Gouge's life his usefulness and reputation as a minister declined. In 1697 he allowed the controversial sectary Joseph Jacob to preach a weekly sermon at his meeting-house. Jacob infuriated some members of the congregation, including the MP Arthur Shallet, by introducing politics into his sermons, but, when dismissed, he took some of the congregation with him to his new meeting-house in Parish Street, Southwark. Shortly afterwards Gouge's congregation was further diminished as a result of a dispute over the admission of a member for communion. These reversals, which reflected badly on Gouge, broke his health and led to a deterioration of both his mental and physical powers. He died in London on 8 January 1700. His funeral sermon was preached by John Nesbitt at Pinners' Hall.

ALEXANDER GORDON, *rev.* M. J. MERCER

Sources W. Wilson, *The history and antiquities of the dissenting churches and meeting houses in London, Westminster and Southwark*, 4 vols. (1808–14), vol. 1, pp. 139–40; vol. 2, pp. 69–72 • J. Nesbitt, *Funeral sermon preached at Pinners' Hall upon the death of Mr Thomas Gouge* (1700) • E. Calamy, *An historical account of my own life, with some reflections on the times I have lived in, 1671–1731*, ed. J. T. Rutt, 1 (1829), 181 • T. W. Davids, *Annals of evangelical nonconformity in Essex* (1863), 618–19 • A. Gordon, ed., *Freedom after ejection: a review (1690–1692) of presbyterian and congregational nonconformity in England and Wales* (1917), 273 • *Calamy rev.*, 229 • *Transactions of the Congregational Historical Society*, 5 (1911–12), 135–7 • *Transactions of the Congregational Historical Society*, 7 (1916–18), 302–5

Gouge, William (1575–1653), Church of England clergyman and author, was born in the parish of St Mary, Stratford Bow, Middlesex, on 1 November 1575 and baptized there on 6 November, the third child and eldest son of Thomas Gouge (d. 1616) and his wife, Elizabeth, *née* Culverwell (*bap.* 1550, *d.* 1591). His grandfather William Gouge (d. 1592), a master baker, had passed into the ranks of the yeomen-gentry and was a leading parishioner of Stratford Bow. Although technically a hamlet within the parish of Stepney, Stratford had during the 1530s become a self-regulating community whose chapel of St Mary was effectively an independent parish church.

Education Gouge was first sent to St Paul's School but in 1586 or early 1587, when his uncle Ezekiel *Culverwell [see under Culverwell family (per. c.1545–c.1640)] became chaplain to Robert, third Lord Rich, at Little Leighs, Essex, he was transferred to nearby Felsted School, where Culverwell apparently acted as chaplain; there, according to the memoir by Gouge's eldest son Thomas *Gouge (1605–1681), on which all later biographers have relied, he was 'trained up three years under the publick Ministry of his Uncle' before spending six years at Eton and matriculating as a scholar at King's College, Cambridge, in 1595 (Gouge, 95). Thomas further states that Gouge was admitted fellow three years later, spending nine years at Cambridge altogether, and had been 'two or three years Master

William Gouge (1575–1653), by William Faithorne the elder, pubd 1654

of Arts' when he married (Gouge, 100). Since he is known to have married in 1604 there seems no reason to doubt that he graduated BA in 1598, was admitted fellow thereafter, and proceeded MA in 1601 or 1602. Unfortunately the Cambridge records for these years are so scanty that Gouge was omitted from the Coopers' *Athenae Cantabrigienses*, whilst in the Venns' *Alumni Cantabrigienses* it was proposed that he did not matriculate until 1598, graduating in 1601. Thomas's testimony is undoubtedly to be preferred.

Gouge's strictness of life and rigid self-discipline, described in detail by Thomas, earned him 'the name of an *Arch-Puritan*': he became a skilful logician, a defender of Peter Ramus, a college lecturer, and 'an excellent Hebrician' (Gouge, 99). Thomas implies that, as the only steadfast pupil of a Jew (Philip Ferdinand) who visited Cambridge to teach Hebrew, Gouge was subsequently the only university graduate capable of teaching the language. Since his uncle by marriage Laurence Chaderton, master of Emmanuel College, was to be appointed one of the translators of the Authorized Version of the Old Testament this was clearly an overstatement.

It was probably Ezekiel Culverwell and his second wife, Winifred (*née* Hildersham), who provided Gouge with a bride, bringing to his father's attention a seventeen-year-old orphan, Elizabeth Calton or Caulton (1586/7–1625), who was at a school in Hatfield Broad Oak (Winifred's native parish) run by the wife of an old friend of Ezekiel. His father summoned him from Cambridge to meet her. He obeyed with reluctance but 'they took such liking one of another' that they were married on 11 February 1604 (Guy, 40).

Public ministry, 1607–1640 Enforced wedlock nevertheless appears to have induced a spiritual crisis or at least a dark night of the soul. Having had to resign his fellowship upon marriage Gouge shut himself away in Stratford 'committing the whole care of his Family affairs to the management of his wife'—a strange thing to do to a girl of seventeen—and continuing with his studies (Gouge, 100). He emerged from this semi-seclusion in 1607, when he was ordained, thereafter perfecting his preaching abilities at Stratford without taking payment. In June 1608 he was recommended by Arthur Hildersham (probably Winifred Culverwell's brother) to the parishioners of St Ann Blackfriars, London, whose minister, the once-eloquent Stephen Egerton, seems to have maintained a self-imposed silence after 1605.

Retaining many ancient privileges, the precinct of the Blackfriars was not a city parish under the full control of the bishop. Its church, rebuilt in 1597, remained a donative in the gift of the More family until in 1607 Sir George More handed it over, with all its property (including the house occupied by Egerton) to the parishioners, with the right to elect (and finance) their clergy. Thus, although unanimously elected preacher and subsequently minister, Gouge was never formally instituted. The diocesan authorities had, however, established the right to regulate the spiritual life of Blackfriars during the bishop's triennial visitations.

Gouge's pulpit became the most celebrated in London. He preached twice every Sunday and his Wednesday morning lectures continued for thirty-five years, attracting huge congregations. Country clergy and 'godly Christians' visiting the capital 'thought not their business fully ended, unless they had been at Black-Friers Lecture' (Gouge, 105). Although until Egerton's death Gouge remained technically his assistant he evidently dominated the life of the precinct almost from the moment of his arrival. He was incorporated MA at Oxford on 11 July 1609 and proceeded BD at Cambridge in 1611. He was eventually admitted DD in 1628.

Gouge first surfaces in the London diocesan records (as 'curate') on 22 January 1611, accused of allowing standing communions. He replied that he had received, and administered, both standing and kneeling, 'knowinge it in itselfe to be indifferent' (LMA, DL/C/309, p. 275). On 18 October that year he and his churchwardens were summoned because it was alleged that strangers were allowed to communicate and that 'they receyve the bread or the cup after the words of consecration are used one from another & not eu[eryone] ymediately from the hand of the minister contrary to the lawes of this land' (LMA, DL/C/308, p. 616). It must be doubted whether he ever truly conformed or refused those who wished to receive at his hands. His successor, William Jenkyn, who preached his

funeral sermon, observed that 'during the time of Prelatical Innovations' he was 'a sweet refreshing shade and shelter ... to the old godly Puritanes' who wished to receive 'purely' (Jenkyn, 42). It is said that he always refused to read King James's Book of Sports.

By 1615 Gouge was a force to be reckoned with, an upholder of that brand of Calvinist orthodoxy which was now increasingly coming under siege. That year he published *The Whole-Armour of God* and (anonymously) *A Short Catechisme*, which reached a sixth edition by 1636. He also saw through the press and furnished a preface to Sir Henry Finch's *An Exposition of the Song of Solomon*. This likewise appeared anonymously, Gouge explaining that the author was 'a man of great place and note' whose 'humility will not suffer him to have his name made known' (sig. [A3]). By 1617 his popularity was such that the old Blackfriars Church proved inadequate and £1500 was raised to enlarge it and acquire further property, including 'the house wherein he himself dwelt so long as he lived' (Gouge, 105).

In March 1621 Gouge again acted as midwife to a work by Henry Finch, *The Worlds Great Restauration, or, The Calling of the Jewes*. Finch's anonymity did not save him from eight weeks' imprisonment, King James finding unpalatable the notion that a Jewry converted *en masse* to Christianity would be accorded sovereignty over the rest of the world. Gouge was likewise imprisoned—according to Thomas Gouge for nine weeks, at the instigation of Richard Neile, bishop of Durham—and was released only after presenting six propositions on the subject which George Abbot, archbishop of Canterbury, considered satisfactory. In 1622 appeared Gouge's most celebrated work, *Of Domesticall Duties*, and on Egerton's death in May he took sole charge of Blackfriars. With three other overseers he received 20s. in Egerton's will for a memorial ring 'in remembrance of my love and of the friendship that hath been long between us' (LMA, DL/C/361, fol. 109r). In 1623 he and Richard Sibbes contributed prefaces to Ezekiel Culverwell's *A Treatise of Faith* (1623), in which Gouge acknowledged his uncle's early influence. In October that year a crowded upper room in Blackfriars collapsed during a Catholic meeting there. Gouge preached on the subject the following week, reporting that ninety-one bodies had been recovered. In 1624 he was appointed sole overseer in the will of Egerton's widow.

On 26 October 1625 Elizabeth Gouge died in Edgware after giving birth to their thirteenth child; the minister, Nicholas Guy, preached her funeral sermon at Gouge's 'importunity ... (though sore against my will)' (Guy, sig. A3). Gouge never remarried. About this time he and Sibbes became the leading clerical members of the voluntary committee known as the feoffees for impropriations. Dedicated to the task of raising money to buy back church tithes that had passed into lay hands, the feoffees were vehemently suspected by William Laud, bishop of London, of deliberately encouraging 'a Puritan faction to undo the church' (*Works*, 3.216–17) and at his insistence they were on 13 February 1633 adjudged by the court of exchequer to be an illicit corporation.

Perhaps it was Laud's mounting hostility to the feoffees that had in October 1631 prompted a letter which, given Gouge's temperament and views, is strikingly out of character. Defending himself against reports that he had maligned the bishop he professed to value Laud's goodwill highly, having always regarded him as prudent, moderate, and courteous. Altogether it furnishes a portrait 'which one suspects even the bishop's best friends would not recognize' (Burch, 29).

In 1630 Gouge brought out an exposition of St John's gospel, in 1631 *God's Three Arrows*, and in 1632 *The Saints Sacrifice*. That nothing is known of his activities during Laud's years as archbishop of Canterbury is suggestive, as is his successful petition in December 1633 to be admitted freeman of the Society of Apothecaries, whose hall was in Blackfriars and one of whose senior members, Gideon Delaune, was also a leading parishioner. Perhaps put on notice by Laud's aggressive tactics since 1631, Gouge seems to have settled down to a period of quiescence under the protection of city business interests.

Parliamentary campaigns, 1640–1653 Although no politician Gouge emerged from obscurity on the eve of civil war, perhaps as the protégé of Robert Rich, second earl of Warwick, whose long-standing patronage he had already acknowledged in his dedication of *God's Three Arrows*. Between 1639 and 1648 a spate of nine short tracts left the London presses, while following the parliamentary ordinance of 12 June 1643 Gouge was nominated a member of the Westminster assembly. Despite failing health he was scrupulous in attending. In 1644 he was appointed to the committee for the examination of ministers and on 12 May 1645 to that responsible for drafting a confession of faith. On 26 November 1647 he was elected one of the assembly's two assessors. On 8 December he and his co-assessor, Cornelius Burges, were appointed to fill the prolocutor's chair by turns. In 1645 Gouge had refused the provostship of King's College, Cambridge.

Gouge endorsed the *iure divino* theory of presbyterianism, from 21 June 1648 serving on a committee responsible for marshalling evidence in its support. He took the covenant without hesitation and was chosen prolocutor of the first meeting of the London provincial assembly on 3 May 1647. Yet like many leading presbyterians he was monarchical in principle and regarded the trial of Charles I as a breach of the covenant and of the constitution. He subscribed *A Vindication of the Ministers of the Gospel, in and about London* (1648), drawn up by Burges on the eve of the trial, and would therefore have regarded Charles's execution as a betrayal of the aims with which the parliamentarian party had begun its opposition to his policies. It is perhaps no coincidence that *The Right Way* (1648) was the last work published in his lifetime.

Gouge suffered increasingly from asthma and the stone, eventually abandoning regular preaching, yet until within weeks of his death he worked at a commentary on the epistle to the Hebrews. He died on 12 December 1653 at Blackfriars and was buried at St Anne Blackfriars four days later. His funeral sermon was preached by William Jenkyn before 'unwonted and great numbers' (Jenkyn, 34) and a

memorial was erected by his great-granddaughter, Meliora Prestley.

Of Gouge's thirteen children, six sons and two daughters reached maturity: Thomas, Nicholas (*b*. 1608), Ezekiel (*b*. 1610), Mary (*b*. 1615), James (*b*. 1619), William (*b*. 1622), Elizabeth (*b*. 1624), and the unnamed son whose birth in 1625 resulted in the death of his mother. Ezekiel was murdered in 1637 and Mary, wife of Christopher Doddington, died in January 1653.

Gouge had written his will on 13 August 1652, making Thomas his executor and principal legatee. Houses in Blackfriars went to Nicholas. James received £1000 and a house in Paternoster Row 'knowne by the signe of three Cranes'. The 'rest of my sonnes' (that is, William and the unnamed youngest) had already received their patrimony and were left only £7 for mourning apparel, and William's wife £5. Three surviving sisters and his daughters Mary Doddington and Elizabeth Roberts likewise received £5 for mourning and his sisters Judith Dawson and Elizabeth Hitchcock annuities of £5 and £10 respectively. Only one 'Auncient Seruant' was remembered and his sole charitable bequests were £20 to the poor of Blackfriars, £10 to those of Stratford Bow, and £10 to Bridewell Hospital. His remaining property in London, Middlesex, and Essex, with all his goods, went to Thomas, who was granted probate on 11 January 1654.

Retrospective Gouge published comparatively little, preferring to distil his workaday efforts into longer, more finished productions. His *Commentary on Hebrews*, complete but for half a chapter at his death, ostensibly preserves the gist of over 1000 sermons. Above all Gouge is remembered for *Of Domesticall Duties*, a penetrating analysis of the godly household. Too frequently cited as an old-fashioned patriarch who advocated the indiscriminate physical punishment of children, Gouge has latterly (although still insufficiently) been recognized as one of the subtlest of early modern writers to articulate the concept of 'companionable' marriage—his own was regarded as exemplary—and of considerate, rather than merely prescriptive, parenthood. His psychological insights into the nature of childhood and adolescence can be breathtaking in their modernity. He even touches on the question of child abuse, a subject effectively taboo until the 1970s.

Despite the esteem in which he was held, Gouge's relations with his flock were not always harmonious. Some passages in *Of Domesticall Duties* suggest that he had difficulty persuading husbands to accept his more enlightened views (for example, that they must not beat their wives) whilst conversely, although he strove ingeniously to neutralize the Pauline injunction that wives must submit to their husbands in all things, some of his female parishioners were offended that he mentioned it at all. His habit of taking a summer vacation likewise aroused criticism. He countered that he was not idle in the country (by which he probably meant Stratford Bow), devoting his time there to his writings. As a palliative he dedicated *A Guide to Goe to God* (1626), his exposition of the Lord's prayer, to his parishioners.

More surprising are the careful sentences which Jenkyn

felt obliged to devote to rebutting charges that Gouge was richer than was expedient for a godly minister and had in his time lent money at interest. The latter charge is unlikely to have been true and whilst he had inherited a substantial estate from his father and amply provided for his sons, Jenkyn observed that Gouge's liquid assets were 'found short, by some hundreds of pounds, of his Legacies and gifts' (Jenkyn, 35). Thus, whilst charitable bequests in his will were modest, Thomas's assertion that throughout his life he had generously supported dependent members of his large family, maintained poor scholars at university, and never turned away deserving supplicants is probably to be trusted.   Brett Usher

Sources T. Gouge, 'The life and death of Dr. Gouge who dyed *anno Christi* 1653', *A collection of the lives of ten eminent divines*, ed. S. Clark (1662), 95–125 · W. Jenkyn, *A shock of corn coming in its season* (1654) · N. Guy, *Pieties pillar* (1626) · Venn, *Alum. Cant.* · parish register, Stratford Bow, St Mary, 6 Nov 1575, LMA, P88/MRY 1 [baptism] · B. Burch, 'The parish of St Anne's Blackfriars, London, to 1665', *Guildhall Miscellany*, 3 (1969–71), 1–54 · W. R. Prest, 'The art of law and the law of God: Sir Henry Finch (1558–1625)', *Puritans and revolutionaries*, ed. D. Pennington and K. Thomas (1978), 94–117 · L. L. Shucking, *The puritan family* (1969) · A. Fletcher, 'The protestant idea of marriage in early modern England', *Religion, culture and society in early modern Britain*, ed. A. Fletcher and P. Roberts (1994), 161–81 · C. Hill, *Society and puritanism in pre-revolutionary England* (1964) · C. Hill, *The English Bible and the seventeenth-century revolution* (1993) · W. Hunt, *The puritan moment: the coming of revolution in an English county* (1983) · G. Lloyd Jones, *The discovery of Hebrew in Tudor England: a third language* (1983) · P. S. Seaver, *The puritan lectureships: the politics of religious dissent, 1560–1662* (1970) · A. F. Mitchell and J. Struthers, eds., *Minutes of the sessions of the Westminster assembly of divines* (1874) · N. Tyacke, *The fortunes of English puritanism, 1603–1640* (1990) · *The works of the most reverend father in God, William Laud*, ed. J. Bliss and W. Scott, 7 vols. (1847–60) · will, PRO, PROB 11/239, fols. 41v–42r · London diocesan records, LMA, DL/C/308; DL/C/309; DL/C/361
Archives PRO, letter to William Laud, SP 16/202/3
Likenesses J. Dunstall, line engraving, BM, NPG; repro. in W. Gouge, *A learned and very useful commentary on the whole epistle to the Hebrews* (1655) · W. Faithorne the elder, line engraving, BM, NPG; repro. in Jenkyn, *Shock of corn* (1654) [*see illus.*] · engraving, repro. in S. Clarke, *A general martyrology*, 3rd edn (1677)
Wealth at death £1100 in cash legacies; several houses in London; family estate in Stratford Bow, Middlesex; property in Essex: will, proved, 11 Jan 1654, PRO, PROB 11/239, fols. 41v–42r

Gough. *See also* Goff, Goffe.

Gough, Alexander Dick (1804–1871), architect and engineer, was born on 3 November 1804. Of his parents nothing is known. With his wife, Mary Ann, he had two sons: Charles H. Gough and Hugh Roumieu Gough. At the age of nineteen, after some foreign travel, he became a pupil of Benjamin Dean Wyatt, the architect. He was entrusted with the superintendence of several of Wyatt's more important works, including Apsley House (1828–9) and the duke of York's column (1831–4).

In 1836 Gough formed a partnership with his fellow pupil Robert Lewis Roumieu (1814–1877) and commenced practice. Between 1837 and 1847 he and his partner exhibited at the Royal Academy fourteen architectural drawings, chiefly of buildings in course of erection by them. In 1837–8 they built the Islington Literary and Scientific Institution (now the Almeida Theatre) in a severe Grecian style. In 1840–41 they much extended The Priory, Roehampton, a stuccoed Gothic villa of *c*.1800, for Sir James Knight Bruce, in an elaborately unarchaeological but appealing manner. Most of their work was in north London, and included new schools for St Peter's, Islington (1839–40), St Pancras (1841–2), and St Stephen's, Islington (1843), as well as a free church and schools in Paradise Street, St Pancras, in Tudor style (1842; dem.). In 1842–3 they enlarged Sir Charles Barry's church of St Peter, Islington, with a new west front and spire, transepts, and a sanctuary. The work was approved by Barry, despite the fact that it is so 'crazy' that Nikolaus Pevsner (who so described it) attributed it to E. B. Lamb (Pevsner, 229). In 1841–3 they built Milner Square, Islington, whose endless narrow bays are flanked by pilasters: 'it is possible to visit Milner Square many times and still not be absolutely certain that you have seen it anywhere but in an unhappy dream' (J. Summerson, *Georgian London*, 1962, 283). In 1847–8 they rebuilt and 'crudely Normanised' (Pevsner) St Pancras Old Church, lengthening the nave and adding a new tower. 'The historical interest of the ancient building was largely destroyed' (Lovell and Marcham, 76). Pevsner attributes to Roumieu and Gough semi-detached villas in De Beauvoir Square, Hackney (Pevsner, 169).

In 1848 the partnership between Gough and Roumieu was dissolved. Roumieu's most celebrated later building is the former vinegar warehouse at 33–5 Eastcheap, London, of 1868. Its wild Gothic suggests that it may have been Roumieu who was responsible for the more extreme examples of the partnership's work. Gough afterwards built a number of churches in north London, including: St Matthew's, Islington (1850–51; dem.) and St Jude's, Mildmay Park (1855; enlarged), both in the late Decorated style; St Mark's, Tollington Park (1853–4; much altered), in the Early English style; the Norman style St Philip's, Arlington Square (1855–7; dem.); St Mary's, Hornsey Rise (1860–61; much altered) in the Decorated style; and the Romanesque St Anne's, Poole's Park (1870; dem. 1965).

Pevsner described Gough's churches as 'characterised by rather wild rock-facing and asymmetrically placed thin spires' (Pevsner, 228), and pointed out that the writers of *The Ecclesiologist* disapproved of his work. His churches outside north London included St Paul's, Chatham, Kent (1853–4; dem. 1974); St John's, Tunbridge Wells, Kent (1857–8; much enlarged); St John's, Marchington Woodlands, Staffordshire (1858–9; tower and spire added 1860); Christ Church, Hastings, Sussex (1858–9); St Barnabas's Mission Church, South Kennington (1864–5; dem.); St John the Evangelist, Hull, Yorkshire (1865–6; dem. *c*.1920); and the nave and aisles of St Saviour's, Herne Hill Road, Camberwell (1866–7; dem.). He also built the girls' industrial schools, Cardington, Bedfordshire (1860–61) and the classical Soldiers' Institute, Chatham, Kent (1861). He reconstructed the interiors of St Mary's, Brampton, Huntingdonshire; St Nicholas's, Rochester, Kent, with parsonage (1860–62); St Giles's, Pitchcott, Buckinghamshire (1863–4); and St Margaret's, Rainham, Kent. He erected schools for St Lawrence's Church, Effingham, Surrey, besides executing many private commissions.

As an engineer, Gough made surveys in 1845, partly on his own account and partly in conjunction with R. L. Roumieu, for the Exeter, Dorchester, and Weymouth Junction Coast Railway; for the Direct West-End and Croydon Railway; and for the Dover, Deal, Sandwich, and Ramsgate Direct Coast Railway. From 1845 to 1848 he was occupied in numerous surveys for compensation claims against the South-Eastern Railway, and the Great Northern, the London and North-Western, and the Eastern Counties railways. He was a man of great industry, and most precise and methodical in his manner of working. He died on 8 September 1871, aged sixty-six, at his home, 6 Second Grove, Tollington Park, London, and was buried in Highgate cemetery five days later. His wife survived him. His obituary in *The Builder* announced that his practice would be continued by his sons Charles H. Gough and Hugh Roumieu Gough (1842/3–1904), 'both for many years associated with him in his professional career' (*The Builder*, 749), but it was the latter of the two alone who actually succeeded him.   PETER HOWELL

Sources *The Builder*, 29 (1871), 749 · *The Architect*, 6 (1871), 173 · *Dir. Brit. archs.* · Graves, *RA exhibitors* · *London: except the cities of London and Westminster*, Pevsner (1952) · B. F. L. Clarke, *Parish churches of London* (1966) · *CGPLA Eng. & Wales* (1871) · P. W. Lovell and W. M. Marcham, *The parish of St Pancras*, 2, Survey of London, 19 (1938), 76 · J. Lever, ed., *Catalogue of the drawings collection of the Royal Institute of British Architects: O-R* (1976) · H. R. Hitchcock, *Early Victorian architecture in Britain*, 1 (1954), 125, 158, 240 · H. S. Goodhart-Rendel, 'Rogue architects of the Victorian era', *RIBA Journal*, 56 (1948–9), 251–9, esp. 255 · H. A. M. Roberts, 'The Gough and Roumieu families', *Blackmansbury*, 7/1 and 2 (1970), 22–5
Wealth at death under £200: administration, 1 Nov 1871, *CGPLA Eng. & Wales*

Gough, Sir Charles John Stanley (1832–1912), army officer, was the second son of George Gough of Rathronan, Clonmel, co. Tipperary, a judge in the service of the East India Company, and Charlotte Margaret Becher, daughter of Charles Becher of Tonbridge, Kent, also of the company. The family had a long military tradition and connection with India, George Gough's uncle being Hugh, first Viscount Gough.

Charles Gough was born on 28 January 1832 at Chittagong, and in March 1848 he was commissioned into the 8th Bengal light cavalry with which he served in the Second Anglo-Sikh War, where his great-uncle commanded the British forces. Following the outbreak of the Indian mutiny in 1857 the 8th was disbanded at Lahore and he served throughout the mutiny in the Guides Cavalry and Hodson's Horse, being present at the siege and capture of Delhi, the first relief of Lucknow, and the capture of Lucknow in March 1858. He received the Victoria Cross for acts of bravery, including saving the life of his younger brother, Hugh Henry *Gough. After the mutiny he served with the 5th European light cavalry. Following the reconstruction of the Bengal army he commanded the 5th Bengal cavalry from 1864 until 1881, taking part in the Bhutan expedition of 1864–5. On 16 June 1870 he married Harriette Anastasia de la Poer (d. 26 March 1916), daughter of John William Power, styled seventeenth Baron Le Poer, a

former MP for Waterford, and they had six children, of whom only two, Hubert de la Poer *Gough and John Edmond *Gough, survived to adulthood.

On the outbreak of the Second Anglo-Afghan War in November 1878 Gough was appointed to command an infantry brigade in the force under Sir Sam Browne which invaded Afghanistan via the Khyber Pass. At Fatehabad on 2 April 1879 he inflicted a crushing defeat on the Khugiani. When the war recommenced in September 1879 Gough commanded the advanced brigade of the Khyber line of communication force under Major-General R. O. Bright. On 12 December 1879 he was ordered to advance from Jagdalak to Sherpur, outside Kabul, 70 miles away, where Sir Frederick S. Roberts and his army were besieged. After a difficult and hazardous march through thick snow Gough reached Sherpur on 24 December to find that news of his advance had precipitated an Afghan attack which Roberts had decisively defeated, thus lifting the siege. Gough was warmly commended by the commander-in-chief, Sir Frederick Haines and was created KCB in 1881. Roberts however thought that he had been unnecessarily slow and did not include him in the force which made the celebrated march from Kabul to Kandahar in August 1880.

Gough commanded the Hyderabad contingent from 1881 to 1885, and the Allahabad division from 1886 to 1890. In the large-scale manoeuvres round Delhi in the winter of 1885–6 he commanded the southern force, but his performance was judged by Roberts to have been disappointing. He was promoted major-general in 1885, lieutenant-general in 1889, and full general in 1891. He applied unsuccessfully to succeed the duke of Connaught as commander-in-chief of the Bombay army and retired to Ireland in 1895, receiving the GCB the same year. In 1897 he published, in collaboration with A. D. Innes, *The Sikhs and the Sikh War*, which was in part a defence of his great-uncle's performance as commander. He died at Innislonagh, Clonmel, Ireland, on 6 September 1912. He was an able, if exacting, soldier and would very probably have gone further but for Roberts's coolness towards him.

R. S. RAIT, *rev.* BRIAN ROBSON

Sources NAM, Charles Gough MSS, 8304–8332 · B. Gough, *A history of the Gough family* (c.1978) · Bengal Army Lists · NAM, Roberts MSS, 7101–7123 · C. M. MacGregor, *The Second Afghan War*, 6 vols. (1885–6) · S. N. Sen, *Eighteen fifty-seven* (Delhi, 1958) · *The Times* (7 Sept 1912) · Lord Roberts [F. S. Roberts], *Forty-one years in India*, 2 vols. (1897) · R. S. Rait, *The life of Field-Marshal Sir Frederick Paul Haines* (1911) · B. Robson, *The road to Kabul: the Second Afghan War, 1878–1881* (1986) · Burke, *Gen. Ire.* · I. F. W. Beckett, *Johnnie Gough, VC: a biography* (1989)
Archives NAM, corresp. and papers; corresp. mainly with his son John
Likenesses photographs, NAM
Wealth at death £32,455 5s. 3d.: Irish administration sealed in England, 19 Oct 1912, *CGPLA Eng. & Wales*

Gough, Herbert John (1890–1965), mechanical engineer and expert on metal fatigue, was born in Bermondsey, London, on 26 April 1890, the second son of Henry James Gough, a civil servant in the Post Office, and his wife, Mary

Herbert John Gough (1890–1965), by Bassano, 1938

Anne Gillis. Gough attended the Regent Street Polytechnic Technical School and won a scholarship to University College School. After a brief interlude as a pupil teacher, he was an apprentice at Messrs Vickers, Sons, and Maxim from 1909 to 1913, when he was appointed a designer draughtsman. During this period he obtained a BSc (hons.) in engineering from London University and later received a DSc and PhD.

In 1914 Gough joined the staff of the National Physical Laboratory (NPL), Teddington, Middlesex, in the engineering department, where he stayed until 1938, becoming superintendent of the department in 1930 in succession to Sir Thomas Stanton. During the First World War Gough served in the Royal Engineers (signals) from 1914 until May 1919, rose to the rank of captain, and was twice mentioned in dispatches. He was appointed MBE (military) in 1919.

During his period at the NPL Gough established the science of the behaviour of materials under fatigue conditions. Fatigue failure is failure due to repeated application of a load much lower than that necessary to produce failure in a single application and is one of the most frequent causes of breakage in service. Gough, working initially under the inspiration of Stanton and with many able young scientists and engineers such as D. Hanson, H. L. Cox, A. J. Murphy, C. E. Elam, and W. A. Wood, established that fatigue failure occurs because the metal undergoes plastic deformation. He discovered that this was due to slippage inside the metal crystals and, using X-rays (a new tool at the time), showed how safe ranges of stress could

be forecast. He also attacked the problem of fatigue under conditions when differently directed stresses are applied simultaneously, explaining how to predict 'lives' under these conditions. Having developed means of estimating stresses in chains, hooks, and rings, Gough applied the principles to the design of lifting gear. He also demonstrated how the designer of mechanical structures needs to allow for the increased stresses arising at fillets, lubrication holes, keyways, and splines. All of this work was of immense practical significance for it enabled designs to be much more economic, replacing rule of thumb by quantitative procedures. Gough also investigated fretting corrosion where moving metal parts touch, cold pressing of metals, lubrication, and welding. He published *The Fatigue of Metals* in 1924 but much of his later work was not widely known until the publication of his presidential address to the Institution of Mechanical Engineers in 1949.

Gough entered the War Office in 1938 as the first director of scientific research. In 1942 he was appointed CB and became director-general of scientific research and development at the Ministry of Supply, remaining there until 1945 when he joined Lever Brothers and Unilever Ltd as engineer-in-chief. Gough's responsibilities at the ministry were very wide, for they concerned physical research, signals, and chemical research, and included the Radar Research Station at Malvern, under John Cockcroft, the chemical station at Porton Camp, Wiltshire, under Davidson Pratt, and the rocket station at Aber-porth, Cardiganshire, under Alwyn Crow. Gough handled the obvious problems of demarcation very well. Although director-general, he took an active personal interest in unexploded bomb disposal.

During the period 1945–50, as a member of the Guy committee, Gough took an active interest in the establishment at East Kilbride of the Mechanical Engineering Research Laboratory (later the National Engineering Laboratory) by the transfer of his old division from the NPL, and assisted in defining its first research programme.

As well as being made CB, Gough was decorated with the medal of freedom with silver palm by the United States government for his work as chief liaison officer on scientific research and development for the United Kingdom, and he received many medals and prizes from the institutions of Mechanical Engineers, Civil Engineering, and Automobile Engineers, and the Royal Aeronautical Society. He was elected to the fellowship of the Royal Society in 1933, and served on its council in 1939–40.

Gough retired from Unilever in 1955 but retained his interests and in particular helped to organize a number of large international scientific conferences. He died suddenly at the Royal Sussex County Hospital, Brighton, on 1 June 1965 after a round of golf, a game of which he was very fond. He was survived by his wife, Sybil Holmes, whom he had married in 1918; they had a son and a daughter.

Gough's colleagues speak of the energy, drive, and enthusiasm that he brought to all that he did. He was by all accounts a strong and forceful personality and applied himself with equal energy to the study of the fatigue of metals and to an analysis of his golf score.

ANTHONY KELLY, rev.

Sources S. F. Dorey, *Memoirs FRS*, 12 (1966), 181–94 · *The Times* (4 June 1965) · *CGPLA Eng. & Wales* (1965)

Likenesses W. Stoneman, two photographs, 1933–47, NPG · Bassano, photograph, 1938, NPG [*see illus.*] · photograph, *c*.1950–1955, Unilever Ltd, London

Wealth at death £20,741: probate, 5 Aug 1965, *CGPLA Eng. & Wales*

Gough, Sir Hubert de la Poer (1870–1963), army officer, was born in London on 12 August 1870, the eldest son of Sir Charles John Stanley *Gough GCB, VC (1832–1912), and his wife, Harriette Anastasia de la Poer (*d.* 26 March 1916), daughter of John William Power, styled seventeenth Baron Le Poer, of Gurteen, co. Waterford, formerly MP for co. Waterford. Brigadier-General John (Johnnie) Edmond *Gough VC (1871–1915) was his brother; a younger brother and sister died of scarlet fever in London in 1879 and two other siblings also died in childhood. He grew up largely in Ireland where 'all our relations were anti-Home-Rulers' (Gough, *Soldiering On*, 23) and where he frequently hunted. He was educated until about 1883 at the Revd Matthew Buckland's private school at Laleham, near Staines, and at Eton College (1884–6); later in 1886 he had a private tutor in Versailles, France, and—after attending a 'crammer' under the tuition of Captain W. H. James of Lexham Gardens, Kensington—he attended the Royal Military College, Sandhurst, in 1888, where he acquired his nickname, Goughie.

Early career In March 1889 he was commissioned second lieutenant in the 16th lancers, a fashionable and expensive regiment (lieutenant July 1890, captain December 1894, major October 1902, lieutenant-colonel October 1902). Regimental service in India in the 1890s provided ample leisure to display his first-class horsemanship in racing, polo, and pigsticking, and he also took part in the Tirah expedition in 1897. On 22 December 1898 Gough married Margaret Louisa Nora, known as Daisy (*d.* 23 March 1951), younger daughter of Major-General H. C. Lewes RA; they had a son who died in infancy and four daughters. In 1899 he attended Staff College, Camberley, and was briefly master of the draghunt; he passed Staff College even though he left for South Africa before completing the course. In the Second South African War he displayed characteristic dash and impulsiveness when, disobeying Lord Dundonald's orders, he led the advance guard of the relief force into Ladysmith (28 February 1900). However these same qualities cost his column heavy casualties at Blood River Poort, Natal, on 17 September 1901. Disregarding intelligence reports, and without adequate reconnaissance, his force charged a small Boer detachment but was then attacked by a larger Boer force. Gough and others were taken prisoner but Gough escaped that night. Nevertheless he ended the war with an enhanced reputation. From 1904 to 1906 he was an instructor at the Staff College and from December 1906 he

Sir Hubert de la Poer Gough (1870–1963), by Francis Dodd, 1917

commanded the 16th lancers. In 1911 he returned to Ireland as a brigadier-general commanding 3rd cavalry brigade, which included the 16th lancers, at the Curragh.

The Curragh incident Gough had a crucial role in the Curragh incident (sometimes misnamed the Curragh mutiny) of March 1914. Most army officers sympathized with Ulster and its opposition to the imposition of home rule. In March 1914 Colonel J. E. B. Seely (secretary of state for war)—of whom it was said that 'if he had just a little more brains, he'd be half-witted' (Fergusson, 29)—and Winston Churchill (first lord of the Admiralty), both former Conservatives with high opinions of their military abilities, initiated ostensibly precautionary but possibly intimidatory and provocative military and naval movements. Lieutenant-General Sir Arthur Paget, general officer commanding-in-chief, Ireland, returned from meetings at the War Office and—apparently misunderstanding and exceeding his mysteriously unwritten instructions—on 20 March told his senior officers that operations were intended against Ulster and gave them an 'ultimatum': operations in Ulster or dismissal, though Ulster-domiciled officers could temporarily 'disappear'.

In answer to a question from Gough, Paget replied that 'domiciled in Ulster' was to be strictly interpreted, and added 'You cannot be held to come under that clause. You need expect no mercy from your old friend in the war office' (Sir John French, chief of the Imperial General Staff). Gough left the meeting angry at his personal treatment and under the impression that the army was to be used to coerce Ulster prior to the passing of the Home Rule

Bill. He decided to offer his resignation, and though he did not attempt to influence his officers, the great majority decided likewise. Reporting this to Paget, Gough wrote that while he and his officers were prepared to maintain law and order they were not willing to *initiate* military operations against Ulster.

Paget addressed the 3rd cavalry brigade officers on 21 March, but failed to convert them: 'Regret to report brigadier and fifty-seven officers 3rd Cavalry Brigade prefer to accept dismissal if ordered North'.

Gough and his regimental commanding officers were summoned to the War Office to be reprimanded by Seely, but by the time they arrived on the Sunday morning, 22 March, Asquith had become aware of the muddle and insisted that order be promptly restored. He told Seely that there were no grounds for punishing or dismissing Gough and the others, who had only taken a choice forced on them by Paget. Meanwhile Lord Roberts had discovered that Seely now repudiated the alternatives presented by Paget and Roberts informed Gough. Gough therefore reported to the War Office on the Monday morning, 23 March, fortified in the integrity of his position. He first saw French, who assured him that there had been a misunderstanding and offered his word that the army would not be asked to enforce the current Home Rule Bill on Ulster. But he felt unable to put his assurance in writing. French then took Gough to see Seely, Paget and the Adjutant-General Sir (John) Spencer Ewart also being present. Seely vainly attempted to browbeat Gough, who stubbornly demanded a written assurance.

French broke the deadlock by suggesting that Gough needed documentary proof to convince his own officers. Seely capitulated and left for a cabinet meeting while Ewart drafted a statement. After lunch Seely received the statement as revised by the cabinet in Asquith's handwriting, but when Gough called to see it only Seely and Lord Morley were present. Seely then, with Morley's assistance, added two paragraphs, the latter affirming that the government had 'no intention whatever of taking advantage of this right [to maintain law and order] to crush political opposition to the policy or principles of the Home Rule Bill' (Fergusson, 151). When the statement had been copied French handed it to Gough, who requested a quarter of an hour to study it together with his two colonels, his brother (brigadier, general staff, to Haig at Aldershot), and Sir Henry Wilson, the director of military operations. They were still not entirely satisfied, so Gough wrote on a sheet of War Office paper, 'I understand the reading of the last paragraph to be that the troops under our command will not be called upon to enforce the present Home Rule Bill on Ulster, and that we can so assure our officers' (ibid., 152). French added, 'This is how I read it. J. F.' (ibid., 153). The government repudiated the two 'peccant paragraphs' and Seely, shortly followed by French and Ewart, resigned. Gough had apparently triumphed.

On his return to the Curragh, Gough was welcomed by cheering troops. With some exceptions, notably Wavell and Sir Charles Fergusson, officers throughout the army sympathized with Gough, as did many Royal Navy and Territorial Force officers. He received many letters and telegrams, mostly eulogistic. The Unionist press was jubilant, while Liberal papers attacked 'Tory cavalry officers' and the Liberal *Daily Chronicle* claimed 'the sinister attempt by a military cabal to intimidate the government has signally failed' (Fergusson, 159). The Curragh incident and Gough's role have since been variously interpreted. According to Hew Strachan the incident was the denouement to the army's nineteenth-century politization through involvement in the empire.

The First World War In the short term Gough's career suffered no ill effects from the Curragh incident. He led his brigade with distinction during the opening weeks of the war in 1914 and was promoted major-general in command of the newly formed 2nd cavalry division in the first battle of Ypres. Further promotions followed in rapid succession: after the battle of Neuve Chapelle in March 1915 he was given command of 7th division and in July he was promoted lieutenant-general in command of 1st corps, which played a prominent part in the battle of Loos, though Gough himself was in no way to blame for the disaster. Jealousy at his rapid rise was offset by his wide reputation for moral as well as physical courage. His chief failings were his hot temper and his tendency to quick, impulsive judgements. A fighting general *par excellence*, Gough discovered that as a corps commander he was remote from the battle and could not visit the front frequently without arousing the resentment of his divisional commanders. This frustration was intensified before the battle of the Somme in 1916 with his promotion to command of the Reserve (soon to be titled Fifth) Army. 'It was not that he enjoyed pitching men into battle to be killed or wounded', a biographer remarks, 'simply that he was confident of his ability to lead soldiers successfully in the dreadful tasks to which they were committed'.

In the third Ypres campaign in 1917 Gough's Fifth Army was placed on the left wing and given the major role in the first phase of the offensive. Gough was never sanguine about the prospects of a complete breakthrough into open country, but he differed from general headquarters in believing that it was essential to secure all short-range objectives on the first day rather than by a series of short advances. Fifth Army was initially successful on its left but made little progress on the right. When heavy rain and stubborn resistance held up the second and third attacks in mid-August, Gough vainly asked Haig to call off the offensive. Second Army took over the major role in September and Fifth Army's reputation declined. Gough's personal relations with his subordinate commanders remained good but his chief of staff, Neill Malcolm, had a brusque manner which caused resentment and uncertainty about his general's real feelings. By the end of the campaign Haig had gained the impression that units had become reluctant to serve in Fifth Army. Personally brave and an aggressive commander, Gough in 1918, according to Sir James Edmonds, complained that his troops lacked blood lust and his officers lacked offensive spirit, and said,

'I want to shoot two officers as an example to the others' (Travers, 20).

In March 1918 the Germans were expected to launch an all-out spring offensive with an army strongly reinforced from the eastern front. Haig and general headquarters were over-confident of British ability to halt a German offensive, and expected it to the north, and general headquarters was apparently biased against Fifth Army. To the south Fifth Army was holding a vulnerable 42 mile sector between Gouzeaucourt and La Fère with a fully stretched front line and very meagre reserves. Haig was aware of this weakness but gave the Third Army of Sir Julian Byng, on Gough's left, priority because of the vital need to protect the channel ports, and because he assumed that the French would quickly reinforce Gough's sector in a crisis. Gough and his chief of staff became convinced that there would be a major offensive against their sector, and increasingly concerned at the thinness of their line and their lack of reserves, and Gough requested reinforcements, in vain. Feeling intimidated by Haig, Gough did not request an interview with him. Gough later said his greatest mistake had been not seeking an interview with Haig before 21 March.

When on 21 March Ludendorff launched his main blow against Fifth Army's front he enjoyed a local superiority of about eight to one. Gough decided he could not hope to hold out in the forward battle zone but must fight a delaying action to save his army from complete destruction while preserving an intact line until British and French reinforcements arrived in strength. Unfortunately for Gough, Pétain and Foch both proved reluctant to commit reserves to the British sector for several days, and to make matters worse one of his corps commanders, Ivor Maxse of 18th corps, interpreted Gough's orders as permitting disengagement and withdrawal to the Somme. This precipitate action forced the two adjacent corps to conform and by 24 March leading German units were already across the river. Nevertheless the German offensive was already losing momentum in the face of Fifth Army's resistance, an organized battle of retreat, when Gough was informed, on 27 March, that he was to be replaced by Sir Henry Rawlinson and the staff of Fourth Army next day. Haig attempted to keep him employed in France but Lloyd George and Lord Derby, the war minister, insisted (3 April) that he be sent home immediately. Gough's career abruptly ended and the promised official inquiry was never held. He may not have been responsible for Fifth Army's defeat, but after his ill conduct of operations in 1917 he had no credit balance to fall back on, and he was made the scapegoat. 'His treatment', Haig admitted to a brother officer of them both in February 1919, 'was harsh and undeserved: but after considerable thought I decided that public opinion at home, whether right or wrong, demanded a scapegoat, and that the only possible ones were Hubert or me. I was conceited enough to think that the army could not spare me.'

Later years In 1919 Gough accepted the thankless appointment of chief of the allied military mission to the Baltic but he was speedily recalled by Lloyd George. He was

appointed GCMG in 1919. No further employment followed and in October 1922 he was retired with the rank of full general. He had been created KCB in 1916, and KCVO in 1917. In March 1922 he was the Asquithian Liberal candidate at a by-election in the Chertsey division of Surrey but was narrowly defeated by the Conservative. After a few years farming in Surrey he took up a successful career in business.

However, Gough remained determined to vindicate his and his army's reputation against the slurs over March 1918. In 1924 he was reconciled to Haig and with Lady Gough stayed with the Haigs at Bemersyde. In 1928 he was a pall bearer at Haig's funeral. In 1931 he published his version of the events of spring 1918 in *Fifth Army*, claiming 'there was no defeat' and 'no other troops … did more to win the War' (Gough, *Fifth Army*, 327–8). However, many in the Fifth Army felt it should have done better and were puzzled why it had not. As the episode began to be viewed more objectively and new evidence appeared Gough's conduct of the retreat tended to be exonerated and even praised. This trend in various histories and memoirs culminated in the belated but none the less welcome amends made by Lloyd George in 1936 in his *War Memoirs*. The 1918 volumes of Sir James Edmonds's *History of the Great War* defended and exonerated Gough. In awarding Gough the GCB in 1937 George VI indicated that Gough's and Fifth Army's honour were fully restored. From 1936 to 1943 he was colonel of the 16th battalion 5th lancers. Gough was a small, slight, wiry man, quick in his movements and with bright eyes, and reportedly a charming personality.

In 1939 Gough was still in vigorous health and eager to serve in a military capacity. He formed the Chelsea branch of the Home Guard in 1940 and later commanded a London zone until he was finally retired in 1942. He was president of the Fifth Army Old Comrades Association and the Combined Cavalry Old Comrades. At the age of eighty he was still an active director of Siemens and nine other companies. Gough published his memoirs *Soldiering On* (1954). He long outlived other First World War senior commanders and, after suffering from influenza and pneumonia, died at his home, 14 St Mary Abbots Court, Kensington, London W14, on 18 March 1963.

BRIAN BOND, rev.

Sources A. Farrar-Hockley, *Goughie: the life of Sir Hubert Gough GCB, GCMG, KCVO* (1975) · H. Gough, *Soldiering on: being the memoirs of General Sir Hubert Gough G.C.B., G.C.M.G., K.C.V.O.* (1954) · H. Gough, *Fifth Army* (1931) · Burke, *Peerage* (1959) · Burke, *Gen. Ire.* (1958) · *WWW* · *Hart's Army List* (1913) · J. Fergusson, *The Curragh incident* (1964) · I. F. W. Beckett, ed., *The army and the Curragh incident* (1914) · T. Travers, *The killing ground* (1990) · *The Eton register*, 5 (privately printed, Eton, 1908) · T. Wilson, *The myriad faces of war: Britain and the Great War, 1914–1918* (1986); repr. (1988) · A. P. Ryan, *Mutiny at the Curragh* (1956) · G. Brooke, *Good company* (1954) · private information (c.1981) · Marquess of Anglesey [G. C. H. V. Paget], *A history of the British cavalry, 1816 to 1919*, 4 (1986) · *CGPLA Eng. & Wales* (1963) · I. F. W. Beckett, *Johnnie Gough, VC: a biography* (1989)
Archives NAM, corresp. and papers · NAM, family corresp., letters to his sister-in-law and niece [some copies] | BL, corresp. with W. Shaw Sparrow, Add. MSS 48203–48208 · HLRO, letters to R. D. Blumenfeld · IWM, corresp. with H. A. Gwynne · IWM, corresp. with Sir Henry Wilson · King's Lond., Liddell Hart C., letters to Sir

J. E. Edmonds; corresp. with Sir B. H. Liddell Hart | FILM IWM FVA, actuality footage | SOUND IWM SA, oral history interview **Likenesses** F. Dodd, charcoal and watercolour drawing, 1917, IWM [*see illus.*] · W. Rothenstein, sanguine drawing, 1918, Birmingham Museums and Art gallery · W. Rothenstein, chalk drawing, 1932, NPG · P. Kahn, ciment fondu, 1961, NPG **Wealth at death** £16,056 17s. 5d.: probate, 4 June 1963, CGPLA Eng. & Wales

Gough, Hugh, first Viscount Gough (1779–1869), army officer, was born on 3 November 1779 at Woodsdown, co. Limerick, Ireland, fourth son of George Gough of Woodsdown and his wife, Letitia, daughter of Thomas Bunbury of Lisnavagh and Moyle, co. Carlow. In 1793 he received a commission in the new Limerick city militia, of which his father was lieutenant-colonel, and on 7 August 1794 was promoted ensign in Hon. Robert Ward's regiment of foot, from which he was transferred in October to the 119th, of which he was adjutant at the age of fifteen. On 6 June 1795 he was promoted lieutenant in the 78th Highlanders, on the formation of its 2nd battalion, and was present with it at the capture of the Cape of Good Hope that year, and at the surrender of the Dutch fleet in Saldanha Bay in 1796. His friends had meanwhile procured his transfer to the 87th Prince of Wales's Irish, with which he served against the brigands in St Lucia, at the capture of Trinidad, the attack on Puerto Rico, and the capture of Surinam, serving with it in the West Indies and at Curaçoa until 1803. In 1803 he obtained command of a company in a second battalion of the regiment formed at Frome, Somerset, by Sir Charles William Doyle from men enrolled in the army of reserve in the counties of Tipperary and Galway. Gough became major in the battalion in 1805, and in 1807 he married Frances Maria, daughter of General Edward Stephens, Royal Artillery. They had a son, the second viscount, and four daughters. Lady Gough died in 1863.

Doyle having been sent to Spain, Gough commanded the battalion when it embarked for Portugal on 28 December 1808, and at the battle of Talavera on 28 July 1809, where the 'Faugh a Ballaghs' ('Clear the Ways'), as this regiment was called from its Erse battle-cry, sustained heavy losses. Gough was severely wounded, and had his horse shot under him. At Wellington's request Gough's commission as lieutenant-colonel was antedated to the battle, the first British officer to receive brevet promotion in action at the head of a regiment. In 1810 the battalion was with Graham at Cadiz, and formed part of the force that disembarked at Algeciras, and fought the battle of Barossa on 5 March 1811, when Gough, with the 87th and three companies 1st guards, made a famous charge on the French 8th light infantry. An 'eagle'—the first taken in the Peninsular War—was captured by Sergeant Patrick Masterson of the 87th, and an eagle with collar of gold and the figure 8 was thereafter worn as a badge of honour by the regiment. Graham wrote to its colonel: 'Your regiment has covered itself with glory' (Cannon, 52). The battalion afterwards went to Cadiz and Gibraltar, and in October 1811 to Tarifa, and, when the French under Laval attacked, it defended the breach in the south-east front. In a desperate assault on 31 October 1811 the heroic leader of the French fell, dying against the portcullis which closed the

Hugh Gough, first Viscount Gough (1779–1869), by Maull & Polyblank

breach, yielding his sword to Gough through the bars. An open breach between two turrets, with the British colours flying, and the word Tarifa, are among the augmentations to the Gough family arms.

The battalion with Gough in command joined Wellington's army in October 1812, and fought at the battle of Vitoria and in the subsequent campaigns. Gough was disabled by a severe wound received at the battle of Nivelle on 10 November 1813. His application for a company in the guards was unsuccessful. He was knighted at Carlton House on 4 June 1815 and received the freedom of the city of Dublin. He was in command of the 2nd 87th when it was disbanded in February 1817. Gough remained on half pay until 1819, when he was appointed to the 22nd foot, and commanded it most of the time in the south of Ireland during a period of civil unrest, until 1826. He then again retired on half pay. When not in regimental employment he was chiefly on his estate in co. Tipperary, where he was a magistrate and popular with the gentry.

Gough became a major-general in 1830, was made KCB in 1831, and in 1837 appointed to command the Mysore division of the Madras army. In the First Opium War Gough was sent to command the troops at Canton (Guangzhou), where he arrived on 2 March 1841. The forts defending Canton were captured on 26–7 May 1841, and Gough was made GCB. After the arrival of Admiral Sir William Parker in July, Gough commanded the troops in the combined operations which ended with the capture of the great fortified city of Chinkiang (Zhenjiang) and the signing of the treaty at Nanking (Nanjing) in 1842. For his part in these events Gough was created a baronet, and received the thanks of parliament and of the East India Company. He returned to Madras, having been made presidency commander-in-chief on 16 June 1841, and on 11 August 1843 was appointed commander-in-chief in India.

Soon after his arrival in Bengal, Gough assumed command of the 'army of exercise' assembled at Agra in view of difficulties over the Gwalior succession. The army entered that state and firm government was established there, but this was unpopular with the Maratha army. Conflict with it appearing inevitable, the Maratha army was attacked and routed by Gough at Maharajpur on 29 December 1843, suffering heavy loss. Gough was again thanked by parliament. Lord Ellenborough, then governor-general, apparently doubted Gough's fitness for the command. He wrote to Wellington on 20 April 1844, just before his own removal, that Gough, 'despite his many excellent qualities, had not the grasp of mind and the prudence essential to conduct great military operations' (*Indian Administration*, 435).

On 11 December 1845 Sikhs invaded the company's territory, starting the First Anglo-Sikh War. Gough, loyally supported by Hardinge, the new governor-general, who placed himself under Gough's orders as second in command, defeated the invaders by sheer hard fighting at Mudki, Ferozeshahr, and Sobraon, and was able to dictate terms to the Sikhs. He was then raised to the peerage as Baron Gough of Ching-keang-foo (Qingjiangfu), China, Maharajpur, and the Sutlej in the East Indies. In the Second Anglo-Sikh War three years later Gough defeated the enemy at Ramnagar, and again on 13 January 1849 at Chilianwala—a victory, despite heavy losses, which contributed to the destruction of Sikh power. The severe loss at Chilianwala has been attributed to the failure of a subordinate, but Gough's failure to reconnoitre the Sikhs' position properly before attacking was also blameworthy. When the news reached Britain there was a public outcry against him and his 'Tipperary tactics'. Gough made no public response. The presence on the battlefield of the governor-general at Mudki, Ferozeshahr, and Sobraon must have added to Gough's problems, for Hardinge, also a soldier, had made himself second in command. He largely shared Ellenborough's doubts as to Gough's fitness for command and was greatly disturbed by the casualties incurred. After Sobraon, Hardinge wrote: 'sometimes I am almost in despair at his want of method & combination & discipline. He has a great many fine qualities of bravery & kindness of heart & is a gentleman but is very jealous' (*Letters*, 146). Sir Charles Napier was sent out to supersede him, but before the change could take place Gough had re-established his reputation by his crushing defeat of the Sikh armies at Gujrat on 21 February 1849, followed by their unconditional surrender to the pursuing force under General Gilbert. He vacated the command on 7 May 1849.

On his return to England, Gough was made a viscount, and awarded a pension of £2000 a year to himself and the next two heirs to the title. The East India Company voted him thanks and a pension, and the City of London conferred its freedom on him. He became a full general in

1854, and was appointed colonel-in-chief of the 60th rifles. He was made colonel of the Royal Horse Guards in 1855. In 1856 he was sent to Sevastopol to invest Marshal Pélissier and other officers with the insignia of the Bath. In 1857 he was made KP (the first non-Irish peer to be such). In 1859 he was sworn of the privy council and in 1861 was made GCSI. On 9 November 1862 he became field marshal. In politics he was a Conservative.

Gough, a man of noble presence, was said to have commanded in more general actions than any other British officer of the nineteenth century except the duke of Wellington. His courage, chivalry, and racy brogue all contributed to his popularity with his soldiers, despite his bull-headed tactics. Wellington described him as 'affording the brightest example of the highest qualities of the British soldier' (Fortescue, *Brit. army*, 12.473). He could however be vindictive, as was shown by his harsh treatment of Henry Havelock after the Anglo-Sikh wars. Gough died at his seat, St Helens, near Booterstown, co. Dublin, on 2 March 1869, and was buried on 9 March at Stillorgan.

H. M. CHICHESTER, rev. JAMES LUNT

Sources R. S. Rait, *The life and campaigns of Hugh, first Viscount Gough*, 2 vols. (1903) · W. Broadfoot, *The career of Major George Broadfoot … in Afghanistan and the Punjab* (1888) · C. Gough and A. D. Innes, *The Sikhs and Sikh wars* (1897) · H. C. Wylly, *Memoirs of the life of Lieut.-Gen. Sir Joseph Thackwell* (1908) · E. J. Thackwell, *Narrative of the Second Seikh War, in 1848–49* (1851) · R. G. Burton, *The First and Second Sikh wars* (1911) · W. F. P. Napier, *The life and opinions of General Sir Charles James Napier*, 4 vols. (1857) · *The Times* (3 March 1869) · Fortescue, *Brit. army*, vol. 12 · H. C. B. Cook, *The Sikh wars: the British army in the Punjab, 1845–1849* (1975) · *The letters of the first Viscount Hardinge of Lahore … 1844–1847*, ed. B. S. Singh, CS, 4th ser., 32 (1986) · R. Cannon, ed., *Historical record of the eighty-seventh regiment, or royal Irish fusiliers* (1853) · W. F. P. Napier, *History of the war in the Peninsula and in the south of France*, 6 vols. (1828–40) · *Hart's Army List* · C. S. Hardinge, *Viscount Hardinge* (1891) · *History of the Indian administration of Lord Ellenborough: in his correspondence with the duke of Wellington*, ed. Lord Colchester (1874) · A. J. Webb, *A compendium of Irish biography* (1878) · J. C. Pollock, *Way to glory: the life of Havelock of Lucknow* (1957) · GEC, *Peerage*

Archives Bodl. Oxf., corresp. and papers · NAM, corresp. and papers · NAM, corresp. and papers as commander-in-chief in India · NL Ire., dispatches and letter-book [copies] | BL, corresp. with Lord Ellenborough, Lord Hardinge, etc., Add. MSS 40864–40877, *passim* · NA Scot., letters to Lord Dalhousie · NAM, letters to Jasper Nicolls · PRO, letters to Lord Ellenborough, PRO 30/12 · PRO, letters to Henry Pottinger, FO 705 · U. Southampton, letters to first duke of Wellington

Likenesses G. G. Adams, plaster bust, 1850, NPG · J. H. Lynch, lithograph, pubd 1850 (after E. Long), NPG · L. Dickinson, oils, c.1851, Oriental Club, London · J. Harwood, oils, c.1851, NG Ire. · F. Grant, oils, c.1853; formerly United Services Club, London, in care of Crown Commissioners · S. Cousins, mezzotint, pubd in or after 1866 (after oils by F. Grant, exh. RA 1854), NG Ire. · J. H. Foley, bronze statue, 1874–80, Phoenix Park, Dublin · F. Grant, pen-and-ink drawing (after his oil painting, 1853), NPG · Maull & Polyblank, hand-coloured albumen print photograph, NPG [*see illus.*] · H. B. Nall, stipple (after J. R. Jackson), BM, NPG · A. Y. Shortt, oils (after E. Long, c.1850), East India and Sports Club, London · bust, BL OIOC · oils, East India and Sports Club, London · photograph, NPG · portrait, NAM; owned by Royal Irish Regiment

Wealth at death under £12,000 (effects in England): Irish probate sealed in London, 24 April 1869, CGPLA Eng. & Wales

Gough, Sir Hugh Henry (1833–1909), army officer, was born in Calcutta on 14 November 1883, the third son of

George Gough of Rathronan, Clonmel, co. Tipperary, a judge in the service of the East India Company, and his third wife, Charlotte Margaret Becher, daughter of Charles Becher of Tonbridge, Kent, also of the company. The Gough family had a long military tradition and connection with India, George Gough's uncle being Hugh, first Viscount Gough. Hugh Gough's elder brother was Charles *Gough.

Gough was educated privately and at the East India College, Haileybury (1851–2), and was commissioned ensign in the 3rd Bengal light cavalry, stationed at Meerut, in September 1853. On the evening of 9 May 1857 he was warned by an Indian officer that the sepoys would mutiny next day. He told his commanding officer and the brigadier commanding the station, Archdale Wilson, but the warning was not believed. The sepoys mutinied next evening, starting the Indian mutiny. Gough was fortunate to escape with his life. He was attached to the 6th dragoon guards (Carabiniers), then in July 1857 was appointed adjutant of Hodson's Horse, with which he served until the end of 1858, when he was appointed second in command of the 2nd Maratha horse. He was present at the siege and capture of Delhi, the relief of Cawnpore, the second relief of Lucknow, and its capture in March 1858. He was prominent in several cavalry actions, notably at Kharkhauda (where his life was saved by his brother) and at Rohtak in August 1857, at Agra in October 1857, and around Lucknow in November 1857 (for which he was awarded the Victoria Cross) and in February 1858, when he was severely wounded. He was mentioned in dispatches and received the brevet of major. After the mutiny he served briefly in the 1st European light cavalry and, after it was disbanded, in the 19th hussars from 1862 until 1867. He married Anne Margaret, daughter of Edward Eustace Hill and his wife, Lady Georgiana Keppel, on 8 September 1863; she survived him and they had five sons and four daughters.

In 1867 Gough was given command of the 12th Bengal cavalry, and he commanded it in the 1868 Abyssinian expedition, being present at the capture of Magdala. He was mentioned in dispatches and received the CB in August 1868. Promoted lieutenant-colonel in 1869 and brevet colonel in 1877, he commanded the cavalry in the force under Major-General Frederick Roberts which invaded Afghanistan via the Kurram valley on the outbreak of the Second Anglo-Afghan War in November 1878. He played a prominent part in the seizure of the Peiwar Kotal in December 1878 and at the action around Matun, in Khost, in January 1879. When the war recommenced after the massacre of Cavagnari's mission at Kabul in September 1879 Gough commanded the cavalry in Roberts's force that captured Kabul in October 1879. He was present at the action at Charasia on 6 October 1879 and in the actions around Kabul in December 1879. When Roberts marched from Kabul to Kandahar in August 1880 Gough again commanded the cavalry brigade, and after the defeat of Ayub Khan outside Kandahar on 1 September 1880 he commanded the unsuccessful pursuit. He was mentioned in dispatches and made KCB in 1881.

Gough remained in command of the 12th cavalry until 1884, when he was appointed to command the Sialkot brigade, an appointment that he held until 1886. In the following year he was appointed to command of the Lahore division, his last active appointment, which he held until 1892. Promoted major-general in 1887, lieutenant-general in 1891, and general in 1894, he retired in 1897, having been made GCB the year before. In 1897 he published his mutiny reminiscences, *Old Memories*, containing his important eye-witness account of the events at Meerut in May 1857. He was appointed keeper of the regalia at the Tower of London in 1898 and died at his residence there, in St Thomas's Tower, on 12 May 1909; he was buried at Kensal Green cemetery. Roberts had no great opinion of his intelligence but rightly valued him as a bold, determined cavalry leader.

H. M. VIBART, rev. BRIAN ROBSON

Sources H. Gough, *Old memories* (1897) · B. Gough, *A history of the Gough family* (c.1978) · J. A. B. Palmer, *The mutiny outbreak at Meerut in 1857* (1966) · *The Bengal army lists* · C. M. MacGregor, *The Second Afghan War*, 6 vols. (1885–6) · *Roberts in India: the military papers of Field Marshal Lord Roberts, 1876–1893*, ed. B. Robson (1993) · *The Times* (14 May 1909) · *The Times* (19 May 1909) · Lord Roberts [F. S. Roberts], *Forty-one years in India*, 2 vols. (1897) · S. N. Sen, *Eighteen fifty-seven* (Delhi, 1958) · W. Forrest, *History of the Indian mutiny*, 2 (1904) · L. J. Trotter, *Hodson of Hodson's horse* (1901) · [S. P. Oliver], *The Second Afghan War, 1878–80; abridged official account*, rev. F. G. Cardew (1908)
Archives NAM, Roberts MSS · NL Wales, letters to Sir James Hills-Johnes
Likenesses Spy [L. Ward], caricature, mechanical reproduction, NPG; repro. in *VF* (15 Feb 1906) · photographs, NAM
Wealth at death £1728 5s. 9d.: administration with will, 12 June 1909, *CGPLA Eng. & Wales*

Gough, John (d. 1543/4), bookseller and translator, first appears in 1523 as a bookseller in the parish of St Bride's, Fleet Street, London. He was associated with the printer Wynkyn de Worde, and was both an overseer and a significant beneficiary of de Worde's will of 1535. He was also one of the first figures in the English book trade to be associated with heterodox beliefs. By his own account, reading the New Testament sparked a dramatic conversion experience, and gave him zeal for spreading his new-found evangelical faith. Accordingly, in 1525 he translated into English *The Ymage of Love*, a devotional work with anticlerical undertones by the Franciscan John Ryckes, for publication by de Worde. As a consequence, in October 1525 Gough and de Worde were indicted for disobeying Bishop Tunstall's strictures on heretical literature. In March 1528 Gough was again arrested, on suspicion of supplying the heretical books which Thomas Garrett was circulating in Cardinal College, Oxford. However, he managed to convince Tunstall of his innocence and was quickly released. His reformist zeal was undaunted; when he bound the Pewterers' Company's account books in 1530, he left evangelical messages on the endpapers. By 1532 he had moved to Paul's Gate in Cheapside. It may have been in the same year that he was arrested together with a group of Anabaptists in London; he was accused of printing a book described mysteriously as 'the Confession of the citie of Geneva' (PRO, SP 1/237, fol. 290v). It is unlikely, however, that Gough himself had Anabaptist sympathies; if he did, he had abandoned them by 1539, when he went out of his way to insert an attack on Anabaptism into a text he translated for publication.

From 1532 onwards Gough began to publish under his own name. His output, never large, consisted almost entirely of religious works, many of which were written or translated by evangelicals including Miles Coverdale, William Turner, and Hugh Latimer. He also edited and translated several reformist texts himself (in the process stretching his linguistic abilities to the limit). These included another edition of *The Ymage of Love*, and an edition of the prologue to the Wycliffite Bible; Gough brought the latter up to date by inserting references to the protestant doctrine of justification. Nor was his support for the reformist cause limited to the professional sphere; in May 1538 he was one of a mob accused of tearing down a rood at St Margaret Pattens. By 1539 he had moved to the sign of the Mermaid in Lombard Street. In July 1540 he was arrested as part of a general purge of London heretics, accused of deprecating an anthem to the Virgin and of assisting the book-smuggler Thomas Lancaster, but he was quickly released. Later the same year, however, he published a broadsheet ballad posthumously defending Thomas Cromwell, and as a consequence was imprisoned again in January 1541. Soon after his subsequent release, his establishment moved again, to Smart's Quay near Billingsgate, and he entered into a partnership with the evangelical printer John Mayler. The next two years were much the most prolific of Gough's career. He published at least two dozen books in 1541–3, mostly with Mayler; the most important of these were the early works of the moderate evangelical Thomas Becon. In 1543 Gough was again arrested, as part of a broader crackdown on reformist printing; he was accused of harbouring a heretical scholar, Stephen Cobbe, in his house. Although he was released on recognizance, this was apparently the end of Gough's publishing career. His will, dated 25 September 1543, affirmed justification by faith alone in forthright and idiosyncratic terms; it also provided for a mass and *Dirige* to be said 'to the laude and prayse of god', suggesting that, at least by this date, Gough's faith leaned more towards Lutheran than Reformed theology (Guildhall Library, London, MS 9171/11, fol. 133r). The will was proved on 14 October 1544. He left a widow, Margaret, and three children, John *Gough (1521/2–1572), Francis, and Joan.

ALEC RYRIE

Sources STC, 1475–1640 · GL, MS 9171/11, fols. 132v–133r · S. Brigden, *London and the Reformation* (1989) · PRO, SP 1/47, fol. 99r; SP 1/237, fol. 290v [LPH, 4, no. 4073; addenda no. 809] · J. Foxe, *The first volume of the ecclesiasticall history contayning the actes and monumentes of thynges passed*, new edn (1570) · N. H. Nicolas, ed., *Proceedings and ordinances of the privy council of England*, 7 vols., RC, 26 (1834–7), vol. 7 · APC, 1542–7 · J. Britnell, 'John Gough and the *Traité de la différence des schismes et des conciles* of Jean Lemair de Belges: translation as propaganda in the Henrician reformation', *Journal of Ecclesiastical History*, 46 (1995), 62–74 · E. G. Duff, *A century of the English book trade* (1905) · repertory, CLRO, 10, fol. 34v · E. R. Harvey, 'Appendix A: The image of love', in T. More, *A dialogue concerning heresies*, ed. T. M. C. Lawler, 2 (1981), 727–59 · D. S. Dunnan, 'A note on John Gough's *The dore of holy scripture*', N&Q, 234 (1989), 309–10 ·

J. G.[ough?], *The myrrour or lokynge glasse of lyfe, for comfortyng of the soule* (1532?)
Wealth at death left 10s. for funeral expenses: will, GL, MS 9171/11, fols. 132v–133r

Gough, John (1521/2–1572), Church of England clergyman, was born in London, son of the printer John *Gough (d. 1543/4). According to John Stowe, the younger John Gough was a professional scrivener before ordination, and his will, written in a beautiful hand, amply supports the contention.

One of several evangelical laymen encouraged into the ministry by Edmund Grindal, bishop of London, at the beginning of Elizabeth I's reign, Gough gave his age as thirty-eight when Grindal ordained him deacon, then priest, on 13 and 25 January 1560. On 15 November following, presented there by the mayor (Sir William Chester) and aldermen, he was instituted rector of St Peter Cornhill, a London parish with radical traditions. In a report submitted in 1561 John Mullins, archdeacon of London, described Gough as resident there, holding no other benefice. Though no graduate he was a licensed preacher, was proficient in Latin, and supported a family. During the plague year of 1563 two of his sons were buried at St Peter: Matthew in July and John in September.

A leader of nonconformity in London from the beginning, Gough contributed the prologue to a 'paraphristic abridgement' of the second edition of Erasmus's *Enchiridion*, entitled *A godly boke wherein is contayned certayne fruitfull rules, to bee exercised by all Christes souldiers*, published by William Seres in 1561. He perhaps inaugurated the 'exercise named prophesying … at St Peter's' mentioned by Thomas Wood (Collinson, 'Letters', 1), and with Robert Crowley and John Philpot organized daily lectures at St Antholin. All three signed a petition requesting forbearance over the canonical habits, which Miles Coverdale submitted on 25 March 1565 to Matthew Parker, archbishop of Canterbury, and the rest of the ecclesiastical commissioners. In the ensuing months they mounted a strenuous campaign, both vocal and literary, against Parker's proceedings, and when in March 1566 Parker finally demanded unconditional conformity from the city clergy they were among the thirty-seven who, on refusal, were suspended and threatened with deprivation three months later. Although their lectures and exercises were suppressed they continued, with the lecturer John Bartlett, to oppose Parker's demands: Stowe describes Gough and Philpot as 'the greatest animators of the whole city'. On 4 June they were therefore dispatched to the custody of Robert Horne, bishop of Winchester. A large crowd of women accompanied them over London Bridge into Southwark, offering gifts and exhorting them 'most earnestly to stand fast in … their doctrine' (Gairdner, 139–40).

A letter from Horne to William Cecil, dated 21 June, suggests that Gough showed no inclination to compromise. Since the commissioners deprived Crowley on 25 June, Gough probably suffered at the same time. When his daughter Ruth was baptized at St Peter on 23 November 1566 he was described in the register only as 'preacher', not 'parson', as in earlier entries. That his successor was not instituted until 26 January 1568 suggests that the mayor and aldermen simply refused in the interim to acknowledge the legality of his removal.

Horne was soon 'desirous to be discharged' of his house guest, and on 28 November the privy council handed Gough back to Parker, professing his case 'more fit to be … determined by you than by us' (LPL, MS 3470, fol. 18r). Since three of the five signatories were Cecil, Nicholas Bacon, and Robert Dudley, earl of Leicester, this was perhaps an attempt by Parker's critics to make him face the consequences of his actions.

Certainly Parker appears to have released Gough, who may have gravitated to Essex. In November 1568 'Mr Goofe' was one of four preachers, including Richard Alvey and Thomas Brice, who were each bequeathed £2 to provide a series of eight sermons in Vange.

Gough was back in London by February 1569 when he preached at Holy Trinity Minories, where many radicals enjoyed the protection of Katherine Bertie, duchess of Suffolk. He occupied the pulpit again in June, and then in April and May 1570. Meanwhile, on 15 January 1570, he had preached at the Tower of London where John Feckenham, former abbot of Westminster, remained in confinement. Feckenham managed to issue a rejoinder, to which both Gough and Laurence Tomson replied in print, Gough with *The aunswer of John Gough preacher, to maister Fecknam's obiections against his sermon, lately preached in the Tower* (1570).

On 4 June 1571, with Christopher Goodman and others, Gough again faced examination by Parker during the renewed drive for conformity which followed Thomas Cartwright's Cambridge lectures in 1570. He had perhaps entered a long, final illness: his brief will is dated 27 March 1571. Mentioning no parish he described himself simply as 'preacher of the word of God' (LMA, DL/C/358, fol. 161v), leaving everything to his wife, Mary. No children, friends, or overseers are named.

John Gough, 'preacher', was buried at St Bartholomew by the Exchange on 1 February 1572. Mary was granted probate by the London consistory court on 9 February. On 15 October 1581 'Elizabeth' Gough was 'buried in the same grave her husband John Gough was buried' (Guildhall Library, MS 4374/1, unfoliated).   BRETT USHER

Sources GL, MS 9535/1 [ordination] · J. Gairdner, ed., *Three fifteenth-century chronicles*, CS, new ser., 28 (1880) [with historical memoranda by John Stowe] · P. Collinson, *The Elizabethan puritan movement* (1967) · P. Collinson, *Archbishop Grindal, 1519–1583: the struggle for a reformed church* (1979) · 'Letters of Thomas Wood, puritan, 1566–1577', ed. P. Collinson, BIHR, special suppl., 5 (1960) [whole issue] · CCC Cam., MS 122, pp. 86–7 [Mullins's report] · LPL, Fairhurst MS 2019 [1565 petition] · LPL, Fairhurst MS 3470 [letters of Horne and privy council] · G. W. G. Leveson Gower, ed., *A register of … the parish of St Peeters upon Cornhill*, 2, Harleian Society, register section, 4 (1879) · F. G. Emmison, ed., *Essex wills*, 2: *1565–1571* (1983), no. 248 · churchwardens' accounts and vestry minutes of Holy Trinity Minories, LPL, MS 3390 · *Correspondence of Matthew Parker*, ed. J. Bruce and T. T. Perowne, Parker Society, 42 (1853) · registered will, LMA, DL/C/358, fols. 161v–162r · parish register, St Bartholomew by the Exchange, GL, MS 4374/1

Wealth at death everything left to wife: will, LMA, DL/C/358, fols. 161v–162r

Gough, John (1720–1791), religious writer and schoolmaster, was born on 30 December 1720 at Kendal in Westmorland, youngest of the four children of John Gough (1686–1737), a Quaker and tobacconist, and his wife, Mary Mansergh (d. 1747). On his father's side he was descended from the regicide General William Goffe (1619–1680) and was a cousin of the naturalist John Gough (1757–1825). He was educated at the Friends' school at Kendal, and while still only fourteen became an assistant in the school kept by Thomas Bennet, a Quaker, at Pickwick in Wiltshire, where he remained until 1740. He then went to Ireland to take charge of the school at Cork established by his only brother, James Gough (1712–1780), who was absent on a religious journey in England until 1742. John then became tutor to the children of Benjamin Wilson, near Edenderry, King's county. Eighteen months later he again took his brother's place at Cork, in his absence, and continued to hold it on his brother's moving to Mountmellick School, Queen's county.

On 18 November 1744 Gough married Hannah Fisher (1721–1798) of Youghal, with whom he had ten children, and in 1748 he moved to Mountmellick to assist his brother, whose wife died that same year. In 1752 he accepted the mastership of the prestigious Friends' school at Dublin, which he held until 1774. He combined this appointment, at a joint salary of £80 per annum, with being paid clerk of the yearly meeting in Dublin; his wife supplemented their income by selling linen. In the 1760s he published two valuable text-books: *Practical Grammar* (1764), based on a work by his brother, and *Practical Arithmetic* (1767), which ran to over sixteen editions before being superseded by *Thompson's Arithmetic*. He also wrote poetry, as did his brother, who was himself the author of books of pious biography and the translator of the *Life of Lady Guion* (1772), which was widely read by quietist Quakers.

In 1774, attracted by the prospect of more freedom and a salary of £150 per annum, Gough moved to Lisburn, co. Antrim, to be the first headmaster of the new Friends' boarding-school. In 1777 he published a much reprinted tract on non-payment of tithes, and in 1781, following his brother's death, *Memoirs of the Life of James Gough*. He also took a more active part as a minister, accompanying the American John Pemberton around the north of Ireland in 1783, and subsequently working in Munster and Leinster. In 1785 he visited meetings in various English counties, and several times attended the London yearly meetings. The last eight years of his life were occupied in writing *A History of the People called Quakers from their First Rise to the Present Time* (1789–90), which, though long accepted as a textbook, is now regarded as a 'mere compilation' (Braithwaite, v). He and his brother, James, were both, however, 'excellent teachers and genuine promoters of education in Ireland' (Jones, 668). His son John (1758–1818) became a printer in Dublin, where his great-grandson, another John (1835–1900), became a bookseller.

Gough died in Lisburn, of apoplexy, on 25 October 1791, and was buried in the local Quaker burial-ground three days later. The testimony of the Lisburn Friends records the sobriety and gravity for which he had been distinguished from childhood. PETER LAMB

Sources N. H. Newhouse, *A history of Friends' School, Lisburn* (1974) · *Some Ulster yesterdays … extracted from papers left by the late Joseph Radley*, ed. M. L. Waterfall [1935] · J. Gough, *Memoirs of the life of James Gough* (1781) · R. M. Jones, *The later periods of Quakerism*, 2 vols. (1921) · M. J. Wigham, *The Irish Quakers* (1992) · R. S. Harrison, *A biographical dictionary of Irish Quakers* (1997) · M. Pollard, *A dictionary of members of the Dublin book trade 1550–1800* (2000) · W. C. Braithwaite, *The beginnings of Quakerism* (1912) · J. Smith, ed., *A descriptive catalogue of Friends' books*, 2 vols. (1867), suppl. (1893); repr. (1970) · *DNB* · J. Gough, 'An epistle from John Gough to Richard Shackleton', Dublin Friends Historical Library, PORT 47, b 52 · C. G. Brannigan, 'Quaker education in Ireland, 1680–1840', MEd diss., National University of Ireland, 1982, 213–19 · A. Webb, 'The "Webb" Irish Quaker family Pedigrees, in particular the Gough/Goff family', Dublin Friends Historical Library
Archives RS Friends, Lond., letters, material intended for a continuation of his *History of the Society of Friends*

Gough, John (1757–1825), natural and experimental philosopher, was born in Kendal, Westmorland, on 17 January 1757, the eldest child of Nathan Gough (d. 1800) and his wife, Susannah (1731–1798), at their home at Yard 77, Stramongate. His father, a shearman-dyer, was described as a 'wealthy tradesman' (Henry, 9) and his mother was the eldest daughter of John Wilson, a prosperous farmer with a good estate on the west bank of Lake Windermere. Nathan and Susannah Gough had three sons and four daughters, one of whom died in infancy. The family belonged to the Society of Friends, whose communities flourished in Cumberland and Westmorland during this period. The Goughs had deep roots in the history of English dissent: John Gough's great-great-grandfather, General William Goffe, had been one of the judges at Charles I's trial in 1649 and later found refuge among the puritans of New England.

Before he was three years old, Gough was attacked by smallpox and lost his sight. In his childhood he expended much effort in developing his sense of touch and hearing, and appears to have been especially eager to learn to recognize animals by touch. When a travelling menagerie passed through Kendal he reportedly 'ran his fingers over all the carnivorous animals, nothing daunted by their expressions of disapprobation' (Gough, 356). He was given a good education with extensive coverage of the natural sciences. His father's generosity, unusual for a tradesman at the time, allowed Gough to continue his education until well over the age of twenty. According to John Dalton (Henry, 9), Nathan Gough would also have paid for a university education, had his son desired it. Attending the Friends' school in Kendal from the age of six, Gough was initially given classes in Latin in the conventional manner and without great success. His education improved considerably around the year 1769, with the arrival of a new master, George Bewley (1749–1828), who introduced him to natural philosophy. In the following years Gough took a leading part in the developing scientific culture of this school. In his early teens he formed a botanical club with his schoolmates, who would read to him from the text of John Wilson's *Synopsis of British Plants* (1744) while he subjected each individual specimen to minute tactile examination. He also gained an interest in experimental philosophy, and used his father's dye-house to perform basic experiments.

At the age of eighteen Gough sought to acquire a more systematic mathematical education, and in 1778, at twenty-one, he went to live with John Slee, a mathematical master at Mungrisedale, Cumberland, as a resident pupil. He stayed at Mungrisedale for eighteen months, following the traditional curriculum up to the elementary principles of the calculus. Returning home he took up the calculus in earnest, with his second sister, Dorothy Gough (b. 1768), acting as his reader. From around 1782 to 1790 he enjoyed the acquaintance of John Dalton, a cousin of George Bewley and also a lakeland Quaker, who had come to Kendal to take up a position in Bewley's school, and who assisted him by reading, writing, and making calculations and diagrams on his behalf. In return Dalton, later to become one of the most eminent figures in nineteenth-century science, was tutored by Gough in Latin and Greek free of charge. In the relative isolation of Kendal, Dalton served as a willing auditor for Gough's scientific enthusiasms, 'participating with him in the pleasure resulting from successful investigations' (Dalton, *Meteorological Observations*, 2nd edn, 1834, xvii).

Gough, the blind philosopher of Wordsworth's 'Excursion', had wide-ranging scientific interests. He published papers in natural history, mechanics, mathematics, chemistry, and what would now be called experimental physics. His most interesting work related directly to his disability and comprised a series of researches into the properties of sound. He had a special interest in the phenomenon of ventriloquism. He was a corresponding member of the Manchester Literary and Philosophical Society, in which his friend and pupil John Dalton was a leading activist, and he contributed a number of papers to their *Memoirs*; he also published papers in *Nicholson's Journal*. The most original of his works appeared in the decade 1796–1805. Nevertheless he remained an essentially local figure and his reputation did not much exceed the bounds of north-west England. A mathematical conservative, Gough was not shy of polemic, and published repeated criticism of Dalton's model of the composition of the atmosphere, which he felt was 'repugnant to the principles of the mechanical philosophy' (*Memoirs of the Manchester … Society*, 2nd ser., 1 1805, 297).

In 1800 Gough married Mary (d. 1858), daughter of Thomas Harrison of Crosthwaite, Cumberland, at the parish church of Kendal. On their marriage they moved to Middleshaw in the hamlet of Old Hutton, 4 miles southeast of Kendal. On 5 December 1800 he was formally disowned by the Kendal meeting of the Society of Friends for marriage before the priest. For someone who had been considered a Quaker all his life this status was not lacking in ambiguity. Coleridge, in an essay published in 1812, said of Gough that 'he is a quaker, with all the blest *negatives*, without any of the silly and factious *positives*, of that sect'

(Coleridge, 17–18). In later years Gough worshipped at the Unitarian Market Place Chapel, where he met Wordsworth; and in 1815 he became one of their trustees. His connection with Unitarian circles however dates back to before 1800, for his papers to the Manchester 'Lit and Phil' were communicated by Edward Holme (1770–1847), a physician in Manchester who came from Kendal and maintained strong connections with the Unitarian chapel there.

Gough's most substantive enquiry was 'An investigation of the method whereby men judge by the ear of the position of sonorous bodies relative to their own persons', which appeared in 1802 (*Memoirs of the Manchester ... Society*, 5/2, 622–52) during an ongoing controversy with another former Quaker, the noted natural philosopher Thomas Young, over the nature of 'compound sounds'. In 1800 Young had published his famous analogy between sound and light ('Outlines of experiments and inquiries concerning light and sound', *PTRS*, 90, 106–50), one of whose propositions was that 'compound sounds', such as beats and combination tones, should be understood as the coalescence of the motion of the two separate sounds. By the time these sounds reach the ear they are physically one, despite their separate points of origin. This proposition contradicted a theory which Gough had put before the Manchester 'Lit and Phil' in 1796, where he had maintained that the unison of compound sounds resided in the limits of the discriminatory powers of the human ear ('The variety of human voices', *Memoirs of the Manchester ... Society*, 5/1 1798, 58–69). According to Gough, the sense of hearing is so constructed that it can discriminate sufficiently to perceive the mixture of sounds but not to separate them into their constituent elements. Hence the amazing variety among human voices, which makes it possible for a sightless person to distinguish speakers with the same discrimination others use in distinguishing faces. In the polemic that followed, Gough made it clear that what he objected to was Young's specific failure to consider the structure of sense discrimination in common with the physical nature of the sensed object. In this respect his line was curiously anticipatory of the physico-psychological concerns of Ernst Mach and his contemporaries in the 1860s and 1870s.

In 1812 Gough had a house built for himself and his family on the south-west slope of Benson Knot (a hill 2 miles north-east of Kendal), which he named Fowl Ing. At about the same time he began to act as a private tutor of mathematics to a select group of pupils from northern England, whom he prepared for university. The subsequent fame of his students superseded his own celebrity. A number of them went on to achieve high distinction in the mathematical tripos, and subsequently in the hierarchies of university and church. One of his first students was William Whewell, who was with him in 1812.

John and Mary Gough had nine children, one of whom, Thomas Gough (1804–1880), was a local notable; a surgeon in Kendal and a specialist in local natural history, he was co-founder of the Kendal Literary and Scientific Society

and curator of the local museum. From 1823 Gough suffered repeated attacks of epilepsy, and he died on 28 July 1825, leaving his wife Mary, and seven of their children. He was buried in the parish churchyard of Kendal.

JOSEPH GROSS

Sources T. Gough, 'John Gough', in C. Nicholson, *The annals of Kendal*, 2nd edn (1861), 355–68 · W. C. Henry, *Memoirs of the life and scientific researches of John Dalton* (1854) · J. F. Curwen, *Kirkbie-Kendal* (1900), 308–9, 349, 407, 424 · J. Foster, *The pedigree of Wilson of High Wray and Kendal*, rev. S. B. Foster, 2nd edn (1890) · F. Nicholson and E. Axon, *The older nonconformity in Kendal* (1915), 374–5, 378, 418–19 · private information (2004) · S. T. Coleridge, 'On the soul and organs of sense', in R. Southey, *Omniana*, 2 (1812), 17–18 · *The letters of William and Dorothy Wordsworth*, ed. E. De Selincourt, 2nd edn, rev. C. L. Shaver, M. Moorman, and A. G. Hill, 8 vols. (1967–93), vol. 3 · J. M. Douglas, *The life of William Whewell* (1881) · E. T. Bewley, *The Bewleys of Cumberland* (1902) · J. Dalton, *Meteorological observations and essays*, new edn (1834), xvi–xviii

Archives Cumbria AS, Kendal, meteorological journal and autobiography | Wellcome L., corresp. with Luke Howard

Likenesses bust, Kendal Museum of Natural History

Gough, John Bartholomew

Gough, John Bartholomew (1817–1886), temperance lecturer, was born at Sandgate, Kent, on 22 August 1817. His father was a foot soldier of the 40th and 52nd regiments, pensioned in 1823 because of a neck injury. Gough was educated first by his mother, who was the village schoolmistress for twenty years, and later (*c*.1825) attended a private school in Folkestone run by a Mr Davis. On account of the poverty of his family, at the age of twelve he went out to America with a family who for 10 guineas agreed to teach him a trade and take care of him until he was twenty-one. He spent two years working on a farm in western New York state, and in December 1831, with his father's permission, went alone to New York city, where he learned the business of a bookbinder at the Methodist Book Room. He acquired a love of drink, left his employment, and for a number of years lived recklessly, moving around the eastern seaboard states and working at various jobs, including acting and singing. He married and had a child during this period, but soon after settling in Worcester, Massachusetts, both his wife and his child died.

In October 1842 a well-known temperance advocate, Joel Stratton, induced him to take the pledge. He began to attend temperance meetings and to recommend abstinence, when his ability as a speaker attracted notice. After giving up his trade in 1843, he became a temperance lecturer, and was soon the foremost speaker on temperance in the United States. On 24 November 1843 he married Mary Whitcomb, the daughter of Captain Stephen Flagg of Boylston.

In 1853–5, and again from 1857 to 1860, Gough lectured widely in Britain, attracting large audiences and reviving the fortunes of the National Temperance League. During the two years of his first visit he delivered 438 lectures and travelled 23,224 miles; during the three years of his second, he gave 605 lectures and travelled 40,217 miles. In 1857 he became embroiled in a public dispute between the London-based moral suasionist National Temperance League and the Manchester-based prohibitionist United Kingdom Alliance (UKA). He offended the UKA by suggesting that prohibition was 'a dead letter', and was, in turn, offended by UKA champion F. R. Lees, who implied that Gough had not given up using alcohol entirely. In a highly publicized case Gough sued Lees, and Lees was made to apologize to him in public.

In 1878 Gough paid a third visit to Britain. He was welcomed by a distinguished assembly in the gardens of Westminster Abbey at the invitation of Dean Stanley. After a month spent on the continent, Gough began his public work in the tabernacle of the Baptist leader C. H. Spurgeon. Advancing years told adversely on his oratory, but his audiences were not less enthusiastic.

Gough returned to America in 1879 and continued his work. When lecturing in the Franklin Presbyterian Church, Philadelphia, he was seized with a paralytic stroke, and he died, after a short illness, on 18 February 1886. He left no family. His widow, Mary, died on 20 April 1891. Gough was a highly successful public speaker, known for his theatrical style. He published many temperance addresses and issued several versions of his autobiography, first published in 1846. MARK CLEMENT

Sources J. B. Gough, *Autobiography and personal recollections of J. B. Gough*, rev. edn (1879) • B. Harrison, *Drink and the Victorians: the temperance question in England, 1815–1872* (1971) • P. T. Winskill, *The temperance movement and its workers*, 4 vols. (1891–2), vols. 2–3 • P. T. Winskill, *Temperance standard bearers of the nineteenth century: a biographical and statistical temperance dictionary*, 1 (1897) • *DNB*
Archives U. Glas. L., orations on temperance
Likenesses E. Burton, mezzotint (after D. Macnee), BM, NPG • R. Cruikshank, pencil drawing, BM • A. Haehnisch, lithograph (after photograph by Ross & Thompson), NPG • D. J. Pound, stipple and line print (after photograph by Mayall), NPG

Gough, Sir John Edmond [Johnnie] (1871–1915), army officer, was born at Murree, Punjab, India on 25 October 1871, the second son of General Sir Charles John Stanley *Gough VC (1832–1912), of Rathronan, Clonmel, co. Tipperary, and his wife, Harriette Anastasia de la Poer (*d.* 1916), daughter of John William Power, styled seventeenth Baron Le Poer, of Gurteen, co. Waterford, a Liberal MP. His elder brother was General Sir Hubert de la Poer *Gough: four other children of the marriage died in infancy. Sir Charles had won his VC during the Indian mutiny for a number of acts of gallantry, including saving the life of his brother, Sir Hugh Henry Gough, who had also won the VC in the mutiny. Always known as Johnnie, Gough was educated at Buckland's School, Laleham (1881–5), and Eton College (1885–7). He was commissioned second lieutenant in the Westmeath militia in April 1890, secured an honorary queen's India cadetship at the Royal Military College, Sandhurst, in February 1891, and was commissioned second lieutenant in the rifle brigade on 12 March 1892.

Gough served with the 1st battalion in India and Hong Kong, and was promoted lieutenant in December 1893. He transferred to the 2nd battalion in Ireland in May 1895 but then volunteered for service in British Central Africa. Gough rejoined his regiment in Malta in December 1897 and served with it in the Sudan, being present at Omdurman. The battalion was then detailed to join the international peacekeeping force on Crete, Gough receiving

promotion to captain on 5 December 1898 and being employed to administer a district. The 2nd rifle brigade was ordered to South Africa in October 1899 and was promptly shut up in Ladysmith. Gough distinguished himself in the defence and received his brevet majority in November 1900. He was district commissioner for Lydenburg, Transvaal, from October 1900 to July 1902. Gough anticipated going to the Staff College, Camberley, but in October 1902 was ordered on special service in Somaliland. When commanding a flying column at Daratoleh on 22 April 1903 Gough ran into the vastly superior force of Muhammad 'Abdullah Hasan, the 'mad mullah'. In conducting a fighting retreat Gough and two others rescued a mortally wounded colleague under fire. Gough concealed his own part in the rescue for which both his companions received the VC, but on 16 January 1904 his own gallantry was similarly recognized by the award of the VC and a backdated brevet lieutenant-colonelcy. Uniquely the VC was thus held by father, son, and uncle simultaneously.

Gough attended the Staff College and, upon graduation in December 1905, was appointed deputy assistant adjutant general in Ireland. There he met Dorothea Agnes (1874–1961), a private secretary, daughter of the late General Sir Charles Patton Keyes and sister of Roger (later Lord Keyes, admiral of the fleet). The couple married on 29 June 1907 and Dorothea accompanied her husband on his next posting in October 1907, as inspector-general of the King's African rifles, Gough having been promoted brevet colonel and appointed aide-de-camp to the king in August. A daughter was born to the Goughs in October 1908. Gough went to report on the situation in Somaliland in January 1909, arguing against a British withdrawal, but contracted hepatitis and was invalided home in June 1909; he was created CMG for his services in 1910. In December 1909 he was appointed general staff officer, grade 1, with rank of substantive colonel at the Staff College, where he remained until January 1913. Gough proved an accomplished instructor, publishing three articles based on his lectures in the *Army Review* and also *Fredericksburg and Chancellorsville* (1913), which demonstrated his belief in the illustrative uses of military history but also in the value of the 'offensive spirit'. After a brief period of half pay while he endeavoured to shake off the ill health that had dogged him since Somaliland, Gough was appointed brigadier-general, general staff, to Sir Douglas Haig at Aldershot on 9 October 1913. Gough proved strong enough to stand up to Haig and was able to suggest and to criticize without creating friction.

Gough's attentions were increasingly drawn to the growing home rule crisis and, at the suggestion of Sir William Robertson, he met the king's private secretary in November 1913 to express his misgivings over government policy. By December he had resolved to resign his commission should Ulster be coerced. Thus, when the Curragh incident occurred in March 1914 Gough strongly supported his brother, Hubert. Indeed it was Gough who played the key role in the negotiations with the War Office which resulted in the celebrated guarantee of the army's non-employment in coercion. In May 1914, as the repercussions of the Curragh persisted, Gough suffered a serious physical illness, but on the outbreak of war he managed to persuade the medical authorities of his fitness and accompanied Haig as chief of staff to the 1st corps. Gough proved a noticeably calming influence amid the turbulence of the retreat from Mons, especially at Landrecies on 25/26 August, and again at Ypres, not least on the critical day of 31 October. According to Neill Malcolm, Gough 'had a wonderful instinct for the essential, and always seemed to have a solution for every difficulty' (*Eton College Chronicle*, 30 March 1915). In December 1914 Gough moved with Haig to the First Army and played an important part in developing the plans for the forthcoming offensive at Neuve Chapelle. On 13 February 1915 Gough was offered command of a division and on 18 February he received the CB. Prior to returning home he was invited to visit his old battalion at Fauquissart, and on 20 February he was hit by a ricochet. He died of heart failure following surgery at Estaires on 22 February 1915, and was buried in the Estaires communal cemetery on the same day. On 22 April he was the recipient of a posthumous KCB. By Gough's death the army had also lost, as described by Sir John French, 'one of our most promising military leaders of the future' (Beckett, *Gough*, 2). IAN F. W. BECKETT

Sources I. F. W. Beckett, *Johnnie Gough, VC: a biography* (1989) · H. Gough, *The Fifth Army* (1931) · H. Gough, *Soldiering on* (1954) · F. S. Oliver, *Ordeal by battle* (1915) · I. F. W. Beckett, ed., *The army and the Curragh incident, 1914* (1986) · *The anvil of war: letters between F. S. Oliver and his brother, 1914–1918*, ed. S. Gwynn (1936) · *Army List* · *CGPLA Eng. & Wales* (1915)
Archives NAM, corresp., diaries, and papers | IWM, Wilson MSS · NAM, Sir Charles Gough MSS · NL Scot., Haig MSS · NL Scot., Oliver MSS · priv. coll., Hubert Gough MSS · priv. coll., Keyes family MSS · Royal Greenjackets, Winchester, Thesiger MSS · U. Durham L., corresp. with Sir Reginald Wingate
Likenesses portrait, 1914, repro. in *ILN* (28 March 1914) · E. Gill, memorial tablet, Winchester Cathedral · photographs, repro. in Beckett, *Johnnie Gough*; priv. coll. · photographs, IWM; repro. in Beckett, *Johnnie Gough* · portrait, repro. in 'Portrait gallery', *United Service Gazette* (Dec 1912)
Wealth at death £2860 2s. 7d.: probate, 12 June 1915, *CGPLA Eng. & Wales*

Gough [*married names* Miller, Aberle], (**Eleanor**) **Kathleen** (1925–1990), social anthropologist and feminist, was born on 16 August 1925 at Hunsingore, near Wetherby, Yorkshire, daughter and youngest child of Albert Gough (1888–1970) and his second wife, Eleanor, *née* Umpleby (1892–1965), a devout Methodist who sang and recited in local chapels. Her father became village blacksmith in 1914 and played a major role in introducing combines to west Yorkshire after the Second World War. Her brother, Clifford Arthur (b. 1920) subsequently joined the business; she also had an older half-sister, Laura Margery Howe (1915–1998).

Kathleen Gough attended the church school in Hunsingore (population 100, no piped water, no electricity). She gained scholarships to King James's Grammar School, Knaresborough, and in 1943 to Girton College, Cambridge, where she gained a 2.1 in English (1945) and a first in archaeology and anthropology (1946). She was awarded the Barrington prize, became Girton research scholar for

1946–7, and held two university-awarded social anthropology studentships. On 5 July 1947 she married her fellow student Eric John Miller in St John the Baptist Church, Hunsingore, and they did fieldwork together in Kerala, south India. She was supervised by Professor J. H. Hutton, an old-style anthropologist, and after he retired, by Meyer Fortes. With Evans-Pritchard and Gluckman he introduced her to twentieth-century British social anthropology. Both Eric and Kathleen obtained doctorates, but the strains of fieldwork ended their marriage and they divorced with minimal bitterness in 1950.

Gough, as she was now again called, had abandoned Christianity and declared herself socialist and anti-imperialist as a student of eighteen, but she later said that she found peace in church services and that her socialism arose from the deep sense of moral justice gained from her mother and school. Having returned alone to India in 1951 to continue her work there, she compared the extreme patriarchy of Tamil Brahmans with the 'more free-wheeling [polyandrous and matrilineal] Nayars'. She sought to make the villagers historically intelligible and meticulously collected information on contemporary social change. Ahead of her time, she backed observation and insights from psychology with modern quantitative methods. She situated the local, political and present within national and international frameworks, in political economy and in the historical past and, unusually, in the desirable future. Her identification with oppressed landless villagers and her perceptions of Congress Party corruption led her to support Indian communists. Her doctoral thesis was long, but she published immediately only two short papers in the *Journal of the Royal Anthropological Institute*, one of which was the Curl bequest prize essay in 1953. She spent a year at Harvard (with a Wenner-Gren fellowship), and on Audrey Richards's recommendation David Schneider invited her to help them to produce their massive *Matrilineal Kinship* (1961), of which she wrote more than half. It remains an indispensable introduction to the subject, even though some reviewers disliked the editors' controversial comparative and historical materialist approach. Gough's Nayar chapter breaks new ground in the understanding of the past and possible future of matriliny and polyandry. She lectured in Gluckman's department at Manchester in 1954–5 and 1960.

Gough married David Friend Aberle (b. 1918), whom she had met at Harvard, at Manchester All Saints registrar's office on 5 September 1955. An esteemed American anthropologist, he shared the rest of her life as comrade-in-arms, companion, and constructive critic. They had one son, Stephen (b. 1956). After Manchester there followed a series of short but sometimes prestigious university appointments held by Kathleen or David at Stanford, Berkeley, Wayne State, Michigan, and again at Manchester. While David was working at Wayne State University in Detroit, Kathleen began to work with the group running the newspaper *Correspondence*, including Grace Lee, James Boggs, and C. L. R. James, the Caribbean Marxist historian, revolutionary, and cricket authority. She became both politically sophisticated and a self-styled 'agitator', a term she proudly traced back to Cromwell's army. While back in Manchester in 1960, she quietly informed colleagues on her return from an anti-Polaris demonstration at Holy Loch that she had been arrested, held overnight, and released with a caution.

In 1961 David and Kathleen planned to settle at Brandeis University in Massachusetts, where they were both appointed to tenured posts. As a result of their involvement in anti-nuclear protest, their support for Cuba, and exaggerated accounts of her criticism of J. F. Kennedy to students, complicated by the fact that David was her head of department, they were both forced to resign in 1963. They moved to the University of Oregon, where they played a major part in organizing protests and sit-ins against the Vietnam war. David's actual (and Kathleen's intended) refusal to grade papers that would have caused students to be drafted into the army forced his resignation four years later. They went next to Vancouver, where David took Canadian citizenship. He remained at the University of British Columbia until his retirement in 1984. Kathleen, who retained her UK nationality, joined Simon Fraser University at Burnaby, British Columbia, where her participation in an attempt to democratize the department and the university led to her being manoeuvred out. This led to a worldwide boycott of the university in 1971. In the same year she published a celebrated article on Engels's *The Origin of the Family* in the *Journal of Marriage and the Family*. She obtained grants enabling her to continue her work on India and, additionally, south-east Asia. She published two books on imperialism in south-east Asia and Vietnam (1973, 1978) and, after work in British libraries (1974) and fieldwork in India (1976), two major books on south-east India (1981, 1989). She was elected a fellow of the Royal Society of Canada in 1988. In her last days she saw the first copies of her *Political Economy in Vietnam* (1990), with a preface by Ved Prakash Vatuk in which he described her as 'soft as a lotus, firm as a rock'—a true Indian whose life had combined the activities of all four Hindu castes: seeking and imparting knowledge, struggle, speaking for the voiceless, and service to others. She was still studying Vietnamese to facilitate the long-term studies in Vietnam she was planning. The *Economic and Political Weekly* in Delhi (a favourite vehicle) published, during her last weeks, her self-critical article on imperialism acknowledging Soviet and Chinese depredations. But she never abandoned socialism or her hopes for a better future for poor villagers.

After four months' illness with cancer, Kathleen Gough died in Vancouver on 8 September 1990, and was buried on 13 September in Capilano View cemetery, Vancouver, after a service which she has herself devised, including psalms and the Hebrew kaddish. She loved India and enjoyed and admired Canada but she was proud of her roots in Yorkshire and maintained ties with her family and former teachers there, and a devotion to the quiet beauty of its countryside. RONALD FRANKENBERG

Sources K. Gough, autobiographical notes, 1990, Girton Cam. · curriculum vitae for University of British Columbia, 1990, Girton Cam. · R. Frankenberg, 'Kathleen Gough Aberle', *Anthropology Today*, 7/2 (1991), 23–5 · *The Independent* (3 Oct 1990) [see also comment by R. Frankenberg, 8 Oct 1990, and correction by D. Aberle, 21 Nov 1990] · G. Berreman, letter to colleagues and students, 11 Sept 1990, U. Cal., Berkeley, department of anthropology · D. Aberle and S. Aberle, 'Kathleen Gough Aberle', 1990 [obit.] · K. T. Butler and H. I. McMorran, eds., *Girton College register, 1869–1946* (1948) · V. P. Vatuk, 'Soft as a lotus, firm as a rock', in K. Gough, *Political economy in Vietnam* (Berkeley, CA, 1990) · personal knowledge (2004) · private information (2004) [Clifford Gough, brother]
Archives Girton Cam. · University of British Columbia Library, textual material, maps, and charts
Likenesses group portrait, photograph, 1943, Girton Cam.

Gough, Mary Fisher (1832–1896), women's activist, was born on 9 May 1832, probably in Dublin; she was one of the five children of Josiah Richard Gough and Deborah Fisher. An Irish Quaker, she lived and died, unmarried, in Dublin. Gough was a signatory to the 1866 petition for women's suffrage (as, it would appear, were her mother, Deborah, and one of her sisters, Susanna Josiah Gough). Sources suggest that she may also have signed later petitions for female enfranchisement. However, evidently a woman of considerable pride, she eventually refused to sign future petitions for the suffrage because, according to her obituarist, 'she would not condescend to go on begging for it' (*Englishwoman's Review*).

Nevertheless, Gough remained a steadfast supporter of the women's movement. She was particularly involved in the cause of women's education and was closely associated with the Queen's Institute in Dublin—an institution devoted to female education. She taught the scrivenery class throughout the life of the institute (1860–80). Her teaching of such a vocational course is suggestive of her progressive ideas concerning female employment. Towards the end of her life Gough had to retire from her active interests due to paralysis. She died on 29 December 1896 at her home, 15 Windsor Avenue, in Fairview, Dublin. KATHRYN GLEADLE

Sources *Englishwoman's Review*, 28 (1897), 63 · pedigree, Religious Society of Friends Historical Library, Dublin, Gough MSS
Wealth at death £201 10s. 6d. effects in England: Irish probate sealed in London, 12 March 1897, CGPLA Eng. & Wales

Gough, Matthew [Mathau Goch, Matago] (d. 1450), soldier, was a native of Hanmer in Flintshire. According to William Worcester he was the son of Owen Gough, bailiff of Hanmer, and his wife, Hawise, daughter of David Hanmer, who had been the nurse of John Talbot, earl of Shrewsbury; but there is more than one version of his pedigree.

Gough fought at Cravant in 1423 and at Verneuil in 1424 and was captain of several fortresses in subsequent years. In 1425 he took part in the earl of Salisbury's expedition to Anjou and in June 1429 he was obliged to surrender Beaugency just before the arrival of a relief force. He was taken prisoner in the summer of 1432 while besieging St Céneri near Alençon; by 1435 he had been released and was joint commander of Le Mans under Sir John Fastolf. From 1439 to 1442 he was captain of Bayeux and in 1440 he took part in the siege and recapture of Harfleur. After the truce of Tours in 1444 Gough was one of the commanders of a joint Anglo-French force with the task of suppressing the bands of brigands who were plaguing the country and in 1446 he was ordered to join the French in expelling the Swiss from Alsace.

Henry VI had undertaken to hand Maine over to his father-in-law René of Anjou and on 28 July 1447 Gough and his fellow Welshman Fulk Eyton were commissioned to receive the towns and fortresses of the county from the king's lieutenant-general, the marquess of Dorset, and to transfer them to the French. The transfer was to be completed by 1 November 1447 but the delaying tactics of Gough and Eyton and other English leaders meant that final agreement was not reached, in the face of growing French impatience, until 11 March 1448.

The renewal of war in the summer of 1449 was followed by a steady French advance. Gough and William Herbert had to surrender Carentan to the duke of Brittany on 30 September and on 30 November Gough himself surrendered Bellême in Perche to the duke of Alençon. On 10 April 1450 Gough and Sir Thomas Kyriell took Valognes, but on 15 April they were defeated by the French at Formigny. Gough succeeded in cutting his way through the French lines and reached Bayeux, but he was forced to surrender the town on 16 May and returned to England. He was stationed in the Tower of London with Lord Scales when, on 2 July 1450, the Kentish rebels, led by Jack Cade, entered the city. The authorities sought the aid of Scales and Gough and on the night of 5–6 July they seized London Bridge. In the ensuing action Gough was killed; he was buried in the church of the white friars in London.

Matthew Gough was one of the outstanding professional soldiers in English service in the fifteenth-century wars in France. William Worcester described him as 'surpassing all other esquires who engaged in war at that time in bravery, hardihood, loyalty and liberality' and Sir John Fastolf left money in his will for masses for his soul. To the French he was known as 'Matago' and this name became a synonym for courage, although in Perche, which had suffered at his hands, it was a term of abuse and many effigies of him were burnt there to celebrate his departure in 1449. The Welsh were well aware of his achievements and one poet, Guto'r Glyn, who may himself have served in France under him, composed a poem in his praise.

Gough's service did not go unrewarded: he was granted extensive lands in Normandy. According to one pedigree his wife was Margaret, daughter of Rhys Moythe of Castell Odwyn in Cardiganshire, but this is not confirmed elsewhere; his descendants are said to have been the Gough family of Alvington in the Forest of Dean.

A. D. Carr

Sources J. Stevenson, ed., *Letters and papers illustrative of the wars of the English in France during the reign of Henry VI, king of England*, 2 vols. in 3 pts, Rolls Series, 22 (1861–4) · *Recueil des croniques … par Jehan de Waurin*, ed. W. Hardy and E. L. C. P. Hardy, 5 vols., Rolls Series, 39 (1864–91) · H. T. Evans, *Wales and the Wars of the Roses* (1915) · I. Williams and J. Llewelyn Williams, eds., *Gwaith Guto'r Glyn* (1961), 8–10 · A. D. Carr, 'Welshmen and the Hundred Years' War', *Welsh History Review / Cylchgrawn Hanes Cymru*, 4 (1968–9), 21–46 · R. A. Griffiths, *The reign of King Henry VI: the exercise of royal authority, 1422–1461* (1981)

Gough, Richard (*bap.* 1635, *d.* 1723), local historian, was born in Newton on the Hill in the parish of Myddle, Shropshire, and baptized on 18 January 1635, the son of Richard Gough and his wife, Dorothy Jenks, formerly of Cockshutt. He was the fifth Richard Gough in succession to live as a small freeholder and yeoman farmer at Newton, though his younger sister, Dorothy, married Andrew Bradocke, of Cayhowell, a gentleman. In 1661 his father died at Cayhowell. About this time Gough married Joan Wood (*d.* 1694), of Peplow, with whom he had eight children between 1663 and 1678.

As a young man Gough served as a clerk to Robert Corbett of Stanwardine, *custos rotulorum* of Shropshire and MP in 1654–5. He continued to serve the Corbetts, for example, as manorial steward, after he had inherited the Newton freehold. He was a member of the Shropshire grand jury and frequently acted on behalf of his parish in legal matters. In 1700 he wrote 'The antiquityes and memoyres of the parish of Myddle'. During 1701–2 he added his 'Observations concerning the seates in Myddle and the familyes to which they belong', in which he systematically recorded the personal histories of each family in the parish. He was buried on 12 February 1723, having outlived his wife and all but two of his children. His manuscript was preserved by the descendants of his daughter Anne. An imperfect version was printed in 1834; the full manuscript was published in 1875. With its uniquely detailed account of all the members of a rural community, the book has established Gough as the most important of the early parish historians.   DAVID HEY, *rev.*

Sources R. Gough, *The history of Myddle*, ed. D. Hey (1981)

Gough, Richard (1735–1809), antiquary, was born on 21 October 1735 in Winchester Street, London, the only son and heir of Harry Gough (1681–1751), merchant and MP, of Perry Hall, Staffordshire, and Elizabeth (*d.* 1774), daughter of Morgan Hynde, a wealthy London brewer. He had three sisters, Judith, Anne, and Elizabeth, two of whom died young. His father had gone to China with his uncle, Sir Richard Gough, when only eleven years old. Harry Gough commanded the ship *Streatham* from 1707 to 1715, after which he retired from the East India Company. He subsequently became a director in 1731 and was MP for Bramber from 1734 until his death.

Education and early works Richard Gough the younger was educated at home by tutors, firstly by a Courlander named Barnewitz, and after his death by Roger Pickering, reputedly one of the most learned dissenting ministers of his day. He finished his Greek studies under Samuel Dyer, the friend of Samuel Johnson. Gough was a precocious child, writing poetry, history, and translations of French works, some of which were privately printed with his mother bearing the costs. The influence of French scholarship and some of the future directions in his adult research were already indicated in this juvenilia, which included *The History of the Bible Translated from the French* (1747), *The Customs of the Israelites Translated from the French of*

RICHARD GOUGH ESQ.ᴿᴱ ANTIQUARY.

Richard Gough (1735–1809), by R. Sawyer, pubd 1822 (after unknown artist, 1786)

Abbé Fleury (1750), and *Atlas renovatus, or, Geography Modernized* (1751). His childhood, however, left him socially ill-equipped and dominated by the influence of his mother.

Gough's father died in 1751, leaving him the reversion of the Middlemore estate in Warwickshire and extensive property holdings in other counties. He was admitted a fellow-commoner at Corpus Christi College, Cambridge, under the tutorship of Dr John Barnardiston, with whom he struck up a close relationship. Gough's maternal family were dissenters and William Cole claimed that at Cambridge his tutor was particularly requested 'not to suffer him to be matriculated, by which he avoided taking the oaths, and not to let him receive the sacrament, otherwise he was to go to the college chapel as others' (Cole MSS, BL, Add. MS 5870, fol. 113). Gough himself, however, in later life, rejected this Presbyterian heritage and appears to have transferred his loyalties to the Anglican church instead. 'Tho' bred a dissenter Mr Go was equally disgusted with their narrow and their liberal principles' (Enfield local history unit, D1624, Gough MSS, no. 16). Gough found it hard to fit in with the social life of Cambridge—a view confirmed by Cole's rather waspish comment that he 'was very shy and awkward and much the joke of his fellow-collegians; and hardly ever stirred out of

college but with his tutor' (Cole MSS, BL, Add. MSS 5824, fol. 62b). This social awkwardness appears to have stayed with him throughout his life. Nevertheless, Gough was extremely receptive to the antiquarian traditions of scholarship established in Corpus Christi College by Archbishop Parker and carried on by eighteenth-century antiquaries such as William Stukeley, and while at Cambridge he formed a number of acquaintances with other similarly minded individuals which he maintained long after he had left the alma mater.

Gough went down from Cambridge without a degree in 1756, marking the end of his years there with an antiquarian tour to Peterborough, Stamford, and Croyland Abbey—following in the footsteps of his Benedictine predecessor, William Stukeley. In later life he singled this trip out as the moment when he was inspired to devote himself to antiquities. This tour proved to be the first of many, which were annual events for a number of years, and provided the basis from which his later major publications would be drawn. Over the years he covered most of England, parts of Wales, and Scotland, taking detailed notes and making sketches as he went. His last regular tour was through Cumberland and Scotland in 1771, but he continued to make excursions, often in the company of John Nichols, until within two years of his death.

Gough's first antiquarian publication was *The history of Carausius, or, An examination of what has been advanced on that subject by Genebrier and Dr Stukeley* (1762), in which he took issue with some of Stukeley's more fanciful arguments. Gough's early admiration for the 'archdruid' had already become tempered with a fair degree of critical scepticism, and although he maintained a profound respect for Stukeley's work with respect to Roman antiquities, he became sharply critical of the latter's methods of arguing and use of evidence. In 1767 he was elected to the Society of Antiquaries and by the partiality of the president, Dean Jeremiah Milles, he was nominated as director in 1771, a post which he held until 12 December 1797. He was a fellow of the Royal Society from 1775 to 1795. He corresponded regularly with the *Gentleman's Magazine* from 1767, using the initials DH, and in 1786 he succeeded his fellow Benedictine John Duncombe as the leading reviewer, judging authors against a rigorous yardstick of accuracy and scholarship.

Marriage and character In 1774 Gough's mother died and he inherited the Enfield estates, and in the same year married, on 18 August, Anne, fourth daughter of Thomas Hall of Goldings, Hertfordshire. It would seem that there was some opposition to this marriage from his friends and family, on the grounds of his wife's having little in the way of a fortune, and he deliberately delayed marriage until he was financially independent. The wedding was certainly performed extremely quietly without the knowledge of his friends. The marriage was a happy one, albeit childless. Gough enjoyed a retired lifestyle with his wife, spending most of the year on the Enfield estate, while wintering in the house in Winchester Street and touring in search of antiquities in the summer. Apart from his activities as director for the Society of Antiquaries he showed little inclination for activity in public life. In his own parish in Middlesex he was involved in the raising of the militia in 1794 and was a trustee for the parish free school, but he always insisted that he was not suited for public life. He used to describe himself as a firm friend to the house of Brunswick and his reviews showed little sympathy for those of a more radical cast of mind. William Cole, however, insisted on referring to him as a Presbyterian and accused him of interpolating republican principles into his published works (BL, Add. MS 5834, fol. 108). Cole may have been influenced in his opinions by Gough's family background and his friendship with a number of leading dissenters, such as John Howard the philanthropist (whose obituary he wrote for the *Gentleman's Magazine*) and Andrew Kippis, editor of the *Biographical Dictionary*, for which he contributed a number of articles. Horace Walpole described him as a bore, but others emphasized his good company and hospitality, his lively conversation, his humour, and his generosity in sharing and communicating knowledge. He had a considerable reputation for philanthropy in his own parish of Enfield. Aside from his antiquarian pursuits he interested himself in the management of his Enfield estates and the improvement of Gough Hall, and was also the author of copious amounts of rather bad verse. A sketch of Gough, taken at the duchess of Portland's sale in 1786, indicates that in physical appearance he was short and inclined to corpulence.

Major works Gough's first major publication was his *Anecdotes of British Topography*, published anonymously in 1768, on credit, by the publisher Richardson—although after 1774 Gough became a man of considerable independent means, at this stage his allowance would not cover the costs of publication. However, rapid sales ensued and he ultimately made a profit of £7 from the enterprise. This was essentially a gazetteer of published and unpublished work of local history and topography for the whole of Great Britain and Ireland, which he had been planning since his days at Cambridge, including all the public records, chronicles, heralds' visitations, printed books, manuscript collections, maps, charts, engravings, articles, and any other material which related to the antiquities or topography of Great Britain. It was well received at the time, although the scope of the enterprise meant that there were a number of inaccuracies, and in 1780 it was reissued in a much larger second edition of two volumes under the title *British Topography*.

In 1786 the first volume of Gough's *Sepulchral Monuments* was published (followed by the second volume in 1796, and an introduction in 1799). Together the two volumes covered the eleventh to the fifteenth centuries. The third volume which would have extended the coverage to the sixteenth century was never completed. In this series he sought, as he stated in his preface, to illustrate the 'History of the Families, Manners, Habits and Arts from the Norman Conquest', and to provide Britain with an equivalent to the *Monuments de la monarchie françoise* of the French antiquary Montfaucon. Gough's interest in tombs and funeral monuments was scarcely novel, but his approach, which concentrated on the artistic form of the monuments and their potential as sources for the study of the manners and customs of the time, represented a new direction in antiquarianism, which no longer relied solely upon the authority of the written word. Careful though Gough's scholarship was, these volumes are now valued chiefly for the illustrations—many of which were of excellent quality, engraved by Basire. Gough always planned a second edition and had commissioned many additional plates and illustrations in preparation; these now form part of the Gough collection at the Bodleian Library, Oxford.

Gough's other major publication was the revision of Camden's *Britannia*, published in 1789, printed by Payne and Nichols. He gave the copyright of the volume to his bookseller, Thomas Payne. In this work Gough translated Camden's entire text anew, a task that took him seven years. The actual printing took a further nine. He was criticized by some for the method which he employed in retaining the original text entire and relegating all his own and Gibson's additions to cumbersome footnotes at the bottom, and also for the accuracy of some of his translations and additions. He professed himself disappointed by the level of public interest. It was on the whole, however, agreed to be a work of immense value and the product of enormous labour. He had planned the enterprise since 1773 and collected new material assiduously from that date. As well as visiting every county himself, he called upon a network of antiquarian friends and correspondents to seek out information, check proofs, and offer suggestions. In 1806 it was reprinted in four volumes, with corrections and additions to the first volume only. A third edition was due to be published but was set back by the fire at Nichols's printing office in 1808, and Gough's health thereafter declined too rapidly to see the project through. The plates and the notes were left to the Bodleian Library along with Gough's other papers, and it was hoped that the syndicates of Oxford University Press would oversee the publication of the revised edition, but the volumes with the notes and additions still remain in the Bodleian's manuscript collection, unpublished.

The Society of Antiquaries Gough was also the author of numerous other essays and papers. Many of his papers were published in the pages of *Archaeologia*, the periodical of the Society of Antiquaries, whose publication he oversaw, and the *Bibliotheca Topographica Britannica*. He was a competent medievalist and regularly contributed papers of value to the Society of Antiquaries. His skills, however, were not those of the original thinker or the literary stylist. His talents were best displayed as an editor and co-ordinator of research. His three major publications were essentially works of an editorial nature, and he was also heavily involved in the publication of a number of other antiquarian works. He became involved in the publication of Hutchins's *History of Dorset*, having met Hutchins, who was quailing before the prospect of committing himself to publication, on one of his tours through Dorset. Gough contributed his greater experience of the publishing world and his extensive contacts, and, following Hutchins's death in 1773, he and Hutchins's friend Dr William Cuming saw the volume through the press, ensuring that there were sufficient proceeds from the profits of sale to provide a fund for Hutchins's widow and daughter (who was made Gough's ward). A second edition, with considerable additions, was planned by Hutchins's son-in-law, Major-General Bellasis, from 1792, but Gough died before this project was completed. In 1775 he had acquired much of the manuscript collections of Thomas Martin (who had died in 1771) and took it upon himself to publish Martin's *History of Thetford* in 1779, with engravings by Francis Grose. He similarly oversaw the publication of Thomas Nash's *History of Worcestershire* (1781–2), and assisted with Manning and Bray's *History of Surrey*, following Manning's death in 1801. Always closely involved in many projects with John Nichols, he was of great assistance in the compilation and publication of the monumental *History of Leicestershire* (1795–1815).

Gough was an active director of the Society of Antiquaries, if not always happy with the direction the society's affairs were taking. He and a coterie of close friends, including Michael Lort, Jeremiah Milles, and Samuel Pegge, were often highly critical among themselves of the quality of the papers presented there and the learning of their fellow members. He disapproved of those who joined for social reasons or who displayed dilettante leanings towards virtu rather than antiquarian rigour. He had firmly held views about the society's role as a public body and custodian of the nation's antiquarian heritage, and was opposed to what he saw as some of its more extravagant and self-indulgent projects, such as the engraving of large historical prints in the 1770s (Basire's *Field of the Cloth of Gold*, 1774, was at the time the largest print ever published) and the move to more grandiose apartments in Somerset House in 1780. Always strongly patriotic, he saw the recovery and preservation of the nation's antiquities as an act of public service which should not be compromised by private interest or pandering to modish taste. His final split with the society came over the election of the fashionable architect James Wyatt in 1797, events described in some detail by Joseph Farington in his diary. Gough vehemently opposed the election of Wyatt on account of the damage which, he argued, Wyatt had inflicted upon the medieval fabric of Durham and Salisbury cathedrals. As director Gough was responsible for the publication of *Archaeologia* and for overseeing the series of engravings sponsored by the society and published as *Vestuta monumenta*. In this capacity he was able to advance the careers of a number of highly skilled draughtsmen such as James Essex, John Carter, Jacob Grimm, Joseph Halfpenny, and Joseph Schnebbelie. He was also involved in the publication of Carter's *Specimens of Ancient Sculpture and Painting* and Schnebbelie's *Antiquaries Museum*. He was a discerning patron and appreciated the potential for architecture and sculpture as historical documents in their own right: hence the importance of securing accurate engravings of buildings and monuments of any historical or antiquarian interest. He belonged to the circle of early Gothic enthusiasts and architectural historians who hoped to put the history of Gothic architecture on a systematic footing, a circle that arose around Charles Lyttelton, bishop of Carlisle, Smart Lethieullier, Jeremiah Milles, James Bentham, and James Essex and later included Gough, John Carter, Michael Tyson, and Michael Lort.

Death and reputation Gough died on 20 February 1809 (*GM*), having suffered a series of epileptic fits which had impaired his mental faculties. He was buried at Wormley church, Hertfordshire, on 28 February; his wife survived him. His will reveals more of the private side of Gough than do any of his letters or published works: in addition to a life interest in his property for his wife he bequeathed numerous legacies to charitable causes, friends, and the children of his friends. His bequest to the Nichols family was particularly generous.

Gough was undoubtedly the leading antiquary of his day, and showed unusual single-mindedness in his approach, having little interest in natural history or geology, unlike many of his fellow antiquaries. Having been never on the grand tour, or even travelled abroad, he resisted the lure of Rome and classical antiquities, concentrating instead almost exclusively upon the native antiquities of Britain. Although he was extremely interested in British Roman antiquities, one of his main concerns was to put the study of the Saxon era of British history on a stronger footing, as he explained in the preface to *Anecdotes of British Topography*. Although not a Saxonist himself, he actively encouraged such scholarship and the publication of Anglo-Saxon texts. Unlike a number of his contemporaries he had little speculative interest in druidical remains and was not drawn into the debates over the authenticity of Ossian or Rowley, or the issues of ethnicity, which drove the researches of many of the Celtic antiquaries. Horace Walpole was always highly critical of the content and direction of Gough's researches, finding native antiquities barbaric and boring: relations between the two men were never easy. On more than one occasion Gough was forced to go through Walpole's friend and fellow antiquary William Cole, in order to secure information or the loan of books. Cole also provides an anecdote which offers a novel slant on Gough's character. He claimed that their mutual friend Michael Tyson had told him that when Gough, Ayloffe, and Milles had been present at the exhumation of Edward I in Westminster Abbey in 1778, Gough had attempted to slip a finger from the dead monarch into his waistcoat pocket, but was caught in the act and forced to return it (Cole MSS, BL, Add. MS 5870, fol. 113).

Gough's independent fortune allowed him to pursue his researches wholeheartedly and enabled him to assist many others in the antiquarian enterprise. As a result of his massive editorial compilations he built up an unrivalled network of correspondence, which enabled him to act as a broker and communicator of antiquarian knowledge for the country at large. His standards were high: textual accuracy, fieldwork, and strict empiricism; his caustic comments on those who failed to match his standards pepper the review pages of the *Gentleman's Magazine*. As befitted a man with such a highly developed view of the public utility of his researches, he had at one time intended to leave his collections to the British Museum. He was, however, disappointed on two counts: he was never appointed a trustee (an honour he felt he deserved) and the museum failed to come to an agreement with him over storing the valuable collection of copperplate-engravings from *Sepulchral Monuments* during his lifetime, while granting him access. As a result he left his entire topographical collection to the Bodleian Library, with the intention of forming an 'Antiquaries Closet' for the study of topography and antiquities. He also left his entire collection of printed books and manuscripts on Saxon and northern literature for the use of the Saxon professor. The remainder of his library was sold for £3552 in 1808 and the prints, drawings, coins, and medals were sold in 1810 for £517.   R. H. SWEET

Sources Nichols, *Lit. anecdotes*, 6.262–343 · A. Chalmers, biographical memoir of Gough, Bodl. Oxf., MS Ger. c. 7 · *GM*, 1st ser., 79 (1809), 195–7, 317–21, 491–3 · J. Evans, *A history of the Society of Antiquaries* (1956) · S. Shaw, *The history and antiquities of Staffordshire*, 2 (1801) · R. Sweet, 'Antiquaries and antiquities in eighteenth-century England', *Eighteenth-Century Studies*, 34 (2000–01), 181–206 · [R. Gough], preface, *Anecdotes of British topography* (1768), i–xxxv · S. F. Badham, 'Richard Gough and the flowering of Romantic antiquarianism', *Church Monuments*, 2 (1987), 32–43 · BL, William Cole MSS, Add. MSS 5870, fol. 113; 5824, fols. 62b, 64; 5825, fol. 11 · G. H. Fordham, 'Richard Gough: an address', *Bodleian Quarterly Record*, 5 (1926–8) · *DNB*
Archives BL, memorandum book and antiquarian collection, Add. MS 29309 · Bodl. Oxf., corresp. · Bodl. Oxf., commonplace books, account of tour of Wales, catalogue of his library, corresp. and papers · Bodl. Oxf., MS collections and papers · Bodl. Oxf., remarkable events of Saxon heptarchy · Bodl. Oxf., papers relating to the Society of Antiquaries, incl. notes relating to its history · CUL, copy of *Literary memoirs of living authors* interleaved with MS notes · Derbys. RO, antiquarian papers and notes relating to Derbyshire · Enfield local history unit, Southgate Town Hall, corresp. and papers · Lincoln Cathedral, accounts by him and John Carter of archaeological discoveries at Lincoln · LPL, papers · Norfolk RO, corresp. | BL, letters to John Carter, Add. MS 29944 · BL, corresp. with Sir Henry Ellis, Add. MSS 36987, 38626, 41312, *passim* · BL, corresp. with Foote Gower, Add. MS 22936 · BL, corresp. with Samuel Pipe Wulfreston, Add. MS 73524 EE · Bodl. Oxf., letters to John Nichols and J. B. Nichols · Bodl. Oxf., letters to Samuel Pegge · Mitchell L., Glas., corresp. with George Paton · NL Scot., corresp. with George Paton and others · NL Wales, letters from F. Leighton · priv. coll., corresp. with Sir Joseph Barker · S. Antiquaries, Lond., corresp. relating to the Society of Antiquaries · S. Antiquaries, Lond., corresp. with J. Schnebbelie · Warks. CRO, letters to Thomas Pennant · Yale U., Beinecke L., letters from J. Halfpenny
Likenesses sketch, 1786 · R. Sawyer, engraving, pubd 1822 (after unknown artist, 1786), NPG [*see illus.*] · silhouette, NPG · woodcut, BM
Wealth at death life interest in property left to wife and bequests of over £30,000; part of library sold for over £4000: *GM*; Nichols, *Lit. anecdotes*; will, PRO

Gough [Goughe], **Robert** (*d.* 1625), actor, was one of the principal performers in Shakespeare's plays, as is known from his inclusion on the list of actors which prefaces Shakespeare's first folio. He was a long-serving member of the King's Men and almost certainly of that company's predecessors, Strange's Men and the Lord Chamberlain's Men.

Nothing is known of Gough's parentage or his date or place of birth. On 13 February 1603 he married Elizabeth, the sister of Augustine Phillips, a fellow actor with the Lord Chamberlain's Men and King's Men. She was left £10 in her brother's will, which was witnessed by her husband on 4 May 1605. Gough and his wife spent all their married life in Southwark, London. Between 11 December 1603 and 7 August 1614 the parish registers of St Saviour, Southwark, record the baptisms of three daughters, Anne, Elizabeth, and Dorothy, and two sons, Nicholas and Alexander. Dorothy died in infancy. Alexander followed his father into the theatre.

Robert Gough may have begun his acting career as an apprentice to a member of Strange's Men and the Lord Chamberlain's Men, Thomas Pope. In his will Pope left him and another player 'all my wering apparrel and all my armes to be equally deuided betwene them' (Honigmann and Brock, 70). As a young actor, Gough played the female role of Aspatia in *The Second Part of the Seven Deadly Sins* (*c.*1592). The 'G' used as a speech heading for the Lords in the text of *All's Well that Ends Well* (1602–4) has been identified, though not without dissent, as denoting Gough. By 1611, when he played Memphonius in *The Second Maiden's Tragedy*, he was probably a Globe shareholder. In 1619 a King's Men licence and a livery allowance both named Robert Gough. The manuscript of *Sir John Van Olden Barnavelt* dating from the same year assigns him only minor roles. He was still a member of the King's Men in April 1621, but in October he was appointed a messenger of his majesty's chamber.

In 1623 Gough was living on Bankside, Southwark, the address given in a bill of complaint brought against him and others by Gervase Markham. Robert Gough was buried in the parish of St Saviour, Southwark, on 19 February 1625. Five days later a commission for the administration of his estate was issued to his widow, Elizabeth.

M. E. WILLIAMS

Sources parish register, St Saviour, Southwark, LMA, MSS X097/270, X097/284 [marriage, burial] · E. K. Chambers, *The Elizabethan stage*, 4 vols. (1923) · G. E. Bentley, *The Jacobean and Caroline stage*, 7 vols. (1941–68) · E. A. J. Honigmann and S. Brock, eds., *Playhouse wills, 1558–1642: an edition of wills by Shakespeare and his contemporaries in the London theatre* (1993) · W. W. Greg, *Dramatic documents from the Elizabethan playhouses* (1931) · T. J. King, *Casting Shakespeare's plays: London actors and their roles, 1590–1642* (1992) · S. Wells and others, *William Shakespeare: a textual companion* (1986) · A. Lancashire, ed., *The second maiden's tragedy* (1978) · A. Munday and others, *Sir Thomas More*, ed. V. Gabrieli and G. Melchiori (1990) · *Henslowe's diary*, ed. R. A. Foakes and R. T. Rickert (1961) · A. Gurr, *The Shakespearian playing companies* (1996) · E. Nungezer, *A dictionary of actors* (1929)
Wealth at death see administration, PRO, PROB 6/11, fol. 145*v*

Gough, Strickland (*d.* 1752), religious controversialist, was born at Bristol, the son of Strickland Gough (*d.* 1718?), Presbyterian minister, and his wife, Elizabeth Comeper. His father served as assistant minister to the Lewin's Mead congregation in Bristol from 1699 until his dismissal, in 1708. He assisted John Catcott in the Tucker Street Presbyterian congregation in Bristol from 1710 to 1717, and died soon afterwards. He published a number of occasional sermons, principally proclaiming his loyalty to the new Hanoverian regime, and a collection, *Sermons on Effectual Calling* (1709).

The younger Strickland Gough was educated for the ministry at Henry Grove's dissenting academy at Taunton. He became a preacher in London but was probably not ordained and held no charge. In 1730 he published anonymously *An Enquiry into the Causes of the Decay of the Dissenting Interest*, which was reprinted in that year. In it he controversially attributes the decline to dissenting ministers, whose '*ignorance* of their own principles, and *ill conduct* and management of their own interests' were principally to blame (p. 5). He argues that the divisive theological debates at Salters' Hall in 1719 had damaged the dissenting interest more severely than any attack from its enemies and warns his co-religionists against bigotry. In clearly justifying his position as a non-subscriber in the debate concerning subscription to the Westminster confession Gough states:

> the fundamental principle of the dissenters is ... a *liberty* for every man to form his own sentiments, and to pursue them by all lawful and regular methods; to disclaim the *impositions* of men, and to worship God according to the dictates of his own conscience. (p. 6)

He criticizes ministers for preaching overlong and unintelligible sermons, and suggests that the Presbyterian Fund was being spread too thinly and used to sponsor candidates who were not suitable for the ministry.

Though Gough has been described as 'a somewhat shallow young man ... with excessive self-confidence and an imperfect knowledge of Dissenting history' (Watts, 382), his measured arguments sparked off one of the more important debates concerning dissent of the first half of the century. It provoked a considerable response from both dissenters and members of the Church of England, and at least nine works were published in reply between 1730 and 1733. Among the more significant participants were Philip Doddridge, Abraham Taylor, and Isaac Watts. Doddridge, who praised Gough for his candour and humanity, agreed with his analysis of the causes of dissent yet argued that only a revival of practical religion would reverse the decline. By contrast Taylor accused Gough of exaggerating the extent of the decline and of writing as an enemy of dissent. Attached to the end of Taylor's *Letter to the Author* was a letter dated 2 December 1730 in which he stated how Gough had conformed to the Church of England. The precise timing of Gough's conformity is not known but it coincided with that of a number of younger ministers, which together caused a great deal of concern among dissenters.

Gough took holy orders and was awarded the degree of MA. On 5 November 1733 he preached before the lord mayor and corporation of London at St Paul's Cathedral; the sermon was published in that year. He held the rectory of Swayfield and the vicarage of Swinstead, in Lincolnshire, where he appears to have been non-resident, as his name does not appear in the parish registers. He is reputed to have written a defence of Benjamin Hoadly's *Plain Account of the Nature and End of the Sacrament of the Lord's Supper* in 1735, in response to critical *Remarks* supposedly by Richard Biscoe. A collection of his sermons appeared in 1751. Gough died, unmarried, on 12 December 1752. ALEXANDER GORDON, *rev.* MARILYN L. BROOKS

Sources E. Calamy, *An historical account of my own life, with some reflections on the times I have lived in, 1671–1731*, ed. J. T. Rutt, 2nd edn, 2 (1830), 504 · J. Murch, *A history of the Presbyterian and General Baptist churches in the west of England* (1835) · A. Gordon, ed., *Freedom after ejection: a review (1690–1692) of presbyterian and congregational nonconformity in England and Wales* (1917), 273 · C. G. Bolam and others, *The English presbyterians: from Elizabethan puritanism to modern Unitarianism* (1968) · Foster, *Alum. Oxon.* · *GM*, 1st ser., 22 (1752), 584 · M. Watts, *The dissenters*, vol. 1 (1978), 382–4 · private information (1890; 2004) · IGI

Archives BL, letters to Thomas Birch, Add. MSS 4308, 4475

Gough, William (1653/4–1682), antiquary, was one of at least two sons of William Gough (*c.*1626–*c.*1692), rector of Inkpen, Berkshire, and was probably the William Goff baptized there on 30 August 1654. His father, a Cambridge graduate, was ejected from the Church of England in 1662, and following the Five Mile Act removed to Earl Stoke, Wiltshire, where he was licensed as a Presbyterian preacher in May 1672; his brother, Strickland Gough (*d.* 1718?), father of Strickland *Gough (*d.* 1752), was also a dissenting minister. William entered Exeter College, Oxford, aged seventeen, in 1671. In 1673 he moved to St Alban Hall when his tutor, Marsh, became its principal, and graduated BA in 1675.

Gough then moved to London, 'where', says Wood, 'he sided with the whiggish party upon the breaking out of the Popish plot, an. 1678, [and] industriously carried on the cause then driven on' (Wood, *Ath. Oxon.*, 4.61). In 1682 he published *Londinum triumphans, or, An historical account of the grand influence the actions of the city of London have had upon the affairs of the nation for many ages past*. The volume was dedicated to the aldermen, sheriffs, and citizens of London. It recounts the city's history from the mythological Troynovant through to 1660, in order to secure 'an uninterrupted enjoyment of her just Rights, Liberties, Priviledges and Franchises' (p. 373). He died in London of smallpox in November 1682 and was buried in the same month at St Dunstan-in-the-West, Fleet Street, London. GORDON GOODWIN, *rev.* PETER SHERLOCK

Sources Wood, *Ath. Oxon.*, new edn, 4.61 · Foster, *Alum. Oxon.* · Venn, *Alum. Cant.* · *Calamy rev.*, 230 · *DNB* · Inkpen parish register, Berks. RO

Goughe, Robert. *See* Gough, Robert (*d.* 1625).

Goulburn, Edward (1787–1868), serjeant-at-law, was the second son of Munbee Goulburn (*d.* 1793), of Amity Hall, co. Vere, Jamaica, and Portland Place, London (where Edward was born), and his wife, the Hon. Susannah

Chetwynd (d. 1818), eldest daughter of William, fourth Viscount Chetwynd. He became a cornet in the Royal Regiment of Horse Guards on 9 July 1803 and a lieutenant on 15 December 1804.

In 1805 Goulburn published *The Blueviad, a Satyrical Poem*; it contained some unfavourable reflections on his fellow officers, which led to his prosecution for libel. Goulburn resigned his commission and entered himself at the Middle Temple. Surprisingly, he published another satirical poem, entitled *The Pursuits of Fashion* (1809), which reached a fourth edition in 1812. He also published a novel, *Edward de Montfort* (1812). In 1815 he was called to the bar and chose the midland circuit. In the same year he married Harriette (d. 1823), third daughter of Philip Nathaniel de Visme, of Notting Hill House, Kensington; they had two sons, Edward Meyrick *Goulburn, who was later headmaster of Rugby School and dean of Norwich, and Frederick Anderleet Goulburn, who became a fellow of All Souls College, Oxford. After his first wife's death, Goulburn married, on 13 August 1825, his cousin the Hon. Esther Chetwynd, second daughter of Richard, fifth Viscount Chetwynd; they had a daughter, Esther, who married Henry Chetwynd-Stapylton.

Goulburn's professional promotion was due largely to the influence of his elder brother Henry *Goulburn, a prominent Conservative politician. He was appointed successively a Welsh judge and a recorder of the boroughs of Leicester, Lincoln, and Boston. In 1829 he was made a serjeant-at-law, and afterwards gained a patent of precedence. He unsuccessfully contested the parliamentary seat of Ipswich in 1832, but represented Leicester as a Conservative from 1835; however, he was defeated again at the general election of 1837. On 21 October 1842 he was nominated a commissioner of the court of bankruptcy in London and he discharged the duties of the office until very shortly before his death. He was created an honorary DCL at Oxford on 4 June 1845. He died at 5 Seymour Street, Portman Square, London, on 24 August 1868. His third wife, Katherine Montagu, second daughter of Matthew, fourth Lord Rokeby, whom he had married in 1831, predeceased him. GORDON GOODWIN, rev. JOANNE POTIER

Sources Law Times (29 Aug 1868), 325, 335; (10 Oct 1868), 419 · [J. Watkins and F. Shoberl], *A biographical dictionary of the living authors of Great Britain and Ireland* (1816) · *Army List* (1804) · Burke, *Gen. GB* · J. B. Atlay, *The Victorian chancellors*, 2 vols. (1906–8) · WWBMP, 1.161–2
Archives Surrey HC, corresp. and papers | St Deiniol's Library, Hawarden, letters to Sir Thomas Gladstone
Wealth at death under £6000: resworn probate, Nov 1868, CGPLA Eng. & Wales

Goulburn, Edward Meyrick (1818–1897), dean of Norwich and headmaster, was born in Chelsea on 11 February 1818, the eldest son of Edward *Goulburn (1787–1868), DCL, serjeant-at-law, commissioner in bankruptcy, and recorder, and briefly (1835–7) MP for Leicester, and his first wife, Harriette (d. 1823), third daughter of Philip Nathaniel de Visme. His mother, who came from a Huguenot family, died young, and he was brought up by his maternal aunt. Henry Goulburn, chancellor of the exchequer, was

his uncle. Goulburn was educated at Rottingdean and at Eton College, before being elected scholar of Balliol College, Oxford, where he matriculated in 1834, and graduated BA with a first class in *literae humaniores* in 1839, MA in 1842, DCL in 1850, and DD in 1856. From 1841 to 1846 he was fellow, and from 1843 to 1845 tutor and dean, of Merton College. He relinquished these positions on his marriage on 11 December 1845 to Julia (d. 1903), daughter of Ralph William Cartwright (1771–1849), MP for Northamptonshire, and his second wife, Julia Frances, sister of Sir Thomas Digby Aubrey, bt. Ordained deacon in 1842 and priest in 1843, he was perpetual curate of Holywell, Oxford, from 1844 to 1850. In February 1847 he was appointed chaplain to Samuel Wilberforce, bishop of Oxford. On 18 November 1849 he was elected headmaster of Rugby School in succession to Archibald Campbell Tait, his former tutor at Balliol, his rival being his friend William Charles Lake, who had been elected scholar of Balliol at the same time as Goulburn. His associations with the county families of the midlands recommended him to the Rugby trustees, who wished to restore the school's links with the gentry.

Goulburn remained headmaster of Rugby for seven years after taking up office in the summer of 1850, but he was antipathetic to the liberal traditions of the place initiated by Arnold and carried on by Tait. He built a new boarding-house at his own expense in 1851 and presented a new field to the school in 1854. Science teaching was introduced in 1851. Though the last year of his headmastership was unrivalled for the brilliance of the scholars turned out by Rugby, its numbers had dwindled, and Goulburn felt himself compelled to resign in 1857. He did not find in schoolmastering a fulfilment of his desire for parochial work, and in July 1857 he accepted the ministry of Quebec Chapel, later known as the church of the Annunciation, St Marylebone. Two years later he accepted the vicarage of St John's, Paddington, which he held from 1859 until his selection by Lord Derby for the deanery of Norwich; he was installed on 4 December 1866.

Goulburn was dean of Norwich for twenty-three years; during the whole period his bishop was John Thomas Pelham, with whom he worked harmoniously, although the temperament and views of the two were very different. He had equally good relations with his canons. Goulburn was a conspicuous representative of a generation of churchmen who transformed cathedral life in the late nineteenth century. His own ideal was set out in his response to the archbishops' inquiry into cathedral reform, which he published as *The Functions of our Cathedrals* (1869). Rather than opening the cathedrals up for large, popular services, he saw them as places for quiet contemplation, study, and prayer. He opposed turning them into 'vast parish churches', stressing instead that their true function was the carrying out of sacred offices in a dignified and reverent way (Barrett, 291). Between 1881 and 1883 he campaigned successfully to prevent a proposed railway line cutting through the cathedral close.

An edition (1996) of the surviving portions of Goulburn's diary provides a detailed record of his activity at Norwich. He took great interest in the fabric of the cathedral, on which he lectured and wrote. Originally an evangelical he gradually became more of a high-churchman, but he was never a ritualist. He regarded with abhorrence latitudinarianism and rationalism and his Oxford Bampton lectures entitled *The Doctrine of the Resurrection of the Body* (1851) were an uncompromising defence of orthodox views on the subject. A deeply spiritual man, he published many devotional works. His *Introduction to the Devotional Study of the Holy Scriptures* (1854) reached a tenth edition in 1878, and his *Thoughts on Personal Religion* (1862) also went through many editions. On ecclesiastical, political, and university questions he was thoroughly conservative, regarding John William Burgon as his leader. Like Burgon he protested against the appointment of Dean Stanley as select preacher of the University of Oxford in 1872, and resigned his own position as select preacher when his protest was disregarded. But he had none of the truculent asperity of Burgon, who refused to 'break bread' with Stanley, and he remained a personal friend of Stanley from the time they visited Greece together in 1842 to Stanley's death. The sermon Goulburn preached on that occasion excited some comment; Stanley's friends were offended by Goulburn's denunciation of his theology, while Burgon objected to his appreciation of Stanley's personality.

Goulburn resigned the deanery on 23 April 1889 and retired to Brighton and then to Tunbridge Wells, where he busied himself in writing Burgon's biography (2 vols., 1892). In December 1891 he was one of the thirty-eight churchmen who signed a declaration asserting the historical truth of the Bible in response to the controversial work *Lux mundi* (1889). Goulburn died at his home, 12 Calverley Park Gardens, Tunbridge Wells, on 2 May 1897, and was buried at Aynho, Northamptonshire. A memorial window was erected to him in Rugby chapel. He was survived by his wife. They had no children, but adopted in 1863 Augusta Cartwright, orphan daughter of Goulburn's brother-in-law, Stephen Cartwright.

A. F. POLLARD, rev. M. C. CURTHOYS

Sources B. Compton, *Edward Meyrick Goulburn* (1899) · *The Times* (4 May 1897) · Boase, *Mod. Eng. biog.* · *The Goulburn Norwich diaries: selected passages from the ten remaining Norwich diaries of Edward Meyrick Goulburn*, ed. S. J. N. Henderson (1996) · P. Barrett, *Barchester: English Cathedral life in the nineteenth century* (1993) · O. Chadwick, *The Victorian church*, 2 (1972) · J. B. H. Simpson, *Rugby since Arnold* (1967) **Archives** Norfolk RO, letter-book, notes on chapter proceedings, corresp. and papers · Norwich Cathedral, engagement diaries and sermons | LPL, letters to Charles Golightly **Likenesses** Lock & Whitfield, woodburytype photograph, NPG; repro. in T. Cooper, *Men of mark: a gallery of contemporary portraits* (1880) · Poulton, carte-de-visite, NPG · carte-de-visite, NPG · oils, Norwich Cathedral · photograph, repro. in Compton, *Edward Meyrick Goulburn* **Wealth at death** £33,770 15s. 5d.: resworn probate, 23 July 1898, *CGPLA Eng. & Wales*

Goulburn, Henry (1784–1856), politician, was born in London on 19 March 1784, the eldest of three sons of Munbee Goulburn (1756/7–1793) and his wife, Susannah (d. 1818), eldest daughter of William Chetwynd, fourth Viscount Chetwynd. His childhood was punctuated by crises. While

Henry Goulburn (1784–1856), by Abraham Wivell

he was still an infant his nurse inadvertently sat on the young Goulburn, leaving him with an indentation of the head and permanently defective vision in his right eye. His father habitually overestimated income from his West Indian sugar plantations, and lived comfortably beyond the family's means, retaining the country residence of Prinknash Park in Gloucestershire and a town house in Great Cumberland Place, Marylebone. When he died suddenly on 29 November 1793, indebted and intestate, he left Henry fatherless and his mother facing vigorous domestic retrenchment and a decade of litigation to secure what remained of the family's assets.

Education At the age of seven Goulburn was sent to Dr Moore's school at Sunbury, where he appears to have been wilful, ill-disciplined, and the subject of hostility from fellow pupils; he was nevertheless an accomplished linguist and Latinist. An eye infection led to his withdrawal from Sunbury and convalescence at Worthing. His father's death and mother's ill health resulted in his brothers Edward *Goulburn and Frederick also being withdrawn from Sunbury. Henry assumed responsibility for their education. His mother hired a tutor for her sons, but her limited means bought teaching which rarely aspired even to mediocrity, and after two years this arrangement was terminated and the adolescent Goulburn resumed the life of an autodidact. In 1800 it was decided that he should seek admission at Trinity College, Cambridge, and a rheumatic college fellow residing in London for a cure was retained as his tutor. This sudden exposure to serious scholarship made a lasting impression on Goulburn, and he spent much of the summer reading Horace. He matriculated at the age of seventeen and entered Trinity as a fellow commoner in 1801.

Goulburn's first two years at Cambridge were not undistinguished. He won a declamation prize and was placed in the first class of each of the annual college examinations. In his third year he relaxed, abandoned the study of mathematics, and devoted his vacation to the newly fashionable tour of north Wales and the Lake District. His decision to spend an additional year at Trinity was insufficient atonement for social indulgence, and he graduated BA in 1805 without great distinction, followed by MA in 1808. During his years at Cambridge he became a competent oarsman and, like his eventual mentor Robert Peel, an outstanding shot. Cambridge was crucial, too, to Goulburn's religious formation. Like many undergraduates he came under the influence of Charles Simeon, who had been a contemporary of his father's at Eton College, and now preached regularly at Holy Trinity Church and taught from his rooms in King's. Goulburn's encounter with Simeon led to his praying for a deeper and more serious faith, and left him with a serious, if quietly articulated, evangelicalism, and a firm commitment to the established church.

Politics and junior office Some, at least, of Goulburn's student friendships became political friendships, and he numbered F. J. Robinson and Henry Temple (Viscount Palmerston) among his closest Cambridge friends. Within two years of graduation the pattern of Goulburn's adult life had been established. On his coming of age in 1805 he undertook full responsibility for managing the family estates in Jamaica, the most important of which was centred on Amity Hall. Goulburn's intention of visiting his estates in person were frustrated by ill health or political commitments, and this left him with the challenge of managing estates with which he was personally unfamiliar through agents whom he did not know personally. Like many slave owners Goulburn was reconciled to slavery as a social institution and accepted a version of the humanitarians' argument that the most appropriate indicator of slaves' conditions was their ability at least to sustain their numbers. The fluctuating numbers on the Goulburn estates suggests that, even by this narrow humanitarian measure, his management sometimes fell short, but this was not for want of his willingness to invest time in estate administration or capital in improving projects.

Although enjoying far from abundant financial means, Goulburn was strongly drawn to a political career, and in the 1807 general election offered himself for the Irwins' burgage borough of Horsham, for which the going rate was said to be 4000 guineas. Although unsuccessful at the poll he was seated in February in 1808 on petition to the house. Predictably Goulburn attached himself to the leading evangelical tory, Spencer Perceval, and self-consciously embarked on a career of political and public service. The extent of Goulburn's loyalty was apparent from his maiden speech on 24 February 1809, in which he offered a partisan defence of the government's Spanish policy; the limits of his loyalty, influenced no doubt by his evangelicalism, were signalled when he refused to support the government over the duke of York's tangled involvement with Mrs Clarke and the sale of commissions. Goulburn was also forging a close friendship with Arthur Wellesley, and on 3 July he set out for Portugal and spent the next few months exploring the war zone at first hand. He returned to London on 18 February 1810 and was immediately offered and accepted an under-secretaryship at the Home Office, finding himself in the junior ranks of a government which included Peel, Palmerston, Croker, Robinson, and Manners Sutton.

In so far as Goulburn had a patron at this stage, it was probably Matthew Montagu, a close ally of Perceval and a critic of Catholic relief. Montagu had supported Goulburn's mother, advised on his education, and frequently welcomed Goulburn into his home. On 20 December 1811 Goulburn married Montagu's third daughter, Jane, and in 1812 succeeded to Montagu's Cornish seat of St Germans. His marriage was firm, committed, and supportive. As under-secretary Goulburn's first piece of legislation was the well-conceived Militia Interchange Act of 1811 which integrated the militias of Britain and Ireland. More dramatic was his role in the aftermath of Perceval's assassination on 11 May 1812. Goulburn, the only Home Office official available in London, hurried to Whitehall, and found himself in his office alone with John Bellingham, the prime minister's assassin.

Lord Liverpool's accession to the premiership led to a ministerial reshuffle, with Peel moving to the chief secretaryship of Ireland and Goulburn replacing him in August 1812 as under-secretary for war and colonies. Appropriately, given Goulburn's colonial interests, he was principally responsible for colonial administration. His style can appropriately be described as that of a managerially minded liberal tory. He soon embarked on an imaginative, but unavailing, attempt to Anglicize the legal system of Trinidad. More constructive was his key role as a negotiator at Ghent in July 1814 charged with negotiating the final arrangement of frontiers, fisheries, and maritime rights at the cessation of the Anglo-American War of 1812–14. This was the kind of technical but politically charged statesmanship at which Goulburn excelled.

In 1818 Goulburn's annual income from his Jamaican estates halved to somewhere under £3000. Managerial changes initiated by Goulburn had failed, although he did console himself that the condition of his slaves had probably improved. This diminution of income had political as well as personal consequences. On Peel's resignation in 1818, Liverpool offered Goulburn the post of chief secretary of Ireland. Goulburn refused what was undoubtedly an elevation partly because he felt he could not relinquish the official salary he enjoyed as an under-secretary and partly because he was reluctant to move his young family across to Dublin or face lengthy periods of separation from them. At the general election of June 1818 Goulburn was returned for West Looe and remained devoted to his ministerial office, willingly handling a massive correspondence, and labouring, with some success, to modernize the internal administration of the Colonial Office.

Ireland, the exchequer, and reform In 1821 Lord Liverpool began to reshape his administration and one consequence was the reshaping of Goulburn's political and domestic life. Having installed the pro-Catholic Richard Wellesley as viceroy, Liverpool sought a protestant chief secretary as a counterpoint. Liverpool turned again to Goulburn, offering him a modest annual pension of £1000 both as a *douceur* and as recognition for long years of service as an under-secretary. On this occasion Goulburn accepted, welcoming his elevation to the privy council on 10 December 1821, but rather less happily seeing the cost of maintaining Irish and English establishments drain his personal fortune at the rate of around £2000 per annum. Goulburn's willingness to take the chief secretaryship owed much to his pleasure at Peel's imminent return to the administration. Goulburn's intimacy with Peel was personal as well as political, and was warmly reciprocated. Peel happily acknowledged that he valued Goulburn's friendship 'as much as that of any *man* on earth', and that, of all his friends, Goulburn approached 'nearest to perfection' (Jenkins, *Goulburn*, 101). The Wellesley–Goulburn administration of Ireland was uneasy, bringing Goulburn to the brink of resignation in 1823. His resignation was averted in part by his wife who had settled happily into life in Dublin. The public face of Goulburn's approach consisted in firm policies discreetly enforced, and he always strove to prevent his protestantism becoming Orangeism. He reconfigured the police force to serve as flying squadrons in disturbed districts, and offered limited support for public works schemes. In 1823 he successfully steered his Irish Tithe Composition Bill through parliament, thereby securing a modest abatement of social tension in the Irish countryside. In March 1825 he carried a bill for the suppression of unlawful societies, which Daniel O'Connell's Catholic Association successfully circumvented. His public commitment to education as a means of ameliorating the social condition of Ireland was undergirded by a private conviction that non-denominational public education would subvert the position of the Catholic church.

At the general election of 1826 Goulburn decided to contest Cambridge University, an abortive attempt to secure a prestigious seat which cost him £1500. He took refuge in sitting for Armagh City between 1826 and April 1831. Liverpool's stroke in 1827 caused Goulburn political and personal dismay. He feared the passage of Catholic emancipation and anticipated a bleak political future for himself. Goulburn was unwilling to serve in a Canningite administration, resigning the chief secretaryship in April 1827; his wife left Dublin in 1827 with deep regrets. In the event, the political upheavals of 1827 enhanced Goulburn's political status, and in January 1828 he was swiftly appointed chancellor of the exchequer by his old friend and new prime minister, the duke of Wellington. Goulburn's energies were largely monopolized by financial policy but one ironic consequence of Peel's being unseated by Oxford University was that it fell to the staunchly protestant Goulburn on 12 February 1829 to announce the government's timetable for emancipation.

Goulburn's conception of economic and fiscal policy appears to have been heavily influenced by his evangelicalism, not least in his imagining the trade cycle as regulated by essentially providential rhythms. 'It seemed', he told the house in May 1829, 'to be a rule of affairs of mankind that blessings should not be showered down, without a corresponding visitation of depression' (*Hansard 2*, 21, 1829, 1175). This was wholly consonant with his strong preference for limiting the circulation of paper currency. The general thrust of Goulburn's policy at the exchequer was a retrenchment in the public finances which was technically well managed but unimaginatively conceived. His 1828 budget summoned up savings of around £1 million, and in May 1829 he managed to convert some £3 million of unfunded debt into funded debt by offering a small premium to holders of the unfunded debt to accept 4 per cents instead. Not surprisingly there was resistance in the City and elsewhere to his move a year later to cut the interest on consols by half a per cent. Most conservative was Goulburn's 1830 budget where he revealed that the reintroduction of an income tax had been discussed in cabinet and rejected. Although a further £2.4 million was committed to debt redemption, had Goulburn been more resolute he might well have carried Peel and Herries, and thereby secured cabinet approval for a new income tax. As the whigs were to discover, Goulburn had taken retrenchment as far as the public finances would allow, and the structural deficit in government income was becoming all too apparent. Of considerable significance, however, was his abolition of existing taxes on leather, cider, and beer. His abolition of the beer duty and introduction of a licensing system effectively deregulating the beer trade were populist measures which also granted the industry much of what it had been pressing for in the 1820s.

The fall of Wellington's administration in November 1830 was greeted by Goulburn with some relief. He had been in office since 1810, with a break of a few months in 1827, and the general direction in which public policy was moving was one with which he felt distinctly uncomfortable. As the Swing riots took hold from November 1830, Goulburn hastened to Betchworth House (the seat in Surrey which he had purchased in 1816) to play the squire and lead his farmers against the rioters. After a lifetime on the government benches, Goulburn found that opposition was not without its compensations. His speech savaging Althorp's 1831 budget was perhaps his most effective parliamentary performance yet, destroying not only Althorp's ill-conceived transfer tax but much of what remained of the whigs' fiscal reputation. During the debates on parliamentary reform, Goulburn sought to steer a course between reform and embracing the extravagant political gestures of the ultras. When the first Reform Bill passed its second reading, Goulburn spoke gloomily of 'a disposition in favour of the abolition of our existing constitution' (Jenkins, *Goulburn*, 225). He found modest consolation at the May 1831 general election, where he withstood a sustained attack on his reputation as a slave owner and was returned a member for Cambridge University, a seat he retained until his death.

Goulburn's stance throughout the remainder of the reform crisis was resolutely Peelite, eschewing the ultras and urging Wellington not to form an administration in May 1832. After the 1832 election his position shifted in important ways, and he urged Peel, largely in vain, to build bridges with the ultras. Goulburn's ideal of cordial co-operation with the ultras was built around a commitment to the party's being led by Peelites, and it was in such a minority administration that he returned to office in December 1834. With Peel determined to take the exchequer himself, Goulburn was offered the Home Office, where his presence offered some reassurance to Irish protestants. Even in the government's short life Goulburn's solid political virtues were again apparent with his playing a key role in drafting the Dissenters' Marriages Bill, which succeeded in wrong-footing the whigs and conciliating dissenting opinion. By 1837 Goulburn's domestic finances were again straitened. Purchasing a commission for his son Edward cost him £1400, and the liquidation of £3600 worth of exchequer bills and consols did not prevent him resigning from White's to save money.

Peel's chancellor of the exchequer Throughout the 1830s Goulburn's political ambitions were focused on the speaker's chair. He had hoped he might succeed in 1830, but nothing came of this. In 1838 he was confident of victory until the whigs put up the popular Shaw Lefevre who narrowly defeated Goulburn by 317 to 299 (Hansard 3, 47, 1838, 1050). Goulburn's final hope of the speakership was dashed in 1841 when Peel decided not to try to unseat Shaw Lefevre. In the summer of 1839 a depressed and ill Goulburn travelled to Italy; en route in Paris he encountered Disraeli whom he found personally agreeable. On Peel's return to office in 1841, Goulburn again found himself at the exchequer, although with a limited domain of action. The great reforming budgets of 1842 and 1845 were presented by Peel himself, with much of the preparatory work done by Gladstone at the Board of Trade. Goulburn's characteristic timidity was apparent in 1842 when he responded cautiously to Peel's proposal to revive the income tax. Nevertheless, when the decision to reintroduce an income tax was taken, Goulburn was happy to commend it to the house as a fiscally progressive and financially necessary measure, and his 1844 budget carefully laid the ground for the continuation of the income tax from 1845. Similarly impressive was his reduction of 3.5 per cent stock to 3.25 per cent in the same budget, a move taken after careful preparation of the City for the event. Like Peel, Goulburn privately favoured a single bank of issue, but followed the compromise solution of dividing the functions of the Bank of England in the 1844 Bank Charter Act. Goulburn was rightly alarmed in 1845 by the boom in railway speculation and shares, which he feared would inhibit investment and growth in the manufacturing sector more generally. His attempt to moderate the railway boom was overtaken by the crisis in Ireland.

Despite their personal intimacy, there were perceptible political differences between Peel and Goulburn in 1845–6. In private Goulburn was sceptical of the value of large-scale public works schemes in Ireland, and only found the money to fund Peel's ambitious public works programme under pressure from the prime minister. In opposition after 1846 he willingly supported the whigs' notably harsher line, bolstered by his underlying commitment to a sternly evangelical political economy. Goulburn was equally sceptical of Peel's conversion to unilateral corn law repeal. He had always preferred radical tariff reform to doctrinaire free trade, insisting on the importance of government's protecting the interests of all trading communities. Moreover, he repeatedly told Peel what the prime minister privately knew but publicly conceded only reluctantly: that corn law repeal would do nothing to help, and might well worsen, the Irish crisis. Nevertheless Goulburn's loyalty to Peel was undiminished. He still maintained, as he wrote to Peel on 27 November 1845, that Peel and Peelite Conservatism were the only barriers to 'the revolutionary effects of the Reform Bill' and to 'unrestrained democracy' (Jenkins, Goulburn, 323). Goulburn therefore set aside private doubt and unflinchingly supported corn law repeal, willingly fleshing out the details of Peel's substantial package of agricultural relief, designed to help reconcile the landed interest to repeal. Characteristically Goulburn's parting financial statement to the Commons on 29 May 1846 laid emphasis on the debt's having been reduced by £7 million and annual charges by £1.5 million. To the last he was a man who luxuriated in the technical vocabularies of politics.

Peel's fall from office marked the end of Goulburn's prominence as a public figure. His life had already been overwhelmed by domestic sadness when his eldest son **Henry** [Harry] **Goulburn** (1813–1843) died, unmarried, at 8 Downing Street, London, on 8 June 1843 following a severe chest infection. Born in London on 5 April 1813, Harry was always a frail child. He was educated privately at Brighton by the evangelical clergyman Henry Venn Elliott and then by the Revd William Jackman at Clapham; 'a tone of deep earnest piety' was said to have been his distinguishing characteristic (GM, 2nd ser., 20, 1843, 98). His career at Trinity College, Cambridge, where he graduated as senior classic and second wrangler in 1835 was 'one of continued triumph'. He was elected a fellow in 1835, was Greek grammar lecturer in 1840 and Latin lecturer in 1841, and was called to the bar by the Middle Temple in 1840. His death all but destroyed a devoted father. In 1844 Goulburn secured a vacant commissionership of customs for his third son, Frederick (1818–1878), also of Trinity College, Cambridge; he rose to chair the customs board. The second son, Edward (1816–1887), of the Grenadier Guards, succeeded to Betchworth House. His only daughter, and youngest child, Jane was born in 1820.

After his retirement from political office in June 1846, Goulburn continued to serve as a church commissioner, for which he received a salary of £1000 per annum. When Peel fell from his horse in 1850 Goulburn hurried back to London from Cambridge, and was with the family when he died. Appropriately Goulburn was a pallbearer at Peel's funeral; he was also an executor of his will. By the time the Peelites returned to office in the Aberdeen coalition in 1852, Goulburn was disqualified from serving by age and a now rigid Conservatism. His own death, from pleurisy, on 12 January 1856 at Betchworth, attracted little public attention. He had outlived most of his generation, and was buried in the family vault at Betchworth.

G. F. R. BARKER, rev. DAVID EASTWOOD

Sources B. Jenkins, *Henry Goulburn* (1996) · B. Jenkins, *Era of emancipation: British government of Ireland, 1812–1830* (1988) · S. Northcote, *Twenty years of financial policy* (1862) · *The Croker papers: the correspondence and diaries of … John Wilson Croker*, ed. L. J. Jennings, 3 vols. (1884) · D. R. Fisher, 'Goulburn, Henry', HoP, *Commons* · N. Gash, *Mr Secretary Peel: the life of Sir Robert Peel to 1830*, new edn (1985) · N. Gash, *Sir Robert Peel: the life of Sir Robert Peel after 1830*, new edn (1986)
Archives Surrey HC, corresp. and papers · U. Mich., Clements L., diplomatic corresp. | BL, corresp. with Lord Aberdeen, Add. MS 43196 · BL, letters to Lord Bathurst, loan 57 · BL, corresp. with W. E. Gladstone, Add. MS 44162 · BL, corresp. with John Charles Herries, Add. MS 57401 · BL, corresp. with William Huskisson, Add. MSS 38739, 38741, 38755 · BL, corresp. with Lord Liverpool, Add. MSS 38247, 38290–38302, 38572–38576 · BL, letters to Lord Liverpool, loan 72 · BL, corresp. with Sir Hudson Lowe, Add. MSS 20114–20233 · BL, corresp. with Sir Robert Peel, Add. MSS 40328–40333, 40443–40445 · BL, corresp. with Lord Ripon, Add. MS 40877 · BL, letters to Lord Wellesley, Add. MSS 37298–37311 · Cumbria AS, Carlisle, letters to first earl of Lonsdale · Derbys. RO, letters to Sir R. J. Wilmot-Horton · LPL, letters to Christopher Wordsworth · Lpool RO, letters to fourteenth earl of Derby · NA Scot., letters to Sir George Clerk · NA Scot., letters to Lord Dalhousie · NA Scot., letters to G. W. Hope · priv. coll., corresp. with Maurice Fitzgerald · PRO, corresp. with Lord Cardwell, PRO 30/48 · PRO, corresp. with Lord Ellenborough · PRO NIre., corresp. with J. G. Beresford · St Deiniol's Library, Hawarden, corresp. with Sir John Gladstone · Trinity Cam., letters to William Whewell · U. Southampton L., letters to duke of Wellington
Likenesses G. Richmond, watercolour, 1848 · J. Doyle, sketches (for political caricatures), BM · G. Hayter, group portrait, oils (*The House of Commons, 1833*), NPG · F. Holl, stipple (after H. W. Pickersgill), NPG · A. Wivell, drawing, priv. coll. [*see illus.*] · portrait, repro. in H. T. Ryall?, ed., *Portraits of eminent conservatives*, 2nd ser. (1846) · portraits, repro. in Jenkins, *Henry Goulburn*

Goulburn, Henry (1813–1843). *See under* Goulburn, Henry (1784–1856).

Gould, Arthur Joseph (1864–1919), rugby player, was born on 10 October 1864 at 4 Bridge Street, Newport, Monmouthshire, the fourth of the twelve children of Joseph Gould (1833–1892), brass-founder, of Oxford, and his wife, Elizabeth, *née* Richards, of Newport. He was born into an athletic family. Six of the boys played rugby for Newport, three of them for Wales: Robert (Bob) won eleven international caps (1882–7), George Herbert (Bert) won three (1892–3), and Arthur captained both club and country.

Nicknamed Monkey because of his agility as a boy in climbing trees, Arthur Gould captained the Newport junior side at fourteen, and played his first game for the senior team two years later, on 20 October 1882 against Weston-super-Mare. Having been selected at full-back, he ignored instructions to kick for safety and twice ran through the entire opposition to score. He was elusive and fast, and by 1890 he had scooped £1000 in prize money at

athletics' meetings; he was the midland counties Amateur Athletic Association sprint and hurdles champion in 1893. His employment as a public works contractor took him to various parts of the country, and he played rugby for Southampton Trojans, London Welsh, Richmond, Hampshire, and Middlesex, as well as Newport.

Gould's playing career was interrupted in 1890, when work took him to the West Indies. On his return, appearing regularly now at centre, he became Newport's highest scorer in their invincible season of 1891–2, and between 1893 and 1895 under his captaincy the team lost only four games out of fifty-five. He was also a successful captain at international level, leading Wales to its first triple crown in 1893 by adopting the 'Welsh' formation of four three-quarters. This style of play, pioneered by the Cardiff club, had not been a success in international rugby and Gould was not initially enamoured of it, but he recognized its potential for the kind of attacking game he favoured. Capped twenty-seven times for Wales between 1885 and 1897, Gould was one of the outstanding sportsmen of the late Victorian era. His brilliant all-round play was crucial to Wales's emergence as a force in international rugby, while his striking good looks—penetrating eyes, dark curly hair, and a lithe 5 foot 11 inch frame—earned him widespread adulation. Yet his admirers' determination to reward his achievements plunged British rugby into crisis from 1896 to 1898.

In 1896 a public subscription was opened in Gould's honour, and this received the blessing of the Welsh Rugby Union (WRU) and drew contributions from as far afield as Australia and America. However, since Gould was still playing, the other home unions, contrary to the wishes of their own member clubs and hostile to any notion of rewarding players, broke off fixtures with Wales and demanded that the WRU declare the testimonial illegal. The Welsh union, however, asserted its right to manage its own affairs by participating fully in a gala occasion at the Drill Hall, Newport, on Easter Monday 1897. Here the president of the WRU, Sir J. T. D. Llewelyn, in the presence of 250 guests including civic and national dignitaries, presented Gould with the deeds of the house in which he lived, purchased with money raised by the subscription. The other unions were horrified. Seeking to defuse the situation, in January 1898 Gould announced his retirement and Wales was readmitted to the international fold, although it was not until 1899 that Scotland agreed to resume fixtures. Gould became a referee and a Welsh team selector, and kept his house.

In 1900 Gould married Lilian Augusta Smith, daughter of Samuel Smith, corn merchant, of Newport, and they had four children: Arthur Jack, Mary, Josephine, and Gwen. After his rugby career came to an end, he worked as a brewery clerk. He died of a haemorrhage on 2 January 1919 at home, Thornbury, 6 Llanthewy Road, Clytha Park, Newport, the house which had once caused such controversy. His funeral took place on 6 January at St John's Baptist Church, Newport, where he was a sidesman.

GARETH WILLIAMS

Sources D. Smith and G. Williams, *Fields of praise: the official history of the Welsh Rugby Union, 1881–1981* · G. Williams, 'How amateur was my valley: professional sport and national identity in Wales, 1890–1914', *British Journal of the History of Sport*, 2/3 (1985), 248–69 · W. J. T. Collins, *Rugby recollections* (1948) · W. J. T. Collins, *Newport Athletic Club, 1875–1925* (1925) · *South Wales Argus* (3 Jan 1919) · *Western Mail* [Cardiff] (3 Jan 1919) · J. M. Jenkins and others, *Who's who of Welsh international rugby players* (1991) · OPCS marriage registrations, Dec quarter, 1900

Likenesses photograph, repro. in Collins, *Rugby recollections*, frontispiece

Wealth at death £987 17s. 8d.: probate, 10 March 1920, *CGPLA Eng. & Wales*

Gould, Barbara Bodichon Ayrton (1886–1950), suffragist and politician, was born on 3 April 1886 at 25 Hornton Street, Kensington, London, the only daughter of William Edward *Ayrton (1847–1908), engineer and physicist, and his second wife, Phoebe Sarah (later Hertha) *Ayrton *née* Marks (1854–1923), physicist. Hertha was committed to women's rights and was a close friend of Barbara Bodichon (benefactress of Girton College, Cambridge, and associate of George Eliot) after whom she named her daughter. Barbara Ayrton had a stepsister, Edith, from William Ayrton's first marriage.

Barbara Ayrton was educated at Notting Hill high school and University College, London. However, her university career was cut short by the serious illness and death in 1908 of her father, and also by her growing interest in the militant suffrage movement. In 1906 Barbara Ayrton and her mother joined the militant organization, the Women's Social and Political Union (WSPU) run by Emmeline and Christabel Pankhurst. Hertha supported the movement financially and Barbara became a WSPU organizer in 1909. In 1912 she was active in the window-breaking campaign, afterwards spending a brief period in Holloway prison having refused bail, and a year later fled to France, disguised as a schoolgirl, in order to avoid the police. In July 1910 Barbara married Gerald Gould (d. 1936), a former fellow student at University College but at the time of their marriage a fellow of both Merton College, Oxford, and University College, London. He was a committed supporter of the suffrage movement and campaigned actively on its behalf. By 1914 Barbara Gould and her mother had both became disillusioned with the WSPU and joined the United Suffragists, an organization which included both women and men as members. Barbara was its first secretary, her mother one of the vice-presidents. It was this organization that helped to keep the suffrage issue alive during the war when the WSPU was disbanded, and Barbara Gould remained active in the movement until a small percentage of women was granted the vote in 1918.

After the war Barbara Gould began her extensive involvement with the Labour Party, motivated principally by her growing interest in international affairs and an increasing concern for neglected children. She joined the *Daily Herald* in 1919 as publicity manager and held the post until the birth in 1921 of her only son, the sculptor and writer Michael *Ayrton (1921–1975). She served for a short time as the chief officer for women of the Labour Party

Barbara Bodichon Ayrton Gould (1886–1950), by unknown photographer, 1909 [left, as conductor on the suffragette bus]

and in 1932 edited the *Labour Woman* for several months. From 1936 to 1937 she was a member of the Labour Party's distressed areas committee and was particularly interested in the effect of unemployment on the family. In 1938 she was the vice-chair of the Labour Party, taking over as chair from 1939 to 1940.

Although not elected to parliament until 1945, Barbara Gould was the parliamentary candidate for the Labour Party for Lambeth North in 1922, for Northwich, Cheshire, in 1924, 1929, and again in 1931, and for Hulme, Manchester, in 1935. She became an MP in the 1945 general election and until 1950 represented Hendon North in London. Once in parliament she focused her immediate attention on the rationing system and on food supplies and in the 1948–9 session she succeeded in introducing a resolution which called for a government enquiry into child neglect. By 1950 she was in poor health and when she was narrowly defeated in the election of that year she decided not to stand again.

Barbara Gould was also active in public life outside the Labour Party. Until 1923 she was organizing secretary of the National Society of Lunacy Reform. From 1929 to 1931 she was a member of the royal commission on the civil service and was one of the members who strongly supported equal pay. She served on the standing joint committee of working women's organizations, becoming chair in 1931. For a time she was an executive member of the National Peace Council and served on the executive of the Women's International League for a number of years. In 1950 she was appointed to the Arts Council and was vice-chair of the British Council.

Barbara Gould's husband predeceased her in 1936, and she died at her home, 74A Philbeach Gardens, London, on 15 October 1950.   SERENA KELLY

Sources O. Banks, *The biographical dictionary of British feminists*, 2 (1990) • E. Sharp, *Hertha Ayrton, 1854–1923: a memoir* (1926) • *WWW, 1941–50* • b. cert. • d. cert.
Likenesses photograph, 1909, Museum of London [*see illus.*] • photograph, *c*.1910, Hult. Arch.
Wealth at death £7852 16s. 4d.: probate, 5 Dec 1950, *CGPLA Eng. & Wales*

Gould, Charles. *See* Morgan, Sir Charles, first baronet (1726–1806).

Gould, Sir Francis Carruthers (1844–1925), cartoonist and stockbroker, was born at Barnstaple, Devon, on 2 December 1844, the second son of Richard Davie Gould (1816/17–1900), architect, and his wife, Judith Carruthers, daughter of William Ford. Educated first at Mr Sharland's school and then at Mr Snow's school in Barnstaple, he entered a bank there at the age of sixteen. From childhood he had been skilled at drawing in pencil, chiefly making studies of birds and animals—he recalled 'having two absorbing interests, pets and politics' (Gould, 9)—and while at the bank he drew, purely for amusement, caricatures of various colleagues, customers, and well-known persons in the town. He was a member of the Barnstaple volunteers and later of the London Irish Rifles. In 1865 he went to London to work in a stockbroker's office, and after a few years he became a member of the stock exchange, operating first as a broker and later as a jobber. In 1869 he married Emily (*d.* 1920), the daughter of Hugh Ballment of Barnstaple, a shipbuilder and -owner and later a tanner. They had three sons and two daughters.

In the stock exchange Gould's pencil was soon busily at work, and his caricatures were in great demand among business acquaintances and friends. Large numbers of them were issued for private circulation. He found the 'House' (that is, the stock exchange) an excellent school, for, as he said, 'there was every variety of personality and very marked individuality among the members'; but for many years he looked upon these drawings solely as distractions and had no idea of embarking on the career of a professional cartoonist.

In 1879, however, Gould was asked by Horace Voules to illustrate the Christmas number of *Truth*, and the work he did was so much appreciated that he was asked to contribute regularly to the journal's subsequent Christmas issues up to 1895. From 1887 he became a fairly constant contributor of cartoons and sketches to the *Pall Mall Gazette*. In 1890, when W. T. Stead was succeeded in the editorship by E. T. Cook, Gould became a member of the staff. Early in 1893, after the paper had passed to the control of William Waldorf Astor (changing its politics from Liberal to Conservative in the process), Gould joined, with Cook and J. A. Spender, the staff of the newly founded *Westminster Gazette*, an evening paper with which he worked until 1914, becoming assistant editor in 1896. His daily cartoon usually occupied a prominent position on the front page—the

Sir Francis Carruthers Gould (1844–1925), by Olive Edis, 1903

first political cartoonist to be given so central a position— and he soon showed a remarkable ability to link quotations from the speeches of the politicians of the day to witty caricatures. For several years from the late 1890s an annual album of his *Westminster* cartoons was published, a mark of his popularity. From 1894 to 1914 he also edited his own paper, *Picture Politics*.

Gould's best years as a cartoonist were those of the long period of Unionist government between 1895 and 1905. A staunch Liberal working for a Liberal paper which was widely read by people of all parties, his best targets were Unionist politicians, notably A. J. Balfour, Lord Salisbury, and Joseph Chamberlain. Although by his own admission he was no more than a competent draughtsman, his pencil was employed with exceptional fertility in the suggestion of a likeness and the features of a face. 'I accentuate', he said, 'the salient features of the political situation of the moment' (*DNB*). He showed a strong sense of the character of his subjects, and he was especially adept at portraying them as animals or, especially, birds (the result of his lifelong fascination for wild creatures), or in female costume: 'Clara' Balfour and Chamberlain the milkmaid were two repeated themes. Sir William Harcourt, Lord Rosebery, John Morley, and the duke of Devonshire were frequent targets. Gould succeeded in being witty both in his drawings and in his captions; he parodied John Tenniel's 'Alice' characters and made copious allusion to the works of Dickens and Joel Chandler Harris's Uncle

Remus stories. He had a large repertory of subjects but, as often with political cartoonists, he was happiest when caricaturing the opposition. Although the political temperature ran very high in these years, his approach was never savage, and when he tried to deal with a serious topic seriously—the death of Gladstone or the concentration camps in South Africa—the result was uneasy, and he could not match the portentous style of Tenniel or Bernard Partridge, though he sometimes tried to do so. But on his own ground he was unrivalled and may be said, with his contemporary Harry Furniss, to have founded an influential style in British cartoon drawings. Despite his undoubted Liberal commitment, his was essentially the cartoon of clubland (and Osbert Lancaster owed something to him): politicians, however ferocious, were for Gould essentially humorous, benign personalities. Many Unionists collected his cartoons of them. He felt that the political caricaturist must have 'a creed and a purpose', with the 'desire to convey some definite teaching'; on the other hand, 'care must be taken that a continuity of criticism does not mean a continuity of malice' (Gould, 83).

Gould helped keep Liberal spirits cheerful during a period when the party was disunited and weak; Lord Rosebery saw him as one of the few remaining political assets of the party. When the party returned to power in 1906 he was rewarded by a knighthood for his political services, the only precedent among cartoonists for this honour being Tenniel.

Gould was a prolific book illustrator, his first notable contribution being *Fairy Tales from Brentano* (1885). With H. W. Lucy, with whose prose he was in happy alliance, he produced *Peeps at Parliament* (1903) and *Later Peeps* (1904). He wrote and illustrated *Froissart's 'Modern Chronicles'* (3 pts, 1902, 1903, 1908), which set a new standard for witty history books. He published several volumes of parody of Tenniel and Lewis Carroll, Indian fables collected by P. V. Ramaswami Raju (1901), humorous accounts of the stock exchange ('the Sit-tee Desert'), and the like. Some were written with his son Frank Herbert Gould, also a stockbroker. He illustrated Liberal election booklets and propaganda and experimented in different kinds of ephemera, such as albums and illustrated pamphlets on the past parliamentary session.

In 1914 Gould retired from regular work and lived in Upway, Porlock, Somerset, where he died on 1 January 1925. Collections of his works are in the British Museum, the Victoria and Albert Museum, and the National Portrait Gallery, London. He left an autobiography, now in the House of Lords Record Office, the early chapters of which were published in the *North Devon Journal*.

H. C. G. MATTHEW

Sources F. C. Gould, autobiography, HLRO [unpublished MS] · *The Times* (2 Jan 1925) · 'Studio-talk', *The Studio*, 23 (1901), 196–220, esp. 196–201 · A. Watson, *'F. C. G.', caricaturist* (1903) · *DNB*
Archives HLRO, autobiography
Likenesses G. C. Beresford, photograph, 1902, NPG · O. Edis, photograph, 1903, NPG [*see illus.*] · M. Beerbohm, sketch, *c.*1908, U. Texas · E. Kapp, chalk drawing, 1919, NPG · R. G. Jennings, oils, National Liberal Club, London · Lib [L. Prosperi], cartoon, watercolour study, NPG; repro. in *VF* (22 Feb 1890)
Wealth at death £14,154 6*s.* 1*d.*: probate, 25 March 1925, *CGPLA Eng. & Wales*

Gould, Frederick James (1855–1938), educationist and secularist author, was born on 19 December 1855 at 17 Portland Street, Brighton, the last of the three children of William James Gould, a jeweller and part-time opera singer, and his wife, Julia, *née* Wilson, a dressmaker.

Gould went to a local academy at the corner of Little James Street and Gray's Inn Road, London, but his rise from genteel poverty began with his election in 1865 as a chorister of St George's Chapel, Windsor Castle. There he was befriended by the devout evangelical Canon Wriothesley Russell, who underwrote his further education at the village school at Chenies, Buckinghamshire, which he attended from 1868, becoming a teacher there in 1871. He secured a post in 1877 as head teacher of the church school at Great Missenden, Buckinghamshire, but by 1879, having lost his faith, he resigned. On 1 November 1879 he married Mahalah Elisabeth, the daughter of Robert Lash, a ship steward, at St James's Church, Bermondsey; they later had three children. The newly married couple moved to London, where he taught for the London school board at the Turin Street School, Bethnal Green, and later at Northey Street School, Limehouse. There he also became involved with a variety of secularist reform causes, notably Frederic Harrison's positivist chapel and the Rationalist Press Association, of which he was a founding member. After a stormy controversy with school board officials over the right of a secularist teacher to deliver daily biblical instruction Gould resigned his position in 1896, criticizing religious education in the schools as being arid and neglectful of meaningful moral instruction.

After leaving the school board Gould became a full-time organizer for the Ethical Culture movement, developed in England by the American expatriate Dr Stanton Coit. He assisted in the formation of the Union of Ethical Societies, helped with its weekly publication, the *Ethical World*, and was involved in the Moral Instruction League, the leading lobby group for non-theological moral instruction in Britain prior to the First World War. In 1899 differences with Coit and reduced financial circumstances led him to move to Leicester, where he had been offered the position of secretary of the town's Secular Society. From 1900 to 1902 he served on the Leicester school board and from 1904 to 1910, with the support of the Labour Party, on the town council.

Gould had maintained his association with the Moral Instruction League (after 1909 the Moral Education League), which in 1910 offered him a position as a demonstrator. Drawing on his extensive teaching experience he travelled across Britain, as well as to the United States and India, lecturing to teachers, teacher-training students, and members of the general public, conducting demonstration lessons with children, and promoting the cause of systematic non-theological moral instruction. With the league's decline during the First World War his services were terminated in 1915, but a small group of supporters from around the world, known as the Gould Committee, volunteered funds substantial enough to support his writing and lecturing until his death. Having gained international attention at the First International Congress on Moral Education in London in 1908 he played a major role in the organization of the next five congresses, and his books were used in schools in every English-speaking country; they were also translated for use in India, Ceylon, Brazil, and several European countries. He continued to involve himself in a variety of reformist causes, including the League of Nations Union, the Social Democratic Federation, and the Social Credit Campaign.

Gould's major contributions to the movement for moral education include nearly fifty books, most notably *Youth's Noble Path* (1911), a collection of edifying tales drawn from a variety of religious and cultural traditions, *Moral Instruction: Theory and Practice* (1913), an explication of his story-based methodology for systematic moral education, and *Hyndman: Prophet of Socialism* (1928), a biography of his friend and political idol Henry Mayers Hyndman. He also published hundreds of pamphlets, articles, curriculum guides, and teaching materials.

Central to Gould's educational thought was his commitment to inclusive, service-oriented humanism as developed by Auguste Comte. Unlike most secularists, who objected to any religious instruction in schools, he sought to incorporate every religious tradition in the construction of an ecumenical and synthetic approach to moral instruction which would place above all creeds a desire for selfless service to others. The passion for social unity which marked his educational writing led him to embrace Hyndman's peculiarly national vision of socialism and to campaign for the Social Credit philosophy of Major C. H. Douglas and the national guilds scheme of A. R. Orage. Although his educational programme was never formally adopted in Britain, it became known, through his lectures, writing, and demonstration lessons, to a significant number of teachers. He also contributed to a shifting of the focus of moral education from a personal morality grounded in religious sanctions to a common civic morality, defined by the state.

Gould lived simply, never drawing more than £500 per year from the Gould Committee, which he supplemented with the modest income from his journalism. Although one daughter, Romola, survived, his other daughter, Eva Minna, died aged six, and his son, Julian, was killed in France in 1917; his wife also seems to have predeceased him. After a severe attack of gastritis in March 1937 his own health deteriorated, and he died at his home, Armorel, Woodfield Avenue, Ealing, London, on 6 April 1938. He was cremated on 11 April at Golders Green crematorium. ROBERT NICHOLAS BÉRARD

Sources F. J. Gould, *The life story of a humanist* (1923) · F. H. Hayward and E. M. White, *The last years of a great educationist: a record of the work … of F. J. Gould* (c.1942) · R. N. Bérard, 'Frederick James Gould and the transformation of moral education', *British Journal of Educational Studies*, 35 (1987), 233–47 · b. cert. · m. cert. · d. cert.
Likenesses G. C. Beresford, photograph, 1921, repro. in Gould, *Life story of a humanist* · photograph, repro. in Hayward and White, *Last years of a great educationist*
Wealth at death £1107 3s. 4d.: probate, 18 May 1938, CGPLA Eng. & Wales

Gould, George (1818–1882), Particular Baptist minister, the eldest son by a second marriage of George Gould, a Bristol china and glass dealer, was born at Castle Green, Bristol, on 20 September 1818. After attending a strict boarding-school (1826–32), he became clerk to a wine merchant at the end of 1832, and in 1836 was articled to an accountant. A serious illness in the winter of 1836–7, and the example of a friend who was preparing for the ministry of the Church of England, led his thoughts in the same direction. To his disappointment he found that he could not conscientiously subscribe to the Thirty-Nine Articles. His father had for many years been a deacon at Counterslip Baptist Chapel, Bristol, and resolving after enquiry to join the same denomination, Gould was baptized there on 5 November 1837. On the following 24 December he preached his first sermon, at Fishponds, near Bristol, and in September 1838 he became a student of the Bristol Baptist college.

In 1841 Gould was chosen pastor of a small Baptist congregation in Lower Abbey Street, Dublin. In May 1843 he married Elizabeth, the younger daughter of Samuel Pearce of South Molton, Devon, and in 1846 he moved to South Street Chapel, Exeter. The Exeter church was at that time in some disarray, and his stay was brief. On 29 July 1849 he succeeded William Brock as pastor of St Mary's Chapel, Norwich. Tall, and with a commanding presence, Gould's preaching showed strong thought and much biblical knowledge; although sometimes hard to follow, at his best he displayed remarkable eloquence. In 1857 long-standing divisions at St Mary's on the question of admitting the unbaptized to communion came to a head; a secession followed, and a bill in chancery (May 1858) was filed by a trustee, the Revd William Norton of Egham Hill, Surrey. In what was, for Particular Baptists, an important test case, the master of the rolls gave judgment (28 May 1860) in favour of Gould and the majority of his church, who had advocated open communion. Gould's meticulous research for the case, subsequently published, showed that from the earliest times individual Particular Baptist congregations had made their own decisions about access to communion. His work is an important contribution to the earlier history of dissent, being filled with extracts from original records. In 1868 new schoolrooms and a lecture room were built at St Mary's, at a cost of £3700.

Gould was active in public affairs, and encouraged his church members to participate in them. In 1861–2 he was at the forefront of moves to reform Norwich's system of poor relief, and in 1874 he was elected to the city's first school board, of which he was chairman from 1880 until his death. During the floods of November 1878 he helped to orchestrate the relief effort. He was president of the

Baptist Union in 1879, and sat for nearly twenty years on the committee of the Baptist Missionary Society. His nonconformity was uncompromising; he was one of the original committee of the Anti-State Church Association, the forerunner of the Liberation Society, and campaigned on many issues. Although Gould was naturally reserved, his friendships were wide and generous. He had a large library: one of his favourite books was Sir Thomas Browne's *Religio medici*. He lost the sight in his left eye in 1873. Having preached for the last time on 5 February 1882, he died of erysipelas on 13 February and was buried on the 16th at the Rosary, Norwich. W. N. Ripley, the rector of St Giles, took part in the funeral service.

Some of Gould's published writings were collected by his son, George Pearce Gould, and appeared as *Sermons and Addresses … with a Memoir by … G. P. Gould* (1883). Gould's other publications included an *Outline of the Ecclesiastical History of Ireland*, which prefaced and rather overshadowed Belcher's and Fuller's history of *The Baptist Irish Society* (1845); an anonymous pamphlet on India, prompted by the mutiny of 1857; and a collection of documents to mark the 1862 bicentenary of the Act of Uniformity.

Elizabeth Gould survived her husband, as did four of their eight children. Of their three surviving sons, the eldest son, George Pearce, went into the Baptist ministry, becoming tutor and later principal of Regent's Park College. Alfred became a distinguished London surgeon, and Harry a respected Norwich accountant and JP; Alfred and Harry were leading Baptist laymen and successive treasurers of the Baptist Missionary Society.

ALEXANDER GORDON, rev. ROSEMARY CHADWICK

Sources G. Gould, *Sermons and addresses … with a memoir by G. P. Gould* (1883) • S. V., 'Memoirs of ministers deceased', *Baptist Hand-Book* (1883), 261–5 • memoir of the Rev. Geo. Gould, late minister of St. Mary's Chapel, 1882 • C. B. Jewson, 'St. Mary's, Norwich [pt 6]', *Baptist Quarterly*, 10 (1940–41), 398–406, esp. 402–6
Likenesses photograph, St Mary's Chapel, Norwich • portrait, repro. in Gould, *Sermons and addresses*
Wealth at death £2726 1s. 1d.: probate, 28 March 1882, *CGPLA Eng. & Wales*

Gould, Sir Henry (1643/4–1710), judge, was the son and heir of Andrew Gould (d. in or after 1676), of Winsham, Somerset, and Magdalen Beard. He matriculated at Exeter College, Oxford, on 13 July 1659. However, he was destined for the law; he entered the Middle Temple on 24 May 1660, and was called to the bar on 17 May 1667. The visitation of 1672, in which he was described as twenty-eight years old, indicates that he had married Anne Trencher of Somerset, but other sources show that he married Sarah (c.1654–1733), daughter of Richard Davidge, a merchant, and indeed a son named Davidge was born about 1680.

Gould was made a bencher of his inn on 7 February 1689. He was appointed a serjeant-at-law in April 1692, a king's serjeant on 20 February 1694, and was knighted two days later. He was sent into Lancashire and Cheshire to prosecute suspected Jacobites in October 1694. As a leading lawyer he prosecuted Sir John Fenwick in 1696. He became a judge of king's bench on 30 January 1699 and on his first circuit he fined Sir John Bolles £100 at Lincoln for accusing

him of coming down with the king's commission to enslave the people and also for kicking the sheriff. Gould was reappointed at the start of Queen Anne's reign, and served in the queen's bench during such controversial party causes as the *Ashby v. White* case. In November 1709 it was reported that he would resign from the bench but have his salary continued. In the event he died in his chambers at Serjeants' Inn, Chancery Lane, on 26 March 1710, leaving two sons, William and Davidge, father of Sir Henry *Gould (1710–1794), and a daughter, Sarah, who was the mother of Henry *Fielding.   STUART HANDLEY

Sources Sainty, *Judges*, 35 • Baker, *Serjeants*, 451, 514 • Foss, *Judges*, 7.384–5 • Sainty, *King's counsel*, 23 • Foster, *Alum. Oxon.* • H. A. C. Sturgess, ed., *Register of admissions to the Honourable Society of the Middle Temple, from the fifteenth century to the year 1944*, 1 (1949), 163 • N. Luttrell, *A brief historical relation of state affairs from September 1678 to April 1714*, 3 (1857), 381; 4 (1857), 545; 5 (1857), 358, 380, 519; 6 (1857), 509, 558, 562 • will, PRO, PROB 11/516, sig. 138 • *State trials*, 3.546 • G. D. Squibb, ed., *The visitation of Somerset and the city of Bristol, 1672*, Harleian Society, new ser., 11 (1992), 161 • *DNB*

Gould, Sir Henry (1710–1794), judge, was the fourth son of Davidge Gould of Sharpham Park, Somerset, a barrister of the Middle Temple, and grandson of Sir Henry *Gould (1643/4–1710), a judge of the king's bench. His mother was Honora Hockmore of Buckland Baron, Devon.

Gould the younger was admitted a member of the Middle Temple on 16 May 1728, called to the bar on 13 June 1734, and elected a bencher in 1754, in which year he also became a king's counsel on 3 May. He had the reputation of being a sound but not an eloquent lawyer. In Michaelmas term 1761 he was appointed a baron of the exchequer, and on 24 January 1763 was transferred to the common pleas in succession to Mr Justice Noel, who had recently died. He proved to be a good judge. During the Gordon riots of 1780 he refused the military protection for his house which was offered to all the judges. He frequently went the northern circuit.

Gould married Elizabeth, daughter of Dr Walker, archdeacon of Wells. They had a son, who predeceased his father, and two daughters. One daughter married Richard Ford William Lambart, seventh earl of Cavan, to whose children Gould left the bulk of his fortune. The other married the Hon. Temple Luttrell.

Gould died at his house in Lincoln's Inn Fields, London, on 5 March 1794. Though his donations to charities were numerous, he left £100,000. He was buried at Stapleford Abbots in Essex, of which parish his brother William was rector. Gould was survived by his wife.

J. A. HAMILTON, rev. ROBERT BROWN

Sources E. Foss, *Biographia juridica: a biographical dictionary of the judges of England … 1066–1870* (1870) • J. Hutchinson, ed., *A catalogue of notable Middle Templars: with brief biographical notices* (1902) • J. Collinson, *The history and antiquities of the county of Somerset*, 3 vols. (1791) • J. Redington and R. A. Roberts, eds., *Calendar of home office papers of the reign of George III*, 3: 1770–1772, PRO (1881); 4: 1773–1775, PRO (1899) • *GM*, 1st ser., 64 (1794), 283–4
Likenesses T. Hardy, mezzotint, pubd 1794, BM, NPG • oils, Harvard Law Library, Cambridge, Massachusetts
Wealth at death wealthy; left £100,000 (after many donations to charity in life)

Gould, James Alipius. *See* Goold, James Alipius (1812–1886).

Gould, John (1804–1881), ornithologist and publisher, was born at Lyme Regis, Dorset, on 14 September 1804, the son of John Gould, a gardener, and his wife, Elizabeth Clatworthy. Very early in Gould's life the family moved to Stoke Hill near Guildford, where three younger sisters were born and where he probably went to school. When Gould was thirteen his father was appointed a foreman gardener at Windsor Castle, where he was in charge of 'the Slopes'. Young Gould was employed at Kew Gardens for a short time, then as a gardener at Ripley Castle in Yorkshire.

Early career and marriage In 1825 Gould moved to London and set up a taxidermy shop (when the family had lived in the Windsor area, Gould had stuffed birds for the boys at Eton College). There is an extant receipt in the Windsor Castle Royal Archives dated 1825 'For preserving a Thick kneed bustard' for George IV. The king employed Gould to do additional taxidermy work, including stuffing the first giraffe that had arrived in England. In 1828, after a competitive exhibition of the skill of several applicants, Gould was appointed animal preserver at the museum of the newly formed Zoological Society of London. In 1833 he was promoted to superintendent of its ornithological department. He went on half pay in 1836 to concentrate on his bird paintings, but continued in the position until 1838 when he resigned to prepare for his journey to Australia. On 5 January 1829 Gould married Elizabeth Coxen (1804–1841). She was the daughter of a sea captain from Ramsgate and lived in the Golden Square area of London near to Gould; a letter to her mother in 1828 showed she was then employed as a tutor of French, Latin, and music.

As the 'bird-stuffer' of the Zoological Society, Gould was soon corresponding with the prominent naturalists of the time, Sir William Jardine, Prideaux John Selby, William Swainson, Edward Smith Stanley (later thirteenth earl of Derby), and many others, both in England and abroad.

Ventures in publishing In the late 1820s a collection of birds from the Himalayan mountains arrived at the society's museum and Gould conceived the idea of publishing a volume of imperial folio sized hand-coloured lithographs of the eighty species, with figures of a hundred birds (*A Century of Birds Hitherto Unfigured from the Himalaya Mountains*, 1830–32). Gould's friend and mentor N. A. Vigors supplied the text. Elizabeth Gould made the drawings and transferred them to the large lithographic stones. Having failed to find a publisher, Gould undertook to publish the work himself; it appeared in twenty monthly parts, four plates to a part, and was completed ahead of schedule.

With this volume Gould initiated a format of publishing that he was to continue for the next fifty years, although for future works he was to write his own text. Eventually fifty imperial folio volumes were published on the birds of the world, except Africa, and on the mammals of Australia—he always had a number of works in progress at the

John Gould (1804–1881), by Ernest Edwards, pubd 1864

same time. Several smaller volumes, the majority not illustrated, were published, and he also presented more than 300 scientific papers.

His hand-coloured lithographic plates, more than 3300 in total, are called 'Gould plates'. Although he did not paint the final illustrations, this description is largely correct: he was the collector (especially in Australia) or purchaser of the specimens, the taxonomist, the publisher, the agent, and the distributor of the parts or volumes. He never claimed he was the artist for these plates, but repeatedly wrote of the 'rough sketches' he made from which, with reference to the specimens, his artists painted the finished drawings. The design and natural arrangement of the birds on the plates was due to the genius of John Gould, and a Gould plate has a distinctive beauty and quality. His wife was his first artist. She was followed by Edward Lear, Henry Constantine Richter, William Matthew Hart, and Joseph Wolf.

A vital member of Gould's team was Edwin C. Prince, his faithful secretary and office manager from 1830 until Prince died in 1875. There are more than 4500 extant letters to and from Gould, and Prince's annotation of the authorship of the letters and the date is on 99 per cent of them.

The publication of the *Century* was quite successful. Subscribers included royalty, nobility, and gentlemen naturalists. Because of the cost, less affluent naturalists complained that smaller-sized works should be made available. As a result, two works on the birds of Australia were published in a smaller format. Pleased with the success of his first publishing venture, Gould immediately launched into the publication of his five-volume *The Birds of Europe* (1832–7, 448 pl.), followed by a monograph on the large-billed toucans (1833–5, 33 pl.), and one on the trogons (1835–8, 36 pl.).

Charles Darwin returned from his epic voyage on HMS *Beagle* in the autumn of 1836. Darwin selected several scientists to describe his collected specimens, and Gould was presented with Darwin's birds. In January 1837 Gould pronounced a group of twelve birds from the Galápagos Islands, which Darwin had thought to be 'blackbirds, warblers, wrens and finches', as all one family of finches, with variations in their beaks and size. This was the crucial piece of evidence that enabled Darwin to come to his theory of island speciation. The 'bird' volume of Darwin's *Zoology of the Voyage of H.M.S. Beagle* was contributed by Gould (1838–41, 50 pl.).

Australian travels and personal loss Two brothers of Gould's wife had emigrated to Australia. They sent bird specimens to Gould and he began publishing parts for a work on Australian birds including a *Synopsis of the Birds of Australia* (1837–8, 73 pl. of heads of birds). He soon realized that the 'natural productions' of the country were untapped and embarked for Australia on 16 May 1838 on the sailing barque *Parsee*. Accompanying him were his wife, his son John Henry, his nephew Henry Coxen, two servants, and his very competent and valuable assistant John Gilbert.

Gould remained in Australia for eighteen months and collected hundreds of specimens of birds, mammals, plants, and insects. 300 new species of birds were named by him, but 100 were later relegated to subspecies types. Gould travelled in eastern Australia, and he sent Gilbert to Western Australia and to Port Essington in the north.

Gould and his family returned to England in August 1840 having travelled round the world. During eight months at sea, coming and going, Gould collected many seabirds and added greatly to the knowledge of these families. Within three months of his return Gould issued part one of his seven-volume *Birds of Australia* (1840–48), which eventually contained 600 plates and text. A supplement with eighty-one plates was published from 1851 to 1869, and a valuable *Handbook to the Birds of Australia* in two volumes in 1865.

On 15 August 1841 Gould's wife Elizabeth died from puerperal fever following delivery of her eighth child; two children had previously died in infancy. It was a severe blow to Gould to lose his wife, the mother of his children, and his artist. Of his six surviving children, two of his sons who were physicians died on voyages from India; Gould's remaining family feared for his health after these tragedies.

Gould was elected FRS in 1843 and given honorary memberships in many British and foreign ornithological societies. Two years after Gould's election to FRS, John Gilbert was killed by Aborigines in a second journey to Australia—while on Leichhardt's expedition—yet another severe loss for Gould.

Humming-Birds and further works Many collectors sent bird specimens to Gould to be identified, and he was a well-recognized systematist. He also travelled to the continent several times, and to North America once, in 1857, when he dined with President Buchanan. The purpose of these journeys was to examine specimens in museums or in private collections, and to obtain subscribers to his works.

The humming-birds of the Americas intrigued Gould and he became an authority on them. He displayed them in a special building he was allowed to build in the zoological gardens at the time of the 1851 Great Exhibition at the Crystal Palace. More than 80,000 people visited his display, including Queen Victoria. The following year Gould obtained permission to continue the exhibit. His *Introduction to the Trochilidae or Humming-Birds* was published in five volumes from 1849 to 1861, with 360 plates, in which the brilliant natural iridescence of the humming-birds was portrayed by the application of gold leaf.

Another work that Gould was especially proud of was his five-volume *Birds of Great Britain* (1862–73, 367 pl.) where he pictured many of the birds with their young. This was his best-selling work. Additional works published by the prolific Gould and his team included *Icones avium* (2 pts, 1837–8, 18 pl.), which Gould called his 'general work', a *Monograph of the Odontophorinae or Partridges of America* (1844–50, 32 pl.), and his scientifically valuable but poorly subscribed *Mammals of Australia*, (3 vols., 1845–63, 182 pl.). Gould's massive work, the *Birds of Asia*, in thirty-five parts which bound to seven volumes, with 530 plates, took thirty-three years to complete, from 1849 to 1883 (and was completed by R. B. Sharpe). The *Birds of New Guinea* (5 vols., 1875–88, 320 pl.) was also finished by Sharpe. This latter work had spectacular hand-coloured lithographs of the birds of paradise.

With new birds constantly being discovered in the 1800s, Gould found it necessary to issue supplements or second editions to *Toucans*, *Trogons*, the *Birds of Australia*, and *Humming-Birds* (completed by Sharpe). As perks to subscribers and for friends such as Charles Darwin, Gould ran off octavo sized introductions for the *Birds of Australia*, *Mammals of Australia*, *Humming-Birds*, and *Birds of Great Britain*.

Gould has received some unfavourable criticism. Edward Lear drew about eighty-one plates for three of Gould's early works, and through error, Gould failed to acknowledge his artistry on some five of them. Joseph Wolf, one of his artists, thought Gould 'shrewd … but uncouth' (Palmer, 70), but also related some humorous moments with Gould. Lady Jane Franklin spoke of Gould's 'good humour' (Mackaness, 1.49), when the Goulds stayed with them in Tasmania. Gould's close associates worked loyally for him for long periods—Edwin Prince for forty-five years, Richter for forty, and Hart for thirty; except for his time in Australia, Gould took pride in paying his workers promptly.

Gould gave or sold most of his bird and mammal specimens to the British Museum but the museum turned down the chance to buy his very valuable collection of

Australian birds and eggs for £1000 in 1847. The collection was immediately purchased by Edward Wilson for the Academy of Natural Sciences of Philadelphia.

Later years Gould was a frequent guest at the home of many friends, naturalists, and subscribers. He was a good shot and a respected fisherman. In his later years he became a close friend of R. Bowdler Sharpe, a prominent ornithologist at the British Museum. Sharpe wrote that Gould could be 'brusque' but 'concealed a very kind heart' (Sharpe, xxiii).

Gould died at his home, 26 Charlotte Street, Bedford Square, London, on 3 February 1881 after a long, painful illness. He was buried in Kensal Green cemetery. The sheer number of imperial folio volumes on birds published by Gould has never been surpassed. He was the entrepreneurial naturalist of the 1800s in England, and the pioneer naturalist of Australia.

GORDON C. SAUER

Sources G. C. Sauer, *John Gould the bird man: a chronology and bibliography* (1982) · R. B. Sharpe, *An analytical index to the works of the late John Gould* (1893) · *John Gould the bird man: correspondence*, ed. G. C. Sauer, 1–2 (1998) [for periods 1838, 1839–41] · C. E. Bryant, ed., 'Gould commemorative issue', *Emu*, 38 (1938), 89–244 · A. McEvey, 'Collections of John Gould manuscripts and drawings', *La Trobe Library Journal*, 1 (1968), 17–31 · A. McEvey, *John Gould's contribution to British art: a note on its authenticity* (Sydney, [1973]) · M. Lambourne, *Birds of the world* (1992) · M. Lambourne and C. Jackson, 'Mr. Prince: John Gould's invaluable secretary', *Naturae*, 4 (1993), 1–23 · G. C. Sauer, *John Gould's prospectuses and lists of subscribers to his works on natural history: with an 1866 facsimile* (Kansas, privately printed, 1980) · G. C. Sauer, 'John Gould in America', *Contributions to the history of North American natural history*, ed. A. Wheeler (1983), 51–8 · A. McEvey, 'John Gould's ability in drawing birds', *Art Bulletin of Victoria* (1967), 13–24 · A. Chisholm, *The story of Elizabeth Gould* (1944) · I. Tree, *The ruling passion of John Gould* (1991) · A. H. Palmer, *The life of Joseph Wolf* (1895) · G. Mackaness, *Some private correspondence of Sir John and Lady Jane Franklin* (1947) · parish register (baptism), 7 Oct 1804, Lyme Regis · private information (2004)

Archives McGill University, Montreal, drawings and papers · Mitchell L., NSW, corresp. and papers · NHM, corresp. and papers · NL Aus., corresp. and papers · NRA, priv. coll., drawings and papers · RCS Eng., papers · State Library of Victoria, Melbourne, corresp. and papers · U. Cam., department of zoology, notes and drawings · University of Kansas, Lawrence, Kenneth Spencer Research Library, drawings · Yale U., letters and drawings, corresp., and papers | Auckland Public Library, letters to Sir George Grey · Royal Museum, Edinburgh, letters to Sir William Jardine · South Australian Museum, Adelaide, letters to F. G. Waterhouse · State Library of Victoria, Melbourne, letters to Sir Frederick McCoy · U. Cam., department of zoology, letters to Sir William Jardine

Likenesses plaster plaque, *c*.1840, priv. coll. · T. H. Maguire, lithograph, 1849, BM, NPG; repro. in T. H. Maguire, *Portraits of honorary members of the Ipswich museum* (1852) · six photographs, *c*.1855–1865, repro. in Sauer, *John Gould the bird man* · J. E. McClees, photograph, 1857, Academy of Natural Sciences of Philadelphia · Maull & Polyblank, carte-de-visite, *c*.1860, Sauer Coll., Kansas City, Missouri · Maull & Fox, two photographs, 1875, priv. coll. · Robertson, portrait, 1878, priv. coll. · E. Edwards, photograph, NPG; repro. in L. Reeve, ed., *Portraits of men of eminence in literature, science and art* (1864), vol. 2 [*see illus.*] · portraits, repro. in Sauer, *John Gould the bird man*

Wealth at death under £70,000: probate, 12 March 1881, *CGPLA Eng. & Wales*

Gould, Sir Nathaniel (1661–1728), merchant and politician, was born on 3 December 1661, the third (but first surviving) son of John Gould, a wealthy nonconformist merchant of London, and his wife, Mary. In 1688 Gould married Frances, daughter of Sir John Hartopp, third baronet, of Freathby, Leicestershire; there were two daughters of the marriage. He was knighted on 14 April 1721.

It was after the revolution of 1688 that Gould first came to prominence when he became one of the largest suppliers of hemp, pitch, and tar to the Royal Navy; and in this capacity, immediately before the War of the Spanish Succession, he played an important part in providing the navy with Russian hemp from Archangel in place of the supplies that could no longer be obtained from Riga (beleaguered by the Russians). In 1694 Gould invested £2000 in the newly founded Bank of England and he was one of those instructed to draw up its by-laws. In 1697 he became a director of the bank and served continuously (with statutory intervals) down to his death. He was deputy governor of the bank from 1709 to 1711 and governor from 1711 to 1713. It was in the former role that, with the governor and two other directors, he attended the queen on 15 June 1710 to desire on the bank's behalf that she make no further ministerial changes following the replacement (as secretary of state) of Charles Spencer, third earl of Sunderland, by William Legge, first earl of Dartmouth.

Gould was a member of the group of so-called tobacco contractors who in 1698 had secured from Peter the Great the right to export tobacco from England to Russia. But to be able to do this the contractors needed to gain admission to the Russia Company and Gould played his part in the attack on the company. Eventually he gained admission to the company and became a director and sometime governor. After having been an interloper in the East India trade in 1696, he was a major investor in the 'new' East India flotation of 1698, and was both a director of the company and manager for the united East India trade over the years 1699–1708.

It was probably the affairs of the East India trade that propelled Gould into politics; with the 'old' East India Company still in existence, many members of the 'new' company sought election to parliament to protect the company's interests. Accordingly, he contested New Shoreham, a venal borough in Sussex, and won it in both of the 1701 elections. (Following the first election, however, he was successfully petitioned against and had to withdraw, but he survived the petition that followed the second.) He represented New Shoreham from 1701 to 1708 and from 1710 until his death. In parliament Gould's career was of little note until the later years of Anne's reign when, in 1713, he spoke three times (and very effectively) against the treaty of commerce with France. Following the accession of George I, he seconded a motion of 12 April 1717 that English trade to the Baltic could not be carried on unless the king of Sweden was brought to reason, and during the South Sea crisis he advocated strong measures against the directors.

Thereafter Gould spoke on two occasions (1723 and 1725) on customs matters, and in 1726 he published a pamphlet entitled *An Essay on the Public Debts*, which in 1727 prompted a rejoinder, *A State of the National Debt*, reputedly by William Pulteney, earl of Bath. It was on this subject that Gould made his last recorded parliamentary speech in February 1728. He died five months later, on 21 July 1728.

D. W. JONES, *rev.*

Sources J. M. Price, *The tobacco adventure to Russia: enterprise, politics, and diplomacy in the quest for a northern market for English colonial tobacco, 1676–1722* (1961) · HoP, *Commons, 1715–54* · will, PRO, PROB 11/623, sig. 208 · 'Gould, Nathaniel', HoP, *Commons, 1690–1715* [draft]

Gould, Nathaniel [Nat; *pseud.* Verax] **(1857–1919)**, novelist, was born at 27 York Street, Cheetham, Manchester on 21 December 1857, the only surviving child (two brothers died in infancy) of Nathaniel Gould, a Manchester tea merchant, and his wife, Mary Wright (*d.* 1897). Educated at Strathmore House, a private school in Southport, Gould excelled at sport and was already writing what he called 'blood-curdling' dramas. After his father died leaving insufficient funds to support his family, Gould left school and was apprenticed to his father's partner. Restlessness and a headstrong nature, which coloured much of his later professional career, also shaped his early years. Clashing with his employer, he left Manchester for his uncle's farm in Derbyshire. He returned briefly to the tea trade but in 1877 he became a journalist on the staff of the *Newark Advertiser* under the editorship of Cornelius Brown.

In 1884 Gould sailed for Australia and for the next eleven years he worked for the press. On the *Brisbane Telegraph* he wrote theatrical notices and was then put in charge of the racing page. While in Brisbane he married Elizabeth Madeleine, daughter of Francis Ruska; the couple had three sons and two daughters. Moving to the *Sydney Referee*, he was made chief racing correspondent under the name Verax. After resigning owing to a personal quarrel, Gould joined the *Bathurst Times* as leader writer. During this time he was commissioned to write a few chapters of a racing serial which were eventually published in the *Referee*. He followed its success back to Sydney and the serial was published in novel form as *The Double Event* by Routledge in 1891. Gould ascribed the immense success of this first book to the coincidence of its publication with the Melbourne Cup meeting—the great racing event of the year in Australia. The novel was dramatized in April 1893. Gould wrote seven or eight novels while in Sydney which were published by Routledge; they were all best-sellers.

In May 1895 Gould brought his family to England, settling in Bedfont, Middlesex. First with Routledge and then, in 1903, with John Long, Gould entered into, and kept, engagements to supply four novels and one shorter story each year. At his death he had written about 130 books, of which twenty-two were still waiting to be published at the rate of five each year. At that time the figure for his total sales was given as 24 million.

In later life Gould was on easy terms with his publishers, and with his work. He never haggled for terms nor exaggerated his importance; he disclaimed any literary pretensions and resolved to write stories that would hold the attention of a mass public from beginning to end. He was proud of the verdict of a clergyman that they 'could be safely put into the hands of any youth or girl'. With the exception of two books on Australia, *On and Off the Turf in Australia* (1895) and *Town and Bush* (1896), and his autobiography, *The Magic of Sport* (1909), Gould's stories were always 'novels of the turf', as he termed them, despite the fact that he rarely rode himself. He was attacked at the time for his caricatures of the aristocracy, but was always technically flawless on racing matters. Gould had a clear and economical prose style, if a tendency for melodramatic plotting; but increased sophistication in the popular fiction market as a result of improvements in education in the 1920s meant that Gould's novels had limited appeal much beyond his death. Gould died on 25 July 1919 at Newhaven, Bedfont, Staines, and was buried at Ashbourne, Derbyshire.

FREDERICK PAGE, *rev.* CLARE L. TAYLOR

Sources N. Gould, *The magic of sport: mainly autobiographical* (1909) · J. Welcome, 'Nat Gould: novelist of the turf', *London Magazine, a Monthly Review of Literature*, new ser., 7/5 (1967), 54–9 · WWW · private information (1927) · b. cert. · d. cert.
Likenesses Elliott & Fry, photograph, repro. in Gould, *Magic of sport*
Wealth at death £7794 17s. 11d.: probate, 10 Sept 1919, CGPLA Eng. & Wales

Gould, Robert (*b.* 1660?, *d.* in or before **1709**), poet, was left an orphan at an early age by parents of whom nothing is known. Information about his life must be gathered from his poetry, which is frequently autobiographical in character (see Sloane, who also has a fuller account of Gould's twenty-one publications). Having spent his youth toiling as a servant in London, Gould by some means acquired an education and in 1680 wrote *Love Given O're* (published 1683), a lively, coarse satire on the inconstancy of woman that was to be his most popular piece, the latest of its several editions being printed in 1710. On 17 June 1683, in London, he married Martha Roderick, with whom he had a daughter, Hannah. About this time he became connected with the household of his chief patron, James Bertie, earl of Abingdon, who in 1685 gave him employment on his estate at West Lavington, Wiltshire. Gould later became a schoolmaster in that county.

In 1689 Gould published *Poems*, which contained, along with verse epistles and occasional poetry, the potent 'Satire Against Man'. Gould was never afraid to speak his mind and railed also against the 'Stupid, Obstinate, Illiter'ate Race' of rural England (*Works of Mr. Robert Gould*, published posthumously by his widow in 1709, 2.159) and the upper classes, 'So vile, so loose, so profligate a crew' (ibid., 1.140); his censure of the latter was motivated in no small measure by the treatment he had endured as a servant. Of his two tragedies, *Innocence Distress'd* and *The Rival Sisters*, only the second was acted, appearing with some success at Drury Lane about October 1695, with music by Henry Purcell, John Blow, and others. Its performance had been opposed by Elizabeth Barry and Thomas Betterton, both of whom Gould had insulted in his caustic 'Satyr Against the Playhouse', published in *Poems*.

Gould's satires, which were chiefly influenced by his friend John Oldham (1653–1683), comprise about one half of Gould's output and were his most important work. Their subjects range from love and marriage to religion and politics, and often anticipate the satirical writings of Swift. As well as contributing a valuable illustration of the period, Gould's poetry is vigorous and well written; it continues to languish in undeserved neglect.

Ross Kennedy

Sources E. H. Sloane, *Robert Gould: seventeenth-century satirist* (1940) · *The works of Mr. Robert Gould* (1709) · W. Van Lennep and others, eds., *The London stage, 1660–1800*, pt 1: *1660–1700* (1965), 453 · *IGI*

Gould, Sir Ronald (1904–1986), schoolteacher and trade unionist, was born on 9 October 1904 in Midsomer Norton, a Somerset mining village. He was the eldest in the family of two sons and a daughter of Frederick Gould, shoe worker, active trade unionist involved in local politics, and later MP for Frome, and his wife, Emma Gay, who was 'in service' until her marriage. It was a close-knit Methodist family. Gould was educated, as a scholarship pupil, at Shepton Mallet grammar school; his parents struggled to pay for his books and daily travel. He then trained at the Methodist Westminster College in London, and gained his teaching certificate in 1924. He taught at Radstock council school in Somerset from 1924 to 1941. His career in local politics as a councillor began in 1924 and he became vice-chairman of Norton Radstock's urban district council four years later, serving as chairman from 1936 to 1946. In 1928 he married Nellie Denning (*d.* 1979), daughter of Joseph William Fish, a railway wagon repairer for the Great Western Railway. They had two sons. In 1941 Gould was appointed headmaster of Welton council school in Somerset, a post he held until 1946.

Active in the National Union of Teachers (NUT) from the start of his teaching career, within twelve years Gould was elected to the union's executive at the first attempt, and was its president in 1943–4. His talents had not gone unnoticed elsewhere. The post-war Labour government appointed him a member of the committee on conditions in the mining industry chaired by Sir John Forster. This was greeted with delight by his local mining community, who believed he would ensure the committee knew about the real conditions in the industry. He was also a founder member of the English advisory committee set up under the 1944 Education Act by the minister for education and architect of the act, R. A. Butler. The act was the subject of lengthy consultation between the government and its partners in education, not least the NUT, in which Gould was so prominent.

From 1947 to 1970 Gould was general secretary of the NUT, the oldest, largest, and most influential teachers' organization. Under his leadership the union's influence grew further. Gould and the union argued in favour of comprehensive education, having recognized early on that every child had talent which was too often left dormant or underdeveloped. Gould did not define ability narrowly: in his opinion every child developed at different rates in different areas of knowledge. His underlying philosophy was that 'man can be improved'. This principle encouraged him to extend the 'professional' education work of the NUT, and to help establish the international teachers' organization, the World Confederation of Organizations of the Teaching Profession (WCOTP). He was unanimously elected president of WCOTP in 1952, and was regularly re-elected to this post until he retired in 1970. By then WCOTP represented six million teachers and was the teachers' voice in UNESCO. In his last year as NUT general secretary he backed to the hilt a teachers' strike, which led to a raising of their salaries.

Gould and his counterpart Sir William Alexander, chairman of the Association of Education Committees, dominated post-war education. Gould described their relationship as that of two boxers: 'He's only another brother earning a living', he said. Together they averted the postponement of the raising of the school leaving age to fifteen in the late 1940s. But even they failed to convince a later Labour government, faced with another financial crisis combined with a teacher shortage, not to postpone its raising again, this time to sixteen. That reform had to wait until after Gould's retirement. However, they did prevent uncertificated staff from being brought in to ease the teacher shortage.

Gould was knighted in 1955 and held honorary degrees from Bristol (1943), British Columbia (1963), McGill (1964), St Francis Xavier (1969), Leeds (1971), and York (1972). A tall, warm-faced man, he was well aware of his own abilities but did not fail to recognize the talents of those around him. His upbringing and his years in education had taught him that wealth—or the lack of it—had nothing to do with intelligence or ability. Following his first wife's death, in 1985 he married Evelyn Little, daughter of Frederick Box, Salvation Army officer. Gould died in his sleep on 11 April 1986 at his home, 12 St John's Avenue, Goring by Sea, Worthing, Sussex.

Doug McAvoy, *rev.*

Sources R. Gould, *Chalk up the memory: an autobiography* (1976) · *Teacher* [newspaper of the National Union of Teachers], *passim* · *The Times* (16 April 1986) · *CGPLA Eng. & Wales* (1986) · private information (1996)
Wealth at death £210,475: probate, 19 Aug 1986, *CGPLA Eng. & Wales*

Gould, Rupert Thomas (1890–1948), horologist and broadcaster, was born on 16 November 1890 at St Edward's Road, Southsea, Hampshire, the second son of William Monk Gould (*d.* 1923), composer and musician, and Agnes Hilton (*d.* 1937), daughter of Thomas Skinner, medical doctor of Edinburgh. After a period at Eastman's Royal Naval Academy he was sent as a fifteen-year-old cadet to Britannia Royal Naval College at Dartmouth in 1906, with the intention of providing him with a career in the Royal Navy. The boy's intelligence was quickly apparent and he was top of his class almost throughout his schooling. He seems to have had an almost photographic memory, enabling him to amass considerable learning as a young man; he was especially interested in mechanical things, discovering a fascination for clocks and watches at a very early age. From May 1907 he began service as a midshipman and in the following seven years, during which time he underwent specialist training as a navigation officer, he served, among others, under captains Beatty and Jellicoe in the Mediterranean and home fleets and on the Yangtze (Yangzi) in China.

Although he looked the part—he was strikingly handsome, blond, blue-eyed, and 6 feet 4 inches tall—Gould's nature was actually quite unsuitable for a naval officer. His knowledge caused him to be rather pedantic; although he was generally kindly in demeanour, he was not a team player nor a good leader of men. He was, however, a talented artist, especially in pen and ink, was socially and intellectually assured, and had a ready wit, especially when he had a large audience. In spite of great self-confidence, he was unfortunately prone to violent nervous disorders, usually provoked by the stress of national crises. Thus, at the outbreak of the First World War, Gould suffered a severe mental breakdown and was invalided out of active service. During convalescence in Yorkshire in 1915 he met his future wife, Muriel Hilda (1894–1980), daughter of Thomas and Emily Estall; they were married on 9 June 1917. A son, Cecil, was born in 1918, followed by a daughter, Jocelyne, in 1920. In 1916 Gould had been found a job as one of the assistants to the hydrographer at the Admiralty, receiving promotion to lieutenant-commander in 1919.

In that year Gould decided to devote his spare time to writing a history of the marine chronometer, an essential navigational instrument for which he had developed a fascination during his training. This led him, in 1920, to discover the great marine timekeepers by John Harrison (1693–1776), decaying in the cellars of the Royal Observatory at Greenwich, and he vowed one day to restore them to their former glory. In the same year Gould was introduced by his friend the author Ralph Straus to the dining club the Sette of Odd Volumes (founded by the antiquary Bernard Quaritch in 1878) and over the next two decades the printed menus for the Sette often featured Gould's fine caricatures of members. The menus always included a distinguished selection of fine wines, and regular dinners with the Sette, which Gould evidently enjoyed to the full, combined with the stress of late nights writing his book, soon began to tell on the Goulds' marriage.

The year 1923 saw the publication of *The Marine Chronometer*, a book so thoroughly researched and well written that it still had no equal seventy-five years later. By this time Gould had sought, and received, permission to restore the Harrison timekeepers and this next Herculean task, to be done in his 'spare time', had already begun at his home in Epsom. Three years later, by which time his wife was finally losing patience with his obsession, Gould's overwork, combined with news of the general strike, precipitated a second nervous breakdown. On his discharge from hospital Gould found, to his dismay, that she had left him. After a vain attempt by Gould's mother (who had recently moved to nearby Ashtead) to reunite them, Muriel petitioned for judicial separation on grounds of cruelty (they were never divorced). She cited as

particularly distressing his excessive drinking, certain sexual predilections, and a series of fits associated with his breakdowns, during which she stated that he terrified her. The case, which was heard in 1927 at the High Court in the full glare of the national press, was won by Muriel and Gould lost everything: the custody of the children, his home and, because of the adverse publicity, his job at the Admiralty. He had no option but to go and live with his mother in Ashtead, at Downside, a large house in Woodfield Lane.

Once Gould had recovered from the stress of separation, the following ten years proved to be the most settled and prolific of his life. At Downside, in a specially converted loft workshop, he completed the restoration of all the Harrison timekeepers, during which time he also wrote many articles for the horological and maritime press and compiled extensive notes for a history of the typewriter, an instrument he amassed a very large collection of at Downside. His major publications at this time, however, consisted of a series of books about unsolved scientific mysteries; *Oddities* (1928) and *Enigmas* (1929) were followed by *The Case for the Sea Serpent* (1930). Gould was one of the first people to investigate the Loch Ness monster mystery systematically, and published his work *The Loch Ness Monster and Others* in 1934. He had always been interested in the history and the rules of tennis (he was an active player himself, though by all accounts not very sporting), and on many occasions in the 1930s he was engaged to umpire at Wimbledon, often on the centre court.

In 1934 Gould was asked by the programmers for BBC radio to speak every week on *Children's Hour* under the name Stargazer, giving a fifteen-minute chat on any subject which he felt might interest the young 'listeners in'. His broadcasts, live and (until wartime) without any script, continued, off and on, for over ten years and included at least one early television broadcast from Alexandra Palace. In 1935, as well as writing a fine small biography of Captain Cook, Gould completed his restoration of all the Harrison timekeepers and gave a historic presentation on John Harrison and his timekeepers to the Society for Nautical Research at the Drapers' Hall in London in that year.

Two years later his mother died, and Gould was obliged to sell up and leave Downside, the estate passing directly to his children, with a small income only to Gould. It is probably for this reason that he was remembered by many of his contemporaries as being decidedly mean with money.

In 1937 Gould had tried hard to gain a curatorial position at the newly opened National Maritime Museum at Greenwich, where the Harrison timekeepers were on display, but the scandal of 1927 was not forgotten and he was refused any employment. Until 1939 he lived at the Red House, a residential hotel in Leatherhead, but the looming international crisis pushed him into his last and worst mental breakdown. One of the few things he had inherited was his mother's car, and on the day war broke out in September that year he packed what effects he still had and drove aimlessly west—away from Europe and war—arriving at Shaftesbury before finally collapsing. During a stay in a nursing home there he fell in love with Grace Ingrams, one of the nurses, and moved in with her and her mother in Wiltshire for the duration. During the war, after convalescence, Gould was employed again by the BBC to broadcast as the Stargazer, and, in October 1942, he was invited to join *The Brains Trust*. He was remembered for being the most frequent sparring partner of another *Brains Trust* panellist, the well-known philosopher Professor Cyril Joad. Gould was noted for his ability to answer even the most esoteric factual questions with his characteristic eloquence and pungent wit. When the panel was once asked, tongue in cheek, 'What is the difference between "fresh air" and "a draught"?' it was Gould who immediately replied: 'it's fresh air when you open the railway carriage window yourself and a draught when somebody else does!'

Since the late 1930s Gould had become very overweight and in 1944, probably owing to the vigorous tennis matches he still played, and perhaps also to his lifelong habit of pipe smoking, he suffered a severe heart attack, compounded by the appearance of Parkinson's disease. In 1945 Grace Ingrams and Gould separated. After a hopeless attempt to reunite with his wife which lasted just two weeks, Gould, now an increasingly sick man, went to live with friends at Harbledown near Canterbury. Ironically, at this late stage the National Maritime Museum decided, in 1945, that it would employ Gould as a curator after all, only to find that, within just seven days of having started, he had to resign owing to ill health. Realizing that this truly great horologist was not long for this world, in 1947 Gould's colleagues in the British Horological Institute awarded him their gold medal, the highest honour the institute can bestow. He described it as the crowning moment of his career. He died on 5 October 1948 at the Kent and Canterbury Hospital, Canterbury, of a combination of Parkinsonism and paroxysmal tachycardia. Only his son and a handful of others were at his funeral in Ashtead parish church when he was buried on 11 October, alongside his mother.

Gould's part in the restoration of Harrison's chronometers was dramatized to good effect in Dava Sobel's bestselling book *Longitude* (1996) and in its subsequent television adaptation (1999), where he was played by Jeremy Irons.   JONATHAN BETTS

Sources private information (2004) · C. Gould, 'Tosca's creed: autobiography of an art historian', 1992 [unpubd MS] · H. A. Lloyd, F. Hope-Jones, and D. W. Evans, *Horological Journal*, 90 (1948), 655–6 · *Navy Lists* (1906–27) · judicial separation papers, PRO, XC6129 J77/2421/5570 · b. cert. · m. cert. · d. cert. · *CGPLA Eng. & Wales* (1949)
Archives British Horological Institute, Upton Hall, Newark, Nottinghamshire, Gould collection of lantern slides and glassplate negatives of clocks and watches · NMM, Gould relics and MS notebooks of Harrison restorations · NMM, papers relating to naval chronometers · priv. coll., drawings and photographs · Scott Polar RI, corresp. and papers | priv. coll., Stewart corresp. | SOUND BBC Sound Archives, London, Brains Trust recordings
Likenesses photographs, priv. coll.
Wealth at death £900 2*s*. 7*d*.: probate, 21 Jan 1949, *CGPLA Eng. & Wales*

Gould, Sabine Baring- (1834–1924), Church of England clergyman, author, and folksong collector, born at Dix's Field, Exeter, on 28 January 1834, was the elder of two sons of Edward Baring-Gould, a captain in the armed forces of the East India Company, invalided out in 1830 as the result of an accident in India when still a young man. He returned home to the uneventful life of squire of Lew Trenchard, Devon, and in 1832 married his first wife, Sophia Charlotte, daughter of Admiral Francis Godolphin Bond RN. Cold, stern, and with a low threshold of boredom, Captain Baring-Gould in 1837 took his wife, young son, and servants to the continent until 1844, when they returned home to begin Sabine Baring-Gould's English education. He boarded at King's College, London, from 1844 to 1846, and in 1847 he attended Warwick grammar school.

Sabine's delicate health persuaded his willing father to resume the family sojourns in Europe, visiting France, Belgium, Italy, Germany, and Austria. The sons, Sabine and William, were educated by tutors and travel. Sabine Baring-Gould had a photographic memory, read voraciously, and picked up languages with ease. At sixteen he organized the excavation of a buried Roman pavement at Pau, and at seventeen he determined his three tasks in life: to help in the spiritual rousing of the people, to restore the family home of Lew House, and to restore Lew Trenchard church. In 1852 the Baring-Goulds settled in Tavistock, near Dartmoor, and in 1853 Baring-Gould entered Clare College, Cambridge, as a student of the classics, in which he was poorly versed. Tall, handsome, and romantically religious, he was attracted by the Tractarian movement, and hoped to become a priest, but in 1856, after graduating BA with a pass degree, he encountered parental opposition. As elder son he had to become squire, thus leaving the family living for his brother.

Disappointed, Baring-Gould turned to teaching, starting at the choir school of St Barnabas, Pimlico, where he met the Revd C. F. Lowder, a well-known Tractarian. He moved to Lancing, a Woodard school, and then to its associate school, Hurstpierpoint College. But in 1863 his parents changed their minds about his ordination, for William refused to go into the church; in 1864 Baring-Gould was made deacon at Ripon, and became curate to the Revd John Sharp, rector of Horbury, Yorkshire. In 1865 Baring-Gould was ordained priest and dispatched to the rough district of Horbury Brig to organize a church mission.

Baring-Gould relished the task, worked day and night, set up an evening school, and won all hearts by his storytelling. Four of his hymns, 'On the Resurrection Morning', written in December 1863 on his mother's death; 'Onward, Christian soldiers', written at Hurstpierpoint College in 1864; and 'Through the night of doubt and sorrow', translated from the Danish, and 'Now the day is over', both written at Horbury Brig, became favourites at the mission.

In 1866 Baring-Gould met his future wife, Grace Taylor, at Horbury Brig. She was a beautiful factory girl of sixteen, who had been working since she was ten years old. Both sets of parents (in 1865 Captain Baring-Gould had married

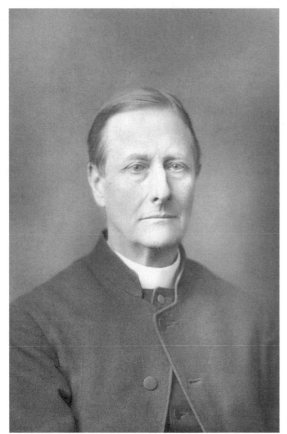

Sabine Baring-Gould (1834–1924), by W. & D. Downey, pubd 1893

began the *Lives of the Saints*, published in fifteen volumes; it comprised 3600 biographies arranged in order of the saints' days, Baring-Gould working at them from 1872 to 1877. The Roman Catholic church put them on the Index. The *Lives* was reprinted in 1897–8 and again in 1914. Three volumes—the British, the English, and the Northumbrian saints—were reprinted in 1990. He also wrote a powerful novel, *Mehalah* (1880), likened by the poet Swinburne to *Wuthering Heights*.

When his father died in 1872, Baring-Gould inherited the Devon estate, but his elderly uncle remained the incumbent at Lew Trenchard. In addition, Baring-Gould had to support his brother, William, his stepmother, his young half-brother, Arthur, and his half-sister, Lilah. He therefore let Lew House, remained at East Mersea, and frequently took his family abroad, partly for health reasons and partly for research. In his absence the parish was looked after by the Revd J. M. Gatrill. His uncle died in 1881, whereupon Baring-Gould presented himself to the family living and moved into Lew House.

Baring-Gould was a popular parson whose forceful sermons attracted people from outside the parish. He revived harvest festivals and encouraged activities for children. His books paid for new cottages, repairs to farms, and the restoration of the manor house and the church. He wrote over forty novels; over sixty theological volumes of sermons, hymns, and devotional books; twenty-four guide and travel books; a score of general interest books; and collections of folksongs. His books were constantly reprinted, many remaining in print at the end of the twentieth century.

Baring-Gould's folksong collecting began in earnest in 1888, with help from the Revd H. Fleetwood Sheppard and Dr. K. A. Bussell. He recorded the tunes accurately but did not hesitate to write fresh words if he considered the existing ones to be indecent. Thus 'Kit has Lost her Key [Cow]' became 'Strawberry Fair'. The words of 'Widecombe Fair' are believed to be authentic. He encouraged his daughter Joan to teach folk dancing in the village. From 1904 he was a friend and collaborator of Cecil Sharp, the folksong and dance collector. Baring-Gould believed his most important work to have been the folksong collecting. He hoped it would 'resuscitate the traditional music of the English', and to that end he deposited copies of the songs and tunes he collected in the Free Municipal Library in Plymouth, thus making them available to all.

Baring-Gould and the Revd Robert Burnard examined Dartmoor's past, and were founder members of the Dartmoor Exploration Committee in 1894. Baring-Gould also belonged to the Devonshire Association and was president in 1895. He was a member of the Royal Institution of Cornwall, and president for ten years from 1897. He won the Henwood gold medal for his presidential addresses on the 'Early history of Cornwall' and on 'The Celtic saints'. In 1918 Clare College made him an honorary fellow.

Baring-Gould spent his last years writing his *Reminiscences* and two religious books, *The Church Revival* (1918), and *The Evangelical Revival* (1920). He died at Lew House on 2

Lavinia Snow, a younger family friend who, with her mother, had accompanied the Baring-Goulds to the continent in 1847) opposed the marriage, but Baring-Gould persisted. Grace Taylor lived for two years in York with a female relative of John Sharp, acquiring an education. On 25 May 1868 the couple were married by Sharp at Horbury Brig, no relatives of bride or groom being present. Five sons and ten daughters were born, one daughter dying in infancy. Grace Baring-Gould was self-possessed and much loved. She died on 8 April 1916, and the words 'Dimidium animae meae' (Half my soul) were inscribed over her tombstone. Baring-Gould's first novel, *Through Flood and Flame* (1868), is held to be partly autobiographical.

In 1867 Baring-Gould became perpetual curate at Dalton, Yorkshire, where he wrote steadily, following his *Book of Were-Wolves* (1865) and *Curious Myths of the Middle Ages* (1866, 1868). His *Origin and Development of Religious Belief* (1869, 1870), suggested by Darwin's theories, was condemned by Roman Catholics, Anglicans, and extreme protestants, but W. E. Gladstone liked the book, and in 1871, when prime minister, he offered Baring-Gould the crown living of East Mersea, Essex. There Baring-Gould wrote *The Vicar of Morwenstowe: a Life of Robert Stephen Hawker* (1876), criticized for glaring inaccuracies but loved for its true flavour of Hawker and the west country. He

January 1924, and was buried in Lew Trenchard churchyard next to his wife. Above his tombstone was inscribed 'Paravi lucernam Christo meo' (I have prepared a lantern for my Christ). BRENDA COLLOMS

Sources B. H. C. Dickinson, *Sabine Baring-Gould* (1970) · W. E. Purcell, *Onward Christian soldier* (1957) · B. Colloms, 'Rev. S. Baring-Gould', *Victorian country parsons* (1977), 236–48 · W. Addison, 'Sabine Baring-Gould', *The English country parson* (1947), 204–14 · D. Roberts, 'If one had to pick the strangest Victorian …', *The Smithsonian*, 24/4 (1993), 74–82 · S. Baring-Gould, *Early reminiscences, 1834–1864* (1923) · S. Baring-Gould, *Further reminiscences, 1864–1894* (1925) · M. Karpeles and A. H. Fox-Strangways, *Cecil Sharp: his life and work*, rev. edn (1967)
Archives Devon RO, corresp. with publishers and papers relating to his appointments; corresp., notebooks, diary, literary MSS, etc. · Plymouth and West Devon RO, sermon notes; letters and photographs | Bodl. Oxf., letters to Hannah Taylor · Devon RO, letters to Mason · Gwent RO, Cwmbrau, corresp. with Sir Joseph Bradney relating to history of Caerwent · NL Scot., letters to Blackwoods · NL Wales, letters to D. R. Daniel · NYPL, letters to F. Bligh Bond · Ransom HRC, corresp. with John Lane · University of Bristol Library, letters to James Baker
Likenesses W. & D. Downey, photograph, pubd 1893, NPG [*see illus.*] · M. Fisher, portrait, 1920, priv. coll. · S. Carter, portrait, Exeter City Library · C. Montimore, pencil sketch, NPG · A. Woolfitt, photographs, repro. in Roberts, 'If one had to pick the strangest Victorian …' · photograph, Vaughan Williams Memorial Library, London · photographs, repro. in Dickinson, *Sabine Baring-Gould* · photographs, repro. in Purcell, *Onward Christian soldier*
Wealth at death £16,132 11s. 6d.: probate, 3 March 1924, CGPLA Eng. & Wales

Gould, Thomas (1657–1734), Roman Catholic priest, was probably born in Cork. He arrived in France about 1678, settled in Poitiers, and studied theology at the Irish Jesuit college there. He quickly came to the notice of the local bishop, Hardouin Fortin de la Hoguette, who appointed him chaplain to the Ursulines in Thouars in 1681 or 1682. Thouars was home to a community devoted to the conversion of Huguenot gentlewomen and Gould became involved in its activities. His zeal won him the admiration of the duke de la Trémoille who made him a canon and treasurer of the Sainte-Chapelle at Thouars. It also brought him to the notice of the chancellor and the solicitor-general to such an extent that about 1687 he was appointed *missionaire du roi pour le Poitou*. His eirenic, scripture-based conversion tactics were directed mostly at upper-class Huguenots and gained many converts. He recognized the importance of integrating new converts not only into the doctrine but also into the social and cultural fabric of Catholicism. Though he tacitly approved of force as a means of conversion he himself preferred to rely on persuasion, good example, and practical inducements. He did not always receive the co-operation of local Catholic clergy. Critical of their educational standards, he complained that badly educated clergy were bound to alienate new converts. After his death a family member was commissioned to continue his missionary work.

While Gould's practical approach to conversion work won him the admiration of church and crown it also excited the enmity of some of his stricter co-religionists. In 1705 he published *Lettre d'un missionaire à un gentilhomme du Bas Poitou, touchant la véritable croyance de l'église catholique contre les dogmes qui luy sont faussement imputez dans les escrits des ministres*, in which he defended himself against charges of heresy, stoutly criticizing the superstition of certain Catholic preachers. Pierre Rival wrote a response, which was translated into English and published in London in 1724. In his work Gould based his arguments almost exclusively on scripture and followed Bossuet's example of citing non-Catholic theologians. The 1705 text was revised and republished in 1709 as *La véritable croyance de l'église catholique et les preuves de tous les points de sa doctrine, fondées sur l'escriture sainte*. It enjoyed great success. To the 1720 edition of the work he appended a new text entitled *Les preuves de la doctrine de l'église, fondées sur l'escriture sainte. Pour servir de réponse à un libelle intitulé, Antidote, contre la lettre d'un missionaire touchant la croyance de l'église Romaine*. In this he responded to criticism of his orthodoxy. In 1724 he published, with the help of a government subvention, a text on the eucharist entitled *Traité du saint sacrifice de la messe, avec l'explication des cérémonies qui s'y observent, et la maniere d'y assister dévotement, selon l'esprit de la primitive église. Adressé à une dame de qualité nouvellement convertie*. All his works enjoyed great popularity and were widely circulated to new converts. In 1727 the French crown assumed the publication costs of his *Entretiens où l'on explique la doctrine de l'église catholique par la sainte ecriture*. In this work Gould drew heavily on his knowledge of the Anglican establishments in Ireland and England. His last work appeared in 1733 entitled *Recueil des opérations que font les protestants aux catholiques sur quelques articles de foi controversés*. He was also the author of *Abrégé des Psaumes de David*. Apart from his published work his regular reports to Paris on the progress of his missionary activities provide a unique insight into the religious policies of the French *ancien régime*. He died in France in 1734.

THOMAS O'CONNOR

Sources Y. Krumenacker, *Les protestants du Poitou au XVIIIᵉ siècle, 1681–1789* (1998) · R. Hayes, *Biographical dictionary of Irishmen in France* (1949) · J. F. Dreux-Duradier, *Histoire littéraire du Poitou* (Niort, 1842–9); repr. (Geneva, 1969)
Archives Archives Nationales, Paris, series O' · Bibliothèque Nationale, Paris, MS Joly de Fleury

Goulding, Edward Alfred, Baron Wargrave (1862–1936), politician and financier, was born in Cork on 5 November 1862, the second son in the family of three sons and four daughters of William Goulding (1817–1884), businessman and MP, and his second wife, Maria Heath (d. 1892), daughter of Edward Manders of Dublin and his wife, Ann. Sir William Joshua Goulding, first baronet (1856–1925), was his elder brother. He was educated at Clifton College and at St John's College, Cambridge, where he was president of the Cambridge Union in 1885, the year of his graduation. He was admitted to the Inner Temple in 1884 and called to the bar in 1887, but his real interests lay in politics. A member of the London county council between 1895 and 1901, where he acted as a whip for the moderates, he was Conservative MP for Devizes from 1895 to 1906 and for Worcester from 1908 until his elevation to the peerage, as

Baron Wargrave, in November 1922. He was created a baronet in June 1915, and was sworn of the privy council in June 1918.

Goulding never held ministerial office, although Bonar Law claimed to have considered him for promotion in 1915. Unimpressive in parliamentary debate, with, according to the *Evening Standard*, 'a nervous hurried manner [and] little sense of humour' (18 July 1936), he was also a constant critic of the inactivity of his own party leadership. He condemned in turn Salisbury's caution in resisting Russian expansion into China in 1898 and his government's proposals for army reform in 1901, Balfour's hesitation on tariff reform, and Baldwin's entire lacklustre leadership. Committed to social reform and imperialism, he was an early champion of old-age pensions, fought for the extension of workmen's compensation and shorter hours for shopworkers, supported the payment of MPs and Conservative working-class candidates, and was a member of the Unionist Social Reform Committee. But above all he was a dedicated supporter of the tariff reform programme launched by Joseph Chamberlain in 1903.

Goulding was a founder member of the Tariff Reform League and from 1904 to 1911 chairman of its organization committee, where his role as 'Joe's Man Friday' provided the opportunity to show his outstanding gifts as a political organizer and wire-puller. Chamberlain thought him the best organizer he had ever known. Tall, slim, and genial, his personal qualities allied with his wealth, energy, and flair for intrigue enabled Goulding to build up a position of exceptional influence in a divided and weakly led party. His house, Wargrave Hall, on the banks of the Thames in Berkshire, where Goulding indulged his enthusiasm for gardening, was a regular weekend retreat for senior tariff reformers and Conservatives; his position in the Tariff Reform League gave him influence in the constituencies and on the selection of candidates; as a member of the Compatriots Club and chairman of the Constitutional Club, which served as his political base, he had close contact with the younger generation of tariff reform enthusiasts, including the extremist 'confederacy'. 'But for him', J. L. Garvin wrote with slight exaggeration on the death of his old friend and fellow campaigner, 'Bonar Law's surprising succession to the Unionist leadership [in 1911] could not have been brought about … Its success was ensured by EDWARD GOULDING as the prince of backbenchers, and by his influence in the lobbies' (*The Observer*, 19 July 1936).

Accused of extremism himself, Goulding's power rested in reality on his pragmatism. He led the negotiations in January–February 1909 with the most prominent Conservative free-traders for a compromise that would allow them to remain in parliament, and took a leading role in proposing, drafting, and securing signatures for the memorial to Bonar Law in 1913 that enabled Law to retain the party leadership while abandoning preferential tariffs on foodstuffs, even though Goulding recognized that this meant the end of the tariff reform crusade. The stigma of factional extremism nevertheless remained, and he was never offered a position in the official Conservative Party

Organization. He was a founder member of the Unionist Business Committee in 1915 and acted as intermediary between the breakaway National Party and Bonar Law in 1918, but with the demise of tariff reform Goulding increasingly turned his attention to his business interests.

Those interests, apart from his directorship of the family firm, W. and H. M. Goulding, manufacturers of chemical fertilizers, were nevertheless often extensions of Goulding's political connections. J. F. Remnant, a friend from the bar, the LCC, and the tariff reform campaign, was co-director of the Assam Company, the Central Electricity Supply Company, Continental Union Gas, St John del Rey, the Trustees' Corporation, and the Westminster Electric Supply Corporation. At the end of the war, the merger operations of another tariff reform associate, Dudley Docker, brought Goulding onto the boards of the Metropolitan Carriage Wagon and Finance Company, Metropolitan Vickers Electrical (Associated Electrical Industries), and Anglo-Argentine Tramways. The connection drew Goulding briefly back into politics as the first chairman of the parliamentary industrial group, formed in February 1919.

But the key figure in Goulding's second career was the Canadian financier Max Aitken (Lord Beaverbrook), whom he met in 1910. Goulding introduced Aitken into British politics, and Aitken, who later acknowledged Goulding as his political mentor, became a close friend and business adviser. In 1912 he made Goulding a director of Rolls-Royce, of which Goulding became chairman in 1921, and subsequently of London Express Newspapers and the Colonial Bank. A shared commitment to empire and hostility to Baldwin led both to draw satisfaction from the Conservative Party's defeat in 1929. Goulding's last political venture was to support Beaverbrook's Empire Free Trade Crusade from 1929 to 1931, although he feared that food duties would preclude success. Actively involved behind the scenes, he excused himself as too old and too busy for public campaigning. His final public duty was to become chairman in 1934 of the Central London Electricity Distribution Committee, established, like the earlier Central Electricity Supply Company, of which he was deputy chairman, to consolidate London's electricity supply.

In the mid-1920s Goulding moved to Shiplake Court, Shiplake, Henley-on-Thames, Oxfordshire, where he died on 17 July 1936. He was buried at Ruscombe after a funeral at Twyford parish church on the 21st. He never married, and the title became extinct with his death. The bulk of his estate, after minor dispositions, including £10,000 to R. H. Cale, secretary of the Constitutional Club, passed to his great-nephew Sir (William) Basil Goulding, third baronet (1909–1982).　　　　　　　　ALAN SYKES

Sources HLRO, Wargrave MSS · HLRO, Beaverbrook MSS · HLRO, A. Bonar Law MSS · A. Chisholm and M. Davie, *Beaverbrook: a life* (1992) · R. P. T. Davenport-Hines, *Dudley Docker: the life and times of a trade warrior* (1984) · Burke, *Peerage* · Venn, *Alum. Cant.* · *Directory of Directors* · W. A. S. Hewins, *The apologia of an imperialist: forty years of empire policy*, 2 vols. (1929) · *Stock Exchange Official Intelligence* · *Stock*

Exchange Year Book • A. S. T. Griffith-Boscawen, *Fourteen years in parliament* (1907) • *Real old tory politics: the political diaries of Robert Sanders, Lord Bayford, 1910–35*, ed. J. Ramsden (1984) • Rolls-Royce PLC Archives • *The Times* (18 July 1936) • *The Times* (22 July 1936)

Archives HLRO, corresp. and papers | CAC Cam., corresp. with Lord Fisher • CAC Cam., Croft MSS • HLRO, corresp. with Lord Beaverbrook • HLRO, letters to Ralph Blumenfeld • HLRO, corresp. with Andrew Bonar Law • U. Birm., Joseph and Austen Chamberlain MSS • W. Sussex RO, Maxse MSS

Likenesses photograph, HL, Wargrave MSS, obits.

Wealth at death £253,407 8s. 9d.: probate, 23 Sept 1936, *CGPLA Eng. & Wales*

Goulding, Frederick (1842–1909), printer of etchings and lithographs, was born at Holloway Road, Islington, London, on 7 October 1842. His father, John Fry Goulding, foreman printer to Day & Son, was married in 1833 to Elizabeth Rogers, who belonged to an old family of Spitalfields weavers, and his grandfather, John Golding, also a copper-plate printer, was apprenticed in 1779 to a still earlier William Golding, a copper-plate printer of St Botolph without Bishopsgate, London. In 1854 Frederick Goulding was sent to a day school conducted at the National Hall, Holborn, by William Lovett, a well-known Chartist. On 24 January 1857 he was apprenticed to Day & Son, at 6 Gate Street, Lincoln's Inn Fields, London, originally a firm of lithographic printers, but at this date concerned chiefly with the printing of engravings, to which branch of their business Goulding was attached. In his spare time during his apprenticeship he studied at the schools of art in Wilmington Square, Clerkenwell, and Castle Street, Long Acre, while also attending lectures at the Royal Academy Schools. In 1859 he acted as 'devil' to James McNeill Whistler in the printing of some of his etchings, and in the same year assisted his father in the printing of a series of etchings by Queen Victoria and Prince Albert. At the Great Exhibition of 1862, from May until November, he gave daily demonstrations of copper-plate printing for Day & Son, and began there a close friendship with Sir Francis Seymour Haden which lasted to the end of his life. On 16 December 1865 he married Melanie Marie Alexandrine Piednue; they had three sons and a daughter.

By this time Goulding was a master of his craft, and began to use his spare time in the evenings and on Saturdays working for private clients at his own home, Kingston House, 53 Shepherd's Bush Road, London. Among the artists for whom he printed were Seymour Haden, Legros, Whistler, and Samuel Palmer. In 1881 he felt justified in launching a printing business of his own, and built a studio, much extended later, in the garden at the back of Kingston House. Among artists whose etchings he printed were Frank Short, William Strang, Joseph Pennell, Rodin, Tissot, Jongkind, and R. W. Macbeth; indeed, there were few etchers or engravers who did not call for Goulding's assistance. In *About Etching* (1879) Haden described Goulding as 'the best printer of etchings in England just now'. From 1876 to 1882 he acted as assistant to Alphonse Legros in an etching class held weekly at the National Art Training School, later the Royal College of Art, and from 1882 to 1891, when he was succeeded by Sir Frank Short, was entirely responsible for running the class. From 1876 to

1879 he also assisted Legros in an etching class held at the Slade School. On 7 February 1890, at a full meeting of the council of the Royal Society of Painter-Etchers, he was unanimously elected the first master printer to the society.

In Goulding's case the craft of plate printing depended on something more than mere handicraft. He combined with remarkable dexterity of workmanship a singular understanding of each artist's aim, and so played a major part in the etching revival of the second half of the nineteenth century. He also produced over thirty etchings of his own. Mostly landscapes in Amsterdam and Bruges, they are datable to the 1870s and 1890s.

After five years' continuous ill health, Goulding died of influenza at his home on 5 March 1909, and was buried in Kensal Green cemetery.

MARTIN HARDIE, rev. PAUL GOLDMAN

Sources M. Hardie, *Frederick Goulding, master printer of copper plates* (1910) • Thieme & Becker, *Allgemeines Lexikon*, vol. 14 • R. Lister, *Samuel Palmer and his etchings* (1969) • K. Lochnan, *The etchings of James McNeill Whistler* (1984) • *CGPLA Eng. & Wales* (1909) • d. cert.

Likenesses J.-E. Lacretelle, pencil drawing, 1880, BM • W. Strang, drypoint, 1906, BM • A. Hartley, oils; known to be in family possession in 1912 • E. Walker, three photo-engravings, BM • two photogravures, BM

Wealth at death £25,356 2s. 5d.: resworn probate, 20 April 1909, *CGPLA Eng. & Wales*

Gouldman, Francis (c.1607–1688/9), Church of England clergyman and lexicographer, was the son of Richard Gouldman of Norfolk. Having been educated in London, by Thomas Farnaby, Francis matriculated as pensioner of Christ's College, Cambridge, in 1623; he proceeded BA in 1626–7 and MA in 1630. On 26 March 1634 he succeeded George Gouldman as rector of South Ockendon, Essex. In April 1644 he appeared at Ongar before the commission for scandalous ministers for Essex, having been denounced for a range of crimes, including preaching but once on the sabbath, never praying for the parliament, and saying that it went against his conscience to pay the rates to that parliament and to lend money to Lord Fairfax: 'shall I take my children's bread, and give it to the Lord Fairfax'. The committee adjudged him 'ill affected, and an Idle Minister', and he was duly ejected from his living, worth about £120 p.a., his annual personal estate being estimated 'near 50 lb' (Baker MS 27, 24(a), fol. 464). A year later financial support of a fifth was awarded to his wife, Abigail, to support her and five children.

On ejection Gouldman appears to have moved to London; his daughter Jane married in St Margaret Pattens in 1648. At the Restoration, Gouldman regained possession of his living. Meanwhile, he had engaged in the editing and collaborative authorship of theological works. John Worthington names him as publisher of John Bois's posthumous *Veteris interpretis* (1655). He also collaborated with John Pearson and other dispossessed clergy on the nine-volume *Critici sacri* (1660).

Gouldman's last publication, and that for which he is best known today, was in the very different field of bilingual lexicography, namely *A copious dictionary in three parts: (I) the English before the Latin … (II) The Latin before the English*

... (III) *The proper names of persons, places, and other things necessary to the understanding of historians and poets* (1664). Worthington in 1662 had reported this as a revision of Thomas's Latin dictionary, and indeed Gouldman acknowledges Thomas as a key source, ending a résumé of the history of Latin lexicography, with special reference to 'our own Writers of Dictionaries', with the claim that 'nothing considerable, nothing desireable, nothing profitable in Thomasius, Rider, or [Francis] Holyoak ... be said to be wanting', and finding Christopher Wase's *Dictionarium minus* (1662) 'a book of good use' (preface). Thomas and Rider–Holyoke indeed provided the material for the bulk of Gouldman's Latin-English entries, as well as for his geographical and poetical dictionary, while for the English-Latin section he used Rider–Holyoke, supplemented from Wase and thus ultimately from the English–French lexicographical tradition of Cotgrave–Sherwood (he estimates his dictionary to contain more 'by a third or fourth part' than those of his predecessors). Innovations included putting 'leading words generally into their natural order and due place' (preface). Second, third, and fourth editions of the dictionary followed in 1669, 1674 (with additions by William Robertson), and 1678 (enlarged by Anthony Scattergood, fellow contributor to *Critici sacri*). However, by 1678 it had significant competition in the shape of dictionaries by Thomas Holyoke (1677), Elisha Coles (1677), and Adam Littleton (1678), all of whom were heavily indebted to it—in the case of Holyoke without acknowledgement. Gouldman himself was already 'sick and weake in body' (will, dated 26 September 1677) and no further editions were published. Gouldman died in Lancashire either at the close of 1688 or early in 1689, and was buried there. His successor in the rectory, Offspring Blackall, was appointed on 24 January 1689, and Gouldman's will was proved on 12 May 1690 by his daughter Jane Frost.   JANET BATELY

Sources 'An account of ejections of the parochial clergy, taken from the books of the committee for plundred ministers', CUL, Mm 1.38, Baker MS 27, 21(b), fol. 427 · 'Ejections of parochial clergy: witnesses against Fras. Gouldman, rector of S. Okenden', CUL, Mm 1.38, Baker MS 27, 24(a), fol. 464 · R. Newcourt, *Repertorium ecclesiasticum parochiale Londinense*, 2 (1710), 447–9 · J. Worthington, *Miscellanies ... also a collection of epistles*, ed. E. Fowler (1704), Epistle 22 (9 Jan 1662), 308 · *The diary and correspondence of Dr John Worthington*, ed. J. Crossley, 2/1, Chetham Society, 36 (1855), 96–7 · J. Walker, *An attempt towards recovering an account of the numbers and sufferings of the clergy of the Church of England*, pt 2 (1714), 251 · J. Peile, *Biographical register of Christ's College, 1505–1905, and of the earlier foundation, God's House, 1448–1505*, ed. [J. A. Venn], 1 (1910), 350 · J. E. B. Mayor, 'Francis Gouldman the lexicographer', *N&Q*, 2nd ser., 3 (1857), 86 · De W. T. Starnes, *Renaissance dictionaries: English–Latin and Latin–English* (1954), 278–90 · *DNB* · parish register, South Ockendon · will, PRO, PROB 11/399, sig. 70
Wealth at death money, debts, goods, and chattels to daughter: will, PRO, PROB 11/399, sig. 70

Goulston, Theodore (*bap.* **1575**, *d.* **1632**), physician, the eldest son of William Goulston, rector of Thrapston, Northamptonshire, and his wife, Elizabeth, was baptized on 6 March 1575. He matriculated at Peterhouse, Cambridge, as a sizar in 1591, taking his BA in 1595. He then transferred to Merton College, Oxford (BA 1595), and was

elected a fellow in 1596. He graduated MA in July 1600, and held the junior Linacre fellowship in medicine at Merton from 1604 to 1611. In 1606 Goulston left to pursue the study of law at Gray's Inn, London, but soon returned to medicine, practising in his father's parish at Wymondham, Leicestershire. In 1610 he was allowed the privilege of taking simultaneously his Oxford MB, his MD, and his licence to practice, 'being now much in esteem for his knowledge [of physic]'. He then moved to London, where he was examined before the College of Physicians in 1610 and elected a fellow in 1611. Goulston was a talented classical scholar, publishing in 1619 at London his *Versio Latina et paraphrasis in Aristotelis Rhetoricam*, whose notes and translation were reprinted along with a Greek edition of the text at Cambridge in 1696. In 1623 he published in London his *Aristotelis de Poetica liber conversus et analytica methodo illustrata*. Both works were dedicated to Prince Charles.

In medicine Goulston continued the work of John Caius in seeking to improve contemporary medicine by refining the text and interpretation of its major classical authority, the Greek physician Galen. Goulston took over into his medical books, especially into his copy of the 1538 Greek edition of Galen (partially preserved in Dublin, Marsh Library, P.3, fols. 2, 18, 19, 21 and 22) notes and readings taken from other sources. He had collated in London Caius' own notes on Galen (now Eton College, Fc 2, 6–8), as well as a manuscript from the royal library and a lost Codex Adelphi. Some, but by no means all, of his notes were incorporated in his *Versio, variae lectiones, et annotationes criticae in opuscula varia Galeni*, published posthumously in 1640 through the good offices of his friend the puritan divine Thomas Gataker. In this edition Goulston edited and translated mainly Galen's smaller philosophical and moral writings, but his notes on the *Administrationes anatomicae* of Galen, preserved among the books given by his widow, Helena, to Merton College, Oxford, suggest that he had contemplated a similar edition of this medical tract. Although his attempts at textual emendation are often crude, and the printed reports of his sources do not always correspond to his marginalia, his notes on variant readings cannot be neglected by a modern editor of Galen, and his emendations are occasionally superior to those found in later editions.

Goulston's adherence to Galen and his polite learning made him a prosperous London physician and a worthy member of the College of Physicians. Its entry requirements demanded an extensive acquaintance with Galen and Hippocrates, and as censor in 1615–16 and 1625–6 he was responsible for conducting the entrance examination. He was, like William Harvey, a believer in the importance of anatomy as the basis of medical knowledge, following Galen, who had stressed again and again the need for the true doctor to dissect for himself. In 1624 Goulston was behind a proposal to hold a lecture at the college on morbid anatomy, and he was probably the anonymous benefactor who paid for it, year by year, and who requested in 1629 that it should be made permanent. Certainly, in his will he left £200 to the college (later turned to a rent-charge of £12 a year) for an annual lecture to be given by one of the four youngest fellows of the college, who were to treat of two or more diseases on the morning and afternoon of three successive days. Although the lecture may have taken place in 1633 and 1635, when the diseases of the lower belly were agreed as the topic, the earliest Goulstonian lecture known to have been delivered was in 1639, by William Rant.

Goulston's medical practice in London, which included his removal of a fishbone from the throat of Archbishop Abbott in 1614, made him a very wealthy man. He had married before 1608 Helena Sotherton (d. 1637), daughter of George Sotherton MP (d. 1599), and his London connections added to his wealth. Goulston became a free brother of the East India Company in 1614, and held shares in the Virginia Company, whose committee he joined in 1619. Having no children himself, he was a charitable benefactor of the children of his London parish, St Martin Ludgate, and made an annual gift of 40s. for the parish poor. He died at his house in St Martin Ludgate, on 4 May 1632, having made his will (PRO, PROB 11/161/64) on 26 April. He made substantial bequests to the College of Physicians, as well as to his family, his apothecary, his parish, and the lecturer and incumbent of St Martin's. Many of his books were, at his request, later given to Merton by his widow.

VIVIAN NUTTON

Sources Munk, *Roll* · Venn, *Alum. Cant.* · J. J. Keevil, 'Theodore Goulston, 1574–1632', *Bulletin of the History of Medicine*, 27 (1953), 201–12 · G. Clark and A. M. Cooke, *A history of the Royal College of Physicians of London*, 1 (1964) · W. J. Birkin, 'The fellows of the Royal College of Physicians of London, 1603–1643: a social study', PhD diss., University of North Carolina at Chapel Hill, 1977 · D. Béguin, 'L'édition Goulston et les prétendus manuscrits perdus de Galien', *Revue d'Histoire des Textes*, 19 (1989), 341–9 · V. Nutton, 'The Galenic codices of Theodore Goulston', *Revue d'Histoire des Textes*, 22 (1992), 259–68 · *DNB* · will, PRO, PROB 11/161, sig. 64

Goupy, Joseph (b. 1678×89, d. before 1770), painter and etcher, was born in London between 1678 and 1689. His parents are unknown, but he was a pupil of his uncle, the French painter Louis *Goupy. He was also related to William Goupy, a London fan painter. As a young man Goupy visited Rome and Malta. In 1711 he was one of the original subscribers to the drawing academy in Great Queen Street. He developed a fashionable clientele for his reduced copies in body colour (gouache) of old master paintings for which he was paid as much as 50 guineas. Before 1717 he was commissioned by Baron Kielmansegg for a fee of 220 guineas to copy the Vatican tapestry cartoons of Raphael then at Hampton Court. Kielmansegg also employed Goupy to paint pictures in snuff-boxes for George I. Goupy made other copies of the cartoons for clients including Frederick, prince of Wales. In 1717 he was paid £200 to restore four of the subjects in the other great Renaissance masterpiece of the Royal Collection: Mantegna's *Triumph of Caesar*. He claimed that by that period his status was such that he was able to earn £600 per annum.

From 1717 to 1737 Goupy worked regularly for John Hedges, treasurer to the prince of Wales, painting both original compositions and copies, and purchasing works of art including pictures by his friend Marco Ricci. He also taught Hedges to draw. Other pupils included Dorothy Boyle, countess of Burlington, Mrs Dorothy Chabeny (in return for presents worth 4 guineas a month), Matthew Robinson, Brook Taylor, the princess of Wales, and members of her family. About 1719 Goupy worked with the portrait painters James Thornhill and Michael Dahl. Portraits painted on his own account include those of Dr Jean Misaubin and his family, the castrato Francesco Bernardi, known as Senesino, and George Frideric Handel.

From 1724 Goupy published a number of prints of landscapes and classical subjects, including several after Salvator Rosa. In 1724 he designed scenery with Peter Tillemans at the King's Theatre, Haymarket, and three years later he worked there on the scenery for Handel's *Riccardo I*. In 1730 his sketch of John James Heidegger, manager of the King's Theatre, appeared in the background of *The Tuneful Scarecrow*, a caricature by Marco Ricci of the singers Francesca Cuzzoni and Carlo Broschi, known as Farinelli. *The Harmonious Boar*—Goupy's later caricature of Handel as a gigantic pig playing the organ (after a pastel in the Fitzwilliam Museum, Cambridge)—reflects operatic rivalries in the 1730s and 1740s.

By 1728 Goupy was married, and he referred to his wife, whose name is not recorded, in a letter to Dr Cox Macro of 30 July. In the same letter he referred to the gout from which he had suffered for at least two years. In 1727 Goupy offended fellow artists by absenting himself when his duty as steward required him to pay the expenses of the annual dinner of the Virtuosi of St Luke, but in 1735 he appeared with other members of the club in a group portrait by Gawen Hamilton (NPG). He was also one of several artists who joined with Hogarth in the campaign that led to the act of 1735 granting copyright to the designers of prints.

In 1736 Goupy was appointed cabinet painter to the prince of Wales, and until the prince's death in 1751 was regularly employed to produce paintings for Leicester House and to restore pictures. He also painted fans, made at least two trips to France (in 1748 and 1750) to acquire paintings for the prince, and made drawings for garden buildings and furniture for Kew. In 1750 Goupy advertised four landscape prints at 1½ guineas the set, or 8 shillings each, as well as four views of Malta at half a guinea; he gave his address as King's Row, opposite Grosvenor Gate. In 1755 his copperplates were acquired by John Boydell. In 1765, giving his address as Kensington, Goupy exhibited two paintings at the Society of Artists of Great Britain and was elected a fellow of the society. He signed the society's roll in 1766 and appeared in the lists of non-exhibitors for 1767 and 1768. He was said to have been granted a pension of a guinea a week by George III shortly before his death. A correspondent to the *St James's Chronicle* (31 August–3 September 1776) recorded that Goupy died before 1770 at the age of eighty-six, 'in very indigent circumstances' owing to the 'Expence of Attendance [on a] Mistress of his Youth, who became mad [and whom he took] to his own house'. A posthumous sale of his collection (Langford & Son, 3 April

1770) included examples of his own landscapes, topographical views, and copies after other masters, as well as watercolours by Marco Ricci and four oil sketches by Sebastiano Ricci.   SHEILA O'CONNELL

Sources C. R. Grundy, 'Documents relating to an action brought against Joseph Goupy in 1738', *Walpole Society*, 9 (1920–21), 77–8 · Vertue, *Note books*, vols. 3, 6 · Frederick, prince of Wales, accounts, 1735–49, Duchy of Cornwall Office, MSS · letter from Joseph Goupy to Dr Cox Macro, 30 July 1728, BL, Add. MS 32556 · E. Croft-Murray, 'Catalogue of British drawings in the British Museum', vol. 2, BM, department of prints and drawings [incl. biography of Joseph Goupy] · B. Robertson, 'Joseph Goupy and the art of the copy', *Bulletin of the Cleveland Museum of Art*, 75 (1988), 354–82 · I. Bignamini, 'George Vertue, art historian, and art institutions in London, 1689–1768', *Walpole Society*, 54 (1988), 1–148 · Royal Arch. · *General Advertiser* (26 April 1750) · *General Advertiser* (27 April 1750) · *General Advertiser* (28 April 1750) · *Daily Advertiser* [London] (28 Feb 1755) · exhibition catalogue (1765) [Society of Artists of Great Britain] · NPG, Heinz Archive and Library, Society of Artists papers · *St James's Chronicle* (31 Aug–3 Sept 1776) · *European Magazine and London Review*, 1 (1782), 83–4 · private information (2004) [C. Lloyd-Jacob, K. Rorschach]
Likenesses G. Hamilton, group portrait, oils, 1735 (*A conversation of virtuosi … at the King's Arms*), NPG · R. Bean, line engraving (after M. Dahl?), NPG
Wealth at death poor: *St James's Chronicle*

Goupy, Louis [Lewis] (*c.*1674–1747), painter, was born in France and by 1710 had come to London, where his brother William Goupy was already resident as a fan painter. In 1711 he was listed as 'Mr Goupee, senʳ', a subscriber to the new academy of painting started under Sir Godfrey Kneller in Great Queen Street. In 1720 he was one of the seceding members who started the academy in St Martin's Lane under Louis Chéron and John Vanderbank. He painted miniatures and portraits in oil, worked in crayons and tempera, and was an etcher. He was also a fashionable teacher of crayons and watercolour painting as well as miniature painting. He was patronized by Richard Boyle, third earl of Burlington, whom he attended on his journey to Italy in 1714. His own portrait, painted by himself, was engraved in mezzotint by G. White and, later, in line by J. Thomson. White also engraved after him a portrait of Mr Isaac, the dancing-master.

Goupy died in London on 2 December 1747, and in February 1748 his collections were sold by auction; they comprised numerous drawings of his own. He is said to have been a pupil and nephew of Bernard Lens, and he was the uncle of Joseph *Goupy, who was also his pupil.

L. H. CUST, rev. EMMA RUTHERFORD

Sources B. S. Long, *British miniaturists* (1929) · D. Foskett, *A dictionary of British miniature painters*, 2 vols. (1972) · H. Walpole, *Anecdotes of painting in England: with some account of the principal artists*, ed. R. N. Wornum, new edn, 3 vols. (1849) · G. Vertue, BM, Add. MS 23068 · D. Foskett, *Collecting miniatures* (1979) · J. Ingamells, ed., *A dictionary of British and Irish travellers in Italy, 1701–1800* (1997) · Waterhouse, *18c painters*
Likenesses J. Thomson, line engraving (after self-portrait by L. Goupy) · J. Thomson, stipple (after self-portrait by L. Goupy), BM, NPG; repro. in H. Walpole, *Anecdotes of painting in England: with some account of the principal artists*, ed. J. Dallaway, rev. and enl. edn, 5 vols. (1826–8) · G. White, engraving (after self-portrait by L. Goupy), repro. in Walpole, *Anecdotes* · G. White, mezzotint impressions (after self-portrait by L. Goupy), BM, NPG

Gourdon [Gorden], **William** (*fl.* 1603–1616), mariner and travel writer, was born at Hull; nothing is known of his parents and he subsequently found employment on the merchant vessels of the Russia Company trading to northern Russia. He is probably the W. Gorden, factor and overseer, who recorded his experiences between April and September 1603 as *A voyage performed to the northwards, Anno 1603 … in … the 'Grace', being the first voyage to Cherie Island*. After some years of trading inactivity the Russia Company decided on another voyage, to extend its territorial reach. Gourdon sailed from Blackwall in April 1611 in the *Amitie*, with Richard Finch. Off the North Cape they met other company ships, and together struggled past the stormy ice-bound coast, landing from time to time to collect wood. They reached the Pechora River on 9 July and were guided over the river bar by Russians, arriving at the upstream market town of Pustozera on 16 July. After negotiations a house was allocated to them, where they installed Josias Logan, their factor, whose task would be the purchase of furs, skins, and other products of the region. They departed on 1 August, and after twelve days at Cherie Island arrived back in the Thames on 12 September. Richard Finch also submitted an account of this voyage in the form of a letter to Thomas Smith, governor of the Russia Company.

Gourdon was also in the crew who pressed further east in 1614, overwintering in the region of the River Ob; this was published in his *Later observations of William Gourdon in his wintering of Pustzera in the yeeres 1614 and 1615, with a description of the Samoyeds*. On this, and a similar expedition in 1615–16, the crews energetically gathered intelligence on the regional geography, land and sea routes, the available commodities, and potential locations for trade. Milton, in his history *Of the Russe Commonwealth* (1643), drew on these accounts and especially on Gourdon's details concerning the Samoyed people. Nothing is known of Gourdon's personal life, nor of the circumstances of his death.   ANITA MCCONNELL

Sources S. H. Baron, 'The Muscovy Company, the Muscovite merchants, and the problem of reciprocity in Russian foreign trade', *Muscovite Russia: collected essays*, ed. S. H. Baron (1980), 133–55 · L. E. Pennington, ed., *The Purchas handbook: studies of the life, times and writings of Samuel Purchas, 1577–1626* (1997), 1.285–7

Gourlie, William (1815–1856), calico printer and botanist, was born in Glasgow in March 1815, the son of William Gourlie, merchant, and his wife, Agnes (*née* Bankier). He was educated at the public school and university of Glasgow, studying botany under W. J. Hooker and J. H. Balfour. Although a businessman in partnership with his father, he had sufficient spare time for the study of science, for which he had an ardent love. He initially collected British plants, especially mosses, but his mercantile connections enabled him to obtain specimens from around the world, including shells and fossil plants. In 1836 he joined the Edinburgh Botanical Society, acting as its local secretary in Glasgow. In 1841 he became a member of the Glasgow Philosophical Society, and in 1855 was elected a fellow of the Linnean Society. He took an active part in the promotion of various benevolent institutions, and acted as local secretary in connection with the Glasgow meeting of the British Association in 1855. He developed cancer and died at his brother's house at Pollokshields on 24 June 1856, leaving a widow and two children. He was buried at Glasgow necropolis. G. S. BOULGER, *rev.* PETER OSBORNE

Sources J. F. Waller, ed., *The imperial dictionary of universal biography*, 3 vols. (1857–63) · *Proceedings of the Linnean Society of London* (1856–7), xxvii · Desmond, *Botanists*, rev. edn · d. cert.

Archives NL Scot., letters from Joseph Hooker

Gournay [Gourney], **Sir Matthew** (*d.* 1406), soldier, was the fourth son of the regicide, Sir Thomas Gournay (*d.* 1333) of Inglescombe, Somerset, and Joan Furneaux. The date of his birth, traditionally given as *c.*1310, and most details on his early life in previous accounts, ultimately derive from an epitaph once found at Stoke-sub-Hamdon, Somerset, copied by John Leland. This stated that he was ninety-six years old at his death and had fought at the battles of Sluys (1340), Benamarin and Crécy (1346), 'Yngenesse' (probably Winchelsea, 1350), Poitiers (1356), Auray (1364), and Nájera (1367), as well as at the siege of Algeciras (1342–4). But no corroborative evidence has been found before he accompanied Edward, prince of Wales, to Bordeaux in 1355–6, by which time he was already a knight. From this date, however, he enjoyed one of the most remarkable military careers of his day, his name seldom being absent from military or civil records, and there is no doubt that he remained active to a ripe, if exaggerated, old age.

Whether Gournay was at Poitiers remains problematic: land transactions in England in the first half of 1356 suggest that he may have returned from Guyenne before the battle, though he was still being paid as one of the prince's bachelors in 1358. He was active in Brittany in 1357, where he took various prisoners, and became captain of Brest in November, a post retained through the summer of 1358. He returned to the prince's service for the Rheims campaign of 1359–60 and was a conservator of the treaty of Brétigny which concluded it. By then he held several castles in Normandy, over the financing of which dispute arose with Edward III. He was detained for a period in the Tower of London until, with John de St Loo, he paid a fine of 3600 écus in early 1362. Although peace nominally existed between England and France, fighting continued in many areas and Gournay returned to help John de Montfort contend for the ducal throne of Brittany. He was a surety for the truce agreed at Landes d'Evran (24 July 1363) between Montfort and Charles de Blois and, displaying a financial acumen that never deserted him, undertook in March 1364 to farm the ducal *brefs de mer* (safe conducts for passage around the dangerous Breton coast), granted to shipping leaving Bordeaux and La Rochelle for the channel. But his major service was at Auray (29 September 1364), when Montfort finally vindicated his claim by defeating and killing Blois, and Gournay took Jean de Châtillon prisoner.

Gournay's presence in Brittany at this juncture may

have been against Edward III's orders and Gournay continued his defiance when, with Hugh Calveley, he joined an erstwhile opponent at Auray, Bertrand du Guesclin, to lead a force of freebooters in support of Enrique da Trastamara's bid for the Castilian throne. On 1 January 1366 they were at Barcelona, and Pedro IV of Aragon conferred a pension of 2000 florins on him; shortly afterwards Trastamara granted him 1000 florins p.a. in return for a loan of 10,000 florins, though instalments of both pensions were paid irregularly and as late as 1402 Gournay was still in dispute over arrears. In his verse-life of du Guesclin, Jean Cuvelier relates that Gournay was then sent on embassy to the Portuguese court where his chivalric exploits won great praise. Eventually, however, heeding royal demands to return to English service, in late 1366 he joined the prince of Wales's expedition in support of Pedro the Cruel of Castile and distinguished himself at Nájera (3 April 1367).

Gournay's whereabouts for the next few years are uncertain: Froissart and other chroniclers attribute various exploits in Artois and the Bourbonnais to him at this point which, if based on actuality, must have occurred later. He probably remained chiefly with Prince Edward in Guyenne; he was at Angoulême on 15 June 1370 and at Bordeaux on 21 July 1371. By then he was already styled seneschal of the Landes, a long thin coastal administrative district running from Arcachon to Bayonne. He exercised this position intermittently for the rest of his life. He also came to possess there considerable baronial estates forfeited by the lord of Albret. Spanish claims also continued to interest him. He became lord of Mola when Calveley sold his Aragonese castles to him in 1371–2; later his right to the lordship of Asp in Valencia was acknowledged by Pedro IV.

Returning to England, Gournay joined the army led by John of Gaunt, duke of Lancaster, that landed at Calais in July 1373. During this *chevauchée*, probably near Soissons, he was taken prisoner. It was not until the Commons in the Good Parliament (1376) petitioned on his behalf, and that of other Englishmen recently put to extortionate ransom, that he was finally liberated. He quickly returned to Guyenne as seneschal of the Landes and captain of Bayonne and Dax, cities threatened by the duke of Anjou and his former employer, now Enrique II of Castile. Here he was joined by his nephew, Sir Thomas Trivet, *en route* for Navarre in late 1378, whom he diverted to attack local enemy garrisons. In England again by October 1379 he was named to a commission investigating the disputed ransom of Olivier du Guesclin, the first instance of what became a major aspect of his later career as a deputy of the constable of England: the adjudication of cases in the court of chivalry, acknowledgement of his expertise in the theory and practice of the law of arms.

It was not long, however, before Gournay enlisted for further active service. With a retinue of 250 men-at-arms and 250 archers he indented to go as marshal with the earl of Cambridge to Portugal in 1381, leaving England in late June after a delay occasioned by the peasants' revolt. On reaching Lisbon the army moved to the Castilian border but the ensuing campaign was a disaster and the demoralized remnants of the expedition eventually limped home in December 1382. There followed a longer spell at home during which, following the death (1383) of his first wife, Alice Beauchamp, sister of Thomas, earl of Warwick, and widow of Sir John Beauchamp of Hatch Beauchamp (to whom he was married by 1374), Gournay married Philippa (d. 1417), sister of John Talbot of Richards Castle, Herefordshire, and took his share in local administration.

In 1385 Gournay was confirmed in possession of various estates in the Landes, personally reconquered from the French and of which he had been briefly deprived, perhaps on his return from Portugal, by a further short spell in prison about which little is otherwise known. Renewed royal favour was signalled in 1386 when his promotion to the Garter seemed likely, but threats to Calais saw him take a small company to its defence and he probably remained on the garrison strength over the next few years. He seems to have fallen once again, at least briefly, into French hands for in 1389–90 he was in dispute with Louis de Sancerre, marshal of France, to whom he had given a bond for 6000 francs, which led to a dispute in the court of the captain of Calais and an appeal to the king. To pay this sum he borrowed money from John of Gaunt, duke of Lancaster, among others, though it was only with difficulty that the duke's executors finally recovered it.

Gournay's relations with Gaunt nevertheless became progressively closer, being strengthened when the latter in 1390 received the duchy of Guyenne, where Gournay maintained his interests. In November 1391 he was present at Westminster to witness the reconciliation of Sir Richard Scrope and Sir Robert Grosvenor mediated by Gaunt. Preparations were by now afoot for Gaunt to visit his duchy. Letters from Richard II to the king of Aragon in 1392–4 revived Gournay's Spanish claims and in August 1394 he was retaining men for service in Guyenne for a year with Gaunt. He was still there in February 1397, and although he returned intermittently to England, where he was named on many commissions, much of his last decade was spent abroad. Henry IV reaffirmed his position as seneschal of the Landes in July 1401 as he recruited a company of almost a hundred men, which he led to the duchy in September to meet, with other captains, increasing French military pressure. From 1402–5 this was intense. A letter of December 1403 survives from Gournay as seneschal, informing the king of countermeasures taken; in August and September 1404 he parried a raid led by the count of Clermont, remarkable feats indeed for a man certainly into his mid-seventies if not older!

When Gournay finally returned to England, or how much peace he enjoyed at his principal manor of Stoke-sub-Hamdon, is unknown. His epitaph states that he died on 26 September 1406; other evidence supports this. For many years it had been clear he would have no direct heir and he drew up many deeds to maximize his income by granting reversions during his lifetime to various feoffees. After delivery of dower most of his English lands passed at first to Henry IV's youngest son, Humphrey, while those in

Guyenne went to Sir John Tiptoft, his widow's second husband. Gournay's brass, tomb, and the stained glass armorial windows that Leland saw commemorating his eventful life have now disappeared, but a French Bible he once owned survives (BL, Royal MS 19 D.iv-v).

MICHAEL JONES

Sources *Chancery records* · PRO · M. C. B. Dawes, ed., *Register of Edward, the Black Prince*, 4 vols., PRO (1930–33) · *John of Gaunt's register*, ed. S. Armitage-Smith, 2 vols., CS, 3rd ser., 20–21 (1911) · F. Devon, ed. and trans., *Issues of the exchequer: being payments made out of his majesty's revenue, from King Henry III to King Henry VI inclusive*, RC (1837) · Rymer, *Foedera* · *The itinerary of John Leland in or about the years 1535–1543*, ed. L. Toulmin Smith, 11 pts in 5 vols. (1906–10), vol. 1, p. 159 · V. H. Galbraith, ed., *The Anonimalle chronicle, 1333 to 1381* (1927) · *The diplomatic correspondence of Richard II*, ed. E. Perroy, CS, 3rd ser., 48 (1933) · G. de Saint-André, *Chronique de Bertrand du Guesclin, par Cuvelier, trouvère due XIVeme siècle*, ed. E. Charrière, 2 vols. (Paris, 1839) · *Œuvres de Froissart: chroniques*, ed. K. de Lettenhove, 25 vols. (Brussels, 1867–77) · *Chroniques de J. Froissart*, ed. S. Luce and others, 15 vols. (Paris, 1869–1975) · M. Jones, ed., *Recueil des actes de Jean IV, duc de Bretagne*, 1–2 (Paris, 1980–83) · F. C. Hingeston, ed., *Royal and historical letters during the reign of Henry the Fourth*, 1, Rolls Series, 18 (1860) · J. Batten, 'Stoke under Hamdon in connection with Sir Matthew de Gournay, kt. and the duchy of Cornwall', *Proceedings of the Somersetshire Archaeological and Natural History Society*, 40/2 (1894), 236–71 · D. Gurney, ed., *The record of the house of Gournay*, 4 vols. (1848–58) · A. Goodman, *John of Gaunt: the exercise of princely power in fourteenth-century Europe* (1992) · P. E. Russell, *The English intervention in Spain and Portugal in the time of Edward III and Richard II* (1955) · S. Walker, *The Lancastrian affinity, 1361–1399* (1990) · M. G. A. Vale, *English Gascony, 1399–1453: a study of war, government and politics during the later stages of the Hundred Years' War* (1970) · Archivo de Corona de Aragón, Barcelona, registers · BL, MS Cotton Caligula D IV · BL, Royal MS 19 D.iv-v · grant of Albret lands, 1374, Archives départementales des Pyrénées-Atlantiques, Pau, E 169

Gouter, James. *See* Gaultier, Jacques (*fl.* 1617–1652).

Gouzenko, Igor Sergeievich [Igor Sergeyevich Guzenko] (1919–1982), defector from the USSR and author, was born on 26 January 1919 at Rogachovo, near Moscow, the son of Sergey Davidovich Guzenko, and his wife, Praskoviya Vasilyevna Filkova. He was the third son and youngest of four children, and was named after his deceased older brother. His father, a native of Rostov on Don, was a bank accountant who died while serving with the Red Army. His mother, whose father was a building contractor, attended university, which was unusual in tsarist Russia. Gouzenko commenced his primary school education in Rostov on Don, continued his studies at the Maksim Gorky School in Moscow, and graduated in June 1937 with high honours. However, before matriculating at the University of Moscow he studied drawing and drafting for one year in Moscow's prestigious Art Studio Chemko. In September 1938 he entered the Architectural Institute of the University of Moscow (the pre-revolutionary Strogonov School of Art). There he met his future wife, Svetlana Borisovna Guseva, whom he married on 20 November 1942. They had four boys and four girls, most of whom attended a university specializing in the sciences. Svetlana Gouzenko's father was a mining engineer and a member of the faculty of the Mining Institute of the University of Moscow, and her mother, Anna Konstantinovna Kosciuszko, was a lineal descendant of General Tadeusz Kościuszko, the Polish revolutionary.

In June 1941 Gouzenko was nominated for a lucrative Stalin fellowship because of his outstanding academic record, but the German surprise attack on 22 June ended his formal education and his hopes of becoming an architect. He was posted to the Kuibyshev Engineering Academy and was then selected to study ciphering. In spring 1942 he was assigned to the Moscow headquarters of military intelligence, the Glavnoye Razvedyvatelnoye Upravleniye (GRU), where he worked as a cipher clerk until spring 1943, when he was transferred to the office of the military attaché at the legation in Ottawa.

From the moment of his arrival Gouzenko experienced the exhilaration and freedom offered by an open society. The material comforts available even in wartime Canada seemed unimaginable, considering the deprivations that he had experienced as an ordinary Russian citizen before the outbreak of war. The ambience of the legation was oppressive, and when his return to Moscow could no longer be delayed Gouzenko decided to defect. As described in his memoirs, *This Was my Choice* (1948), he carefully prepared the documentation that he would take with him to alert the Canadian authorities and the West that Moscow was involved in blatant spying activities directed against its allies. He walked out of the Soviet embassy in Ottawa on 5 September 1945 with over one hundred classified documents under his shirt. Initially no one in Ottawa believed him but an attempt by legation personnel to kidnap him and his wife and child convinced the Canadian authorities of his sincerity.

Gouzenko's defection in September 1945, together with Russian activities in other parts of the world, contributed to intensify the cold war. His testimony in Canada before the royal commission of inquiry established to investigate his charges of Russian espionage in Canada, plus the documentation that he brought with him, led to the prosecution and conviction of eleven people, including Fred Rose, a Communist member of the Canadian parliament. In particular Gouzenko was able to give a detailed picture of the Soviet spy network directed against the Chalk River atomic research establishment in Ontario. According to one obituarist Gouzenko's testimony enabled the federal bureau of investigation to uncover 'the Gold–Greenglass–Rosenbergs network which had penetrated the Manhattan Project engaged on the first atomic weapons' (*The Times*).

In Britain, Gouzenko's information led to the arrest of the atomic physicist Allan Nunn May, a former employee at Chalk River. He maintained that a Soviet agent, 'Elli', was at work in MI5. Though Gouzenko's information dealt with only a narrow spectrum of the GRU's espionage, H. A. R. (Kim) Philby subsequently admitted that his defection had been a counter-intelligence 'disaster' for Moscow. In particular the telegrams and other materials that he removed from the legation proved of enormous assistance to western decrypters in unravelling the GRU codes. That no further arrests followed can probably be explained by the fact that it was impossible to fathom the cryptonyms assigned to those working for the GRU. Fearing Stalin's retribution Gouzenko was given Canadian citizenship and a new identity, and was closely guarded by the royal Canadian mounted police. In 1954 his best-selling novel, *The Fall of a Titan*, which dealt with the inhumanity and brutality of the Stalinist regime, won the governor-general's award. In the 1950s Gouzenko appeared frequently on television, but to disguise his identity he wore a bag over his head.

Gouzenko was of medium height, broad-shouldered, had a military posture, and dressed conservatively. He was partial to classical music, was an avid photographer, enjoyed doing drawings and paintings, many of which he sold, wrote several unpublished works, including a novel, *Ocean of Time*, and was interested in astronomy and gymnastics. His diabetes led to blindness but he read and wrote Russian and English in braille. He died suddenly on 25 June 1982 near Toronto, thirty-nine years to the day after arriving in Canada.   JAMES BARROS, *rev.*

Sources I. Gouzenko, *This was my choice* (1948) · S. Gouzenko, *Before Igor* (1961) · C. Andrew, *The Mitrokhin archive: the KGB in Europe and the West* (1999) · *The Times* (2 July 1982) · private information (1990, 2004) · *Report of the royal commission … the communication, by public officials and other persons in positions of trust, of secret and confidential information* (Ottawa, ON, 1946)

Gove, Richard (1586/7–1668), Church of England clergyman, was born in the parish of South Tavistock, Devon, the son of a gentleman. He matriculated at Magdalen Hall, Oxford, on 1 March 1605, aged eighteen, graduated BA on 31 May 1608, and proceeded MA on 4 July 1611. He was then ordained and became chaplain to John Paulet, Lord Paulet, who on 25 August 1618 presented him to the living of Hinton St George next to his own Somerset seat. Here Gove also taught in a grammar school.

During the Commonwealth, Gove was deprived of his living, and by 1652 he was living at East Coker, Somerset. Between 1650 and 1658 he published four devotional and pastoral works. *The Saints Hony-Comb Full of Divine Truths* (1652) manifested conventional godly piety, emphasizing prayer, assurance of salvation and the availability of God's mercy, the importance of preaching, and the intrinsic authority of scripture. Although avowedly couched in plain terms and addressed to 'the Well-affected Reader, whether learned or unlearned', it is sprinkled with Latin quotations and shows evidence of wide reading, citing the works of, among others, Lancelot Andrewes, John Bois, John Donne, Joseph Hall, William Perkins, and James Ussher. *The Communicants Guide* (1654) was a similarly mainstream work, directed at the young and dealing carefully and systematically with the receiving and the significance of the sacrament of the Lord's supper.

At some point in the 1650s, according to Anthony Wood, Gove was made minister of St David's, Exeter, and 'for several years much frequented' by the presbyterians there (Wood, *Ath. Oxon.*, 3.823), but later turned out. About the time of the Restoration he returned to East Coker, where he taught in the grammar school and where he was instituted rector on 26 September 1661. He died there on Christmas eve 1668, and was buried in the chancel of his church.   E. T. BRADLEY, *rev.* VIVIENNE LARMINIE

Sources R. Gove, *The saints hony-comb full of divine truths* (1652) · Wood, *Ath. Oxon.*, new edn, 3.822–3 · Foster, *Alum. Oxon.* · *Walker rev.*, 313 · Wing, *STC* · F. W. Weaver, ed., *Somerset incumbents* (privately printed, Bristol, 1889), 67, 377

Gover, Charles Edward (1835/6–1872), writer on Indian folklore, was the son of Thomas Gover of Poplar, Middlesex. He became a schoolmaster in Madras in 1863 and was appointed principal of the Madras Military Male Orphan Asylum in 1864. He remained there until its amalgamation with the Lawrence Asylum in Ootacumund in 1872. He was subsequently employed as a municipal sanitary inspector and census officer. In 1863, he married Clara Gertrude (*b.* 1844/5), daughter of William Taylor; they had five children.

Gover took a deep interest in India beyond the confines of his professional work. His first concern was with the problems posed by the diversity of Indian weights and measures; in 1865 he published in Madras *Indian Weights and Measures: their Condition and Remedy*, followed two years later by *An Uniform Metrology for India*. His greatest enthusiasm, however, was for the way of life and culture of the Dravidian peoples of south India, about whom he collected copious material. In addition to being a member of the Society of Arts and a fellow of the Anthropological Society, he became a member of the Royal Asiatic Society in 1868, and in 1869–70 presented two papers, one entitled 'The Pongol festival in southern India', and the other illustrating the lifestyle and religious views of the lower classes in south India. The latter was chiefly based on a large collection of popular songs in ancient Kanarese, specimens of which were rendered in English verse. Both papers were subsequently printed in the society's journal, while the collection of popular songs, and accompanying explanatory text, was greatly expanded and published as *The Folk-Songs of Southern India* in Madras in 1871, and London the following year.

One of Gover's aims was to draw the attention of the general public to the way of life of south India's peoples, and their extensive folk literature. This he helped achieve by the publication of several of his papers in the popular *Cornhill Magazine*, while his book, *The Folk-Songs*, also drew praise for its accurate and spirited picture of peasant life. However, his venture into philological terrain, with his claim that the Dravidian languages reflected the purity of their ancient Aryan roots, was strongly criticized. His stilted versification of the folk-songs was compared unfavourably to his vigorous prose. Nevertheless, his collection of fast-disappearing indigenous material has continued to be of great value to scholars, as testified in the 1959 reprint in Madras of *The Folk-Songs*. Gover died of a haemorrhage on 18 September 1872 in Madras and was buried at St Andrew's Church there the following day.

    GORDON GOODWIN, *rev.* ROSEMARY CARGILL RAZA

Sources *The Asylum Press Almanac and Compendium of Intelligence* [Madras] (1862–72) · *The Athenaeum* (27 July 1872), 111–12 · *Journal of the Royal Asiatic Society of Great Britain and Ireland*, new ser., 3 (1868), i · *Journal of the Royal Asiatic Society of Great Britain and Ireland*, 5 (May 1870), x–xi · 'Hindu festival of the Pongol', *Cornhill Magazine*, 17 (1868), 349–56 · 'Dravidian folk-songs', *Cornhill Magazine*, 24 (1871), 570–87 · Madras marriage records, BL OIOC, N/2/44, fol. 196 · Madras burial records, BL OIOC, N/2/53, fol. 17
Wealth at death everything to wife (sole executor): will, 21 July 1863, probates granted by high court of judicature at Madras, 1873, BL OIOC L/AG/34/29

Gow, Andrew Sydenham Farrar (1886–1978), classical scholar, was born on 27 August 1886 at 100 Gower Street, London, the eldest of the three sons (there were no daughters) of the Revd Dr James Gow (1854–1923), who, after being a fellow of Trinity College, Cambridge, was headmaster of Nottingham high school and later of Westminster School, and his wife, Gertrude Sydenham Everett-Green. He was educated at Nottingham high school, at Rugby School, and at Trinity College, Cambridge, where he obtained first classes in both parts of the classical tripos (1908 and 1909), in part two specializing in archaeology, and won several classical prizes.

In 1911 Gow won a Trinity prize fellowship with a dissertation consisting of a miscellany of papers, several of which were later expanded into valuable articles. He applied four times for permanent posts in Cambridge, but was each time unsuccessful; it was feared that he would alarm and discourage his pupils, particularly the weaker sort. Indeed Gow's appearance was formidable, an uncompromisingly Scottish kind of countenance being set off by bushy eyebrows and side-whiskers, and anything like conceit or pretentiousness on the part of a pupil might provoke a wounding sarcasm. In 1914 he became a master at Eton College, where he remained during the First World War, a heart murmur having disqualified him for military service. Some pupils were indeed alienated by his dryness and his caustic wit; his frequent comment on an exercise shown up to him was 'Oh, death, boy!', and his highest expression of praise was 'Not wholly bad!' But some of the boys appreciated his solid scholarship and the great pains he took to help them, and the nickname Granny Gow was bestowed upon him not without affection.

In 1925 Gow returned to Cambridge as a teaching fellow of Trinity. He was better placed in a university than in a school, and enjoyed more than he could have done in any other society the life of that great college, which was to be his home for the remainder of his life. He was a congenial colleague to A. E. Housman, and in 1936, the year of Housman's death, brought out a brief memoir which, though mainly concerned with Housman's scholarship, throws more light upon him than almost any of the studies by literary persons. Gow acted as Housman's literary executor, and supervised a reprint of his edition of Manilius.

Gow lectured effectively, particularly on Theocritus, and used the material collected for his lectures to compose a number of articles, all of solid merit. He sacrificed precious time by taking on the onerous administrative post of tutor, which he held from 1929 to 1942, and also the pious labour of bringing out volume two of the posthumously published *Early Age of Greece* (1931) of Sir William Ridgeway. In 1943 he became a fellow of the British Academy, and in 1947 Brereton reader in classics in Cambridge. He had honorary degrees from the universities of Durham (DLitt) and Edinburgh (LLD).

In 1950, a year before his retirement from the latter post, Gow published a memorable edition of Theocritus, a second edition following three years later. The editor's massive learning, unusual accuracy, and sober judgement render this book indispensable to scholars. In 1952 Gow followed the Theocritus with an admirable edition of the Greek bucolic poets in the series of Oxford Classical Texts, and a year later he brought out a valuable translation of these writers with a useful introduction. The year 1953 saw also the appearance of an edition of the difficult Hellenistic didactic poet Nicander, in which Gow collaborated with A. F. Scholfield.

Gow next began work on the Hellenistic epigrams contained in the Greek anthology. A monograph called *The Greek Anthology: Sources and Ascriptions* appeared in 1958, and in 1965 it was followed by the two-volume *Hellenistic Epigrams: the Garland of Meleager*, in which Gow collaborated with Denys Page, Page being primarily responsible for the poems of Meleager and Gow for all the rest. The same year saw the appearance of Gow's edition, with commentary, of the fragments of the Alexandrian iambic poet Machon; none of his productions makes more entertaining reading than his edition of this scurrilous but amusing author. In 1968 Gow and Page followed up their first volume by bringing out *Hellenistic Epigrams: the Garland of Philip*, again in two volumes; this time Gow was primarily responsible for the 650 epigrams which were either attributed to Antipater of Thessalonica or left over as being either his work or that of Antipater of Sidon. Gow's work on Hellenistic epigrams has the same qualities as his *Theocritus*, and like that book will remain an essential instrument of scholarship.

The fears expressed early in Gow's career regarding the possible effects of his teaching did not prove entirely vain; his dryness and severity antagonized a number of his pupils, and the austerity of the regime at Trinity encouraged alarming departures from that quality by lesser scholars in certain other places. But pupils of the more pertinacious sort profited greatly from his teaching and his company. During the Second World War he regularly sent to pupils who were on active service a circular newsletter of a highly characteristic kind; these letters were published in 1945 in a book called *Letters from Cambridge*.

Gow also did much to interest undergraduates in art, a subject by no means popular among the Cambridge dons of his generation. Several members of his family had been artists or lovers of art, and Gow himself became no mean collector and connoisseur. From about 1909 he was a friend of John Beazley, with whom he once combined to buy a Sienese picture they had discovered in a dealer's;

and he often travelled in Italy to look at pictures, sometimes in the company of his friend Scholfield. Although in theory Gow disapproved of all art later than 1500 except for Rembrandt, Velázquez, and, with some reservations, Rubens, he left to the Fitzwilliam Museum, of which he had been a syndic from 1934 to 1957, twenty-four works by Degas and six each by Rodin and Forain. From 1947 to 1953 he served as a trustee of the National Gallery, to which he left a fine collection of photographs of paintings which he had often used to stimulate a love of art in undergraduates. They were accustomed to drop in on him between ten and eleven in the evening, when he could be an agreeable companion; and he, who had spent so little of his life with women, surprised his colleagues by making friends with the celebrated actress Dorothy Tutin.

In his last years Gow's health became impaired, and in 1965 he left his rooms in Nevile's Court, with a fine Athena for a door knocker, for a set in the King's Hostel, where there was a lift. After breaking a thigh in 1973 he moved to the Evelyn Nursing Home, where he died on 2 February 1978. He was unmarried.   HUGH LLOYD-JONES, *rev.*

Sources F. H. Sandbach, 'Andrew Sydenham Farrar Gow, 1886–1978', *PBA*, 64 (1978), 427–41 · personal knowledge (1993)
Archives Trinity Cam., corresp. and papers
Likenesses A. C. Barrington Brown, photograph, repro. in Sandbach, 'Andrew Sydenham Farrar Gow', facing p. 427
Wealth at death £367,912: probate, 15 March 1978, *CGPLA Eng. & Wales*

Gow, Ian Reginald Edward (1937–1990), politician, was born at 3 Upper Harley Street, London, on 11 February 1937, the younger son in the family of two sons and one daughter of Alexander Edward Gow FRCP (1884–1952), a consultant physician at St Bartholomew's Hospital, London, and his wife, Helen Gordon, *née* Rannie. A highly intelligent child, he attended Winchester College but did not proceed to university. He undertook his national service in the 15th and 19th hussars, being commissioned in 1956, and rose to the rank of major. His tours of duty included Malaya, but the crucial posting was to Northern Ireland. This coincided with an upsurge in IRA activity, although the level of violence was insignificant compared with the later campaigns conducted by the group's 'provisional' successors after 1970. The Northern Ireland government introduced internment, and its counterpart in Éire followed suit. On this occasion a tough co-ordinated response stamped out the violence. But if anything, Unionist feeling in the north became even more hostile towards the Catholic minority, and more determined to resist absorption by the south. Gow himself, who was stationed on the border at Omagh, co. Tyrone, was strongly influenced by these views.

After returning to civilian life, Gow qualified as a solicitor in 1962, eventually taking a partnership in the distinguished firm Joynson Hicks & Co. Even as a child he had regarded himself a Conservative. After his national service, and the successful beginning of his legal career, he decided to run for parliament. He stood unsuccessfully against Richard Crossman at Coventry East in 1964, and lost again at Clapham in 1966. A few months after this second reverse he married, on 10 September 1966, Jane Elizabeth (*b*. 1943/4), daughter of Charles William Christopher Packe, an army officer. It was a very happy marriage, and produced two sons.

Gow did not contest a seat in 1970, but at the general election of February 1974 he fought and won the safe Conservative constituency of Eastbourne, which he held until his death. Thus he joined the Commons just as the Heath government fell; significantly for him, that election also ended the traditional alliance between the tories and the Ulster Unionists. At Westminster, Gow established close links of his own with the Unionists; he was a friend of Enoch Powell, who sat for the Ulster Unionist Party after October 1974. But there were still kindred spirits within his own party, notably the war hero Airey Neave. After masterminding Thatcher's successful bid for the Conservative leadership in February 1975, Neave became shadow spokesman on Northern Ireland. The prospects were bright for a radical shift in tory policy; Neave (and Gow) shared Powell's desire for the full integration of Northern Ireland within the United Kingdom. As a relative newcomer to the house, Gow himself could not expect immediate promotion (he had, in fact, voted for Geoffrey Howe in the leadership election). But in 1978 Neave asked him to share his front-bench duties, and they worked together on the new policy until Neave's murder by the INLA (Irish National Liberation Army) shortly before the general election of May 1979.

Thatcher might have considered Gow the perfect substitute for Neave when she took office. Instead she appointed her former chief whip, Humphrey Atkins, who soon abandoned Neave's plan for integration. Gow had no direct ministerial authority in Northern Ireland. Thatcher instead appointed him her parliamentary private secretary straight after the election. This proved one of her most inspired appointments. Gow was 'one of us' on a range of issues. Like Thatcher, he fully shared Enoch Powell's zeal for free-market economics; during the 1970s he had introduced an anti-union private member's bill. But more important than this ideological kinship was Gow's profound sense of personal loyalty to his leader. For four years he was an unusually assiduous and influential parliamentary private secretary. All his energies were placed at Thatcher's service. Based in a small office beside the cabinet room in 10 Downing Street, he was a channel of communication between ministers and Thatcher. She appreciated his 'combination of loyalty, shrewdness and an irrepressible sense of fun' (Thatcher, 29–30). His visibility in the Commons as Mrs Thatcher's 'eyes and ears' made him deeply unpopular in some quarters. He was nicknamed 'Supergrass' by the prime minister's opponents, who were irritated by what seemed an obsequious manner. In fact, Gow was simply modest and unfailingly polite. Although occasionally he sounded pompous, his sense of humour went far beyond the self-deprecation for which he was best-known, and he was a delightful companion.

Gow would have been unpopular enough in some quarters even if he had merely devoted himself to his controversial boss. As it was, Atkins's successor as Northern Ireland secretary, James Prior, felt that his position was constantly undermined by Gow, whose 'hard-line Unionist advice' to Thatcher was 'utterly disastrous' (Prior, 197). In 1982 Prior made another attempt to build devolved institutions in Northern Ireland. To his disgust he learned that Gow was co-operating with the bill's opponents; subsequently he felt that the impression of government disunity was a key factor in the failure of his initiative.

Gow ceased to be Thatcher's parliamentary private secretary in June 1983 when he became a junior minister in the Department of the Environment. There he earned mixed reviews for his administrative performance. His area of special responsibility was housing, where practical considerations had clashed with his free-market instincts. Indeed, some of his allies thought that he had 'gone native'. For example, while he had always backed the sale of council houses he was outraged by the government's refusal to allow councils to spend the proceeds as they chose.

In a government reshuffle in September 1985 Gow moved to the treasury as minister of state. By then he had become a more flexible operator, and future promotion looked certain. But he was still immoveable on one subject, at least. He had been at the treasury for only two months when he suddenly resigned over the Anglo-Irish agreement. He felt that the deal was one-sided: Éire had secured influence over the north without offering any meaningful concessions. His resignation statement was a typical effort from this eloquent orator; Thatcher's personal commitment to the agreement made his departure even more painful. But Gow never regretted his stance, feeling to the end that he had been proved right.

Despite this blow Gow remained very active in the Commons. He served on the public accounts committee, and in 1988 he resumed the chairmanship of the back-bench Conservative Northern Ireland committee, which he had relinquished in 1979. He was a frequent contributor to debates—impassioned on Northern Ireland, often witty on other subjects, although his contributions reflected a 'traditionalist' viewpoint (for example, as a high Anglican he opposed the ordination of women and divorced men). Bald and bespectacled, he had in his dress, bearing, and manner a slightly old-fashioned air.

Gow's ideas on Northern Ireland had been noted by republican terrorists. His name was on a death list which was discovered in Clapham. He scorned the idea of hiding from his enemies; unusually, his address and telephone number were both published in *Who's Who*. On 30 July 1990 he was murdered outside his home, The Dog House, Hankham, Pevensey, Sussex, by an IRA bomb planted under his car.

Geoffrey Howe, who regarded Gow as his 'oldest and closest political friend', described him as 'one of the most respected, warm-hearted, and courageous politicians of his generation' (Howe, 633, 695). To Alan Clark, who owed his place in the Thatcher government to Gow's influence, he 'remained always witty, clever, industrious, affectionate, and almost *painfully* honourable' (Clark, 319). Gow's murder was terrible proof that even in a democracy a little knowledge can be a deadly thing. He might have comprehended the Unionist case, but he rarely showed any understanding of those who despised Northern Ireland as an artificial creation which had legitimized the injustices of one section of the community. Essentially a romantic man, he tended to see questions in primary colours where most of his colleagues could detect only shades of grey. At the time of his death he was still urging the integrationist solution, but his chances of persuading ministers were slim; he had also protested in vain at the release of the IRA bomber Gerard Kelly.

The motives of Gow's assassins are even more obscure than in most such cases. Ironically, the by-election which followed in October 1990 resulted in a dramatic victory for the Liberal Democrats. The economy was struggling, and the poll tax had proved deeply unpopular. If the Conservatives could not win even Eastbourne under these tragic circumstances, something dramatic had to be done to revive their fortunes. The prime minister was deposed within weeks. But it is unlikely that the terrorists who selected Gow as a worthwhile target were thinking on these lines. Presumably, given the victim's long (and continuing) friendship with Thatcher, the murder was an act of pure vindictiveness. It certainly did not force a change in government policy. At most, the manner of his death merely forced on Gow's civilized opponents the belated realization that, for all his frailties, he had been a brave and charming man.   MARK GARNETT

Sources *The Times* (31 July 1990) [obit., tributes, and reports of murder] · private information (2004) · *WWW* · b. cert. · m. cert. · d. cert. · J. Prior, *A balance of power* (1986) · G. Howe, *Conflict of loyalty* (1994) [incl. memorial address, appx 1] · A. Clark, *Diaries* (1993) · M. Thatcher, *The Downing Street years* (1993) · H. Young, *One of us: a biography of Margaret Thatcher*, 2nd edn (1991)
Likenesses photograph, repro. in *The Times*
Wealth at death £787,486: probate, 26 Sept 1990, *CGPLA Eng. & Wales*

Gow, John (1698–1725), pirate, was born either at Scrabster, near Thurso, or at Wick. Details of his background and upbringing are unknown until September 1699, when he moved with his merchant father's family to Stromness in the Orkney Islands. It is believed that Gow ran away to sea, and may have manifested piratical intentions before the seizure for which he is now known. To Daniel Defoe, Gow was

> a superlative, a Capital Rogue ... even before he came to Embark in this particular ship. And he is more than ordinarily remarkable, for having form'd the like Design of going a Pirating when he serv'd as Boatswain on board an English Merchant Ship, Bound Home from Lisbon to London, in which he form'd a Party to have seiz'd on the Captain and Officers, and to run away with the Ship. (Defoe, introduction)

On this occasion Gow's attempt came to nothing because recruits were lacking. He was paid off in London and news of his enterprise having got round, embarked quickly for the Netherlands to avoid prosecution.

In August 1724 Gow joined the *Caroline* in Amsterdam as a foremast hand, and was subsequently promoted to second mate and gunner. The galley was employed to carry a cargo of beeswax, leather, and woollen clothes from Santa Cruz in the Canary Islands to Genoa. She arrived in Africa in September, and after two months' lading sailed for Italy on 3 November. It seems clear that complaints about conditions and food aboard the vessel were pretexts for a planned seizure; on their first evening out, Gow and his seven co-conspirators determined to take the vessel and go on the account. During the night the mutineers murdered the chief mate, supercargo, surgeon, and Captain Ferneau, throwing the bodies overboard. The galley was renamed the *Revenge* and her course set for Spain and Portugal. The pirates seized a sloop bound from Newfoundland to Cadiz with fish, and subsequently captured a Scottish vessel, both of which were scuttled. Having failed to take a French ship or to cut out a vessel at Madeira, Gow and his men had better luck at Porto Santo, where they obtained water and provisions after allegedly holding the Portuguese governor hostage. The *Revenge* subsequently seized a New England and a French vessel, 'compensating' some of the victims with the cargo of others, presumably to allay any future charges of piracy. When Gow refused to attack a much stronger West Indian merchantman, he was upbraided by Lieutenant Williams, who was wounded in the altercation, imprisoned, and subsequently shipped off on a capture in the hope that he would be hanged in England.

It was Gow who now suggested that the *Revenge* sail for Orkney as the best location to satisfy their victualling and careening needs while avoiding detection by the authorities. The *Revenge*, now renamed the *George*, arrived in January 1725, where the pirates gave out a story of delays and adverse weather and bartered with several vessels. Their subterfuge began to unravel when several pressed sailors defected and alarmed the countryside. Gow and his remaining crew responded by raiding the residence of Mr Honeyman, the county sheriff. Honeyman's wife and daughter escaped with gold and estate papers, but the brigands plundered the house of plate and valuables 'and forced one of the Servants, who played very well on the Bagpipe, to march along, Piping before them, when they carryed them off to the Ship' (Defoe, 34). Subsequently, although they had cleaned only half of the *George*, Gow and his crew removed to Cava, where they abducted and apparently raped three local women. Moving on to Eday, Gow hoped to plunder the house of Mr Fea, a former schoolmate, but lacking a local pilot, the *George* grounded on 13 February and Gow and his men were forced to request Fea's assistance in refloating their vessel. On the pretext of entertaining the pirate delegation, Fea first seized the boatswain and then captured his four companions at an alehouse to which he had invited them for a drink. Gow and the remaining crew were isolated and when their ship ran further aground, the captain 'with an Air of Desperation, told them they were all dead Men' (ibid., 41).

In this Gow was prophetic. After some initial 'fencing'

between the groups (Gow hoped to use his ship and its cargo to bribe his way to freedom), both he and his crew were seized by local landowners. Defoe notes acidly that 'Nothing but Men infatuated to their own Destruction, and condemn'd by the visible Hand of Heaven to an immediate Surprise, could have been so stupid' (Defoe, 50). Gow and his fellow prisoners were transported by sea to London, where they arrived on 26 March and were imprisoned in the Marshalsea. In his trial on 8 May Gow initially refused to plead, but being threatened with pressing, he declared himself not guilty. As four of the crew had turned king's evidence, this only delayed the inevitable judgment. Convicted of murder and piracy, Gow was hanged on 11 June 1725. The rope breaking at the first attempt, Gow, 'still alive and sensible, tho' he had Hung four Minutes, … was able to go up the Ladder the second Time, which he did with very little Concern'd, and was Hang'd again' (Defoe, 63). Gow appears to have died unmarried, though tradition has identified him as a suitor of Katherine Rorieson of Thurso (whom he allegedly intended to carry off from her husband) and Hilda Gordon of Stromness (who is claimed to have plighted her troth to Gow at Orkney's Stone of Odin and, subsequently, to have journeyed to London at the time of the pirate's execution to renew her vows). Following his execution Gow was the subject of Defoe's *Account of the Conduct and Proceedings of the Late John Gow, alias Smith* (1725) and was fictionalized as Captain Cleveland in Sir Walter Scott's *The Pirate* (1822). Orkney islanders commemorated Gow with a folly, said to be built from the ballast stones of the *George*, near Bridge Street, Kirkwall, and, more recently, with Pirate Gow's inn—a pub and chalet complex—on Eday.

SAMUEL PYEATT MENEFEE

Sources D. Defoe, *Account of the conduct and proceedings of the late John Gow, alias Smith* (1725); repr. (1978) · D. Cordingly, *Life among the pirates: the romance and the reality* (1995) · A. Fea, *The real Captain Cleveland* (1912)

Gow, Nathaniel (1763–1831), fiddler and composer, was born on 27 May 1763 at Inver, near Dunkeld, Perthshire, and baptized at Little Dunkeld two days later, the fourth of the five sons of Niel *Gow (1727–1807) and his first wife, Margaret Wiseman. The date of his birth, which has often been given wrongly, is established by the baptismal register for Little Dunkeld parish. As a child he was given fiddle lessons by his father before being sent to Edinburgh, where his teachers included the violinists Robert Mackintosh and Alexander McGlashan and the trumpeter Joseph Reinagle. In August 1782 he was appointed one of the king's trumpeters for Scotland and in the same year was engaged as a professional violinist in the orchestra of the Edinburgh Musical Society. He also played for fashionable dances, working his way up from cellist in McGlashan's band to leader of his own (following the death of his eldest brother, William Gow, in 1791). The first of his annual balls was held in 1797; these became major events of the Edinburgh social calendar and enjoyed noble patronage. By the turn of the century Gow's band was in wide demand and his fame had spread to London, where George Gordon, marquess of Huntly, arranged a

Nathaniel Gow (1763–1831), by John Kay

ball for his benefit in 1797. On 17 August 1784, in Edinburgh, Gow married Janet (d. 1808), the daughter of Francis Fraser, a sheriff officer who became a solicitor in the supreme court of Scotland; they had five daughters (Margaret, Janet, Catharine, Mary, Jean) and one son, **Niel Gow** (1794–1823), music-seller and composer, who was born in Edinburgh on 17 February 1794. In 1786 the family was living in Bailie Fyfe's Close, where they remained until moving to Princes Street in the New Town in 1800.

Nathaniel Gow contributed pieces to his father's first three collections of strathspey reels (1784, 1788, 1792; the third book includes a lament for the death of his brother William), and he was largely responsible for the 'considerable additions and valuable alterations' in their later editions. In 1796 he went into business in partnership with the cellist William Shepherd as a seller of music and musical instruments and a publisher specializing in dance music composed or arranged by members of the Gow family. They had a shop at 41 North Bridge Street, Edinburgh, before moving to Princes Street. Gow and Shepherd were the chief suppliers of Broadwood pianos in Scotland and maintained close links with the London firm of John Gow, Nathaniel's brother. Among their publications were the fourth and fifth collections of strathspey reels by Niel Gow & Sons (1801, 1809), the first three parts of the *Complete Repository of Original Scots Slow Strathspeys* (1799–1806), and, reflecting current international fashion, *A Complete Collection of Originall German Valtz* (c.1800). Each season new dance tunes introduced by Gow's band would appear in print; there were also his popular arrangements of Edinburgh street cries—'Caller Herring', 'The Mad (or Poor) Boy', 'Pease and Beans and Rock Partens'. Following

Shepherd's death on 19 January 1812, however, the firm went into decline, and on 11 October 1813 it was wound up.

Gow's first wife died in 1808, and on 30 August 1814 he married Mary (1786–1838), the daughter of William Hogg of Prestonpans. Two years previously she had successfully sued him in the court of session for breach of promise. The eldest of their five children, Augusta, was born on 13 July 1815. The family lived at 19 Queen Street in 1814–16, and afterwards at 2 Hanover Street. After the firm of Gow and Shepherd was dissolved, Gow continued to work as a private teacher and as the leader of his band. The patronage of the prince regent, for whom he played several times in London, added to his prestige.

In 1818 Gow resumed business as a publisher and retailer, this time in partnership with his son Niel. The latter, of whom his father had high hopes, had studied medicine at the University of Edinburgh (1811–15) and in Paris, and in 1815 was admitted as a licentiate of the Royal College of Surgeons of Edinburgh; it was to him that the 'active management' of the new shop at 60 Princes Street was entrusted (*Edinburgh Advertiser*, 21 July 1818). Niel's musical taste is apparent in his settings of poems by James Hogg ('The Lament of Flora Macdonald', 'Bonny Prince Charlie') and in his editing of *The Edinburgh Collection* (1824). The presence of English and Italian madrigals in the latter was perhaps the first sign in Scotland of an awakening interest in such 'ancient' music.

For five years things went well. The firm's publications included *The Vocal Melodies of Scotland* (1819), a sixth collection of *Strathspeys, Reels, and Slow Tunes* (1822), and *The Ancient Curious Collection of Scotland* (1823), which was dedicated to Sir Walter Scott. Scott repaid the compliment in *St Ronan's Well* (1824), where he imagined Gow's band playing for theatricals at Shaws-Castle:'"He is his father's own son," said Touchwood … "I never expected to hear his match in my lifetime"' (vol. 2, chap. 7). For the royal visit to Edinburgh in August 1822 Nathaniel Gow composed *King George the Fourth's Welcome to Auld Reekie*, and at the banquet at Dalkeith House was singled out by the king 'with some marks of Royal condescension' (*Edinburgh Advertiser*, 21 Jan 1831).

But Niel Gow fell ill with 'a lingering disease', and on 7 November 1823 he died in Edinburgh, aged twenty-nine. Nathaniel, too, was struck down with apoplexy. Suddenly the family faced financial problems; these were exacerbated by a loss of 'upwards of eight thousand pounds' which Nathaniel had lent to his son-in-law Adam Armstrong, the proprietor of Drum colliery, who had married Mary Gow in 1810. Nathaniel's business struggled on, with help from his brother John's firm in London, and he still gave lessons 'to young Ladies at his own house' (*Edinburgh Advertiser*, 28 May 1824). On 14 February 1826 he announced he was entering into partnership with John Murray Galbraith, an experienced tradesman and piano-tuner who had worked for John Broadwood & Sons in London. But in 1826 he was compelled to abandon his annual ball, and by September 1826 he was largely bedridden. In October the partnership with Galbraith was dissolved, and on 4 May 1827 Gow was declared bankrupt and his firm's stock sequestrated. A petition to the king for a pension (NL Scot., MS 573, fols. 32–47, dated 4 May–7 Nov 1826) was successful, however; the Royal Caledonian hunt voted him an annuity of £50, and special benefit balls 'for behoof of Gow and Family' were held in 1827–30. Gow died at his home, 2 Hanover Street, Edinburgh, on 19 January 1831, and was buried on the 24th near his son in Greyfriars churchyard.

Some of Gow's slow airs, strathspeys, and reels—such as 'Largo's Fairy Dance', composed for the Fife hunt in 1802—have remained favourites of their kind. Of his skill as a fiddler Joseph McGregor wrote:

> he had all the fire and spirit of his celebrated father in the quick music, with more refined taste, delicacy, and clearness of intonation in the slow and plaintive melodies … which placed him, by general and ungrudging consent, as the master spirit of that branch or department … in which, for a long course of years, he walked in unapproachable triumph.

McGregor characterized him as a man of:

> good understanding—generally of a lively companionable turn, with a good deal of humour—very courteous in his manners; though, especially latterly, when misfortune and disease had soured him, a little hasty in his temper … and faithful in his duties to his family. In his person he was tall and 'buirdly'—and he dressed well, which, added to a degree of courtliness of manner on occasions of ceremony, gave him altogether a respectable and stately appearance. (McGregor, 6–7)

He records that a 'spirited likeness' of him was painted by John Syme.   CHRISTOPHER D. S. FIELD

Sources J. McG. [J. McGregor], 'Memoir of Nathaniel Gow', in *A collection of airs, reels and strathspeys, being the posthumous compositions of the late Niel Gow* (1837), 4–7 · J. Glen, 'Nathaniel Gow', *The Glen collection of Scottish dance music*, 2 (1895), x–xiv · M. A. Alburger, *Scottish fiddlers and their music* (1983) · J. L. Cranmer, 'Concert life and the music trade in Edinburgh, c.1780 – c.1830', PhD diss., U. Edin., 1991 · N. Gow, 'To his royal and gracious majesty the king, the petition and solicitation of your majesty's loyal subject and servant', 1826, NL Scot., MS 573, fos. 32–47 · *Edinburgh Advertiser* (21 July 1818) · *Edinburgh Advertiser* (28 May 1824) · *Edinburgh Evening Courant* (23 Oct 1813) · *Edinburgh Evening Courant* (18 Feb 1826) · *Edinburgh Evening Courant* (5 March 1827) · *Edinburgh Evening Courant* (1 March 1828) · *Edinburgh Evening Courant* (15 March 1828) · *Edinburgh Advertiser* (21 Jan 1831)
Archives NL Scot., MS petition and letters
Likenesses photolithograph, 1895, repro. in Glen, 'Nathaniel Gow' · J. Kay, drawing, NPG [*see illus.*] · J. Syme, oils; untraced since 1837
Wealth at death declared bankrupt (4 May 1827): *Edinburgh Evening Courant*

Gow, Niel (1727–1807), fiddler and composer, was born at Inver, by Dunkeld, Perthshire, on 22 March 1727, the son of John Gow and his wife, Catherine McEwan. He married Margaret Wiseman presumably before 1759; they had five sons, including the fiddler Nathaniel *Gow, and at least two daughters. After his first wife's death Gow married Margaret Urquhart (or Orchard) on 17 June 1768; they had no children.

Scotland's most famous fiddler, and the author of

Niel Gow (1727–1807), by Sir Henry Raeburn

approximately eighty-seven compositions, Gow was enormously popular, and played for dances throughout Scotland (often with his cellist brother Donald) and, in London, at balls given by his patron, the duke of Atholl. 'His bow-hand … was uncommonly powerful [when playing strathspeys]', a contemporary wrote:

> The up-bow, … often feeble and indistinct in other hands, … was struck … with a strength and certainty which never failed to surprise and delight the skilful hearer … The effect of the sudden shout with which he frequently accompanied … the quick tunes … seemed to electrify the dancers, inspiring them with new life and energy.   (Alburger, 97–8)

A Collection of Strathspey Reels (1784) was the first of four volumes that Gow published under his own name. His sons William (*d.* 1791) and Nathaniel, musicians in Edinburgh, prepared the music and dealt with the printers; later publications were 'by Niel Gow and Sons'. All included traditional dance music, which Gow had probably learned by ear from other players; this encouraged further collecting while helping his family's and his own compositions reach wider audiences.

'Niel Gow plays', wrote Robert Burns when he visited Gow at home in Inver in 1787. 'A short, stout-built, honest Highland figure, with his greyish hair shed on his honest social brow—an interesting face, marking strong sense, kind open-heartedness, mixed with unmistrusting simplicity' (Fitzhugh, 162), Gow played two of his published compositions, 'Loch Erroch-Side' (to which Burns later set verses) and 'Lament for Abercairney', 'McIntosh's Lament' (a 'fiddle pibroch'), and the reel 'Tullochgorum'. The music Gow chose encapsulates his life and career: a living source of traditional music, unequalled performer of

Scottish dance music (especially strathspeys and reels), composer, publisher; generous-natured, respected, and comfortable with all who sought his company, showing 'a high degree of … humour, strong sense and knowledge of the world' (*Scots Magazine*, 4). In personal habits he was temperate, though some said he drank too much; 'he was constant in his attendance at divine worship, and had family prayers evening and morning in his own house' (Chambers, *Scots.*, 2.140). He was equally renowned for his

> fidelity, generosity and kindness … Though he had raised himself to independent and affluent circumstances … he continued free of every appearance of vanity or ostentation. He retained to the last, the same plain and unassuming simplicity in his carriage, his dress and his manners, which he had observed in his early and more obscure years.
> (Alburger, 116)

The most enduring image of Gow remains Sir Henry Raeburn's portrait, which shows him in tartan knee-breeches and hose, seated, playing his fiddle. Gow died on 1 March 1807 in Inver, where he lived all his life, and was buried in the Little Dunkeld churchyard; his gravestone was later moved to Dunkeld Cathedral. He left his daughter Margaret the majority of his estate, 'over 1000 pounds st[erlin]g and under 1500 st[erlin]g', including an eight-day clock and two bibles.   MARY ANNE ALBURGER

Sources M. A. Alburger, *Scottish fiddlers and their music* (1983); repr. (1996), 93–117 · J. Glen, *The Glen collection of Scottish dance music*, 1 (1891), vii · Chambers, *Scots.* (1835) · [McKnight], 'A brief biographical account of Neil [sic] Gow', *Scots Magazine and Edinburgh Literary Miscellany*, 71 (1809), 3–5 · settlement of Niel Gow, 14 May 1808, NA Scot., CC7/9/1 · OPR records of marriages, births, and christenings, Aberdeen Family History Society [also at Edinburgh] · R. T. Fitzhugh, *Robert Burns: the man and the poet* (1971) · J. McG. [J. McGregor], 'Memoir of Neil (sic) Gow', in *A collection of airs, reels and strathspeys, being the posthumous compositions of the late Niel Gow* (1837) · D. Baptie, ed., *Musical Scotland, past and present: being a dictionary of Scottish musicians from about 1400 till the present time* (1894), 67
Likenesses D. Allan, double portrait, *c.*1780 (with his brother), Scot. NPG · J. Jenkins, engraving, repro. in *Edinburgh curiosities* (1801) · H. Raeburn, oils, Scot. NPG [*see illus.*]
Wealth at death £1000–£1500: settlement of Niel Gow, 14 May 1808, NA Scot., CC 7/9/1, 28 June 1808, confirmation

Gow, Niel (1794–1823). *See under* Gow, Nathaniel (1763–1831).

Gowan, Ogle Robert (1803–1876), politician in Canada, was born on 13 July 1803 at Mount Nebo, co. Wexford, Ireland, the second of the four children of John Hunter Gowan (*d.* 1825), a landlord and magistrate, and Margaret Hogan. The illegitimate younger son in the second family of an important Wexford Orangeman, Gowan was educated at home. His godfather was one of the grand masters of the Orange order in Ireland, and he joined the order in 1818. After moving to Dublin he published an anti-Catholic newspaper, anti-Catholic pamphlets, and *The Annals and Defence of the Loyal Orange Institution of Ireland* (1825). On 20 August 1823 he married Frances Anne Turner of Wexford; they had eleven children. Frances died in 1852, and in 1866 Gowan married Alice Hitchcock. Upon his father's death, Gowan engaged in a bitter court battle over the estate, a dispute which he lost, and which harmed his reputation. In 1829, perhaps influenced by the passage of Catholic emancipation, he emigrated to Upper Canada with his wife, seven children, and two servants, and acquired land in Leeds county. On 1 January 1830 he was responsible for the meeting at the Brockville court house at which a number of local lodges founded the grand Orange lodge of British North America. Gowan was chosen deputy grand master and, when the duke of Cumberland declined the position, became the grand master.

Gowan ran for the assembly in 1830 as an independent. He was defeated, but, as Irish protestant immigrants continued to flow into Upper Canada, the influence of the Orange lodge grew. In 1834 and 1835 Gowan was elected to the assembly for Leeds county, but both elections were overturned because of Orange violence at the polls. He was defeated in a by-election in 1836 but later in the year was successful in the general election, when he rallied Orangemen against the reformers. During 1837 and 1838 Upper Canada was threatened not only by a small and easily suppressed rebellion but by raids from across the American border. Gowan became a captain in the Leeds militia, commanded a company of the Queen's Own Rifles during the capture of Hickory Island, was raised to the rank of lieutenant-colonel, and was twice wounded at the battle of the Windmill, near Prescott. Yet his relationship with Lieutenant-Governor Sir Francis Bond Head and his successor, Sir George Arthur, was strained. In 1836 the Orange order in the United Kingdom was dissolved, but Gowan refused to disband the order in Canada and resented the fact that neither Head nor Arthur was willing to recognize the services performed by Orangemen during the rebellion. In 1839 he was dismissed from his post as an agent for crown lands for publishing a letter advocating responsible government and in 1841 was defeated in the first election to the assembly of the united province of Canada. By 1843, however, Governor-in-Chief Sir Charles Metcalfe was desperately seeking to build an anti-Reform alliance, and one of the colonial politicians to whom he turned was Gowan. Gowan was elected in 1844 as a government supporter, but because of his Orange ties he remained an outsider and had to be content with the minor position of supervisor of tolls on canals, a post he lost in 1849 after the Reformers returned to power.

Gowan also lost his position as grand master in 1846 and his seat in the assembly in the elections of 1847–8. For participating in the demonstrations against the Rebellion Losses Bill and writing abusive articles about the governor-general, Lord Elgin, he was dismissed as a justice of the peace and as a lieutenant-colonel in the militia. In 1853 Gowan moved from Brockville to Toronto, acquired a newspaper, *The Patriot*, and was elected as an alderman. In the same year he was again elected grand master of the Orange order, although the contest was so bitter that more than a hundred lodges temporarily withdrew from the grand lodge, and in 1856 Gowan agreed to step down. In 1854 he threw his support behind the Conservatives, led in Upper Canada by his friend and fellow Orangeman John Alexander Macdonald, but, since the Conservatives were allied with the French-Canadian Catholic bloc, Gowan could not get unanimous Orange support. He was

defeated in 1854 and 1857, and finally won a seat at a by-election only in 1858. Faced with recurrent financial difficulties, in 1861 he retired from politics to become an inspector in the money order department of the post office of Upper Canada. From 1869 to 1874 he was issuer and inspector of licences for the city of Toronto, but his main interest remained the Orange movement, and he represented Canada at the foundation of the Imperial Grand Council in Belfast in 1866. In 1859–60 he published three volumes on *Orangeism: its Origin and History*. He was apparently working on a fourth volume when he died in Toronto, on 21 August 1876.

In his biography of Gowan, written over a century later, Don Akenson claims that the motivating factor in Gowan's life was the search for respectability. It is doubtful whether he ever fully achieved this goal, but his children certainly did. His daughters in particular married well, and one of his grandsons, Howard Ferguson, became premier of Ontario. Gowan's greatest achievement was his work on behalf of the Orange order. By the end of his life the order which he had done so much to organize had outgrown its Irish roots and had become one of the most important voluntary organizations in Canada: indeed, there were more Orangemen in Canada than there were in Ireland.

PHILLIP BUCKNER

Sources H. Senior, 'Gowan, Ogle Robert', *DCB*, vol. 10 · D. Akenson, *The Orangeman: the life and times of Ogle Gowan* (1986) · D. H. Akenson, *The Irish in Ontario: a study in rural history* (1984) · H. Senior, *Orangeism: the Canadian phase* (1972) · H. Senior, 'Ogle Gowan, Orangeism and the immigrant question, 1830–1833', *Ontario History*, 60 (1968), 13–24
Archives Ontario Archives, MSS

Gowan, Thomas (1631–1683), Presbyterian minister and philosopher, was born at Caldermuir in western Edinburghshire. His parentage is unknown. He studied at Edinburgh under the regent James Wyseman, graduating MA in 1655. After training for the Presbyterian ministry he settled in Ireland. Gowan was ordained to the parish of Donnagh, co. Monaghan, in 1658, and received £30 in tithe income. With the return of episcopacy in 1661 he lost the tithe but remained minister to the Presbyterian community at Glaslough. In 1666 he obtained leave in order to establish an academy for dissenters at Connor, co. Antrim, at the same time as the academy movement was developing in England. Gowan provided supply preaching at Connor, and participated in the business of the Antrim 'meeting', the precursor of the later presbytery, even though not formally installed as minister.

A call to the larger congregation of Antrim in 1671 offered a better location for the academy. Gowan was released from Glaslough about July 1672 but must already have taken up provisional residence in Antrim, since the 'little maintenance' provided for him there was already 'not well payed' (Belfast, Union Theological College, Antrim minutes, 3 July 1672). The congregation could offer neither manse nor meeting-house. His stipend, which was ruled to be too low at £40 per annum in 1674, seems never to have been paid in full or on time, and on his death his widow received only a portion of several years' arrears.

Information on his wife's family is unavailable. She must have been the younger partner, and they had at least one daughter and one son; the latter, a long-serving minister at Leiden, was born in the year of Gowan's death.

The English dissenter John Howe had since 1671 been chaplain in the household of John Skeffington, Viscount Massarene, at Antrim Castle, and had a dispensation from the episcopal authorities to preach in the parish church after the conclusion of the legal service. Massarene negotiated a similar concession for Gowan and his congregation. The Antrim meeting sanctioned the arrangement on the understanding that their adherents would not be 'ensnared' or 'profane the Sabbath' by being within earshot during the liturgy (Belfast, Union Theological College, Antrim minutes, 11 March 1673); nevertheless, some consciences were offended and Gowan could not enforce attendance. By 1677 he was preaching in a modest 'thatchd house' outside the town (Massarene to Ormond, 18 Jan 1678, *Sixth Report*, HMC, 746–7) and had succeeded Howe as domestic chaplain. In 1679, with the government nervous over renewed covenanting activity across in Scotland, he was one of two ministers sent from the Antrim meeting to present a loyal address to the lord lieutenant.

By 1675 Gowan had an official monopoly in philosophy teaching within Ulster. The academy provided his main income. It saved the sons of dissenters from crossing to Glasgow for classical and philosophical instruction and probably provided a more progressive curriculum. Gowan, as Goveanus, published two textbooks. In *Ars sciendi* (1681), dedicated to Massarene's son, who had apparently been his student, he expounded a traditional logic on the model of the Reformed scholastics Keckermann and Burgersdijk, but also offered an extensive analysis of logical and metaphysical topics, and practical instruction on hermeneutics and public presentation for prospective teachers and preachers. He studied the continental debate over Cartesianism, and knew the work of Johann Clauberg (whose anti-Catholic agenda he shared) and of the Port-Royalists, who together aimed at harmonizing traditional logic with the psychology and metaphysics of Descartes. Gowan retained an Aristotelian view of universals and of the sensory foundations of knowledge, while expressing it in the new language of 'ideas'. He denied the procedural value of doubt where there is no reason to doubt, but accepted much of Cartesian natural philosophy. *Logica elenctica* (1683) provided specimen theses, objections, and responses for student disputants; a brief compendium of *Elementa logicae* was added. Representatives of the Scottish universities in 1695 judged Gowan 'prolix in his Didacticks and obscure in his Elenticks bringing in many heterogeneous things' (*Munimenta alme universitatis Glasguensis*, 2.531), but his texts were studied in English academies, such as Rathmell and Bethnal Green, where Cartesianism had made an inroad. As late as 1723 *Ars sciendi* was the most recent philosophy text in the library of Harvard College.

In 1675 the Tyrone meeting recommended the establishment of a divinity school for Ulster dissenters. The Antrim meeting sought to have this too brought under Gowan's control, proposing that Howe should help with the additional burden (Belfast, Union Theological College, Antrim minutes, 1 June 1675). There is no evidence that this arrangement was implemented. Howe was soon in negotiation to return to England, and the divinity school was established under William Leggat at Dromore, co. Down (Bodl. Oxf., MS Carte 221, item 194). Gowan died at Antrim on 13 September 1683 and was buried in Antrim churchyard. Two works unfinished at his death are lost: a natural philosophy text, and a treatise against the Quakers, the latter originally planned jointly with Howe in response to a commission from the Antrim meeting.

M. A. STEWART

Sources minutes, Antrim meeting, 1671–91, Union Theological College, Belfast • J. McConnell and others, eds., *Fasti of the Irish Presbyterian church, 1613–1840*, rev. S. G. McConnell, 2 vols. in 12 pts (1935–51) • *Sixth report*, HMC, 5 (1877–8), 746–7 [Viscount Massarene to duke of Ormond, 18 Jan 1678] • letter, correspondents unidentified, [1675–83], Bodl. Oxf., MS Carte 221, item 194 • J. Ware, 'The writers of Ireland', ed. and trans. W. Harris, *The whole works of Sir James Ware concerning Ireland*, 2/2 (1746), 351–2 • D. Laing, ed., *A catalogue of the graduates … of the University of Edinburgh*, Bannatyne Club, 106 (1858), 76 • C. Innes, ed., *Munimenta alme Universitatis Glasguensis / Records of the University of Glasgow from its foundation till 1727*, 2, Maitland Club, 72 (1854), 531 • H. McLachlan, *English education under the Test Acts: being the history of the nonconformist academies, 1662–1820* (1931), 69, 87 • *Catalogus librorum bibliothecae collegii Harvardini* (Boston, MA, 1723) • T. Witherow, *Historical and literary memorials of presbyterianism in Ireland, 1623–1731* (1879), chap. 6 • W. T. Latimer, 'The Rev. Thomas Gowan and Antrim congregation', *Annual Report*, 1910 [Presbyterian Historical Society of Ireland] (1911), 6–9 • P. Kilroy, *Protestant dissent and controversy in Ireland, 1660–1714* (1994)

Gowdie, Isobel (*fl.* 1662), alleged witch, first appears as the wife of John Gilbert and an inhabitant of the farmstead at Loch Loy, near Auldearn, in highland Scotland. Although she was later supposed to have begun practising witchcraft in 1647, it was in spring 1662 that she was implicated in a plot to harm Henry Forbes (*fl.* 1655–1678), the minister of the kirk at Auldearn, and appears to have come forward—on her own account—to confess her guilt before the local authorities of having been 'over long' in the service of witchcraft (*Fasti Scot.*, 4.436; Pitcairn, 3, part 2, 603, 614). She gave four separate confessions at Auldearn between 13 April and 17 May 1662 in which the list of her crimes and accomplices was constantly refined and clarified by her examiners. She described how, in 1647, she had met the devil while out walking and had entered into a covenant with him. That same night she went to the kirk at Auldearn, where she denied her Christian baptism before the devil and received his mark on her shoulder. While she was held fast by her neighbour, Margaret Brodie, the devil supposedly sucked the blood from out of the mark and sprinkled it upon her head, declaring: 'I baptise thee, Janet, in my own name!' (Pitcairn, 3, part 2, 603). Having given herself in spirit to the devil Gowdie proceeded to give him exhaustive use of her body, and in her second confession provided lurid details of their sexual relationship.

Equipped with her new name and backed by a strong network of covens, Gowdie then supposedly began to wreak havoc upon her local community with the aid of her familiar spirit, known as the 'Read Reiver'. She claimed to have ruined crops and to have soured milk, to have transformed herself—at will—into jackdaws, hares, and crows, and to have stolen into the houses of the local gentry in order to 'eat and drink of the best' (Pitcairn, 604). Indeed, the procuring and consumption of rich foods is a constant theme in all her confessions and seems to have been one of the greatest benefits that she felt she had received during her service to her dark master. However, it is clear that Isobel, in 'professing [her] repentance' and her 'great grief and shame', was keen to please her interrogators and that her spoken testimony was heavily edited and led by them. Thus, her initial enthusiasm to tell of her meetings with the king and queen of the fairie, up in the 'Deunie-Hills', and to describe their appearances, together with the fearsome activities of the herds of 'elf-bulls' that milled about them, was brusquely cut short and went largely unrecorded in the official case notes (ibid., 604).

Demonology and not folklore was what concerned and motivated the authorities, and consequently the cataloguing of Gowdie's murderous crimes as a witch was what was demanded of her, and was what was duly revealed in her subsequent depositions. She had raised an unbaptized child from its grave at Nairn, caused the heirs of John Hay, laird of Park, to sicken, wither, and die, and had killed many men by flying through the air above them upon straws and shooting them down with special 'elf arrows' that came to her straight from the hands of the devil himself (Pitcairn, 615). Minister Forbes seems to have been singled out by the coven for particular attention and an underlying antagonism between him and Gowdie appears to have existed. Gowdie claimed to have begged the devil to be allowed to shoot at him again, after another witch's arrow fell short of its intended target. Moreover, she maintained that in winter 1660 the coven had sought to make his illness fatal by uttering incantations over a bag containing the 'galls, flesh and guts of toads', together with barley grains and nail and hair clippings, before hacking it to pieces and throwing the remains into water (ibid., 610, 612). However, in repeatedly expressing her profound sorrow for killing her neighbour, William Brower of Milltown Moynes, Gowdie appears to have seen herself as having acted against her own will, and to have genuinely believed that she had been directly responsible for his death through her use of demonic magic. It is conceivable that this powerful sense of guilt was a major factor in prompting Gowdie to make her confessions and to demand that an exemplary sentence should be passed upon her, desiring that she should be riven upon iron harrows or 'worse, if it could be devised' (ibid., 613–14).

Though Robert Pitcairn believed that Gowdie was probably convicted of witchcraft and subsequently burnt at the stake—together with her accomplice, Janet Breadheid—there is no record of her eventual fate. Her papers were forwarded to the Scottish privy council in summer 1662, and Sir Hew Campbell of Calder, together with eight others, was empowered to try the case, on 10 July 1662. However, it was recommended that the death sentence was to be passed only if a whole list of conditions regarding the prisoner's physical wellbeing and the state of her mental health was met in full. Not only was it important to prove beyond all doubt that Gowdie had confessed voluntarily and 'without any sort of torture', but, significantly, solid evidence was also required that 'at the tyme of their confessions … [Gowdie and Breadheid] were of sound judgment, nowayes distracted or under any earnest desyre to die'. Only if Gowdie insisted upon reiterating and renewing her former confessions before the judiciary, 'then and in that case and no otherwayes' should the death sentence be invoked (*Reg. PCS*, 1.243). Given so many provisions for allowing an acquittal—and no evidence of either a trial or an execution—it would appear likely, though by no means certain, that Gowdie was eventually discharged and allowed to slip back into the quiet obscurity whence she came. Her husband had never been implicated in the witchcraft allegations.

The case has been recognized by successive generations of writers, from Sir Walter Scott onwards, as being both sensational and atypical, bringing the term 'coven'—to denote a group of witches—into popular usage and attesting to a wealth of fairy lore in the highlands of Scotland that was far removed from the learned traditions of élite demonologists. Unfortunately, the desire to make this one, particularly detailed, account general and to apply it, uncritically, to the *modus operandi* of English witches has been both misleading and unhelpful. In particular Margaret Murray's attempts to prove that Gowdie represented a powerful and enduring underground pagan tradition at work within the British Isles, by selectively quoting from her confessions, has been subjected to increasing scholarly criticism from the 1970s onwards and has largely been discredited. Rather than speaking for a prior folk culture Gowdie's wild imaginings can be more accurately viewed as articulating the concerns and frustrated desires of a poor and frequently hungry woman who wished for plentiful meat to feast upon, and a level of social and sexual freedom that was all too lacking in the hierarchical, and kirk dominated, Scotland of the mid-seventeenth century. *The confession of Isobel Gowdie*, an orchestral 'requiem' by the Scottish composer James MacMillan, was premiered at the BBC Proms in 1990 and has been performed many times since. JOHN CALLOW

Sources R. Pitcairn, ed., *Ancient criminal trials in Scotland*, 3, pt 2 (1833) · *Reg. PCS*, 3rd ser., vol. 1 · C. Larner, C. Hyde Lee, and H. V. McLachlan, eds., *A source book of Scottish witchcraft* (1977) · W. Scott, *Letters on demonology and witchcraft* (1830) · C. O. Parsons, *Witchcraft and demonology in Scott's fiction* (1964) · M. A. Murray, *The god of the witches* (1931) · D. Purkiss, *Troublesome things: a history of fairies and fairy stories* (2000) · N. Cohn, *Europe's inner demons*, rev. edn (1993) · C. Larner, *Enemies of God: the witch-hunt in Scotland* (1981) · M. A. Murray, *The witch-cult in western Europe: a study in anthropology* (1921) · G. Watson, *Bothwell and the witches* (1975) · R. Hutton, *The triumph of the moon* (1999) · C. Larner, *Witchcraft and religion: the politics of popular belief* (1984) · *Fasti Scot.*, new edn

Gowdie [Goldie], **John** (*c*.1682–1762), Church of Scotland minister and university principal, was probably born at

Jedburgh, Roxburghshire, where his father was then schoolmaster. His parents were Agnes Aberneathy and John Gowdie (d. 1702), who became minister of Sprouston, Roxburghshire, in 1691. After graduating MA from Edinburgh on 30 April 1700 Gowdie was licensed by the presbytery of Kelso on 27 January 1702 and ordained to Earlston, Berwickshire, on 9 August 1704. On 3 January 1706 he married Jean Deas or Daes (d. 1736), with whom he had a son and a daughter. Serious and bookish, he distanced himself from evangelical fellow ministers over issues like the abjuration oath, and actively opposed them in the controversy over the *Marrow of Modern Divinity* during the years 1718–23. His sincerity won respect from the 'marrow man' Thomas Boston, however, even when he delivered a two-hour defence of the supposedly heretical John Simson in the general assembly of 1728.

Such performances, coupled with his solid adherence to moderate principles, drew the attention of the Argyll administration. Noting that Gowdie had fallen into 'unlucky circumstances' (probably a reference to his wife, Jean, who became deranged), Lord Drummore recommended to Lord Milton on 9 September 1729 that he be translated to Edinburgh, followed by a presentation for his son to Earlston, all of which would earn 'honest Goudie's prayers, and I am certain his obsequious services' (NA Scot., Saltoun MS 16540). Gowdie was accordingly translated to Lady Yester's Church in Edinburgh on 23 July 1730 (and was immediately replaced at Earlston by his son), and then to West St Giles or New North Kirk on 14 December 1732. The following May he was elected moderator of the general assembly, and in November 1733, ever wary of evangelical fervour, he used his casting vote at the meeting of the assembly's commission to depose, in effect, Ebenezer Erskine and his supporters, thus triggering the secession.

Gowdie demitted his parish charge after the Argathelian interest arranged his election as professor of divinity at Edinburgh University on 18 July 1733. The sermon that he preached before the general assembly of 1734 appeared in print soon afterwards, and he published other sermons in 1735 and 1736. Although his divinity lectures were considered dull and unoriginal, he continued to receive patronage, becoming king's chaplain and dean of the Chapel Royal in 1735. Deprived of these offices in 1744, during the brief squadrone administration that lasted from 1742 to 1746, he was rewarded for his loyalty to the Argathelians on 6 February 1754, when he became principal of Edinburgh University, which had made him a DD on 13 March 1759. As principal he was weak and indolent, and the university's reputation declined. Disliked for his conduct over Simson and Erskine, and derided for his paucity of talent, Gowdie represented, for many churchmen, the deleterious effects of political patronage upon ecclesiastical affairs.

On 28 August 1743, while in his sixties, he married his second wife, Anne Ker, with whom he had one child. Two years after his marriage he inherited from his niece a Roxburghshire estate called Whitmuirhall, but the inheritance was not confirmed until 1758, and his son sold it in 1761. Gowdie died in Edinburgh on 19 February 1762, and was buried in Greyfriars churchyard. He was survived by his wife, who died on 21 April 1764.

LAURENCE A. B. WHITLEY

Sources *Fasti Scot.*, new edn, 7.382 · R. Wodrow, *Analecta, or, Materials for a history of remarkable providences, mostly relating to Scotch ministers and Christians*, ed. [M. Leishman], 4 vols., Maitland Club, 60 (1842–3), vols. 3–4 · NL Scot., Saltoun MSS 1729–1758, Saltoun MSS 16540–17601 · NL Scot., Yester MSS 1742–1744, 7046–7062 · m. reg. Scot. [Jean Deas] · m. reg. Scot. [Anne Ker] · m. reg. Scot. [parents] · R. B. Sher, *Church and university in the Scottish Enlightenment: the moderate literati of Edinburgh* (1985) · J. Warrick, *The moderators of the Church of Scotland from 1690 to 1740* (1913) · D. Laing, ed., *A catalogue of the graduates … of the University of Edinburgh*, Bannatyne Club, 106 (1858) · *Memoirs of the life, time and writings of … Thomas Boston*, ed. G. H. Morrison, new edn (1899) · H. Sefton, 'The early development of "moderatism" in the Church of Scotland', PhD diss., U. Glas., 1962 · J. Brown, *The epitaphs and monumental inscriptions in Greyfriars churchyard, Edinburgh* (1867), 307

Likenesses pencil drawing, repro. in Warrick, *Moderators*, 304

Gower, Elizabeth Leveson- [*née* Lady Elizabeth Sutherland], **duchess of Sutherland and *suo jure* countess of Sutherland (1765–1839)**, landowner, was born on 24 May 1765 at Leven Lodge, near Edinburgh, the youngest and only surviving child of William Sutherland, eighteenth earl of Sutherland (1735–1766) and his wife, Mary (c.1740–1766), daughter and coheir of William Maxwell. Both parents died of 'putrid fever' in Bath in 1766, leaving the family, for the first time in five and a half centuries, with no direct male heir. Lady Sutherland was brought up by her maternal grandmother, Lady Alva; her interests, as an orphan, were placed in the care of tutors whose directives were executed by the general commissioner of the Sutherland estates. The succession to the title was disputed by several claimants but her tutors successfully defended her case in the House of Lords in 1771, tracing her descent from William, earl of Sutherland, in 1275. She thus inherited, under an entail of 1706, the ancient earldom and estate of Sutherland, as well as lands acquired subsequently, notably the barony of Assynt.

Between 1779 and 1782 Elizabeth Sutherland was educated in London, and she lived mainly there and in Edinburgh. She married on 4 September 1785 George Granville Leveson-*Gower, Viscount Trentham (1758–1833), known as Earl Gower from 1786, who in 1803 succeeded his father as second marquess of Stafford. The marriage settlement instituted a fresh enfeoffment in terms of the entail on the Sutherland estates, which were arranged on life rent to her husband. This was a prelude to further acquisitions of land in the county, including the Skelbo estate, so that by 1816 two-thirds of the county of Sutherland was in the hands of the Sutherland family. Further purchases of land continued to be made until the death of her husband in 1833, just six months after he was created duke of Sutherland. The huge highland estate had been heavily tied up in the hands of mortgagors who, from the 1790s, were progressively displaced to make way for a new management regime. A new philosophy of modernization and improvement (from the landowners' perspective) was inaugurated. Lady Sutherland (as she continued to be known) was the driving force behind much of the change, having shown interest in management questions since before her marriage. After 1803 the policy was accelerated, leading to a radical agrarian transformation of the estate which drew heavily on her husband's great wealth. Ambitious building and industrial projects grew as highland small tenants were removed from the interior to settlements on the coast. The family employed professional managers, notably James Loch, to undertake and shape the massive changes (and to bear the brunt of the vociferous criticisms of the policy). The countess visited Sutherland regularly and was fully apprised of the nature and consequences of these highly controversial changes. She was the target of great hatred in the northern highlands, though the policy of highland clearance also had its supporters, who considered the changes necessary, inevitable, and benevolent. Lady Sutherland endeavoured to counteract the adverse publicity surrounding the clearances, but with little success.

Like many aristocratic women of the period, Elizabeth Sutherland's interests were not confined to her estates. She accompanied her husband to Paris in May 1790 on his appointment as ambassador, at the height of the French Revolution, and wrote interesting descriptions of the political turbulence. She sent clothing to the imprisoned Marie Antoinette, an act which was reputed to be the last gesture of kindness shown to the doomed queen. The family experienced some difficulty in leaving France, finally departing in 1792. At the time Lady Sutherland's passport described her as 'five feet in height, hair and eyebrows light chestnut, eyes dark chestnut, nose well-formed, mouth small, chin round, forehead low, face somewhat long'. In 1793 she raised a regiment, the Sutherland fencibles, which in 1798 was employed in quelling the Irish rising. In the 1790s, she and her husband were closely connected with George Canning, one of her many male admirers, who regarded her as beautiful, intelligent, and charming. Other women regarded her as rather overbearing. She became a leading hostess in London, where she gave sumptuous dinners attended by royalty, aristocrats, and statesmen from Britain and abroad.

Privately, Lady Sutherland spent much of her time raising her four children, sketching (she was a gifted watercolourist, and was especially accomplished in her landscapes of the Sutherland coast and of Dunrobin Castle), corresponding with Sir Walter Scott, and consuming snuff. She dominated her sons and probably her husband as well. One of the main aims of her life was to maximize the personal fortunes of both of her sons, George Granville (1786–1861), who became second duke of Sutherland, and Francis *Egerton (1800–1857), created earl of Ellesmere, and to make the best marriages for her daughters, Charlotte Sophia (1788–1870), who became duchess of Norfolk, and Elizabeth Mary (1797–1891), who became marchioness of Westminster. From the death of her husband until her own death, the Scottish estates were administered separately on her behalf.

The duchess-countess of Sutherland, as she was known after her husband's elevation to a dukedom, died tranquilly on 29 January 1839 at Hamilton Place, Hyde Park, London. She was buried on 20 February, with great state, at Dornoch, in Sutherland.   ERIC RICHARDS

Sources GEC, *Peerage* · R. J. Adam, ed., *Papers on Sutherland estate management, 1802–1816*, 2 vols., Scottish History Society, 4th ser., 8–9 (1972) · E. Richards, *The leviathan of wealth: the Sutherland fortune in the industrial revolution* (1973) · *The Huskisson papers*, ed. L. Melville [L. S. Benjamin] (1931) · C. R. Fay, *Huskisson and his age* (1951) · *Lord Granville Leveson Gower: private correspondence, 1781–1821*, ed. Castalia, Countess Granville [C. R. Leveson-Gower], 2nd edn, 2 vols. (1916) · *The Farington diary*, ed. J. Greig, 2 (1923) · W. Hinde, *George Canning* (1973) · [C. K. Sharpe], *Letters from and to Charles Kirkpatrick Sharpe*, ed. A. Allardyce, 2 vols. (1888) · Duke of Sutherland [G. G. Sutherland-Leveson-Gower], *The story of Stafford House* (1935) · J. Loch, 'Dates and documents relating to the family and property of Sutherland', 1859, NA Scot.
Archives NL Scot., corresp. and papers · Staffs. RO | Keele University Library, letters to Ralph Sneyd · NA Scot., Loch collection · NL Scot., corresp. with Sir Walter Scott · NL Scot., corresp. with J. P. Wood
Likenesses Hoppner, portrait · Lawrence, portrait · Reynolds, portrait · Romney, portrait
Wealth at death wealthy

Gower, Sir Erasmus (1742–1814), naval officer and colonial governor, was born on 3 December 1742, eldest of the nineteen children of Abel Gower of Glandovan, Pembrokeshire, and his wife, Laetitia Lewes, only daughter of the Revd Erasmus Gower. 'Destined for the sea', he sailed in 1755 as captain's servant with his uncle Captain John Donckley (who died at sea in 1756) before moving to the *Coventry* (28 guns), *Winchester* (50 guns), and *Superb* (74 guns) as a midshipman. In 1762 he passed for lieutenant and was one of the officers 'deemed expedient to send into the Portuguese service' (*Naval Chronicle*, 4, 1801, 257). Two years later he joined *Dolphin* (20 guns) as an able seaman under Commodore John Byron. Promoted to midshipman during this voyage of discovery, on 9 July 1766 (PRO, ADM 6/20, fol. 27), Gower received his commission as lieutenant of *Swallow*, the 'miserable tool' commanded by Philip Carteret for a second and more fruitful circumnavigation, partly thanks to the continuity afforded on a second voyage by survivors of the first. To Gower's 'meritorious behaviour', said Carteret, 'I am incapable to do sufficient Justice' (Wallis, 1.131, 133). In 1769 Gower went as first lieutenant to the *Swift*, on the Falklands station. On 13 March 1770 *Swift* grounded on an unmarked rock and sank in Port Desire, Patagonia, leaving the crew stranded until the sloop's cutter sailed to the Falklands to bring succour. The subsequent court martial acquitted the captain and officers, who 'had behaved exceeding well' (PRO, ADM 1/5304), and Gower went to *Princess Amelia* (80 guns), flying the flag of George Rodney, as second lieutenant. Disappointed in expectation of a command, he became first lieutenant in *Portland* (50 guns) in May 1773, returned to England in 1774, and in March 1775 joined *Levant* (28 guns) for service in the Mediterranean.

In 1779 Rodney, restored to command in the West Indies, made Gower first lieutenant of his flagship, *Sandwich*

(94 guns), and in January 1780 he placed Gower in command of *Prince William* (64 guns), the beautifully built captured provision ship *Guipuzcoana*. In 1781 Gower briefly went to *Edgar* (74 guns) as flag captain to Commodore John Elliot in Gibraltar, before getting the *Medea* (28 guns) in November 1781. 'Lord Sandwich', he wrote, 'has made a most effectual sacrifice of me by forceing me to go to the East Indies' (Wallis, 2.510), but he distinguished himself and returned in 1784 with £5000, which 'added to a little I had before, and the half pay will make me very comfortable' (ibid., 2.518). In 1786, when an offer to command a squadron in India had not been followed up with an appointment, he went as Commodore John Elliot's flag captain in *Salisbury* (50 guns) to the Newfoundland station, where he served for three seasons. In 1787 Gower, had he not been in Newfoundland, would have commanded *Vestal* (28 guns), which because of storms and disease had to return without achieving its object of a diplomatic mission to China, but he was available when the project revived in 1791. Now knighted (1792), he assumed command of the *Lion* (74 guns) in 1792, and for the next two years conveyed the ambassador, George, Earl Macartney, his colourful suite, and all their accoutrements, to and from often dangerous destinations, losing hundreds of men to disease. If the mission did not have the success hoped for, it was no fault of Gower's. War with France having broken out, in 1794 he brought back to England a convoy of extraordinary value and assumed command of *Triumph* (74 guns), in the channel squadron. On 17 June 1795, when *Triumph* and *Mars* were bringing up the rear of five ships of the line and two frigates under Cornwallis, pursued by thirteen French ships of the line, fourteen frigates, two brigs, and two cutters, his masterly defence earned particular recognition, but in June 1797, as a result of the Spithead mutiny, Gower suffered the 'unprovoked and very unexpected insubordination of the people, whose comfort was always my first object, and whose promptitude of obedience had hitherto been my greatest Pride' (Gower to Evan Nepean, 2 June 1797, PRO, ADM 1/1844). Forced off the ship with all his officers, he was ordered by their lordships to hoist a broad pendant in *Neptune* (90 guns), on the Thames, to deal with mutineers on the Nore, which he did firmly and promptly. Plagued by ill health, he remained as a private captain in *Neptune* until, promoted to rear-admiral of the white on 22 February 1799, he went ashore. In 1801 he hoisted his flag in *Princess Royal* (98 guns), and he served with Lord Cornwallis in the channel squadron until 13 February 1802. Promoted rear-admiral of the red in 1801 and vice-admiral of the white three years later, he hoisted his flag that year in *Isis* (50 guns), and, for the next three seasons, becoming vice-admiral of the red in October 1805, served as governor of Newfoundland. His measures to improve the judicial system, his astute appraisals of changing shipping patterns which led him to argue for the positive effects upon Newfoundland's fishery, his challenge to American attempts to interfere with the fishery in Labrador, and his bid to enhance the condition of the poor and to establish schools marked the recognition that Newfoundland, in spite of official British attitudes, had at last become, as Lord Liverpool maintained, a sort of colony.

Gower never married, though the terms of his will include an unexplained legacy of £1000 to Henry Clark, 'the son or reputed son of Matilda Clark' (PRO, PROB 11/1558, fols. 351–352v), baptized in St John's Chapel, Portsea, in 1801. Promoted admiral of the blue in 1809 and admiral of the white in 1810, Gower died on 21 June 1814 at his home, The Hermitage, Hambledon, Hampshire, and was buried in Hambledon parish church graveyard. His character and personality, as indicated by his correspondence and actions, find an accurate description in his epitaph:

> in domestic life … consistent, and affectionate, in command prompt, indefatigable and brave, a patron of merit; unbiassed by favour, or connections in society, friendly, placid, conciliating and firm, under long and severe affliction [he was] respected by his friends and lamented by the poor. (*Naval Chronicle*)

W. A. B. DOUGLAS

Sources DNB · 'Biographical memoirs of Sir Erasmus Gower, knight', *Naval Chronicle*, 4 (1801), 257–89 · 'Additional biographical memoir', *Naval Chronicle*, 30 (1813), 265–301 · PRO, ADM 1, vols. 472–6, vol. 727, vols. 1838–1844, vol. 5304 · PRO, PROB 11/1558 · *Lion* (journal), NMM, Gow/3 · *Carteret's voyage around the world, 1766–1769*, ed. H. Wallis, 2 vols., Hakluyt Society, 2nd ser., 124–5 (1965) · *Steel's Original and Correct List of the Royal Navy* (1774–1810) · C. G. Head, 'Gower, Sir Erasmus', *DCB* · A. Peyrefitte, *The immobile empire* (1992) · D. Spinney, *Rodney* (1969) · C. G. Head, *Eighteenth century Newfoundland: a geographer's perspective* (1976) · H. H. Robbins, *Our first ambassador to China* (1908) · D. Syrett and R. L. DiNardo, *The commissioned sea officers of the Royal Navy, 1660–1815*, rev. edn, Occasional Publications of the Navy RS, 1 (1994)

Archives BL, journal of voyage to China, Add. MS 21106 · NMM, journal, letter-book, and notebook | NMM, letters to Sir Philip Carteret

Likenesses R. Livesay, oils, NMG Wales · R. Livesay, portrait, NMM; repro. in 'Biographical memoir' · W. Ridley, stipple (after R. Livesay), BM, NPG; repro. in *Naval Chronicle* (1800)

Wealth at death approx. £15,000–£16,000 in legacies: will, PRO, PROB 11/1558

Gower, Foote (1725/6–1780), Church of England clergyman and antiquary, was baptized on 1 June 1726 at the church of St John the Baptist, Chester, the eldest of at least six children of the Revd Foote Gower, a physician in the town, and his wife, Anna Maria. Educated at Brasenose College, Oxford, whence he matriculated on 15 March 1744, aged eighteen, he graduated BA (1747) and proceeded MA (1750), MB (1755), and MD (1757); he was elected a fellow of his college in 1750. He married Elizabeth, a sister of John Strutt MP (*bap.* 1727, *d.* 1816), and they had three sons: the Revd Thomas Foote Gower (*d.* 1849), Dr Charles Gower (*d.* 1822), and Richard Hall *Gower (*bap.* 1767, *d.* 1833).

It is not known whether Gower practised as a physician but he served as rector of the parishes of Chignan St James and Mashbury from 1761 to 1777, and also Woodham Walter from 1769 until his death, but resided at Chelmsford. Outside his priestly duties his abiding interest was county histories. In 1771 he published *A Sketch of the Materials for a New History of Cheshire, in a Letter to Thomas Falconer*, the contents of which included a list of manuscripts from Roger

Wilbraham for the Nantwich area, as well as the medical papers of his father. His aim was to issue the work in folio form at a subscription of 10 guineas, but this never materialized, though he published another prospectus in 1772. He was elected fellow of the Society of Antiquaries in 1768. Gower had hoped to prepare a history of Essex and his letters to a fellow antiquarian, Richard Gough, preserved in the British Library (Add. MS 22936), contain a great many references to his own life in Essex between 15 March 1765 and 22 August 1775. The 220 letters give a detailed portrait of him, ordering books from London, and asking Gough to carry out tasks for him, as well as references to the churches of the county and its historians. He also made collections for a new edition of John Horsley's *Britannia Romana*.

Gower's health deteriorated about 1772, which would explain his failure to write his projected county histories. He died of a 'rheumatick attack' on 27 May 1780 on a visit to Bath, a town which had connections with his patron at Woodham Walter, Thomas Fytche of Danbury Place. He was buried at Bath Abbey, probably on 2 June; he and the Revd Nathaniel Gower (*d.* 16 March 1726) are the only Gowers in the register of the cemetery. He was survived by his wife. His collection of Cheshire manuscripts was sold to Dr J. Wilkinson of London, who reissued his prospectus (7 June 1792) and resold to William Latham, who had connections with Sandbach and also expressed an interest in compiling a history. Like Gower and Wilkinson, Latham was unable to achieve his ambition.   D. BEN REES

Sources M. Christy, 'The Gower–Gough correspondence, 1765–1775', *Essex Review*, 8 (1899), 50–51 · 'Essex churches', *Essex Review*, 1 (1892), 95–6 · 'Essex churches', *Essex Review*, 2 (1893), 34–5 · G. Ormerod, *The history of the county palatine and city of Chester*, 2nd edn, ed. T. Helsby, 1 (1882), xxxiii–iv · D. Lysons and S. Lysons, *Magna Britannia: being a concise topographical account of the several counties of Great Britain*, 2 (1808), 466 · parish register, Bath Abbey [burials], 2 June 1780 (?) · *DNB* · Foster, *Alum. Oxon.* · will, PRO, PROB 11/1067, sig. 357 · *IGI*
Archives BL, collections relating to Cheshire, Add. MSS 11334, 11338 · Bodl. Oxf., collections for history of Cheshire · Bodl. Oxf., collections for history of Essex · Ches. & Chester ALSS, corresp. and papers relating to history of Cheshire | BL, corresp. with Richard Gough, Add. MS 22936
Likenesses W. Skelton, line engraving, pubd 1790 (after J. Taylor), NPG

Gower, Francis Leveson-. *See* Egerton, Francis, first earl of Ellesmere (1800–1857).

Gower, (Edward) Frederick Leveson- (1819–1907), politician and autobiographer, the third son of Granville Leveson-*Gower, first Earl Granville (1773–1846), diplomat, and his wife, Lady Henrietta, or Harriet, Cavendish (1785–1862) [*see* Gower, Henrietta Elizabeth Leveson-], daughter of the fifth duke of Devonshire, was born on 3 May 1819. He was always called by his second forename and usually 'Freddy'. His early years were partly spent with his parents at the British embassy, Paris. As a boy he was a frequent visitor at Holland House. Educated at Eton College and at Christ Church, Oxford, he graduated BA in 1840; he was judge's marshal to Lord Denman and Lord

(Edward) Frederick Leveson-Gower (1819–1907), by Charles Holl and A. Roberts (after Henry Tanworth Wells, 1871)

Parke, and was called to the bar at the Inner Temple in 1845. In 1846 he was elected as a Liberal for Derby at a by-election, and was re-elected at the general election the next year, but was unseated on petition, his agent having illegally engaged voters as messengers. Elected for Stoke-on-Trent in 1852, he was at the bottom of the poll at the election five years later, the Chinese war having divided the Liberals in the constituency. In 1859 he was elected for Bodmin, and he held the seat until 1885, when he retired from political life.

Leveson-Gower's speeches in the House of Commons were not numerous, though he seconded the address on the meeting of parliament in the autumn of 1854. Gladstone offered him the posts of chief whip and postmaster-general, but he refused both, thinking that there were others more deserving of promotion. He was for several years chairman of railway committees, a tribunal of which he formed no high opinion. In 1874 he became the first chairman of the National School of Cookery, and held the position until 1903, when he became vice-chairman. He acted for some twenty years as a director of Sir W. G. Armstrong & Co.

Leveson-Gower took much pleasure in foreign travel. In 1850–51 he visited India. In 1856 he went to Russia as attaché to his brother, Lord Granville Leveson-*Gower, the special envoy at the coronation of Tsar Alexander II. But it was as a social figure that he was most conspicuous. Gifted with agreeable manners, conversational tact, and a good memory, he excelled as a diner-out and giver of dinners. These qualities are reflected in his *Bygone Years* (1905), a pleasant volume of reminiscences, which contains many well-told anecdotes. His editing of his mother's *Letters* (1894) also shows an intimate knowledge of several generations of society. He was a member of Grillion's Club, and also of the Political Economy Club (he made a serious study of political economy). He was JP for the county of Surrey and deputy lieutenant for Derbyshire.

Leveson-Gower married, on 1 June 1853, Lady Margaret Mary Frances Elizabeth, second daughter of Spencer Joshua Alwyne Compton, second marquess of Northampton; she died on 22 May 1858, three days after bearing their only child, George Granville Leveson-*Gower (who was one of Gladstone's secretaries, 1880–85). After her death, Freddy Leveson-Gower lived with his mother at Chiswick House, Chiswick, until she died in 1862, when he took 14 South Audley Street. In 1870 he also purchased Holmbury, near Dorking. There Gladstone visited him at least annually and often for weekends during the session. Other frequent guests were his brother, Lord Granville, to whom he was much attached, Harriet Grote, Bishop Wilberforce, Tennyson, and Russell Lowell. Leveson-Gower died at 11 Duchess Street, London, on 30 May 1907, and was buried at Castle Ashby, Northamptonshire.

L. C. SANDERS, rev. H. C. G. MATTHEW

Sources F. Leveson-Gower, *Bygone years: recollections* (1905) · *The Times* (31 May 1907) · H. E. Gower, *Letters, 1810–1845*, ed. F. Leveson-Gower, 2 vols. (1894) · Gladstone, *Diaries* · G. W. E. Russell, *Sketches and snapshots* (1910) · CGPLA Eng. & Wales (1907)
Archives BL, corresp. with W. E. Gladstone, Add. MSS 44440–44519, *passim* · PRO, letters to Granville, PRO30/29
Likenesses De Caraman, portrait, 1836–7, priv. coll. · H. T. Wells, chalk drawing, 1871, priv. coll. · C. Holl and A. Roberts, stipple (after H. T. Wells, 1871; Grillion's Club series), BM, NPG [*see illus.*] · O. Manara, oils, Hardwick Hall, Derbyshire
Wealth at death £40,474 18s. 5d.: probate, 24 July 1907, CGPLA Eng. & Wales

Gower, George (d. 1596), portrait and decorative painter, son of George Gower, came of a Yorkshire gentry family. His date of birth and the nature of his training are unknown, although he may have been the George Gower who became a freeman of York in 1555/6 as a merchant. In the 1570s and 1580s he was probably the leading portrait painter in London, where many of his rivals were born and trained overseas. His linear, typically English style conveys a firm sense of character.

Gower's earliest surviving paintings are portraits of Sir Thomas Kytson and Elizabeth Cornwallis, Lady Kytson (both 1573; Tate collection). This commission is documented in the Kytson accounts (formerly at Hengrave Hall, Suffolk) for the couple's visit to London in March–June 1573: 'Payed to Gower of London paynter for v pictures vjli.vs' (Cambridge University, Hengrave MS 82(3)). The three other works have not been convincingly identified and are probably lost. The Willoughby family archives (now at Nottingham University) for the same year record a payment to an unnamed artist for the portraits of Sir Francis Willoughby and Elizabeth, Lady Willoughby (priv. coll.), which are plausibly attributed to Gower.

Gower's self-portrait (priv. coll.) of 1579 also survives, and together with the Kytson portraits has been used as a basis for attributing at least a dozen further works to him. It is unique in being the only known surviving self-

George Gower (d. 1596), self-portrait, 1579

portrait in large by a British sixteenth-century artist. Gower depicted himself holding a brush and a palette charged with paint; above these, in the pans of a meticulously delineated metal balance, a pair of dividers is shown outweighing the Gower family coat of arms. Over this allegorical device, an eight-line verse testifies to Gower's personal pride in his professional skill, which it compares with the military feats that had gained his forebears the status of gentlemen. The arms confirm that Gower was a grandson of Sir John Gower of Stettenham, Yorkshire, and his wife, Elizabeth Goldsborough, and that his mother was a Statham of Northamptonshire.

On 5 July 1581 Gower was appointed sergeant-painter to Elizabeth I, with an annuity of £10, and from that date until the year of his death he is named in the royal accounts in connection with decorative, heraldic, and *trompe-l'œil* painting at Eltham, Greenwich, Westminster, Whitehall, and Richmond palaces, all now lost. In 1583–4 he was in charge of such work at Whitehall as painting 'ij Personadges done about the Arches & Pillers of the Bankett house' (Edmond, 180). Other official commissions included cleaning the celebrated astronomical clock (still extant) in 1584–5 and in 1591–2 gilding the great lost fountain topped with the figure of Justice, both at Hampton Court Palace, as well as decorating such items as coaches, furniture, and textiles for the queen. He seems to have been the first portraitist to become sergeant-painter, and there is no evidence that portrait painting had been a part of his predecessors' duties, which had been principally of an applied nature. In 1588–9 he was paid for cleaning and varnishing earlier royal paintings. By 1593 he was painter to the navy. In 1596 the privy council appointed the sergeant-painter to oversee the queen's portraits.

A draft patent of 1584, which was apparently never executed, would have granted Gower the monopoly of all painted and engraved portraits of the queen, while allowing Nicholas Hilliard the monopoly of her portraits in miniature; as sergeant-painter, Gower would also have gained exclusive rights in purveying art materials. In spite of this document, it has not proved possible to identify with confidence any portraits of the queen painted by him, although he has been proposed as the author of two of the 'Armada' portraits of about 1588–9 (Woburn Abbey, Bedfordshire; National Portrait Gallery on loan to Montacute House). A patent of February 1589, granting him properties in Devon, Essex, and Leicestershire, indicates that he merited a special reward.

Gower was twice married: his first wife was Katherine Cotton, and his second wife, Grace Hughson, outlived him. Her identity is known through a prerogative court of Canterbury sentence delivered in June 1597, settling a dispute over the administration of Gower's property with a kinsman called 'Walter Gower alias Wainewright', and which may suggest that Gower was incapacitated for some time before his death (PCC sentence 1597, 50). While often resident at court, Gower was domiciled from 1585 until his death in the London parish of St Clement Danes, where he was buried on 30 August 1596.

KAREN HEARN

Sources J. W. Goodison, 'George Gower, serjeant painter to Queen Elizabeth', *Burlington Magazine*, 90 (1948), 261–5 • E. K. Waterhouse, 'A note on George Gower's self-portrait at Milton Park', *Burlington Magazine*, 90 (1948), 267 • E. Auerbach, *Tudor artists* (1954), 52, 107–11, 113–15, 118, 130, 142, 147 • E. Croft-Murray, *Decorative painting in England, 1537–1837*, 1 (1962), 179–80 • R. Strong, 'A painting by Queen Elizabeth I's serjeant-painter', *Art Association of Indianapolis Bulletin* (Dec 1963), 52–8 • R. Strong, *The English icon: Elizabethan and Jacobean portraiture* (1969), 15–16, 167–84 • M. Edmond, 'Limners and picturemakers', *Walpole Society*, 47 (1978–80), 60–242, esp. 178–82, 212 no. 541 • E. Waterhouse, *Painting in Britain, 1530–1790*, 5th edn (1994), 34–5 • K. Hearn, ed., *Dynasties: painting in Tudor and Jacobean England, 1530–1630* (1995), 102–3, 107–8 [exhibition catalogue, Tate Gallery, London, 12 Oct 1995 – 7 Jan 1996] • C. Gapper, '"Trompe l'oeil" architectural painting on plaster in the royal works, 1582–89', *Traditional Paint News*, 1/2 (1996), 16–20 • J. Foster, ed., *The visitation of Yorkshire made in the years 1584/5 … to which is added the subsequent visitation made in 1612* (privately printed, London, 1875) • sentence, 1597, PRO, PROB 11/89, sig. 50

Likenesses G. Gower, self-portrait, oil on panel, 1579, priv. coll. [*see illus.*] • J. Basire, line engraving, 1800 (after G. Gower), BM, NPG; repro. in R. Gough, 'Parochial history of Castor', in K. Gibson, *A comment upon part of the fifth journey of Antoninus through Britain* (1800)

Gower, George Granville Leveson-, first duke of Sutherland (1758–1833), landowner, eldest son of Granville Leveson-*Gower, second Earl Gower and later first marquess of Stafford (1721–1803), and his second wife, Lady Louisa Egerton (1723–1761), daughter of Scroop Egerton, first duke of Bridgewater, was born in Arlington Street, London, on 9 January 1758. He claimed descent in the male line from Sir Alan Gower of Stittenham, supposedly sheriff of York at the time of the conquest. Until 1786 he was known as Viscount Trentham. His mother died in 1761 and he spent much of his childhood in the care of his maternal aunt, Lady Caroline Egerton. The Leveson-Gowers had

George Granville Leveson-Gower, first duke of Sutherland (1758–1833), by Thomas Phillips, 1805

accumulated wealth in Staffordshire and Shropshire and had established considerable political and industrial interests. But the talent of the family to make good marriage alliances helped its rise to the highest rank of wealth, most spectacularly when his father had married the sister of the heirless duke of Bridgewater, the 'canal duke'.

Family alliances and wealth Trentham was delicate as a child and though studious made only slow progress at school at East Hill, near Wandsworth in London, after which he attended Westminster School from 1768 to 1774. Edmund Burke suggested he be sent to Auxerre, where he acquired a good knowledge of French. In May 1775 he entered Christ Church, Oxford, where he mainly cultivated his interest in languages.

After Oxford Trentham travelled to Scotland and then to Ireland in 1780, to France, Germany, Austria, and the Low Countries in 1781, and to Italy in 1786. On 4 September 1785 he married Elizabeth Sutherland (1765–1839) [*see* Gower, Elizabeth Leveson-, duchess of Sutherland], who, as duchess of Sutherland, had inherited arguably the most ancient subsisting peerage in Great Britain and was proprietor of the greater part of the county of Sutherland. Her territories in the northern highlands were immense in scale but small in income. It was a territorial empire which eventually expanded to more than a million acres. Her husband took great pleasure in these highland properties but actively disliked the sound of the bagpipes. In March 1803 he inherited the annual net income of the Bridgewater Canal and estates from his maternal uncle. Six months later his father, the marquess of Stafford, died, and thus he also came into the marquessate and possession of the family estates at Trentham and Wolverhampton in Staffordshire, Lilleshall in Shropshire, and Stittenham in Yorkshire. Charles Greville described him as 'a leviathan of wealth' (*Greville Memoirs*, 20). He became 'abominably rich' (*Private Correspondence*, 2.20).

At the time of his death the duke of Sutherland, as he had become, was the greatest landowner in the country. He was the largest canal and railway proprietor too. As the *Quarterly Review* put it, his was 'a single estate certainly not in these days equalled in the British Empire' (*QR*, 69, 1841, 42). In the late 1820s he had a gross income of almost £200,000 per annum. His expenditures were enormous, especially those entailed in maintaining the style of Stafford House in London and the other substantial family houses at Trentham, Lilleshall, and Dunrobin. As early as 1806 his living standard was said to have 'exceeded everything in this country, no one could vie with it' (J. Farington, *The Farington Diaries*, ed. J. Grieg, 1924, 3.189, 236). There were large expenditures on reconstruction and refurbishment of each of the country houses. Eventually a large proportion of his enormous wealth was invested in the great estates in the northern highlands, consequent upon his marriage to the countess of Sutherland.

Politics and influence Just before he was twenty-one Viscount Trentham was selected MP for Newcastle under Lyme in Staffordshire; he was re-elected in 1780 though not in 1784. In 1787 (by which time he was known as Earl Gower) he was back in the House of Commons sitting for the county of Stafford, which he represented until 1798 when he entered the House of Lords as Baron Gower of Stittenham.

In 1790, though without previous diplomatic experience, Gower went as ambassador to Paris, a post of extreme importance and difficulty in the days of the French Revolution. He arrived in July, aged thirty-two, with his wife. His instructions and dispatches became interesting historical documents of the time and were published under the editorship of Oscar Browning in 1885. He stayed on in Paris until the hurried withdrawal of the embassy in August 1792, having experienced difficulties in obtaining passports for himself, his wife, and their young son, George Granville (*b.* 1786), later second duke of Sutherland. Lady Sutherland was held up at Abbeville, during her journey, by the local revolutionary council but was released after a short detention. These events terminated Gower's diplomatic career.

Afterwards Gower was offered posts which included that of lord steward and the lord lieutenancy of Ireland. He declined, apparently on the grounds of poor eyesight, but in 1799 became joint postmaster-general and he held this position until 1810. In the 1790s he was closely associated with George Canning and also with William Huskisson, who was his secretary from 1790 and whose political career was much promoted by the Leveson-Gower interest. In 1803, Gower succeeded his father as second marquess of Stafford. He was evidently still involved in politics and was one of the leaders in the attack on Addington's administration in 1804. He gave notice of a motion in the House of Lords regarding 'the defence of the country', but the ministry meanwhile chose to resign. He attached himself to Grenville rather than Pitt and received the Garter in 1806. In April 1807 he moved a motion, condemning the king's conduct on the Roman Catholic question, which was easily defeated. Thereafter he took little part in politics even though he possessed great political leverage. Creevey in 1819 said he was worth ten votes in the House of Commons, but he did not exercise the influence with any energy and let much of it slip away in the 1820s. In politics he supported Catholic emancipation, Huskisson's liberal trade policies, and the Reform Bill.

Spending a fortune Stafford enlarged Cleveland House which he inherited from the duke of Bridgewater with a remainder to his second son, Lord Francis. He augmented its great collection of paintings and was one of the first owners of private galleries in London to permit public access. He was an astute and enthusiastic art collector and as president of the British Institution he presented the National Gallery with many pictures, including the celebrated *Doria Rubens*, which he had bought in Genoa for £3000. In December 1827 he purchased the incomplete Stafford House which had been begun by the duke of York, for which he paid £72,000, and on which a further £200,000 was lavished in the following decade or so. It later became Lancaster House and then the London Museum. It was host to many great displays of wealth and prestige, and was later to be the model for Crécy House in the work of Disraeli. He gave his first son, George Granville, the estate of Lilleshall as a wedding present in 1825, worth £25,000 per annum. He was expected to learn how to live off its income. The Sutherland estates in Scotland reverted to the second duke in 1839, on the death of his mother.

In 1804 Stafford was described as

> a very good man to have in a house in the country, as he goes on quietly in his own way and has a hundred little pursuits of his own, such as poking into all the ponds for weeds, and examining all the cobwebs for insects … he is good-humoured and ready to oblige. (H. Cavendish, *Hary-O: the Letters of Lady Harriet Cavendish, 1796–1809*, ed. G. Leveson-Gower, 1940, 99)

He was thought to be somewhat ponderous and other-worldly, but his wife supplied all the socializing energy that his position required. From 1803 he devoted himself increasingly to patronage of the arts and the improvement of his estates. A large proportion of his princely income was devoted to radical agricultural change and the expansion of the territorial empire in the northern highlands. The strategy of the family involved the consolidation and modernization of its landed estates and the maintenance of a dynastic balance between their two sons. There was a particular concern that the second son, Lord Francis [*see* Egerton, Francis, first earl of Ellesmere], heir to the Bridgewater fortune, would be wealthier than his elder brother, Lord Gower.

In October 1806 Stafford was said by his wife to be already well pleased with the improvements under way in the north of Scotland: 'He is seized as much as I am with the rage of improvement, and we both turn our attention with the greatest energy to turnips, but cannot settle whether they ought to be broadcast or drilled' (Allardyce, *Letters*, 1.281). The countess herself contributed much of the energy and initiative for these changes. In October 1808 she said that they were

> much occupied in plans for improvement. This country is an object of curiosity at present, from being quite a wild quarter inhabited by an infinite multitude roaming at large in the old way, despising all barriers and regulations, and firmly believing in witchcraft.   (ibid., 1.346)

The highlanders would receive civilization and improvement. The grand plans for improvement, were, however, constrained by difficulties in the management of the far-flung estates.

At a dinner party in 1812 Lord Stafford remarked that it was impossible for a gentleman to administer an estate, to which proposition the Scottish lawyer James *Loch expressed disagreement. From this discussion Loch was soon offered the commissionership of the family estates, which he held until his death in 1855. At that time it was remarked that 'The Staffords seem to have turned their thoughts entirely to economy and the society of Scotch agents' (Richards, 19). Lord Gower was also recruited into a more direct managerial role in rural affairs, but Loch was at the helm.

On the English estates an ambitious programme of rationalization, greater accountability, and efficiency, was instituted under Loch. Rents rose and better farming practices were introduced, down to such fine detail as the abolition of beer payments. It was claimed that the severity and rapidity of these changes damaged the local popularity of the Stafford family. In 1820 the family was so surprised at the rebellion of the freeholders of Staffordshire against the Trentham interest that Lord Gower retired ignominiously from the electoral contest. Soon the interest was relinquished and in 1825 the Staffords' political property at Newcastle was sold off to Lord Anson. Thomas Bakewell, a local critic of these changes, complained that, unlike his father, Lord Stafford was little seen among his English tenantry and had become 'reserved and secluded'.

The Sutherland clearances In Sutherland the improvement policies were revolutionary in scale and impact. They entailed a thoroughgoing commercial redeployment of the land. The twin objectives were to raise rents and to reduce the vulnerability of the much-increased population to famine. Loch claimed that the progress on the estates had been impeded by the existence of long leases which had preserved the old ways and held back landlord-initiated improvements. These leases expired, on both the Scottish and the English estates, at the time when Lord Stafford had income enough to fund massive investment in change.

The comprehensive changes in Sutherland were planned in great detail. They included unprecedented expenditures on communications designed to end the isolation of Sutherland. There had been no coach traffic beyond Aberdeen until 1811, when parliament offered half the cost of road building in the northern counties of Scotland if proprietors found the rest. Stafford took advantage of this arrangement. In the following twenty years the family completed 450 miles of roads and 134 bridges, including the great iron structure at Bonar Bridge, its 150 feet span connecting Ross and Sutherland. In 1818 Stafford extended the mail service from Inverness to Thurso.

Simultaneous large investments were made in harbour construction, fishing facilities, house and inn building, and new industrial development along the eastern and northern coasts. These developments were designed to rejuvenate the economy, increase the rental income of the estate, and create employment for the population displaced from the interior. In addition the family bought adjoining estates which consolidated the family's holdings in the highlands. The purchase of tens of thousands of acres in the Reay country (1829), Bighouse (1830), Armadale (1813), and Carroll (1812), was regarded not only as an investment but also as the reunification of lands lost by the family in previous centuries. This territorial aggrandizement gave the family almost total control of the county of Sutherland by 1830.

The main source of new income on the Sutherland estate derived from the re-leasing of most of the inland territory to great capitalist sheep farmers, some of whom were drawn from southern Scotland and from England. Their farms reaped economies of large-scale, commercial wool and meat production, against which the resident population could not compete. The new sheep farms required the removal and relocation of the interior communities.

The inland populations were removed *en bloc* and offered resettlement on coastal lots, on lands some of which had been bought expressly for their reception. The plans were contingent on the concomitant development of industries and fishing along the sea coast which, by their design, would enable the people to live more comfortably and with greater security of income. They would be liberated from feudal obligations and placed in a position to divide their labour according to the principles of Adam Smith.

Most of all, the plans required the ousting of several thousand people at a time, in a series of great 'removals' from 1812 to 1815 and 1819 to 1821. The execution of these policies inevitably led to much manhandling of the reluctant or resistant small tenantry. Moreover, the estate agents found it necessary to burn many houses and other buildings to prevent their re-occupation. These events were widely reported in the Scottish and London newspapers and created a storm of indignation within and beyond the highlands. There were allegations of general cruelty and specific atrocities. The most serious charges, including that of culpable homicide, were made against Patrick Sellar, who was both agent to the Sutherland estate and sheep farmer in his own interest. He was brought to trial at Inverness in 1816 but was acquitted and subsequently recovered heavy damages against Robert Mackid, the sheriff substitute, who had carriage of the legal process. The removals in Sutherland occasioned great turmoil among the people and there was serious agitation and prolonged resistance in several parts of the county. Eventually, however, the landlord's policies prevailed, leaving a legacy of bitterness which persisted even to the end of the following century.

James Loch was principal apologist for the Stafford family and provided their justification of the Sutherland policies. Once described as 'the Duke's Premier', he published two substantial accounts of the improvements (Richards, 31). He argued that, before the 'vast changes', the population of the estate had lived in extreme poverty under the feudal yoke of tacksmen. The highlands in general and Sutherland in particular had fallen far behind the rest of the country and there had been an imperative for change that made it necessarily both decisive and swift. The middlemen of the previous system had benefited most from the *status quo ante* and had fomented most of the opposition to the improvements. They had been eradicated and the common people had been made direct tenants to the landlord at generally reduced rents. Every effort had been made to provide for their comfort in the resettlement zones along the coasts of the estate. The essential purpose of the changes had been to retain the population in conditions of greater security and liberality. Generous notice had been provided for the removals, and Lord Stafford had spared no expense in creating better facilities for his tenantry. He had spent £60,000 together with all rental income for the period from 1811 to 1833. Most of all, the people would no longer be hostage to recurrent famine since they were re-established in more diversified and secure economic circumstances, notably in the new fishing enterprises and associated activities along the coasts. In parallel, the great inland territory thus relinquished was made over to sheep farmers who utilized the land in a much more commercial fashion, and brought wealth to the county and paid much higher rents. In Loch's view the essential benevolence and common sense of the improvements had been obscured by the malice of self-interested opponents who had attempted to block all progress.

The wider verdict on these policies was less favourable. Lord Stafford's expenditures created substantial employment along the coasts for the duration of the investments. It is clear that the Sutherland policies were originally designed to retain the population on the estate. They were resettlement plans not evictions. While many people left the estate, and some emigrated to Canada, most stayed and were accommodated in small lots on the coasts. The population stabilized until the mid-nineteenth century. But the creation of reception facilities was not well synchronized with the removals. There was less famine than previously and even in the 1840s the estate sustained better levels of welfare among the people than in most parts of the highlands; but few of the original visionary projects came to genuine fruition. They had been extremely expensive but yielded very low rates of return on the outlays. Most of the positive aspects of the policies involving reconstruction and resettlement were ultimately undermined by adverse economic trends, especially those affecting the fishing and kelp, and the mining and manufacturing enterprises. As time went by, many of the small tenantry migrated. Moreover fears of population growth, and Loch's belief that the natural tendency of population was to increase more quickly than the means of subsistence, began to influence the management. Eventually the estate began to encourage emigration and to discourage early marriage among the small tenantry. The original assumptions for large-scale and cumulative development along the coasts proved largely illusory.

The policies in Sutherland were premised on highly optimistic assumptions about the malleability of the people and the future of new investment in the highlands. They grossly under-estimated the dislocation involved and the almost total lack of co-operation of the common people. Towards the end of his life Loch told Lord Shaftesbury that 'the statements regarding the acts of cruelty and oppression either in the former or the present management are so entirely devoid of truth that they can only be met by a bare, but most distinct, denial' (Richards, 277). He claimed that the common people were palpably more comfortable and that the improvements had succeeded. Yet, in truth, Loch was actively encouraging emigration and there was a large demand, in the north-west of the estate, for assistance to leave Sutherland.

The clearance policies gave rise to severe and repeated controversy. Writers as various as Donald McLeod, Sismondi, Hugh Miller, William Cobbett, and Alexander Mackenzie, regarded the Sutherland clearances as the most inhuman example of the economic revolution that raged through the highlands in the early nineteenth century. Karl Marx in *Capital* (1867) regarded it as the classic case in British history of the expropriation of the people by the aristocracy. Harriet Beecher Stowe and Léonce de Lavergne were among a smaller group of writers who saw merit in the Sutherland policies.

The professionalism of Loch's management ensured that his employers were well briefed on the affairs of the estates. Neither Lord Stafford nor his wife was ever ignorant of the programmes instituted in their names. Loch said that the Staffords were perfectly aware of the immense cost of the improvements and the agitation to which they gave rise. 'It is indeed worth all it has cost', remarked Lord Stafford when he examined the installations at Brora (Richards, 283). He took great joy in the improvements, according to Loch. A different view was expressed by his second son, Lord Francis Egerton (1800–1857), heir to the Bridgewater fortune and earl of Ellesmere from 1846, who remarked of his father's great land purchases in the highlands: 'I never could understand my father's policy in buying it, but he was in conditions as to money and expenditure which gave him a privilege of indulging any such caprice' (ibid., 283).

Dynastic adjustments and successors In 1821 Lord Stafford visited Paris for five months. In 1822 he was seized with paralysis from a stroke. He revived but his health did not fully recover and he was unable to visit Sutherland for several years. But in June 1826 he travelled north by steam vessel, and he did so again in the following years. His fortune meanwhile continued to swell. The Bridgewater Canal was extraordinarily profitable and in 1824 alone yielded him a clear income of £120,000. Stafford, however, was placed at the centre of the looming transport revolution. In 1825, for £100,000, he bought a fifth share in the rival Liverpool and Manchester Railway, the value of which rose spectacularly within a few years. This investment was the result of complicated negotiations which were ostensibly opposed diametrically to the interests of the Bridgewater Canal and therefore of Lord Francis. In reality, with the influence of Loch, it was a clever compromise which secured the future income of both of Stafford's sons while also assuring the future co-existence of the two modes of transport.

On 14 January 1833 Stafford was raised to a dukedom and adopted the title of Sutherland at the suggestion of Princess Augusta. The title was thought to be in recognition of his support for Russell's reforms, but Lord Francis claimed that he was a reformer 'out of mere cowardice and dotage' (Richards, 9). Soon after arriving at Dunrobin Castle, the duke fell ill and died, on 19 July 1833. He was buried at the old cathedral of Dornoch after an elaborate highland funeral on 31 July at which there were forty carriages and gigs and 100 mourners on horseback; the road was lined with 3000 people, even though there was no traditional whisky allowance. His son, the new duke, remarked, 'The conduct of the common people is really wonderful, not a sound was to be heard all the way' (Gower, 180).

The duke was survived by two sons. George Granville Leveson-Gower succeeded him to the dukedom; and Lord Francis Leveson-Gower succeeded to the entailed Bridgewater estate. There were also two daughters: Lady Charlotte, afterwards duchess of Norfolk, and Lady Elizabeth, afterwards marchioness of Westminster. His family was thus connected by marriage to some of the other great aristocratic families of the day.

In appearance the duke was tall and slight, a nervous and dull man, burdened with a large beaky nose and a prim mouth. Two great statues of him by Chantrey were erected at Dunrobin Castle and Trentham Hall, and there are portraits by Romney, Phillips, and Opie. Critics in a later generation regarded his vast edifice overlooking Dunrobin as a symbol not of the duke's benevolence but of the inhumanity and unwisdom of the clearances.

The second duke, George Granville Leveson-Gower (1786–1861), left most of the estate management to his agents. He added 'Sutherland' to his surname in 1841. He was married late, to Harriet Elizabeth Georgiana Leveson-*Gower, née Howard (1806–1868), because of his hopeless love for Queen Louise of Prussia, which was said to have blighted his early adulthood. Soon after his father's death he remarked to his mother that 'we are all so well off that there can be no cause for uneasiness in any respect with regard to any of our worldly goods, of which there is such a plentiful abundance for us' (Richards, 17).

The third duke was **George Granville William Sutherland-Leveson-Gower** (1828–1892), styled marquess of Stafford from 1833 to 1861, who succeeded to the dukedom in 1861. Born on 19 December 1828 at Hamilton Place, London, and educated at Eton College and King's College, London University, he was Liberal MP for the county of Sutherland from 1852 to 1861. He was lord lieutenant of the county of Cromarty from 1853 until his death. He attended the special mission to the coronation of Alexander II of Russia in 1856. Stafford House was host to many visiting notables, including sultans, shahs, emperors, and kings. In 1864 Garibaldi was a guest, and on his return the duke took him as far as Caprera in his yacht. He was little interested in politics but was an enthusiastic sportsman and traveller; he attended the opening of the Suez Canal in 1869 and accompanied the prince of Wales on his tour of India in 1876. He spent much of his huge fortune on land experiments on his highland estates, and he also invested £226,300 in the development of the highland railway. He constructed his own private station in Sutherland and famously enjoyed driving his own locomotive engine and coaches along his personal railway. He especially loved watching the work of fire engines. He helped popularize cigarettes over cigars in London society.

He married first Anne, daughter of John Hay-Mackenzie of Cromartie and Newhall, in 1849. She became countess of Cromartie in her own right in 1861 with a special remainder in favour of her second surviving son, Francis, who became earl of Cromartie in 1888. She was mistress of the robes and was very close to Queen Victoria throughout her life. She died in Torquay in November 1888, while the duke was in the United States. Already at odds with his eldest son on questions of estate management, the widowed duke was much criticized in the family for not attending the funeral on the grounds of distance and ill health. Queen Victoria herself was upset.

The duke, amid considerable family controversy, remarried in the following March. The wedding took place in Florida and his new wife was Mary Caroline (née Michell), widow of Arthur Kindersley Blair, who had been found shot in Pitlochry in October 1883. The new duchess was cold-shouldered by the family and there was immediate controversy over the duke's financial arrangements when they returned to England.

The third duke died in Dunrobin on 22 September 1892 and was buried at Trentham, Staffordshire. He left a very large proportion of his great wealth to his widow, and the will, which had been changed many times between 1889 and 1892, was contested by the rest of the family. There was extreme antagonism between the parties and the case grew into one of the great scandals of the late Victorian age. Amid the legal proceedings, during a negotiation with solicitors attending Stafford House, the dowager duchess snatched a vital document and threw it into the fire. She was convicted for the destruction of one of her husband's papers, imprisoned in Holloway for six weeks, and fined £250 for the offence. She claimed that she was following her late husband's wishes. A compromise was arranged in 1894, but the life and death of the third duke had seriously damaged the great fortune of the Sutherlands. ERIC RICHARDS

Sources E. Richards, *The leviathan of wealth: the Sutherland fortune in the industrial revolution* (1973) · J. Loch, *Memoir of George Granville, late duke of Sutherland* (1834) · R. Gower, *Stafford House letters* (1871) · R. J. Adam, ed., *Papers on Sutherland estate management, 1802–1816*, 2 vols., Scottish History Society, 4th ser., 8–9 (1972) · F. C. Mather, *After the canal duke: a study of the industrial estates administered by the trustees of the third duke of Bridgewater … 1825–1872* (1970) · H. Malet, *Bridgewater: the canal duke, 1736–1803* (1977) · J. Loch, *Dates and documents relating to the family and property of Sutherland …* (1859) · J. Loch, *Account of the improvements on the estates of the marquess of Stafford* (1820) · HoP, *Commons* · *The News* (27 Jan 1822) · *The Greville memoirs*, ed. H. Reeve, new edn, 8 vols. (1888) · B. Falk, *The Bridgewater millions: a candid family history* [1942] · *Lord Granville Leveson Gower: private correspondence, 1781–1821*, ed. Castalia, Countess Granville [C. R. Leveson-Gower], 2nd edn, 2 vols. (1916) · GEC, *Peerage*

Archives NL Scot., corresp. and papers · Staffs. RO, corresp. and bank books | BL, letters to Lord Grenville, Add. MS 59021 · Keele University Library, letters to Ralph Sneyd · NA Scot., corresp. with James Loch

Likenesses J. Nollekens, plaster bust, 1805, Dunrobin Castle, Highland region · T. Phillips, oils, 1805, NPG [*see illus.*] · J. Doyle, lithograph, pubd 1833 (*Mutual congratulation*), NPG · J. Francis, bust, 1834, Dunrobin Castle, Highland region · J. Young, mezzotint, pubd 1834 (after T. Phillips), NPG · F. Chantrey, statue, 1838, parish church, Trentham, Staffordshire · F. Chantrey, statue, probably Dunrobin Castle, Highland region · F. Chantrey, two pencil sketches, NPG · G. Hayter, oils (*The trial of Queen Caroline, 1820*), NPG · J. Opie, portrait · G. Romney, portrait · P. C. Wonder, study, oils, NPG

Wealth at death over £1,000,000 · £1,275,088 12s. 7d.—George Granville William Sutherland-Leveson-Gower: will, 1893

Gower, George Granville William Sutherland-Leveson-, third duke of Sutherland (1828–1892). *See under* Gower, George Granville Leveson-, first duke of Sutherland (1758–1833).

Gower, Sir George Granville Leveson- (1858–1951), autobiographer, politician, and private secretary, was born in London on 19 May 1858, the only child of (Edward) Frederick Leveson-*Gower (1819–1907) and his wife, Lady Margaret Mary Frances Elizabeth, *née* Compton. Granville George Leveson-*Gower, second Earl Granville, the foreign secretary and colleague of W. E. Gladstone, was his uncle, and an important influence on his life. His mother died three days after his birth, and he was brought up by his father and uncle. He was educated at Eton College and Balliol College, Oxford, matriculating in 1876. There he made many lifelong friends, including G. N. Curzon. He achieved a second class in moderations (1878) and in Greats (1880), the year of his uncle's return to office with Gladstone. He immediately became one of Gladstone's private secretaries and found himself on the inside of Liberal politics during an especially problematic government.

Mr Leveson, as Gladstone usually called Leveson-Gower, proved a much employed mediator between Gladstone and the many whigs with whom the prime minister was in disagreement. He worked for Gladstone throughout his second government, and in 1881 accompanied a mission to Spain. From 1885 to 1886 he was MP for North-West Staffordshire, a county in which the Granville interest was strong, and was a junior whip; he lost his post and his seat with the home rule defeat in 1886. He persisted in his attempt to pursue a political career, unsuccessfully contesting East Marylebone in 1889, and being elected at a by-election for Stoke-on-Trent in 1890 (a constituency his father had earlier represented). He held the seat in the election of 1892, but lost it in that of 1895. From 1892 to 1895 he was comptroller of the royal household and a church estates commissioner (often the only commissioner taking the Liberal line during the important discussion on Welsh disestablishment). He did not contest another seat. In the long Liberal opposition from 1895 until 1905 he was active in trying to retain whiggish support for the party, and to show his fellow Liberals that whigs could be useful. He served on the London school board 1897–9, representing the City of London ward for the Progressive Party. On 9 June 1898 he married, at St Peter's, Eaton Square, London, (Adelaide Violet) Cicely Monson (d. 1955), daughter of Captain Debonnaire John Monson (1830–1900), also of the royal household, and his wife, Augusta (d. 1936); they had two daughters.

Leveson-Gower had what he recalled as 'a very moderate income' (Leveson-Gower, *Years of Endeavour*, 196) and his political expenses came out of his own pocket, a fact which led him after his marriage to abandon his attempt at a political career. He wrote regularly for the periodicals and in 1899 became European editor of the *North American Review*. His *Poems* were published in 1902. He received no post in the Liberal government formed in 1905, though he became chairman of the Home Counties Liberal Federation. In 1908 he resigned from the *Review* to become commissioner of woods and forests, a post he held until 1924. He was later a director of two railway companies and of the Lillieshall Company. He was knighted in 1921.

Though his political career never matched its initial potential—and, despite his loyalty, he came to be seen as something of a lightweight—Leveson-Gower in old age became an amiable memorialist, publishing *Years of Content* (1940), *Years of Endeavour* (1942), and *Mixed Grill* (1947, enlarged edn 1948). These remain lively volumes, with many entertaining stories, mostly of a political and social sort. Leveson-Gower died on 18 July 1951.

H. C. G. MATTHEW

Sources *Dod's Parliamentary Companion* · Burke, *Peerage* · Foster, *Alum. Oxon.* · Gladstone, *Diaries* · I. Elliott, ed., *The Balliol College register, 1833–1933*, 2nd edn (privately printed, Oxford, 1934) · G. G. Leveson-Gower, *Years of content, 1858–1886* (1940) · G. Leveson-Gower, *Years of endeavour, 1886–1907* (1942) · CGPLA Eng. & Wales (1951)

Archives BL, corresp. with W. E. Gladstone, Add. MSS 44484–44789, *passim* · JRL, letters to *Manchester Guardian*

Likenesses photographs, repro. in Leveson-Gower, *Years of content* · photographs, repro. in Leveson-Gower, *Years of endeavour*

Wealth at death £51,898 9s. 4d.: probate, 4 Sept 1951, CGPLA Eng. & Wales

Gower, Granville George Leveson-, second Earl Granville (1815–1891), politician, was born at Great Stanhope Street, Mayfair, Westminster, on 11 May 1815, the eldest

Granville George Leveson-Gower, second Earl Granville (1815–1891), by George Richmond, 1876

son in the family of three sons and two daughters of Granville Leveson-*Gower, first Earl Granville (1773–1846), and a grandson of Granville Leveson-*Gower, first marquess of Stafford, who had been a colleague of the younger Pitt. (Edward) Frederick Leveson-*Gower was his brother, and Lady Georgiana *Fullerton his sister. From 1833 until his father's death he bore the courtesy title of Lord Leveson. His mother was Lady Henrietta Elizabeth Cavendish (1785–1862) [see Gower, Henrietta Elizabeth Leveson-], second daughter of William *Cavendish, fifth duke of Devonshire, and his first wife, Lady Georgiana Spencer [see Cavendish, Georgiana]. Granville was thus connected to many of the great political families of eighteenth- and early-nineteenth-century England. He jokingly made the point in a parliamentary debate in 1855: 'I have relations upon this side of the House [of Lords], relations upon the cross-benches [and] relations upon the opposite side of the House' (Fitzmaurice, 1.122). His political role was always that of a great whig magnate. The family estates were in Staffordshire, but Granville never lived on them.

Education, parliament, and marriage Leveson-Gower was educated at Mr Bradford's private school in Beaconsfield from the age of eight to thirteen and then went to Eton College. After a spell with a private tutor he proceeded to Christ Church, Oxford, in 1832, and remained there until 1836. His studies were desultory but he successfully presented himself for the BA examination, although he did not formally take the degree until 1839. His father was the British ambassador in Paris (1824–8, 1830–35, and 1835–41) and Leveson spent much time there, becoming fluent in French (which he was said always to speak with the accent of the *ancien régime*) and mingling with French society. Universally judged to be an amiable young man, he attracted a variety of nicknames, of which the one that stuck for life was 'Pussy'. He was himself an attaché at the Paris embassy from May 1835 to August 1836.

Leveson wished to enter parliament and was accommodated in Morpeth, which was still (despite the Parliamentary Reform Act of 1832) virtually a closed borough in the gift of the second Earl Grey, and from which in 1837 the sitting member, Edward Howard, wanted to retire temporarily. Leveson's maiden speech (17 April 1837), on British policy in the Iberian peninsula, was a great success for fortuitous reasons. He had been sitting next to the experienced diplomat Henry Bulwer, who had been explaining the situation to him. Both Bulwer and Leveson rose to speak and, according to precedent, the speaker called the maiden speaker. Leveson used all Bulwer's best arguments, to the latter's amused surprise. Perhaps because of this success, he was called upon later in the year to move the address in reply to the queen's speech (20 November 1837). But otherwise he spoke little, and when Howard wanted Morpeth back in February 1840 he was left without a parliamentary seat.

On 25 July 1840 Leveson married Marie-Louise Pellina (1812?–1860), the only child of Emmerich Josef Wolfgang Heribert, duke of Dalberg, and the widow of Sir Richard Acton, seventh baronet, of Shropshire. Leveson thus became connected with two of the most talented and cosmopolitan families of nineteenth-century Europe. Lady Acton was a Roman Catholic, somewhat older than Leveson, and his family were not happy about the marriage. Leveson was compelled to promise that any daughters would be brought up in their mother's faith but refused to enter into similar undertakings about any sons. Only the threat that they would otherwise content themselves with a protestant marriage persuaded Father Randal Lythgoe, later father provincial of the English Jesuits, to conduct the ceremony. This presumably explains why they were married twice on 25 July 1840, first at the Spanish Chapel and then at Devonshire House in Piccadilly (Granville to Leveson, 15 April 1840, and correspondence between Leveson and R. Lythgoe, 18–20 July 1840, Granville MSS, PRO 30/29/18). Lady Acton had a son from her first marriage, Sir John Acton, the famous historian, but there were no children of her marriage to Leveson.

Just before his wedding Leveson was invited by Lord Palmerston to become under-secretary at the Foreign Office. He found the experience interesting but intimidating, and, apart from Palmerston's reputation for overworking his subordinates, Leveson found his abrasive style uncongenial, and later in his career was often to be critical of it.

Leveson's work at the Foreign Office was terminated by the Conservative victory in 1841. He was roughly handled on the hustings in South Staffordshire in the general election of July 1841 but came in at a by-election for the safe seat of Lichfield in September 1841. He made no particular mark in the Commons in opposition but he consolidated an alliance with Charles Villiers, later earl of Clarendon, first forged in their doubts about Palmerston's policy in 1839–41. He also became a staunch supporter of free trade. His official biographer, Lord Edmond Fitzmaurice, comments on his comparative freedom from the usual prejudices of his class, pointing out that he had been brought up in a very cosmopolitan society and that, significantly, 'his father, though closely allied with the great territorial connection in the country, had never himself resided on his English estates, which were regarded as a source of mining and manufacturing wealth rather than of agricultural enterprise' (Fitzmaurice, 1.38). His father died on 8 January 1846 and Granville made his first speech in the House of Lords in favour of the repeal of the corn laws.

Whig peer and courtier Granville expected office when Lord John Russell replaced Sir Robert Peel as prime minister in 1846 and was disappointed to be offered only the honorary court appointment of master of the buckhounds, which he held until 1848, although he also became, a little later in 1846, a member of the new commission on railways. He was, probably as another consolatory appointment, sworn of the privy council in August 1846. In 1847 he was made paymaster-general in succession to T. B. Macaulay, but without a seat in the cabinet. In the following year he also became vice-president of the Board of Trade, under Henry Labouchere. He finally entered the cabinet, still as paymaster-general, in October 1851. His main work during this period was to assist the prince consort in the organization of the Great Exhibition of 1851, where his foreign contacts and linguistic skills were invaluable.

Nevertheless, Granville's elevation to the Foreign Office, when Russell forced Palmerston's resignation over his unauthorized recognition of Louis Napoléon's *coup d'état* in December 1851, was surprising and reflected the lack of suitably qualified candidates, Lord Clarendon having declined it. Palmerston, though angry with Russell, briefed Granville carefully, but Granville had no time to develop any policies before the Russell government itself fell in February 1852. Russell had been irritated, after the fall of Palmerston, by a request from the court that the new foreign secretary would supply them with a 'programme' of the government's foreign policy objectives. Granville wrote an anodyne, but not uninteresting, analysis, mainly designed to show that the government's policy would henceforth be less abrasive than under Palmerston, but referring to Britain's worldwide role, her support for 'progress', the need to foster her trade abroad, and the desirability of steering a middle course between meddling 'intervention' in the affairs of other states and allowing British interests to go by default (Fitzmaurice, 1.49–52).

Granville, by his wide contacts, did something to bring about the 'fusion' of the whig party and the Peelites, and when the earl of Aberdeen formed his coalition government in December 1852 Granville became lord president of the council at Russell's suggestion in order to strengthen the whig element in the cabinet. This was essentially an honorific office, and though Granville was not inactive—he sat on the cabinet committees to consider the renewal of the East India Company charter and the projected parliamentary reform bill, as well as having departmental responsibility for the intended educational reforms—he made no great mark. He tended to be on the side of the doves in the deepening Eastern crisis which led to the Crimean War, although later giving the opinion that, if the policy of either Aberdeen or Palmerston had been consistently carried through, war could have been avoided.

When the ministry was reorganized in June 1854 and the presidency of the council was required for Lord John Russell, Granville was persuaded to step down and take the chancellorship of the duchy of Lancaster without a seat in the cabinet. He returned to the cabinet as lord president of the council when Palmerston succeeded Aberdeen as prime minister in February 1855. He also became the leader of the Liberal Party in the House of Lords. He remained lord president, except for an interlude when the Liberals were out of office in 1858–9, until July 1866. He was sent as ambassador-extraordinary to Russia to represent the queen at the coronation of Alexander II in the summer of 1856 and was made a knight of the Garter in July 1857.

Education was a major issue in the 1850s and 1860s. Critics were already aware that Britain was falling behind her continental rivals in the provision for the middle classes. The judicial decision in the Leeds grammar school case in 1805 tied the old endowed schools strictly to the terms of their original foundations to teach the classics. By the middle of the century a new generation of schools was springing up to teach science and modern languages, and in 1858 the two ancient universities instituted the Oxford and Cambridge local examinations to try to establish some general standards. In the 1860s the great problem was the so-called 'conscience clause' to allow parents to withdraw their children from religious education in the publicly maintained schools if it offended their own beliefs. As lord president of the council Granville had ultimate responsibility for all these issues; but he seems to have felt little interest in them and was pleased enough, in 1856, to see real responsibility transferred to a newly created vice-president of the committee of the privy council for education, who sat in the Commons. This marked, in effect though not in name, the creation of a ministry of education. Granville similarly distanced himself from Lord Newcastle's commission of 1858, which inquired into elementary education.

Granville's record as chancellor of the University of London, an office he held from 1856 to 1871, was no more impressive. He used his casting vote to block the admission of women to the matriculation examination in 1862, though he seems to have moved to a position of bored acquiescence a few years later. On one occasion a despairing vice-chancellor, George Grote, had to tell him that although he (the vice-chancellor) could be responsible for the detailed management of the university, it was essential that Granville should turn up for ceremonial occasions (Grote to Granville, 14 May n.d., Granville MSS, PRO 30/29/18).

Granville's first wife died on 14 March 1860, and he married as his second wife Castalia Rosalind (1847–1938), youngest daughter of Walter Frederick Campbell of Islay, Scotland, on 26 September 1865 at St Mary Abbots, Kensington. They had two sons, Granville George (1872–1939) and William Spencer (1880–1953), who became successively third and fourth Earl Granville, and three daughters Victoria Alberta (1867–1953), Sophia Castalia Mary (1870–1934), and Susan Katherine (1876–1878).

When Lord Derby resigned the premiership on 11 June 1859 the queen sent for Granville as a compromise candidate to avoid the rival claims of Palmerston and Russell. Palmerston would have served under him but Russell would not. Palmerston formed the government and Granville went back to the presidency of the council. When Palmerston died in October 1865 Granville was again talked of as a possible successor, but this time the queen sent for Russell. Granville remained lord president of the council. Russell also made him lord warden of the Cinque Ports, which entitled him to live in Walmer Castle, but which otherwise, as Russell warned him, was not an altogether desirable appointment: 'The salary is nil, and the expense something' (Fitzmaurice, 1.488).

When William Gladstone became prime minister in December 1868 Granville was only fifty-three, but he belonged by temperament to an older generation of whig peers. He was not an ineffective politician. In June 1866 he had resumed his position as leader of the Liberal Party in the Lords. (Lord John Russell, now Earl Russell, had been leader *ex officio* while prime minister in 1865–6.) As leader he piloted through important legislation, including the disestablishment of the Irish church in 1869, with skill and urbanity. Nor was he a die-hard. Throughout the 1860s he consistently supported further parliamentary reform. But he was ill prepared for the new issues and forces which dominated the late nineteenth century.

Colonial secretary, 1868–1870 Gladstone appointed Granville colonial secretary. Granville had rarely held departmental office before, but in 1868 the secretaryship of state for the colonies was still regarded as a prestigious position, previously held by Lord Stanley, the duke of Newcastle, and Russell himself, but one which seldom involved much real work. Empire, however, was about to become the cause of the future, and Disraeli and the tories were quicker to appreciate the changing public mood than were the whigs. The new interest in empire revealed itself in concern for the old colonies of settlement, which were to evolve into the dominions, before it became identified with the acquisition of new lands, usually described by the short-hand term of the 'new imperialism'.

Gladstone and Granville immediately fell foul of this changing public perception. There were problems in New Zealand, where the 1860s had seen open warfare between the European settlers and the Maori, and in Canada, where Granville himself played an important role in persuading the Hudson's Bay Company to surrender its vast territories to the crown and in the setting up of the first prairie province, Manitoba. The latter resulted in the Red River rebellion, led by Louis Riel, because the métis (people of mixed French-Canadian and Amerindian descent) objected to being transferred without consultation to the jurisdiction of the Canadian government. Gladstone and Granville saw no reason why these crises should delay the implementation of Edward Cardwell's army reforms, even though these involved reductions in, or even the complete withdrawal of, imperial garrisons. Indeed they thought that the colonists should assume greater responsibility for their own defence. Granville tartly told Sir George Bowen, the governor of New Zealand:

> The refusal to retain troops in New Zealand did not proceed from any indifference to the true welfare of the Colony but from a conviction that … the employment of British troops in a Colony possessed of responsible Government was objectionable in principle except in the case of foreign War. (Eldridge, 63–4)

These decisions, however, opened them to Disraeli's charges that they were intent on dismantling the empire for short-term financial reasons. At the same time Granville took some decisions that were to lay the foundations of the new imperialism, though without any clear appreciation of the long-term consequences. He favoured buying out the Dutch possessions on the Gold Coast, though he realized that the House of Commons would be unenthusiastic, and he supported the dispatch of Sir Garnet Wolseley's expedition against the Asante in 1873.

Foreign secretary, 1870–1874 Granville himself was unexpectedly removed from the Colonial Office in July 1870 by the sudden death of the foreign secretary, his old friend Lord Clarendon. Granville returned to the office he had last held in 1852 for much the same reason as on the earlier occasion, the lack of more obvious candidates. He was not particularly familiar with the European situation. He was initially badly briefed by Edmund Hammond, the permanent under-secretary, who told him 'he had never … known so long a lull in foreign affairs, and that he was not aware of any important question that I [Granville] would have to deal with' (*Hansard 3*, 203, 1870, 3). A few hours later Granville learned of the appearance of the Hohenzollern candidate for the Spanish throne, which led directly to the outbreak of the Franco-Prussian War.

The Derby–Disraeli ministry had stood on the sidelines at the time of the Austro-Prussian War in 1866; Gladstone's administration did the same thing as the Franco-Prussian War irrevocably altered the balance of European power in favour of the Germans. There is little evidence that anyone in the cabinet appreciated the significance of what was happening. Palmerston a few years earlier had not been unsympathetic to the cause of German unity, despite his objections to the bullying of Denmark. Granville, perhaps because of old associations, was a little more friendly towards France than some of his colleagues, but generally it was the traditional enemy,

France, and especially the emperor, Napoleon III, who were suspected of being the disturbers of European peace. In 1870 Britain focused her attention on what was essentially a side issue, though one that was both historically and strategically important to Britain—the fate of the Low Countries. Britain was obligated by the treaty of 1839 to concern herself with the neutrality of Belgium. Granville issued a formal question to both France and Prussia as to whether they would respect Belgian neutrality. On receiving assurances from both combatants that they would, Britain stood back to await the outcome of the contest.

Russia took advantage of the Franco-Prussian War to abrogate unilaterally the clauses of the treaty of Paris at the end of the Crimean War, which neutralized the Black Sea. Gladstone and Granville were well aware that they could not prevent this development, especially as Russia had secured the tacit support of Prussia, but both considered it very important that the treaty should be amended in a regular way. A conference was convened in London in January 1871, which duly cancelled the Black Sea clauses but also strengthened Turkey's control of the Dardanelles. As much as possible had been salvaged.

To Gladstone the establishment of a code of international law, which all nations would respect, was vital to ensure worldwide peace and justice. Although the moral fervour came from Gladstone, the concept was entirely congenial to Granville. It was soon to be severely tested by the *Alabama* arbitration. The *Alabama* was one of several ships built in Britain for the southern states during the American Civil War. Although the British government had agreed to the northern request that the *Alabama* should be detained, she slipped away, was armed in the Azores, and did considerable harm to northern shipping. The legal position was by no means clear, but in 1871 Britain agreed to refer the matter to international arbitration. The arbitrators' verdict, delivered in September 1872, while not accepting the whole of the American case, was unfavourable to Britain, which was required to pay over £300,000 in compensation. The arbitration had never been popular in Britain and public irritation probably played some part in the Liberal defeat in 1874, but to both Gladstone and Granville the restoration of friendly relations with the United States and the recognition of the principle of arbitration in international disputes meant more than an unsatisfactory verdict.

When the Conservatives won the 1874 election Gladstone insisted that he wished to retire from politics and devote himself to scholarly studies. It was perhaps a reflection of the fact that few people thought his withdrawal was other than temporary that no proper arrangements were made for a succession to the leadership of the Liberal Party. Some assumed that Granville, as leader in the Lords, had succeeded *ex officio*. Others believed that the leadership must pass to either Lord Hartington or W. E. Forster in the Commons. In the mean time Granville provided a social centre for the party, much as Lord Holland had provided one at Holland House earlier in the century. Until 1873 this was at 16 Bruton Street, then at 18 Carlton House Terrace. Like the earlier great salons, the Granvilles' receptions welcomed distinguished visitors from all walks of life, by no means all of them political supporters.

Even after the 1880 election there was a general public expectation that, in the interests of party unity, the premiership would have to go to a whig, though more probably to Hartington than to Granville. Only Gladstone's declaration that he could not serve in a subordinate capacity, and might even have to oppose the government on certain issues, compelled Hartington and Granville jointly to recommend to the queen that she send for Gladstone. They did not expect to find it easy to persuade her. Granville's relief at their success was recorded by Victoria's private secretary, Henry Ponsonby. After the interview 'Granville kissed his hand with a smile like a ballet girl receiving applause … and exclaimed "No difficulty at all—all smooth"' (Jenkins, 137).

Throughout the ministry Granville supported Gladstone in his efforts to keep the whigs and radicals together, notably at the time of the duke of Argyll's resignation over the Irish Land Act in 1881 and Hartington's threatened resignation over the franchise crisis in 1883, though he was unsuccessful on the first occasion. Granville took some of the burden of routine appointments from Gladstone's shoulders and chaired meetings during Gladstone's frequent illnesses (some genuine, some diplomatic).

Return to the Foreign Office, 1880–1885 Granville himself went back to the Foreign Office in April 1880. The acute phase of the great Eastern crisis of 1875–8 had passed but many problems remained. Russia had replaced France as the national enemy in the mind of the public and was seen as a particular threat to British India. With the rising tide of imperialism, the security of India loomed larger and larger for both economic and prestige reasons. Granville had long had an interest in Indian questions. Charles Canning, who was governor-general during the so-called Indian mutiny of 1857, was a close friend from Eton days. He wrote to Granville constantly during that crisis and Granville stoutly defended him in the Lords. Granville also had to deal with Indian questions during Gladstone's first ministry. In 1868 Russia had occupied Samarkand, the capital of Bukhara. Clarendon began negotiations with the Russian chancellor, Prince Gorchakov, to try to demarcate spheres of influence. Granville continued these discussions and, in January 1873, Gorchakov agreed to respect the neutrality of Afghanistan. But the following spring Russia took possession of Khiva, which the British saw as almost as threatening as an intervention in Afghanistan. The Liberal policy of negotiation had not resolved the central Asian crisis, and the more vigorous forward policy of their Conservative successors involved Britain in war with Afghanistan in 1878.

On their return to office the Liberals negotiated a settlement with the emir, Abdurahman, by which they controlled his foreign policy but did not interfere in domestic affairs. Afghanistan had been stabilized, but another central Asian crisis flared up in 1885. A Russian force defeated an Afghan force at Panjdeh in a disputed border region.

The incident caused intense public excitement. Gladstone's government responded with unusual firmness, immediately securing a vote of credit for £11 million to cover possible military action. But Granville also negotiated. A compromise, acceptable to the Afghans, was reached by which Panjdeh was conceded in return for Afghan control of the Zulfikar Pass.

Panjdeh remained in British folk memory as the point at which Britain and Russia came very close to war. The public was less aware of important disputes in the Balkans, some concerned with interpretations of the treaty of Berlin of 1878, some with the frontiers of Greece and Montenegro. Although Bismarck, the German chancellor, largely called the tune, the British government agreed to a naval demonstration at Smyrna to induce the Turks to cede the agreed territory to Greece and Montenegro. It has been suggested (by W. N. Medlicott in his *Bismarck, Gladstone and the Concert of Europe*, 1956) that the early 1880s were an important turning point in European relations, when Bismarck's policy of tight alliances triumphed over Gladstone's more open policy of a concert of Europe ruled by international law. There is little in Granville's papers to suggest that he was conscious of great decisions being made. Bismarck felt an increasing contempt for the British foreign secretary, which he did not hesitate to express to Lord Rosebery, who entered the cabinet in 1885 (NL Scot., Rosebery MS 10004).

Neither Gladstone nor Granville was prepared for the central role assumed by Africa in the 1880s. The crisis in South Africa, culminating in the battle of Majuba Hill and the independence of the Transvaal, was the concern of the Colonial Office, rather than the Foreign Office; but other crises crowded in. The most significant concerned Egypt. The Suez Canal had been opened in 1869. It was of great strategic importance to Britain, both because of communications with India and because the vast majority of the trade passing through it was British. Neither Gladstone nor Granville had any wish to intervene in Egypt, but the rise of an Egyptian nationalist movement, directed both at the Turks and foreign financial exploitation, led to the British military occupation of Egypt in 1882. The occupation was meant to be temporary but, once involved, the British dared not withdraw lest another power, probably France, should take their place. Granville, in common with most members of the cabinet, found it impossible to comprehend a non-European nationalist movement, particularly one led by an army officer, Arabi Pasha. Characteristically, however, he subsequently showed courteous concern to settle Arabi in comfortable exile in Ceylon (Cabinet opinions 'As to Arabi going to Ceylon', 4–7 Dec 1882, Granville MSS, PRO 30/29/143).

Granville was equally baffled by the sudden German interest in what became South-West Africa. At first he seems to have believed that the Germans wanted the British to protect their nationals there. On discovering that the Germans wanted to establish a protectorate themselves, he had no real objections. But the Angra Pequena incident, as it became known, caused a sharp strain in Anglo-German relations; Bismarck may genuinely have believed that the British wished to thwart German colonial plans worldwide, or he may have wished to create that impression as part of his general international policy.

Britain gave more hostages to fortune when she concluded a treaty with Portugal about the Congo in April 1884. The initiative came from the British ambassador in Lisbon, Sir Robert Morier, rather than from the Foreign Office. The treaty did not find favour with the British business community, who thought the terms unfavourable and organized an elaborate campaign against it. It was also denounced by other European nations, who denied the right of Britain and Portugal to settle the fate of the Congo bilaterally.

The result was the Berlin West Africa Conference of November 1884 to February 1885, which essentially established the ground rules for the 'scramble for Africa', and in practice greatly accelerated the scramble by insisting on the idea of 'effective occupation'. As a result, in the next few months Britain, in order to secure existing or prospective trading interests, acquired protectorates or spheres of influence over the Niger delta and over the areas that became Kenya and Uganda.

By the end of the Berlin West Africa Conference, Bismarck had found that his interests coincided more closely with those of Britain than of France, which he had been trying to conciliate at the beginning, but Britain's continued occupation of Egypt, which rested on no legal foundation, made her uncomfortably dependent on the goodwill of other powers. This was amply demonstrated in 1885 when international consent was required to reorganize Egypt's foreign debt. Britain's involvement with Egypt also dragged her into the Sudan, which had been conquered by Egypt a generation earlier, but which had now developed its own fundamentalist nationalist movement under the Mahdi. Britain decided that withdrawal was the only policy and sent General Charles Gordon, a British soldier of immense prestige, who had served there previously under Egyptian authority, to carry it out. Gordon's death at Khartoum in January 1885 did much to seal the fate of the Gladstone government.

Granville's handling of all these problems attracted severe criticism from a number of diverse quarters. Wilfrid Scawen Blunt, who constituted himself a champion of the Egyptian nationalist movement, subsequently wrote an indictment of British government policy in his *Secret History of the English Occupation of Egypt* (1907). On the other side of the argument Granville's parliamentary undersecretary, Sir Charles Dilke, deplored Granville's inertia and lack of understanding of the new competitive spirit abroad in the world (C. Dilke, diary and journal, BL, Add. MSS 43924–43925, 43935) and accused him of allowing the permanent under-secretary, Lord Tenterden, to draft all the dispatches and then being unable to defend them in cabinet (BL, Add. MS 43935, fols. 110–11). The article in the *Dictionary of National Biography* reproached Granville for missed opportunities and allowing desirable areas of the world 'to slip out of the possession of Great Britain'. It was a widely held contemporary view. In May 1885 Lord Randolph Churchill fiercely attacked him in *The Times* and Lord Hartington told Lewis Harcourt privately that every word was true and that Granville 'was probably the worst Foreign Minister England [has] ever had' (Jackson, 181).

Last years and death When Gladstone returned briefly to power in 1886 Herbert Bismarck, the great chancellor's son, wrote to Rosebery, 'don't put old Granny at the head of this most important office [the Foreign Office]' (H. Bismarck to Rosebery, 31 Jan 1886, Rosebery MS 10004). The queen, who had once liked Granville but had been offended by his criticisms of her proposed assumption of the title of empress of India in 1876, also preferred Rosebery. Rosebery duly went to the Foreign Office and Granville took the Colonial Office—not without some protests to Gladstone that this change would seem to confirm public criticisms and make his position as leader of the Lords difficult.

In fact, Granville was no fool. His urbanity defused many situations, and the deafness of which those who tried to lobby him increasingly complained may well have been, in part, assumed. He also had an ability, from their point of view an irritating one, to turn the conversation from politics to horse-racing and -breeding. At the same time Granville was out of his depth in a rapidly changing world. Nor was he in total control of British foreign policy—he never enjoyed the freedom of action Palmerston had gained for himself. In 1870–74 and again in 1880–85 all important foreign questions were discussed by the cabinet as a whole (see cabinet memoranda in Granville MSS, PRO 30/29/68–9, fols. 143–5). Moreover the prime minister, Gladstone, had strong and developed ideas about the direction that policy should take. John Morley described Granville as Gladstone's 'best friend' (Morley, 3.462) and this seems to be borne out by the immense amount of correspondence between them (A. Ramm, *Political Correspondence of Mr Gladstone and Lord Granville*, 4 vols., 1942–62). But it was an unequal relationship. Granville was experienced, good-humoured, a useful representative of the old aristocracy, but ultimately a loyal lieutenant. He followed Gladstone's lead on Irish affairs, as he had done on foreign policy.

By 1885 Ireland was the most important question on the British political agenda and Gladstone's home-rule proposals were to split the Liberal Party. Granville was one of the few great whig peers to support Gladstone (along with lords Kimberley, Ripon, Rosebery, and Spencer). There is no reason to suppose that Granville did violence to his own views in following Gladstone's lead. In 1885 he had not been enthusiastic about the proposal for limited devolution and a legislative council in Ireland, foreseeing very clearly all the problems of divided jurisdiction, and he accommodated himself readily to Gladstone's more radical proposals.

Few other issues have split English upper-class society as Irish home rule did, and, characteristically, Granville in his last years scored some minor successes in trying to bring about reconciliation, notably in the old whig club, Brooks's, where rival factions so consistently blackballed each other's candidates that members began to fear no one would be admitted at all and it would not be long before the last member would preside over the demise of the ancient institution. Granville intervened to remind members of the divisions the club had survived in the past and sanity was restored.

Granville continued as leader of the Liberal Party in the Lords—though increasing ill health necessitated frequent absences—until his death, which occurred before his party returned to power. He died at his brother's house, 14 South Audley Street, London, on 31 March 1891. Contemporary accounts said he died of gout and an abscess in his face (possibly cancer). He was buried in the family plot at St Michael's Church, Stone, Staffordshire, on 4 April 1891. Granville died in some financial embarrassment and £60,000 had to be raised to save his estate from bankruptcy. Gladstone masterminded the operation, though it came at an awkward moment when he was forming his last administration. Rosebery and Hartington (now the duke of Devonshire), among others, contributed but eventually Gladstone had to find the balance himself. (The story survives in the Gladstone, not the Granville, MSS; see Matthew, 332.)   MURIEL E. CHAMBERLAIN

Sources E. G. Petty-Fitzmaurice, *The life of Granville George Leveson Gower, second Earl Granville*, 2nd edn, 2 vols. (1905) · J. Morley, *The life of William Ewart Gladstone*, 3 vols. (1903) · *The political correspondence of Mr Gladstone and Lord Granville, 1868–1876*, ed. A. Ramm, 2 vols., CS, 3rd ser., 81–2 (1952) · *The political correspondence of Mr Gladstone and Lord Granville, 1876–1886*, ed. A. Ramm, 2 vols. (1962) · P. Jackson, *The last of the whigs: a political biography of Lord Hartington* (1994) · R. R. James, *Rosebery: a biography of Archibald Philip, fifth earl of Rosebery* (New York, 1964) · GEC, *Peerage* · FO List (1891) · Colonial Office List (1891) · C. C. Eldridge, *England's mission: the imperial idea in the age of Gladstone and Disraeli* (1973) · *The Greville memoirs*, ed. H. Reeve, new edn, 8 vols. (1888) · H. E. Gower, *Letters, 1810–1845*, ed. F. Leveson-Gower, 2 vols. (1894) · *The Times* (14 May 1885), 1–6 · *The Times* (16 April 1891) · Gladstone, *Diaries* · W. N. Medlicott, *Bismarck, Gladstone and the concert of Europe* (1956) · W. S. Blunt, *Secret history of the English occupation of Egypt: being a personal narrative of events* (1907) · H. C. G. Matthew, *Gladstone, 1875–1898* (1995) · T. A. Jenkins, *Gladstone, whiggery and the liberal party, 1874–1886* (1988) · NL Scot., Rosebery MSS · PRO, Granville MSS · BL, Dilke MSS

Archives NL Scot., corresp. · PRO, corresp. and papers, PRO 30/29 · PRO, corresp. and papers, FO 362 · PRO, papers, FO 97/621 · UCL, letters · Walmer Castle, manuscripts · Yale U., Beinecke L., travel diary, kept while at sea, d301 | Balliol Oxf., corresp. with Sir Robert Morier · BL, corresp. with Lord Aberdeen, Add. MSS 43250–43255 · BL, corresp. with Sir Francis Adams, partly relating to Tunisia, Add. MS 64796 · BL, letters to John. Bright, Add. MS 43387 · BL, corresp. with Lord Carnarvon, Add. MS 60773 · BL, corresp. with Charles Dilke, Add. MSS 43878–43881, 43901 · BL, letters to T. H. S. Escott, Add. MS 58784 · BL, corresp. with W. E. Gladstone, Add. MSS 44165–44180, 43875–43880, 44901 · BL, corresp. with Sir Edward Walter Hamilton, Add. MS 48617 · BL, letters to Lady Holland, Add. MS 52130 · BL, corresp. with Sir A. H. Layard, Add. MSS 38960–39036; 39121–39140, *passim* · BL, corresp. with Sir Stafford Northcote, Add. MS 50022 · BL, corresp. with Lord Ripon, Add. MSS 43520–43521 · Bodl. Oxf., letters to Lord Clarendon · Bodl. Oxf., letters to Benjamin Disraeli · Bodl. Oxf., corresp. with Sir William Harcourt · Bodl. Oxf., letters to Lord Kimberley · Borth. Inst., corresp. with Lord Halifax · Chatsworth House, Derbyshire, letters to dukes of Devonshire · CKS, letters to Lord Brabourne · CKS, letters to Edward Stanhope · CUL, corresp. primarily with Lord Acton, Add. MSS 8121, 8123 · Glos. RO, corresp. with Sir Michael Hicks Beach · Harrowby Manuscript Trust,

Sandon Hall, Staffordshire, corresp. with Lord Harrowby · Herts. ALS, corresp. with earl of Lytton · Herts. ALS, letters to Lord Lytton · Hunt. L., letters to Lord Aberdare · ICL, letters to Lord Playfair · Keele University Library, corresp. with Ralph Sneyd · King's AC Cam., letters to Oscar Browning · LPL, corresp. with Lord Selborne · LPL, letters to A. C. Tait · LUL, letters to Lord Overstone · NA Scot., corresp. with Sir Charles Murray · NL Scot., corresp. with Sir Henry Elliot · NL Scot., Rosebery MSS · NL Wales, letters to Lord Rendel · priv. coll., corresp. with Lord Hammond · PRO, corresp. with Sir Evelyn Baring, FO 633 · PRO, letters to Lord Cairns, PRO 30/51 · PRO, corresp. with Lord Cardwell, PRO 20/48 · PRO, corresp. with Lord Cowley, FO 519 · PRO, corresp. with Sir Edward Malet, FO 343 · PRO, corresp. with Lord Russell, PRO 30/22 · PRO, letters to Sir William White, FO 364/1–11 · PRO NIre., Blackwood MSS · PRO NIre., corresp. with Lord Dufferin · Shrops. RRC, letters to Lord Acton · St Deiniol's Library, Hawarden, letters to W. E. Gladstone and Catherine Gladstone · St Deiniol's Library, Hawarden, letters to duke of Newcastle · Staffs. RO, letters to Lord Hatherton · Staffs. RO, corresp. with duke of Sutherland · Trinity Cam., letters to Lord Houghton · U. Birm. L., corresp. with Joseph Chamberlain · U. Durham L., corresp. with Charles Grey · U. Durham L., corresp. with third earl Grey · U. Nott. L., letters to J. E. Denison · U. Nott. L., letters to duke of Newcastle · U. Southampton L., corresp. with Lord Palmerston · UCL, corresp. with Sir Edwin Chadwick · W. Sussex RO, corresp. with Richard Cobden · W. Sussex RO, letters to F. A. Maxse · W. Sussex RO, letters to fifth duke of Richmond · W. Sussex RO, letters to sixth duke of Richmond

Likenesses engraving, 1826 (after miniature), repro. in Fitzmaurice, *Life of Granville George Leveson Gower* · R. Doyle, pen-and-ink sketch, 1848, repro. in Fitzmaurice, *Life of Granville George Leveson Gower* · W. Walker, mezzotint, pubd 1853 (after R. Lehmann), BM · Hills & Saunders, photograph, 1863, NPG · G. H. Thomas, pencil drawing, 1863 (after miniature), repro. in Fitzmaurice, *Life of Granville George Leveson Gower* · W. & D. Downey, photograph, 1867, repro. in Fitzmaurice, *Life of Granville George Leveson Gower* · E. Fairfield, pen-and-ink sketch, 1872 (*Waiting for the verdict*; after miniature), repro. in Fitzmaurice, *Life of Granville George Leveson Gower* · J. Brown, stipple prints, pubd 1874–5, BM · G. Richmond, oils, 1876, U. Lond. [*see illus.*] · T. L. Atkinson, mezzotint, pubd 1879 (after G. Richmond), BM · M. Beerbohm, sketches, c.1890, Merton Oxf. · D. A. Wehrschmidt, oils, c.1890, National Liberal Club, London · W. Thornycroft, marble statue, 1895, Palace of Westminster, London · Ape [C. Pellegrini], chromolithograph caricature, NPG; repro. in *VF* (13 March 1869) · Dalziel, woodcut, BM · J. Gilbert, group portrait, pencil and wash (*The coalition ministry, 1854*), NPG · T. Lawrence, portrait (in youth), Kensington Palace, London · G. Richmond, chalk drawing, NPG · F. Sargent, pencil drawing, NPG · T. [T. Chartran], chromolithograph caricature, NPG; repro. in *VF* (5 July 1882) · photographs, NPG · portraits, repro. in Fitzmaurice, *Life of Granville George Leveson Gower* · prints, NPG

Wealth at death £33,283 2s. od.: probate, 5 Nov 1891, CGPLA Eng. & Wales

Gower, Granville Leveson-, first marquess of Stafford (1721–1803), politician and landowner, the third but eldest surviving son of John Leveson-*Gower, first Earl Gower (1694–1754), and his first wife, Evelyn (1691–1727), daughter of Evelyn Pierrepont, first duke of Kingston, was born on 4 August 1721 at Trentham, Staffordshire. He was educated at Westminster School (1731–40), and at Christ Church, Oxford; he matriculated on 30 April 1740 but did not take a degree. His first marriage, on 23 December 1744, to Elizabeth, daughter of Nicholas Fazakerly MP, of Penwortham, Lancashire, and Ann Lutwyche, was terminated by her death from smallpox on 19 May 1746. Their only child predeceased her.

Gower entered politics in 1744, winning a by-election for Bishop's Castle (Shropshire) two years after his father had forsaken the family's tory tradition by accepting office in the Carteret–Newcastle administration. Known by the courtesy title of Viscount Trentham from 1746 until he succeeded his father as second Earl Gower in 1754, he subsequently represented Westminster (1747–54) and Lichfield (1754). Marriage ties brought him into the political orbit of the fourth duke of Bedford. His sister Gertrude had married Bedford in 1737, and this connection was strengthened by Trentham's second marriage, on 12 March 1748, to Bedford's niece Lady Louisa Egerton (1723–1761), daughter of Scroop Egerton, first duke of Bridgewater, and his second wife, Lady Rachel Russell. They had one son, George Granville Leveson-*Gower, later created duke of Sutherland, and three daughters. It was as a follower of the duke that Trentham first obtained office, when he became a lord of the Admiralty in 1749. He was narrowly re-elected at Westminster, with Bedford's support, in an election marked by large-scale violence. He resigned with Bedford in 1751 and in 1755 was made lord privy seal to win Bedford's support for the Newcastle administration. Thereafter Gower remained identified with the Bedford connection, alternating short periods of opposition with longer ones in office: he served as lord privy seal from 1755 to 1757, and again from 1784 to 1794, master of the horse (1757–60), master of the wardrobe (1760–63), lord chamberlain (1763–5), and lord president of the council from 1767 to 1779 and in 1783–4. Though not possessed of exceptional abilities and not attracted to positions of executive responsibility, he became a figure of prominence in the high politics of his era. He frequently attended the House of Lords where he gained a reputation as a creditable speaker. Agreeable to the king and liked by many of his contemporaries, Gower's amiability often led to his being a point of contact between the Bedfords and other parties. In 1767 he played a prominent role in the negotiations that ultimately led to the Bedfords joining the Chatham administration, an important step towards resolving the political instability of the 1760s. On 25 May 1768 he married his third wife, Susanna [*see* Gower, Susanna Leveson- (1742/3–1805)], daughter of Alexander Stewart, sixth earl of Galloway, and his second wife, Catherine Cochrane. She was a woman of the bedchamber to Princess Augusta and earned a reputation for her constant soliciting of office. They had three daughters and one son, Granville Leveson-*Gower, later first Earl Granville.

Gower was at the peak of his political importance in the 1770s and early 1780s. On Bedford's death in early 1771 he assumed the leadership of the duke's followers who by this time formed an important element within Lord North's administration. Gower was not particularly close to North, however, and some suspected that he coveted the premiership for himself. This is unlikely given his preference for positions other than those of business. He was instrumental in 1772 in forcing the resignation of the earl of Hillsborough, the American secretary and one of North's closest allies in the cabinet, when the latter opposed the plans of the Ohio Company (in which Gower had an interest) to create an inland colony in North America. Gower's influence was perhaps most felt in colonial affairs. The Bedfords had typically taken a more coercive view of American policy; Gower joined with the rest of the connection in voting against and then protesting the repeal of the Stamp Act in 1766. As the crisis in relations with the American colonies built from 1773, he maintained the position that submission must precede conciliation in colonial affairs. He helped to shape in the cabinet, and supported in the House of Lords, the measures that brought events to a head, telling the Lords in February 1775 that he had advised every measure taken against the Americans and that 'he did not mean to screen himself from any consequence whatever, but was prepared for the worst, and ready to face the block in such a cause' (Cobbett, *Parl. hist.*, 18.208). The ensuing war he saw as necessary and the only alternative to the abandonment of the colonies, but he became increasingly frustrated with what he regarded as North's indecisive leadership of the war effort. In late 1779 he took the occasion of North's failure to act on Gower's promise to the Lords that the ministry would improve commercial relations with Ireland to resign his office; he openly attacked the ministry in parliament, telling the Lords that while he had 'presided for years at the council table', he had 'seen such things pass there of late that no man of honour or conscience could any longer sit there' (ibid., 20.1175–6). His hope of seeing North replaced by a minister who would be more vigorous in the prosecution of the war went unfulfilled.

When North's administration finally fell in March 1782, Gower was sounded as a possible alternative to calling in the leaders of the opposition. He declined to act, however, and later rebuffed overtures from the second Rockingham administration and its successor under the earl of Shelburne. After Shelburne was driven from office by the combined followers of North and Charles James Fox in early 1783, Gower became deeply involved in attempts to find an alternative to the coalition, at times being put forward as a possible first minister. The king was agreeable to the idea, but Gower ultimately declined when he could not find a suitable leader of the House of Commons. He continued to oppose the coalition, however, and it was at his London house in December 1783 that the opponents of the coalition concerted their strategy, with the king's blessing, to oppose the Fox–North India Bill in the House of Lords by invoking the king's hostility to it. When the bill was defeated and the coalition dismissed, Gower agreed to take office as lord president of the council in the administration formed by William Pitt the younger. He exchanged this for the privy seal in 1784, making way for Lord Camden to join the cabinet. As Pitt's ministry became more secure, he became less active in its affairs, attending the cabinet less regularly and speaking less frequently in parliament. He did, however, provide Pitt with solid support during the Regency crisis in 1788. In 1786 he was rewarded for his past services by being created marquess of Stafford. In 1794 he resigned the privy seal and largely retired from public life.

Stafford's success in politics was matched by, and at least partly based on, the successful exploitation of his lands in Staffordshire, where he was one of the largest landowners, and in Shropshire. In addition to increasing his agricultural rents by careful management, he obtained a growing income from mining. His efforts also extended to the economic development of both counties, for he was an enthusiastic patron of canal building, an interest he shared with his brother-in-law, Francis Egerton, the 'canal duke' of Bridgewater. It was through Stafford's land agent that Bridgewater was introduced to the engineer James Brindley. Instrumental in obtaining the necessary legislation for the Trent and Mersey and other canals, Stafford also used his political influence for the advantage of local industries, particularly the Staffordshire potters, and he enjoyed a mutually beneficial relationship with Josiah Wedgwood. Not surprisingly, Stafford was one of the most influential figures in Staffordshire, where he served as lord lieutenant of the county from 1755 until 1800 and as high steward of Stafford from 1769 until his death. He exercised considerable electoral influence, controlling one of the parliamentary seats for Lichfield and strongly influencing both seats at Newcastle under Lyme.

Stafford's long career was marked by a variety of honours. He was named to the privy council in 1755 and became a knight of the Garter in 1771 (in succession to the duke of Bedford). He was also a governor of Charterhouse (1757) and elected a fellow of the Society of Arts in 1784. He was one of his generation's most durable and successful political figures: in an active political career that spanned fifty years, he spent thirty-six years in office, though never in a post of departmental responsibility, and twenty-seven years in cabinet, including his time as lord chamberlain when he attended cabinet meetings. He was also markedly successful in obtaining patronage for his family and followers. Sir Nathaniel Wraxall's characterization of him was not far off the mark:

> His abilities were moderate, but his person and manners had great dignity. His vast property, when added to his alliances of consanguinity or marriage with the first ducal families in this country ... rendered him one of the most considerable subjects in the kingdom.   (*Historical and Posthumous Memoirs*, 4.66)

Spending a half-century at the centre of British politics, he was if not quite a figure of the first rank himself the sort of noble magnate that figures of the first rank had to take into account. Stafford died on 26 October 1803 at Trentham Hall, Staffordshire, and was buried there on 3 November.   WILLIAM C. LOWE

Sources J. Cannon, *The Fox–North coalition: crisis of the constitution, 1782–4* (1969) · *The correspondence of King George the Third from 1760 to December 1783*, ed. J. Fortescue, 6 vols. (1927–8), also *The later correspondence of George III*, ed. A. Aspinall, 5 vols. (1962–70) · B. Donoghue, *British politics and the American revolution: the path to war, 1773–75* (1964) · Cobbett, *Parl. hist.*, vols. 18, 20 · *The historical and the posthumous memoirs of Sir Nathaniel William Wraxall, 1772–1784*, ed. H. B. Wheatley, 5 vols. (1884) · C. Hadfield, *The canals of the west midlands*, 2nd edn (1969) · E. Richards, *The leviathan of wealth: the Sutherland fortune in the industrial revolution* (1973) · M. W. McCahill, *Order and equipoise: the peerage and the House of Lords, 1783–1806* (1978) · I. R. Christie, *The end of North's ministry, 1780–82* (1958) · *Fifth report*, HMC,

4 (1876) • GEC, *Peerage* • E. Cruickshanks, 'Leveson Gower, Granville', HoP, *Commons, 1715–54* • J. C. D. Clark, *The dynamics of change: the crisis of the 1750s and English party systems* (1982) • DNB • *Court and city calendar* (1785)

Archives PRO, family and political corresp. and MSS, PRO 030/29 • Staffs. RO, corresp. and MSS; papers as lord lieutenant of Staffordshire and lord privy seal; political corresp. • Staffs. RO, family MSS | Castle Howard, Yorkshire, corresp. with Lord Carlisle

Likenesses G. Romney, oils, *c*.1776–1778, Dunrobin Castle, Highland region • E. Fisher, mezzotint (after J. Reynolds), BM, NPG • attrib. Hackwood, Wedgwood medallion, Wedgwood Museum, Stoke-on-Trent • C. Warren, line print (after J. Brown), BM; repro. in *The Senator* (1792)

Wealth at death income over £20,000: N. A. M. Rodger, *The insatiable earl: a life of John Montague, 4th earl of Sandwich* (1993), 74, citing Edward Johnson, 'The Bedford connection: the fourth duke of Bedford's political influence between 1732 and 1771', Cambridge PhD thesis (1979), 21, 51

Gower, Granville Leveson-, first Earl Granville (1773–1846), diplomatist, was born on 12 October 1773 at Trentham, Staffordshire, the only son of the marriage between Granville Leveson-*Gower, then second Earl Gower and later first marquess of Stafford (1721–1803), and his third wife, Lady Susanna Stewart (1742/3–1805) [see Gower, Susanna Leveson-], daughter of the sixth earl of Galloway. He had three full sisters, and three half-sisters and a half-brother from his father's second marriage. These siblings subsequently became the countesses of St Germans, Harrowby, and Carlisle, the duchess of Beaufort, the wives of a chief baron and the archbishop of York, and the first duke of Sutherland. Lord Granville (as he was known from 1786 through several changes of rank) was thus exceedingly well connected. He was educated at Dr Kyle's school at Hammersmith, and then by the Revd John Chappel Woodhouse, before matriculating at Christ Church, Oxford, in April 1789. He took no degree, but became a DCL in 1799.

Following Oxford, in 1794 Lord Granville undertook a European tour, which was restricted by the events in France to travels in Italy. In Florence he met the future Lady Holland, who recorded

> He is remarkably handsome and winning; a year or two ago he created a great sensation at Paris, when Ly. Sutherland introduced him as her *beau beaufrère*; she also initiated him into orgies of gambling, an acquisition he has maintained. (*Journal*, 1.116)

More significantly, in Naples he met Henrietta Frances (Harriet) *Ponsonby, countess of Bessborough (1761–1821), and began a liaison that was to produce two children and to last until his marriage to Lady Bessborough's niece Lady Henrietta, or Harriet, Elizabeth Cavendish (1785–1862) [see Gower, Henrietta Elizabeth Leveson-], on 24 December 1809. With her he was to have five legitimate children: his heir and successor, Granville George Leveson-*Gower, the foreign secretary; a son who died young; (Edward) Frederick Leveson-*Gower, MP and author; Susan, Lady Rivers; and Lady Georgiana *Fullerton, the Roman Catholic novelist. The son of his liaison with Lady Bessborough, George Stewart, became his private secretary, while their daughter, Harriet Stewart, became duchess of Leeds. Described

variously as an Apollo, an Adonis, and an Alcibiades, Granville Leveson-Gower was widely considered one of the most handsome men of his time: his curly brown hair, blue eyes, and sensuous features brought him strings of female admirers, including William Pitt's niece and hostess, Lady Hester Stanhope.

Granville was always intended by his parents for a career in politics. He entered parliament in 1799 for the family borough of Lichfield, and in 1799 was returned unopposed for the county of Staffordshire, which he continued to represent until his elevation to the House of Lords in 1815. In politics he generally followed George Canning, whose friend he had become at Christ Church, although his marriage brought him firmly within the ambit of the 'whig cousinhood', and his party allegiances were seldom firm. In 1803 he acted as an intermediary between Pitt and Fox. He was appointed a lord of the Treasury by Pitt in July 1800, but refused to serve under Addington and resigned in February 1801. But his career was to be predominantly in diplomacy: his first official employment saw him attached to Lord Malmesbury's missions to France in 1796–7, and as envoy-extraordinary to Prussia in 1798. In 1804 he was sworn of the privy council and appointed ambassador to St Petersburg (1804–6 and 1807); his attempts to maintain peace failed, and on Russia declaring war in October 1807 he returned again to Britain, having also failed to obtain the peerage which was the object of his personal ambition. In July 1809 he was brought into the Portland cabinet as secretary at war, but he resigned when the cabinet broke up the same October. It is believed that Granville was the intended victim when John Bellingham assassinated the prime minister, Spencer Perceval: Bellingham apparently had a grudge against Granville dating back to his time in Russia. In August 1815 he finally obtained a viscountcy from Lord Liverpool. He served as minister at Brussels in 1815.

Estranged from Canning at this time, for several years Granville's circle was predominantly that of the whigs. But his friendship with Canning was restored with the latter's political fortunes, and it was Canning who sent Granville as ambassador to The Hague in 1823–4, and then as ambassador to Paris from 1824 to 1828. He was recalled after Canning's death, but was reappointed by Lord Grey's ministry in 1830, and remained in Paris (with a short interval during Peel's ministry of 1834) until Melbourne's fall in 1841. As a Canningite, he was generally in sympathy with his Foreign Office chief, Palmerston, and diligently pursued his policies, although their relationship was strained by the Mehmet Ali crisis of 1839–40, when Granville favoured a more conciliatory line towards France. His ties with the whigs confirmed, in 1832 he returned from France in order to vote in support of the Reform Bill. He was rewarded with an earldom in 1833.

In later life Granville suffered badly from gout; in 1823 he had been inadvertently shot in the face by the duke of Wellington (a notoriously bad shot), and several of the seven pellets were never removed. In 1841 he suffered a massive stroke, but, with the collapse of the ministry imminent, he stayed in post until the government fell. For two years the Granvilles travelled the continent and arrived back in Britain only in November 1843. They eventually settled back in Bruton Street, London, but Granville's health never recovered, and he died there on 8 January 1846, and was buried at Stone, Staffordshire.

K. D. REYNOLDS

Sources DNB · GEC, *Baronetage* · HoP, *Commons* · *Lord Granville Leveson Gower: private correspondence, 1781–1821*, ed. Castalia, Countess Granville [C. R. Leveson-Gower], 2nd edn, 2 vols. (1916) · *The journal of Elizabeth, Lady Holland, 1791–1811*, ed. earl of Ilchester [G. S. Holland Fox-Strangways], 2 vols. (1908) · B. Askwith, *Piety and wit: a biography of Harriet Countess Granville, 1785–1862* (1982) · K. Bourne, *Palmerston: the early years, 1784–1841* (1982) · A. Foreman, *Georgiana, duchess of Devonshire* (1998) · *Hary-O: the letters of Lady Harriet Cavendish, 1796–1809*, ed. G. Leveson-Gower and I. Palmer (1940) · Earl of Bessborough and A. Aspinall, eds., *Lady Bessborough and her family circle* (1940) · E. Longford [E. H. Pakenham, countess of Longford], *Wellington, 2: Pillar of state* (1972)

Archives Christ Church Oxf., dispatches and papers · PRO, corresp. and papers, PRO 30/29 | Balliol Oxf., corresp. with David Morier · BL, corresp. with John Bellingham, Add. MS 48216 · BL, corresp. with Lord Holland, Add. MSS 51604–51608 · BL, corresp. with William Huskisson, Add. MSS 38739–38758 · BL, corresp. with third Viscount Melbourne, Add. MSS 60443–60444 · BL, corresp. with Lord Morley, Add. MSS 48222–48223 · BL, letters to Sir Arthur Paget, Add. MSS 48413–48415, *passim* · Castle Howard, letters to Lady Carlisle · Derbys. RO, Matlock, corresp. with Sir R. J. Wilmot-Horton · Duke U., Perkins L., letters to Lord Holland · Harrowby Manuscript Trust, Sandon Hall, Staffordshire, corresp. with Lords Harrowby · Keele University Library, letters to Sneyd family · PRO, corresp. with Strafford Canning · PRO, corresp. with Francis Jackson, FO 353 · PRO, corresp. with H. M. Pierrepont, FO 334 · U. Durham L., corresp. with second Earl Grey · U. Southampton L., Broadlands MSS · U. Southampton L., letters to Lord Palmerston

Likenesses G. Romney, group portrait, oils, 1776–7 (*The Gower children*), Abbot Hall Art Gallery, Kendal · J. S. Agar, stipple (after T. Phillips), BM, NPG; repro. in *The British gallery of contemporary portraits* (1813) · G. Hayter, group portrait, oils (*The trial of Queen Caroline, 1820*), NPG · portrait (after T. Lawrence), Sutherland Trust; repro. in Foreman, *Georgiana*

Wealth at death under £160,000: GEC, *Baronetage*

Gower, Harriet Elizabeth Georgiana Leveson- [*née* Harriet Elizabeth Georgiana Howard], **duchess of Sutherland** (1806–1868), courtier, was born on 21 May 1806, the third daughter and fifth of the twelve children of George *Howard, later sixth earl of Carlisle (1773–1848), and his wife, Lady Georgiana Dorothy Cavendish (1783–1858). She was thus born into the 'whig cousinhood': her maternal grandmother was the celebrated Georgiana *Cavendish, duchess of Devonshire, and her immediate family connections also included the Granvilles, Spencers, Ponsonbys, and Greys. Large, boisterous, and charming, Harriet Howard made her official début in London society on 25 April 1823. Precisely one week later she accepted a proposal of marriage from one of the most eligible bachelors of the day: her cousin George Granville Leveson-Gower (1786–1861), then Earl Gower and heir to his father's marquessate of Stafford. Harriet was not yet seventeen; Gower was twenty years her senior. The marriage took place on 28 May and was a happy and enduring one. Harriet had four sons, including Ronald Charles Sutherland-Leveson-*Gower, and seven daughters, three of whom died in infancy.

Harriet Elizabeth Georgiana Leveson-Gower, duchess of Sutherland (1806–1868), by Franz Xaver Winterhalter, 1849

Lady Gower threw herself into her new role with the exuberance of her grandmother. Despite her frequent pregnancies she soon established herself as a hostess, especially after Gower's father purchased the lease on the unfinished York House (speedily renamed Stafford House), London, in 1827. She came into her own in the 1830s, for in January 1833 her father-in-law was raised to the dukedom of Sutherland, and died six months later. As duchess of Sutherland, and with a compliant husband, Harriet had huge resources at her command. There is no doubt that she was the driving force behind their vast building and refurbishment programme: Lilleshall Hall in Shropshire was rebuilt in Tudor style in the 1820s, and in subsequent years Stafford House was extended and completed by Benjamin Wyatt; Trentham Hall in Staffordshire was rebuilt in Italianate style by Sir Charles Barry, who also altered the family's Scottish seat, Dunrobin Castle in Sutherland. Finally, in 1849 they also purchased Cliveden Manor, on the Thames in Buckinghamshire, and rebuilt it after a fire. The expense was phenomenal, and, especially in the context of the highland clearances, brought down some unfavourable reflections on the duchess's head.

But the duchess was no thoughtless socialite. She had been brought up with strong religious principles, and as she matured she became a firm high-churchwoman. She gave substantially, although unsystematically, to charity, and had an extensive list of pensioners from the family estates. Her enthusiasm for the cause of anti-slavery aroused mockery both from within the movement (where some doubted her sincerity) and among its opponents (Thomas Carlyle referred to Stafford House as 'Aunt Harriet's Cabin' (Reynolds, 127)), but the patronage she lent to the movement's activists, notably Harriet Beecher Stowe, was of material use. On 26 November 1852 she held a meeting at Stafford House in support of the movement, breaking with all precedent by addressing the meeting herself to propose a memorial from the women of England to the women of the United States urging the abolition of slavery, and heading the list of signatories. The meeting and memorial were not particularly important in bringing about the end of slavery, but they served to draw public attention to the cause in a way that meetings of provincial worthies must have envied.

On Queen Victoria's accession in 1837 the duchess was appointed mistress of the robes. This placed her at the head of the queen's aristocratic female household, and entailed attendance on the queen on ceremonial occasions, as well as some formal administrative duties (carried out for the most part by the groom of the robes). The duchess's magnificence made her in some ways an unlikely courtier (Princess Lieven asked from France 'I hear that she is a little too humble, a little too much like a head-housemaid; can that be possible?' (Sudley, 180), and the queen is famously supposed to have said on visiting Stafford House from Buckingham Palace 'I have come to your palace from my house' (Stuart, 57)). The proposal by Sir Robert Peel to remove the duchess from her office along with several others of the female household in 1839 was the cause of the 'Bedchamber' crisis; on this occasion Harriet retained her position, but she resigned in 1841 when Melbourne's government fell. She was reinstated, however, in 1846, and served as mistress of the robes under all the whig–liberal governments until the death of her husband. In so far as the queen had friends, the duchess was one of them, her acceptance being ensured by the high value she placed on the prince consort. In 1850 the queen wrote

> I must ever love the Duchess of Sutherland for her very great and sincere admiration of the Prince. … There is not a work he undertakes … which she does not follow with the greatest interest, being herself so anxious to do good, so liberal-minded, so superior to prejudice, and so eager to learn, and improve herself and others.   (T. Martin, *Life of the Prince Consort*, 5 vols., 1875–80, 2.245)

Indeed, she was with the queen at Windsor when Albert died, and was her sole companion for some time afterwards. The death of the duke of Sutherland earlier in 1861 made her still more acceptable as a companion in the queen's misery. The friendship survived attempts by the duchess to encourage Victoria to resume some kind of public life and the queen's disapproval of Harriet's patronage of the Italian patriot Garibaldi (she entertained

him at Chiswick House and Trentham in 1864). The duchess has been described as 'perhaps the last of the Whigs to be on genuinely confidential terms with the Queen' (Matthew, 150).

Outside the queen and her own family, the duchess's most significant relationship was with the rising politician W. E. Gladstone. From 1853, when he was taken ill while staying at Dunrobin, Gladstone was taken under the duchess's wing, and it can fairly be said that she sponsored his acceptance by the whigs as he moved away from the tory party. Particularly in the decade after 1858 they carried on a confidential correspondence (Gladstone's letters are unfortunately missing, although the duchess's are in the British Library), and Gladstone was a regular at the weekend gatherings of politicians, churchmen, and literary figures that the duchess held at Cliveden. (The country weekend in the home counties was just coming into vogue thanks to the advent of the railways; the duchess, if not its inventor, was certainly in the vanguard.) They shared a religious perspective on public events, an interest in literature, and after 1863 the conviction that the queen was endangering the monarchy by her prolonged seclusion.

In her own widowhood, the duchess (whose health declined from 1863 and who was afflicted by cataracts) retired from public life, living mostly at Cliveden and at Chiswick House near London; her last official engagement was to attend the queen at the wedding of the prince of Wales and Princess Alexandra in 1863. Her own sons caused some anxieties (the second son, Lord Frederick, died during the Crimean War; marital difficulties affected the heir, Lord Stafford; and scandal threatened the security of Lord Ronald), but her four daughters made grand matches in the whig manner, becoming duchess of Argyll, Lady Blantyre, duchess of Leinster, and duchess of Westminster. Harriet Sutherland died at Stafford House on 27 October 1868. Gladstone was among the pallbearers at her funeral at Trentham church, and composed the Latin epitaph on her tomb. The important connections of her life persisted in succeeding generations: her daughter Elizabeth Argyll and daughter-in-law Anne Sutherland both succeeded her as mistress of the robes; one granddaughter married Gladstone's eldest son; and her grandson married the queen's daughter Princess Louise.

K. D. REYNOLDS

Sources Staffs. RO, Sutherland papers · NL Scot., Sutherland MSS · BL, Gladstone MSS · K. D. Reynolds, *Aristocratic women and political society in Victorian Britain* (1998) · H. C. G. Matthew, *Gladstone, 1809–1874* (1988) · D. Stuart, *Dear duchess: Millicent duchess of Sutherland, 1867–1955* (1982) · *Three Howard sisters: selections from the writings of Lady Caroline Lascelles, Lady Dover, and Countess Gower, 1825 to 1833*, ed. Maud, Lady Leconfield, rev. J. Gore (1955) · *The Lieven–Palmerston correspondence, 1828–1856*, ed. and trans. Lord Sudley [A. P. J. C. J. Gore] (1943) · Burke, *Peerage* (1901) · J. S. Lewis, *In the family way* (1986) · W. A. Lindsay, *The royal household* (1898) · *CGPLA Eng. & Wales* (1868)

Archives BL, diary of a journey to Berlin, Add. MS 45109 · NL Scot., commonplace book and corresp. · Staffs. RO, corresp. and MSS | BL, corresp. with W. E. Gladstone, Add. MSS 44324–44329 · Bodl. RH, Buxton MSS · Keele University Library, corresp. with R. Sneyd · St Deiniol's Library, Hawarden, letters to C. Gladstone

Likenesses W. R., pencil drawing, 1818, Castle Howard • T. Lawrence, oils, exh. RA 1828, Dunrobin Castle • G. Hayter, group portrait, oils, 1838 (*The coronation of Queen Victoria*), Royal Collection • G. Hayter, pencil study, c.1838, BM • C. R. Leslie, group portrait, oils, 1838 (*Queen Victoria receiving the sacrament at her coronation*), Royal Collection • C. R. Leslie, oils, c.1839, Wolverhampton Art Gallery • S. F. Diez, drawing, 1841, Staatliche Museen zu Berlin • F. X. Winterhalter, oils, 1849, priv. coll. [*see illus.*] • M. Noble, effigy, 1868, St Mary and All Saints Church, Staffordshire • M. Noble, marble bust, c.1869, Alnwick Castle, Northumberland; related plaster bust, NPG • M. Noble, statue, 1869, Dunrobin Castle • H. P. Bone, enamel miniature (after Mrs Mee), Arundel Castle, West Sussex • T. Lawrence, portrait, repro. in *Three Howard sisters*, ed. Leconfield • H. Robinson, stipple (after A. E. Chalon), BM, NPG • W. C. Ross, miniature, London, Wallace collection • F. X. Winterhalter, oils, copy, Royal Collection

Wealth at death under £8000: administration, 24 Dec 1868, *CGPLA Eng. & Wales*

Gower, Henrietta Elizabeth [Harriet] **Leveson-** [née Lady Henrietta Elizabeth Cavendish], **Countess Granville** (**1785–1862**), society hostess, was born at Devonshire House, Piccadilly, London, on 29 August 1785, the younger daughter of William *Cavendish, fifth duke of Devonshire (1748–1811), and his first wife, Georgiana *Cavendish (1757–1806), eldest daughter of John *Spencer, first Earl Spencer. Her devotion to her mother, 'the beautiful duchess', was the mainspring of her happy childhood, while her elder sister, Georgiana (known as 'G'), and her young brother, Lord Hartington, were the focus of her liveliest affections. The duke was aloof and rarely seen. The Chatsworth schoolroom, under the supervision of Selina Trimmer, had other pupils, including the natural son and daughter of her father and his mistress, Lady Elizabeth Foster, who herself lived with the Devonshires in perfect amity. Moreover, the flock of cousins from the family of her aunt, Henrietta, Lady Bessborough, often stayed at Chatsworth.

Patrician by birth, the scion of a great whig family, Hary-O (as she was known in the family before her marriage) spoke in the 'bleating drawl' of the Devonshire House set. Although no beauty, she had wit, intelligence, and shrewdness; her sharp eye missed little but 'in high croak and spirits' viewed with tolerance the world of drums, dandies, gossip, and matchmaking in which she moved. After her sister's marriage in 1801 to George Howard, later sixth earl of Carlisle, she wrote to her almost daily, until Lady Carlisle's death in 1858. These letters to 'G', observant, critical, aware of the ridiculous but always amused, treating of subjects engrossing to both, are endearing indications of the sisters' deep attachment. Their affection surmounted their differing interests: Harriet's eldest son was to remark that his mother did not 'care a rap about politics' while Lady Carlisle thought of 'nothing else' (Fitzmaurice, 1.180).

With her mother's death in 1806, Lady Harriet's position at home became as unhappy as it was awkward. Lady Elizabeth Foster took over the direction of Devonshire House where she, the unmarried daughter, should have reigned. It was an invidious position: for three years she made the best of the absurdities and the vexations caused her by Lady Elizabeth. When it became apparent, in 1809,

Henrietta Elizabeth [Harriet] **Leveson-Gower, Countess Granville** (1785–1862), by Thomas Barber

that the duke would shortly bestir himself into making his liaison lawful, Lady Bessborough set about finding a suitable husband for her niece. Lord Granville Leveson-*Gower (1773–1846) had for seventeen years been her own lover, with whom she had two children. None the less, she encouraged his courtship of her niece, who had known him all her life and had never cared much for him. Now she was captivated by this exceptionally handsome man, a member of parliament, who was intelligent and had every advantage of birth. The handkerchief was tossed in July, his proposal made in November, and she married him on 24 December 1809 and loved him to the end of her life. 'Granville, adored Granville, who would make a barren desert smile', she wrote. There were five children of this very happy marriage, including Georgiana [*see* Fullerton, Lady Georgiana Charlotte] and Granville George Leveson-*Gower (1815–1891), second Earl Granville, the foreign secretary. The two illegitimate children of Lady Bessborough and Granville were absorbed into the family and loved. In 1815 a viscountcy for Granville, and in 1833 an earldom, gave Lady Granville the name by which she is most widely known. Perhaps the zenith of her days was reached when Lord Granville was appointed ambassador to France (in 1824–8, in 1830–35, and again in 1835–41), where she acted as his hostess, entertaining the cosmopolitan Parisian society. Her fond descriptions of the Paris embassy house and the caustic accounts of daunting receptions, of people, of dress and manners make irresistible reading in the volumes of her letters published in 1894, 1940, and 1990.

Lord Granville died in 1846. In her desolation his widow

turned to her brother, now the sixth duke, in the 'utter and hopeless breaking of my heart'. Much of her time was spent at Chiswick finding a new consolation in evangelical piety. She died of a stroke on 25 November 1862 at her home, 13 Hereford Street, Park Lane, London.

VIRGINIA SURTEES

Sources H. E. Gower, *Letters, 1810–1845*, ed. F. Leveson-Gower, 2 vols. (1894) • B. Askwith, *Piety and wit: a biography of Harriet Countess Granville, 1785–1862* (1982) • *Hary-O: the letters of Lady Harriet Cavendish, 1796–1809*, ed. G. Leveson-Gower and I. Palmer (1940) • V. Surtees, *A second self* (1990) • J. Lees-Milne, *The bachelor duke* (1991) • GEC, *Peerage* • E. G. Petty-Fitzmaurice, *The life of Granville George Leveson Gower, second Earl Granville*, 2nd edn, 2 vols. (1905)
Archives Chatsworth House, Derbyshire • PRO | Castle Howard, Howard MSS • Keele University, Sneyd MSS • Sandon Hall, Staffordshire, Harrowby MSS
Likenesses R. Cosway, double portrait, miniature, 1789 (with her sister) • J. Notz, watercolour, *c.*1830, Chatsworth House, Derbyshire • T. Barber, portrait, Hardwick Hall, Derbyshire [*see illus.*] • E. Surtees, oils (after pastel portrait by J. Russell, *c.*1789), Chatsworth House, Derbyshire
Wealth at death under £16,000: probate, 19 March 1863, *CGPLA Eng. & Wales*

Gower, Henry (1277/8–1347), bishop of St David's, was descended from a noble family, and his surname, possessions in Gower, and evident interest in Swansea suggest that his roots were in the English-speaking peninsula of Gower. He matriculated at Merton College, Oxford, and became master of arts, doctor of both civil and canon law, and fellow of Merton *c.*1307. His election as chancellor of the university was confirmed on 18 October 1322, and he vacated the office in 1325. As chancellor he is claimed to have rebutted the archdeacon of Oxford's claims to jurisdiction over the university, but this dispute between archdeacon and university was not raised in its final form until 1325, and not settled until 1345. About 1314 he became canon of St David's and some time after 1319, certainly by 1323, archdeacon of St David's. Gower was distinguished for his knowledge of several languages, probably including Welsh, since his fitness for a Welsh appointment was specially noted. Letters written in Edward III's name describe him as a man of foresight and unblemished character.

Bishop David Martin of St David's (1293–1328) died on 9 March, leaving his diocese vacant during the disturbances caused in south Wales by the fall of Edward II. The precentor and canons, using Gower as their emissary to inform the king of Martin's death, recommended him as the latter's successor. On 26 March the *congé d'élire* was issued; Gower was elected on 21 April at the age of fifty, and on 12 June was consecrated at Canterbury by Stephen Gravesend, bishop of London. His election was confirmed by Pope John XXII in December 1328. Gower's was the last election in fourteenth-century Wales in which neither king nor pope interfered to secure the choice of a bishop.

Gower wished to proceed to the papal court at Avignon, but a general order prohibited all magnates from leaving the country, and he seems to have received a special appointment to calm the 'whirlwinds of war' in his own diocese. This may indicate that he was in the confidence of Mortimer and the queen. Mortimer was the tenant of some lands belonging to the diocese of St David's, and

Gower, having been appointed by Edward III to hear complaints concerning Mortimer's misconduct within them, was rewarded by the king for his loyalty. Letters of a most favourable kind concerning Gower's learning and character were sent in Edward's name commending him and his business to the pope and cardinals. Before 1328 was out Gower and his household were attacked when reconciling the church of Llanbadarn Fawr, near Aberystwyth, for which he successfully petitioned for a writ in chancery to give him redress.

Gower played only a limited part in the general business of the realm. In 1329 he received letters of protection to cross the sea with the king, who was to perform homage to Philip VI of France at Amiens. In 1334 he was a member of a commission to renew the truce with France in the south, and in January 1342 he was one of the negotiators of a peace treaty at Antoing near Tournai. He was present at the parliaments held in 1329, 1341, and 1343. In 1346 he lent the king 300 marks.

Entries in the statute book of St David's show Gower to have been a conscientious diocesan. Three sets of his statutes and constitutions, issued in 1332, 1342, and 1344, reveal his concern to improve worship, discipline, and financial administration at his cathedral, and also at the collegiate church of Abergwili, near Carmarthen. The statute book also contains the foundation charter of his large hospital, that of the Blessed David at Swansea, founded in 1332. It was intended to support six chaplains to celebrate daily service and to maintain 'priests, blind, decrepit, or infirm, and other poor men … destitute of food and begging'. It was amply endowed with churches and lands in Swansea and Gower. In 1338 and 1339 he negotiated agreements between the canons of Abergwili and the Cistercian abbeys of Whitland and Strata Florida in his diocese over the highly contentious question of the tithes to be paid to either party in a number of appropriated livings.

Gower's fame rests chiefly on his munificent benefactions and his distinction as an architect. Often referred to as the 'Welsh Wykeham', he has strong claims to be the outstanding builder among medieval Welsh bishops. He was the originator of an attractive local form of 'decorated' Gothic architecture, and 'has left more extensive traces of his mind at St David's than any other bishop before or since' (Jones and Freeman, 302–3). In 1334 he established a chantry in the lady chapel of his cathedral, and appropriated the church of Manorowen near Fishguard to the sub-chanter and vicars-choral as its endowment. Probably at this time, he carried out considerable alterations to the fabric of the lady chapel and installed there a handsome tomb for his predecessor. Before the high altar he built a magnificent stone rood screen, which still dominates the cathedral. Having built a second stage to the tower and raised the aisles to their present height, he had intended to vault over the whole building in stone, but was obliged to leave the work incomplete.

The most notable manifestation of Gower's genius as an architect is to be seen in the superb episcopal palace at St David's, 'altogether unsurpassed by any existing English (or Welsh) edifice of its kind' (Jones and Freeman). He built the precinct wall around St David's and strengthened the fortifications at Porth-y-twr, thus making it possible to turn the palace into a more peaceful residential abode. To the existing buildings there he added a second hall and a delightful arcaded parapet, researches on the masonry of which show him to have rebuilt at first-floor level over a long period. The statute book records an order issued by Gower in 1342 (BL, Harley MS 6280, fol. 13) for bringing seven episcopal residences within his see into good repair. At three of these, besides St David's, he is believed to have been responsible for major alterations. He is credited with having created a second hall and an arcaded parapet at Lamphey and Swansea. The masons at Lamphey were inferior in skill to those at St David's and used local materials, but worked to Gower's commission. Some doubt has been cast on Gower's responsibility for the building at Swansea, though the architectural style is thoroughly typical of him. Any palace he built at Llanddewi, Gower, has long since disappeared.

Claims made for Gower's being responsible for 'decorated' features in other churches within his diocese are not all reliable. Work carried out at Carew, Hodgeston, and Monkton, all in Pembrokeshire, may have been executed by masons brought into his diocese by Gower, but working for other patrons. However, the church at Llanddewi and old St Mary's Church, Swansea, may have been directly indebted to him.

Gower died on 25 April 1347, and was buried at his cathedral in a large altar tomb in the south-west corner of the rood screen he had built. It bears an effigy of a bishop in eucharistic vestments, possibly a likeness of him, but now sadly mutilated.   GLANMOR WILLIAMS

Sources G. Williams, 'Henry de Gower', in G. Williams, *The Welsh and their religion* (1991), 93–116 · W. Greenway, 'Henry de Gower: bishop of St David's, 1328–47', *Gower*, 11 (1958), 13–17 · Emden, *Oxf.* · *Fasti Angl.*, *1300–1541*, [Welsh dioceses] · *RotP*, vol. 2 · Rymer, *Foedera*, 2nd edn · E. Yardley, *Menevia sacra*, ed. F. Green (1927) · W. B. Jones and E. A. Freeman, *The history and antiquities of St David's* (1856) · C. A. R. Radford, *The bishop's palace, St David's* (1953) · C. A. R. Radford, 'The palace of the bishops of St David's at Lamphey, Pembrokeshire', *Archaeologia Cambrensis*, 93 (1935), 1–14 · G. Williams, *The Welsh church from conquest to Reformation*, rev. edn (1976) · Statute Book of St David's, BL, MS Harley 6280
Archives BL, Harley MS 6280
Likenesses tomb effigy, St David's Cathedral; now mutilated

Gower, Sir Henry Dudley Gresham Leveson (1873–1954), cricketer, was born on 8 May 1873 at Titsey Place, Limpsfield, Surrey, the seventh of the twelve sons of Granville William Gresham Leveson Gower (1838–1895), whose estates amounted to nearly 7000 acres of land in Surrey, and who sat briefly (1863–5) as Liberal MP for Reigate, and his wife, Sophia (*d.* 1926), daughter of Chandos Leigh, first Baron Leigh. Sophia was the sister of Sir Edward Chandos Leigh QC, who was president of the Marylebone Cricket Club (MCC) in 1887. Leveson Gower (pronounced 'Loosen Gore' and always known by both names) was educated at Winchester College, where he was in the eleven for three years. As captain in 1892, he led his side to victory against Eton College by making 99 runs and taking eight for 33 in

the match. He then went up to Magdalen College, Oxford, and played against Cambridge at Lord's four times (1893–6). As captain, in his last year, he took Oxford to a remarkable victory after being set 330. He did not take a degree.

Short in stature and slight in physique, Leveson Gower was an outstanding fielder and a good cutter of the ball. He made his début for Surrey in 1895 and four years later made 155 for the county—his highest score in first-class cricket—against his old university. He played 122 matches for Surrey between 1895 and 1920, and captained the county to third, fifth, and second place in the championship in the seasons 1908–10. It was his personal qualities of leadership off and on the field (as, indeed, the title of his autobiography indicates) which marked him out rather more than his talents as a performer. Compared with his university contemporaries such as C. B. Fry and Pelham Warner, he did not fulfil expectations.

Although he embarked on a career as a stockbroker, Leveson Gower was able to find time to tour both the West Indies with Lord Hawke's eleven and America under Warner in 1897–8. In 1898 he was asked to take over the administrative responsibilities of running the Scarborough cricket festival in Yorkshire, already well established by its founder, C. I. Thornton. He had shown signs of his abilities in raising elevens against the two universities in the Eastbourne cricket week. Soon the Scarborough festival became almost synonymous with H. D. G. Leveson Gower's eleven, and attracted the annual visiting tourists as opponents. In 1909–10 Leveson Gower led the MCC in South Africa, where he captained England in the first three tests before standing down from the side. His last appearance in first-class cricket was in 1931, for his eponymous eleven, the end of a career in which he had made 7638 runs (average 23.72).

Leveson Gower married on 23 April 1908 Enid Mary, daughter of Robert Sharp Borgnis Hammond-Chambers KC; they had no children. He served in the Royal Army Service Corps during the First World War, attained the rank of major, and was mentioned in dispatches.

Leveson Gower had been elected a member of the MCC committee as early as 1898. Eleven years later he became an England selector, before becoming chairman of the selectors in 1924 and in 1927–30. He was also treasurer of Surrey (1926–8) and president (1929–39). For his services to the Scarborough festival he was given the freedom of the borough in 1930 and eventually completed an association of over fifty years. While the festival proved an enjoyable annual event for players and spectators alike, Leveson Gower maintained the divisions between amateurs and professionals and their wives even after the close of the day's play. He was a man of his time—an 'Establishment' figure—but his overall qualities of humour, kindness, and vitality were central to his character. His schoolboy nickname of Shrimp stuck with him throughout his life and remained apt. Leveson Gower was knighted in 1953 and died at his home, 30 St Mary Abbots Court, Kensington, in London on 1 February 1954. He was survived by his wife.

R. H. HILL, *rev.* GERALD M. D. HOWAT

Sources *The Times* (2 Feb 1954) · *Wisden* (1955) · H. Leveson Gower, *Off and on the field* (1953) · personal knowledge (1971) · Burke, *Peerage* (1939) [Sutherland] · *CGPLA Eng. & Wales* (1954)

Wealth at death £7158 0s. 11d.: administration, 28 June 1954, *CGPLA Eng. & Wales*

Gower, Humphrey (1638–1711), college head, was born at Brampton Bryan, Herefordshire, the son of Stanley Gower (b. 1603) and his wife, Sarah Hyde. Stanley Gower, who was born in Dublin, was a member of the Westminster assembly from 1643 and rector at Brampton until 1650, when he became rector of Holy Trinity, Dorchester. Gower attended St Paul's School, London, from about 1647 to 1651, and then Dorchester School until 1655. He entered St John's College, Cambridge, on 21 May 1655, and was elected to a scholarship on the foundation of William Spalding on 7 November. Having graduated BA in 1659, on 23 March 1659 he was admitted to a foundress fellowship and proceeded MA in 1662, BD in 1669, and DD in 1676. He was rector successively of Hamoon, Dorset (1663–7), Paglesham, Essex (1667–75), Newton (1675–7) and Fen Ditton, Cambridgeshire (1677–9), and Terrington, Norfolk (1688–1711); he was also prebendary of Ely in 1679–1711.

Gower had been reputed one of the best scholars of his year and styled 'eruditus juvenis' ('learned young man'). In 1667 or 1668 he preached before the king and was offered a royal chaplaincy which he declined, preferring the academic environment. Gunning, master of St John's, as bishop of Ely promoted him to the mastership of Jesus College on 11 July 1679, and he was elected master of St John's on 3 December. In 1680–81 Gower was vice-chancellor, and received the king at Newmarket, where on 18 September 1681, in the wake of both the fears of a 'popish plot' fuelled by Titus Oates, and the royal victory over the whig exclusionists after the dissolution of the parliament at Oxford, he made a speech affirming the loyalty of the university to the Anglican establishment and the divinely ordered power of the throne. On 27 September Gower excelled himself in a further entertainment of the king and queen to dinner in the master's long gallery (the present combination room) at St John's, having already in the university schools made one Latin and one English speech and presented a Bible to the king and Sir William Dugdale's *A View of the Late Troubles in England* to the queen. Despite his courtly skills, however, he refused the promises of preferment made on that occasion by a grateful king, writing to the bishop of Peterborough on 18 January 1682 that he was 'wedded to St John's College'. On 29 June 1688 he was elected Lady Margaret professor of divinity.

Gower did not escape political involvements. On 25 July 1693 the court of king's bench ordered him to eject twenty fellows who had refused the oath of allegiance to William III and Queen Mary, and he was indicted at Cambridge assizes on 10 August for not having done so. An anonymous legal opinion preserved at St John's contends that the order had violated due process of law and Magna Carta. The jury at the assizes threw out the indictment, and the case against Gower also failed when heard in king's bench itself in Trinity term 1694. His stand saved the college from the spectacle of mass ejectment during his mastership.

Gower's concern for the externals of the college is revealed in the proposal, the subject of letters to him by Wren and Hawksmoor in 1697 and 1698, to build a new bridge over the Cam—the present Kitchen Bridge completed by Robert Grumbold in 1711. His college loyalty, and care for friendship and for his own standing in the university, are all reflected in a judicious letter of 11 December 1700 to the poet Matthew Prior, a fellow of the college, who sought support for election as a university member of parliament. While protesting existing obligations to Henry Boyle and Anthony Hammond (the latter, unlike Prior, a resident of the college for many years and Gower's personal friend), Gower also made clear that he would not be an active opponent. On 9 August 1706 he cordially acknowledged an ode which the poet had sent him.

Friendship also influenced Gower's benefactions to his college. By his will of 10 July 1708 he bequeathed it the first choice of his books. Edmund Brome, fellow, Gower's friend and fellow resident in the master's lodge, was to choose books to the value of £50 from the remainder, although the college actually gave him the use of nearly 400 books worth in total much more. After his fellowship had expired Brome's books were to come to the college, or could be sold to help needy scholars. Fifty-eight items were sold to Brome himself for £20 2s.

Gower in 1696 bought the manor of Barrington in Thriplow, an estate of some 200 acres, from Sir Christopher and Dame Elizabeth Hatton. He used it as a place of retirement and recreation with friends, and presented it in his will for the use of the master of the college. The bequest was subject to the life interest of his nephew, and to the previous accumulation of rents to the value of £500, which should be used by the college to buy an advowson. The living of Lilley, Hertfordshire, was bought by this means. The estate was sold in 1914. He also provided for charity. The Thriplow estate was subject to a charge of £20 a year to be devoted to exhibitions for two sons of clergy who had attended St Paul's School, London, and Dorchester School, of the rank of sizar. Legacies included those to the poor and to the church at Brampton Bryan, to the newly formed Society for the Propagation of the Gospel in Foreign Parts, and for books for the library of the church of Ely. He also remembered, besides his relatives, named individuals who had lived with, or were dependent on him. Gower died on 27 March 1711 at the master's lodge in St John's; he was buried on 7 April in the college chapel.   MALCOLM G. UNDERWOOD

Sources T. Baker, *History of the college of St John the Evangelist, Cambridge*, ed. J. E. B. Mayor, 2 vols. (1869) · Venn, *Alum. Cant.* · *Calendar of the manuscripts of the marquis of Bath preserved at Longleat, Wiltshire*, 5 vols., HMC, 58 (1904–80), vol. 3 · will, 10 July 1708, PRO, PROB 11/520 · St John Cam., M1.2, fols. 21–4; printed in *The Eagle*, 24/131 (June 1903), 310–12 · St John Cam., D105.219; printed in *The Eagle*, 25/163 (March 1914), 172–5 · C. H. Cooper, *Annals of Cambridge*, 3 (1845) · J. E. B. Mayor, ed., *Admissions to the College of St John the Evangelist in the University of Cambridge*, pts 1–2: Jan 1629/30 – July 1715 (1882–93) · register of fellows, St John Cam., C3.2 · E. A. Fry, *Dorset clergy*, ed. J. C. Sherbourne and A. T. Sawtell (1901) · M. McDonnell, ed., *The registers of St Paul's School, 1509–1748* (privately printed, London, 1977) · A. Sidebotham, *Brampton Bryan church and castle* (privately printed, Leominster, 1990), 13

Likenesses follower of J. Riley, oils, 17th cent., St John Cam. · oils, *c.*1679, St John Cam. · oils, *c.*1700, St John Cam. · G. Vertue, line engraving, 1719 (after J. Fellowes), BM, NPG, St John Cam. · oils, St John Cam.

Wealth at death £551 10s. 0d.—plus an estate valued at £10 13s. 4d. p.a.: will, PRO, PROB 11/520

Gower, John (*d.* 1408), poet, may have been born in the 1330s or 1340s. Although the date of his death can be fixed, and his tomb still survives in Southwark Cathedral (formerly the priory of St Mary Overie), that of his birth is unknown. In a letter to Archbishop Arundel (*c.*1400) accompanying his Latin poem the *Vox clamantis*, Gower describes himself as 'old'. How old he was is not revealed, but it has been assumed that this and similar references indicate that he was probably over sixty by the turn of the century.

Family origins That the name Gower is a common one has made the identification of his family difficult. There is nothing to support Caxton's assertion in his edition of Gower's long English poem, the *Confessio amantis* (1483), that Gower was 'a squyer borne in Walys in the tyme of kyng Richard the second'. This was perhaps suggested by the region of Gower in south Wales. A birth date as late as the reign of Richard II is impossible: perhaps Caxton meant Edward II. However Caxton was correct in calling him a squire, and not a knight as John Leland did. Leland's remark that he came from Stittenham in Yorkshire 'so I understand', began a long controversy over his family. Thynne in his *Animadversions* objected that the poet's arms on his tomb were different from those of the Stittenham Gowers. Weever in his *Ancient Funeral Monuments* (1631) noted the similarity with those on the tomb of Sir Robert Gower (*d.* 1349), a considerable landowner in Kent and Suffolk, at Brabourne in Kent, but the supposed connection with the Stittenham Gowers continued to be repeated until the nineteenth century, when Sir Harris Nicolas showed that the seal of John Gower on a deed of 1373 had the same arms as on his and Sir Robert's tombs, and that he came from the Kentish rather than the Yorkshire family. This argument, now long accepted, is supported by the documentary evidence of the poet's close connection with Kent and by the presence of some Kentish features in his English. However, it has been suggested that there was also a Yorkshire connection, but with the Gowers of Langbargh, who had arms similar to those of the Kentish Gowers, and with whom Sir Robert was related through marriage. That John Gower had some family connection with Sir Robert Gower is suggested by the fact that on 28 June 1368 he received the manor of Kentwell at Long Melford, Suffolk, from Thomas Syward and his wife, Joan, the daughter of Sir Robert.

Life to c.1400 The documentary evidence relating to Gower's life is less extensive than that available for his friend Chaucer, whose social position was similar, but who had a varied and more public administrative career. Moreover, it is sometimes difficult to be sure that the John Gower of

John Gower (*d.* 1408), illuminated miniature [kneeling]

the records is in fact the poet. His appearance in one of the earliest series that seem to associate him with Kent was questioned by his modern editor, G. C. Macaulay. This concerns the manor of Aldington Septvauns in Kent (between Sittingbourne and Maidstone), which in 1365 was purchased by John Gower from the heir, William Septvauns. This proved to be a messy affair, and it seems that Gower had some premonition that it might be so, since he took care to have the writs and charters recorded in chancery. On 13 April 1366 a commission was set up to look into the question of the heir's age—whether the original testimony was incorrect and if the heir was below age and had been led and counselled to alienate his lands, what waste and destruction had been done to the lands, and what profit the king had lost. It turned out that he was under age, that there was no waste, and that his lands should be recovered, but not from those to whom he was legally obligated through debts, recognizances, and charters. In 1368 a special licence was recorded allowing Septvauns to enfeoff John Gower with a moiety of the manor of Aldington. Five years later Gower disposed of it, together with Kentwell. Macaulay found it impossible to believe that the poet could be identical with this 'villainous misleader of youth' (*Complete Works*, 4.xv). But everything seems to point towards the identification, and although the affair turned out to cause problems it does not seem to have been nefarious.

Probably Gower had some legal or civil office. A reference in his French poem, the *Mirour de l'omme*, seems to imply that he may have been connected with the law. Apologizing for not being a clerk, and knowing but little French or Latin, he remarks that he 'wore the striped sleeve' ('ai vestu la raye mance'; *Mirour*, l. 21,774), apparently the distinctive dress of serjeants-at-law and certain court officials. It is notable that illustrations in fifteenth-century manuscripts show all of the court officials except judges and registrars wearing 'rayed' gowns. That in the *Mirour* (ll. 24,181 ff.) he is highly critical of contemporary lawyers and the way they feather their nests need not rule out some kind of personal connection: he shows a good knowledge of legal privileges and terminology. Probably he was, as J. A. W. Bennett wrote, 'a Londoner versed in the law who was in touch with Kentish gentry, chose his friends chiefly from the legal and ecclesiastical professions, and had some knowledge of life at court' (*Selections*, xix).

Gower was certainly living in Southwark, in the priory of St Mary Overie, from 1398 until his death, and it is quite likely that he had moved there some years before. He may have had a house in the close, perhaps because of benefactions towards the repairing of the priory. The priory probably provided him with a library and a scriptorium. It has been suggested that he lived there for much of the time from as early as about 1377—about the time that there is the first documentary evidence of his connection with Geoffrey Chaucer, then living at Aldgate—but there is no certain proof of this. What is known is that Chaucer, about to leave for Italy in May 1378, appointed as general attorneys (a precaution against losing a lawsuit by default because of absence) John Gower and Richard Forester. It seems almost certain that this John Gower (who is simply named in the document) is the poet; the appointment does not throw light on his place of residence, but presumably indicates that by then he was a trusted friend of Chaucer. Some years later, in *Troilus and Criseyde* (written in the 1380s), Chaucer names him, in the famous phrase 'moral Gower' (Chaucer, *Troilus and Criseyde*, book 5, l. 1856), and asks him to correct the work if there is need.

John Gower appears in the records of a number of transactions from 1378 onwards. He bought land in Throwley and Stalesfield in Kent (near Brabourne) from Isabel the daughter of Walter Huntingfeld. In 1382 he acquired from Guy Rouclif, clerk, two manors—Feltwell in Norfolk and Multon in Suffolk. In this transaction (1 August 1382) he is called 'esquier de Kent'. He leased these for the duration of his life, making them over to Thomas Blakelake, parson of St Nicholas, Feltwell, and others, on condition that £40 was paid to him annually in the conventual church of Westminster (6 August 1382; confirmed on 24 October 1382 and 29 February 1384). He evidently kept some interest in it, since in 1396 one John Cook of Feltwell was pardoned for not appearing to answer to him concerning a debt. Gower is listed in 1401–2 as the owner, and the two manors are mentioned in his will. An event of a quite different kind is recorded in 1393, when Henry of Lancaster, earl of Derby, gave 'un esquier John Gower' a collar, which is presumably the collar with SS depicted on his tomb. Whether or not this represents an act of gratitude for some particular service (such as the giving of a presentation copy of the *Confessio amantis* with its altered dedication to Henry), it is certainly a sign of favour. On 21 November 1399, soon after he was crowned, Henry IV made an annual grant to Gower of two pipes of Gascon wine. Possibly he alludes to this in one of his Latin poems (urging Henry to rule wisely and justly) when he describes himself as 'drinking your dutiful respects' (*Complete Works*, 4.345).

Marriage Late in life Gower married. On 2 January 1398, the bishop of Winchester granted a licence for his marriage to Agnes Groundolf, a fellow parishioner of St Mary Magdalene, Southwark, in Gower's oratory within his lodging in the priory. Nothing more is known about the circumstances or the nature of the marriage: to describe it as a marriage of convenience between an ailing man and his nurse must remain speculation. His description of her in an epitaph he wrote for her tomb (recorded in Bale's papers) as *uxor amans humilis Gower … Ioannis* ('the loving wife of humble John Gower') may be conventional but may well suggest genuine affection. She outlived him. Of his life in the priory virtually nothing is known. A mysterious incident in which three Londoners are mainprisors for one of the canons, Thomas Caudre, that he would do or procure no harm to John Gower, remains unexplained: it may refer to a private quarrel, or to some financial dealing, or to some political disagreement.

Literary career Gower wrote extensively, and with fluency and distinction, in three languages. His lyrical poetry is hardest to date. In the *Mirour*, speaking of his misspent youth, he says that, abandoned to wantonness and vain joy, he disguised himself, and made foolish love songs and danced as he sang them—apparently *caroles* or dance songs:

> les fols ditz d'amours fesoie,
> Dont en chantant je carolloie.
> (*Mirour*, ll. 27,337 ff.)

He probably did write courtly songs in his youth, but whether any of his *Cinkante balades* represent these early poems is still an open question. Thomas Warton, who first drew attention to them, and praised them warmly—'they are tender, pathetical, and poetical … Nor had yet any English poet treated the passion of love with equal delicacy of sentiment and elegance of composition' (Warton, 333)—thought that they were probably the work of a young man. Others have echoed this opinion, though not their modern editor, Macaulay, who remarked sensibly that:

> for this kind of work it is not necessary, or perhaps even desirable, to be a lover oneself; it is enough to have been a lover once: and that Gower could in his later life express the feelings of a lover with grace and truth we have ample evidence in the *Confessio amantis*. (*Complete Works*, 3.lxxii–lxxiii)

Although it may be that some come from earlier in Gower's life, there is no doubt that the manuscript in which they survive (with other, later works) was intended for Henry IV, probably soon after his accession in 1399, perhaps to entertain his court ('por desporter vo noble court roial'; *Balade* 2). The *Cinkante balades* can hardly be described as 'fols ditz d'amours'. The sequence is a varied one (with some poems placed in the mouth of the lady), and although Gower is indebted to the French courtly tradition (he is fond, for instance, of the phrase *fin amour*) he does not follow it slavishly. Love does not always run smoothly—there are many false lovers nowadays (*Balade* 41), more treacherous than Jason, Hercules, Aeneas, and their like (*Balade* 43)—but what is celebrated is a noble and idealized love, characterized by constancy and honour, something very like the 'honeste love' of the *Confessio amantis*. Like Chaucer he marvels at the paradoxes and the mysteries of love: it is a wondrous thing ('Amour est une chose merveilouse'), a dangerous road where the near is far, and the far remains near (*Balade* 48), but it accords with nature and reason (*Balade* 50). The *Balades* are impressively eloquent and graceful.

The *Mirour de l'omme*, a long didactic poem (of nearly 30,000 lines), written *c*.1376–9, is Gower's first major work that can be dated. Probably begun at the very end of Edward III's reign, its reference to the evils that arise in a land when a king is ruled by a woman may well be an allusion to the influence of Alice Perrers. There is a clear allusion to the great schism of 1378 (ll. 18,817–40). The poem survives in a single incomplete copy discovered in the Cambridge University Library by Macaulay in 1895. The title, *Mirour de l'omme*, given in the manuscript accords with Gower's description, in a colophon found in a number of manuscripts of the *Confessio amantis*, of the first of his three books, that written in French, called *Speculum hominis* (or in a later revised version, *Speculum meditantis*), which treats the vices and virtues, and the classes of society, and shows how a sinner who has transgressed ought to return to the knowledge of his creator. The ten sections listed in the manuscript rubric form three larger divisions. The first, and by far the longest (ll. 1–18,420), presents the origin and nature of sin in the form of a religious cosmological allegory. The vices are the offspring of Sin, the daughter of the Devil, and Death, her son. Sin and her seven daughters, the Seven Deadly Sins, are sent to win over the World and to destroy Man's hope of salvation. Man is invited to the Devil's council, and is tempted. While the Flesh succumbs, the Soul resists. Reason, summoned by the Soul, cannot overcome Temptation, but the Flesh is moved by Fear's revelation of the terrible sight of Death, and is reconciled for a time with the Soul. The Seven Deadly Sins (riding on symbolic animals in a grotesque procession) are married in turn to World, and in turn each produce five children (thus Pride, the first, produces Hypocrisy, Vainglory, Arrogance, Boasting, and Disobedience). Man is attacked by the whole brood and forced to submit to Sin. Now Reason and Conscience pray to God for help, and are given seven corresponding Virtues, who are married to Reason and in her turn each produces five daughters. This symmetrical scheme is enlivened by vivid descriptions and by being set against the spiritual battle for Man, whose Flesh inclines to the Vices and whose Soul inclines to the Virtues.

The second part (ll. 18,421–27,360) demonstrates the power of sin throughout the world. Every estate is full of corruption: ecclesiastics and religious, lords, knights, lawyers and judges, merchants and traders, craftsmen and labourers. Much is traditional 'estates satire', but it is sharp and pointed—the friars 'preach poverty to us, and always have their hands out to receive riches'—and often local, as in the address to Wool, 'noble lady, the goddess of merchants, born in England'. Since everyone blames

someone or something else, the poet asks the World where all this evil comes from. The answer is that it comes from Man, to whom God has given reason and dominion over all things on earth, but who has transgressed against God. Man is a microcosm, and when he transgresses all the elements are disturbed. However, it is possible for him to repent so that the world may be amended. In the brief third part (ll. 27,361–29,945) the sorrowful poet calls on the Virgin Mary, the Lady of Pity, to aid him. He tells the story of her life, and begins an ecstatic prayer rehearsing her names and symbols. This vast encyclopaedic poem has passages of real power, and foreshadows ideas and themes found in Gower's later works. It has been rightly called 'the swan-song of Anglo-Norman literature' (Legge, 220).

The *Vox clamantis*, a Latin satirical poem of 10,265 lines in unrhymed elegiac couplets, must have been completed some time after 1381, the year of the peasants' revolt (of which it gives a memorable description), but probably when Richard II was still a young king—it contains a section of advice to him which is couched in friendly and hopeful terms. Gower revised some of it later to make it appear more clearly a foreshadowing of Richard's later downfall. Eleven manuscript copies survive. The first book is a long introductory *Visio*. A bright June day in the fourth year of King Richard is followed by a night that brings a strange sense of terror. At dawn the poet falls asleep and dreams. Going out to pick flowers, he sees bands of peasants going over the fields. Suddenly they are transformed by God's curse into various animals—asses, oxen, swine, dogs, foxes and cats, domestic fowl, flies, and frogs—some of them misshapen, all of them hostile and rebellious: domestic animals are disobedient, tame animals become wild; the world is turned upside down. Urged on by the Jay (Wat Tyler) the peasants advance, armed with rustic weapons and implements, and enter New Troy (London), furiously killing and sacking. Helenus the chief priest (Archbishop Sudbury) is murdered. Death is everywhere, and in horror the poet flees. He boards a ship, but it is assailed by storms and a sea monster. The proud Jay is killed by William (William Walworth) and the storm is calmed. The ship drifts until it reaches an island. It is, he is told, the island of Brutus, inhabited by savage and lawless men. Terrified once more, the poet hears a heavenly voice which tells him to record his dreams. He awakes, amazed, not knowing whether what he had seen was outside him or within him.

The *Visio* is a powerful and imaginative piece of writing, which has a genuinely nightmarish quality. The complaint on the state of England that follows in books 2–7 uses satire of a more traditional kind. Men blame Fortune for the country's decline, but it is human vice that is responsible. Each man makes his fate for himself ('sibi quisque suam sortem facit'). The similarity of outlook with the *Mirour* becomes more marked as Gower details the failings of the three estates and their various subcategories: the sins of the clergy (books 3–4); knights and labourers (book 5); and lawyers (book 6). Although lawyers are corrupted, law is necessary, and must be enforced by the king, who is advised to rule himself well, defend his people, rule them with wisdom and love, and destroy the evils that beset the land in this depraved time. The final book begins with the statue seen by Nebuchadnezzar in his dream (Daniel 4). Now gold has given way to the iron of avarice and the clay of lechery. Man, created for the service of God, should repent and live virtuously. 'The spirit spoke to me in my sleep', says the poet, 'and I have spoken as the voice of the people' ('Quod scripsi plebis vox est').

Some years after the composition of the *Vox clamantis* Gower wrote his major English poem, the *Confessio amantis*, of over 30,000 lines in octosyllabic couplets. The forty-nine surviving manuscripts seem to indicate three stages of revision. The original prologue and conclusion have a dedication to King Richard. Gower says that while rowing on the Thames he met the king's barge, and the king invited him to an audience and bade him write 'some newe thing'. (But already some Latin lines at the end of the poem contain a kind of dedication to Henry of Lancaster, then earl of Derby.) No date is given in the text, but the date 1390 is written in the margin at line 331 of the prologue, and it is usually assumed that this is the date of the work's completion. The plan must have been conceived earlier, perhaps *c*.1386, about the time that Chaucer was completing *The Legend of Good Women*. The epilogue seems to have been revised within a few months: a section beginning with a prayer to the Creator for King Richard, who is spoken of in a laudatory vein, is changed to a prayer to set the land 'in siker weie … upon good governance'. The date of this revised section is given in a marginal note as the fourteenth year of King Richard (21 June 1390–21 June 1391). Finally, no later than June 1393, the prologue was revised, with the story of the meeting with the king removed, and the statement that the poet proposed to make 'a bok for king Richardes sake' changed to:

a bok for Engelondes sake,
The yer sextenthe of kyng Richard.

Gower now says that he will send the book:

unto myn oghne lord,
Whiche of Lancastre is Henri named.
(*Complete Works*, 1.2)

It is not clear that any particular event occasioned this shift. It may well reflect some loss of confidence in Richard, but it would be rash to interpret it as a defiant act of disloyalty. Double dedications were not unknown, and the first version of the poem continued to circulate—in a larger number of copies (thirty-two manuscripts) than the other versions.

The prologue announces that the book will be of love, 'which doth many a wonder'. The world nowadays is not as it was, and love has fallen into discord. In the manner of his earlier works Gower laments the depravity of rulers, clergy and commons, again using Nebuchadnezzar's dream, but giving it a slightly different emphasis in his insistence that division is the cause of evil—in man and in society. In the first of the eight books that follow, the Lover, the Amans of the title, is pierced by a fiery dart from Cupid. Venus instructs him to make his confession to her priest, Genius, who instructs him on the proper use of the senses and on the seven deadly sins, illustrating each in its

various categories by a series of short tales—over 100 in all, deriving from Ovid and other sources. The adapting of the deadly sins to the doctrine of love requires a certain ingenuity. It is done in a way that is witty and entertaining for his courtly readers and also instructive. Like his other long poems it is encyclopaedic, containing material on the religions of the ancient world, on philosophical knowledge, on the duties of kingship. It is educative, presenting a course of instruction for the Lover, for man, and for society. The stories present the extremes and the paradoxes of Love, which may ennoble its servants, or, if moderation is lacking, destroy them. An ideal of 'honeste love' emerges, with its proper part in nature, restoring concord and peace. The elegantly written tales (especially those that treat the pathos of love) show Gower's mastery of the art of narrative. The ending of the poem, in which Amans is healed by Venus and the fiery dart is removed is a haunting scene: he sees Cupid and his rout surrounded by companies of the famous lovers whose stories he has heard. His face is wrinkled by age, and Venus tells him to go 'ther moral vertu duelleth'. He goes 'homward a softe pas' and prays for the state of England.

One of the passages removed from the ending in the revision concerns Chaucer. In the first version Venus asks the poet to:

gret wel Chaucer whan ye mete,
As mi disciple and mi poete

and makes complimentary remarks about him (*Complete Works*, 2.466). The reasons for the omission of this passage have been the subject of fierce, but inconclusive, argument. There has been much speculation about a quarrel between the two poets, or at least a cooling of their earlier friendship. It is possible that Gower may not have approved of the bawdy fabliaux that Chaucer was now reworking for *The Canterbury Tales*, and possible, though less likely, that he was offended at what may be a joking allusion in the introduction to *The Man of Law's Tale* to his telling of the stories of Canace and Apollonius, which involve incest. However, some 'revised' manuscripts still have the lines on Chaucer, and it is at least as likely that the omission is due to technical or structural considerations—it may be, for instance, that Gower perhaps thought that this slightly humorous personal digression was not appropriate at this point.

A number of shorter poems come from the last years of the century. In Latin, there is, for instance, the *Carmen super multiplici viciorum pestilencia* (1396–7), an attack on Lollardy and other sins; *De lucis scrutinio* on the shortcomings of the estates (light destroys the evils that flourish in the shadows); and several in praise of Henry IV. In French, there is a group of eighteen *balades* now usually called the *Traitié pour essampler les amantz marietz*, after its head-note which describes it as a treatise to provide examples for married lovers so that they may guard and maintain their faith through noble loyalty to the honour of God. In them Gower takes a grave and serious view of marriage and of *honest amour*, stressing fidelity and loyalty. It is founded on reason not sensuality or passion. A number of examples of lovers who for various reasons came to disaster are given, mostly ones which he had used in the *Confessio amantis*—Hercules, Jason and Medea, Philomela, and so on. Foolish Love is as unstable as Fortune. (These *balades* were translated into northern English by one Quixley at the beginning of the fifteenth century.) Some Latin verses (*Est amor in glosa*) which accompany them list the paradoxes of love, and end with a praise of married love and a couplet that seems clearly linked to Gower's own marriage:

> Hinc vetus annorum Gower sub spe meritorum
> Ordine sponsorum tutus adhibo thorum.
> (Now old in years, in hope of what I've earned
> Now wed, my bed I seek, quite unconcerned.)
> (Rigg, 290)

Finally, there is the English poem *In Praise of Peace*. Addressed to King Henry, it is an eloquent statement of one of Gower's favourite themes.

Gower's last major work is the Latin *Cronica tripertita*, a poem of 1062 leonine hexameters, which gives an account (from a fervently Lancastrian point of view) of Richard's reign and downfall. 'The king always had an obdurate heart' (l. 13): the first part (using the heraldic animal imagery of political prophecy and invective) praises the nobles against whom he plotted and who opposed him—Gloucester, Warwick, Arundel—and records Richard's humiliation in 1387, when his forces were defeated by the earl of Oxford. Ten years later (part 2), in 1396–7, Richard took his revenge, treacherously attacked the three nobles, and deposed Thomas Arundel, the archbishop of Canterbury. Part 3 tells how the king like a mole dug traps for his enemies, and exiled Henry of Derby, the duke of Lancaster, how he returned, and how eventually Richard was captured and deposed, and died of grief in the Tower. The poem ends by contrasting the two kings. It seems as if Gower thought of the *Cronica tripertita* as a summation of and an epilogue to his commentary on the tragic reign of Richard which he had begun in the *Vox clamantis*.

Last years, death, and reputation The introductory verse letter to Archbishop Arundel in his presentation copy of the *Vox clamantis*, the *Cronica tripertita*, and other Latin poems describes the author as blind, and 'sick in body, aged and totally miserable'; another reference to his blindness is found in one of his last verses, *Quicquid homo scribat* (*Complete Works*, 4.365):

> A man may write, but Nature writes the end;
> She, like a shadow, flees without return.
> She wrote the end for me, and so I can
> No longer write a thing, for I am blind.
> (Rigg, 292)

Gower died in 1408. His will was proved on 24 October. He left bequests to his wife, Agnes, who was one of his executors, to the prior, sub-prior, canons, and servants of St Mary Overie, and to the churches and hospitals of Southwark and the neighbourhood. Among the gifts to the priory was a large book, a *martilogium* 'newly composed at my expense', in which a memorial for him was to be recorded every day. He was buried in the chapel of St John the Baptist. Though his tomb and effigy is still to be seen, it has been moved twice since 1800, and the chapel has now disappeared. The painting and lettering on the tomb have been restored from earlier descriptions (by Thomas Berthelette, who printed the *Confessio amantis* in 1532, Leland, and Stow). Under his head was the likeness of three books—the *Speculum meditantis*, the *Vox clamantis*, and the *Confessio amantis*. A Latin inscription identified him as an esquire (*armiger*), a famous poet, and a benefactor. According to Stow he was represented with long curling auburn hair and a small forked beard. This seems likely to have been an idealized recollection of the poet in more youthful days (as perhaps are the pictures of him shooting the arrows of satire against the world that appear in two manuscripts of the *Vox clamantis*). An explicitly identified portrait (*effigies Gower esquier*) appears in the duke of Bedford's psalter-hours (after 1414; BL, Add. MS 4213). It shows him as an elderly, almost bald man with white curling hair and a forked beard (Wright, 191); it may have been done from memory. It is one of a series of ten depictions of him in the initials of this Lancastrian manuscript, and some care seems to have been taken in the placing of them with psalms in a way that could recall the *Vox clamantis*. The figure is similar to the elderly, balding Amans sometimes depicted in manuscripts of the *Confessio amantis*, for instance in Bodl. Oxf., MS Bodley 902; in others, however (BL, MS Egerton 1991 provides a good example), the penitent is represented as an elegant and youthful figure. Such portraits are meant probably to be general rather than exact 'likenesses'.

Gower's poetic reputation has rested almost exclusively on the *Confessio amantis*. The number of manuscripts testify to its popularity. Uniquely, it seems, for a Middle English poem it was translated into Portuguese (probably in 1433–8) by Robert Payn, an Englishman in the household of Queen Philippa, the daughter of John of Gaunt, duke of Lancaster, and later a canon at Lisbon, and from that into Castilian prose (after 1428) by Juan de Cuenca. In the fifteenth century Gower's name is linked with that of Chaucer, and later Lydgate, as one of the 'masters' of English poetry. He continued to be praised in the sixteenth century: in *Pericles* 'ancient Gower' is brought back from his ashes to introduce a play based on his story of Apollonius. But his fame did not last, and in spite of Thomas Warton's full and generous account—'If Chaucer had not existed, the compositions of John Gower … would alone have been sufficient to rescue the reigns of Edward III and Richard II from the imputation of barbarism' (Warton, 311)—some nineteenth-century critics simply abused him—he 'raised tediousness to the precision of science', according to James Russell Lowell (*My Study Windows*, 1871). The Macaulay edition laid the foundation for serious study, and gradually modern criticism has done more justice to his poetic excellence. Chaucer's epithet 'moral' was a very exact one. Gower had a coherent and serious view of the need for love and concord and peace, but he was not always solemn: in his *Confessio amantis* especially he brilliantly combined entertainment with doctrine—'somwhat of lust, somwhat of lore'.

DOUGLAS GRAY

Sources *The complete works of John Gower*, ed. G. C. Macaulay, 4 vols. (1899–1902) · J. H. Fisher, *John Gower: moral philosopher and friend of Chaucer* (1964) · H. Nicholas, 'John Gower the poet', *Retrospective*

Review, 2nd ser., 2 (1828), 103–17 • S. Wright, 'The author portraits in the Bedford Psalter-Hours: Gower, Chaucer and Hoccleve', *British Library Journal*, 18 (1992), 190–201 • *The major Latin works of John Gower*, trans. E. W. Stockton (1962) • H. N. MacCracken, *Quixley's 'Ballades royal'* [1908]; repr. in *Yorkshire Archaeological Journal*, 20 (1908–9), 33–50 • R. F. Yeager, 'A bibliography of John Gower materials through 1975', *Medievalia*, 3 (1977), 261–306 • *DNB* • P. E. Russell, 'Robert Payn and Juan de Cuenca, translators of Gower's *Confessio amantis*', *Medium Ævum*, 30 (1961), 26–32 • B. S. Moreno, 'Some observations on the dates and circumstances of the fifteenth-century Portuguese and Castilian translations of John Gower's *Confessio amantis*', *SELIM. Revista de la Sociedad Española de Lengua y Literatura Inglesa Medieval*, 1 (1991), 106–22 • T. Warton, *The history of English poetry*, 4 vols. (1774–81) • M. D. Legge, *Anglo-Norman literature and its background* (1963) • A. G. Rigg, *A history of Anglo-Latin literature, 1066–1422* (1992) • *Selections from John Gower*, ed. J. A. W. Bennett (1968) • J. Stow, *A survey of London* (1598) • J. Stow, *The annales of England … from the first inhabitation untill this present yeere 1600* (1600) • *Commentarii de scriptoribus Britannicis, auctore Joanne Lelando*, ed. A. Hall, 2 vols. (1709) • F. Thynne, *Animadversions upon the annotacions and corrections of some imperfections of impressions of Chaucers workes* (1598) • J. Weever, *Ancient funerall monuments* (1631)

Archives Yale U., Beinecke L., MS of 'Confessio amantis'
Likenesses illuminated miniature, BL, Egerton MS 1991, fol. 7*v* [*see illus.*] • tomb effigy, Southwark Cathedral, London

Gower, John Leveson-, first Baron Gower (1675–1709), politician, was born on 7 January 1675 at Trentham Hall, Staffordshire, the eldest son of Sir William Leveson-Gower, fourth baronet (*c*.1647–1691), of Stittenham, Yorkshire, whose principal estate was Trentham, and his wife, Lady Jane Grenville (*c*.1653–1697), the eldest daughter of John *Grenville, first earl of Bath. He had a younger sister, Jane [*see* Hyde, Jane, countess of Clarendon and Rochester]. After an education at James Linfield's school at St James's, Westminster, he married in September 1692 Lady Katherine Manners (1675–1722), the daughter of John Manners, first duke of Rutland. The marriage produced four sons and three daughters. Also in 1692 Leveson-Gower succeeded his father as MP for Newcastle under Lyme, a seat which he held unopposed until he was elevated to the peerage. A critic of the ruling whig junto, he voted against Sir John Fenwick's attainder in 1696, and was one of a hundred tories who refused to sign the resulting association which identified William III as the 'right and lawful king'. He showed acrimony in proposing the impeachment of Lord Somers on 8 April 1700, the motion being lost by 167 votes to 101. On 10 February 1701 he was called on by the clerk, Paul Jodrell, to second Sir Edward Seymour's proposal that Harley be appointed speaker. On this occasion, and in his bid to impeach the earl of Portland in April, Leveson-Gower was successful. He became a privy councillor on the accession of Queen Anne, and in April 1702 replaced the earl of Stamford as chancellor for the duchy of Lancaster. On 16 March the following year he was created Baron Gower of Stittenham to secure the tory majority in the Lords. From this point his political career began to suffer set-backs: in May 1706 he was dismissed from the commission to conclude the union between England and Scotland and failed to be appointed to the first privy council for the united kingdom.

Away from politics, Leveson-Gower was engaged in redesigning the gardens and, between 1701 and 1709, the house at Trentham according to the designs of William Smith of Tettenhall. Having long suffered from the disease, he died from gout at Belvoir Castle, Leicestershire, on 31 August 1709 and was buried at Trentham on 10 September; the title then passed to his eldest son, John Leveson-*Gower, first Earl Gower. He was survived by his wife, who died on 7 March 1722 and was buried with her husband on 15 March. Of their younger sons, William was MP for Staffordshire from 1720 to 1756 and Thomas MP for Newcastle under Lyme from 1722 to 1727, while Baptist held that seat from 1727 to 1761.   RICHARD WISKER

Sources T. Pape, *Newcastle-under-Lyme from the Restoration to 1760* (1973) • R. Walcott, *English politics in the early eighteenth century* (1956) • A. Browning, *Thomas Osborne, earl of Danby and duke of Leeds, 1632–1712*, 3 vols. (1944–51) • H. Horwitz, *Parliament, policy and politics in the reign of William III* (1977) • *The parliamentary diary of Sir Richard Cocks, 1698–1702*, ed. D. W. Hayton (1996) • J. R. Wordie, *Estate management in eighteenth-century England: the building of the Leveson-Gower fortune* (1982) • J. C. Wedgwood, 'Staffordshire parliamentary history [2/1]', *Collections for a history of Staffordshire*, William Salt Archaeological Society, 3rd ser. (1920) • Staffs. RO, Sutherland papers, D. 593 • letter-books, Staffs. RO, Sutherland papers, D. 868 • GEC, *Peerage* • *DNB* • parish register (burial), Trentham, 10 Sept 1709

Archives Staffs. RO, papers • William Salt Library, Stafford | HMC, Cowper MSS • HMC, Portland MSS • HMC, Rutland MSS • Staffs. RO, Sutherland letter-books

Wealth at death £6238 3*s*. 1*d*. rental *c*.1710; £7795 12*s*. 6*d*. personal estate, incl. furniture, valuables, and livestock, 12 Mar 1710; rental at twenty-three years' purchase capital value £143,478: Staffs. RO, Sutherland MSS, D. 593 14/1/4; inventory, D/ 593 C/19/2

Gower, John Leveson-, first Earl Gower (1694–1754), politician, was born in London on 9 August 1694, the eldest son of John Leveson-*Gower, first Baron Gower (1675–1709), and his wife, Lady Katherine Manners (1675–1722). He was educated at Westminster School and, from 1710, at Christ Church, Oxford; he was made DCL of Oxford on 19 August 1732. On 13 March 1712 he married Lady Evelyn Pierrepont (1691–1727), the third daughter of Evelyn *Pierrepont, first duke of Kingston. The marriage produced eleven children, the third son being Granville Leveson-*Gower, first marquess of Stafford; the eldest daughter, Gertrude (1714–1794), married in April 1737 John Russell, fourth duke of Bedford.

As a young man Gower was sympathetic to Jacobitism but was initially uninterested in politics, preferring to spend his time hunting and at the races. From 1720 he began to cultivate his political interest in Staffordshire. With Newcastle under Lyme in his control, he built up support in Stafford, Cheadle (where he was mayor in 1721), and Lichfield. During this period he suffered a series of personal tragedies. His first wife died on 26 June 1727; on 31 October 1733 he was married to Penelope Atkins, Lady Atkins, *née* Stonhouse, the widow of Sir Henry Atkins, bt, but she died on 19 August the following year. He married his third wife, Lady Mary Grey, the daughter and coheir of Thomas Tufton, earl of Thanet, and the widow of Anthony Grey, earl of Harold, on 16 May 1736.

In political terms the 1730s saw Gower's emergence as the leader of the tories in the Lords. He served as lord justice in 1740 and, after Walpole's fall, was the one tory to take high office as lord privy seal and a privy councillor (12 May 1742) in the new whig ministry. His alliance with his political opponents, a move of considerable party political importance, was short-lived, however. He resigned in December 1743, only to be reappointed as lord privy seal under the Broadbottom administration in December the following year, a position he held until his death in 1754. He personally assured the king of his loyalty during the Jacobite rising of 1745, and raised one of the fifteen recruited regiments, for which he was created Viscount Trentham and Earl Gower on 8 July 1746. In 1748, 1750, and 1752 he again acted as one of the lords justices.

Gower's proximity to the administration provoked criticism from many who saw his actions as desertion of the tory cause. Samuel Johnson included him in his definition of 'renegado' in his *Dictionary* (1755), though the reference was removed by the printer. However, despite fierce attacks, the Gower interest, comprising seven constituencies in Staffordshire and Westminster, retained both its Staffordshire and Lichfield seats in the 1747 election. The considerable financial cost of preserving his interest was met in part by income from Gower's estate, some of which was given over to industrial production, and from shares in eight other estates, including those of Bath and Albemarle. Unmoved by tory criticisms, he emerged as a loyal Pelhamite in the late 1740s and early 1750s. In June 1751 he refused to follow the lead of his son Lord Trentham, and son-in-law Bedford, and resign in support of the recently dismissed fourth earl of Sandwich. He again refused to give up office on the death of Pelham in March 1754. He himself died on 25 December 1754 at 6 Upper Brook Street, London. Election and family expenses had eaten away at his fortune and at his death there were outstanding debts of £37,861 and over £36,000 in legacies. He was survived by his wife, who died on 9 February 1785, and his second son from this marriage, Rear-Admiral John Leveson-*Gower (1740–1792).   RICHARD WISKER

Sources Staffs. RO, Sutherland papers, D. 593 · letter-books, Staffs. RO, Sutherland papers, D. 868 · J. C. Wedgwood, 'Staffordshire parliamentary history [2/2]', *Collections for a history of Staffordshire*, William Salt Archaeological Society, 3rd ser. (1922) · J. R. Wordie, *Estate management in eighteenth-century England: the building of the Leveson-Gower fortune* (1982) · HoP, *Commons* · GEC, *Peerage*, new edn, vol. 6 · William Salt Library, Stafford, Plaxton MSS, 356/40
Archives Staffs. RO, Sutherland MSS; Sutherland letter-books | BL, letters to Lord Essex, Add. MSS 27732–27735 · HMC, Hastings MSS; Portland MSS; Rutland MSS · PRO, corresp., papers, and accounts · William Salt Library, Stafford
Likenesses S. Slaughter, oils, after 1742, Dunrobin Castle, Sutherland · J. Faber junior, mezzotint (after J. B. Vanloo, 1742–5), BM, NPG

Gower, John Leveson- (1740–1792), naval officer and politician, was born on 11 July 1740, the second son of John Leveson-*Gower, first Earl Gower (1694–1754), politician, and his third wife, Mary Grey (1701–1785), the daughter of Thomas Tufton, earl of Thanet, and the widow of Anthony Grey, earl of Harold. After being educated privately, Leveson-Gower entered the navy, and was commissioned

lieutenant in 1758. He commanded the fireship *Salamander* at Lagos under Admiral Edward Boscawen on 18 August 1759. Having been promoted captain on 30 June 1760, he took the newly built frigate *Quebec* (32 guns) to the Mediterranean, serving under Sir Charles Saunders, a good friend to him, until the end of the war. In December 1760 he captured the French privateer *Phoenix* (18 guns) off Cape Palos. Leveson-Gower benefited throughout his career from the political influence of his half-brother, Granville Leveson-*Gower, second Earl Gower. John took the *Africa* to Guinea and the West Indies in 1765; later he commanded the *Aeolus* and the *Pearl*, and finally the guardship *Albion* at Plymouth in 1774 in a period of peace when few captains were employed. On 5 July 1773 he had married Frances (1746–1801), eldest daughter of Admiral Edward Boscawen. He commanded the *Valiant* (74 guns) in the channel in 1775, capturing several American ships with valuable cargoes. At Ushant on 27 July 1778 he gave stalwart support to Admiral Keppel, losing six killed and twenty-six wounded on the *Valiant*. A defence witness at Keppel's court martial, he resigned when the vindicated admiral struck his flag (1779). His half-brother Granville did not support him but resigned from Lord North's ministry later that year.

After this Leveson-Gower was unemployed until April 1782 when he was appointed first captain to Lord Howe in the *Victory* in the channel. In October he took part in the relief of Gibraltar and in the action off Cape Spartel, being commended by Howe for his skilful navigation. In January 1783 he was appointed a junior lord of the Admiralty under Howe as first lord. Both resigned with the Shelburne ministry in April. Granville returned to the cabinet when the Pitt ministry was formed in December 1783, while John and Lord Howe returned to their former posts. He was successively MP for Appleby, nominated by his cousin Lord Thanet, and for Newcastle under Lyme, backed by Granville, now Lord Stafford. He spoke four times on Admiralty matters and was ridiculed by Nauticus Junior for his support of the ministry, though the writer conceded his ability in naval matters. In 1785 he took the *Hebe* on a circumnavigation of Great Britain with Prince William Henry, satisfying George III and winning the prince's respect. Flying his flag as commodore in the *Edgar* he commanded the channel squadron in 1787, and was promoted rear-admiral of the blue in that year.

In 1788 Leveson-Gower took an enlarged squadron to the West Indies. James Anthony Gardner has left a vivid picture of him in command: getting up at three in the morning to check on the watch, 'he used to play hell … and would spare no one' (*Recollections*, 65). Gardner admitted he was a good officer and a good friend, but fiercely hostile to his enemies. When Howe resigned from the Admiralty, Leveson-Gower remained under Lord Chatham, resigning in August 1789. During the Nootka crisis in 1790 he served again as Howe's first captain. He was one of the rear-admirals chosen to serve under Lord Hood in the considerable fleet prepared in 1791 to counter Russian aggression. His naval career ended with the disbandment of that fleet. He died suddenly on 15 August 1792 of apoplexy at his house at Bill Hill, Wokingham, and was buried on 23 August at Barkham parish church, Berkshire. Demanding of his subordinates, loyal to his friends, and harsh to his enemies, Admiral John Leveson-Gower showed himself a resourceful and thoroughly competent officer in every command he held. He was survived by his wife, who died in July 1801. Of their sons, John, a general, was second in command in the La Plata expedition of 1807, while Edward, a rear admiral, and Augustus, a captain, had naval careers.   RICHARD WISKER

Sources J. Charnock, ed., *Biographia navalis*, 6 (1798), 394–6 · *Recollections of James Anthony Gardner*, ed. R. V. Hamilton and J. K. Laughton, Navy RS, 31 (1906), 65–67, 92 · C. Aspinall-Oglander, *The admiral's widow* (1942), 40, 47, 93, 133, 152 · *Report on manuscripts in various collections*, 8 vols., HMC, 55 (1901–14), vol. 8, pp. 314–15, 329, 336, 347, 381 · P. Webb, *Naval aspects of the Nootka Sound crisis* (1975), 141–5 · C. King, *The Russian armament* (1938), 176, 182–3 · Nauticus Junior [J. Harris], *The Naval Atalantis* (1788) · W. L. Clowes, *The Royal Navy: a history from the earliest times to the present*, 7 vols. (1897–1903), vol. 3, pp. 217n, 415, 567 · J. Brooke, 'Leveson Gower, Sir John', HoP, *Commons, 1754–90* · *Letters and papers of Admiral of the Fleet Sir Thos. Byam Martin, GCB*, ed. R. V. Hamilton, 3, Navy RS, 19 (1901), 290–92 · *Lord Granville Leveson Gower: private correspondence, 1781–1821*, ed. Castalia, Countess Granville [C. R. Leveson-Gower], 2nd edn, 1 (1916), 51, 54 · Walpole, *Corr.*, 25.590; 31.9; 34.373–4 · parish register (burial), Barkham parish church, 23 Aug 1792

Archives Berks. RO, Leveson-Gower of Bill Hill MSS · Staffs. RO, Sutherland MSS

Likenesses G. Stuart?, oils, 1763–7, Titsey Place, Oxted, Surrey · J. Reynolds, portrait, 1782–3; formerly at Bill Hill, Wokingham, Berkshire · D. Gardner, pastel, Titsey Place, Oxted, Surrey · G. Romney, double portrait (with his wife); formerly at Bill Hill, Wokingham, Berkshire

Wealth at death £71,000—incl. £10,080 rental; £12,900 acquired estates; £48,000 paid to him and his mother

Gower, Laurence Cecil Bartlett [Jim] (1913–1997), jurist, was born on 29 December 1913 at 22 Disraeli Road, Forest Gate, Essex, the elder child and only son of Henry Laurence Gower, businessman, and his wife, Daisy Ethel, *née* Lee. Jim Gower (as he was known throughout his life) was educated at Lindisfarne College and University College, London, from where he graduated with first-class honours in law in 1933. After taking the LLM in 1934, and serving articles with the five-partner Bedford Row firm of Smiles & Co., he was admitted a solicitor in 1937. On 7 September 1939 he married Helen Margaret Shepperson (Peggy) Birch (1910/11–1999), secondary school teacher, the daughter of George Francis Birch, corn merchant. They had three children, Jenny, James, and Richard. Gower served in the army throughout the Second World War (latterly in the Royal Army Ordnance Corps), and played a significant part in the planning of the allied landings in France in June 1944. He ended the war as a lieutenant-colonel (having joined the army as a private).

In 1948 Gower was invited to accept the Sir Ernest Cassel chair of commercial law at the London School of Economics. His fourteen-year tenure of this prestigious post was exceptionally distinguished. In particular, the publication of his *Principles of Modern Company Law* in 1954 demonstrated that subjects at the time often regarded as so dominated by the concerns of legal practice as to be unsuitable for academic study could in reality be properly understood only if put into historical and economic context. Gower's own experience and continued involvement in both legal practice and academic life made him well aware of the deficiencies in English legal education; and the reform proposals he made in his inaugural lecture set the terms for debate over the next quarter of a century. In 1962 he saw the possibility of putting his ideas into practice. He resigned the Cassel chair, was appointed adviser on legal education to the Nigerian government and dean of the faculty of law in Lagos, and threw himself energetically into the task of providing Nigeria and other anglophone African territories with their own systems of legal education putting appropriate emphasis on the skills needed for routine legal practice. But in 1965, as Nigeria moved towards civil war, Gower took a stand on an issue of principle in the university and, in an atmosphere of inter-tribal tension, was summarily sacked from his office as dean.

At this time, the Law Commissions Act of 1965, giving effect to the Labour Party's pledge to establish a body charged with the systematic development and reform of English law, was going through the United Kingdom parliament; and Gower's experience as a practising solicitor and teacher of law, coupled with his radical (but realistic) approach to the legal system, made him exceptionally well qualified for appointment as one of the five founding law commissioners, who took up office in June 1965.

Gower had had experience (not only in his solicitor's practice but also in the poor man's lawyer clinic, which he and his lifelong friend Arnold Goodman organized in deprived areas of London) of the hardship to which English divorce law gave rise. In 1952 he had given outspoken evidence about the reality of bogus hotel adultery and simulated desertion divorces to the royal commission on marriage and divorce, which had not endeared him to the conservatively minded. But as a law commissioner he was able to suppress his naturally somewhat rebellious and irreverent personality, and his diplomatic skills enabled him to take the lead in successfully negotiating the compromise which became the basis of the Divorce Reform Act of 1969: the sole ground for divorce was to be that the marriage had irretrievably broken down, although such breakdown was to be inferred from facts akin to the traditional matrimonial offences or from the fact that the parties had lived apart for five years (or two years if they agreed to the divorce). Gower also took the lead in formulating many other proposals made by the Law Commission and in due course enacted, ranging from reform of the law of nullity of marriage to abolition of outdated forms of action, such as breach of promise of marriage, restitution of conjugal rights, and the husband's right to claim damages against the person with whom the wife had committed adultery.

From the many opportunities available to him at the end of his term as a law commissioner, in 1971 Gower accepted the offer of appointment as vice-chancellor of Southampton University. He and his wife, Peggy—who for nearly sixty years shared and unfailingly supported him in all his activities—threw themselves vigorously into the life of the university. Gower was a skilled fund-raiser, and a highly effective administrator (not least in promoting the interests of the university's newly opened medical school); but perhaps the Gowers' greatest achievement was in building up an atmosphere of trust and shared enthusiasm with the student body and academic and administrative staff.

Gower retired from the vice-chancellorship in 1979, but his intellectual (and physical) energy remained undiminished. He had been appointed a trustee of the British Museum in 1968 and continued to give the museum not only sagacious advice about financial and legal issues but also enthusiastic support to extending its wider educational role. He remained a much sought-after lecturer.

By 1981 a number of scandals in the futures, investment, and banking industries had demonstrated the inadequacy of the legislative framework intended to protect investors from fraud; and in that year Gower was appointed by Margaret Thatcher's administration to consider the statutory protection required by private and business investors, and the need for statutory control of dealers and investment consultants and managers. Gower carried out an intensive programme of consultation and research. This not only helped to establish a larger measure of agreement than would previously have been thought possible, but also created a powerful momentum for legislation. If he had had the power to decide policy he would no doubt have recommended the creation of a securities and exchange commission on the United States model (of which he had over the years acquired a profound knowledge). But he recognized that personal conviction had to yield to practical politics, and he drew back from making such a recommendation. The Financial Services Act of 1986 owed much to his report. His work on investor protection was a fitting climax to a distinguished career as teacher, scholar, and law reformer. His standing is evidenced by the award of eight honorary degrees from universities both in the United Kingdom and elsewhere in the Commonwealth, his election as a fellow of the British Academy in 1965, and his appointment as one of the first queen's counsel *honoris causa* in 1991.

A man of tall, spare, and angular build, Gower had enormous physical as well as intellectual energy, and his capacities remained undimmed until the last year of his life. He died on Christmas day 1997 in a nursing home at 31 Eton Avenue, Camden, London. He was survived by his wife and their three children.   S. M. CRETNEY

Sources S. M. Cretney, 'Laurence Cecil Bartlett Gower, 1913–1997', *PBA*, 101 (1999), 379–404 · L. C. B. Gower, 'Memoirs of a maverick lawyer', MS, priv. coll. · W. R. Cornish, 'Jim Gower: an appreciation', *Modern Law Review*, 61 (1998), 127–31 · *The Times* (5 Jan 1998) · *Daily Telegraph* (7 Feb 1998) · *The Independent* (12 Feb 1998) · *WWW* · personal knowledge (2004) · private information (2004) · b. cert. · m. cert. · d. cert.
Archives priv. coll. | U. Southampton L., papers relating to Royal Commission on the Press · U. Southampton L., corresp. with James Parkes
Likenesses photograph, repro. in *The Times* · photograph, repro. in *The Independent*

Gower [*married name* Beaton]**, Lilias Mary** [Lily] (1877–1959), croquet player, was born at Castle Malgwyn, Pembrokeshire, the eldest daughter in the family of four daughters and two sons of Erasmus Gower (1833–1914), landowner and formerly captain in the 12th lancers, and his wife, Catherine van Agnew. Her mother was a keen croquet player who 'passed on her zeal to her daughter' (Lillee, 86); she taught her the game at home, and the two played at the Newcastle Emlyn lawn tennis and croquet club near the family seat in Pembrokeshire. From a book on croquet published by Longmans, one of many contemporary guides to croquet rules and techniques, she acquired an understanding of the mechanics of the game, which she combined with her own aggressive style of play.

Lily Gower startled the croquet world in July 1898, when, in her first competitive match, she won the challenge cup at Budleigh Salterton lawn tennis and croquet club, beating C. E. Willis (one of the top male competitors of the time) in the final. In the following September she repeated her triumph at the Maidstone club's championships, held at Wimbledon. The sports paper *Ladies Field* considered her success 'epoch-making' and proof that 'a woman, if armed with up-to-date implements, can compete with success in the severe and prolonged conflict of nerve, endurance, and hard work which a week of match croquet requires' (Lillee, 91). She was at her peak between 1899 and 1907, when she challenged for and won the major events in both singles and doubles, against both men and women. These included the ladies' championship of England, 1899, 1900, and 1901. In 1904 she won the open champion cup and in 1905 the open championship, a feat which only one other woman achieved in the next fifty years.

Lily Gower's emergence as the most successful female croquet player of her generation coincided with a renaissance of the game following the revival of the championships in 1895 and the foundation of the All England croquet association in the same year, and its transition from being little more than a charming leisure activity. Young, tall, and beautiful, she initially upset the croquet establishment by her uncompromising approach to the game. Her technique was described by a contemporary writer:

> She stands quite upright to her stroke, and takes aim by putting the mallet in the first instance over the ball. She then strikes with confidence, careless, apparently, whether the object ball is six feet or six yards away. Her tactics are simple—to scheme for the four ball break at all seasons. (Lillee, 90)

In 1900 she was invited to contribute to a manual on the game an account of the tactics which had made her famous. As a player and later as an official, she played a significant part in developing croquet as a serious competitive sport. Most importantly, however, she was a role model for other women and girls interested in this and other sports.

On 24 January 1906 Lily Gower married Reginald Charles John Beaton (b. 1870/71), an underwriter at Lloyd's, son of Walter Hardy Beaton, a merchant. They had a son.

Her husband was an accomplished player with whom she formed a formidable doubles partnership, winning the open mixed doubles in 1904–6, 1907, and 1920. She does not appear to have truly retired from the game, for she was winning events as late as 1948. She died at 38 Cheniston Gardens, Kensington, London, on 29 July 1959; her husband had predeceased her. RACHEL CUTLER

Sources 'Miss Lily Gower, lady champion of England', *Croquet up to date: containing the ideas and techniques of the leading players and champions*, ed. A. Lillee (1900), 84–115 · *Burke's Who's who in sport* (1922) · *Croquet Annual* (1901–2) · D. M. C. Pritchard, *The history of croquet* (1986) · Straw Hat, *Croquet* (1899) · K. E. McCrone, *Sport and the physical emancipation of English women, 1870–1914* (1988) · Burke, *Gen. GB* (1937) · *The Times* (7 Aug 1959), 14 · m. cert. · d. cert. · CGPLA Eng. & Wales (1959)

Likenesses J. Mathias, photograph, c.1900, repro. in Lillee, ed., *Croquet up to date*, frontispiece · Russell & Sons, photograph, c.1900, repro. in Lillee, ed., *Croquet up to date*, facing p. 86

Wealth at death £10,542 14s. 5d.: probate, 19 Oct 1959, CGPLA Eng. & Wales

Gower, Millicent Fanny Sutherland-Leveson- [*née* Millicent Fanny St Clair-Erskine], **duchess of Sutherland (1867–1955)**, society hostess and social reformer, was born on 20 October 1867 at Dysart House, Fife, the eldest child of Robert St Clair-Erskine, fourth earl of Rosslyn (1833–1900), and his wife, Blanche (d. 1933), daughter of Henry Fitzroy and widow of the Hon. Charles Maynard. Frances Evelyn (Daisy) *Greville, countess of Warwick, was her half-sister. On her seventeenth birthday she married Cromartie Sutherland-Leveson-Gower, marquess of Stafford (1851–1913), and rapidly established herself as one of the most successful London hostesses, one of the few who was at home with both the Marlborough House set and the Souls. Her first book, *How I Spent my Twentieth Year*, was published in 1889. Two sons and two daughters were born between 1885 and 1893; the eldest child, a daughter, died at the age of two and a half. In 1892 her husband succeeded to the title of fourth duke of Sutherland, and to extensive estates in Scotland, Staffordshire, and Shropshire. Their London residence, Stafford House, became (as it had been under Sutherland's grandmother, the Duchess Harriet) a great venue for social and political receptions. Millicent's fame as a society beauty was captured about 1904 in John Singer Sargent's portrait of her.

But Millicent Sutherland was not content to be merely a society hostess. She had a serious outlook on life and became active as a social reformer, earning the nicknames the Democratic Duchess and Meddlesome Millie; she did not travel as far down the road to socialism as her half-sister, Daisy Warwick. She campaigned successfully for the elimination of the use of lead in pottery glazing in the Staffordshire potteries, for which she was caricatured by Arnold Bennett in his Five Towns novels as the Countess of Chell. She contributed a chapter, 'On the dangerous processes in the potting industry', to a local study of workers in pottery manufacture. She also founded the North Staffordshire Cripples' Aid Society, attempted to revive the home-spun woollen industry in the Scottish highlands, and helped to found a rural technical school at Golspie in Sutherland. She served as president of the Scottish Home

Millicent Fanny Sutherland-Leveson-Gower, duchess of Sutherland (1867–1955), by Charles Lallie, c.1906

Industries Association. The duchess also had ambitions to be a writer. Her first novel, *One Hour and the Next* (1899), reflected her growing political awareness and surging romanticism; a volume of short stories, *The Winds of the World* (1902), was scathingly reviewed but was avidly read by a less critical public. She commissioned and edited a volume of poetry by leading poets of the day and wrote a play in blank verse, *The Conqueror*, which received a dozen performances at the Scala Theatre in London in 1905. In 1924 a semi-autobiographical novel, *That Fool of a Woman*, was to appear, revealing much about her marital misadventures.

The duke died in 1913, and on 17 October 1914 Millicent married Percy Desmond Fitzgerald (d. 1933), an army officer. On the outbreak of the First World War she organized a Red Cross ambulance unit, and served in France throughout the war. She was captured at Namur in the German advance in 1914, but managed to escape. She became director of No. 9 British Red Cross Hospital at Calais, and moved with it to Roubaix in June 1918, where it became a front-line casualty clearing station. She was awarded the Croix de Guerre, the Belgian Royal Red Cross, and the British Red Cross medal.

The duchess divorced Fitzgerald, a philanderer, in 1919. Her third marriage, to Colonel George Ernest Hawes (d. 1945), on 27 October 1919, was equally unfortunate: he was a homosexual, and she divorced him in 1925. Thereafter she drifted from one house to another in France, and travelled extensively. In 1940 she was living near Angers, and when the French capitulated she found herself once more to be a prisoner in German hands. She escaped, through Spain and Portugal, to the United States, and was one of the first foreign civilians to return to liberated Paris in 1945. To a friend, Princess Marthe Bibesco, she confessed that she now felt she had lost all her usefulness. She died on 20 August 1955 at La Maizou, Orriule, near Sauveterre-de-Béarn, Basses Pyrénées, France, and was cremated at the Père Lachaise cemetery in Paris. Her ashes were returned to the Sutherland private cemetery at Dunrobin. Her younger son and daughter had predeceased her.

DENIS STUART

Sources D. Stuart, *Dear duchess: Millicent duchess of Sutherland, 1867–1955* (1982) · J. Abdy and C. Gere, *The Souls* (1984) · Burke, *Peerage* **Archives** IWM, 'Benevolent Org.', box 4, file xii · L. Cong. · NA Scot., CTD/318/22, 32 · Ransom HRC · Staffs. RO | Herts. ALS, letters mainly to Lady Desborough · NA Scot., letters to Alex Mackenzie **Likenesses** E. Roberts, *c.*1892–1894 (*Millicent, duchess of Sutherland*), Dunrobin Castle, Highland region · J. S. Sargent, before 1904 (*Millicent, duchess of Sutherland*) · C. Lallie, photograph, *c.*1906, NPG [*see illus.*] · photograph, repro. in Abdy and Gere, *The Souls* **Wealth at death** £40,384 9s. 10d.: probate, 29 Dec 1955, *CGPLA Eng. & Wales*

Gower [*married name* Fahie], **Pauline Mary de Peauly** (1910–1947), aviator, was born on 22 July 1910 at Tunbridge Wells, Kent, the younger of two daughters of Sir Robert Vaughan Gower (1880–1953), solicitor and Conservative MP, and his first wife, Dorothy Susie Elenor (1882–1936), the only daughter of Herbert McClellan Wills JP. As her father had considerable financial resources the family lived comfortably in a large house close to Tunbridge Wells. Pauline and her sister were educated at the Sacred Heart Convent in Tunbridge Wells, initially as day students and then later as boarders, although their home, Sandown Court, Pembury, was only 3 miles away. The family was not Roman Catholic but the school's principal, Mother Ashton Case, was a cousin of Pauline's mother, which, along with the school's excellent reputation, may have influenced the parents' choice. Pauline fitted into school life easily and well. She was talented and able, which, combined with her sunny personality, made her popular with both staff and her fellow students. By the time she was in her mid-teens she had developed an abiding affection for both the institution and the religion. On 16 July 1926, just before her sixteenth birthday, she was received into the Catholic church.

After leaving school at eighteen Pauline Gower went through a London season as a débutante and was presented at court. Unsure what to do with her life, she played with ideas of furthering her interests in such things as music, Greek mythology, photography, horse riding, and politics, but she soon settled on the notion of becoming a pilot. Her interest in aviation was kindled when she went for a joyride during her last year at school. When she was nineteen her decision had been made: she would do all she could to make a career in aviation and, in the face of her father's vehement disapproval, she proceeded to arrange flying lessons. Her parents refused all financial help so she raised the necessary money by giving violin lessons. After only seven hours of instruction she

Pauline Mary de Peauly Gower (1910–1947), by Bassano, 1937

made her first solo flight and by 4 August 1930, after fifteen hours and fifteen minutes flying time, was granted an A (private pilot's) licence. She was the first woman to obtain a flying certificate from Phillips and Powis School of Aviation and the first woman to fly solo after such a short period of instruction. So as to fulfil her ambition of earning a living from flying she enrolled at the London aeroplane club, Stag Lane, in order to train for a B (commercial) licence. It was here that she became friends with Amy Johnson, recently returned from a record-breaking solo trip to Australia, and met Dorothy Spicer, who was to become her partner in various aviation ventures. On 13 July, having successfully completed the night-flying test, she was awarded a B licence, becoming the third woman in the world to do so.

While training, Pauline Gower and Dorothy Spicer had decided to establish a joyriding business, with Pauline as the pilot and Dorothy as the engineer. This they did, initially with a hired Gipsy Moth and later with a secondhand Simmonds Spartan two-seater, a twenty-first birthday present given to Pauline by her father, who had by this time become supportive of her activities. With Wallingford, Berkshire, as their headquarters they flew to various parts of the country to provide joyrides and air-taxi trips. Initially they took a light-hearted approach to flying, but their attitude changed when one day Pauline discovered that she had carelessly taken off without adequately bolting the aircraft's folding wings in position. They both settled down and studied their respective areas with great diligence and considerable aptitude. Pauline eventually obtained every flying certificate possible and Dorothy every one in aeronautical engineering.

In 1932 the pair joined the Crimson Fleet air circus of Modern Airways Ltd and, later, British Hospitals Air Pageant. At the time Britain had gone 'air mad' and several air circuses were operating around the country, which, much like traditional circuses, would travel from town to town. After the rigours of air-circus life the partners decided to establish Air Trips Ltd, an aerial-taxi and joyriding business operating from the holiday town of Hunstanton, Norfolk. It was the first aviation company to be wholly owned and staffed by women. By 1936 they were touring again, this time with Tom Campbell Black's British Empire Air Display. Pauline was appointed the chief pilot and Dorothy the senior engineer.

While she was with the circus in Scotland, Pauline learned of her mother's sudden and tragic death. Feeling that she should support her father she gave up touring. Air Trips Ltd moved into its final phase when the partners established an aerial garage at an airfield on Hayling Island in Hampshire. They found the work dissatisfying and as both had many other irons in the fire they decided to end the business. Their final task was to write a book, *Women with Wings*, published in 1938. Amy Johnson wrote the foreword, Pauline the body of the text, and Dorothy the prologue and epilogue.

In the second half of 1938 Pauline's many and varied activities were recognized with a variety of honours and appointments, including her election as a fellow of the Royal Meteorological Society and the conferment of the dignity of officer of the venerable order of St John of Jerusalem. She became sought after as a speaker and was asked to serve on various committees, among them the Gorrell committee, set up to look into the matter of air safety, upon which she was not only the youngest member but also the only woman. In 1939 she was appointed a commissioner of the Civil Air Guard.

War seemed inevitable and Britain was particularly vulnerable as the Royal Air Force was small with an insufficient number of pilots. So that RAF pilots could concentrate on combat duties, such tasks as ferrying new aircraft from the factories to the squadrons and returning with damaged ones were delegated to the Air Transport Auxiliary (ATA). On 1 December 1939 Pauline was appointed as an ATA second officer and given the job of forming a women's section. At the beginning there were only nine women pilots flying light trainers; as the war progressed more were appointed until the number of women serving in the auxiliary exceeded 150. The women pilots eventually flew all types of aircraft, from light trainers to four-engined bombers. The value of their contribution was finally recognized when Pauline obtained the same pay for her women pilots as the men received for doing the same work. Pauline herself achieved the rank of commandant, and in 1942 she was appointed MBE. Pauline Gower's leadership abilities, organizational skill, and contribution to aviation were further recognized when she was appointed a director of British Overseas Airways on 26 May 1943, thereby becoming the first woman to obtain such a position in any national airline. Her workload increased enormously as she was still responsible for the women's section of the ATA. However, she was able to find the time for a personal life: during Easter 1945 she became engaged to Wing Commander William Cusack Fahie (1918–1972) and they were married on 2 June 1945 at the Brompton Oratory, London. Her life suddenly and unexpectedly ended on 2 March 1947, at her home, 2 The Vale, Chelsea, when she died of a heart attack, having just given birth to twin boys, Paul and Michael. She was buried on 7 March at the new cemetery, Tunbridge Wells.

MICHAEL FAHIE

Sources M. Fahie, *A harvest of memories* (1995) · C. B. Smith, *Amy Johnson* (1967) · D. B. Walker, *Spreading my wings* (1994) · E. C. Cheesman, *Brief glory* (1946) · L. Curtis, *The forgotten pilots: a story of the Air Transport Auxiliary, 1939–45* (1971) · P. Gower, *Women with wings* (1938) · A. King, *Golden wings: the story of some of the women ferry pilots of the Air Transport Auxiliary* (1956) · A. H. Narracott, *Unsung heroes of the air* (1943) · personal knowledge (2004)

Archives NRA, priv. coll., MSS · Royal Air Force Museum, Hendon, London, MSS · Royal Society for the Prevention of Cruelty to Animals, London, MSS · Society of the Sacred Heart, London, provincial archives, MSS · Tunbridge Wells Library, MSS

Likenesses double portrait, photograph, 9 Sept 1931 (with Dorothy Spicer), Hult. Arch. · Bassano, photograph, 1937, NPG [*see illus.*]

Wealth at death £12,725 0s. 9d.: probate, 19 Oct 1948, CGPLA Eng. & Wales

Gower, Richard Hall (*bap.* 1767, *d.* 1833), naval architect, youngest son of the Revd Foote *Gower MD, was baptized at Chelmsford on 26 November 1767, and after spending some time at Ipswich grammar school obtained a scholarship at Winchester College in 1778. In 1780 he entered as midshipman on board an East India Company ship. Returning to England in 1783, Gower was taught for a short time by a navigation master at Edmonton, and upon rejoining his ship was nicknamed the Young Philosopher. In 1787 he devised an instrument which measured a vessel's way through the water with greater accuracy than had previously been possible. Gower next turned his attention to the design and construction of ships, and eventually left the service altogether in order to devote himself fully to this work. In 1800 the *Transit*, a ship intended for the packet service, was built to his designs at Itchenor, Sussex: she was four-masted, with sails designed for easy handling. She beat the government sloop *Osprey* out of all comparison in a trial of speed; but, greatly to Gower's disappointment, the East India Company did not purchase her, although she later proved a successful trading ship and attracted the attention of the Admiralty and private yachtsmen. Subsequently the Admiralty built a cutter, also called the *Transit*, from Gower's plans: it proved unsuccessful as a naval vessel. In the meantime Gower had married, and in 1793 had published *A Treatise on the Theory and Practice of Seamanship* (2nd edn, 1796), which long remained a standard work. He wrote a separate supplement containing a description of the *Transit* (1807; 2nd edn, 1810). He then considerably altered her lines, and in 1819 built a yacht on his improved plan (with three masts instead of four) for Lord Vernon, a pioneer patron of yachting. This vessel's behaviour in the water was much admired by nautical and engineering authorities, her speed and ease of handling being remarkable.

Gower also wrote *A Treatise on Signals* (1801), advocating a set of signals formed of shapes instead of flags; *A narrative of a mode pursued by the British government to effect improvements in naval architecture* (1811), describing the altered lines of the *Transit*; and *Remarks relative to the danger attendant upon convoy, with a proposition for the better protection of commerce* (1811), an ill-conceived plan for cruisers to be stationed along the coast, in communication with signal stations. In 1812 he competed unsuccessfully for a 100 guinea prize offered for an improved lock in the Regent's Canal; some years later locks similar to those suggested by him were, in fact, erected in the canal. Gower next constructed a further improved yacht, the *Unique*, economizing on timber and securing light draught. He also invented an ingenious fly-boat intended for use against American cruisers. Other valuable inventions of Gower, brought out in the face of much discouragement, were the long-useful catamaran for forming a raft; a lifeboat of a nove! design for employment at Landguard Fort; a sound tube connecting top and deck; a propeller or floating anchor; and numerous ingenious minor articles. Gower died towards the end of 1833 near Ipswich, where he seems to have had his residence. He was a man of considerable talent and ingenuity whose claims were, sadly, greater than his achievements.

JAMES BURNLEY, *rev.* ANDREW LAMBERT

Sources J. Fincham, *A history of naval architecture* (1857) · D. Lyon, *The sailing navy list: all the ships of the Royal Navy, built, purchased and captured, 1688–1860* (1993) · W. G. Arnott, *Orwell estuary* (1954)
Archives NMM, journal
Likenesses lithograph, BM, NPG

Gower, Lord Ronald Charles Sutherland-Leveson- (1845–1916),

sculptor and author, was born on 2 August 1845 at Stafford House, London, the youngest of eleven children of George Granville Leveson-Gower (Sutherland-Leveson-Gower from 1841), second duke of Sutherland (1786–1861), and his wife, Harriet Elizabeth Georgiana Leveson-*Gower (1806–1868), mistress of the queen's robes, daughter of George *Howard, sixth earl of Carlisle, and his wife, Georgiana. After being educated privately and at Eton College from 1859, he matriculated from Trinity College, Cambridge, in 1865, but his studies were much interrupted by social activities and foreign travel, including a visit to Garibaldi's camp at Rocco d'Anfo in July 1866. A taste for travel and a cosmopolitan interest in art were inherited from his parents, whose frequentation of European studios had assisted them in decorating their substantial properties: Dunrobin Castle (Sutherland), Trentham Hall (Staffordshire), Cliveden House (Buckinghamshire), and Stafford House (later Lancaster House) in London. Lord Ronald's cultural interests had no such practical application, and indeed were at first accompanied by a feeling of vocational vacuum, the dilemma of aristocratic younger sons. Among the conventional alternatives the church was discounted, since promotion was dependent on marriage, and Gower was attracted to his own sex. The army was a more inviting prospect, but his brother

Lord Ronald Charles Sutherland-Leveson-Gower (1845–1916), by Sir John Everett Millais, 1876

Frederick's death from fever during the Crimean War caused his mother to dissuade him from taking this step. Instead, he decided not to graduate, and entered parliament, elected as a Liberal for Sutherland in 1867. In a parliamentary career lasting eight years he spoke only once (28 May 1869), in the debate on the Scottish Reform Bill, and then only to defend his constituency against the threat of amalgamation with neighbouring counties. However, as a diarist, Gower was a dedicated spectator of events both in and outside the house. In 1868 he paid another visit to Garibaldi in self-imposed exile on the island of Caprera, and in 1870 accompanied the *Times* correspondent W. H. Russell on a journey from Berlin to Paris via the front, witnessing some of the carnage of the Franco-Prussian War and the confusion of Paris after the flight of Napoleon III.

During his years in the house, what seemed more suitable activities presented themselves to Gower, in the form of sculpture and historical research. It was while supervising the execution by the sculptor Matthew Noble of a tomb effigy for his mother in 1868 that Gower conceived the possibility that he might do such things himself. At the same time, the collecting habits of his extended family, and his father's and grandfather's experiences in France immediately before the terror, were to inspire a series of art historical and biographical projects. Lord Ronald was an avid researcher and collector of memorabilia relating to his preferred subjects, in particular Marie Antoinette, Joan of Arc, and Shakespeare. In 1874 he did not stand at the general election so as to devote himself full-time to these activities. Spending long periods in Paris over the ensuing decades, he worked as a sculptor, first in the studio of the prolific French sculptor and decorator Albert-Ernest Carrier-Belleuse, then in studios of his own. With the assistance of one of Carrier's *praticiens*, Luca Madrassi, he created a number of original pieces, exhibited at the Royal Academy, the Grosvenor Gallery, and the Paris Salon. He contributed reviews on artistic topics to the magazine *Vanity Fair*, under the anagrammatical pseudonym Talon Rouge, made the acquaintance of prominent figures in Parisian artistic life, such as Gustave Doré and Sarah Bernhardt, and in England entered a circle of young 'aesthetes', including Oscar Wilde. Friends were entertained by him in his 'house beautiful', Gower Lodge, Windsor, the furnishings of which were comprehensively described by Lord Ronald in *Bric-a-Brac* (1888).

In 1877 Lord Ronald made his Royal Academy début with the marble statue *Marie Antoinette Leaving the Conciergerie*. He had already started work on what he habitually described as his *magnum opus*, the Shakespeare monument. In the following year, returning from a tour around the world, he found that his 'moral character' had been impugned in the press. He was dissuaded by the lawyer Sir Henry James from initiating a libel action, and returned to work on his sculpture. The Shakespeare monument took him ten years to complete, and cost its author, at his own estimate, £500 annually. In its original form, the plaster model exhibited at the Paris Salon in 1881, it differed greatly from the version finally erected. Its central feature, instead of the eventual full-length seated figure of the playwright, consisted of an allegorical group, with Shakespeare's bust crowned by figures of Comedy and Tragedy. In this form it was memorably written off by the caustic Emilia Pattison (the future Lady Dilke) as a 'Brobdingnagian Twelfth-cake' (*Academy*, 11 June 1881, 439). Oscar Wilde gave a far more generous account of the final version when speaking at the unveiling ceremony in Stratford upon Avon on 10 October 1888. Of the sculptor himself, Wilde claimed in his speech that 'there were few things he did not touch, and everything he touched he adorned' (*Birmingham Daily Post*). The monument remained in Stratford, though not on its original site in the Memorial Gardens. In 1933 it was removed to a more accessible position in Bancroft Gardens. It consists of the seated figure of Shakespeare and accompanying statues of Prince Hal, Lady Macbeth, Falstaff, and Hamlet, all in bronze.

After the unveiling Lord Ronald bade farewell to sculpture and turned his attention to writing. In 1883 he published *My Reminiscences* in two volumes and in 1902 *Old Diaries, 1881–1901*; these were consolidated as *Records and Reminiscences* (1903). His lively pen and wide experience of the court, liberal politics, and artistic circles made him an attractive observer of the Victorian scene. He also wrote such popular historical works as *The Last Days of Marie Antoinette* (1885) and *Joan of Arc* (1893), and was the author of a series of art historical monographs, including *Michelangelo Buonarroti* (1899) and *Sir David Wilkie* (1902). From 1874 he had been a trustee of the National Portrait Gallery,

and on 4 May 1896, as the only trustee present on the occasion of the opening of its new premises, he personally unlocked the bronze doors to admit the small crowd waiting outside.

In 1898 Lord Ronald adopted as his son a young journalist Frank Hird, who was his companion in his remaining years. When not travelling, Lord Ronald and Hird resided at Hammerfield, Penshurst, Kent, until 1911. In that year, with his mental powers already impaired by falls suffered during epileptic fits, Lord Ronald was bankrupted after entrusting his financial affairs to a confidence trickster. He was obliged to sell his home and collections, and ended his life in greatly reduced, though still comfortable, circumstances at 66 Mount Ephraim, Tunbridge Wells. In his later years he had been a crusader for cremation, and after his death on 9 March 1916 his body was cremated at Golders Green, and his ashes were interred at Rusthall, Kent, on 14 March 1916. P. WARD-JACKSON

Sources R. Gower, *My reminiscences*, 2 vols. (1883) · R. S. Gower, *Old diaries, 1881–1901* (1902) · P. Ward-Jackson, 'Lord Ronald Gower, Gustave Doré and the genesis of the Shakespeare memorial at Stratford-upon-Avon', *Journal of the Warburg and Courtauld Institutes*, 50 (1987), 160–70 · G. C. Williamson, 'The Lord Ronald Sutherland Gower', *Khaki* (1916) · *The Times* (1911) · *The Times* (1913) · *The Times* (1916) · *Birmingham Daily Mail* (11 Oct 1888) · *Birmingham Daily Post* (11 Oct 1888)
Archives BL, diary and papers, Add. MS 45110 · priv. coll. | BL, corresp. with W. E. Gladstone, Add. MSS 44397–44525, *passim* · Bodl. Oxf., letters to Benjamin Disraeli · King's AC Cam., letters to Oscar Browning
Likenesses A.-E. Carrier-Belleuse, bronze statuette, 1852, Dunrobin Castle, Sutherland · J. E. Millais, oils, 1876, Royal Shakespeare Theatre, Stratford upon Avon [*see illus.*] · Walery, photograph, *c*.1895, NPG · H. S. Tuke, oils, 1897, NPG · Spy [L. Ward], chromolithograph caricature, NPG; repro. in *VF* (Aug 1877) · G. J. Stodart, stipple (after photograph by Negretti and Zambra, 1882), NPG
Wealth at death £2241 8*s*. 0*d*.: probate, 13 April 1916, *CGPLA Eng. & Wales*

Gower, Stanley (*bap.* 1600?, *d.* 1660), Church of England clergyman, was possibly the child of that name baptized at Chesterfield, Derbyshire, on 29 March 1600. It is certain that for eight years he was a pupil of the famed puritan minister Richard Rothwell, at that time chaplain to the Derbyshire magnate William Cavendish, Baron Cavendish and from 1618 earl of Devonshire. Rothwell, who prepared Gower for university, had once been a regimental chaplain under the earl of Essex in Ireland. This may explain why on 27 October 1621 Gower was admitted as a scholar to Trinity College, Dublin, from where he graduated BA in 1625. In 1627 he was ordained and on the same day admitted as chaplain-in-ordinary to James Ussher, archbishop of Armagh. Ussher had examined Gower on his admittance to Trinity College and had taken a particular interest in Gower's progress.

About 1629 Gower went to England and served a congregation in Sheffield, where he and his wife, Sarah, formed a strong attachment to John and Mary Stainforth. In 1634 Gower was preferred to the rectory of Brampton Bryan in the gift of Sir Robert Harley. Three of Gower's children were born at Brampton and two of them were named after his patron and his wife. Robert was baptized on 11 October 1635, Humphrey *Gower on 11 January 1638, and Brilliana on 5 May 1639. Gower's ministry at Brampton was distinguished by his nonconformity and his career illustrates the continuities between Elizabethan puritanism and the demands made for church reform in the civil-war period. Gower's endurance as a preacher was impressive: on fast days he entered the pulpit at eight or nine o'clock in the morning to pray and preach extempore until after five o'clock 'if daylight continue soe longe' (PRO, SP 16/381/92). In 1638 charges were prepared against him for neglecting parts of the liturgy, not wearing the surplice or using the sign of the cross at baptism, and other puritan practices, but he escaped censure through the influence of his patron.

In 1640 Gower signed two diocesan petitions against the etcetera oath and against the irregular elections to convocation in the diocese of Hereford. He also prepared the survey of the state of the ministry in Herefordshire drawn up for the parliamentary committee for scandalous ministers, of which his patron was a member. In the survey Gower blamed episcopal government for the poor state of the ministry, 'bringing all most every godly exercise which ministers would use to edifie their people within the compasse of a conventicle' (Corpus Christi College, MS 206, fol. 11r). In January 1641 Gower supported an anti-episcopal petition to parliament from the county, which was not however presented, because of a lack of local support. From the meeting of the Long Parliament until the autumn of 1642 Gower was corresponding with Sir Robert Harley at Westminster about church reform. He also forwarded notes of royalist sermons preached in Hereford Cathedral to Sir Robert and denounced the royalist clergy as the 'devills orators' (BL, Add. MS 70003, fol. 256r). Gower was staunchly anti-Catholic and anti-Arminian and favoured the abolition of episcopacy, which he regarded as an antichristian institution.

In 1643 Gower was chosen as one of the two Herefordshire representatives to the Westminster assembly of divines, where he was active in promoting a presbyterian church settlement. In that year, after his arrival in London, he was appointed as preacher in the staunchly presbyterian parish of St Martin Ludgate and was invited to preach before the houses of parliament on several occasions. His sermon to the Commons of 31 July 1644 was printed as *Things Now-a-Doing* (1644); it was millenarian in tone and predicted that the year 1650 would see the downfall of the Church of Rome. Gower also praised his auditors for their church reforms and urged them to ensure that the clergy were given sufficient wages and ministerial authority 'to tell the people their transgressions and the house of Jacob their sins' (Gower, *Things*, 24). In October 1644 he was appointed by parliament to be one of the ministers authorized to ordain clergymen in London. In 1648 he was in the Isle of Wight, as a member of the delegation of ministers sent to persuade the king to accept a presbyterian settlement, when he was approached by the townsmen of Dorchester to be their minister.

Early in 1649 Gower was instituted as rector of Holy Trinity, Dorchester, Dorset which has been described as 'the most "puritan" place in England' (Underdown, ix). There he took on the mantle of his predecessor, the great presbyterian patriarch John White. Gower's life of Richard Rothwell appeared in Samuel Clarke's *A Generall Martyrologie* (1651). Later he wrote the preface to the 1660 edition of his former mentor James Ussher's sermons preached in Oxford in 1640, published as *Eighteen Sermons*. Gower died at Dorchester in 1660 and his wife died the following year.   JACQUELINE EALES

Sources S. Gower, *Things now-a-doing* (1644) • S. Clarke, 'The life of Master Richard Rothwel, who died, anno Christi, 1627', *A generall martyrologie … whereunto are added, The lives of sundry modern divines* (1651), 452–61 • S. Gower, preface, in *Eighteen sermons preached in Oxford 1640 … by the right reverend James Ussher* (1660) • J. Eales, *Puritans and roundheads: the Harleys of Brampton Bryan and the outbreak of the English civil war* (1990) • J. Fletcher, 'A trio of Dorchester worthies', *Proceedings of the Dorset Natural History and Antiquarian Field Club*, 47 (1926), 129–47 • survey of the ministry in Herefordshire, 1640–41, CCC Oxf., MS 206 • D. Underdown, *Fire from heaven: life in an English town in the seventeenth century* (1992) • *IGI* [Chesterfield parish register] • Burtchaell & Sadleir, *Alum. Dubl.*, 2nd edn, 337 • C. H. Mayo, ed., *Municipal records of the borough of Dorchester, Dorset* (1908) • Tai Liu, *Puritan London: a study of religion and society in the City parishes* (1986)
Archives BL, letters to Sir Robert Harley and papers, Add. MSS 70002–70003, 70105 • Folger, letters to John and Mary Stainforth, x. d. 428/196–200

Gower, Susanna Leveson- [*née* Lady Susan Stewart], **marchioness of Stafford** (1742/3–1805), politician, was the third daughter of Alexander Stewart, sixth earl of Galloway (1694–1773), and his second wife, Lady Catherine Cochrane (d. 1786), daughter of John Cochrane, fourth earl of Dundonald. As one of thirteen children, Lady Susan Stewart (as she was known until her marriage) could easily have become a maiden aunt shuttling between the homes of her brothers John Stewart, Lord Garlies (later seventh earl of Galloway) and Keith Stewart, eventually an admiral; however, her father was eager to have some of his children placed where they could develop the necessary connections to secure patronage and advance the others' careers and economic prospects. Lady Susan appears to have internalized this sense of duty to familial advancement early; it was to form one of the chief themes of her life. By her teens she was being groomed for a position at court, a good marriage, or both. She was encouraged to be socially active and independent. She spent long visits with friends such as the beautiful Elizabeth Gunning, then duchess of Hamilton, where she could mix with the best society and meet the most eligible *partis*. As an attractive, intelligent, sensible, and warm-hearted young woman whose birth exceeded her fortune, she was an ideal candidate for a court appointment. Moreover, the Galloways were supporters of George III's favourite, John Stuart, third earl of Bute (to whom she would remain loyal well after he fell from favour), and in 1761 Bute's influence over appointments to the royal households was unchallenged.

In that year, Lady Susan was appointed woman of the bedchamber to George III's sister, Princess Augusta. She became genuinely fond of the princess, not only accompanying her to Germany when she married in 1764 but also maintaining contact with her throughout her life. Horace Walpole, who disliked ambitious, self-assured political women, condemned her to posterity as someone who manipulated and exploited people in a never-ending quest for patronage (especially after her marriage): 'her life was a series of jobs and solicitations, and she teazed every Minister for every little office that fell in his department. She made a thousand dependents and enemies, but no friend' (*Last Journals of Horace Walpole*, 1.223). While her correspondence confirms that she definitely was ambitious and kept a very close eye on opportunities to secure patronage, Walpole was wrong in his overall judgement: she had a real talent for friendship and was liked and respected by the women and men in her extensive personal networks. Political differences put paid to a few of her early friendships, such as those with Mary Watson-Wentworth, marchioness of Rockingham, and Georgiana, Countess Spencer, but many proved enduring. Moreover, in using her connections to pursue her goals she was not doing anything at all unusual for the time. In turn her services as a patronage broker were frequently requested by family members, friends, or clients, particularly after her marriage gave her direct access to leading politicians.

When it came to patronage, family concerns took precedence, whether Lady Susan was seeking patronage for her son and sons-in-law, or, as she did in her early years in London, her brothers. Her correspondence with her father is shot through with references to various attempts to secure patronage for her brothers. Conducting multiple campaigns at once could leave her in a somewhat difficult position, however, if more than one request looked set to be granted at the same time. In 1766, for instance, her father decided that she would have to turn down the offer of another ship for her brother Keith from the first lord of the Admiralty, John Perceval, second earl of Egmont, so that he could remain at home to stand for parliament and be at hand in case the place that she was trying to secure him in the household of George III's brother the duke of Gloucester materialized:

> I desire, you may assure his Lop. that I'm perfectly sencible of the honour he has done me & of his goodness to my Son, & that I beg the continuance of his favour & protection to him; … I heartily wish you may succeed, in your scheme of getting him, into the Duke of Glochesters family, it would be greatly, both for his honour & interest, & would make me very happy. (Galloway to Lady Susan Stewart, 19 June 1766, PRO 30/29/4/3, no. 70, fol. 403)

On 25 May 1768, at the age of twenty-five, Lady Susan married, as his third wife, Granville Leveson-*Gower, second Earl Gower, after 1786 first marquess of Stafford (1721–1803). Although he was a widower more than twenty years her senior, with four children aged under eleven, theirs was a marriage of love, not of convenience. Its success was due, in no small part, to her efforts. As she told her daughter Charlotte years later, she devoted herself to it: 'When I was a girl, I made it my Study & Ambition to be the best of Daughters—When I became a Wife, it was the study & ambition of my Heart to be the best of Wives'

(Lady Stafford to Lady Worcester, *c*.1800, University of Birmingham Library, MS 14/v, letters of Lady Stafford, no. 93). Her efforts paid off handsomely with both Gower and his children: even after she had four children of her own—and her son, Granville Leveson-*Gower, later first Earl Granville (1773–1846), was easily the family favourite—she maintained close ties with the other children. Gower was handsome, sociable, and generally well-liked; he was also an important if frustratingly reluctant politician. As the calm voice of the Bedford faction, he had by 1768 already served as an MP, lord privy seal, and lord chamberlain, and was currently serving as lord president of the council.

Gower held high office off and on for the next thirty years, but spurring him into political action required continual effort. The part that Lady Gower played in doing this was recognized at the time, and in later years her stepdaughter Louisa and Louisa's husband, Archibald *Macdonald, later first baronet, proved to be her able accomplices. In 1779, with the American War of Independence going badly and Lord North's government becoming increasingly fragile, some people began to see in Gower a potential replacement for North. Macdonald was one of these. He knew, though, that the only way to put pressure on Gower was to work through Lady Gower. Consequently it was to her that he turned when he wanted to get Gower to come to London and it was to her that he laid out his hopes of becoming Gower's private secretary if he chose to head the administration: 'You shall be my Plenipotentiary, & dispose of me for my Lords advantage in any way you see fit' (Archibald Macdonald to Lady Gower, 23 June 1779, PRO 30/29/4/4, no. 12, fol. 625*v*).

Fortunately Lady Gower's political opinions coincided with those of her husband: both were supporters of the king and his ministers. If anything, she became more interested in politics as she got older. She was a particular supporter of William Pitt the younger and her letters to Granville when he was at university frequently present Pitt as a role model to follow. Most of all she revelled in being at the heart of the political world. When, in 1794 at age seventy-three, her husband decided to resign the privy seal despite all her efforts to persuade him to stay on, she was left feeling decidedly 'Glum' (3 July 1794, PRO 30/29/4/4, no. 77).

While social politics and patronage were central concerns throughout Lady Gower's life, they became increasingly interwoven with maintaining the family's electoral interest after her marriage. She followed every election energetically, participating in processions and triumphal entries, taking part as necessary in the fatigues of election entertainments, and ensuring—always—that the family was well and properly represented at influential sociopolitical events such as the annual race meetings. She was convinced that the social dimension of politics mattered. In London she attended court, entertained frequently at home, and used social situations of all sorts to secure support for her latest causes. She approached her political involvement with energy and humour, whether she was actively canvassing peers at a drawing room, as she did during the Douglas cause when she left Lady Mary Coke worrying that 'Lady Gower's influence wd have carried all that party [the Bedford faction] against Mr Douglass' (*Letters and Journals*, 3.12), or trying to secure a patronage appointment for a tenant in one of the family boroughs.

Lady Gower's enthusiasm for politics did not prevent her from paying careful heed to her children and their education. She was a fond and encouraging mother, quick to praise and careful in her criticism, and while perhaps too likely to overlook Granville's dalliances with women such as Harriet Ponsonby, countess of Bessborough, she did occasionally take him to task over his gambling. She did not, however, favour him to the detriment of her daughters. The three all made marriages which extended Lady Gower's political dynasty: Georgiana Augusta (1769–1806) married William Eliot, second earl of St Germans (*d.* 1845), and was the mother of Edward Granville *Eliot, third earl of St Germans (1798–1877); Charlotte Sophia (1771–1854) married Henry Charles Somerset, marquess of Worcester and subsequently sixth duke of Beaufort (1766–1835), and was the mother of Henry *Somerset, seventh duke of Beaufort (1792–1853) [*see under* Somerset, Lord Granville Charles Henry], and Lord Granville Charles Henry *Somerset (1792–1848); and Susan (1772–1838) married Dudley *Ryder, first earl of Harrowby (1762–1847), and was the mother of Dudley *Ryder, second earl of Harrowby (1798–1882). Lady Gower's close relationships with her daughters, and especially with Charlotte, are preserved in her extensive correspondence. A genuinely religious woman herself, she emphasized the importance of religion to her daughters from their youth. Charlotte, who became known for her evangelical Methodism, undoubtedly received the framework for her strong convictions at home. Lady Gower's aspirations for her daughters were very much of their time: she laid them out in a letter to the fourteen-year-old Charlotte in 1785:

> I think with inexpressible Pleasure that you will be a sensible, pleasing, kind, delightful good little Wife, that you will make your Husband happy, & be an Example to my Grand-Children—Let no Dissipation, no Happiness in this World make you ever neglect your Duty to God in every Situation of Life, that is the Foundation of all good. (University of Birmingham Library, MS 14/v, Stafford letters, no. 13 [1785?])

What she advocated for her daughters was no less than what she had tried to achieve in her own life. At a time when being an excellent wife and mother was highly valued, and wives were expected to devote themselves to their husbands, children, and the family's concerns, she appears to have justly succeeded in becoming one of the 'best' of wives. Archibald Macdonald, writing about 1783 to thank her for her trouble in trying to secure him an East India Company directorship, gave her well-earned praise:

> One passage in your kind Letter will not let me sleep till I write to you—I never in my Life knew a stronger instance of true attachment to a husbands family, & the resolute performance of duty, than to that to which you allude, for which I have ever admired you. (Archibald Macdonald to Lady Gower, *c.*1783, PRO 30/29/4/5, no. 38)

The most active political period in the life of Lady Stafford (as she had become in 1786) ended with her husband's retirement from politics. However, she continued to follow her son Granville's career with pride. Her last years were spent quietly with her husband, who became increasingly blind, and with her growing extended family. She survived her husband by nearly two years, and died at her home in Stanhope Street, Mayfair, Westminster, on 15 August 1805. She was buried at Trentham, Staffordshire, on 25 August.   E. H. CHALUS

Sources C. Penny, 'Catalogue of Lady Stafford's letters, 1774–1805', bound typescript, 1986 • GEC, *Peerage*, new edn • N. B. Smith, 'West country genealogy, heraldry and history', www.uk-genealogy.org.uk/, 25 Feb 2002 • freespace.virgin.net/john.elkin/levgower001.htm#ref7 [the Leveson Gower family], 25 Feb 2002 • *Lord Granville Leveson Gower: private correspondence, 1781–1821*, ed. Castalia, Countess Granville [C. R. Leveson-Gower], 2nd edn, 2 vols. (1916) • U. Birm. L., Stafford letters, MS 14/v • PRO, Granville papers, 30/29 • *The last journals of Horace Walpole*, ed. Dr Doran, rev. A. F. Steuart, 2 vols. (1910) • Walpole, *Corr.* • *The letters and journals of Lady Mary Coke*, ed. J. A. Home, 4 vols. (1889–96) • *GM*, 1st ser., 75 (1805), 782 • IGI

Archives PRO, Granville papers, 30/29 • U. Birm. L., letters to her daughter Charlotte

Wealth at death £10,000 bequeathed her by husband: will, PRO, PROB 11/1450, sig. 815

Gower, Sir Thomas (*fl.* 1530–1577), soldier, was the son of Sir Edward Gower of Stittenham, Yorkshire, and Margery, daughter of Sir Robert Constable. By 1530 he had married Anne Muleverer; his second wife, Barbara Baxter, was probably the mother of his son Thomas. In 1541 he was given responsibility for overseeing the construction of new fortifications at Carlisle. However, he quarrelled with Stefan von Haschenperg, the German engineer designing the works, and was sent instead to Berwick. Progress on new fortifications there was slow, in part because Gower had argued with John Forman, the master mason. Nevertheless he appears to have been highly regarded as a soldier, and played an important role in supplying the earl of Hertford's foray into Lothian in 1544. The following year he was taken prisoner at the battle of Ancrum Moor (27 February 1545). Upon his release he failed to prove a serious accusation he had made against Lord Ralph Eure before the privy council. Subsequently Gower was himself committed to the Fleet prison in June 1546. Released early in the reign of Edward VI he was appointed marshal of Berwick, surveyor of the royal estates in Northumberland, and captain of the new fort at Eyemouth (1 September 1547). He led a band of light horsemen in the army with which Protector Somerset invaded Scotland. The evening before the battle of Pinkie Cleugh (10 September), Gower was one of three cavalry officers taken prisoner following a skirmish on Fawside Brae.

Gower had to pay a considerable ransom, and additionally was much burdened by expenses at Eyemouth. In 1549 he went to London to claim eighteen months' arrears of sums due for Eyemouth. Three years later (9 June 1552) £100 of his debt of £300 to the crown was remitted by the king through Northumberland's influence. Yet Gower's abrasive personality continued to create problems. In

October 1552 he lost his post as surveyor. Early in Mary's reign he managed to offend the new queen, and he was again committed to the Fleet, accused of sedition. Duly penitent, he was discharged and he kept an uncharacteristically low profile until the renewal of conflict with Scotland in 1558, in which year he was mentioned as master of the ordnance in the north parts. He was subsequently knighted. In 1560 he was made master of the ordnance in the army sent to besiege Leith. In 1569 the earl of Sussex sent him to assist in the fortification of Newcastle. In 1577 he is last mentioned in a letter sent to the council from the earl of Huntingdon, enclosing a report from Gower on Kingston upon Hull, where he had been sent to survey the castle and forts.

E. T. BRADLEY, *rev.* GERVASE PHILLIPS

Sources M. Merriman and J. Summerson, 'The Scottish border', *The history of the king's works*, ed. H. M. Colvin and others, 4 (1982), 607–728 · *CSP dom.*, 1601–3; addenda, 1547–65; addenda, 1566–79 · J. Foster, ed., *The visitation of Yorkshire made in the years 1584/5 ... to which is added the subsequent visitation made in 1612* (privately printed, London, 1875) · *Heraldic visitation of the northern counties in 1530, by Thomas Tonge*, ed. W. H. D. Longstaffe, SurtS, 41 (1863) · [F. W. Dendry], ed., *Visitations of the north*, 2, SurtS, 133 (1921) · A. Collins, *The peerage of England: containing a genealogical and historical account of all the peers of England*, 3rd edn, 5 vols. in 6 (1756) · J. Stow, *The annales of England ... untill this present yeere 1592* (1592) · R. Holinshed and others, eds., *The chronicles of England, Scotlande and Irelande*, 2 vols. (1577) · *CSP for.*, 1558–60 · W. Patten, 'The expedition into Scotland ... 1547', *Tudor tracts, 1532–1588*, ed. A. F. Pollard (1903), 53–157; repr. (1964)

Gower, Sir Thomas, first baronet (1584–1651), local politician, was born in Stittenham, Yorkshire, the son of Thomas Gower and Mary, daughter of Gabriel Fairfax of Steeton. Stittenham had been the family estate since the twelfth century. Gower married Anne, daughter of John D'Oyley, on 28 May 1604, and the couple had five sons, Thomas *Gower (1604/5–1672), D'Oyley, Howard, William, and Edward, and one daughter, Margaret. In 1620 Gower was high sheriff of Yorkshire, and he was created baronet on 2 June 1620. Anne, Lady Gower, died on 28 October 1633, and he later married Mary, a widow with a daughter and a granddaughter, both also called Mary.

In the decade of unrest before the civil war the Gower family appeared to be co-operating with the king's opponents. In 1629 Sir Thomas was fined £50 in the court of Star Chamber. In 1632 he made some critical remarks about Sir George Radcliffe, the king's attorney for the council of the north and a friend of Thomas Wentworth, the lord president. Wentworth attempted to cite Gower for contempt but Gower fled with his family to London and established himself in Holborn. Wentworth's officers attempted to arrest him but he claimed that the council of the north had no authority to arrest him outside its jurisdiction. Gower became somewhat of a hero in Holborn for his defiance of the king's prerogative court. Wentworth appealed to the privy council in December, accusing Gower of 'many contempts' and 'scandalous words' to Radcliffe, and claiming that the council could not rule in the north without 'coercive power ... to compel the parties to an answer' (*CSP dom.*, 1631, 450–51). Gower was returned to

York by the privy council and he spent several months in confinement. In 1640 he and his son Thomas signed a petition drawn up by Yorkshire gentry requesting the king to cease billeting soldiers in citizens' homes without their consent. The document cited the petition of right as justification for the protest.

Despite their previous activities Gower, with his five sons, joined the royalist forces in June 1642. He also lent the king £1500. During the confusion of the war that year Sir Thomas Gower and Lord Thomas Savile were arrested by the earl of Newcastle on suspicion of complicity in a plot to seize Queen Henrietta Maria on her journey from the coast to York, and to deliver her to parliament as a hostage. Savile was confined in Newark Castle for six months, but he later refuted the charge before the king at Oxford. Savile was repudiated, and Newcastle publicly apologized for arresting him. Gower was not convicted or punished, and there is general doubt concerning the validity of the charges. The *Journal of the House of Lords* recorded in 1647 an order in parliament that the treasurers of Weavers' Hall were to repay Thomas Gower £6000 'for the payment of private soldiers' (*CSP dom.*, addenda, 1625–49, 707). In the latter years of the conflict the elder Gower served in Newark garrison for the king.

During the interregnum both Gower and his son were declared delinquent and were forced to compound, the father paying a £200 fine. On 13 June 1651 Gower's wife, Mary, at that point in good health, following the agreement in their marriage settlement, made a will leaving her estate to her daughter, Mary, wife of Francis Topham of Upper Bradley, Yorkshire, and giving substantial bequests to five great-granddaughters, daughters of Mary and George Spencer. She died within a few weeks, however, and the will was proved on 13 August. Gower himself died on 20 October that year and was buried at St Margaret of Huttons Ambo, North Riding of Yorkshire.

W. CALVIN DICKINSON

Sources *CSP dom.*, 1631–51 · *Fifth report*, HMC, 4 (1876) · J. T. Cliffe, *The Yorkshire gentry from the Reformation to the civil war* (1969) · S. R. Gardiner, *History of England from the accession of James I to the outbreak of the civil war*, 7 (1884) · M. A. E. Green, ed., *Calendar of the proceedings of the committee for compounding ... 1643–1660*, 5 vols., PRO (1889–92) · *VCH Yorkshire North Riding* · J. W. Clay, 'The gentry of Yorkshire at the time of the civil war', *Yorkshire Archaeological Journal*, 23 (1914–15), 349–94, esp. 361 · will of Mary, Lady Gower, PRO, PROB 11/218, fols. 30v–31r · Burke, *Peerage*

Gower, Sir Thomas, second baronet (1604/5–1672), politician, was the eldest son of Sir Thomas *Gower, first baronet (1584–1651), of Stittenham, Sheriff Hutton, Yorkshire, and Anne Doyley (*d.* 1633). He went to Wadham College, Oxford, in 1617, aged twelve, and was admitted to Gray's Inn in 1621; he could be considered a scholar and linguist as well as an active politician. He was knighted in 1630 and the next year, following the death of his first wife, Elizabeth Howard, he married Frances Leveson (1614–1661), a marriage which led to the future aggrandizement of his family. As sheriff of Yorkshire in 1642 he vainly strove to achieve consensus among the Yorkshire gentry as civil war approached. After diligently carrying out the orders of parliament, he was named in the king's commission of array together with Sir Marmaduke Langdale and others previously sympathetic to the parliamentary cause. He, his father, and his five brothers all fought for the king. Having raised a regiment, he lent Charles £2250, eventually receiving repayment in 1665. He criticized the management of the siege of Hull and the damage it did the king's cause and later, in October 1642, commented on the problems Sir John Hotham's success caused the royalists in Yorkshire. He surrendered at Oxford in 1646 and, with Sir Thomas Fairfax's assistance, made his peace with parliament. Compounding cost him £730, which he paid in 1650.

During the interregnum Gower maintained his wife's interest in the great estate of her uncle Sir Richard Leveson of Trentham, Staffordshire, and opposed the machinations of her nephew and rival, Sir Richard Temple of Stowe, Buckinghamshire. The officials of the protectorate regarded him with suspicion and confined him to within a narrow radius of his house in 1657, when two of his brothers were imprisoned; he used this detention to study medicine to help his poor neighbours. Gower's letters to Sir Richard Leveson describe how Fairfax, the duke of Buckingham, and many Yorkshire gentry including the Gowers took York from Lambert at the beginning of 1660.

The Restoration brought Gower into national politics. Although Thomas Danby defeated him in the election for Malton in 1661 Gower won the seat on appeal, and his elder son, Edward, was active in the Scarborough election. Gower served the government in Yorkshire as JP, as deputy lieutenant for the North Riding, as collector of taxes, and as an invaluable source of intelligence on dissident activities. He learned early on of the Yorkshire, or Farmley Wood, plot of 1663, which drew on the large number of disaffected parliamentarians in Yorkshire, and ensured that two of his spies attended the plotters' preliminary meeting at Harrogate on 9 June. He informed the government, who promptly sent the duke of Buckingham north with a troop of horse, and himself began the series of arrests which soon rounded up 100 or so suspects. He continued to monitor developments closely, making use of the informer, Major Joshua Greathead. The planned uprising petered out in October, though the government response was relatively harsh. Gower's deployment of numerous agents had been of considerable value, and he would remain a source of information on suspicious activities in Yorkshire up to 1670.

Gower was a conscientious member of the Cavalier Parliament, serving on 389 committees. He was considered an ally of Buckingham or of Ormond and was not a supporter of Clarendon; indeed, he was far from uncritical of government proceedings. A major disappointment for him was the fate of the Leveson inheritance—for Sir Richard Leveson, who had considered Gower's son Edward as his heir for a time, left the estate to another relation. In 1668, united with his enemy Sir Richard Temple, another disappointed heir, Gower opposed a bill to settle the Leveson estate. An unexpected death in September 1668, however, gave the estate to the next heir, his younger son William, who took the name of Leveson-Gower. Gower continued active in the House of Commons, which instructed him to look into the historic precedents when trade between England and Scotland was being debated in 1668. He spoke in the debate about the assault on Sir John Coventry in 1671 and was serving on a committee enquiring into the growth of popery when he died, at Stittenham Manor, Sheriff Hutton, after a short illness, on 3 September 1672. He was deemed 'a right valiant and learned knight and true patriot of his country' (Plaxton). Gower was buried at Sheriff Hutton church.

RICHARD WISKER

Sources Leveson and Leveson-Gower letter-books, Staffs. RO, Sutherland-Leveson-Gower family papers, D868, vol. 8, letters 1–25, 44–51, 57–71 · *Fifth report*, HMC, 4 (1876), esp. 191–204 [Duke of Sutherland (Trentham MSS)] · G. Plaxton, 'History of Lilleshall', William Salt Library, Stafford, 356/40 · P. A. Bolton and P. Watson, 'Gower, Sir Thomas', HoP, *Commons, 1660–90* · Staffs. RO, Sutherland papers, D593, F/2/44, H/5/1, P/16/2/4/2, S/16/1–4 · J. R. Wordie, *Estate management in eighteenth-century England: the building of the Leveson-Gower fortune* (1982), 5–9, 24, 228 · J. Walker, 'The Yorkshire plot, 1663', *Yorkshire Archaeological Journal*, 31 (1932–4), 348–59 · J. T. Cliffe, *The Yorkshire gentry from the Reformation to the civil war* (1969), 301–2, 330, 334–5 · A. Fletcher, *The outbreak of the English civil war* (1981), 192, 194, 314, 316 · E. F. Gay, 'Sir Richard Temple, the debt settlement and estate litigation, 1653–1675', *Huntington Library Quarterly*, 6 (1942–3), 255–91, esp. 274, 277, 288 · A. H. Woolrych, 'Yorkshire and the Restoration', *Yorkshire Archaeological Journal*, 39 (1956–8), 483–507, esp. 492–5 · *CSP dom.*, 1641–3, 365; 1664–5, 142, 201, 401, 437; 1665–6, 39, 476; 1670, 227, 316 · Foster, *Alum. Oxon.* · R. L. Greaves, *Deliver us from evil: the radical underground in Britain, 1660–1663* (1986) · A. Marshall, *Intelligence and espionage in the reign of Charles II, 1660–1685* (1994) · GEC, *Baronetage* · T. Brayshaw, 'The Yorkshire portion of Leland's "Itinerary" [pt 2]', *Yorkshire Archaeological and Topographical Journal*, 10 (1887–9), 313–44, esp. 325

Archives Hunt. L., legal papers and letters | Staffs. RO, Leveson and Leveson-Gower letter-books, D868 · Staffs. RO, Sutherland MSS, D543

Wealth at death rental £500 p.a., wife's portion £3000; estate of 1537 acres: Wordie, *Estate management*, 8; 1631 settlement, Staffs. RO, Sutherland MSS, D593 C/14/2, *c*.1700 survey D593 H/5/1

Gowers, Sir Ernest Arthur (1880–1966), public servant and writer of reference works, was born in London on 2 June 1880, the younger of the two sons among the four children of Sir William Richard *Gowers (1845–1915), physician, and his wife, Mary (d. 1913), daughter of Frederick Baines, of Leeds. He was educated at Rugby School and at Clare College, Cambridge, of which he was a scholar and, from 1949, an honorary fellow. Having gained a first class in the classical tripos in 1902, he entered the civil service and was posted to the Inland Revenue, later transferring to the India Office. He married, in 1905, Constance (MBE 1946; d. 1952), daughter of Thomas Macgregor Greer, solicitor and politician, of Ballymoney, co. Antrim, with whom he had one son and two daughters.

Gowers was called to the bar (Inner Temple) in 1906. He acted as private secretary to several parliamentary undersecretaries, including Edwin Montagu, and in 1911 moved to the Treasury as principal private secretary to David

Lloyd George, then chancellor of the exchequer. In the following year Lloyd George made him chief inspector in the National Health Insurance Commission (England), the establishment of which in that year under the terms of the National Insurance Act of 1911 was the most complex task which had yet faced the civil service. He held this post for five years.

In 1917 Gowers became secretary to the Conciliation and Arbitration Board for government employees. In 1919 he was made director of production at the mines department (Board of Trade), and a year later he was promoted to take charge of the department as permanent under-secretary for mines. In 1927 he became chairman of the Board of Inland Revenue, and in 1930 he retired from the civil service although not from public service.

Gowers renewed his association with mining by becoming chairman of the Coal Mines Reorganization Commission, established by the Coal Mines Act of 1930. After five years the commission acknowledged failure because of the opposition of colliery owners to the amalgamation of mines. Despite this setback Gowers went on to become chairman of the Coal Commission set up in 1938, and by 1942 such progress had been made that he was able to announce that all unworked coal in Britain had become the property of the Coal Commission.

Gowers was chairman of the manpower subcommittee of the committee of imperial defence, the body which produced the famous schedule of reserved occupations. In 1939 he was appointed regional commissioner for civil defence for the London region, and in 1941 was promoted to senior regional commissioner. From then on he bore the main responsibility for civil defence in London until the end of the war, co-operating successfully with the leader of the London county council, Charles Latham.

After the war Gowers undertook a number of public tasks, such as the chairmanship of the Home Office committee of inquiry into the closing hours of shops (1946–7) and the chairmanship of the royal commission on capital punishment (1949–53). From 1948 to 1957 he was chairman of the National Hospitals for Nervous Diseases (headquarters in Queen Square, London), an institution which his father and other pioneers of modern neurology had made world-famous towards the end of the nineteenth century.

Gowers may be regarded as one of the greatest public servants of his day. He presided over numerous official bodies and committees of inquiry besides those already mentioned. Among the matters he investigated were the admission of women into the senior branch of the foreign service, and the preservation, maintenance, and use of houses of outstanding historical or architectural interest. His courtesy, his fine sense of humour, and his unfailing clarity of expression explain why his services were so frequently sought.

Gowers's literary style was lucid and urbane. His writings include a two-shilling booklet, *Plain Words: a Guide to the Use of English*, issued in 1948; its sequel, *An ABC of Plain Words* (1951); *The Complete Plain Words* (1954), which combined the two earlier works; *A Life for a Life? The Problem of*

Capital Punishment (1956); and a revision of *Modern English Usage* (1965) by H. W. Fowler. The first of these, *Plain Words*, was written at the invitation of Sir Edward Bridges, then head of the civil service, to serve as an introduction to a course of instruction for entrants to the service in the writing of simple and unambiguous English, on which Gowers was known to be insistent. The books on 'plain words' show his regard for brevity and precision as the leading virtues in factual writing. Throughout his life he crusaded against the faults which have made 'officialese' a term of opprobrium and in favour of simple and direct English. His customary mood of amiable scepticism is revealed in many passages, for example in his remark about the fashionable use of the word 'repercussion': 'Many officials must have echoed in their own way the cry of Macbeth, who knew more about repercussions of this sort than most people, "Bloody instructions which being taught return To plague th'inventor"'.

Since *Plain Words* exhibited the profound influence of H. W. Fowler, it was natural that the Oxford University Press should have turned to Gowers to revise *Modern English Usage*, a task which he completed in his eighty-fifth year. One of his principal aims was to leave unimpaired the peculiar flavour that had endeared Fowler to so many people. Here and there he softened some of Fowler's astringency and removed some of his more idiosyncratic remarks. The revised *Modern English Usage*, characterized by the same fastidious care for 'proper words in proper places' that the first author had displayed, nevertheless showed much originality, both in newly written articles (for example 'abstractitis', 'sociologese') and within the articles on older topics. In an age of possibly declining standards of written English, Gowers provided clear guidance to anyone who turned to him for a ruling on matters of linguistic dispute.

Gowers's work with the royal commission on capital punishment made him a convinced abolitionist: his personal views were set down in his book *A Life for a Life?*

Gowers was made an honorary DLitt of Manchester University and was elected an honorary associate of the Royal Institute of British Architects. He was appointed CB in 1917, KBE in 1926, KCB in 1928, GBE in 1945, and GCB in 1953. He spent his later years pig-farming in west Sussex and he died at King Edward VII Hospital, Midhurst, Sussex, on 16 April 1966.   R. W. BURCHFIELD, *rev.*

Sources *The Times* (18 April 1966) · R. W. Burchfield, review, *The Listener* (6 May 1965) [H. W. Fowler, *A dictionary of modern English usage*, 2nd edn, rev. E. A. Gowers (1965)] · *CGPLA Eng. & Wales* (1966) **Archives** NL Wales, corresp. with Thomas Jones **Likenesses** W. Stoneman, photograph, 1930, NPG · M. Frampton, oils, 1943, IWM · L. Rey, bronze bust, exh. RA 1943 · W. Stoneman, photograph, 1953, NPG **Wealth at death** £106,265: probate, 19 Aug 1966, *CGPLA Eng. & Wales*

Gowers, Sir William Richard (1845–1915), physician, born in London on 20 March 1845, was the only son of William Gowers, of Hackney, and his wife, Ann Venables. He was educated at Christ Church School, Oxford, and at sixteen was apprenticed to Dr Simpson at Coggeshall in

Essex. He completed his medical training at University College, London, as a pupil of Sir William Jenner. After qualifying MRCS in 1867, he became house physician, and subsequently private secretary to Jenner—'the daily intercourse with that mind was a privilege inestimable'. At the early age of twenty-five he was appointed medical registrar, and, three years later (1873), assistant physician to the National Hospital for the Paralysed and Epileptic, Queen Square, London. He regularly acknowledged the inspirational example of his senior colleague Hughlings Jackson. Jackson's original research contributions were essentially analytical and physiological, while Gowers acquired his knowledge of the nervous system by the meticulous observation of clinical phenomena and of the pathological changes underlying them.

In 1872 Gowers was appointed assistant physician at University College Hospital, becoming physician in 1883 and, later, professor of clinical medicine. He was elected a fellow of the Royal College of Physicians, London, in 1879, and in 1887 was elected fellow of the Royal Society. He delivered the Goulstonian lectures at the Royal College of Physicians in 1880, and the Bradshaw lecture in 1896. Pressure of work led to his early retirement from University College in 1888. In 1875 he married Mary (d. 1913), daughter of Frederick Baines, of Leeds, and had two sons and two daughters. One of his sons was Ernest *Gowers, author of *Plain Words* (1948).

While Gowers was always interested in diseases of the nervous system, his earliest contributions to medical literature dealt with the blood. He invented a haemoglobinometer for measuring haemoglobin, and also improved the haemocytometer, an instrument for counting blood cells. His first important book was *Medical Ophthalmology* (1879), in which he emphasized the use in medical diagnosis of the ophthalmoscope, which 'gives information not often otherwise obtainable regarding the existence and nature of disease elsewhere than in the eye'. The accuracy and clarity of the illustrations, drawn by himself, were outstanding and the book became a standard work, being translated into Italian and German. In 1880 he published *Diagnosis of Diseases of the Spinal Cord*, describing for the first time the nerve fibre tract in the cord, later known as Gowers's tract, somewhat to his dismay. He also published many of the earliest, often original, descriptions of dystrophia myotonica, ataxic paraplegia, vasovagal attacks, musicogenic epilepsy and palatal myoclonus, among others. His descriptions of posthemiplegic movement disorders (1876) and muscular dystrophy (1879 and 1902) are regarded as classics. The sign of a boy with pseudohypertrophic muscular dystrophy 'climbing up his legs' in order to rise from the floor is still known in 2004 as Gowers's sign.

Gowers's greatest book, *A Manual of Diseases of the Nervous System* (1886–8), became a work of international repute, being generally known as 'the bible of neurology'. His *Epilepsy* (1881) and *The Borderland of Epilepsy* (1907) were among his other prolific, clear, and notable writings.

Gowers made daily use of his skill in shorthand and urged his pupils, at times obsessively, to learn the method in order to take notes of cases and lectures. He was a considerable artist, etching and drawing general subjects as easily as medical. Many of his works were exhibited, once, at the Royal Academy.

In the 1880s Gowers's teaching at Queen Square achieved an international reputation. He was a fluent and lucid lecturer and a bold and incisive clinical teacher. But, often strained and tired by overwork, he sometimes seemed dogmatic and impatient of criticism, and was even given to occasional sardonic if humorous invective. The immense labour of writing the *Manual* permanently impaired his enthusiasm and energy. If he lacked the originality and inspiration of Hughlings Jackson, Gowers was nevertheless a great clinical neurologist and through his writings enriched the wider understanding of scientific neurology in the medical world of his time. He was an honorary fellow of RCPI, honorary MD (Dublin) and LLD (Edinburgh). He was knighted in 1897. Gowers died at his home at 34 Ladbroke Square, London, on 4 May 1915.

E. G. T. LIDDELL, rev. WALTON OF DETCHANT

Sources *BMJ* (15 May 1915), 1055–6 · *The Lancet* (8 May 1915), 828–30 · Munk, *Roll* · W. Haymaker, ed., *The founders of neurology* (1953) · L. C. McHenry, ed., *Garrison's history of neurology* (1969)
Archives RS | UCL, corresp. with Sir Victor Horsley
Likenesses photograph, 1887, RS · portrait, repro. in Haymaker, ed., *Founders of neurology*
Wealth at death £13,988 2s. 5d.: administration with will, 28 May 1915, *CGPLA Eng. & Wales*

Gowing, Sir Lawrence Burnett (1918–1991), painter and art historian, was born on 21 April 1918 at 53 Stamford Hill, London, the son of Horace Burnett Gowing (d. 1944), master draper, and his wife, Clara Louise Lawrence. His grandfather was a treasurer of the Pawnbroker's Benevolent Society. Gowing's oil painting *Mare Street, Hackney* (1937–8) shows a no. 31 double-decker tram going past the family drapery shop as well as the newly introduced Belisha beacon. He attended the Quaker preparatory school the Downs, Colwall, from 1927 to 1932, where the ex-Slade student Maurice Feild arrived to teach art in 1928 and encouraged the boys to paint outdoors in oil on 15 by 11 inch strawboard during their Wednesday afternoon hobby time. From 1932 he studied at another Quaker school— Leighton Park, Reading—until in 1935 he was privately coached for matriculation, living at home at Oakleigh Park, London. At this stage his parents intended him to become an insurance clerk. But at Leighton Park he had heard Feild's friend W. H. Auden (who taught at the Downs from 1932 to 1935) lecture on film as a career, and Gowing wrote to him for advice. Auden replied from Iceland: 'You only want to become a film director because you think it is the art of the future. It isn't. Art is the art of the future' (Laughton, 176). Auden introduced Gowing to the painter William Coldstream, whose pupil he became in 1936 at 12 Fitzroy Street, London.

This location became the home of the School of Drawing and Painting, set up by Coldstream, Claude Rogers, Victor Pasmore, and Graham Bell. It became known eponymously, after its move in February 1938 to a vacant motor showroom at 314/316 Euston Road, as the *Euston

Sir Lawrence Burnett Gowing (1918–1991), by Lucian Freud, 1982

Road School. Inspired by Cézanne and Degas, and rejecting what they saw as the false realism of the Royal Academy, the pupils struggled to find an objective, verifiable, and, indeed, measurable approach to the painting of their everyday surroundings. Gowing closely identified with Coldstream's penchant for discrete paint strokes, *tache* against *tache*. He befriended another pupil, the ballet critic and writer on art Adrian Durham *Stokes, whose literary executor and editor of his collected works Gowing became. Stokes's *Colour and Form* (1936–7) profoundly influenced Gowing, not only for its discussion of 'surface colour' and the carving and modelling of space, but also for its championing of Cézanne. Stokes's concern for a 'sense of the existent world' was equally influential (*Critical Writings*, 11). Both contributed to Coldstream's retrospective exhibition at the South London Art Gallery, Camberwell, in 1962.

The sale of *Self-Portrait in Oakleigh Avenue* (1936) to Kenneth Clark, director of the National Gallery and also a backer of the School of Drawing and Painting, persuaded Gowing's father to let him become a painter. Having moved into Stokes's old top-floor studio at 6 Fitzroy Street at a rent of £78 a year, Gowing painted chest patients lying out on the iron balconies of University College Hospital, theatrical backdrops, nudes, and portraits, including one of a young Alfie Bass. He survived by selling work and writing for the *Dancing Times*. He was drawn into the life of adjacent Bloomsbury and met Julia Frances Strachey (1901–1979), daughter of Oliver Strachey, codebreaker, widow of Stephen Tomlin, and author of the minor novel *Cheerful Weather for the Wedding* (1932). She was seventeen years his senior. Julia's impression of Gowing—'With his long, slender legs and arms, Lawrence reminded me of a

daddy-long-legs' (Partridge, 162)—did not prevent them moving into 88 Charlotte Street and living together from 1940 to 1948. They married on 28 March 1952, although they then spent much time apart. *Lady with Book* (1941–2), now in the Ashmolean Museum, Oxford, is a portrait of Julia reading Percy Lubbock's *Art of Fiction* in the sitting room at Chilton Foliat, Wiltshire, warmed by a slender white enamel oil stove.

The Second World War broke up the Euston Road School. Gowing's Quaker schooling and Bloomsbury connections lay behind his conscientious objection: remarkably, the tribunal gave him total exemption on condition that he continued to paint! Bombing led to his abandoning London in favour of, first, Chilton Foliat, then Shalbourne, Wiltshire, where the countryside became his prime subject matter. This engagement with landscape was fuelled not only by his various reading of Sturt, Grigson, Piper, and Gilbert White, but by his admiration for Cézanne and Courbet. Writing too became the adjunct to painting: he contributed anonymously *Notes of a Painter* to John Lehmann's Penguin New Writing series, and in 1945 the eccentric dialogue 'Painter and apple', based on a series of fourteen still lifes entitled *Green Apples* (1940–46), to *Arts*. Gowing and his wife returned to London in 1943, first to Paulton Square, then 25 Wellington Square, Chelsea; they were fire-watchers based at Chelsea Public Library.

Before the end of the war, Gowing started to teach at Camberwell School of Arts and Crafts, where Coldstream and Pasmore were recreating the Euston Road School. In 1945 he received his first portrait commission, *Lord Lindsay*, for Balliol College; other portraits included *Cecil Day-Lewis*, *Lord Halifax*, and *Clement Attlee*. The summers of 1946 and 1947 were spent landscape painting in Sutton, between Pulborough and Petworth; he later described his confrontation with nature, stripping off his clothes to make himself 'defenceless against the place' (*Lawrence Gowing*, 30). In 1947, after a chance encounter with Robin Darwin on a bus, he applied for, and in 1948 was somewhat surprisingly appointed to, the post of professor of fine art, Newcastle, where he remained until 1958. In 1948 he had a very successful one-man exhibition at the Leicester Gallery, run by Oliver Brown. In 1949 he was diagnosed as tuberculous and underwent sanatorium treatment. He used this opportunity to write a book on Vermeer, published in 1952, that established his reputation as an art historian. John Pope-Hennessy remarked that the difference between the unrevised and revised versions was that 'in the interval … Lawrence had transposed his text into the key of Adrian Stokes' (Wollheim, 22). In 1954 he organized a major Cézanne exhibition, shown in Edinburgh and the Tate Gallery, in which he controversially challenged the conventional dating of several major works.

In 1959 Gowing became principal of the new Chelsea School of Art, formed from the merger of the Chelsea and Regent Street polytechnics. Under Gowing, Chelsea became a model for art education: art history was integrated with studio practice; an option programme ranging across science, music, philosophy, and literature was introduced; and with Michael Doran's help the foundations of a specialist modern art history library were laid. His lectures were always engaging: for example, he divided, Ruskin-style, painters into those who used red and blue (expressionists) or green and yellow (himself).

Gowing resigned from Chelsea in 1965 in order to become keeper of the British collections and deputy director of the Tate Gallery. The highlights of this period were his re-hanging of Turner's work and two exhibitions in America, 'Turner: imagination and reality', connecting the colour explorations of Turner's later works with the abstract expressionists through the simple expedient of removing their frames, and 'Matisse', both shown at the Museum of Modern Art, New York, in 1966. A preoccupation with Matisse also resulted in an exhibition at the Hayward Gallery (1968) and a film for the Arts Council, *Matisse, a Kind of Paradise* (1969). During this period Gowing's own painting attained its most abstraction in such works as *Wood: Parabolic Perspective* (1963) or *Track through Willis's Wood V* (1964): the abstract qualities were translated into his later, much looser landscapes, which seemed to imitate the effects of watercolour in oil paint.

In 1967, chagrined by his failure to become director of the Tate Gallery, Gowing resigned to become professor of fine art at Leeds University, where he remained until 1975. Having divorced his first wife earlier in the year, on 22 December 1967 he married Jennifer Akam Wallis (b. 1927), lecturer, and daughter of Sydney Herbert Wallis, civil servant with the Board of Trade. He and his second wife set up home at 49 Walham Grove, Fulham, where they brought up three daughters.

After arranging the Hogarth exhibition at the Tate in 1971, Gowing organized in 1973 the 'Watercolours by Cézanne' exhibition at Newcastle and London, which led to his involvement in 'Cézanne: the Late Works', an exhibition (accompanied by a book) at the Museum of Modern Art, New York, the editorship of Cézanne's Basel sketchbooks, and *Cézanne: the Early Works* (1988). He was a member of the Arts Council from 1970 to 1972 and from 1977 to 1981. In 1975 he began a ten-year spell as Slade professor of fine art. This coincided with a stylistic development in his own painting: in 1976 he embarked on a series of figurative painting, using his students and studio assistants to cover his body with paint or spray paint around its naked Vitruvian shape: these were shown to less than critical acclaim at his 1982 retrospective at the Serpentine Gallery. On retirement in 1985 he went to the National Gallery, Washington, as a research fellow, later becoming a curator at the Phillips Collection. Appointed a CBE in 1952, he was made a knight in 1982. He was elected an associate of the Royal Academy in 1978 and a Royal Academician in 1989. He died on 5 February 1991 at Charing Cross Hospital, Fulham, London; he was survived by his second wife and three daughters.

Gowing's enthusiasms were catholic and sometimes eccentric—the minor Welsh landscape painter Thomas Jones, Joseph Beuys, Francis Bacon's use of medical illustration, Lucian Freud, as well as Matisse and Cézanne. His visible and audible enthusiasm, emphasized by his peculiar taste for black leather trousers and a rhetorically effective expectorative stutter, made him a remarkable advocate for painting as seen by a painter: this proved attractive to the wider audience of his two BBC television series, *Three Painters* (1984 and 1986), on Massaccio, Vermeer, Brueghel, Goya, Matisse, and, inevitably, Cézanne.

STEPHEN BURY

Sources *Lawrence Gowing* (1983) · F. Partridge, *Julia: a portrait by herself* (1983) · B. Laughton, *The Euston Road School* (1986) · R. Wollheim, 'In the cause of creativity: a memoir of Lawrence Gowing', *TLS* (5 April 1991) · *The Times* (7 Feb 1991) · *The Independent* (7 Feb 1991) · *The Guardian* (8 Feb 1991) · C. Parry-Crooke, ed., *Contemporary British artists* (1979) · *Lawrence Gowing* (1982) · *WWW*, 1991–5 · *The critical writings of Adrian Stokes*, 1 (1978) · b. cert. · m. cert. [J. A. Wallis] · d. cert.

Archives Chelsea College of Art and Design · Tate collection, corresp. · U. Sussex | Tate collection, corresp. with Lord Clark | FILM Arts Council · BFI NFTVA · BFI NFTVA, documentary footage | SOUND BL NSA, oral history interviews · BL NSA, performance recordings

Likenesses R. Moynihan, oils, 1938, NPG · L. Freud, etching, 1982, priv. coll. [*see illus.*] · Walia, photograph, repro. in Parry-Crooke, ed., *Contemporary British artists*, pl. 19 · photograph, repro. in *The Times*

Wealth at death £814,348: probate, 1991, *CGPLA Eng. & Wales*

Gowing [*née* Elliott], **Margaret Mary** (1921–1998), historian, was born on 26 April 1921 at 58 Tavistock Road, Kensington, London, the youngest among the three children of Ronald Elliott, motor engineer, and his wife, Mabel Donaldson. She was educated at the Portobello Road elementary school in North Kensington before winning a London county council scholarship to Christ's Hospital, Hertford, in 1932. With the aid of further scholarships she went on in 1938 to the London School of Economics, where she took first-class honours in economic history. On 7 June 1944 she married Donald James Graham Gowing (1920/21–1969), a musician; they had two sons. After wartime appointments in the Ministry of Supply and the Board of Trade, her vocation as a historian was fashioned by her work as assistant to Sir Keith Hancock in the Cabinet Office's project for a series of civil histories of the Second World War, a series (begun in 1941) that eventually ran to twenty-seven volumes. While in the Cabinet Office, where she stayed from 1945 to 1959, she published two books: *British War Economy* (1949, with Hancock) and *Civil Industry and Trade* (1952, with Eric Hargreaves). As a member of Sir James Grigg's committee on departmental records, she also made the first of her many contributions to improving procedures for the collection and management of public records in the United Kingdom.

When, in the wake of the Grigg committee's report (1954) and the resulting Public Records Act (1958), the UK Atomic Energy Authority decided to appoint a historian and archivist, Gowing was an ideal candidate and she joined the authority in 1959. Her first task was the ordering, from scratch, of the scientific, technical, and administrative archives of an organization which, though only five years old, presented daunting challenges of size (it had 40,000 employees at the time) and of decentralization (aggravated by dispersion over ten sites). The work gave her unfettered access to unexploited papers, most of them still classified, relating not only to the Atomic Energy Authority but also to the British wartime atomic project and the Ministry of Supply's involvement in the development of atomic energy between 1945 and 1954. It also brought her into contact with many of the scientists and policy makers who had led the various British initiatives, and she seized the opportunity. She once said that at the time of her appointment she 'didn't know an atom from a molecule', but she soon rectified that weakness and won the respect of physicists of the stature of Niels Bohr, Sir James Chadwick, and Rudolf Peierls.

Three large and widely acclaimed volumes followed. The first, published in 1964, was *Britain and Atomic Energy, 1939–1945*. The other two, written with Lorna Arnold, were published as *Independence and Deterrence* in 1974. Together, the volumes offered a meticulously researched account of the making and execution of British nuclear policy in war and peace until 1952, when operation Hurricane, the test of a rather primitive atomic device at Monte Bello off the coast of Australia, finally raised Britain to the rank of the world's third nuclear power. Epitomizing Gowing's belief that official histories could and should achieve the highest academic standards, they also went far beyond the analysis of public documents to lay bare the tensions and suspicions that lurked behind domestic party politics and the vicissitudes of Anglo–American co-operation. They made sense, to a degree unmatched before or since, of the determination, shared by Clement Attlee, Winston Churchill, and many leading scientists and politicians of all parties (though challenged by Henry Tizard and Patrick Blackett), that Britain should have its own bomb. The motives for this determination included defence and more distant aspirations for a civil programme for nuclear power. But an important auxiliary aim was that a British voice should be as powerful as any in international debate. This particular aim, as Gowing described it, was not easily achieved. The leaders of the American atomic energy programme remained unimpressed by Hurricane, and it was only in 1958, after the successful tests of a British hydrogen bomb, that the special relationship with the United States was restored. Growing concern about Soviet scientific and technological expertise, manifested in the launch of the sputnik satellite in 1957, and the personal friendship between President Eisenhower and Harold Macmillan both played their part in this change of heart, following twelve years in which the exchange of information between the two countries had been virtually nonexistent.

By the time when *Independence and Deterrence* appeared Gowing had spent six years as reader in contemporary history at the University of Kent (1966–72) and, in January 1973, she had taken up the newly created chair of the history of science at the University of Oxford. Her time at Kent had been clouded by the death of her husband, Donald Gowing, in 1969 after twenty-five years of marriage, and by disagreements within the university that made a move attractive to her. Although her chair in Oxford was in the modern history faculty, she was never closely involved in faculty affairs, and her closest contacts were with scientists. It was with the support of one of these, the physicist Nicholas Kurti, that she established the Contemporary Scientific Archives Centre; here, as honorary director, she oversaw the cataloguing and deposit in suitable locations of over a hundred collections of the papers of twentieth-century scientists. The venture was of a piece with her wish to see science and technology given a more respected place in British culture. As she insisted in her inaugural lecture at Oxford, published as *What's Science to History or History to Science?* (1975), the frontiers that had set the history of science apart from conventional history were man-made and distorting; and it was the function of the kind of history she wrote to bring the two realms together. Her Wilkins lecture to the Royal Society (1976) developed a different perspective on the problem, tracing a history of British prejudice against science and, more particularly, industrial science going back to Victorian times.

Politically, Gowing was firmly of the left. Her lifelong socialism originated in her memories of a far from comfortable early life and in a keen appreciation of the opportunities that London had offered even to a poor child like herself. That appreciation made her a prominent champion of free entry to national museums and fired her anger at the introduction of charges at the Imperial War Museum (from whose board of trustees she resigned in protest) and the Science Museum in the 1980s. On this as on other matters she was not by nature a compromiser, and her convictions were held with a tenacity that marked equally her belief in the merits of enlightened central government, her dislike of the policies of Margaret Thatcher's administrations, and her judgements of people, both favourable and unfavourable. Within Oxford she never took to the more grandiose facets of college life, but she maintained a special fondness for her own college, Linacre, a modern foundation whose informality squared with her hatred of pomposity in any form.

During her thirteen years in the Oxford chair, Gowing received many honours. These included her appointment as CBE in 1981, invitations to give major public lectures throughout the world, honorary doctorates from the universities of Leeds, Leicester, Manchester, and Bath (where the Contemporary Scientific Archives Centre was housed from 1986), and a Festschrift (*Science, Politics and the Public Good*, 1988, edited by Nicolaas Rupke). But the rarest accolade of her career was her election as a fellow of both the British Academy (1975) and the Royal Society (1988), one that she shared only with Sir Karl Popper and Joseph Needham.

Gowing worked quickly and with an energy that allowed her to balance family life (including raising two sons) with an active involvement in a wide range of organizations whose ideals appealed to her. These organizations included the Labour Party, the Campaign for the Advancement of State Education, of which she was a founder member in the early 1960s, the BBC archives advisory committee, and the National Portrait Gallery, where, as a trustee from 1978 to 1992, she argued for the acquisition of more portraits of scientists and engineers. Between 1978 and 1980, by which time the Grigg system was in need of review, she also served as one of the three members of the inquiry on public records chaired by Sir Duncan Wilson. Such commitments were time-consuming, and they help to explain why she never completed the intended sequel to *Independence and Deterrence*, a sequel that would have covered the years to 1958 in which Britain advanced from the status of a fledgeling nuclear power to one of international importance on both the civil and the military fronts. At the time of her retirement from the Oxford chair in 1986, completion still seemed possible, and she continued until 1993 the part-time association with the UK Atomic Energy Authority that she had maintained at both Kent and Oxford. But it was left for her collaborator Lorna Arnold, in three separate books published between 1987 and 2002, to treat particular aspects of what Gowing had always hoped to produce as an ambitious single volume.

In Gowing's last years advancing illness diminished her capacity for work, leaving her profoundly frustrated. By the time of her death, in Kingston Hospital, Kingston upon Thames, on 7 November 1998, her main legacy remained the magisterial works she had published more than twenty years earlier, analysing a period in which war and post-war rivalries between the great powers had set the relations between science and politics on a new footing.   ROBERT FOX

Sources R. Fox, *The Independent* (20 Nov 1998) · *The Times* (11 Nov 1998) · R. Norton-Taylor, *The Guardian* (9 Nov 1998) · *Daily Telegraph* (23 Nov 1998) · Margaret Gowing's personal papers, MHS Oxf. · papers, Linacre College, Oxford · b. cert. · m. cert. · d. cert. · personal knowledge (2004) · private information (2004)
Archives Linacre College, Oxford, documents · MHS Oxf., corresp. and papers
Likenesses photograph, U. Oxf., faculty of modern history · photograph, priv. coll.; repro. in *The Times* · photograph, priv. coll.; repro. in Norton-Taylor, *The Guardian* · photographs, priv. coll.; repro. in Fox, *The Independent*

Gowland, John (*d.* 1776), apothecary and inventor of Gowland's lotion, was the grandson of Ralph Gowland, attorney and antiquary of Durham, his first cousin being Ralph Gowland (*c.*1722–*c.*1782), an undistinguished MP successively for Durham and Cockermouth. John Gowland did not follow the family tradition of the law; he may have been the John Gowland who was apprenticed to John Marsden, an apothecary at York, on 27 September 1720. Possessing good social connections, about 1736 Gowland secured the post of apothecary in the household of Frederick, prince of Wales.

Gowland clearly prided himself on his professional integrity, and chafed at having to dispense medicines prescribed by court physicians all too ready to blame most ills on impure blood and to rely mainly on sudorifics, purges, and emetics. In 1743 Elizabeth Chudleigh, the future countess of Bristol, was appointed maid of honour to Frederick's wife, Augusta, princess of Wales. Miss Chudleigh had from a precociously early age realized that her face, and other bodily parts that she was not shy of exposing as the occasion called for, were her fortune. When her

skin became blotchy and opaque, the royal doctors subjected her to purging, sea-bathing, and other ineffectual treatments, while she attempted to disguise her blemishes with patches and paints. Gowland's diagnosis was that the pores had become clogged from make-up or other causes, and he therefore devised a lotion with which to bathe regularly the face, hands, or any other affected area. Its action would release a form of scurf that could be rubbed away, allowing the skin to breathe naturally and so recover its customary bloom. Freckles and other disfigurements would likewise vanish, and pallor be corrected by a renewed supply of blood to the face. In reality the lotion contained not only bitter almonds and sugar but also a small quantity of corrosive sublimate, a derivative of sulphuric acid and thus powerful enough to remove the top skin. John Corry, in *Quack Doctors Dissected* (1801, 45), condemned its action as follows:

> There's the lotion of Gowland that flays ladies' faces,
> Distorting the features of our modern graces.

In spite of containing a noxious and poisonous substance the lotion restored Miss Chudleigh almost instantly to pulchritude, and society ladies anxious to emulate her schoolgirl complexion beat a path to the door of Gowland's residence in Bond Street, London, where the lotion was concocted and sold. However, he refused to add a hyperbolic adjective to what he named simply Gowland's lotion, or to advertise it in the press, relying entirely on personal recommendation. That celebrity led to his appointment in 1760 as apothecary to George III, an office he held until his death. For her part, once she embarked on her undulating career as a gold-digger *par excellence*, Miss Chudleigh was by no means happy about the story of her cure being publicized, and it did not appear in print until after her death.

The demand for Gowland's lotion, and its high price of 10*s.* 6*d.* a quart bottle, made him a wealthy man; in later life he owned much property and had £23,000 out in personal loans. As he and his wife, Elizabeth, left no children, he bestowed handsome legacies on his cousins Ralph Gowland and Thomas Gowland, and their families. The secret formula of his lotion he entrusted to Thomas Vincent, clerk to the royal music closet and principal oboist in the king's band, who had been his close friend since early in their court days. When Gowland died at Bath on 3 August 1776 Vincent took over the making of the lotion and inherited the business on Elizabeth Gowland's death just over three years later.

Vincent's troubles began when he married as his second wife Maria Elizabeth, a glazier's widow. Having moved into her house in Davies Street, London, he bought the lease and the contents, which he injudiciously placed in her sole name. During his absence abroad she and some confederates began to make their own variety of the lotion, clearly inferior, as she did not know the exact formula. In order to end relations with her Vincent had to leave home; together with his son-in-law, Robert Dickinson, he started up production at 55 Long Acre. A war of pamphlets between husband and wife ensued. He was compelled to begin advertising, and strove to build up a network of retailers in all cities and towns of Britain. Vincent died apparently in 1800, and Dickinson clearly lacked his entrepreneurial vigour, so Mrs Vincent's counterfeit version captured most of the trade.

The name of Gowland might have been entirely forgotten, had not Jane Austen in *Persuasion* (1818) made Sir Walter Elliot compliment his neglected daughter Anne for her greatly improved complexion, which had become cleaner and fresher. 'I should recommend Gowland, the constant use of Gowland, during the spring months. Mrs Clay has been using it at my recommendation, and you see what it has done for her. You see how it has carried away her freckles' (*Persuasion*, ed. R. W. Chapman, 145–6). Jane Austen may have read the puffing pamphlets, with their emphasis on curing pallor and freckles, one having been published in 1792 by the retail agent R. Cruttwell in Bath. Curiously enough, Emma Elizabeth Chamberlayne, her second cousin once removed, in 1766 had married John Gowland's second cousin Thomas Gowland junior, a West India merchant. Fascinated though she was by the ramifications of her extended family, Jane Austen probably never knew of this distant kinship with the man she had immortalized.   T. A. B. CORLEY

Sources T. Corley, 'The shocking history of Gowland's Lotion', *Jane Austen Society Report* (1999), 37–41 · T. Vincent and R. Dickinson, *On the power and effect of Gowland's lotion* [n.d., c.1793] · T. Vincent and R. Dickinson, *An account of the nature and effects of Gowland's lotion* (c.1792) · HoP, *Commons* · J. Austen, *Persuasion* (1933), vol. 5 of *The novels of Jane Austen*, ed. R. W. Chapman, 145–6, 272 · *GM*, 1st ser., 46 (1776), 386 · *Town and Country Magazine*, 8 (1776), 503 · *Bath Chronicle* (6 Jan 1814); repr. in J. Austen, *Persuasion*, ed. R. W. Chapman (1933), 272 · PRO, PROB 11/1022, 1058/456 · P. J. Wallis and R. V. Wallis, *Eighteenth century medics*, 2nd edn (1988)

Gowran. For this title name *see* Fitzpatrick, Richard, first Baron Gowran (c.1662–1727).

Gowrie. For this title name *see* Ruthven, William, fourth Lord Ruthven and first earl of Gowrie (c.1543–1584); Ruthven, John, third earl of Gowrie (1577/8–1600); Ruthven, Alexander Gore Arkwright Hore-, first earl of Gowrie (1872–1955).

Goyder, George Woodroffe (1826–1898), surveyor, was born on 29 January 1826 in Liverpool, third son and fourth of eight children of David George Goyder (1796–1878), doctor and Swedenborgian minister, and his wife, Sarah Etherington (1794–1886). Educated at Glasgow high school, Goyder worked for firms making precision and surveying instruments in Glasgow, Liverpool, and Warrington. He migrated to Sydney, New South Wales, in 1848, and to Adelaide, South Australia, in 1850, as a government draughtsman. In January 1851 he joined the lands and survey department, and on 10 December married, in the Anglican pro-cathedral, Christ Church, North Adelaide, Frances Mary Smith (1825–1870), daughter of John Smith, who had come to Adelaide from Bristol in 1849. His dedication to his work often parted them. About August 1853 he became a chief clerk, in January 1857 assistant surveyor-general, and on 29 May 1861 surveyor-general. He held this post for thirty-three years, and was thus 'king of the Lands Department' when it was South Australia's most important department, and when the colony's chief public activities were land exploration and settlement, and debating whether to favour large landholders or small.

Goyder travelled tirelessly, each year riding thousands of miles, often at his own expense, to supervise his field staff and to value or survey land. In June 1857 he wrongly reported the Lake Torrens region in South Australia's north to be well watered; he was misled by floodwaters from further north. In 1866 he published a map showing the southern limit of those pastoral runs which needed rent relief because of recurrent drought. 'Goyder's line' still effectively divides South Australia into agricultural and pastoral land, but from 1874 aspiring farmers crossed it to grow wheat in the north. In the few wet years that followed they did well; when the normal dry years returned they were forced from their farms.

In 1868–9 Goyder took 131 men by sea to the Northern Territory, then under South Australia's jurisdiction, to select a site for a capital. He recommended Palmerston (now Darwin) on Port Darwin, surveyed the site and a further 665,000 acres, and wrote an extensive report on the region's pastoral, agricultural, and mineral potential. He was by then considered the colony's ablest public servant. His travelling, voluminous official writing, and command of his multiplying tasks earned him the nickname Little Energy. He had been inspector of mines and valuator of runs since 1861. In 1874, as the colony's railway system began a rapid expansion, he became chairman of the railways commission. In 1875 he was chief of those who established a forest board, perhaps the first in the empire, for the economic management of trees, and until 1881 was its chairman. He saw the value of water regulation, introducing a wide range of storage and drainage measures. He drew a model town plan, based on Adelaide's, on which most of the 160 South Australian towns laid down in his time were established. He combined such wide-ranging activities with meeting ceaseless demands for closer settlement surveys until he retired on 30 June 1894.

Goyder possessed the essential qualities of a pioneer: energy, judgement, health, and a good eye for ground. He was strict but fair, and most of his subordinates liked him; and while anyone connected with the disposal of public land will make enemies, in October 1894 his fellow colonists showed their regard by giving him 1000 sovereigns. He was appointed CMG in January 1889. His wife died on 8 April 1870 in Bristol, England, of an accidental overdose of laudanum; they had nine children. On 20 November 1871 he married, in St Luke's Church, Adelaide, her sister, Ellen Priscilla Smith (1834–1899); they had a son and twin daughters. Goyder died of cerebral embolism at Warrakilla, his home at Biggs Flat, near Adelaide, on 2 November 1898, and was buried in Stirling cemetery, Adelaide.

BILL GAMMAGE

Sources private information (2004) · M. Williams, 'George Woodroffe Goyder', *Proceedings of the Royal Geographical Society of Australasia, South Australian Branch*, 79 (1978), 1–21 · *AusDB* · M. Kerr, *The surveyors* (1971) · m. certs. · d. cert.

Likenesses photographs, 1861–80, State Library of South Australia, Adelaide, Mortlock Library of South Australiana, South Australia archives · portraits, priv. coll.

Wealth at death £4000: *AusDB*

Grabe, John Ernest (1666–1711), patristic and biblical scholar, was born at Königsberg, east Prussia, on 30 June/10 July 1666, the son of Martin Sylvester Grabe (1627–1686), professor of theology and history at the University of Königsberg, and Sophia Behmen (*d.* after 1686), daughter of Michael Behmen, professor of theology at the same university. On 2 November 1682 he matriculated at the University of Königsberg and received his MA on 26 April 1685.

Until 1694 Grabe was lecturer in history and rhetoric, but soon became involved in the controversies about the eirenic theology of George Calixtus (so-called syncretism) then raging in the Lutheran church in east Prussia. This instilled doubts about Lutheranism in his mind and he became inclined towards joining the Roman Catholic church. He first, however, in 1694 presented a statement of his difficulties to the ecclesiastical consistory of Samland in Prussia. The replies to this memorial by three Lutheran divines commissioned by the elector of Brandenburg were printed in 1695. Meanwhile Grabe was arrested and brought to the fortress of Pillau and was subsequently detained in Königsberg until May 1695, when he found it safer to seek refuge in Breslau. Unsettled by the reply of Philipp Jacob Spener, one of the three Lutheran theologians, Grabe eventually found his way to Berlin and conferred with Daniel Ernst Jablonski, bishop of the Moravians, about his future. He took Jablonski's advice and turned to England in spring 1697 where he was supported by Jablonski's friends.

Eventually Grabe settled in Oxford, and there in 1698 published the first volume of his *Spicilegium ss. patrum ut et haereticorum seculi i–iii post Christum natum*. In July 1700 he was ordained deacon by Dr William Lloyd, bishop of Worcester. In the same year he was made chaplain of Christ Church by way of maintaining him; it is probable he never performed the office. In 1700 he published Justin Martyr's *First Apology*, and in 1702 St Irenaeus's *Contra omnes haereses libri quinque*. Grabe held his chaplaincy at Christ Church until 1703 when he began to reside at St Edmund Hall, then a favourite resort of the nonjurors. During the reign of Queen Anne a pension was settled on him, and he was employed upon printing the Alexandrine manuscript of the Septuagint, then in the Royal Library at St James's. At Harley's suggestion, Queen Anne presented £60 towards the printing costs.

In 1703 Grabe revised the scholia for John Gregory's Greek Testament, which was printed at Oxford, and in the same year he published a beautiful edition in folio of Bishop George Bull's Latin works. He now set to work upon the publication of the Codex Alexandrinus, and in 1705 he published an account of the manuscript, giving it preference to the Vatican manuscript, together with three specimens of his intended edition. The University of Oxford conferred on him the degree of DD on 27 April

1706. The king of Prussia sent him a present, and subscriptions came in from all parts.

In 1707 Grabe published *Septuaginta interpretum tomus I*, the first volume of his edition of the Septuagint based on the Alexandrine codex and improved by the Hexapla of Origen. In 1709 he published the fourth and last volume. The second volume, edited by Francis Lee MD, a learned physician, from Grabe's manuscript, was published in 1719. Lee died in that year, and the third volume, under the editorship of George Wigan DD, of Christ Church, came out in 1720. All the volumes were from Grabe's transcript. This edition remained one of the standard editions of the Septuagint before the discovery of the Codex Sinaiticus and the Chester Beatty papyri and was reprinted several times, even in Russia. In 1710 he published a *Dissertatio de variis vitiis LXX interpretum ante B. Origenis aevum illatis*, and explained why he had departed from the original plan of his publication.

Shortly before his death Grabe had a controversy with the antitrinitarian William Whiston, who had claimed Grabe's assent to his views as to the authority of the apostolic constitutions. Grabe therefore published in 1711 *An Essay upon Two Arabic MSS. in the Bodleian Library*, in which he expressed doubts about the value of the apostolic constitutions.

On 22 August 1711 Grabe wrote to Robert Harley complaining of his broken health, the non-payment of his pension for the past twelve months, and consequently his having run into debt of £60. His pension was paid, together with a gift of £50 from Harley. He died in London on 3 November 1711. He wished upon his deathbed that it should be known that he died in the faith and communion of the Church of England. He inclined to nonjuring views and in his last illness received communion from the nonjuror bishop George Hickes. He also supported a plan for the introduction of episcopacy into Prussia, and the adoption of a liturgy after the English model. He was buried on 8 November 1711 in the church of St Pancras, not, as is frequently stated, in Westminster Abbey, where Harley afterwards erected a cenotaph. He left a great mass of manuscripts, which he bequeathed to George Hickes for life, and afterwards to George Smalridge, from whom they passed to the Bodleian.

There are two small but interesting pieces by Grabe that were published after his death, namely 'Liturgia Graeca', his own attempt to revise the Anglican liturgy, published by Christoph Matthaeus Pfaff at the end of *Irenaei fragmenta anecdota* (1715); and *De forma consecrationis eucharistiae* (1721), a defence of the Greek Orthodox church against the Roman Catholic church, which was edited by an anonymous nonjuror (probably Thomas Wagstaffe) in both Latin and English. Grabe was certainly the most outstanding patristic and biblical scholar of late seventeenth-century England.

G. H. Thomann

Sources G. Thomann, 'John Ernest Grabe (1666–1711): Lutheran syncretist and Anglican patristic scholar', *Journal of Ecclesiastical History*, 43 (1992), 414–27 · M. S. Grabe, 'D. J. E. Graben Leben Tod und Schrifften', *Acta Borussica*, 1 (1730), 1–27 · G. Hickes, 'Preface', in J. E. Grabe, *Some instances of the defects and omissions in Mr Whiston's* *collection* (1712) • *Reliquiae Hearnianae: the remains of Thomas Hearne*, ed. P. Bliss, 2 vols. (1857) • *Remarks and collections of Thomas Hearne*, ed. C. E. Doble and others, 11 vols., OHS, 2, 7, 13, 34, 42–3, 48, 50, 65, 67, 72 (1885–1921), vols. 1–3 • C. F. Secretan, *Memoirs of the life and times of the pious Robert Nelson* (1860), 219–25 • G. Smalridge, *Two speeches made in the theatre at Oxford* (1714) • 'Einige Zweifel', *Bremische und Verdische Bibliothek*, 2 (1756), 43–56 • G. Thomann, 'John Ernest Grabe's liturgies: two unknown Anglican liturgies of the seventeenth century', *Studies in English church history* (1993), 89–126 • W. Jardine Grisbrooke, *Anglican liturgies of the seventeenth and eighteenth centuries* (1958) • D. H. Arnoldt, *Ausführliche und mit Urkunden versehene Historie der Königsbergischen Universität*, 2 (Königsberg, 1746) • *DNB*

Archives BL, Add. MS 4253, fol. 44 • Bodl. Oxf., corresp. and papers • Geheimes Staatsarchiv, Berlin, Preussischer Kulturbesitz, MS Etatsministerium 38, Geistliche Sachen Königsberg, EM 38e, EM 139: Univ. Königsberg • LPL, MS ARC L40.2.L.29 | BL, MS Harl. 3985 • Bodl. Oxf., MS Rawl. C851

Likenesses F. Bird, marble effigy, 1711, Westminster Abbey, London • engraving, repro. in Grabe, 'D. J. E. Graben Leben Tod und Schrifften', frontispiece • engraving, repro. in J. E. Grabe, ed., *Septuaginta interpretum*, 1 (1700), frontispiece

Wealth at death see Thomann, 'John Ernest Grabe', 424; Grabe, 'D. J. E. Graben', 22; BL Add. MS 4253, fol. 44, copy, 22 Aug 1711

Grabham, Elizabeth. *See* Surr, Elizabeth (*b.* 1825/6, *d.* in or after 1898).

Grabu, Louis (*fl.* 1665–1694), composer and musician, was described as 'of Shalon [possibly Cape Salou] in Catalunnia', though he always seems to have been regarded as a Frenchman. He was appointed composer to Charles II on 31 March 1665, soon after his arrival in England. Three days later he was married in St James's Palace to Catherine de Loes 'of Paris'. Almost a year later (25 March 1666) he was made master of the king's musick at the usual salary of £200 a year, and successively displaced John Banister, first as leader of the king's band of twenty-four violins (24 December 1666), then as leader of the select band of twelve violins (14 March 1667). The reason for this rapid advancement is not clear, but it may have had something to do with complaints (which were upheld) that Banister had held back money due to the band and, according to Anthony Wood, 'for some saucy words spoken to his maj[esty], viz. when he [the king] called for the Italian violins, he made answer that he had better have the English' (Ashbee and Lasocki, 502). Not surprisingly Banister was peeved, and Pelham Humfrey gave his opinion to Samuel Pepys on 15 November 1667 that Grabu 'understands nothing nor can play on any instrument and so cannot compose' (Pepys, 8.530). Pepys was in two minds about him. The previous month, having heard an English song by Grabu he 'was never so little pleased with a consort of music in my life—the manner of setting of words and repeating them out of order ... makes me sick'. On the other hand he had to admit that 'the instrumental music he had brought by practice to play very just' (ibid., 8.458).

For the marriage of the duke of York and Mary of Modena on 30 March 1674, Grabu seems to have rewritten and expanded the music for *Ariadne, or, The Marriage of Bacchus*, originally composed by Pierre Perrin; this was acted by the Royal Academy of Music at the Theatre Royal, Covent Garden. The opera, however, was not a success, though whether this had anything to do with the quality of the music cannot be said since the music does not survive. For whatever reason (possibly as a result of the Test Act), Grabu was replaced as master of the king's musick by Nicholas Staggins on 29 September 1675. He successfully petitioned the king for £627 9s. 6d. arrears of salary (5 May 1677), and, together with his wife and three small children, was granted a pass to go to France on 31 March 1679.

With the support of the duke of York, Grabu was back in England in the autumn of 1683, and wrote music for *A Pastoral in French*, engraved and published in 1684. He was also engaged to provide the music for John Dryden's opera *Albion and Albanius*, written to celebrate twenty-five years of the Restoration but thwarted by Charles II's death in February 1685, three months short of the anniversary. The fact that its performance in early June coincided with the duke of Monmouth's rebellion took some of the shine off the occasion; nor could the quality of the music—or Dryden's treatment of the subject for that matter—prolong the run beyond six nights. The music (published in 1687) is thoroughly French and outside the musical traditions of the English stage. At different times, however, Grabu did contribute songs and instrumental pieces to various plays, including Shadwell's *Timon of Athens* (1678), Lee's *Mithridates* (1678), *Oedipus* (1678) by Dryden and Lee, and Rochester's *Valentinian* (1684). Grabu remained in London until 3 December 1685, when he returned to Paris, but he was back in England again in 1687. His name appears in advertisements for a concert at 'Mr Smith's in Charles-Street, Covent Garden' in 1694, but on 4 December that year he and his family were given passes to travel to either Holland or Flanders. Thereafter nothing is known about him.

Most writers, echoing Edward J. Dent, have been dismissive of Grabu as a composer, and although he came in for some public ridicule in his own time he was probably, all things considered, not so incompetent as has been suggested. Indeed, given that Locke was dead and Purcell had yet to prove himself as an opera composer, Dryden was perhaps no more than fair when he said: 'When any of our countrymen excel him, I shall be glad, for the sake of old England, to be shown my error; in the meantime, let virtue be commended, though in the person of a stranger' (*Albion and Albanius*, 1685, preface). IAN SPINK

Sources Highfill, Burnim & Langhans, *BDA*, 6.290–94 • A. Ashbee and D. Lasocki, eds., *A biographical dictionary of English court musicians, 1485–1714*, 1 (1998), 502–5 • Pepys, *Diary*

Grace, Edward Mills (1841–1911), cricketer, was born on 28 November 1841 at Downend, near Bristol. He was the third of five sons (W. G. *Grace being the fourth) of Dr Henry Mills Grace (1808–1871) and his wife, Martha, daughter of George Pocock, a schoolmaster and evangelist. Both his father and his maternal uncle fostered an interest in cricket, and all the family practised from early childhood in the orchard of their home, Chestnuts, in Downend. After his early education at Kem Goodenough House School, Ealing, Middlesex, and Mr Kemp's academy, Long Ashton, near Bristol, Grace studied medicine at the Bristol medical school and qualified MRCS (London) and LRCP

Edward Mills Grace (1841–1911), by Barraud & Jerrard

(Edinburgh) in 1865 and LSA in 1866. In 1869 he began practice in Thornbury, Gloucestershire, where he remained all his life, holding a number of local offices. He was coroner for west Gloucestershire from 1875 to 1909. He was married four times, in 1868, 1885 (to Annie Louise Robinson), 1902, and 1907; three of his wives predeceased him. From his four marriages there were five sons and four daughters.

In his youth a good athlete and fast runner, Grace was the first of his family to become famous at cricket. On 7 August 1855, at the age of thirteen, he was included in the 22-man team for West Gloucestershire against the All England eleven, a travelling side who played against 'odds' (teams of more than eleven players). William Clarke, its secretary and manager, acknowledged Grace's promise by presenting him with a bat. He first appeared at Lord's in July 1861, playing for an invitation side called South Wales against the MCC, and in the next year he very briefly established a position as one of the finest all-rounders in England. For the MCC against the Gentlemen of Kent, at Canterbury in 1862, he carried his bat through the innings, scoring 192 not out, and took all ten wickets in the Kent second innings with his slow underarm bowling. He also made the first of many appearances (1862–86) for the Gentlemen against the Players, often playing with his brothers W. G. Grace and George Frederick Grace.

In 1863, when he made over 3000 runs and took over 300 wickets, Grace played an all-round part in the defeat of the All England eleven, by an innings and 20 runs, by a Bristol twenty-two. This led to an invitation to tour Australia in 1863–4 with George Parr's team. His century for a Lansdown eighteen at Bath in 1865 against the All England eleven was 'an epoch-making event, as such achievements against the All England team were almost unheard of'. These were the words of his brother W. G., who from now on eclipsed him in fame and performance. The three Graces played for England against the Australians in 1880, in what was later regarded as the first test match in England. It was Edward's only international match.

With his two brothers, Grace helped to establish Gloucestershire as a first-class county and to win the county championship in 1876 and 1877. He was an efficient but autocratic secretary of Gloucestershire (1871–1909), for which he was paid about £60 a year in expenses. One committee minute recorded: 'Present: E. M. Grace and that's all.' On his retirement he received a testimonial of £600 and a walking-stick, which his increased lameness necessitated. His reward was well earned: he had worked for many years without any secretarial help and his prodigious memory allowed him to collect subscriptions as he walked around the ground and—without making notes—send off receipts the following morning.

Grace was a rapid scorer and forceful hitter, although unorthodox in style and cross-batted. He was one of the first to employ the 'pull' stroke, hitting good-length balls from off stump or outside to the on boundary with consummate ease. His defence was less sound. His nerve, judgement, and speed made him the best fielder at point of his day, taking the ball almost off the bat. Grace ceased to play in first-class cricket in 1896, but played almost until his death for the Thornbury team, which he managed and captained for thirty-five years. For twenty-five of those years the committee never met. In 1909, at the age of sixty-eight, he took 119 wickets for them, but in a game a year later had to be taken off the field, exhausted. He scored just over 10,000 runs in first-class cricket and took 305 wickets. In all cricket he made over 76,000 runs and secured over 12,000 wickets. He was a small man, bewhiskered rather than bearded, sometimes obstreperous and never quite able to come to terms with the greater success of his brother. Nevertheless, the abiding memory of his contemporaries was of his kindness and humour. He died of a cerebral haemorrhage on 20 May 1911 at his home, Park House, in Thornbury, the scene of so many of his successes, and was buried in Downend parish churchyard.

W. B. OWEN, rev. GERALD M. D. HOWAT

Sources F. S. Ashley-Cooper, *Edward Mills Grace* (1916) • A. G. Powell and S. C. Caple, *The Graces, E. M., W. G. and G. F.* (1948) • A. Haygarth, *Arthur Haygarth's cricket scores and biographies*, 15 vols. (1862–1925) • *Wisden* (1890) • *Wisden* (1900) • *Wisden* (1912) • 'Chats on the cricket field', *Cricket Field* (2 June 1894), 143–5 • E. M. Grace, *The trip to Australia* (1864) • *The Lancet* (27 May 1911)

Likenesses photographs, *c.*1870–1888, Marylebone Cricket Club, Lord's, London • double portrait, photograph, *c.*1880 (with W. G.

Grace), Marylebone Cricket Club, Lord's, London · photograph, c.1900, repro. in Ashley-Cooper, *Edward Mills Grace* · Barraud & Jerrard, photograph, Marylebone Cricket Club, Lord's, London [*see illus.*]

Wealth at death £6721 2s. 5d.: resworn probate, 11 July 1911, *CGPLA Eng. & Wales*

Grace [*née* Hodgkiss], **Mary** (*d.* 1799/1800), painter, was the daughter of a shoemaker named Hodgkiss. She appears to have been self-taught and, possibly with the help of Stephen Slaughter, a picture conservator, attained proficiency as a portrait painter. Like many women artists in London in this period, she seems to have worked as a copyist but she also exhibited ambitious works in her own name, all of which are untraced. On 10 December 1744 she married Thomas Grace in London. In 1762, as Mrs Grace, she exhibited with the Incorporated Society of Artists, sending a portrait of herself, a whole-length of a young lady, *A Ballad Singer*, and *An Old Woman's Head*. In 1763, as well as a portrait of Mr Grace, she showed *Beggars* and *Five Senses*. She continued to exhibit up to 1769, sending in 1765 *The Death of Sigismunda*, and in 1767 *Antigonus, Seleucus, and Stratonice*.

In 1770 Mary Grace's husband owned property in Hommerton, Hackney, Middlesex; after his death (in late 1770 or in 1771) she took responsibility for this but when she died (in late 1799 or in 1800) she was living in central London in Weymouth Street. She left a substantial bequest to her daughter (£1300) and property in England and Ireland to her son. Her own portrait was engraved and published in 1785. A portrait by her of the Revd Thomas Bradbury was engraved in mezzotint by John Faber in 1749, and again by Jonathan Spilsbury. With Mary Moser, Angelica Kauffmann, and Maria Cosway she was adjudged by contemporaries as exemplary of the view that women could acquire independence as professional artists.

L. H. CUST, *rev.* MARCIA POINTON

Sources M. Pointon, *Strategies for showing: women, possession and representation in English visual culture, 1665–1800* (1997) · F. Fitzgerald [C. Taylor], ed., *The artist's repository and drawing magazine, exhibiting the principles of the polite arts in their various branches*, 4 (1788), 137–41 · Hackney parish church rate books, Hackney Archives Department, London · will, 28 May 1800, PRO, PROB 11/1342, sig. 366 · Graves, *Artists*, 3rd edn · Graves, *Soc. Artists* · Anderton catalogues [exhibition catalogues, Society of Artists, BM, print room] · E. Edwards, *Anecdotes of painters* (1808); facs. edn (1970) · IGI

Likenesses M. Grace, self-portrait, stipple, pubd 1785, BM, NPG; repro. in *The artists' repository* (1770–80), vol. 4

Wealth at death £1300: will, PRO, PROB 11/1342, sig. 366

Grace, Richard (*c.*1616–1691), army officer, was born probably at Courtstown, Tullaroan, co. Kilkenny, the third son of Robert Grace (*d. c.*1640), sometimes described as twenty-third baron of Courtstown, and his wife, Eleanor, daughter of David Condon of co. Cork. In 1637 he purchased an estate of 600 Irish acres at Moyelly, King's county. His family was Roman Catholic, but allied to their relative Ormond, the Irish royalist leader. After rebels plundered his estate in the wake of the 1641 rising, he went to England, probably with one of the first contingents of Irish troops sent by Ormond in 1643 to reinforce

Charles I. By 1644 he was a captain in command of a troop in Prince Rupert's cavalry regiment. In 1645 he transferred to the command of Colonel William Legge, with whom he saw frequent action, some of it of a partisan character. Returning to Ireland after the fall of Oxford in 1646, he joined Ormond. In 1648, with the rank of major, he was appointed governor of Birr. In 1649–50, as lieutenant-colonel of a cavalry regiment, he participated in Ormond's lacklustre manoeuvres to obstruct Cromwell's advance through south Leinster and north Munster. In 1651–2 he played a leading role in the conduct of an effective partisan war against the Commonwealth army. His forces ranged through Leinster, making good use of the bogs as places of refuge, from which to attack outposts and small parties of the enemy, drive stock, and burn stores. Promoted colonel in 1652, he took an oath to 'uphold the Roman Catholic religion, his majesty's just prerogatives and the liberty of my nation' (Kelly, 26.242). He defied orders to surrender to the parliamentarians, who placed a reward of £300 on his head. After several skirmishes he suffered a heavy defeat while west of the Shannon at Loughrea, and in August 1652 finally surrendered on terms to Colonel Hierome Sankey at Birr. He was the last Irish commander of importance to submit.

Grace was permitted to bring 1200 men into the service of Spain. Posted to Catalonia, he defected with his regiment to the French army in the summer of 1653. This move infuriated the Spaniards and greatly embarrassed the remainder of the Irish officers in Spain, who denounced him in the strongest terms. Possibly he acted at the behest of Charles II, who was then in Paris, although it was afterwards alleged that his defection was prompted by the bad treatment his regiment had endured in Spain. In the French army he served under Turenne at the siege of Senay in 1654. At the duke of York's request he changed allegiance once again in 1656 by transferring to Flanders with his regiment, by then much depleted, to form part of a new royalist force in the Spanish service. Spanish reluctance to re-employ him was overcome by incorporating his men into Ormond's Irish regiment, which Grace, with the rank of lieutenant-colonel, in reality commanded. In 1658 he fought at the battle of the Dunes. His regiment formed part of the reserve, and he succeeded in preserving it from destruction when the Spaniards and their allies were defeated. In November of that year he succeeded Ormond as colonel of the Irish regiment. Charles II praised his 'faithful and constant adherence and his important services beyond the seas' (Kelly, 26.259). He was close to the duke of York, the future James II, who favourably noticed him in his memoirs. He became the duke's chamberlain, accompanying him to England at the restoration. Thereafter his time was divided between Ireland and London, where he seems to have been a minor figure at court.

Named in Charles II's 1660 declaration as one of those who had served him in exile, Grace was pardoned and granted an immediate pension of £100 per month, pending the recovery of his confiscated property. He crossed to

Ireland with a coach and six horses in 1662. His connection to the royal family and his links to Ormond ensured that Moyelly was restored to him in 1664, and a decade later he survived a legal challenge aimed at ejecting him from his estate. In 1666 he was active in negotiating an end to tory activity in co. Kilkenny. He acquired further property in King's county, Kildare, and Dublin. He was granted the remission of all quit rents. He gained lucrative rights to establish manors, and to hold fairs and weekly markets. His wife was Sarah Tucker, a native of Kent. In 1665 Frances (d. 1717), their only child, married Robert Grace, heir to John Grace of Courtstown, his grandnephew. He used his influence to assist his Carroll cousins, including Charles Carroll, founder of the distinguished Maryland dynasty, who is thought to have benefited from his support and connections before moving to America. An annuity of £300 per annum, bestowed on him in 1676, was confirmed to him and his son-in-law on the accession of James II in 1685 for 'his long and faithful service to the crown' (CSP dom., 1685, 217).

In 1687, with the widespread introduction of Catholic officers into the Irish army, 'old Dick Grace' was given a company in Sir Thomas Newcomen's regiment of foot, later transferring to the infantry regiment raised by his kinsman Colonel John Grace. His principal military responsibility was the security of the strategically important fortress town of Athlone, of which he was appointed governor in 1687. He dealt firmly with local protestants, levying money on them for the repair of Athlone Castle. However, he treated the Quaker William Edmundson with kindness when he was brought a prisoner to Athlone by Irish rapparees (partisans), and released him from confinement at the first opportunity. In the summer of 1690, after the Boyne defeat in July, Athlone moved to the front line of hostilities when the Jacobite army withdrew behind the Shannon. King William sent the Scottish general James Douglas with 7500 troops to capture Athlone. Grace burned the part of Athlone on the east bank of the river at Douglas's approach, retiring with the garrison of 2000 across the river to the west town and breaking down the bridge. When Douglas arrived, Grace defiantly fired his pistol over the head of the Williamite drummer sent to summon his surrender, declaring it to be the only terms he would make and promising to eat his boots when his rations were exhausted. An artillery bombardment by the Williamites caused little damage, and Douglas's men could make no headway in their attempts to find a way across the river. With Grace showing no sign of capitulation, Douglas broke off the siege after a week and withdrew, accompanied by the remaining protestants of the locality. Grace's defence of Athlone was widely acclaimed. He had preserved the line of the Shannon, and after many other garrisons had surrendered, his determined resistance helped to shore up the flagging Jacobite morale immediately prior to the critical first siege of Limerick. It was a considerable achievement, which won the praise of contemporaries and demonstrated the courage, determination, and professional competence which were the hallmarks of his military career.

During the following winter Grace ceased to be governor of Athlone, probably because of his advanced years. He was present in the town during the great siege of 1691, where, defiant to the end, he was killed on 28 June, two days before the final successful Williamite assault. According to local tradition he was buried in St Mary's Church. As an attainted Jacobite his property was confiscated after the war. The death of his son-in-law from wounds received at the battle of Aughrim (1691) resulted in the confiscation of the 7500 acre Courtstown estate, although Frances Grace was allowed to retain her jointure house at Inchmore Castle, co. Kilkenny, until her death in 1717.   HARMAN MURTAGH

Sources J. J. Kelly, 'Colonel Richard Grace, governor of Athlone [6 pts]', *Irish Ecclesiastical Record*, 4th ser., 26 (1909), 39–53, 127–45, 240–60; 4th ser., 32 (1912), 399–415, 490–504; 5th ser., 2 (1913), 22–52 • S. Grace, *Memoirs of the family of Grace*, 2 vols. (1823), 1.1–48, and pl. • D. Murtagh, 'Colonel Richard Grace', *Irish Sword*, 1 (1949–53), 173, and pl. • D. Bryan, 'Colonel Richard Grace, 1651–1652', *Irish Sword*, 4 (1959–60), 43–51 • J. Barratt, 'The last cavalier', *Military Illustrated*, 138 (Nov 1999), 34–41 • H. Murtagh and M. O'Dwyer, eds., *Athlone besieged: eyewitness and other contemporary accounts of the sieges of Athlone, 1690 and 1691* (Athlone, 1991), 10–14, 75, 77 • H. Murtagh, 'The siege of Athlone, 1690', *Journal of the Old Athlone Society*, 1/2 (1970–71), 84–7 • M. K. Walsh, 'The Wild Goose tradition', *Irish Sword*, 17 (1987–90), 4–15 • *The life of James the Second, king of England*, ed. J. S. Clarke, 1 (1816), 268–9, 345, 354; 2 (1816) • L. Cox, 'Historic Moyelly, home of Colonel Richard Grace', *Journal of the Old Athlone Society*, 1/2 (1970–71), 238–41 • B. Jennings, ed., *Wild geese in Spanish Flanders, 1582–1700*, IMC (1964), 441, 612–13, 616–17, 621 • J. Barratt, 'King Charles' forgotten army', *Military Illustrated*, 110 (July 1997), 42–7 • *The manuscripts of the marquis of Ormonde*, [old ser.], 3 vols., HMC, 36 (1895–1909), vol. 1, p. 17 • *Calendar of the manuscripts of the marquess of Ormonde*, new ser., 8 vols., HMC, 36 (1902–20), vol. 3, pp. 215, 239; vol. 7, pp. 105, 415 • *CSP dom.*, 1685, 137, 217, 316–17, 322–3; 1686–7, 339, 399 • W. Edmundson, *A journal of the life, travels, sufferings and labour of love in the work of the ministry* (1715), 126–36 • *A short view of the methods made use of in Ireland for the subversion and destruction of the protestant religion and interest in that kingdom … by a clergyman* (1689), 22–3
Likenesses M. Cogan, oils, 1951 (after print, 1652), priv. coll. • R. Grace, line engraving (after facsimile of *The pourtraiture of Collonell Richard Grace now utterly routed by the coragious Coll: Sanckey*, 1652), repro. in Grace, *Memoirs* • line engraving (after print, 1652), BM, NPG; repro. in Grace, *Memoirs*
Wealth at death estate of 1684 acres: J. G. Simms, *The Williamite confiscation in Ireland, 1690–1703* (1956), 179

Grace, Sheffield (1788–1850), historian, was born in Boley, Queen's county, Ireland, the second son of Richard Grace (d. 1801), MP for Baltimore, and his wife, Jane, daughter of John Evans, son of George, first Lord Carbery. He studied at Winchester College, became a member of Lincoln's Inn in 1806, matriculated at St Mary Hall, Oxford, on 2 July 1813, aged twenty-five, and was elected a fellow of the Royal Society and of the Society of Antiquaries, London. He was a founder member of the Union Club in London in 1821. He was created DCL at Oxford on 27 June 1827. In 1829 he married Harriet Georgiana, daughter of Lieutenant-General Sir John Hamilton; they had a son and two daughters. Grace befriended the novelist John Banim, and his work was highly praised by Samuel Carter Hall. He died at Knole House, Tunbridge Wells, on 5 July 1850.

Grace's most interesting publication was *A Descriptive and Architectural Sketch of the Grace-Mausoleum, in the Queen's County*, originally contributed to the third volume of William Shaw Mason's *Statistical Account or Parochial Survey of Ireland* (1819), and reprinted separately in the same year. It contains a great number of illustrations, portraits, and pedigrees, including a portrait of the author. He also published a fictionalized *Memoirs of the Family of Grace* (1823), with a dedication to the duchess of Buckingham and Chandos; this contained many portraits and sketches, mainly from plates which had been used for other books. In addition he published other works of family history and biography, and a short volume of poetry.

J. T. GILBERT, *rev.* MYFANWY LLOYD

Sources *GM*, 2nd ser., 33 (1850) · W. S. Mason, *A descriptive and architectural sketch of the Grace-mausoleum, in the Queen's county*, ed. S. Grace (1819) · S. C. Hall and Mrs S. C. Hall, *Ireland, its scenery, character …*, 3 vols. (1846) · Foster, *Alum. Oxon.* · D. J. O'Donoghue, *The poets of Ireland: a biographical dictionary with bibliographical particulars*, 1 vol. in 3 pts (1892–3) · J. S. Crone, *A concise dictionary of Irish biography*, rev. edn (1937)

Archives TCD, corresp. with William Shaw Mason · U. Nott. L., corresp. with fourth duke of Newcastle · W. Sussex RO, letters to duke of Richmond

Likenesses R. Grave, line engraving, 1746 (after miniature), repro. in Grace, *Descriptive and architectural sketch*, pl. 8 · F. Deleu, line print (after A. Robertson), BM; repro. in S. Grace, *Memoirs of the family of Grace* (1823) · F. Manskirsch, miniature

William Gilbert [W. G.] **Grace** (1848–1915), by Archibald James Stuart Wortley, 1890

Grace, William Gilbert [W. G.] **(1848–1915)**, cricketer and medical practitioner, was born on 18 July 1848 at Clematis House, close to the family home of Downend House, Downend, Mangotsfield, near Bristol. He was the fourth son, in a family of nine, of Dr Henry Mills Grace (1808–1871) and his wife, Martha, who was the daughter of George Pocock, a schoolmaster and evangelist. She survived a flight across the Avon in a chair powered by her father's invention of a box kite to become a great influence on her cricketing sons and win her own unique place in *Wisden Cricketers' Almanack*.

Education and early cricketing career Soon after he could walk, Gilbert joined his family in practising in the orchard at Chestnuts, his home in Downend from 1850 to 1875. When he was six, his mother took him to see the All England eleven play a local twenty-two, which included his father, uncle, and brother. His early education, at a dame-school and two private ones, ended at fourteen, though he subsequently had a private tutor. He made his début in men's cricket on the day after his ninth birthday. Although he did nothing spectacular until he was fifteen, his mother kept faith with him. He would 'make a better batsman than any of his brothers for his back play is superior to theirs' (Bax, 24). She was rewarded when he made 32 for Bristol eighteen against the All England eleven and was invited to play for his illustrious opponents in the following year. Later, in that summer of 1864, came his débuts at Lord's and the Oval together with 170 (his first century) for an invitation side called South Wales against the Gentlemen of Sussex. *Lillywhite's Annual* (1865)

conceded that he promised 'to be a good bat'. His appearance for the Gentlemen at Lord's brought their first success against the Players in nineteen matches and, symbolically, asserted an authority he would exercise in that fixture for forty years.

In scoring 224 not out for the All England eleven against Surrey a few days after his eighteenth birthday, Grace recorded what was then the highest score to have been made at the Oval, a ground record he would break in 1871. Shortly after his All England performance, his 173 not out for the Gentlemen of the South against the Players of the South, on a wicket dangerous even by the standards of the day, established a reputation that his performances in the 1870s enhanced. He would make runs far in excess of contemporary accepted standards and *Lillywhite* now hailed him as 'the most wonderful cricketer that ever held a bat'.

Money, marriage, and medicine Some of Grace's cricket was for the United South of England eleven—the last of the travelling 'circuses' which played against odds. His performances included 210 not out against eighteen of Hastings in 1875 and 400 not out against twenty-two of Grimsby in the following year. Grace would often organize both the team and the finances himself and was contractually paid about £50 a match. To call him a 'shamateur' is an anachronism. His contemporaries accepted that participation in these games and in overseas tours could command a price, while his cricket for Gloucestershire would be as an amateur. How much the MCC knew about all this when they elected him to membership in

1869 can only be guessed at. A body whose members at that time were men of a different social milieu from Grace acted wisely if unusually. Grace, brought up in a modest professional home, needed financial support.

In 1867 Grace had followed in the family tradition by embarking on a course at Bristol medical school. The death of his father in 1871 further reduced his resources, although his marriage to his cousin Agnes Nicholls Day (1853–1930) on 9 October 1873 brought a settlement. The honeymoon was spent touring Australia, whose press hailed Grace as 'a cricketing phenomena' (*Melbourne Age*, 1874). In return for playing in every match he was paid a fee of £1500 with expenses. William Gilbert Grace, jun., was born in 1874. Saddled with his father's names, he never remotely matched his talents, although a Cambridge blue and a few appearances for Gloucestershire put his abilities into perspective before his early death in 1905. Another son, Henry Edgar (1876–1937), became an admiral.

Grace eventually completed his studies at St Bartholomew's Hospital, London, and qualified in 1879 as MRCS (London) and LRCP (Edinburgh). Thereafter he worked for twenty years both as a parish doctor for the Bristol Poor Law Union and in his own largely working-class practice. In the year he had qualified, the MCC presented him with £1500 from a national testimonial the club itself had instigated. Rather than purchase him a practice, the MCC gave him the money as he 'was old enough to take care of himself' (*Wisden*, 1880, 84). He was always conscious of his obligations to both family and patients. The one saw the firm but devoted Victorian paterfamilias, the other his unstinted generosity in time and concern. He was, remembered a friend, 'ever ready to lend a helping hand'. At a time when medicine was still more an art than a science, Grace's approach was a practical and common-sense one. To a chimney-sweep asking for a tonic, he offered, instead, a few rounds of boxing against himself. On one occasion he saved the life of a player (A. C. M. Croome) by compressing his throat for an hour after he had been spiked on the railings. Grace was not pleased when a wicket-keeper, whose eye he had just stitched up, promptly stumped him.

Becoming 'The Champion' In four successive seasons in first-class cricket (1868–71) Grace averaged over 50 and made twenty-three centuries. For the Gentlemen against the Players he made double-centuries at the Oval in 1870 and at Brighton in 1871. This was the year in which he was hailed by the press as 'The Champion'. He averaged 78.25 and became the first player to make over 2000 runs in a season. He had also assumed the captaincy of the new county club of Gloucestershire, which he retained until 1899. The county gave him expenses, often of £50 a season, which stretched their resources and also assisted him in paying a medical locum.

In August 1876 there were eight outstanding days in which Grace compiled 344 for the MCC against Kent, 177 for Gloucestershire against Nottinghamshire, and 318 not out for Gloucestershire against Yorkshire. He had also bowled 181 (four-ball) overs, opening the bowling in each

match and taking fifteen wickets for 302. His achievements, together with those of his brothers E. M. *Grace and G. F. Grace (1850–1880), made Gloucestershire one of the strongest sides in the newly established county championship. Outstanding as was Grace's batting, he was also regularly taking over a hundred wickets a season, and reached 191 in 1875.

Grace's batting was orthodox and uncomplicated. He saw the ball early and his timing was perfect, and he played equally well off front and back foot: these achievements were compounded by his immense stamina and powers of concentration. He preferred fast bowling and the measure of his success has to be set against the rough wickets on which he played so much of his early cricket. He advanced the game technically by his range of strokes and his ability to score all round the wicket. His round-arm bowling belonged to an earlier age, at first medium-paced and later, with increasing girth, becoming slow. He commanded length and variety in flight, with the ball coming in from the leg. Many of his wickets were caught and bowled and his total of 2876 wickets in first-class cricket far outstripped his contemporaries. Alfred Shaw, the most economical professional bowler of his generation, stood some 800 wickets behind him.

Playing against Australia Grace had been playing for seventeen years before he made a century against Australia at the Oval in 1880 in what was later regarded as the first test match in England. It was the only one in which three Grace brothers played together: George Frederick died two weeks after the match. From then until 1899, Gilbert played in every test in England against Australia. Appropriately, he played at the Oval in 1882 in the match which England lost to Australia by seven runs and which gave rise to the saga of the 'Ashes'. He recorded 170 against them at the Oval in 1886 which stood for some years as an England record, an innings he called 'not altogether faultless but a pretty good performance' (Midwinter, 92). Grace paid his second visit to Australia in 1891–2, a tour organized by the earl of Sheffield, who paid him £3000 together with expenses and the cost of a locum. Overseas tours were seen as financial enterprises and no eyebrows would have been raised at the England captain (as Grace had become in 1888) negotiating terms.

Later career and retirement from first-class cricket That the tour proved a financial failure, that England lost the test series, and that Grace performed fairly modestly were disappointing returns for the promoter. Grace, controversial though he could be over umpiring decisions, was nevertheless welcomed by the Australian press and public. He was by then in his forties. Burdened by weight, family commitments, and a demanding practice, he performed for several seasons below his own high standards. But 1895 heralded an 'Indian summer' to which national acclaim and public esteem brought him the reward of three testimonials exceeding £9000. 'He has drained the language of eulogy' (*Pall Mall Gazette*), said a press report. Two hundred and eighty-eight runs against Somerset made him the first man to score a hundred hundreds. Subsequently, 257 against Kent and 169 against Middlesex helped to make him the first to achieve 1000 runs in May—only two have done so since, W. R. Hammond and C. Hallows. By the end of the season he had scored 2346 runs (average 51.00), made nine centuries, and helped Gloucestershire to fourth place in the county championship. Both *The Times* and *Punch* pleaded for his recognition in the honours list but there would be no cricketing knight until eleven years after his death—and that award would go to an administrator. Instead he had earned the sobriquet the Old Man and other plaudits came his way. In 1898, on his fiftieth birthday, he captained the Gentleman against the Players at Lord's, an event marked by a jubilee medal and recorded for posterity on moving film.

Grace's playing connection with Gloucestershire ended abruptly in 1899. The essence of an ongoing dispute lay in who picked the sides, Grace or the committee. Grace had become autocratic over the years, favouring public school and university men such as G. L. Jessop and C. L. Townsend rather than local club cricketers. It was an educational and cricketing heritage not his own, but one that he admired and to which he had entrusted his eldest son. Matters were brought to a head when the committee learned that he had accepted an invitation from the Crystal Palace Company to manage the new London county club at a salary of £600. To the committee's understandable request as to 'what matches he intend(ed) playing' (Midwinter, 131) for Gloucestershire Grace took offence and resigned with the comment that he held the committee in 'the greatest contempt'.

Grace was already living in London, having moved there in 1898 because of the death of his daughter Bessie, the end of his Bristol parish medical work (through reorganization), and the winding-up of his own practice. The time had come for change. Within a week of writing to Gloucestershire, he had also played his last test match for England. The London county years (1899–1906) provided a dignified, if low-key, end to his playing days. Peace was made and honour restored with Gloucestershire in 1903, when he accepted life membership and entertained the county at the Crystal Palace. Grace made 150 and took six wickets in London county's seven wickets' victory.

Grace's last important first-class match was for the Gentlemen against the Players at the Oval in 1906, in which he made 74 on his fifty-eighth birthday. None of his fellow players had been born when he had first appeared there in that fixture in 1865. His final game at first-class level was in 1908. In scoring 54,896 runs (average 39.55) and taking 2876 wickets (average 17.92), Grace has been (by 1996) eclipsed by only four batsmen and five bowlers. The figures are those traditionally accepted by their inclusion in *Wisden*, though statisticians have offered minor variants.

A true celebrity, and his death Grace was a quintessential Victorian in his commitment to work and play, his entrepreneurial approach to money-making, his self-assurance, his competitiveness, and his paternal authoritarianism. His contributions to cricket were manifold. In his person he symbolized the game's progress from the loosely organized structure of his youth to the formalism of test matches and the county championship, its links with empire and Commonwealth, and its technical advances, which set the pattern for the twentieth century. His public image and performances were widely reported in the expanding journalism of his day; his presence attracted supporters in huge numbers and sometimes doubled the entrance-charge to grounds. A legend in his lifetime, 'W. G.' remains, a century later, one of the best-known British sportsmen. He is commemorated at Lord's by the Grace gates, erected in 1923.

Grace's physical appearance was as recognizable as that of anyone in Britain. Photographs taken when he was seventeen show the first hints of the beard which would become thick, black, and later grey. Not until he was thirty did his figure take on its familiar Falstaffian proportions, which sometimes led to confusion with the similarly proportioned and bearded prime minister, Lord Salisbury. A personality dominated by height and weight was softened by a high piping voice with a mild, west-country burr.

Two professional bowlers, Tom Emmett and Alfred Shaw, have bequeathed their experience of bowling to Grace. Emmett lamented that 'He dab 'em but seldom, and when he do dab 'em, he dabs 'em for four' (Midwinter, 34). Shaw allegedly remarked that he put the ball where he pleases but 'Mr Grace puts it where *he* pleases' (ibid.). His wicket was highly prized and there were those who murmured that it called for something more than the bowler's skill. A press comment in 1912 of 'the weakness of W. G. for dwelling at the wicket after the umpire's decision' (Midwinter, 158) spoke no more than a widely accepted belief. Grace could intimidate both umpires and players by his presence and by his incessant talking. Some Australians resented his arrogance and 'thought him too apt to wrangle'. S. M. J. Woods called him 'an artful old toad'.

There were those who saw Grace—as one of his biographers, Bernard Darwin, was told—as 'just a great big schoolboy' (Midwinter, 163). It explains, if it does not always excuse, his childish humour, his gluttony in seeking to be centre-stage, his sulkiness, and even (for a medical man) a reluctance to wash. Yet much could be forgiven him for his kindness, especially to the old, to children, and to those less talented or fortunate than he. What he could achieve on the cricket field jealously mattered to him on the day itself but was modestly dismissed to oblivion afterwards, consigned to history and to the occasional winter reading of his *Wisdens*. Averages and records were not to be set in tablets of stone.

Grace could excel at any sport he chose to pursue. As a young man he had been a hurdler and a sprinter. Most of his life he beagled, fished, and shot. Both golf and bowls claimed his interest in his later years. He played golf to a handicap of nine and captained England against Scotland in the first bowls international in 1903.

Apart from his textbooks and his *Wisdens*, Grace had neither the time nor the inclination to be a reader. With considerable help from his ghost writers he published four books, including *Cricket* (1891) and *W. G.: Cricketing Reminiscences* (1898). Four years after his death a *Memorial Biography* (1919) appeared, whose editors had received 500 letters and conducted over a hundred interviews.

Grace played cricket almost to the end of his life. His final game, on 25 July 1914, brought him an undefeated 60 for his local club, Eltham. In all his cricket he had made nearly 100,000 runs and taken well over 7000 wickets.

Ten days after that match the First World War broke out. Grace wrote a rare letter to the press, urging cricketers to 'come to the help of their country without delay in its hour of need' (*The Sportsman*, 27 Aug 1914). Although horrified at the unfamiliar concept of total war, he had a sure sense of where patriotism and duty lay. Through his influence cricket was sacrificed and scarcely any was played. On 23 October 1915 he died, after a stroke, at Fairmount, his home in Mottingham in Kent. He was buried three days later at Elmers End cemetery in London. Many of the cricketers who might have been there had heeded his words and gone to war.   GERALD M. D. HOWAT

Sources M.B. Hawke [Lord Hawke], G. R. C. Harris [Lord Harris], and H. Gordon, eds., *The memorial biography of Dr. W. G. Grace* (1919) · E. C. Midwinter, *W. G. Grace: his life and times* (1981) · W. G. Grace, *Cricket* (1891) · R. Low, *W. G.* (1997) · W. G. Grace, *W. G.: cricketing reminiscences and personal recollections* (1899) · *Wisden* (1896) · *Wisden* (1916) · *James Lillywhite's Cricketers' Annual* (1872–1900) · F. S. Ashley-Cooper, *W. G. Grace: a record of his performances in first-class cricket* (1916) · B. Darwin, *W. G. Grace* (1934) · A. A. Thomson, *The great cricketer* (1957) · C. Bax, *W. G. Grace* (1952) · W. M. Brownlee, *W. G. Grace* (1887) · A. Wye, *Dr. W. G. Grace* (1901) · P. J. Toghill, 'Dr W. G. Grace', *BMJ* (12 May 1979), 1269–70
Archives Marylebone Cricket Club Library, London, letters [copies] | FILM BFI NFTVA, 'Grace in 1898' · Marylebone Cricket Club, Lords, London, Grace in nets, *c*.1890s
Likenesses photograph, *c*.1870, priv. coll. · photograph, 1874, Marylebone Cricket Club, Lord's, London · W. Tyler, plaster of Paris bust, 1888, Marylebone Cricket Club, Lord's, London · G. W. Beldam, photograph, *c*.1890, Beldam Collection, Guildford, Surrey · A. J. S. Wortley, oils, 1890, Marylebone Cricket Club, Lord's, London [*see illus.*] · M. Beerbohm, pen-and-ink caricature, 1895, Marylebone Cricket Club, Lord's, London · C. Cutler, watercolour, 1895, Burlington Gallery, London · photograph, 1895, Marylebone Cricket Club, Lord's, London · Barraud, photograph, NPG; repro. in *Men and Women of the Day*, 1 (1888) · H. Furniss, caricature drawings, Marylebone Cricket Club, Lord's, London; repro. in H. Furniss, *A century of Grace* (1985) · Spy [L. Ward], chromolithograph caricature, NPG; repro. in *VF* (9 June 1877); also at Marylebone Cricket Club, Lord's, London · oils, NPG · stipple, NPG; repro. in *Baily's Magazine* (1870)
Wealth at death £7278 10s. 1d.: probate, 7 Dec 1915, CGPLA Eng. & Wales

Gracedieu, Sir Bartholomew (*c*.1657–1715), merchant and colonial agent, was the son of Thomas Gracedieu (*d. c*.1679), 'citizen and dyer' of St Botolph without Bishopsgate, London. In September 1671 he was apprenticed to Thomas Collet, a salter by trade and a member of the Vintners' Company. He became a freeman of London in 1679, and, although he found considerable success as an overseas merchant, he appears to have maintained an interest in salting. His master's influence also extended to his choice of domicile, since he became a long-term resident of Collet's parish, St Magnus the Martyr. By 1692 he had

married Frances (*d.* 1720), with whom he had at least three children, including two daughters.

By March 1686 Gracedieu had entered the trade to Jamaica, thereby consolidating his family's connections with the island—his brother Daniel having resided there in 1678. He dealt extensively in sugar, indigo, and logwood, the colony's main exports, and also invested in shipowning. By 1692 the council of Jamaica was prepared to use him for the remittance of its payments to England, and his standing with the planters and merchants of the island led to his eventual appointment as official agent, a role in which he served from 1693 to 1704.

Gracedieu's prominence in the capital was clearly a recommendation for such office. He was a notable figure in the nonconformist community, having been appointed as one of the managers of the Presbyterian Fund in 1690, and he later became a member of the New England Company, which maintained strong links with London dissenters. Despite his religious beliefs he made rapid strides in political circles, serving as a common councillor for Bridge ward in 1693, and being chosen a City lieutenant in 1694. The following year his income was assessed at more than £600 per annum, and his commercial prominence was recognized by the government in 1696, when he was nominated as one of the commissioners for taking subscriptions to the ill-fated land bank. In June 1697 he was elected sheriff, and in that capacity attended the king to offer the City's congratulations on the signing of the treaty of Ryswick. Such was the king's gratitude that Gracedieu and his fellow sheriff were knighted in the royal bedchamber at Kensington. In 1698 he assumed the mastership of the Vintners' Company, but his hopes for greater civic status went unfulfilled, for he lost an aldermanic election at Bridge ward in June 1700 'by a majority of three to one' against the tory Charles Duncombe (Luttrell, 4.651). This defeat did not blunt his political ambition, and in July 1701 he helped to stage a City welcome for the Kentish petitioners, who had embarrassed the ministry by urging parliament to pursue a more aggressive policy against the French.

Gracedieu's fear of French aggrandizement may well have been animated by his interest in Jamaican affairs, especially as the island was perceived to be vulnerable in the wake of a series of natural catastrophes. Indeed, in 1701–2 Gracedieu headed the cartel which undertook the remittance of payments for the island's newly strengthened garrison. With the advent of renewed Anglo-French conflict, he campaigned hard for more efficient convoys and better fortifications to protect the island and its trade, with some success. However, in these fraught times he even managed to fall out with fellow agent and vintner Sir Gilbert Heathcote, when a major controversy arose concerning a proposed removal of trade from Port Royal to Kingston. Gracedieu and his allies feared this innovation would weaken the island even further, and after much acrimony their arguments prevailed to save Port Royal.

Gracedieu's status was further enhanced in 1705 when he was returned to parliament for the Cornish borough of

St Ives. Although trading connections may have recommended his candidacy, he could not boast any obvious association with the town or its electoral patrons. Nevertheless, he performed very strongly, topping the poll. Given his nonconformist credentials, it is unsurprising that he was subsequently regarded as a supporter of the whig ministry, and backed the administration in divisions concerning the election of the speaker and the Regency Bill. He proved an inactive member, although in July 1706 he presented an address on behalf of his constituents to the queen in recognition of the victory at Ramillies. His unspectacular Westminster career ended in 1708 when he chose not to seek re-election, a decision perhaps influenced by the financial problems which bedevilled his last years.

Following his retirement from parliament Gracedieu limited his public role to colonial affairs. In 1709 he lent his support to a campaign for the settlement of impoverished palatine refugees in Jamaica, an issue which again stirred up divisions between rival island interests. Thereafter he even ceased to figure in the West Indian theatre, an anonymity which can be attributed to business difficulties, it being reported in January 1710 that 'Sir B——Grace——, a great merchant in the City, has stopped payments' (newsletter, 19 Jan 1710, BL, Add. MS 70421). The precise cause of his commercial downfall is unclear, although he had suffered the misfortune of losing a ship to privateers in 1699, and as recently as 1707 he had complained of the inadequate protection afforded to colonial shipping. Electioneering expenses may also have further stretched his personal resources. One contemporary simply described him as 'broke', and by early February 1710 a commission of bankruptcy had been served against him (*Le Neve's Pedigrees of the Knights*, 459). Such penury effectively undermined his public career, and it is probably significant that as early as 1708 he had ceased to play an active role on the vestry of St Magnus the Martyr. Although a spent political force, he remained true to his party, voting for the four whig candidates at the bitter London election of 1710.

The exact date of Gracedieu's death has not been ascertained, but doubtless occurred shortly before 30 March 1715, when his body was 'carried away' from the parish of St Andrew, Holborn, in preparation for burial in the nonconformist cemetery at Bunhill Fields on 3 April (Guildhall Library, MS 6673/6). Letters of administration over his estate were granted to his widow, Lady Frances, who in turn was succeeded in 1720 by the couple's only surviving daughter, Eleanor. Both mother and daughter were interred at Bunhill.   PERRY GAUCI

Sources *Le Neve's Pedigrees of the knights*, ed. G. W. Marshall, Harleian Society, 8 (1873), 459 · GL, MS 15220/2, p. 79 · GL, MS 15212/1, p. 63 · *CSP col.*, vols. 15–24 · W. A. Shaw, ed., *Calendar of treasury books*, 8, PRO (1923), 644–5; 9 (1931), 1946; 10 (1935), 900, 1155; 16 (1938), 95–6; 17 (1947), 46–8, 126, 338; 18 (1936), 488; 20 (1952), 211 · *Journal of the commissioners for trade and plantations*, [vol. 1]: *From April 1704 to February 1708/9* (1920) · *Journal of the commissioners for trade and plantations*, [vol. 2]: *From February 1708/9 to March 1714/15* (1925),

57–9 · Thomas Gracedieu, will, PRO, PROB 11/360, sig. 116 · Bartholomew Gracedieu, administration, 20 May 1715, PRO, PROB 6/91 · Bartholomew Gracedieu, administration, 15 Feb 1720, PRO, PROB 6/96 · 'London within the walls, 1695', *London Records Society*, 2 (1966), 125 · N. Luttrell, *A brief historical relation of state affairs from September 1678 to April 1714*, 4 (1857) · L. M. Penson, *The colonial agents of the British West Indies* (1924) · newsletter, 19 Jan 1710, BL, Add. MS 70421 · F. Cundall, *The governors of Jamaica in the first half of the eighteenth century* (1937), 30–31, 33, 44 · PRO, C 24/1150, case 37 [*Mingham v. Mingham*] · minutes of the managers of the Presbyterian Fund, DWL, D.D.67, fol. 10 · PRO, RG 4/3974

Wealth at death probably in financial trouble; stopped payments to creditors five years before death: newsletter, 19 Jan 1710, BL, Add. MS 70421

Graddon [*married name* Gibbs]**, Margaretta** (*b.* 1804), singer, was born at Bishop's Lydeard, near Taunton. After receiving lessons from Tom Cooke and gaining some experience in provincial concert rooms, she sang at Vauxhall in 1822, in Dublin the following year, and at Drury Lane for the first time in October 1824, as Susanna in *The Marriage of Figaro*. On 10 November 1824 she made her mark as the heroine in Henry Bishop's version of *Der Freischütz*. Her portrait in this character illustrates the title-page of a polka, *Le bal costumé*, composed by her, and published in 1854. She appeared at the same theatre as Amanda in Bishop's *The Fall of Algiers* (1825), as Zulema in Weber's *Abu Hassan*, and as Maria in Wade's *Two Houses of Granada* (1826). On 18 March 1830 she married Alexander Gibbs, of the piano-making firm Graddon and Gibbs. The critics disagreed among themselves as to the limits of her musical and dramatic talents. The couple went to America, where Mrs Gibbs made her début in New Orleans on 23 December 1835 in *The Marriage of Figaro*; it was commented that her matronly figure was unsuited to the part of Susanna, although her singing was brilliant. She was in New York the following year, and again in 1855, when she appeared in *The Lakes of Killarney*, an 'entertainment of song and anecdote'. There is no record of her life after this, nor is the date of her death known.

L. M. MIDDLETON, *rev.* J. GILLILAND

Sources Brown & Stratton, *Brit. mus.* · J. N. Ireland, *Records of the New York stage, from 1750 to 1860*, 2 (1867), 180–81 · Boase, *Mod. Eng. biog.* · Adams, *Drama* · W. T. Parke, *Musical memoirs*, 2 vols. (1830) · Mrs C. Baron-Wilson, *Our actresses*, 2 vols. (1844) · Hall, *Dramatic ports.* · IGI

Likenesses portrait, repro. in *Ladies Monthly Museum* (1825) · portrait, repro. in *Cumberland's minor theatre*, 3 (*c.*1831) · portrait, repro. in Mrs A. Gibbs [M. Gibbs], *Le bal costumé* [1854], title-page [polka] · prints, Harvard TC, NPG

Grade, Lew, Baron Grade (1906–1998), theatrical agent, television executive, and film producer, was born Louis Winogradsky on 25 December 1906 at Tokmak, near Odessa, Ukraine, the eldest of four children, three boys and a girl, of Isaac Winogradsky (*c.*1879–1935), and his wife, Golda (later Olga) Eisenstadt (*c.*1887–1981). Isaac was a businessman who tried many ventures and failed in several, and the driving force of the family was Louis's redoubtable mother. Although the Winogradskys enjoyed a moderately comfortable life and suffered less than some Jews from the antisemitism rife in Russia, Isaac decided to

Lew Grade, Baron Grade (1906–1998), by Cornel Lucas, 1996

emigrate and the family settled in the East End of London in 1912. Louis was then five years old and spoke only Russian. He attended Rochelle Street School in Shoreditch, where he was put in a class with much younger children because of his lack of English. Thanks to a photographic memory and an ability to read quickly, he was soon speaking the language better than his parents. A talent for arithmetic helped to win him scholarships which would have taken him on to college, but having decided to pursue a business career he left school at the age of fifteen and took a job in a clothing company. Rapidly mastering the essentials of the trade, he left after a couple of years and, still in his teens, set up an embroidery factory with his father. Although some of the proceeds had to pay off Isaac's gambling debts, the company prospered.

From dancer to theatrical agent As a boy Louis was a devotee of Saturday morning cinema and music-halls, but beyond that had no interest in show business. He took his first steps in it, literally, as a dancer. The Charleston had arrived as the new craze from America and Louis Grad, as he now styled himself, proved so adept at it that he won the British championship. The climax to his act was a frenzied routine on the top of a small table. In 1926 he styled himself world champion after winning a contest at the Albert Hall judged by the impresario C. B. Cochran and Fred Astaire. Louis decided to leave the rag trade and take up dancing as a profession. In a double act with another refugee from Ukraine, Al Gold, and as a solo performer, he toured Britain and the continent. An article in a Paris newspaper just before his opening night at the Moulin Rouge mis-spelt his name as Grade. He decided to stick with it.

During the early 1930s, as the Charleston's appeal faded and Grade's knees could no longer take the strain, his dancing career ended and he took up the new one of theatrical agent. Through a stalwart of the business, Joe Collins (father of the actress Joan), Grade helped to get British dates for acts he had seen while performing abroad. From scouting for Collins, Grade became an agent himself. He had an instinct for spotting talent and once more he learnt a new business quickly. He and Collins joined forces, setting up the Collins and Grade Agency. Grade's speciality was booking acts from the continent, from circus performers to the jazz musicians Django Reinhardt and Stephane Grappelli.

Early in the Second World War, Grade was briefly and unhappily in the army as an entertainment officer, before being discharged because of his damaged knees. On 23 June 1942, at Caxton Hall register office in London, he married Kathleen Sheila Moody (b. 1921), a singer and dancer whom he had first encountered when he booked her into the Winter Gardens at Morecambe as part of an act called Beams' Breezy Babes. Because Kathleen was a Roman Catholic, Grade's mother declined to attend the wedding, but the two women afterwards became close. It proved the happiest of matches (according to Grade, the best deal he ever made) and lasted fifty-six years, though his long working hours, frequent absences abroad on business, and refusal to take holidays demanded considerable forbearance on her part. After she had several miscarriages they adopted a son, Paul, in 1952.

In January 1943 Grade parted from Collins and agreed to look after the agency business of his younger brother Leslie, who had been called away to the forces and was not discharged until the end of the war. When he returned the brothers went into business as Lew and Leslie Grade Ltd. The middle brother, who took the name Bernard Delfont, was also an agent, but became better known as a theatrical producer. Lew Grade was now moving into a bigger league, dealing with established stars and formidable impresarios such as Val Parnell. To calm his nerves during important negotiations he took up the long, handmade Havana cigars which became his trademark. For many years he smoked, or partly smoked, fifteen a day, without apparently damaging his health.

After the war the Grades expanded the business by taking over other companies, becoming the second largest agency in Europe after William Morris. Lew was still busy on the continent, booking French artists such as Edith Piaf, Charles Trenet, and Jean Sablon, but the agency had no connections in the United States. A first, dispiriting trip to New York convinced Grade that America was not for him, but on a second visit in 1948 he concluded an agreement with MCA to be their exclusive representative in Europe. By November 1948 MCA was trying to buy the Grade agency. The Grades resisted the approach and set up in New York themselves, later opening an office in Los Angeles as well. There followed a busy traffic across the Atlantic as Lew signed Lena Horne, Jack Benny, Dorothy Lamour, Danny Kaye, Bob Hope, and Louis Armstrong to appear in Britain and secured bookings for British acts such as Tommy Trinder, Norman Wisdom, and Tommy

Cooper on American television shows. Lew and Leslie Grade became even bigger by merging with London Artists, the agency which represented Laurence Olivier, John Gielgud, and Ralph Richardson.

The move into television In the 1950s Grade decided, after initial reluctance, to seize the opportunities offered by the new Independent Television. With leading figures in the theatre such as Prince Littler and Val Parnell, who ran the Stoll Moss group, and the West End impresario Binkie Beaumont, he put together a consortium called Independent Television Corporation (ITC) with backing from Warburgs. Initially they were turned down by the Independent Television Authority as having too much power in the industry. Later, however, Grade and his consortium were invited to join a group headed by Norman Collins and Sir Robert Renwick which had been granted the franchise for weekends in London and weekdays in the midlands. The new company, in which ITC had a 50 per cent stake, was ABC, but soon became ATV because of the name clash with the ABC cinema group. ITC continued as a production company. Grade admitted that he knew nothing about television but he recruited astutely and, as always, mastered a new business quickly.

ATV's early schedule for the London weekend slot, which started transmitting in September 1955, included *Sunday Night at the London Palladium* hosted by Tommy Trinder, *Val Parnell's Saturday Spectacular*, and *The Adventures of Robin Hood*, a series of half-hour shows made by ITC which ran for 165 episodes and were sold to the CBS network in the United States. Thanks largely to Grade, ATV was one of the first British television companies to exploit the American market. But ATV's output also contained a regular Sunday religious programme, which Grade introduced to fill an early evening gap.

After a few months Grade was devoting himself to television almost full time, becoming deputy managing director to Parnell, and by 1956 he had left the agency altogether. ATV set up a distribution company in the United States and bought the British national film studios at Elstree. In 1962 Grade displaced Parnell to become managing director. In 1965 he was instrumental in helping ATV to take over Stoll Moss, Britain's biggest theatre chain. The company also went into the music business by acquiring Northern Songs, which had the rights to the Beatles' songs, and Pye Records. With Leslie still running Britain's biggest agency and Bernard established as the leading London theatre impresario, the Grades' grip on show business was immense. Critics spoke of a 'Gradopoly'.

In television ATV built a reputation for wholesome family entertainment (Lew would countenance no descent, as he saw it, into sex, violence, or bad language) aimed at the popular mainstream. Typical of the output were *Emergency Ward Ten*, a twice-weekly hospital drama, *The Saint*, starring Roger Moore, which ran for six years and more than 150 episodes, *The Power Game*, with Patrick Wymark, and *Danger Man*, whose star, Patrick McGoohan, went on to make *The Prisoner*. Filmed in Clough Williams-Ellis's Portmeirion in north Wales, *The Prisoner* mystified audiences on first release but became a cult classic. ATV's most durable drama, though the most derided, was the soap opera *Crossroads*, which started in 1964 and ran for twenty-four years before being revived in 2001. Grade backed Gerry Anderson's ground-breaking puppet series, including *Stingray*, *Thunderbirds*, *Captain Scarlet*, and *Space 1999*, but was less successful with British-made vehicles for the Hollywood stars Tony Curtis (*The Persuaders* with Roger Moore) and Shirley MacLaine.

Among the many remarks attributed to Grade was his comment on a television programme, 'that must be culture, it certainly wasn't entertainment'. He denied saying it and in any case it was a distinction he did not always make. He brought Maria Callas to peak-time television from the Royal Opera House, backed television versions of productions from the National Theatre, engaged Sir Kenneth Clark to do a series on art, and put on A. J. P. Taylor's live and unscripted history lectures. In 1976, in a joint project with Italian television, he produced a lavish biblical epic, *Moses the Lawgiver*, starring Burt Lancaster. He followed it with the even more ambitious *Jesus of Nazareth* (1977), claiming that the subject had been suggested to him by Pope Paul VI during an audience at the Vatican. Grade secured sponsorship from General Motors (though they later withdrew in favour of Procter and Gamble) and sold the programme to the NBC network. He signed up Franco Zeffirelli as director and assembled a star cast, starting with Olivier, though the leading role went to the relatively unknown Robert Powell. It was a handsome and by no means unintelligent production and the new pope, John Paul II, signified his approval by making Grade a papal knight, a rare honour for a Jew.

In the early 1970s Grade persuaded the singer and actress Julie Andrews to star in a television series, making the programmes in London and selling them to America. *The Julie Andrews Hour* won seven Emmy awards and had two important by-products. One of the guest spots on the show was filled by Jim Henson's Muppets. Grade saw their potential and promoted them to a series of their own, produced at Elstree, which ran for 120 episodes over five years. Second, as part of the deal with Andrews, Grade agreed to back two films directed by her husband, Blake Edwards, *The Tamarind Seed* (1974) and *The Return of the Pink Panther* (1974). Although Grade had dabbled in the cinema before, this was his first serious taste of the business.

The move into cinema In 1977, at the age of seventy, Grade was obliged under Independent Broadcasting Authority rules to give up as chairman of ATV, though he became chairman and chief executive of its holding company, Associated Communications Corporation (ACC). Already, however, he felt he had gone as far as he could in television and needed a new challenge. He sought it in films, and though he played the cinema mogul with characteristic swagger, boasting that he would take on Hollywood, there were more misses than hits. Although intended to boost the British cinema industry, his films lacked a clear national identity while an old man's tastes were not always those of a mainly young audience. He backed two

Raymond Chandler remakes, *Farewell my Lovely* (1975) and *The Big Sleep* (1978), as well as an assortment of pictures of varying distinction including *The Cassandra Crossing* (1976), *The Boys from Brazil* (1978; with Olivier as the Nazi-hunter Simon Wiesenthal), and *The Eagle has Landed* (1976).

Grade had a huge money-spinner with *The Muppet Movie* in 1979 and a costly flop with *Raise the Titanic* (1980), prompting one of the few Gradeisms its author acknowledged: 'It would have been cheaper to lower the Atlantic' (Grade, 262). His happiest film was *On Golden Pond* (1981), which teamed Henry Fonda (in his last screen role) with his daughter Jane and Katharine Hepburn, and won three Oscars. A worthy venture, if a long way from Grade's idea of mainstream entertainment, was *Sophie's Choice* (1982), which had an Oscar-winning performance by Meryl Streep as a Polish woman haunted by the Holocaust.

In December 1981, with ACC weakened by heavy losses from film-making, an Australian entrepreneur, Robert Holmes à Court, became principal shareholder and joined the board. In January he decided to make a bid for the company. Grade initially welcomed Holmes à Court's involvement and gave his support. Holmes à Court bought ACC cheaply and became chairman and chief executive. Although Grade was executive deputy chairman of ACC's entertainment division he was no longer on the board and relations with Holmes à Court quickly deteriorated. Grade was angry when Holmes à Court starting sacking long-time staff, including a favourite tea lady, and matters came to a head in a dispute over the funding for *Sophie's Choice*. Grade left the company, amid some bitterness, in June 1982.

Grade became chairman and chief executive of the London-based Embassy Communications International, but he was reporting to an American boss. His only notable project for Embassy was the film *Champions* (1984), the story of the jockey Bob Champion who overcame cancer to win the Grand National. In 1985 Embassy was sold and Grade was once more on his own. He formed the Grade Company and made a series of television films based on Barbara Cartland's romantic novels. He also co-produced the Broadway production of Andrew Lloyd Webber's *Starlight Express*. He embarked on his last venture, the film *Something to Believe in* (1998), when he was in his nineties, though its old-fashioned sentimentality was out of touch with the times.

An incomparable maker of deals and a great showman, Grade was one of the most important figures in British show business in the twentieth century. A short tubby man with sharp blue eyes, he was ebullient and extrovert and eternally bullish. He insisted that money was unimportant to him. He acquired the trappings of success, including Rolls-Royces, but left himself little time to enjoy them. His hobby was his work. He was in the office by 7 a.m. and often worked well into the evening. He undertook a punishing schedule of overseas trips, prepared to fly half way across the world to clinch a sale. Holidays bored him and he avoided taking them whenever possible.

Blessed with enormous self-confidence, prodigious energy, and an abundance of cheek, Grade relished the challenge of the near impossible. He was a consummate negotiator, with the knack of disarming the most difficult opponents. Told that a performer was unattainable or an executive unpersuadable, Grade, with his myriad contacts and large fund of goodwill in the business, usually won them round. What fascinated and absorbed him was brokering a deal, and the persuasion and cajoling this entailed. He prided himself on sticking to agreements, preferring handshakes to written contracts, and expected others to behave similarly. Sometimes he was let down, though he did not bear grudges. He was shrewd, and drove a hard bargain, but was never devious.

Grade was no intellectual, declaring that his tastes were those of the average person, and assessed projects for their popular appeal rather than artistic merit. At the same time, he backed ventures into opera or classical theatre which he thought worthwhile in themselves and had their reward in prestige rather than audience ratings. He denied uttering a remark often attributed to him: 'All my shows are great. Some of them are bad, but they are all great.' Nevertheless, it contained much truth. Whatever their merits, his shows were stamped by the flamboyance he brought to them. His 1987 autobiography, *Still Dancing*, was typically exuberant, if not always reliable.

Grade's salesmanship won ATV two queen's awards for export and it was for services to export that he was knighted in 1969. He was made a life peer in 1976. His profession honoured him with a fellowship of the British Academy of Film and Television Arts (1979). He kept his promise never to retire and was working until his final illness. He died of heart failure in the London Clinic, 20 Devonshire Place, on 13 December 1998, just short of his ninety-second birthday, and was buried three days later in the Liberal Jewish cemetery in Willesden, north London.

PETER WAYMARK

Sources L. Grade, *Still dancing* (1987) · H. Davies, *The Grades* (1981) · Q. Falk and D. Prince, *Last of a kind: the sinking of Lew Grade* (1987) · *The Times* (14 Dec 1998) · *The Independent* (14 Dec 1998) · *The Guardian* (14 Dec 1998) · *Daily Telegraph* (14 Dec 1998) · R. Grade Freeman, *My fabulous brothers* (1982) · *The Independent* (17 Dec 1998)
Likenesses photographs, 1955–81, Hult. Arch. · A. Newman, photograph, 1978?, NPG · F. Goldstein, chalk drawing, 1986, NPG · A. Morrison, photograph, 1989, NPG · C. Lucas, photograph, 1996, NPG [*see illus.*] · R. Spear, oils, NPG
Wealth at death £8,560,493—gross; £8,423,342—net: probate, 19 March 1999, *CGPLA Eng. & Wales*

Gradidge, (John) Roderick Warlow (1929–2000), architect, was born on 3 January 1929 at Hunstanton, Norfolk (although conceived in Baghdad), the eldest of the three children of Brigadier John Henry (Reggie) Gradidge (1894–1969), of Cornish descent, and his wife, Lorraine Beatrice, *née* Warlow-Harry (1908–1999). As his father commanded the corps of guides cavalry regiment on the north-west frontier, Gradidge was first educated in India, in Kashmir and at Dehra Dun, until he was sent home to Stowe School in 1943. When young, he seemed academically indifferent to the point of delinquency, but the headmaster, J. F. Roxburgh, encouraged his incipient love of architecture and, after two years of national service, mostly in Palestine, he attended the Architectural Association School of Architecture from 1949 to 1953. There he came into conflict with Robert Furneaux Jordan, who told Gradidge that he would never be an architect and so encouraged his hostility to modernism and to those he would invariably describe as 'doctrinaire' modern architects.

After a period in Cambridge working on designs for petrol stations, Gradidge found his métier as an architect working for brewers, first Benskins and then Ind Coope, restoring or altering pubs in a sympathetic Victorian manner. His most celebrated pub interior was in London, that of the Markham Arms in the King's Road, Chelsea (1972). Insistent that colour and decoration were important and that 'modernism never sold a pint of bitter' (*Daily Telegraph*, 26 Aug 1987), he transformed the interior of the Three Greyhounds in Soho, London, in the manner of J. N. Comper by using the church decorators Campbell Smith. Real church work followed. An early and active member of the Victorian Society, he could be trusted to alter nineteenth-century interiors with tact and intelligence. He reordered the interior of A. W. N. Pugin's church of St Augustine at Ramsgate so that no fittings were lost, and he again came to the rescue of Pugin when in 1969 he installed the screen ejected from St Chad's Roman Catholic Cathedral, Birmingham, in the Anglican church of Holy Trinity, Reading, for his friend the Revd Brian Brindley.

Gradidge wrote his dissertation at the School of Architecture on the 'Vigorous Style' of such Gothic revivalists as George Edmund Street and he argued that their approach to architectural form influenced his greatest hero, Edwin Lutyens, whose faded reputation he helped to rehabilitate by leading pioneering tours for the Victorian Society. When asked to add a swimming pool wing to Lutyens's Fulbrook in Surrey in 1974–6, Gradidge did so in a sympathetic half-timbered manner. This exemplified his belief in 'keeping in keeping' in contrast to the modernist insistence that an addition to a historic building must be, as he contemptuously put it, 'frankly of our day and age' (personal knowledge). Many commissions followed to adapt or enlarge other late Victorian and Edwardian houses, often in Surrey. He also restored the interior of Northampton Guildhall by E. W. Godwin (1992–3) and wittily and sensitively decorated the interior of Bodelwyddan Castle in Wales for the National Portrait Gallery (1986); his transformation of the National Portrait Gallery's home in London was destroyed within his lifetime, to his distress and fury. Perhaps his most successful new interior was the library at Easton Neston, Northamptonshire, carried out with David Hicks for Lady Hesketh in 1964.

To the surprise of his older friends, Gradidge showed great flair as a writer. Forceful and opinionated journalism led to commissions for books. *Dream Houses* (1980), written on the last scheduled boat to South Africa, was a celebration of the arts and crafts houses of the 1890s he so admired; his study *Edwin Lutyens: Architect Laureate* (1981) further demonstrated the strengths of his approach as an architect rather than as a historian; while his book *The*

Surrey Style (1991) extolled the half-timbered and tile-hung vernacular in his favourite county.

Gradidge was a complicated and consciously eccentric figure, either loved or loathed. His penetrating and combative upper-class accent reflected the background he often seemed in reaction against, and causing offence seemed to be as much a duty as a pleasure. Proudly independent and single, he was happy to refer to himself as a 'pervert', and an interest in tattooing was manifested both in the adornment of his own conspicuously large person and the company he sometimes kept. He demonstrated originality in his defiance of convention both architectural and sartorial. In the 1960s he adopted the 'drape' of a Teddy boy, which reflected his enthusiasm for rock and roll music and jiving (at which he was adept). Daniel Farson, who employed him to revive the Waterman's Arms on the Isle of Dogs, recorded that 'he was once a deb's delight and impresses some people as "a proper English gentleman", but to others he is less easily definable, perhaps the successful proprietor of a fairground'. Later, when fashion caught up with his interest in pierced bodies, earrings were superseded by a plaited pigtail, while trousers were replaced by an English tweed kilt which its wearer called a 'skort' and insisted was comfortable 'rational dress'.

In 1987 Gradidge was delighted to be able to wear the robes of the master of the Art-Workers' Guild, the society founded in 1884 to sustain the arts and crafts approach he admired and to which he eventually left his estate. Profoundly religious, his spiritual home was the Anglo-Catholic church of St Mary, Bourne Street, London, for which he designed a columbarium shortly before his sudden death, at his home, 21 Elliott Road, Chiswick, London, from heart failure on 20 December 2000. A requiem mass was celebrated at St Mary's on 3 January 2001, and his ashes were subsequently placed in the church.

GAVIN STAMP

Sources *Daily Telegraph* (22 Dec 2000) · *The Times* (1 Jan 2001) · *The Independent* (2 Jan 2001) · *The Guardian* (25 Jan 2001) · personal knowledge (2004) · private information (2004) [Penelope Kirk, sister]
Archives Art Workers' Guild, London, articles and papers · RIBA BAL, job corresp.
Likenesses photograph, 1992, repro. in *Daily Telegraph* · G. Boyd Harte, portrait, Art-Workers' Guild · G. Stamp, photograph, repro. in *The Independent* · G. Stamp, photographs, priv. coll. · photograph, repro. in *The Guardian*
Wealth at death £591,929—gross; £573,459—net: probate, 22 May 2001, CGPLA Eng. & Wales

Gradwell, Robert (1777–1833), college head and Roman Catholic bishop, third (and twin) son of John Gradwell of Clifton-cum-Salwick in the Fylde, Lancashire, and his wife, Margaret, daughter of John Gregson of Balderston, was born at Clifton-cum-Salwick on 26 January 1777 and baptized in the Catholic chapel there on the same day. He was sent to the English College at Douai in 1791, and upon its suppression remained for some time in confinement with the other students. A French *laissez-passer* for Citizen

R. Gradwell, who was then eighteen years old, describes him as 5 feet 2 inches tall, with chestnut hair and eyebrows and grey eyes. He had an oval face with two small warts, a high forehead, and a large nose.

On regaining his liberty in 1795, Gradwell proceeded to Crook Hall, near Durham, where the majority of the refugees from the English College had assembled. On 4 December 1802 he was ordained priest, and for seven years he taught poetry and rhetoric at Crook Hall and the new college at Ushaw. In 1809 he was stationed as priest at Claughton, Lancashire. When the English College at Rome was restored to the English secular clergy, the English vicars apostolic recommended Gradwell as rector. They did this mainly on the suggestion of the historian John Lingard, with whom Gradwell had formed a close friendship at Ushaw. Gradwell was first appointed agent for the vicars apostolic, and arrived in Rome on 2 November 1817; then (by letters dated 8 March 1818) Cardinal Consalvi, secretary of state, appointed him rector. He was formally installed on 10 June, and a group of ten students soon afterwards arrived from England.

Gradwell successfully re-established the college after its twenty-year closure during the French occupation of Rome. He was concerned that the studies should be not only of a high academic standard but also suitable for those who were to spend their lives as priests in England. The college quickly gained respect at home and abroad, and six of the students who studied under his rectorship became bishops in England. As agent he gave active support to the vicars apostolic in their dispute with the Jesuits and in their dealings with the egregious Dr John Milner. He entered into correspondence with his friend Lingard, and was able to assist him in his researches by providing information about documents in various Roman archives and libraries. On 24 August 1821 the pope conferred on him the degree of DD, in recognition of his services as rector of the English College and agent for the vicars apostolic.

On 19 May 1828 the Congregatio de Propaganda Fide elected Gradwell coadjutor *cum futura successione* to Bishop James Yorke Bramston, vicar apostolic of the London district. He was accordingly consecrated on 24 June to the see of Lydda *in partibus infidelium*. He resigned the rectorship of the English College and was succeeded by his vicerector, Nicholas Wiseman. The following August he arrived in London. In 1832 he and Bishop Bramston jointly issued a pastoral letter to the clergy and laity of the London district prohibiting wakes during the cholera epidemic of that year.

Gradwell died at 35 Golden Square, London, on 18 March 1833. His eulogy was inscribed on a marble monument in the church of St Mary Moorfields, where he was buried. When the church was sold in 1903 his remains and his monumental inscription were taken to Old Hall, near Ware. Gradwell published little during his lifetime, but left a number of manuscripts on his death, including his journal of his time in Rome and his correspondence as agent. Other manuscripts include a scrapbook and diary,

and an incomplete history of the English College at Rome, where his most significant contribution to the life of the Roman Catholic church had been made.

THOMPSON COOPER, rev. MICHAEL E. WILLIAMS

Sources *GM*, 1st ser., 103/1 (1833), 378, 652 · *Catholic Magazine and Review*, 3 (1833), 332 · *Laity's Directory* (1834) · G. Anstruther, *The seminary priests*, 4 (1977), 115–16 · Gillow, *Lit. biog. hist.* · M. E. Williams, *The Venerable English College, Rome* (1979), 68–89
Archives Lancs. RO, corresp. and papers · Venerable English College, Rome, corresp. and papers · Westm. DA, corresp. and papers | Ushaw College, Durham, letters to Nicholas Wiseman
Likenesses J. Holl, stipple, pubd 1833, repro. in *Laity's directory* · portrait, English College, Rome, Italy

Graefer, John Andrew (*d.* 1802), horticulturist and landscape gardener, was born in Vienna but at an early age came to England, where he became a pupil of the gardener Philip Miller. He was subsequently employed as a gardener by the earl of Coventry, and then by James Vere at Kensington Gore. About 1776 he established a nursery at Mile End, London, in partnership with another gardener and a seedsman. According to W. Aiton, in the *Hortus Kewensis* of 1810, between 1783 and 1784 Graefer introduced in England, possibly with seeds provided by the Swedish botanist and medical doctor Carl Peter Thunberg (one of the few foreigners who had been allowed to visit Japan), the *Aucuba japonica*, the *Ophiopogon japonica*, the *Orontium japonica*, and the *Eucomis punctata*. He also reintroduced in England the *Eleagnus angustifolius orientalis*.

In 1786 Sir William Hamilton had persuaded the queen of Naples, Maria Carolina, to have an English garden laid out at the royal palace at Caserta. Graefer, whose name had been suggested by Sir Joseph Banks, thus entered the service of the queen, and moved to Naples with his three sons, John, Charles, and George. On his journey, while his ship was obliged to halt in the harbour of Ponza, Graefer had the opportunity to spend some time on the island, and drew up a detailed *Flora insulae Ponza*. In Caserta, Graefer laid out a charming (although rather small) English garden and stocked it with a large variety of plants. As Loudon says: 'Every exotic, which at that time could be furnished by the Hammersmith nursery, was planted …. Among these the Camellias, Banksias, Proteas, Magnolias, Pines, etc.' (Loudon, 19). At the same time Graefer, according to Loudon, also laid out several other gardens in Naples, including one for the duca di San Gallo. In Caserta, however, he met with many unforeseen difficulties; the Neapolitans did not seem to appreciate his work and his subordinates cheated him shamelessly. In 1788 the queen became tired of the project and the English garden was taken over by the king, Ferdinando IV. As a result Graefer had to accept a drastic cut in salary and was obliged to work under the supervision of the architect Carlo Vanvitelli.

In 1789 Graefer published *A descriptive catalogue of upwards of eleven hundred species and variations herbaceous and perennial plants*, which was reprinted at least four times (4th edn, 1804). In its foreword the 'Editor' informed the reader, among other things, that 'the Author of the following Catalogue is publicly celebrated, in the Annals of the Admiralty, for his *Invention of Prepared Vegetables*'. This consisted of the preparation of dried vegetables, which permitted ships' provisions of greens, such as broccoli, to be preserved for over a year. According to a 1793 work by N. Hadrawa, Graefer also drew up a *Flora dell'isola di Capri* and sent it for publication to a natural history society in Berlin. The book apparently was not published and the manuscript was lost (Norman Douglas made an extensive, but unsuccessful, search for it in 1930).

In 1791 Graefer (who by then must have been a widower), married Elizabeth Dodsworth, a young woman from Chester. In 1792 she gave birth to a son, Ferdinando, who died shortly afterwards; a second child, Maria Carolina, was born in 1794. In December 1798, when the French invasion became imminent, the royal family and the Neapolitan court escaped to Sicily. Graefer was taken along with them and became employed by Lord Nelson as steward of his estate, Bronte. Unfortunately Graefer's competence as an administrator did not match his skill as a gardener. After complaining about the squandering and prodigality of his steward ('Graefer thought that I approved giving to the poor'), Nelson, in 1802, felt somehow relieved by Graefer's death: 'I have lost Graeffer [*sic*], my Governor of Bronte: he died August 7. It embarrasses me a little, but I endeavour to make the best of things, and it may possibly turn out to my pecuniary advantage' (*Dispatches and Letters*, 30).   CARLO KNIGHT

Sources C. Knight, *Il giardino Inglese di Caserta, un'avventura settecentesca* (1986) [with an introduction by H. Acton] · G. W. Johnson, *A history of English gardening* (1829) · Desmond, *Botanists* · J. C. Loudon, *An encyclopedia of gardening* (1822) · J. A. Graefer, *A descriptive catalogue of upwards of eleven hundred species and variations herbaceous and perennial plants* (1789) · N. Douglas, *Capri, materials for a description of the island* (1930) · A. M. Coats, 'Forgotten gardeners: John Graefer', *Garden History Society Newsletter*, 16 (1972), 4–7 · N. Hadrawa, *Ragguagli di varii scavi e scoverte di antichità fatte nell'isola di Capri* (1793) · T. J. Pettigrew, *Memoirs of the life of Vice-Admiral Lord Viscount Nelson*, 2 vols. (1849), vol. 2 · *The dispatches and letters of Vice-Admiral Lord Viscount Nelson*, ed. N. H. Nicolas, 7 vols. (1844–6), vol. 5

Graeme, James (1749–1772), poet, born on 15 December 1749 at Carnwath in Lanarkshire, was fourth and youngest son (there were also two daughters) of William Graeme, a farmer of the 'middling class' (Davenport, 221). As a child he was delicate and he became the focus of his parents' attention. After being taught to read in a dame-school, he was sent to the grammar schools of Carnwath, Libberton, and in 1763, Lanark, where he was taught by Robert Thomson, brother-in-law of the poet James Thomson. Graeme's scholarly achievements caused his parents to consider educating him for the church and in 1767 he went to Edinburgh University, where he studied for three years. His friend and biographer, Robert Anderson (1750–1830), says that Graeme excelled in the classics and had a keen interest in philosophy, besides reading widely in general literature. Graeme also wrote poetry in his spare time. In 1769, on the recommendation of Andrew Lockhart, he was presented to a bursary at St Andrews University, but he soon resigned it and he returned to Edinburgh the next year,

where he entered the theological class, although his studies were hindered by ill health. In 1771 he became tutor to the sons of Major Martin White of Milton, near Lanark, but he became depressed by the dependent nature of his position. By September his consumption had worsened. His 'playful wit and humour never [forsook] him' during his final illness, 'till he was no longer able to smile, or even to speak' (Davenport, 227). He died at Carnwath on 26 July 1772. Graeme was a man of amiable character, but his poems, consisting of elegies and miscellaneous pieces, show little talent. His reputation as a poet is due to the partiality of Anderson, who printed his friend's poems after his death, together with some of his own, in *Poems on Several Occasions* (1773). They reappeared in volume 11 of Anderson's *Poets of Great Britain*, and in R. A. Davenport's *British Poets*, volume 71.

C. L. KINGSFORD, *rev.* MICHAEL BEVAN

Sources R. A. Davenport, 'The life of James Graeme', *The British poets*, 71 (1822), 221–8 · *GM*, 1st ser., 52 (1782), 425–30

Grafton. For this title name *see* FitzRoy, Henry, first duke of Grafton (1663–1690); FitzRoy, Augustus Henry, third duke of Grafton (1735–1811); Fitzroy, George Henry, fourth duke of Grafton (1760–1844).

Grafton, Richard (*c.*1511–1573), printer and historian, probably came from a Shrewsbury family. He was the son of Nicholas Grafton, who may have been a skinner, and the grandson of Adam Grafton, perhaps to be identified with the man of that name recorded in 1473 as vicar of St Alkmund's, Shrewsbury. Richard was apprenticed in 1526, so he was probably born about 1511.

Working for the reformers Grafton's master, John Blage, was a member of the Grocers' Company and grocer to Thomas Cranmer. He was also a man who had both evangelical sympathies in religion and commercial links with Antwerp. Grafton himself became free of the Grocers' Company in 1534, although there is no evidence of any involvement in the grocery trade itself. However, he is known to have been a merchant adventurer with connections in Antwerp, and he engaged in commerce under the patronage of Cranmer, who also employed him to put into practice a project for a new English translation of the Bible. Grafton's letters associated with this venture demonstrate his own reforming standpoint, and also show how prominent reformers put his commercial know-how and capital to their own uses. He was involved in the financing and production of the Matthew Bible of 1537 (printed under the name of 'Thomas Matthew', it was the work of Miles Coverdale and William Tyndale, edited by John Rogers), even though he was briefly imprisoned for debt during that year. And when in 1538 Thomas Cromwell obtained a commission from the king by letters patent to produce an official English Bible—the future Great Bible of 1539—Grafton and his associate Edward Whitchurch were charged with the task of its publication. Grafton acted as the merchant who oversaw the project; Miles Coverdale was the editor. The extent of Whitchurch's involvement at this point is unclear.

Grafton was at this stage still only the commercial agent

in charge of implementing the project, while the actual printing was done in Paris by François Reynault, on whose behalf Grafton had petitioned Cromwell in early 1538 to protect Reynault's interests in the London book trade. Unfortunately, in the late summer and autumn of 1538 worsening diplomatic relations between France and England began to put the project in danger. In December the French inquisitor-general was turned on it, and Reynault was singled out in an edict designed to suppress the English Bible. The bibles were confiscated, and Grafton fled back to London.

In July 1539 Cromwell began trying to persuade the French to return those bibles that had not yet been destroyed. At the same time he obtained a grant by letters patent in which the king forbade anyone except Cromwell, or whoever had his special licence, to print English translations of the Bible. In November 1539 the types, forms, and presses being used for the Great Bible were transported from Paris to London, probably straight into the empty Greyfriars buildings just north of St Paul's Cathedral. The bibles were printed there and on Whitchurch's premises. Grafton and Whitchurch continued to work together regularly, and in 1540 they shared the printing of a new edition of the Bible that included a preface by Thomas Cranmer, and so became known as Cranmer's Bible (STC 2070). Grafton lived in Greyfriars for the rest of his life, long after he gave up printing and publishing.

Political insecurity and commercial influence On 28 July 1540 Grafton's patron Thomas Cromwell was executed without trial. During the two years that followed Grafton was in prison three times—twice in 1541, for publishing material hostile to the religiously conservative new regime and for an offence against the Act of Six Articles (for which his old master Blage was also in trouble); and once in 1543 'for printing off such bokes as wer thought to be unlawfull' (Kingdon, 91). He was released on 2 May by order of the king.

On 28 January 1543 Grafton and Whitchurch obtained a privilege by letters patent which gave them the sole right to publish church service books; it was renewed on 22 April 1547 because the original one had been lost. In 1545 they became printers attached to the household of Prince Edward, the heir to the throne. Soon afterwards Grafton began to operate as sole printer to the young prince, and on Henry VIII's death in 1547 he succeeded Thomas Berthelet as printer to the new king, an office he held throughout the reign. The texts he published included the Book of Common Prayer in March 1549 (STC 16268) and John Marbeck's pioneering *Concordance* to the Bible (STC 17300) in 1550.

In 1547–8 the city of London had come into possession of most of the Greyfriars buildings, by now called Christ's Hospital, and confirmed Grafton in his holdings within the precincts. The city's court of aldermen allowed him the buildings and grounds that he wanted and he was never disturbed. Probably some time between 1545 and 1547 he had married Anne Crome, a relation of Dr Edward Crome, a leading figure among the London godly. They

had at least four sons, Robert, Edward, Richard, and Gregory, and a daughter, Joan, who married the stationer Richard Tottel. Anne died in 1560, and in January 1562 Grafton remarried, his second wife being Alice Aylyffe; two sons are recorded as born of his second marriage. In the late 1540s Grafton seems also to have supported a number of younger writers, including the scholar and future diplomat Thomas Wilson, who acknowledged Grafton's help in the 'Epistle Dedicatory' to the *Rule of Reason*, published by Grafton himself in 1551 (STC 25809). In August 1551 the city acquired St Thomas's Hospital in Southwark, and Grafton became one of its governors, and also its deputy treasurer.

Fall from favour On the death of Edward VI in 1553 Grafton sided with the faction that attempted to make Lady Jane Grey queen, and he printed the proclamation announcing her as such. Even though he also printed the proclamation declaring Princess Mary to be queen, his sympathies must have been clear and he lost his position of royal printer. Nevertheless in 1553–4 he sat in parliament as a London MP. Although he had fallen from favour at court he was still influential in the city. It was probably for this reason that he was among those commissioned in 1554 to arrange the pageants for Philip and Mary's triumphal entry into London on 18 August after their marriage in the previous month. The city seems to have tried to use these pageants to articulate its fears and hopes for the new regime; one pageant station caused controversy because it depicted Henry VIII passing a Bible to Edward—the bishop of Winchester ordered that the book be painted out.

Grafton became warden of the Grocers' Company in 1555, and in October was appointed for a second term as a governor of the city's hospitals. In 1556, after the end of his wardenship, he was once again the hospitals' treasurer. He sat as a London MP in parliament again in 1557. By this time he was no longer printing; his son-in-law Richard Tottel had inherited his types and woodcuts. Following the accession of Elizabeth in 1558 he was once more engaged in pageant making, as part of the new queen's coronation celebrations, staged on 14 January 1559. In June 1561 he was one of a committee that oversaw repairs to the lightning-damaged steeple of St Paul's Cathedral. He was MP for Coventry in 1563, and in 1563–4 warden of the Grocers' Company for the second time.

None the less Grafton was now in financial difficulties. His first wife, Anne, had died in 1560, and her money seems to have been entailed to her children. In November 1561 two aldermen were sent to investigate his conduct as treasurer of the city hospitals, and when he stepped down as warden of the Grocers' Company in June 1564 the full extent of his problems began to emerge. At the sitting of the company's court of assistants on 29 January 1565 he confessed that he was in debt to the company to the sum of more than £40. There is no evidence that this indicates financial improprieties rather than disastrous mismanagement. The company investigated his circumstances further over the next two years, and on 26 September 1566 the court agreed to buy his house in Greyfriars to cover part of the debt. Nevertheless in 1569 he still owed £20.

Grafton's chronicles In January 1544 Grafton had issued an edition of John Hardyng's mid-fifteenth-century metrical *Chronicle* (STC 12766.7), to which he added a verse dedication to the duke of Norfolk praising the latter's Scottish campaign of 1542 and a substantial prose continuation recounting the history of England up to the year of publication. In 1548 he printed the *Union of the Two Noble and Illustre Families of Lancastre and Yorke* (STC 12721) by his friend Edward Hall, and reissued it with a new preface in 1550 (STC 12723). However, he did not produce any further historical writing of his own until many years later.

It was in 1562–3, while the Grocers' inquiries were under way, that Grafton's son-in-law Richard Tottel, a well-known printer–publisher in his own right, issued the first edition of Grafton's *Abridgement of the Chronicles of England* (STC 12148). Its preface speaks scathingly of other previous abridgements of chronicles, and it was probably in reaction to this that Thomas Marsh—stationer and printer of such books for a number of years—approached John Stow to write a new one, what was to be the *Summarie of English Chronicles* of 1565 (STC 23319).

The ensuing literary quarrel, which is preserved in the prefaces to both Grafton's and Stow's chronicle–histories, represents an early (and illuminating) disagreement between scholarly authors, even though it had its origins as much in the commercial concerns of the initial publishers as in the authors' concerns for their literary 'property'. Marsh had been printing abridged chronicles since 1556, including two editions of the *Breviat Chronicle* (STC 9972, 9976) first printed by J. Mychell (STC 9968). In 1561–2 he had been fined for printing an edition of a chronicle without licence—perhaps the Mychell one or another similar (STC 9989.5). Grafton's new chronicles would have posed a commercial threat.

Further conflict arose in 1565 when John Kingston published Grafton's *Manuell of Chronicles* (STC 12167), dedicated 'To his loving frendes the Master and Wardens of the companie of the moste excellent Arte and science of Impryntyng', and asking in its preface that the Stationers' Company should print no abridgements other than Grafton's own. In an attempt to secure protection he offered the rights for the *Manuell* freely to the company. Stow and Marsh retaliated in 1566–7 with a small chronicle of their own, the *Summary of English Chronicles Abridged* (STC 13325.4). It was uncomplimentary about Grafton and his work and asked for protection from the lord mayor and aldermen of London lest 'thorough the thu[n]dryng noyse of empty tonnes, & unfruitful graffes of Momus offsprynge, it be not ... defaced and overthrowne' (Stow, *Summary*, 16–17). Stow used his rival's name and his printer's device (a 'tun' around a 'grafted' fruit tree) to make cruel jokes at his expense. At this, according to Stow, Grafton 'marvelously stormyd & cawsyd the master & wardens of the stacionars to threaten Thomas Marche' (Stow, *Survey*, lii). The Stationers asked Stow to come to their court and face Grafton; according to Stow, Grafton did not appear. It should be remembered that at this time he was still in financial difficulties.

The quarrel continued in 1568 with the publication by Tottel in that year of Grafton's *A Chronicle at Large ... of the Affayres of Englande* (STC 12147), and the angry competition might have lasted longer, but in 1573 (probably in late April or early May) Grafton died. He was buried on 14 May in Christ Church Greyfriars, London. Stow's response to the *Chronicle at Large*, the *Chronicles of England* (STC 23333), did not appear until 1580. There is no authentic portrait of Richard Grafton, and apparently no surviving will—possibly because by the end of his life he was too much in debt to have anything to leave.

Assessment Although Grafton's chronicles are not as well written as Stow's, they stand as a good example of their genre. In terms of composition and presentation they are certainly far better than the earlier abridgements published by Marsh and others. These writings apart, however, Grafton does not seem to have been the initiator of any of the influential projects to which he gave so much of his time, energy and financial support. Although his choice of activities shows that he was a committed reformer and protestant, he did not suffer the painful fate of many of his friends, acquaintances, and allies. Always the right-hand man, implementing rather than instigating policies, he seems to have managed to appear relatively harmless to unfriendly regimes. During the first half of his life he suffered set-backs and spells in prison, but he always seems to have had a patron who could pull strings on his behalf, while from 1553 his connections within the city of London served him in good stead, even in the times of greatest political and financial hardship. The dual influence of city and court shaped his life, and the dynamic tensions between them both probably buffered him, too, against the worst dangers that either could offer. His links with the court helped his business, and his city connections protected him when others were dying for their beliefs at the hands of the Marian regime—a regime that, fortunately for Grafton, was prepared to make compromises with the city in order to maintain its hold on power. Finally the quarrel resulting from his publication of chronicle–histories is a valuable source for the attitudes of sixteenth-century publishers and writers to their work, and to their rights over it.

MERAUD GRANT FERGUSON

Sources J. A. Kingdon, *Incidents in the lives of Thomas Poyntz and Richard Grafton* (1895) · J. A. Kingdon, *Richard Grafton, citizen and grocer of London* (1901) · J. Nichols, *The progresses and public processions of Queen Elizabeth*, new edn, 3 vols. (1823) · J. G. Nichols, *London pageants* (1831) · J. Ames, T. F. Dibdin, and W. Herbert, eds., *Typographical antiquities, or, The history of printing in England, Scotland and Ireland*, 4 vols. (1810–19) · A. W. Pollard, ed., *Records of the English Bible: the documents relating to the translation and publication of the Bible in English, 1525–1611* (1911) · J. G. Nichols, ed., *The chronicle of Queen Jane, and of two years of Queen Mary*, CS, old ser., 48 (1850) · J. G. Nichols, ed., *The chronicle of the grey friars of London*, CS, 53 (1852) · *The acts and monuments of John Foxe*, ed. J. Pratt, [new edn], 8 vols. in 16 (1853–70) · J. Stow, *A survey of London*, rev. edn (1603); repr. with introduction by C. L. Kingsford as *A survey of London*, 2 vols. (1908); repr. with addns (1971) · J. F. Mozley, *Coverdale and his bibles* (1953) · J. M. Osborn, ed., *The quenes majesties passage through the citie of London to Westminster the day before her coronation*, Elizabethan Club, 1 (1960) **Likenesses** woodcut, 1749, BM, NPG; repro. in Ames, Dibdin, and Herbert, eds., *Typographical antiquities*

Wealth at death negligible if any; in debt to Grocers' Company: Kingdon, *Richard Grafton*

Graham family (*per. c.*1250–1513), nobility, was descended from Anglo-Norman immigrants who came to Scotland under William the Lion and increased in importance from the twelfth century, particularly through the patronage of the Comyns, securing the lordships of Dalkeith and Eskdale in Edinburghshire. David Graham, a member of a junior branch of the family, served Patrick, fifth earl of Dunbar, and was deputy justiciar of Lothian in 1248. A notable accumulator of estates, in 1253 he obtained royal confirmation for eighteen grants of land, including Eliston and Kinpunt in the west of Lothian, Dundaff and Strathcarron in Stirlingshire, and lands in Cunningham and Carrick. Substantial grants from the earl of Lennox were to form the basis of the Graham barony of Mugdock, and grants of land in Perthshire by Malise, earl of Strathearn, were to form the barony of Kincardine. Graham supported the Comyns in 1255, and shared their political eclipse, but was back in favour as sheriff of Berwick by 1264. He died *c.*1272 and was succeeded by his son, Patrick, who consolidated his father's estates in Lennox and Strathearn and took an active part in national politics following the death of Alexander III. Sheriff of Stirling by 1289, he served as one of the Scottish auditors in 1291, and was a steadfast supporter of John Balliol until he met his death at Dunbar in 1296. He married Annabella, sister of Malise, earl of Strathearn (*d.* 1293).

Patrick Graham's son, David, who had fought with his father at Dunbar and was taken prisoner after the battle, succeeded. He continued to uphold the Balliol cause, and it was the killing of his patron, Sir John Comyn, by Robert Bruce, that explains his reluctance to espouse Bruce's cause and led to a period of English service. Following Bannockburn, however, Graham accepted the political situation and returned to serve Robert I, appending his seal to the declaration of Arbroath in 1320. In 1325 he exchanged lands in the earldom of Carrick with the king, for which he received lands including Old Montrose in the sheriffdom of Forfar. He died *c.*1330, and was succeeded by his son, also David, who was one of those who submitted to Edward Balliol after the battle of Dupplin and Balliol's coronation at Scone in 1332. But Graham made his peace with David II, and in 1346 accompanied the king into England and was taken prisoner with him at Nevilles Cross on 17 October, but he had returned to Scotland by 1348, and was later appointed as one of the commissioners to negotiate David II's release. His continuing career in royal service is demonstrated by his frequent appearances as a witness in official records until his death *c.*1376. He was succeeded by his son, Sir Patrick Graham, who in 1357 had been a hostage for the ransom of David II. Active as a diplomat in negotiations with England, and in financial administration, Graham was a staunch supporter of Robert Stewart, earl of Fife and later duke of Albany, from whom he received lands in the Lennox. It was on Albany's behalf that in 1399 Graham was appointed to the council established to advise, and restrain, the duke of Rothesay, the king's lieutenant. But he died in 1400, and was succeeded

by his son William, born of his first marriage, to a woman named Matilda. His second wife, Euphemia Stewart, was the daughter of a half-brother of Robert II.

Sir William Graham (*d.* 1424) formed links with the Douglases. He received a grant of lands in Stirlingshire from Archibald, fourth earl of Douglas, while, following the forfeiture of George Dunbar, earl of March, in 1400, Douglas influence may have led to Graham's holding March's barony of Dundaff, as tenant-in-chief of the crown. He took part in the earl of Douglas's invasion of England in September 1402, and was captured at Homildon Hill, but ransomed soon after. He was also the principal vassal of Duncan, earl of Lennox, whereby he augmented Graham estates in the Lennox, acquiring the superiority of Mugdock, his chief residence and centre of administration, which he was to hold directly of the crown. This considerable landed influence, coupled with his support for Earl Duncan's grandson, the duke of Albany, earned him substantial patronage, above all his prestigious marriage to Mary Stewart, daughter of *Robert III. This was a palpable demonstration of Graham's high favour, notwithstanding the fact that he was Mary's third husband. Sir William's brother, **Patrick Graham**, second earl of Strathearn (*d.* 1413), also benefited from Albany patronage, through his marriage about 1406 to Euphemia Stewart, Albany's niece and the heir of David, earl of Strathearn (*d. c.*1389). As a result Patrick himself became earl of Strathearn, but on 10 August 1413 he was murdered near Crieff by John Drummond of Concraig, a close associate of Walter Stewart, earl of Atholl, who had ambitions to control Strathearn. He was succeeded as earl of Strathearn by his son, Malise *Graham.

From 1407 Sir William Graham appears on official documents as William, lord of Graham, a style which underlines his political status, as there was no territorial lordship of Graham. After Albany's death in 1420 he switched his support to Walter Stewart, earl of Atholl. Atholl had built up considerable support in Lennox, and it was on Graham's lands of Mugdock and Killearn that the Lennox men assembled in August 1423, to press their grievances just before the general council which resolved to negotiate the release of James I from English captivity. Not surprisingly, concern about the Albany Stewarts and their adherents exercised James I on his return to Scotland in 1424, Graham possession of the earldom of Strathearn being one bone of contention. Malise Graham was sent to England as a hostage for the payment of the king's ransom, fated to be the longest-serving hostage, not returning to Scotland until 1454, and James reclaimed the earldom of Strathearn for the crown, substituting for it the less valuable earldom of Menteith. Late in 1424 James I felt secure enough to move against the Albany Stewart faction. William Graham was arrested and held in Dunbar Castle, in the custody of George, earl of March, but he was dead by November 1424, having been predeceased by his son Alexander. His death dealt a severe blow to the men of Lennox, as William's younger brother, Sir Robert *Graham, lacked the older man's experience, connections, and influence, notwithstanding the major role he was to play in the murder of James I in 1437.

Sir William Graham was succeeded by his grandson, **Patrick Graham**, first Lord Graham (d. 1466), who served as a hostage for James I's ransom from 1427 until 1432. His absence in England, and the lack of any noteworthy record of activity during the reign of James I, suggest a waning in the fortunes of the Grahams, but Patrick Graham's position recovered during the minority of James II, through the patronage of the Black Douglases, who exercised a considerable degree of control over the minority administration. The title lord of Graham, used by his grandfather William (except during the personal rule of James I), had been adopted by him by 1443; again, this was a designation of convenience rather than an officially conferred title; but in 1445 Graham was recognized as a lord of parliament, as Patrick, first Lord Graham. His status had been affected by James I's repossession of the earldom of Strathearn, in that his lands of Kincardine became a crown fief; now he took advantage of Douglas favour during the royal minority to obtain a new charter of infeftment which erected Kincardine into a barony. He pursued a career of royal service, appearing as one of the most frequent royal charter witnesses during the reign of James II, particularly after the Black Douglas crisis, when he was almost continuously at court, possibly to demonstrate his loyalty in spite of previous Douglas connections. In 1458 he had his lands in the Lennox erected into the barony of Mugdock. Several times an ambassador to England, he also held the keepership of Dumbarton Castle, and was sheriff of Perth in 1462 and 1464. He died in 1466 and was succeeded by his son, born of his marriage to Christian, daughter of Sir Robert Erskine.

William Graham, second Lord Graham (d. 1471), is recorded as sitting in parliament on 9 October 1466. On 23 November following he received a safe conduct from Edward IV to accompany his relative, Patrick Graham, bishop of St Andrews, on his journey through England to France and Flanders, although there is no evidence that he used it. He sat in parliament again in 1467 and 1469, but died in 1471. He had married Helen Douglas, daughter of William Douglas, earl of Angus (d. 1437), and was succeeded by their son. **William Graham**, first earl of Montrose (1462/3–1513), was a minor at the time of his father's death, his ward and marriage being granted by James III to Thomas, Lord Erskine. As third Lord Graham, William sat in parliament between 1479 and 1487, and he was a steadfast supporter of the king, appearing with him in Edinburgh at the end of May 1488, possibly going on to Sauchieburn with him in June. A pragmatic switch of allegiance saw Graham sitting in James IV's first parliament, on 6 October 1488, and he subsequently received grants of the lands of Aberuthven and Inchbrakie in Perthshire. On the occasion of James IV's marriage to Margaret Tudor in 1503, an earldom was created for Graham out of the Lindsay dukedom of Montrose, which had lapsed to the crown on the death of David Lindsay, and possibly in recognition of his hereditary charter for the lands of Old Montrose. This rewarded Graham for his loyalty and sought to counter the influence of the Lindsays, whose bitter feuding had destabilized Angus. Montrose was killed at Flodden in 1513, having married, first, Annabel Drummond, second, Janet, daughter of Sir Archibald Edmonston of Duntreath, and, third, Christian, widow of Patrick, Lord Haliburton. The subsequent earls of Montrose were the descendants of the first earl's first marriage.

C. A. McGLADDERY

Sources M. Brown, *James I* (1994) • S. I. Boardman, *The early Stewart kings: Robert II and Robert III, 1371–1406* (1996) • J. M. Thomson and others, eds., *Registrum magni sigilli regum Scotorum / The register of the great seal of Scotland*, 11 vols. (1882–1914), vol. 2 • *CDS*, vol. 4 • G. Burnett and others, eds., *The exchequer rolls of Scotland*, 5 (1882) • *Scots peerage*, 6.193–224; 8.260 • R. Nicholson, *Scotland: the later middle ages* (1974), vol. 2 of *The Edinburgh history of Scotland*, ed. G. Donaldson (1965–75) • A. A. M. Duncan, *Scotland: the making of the kingdom* (1975), vol. 1 of *The Edinburgh history of Scotland*, ed. G. Donaldson (1965–75)

Graham, Andrew (1815–1908), astronomer, was born on 8 April 1815 in co. Fermanagh, Ireland. He was trained by T. R. Robinson at Armagh observatory, and on 1 March 1842 became assistant to Edward Joshua Cooper (1798–1863) at the latter's lavishly equipped Markree observatory. His annual stipend of £100 with free accommodation remained unchanged for eighteen years. In 1847 Graham devised an improvement to the bar micrometer and the following year he discovered a ninth asteroid, Metis; he was said to be the only astronomer of his day also to compute the orbit and analyse the irregularities himself. Between 1848 and 1856 he and an assistant made meridian observations of 60,066 stars along the ecliptic (the sun's apparent annual path across the sky), of which only 8965 were previously determined. Their catalogue, published in four volumes, met a real need, providing reference stars for planets, new minor planets, and comets. Graham was considered an extraordinary observer, and also computed the orbits of 198 comets for a book published by Cooper in 1852.

John Couch Adams (1819–1892) had assumed direction of the Cambridge University observatory in September 1861. When he met Graham in December 1862, Cooper was aged sixty-four and ailing, and Graham's situation looked precarious. Adams offered £150 with £10 increments every three years (to £230 by 1903), and free accommodation, coal, and light at the observatory (latterly worth £70 per year); Graham would have a powerful new 8 inch transit circle, a better climate, more assistance, and better prospects. Graham accepted, completed his work for Cooper in June 1863, and moved to Cambridge. From April 1864 Adams delegated all the routine work to Graham: he laboured for thirty-nine years, taking a vacation only on urgent family business. A staunch Wesleyan Methodist, his recreation was chapel meetings and events. In 1871 he declined to assist a visit from Le Verrier and William Lassell because he had a chapel commitment. Graham and his wife Mary (c.1813–1883) had two sons and two daughters, Emma and Harriott, who became engaged while visiting Ireland; after her marriage Harriott emigrated to Queensland, and died there in 1876. Mary Graham died at the observatory on 20 August 1883.

In 1882 **Anne Walker** (b. c.1864), a computer and effectively Graham's second assistant, was allocated a vacant room at the observatory. The transit circle required two observers. From 1872 Graham worked with his assistant Henry Todd, until Todd's health necessitated that Walker regularly substitute for him; in 1892–3 only Graham and Walker observed, and from 1894 to 1896 'Miss Walker alone observed' (Eddington, *Astronomical Observations*, vi). The Cambridge zone of 14,464 stars for the international *Astronomische Gesellschaft* (AG) scheme was published in 1897. On Graham's retirement in 1903, after more than sixty years' work in astronomy, Adams's successor R. S. Ball petitioned senate: 'No one without his spirit and dignity would have done such work … at so low a stipend for all those years' (Ball, 829–30). He was voted a £200 pension and moved to Maid's Causeway, off the Newmarket Road, where he died on 5 November 1908.

Anne Walker was born at Wickham, Suffolk. At the age of fifteen, in 1879, she joined the Cambridge observatory as a part-time computer. From 1882, having distinguished herself in the local senior exams, she was employed full-time (9 a.m. to 2 p.m. for a six-day week) at £10 per quarter, with a month off at Christmas. From the beginning she did some observing, but was chiefly engaged on reduction of the zone observations. When Todd moved out, Walker obtained the perquisite worth £30 yearly of moving into the observatory. In 1884 her salary was £60, with free accommodation. She was more than 'a good observer and an expert calculator' (observatory report, 26 May 1885, 1): with her energy, zeal, and skill, she was invaluable among the ageing staff. In her free afternoon time she helped Adams collate Newton's mathematical papers. It was too cold to work in the calculating room in the winter of 1889; a gas stove was not installed until 1891, when gas lighting replaced paraffin lamps. With Todd unable to observe at night, Walker helped Graham complete the AG zone in 1896. In 1899 hers were the first, and until April 1903 the only, observations for the new *Catalogue of Zodiacal Stars* (1928).

Ball became director of the observatory in 1892, and he retired Todd that June. Walker's position was anomalous. Officially only a computer, she actually did all the work of a third assistant; this had been tacitly recognized by Adams, who had raised her salary by £10 every three years since 1884. When Ball advertised for a new assistant she wrote for clarification, adding: 'I am very desirous to contribute astronomical work' (Walker to Ball, 21 March 1885, letter-book, 89). This suggests that Ball had not spoken to her about it, although they lived in the same building. But Ball engaged younger men at more money—P. Morris for 1893–6, then A. R. Hinks, a 23-year-old first-rate mathematics graduate of Trinity College, in 1896 at £150. Walker's salary had not risen after 1895; the writing was on the wall. In 1899 she officially became the meteorological observer, worth an additional £3 5s. a quarter. With free accommodation she was on the equivalent of £190 per year, surely the best paid woman astronomer in the country.

Graham retired on 27 April 1903, aged eighty-eight.

Hinks was appointed chief assistant, another graduate was appointed second assistant. Walker gave her notice to leave on the same day, after twenty-four years, which suggests her frustration, as well as her loyalty to and affection for Graham. A spinster one year short of her fortieth birthday, she was a late practitioner of the antiquated eye and ear method of observing in an observatory lacking electricity until 1909. Since she did not qualify for a pension, only frugality would have enabled her to save enough to preserve her dignity. As there is no photograph of her among those of the observatory staff, Walker disappeared with even less trace than the meagre formal notes in reports and catalogues that alone mark her quarter century as an observing assistant at a major observatory.

ROGER HUTCHINS

Sources [R. S. Ball], 'Retirement of Mr Graham', *Cambridge University Recorder*, 33 (1903), 828–30 · *The Observatory*, 31 (1908), 467 · 'Cooper, Edward Joshua', *DNB* · St John Cam., John Couch Adams MSS, box 2 · Observatory syndicate annual reports, Cambridge University Observatory · minute books, Cambridge University Observatory · [A. Eddington], introduction, *Catalogue of zodiacal stars* (1928) · letter-book, 1888–1900, Cambridge University Observatory, 89 · W. Doberck, 'The Markree observatory [pt 1]', *The Observatory*, 7 (1884), 283–8 · A. S. Eddington, *Astronomical observations made at the observatory of Cambridge*, ed. J. C. Adams, 25 (1919), v–ix · d. cert. [Mary Graham] · census returns, 1891 [Anne Walker]
Archives St John Cam., John Couch Adams MSS, letters
Likenesses photograph, c.1900, U. Oxf., Astrophysics Library · photograph, Cambridge Observatory Library

Graham, (James) Angus, seventh duke of Montrose (1907–1992), farmer and politician, was born on 2 May 1907 at 19 Manchester Square, London, the elder son and eldest of the four children of James *Graham, marquess of Graham, later sixth duke of Montrose (1878–1954), and his wife, Lady Mary Louise (1884–1957), the only child of William Alexander Louis Stephen Douglas-Hamilton, twelfth duke of Hamilton. He inherited the courtesy title Lord Fintrie, by which name he was known until 1925, when his father became sixth duke of Montrose and he became marquess of Graham. He was heir to a clutch of ancient and illustrious titles, but his father possessed no great wealth, despite having invented the aircraft-carrier.

Graham was educated at Eton College and Christ Church, Oxford, where he read agriculture and gained a blue for boxing. He then travelled around Canada helping with the harvest before returning to Britain to work for Imperial Chemicals in Newcastle upon Tyne. On 20 October 1930 he married Isobel Veronica (d. 1990), younger daughter of Lieutenant-Colonel Thomas Byrne Sellar, army officer. They had a daughter, Fiona (b. 1932), and a son, James (b. 1935). Soon after their marriage he and his wife emigrated to southern Africa, where he found work as a seed salesman in Johannesburg and Southern Rhodesia, before being appointed as an agronomist in the latter colony in 1931. Soon afterwards he bought a 1600 acre farm near Salisbury. Powerfully built, sporty, with a strong singing voice, he became a popular member of the small settler community. His white supremacist ideas soon became manifest in letters to the local press asserting the physical and mental superiority of Europeans, though he was keenly interested in learning African languages and customs. A convinced British Israelite, he believed that the 'Anglo-Celtic' peoples were literally descendants of the lost tribe of Israel. It was later alleged that he had attended the Nuremberg rallies and met a number of Nazi leaders. Nevertheless, as an officer in the Royal Naval Volunteer Reserve he immediately reported for duty in September 1939, and served on destroyers in the battle of Crete and on Atlantic convoys; he ended the war with the rank of lieutenant-commander. After returning to Rhodesia in 1945, he was divorced from his first wife in 1950, and on 17 April 1952 he married Susan Mary Jocelyn Gibbs, widow of Michael Raleigh Gibbs, of Nakuru, Kenya, and daughter of Dr John Mervyn Semple, of Gilgil, Kenya. They had two daughters, Cairistiona (Kirstie; *b.* 1955) and Lilias (*b.* 1960), and two sons, Donald (*b.* 1956) and Calum (*b.* 1958).

Graham rapidly became disillusioned with what he regarded as Britain's faltering imperial conviction, and particularly with the policy of central African federation, which he opposed on the grounds that it would, however slowly, draw Africans into the political system. He stood unsuccessfully for the Confederate Party in the general election of 1953, but was elected in 1958 as Dominion Party MP for Hartley-Gatooma in the federal assembly. In 1954 he succeeded his father as seventh duke, and, while preferring to be known in Southern Rhodesia as Lord Graham, he began to attend House of Lords debates on Britain's African policy, which he invariably opposed. During one debate Lord Hailsham recalled having been bitten by Montrose while playing the Eton wall game.

As the Central African Federation began to disintegrate Graham re-entered Southern Rhodesian politics, becoming a founding member and vice-president of the Rhodesian Front. Following the Front's electoral victory in 1962, he became minister of agriculture, lands, and national resources, although he was regarded in cabinet as slow-witted, a common charge despite the fact that he was a progressive scientific farmer. He was a leading champion of a unilateral declaration of independence from Britain (UDI), in order to preserve white minority rule. It was rumoured at the time that the prime minister, Ian Smith, planned to replace the governor, Sir Humphrey Gibbs, with Graham, who would assume the title of regent, thus preserving some semblance of monarchical continuity. If such a scheme existed, it was undermined during a visit by Harold Wilson just before UDI, when, as light relief after an official dinner, Graham used his great frame and a coin to illustrate a lewd yarn about a female belly dancer. Wilson was not amused, regarding this as a wasted opportunity for urgent political discussion, and momentarily offended his hosts when he said, 'I see … now I understand what qualifications you have to have to become the Regent of Rhodesia' (Wilson, 216). Wilson believed that this episode effectively ruled out any such viceregal role, though it may also have persuaded the British to underestimate the determination of their opponents.

Graham remained a powerful figure in the Rhodesian Front. Undeterred by accusations of treason, for which crime an ancestor had been executed, he signed the independence declaration in November 1965 as 'Montrose', lending the rebellion an eccentric respectability. None the less he declared that any attempt to harm the governor, Sir Humphrey Gibbs, a fellow Etonian, would be over his 'dead body' (Flower, 60). Although banned from returning to Britain (and unable to attend the weddings of his two eldest children), he still received the sovereign's command to attend the House of Lords. He was minister of external affairs and defence from 1966 to 1968, retaining his belief in permanent white supremacy. He advocated territorial segregation on South African lines and opposed doggedly any settlement with Britain, famously declaring: 'If we have to eat sadza [African maize porridge], then we'll eat sadza' (Dupont, 180). Despite his ribald sense of humour, he attributed Britain's decline to sexual permissiveness, and was attracted to bizarre conspiracy theories. By 1968 he was becoming too extreme for the Rhodesian Front and resigned his office in protest against compromise with Britain. After a failed attempt to unseat Smith as president of the Rhodesian Front and stand for the new senate, he withdrew from politics and began to indulge his hobbies as a watercolourist and Gaelic poet of not inconsiderable talent.

In 1980 Graham emigrated to Natal before returning in 1988 to Britain, where he resumed his seat in the Lords and the hereditary sheriffship of Dunbartonshire, making his seat at Nether Tillyrie, Milnathort, Kinross-shire. He died of cancer of the prostate at St Columba's Hospice, Edinburgh, on 10 February 1992. He was survived by his second wife and the six children of his two marriages, and was succeeded as eighth duke by his eldest son, James.

DONAL LOWRY

Sources *Daily Telegraph* (12 Feb 1992) · *The Times* (13 Feb 1992) · *The Independent* (18 March 1992) · *WWW*, 1991–5 · Burke, *Peerage* · J. Barber, *Rhodesia: the road to rebellion* (1967) · R. Blake, *A history of Rhodesia* (1978) · L. W. Bowman, *Politics in Rhodesia: white power in an African state* (1973) · F. Clements, *Rhodesia: the course to collision* (1969) · T. Creighton, *Southern Rhodesia and the Central African Federation: the anatomy of partnership* (1960) · C. Dupont, *The reluctant president* (1978) · M. Evans, 'The role of ideology in Rhodesian front rule, 1962–1980', PhD diss., University of Western Australia, 1993 · K. Flower, *Serving secretly: an intelligence chief on record: Rhodesia to Zimbabwe, 1964 to 1981* (1987) · J. Greenfield, *Testimony of a Rhodesian federal* (1977) · P. Joyce, *Anatomy of a rebel. Smith of Rhodesia: a biography* (1974) · L. J. McFarlane, 'Justifying rebellion: black and white nationalism in Rhodesia', *Journal of Commonwealth Political Studies*, 6 (1968), 54–79 · P. Murphy, *Party politics and decolonization: the conservative party and British colonial policy in tropical Africa, 1951–1964* (1995) · A. R. W. Stumbles, *Some recollections of a Rhodesian speaker* (1980) · H. Wilson, *The labour government, 1964–1970* (1974) · J. R. T. Wood, *The Welensky papers: a history of the Federation of Rhodesia and Nyasaland* (1983) · K. Young, *Rhodesia and independence: a study in British colonial policy* (1967) · b. cert. · d. cert.

Graham, Angus Charles (1919–1991), Sinologist and philosopher, was born on 8 July 1919 at 31 Clive Place, Penarth, Glamorgan, the elder of two sons of Charles Harold Graham (1893–1928) and his wife, Mabelle, *née* Booker. At the time of his birth, his father was a coal exporter, but in 1925 he moved to Malaya to work as a rubber planter; he died of malaria three years later. From 1932 to 1937 Graham attended Ellesmere College in Shropshire, and in 1937 he went to Oxford University to read theology at Corpus Christi College, graduating with a second-class degree in 1940. He then joined the Royal Air Force for his compulsory wartime service and in 1944 he was put on a Japanese language course at London University; he served as a Japanese interpreter in Malaya and Thailand until he was released from the air force in 1945 with the rank of flying officer.

Graham had lost his religious faith a few months after leaving Oxford and in any case had never intended to enter the church. In 1946 he enrolled at the School of Oriental and African Studies (SOAS) at London University for a three-year course in Chinese, graduating with first-class honours in 1949, followed by a PhD in 1953. It was not modern Chinese but the Chinese classical language and the classical texts which profoundly interested him and which he continued to study for the rest of his life. In 1950 he was appointed a lecturer at SOAS and in 1971 professor of classical Chinese; he remained in that post until his retirement in 1984. During those years and in retirement he also held a number of visiting fellowships and professorships both in America and the Far East, which took him abroad for parts of the year. On 23 January 1956 he married Der Pao Chang (*b.* 1932/3), daughter of Yuan-po Chang, general merchant; their daughter, Dawn, was born in 1964.

Graham regarded the two greatest periods in the history of Chinese thought as being the last years of the Zhou dynasty, 500–200 BC, and the period of the Song dynasty, AD 960–1279. For the subject of his PhD, which he expanded and published as his first book in 1958, he chose two Chinese philosophers of the eleventh century, the Cheng brothers, who questioned orthodox Confucianism and whose ideas influenced the leaders of neo-Confucianism. He then turned to the earlier period, when the loss of power of the Zhou kings had led to a breakdown of the traditional feudal system. The sage-kings of old had claimed the authority of heaven, whose Dao, or 'way', they confidently followed, but now every school of thought proposed its own way, and Graham decided to study 'the variety of modes of thinking inside the tradition' (Graham, 4). In 1960 he published a new and for the first time complete translation of the *Book of Liezi* (Lieh Tzŭ), drawing attention to the Daoist concept of 'spontaneity', the importance of responding to circumstances without prior thought, spontaneously following the way. He also worked for many years on the text of the anti-rationalist Zhuangzi (Chuang-tzŭ); he disentangled and then reunited the different strands of philosophical ideas by comparing the grammatical structure of the passages, and when he had completed the textual revision he re-translated the whole work and published it in 1981.

Graham's interest in the structure and use of the classical Chinese language was always an important part of his studies: he believed that an understanding of the language was the way to gain access to the meaning of a text. He was especially respected for his work on the rationalist Mozi (Mo-Tzŭ), the logical and scientific chapters of whose text had for 2000 years been known to be incorrect because the manuscript had been damaged and the bamboo strips left in the wrong order. By patient study and devotion to the task Graham succeeded in revealing the correct text, which he then translated and analysed for its scientific value and published in 1978, with the title of *Later Mohist Logic, Ethics and Science*.

Poetry was a further interest and Graham reached a wide audience with his *Poems of the Late T'ang*, first published in 1965 and continually in demand since then; he felt that the increasing complexity of language in the seventh and eighth centuries made the poets of that period the most interesting of all Chinese poets and that late-Tang poetry 'explores the Chinese language to the limit of its resources' (*Poems of the Late T'ang*, 22).

In 1989 Graham published his most acclaimed and popular book, *Disputers of the Tao* [Dao], a general history of philosophy in China during the classical age, 500–200 BC, providing a wealth of information about the wide variety of philosophers and schools of thought of that period. In a book of essays written to celebrate his seventieth birthday, *Chinese Texts and Philosophical contexts* (1991), Graham himself was invited to contribute by writing a commentary on each essay: this he was glad to do, showing not only his continuing lively interest in the discussion but also the warmth of feeling between him and his former students. He was widely respected as the leading Western authority on classical Chinese when he died of cancer in the City Hospital, Nottingham, on 26 March 1991. He was survived by his wife, Der Pao, and their daughter, Dawn.

ANN GOLD

Sources A. C. Graham, introduction, *Unreason within reason* (1992) · H. Rosemont, ed., introduction, *Chinese texts and philosophical contexts: essays dedicated to Angus C. Graham*, ed. H. Rosemont (1991) · *The Independent* (5 April 1991) · *The Times* (17 April 1991) · *WWW* · private information (2004) · personal knowledge (2004) · b. cert. · m. cert. · d. cert.
Likenesses photograph, repro. in *The Independent*

Graham [*née* Horsley-Beresford], **Caroline Agnes**, duchess of Montrose (1818–1894), racehorse owner, was the third and youngest daughter of John Horsley-Beresford, second Baron Decies (1774–1855), and his wife, Charlotte Philadelphia (*d.* 1852), only daughter and heir of Robert Horsley of Bolam House, Morpeth. On 15 October 1836 she married James *Graham, fourth duke of Montrose (1799–1874) and Conservative politician, at St George's Church, Hanover Square, London, and entered on a career as a prominent society hostess. They had three sons and three daughters; the youngest son, Douglas Beresford Malise Ronald Graham (1852–1925), succeeded to the dukedom.

It was while married to Montrose that Caroline began her long association with the turf. Although she was thoroughly knowledgeable on all aspects of thoroughbred racing and breeding, she was obliged to race under the pseudonym of Mr Manton, as racing was not then considered a suitable pastime for a lady. (The actress Lily Langtry raced under the name Mr Jersey.) Her interest was, however, no secret: her association with the Manton trainer Alec Taylor was well known.

Caroline was widowed in 1874, but in 1876 she married the celebrated owner, Jockey Club member, and dandy William Stuart Stirling Crawfurd (1819–1883). It was largely as a result of this second marriage that her turf career really developed. Together with Craw, as her husband was known, the duchess (who still preferred to be addressed by her title) patronized not only Taylor at Manton but also Joe Dawson's Bedford Lodge stables at Newmarket, which they later bought and turned into a private stable under the supervision of Buck Sherard.

The couple's scarlet racing colours which, with the duchess's bright red hair—usually crowned with a large Homburg hat—earned her the nickname Carrie Red, were highly successful, winning a number of England's classic races. Their most famous racehorse was the 1878 Epsom Derby winner, Sefton, after whom the duchess named the purpose-built stables to which she moved her interests in the winter of 1882–3. Their other classic winners included Craig Millar (winner of the St Leger) and Moslem (joint winner in a dead heat for the 1868 Two Thousand Guineas). In addition Craw's filly Thebais won both the One Thousand Guineas and the Oaks in 1881 and the couple together enjoyed further One Thousand Guineas success with St Marguerite and Mayonnaise.

The duchess was shattered by Craw's death at Cannes in 1883. She had his body brought back to England and buried at St Agnes's Church, Newmarket, which she had built and endowed in his memory. All Craw's horses were kept in training, many of them ridden by the most brilliant jockey of the times, Fred Archer. Archer's ease with his social superiors was often remarked upon and he certainly enjoyed a close relationship with the duchess. It was rumoured that the two were planning to marry, until Archer found out that marriage to a duchess was not enough to make him a duke and cried off.

But Caroline did marry again. Her third husband, Marcus Henry Milner (1864–1939), whom she married in 1888 at the age of seventy, was forty-six years her junior and the couple were widely believed to be unhappy. The duchess, however, who continued to live at Sefton Lodge, was unlikely to be troubled by gossip. A number of her contemporaries, most notably the Hon. George Lambton, testified to her strength of personality and grand disregard for the opinions of others. She was said to have threatened the vicar of St Agnes's with dismissal for uttering a prayer for a fine, dry harvest time shortly before one of his patroness's horses, with a known fondness for heavy going, was due to race in a big handicap.

Caroline died on 16 November 1894 at her home at 45 Belgrave Square, London; she was buried four days later, near to her beloved Craw at St Agnes's. The dispersal sale of her stud on 11 December 1894 had far-reaching results for the British turf: the mare Canterbury Pilgrim, sold to the earl of Derby, went on to establish one of the most influential strains in British racing.   EMMA EADIE

Sources C. Ramsden, *Ladies in racing: sixteenth century to the present day* (1973), 21–6 • R. Onslow, *Headquarters: a history of Newmarket and its racing* (1983) • G. Lambton, *Men and horses I have known* (1924) • J. Welcome [J. N. H. Brennan], *Fred Archer: his life and times* (1967) • GEC, *Peerage* • Boase, *Mod. Eng. biog.* • *Debrett's Peerage*
Archives Herts. ALS, Bulwer-Lytton MSS, letters to E. B. Lytton
Wealth at death £181,325 17s. 5d.: administration with will, 15 Feb 1895, CGPLA Eng. & Wales

Graham, Clementina Stirling (1782–1877), hostess and author, born on 4 May 1782 at Seagate, Dundee, was elder daughter of Patrick Stirling of Pittendriech, merchant, and his wife, Amelia Graham of Duntrune, Forfarshire. Her mother succeeded to the small estate of Duntrune, near Dundee, in 1802, and the family then assumed the surname of Graham. Through her mother, Miss Graham was a descendant of John Graham of Claverhouse, Viscount Dundee, and a fine portrait and valuable papers of the great viscount were cherished heirlooms. Her own opinions were whig. An honoured member of the circle of Edinburgh whigs led by Jeffrey and Cockburn, she was entirely without party animosity, and her relations with them were social. Her character was of the playful and mild, not of the severe and sarcastic order. Spending her time partly in Edinburgh and partly at Duntrune, Miss Graham shared the tastes of both country and town. She had little of the literary lady about her except a liking for the society of men of letters and of art. Although without sparkling wit herself, she had a great deal of quiet humour and a keen appreciation of wit in others. Peers, lairds, and merchants, doctors, lawyers, and artists all met at her house, which in France would have been called a *salon*. It had none of the exclusiveness of a clique, however, but rather the feeling of a family of friends. Genius and wit were sufficient introduction to her hospitality, although she had a Scottish partiality for her kinsfolk and her neighbours. She died, unmarried, on 23 August 1877 at Duntrune.

In early life Miss Graham displayed remarkable powers of impersonation, and often successfully mystified her acquaintance by presenting herself to them disguised as somebody else. One of her most successful creations was Lady Pitlyal, a countrified old lady, with the habits and manners of forty years before. In her old age, at the request of her friend, Dr John Brown, she recorded the pranks she had played on Jeffrey and others in a little volume entitled *Mystifications*, first privately printed in 1859 together with a few poems and prose sketches. Dr Brown edited the first published edition of *Mystifications* in 1865 and it remained in print until 1911. She also translated from the French and published in 1829 *The Bee Preserver* by Jonas de Gelieu, a Swiss author, for which she received a medal from the Highland Society; to her last days she was an ardent lover of bees. She wrote a few pleasing songs, including 'The Sailor Boy', which enjoyed some popularity in the middle of the nineteenth century.

A. J. G. MACKAY, rev. K. D. REYNOLDS

Sources John Brown, 'Memoir', in C. S. Graham, *Mystifications* (1865) • Boase, *Mod. Eng. biog.* • Ward, *Men of the reign* • Irving, *Scots.* • D. Baptie, ed., *Musical Scotland, past and present: being a dictionary of Scottish musicians from about 1400 till the present time* (1894)
Archives NL Scot., corresp. with George Combe • University of Dundee, archives, corresp. with Lady Airlie [copies]

Clementina Stirling Graham (1782–1877), by unknown artist

Likenesses watercolour drawing, Scot. NPG [*see illus.*]

Wealth at death £8548 13s. 4d.: confirmation, 8 Nov 1877, CCI

Graham, Dougal (*bap.* **1721**, *d.* **1779**), poet and chapbook writer, was born in St Ninian's parish, Stirling, son of Dougal Graham and Barbara Stewart, and baptized there on 5 February 1721. Little is known of his life. He had at least some formal education, but his parents were poor and he early entered service at Campsie in southern Stirlingshire. Graham was hunchbacked, lame, and less than 5 feet tall. On 8 September 1749 he was admitted to the Fraternity of Stirlingshire Chapmen. About 1770 he was appointed Skellat bellman (town crier) of Glasgow.

During his lifetime Dougal Graham's main fame was as a poet. Although only two works, *A Full, Particular and True Account of the Rebellion in the Years 1745–6* (1746) and a song, 'The Battle of Drummossie-Muir' (1746) were acknowledged, a number of other poems including 'The Turnimspike' (Eyre-Todd, 40–42) and 'John Highlandman's Remarks on Glasgow' (Eyre-Todd, 42–6) have also been ascribed to him. His *Account of the Rebellion* went through at least three editions during his life (1746, 1752, and 1774), the third being substantially rewritten to include the wanderings of Charles Edward Stuart after the battle of Culloden. Graham is thought to have accompanied the Jacobite army virtually throughout the campaign, acting in effect as war correspondent for the Glasgow booksellers. His poem was basically metrical journalism, a racy and detailed account of more than 5000 lines drawn from a mixture of written and personal sources. He used the 'low' style, one of the established registers in Scotland, which was particularly useful for colloquial verse narrative and political poetry of the more rumbustious sort:

> The Camrons rose, headed by Lochiel,
> And Stewarts did under Appin dwell,
> With the Macdonalds of Glengary …
> Numbered one thousand, eight hundred men,
> But badly arm'd, as you may ken;
> With lockless guns, and rusty swords,
> Durks and pistols of ancient sorts …
> Some had hatchets upon a pole,
> Mischievous weapons, antick and droll …
> Their uniform, was belted plaids,
> Bonnets of blew upon their heads,
> With white cockade and naked thie
> Of foot, as nimble as may be.
> (MacGregor, 1.87)

Dougal Graham was also identified posthumously as author of nearly two dozen classic chapbooks, including *The Whole Proceedings of Jocky and Maggie's Courtship*, *John Cheap the Chapman*, *The History of the Haverel Wives*, *Simple John and his Twelve Misfortunes*, and *The Coalman's Courtship to the Creelwife's Daughter*. Chapbooks formed the staple secular reading matter of the common people of Scotland until well into the nineteenth century. They were published in pamphlet form on coarse paper, adorned with crude illustrations, and were sold in country districts by pedlars of the lower sort and in the cities by professional 'patterers'. They covered a wide range of matter: popular history and biography, manuals of instruction, almanacs, devotional works, and imaginative literature including poems, tales, jokes, and songs. Piracy was universal, and anonymity the rule, so that attribution is uncertain. It seems quite possible, however, that the author of the *Account of the Rebellion* could also have created texts such as *Jocky and Maggie* and *The Coalman's Courtship*, which present a series of bawdy and anarchic scenes of love and marriage. In the past these have tended to be treated as sources of folklore and social history, and assumed to possess a photographic accuracy, but their fundamentally ironical stance now seems obvious. In *Jocky and Maggie* the parents consent to the wedding with a reasonableness that implies their attitude is anything but normal, while the drunken, chaotic wedding night is itself a trope, long established in popular literature. Language is also subject to artistic heightening, as can be seen when Jocky is summoned before the kirk session for fornication and bastardy:

> Mither: … what way could the warld stand, if fouks wadna make use o' ither, it's the thing that's natural, bairns getting, therefore, it's no to be scunnert at … The minister is but a mortal man, and there's defections in his members as well as mine.
> Maggie: Ay, but fouk should ay strive to mortify their members.
> Mither: An is that your Whigry? Will you or any body else, wi' your mortifying o' your members, prevent what's to come to pass … we sall sell the cauf an foster the wean on the cow's milk: That's better mense for a fault, than a' your mortifying o' your members, an a' your repenting-stools; a wheen papist rites an rotten ceremonies, fashing fouks wi'

sack gown and buttock-males an I dinna ken what, but bide you yet till I see the minister … I hae a pokfu' o' perfect petitions to louse an put to him an his elders, and if thou maun gae to their black-stool, it's no be thy lane sall sit upon't.
(MacGregor, 2.21–3)

The enormous scale of the chapbook business was such that if even half of the attributions are accurate Dougal Graham must have been, by some distance, the biggest-selling author in eighteenth-century Scotland. Yet his readers had to be able to process complex non-standard language which was also richly figurative and highly charged and the judgement that his tales were 'level to the meanest capacity' (Fairley, 9) seems misplaced. Whoever wrote these pieces was a master of demotic Scots prose. Dougal Graham died at Glasgow on 20 July 1779.

WILLIAM DONALDSON

Sources J. A. Fairley, *Dougal Graham and the chap-books by and attributed to him, with a bibliography* (1914) · *The collected writings of Dougal Graham, 'Skellat' bellman of Glasgow*, ed. G. MacGregor, 2 vols. (1883) · W. Harvey, *Scottish chapbook literature* (1903) · *John Cheap the chapman's library: the Scottish chap literature of last century, classified with life of Dougal Graham*, 3 vols. (1877) · J. Strathesk, *Hawkie: the autobiography of a gangrel* (1888) · J. Fraser, *The humorous chap-books of Scotland* (1873) · G. Eyre-Todd, ed., *The Glasgow poets: their lives and poems* (1903) · W. Donaldson, *The Jacobite song: political myth and national identity* (1988) · W. Donaldson, 'Popular literature: the press, the people, and the vernacular revival', *The history of Scottish literature*, ed. C. Craig, 3: *Nineteenth century*, ed. D. Gifford (1988), 203–15 · A. Fenton, 'Dougal Graham's chapbooks as a mirror of the lower classes in eighteenth-century Scotland', in A. Gardner-Medwin and J. H. Williams, *A day estivall: essays on the music, poetry, and history of Scotland and England* (1990), 69–80 · bap. reg. Scot.

Likenesses engravings, repro. in MacGregor, *Collected writings of Dougal Graham*

Graham, Eleanor (1896–1984), publisher and children's writer, was born at 18 Grosvenor Park Road, Walthamstow, Essex, on 9 January 1896, the youngest child of Peter Anderson Graham (d. 1925), a reporter for the *Edinburgh Courant* and, after 1900, editor of *Country Life*, and his wife, Jane, née McLeod (d. 1926?), who had been the librarian of a private lending library in Edinburgh. P. Anderson Graham was one of '[W. E.] Henley's young men' in the 1890s, the literary set that included Kenneth Grahame, whose biography Eleanor later wrote. When she was six her parents separated, which upset her deeply. She was very close to her Scottish grandmother, whose country ways she captured in her semi-autobiographical book, *Head O'Mey* (1947).

Eleanor Graham was educated at Chingford high school in Essex, at the North London Collegiate School for Girls, and at the London School of Medicine. She decided against a career in medicine, and left the school in 1916. She joined Lady Muriel Paget's mission to Czechoslovakia in the early 1920s, travelling widely to distribute aid in the countryside until she caught typhoid fever and had to return home. She settled in London, attending poetry readings at the Poetry Bookshop, where for a penny she heard Yeats read 'Innisfree'. Although she published her first children's book in this period, she never made her living by writing. In 1927 she was hired by the Bumpus Bookshop in Oxford Street to run its new children's room. She confided to her employer that she knew nothing of children's books and received the comforting reply that no one else did either.

Very little critical or scholarly attention was paid to children's books before the 1930s, much rubbish was sold for children, and the good that came their way did so unheralded and often by chance. Graham was one of the first to see that a critical apparatus was needed for the evaluation of children's books and, as head of the respected Bumpus children's room, she was in an ideal position to make good the deficiency. During the late 1920s the first children's rooms in public libraries were established and Graham learned a great deal from watching children and librarians select books. She was convinced that children deserved books of the highest quality, and was ahead of her time in believing that any child was capable of responding to great writing, no matter how underprivileged his or her background. The period was a golden age for children's fiction but Graham felt the need for improvement in non-fiction for children, especially in science and history. She lamented that so little poetry was published for children, and raided the Bumpus stockroom for suitable collections. She was responsible for introducing Walter de la Mare, previously seen as an adult writer, to children. She worked at Bumpus until 1931 and took a proper pride in the influence she exercised through the job. She was not in awe of authors, and once advised Arthur Ransome that his new book *Swallows and Amazons* would sell better if he gave it some illustrations. He took her advice.

In the 1930s Graham worked as a children's book editor for William Heinemann and for Methuen, and briefly as the librarian for a private lending library that operated from a garage in Kensington, where she continued to observe children's reading habits. She reviewed children's books for the *Sunday Times*, the *Bookman*, and later for the new *Junior Bookshelf*. In 1938 she published her best-known book, *The Children who Lived in a Barn*. It was a worthy attempt to inject a little reality into the implausible holiday story genre spawned by Ransome's imitators, and as such is of interest more as a document than as a work of fiction.

In 1940 Graham, who had taken a wartime job with the Board of Trade, was summoned by Allen Lane, publisher of the new Penguin Books, to his country house to discuss a new series for children. She arrived late and they spoke until two o'clock in the morning; Lane made her the editor of his new children's paperback series, Puffin Books, a position she held until her retirement in 1961. She was determined that the Puffin imprint should always signify quality and that it should not confine itself to well-established children's classics but should seek out modern classics. Despite the paper shortage and booksellers' doubt about the cheap new series, Puffin achieved a list of thirty-two titles by 1946, the first being Barbara Euphan Todd's *Worzel Gummidge*. The series was a huge success and contributed greatly to children's literature, first by providing an affordable format for high-quality children's books, and secondly by the work it commissioned: Roger Lancelyn Green's *King Arthur and his Knights of the Round*

Table (1953), for example, or Graham's own anthology, *A Puffin Book of Verse* (1953). The latter, drawing heavily on Graham's favourite poet Robert Herrick, reflected her interest in putting into children's hands poetry originally written for adults. She addressed the lack of historical writing for children, starting the Story Biography series for Methuen and contributing to it *The Story of Charles Dickens* (1952).

Eleanor Graham retired from Puffin in 1961. She had always worked from her London flat, and now she moved to Loughton, a country village, but she kept an approving eye on Kaye Webb, her young successor at Puffin. Children's literature entered a period of rapid change in the 1960s, and the book list Graham had built up was beginning to look a little fusty. The 1960s and 1970s put an end to the popularity of many of the titles Graham had selected, but they also saw the rise of young authors to whom she had given their first commissions, such as the artist Brian Wildsmith, who had illustrated Graham's *The Story of Jesus* (1960). She continued to review children's books and remained a respected authority on them for the rest of her life. In 1973 she received the Children's Book Circle Eleanor Farjeon award for services to children's literature. She died at Hereford Lodge, Hereford Road, Westminster, London, on 8 March 1984.

Eleanor Graham was a soft-spoken woman whose wide-apart shining eyes gave her a childlike appearance. There was nothing naïve, however, about her critical faculties. She helped to elevate children's writing to a respected genre of English literature and assisted the numerous talented authors who emerged after about 1930 both as a publisher, by making their work available to the widest possible audience, and as a reviewer, by holding them accountable. Children, to her, were readers to be treated with the greatest respect, for them 'nothing but the best is good enough' (Clark, 91).   ELIZABETH J. MORSE

Sources M. Clark, 'Eleanor Graham', *Signal: Approaches to Children's Books*, 9 (Sept 1972), 91–6 · E. Graham, 'The Bumpus years', *Signal: Approaches to Children's Books*, 9 (Sept 1972), 97–108 · T. Chevalier, ed., *Twentieth-century children's writers*, 3rd edn (1989) · E. Graham, *Kenneth Grahame* (1963) [incl. note about the author] · H. Carpenter and M. Prichard, *The Oxford companion to children's literature* (1984) · B. Doyle, *The who's who of children's literature* (1968) · K. Webb, *The Times* (13 March 1984), 16 · R. L. Green, *Tellers of tales* (1946) · M. Crouch, *Treasure seekers and borrowers: children's books in Britain, 1900–1960* (1962) · J. E. Morpurgo, *Allen Lane, King Penguin: a biography* (1979) · b. cert. · d. cert. · *WWW*, 1916–28
Likenesses photograph (in middle age), repro. in Clark, 'Eleanor Graham', 94
Wealth at death £25,125: probate, 24 July 1984, *CGPLA Eng. & Wales*

Graham, Sir Fortescue (1794–1880), Royal Marines officer, was born at Tintinhall near Yeovil, the son of Colonel Richard Graham, Royal Marines (a descendant of the Grahams of Platten, co. Meath), and his wife, Catherine, daughter of Captain Philip Walsh RN. He was educated at Martock College, Somerset, and on 17 November 1808 was appointed second lieutenant in the Royal Marine Artillery, in which rank he remained seventeen years, twelve of them in the artillery branch of the marine forces. He

was with the battalion formed of marines of the squadron which served with the army ashore at Walcheren in 1809, and subsequently served with the 1st battalion of marines in Portugal and in the north of Spain, including the capture and defence of Castro.

Graham went with the battalion to America, and was present under Sir Sydney Beckwith at the attack on Norfolk and taking of Hampton in 1814. When the brigade was broken up, Graham accompanied the battalion to Canada, and was sent in charge of a division of gunboats to attack an American battery at the head of Lake Champlain, with which he was engaged for several hours. Afterwards he returned with the battalion to the east coast of America, and was present at the attack and capture of Fort Point Peter and the town of St Mary's, Georgia.

Graham became first lieutenant in the Royal Marines on 6 May 1825, and after almost thirty years' service as a subaltern obtained his company on 10 July 1837. Soon after, he joined the battalion of marines serving in Spain during the Carlist War, and subsequently went to China, where he commanded the marine battalion in the demonstration against Nanking (Nanjing) at the close of the First Opium War.

Graham became major on 11 November 1851, lieutenant-colonel on 26 November the same year, and colonel on 20 January 1854. He commanded a brigade of marines at the capture of the fortress of Bomarsund, on the Åland Islands, during the Crimean War in 1855, and was made CB. He was commandant of the Portsmouth division of Royal Marines from 1855 to 1857 and aide-de-camp to the queen from 1854 to 1857. He was made major-general in 1857, lieutenant-general and KCB in 1865, and general and colonel of the Royal Marine Artillery in 1866; he retired in 1870.

Graham married first, in 1828, Caroline, daughter of G. Palliser; she died in 1859. Second, he married Jane Mary, daughter of Captain Lowcay RN, and widow of Admiral Blight; she died in 1866. Graham died at his residence, 69 Durnford Street, East Stonehouse, Plymouth, on 9 October 1880.   H. M. CHICHESTER, *rev.* JAMES LUNT

Sources *Dod's Peerage* (1879) · *Navy List* (1879) · *LondG* · P. H. Nicolas, *Historical record of the royal marine forces*, 2 (1845) · *Prof. Papers of Royal Engineers*, 1 [account of operations at Bomarsund] · Fortescue, *Brit. army*, vols. 9–10 · E. W. Sheppard, *Short history of the British army to 1914* (1926) · Boase, *Mod. Eng. biog.*
Wealth at death under £12,000: probate, 29 Oct 1880, *CGPLA Eng. & Wales*

Graham, George (c.1673–1751), horologist and maker of scientific instruments, was the eldest of three children of George Graham (c.1615–1679), a husbandman, and his second wife, Isobel. His baptism has not been traced and it is uncertain whether he was born at Horsegills in Kirklinton or at Fordlands in Irthington, farms barely a mile apart lying 6 miles north-east of Carlisle, Cumberland. Graham had a brother John and a sister Isobel and he was also half-brother to six offspring from his father's first marriage. Evidence indicates a religious rift in the family and Graham's father certainly changed faiths—he was of the Church of England in 1675 but was a Quaker when he died

George Graham (c.1673–1751), by Thomas Hudson, c.1739

in 1679. The younger George, then aged about six, went to live with his half-brother William at nearby Sikeside.

Apprenticeship and the Tompion family In 1688 Graham was sent to London where he was apprenticed to Henry Aske in the Clockmakers' Company for seven years on 2 July. He signed his indenture in a bold and confident hand. His other half-brother Richard and half-sister Mary were also in London, in 1690, in the parish of St Andrew's, Holborn. Richard and Mary were also Quakers but there is no evidence that Graham was ever of that faith. Richard and his wife, Alice, had six children of whom two survived infancy—William, later associated with his uncle George in the horological trade before emigrating to Philadelphia, and Ann, the residual legatee in Graham's will written in 1747.

Aske's recorded work—'lantern' clocks—is not of the quality expected of the master of such a celebrated pupil and Graham may have been unofficially turned over to another master; Aske lived in Naked Boy Alley, Ludgate Hill, but assessments do not prove that Graham was ever present there. Made free on 30 September 1695, Graham joined Thomas *Tompion's household and workshop about 1696, aged about twenty-two, and would then have received further tuition. Tompion, however, instigated a house style in which his employees were trained and Graham's hand cannot, therefore, be identified in any Tompion timepiece. Tompion and/or Ambrose Gardner, his principal clockmaker during the 1690s, probably acquainted Graham with the styles required. In December 1697, after a two-year journeyman period, Graham enrolled the first of at least fifteen apprentices, Joseph Ward, probably the son of the Water Lane plate-worker of the same name; his second pupil, bound in December 1700, was Obadiah Gardner, son of Ambrose whose family were also members of Tompion's household.

Graham married a niece of Tompion's, Elizabeth Tompion (b. 1687) of Ickwell, Bedfordshire, at St Mary-le-Bow Church on 25 September 1704; Elizabeth was nearly eighteen, and Thomas Tompion witnessed the marriage allegation. With the future of the business in mind, about 1701 Tompion had taken into partnership Edward Banger, a former apprentice who had married Tompion's niece Margaret Kent. Following Banger's apparent dismissal from the premises about 1708 the business ran under Tompion's name alone until about 1711, when Graham was taken into partnership; when Tompion died in November 1713 George and Elizabeth inherited London's leading clock and watchmaking concern. Graham advertised his succession in *The Englishman* on 28 November 1713:

> GEO. GRAHAM, Nephew of the late Mr. Tho. Tompion, Watch-maker, who lived with him upwards of 17 Years, and managed his Trade for several Years last past; whose Name was joined with Mr. Tompion's for some Time before his Death, and to whom he hath left all his Stock and Work, finished and unfinished; continues to carry on the said Trade, at the late Dwelling-house of the said Mr. Tompion, at the Sign of the Dial and Three Crowns, at the Corner of Water-lane in Fleetstreet, London; where all persons may be accomodated as formerly.

Little is known of life within the Graham household but the marriage may not have run smoothly: Elizabeth is reputed to have had two sons whose legitimacy George refused to acknowledge.

The post-Tompion business Graham emulated Tompion by becoming London's most skilled and influential maker, continuing the refinement of techniques and gaining international renown in his own right. Apart from his major contributions to the improvement of precision clocks he can be credited with the introduction of the cylinder escapement for watches and improvements in the production and design of scientific instruments. After Tompion's death, however, the firm's production rate—or at least the retail rate—of standard clocks and watches fell quite dramatically, consistently averaging about fifty timepiece watches a year compared to Tompion's 140, and twelve repeating watches to Tompion's seventeen. Consistency of clock production cannot be judged but he averaged just six standard retail clocks a year to Tompion's seventeen. Various factors accounted for this drop in output: more time was spent on finishing items, Graham was apparently indifferent to financial success, he had an overriding interest in scientific matters, and he probably lost trade in the increasingly competitive market. He continued numbering in Tompion's four principal series, for clocks, timepiece watches, repeating watches, and clockwatches. The latter series also accommodated alarm watches but Graham abandoned it about 1720 (perhaps upon moving premises) when these types were included with either the timepieces or the repeating watches.

Under Graham's management the business continued

to produce standard retail clocks in the tradition of Tompion's austere reliability though his merchandise did not include quite as wide a range; for instance, no Graham clock is recorded of longer duration than two months. Very few profusely decorated examples are recorded although he occasionally supplied replacement movements for French cases such as the superb pedestal clock at Waddesdon Manor, Buckinghamshire. There is no record of his supplying items to the royal family, and he is not known to have supplied turret clocks.

Roughly half of Graham's extant numbered clocks are weight-driven longcase clocks, 35 per cent are table/bracket clocks or timepieces, sometimes with alarm, 10 per cent are longcase regulators, and 5 per cent are various items, chiefly of 30 hour duration. The regulators excepted, most numbered items are standard retail models though several unusual commissions are recorded including a 'tavern timepiece' (no. 575), a longcase clock with regulator in dial arch (no. 587), a monumental longcase 10 ft high at Dunham Massey in Cheshire (no. 629), two three-train *grande-sonnerie* clocks (nos. 488 and 721), the earlier being part of Tompion's unfinished stock, and an extraordinary table-clock (no. 521), his most highly decorated, in the National Palace, Madrid. Graham also supplied bedroom clocks with a silent escapement devised about 1715, incorporating an escape-wheel in the form of a lantern pinion whose three rollers act as 'teeth' impulsing gut pallets. Comparison between late Tompion and late Graham clock-case designs reveals surprisingly few changes in the standard retail models or in the choice of woods and decoration, and apart from the major advances in precision work, improvement of mechanisms was limited to the refinement of existing techniques and models. Though the dead-beat escapement was used in his regulators from about 1720, it did not supersede the recoil escapement in domestic longcase clocks until about 1729.

Graham's dead-beat and other inventions Improvements in workmanship and movement design, most evident in the work of leading makers, highlighted temperature errors and the need for an improved escapement; Graham applied himself to both requirements. About 1720 he introduced the escapement named Graham's dead-beat, which, though more efficient because it had no recoil, required greater care in its construction because of the more precise nature of its action. Graham never claimed priority, possibly because he knew of Tompion's use of almost identical pallets, albeit with pin-wheel escapement, about 1675, but he improved the design by using an escape-wheel with peripheral teeth and pallets working above the plane of the wheel rather than at its side. Its earliest use is reputed to have been in a clock Graham made for the Revd John Whiteside, keeper of the Ashmolean Museum, Oxford. It was adopted by many other makers for use in the majority of precision clocks until the twentieth century and although other escapements, by such makers as Lepaute, Mudge, Vulliamy, Hardy, and Grimthorpe, challenged Graham's for accuracy, it was not superseded until the advent of electrical timekeeping. At the time of its introduction, however, the dead-beat was capable of an accuracy which without temperature compensation was wasted, but within two years Graham contrived a pendulum to complement the escapement and so the true regulator was born. He had experimented about five years earlier with a view to producing a temperature compensated pendulum but found no convenient answer and had no further encouragement until December 1721 when, using mercury for another purpose, he noticed the large degree of expansion when a jar of the metal was placed by the fire. Recognizing its potential he produced a pendulum with a glass jar of mercury for a bob and by June 1722 was testing its accuracy against transits of fixed stars. This type of pendulum is still used today.

Over two dozen regulators by Graham are known, the finest of which, now in the Time Museum, Rockford, Illinois, USA, is no. 634, made about 1723; it shows both sidereal and mean solar time. One of the earliest and most interesting is no. 631 of about 1721, its trunk door having two apertures to show a thermometer (missing) and the mercury pendulum. It is the earliest with square dial silvered all over to provide clarity, which was further enhanced by a large subsidiary second hand and a single central minute hand, the hours appearing in an aperture. With the exception of its up-and-down indication, Graham used this style of dial for most of his later regulators, including nos. 728 and 767, displayed in the Royal Scottish Museum, Edinburgh, and the Time Museum, Rockford, and it was adopted by many other eighteenth- and nineteenth-century regulator makers. James Short described John Shelton as 'the principal person employed by Mr Graham in making astronomical clocks'. A small group of unnumbered equation regulators signed by Graham, an example of which is in the British Museum, were probably Shelton's work, along with nearly identical examples bearing the names Thomas Mudge, Eardley Norton, and Shelton himself, one dated 1736. Graham published at least one *Table of the Equation of Days*, about 1750.

Recognition and further innovation Apart from witnessing the introduction of two of the advances for which Graham is most famed—the dead-beat escapement and the temperature-compensated mercury pendulum—the period 1719–22 was most important to him in other respects. He was elected junior warden of the Clockmakers' Company in September 1719 and subsequently rose through the ranks of renter and senior warden to become master for the year beginning 29 September 1722. In addition he was admitted a fellow of the Royal Society on 16 March 1721 and a fortnight later advertised the move of his business in the *London Gazette* (26 March). His new premises, with the old name, the Dial and Three Crowns, retained, were on the north side of Fleet Street on the eastern corner of Peterborough Court, 100 yards east of Water Lane, and he remained in business there until his death. Polls list Thomas Wright the instrument maker 'in shop' for the first eight years, presumably paying rent to Graham.

After Tompion's death Graham continued to offer a

wide range of watches of the very best quality, from plain silver cased timepieces at £11 to gold cased repeating watches from about £60. He was one of the first, about 1728, to supply watches in single cases, perhaps to reduce cost, but he also employed leading chasers such as Parbury and Moser to supply the finest repoussé outer cases, especially for repeating watches. An example enamelled by Moser is also recorded. Apart from improving mechanisms introduced during Tompion's era Graham instigated other new features and kept apace with advances being made elsewhere: following Tompion's death he introduced a repeating mechanism reputed to have been devised by an employee, Matthew Stogden, which was adopted by many of London's leading contemporary watchmakers; about 1714 he combined the dust-ring and cock-cap as used by Tompion to form a single dust-cap to enclose the movement of a striking watch with pierced cases, and this became a standard component of English watches; four years later he was probably the first English maker to produce a watch with centre-seconds hand and stop mechanism to enable more accurate timings. About 1726 he suddenly abandoned the verge escapement in favour of the cylinder which he then used exclusively. This escapement, perhaps influenced by Tompion's 'virgule' patented in 1695, was used by many leading British makers during the eighteenth and nineteenth centuries and it was adopted, on account of the thinness of movement it enabled, by French and Swiss mass producers of the nineteenth and twentieth centuries. It was an alternative to the verge but it was not capable of consistent accuracy. About 1730 Graham was the first to use 'dumb-repeat' whereby the hammers strike the inside of the dust-cap, or against blocks instead of a bell, thus dispensing with the need for a pierced case, and six years later he was among the first in this country to use white enamel dials.

Graham is not known to have contemplated competing for the board of longitude prize offered in 1714 for the invention of a timekeeper capable of sustaining accuracy at sea, and this may have been due, in part, to his acceptance that John Harrison's ideas were further advanced than his own. Graham became a lifelong admirer of Harrison's work from the time of their meeting, about 1725, in Graham's shop, and Harrison later paid generous tribute to Graham's moral and financial support.

Contribution to astronomy Graham is renowned for his clocks and watches but his contribution to the study of astronomy was of greater importance and significance. The earliest evidence of this interest occurs about 1710–15 with the production of tellurions—instruments to display the relative motions of sun, moon, and earth by geared models; two are recorded—one signed Tompion and Graham, now in the Museum of the History of Science, Oxford, the other signed Graham alone, now at the Adler Planetarium, Chicago, USA. It is reputed that when the first of these was in John Rowley's hands awaiting shipment to Prince Eugene of Savoy along with instruments of his own making, Rowley noted its detail and about 1712 produced an improved model. Sir Richard Steele saw this

instrument and, being ignorant of those made by Graham, misguidedly named it an orrery in honour of Charles Boyle, earl of Cork and Orrery. Tellurions and planetariums subsequently became known as orreries.

Graham probably carried out astronomical observations from the roofs of both Tompion's old shop and from his new premises, and his first-hand experience of deficiencies in instruments currently in use together with his broad knowledge of mechanics and production techniques resulted in the manufacture of several historically important instruments for astronomers such as Halley, Bradley, and Molyneux. The friendships forged in the pursuit of this interest doubtless brought about his election to the Royal Society, and the high regard in which he was held by that body is reflected in his election to their council no fewer than twelve times in 1722–47. He presented over twenty papers on a variety of subjects, chiefly the results of astronomical observations—eclipses of sun and moon, transits of Mercury over the sun, occultations of Jupiter and satellites, of Mars and of Aldebaran by the moon, barometric levels, variations of the magnetic needle, pendulum experiments, Colonel Molesworth's hourglass, and weights and measures. Some of the astronomical observations were made from his own premises where he was occasionally joined by friends such as Bevis, Bradley, and Short.

Edmond Halley who succeeded Flamsteed as astronomer royal at Greenwich observatory in 1720 had been deprived of instruments following Mrs Flamsteed's successful claim to their ownership. During 1721–5 Graham supplied three regulators which, curiously, had plain pendulums, though during the 1740s he supplied two compensated pendulums, presumably for two of these clocks. In 1721 Halley ordered from Graham a transit telescope which was in use until 1750 and is now displayed at the observatory, although only the mounting survives of Graham's work. In 1725, with Jonathan Sisson's assistance, Graham constructed an iron mural quadrant of 8 ft radius which was mounted facing north on the meridian wall erected by Halley in 1721. This celebrated quadrant was the first with Graham's more accurate 90° arc of ninety-six divisions. Hitherto, precise division could not be attained because a right angle cannot be divided geometrically into its 90 degrees but Graham realized that greater accuracy would be achieved by dividing the scale into ninety-six parts entirely by bisection. Each of the divisions was then further subdivided into eight and a vernier gave readings to one thirty-second of a subdivision, that is, to 0·0036°. Conversion tables were used to translate divisions into degrees, though an arc of 90 degrees was engraved alongside that of ninety-six divisions. This instrument remained in use at the observatory until 1812 and it may still be seen there.

Hooke and Flamsteed had both tried to determine parallax in fixed stars but their results were inconclusive. So matters stood until Samuel Molyneux, a wealthy amateur astronomer with an observatory at Kew, decided to investigate and employed Graham to make a zenith sector of over 24 feet focal length. The first observations were made in November 1725, Molyneux's memorandum noting occasions when he was joined in his observations by Bradley, and by Graham who carried out checks and minor alterations. An apparent change in the position of stars was soon noticed but it was not a discrepancy which could be explained by parallax and the implication was not immediately realized. In curiosity Bradley ordered another sector of modified design from Graham, his intention still being to determine parallax. This instrument was set up at Wanstead in August 1727 and the results of Bradley's observations were outlined in a paper delivered to the Royal Society—'A new apparent motion of the fixed stars discovered'—published in 1734. He had failed to determine parallax in fixed stars but could now explain one of the reasons for the apparent shifting of stars, the phenomenon being caused by the aberration of light. Bradley then changed the focus of his researches to the annual change of declination of some of the fixed stars, and observations using Graham's sector continued until 1747 when he published *A letter to the Rt. Hon. George earl of Macclesfield concerning an apparent motion observed in some of the fixed stars*. He had made his second great discovery—the nutation of the earth's axis. In 1749 Bradley had Graham's sector moved from Wanstead to Greenwich observatory where it remained in use until 1812 and where it is now exhibited. Graham also made a 2½ ft equatorial sector for Bradley which was in use in 1748–79, but was last heard of in 1933. About 1750 Graham supplied Bradley with a regulator with gridiron pendulum.

The team of scientists sent to northern Sweden in 1736 by the French Academy to measure an arc of meridian relied upon:

> a Sector of about 9 foot Radius … made at London under the Direction of that ingenious artist Mr Graham … who had exerted himself to give it all the Advantages and all the Perfection that could be wished for. He had even taken the trouble to divide the Limb with his own hands. We had a Clock of Mr Graham's, and an instrument which we owed to the same gentleman, consisting a Telescope perpendicular to, and moveable about a horizontal Axis. (Rigaud, xxvii)

Their calculations helped confirm Newton's theory of the figure of the earth.

In 1741 Graham supplied a regulator and a 12 foot zenith sector to Uppsala observatory, Sweden, newly built under the direction of Andrew Celsius. The regulator, one of the first with temperature compensation to be used on the continent, was delivered in 1741 by Daniel Eckström, the Stockholm clockmaker, on his return home after spending time with Graham in London. Eckström was strongly influenced by Graham's work.

In November 1742 the Royal Society in London and the Royal Academy of Sciences in Paris proposed that accurate standards of the weights and measures of both countries be examined and unified. Graham was appointed to represent the Royal Society and though the comparison was carried out no action was taken. In 1748 Graham was among contributors who supplied details to Dr Richard Davies for tables of specific gravities, having weighed gold and silver.

Of Graham's fifteen apprentices at least ten gained their freedom including Thomas Mudge (1715–94) who went on to achieve great fame as the inventor of the lever escapement for watches (the most significant advance since the application of the balance-spring) and as the maker of a celebrated group of marine timepieces. Also among them were William Dutton, who partnered Mudge in business, Samuel Barkley, John Priest, and Henry Hull the specialist cylinder escapement maker employed by other leading makers, notably Ellicott.

Death and reputation Graham died during the evening of 16 November 1751, probably at his premises in Fleet Street, and was buried on 23 November at Westminster Abbey in the same grave as Thomas Tompion. He wrote his own will, dated 23 June 1747, and appointed Samuel Barkley and Thomas Colley as executors. Half of his personal estate went to his wife, Elizabeth, who survived him. Ann Graham, a spinster aged fifty-five when Graham died, had already been named residual legatee; she may have lived with George and Elizabeth, caring for them in their old age. Mary Puckeridge (*née* Hall) and a maidservant each received 20 guineas; Mary Puckeridge's connection with Graham's family is unknown.

Barkley and Colley continued Graham's business at the same address while Thomas Mudge advertised that he 'carries on Business in the same Manner Mr. Graham did' at his shop opposite the Bolt and Tun—nearly opposite the former Tompion–Graham premises. Barkley survived Graham by less than two years but Colley continued until the 1760s when he formed a brief partnership with John Priest; Colley died in 1771.

None of Graham's business ledgers is known to have survived but some correspondence, with Bernard Howard (Norfolk archives, Arundel Castle), and with the Revd John Whiteside and the Revd Professor Bradley, both of Oxford, is recorded. The Royal Society possesses the papers he delivered. At least one clock survives with its original bill, longcase no. 681, supplied to Mr Robert Cay of Northumberland in 1728. Graham's portrait by Thomas Hudson, now in the Science Museum, London, was painted about 1735–40, possibly for George Parker, second earl of Macclesfield, who owned it when it was copied in mezzotint by Thomas Ryley about 1750; the earl also had a sidereal regulator by Graham in his library at Shireburn Castle.

Graham, who came to be known as Honest George, was of exemplary character as the following extract from his obituary attests:

> His temper was not less communicative than his genius was penetrating, and his principal view was not either the accumulation of wealth, or the diffusion of the same, but the advancement of science and the benefit of mankind. As he was perfectly sincere, he was without suspicion; as he was above envy he was candid, and as he had a relish for true pleasure he was generous. He frequently lent money, but never could be prevailed upon to take any interest; and for that reason he never placed out any money on government securities. He had bank-notes which were thirty years old by him when he died; and his whole property, except his stock-in-trade, was found in a strong-box, which, though it was less than would have been heaped up by avarice, was yet more than would have remained to prodigality. (*GM*, 523)

Hudson's portrait shows him with an expression of calm resignation, not without pride, seated, bewigged and wearing a long-tailed coat, his hat and gloves in his lap. His finely boned features contribute to an impression that he was of small stature.　　JEREMY LANCELOTTE EVANS

Sources J. B. Penfold, 'The Cumbrian background of George Graham', *Antiquarian Horology and the Proceedings of the Antiquarian Horological Society*, 8 (1972–4), 600–13 · J. B. Penfold, 'The London background of George Graham', *Antiquarian Horology and the Proceedings of the Antiquarian Horological Society*, 14 (1983–4), 272–80 · C. D. Hellman, 'George Graham, maker of horological and astronomical instruments', *Vassar Journal of Undergraduate Studies*, 5 (1931), 221–51 · J. B. Penfold, 'The marriages of George Graham and Edward Banger', *Horological Journal*, 94 (1952), 798–800 · F. Baily, *An account of the Revd John Flamsteed, the first astronomer-royal* (1835) · *Miscellaneous works and correspondence of the Rev. James Bradley*, ed. [S. P. Rigaud] (1832) · J. R. Millburn, 'The Fleet Street address of Graham and his successors', *Antiquarian Horology and the Proceedings of the Antiquarian Horological Society*, 8 (1972–4), 299–301 · W. Hutchinson, *The history of the county of Cumberland*, 2 vols. (1794); facs. edn (1974) · *An inventory of the navigation and astronomy collections in the National Maritime Museum*, National Maritime Museum, 3 vols. (1970) · M. Daumas, *Scientific instruments of the seventeenth and eighteenth centuries and their makers*, ed. and trans. M. Holbrook (1972); repr. (1989) [Fr. orig., *Les instruments scientifiques aux xvii et xviii siècles* (1953)] · E. G. R. Taylor, *The mathematical practitioners of Hanoverian England, 1714–1840* (1966) · G. H. Baillie, *Clocks and watches: an historical bibliography* (1951) · Johan Horrins [J. Harrison], *Memoirs of a trait in the character of George III … authenticated by official papers and private letters* (1835), appx 6, n. · G. Pipping, 'The Graham clock of Uppsala observatory in Sweden', *Antiquarian Horology and the Proceedings of the Antiquarian Horological Society*, 18 (1989–90), 411–16 · N. Goodison, *English barometers, 1680–1860*, rev. edn (1977), 153–6 · R. W. Symonds, *Thomas Tompion, his life and work* (1951) · J. L. Evans, 'The numbering of Tompion's watches—series and system', *Antiquarian Horology and the Proceedings of the Antiquarian Horological Society*, 14 (1983–4), 585–97 · parish rate books, London, St Bride, and London, St Dunstan, GL · C. E. Atkins, ed., *Register of apprentices of the Worshipful Company of Clockmakers of the City of London* (privately printed, London, 1931) · B. Hutchinson, 'Guardians of Greenwich time', *Vistas in Astronomy*, 28 (1985), 87–94 · *GM*, 1st ser., 21 (1751), 523–4 · *The Englishman* (28 Nov 1713) [advertisement]
Archives BM, clocks, watches, barometers, and other instruments · FM Cam., clocks, watches, barometers, and other instruments · GL, Clockmakers' Company collection, clocks, watches, barometers, and other instruments · MHS, Oxf., clocks, watches, barometers, and other instruments · NMM, Greenwich, Royal Observatory, clocks, watches, barometers, and other instruments · Sci. Mus., clocks, watches, barometers, and other instruments · Time Museum, Rockford, Illinois, clocks, watches, barometers, and other instruments | Bodl. Oxf., Bradley MSS; Graham–Whiteside MSS [Ashmole] · GL, Sully–Graham MSS · Norfolk archives, Arundel Castle, West Sussex, Graham–Howard MSS · RS, society archives, papers delivered before the society
Likenesses T. Hudson, oils, c.1739, Sci. Mus. [*see illus.*] · T. Ryley, mezzotint, c.1750 (after Hudson), NPG; repro. in Symonds, *Thomas Tompion* · J. Faber junior, mezzotint (after Hudson), BM, RS · T. Hudson, drawing (sketch for his oil painting, 1739) · J. Tookey, engraving (after Hudson), RS
Wealth at death over £1500: GM; *Historical Chronicle*, 21 (1751), 523–4; will

Graham, George (*bap.* 1728, *d.* 1767), playwright, the son of the Revd Andrew Graham, a private tutor, and his wife, Jane, 'a boarding-dame at Eton', was baptized on 30 October 1728 at Blankney, Lincolnshire. His family was related to the duke of Montrose on his father's side. He had at least one older brother, David. Graham studied at Eton

College from 1740 to 1746, and on 20 December 1746 was admitted as a scholar at King's College, Cambridge. He proceeded BA (1751) and MA (1754); he was a fellow of the college between 1749 and 1767, and assistant at Eton between 1753 and 1767. In the latter capacity he was credited with having encouraged Joah Bates 'in his love of music' (Austen-Leigh, 145).

Graham's own musical inclination explains, perhaps, why he chose to write a masque at a time when the genre was out of fashion: *Telemachus* was published in 1763, and reprinted in 1767, while a version which P. Hayes had adapted appeared in 1765. Graham's masque received mixed responses. In Cooper's *Memorials of Cambridge* it is reported to have 'received high commendation'; Baker is less enthusiastic and pronounces it 'coldly correct, with little to censure, but less to applaud' (Baker, 3.323), whereas Genest finds it 'not badly written, but … very dull' (Genest, *Eng. Stage*, 10.181). Samuel Johnson, with whom Graham was on friendly terms, was more generous in his (unsigned) review, which gives a summary of the plot and concludes by recommending the 'fertility of imagination, the depth of sentiment, and the knowledge of passion' to the discerning reader (*Critical Review*, 15, 1763, 314–18). In his dedication to Lord Lyttelton, Graham makes it clear that he was keen to attract 'several readers', discerning or otherwise, and sanguine that Lord Lyttelton's patronage would make for good publicity. Although *Telemachus* may have been privately staged, as was common with masques, its inclusion in the section 'Plays printed but not acted, between 1660 and 1830' in Genest suggests that it never achieved substantial popularity.

As the title-page proclaims, Graham's masque was inspired by Fénelon's *Les aventures de Télémaque* (1699). The plot is based on the classic 'contention between pleasure and virtue' (*Critical Review*, 15, 1763, 314), pleasure in this case being personified by the demi-goddess Calypso and her less illustrious nymph Eucharis, over whose combined temptations Telemachus's virtue eventually manages to triumph. In the process, the usual (for the time) struggle between 'irrational', feminine sensibility and 'sound', masculine reason is settled, once Telemachus gets over his irritation at Mentor's assurances that:

> What reason warrants, stands for-ever fixed,
> Like the foundations of the Hesperian coast.
> (Graham, *Telemachus*, 1763, 36)

Apart from another play, *The Duke of Milan*, which David Garrick turned down, Graham also wrote a collection of edifying stories interspersed with so-called 'poetic essays' in the same spirit. The book, *The Virtuous Novelist, or, Little Polite Court Tales* (1750; repr. in microfiche, Opie Collection of Children's Literature, 1992, no. 006:167), was intended for 'the amusement & instruction of our British youth of both sexes' (title-page). The ten stories are variations on the same theme: the superiority of virtuous poverty, humbleness, and homeliness over vacuous beauty, riches, and hedonistic pleasures.

Graham died in February 1767 and was buried at Eton College on 7 February.

ARTEMIS GAUSE-STAMBOULOPOULOU

Sources R. A. Austen-Leigh, ed., *The Eton College register, 1698–1752* (1927), 145 · C. H. Cooper, *Memorials of Cambridge*, 1 (1860), 229 · D. E. Baker, *Biographia dramatica, or, A companion to the playhouse*, rev. I. Reed, new edn, rev. S. Jones, 3 (1812), 323 · Genest, *Eng. stage*, vol. 10 · *GM*, 1st ser., 37 (1767)

Graham, George Farquhar (1789–1867), writer on music, was born on 28 December 1789 in Edinburgh, the eldest son of Lieutenant-Colonel Humphrey Graham. He was educated at Edinburgh high school and the University of Edinburgh, and taught himself music. He was one of the secretaries of the first Edinburgh music festival in 1815 and composed an overture for one of the concerts. In 1816 he published *An account of the first Edinburgh musical festival, to which is added some general observations on music*. Soon after this he visited France and Italy and heard Paganini play in Florence. Graham was a talented violinist, and was one of a group of musicians in Edinburgh who played quartets together. When Sir Henry Bishop retired in 1843, Graham stood unsuccessfully for the chair of music at Edinburgh University.

Throughout his life Graham wrote about music. He contributed the article on music to the seventh edition of the *Encyclopaedia Britannica*. This was reprinted separately in 1838, with an introduction and appendix, as *An Essay on the Theory and Practice of Musical Composition*. He became an expert at deciphering manuscript music written in lute tablature, and helped William Dauney to transcribe and edit the Skene manuscript, published in 1839 as *Ancient Scottish Melodies: a Selection from Skene MS*; he also contributed a paper to the appendix. He helped to edit Wood's *Songs of Scotland* (1848–9), for which he wrote historical, biographical, and critical notes and harmonized twenty-eight of the songs. He also wrote on music for the *Edinburgh Review* and *The Scotsman*.

Graham's first composition, in 1811, was a grand divertimento for piano, *The Battle of Barrosa*. His anonymous *Twelve Pieces of Vocal Music* (1811) were dedicated to Haydn. He wrote *The Elements of Singing* (1817) for the Edinburgh Institution of Sacred Music, and two of his doxologies were included in R. A. Smith's *Edinburgh Sacred Harmony* (1829). His best-known songs were 'Ah, County Guy' (supposedly written at the request of Sir Walter Scott), 'You never longed nor loved', 'The Mariner's Song', and the glee 'A Wet Sheet in a Flowing Sea'.

Graham died on 12 March 1867 at Gilmore Place, Edinburgh.   ANNE PIMLOTT BAKER

Sources H. G. Farmer, *A history of music in Scotland* (1947) · Grove, *Dict. mus.* · D. Baptie, ed., *Musical Scotland, past and present: being a dictionary of Scottish musicians from about 1400 till the present time* (1894) · Boase, *Mod. Eng. biog.* · DNB
Archives NA Scot., corresp. and papers | U. Edin. L., letters to David Laing

Graham, Sir Gerald (1831–1899), army officer, was born at Acton, on 27 June 1831, the only son of Robert Hay Graham (1789–1859) MD, of Eden Brows, Cumberland, and his wife, Frances (1797–1898), daughter of Richard Oakley (1763–1833) of Oswaldkirk, Yorkshire, and Pen Park, Bristol. He was educated at schools at Wimbledon and Dresden. He entered the Royal Military Academy, Woolwich, in

Sir Gerald Graham (1831–1899), by Sir Edward John Poynter, exh. RA 1886

May 1847, passed out third of his batch, and was commissioned second lieutenant Royal Engineers on 18 June 1850. His promotions followed the usual pattern and he reached major-general on 19 October 1881, aged fifty. Along the way he became friendly with two rising stars, Charles Gordon and Garnet Wolseley. Gordon he met at the Royal Military Academy, and they became close friends in the Crimea, when they were demolishing the Sevastopol dockyard in the winter of 1855–6. To Wolseley, with whom he served in the Crimea and China, he was less close, and he was never a member of the Wolseley 'ring'.

Graham was an impressive figure: tall (6 feet 4 inches), massively built, with a handsome face, steel-blue eyes, and dark hair. He first came to notice in the Crimea where he served at the Alma and Inkerman and the siege of Sevastopol. He was seriously wounded, twice mentioned in dispatches, awarded the Mejidiye (fifth class), and the French Légion d'honneur. For his conduct at the assault of the Redan, and for his heroism in bringing in wounded officers and men, he was awarded the Victoria Cross. He was decorated by Queen Victoria at the review in Hyde Park to inaugurate the VC on 26 June 1857. He was also made brevet major.

In the spring of 1860 the 23rd field company Royal Engineers, which he was then commanding, joined at

Hong Kong the force assembling under Sir Hope Grant for the Anglo-French expedition against China. Graham was severely wounded on 21 August 1860 in the victorious assault on the Taku (Dagu) forts. In spite of his wound he remounted his horse (also wounded) until his horse was again wounded and he was compelled to leave the field. As soon as he was convalescent he rejoined his sappers and marched with them to Peking (Beijing) where they occupied the Anting (Anding) gate. He was present at the entry of Lord Elgin into Peking and the signing of the treaty on 24 October 1860. He was mentioned in dispatches and made brevet lieutenant-colonel.

Graham was serving as commanding royal engineer at Shorncliffe camp when on 29 April 1862 he married at St Peter's, Eaton Square, London, Jane Dinah, daughter of George Durrant (d. 1877) of Elham Hall, Suffolk, and widow of the Revd G. B. Blacker (d. 1858), rector of East and West Rudham, Norfolk. They had six children.

From May 1866 to 1869 Graham was commanding royal engineer at Montreal, and while in Canada his previous war services were rewarded by the CB and a brevet colonelcy. From 18 December 1877 he was assistant director of works for barracks at the War Office, until promoted major-general in 1881. In 1882 Sir Garnet Wolseley, the adjutant-general, selected Graham to command the 2nd infantry brigade in the 1st division of the expeditionary force for Egypt.

Graham distinguished himself in the subsequent operations. He commanded at the victory of Qassasin (26 August) against greatly superior numbers, for which he was praised by Wolseley. At the battle of Tell al-Kebir, on 13 September, Graham led his brigade in the assault and was praised by Wolseley. He was mentioned in dispatches, thanked by both houses of parliament, received the Mejidiye (second class), and was made KCB. He commanded a brigade in the army of occupation in Egypt.

By the beginning of 1883 the rebellion led by the Mahdi, Mohammed Ahmad, had spread through much of the Sudan. In the eastern Sudan the strategically important Red Sea port of Suakin was threatened by the Mahdist tribes, especially the Hadendowa (the 'Fuzzy Wuzzies'), dedicated Muslims and extremely brave. Their leader was Osman Digna (Uthman ibn Abu Bakr Dignai), a devoted Mahdist and clever tactician. He routed the Egyptian force sent under Valentine Baker Pasha to relieve Suakin at al-Teb on 2 December 1883. Suakin, temporarily held by a British naval force, was nightly subjected to small arms fire and appeared vulnerable.

The British, as the occupying power, made the reluctant khedive agree to Egyptian withdrawal from the Sudan. Major-General Charles Gordon was lent to the Egyptian government to supervise this. In late January and early February 1884 Graham accompanied Gordon up the Nile to Korosko on the way to Khartoum. On parting Gordon gave Graham a silver-mounted kourbash (rhinoceros-hide whip), and took Graham's white umbrella, having lost his own. Later Graham recorded his sense of foreboding as they bade farewell.

Graham was appointed to command an expedition to the eastern Sudan to relieve the Egyptian garrison besieged at Tokar and to destroy Osman Digna, who was threatening Suakin. Acting quickly he arrived at Suakin on 22 February with some four thousand British troops and fourteen guns, a considerable logistic feat. The climate was abominably hot, water was scarce, and the barren desert plain was covered with a vicious thorn-covered mimosa scrub (Acacia arabica), often higher than a man. The coastal plain was seamed with innumerable wadis and distant observation was difficult. Nevertheless Graham acted promptly. He moved the bulk of his force by sea to Trinkitat, farther down the coast, marched inland to Tokar, and defeated Osman Digna in the third battle of al-Teb on 29 February.

Having moved back by sea to Suakin, Graham kept up the impetus by attacking Tamai, south-west of Suakin, and the main Hadendowa village. He burnt the village, destroyed a considerable quantity of ammunition, and returned to Suakin. The Hadendowa had fought ferociously; Graham's casualties were 100 killed and 112 wounded. The Mahdists lost about two thousand from an estimated twelve thousand. As early as 5 March, Graham was urging the importance of opening up the Suakin–Berber route to Khartoum and Gordon, who strongly supported the proposal. Although it was turned down, a scheme was prepared and a reconnaissance made as far as Tambouk. After Tamai, Graham again urged the importance of sending troops from Suakin to Berber. He was strongly supported by Sir Evelyn Baring (afterwards Lord Cromer), the British agent in Egypt, but to no avail. After Graham had occupied and destroyed Tamanieb on 27 March, he was ordered to end the campaign and return to Cairo, leaving a garrison in Suakin.

Graham returned to England at the end of April to something of a hero's welcome. He was again thanked by both houses of parliament, received the grand cordon of the Mejidiye, and was promoted lieutenant-general. He chose this in preference to a baronetcy, presumably with his pension in mind. He was also presented with a sword of honour by the 1st Newcastle and Durham volunteer engineers, whose inspecting officer he was.

Two possible routes were considered for a Gordon relief expedition: first, up the Nile, and second, from Suakin to Berber—much shorter, but with great problems over water. In February 1885 the government, after much delay, decided to use both routes, but with the Nile (which Wolseley favoured) the main route on which resources were concentrated. Wolseley was to command the Nile column and Graham the force from Suakin.

Graham arrived there on 12 March 1885 after personally receiving instructions from Lord Hartington, the secretary of state for war. He was to destroy Osman Digna, then to push forward the construction of a railway from Suakin to Berber. It took some time to assemble the necessary troops, of which a brigade came from India. The Mahdists captured Khartoum and killed Gordon on 25 January 1885: Wolseley's relief force arrived too late. There was a public outcry in Britain. Wolseley was told he could continue his operations, and in reply recommended an immediate expedition to Suakin to crush Osman Digna and to push forward the railway to Berber as rapidly as possible. A considerable force was assembled at Suakin amounting to some thirteen thousand troops and as many followers. In addition to an Indian brigade the force included a New South Wales contingent.

Graham, who had not been Wolseley's first choice to command the second Suakin expedition, wasted no time after his arrival. Osman Digna had gathered a large number of the Hadendowa at Tamai and Hashin. Graham moved against Hashin on 20 March, stormed the position, and dispersed the enemy. He next operated against Osman Digna at Tamai, constructing intermediate posts *en route*. At the first of these at Tofrek, some 6 miles from Suakin, in thick bush that restricted observation, the leading brigade under Major-General John McNeill was constructing zaribas of thorn bushes when it was suddenly taken by surprise, attacked, and almost overwhelmed. McNeill lost 141 killed and 155 wounded before the situation was restored. He also lost 501 camels, a third of his transport. Continuing the advance to Tamai on 2 April, pushing back Osman Digna who escaped to the mountains, Graham burnt the village and destroyed large stocks of ammunition. He then returned to Suakin.

Graham's second important task was the construction of a railway to Berber, over 200 miles distant. The government had put the construction out to civilian contract rather than employ the Royal Engineers. As local labour was virtually unattainable some 750 highly paid British labourers were recruited. They were difficult to discipline, and neither the soldiers nor the officers approved of them.

Work began on 13 March. It was planned to build the railway in 50 mile blocks, and it was reckoned it would take a year to complete. It was of course vulnerable to attack by Osman Digna. Huge quantities of material were offloaded at Suakin, much of it useless. About 10 miles had been roughly completed when on 20 April Graham was informed that the government was considering suspension of the expedition, ostensibly because of the Panjdeh incident and the possibility of war with Russia. The decision led to an outcry, and Wolseley was sent to Suakin to report, arriving on 2 May.

Wolseley was not impressed with the conduct of the campaign. Graham had had too many casualties for too little gain. Wolseley wrote, 'I am afraid that I must give Graham up as incorrigibly stupid. I shall not take him on service any more' (Robson, 171). Never an enthusiast for the railway, Wolseley reckoned it would require at least two brigades to protect it. On 11 May he recommended to Hartington its discontinuation. Two days later Hartington authorized the dismantling of the track and the shipping back of the material. By the end of the campaign Graham's reputation with his own officers was low and Wolseley had lost confidence in him. He was criticized in the press and parliament. His strategy had been faulty, he had been careless and incompetent, misused his staff, and, despite the large scale and cost of the 1885 expedition, had failed to subdue Osman Digna, had suffered

heavy losses, and had achieved only 18½ miles of badly built railway. Brian Robson, in his 1993 study of the eastern Sudan campaigns, concluded that Graham 'was not really up to command of the expedition in 1885' (Robson, 185).

Graham arrived back in England on 14 June. He received the thanks of both houses of parliament, and was made GCMG. Although only fifty-four he was not offered further employment, except for the governorship of Bermuda in 1888, which he declined. On 14 June 1890 he retired from the army. He was made GCB on 20 May 1896 and appointed a colonel-commandant of the Royal Engineers in 1899. Retired, he lived in various places and finally, from 1898, at Bideford, and spent much time golfing. He was involved in an unfortunate speculation, a white-lead company of which he became a director, and in which he lost money. He was also a director of the Maxim-Nordenfeldt Company.

General Sir Richard Harrison, who served with Graham, called him 'the bravest man I ever met' (Vetch, 363), and Wolseley wrote that he was 'the most imperturbable of men' (Wolseley, *Story of a Soldier's Life*, 2.33) and 'a man with the heart of a lion and the modesty of a young girl' (quoted in *DNB*). He was reserved, kind, loved children and dogs, and was described by his biographer, Colonel R. H. Vetch, as 'somewhat slow in assimilating both facts and theories' (Vetch, 361). His generalship was questionable. Wolseley had no high opinion of him and thought him up to commanding only a brigade. He was criticized in and outside parliament for the heavy losses he incurred in what was considered to be only 'savage warfare', but few of his critics took into account the ferocity of the Hadendowa. However some of Graham's planning is hard to fathom and he was accused of playing his cards too close to his chest. He was brave and unflappable, but his tactical ability was criticized by other officers. Apparently he was promoted above his ceiling.

Graham contributed several pieces to the *Royal Engineers Professional Papers* and translated Captain Adolphe Goetze's German official account of the *Operations of the German engineers and technical troops during the Franco-German War of 1870–1*. He also wrote 'Last words with Gordon', first published in the *Fortnightly Review* (January 1887), then published separately the same year with additions and appendices. In 1886 he lectured at the Royal United Service Institution on infantry fire tactics and squares. Graham caught a chill, then pneumonia, and died, after a few days' illness, on 17 December 1899, at his residence, Springfield, Bideford, Devon, and was buried in the parish churchyard there on 22 December.

JAMES LUNT

Sources B. Robson, *Fuzzy-wuzzy: the campaigns in the eastern Sudan, 1884–85* (1993) · R. H. Vetch, *Life, letters and diaries of Sir Gerald Graham VC* (1901) · *Royal Engineers Journal* (Feb 1900) · *Royal Engineers Journal* (March 1900) · A. W. Kinglake, *The invasion of the Crimea*, 8 vols. (1863–87) · W. Porter, *History of the corps of royal engineers*, 2 vols. (1889) · E. A. De Cosson, *Days and nights of service with Sir Gerald Graham's field force at Suakin* (1886) · W. T. Willcox, *A history of the 5th (royal Irish) lancers* (1908) · earl of Cromer [E. Baring], *Modern Egypt*, 2 vols. (1908) · M. Mann, *China, 1860* (1989) · J. Pollock, *Gordon: the man* *behind the legend* (1993) • *In relief of Gordon: Lord Wolseley's campaign journal of the Khartoum relief expedition, 1884–1885*, ed. A. Preston (1967) • J. H. Lehmann, *All Sir Garnet: a biography of Field-Marshal Lord Wolseley* (1964) • Viscount Wolseley [G. Wolseley], *The story of a soldier's life*, 2 vols. (1903), vol. 2 • M. Barthorp, *War on the Nile: Britain, Egypt and the Sudan, 1882–1898* (1984) • *DNB*

Archives NAM, corresp.

Likenesses E. J. Poynter, oils, exh. RA 1886, Royal Engineers, Brompton barracks, Chatham, Kent [*see illus.*] • wood-engraving, NPG; repro. in *ILN* (12 Aug 1882)

Wealth at death £4625 15*s*. 4*d*.: probate, 19 April 1900, *CGPLA Eng. & Wales*

Graham, Gerald Sandford (1903–1988), imperial and naval historian, was born on 27 April 1903 in Sudbury, Ontario, Canada, the son of Henry Sandford Graham (1868–1951), Presbyterian minister, and his wife, Florence Marion, *née* Chambers (1873–1961). The father, though born in Monmouth, was of Scottish descent, and the mother was an Irish Protestant.

An outstanding student, Gerald Graham took his BA at Queen's University in Kingston, Ontario, in 1924, and his MA a year after, winning a scholarship to Harvard for his AM (1927), and another to Trinity College, Cambridge, where he completed his PhD in 1929, with the thesis which became his first book, *British Policy and Canada, 1774–1791*, published in 1930 and still cited by scholars. A Rockefeller fellowship for 1929–30 allowed him to spend the year in Germany before beginning his teaching career as an instructor at Harvard in 1930.

The 1930s were a formative period of Graham's life. At Harvard he made a number of lifelong friends, including T. S. Eliot. In 1936 Queen's University received him back, and rapidly promoted him to full professor. In Canada he became part of a circle of able historians, including A. L. Burt, Donald Creighton, George V. Ferguson, and Harold Innis, whom Graham revered as the most brilliant historian Canada had produced. He also began a close friendship with the philosopher George Grant, and was deeply influenced by his ideas.

The Second World War helped to shape Graham's future academic life. A Guggenheim fellowship in 1941 took him back to the USA, where his book *Sea Power and British North America, 1783–1820* (1941) showed the shift of his interests to naval power and its relationship to empire. Late in 1941 he joined the Canadian army but was soon shifted to the Canadian navy's officer training school at Royal Roads in British Columbia as an instructor with the rank of lieutenant-commander. Anxious to experience the battle of the Atlantic at first hand, he wangled his way into service on Canadian destroyers during the college vacations, and spent some time on torpedo boats based in Dover. After D-day he was moved back into the historical section of the Canadian Army Overseas in London with the rank of major.

The move proved to be permanent. In 1946 Graham was appointed lecturer, and in 1947 reader in history at Birkbeck College, London. In 1949 he was appointed Rhodes professor of imperial history at the University of London, King's College, and began publishing a magisterial series of deeply researched books analysing the links between sea power and imperial policy in all the oceans, *Empire of the North Atlantic* (1950), *The Politics of Naval Supremacy* (1965), *Great Britain in the Indian Ocean* (1967), and, after his retirement, *The China Station: War and Diplomacy, 1830–1860* (1978), as well as a steady yearly output of articles, chapters in joint works, documentary editions, and published lectures on themes from Canadian history, imperial finance and trade, and imperial constitutional history.

Graham's tenure of the Rhodes chair coincided with the explosions of Asian and African nationalism and the transfers of power to independent states in Asia, Africa, and the Caribbean. His seminar at the Institute of Historical Research became an engine for the decolonization of imperial history, influencing the profession in every country of the Commonwealth. It was a miniature commonwealth in itself, attracting students from the old dominions and the USA, and increasingly from Africa and the Caribbean, many of whom laid the basis for 'national' schools of historical research in their own countries. After his retirement a list of his former postgraduate students occupying university positions contained over two hundred names. They taught in every province of Canada, most states of Australia, in New Zealand, South Africa, Uganda, Nigeria, Ghana, Sierra Leone, India, Sri Lanka, Malaysia, Singapore, and Hong Kong, as well as in Britain and the USA. Many of them rose to senior positions in their own countries, and as a group they played an important role in the foundation and development of the new post-war colonial universities which became the national universities of independent states.

Yet there was no 'Graham school' of imperial history. Graham shared George Grant's pessimistic conservatism and the sense that mankind was losing its humanity in the face of technology and materialism. He did not share in the euphoria of most of his students, eager for the brave new world of colonial independence, but held the gloomy view that, in Africa especially, independence was premature, and would usher in decay and corruption. Yet he had a special kind of scholarly integrity which allowed him to act as midwife to major nationalist revisionism such as that of his students like Kenneth Dike, Jacob Ajayi, and West Indian scholars, by emphasizing their freedom to propound any thesis, provided it could work as an explanation of evidence and was written with clarity and elegance.

In 1929 Graham married Winifred Emily Ware (1907–1990), with whom he had a son, John Ware Graham. The marriage was dissolved in 1950. In that year he married Constance Mary, *née* Greey, with whom he had two daughters, Laura and Constance, and a son, James. Graham died at the Sussex Clinic, St Leonards, Sussex, on 5 July 1988 from bronchial pneumonia in the aftermath of major surgery. He was buried at St Leonard's Church, Beckley, Sussex, on the 9th. JOHN FLINT

Sources K. O. Dike, 'Gerald S. Graham: teacher and historian', in J. E. Flint and G. Williams, *Perspectives of empire: essays presented to Gerald S. Graham* (1973), 1–8 • J. E. Flint, 'Gerald Sandford Graham, 1903–1988', *Journal of Imperial and Commonwealth History*, 17 (1988–9), 297–300 • G. S. Graham, 'Convoy Diary', *University of Toronto*

Quarterly, 13 (1943), 102–16 • G. S. Graham, 'The room in Dover', *Queen's Quarterly*, 53 (1943), 12–14 • personal knowledge (2004) • private information (2004) • *CGPLA Eng. & Wales* (1988) • d. cert.

Archives King's Lond., corresp. and papers • priv. coll., corresp. with T. S. Eliot • Queen's University, Kingston, Ontario, corresp. and papers

Likenesses T. Marlborough, photograph, repro. in Flint and Williams, *Perspectives of empire*, frontispiece

Wealth at death £24,649 in England and Wales: probate, 22 Dec 1988, *CGPLA Eng. & Wales*

Graham, Henry Grey (1842–1906), historian, born in the manse of North Berwick on 3 October 1842, was the youngest of the eleven children of Robert Balfour Graham DD, minister of the established church of North Berwick, and his wife, Christina, daughter of Archibald Lawrie DD, minister of London. At an early age he showed a great love of reading and spent most of his pocket money on books. On the death of his father in 1855, his mother took him and her youngest daughter to Edinburgh, where, two years afterwards, he entered the university. Although he showed no absorbing interest in the work of the classes and acquired no university distinctions, Graham was a prominent and clever speaker in the debating societies. After being licensed as a probationer of the Church of Scotland in 1865, he was assistant at Bonhill, Dunbartonshire, until he was appointed in March 1868 to the charge of Nenthorn, Berwickshire. Here he made the acquaintance of Alexander Russel, editor of *The Scotsman*, who was accustomed to come to Nenthorn in summer; and he became a frequent contributor to *The Scotsman* of reviews and leading articles. Of non-theological tendencies and widely tolerant in his opinions, he was asked, after the death of Dr Robert Lee of Old Greyfriars Church, Edinburgh, to become a candidate for the vacancy, but declined. In 1878 Graham married his first cousin Alice, daughter of Thomas Carlyle of Shawhill, advocate; they had a son, Nigel Carlyle, who died in Egypt, and a daughter, Ada Carlyle. In 1884 he was translated to Hyndland parish church, Glasgow, where he remained until his death on 6 May 1906.

Graham's principal work is *Social Life of Scotland in the Eighteenth Century* (2 vols., 1899; 3rd edn, 1906). In this work he sought to show the 'continuous revolution' going on in the eighteenth century, as witnessed by the 'gradual transformation in manners, customs, opinions, among every class … the rise and progress of agricultural, commercial and intellectual energy' (preface). It was in these facts that he saw the true history of the Scots in the eighteenth century. The work is still considered a classic. His *Scottish Men of Letters of the Eighteenth Century* (1901; 2nd edn, 1908) led to a correspondence with Frances Balfour on behalf of A. J. Balfour, who wished to put questions to Graham about the work. For Blackwood's series of Foreign Classics he wrote a monograph on Rousseau (1882), and his *Literary and Historical Essays* (published posthumously in 1908) include 'Society in France before the Revolution' (taken from the Royal Institution lectures given in February 1901) and a paper entitled 'Russel of *The Scotsman*'.

T. F. HENDERSON, *rev.* MYFANWY LLOYD

Sources *The Scotsman* (8 May 1906) • *Glasgow Herald* (8 May 1906) • T. C. Smout, *A history of the Scottish people, 1560–1830* (1969) • H. G. Graham, *Literary and historical essays* (1908)

Wealth at death £2529 8s. 2d.: confirmation, 22 June 1906, *CCI*

Graham, Henry Grey (1874–1959), Roman Catholic bishop, was born on 8 March 1874 at the manse, Maxton, Roxburghshire, the fifth son and last of the ten children of Manners Hamilton Nisbet Graham (1830–1911), minister of Maxton, and his wife, Margaret Jane Ritchie (d. 1891). He was descended from a long line of Presbyterian ministers and his father's brother, the Revd Henry Grey Graham, was a well-known historian. Having attended Kelso burgh school, Henry, aged fifteen, went to St Andrews University in 1889, graduated master of arts in 1893, and went on to study divinity. Repeatedly a prizewinner, he graduated bachelor of divinity in 1896 and for a year was assistant to the professor of Hebrew. Licensed by the presbytery of Selkirk, he became assistant minister at Dalserf, Lanarkshire, in 1897 and three years later assistant at the Park Church in Glasgow. Then in November 1901 he was ordained as assistant and successor in the parish of Avendale (Strathaven), Lanarkshire.

For some time Grey Graham (as he was usually known) had been attracted to the Roman Catholic church and its worship, an attraction strengthened by his visiting Catholic families in Dalserf and Strathaven and by visits to Ireland and Belgium. He was involved in the movement to promote 'Catholic' worship in the Church of Scotland, and the question of the church's authority likewise concerned him greatly. From 1900 Graham and another young minister, John Campbell McNaught, were much influenced by an older minister, John Charleson, who changed Graham's fascination with Catholic externals into a more reasoned understanding of Catholicism.

Late in 1901 Charleson finally became a Roman Catholic. After further agonizing Graham resigned his ministerial charge in July 1903, was received into the Roman Catholic church at Fort Augustus Abbey on 15 August, and in October joined Charleson at the Scots College at Rome. The whole episode received much publicity in the context of the Scoto-Catholic movement and the impeccable ministerial background of Graham's family.

Ordained priest at Rome for the archdiocese of Glasgow on 12 December 1906, Graham returned to Scotland the following July and was appointed assistant priest at Motherwell. Eight years later, in 1915, he became parish priest at Longriggend, Lanarkshire. At this time the Roman Catholic church in Scotland was experiencing complex problems which the bishops, all of them elderly and some infirm, could hardly solve. Accordingly Monsignor William Brown was commissioned by Rome to conduct a visitation and arrived in Scotland in June 1917. On 30 August, Graham was nominated titular bishop of Tipasa in Namibia and auxiliary to the infirm archbishop of St Andrews and Edinburgh, and on 16 November he received episcopal ordination in Edinburgh.

Graham's appointment was unexpected and unwelcome and, though he was given full powers by Rome to administer the diocese, there were difficulties from the outset. A mensal fund and dwelling had to be found for him and much that he did was contentious, for discretion was not his strong suit and he was somewhat scrupulous, always seeking the flawless solution and arrangement. In 1918 the Scottish Education Act was being negotiated, whereby local authorities would take over responsibility for the dilapidated Catholic schools and their underpaid teachers, with the church's rights duly safeguarded. Graham opposed the act implacably until ordered by Rome to conform with the other bishops in supporting it. Later Rome instructed him to act moderately and not according to the strictest letter of the law over the sale of these schools.

In 1919 Graham was appointed administrator of Glasgow diocese but its ailing archbishop refused to accept him. In 1921, when Archbishop Mannix, in the teeth of the British government's opposition, came to Scotland to advocate Irish independence and no hall in Edinburgh could be booked for him, Graham arranged an open-air meeting in the playground of a Catholic school. When the aged archbishop in Edinburgh died in November 1928, Graham took charge of the diocese as vicar capitular (Scottish Catholic Archives, ED 19/11/8) until a new archbishop was appointed less than a year later.

Graham's episcopal appointment had terminated. Although in bishop's orders, he now became parish priest of Holy Cross parish in Glasgow, where he remained for the next thirty years and was rarely in the public eye. His tall, thin figure was a familiar sight locally as he conscientiously visited parishioners' homes. After a short illness he died on 5 December 1959 in the Bon Secours Nursing Home, Glasgow; he was buried at St Peter's cemetery, Dalbeth, Glasgow, on 10 December 1959.

In 1904 Graham had begun to write articles for the Scottish Catholic press about his impressions as a convert and as a student in Rome. From about 1911 he published religious pamphlets, mostly for the Catholic Truth societies of Scotland and London. His aim was to refute error and proclaim truth and, being a single-minded man, he tended to see things in black and white and was perhaps not always fair to the church he had left. His determination, verging on imprudence, was shown when he embarked on twelve public lectures on the truth of Catholicism at Motherwell in 1909 and, despite opposition and even street violence, delivered them all.

Graham was patently upright and sincere, endowed with a sense of humour, but his meticulousness and attention to detail led to scrupulosity. The story is told that when a young woman approached him in church with her head uncovered, he took the biretta off his own head and put it on hers. In his old age his scrupulosity increased, but when he died his parishioners felt that 'a holy pastor had gone to his reward' (McEwan, 128).   MARK DILWORTH

Sources H. G. McEwan, *Bishop Grey Graham, 1874–1959* (1973) · H. G. Graham, *From the kirk to the Catholic church*, new edn (1960) · J. Darragh, 'The apostolic visitations of Scotland, 1912 and 1917', *Innes Review*, 41 (1990), 7–118 · J. Darragh, *The Catholic hierarchy of Scotland: a biographical list, 1653–1985* (1986) · D. M. Murray, 'Scoto-Catholicism and Roman Catholicism: John Charleson's conversion of 1901', *Records of the Scottish Church History Society*, 24 (1990–92), 305–19 · *Catholic directory for Scotland*, 1908–61 · *Fasti Scot.*, new edn, vols. 2, 3 · Scottish Catholic Archives, Edinburgh, ED 19/11/8
Archives Scottish Catholic Archives, Edinburgh, notes
Likenesses photographs, repro. in McEwan, *Bishop Grey Graham*
Wealth at death £9188 0s. 1d.: confirmation, 10 Feb 1960, *CCI*

Graham, Hugh, Baron Atholstan (1848–1938), newspaper proprietor in Canada, was born of Scottish parents at Athelstan, Huntingdon county, eastern Quebec, on 18 July 1848, the eldest son of Robert Walker Graham and his wife, Marion, the daughter of Colonel Thomas McLeay Gardner. At the age of fifteen his scanty education at Huntingdon Academy ended when an uncle, E. H. Parsons, editor of the Montreal *Evening Telegraph*, gave him employment, first as office boy, later as business manager. After gaining varied experience in journalism, in January 1869 he founded the Montreal paper *The Star*, which appeared first as an evening, later as a daily paper. Initially devoted to scandal and sensation, it acquired a good circulation, enabling Graham, who had great business ability, to transform it into a reputable, influential, and prosperous paper. Later he established the *Family Herald and Weekly Star*, 'Canada's national farm magazine', and the *Montreal Standard*, for the urban population of Montreal; he also acquired control of the *Montreal Herald*, a Liberal daily, and became president of the Montreal Star Publishing Company. A man of great vitality and energy, he retained active direction of his newspapers until he was well into his eighties, when he disposed of them. With little education, he made no pretence of being a writer or editor, and his remarkable success as a newspaper publisher was due to his striking ability to foresee what the public would regard as important news, and to his energy, skill, and willingness to spend money freely in catering for its appetite.

Since Graham was a strong protectionist and keen imperialist, his papers usually, but not always, supported the Conservative Party. In political circles, however, he was regarded as a maverick, and his habit of sending communications to political leaders in a curious cipher of his own invention exposed him to the charge of being an intriguer. He unerringly sought closer consolidation of the British empire/Commonwealth, and took a leading part in the organization of the Empire Press Union, of the Canadian section of which he was president for many years.

On 17 March 1892 Graham married Annie Beekman, the second daughter of Edward Hamilton of Exeter, Devon, and Montreal. They had one daughter, later Mrs B. M. Hallward of Montreal.

In later life Graham used his great wealth for philanthropic purposes, particularly to maintain a soup kitchen each winter in Montreal and to support medical research and hospitals, especially the Montreal Children's Memorial Hospital, of which he was vice-president. It was largely for his philanthropy that he was created knight bachelor on 9 November 1908 and was raised to the peerage on 5

May 1917 as Baron Atholstan of Huntingdon, Quebec, and Edinburgh (the first Canadian journalist thus recognized). He was made honorary LLD of Glasgow University in 1909. He died at Montreal on 28 January 1938. His title lapsed at his death. His chosen motto—'Onward'—sums up his approach to the newspaper business, if not his traditional political views.

J. A. STEVENSON, *rev.* ELIZABETH BAIGENT

Sources *The Times* (29 Jan 1938) · H. J. Morgan, ed., *The Canadian men and women of the time*, 2nd edn (1912) · *Who's who in Canada* (1937–8) · private information (1949) · W. S. Wallace, ed., *The Macmillan dictionary of Canadian biography*, 3rd edn (1963) · *WW* · Burke, *Peerage*
Likenesses A. Jongers, portrait; formerly in possession of his daughter, Mrs B. M. Hallward, 1949
Wealth at death rich: *DNB*

Graham, James, first marquess of Montrose (1612–1650), royalist army officer, was the son of John *Graham, fourth earl of Montrose (1573–1626), and Margaret Ruthven, daughter of William *Ruthven, first earl of Gowrie.

Early life and education James's mother died in 1619, and in 1624 he was sent to Glasgow to study under Mr William Forrett, living in the house of Sir George Elphinstone of Blythswood, the justice clerk of Scotland. On his father's death on 14 November 1626 Montrose's uncle Archibald *Napier, first Lord Napier, became his guardian and in January 1627 Montrose enrolled as a student at the University of St Andrews. There he is recorded enjoying hunting, hawking, archery, golf, and chess, as well as studying. Even without the benefit of hindsight it seems that he was particularly inspired by the tales of military glory in ancient writers such as Xenophon, Lucan, and Caesar, musing (now or soon afterwards):

> Though Caesares Paragon I cannot be,
> In thought yet shall I sore as high as he.
> (Napier, *Memorials*, 1.263n.)

On 10 November 1629 he married Magdalene Carnegie (d. *c*.1648), daughter of Lord Carnegie of Kinnaird, and (in view of their youth) the couple lived at Kinnaird Castle for the following three years. During these years their first two sons were born and then, once Montrose had come of age and provided for the succession to his earldom, he completed his education by foreign travel. On 6 September 1632 he received a licence to travel abroad for three years, and from then until 1636 he studied in France and Italy, and that he spent some months in 1633–4 at Angers suggests he attended the French military school there.

Montrose was in England in 1636, and it is said that he was slighted at a meeting with Charles I, and thus turned against the king, through the machinations of the marquess of Hamilton (Napier, *Memorials*, 1.94). This sounds like a story designed to explain the royalist hero's initial support for the covenanters. However, Hamilton himself noted that when the revolt against Charles I began in Scotland (July 1637) Montrose had 'very lately returned thither much miscontented out of England' (*The Hamilton Papers*, ed. S. R. Gardiner, 1880, CS, new ser., vol. 27, 259), so it may

James Graham, first marquess of Montrose (1612–1650), attrib. Willem van Honthorst

well be true that he believed his talents had not been sufficiently recognized at court.

The covenanter and disillusionment After his arrival in Scotland, Montrose avoided involvement on either side in the early months of the revolt, but on 15 November 1637 he was at a meeting of those leading opposition to the king. Robert Baillie later credited 'the canniness of [the earl of] Rothes' with having 'brought in Montrose to our party' (*Letters ... Baillie*, 2.261), and Montrose himself acknowledged to Robert Murray, parish minister of Methven, that 'you were an instrument of bringing me to this cause' (Napier, *Memoirs*, 1.136). He soon became one of the most active leaders of the opposition, though anecdote suggests that from early on his determination to gain public prominence was noted and resented. The tale that, in February 1638 when on a scaffold erected to issue a protestation Montrose stood on a barrel to make himself more conspicuous, Rothes remarked, 'Jamie, you will not be at rest till you be lifted upp ther above the rest in three fathoms of a rope' is perhaps too neatly prophetic to be entirely credible (J. Gordon, *History of Scots Affairs*, ed. J. Robertson and G. Grub, 3 vols., 1841, 1.33n.). In 1638 Montrose took a leading part in securing signatures to the national covenant and in negotiations with the marquess of Hamilton, the king's representative, and he sat in the Glasgow Assembly which established presbyterian church government in place of episcopacy. Hamilton, however, did not list him among the seven nobles he regarded as the leading contrivers of the covenanting movement, though he added sourly that 'There are many others as forward in show; amongst whom none more vainly foolish than Montrose' (*Miscellaneous State Papers, 1501–1726*, ed. P. Yorke, 2 vols., 1778, 2.117).

By the end of 1638 the earl of Argyll was increasingly becoming recognized as the outstanding leader of the covenanters. In terms of land and power he was much superior to Montrose, and his gravity, piety, and intellect made him seem to many covenanters a more suitable leader than the flamboyant Montrose. When the covenanters raised an army in 1639 Montrose was given command of forces sent to the north-east to counter the raising of men by the royalist marquess of Huntly. The allegation that he felt slighted at not being appointed commander-in-chief of all the covenanters' armies comes from his enemies, but the later evidence of his determination to gain preeminence gives it some plausibility. Certainly Montrose, whose 'more than ordinare and civill pride made him very hard to be guided' (*Letters … Baillie*, 2.261), soon overstepped his authority in his new command and was forced to back down, humiliatingly and even dishonourably, by his colleagues. After leading his men into Aberdeen on 30 March 1639 he had promised Huntly a safe conduct without exacting concessions from him sufficient to satisfy the other covenanter leaders, and Huntly was, in effect, arrested. Montrose took part in forcing Huntly into submission, preferring to retain his credit with his colleagues to insisting that his safe conduct be honoured.

When a royalist rising followed Huntly's detention, Montrose led the covenanters in the confused manoeuvrings that culminated in his success at Brig of Dee on 18 and 19 June and the occupation of Aberdeen. On 16 July he was a member of a covenanting delegation which met Charles I at Berwick, a meeting that was probably central to the process whereby Montrose, feeling himself undervalued by the covenanters, began to move towards a change in allegiance. When the Scottish parliament met in August 1639 and the covenanters demanded sweeping constitutional changes, it was said that 'Montrose argued somewhat against those motions, for which the zealots became suspicious of him, that the king had turned him at his being with his majesty in Berwick; yet they seemed to take little notice thereof' (*Memoirs of Henry Guthry*, 65). By the end of 1639 he was in secret correspondence with the king.

The emergence of the royalist   Parliament was due to meet on 2 June 1640, and the covenanters resolved to proceed with the session though Charles had not sent a royal commissioner to preside. At a preliminary meeting on 1 June the implications of this were debated, and Montrose took a lead in arguing that 'as long as we had a King' parliament could not meet without his authority (Napier, *Memorials*, 1.255n.), and the issue of whether subjects could depose a king was raised, though perhaps only implicitly. This— and the subsequent meeting of parliament in defiance of the king—confirmed to Montrose that the covenanting movement had become more radical in its intentions than he was ready to accept. When it came to renewed military action it became clear that Montrose was no longer regarded as one of the leaders of the movement. Whereas in 1639 he had been entrusted with suppressing

northern royalists, in 1640 this role was assigned to the man he saw as his rival, Argyll. Montrose 'became somewhat capricious for his own fancies' (*Letters … Baillie*, 1.247), and reacted with a gesture of defiance. One of Argyll's targets was the royalist Ogilvies of Airlie, but Montrose intervened and in July reached an agreement with Lord Ogilvie whereby he himself placed a garrison in the house of Airlie. Argyll reacted by expelling Montrose's men and burning the house. To Montrose this was a humiliation, while to his fellow covenanters the incident was a further sign that, as in his lenient treatment of Huntly in 1639, his heart was not in the harsh repression of royalist nobles that was deemed necessary.

Montrose was not alone in his dislike of Argyll and fear that he was moving towards domination of Scotland, and in August 1640 he and nineteen other nobles signed the Cumbernauld bond. Who drafted the document is unknown, and its wording is deliberately vague, but it bound its signatories to work to uphold the covenant against 'the particular and indirect practickings of a few' and indicated belief that Argyll and his supporters were inflicting unnecessary suffering on the country out of personal ambitions (Napier, *Memorials*, 1.254–5). The bond was not overtly royalist, for the intention was to try to form a moderate alliance against Argyll rather than to undermine the covenanters' cause. Montrose was still ready to identify himself with that cause on 20 August, when he initiated the covenanters' invasion of England by leading his regiment across the River Tweed after his name was chosen for this honour by lot. However, when the existence of the Cumbernauld bond became known in November he and his fellow 'banders' were denounced, and he lost any hope of further influencing the covenanting movement from within. Resolving that the only effective way of opposing Argyll was through secret co-operation with the king, rather than by trying to form a political faction, Montrose warned Charles that deposing him was being discussed and urged him to make limited concessions which would bring him renewed support in Scotland. However, news of his activities leaked out, and Montrose, 'whose pryde was long ago intollerable, and meaning verie doubtsome' (*Letters … Baillie*, 1.262), was imprisoned in Edinburgh Castle on 11 June 1641 as a 'plotter'. When summoned to appear before the committee of estates on 22 June he refused, and insisted on a public trial of allegations against him. The next day he was forced to appear, but refused to answer questions and was pronounced 'disobedient and contumacious' (Napier, *Memorials*, 1.289). On 5 August he was more co-operative, confirming that he and others had feared that Argyll aimed at being a dictator (which should be interpreted in the Roman sense of someone granted exceptional temporary powers to deal with an emergency). Montrose's decision now to answer at least some questions was probably motivated by his desperation to be allowed to appear before parliament and the king (who had gone to Scotland to try to negotiate a settlement) so that he could defend himself and denounce his enemies publicly, but the covenanters were careful to deny him such an opportunity to vindicate himself. He also tried to persuade Charles to meet him so he could reveal things 'which not only concerned his honour in a high degree, but also the standing or falling of his crown', and in a letter of 11 October Montrose told Charles that he could prove a case of treason against his enemies (Buchan, 132). He was never given the chance to state his case, however, and was not released from Edinburgh Castle until 17 November, after the king had agreed a settlement with the covenanters which greatly weakened royal power in Scotland.

Up to the time of his arrest Montrose had retained hopes that a moderate settlement could reconcile his loyalty to the crown with his support for satisfaction of the grievances which had led to revolt in 1637. By the time he was released, however, Charles's priorities lay in dealing with Catholic rebellion in Ireland and a growing crisis in England, and this had forced him to leave Scotland in the control of the faction dominated by Argyll. Montrose, denounced as a 'bander' and 'plotter', was excluded from power. When civil war broke out in England and the English parliament began to seek military help from the covenanters Montrose took this as confirmation of his judgement that Charles had made a disastrous mistake in leaving Scotland in potentially hostile hands. He saw it as his mission to rally Scottish royalists, to deter the covenanters from attempting intervention in England. However, the king preferred the advice of those, led by Hamilton, who argued that a demonstration of royalist strength would provoke rather than prevent intervention. Montrose's isolated attempts to organize opposition in Scotland to the invasion of England failed, and he then joined the king in England, rejecting approaches from the covenanters designed to win his renewed support for them.

The year of victories, 1644–1645   Only after the covenanters' army had entered England did Charles recognize the failure of his previous policy and issue a commission to Montrose as his lieutenant-general in Scotland (1 February 1644). Montrose had at first hopes of combining a rising in Scotland with an invasion of the highlands planned by the earl of Antrim, but on the collapse of that project he determined to act on his own, and crossed the border with a small force on 14 April. He occupied Dumfries briefly, but was forced to retreat immediately, failing to win significant local support. News that the king had created him a marquess (6 May) was doubtless an encouragement, however, and he resolved on a new strategy. He now accepted that the hold of the covenanting regime on the south of Scotland was too strong for local royalists to risk a rising, and calculated that the only course of action that had any hope of success was to attempt to rouse the royalists of the north-east lowlands and the clans of the highlands.

However, there were few who would not have judged that the journey that Montrose now undertook, in disguise and with only two companions, through the lowlands to the highlands, was folly. It was a huge risk taken by a young man with an immense confidence in his own abilities, with a determination to show that under his leadership the king's supporters in Scotland could contribute to his cause after years of demoralization and division, and with a desire for glory arising from the deeds of ancient heroes. His daring was rewarded by remarkable good fortune. Antrim's efforts had finally led to the landing in the west highlands of a force of about 1600 men, Irish and highlanders, led by Alasdair MacColla (Alexander MacDonald), and when Montrose heard of this he made his way to Atholl and took command of the little Irish force and its highland allies. In the year that followed, Montrose, with these men forming the core of his army, won six remarkable victories, defeating the covenanters at Tippermuir or Tibbermore (1 September 1644), Aberdeen (13 September), Inverlochy (2 February 1645), Auldearn (9 May), Alford (2 July), and Kilsyth (15 August). In all these battles the defeated covenanters were superior in number to Montrose's army, which never numbered much more than 2000 men except at Kilsyth, where he commanded perhaps 5000. After Kilsyth the covenanting regime in Scotland temporarily collapsed. This was an astonishing achievement. Montrose had identified and successfully exploited a weakness in the covenanters' strategy in Britain's wars. They had dispatched large armies into England and Ireland, and were over-confident of their ability to control resistance to them within Scotland. That they were correct to dismiss the royalist threat seemed confirmed when an incompetent attempt at royalist revolt in the north-east by the marquess of Huntly in March and April 1644, and Montrose's own raid on Dumfries, had easily been crushed. They had stripped Scotland of troops to fight in the other kingdoms. Montrose thus took his enemies by surprise, with no effective response to his advance. In his first battles he faced mainly ill-trained levies, hastily raised, and even after his initial successes the covenanters were reluctant to withdraw large numbers of troops from England to face him, regarding his victories as severe embarrassments rather than a major threat.

Taking full advantage of the difficult terrain of the highlands, Montrose fought a campaign of movement, seeking to keep his enemies guessing as to where he would strike next. Most of his victories were won on lowland battlefields close to the edge of the highlands, as he sallied out, fought when favourable opportunity offered, and then withdrew to highland safety when his enemies threatened to concentrate against him. To some extent his strategy was dictated by the Irish and highlanders on whom he relied, for though they served him well in battle their objectives differed from his. Whereas he saw the fighting in Scotland as a preliminary to helping the king in England, they had more limited ambitions, seeking to force the withdrawal of the Scottish army in Ireland and to conquer former clan lands from the Campbells. Their war was as much or more a war against Argyll, as chief of the Campbells, as a war for the king. On occasion, therefore, Montrose was forced to divert resources to a west highland war, though on one occasion he took brilliant advantage of his men's insistence on continuing the war in the west. He had intended, conventionally, to settle into winter quarters late in 1644, but Alasdair MacColla demanded that the onslaught on the Campbells continue. Montrose agreed to lead the campaign, and it brought him his great defeat of the marquess of Argyll at Inverlochy. Thus though Montrose's determination to help the king and his daring and skill were the keys to his year of victories, he also showed flexibility, accepting the need to adapt his plans on occasion to allow for the ambitions of the Irish and highlanders. The one flaw that can be detected in his skills as a commander was a degree of carelessness in monitoring the movement of enemy troops. In a raid on Dundee (4 April 1645) he escaped only just in time to flee to the hills, and at the battle of Auldearn his victory came after his army had almost been overwhelmed by an unexpected enemy night march. Great risk was central to his whole enterprise, but failure at intelligence-gathering added unnecessary risk.

By the summer of 1645 Montrose had won five impressive victories, but he was increasingly frustrated. He had won glory, but done nothing which was of direct help to Charles I in the war in England, and by 1645 it was increasingly clear that Charles was facing defeat there. On 3 February, Montrose had confidently urged the king to come to Scotland 'after I have reduced this country to your Majesty's obedience' (Napier, *Memorials*, 2.179), seeing himself as the one man who could restore the king's fortunes. At last, after Kilsyth, it seemed that he had indeed won control of all Scotland. With no army in the field to oppose him, he set about establishing a royalist regime, instead of making a tactical withdrawal to the highlands as he had done after previous victories. A commission of May 1645 had made him lieutenant-governor and captain-general of Scotland, and he used his new powers to summon parliament to meet in Glasgow. But his triumph was fragile. Throughout his campaign few lowland royalists had rallied to his cause, though he had gained valuable support from the Gordons in the north-east, and even after his final victory few were willing to join him. His use of Irish Catholic troops, regarded as barbarians as well as enemies of true religion, alienated many. His covenanting past had left lingering mistrust among royalists. Moreover, Kilsyth forced the covenanters at last to make defeating Montrose their first priority, and few believed that if the Scottish army in England returned home he could withstand it. Finally, an outbreak of plague made it impossible for him to enter the capital, denying credibility to his attempts to establish a government. There was no possibility of the king joining him in Scotland, and most of his men were unwilling to further his wider ambitions. After Kilsyth many highlanders, Irish, and Gordons insisted on returning north rather than risk being cut off and defeated in the lowlands.

Montrose was determined not to retreat, for the king was now on the verge of complete defeat in England: there would be no later opportunity to help him. Perhaps too Montrose's pride made it impossible for him to admit the failure of his vision after having achieved so much. He loitered indecisively on the borders with his remaining men. Though warned that enemy troops were approaching, he was not even with his army when it came under attack on 13 September at Philiphaugh by cavalry sent home from the Scottish army in England. Reaching the battlefield too late to prevent complete defeat, he accepted the inevitable and fled back to the highlands.

Defeat and frustration, 1645–1649 Montrose's victories had been spectacular, but they had not been sufficient to bring him widespread support, and even the limited credibility he had built up had depended on unbroken success. One defeat had cancelled out all his victories, and he had brought no real advantage to his king. As Lord Jermyn had remarked in August 1645, Montrose had failed 'to make his victoryes profitable, as well as miraculous' (*The Lord George Digby's Cabinet*, 1645, 41–2). In the months that followed Philiphaugh, Montrose fought unsuccessfully to rebuild an army, hindered by the efforts of the marquess of Huntly, who now led the Gordons in the king's name but refused to co-operate effectively with the man who had betrayed him in 1639. In July 1646, on the orders of Charles I (now a prisoner of the Scottish army in England), he disbanded his men, and in September sailed into exile.

Far from being crushed by failure, however, Montrose's experience of success in 1644–5 encouraged him to propose a new campaign. He submitted plans to Queen Henrietta Maria in Paris for another Irish invasion of Scotland which, when joined by highlanders, would produce an army of 30,000 men to rescue her husband. Not surprisingly this grandiose project was ignored as unrealistic. However, his year of victories, as an example of what one man could achieve against great odds through resolution and courage, roused widespread admiration in Europe. Publication of an account of his deeds in Latin by George Wishart in 1647 gained him an international reputation as a heroic figure. The French offered him an appointment as lieutenant-general, but he rejected it as 'any imployment below ane Marischall of France was inferiour to him' (Napier, *Memorials*, 2.307). Instead, he stole out of France to join that country's enemies, who were evidently more willing to appreciate his value. In 1648 he was awarded the rank of field marshal by Emperor Ferdinand III in Prague. However, while he sought honours from foreign rulers, Montrose did not intend active service for them, for he remained determined to find some way to help Charles I. His wife's death in Scotland about 1648 is not mentioned in his surviving correspondence, but Charles I's execution in January 1649 roused him to vengeful fury:

I'll sing thine obsequies with trumpet sounds
And write thine epitaph in blood and wounds.
(Napier, *Covenanters*, 2.573)

He now turned his passionate loyalty to the exiled Charles II, who renewed his commission as lieutenant-governor and captain-general of Scotland (4 March 1649) and authorized him to negotiate with all kings and princes for military aid (23 April). Montrose travelled widely, seeking help for the cause in many German states and in Poland and Scandinavia. His frustration at not having the resources to renew the war were intensified when Charles

II opened negotiations with the covenanters for an agreement under which they would help him regain his thrones. To Montrose this was a move towards the fatal mistake of compromise that Charles I had made in 1641, and again in his 1647–8 attempt to regain his throne with the help of the Scottish engagers. Scotland, in Montrose's eyes, must be won by military force if royal power was to be re-established in Britain and the death of Charles I revenged. Personal considerations as well as loyalty to the crown doubtless influenced him. In any negotiated settlement the covenanters would insist on his exclusion from Scotland, and would thus condemn him to the life of an isolated exile, his brief moment of glory forgotten.

The last campaign 1649–1650 In May 1649 Charles II's discussions with the covenanters collapsed, however, and he authorized Montrose to take military action against them, adding a commission as lord high admiral of Scotland to his other offices (NA Scot., GD220/3/135). It was, however, almost entirely left to Montrose himself to find the resources necessary for a new war, and though many princes promised aid almost nothing materialized. All that he could muster was an advance force of a few hundred men which he dispatched from Norway to occupy the Orkneys in September 1649. He himself joined them with reinforcements in March 1650, but by this time the changing political situation had altered the nature of his venture. His intention from the start had undoubtedly been to repeat the miracle of 1644, to conjure an army out of nowhere and conquer Scotland. But he knew that in 1649–50 neither Charles II nor his advisers believed this credible. They saw Montrose's venture as sideshow, a tactic to help to force the covenanters back into negotiations for a settlement by raising their fears of his military prowess. By the time he left for the Orkneys, Montrose knew that Charles had reopened talks with the covenanters, and after he arrived he received a letter confirming what he already feared. He was not expected to attempt conquest but to pose a potential military threat to gain concessions from the covenanters. As a consolation, the king awarded him the Order of the Garter. In the circumstances the sensible thing to have done would have been to remain in the Orkneys, ready to withdraw if a settlement was reached, or perhaps make threatening pin-prick landings on the mainland if the covenanters needed to be further alarmed. Such a policy was unbearable to Montrose. A compromise settlement would leave him without a future and would, he believed, be disastrous to the king. As in 1644, he resolved that a wild gamble was better than inglorious passivity. He therefore landed his men on the mainland and advanced south through Caithness and Sutherland. Failing to gain significant numbers of local recruits, he had only about 1200 men when he was attacked by about 220 covenanting cavalry at Carbisdale (27 April). His levies—Danes, Germans, and Orkney men—collapsed and fled before a determined surprise assault, Montrose's old weakness of failure to monitor the movements of enemy troops being central to disaster as at Philiphaugh.

Execution Montrose himself escaped, fleeing to Assynt, but was taken prisoner there and handed over to the covenanters. Reaching Edinburgh on 18 May 1650 he was led through the streets in a cart driven by the hangman. There he heard that on 1 May the king had signed a draft agreement with the covenanters. Had he not been defeated, he and his men would probably have been allowed to withdraw from Scotland, but now that he was in the covenanters' hands there was no hope that he would escape their vengeance for the immense damage he had inflicted on them in 1644–5. Already under sentence of death, he was brought before parliament, where after being denounced he made a speech asserting that he had remained loyal to the national covenant of 1638. In his campaigns he had acted under commissions from his kings. His landing in Caithness had been 'in order to the accelerating of the treaty betwixt him [Charles II] and you' (Napier, *Memoirs*, 2.795), and he would have retired as soon as the king had ordered him to do so. He was sentenced to be hanged for three hours (being denied more honourable death by the axe), with Wishart's memoir of his deeds and a declaration he had issued strung around his neck. His head was then to be displayed on the Tolbooth, his limbs sent for display in other burghs. 'Let them bestow on every airth [part] a limb', he wrote defiantly (Napier, *Covenanters*, 2.573). On 21 May, on a tall scaffold erected in the High Street of Edinburgh, he died with dignity, finely dressed in a scarlet cloak 'moir beseiming a brydegrome, nor [than] a criminall going to the gallowis' (J. Nicoll, *A Diary of Public Transactions and other Occurrences*, ed. D. Laing, Bannatyne Club, no. 52, 1836, 13). In a brief statement he described Charles I as having 'lived a sanctt and died a martyre: I pray God I may end so: if ever I would wish my soule in another manis stied [man's stead] it is in his' (*Miscellany of the Maitland Club*, vol. 2, pt. 2, ed. A. Macdonald and J. Dennistoun, 1840, 488).

Montrose had known that his last expedition had little hope of success, and that even if he won victories he was likely to be ordered to abandon them by a king who was using him as a disposable pawn in his negotiations. In the event his death on the scaffold must have been, if not welcome, at least a better end than the life of futile exile that otherwise awaited him. It was a last service for the crown, and as it paralleled the martyrdom of Charles I it was an honourable and heroic death. To Scottish royalists, demoralized by failure, division, and weak leadership, he became a symbol of determination and loyalty until death. The potency of Montrose as a symbol of indomitable martyrdom was evident immediately after his death. His dismembered body was buried on the burgh muir of Edinburgh, but Jean, Lady Napier, his nephew's wife, had it disinterred by night and the heart removed. This was embalmed, placed in a casket, and sent to Montrose's son and heir in the Netherlands. When the restoration of monarchy came in 1660 its most potent ceremonial celebration in Scotland was the reassembling of Montrose's body. The embalmed heart was added to his bones and lay in state at Holyrood Abbey. On 11 May 1661 an elaborate procession took the body from the abbey to St Giles's, fourteen earls carrying the coffin. Thus the hero was buried 'with a greater solemnitie than any of our Kings ever had at their buriall in Scotland' (*Letters … Baillie*, 3.466). Yet myth would not accept that his heart had had so quiet a fate, and elaborate stories emerged of its being taken by sea to India, stolen by an Indian prince, brought back to Europe by land, and disappearing in revolutionary France. As with Robert the Bruce, a heroic heart required an epic afterlife.

The character and beliefs of a self-defined hero Montrose had consciously seen himself in terms of the great heroes of ancient times. A small circle of relatives and friends had followed him with devoted loyalty, but he never succeeded in cultivating the arts of the politician, of persuasion and compromise—and indeed at heart he despised them. Action, with himself in command, and the recognition that would follow, were what he craved. Edward Hyde, earl of Clarendon, recognized Montrose's conviction that he had some special destiny: he 'did believe somewhat [something] to be in him, which other men were not acquainted with'. While he had a 'wonderful civility and generosity' towards inferiors, he was less at ease with equals or superiors, for 'He was naturally jealous, and suspected those who did not concur with him' (Clarendon, *Hist. rebellion*, 5.122). A man who would be pre-eminent cannot tolerate rivals. His cult of individual power and pre-eminence is expressed most openly in verse, where he combines celebration of monarchical power, of the military hero, and of the power of the dominant lover. 'Be govern'd by no other sway, than purest monarchy', for:

Like Alexander I will reign,
And I will reign alone,
My thoughts shall ever more disdain
A rival on my throne;
He either fears his fate too much,
Or his deserts are small,
Who puts it not unto the touch
To win or lose it all.

In the seal that he adopted for his last campaign he gave visual form to his recognition that it was certain to end in complete triumph or total failure, with no other options possible. The motto 'Nil medium' ('No compromise' or 'No middle way') surmounted a lion poised to leap from one pinnacle of rock to another, over a deep ravine. Success or death are the only possible outcomes (Napier, *Memoirs*, 2.746–7). Elsewhere he asked rhetorically:

Can little beasts with lions roar,
And little birds with eagles soar?
(Napier, *Memorials*, 1.239)

It was his ambition to soar with the eagle, and to achieve this he was prepared for death. At the point of death he presented his execution as a matter of winning rather than losing it all. His death was a culminating declaration of loyalty.

The example of Montrose was in later ages to be an inspiration to generations of Jacobites. He was the prototype of Bonnie Dundee and Bonnie Prince Charlie, heroic figures who like him dared and lost. Between the 1830s

and the 1850s the obsessive Jacobite Mark Napier published seven volumes of biography and sources on Montrose's life, raising a monument of documentary research which forms the basis for all later study of the man, but his interpretations, and indeed his attributions of authorship of documents, are distorted by uncritical hero-worship. He sought to add to Montrose the hero and Montrose the poet a third dimension, Montrose the scholar, hailing him as an important political thinker. However, the papers on which the claim is based all appear to be the work of Lord Napier, Montrose's brother-in-law—and anyway are mainly reworkings of the writings of Jean Bodin.

Mark Napier was unintentionally ambiguous when he wrote of Montrose's 'meteor-like career of self-devotion' (Napier, *Covenanters*, 1.vii). Napier meant devotion to the crown, but a cynic might interpret it as devotion to himself. To talent, education, energy, and high birth Montrose added driving ambition, a determination to be great. The first vehicle for achieving this that emerged was the covenanting movement, and Montrose flung himself into the cause with more youthful enthusiasm, perhaps, than considered thought, swept along by the excitement and danger. Second thoughts as to the likely consequences of the movement coincided with recognition that he could not gain primacy within it. The emergence of Argyll coincided with the disillusionment of Montrose, and there is perhaps a suspicion that Montrose would not have been so horrified at the talk of appointing an emergency 'dictator' if the post had been within his own rather than Argyll's grasp. None the less, his revulsion against aspects of the covenanters' programme, and his growing conviction that only strong monarchy could prevent anarchy, were genuine—and were shared by other nobles—rather than just an egotistic response to rejection. Once committed to the dynasty, serving it against his former colleagues became the centre of his life, but his qualities of single-mindedness and insistence on the need for decisive action alienated the more cautious royalists. He, in turn, was contemptuous of those who did not share his vision, tending to see them not just as weak but as traitors. Even when he was victorious in 1644–5 there was resentment at his tendency to attribute triumph to himself alone. Partly, no doubt, this was the inevitable jealousy of lesser men, but the Irish, highlanders, and Gordons all came to feel that their contributions were insufficiently recognized as Montrose was arrogantly 'ascrybing to himselfe the glory of all that was done' (R. Gordon, *Genealogical History of the Earldom of Sutherland*, 1813, 531). Certainly his sense of personal accomplishment and worth is notable in his dispatches. After Inverlochy he exultantly wrote to Charles I, 'Only give me leave, after I have … conquered from Dan to Beersheba, to say to your Majesty then, as David's General said to his master, "Come thou thyself, lest this country be called by my name"' (Napier, *Memorials*, 2.179). Scotland would soon be in his possession, and people might call it after him. This is of course a mere rhetorical flourish, but none the less it is revealing of the man.

It was, however, this egotism that enabled Montrose to

achieve what he did. His intensity of self-belief drove him on. In comparing himself to biblical and classical heroes, the fact that he fought in an obscure war in one corner of Britain did not dismay him, nor did the fact that the battles he fought were tiny in scale. It was striving for the all but impossible by the exceptional individual that brought renown, and ultimate failure was not disgrace if he had acted heroically. The fascination with which the story of his brief flash of glory has been told and read down the generations is an indication of the power of this vision.

DAVID STEVENSON

Sources GEC, Peerage · Scots peerage · M. Napier, Montrose and the covenanters, 2 vols. (1838) · M. Napier, ed., Memorials of Montrose and his times, 2 vols., Maitland Club, 66 (1848–50) · M. Napier, Memoirs of the marquis of Montrose, 2 vols. (1856) · G. Wishart, The memoirs of James, marquis of Montrose, 1639–1650, ed. and trans. A. D. Murdoch and H. F. M. Simpson (1893) · J. Buchan, Montrose (1928) · E. J. Cowan, Montrose: for covenant and king (1977) · The letters and journals of Robert Baillie, ed. D. Laing, 3 vols., Bannatyne Club, 73 (1841–2) · The memoirs of Henry Guthry, late bishop, ed. G. Crawford, 2nd edn (1748) · DNB · D. Stevenson, 'The "Letter on sovereign power" and the influence of Jean Bodin on political thought in Scotland', SHR, 61 (1982), 25–43 · J. C. Robbie, 'The embalming of Montrose', Book of the Old Edinburgh Club, 1 (1908), 31–46 · NL Scot., Adv. MS 31.3.10, fol. 43

Archives NA Scot., corresp. and papers, GD220/3 · NA Scot., letters to Sir William Moray · NL Scot., letter to laird of Inchbraikie; letters to Prince Rupert · W. Sussex RO, letters to Marquess of Huntly

Likenesses R. C. Bell, line engraving, 1629 (after G. Jamesone), BM; repro. in Napier, ed., Memorials of Montrose, 2 (1850) · G. Jamesone, oils, 1629, repro. in D. Thomson, The life and art of George Jamesone (1974); priv. coll. · G. Jamesone, oils, 1640, priv. coll. · W. Dobson, oils, 1643–1644?, Scot. NPG; repro. in P. Buchan, William Dobson (1983), 44 · medal, 1650, BM · W. H. Geissler, version of portrait attrib. W. van Honthorst, commissioned 1924, Scot. NPG · R. C. Bell, engraving (after oil painting by G. Jamesone, 1640), repro. in D. Thomson, The life and art of George Jamesone (1974) · R. Cooper, stipple (after W. Dobson), BM; repro. in E. Lodge, Portraits of illustrious personages of Great Britain, 2 vols. (1821) · attrib. W. van Honthorst, oils, Scot. NPG [see illus.] · J. Houbraken, line engraving, BM, NPG; repro. in J. Birch, The heads of illustrious persons of Great Britain (1740) · oils (after van Honthorst), NPG · wash drawing (after W. Dobson), Scot. NPG

Graham, James, second marquess of Montrose [called the Good Marquess] (1633–1669), nobleman, was the second son of James *Graham, fifth earl and first marquess of Montrose (1612–1650), known as the Great Marquess, and his wife, Magdalen (d. c.1648), daughter of David Carnegie, Lord Carnegie, later fifth earl of Southesk. After the death of his elder brother, John, in February 1645 Graham was seized together with his tutor from Old Montrose and imprisoned in Edinburgh Castle by order of the committee of estates. He was released in August 1645 because of the pestilence and placed under the care of the earl of Dalhousie. On 4 December 1648 he petitioned the general assembly for liberty in order to pursue his education. Consequently he was in Flanders when his father was executed on 21 May 1650 and he succeeded as second marquess. While abroad he lived with his cousin Captain Harry Graham, an officer of a Scottish regiment in Dutch service.

Montrose returned to England in 1652 but Edward Nicholas recorded that 'young Lord Montrose had much cause of discontent for being neglected' (Warner, 302). Upon his return to Scotland some of his estates were returned to him. Nevertheless he joined the earl of Glencairn's highland rising in 1653. The presence on the same side of Archibald Campbell, Lord Lorne, eldest son of the marquess of Argyll, who had presided over his father's execution, provoked him and it was reported 'young Montrose had like to have killed Lord Lorne' (Whitelocke, 4.87). When the rising failed Montrose was, on 23 September 1654, able to agree terms for a surrender with General George Monck. Several marriage contracts exist dated between 15 November and 20 December 1656 for his marriage to Lady Isabel Douglas (d. 1672), fifth daughter of William Douglas, fifth earl of Morton, and widow of Robert *Ker, first earl of Roxburghe (d. 1650). They had two sons, the elder, James, being born on 20 October 1657, and three daughters.

Montrose's name was the first signature appended on 29 November 1659 to the address from Stirlingshire to General Monck. Montrose journeyed to London at the Restoration and Charles II granted him £10,000 on the customs of Glasgow. On 12 October 1660 his marquessate was confirmed, and on 8 February 1661 parliament rescinded the forfeiture of his father. He refused to vote at the trial of Argyll in May 1661, claiming 'he owned, he had too much resentment to judge in that matter' (Bishop Burnet's History, 1.226). On 11 May he attended the state funeral of his father in Edinburgh.

It was not until 1666 that Montrose came to an agreement with his father's creditors, which led to the sale of some estates, including Old Montrose. In February 1667 he came to an agreement with the ninth earl of Argyll (the former Lord Lorne) over their outstanding differences. On 25 June 1668 he was appointed an extraordinary lord of session. He died at Mugdock, Stirlingshire, in February 1669 and was buried on 23 April at Aberuthven, Perthshire, even Argyll attending his funeral. He was succeeded as third marquess by his son James (1657–1685). His widow died on 16 December 1672.

STUART HANDLEY

Sources GEC, Peerage · Scots peerage · G. Brunton and D. Haig, An historical account of the senators of the college of justice, from its institution in MDXXXII (1832), 393–4 · E. J. Cowan, Montrose for covenant and king (1977) · M. Hastings, Montrose: the king's champion (1977) · The Nicholas papers, ed. G. F. Warner, 1, CS, new ser., 40 (1886), 302 · B. Whitelocke, Memorials of English affairs, new edn, 4 vols. (1853) · Bishop Burnet's History, 1.226 · Report on manuscripts in various collections, 8 vols., HMC, 55 (1901–14), vol. 5, p. 169 [Edmondstone of Duntreath] · CSP dom., 1654; 1661–2

Archives NL Scot., corresp. and commission | BL, letters to Lord Lauderdale and Charles II, Add. MSS 23115–23129

Graham, James. See Grahme, James (1650–1730).

Graham, James (1676–1746), judge, was born on 8 December 1676 at Airth, Stirlingshire, the son of James Graham of Polton, baillie of Edinburgh. He studied at Leiden and was admitted member of the Faculty of Advocates on 14 June 1698. He was appointed a judge of the Scottish court of Admiralty (1702), and served as dean of the Faculty of

Advocates (1737–46). He was founder of the family of Graham of Airth Castle, Stirlingshire. He was married twice. On 4 December 1700 he married his cousin Marion Hamilton, daughter of Lord Pencaitland. Then, in 1717, he married Lady Mary (d. 1734), daughter of James Livingston, third earl of Callendar; they had two sons, James and William (1730–1790), who succeeded him, and two daughters. Graham died at Edinburgh on 5 November 1746.

FRANCIS WATT, rev. ANITA MCCONNELL

Sources Anderson, *Scot. nat.* · *Scots Magazine*, 8 (1746), 550 · Burke, *Gen. GB* (1858) · F. J. Grant, ed., *The Faculty of Advocates in Scotland, 1532–1943*, Scottish RS, 145 (1944)
Likenesses G. Chalmers, line engraving, 1739, BM · G. Chalmers, pencil miniature, V&A

Graham, James, first duke of Montrose (1682–1742), landowner and politician, the eldest son of James Graham, third marquess of Montrose (d. 1685), and his wife, Christian Leslie (1661–1710), second daughter of John *Leslie, first duke of Rothes (c.1630–1681), chancellor of Scotland, was born about April 1682. He became fourth marquess on his father's death on 18 February 1685, and there was a lengthy minority during which the estates were administered by James Graham of Orchill, a relative, who was tutor-at-law from 1688 until 1696, when the marquess chose his own curators. During his minority Montrose added greatly to his lands by succeeding to the estate of Braco, on the death of Sir James Graham, and in 1694 to the lands of the childless earl of Menteith. In 1702 he married Christian Carnegie (d. 1744), second daughter of David Carnegie, third earl of Northesk; they had ten children, many of whom, including the eldest son, James, died in infancy. Montrose's already large property was further augmented in 1703 when he purchased the estates of Lennox and Darnley in Dunbartonshire and Stirlingshire through the good offices of his friend and kinsman Mungo Graeme of Gorthie, though in order to effect such a purchase he was obliged to feu much of his Perthshire lands, including Braco.

Embarking upon a political career, the marquess began to exert his considerable influence among the freeholders and burgh councillors of west central Scotland. There he was a grave disappointment to the Jacobite faction, who had hoped for much from this young great-grandson of James *Graham, first marquess of Montrose (1612–1650), the civil war general, for he was a steady supporter of the protestant succession. Lockhart of Carnwath, the Jacobite writer, remarks of Montrose that he could have been the leader of the cavaliers, 'but being of an easy, mean-spirited temper, governed by his mother and her relatives … and extremely covetous, he could not resist the first temptation the Court threw in his way' (Lockhart, 1.119). Queen Anne named the marquess to the office of high admiral of Scotland on 23 February 1706, and on 28 February he was advanced to the presidency of the council. His services in connection with the parliamentary union were rewarded by the queen when Montrose was advanced to the rank of duke by a patent dated 24 April 1707. He was included in the sixteen peers elected by the last Scottish parliament on 13 February 1707, and successfully retained his seat in the House of Lords at several subsequent elections. His position in government was recognized on 28 February 1709 when he was made keeper of the privy seal of Scotland, an office which he retained until 1713, when he was removed by Oxford's tory administration.

Upon the death of Queen Anne in 1714 Montrose was one of those named by George I to administer a regency. He was in London to receive the new king, who appointed him keeper of the signet and one of the secretaries of state; he briefly replaced the dismissed earl of Mar before resigning in August 1715. During that year's Jacobite rising Montrose was one of the officials in charge of the civil administration of Scotland. Subsequent to the rising the duke showed marked reluctance to accept forfeited offices of rebels, such as the earl of Linlithgow, his cousin, but he was ultimately prevailed upon to accept the sheriff-principalship of Stirling lest it fall into the hands of his political rival the duke of Argyll. Montrose exerted himself to obtain leniency for many of those who had participated in the rebellion, and wrote to Graeme on 10 December 1715 that he feared the government would be overly harsh and that punishment 'extended much further than either you or I would wish, the consequence of which … can never be pleasing to us as Scots men and will not do the K[ing] service' (Montrose to Graeme, 10 Dec 1715, NA Scot., GD 220/5/9/1).

The seeking of office and the salaries of office governed Montrose's life, for he needed a steady flow of money, not merely to finance his land purchases but to pay debts incurred by bad investment decisions. Like so many Scottish gentlemen he had lost money in the Darien scheme in his early youth, and he compounded his difficulties with substantial bad investments in the York Buildings Company and the South Sea Company. In 1722 he reported to his man of business that as he had 'been obliged to sell out of Y[ork] Buildings att sad low prices, my loss in those cursed stocks makes it the more necessary for you below to be verie exact in gathering in the rents' (Montrose to Graeme, 1 March 1722, NA Scot., GD 220/5/8). The duke claimed to have lost in his York Buildings venture 'above thirtie thousand pound which … makes a considerable blank in my profits', and admitted that his investment in the South Sea Company 'goes exceeding heviely' (Montrose to Graeme, 23 Aug 1720, NA Scot., GD 220/5/9).

The duke's financial difficulties were not eased by his ill-advised quarrel with the notorious Rob Roy Macgregor, with whom he engaged in several profitable cattle-trading ventures before one of Rob's drovers absconded with £1000 of the duke's money. Montrose demanded repayment and, though Rob Roy attempted to pay some of his losses, perhaps hoping for evidence from Rob that the duke of Argyll had been corresponding with the Old Pretender, he began to exert judicial pressure on his unfortunate partner. However, the end result was open warfare, with Rob Roy maintaining himself by robbing the duke and his tenants from a secure refuge in the neighbouring Campbell country. The local war was clearly won by the outlaw, who did not hesitate to rob the officer charged with collecting Montrose's rents. Rob Roy's 'insolences are insupportable', the duke wrote:

> it were verie easie for me to procure ane order for a detatchment of foot or dragoons to be sent to that countrie, but is this a proper time for me to be saying that I can't suppress or defend my self agst such a fellow? … I can not enter into yr thought that I must lay down a scheme for living in warr to possess my owen, which is planely the import of keeping dragoons att my house.   (Montrose to Graeme, 2 Dec 1721, NA Scot., GD 220/5/8)

Troops were, however, required before rents could be safely collected in the highland portions of the duke's estate. The struggle, which the duke had brought upon himself, lasted until he accepted his defeat and compromised with the outlaw.

The duke spent two-thirds of each year in England; until 1719, when his quarrel with Rob Roy made it hazardous, his Scottish residence was Buchanan House, near Drymen in Stirlingshire. The duke then constructed a new home in the Drygate in Glasgow, long known as Montrose's lodging. This in turn gave considerable influence in Glasgow's politics, for in 1714 he had been appointed to his father's office of bailie and justiciar of the barony and regality of Glasgow at the king's pleasure, and he was reappointed for life in 1717, his growing influence having been recognized by his election on 1 October 1714 as chancellor of the university.

Montrose was named lord lieutenant of Dunbartonshire, sheriff-principal of Stirling, and keeper of the great seal of Scotland upon the accession of George II, by a commission dated 24 October 1727. However, in April 1733 when he joined the opposition to Sir Robert Walpole's Excise Bill he was dismissed from office, and at the general election of 1734 he was defeated in the peers' election and did not again sit in parliament. Montrose and another five Scottish peers petitioned parliament in 1735 on the ground of undue interference by the government in the peers' election, no doubt correctly, but quite predictably the petition was rejected. The duke died in London on 7 January 1742, and was buried at Aberuthven, Perthshire, on 12 February.

Montrose was survived by his wife, who died at Edinburgh on 25 May 1744. Their second child, David, Lord Graham (1705–1731), known as the marquess of Graham from 1707, was created a peer of Great Britain by the titles of Earl Graham and Baron Graham of Belford in Northumberland, and took his seat in the House of Lords on 19 January 1727. He died of a rapid consumption at Cleay House, Norfolk, on 30 September 1731, and was buried at Aberuthven. His siblings who reached adulthood were William (1712–1790), who succeeded as second duke of Montrose, and George (1715–1747), who became a captain in the Royal Navy and was appointed governor of Newfoundland in 1740; he died unmarried at Bath on 2 January 1747.

RONALD M. SUNTER

Sources GEC, *Peerage* • G. Lockhart, *The Lockhart papers: containing memoirs and commentaries upon the affairs of Scotland from 1702 to 1715*, 2 vols. (1817) • NA Scot., Montrose MSS, GD 220/5/9/1, GD 220/5/8, GD 220/5/9 • W. H. Murray, *Rob Roy Macgregor: his life and times*

(1982) • M. A. Thomson, *The secretaries of state, 1681–1782* (1932) • P. W. J. Riley, *The English ministers and Scotland, 1707–1727* (1964) • W. Ferguson, *Scotland's relations with England: a survey to 1707* (1977) • G. S. Holmes, *British politics in the age of Anne* (1967) • *Scotland and Scotsmen in the eighteenth century: from the MSS of John Ramsay, esq., of Ochtertyre*, ed. A. Allardyce, 2 vols. (1888) • *Scots peerage*
Archives NA Scot., corresp. | Hunt. L., letters to earl of Loudon • NA Scot., letters to Cornelius Kennedy • NA Scot., letters to Lord Leven • U. Glas. L., letters to John Stirling • U. Glas. L., letters to Lord Polwarth

Graham, James (1745–1794), quack, was born the son of William Graham (*b*. 1710), saddler, and his wife, Jean (*b*. 1715), in the Cowgate, Edinburgh, on 23 June 1745. He studied medicine in the heyday of Edinburgh University under Monro primus, Cullen, Black, and Whytt, but, though later calling himself Dr Graham, he did not take a degree. In 1770 he began practice in Pontefract, Yorkshire, and in the same year married a Miss Mary Pickering; they had three children (of whom a son and a daughter survived him). Graham moved to the American colonies, and began to specialize in New York as an oculist and aurist. He also went to Philadelphia, where he grew familiar with Benjamin Franklin's electrical discoveries. In 1774 he returned to England, to practise first in Bristol and then in Bath, developing the singular cures that made his name. He moved to London in 1775 and established himself in Pall Mall, before returning in January 1777 to Bath, where he met, treated, and hobnobbed with the historian Catharine Macaulay. She afterwards married his younger brother, William.

Concentrating on valetudinarians who were suffering from newly fashionable 'nervous disorders', Graham's treatments included so-called aethereal and balsamic medicines, milk baths, dry friction, and a technique of placing patients either on a 'magnetic throne' or in a bath through which electrical currents were passed. Although he was attacked as a quack, his cures won accolades. In the winter of 1778–9 he visited Newcastle to superintend the construction of some glasswork he required for his next venture in London. In the summer of 1779 he met Franklin in Paris, and visited Aix-la-Chapelle, where he claimed he received testimonials from many well-born patients, including Georgiana, duchess of Devonshire. That autumn he settled in what he designated his Templum Aesculapium Sacrum, which was housed in the Adelphi Buildings, on the riverside by the Strand; from there he advertised his wonderful nostrums and cures, including earth-bathing. A succession of self-promoting pamphlets, including *Sketch of the Plan, &c. of the Temple of Health!* (1780), described his house and apparatus, boasting they had cost him at least £10,000. *A Sketch or Short Description of Dr Graham's Medical Apparatus* (1780) explained how the temple was decked out with elaborate electrical machines, jars, conductors, and an 'electrical throne' insulated on glass pillars, together with chemical and therapeutic apparatus. Statues, paintings, stained glass windows, music, perfumes, and gigantic 'footmen' were among the attractions in this multimedia spectacle. In the 'great Apollo

James Graham (1745–1794), by John Kay, 1785 [*Dr James Graham Going Along the North Bridge in a High Wind*]

apartment' he displayed his apparatus, conducted consultations, sold his medicines, and delivered health advice, including his 'Lecture on the generation, increase and improvement of the human species', published in 1780. This kept him in the public eye for the next decade, as he explained the secrets of a happy sex life—productive of healthy living for individuals and the repopulation and rejuvenation of the nation at large. To illustrate his performance he may have displayed barely draped young models as Hebe Vestina, or goddesses of health, including, according to subsequent legend, Emma Lyon, later to become Lady Hamilton.

Graham also promised relief from impotence and sterility to those who hired his 'celestial bed', which was 12 feet long by 9 feet wide and 'supported by forty pillars of brilliant glass of the most exquisite workmanship'; it was also engraved with the legend, 'Be fruitful, multiply and replenish the earth', and linked up to 15 cwt of magnets and electrical machines. Apparently he charged £50 a night for the privilege of slipping between the sheets. The temple attracted large audiences, the ladies going 'incog', according to Henry Angelo. Sightseers included Horace Walpole, who remarked on 23 August 1780 that Graham's was 'the most impudent puppet-show of imposition I ever saw, and the mountebank himself the dullest of his profession, except that he makes the spectators pay a crown apiece' (H. Walpole, *Correspondence*, ed. W. S. Lewis, 33, 1965, 217). Graham became a celebrity, and on 2 September 1780 George Colman the elder produced at the Haymarket Theatre an extravaganza, *The Genius of Nonsense*, in which John Bannister appeared as Emperor of the Quacks, mimicking Graham's absurdities. The farce had

received twenty-two performances by July 1781. Various squibs and burlesques satirizing Graham were also published, notably *Il convito amoroso*, assumed to be by Graham himself.

In the spring of 1781 Graham was forced to sell up and move to Schomberg House, Pall Mall, where he operated at lower charges. On 25 November 1782 his property was seized for debt, being advertised for sale on 20 December and on subsequent days. On 6 January 1783 he inserted a notice in the *Public Advertiser* that he would that day pay 20s. in the pound on all his lawful debts. He continued to lecture on sexual health, and in March 1783 he informed the public that the 'high priestess' at his temple read lectures to ladies, and that 'the rosy, athletic, and truly gigantic goddess of Health and of Hymen, on the celestial throne', assisted in the course of the reading of the lecture.

Refused a licence to practise in Norwich, on 29 July 1783 Graham delivered his lecture on generation at Edinburgh in Mary's Chapel, Niddry's Wynd. When a further performance was prohibited on the grounds of indecency, Graham continued to offer it for some days in his rooms, publishing in his defence *An appeal to the public, containing the full account of the ignorant, illegal, and impotent proceedings of the contemptible magistrates of Edinburgh*. On 6 August he was committed to the Tolbooth to be tried for 'his late injurious publications in this city'; he retorted with *A full circumstantial and most candid state of Dr. Graham's case, giving an account of proceedings, persecutions, and imprisonments, more cruel and more shocking to the laws of both God and man than any of those on record of the Portuguese Inquisition*. On 10 August he preached in the Tolbooth to the prisoners, entertaining his audience and the prison chaplain with 'a mellow bottle and a flowing bowl' (*Caledonian Mercury*, 11 Aug 1783). On 19 August he was released on bail for 300 marks Scots (ibid., 20 Aug 1783). After he continued to lecture in a large room in Bailie Fyfe's Close, he was sentenced on 22 August to a fine of £20 sterling, which was paid by his audience. Shortly afterwards he left Edinburgh and lectured in various towns, with occasional prohibitions. In the autumn of 1783 Mrs Siddons's youngest sister, Mrs Curtis, read lectures on the state and influence of women in society at Graham's house in London before his own lectures followed. In December he gave out that he possessed the secret of living to at least the age of 150. In 1786 he was in Paris and afterwards at Newcastle; 1788 found him in the Isle of Man. From around 1783 he played down the use of 'medical electricity' in favour of natural cures. In 1789 he informed audiences in Bath that he regretted the extravagances of youth and a warm imagination uncurbed by Christianity, but that he was passing into 'the mild serenity of an evening natural, and of an autumn intellectual sun'.

In 1790 Graham's *Short treatise on the all-cleansing, all-healing, and all-invigorating qualities of the simple earth* gave the fullest description of the techniques of earth-bathing he had practised from the late 1770s. Mud-bathing exemplified his faith in simple cures and the healing powers of nature. Henry Angelo described one of his performances:

After making his bow he seated himself on the stool; when two men with shovels began to place the mould in the cavity: as it approached to the pit of the stomach he kept lifting up his shirt, and at last he took it entirely off, the earth being up to his chin, and the doctor being left *in puris naturalibus*. He then began his lecture, expatiating on the excellent qualities of the Earth Bath, how invigorating etc. quite enough to call up the chaste blushes of the *modest* ladies.   (Angelo, 2.61)

From the mid-1780s, Graham became a religious enthusiast, defending the divinity of Jesus Christ against Unitarians such as Joseph Priestley. From 1787 he styled himself 'the Servant of the Lord O.W.L.' (Oh, Wonderful Love), and dated his publications 'in the first year of the New Jerusalem Church'. Wandering round the country as a preacher, he explicitly harmonized his new theology with his vegetarianism. In 1790 he claimed that upon the illness of George III he had hurried from Liverpool to Windsor, to give his opinion to the prince of Wales, who (Graham stated) confessed he too would suffer in the same way unless he married a certain princess. Robert Southey saw this 'half knave, half enthusiast' twice, once in his mudbath. He recorded that Graham 'would madden himself with opium, rush into the streets, and strip himself to clothe the first beggar he met' (*Commonplace Book*, 4.360). At Edinburgh he was for some time confined in his own house as a lunatic.

Graham's last pamphlet opens with an affidavit made on 3 April 1793, that from the last day of December 1792 to 15 January 1793 he neither ate nor drank, nor took anything but cold water, sustaining life by wearing cut-up turfs against his naked body and by rubbing his limbs with his own nervous aethereal balsam. He died suddenly, at his house opposite the Archer's Hall, Edinburgh, on 23 June 1794, and was buried in Greyfriars churchyard, Edinburgh.

Though an exhibitionist and entrepreneur, a self-confessed eccentric, and possibly finally mad, Graham was also a man of significant medical ideas. He opposed flesh-eating and excess in food and drink, and advocated cold bathing, fresh air, sleeping on hard beds, and other aspects of a Spartan regime. Hostile to 'luxury', he asserted that illness was caused by wearing too much clothing, and he wore nothing woollen. In particular he believed that energetic sexual performance was the secret and the sign of a healthy existence. While advocating the use of erotica as sex aids, he was a fierce critic of practices he regarded as depraved, in particular prostitution (though wives could learn from whores the erotic arts) and masturbation—he stated that 'every act of self-pollution is an earthquake—a blast—a deadly paralytic stroke' (J. Graham, *Lecture on … Generation*, 1780, 20). Though often treated by historians as a mere charlatan, in truth Graham was an enthusiast whose views, albeit carried to extremes, were actually highly typical of his age.   ROY PORTER

Sources J. Paterson, *Kay's Edinburgh portraits: a series of anecdotal biographies chiefly of Scotchmen*, ed. J. Maidment, 2 vols. (1885), 38–44 • R. S. Porter, 'The sexual politics of James Graham', *British Journal for Eighteenth-Century Studies*, 5 (1982), 199–206 • R. S. Porter, 'Sex and the singular man: the seminal ideas of James Graham', *Stud. Voltaire Eighteenth Century*, 228 (1984), 1–24 • N. O. Scarpi, 'Emma Lyon and Dr Graham', *Ciba Symposium*, 11 (1963), 43–8 • B. B. Schnorrenberg, 'A true relation of the life and career of James Graham, 1745–1794', *Eighteenth-Century Life*, 15 (1991), 58–75 • W. L. Whitwell, 'James Graham, Master Quack', *Eighteenth-Century Life*, 4 (1977–8), 43–9 • 'Some notable quacks', *BMJ* (27 May 1911), 1264–74 • H. Angelo, *Reminiscences*, 2 vols. (1828–30) • J. Grant, *Cassell's old and new Edinburgh*, 3 vols. [1880–83] • *DNB*

Archives NL Scot., papers • Wellcome L.

Likenesses double portrait, etching, 1783 (*The quacks*; with G. Katerfelto), Wellcome L. • J. Kay, etchings, 1783–5, BM, NPG, Wellcome L. [*see illus.*] • J. Kay, double portrait, etching, 1785 (with Miss Dunbar), Wellcome L. • T. Rowlandson, pen, watercolour, and pencil caricature (*Dr Graham's earth bathing establishment*, *c.*1790–95), Yale U. CBA • print, repro. in W. Wadd, *Nugae chirurgicae* (1824) • woodcut (*The doctor himself*), repro. in *Rambler's Magazine* (Feb 1783)

Graham, James, third duke of Montrose (1755–1836), politician, was born on 8 September 1755, the only son of William, second duke of Montrose (1712–1790), soldier and landowner, and Lady Lucy Manners (1716/17–1788). He was educated at Eton College (1765–72) and at Trinity College, Cambridge, from where he matriculated in January 1773 and graduated MA two years later. On his return from the grand tour in February 1778 he became involved in the debate over what he saw as the government's ineffectual and irresponsible handling of the war with America. On 11 September 1780 Graham was elected MP for Richmond, Yorkshire, and was described at the time as a skilled speaker with a promising political career ahead of him. In the same year he was appointed chancellor of the University of Glasgow, an office that he held for the rest of his life. Initially Graham remained independent of party allegiance, voting with the government or the opposition, moving an unsuccessful motion for a Scottish militia, and succeeding in his bid to repeal the act banning the wearing of highland dress. A stern critic of Fox's East India Bill, he was appointed by Pitt as a lord of the Treasury in December 1773.

From 1784 Graham sat as MP for Great Bedwyn, Wiltshire, and developed his reputation as an eloquent commentator on Scottish issues. Having previously spoken on the need for famine relief and aid for the linen and cotton industries, he now championed the cause, among others, of Scottish fishermen and distillers. On 3 March 1785 he married, at his father's house in Grosvenor Street, London, Lady Jemima Elizabeth Ashburnham (1762–1786), daughter of John, second earl of Ashburnham; she died in childbirth in September of the following year, an infant son died soon after. His political career in the late 1780s was marked by several clashes with Fox over the regency crisis, the trial of Warren Hastings, and Graham's nomination of Henry Addington as speaker. From August 1789 to February 1791 he served with Lord Mulgrave as paymaster-general of the forces, and was also vice-president of the Board of Trade and a member of the privy council. On 24 July 1790 Graham married Lady Caroline Maria Montagu (1770–1847), daughter of George, fourth duke of Manchester. The marriage, which took place at Kensington Palace, produced five sons and two daughters. On 23 September of the same year he inherited the family title, and it was as third duke of Montrose that he became a knight of the

Order of the Thistle on 14 June 1793 and a knight of the Garter on 26 March 1812.

In mid- to later life, Montrose held a number of offices. He was master of the horse from 7 December 1790 to 1795 (a position he held again from April 1807 to 1830); commissioner for Indian affairs from 16 May 1791 to 22 October 1803; lord lieutenant of Stirling (from 1794 to 1836) and of Dumbarton (1813–36); lord justice general of Scotland (from 14 January 1795 to 1836); president of the Board of Trade under Pitt between June 1804 and 1806; and lord chamberlain on two occasions (December 1821 to May 1827 and February 1828 to July 1830). He died at his house on Grosvenor Square, London, on 30 December 1836, and was buried in the mausoleum of the earls of Montrose at Aberuthven, Perthshire. He was survived by his second wife, who died on 24 March 1847, and, among other children, his eldest son, James *Graham, fourth duke of Montrose.   PHILIP CARTER

Sources GEC, *Peerage*, new edn · E. Haden-Guest, 'Graham, James', HoP, *Commons* · *GM*, 2nd ser., 5 (1836) · R. M. Souter, *Patronage and politics in Scotland, 1707–1832* (1986) · M. Fry, *The Dundas despotism* (1992)
Archives NL Scot., corresp. | BL, corresp. with Sir Robert Peel, Add. MSS 40348–40422, *passim* · City Westm. AC, corresp. with Herries, London and Westminster light horse volunteers · NA Scot., letters to Lord Balgonie; corresp. with William Cunningham Graham; corresp. with first and second Lords Melville · NL Scot., corresp. with Lord Lynedoch · NRA Scotland, priv. coll., letters to Stirling family · U. Glas., Archives and Business Records Centre, corresp. with Duncan Macfarlan
Likenesses J. Kay, caricature etching, 1784, BM, NPG · D. Wilkie, group portrait, oils, 1828 (*The entrance of George IV at Holyroodhouse*), Scot. NPG

Graham, James (1765–1811), poet, was born on 22 April 1765 at Glasgow, the son of Thomas Graham (*d.* 1791) a prominent lawyer and committed whig, and Jean Robertson. He was educated at Glasgow grammar school and at Glasgow University. Against his own inclination to study for the church, he was then apprenticed to his cousin, Laurence Hill, a writer to the signet, in Edinburgh. Despite his dislike of the work and uncertain health, he completed his apprenticeship, and on 11 December 1788 was admitted a member of the Society of Writers to the Signet. On the death of his father in 1791 he contemplated a change of profession, and he eventually became an advocate in 1795.

Over the following few years, Graham pursued his profession, while writing verse as a means of recreation. He published a *Rural Calendar* in 1797, *Wallace: a Tragedy* in 1799, and a dramatic poem, *Mary, Queen of Scots*, in 1801. On 17 March 1802 he married Janet (*d.* 1815), the eldest daughter of Richard Graham, town clerk of Annan. They had two sons and a daughter.

In 1804 Graham published a descriptive and meditative poem entitled *The Sabbath*. Within a year it had come out in three new editions, which included a sequel, *Sabbath Walks*. *The Sabbath* won Graham the admiration of Sir Walter Scott, and made him the victim of one of Byron's barbed comments in his *English Bards and Scotch Reviewers* (1809). In 1806 Graham published *Birds of Scotland* and a

pamphlet advocating trial by jury in civil causes. A collection of his poems appeared in two volumes in 1808, followed by *British Georgics* (1809) and *Poems on the Abolition of the Slave Trade* (1810). A rare work of Graham's, *Fragments of a Tour through the Universe* was suppressed after its publication by his relatives, who were worried about its political tendencies, as it attacked not only slavery and the press-gang, but also war and even the monarchy. The only known existing copy is held in the rare-book collection of the Newberry Library, Chicago.

Graham found limited success as an advocate, and resolved to realize his early ambition of becoming a clergyman. In 1809 he went to London, and shortly afterwards was ordained by the bishop of Norwich and appointed curate of Shipton Mayne, Gloucestershire. In August 1810 he became sub-curate of St Margaret's, Durham; in May 1811 he was transferred to Sedgefield in the same diocese. He was forced to leave soon afterwards because of his declining health, and travelled with his wife to Edinburgh, and then to his brother's home at Whitehill, Glasgow. He died there on 14 September 1811. Kenneth *Grahame, the children's writer, was his great-grand-nephew.

T. W. BAYNE, *rev.* DOUGLAS BROWN

Sources *Register of the Society of Writers to Her Majesty's Signet* (1983) · Chambers, *Scots.* (1855) · Anderson, *Scot. nat.* · J. G. Lockhart, *Memoirs of the life of Sir Walter Scott*, 7 vols. (1837–8) · R. A. Davenport, *A dictionary of biography: comprising the most eminent characters of all ages, nations, and professions* (1831) · *Edinburgh Annual Register* (1812) · *Memoir and correspondence of Mrs Grant of Laggan*, ed. J. P. Grant, 1 (1844), 136, 243 · T. Royle, *The mainstream companion to Scottish literature* (1993)
Archives NL Scot., letters, corresp. and MSS, MS 3519 | Bodl. Oxf., letters to Lady Byron · NL Scot., letters to Archibald Constable, MS 327 · NL Scot., letters to Robert Lundie, MSS 1675–1676
Likenesses J. Henning, porcelain medallion, *c.*1810, Scot. NPG · S. Freeman, engraving (after miniature), BM, NPG; repro. in Chambers, *Scots.*

Graham, James (1791–1845), one of the recipients of the Norcross annuity to Waterloo soldiers, was born at Cloona, co. Monaghan, Ireland, and in 1813 joined the Coldstream Guards, in the 2nd battalion of which regiment he greatly distinguished himself as a lance-sergeant at the battle of Waterloo. In August 1815 the Revd John Norcross (*c.*1762–1837), formerly fellow of Pembroke College, Cambridge, rector of Framlingham, Suffolk (1813–37), wrote to the duke of Wellington, offering to settle an annuity of £10 for life, to be called the Wellington pension, and paid annually on 18 June, 'on any one of my brave countrymen who fought under your grace in the late tremendous but glorious conflict' (*Supplementary Despatches*, 11.35). The duke cordially accepted the offer (*Despatches*, 8.222, 249). Eventually, after reference to Colonel (afterwards General Sir James) Macdonell, who had commanded at Hougoumont, the key of the duke's position at Waterloo, two annuitants were selected: Lance-Sergeant James Graham, Coldstream Guards, and Private Joseph Lester, 3rd foot guards. Graham's claim was stated thus:

Assisted Lieutenant-colonel Macdonell in closing the gates, which had been left open for the purpose of communication, and which the enemy were in the act of forcing. His brother, a corporal in the regiment, was lying wounded in a barn, which was on fire, and Graham removed him so as to be secure from the fire, and then returned to his duty. He had been 3²⁄₁₂ years in the regiment. (*Supplementary Despatches*, 11.121)

The annuities were paid for two years, and then ceased on the bankruptcy of Mr Norcross, who died on 10 April 1837. Graham continued in the Coldstream, and is stated (*Naval and Military Gazette*) to have been the man who saved the life of Captain (afterwards Lord Frederick) Fitzclarence at the seizure of the Cato Street conspirators in 1820. Graham was discharged from the guards after eight and a half years' service. He re-enlisted in the 12th royal lancers, and served nine and a half years as private. He was discharged 'with an injured chest and worn out', to a Chelsea out-pension of 9*d*. per day, on 13 July 1830, his character being 'very good, and distinguished by gallant conduct at Waterloo'. He was admitted an in-pensioner at the Royal Hospital, Kilmainham, Dublin, on 1 July 1841, and died there on 28 April 1845. Various apparently incorrect versions of the Norcross gift have been published.

H. M. CHICHESTER, *rev.* JAMES LUNT

Sources Fortescue, *Brit. army*, 10.357 • D. Howorth, *A near run thing* (1968), 80 • *Supplementary despatches (correspondence) and memoranda of Field Marshal Arthur, duke of Wellington*, ed. A. R. Wellesley, second duke of Wellington, 15 vols. (1858–72), vol. 11, pp. 35, 121 • *The dispatches of … the duke of Wellington … from 1799 to 1818*, ed. J. Gurwood, 13 vols. in 12 (1834–9), vol. 8 • W. Siborne, *History of the war in France and Belgium in 1815*, 1 (1844), 391–2 • *Naval and Military Gazette* (May 1845) • Venn, *Alum. Cant.* • *GM*, 2nd ser., 24 (1845), 101
Likenesses watercolour, NG Ire.

Graham, James, fourth duke of Montrose (1799–1874), politician, born in London on 16 July 1799, was the elder son of James *Graham, third duke of Montrose (1755–1836), politician, and his second wife, Lady Caroline Maria Montagu (1770–1847), daughter of George, fourth duke of Manchester. He was educated at Eton College from about 1810 until 1814, and at Trinity College, Cambridge, where he graduated MA in 1819. As marquess of Graham he represented Cambridge in parliament from 1825 to 1832, and opposed the repeal of the Test Acts, Catholic emancipation, and the Reform Bill. He was created a privy councillor (23 February 1821), and was a commissioner of the India board (4 February 1828 to November 1830). Graham succeeded to the dukedom in 1836. On 15 October 1836 he married Caroline Agnes (1818–1894) [*see* Graham, Caroline Agnes, duchess of Montrose], third daughter of John Horsley-Beresford, second Lord Decies, and his wife, Charlotte Philadelphia, *née* Horsley.

Montrose was a tory of the old school, and opposed the free-trade measures of Robert Peel in 1846. He was lord steward of the queen's household during Derby's administration of 1852–3, and chancellor of the duchy of Lancaster in Derby's government of 1858. From July 1866 to December 1868 he was postmaster-general, concluding a postal convention with the United States, India, and China, and improving mail contracts with the East held by the Peninsular and Oriental Company. In the session of 1868 Montrose brought forward in the House of Lords the Electric Telegraphs Bill, which nationalized the telegraphs. He was elected chancellor of the University of Glasgow in 1837, and from 1827 was honorary colonel of the Stirling, Dumbarton, Clackmannan, and Kinross militia. He was also major-general of the royal archers (the queen's bodyguard in Scotland) and was appointed lord lieutenant of Stirlingshire (28 February 1843). His principal seat, Buchanan Castle, Stirlingshire, was destroyed by fire in January 1850, but between 1854 and 1857 he built another castle on the same site. Montrose died at Cannes on 30 December 1874 and was buried there. He was succeeded in the dukedom and estates by his only son, Douglas Beresford Malise Ronald Graham (1852–1925). Montrose's widow, who ran racehorses under the name 'Mr Manton' was married twice more—first to William Stuart Stirling Crawfurd, and then, after his death at Cannes in 1883, to M. H. Milner. She died in 1894.

G. B. SMITH, *rev.* H. C. G. MATTHEW

Sources GEC, *Peerage* • *Annual Register* (1874)
Archives BL, corresp. with Sir Robert Peel, Add. MSS 40446–40532, *passim* • Lpool RO, letters to fourteenth earl of Derby • NRA Scotland, priv. coll., letters to J. J. Hope Johnstone • NRA, priv. coll., letters to S. H. Walpole • U. Glas., Archives and Business Records Centre, corresp. with Duncan Macfarlan • U. Glas. L., Macfarlan MSS
Likenesses Ape [C. Pellegrini], lithograph • W. J. Edwards, stipple (after W. C. Ross), BM, NPG • oils, Eton
Wealth at death £181,325: confirmation, 29 July 1875, *CGPLA Eng. & Wales*

Graham, James, sixth duke of Montrose (1878–1954), marine engineer and Scottish nationalist, was born on 1 May 1878 at 35 Chester Square, London, the eldest of five children of Douglas Beresford Malise Graham, fifth duke of Montrose (1852–1925), and his wife, Violet Hermione (1854–1940), daughter of Sir Frederick Graham, third baronet, of Netherby, Cumberland, and of his wife, Jane Hermione, daughter of Edward Seymour, twelfth duke of Somerset. The two families of Grahams had no previous connection.

Graham was educated at Warren Hill School, Eastbourne, from 1889 to 1892, then at Eton College until 1895. After a leisurely voyage to Australia and back, he became a naval midshipman in the following year. During his service he took from Ceylon the first continuous moving photographic record of a total solar eclipse. He transferred to the merchant marine in order to broaden his experience, and earned a master mariner's certificate at Glasgow Navigation School. In 1900 he went to serve in the Second South African War in the royal naval detachment, engaged in various auxiliary tasks. On his return Lloyd's of London commissioned him to go back and inspect sites for signal stations in South Africa while also negotiating with the authorities there the introduction of wireless telegraphy.

Graham next tried politics. In the last months of A. J. Balfour's government he was an unpaid assistant private secretary to the chancellor of the exchequer, Austen Chamberlain. As a Unionist he fought Stirlingshire in the general election of 1906, then Eye, Suffolk, at a by-election later that year, and again at the general election of January 1910. He was beaten in each case.

On 14 June 1906 Graham married at St George's, Hanover Square, London, Lady Mary Louise (1884–1957), only child of William Douglas-Hamilton, twelfth duke of Hamilton, and of his wife, Mary, daughter of William Montagu, seventh duke of Manchester. They had two sons and a daughter. They lived at Buchanan Castle, Stirlingshire, at Brodick Castle, Arran, and at Easton Park, Suffolk.

Graham turned back to the sea and ships. In 1911 he became president of the British Institute of Marine Engineers. He conceived and designed the first aircraft-carrier, the *Argus*, as well as, for himself, the first seagoing heavy oil motor ship. Appointed a director of William Beardmore & Co., Glasgow, in time for the First World War, he then chaired the engineering section of the Admiralty board of inventions. He served besides in the auxiliary naval service, winning two medals. He mobilized and commanded the Royal Naval Volunteer Reserve both on the River Clyde and on the east coast of Scotland, mainly engaged in minesweeping. He became commodore of reserve in 1921, then naval aide-de-camp to the king. He went on the retired list in 1927.

In 1925 Graham succeeded as duke and took the Unionist whip in the House of Lords. He had lost his hearing, and spoke whenever possible on behalf of the deaf. In between, other interests engaged him. He served as president of the International Scottish Home Rule League, a shadowy body which sought to interest businessmen in the case for a parliament in Scotland, now stricken by severe economic problems. As a result of these contacts he led in 1932 a Scottish mission to Canada aiming to revive trade at the depth of the depression. He was in touch also with the Scottish Home Rule Association, though reluctant to speak at its meetings because he considered it too 'Communistic' (Brand, 176). He displayed equal caution towards its more separatist successor, the National Party of Scotland. The *Glasgow Herald* of 30 October 1928 reported his presiding over a rally of 3000 people for the NPS soon after its foundation. Yet in that year he refused to come out for a man of his own name—the novelist Cunninghame Graham—as nationalist candidate in the rectorial election at the University of Glasgow, on the grounds that the other candidate was the Conservative prime minister, Stanley Baldwin, whom Montrose felt bound to back.

Liberals and Unionists supporting self-government for Scotland did not want the cause tainted by links with the left. Several came together in the Scottish Party, inaugurated on 21 September 1932. Montrose was its best-known figure. Moves followed, however, to end the fragmentation dogging Scottish nationalism. The obvious way forward lay through merger of the NPS with the Scottish Party, which took place on 7 April 1934. It brought into being the modern Scottish National Party (SNP) under that name. It shortly elected Montrose as its president. Still then taking the Unionist whip at Westminster, he resigned it to become a Liberal early in 1935. On 4 May a letter from him in the *Glasgow Herald* proposed a further merger, between the SNP and the Scottish Liberal Party. But he had not consulted nationalist colleagues, who

reminded him that the SNP did not permit dual membership with other parties. Still, his innocence of political sectarianism suited the consensual approach of the party's leader, John MacCormick, who continued to treat Montrose as its principal grandee. This role he enhanced as lord high commissioner to the general assembly of the Church of Scotland in 1942–3.

After the war MacCormick organized the covenant movement to draw up a petition for home rule, which at length attracted 2 million signatures. It was launched at a ceremony in Edinburgh on 29 October 1949. Of the 1200 present Montrose stepped forward as the first to sign, in a climax of sorts to the political career of a well-meaning but ineffectual nobleman. Montrose died of heart failure, at Buchanan Castle, on 20 January 1954 and was buried on 23 January at Buchanan kirkyard, Stirlingshire. His elder son, (James) Angus *Graham, succeeded him as seventh duke of Montrose.   MICHAEL FRY

Sources J. Graham, sixth duke of Montrose, *My ditty box* (1952) · J. Brand, *The national movement in Scotland* (1978) · A. Marr, *The battle for Scotland* (1992) · Burke, *Peerage*
Likenesses photographs, *Glasgow Herald* Archives · photographs, *The Scotsman* Archives
Wealth at death £28,632 8*s*. 8*d*.: confirmation, 12 May 1954, *CCI*

Graham, James Gillespie (1776–1855), architect, was born on 11 June 1776 in Dunblane, where he was baptized on 17 June, the elder son of Malcolm Gillespie, sheriff-substitute of Dunblane. Of his early life and education, nothing is known. Possibly involved in the pre-1800 remodelling of Lanrick Castle, Perthshire, he became superintendent of Lord Macdonald's extensive works in Skye and North Uist by 1800, and designed churches at Snizort and Kilmuir, feuing plans for Portree and Kyleakin, and other buildings. Probably self-taught, he opened his architectural office in 1801, and designed the house of Achnacarry for Lochiel (1802), a sub-Adam castellated façade on an otherwise straightforwardly classical plan. His house designs changed and became more three-dimensional—particularly Culdees Castle, Perthshire (1810), Drumtochty, Kincardineshire (1815), Cambusnethan, Lanarkshire (1816), and Dunninald, Forfarshire (1823), after a visit in 1808 to London, where he could have seen the designs by Robert Lugar for Balloch, Dunbartonshire, in the Royal Academy. His highland connection served him well and led to 'baronial or castellated' proposals for a new house for Campbell of Barcaldine in 1813–14 (possibly the first use of the term 'baronial'), a scheme for Macdonald of Clanranald at Arisaig in 1813, and the Glenfinnan monument for Macdonald of Glenalladale (1815). Seventy-one of over 120 projects that can be confidently attributed to Graham occurred between 1810 and 1825 in locations as scattered as Skye, the borders, Inverness, Kincardineshire, and Aberdeen, which implies that some of them—churches such as Channelkirk (1817) and Kilmuir (1810)—were undertaken by providing drawings only.

Graham's sixteen public buildings included the weighty classical court houses in Inveraray (1816) and Dumbarton (1822), while the most distinguished of his few classical

James Gillespie Graham (1776–1855), by Sir John Watson-Gordon, 1841

(unsuccessfully) his appointment as architect and surveyor of the churches to be built in Scotland, when he claimed the title 'architect to the Prince Regent'. Graham was a governor of George Heriot's School, Edinburgh, in 1833, an Edinburgh city councillor in 1838, and was elected fellow of the Society of the Antiquaries of Scotland. He had a house at 34 Albany Street (later Castle Street), Edinburgh, chambers at 5 Duke Street, and a house in Portobello—thought to have been the location of his meeting with the young A. W. N. Pugin in 1829. With Pugin he designed alterations to Orchill, Perthshire, submitted a widely remarked entry to the houses of parliament competition in 1835, and made abortive proposals for remodelling Glasgow Cathedral, Victoria Hall, Edinburgh (now Tolbooth St John's), works to Taymouth and Murthly, and further proposals to restore Holyrood as an assembly hall for the Church of Scotland. Graham signed Pugin's drawings.

Graham designed over twenty-seven churches and chapels, preponderantly standardized neo-Perpendicular 'god boxes' of three to five bays and a horseshoe gallery, with occasional lacy decoration or a stumpy tower. In Alloa and Montrose he produced magnificent steeples modelled on Louth. His Catholic chapels (later cathedrals) in Glasgow and Edinburgh were ornate structures, that in Glasgow being unusually ambitious. Alterations to existing buildings—at Holy Rude, Stirling, Dunblane Cathedral, and St Michael's, Linlithgow—were generally unscholarly and damaging. St Margaret's Convent, Edinburgh (1835), and the chapel of St Anthony the Eremite at Murthly (consecrated November 1846), both Catholic, are in a thickset Romanesque style. Engravings of St Anthony's Chapel, lithographed by F. Schenk and M. Ghemar, were published in Edinburgh in 1850.

Graham was essentially a visually driven architect, and showed a remarkable ability to pick up styles and details from others and then remodel them according to his own taste for picturesque effect. Given that his first commission at Achnacarry was in the revivalist style, that he was painted by his friend Sir John Watson Gordon in the baronial style, and that his last major works (in Brodick and Aytoun) were overtly baronial—a style 'lately revived by me' (PRO, MS GD 121/67/1/409)—he is revealed as a romantic historicist, although not, compared to David Bryce, an academic one. In 'A memorandum on the Scottish baronial style of architecture', prepared in 1848 to persuade the admiring Grand Duke Constantine 'to introduce this style of architecture in the Russian Empire', Graham noted that he had 'studied at once to adapt it for modern habitation, and to preserve and even increase its grandeur of effect' (ibid.). Grandeur of exterior and interior effect was, indeed, Graham's principal grail. One of the most prolific architects of early nineteenth-century Scotland, he was the creator not so much of great architecture as of magnificent experience, as the romanticism of his exteriors was matched by an interior landscape with a brilliant use of light. His architecture matured from the cake-box gothick remodelling of Kincardine (1805) into a personal language that closed at Aytoun with an architectural

country houses was Blythswood, Glasgow (1821), and his five commercial banks included Stirling (1825) and Aberdeen (1836). His ten town planning or urban building schemes included the layout of Blythswood Holm, Glasgow (1820), the outstanding plan of circus and ellipse combining tenement and terraced house of the Moray estate, Edinburgh (1822–31), the majestic Hamilton Square, Birkenhead (1824), and the *rus in urbe* of Blacket Place, Edinburgh (1825). He designed twenty-three historicist or revivalist houses, exemplified by Duns, Berwickshire (1818–20); the largest, in what he called a 'James 1st' style, was Murthly, Perthshire (from 1827)—unusually early for neo-Jacobean. On 30 May 1815 he married into the Episcopalian gentry, by taking as his wife Margaret Anne (*d.* 1826), daughter of William Graham of Orchill. Advised by his wife's relatives, he had added the name Graham to his by the early 1820s. Margaret Gillespie Graham died in 1826, leaving two daughters. Graham married secondly in March 1830, in Edinburgh, Elizabeth Marjorie, elder daughter of the late Major John Campbell of the 76th regiment of foot. In March 1834 Graham's finances were put under trusteeship, which was only released in 1843.

Using a combination of charm and opportunism, in 1818 Graham persuaded the lord clerk register to support

Scottish symphony. After four years of illness he died on 21 March 1855, aged seventy-eight, and was buried in Greyfriars kirkyard, Edinburgh. CHARLES McKEAN

Sources Colvin, *Archs.* · J. Macaulay, 'James Gillespie Graham in Skye', *Bulletin of the Scottish Georgian Society*, 3 (1974–5), 1–14 · J. Macaulay, 'Graham and Pugin: some Perthshire connections', *Architectural Heritage*, 8 (1997), 22–36 · J. Macaulay, 'The architectural collaboration between J. Gillespie Graham and A. W. N. Pugin', *Architectural History*, 27 (1984), 406–20 · J. Macaulay, *The Gothic revival, 1745–1845* (1975) · J. P. Neale, *Scotch seats: Jones' views of seats, mansions, castles, etc* (c.1824) · T. Annan, J. O. Mitchell, and others, *The old country houses of the old Glasgow gentry* (1870) · [G. M. Kemp], *Plans of the proposed restorations and alterations to the cathedral of Glasgow* (1836) [Kemp's signed copy, RIAS library] · [W. Papworth], ed., *The dictionary of architecture*, 11 vols. (1853–92) · M. Glendinning, R. MacInnes, and A. MacKechnie, *A history of Scottish architecture* (1996) · *Edinburgh*, Pevsner (1984) · T. Bonnar, *Biographical sketch of George Meikle Kemp* (1892) · J. Cullen, *Glasgow illustrated* (1834) · G. Cumming, *Forfarshire illustrated* (1848) · M. Davis, *Scots baronial* (1996) · M. C. Davis, *The castles and mansions of Ayrshire* (1991) · T. A. Markus, ed., *Order and space in society* (1982) · J. Macaulay, 'The demolition of the western towers of Glasgow Cathedral', *The architecture of Scottish towns and cities*, ed. D. Mays (1997), 115–24 · J. M. Leighton, *Select views of Glasgow and its environs* (1828) · J. M. Leighton, *Select views on the River Clyde* (1830) · C. McKean, ed., *Illustrated architectural guides to Scotland* (1982–) · *Tolbooths and town houses: civic architecture in Scotland to 1833*, Royal Commission on the Ancient and Historical Monuments of Scotland (1996) · b. cert. · m. certs. · sheriff court records, Commissariat of Edinburgh, SC 70/87, p. 721 · parish records, Dunblane, Perthshire · inventory of Dalguise Muniments, NA Scot. · tombstone, Greyfriars' kirkyard, Edinburgh

Archives NA Scot., drawings · National Monuments Record of Scotland, Edinburgh, drawings · priv. colls., drawings · RIBA, scheme · Royal Incorporation of Architects in Scotland, drawings | Armadale Trust, Skeat, Clan Donald Lands Trust, MSS rel. to work in Skye · priv. coll., designs · priv. coll., letters to Robert Stuart · Scot. RO, Breadalbane Muniments · Scot. RO, Strathearn and Blair MSS · Scot. RO, Melville Castle Muniments · Scot. RO, Murthly Castle Muniments · Scot. RO, Campbell of Barcaldine Muniments · Scot. RO, Lochnaw Muniments · Scot. RO, MacDonald of Clanranald Muniments · Scot. RO, inventory of Dalguise Muniments

Likenesses H. Raeburn, portrait, 1823, priv. coll. · J. Watson-Gordon, portrait, 1841, priv. coll. [*see illus.*] · B. W. Crombie, etching, 1847 (after Kay), Witt

Sir James Robert George Graham, second baronet (1792–1861), by Mayall & Co.

Graham, Sir James Robert George, second baronet

(**1792–1861**), politician, was born on 1 June 1792 at the family home of Netherby, near Carlisle, the eldest of the twelve children of Sir James Graham of Netherby, first baronet (*d.* 1824), and Lady Catherine Stewart, daughter of John, seventh earl of Galloway.

Background and early career Graham's father was a follower of the duke of Portland, who secured the revival of the family baronetcy in 1783, and was later a Pittite MP for Ripon. His mother was a devout evangelical, a disciple of Isaac Milner and a friend of William Wilberforce, whose influence on her son's religion was profound. Graham was educated at a private school at Dalston, kept by the Revd Walter Fletcher, chancellor of the diocese of Carlisle, and at Westminster School, and was afterwards a pupil of the Revd G. Richards of Bampton, Oxfordshire. He entered Christ Church, Oxford, in June 1810. Here he appeared a typically supercilious dandy, with a fine string of horses but no interest in academic work. Eventually, bored with the constraints of university life, he left without taking a degree in the spring of 1812. Excited by the struggle against Napoleon, and anxious to see it for himself, he left for the Iberian peninsula. He later moved on to Sicily, where in 1813–14 he acted as private secretary to Lord William Bentinck, commander-in-chief of the British army there. In early 1814 he conducted a mission for Bentinck which involved a clandestine journey through Italy in order to ascertain the British government's policy towards Murat, king of Naples. Graham concluded an armistice with Murat, and was commended for good judgement by Bentinck and by Lord Aberdeen for the government.

Graham's wartime experience intensified his already strong political ambition, his enthusiasm for national liberty, and his disapproval, tinged with condescension, of the narrow vision of the British tory government. Sensitive to the need to assert the leadership of the landed classes, he had declared himself a whig in joining Brooks's Club in 1812, and rashly became heavily indebted by spending £6000 to become MP for Hull at the 1818 election. At the next election, in 1820, he was returned for St Ives, but when a petition was issued against his return, he declined to contest it on the grounds that this would weaken his finances further. He therefore withdrew from parliament in 1821, and went to live at Croft Head, the home farm on the Netherby estate, with his wife, Fanny, youngest daughter of Colonel Callander and Lady Elizabeth McDonnell. They had married on 8 July 1819, after

Graham, who in youth was notably tall and handsome ('a very Apollo in form', according to Harriette Wilson's *Memoirs*), had had a number of affairs. They had three sons and three daughters.

Graham devoted the next few years of his life to improving the 25,000 acres of the Netherby estate, which he inherited on the death of his father in April 1824. The land was not rich, and had been neglected; but between 1818 and 1845 he spent £93,000 on it. With his new steward, John Yule, he undertook major drainage schemes, built good roads, greatly improved the quality of stock, and educated tenants in detailed rotational techniques. As tenancies fell in, he increased their size and efficiency. The work took long to bear fruit, and rents rose only slowly before the 1840s. In the 1820s Graham was frequently pessimistic about the estate's survival, and sometimes considered selling. In consequence, he became extremely critical of the government's economic policy, particularly the return to the gold standard in 1819 which, in retrospect, he blamed for lowering rents and trapping wartime debtors in high interest payments. In 1826 he published a pamphlet, *Corn and Currency*, which advocated a loosening of monetary policy and a corn tariff low enough to keep down prices and wages and hence maintain the productivity of the general economy. He also called for lower taxes, arguing that the government should have reduced official salaries and other expenditure in line with the rent and wage reductions enforced in 1819. He fought for lower rates in his locality, attacking the mismanagement of the poor law and prisons and working to reduce official salaries. When he returned to parliament as MP for Carlisle in 1826, it was not as a snobbish whig dandy but as a knowledgeable landowner and an advocate of retrenchment and reform in local and national politics.

In the next four years Graham made an impressive reputation for himself at Westminster as a leading representative of the independently minded cost-cutting gentry critics of government. He belonged to the strand of whiggism which came to accept Althorp as its figure-head and which had close affinities with the least partisan members of parliament, principally county members and Canningites. (Graham himself achieved a great ambition in becoming a county MP, for Cumberland, in January 1829.) His first loyalty was never to party; it was to his estate, and to the defence of property. So his fervent espousal of the cause of economy was married with an anxiety for the preservation of social order. This combination of views fitted him well for the fluid political situation of 1828–30, as fixed party divisions disintegrated, the economy went into depression, and many MPs succumbed to a mood of restless apocalypticism. Graham made a series of motions which caught the public imagination, on the currency question in 1828, and on official salaries in 1830. He served on a number of select committees and won a reputation for efficiency and industry. He also argued that 'moderate but effective' parliamentary reform was required in order to facilitate the necessary reduction in government expenditure and patronage. By

the autumn of 1830, with Wellington's government too weak to survive unaided and a new coalition of some sort inevitable, Graham, like Althorp and Palmerston, had come to articulate so many of the views of respected middle-of-the-road gentry MPs that he would have been a candidate for high office whatever the nature of the emerging coalition. He played an important role in the negotiations between the whigs and Canningites which led to the formation of Grey's reform government in November 1830, and was given a seat in the new cabinet as first lord of the Admiralty. He became a privy councillor.

The 1830s Graham's job at the Admiralty was to realize the reformers' promises of more economical and efficient administration of this high-spending department. During his tenure, the navy estimates were reduced from £5.84 million to £4.66 million, despite the expenditure incurred in dispatching extra ships to Portugal, the Netherlands, the Ottoman empire, and the West Indies in order to assert British interests. He also sent ships to Ireland in 1832 'to create a moral effect' during the tithe disturbances there. He worked hard to root out inefficiencies in the Admiralty, lengthening hours of work and reducing salaries. Believing that existing accounting procedures minimized its accountability to parliament, he established the navy appropriation account, which explained how the money voted in the estimates had actually been spent, and was to be presented to the Commons each year. This important reform was the model for the general government appropriation accounts established later in the century. In the interests of rationalization, centralization, and parliamentary accountability, he also abolished the semi-autonomous navy and victualling boards and reorganized the civil departments of the navy under the responsibility of individual members of the Admiralty board, over which the first lord presided. This greatly increased the power of the first lord himself, and so eased Graham's task in superintending reforms throughout the administration. But it created difficulties for the future, especially in wartime when the enormous burden of mundane civil business borne by the board members left them with insufficient time to devise battle strategy.

Graham's standing among gentry MPs explains his selection for the 'committee of four' government ministers charged with drafting the 1831 Reform Bill. Though his independence from the whig family cliques gave him the confidence of some advanced reformers, radical cartoonists still tended to depict him as the brakeman on the reform coach. In some respects this was justified: he opposed the inclusion of the secret ballot in the bill, and advocated a sizeable increase in the number of county seats, so as to defend propertied interests. But paradoxically his concern for the maintenance of public order made him anxious to settle the reform question quickly, and so he was to the fore in pressing the cabinet to ask the king to threaten the mass creation of whig peers in order to force the Lords to pass the bill. Had his advice been taken in the autumn of 1831, six months of agitation would have been avoided. Once the Reform Act passed, Graham was frequently gloomy about social turbulence and the prospects for upholding the authority of government. As a staunch Anglican, he was particularly concerned about the dissenters' campaigns against privileges of the established church, which he regarded as a great bulwark of social order.

In 1833–4 Graham became unsympathetic to those whigs, such as Lord John Russell, who wished to identify the government with a policy of religious radicalism, especially in Ireland in response to the campaign of Daniel O'Connell against the protestant church. In May 1834 Graham resigned from the cabinet with three other ministers in protest at its drift towards accepting the principle of appropriating some of the revenues of the Church of Ireland for secular Irish purposes. He feared the consequences for protestantism and British rule in Ireland, and for the established churches in Britain, especially in view of the number of vocal radical pressure groups in the reformed parliament.

Graham, with Lord Stanley, now formed an informal grouping in the political middle ground, known to some as the 'Derby Dilly'. They hoped to exploit the increasing alarm of the king, the Lords, and many propertied people at the perceived extremism and partisanship of the government. The Conservative Party, in opposition, was at this time weak in numbers, and when the king removed the whigs in November 1834 and asked the Conservatives to form a ministry, there was a widespread view that it could not prosper without support from the Dilly. But Graham and Stanley would not join the new government, not wishing to associate with opponents of the Reform Act; Graham was re-elected in East Cumberland at the election of January 1835 by stressing to his constituents that he remained a reformer. Instead, they sought a realignment in the centre, embracing moderate whigs, Peel, and themselves. But this did not materialize. When Peel's government was defeated in April 1835, the whigs returned to power on the principle of appropriation, while the Conservatives reverted to opposition much stronger and more confident than they had been a year before. Lacking a numerous body of supporters, Graham and Stanley were forced into alliance with the Conservatives; Graham, stung by constant barracking from his former colleagues, moved his place to the opposition side of the Commons in June 1835. At the next election for East Cumberland, in 1837, he was defeated by a whig and a radical in a very bitter contest, and in 1838 was returned instead for the small borough of Pembroke, on the nomination of Earl Cawdor.

This shift of constituency symbolized Graham's evolving relationship with extra-parliamentary opinion. Not until he returned to Carlisle as a Liberal in 1852 was he again to sit for a remotely popular seat, or face a contest (he sat for Dorchester, then Ripon, between 1841 and 1852). Although he had been critical of the old tory regime of the 1810s and 1820s, and had taken the popular side against it, this was on account of its inefficiency and extravagance rather than because of an enthusiasm for 'the people'. He had rarely cultivated popularity, and had always appeared grand in his bearing and self-conscious about his social status. Together with his sarcastic manner, directness of expression, and inability to suffer those less competent at administration than himself, this had already won him a reputation for disdainful vanity and ensured him much hostility in press and parliament, especially from whig partisans whom he had deserted. In addition, his evangelical upbringing and natural pessimism led him to reflect gloomily on the difficulty of disciplining mankind; so did his economic studies, which convinced him that a manufacturing economy was an 'artificial' one, in which production would naturally tend to exceed consumption, placing inexorable downward pressures on profits and wages and thus stirring up social tension. The consequence was that by the late 1830s any suggestion of radicalism in his political outlook had disappeared. His sympathies seemed to lie with the cause of 'order' instead. He was extremely sensitive to the need to maintain executive authority, and anxious also to return to office in order to continue the work of retrenchment and administrative reform which he believed was a necessary prerequisite of social stability. These views were similar to those of the Conservative leader, Sir Robert Peel, and Graham became Peel's close confidant. (He also succeeded Peel as lord rector of Glasgow University in 1837.) As a result, when the Conservatives returned to office in September 1841, Graham became Peel's home secretary and most intimate counsellor in government, who should share with him the credit for the ministry's achievements. However, there was no natural sympathy between Graham and Conservative back-benchers, and he never attempted to cultivate their support. This was a problematic position for a home secretary, and explains much of Graham's difficulty over the following five years.

Home secretary Graham brought indefatigable industry and a powerful administrative brain to the Home Office. He was faced with great problems: social unrest, Chartism, the emergence of the 'condition of England' problem, and a campaign in Ireland for the repeal of the Union. He reacted with great conscientiousness and zeal, but with distinctly mixed success. His record of legislative success was poor and his parliamentary reputation declined.

Graham described the strikes and Chartist activity of 1842 as 'the mad insurrection of the working classes', and sought to intimidate the agitators by a display of state power. He ordered troops to turn out around the country, urged magistrates to use their powers to suppress meetings, and presided over a policy of widespread arrests and special trials. Radical antagonism was naturally excited against him, and this was exacerbated in 1844 by an incident involving the Italian nationalist Giuseppe Mazzini, who was living in exile in London. In the autumn of 1843 the Austrian ambassador in Britain, Baron Philipp von Neumann, had met Graham and asked him to locate Mazzini's hiding-place. In March 1844, after further pressure from Neumann, Graham issued a warrant for the copying of Mazzini's mail by the Post Office, and agreed to pass to Lord Aberdeen, the foreign secretary, any information about suspected risings against the Austrian and other conservative regimes in the various Italian states, which Aberdeen could then communicate to the Austrians. By accommodating Austria in this way, Graham and Aberdeen hoped to get the pope to use his influence to dissuade the Irish Catholic clergy from fomenting the campaign for the repeal of the corn laws. Mazzini and his friends discovered that their mail was being tampered with, and in June a parliamentary furore arose. Graham defended the right of governments to open mail for political purposes. This right was upheld by a secret committee which investigated precedents, though it also revealed that Graham had been unusually assiduous in opening mail, and in the summer of 1842 had issued twenty warrants to inspect Chartists' letters. The affair excited public revulsion at ministers' behaviour; tampering with correspondence, especially at the behest of an illiberal foreign government, was deemed despicable and un-English. Although he was less to blame than Aberdeen, Graham suffered much more opprobrium because of his autocratic reputation; there was a fad for correspondents to write 'Not to be Grahamed' on their envelopes.

While Graham's zeal in defending order upset Liberals, it also managed to offend many propertied Conservatives. He criticized magistrates for their complacency and inefficiency during the unrest of 1842, and unsuccessfully proposed to the cabinet the appointment of salaried assistant barristers at quarter sessions in order to quicken and tighten up the law and order process in the localities. Back-benchers retaliated, interpreting much of his legislation as overbearing and destructive of traditional liberties. With personal sympathy for him among MPs scant, his controversial bills foundered, such as his measure to establish a central council to standardize qualifications for the medical profession (the British Medical Association accused him of seeking despotic control). His worst set-back came in the field of education. Graham saw the promotion of religious education as one of the principal means by which the state could combat the threat of social unrest. In particular, he sought to reduce the danger of disorder in the turbulent industrial districts by establishing a better education for factory children. In 1843 he introduced a bill requiring factory employees under thirteen to be given three hours of instruction daily. But he included securities for an Anglican presence in the schools. Dissenters were indignant, a vast petitioning campaign ensued, and the bill was withdrawn.

In Ireland the repeal movement revived in 1842 and a series of monster meetings was planned for 1843. Graham's initial response was one of intense alarm at 'the reign of Terror', the failure of juries to convict offenders, and the unwillingness of the Irish executive to assert itself to uphold the law. This anxiety helps to explain the government's decision to proclaim the biggest repeal meeting, scheduled for Clontarf in October 1843, and, a week later, to arrest the repeal leader Daniel O'Connell on a charge of conspiring to incite disaffection. Unwisely the prosecuting authorities had Catholics removed from the trial jury. O'Connell appealed against the conviction and

eventually, in September 1844, the House of Lords overturned it, on the votes of Liberal judges. Graham was very bitter and believed that the authority of government in Ireland had been gravely wounded. By this time, assisted by Peel's influence, he had come to see the need for legislative activity in order to counter the propaganda of the repealers. Strongly convinced of the potency of religion as a bulwark of social order, he was particularly keen to increase the Catholic priests' confidence in British rule. The Charitable Bequests Act of 1844 aimed to improve the Catholic church's financial position and to draw the bishops into the habit of communication with government through membership of a board of commissioners. The same strategy can be discerned in the educational policy of 1845, featuring an increased grant to the Catholic seminary of Maynooth and the establishment of the Queen's colleges, non-denominational university colleges for Catholics and protestants to use together. However, only a minority of bishops, from the older generation, defied O'Connell's wishes and participated in the running of the charitable bequests board and the colleges. By the autumn of 1845 the government still did not feel confident of the loyalty of the Irish people, and this was to be of major significance in the corn tariff crisis of 1845–6.

Graham and Peel shared a staunch but controversial loyalty to the principles of political economy. When factory reformers called for reductions in the length of the adult working day to ten hours, the government resisted, arguing that it would make British factories uncompetitive internationally. In 1844 the factory reformers defeated the government, and the twelve-hour day had to be reasserted by the calling of a vote of confidence in government, a manoeuvre which embittered relations with back-benchers. Graham's refusal to compromise with those who criticized the severity of the 1834 poor law was similarly contentious.

Into this fraught atmosphere, in the autumn of 1845, came news of the failure of the Irish potato crop. Graham saw the famine as a dispensation of providence which it was man's duty to rectify in order to preserve social peace. Moreover, on political grounds some gesture was necessary in order to reassure sceptical Irishmen of the government's concern for their survival. But if the corn laws were suspended temporarily, the strength of public agitation would prevent their reimposition, giving the impression that government had surrendered to popular pressure. Though in the 1830s Graham had defended the sliding scale, he and Peel had agreed since 1842 that the corn laws were politically and economically counterproductive and that, despite their talismanic significance for most Conservative back-benchers, they must be repealed in the near future if economic stagnation was to be averted. The famine provided the occasion. The decision to press ahead with the repeal of the corn laws demonstrated great long-term administrative wisdom and great short-term political inflexibility. It reveals the extent to which the experience of government since 1841 had engendered in both Peel and Graham a conviction of the superiority and sufficiency of their judgement, a condescension towards those who lacked their knowledge of affairs, and an overpowering concern with public order. Throughout the crisis, they seemed, in *Punch's* words, 'two persons with only one intellect'. After months of high drama, the corn laws were repealed in June 1846, the Conservative Party split, and Peel fell from office. Lord John Russell formed a Liberal government, which was kept afloat by the hundred or so Conservative MPs who remained loyal to Peel. Inevitably these included Graham, who became the leading member of the group in the Commons after Peel's death in 1850.

Graham and the Liberal Party The Peelites, and Graham in particular, were in an unenviable political position after 1846. Politics since 1841 had filled him with loathing for the constraints of party; he had no desire to shackle himself with back-benchers who in his eyes were dogmatic, unimaginative, and ungrateful. In any case, there was hostility to him on both sides of the Commons, from protectionist Conservatives and (as he believed) from Liberals who remembered his defection of 1834–5. His reputation for aloofness, mistrustfulness, sarcasm, and unpopularity was now unshakeable. To join the Liberals would inevitably prompt charges of chronic vacillation and lack of principle; it was also unappealing, given Graham's great distrust of Palmerston's ebullient and reckless foreign policy. And in view of the government's weakness, it might achieve little. So Graham rejected offers to join Russell's cabinet in 1849 and 1851. Yet the Peelites were a major source of weakness in the political system, preventing the establishment of a firm executive government able to deal with the social, economic, religious, and international tensions which abounded in the late 1840s. And Graham naturally believed that his talents were required in office. What should he do? The death of Peel, who had been his counsellor for fifteen years, left him rudderless.

Graham had no wish to be another Peel, or a party leader, even had he had the necessary standing. None the less, his administrative skills and political experience made him an indispensable figure in the political manoeuvring of the 1850s. His role in the final decade of his career was to be an *éminence grise* in the formation of the great Liberal coalition which endured for thirty years. He was the first Peelite to accept the logic of an alliance with the Liberal Party, and the most important advocate of it. In 1852 he stood successfully at Carlisle as a Liberal, defeating a protectionist; he was to hold the seat until his death. Graham's past association with Liberals made him more attuned than his younger colleagues to the continuing potency of the cause of peace, retrenchment, and reform, and less susceptible to notions of Liberal extremism and unsoundness.

The idea of a Liberal–Peelite alliance developed in fits and starts in the early 1850s, and ran in tandem with continuing prejudices and rivalries on both sides. The Peelites sought to maximize their strength, relative to the Liberals, by highlighting the aspects of their identity most attractive to middle England. They stressed their commitment to administrative efficiency, low expenditure, and low taxes on land, income, and consumption. Graham also emphasized their support for modernizing legislative activity in Ireland, and was dealt a propaganda gift when Russell, who had previously been much more successful than Graham in portraying himself as the friend of religious toleration in Ireland, stirred up Catholic hostility with the Ecclesiastical Titles Act of 1851, which the Peelites opposed. At the 1852 election Graham also advocated further parliamentary reform. One may see this as a defensive move, born of his characteristic timidity about social change; he argued that once Russell had revived the issue, it could not be stopped, and ought to be settled quickly and peacefully. Diminishing the number of small boroughs also promised to weaken protectionist forces. But, in addition, reform was a useful ploy in advertising Graham's Liberalism. Most significantly, it brought him increasingly into alignment with the agenda associated with Russell, the other survivor of the committee of four. After Russell's fall from office in early 1852, Graham and he were to operate a rough-and-ready alliance, based on a vigorous domestic policy, retrenchment, reform, and scepticism about Palmerston. This ended only with Graham's death.

The other leading Peelites were more hesitant about a Liberal coalition than Graham was, and it was not until the experience of a minority Conservative government in 1852 that the anti-protectionist forces could see their way to a coalition. Graham's tactics paid off, in that the Peelites were the major victors of the negotiations which led to the Aberdeen coalition of December 1852, whereas other, equally plausible political combinations would have left them marginalized. Graham was much involved in the government's formation, and was offered the exchequer or the Home Office. But he returned to the Admiralty as first lord, a lower-profile appointment which probably reflected his own doubts about his popularity and nerve. However, cabinet disputes created too much indecision in foreign policy, and this contributed to the outbreak of the Crimean War in 1854. So great responsibility was again thrust on Graham.

As a keen advocate of low expenditure, Graham disliked the half-hearted forward moves which increased tension in the East in 1853, but, like many others, he was ambivalent about the broader issues involved. He had always been a staunch patriot: he had liked Palmerston's bold anti-Russian policy of 1833, had urged the revival of the militia during the French invasion scare of 1845, and had called for a bigger army after Napoleon III's *coup d'état*. Once he saw that war with Russia was inevitable, he urged its prosecution 'with decision and promptitude'. He played a crucial part in war management (he was made GCB in April 1854), and was primarily responsible for the choice of naval strategy. This aimed to strike a knock-out blow against the Russian naval force at Sevastopol, 'which would settle the affairs of the East for some time to come'. Meanwhile, the Baltic fleet, commanded by Sir Charles Napier, would play a secondary role, operating a close blockade to hinder Russian trade and to prevent Russian ships from escaping to menace British and French waters.

There was no alternative to this initial emphasis on the Crimea. The Admiralty, having long concentrated its planning against a French rather than a Russian threat, had made little provision for a Baltic campaign; intelligence on the area was scanty, and the fleet lacked small cruisers capable of navigating the Baltic shallows. Considerations of economy led Graham to delay mobilizing the fleet until war was inevitable, and to reject a policy of bounties, so the men assembled for the Baltic were mostly unskilled and untrained. However, Russia's Baltic fleet was her pride, and would have to be tackled if the war was to be prolonged. Hence the importance of the swift attack on Sevastopol; resources could then be transferred northwards if appropriate.

The strategy did not unfold as planned. Sevastopol was not taken until September 1855, after the army had endured bloody battles and a winter of terrible privation and disease, all graphically reported back home. Meanwhile, public opinion had become restless at the failure of the Baltic fleet to attack the great Russian fortifications of Sveaborg and Kronstadt. In the autumn of 1854 the Admiralty started to communicate this restlessness, leading to an unfortunate misunderstanding with Napier and his withdrawal from the campaign. It would have been foolish for the fleet in its current state to attack the fortifications. The economy-conscious Graham had hoped that Sweden would enter the war and supply the seamen and cruisers needed for a forward policy, but when this possibility lapsed, and stalemate threatened in the Crimea, an extra £600,000 was found for improving the Baltic fleet in October 1854. Even so, these plans were later criticized for their diffuseness, which was blamed on the lack of a permanent naval staff with the time to consider strategy. Although the Admiralty assembled and equipped its fleets expeditiously, and rightly escaped the intense public condemnation visited on the army administration in 1854–5, it too had been found wanting under wartime conditions.

Graham's war role ended in February 1855, when he resigned from the government with some other Peelites. The Aberdeen coalition had fallen in January, the prime minister and the duke of Newcastle acting as scapegoats for the failings of the war machine. Palmerston became prime minister; Graham, citing patriotism, agreed to serve under him. But Graham failed to extract from Palmerston a pledge that the new government would resist the establishment of a parliamentary select committee to inquire into war administration, a move which the Peelites considered was likely to undermine military morale and weaken executive authority. When Palmerston consented to the formation of the committee, Graham resigned, with Sidney Herbert and W. E. Gladstone. For the next three years he was free to criticize Palmerston's foreign policy and the extravagance, recklessness, and inefficiency of his domestic administration. He sometimes acted with Russell, most importantly in helping to defeat Palmerston on the China question in March 1857, triggering an election. The Peelites suffered in the public mind from their coolness towards the war and to Palmerston, and were reduced to a rump at the election.

Graham never held office again. He was not offered it when Palmerston returned as prime minister in 1859, though it was known that he would not accept it. He was depressed after the death of his wife at Cowes in October 1857, and ill with sciatica and diseased arteries. He died at Netherby on 25 October 1861 and was buried in Arthuret churchyard. But to the end of his life he had remained an important politician. He chaired a number of useful parliamentary inquiries in these last years. And, despite his distrust of Palmerston, he continued to prefer Liberal to Conservative government. He discerned that Conservatives tended to be warlike, extravagant on defence spending, and illiberal in Ireland, while he approved of Russell's and Cobden's influence on the Liberal Party. He helped to dissuade Gladstone from taking office under Derby in 1858. The Liberal government of 1859 had his strong support, and was in a sense the culmination of his strategy over the previous ten years.

Assessment Temperamentally and in political allegiance, Graham was a man of superficial contradictions. Arthur Gordon described him as 'rash and timid', and belittled his judgement on both grounds. This was a widely held view. Graham's outlook was dominated by an often immoderate concern with the maintenance of public order, property, and government authority. But his arrogant executive hauteur sat uneasily with an evangelically inspired tendency to overreact to social turbulence, an ambivalence about responsibility, and a susceptibility to depression, self-doubt, and *anomie*. Distrusting the excesses of public opinion, he was inclined to exaggerate its radicalism and force. He was an efficient manager of a desk, a major influence on the professionalization of Victorian administration, and a contributor to the Peelite–Gladstonian fiscal tradition, but he lacked the character, the vision, and the warmth to be a successful political leader. Although he had the advantage of a large and powerful frame, and the detail of his parliamentary speeches was often forceful, their delivery could be monotonous and feeble, while his wit rarely rose above biting sarcasm and he disdained to cultivate either fashionable society or the political small fry. He disliked country-house visiting, travelled strikingly little, and had few hobbies. Assiduous and austere, he seemed to believe that political power could rest entirely on administrative ability. Disinterested, devout, and genuinely alarmed for the future of his class, his religion, and his civilization, he threw himself into public service. He did not intend to belittle party, but party kept belittling him, as he saw it, and this he found insufferable. In the course of twelve years he alienated the bulk of both sides of the Commons.

But it is important to remember that he was a major force not only in dismantling the two strongest governments of the first half of the nineteenth century, but also in creating them in the first place. And again after 1846 he came to see, however reluctantly, that some compromise with party discipline was necessary if the administrative, financial, and legislative efficiency which was his political goal was to be promoted. Behind the scenes, he was an effective political operator. Graham, with Russell and Palmerston, should take most of the credit for the painful but inexorable evolution to maturity of the broad Liberal governing coalition which was to dominate British politics from the 1850s to the 1880s. It was no accident that these three men were the major survivors of the reform government of 1830, for the continuities between the two coalitions significantly outweighed the differences. This fact among others demonstrates how small were the inconsistencies which at first sight seem to litter Graham's career. JONATHAN PARRY

Sources C. S. Parker, *Life and letters of Sir James Graham, 1792–1861*, 2 vols. (1907) · J. T. Ward, *Sir James Graham* (1967) · A. B. Erickson, *The public career of Sir James Graham* (1952) · A. P. Donajgrodzki, 'Sir James Graham at the home office', *HJ*, 20 (1977), 97–120 · F. B. Smith, 'British post office espionage, 1844', *Historical Studies*, 14 (1969–71), 189–203 · D. A. Kerr, *Peel, priests, and politics: Sir Robert Peel's administration and the Roman Catholic church in Ireland, 1841–1846* (1982) · J. B. Conacher, *The Peelites and the party system* (1972) · J. B. Conacher, *The Aberdeen coalition, 1852–1855* (1968) · A. D. Lambert, *The Crimean War: British grand strategy, 1853–56* (1990) · C. I. Hamilton, 'Sir James Graham, the Baltic campaign and war-planning at the admiralty in 1854', *HJ*, 19 (1976), 89–112 · D. Spring, 'A great agricultural estate: Netherby under Sir James Graham, 1820–1845', *Agricultural History*, 29 (1955), 73–81 · Gladstone, *Diaries*

Archives BL, corresp. and papers, Dep. 9374 · Cumbria AS, Carlisle, corresp. with Queen Victoria [microfilm version available in Bodl. Oxf., CUL, NL Ire., and Newberry Library, Chicago] | Beds. & Luton ARS, corresp. with second Earl de Grey · BL, corresp. with Lord Aberdeen, Add. MSS 43190–43192, 43329–43331 · BL, corresp. with W. E. Gladstone, Add. MSS 44163–44164 · BL, corresp. with F. R. Bonham, Add. MS 40616 · BL, corresp. with Lord Holland, Add. MS 51542 · BL, corresp. with Sir Thomas Byam Martin, Add. MSS 41369–41370 · BL, corresp. with Sir Charles Napier, Add. MSS 40023–40026, 40037 · BL, letters to Sir Robert Peel, Add. MSS 40318, 40446–40452 · Bodl. Oxf., corresp. with Lord Clarendon · Bodl. Oxf., letters to Samuel Wilberforce · Borth. Inst., corresp. with Sir Charles Wood · Bucks. RLSS, corresp. with Lord Cottesloe · CKS, letters to Lord Stanhope · Cumbria AS, Carlisle, corresp. with Lord Aberdeen · Cumbria AS, Carlisle, corresp. with William IV · Cumbria AS, Carlisle, corresp. with Lord Brougham · Cumbria AS, Carlisle, letters to J. W. D. Dundas · Cumbria AS, Carlisle, corresp. with Sir Edward Eliot · Cumbria AS, Carlisle, corresp. with Sir Thomas Fremantle · Cumbria AS, Carlisle, corresp. with W. E. Gladstone · Cumbria AS, Carlisle, corresp. with third Earl Grey · Cumbria AS, Carlisle, corresp. with Lord de Grey · Cumbria AS, Carlisle, corresp. with Sir Henry Hotham · Cumbria AS, Carlisle, corresp. with Lord Hyterbury · Cumbria AS, Carlisle, corresp. with Sir Pulteney Malcolm · Cumbria AS, Carlisle, corresp. with Lord Palmerston · Cumbria AS, Carlisle, corresp. with Sir William Parker · Cumbria AS, Carlisle, corresp. with Sir Robert Peel · Cumbria AS, Carlisle, corresp. with Lord Raglan · Cumbria AS, Carlisle, corresp. with Sir John Russell · Cumbria AS, Carlisle, corresp. with Lord Stanley · Cumbria AS, Carlisle, corresp. with Sir Edward Sugden · Cumbria AS, Carlisle, corresp. with duke of Wellington · Devon RO, letters to Sir Thomas Dyke Acland · Durham RO, letters to Lord Londonderry · Glamorgan RO, Cardiff, corresp. with Lord Lyndhurst · McGill University, Montreal, McLennan Library, letters to Lord Hardinge · Mount Stuart Trust, Isle of Bute, corresp. with Lord Bute · NA Scot., letters to Lord Dalhousie · NA Scot., letters to George William Hope · NA Scot., corresp. with Lord Melville · NL Scot., corresp. with Sir Thomas Cochrane · NL Scot., corresp. with Edward Ellice · NL Scot., corresp. with Lord Melville · NL Wales, letters to George Cornewall Lewis · NL Wales, corresp. with earl of Powis · NMM, letters to Sir Edward Codrington · NMM, letters to Sir Thomas Foley · NMM, letters to Sir Alexander Milne · NMM, letters to Sir William

Parker · Norfolk RO, letters to John Wodehouse · NRA Scotland, priv. coll., letters to Henry Duncan · NRA Scotland, priv. coll., letters to Sir George Sinclair · PRO, corresp. with Lord Cardwell, PRO 30/48 · PRO, letters to Sir George Murray, WO 80 · PRO, corresp. with Lord John Russell, PRO 30/22 · PRO NIre., letters to Lord Dufferin · Sheff. Arch., corresp. with Lord Fitzwilliam · St Deiniol's Library, corresp. with Sir John Gladstone · St Deiniol's Library, corresp. with Sir Thomas Gladstone · St Deiniol's Library, corresp. with W. E. Gladstone · St Deiniol's Library, letters to duke of Newcastle · U. Durham L., corresp. with third Earl Grey · U. Glas., Archives and Business Records Centre, corresp. with Duncan Macfarlan · U. Nott. L., corresp. with Lord William Bentinck · U. Nott. L., corresp. with duke of Newcastle · U. Southampton L., corresp. with Lord Palmerston · U. Southampton L., letters to duke of Wellington · UCL, letters to Lord Brougham · UCL, corresp. with Sir Edwin Chadwick · W. Sussex RO, letters to duke of Richmond · Wilts. & Swindon RO, corresp. with Sydney Herbert and Elizabeth Herbert · Woburn Abbey, letters to duke of Bedford · Port Eliot, letters to earl of St Germans

Likenesses Raeburn, portrait, c.1797, repro. in Ward, *Sir James Graham*, facing p. 44 · E. Desmaisons, lithograph, pubd 1842 (related to S. F. Diez, 1842), BM, NPG · S. F. Diez, drawing, 1842, Staadliche Museen zu Berlin, Germany · Brown, stipple, pubd 1863 (after Doyle), NPG · B. W. Crombie, pencil caricature, Scot. NPG · J. Doyle, drawings, BM · J. Gilbert, group portrait, pencil and wash (*The coalition ministry, 1854*), NPG · G. Hayter, group portrait, oils (*The House of Commons, 1833*), NPG · Mayall & Co., photograph, NPG [*see illus.*] · J. Partridge, group portrait (*The Fine Arts commissioners, 1846*), NPG · sketch, repro. in T. M. Torrens, *Life and times of Sir James Graham* (1863)

Wealth at death £35,000: probate, 12 Nov 1861, *CGPLA Eng. & Wales*

Graham, Janet (1723–1805), poet, was born at Shaw, Hutton parish, Annandale, Dumfriesshire, the eldest daughter of William Graham of Shaw; she was possibly the Janet Graham baptized on 3 May 1723 in Kirkpatrick Juxta parish. She lived in Dumfries for a time and latterly in Edinburgh; like many genteel maiden ladies of the period she stayed with different families. Her only work to have survived in print is the humorous song '[The] wayward wife', to the tune of 'Bide ye yet' (no. 97 in Johnson's *Scots Musical Museum*, 1787). It appeared in David Herd's *Ancient and Modern Scottish Songs* (1776), with the first two lines of the second stanza omitted; in *The Charmer: a Collection of Songs* (1782); and in Allan Cunningham's *The Songs of Scotland* (1825). It begins 'Alas! my son, you little know' and is a (decidedly non-feminist) piece of advice from father to son on 'the sorrows that from wedlock flow':

> Great Hercules and Samson too,
> Were stronger men than I or you;
> Yet they were baffled by their dears,
> And felt the distaff and the sheers.

Cunningham apparently misread the song, calling it 'A mother's advice to her son' (Cunningham, 1.220); 'a beautiful song' was Burns's opinion (R. H. Cromek, *Reliques of Robert Burns*, 1808, 231).

Miss Jenny was relished by society for her lively conversation and sense of humour. She once cured a major of the habit of publicly berating his servants by following his example, loudly (Johnson, 143); Cunningham relates how when Lord Hopetoun, taken with her dancing, asked where she had been taught, she replied, 'In my mother's wash-tub.' Afterwards she commented, 'Guid forgie me for saying so! I was never in a wash-tub in my life!' (*The Works of Robert Burns*, ed. A. Cunningham, 1834, 8.59). Graham died in Edinburgh in April 1805, possibly from the asthmatic complaint from which she had long suffered. She was probably buried in Hutton churchyard, Boreland village. HAMISH WHYTE

Sources R. Burns and others, *The Scots musical museum*, ed. J. Johnson and W. Stenhouse, new edn, 4 (1853), 101, 142–4, 408 • [D. Herd], ed., *Ancient and modern Scottish songs*, 2nd edn, 2 (1776), 120–21 • A. Cunningham, ed., *The songs of Scotland, ancient and modern*, 1 (1825), 217–20; 3 (1825), 284 • F. Miller, *The poets of Dumfriesshire* (1910), 159–60 • W. Rogerson, *Hutton under the Muir: notes on the past of an Annandale parish*, reprinted for private circulation by the *Dumfries and Galloway Courier and Herald* (1908), 37–9 • private information (2004)

Graham, Jocelyn Henry Clive [Harry] (1874–1936), author, was born on 23 December 1874 in London, the second child of Sir Henry John Lowndes Graham (1842–1930), clerk of the parliaments, and his first wife, Lady Edith Elizabeth Gathorne-Hardy (*d.* 1875), daughter of the first earl of Cranbrook. Graham's mother died when he was two weeks old, but he later felt himself fortunate in having in Sir Henry 'the most perfect of fathers' (family papers). In 1884 Sir Henry married Lady Margaret Georgina Compton, daughter of the fourth marquess of Northampton, and had three further children. Harry Graham was educated at Eton College and at the Royal Military College, Sandhurst, and joined the Coldstream Guards in 1895. Between 1898 and 1904 he was aide-de-camp to the earl of Minto, governor-general of Canada, with a gap in 1901–2, when he served in the Second South African War.

Under the pseudonym 'Col. D. Streamer', a pun on his regiment, in 1899 Graham published *Ruthless Rhymes for Heartless Homes*, for which he is best known. Forerunners of the sick joke, unlike *Struwwelpeter* they contain no moral to mitigate the enjoyable beastliness. Whereas Hoffmann's Pauline goes up in flames because she disobeys her mother, in 'Tender-heartedness' Graham visits the same fate on Billy without any attempt to edify:

> Billy, in one of his nice new sashes,
> Fell in the fire and was burnt to ashes;
> Now, although the room grows chilly,
> I haven't the heart to poke poor Billy.

Ruthless Rhymes reflected an upbringing in which almost nothing was off-limits as a subject for humour. 'My family would think me very ill if I ever said anything in a letter that wasn't absolutely flippant', the nineteen-year-old Graham wrote to a friend (family papers). Sir Henry was a pianist, singer, and songwriter whose *Six Drawing-Room Ditties*—'Oh, what a shape hers! Cutting her capers.'—were an early influence. Graham impressed Lady Minto by writing, producing, and starring in musical shows. The governor-general was less happy when his aide-de-camp published a comic poem about Theodore Roosevelt that included the lines:

> Though jealous rivals dared to scoff,
> He wore the smile-that-won't-come-off.

Lord Minto commented, 'I am furious … it's all wrong for

one of my staff to be making fun of the President'. But he later wrote: 'Harry quite awful and makes me hysterical he is so amusing' (Bowles, xi–xiii).

Graham was private secretary to the former prime minister Lord Rosebery from 1904 to 1906, when he became a full-time writer. He was briefly engaged to the American actress Ethel Barrymore, who found him 'a gay, brilliant creature' but decided not to marry him (Barrymore, 144–6). He tried biography—*Splendid Failures* has sympathetic portraits of Wolfe Tone, Toussaint L'Ouverture, and Hartley Coleridge—but his speciality was the comic poem, without the brutal succinctness of *Ruthless Rhymes* but dotted with biting observations, as in 'Forms of address', which appeared in *Deportmental Ditties* (1909):

> Then make it a rule, if you're bent on succeeding,
> To show every sign of good birth and good breeding,
> To do what is thought *comme-il-faut* and *de rigueur*,
> To browbeat the poor and to bully the nigger.

On 8 February 1910 Graham married Dorothy (1879–1942), daughter of Sir Francis Hyde Villiers, British ambassador in Brussels, and widow of Captain Hugh Keith-Fraser. When war was declared in 1914 he was nearly forty, but he rejoined his regiment, dealing with disciplinary lapses such as 'the glorious crime' of 'looking at the sergeant-major in an old-fashioned manner' (Graham papers). From 1917 he served in France, and saw many horrors. But he continued writing and following the progress of musical comedies to which he had contributed lyrics. *The Maid of the Mountains* (1917) ran for a record 1352 performances at Daly's, in London; its best-known song, 'Love will Find a Way', is characteristic of dozens of lyrics turned out by Graham over the next fifteen years. At one point, in 1924, there were seven productions in which he was involved (Bowles, xvi). Many were set in 'that imaginary country in Central Europe, which has to be imaginary because no actual country ever could be governed on such pleasantly frivolous lines' (*The Times*, 11 Feb 1931).

Graham's facility allowed him to ring innumerable changes on the theme of young love, although he used his comic gift when he could. In the Gilbertian 'I understood' the narrator tells of his failed attempts at love, borrowing, and insurance selling with the refrain:

> He didn't say he wouldn't and he didn't say he would,
> He didn't have to say a single word—I understood.

Graham's most popular song, made famous by Richard Tauber, was 'You are my heart's delight', from *The Land of Smiles*, with music by Franz Lehár. *White Horse Inn*, also translated by Graham from the German, had hits with the title-song and 'Goodbye' ('I'll be sometimes missed by the girls I've kissed'). In his comic prose there is evidence that Graham influenced P. G. Wodehouse, who is on record as an admirer (private information). In *The Bolster Book* (1910) he invented a club for rich young boneheads, the Celibates, with dialogue that pre-echoed Wodehouse's 'Drones'.

In 1930, with *More Ruthless Rhymes*, Graham revisited what the poet Gavin Ewart called the 'epigrammatic squib' (Ewart, 91). 'Indifference' finds him as casually mordant as ever:

> When Grandmamma fell off the boat,
> And couldn't swim (and wouldn't float),
> Matilda just stood by and smiled.
> I almost could have slapped the child.

Ewart believed Graham 'was not much inferior' to Gilbert as a versifier. When he died a fourth leader in *The Times* (31 October 1936) described *Ruthless Rhymes* as 'that enchanted world where there are no values nor standards of conduct or feeling, and where the plainest sense is the plainest nonsense'.

Despite his sharpness with the pen Graham was widely liked. He lunched at his clubs—the Beefsteak and the Garrick—and did his best work in the small hours. 'Tall, lean and soldierly' (*The Times*, 2 Nov 1936), he accentuated his military bearing with a Kitchener-style moustache. His only child, Virginia Graham (1910–1993), followed him as a writer, contributing many articles to *Punch*. Graham died of cancer in London on 30 October 1936.

JAMES HOGG

Sources F. Bowles, 'Introduction', in Col. D. Streamer [H. Graham], *Across Canada to the Klondyke*, ed. F. Bowles (1984) · *The Times* (8 Dec 1930), 14 · *The Times* (11 Feb 1931), 10 · *The Times* (31 Oct 1936), 13–14 · *The Times* (2 Nov 1936), 19 · G. Ewart, 'Light verse and Harry Graham (1874–1936)', *London Magazine* (Sept 1964), 84–91 · IWM, H. J. C. Graham papers · priv. coll., family papers · J. Parker, ed., *Who's who in the theatre*, 6th edn (1930) · E. Barrymore, *Memories* (1955) · *Joyce and Ginnie: the letters of Joyce Grenfell and Virginia Graham*, ed. J. Hampton (1997) · private information (2004) [Laura Dance, niece] · *CGPLA Eng. & Wales* (1936) · Burke, *Gen. GB* (1965)

Archives IWM, military papers

Wealth at death £26,885 11s. 8d.: probate, 30 Dec 1936, *CGPLA Eng. & Wales*

Graham, Sir John (d. 1298), soldier, owes his fame, and very probably his existence, to the late fifteenth-century poet Blind Hary, who recounts his exploits as a friend and follower of Sir William Wallace. It is possible that there is a tenuous connection between the heroic warrior of Hary's *Wallace* and a Sir John Graham of Abercorn who died in 1337, and who may in turn have been identical with a man of that name who was reportedly active against the English in 1298. But it is just as likely that Graham is entirely Hary's invention, begotten of the poet's desire to sing the praises and enjoy the patronage of the Stirlingshire family of Graham of Dundaff.

According to Hary, Graham is brought to enlist under Wallace's banner by his father, another Sir John. The two men thereafter campaign together in Scotland and England, with Graham acting sometimes as a sober foil to his fiery leader, an Oliver to his Roland, in a manner characteristic of chivalric epic—for instance, he rebukes Wallace for taking the risk of going among the English in disguise. Nevertheless, Graham's own prowess is such that, like Wallace himself, he can only be brought down by underhand means, being finally slain at the battle of Falkirk in 1298 by a soldier who stabs him from behind. Eulogized by Wallace as 'My best brothir in warld that evir I had' (Hary, 2.58), Graham is laid to rest in Falkirk churchyard, where he is still commemorated by an early

nineteenth-century monument with inscriptions in Latin and Scots, the latter taken from an early seventeenth-century edition of Hary's poem.

HENRY SUMMERSON

Sources *Hary's Wallace*, ed. M. P. McDiarmid, 2 vols., STS, 4th ser., 4–5 (1968–9)

Graham, John, third earl of Montrose (1548–1608), magnate and lord chancellor of Scotland, was the posthumous son of Robert Graham, master of Graham (*c*.1518–1547), and his wife, Margaret Fleming (*d*. 1584x7), daughter of Malcolm, third Lord Fleming. His father, who was killed at the battle of Pinkie on 10 September 1547 by a ship's cannon-shot, was the eldest son and heir of William Graham, second earl of Montrose (*c*.1495–1571). The latter became responsible for his grandson's upbringing and education, and in 1566 granted to the eighteen-year-old John Graham his father's former barony of Mugdock in Lennox. Three years earlier, on 24 August 1563, John Graham had married his second cousin Jean Drummond (*c*.1550–1598), daughter of David, second Lord Drummond, with whom he had three sons and a daughter. In his grandfather's later years he was increasingly called on to take charge of the Montrose estates, and he was also active politically: as master of Graham he sat in parliament (as earl he also attended the general assembly of the kirk), and on 24 July 1567 he was one of the procurators authorized by Queen Mary at Lochleven to receive her renunciation of the crown in favour of her son James VI. He was present on the side of Regent Moray at the battle of Langside against Mary on 13 May 1568, and in 1569 the regent directed him to secure Dumbarton Castle from his uncle Lord Fleming (the attempt was unsuccessful). On the death of his grandfather on 24 May 1571, John Graham succeeded as third earl of Montrose.

Montrose was present at Stirling Castle on 4 September 1571 when Regent Lennox was fatally shot in a skirmish during the civil war. On the consequent election to the regency of John Erskine, seventeenth earl of Mar, Montrose was appointed a privy councillor, and in July 1572 he was one of the commissioners sent by the fourth earl of Morton to conclude the pacification of Perth with the Hamilton party. Thereafter he was appointed one of the judges for the restitution of goods taken or spoiled during the civil war in Scotland north of the Forth. In 1575, along with John Stewart (later fifth earl of Atholl), his maternal half-brother (Margaret Fleming had subsequently wed Thomas, master of Erskine and then John, fourth earl of Atholl), he was given responsibility for holding wapinshawings (military musters) in Strathearn. A year later, having had his own kinsman Andrew Graham installed as bishop of Dunblane, Montrose received from him a feu of all the lands of the see, causing the sitting tenants to petition parliament against what they saw as a threat of 'uter heirschip and extreme beggartie' (Kirk, 409). Although a leading member of the reformed party throughout the 1570s, Montrose grew increasingly estranged from Morton, who had been regent since

November 1572, and on 8 March 1578 he attended the Stirling convention called by Argyll and Atholl at which the king accepted Morton's demission of the regency and took government into his own hands. Montrose was one of a council of twelve appointed to assist the king; he was warded briefly on Morton's resumption of authority in July, but soon engineered his escape. Besides his interests in Perthshire and Strathearn (where his chief residence was Kincardine), Montrose maintained his interest in his Lennox barony of Mugdock. None the less, his power at this time was limited. His annual income from his estates was not great and he was considered 'of small power, having but few gentlemen of his surname' (Rogers, 12). When the earls of Atholl and Argyll opposed Morton in arms in July and August 1578, Montrose could raise only 300 men in their support.

In 1579 Montrose attended the teenage King James on his formal entry into his capital, and at this time he was considered to be a strong supporter of Esmé Stewart, duke of Lennox, in opposing Morton. In 1581 he escorted the latter from custody in Dumbarton Castle to his trial in Edinburgh, and then served as the chancellor of the assize that condemned Morton to death in June that year. Despite this, in August 1582 Montrose initially joined with pro-Morton lords and supported the Ruthven raid against the king and Lennox (his political *volte face* is generally attributed to his growing jealousy of the duke's supremacy at court). Soon after, however, he altered his position and joined a group of lords opposed to the Ruthven regime. Montrose attended the king in June 1583 at St Andrews following James's 'escape' from the Ruthven lords, and thereafter he actively supported the subsequent regime led by James Stewart, fifth earl of Arran. Although this too was seemingly at odds with his considered political and religious beliefs, the root cause may again have been of a more personal nature: Montrose was regarded as the opponent of any actions supported by the earl of Angus 'whose wyef he is charged to have dishonoured' (Rogers, 32). After the fall of the Ruthven regime Montrose was given keepership of Glasgow Castle, and he briefly acquired some of the estates forfeited by the first earl of Gowrie, executed in 1584. Under a contract dated 12 December 1593 his eldest son and heir, John *Graham, later fourth earl of Montrose, married Gowrie's daughter Margaret Ruthven. Following the death of her brother, the third earl, for his involvement in the Gowrie conspiracy of 1600, Montrose was again the beneficiary of a grant of Ruthven lands.

During Arran's administration, on 12 and 13 May 1584 Montrose was appointed first an extraordinary lord of session and then treasurer of the realm, replacing Gowrie on both occasions. He held both positions only briefly, and by February 1586 had been replaced in them by Thomas Lyon, master of Glamis. Montrose also accepted responsibility as guardian for the ten-year-old Ludovick Stewart, second duke of Lennox, who had arrived in Scotland shortly after the death of his father in 1583. Montrose's close association with the dukes of Lennox and the earl of Arran led to speculation concerning the strength of his commitment to the protestant faith, but though his political stance was generally pro-French he remained notionally protestant throughout his life (in 1581 he was named as responsible for the erection of presbyteries within Strathearn). In support of Arran's administration Montrose plotted the murder of such prominent opponents as the earls of Angus and Mar, and Adam Erskine, commendator of Cambuskenneth (the latter two being respectively the nephew and the illegitimate son of his mother's second husband). Following Arran's removal from power at the end of 1585 Montrose was placed in the custody of John, Lord Hamilton, but in May 1587, at a reconciliation banquet hosted by the king, Montrose and Angus joined hands and swore an end to their feud.

In the later 1580s and early 1590s Montrose pursued policies at odds with those of the king: he was in frequent communication with the 'renegade' earls of Huntly and Bothwell, and like many of the Scottish nobility he was on varying terms with Chancellor John Maitland of Thirlestane. He sympathized with, and was an accessory to, the Brig o' Dee conspiracy against Maitland and the king in 1589, and he was extremely active in the faction seeking to revenge the murder of James Stewart, second earl of Moray, throughout 1592. At Maitland's recommendation he was again appointed an extraordinary lord of session in November 1591, a position he retained until May 1596, but during the 1590s he was also intermittently considered to be one of the 'discontented' faction at court, and some suspected him of secret Catholicism. Montrose sided with his half-brother Atholl and Francis Stewart, first earl of Bothwell, during the latter's rebellion in October 1593, and when Bothwell was briefly reconciled with the king Montrose sat on the assize that acquitted him of witchcraft and attempted regicide. In 1594, despite his past, Montrose attended the baptism of Prince Henry Frederick at Stirling Castle. He was also granted commissions to pursue the lawless MacGregor clan, who frequently raided his estates for cattle.

In the later 1590s Montrose retained the confidence of the king within the chamber, where he supported the faction headed by his former ward, the duke of Lennox, and by the earl of Mar, and also proved his worth as an administrator. He hoped either to recover the office of treasurer or to be chosen as chancellor, but in 1595 he had to be content with appointment as an auditor of the exchequer. In January 1597 he was one of a group of noblemen chosen to oversee the reforming accounting work of the Octavians, and in December 1598 he was appointed president of the privy council. On 18 January 1599 Montrose was elevated to the position of lord chancellor (vacant since the death of John Maitland on 3 October 1595), and later that year James (unsuccessfully) proposed him as provost of Edinburgh. In 1599 he was made chancellor of the University of St Andrews.

Montrose remained in favour after James journeyed south to succeed to the English throne in 1603, and in February 1604 he accepted appointment as commissioner-general to represent the absent king in the Scottish parliament. He subsequently travelled to London as chief commissioner for the negotiation of full union between Scotland and England, but, though he signed the proposed act of union in December 1604, neither the Scottish nor the English parliament would endorse the legislation. In that same month Montrose demitted his office of chancellor in favour of Lord Fyvie, but remained royal commissioner (with an annual pension of £2000 Scots). As commissioner he presided at the Perth 'red' parliament of July 1606 and at the Linlithgow convention of December 1606, but by 1607 his health was failing and he became less active in public affairs. He died at New Montrose on 9 November 1608. His political stature was such that he was granted a state funeral and buried in St Giles's, Edinburgh, with great ceremony. King James reportedly promised 40,000 merks to help cover his funeral expenses, but if he did so the money was never received, and the financial burden fell on the late earl's estate.

ROB MACPHERSON

Sources CSP Scot., 1547–1603 • G. Brunton and D. Haig, An historical account of the senators of the college of justice, from its institution in MDXXXII (1832) • G. Crawfurd, The lives and characters, of the officers of the crown, and of the state in Scotland (1726) • Scots peerage, 6.230–39 • Reg. PCS, 2nd ser. • Reg. PCS, 1st ser. • APS, 1424–1625 • T. Thomson, ed., Acts and proceedings of the general assemblies of the Kirk of Scotland, 3 pts, Bannatyne Club, 81 (1839–45) • D. Calderwood, The history of the Kirk of Scotland, ed. T. Thomson and D. Laing, 8 vols., Wodrow Society, 7 (1842–9) • A. Hay, Estimate of the Scottish nobility during the minority of James the Sixth, ed. C. Rogers, Grampian Club (1873) • J. B. Paul and C. T. McInnes, eds., Compota thesaurariorum regum Scotorum / Accounts of the lord high treasurer of Scotland, 9–13 (1911–78) • M. Livingstone, D. Hay Fleming, and others, eds., Registrum secreti sigilli regum Scotorum / The register of the privy seal of Scotland, 4–8 (1952–82) • G. Burnett and others, eds., The exchequer rolls of Scotland, 23 vols. (1878–1908), vols. 18–23 • J. M. Thomson and others, eds., Registrum magni sigilli regum Scotorum / The register of the great seal of Scotland, 11 vols. (1882–1914), vols. 4–6 • J. Spottiswood, The history of the Church of Scotland, ed. M. Napier and M. Russell, 3 vols., Bannatyne Club, 93 (1850) • GEC, Peerage, new edn, 9.147–9 • J. Kirk, Patterns of reform: continuity and change in the Reformation kirk (1989)

Graham, John, fourth earl of Montrose (1573–1626), nobleman, was the son of John *Graham, third earl of Montrose (1548–1608), an extraordinary lord of session, lord high treasurer, chancellor, and commissioner-general under James VI, and Jean (d. 1598), daughter of David Drummond, Lord Drummond. He received a charter of lands from his father in 1581. He married (contract of 12 December 1593) Lady Margaret, daughter of William *Ruthven, first earl of Gowrie. She predeceased him, and was buried on 15 April 1618. They had one son, James *Graham, fifth earl and first marquess of Montrose (1612–1650), the covenanting and later royalist leader, and there may have been another son, called John, who died in infancy. At least four of their six daughters survived into adulthood, marrying into various landed families. With an unknown mistress he had a son, John, who was involved in the covenanting wars and was last recorded at his half-brother's funeral in 1661.

Montrose was involved in national politics from the age of about twenty-three, attending a convention of estates at Perth in 1597 as master of Montrose. Under that title he was admitted to the privy council in March 1604, the king noting 'that it is expedient that men of his rank and qualitie sould in thair youth be trayned up in imployment in our affairis, that, being of rype age, they may be the mair capable' (Reg. PCS, 1st ser., 6.605). He carried the great seal at the parliaments of 1604 and 1606, presided over by his father, and succeeded to the earldom on his father's death in November 1608. He was soon after placed in an embarrassing predicament by James VI who had promised 40,000 merks (£26,666 13s. 4d. Scots) for the funeral expenses 'but the promise was not performed, which drew on the greater burthein of his sonne' (Calderwood, 7.38). Although he received licence from the privy council to travel abroad in 1609 and 1613, he remained in Scotland.

Montrose attended the parliaments of 1609 and 1617, was elected one of the lords of the articles on both occasions, and was appointed to a parliamentary commission on heritable offices in 1617. He was a member of the archiepiscopal court of high commission for the province of St Andrews from 1610 and was reappointed to the unified high commission in 1615. As the king's commissioner to the general assembly at Aberdeen in 1616 he was commanded to 'order the laitie' who attended. He was given the same task in the following year, 'but excused himself with sickeness' (Calderwood, 7.222, 284). In March 1626 Charles I appointed him to the newly established commission for grievances and he was named president of the privy council. Thereafter he attended meetings of the council rarely, probably because of failing health, and was summoned to attend on a number of occasions. He died at Kincardine Castle on 14 November 1626 and was buried at Aberuthven on 3 January 1627.   ALAN R. MACDONALD

Sources Scots peerage • D. Calderwood, The history of the Kirk of Scotland, ed. T. Thomson and D. Laing, 8 vols., Wodrow Society, 7 (1842–9), vol. 6 • APS, 1593–1625 • Reg. PCS, 1st ser., vol. 6 • Reg. PCS, 2nd ser., vol. 1 • NA Scot., Montrose MS GD220
Archives NA Scot., muniments, GD220 | NL Scot., letters to laird of Inchbraikie
Wealth at death £17,420 15s. 0d. Scots—incl. £12,622 15s. 0d. owed by debtors, plus assets of £4798: NA Scot., 3 Aug 1627, GD220/1/B2/3/1

Graham, John, first viscount of Dundee [known as Bonnie Dundee] (1648?–1689), Jacobite army officer, was the eldest son of William Graham (d. 1653), of Claverhouse, and Lady Magdalene Carnegie (d. 1675), fifth daughter of John *Carnegie, first earl of Northesk.

Family background and education John Graham was descended from the Grahams of Kincardine, who were also ancestors of the Montrose family. In the early fifteenth century Sir William Graham of Kincardine married, as his second wife, Lady Mary Stewart, daughter of King Robert III. The eldest son of this union, Sir Robert Graham of Fintry and Strathcarron, married Matilda, daughter of Sir James Scrymgeour of Dudhope, on the outskirts of Dundee, and it was from this marriage, which brought together royal blood and strong links with the city and title of Dundee, that the Grahams of Claverhouse were

John Graham, first viscount of Dundee (1648?–1689), by David Paton

descended. The Scrymgeours were not only Scotland's hereditary standard-bearers, but constables of Dundee and owners of Dudhope Castle. In the seventeenth century they became the earls of Dundee.

The Grahams acquired property around Dundee, including Claverhouse, an estate some 3 miles north-east of the city, alongside the Dighty Water, later known as the Barns of Claverhouse; Claypotts Castle, a small sixteenth-century keep, near Broughty Ferry; and the lands and barony of Glen Ogilvie, in the parish of Glamis, known as the Glen. The family's connections with the Montrose branch remained strong: John's grandfather, Sir William Graham, became a curator or tutor to the first marquess during his minority years, but died in 1642, too early to be caught up in Montrose's highland war. John's parents married in 1645 and in addition to John had a son and two daughters. The family was spared when Cromwell's army came north and sacked Dundee in 1650 and in the following year General Monck gave 'Lady Carnigges of the Glen' an order of protection (Linklater and Hesketh, 17). At his father's death two years later John was officially declared heir with the title of Graham of Claverhouse, but his mother acted as guardian or 'tutrix' until the end of his pupillage at the age of fourteen. On 22 September 1660 both he and his younger brother, David, were admitted as 'burgesses and brethren of the guild of Dundee, by reason of their father's privilege' (ibid., 18). By that date Claverhouse had probably been at university for two years. He was admitted to St Salvator's College at St Andrews University and undertook a full course in the liberal arts, philosophy, and mathematics. A later account of his

time at university, given in the memoirs of Sir Ewen Cameron of Lochiel, said:

> He had made considerable progress in the mathematics, especially in those parts of it that related to his military capacity; and there was no part of the Belles Lettres which he had not studied with great care and exactness. He was much master in the epistolary way of writing; for he not only expressed himself with great ease and plainness, but argued well, and had a great art in giving his thoughts in few words. (ibid., 19)

Claverhouse's letters, many of which survive, suggest this to be true, and though Sir Walter Scott wrote that he spelled 'like a chambermaid', he seems to have been no worse in this regard than many contemporaries. In 1661, his final year at university, James Sharp, later archbishop of St Andrews, became master of St Mary's College. A contemporary, the Revd Thomas Morer, wrote later that Claverhouse 'was admired for his parts and respects to churchmen, which made him dear to the Archbishop, who ever after honoured and loved him' (ibid., 19–20).

Early military service Claverhouse's teenage years were spent at Glenogilvie, where he and his brother managed the family estates. In February 1669 he was appointed a commissioner of excise and a JP for Forfarshire. Then on 25 July 1672 he volunteered for military service abroad. The commander, whose regiment of foot he joined as a junior lieutenant, was Sir William Lockhart, another Scot, whose men formed part of the army commanded by the duke of Monmouth in the service of Louis XIV's general Marshall Turenne. Among Graham's fellow officers was John Churchill, later duke of Marlborough; leading the opposing Dutch army was another young man, Prince William of Orange, captain general and stadholder of the Dutch United Provinces.

Two years after he joined Lockhart's regiment it returned to England, and Claverhouse switched sides, 'wishing', as his contemporary, Sir John Dalrymple put it, 'to know the services of different nations' (Linklater and Hesketh, 22). Religious reasons may also have played a part, with the end of the second Anglo-Dutch war and the withdrawal of the official British corps from French service providing the opportunity of serving with a protestant army. Claverhouse volunteered and became a cornet in the prince's own company of guards, where he saw almost continuous action over the next three years. At some point during this time he is alleged to have saved William's life. In the course of one of his battles William was supposedly knocked from his saddle and Claverhouse rode to his aid, pulled him on to his own horse, and carried him away from danger. Cameron of Lochiel claimed this occurred at the battle of Seneffe, but there is no record that William was unhorsed at Seneffe. In any event Claverhouse was promoted to captain of horse in November 1676, where he is recorded as the 'baron de Claverhous'. He may have had even greater ambitions, since at some point he appears to have had a public row with a rival officer, David Colyear, later earl of Portmore, whom he accused of intriguing behind his back for a promotion which Claverhouse regarded as rightfully his.

They came to blows, and Lochiel records Claverhouse as striking Colyear with a cane. He was seized by guards and brought before William for what was at that time a serious crime: attacking a fellow officer could be punished by the loss of the striking arm. Claverhouse apologized, but went on to bring up the question of his promotion, to which William, in dismissing him, responded: 'I make you full reparation for I bestow on you what is more valuable than a regiment—I give you your right arm' (ibid., 25).

Claverhouse's name was brought to the attention of Charles II's brother, James, duke of York, perhaps by William himself, and in February 1678 after returning to Scotland, he was, on James's personal recommendation, given command of one of three independent troops of horse, raised to deal with growing ferment from covenanters in the south-west of Scotland. On 23 September he was gazetted as captain, on pay of 14s. a day, with an allowance of 4s. for two horses. His brief was to patrol the extreme south-west area of Dumfriesshire and Annandale, to break up the field conventicles being held there by covenanting ministers, and to maintain law and order.

Defeat at Drumclog A number of Claverhouse's letters sent at this time to his commanding officer, the earl of Linlithgow, reveal frustration at his lack of resources, but also the punctiliousness of a junior officer determined not to put a foot wrong. On 28 December 1678 he wrote:

> my Lord, they tell me that the one end of the bridge in Dumfries is in Galloway and that they may hold conventicles at our nose, we do not dare to dissipate them seeing our orders confines us to Dumfries and Annandale. Such an insult as that would not please me and on the other hand I am unwilling to exceed orders. So that I may expect from your lordship orders how to carry in such uses? (Linklater and Hesketh, 33)

Among his early actions was the destruction of a barn suspected of being used for a conventicle, and the disciplining of one of his soldiers for shooting a horse. In February 1679 he was given extra powers by an act of parliament conferring on him the role of sheriff depute of Dumfries, Annandale, Wigtown, and Kirkcudbright. Along with the title went rights to arrest, impose fines, and prosecute anyone failing to attend church services. These civil duties brought him into conflict not only with local people but with William Douglas, third earl of Queensberry, and sheriff of Dumfriesshire, who became a political opponent. In March, Claverhouse wrote to Linlithgow, warning of open rebellion. His predictions were borne out following the murder on 3 May of Archbishop Sharp, the escape of his assassins to the west, and the burning, on 29 May—the king's birthday—of anti-covenant acts of parliament on the streets of Rutherglen. Although Claverhouse and his fellow-officer, Lord John Ross, had fewer than 500 officers and men between them, Claverhouse rode out immediately to Rutherglen, leaving Ross with his troops in Glasgow.

Learning that another large conventicle was due to take place that Sunday, 1 June, near Loudon Hill, south-west of Hamilton, Claverhouse made for the little village of Strathaven, east of Loudon. As he wrote later: 'I thought we might make a little tour, to see if we could fall upon a conventicle; which we did, little to our advantage' (Linklater and Hesketh, 42–3). It was something of an understatement. The battle of Drumclog, which took place that day, was to be his first and only military defeat. The covenanting force outnumbered his men by as much as two to one, and though they were poorly armed, their commander was the remarkable William Cleland, just nineteen years old, a poet as well as a soldier, with military skills beyond his age. Taking advantage of the ground, a hill overlooking a boggy marsh which prevented Claverhouse's horse from charging, Cleland's men closed in for hand-to-hand combat, causing some of the dragoons to lose their nerve and fall back. Claverhouse's own mount was attacked by a pitchfork, which 'made such an opening in my sorrel horse's belly, that his guts hung out half an ell' (ibid., 46). Maddened by the wound, the horse bolted, taking Claverhouse from the field. The retreat became headlong, and the beaten and dispirited dragoons fled back towards Glasgow. Drumclog was, in reality, no more than a skirmish, but it was still a defeat. As Claverhouse admitted in a report that night: 'I saved the standards; but lost on the place about eight or ten men … the dragoons lost many more … I made the best retreat the confusion of our people would suffer' (ibid., 46). He seems not to have been censured for this defeat by the privy council, but his independent command now came to an end, and his troop of horse guards were absorbed into the duke of Monmouth's army which defeated the covenanting force on 22 June at the battle of Bothwell Bridge.

The king's servant Claverhouse was now summoned to London to attend the court, and it was during the three years from 1679 to 1682 that his close association with James, duke of York, later James II (James VII of Scotland) began. He was a regular visitor to the court, both in London and at Windsor, and on one occasion travelled to France with the duke's party. When James was appointed high commissioner in October 1679, as Charles II's representative in Scotland, Claverhouse accompanied him north. He continued his policing duties in the west, but was again summoned to join the duke on his return journey to England in February 1680. It is clear that he was much favoured by James, who rewarded his loyalty with the small estate of Freuch in Galloway. Claverhouse also, at this time, began a lengthy correspondence with the earl of Menteith with a view to winning the hand of the earl's niece Helen Graham, the heir to his estates; his suit, however, was unsuccessful. In 1681 he was a member of the assize (or jury) in the trial of the duke of Argyll who had been unable to swear the newly drafted oath of loyalty brought in under the Test Act. He was also granted two newly vacant titles, the heritable sheriffdom of Wigtown and the heritable regality of Tongland, north of Kirkcudbright, and commissioned to act as sheriff depute in the neighbouring districts of Dumfries, Annandale, and Kirkcudbright. He reported directly to Queensberry, who was now lord justice-general.

To bring order to a troubled area Claverhouse devised a scheme whereby dissenters who agreed to attend their local church were offered an amnesty, while ringleaders who continued to hold illegal conventicles were severely punished. He asked for government funds to raise a hundred dragoons and establish a permanent garrison in the area. The plan appears to have worked. Two known ringleaders were captured and sent to Edinburgh for trial, while local landowners were told to ensure their tenants attended church. By April 1682 he was able to report to Queensberry:

> [T]his country is now in perfect peace; all who were in rebellion are either seized, gone out of the country, or treating their peace; and they have already conformed, as going to the Church, that is beyond my expectation. In Dumfries, not almost all the men are come, but the women have given obedience … I do expect to see this the best settled part of the Kingdom on this side the Tay.　(Linklater and Hesketh, 76–7)

The privy council recognized the success of Claverhouse's efforts and on 15 May 1682 he was summoned before it to be thanked for his 'diligence' in fulfilling his commission in Galloway. However, his methods brought him into conflict with Sir James Dalrymple, the lord president and a powerful local laird, who, together with his son, Sir John Dalrymple, resented Claverhouse's jurisdiction. Claverhouse responded by arresting a number of Dalrymple tenants. When Sir John protested he was forcibly removed from a courtroom in Strathaven, where Claverhouse had been taking evidence. Sir John described the events in a letter:

> Claverhouse became so rude and enraged that though there were an hundred present who were not members, yet Claverhouse did cause his soldiers and officers take [me] by the shoulders from the table, which was an indignity that his Majesty's justice, and princely generosity, does not allow to be offered to a gentleman.　(Linklater and Hesketh, 87)

Sir John instituted legal action and Claverhouse responded by mounting a case for criminal libel. On 14 December the privy council found Dalrymple guilty, stripped him of judicial office, fined him £500, and committed him prisoner in Edinburgh Castle during the council's pleasure. Claverhouse, on the other hand, was acquitted of any wrongdoing and complimented for his faithful and diligent service to the king. On Christmas day 1682 a commission gazetted 'our right trusty and well beloved John Graham of Claverhouse' to be colonel of a newly formed regiment, 'His Majesty's Regiment of Horse' (ibid., 89).

Claverhouse's close connections with the duke of York were cemented by two months in spring 1683 spent in royal circles in London, Newmarket, and Windsor. He also acquired the lands and castle of Dudhope, not far from the Claverhouse estates near Dundee. On 11 May 1683 he was sworn of the privy council. His immediate duty was to accompany the circuit court which opened in Stirling and whose task was to ensure that the local citizenry swore oaths of loyalty according to the test acts. Most did so, though one man, William Bogue, prevaricated, was put on trial, and sentenced to death for high treason. Claverhouse's verdict on the affair is a fair summary of his own philosophy:

> I am as sorry to see a man die, even a whig, as any of themselves. But when one dies justly, for his own faults, and may save a hundred to fall in the like, I have no scruple.
> (Linklater and Hesketh, 100)

Claverhouse now contracted a marriage which could hardly have been less suitable. Jean Cochrane (c.1664–1695) was barely twenty years of age and came from a prominent whig family who were fervent supporters of the covenant. Claverhouse took the precaution of asking for the king's permission, which was granted, and on 10 June 1684 the couple were married at Paisley, with a guard of honour formed by Claverhouse's own troopers. In mid-celebration the bridegroom was called away to break up a conventicle in Lanarkshire. The search was fruitless, but subsequent incidents suggested that trouble might be flaring up again in the west, and harsh reprisals began to be taken. Six men, captured by Claverhouse's troop near Closeburn in Dumfriesshire, were taken prisoner and sent to Edinburgh where they were summarily tried and executed.

The killing time　These incidents mark the beginning of a period sometimes known as the 'killing time', with which Claverhouse's name, in the form of 'bluidy Clavers', has long been associated. According to some historians of the covenant he was the principal protagonist in imposing a brutal regime, which involved summary execution, torture, imprisonment, and banishment. He was said to be 'imbued with a disregard of individual rights', as well as being 'careless of death', and 'ruthless in inflicting it on others' (Wodrow, 3.68). He is variously said to have terrorized children into identifying the whereabouts of their parents by lining them up and firing over their heads, wrecking the homes of suspects, and extorting money by threat. Daniel Defoe, who came to Scotland some years later, accused him of murdering above a hundred of the persecuted people, 'several with his own hand' (Owens and Furbank, 6.194). These accounts are grossly exaggerated. Careful analysis of the evidence suggests that Claverhouse was directly involved in only three executions at the most, though he was undoubtedly rigorous in the pursuit of his duties. Early in September 1684 he was assigned to another itinerant court, set up by the privy council, which had wide powers to summon suspects and hand down draconian sentences. In November two life guards were attacked and killed, prompting the privy council to pass a resolution which was, in effect, a licence for summary execution. Claverhouse was later accused of carrying out just such an execution, in early December, against one William Graham, a tailor from Crossmichael in Kirkcudbright, whose gravestone claims that he was 'instantly shot dead by a party of Claverhouse's troops' (Linklater and Hesketh, 119). Yet, the date (1682) is wrong, and the details were not written down until six years later. Claverhouse was, however, involved in direct action following an attack by a large party of rebels on the town of Kirkcudbright on 16 December. He caught up with a small band of rebels on Auchencloy Moor, killed five men and took three prisoner. Later he presided at the trial of two of the prisoners, Robert Smith of Glencairn and Robert

Hunter, and passed sentence of death upon them. The two were immediately executed. He also ordered that one of those killed in the skirmish, James Macmichael, should be disinterred from the graveyard at Dalry church and hanged on the local gibbet under the law of *laesa majestas*, intended as a demonstration that justice had been done, even after death.

Meanwhile, the resentment of Queensberry towards Claverhouse and his alleged arrogance grew into an open quarrel. Complaints were sent to the duke of York amid rumours that Claverhouse was not being tough enough on the rebellious whigs in Ayrshire because of his wife's connections. He was ordered to move his court to Fife, and requested to pay back fines which he had spent on his soldiers' expenses. A month after the death of Charles II and the succession of James, he was summoned before the privy council by Queensberry and ordered to account for the fines he had collected. On 2 March 1685 he was stripped of his place on the council. Less than two months later, however, he was reinstated after formally apologizing to Queensberry, and by May was back in the saddle in Ayrshire.

Within days Claverhouse was involved in one of the most controversial incidents of his military career, when he rode into the village of Priesthill and questioned a man called John Brown, suspected of being a rebel. When Brown refused to take the oath, he was executed on the spot. Later covenanting versions claimed that Brown and his wife had been treated with great cruelty. Claverhouse's own report to Queensberry says only that after Brown had refused to acknowledge the king and following the discovery of arms and incriminating papers in his house, 'I caused shoot him dead, which he suffered very unconcernedly' (Linklater and Hesketh, 129). A second incident involved a young man, Andrew Hislop, from Gillesby in Annandale, accused of sheltering a wounded rebel. He was found by Claverhouse and his troops, and brought before the local steward depute, Sir James Johnstone of Westerhall, who ordered his execution. When the commander of a highland infantry company in the area refused to carry it out, Claverhouse ordered his own troops to do the job.

Another execution connected to Claverhouse is described on a tombstone in the churchyard of Colmonell in Carrick, which records the death, at Claverhouse's hand, of one Matthew McIlwraith. There is no record to confirm this statement, though the name Matthew Meiklewraith is listed on the lengthy roll of wanted men published in May 1684, so he may have met the same fate as John Brown. These three cases are the only ones that can be ascribed directly to Claverhouse and his soldiers. He may well have been severe in interrogation and zealous in pursuit of rebels, but he cannot, despite the subsequent covenanting mythology, be accused of unnecessary cruelty.

Fugitive and rebel In the aftermath of the invasion by Argyll in May 1685 Claverhouse was promoted to the rank of brigadier. Later he journeyed south to see the king, and found himself sufficiently in favour to have the fines extracted from him by Queensberry repaid in full. On 21 December his regiment was given the title 'His Majesty's Own Regiment of Horse', and later he became a major-general with a pension of £200 sterling a year 'during pleasure' (Linklater and Hesketh, 137, 141). Records in Dundee show that with the return of relative peace to the west of Scotland he was able to spend more time on his estates at Dudhope, taking his seat on the local bench, and extracting local tolls and taxes on behalf of the town. In the course of the next two years he also journeyed south to Bath, where he took the waters, and London, where his portrait was painted by Sir Godfrey Kneller.

At the end of October 1688 Claverhouse, with his 357-strong regiment, joined the king and was with him in the days following the landing at Torbay of William of Orange on 5 November. One week later he was raised to the Scottish peerage as viscount of Dundee and Lord Grahame of Claverhouse, in recognition of 'good and eminent services … together with his constant loyalty and firm adherence (on all occasions) to the true interests of the Crown' (Linklater and Hesketh, 145). He was among those who attempted to persuade James to resist William's advance, and was said to have been so shocked at hearing news of the king's flight that he broke down in tears. While with his cavalry at Watford he received a letter from William inviting him to join the invading forces. He refused, and on 13 December met leading Scots figures in London to discuss the future. He was to see the king only once more, when James unexpectedly returned to London, having failed to cross the Channel. He promised that once he was in France he would commission Dundee lieutenant-general and commander-in-chief of the Scottish army.

Early in February 1689 Dundee and the earl of Balcarres, accompanied by their troops, headed back to Scotland and the temporary security of Dudhope Castle, where Lady Dundee was expecting her first child. On 14 March the two peers attended the convention set up in Edinburgh to determine whether Scotland would back James or William. When it became clear that the convention would side with William, Dundee, with fifty troopers, rode out of Edinburgh, stopping only at the castle, where he spoke to the duke of Gordon who held it for the king. According to legend Gordon asked him where he was heading, to which Dundee replied 'Wherever the spirit of Montrose shall direct me' (Linklater and Hesketh, 159). He reached Stirling on 19 March, but found it no longer in friendly hands. He therefore rode on to Dunblane, where he met the first of his highland supporters, Alexander Drummond of Balhaldie, son-in-law of the influential highland chief Sir Ewen Cameron of Lochiel. Next day he returned to Dudhope to wait for news from James and to be with his wife for the birth of their child. A herald was sent to demand his surrender, and when he refused a proclamation was drawn up condemning his actions and pronouncing 'the said Viscount Dundee fugitive and rebel' (ibid., 163). Towards the end of March Lady Dundee gave birth to a son, James, who was baptized on 9 April at the church of Mains near Dundee. On 16 April, Dundee raised the royal standard on the heights of Dundee Law, and set out for the highlands.

The general who opposed Dundee was Hugh Mackay of Scourie. He arrived at Leith on 24 March with troops of the Scots brigade from Holland and was commissioned commander-in-chief of the forces under the convention. Mackay's army, amounting to no more than 1100 men, marched north to Brechin and Fettercairn, hoping for the support of prominent highlanders, including Ludovic Grant of that ilk, sheriff of Inverness, the master of Forbes, and the earl of Atholl. Unlike Mackay, Dundee understood instinctively how to win the loyalty and enthusiasm of the highlanders, and weld them into a potent force. He also knew how to move swiftly through the straths and hills of north-east Scotland, keeping well ahead of Mackay's more ponderous army. His strength at this stage was barely more than 200 men, though he hoped to recruit more in Lochaber, from what Lochiel described as 'the confederacy of clans' (Linklater and Hesketh, 161). In early May he issued a royal letter asking the clans to gather on 18 May.

Before then Dundee made a surprise move south to Blair Castle, a key stronghold which commanded the route south to Stirling and north to Inverness. There he received a warm welcome from Atholl's factor, Patrick Steuart of Ballechin, before striking further south, and capturing the city of Perth. He approached, but did not attack Dundee, and then turned back to the highlands after spending a night at Glenogilvie with his wife. The whole exercise had been a brilliant stroke of propaganda, and when on 18 May the clans gathered at Dalcomera, on the north bank of the River Spean, he was able to recruit an army of some 2000, led by clan chiefs including MacDonnell of Glengarry, Cameron of Lochiel, MacDonald of Morar, and MacIain of Glencoe. Later adherents came from the MacDonalds of Sleat, the captain of Clanranald, Sir John Maclean of Duart, MacNeil of Barra, Macleod of Raasay, and the MacGregor clan. Dundee hoped that reinforcements and supplies would come also from James, whose armies were now in Ireland, but despite promises, none was forthcoming. After a week spent drilling his clan army he marched east.

On 26 May, Mackay moved south from Inverness with 100 troopers, 140 dragoons, 200 foot, and 200 highland supporters. Over the next ten days the two armies crisscrossed northern Scotland. A few small skirmishes between stragglers, a castle or two sacked, and some booty seized was the sum total of military activity. Both leaders, Mackay and Dundee, suffered illness in the course of the campaign, and both found difficulty in keeping their armies up to strength. Finally, Dundee pulled back to Lochaber to recoup, while Mackay took his army north to Inverness. It was now augmented by 300 dragoons commanded by Colonel Berkeley, 700 foot under Sir James Leslie, 300 men of the earl of Leven's and Colonel Hastings's regiments, three regiments of the Scots brigade, and 200 highlanders.

On 18 July a reward of 18,000 merks was offered for Dundee dead or alive, and this was supplemented by another,

more generous one of £20,000 sterling. But Dundee was not betrayed. He had received documents from James, who was laying siege to Londonderry, commissioning him officially as lieutenant-general of the king's forces in Scotland, and giving him authority to offer commissions to the clan chiefs and proclaim war against the government in Edinburgh. There was also a promise of reinforcements. However, instead of the 5000 troops promised from Ireland, Dundee eventually received 300 poorly trained Irishmen, under the command of Colonel Alexander Cannon, who knew little of the highlands, and nothing of clan warfare. Nevertheless, the king's letter encouraged Dundee to send out messages to wavering clans that they should join the cause or suffer the consequences. His army still numbered fewer than 2000, together with a small troop of no more than fifty horse, but on hearing news that Steuart of Ballechin had taken control of Blair Castle, a vital garrison controlling the route south towards Stirling, he marched out from Lochaber on 22 July and headed south. Despite the lack of support, morale among the clansmen was high. As Drummond of Balhaldie later wrote: 'he had gained so upon the affections of his small army that, though half-starved, they moved forward as cheerfully as if they had not felt the least effects of want' (Linklater and Hesketh, 202). Late on the night of 26 July they reached Blair Castle, where Dundee held a council of war.

Victory and death Meanwhile, Mackay's army had regrouped in Edinburgh before setting out north again. On the morning of Saturday 27 July the troops, with their long baggage train, came through the Pass of Killiecrankie, emerging on low ground beside the River Garry, with the rising slopes of the Creag Eallaich Hill to their right. Here Mackay first spotted some detachments of the highlanders. Ordering his troops to march some way up the hill to their right, he halted his battalions above Urrard House, then deployed them in a long line, three men deep, with their backs to the river. He dropped his troops of horse back from a gap in the centre, with the cannon in front of them. In hot sunshine, they awaited the enemy.

Dundee and his force had left Blair Castle at dawn, taking the highlanders in a circling movement southwards, behind the Hill of Lude, emerging on the heights of Creag Eallaich, overlooking Mackay's army. Seeing the length of the enemy's line he spaced the highlanders along the ridge, keeping the clans well packed, but with wide intervals between them. Each was assigned to aim for one of Mackay's battalions. He placed the cavalry in the centre. There were some small skirmishes in the course of the afternoon, but it was not until around eight o'clock in the evening, as the sun was beginning to set, that Dundee gave the order to charge. The clansmen set off down the slopes, screaming their battle-cries 'like one great clap of thunder' as Balhaldie put it (Linklater and Hesketh, 215). As they did so, they threw aside their plaids. Clutching only their muskets, swords, and targes, they headed straight for the enemy lines, pausing only to discharge their muskets—too early, as it happened, to cause much damage. A withering volley from Mackay's musketeers opened up some gaps among the highlanders, but they came together, and, drawing their broadswords, charged straight into the enemy lines. Mackay's left wing broke and fled almost immediately, but Leven's and Hastings's battalions loosed off musket fire into the flanks of the charging Camerons, inflicting great damage. Viscount Kenmure's foot soldiers in the centre also brought down a number of Glengarry's men. But then a troop of horse under Lord Belhaven, ordered forward by Mackay to attack Glengarry in the flank, wheeled suddenly left, panicked, and careered back onto Kenmure's men, scattering them as they galloped through the ranks. The combination of Glengarry's charge and the panicking horses was enough to break the battalion, which turned and fled. At the same time Annandale's troop, which had wheeled right to attack Cameron of Lochiel's men, also scattered, taking part of Leven's battalion with them. Mackay rode forward to steady his line, but it had already broken, with soldiers fleeing back down the hill towards the river and the Pass of Killiecrankie, pursued by the clansmen, who caused great slaughter as they trapped them in the mouth of the pass. Only Leven's battalion, and half of Hastings's, remained where they were.

Dundee himself had waited briefly on the ridge before the highlanders set off, then spurred his horse downhill, heading straight for the centre of Mackay's line. As he approached, the cavalry troop behind him under the command of one of King James's officers, Sir William Wallace, swerved left, perhaps to avoid a patch of marshy ground, leaving Dundee isolated. A small group of mounted officers, including Dunfermline and Pitcur, galloped forward to fill the gap, but Dundee was lost in a cloud of smoke. One report has it that Dunfermline saw him turn in his saddle and raise his arm to signal for Wallace's men to come up and join him. At this point he was struck in the left side by a bullet, which may have hit him in the gap exposed beneath the armour as he raised his arm. He fell from his horse and died soon afterwards, attended by a soldier called Johnston. His last words were reported by Lieutenant John Nisbet of Kenmure's regiment, who was taken prisoner, and heard later at Blair Castle what happened. Dundee is said to have asked Johnston, 'How goes the day?', to which Johnston replied, 'Well for the King, but I am sorry for your Lordship'. 'It is the less matter for me', said Dundee, 'seeing that the day goes well for my master' (Linklater and Hesketh, 220). That night his body was stripped of its armour, possibly by men from clan Cameron. Next day it was wrapped in a plaid and taken to the church at Blair Atholl where it was placed in a rough coffin and buried on 29 July in a vault alongside that of Pitcur, who had also been killed in the battle. Dundee's armour and some of his clothes were later recovered by his brother. Today the breastplate can be seen at Blair, with a fake hole drilled in the centre of it on the instructions of the fourth duke of Atholl 'to improve its warlike

appearance' (ibid., 221). A tablet marks the site of Dundee's burial place.

Although Killiecrankie was a total victory for Dundee's forces, with Mackay's losing up to a third of its strength—perhaps 1200 men and 500 prisoners—the general himself escaped, together with most of Leven's regiment and half of Hastings's. Losses on the highland side were far smaller—perhaps 700 dead and 200 wounded—but the clan chiefs, at the head of their men, suffered disproportionately, with MacDonalds of Sleat, Macleans, and Camerons losing some of their best men. Following Dundee's death leadership of the clan army passed to Colonel Cannon, who was to prove an ineffective commander. He was defeated three weeks later at the battle of Dunkeld, by a small force of Cameronians under the command of the soldier-poet William Cleland. Within a year the highland rising was effectively over.

For Dundee's family reprisals were inevitable. On his death the title passed to his infant son, James, but in early December the child died, and Dundee's brother, David, succeeded to the viscountcy. David was taken prisoner in September 1689 and, though released later that year, was stripped of the Dudhope estates and the title. Dundee's widow, who had left Dudhope to go to her Cochrane relatives in the west, returned to Edinburgh, and later married Colonel William Livingstone of Kilsyth, with whom she had a son. Both mother and child died in a freak accident on 15 October 1695 when the roof of an inn at Utrecht in Holland, where they were staying, collapsed, killing them both. They were brought back to Scotland for burial in the Livingstone's family churchyard at Kilsyth.

Reputation Dundee's reputation as a military commander rests on his brilliant campaigning skills, the loyalty he engendered among the highland clansmen, and his victory at Killiecrankie. His qualities of leadership and his youthful good looks meant that to his supporters, and to historians of the romantic school, he was celebrated as Bonnie Dundee. But his earlier military career in the west of Scotland is seen in a very different light; there he is still remembered as bluidy Clavers. Sir Walter Scott did much to reinforce the image of Dundee as a vengeful persecutor in his novel *Old Mortality*; while Lord Macaulay described him as: 'Rapacious and profane, of violent temper and obdurate heart, [he] has left a name which, wherever the Scottish race is settled on the face of the globe, is mentioned with a peculiar energy of hatred' (Macaulay, 498). Later historians have presented a more balanced picture, and it would be fair to say that close study of his life reveals a man guided rather by obedience to an unsatisfactory monarch than by any notably vindictive qualities. His loyalty to James was fundamental, both as a subject, an officer, and a friend. Dundee's letters are studded with references to the royal service, the importance of discipline and good order, and his abhorrence of lawlessness. For him the king was the ultimate commanding officer. It was, therefore, by a natural, and to him quite unsurprising logic that Dundee, the great disciplinarian, eventually found himself a rebel. The fact that his dedication was to drive him, against all his soldierly instincts, into open revolution, makes him at once an intriguing and courageous human being.   MAGNUS LINKLATER

Sources L. Barbé, *Viscount Dundee* (1903) · M. Barrington, *Graham of Claverhouse, Viscount Dundee* (1911) · G. Daviot, *Graham of Claverhouse* (1937) · A. Taylor and H. Taylor, *John Graham of Claverhouse* (1939) · M. Morris, *Claverhouse* (1887) · M. Napier, *Memorials and letters illustrative of the life and times of John Grahame of Claverhouse, Viscount Dundee*, 3 vols. (1859–62) · M. Linklater and C. Hesketh, *Bonnie Dundee: John Graham of Claverhouse: for king and conscience* (1992) · T. C. Stanford, *John Graham of Claverhouse, Viscount of Dundee* (1905) · GEC, *Peerage* · archives of the Duke of Buccleuch, Queensberry MSS · NL Scot., Wodrow MSS · NL Scot., Balcarres MSS · APS, vols. 8–9 · *Reg. PCS*, 3rd ser., vols. 6–13 · C. Lindsay [earl of Balcarres], *Memoirs touching the revolution in Scotland*, ed. A. W. C. Lindsay [earl of Crawford and Balcarres], Bannatyne Club (1841) · J. Graham, letters, NL Scot. · *Memoirs of the Lord Viscount Dundee* (1714) · *Historical notices of Scotish affairs, selected from the manuscripts of Sir John Lauder of Fountainhall*, ed. D. Laing, 2 vols., Bannatyne Club, 87 (1848) · J. Lauder, *Historical observes of memorable occurrents in church and state, from October 1680 to April 1686*, ed. A. Urquhart and D. Laing, Bannatyne Club, 66 (1840) · H. Scourie, *Memoirs of the war carried on in Scotland and Ireland, 1689–1691* (1833) · W. Aiton, *A history of the encounter at Drumclog* · J. Dalrymple, *Memoirs of Great Britain and Ireland*, 3 vols. (1790) · *Memoirs of Sir Ewen Cameron of Locheill*, ed. J. Macknight, Abbotsford Club, 24 (1842) · W. Fraser, *The red book of Mentieth*, 2 vols. [n.d.] · W. Fraser, ed., *The Red Book of Grandtully*, 2 vols. (1868) · J. Kirkton, *Secret and true history of Scotland* (1817) · G. Mackenzie, *Memoirs of the affairs of Scotland* (1821) · J. Philip, *The Grameid*, trans. A. Murdoch (1888) · R. Wodrow, *The history of the sufferings of the Church of Scotland from the Restoration to the revolution*, ed. R. Burns, 4 vols. (1828–30) · W. R. Owens and P. N. Furbank, eds., *Political and economic writings of Daniel Defoe*, 8 vols. (2000) · T. B. Macaulay, *The history of England from the accession of James II*, 2nd edn, 5 vols. (1849–61)
Archives RO, letters to duke of Queensberry
Likenesses J. S. Agar, stipple (after P. Lely), BM, NPG · D. Allan, red chalk drawing, Scot. NPG · W. H. Geissler, oils, Scot. NPG · D. Paton, ink drawing, Scot. NPG [*see illus.*] · ink drawing, Scot. NPG · oils, Scot. NPG

Graham, John (*fl.* **1719–1775**), portrait painter, was born in Britain but moved abroad some time before 1719; he studied in Antwerp under Jacques Ignatius de Roore and in The Hague under Arnold Houbraken and Mattheus Terwesten. Baron Philip von Stosch described Graham as 'peintre du Duc de Richmond' (Ingamells, 418); Graham may have met Charles Lennox, second duke of Richmond, while the latter was in The Hague between 1719 and 1722. It is possible that Graham travelled to Italy; in 1726 Sir Edward Gascoigne met 'Graham peintre' in Bologna and Stosch said he was exiled from there by the cardinal legate of Bologna early in 1727 (ibid.). Graham was a subscriber to the painters' confraternity Pictura at The Hague in 1727, rejoined this body in 1738, and continued membership between 1742 and 1761. At The Hague he lived with his sister in a house which he adorned with ceiling and other paintings from his own hand. Two works by Graham are known. One is a badly drawn full-length oil portrait of Simon Fraser, a junior officer serving with a loyal Scottish regiment in the Netherlands between 1748 and 1755. The other is a miniature of an unknown man, dated The Hague, 1737, and possibly related to the miniature on enamel inscribed on the reverse 'J. Hage/I. Graham/F.1737' in the Rijksmuseum, Amsterdam (Foskett, 549). On 24–5 July 1775 'Jan

Graham, peintre' sold a collection of 136 paintings in The Hague (Lugt). It is generally assumed that this man was John Graham, and that he subsequently moved back to Britain with his sister.

L. H. CUST, *rev.* NICHOLAS GRINDLE

Sources Waterhouse, *18c painters* · J. Ingamells, ed., *A dictionary of British and Irish travellers in Italy, 1701–1800* (1997) · F. D. O. Obreen, ed., *Archief voor Nederlandsche kunstgeschiedenis*, 7 vols. (Rotterdam, 1877–90) · Thieme & Becker, *Allgemeines Lexikon* · P. J. J. Van Thiel and others, *All the paintings of the Rijksmuseum in Amsterdam: a completely illustrated catalogue* (1976) · F. Lugt, *Répertoire des catalogues de ventes publiques*, 1 (The Hague, 1938) · D. Foskett, *Miniatures: dictionary and guide* (1987)

Graham, John (1754–1817), painter and teacher of art, was born in Edinburgh. He was apprenticed to a coach-painter in Edinburgh, George MacFarquhar (*fl.* 1763–1799), and later pursued that trade in London. He then undertook study at the Royal Academy Schools and he exhibited at the academy fairly regularly between 1780 and 1797. His paintings included *Murder of David Riccio* and *Mary, Queen of Scots the Morning before her Execution*. He also painted *Othello and Desdemona* for John Boydell's Shakspeare Gallery, that short-lived attempt to establish a national school of history painting which opened in Pall Mall in 1789. In these years he lived at a variety of addresses in the West End of London, and latterly in Leicester Square, which may indicate a widening of his aspirations.

In 1795, three years after the move to Leicester Square, Graham painted a subject that was popular with a number of artists at the time—*The Marriage of George, Prince of Wales, and Princess Caroline in the Chapel Royal*. His painting (ex Christies, 5 June 1987, lot 150) is similar in composition to one by Henry Singleton (Royal Collection) but the perspective is poor and the effect rather feeble. The mezzotint by John Daniell, which was published in the following year and for which the painting was no doubt made, is considerably livelier.

On four occasions between 1793 and 1797 Graham was a candidate for associate membership of the Royal Academy, but received very few votes in the ballots. Prior to the election of 1794 Joseph Farington, that obsessive observer of such things, went so far as to tell Sir Thomas Lawrence that Graham was a candidate he would certainly not vote for, in what he considered a very weak field. Such rebuffs no doubt played a part in Graham's thoughts of returning to Scotland. Perhaps as a preliminary, he arranged the exhibition of his *King James I of Scotland, Playing on the Harp Attended by his Queen and Court* at the Assembly Rooms in Edinburgh in 1796. The showing was accompanied by an attractively printed but rather pretentious leaflet addressed to 'Lovers of the Fine Arts' which, despite its high-minded tone, did not fail to point out that the painting was for sale.

Early in 1798, on the recommendation of the influential banker Sir William Forbes, Graham was invited by the board of trustees for fisheries, manufactures, and improvements in Scotland to settle in Edinburgh as a 'public Teacher of Art'. As Farington records, Benjamin West, who considered Graham 'an ingenious man', felt he was ideally suited for the position. The board of trustees (the forerunners of the trustees of the National Galleries of Scotland) had established an academy in 1760 to teach drawing to artisans, with the intention of improving industrial design. The new drawing academy had the rather more elevated aims of teaching 'the Principles of Art, and of assisting those who aim at being Professional Artists' (*Edinburgh Evening Courant*, 1 July 1799). Before taking up his duties, Graham felt obliged to hold a second public exhibition of his work in Edinburgh, 'as specimens of his abilities' (ibid., 3 Jan 1799). This took place in temporary premises opposite the main entrance of the college in South Bridge (now called Old College).

The academy which Graham set up was furnished, at the board's expense, with statues and busts from the antique, and the teaching followed the system of the Royal Academy Schools. At this stage the curriculum did not include drawing from life. The rooms were initially at 4 St James's Square but from about 1811 seem to have been relocated at no. 7. In the earlier years particularly, Graham was worried that he was perceived only as a teacher of artists sponsored by the board, and he advertised on a number of occasions that he also took private pupils, each sex at a separate time of day, at a cost of 2 guineas for twelve lessons.

This new academy and the older Trustees' Academy were effectively merged early in 1800, with Graham as master, an appointment he held until his death. He proved to be inspirational and effective, and a number of important nineteenth-century Scottish artists benefited from his teaching—David Wilkie, William Allan, Alexander Fraser, and John Watson Gordon. It was as a 'Master to whom Scottish Art had been considerably indebted' that the Royal Scottish Academy bought his 'large Gallery Picture', *The Disobedient Prophet*, in 1859 (minutes of the general meetings of the Royal Scottish Academy, 1857–73, Royal Scottish Academy library). This vast painting was then hung in the National Gallery of Scotland, Edinburgh, which opened in the same year. It remained on show there until 1896, but has since disappeared. His *David Instructing Solomon*, bought by the earl of Wemyss in 1797, has suffered a similar fate.

Besides subject paintings, Graham painted rather pedestrian portraits, including one of Alderman John Boydell (Stationers' Hall, London). He is also known as an animal painter, having made a series of studies of lions and tigers in the menagerie at the Tower of London. Two of these were exhibited with the Free Society of Artists in 1782. Although Graham now has little reputation as a painter, Wilkie retained the greatest respect for him and is said to have always had a print from his *Funeral of General Fraser* (exhibited at the Royal Academy in 1791) hanging in his study. Allan Cunningham described his personality in these terms: 'a kind and ardent-minded man, and had the tact of inspiring the scholars with his own enthusiasm' (Cunningham, 1.35). Graham died at his home, 7 St James's Square, 'after a severe and lingering illness', on 1 November 1817. The writer of his obituary notice remarks

that he was 'friendly, honest, sincere, and independent, and highly regarded by those who knew his worth' (*Edinburgh Magazine and Literary Miscellany*).

DUNCAN THOMSON

Sources *DNB* · artists' files, Scottish, Scot. NPG, section 4 · Farington, *Diary*, vols. 1–3 · *Exhibition of Mr. Graham's historical picture of King James I of Scotland … George Street [Edinburgh], 1796* (1796) · W. B. Johnston, *Catalogue, descriptive and historical, of the National Gallery of Scotland* (1859) · O. Millar, *The later Georgian pictures in the collection of her majesty the queen*, 2 vols. (1969) · Graves, *RA exhibitors* · Graves, *Soc. Artists · English pictures* (1987) [sale catalogue, Christies, 5 June 1987] · *Engraved Brit. ports.*, vol. 5 · *Summary catalogue of British paintings*, V&A (1973) · M. Wood, ed., *Register of Edinburgh apprentices, 1756–1800*, Scottish RS, 92 (1963), 40 · C. B. B. Watson, ed., *Roll of Edinburgh burgesses and guild-brethren, 1761–1841*, Scottish RS, 68 (1933), 99 · F. J. Grant, ed., *The Commissariat record of Edinburgh: register of testaments, 1761–1841*, Scottish RS, 3 (1899), 171 · *Edinburgh Magazine and Literary Miscellany*, 1 (1817), 500 [a new series of the *Scots Magazine*] · A. Cunningham, *The life of Sir David Wilkie* (1843), vol. 1, p. 35

Archives Royal Scot. Acad., minutes of the general meetings of the Royal Scottish Academy

Graham, John (1776–1844), historian, born in co. Fermanagh, was the grandson of Lieutenant James Graham of Clones, and great-grandson of James Graham of Mullinahinch, who was a cornet at the defence of Enniskillen in 1689. The family was transplanted to Ulster from Cumberland in the early seventeenth century. Graham graduated BA in 1798 and MA in 1815 at Trinity College, Dublin, was ordained in the established church of Ireland, and obtained the curacy of Lifford, co. Donegal.

Graham's interest in historical research first became evident when he compiled an account of the town and parish of Maghera in the diocese of Derry. Drawn up for the first volume of Shaw Mason's *Statistical Account or Parochial Survey of Ireland*, Graham's work was published in Dublin in 1813. He continued his study of the Derry area and compiled notes for a history of the diocese. In 1819 he published, by the aid of Lord Kenyon, in London, *Annals of Ireland, Ecclesiastical, Civil, and Military*, an account, compiled from numerous authorities, of the wars in Ireland, which began in October 1641. Graham had witnessed in 1788 the celebration of the centenary of the siege of Londonderry, and had been brought up in admiration of its heroes; in 1823 he published *Derriana*, a history of the siege of Londonderry and defence of Enniskillen in 1688 and 1689, with historical poetry and biographical notices. It is a clear and interesting account of the siege, based on the journals of the defenders and other contemporary records. A second edition of the book, without the poems, was published in Dublin in 1829, and several editions of the poems alone were printed.

In April 1824 Graham obtained the rectory of Tamlaghtard, commonly called Magilligan, on the coast of co. Londonderry, and here he lived until his death on 6 March 1844. In 1839 he published in Dublin *A History of Ireland from the Relief of Londonderry in 1689 to the Siege of Limerick in 1691*, and two years later he produced *Ireland Preserved*, containing his editions of dramatic pieces on the siege of Londonderry and the battle of Aughrim, as well as poems of his own. A zealous and even fanatical participant in protestant commemorations of the Williamite period, Graham nevertheless regretted that sectarian divisions prevented Catholics from taking part in civic celebrations. Walter Scott wrote to him on the subject of the Graham clan, and is believed to have admired his ballads. Graham was also acquainted with the Irish novelist Maria Edgeworth.   NORMAN MOORE, *rev.* COLM LENNON

Sources J. Graham, *An account of the town and parish of Maghera* (1813), preface · J. Graham, *Annals of Ireland* (1819), preface · J. Graham, *Ireland preserved* (1841), preface · W. Scott, *Dublin University Magazine*, 1 (1833), 325–7 · *Derry Journal* (12 March 1844) · A. T. Q. Stewart, *The narrow ground: aspects of Ulster, 1609–1969* (1977), 71–2 · *The letters of Sir Walter Scott*, ed. H. J. C. Grierson and others, centenary edn, 12 vols. (1932–79), vol. 5, pp. 118–19
Archives BL, letters to Sir Robert Peel, Add. MSS 40228–40613, *passim* · NL Scot., letters to Sir Walter Scott · Representative Church Body Library, Dublin, MS J 32 · TCD, corresp. with William Shaw Mason

Graham, John (1794–1865), bishop of Chester, was born in Claypath, Durham, on 23 February 1794, the only son of John Graham, managing clerk to Thomas Griffith of the Bailey, in the city of Durham. He was educated at the grammar school in Durham and matriculated at Christ's College, Cambridge, in 1812, being elected to a scholarship in 1813. In 1816 he graduated as fourth wrangler, and was bracketed with Marmaduke Lawson as chancellor's medallist, proceeding BA in 1816, MA in 1819, BD in 1829, and DD by royal mandate in 1831. He was elected a fellow and tutor of his college in 1816, was ordained deacon and priest (Salisbury) in 1818, and in 1828 was collated to the prebend of Sanctae Crucis in Lincoln Cathedral.

In 1830 Graham was elected master of Christ's College in succession to John Kaye. A liberal, he declared himself, in 1834, in favour of the movement at Cambridge led by Connop Thirlwall and Adam Sedgwick to repeal the religious tests which prevented dissenters from taking degrees. In 1838 he failed in an attempt to reform his college's statutes to permit non-Anglicans to become members of the foundation (that is, to hold scholarships or fellowships) and to allow the fellows to marry. As master he married in 1833 Mary, daughter of the Revd Robert Porteous; they had four sons and four daughters.

Graham was vice-chancellor of the university in 1831 and again in 1840. He promoted university reform on a committee appointed by the heads of houses in 1838 to revise the university's statutes and, in 1848, as a member of a syndicate to broaden the curriculum. In 1842–3 he was a candidate for the regius professorship of divinity, in opposition to Christopher Wordsworth, but withdrew in the face of criticism and the threat of litigation on account of his also being an elector to the chair.

Graham became rector of Willingham in Cambridgeshire in 1843. He was nominated chaplain to Prince Albert on 26 January 1841, and in the contest for the chancellorship of Cambridge University, on 27 February 1847, he acted as chairman of the prince's committee. He was well regarded by the royal family, and on 25 September 1849 was appointed clerk of the closet to the queen, an appointment which he held until his death.

In 1848, on the translation of John Bird Sumner to the see of Canterbury, Graham received, on Lord John Russell's recommendation, the vacant bishopric of Chester. His consecration took place in the Chapel Royal, Whitehall, on 14 May 1848, and on 16 June he was installed in Chester Cathedral. On the occasion of his leaving Cambridge the mayor and council of the town tendered him an address of congratulation on his appointment, the only instance in which a tribute of the kind had ever been offered by that body. The bishop was a Liberal in politics, but seldom spoke or voted in the House of Lords, and though of evangelical sympathies he was not a party man. His leading idea was to preserve peace in the diocese; he could, however, be firm when occasion required. His conciliatory manner was extended to the dissenters of Chester. He thus gave some offence to the high-church party. He published little other than sermons, contributing them to publications of the Church Missionary Society and the SPCK.

As bishop Graham maintained his interest in university reform. Russell made him chairman of the royal commission appointed in 1850 to inquire into the state of Cambridge University. The report of the Graham commission, as it was known, was 'kind to the university and kinder still to the colleges' (Searby, 526); Graham was one of the statutory commissioners appointed under the 1856 Cambridge University Act to carry these rather cautious recommendations into effect by negotiation with the university and colleges.

Graham died at the bishop's palace, Chester, on 15 June 1865, and was buried in Chester cemetery on 20 June.

G. C. BOASE, *rev.* ELLIE CLEWLOW

Sources GM, 3rd ser., 19 (1865), 240–42 · *Chester Courant* (21 June 1865), 7–8 · Venn, *Alum. Cant.* · P. Searby, *A history of the University of Cambridge*, 3: 1750–1870, ed. C. N. L. Brooke and others (1997) · D. A. Winstanley, *Early Victorian Cambridge* (1940) · J. Peile, *Biographical register of Christ's College, 1505–1905, and of the earlier foundation, God's House, 1448–1505*, ed. [J. A. Venn], 2 (1913) · O. Chadwick, *The Victorian church*, 1 (1966) · D. W. Bebbington, *Evangelicalism in modern Britain: a history from the 1730s to the 1980s* (1989) · R. Brent, *Liberal Anglican politics: whiggery, religion, and reform, 1830–1841* (1987) · J. Prest, *Lord John Russell* (1972)
Likenesses pencil sketch, Christ's College, Cambridge
Wealth at death under £18,000: resworn probate, Feb 1866, CGPLA Eng. & Wales

Graham, John (1805–1839), botanist, was born in Dumfriesshire. Nothing is known about his early life or education. About 1828 he went to India, under the patronage of Sir John Malcolm, governor of the Bombay presidency. He lived with the governor's family until Malcolm obtained for him the appointment of deputy postmaster-general of the presidency. He became superintendent of the botanical garden at Bombay soon after its establishment in 1830 by the Agri-Horticultural Society of Western India. He aimed to fill it with exotic and indigenous plants, many of which he himself collected. Graham died at Khandala on 28 May 1839, after a few days' illness. At the time of his death he was engaged in printing *A Catalogue of the Plants Growing in Bombay and its Vicinity*. It was finished by his friend Joseph Nimmo and published under the auspices of the Agri-Horticultural Society of Western India in 1839.

Graham had based his compilation on *Prodromus florae peninsulae Indiae orientalis* by Robert Wight and G. A. W. Arnott (1834) and, furthermore, referred the reader to this book for descriptions of the plants he cited. However, the value of Graham's catalogue, one of the earliest Indian floras, lay in its recording the localities where the plants had been collected, both by Graham and by his botanical friends. B. D. JACKSON, *rev.* RAY DESMOND

Sources J. Graham, *A catalogue of the plants growing in Bombay and its vicinity* (1839), ii–iv [preface] · J. W. Hooker, *Journal of Botany*, 3 (1841), 300–01 · I. H. Burkill, *Chapters on the history of botany in India* (Calcutta, 1965)

Graham, John Anderson (1861–1942), Church of Scotland minister and missionary, was born on 8 September 1861 in De Beauvoir Town, Hackney, London, the second of four sons of David Graham (*d.* 1887), customs officer, and his wife, Bridget Nolan, who was of Irish descent. His father retired the following year, returned with the family to his Scottish homeland in Cardross, Dunbartonshire, and took up farming on Glenboig Farm. John's early education was at Cardross parish school until 1874, when at thirteen years of age he became a clerk in a law firm in Glasgow to supplement family income, and continued his education by attending night classes at the Andersonian Institute. He then spent two years at the prestigious high school in Glasgow before entering the civil service in Edinburgh at the age of sixteen, as a stepping-stone to a career in law, and where he served in various posts for five years.

Under the influence of his parish minister, the Revd John McMurtie, John was increasingly drawn to a deeper personal spirituality and involvement in the church, as testified by entries in his diary on his twenty-first birthday (Minto, 7), until he finally resigned from government service to prepare for the ministry. He graduated MA from Edinburgh University in 1885 and went on to three years at Divinity Hall, after which he was ordained on 13 January 1889 at St George's Church, Edinburgh. During this period he came under the further influence of the Very Revd Professor W. Charteris and his teaching on 'applied Christianity', became clerk to *The Christian Life and Work* committee, and secretary of the Young Men's Guild of the Church of Scotland, all of which propelled him into his final career choice of being a foreign missionary, the first to be appointed by the guild. The field chosen was the remote hill station of Kalimpong, India, situated at 4000 feet on a ridge in the eastern Himalayas.

Two days after his ordination John was married to Katherine McConachie (*d.* 1919), a native of Edinburgh whom he had met and worked with among slum children. They departed for India a few days later to embark on a work that was to stretch them to the utmost and expose a breadth of vision and compassion seldom matched, while raising a loving tight-knit family of two sons, David and Jack, and four daughters, Peggy, Isa, Bunty, and Betty. Through their combined efforts, not only was the small mission outpost of the Church of Scotland's Eastern Himalayan Mission (EHM) at Kalimpong developed into the 'power station' (Ogilvie, 118) of the Himalayas, but the

primitive town itself was transformed beyond recognition.

John and Katie (as affectionately called by her family and friends) worked together as a fine-tuned team. Responsible for EHM's Kalimpong district work, they organized the indigenous church, and the initial four congregations grew to fourteen; a magnificent neo-Gothic church was built and became the pride of the community; schools were started throughout the surrounding hills and a teacher training institute established which drew students from the neighbouring closed countries of Bhutan and Nepal; work was extended into the nearby neglected Duars tea-growing region; and a co-operative credit society was formed to give relief from the punitive rates of local moneylenders. Through Katie's initiative Charteris Hospital was founded in 1892 with a chain of village dispensaries, the first girls' school opened in 1891, and female teacher training was introduced. Cottage industries were championed, resulting in the foundation of Kalimpong Homes Industries, which employed 1000 local people by 1922 and had trained many more in lacework, weaving, silk cultivation, carpentry, and wood-carving. All of this reflected their great love and concern for the spiritual and practical welfare of the indigenous Lepcha, Nepali, and Bhutia people, among whom the Grahams left a lasting legacy, and Dr Graham's outstanding administrative gifts, excellent relations with government officials, and ability to secure their co-operation, as well as his powers of communication with his constituency back in Scotland. Numerous letters and articles were printed in *Life and Work*, and the first edition of 10,000 of *On the Threshold of Three Closed Lands* (1897) soon sold out, necessitating a second in 1905. This was followed by a much broader work, *The Missionary Expansion of the Reformed Churches* (1898).

However, the Grahams are most remembered for the work they pioneered among 'the lost tribe' of Anglo-Indian children after their first furlough. In 1900 a hundred acres were secured from the government for the establishment of St Andrew's Colonial Homes (renamed Dr Graham's Homes in 1947), and the first cottage was opened on 4 November 1901. This model village, which grew to house more than 600 children, rescued many from tea plantations and the slums of Calcutta, contained all the requisite facilities including school, industrial training, infirmary, and chapel, and became famous around the world. Here Daddy Graham, as he was affectionately labelled by the children he had taken into his heart, found full scope for the exercise of his strong faith in God and the magnetic power of his personality, securing co-operation and wholehearted support across denominational, national, class, and racial lines, for establishment of a work which was still going strong 100 years later.

Mrs Graham was awarded the gold kaisar-i-Hind medal in 1916, three years before her untimely death on 15 May 1919, after which the Katherine Graham Memorial Chapel was built in her memory in the grounds of the homes, dedicated on 24 December 1925. Her insight and companionship were sorely missed while John Graham continued to expand his sphere of influence.

Non-sectarian, Dr Graham worked hard for church union and formation of the United Church of North India. In 1921 he was elected moderator of the general assembly of the Presbyterian Church of India, and in 1931 was called to preside as moderator of the general assembly of the Church of Scotland, the first missionary to be so honoured. His humanitarian service was fêted by both the Indian and the British governments; he was awarded the gold kaisar-i-Hind medal in 1903, and made a companion of the Indian Empire at the coronation durbar of George V in 1911. He was awarded the honorary degrees of DD by Edinburgh University in 1904 and LLD by the University of Aberdeen. He was invited by royalty to visit the surrounding closed kingdoms of Nepal, Sikkim, and Bhutan; he took a specially keen interest in the last, and functioned as virtual intermediary between the British government and the maharaja of Bhutan. In 1932 Dr Graham retired from the guild mission and returned to Kalimpong, where he served as honorary superintendent of the homes until his death on 15 May 1942. He was buried the same day, beside his beloved wife in the homes cemetery.

CINDY L. PERRY

Sources J. R. Minto, *Graham of Kalimpong* (1974) · Church of Scotland, minutes of Foreign Missions Committee, May 1931–1932, Centre for the Study of Christianity in the Non-Western World, Edinburgh, Andrew F. Walls Library, note 1350, 260 · A. Fleming, *Dr Graham of Kalimpong*, Church of Scotland Foreign Mission Committee [n.d., 1930?] · N. Maclean, 'Ave atque vale', *Life and Work* (July 1942), 109 · D. G. Manuel, *A gladdening river* (1914) · C. L. Perry, *Nepali around the world* (1997) · D. A. Dewan, *Education in the Darjeeling hills* (1991) · J. N. Ogilvie, *An Indian pilgrimage* (1922) · *Mission News*, 58/2 (June 1942), 17–26 · J. A. Graham, *On the threshold of three closed lands*, 2nd edn (1905) · CGPLA Eng. & Wales (1942)
Archives NL Scot., corresp., diaries, and papers | Bishop's Lodge, Darjeeling, India, east Himalayan mission records · New College, U. Edin., CSCNWW, Himalayan collection · New College, U. Edin., CSCNWW, Andrew F. Walls Library, Church of Scotland printed foreign mission records
Likenesses J. Dobbie, oils, 1930–39, Church of Scotland offices, Overseas Council, Edinburgh · Clark, pastels, 1931, England · N. Hutchinson, portrait, Dr Graham's Homes, Kalimpong, Jarvie Hall · photograph (after portrait), Secretary Graham's Homes Committee, Edinburgh
Wealth at death £2851 9s. od.: confirmation, 23 Oct 1942, CCI

Graham, John Murray (1809–1881), historian, was born on 15 October 1809 in Aberdeenshire, the eldest son of the eight children of Andrew Murray (1782–1847) of Murrayshall, Perthshire, advocate and sometime sheriff of Aberdeenshire, and his wife, Janet, only daughter of Oliver Thomson of Leckiebank, Fife. He was educated at Edinburgh University, where he graduated MA in 1828. He became an advocate in 1831. On 22 November 1853 he married Robina, youngest daughter of Thomas Hamilton. Closely related to Thomas *Graham, Lord Lynedoch, Murray succeeded in 1859 to Bertha Park, part of the Balgowan estate, under a trust settlement established by his kinsman; he assumed in addition to those of Murray, the name and arms of the Graham family.

John Murray Graham wrote several works, of which the most notable were his *Memoir of General Lord Lynedoch* (1869), compiled from family papers, and his *Annals and Correspondence of the Viscount and the First and Second Earls of Stair* (1875). He died at his estate at Murrayshall, Perthshire, on 18 January 1881, and was succeeded by his nephew, Henry Stewart Murray-Graham (1848–1913).

C. L. KINGSFORD, *rev.* G. MARTIN MURPHY

Sources Boase, *Mod. Eng. biog.* · *The Times* (19 Jan 1881) · *The Athenaeum* (29 Jan 1881), 167 · *The Antiquary*, 3 (1881), 136 · *The Academy* (29 Jan 1881), 81 · Burke, *Gen. GB*
Wealth at death £4065 3s. 10d.: confirmation, 7 May 1881, CCI

Graham, Malise, third earl of Strathearn and first earl of Menteith (1406x13–1490), landowner, was the only son of Patrick *Graham, second earl of Strathearn (d. 1413) [see under Graham family], and Euphemia, daughter and heir of David Stewart, earl of Strathearn, fourth son of Robert II. The marriage of his parents was arranged by 1401 and took place about 1406. Graham was born between that date and his father's murder in 1413. At first Strathearn was administered by his mother, but by 1416 power over Graham and his lands had passed to Walter Stewart, earl of Atholl (d. 1437), his great-uncle. Atholl remained his tutor for the next decade and gradually secured authority in Strathearn. In 1424 Graham was named as a hostage for the release of James I, though he did not go to England until arrangements were finally made in 1427. In September of that year he was deprived of Strathearn, which was given to Atholl, receiving in compensation from the king a truncated earldom of Menteith. But his custody of this was purely nominal, and within two months of the grant he was sent to England as a hostage for the king's ransom.

The treatment of Graham by the king was probably resented by his Graham kinsmen, including Sir Robert *Graham (a landowner in Strathearn), and by Archibald Douglas, fifth earl of Douglas (d. 1439), husband of his sister Euphemia. It was hardly the major issue claimed by some historians, however. Douglas had his own problems with James I, and Robert Graham continued to work closely with Atholl in Strathearn. By comparison with the royal attack on the Albany Stewarts, Malise's fate was insignificant. For the next quarter of a century he resided as a forgotten hostage at Pontefract Castle. His re-emergence came at the critical point in relations between James II and the Black Douglases in 1453. The Douglases and James Hamilton, second husband of Graham's sister, negotiated his release—an act which has been alleged as having the intention of making the exile a rival royal claimant. As a descendant of Robert II's second and unquestionably legal marriage, historians have suggested that Graham could have had a right to the throne over the dubious legitimacy of James II. There is no evidence of this as the motive for Graham's release. Rather the Douglases probably sought to embarrass James II by drawing attention to his father's abandonment of the hostages. Graham certainly made no attempt to establish himself as a pretender. He appeared at parliament in 1455 to forfeit his Douglas redeemers, and for the next thirty-five years was the least active of the Scottish earls. He was married twice, first to Jane Rochford and then to Marion, whose surname is unknown. He died before May in 1490.

M. H. BROWN

Sources M. Brown, *James I* (1994) · A. I. Dunlop, *The life and times of James Kennedy, bishop of St Andrews*, St Andrews University Publications, 46 (1950) · W. Fraser, ed., *The Red Book of Menteith*, 2 vols. (1880) · C. McGladdery, *James II* (1990) · G. Donaldson, *All the queen's men* (1983) · E. W. M. Balfour-Melville, *James I, king of Scots, 1406–1437* (1936) · *Scots peerage*, vol. 6

Graham, Maria. *See* Callcott, Maria (1785–1842).

Graham, Patrick, second earl of Strathearn (d. 1413). *See under* Graham family (per. c.1250–1513).

Graham, Patrick, first Lord Graham (d. 1466). *See under* Graham family (per. c.1250–1513).

Graham, Patrick (c.1435–1478), archbishop of St Andrews, was the son of Robert Graham of Fintry and grandson of Mary Stewart, Robert III's daughter. Mary and her second husband, Sir James Kennedy of Dunure, had a son James, who became bishop of St Andrews. She later married Sir William Graham of Montrose, and their son Robert was Patrick's father. With such powerful connections, Patrick Graham's preferment in the church was accomplished rapidly. At the age of fifteen canonries and prebends of Glasgow and Aberdeen were reserved for him, and five years later he was dispensed to receive two further benefices. He was educated at the University of St Andrews, graduating in arts in 1456; he had become dean of the faculty of arts by 1457 and an examiner of bachelors by the following year.

Graham's appointment to the bishopric of Brechin came before 29 March 1463 and, following the death of his uncle James Kennedy in May 1465, Graham succeeded him as bishop of St Andrews. The papal bull from Paul II appointing Graham to St Andrews was issued in Rome on 4 November 1465, but his elevation to the senior Scottish bishopric created considerable resentment. He was only thirty years old, and both bishops Andrew Muirhead of Glasgow and Thomas Spens of Aberdeen were senior ecclesiastics with demonstrable skill as statesmen and administrators. Graham's subsequent acquisition of the abbey of Paisley and the priory of Pittenweem *in commendam*, whereby he enjoyed the revenues of these houses as their non-resident head, placed a significant financial strain on him since, as with Brechin and St Andrews, the apostolic camera required over 3000 gold florins in common services.

A period of litigation concerning Brechin added to Graham's problems when, driven by his financial difficulties, he challenged bequests made by his late uncle, Bishop Kennedy, a course of action which caused widespread dismay to the foundations involved, including the University of St Andrews. In the turmoil of faction struggles during the minority of James III alliances were sought for mutual assistance, and Graham entered into bonds with his uncle Gilbert, Lord Kennedy, and Sir Alexander Boyd. Also, shortly before the seizure of the young king in 1466, James

Douglas, earl of Morton, entered into a contract with Graham and his father and brother for the marriage of the bishop's niece to Morton's son, John, although this careful political manoeuvring collapsed with the ousting of the Kennedy faction later that year. A statute of 1466 threatening any holder of a commend with the loss of his temporality and the penalties of rebellion made Graham particularly vulnerable, as he had been granted the abbey of Paisley *in commendam* following the deprivation of its abbot for failing to pay a pension to a cardinal. By 1469 Graham had resigned his commend of Paisley, but he was granted a commend of the priory of Pittenweem by the pope on 28 April 1467, restoring his vulnerability. A further weakness in Graham's position was the fact that his ecclesiastical preferment had occurred during the minority of James III, and although there is nothing to suggest that Graham was incompetent, his rise was based on family connections rather than proven court service in either diplomatic or administrative capacities.

When the king took over the reins of government in 1469, he demonstrated a determination to bring the Scottish church under greater royal authority and to limit papal interference in taxation and provisions within Scotland. To this end, James III was prepared to use the Scottish parliament, and in November 1469 an indult of Nicholas V to Bishop Kennedy was revived, whereby the bishop of St Andrews was permitted to confirm elections in the monastic houses of his diocese, including Coldingham and Dunfermline. This move by the king was intended to exclude papal patronage from the premier Scottish diocese, infuriating the papacy in the process and placing Graham, who owed much to papal support, in an extremely difficult position. Paul II promptly revoked the indult, but the Scottish parliament fought back in May 1471 by challenging papal taxation. By 2 July 1471 Graham was in or on his way to Rome, forestalling Abbot Henry of Cambuskenneth, who in June had been appointed procurator by James III to travel to Rome in order to explain the Scottish king's stance to the new pope, Sixtus IV. However, Graham succeeded in ingratiating himself with Sixtus, who no doubt saw in him an ally for the papacy in its fight against the erosion of papal influence in Scotland.

Sixtus issued a bull on 17 August 1472 erecting St Andrews into an archbishopric with metropolitan authority over the other twelve Scottish bishops, bringing Galloway, hitherto very tenuously under the control of York, and the Isles and Orkney, claimed by the archbishop of Nidaros in Norway, under the jurisdiction of the Scottish church. Notwithstanding previous concerns over attempted meddling by the archdiocese of York in Scottish church affairs, the elevation of St Andrews was not a popular development. The Scottish church had arrived at a position where the clergy managed their affairs without too much interference; for a bishop concerned about the violation of his rights, direct recourse to Rome was preferable to having to refer his plea to a metropolitan authority, a move that implied a loss of status. Nor would the prospect of Graham as an archbishop prepared to enforce papal policies against the wishes of the crown have been welcomed by James III, given the king's attempts to limit papal influence in the area of ecclesiastical patronage. Such was the outrage and alarm generated by his elevation that it is not surprising that Graham did not return to Scotland until at least September 1473.

It was difficult for Graham to exercise the powers and offices conferred on him by an enthusiastic pope in the face of the mounting domestic hostility towards him, but he was described nevertheless as legate a latere and apostolic internuncio for the purpose of collecting money and levying men for a crusade against the Turks, with the power to exact a tithe of the incomes of the Scottish clergy. In addition, Graham was the beneficiary of the revenues of the priory of Pittenweem and seven parish churches in spite of the parliamentary statute of 1471 forbidding such possessions. He was appointed monastic visitor and empowered to impose reforms even on the houses of Kelso and Holyrood, hitherto exempt from such visitations, and he was to hold the office of commendator of the abbey of Arbroath for five years. Such a trampling upon vested interests could not be ignored, and with the new archbishop still absent in Rome, James III moved swiftly against his interests in Scotland, supported by a clergy alarmed by the implications of Graham's metropolitan status.

By August 1473 Graham's goods and money had been restrained, and a general council was summoned in November 1473, probably convening the following January, at which plans were set in motion that resulted in the seizure of the temporalities of St Andrews by February 1474. In April, James paid Andrew Mowbray for pleading the king's business at the papal court, probably advancing a justification of Graham's deposition, and in May mention is made of a tax granted to the king by the clergy, which may bear out the statement by Bishop John Lesley in his *History* that the Scottish bishops had offered the king 12,000 merks to help against the archbishop. Graham was finished, effectively, before he returned to Scotland, and that he took no part in active government in terms of attending parliament or witnessing charters indicates the extent of his ostracism. Yet this did not end the matter, for he remained under sustained attack which left him, by September 1476, heavily in debt and discredited, deserted even by the papacy now that he no longer had the value of influence. In 1475 he incurred excommunication, and he suffered a breakdown in his health described as insanity.

During the period of Graham's disgrace James III had been advancing his favourite, William Scheves, securing for him the archdeaconry of St Andrews by 15 April 1474. It was Scheves who was appointed coadjutor of the see of St Andrews by a papal bull issued by Sixtus IV on 13 July 1476, on the grounds of Graham's excommunication and insanity, although it was not until 5 December 1476 that the pope commissioned Johann Husemann, dean of the church of St Patroclus in the diocese of Cologne and a practitioner of canon law, to inquire into charges made against Graham. The findings of the inquiry were couched in virulent terms, accusing Graham of being a heretic, schismatic, falsifier, simoniac, person of irregular life, blasphemer, and excommunicate. He was accused further of claiming to have been chosen by God to reform the church, taking to himself papal powers. The bull of condemnation and the official deprivation of Graham on 9 January 1478 were merely official confirmation of a long established fact, and the provision of William Scheves to the archbishopric followed speedily on 11 February. The terms of Graham's deposition condemned him to perpetual confinement in a monastery 'or other place', and he was held first at Inchcolm, then at Dunfermline, and eventually at the castle of Lochleven, where he died during 1478; he was buried at St Serf's Inch, Lochleven.

C. A. McGLADDERY

Sources J. Herkless and R. K. Hannay, *The archbishops of St Andrews*, 5 vols. (1907–15), vols. 1–3 · J. Dowden, *The bishops of Scotland ... prior to the Reformation*, ed. J. M. Thomson (1912) · *APS*, 1424–1567 · J. M. Thomson and others, eds., *Registrum magni sigilli regum Scotorum / The register of the great seal of Scotland*, 11 vols. (1882–1914), vol. 2 · A. Theiner, *Vetera monumenta Hibernorum et Scotorum historiam illustrantia* (Rome, 1864) · [G. Buchanan], *The history of Scotland translated from the Latin of George Buchanan*, ed. and trans. J. Aikman, 6 vols. (1827–9) · T. Dickson and J. B. Paul, eds., *Compota thesaurariorum regum Scotorum / Accounts of the lord high treasurer of Scotland*, 1–4 (1877–1902) · A. I. Dunlop, ed., *Calendar of Scottish supplications to Rome*, 3: 1428–1432, ed. I. B. Cowan, Scottish History Society, 4th ser., 7 (1970) · L. J. Macfarlane, 'The primacy of the Scottish church, 1472–1521', *Innes Review*, 20 (1969), 111–29, esp. 111–12 · N. Macdougall, *James III: a political study* (1982) · J. Lesley, *The history of Scotland*, ed. T. Thomson, Bannatyne Club, 38 (1830)

Graham, Richard, first Viscount Preston (1648–1695), politician and Jacobite conspirator, was born at Netherby, Cumberland, on 24 September 1648, the eldest son of Sir George Graham, second baronet (*d.* 1658), of Netherby and Ersk, and his wife, Lady Mary, daughter of James Johnston, first earl of Hartfell (1602–1653). He succeeded his father as third baronet on 19 March 1658 and two years later was a pupil at Westminster School under Richard Busby. Admitted to the Inner Temple in 1664, on 20 June that year he matriculated from Christ Church, Oxford, where he studied under the supervision of the dean, John Fell. Distinguished as a thoughtful and scholarly youth, fully versed in the classics, he imbibed the high Anglican and ultra-royalist ethos prevalent among the student body. Having been created MA on 4 February 1667, he published anonymously *Angliae speculum morale* (1670), in which he attempted to diagnose the ills that afflicted society and to offer a solution to them, through the lasting reformation of manners and an adherence to a truly Christian form of life. Significantly, in the light of his later career, he justified the status of the nobility on the grounds that their 'fidelity to their Prince renders them worthy of those advantages they enjoy', and dwelt at length upon the conduct and role of the courtier. 'He who truly intends to make a Court the Scene of his life', Graham concluded, in somewhat priggish terms, 'ought above all to practice sincerity ... for the addresses of the people to their Sovereign ... [are] convey'd through him as a conduct, [and] it should be his care that they arrive at the Royal Ear without addition or dimunition' (pp. 17–18). On 2 August 1670 he married Lady Anne (*d.* in or after 1707), second daughter of Charles *Howard, first earl of Carlisle (1628–1685); they had three sons and four daughters.

Having determined upon a political career, Graham secured election on 8 June 1675 as MP for Cockermouth, Cumberland, taking advantage of his family's strong connections and concentration of patronage in that area. He continued to represent that borough in the successive parliaments of 1678–9, 1679, and 1680–81. His authoritarianism and abrasive toryism, when coupled with his high Anglican religious beliefs, made him a natural supporter of both the hereditary principle and of the duke of York's right to succeed to the throne. Consequently, in December 1679 Graham was one of the few northern gentlemen who turned out to welcome James's progress to Scotland and subsequently entertained the duke and his wife at his home at Norton-Conyers. At the York assizes in 1680 Graham refused to sign a petition to the king which demanded the calling of frequent parliaments, and on 2 November 1680 he moved a parliamentary motion, on behalf of the duke of York, which opposed the passing of the second Exclusion Bill. His reward was not slow in coming, and on 11 March 1681 Charles II opened up to him the possibility of his further advancement, including becoming a viscount. Journeying north, he attended upon the duke of York at Edinburgh, which was fast becoming a 'hothouse' for experiments in absolutist governance, and on 30 July 1681 received his patent for a Scottish peerage during a session of James's privy council. It was as Viscount Preston of Haddington and Lord Graham of Eske that two days later he took his place in the Scottish parliament. Having gained the full confidence of the duke of York, Preston travelled in his company to Leith before delivering on 26 August a rousing speech to the Scottish parliament which fully supported James's succession to the English throne.

On the following morning Preston set off for his estates in Cumberland, but by September he was back in London and attending the king. Charles II entrusted him with meeting and greeting, on 5 January, 1682, Hamet ben Hamet ben Haddu, the ambassador of the emperor of Morocco, and conveying him from Tower Wharf to his lodgings in the Strand. Preston himself was appointed ambassador to the court of France shortly afterwards, and landed at Dieppe on 11 May 1682. He was soon to prove his worth to his sovereign, gathering evidence about supposedly whig-inspired plots against the life of Charles II and uncovering in August what he believed to be a plan for a major French descent upon the coast of Ireland. Despite this discovery, he won the respect and friendship of the French king, and through his forceful complaints to Louis XIV ensured the consignment to the Bastille of Abbot Primi, whose writings threatened to expose the terms of the secret treaty of Dover to general scrutiny. In September 1682 Preston 'presented a sharp memorial to the French King touching his seizeing the citty of Orange'

(Luttrell, 1.221), and a year later was instrumental in blackening Bishop Gilbert Burnet's name at the court of Versailles. Having recorded a laconic description in his diary of a man broken 'on the wheel upon the Pont Neuf … for cheating the Marquis de Bouillon' (*Sixth Report*, HMC, 261), and having vigorously defended the merchants of the Hudson's Bay Company from French encroachments, he returned to England upon the accession of James II.

Elected MP for Cumberland on 2 April 1685, Preston rapidly asserted his parliamentary authority as with Charles Middleton, earl of Middleton, he acted as the manager of the king's interest in the two sessions of the Commons which met between 19 May and 2 July and on 9–20 November 1685. He was admitted to the privy council on 21 October 1685, and was appointed keeper of the great seal to the dowager queen, Catherine of Braganza, just five days later. His local dominance in the north of the kingdom was assured in 1687, when he was made lord lieutenant of Cumberland and Westmorland, and he reached the zenith of his career in October 1688 when, after the dismissal of the earl of Sunderland, he was chosen by James II to be the lord president of the privy council. After the landing of William of Orange in November 1688 Preston was one of the committee of five appointed to govern the capital in the absence of the king, and his correspondence provides a graphic and authoritative description of the sudden unravelling of royal power over the following days and weeks. At the very point when the crown and sceptre were slipping from his grasp, and when his senior officers were deserting him in droves, James II still found the time to order Preston to seize John Churchill's goods and furniture from his lodgings in Whitehall and St Albans, an incident which points both to the king's vengeful animus and to his lack of any clear set of priorities.

It would appear that Preston considered following his master into exile in December 1688, but was repeatedly urged by the fallen king to stay in England in order to gather information about the debates in the Convention Parliament. In March 1689 Narcissus Luttrell reported that he was fomenting trouble in the north and it is evident that he received considerable subsidies from the French treasury with which to finance covert action and promote the Jacobite cause. Furthermore, he had had the presence of mind to retain his seals of office and continued to be regarded by many Jacobites as the real secretary of state. Arrested in May 1689 and confined to the Tower on suspicion of attempting to raise a rebellion, he was bailed in late October. However, in spite of his intelligence and real skill as a diplomat and politician, Preston had neither the guile to avoid trouble nor the steadfastness of character necessary to make him a successful coup conspirator: he continued to insist upon drawing the attention of the authorities to himself and his activities. Consequently, in November 1689 he forced a test case upon the House of Lords, hoping to prove the validity of a patent for a new English baronetcy, conferred upon him by James II from his place of exile. Had he won his argument in the Lords, Preston would have effectively given the lie to the myth of James II's voluntary abdication and would have paralysed

William III's ability to direct the administrative machine. However, the judiciary quickly ruled against him and on 11 November 1689 he was committed to the Tower, 'for pretending to the peerage of England' (Luttrell, 1.603). With little stomach for a life spent behind bars, Preston penned a grovelling apology to the house and withdrew his claim. Released on 28 November 1689, after an appearance before the king's bench, he then became embroiled in a bitter dispute with Lord Montague over the division of profits from the office of the king's wardrobe. Preston's claims to a life tenure of his sinecure, granted by the former monarch, were also rejected in court, and on 28 May 1690 he was fined £1300 in damages.

Undismayed, Preston organized a meeting of leading protestant Jacobites in Covent Garden in December 1690, and had several conferences with members of both houses of parliament as to the best ways of restoring the Stuarts with French help. As a prelude to a planned invasion in 1691, it was argued that James II should persuade Louis XIV to re-establish toleration for protestants in France, and that upon landing he should keep the accompanying French in the background and resolve to protect the Church of England and to govern according to the law, through parliament. Moreover, it was determined that given his diplomatic service and splendid contacts at the courts of Versailles and St Germain, Preston should go to France 'in order to accommodate these seeming contradictions' and to negotiate directly with the exiled king (Clarke, 2.442). Along with his own minutes of the negotiations, Preston also took a parcel of letters from those protestant statesmen—including the bishop of Ely and Lord Clarendon—with whom he had consorted, and lists of the strength and disposition of the Royal Navy, provided by its former commander, Lord Dartmouth.

Pretending to represent a gang of smugglers, John Ashton, who had been a servant to Mary of Modena, hired a fishing smack, the *James and Elizabeth*, in order to carry Preston and Major Edmund Elliott to France. As the little boat sailed safely up the Thames on the stroke of the new year of 1691 passing both a government frigate lying off Woolwich and the blockhouse at Gravesend, the mood of the conspirators visibly lightened and Preston left his secret correspondence in the hold in order to unpack a hamper and to hand out seasonal roast beef, mince pies, and wine to his friends. However, just as they were sitting down to eat the alarm was given that a swift vessel had set out from Tilbury and was pursuing them. The letters had been tied together with a lead weight so that they might be jettisoned in the event of just such an occurrence, but Preston appears to have lost his head and did nothing to retrieve them while the vessel was being boarded by a search party. Ashton, made of sterner stuff, tried to pick them up and hide them under his coat, but he was seized before he could throw them overboard. After trying, and failing, to bribe his captors into releasing them, Preston and his two companions were brought to Whitehall to be questioned before being committed to the Tower of London on 3 January.

Each of the defendants opted for an individual trial, and Preston argued for the right to be tried before the House of Lords. However, on 4 January John Evelyn recorded the reprise of the earlier judgment against him, that he was 'not an English Peer' and his trial was 'hastn'd at the Old Bailey' (*Diary and Letters*, 543). With the letters bearing his own private seal, there was little chance of an acquittal on the charges of treason and he was duly condemned to death on 19 January, with his estates and titles being held forfeit to the crown. However, it was observed that 'Preston's mind [had] sunk so visibly that it was concluded he would not die, if confessing all he knew could save him'. Even though his life hung in the balance, he still vacillated, for:

> he had no mind to die, and yet was not willing to tell all he knew … when he was heated by the importunities of his friends … and when he had dined well, he resolved he would die heroically; but by the next morning that heat went off; and when he saw death in full view, his heart failed him. (*Bishop Burnet's History*, 4.125–7, 2.70–71)

Transferred to Newgate gaol on 1 May 1691, Preston provided the authorities with a full confession and testified that the earls of Clarendon and Dartmouth, Bishop Francis Turner of Ely, the countess of Dorchester, and William Penn had all been among his accomplices. His testimony, corroborated by Matthew Crone, another former Jacobite agent, gained him a pardon in late May and his freedom, upon a bail of £2000 and the surety of his estates, on 13 June. Though his conduct had gained him the opprobrium of his former comrades—for Ashton had remained silent and gone to the scaffold for his part in the plot, and Dartmouth had died a prisoner in the Tower—Preston still attempted to retain some dignity and was again remanded in Newgate, on 4 August 1691, for refusing to turn king's evidence on another group of his friends. However, the authorities had finished with him. He was of no more use or interest to them, the object of hatred and mockery to his foes, and of contempt, or at best pity, to his erstwhile friends. Allowed to retire to the seclusion of his northern estates, he spent his latter years and 'many Hours of leisure' quietly revising a translation of Boethius, originally begun in 1680, which appeared as *Of the Consolation of Philosophy* in 1695. He appears to have identified closely with Boethius, 'a Man of comprehensive Learning … of great Piety and Devotion … [whose] constancy in suffering makes him appear to have been of … great vertue and courage' (p. iv) and retained his intellectual pride to the end, adding copious notes to the commonplace book that had once belonged to John Milton. Having lost all hope, he died, largely unnoticed and unmourned, at his home at Nunnington Manor on 22 December 1695, and was buried in the neighbouring church. He was survived by his wife, who was still alive on 5 February 1707. Their son Edward (1679–1709) succeeded his father as second Viscount Preston, as the attainder had not affected his Scottish peerage.   JOHN CALLOW

Sources N. Luttrell, *A brief historical relation of state affairs from September 1678 to April 1714*, 1–3 (1857) · *Relation de ce qui s'est passé au procez de Mylord Preston et du sieur Jean Ashton … publiée par le commandement de la reine* (Paris, 1691) · *The arraignment, trials, conviction and condemnation of Sir Rich. Grahme, bart., Viscount Preston*

(1691) · W. Wake, *A sermon preached upon the XXX*[th] *of January … 1684–5 at Paris in the chappel of … the Lord Viscount Preston: his majesties envoy extraordinary in the court of France* (1685) · [D. Defoe (?)], *An account of the late horrid conspiracy to depose their present magesties K. William and Q. Mary* (1691) · *Bishop Burnet's History* · *The life of James the Second, king of England*, ed. J. S. Clarke, 2 (1816) · W. C. Braithwaite, *The second period of Quakerism*, ed. H. J. Cadbury, 2nd edn (1961); repr. (1979) · P. K. Monod, *Jacobitism and the English people, 1688–1788* (1989) · E. Cruickshanks and E. Corp, eds., *The Stuart court in exile and the Jacobites* (1995) · J. Garrett, *The triumphs of providence: the assassination plot, 1696* (1980) · *Diary and letters of John Evelyn*, ed. W. Bray, 2nd edn (1819); repr. (1871) · T. B. Macaulay, *The history of England from the accession of James II*, new edn, ed. C. H. Firth, 6 vols. (1913–15) · R. Douglas, *The peerage of Scotland* (1764) · GEC, *Peerage* · *Sixth report*, HMC, 5 (1877–8), 319–21 · *Seventh report*, HMC, 6 (1879), 261–404 · E. Cruickshanks, 'Grahme, Sir Richard', HoP, *Commons, 1660–90* · BL, Add. MS 4637

Archives Berks. RO, letter-books as ambassador at Paris · BL, corresp. and papers, Add. MSS 63752–63781 · BL, genealogy, Add. MS 4637 · BL, trial for treason, Add. MS 27402, fol. 187 · Yale U., Beinecke L., letter-book in an unidentified hand with copies of letters from Paris, FB 83 | BL, letters to Lord Middleton, Add. MS 41805, fols. 266, 273, 277 · BL, entries in John Milton's commonplace book, Add. MSS 36354, fol. 28, *passim* · BL, letters read at his trial, Add. MS 28005, fol. 306

Likenesses oils, *c.*1687–1690, NPG

Wealth at death man of considerable estate in Yorkshire; also owned a London townhouse; was drawing £100 p.a., from 10 Nov 1685, for services to James II: *Sixth report*, 321

Graham, Richard (*fl.* 1695–1727), author, of whose birth or parentage nothing is known, wrote 'A short account of the most eminent painters, both ancient and modern', which was appended as a supplement to John Dryden's translation of Charles Alphonse Du Fresnoy's *De arte graphica*, published as *The Art of Painting* in 1695. An acknowledged digest of foreign biographical works, Graham claimed that the 'Short account' was more accurate than previous biographies in English, because of the chronological arrangement of the material, 'to preserve the order of the time, which indeed was the thing principally intended in these papers' (Graham, 'Short account', 232).

Graham was a member of the Virtuosi of St Luke, a London club of artists and art experts, from 1697 to 1727, and his involvement with the translation and publication of Du Fresnoy was in collaboration with other members of the Virtuosi. He was regarded as an art expert by artists and authors alike. In his 1706 translation as *The Art of Painting and the Lives of the Painters* of Roger de Piles's 1699 treatise *L'abrégé de la vie des peintres … avec une traité du peintre parfait*, John Savage acknowledged that he imitated Graham. The engraver George Vertue copied material from notes and catalogues kept by Graham of art sales material that in turn formed part of the information used by Horace Walpole for his *Anecdotes of Painting*. Graham had his own collection, including pieces by native painters, which was sold for reasons unknown on 6 March 1712.

Little else is known with certainty about Graham. He may be identical with the R. Graham, esquire, who published *Poems upon the Death of the most Honourable the Marchioness of Winchester* in 1680, and with the Richard Graham who matriculated at Trinity College, Cambridge, as a fellow-commoner in 1680, and was perhaps admitted to the Middle Temple in 1682 and the Inner Temple in 1684, and who had a son, Richard, born in March 1693. Graham may also be identical with the Richard Graham who died in London in September 1727, but as the Virtuosi's annual feast that year (at which Graham was present) was possibly held between October and December, this cannot be proved. NICHOLAS GRINDLE

Sources [R. Graham], 'A short account of the most eminent painters, both ancient and modern', in C. A. Du Fresnoy, *De arte graphica / The art of painting*, trans. J. Dryden (1695), 227–355 · I. Bignamini, 'George Vertue, art historian, and art institutions in London, 1689–1768', *Walpole Society*, 54 (1988), 1–148 · Vertue, *Note books*, vols. 1, 5–6 · R. de Piles, *The art of painting, and the lives of the painters* (1706) · R. Graham, *Poems upon the death of the most honourable the marchioness of Winchester* (1680) · Venn, *Alum. Cant.* · administration, PRO, PROB 6/103 · J. C. Davies, ed., *Catalogue of manuscripts in the library of the Honourable Society of the Inner Temple*, 3 vols. (1972)

Graham, Ritchie (d. 1592). *See under* North Berwick witches (act. 1590–1592).

Graham, Sir Robert, of Kinpont (d. 1437), landowner and assassin, was the third son of Patrick Graham of Kincardine and his second wife, Euphemia, daughter of John Stewart of Ralston. Possibly intended for the church, he was educated at the University of Paris in the 1390s; he had returned to Scotland by 1399 and he married Marion, daughter of John Oliphant of Aberdalgie, about that time. The match may have been designed to further the Grahams' ambitions in Strathearn, where Robert's elder brother, Patrick, was to become an earl by marriage. The family's promotion was perhaps the work of Robert Stewart, duke of Albany (d. 1420), and the Grahams remained adherents of the Albany Stewarts after his death [*see* Graham family]. In 1424, following the death of his eldest brother, William, Robert probably led the support which the Grahams gave to Albany's grandson Walter Stewart of Lennox (d. 1425). As a result Robert was imprisoned by James I, who was preparing a general assault on the house of Albany. His imprisonment in Dunbar Castle did not lead to trial, however, and he appears to have been released by 1428. In Strathearn he was forced to accept the disinheritance of his nephew Malise *Graham in favour of Walter Stewart, earl of Atholl, and was acting as bailie for the earl by 1433. A troublesome minor landowner seemed to have been absorbed into the political structures of James I's regime.

Graham's service with Atholl proved crucial to both men. When the earl's relations with the king soured, he had a man in his household with grievances against James I which apparently outweighed Graham's likely reservations about Atholl himself. Although Graham may have encouraged Atholl to take action, it is more likely that the earl used Graham to spearhead his attack on the king. In October 1436 Sir Robert Graham, as he was by this date, was chosen by the estates to articulate their opposition to royal policies in general council. Atholl's influence, and his own previous antagonism towards the king, secured him this role, but in attempting to arrest James he overplayed his hand and was forced into hiding. It would appear that Atholl began to prepare a full *coup d'état* in February 1437 and again turned to Graham, who assembled a group of other irreconcilable Albany Stewart adherents—men who, like him, were prepared to kill the king and could be presented by Atholl as acting from their own sense of grievance. The plan won initial success. On the night of 20–21 February Graham led a small band, including the eldest of his five sons, Thomas, into the royal residence at the Dominican friary in Perth. A short search revealed the king hiding in a drain and they stabbed him to death. They were able to escape without pursuit, but the failure of the assassins to kill Queen Joan left the king's chosen regent alive to lead his supporters. After a brief civil war she assumed power and, following the capture of Atholl, Graham was seized, probably in northern Perthshire, by two local lords. He was taken to the court at Stirling and executed there with exemplary brutality in April 1437.

One account of the events of 1437 depicts Graham as more than just a pawn in the clash between the king and Atholl. In *The Dethe of the Kynge of Scotis*, a near contemporary English description of the murder of James, Sir Robert Graham is the central personality. His case against the king, that he was a tyrant who had killed his lords and taxed his subjects against custom, is put forward with sympathy. Graham's actions, first challenging James to reform, then seeking to detain him, and only finally resorting to regicide, are justified, and the deed is portrayed as tyrannicide, an act defended by political theorists such as Jean Gerson and Jean Petit in contemporary France. A man trained in law at Paris, Graham may have presented the king's murder in this way, and whether as idealist or aristocratic agent, his motives struck a chord within the community which was consistently vocal in opposition to the demands of James I. If that were so, the ferocity of Graham's execution could be construed as reflecting the wider community's response to his deed.

M. H. BROWN

Sources M. Brown, *James I* (1994) • M. H. Brown, '"That old serpent and ancient of evil days", Walter earl of Atholl and the death of James I', *SHR*, 71 (1992), 23–45 • M. Connolly, '*The dethe of the kynge of Scotis*: a new edition', *SHR*, 71 (1992), 46–69 • W. Drummond, *The genealogy of the most noble and ancient house of Drummond*, ed. D. Laing (1831); repr. (privately printed, Glasgow, 1889)

Graham [Grimes], **Robert** [*name in religion* Alexis] (d. **1701**), army officer and Trappist monk, was the second son of a certain 'Colonel' William Grimes, a cousin of the earl of Montrose, who is described in Lord Manchester's correspondence as a cavalry officer serving under Viscount Dundee, and later commander of the Bass Rock, recipient of Jacobite bounty in Edinburgh, and (in 1701) an alleged would-be assassin of William III. Graham had a stormy childhood and adolescence in Scotland. Despite being brought up in a protestant household, he professed a desire to become a Roman Catholic from an early age, and was whipped by his Presbyterian tutor for attending a Catholic service in Edinburgh. He was transferred to the guardianship of a kinsman, Lord Perth, and later passed into the hands of an austere Presbyterian uncle.

Graham then commenced a life of libertinism, which earned him considerable notoriety. His movements are difficult to trace, but he appears to have served in Flanders under William III. His excesses are said to have been well known in London, Flanders, and Paris. He was confirmed as a Roman Catholic at Bruges, but apparently relapsed into his profligate ways. He was presented to James II at the exiled Jacobite court at St Germain, before spending some time in the seminary at Meaux. Like his brother, who had become a Capuchin friar as Brother Archangel, Robert finally entered religious orders, taking the habit at the monastery of La Trappe in 1699 and the name Brother Alexis. His extreme acts of penitence, including fasting, hard labour, and sleep deprivation, became well known; James II, courtiers, and court ladies were regular visitors at his cell. He died early in 1701 after a protracted illness.

H. M. CHICHESTER, *rev.* DAVID TURNER

Sources *Relation de la vie et de la mort du Frère Alexis, religieux de la Trappe, nommé dans le monde Robert Grême, gentilhomme écossais* (Paris, 1705) • Lord Manchester [W. D. Montagu], *Court and society from Elizabeth to Anne*, 2 vols. (1864)

Graham [*later* Cunninghame Graham], **Robert**, of **Gartmore** (**1735–1797**), politician and poet, was born at Gartmore, Perthshire, the second son of Nicol or Nicolas Graham (1694/5–1775), laird of Gartmore, and Lady Margaret Cunninghame (1703/4–1789), daughter of William, twelfth earl of Glencairn. Robert and his elder brother William were educated at Glasgow University, having matriculated under Professor Andrew Ross; their tutor was Professor William Richardson (a native of their local district of Menteith), who was to be a lifelong friend. Their younger brother John (Jack) went to India, and reputedly fought at the battle of Assaye (1803).

In 1752 Robert left for Jamaica, where he was to stay as landowner, planter, politician, and public servant until 1770. By 1753, at the age of eighteen, he already held the office of receiver-general of the taxes. He married Anne (Annie) Taylor (d. 1781?) in 1764; they had five children, two sons and three daughters. The following year he was elected to the national assembly for the district of St David. By 1770, with his wife ill and with vague political aspirations in Britain, he was preparing to leave Jamaica. He arrived in Britain as laird of Ardoch in Dunbartonshire, having succeeded to the estate, which had been entailed upon him in 1757, on the death of his kinsman Bontine in 1767 or 1768. William was married but died in 1774 without sons, so Robert inherited Gartmore on their father's death on 16 November 1775 at the age of eighty. Following the death of his wife, probably in 1781, he married in 1786 or 1787 Elizabeth Buchanan Hamilton, the daughter of a neighbouring laird, Thomas Buchanan Hamilton of Spital. This was an unhappy, short-lived union; it ended by separation in early 1789, the year of his mother's death.

Now involved in local and national politics, including reform of the internal government of the royal burghs of Scotland, Graham was elected lord rector of Glasgow University (1785–7), replacing Edmund Burke; he was very active in the post. His political interests broadened and, partly through the influence of his friends Charles James

Robert Graham of Gartmore (1735–1797), by Sir Henry Raeburn, c.1794

Fox and Thomas Sheridan, he represented Stirlingshire in parliament between 1794 and 1796, replacing Sir Thomas Dundas. His support for political reform was evident in his (unsuccessful) attempt to introduce a bill of rights, which to some extent foreshadowed the Reform Bill of 1832. An earnest advocate of the principles of the French Revolution, he lost his seat in June 1796, being replaced by Sir George Keith of Elphinstone. In the same year, owing to the death of John Cunninghame, fifteenth and last earl of Glencairn, he succeeded to the Finlaystone estates in Renfrewshire, and assumed the additional surname of Cunninghame.

In the last two decades of his life Graham devoted himself also to literary matters. He wrote various lyrical pieces, the best known of which, 'If doughty deeds my lady please', is deservedly famous, much praised by Burns, Scott, and others. Towards the end of his life he was in ill health (gout and the effects of tropical diseases), and he died on 4 December 1797 at Gartmore, where he was buried beside his parents and first wife in the family cemetery. He was survived by his two sons: William, his heir, who was educated at Neuchâtel from at least 1790 to 1793, and Nicol, who may have been maréchal-de-camp in the Austrian service, who died, date unknown, at the estate of Jarbrook in Dumfriesshire.   JOHN WALKER

Sources R. B. C. Graham, *Doughty deeds: an account of the life of Robert Graham, 1735–1797* (1925) · J. Stewart, *The Grahams* (1958) · C. Watts and L. Davies, *Cunninghame Graham: a critical biography* (1979) · H. F. West, *A modern conquistador: Robert Bontine Cunninghame Graham, his life and works* (1932) · *The Scottish sketches of R. B. Cunninghame Graham*, ed. J. Walker (1982) · A. F. Tschiffely, *Don Roberto* (1937)

Archives NA Scot., corresp.
Likenesses H. Raeburn, oils, *c.*1794, Scot. NPG [*see illus.*] · Bone?, portrait, repro. in Graham, *Doughty deeds* · D. Martin, oils, Scot. NPG · attrib. H. Raeburn, oils, Scot. NPG

Graham, Sir Robert (1744–1836), judge, was born at Hackney, Middlesex, on 14 October 1744, the son and heir of James Graham (1703/4–1782), schoolmaster, who was descended from George Graham of Callander, second son of William, Lord Graham, and brother of the first earl of Montrose.

Graham was educated nearby at Dalston, where his father kept a school, and went up to Trinity College, Cambridge, on 28 January 1762, matriculating at Easter and becoming a scholar in the same year. He graduated BA as third wrangler in 1766, also coming out high in classics, was made a fellow in 1767, and took his MA in 1769. He was afterwards auditor to the college (1778–91) and counsel to the university (1787–91).

Graham entered at the Inner Temple on 8 April 1766 and was called to the bar on 13 May 1771. By 1769 he was already well enough established to be one of the counsel appearing before the Commons on the celebrated Middlesex election petition which followed the contest between Wilkes and Colonel Luttrell. Burke wrote that Graham was 'below his usual par' (*Correspondence*, 2.23); and Lord Mountmorres noted that 'Graham performed wonders, and like the sage of old would have moved the world if they had given him but a place to stand upon' (*Charlemont MSS*). He gained the favour of the prince of Wales, becoming his attorney-general and a KC in the same month, February 1793, and a bencher in the same year. Despite this promotion he was apparently not in the front rank of lawyers, for when he was made a baron of the exchequer on 16 June 1800, Sir Edward Law (the future Lord Ellenborough) caustically remarked that his appointment placed even the famously mediocre Mr Justice Rooke 'on a pinnacle' (Foss, *Judges*, 23). He was knighted in the same month.

By this time Graham had acquired most of the still rural hamlet of Dalston and some lands adjacent to it. With his wife, Margaret (*d.* 1832), he lived first in Guilford Street, London, and then in Bedford Square; they had no children.

Though courteous and affable, Graham was at first a chatterbox on the bench, according to Chief Baron Thomson, and was never held in high esteem as a judge, though he acquired adventitious fame in the north-east by narrowly escaping drowning when he fell into the Tyne while on the assize in Newcastle, an incident popularized locally in the song 'My Lord 'Size'. Graham was eighty-two when he retired on a pension, on 19 February 1827, having pronounced innumerable death sentences with the same incongruous but artless 'extreme civility which he exhibited to everybody and upon all occasions, especially to the prisoner' (Hawkins, 73). He was sworn of the privy council in the reign of William IV but did not sit on the judicial committee constituted in 1833.

Graham's wife died at Kingston upon Thames, Surrey, on 1 March 1832 and he died at his sister Charlotte's house close by at Long Ditton, on 28 September 1836; he was buried with some pomp in All Saints' Church, Kingston, on 7 October, and memorials to both of them were erected there. After the death in 1840 of Charlotte, his last surviving sister, the Graham estates at Dalston passed to his niece Catherine Massie and her brother.

PATRICK POLDEN

Sources Foss, *Judges*, 9.53–4 · Venn, *Alum. Cant.*, 2/3.109 · *VCH Middlesex*, vol. 10 · [H. Hawkins], *The reminiscences of Sir Henry Hawkins, Baron Brampton*, ed. R. Harris, 2 vols. (1904), 73 · [J. Grant], *The bench and the bar*, 1 (1837), 75–80 · *GM*, 2nd ser., 6 (1836), 653 · *The correspondence of George, prince of Wales, 1770–1812*, ed. A. Aspinall, 8 vols. (1963–71) · [E. Burke], *The correspondence of Edmund Burke*, 2, ed. L. S. Sutherland (1960) · W. D. Biden, *The history and antiquities of … Kingston-upon-Thames* (1852), 47 · J. C. Bruce, *A hand-book to Newcastle-on-Tyne* (1863), 72–3 · *GM*, 1st ser., 52 (1782), 262 · *GM*, 2nd ser., 14 (1840), 221 · Sainty, *Judges* · Sainty, *King's counsel* · *IGI* · *The manuscripts and correspondence of James, first earl of Charlemont*, 1, HMC, 28 (1891), 294 · PRO, IR 26/1417
Likenesses J. S. Copley, oils, 1804, National Gallery of Art, Washington DC
Wealth at death under £5000 personal estate: PRO, death duty registers, IR 26/1417; *VCH Middlesex*

Graham, Robert (1786–1845), physician and botanist, was born at Stirling on 7 December 1786, the third son of Robert Graham (d. 1819), physician, and his wife, Anne, daughter of Charles Stewart of Ardshiel. In 1792 Robert Graham senior inherited the estate of his relative George Moir at Leckie, near Stirling, whereupon he retired from practice and changed his name to Moir.

Graham was educated at Stirling grammar school and then at Edinburgh University, before being apprenticed in 1804 to Andrew Wood, a surgeon. He graduated from Edinburgh in 1808 and was licensed by the Royal College of Surgeons in the same year. He studied for a year at St Bartholomew's Hospital, London, and then set up in practice in Glasgow; he secured an appointment as physician to Glasgow Royal Infirmary in 1812. He married on 29 December 1817 Elizabeth Belsches, youngest daughter of David Buchanan. Thirteen children were born to them, of whom six daughters and four sons, and his wife, survived him.

Before Glasgow had a separate chair of botany Graham gave occasional lectures in the subject; in 1818, however, a chair was established and he became the first professor of botany. He transferred to Edinburgh University in 1820, having been appointed regius professor of botany and keeper of the king's garden, and he was elected fellow of the Royal Society of Edinburgh in 1821. He also lectured on clinical medicine and was one of the physicians to the Royal Public Dispensary.

Graham immediately set about establishing a new botanical garden in Inverleith Row to replace the existing small and unsatisfactory one in Leith Walk. Over a period of two years he supervised the removal of all trees, shrubs, and plants to the new site. The government grant was insufficient to meet all the wages and expenses of the garden, and Graham subsidized it from his own pocket; however, a grant of over £1500 enabled him to open in 1834 the largest palm house of its kind in Britain. In 1836 he was the first president of the Botanical Society of Edinburgh; in 1840 he was president of the Royal College of Physicians of Edinburgh and in 1842 he became president of the Medico-Chirurgical Society.

In time Graham's lectures attracted more than 200 students; to encourage them he presented gold medals for the best herbarium and the best essay. He was the first to lecture on botany during the winter months, and he gave many popular lectures in the garden. Each year during August and September he took groups of friends and students to different parts of Great Britain and Ireland. After a small treatise, *Practical Observations on Continued Fever* (1818), Graham published only on botanical matters. He described all new species on their first flowering in the garden, and his travels yielded several additions to the British flora. He embarked on, but never completed, a flora of Great Britain. After a long illness he moved to Coldoch, Perthshire, where his younger brother and sisters lived, in July 1845. He died there soon afterwards, on 7 August, and was buried at Leckie on 13 August.

ANITA McCONNELL

Sources C. Ransford, *Biographical sketch of the late Robert Graham MD, FRSE* (1846) · H. R. Fletcher and W. H. Brown, *The Royal Botanic Garden, Edinburgh, 1670–1970* (1970), 99–112 · J. Duns, *Memoir of Sir James Y. Simpson, bart.* (1873), 108–10 · I. B. Balfour, 'A sketch of the professors of botany in Edinburgh from 1670 until 1887', *Makers of British botany: a collection of biographies by living botanists*, ed. F. W. Oliver (1913), 280–301, esp. 291–3 · *Transactions of the Botanical Society* [Edinburgh], 2 (1846), 59–63
Archives Royal Botanic Garden, Edinburgh, corresp. and lecture notes
Likenesses C. Smith, oils, U. Edin. · lithograph, NPG

Graham, Robert Bontine Cunninghame (1852–1936), traveller, author, and politician, was born at 5 Cadogan Place, London, on 24 May 1852, the eldest of the three sons of William Cunninghame Bontine (1825–1883), of Gartmore, Perthshire, and Ardoch, Dunbartonshire, a major in the Scots Greys, and his wife, Anne Elizabeth (1828–1925), youngest daughter of Admiral Charles Elphinstone Fleeming, of Cumbernauld and Biggar, Dunbartonshire. Under the terms of an entail linked to ownership of the estate of Ardoch, the eldest son had to bear the surname and arms of Bontine during the lifetime of his father. Robert's full name reflects his descent from two ancient families, the Cunninghams, earls of Glencairn, and the Grahams, earls of Menteith, through whom he could claim descent from King Robert II. 'I ought, madam, if I had my rights', he once remarked in Scotland, 'to be king of this country' (Ford Madox Ford, *Return to Yesterday*, 1931, 38). Andrew Lang and Morrison Davidson, postulating the illegitimacy of the Stuart line, claimed that he was really Robert IV of Scotland and Robert I of Great Britain and Ireland. Known to friends and South Americans as Don Roberto, described in *The Times* as the 'cowboy dandy', to socialists he was 'Comrade', while to Galsworthy and Epstein he was 'the modern Don Quixote'. He was picturesque, bold, erratic, and adventurous, yet also pessimistically meditative; in some respects 'ahead of his times', he retained nostalgia for 'vanished Arcadias', those exotic sunny regions which to him seemed relatively untainted

Robert Bontine Cunninghame Graham (1852–1936), by Sir John Lavery, 1893

by 'progress' and commercialism. He defended the victims of imperialism, of racial prejudice, and of social injustice.

After schooling at Hill House, Leamington Spa (1863–5), followed by two years at Harrow School (1865–7) and private tuition in London and Brussels, he set out for South America at the age of seventeen. This was the first of several lengthy visits to America, during which he attempted cattle ranching and horse dealing; he rode with gauchos in Argentina, explored the forests of Paraguay, and trekked with a wagon train to Mexico City. During the First World War he worked in Uruguay, selecting horses for the British army; and it was in Buenos Aires, where he was widely respected, that he died on 20 March 1936. The South American journeys provided him with material for many of his tales and essays, and his historical studies include an account of the Jesuit missions in Paraguay, *A*

Vanished Arcadia (1901), biographies of various *conquistadores*, and a life of Francisco Solano López (president of Paraguay, 1865–70).

Cunninghame Graham's political career in Great Britain was characterized by that sympathy for the underdog which led him to advocate both socialism and Scottish nationalism. Elected as Liberal MP for North-West Lanarkshire in 1886, he soon revealed the extent of his radicalism. During his time in the house (until 1892), he condemned imperialism, racial prejudice, corporal and capital punishment, profiteering landlords and industrialists, child labour, and the House of Lords; he advocated the eight-hour working day, free education, home rule for Ireland and Scotland, and the general nationalization of industry. Asked in parliament (6 March 1889) whether he preached 'pure unmitigated Socialism', he replied, 'Undoubtedly.' He was certainly the first socialist in parliament, for Keir Hardie, whom he advised and guided, did not enter until 1892. In 1888 he became founding president of the Scottish Labour Party; Hardie was its secretary. Their programme included a graduated income tax, national health insurance, and nationalization of transport, mining, and banking. The notion that Cunninghame Graham was a flitting amateur of politics is refuted by the long record of his tireless campaigning. During his parliamentary years he campaigned up and down the country on behalf of the exploited chainmakers of Cradley Heath; with John Burns and Prince Kropotkin he helped the dockworkers in their struggle for 'the docker's tanner'; he spoke alongside Friedrich Engels, Sergey Stepniak, and George Bernard Shaw at demonstrations for the eight-hour working day; and he travelled to Paris with Hardie and William Morris (whom he greatly admired) to become a lively multilingual participant in the Marxist congress of the Second International. In the period 1889 to 1900, he contributed numerous pieces to such left-wing periodicals as the *People's Press*, the *Labour Elector*, the *People's Prophet*, Hardie's *Labour Leader*, and H. M. Hyndman's Marxist organs, the *Social-Democrat* and *Justice*.

At the turbulent 'bloody Sunday' demonstration at Trafalgar Square on 13 November 1887 (an event magnified in Morris's *News from Nowhere*), Cunninghame Graham and John Burns led an assault on the police lines; both leaders were arrested and subsequently found guilty of unlawful assembly; both were sentenced to six weeks' imprisonment at Pentonville. The experience did nothing to diminish Cunninghame Graham's radical ardour: repeatedly he argued for the formation of a national labour party and for militant trade unionism. In 1892 he contested the Camlachie division of Glasgow unsuccessfully as a Labour candidate. After 1900, as the Labour Party grew in numbers in parliament, he became increasingly critical of Labour MPs, feeling that they were too often tame and moderate; and, though he supported Labour candidates at elections, he emphasized that he sought a full-scale social revolution. During the war, his views changed: he stood unsuccessfully as a Liberal at Western Stirling and Clackmannan in 1918, and thereafter devoted his political energies mainly to the cause of Scottish home rule. He was president of the Scottish Home Rule Association and of its successor, the National Party of Scotland. In 1934 the National Party was amalgamated with the duke of Montrose's relatively right-wing Scottish Party to become the Scottish National Party; Cunninghame Graham remained president until his death.

After his early years in Central and South America, Cunninghame Graham had continued to travel adventurously abroad. In 1894 he prospected unsuccessfully for gold in Spain, and in 1897 he travelled into the Atlas Mountains of Morocco disguised as a sheikh or *sharif*. The latter journey might have been a fiasco, for he was arrested and held captive by the kaid of Kintafi, but it was redeemed by what is probably his finest travel book, *Mogreb-el-Acksa* (1898). This provided the basis for Shaw's *Captain Brassbound's Conversion*; and Cunninghame Graham himself was the model, Shaw avowed, for the dashing and impetuous Sergius Saranoff in *Arms and the Man*. Cunninghame Graham was patrician, flamboyant, handsome, athletic, lean, and wiry; neatly bearded and with flowing hair, he resembled a Spanish hidalgo. Indeed, his maternal grandmother, Catalina Paulina Alessandro de Jiménez, was a Spanish lady who married Charles Elphinstone Fleeming and, when her husband was an admiral, gave birth to Cunninghame Graham's mother in a cabin of Fleeming's flagship off La Guaira. Cunninghame Graham proved a striking model for authors, artists, sculptors, and photographers. His appearance and South American travels made him the model for Charles Gould in *Nostromo*, the greatest novel by his friend Joseph Conrad. (He had been prompt to hail the Polish-born novelist, and their friendship extended from 1897 until Conrad's death in 1924. The essay 'Inveni portum' is a moving obituary.) He contributed elements to Etchingham Granger, the central character in *The Inheritors* (1901), by Conrad and F. M. Hueffer; to Graham, the hero of H. G. Wells's *When the Sleeper Wakes* (1899); and to Mr Courtier, the quixotic 'champion of lost causes' in John Galsworthy's *The Patrician* (1911).

As this suggests, one special 'career' of Cunninghame Graham was that of cultural go-between, linking and aiding the most heterogeneous groups of people. His friends, acquaintances, and correspondents ranged from Buffalo Bill to the rani of Sarawak; they included artists and sculptors (John Lavery, William Strang, J. M. Whistler, William Rothenstein, Augustus John, Jacob Epstein); political individualists (Wilfrid Scawen Blunt, Charles Stewart Parnell, Roger Casement, Lawrence of Arabia); naturalists (W. H. Hudson, Henry Salt); pioneer socialists and militant trade unionists (Ben Tillett, Will Thorne, Keir Hardie, Tom Mann, John Burns, Jim Larkin); revolutionaries (Engels, Hyndman, Morris, Kropotkin); fiction writers (Bret Harte, Henry James, Wells, Conrad, Ford, Galsworthy, Compton Mackenzie); critics (Edward Garnett, Arthur Symons, Edmund Gosse); explorers (Up de Graff, C. H. Prodgers); poets (Thomas Hardy, John Masefield, Ezra Pound); prime ministers (Herbert Asquith, Ramsay MacDonald); editors (Frank Harris, W. T. Stead, A. R. Orage); playwrights and actors (Shaw, Wilde, Henry Arthur Jones, Sir John Martin-Harvey); scholars, convicts, historians, naval men, circus hands, cowboys, and gauchos. Conrad exclaimed: 'What don't you know! From the outside of a sail to the inside of a prison!' (*Joseph Conrad's Letters to R. B. Cunninghame Graham*, ed. C. T. Watts, 1969, 64).

Cunninghame Graham's own literary output was full and diverse. During his lifetime he was often praised highly for writing which was sharply realistic, ironic, and quirkily personal. In addition to eleven histories and biographies concerned with the Spanish conquest and subsequent South American events, there are *Notes on the District of Menteith* (1895) and *Doughty Deeds* (1925, the life of an ancestor, Robert Graham of Gartmore). But most of his volumes are collections of tales and essays, many of which had previously appeared in magazines. Their ratio of reminiscence to invention is usually high; meditative recollection of his past travels and encounters often provides the basis. The more elegiac writing may now seem dated, but his sceptical wit and his eye for the incongruous provide ample pleasures. His most famous short pieces included 'Bloody Niggers' (a satiric foray published in the *Social-Democrat*, vol. 1, April 1897), *Aurora la Cujiñi* (first published as a booklet in 1898), 'A Hegira' and 'The Gold Fish' (in *Thirteen Stories*, 1900), and the frequently anthologized 'Beattock for Moffat' (in *Success*, 1902). Since the 1950s, his literary reputation has markedly declined: the enthusiasm for his work expressed by Conrad, Ford, Garnett, and Shaw was certainly influenced by their personal knowledge of a particularly picturesque, adventurous, and humane personality. Many of his shorter works were aptly called 'sketches', a term which may imply not only deft rapidity but also slightness. His histories and biographies are protracted by digressions and sprinkled with inaccuracies and proof errors (his handwriting was notoriously illegible). As D. H. Lawrence complained, he could be self-indulgent, repetitive, and slapdash (*The Calendar*, 3, 1927, 322–6). Today, his most rewarding longer works are probably *Mogreb-el-Acksa* and *A Vanished Arcadia*; the strongest of his collections is *Thirteen Stories*; and a convenient posthumous gathering is *Selected Writings of Cunninghame Graham* (1981). All of these manifest his sense of sympathy with the underdog and his desire to memorialize ways of life threatened by 'progress'. His writings as a whole constitute an immense and complex autobiography of a man whose combinations of radicalism and scepticism, of nostalgia and witty shrewdness, can often be engaging. He offers distinctive insights into past ways of life, whether on the heathland, on the pampas, in the desert, or at sea. As W. H. Hudson declared in his dedication of *El ombú*, he was 'singularísimo escritor inglés'—a most individualistic writer in English. Contemporaries were sometimes dazzled by him. G. K. Chesterton asserted: 'Cunninghame Graham achieved the adventure of being Cunninghame Graham … It is an achievement so fantastic that it would never be believed in romance' (G. K. Chesterton, *Autobiography*, 1936, 269). John Lavery, whose paintings Cunninghame Graham helped to promote, remarked: 'I think I did something to help Graham in the creation of his masterpiece—himself' (J. Lavery, *The Life of a Painter*, 1940, 92). The truth within the hyperboles is that though Cunninghame Graham was not pre-eminent as a writer, a politician, or an explorer, he was pre-eminent as a mercurially versatile personality whose direct and indirect contributions to literature and to British political evolution were substantial. If his friends and early biographers connived with him in exaggerating the romantic aspects of his life, those aspects (the exploratory energy, the combative panache, and the humane idealism) were genuinely there.

Cunninghame Graham had no children. On 24 October 1878 he married the young woman known as Gabrielle (or Gabriela) de la Balmondière, who claimed to be the Chilean-born daughter of a French father and a Spanish mother. Not until the 1980s did biographers learn that she was really Caroline Horsfall (*b.* 1859), from Masham in the North Riding of Yorkshire. Her writings include essays, poetic translations, and a substantial biography, *Santa Teresa* (1894). She died in 1906; her widower was eventually buried beside her in the grounds of the ruined Augustinian priory on Inchmahome in the Lake of Menteith in April 1936.

Among the many portraits of R. B. Cunninghame Graham are the full-length painting by John Lavery (1893) in the Art Gallery and Museum, Glasgow, and the portrait showing him on his horse Pampa, also by Lavery, in the Museo de Bellas Artes, Buenos Aires. The Dunedin Public Art Gallery, New Zealand, displays William Rothenstein's portrait of him as a fencer. There is a fine etching by William Strang (1898), who depicted him as Don Quixote in 1902. Two casts of a bronze head and shoulders by Albert Toft (1891) are displayed in Edinburgh and Glasgow, and two casts from a head vigorously sculpted by Jacob Epstein (1923) can be seen in Manchester City Galleries and in the Scottish National Portrait Gallery.   CEDRIC WATTS

Sources C. Watts and L. Davies, *Cunninghame Graham: a critical biography* (1979) · C. Watts, *R. B. Cunninghame Graham* (1983) · private information (2004) · H. F. West, *A modern conquistador: Robert Bontine Cunninghame Graham, his life and works* (1932) · A. F. Tschiffely, *Don Roberto* (1937) · H. MacDiarmid [C. M. Grieve], *Cunninghame Graham: a centenary study* [1952]
Archives Dartmouth College, Hanover, New Hampshire, Baker/Berry Library, corresp. and papers · London Library · NL Scot., corresp. and literary papers · NL Scot., letters · priv. coll. · Ransom HRC, papers · U. Mich., letters and MSS | BL, corresp. with J. E. Burns, Add. MSS 46284 · BL, letters to George Bernard Shaw, Add. MS 50531 · Harvard U., Houghton L., letters to Sir William Rothenstein · Mitchell L., Glas., letters to Frederick Niven · NL Scot., letters to John Macintyre · U. Leeds, Brotherton L., letters to Sir Edmund Gosse · U. Reading L., letters to the Bodley Head · University of Essex, Colchester, letters to S. L. Bensusan · W. Sussex RO, letters to Wilfrid Scawen Blunt
Likenesses T. Merry, cartoon, 1888, repro. in *St Stephen's Review* (23 Jan 1888) · A. Toft, bronze bust, 1891, Kelvingrove Art Gallery, Glasgow, Scot. NPG · J. Lavery, oils, 1893, Art Gallery and Museum, Glasgow [*see illus.*] · W. Rothenstein, lithograph, 1898, NPG · W. Strang, etching, 1898, NPG · W. Strang, etching, 1902, repro. in W. Strang, *Series of thirty etchings … illustrating subjects from 'Don Quixote'* (1902) · T. B. Wirgman, chalk drawing, 1918, NPG · E. Kapp, drawing, 1919, Barber Institute of Fine Arts, Birmingham · M. Beerbohm, six caricature studies, 1921, Dartmouth College, Hanover, New Hampshire · J. Epstein, bronze heads, 1923, Aberdeen Art Gallery, Man. City Gall., Scot. NPG · J. McBey, oils, 1934, NPG · M. Beerbohm, caricature, repro. in *Academy*, 56 (1899), 117 · M. Beerbohm, oil caricature, U. Texas · H. Furniss, pen-and-ink sketch, NPG · L. Hunter, crayon and wash drawing, Scot. NPG · G. W. Lambert, pencil drawing, NPG · J. Lavery, oils, Museo de Bellas Artes de la Boca, Buenos Aires, Argentina · F. Pegram, pencil sketch, V&A; repro. in *Pictorial World* (6 Dec 1888) · W. Rothenstein, portrait, Dunedin Public Art Gallery, New Zealand · Spy [L. Ward], caricature, chromolithograph, NPG; repro. in *VF*, 20 (1888), 549 · Stuart, photograph, NPG
Wealth at death £100,647 1*s.* 6*d.*: confirmation, 19 July 1936, *CGPLA Eng. & Wales* · £1—additional estate: 22 Oct 1936, *CCI*

Graham, Sir Ronald William (1870–1949), diplomat, was born in London on 24 July 1870, the elder son of Sir Henry John Lowndes Graham, who became clerk of parliaments, and his first wife, Edith Elizabeth, daughter of Gathorne Gathorne-*Hardy, first earl of Cranbrook (1814–1906). Graham was educated at Eton College, where he won the prince consort's prize for French, and then studied abroad for two years. Nominated attaché in the diplomatic service early in 1892, he passed a competitive examination three months later and in the following year was posted for duty to Paris. In 1894 he was promoted third secretary and passed an examination in public law. He transferred to Tehran in 1897 as second secretary, and to St Petersburg two years later. He then spent four years in the eastern department of the Foreign Office, during which he served as British agent before the Muscat arbitration tribunal at The Hague (1905) and went on special service to Crete in 1906. In April 1904 he was one of seven old Etonians to attain the rank of first secretary.

Graham was appointed to Cairo in 1907 with the rank in the diplomatic service of counsellor of embassy. For the following seven years he helped to pilot British interests through a complicated period in Anglo-Egyptian relations, and for several periods acted as British agent and consul-general. After the political crisis marked by the assassination of the Coptic prime minister, Boutros Pasha, in 1910 he was seconded as adviser to the ministry of the interior in the Egyptian government. He was faced with new problems on the outbreak of war in 1914 when Egypt was still nominally under the suzerainty of Turkey but occupied by the British. In November 1914 Graham was appointed by Sir John Maxwell, the general officer commanding troops in Egypt, to act for him with the Egyptian administrative authorities with the rank of a chief staff officer. Graham continued in these duties until the safety of the Suez Canal had been assured. He was mentioned in dispatches and received the grand cordon of the order of the Nile.

In 1912 Graham married Sybil (*d.* 1934), daughter of (William) St John Fremantle *Brodrick, ninth Viscount (later first earl of) Midleton (1856–1942), and the first four years of their happily married life were spent in Egypt where his wife began social services which were to play an important part in Graham's diplomatic missions throughout his career. He returned to London in 1916 to take up duties at the Foreign Office as assistant under-secretary of state. He was a member of the empire cotton-growing committee (1917–19) and was acting permanent under-

Sir Ronald William Graham (1870–1949), by Walter Stoneman, 1933

secretary of state while Lord Hardinge of Penshurst attended the Paris peace conference in 1919. Later in that year he was sent as minister-plenipotentiary to The Hague, serving also as minister to the duchy of Luxembourg.

In November 1921 Graham was sworn of the privy council and went as ambassador to Rome, where he remained until he retired from the diplomatic service in 1933. During this unusually long tenure of office he was confronted by problems arising out of one of the more turbulent periods in the history of the kingdom of Italy. He found a nation bitterly disillusioned with the interpretation of the treaty of Versailles so far as Italy's share of the spoils of war was concerned; a people distracted by a succession of governments unable to curb sanguinary conflicts between communists and fascists; while Fiume was still defiantly occupied by partisans of the militant poet Gabriele d'Annunzio. When the king of Italy as a desperate resolve called Mussolini to the premiership after the fascist 'march on Rome' in 1922, Graham had the delicate task of seeking a renewal of Italian confidence in her wartime allies, Britain and France. Mussolini was persuaded to visit London at the end of 1922 for allied talks on reparations, when he informed the other premiers that Italy would consider reparations and war debts as one inseparable problem. Graham saw Anglo-Italian friendship popularly confirmed in the following year by the visit to Italy of King George V and Queen Mary, when he was invested with the GCVO and received the order of St Maurice and St

Lazarus from the king of Italy. But the progressively dictatorial methods of Mussolini in both home and foreign affairs made Graham's mandate to maintain and safeguard friendship with Italy increasingly difficult—and, as far as foreign alliances were concerned, essential. The strain of these relationships was deftly concealed in the social life which he and Lady Graham developed at the embassy, where Mussolini was several times guest in the earlier years of his regime.

Graham was active in negotiations which led to a pact of entente and collaboration between the four western powers of Britain, Italy, France, and Germany. The proposal for such a four-power pact was formally put forward by Mussolini in March 1933. Four months later a text acceptable to all the powers concerned was successfully negotiated. One of Graham's last acts was to sign on behalf of his country on 15 July, for he retired in November of the same year.

Six months after leaving Rome, Graham was left a widower. There were no children. He was British government director of the Suez Canal Company from 1939 to 1945 and chairman of the Lincolnshire and Central Electricity Supply Company from 1939 to 1948. A trustee of the British Museum from 1937, he was on its standing committee until his death in London on 26 January 1949. In addition to his other honours he was appointed CB (1910), GCB (1932), KCMG (1915), and GCMG (1926).

I. S. MUNRO, *rev.*

Sources *The Times* (27 Jan 1949) · personal knowledge (1959) · *WWW* · *CGPLA Eng. & Wales* (1949)
Archives Bodl. Oxf., corresp. with Rumbold · CUL, corresp. with Lord Hardinge | FILM BFI NFTVA, documentary footage
Likenesses W. Stoneman, photograph, 1933, NPG [*see illus.*]
Wealth at death £79,953 7s.: probate, 25 March 1949, *CGPLA Eng. & Wales*

Graham, Rose (1875–1963), historian, was born into a cultured Victorian family (her mother had been acquainted with William Makepeace Thackeray in her youth) on 16 August 1875 at 5 St Andrew's Place, Marylebone, London, the only daughter of William Edgar Graham, a decorator, upholsterer, and furniture maker, and his wife, Jane, the daughter of Thomas Newton. Jane Graham was much concerned with the foundation of girls' high schools, and sent her daughter to Notting Hill high school (1887–94), which was then led by a progressive headmistress who encouraged her more capable pupils to continue their education at university. With her mother's approval, she went on to Somerville College, Oxford (1894–8), where she took a second in the school of modern history in 1897. After Oxford degrees were opened to women, she took her BA and MA in 1920. She became a DLitt of Oxford in 1929, and was elected an honorary fellow of Somerville in 1933. Her years at Oxford were very happy, and she retained a deep affection for Somerville College all her life, regaling students in her later years with stories of life in a women's college in the 1890s.

When Graham came down from Oxford, her mother,

who was proud of her work, persuaded her not to take a teaching post but to continue with historical research. In her last year at Oxford she had begun working under the direction of Reginald Lane Poole, and in 1901 she published a book on St Gilbert of Sempringham and the Gilbertines. This was the first of her many books on medieval ecclesiastical history (her article 'The annals of the monastery of the Holy Trinity at Vendôme' appeared in the *English Historical Review* in 1898). That subject, and in particular English and continental monastic history, became her life interest.

Graham was widely travelled, and her frequent visits to the continent, many of them in the company of her mother, led to a number of important studies on the orders of Cluny and Grandmont and their English houses. Her second book, *An Abbot of Vézelay*, was written after a series of visits to France immediately before the First World War, and was published in 1918. She returned to France many times, particularly to southern Burgundy and to Alsace (her article 'The order of St. Antoine de Viennois and its English commandery, St. Anthony's, Threadneedle Street', which appeared in the *Archaeological Journal* in 1927, was the result of several visits to the museum in Colmar).

In 1924 Graham attended a council meeting of the Canterbury and York Society. To her surprise and consternation she came away as its honorary general editor (she had not been consulted). Nevertheless, she remained editor until 1958. In 1952, under the aegis of the society, she published the first volume of an edition of *Archbishop Winchelsey's Register*, the object of many years' work. The second and final volume appeared in 1956. She served as president of the British Archaeological Society from 1945 to 1951 and as vice-president from 1952 to 1963. In addition to her scholarly talents, she proved a capable administrator with a keen business acumen.

Graham accumulated a number of awards and honours throughout her life. In 1903 she was awarded the Royal Historical Society's Alexander prize for her essay 'The intellectual influence of English monasticism between the tenth and twelfth centuries'. On 3 June 1920 she was one of the first two women (the other was Eugénie Sellers Strong) to be elected a fellow of the Society of Antiquaries *honoris causa*. She served several times on the society's council, and contributed at least two papers, subsequently published in *Archaeologia*. In 1934 she was appointed a member of the Royal Commission on Historical Monuments, and in 1939 she was made CBE. Out of admiration for her work and the friendships she inspired and maintained, twelve of her colleagues contributed essays to a Festschrift, *Medieval Studies Presented to Rose Graham* (1950).

Graham cultivated friendships with many of the most important early and mid-twentieth-century medievalists, including F. M. Powicke, David Knowles, and E. F. Jacob. She is especially remembered for her kindness and encouragement of younger scholars. Known affectionately as Auntie Rose for her approachability and keen interest in her students' work, she none the less intimidated many with her immense learning, and also with her deafness. A lifelong resident of London, she died there in St Bartholomew's Hospital on 29 July 1963.

EMILY J. HORNING

Sources *The Times* (31 July 1963) · *The Times* (2 Aug 1963) · A. W. Clapham, foreword, *Medieval studies presented to Rose Graham*, ed. V. Ruffer and A. J. Taylor (1950) · L. E. Tanner, memorial address, delivered 25 Oct 1963, *Journal of the British Archaeological Association*, 3rd ser., 27 (1964), 1–3 · private information (2004) [former student of Rose Graham] · *Somerville College register, 1879–1971* [1972] · b. cert. · d. cert.
Archives Somerville College, Oxford
Likenesses Bassano, photograph, *c*.1950, repro. in Ruffer and Taylor, eds., *Medieval studies*

Graham, (William) Sydney (1918–1986), poet, was born in Greenock, Renfrewshire, on 19 November 1918, the elder child and elder son of Alexander Graham (1884–1954), marine engineer, of Greenock, and his wife, Margaret McDermid (1882–1940), shopkeeper. After leaving Greenock high school at fourteen, he completed an apprenticeship in engineering. In 1938–9 he attended Newbattle Abbey Adult Education Residential College, near Edinburgh, where he responded enthusiastically to the literature and philosophy courses. Early Scottish and Anglo-Saxon literature, modern writers including James Joyce, Ezra Pound, and T. S. Eliot, pre-Socratic philosophers, and Martin Heidegger were important influences, to which he later added Arthur Rimbaud, Marianne Moore, and Samuel Beckett.

After casual jobs in Ireland, Graham became a munitions engineer in Glasgow for a time during the Second World War, when he wrote *The Seven Journeys* (published later in 1944). David Archer, a publisher and philanthropist, provided him with practical support, publishing *Cage without Grievance* (1942) and facilitating lively friendships in Glasgow and London with, among others, Jankel Adler, Robert Colquhoun, Robert MacBryde, Dylan Thomas, and (F.) John Minton. Bohemian life promoted both Graham's development and heavy drinking. Published in 1945, *2ND Poems* (a play on the words 'To Nessie Dunsmuir') continued the intense, romantic, semi-surreal language which both he and Dylan Thomas had derived in part from Joyce. Graham valued his early work (omissions from the *Collected Poems, 1942–1977*, 1979, arose from misunderstandings about available space), which was intelligently evaluated by the critic Vivienne Koch in American journals. She became a close friend. His Atlantic award for literature in 1947 and his teaching at New York University in 1947–8 increased his circle of friends. He also visited Greece in 1964 and 1977 and Iceland in the 1960s; some of his poems drew on those experiences.

Faber and Faber accepted *The White Threshold* (1949) and became Graham's principal publishers. T. S. Eliot, a director there, admired his excellent knowledge and craftsmanship and said at one of their meetings that Graham's poetry was difficult and would sell slowly because people did not like to think. His work certainly required the reader's full attention, which he gained at his impressive public readings in Britain and abroad, by the moving dramatic art and clarity of his definitive delivery. *The Nightfishing* (1955), *Malcolm Mooney's Land* (1970), and *Implements in their Places* (1977), the last two both Poetry Book Society choices, deployed a language increasingly transparent and exactly tuned to explore the essential separateness of each human experience in a world of flux. They displayed the desperate need to communicate, and the obdurate strangeness of language itself as medium and metaphor. Graham's themes were developed through sharply observed images, highly personal and presented with urgency through a musical poetry rich in structure and feeling. The work, like his own voice, had a Scottish timbre. The originality with which he enlivened and disturbed language was that of a thoroughly radical, modern, international tradition. This work, taken together with his simpler, lyrical pieces, made his achievement outstanding and of permanent importance.

Graham's poems, which did not fit any of the prevailing fashions, but nevertheless attracted a constant interest among serious readers, were published by several magazines in Britain, North America, and Europe, and were broadcast by the BBC. After 1944 Graham lived chiefly in Cornwall, often writing during the night after evenings spent with friends or literary visitors in his local pub. His work's excellence, together with his own professional integrity, inspired support from a number of friends, poets, and painters who gave practical help or bought manuscripts. His remarkable letters, mostly in private hands, run parallel to his poetry, showing his loneliness, need to communicate, and deep feeling for his many friends. They throw light on his working methods, often containing verse and detailed criticism. Full of word play, they are startling, honest, sharp, and deeply humorous. He concentrated on poetry almost exclusively, having worked only very briefly on the land, as a copywriter, fisherman, or auxiliary coastguard when living at Gurnard's Head in Cornwall. Small grants from the Arts Council helped and a civil-list pension of £500 a year was granted him in 1974.

Graham had curly dark hair, very piercing blue eyes, and was 5 feet 8 inches in height with a slim physique. He loved music and had a good singing voice. Proud to be Scottish, he was witty, positive, and assertive, dominating conversations and demanding patience from his friends, which was usually freely given. His generosity of spirit inspired much affection and respect. In October 1954 he married Agnes (Nessie) Kilpatrick (1909–1999), daughter of David Dunsmuir, miner, of Blantyre. They had no children, but Graham acknowledged a daughter, Rosalind, born in 1944 to Mary Harris. Agnes had been a fellow student at Newbattle. During their close relationship they lived in distinctly spartan conditions; she provided material as well as moral support and always steadfast encouragement. From 1967 they lived at 4 Mountview Cottages, Madron, Cornwall, where Graham died from cancer, after a long illness, on 9 January 1986. He was cremated at Truro crematorium, Cornwall, and his ashes were scattered on the River Clyde, Scotland.

MICHAEL SEWARD SNOW, *rev.*

Sources J. Davidson and R. Duncan, *The constructed space: a celebration of the poet W. S. Graham* (1994) · T. Lopez, *The poetry of W. S. Graham* (1989) · *The nightfisherman: selected letters of W. S. Graham*, ed. M. Snow and M. Snow (1999) · personal knowledge (1996) · private information (1996) [Nessie Graham] · *The Times* (14 Jan 1986) · *The Guardian* (14 Jan 1986) · *Glasgow Herald* (15 Jan 1986) · *The Cornishman* (16 Jan 1986) · *Irish Times* (20 Jan 1986) · *The Scotsman* (25 Jan 1986)
Archives National Archives of Canada, Ottawa · NL Scot., corresp. and literary papers · Ransom HRC · Royal College of Art, London · UCL | JRL, corresp. with Michael Schmidt · NL Scot., letters to Sven Berlin · NL Scot., letters to J. F. Hendry · NL Scot., letters to William Montgomerie and Norah Montgomerie · NL Scot., letters to Ruth Rosen with associated corresp. · NL Scot., letters to R. Crombie Saunders · University of Victoria, British Columbia, Macpherson Library, MSS and literary papers |SOUND BBC Sound archives, poetry readings 1960, 1968, 1978
Likenesses M. Snow, photographs, repro. in *The nightfisherman*, ed. Snow and Snow · photograph, repro. in C. Barker, ed., *Portraits of poets* (1986)

Graham, Thomas, Baron Lynedoch (1748–1843), army officer, was born on 19 October 1748, reportedly at Newton of Blairgowrie, Perthshire, the mansion house of a property belonging to his father; he was the third son and only surviving child of Thomas Graeme, of Balgowan (d. 1766), and his wife, Lady Christian Hope, the sixth daughter of Charles, first earl of Hopetoun. Educated at home by private tutors, one of whom was James Macpherson, the translator of *Ossian*, in November 1766 Graham entered Christ Church, Oxford, as a gentleman commoner, but he left in 1768 without having taken a degree. After making a grand tour of Europe between 1768 and 1771, in 1772 Graham was a parliamentary candidate for Perthshire at a by-election on the independent list against the dominant Atholl interest, but he was defeated by a brother of the duke of Atholl. On 26 December 1774, in a joint ceremony, he married Mary (1757–1792), the second daughter of Charles, ninth Lord Cathcart, while her eldest sister, Jane, married John Murray, fourth duke of Atholl.

When not touring the continent the Grahams lived in Leicestershire. However, although Mary was admired for her beauty and was twice painted by Gainsborough in the mid-1770s, her constitution was so delicate that, from 1780, hoping that the climate would improve it, the Grahams resided some years in the Iberian peninsula. They then returned to Scotland, where, on 3 September 1785, Graham participated in the first recorded cricket match there, scoring forty runs over two innings, the highest tally. In 1787 he bought the small estate of Lynedoch (or Lednoch) in Methven parish, 8 miles from Perth, and invested heavily in its development. A country sports enthusiast and keen agriculturalist, he greatly improved the local husbandry, introducing Cleveland horses and Devon cattle. In the 1780s he developed strong whig sympathies, and he joined Brooks's in 1783 and the Whig Club in 1785.

Mary's health, however, continued to weaken, and the Grahams—a loving but childless couple—returned to the

Thomas Graham, Baron Lynedoch (1748–1843), by Sir Thomas Lawrence, 1813

continent in 1790. She died of consumption at sea off Hyères on 26 June 1792, and he never ceased to mourn her. The disrespectful treatment of her body by the French revolutionary authorities—at Toulouse her coffin was broken open by drunken officials in search of contraband—embittered Graham, who became an ardent Francophobe and supporter of the war. He joined Lord Hood's fleet as a volunteer when it docked at Gibraltar in July 1793 and acted as Lord Mulgrave's aide during the siege of Toulon (1793). On returning to Scotland he raised the Perthshire Volunteers, the 90th foot, who were styled light infantry, albeit unofficially. Graham was commissioned as the regiment's lieutenant-colonel commandant on 10 February 1794, and Rowland (later Lord) Hill was designated its lieutenant-colonel. Kenneth Mackenzie, later Sir Kenneth Douglas, was one of the unit's majors; during the Napoleonic wars he acquired the reputation of being Britain's premier trainer of light infantry, and his early work with the 90th was widely admired, not least by Sir John Moore.

In April 1794 Graham was elected MP for the county of Perth, though his military service continued to preoccupy him, and he is not known to have spoken or voted in the house between 1794 and 1803. After serving with the 90th in the defence of southern England and in the Quiberon and Isle Dieu operations under Sir John Doyle, he accompanied it to Gibraltar. Appointed brevet colonel on 22 July 1795, he served as British military commissioner with the Austrian army in Italy and found himself trapped with General Wurmser's forces when Mantua came under siege. Having volunteered to go in search of help, Graham managed to slip through the French lines on 29 December 1796 and—through courage, perseverance, and luck—reached the Austrian headquarters five days later. Following a period at home he returned to active service with the 90th, distinguishing himself during the capture of Minorca (1798) before taking command of the garrison of Messina. Appointed brigadier-general, he then conducted the siege of Valletta, Malta, for most of its two-year duration. Superseded by Major-General Pigot, he witnessed the city's surrender (1799) before leaving Malta for Egypt and the 90th. His regiment had performed well in recent fighting. With the Egyptian campaign all but concluded, he returned home via Constantinople and, following the peace of Amiens, Paris.

After a period in Ireland, the 90th was sent to the West Indies. Graham, meanwhile, concentrated on his parliamentary activities. His first recorded speech was delivered on 3 April 1806 and concerned the terms of military service. He voted against Addington's ministry in the divisions which defeated it (April 1804), and supported Pitt's second ministry. Predictably, his whiggish independence did little to help the furtherance of his career in either politics or the army. Atholl turned against him and brought forward his son, so Graham did not stand in the 1807 election, and his seat passed to James Drummond, who retained it in 1812. For much of the intervening period Graham strove to get his military rank made permanent; having acquired it by raising a regiment, his commission was temporary and, despite his achievements, he was not entitled to the privileges enjoyed by regular officers, such as half pay during periods of leave. However, he had a formidable opponent at the horse guards: Frederick, duke of York, the commander-in-chief, not only was wary of deviating from the established principles on granting commissions but had also apparently been offended by Graham's perceived or actual opinions. Although he assured him that he was acting purely in keeping with his sense of public duty, York repeatedly rejected Graham's petitions for a permanent commission and, during the ephemeral peace of Amiens, came close to removing him from the army altogether.

Whether rooted in personal and political animosity or purely in professional considerations, York's resistance was not overcome until 1809, and then only because of a plea attributed to Sir John Moore, an old admirer of the 90th, who had turned to Kenneth Mackenzie for assistance in training the prototype light infantry regiments he had forged at Shorncliffe camp. Graham accompanied Moore to Sweden and Spain in 1808 and was among the few who witnessed Moore's heroic death and burial in the wake of the battle of Corunna (January 1809). Moore's successor, Lieutenant-General John Hope, told York that it was Sir John's dying wish that Graham's services be acknowledged by the granting of a full commission. Although Moore was more of a whig than Graham, and there were those in the cabinet who had been plotting his replacement as commander of the forces in the Iberian peninsula by Lord Moira, in the light of the circumstances surrounding his death, and the political storm that erupted in the aftermath of the Corunna campaign's failure, York acceded to the request. In 1809 Graham may have been informally offered, and declined, command of the Portuguese army.

His rank of major-general made permanent in 1809 (antedated to 1803), Graham was entrusted with a brigade in the disastrous Walcheren expedition (1809). Invalided home, he was subsequently sent, as a lieutenant-general (1810), to Cadiz to command the garrison's British contingent, at the head of which he attacked the investing French forces under Marshal Claude Victor. This foray culminated, on 5 March 1811, in the battle of Barrosa, which, though a significant tactical victory, yielded no strategic results, just bitter recriminations within the allied camp. Graham complained, with some justification, that the 10,000 strong Spanish contingent under General Manuel La Peña, who was supposed to be in command of the joint force, should have assisted the British in attacking the French rather than staying timidly on the defensive. This was not the first time that La Peña had abandoned a colleague, and the episode added to the acrimony in Anglo-Spanish relations. Indeed, Graham now invoked the discretionary instructions given him by his government not to commit his own soldiers to operations in which he did not enjoy supreme command. He also declined a Spanish dukedom.

Having eventually relinquished command of the British at Cadiz to General Cooke, Graham joined the main body of Wellington's army in June 1811. Initially he had been rather critical and dismissive of Wellington, a tory, suspecting that his appointment as commander of the British forces in the peninsula owed more to political connections than to his martial skill. By this time, however, Wellington was emerging as the most adroit British general since Marlborough, and Graham's admiration steadily increased; Wellington reciprocated. Graham was brave, charming, popular with his troops—an address from the guards after Barrosa called him 'Our Father and our Friend' (Delavoye, 509)—an intrepid rider and keen fox-hunter, and, despite his ill health and poor eyesight, one of the best among Wellington's peninsular subordinates, though he had limitations as a commander.

At the head of the first division, Graham participated in the siege and capture of Ciudad Rodrigo (January 1812). His investiture as KB in March 1812 (on the extension of the order he became GCB in 1815) and the decision to entrust him with control of a corps of three infantry divisions and two cavalry brigades testified both to his abilities and to Wellington's confidence in him. However, a painful eye complaint—reportedly from repeatedly using a spyglass in bright sunlight and much writing by candlelight—obliged him to leave for Britain in July 1812. Six months later he returned, though still not fully cured, and assumed command of Wellington's left wing, some 40,000 troops, seeing action at Vitoria (21 June 1813) and at Tolosa. He was wounded at the latter, while at the former he was curiously quiescent. Despite being urged to press his adversaries vigorously, he failed to commit many of his 20,000 men to the fighting, contenting himself with a very limited attack in the vicinity of the Gamarra bridge. He later maintained that the enemy's position and forces appeared too strong to risk a serious assault here, but this does not explain why he neglected to explore other, easier avenues of approach. Certainly he allowed himself to be contained by a force much weaker than his own. He failed to cut the easterly road out of Vitoria and so cut off 50,000 French troops: according to Michael Glover, 'if he had done so Vitoria would have been one of the most overwhelming victories of all time' (Glover, 205). His eyesight, which still seems to have been impaired, doubtless played a part in his failure fully to comprehend the situation before him, as did the complexity of Wellington's strategy and the insufficient clarity of Wellington's orders. Wellington called for the timely co-ordination of the movement of several columns, some of which had to advance over very difficult countryside. In fact Graham was not the only senior subordinate who did not fulfil all Wellington's expectations that day. As a result of delays imposed by adverse terrain and compounded by hesitancy, the force under Lord Dalhousie also failed to conform with both the spirit and the letter of Wellington's original plan.

Such 'friction', as Clausewitz termed it, was part of the sheer intractability of war. Yet, for all these shortcomings Vitoria was a great victory that all but ousted the French from northern Spain and exposed the south of France to invasion. Entrusted with capturing French-held San Sebastian, Graham sustained a serious reverse in his first attempt and was saved from defeat a second time only by the close support his siege batteries gave to the attack columns. Seeing the assault stalling, he ordered his heavy guns to fire over the infantry at the fortress's high curtain wall, then crowded with French troops. This dangerous venture was undertaken with consummate skill; the defenders sustained terrible losses, whereas few if any allied soldiers were killed. With insufficient manpower left to hold the breaches or their internal defences, the remaining French were pushed back into the citadel on Monte Urgall, to which they clung for a few days more before capitulating on 8 September 1813.

The allies pressed on over the River Bidassoa. Barely had Graham led his troops across, however, than his health again failed and he returned once more to Britain. In November 1813 the Dutch revolted against the French, and invited back William, the prince of Orange, who in December returned, with British support, from exile in England. Graham, recuperated, had agreed to command a British force for the Netherlands, but very reluctantly, as he saw little hope of glory and considerable risk of disgrace in an expedition whose task was as much political as military. He was given an improvised force of mostly inferior units, 'a very bad army' (Muir, 308), which reached the Netherlands on 17 December. He was victorious at Merxem, but was repulsed with heavy losses in the assault on the fortress of Bergen-op-Zoom in March 1814. He was mortified by this defeat, but the ministers and army exonerated and praised him.

After Napoleon's first abdication in 1814, Graham

returned home to great acclaim. He received Portuguese, Spanish, and Netherlands honours, and in May 1814 he was made Baron Lynedoch of Balgowan, in the county of Perth, with a pension of £2000 a year. He was rector of Glasgow University from 1813 to 1815. A full general from 1821 and governor of Dumbarton Castle from 1829, he also became colonel of, successively, the 58th foot in 1823, the 14th foot from 1826, and the 1st foot in 1834. From 1815 onwards he was active in the establishment and promotion of a London club for naval and army officers. Although this was dismissed as a politically dangerous notion by the earl of St Vincent, among others, a branch committee was created at Lord Hill's headquarters with the army of occupation in France, and, crucially, Wellington's support was secured. The United Service Club was duly established and purchased its first premises in Pall Mall in 1817.

After another lengthy visit to the continent, which included receptions in St Petersburg, Moscow, and Vienna—he was a friend of Marshal Johann Joseph Radetsky—Graham acquired Cotsgrove Lodge in Leicestershire, from where he pursued his love of country sports and European travel. He regularly voted in the House of Lords, in person or by proxy, in support of Catholic emancipation, parliamentary reform, and other liberal legislation, and acted as the duke of Bedford's second in his duel with the duke of Buckingham in 1822. When aged eighty-five he was offered command of the Portuguese army. In May 1837 he was made GCMG. His interest in farming and stock-breeding also persisted; he spent a part of each autumn at Lynedoch and he was regularly a prize winner of the Highland and Agricultural Society of Scotland. Queen Victoria was among those who congratulated him on his success at Epsom in 1839, where Jeffy, a two-year-old colt he had bred, won a plate, a feat he was to repeat at Newmarket in 1842. When the queen visited Scotland shortly after her marriage, Graham hurried back from Switzerland to join in formally welcoming her to Edinburgh.

Graham had now suffered from poor health in general and from cataracts in particular for some time; he sought relief in homoeopathy and, increasingly, in Italy's climate. However, he died at his town house, 12 Stratton Street, Piccadilly, London, on 18 December 1843. At his request, his funeral was simple. A steamer carried his coffin to Dundee, whence it was taken through Perth to Methven churchyard. There he was laid to rest in the mausoleum that already contained the remains of his mother and his beloved wife.   DAVID GATES

Sources J. Philippart, ed., *The royal military calendar*, 3rd edn, 2 (1820) · *GM*, 2nd ser., 21 (1844), 197 · D. Gates, *The British light infantry army* (1987) · A. Brett-James, *General Graham* (1959) · A. M. Delavoye, *Life of Thomas Graham, Lord Lynedoch* (1880) · C. Aspinall-Oglander, *Freshly remembered: the story of Thomas Graham, Lord Lynedoch* (1956) · HoP, *Commons, 1790–1820* · M. E. Graham, *The beautiful Mrs Graham and the Cathcart circle* (1927) · C. T. Atkinson, ed., *Supplementary report on the manuscripts of Robert Graham esq. of Fintry*, HMC, 81 (1940) · M. Glover, *Wellington as military commander* (1973) · R. Muir, *Britain and the defeat of Napoleon, 1807–1815* (1996) · M. I. Fry and G. Davies, 'Wellington's officers in the D.N.B.', *Journal of the Society for Army Historical Research*, 33 (1955), 126–7 · C. D. Hall, *British strategy in the Napoleonic War, 1803–15* (1999)

Archives Duke U., Perkins L., letters · NA Scot., corresp. and papers · NL Scot., corresp. and papers · NRA, priv. coll., corresp. · U. Edin. L., letter-book | All Souls Oxf., letters to Sir Charles Vaughan · BL, corresp. with Lord Hill, Add. MSS 35059–35060 · BL, letters to Sir John Moore, Add. MS 57541 · BL, letters to Lord Nelson, Add. MSS 34911–34917, *passim* · BL, letters to Lord Spencer · NA Scot., letters to Sir Alexander Hope · NA Scot., letters to lords Melville · NL Scot., corresp. with Kenneth Mackenzie [copies] · NL Scot., letters to Lord Methven · NMM, letters to Sir Watkin Pell · NRA, priv. coll., corresp. with Lord Cathcart · PRO NIre., corresp. with Lord Castlereagh · U. Durham L., letters to second Earl Grey · Woburn Abbey, Bedfordshire, letters to Lord George William Russell

Likenesses P. Batoni, oils, 1772, Yale U. CBA · S. W. Reynolds, mezzotint, pubd 1802 (after J. Hoppner), BM, NPG · T. Lawrence, portrait, 1813; Christies, 15 Nov 1996, lot 35 [*see illus.*] · coloured etching, pubd 1816, NPG · T. Lawrence, oils, 1817, Wellington Museum, Apsley House, London · G. Hayter, oils, *c.*1820, NPG · T. Lawrence, oils, *c.*1820; formerly at United Service Club, London · T. Webb and G. Mills, copper medal, 1820 (after P. Rouw junior), Scot. NPG · G. Hayter, oils, 1822, Scot. NPG · plaster medallion (after T. Webb), Scot. NPG

Graham, Thomas (1805–1869), chemist, was born on 21 December 1805 at 55 St Andrew's Square, Glasgow, the second of the seven children of James Graham (1776–1842), a prosperous Glasgow merchant and manufacturer of light woven fabrics for the West Indies, and his wife, Margaret (1775–1830), *née* Paterson. He remained close to his family and never married. His education started in 1811 at Angus's 'English' preparatory school in Glasgow. In 1814 he entered Glasgow grammar school and at the age of thirteen he proceeded to Glasgow University to study arts. His course concluded in 1823/4 with chemistry under Thomas Thomson, from whom Graham first imbibed a relish for the subject, and natural philosophy under William Meikleham. In April 1824 Graham graduated MA and remained at Glasgow University for a further two years.

Graham's father wanted him to follow in the footsteps of his uncle John and great-uncle James, who were both Church of Scotland ministers at Killearn, Stirlingshire. He therefore enrolled from 1824 to 1826 in divinity classes, but in fact worked at natural philosophy and chemistry, presenting a paper on the absorption of gases by liquids to the university chemical society in September 1825. Determined to make chemistry his career despite strong opposition from his father, he persuaded him that divinity was taught better at Edinburgh University so that he could attend that university as a medical student. He began studying medicine at Edinburgh in May 1826 with the covert acquiescence of his mother and of his devoted sister Margaret (1803–1865).

Graham worked in the Edinburgh University chemical laboratory under his friend G. D. Longstaff. In 1828 he became a fellow of the Royal Society of Edinburgh and he deputized for the extramural chemistry lecturer, Edward Turner. However, Graham's father became impatient at his son's failure to take up preaching and cut off all his financial support. Graham returned to Glasgow in November 1828 and supported himself by teaching mathematics extramurally. In February 1829 he started to offer classes

Thomas Graham (1805–1869), by Maull & Polyblank, *c*.1855

in practical chemistry at Portland Street. With the availability of a laboratory he was able to investigate gaseous diffusion, platinum catalysis, the glow of phosphorus, and the action of charcoal on solutions. He also gave evening lectures on chemistry and mechanics at the Glasgow Mechanics' Institution.

To become a university teacher in chemistry (for which he required medical recognition) Graham submitted an essay on gaseous diffusion to the faculty of physicians and surgeons of Glasgow, and was elected a member of the faculty in August 1830. He became professor of chemistry at Anderson's Institution, Glasgow, in September 1830. Thus he attained secure employment and reconciliation with his father. He lectured on chemistry to a wide audience including medical students, ladies' classes, and mechanics. Graham possessed a quiet, rather stiff, and hesitant manner but he was an enthusiastic and ambitious chemist.

In 1831 Graham read a paper to the Royal Society of Edinburgh in which he showed that, at constant pressure, the rate of diffusion of a gas was inversely proportional to the square root of its density. For this discovery he won the society's Keith prize; the principle has become known as 'Graham's law'. He then examined the different roles of water in compounds. Following Berzelius's lead that water might assume the role of an acid or a base Graham distinguished the three phosphoric acids by their different degrees of hydration or basicity. Turner read Graham's paper to the Royal Society of London in June 1833. Significantly, this was the first paper in *Philosophical Transactions* to use Berzelian symbols. Berzelius praised it, but preferred to explain the existence of three phosphoric

acids by isomerism. Graham believed this interpretation was wrong and he attacked Berzelius's theory at the 1834 Edinburgh meeting of the British Association for the Advancement of Science. However, he supported Berzelian symbolism despite the fierce opposition of the senior English chemist, John Dalton. He also discussed the spontaneous flammability of phosphine and the role of water in the constitution of salts. Graham became a fellow of the Royal Society of London in December 1836, by which date he was recognized as a chemist of European stature. He was awarded its royal medal in 1838 and 1850, and the Copley medal in 1862.

In June 1837 Graham was appointed professor of chemistry at University College, London. He gave 150 lectures annually and by 1855 had taught chemistry to more than 2700, mainly medical, students. His carefully written and influential text book *Elements of Chemistry* was issued in six parts between 1837 and 1841 and it was translated into German by Otto in 1844.

Graham actively promoted chemistry within the British Association from 1837 to 1845, and was secretary from 1839 of the influential chemical committee of the Royal Society. In 1841 he helped to establish the Chemical Society of London, and he was its president in 1841–3 and 1845–7. He also presided over the Cavendish Society, founded in 1846 to publish translations of foreign chemical works.

From 1842 Graham acted as unofficial chemical adviser to the government. He analysed tobacco for possible adulteration and after several prosecutions he claimed that the duty from tobacco had risen by about £300,000. He also reported on malt duty, ventilation of parliament, casting iron guns, disinfectants, sugar refining, London's water supply, chemistry at the Great Exhibition, the fire on the steamship *Amazon*, the original gravity of beer, coffee adulteration, methylated spirit, and Dundonald's Crimean War plan. He was a chemical witness at patent trials of paraffin oil and rubber vulcanization. In his chemical researches he attempted to understand the chemistry of diabetes. He concluded that the disease was caused by deficient oxidation of sugar during respiration, but the ultimate cause eluded him.

Graham was a pioneer in physical chemistry. He extended his researches on gaseous diffusion and he was able to make a clear distinction between effusion and transpiration (or viscous flow) of gases. In 1848 he began his liquid diffusion studies and found that there was no simple connection between diffusion speed and molecular weight for liquids. In 1852, faced with a wilderness of facts on osmosis, he coined the neologisms osmose, osmotic force, and osmometer. He explained that osmosis was liquid diffusion accompanied by osmose, or water, flowing in the opposite direction through a membrane.

In 1857 Bunsen disputed Graham's diffusion law. Belatedly, in 1863, the latter showed that Bunsen was mistaken. Graham now used graphite instead of stucco for diffusion and emphasized the essential differences between the three modes of gas motion—diffusion, effusion, and transpiration. He also developed atmolysis to separate gaseous mixtures through rubber, clay, and metals, which led to his discovery of the occlusion of gases. In 1861 Graham distinguished between 'colloids', which diffused slowly through water but were stopped by gelatine, and 'crystalloids', which diffused rapidly through both water and gelatine. He accurately measured their respective diffusion speeds in jars and suggested that osmosis was caused by unequal hydration on opposite sides of a membrane. Using parchment paper in osmometers he introduced 'dialysis' to separate colloids from crystalloids.

From 1851 Graham was a non-resident scientific assayer of silver and gold for the Royal Mint under Sir John Herschel, then master of the mint. Following Herschel's retirement, Palmerston appointed Graham as master in March 1855, and he resigned his chair at University College. By 1858 he had made substantial savings in the coinage of silver and gold. He then replaced copper coins by harder bronze coins. From November 1860 Graham's brother John (1812–1869) assisted with the distribution of bronze coins and in 1866 he became chief coiner. There was a handsome net profit by 1869 of £290,000 on the bronze coinage.

Graham died on 16 September 1869 of pleuropneumonia at his home, 4 Gordon Square, London, aged sixty-three. He was buried on 23 September at Glasgow Cathedral.   MICHAEL STANLEY

Sources M. Stanley, 'The chemical work of Thomas Graham', PhD diss., Open University, 1980 · M. Stanley, *The making of a chemist: Thomas Graham in Scotland* (1987) · M. Stanley, 'Thomas Graham, 1805–69', *Chemistry in Britain*, 27 (1991), 239–42 · E. Frame, 'Thomas Graham: a centenary account', *Philosophical Journal*, 7 (1970), 116–27 · R. A. Smith, *The life and works of Thomas Graham* (1884) · 'Dinner to Professor Graham', *Glasgow Courier* (9 Sept 1837), 4d · class registers, divinity, 1818–42, U. Glas. · J. G. Smith, *The parish of Strathblane and its inhabitants from early times* (1886), 163 · T. Graham, 'Adulteration of tobacco', *Daily News* (11 Oct 1849), 7 · R. W. Bunsen, *Gasometry* (1857), 203 · J. R. Partington, *A history of chemistry*, 4 (1964), 265–76 · Glasgow city parish births, p. 286, St Andrews · d. cert. · *Glasgow Evening Journal* (23 Sept 1869)

Archives ICL, letters to Lord Playfair · PRO, Royal Mint records [Mint 1 vols. 42–6, etc.] · RS, corresp. with Sir John Herschel · UCL, corresp. relating to University College London · University of Strathclyde, Glasgow, laboratory notebooks · Wellcome L., notebooks and papers

Likenesses J. G. Gilbert, oils, 1837, University of Strathclyde, Glasgow · W. Bosley, lithograph, pubd 1849 (after daguerreotype), BM · W. Trautschold, oils, 1850–75, NPG · Maull & Polyblank, albumen print, c.1855, NPG [*see illus.*] · Maull & Polyblank, albumen print, 1855, NPG · A. Craig, oils, 1859, Sci. Mus. · W. Brodie, bronze statue, 1872, George Square, Glasgow · Maull & Polyblank, photograph, 1886 · H. A. Budd, oils, 1931 (after engraving by Cook), Royal Society of Chemistry, London · S. Bellin, mezzotint, BM · C. Cook, engraving (after photograph by Maull & Polyblank) · C. Cook, stipple (after daguerreotype by Claudet), NPG · E. Edwards, photograph, NPG; repro. in L. Reeve, ed., *Men of eminence*, 3 (1864) · J. Faed, engraving (after Gilbert), Wellcome L. · G. F. Watts, oils, RS

Wealth at death under £18,000 (effects in UK): resworn administration, 16 Oct 1869, CGPLA Eng. & Wales

Graham, Thomas Alexander Ferguson (1840–1906),

genre painter, was born on 29 October 1840 in Kirkwall, Orkney, the only son of Alexander Spiers Graham, writer to the signet and crown chamberlain of Orkney, and his wife, Eliza Stirling; he was baptized on 4 February 1841. After the death of his father, he and his sister moved to Edinburgh to live with their grandmother. In January 1855 he enrolled as a student at the Trustees' Academy where, with William McTaggart, William Quiller Orchardson, John Pettie, and George Paul Chalmers, he was a pupil of Robert Scott Lauder. All these young artists were taught the primary importance of drawing, of light and shade, and of colour, but were to produce paintings which, especially if placed in the context of finely detailed Pre-Raphaelite works, were to be criticized as lacking 'finish'.

Friendships formed at the Trustees' Academy formed the backbone of Graham's early professional and personal life. Encouraged by the teaching of Scott Lauder, Graham travelled abroad from the age of twenty, when—in the company of McTaggart and Pettie—he visited Paris for the first time; in 1862 he first visited Brittany, this time with Pettie and Chalmers. In 1863 he settled in London, where he initially shared a house in Fitzroy Square with Orchardson and Pettie; the following year he spent time sketching in Venice. These foreign travels further induced him to portray a sense of local atmosphere in his work through a combination of relatively small scale, subtle light and shadow, and—in sharp contrast to the more historicist genre work of his friends—a deliberate choice of modern subjects. His early oil paintings, such as *A Young Bohemian* (1864; National Gallery of Scotland, Edinburgh), clearly show the impact of Scott Lauder's teaching of tonal values, but, unusually for a pupil, the choice of a contemporary, purely decorative subject. Its modernity of composition, colour, and brushwork appealed to its one-time owner, the portrait painter John Singer Sargent.

Graham's works of the 1880s, such as *Alone in London* (Perth Art Gallery, Scotland) and *The Landing Stage* (Bradford Art Gallery, Yorkshire), are essentially concerned with the modern British urban context. Here, the figures, while engaging the viewer and evoking sentiment, become almost subservient to the townscape. Graham was skilled at adapting aesthetics derived from Whistler to Eugène Boudin for his own means. His oil landscapes, whether of Scottish east coast fishing villages or life in Morocco, which he visited in 1885, are thus executed in pastel colours, thin paint, and hatching techniques, and use a low tonality sharpened by a dash of fresh colour. In this way, Graham's style and romantic subjects may be said to be both Scottish and international in their aspirations. None the less, Tom Graham has always been ranked as one of the Scottish high Victorian artists of 'the Scott Lauder school'. His paintings, popular both with artists and the public of his day, have been said by Lindsay Errington to be 'gentle and sensitive', possessing a 'quiet charm' (109, 72); they certainly lack the slick panache of the mature work of such friends as Orchardson or Pettie.

Graham first exhibited at the Scottish Academy in 1859, but he also showed at the British Institution and the Royal Academy after his move south. Always committed to exhibiting in Edinburgh, he contributed to the Scottish Academy almost annually from 1867, and in 1883 he was elected an honorary member of the Royal Scottish Academy. In appearance, he was finely featured, with brown hair and a beard. Unmarried, he had a wide circle of friends who regarded him as having—like his paintings—a 'fine presence and singular charm of personality'. He died during a visit to Edinburgh at 20 Torphichen Street on 24 December 1906. His works are held in the National Galleries of Scotland and the Royal Scottish Academy, Edinburgh, the McManus Galleries in Dundee, the Victoria and Albert Museum, London, and Bradford City Art Gallery.   ELIZABETH S. CUMMING

Sources [Iconoclast], *Scottish art and artists in 1860* (1860) · *Report of the Royal Scottish Academy* (1907) · L. Errington, *Master class: Robert Scott Lauder and his pupils* (1983) [exhibition catalogue, NG Scot., 15 July – 2 Oct 1983, and Aberdeen Art Gallery, 15 Oct – 12 Nov 1983] · J. L. Caw, *Scottish painting past and present, 1620–1908* (1908) · D. Macmillan, *Scottish art, 1460–1990* (1990) · D. Irwin and F. Irwin, *Scottish painters at home and abroad, 1700–1900* (1975) · W. Hardie, *Scottish painting, 1837–1939* (1976) · old parish registers and registers of births and baptisms, marriages and deaths, General Register Office for Scotland, Edinburgh
Archives Royal Society of Arts, Edinburgh, MSS and corresp.
Likenesses T. A. F. Graham, self-portrait, oils, 1882, Aberdeen Art Gallery · R. W. MacBeth, oils, 1887, Royal Society of Arts, Edinburgh · J. Archer, oils, Scot. NPG · W. Q. Orchardson, oils, Scot. NPG
Wealth at death £1134 4s. 1d.: confirmation, 14 March 1907, *CCI* · Scottish confirmation sealed in London, 27 March 1907, *CCI*

Graham, Sir William (d. 1424). *See under* Graham family (*per. c.*1250–1513).

Graham, William, second Lord Graham (d. 1471). *See under* Graham family (*per. c.*1250–1513).

Graham, William, first earl of Montrose (1462/3–1513). *See under* Graham family (*per. c.*1250–1513).

Graham, William, first earl of Airth and seventh earl of Menteith (1591–1661), politician, was the eldest son of John Graham, sixth earl of Menteith (1574–1598), and Mary (d. in or after 1618), daughter of Sir Colin Campbell of Glenorchy. Following the death of his father he succeeded to the earldom at the age of seven, and was served heir on 7 August 1610, when not yet of full age. On 26 February 1612 he married Agnes Gray (d. in or after 1667), daughter of Patrick *Gray, sixth Lord Gray (d. 1611), and his second wife, Mary. They had eleven children in all: seven sons, four of whom died young, and four daughters. In 1618, owing to a dispute with his mother over the lands of Kinpont, Menteith had occasion to inventory the contents of the earldom's charter chests. In the following year he set out to recover the lost properties and rights of the earldom, a process which became a passion with him. He sat in the parliament of 1621, where he voted against the five articles of Perth. Prior to the death of James VI he showed very little interest in public affairs. His political career seems to have come about by accident.

In the autumn of 1625 Charles I issued an act of revocation annulling all grants of land belonging to either the crown or the kirk which had been made since 1540. An

William Graham, first earl of Airth and seventh earl of Menteith (1591–1661), by George Jamesone, 1637

immense amount of property was involved, and the uproar was equally immense. Charles's explanatory statements failed to placate the panicked landholding classes; still another in a series of aristocratic delegations was on its way to court in December 1626. Charles was angry and threatened not to receive them. Menteith, who happened to be at court, intervened, through the good offices of his friend the secretary of state, Sir William Alexander. He persuaded Charles not only to receive the delegation but also to listen to them and change his policy respecting the implementation of the revocation. Instead of legal action Charles appointed a very large commission with an agenda that made it clear that the consequences for the landholding classes would be minimal, and that nothing was going to happen quickly. The panic gradually subsided. In that December Charles made Menteith a privy councillor and a member of the exchequer commission. His rise had begun.

It took about a year for Menteith to become Charles's principal adviser in Scottish affairs. In January 1628 Charles made him president of the privy council, and of the exchequer in the absence of Archbishop Spottiswoode. Charles had come to trust his judgement, in the matter of the revocation and in much else. For the next five years Menteith was the king's chief agent in Scottish affairs. He was not a policy maker; he was concerned chiefly to carry out Charles's wishes, even those of which he disapproved. Like Lord Treasurer Dunbar in the reign of James VI, he travelled back and forth between Edinburgh and London at least twice a year in order to explain the king's wishes to his Scottish subjects and vice versa.

The result was the creation of an atmosphere in which the interests of the people who counted received consideration and complaints could be heard. Menteith's great value to Charles was that the landholding classes, especially the higher aristocracy, trusted him. He was one of them, and shared their prejudices and interests. As a group they were feeling shut out and neglected, with the death of James, whom they knew and who knew them, and Charles's obvious disregard of James's old officials and advisers. Menteith reassured them: they felt that as long as he had Charles's ear their interests would be safeguarded.

Menteith's value to Charles extended far beyond the defusing of the tension the revocation had caused. He was the king's troubleshooter. He headed a committee to look into the dilapidated condition of Dumbarton Castle and also helped to arrange the removal of the venal Sir Archibald Napier of Merchiston from the office of treasurer-depute. He and Lord Treasurer Morton were co-chairs of a commission to implement the king's policy with respect to the Association for Fishing, an Anglo-Scottish fishing company which Charles created in order to compete with the immensely successful Dutch fishing fleet. Many Scots regarded this as an English scheme to open Scottish waters to English fishermen; Menteith and Morton were concerned to keep the area reserved exclusively for Scots as large as possible, and they were reasonably successful. Menteith presided effectively over a difficult meeting of the convention of estates in the summer of 1630. The convention voted a tax and, at Menteith's behest, ratified the four decreets arbitral on the revocation which Charles had issued in 1629. Menteith also successfully stifled efforts on the part of some lay patrons of benefices to attack the bishops and of some clergy to attack the five articles of Perth. Charles was very pleased, and rewarded him in September 1630 with a seat on the English privy council.

In April 1628 Lord Lorne, the *de facto* head of the house of Argyll in the absence of his father the earl, surrendered the office of hereditary justice-general of Scotland in return for cash and the retention of his hereditary authority in Argyll and the Isles. In July Charles appointed Menteith justice-general and instructed him to revive the system of justice ayres in criminal cases, which had fallen into desuetude in the 1590s. The effort failed, owing to the opposition of the lords of regality, who protested that their right to try accused inhabitants of the regality in the regality court was being undermined. Menteith's memorandum on the subject indicates that he believed that regality jurisdiction should be confined to cases of life and limb; otherwise the circuit courts would be hamstrung. Since the king was not prepared to enforce such a limitation, Menteith and the lord advocate, Sir Thomas Hope, recommended that the ayres be abandoned, and Charles acquiesced. Menteith disliked judicial innovations, another indication of his essentially conservative outlook.

In 1629 Menteith launched a genealogical initiative that was to ruin him. He believed that his ancestor Malise *Graham, first earl of Menteith (1406x13–1490), had been wrongfully deprived of the earldom of Strathearn by James I on the ground that Strathearn was a male fee; Malise's claim lay through his mother, the heir of her father, David, earl of Strathearn, the eldest son of King Robert II by his second wife, Euphemia Ross. The earldom had been annexed to the crown; Menteith carefully explained to Charles that he wanted none of the lands or rights of the earldom now in the crown's hands. All he wanted was to be recognized as heir to Earl David, with the title of earl of Strathearn, and to be allowed to recover whatever lands Earl David possessed which were not in the crown's possession. Charles was happy to reward his good servant and friend in this apparently harmless way. He even made a grant of £3000 sterling as 'satisfaction' for Menteith's 'renunciation' of the lands and rights of Strathearn to the crown, and in July 1631 created him earl of Strathearn.

Menteith was on an antiquarian ego trip in all this; he showed no interest in seeking out Earl David's holdings and laying claim to them. In 1631 and 1632 he acquired two pieces of property, one being the barony of Airth, that had no connection with Strathearn, and went heavily into debt in the process. But his ability to pursue those claims alarmed a number of major landholders, who now combined with Menteith's many enemies at court to ruin him. The accusation they made was startling. They described Earl David, Menteith's ancestor, as the eldest son of Robert II's first marriage. This was nonsense, but what was not nonsense was that Robert II had married his first wife after their children were born, and that she had been precontracted as a child. Charles's ancestor Robert III might, therefore, not be the rightful king. Why should Menteith not declare himself to be the rightful heir of Robert II? This worst-case scenario was laid before Charles, along with the accusation, which Menteith steadily denied, that Menteith had boasted of having the reddest blood in Scotland.

Charles at first refused to believe ill of his friend, though he did insist that Menteith surrender the title of Strathearn, and even that of Menteith. He was created earl of Airth in January 1633 and would henceforth be known as earl of Airth and Menteith (a secondary title), though with the precedence accorded the Menteith earldom, and without loss of property. Menteith's enemies were far from satisfied. They chipped away at Charles's confidence in Menteith with new charges, among them that Menteith had said that he should rightfully be king of Scotland. In May 1633 Charles appointed a committee to investigate these charges and ordered Menteith to withdraw to one of his houses pending the investigation. Menteith was thus unable to appeal personally to Charles while the latter was in Scotland in the summer of 1633. Eventually Menteith signed a submission which was little better than a confession, and in October 1633 Charles deprived him of his offices and his pension. His political career was over.

Menteith fell from power so rapidly in part because he

had no following. He was nothing of a politician, and was rather proud of it—he once boasted to Lord Treasurer Morton of his lack of a courtier's tongue. He was a bad correspondent and a haphazard administrator; he was careless and slow about doing favours even for his two closest political allies, Secretary Alexander and Lord Advocate Hope. He had no great office which he might have used as a power base, and showed no interest in getting one. He made no effort to intimidate his colleagues, as had King James's agent Lord Treasurer Dunbar. He was not a consensus-builder and had no network of kinfolk to sustain him, like Lord Chancellor Dunfermline, Dunbar's successor as James's principal agent in Scottish affairs. Like his master, Menteith was something of a loner. He depended entirely on the king's favour; when he lost that, he lost everything. The king's loss was equally great, although Charles did not realize it. The king never understood how useful Menteith was in creating political calm in Scotland. It is no coincidence that only four years after Menteith's fall Charles provoked the confrontation that would eventually lead him to the block. Menteith's career is one of the great might-have-beens in the history of the Stuart monarchy.

The last twenty-eight years of his life were a long twilight for Menteith. His creditors beset him; the king's efforts to help him were ineffectual. In December 1637 he was finally released from house arrest and, because he was a royalist in spite of all that had happened, Charles restored him to the privy council in 1639. Menteith's lands were devastated by fighting in the late 1640s; in the end he had to sell most of them. He lived to see the Restoration, and died early in 1661. His grandson William Graham succeeded him as earl of Airth and Menteith.

MAURICE LEE JUN.

Sources W. Fraser, ed., *The Red Book of Menteith*, 2 vols. (1880) • M. Lee, *The road to revolution: Scotland under Charles I, 1625–1637* (1985) • A. I. Macinnes, *Charles I and the making of the covenanting movement, 1625–1641* (1991) • G. Donaldson, *Scotland: James V to James VII* (1965), vol. 3 of *The Edinburgh history of Scotland* (1965–75) • *Reg. PCS*, 1st ser. • *Reg. PCS*, 2nd ser. • W. Fraser, *Memorials of the earls of Haddington*, 2 vols. (1889) • C. Rogers, ed., *The earl of Stirling's register of royal letters relative to the affairs of Scotland and Nova Scotia from 1615 to 1635*, 2 vols. (1885) • *The historical works of Sir James Balfour*, ed. J. Haig, 4 vols. (1824–5) • H. Nicolas, *History of the earldoms of Strathearn, Menteith, and Airth* (1842) • *CSP dom.*, 1625–49 • J. Spalding, *Memorialls of the trubles in Scotland and in England, AD 1624 – AD 1645*, ed. J. Stuart, 2 vols., Spalding Club, [21, 23] (1850–51) • J. Scot, 'Scotstarvet's "Trew relation"', ed. G. Neilson, *SHR*, 11 (1913–14), 164–91, 284–96, 395–403; 12 (1914–15), 76–83, 174–83, 408–12; 13 (1915–16), 380–92; 14 (1916–17), 60–67 • J. Scott, 'Trew relation of the principal affaires concerning the state', ed. G. Neilson, *SHR*, 14 (1916–17) • GEC, *Peerage*
Archives NA Scot., corresp.
Likenesses G. Jamesone, oils, 1637, Scot. NPG [*see illus.*]
Wealth at death in debt

Graham, William (1737–1801), minister of the Secession church, was born on 16 March 1737 at Carriden, Linlithgowshire, where his father was steward to the earl of Hopetoun. Following an early education at the local grammar school in Borrowstounness, Graham studied law in Edinburgh from 1751 to 1754. In these years the Church of Scotland experienced various divisions over the subject of patronage, and Graham attached himself to the Secession church. In 1754 he moved to Abernethy to study divinity with Alexander Moncrieff, minister of the Anti-Burgher branch of seceders. Moncrieff appointed Graham to the post of tutor in philosophy at the age of eighteen.

In 1758 Graham married Mary Johnston of Whitenow, Dumfriesshire. In the same year he was licensed to preach and on 19 November 1758 was ordained to the pastoral charge in Whitehaven, Cumberland, where he stayed for twelve years, taking the opportunity to write critically against ecclesiastical patronage. In June 1770 he moved to Newcastle upon Tyne, where he remained for the rest of his life. An excellent mathematician, Graham spent a great deal of his time and money trying to discover an exact method of finding longitude at sea. However, his main concerns were ecclesiastical and theological. He was a strong advocate of the secession movement which he defended in *A Candid Vindication of the Secession Church* (1790). His commitment to protestantism led him to oppose moves to remove certain Roman Catholic disabilities and in 1780 he published *False Prophets Unmasked, as Sermon Against Popery*. He was a supporter of foreign missions, preaching the first sermon on behalf of the London Missionary Society in Newcastle in 1796, and defending the missionary movement against its detractors in *An Essay … to Remove Certain Scruples Respecting Missionary Societies* (1796). Graham attracted a wide readership through his opposition to any formal connections between church and state (*A Review of Ecclesiastical Establishments in Europe*, 1792), a move which brought support from many English dissenters and opposition from members of the Church of England. In October 1800 he suffered a stroke which left him paralysed for three months and which resulted in his death, at Newcastle, on 19 January 1801.

KENNETH B. E. ROXBURGH

Sources DNB • J. Baillie, *A funeral sermon occasioned by the death of Francis Baillie to which is subjoined An elegy on the death of the late Rev. Mr W. Graham of Newcastle* (1802) • J. M'Kerrow, *History of the Secession church*, rev. edn (1841), 899–902 • W. Mackelvie, *Annals and statistics of the United Presbyterian church*, ed. W. Blair and D. Young (1873), 119, 524–5

Graham, William (1800–1886), schoolmaster and educationist, was born at Dunkeld, Perthshire, on 7 October 1800 to Alexander Graham (*c.*1774–1833), teacher, and his wife, Margaret Bell, apparently their only child. Alexander Graham moved to Perth to open a Latin academy, and there William had most of his early education before being, at the age of twelve, enrolled at Edinburgh University. After university he became an assistant to his father, besides teaching elocution and giving public readings. On 14 October 1828 he married Christina Drummond (*b.* 1805) at Kettle, Fife.

In 1823 Graham was English master at the Academy of Cupar, and in 1831 was appointed teacher of history, English literature, and elocution in the Scottish Naval and

Military Academy in Edinburgh, an appointment of which he was always most proud. It was a bitter blow for all when in 1858 the government withdrew its support, leading to the academy's closure. In 1833 some of its masters gave occasional lectures which led, the following year, to the formation of a school to offer girls an affordable education equal to that of boys, being the first in the country to offer girls secondary education. The school opened on 7 November 1834 in a small flat in Queen Street, Edinburgh. Because of the demand for places it moved to 15 Great Stuart Street as the Scottish Institution for the Education of Young Ladies. It was successful, and in 1840 moved to 9 Moray Place, Edinburgh, with its boarding-house at 46 Moray Place. William Graham went to live in 1 Moray Place in 1856.

In 1846 Dr Schmitz, rector of the Edinburgh high school, called a meeting of a few Edinburgh teachers to consider a suggestion made by an educational association in Glasgow to elevate and improve teachers in Scotland. Graham and others from the Scottish Naval and Military Academy were among the founders of the Educational Institute of Scotland, which held its first meeting on 1 September 1847, with Dr Schmitz giving the first presidential address. In 1850 Graham's outstanding qualities as an educationist were recognized when the University of Aberdeen conferred on him the degree of doctor of laws. In 1851 he was elected the fifth president of the Educational Institute of Scotland. For many years he edited the Educational Institute's *Journal*, contributing many articles to it, and to other publications.

In 1867 Graham was appointed teacher of history, English literature, and elocution at New College, Edinburgh, and was at one time president of the Watt Club in connection with the School of Arts. In 1870 the Merchant Company opened in Queen Street its Ladies' Institution for Young Ladies, resulting in the closure of the Scottish Institution for the Education of Young Ladies, and some small private schools. Graham's own small academy at the west end of Queen Street, which had existed since before 1834, continued, and there he prepared boys for English public schools. Following requests from old pupils Graham published in 1873 *Lectures, Sketches and Poetical Pieces*. Throughout his life in Edinburgh he was a 'visiting master', walking from boarding-school to boarding-school instructing girls in English and history. Dr Pryde, first principal of the Merchant Company's Queen Street institution, said Graham was a born teacher, so that no matter how often he repeated a lesson, if it was new to the pupils then it was as if new to him. In 1879 he received a testimonial of £600 presented to him by Professor Douglas Maclagan.

Graham continued to teach until within two years of his death. Latterly he assisted his two unmarried daughters in their private school in Inverleith, a suburb of Edinburgh. He died at 7 Inverleith Terrace, Edinburgh, on 22 November 1886, and was buried at Warriston cemetery. He had five daughters, three of whom married, and two sons. His son William (*b.* 1836) emigrated to Australia, and became a partner in an eminent Australian firm and a member of the upper house of representatives in Queensland. Graham was commemorated by a plaque at 1 Moray Place, Edinburgh.   MURIEL A. N. HOPE

Sources D. H. Edwards, *Modern Scottish poets, with biographical and critical notices*, 3 (1881), 188–90 · *The Scotsman* (23 Nov 1886) · M. Macdonald, 'The Scottish Institution: a pioneer venture', *History of Education Society Bulletin*, 52 (1993) · D. Pryde, *Pleasant memories of a busy life* (1893), 103–5 · *Report of the Scottish Institution for the Education of Young Ladies* · E. Blishen, ed., *Blond's encyclopaedia of education* (1969) · Jessie Carrick to Francis A. Forbes, 1858–9, Edinburgh Room Central Library, Edinburgh · *The Scotsman* (1834–70) · *Edinburgh Evening Courant* (1834–70) · *CCI* (1887) · d. cert. · private information (2004) [family]
Likenesses oils (aged about forty-five), priv. coll.
Wealth at death £501 11s. 6d.: confirmation, 23 Feb 1887, *CCI*

Graham, William (1810–1883), missionary and religious writer, was the youngest of seven children of a farmer at Clogh, co. Antrim, where he was born. A local school gave him his early education, and his college training was obtained at the Royal Belfast Academical Institution. After being licensed, he was sent on missionary service to the west of Ireland. In August 1835 he was ordained as minister of Dundonald, co. Down, but on 1 November 1842 he resigned his charge, having been appointed by the general assembly as one of its first missionaries to the Jews. In this capacity he was stationed first at Damascus, then at Hamburg, and finally at Bonn, where he built a church and worked for thirty years, returning to Belfast in 1875. Graham was married, but nothing is known of his wife. In 1883 he resigned, and on 11 December of that year he died at his home, Nursery Cottage, Malone, co. Antrim.

Graham was widely known as an author of commentaries. These included *The Spirit of Love, a Commentary on the First Epistle of John* (1857), *A Commentary on the Epistle to Titus* (1860), and one on Ephesians (1870). He also published two works connected with his missionary activities, *An Appeal to the People of Israel* (written in four languages, 1865) and *The Jordan and the Rhine* (1854).

THOMAS HAMILTON, *rev.* DAVID HUDDLESTON

Sources *The Witness* (14 Dec 1883), 5 · *A history of congregations in the Presbyterian Church in Ireland, 1610–1982*, Presbyterian Church in Ireland (1982) · *Irish Presbyterian Missionary Herald* (1843–86) · R. Allen, *The Presbyterian College, Belfast, 1853–1953* (1954) · *CGPLA Ire.* (1884)
Likenesses silhouette, repro. in *A history of Dundonald Presbyterian Congregation, 1645–1945* (1945)
Wealth at death £1170 1s. 8d.: probate, 29 Feb 1884, *CGPLA Ire.*

Graham, William (1817–1885), collector and art patron, was born on 25 August 1817 in Glasgow, the eldest son of William Graham (1795/6–1855), a merchant of Burnshiels, Renfrewshire, and Catherine, daughter of J. Swanston. He was educated privately and at Glasgow University, and succeeded his father as senior partner in the family business, W. and J. Graham & Co., which imported dry goods from India and port from Portugal. He settled in London in 1866, living at 54 Lowndes Square and then at 44 (renumbered 36 in 1876) Grosvenor Place, and renting houses in Perthshire for the summer.

In 1865 Graham was elected Liberal MP for the city of

Glasgow. He spoke mainly on Scottish and religious questions (he was a devout Presbyterian) and advocated moderate parliamentary reform. He was a friend of Gladstone (who appointed him a trustee of the National Gallery in 1884), but was not active politically and stood down with some relief in 1874 because of illness.

Graham was one of the most important art patrons and collectors of the 1860s and 1870s, playing a key role in the careers of Dante Gabriel Rossetti and Edward Burne-Jones. His attitude to art was essentially emotional rather than intellectual: he was so taken with one painting by Burne-Jones that he kissed it; he was suspicious of connoisseurs. He may have been encouraged to begin collecting, in the 1860s, by his uncle, John Graham of Skelmorlie, whose fine collection included J. E. Millais's *Sir Isumbras at the Ford* (1857; Tate collection). He bought his first Rossetti—*Morning Music* (1864; Fitzwilliam Museum, Cambridge)—in 1866, and first met the artist in 1868. He soon became Rossetti's principal patron (rivalled only by F. R. Leyland) and a friend, taking care of the artist in Scotland following his suicide attempt in 1872. Graham preferred Rossetti's early work, owning both *The Girlhood of Mary Virgin* (1849) and *Ecce ancilla domini!* (1850) (both Tate collection), and expressed reservations about those later paintings inspired by Jane Morris, but would buy whatever the artist wanted to sell him. His principal commission was *Dante's Dream at the Time of the Death of Beatrice* (1871; Walker Art Gallery, Liverpool), which proved too large for its intended position at Grosvenor Place, and had to be replaced by the version now in Dundee Art Gallery. Delays in completing commissions and disagreements about money somewhat soured their friendship in Rossetti's final years, but in 1881 the artist could still call him 'a friend who has shown me such marks of brotherly attachment as deserve every consideration from me' (Rossetti to Graham, September 1881, *Letters of Dante Gabriel Rossetti*, no. 2552).

Graham enjoyed a calmer and more fruitful relationship with Burne-Jones, who wrote, 'I used to think one could use no other word but genius for his perception and instinct for painting. It was infallible. He was never wrong' (Burne-Jones to Frances Horner, July 1892, FM Cam., Burne-Jones papers, xxvii, 13). Burne-Jones was particularly devoted to Graham's daughter Frances, one of eight children from his marriage to Jane Catherine Loundes (1819/20–1899) of Arthurlie, Renfrewshire, on 1 January 1845. Graham owned both the watercolour and oil versions of *Laus Veneris* (watercolour, 1861; priv. coll.; oil, 1873–5, 1878; Laing Art Gallery, Newcastle) and *Chant d'amour* (watercolour, 1865; Museum of Fine Arts, Boston; oil, 1868–73; Metropolitan Museum of Art, New York), favouring the warm Venetian colouring of the latter. In the 1880s Graham acted as Burne-Jones's agent, negotiating the sales of *King Cophetua and the Beggar Maid* (1880–84; Tate collection) to Lord Wharncliffe and of the large *Briar Rose* cycle (1874–90; Buscot Park, Oxfordshire) to Agnews.

Graham owned major paintings by J. E. Millais, W. Holman Hunt, Lord Leighton, G. F. Watts, Fred Walker, and Arthur Hughes. He also bought old masters for smaller sums, but in even greater quantities. Encouraged by Rossetti and Burne-Jones, he concentrated on acquiring paintings produced in central and northern Italy during the late fifteenth and early sixteenth centuries. They included Antonello's *Virgin and Child*, Dosso Dossi's *Circe and her Lovers* (both National Gallery of Art, Washington, DC), Pesellino's *Virgin and Child with St John* (Toledo Museum of Art, Ohio), and Piero di Cosimo's *The Discovery of Vulcan* (Wadsworth Atheneum, Hartford, Connecticut).

From the late 1870s Graham collected less, because of ill health, financial constraints, and the tragic deaths of his two sons, Rutherford and Willy. Burne-Jones's chalk portrait of 1880 (priv. coll.) bleakly depicted the physical consequences of these events. According to Georgiana Burne-Jones, 'His face was that of a saint, and at times like one transfigured' (Burne-Jones, 1.296), and indeed he came to resemble Jacopo Bellini's *San Bernardino of Siena* (priv. coll.), in his own collection.

Graham died of stomach cancer on 16 July 1885, while staying with his daughter Agnes Jekyll [*see* Jekyll, Dame Agnes] at Oakdene near Guildford in Surrey, and was buried in the necropolis of St Mungo's Cathedral, Glasgow, together with several small paintings by Burne-Jones. The bulk of his collection was sold at Christies in London on 2–3 and 8–10 April 1886, realizing £69,168. Today it is best represented in the Walker Art Gallery, Liverpool.

OLIVER GARNETT

Sources O. Garnett, 'The letters and collection of William Graham: Pre-Raphaelite patron and pre-Raphaelite collector', *Walpole Society*, 62 (2000), 145–343 · F. Horner, *Time remembered* (1933) · *Letters of Dante Gabriel Rossetti*, ed. O. Doughty and J. R. Wahl, 4 vols. (1965–7) · J. S. Jeans, *Western worthies* (1872), 42–7 · G. Burne-Jones, *Memorials of Edward Burne-Jones*, 2 vols. (1904) · *The Owl and the Rossettis: letters of Charles A. Howell and Dante Gabriel, Christina and William Michael Rossetti*, ed. C. L. Cline (1978) · m. reg. Scot. · W. I. Addison, ed., *The matriculation albums of the University of Glasgow from 1728 to 1858* (1913) · gravestone, Glasgow Cathedral necropolis

Archives priv. coll., MSS | FM Cam., Burne-Jones MSS · priv. coll., letters to Burne-Jones · Sheff. Arch., letters to Lord Warncliffe · University of British Columbia, Vancouver, Rossetti–Angeli MSS, letters to Rossetti

Likenesses D. G. Rossetti, pastel drawing, 1870, priv. coll. · E. Burne-Jones, chalk drawing, 1880, priv. coll. · E. Burne-Jones, oils, 1880, priv. coll. · F. Walker, pen-and-ink sketch, repro. in J. G. Marks, *Life and letters of Frederick Walker, A.R.A.* (1896)

Wealth at death £149,526 4s. 8d.: confirmation, 24 March 1886, *CCI* · £34,795 9s. 5d.: additional estate, 25 Nov 1886, *CCI*

Graham, William (1839–1911), philosopher and political economist, was born in Saintfield, co. Down. He was a younger son of Alexander Graham, farmer and horse-dealer, and his wife, Maria Crawford, a descendant of a Scottish Presbyterian family which moved to Ireland in Charles II's time to escape religious persecution. The father died poor while his son was very young, and it fell to the mother, a woman of spirit and intelligence, to bring up the children—four sons and a daughter—amid many hardships.

Graham obtained a foundation scholarship at the Educational Institute, Dundalk, and being well grounded there in mathematics and English was soon engaged as a teacher in the royal school at Banagher, where he remained until he entered Trinity College, Dublin, in July 1860. At Trinity College, Graham won distinction in mathematics, philosophy, and English prose composition. During most of his college course he worked outside the university as headmaster successively of two important schools in or near Dublin. But a foundation scholarship in mathematics which he won in 1865 gave him an annual stipend together with free rooms and meals. He graduated BA in 1867, and thereupon engaged in coaching students in mathematics and philosophy. His success as a private tutor enabled him to give up his school work. He devoted much time to the study of philosophy, and in 1872 he published his first book, *Idealism, an Essay Metaphysical and Critical*, a vindication of Berkeley against Hamilton and the Scottish school.

Graham, who had proceeded MA in 1870, left Dublin in 1873 to become private secretary to Mitchell Henry MP, but resigned the post in 1874 and settled in London. In 1875 he was appointed lecturer in mathematics at St Bartholomew's Hospital, and he engaged at the same time in literary and tutorial work; but the best part of his time for some years was given to the preparation of the most important of his books, *The Creed of Science*, which appeared in 1881. This was a discussion concerning how far the new scientific doctrines of the conservation of energy, evolution, and natural selection necessitated a revision of the accepted theories in philosophy, theology, and ethics. It was well received, running to a second edition in 1884, and it evoked the admiration of Darwin, Gladstone, and Archbishop Trench. In some circles Graham's argument was credited with atheistic tendencies. This suspicion caused the Irish chief secretary, Sir Michael Hicks Beach, to withdraw an offer which he made to Graham of an assistant commissionership of intermediate education in October 1886.

In London Graham was soon a welcome figure in the best intellectual society, where his conversational gift was valued. His many friends included Carlyle, Lecky, and Froude. Meanwhile his increasing reputation had led to his election in 1882 to the chair of jurisprudence and political economy in Queen's College, Belfast. This post he held until 1909, when ill health compelled his retirement. At Belfast he enjoyed the enthusiastic regard of a long succession of pupils. He was professor of law for ten years before he joined the legal profession. In 1892 he was called to the bar at the Inner Temple without any intention of practising.

Graham's duties at Belfast allowed him still to reside most of the year in London, and in his leisure he produced a succession of works on political or economic subjects, contributing to the *Nineteenth Century*, *Contemporary Review*, and *Economic Journal*. He was for many years examiner in political economy and also in philosophy for the Indian Civil Service and the Royal University of Ireland, and in English for the Irish intermediate education department.

Graham received the honorary degree of LittD from Trinity College, Dublin, in 1905. His health began to fail in 1907, and he died unmarried in a nursing home at 12 Hume Street, Dublin, on 19 November 1911. He was buried in Mount Jerome cemetery there.

JOHN RAE, *rev.* C. A. CREFFIELD

Sources *The Times* (21 Nov 1911) · *Irish Times* (20 Nov 1911) · *The Athenaeum* (25 Nov 1911), 660 · Graham's autobiographical MS notes · personal knowledge (1912) · *CGPLA Eng. & Wales* (1912)

Wealth at death £1036 15s. 6d.: probate, 23 Jan 1912, *CGPLA Eng. & Wales*

Graham, William (1887–1932), politician, was born at Peebles on 29 July 1887, the eldest of the seven children of George Graham (*d*. 1931), master builder, and his wife, Jessie Newton, only daughter of an Edinburgh baker. The family later moved to Innerleithen, where Graham began elementary school, and then to Edinburgh, where he won a scholarship to George Heriot's School. While at school he also worked as an errand boy and took a correspondence course in order to pass the examination for the clerical civil service. The pattern of his life was set early: hard work, long hours, endless study, and relentless self-improvement, later expanded into commitments to social improvement and public duties. In 1903 he obtained a junior clerkship at the War Office in London and took evening classes in bookkeeping and shorthand at Pitman's College. Two years later, lacking adequate income to afford living in London, he returned to Edinburgh. In 1906 he became a journalist with the Selkirk *Southern Reporter*, a modest Liberal newspaper. Although aged only nineteen he was soon appointed editor, and began also to contribute to larger Scottish newspapers. After a disagreement with his proprietor he became Selkirk representative of the rival *Border Standard*. This was a Conservative newspaper, but Graham kept a distinction between his regular journalism and his politics. Under the influence of Ruskin and other radical writers he moved from Liberalism to more progressive social causes, and in January 1908 he joined the Independent Labour Party (ILP) as founding secretary of its Selkirk branch.

By supplementing his regular income with freelance journalism and as a court reporter Graham earned enough to become a student at the University of Edinburgh, where he matriculated in 1911. He won medals in four subjects, graduated with a second-class MA in economic science in 1915, and proceeded in 1917 to an LLB, with honours in statistics, mathematical economics, forensic medicine, and administrative law. These successes were the more remarkable not only because he continued to sustain himself by journalism but also because he now undertook further activities. From 1913 to 1919 he was an ILP member of Edinburgh town council, serving on its law, tramways, parks, and public health committees, and he became a JP. Though sharing some of the ILP distaste for the First World War, he volunteered for military service but was rejected on medical grounds. His chief war work was as a member of the Edinburgh distress committee, as vice-chairman of the city's advisory committee on juvenile unemployment, and as chairman of its war disablement committee. From 1915 he lectured on economics for the Workers' Educational Association. In 1919 he married Ethel Margaret Dobson (*d*. 1947), daughter of Henry Beardmore Dobson, cashier, of Harrogate; they had no children.

Graham's local ubiquity and public diligence assisted him at the 1918 general election, when as an ILP candidate he overcame an entrenched Liberal majority to become MP for Central Edinburgh, the seat he held at successive elections until 1931. In a Parliamentary Labour Party consisting largely of trade unionists his knowledge of higher education, local government, economics, law, and medicine was unusual and offset what was, among MPs, his relatively young age. He became an obvious Labour representative for various bodies. He was a member of the royal commission on income tax (1919), the speaker's conference on devolution (1919–20), Lord Colwyn's committee on railway agreements (1920), the royal commission on the universities of Oxford and Cambridge (1920–22), and a department committee on grants to local authorities (1922). He served on the Medical Research Council from 1920 to 1928 and was chairman of the Industrial Fatigue Research Board from 1921. He chaired his party's education committee from 1919. In 1921 he published *The Wages of Labour*, which was characteristic of its time in trying to show that Labour politicians possessed economic competence alongside their reforming intentions.

With the return to parliament in 1922 of more experienced Labour politicians Graham's skills for a time became less significant. Nevertheless in the first Labour government of January to November 1924 he was appointed financial secretary to the Treasury. Here he formed a close partnership with the chancellor of the exchequer, Philip Snowden, whom he admired both as an old socialist hero and as the upholder of a shared economic outlook whose radicalism paradoxically lay in its stern orthodoxy: free trade, sound money, and balanced budgets. Graham found a mentor, and Snowden a protégé. Graham was a good minister: an effective administrator who commanded his material, and a lucid speaker who emulated the former Conservative leader, Bonar Law, in expounding complex financial details without notes, from memory. He was also respected and well liked in all parties. Though teetotal and a non-smoker, small in stature, insignificant in appearance, and efficient rather than imaginative, he had a quiet charm and gentle humour, which made him good company. Out of government Graham resumed his journalism, principally for the *Edinburgh Evening News*. His financial reputation brought him both a directorship of the Abbey National Building Society and chairmanship of the House of Commons public accounts committee (1924–9). He served on the joint select committee on the BBC's charter (1925–6) and was chairman of a departmental committee on native welfare in Kenya (1926). As a member of the Parliamentary Labour Party executive, in 1928–9 he helped to produce a draft programme for the first year of the next Labour government.

On MacDonald's formation of the second Labour government after the 1929 general election Graham joined the cabinet as president of the Board of Trade. He again showed himself highly capable but, like other cabinet members, was both overwhelmed by the scale of the international economic recession and hampered by the inadequacies of Labour economic doctrines and the institutional constraints upon a minority government. He had two main strategies for coping with the decline of British exports: restoration of easier international trade and reorganization of domestic industries. At the Hague conference on German reparations in August 1929 he achieved readjustments of deliveries in kind that had damaged British trade. Following his proposal at the League of Nations assembly in September 1929 a conference on concerted economic action in February and March 1930 produced a tariff truce as a prelude to future tariff reductions. But the pressures for trade protectionism were inexorable. Few foreign governments signed the truce and the Labour cabinet itself was now divided on trade issues, and only ratified the truce in September after two postponements. Further sessions of the conference failed to win new adherents, and by March 1931 the tariff truce had collapsed. Graham's creation of an overseas trade development council and dispatch of trade missions overseas could now make little impression. At home his Coal Mines Act, a hard-won compromise between pressures from the coal owners, the miners' union, and the Conservative and Liberal parties, had limited practical effect. Committees to consider rationalization of the cotton and iron and steel industries met employers' resistance, to the extent that Graham shifted from his pragmatic reformism towards proposals for public corporations and compulsory reorganization, only to face Bank of England resistance.

Graham's political re-education was soon accelerated, producing a bitter and painful personal breach. Now Snowden's designated heir, he was appointed to the cabinet economy committee which, amid the sterling crisis of August 1931, reviewed the May committee report on national expenditure. Although retaining conventional financial assumptions, the threat of reduced unemployment benefits pushed him in unexpected directions. He horrified Snowden by supporting a revenue tariff as an alternative and was among the cabinet minority that ultimately rejected MacDonald's and Snowden's proposed benefit cut. After the cabinet split and the formation of the emergency National coalition government he became joint deputy leader of the Parliamentary Labour Party and chairman of its finance and trade committee, which enraged MacDonald and Snowden by repudiating proposals accepted during the August meetings, and then replacing them with increasingly radical socialist policies. In an astonishingly opportunistic newspaper statement (*Daily Express*, 31 Aug 1931), Graham declared that the Labour Party could bury its recent past and win the next election by exploiting the short memories of working-class voters—an attitude which backfired by helping to convince the coalition partners to perpetuate their alliance and call an early election. Graham was among the many former ministers defeated at this October 1931 election.

The furious controversies of the previous months left Graham in financial difficulties after he left government, denied a return to his building society directorship, and unable to regain his journalistic earnings. Stafford Cripps found him a post as economic and statistical adviser to the stockbrokers Schwab and Snelling. During the winter, however, he fell ill with pneumonia and died at his home, 29 Sunningfields Road, Hendon, Middlesex, on 8 January 1932; he was buried four days later at Hendon Park cemetery. Aged only forty-four he had seemed set to become a dominant Labour politician; many who knew him thought a future party leader had been lost.

PHILIP WILLIAMSON

Sources DNB · *The Times* (9 Jan 1932) · *The Times* (11 Jan 1932) · *The Times* (13 Jan 1932) · T. N. Graham, *Willie Graham* (1948) · W. Knox, 'Graham, William', *Scottish labour leaders, 1918–39: a biographical dictionary*, ed. W. Knox (1984) · R. Skidelsky, *Politicians and the slump: the labour government of 1929–1931* (1967) · P. Williamson, *National crisis and national government: British politics, the economy and empire, 1926–1932* (1992) · R. W. D. Boyce, *British capitalism at the crossroads, 1919–1932* (1987) · CGPLA Eng. & Wales (1932) · WWW, 1929–40

Archives PRO, corresp. with Ramsay MacDonald, PRO 30/69/1/193

Likenesses T. Cottrell, cigarette card, NPG

Wealth at death £11,907 0s. 1d.: resworn probate, 16 March 1932, CGPLA Eng. & Wales

Grahame, James. *See* Graham, James (1765–1811).

Grahame, Kenneth (1859–1932), writer and secretary of the Bank of England, was born on 8 March 1859 at 32 Castle Street, Edinburgh, the second son and third of four children of James Cunningham Grahame (1830–1887), advocate, and his wife, Elizabeth (Bessie; 1837–1864), daughter of David and Mary Ingles of Heriot Row, Edinburgh. R. B. Cunninghame *Graham was a distant relative.

Early life and education In 1860 Cunningham Grahame moved his family (now including Helen, born in 1856, and Thomas William, 1858–1874) to Argyll on being appointed sheriff-substitute. There, on 16 March 1864, a third son, Roland, was born, and on 4 April Bessie died of scarlet fever; Kenneth was also seriously ill, and he was left with bronchial problems which affected him throughout his life. Cunningham Grahame never recovered from the loss of his wife, and spent most of the rest of his life in France, leaving his children to be supported by his brother, John, and raised by their maternal grandmother, first at The Mount, Cookham Dene, Berkshire, and from 1867 at Fernhill Cottage, Cranbourne.

Kenneth was sent to St Edward's School, Oxford, in 1868, where, despite some traumatic experiences, he became head boy and captain of the rugby fifteen; he won the divinity prize and the prize for Latin prose in 1874, and the sixth-form prize in 1875. His brother Willie died on new year's eve, 1874. The events of this period were reflected in the books on childhood which made his name, and the love that he developed for Oxford and the river remained with him. His uncle, John Grahame—whether for financial reasons or as a matter of principle is not clear—refused to pay for his entry to the university, and

Kenneth Grahame (1859–1932), by John Singer Sargent, 1912

this scarred Kenneth for life. Instead of being permitted to pursue his education, in 1876 he moved to London to work in his uncle's firm of parliamentary agents (Grahame, Currie, and Spens), while waiting for a vacancy in the Bank of England. He lived at Draycott Lodge, Fulham, in a house belonging to another uncle, Robert Grahame, and his wife, Georgina.

Banker and writer Much of Grahame's life for the next thirty years can be seen as representing a tension between two sides of his character: the unconventional writer and traveller, and the conventional bank employee—between his intellectual and aesthetic leanings, and the career imposed upon him. As an example, he met Frederick James Furnivall and joined the New Shakespere Society on 9 June 1877 and in 1880 became its honorary secretary, a post which he held until 1891. He also joined the London Scottish (volunteer) regiment, became a sergeant, and in 1887 was on duty for Queen Victoria's Golden Jubilee.

On 1 January 1879, he had entered the Bank of England as a 'gentleman clerk'—being the only clerk ever to have scored 100 per cent in the essay which was part of the qualifying test. He took a flat in Bloomsbury Street which he later shared with his brother Roland. In 1884 he took up voluntary work with the poor at Toynbee Hall, Stepney, and joined his sister Helen for a holiday on the Lizard peninsula in Cornwall, where he developed a lifelong affection for the area, and for sailing and deep-sea fishing. Mary Richardson, a friend of Helen's, described him at this period:

He was a tall [according to his passport, 5 feet 11 inches] … fine looking young man, a splendid head, broad and well-proportioned—carried himself well—a good healthy complexion, large widely opened rather light grey eyes, always with a kindly expression in them. Not exactly handsome but distinctly striking-looking—sensitive hands and mouth, rather short clever nose.   (Green, 94)

Despite his reserved character, Grahame's involvement with Furnivall led to his acting the part of Giacomo in a performance of *The Cenci* at the Grand Theatre, Islington, for the Shelley Society, on 7 May 1886. This was a very scandalous production, and Kenneth may well have been relieved to leave for a visit to Tuscany; he stayed at the Villino Landau, near Florence, with his sister. This visit began an affection for Italy and the Mediterranean which lasted all his life. In this year he moved to a top floor flat at 65 Chelsea Gardens, London.

Cunningham Grahame died at Le Havre on 27 February 1887. Kenneth arranged the funeral and wound up his father's affairs; his diary entries show no emotion. At the end of 1887 Grahame had his first literary acceptance: 'By a Northern Furrow' was taken by the *St James's Gazette*, although it was not published until 26 December 1888.

Grahame's career at the bank progressed rapidly. In 1888 he transferred to the chief cashier's office where Frank May was the incumbent. Here he became friends with Gordon Nairne, later to become chief cashier. After a few months he transferred, in 1889, to the secretary's office. Here he met Sidney Ward, who became one of his companions for hearty country weekends. The fashion for rural quasi-mysticism, neo-paganism, and walking and 'manly' pursuits appealed to the escapist side of Grahame. Such escapes from City life were reflected in his first essays, influenced by the work of R. L. Stevenson. On 18 October 1890 his first contribution to the *Scots Observer* (later the *National Observer*), 'Of smoking', appeared. The editor, the idiosyncratic W. E. Henley, encouraged Grahame, but when it was suggested that he leave the bank in order to write full-time, he observed, 'I am a spring, not a pump' (Chalmers, 48).

The Golden Age A major change in direction in Grahame's writing, which was to make him famous, came with the short piece 'The Olympians', published in the *National Observer* on 19 September 1891. This elegantly ironic picture of childhood avoided the tendency towards pretension and preciousness evident in his 'Stevensonettes'. It was republished in his first book, *Pagan Papers*, which he submitted to John Lane, on 19 January 1893, and which appeared in October. Five more stories about the same children were written between February and September and included in the first edition, although they were later extracted to form the basis of *The Golden Age* (1895). The other essays, with titles such as 'Loafing', 'The Fairy Wicket', and 'The Lost Centaur', lamenting the decay of rural life, and leaning towards pantheism, appealed to the popular taste. The first edition has a frontispiece by Aubrey Beardsley (whom Grahame knew). The book received mixed reviews, but Grahame had established a reputation, and was invited by Henry Harland to contribute to *The Yellow Book*. For its second issue, in 1894, he wrote 'The Roman road', a conversation between child and adult

which implies that only the footloose artist and the innocent child can have true insights. The story was a *succès d'estime*, and Grahame's contributions became notable events. He was a somewhat unusual member of the bohemian set that produced the magazine, as Netta Syrett noted, commenting on 'his complete freedom from the affectations which so puzzled me in the other men of the set' (Prince, 112).

Both sides of Grahame's life were flourishing. With Tom Greg, a barrister, he took a lease on 5 Kensington Crescent, London, and he became acting secretary at the bank between the incumbencies of Hammond Chubb and G. F. Glennie. He also mined his new vein of writing, producing eleven new stories from December 1893 to January 1895. These, together with the six from *Pagan Papers*, and 'The Roman road', were published by John Lane in February 1895 as *The Golden Age*. The book was a great success; the stories were seen as a breakthrough in writing about childhood, debunking the cult of the 'beautiful child'. A. C. Swinburne, in the *Daily Chronicle*, called *The Golden Age* 'well-nigh too praiseworthy for praise', while *The Academy* noted: 'So typical are their thoughts and actions, misgivings and ambitions, that *The Golden Age* is to some extent every reader's biography' (Prince, 127). It was to be followed by *Dream Days* (1899), another collection of stories of childhood.

In 1897, at 57 Onslow Square, London, Grahame met Elspeth Thomson (1862–1946), stepdaughter of John Fletcher *Moulton, barrister and sometime Liberal MP. Elspeth was the daughter of Robert William *Thomson (1822–1873), the inventor of the pneumatic tyre and the first floating dock, and his wife, Clara Hertz. She was a favourite of Sir John Tenniel, who wrote her annual valentines, and a friend of Tennyson. Grahame's childhood illness reasserted itself in 1899, however, when he was very seriously ill with pneumonia and a chest infection. He began a series of letters to Elspeth in baby talk which demonstrate a certain ambivalence in his feelings towards her. Despite this, they were married on Saturday 22 July 1899, at St Fimbarrus's Church, Fowey, in Cornwall. His cousin Anthony Hope Hawkins was best man. Grahame had formed a lasting friendship with Arthur Quiller-Couch (Q) at Fowey.

Family life The Grahames moved to 16 Durham Villas, Campden Hill, London, and on 12 May 1900 their son Alastair (Mouse) was born, prematurely; he had a congenital cataract in his right eye, which was completely blind, and a squint in the left eye. He was idealized by Elspeth; as he grew older, Grahame told him a series of bedtime stories. Some of these, told in 1904, may have formed the basis of Grahame's most famous book, *The Wind in the Willows* (although the evidence for this comes from the romantic and not always reliable Elspeth).

Grahame was well-liked and respected at the Bank of England, but appears to have taken his duties rather lightly. In 1898 he had reached the peak of his City career, having been appointed secretary of the bank, succeeding Glennie. The quiet tenor of life was interrupted on 24 November 1903, when one George H. Robinson entered the bank and fired at Grahame with a revolver. Grahame was unhurt and was instrumental in Robinson's capture. As the humorous journal *Punch* observed: 'Mr Kenneth Grahame is wondering what is the meaning of the expression "As safe as the Bank of England".' On 27 April 1907, he entertained the children of the prince of Wales (later George V) to tea at the bank. However, Grahame's record of ill health and short hours had come to the attention of the new governor, William Middleton Campbell (appointed in 1907), and in June 1908 he resigned from the bank, with a relatively low pension of £400 p.a.

In 1906 the Grahames had moved to a country house, Mayfield, Cookham Dene, Berkshire, near his childhood home. Although he had not published anything since *Dream Days*, his reputation remained high, and in June 1907 he received an admiring letter from the president of the United States, Theodore Roosevelt. His most enduring book, *The Wind in the Willows*, was developing. In 1907 he wrote 'Bertie's Escapade' for the *Merry Thought*, a nursery magazine, written for (and by) Alastair. This story suggests some of the episodes in the book. Between May and September the Grahames were either on holiday away from their son, or Kenneth was living in London, and he wrote a series of letters to Alastair containing much of the material of five chapters of the book (the adventures of Toad). 'The Wind in the Reeds' (as it was originally known) was finished by December, but it was rejected by Grahame's publisher, the Bodley Head, and by an American magazine, *Everybody's*. Finally, Grahame's agent, Curtis Brown, persuaded Methuen to publish it; such was the firm's lack of confidence in the book that they offered no advance, and Brown negotiated 'excellent rising royalties' (Green, 291). *The Wind in the Willows* was published in October 1908 to mixed reviews; there was some regret that the formula of *The Golden Age* had not been repeated. However, the book was widely and rapidly successful; in the United States it was published by Charles Scribner (who had previously rejected it) after a recommendation from Roosevelt.

Grahame was now both financially secure and world-famous, and in May 1910 the family moved to Boham's, Blewbury, a village near Didcot, Berkshire. On 7 June he met Roosevelt in Oxford. An American scholar, Clayton Hamilton, who was researching Stevenson, was invited for the weekend to Boham's and elicited some significant comments from Grahame about his writing: 'I am not a professional writer. I never have been, and I never will be, by reason of the accident that I don't need any money. I do not care for notoriety' (Prince, 256). Of *The Wind in the Willows* Grahame is reported to have said: 'They liked the subject matter ... They did not even notice the source of all the agony, all the joy. A large amount of what Thoreau called life went into the making of many of those playful pages' (ibid., 257).

Later life and reputation Grahame did little more literary work. He contributed an article, *The Felowe that Goes Alone*, in 1913 to his old school's magazine, *St Edward's Chronicle*, and also in 1913 began editing *The Cambridge Book of Poetry for Children*, which was published in 1916. Meanwhile, his son, Alastair, labouring under excessive parental expectations, was pursuing a very unhappy school career. After preparatory school at the Old Malt House, Weymouth, Dorset, from 1911, he spent six months at Rugby School in 1914, and a year at Eton College. Early in 1916 he was removed from that school and sent to a private tutor. In 1918 he entered Christ Church, Oxford, but was no happier; he was isolated, and struggled with his examinations; and on 13 May 1920 he was killed by a train at Port Meadow on the edge of the city. The evidence strongly suggests a suicide, although the illusion was maintained by family and friends that it had been an accident.

The Grahames stripped Boham's of personal effects, let it, and on 28 October departed for Italy, where they travelled for four years. They spent much of their time in Rome, where, in 1921, Kenneth gave a lecture, 'Ideals', to the Keats–Shelley Society. In June 1922, they returned to England to put Boham's on the market, and in 1924 bought Church Cottage, Pangbourne, Berkshire, although their travels continued until 1930. In their later years, the Grahames became reclusive, and, in Elspeth's case, somewhat eccentric, although they took an interest in village matters. Kenneth's health declined, with high blood-pressure, arteriosclerosis, and fatty degeneration of the heart. As a result his chief pleasures in life, walking, and good food and drink, were restricted.

Kenneth Grahame died just before 6 a.m. on Wednesday 6 July 1932, of a cerebral haemorrhage, at Church Cottage. He was buried on Saturday 9 July at St James-the-Less, Pangbourne, but his body was later moved to Holywell cemetery, Oxford, where Alastair was buried. The inscription on the headstone is by Anthony Hope: 'To the beautiful memory of Kenneth Grahame, husband of Elspeth and father of Alastair, who passed the River on 6th July 1932, leaving childhood and literature through him more blest for all time.'

Elspeth supervised, and, it seems, strongly edited, the biography by Patrick Chalmers (1933), and in 1944 published an inaccurate and idealized account, *First Whisper of 'The Wind in the Willows'*, which contains some unpublished writings by Grahame. She died on 19 December 1946.

Grahame's achievement as a writer is paradoxical. *The Golden Age* and *Dream Days*, books about childhood for adults, have not retained their popularity, but their style and approach provided a model—through writers such as Edith Nesbit and Rudyard Kipling—for much of twentieth-century children's literature. *The Wind in the Willows*, on the other hand, remains one of the most famous books in the English language, and it can be seriously argued that it is not a children's book at all. Despite the presence of Rat, Toad, Mole, and Badger as central characters, it can be read as an account of threat of social change and the destruction of rural England, and of the response of a generation. Grahame's own life is clearly reflected in its attitude to women, to religion, to retreatism, to food and drink, to rebellion, and to home and friendship, among many other things.

In 1929 the book was adapted for the stage by A. A. Milne as *Toad of Toad Hall*; an animated version entitled *Ichabod and Mr Toad* was produced by Disney Studios in 1949; and an uneven Terry Jones film adaptation appeared in 1996. Its varying and continuing manifestations serve to reinforce Milne's original view of *The Wind in the Willows* as a 'household book', a cultural icon, and part of the world's literary heritage. The Kenneth Grahame Fund, to which Grahame bequeathed his royalties, is the chief purchasing fund of the Bodleian Library, Oxford.

PETER HUNT

Sources P. Green, *Kenneth Grahame: a biography* (1959) · A. Prince, *Kenneth Grahame: an innocent in the Wild Wood* (1994) · P. R. Chalmers, *Kenneth Grahame: life, letters and unpublished work* (1933) · L. R. Kuznets, *Kenneth Grahame* (1987) · P. Hunt, 'The wind in the willows': a fragmented Arcadia (1994) · E. Grahame, *First whisper of 'The wind in the willows'* (1944)
Archives Bodl. Oxf., corresp., papers, and literary MSS | Bodl. Oxf., notes to John Lane · Bodl. Oxf., letters to Evelyn Sharp · Burnham, Dorneywood, Courtauld-Thomson collection · Ransom HRC, corresp. with John Lane · U. Reading L., letters to Bodley Head Ltd
Likenesses J. S. Sargent, charcoal drawing, 1912, Bodl. Oxf. [*see illus.*] · A. Wysard, pen and ink with bodycolour, NPG · photograph (as a boy), St Edward's School, Oxford · photographs, repro. in Green, *Kenneth Grahame* · photographs, repro. in Prince, *Kenneth Grahame*
Wealth at death £41,750 10s. 10d.: probate, 8 Sept 1932, CGPLA Eng. & Wales

Grahame, Simion (*c.*1570–1614), author and Franciscan friar, was born in Edinburgh, the son of Archibald Grahame, a burgess of that city. James VI in 1580 presented him to the prebend of Brodderstanis for his 'sustentatioun at the scholis, for sevin yeiris'. In 1587 the king again presented Grahame to the same prebend 'for all the dayes of his lyftyme'. Some details of Grahame's life can be gleaned from his two extant works. The first is a collection of eight poems dedicated to James VI and I, ornamentally printed and published at London in 1604, entitled *The Passionate Sparke of a Relenting Minde*. The second is a collection of prose and verse entitled *The Anatomie of Humours*, printed at Edinburgh in 1609. In the verse epistle to the earl of Montrose that begins *The Anatomie* Grahame states that his 'peregrinations enlarged my curiousitie, my souldiers estate promised to prefere mee, and the smiles of court stuffed my braine with manie idle suppositions'.

Grahame's circumstances underwent a change for the worse, despite his early favour with James and his hopes for further preferment. He appears to have wandered 'in exile' ('From Italy to Scotland his Soyle', a poem found in both collections) for some time, though the date and circumstances of this are unknown. This is perhaps not unconnected to Sir Thomas Urquhart's statement that Grahame was 'too licentious and given over to all manner of debordings' (Urquhart, 122). According to Dempster, however, Grahame was called by the Holy Spirit later in life and became a Franciscan (*Historia ecclesiastica*, 1.328). The final poem of both *The Passionate Sparke* and *The Anatomie*, 'His Dying Song', indicates that Grahame was drawn from a worldly life to a spiritual one as early as 1604. This movement is also seen throughout *The Anatomie*, which contains a lengthy prose treatise satirizing the three estates and a variety of human follies, and advising repentance and spiritual devotion. Titles of poems in *The Anatomie* such as 'The Spirit of Grace to a Wicked Sinner' and 'The Sorrowful Song of a Converted Sinner' support this conversion pattern. It is unclear when Grahame returned from exile to England, though he was probably there for the 1604 publication of his *Passionate Sparke*. He seems to have returned to the continent, and Dempster claims that Grahame died in Carpentras, France, while returning once more to Scotland in 1614.

GORDON GOODWIN, rev. S. BELL

Sources *Thomae Dempsteri Historia ecclesiastica gentis Scotorum, sive, De scriptoribus Scotis*, ed. D. Irving, rev. edn, 1, Bannatyne Club, 21 (1829), 328 · T. Urquhart, *Ekskubalauron, or, The discovery of a most exquisite jewel* (1652) · Anderson, *Scot. nat.*

Grahme, James (1650–1730), courtier and politician, was born at Norton Conyers, Yorkshire, in March 1650 and baptized on 3 April, the second son of Sir George Grahme, baronet (*c.*1624–1658), of Netherby, Cumberland, and his wife, Lady Mary Johnston, second daughter of James, first earl of Hartfell in the peerage of Scotland. He was educated under Richard Busby at Westminster School. On 16 July 1666 he matriculated from Christ Church, Oxford, and was entered at the Inner Temple, though he never pursued a legal career. In 1671 he became a captain in Douglas's Foot, one of the Scottish regiments in French service, and from 1673–4 he served with the English regiment in Louis XIV's forces. He fought in the Netherlands under Turenne and Monmouth. He was appointed captain to the Earl of Carlisle's Foot in 1674, and captain in the Admiralty regiment in 1675. He was with the Coldstream Guards from 1675 to 1678, and served as lieutenant-colonel of foot in Lord Morpeth's regiment in 1678–9. Attractive in person and manners, Grahme was something of a favourite at court and in 1675 (licence 23 November) he married one of the queen's maids of honour, Dorothy (d. 1700), daughter of the Hon. William Howard of Rivensby, Lincolnshire, and granddaughter of the first earl of Berkshire—this despite opposition from her family. They had three sons and two daughters. The marriage was happy and it was probably through her influence that by 1679 Grahme had obtained the household post of keeper of the privy purse to Charles II's brother, the duke of York, with apartments in St James's Palace. He was sent to France in 1682 with Lord Feversham on a mission to compliment Louis XIV, who presented him with a portrait of himself set in diamonds.

On the accession of James II, Grahme was appointed keeper of the privy purse and master of the buckhounds. He was also granted a lease of Bagshot Park in Surrey. He was elected MP for Carlisle, where his brother Richard *Graham, Viscount Preston, had been chosen recorder, and he was suggested as court candidate for Carlisle in James's proposed parliament of 1688. In 1685 Levens Hall in Westmorland had been mortgaged for £13,000 by the MP Alan Bellingham and placed with trustees. Grahme, who was probably the mortgagor, bought Levens for £24,000 in 1688. After the revolution in December 1688,

Grahme accompanied James II to Rochester on his way to exile. Soon after leaving England, James transferred £10,000 of East India Company stock and £13,000 of Royal Africa Company stock to Grahme in lieu, Grahme claimed, for the loan of £8000 which he made to the king shortly before his departure. It seems, however, that Grahme sold these shares and forwarded the money to James in France. The disposal of these shares brought Grahme a good deal of trouble as he was prosecuted in the exchequer for their recovery. He was even prosecuted for a debt of £1250 incurred in the issue of medals for touching for the king's evil in James's reign, a debt later cancelled by Queen Anne. In 1689 Grahme sent his eldest son, Henry, to the Stuart court at St Germain-en-Laye, where his younger brother Fergus Grahme had succeeded him as privy purse.

Acting with his brother Viscount Preston, Grahme was engaged in 1690 in a high Anglican scheme involving Lord Clarendon, Sir Edward Seymour, and his brother-in-law Sir John Fenwick to restore James II, while providing for the security of the Church of England. In June a proclamation for Grahme's arrest was issued but he could not be found. The following month Nottingham, the secretary of state, had an offer of information about French designs from Grahme, though he would not name those involved in Britain. He was allowed to take the oaths privately, lest he be suspected. Viscount Preston was arrested while travelling to France to resume his post as secretary of state to James II. In his papers was found incriminating evidence against Grahme, whose arrest was ordered in February 1691. Again, Grahme offered to make disclosures, telling Nottingham that he had acted as he did because his prosecution in the exchequer would ruin him. He was granted a royal pardon. Arrested again at the time of the Franco-Jacobite invasion from La Hogue in 1692, Grahme does not appear to have given valuable information, for Nottingham thought he deserved no mercy. Grahme's conduct, however, made Lord Middleton, the secretary of state at St Germain, suspicious and nothing of importance was entrusted to him. He was again arrested at the time of Sir John Fenwick's plot to restore James in 1696.

Meanwhile, Grahme lived quietly at Levens as his brother and lifelong correspondent, Fergus, had advised him to do. His extensive Westmorland and Cumberland estates were said to be worth £1000 a year, and the selling of the lease of Bagshot Lodge to Sir Edward Seymour eased his financial worries. This enabled Grahme to carry out improvements at Levens Hall and to lay out its celebrated gardens in the French style under the supervision of William Beaumont, who had designed Hampton Court gardens for James II. By 1700 Grahme had so far secured his power base in Westmorland that he was able to put up his son Henry (who had returned from France two years earlier) for Westmorland and, despite accusations that Henry was a papist and was disaffected, he was returned to the first 1701 parliament.

In 1702 (licence 4 March) Grahme married for a second time. His new wife was Elizabeth (d. 1708), daughter of Isaac Barton of All Hallows, Barking, and widow of George Bromley of the Middle Temple; there were no children. The accession of Queen Anne opened a new world for Grahme, who was returned for Appleby, where he held burgages, at the 1702 election. He had wide-ranging connections among the tories at court, who nicknamed him 'Sir Humphrey Polesworth', and he was close to Robert Harley and Henry St John. Grahme's son Henry became groom of the bedchamber to Prince George of Denmark. Grahme was also on good terms with William Nicolson, bishop of Carlisle, who described him as entirely influenced by Harley; this would explain Grahme's voting against the tack in 1704 (to tack the bill to prevent occasional conformity to a money bill so that the Lords could not reject it). His repeated pleas to Harley for financial assistance, however, resulted only in a loan of £200. Again returned for Appleby in 1705, he was torn between his loyalties to the court, who put up the whig John Smith for speaker and his friend William Bromley as the tory candidate. Grahme's tory loyalties were still strong, as his association with the nonjuring writer Charles Leslie show, and on 15 October he and his son voted against Smith, which caused his son to lose his place. Returned for Westmorland, which he represented until 1727, Grahme won popularity by voting against the impeachment of Sacheverell in 1710. Although he was a member of the October Club, in 1712 he defended Marlborough, to whom his family had obligations, against accusations of corruption.

Grahme's financial difficulties deepened after 1715. His speaking and voting for the Septennial Bill in 1716 might be interpreted as a gesture towards the whig regime, but he voted against the repeal of the Occasional Conformity and Schism Acts and Sunderland's Peerage Bill in 1719. He was one of the MPs who in 1720 took a bribe of unpaid South Sea stock worth £2000. In 1721 Grahme was involved in the negotiations with Sunderland, who sought tory support to save himself from impeachment after the bursting of the South Sea Bubble. Grahme corresponded with James Francis Edward Stuart, the exiled Stuart 'Pretender', at the time of the Atterbury plot and was sent a commission of colonel by James to take part in the proposed Jacobite rising in 1722. Grahme died on 16 January 1730, and was buried at Charlton in Wiltshire, the seat of the fourth earl of Berkshire, who had married his daughter and sole surviving heir. Grahme's monumental inscription describes him as a faithful servant of Charles II and James II, 'an unworthy but true member of the Church of England' and 'a sincere lover of monarchy'.

EVELINE CRUICKSHANKS

Sources HoP, *Commons, 1660–90,* 1.617–18; 2. 428–9 · HoP, *Commons, 1690–1715* [draft] · HoP, *Commons, 1715–54,* 2.76–7 · J. Bagot, *Colonel James Grahme of Levens* (1886) · J. V. Beckett, 'The finances of a former Jacobite: James Grahme of Levens Hall', *Transactions of the Cumberland and Westmorland Antiquarian and Archaeological Society,* [new ser.], 85 (1985), 131–42 · J. F. Munby, 'The finances of James Graham: a reply', *Transactions of the Cumberland and Westmorland Antiquarian and Archaeological Society,* [new ser.], 86 (1986), 274–6 · *Report on the manuscripts of Allan George Finch,* 5 vols., HMC, 71 (1913–2003), vol. 2, pp. 195, 310, 390–92; vol. 3, pp. 9–10, 149, 315–16, 330, 351–5 · E. Cruickshanks and E. Corp, eds., *The Stuart court in exile and the Jacobites* (1995), 1–13 · C. Cole, *Historical and political memoirs*

(1735), 195–235 • A. Bagot, 'Monsieur Beaumont and Colonel Grahme: the making of a garden, 1689–1710', *Garden History*, 3/4 (1975), 66–78 • {}, A. Bagot, and J. Munby, eds. *'All things is well here': letters from Hugh James of Levens to James Grahme, 1692–95*, Cumberland and Westmorland Antiquarian and Archaeological Society, record ser., 10 (1988) • Bagot MSS, Historical Manuscripts Commission, London, 342 • *The London diaries of William Nicolson, bishop of Carlisle, 1702–1718*, ed. C. Jones and G. Holmes (1985), 24, 237, 247, 303 • E. Cruickshanks, 'Charles Spencer, third earl of Sunderland, and Jacobitism', *EngHR*, 113 (1998), 65–76, esp. 74 • J. F. E. Stuart, letter to J. Hamilton, 31 Jan 1722, Royal Arch., Stuart papers, 57/110; J. F. E. Stuart, letter to A. Urquart, 31 Jan 1722, Royal Arch., Stuart papers, 57/112 • Foster, *Alum. Oxon.*

Archives NRA, priv. coll., corresp. | Royal Arch., Stuart papers
Likenesses P. Lely, portrait, Levens Hall, Cumbria • drawing, Elford Hall, Staffordshire
Wealth at death over £1000 a year in 1690s: *Transactions of the Cumberland and Westmorland Antiquarian and Archaeological Society*, 85.132, 133; 86.275

Graile, Edmund (1575/6–1643), poet and physician, was born at Wotton under Edge, Gloucestershire, according to a deposition dated 12 October 1640 (in which he gave his age as sixty-four). He was the eldest son of Thomas Graile (*d.* 1608), a yeoman with extensive land-holdings in Wotton and North Nibley, and his wife, Agnes (*d.* 1619). He matriculated at Magdalen College, Oxford, in 1593, and took his BA in 1595 and his MA in 1600. In 1607 he was appointed physician at St Bartholomew's Hospital in Gloucester, at an annual salary of £3 6s. 8d. The hospital, a religious house before the dissolution of the monasteries, had been established in the previous century.

Graile was the author of *Little Timothie his lesson, or, A summary relation of the historicall part of holy scripture, plainely and familiarly comprized in meeter, for the helpe of memory, and instruction of the ignorant in the writings of God*, first published in 1611; a third impression, augmented by some original prayers, was issued in 1632. In a dedicatory epistle, addressed to the president and governors of St Bartholomew's, Graile explains that a former bishop of Gloucester had encouraged him to publish 'this little Pamphlet'. He also expresses concern for the hospital and its forty inmates, urging in particular the raising of funds for the provision of a hospital chaplain. Graile's verse is simple stuff but not without charm. According to some prefatory lines entitled 'The Author to the Curious Reader' he had no desire to achieve 'perfection of a Poets skill (which doth with silver raies poor rusticks daunt)'; that was the preserve of more sophisticated writers. Simplicity and honesty were his touchstones:

> There needes no garland where the wine is good
> nor colours where the substance is most pure.
> Sinceritie by truth hath ever stood,
> and shall, so long as doth the Truth indure.

Verses in honour of Sir William Throckmorton and his wife also appear in the opening pages. Graile evidently remained on good terms with the Throckmortons, for he acted as trustee of a family settlement in 1632.

Despite inheriting some of his father's property at Wotton, Graile and his family lived most of the time at St Bartholomew's; indeed he was obliged to reside there under the terms of an ordinance of 1635, which also required the hospital to accommodate twenty men and thirty women and included elaborate rules for their conduct, laying particular emphasis on sobriety, piety, and cleanliness.

The minutes of Gloucester corporation record, *inter alia*, that Graile installed hot baths in the hospital in 1641. He remained its physician until his death, from an attack of fever, on 24 September 1643; his wife, Elizabeth, had predeceased him, on 13 February 1638. They had four sons and three daughters. A monument in the hospital chapel commemorating Graile, his wife, and his youngest son was removed on the demolition of the chapel in 1788 to Corse church (where one of his descendants was vicar).

Verse was not Graile's only tangible legacy: in 1708 Thomas Graile, rector of Lassington, bequeathed to his cousin John Graile 'the skeleton in a box being the work of his and my grandfather Mr. Edmond Graile Master of Arts and Professor of Chirurgery Famous in his time' (Glos. RO, wills, 1709/140).   P. L. DICKINSON

Sources *N&Q*, 11th ser., 7 (1913), 46 • R. Bigland, *Historical, monumental and genealogical collections, relative to the county of Gloucester*, ed. B. Frith, 1 (1989), 442 • wills, Glos. RO, Gloucester, 1608/123; 1629/105; 1709/140 [first also recorded in PRO, PROB 11/112, sig. 97; third also recorded in PRO, PROB 11/569, sig. 106] • Glos. RO, MSS GDR 205; GBR, B3/1/222; GBR, J3/16; GBR, B3/2/190 and 287; D225/F47; D1677/GG776 • Foster, *Alum. Oxon.*, 1500–1714, 2.595 • PRO, E115/180/93 • parish registers, Wotton under Edge, Glos. RO [transcript in Gloucester City Library] • *Transactions of the Bristol and Gloucestershire Archaeological Society*, 67 (1948), 123
Wealth at death land at Huntingford, Wotton under Edge; family fairly prosperous

Grailly, Jean (III) de [known as Captal de Buch] (*d.* 1377), soldier, was a member of a Gascon noble family, albeit of Savoyard origins, which served the English crown with some consistency over many generations. Son of Jean (II) de Grailly (*d.* 1343) and Blanche de Foix, daughter of Gaston (I), count of Foix and vicomte of Béarn (1302–15), Jean held the important lordship of Buch (Gironde) as well as those of Castillon, Bénauges, and other strongholds in the Plantagenet duchy of Aquitaine. He was descended in the female line from the ancient Gascon family of Bordeaux, who held the lordships of Buch and Puy-Paulin. Pierre (II) de Grailly (or Grilly), grandson of Jean (I) de Grilly (*d.* 1303), lieutenant and seneschal of Edward I in Aquitaine in 1266–8 and 1278–87, had married Assalhide de Bordeaux, lady of Puy-Paulin, and inherited her lands, including the *captalat* of Buch. In her will of 2 April 1329 Assalhide instituted their son Jean (II) de Grailly as her universal heir to all her lordships. Jean (III), who succeeded to his father's inheritance in 1343, became perhaps the foremost of those Gascon nobles whose loyalty to the English king–dukes of Aquitaine did much to maintain and further Edward III's war efforts against France.

Grailly's loyalty was rewarded on a number of occasions—by his nomination as a founder member of the Order of the Garter (1348), one of three non-English knights in the first election, and by gifts of lands and money from Edward, the Black Prince. He served in the Gascon campaign of 1345–6 of Henry of Grosmont, earl of

Lancaster, and afterwards achieved distinction under the Black Prince, for whom a Gascon principality was created by Edward III. Jean was one of the three Gascon lords responsible for requesting Edward III to send the prince to Gascony in 1355, and played a crucial role in the events that led to the victory at Poitiers on 19 September 1356. During that battle Grailly's flanking manoeuvre greatly contributed to the French defeat and he benefited from his capture of the duke of Bourbon, who was bought from him by the Black Prince for 25,000 couronnes. Jean de Grailly journeyed to Prussia with his kinsman Gaston (III) de Foix (Phébus), count of Foix and vicomte of Béarn, in 1357–8, fighting the heathen Lithuanians at the request of the grand master of the Teutonic order. On his return he aided Gaston de Foix in the suppression of the peasant revolt known as the *jacquerie* (1358) in the countryside around Meaux. Grailly went on to serve Edward III and the Black Prince in the French expedition of 1359–60, but was captured, as lieutenant of the prince's ally Charles, king of Navarre, at the battle of Cocherel (May 1364). Such was the anxiety of Charles V, king of France, to win him to the French cause that he released him without ransom and offered him the lordship of Nemours in return for his homage. On his return to Aquitaine his loyalty was challenged by the Black Prince and he renounced both his French homage and possessions. He then fought for the prince during the Castilian campaign of 1366–7, commanding one of the victorious divisions at the battle of Nájera (3 April 1367).

The French military and diplomatic recovery, after the renewal of hostilities in 1368–9, contributed substantially to Grailly's misfortunes in the 1370s. He was rewarded for his continuing loyalty to the English cause by the grant to him of the *comté* of Bigorre by the Black Prince in June 1370, and he participated in the campaign that was to lead to the notorious sacking and massacre at Limoges (19 September 1370). In the aftermath of the defeat of John Hastings, earl of Pembroke, at sea off La Rochelle (22 June 1372), Grailly was again captured by the French at Soubise on 23 August and imprisoned by them. He was never released. Charles V again offered him material incentives to embrace French allegiance, but he refused them. Froissart recounts that he was the Gascon noble whom the French feared the most, and was therefore kept in close confinement at Paris. He died in captivity in 1377.

Grailly had married Rose, daughter of Bernard-Ezi (II), sieur d'Albret (d. 1359), and had drawn up an interesting will in March 1369. This stipulated the celebration of no less than 50,000 masses during the year following his death and the foundation of numerous chapelries, as well as a gift of the large sum of 1000 écus d'or to the fabric of the Franciscan convent at Bordeaux. His pious gifts and benefactions totalled 40,000 écus d'or. He was succeeded by his son Archambaud de Grailly, who became count of Foix and vicomte of Béarn (d. 1412) through his marriage with Isabelle, sole heir of Count Mathieu de Castelbon. The *captalat* of Buch, and other Grailly lands within English Gascony, were subsequently detached from the Foix-

Béarn inheritance, to be held by a cadet branch of the family until the end of English rule in the mid-fifteenth century.   MALCOLM VALE

Sources *Chroniques de J. Froissart*, ed. S. Luce and others, 3–7 (Paris, 1869–1975) · *La vie du Prince Noir by Chandos herald*, ed. D. B. Tyson (1975) · R. Barber, *Edward, prince of Wales and Aquitaine: a biography of the Black Prince* (1978) · R. Boutruche, *La crise d'une société* (1947) · *Archives historiques de la Gironde*, 58 (1932), 1–18 · L. Babinet, 'Jean III de Grailly, captal de Buch', *Mémoires de la Société des Antiquaires de l'Ouest*, 2nd ser., 18 (1896) · M. Vale, *The Angevin legacy and the Hundred Years War, 1250–1340* (1990) · P. Capra, *L'administration anglo-gasconne au temps du Prince Noir* (1972) · Y. Renouard, ed., *Bordeaux sous les rois d'Angleterre* (1965) · K. Fowler, *The king's lieutenant: Henry of Grosmont, first duke of Lancaster, 1310–1361* (1969) · P. Tucoo-Chala, *Gaston Fébus et la vicomté de Béarn, 1343–91* (1954) · Rymer, *Foedera*, new edn, 2/2; 3/1 · *Le livre des hommages d'Aquitaine*, ed. J.-P. Trabut-Cussac (1959) · M. C. B. Dawes, ed., *Register of Edward, the Black Prince*, 4 vols., PRO (1930–33) · F. Pasquier and H. Courteault, eds., *Chroniques romanes des comtes de Foix* (1895) · PRO, C 61, SC 1, E 101 · *Chancery records*
Archives Archives Départementales de la Gironde, Bordeaux · Archives Départementales des Pyrénées-Atlantiques, Pau

Grain, Richard Corney (1844–1895), entertainer, the youngest son of John Grain, a farmer, and his wife, Mary Anne, was born on 26 October 1844 at Teversham, Cambridgeshire. He received what he called 'an average middle-class education', partly in Germany, where he went at the age of fourteen. He became a student of the Inner Temple on 27 April 1863, and was called to the bar on 30 April 1866. For a short period he went on the western circuit. Having more musical than histrionic proficiency, he sang and acted in private, and on 16 May 1870 he joined what was known as the German Reed entertainment, at the Gallery of Illustration, appearing in a sketch of his own called *The School-Feast*.

Grain remained with this company until the end of his life, and eventually became its principal support. He moved with it to St George's Hall, toured with it in the provinces, and in 1877 became the partner of Alfred German Reed in its management. Over twenty-five years Grain wrote for the company between fifty and sixty entertainments consisting of social sketches and songs with piano accompaniments. At times he took part in comediettas or other dramatic performances, but, as he owned, had little taste or capacity for acting. His comic sketches were fashionable, and were frequently performed in private houses. His last sketch was entitled *Music à la mode*.

Grain had a large frame and exceptionally large and expressive hands. He wrote an autobiography, *Corney Grain, by Himself*, which first appeared in *Murray's Magazine* before being issued as a book in 1888. His death, from 'epidemic influenza' on 16 March 1895, at his home, 8 Weymouth Street, Marylebone, London, six days after the death of German Reed, broke up what had been for forty years a very successful and popular entertainment.

JOSEPH KNIGHT, *rev.* NILANJANA BANERJI

Sources Adams, *Drama* · J. Foster, *Men-at-the-bar: a biographical hand-list of the members of the various inns of court*, 2nd edn (1885) · M. Watson, 'Alfred German Reed and Corney Grain', *The Theatre*, 4th ser., 25 (1895), 221–3 · J. Hollingshead, *Gaiety chronicles* (1898) · *The life and reminiscences of E. L. Blanchard, with notes from the diary of*

Wm. Blanchard, ed. C. W. Scott and C. Howard, 2 vols. (1891) • Hall, *Dramatic ports.* • personal knowledge (1901) • d. cert. • b. cert.

Likenesses Bassano, cabinet photograph, NPG • H. Furniss, pen-and-ink caricature sketch, NPG • P. Naumann, wood-engraving, BM; repro. in *ILN* (23 March 1895) • Spy [L. Ward], chromolithograph caricature, NPG; repro. in *VF* (22 Aug 1885) • caricature, repro. in *The Hornet* (5 April 1876) • caricature, repro. in *Entr'acte* (Feb 1881) • lithograph (after photograph by Elliott & Fry), repro. in A. Cecil, *Her mother!* (c.1890) [sheet music]

Wealth at death £16,822 1s. 2d.: probate, 20 April 1895, *CGPLA Eng. & Wales*

Grainger, Edward (1797–1824), anatomist and lecturer, the elder son of Edward Grainger, surgeon and author of *Medical and Surgical Remarks* (1815), and brother of Richard Dugard *Grainger (1801–1865), was born in Birmingham on 28 April 1797. After being educated at the free school, Birmingham, and trained by his father, Grainger entered as a student at the united hospitals of Guy's and St Thomas's, London, in October 1816 where he was regarded as a 'most industrious student, and especially diligent in anatomical pursuits' (Feltoe, 107).

Grainger hoped to be appointed demonstrator of anatomy at Guy's and St Thomas's, but the post went to Charles Aston Key, a relative of Sir Astley Cooper, surgeon and lecturer at the hospitals, on the grounds 'that such an appointment could only be given to one who was a hospital apprentice, or in other words, to one who had paid him [Cooper] or his colleagues' the necessary fees (*An Account*, 19). Cooper advised Grainger that the best course would be for him to open an anatomy school in Birmingham. Grainger, who 'was of a rather staid and quiet demeanour, but strong-willed, and not easily diverted from any opinions which he had taken up' (Feltoe, 107), ignored Cooper, and in the summer of 1819 (at about the time that he became a member of the Royal College of Surgeons) he began to offer a course in practical anatomy in a large attic in a tailor's house in St Saviour's churchyard, Southwark. Grainger was a knowledgeable, clear, and concise teacher, and his courses soon proved popular with students, so much so that in the following autumn he moved to new premises in a former Roman Catholic chapel in Webb Street, Maze Pond, near the hospitals. The size of the classes had increased enough by 1821 for Grainger to have a theatre built in Webb Street, where he was joined by John Armstrong, Richard Phillips, a chemist, and Thomas Southwood Smith. By October 1823 the school had attracted some 300 pupils, and a larger theatre was built. Grainger's establishment had become a rival to the hospital schools.

Grainger's success brought him into conflict with the nearby hospitals and with Sir Astley Cooper in particular. The school required a supply of corpses and Grainger was willing to pay the body snatchers a higher fee than some of his competitors, thereby breaking the control over the price of bodies maintained by a combination of anatomists known as the Anatomical Club. This infuriated Sir Astley Cooper, and following the arrest of William Millard, a resurrectionist employed now by Grainger, but formerly by Sir Astley, Millard's wife was told that Cooper 'would be ready to hang your husband if he thought he

had anything to do with that young man; Sir Astley would give £10,000 if he could ruin Grainger' (*An Account*, 33).

As it happened Sir Astley did not get the opportunity to carry out his threat. Grainger died from consumption at his father's house in Birmingham on 13 January 1824. The Webb Street school was then taken over by Richard Grainger. MICHAEL BEVAN

Sources *Memorials of John Flint South*, ed. C. L. Feltoe (1884) • *The Lancet* (18 Jan 1824), 94–5 • *GM*, 1st ser., 94/1 (1824), 183–4 • *An account of the circumstances attending the imprisonment and death of the late William Millard* (1825) • R. Richardson, *Death, dissection and the destitute*, pbk edn (1988) • A. Desmond, *The politics of evolution: morphology, medicine and reform in radical London* (1989) • *A catalogue of engraved portraits of nobility … connected with the county of Warwick* (1848)

Archives Wellcome L., lecture notes

Likenesses P. Hollins, bust, 1848, Theatre of the Webb Street school • P. Hollins, marble bust, RCS Eng.

Grainger, James (1721x4–1766), physician and poet, was born at Duns, Berwickshire, between 1721 and 1724, the son, from the second marriage, of John Grainger of Houghton Hall, Cumberland, who, in consequence of some unsuccessful mining speculations, and, it is said, his Jacobite leanings in 1715, was forced to sell his estate, and take a post in the excise at Duns. On the death of his father, Grainger's half-brother, William Grainger, sent him to school at North Berwick, after which he studied medicine at Edinburgh University for three years, and was apprenticed to George Lauder, a surgeon in the city. Entering the army as a surgeon, he served in Lieutenant-General Pulteney's infantry regiment during the rebellion of 1745, and in the Netherlands in 1746–8.

After leaving the army following the peace of Aix-la-Chapelle in 1748, Grainger toured Europe, and, having returned to Scotland, graduated MD at Edinburgh in 1753. In the same year he printed his *Historia febris anomalae Batavæ annorum 1746, 1747, 1748, … Accedunt monita siphylica*, giving an account of his military medical experiences during an epidemic among the troops in Holland. Sir John Pringle's elaborate work on the same subject had appeared a year earlier, and Grainger's effort failed to attract attention.

Grainger settled in London after 1753, established a practice in Bond Court, Walbrook, and met literary figures such as Samuel Johnson, William Shenstone, John Armstrong, Tobias Smollett, and Thomas Percy. Grainger held regular consultations at the Temple Exchange Coffee House, near Temple Bar, and there met Oliver Goldsmith. In spite of his reputed ability, Grainger failed to obtain patients, and depended chiefly on his writing for a livelihood. In 1755 his 'Ode on Solitude' was published in Robert Dodsley's *Collection*, IV, winning praise from his contemporaries; Johnson considered the opening lines 'very noble' (Boswell, *Life*, 3.197). From May 1756 to May 1758 he wrote on poetry and drama in the *Monthly Review*, and, not wholly neglecting medicine, he published a paper on 'An obstinate case of dysentery cured by lime water' in *Essays Physical and Literary* (2, 1756, 257). He became a licentiate of the Royal College of Physicians in 1758. With Percy and others he became connected with the *Grand Magazine of Universal Intelligence*, a short-lived journal started in 1758;

and about the same time he translated 'Leander to Hero' and 'Hero to Leander' for Percy's projected version of Ovid's *Epistles*. In November 1758 he published a *Poetical Translation of the Elegies of Tibullus, and of the Poems of Sulpicia* (dated 1759), which he had begun while in the army. The book was harshly reviewed by Smollett, then editor of the *Critical Review*; this led to a literary feud with a series of attacks from both sides. Grainger addressed Smollett throughout as 'good Dr Tobias' and 'Dr Toby', because Smollett detested his baptismal name. Smollett, in his *Review* for January, contemptuously referred to Grainger as 'one of the Owls belonging to the proprietor of the "M**thly R****w"', and in the *Review* for February, Grainger was furiously attacked as a contemptible hack-writer. Reference was made to his having compiled from materials left by the author the second volume of William Maitland's *History and Antiquities of Scotland* (1757) (cf. *GM*, 1791, 2.614), and to the failure of his application to write for the *Biographia Britannica*. Grainger did not reply. With many others he assisted Charlotte Lennox with her translation of Pierre Brumoy's *Théâtre des grecs* (1759).

In April 1759 Grainger left England on a four-year tour of the West Indies with John Bourryau, a former pupil and heir to property there. Grainger was to receive a life annuity of £200 for undertaking the trip. Their first destination was the island of St Kitts. Soon after their arrival Grainger married Miss Burt, daughter of William Burt, a Nevis planter and former governor of the island, whose widow Grainger attended for smallpox on the voyage out. They had two daughters, Louise Agnes and Eleanor. Grainger started practising as a physician on the island, and was entrusted by his wife's uncle, Daniel Mathew, with the management of his estates. Unable to afford to become a planter himself, he indulged in his favourite study of botany, and his scanty savings were invested in the purchase of slaves.

While travelling to different parts of the island to visit his patients, Grainger composed his principal work, *The Sugar-Cane*, a 2560-line poem in four books on the cultivation of the crop. He sent the manuscript to Percy in June 1762 for his and Shenstone's revision, and in the autumn of 1763, following the death of his brother, he returned to England and submitted his poem to his friends. James Boswell relates that *The Sugar-Cane* was read in manuscript in Sir Joshua Reynolds's drawing-room, and that the 'assembled wits' were much amused by Grainger's account of the havoc wrought by rats in the sugar-fields. Dr Johnson spoke of the time when Grainger read the poem to him, and that when he came to the line, 'Say, shall I sing of rats?' Johnson cried 'no' with great vehemence (J. Boswell, *Life of Johnson*, ed. J. W. Croker, 1848, 834). The poem was published in 1764, with copious notes, and was favourably reviewed by Percy in the *London Chronicle* and, as Smollett was by that time on his travels, by Johnson in the *Critical Review*; the latter, however, censured Grainger for not denouncing the slave trade, even though Grainger recommended throughout a humane treatment of slaves.

Just before the publication of his poem in May 1764, Grainger returned to St Kitts, where his affairs had become involved in his absence. However, he had acquired some property on the death of his brother, and was partly able to meet his difficulties. He expanded the notes of *The Sugar-Cane* into an *Essay on the more common West India diseases; and the remedies which that country itself produces: To which are added some hints on the management of negroes*, which was published in 1764. He also contributed to the first volume of Percy's *Reliques of Ancient English Poetry* (1764) a ballad of West Indian life called 'Bryan and Pereene'. Grainger died at St Kitts on 24 December 1766 of 'West Indian fever'.

'Grainger was a man', said Johnson, 'who would do any good that was in his power.' He was the 'ingenious acquaintance' whose 'singular history' Johnson related (not quite correctly) to Boswell in 1776 (Boswell, *Life*, 2.455). In person he was tall and of 'a lathy make', plain-featured, and deeply marked with the smallpox. He managed to retain his broad provincial accent and was known as a good conversationalist. An attack on Mrs Grainger, imputing her husband's premature death to grief at the discovery of her immorality, was published during her lifetime in the *Westminster Magazine* for December 1773. Percy sent an indignant denial to the *Whitehall Evening Post*, and threatened legal proceedings, upon which the libel was withdrawn and apologized for in January 1774. Grainger bequeathed his manuscripts to Percy, and in accordance with his wish a complete edition of his poetical works was suggested by Percy to Dr Robert Anderson in 1798, and was printed in 1801, with the addition of an index of the Linnaean names of plants, by William Wright. Anderson deferred the publication until Percy supplied him with materials for a life of Grainger, and the book, later extremely scarce, did not appear until 1836.

GORDON GOODWIN, rev. CAROLINE OVERY

Sources A. Chalmers, ed., *The general biographical dictionary*, new edn, 16 (1814), 164–71 · Munk, *Roll* · B. Hill, 'Let's sing of rats: James Grainger MD', *The Practitioner*, 177 (1956), 627–31 · W. B. Ober, 'James Grainger, MD, 1721? to 1766', *New York State Journal of Medicine*, 65 (1965), 1257–60 · D. K. McE. Kevan, 'Mid-eighteenth-century entomology and helminthology in the West Indies: Dr James Grainger', *Journal of the Society of the Bibliography of Natural History*, 8 (1976–8), 193–222 · *Boswell's Life of Johnson*, ed. G. B. Hill, 6 vols. (1887) · D. P. Henige, *Colonial governors from the fifteenth century to the present* (1970) · *GM*, 1st ser., 37 (1767), 95

Archives BL · Bodl. Oxf., prescriptions and translations of Ovid's *Epistulae heroidum* · NL Scot. | A. K. Bell Library, Perth, Perthshire, letters to Lord Kinnaird · Bodl. Oxf., letters to Bishop Percy

Grainger, Percy Aldridge (1882–1961), composer, was born George Percy Grainger at Brighton, Victoria, Australia, on 8 July 1882, the son of John Harry Grainger (1855–1917), architect and engineer, and his wife, Rosa Annie (Rose) Aldridge (1861–1922). He spent his childhood in Melbourne, Victoria, where he was privately educated under the guidance of his musically gifted mother. He received supplementary lessons in languages, art (with Frederick McCubbin), elocution and drama (with Thomas A. Sisley), and the piano (with Louis Pabst and Adelaide Burkitt). His early readings of classical legends and Icelandic sagas influenced him towards a muscular, even drastic approach to life.

Percy Aldridge Grainger (1882–1961), by Elliott & Fry

By 1895 Grainger's pianistic accomplishments led him to pursue studies at the Hoch Conservatorium in Frankfurt am Main, where he learned from James Kwast and took theory and composition classes with Iwan Knorr. At the Hoch Conservatorium he fell in with several older British students—Cyril Scott, Henry Balfour Gardiner, Roger Quilter—who, with Norman O'Neill, were later dubbed the Frankfurt group. While in Frankfurt, Grainger fell under the spell of Rudyard Kipling, settings of whose verses he worked on between 1898 and 1956, and Walt Whitman, who inspired his *Marching Song of Democracy* (1901–15) and many aspects of his life philosophy.

From 1901 to 1914 Grainger based his career as a concert pianist and private teacher in London, whence he undertook frequent tours of northern Europe and two lengthy Antipodean visits in the touring party of the Australian contralto Ada Crossley (1903–4, 1908–9). During the first half of his residence in London, when often fulfilling subsidiary musical roles, Grainger depended upon sponsorship by such leading musicians as Hans Richter, Sir Charles Villiers Stanford, and Sir Henry Wood. He also benefited from the patronage of such society figures as Sir Edgard and Lady Speyer, through whom he first met Edvard Grieg, and Lilith Lowrey, at whose 'at homes' in Chelsea Grainger was a particular favourite. Lowrey was so taken with the golden-haired Grainger that, in return for sexual favours and music lessons, she vigorously helped to promote his performing career. This 'love-serve-job', as Grainger termed it, ceased about 1904, when his mother felt it was no longer to his professional advantage. From 1910 onwards Grainger established himself more solidly in the virtuoso recitalist class and as performer of landmark Romantic concertos. He particularly promoted

the piano concerto of Grieg, with whom he had studied the work in Norway during the composer's final months. Building on this new regard, Grainger finally relented in allowing his major compositions to be published, through Schott & Co., and in 1912 arranged the first London concert dedicated entirely to his compositions. Many of these early released and well-received works, such as *Shepherd's Hey* and *Molly on the Shore*, were based on English folk-songs, some of which Grainger himself had collected and edited in 1905–8. Others, such as *Mock Morris* and *Handel in the Strand*, were in a similarly jaunty style but were not direct settings of folk-songs. In 1911 he changed his name to Percy Aldridge Grainger.

With the outbreak of war in 1914 Grainger and his mother moved to New York. He took American citizenship in 1918, while serving in a US army band, and in 1921 settled in White Plains, New York, where he saw out his days. The years 1914–22 constituted the peak of Grainger's musical career. As a pianist he entered into lucrative piano-roll and gramophone recording contracts, and performed as a Steinway artist across the country with leading orchestras and conductors. In his concerts and recordings he played a wide variety of works from Bach to contemporary music, including lesser-known works by Stanford, Cyril Scott, Nathaniel Dett, and David Guion. In 1916 he undertook concerts with the soprano Nellie Melba, a compatriot, in aid of field ambulances, but did not avoid the accusation of his British friends that he was lurking in America to avoid his patriotic duty. Robin Legge, music critic of London's *Daily Telegraph*, charged Grainger with cowardice, and warned him that 'England is no place for you after the war I fear'. During the war years his compositions, such as the *In a Nutshell* suite, the *Marching Song of Democracy*, and his 'music to an imaginary ballet' *The Warriors*, gained notable premières. His setting of a morris dance tune, *Country Gardens*, became an instant hit on its publication in 1919. Through dozens of arrangements, it remains his best-known work.

The suicide of his beloved mother in 1922, by leaping from a New York skyscraper, proved a watershed in Grainger's career. He became shy of the more challenging musical platforms and nostalgic for the simple enthusiasms of his youth. During 1922–8 he renewed his folk-song collecting expeditions; his work in Jutland with the Danish ethnologist Evald Tang Kristensen led to the composition of his *Danish Folk-Music Suite*. He undertook several visits to Europe, where he resuscitated his friendship with Frederick Delius, and to Australia, where he sought solace among his mother's relatives. During his return from one Australian trip, in 1926, he met the Swedish artist Ella Viola Ström-Brandelius (1889–1979), who on 9 August 1928, to the strains of his musical 'ramble' *To a Nordic Princess*, became his wife during one of his Hollywood Bowl appearances.

Although Grainger continued to perform for several decades after his marriage, he did so increasingly in an educational rather than fully professional role, preferring to trade appearances as a concerto soloist for performances of his own or his friends' new works. He relished the chance to perform in high-school auditoria, and during the Second World War saw his career as a solo pianist partially resurrected through numerous concerts at army and air force camps. Between 1919 and 1930 he taught in the summer school of the Chicago Musical College, and during 1937–44 at the National Music Camp, Interlochen. He gave his last official American concert tour in 1948, but continued, despite worsening health from 1952, to give occasional lectures and educational concerts until he was in his late seventies. Grainger died in White Plains Hospital, New York, on 20 February 1961. He was buried alongside his mother in the West Terrace cemetery, Adelaide, on 2 March 1961.

In 1911 Grainger concisely defined his enthusiasms in life as sex, race, athletics, speech, and art. In others' opinions, he was variously avant-garde, eccentric, or merely a poseur in these fields. He early realized the social utility of sex and over five decades enthusiastically practised flagellation with his wife, several earlier lovers, and by himself. 'He was one of the century's more practised flagellants, equally at home in giving or receiving the lash', having with the onset of puberty 'started to associate the whipping with sexual pleasure, consequent upon acts of cruelty to women' (*All-Round Man*, 9). Grainger was also obsessed with the idea of incest, considering it the most efficient way of maintaining racial purity.

On matters of race Grainger was an avowed proponent of Anglo-Saxonism and Nordicism, moving from a more racial intent in writings of the 1910s and 1920s to a more openly racist frame of mind in writings of the 1930s and early 1940s. He rejected all effete notions of the artist in favour of a muscular, open-air approach which he himself advertised through carrying of his own suitcases, long hikes, and vigorous on-stage antics. One of his most famed feats was to leap from the stage during the orchestral section of a concerto, run to the back of the hall, and return just in time to catch his next entry as soloist. His fascination with languages—he knew half a dozen to a reasonable level of competence—led to a quest to free the English language of Graeco-Latin contaminations supposedly introduced by the Normans in 1066. The resultant 'blue-eyed', or Nordic, English came to prominence from 1926 onwards in his voluminous autobiographical writings and his letters to friends. 'Education' became 'mind-tilth', 'music' became 'tone-art', and 'telephone' became 'thor-juice-talker'.

It was, however, in Grainger's fifth field, that of art, that his ideas were most profound. Apart from keen promotion in his essays and musical editions of Nordic music, early music, percussion instruments, and the piano's more robust features, he lived his life in search of 'free music', desiring to float through musical space, unimpeded by 'this absurd goose-stepping' which he believed bedevilled music. Grainger likened music's contemporary condition to Egyptian bas-reliefs with their regularized shapes, while he yearned for the twists and curves of Greek sculptures. Early examples of Grainger's free experimentation include his *Train Music* (1900–01) and his *Sea-Song* (1907). His *Random Round* (1912–14), inspired by

Pacific islander improvisatory practice, experimented with 'concerted partial improvisation', while his two 'free music' pieces of 1935–7 introduced the first consistently gliding tones in his output, achieved firstly by string quartet and then by a quartet of theremins.

In later life Grainger invented several 'free music' machines, with the intention of cutting out the role of the performer as interpreter of the composer's work. Rather, the composer would speak directly to the audience through the machine's exact reproduction of a work's features. The Estey-reed tone-tool (1950–51) was a form of giant harmonica, while the kangaroo-pouch tone-tool (1952) introduced a 'hills and dales' form of music which, to Grainger's mind, reflected Hogarth's 'curve of beauty'. A further machine, the electric-eye tone-tool, incorporated photocells into its design, but remained incomplete at the composer's death.

As a composer Grainger was relatively prolific, producing over 400 works, either original compositions or folk-music settings. He was, however, most comfortable as a miniaturist: few of his works take more than seven or eight minutes to perform. Grainger's style was highly distinctive, almost baroque in its rhythm, with a 'half-horizontal, half-perpendicular' chordal sense, and an intertwining of parts owing much to Brahms. He considered himself a musical democrat, in both the way he wrote his music and the way he wanted it performed. In 1955 he professed to 'like each voice, at all times throughout my music, to enjoy equal importance and prominence' (*Grainger on Music*, 375). So, too, he sought through the 'elastic scoring' of many of his later compositions to establish simple groupings of instruments which would allow as many players as possible to take an effective part in the musical performance of his music. When asked late in life what his most important and characteristic works were, he listed nine works or collections, all but one of which he had started to compose by his mid-twenties. Among them were some fifty British folk-music settings, the orchestral *English Dance* (1901–9), and his two 'Hillsongs' (1901–7), inspired by a three-day hike in western Argyll (ibid., 374).

Grainger's legacy has been colourful. Among his five professed enthusiasms, his views on race are now considered abhorrent, while his attempts to reform the English language are taken as cranky, if not just bizarre. His sexual gusto has been kept well alive by occasional exposés in the Australian tabloid press, and sometimes linked with his notable athleticism. Late in life Grainger deposited a package with his bank that was to be opened ten years after his death: it held an essay and 'a large collection of photographs giving full details of his sex life' in the hope that 'the world would be broadminded to accept such things without guilt or shame' (Bird, 245). However, Max Harris in 1983 claimed Grainger as 'one of the great embarrassments to the residual puritanism of the nation' (*The Unknown Great Australian*, 1983, 58).

Within the realm of art, Grainger was a significant influence upon the emergence in the 1960s of a distinctively Australian art music, but more so in concept and theme than in actual style. While his band music, in particular *Lincolnshire Posy* (1937), was an important milestone in the development of American band repertory, his 'free music' experiments were rapidly overtaken by the development of electronic sound synthesis. Perhaps Grainger's most enduring legacy was in the setting of folk-music, where he was a popular model for following generations of British composers. Benjamin Britten, for instance, acknowledged Grainger as his 'master' in this regard. In 1934 Grainger established his own museum in the grounds of the University of Melbourne, where most of his papers, compositions, memorabilia, and recordings are housed.

MALCOLM GILLIES

Sources J. Bird, *Percy Grainger* (1976) · K. Dreyfus, *Music by Percy Aldridge Grainger* (1978) · *The farthest north of humanness: letters of Percy Grainger, 1901–14*, ed. K. Dreyfus (1985) · W. Mellers, *Percy Grainger* (1992) · *The all-round man: selected letters of Percy Grainger, 1914–61*, ed. M. Gillies and D. Pear (1994) · *Grainger on music*, ed. M. Gillies and B. Clunies Ross (1999) · private information (2004) [family] · autopsy report, White Plains Hospital, New York · M. Gillies and D. Pear, *Portrait of Percy Grainger* (2002)
Archives University of Melbourne, Grainger Museum, papers | NL Scot., letters to D. C. Parker | SOUND University of Melbourne, Grainger Museum, cylinder recordings, piano rolls, early gramophone recordings
Likenesses R. Bunny, sketch, c.1902–1904, University of Melbourne, Grainger Museum · J. S. Sargent, chalk drawing, c.1907, University of Melbourne, Grainger Museum · Elliott & Fry, photograph, NPG [*see illus.*] · G. W. Lambert, double portrait, pencil drawing (with H. Tonks), NPG · J. S. Sargent, portrait, National Gallery of Victoria, Melbourne · photographs, University of Melbourne, Grainger Museum · photographs, Percy Grainger Library Society, White Plains, New York · photographs, Hult. Arch.
Wealth at death £2725 6s.—in England: administration with will (limited), 18 Dec 1962, *CGPLA Eng. & Wales*

Grainger, Richard (1797–1861), builder and property speculator, was born on 9 October 1797 in High Friar Lane, Newcastle upon Tyne, the youngest of the six children of Thomas Grainger (d. c.1810), a quayside porter, and his wife, Amelia, *née* Burt or Brunt (1755–1835), a seamstress and glove maker. He was educated at St Andrew's charity school in Newgate Street, Newcastle, before being apprenticed to a carpenter at the age of twelve and in 1816 setting up as a builder with his brother George (d. c.1817). He soon became connected with influential Methodists, including the solicitor John Fenwick, who later backed him, and William Batson, for whom he built houses in Higham Place, Newcastle (c.1819–1820), before purchasing property for the first time in Percy Street. On 7 October 1821 he married Rachel Arundale (d. 1842), the daughter of a prosperous leather merchant; she assisted in his business and they had six sons and seven daughters.

In the centre of Newcastle were 13 acres of vacant ground occupied by the historic manor of Anderson Place (which were eventually purchased by Grainger for £50,000 in 1834). Grainger's first major developments, all designed either by John Dobson or Thomas Oliver, had been necessarily peripheral to this: Blackett Street (1824), financed by a £5000 dowry from his wife; Eldon Square (1825–31); Leazes Terrace (1829–34); and the Royal Arcade, Pilgrim Street (1831–2). The air of fashionable elegance

Grainger was bringing to Newcastle culminated in the new commercial and residential city centre, involving several architects, which he planned and laid out on the former Anderson Place site between 1834 and 1840. This was based on Grey Street—an innovative north–south route—and Upper Grainger Street. Crucial to his schemes had been the support of the council, which insisted on the provision of a new market, and that of the town clerk, John Clayton (1792–1890), who arranged loans and supervised Grainger's continual mortgaging of newly built property to finance further development.

Grainger was now at the peak of his career, but he overreached himself and was saved from bankruptcy only by Clayton's manoeuvrings behind the scenes. In 1839 he had bought the Elswick Hall estate, in Newcastle's west end, but had to leave within three years and his over-complex ideas for its redevelopment largely failed to materialize. He was able to carry on business in a modest way at 9 Clayton Street West while living at no. 5, where he died on 4 July 1861. He was buried six days later at St James's Church, Benwell, Newcastle.

T. E. FAULKNER

Sources L. Wilkes and G. Dodds, *Tyneside classical* (1964) · I. Ayris, *A city of palaces: Richard Grainger and the making of Newcastle upon Tyne* (1997) · T. E. Faulkner, 'The early nineteenth-century planning of Newcastle upon Tyne', *Planning Perspectives*, 5 (1990), 149–67 · T. E. Faulkner, 'Conservation and renewal in Newcastle upon Tyne', *Northumbrian panorama: studies in the history and culture of north east England*, ed. T. E. Faulkner (1996), 123–48 · L. Wilkes, *Tyneside portraits* (1971) · *CGPLA Eng. & Wales* (1861)
Archives Newcastle Central Library, MSS · Northumbd RO, MSS · Tyne & Wear Archives Service, Newcastle upon Tyne, MSS
Likenesses portrait, c.1830, Laing Art Gallery, Newcastle upon Tyne · G. H. Phillips, mezzotint, pubd in or before 1840 (after T. Carrick), BM, NPG · D. Mossman, oils, c.1855, Laing Art Gallery, Newcastle upon Tyne
Wealth at death £20,000: probate, 27 Nov 1861, *CGPLA Eng. & Wales*

Grainger, Richard Dugard (1801–1865), anatomist and physiologist, younger son of Edward Grainger, surgeon, was born in Birmingham. He attended the grammar school there and subsequently entered the Royal Military Academy at Woolwich as a cadet. He then trained as a surgeon at St Thomas's Hospital, London, and his brother Edward *Grainger's anatomy school in Webb Street, qualifying MRCS in 1822. As Edward suffered poor health Richard joined him in running Webb Street, and in 1823 inherited it on his brother's death. Although less controversial than Edward, Richard played his part in breaking the hospital schools' monopoly on corpses for dissection, and under his direction Webb Street remained successful until the mid-1830s. The animus against Edward continued after his death, and in 1824 the royal college issued new regulations refusing to accept certificates of attendance at Webb Street lectures as a basis for entry to the college. Richard's less confrontational approach attracted the support of Astley Cooper, his brother's nemesis, and saved Webb Street.

Richard Grainger was a zealous prosecutor of anatomical and physiological research. In 1829 he published *Elements of General Anatomy*, which reflected his wide reading of continental sources, and which was intended as a manual

Richard Dugard Grainger (1801–1865), by unknown artist

for students. It was one of the earliest attempts to present a general view of physiology linked to proper study with a microscope. In 1837 he published *Observations on the Structure and Functions of the Spinal Cord*, in which his dissections provided anatomical support for Marshall Hall's doctrine of reflex action, which had been postulated from physiological experimentation. The above led to his election as a fellow of the Royal Society that year.

Grainger was an early member of the London Phrenology Society, and appointed John Elliotson as a lecturer at Webb Street. By 1840 he had abandoned phrenology recognizing that it had no basis in physiology, and that its radical connections were an impediment to professional progress. Although not a radical by inclination, his opposition to the London hospital schools' monopoly, passionate belief in the benefits of anatomical research, and interest in social reform all reflected liberal views. One of his partners, Thomas Southwood Smith, performed the public dissection and funeral oration on the utilitarian Jeremy Bentham at Webb Street, and Grainger did the same for the radical Richard Carlile, seizing the opportunity to highlight the failure of the Anatomy Act to supply sufficient corpses for dissection.

By the 1830s the main teaching hospitals were insisting, on the grounds of professional regulation, that private anatomy schools close. In 1842 St Thomas's appointed Grainger lecturer in general anatomy and physiology, and Webb Street closed. The following year he qualified FRCS, and from 1846 to 1850 he was a member of the council. Grainger lectured successfully at St Thomas's, and also contributed to the life of the hospital by helping catalogue the museum collection, standing in when the quality of

demonstrating in the dissecting room fell, and by becoming dean in 1852. He retired in 1860 and his pupils subscribed a £500 testimonial which he donated to provide an annual prize for the best physiological essay.

On 26 July 1841 Grainger, a widower, had married for the second time; his wife was Martha Blissett Maurice (1812–1893), eleventh and youngest child of Thelwall and Ann Maurice, from Marlborough, Wiltshire. That year Grainger was appointed an inspector under the royal commission on children's employment, at Edwin Chadwick's instigation. Grainger was an early adherent of public health administration, and in 1844 became involved in the Health of Towns Association with Southwood Smith, Chadwick, and Sir John Simon. As a central committee member he harangued sanitary meetings in Liverpool and Manchester, wrote tracts, and helped with organization of the movement. In 1849 he was appointed a medical inspector under the General Board of Health to inquire into the origin and spread of cholera. He produced a major report on epidemic cholera, and also one on the state of the metropolitan workhouses. Grainger, together with Gavin Milroy, another temporary public health inspector, was proprietor and editor of the *Medico-Chirurgical Review*. He was also a member of the Epidemiological Society, where he read papers on sanitary reform.

With the demise of the General Board of Health in 1854 Grainger was too valuable an asset to public health to lose, and was appointed an inspector under Chadwick's Burials Act. In 1862 he was appointed one of the commissioners on a second children's employment commission. Aside from work he had a number of social interests. He was involved in improvement of the working conditions of young women employed in millinery and dressmaking, and was prominent in the formation of the Christian Medical Association. He also took an interest in medical education, and in 1864 published a paper criticizing the extant syllabus.

Grainger was a tall, spare man, with a habitual stoop. He was lively, energetic, and earnest, but also courteous and retiring. A person of great convictions, he fought many battles as a sanitary reformer with recalcitrant local vested interests. Grainger was an evangelical and a sabbatarian. As a scientist he was also anxious to promote that which had been shown to be useful, and in his 1848 Hunterian oration promoted the cultivation of organic science. He devoted much of his time to the study of the Bible and was anxious that students should understand that the claims of revealed truth were not antagonistic to those of scientific truth. In his address to the Christian Medical Association at its first meeting on 10 November 1854 he claimed that:

> Instead of attempting to penetrate the veil, which it has pleased the Almighty to interpose between our finite capacity and his infinity, the best physiologists are agreed to regard as among the inscrutable facts of nature, those very questions, such as the relation of mind and matter, of the soul and its instrument, the brain, which formerly engaged … so large a share of scientific writing. (Grainger, 12)

Grainger died on 1 February 1865 at his home, 6 Hornsey

Lane, Highgate, after suffering from Bright's disease for several years, and was buried at Eltham, Kent. Martha was Grainger's sole legatee.   NICK HERVEY

Sources BMJ (18 Feb 1865), 176 · The Lancet (18 Feb 1865), 190 · D'A. Power, 'The rise and fall of the private medical schools in London', BMJ (22 June 1895), 1389–91 · D. Roberts, Victorian origins of the British welfare state (1960) · R. Lambert, Sir John Simon, 1816–1904, and English social administration (1963) · S. E. Finer, The life and times of Sir Edwin Chadwick (1952) · R. Richardson, Death, dissection and the destitute (1987) · R. D. Grainger, An address delivered to the Christian Medical Association (1855) · The Lancet (27 Feb 1836), 883–6 · Boase, Mod. Eng. biog. · Medical Times and Gazette (11 Feb 1865), 157–8 · F. G. Parsons, The history of St Thomas's Hospital, 3 (1936) · d. cert. · m. cert. · IGI · CGPLA Eng. & Wales (1865) · index of deaths, Family Records Centre
Archives Wellcome L., lecture notes
Likenesses G. F. Ferriswood and J. H. L. Athey, lithograph (aged fifty), RCS Eng. · Lupton, engraving (after Wageman), Wellcome L. · J. H. Lynch, lithograph (after G. F. Teniswood), Wellcome L. · watercolour, RCS Eng. [see illus.]
Wealth at death under £7000: probate, 18 Feb 1865, CGPLA Eng. & Wales

Grainger, Thomas (1794–1852), railway engineer, was born on 12 November 1794 at Gogar Green, Ratho, near Edinburgh, where his father had a small farm. He was educated at the University of Edinburgh and by 1816 had begun business as an independent civil engineer and surveyor. In 1823 he employed John Miller and they became partners two years later. They designed much of the early Scottish railway network, starting with a commission for the Monkland and Kirkintilloch Railway, which opened in 1826 to deliver coal from the Cairnhill colliery to the canal 10 miles away.

Grainger and Miller were employed to plan the route for a Glasgow to Edinburgh line sponsored by Glasgow mercantile interests, some coal and iron companies, and directors of the Glasgow to Garnkirk Railway. Their route followed Slamannan, Bathgate, and Midcalder, while a rival scheme proposed running through Bellshill and Whitburn. Grainger's plan was the cheaper of the two, although the cost was estimated at £410,000. The eventual line did not receive parliamentary authorization until several years later, in 1838, and then followed a different route to the north of Grainger's original proposal, passing through Linlithgow and Falkirk. Grainger and Miller were again employed on the project although their plans had to be endorsed by a group of eminent engineers.

Grainger and Miller also worked on the Edinburgh, Leith, and Newhaven Railway, and were responsible for the tunnel outside Waverley Station in Edinburgh which caused some controversy. Vigorous opposition was led by Dr Patrick Neill, printer, conservationist, and chief founder of the Edinburgh Horticultural Society. Neill forced a deviation round his own property, and continued to carp at the spoliation caused by the line's progress. Grainger also undertook commissions in Forfarshire, exploring possible links from Brechin to Montrose and Forfar to Arbroath, and planning the Dundee to Arbroath Railway. He was involved in attempts to link Edinburgh to the north through Fife via a ferry from Granton to Burntisland, although this scheme failed to reach fruition.

Grainger and Miller used a variety of track gauges on their railway projects which indicates that they entertained no thoughts of creating an integrated railway network even within Scotland.

In the later part of his career Grainger was engaged in railway construction in Yorkshire, including time with the East and West Yorkshire Junction Railway and the Leeds, Dewsbury, and Manchester Railway. He was the engineer in charge of the Leeds to Thirsk line, which opened in 1849 and included some remarkable achievements with four major viaducts and the Bramhope Tunnel, the construction of which required the solution of considerable drainage problems. Grainger also built the great viaduct at Yarm over the Tees, completed in 1849, which was 760 yards long.

Thomas Grainger served as a member of Edinburgh city council and the improvement commission and was, for two years, president of the Royal Scottish Society of Arts. His early death probably deprived him of the opportunity to serve as lord provost of Edinburgh. He was reported to have made a handsome fortune and owned an estate at Craig Park near Ratho, as well as iron, mining, and smelting business interests in Fife. He was injured in a railway accident at Norton Junction near Stockton-on-Tees and died four days later on 25 July 1852 at Craig Park.

C. H. LEE

Sources C. J. A. Robertson, The origins of the Scottish railway system, 1722–1844 (1983) · W. W. Tomlinson, The North Eastern railway: its rise and development [1915] · DNB · The Scotsman (28 July 1852)
Likenesses J. Watson-Gordon, oils, Inst. CE

Gramont, de. For this title name see Hamilton, Elizabeth, Countess de Gramont (1641–1708).

Granard. For this title name see Forbes, Arthur, first earl of Granard (1623–1695); Forbes, George, third earl of Granard (1685–1765); Forbes, George, sixth earl of Granard (1760–1837).

Granby. For this title name see Manners, John, marquess of Granby (1721–1770).

Grand, Lawrence Douglas (1898–1975), soldier and intelligence officer, was born on 10 August 1898 at 7 Rose Lane, Wavertree, Liverpool, the elder son of Douglas Henry Grand of Beckenham, a commission merchant, and his wife, Emma Gertrude Chamberlain. He left the sixth form at Rugby School in mid-1916 for a year at Woolwich, and was commissioned second lieutenant in the Royal Engineers on 28 September 1917. He saw no active service in the First World War, as he went on to the School of Military Engineering at Chatham, but saw plenty soon after it. He served briefly in north Russia in 1919, in 384 field company; on the north-west frontier of India and in the Iraq revolt in 1920; and with the Iraq levies in Kurdistan in 1923. For his work in this last campaign he was appointed MBE.

Grand matriculated at Christ's College, Cambridge, in October 1923, but never went into residence and took no degree. After five years' routine soldiering in England he was promoted captain on 28 September 1928; he became major on the same date in 1937. He married on 6 November 1930 Irene Lola Hilda (*b.* 1902/3), daughter of Charles Theobald Mathew, a captain in the Indian army. They had a son, and a daughter who married the heir of the tenth earl of Bessborough.

In April 1938 Grand was seconded to the Secret Intelligence Service to start up a new section, at first called IX, later known as D. His task was 'to investigate every possibility of attacking potential enemies by means other than the operations of military force' (Foot, 2), yet he was at first forbidden to instigate any overt action. 'Examining such an enormous task', he wrote in 1946, 'one felt as if one had been told to move the Pyramids with a pin' (ibid.).

Grand had a country headquarters at The Frythe, near Welwyn, and set up an office in 2 Caxton Street, Westminster, where he accumulated friends, mostly from the City of London. One of them has testified to his fertility of ideas and powers of leadership (Sweet-Escott, 20), but results were meagre. He was tall, good-looking, elegantly dressed, with a heavy dark moustache, and exuded an air of mystery and command at once. He sent an agent out to reconnoitre the middle Danube, aiming at blocking the flow of Romanian oil to Germany, and had a few leaflets prepared by émigrés aimed at seducing German voters from allegiance to the Nazis. Attempts to interfere with the supply of Swedish iron to Germany misfired. For some months J. C. F. Holland, who was preparing comparable tasks for the War Office, worked alongside him in Caxton Street, but while Holland thought Grand rash, Grand thought Holland over careful. Holland went back to the War Office when the Second World War began.

Grand took over three upper floors of the St Ermin's Hotel next door, and expanded his section, but combining haste with secrecy led too often to muddle. D section's attempts in midsummer 1940 to arrange stay-behind parties, to disrupt the communications of a German invasion that was expected shortly, caused such confusion that the whole project was handed over to Holland. Grand had seventy-three officers under him by July (and claimed 140). His section, Holland's section, and a propaganda branch of the Foreign Office were all then absorbed into the new Special Operations Executive. He was not: he and his new master, Hugh Dalton, fell out irretrievably. Dalton thought him disloyal, dishonest even, and shed him back to the army in September, on condition that he was at once posted abroad.

Grand went to India and resumed more professional engineering. In 1943, advanced to CBE, he became director of engineer resources at general headquarters in India. Not even Indian heat could dim his energies and he was created CIE in 1946. He returned home to become chief engineer, home counties district, in 1946–9. In 1949 he was promoted major-general and held his last army post, as director of fortifications and works in the War Office; he retired as a CB in 1952. In 1951 he joined the Institution of Civil Engineers. He worked in the 1960s with Epar (Engineer Planning and Resources) Limited, an engineering firm at 50 Pall Mall, and was involved with the construction of large hotels in the Levant. When posted to the War Office, he moved his home from Trebetherick on Padstow Bay in Cornwall to Delaford Manor, Iver, Buckinghamshire, where he lived until his death, from a motorway accident. He was declared dead on arrival at Putney Hospital, London, on 22 November 1975.

M. R. D. FOOT

Sources B. Sweet-Escott, *Baker Street irregular* (1965) · M. R. D. Foot, *SOE in France: an account of the work of the British Special Operations Executive in France, 1940–1944*, 2nd edn (1968) · D. Lampe, *The last ditch* (1968) · *The Second World War diary of Hugh Dalton, 1940–1945*, ed. B. Pimlott (1986) · *WWW* · b. cert. · private information (2004) · m. cert. · d. cert.
Archives PRO, MSS
Likenesses photograph, 1939–45, Special Forces Club

Grand, Sarah. *See* McFall, Frances Elizabeth Bellenden (1854–1943).

Grandison. For this title name *see* St John, Oliver, first Viscount Grandison of Limerick (1559–1630).

Grandison, John (1292–1369), bishop of Exeter, was the second son of Sir William Grandison (*d.* 1335), and of Sybil (*d.* 1334), younger daughter and coheir of Sir John de Tregoz, knight, William being heir of Otto Grandson (*d.* 1328), head of the English branch of a noble Savoyard family whose principal residence was Grandson Castle near Lake Neuchâtel. John Grandison was born at Ashperton, Herefordshire, in a family of five sons (three of them clerics) and four daughters. He studied at Oxford, first in 1306 and later in 1326–7; and at Paris from 1313 to 1317 he studied theology under Jacques Fournier, later Pope Benedict XII (*r.* 1334–42); at Avignon he became the protégé, friend, and chaplain of Pope John XXII (*r.* 1316–34), for whom he performed diplomatic missions. He was rewarded by prebends at York, Wells, and Lincoln, and in 1310 by the archdeaconry of Nottingham. He was made bishop of Exeter by papal provision on 10 August 1327, consecrated at Avignon on 18 October, and enthroned in Exeter on 22 August 1328.

Grandison's background was thus wealthy, noble, cultivated, and learned. He was lavish in expenditure, even though not enriched by inheritance from his family estates until after the death of his elder brother Peter without a direct heir in 1358. His pride of birth is indicated in the use of his family arms (paly of six argent and azure, on a bend gules a mitre between two eaglets displayed or). With these he caused the buildings, books, metalwork, jewellery, ivories (whose provenance is thereby uniquely established), and textiles (witness some surviving orphreys for a chasuble) that he so magnificently commissioned to be extensively adorned. His cosmopolitan taste is illustrated by the descriptions in his will of artefacts 'in the Roman manner' or bought in Paris (though his ivories were commissioned locally). Grandison's learning was directed above all to the study of liturgy and the lives of saints. His own remarks about his version of the life and miracles of St Thomas of Canterbury display his methods: he described it to Pope Benedict XII as condensed from the work of many writers and intended as a subject of contemplation; more than fifteen years later, in 1357, still preoccupied with its accuracy, he asked the prior of Christ Church, Canterbury, to correct errors and supply defects in it. Besides this respect for Thomas Becket, he was also particularly devoted to the Blessed Virgin Mary, and composed a series of her masses. The culmination of his work was his production of the *Legenda de tempore et de sanctis*, the presentation copy of which, in two volumes and annotated in his own hand, he gave to his cathedral in 1366, where it still remains. He prepared new pontificals, but his chief accomplishment was the composition by 1337 of an *ordinale* regulating his cathedral and chapter, which displays masterly erudition and care in liturgy, ceremonial, and polyphony. He presented his church with numerous service books in his lifetime. He amassed a large and valuable library; the books were distributed among several religious houses and foundations after his death, Exeter Cathedral being among the beneficiaries. The surviving books, and the archives he used, display Grandison's enthusiasm for annotation in his unmistakable handwriting.

On his arrival Grandison found his large diocese, which was in considerable disarray following the murder of Bishop Walter Stapeldon in London in 1326, remote and unwelcoming. He was burdened by huge arrears of debt to the papal curia, personal poverty, a hostile chapter, and difficult relations with the locally influential Hugh, Lord Courtenay, future earl of Devon (*d.* 1340). But as a papal nominee he was not greatly involved in affairs of state, and devoted all his energies and passion for order to his cathedral and diocese during an episcopate spanning forty-two years, leaving it only for a week or two at rare intervals, usually to attend parliament or convocation. His principal residence was on his manor of Chudleigh. His episcopal registers display his diligence and severity in enforcing discipline, punishing offenders, and suppressing abuses; and also his care for education, in making new statutes for Crediton and Ottery collegiate churches, extending grammar scholarships at St John's Hospital in Exeter, and, most unusually, sending detailed instructions to schoolmasters. His care for the religion of the laity led him to urge the recording of the lives of Cornish saints and to encourage interest in St Sidwell of Exeter, though he opposed the development of more dubious cults. The registers also illustrate the vehement, sometimes violent, expressions of his seemingly choleric disposition; this is most clearly shown in his armed opposition—with papal approval—to Archbishop Simon Mepham's visitation in 1332. Though confessing that he disliked riding (preferring his books), Grandison nevertheless kept firm control, through his officers, over his whole extensive diocese, even after the pestilence of 1348–9 and its recurrences caused vast mortality, resulting in lack of clergy and extensive poverty.

Grandison found his cathedral half-finished after Stapeldon's death, though he hoped that when completed it would exceed in glory similar churches in England or in France. The eastern arm including the first bay of the nave was complete and already sumptuously furnished with throne, silver reredos, sedilia, and pulpitum. Grandison consecrated the high altar in December 1328, and proceeded to raise funds for completing the nave from his diocese, assisted by materials and cash in hand from Stapeldon's time, and timber from the episcopal estates. Thomas Witney, a celebrated master mason who had been involved with the building and furnishings since *c.*1313, was a respected member of the bishop's household, and continued as consultant architect to complete the nave, including roof and vault, and to design the lower southern range of the exterior western image wall before his death, probably in 1342. This range may have been completed by Witney's younger colleague, William Joy, by 1348. Grandison's most personal concern was for his own chantry chapel, built beside the western entrance to the nave within the outer screen facade, for the westernmost roof bosses (especially that of Becket's murder), and perhaps for the minstrels' gallery, which had not been part of Witney's original plan.

The foundation of the collegiate church of Ottery St Mary in 1337 was Grandison's most lavish project. Every aspect of this institution was his personal concern, and he took particular care for its organization, though members of his family were also involved: his brother Otho (*d.* 1359) was a benefactor, and family heraldry permeated the fabric and fittings. The church's rebuilding during the next ten years appears to have been closely linked with the work on Exeter Cathedral: externally copying its twin towers, while internally the vaults resemble the work of William Joy, and the figured roof bosses the style of some of the nave carvers of the cathedral.

Grandison died at Chudleigh on 16 July 1369, and was buried in the little chantry chapel he had prepared long since in his cathedral. He had endowed an obit for himself, his parents, and Pope John XXII as early as 1338. His tomb was desecrated in the late sixteenth century, and little but an enamelled gold finger-ring survives from it. His will, dated 8 September 1368, provides for his elaborate funeral; but while he made bequests on a munificent scale to a vast range of persons, from the very highest and most powerful to the weakest and poorest, and to many institutions, it demonstrates above all his fundamental desire to bestow glory on his cathedral and his Ottery foundation by making them treasure-houses of precious books, textiles, and artefacts. He finally chose words of the deepest humility to be set on a lead plate with his body: 'piteous bishop, most piteous servant of the Mother of Mercy'.

AUDREY ERSKINE

Sources Emden, *Oxf.* • F. C. Hingeston-Randolph, ed., *The register of John de Grandisson, bishop of Exeter*, 3 vols. (1894–9) • J. N. Dalton, *The collegiate church of Ottery St Mary* (1917) • J. Alexander and P. Binski, eds., *Age of chivalry: art in Plantagenet England, 1200–1400* (1987), 230 (item 95), 463–7 [exhibition catalogue, RA] • N. Stratford, 'Bishop Grandison and the visual arts', *Exeter Cathedral, a celebration*, ed. M. Swanton (1991), 145–56 • N. Sandon, 'Medieval services and their music', *Exeter Cathedral, a celebration*, ed. M. Swanton (1991), 127–36 • A. M. Erskine, ed. and trans., *The accounts of the fabric of Exeter Cathedral, 1279–1353*, 2 vols., Devon and Cornwall RS, new ser., 24, 26 (1981–3) • F. Rose-Troup, *Bishop Grandisson student and art* *lover* (1929) • *Devon*, Pevsner (1989) • N. I. Orme, 'Bishop Grandisson and popular religion', *Report and Transactions of the Devonshire Association*, 124 (1992), 107–18 • N. R. Ker, ed., *Medieval manuscripts in British libraries*, 2 (1977), 800–46 • J. Allen and S. Blaylock, 'The structural history of the west front', *Medieval art and architecture at Exeter Cathedral*, ed. F. Kelly (1991), 94–115 • G. Oliver, *Lives of the bishops of Exeter, and a history of the cathedral* (1861) • S. Pates, *The rock and the plough: John Grandisson, William Langland and 'Piers Plowman': a theory of authorship* (2000)

Archives Bodl. Oxf., MS Bodley 493 • Devon RO, diocesan records, episcopal register, Chanter 3, 4, 5 • Exeter Cathedral Library, MSS and capitular archives **Likenesses** boss on vault (of Grandison?), Ottery St Mary, Devon • boss on vault (of Grandison?), Exeter Cathedral • corbel (of Grandison?), Lady Chapel, Ottery St Mary, Devon • seal, BL **Wealth at death** see will, Hingeston-Randolph, ed., *Register of John de Grandisson*, vol. 3, pp. 1549–57, 1511–23

Grandison, Katharine. *See* Montagu, Katharine, countess of Salisbury (*d.* 1349), *under* Montagu, William, first earl of Salisbury (1301–1344).

Grandmesnil, Hugh de (*d.* 1098), baron and administrator, was the eldest of the three sons of Robert, lord of Grandmesnil (in the canton of St Pierre-sur-Dives, Calvados) in Normandy, and Hawise, daughter of Giroie, lord of Echauffour and Montreuil-l'Argillé (whose family were both vassals and rivals of the Bellême family). Hawise was, secondly, the wife of William, son of Robert, archbishop of Rouen; she eventually became a nun at Montivilliers accompanied by two of her daughters, for whom her son Hugh made provision. When their father died in 1040, Hugh and his brother Robert apparently each inherited part of the family fief. Their youngest brother, Arnold, and their cousin William de Montreuil went to Apulia as mercenaries *c.*1050. Hugh and Robert were immortalized by their decision to found a monastery, according to a fashion then sweeping Normandy, some time about 1050. The site chosen being unsuitable, they followed the advice of their uncle William fitz Giroie and decided to refound the ancient abbey of St Evroult, first compensating the monks of Bec who then owned the ruins. The monk and historian of St Evroult, Orderic Vitalis, tells of the generous endowment of the abbey by the brothers and their maternal kin. In the same year the younger brother Robert entered the abbey as a monk; he became its abbot in 1059.

Falsely accused by Mabel de Bellême, wife of Roger de Montgomery, in the wake of a rebellion by Robert fitz Giroie, Hugh and Robert de Grandmesnil, among others of their maternal kin, were exiled in 1061. Robert became an abbot in Sicily, but Hugh was recalled in 1064 and subsequently fought with Duke William at Hastings. The move undoubtedly made his fortune. During William's absence in Normandy in 1067, Grandmesnil was among those left in charge. By 1086 he was castellan and sheriff of Leicestershire, where he held sixty-seven manors. He also held extensive property in Nottinghamshire, Hertfordshire, Northamptonshire, Gloucestershire, Warwickshire, and Suffolk. Several of his Norman vassals held these lands from him, including Hugh and Robert Burdet, Osbert de Neufmarché, and Walter de Beaumais. He returned to Normandy in 1068 to check on the activities of his beautiful French wife, Adelize or Adeliza (*d.* 11 July 1091), daughter of Ivo, count of Beaumont-sur-Oise. Adelize's English dower lands were recorded separately from her husband's in the Domesday survey of 1086. They included manors in Bedfordshire, which Hugh had acquired by exchange with Ralph Taillebois. After Ralph's death (before 1086) Hugh disputed Ralph's inheritance with Hugh de Beauchamps, Ralph's son-in-law and principal heir, and with the husband of Ralph's niece, Ranulf, brother of Ilger.

Two of Grandmesnil's sons, Ivo and Aubrey, earned their father's disapproval by joining the revolt of the king's son Robert Curthose in 1078. Hugh was among those who helped to effect a reconciliation between the king and Robert in 1079. Although he supported Curthose against William II in 1087–8, Hugh retained his offices under the new king. He was in Normandy in January 1091, assisting Robert de Courcy, husband of his daughter Rohais, against Robert de Bellême. This action provoked conflict with Robert Curthose, but matters were resolved by the appearance of William II in Normandy. Hugh de Grandmesnil was in England when he died, on 22 February 1098, a few days after becoming a monk of St Evroult, whose habit had previously been sent to him for the purpose. His body was buried later the same year at St Evroult, where Orderic Vitalis wrote his epitaph. Hugh and Adelize had ten children: five daughters, Adelina (who married Roger d'Ivry), Rohais (Robert de Courcy), Matilda (Hugh de Montpinçon), Agnes (William de Sai), and Hawise; and five sons, Robert, William, Hugh, Ivo de *Grandmesnil, and Aubrey. William (who later settled in Apulia), Ivo, and Aubrey were among the 'rope-dancers of Antioch' in 1098, who deserted the besieged crusader army in the city by letting themselves down the walls at night. Robert (*d. c.*1136) succeeded to Hugh's Norman estates, which he governed as a supporter of Henry I. The English lands went to Ivo, who seems previously to have acted as his father's steward (*dapifer*).   K. S. B. KEATS-ROHAN

Sources Ordericus Vitalis, *Eccl. hist.* • *ASC*, s.a. 1088 [text E] • GEC, *Peerage*, new edn

Grandmesnil [Grantmesnil], **Ivo de** (*d.* 1101/2), magnate, was the son of Hugh de *Grandmesnil, lord of Leicester in England and Grandmesnil in Normandy, and Adeliza, daughter of Ivo de Beaumont-sur-Oise. Ivo followed Robert Curthose, duke of Normandy, on the first crusade in 1096, but gained discredit from his premature abandonment of the defence of Antioch. With his brothers William and Aubrey, he was among those disgraced as 'rope-dancers' for letting themselves down from the walls of the besieged city by night. When Hugh de Grandmesnil died in 1098, his estates were divided: the Norman lands went to the eldest son, Robert (II) de Grandmesnil (*d. c.*1136), while Ivo took those in England. These consisted of the town and castle of Leicester and a large block of estates in the south and west of the shire; there were other extensive holdings in Warwickshire and Northamptonshire. Ivo appears to have succeeded his father as sheriff of

Leicestershire. He married a daughter of Gilbert de Gant, another midlands baron. However, his career as a baron was short-lived. In 1100 he chose to oppose the succession of Henry I in favour of his crusading captain, Robert Curthose, and in pursuit of the cause he devastated his neighbours' estates in the midlands. When in 1101 King Henry and Robert came to an amicable settlement at Alton, Ivo was exposed to the king's vengeance, despite the king's undertaking to pardon Robert's friends. Ivo was obliged to mortgage his lands to Robert de Beaumont, count of Meulan, the king's chief adviser, for 500 marks for fifteen years to clear a fine imposed on him. A marriage alliance between Ivo's son, also Ivo, and Count Robert's niece was to take place on the return of the lands. Ivo and his wife then set off on pilgrimage, but died *en route* in either 1101 or 1102.

The younger Ivo de Grandmesnil never received his inheritance, and in 1107 the king invested Count Robert as earl of Leicester, thus making the Grandmesnils' dispossession clear to all. Ivo and a brother were brought up in Henry I's court, and received from the king some favour, if no lands. Both died childless in 1120 in the wreck of the *White Ship*. By a curious coincidence, the honour of Grandmesnil in Normandy was also to come to Count Robert's descendants, when his grandson, Robert de Breteuil, earl of Leicester (d. 1190), married Petronilla de *Grandmesnil granddaughter of Robert (II) de Grandmesnil.

DAVID CROUCH

Sources Ordericus Vitalis, *Eccl. hist.* · D. Crouch, *The Beaumont twins: the roots and branches of power in the twelfth century*, Cambridge Studies in Medieval Life and Thought, 4th ser., 1 (1986) · C. W. Hollister, 'The Anglo-Norman civil war, 1101', *EngHR*, 88 (1973), 315–34

Grandmesnil, Petronilla de, countess of Leicester (d. 1212), magnate, was the daughter and heir of Guillaume, lord of Grandmesnil in Normandy. She was the last representative of the great Norman aristocratic house of Grandmesnil. Her father's name is known only from a grant by her to the abbey of St Evroult in his memory. It is assumed that Guillaume was the son of Robert (II) de Grandmesnil (d. c.1136), the last lord of Grandmesnil mentioned by Orderic Vitalis, but this is by no means certain. Petronilla was given in marriage (presumably as a royal ward) by Henry II to Robert de *Breteuil (c.1130–1190), the only son of Robert, earl of Leicester. The marriage had taken place by 1159. The pair initially lived in Normandy, where Robert had the charge of his father's honour of Breteuil and administered in his own right the honour of Pacy and his wife's honour of Grandmesnil in central Normandy. By 1164 they had had several children, among them *Roger, bishop of St Andrews.

In 1168 Robert inherited his father's earldom. When the new earl rebelled against Henry II, he took Petronilla with him into exile at the court of Louis VII. The countess seems by now to have established a reputation as a strong-willed, political figure. She accompanied the earl's invasion of England at the head of a mercenary army in 1173. Jordan Fantosme tells how the earl obliged her to dress in armour and carry shield and lance to ride with him at the head of his force as it marched to encounter the royal army near

Bury St Edmunds. Fantosme puts into her mouth a rather slighting speech directed against the English, and seems to regard her as a bad influence on her husband. She was unhorsed, thrown into a ditch, and captured by Simon de Wahull during the battle, causing her husband to panic, according to Fantosme. She was imprisoned with the earl in Portchester Castle, and doubtless she stayed with him in his various places of confinement until his release in 1177. Between 1179 and 1181 the earl went on pilgrimage to Jerusalem, and it is probable that the countess accompanied him. On the earl's next arrest in 1183, it is significant that she was also kept under surveillance, and lodged with one of her daughters and her household in Bedford Castle. She was imprisoned from April to September of that year.

On the earl's death abroad in 1190 Petronilla did not remarry, and seems to have come under the tutelage of her eldest surviving son, the heir to the earldom, Robert de *Breteuil (d. 1204). He answered for, and eventually paid, her minor debts contracted to Aaron of Lincoln. He seems to have venerated her to the unusual extent of abandoning the paternal surname of Breteuil (which appears on his secret seal before his succession) to take up the matronym *filius Petronille*, by which he was customarily known after 1190. She did not come into full control of her lands until 1204, on the death of her son. Her dower included lands and houses in Leicester and three and three-quarters knight's fees in the county. She also owned Netheravon in Wiltshire. Her centre and habitual residence as a widow was the town of Ware, Hertfordshire (Grandmesnil dower lands in the Domesday Book), where the earls maintained a hall; she acted as advocate of Ware Priory, and at least one prior did homage to her. In 1208 the king granted her a market in the town and control of its bridge for life. Petronilla also exerted rights over the abbey of St Evroult in Normandy, by virtue of her descent. She granted the abbey the cell of Charley in Leicestershire to be a daughter house. She appears to have maintained her claim on Grandmesnil, despite the loss of Normandy. In 1206 she offered 2000 marks for control of Leicester—which indicates a certain wealth—but was outbid by her son-in-law Saer de Quincy (d. 1219). The countess died on 1 April 1212.

DAVID CROUCH

Sources *Pipe rolls* · *Chancery records* · GEC, *Peerage* · Cartulary of St-Evroult, Bibliothèque Nationale, Paris, MS Lat. 11055 · Cartulary of Lyre, Château de Semilly (Manche), Marquise de Mathan MSS, transcripts of Dom Lenoir · Register of Sheen priory, BL, MS Cott. Otho B xiv · PRO, 31/8/140B pt 1 · W. Stubbs, ed., *Gesta regis Henrici secundi Benedicti abbatis: the chronicle of the reigns of Henry II and Richard I, AD 1169–1192*, 2 vols., Rolls Series, 49 (1867) · *Jordan Fantosme's chronicle*, ed. and trans. R. C. Johnston (1981) · R. Howlett, ed., *Chronicles of the reigns of Stephen, Henry II, and Richard I*, 4, Rolls Series, 82 (1889)

Grandson [Grandison], **Sir Otto de** (c.1238–1328), soldier and diplomat, was the eldest son of Pierre de Grandson, lord of Grandson, on the shore of Lake Neuchâtel (now in Switzerland), and his wife, Agnes, daughter of Ulric, count of Neuchâtel. His move away from the family home and into English affairs resulted from his father's position as the household knight and dependent of Peter of Savoy, earl of Richmond (*d.* 1268), uncle of Henry III's queen, Eleanor, and a powerful influence at Henry's court. Occasionally in England between *c.*1245 and his death in 1258, Pierre de Grandson was receiving an annual fee of £20 from Henry by 1249/50, and his son Otto was possibly introduced into the household of Edward, Henry's eldest son and heir, about this time. He first appears, in company with several of Edward's retainers, in October 1265, when he received a grant of confiscated property in London, and by 1268 he was certainly one of Edward's knights. He rapidly became one of the prince's closest friends, accompanying him on his crusade of 1270–72 and appearing as one of his executors in the will that Edward made at Acre in June 1272. When he returned to England as king in 1274 Grandson emerged as 'one of Edward's most trusted henchmen' (Prestwich, 54).

Henceforth Grandson's considerable services to the crown were partly military but mainly diplomatic. He fought as a banneret in the first Welsh war of 1277–8, visited Gascony and Paris on Edward's business in 1278–9, and fought again in the second Welsh war of 1282–3. In March 1284, after its conclusion, he was made justiciar of north Wales. Grandson was essentially viceroy of the newly conquered lands, a position suggestive of the confidence placed in him by Edward; and he may have had some influence, as his Savoyard friends and kinsmen certainly did, on the design of the castles by which Wales was to be held down. In 1286 he joined Edward in Gascony, after an embassy to the papal curia, and in 1289–90 he journeyed once again to the curia to discuss, *inter alia*, the granting of a papal dispensation for the marriage of Edward of Caernarfon, Edward's son, to Margaret of Scotland (the Maid of Norway), and Edward's projected crusade.

Although Edward never again went on crusade, Grandson himself led a small expedition to the east in 1290 and was present at the fall of Acre in May 1291. He may have been the author of a memorandum written between 1289 and 1307 concerning plans for a new crusade. After the débâcle at Acre he retired to Cyprus, whence he visited Armenia and Jerusalem before returning to Grandson and finally to England in 1296. His involvement in the Anglo-Scottish war, then just beginning, followed the pattern of his earlier work for Edward. He was present at the surrender of Dunbar on 28 April 1296, which marked the victorious conclusion of Edward's first campaign, but his main work continued to be high-level diplomacy. He was active in building up Edward's anti-French coalition in the Low Countries in 1296–7, negotiated for a truce with France in 1298, attended the papal curia in 1300–01, helped to settle the terms for a final French peace in 1303, and was among those sent again to the curia by Edward in 1305 to seek the suspension of Robert Winchelsey (*d.* 1313), archbishop of Canterbury.

Grandson was rewarded by Edward with extensive land grants in England, especially in Kent, and also in Ireland, and in 1275 with the wardenship of the Channel Islands, later transformed into a life grant. This last proved a source of constant conflict and friction with the islanders.

After Edward I's death in 1307 he left England for ever, returning to his ancestral home at Grandson. Although he was occasionally called out of retirement to represent English interests at the curia and at the French court, his main interests were now religious. He took the cross again in 1307, and was a notable benefactor to the Franciscans and Carthusians of his homeland. He died in April 1328 and was buried in Lausanne Cathedral. John Grandison, bishop of Exeter (1328–69), was his nephew. It is hard to think of any comparable figure in medieval English history who lived so long, travelled so widely, or had a career so diverse and adventurous. J. R. MADDICOTT, *rev.*

Sources *Calendar of the liberate rolls*, 4, PRO (1959) · C. L. Kingsford, 'Sir Otho de Grandison, (1238?–1328)', *TRHS*, 3rd ser., 3 (1909), 125–95 · E. R. Clifford, *A knight of great renown* (1909) · A. J. Taylor, *Studies in castles and castle-building* (1985) · C. Tyerman, *England and the crusades, 1095–1588* (1988) · M. Prestwich, *Edward I* (1988)

Granet, Sir (William) Guy (1867–1943), railway administrator, was born in Genoa on 13 October 1867, the second son of William Augustus Granet (1818–1878), a banker living in Genoa, and his wife, Adelaide Julia, daughter of E. Le Mesurier. He was educated at Rugby School from 1882 to 1884 and at Balliol College, Oxford, where he obtained a second class in modern history (1889) and was captain of the boat club. He then spent four years in his father's business in Genoa and married, in 1892, Florence Julia (*d.* 1949), daughter of William Court *Gully (later Viscount Selby), with whom he had a daughter. He was called to the bar by Lincoln's Inn in 1893 and practised on the northern circuit.

In 1900 Granet left the bar to become secretary of the Railway Companies' Association, and there he soon showed the qualities which made him one of the central figures in the railway world of his generation. In 1905 he joined the Midland Railway Company as assistant general manager, with the reversion of the general managership a year later. He found the Midland Railway inclined to live on its reputation, but under his vigorous leadership that soon changed. Granet brought to railway problems a keen analytical brain which refused to accept established practice as the last word. He soon saw the possibilities of a scientific study of train movements, and appointed as general superintendent Cecil Walter Paget, who with Granet's wholehearted support completely reorganized operating methods on the Midland and made it outstanding in the economy of its traffic operation. By solving the problem of congestion of freight traffic the company was able to improve the quality of its passenger service, which was vital to its future success.

Granet's mercurial temperament was not always easy for his staff, but he won their loyal support by his readiness to listen, his shrewd judgement, and his human qualities. It was a period of much railway legislation, and here Granet's legal training stood him in good stead. He was said to be one of the most persuasive expert witnesses who ever gave evidence before a parliamentary committee. He had a weight and deliberation of utterance and a massive demeanour which inspired confidence.

Granet took a special interest in labour problems, and

he did much to improve conditions of service. In 1907 he took a leading part in the negotiations which led to the establishment of conciliation boards. He had a leading part again in 1911 in the settlement of the railway strike at the time of the Agadir crisis, when he was authorized to negotiate on behalf of the main companies. He received a knighthood in that year.

In 1912 Granet was appointed a member of the royal commission on the civil service and he signed a minority report in 1914. When war came in that year his energy and organizing ability were in constant demand by the government. In 1915 he was appointed controller of import restrictions and in 1916 deputy director-general of military railways at the War Office under Sir Eric Geddes; he was largely responsible for introducing train ferries to carry traffic across the channel, at the suggestion of Follett Holt. In 1917 he became director-general of movements and railways and a member of the Army Council, and in 1918 chairman of the British and allied provisions commission and representative of the Ministry of Food in the United States and Canada. He was a member of the Geddes committee on national expenditure in 1921–2, and was appointed GBE in 1923.

Granet resigned the general managership of the Midland Railway in 1918 and was elected to a seat on the board, becoming chairman in 1922. On the amalgamation of the railways he became deputy chairman of the London, Midland, and Scottish Railway, succeeding Lord Lawrence of Kingsgate as chairman in 1924. Realizing that some radical changes were needed he persuaded Sir Josiah Stamp to come in 1926 as chief executive with the title of president, to devise a new organization. It was a bold step as Stamp knew nothing of railway problems, but Granet's judgement was justified by the result. In 1927, recognizing the success achieved by Stamp with his executive committee, Granet resigned the chairmanship to him so as to give him wider scope. But Stamp always relied greatly on Granet's experience, and as chairman of the traffic committee of the board Granet continued to exert much influence on the railway company's policy. He was chairman of the South African railways commission in 1933.

In 1919 Granet became a member of the firm of Higginson & Co., merchant bankers, and he was a director of a number of companies, including Lloyds Bank and The Times Publishing Company. When financial reverses came to him towards the end of his life he bore them with the same courage and equanimity with which he fought the five years of his final illness, continuing in active work to the end. He died at his home, Burleigh Court, near Stroud, Gloucestershire, on 11 October 1943.

Granet had a masterful personality, holding strong views to which he gave vigorous expression. Beneath his rather formidable manner there was a warm-hearted affection and loyalty towards individuals and institutions.   HAROLD HARTLEY, rev. MARK POTTLE

Sources personal knowledge (1959) • private information (1959) • *The Times* (12 Oct 1943) • *The Times* (14 Oct 1943) • *Railway Gazette* (22 Oct 1943) • H. Parris, 'Granet, Sir William Guy', *DBB*

Archives U. Warwick Mod. RC, corresp. and papers
Likenesses W. Stoneman, two photographs, 1917–27, NPG • J. S. Sargent, charcoal, priv. coll. • Spy [L. Ward], caricature, Hentschel-colourtype, NPG; repro. in *VF* (11 Nov 1908) • photograph, repro. in *The Times* (14 Oct 1943) • photograph, repro. in Parris, 'Granet, Sir William Guy'
Wealth at death £54,360 13s. 3d.: probate, 13 Dec 1943, *CGPLA Eng. & Wales*

Graney. For this title name *see* Grey, Leonard, Viscount Graney (c.1490–1541).

Grange. For this title name *see* Erskine, James, Lord Grange (*bap.* 1679, *d.* 1754); Erskine, Rachel, Lady Grange (*bap.* 1679, *d.* 1745).

Grange, John (*b.* 1556/7), poet, described his parents as plebeian and his place of origin as London (*Reg. Oxf.*, 2.61). In 1575 he matriculated at the Queen's College, Oxford, aged eighteen; in 1577 he described himself on the title-page of *The Golden Aphroditis* as 'student of the common law of England'; on 15 November 1578 he enrolled at the Roman Catholic seminary at Douai. Grange celebrated the occasion by writing three epigrams in the seminary's diary, but left again a month later. These are the only facts known about his life.

The Golden Aphroditis was Grange's one publication, printed in 1577. The first part is a prose story relating a love triangle between a woman, A. O. (a natural daughter of the goddess Diana), and two suitors, N. O. and I. I., in the course of which the characters conduct a series of dialogues and often give vent to their feelings in inset lyrics. Full of Platonic allegory, it may also constitute a *roman-à-clef* connected with the projected marriage of the Catholic Lord Stourton, an Oxford contemporary of Grange, who is the dedicatee of the book. It concludes with the marriage of N. O. and A. O., attended by the classical gods and goddesses. The second section of the book, subtitled 'Granges Garden', offers a selection of lyric poetry together with prose epistles all on the theme of love.

Whatever contemporary fame Grange achieved seems to have rested upon 'Granges Garden'. William Webbe, writing in 1586, quoted a lyric from it, praising Grange's creative use of the Echo convention, while elsewhere he listed Grange among distinguished poets associated with the inns of court. At least one other lyric attributed to Grange appears in a manuscript miscellany now in the Bodleian Library, Oxford. But subsequently Grange's reputation has depended upon the innovative use of narrative in *The Golden Aphroditis*, which can be set alongside the prose fiction of Gascoigne, Lyly, and others.

MATTHEW STEGGLE

Sources T. F. Knox and others, eds., *The first and second diaries of the English College, Douay* (1878), 147 • B. E. Richardson, 'Two English Francophiles: some French influences on fashionable English fiction', *Proceedings of the Royal Irish Academy*, 84C (1984), 225–35 • Foster, *Alum. Oxon.* • *Reg. Oxf.*, 2/2.61 • W. Webbe, 'A discourse of English poetry', *Elizabethan critical essays*, ed. G. G. Smith, 1 (1904); repr. (1950), 226–302 • M. Crum, ed., *First-line index of English poetry, 1500–1800, in manuscripts of the Bodleian Library, Oxford*, 2 vols. (1969)

Granger, James (*bap.* 1723, *d.* 1776), print collector and biographer, was born in Shaftesbury, Dorset, and baptized

James Granger (*bap.* 1723, *d.* 1776), by John Cornish, 1765

there at St James's on 31 March 1723, the son of William Granger and Elizabeth Tutt, who had married in 1717. Nothing is known of Granger's early life except that he matriculated from Christ Church, Oxford, on 26 April 1743 at the age of twenty. During the next three years he certainly took holy orders and, most probably, married Anne (1714–1790), daughter of Joseph Cane the incumbent of Shiplake parish in the diocese of Oxford. Their wedding can be dated by the fact that following Joseph Cane's death Granger succeeded him as rector of Shiplake on 27 April 1747.

Living with his wife at the vicarage in Shiplake, Granger faithfully conducted his duties and, as he later wrote, enjoyed the 'good fortune to retire early to independence, obscurity and content' (*A Biographical History of England*, 5th edn, 6 vols., 1824, 1.vii). He never aspired to any greater clerical position or fame and published only two sermons; both, however, reveal his characteristic faith, good humour, and liberal beliefs. The first, *An Apology for the Brute Creation, or, Abuse of Animals Censured* (1772), was a plea against cruelty to animals for which Granger was accused of denigrating the pulpit with mention of horses and dogs. The second, entitled *The Nature and Extent of Industry* (1773), was ironically dedicated to members of his parish; to those 'who neglect the Service of the Church, and spend the Sabbath in the worst kind of *Idleness*, this plain Sermon which they never heard, and will probably never read, is inscribed'.

Granger himself eschewed all idleness or pursuit of profit, insisting in the dedication of the first edition of his *History* that 'I write neither for fame nor bread … but …

only to amuse myself.' Between 1764 and 1767 he filled his leisure time in compiling information for his *Biographical History of England from Egbert the Great to the Revolution*, a catalogue of engraved historical portraits. Somewhat ahead of his times in his enthusiasm for portrait print collecting, Granger set about this task by consulting his own modest collection of prints and his work was much enhanced by the support of a few other similarly enlightened antiquarian print collectors. As the existing literature on English prints was then limited to Joseph Ames's rather arbitrary *Catalogue of English Heads* (1748), Granger's fellow collectors welcomed his efforts and consequently he was given free access to the cabinets of Horace Walpole, James West, and Sir William Musgrave, whose collections he reorganized and catalogued in the process. Even though he sold his copyright to his publisher Thomas Davies for the sum of £50, he was keenly interested in the production of the book; the wealth of letters between author and publisher demonstrate Granger's involvement and his part in delicate decisions over the book's title, final appearance, and selling price of 2 guineas. Issued on 16 May 1769, with the endorsement of its dedication 'by permission' to Horace Walpole, Granger's *Biographical History of England* was an immediate and enduring success. Only three weeks after it was issued, Granger was pleased to write to the Revd William Cole that 'My Book sells much better than I expected: Mr Davies the Bookseller tells me that he has already sold … 450 copies' (BL, Add. MS 5992, fol. 185, 1 June 1769). Although sales soon slowed down, by 1824 Granger's *Biographical History* had been through four subsequent editions. Additionally, in 1806 the Revd Mark Noble completed Granger's original plan when he published a continuation of the *Biographical History* down to the reign of George I.

Despite Horace Walpole's original support for the project, he was soon frustrated by the growing fashion for portrait print collecting as 'heads which used to be sold for sixpence or less, were advanced to five shillings' (H. Walpole, 'Book of materials', 1771, Yale University, Lewis Walpole Library, fol. 2) and this he directly attributed to the impact of Granger's catalogue. The success of *A Biographical History of England* and the ensuing rise in 'the taste for collecting and preserving engraved British portraits' was largely due to Granger's development of an innovative taxonomy for 'reducing our Biography to System' (J. Granger, *A Biographical History of England*, 1769). He did this by first organizing the portrait sitters chronologically, according to the reign in which they had lived, and then by subdividing them into twelve hierarchical classes, the first being royalty and the twelfth encompassing 'Persons … of the lowest Order of the People' (ibid.). The other aspect of Granger's work which increased its audience far beyond that of specialist print collectors was his biographical memoirs of each of the subjects listed which answered the readers' desire to be 'acquainted with a man's aspect' (ibid.). Mrs Delany, who is not known to have collected portrait heads, reported how much she enjoyed 'Mr Granger's biographical account' (*Autobiography … Mrs Delany*, 2.58). Not everyone was so laudatory;

Samuel Johnson detected Granger's political bias and complained that 'the dog is a Whig' (Boswell, 5.255) whereas the antiquarian Richard Gough reproached him for his indiscriminate practice of 'having thrown together every picture of every person that deserved or pretended to any connection with Great Britain' (Gough, 1.3).

In keeping with the common interest linking portrait head collectors, other readers who detected mistakes or gaps in Granger's catalogue were moved to write to him offering their own insights. The growing numbers of such print collectors, and their collective desire for an exact and comprehensive reference work, led Davies to commission Granger to produce a supplement to the *Biographical History* in 1770. When it finally appeared in 1774, Granger expressed his gratitude to his many 'worthy Friends [who] had communicated their Observations with a view of improving the work' (Eton College, MS 200, fol. 17). This sociability and decorum is apparent in all of Granger's dealings with his friends who were usually print collectors themselves; his surviving correspondence attests to constant visits to the homes of the duke and duchess of Portland, Joseph Gulston, and Horace Walpole and the regular exchange of duplicate prints between these people. Granger's hospitality and love of fine living is also demonstrated in the many invitations he extended and the regular gifts of food and wine sent out, via the Henley coach, to many of his intimates. He was evidently thought of as a good companion and in 1773 or 1774 he accompanied Lord Mountstuart on a tour of Belgium, Holland, France, and Spain where they both indulged their passion for collecting prints.

Despite his personal popularity and his success as an author, Granger was a modest man. As he himself explained, he desired nothing more in life than to be known as an 'honest man, and a good parish priest' (*A Biographical History of England*, 5th edn, 1.viii). In practice, however, his name has gained far greater fame through his life or publications ever promised. In 1882 the *Oxford English Dictionary* first defined the verb 'to grangerize' as the term for a long fashionable method of print collecting in which published books were embellished and extended by the addition of portraits and other prints. Though Granger himself never indulged in this form of print collecting, preferring instead to store his prints loose in portfolios, some of his closest friends were ardent grangerizers and the several editions of his *Biographical History of England* became one of the most popular titles for this sort of customization, the most impressive being the thirty-six-volume collection made by Richard Bull, which was sold to Lord Mountstuart in 1774 (now in the Huntington Library).

Granger died at Shiplake on the morning of Monday 15 April 1776, after having been seized by an 'Apoplectic fit' (J. Granger, *A Biographical History of England*, 5th edn, 1.xxvii) while celebrating communion, at his parish church of Shiplake, on the preceding day. He left no will but was survived by a brother, John (*d.* 1810), and by his wife, Anne, who inherited her husband's small estate through an administration granted on 10 May 1776. She

died on 28 March 1790 and was buried alongside Granger in his tomb at Shiplake church. Granger's own collection, comprising over 14,000 prints, was sold by Greenwood in 1778.

LUCY PELTZ

Sources 'Buckler drawings', 22, 1830, BL, Add. MS 36377, fol. 44 • D. Bank and A. Esposito, eds., *British biographical archive*, 2nd series (1991) [microfiche] • Foster, *Alum. Oxon.* • R. Gough, *Sepulchral monuments in Great Britain*, 2 vols. (1786–96) • J. Granger, letter of administration, 10 May 1776, PRO, PROB 6/152/93 • *The Granger Society, for the publication of ancient portraits and family pictures* [1841] [prospectus] • Boswell, *Life* • 'Institution books', PRO, PROB E331, 17000–17014 • *The autobiography and correspondence of Mary Granville, Mrs Delany*, ed. Lady Llanover, 1st ser., 3 vols. (1861); 2nd ser., 3 vols. (1862) • J. Granger, correspondence with R. Bull, 1769–74, Eton, MS 200 • T. Davies, letter to J. Granger, 9 March 1769, Folger, MS Y.C. 715 (2) • letters from J. Granger to W. Cole, BL, Add. MS 5992, fols. 184–202 • Walpole, *Corr.* • *Letters between Rev. James Granger … and many of the most eminent literary men of his time*, ed. J. P. Malcom (1805) • Nichols, *Illustrations* • *A biographical history of England, from the revolution to the end of George I's reign: being a continuation of the Rev. J. Granger's work*, ed. M. Noble, 3 vols. (1806) • *N&Q*, 2nd ser., 4 (1857), 22 • *Engraved Brit. ports.* • L. Peltz, 'The extra-illustration of London: leisure, sociability and the antiquarian city in the late eighteenth century', PhD diss., University of Manchester, 1997 • *GM*, 1st ser., 6 (1736), 553 • *GM*, 1st ser., 46 (1776), 192, 313 • *GM*, 1st ser., 52 (1782), 223, 433 • *GM*, 1st ser., 73 (1803), 895 • L. Peltz, 'Engraved portrait heads and the rise of extra-illustration: the Eton correspondence of the Rev. James Granger and Richard Bull, 1769–1774', *Walpole Society*, 66 (2004) [forthcoming]

Archives BL, letters to William Cole, Add. MS 5992, fols. 184–202 • Eton, corresp. Richard Bull, MS 200

Likenesses J. Cornish, miniature on copper, 1765, NPG [*see illus.*] • C. Bretherton, stipple, 1775 (after W. W. Ryland), repro. in J. Granger, *A biographical history of England from Egbert the Great to the Revolution*, 2nd edn, 4 vols. (1775), frontispiece • W. Baillie, chalk drawing, Hunt. L., *Biographical history of England* • D. P. Pariset, stipple (after P. Falconer), BM

Wealth at death see administration, PRO, PROB 6/152/93

Granger, Stewart [*real name* James Lablache Stewart] (1913–1993), actor, was born on 6 May 1913 in Old Brompton Road, London, the second of the two children of Major James Stewart (1861–1938), of the Royal Engineers, and his wife, Frederica, *née* Lablache. His mother hoped that he would emulate her great-grandfather, the celebrated basso profondo Luigi Lablache, but a distinct lack of operatic ability resulted in his enrolment as a pre-medical student at Epsom College. At sixteen, however, a family financial crisis forced him to join the Bell Punch Company. In 1933 he accepted Michael Wilding's invitation to become a film extra in *A Southern Maid*. After training at the Webber-Douglas Theatre School he made his stage début in Hull in *The Cardinal* (1935). On leaving Birmingham repertory he changed his name (adopting his grandmother's maiden name to avoid confusion with the American film star, James Stewart), and he garnered acclaim in the Old Vic's *Serena Blandish* (1939). His full screen début followed in *So this is London* (1939). Meanwhile, on 10 September 1938, he married his regular co-star Jean Elspeth Mackenzie (*b.* 1912), whose stage name was Elspeth March; they had two children, Jamie (*b.* 1944) and Lindsay (*b.* 1946).

In 1940 Granger enlisted in the Gordon Highlanders, transferring to the 6th battalion of the Black Watch after

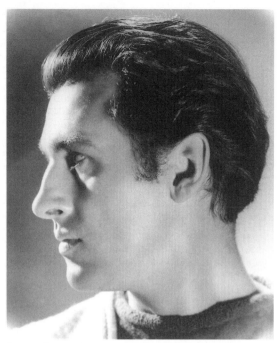

Stewart Granger (1913–1993), by Cornel Lucas, 1946

securing a commission as a second lieutenant. However, he was invalided out of the war with a stomach ulcer in 1942, shortly before his unit was wiped out in north Africa. Resuming his acting career he was cast as the Marquis of Rohan in Gainsborough Pictures' *The Man in Grey* (1943); however, he swapped roles with James Mason and gained matinée idol status with his performance as Peter Rokeby. Signing a seven-year contract, he scored in *Love Story* (1944) as a near-blind pilot, and as a spiv in *Waterloo Road* (1945). But the public preferred him in costume and, either side of proving himself a man of action as Apollodorus in *Caesar and Cleopatra* (1945), he headlined a string of Gainsborough costume dramas, including *Fanny by Gaslight*, *Madonna of the Seven Moons* (both 1944), and *Saraband for Dead Lovers* (1948). Not all of his films met with critical approval, however; his impersonation of the violinist Paganini in *The Magic Bow* (1946) prompted the *Daily Graphic* to opine that 'he appears to be sawing wood with one hand and milking a cow with the other' (Parrish and Starke, 366).

Granger divorced in 1948 and began courting Jean Merilyn Simmons (*b.* 1929), his co-star in the comedy *Adam and Evelyne* (1949). With Granger signed to MGM on a seven-year deal, following his success in *King Solomon's Mines* (1950), the couple married in Tucson, Arizona, on 20 December 1950, with the help of Howard Hughes. However, they were compelled to sue the eccentric tycoon after he bought Simmons's contract against her wishes and, much to Hollywood's astonishment, they won an out-of-court settlement for $250,000, plus $35,000 costs. Unfortunately, the victory only reinforced Granger's burgeoning reputation as a 'difficult' actor. His refusal to play the media gossip game and his brusque on-set manner led

one colleague to compare him to John Barrymore without the booze. Handsome, tall, and athletic, Granger acknowledged his ego, but he was also a hard-working perfectionist, frequently suffering injury while performing his own stunts. After his acrimonious parting from *A Star is Born*, director George Cukor dismissed him as 'just a movie star' (Parrish and Starke, 389). Yet he was offered (and refused) the leads in *Quo vadis?* (1951), *From Here to Eternity* (1953), and *Ben Hur* (1959). Instead, he chose to carry on swashbuckling in the tradition of Douglas Fairbanks and Errol Flynn. He set the record for the longest screen fencing bout with Mel Ferrer in *Scaramouche* (1952), their seven-minute duel requiring eighty-seven separate sword counts and twenty-eight stunts. Next he fought himself as he played both Rassendyll and Rudolf V in *The Prisoner of Zenda* (1952), remaining at court for *Young Bess* (1953), opposite Simmons, and *Beau Brummell* (1954). But, following *Moonfleet* (1955), his fortunes began to wane and only *The Last Hunt* (1956), *Bhowani Junction* (1959), and *North to Alaska* (1960) were positively received. Interviewed in 1968, he confessed:

> I've seldom, if ever, made a film I have really liked or been proud of … To spend a life making even reasonable films is bad enough, but to spend one, as I have, making terrible ones tends to be a little dispiriting. (*The Times*, 18 August 1993)

Granger's private life was also in turmoil. Although he and Simmons had become naturalized Americans in 1956 and had settled on a ranch in Arizona with their daughter, Tracy (*b.* 1956), their constant separations led to Simmons's filing for divorce on the grounds of 'outrageous cruelty' in 1960. Subsisting on Italian epics such as *The Swordsman of Siena* (1961) and *Sodom and Gomorrah* (1962) and a trilogy of Karl May sauerkraut Westerns, Granger married the former Miss Belgium, Viviane Lecerf, on 12 June 1964, only to divorce within a year of the birth of their daughter, Samantha (*b.* 1968). In 1967 he renounced his American citizenship, although he later returned to America for the television series *The Men from Shiloh* (1970–71) and to play Sherlock Holmes in a television adaptation of *The Hound of the Baskervilles* (1972). He ended a decade-long movie hiatus with *The Wild Geese* in 1978, but following the removal of part of his lung in 1981 he worked only occasionally, notably as the duke of Edinburgh in the television-movie *The Royal Romance of Charles and Diana* (1982), and on stage in *The Circle* (1990). He died of cancer on 16 August 1993 in Santa Monica, California.

DAVID PARKINSON

Sources S. Granger, *Sparks fly upward* (1981) • J. R. Parrish and D. E. Starke, *The swashbucklers* (1976) • *The international dictionary of films and filmmakers*, 3: *Actors and actresses*, ed. J. Vinson (1986) • D. Thomson, *A biographical dictionary of film*, 3rd edn (1994) • *The Times* (18 Aug 1993) • *The Independent* (18 Aug 1993) • WWW [forthcoming] • *Army List*

Likenesses C. Lucas, bromide fibre print, 1946, NPG [*see illus.*] • photograph, repro. in *The Times* • photograph, repro. in *The Independent* • photographs, Hult. Arch.

Granger, Thomas (1577/8–1627), Church of England clergyman and author, was born in Epworth, Lincolnshire. He matriculated as sizar at Peterhouse, Cambridge, in 1598, graduated BA in 1602, and proceeded MA in 1605. Between degrees he was tutor to the Leventhorpe family at Shingay Hall, Hertfordshire. In September 1606 Granger was ordained deacon at Lincoln and admitted as curate of Epworth. He became vicar of Butterwick, Lincolnshire, in November, when his age was given as twenty-eight on the presentation deed; he also taught in a school there. He was ordained priest in the following September, although that year he was cited for teaching without a licence, as he was in 1609 for ceremonial offences. By 1609, when their eldest child, Elizabeth, was born, Granger had married Elizabeth, whose previous surname is unknown. They had five other children, Sara, Hester, (a second) Hester, Samuel, and Lucy.

The increasingly divided local context evidenced by Bishop Richard Neile's 1614 visitation report and by John Cotton's troubles in neighbouring Boston may have provided the motivation for Granger, between 1616 and 1621, to publish ten works: seven sermons, an edition of Lily's grammar (*Syntagma grammaticum*, 1616), a practical Ramist logic text for country preachers (*Syntagma logicum*, 1620), and a *Commentarie on Ecclesiastes* (1621). Noting the 'contention about the … chiefe articles of the faith' (T. Granger, *Commentarie on Ecclesiastes*, 1621, 184–5), Granger mounted a strident defence of the English Calvinist theology of the abortive Lambeth articles (1595). Perhaps against Richard Hooker, he subjected human reason to a critique and also insisted that scripture alone, and not the church, was immediately inspired of God. Granger's logic manual used contentious examples, such as 'all [of the elect] persevere not in faith' to illustrate false theology (T. Granger, *Syntagma logicum*, 1620, 341). He promoted assurance, while insisting that salvation was not for faith foreseen or for human co-operation but rather 'according to the good pleasure of [God's] will' (T. Granger, *A Looking-Glasse for Christians*, 1620, sig. A4). Grace was irresistible and God's decree immutable. While sacraments were merely public signifiers for the godly, not the effectual agents of God's division of humanity, accepting the Word as interpreted by a preacher was 'an evident token of true conversion' (T. Granger, *Pauls Crowne of Rejoycing*, 1616, 64).

In Butterwick, Granger may have suffered for recommending 'godly' harmony before traditional neighbourliness. A possibly autobiographical sermon dialogue between godly and ungodly characters included the 'ungodly' complaint that their preacher was 'too precise and curious' and the godly character's complaint of being short-changed on tithes and threatened with removal from office (T. Granger, *Pauls Crowne of Rejoycing*, 1616, 29). Granger recommended social separation: the godly should 'eschew the company of all prophane persons' (T. Granger, *The Blinde-Mans Sermon*, 1616, sig. D8v), including marriage to an 'Idolater' (T. Granger, *The Tree of Good and Evill*, 1616, 7). While the godly should practise financial discrimination, even the idle poor were owed the necessities of life by the 'children of God' (T. Granger, *Commentarie on Ecclesiastes*, 1621, 287–8). His 'Rules for Lending' indicated that any surplus had to be lent 'freely to any that need our helpe', though 'with discretion and judgement' (T. Granger, *The Tree of Good and Evill*, 1616, 54–5). Only when lending was a strain, and where the borrower might profit, could interest be charged. But the godly were obligated to lend among themselves, and without interest. These views, and the £73 in bonds owed to him at his death, suggest that Granger may have developed what Thomas Hooker later labelled an implicit gathered community. During a period of a supposed 'balance' in the church, Granger labelled as 'foolishnesse' the notion that 'a common mediocrity, or meane' comprised 'vertue, or the best profession' (T. Granger, *Commentarie on Ecclesiastes*, 1621, 58).

Granger's apparent exclusivity had its limits, however. He denied any link between preaching and political disloyalty but insisted that the godly had a higher duty to maintain true religion. Aware of the contentiousness of his ideas, Granger offered a partial dedication of *Ecclesiastes* to Bishop George Mountaigne, hoping that it 'might find better passage under your patronage' (sig. A5). He was duly presented by the bishop early in 1622 to the vicarage of Horbling, also in Lincolnshire. There too he combined his ministry with schoolteaching. Granger died at Horbling in 1627 and was buried there on 21 June.

JOHN MORGAN

Sources will, Lincs. Arch., LCC wills, 1627–494 · inventory, Lincs. Arch., INV 132/229 · bishop's transcripts of Epworth, Butterwick, and Horbling parish regsisters, Lincs. Arch. · presentation deed as vicar of Butterwick, Lincs. Arch., PD 1606/10 · archidiaconal visitation book, 1609, Lincs. Arch., Lincoln diocesan archives, Vij 12 [citing Granger for ceremonial offences], p. 318 · Granger's subscription to teach school at Horbling, 1623, Lincs. Arch., Sub 1, fol. 146v · bishop's register, Lincs. Arch., Lincoln diocesan archives, register 30 [Granger's presentation and institution to Butterwick], fols. 291v, 296 · episcopal visitation book, Lincs. Arch., Vj [citing Granger for teaching at Butterwick without a licence], fols. 39v, 110v · T. A. Walker, *A biographical register of Peterhouse men*, 2 (1930), 194 · J. Morgan, *Godly learning: puritan attitudes towards reason, learning and education, 1560–1640* (1986)

Archives Lincs. Arch., presentation of deed to Butterwick, PD 1606/10 · Lincs. Arch., subscription relating to teaching school at Horbling, Sub 1, fol. 146v | Lincs. Arch., archidiaconal visitation book relating to ceremonial offences, Vij 12, p. 318 · Lincs. Arch., bishop's register relating to presentation and institution to Butterwick, register 30, fols. 291v, 296 · Lincs. Arch., episcopal visitation book relating to teaching at Butterwick without a licence, Vj, fols. 39v, 110v · Lincs. Arch., Epworth, Butterwick, and Horbling bishops' transcripts of parish registers

Wealth at death £73 0s. 8d.: inventory, Lincs. Arch., INV 132/229

Grannd, Pàdraig, nan Òran. *See* Grant, Peter (1783–1867).

Grant family of Freuchie (*per.* 1485–1622), chiefs of clan Grant, owned valuable and strategically placed lands in the sheriffdoms of Moray and Inverness. Their fortunes were often influenced by the policies of powerful neighbours, especially the earls of Huntly and Moray, with either of whom the Grants might establish formal or informal relations, while nevertheless aspiring to remain independent and build up their own clan strength. **John Grant of Freuchie** (*d.* 1528), eldest son of John Grant the younger of Freuchie who died before 16 September 1483, succeeded his grandfather Sir Duncan Grant as laird in

1485. He was apparently called the Red Bard, but nothing is known of his poetical work. His mother was probably Muriel, daughter of Malcolm Mackintosh, captain of clan Chattan. During the lifetime of his grandfather he succeeded his father in the lands of Inverallan, and in 1483 he gave a bond of manrent (a contract of mutual obligation) to George Gordon, second earl of Huntly and lord of Badenoch, in return for a grant of lands in Badenoch. On 15 September 1484 he made a bond of friendship with John Ogilvy of Deskford and contracted to marry his daughter Margaret. The bond was repeated by their successors in 1514.

Grant's support of James IV and the earl of Huntly in various commissions to punish wrongdoers and pacify the highlands brought rewards in the shape of further lands to add to the scattered properties in Strathspey, Moray, and Banff which he had inherited from his grandfather. In 1494 these were incorporated into the barony of Freuchie. In 1498 Ballindalloch was added to his estate, and in 1509 the barony and recently royal castle of Urquhart on Loch Ness. On the same day in December 1509 the lands of Corriemony at the head of Glen Urquhart were granted to his second son, John, and the lands of Glenmoriston to his natural son John Mor, both being made into baronies and the bases for powerful cadet families. From at least 1516 he held lands in Abernethy from the earl of Moray. In the confusion following the Scots defeat at Flodden in 1513, Sir Donald MacDonald of Lochalsh, claiming to be the lord of the Isles, seized the castle of Urquhart and plundered the lands around. The invaders were driven out by the end of 1516 and Grant claimed damages before the lords of council, but though he was awarded £2000 he received nothing. John Grant died on 1 May 1528 having considerably advanced the standing of his family. It is from John's time that there occurs the first reference to the 'clan de Grantis', in letters of remission granted under the great seal in 1527–8 for not attending the muster of the army at Solway and Wark in 1523. He left three sons and five daughters, having arranged important marriages for four of his daughters.

James Grant of Freuchie (1485?–1553), called James of the Forays, was served heir in all his father's lands including Freuchie with its castle and fortalice, which may then have been still building, as the earliest evidence of residence there comes only in 1551. Although the castle was also known as Ballachastell, this alternative was never used as the chief's designation. James married first Elizabeth, daughter of John Forbes, sixth Lord Forbes, and second Christian Barclay. He continued his father's support of the earl of Huntly, giving several bonds of manrent to him in the later 1540s, but in 1530 also gave a bond for life to James Stewart, earl of Moray, a half-brother of James V who died in 1544. His relations with his kinsmen the Mackintoshes and clan Chattan were ambivalent: he was included in the 1528 commission to extirpate them following disturbances during the minority of their chief, but later took their part and protected them from the earl of Moray, thereby earning a fine of £1000 Scots from the privy council. James and seven other Grants obtained feus

(hereditary leases) of many church lands in Strathspey, where he was given 40 merks' worth of land and the rest not more than 24 merks each. In July 1543 he joined with Huntly in signing a bond of mutual support with Cardinal Beaton, four bishops, six earls, and many others, in response to the lack of policy and justice following the defeat at Solway Moss and the death of James V late in 1542, and the resulting danger from England. The troubles of the time came nearer home in 1544, when the Grants took part in an expedition under Huntly in support of the Frasers against the Clanranald, in which Urquhart and Glenmoriston were overrun by the Camerons and Urquhart Castle captured. As compensation for this James Grant was given Cameron lands in Lochalsh and Lochcarron, but never occupied them. James died at his castle of Freuchie in 1553 and was buried at Duthil. In his will he left personal property there and at Knockando, Mullochard, Gartenmore, and Kilsanctninian (in Urquhart). He had four sons, John, who succeeded him, William, Duncan, and Archibald, who all received parts of the church lands of Strathspey, and four daughters.

John Grant of Freuchie (d. 1585) succeeded his father as laird of Freuchie in 1553, taking sasine at 'the castle and fortalice of Ballachastell'. In 1562 a document concerning his woods referred to him as laird of Grant but the chiefs continued to call themselves Grants of Freuchie. He acquired further church lands and became justiciar for the whole of Strathspey, in Urquhart and Glenmoriston and in part of Strathavon. John attended the Reformation parliament in 1560, and was evidently sometimes at Queen Mary's court, for he was said to have been present at the time of David Rizzio's murder in 1566, and later supported her. In his time the clan had been built up considerably and in 1585 a bond of the principal men included twenty-seven signatories, of whom sixteen were named Grant and many of the rest used patronymics. John married Lady Margaret Stewart, daughter of John Stewart, third earl of Atholl, and second Lady Janet Leslie, daughter of George Leslie, third earl of Rothes. He had two sons and seven daughters; his second son, Patrick, was given Rothiemurchus but encountered Mackintosh opposition until a final arbitration in his favour in 1586. John's eldest son, Duncan, died at Abernethy in 1582 leaving five sons and one daughter from his marriage to Margaret, daughter of William Mackintosh of Dunachton.

John Grant of Freuchie (1568?–1622), son of Duncan Grant and Margaret Mackintosh, succeeded his grandfather as laird of Freuchie while still a minor. He was a good manager and gave wadsets to his brothers and other clansmen with a view to improving the value of his estate. He was able to consolidate his possession of the whole barony of Freuchie, but finally gave up his claim to any right to the lands and castle of Strome in 1600. A staunch protestant, he signed a bond in defence of true religion with the king and a number of nobles in 1589, and finally broke with Huntly about 1590, after some years of sporadic violence, to side with Argyll at the battle of Glenlivet in 1594. In attempting to bring peace to the highlands he made bonds with Cameron of Lochiel, MacDonald of Glengarry, and Mackintosh of Dunachton, and in 1590 at Balla-chastell there was signed a bond of mutual support whose nine signatories included the earls of Atholl and Moray, Fraser of Lovat, Campbell of Cawdor, Stewart of Grantully, and Grant himself. The last, by a contract dated 15 April 1591, married Lilias (*d.* 1643/4) [*see* Grant, Lilias], daughter of Sir John Murray, created earl of Tullibardine in 1606; she possessed considerable force of character. They had one son, knighted in 1617, and five daughters. John Grant died on 20 September 1622 and was buried at Duthil.   R. W. MUNRO and JEAN MUNRO

Sources W. Fraser, *The chiefs of Grant* (1883) · I. F. Grant, *The clan Grant* (1955) · J. Wormald, *Lords and men in Scotland* (1985) · K. M. Brown, *Bloodfeud in Scotland* (1986)
Archives NA Scot., GD 248

Grant, Albert [*formerly* Abraham Gottheimer], **Baron Grant in the Italian nobility (1831–1899)**, company promoter, was born in Dublin on 18 November 1831, the son of Bernard Gottheimer, a poor Jewish pedlar from central Europe and later a partner in a business in Newgate Street, London, importing fancy goods. Educated in London and Paris, the son later assumed the name of Albert Grant. In 1856 he married Emily Isabella, daughter of Skeffington Robinson, of London and Epsom, and they had at least one son.

Grant began his career as a clerk and then a traveller in wines, entering the financial world in April 1859 when he established the Mercantile Discount Company. This failed during the leather crisis of 1860–61. In February 1864 he established Crédit Foncier and a month later the Crédit Mobilier and then six months later he merged them into Crédit Foncier and Mobilier of England. This institution served as the principal vehicle for his company promotions in the 1860s, nearly all of which were surrounded by allegations of fraud. He worked by trading shares in a company prior to their allotment. These were puffed to extravagant heights and then sold to the general public before they had time to fall to a discount. In this way he rigged the market on a grand scale. Crédit Foncier and Mobilier was finally liquidated in 1872. In the 1870s he operated in partnership with his brother Maurice through a private bank, Grant Brothers & Co.

The secret of Grant's success as a promoter is said to have been his idea of obtaining lists of all the clergy, widows, and other small yet hopeful investors. The public which he discovered in this way was greedy to take up companies more quickly than he could bring them out. 'All sorts of kind individuals were at his elbow, ready to supply him with the means of meeting the demand', and he was tempted into embarking upon schemes without proper investigation. Among the companies floated by him were the Cadiz Waterworks, Central Uruguay Railway, Labuan Coal Company, City of Milan Improvements, Imperial Land Company of Marseilles, Russia Copper Company, and Varna Railway. Perhaps the most notorious of these schemes was that connected with the Emma Silver Mining Company of Utah. The prospectus was issued towards the end of 1871, the capital being fixed at £1 million in shares of £20. The venture looked imposing and

Albert Grant, Baron Grant in the Italian nobility (1831–1899), by London Stereoscopic Co.

the profits were estimated at £800,000 a year. The money was subscribed at a premium but all that the investors ever received was a shilling for each of their £20 shares. Grant, however, received £100,000 as promotion money.

In the meantime Grant had been making a considerable display as a public character. He was returned to parliament for the borough of Kidderminster in 1865 but lost the seat in 1868. He was re-elected in 1874, but this was subsequently declared to be null and void on the grounds of his corrupt practices. In 1868 Victor Emmanuel II of Italy conferred on him the title of baron for services rendered in connection with the Galleria Vittorio Emanuele in Milan. In 1873 Grant purchased a large area of slum land close to Kensington Palace, pulled down the houses and erected Kensington House from the designs of Sir James Knowles, a massive building surrounded by its own grounds. The building was only used once, on the occasion of the bachelors' ball, given there on 22 July 1880. Three years later the house was demolished and the site seized by Grant's creditors; the grand staircase was removed to Madame Tussaud's exhibition in Marylebone Road. During 1873–4 Grant rendered a real service to the London public by purchasing the neglected area of Leicester Fields, occupied by dead cats and other refuse and surmounted by a broken statue of George I. He converted the space into a public garden, which was handed over by him on 2 July 1874 to the Metropolitan Board of Works for the enjoyment of the public. At each angle of the square was placed a bust of a former resident—Reynolds, Newton, Hogarth, and John Hunter. In the centre was a statue of Shakespeare by Signor Fontana, reproduced from the statue in Westminster Abbey. In the same year, after a keen competition at Christies, Grant bought for 800 guineas a fine portrait of Sir Walter Scott by Landseer, which he presented to the National Portrait Gallery at a time when the government confessed that it had no available funds with which to make the purchase. In 1874 he bought *The Echo* newspaper from Messrs Cassell for £20,000 and endeavoured for a very short time to run a halfpenny morning edition. Grant is said to have been the first person to persuade the morning papers to break their columns for advertisement. He soon transferred *The Echo* to Passmore Edwards.

A series of actions and proceedings in the bankruptcy court, which lasted until the very eve of his death, shattered Grant's resources and finally left him comparatively poor. His pictures were sold at Christies in April 1877 for £106,202, some of the more notable ones, such as Landseer's *Otter Hunt*, at a very great loss. In June 1877 it was stated in the Court of Appeal that eighty-nine actions were pending in regard to Grant's affairs. In July 1876, in the court of common pleas before Lord Coleridge, Grant was the defendant in a case in which the plaintiff, Twycross, was a shareholder of the Lisbon Tramways Company. He charged Grant with fraudulent promotion. Grant pleaded his own cause in a very long, cynical, and conspicuously able speech. Judgment was given for the plaintiff for £700, but the charge of fraud was rejected. The case dragged on until February 1879 when Grant's affairs were in liquidation and when the judges of appeal refused the application of Twycross's widow for costs. He made a further effort to rebuild his fortunes in May 1878 by founding the General Banking Company, but such was his reputation by this time that of the 20,000 shares of the company only 3744 were taken up in addition to his own 1000. The company was liquidated in February 1877, a week before Grant himself went bankrupt. An action brought against him in the London bankruptcy court in 1885 showed liabilities of £217,000 and assets of £74,000. He said that in 1867 he had had a surplus in excess of £500,000. A receiving order against him was issued in the same court on the Saturday before he died, of heart failure, at Aldwick Place, Pagham, near Bognor Regis, in Sussex, on Wednesday 30 August 1899.

Albert Grant is widely believed to have served as the model for the corrupt financier Melmotte in Anthony Trollope's novel *The Way we Live Now*, first published serially in 1874–5.

THOMAS SECCOMBE, *rev.* MICHAEL REED

Sources P. L. Cottrell, 'Grant (Gottheimer), Albert (Abraham) Zachariah', *DBB* • D. Kynaston, *The City of London*, 1 (1994) • *The Times* (31 Aug 1899) • *Daily News* (31 Aug 1899) • *The Times* (15 July 1876) • *The Times* (18 July 1876) • *The Times* (13 Feb 1879) • *ILN* (9 Sept 1899) • *Truth* (7 Sept 1899) • T. Taylor and R. Owen, *Leicester Square: its associations and its worthies* (1874) • J. Hollingshead, *The story of Leicester Square* (1892) • *A list of the companies established under the auspices of Mr Albert Grant* (1872) • 'Grant v. the overseers of Pagham', *Law reports: common pleas division*, 3 (1878), 80 • 'Twycross v. Grant and others', *Law reports: common pleas division*, 4 (1879), 40 • d. cert.

Likenesses Ape [C. Pellegrini], chromolithograph caricature, NPG; repro. in *VF* (21 Feb 1874) • London Stereoscopic Co., photograph, NPG [*see illus.*] • Pet, chromolithograph caricature, NPG; repro. in *Monetary Gazette* (31 Jan 1877), suppl. • caricature, repro. in Hollingshead, *Story of Leicester Square* • portrait, repro. in *ILN*

Grant, Alexander, of Grant (1674x9–1719), army officer, was born between 1674 and 1679, probably at Freuchie in Elginshire, the eldest surviving son of Ludovick *Grant of Freuchie (1650?–1716) and his first wife, Janet Brodie (*d.* 1697), only child of Alexander Brodie of Lethen. He studied law on the continent, but had returned by 30 November 1698, when he married Elizabeth Stuart (*d.* 1708), daughter of James Stuart, Lord Doune, at St Bride's, Fleet Street, in London. He then served in the regiment that his father raised at the special request of William III and II in 1700. Grant represented Inverness-shire in the Scottish parliament of 1703–7, and on 4 March 1706 was appointed to the colonelcy of Mar's regiment on the Scottish establishment. Grant was a close confidant of John Campbell, second duke of Argyll, and was one of the commissioners appointed to arrange the union with England.

On 7 February 1707 the duke of Marlborough requested that Grant's regiment be provided for service in Flanders, and on 24 December 1707 it was taken onto the British establishment. Grant's political as well as military alignment with Marlborough was confirmed when he remained member for Inverness-shire in the 1708–10 British parliament. Following the battle of Oudenarde (1708), orders were sent to Grant for his regiment to march to Newcastle upon Tyne for embarkation to the Low Countries. Despite reported problems with discipline, the troops, brigaded with Strathnaver's regiment, arrived at Ostend to take part in the operations against Bruges and Ghent, held at this time by the duke of Vendome. Grant's first wife having died on 22 April 1708, on 8 April 1709, at St Martin-in-the-Fields, Grant married Anne (*d.* 1717), maid of honour to Queen Anne and daughter of John Smith, former speaker of the House of Commons. Grant's regiment was subsequently employed largely on garrison duties in 1709 and 1710. In 1710 he became member of parliament for Elginshire, a seat he retained for the rest of his life. On 4 May 1711 Grant sought replacements for men drafted into those regiments to go with John Hill's expedition to Quebec. Soon afterwards Grant and a party of officers were taken prisoner by the French, but were exchanged after being held captive in Calais for a short time. Grant was removed from his regiment in 1711, apparently because of his Hanoverian sympathies, at a time when anti-Jacobite elements were being purged from the army. In a request dated 9 April 1714 he unsuccessfully sought an appointment as brigadier-general. He was restored to his colonelcy following the accession of George I.

During the 1715 Jacobite rising Grant and his regiment were stationed in England but he sent encouragement to his younger brother, Captain George Grant, to raise the clan Grant for the king. Shortly afterwards the regiment went to Scotland and Grant was appointed constable of Edinburgh Castle. He went with Argyll to Leith in October 1715 to subdue the rebellion there, and served on Argyll's staff at the battle of Sheriffmuir (13 November 1715). Grant's appointment as brigadier-general was confirmed shortly afterwards, and he briefly served as governor of Sheerness. He vacated the colonelcy of his regiment in 1717 and the following year it was disbanded, after brief service in Ireland.

In 1716 Grant's father, Ludovick, died, and he inherited the remainder of the family estate, territory around Loch Ness having been granted to him by his father in 1699. Active in the life of the highlands at this important period, Grant served as justice of the peace for Inverness, Moray, and Banff and was successful in suppressing outlawry and brigandage during the upheavals following the Jacobite insurrections at this time. Grant died on 19 August 1719 and was succeeded by his brother, Sir James Grant of Pluscardine.

By virtue of his close association with the duke of Argyll, Alexander Grant played an influential, if secondary, part in ensuring the accomplishment of the union of Scotland and England. Subsequently convinced that stability was to be achieved only by ensuring the Hanoverian succession he used his influence to blunt Jacobite efforts to cause unrest in the highlands, most particularly in the rebellion in 1715.   JAMES FALKNER

Sources DNB · C. Dalton, ed., *English army lists and commission registers, 1661–1714*, 6 vols. (1892–1904) · *The letters and dispatches of John Churchill, first duke of Marlborough, from 1702 to 1712*, ed. G. Murray, 5 vols. (1845) · C. Dalton, *George the First's army, 1714–1727*, 2 vols. (1910–12) · J. M. Simpson, 'Grant, Alexander', HoP, *Commons, 1715–54* · Burke, *Peerage* (1999) · IGI
Archives NL Scot., legal corresp. and papers | NL Scot., corresp. with Duncan Forbes

Grant, Sir Alexander, fifth baronet (1705–1772), merchant and politician, was born at the Mains of Dalvey, Inverness-shire, on 1 July 1705, the eldest of the three children of Patrick Grant (c.1654–1755), a barber and farmer, and his wife, Lydia, of Borlum, a daughter of William Mackintosh and a sister of Brigadier-General William Mackintosh. Little is known of Grant's childhood. Late in his teens he enrolled in an introductory medical course at the University of Aberdeen and upon its completion left for Jamaica. There, in the mid-1720s, he practised medicine and surgery; later he took up the work of a planter. His first recorded land patent appears in May 1730, when he received 300 acres in St Elizabeth parish; one month later he leased 1 acre in Westmoreland parish and opened a store for medicines and provisions. In the same year he entered into a planting partnership with Peter Beckford of Spanishtown. Over the next few years he continued to buy more land in the outlying parishes and in Kingston, where he transferred his medical practice in 1734. There he met and married Elizabeth Cooke (1717–1792), the daughter of Robert Cooke, who had emigrated from Bristol and become a prominent planter.

By 1740 the profits from Grant's merchandising trade were sufficient for him to return to Britain. He settled in London, operating as a general merchant. Initially he entered into a partnership with the Scottish wholesale druggist Alexander Johnston (1698–1775) and worked out of Johnston's shop in Magpie Alley, Fenchurch Street. Johnston supplied food, medicine, and cloth to West Indians, and Grant marketed their sugar. He lived above the counting-house until 1741, when he moved his family to Hatton Garden and in 1746 to Billiter Lane. The partnership lasted until 1753, when they divided their cash and stock. After the dissolution Grant pushed the sale of sugar and the supply of provisions with new vigour and from 9 Billiter Lane built up a global merchandising empire. In addition he moved into two activities that complemented his West Indies trade: slaving and contracting. In 1748 he joined Richard Oswald, Augustus and John Boyd, John Mill, and John Sargent in establishing a slave 'factory' on Bance Island, near the mouth of the Sierra Leone River in west Africa. Somewhat later, during the Seven Years' War, Grant began to provision the India Company squadrons; at the end of the 1750s he contracted to victual his majesty's ships at the Halifax naval station. And, after the war, he continued to provision the West India squadron. Grant's enterprises were broad: characteristically he plunged heavily into the funds, development of Scottish forests and fisheries, Greenland whaling, and speculation in Scottish, Nova Scotia, Florida, and Jamaica land, even as he pursued more traditional lines of trade.

In 1748 and 1749 Grant claimed the title to a Nova Scotia baronetcy that had been granted to an ancestor four generations before but had fallen dormant. Towards this end he received from the chief of the clan a grant of the barony of Grangehill, which he renamed Dalvey. But confirmation of the title dragged on until August 1752, when his father was retoured heir. When his father died three years later Grant inherited the title. At this time a prosperous merchant in the City and an affluent member of society with close friends at court, Grant felt free to cultivate political interest. He had previously turned to politics in the early 1750s, but had been defeated in the contest over the Inverness burghs in April 1754, due in large measure to the diffidence of the clan chief and the betrayal of supposed friends. Several years later, when George II died, Sir Alexander found himself 'somewhat distinguished' by his friendship with the king and Lord Bute. Helped by such acquaintances, he was unanimously elected as the member for the Inverness burghs in April 1761.

In parliament Grant worked behind the scenes as an adviser and lobbyist. During the 1760s the former sugar planter and navy contractor was widely regarded as one of the best sources on West Indian and Canadian affairs. Yet he was neither vociferous nor visible: he went two years without speaking in the house and, when he did, on 24 March 1763, he merely provided expert testimony on the possible economic effects of the cider tax. He attended the house almost every day that it was in session, and was an inveterate committee-goer. For most of his tenure he was loyal to the ministry in power: initially he sided with Bute and supported Bute's peace; after Bute's fall in 1763, he sided with Grenville, although he maintained close ties to Bute's party; he opposed John Wilkes and the repeal of the cider tax; and after Grenville's fall in 1765 he sided with Rockingham. Yet, in a display of independence, he opposed the repeal of the Stamp Act in February 1766. But by that time he was already under fire in Scotland. Due to the machinations of an aspiring nabob, Colonel Hector Munro, Grant was stripped of the provostship of Nairn in October 1765 and of his seat on the Nairn council one year later. Ultimately he filed a complaint in the court of sessions, but to no avail, and he lost his seat to Munro in the general election of 1768.

In 1770 Grant turned his business over to three relatives, but almost immediately he felt he had made a mistake and one year later returned to the counting-house. Yet his presence was fleeting. In June 1772 he was 'in a dangerous way', and in late July he was speechless. He died on 1 August at his house in Great George Street, Westminster, of 'a total and gradual decay of nature'. His body was carried on a fishing smack to his home at Dalvey House, near Forres, and buried on 1 September alongside his father.

DAVID HANCOCK

Sources D. Hancock, *Citizens of the world: London merchants and the integration of the British Atlantic community, 1735–1785* (1995) · GEC, *Baronetage*, vol. 4 · W. Fraser, ed., *The chiefs of Grant*, 1 (1883), 499–533 · *Journal of the commissioners for trade and plantations*, [14 vols.] (1920–38) [April 1704 – May 1782] · W. L. Grant and J. F. Munro, eds., *Acts of the privy council of England: colonial series*, 6 vols (1908–12) · A. Mackenzie, *History of the Munros of Fowlis* (1898) · F. B. Benger, 'Pen sketches of old houses in this district: 15. Bookham Grove, Great Bookham', *Proceedings of the Leatherhead and District Local History Society*, 1 (1955), 21–5 · Chancery records · Deeds, Island RO, Spanishtown, Jamaica · will, PRO, PROB 11/982, sig. 403 · NA Scot., GD 176/828

Archives NA Scot., GD 248 · NA Scot., GD 345 · Tomintoul House, Inverness-shire | District Council Office, Nairn, burgh council minutes · GL, rate books · Hants. RO, Malmesbury MSS · Jamaica Archives, Spanishtown, Jamaica, land patents and deeds · NA Scot., register of sasines · The Hirsel, near Coldstream, Berwickshire, earl of Home MSS · Mount Stuart, Isle of Bute, Bute MSS

Wealth at death £93,000: sederunt book, Grant papers, Tomintoul House, Inverness-shire; will, PROB 11/1772; NA Scot. GD 176/828

Grant, Sir Alexander, tenth baronet (1826–1884), university principal, eldest son of Sir Robert Innes Grant, the ninth baronet, of Dalvey (1794–1856), and his wife, Judith Tower (1804/5–1884), eldest daughter of Cornelius Durant Battelle of the Danish island, Santa Cruz, West Indies, was born in New York on 13 September 1826. His father had lived in the West Indies, and married the daughter of a planter.

Grant was taken to England soon after his birth, and subsequently accompanied his parents to the West Indies, where he stayed for two or three years. He was sent to England to be educated, attending preparatory schools before entering Harrow in 1839. He won several prizes, and was the first Harrow boy to gain one of the open Balliol scholarships at Oxford. He played twice in the Harrow cricket eleven against Eton and Winchester. In the spring of 1845 Grant went into residence at Oxford. He read widely in modern literature, and was interested in the Tractarian

theological movement, but only gained a second class. In 1849, nevertheless, he was elected, over twelve first-class men, to an open Oriel fellowship.

In 1848–9, by the unexpected emancipation of all the slaves in the island of Santa Cruz, without any compensation, Grant's family was impoverished. He gave up reading for the bar and became a private tutor at Oxford. In 1857 he published his edition of the *Ethics* of Aristotle, then a central text in the Oxford Greats curriculum. Grant was the first British scholar to interpret Aristotle in primarily historical terms. Jowett's influence had led him to the study of German scholarship, and he followed Hegel in adopting an evolutionary picture of the history of Greek philosophy. Grant's edition was republished several times, but his adoption of an administrative career prevented him making further original contributions to classical studies.

In 1855 Grant was nominated one of the examiners of candidates for the Indian Civil Service. In 1856 he succeeded his father as tenth baronet. In 1859 he accepted an offer of Sir Charles Trevelyan to go out to Madras. Before leaving England he married, on 2 June 1859, Susan (d. 1895), second daughter of Professor James Frederick *Ferrier of St Andrews. Trevelyan had drawn up ambitious plans for organizing education in India. On Grant's arrival at Madras, it was found that the only post to which he could be immediately appointed was an inspectorship of elementary vernacular schools, but when in 1860 the Elphinstone Institution was remodelled and affiliated to the University of Bombay, Grant was appointed to the new professorship of history and political economy. The future politician Pherozeshah Mehta was a pupil, and much influenced by him. Two years later he succeeded Dr Harkness as principal of the college and dean of the faculty of arts in the university. Wishing to place greater emphasis on classical study, he instigated the removal of modern Indian languages from the university's examinations, with damaging results for their teaching in schools.

In 1863, on the retirement of Sir Joseph Arnould, Grant was appointed vice-chancellor of the University of Bombay. He became a strong critic of centralization in Indian government. He temporarily resigned the office of vice-chancellor of Bombay University in 1865, but was re-elected shortly afterwards and continued to hold the office for three more years. Also in 1865 he was appointed director of public instruction for the presidency of Bombay, where he proved an energetic administrator. In 1868 he became a member of the legislative council. A government minute of 3 October 1868 affirmed that he had 'undoubtedly set his mark on the history of education in India'.

Anxious to return to Britain to be with his children, one of whom became the notable administrator in India, Sir (Alfred) Hamilton *Grant, Grant became a candidate for the post of principal of Edinburgh University in 1868. The appointment was made by the curators of patronage, a joint body of university and town council representatives. Grant was the 'university' candidate, and won by one vote over the 'town' candidate, the surgeon Sir James Young Simpson. As principal Grant avoided partisanship, and gained the confidence of his colleagues and the respect of the students; he was noted for his urbanity and diplomatic qualities. He was far more active than his elderly predecessor Sir David Brewster, and presided over a period of rapid expansion: student numbers more than doubled during his period of office, and in the medical faculty rose from 517 to 1736. Grant's most important achievement was the construction of a new medical school, with the aid of a government grant and a large public subscription. This was opened in 1884, and coincided with the lavish tercentenary celebrations of the university, the first festival of its kind in Britain, designed by Grant to assert the university's international status. He also compiled a substantial history, *The Story of the University of Edinburgh During its First Three Hundred Years* (2 vols., 1884). These exertions probably contributed to his death from an 'apoplectic seizure' at his home, 21 Lansdowne Crescent, Edinburgh, on 30 November 1884. He was buried in the Dean cemetery, Edinburgh, on 5 December after a public funeral in St Mary's Episcopal Cathedral. He was a fellow of the Royal Society of Edinburgh and a director of the Commercial Bank of Scotland and the Scottish Equitable Insurance Company. Grant was succeeded in the baronetcy by his son Ludovic (1862–1936), then a student at Balliol and later professor of public law at Edinburgh.

Grant's tenure coincided with a period of intense debate on Scottish university reform, and he expressed his views in annual addresses to the students and in his oral evidence to the royal commission on Scottish universities of 1876. He was one of a group of Scottish academics with Balliol connections who sought to introduce higher standards of scholarship, especially in the classics, and to establish a more specialized honours curriculum. He also had to deal with the controversy aroused by the attempt of a group of women led by Sophia Jex-Blake to enter the university as medical students, which was frustrated both by hostility within the medical faculty and by a Court of Session ruling that women were debarred from the Scottish universities. Grant took a cautious line on this issue. While he supported the right of women to higher education, he thought their needs were different from those of men, and advocated the idea of a 'women's university', which was not to find favour in Scotland.

Grant's programme of university reform involved him in wider questions of Scottish education, as it required the extension and strengthening of secondary schooling. He especially supported the controversial reform of Edinburgh's wealthy endowed hospitals, to turn them from residential institutions into middle-class day schools, and wrote an essay advocating this in *Recess Studies* (1870), a collective volume edited by himself. Following the Education (Scotland) Act of 1872, which organized state elementary education, Grant became a member of the Board of Education, a temporary body based in Edinburgh to supervise the implementation of the act and advise on the new education code. Grant and his colleagues argued vigorously for the retention of 'university' subjects such as Latin and

mathematics in the elementary schools, as had been the tradition in Scottish parish schools, but the board obtained only limited concessions on this point before its dissolution in 1878. In this issue as in others, Grant was an instinctive champion of the classically inspired ideal of liberal education, with its élitist social implications, against the utilitarian trends of the age.

R. D. ANDERSON

Sources W. Y. Sellar, *Blackwood*, 137 (1885), 133–43 · *The Scotsman* (1 Dec 1884) · *The Scotsman* (6 Dec 1884) · W. B. Hole, *Quasi cursores: portraits of the high officers and professors of the University of Edinburgh at its tercentenary festival* (1884), 7–17 · F. M. Turner, *The Greek heritage in Victorian Britain* (1981) · R. D. Anderson, *Education and opportunity in Victorian Scotland: schools and universities* (1983) · *The Scotsman* (6 July 1868) · *The Scotsman* (7 July 1868) · *The Academy* (6 Dec 1884), 375 · *Saturday Review*, 58 (1884), 776–7 · W. A. Knight, *Some nineteenth century Scotsmen* (1903) · *Wellesley index* · S. Nurullah and J. P. Naik, *A history of education in India* (1951) · S. R. Dongerkery, *A history of the University of Bombay* (1957) · Burke, *Peerage*
Archives NL Scot., letters to A. C. Fraser · Royal College of Surgeons, Edinburgh, corresp. with Sir James Young Simpson relating to principalship of Edinburgh University
Likenesses W. Hole, etching, NPG; repro. in Hole, *Quasi cursores* · C. McBride, marble bust, U. Edin.
Wealth at death £8340 6s. 11d.: confirmation, 11 Feb 1885, *CCI*

Grant, Sir Alexander, first baronet (1864–1937), biscuit manufacturer and benefactor, was born on 1 October 1864 in Forres, Moray, the eldest son of Peter Grant (1838–1882), a guard with Highland Railway, and his wife, Elizabeth, daughter of James and Elizabeth Norries. While he was a pupil at Forres Academy his father died, and he left school to be trained in the office of a writer to the signet. Unhappy with legal minutiae, he had himself apprenticed to Thomas Stuart, a small but progressive local baker. Once a journeyman, he moved to Edinburgh, where the biscuit manufacturer Robert McVitie engaged him as an assistant at £1 a week.

Grant was both capable and ambitious, and McVitie made good use of his talents, encouraging him to attend lectures on food chemistry at Heriot-Watt College. Grant also tackled all available literature in English on the craft of baking and visited Europe to learn about biscuit manufacture there. On 31 July 1887 he married Elizabeth, daughter of Alexander Norris of Edinburgh; they had one son and two daughters. Shortly afterwards he was promoted to foreman, but he resigned to run a bakery in Inverness. When this venture failed McVitie reluctantly gave him his job back; after the Edinburgh factory was destroyed by fire, Grant was made manager of its temporary replacement in Yorkshire. He returned to manage the rebuilt factory, which was claimed to be the most up to date of its kind in Britain.

When in 1901 McVitie's partner, Charles Edward Price, retired, Grant was appointed general manager. He and McVitie established a branch factory at Harlesden, north London—an audacious foray into the English biscuit-makers' territory. For three months after its start-up Grant travelled between Edinburgh and London on the sleeperless night train, during the week not spending a single night in his bed. The factory failed to become profitable until 1905, but by then its output was three times that of the Edinburgh factory.

McVitie died childless in 1910, and in June 1911 McVitie and Price Ltd was registered as a private limited company with £150,000 capital. Grant became chairman and managing director. In 1914 he opened a further factory, in Manchester; it was soon being used to make army and emergency biscuits for the government. These and other wartime concerns took their toll of Grant, who fell ill with double pneumonia, but his robust constitution pulled him through. He then secured a shareholding control of the company, and by the 1920s was reported to head the largest one-man enterprise in Britain.

Between the wars Grant made some noteworthy benefactions, totalling about £750,000. In 1920 he saved the taxpayer £25,000 by cancelling for five years the interest on £100,000 of war stock held by his firm. He donated a total of £200,000 for the rebuilding and endowment of the National Library of Scotland, where his name is commemorated on the great window, and he gave Edinburgh University £150,000 for various projects, for which he was made an honorary LLD. His most spectacular gesture—originally anonymous, but his name soon leaked out—was to provide Holyroodhouse with banqueting silver, linen, cutlery, and glassware—all Scottish-made—at a cost of £10,000.

Public honours soon followed. In 1923 Grant was given the freedom of the city of Edinburgh, and he later became freeman of Forres and of Nairn. Then in June 1924 he received a baronetcy for public services, apparently mooted before James Ramsay MacDonald had become prime minister the previous January. MacDonald, a native of Lossiemouth near Forres, was a friend of Grant, and his secretary persuaded Grant to meet some of the expenses of living at 10 Downing Street for the first premier who lacked a private income. Grant therefore loaned to MacDonald a Daimler car and £40,000 worth of securities.

In September 1924 the British press heard about the loan and linked it with the award of the baronetcy as the latest example of the 'honours scandals' that had beset earlier administrations. If MacDonald, and indeed his advisers, acted with a mixture of imprudence and unworldliness, Grant was politically quite as naïve in reassuring MacDonald that 'it is only the opinion of good people that matters and that guides public opinion, however loud the others may be' (Marquand, 359). Never a Labour supporter Grant dubbed himself a lifelong conservative, but for some reason he backed a Liberal candidate for an Edinburgh seat in 1924.

Grant had a round face with a full moustache and was of stocky build. He exerted himself quite as hard as he worked his employees, and indeed his son, Robert McVitie Grant. Robert, who was a modernizer like his father, died a bachelor at fifty-two, in 1947. Grant kept clear of society and enjoyed the countryside through motoring and golf. He was not involved in public affairs, apart from serving as a JP, and his religion was that of a good and practical Christian.

A committed supporter of the Industrial Welfare Society, in 1921 Grant suggested to the future George VI the idea of a summer camp jointly for boys from independent schools and from industry. He subsidized the first few 'Duke of York' camps, which continued annually until the Second World War. In business he remained fully active into his seventies. He caught a bad chill on the train back to Edinburgh after attending the king's coronation, and died at his home, 15 Hermitage Drive, Edinburgh, on 21 May 1937 from pneumonia. He was buried at Forres, and was survived by his wife.　　　　T. A. B. CORLEY

Sources T. Barton, 'Grant, Sir Alexander', *DSBB* · J. S. Adam, *A fell fine baker: the story of United Biscuits* (1974), 8–27 · *Glasgow Herald* (22 May 1937) · *The Scotsman* (22 May 1937) · *The Times* (22 May 1937) · *The Times* (25 May 1937) · Burke, *Peerage* · G. R. Searle, *Corruption in British politics, 1895–1930* (1987), 430–32 · D. Marquand, *Ramsay Macdonald* (1977), 357–61 · P. Pugh, *A clear and simple vision* (1991), 1–6 · A. de Courcy, *Circe: the life of Edith, marchioness of Londonderry* (1992), 191–2 · J. H. Wheeler-Bennett, *King George VI: his life and reign* (1958), 174–84 · S. Bradford, *King George VI* (1989), 80–81 · D. Judd, *King George VI, 1895–1952* (1982), 778 · *WWW*
Archives NL Scot., diary, MS 15978 | NA Scot., GD 381 3/1–3 · NL Scot., letters to H. P. Macmillan · PRO, corresp. with Ramsay Macdonald, PRO 30/69/1/194, 30/69/1/34
Likenesses photograph, *c.*1925, repro. in Adam, *Fell fine baker* · photograph, *c.*1930, repro. in Pugh, *Clear and simple vision*, 2
Wealth at death £1,039,976 5*s.* 9*d.*: confirmation, 1 Sept 1937, *CCI*

Grant, Sir Alexander Cray, eighth baronet (1782–1854), planter in the West Indies and politician, was born on 30 November 1782 at Bowring's Leigh, Devon, the eldest son of Sir Alexander Grant, seventh baronet (*d.* 1825), and his wife, Sarah, the daughter and heir of Jeremiah Cray of Ibsley, Hampshire. He entered St John's College, Cambridge, as a fellow-commoner, and graduated MA in 1806. In 1810 and 1811 he was a member of the colonial assembly of Jamaica. The following year he entered the House of Commons as MP for the borough of Tregony, Cornwall, and pursued an ambitious and active political career until his retirement from the house in 1843. He succeeded his father as eighth baronet on 26 July 1825.

Although Grant never returned to Jamaica, he was a prominent proprietor in the colony. He owned two plantations, on which, with a labour force of nearly 700 slaves, he cultivated sugar cane, manufactured rum, and kept a herd of cattle. In June 1833 he estimated his annual income from both plantations to be in the region of £8000 or £9000, nearly three-quarters of which came from sugar. Grant blamed emancipation and increased duty on sugar for the subsequent decline of income from his estates in Jamaica. Although he was awarded £10,702 by the commissioners of compensation in 1835, for 597 slaves, in 1841 he claimed that for several years he had been 'cultivating his property at a great loss' (*Hansard 3*, 1841, 611–12).

Politically ambitious, Grant sat in the Commons for Tregony in 1812, for Lostwithiel in 1818 and 1820, for Aldborough, Yorkshire, in 1826, for Westbury, Wiltshire, in 1830, and for Cambridge in 1840. He failed to get elected for

Grimsby in 1835 and Honiton in 1837. He served as chairman of committees of the whole house in the parliaments of 1826 and 1830, but his attachment to the West Indies interest in parliament may have hindered further advance. He spoke out in support of his fellow planters on many occasions. In 1816 he complained that the treatment of slaves in Jamaica had been unfairly represented to parliament. He defended government compensation for slave owners in 1841 by insisting on their freehold rights in slaves, reminding parliament that the 'sin of slavery was forced on' the colonies 'by the mother country' (*Hansard 3*, 1841, 287).

Grant was a leading figure in the tory party. He was a member of the Carlton Club and a close associate of Sir Robert Peel, who nicknamed him 'the Chin'. In 1834 he was appointed to the Indian Board of Control. Later attempts to exploit his relationship with Peel for personal advance were gently rebuffed, though in 1843 he was appointed one of the commissioners for public accounts, with a salary of £1200, a position he held until his death, at 32 Pall Mall, London, on 29 November 1854. He died unmarried and was succeeded by his brother, Robert Innes Grant.   JOHN C. APPLEBY

Sources *Hansard 1* (1816), 33.252–3, 34.1221–4; (1818), 38.308–11, 1205 · *Hansard 2* (1825), vol. 12; (1826), 16.269; (1828), 18.877; (1830), 22.326, 23.1412, 24.837, 25.312, 1295, 1297 · *Hansard 3* (1830–31), vol. 2; (1840), 54.1407, 55.1407; (1841), 56.610, 57.170–71; (1842), 65.647 · BL, Add. MSS 40345, 40348, 40394, 40403, 40404, 40406, 40409, 40414, 40427, 40486, 40488, 40489, 40506, 40517, 40525, 40536, 40537, 40545, 40602, 40605, 40606 · *The private letters of Sir Robert Peel*, ed. G. Peel (1920) · *British parliamentary papers: papers relating to negro apprenticeship slavery and the abolition of the slave trade, 1837–41* (1969) · *A portion of the journal kept by Thomas Raikes esq. from 1831 to 1847: comprising reminiscences of social and political life in London and Paris during that period*, 4 vols. (1856–8) · C. S. Parker, ed., *Sir Robert Peel: from his private papers*, 2nd edn, 3 vols. (1899) · *The letters of the third Viscount Palmerston to Laurence and Elizabeth Sulivan, 1804–1863*, ed. K. Bourne, CS, 4th ser., 23 (1979) · G. P. Judd, *Members of parliament, 1734–1832* (1955) · K. M. Butler, *The economics of emancipation: Jamaica and Barbados, 1823–1843* (1995) · N. Gash, *Politics in the age of Peel* (1953) · N. Gash, *Mr Secretary Peel: the life of Sir Robert Peel to 1830* (1961) · d. cert. · will, PRO, PROB 11/2204, sig. 30, vol. 1

Archives BL, corresp. with Sir Robert Peel, Add. MSS 40345, 40348, 40394, 40403, 40404, 40406, 40409, 40414, 40427, 40486, 40488, 40489, 40506, 40517, 40525, 40536, 40537, 40545, 40602, 40605, 40606

Grant, Andrew (*fl.* 1809), physician, wrote a *History of Brazil* in 1809, of which a French translation, with additions, appeared at St Petersburg in 1811. No other details of his life are discoverable. The book is dedicated to the merchants of Britain, and much of the work is designed to inform and encourage those engaged in commerce. As well as a history of Brazil since the arrival of the Portuguese, it gives detailed accounts of its geography, ports, and natural resources, as well as hints for health when visiting the country, including an exhortation to avoid dancing on arriving in tropical regions. Throughout the work, Grant was highly critical of the actions and effects of the colonizers and condemned the forced importation of Jews and the continued importation of African slaves. He praised the work of the Jesuits in gaining the esteem of the native people, in contrast to the attempts made by the colonizers to enslave the population.

GORDON GOODWIN, rev. MYFANWY LLOYD

Sources Watt, *Bibl. Brit.*

Grant [*née* MacVicar], **Anne** (1755–1838), author, was born on 21 February 1755 at Glasgow, the only child of Duncan MacVicar (*b.* 1731), farmer and soldier. Her mother, who died in 1811, was a daughter of Stewart of Invernahyle, a cadet branch of the Stewarts of Appin. Anne's father abandoned his farm in 1757 after the outbreak of the Seven Years' War, and, having obtained a commission in the 77th foot regiment, was dispatched to North America. His wife and daughter joined him in New York the following spring when Anne was three. Her father was often away (he took part, for example, in the disastrous expedition to Ticonderoga in 1758) and her early education was very much in the hands of her mother. Anne was a precocious child, and it has been claimed that she read the poems of Blind Harry and 'some of the most uncouth and rugged of the earlier Scottish minstrels' as well as the whole of the Old Testament and half of *Paradise Lost* by her sixth year (Graham, 281). She described these years in her third book, *Memoirs of an American Lady*, a tribute to her Dutch friends, in particular a Madame Schuyler, of whom she wrote 'whatever culture my mind received, I owe to her' (ibid., 282). Anne stayed with Madame Schuyler's family when the regiment was on manoeuvres and clearly owed much of her upbringing to her generous benefactor, who even offered to adopt her.

In 1765 Anne's father retired on half pay and purchased a small estate in Vermont. Poor health compelled him to return to Scotland three years later with his family, and on the outbreak of the American War of Independence his lands were confiscated. He still possessed a modest income and in 1773 was appointed barrack-master at Fort Augustus. It was here that Anne met James Grant (d. 1801), military chaplain to the 90th regiment of foot garrisoned there. They married in 1779, when he was given the charge of the neighbouring parish of Laggan by the fourth duke of Gordon.

From the age of eighteen Anne had kept up a regular and vivacious correspondence with a wide circle of friends. The death of her husband in 1801 left her in extreme poverty, alleviated only by a £30 pension to which she was entitled as a chaplain's widow; this meagre income was stretched to support herself and the eight children remaining of her family of twelve. Her answer to her straitened circumstances was to prepare a collection of the verses she had written over the years for her extensive correspondents, and thanks to the efforts of her friends and admirers, including the notorious Jane Gordon, wife of the fourth duke, no fewer than three thousand subscribers were found, and the volume was published in 1803. The best remembered is the song beginning 'Oh where, tell me where, is your highland laddie gone?'

Encouraged by this success, Anne set out to prepare,

Anne Grant (1755–1838), by William Bewick, 1824

with the help of the antiquary George Chalmers, a selection from her correspondence for publication under the title *Letters from the mountains; being the real correspondence of a lady between the years 1773 and 1807* (1807). From these 'simple and careless letters', as they are described in the advertisement to the first edition, it is possible to reconstruct her busy life 'spent in the most remote obscurity'. The *Letters* describe how she learned Gaelic (all her children spoke nothing else until they were three), 'that emphatic and original language' (*Letters*, 2.94), in order to understand what she called 'the peculiarities of Highland manners' (ibid., 1.17), and how she moved her family from Laggan's tiny glebe to the small neighbouring farm of Gartbeg, 50 miles from Inverness. In addition, the correspondence comments on the disintegration of the highland way of life, on literature from Ossian to Werther and Mary Wollstonecraft—'the empress of female philosophers' (ibid., 2.265)—and on the excesses of the leaders of Revolutionary France, especially Robespierre, whom she hoped 'will meet some enthusiast soon who will send him on a journey he is little prepared for' (ibid., 2.280).

This publication was followed by the *Memoirs of an American Lady* (1808) and *Essays on the Superstitions of the Highlanders* (1811), which is in many respects Anne Grant's most interesting book. As she explained in the preface, she considered that 'this work completes that picture of highland life, of which my other writings presented casual sketches or broken features.' Certainly it would have

been of great interest to those who were still fascinated by the arguments over the authenticity of Ossian or claims that highland peasants were noble savages, as suggested by disciples of Rousseau. As she wrote in the fourth essay: 'Wherever they remain in undisturbed possession of their own language and the prejudices connected with it, they think and act pretty much as they would have done a thousand years ago, unless restrained by religion' (*Essays on the Superstitions*, 117). One other feature of the book was her work on the classic Gaelic poem 'The Owl': she described herself composing her translation and commentary 'by the pencil of pensive recollection and heightened by the colouring of fancy' (ibid., appendix). The success of her publications enabled her to move to a series of prestigious addresses in Edinburgh from 1810: Heriot Row, Kirkbraeshead, Coates Crescent, and finally Manor Place. This was also a time of sadness as she continued to suffer the deaths of her children, until only the youngest remained, John Peter (*b*. 1791), later the editor of his mother's *Memoir and Correspondence* (1844).

Anne certainly derived some compensation from her extended acquaintance with literary friends in Edinburgh during the last thirty years of her life. Thomas De Quincey recalled in his *Literary Reminiscences* how she, 'an established wit and just then receiving incense from all quarters', was particularly kind to him, 'a person wholly unknown' (De Quincey, 1.55). Captain Edward Topham spoke of her as 'blessed with an ample share of that first of national endowments, good sense', with 'a strong and enlightened mind, cultivated by study and observation' (*The Contrast*, 200). Sir Walter Scott, with whom she was good friends, called her 'a stout old girl' (*Journal*), but the best description of her appearance and character at this time, perhaps, is in J. G. Lockhart's *Life of Sir Walter Scott*:

> Mrs. Grant was a tall, dark woman of very considerable intellect, great spirit and the warmest benevolence. She was always under the influence of an affectionate and delightful enthusiasm, which, unquenched by time or sorrow, survived the wreck of many domestic attachments, and shed a glow over the close of a very protracted life. (Lockhart)

Her letters show that she was on familiar enough terms with Scott and Lockhart to have had pronounced views on the vexed question of the authorship of *Waverley*. She wrote in July 1814, the month of its publication: 'I am satisfied from internal evidence that Walter Scott and no other is the author of that true and chaste delineation of Scottish manners, such as they existed at the time he assigns for his drama' (*Memoir and Correspondence*).

These and other distinguished literary contemporaries subscribed in 1825 to a petition to Robert Dundas, second Viscount Melville, urging the government to grant Anne Grant a pension. When she learned that it was to be what she regarded as a paltry £98 per annum, she declined in high dudgeon—which gave Scott the opportunity to comment that she was as 'proud as a Highland woman, vain as a poetess, and absurd as a Blue Stocking'—but nevertheless, as Scott anticipated ('your scornful dog will always eat your dirty pudding'), she eventually accepted (*Journal*, 30 Nov 1825). To the end she was a strong-minded and thrawn lady of distinction: as she exulted in her *Letters from the Mountains*, her first best-seller, 'an enthusiast I was born and an enthusiast I will die' (*Letters*, 3.84). She died intestate at 9 Manor Place, Edinburgh, on 7 November 1838; according to the inventory of her personal effects, she left estate in Scotland valued at £254 16s. 8d. and she was due £11 3s. 4d. on a mortgage taken out in Massachusetts. She was buried alongside four of her daughters in St Cuthbert's kirkyard in Edinburgh.   ANDREW TOD

Sources A. Grant, *Memoirs of an American lady* (1808) · A. Grant, *Letters from the mountains; being the real correspondence of a lady between the years 1773 and 1807* (1807) · *Memoir and correspondence of Mrs Grant of Laggan*, ed. J. P. Grant, 3 vols. (1844) · H. Graham, *A group of Scottish women* (1908) · E. H. Grant, 'Mrs Grant of Laggan: an account of her life', *Stand Fast* [magazine of the Clan Grant Society], 1/2 (1982) · *The journal of Sir Walter Scott*, 2 vols. (1890–91) · J. G. Lockhart, *Memoirs of the life of Sir Walter Scott*, 7 vols. (1837–8) · *The contrast, or, Scotland as it was in the year 1745 and Scotland in the year 1819* (1825) · T. De Quincey, *Literary reminiscences*, 2 vols. (1851) · parish register (marriage), Baleskine and Abertarff, 1779 · *DNB* · inventory of the personal effects of Anne Grant, 24 Nov 1842, NA Scot.
Archives U. Edin. L., corresp. | Edinburgh City Archives, letters to Mrs Wood · NL Scot., letters to Henry Stuart
Likenesses J. Henning, wax medallion, 1810, Scot. NPG · watercolour portrait, 1810, Scot. NPG · W. Bewick, chalk drawing, 1824, Scot. NPG [*see illus.*] · A. Edward, cut-paper silhouette, 1831, Scot. NPG · J. Tannock, oils, Scot. NPG
Wealth at death £254 16s. 8d.: inventory, 1842, NA Scot. · £11 3s. 4d. due on Massachusetts mortgage

Grant, Anthony (1806–1883), Church of England clergyman, was the youngest son of Thomas Grant of Portsea. He was born on 31 January 1806, was sent to Winchester College in 1815, and on 17 February 1825 matriculated as a scholar of New College, Oxford, becoming fellow in 1827. Grant took no undergraduate degree, but won the chancellor's Latin essay in 1830 and the Ellerton theological prize essay in 1832. He proceeded BCL in 1832 and DCL 1842. In 1834 he was ordained, and two years later became curate of Chelmsford. In 1838 he married Julia, daughter of General Peter Carey. From 1838 to 1862 he was vicar of Romford, Essex, and from 1862 to 1877 vicar of Aylesford, Kent. In 1843 he gave the Bampton lectures at Oxford, published as *The Past and Prospective Extension of the Gospel by Missions to the Heathen* (1844). These lectures created a powerful impression, and were important in the history of mission work. He also published on colonial church extension (1852) and the church in China and Japan (1858), but his interest in missions was confined to advice. In 1846 Grant was made archdeacon of St Albans, and the archdeaconry of Rochester was annexed to it in 1863. He was select preacher at Oxford in 1852, and in 1860 became canon of Rochester and in 1877 chaplain to the bishop of St Albans. In 1882 he resigned his archdeaconry of Rochester, but retained that of St Albans and his canonry until his death at Ramsgate, Kent, on 25 November 1883. His wife survived him. His son, Cyril Fletcher Grant, edited his sermons in 1884.

C. L. KINGSFORD, *rev.* H. C. G. MATTHEW

Sources *The Guardian* (5 Dec 1883) · *The Times* (27 Nov 1883) · private information (1890) · Foster, *Alum. Oxon.*
Wealth at death £15,134 19s. 3d.: probate, 12 Jan 1884, CGPLA Eng. & Wales

Grant, Sir Archibald, of Monymusk, second baronet (1696–1778), politician and agricultural improver, was born in Scotland on 25 September 1696. He was the elder son of Sir Francis *Grant (1658x63–1726), lord of session with the judicial title Lord Cullen and, from 1705, first baronet, of Monymusk, Aberdeenshire, and his first wife, Jean, daughter of the Revd William Meldrum of Meldrum. Grant passed advocate of the Scottish bar in 1714 and later was called to the English bar at Lincoln's Inn. He succeeded to the baronetcy on the death of his father in March 1726.

Grant's career fell into two very different phases. The first came to a dramatic end on 5 May 1732 when he was expelled from the House of Commons, where he had represented Aberdeenshire for ten years. The reason lay in his participation in a massive array of speculative activities, unusual even by the standards of the time. Some were linked to identifiable economic enterprises, notably in the exploitation of minerals; others were little more than frauds, even though Grant may have believed that his plans would benefit all concerned.

The final crash in this complex period of Grant's life was linked to his activities in the York Buildings Company, which spread from its initial concern with supplying water in London to the exploitation of estates in Scotland forfeited after the Jacobite rising of 1715, and the Charitable Corporation for the Relief of the Industrious Poor. The latter, which he assisted with small sums upon pledges at legal interest, has been accurately described as a corporate pawnbroker.

Both these concerns were vehicles admirably suited for someone with Grant's bent for questionable financial speculations. In co-operation with other directors and officials, Grant borrowed irregularly from the Charitable Corporation. In the end, to avoid their own and the corporation's collapse, he devised a share-pushing scheme involving some of his mining ventures and the York Buildings Company. Dishonesty among the conspirators themselves made an already serious situation hopeless. The scheme collapsed and with it the Charitable Corporation. Fear that Grant might abscond led to his being taken into custody for a time. After a parliamentary investigation he was found guilty of fraud and neglect. Although he admitted that he was guilty of neglect, he protested strongly that he was innocent of any deliberate fraud, but to no avail, and he was expelled from parliament. An attempt to prosecute him came to nothing, and after protracted litigation he retained his estates. He never returned to national politics, though he was appointed to the minor sinecure of keeper of the register of hornings in 1749.

The second phase of Grant's life was devoted to the improvement of his estates. Monymusk had been bought by his father when he sold his ancestral property in Banffshire in 1713. He paid little attention to his new land, much regretting the purchase, and young Archibald became the factor in 1716. The property was made over to him on his marriage, on 17 April 1717, to Anne, daughter of James Hamilton of Pencaitland.

Even in those early years, when Grant was resident

mainly in Edinburgh and London, his speculative activities did not prevent him from keeping a close watch over the estate, which was in poor shape. It became his main interest only after he took up permanent residence at Monymusk in 1734. He promoted with signal success the usual range of agricultural improvements of the eighteenth century, including the encouragement of rural industry, notably the manufacture of linen. His first main objective was to introduce the fallow system, which, like many other ideas, he brought from England. He quickly followed this up with the introduction of new crops, clover and ryegrass, to give the basis of regular rotations.

Grant's forceful personality and his wider—if not generally successful—experience, allied to the close control that residence at Monymusk entailed, enabled him to force the tenantry to conform to his new ways. According to him their backward ways were the greatest hazard he encountered. His agricultural improvements succeeded: they were emulated by others and gained for him a reputation as an agricultural improver that has largely effaced his early dubious financial practices. He published two pamphlets in Aberdeen on agricultural matters, *The Farmer's New-Year's Gift* (1757) and *The Practical Farmer's Pocket Companion* (1766).

After the death of his first wife, with whom he had two daughters, in 1731 Grant married Anne (*d*. before 1744), daughter of Charles Potts of Castleton in Derbyshire; the couple had one son, also Archibald, who succeeded to the baronetcy. Grant's third marriage, on 18 August 1751, was to Elizabeth (*d*. 1759), widow of James Callander of Jamaica; his final marriage, on 24 May 1770, was to Jane (1706/7–1788), widow of Andrew Millar, the London bookseller. Opinion differed on his matrimonial ventures. David Hume, who thought the planting of trees was 'the only laudable thing he has ever done', was caustic about Grant's marriage to Jane Millar: 'It will be a curious Experiment, whether his sly Flattery or her tenacious Avarice will get the better' (*The Letters of David Hume*, ed. J. Y. T. Greig, 2 vols., 1932, 2.226). Grant died on 17 September 1778, and was probably buried at Monymusk. He was survived by his fourth wife, who died on 25 October 1788.

R. H. CAMPBELL

Sources A. J. G. Cummings, 'The business affairs of an eighteenth-century lowland laird: Sir Archibald Grant of Monymusk, 1696–1778', *Scottish elites*, ed. T. M. Devine (1994), 43–61 · A. J. G. Cummings, 'Industry and investment in the eighteenth-century highlands', *Industry, business and society in Scotland since 1700*, ed. A. J. G. Cummings and T. M. Devine (1994), 24–42 · D. Murray, *The York Buildings Company* (1883) · 'Two reports from the select committee on the petition of proprietors of the charitable corporations for relief of the industrious poor [1732, 1733]', *Reports from Committees of the House of Commons*, 1 (1715–36), 363–442, 537–80 · H. Hamilton, ed., *Selections from the Monymusk papers, 1713–1755* (1945) · H. Hamilton, ed., *Life and labour on an Aberdeenshire estate, 1713–1755* (1946) · DNB · Burke, *Peerage* (1914)
Archives NA Scot., corresp. and papers · NL Scot., legal papers
Likenesses W. Hogarth, double portrait (with his second wife), Monymusk House, Aberdeenshire

Grant, Bernard Alexander Montgomery [Bernie] (1944–2000), politician, was born on 17 February 1944 in Georgetown, British Guiana, the son of Eric Alexander Grant and

Bernard Alexander Montgomery Grant (1944–2000), by Roger Hutchings, 1986

his wife, Lily, *née* Blair. Both parents were schoolteachers, his father subsequently becoming a headteacher. He was named after two British generals then fighting in the Second World War: Sir Bernard Montgomery and Sir Harold Alexander. From St Joseph's Roman Catholic School, Georgetown, he went on to St Stanislaus College, a Jesuit-run secondary school that was, at the time, one of the most prestigious in the region. St Stanislaus was a characteristic colonial institution. Like its great rival, Queen's College, the school had been created in the nineteenth century to accommodate the children of European settlers and expatriates, and took the English public schools of the time as its model. The school offered a 'classical' English education, and during the twentieth century it had become one of the major pools of talent from which the colony drew its civil servants and professionals. In later years Grant spoke with considerable affection about his schooldays, recalling his fondness for Latin verse and nineteenth-century literature. The orderly habits imposed by the school were a constant memory, and he spoke in private with equal nostalgia about being beaten with the ferule—a broad leather strap that the priests habitually carried. Grant's adolescent education took place within the framework of a political atmosphere dominated by the prospects of independence. The 1950s and early 1960s in the colony saw a ferment of argument and agitation around regional and domestic issues, which had its greatest effect on the class of professionals who were consciously preparing themselves to rule an independent Guyana. Families like the Grants, made up from public servants and union officials, wielded considerable influence and were at the centre of the argument.

After leaving St Stanislaus, Grant began work with the mining firm Demerara Bauxite, an occupation that determined his initial career choices. At the time, four years before independence, it was the sort of job—roughly equivalent to the minor rungs of the local civil service— that a well-educated local could obtain without much difficulty, but the higher, managerial, positions would invariably be held by expatriate or native-born whites. For a young man of Grant's background and situation future prospects depended on acquiring the higher qualifications then unobtainable in the region. Inevitably Grant, his mother, and his three sisters joined the wave of migration that was sweeping through the Caribbean.

The family arrived in England in 1963. Grant found a job as a railway clerk, then attended Tottenham Technical College to study for his A levels, before entering a degree course in mining engineering at Heriot-Watt University, in Edinburgh. At the end of the second year he dropped out of the course. Later on he gave as his reason the fact that 'white students were sent on scholarships to South Africa. But the black students had to go into the mines in Dunfermline and work as coal miners' (*Daily Telegraph*). Grant had already become well known among the black students in Edinburgh as a student politician, but when he arrived back in London at the end of the 1960s he was still discussing, with friends, the prospects of resuming his studies as an engineer. In the meantime he took a job as a telephonist at the General Post Office's (GPO's) international telephone exchange in Kings Cross.

In 1970 the GPO was hit by a strike, and Grant was one of the most popular and energetic local organizers. By the time the strike had ended Grant had stopped talking about going back to university, and it was obvious that he was happy and excited by the challenge of trade union politics and organization. In the workplace he had been part of a group of students and graduates who were more or less temporary, but he stayed on as the exchange representative for the telephonists, attended union conferences, pursued a number of trade union courses, and chaired the local branch of the Union of Post Office Workers. With a typical mixture of passionate commitment and shrewdness he had recognized one of the few industrial areas where the colour of his skin would not be a disability. His charm and authority made him a natural representative. At the same time he had his first experience of anti-racist organization in that role. The Chapel Street branch of the union was notorious as a hotspot of National Front (NF) activity, and Grant was a prime mover in the workplace campaign to outlaw racist practices and defeat NF candidates for office.

During this period Grant's politics took on a sharper edge, and he began to forge long-term alliances on the radical and anti-racist left. Initially he joined the Socialist Labour League, forerunner of the Workers' Revolutionary Party. In the mid-1970s, however, he joined the Labour Party, and by 1978 he had left the GPO to become a full-time official for the National Union of Public Employees. His reputation and experience made him a much sought-after activist in local anti-racist campaigns. Haringey, where he had lived and been a student, was an almost inevitable port of call. In the late 1960s and through most of the 1970s the borough's growing ethnic population was confronted by local resentment and hardline racist organization. Grant had not lost his capacity to laugh at himself: 'We set up an organisation called The Haringey Labour Movement Anti-Racist and Anti-Fascist Committee,' he recalled. 'It was one of the longest names of any organisation that I have been involved in' (personal knowledge).

Grant was persuaded to stand as a Labour candidate in the local elections of 1978, 'mainly because I was a genuine trade-unionist and they didn't have many' (*The Independent*). He became a Haringey borough councillor in that year, and leader of the council in 1985. His elevation coincided with a period of intense conflict between the Conservative government and a variety of municipal authorities. A black man with a left-wing trade union background, he was also an anti-apartheid campaigner and a supporter of revolutionary governments, feminist causes, black studies, and a multi-racial school curriculum. The tabloid press, its hackles raised, dubbed him Barmy Bernie. Haringey council, personalized in the form of its leader, was the subject of an endless stream of negative stories for most of the decade. In October 1985 Grant became a figure of enduring controversy after a riot exploded on Tottenham's Broadwater Farm estate. The riot followed the death of a local resident, Cynthia Jarrett, while policemen were searching her house. In the ensuing fracas a policeman, Police Constable Blakelock, was murdered, and in the aftermath of the incident Grant commented that the youths on the estate felt that the police were to blame for Cynthia Jarrett's death and had given them 'a bloody good hiding' (*Daily Telegraph*). The remark made him a hate figure in the right-wing tabloids. His subsequent notoriety, and his support for controversial projects such as the campaign for black sections in the Labour Party, made the Labour establishment nervous and distant, and his political survival stemmed mainly from the respect and affection that large segments of the local electorate felt for him.

In 1987 (following the deselection by Tottenham constituency Labour Party of the sitting MP, Norman Atkinson) Grant was elected Labour MP for Tottenham. He entered parliament dressed in African robes, and his career entered a new, more international phase, pursuing broader causes. Among his other duties he chaired the all-party group on race and community (1995–2000), the Campaign Group of Labour MPs (1990–2000), and the Standing Conference on Race Equality in Europe (1990–2000). He edited the *Black Parliamentarian* magazine from 1990 to 1992. He became the figurehead and tireless activist in cases of official harassment or misconduct, notably that of Joy Gardner, a black woman who died when immigration officers entered her house and put her under restraint. At the same time he became an important resource for Third World governments and campaigners looking for support within the British political culture. When Monserrat's volcano erupted, devastating the island, a row broke out about British aid and policy towards the refugees. Typically the Monserratian chief minister immediately telephoned Grant and invited him in to plead the island's case. Grant caused some embarrassment by arriving on the island before the government's fact-finding mission, but he was never reluctant to break ranks, frequently diverging from some of the most deeply held beliefs of his left-wing allies. For instance in 1993 he created a stir by saying that many in ethnic minorities would welcome government aid that would give them the option of returning home. To ward off the subsequent misunderstanding he felt obliged to hold a press conference to distance himself clearly from the compulsory repatriation advocated by followers of Enoch Powell. Later he defended Harriet Harman's decision to send her children to a selective school, arguing that his own children had suffered from their education in the comprehensive sector. Before that he began the campaign for government reparations for the looting of art objects and other resources from Britain's former colonies. Like his support for Labour Party 'black sections', his views on these issues were often strongly opposed by political allies and enemies alike, but in later years he became a highly respected figure, and while he faced plenty of criticism it was muted by the affection in which he was generally held.

Even those who characterized Grant as rash and hasty with his opinions also acknowledged that he was likeable, charming, generous to friends and enemies, and relentlessly honest. He was a child of the contradictions inherent in his background. He had been born and had grown up in a colony, but was part of a class that challenged and finally threw off colonial rule. He arrived in Britain as a middle-class foreign student—a bird of passage—but stayed to become a central figure in the politics of organized labour. He was a dedicated local politician with an international reach and reputation. Above all he was the product of a long and rebellious confrontation with political repression, and at one and the same time the obedient graduate of a training that privileged moral absolutes. He was confident that he knew right from wrong, he had a passionate devotion to an ideal of justice, and he had faith that these beliefs were the guiding lights of his politics and his everyday life.

During the last decade of his life Grant's chronic diabetes began to disable him. In October 1998 he had a heart bypass operation, and subsequently faced dialysis three times a week. Typically he reacted by becoming a champion of the health service and by taking an active interest in the Commons' All Party Kidney Group. Grant married, on 9 November 1971, Joan Courtney (b. 1952/3), an exporter's clerk, with whom he had three sons. This marriage was dissolved and on 18 December 1998 he married his secretary and personal assistant, Sharon Margaret Lawrence (b. 1951/2), daughter of Phillip Arthur Lawrence, headteacher. Grant died, of a heart attack, in London on 8 April 2000, and was survived by his second wife and the three sons of his first marriage: Steven, Alex, and Jimmy.

MIKE PHILLIPS

Sources *The Times* (10 April 2000) · *Daily Telegraph* (10 April 2000) · *The Guardian* (10 April 2000) · *The Independent* (10 April 2000) · *WWW* · private information (2004) · personal knowledge (2004) **Likenesses** R. Hutchings, photograph, 1986, Network Photographers, London [*see illus.*] · photograph, 1993, repro. in *The Independent* · photograph, 1995, repro. in *The Times* · photograph, 1995, repro. in *Daily Telegraph* · photograph, repro. in *The Guardian* **Wealth at death** under £210,000—gross; £10,000—net: administration, 22 May 2000, *CGPLA Eng. & Wales*

Grant, Cary [*real name* Archibald Alec Leach] (1904–1986), actor, was born on 18 January 1904 at 15 Hughenden Road, Bristol, the only surviving child of Elias Leach (1876–1935), a tailor's presser, and his wife, Elsie Maria, *née* Kingdon (1878–1973), daughter of a shipwright. An elder brother had died before he was born. He became one of the wealthiest and most famous Hollywood film stars of the mid-twentieth century, making seventy-two feature films between 1932 and 1966. A dark, handsome man well over 6 feet tall with thick, wavy hair and an attractively cleft chin, he was a romantic comedian, suave and well dressed, ironic, jaunty, and a touch caustic, but very, very funny. The world accepted this relaxed figure as the real person, and to his many friends he was an amusing and generous individual. But the image was carefully cultivated, and behind it was a complex and troubled man.

The Leach household was not happy and when Archie Leach was nine his mother was suddenly committed to a mental institution. Nobody told the boy what had happened to her and in time he came to believe that she was dead. The sense of abandonment deeply affected his character and left him with a lack of trust which was to ruin all but one of his many marriages and love affairs. He was a lonely child, hanging around backstage doing odd jobs at the local music-halls. Stagestruck, he left school at fourteen and joined a troupe of boy acrobats, stilt walkers, and slapstick comics called Bob Pender's Knockabout Comedians. With them he toured the British music-halls, learning physical skills and a sense of timing which never left him. In 1920 they went to America for a long run at the huge New York Hippodrome, followed by a tour of large American cities. Pender returned to England in the early 1920s but Leach and some of the other young men stayed on and ran their own troupe for several years. He later told colourful stories about the strange jobs he had during the next few years. A charmer, he soon became welcome in New York theatrical circles and appeared in musical shows for both the Hammersteins and the Shuberts. As he grew more sophisticated he acquired mannerisms which became characteristic of him—the well-timed double take, the quizzically raised eyebrow—and modified his working-class accent to one all his own, clipped and jerky but apparently acceptable to American ears as typically

British. A screen test at Paramount's small New York studio was not a success but his first film, a short later shown as *Singapore Sue*, was made there in 1931. He went to Hollywood, where his good looks, charm, and useful contacts easily got him a five-year contract with Paramount, and in 1932 he assumed the more elegant name of Cary Grant. He legally adopted the name in December 1941.

From 1932 to 1936 Paramount used Grant in over twenty films as well as lending him to other companies. He played opposite many well-known stars but the films, although good experience, were stereotyped and undistinguished. To Grant's frustration Paramount made no attempt to promote him as they promoted their big star Gary Cooper. However, his appearance in a star vehicle with Marlene Dietrich and two more with Mae West drew attention to him, and the talented director George Cukor borrowed him to play opposite Katharine Hepburn in *Sylvia Scarlett* (1935). Although this film was a failure, Cukor's sympathetic direction enabled Grant to explore a style of his own and it was a milestone in his development.

On 9 February 1934 Grant married a young actress, Virginia Adler (b. 1908), daughter of James Edward Cherrill, and former wife of Irving Adler. The marriage rapidly fell apart and ended in a bitter divorce the next year. Grant returned to the apartment he had previously shared with a fellow Paramount actor, Randolph Scott. This convenient bachelor arrangement was not uncommon at the time but led to talk of bisexuality. Whatever the truth, Grant's desire for a happy marriage was to prove one of the driving forces of his life. During a pause in his work for Paramount in 1935 he made a film in England with the actress Mary Brian, with whom for a while he contemplated a second marriage. About this time his father died and he was able to settle his mother, whose whereabouts he had discovered, in a house of her own. He was to visit her many times until her death in 1973.

As his reputation grew, Grant decided to leave Paramount and in future negotiate his own contracts for single films or groups of films. He refused to renew his contract in the autumn of 1936, a brave move at the height of the studio system. From then on he was to insist on a share of the box-office take on top of a guaranteed fee. *Topper* (1937), in which he made a debonair appearance as a ghost, was made at MGM and was such a box-office hit that Columbia and RKO eagerly signed overlapping contracts with Grant. By the middle of the war he had made some twenty films for them, more or less on his own terms. He worked with some of the best directors in Hollywood, including Leo McCarey, Howard Hawks, Frank Capra, and George Stevens. *The Awful Truth* firmly established him in 1937 as a leading comedy actor. *Bringing up Baby* (1938) and *Holiday* (1938) were other crazy comedies and *Gunga Din* (1939), an enormous success, was an uproarious version of Kipling's story. His screen image and comic timing were now so polished that success at the box-office was assured, and his departure from Paramount was triumphantly justified. A perfectionist, his apparently casual performances were achieved by meticulous attention to detail.

When war broke out in 1939 Grant remained in Hollywood, reassured by the British ambassador's comforting view that members of the expatriate community were acting as their country's representatives. He became an American citizen in June 1942. The citation for the king's medal for services in the cause of freedom, awarded him in April 1947, was for his contributions to the British War Relief Fund.

Grant continued to make films, mainly comedies, during the war. One which was outstanding as both a critical and a commercial success was *The Philadelphia Story* (1940) for MGM, directed by Cukor and co-starring Katharine Hepburn. James Stewart received an Oscar for his part in this film. Grant, on the other hand, had such a relaxed comedy style that he hardly seemed to be acting at all and was taken for granted by the academy. He was nominated as best actor for his next film, the sentimental *Penny Serenade* (1941), but to his disappointment the Oscar that year went to Gary Cooper. The black comedy *Arsenic and Old Lace* (1942) was another tremendous commercial hit. His next film, *Suspicion* (1941), was the first of four important collaborations with the English director Alfred Hitchcock. Characteristically, the latter saw more in Grant than the urbane charmer. He detected a hidden side, guarded and even with a hint of menace, and cast him as a man plotting to murder his wife. Both Grant and the studio demurred and the ending was changed, but a teasing ambiguity remained, and the film has probably had a greater appeal to later, more sophisticated generations than it had at the time. Joan Fontaine won an Oscar as the wife, but as usual Grant's unostentatiously perfect performance went unrewarded.

On 8 July 1942 Grant married a second time. His wife, Barbara Hutton, formerly Reventlow (1912–1979), was heiress to the Woolworth fortune, and the extravagant and gregarious lifestyle of a wealthy socialite was so much at variance with Grant's lack of security that despite a real affection which lasted until her death in 1979 the marriage could not survive, and ended sadly in 1945. Grant was deeply distressed by this second failure and by his lack of recognition as an actor, and for a while his work suffered. Then, with the unusual production *None but the Lonely Heart* (1944), written and directed by the playwright Clifford Odets, he was again nominated for an Oscar. But again, while a supporting player in his film was honoured, the award for best actor that year went elsewhere. Hurt and depressed, for about a year he made no films.

It was Hitchcock who revitalized Grant with one of the best films of his career, *Notorious*, in 1946. Again Hitchcock cast him as not entirely straightforward, a cool intelligence agent using the woman he loved to entice another man. The film, with Ingrid Bergman, had the usual Hitchcock suspense and was much admired. Refreshed, Grant returned to making light comedies. Among them, *I was a Male War Bride* (1949) was an uncharacteristically broad comedy, with Grant in deliberately unconvincing drag, and rather surprisingly was another huge box-office hit. On 25 December 1949 Grant married for the third time.

Betsy Drake (b. 1932) was another young actress, an intelligent and well-educated girl of wide interests. Desperately anxious to get this marriage right, for a while they lived quietly and for some years Grant read widely and made fewer films. It was through Betsy that he met a doctor who was experimenting with the use of LSD to help patients solve their problems by reliving their pasts. Grant attended a number of sessions and believed they had been beneficial.

By 1950 Grant had been in films for nearly twenty years and his type of sophisticated, screwball comedy was beginning to look dated as gritty realism took over. He talked of retiring. Before long, however, he was again lured back by Hitchcock and in 1954 filmed one of his most popular and glamorous films, the comedy thriller *To Catch a Thief* (1955), with Grace Kelly. Far from retiring, he continued to make films for another twelve years and, though fewer in number and lacking some of the old sparkle, most of them made money. One made in Spain in 1957 co-starred Sophia Loren, with whom he fell madly in love. This wrecked his already faltering marriage to Betsy and he was devastated when Loren married Carlo Ponti. Once more he was rescued from despair by Hitchcock with the last of their four films together, one of Grant's best, the classic comedy thriller with a chase, *North by North West* (1959). His third marriage having ended in divorce in 1962, on 22 July 1965 Grant married another young actress, Dyan Cannon (born Samille Diane Friesen; b. 1939), but despite the welcome birth of his only child the marriage was no more successful than the others and ended in 1968. In a lamentable last film, *Walk, Don't Run* (1966), for the first time Grant did not get the girl.

At sixty-two Grant was still a vigorous and handsome man and had no intention of becoming a silver-haired character actor. Without formally announcing his retirement he simply turned his attention to other things. He had always been interested in business and for some years he now pursued an active business career which included directorships of the big toiletries firm Rayette-Fabergé and of MGM. In 1970 the Academy gave him the survivor's consolation prize, an honorary award 'for his unique mastery of the art of screen acting, with the respect and affection of his colleagues'. Later his films found new life on television and video, and as times changed a new audience's perception of him shifted slightly. A hint of the hidden depths and vulnerability could be detected behind the cool façade so carefully constructed to divert attention from the uncertainty within.

During the last decade of his busy life Grant achieved married happiness at last. He had met Barbara Harris (b. 1951), an English girl forty-seven years his junior, in 1976 when she was a public relations consultant for Fabergé, and after several years of passionate friendship they married on 15 April 1981. As an old man with thick white hair and undimmed charm he toured the small towns of America with a one-man show called *A Conversation with Cary Grant*, reminiscing and chatting with the audience. It was as he prepared for the show in Davenport, Iowa, in November 1986 that he had a severe stroke. He died on 29 November 1986 at St Luke's Hospital in Davenport. He was survived by his wife.   RACHAEL LOW

Sources *The Times* (1 Dec 1986) · *The Independent* (1 Dec 1986) · *The international dictionary of films and filmmakers*, 2nd edn, 3: *Actors and actresses*, ed. N. Thomas (1992) · N. Nelson, *Evenings with Cary Grant* (1991) · G. Wansell, *Cary Grant: haunted idol* (1983) · G. McCann, *Cary Grant: a class apart* (1996) · J. Hyams, *Mislaid in Hollywood* (1973), 87–98 · B. Gill, 'Pursuer and pursued: the still untold story of Cary Grant', *New Yorker* (2 June 1997) · W. C. McIntosh and W. D. Weaver, *The private Cary Grant* (1983) · M. Donaldson and W. Royce, *An affair to remember—my life with Cary Grant* (1989) · A. Britton, *Cary Grant, comedy, and male desire* (1983) · P. Kael, 'The man from dream city', *When the lights go down* (1980) · H. Higham and R. Moseley, *Cary Grant: the lonely heart* (1989) · b. cert. · m. cert.
Archives Academy of Motion Picture Arts and Sciences, Beverly Hills, Margaret Herrick Library, MSS | FILM BFI NFTVA
Likenesses photographs, BFI NFTVA · photographs, Hult. Arch.

Grant, Charles (1746–1823), director of the East India Company and philanthropist, was born in March 1746 at Aldourie farmhouse, Glen Urquhart, his mother's home, on Loch Ness in Inverness-shire in the highlands of Scotland. He was the third of seven children born to Alexander Grant (d. 1762) of the Shewglie line, a soldier in the Jacobite army of Prince Charles Edward Stuart, and Margaret Macbean (d. 1758), daughter of Donald Macbean of Kinchyle. Charles's christening was a dramatic affair in which he was named after the Pretender and swords were clashed over his cradle dedicating him to the prince's service. Shortly afterwards Charles's father, Alexander, was severely wounded at the battle of Culloden. He had to go into hiding and his property at Glen Urquhart was destroyed, leaving the family in very straitened circumstances. In 1756 he joined a highland regiment raised for service in America and died in Havana in 1762. His wife had died in November 1758, leaving Charles and his four younger siblings orphans.

Early career It was not an auspicious start for Charles but he was fortunate in his uncle John, Alexander's younger brother, who worked for the excise at Elgin. John had supported Charles since the age of seven, sending him to school in Elgin. In 1758 Charles was apprenticed to William Forsyth, a Cromarty shipowner and merchant. He was set on the path towards his eventual evangelical Christianity in these early years. His mother was a pious woman and his uncle showed him how to live a prayerful, Christian life. Forsyth was also a 'pious, God-fearing man' (Morris, 3–5). Christian humility, however, was not part of the young Charles's character. At sixteen he complained to his uncle that Forsyth's servant was clothed better than he was and that he found it difficult to bear the reproaches of others about his poverty. In 1763 John prevailed upon a cousin, Captain Alexander Grant, a partner in a mercantile house at Aldermanbury, London, and formerly with Clive in India, to provide him a place. Charles's own letter and a glowing reference from Forsyth clinched the appointment. Forsyth told Alexander Grant that Charles's 'genius' was such that 'he will in a short time … render himself capable of keeping the principal books upon any branch of trade'. More than this, he added that Charles would soon endear himself to his employer (Morris, 67–70). Charles lived up to this commendation. He worked for his cousin for five and a half years, becoming head clerk, and was trusted to the extent that Alexander left Charles in charge of his affairs when he returned to India.

A drive to improve the status of his family to what he felt was its rightful position underpinned the whole of Grant's life. He never forgot his uncle John's support and had, even on his slender salary, sent home what money he could. However, he wanted to be able to do much more. Like so many others at the time, Grant looked to India to provide him with a position that would eventually restore the family fortunes. He cultivated useful friends, such as Richard Becher, who was a close friend of the governor of Bengal, and Luke Scrafton, one of the directors of the East India Company. Eventually they managed to obtain Grant an appointment as a cadet with the company's Bengal army.

Grant set sail at the end of 1767 with his brother Robert, a midshipman on the ship. He arrived in Calcutta in June 1768, to be taken into the household of Richard Becher, who by then was a member of the Bengal council, and given charge of his business. Thus he began a fifty-year connection with India. He remained in India for two and a half years until his health broke down and he had to return home. He tried to set up in business in England but it went badly, and he had to borrow from his friend Becher, taking more than ten years to repay the debt. Grant was therefore desperate to obtain a post in the company's civil service in order to restore his fortunes. His persistence was rewarded, and at the end of 1772 he obtained a Bengal writership. On 23 February 1773, just before he embarked for India, he married Jane (1755/6–1827), the seventeen-year-old daughter of Thomas Fraser of Balnain. The marriage was a step up for Charles and they made a striking couple. Jane was beautiful, cultivated, and refined and Charles was 'tall and dignified, with a clear, fresh complexion, large blue eyes, deeply set under a prominent brow, and a peculiarly pleasing smile' (Morris, 30). It was to prove a long and happy marriage although Jane had to put up with Charles's constant preoccupation with his perceived lack of money.

The board of trade Grant's first appointment in India was as secretary to the board of trade. This appointment at the seat of power in India brought him into contact with many influential people, and he found himself conducting much of the business of the board. Grant gained great influence through his mastery of the enormous volume of documents that passed through his hands. Two daughters, Elizabeth (b. 1774) and Margaret (b. 1775), were quickly born to Charles and Jane. The family lived well—indeed, above their means. Charles lost heavily at gambling. Then came the blow that Charles was to regard as a punishment and warning from God for his ungodly life. Elizabeth and Margaret died of smallpox within nine days of each other in 1776. From this time evangelical Christianity became his driving force. He started a mission at Malda, where he became commercial resident in 1780. He rescued Kiernander's mission church in Calcutta in 1787

at a personal expense of Rs 10,000 and his liberality enabled the building of St John's Church, Calcutta (the old cathedral), also in 1787.

As commercial resident Grant was responsible for the purchase of the goods shipped home each year. The position gave him scope to engage in private trade. By 1784 he was out of debt. He was, however, not without feelings of guilt about the personal profits he had made. He claimed to be the first to start indigo cultivation at Gaumalti. This was an attempt to create a new centre of rural industry which would help diversify the economy and cushion the effects of the decay of the weaving industry. It did not prove a successful venture. In 1787 Lord Cornwallis, the new governor-general, persuaded Grant to accept a seat on the board of trade. Cornwallis charged him with the reform of the company's commercial system and depended on him for virtually all his information regarding the company's trade. This put him in effective control of the board. He saw no conflict between the interests of the company and its servants and the welfare of the people of India. Indeed, he had come to believe that only the continuance of company rule could ensure the happiness of the people, and he became the company's staunchest champion. His experience with indigo manufacture led him in 1787 to frame 'Regulations for weavers' to prevent their exploitation. He also completely reformed the export warehouse system.

During a period of nearly twenty years in India, Grant gained invaluable experience of many aspects of company rule. He made a deep impression as a man of ability and integrity. He was not, however, a comfortable man. Sir James Macintosh, while attributing any good done by the board of trade solely to Grant, criticized 'the sternness of [his] virtue, and the nice scrupulousness of his feelings in matters of right and wrong' (Morris, 40). Joseph Price was not so charitable, describing Grant as 'a most canting Presbyterian, a methodical snivelling Oliverian' (Embree, 52). Grant's scrupulousness was both his strength and his weakness. He refused to support his friend Philip Francis when he was involved in a scandal, and later had no mercy in objecting to grants to Warren Hastings and the marquess of Hastings. On the other hand, he could rationalize his own actions on the few occasions when he found himself sailing close to the 'moral wind'. Over the years much time was spent on writing papers and letters exonerating himself from any taint of moral corruption in his dealings, to an extent that could be regarded as paranoia. There was an unattractive puritanical streak about him that was reinforced once he became an ardent evangelical Christian. On the other hand, those close to him regarded him highly. William Wilberforce, for example, described him as 'one of the best men I ever knew' (R. I. Wilberforce and S. Wilberforce, *The Life of William Wilberforce*, 5 vols., 1838, 5.206).

In 1790 Grant left India because of worries about his family's health. By that time another five children had been born: Maria (b. 1778), Charles *Grant (1778–1866), Robert *Grant (1780–1838), Charity Emilia (Charamile; b.

1785), and Sibylla. Catherine Sophia and William Thomas (*b*. 1793) were born after the Grants' return to England.

Director of the East India Company Grant returned to England bearing Lord Cornwallis's high recommendation to Henry Dundas, president of the Board of Control. With the support of Pitt, Cornwallis, and Dundas, he was elected unopposed in 1794 as a director of the company. His role as champion of company rule in India occupied the rest of his life and was in effect a career, his family referring to him as the Director. By the time he returned to England he had become convinced that even a limited private trade would lead to the colonization of India by multitudes of adventurers who would demand an end to the company's monopoly and their rights as British citizens. He could see that the logical end to granting free trade would be free European settlement and eventually the cessation of the company's monopoly. It was therefore ironic that he should draft the first real breach in the company's monopoly in 1793 which guaranteed 3000 tons annually in the company's ships to private traders. He also opposed the powerful shipping interest in the company whose high freight rates kept trade with India low. In 1796 he and David Scott succeeded in making substantial changes to the company's shipping regulations. In 1800 he wrote a long paper, 'Observations on the question of enlarging the trade of British subjects between India and Europe', which although unpublished was very influential. He also wrote the reports drawn up by the directors' special committee on trade in 1800 and 1801. The settlement reached in 1801 was a triumph for the company because it did not touch its right to control shipping, the management of the sales of all goods brought to Britain from India, and the power to prevent unauthorized persons entering India. Grant was also closely consulted over the permanent settlement which fixed the revenue system in Bengal and established new judicial regulations there; the eventual dispatch ordering it showed many traces of his authorship.

Grant defended the company's monopoly of patronage as vigorously as he defended its monopoly of trade. He believed that the best way to prevent further erosion of the company's privileges was to ensure that no charges of corruption could be laid against company servants. It was largely due to his perseverance that the sale of company patronage finally ceased in 1809. He also believed that the proper training of the company's civil service was necessary if corruption was to be stemmed. While, along with his fellow directors, he had many reservations about Lord Wellesley's proposal for a training college in India, the proposal eventually accepted was based on his revisions. Grant had, however, long believed that the company should have a training college in England rather than in India. He became the driving force behind the founding of the East India College at Haileybury in 1805, which was often referred to as his 'child'.

Grant persuaded both Pitt and Dundas to offer the post of governor-general to John Shore in 1792 and obtained Shore's acceptance. Shore had few political friends and Grant became the channel of communication between him, the court of directors, and the Board of Control. In 1800 Dundas offered Grant a seat on Wellesley's supreme council. He decided not to accept, mainly for family reasons but also because he feared allegations that he had been bought by Dundas. By 1804 it was acknowledged that he had no equal as spokesman for the company and he was elected deputy chairman. He held the post of chairman three times during his long career. He was an effective, if grave, speaker with an imposing presence. With his energy, agile mind, and integrity he increasingly became identified with control of the company's administration. His long experience in Bengal gave his views added weight. Such was his stature that he was brought back to the chair in 1815 at the age of sixty-nine to strengthen the waning powers of the directors against the Board of Control.

Evangelical reformer Grant was also an active politician. His kinsmen persuaded him to stand for the county of Inverness. He bought the Waternish estate on the Isle of Skye, Inverness-shire, with a mortgage of £20,000 and was successful at the 1802 general election. As with all he did, he took seriously his duties as an MP. He pushed through improvements in the locality and used his powers of patronage to the advantage of his constituents. He was an energetic member of the Scottish Society for the Promotion of Christianity in the highlands and islands. Although he generally supported the government of the day, he reserved the right to vote as he saw fit on specific issues.

While for his contemporaries Grant's championship of the company's monopoly gave him his reputation, it was his fervent evangelicalism for which he is most remembered today. On his return to England he became a member of the Clapham sect, moving to Battersea Rise, Surrey. In 1791 he became a director of the Sierra Leone Company. He was a prominent supporter of the campaign to abolish the slave trade and was a founder and a vice-president of both the Church Missionary Society in 1799 and the British and Foreign Bible Society in 1804. His great passion, however, was his mission to Christianize India, which he regarded as Britain's moral and religious duty. There is no doubt that without his energy and persistence the needs of India would not have been at the forefront of the minds of the British religious public. It was Grant who tried to interest the establishment in a missionary proposal for Bengal in 1787 and who succeeded in attracting William Wilberforce to the cause. It was Grant who smoothed the path of the Baptist and London missionary societies, and he who asked Charles Simeon at Cambridge to search out intelligent, energetic young Anglicans to go to India as company chaplains. It was his patronage as a director that ensured their passage. Indeed, without his influence and skill, it is likely that missionaries would have been expelled from India in the aftermath of the Vellore mutiny of 1806.

Grant's views on the role of Christianity in India found their best expression in his tract *Observations of the state of society among the Asiatic subjects of Great Britain, particularly with respect to morals, and the means of improving it*, written in

1792 in an attempt to influence Henry Dundas and published in 1813. His views influenced several generations of Britons. He contrasted the supposed ignorance and immorality of Hindus and Muslims on the one hand with the moral and intellectual superiority of Europeans on the other. He attributed this perceived disparity not to racial differences but to their religions. In his view it was Christianity that had raised Europeans on the scale of nations and Christianity could do the same for India if only the British government would acknowledge its moral and divine duty in this respect. As far as he was concerned, good laws would achieve little without the transformation of the Indian character which he had no doubt that the light of education and Christianity would achieve.

There were, however, deep ambiguities in Grant's attitude to how the company should rule India; these can largely be explained by the tension between his evangelicalism and his position as a senior servant of the company. He was strongly opposed to any territorial expansion, believing not only that it would overextend the company to the point of collapse but also that it was immoral and against former treaties with the native princes. Politically and economically he was extremely conservative. As the defender of the company's monopoly he had to argue that it was impossible to make any significant change in the pattern of either Indian demand or production because the conditions were such that everything worked together to maintain an almost unchanged market which would not provide an outlet for Western goods. As defender of the propagation of Christianity in India he argued that Indian society could be changed. He was against freedom of the press and free entry into India at the same time as insisting on free and unrestricted access for missionaries. At the 1793 and 1813 renewals of the company's charter, he endeavoured to force the company actively to support Christianity. He and Wilberforce failed in 1793. Conventional wisdom has it that they succeeded in 1813 after a massive petitioning campaign forced the government to include a clause setting out Britain's Christian duty to India. However, close examination both of the wording of the clause and of events thereafter demonstrates that the new clause changed very little. Similarly, Grant's efforts to force the company to discontinue its attendance at and support of key Hindu festivals were largely ignored in India. His opponents had no illusions about the radical nature of his proposals, which they believed threatened the continuance of British rule.

Grant continued to work loyally for the company until the day of his death from a heart attack at his London home at 40 Russell Square on 31 October 1823. He died aged seventy-seven after completing a full day's work in Leadenhall Street. The East India Company, in recognition of his thirty years of devoted service in its direction, unusually paid for a marble monument and inscription by Samuel Manning to be placed in St George's, Bloomsbury, where Grant was interred. The fact that he remained in the direction for so long despite considerable differences of opinion with other directors speaks volumes for his ability and integrity. A highly influential public figure, he was also a generous, loving, and faithful friend, husband, and father. His papers existed for some time and were used by Henry Morris for his biography of Grant. They then disappeared and all efforts to trace them have failed.   PENELOPE CARSON

Sources DNB · H. Morris, *The life of Charles Grant* (1904) · A. T. Embree, *Charles Grant and the British rule in India* (1962) · *GM*, 1st ser., 93/2 (1823), 569 · S. Neill, *A history of Christianity in India, 1707–1858* (1985) · D. R. Fisher, 'Grant, Charles', HoP, *Commons, 1790–1820* · P. Carson, 'Soldiers of Christ: evangelicals and India, 1780–1833', PhD diss., U. Lond., 1988 · E. M. Howse, *Saints in politics: the 'Clapham sect' and the growth of freedom*, pbk edn (1971)

Archives BL OIOC, corresp. relating to India, MS Eur. E 93 | BL, corresp. with David Anderson, Add. MS 45431 · BL, Hastings MSS, Add. MSS 29180–29182, 29190 · BL, Liverpool MSS, Add. MSS 38267, 38321 · BL, Lowe MSS, Add. MSS 20134, 20236 · BL, Wellesley MSS, Add. MSS 27275, 37309 · BL OIOC, letters to David Scott, MS Eur. F 18 · Bodl. Oxf., corresp. with Robert Dundas · NA Canada, corresp. with Sir Archibald Campbell · NA Scot., letters to James Grant · NAM, corresp. with James Chisholm · NL Scot., letters to first earl of Minto · NRA Scotland, priv. coll., letters to Hugh Grant of Moy · NRA Scotland, priv. coll., letters to H. M. Wellwood on Scottish Church · priv. coll., letters to his daughter Margaret · PRO, Cornwall MSS 10, 18, 19, 12

Likenesses Argus, coloured engraving, c.1813 (*The storming of Monopoly Fort*), BL OIOC · Miss Lancaster Lucas, oils (after H. Raeburn), BL OIOC · S. Manning senior, marble monument, St George's, Bloomsbury · H. Raeburn, oils, Inverness Library

Wealth at death leasehold house in Russell Square; estate on Skye and other land in Inverness; est. £40,000–£50,000 bequeathed to children: will, PRO, PROB 11/1680

Grant, Charles, Baron Glenelg (1778–1866), politician, the eldest son of Charles *Grant and Jane Fraser, was born probably on 26 October 1778 at Kidderpore, Bengal, and spent his early childhood in India. He entered Magdalene College, Cambridge, an evangelical stronghold, in November 1795 and shared a brilliant student career with his brother Robert *Grant, being fourth wrangler in 1801 and becoming a fellow of Magdalene in 1802. He was a member of the Speculative Society, and was later rated by Hobhouse as 'one of the best speakers I have ever heard' (Broughton, 5.176).

Early political career: Ireland, free trade, and reform Grant was called to the bar (Lincoln's Inn) in 1807 and in 1811 entered parliament—for Inverness burghs until 1818, and from 1818 to 1835 for Inverness-shire. He made an effective maiden speech on 13 July 1812, and in December 1813 was appointed to minor office under Lord Liverpool. His appointment as Irish chief secretary in 1818 in succession to Robert Peel was a major event, since he was the first tory supporter of Catholic emancipation to hold the office. He was sworn of the privy council in 1819, but in 1821 was dismissed after complaints of inefficiency. He returned to office in 1823 as vice-president of the Board of Trade, taking a leading part in the repeal of the Combination Acts the following year. Firmly identified as a Canningite, he entered the cabinet under Lord Goderich in August 1827 as president of the Board of Trade and treasurer of the navy, and remained in office when Wellington became prime minister in January 1828.

Grant caused a brief cabinet crisis in March 1828 over

Charles Grant, Baron Glenelg (1778–1866), by Charles Turner, pubd 1820 (after Thomas Clement Thompson, exh. RA 1819)

proposed modification of the corn laws, when he objected to a compromise agreed by Huskisson. He withdrew his threatened resignation of 25 March to preserve Canningite solidarity but was unenthusiastic in recommending the revised duties to the house. In May 1828, he resigned with the Canningites when Wellington refused to transfer the representation of East Retford to an industrial town.

Grant's defeat of a ministerial candidate at the 1830 election was one of the harbingers of Wellington's downfall. When Earl Grey formed his ministry in December 1830, Grant was one of the Canningite 'men of business' whose experience was vital to the whigs. Yet barely eight years later he was driven from office for incompetence. From 1830 to 1834 he was president of the Board of Control, and was responsible for the renewal of the East India Company charter in 1833. There was speculation in 1834 that he might become governor-general of India.

Colonial secretary When Melbourne became prime minister in April 1835, Grant was made secretary of state for the colonies. He had held Inverness-shire at the 1835 general election by just seven votes and it was believed that he took a peerage to avoid a further contest. He was created Baron Glenelg on 11 May 1835—probably Britain's only palindromic cabinet minister.

In December 1835 he refused to countenance the annexation by Sir Benjamin D'Urban, governor of the Cape, of the Ciskei ('Queen Adelaide Province'), a region thickly settled by Xhosa but coveted by white settlers. Glenelg's contemporaries, and many subsequent historians, found his concern for the rights of indigenous people incomprehensible, and interpreted a principled stand as an obstinate irresolution. Glenelg also opposed the incursion of settlers into New Zealand. Typically, in December 1835, Melbourne urged Howick to 'make up Glenelg's mind' on 'this New Zealand business' (Adams, 101).

By 1835 Glenelg faced two vocal enemies. In 1831 he had opposed a £25,000 payment for the outfit of Queen Adelaide and 'neither the King or Queen ever forgave this and the King could not *bear* Lord Glenelg' (Esher, 1.281–2); and now William IV denounced his conciliatory approach to political discontent in Canada. Lord Howick had been blocked from promotion in November 1834 partly because of antipathy between the two men. Howick set himself up as a rival policy maker towards Canada, a subject on which the king especially distrusted Glenelg, as he made clear in an unprecedented denunciation on 1 July 1836. Howick's interventions made Glenelg 'very sore & jealous'.

On 26 December 1838, shortly after news had arrived of the outbreak of rebellion in Canada, the home secretary, Lord John Russell, offered to exchange offices with Glenelg. Melbourne refused to make Glenelg a scapegoat, but Howick continued to grumble at his 'lamentable inefficiency' (Howick diary, 10 Aug 1838, in Ziegler, 285). Glenelg received a reprieve when Sir William Molesworth moved a censure motion against him on 7 March 1838. Ministers made the motion an issue of confidence, and won by an unexpected margin of twenty-six votes.

Although ministers counted on Glenelg's 'plain, direct, and earnest eloquence' to counter Brougham's attacks in the Lords, he seemed overwhelmed by a 'torrent of invective and sarcasm'. Greville thought him 'benumbed' and terrified by Brougham. By October 1838 Glenelg had 'almost entirely given up' speaking (Sanders, 382).

On 31 July 1838 Glenelg congratulated Durham for 'judiciously and ably' dealing with leaders of the failed Canadian uprising by exiling them to Bermuda (New, 439). In fact, Durham's ordinance was illegal and ministers were forced to accept an indemnity dictated by Brougham. On 18 October Russell urged that Glenelg should succeed the octogenarian Sir John Newport as comptroller of the exchequer. Duncannon reported 'a strong feeling for a change at the Colonial Office, which Glenelg has brought upon himself a good deal by the manner in which he conducts his business'. Two bereavements now intervened. News had just arrived from India of the death of Glenelg's brother, Robert, and there was reluctance to press him while 'suffering under private calamity'. On 1 November Russell was stunned by the unexpected death of his wife. The problem remained: grief made Glenelg still more dilatory. However, Glenelg refused to move while his Canadian policy 'was likely to be a subject of hostile animadversion' (Kriegel, 389). Dr Newbould argues that Glenelg remained in office because the only successor acceptable to Howick, the Irish lord lieutenant, Normanby, was needed in Dublin to dissuade O'Connell from launching a repeal campaign (Newbould, 226).

Resignation In January 1839 ministers faced a confrontation with the Jamaica planters over the last stages of the emancipation of the slaves. Howick objected to entrusting another colonial crisis to Glenelg's management. On 2 February, Russell threatened to resign unless Glenelg was moved. Yet as Poulett Thomson pointed out, Glenelg could hardly be dismissed for 'total incapacity … why that's been known for a year or two' (Esher, 2.113–14).

On 5 February, Melbourne wrote to offer Glenelg the privy seal, promising to delay the change to enable him to defend his Canadian policy in the Lords. Unfortunately Melbourne 'added something more about energy and activity being wanted at the Colonial Office' (Broughton, 5.175). Holland commented that 'Glenelg was hurt at being written and not spoken to'. The incident stirred resentful memories of dismissal in 1821, while the offer of the privy seal was a tactless reminder of the manoeuvre used to remove the ineffectual Goderich in 1833. With 'a sense of ill-usage and a mortified spirit', Glenelg told the Lords on 8 February that Melbourne's 'utterly unforeseen and unexpected' letter forced his resignation. It may be noted that the lifelong whigs, Howick and Russell, were more critical of Glenelg's failings than the former Canningites, Melbourne and Palmerston.

Greville was surprised that 'they ventured to make any changes in such a rickety concern'. Melbourne claimed he would never have sacrificed Glenelg 'if I hadn't known that nothing but that could prevent the dissolution of the Government' (Esher, 2.115–17). Brougham perversely denounced Glenelg's downfall as 'a case for pistoling, an infamous league of eleven men to ruin one' (Trevelyan, 2.1–2). Yet, despite 'some sarcasms' the ministry survived the upheaval unscathed.

Character, religion, and death Both Grant brothers were regarded by Greville as 'forgetful and unpunctual … if you asked Charles to dine with you at six on Monday, you were very likely to have Robert at seven on Tuesday'. His personal crisis in 1828 created an impression of weakness. J. C. Herries complained that 'every thing he says dies in his hands' (*Journal of Mrs Arbuthnot*, 2.181–2). Macaulay felt that his mind 'turns, like ivy, to some support'. Hobhouse thought he was 'by no means a lazy man' (Broughton, 5.176). Glenelg was an early riser, and in four years as colonial secretary was said to have written or revised 30,000 dispatches.

Hard work and frequent ill health took their toll in an unlucky episode. After a cabinet dinner on 29 May 1833, Melbourne and Grant fell asleep, and Grey jokingly suggested blowing out the candles and leaving them. John Doyle ('H.B.') quickly produced a lampoon of the scene. Thereafter Grant was invariably portrayed asleep, and denounced by *The Times* as 'His Somnolency', a characterization which prompted Brougham's devastating gibe that the Canadian uprisings of 1837 'must have cost him many a sleepless day' (C. E. Carrington, *The British Overseas*, 1950, 350–51). Hence Stanley's jocular enquiry, after Glenelg's resignation, 'Who is to have Glenelg's nightcap?'

Grant was capable of firmness: 'We were not justified in having gone so far if we did not go through with our measure,' he told the cabinet on 2 January 1832 in the last stages of the reform crisis (Kriegel, 109). Asked in June 1833 what he would do if the East India Company opposed his terms for renewal of their charter, he replied 'with his usual nonchalence and courage' that he would 'take the whole Management of India into the hands of government'. Although Melbourne had complained that Glenelg was 'too late and never ready', he thought him 'a mild, agreeable man' (Esher, 2.111, 116). Hobhouse thought Glenelg was 'too scrupulous in the choice of his language, and took more time than was necessary in the composing of his despatches' (Broughton, 5.176). Glenelg had the 'consideration, good will, and respect' even of those who felt the Colonial Office was 'ill adapted to his particular talents and character' (Kriegel, 390). Russell admired Glenelg's 'unimpeachable integrity', and Duncannon praised 'his character, firmness, and integrity'. James Stephen concluded that Glenelg's 'real and only unfitness for public life arises from the strange incompatibility of his temper and principles with the rules of action to which we erect shrines in Downing Street' (Stephen, 56). Glenelg spoke occasionally in the Lords as an elder statesman; his last speech, on 5 May 1856, welcomed the end of the Crimean War and called for friendship with Russia. In later life he studied German to read Goethe in the original.

During debates on the Test Acts in 1828, Grant was described as a Presbyterian. He was an enthusiastic evangelical certainly from his Cambridge days. He never married. Macaulay once referred—with apologies to his own sister—to his 'feminine mind'. No conclusion should be drawn from this regarding Glenelg's private life, but the comment may help to explain the irritation he aroused in a masculine world. In 1835 he was named by a scurrilous newspaper as a lover of Emma Murray, Palmerston's mistress.

Melbourne believed that Grant's father left a fortune of £50,000 to £60,000, divided between his two sons (the *Complete Peerage* states that Glenelg bought a Highland estate for about £85,000), and implied steady impoverishment by the expense of contested elections in Inverness-shire. In 1837 it was reported that Glenelg was forced to sell his estate and in 1838 Melbourne thought him 'very poor'. Negotiations in 1838–9 were partly aimed at moving Glenelg into a pensionable post, which probably stung his pride. In later years he lived in France, at Cannes, where he was reconciled to Brougham. He died there on 23 April 1866 and was buried in its cemetery. **GED MARTIN**

Sources Lord Holland [H. R. V. Fox] and J. Allen, *The Holland House diaries, 1831–1840*, ed. A. D. Kriegel (1977) • K. Bourne, *Palmerston: the early years, 1784–1841* (1982) • *The Greville memoirs, 1814–1860*, ed. L. Strachey and R. Fulford, 8 vols. (1938) • S. Walpole, *The life of Lord John Russell*, 2 vols. (1889) • P. Ziegler, *Melbourne* (1976) • Baron Broughton [J. C. Hobhouse], *Recollections of a long life*, ed. Lady Dorchester [C. Carleton], 6 vols. (1909–11) • N. Gash, *Mr Secretary Peel: the life of Sir Robert Peel to 1830* (1961) • N. Gash, *Sir Robert Peel: the life of Sir Robert Peel after 1830* (1972) • G. O. Trevelyan, *The life and letters of Lord Macaulay*, 2 vols. (1876); repr. in one vol. (1978) • P. Adams, *Fatal necessity: British intervention in New Zealand, 1830–1847* (1977) • K. N.

Bell and W. P. Morrell, eds., *Select documents on British colonial policy, 1830–1860* (1928) • *Lord Melbourne's papers*, ed. L. C. Sanders (1889) • *The girlhood of Queen Victoria: a selection from her majesty's diaries between the years 1832 and 1840*, ed. Viscount Esher [R. B. Brett], 2 vols. (1912) • J. Prest, *Lord John Russell* (1972) • E. Dobie, 'The dismissal of Lord Glenelg from the office of colonial secretary', *Canadian Historical Review*, 23 (1942), 280–85 • H. T. Manning, 'The colonial policy of the whig ministers, 1830–37', *Canadian Historical Review*, 33 (1952), 203–36, 341–68 • *The journal of Mrs Arbuthnot, 1820–1832*, ed. F. Bamford and the duke of Wellington [G. Wellesley], 2 vols. (1950) • I. Newbould, *Whiggery and reform, 1830–1841: the politics of government* (1990) • C. W. New, *Lord Durham: a biography of John George Lambton, first earl of Durham* (1929) • C. E. Stephen, *Life of the Right Honourable Sir James Stephen* (1906) • *The letters of the third Viscount Palmerston to Laurence and Elizabeth Sulivan, 1804–1863*, ed. K. Bourne, CS, 4th ser., 23 (1979) • *The correspondence of Lord Aberdeen and Princess Lieven, 1832–1854*, ed. E. J. Parry, 2 vols., CS, 3rd ser., 60, 62 (1938–9) • *The Times* (28 April 1866) • *The Constitution* [Toronto, Ont.] (12 July 1837)

Archives NA Canada, memorandum on Canadian constitution | BL, corresp. with Lord Holland, Add. MS 51543 • BL, corresp. with William Huskisson, Add. MSS 38744–38758 • BL, corresp. with second earl of Liverpool, Add. MSS 38257–38299, 38458, *passim* • BL, corresp. with Sir Robert Peel, Add. MSS 40278–40423 • BL OIOC, letters to Lady Grant, MS Eur. E 308 • Bodl. RH, corresp. with Thomas Buxton • CUL, letters to J. Stephen • Lambton Park, Lambton estate office, Chester-le-Street, co. Durham, letters to Lord Durham • NA Canada, corresp. with Lord Durham • NA Scot., letters to J. Grant • NA Scot., corresp. with Sir Andrew Leith • NAM, corresp. with James Chisholm • NL Scot., corresp. with George Combe • NRA Scotland, priv. coll., corresp. with John Macpherson-Grant • NRA Scotland, priv. coll., letters to Lord Moncreiff • PRO NIre., corresp. with Lord Gosford • Sandon Hall, Staffordshire, corresp. with Lord Harrowby • St Deiniol's Library, Hawarden, corresp. with Sir John Gladstone • TCD, corresp. with William Shaw Mason • U. Durham L., corresp. with second Earl Grey • U. Durham L., corresp. with third Earl Grey • U. Edin., New Coll. L., letters to Thomas Chalmers • U. Nott. L., corresp. with Lord William Bentinck • U. Nott. L., letters to Duke of Newcastle • U. Southampton L., corresp. with Lord Palmerston • W. Sussex RO, letters to duke of Richmond

Likenesses C. Turner, mezzotint, pubd 1820 (after T. C. Thompson, exh. RA 1819), BM [*see illus.*] • J. Doyle, chalk caricature, 1839 (*Playing off a joke upon an old friend*), BM • J. Doyle, chalk caricature, 1839 (*The somnambulist*), BM • F. C. Lewis, stipple (after J. Slater, Grillion's Club series), BM, NPG • portrait, Legislative Building, Fredericton, New Brunswick

Wealth at death under £5000: resworn probate, Nov 1866, *CGPLA Eng. & Wales*

Grant, Sir Charles (1836–1903). *See under* Grant, Sir Robert (1837–1904).

Grant, Charles Jameson (*fl.* 1830–1852), caricaturist, is someone on whom there is very little documentation: nothing is known of his family background, nor of his personal history prior to the beginning of his career. He was one of the most prolific and individual graphic satirists of the 1830s, though for more than a century and a half his significance has been eclipsed by that of contemporaries such as John Doyle (H. B.), Robert Seymour, and William Heath, all of whose lives can be more accurately documented. Throughout his active life he was resident in London, living for a time at the north end of Gray's Inn Road, working for the publishers and print dealers clustered around St Paul's Churchyard, Cheapside, and the Strand.

His career began as a collaborative affair, in which he provided designs for the caricaturists William and Henry Heath, though he soon began to execute the majority of his own designs himself, producing close to a hundred single-sheet satirical prints between 1830 and 1832. His work appeared with the initials C. J. G. or the name C. J. Grant. While his prints of this period often displayed considerable inventiveness and an often bizarre or grotesque comic imagination, they were very much a product of a market in which the artist's individual ideology was subservient to that of his publishers and their audience, being pro moderate electoral reform and anti radicalism and revolution. Despite this, he developed a menagerie of favourite *bêtes noires* who would remain staples of his work for years to come, including Henry Brougham, Ernest, duke of Cumberland, and the duke of Wellington and Lord Grey—principal players in the drama surrounding the Reform Act of June 1832.

Following the passage of the act, however, the market for single-sheet political prints declined rapidly, and from 1833 Grant began to produce more and more prints in lithographic sequentially numbered series, often eschewing politics in favour of a milder form of social satire. Series such as Grant's Oddities, Laughing Made Easy, and Whim-Whams were all short-lived affairs, but the thirty-nine multipanelled issues of *Every Body's Album and Caricature Magazine* (1834–5) form a much more substantial body of work, using the tonal qualities of lithography in an extremely subtle manner, and constituting some of his finest work in the medium. The series often made use of a thematic, though not narrative, unity to picture a world in the grip of folly and distraction and can be read on more than one level—as harmless fun, meaningless nonsense, or social critique.

At the same time, however, Grant was also pursuing what would become his greatest and most characteristic contribution to the history of graphic satire: between 1833 and 1835 he produced 131 numbers of The Political Drama, a weekly series of penny prints engraved on wood and printed on extremely cheap paper. It is this series which captures most fully the spirit of his own political and social vision. Unremittingly anti-authoritarian and crudely executed, these prints were apparently expressly designed to appeal to the social, political, and aesthetic experience of the radical working classes. Politicians, bishops, magistrates, sabbatarians, the monarchy, and the Metropolitan Police force are just some of the characters with which Grant peopled a world of blatant hypocrisy, self-interest, and abuse of power.

From 1836 until the end of his career the majority of Grant's work appeared in radical, pro-Chartist periodicals and in numerous examples of cheap serialized fiction for the working classes which William Thackeray, for one, found quite offensive: in 1838 he noted that: 'Rude woodcuts adorn all these publications, and seem to be almost all from the hand of the same artist—Grant by name. They are outrageous caricatures; squinting eyes, wooden legs, and pimpled noses forming the chief points of fun' (Thackeray, 287).

Grant's later career seems to have been driven largely by financial necessity rather than by any aesthetic or ideological criteria, and after 1840 his productivity began to decline rapidly. In a note written in 1840 he described himself as 'such an obscure object in the background' (*N&Q*, 209), a realistic assessment both of his position at the time and of his subsequent reputation. No known work survives in any major collections from the late 1840s, with only a single lithographic print dated 1852 providing any proof that he continued to work beyond that time. Only in the last decades of the twentieth century, as the subject of an exhibition at University College, London, in 1998, has Grant finally been given some of the recognition he deserves as one of the most unique figures in the history of graphic satire. Examples of his work are in the department of prints and drawings at the British Museum, the Strang print room, University College, London, and the People's History Museum, Manchester.   R. J. POUND

Sources R. J. Pound, *C. J. Grant's political drama: a radical satirist rediscovered* (1998) [exhibition catalogue, University College, London, 22 April–5 June 1998] • C. Fox, *Graphic journalism in England during the 1830s and 1840s* (1988) • C. Fox, 'Political caricature and the freedom of the press in early nineteenth century England', *Newspaper history: from the seventeenth century to the present day*, ed. G. Boyce, J. Curran, and P. Wingate (1978), 226–43 • F. G. Stephens and M. D. George, eds., *Catalogue of political and personal satires preserved … in the British Museum*, 11 (1954) • *N&Q*, 4th ser., 5 (1870), 209–10 • D. Kunzle, 'Between broadsheet caricature and *Punch*: cheap newspaper cuts for the lower classes in the 1830s', *Art Journal*, 43 (1983), 339–46 • W. M. Thackeray, 'Half a crown's worth of cheap knowledge', *Fraser's Magazine*, 17 (1838), 279–90 • L. James, *Fiction for the working man, 1830–1850* (1963), 24, 51–82 • *Robson's directory and court guide* (1839), 516

Grant, Clara Ellen (1867–1949), headmistress and settlement worker, was born on 21 June 1867 in Chapmanslade, Corsley, near Warminster, Wiltshire, the second of at least nine children of Thomas Grant, a painter and plumber, who was proprietor of an interior decoration business, and his wife, Maria, *née* Dredge (*b. c*.1838, *d.* after 1931). Both parents were well read: Thomas Grant was a self-taught musician and for many years a church organist. When Clara was five she became one of the first pupils of Chapmanslade's new national school, where she appears to have been beyond the control of the elderly and ineffectual headmaster. In 1875 the family moved to Frome, where Clara briefly attended a national school and then a seminary for young ladies in Fromefield. From an early age she combined a rebellious streak with a clear ambition: she wished to become a teacher and live in London. At thirteen she became a pupil teacher at Christ Church infants' school and by fourteen she was senior pupil teacher. In later life she called the pupil teacher system a lottery, its outcome dependent on the standard of the head teacher and generally favouring practical skills at the expense of general culture. She was lucky in her head teacher and furthered her general education by reading. In 1885 her apprenticeship came to an end and she gained a first class in the Queen's scholarship examination. She entered Salisbury Diocesan Training College in 1886 and

in 1888 became head teacher of a church school in a small Wiltshire town.

Late in 1890 Grant achieved her goal of a position in London when she became head of a school in Hoxton. Despite Hoxton's reputation as a sink of misery and crime, she spent three happy years there, enjoying the cultural life of London with her sister, a music student. She furthered her own education through university extension courses and lectures at Gresham College. In 1893 she had a brief unhappy spell teaching in a board school, where the severe discipline and rote learning ran counter to her more enlightened inclinations. In later years she satirized the work of Mrs Floyer, an examiner in needlework whose obsessions included the farcical 'needlework drill' which consisted of repetitive practice of the gestures of sewing before graduating to real thread and fabric. The board perceived that Grant was unsuited to the school and arranged a transfer to a school in Wapping.

Grant was a disciple of Froebel, whom she quoted as the source of her determination to live among those she taught. Her pupils and their families were among the poorest in London, but she always respected their dignity and their innate decency. In 1896 she included in her Christmas card a short 'wants list' in the hope of soliciting old clothes and discarded household goods for her pupils' families. Almost by accident, this sideline became the focus of her life's work. She had hoped to go on the universities' mission to central Africa, but the East End claimed her.

In 1900 Grant was appointed head of a school she referred to as the little tin school in Bow Common, one of the most deprived districts in Poplar. Charles Booth's survey had recently branded this one of the most violent districts of London, but again she saw little violence and reacted with compassion and common sense to her pupils' needs. She quickly realized that 'something had to be done to help the children socially if "school education" were not to be both cruel and ineffective' (*Farthing Bundles*, 78). Having participated in Canon Barnett's settlement work at Toynbee Hall and having met Jane Addams while on a tour of Chicago, Grant evolved a small informal settlement based in her own home in Fern Street, Bow Common, where neighbours could buy used clothing cheaply, where women seeking work could find small jobs, and where families could apply for emergency help for practically any problem. Her school pioneered school breakfasts, had the first school nurse in London, and was the first to include a 'sleep time' for the smallest infants. In 1907 the house emerged as the Fern Street Settlement, the focus of social work for the entire neighbourhood.

A supporter of the Liberal Party, Grant was no socialist and believed in promoting parents' responsibility for their families, but she appreciated that, where there were no jobs, it was foolish to deny charity to those who did not have work. She was an opponent of the workhouse, on the ground that it broke up already fragile families, and once briefly served as a parish guardian. A devout member of the Church of England, she advocated tolerance of other religions and *rapprochement* with the Catholic church, whose emphasis on the veneration of Mary she saw as an opportunity for a very cautious kind of sex education. On a practical level she argued that the school was as well placed as the church to handle community welfare and that for the church to enter into such secular affairs was to risk diluting its sacred character.

Grant's interest in the physical welfare of her pupils did not detract from her effectiveness as a teacher. She was proud of her ability to incorporate into her classroom contemporary ideas about learning by doing. She gained the sometimes grudging respect of schools inspectors and published a series of nine manuals for infant school teachers to popularize her methods. Her appreciation of the importance of play and recreation led her to press for the provision of parks, organized sports, and outings for mothers, while the children's grab bags of scraps and trinkets, her 'farthing bundles' became famous throughout London and earned her a humorous verse in the *Daily Herald*.

During the First World War, Grant helped with the local air raid shelter, comforted the bereaved, and reflected that the first blackout of the twentieth century provided many Londoners with their first opportunity to see the stars. She was never jealous of her position, gladly handing over welfare work to other agencies as they became more numerous. In 1927 she retired from teaching but was never able to retire from the settlement. Her memoir, *Farthing Bundles*, written in the early 1930s, indicates a growing interest in religion but shows her lively social conscience undiminished and her political judgment still keen as she watched the rise of fascism in Europe. Clara Grant died at her home, 38 Fern Street, on 10 October 1949.

Grant's seeming indifference to such issues as the promotion of birth control to alleviate poverty and her failure to understand social causes of deprivation have been criticized in later writing. She was probably guilty of the former, although her statement that she simply preferred not to engage with the issue of contraception reads rather more like the reticence of an Edwardian spinster than a failure to comprehend the problem. Of the latter she can certainly be exonerated: all Grant's writings come round to the responsibility of society to act as an employer of last resort and as a mediator of the health, housing, and recreational needs of its poorest citizens. She refused to see poverty itself as a cause for shame. Grant described herself as 'the only plain one of a family of good-looking sisters' (Grant, *Farthing Bundles*, 112). Whether or not this was true, she cultivated other strengths—her intelligence, her sense of humour, and her diplomatic skills—to secure her place at the heart of Bow Common.

ELIZABETH J. MORSE

Sources C. E. Grant, *Farthing bundles*, 2nd edn (1933) · C. E. Grant, *Fern Street Settlement* (1932) · D. Copelman, *London's women teachers: gender, class and feminism, 1870–1930* (1996) · C. Dyhouse, *Girls growing up in late Victorian and Edwardian England* (1981) · b. cert. · d. cert. · census returns, 1881

Wealth at death £1416: probate, 16 Dec 1949, *CGPLA Eng. & Wales*

Grant, Colquhoun (d. 1792), Jacobite soldier and lawyer, was the son of the farmer of Burnside on the estate of Castle Grant, Inverness-shire. In 1745 he joined the army of Charles Edward Stuart, elder son of the Stuart claimant to the throne, in the highlands and was active in obtaining recruits. According to one account of his exploits during the rising of 1745, he was one of those detached by Prince Charles to force an entrance into Edinburgh. Grant pursued some of the guard to the very walls of the castle, where they had just enough time to close the outer gate. Grant then stuck his dirk into the gate and left it there as a gesture of triumph and defiance. Another account connects the dirk incident with his pursuit of the dragoons after the battle of Prestonpans. This account relates that, mounted on the horse of a British officer, Grant chased single-handed a troop of dragoons to Edinburgh Castle and, thwarted in his pursuit, he plunged his dirk into the castle. While the dirk incident is as likely as not a humorous invention, Grant is known to have distinguished himself in an attack on the dragoons at Prestonpans and by capturing two pieces of artillery. For his bravery he received the special thanks of Prince Charles at the first levee held at Holyrood, the prince also presenting him with a profile cast of himself.

Though not of the gigantic size sometimes ascribed to him by tradition, Grant was tall and handsome. His stature led to his being selected by Prince Charles to form one of his life guards under Lord Elcho. He served with the prince in this capacity until the defeat at Culloden on 16 April 1746. Having escaped after the battle to his native district, he remained in hiding until the proceedings against the rebels had been terminated. Subsequently he settled in Edinburgh as a writer to the signet, a profession for which he must have served his apprenticeship before the outbreak of the rising, and was retained from 1773 to 1778 as law agent to his chief, Sir James Grant of Grant.

Grant's confidence in the clarity of his spoken English appears on at least one occasion to have been misplaced: while he was in the House of Lords as an agent in an appeal he asked the clerk to be permitted to read a document aloud to the assembled peers. 'His amazement and vexation may be imagined when the Chancellor (Thurlow), after endeavouring in vain to comprehend what he was uttering, exclaimed—"Mr Col-co-hon, I will thank you to give that paper to the Clerk, as I do not understand Welsh"' (Kay, 1.422).

Grant and Alexander Watson of Glenturke, another highland lawyer, were constant companions and used to dine together in a tavern in Jackson's Close for 'two placks apiece', dividing half a bottle of claret between them. Grant died in Edinburgh on 2 December 1792 and, although unmarried, left several children, who were well provided for on account of the wealth his frugal habits had enabled him to amass.

T. F. HENDERSON, *rev.* ROGER TURNER

Sources J. Kay, *A series of original portraits and caricature etchings … with biographical sketches and illustrative anecdotes*, ed. [H. Paton and others], new edn [3rd edn], 1 (1877), 418–22 · W. Fraser, ed., *The chiefs* *of Grant*, 3 vols. (1883) • E. Evans, *Catalogue of engraved British portraits*, 2 [1853], 175

Likenesses J. Kay, group portrait, etching, BM; repro. in Kay, *Series*, ed. Paton, pl. 165

Grant, Sir Colquhoun (*c.*1764–1835), army officer, belonged to the branch of Grants of Gartonbeg. He joined the 36th foot at Trichinopoly, India, immediately after becoming an ensign in September 1793. He became a lieutenant in 1795, and in 1797 transferred to the 25th (later the 22nd) light dragoons. While with that regiment he was present at the battle of Malavalli and at Wellesley's capture of Seringapatam in 1799.

In 1800 Grant became a captain in the 9th dragoons, and in 1801 a major in the 28th (Duke of York's) light dragoons. When that formation was disbanded in 1802 Grant became a lieutenant-colonel in the 72nd highlanders. He was wounded leading his regiment during the recapture of the Cape of Good Hope in 1806. On 25 August 1808 Grant was transferred to the 15th hussars, and later that year (21 December) he greatly distinguished himself at Sahagun during the retreat to Corunna.

The 15th hussars regiment was deployed in the English midlands during the Luddite and other domestic disturbances before returning to Spain in 1813. Grant, who had been made a brevet colonel and aide-de-camp to the prince regent, commanded a hussar brigade at Morales, where he was wounded, at Vitoria, and at the Nivelle. He now commanded a brigade composed of the 13th and 14th light dragoons. He was made a major-general and KCB in 1814.

At Waterloo, Grant commanded the 5th brigade of the British and King's German Legion cavalry, composed of the 7th and 15th British hussars and the 2nd hussars (King's German Legion). He was wounded and had several horses killed under him. He was appointed a colonel of the 12th royal lancers in 1825, and transferred to his old regiment, the 15th hussars, in 1827. He became lieutenant-general in 1830.

Grant was made a KCH in 1816, and was bestowed with the orders of St Vladimir in Russia and William the Lion in the Netherlands. He was at one time groom of the bedchamber to the duke of Cumberland. He became MP for Queensborough in 1831, but the constituency disappeared under the 1832 Reform Act. In 1833 he was bequeathed large estates at Frampton, Dorset, by his friend Francis John Browne, formerly MP for that county. Grant had married Browne's niece, the daughter of the Revd John Richards of Long Bredy. In 1834 their daughter married Richard Brinsley Sheridan, grandson of the famous playwright. Grant unsuccessfully contested the seat of Poole in 1835, and died at Frampton on 20 December 1835. His daughter inherited the Frampton estates.

H. M. CHICHESTER, rev. S. KINROSS

Sources Fortescue, *Brit. army*, vols. 9–10 • E. C. Joslin, A. R. Litherland, B. T. Simpkin, and others, eds., *British battles and medals*, 6th edn (1988) • J. Haydn, *The book of dignities: containing rolls of the official personages of the British empire* (1851) • W. F. P. Napier, *History of the war in the Peninsula and in the south of France*, 3 vols. (1882) • J. Philippart, ed., *The royal military calendar*, 3rd edn, 3 (1820) • *GM*, 2nd ser., 5

(1836) • H. T. Siborne, ed., *Waterloo letters* (1891) • *United Service Journal* (1838) • D. Gates, *The Spanish ulcer: a history of the Peninsular War* (1986) • R. Muir, *Britain and the defeat of Napoleon, 1807–1815* (1996)

Wealth at death bequeathed major landholdings

Grant, Colquhoun (1780–1829), army officer, was the son of Duncan Grant of Lingieston, Moray, and the brother of Colonel Alexander Grant CB, a distinguished Madras officer of the East India Company. Grant's widowed mother obtained an ensigncy in the 11th foot for her son through General James Grant of Ballindalloch, and he was appointed an ensign on 9 September 1795, while still fourteen, with permission to remain at a military school near London until he was promoted.

In 1796 Grant became a lieutenant, and in 1798 he was taken prisoner, along with the bulk of his regiment, after the unsuccessful descent on Ostend. He was detained for a year at Douai. On 19 November 1801 he obtained the command of a company and served in the West Indies during the capture of the Danish and Swedish possessions there. He was later on the personal staff of Sir George Prevost.

After serving with the 1st battalion of his regiment at Madeira, Grant accompanied it to the Peninsula, and undertook intelligence-gathering missions. These tended to be of an overt nature, and during his periods spent behind enemy lines he was always in uniform. Grant greatly relied on his personal resources of sagacity, courage, and speed. He had a talent for learning languages and dialects and was at home with the Spaniards with whom he liaised, earning the sobriquet 'Granto bueno'. In 1810 he narrowly avoided capture by General Foy in Cáceres, escaping half-dressed, and being forced to leave his horse and papers behind.

Grant was now a deputy assistant adjutant-general on the British staff. He became a brevet-major on 30 May 1811. The historian Sir William Napier, an intimate of Grant's, relates that when Marmont neared Beira in the autumn of 1811, during Wellington's blockade of Ciudad Rodrigo, it was feared that the French marshal might be contemplating a *coup de main* to relieve that citadel. Grant infiltrated the enemy's lines, and succeeded in gathering enough information about Marmont's numbers and supplies to show that he had no such intention. Shortly afterwards, while observing French movements on the banks of the Coa, Grant was surprised by some French dragoons, and taken as a prisoner to Salamanca. His guide was killed. Grant's popularity among his captors there, and his intimacy with Patrick Curtis, the head of the Irish College at Salamanca, moved Marmont to fear that he was actually the spy John *Grant (1782?–1842).

After accepting Grant's word of honour that he would not attempt to escape if paroled, Marmont sent him with an escort of 300 men to Bayonne, with secret orders that he should be re-manacled there. Suspecting duplicity, Grant escaped. He masqueraded as an American officer to the unsuspecting French general, Souham, with whom he travelled to Paris. There he sought out a British secret agent, and with his help remained in the city for several weeks, during which he gathered intelligence for Wellington, just as he had done at Salamanca. Finding Paris too dangerous, he obtained the passport of a recently deceased American, and made to embark for the United States from the Loire, escaping in the guise of a sailor to England. There he arranged for the release of a French officer of equal rank, and then returned to Spain, arriving at Wellington's headquarters within four months of his capture. Wellington had lamented this event, describing it as being tantamount to the loss of a brigade. Grant was employed on intelligence duties during the rest of the Peninsular War, became a brevet lieutenant-colonel on 19 May 1814, and major with his regiment on 13 October 1814.

On Napoleon's return from Elba, Wellington recalled Grant, who had recently joined the senior department of the Royal Military College at Farnham, and placed him in charge of the intelligence department of the army, with the rank of assistant adjutant-general. In some of the staff returns he is incorrectly described as 'Sir' Colquhoun *Grant 11th foot (compare *Army List*, 1815). On 15 June 1815 Grant, who was at Condé, was informed by his spies that a large battle would be fought within three days. The news was accidentally delayed, and did not reach Wellington until delivered to him by Grant on the field of Waterloo. Afterwards Grant was based in Paris, where he ensured that the allies did not appropriate the spoils of war at the expense of British troops.

Grant was placed on half pay as a major in the 11th foot between 1816 and October 1821, when he was made a lieutenant-colonel of the 54th foot, then travelling from the Cape to India. He commanded a brigade under General Morrison in Arakan during the First Anglo-Burmese War (1824–6), for which he was made CB. While in Burma Grant contracted a fever that was to ruin his health. This blow was compounded by his sense that he had been neglected by his superiors. He left the army on 1 October 1829, and died on 20 October at Aix-la-Chapelle (now Aachen), where a monument was erected in his honour in the protestant burial-ground. His brother-in-law, Sir James MacGrigor of the army medical department, who married Grant's youngest sister, described Grant as a kindly, amiable man, possessing in a higher degree than any other officer he had met all the better and brighter attributes of a Christian soldier.

H. M. CHICHESTER, rev. S. KINROSS

Sources W. F. P. Napier, *History of the war in the Peninsula and in the south of France*, 3rd edn, 6 vols. (1834–40) • J. McGrigor, *The autobiography and services of Sir J. McGrigor* (1861) • Chambers, *Scots.* (1835) • Fortescue, *Brit. army*, vols. 7–8, 10 • L. James, *The iron duke* (1992) • C. W. C. Oman, *A history of the Peninsular War*, 4 (1911), 75 • P. J. Haythornthwaite, *The armies of Wellington* (1994) • C. W. C. Oman, *Wellington's army, 1809–1814* (1912) • *Army List* • S. G. P. Ward, *Wellington's headquarters: a study of the administrative problems in the Peninsula, 1809–14* (1957) • D. Gates, *The Spanish ulcer: a history of the Peninsular War* (1986) • R. Muir, *Britain and the defeat of Napoleon, 1807–1815* (1996)

Grant, David (1823–1886), poet, was born in 1823 at Affrusk in the parish of Banchory-Ternan, Aberdeenshire, and baptized there on 29 January 1824, the son of George Grant, farmer, and Eliza Sivewright. He was educated at Aberdeen grammar school, and Marischal College, Aberdeen, where he took no degree. He became a teacher in 1852, and after employment in various Scottish schools, in 1862 he was appointed French master in Oundle grammar school, Northamptonshire. In 1861 he had married a Mrs Allan, who died in the following year. In 1865 he became assistant master of Ecclesall College, a private school near Sheffield. On 23 June 1871 he married Elizabeth Ross (*b.* 1842/3), daughter of Andrew Ross, farmer, with whom he had two children. That same year, he purchased Springvale Academy, a private day school in Sheffield, of which he disposed in 1878. His advanced views on education were noticed and encouraged by Earl Russell.

Already a frequent contributor to the *Aberdeen Herald*, Grant subsequently edited the *Sheffield Post* for a short time, and wrote for the *Aberdeen Free Press*. His first collection, *Metrical Tales*, was published in Sheffield in 1880. In 1883 he left Sheffield for Edinburgh, where he divided his time between literature and tuition. There, he published *Lays and Legends of the North* (1884). These humorous tales written in the Scottish vernacular have been reprinted together or separately many times. He died in Edinburgh on 22 April 1886. WILLIAM BAYNE, rev. S. R. J. BAUDRY

Sources R. C. T. Mair, 'Biographical sketch', in D. Grant, *Lays and legends of the north* (1908) • H. K. Grant, 'Introduction', in D. Grant, *A northern garland* (1936) • L. Spence, 'Introduction', in D. Grant, *A Feughside fairy tale* (1937) • W. Grant, 'Introduction', in D. Grant, *The sounin' o' the kirk* (1935) • D. H. Edwards, *Modern Scottish poets, with biographical and critical notices*, 16 vols. (1880–97) • *IGI* • m. cert. • d. cert. • bap. reg. Scot.

Likenesses photograph, 1880, repro. in Grant, *Lays and legends*

Grant, Duncan James Corrowr (1885–1978), painter and decorative artist, was born in his family's ancestral home, The Doune, at Rothiemurchus, near Aviemore, on 21 January 1885, the only child of Major Bartle Grant and his wife, Ethel McNeil. His early years were spent in India and Burma, where his father's regiment was stationed; he returned to England in 1893, to attend Hillbrow preparatory school, Rugby, where he first met Rupert Brooke, received lessons from an art teacher who aroused his interest in Japanese prints, and was thrilled to discover the work of Edward Burne-Jones. ('For years I would ask God on my knees at prayers to allow me to become as good a painter as he' (Spalding, 13).) In 1899 he became a day pupil at St Paul's School, living for most of this period with his cousins the Stracheys—his aunt Jane Maria Grant having married Richard Strachey (1817–1908). This proved the more significant educational experience. Not only was Lady Strachey an engaging, original, and energetic personality, but her numerous children, in particular Philippa, Lytton, Margery, and James, provided Duncan Grant with an intelligent and very cultivated milieu.

His background gave Grant access to the world of high Victorian art. As a boy he accompanied Lady Strachey to the studios of certain eminent artists on 'picture Sunday'; as a young man he attended one of Sir Lawrence Alma-Tadema's at-homes. Lady Strachey, perceiving that he gained little from St Paul's, had agreed with his parents

Duncan James Corrowr Grant (1885–1978), self-portrait, 1925

that he should leave school early and study at the Westminster School of Art. He did so, also travelling in Italy in 1902 and 1903. His understanding of what it meant to be an artist was developed further when in 1903 his cousin Dorothy Strachey married a French painter, Simon Bussy, who enjoyed friendship with Matisse. On coming of age Grant used a £100 legacy from another aunt, Lady Colvile, to study for one year (1906–7) in Paris, at Jacques-Emile Blanche's La Palette. While there he copied Chardin in the Louvre and ignored, or remained unaware of, the controversy caused by the Fauves. Thus, though an art student in Paris during one of the most revolutionary moments in the history of painting, he continued, for some years yet, to paint with sober colours and formal restraint. A fine example of his early work is his portrait of James Strachey (Tate collection).

On his return to London, Grant began working on his own. He went often to concerts and the theatre, and was frequently in the company of his friends. A brief affair with his cousin Lytton Strachey gave way to a more significant relationship with Maynard Keynes, who was attracted, like many others, by the originality of Grant's mind and by his good looks. As a near neighbour of Virginia Stephen (later Woolf) and her brother Adrian, with whom he also had an affair, Grant swiftly became a central figure within the Bloomsbury group, despite the fact that he lacked the Cambridge education shared by all the other male participants.

The turning point in Grant's career came in 1910, when he responded to the implications of a French post-impressionist exhibition which Roger Fry had mounted at the Grafton Galleries in London. He rid himself abruptly of all the pictorial conventions that had previously governed his art and experimented with an expressive handling of line, colour, and form. Rupert Brooke, in his review of the Second Post-Impressionist Exhibition of 1912–13, observed that Grant was 'roaming … between different styles and methods' (Spalding, 127). Although this continued to hold true of his work for some time yet, his daring innovations quickly earned him a leading position among avant-garde artists in Britain. His eclectic sensibility derived ideas from many sources, which he employed with great imaginative freedom. His most surprising work is his *Kinetic Abstract Scroll* (Tate collection), produced during August 1914. Composed of abstract blocks, grouped in repeated clusters which rise and fall, it was intended to be viewed, like a film, through an aperture, as it was wound past. Grant wanted it to be accompanied by music and specified a slow movement from one of Bach's Brandenburg concertos. This upholds the solemnity of this work, which is rare in Grant's output.

When Roger Fry founded the Omega workshops in 1913, in the hope that the new sense of colour, design, and rhythm animating post-impressionism would spill over into the decorative arts, Grant agreed to become, with Vanessa *Bell (1879–1961), a co-director. He received welcome remuneration for his designs and quickly proved to be an able, original decorator, owing to his nervous, highly personal brushwork and his witty and lyrical invention. He is well represented in the Courtauld Institute collection of Omega items. While working closely together in the lead up towards the opening of the workshops, Grant and Bell moved into an intimate relationship which also marked the onset of an aesthetic partnership. Hitherto Grant's passions had been engaged almost always by members of his own sex and, although this essential aspect of his sexual nature never ceased to affect him, his union with Bell, and his friendship with her husband, played a determining role in the conduct of his life. It was Vanessa Bell who sustained and assisted him in his resolution not to fight in the First World War, making a home for him and David Garnett, first at Wissett Lodge in Suffolk, then at Charleston, at Firle, in Sussex, where he undertook farm work until the end of the war. In 1918 Bell bore Grant a daughter, Angelica, who some twenty years later married David Garnett. Despite various homosexual allegiances in subsequent years, Grant's relationship with Vanessa Bell endured to the end; it became primarily a domestic and creative union, the two artists painting side by side, often in the same studio, admiring but also criticizing each other's efforts. They also continued to work in partnership on many decorative schemes after the Omega closed in 1919.

Ironically, Grant, who became greatly admired as a colourist, produced some of his most integrated compositions immediately after the First World War, when he adopted, temporarily, a sombre, low-toned palette. This work is also characterized by a search for 'solidity', a term often used in Roger Fry's criticism of that period. There was never any serious return to abstraction, though his palette regained a richness and brilliance. This, combined with his painterly fluency, helped bring him to the zenith of his popularity in the 1930s. In 1935 both he and Vanessa Bell accepted commissions to paint decorative panels for the new Cunard liner, RMS *Queen Mary*. Grant's stylized figures did not fit with the more lightweight aesthetic found elsewhere in the ship, and their rejection was the cause of a small scandal. He continued, however, to accept decorative commissions, such as the Russell chantry, which he painted in the 1950s for Lincoln Cathedral. Equally, if not more, significant are the decorations in Berwick church, Sussex, a commission which Grant shared with Vanessa Bell and her son and their daughter, Quentin and Angelica. The unaffected simplicity of these decorations is in keeping with the character of the small church and enables them to fulfil their purpose. This work was carried out during the Second World War at Charleston, which had once again become Grant and Vanessa Bell's permanent home, and remained so from then on. The main part of the work for Berwick church was completed in 1943. In 1941 Grant had been made royal designer for industry for his work on printed textiles.

After the return to peace in 1945 the most significant development in Grant's life was his encounter in Piccadilly with Paul Roche. A young Catholic, Roche at first kept from the older man the fact that he was training for the priesthood, a career he eventually abandoned. He shared Grant's *pied-à-terre* in London, posed for many paintings and drawings, and formed a lasting relationship with the painter, despite their difference in age and the fact that by the late 1950s Roche had married, moved to America, and had five children, one illegitimate.

During this period Grant's reputation as an artist declined and he had difficulty selling his pictures except at very low prices. In 1961 Vanessa Bell died and he was left to live alone at Charleston, with the loyal housekeeper, Grace Higgens, and her husband. He was a forgotten figure by all but a few friends until the late 1960s, when he was rediscovered by a younger generation. He enjoyed friendship with Lindy Guinness (later Dufferin), whom he encouraged to paint; he also attracted the interest, support, and friendship of the Tate curator Richard Morphet and the art historians Richard Shone and Simon Watney; and his career and reputation were regalvanized by the art dealer Anthony d'Offay, whose promotion of Grant helped fertilize the joyous relaxation that informs his late work. He had welcomed the return of Paul Roche and his family to England after Vanessa Bell's death, and in his final years spent much time in Roche's company. Throughout this and all periods of his artistic life painting remained as essential to his well-being as breathing, and he continued to work up until a few days before his death.

Grant is assured of his place in British art history as an innovator of great talent, as an accomplished decorator, and as a painter of large though unequal achievement. At his best, he orchestrates a subtle, often mellifluous and sonorous arrangement of colours and forms, frequently weaving into his work allusions to other artists within the western European tradition of which he was a proud and sensitive inheritor. As a man he was distinguished by great personal beauty and an uncommon sweetness of character; no one who met him could fail to be impressed by his gentle dignity and his faintly ironical vivacity. His enthusiastic generosity as a critic of other artists' work derived from a firm conviction that, of all human activities, painting is the best. He died in Paul Roche's home, at The Stables, Aldermaston, on 8 May 1978.

QUENTIN BELL, *rev.* FRANCES SPALDING

Sources M. Holroyd, *Lytton Strachey: a critical biography*, 2 vols. (1967–8) · P. Roche, *With Duncan Grant in southern Turkey* (1982) · A. Garnett, *Duncan Grant: works on paper* (1981) [exhibition catalogue, Anthony d'Offay Gallery, London] · R. Shone, *Bloomsbury portraits* (1993) · F. Spalding, *Duncan Grant: a biography* (1997) · personal knowledge (1986) · A. Clutton-Brock, *Duncan Grant: a retrospective exhibition* (1959) [Tate Gallery, London] · *The Times* (10 May 1978) · *CGPLA Eng. & Wales* (1978)

Archives King's AC Cam., corresp. and papers · Tate collection, material relating to him · U. Sussex, corresp., incl. letters to Vanessa Bell [copies] | BL, corresp. with John Maynard Keynes and Lytton Strachey, Add. MSS 57930–57933, 58120, 74230 · U. Sussex, corresp. with Virginia Woolf

Likenesses D. Grant, self-portrait, oils, *c.*1909, NPG · D. Grant, self-portrait, 1910, priv. coll. · D. Grant, self-portrait, 1925; Sothebys, 10 May 1989, lot 65 [*see illus.*] · Partridge, photograph, 1930, Hult. Arch. · V. Bell, oils, 1934, Williamson Art Gallery, Birkenhead · F. Man, photograph, 1940, Hult. Arch. · G. Argent, photographs, 1968, NPG · C. Beaton, photograph, NPG · photographs, NPG

Wealth at death £57,490: probate, 26 July 1978, *CGPLA Eng. & Wales*

Grant, Edward (*c.*1546–1601), headmaster and author, was a scholar at Westminster School under both John Passey, headmaster in 1557, and John Randal, head in 1563. He matriculated as a sizar at St John's College, Cambridge, on 22 February 1564, and migrated to Oxford, where he graduated BA on 27 February 1572. On 27 March of that year, as a member of Exeter College, he was awarded his MA, and was incorporated in that degree at Cambridge in 1573. He was awarded his BTh at Cambridge in 1578/9 and, having been made a university preacher in 1580, took his doctorate in 1588. Little is known of Grant's wife, Susan, who survived him, or of his daughter Sarah, but her elder sister Susan married John Dixe, prebendary of Willesden (*d.* 1614). Grant's eldest son, Gabriel, attended Trinity College, Cambridge, from 1593 and was a prebendary of Westminster from 1613 to 1638. A younger son, John, also attended Trinity in 1596.

Between 1572 and 1592 Edward Grant was headmaster of Westminster School, whose reputation had yet to be built. Under his own mastership and that of William Camden, who succeeded him after eighteen years as second master, 'the number of boys rapidly increased and the names of well known families begin to appear in the lists' (Tanner, 26). It seems that Grant found his duties increasingly onerous. On 12 December 1587 he wrote in Latin to the queen asking to be relieved of his stressful position; the request was refused. But Grant's labours bore increasing fruit. When he stepped down in 1592 there were sixty-four minor candidates for election to the school, and in 1599, not long after Camden took over, a larger building had to be found. As one historian of the school records, 'The long periods of office of Goodman as Dean and Edward Grant and William Camden as Schoolmasters won for the school celebrity and success' (Field, 27). Ben Jonson, archbishops Bancroft and Neile, the diplomat Dudley Carleton, and the antiquary Robert Cotton were among his more famous students.

In 1575 Grant published a Greek grammar, *Graecae linguae spicilegium*. In 1597 Camden issued the work in a more accessible and elementary form under the title *Institutio Graecae grammatices compendaria in usum scholae regiae Westmonasteriensis*. This grammar was employed at Westminster School for about half a century, until superseded by that of Busby, but it continued in use at Eton, and became known in later years as the Eton Greek Grammar. Wood thought its original author 'the most noted Latinist and Grecian of his time' (Wood, *Ath. Oxon.*, 1.711), and his scholarly interests were reflected in other ways. Cooper tells of Grant's presentation of books to the library of St John's College, Cambridge, in April 1579 and of his 'zealous efforts to preserve the fame of Roger Ascham, whose orphan family he strongly recommended to the Queen' (Cooper, *Ath. Cantab.*, 2.320), and it was Grant who published a posthumous edition of Ascham's letters.

Both during and after his tenure at Westminster, Grant was able to acquire ecclesiastical preferments to help support himself and his family. On 14 September 1576 he was presented by the queen to the next vacant prebend of Westminster Cathedral, and soon afterwards accepted the canonry of the twelfth prebend, being in residence at the chapter house by 22 September 1577. In April 1586 Dean Goodman reported him to be one of the canons 'most commonly present' (Strype, 3 ii, 416). He became rector of Shenley, Hertfordshire, in 1581, and of South Benfleet, Essex, on 12 December 1584, resigning in the following year. He acquired the rectories of Bintree and Foulsham, Norfolk, from 20 November 1586 to 1594, of East Barnet from 3 November 1591, and of Algarkirk, Lincolnshire, from 1594, appearing in the Lincoln diocesan records of that year as a non-resident and a pluralist. On 22 April 1598 he was instituted to the rectory of Toppesfield, Essex, holding the living until his death, and there is evidence from his will that he lived here for part of the year. But he cannot simultaneously have been in all his far-flung parishes and also at Ely, where he was instituted to the sixth prebend in 1589 and was in occupancy on 10 December 1590.

Grant died on 4 August 1601 and was buried in Westminster Abbey. Despite his many preferments he seems not to have accumulated great wealth, with the exception of a library 'which cost me almost four hundred pounds', and which can surely not have comprised less than a thousand volumes. This he bequeathed to 'my youngest and ever obedient son' for whom, it may be speculated, he nourished special affection (PRO, PROB 11/98, sig. 72); the marriage of Gabriel, his eldest, seems to have aroused his lasting antipathy.   STEPHEN WRIGHT

Sources Wood, *Ath. Oxon.*, new edn, 1.711 · Cooper, *Ath. Cantab.* · *Fasti Angl., 1541–1857*, [Ely] · L. E. Tanner, *Westminster School*, 2nd edn

(1951) · J. Sargeaunt, *Annals of Westminster School* (1898) · J. Field, *The king's nurseries: the story of Westminster School* (1987) · C. W. Foster, ed., *The state of the church in the reigns of Elizabeth and James I*, Lincoln RS, 23 (1926) · will, PRO, PROB 11/98, sig. 72 · J. Strype, *Annals of the Reformation and establishment of religion … during Queen Elizabeth's happy reign*, new edn, 3/2 (1824) · RO Westminst.
Wealth at death total value unknown; incl. library: will, PRO, PROB 11/98, sig. 72

Grant, Elizabeth (1745/6–1828), songwriter, of Carron, Banffshire, was the daughter of 'Lieutenant Joseph Grant (*fl.* 1720–1760), late of Colonel Montgomerie's regiment of Highlanders', and was born near Aberlour, Banffshire. She was married about 1765 to her cousin, Captain James Grant of Carron. Encountering financial difficulties, James Grant was obliged to sell Carron in 1786 or 1787, and on 14 March 1790 he died in the abbey of Holyroodhouse, Edinburgh. They had five sons. Mrs Grant was married on 5 March 1793 to Dr James Thomas Murray of Dungannon, a Bath physician, and she died in Bath on 27 February 1828, aged eighty-two, and was buried at St James's Church, Bath, on 3 March. She is normally referred to as Mrs Grant. She was consulted in Bath by the song collector Cromek about Alexander Ross (1699–1744), the Angus poet who wrote *The Gentle Shepherdess*. A portrait by Allan Ramsay was said to be of her, but this is now thought unlikely.

Grant's reputation as a songwriter rests on 'Roy's Wife of Aldivalloch' to the tune 'The Ruffian's Rant'. It is a young man's lament for his lost love who marries an older man:

How happy I, had she been mine
Or I been Roy of Aldivalloch.

Aldivalloch is a farm near Cabrach, Banffshire, and the *Inverness Courier* located a veritable Roy of Aldivalloch, married to a young bride in 1727. The song collector Peter Buchan (1790–1854) took down a more elaborate, if later, version, suggesting that it was already an established folk song.

'Roy's Wife' was very popular. It awoke the interest of Robert Burns, who suggested that its attractiveness depended on its irregularity, a feature sometimes referred to as a 'Scotch snap' which 'Roy's Wife' exhibits very well. He stated that the song had 'high merit as well as great celebrity', and wrote variants on it for Johnson's *Musical Museum*. He sent George Thomson an English song to the same tune, 'Canst thou leave me thus, my Katy?'. It is, perhaps, a testimony to Mrs Grant's song that it was more successful than those, both polite and impolite, by Burns. An even better indicator of its success is that the tune 'The Ruffian's Rant', used by Burns for a bawdy song which Gershon Legman (*b.* 1917) considered the forerunner 'in form and style' of the notorious 'Ball o' Kirriemuir', became known as 'Roy's Wife'. However, William Montgomerie of the School of Scottish Studies, in an article in the *Burns Chronicle* (1959), shows that Mrs Grant deserves little credit for it.   LOUIS STOTT

Sources W. Montgomerie, 'Roy's wife of Aldivalloch', *Burns Chronicle* (1959), 49–56 · [D. Herd], ed., *Ancient and modern Scottish songs*, new edn, 2 vols in 1 (1791) · D. Laing, *Johnson's musical museum* (1853), 4.368 · J. Johnson, *Musical museum* (1787–1803) · C. Mackay, *Songs of Scotland* (1861) · W. Fraser, ed., *The chiefs of Grant*, 3 vols.

(1883) · Earl of Cassilis, *Rulers of Strathspey* (1911) · E. B. Lyle and others, eds., *The Greig-Duncan folk song collection*, 8 vols. (1981–2000) · private information (2004) [Scot. NPG] · *Bath Chronicle* (28 Feb 1828) · *Bath Chronicle* (17 Dec 1818) · R. Chambers, *Scottish songs before Robert Burns* (1862) · *DNB* · C. Rogers, *The modern Scottish minstrel, or, The songs of Scotland of the past half-century*, 6 vols. (1855–7) · E. Mac-Coll, *Folksongs and ballads of Scotland* (1965) · G. Legman, *The horn book* (1970), 423 · F. J. Grant, ed., *Register of marriages of the city of Edinburgh, 1751–1800*, Scottish RS, 53 (1922), 577

Likenesses engraving, repro. in Chambers, *Scottish songs before Robert Burns*, 433

Grant, Elizabeth. *See* Smith, Elizabeth (1797–1885).

Grant, Sir Francis, first baronet, Lord Cullen (1658×63–1726), judge and writer, was born at Balintomb in the parish of Knockando, Moray, either in 1658, 1660, or 1663, according to differing sources. He was the elder son of Archibald Grant and his wife, Christian, daughter of Patrick Nairne of Cromdale. In 1678 he entered the arts class at King's College, Aberdeen, and after graduation possibly spent a couple of years attending informal law classes in Edinburgh before moving to the Netherlands, where he entered the University of Leiden on 31 August 1684. While the United Provinces provided an important refuge for exiled Scots presbyterian nonconformists during the Restoration, the University of Leiden also remained a popular venue for the education of aspiring Scottish lawyers. At Leiden, Grant received not only a broad humanistic education encompassing classical antiquity, languages, and civil and ecclesiastical history, but also a thorough immersion in civil and canon law. These latter subjects Grant studied under the celebrated jurist Johannes Voet, who was particularly interested in Scots law and, reputedly, considered Grant to be one of his finest pupils.

About 1687 Grant returned to Scotland to undergo private examination for admission to the Faculty of Advocates, but his entry was delayed as the upheavals of the revolution of 1688 intervened. Interested in the constitutional dilemmas posed by recent events, Grant published in 1689 a highly original pamphlet entitled *The loyalists reasons for his giving obedience, and swearing allegiance to the present government*. Here Grant struck a difficult balance, arguing for the legitimacy of the Scots' transfer of their allegiance to King William, without conceding that any popular resistance to the old regime had actually occurred. Grant squared this circle by introducing into the Scottish debate just-war theories derived from the Dutch founder of international law, Hugo Grotius. According to Grant, since James VII had committed a delict against his subjects in breach of the rectoral contract on which his political authority depended, the throne had thereby become vacant, and the prince of Orange had taken possession of it in a just war by law of conquest. An ardent if somewhat conservative whig, Grant carefully avoided any tory traps in this argument by pointing out that William had conquered only the king, and not the kingdom, with the corollary that the Scots remained a free people. Nevertheless, the legitimacy of the prince of Orange did not rest upon international law alone, for, as Grant concluded, William enjoyed his title by 'Birth-right, Conquest, and Election, conjunctly or separatly' (*Loyalists Reasons*, 59).

Sir Francis Grant, first baronet, Lord Cullen (1658×63–1726), by John Smibert

In January 1691 Grant was admitted to the Faculty of Advocates, having been successfully examined in public on the title *De transactionibus* from Justinian's *Digest*. Once qualified he soon established a flourishing practice which evidently attracted attention, not only because his conscience obliged him to serve 'clergymen of all professions' without charging fees, but also because he felt unable to 'suffer a just cause to be lost through a client's want of money' (*Biographia Britannica*, 4.2256). Between 1694 and 1700 he served as curator of the newly established Advocates' Library. His reputation as a man of great learning persisted after his elevation to the judicial bench in 1709, and one of his fellow senators in the court of session later characterized him as 'a living library, and the most ready in citations; when the Lords wanted anything in the Civil or Canon law to be cast up, or Acts of Parliament, he never failed them, but turned to the place' (Wodrow, 3.282).

Grant was also admired as a devout Presbyterian, described by the Revd Robert Wodrow as 'a man of great piety and devotion, wonderfully serious in prayer and hearing the word' (Wodrow, 3.282). Throughout his life Grant's deep religious commitment manifested itself in various ways. Having been involved in the prosecution of the Renfrewshire witches in the late 1690s, he published *Saducismus debellatus* in 1698 to denounce fashionable scepticism about the reality of witchcraft and diabolism. That same year he started 'a praying society' composed largely of fellow lawyers but also including several clergymen, which met weekly for Christian deliberations (ibid., 4.235). This small informal group later spawned the Edinburgh Society for the Reformation of Manners, the inaugural meeting of which occurred at Grant's house in September 1700. In 1709 this latter society in turn evolved into the Society in Scotland for Propagating the Gospel. Grant was made a founding director of this organization, which became notorious for its Anglicizing highland missions. Indeed, the unionist Grant contended that it was very much in England's interest to bind 'to the interest of the Isle, a verry numerous people, because it brings them off from a different both Ecclesiastick and civill head, inconsistent with that established in the great Continent of the United Kingdom' (Grant to James Kirkwood, 29 Oct 1707, NL Scot., MS 821, fol. 144*r*).

During the 1700s Grant published *A brief account of the nature, rise, and progress of the societies for reformation of manners, etc, in England and Ireland; with a preface, exhorting to the use of such societies in Scotland*, and various other tracts dealing with the reformation of manners, sabbatarianism, the execution of laws against profaneness, and the use of informers in effecting such prosecutions. He also issued a pamphlet upholding the legal proscription on lay patronage in the kirk. Amid, and perhaps because of, the heated Presbyterian–Episcopalian wrangling of the reigns of William and Anne, Grant was, however, prepared to tincture his staunch Presbyterian orthodoxy with a measure of latitude, provoking Wodrow's suspicion that he 'seemed a little ambulatory in his judgment as to church government' (Wodrow, 3.282). During the debates over toleration in 1703 Grant published *An Essay for Peace, by Union in Judgement; about Church-Government in Scotland*, in which he advocated presbytery 'where possible, but imparity in exceptional circumstances' (p. 3). At the Reformation 'such Protestant churches as could obtain their choice', observed Grant, 'returned to primitive parity', some to 'mixed superintendency', while others were obliged out of necessity to retain episcopacy (p. 11). Although the Anglican church had retained episcopacy at the Reformation as 'a good design of gaining in the Papists', Grant recognized that this form of church government had now become 'so twisted with the civil constitution; that without a convulsion of this, that cannot be changed' (ibid.).

In the debates which preceded the Anglo-Scottish Union of 1707, Grant extended this argument for ecclesiastical pluralism. In *The Patriot Resolved* (1707) he supported incorporating union as a measure in the best interests of Scottish Presbyterianism, which would now be protected in the Union, not as a mere 'simple' or 'mutable' law, but as a fundamental law constitutive of the new united state. Employing a legal analogy, Grant maintained that so long as the fundamentals of religion, like the principles of justice, were preserved, men could tolerate differences in forms of religion and legal procedure. Just as state formation had not hitherto required the abolition of local customary laws, such as the Scandinavian udal law which prevailed in Scotland's northern isles, the consolidation of the British state need not demand the eradication of permitted variations in religious inessentials. Furthermore, Grant concluded that the passing of Scotland's unicameral, magnate-dominated parliament was no real loss;

despite Scotland's paltry representation in the new British parliament, the rights of the Scottish people would actually be better protected within a bicameral legislature where the commons were less deferential to the nobility.

Not only was Grant a pronounced unionist, he also held an untypical conception of Scottish national identity, though one which was beginning to make headway in juridical circles. Political debate in Scotland had long centred on the question of whether Scotland's original ancient polity had been hereditary, as the Jacobites believed, or elective and accountable, as in the whig version of the nation's Gaelic origin myth. Influenced by the legacy of 'our great Feudist' Thomas Craig, Grant, however, perceived that Scotland's laws and institutions, far from enjoying a direct provenance from an ancient Gaelic past, were feudal and 'Teutonick', and that the people of Scotland, far from being Celtic, were largely of Germanic or Belgic origin (*Law, Religion and Education Considered*, 1715, 1, 'Law', 108). Hence Grant did not fear that the Union would lead to the contamination of Scots law, for he detected a 'Consonancy' across all of Europe's mixed Roman–Gothic institutions, including the laws of Scotland and England, which were 'similar; as ultimately, proceeding from the same Source; whatever was the intermediate Channel' (ibid., 100).

More widely, Grant's writings encompassed a variety of fields, and his ideological contribution, while eclectic, can also often appear opaque. His literary style was later described as 'dark and intricat, and so wer his pleadings at the barr, and his discourses on the bench' (Wodrow, 3.282). One of his pamphleteering opponents, the Reverend James Webster, a fellow Presbyterian of a less eirenic cast, was arguably justified in complaining, in his *Discourse demonstrating that the government of the church which is of divine right is fixed and not ambulatory* (1704), about Grant's 'bad Diction, perplex'd Stile, and entangl'd Expression' (p. 4). Even within his own family it was admitted that Grant's 'Laconick Style' meant that his works were 'the less regarded by those who are more catched by forms than substance' ('Some account of the life', NA Scot., GD 345/789, fol. 9). Nevertheless, certain patterns can be discerned in Grant's œuvre. Throughout his career, Grant retained the aim of 'radicating the Foundations of Christianity; abstract from non-essential Disputes' (*Law, Religion, Education*, 'The design'). An abiding interest in the laws of nature and of nations encouraged a universal perspective on legal problems, and a pluralistic outlook in the legal sphere which paralleled his religious latitudinarianism. While law and religion are inextricably linked throughout his work, at times Grant's lawyerly view of religion verged on self-parody, as in his description of the Bible as 'the Magna Charta of Privileges, for Time and Eternity', or in his identification of the central themes of salvation as 'our Indemnity of bygone forfeitures' and 'a Gift of our new Inheritance' (ibid., 2, 'Religion', 5).

Grant married three times: first, on 15 March 1694, Jean, daughter of the Reverend William Meldrum of Meldrum,

Aberdeenshire; second, on 18 October 1708, Sarah, daughter of the Reverend Alexander Fordyce of Ayton, Berwickshire; and third, in 1718, Agnes, daughter of Henry Hay. With his first wife he had three sons, including Archibald *Grant (1696–1778) and William *Grant, later Lord Prestongrange (1700/01–1764), and three daughters. With his second wife Grant had two daughters. Grant conveyed the benefits of his matrimonial experiences in an extensive letter of advice to his eldest son on the subject of choosing a wife, recommending one who was 'plyabl; nor stiff and opinionate on some singularities' ('Advice to my son, concerning the qualities of a proper match', NA Scot., GD 345/799/1, fol. 2v).

Throughout his career Grant accumulated a range of honours. By patent dated 7 December 1705 he was created a baronet of Nova Scotia with remainder to his male heirs. In 1709 he was appointed an ordinary lord of session, and took his seat on the bench as Lord Cullen, his title derived from the name of his Banffshire estate, which he later sold. In 1713 he purchased the estate of Monymusk in Aberdeenshire. Grant denounced the Jacobite rising of 1715 in *A Key to the Plot* (1716), and served on the post-rising visitation commission to King's College, Aberdeen, where his presence did nothing to hinder his son-in-law, Alexander Garden of Troup, from being appointed professor of civil law (or civilist). On 17 May 1720 Grant obtained a grant of supporters and an addition to his coat of arms, taking as one of his mottoes the words 'Jehovah jireh', the only instance in Scottish heraldry of a Hebrew motto. Grant died 'without a cloud' (Wodrow, 3.282) at Edinburgh on 23 March 1726, and was buried in Greyfriars churchyard on 26 March. COLIN KIDD and CLARE JACKSON

Sources C. Jackson, 'Revolution principles, *jus naturale* and *jus gentium* in early Enlightenment Scotland: the contribution of Sir Francis Grant, Lord Cullen (c.1660–1726)', *European natural law theories: contexts and strategies in the early Enlightenment*, ed. T. Hochstrasser and P. Schröder [forthcoming] · J. Stark, *Lord Cullen, the first of the Monymusk Grants* (1912) · 'Some account of the life and character of Sir Francis Grant', NA Scot., Monymusk papers, GD 345/789 · *Biographia Britannica, or, The lives of the most eminent persons who have flourished in Great Britain and Ireland*, 4 (1757), 2256–7 · R. Wodrow, *Analecta, or, Materials for a history of remarkable providences, mostly relating to Scotch ministers and Christians*, ed. [M. Leishman], 4 vols., Maitland Club, 60 (1842–3), vol. 3, pp. 281–2; vol. 4, pp. 234–5 · F. Grant to J. Kirkwood, 29 Oct 1707, NL Scot., MS 821, fols. 142–4 · F. Grant, 'Advice to my son, concerning the qualities of a proper match', NA Scot., GD 345/799/1 · R. L. Emerson, *Professors, patronage, and politics: the Aberdeen universities in the eighteenth century* (1992), 29–30, 39–40, 113, 137 · 'Register of the resolutions & proceedings of a society for the reformation of manners', Sept 1700–Dec 1707, U. Edin. L., MS La.III.339 · J. Robertson, ed., *A union for empire: political thought and the Union of 1707* (1995), 159, 167, 224–5 · *Album studiorum academiae Lugdon Batavae* (?) MDLXXV–MDCCCLXXV (The Hague, 1875), 670 · J. M. Pinkerton, ed., *The minute book of the Faculty of Advocates*, 1: *1661–1712*, Stair Society, 29 (1976), 92 · matriculation list, 1684, Rijks Universiteit, Leiden, ASF 12, p. 250 · 'Recensielijsten', Rijks Universiteit, Leiden, ASF 55–57 · V. Durkacz, 'The source of the language problem in Scottish education, 1688–1709', *SHR*, 57 (1978), 28–39, esp. 35–6 · W. R. McLeod and V. B. McLeod, *Anglo-Scottish tracts, 1701–1714: a descriptive checklist* (1979) · T. Maxwell, 'The Presbyterian–Episcopalian controversy in Scotland from the revolution settlement till the accession of George I', PhD diss., U. Edin., 1954 · J. Warrick, *The moderators of the Church of Scotland from 1690 to 1740* (1913), 103 · *DNB*

Likenesses J. Smibert, oils, Scot. NPG [*see illus.*]

Grant, Sir Francis (1803–1878), portrait and sporting painter, was born on 18 January 1803 in Edinburgh, the fourth of seven children of Francis Grant (*d.* 1819), laird of Kilgraston, Perthshire, a landowner with estates in Scotland and Jamaica, and his wife, Anne Oliphant. His brother was General Sir James Hope *Grant (1808–1875). From the age of eleven to thirteen, Francis Grant attended Harrow School, and he finished his education at Edinburgh high school in 1818. Sir Walter Scott left the following account of the young Francis Grant in his journal of 1831:

> In youth, that is extreme youth, he was passionately fond of fox-hunting and other sports ... He also had a strong passion for painting, and made a little collection. As he had enough sense to feel that a younger brother's fortune would not last long under the expenses of a good stud and a rare collection of *chef-d'œuvres*, he used to avow his intention to spend his patrimony, about £10,000, and then again to make his fortune by the law. The first he soon accomplished. But the law is not a profession so easily acquired, nor did Frank's talents lie in that direction. His passion for painting turned out better. (*Journal*, 802–3)

Grant did study for the Scottish bar for one year, but he soon decided to make a career as an artist. In 1826 Grant married Amelia Farquharson, the daughter of a Scottish laird; Amelia died in 1827, after the birth of their son. Grant's second wife, Isabella Elizabeth Norman, whom he married in 1829, gave birth to three sons and four daughters during the course of their marriage. Isabella was a niece of the duke of Rutland, the leader of hunting society at Melton Mowbray, Leicestershire. Grant had frequented the hunts at Melton Mowbray since 1820, where he became acquainted with the sporting artist John Ferneley. He studied painting briefly with Ferneley, and possibly with Alexander Nasmyth in Edinburgh.

Grant's second marriage gave him access to many clients among the hunting set in Melton Mowbray, and his first successes were sporting pictures such as *A Meet of the Fife Hounds* (1833; Scot. NPG). In 1834 Grant's *The Melton Breakfast* (priv. coll.) was shown at the Royal Academy, and proved extremely popular as an engraving. In 1837 *The Meeting of his Majesty's Staghounds on Ascot Heath* (ex Christies, 31 May 1918) was accepted to the Royal Academy exhibition, and in 1855 it was awarded a gold medal at the Universal Exhibition in Paris. Grant's next major sporting picture, *The Melton Hunt Going to Draw the Ram's Head Cover* (exh. RA, 1839; Virginia Museum of Fine Arts), was praised for its accurate portrayal of thirty-six different riders, as well as its lively and varied composition. Unlike his earlier cabinet-sized hunting scenes, *The Melton Hunt Going to Draw* featured life-size figures in motion. In 1840, Grant received a commission to paint Queen Victoria. His *Queen Victoria Riding out* (exh. RA, 1840; Royal Collection) shows the queen taking exercise in Windsor Great Park with members of her household. Victoria's diaries provide an invaluable account of the process by which he painted

Sir Francis Grant (1803–1878), self-portrait, *c*.1845

such large, multi-figure equestrian portraits. Grant generally painted the horses in his studio, which was equipped for live animals. For the portraits, he often posed his sitters astride a wooden horse, and the queen described Lord Melbourne sitting to Grant 'on that wooden horse without head or tail, looking so funny, his white hat on, an umbrella in lieu of a stick' (Millar, 84). Many years later Willoughby de Broke contrasted his paintings favourably with photographs: the great painter of the English gentry, 'he was of their class; he knew how a well-bred man ought to sit on a well-bred horse, and he put him there, as few other artists ever could, plumb on the middle of the saddle' (Broke, 11).

The success of *Queen Victoria Riding out* allowed Grant to concentrate primarily on portraiture, as opposed to sporting painting, after 1840. Grant's success in this genre was unmatched by his contemporaries. The portraits he produced in the latter half of his career are notable for their large scale and broad brushwork, anticipating trends in later Victorian and Edwardian portraiture. He painted many of the famous figures of his day, including Queen Victoria and Prince Albert, in equestrian portraits for Christ's Hospital, London (exh. RA, 1846; governors of Christ's Hospital, London), Henry Hardinge, first Viscount Hardinge of Lahore (exh. RA, 1850; NPG), Benjamin Disraeli (exh. RA, 1852; NPG), Edwin Landseer (*c*.1852; NPG), John Russell, first Earl Russell (1853; NPG), and Thomas Babington Macaulay, Baron Macaulay (1853; NPG). Grant's success was often attributed to his good looks and aristocratic background, but his popularity was more probably due to the fact that he tempered the heroic intensity of Thomas Lawrence's windswept, Romantic portraits with

a dose of Victorian sobriety, while never forsaking gentle idealization of the face and figure of his sitter. His style complemented perfectly the aristocratic collections of his patrons, which often contained works by Van Dyck, Gainsborough, and Thomas Lawrence. Grant's portraits of women were particularly popular and well received. Important examples include *The Daughters of the Duke of Norfolk* (exh. RA, 1848; priv. coll.) and *Louise, Marchioness of Waterford* (1857; NPG). His most experimental portraits, such as *Daisy Grant* (exh. RA, 1857; ex Christies, 20 April 1990) and *Elizabeth Grant* (1851; RA), portray his own daughters.

Grant was also a distinguished and influential member of the Royal Academy. In 1866, after his friend Edwin Landseer declined the position, Grant was elected president of the Royal Academy; that same year he was knighted. As president, he negotiated the Royal Academy's 999-year lease on Burlington House, Piccadilly, London, for the rate of £1 a year, and oversaw its renovation. Grant introduced honorary memberships in 1868, and instituted the annual winter loan exhibition in 1870. According to Francis Frith,

> For 'dear old Grant', as we always called him, every member of the Academy … had the warmest affection … There was a rollicking, foxhunting kind of flavour about his speeches, he leapt over art questions, and just shook his whip at the students, or at the shortcoming of the exhibition. (Wills, 'Sir Francis Grant as a sporting painter')

Some critics accused Grant of promoting the interests of portraiture at the expense of other genres. In 1868 Grant lifted the ban on whole-length and half-length portraits being hung at eye level, or 'on the line', in the exhibition galleries. According to G. D. Leslie, 'Coincidentally with the invasion of the line by the life-sized portraits, the patronage hitherto given to subject-pictures began to fall lamentably, and in consequence of this a great number of distinguished painters, who formerly produced important works of figure subjects, began to take to portraiture' (B. Denvir, ed., *The Late Victorians: Art, Design and Society, 1852–1910*, 1986, 35).

After several years of failing health Grant died of heart disease at his country home, The Lodge, at Melton Mowbray, on 5 October 1878. Grant's family declined the honour of interment at St Paul's Cathedral, and Grant was buried on 12 October 1878 in the Church of England cemetery at Melton Mowbray, Leicestershire. He was survived by his wife.   A. CASSANDRA ALBINSON

Sources C. Wills, 'Sir Francis Grant as a sporting painter', *British Sporting Art Trust* (privately published, autumn 1992) · C. Wills, 'Sir Francis Grant's sporting pictures', *Country Life*, 185/44 (31 Oct 1991), 58–68 · C. Wills, 'Grant, Sir Francis', *The dictionary of art*, ed. J. Turner (1996) · J. Steegman, 'Sir Francis Grant, PRA: the artist in high society', *Apollo*, 79 (1964), 479–85 · Boase, *Mod. Eng. biog.*, vol. 6 · H. Valentine, ed., *Art in the age of Queen Victoria: treasures from the Royal Academy of Arts permanent collection* (1999) [exhibition catalogue] · *DNB* · *The Times* (7 Oct 1878), 6c · D. Irwin and F. Irwin, *Scottish painters at home and abroad, 1700–1900* (1975) · O. Millar, *The Victorian pictures in the collection of her majesty the queen*, 2 vols. (1992) · W. Sandby, *The history of the Royal Academy of Arts*, 2 (1862) · G. Jackson-Stops, ed., *The treasure houses of Britain: five hundred years* *of private patronage and art collecting* (1985) [exhibition catalogue, National Gallery of Art, Washington, DC, 3 Nov 1985 – 16 March 1986] · *The journal of Sir Walter Scott*, new edn (1891) · W. Hardie, *Scottish painting, 1837 to the present* (1990) · J. Egerton, *British sporting paintings: the Paul Mellon collection in the Virginia Museum of Fine Arts* (1985) · *Chambers's biographical dictionary*, ed. D. Patrick and F. H. Groome (1897) · Redgrave, *Artists* · W. de Broke, *The passing years* (1924) · *CGPLA Eng. & Wales* (1878)

Archives NL Scot., letters | BL, letters to W. E. Gladstone, Add. MSS 44412–44450 · BL, corresp. with H. Graves & Co., etc., Add. MS 46140 · LPL, letters to C. Longley · NPG, 'Sitters' Book' · RA, letters relating to tenure as president, MIS/GR/1–20 · U. Southampton L., corresp. with W. F. Cowper

Likenesses J. Watson-Gordon, oils, 1822, priv. coll. · J. Ferneley, group portrait, oils, 1823 (with his brothers John and Henry Grant), Leicester Museum and Art Gallery · F. Grant, self-portrait, oils, c.1840, NPG · F. Grant, self-portrait, oils, c.1845, NPG [*see illus.*] · D. O. Hill and R. Adamson, calotype, 1845, NPG · W. C. Ross, miniature, c.1846, priv. coll. · Count D'Orsay, plaster statuette, c.1847, priv. coll. · F. Grant, self-portrait, oils, c.1865, RA · J. Ballantyne, oils, 1866, NPG · M. Grant, marble bust, 1866, RA · M. Grant, plaster bust, 1866, NPG · C. B. Birch, double portrait, pencil drawing, c.1870 (with E. Landseer), NPG · Ape [C. Pellegrini], chromolithograph caricature, NPG; repro. in *VF* (29 April 1871) · Elliott & Fry, photograph, carte-de-visite, NPG · T. Fairland, lithograph (after J. Watson-Gordon, exh. RA 1846), BM, NPG · F. Grant, self-portrait, watercolour, Yale U. CBA · J. P. Knight, oils, Scot. NPG · J. Landseer, pencil sketch, Scot. NPG · D. Maclise, drawing, V&A · J. Noble, Parian ware bust, Royal Collection · J. Watkins and C. Watkins, cartes-de-visite, NPG

Wealth at death under £20,000—in the UK: probate, 27 Dec 1878, *CGPLA Eng. & Wales*

Grant, Sir George Macpherson-, third baronet (1839–1907), cattle breeder, landowner, and politician, was born on 12 August 1839, probably at Ballindalloch, Banffshire. He was the eldest son of Sir John Macpherson-Grant (1804–1850) and his wife, Marion Helen Campbell (1810–1855). His father was the second baronet and grandson of Sir George Macpherson, the first baronet, who had inherited the estate of Ballindalloch, Banffshire, as heir to his father's maternal uncle, General James Grant, adding the additional surname of Grant. George was educated at Harrow School and at Christ Church, Oxford, where he graduated in 1861. On 3 July 1861 he married Frances Elizabeth (d. 1916), daughter of the Revd R. Pocklington, vicar of Wallesby, Nottinghamshire, and returned to take charge of the family's 125,000 acre estates at Ballindalloch and Invereshie on attaining his majority later that year.

When Macpherson-Grant returned to his properties, the roots of breeding polled cattle were already well formed. While the fixation of specific breeds of cattle in England began about 1750, it was not until the beginning of the nineteenth century that Scottish farmers turned their attention to the perfection of pedigree livestock. Both his father and grandfather had been noted for taking a prominent part in improving the local breed of polled cattle at Ballindalloch, along with other landowners— Hugh Watson of Keillor (1789–1860) in the county of Angus and William M'Combie of Tillyfour (1805–1880) in Aberdeenshire. In 1835 his grandfather had employed James Mackay as manager, a post which he held for the next forty-one years, during the whole of which time he was engaged in managing and improving the Ballindalloch herd for three generations of his employers' family. While there was thus already a solid base to build on at Ballindalloch, Macpherson-Grant's and Mackay's purchase of the cow Erica 843, for 50 guineas, at the Kinnaird sale on the dispersion of the Watson herd in 1861, is considered the commencement of the 'Ballindalloch era' for polled or Aberdeen Angus cattle. Erica became, as part of the Ballindalloch herd, the founder of the premier family of the breed, producing eight calves between 1862 and 1872, when she died of an abscess at the age of sixteen. Of these calves four were bulls and four were heifers, and it is from the latter that the three recognized branches of the Erica family are drawn and defined by the bull: the Chieftain Ericas, the Kildonian Ericas, and the Trojan Ericas.

Aside from this breeding success that made Macpherson-Grant a world renowned figure, he was also instrumental in the general public presentation of the breed and in establishing its international reputation as the foremost producer of high-quality beef. About 1857 the *Herd Book* was restarted, the original having been destroyed by fire in 1851, and Macpherson-Grant was the main agent in the formation of the Polled Cattle Society (30 July 1879). Because of the sensitivities of whether to place Angus or Aberdeen in the foremost position, it not being clear where the breed lines first formed, it was not until 1886 that the *Herd Book* name of the breed became the Aberdeen Angus, and not until October 1907 that the society itself finally changed its name. Macpherson-Grant held office as president of the society for two terms in 1882–5 and 1891–3, his first term following Queen Victoria's acceptance of the role of patroness of the society in July 1881. She was followed in this office by successive monarchs. Macpherson-Grant was also president of the Highland and Agricultural Society in 1892, being the first 'commoner' president of that body.

In the 1865 parliamentary election Macpherson-Grant contested the seat for the county of Inverness, losing to the sitting MP by thirty-nine votes, and it was not until 1879 that he was elected as Liberal MP for Elginshire and Nairnshire, defeating the Conservative Brodie of Brodie with a majority of 258 votes. He was re-elected as a Liberal again in 1880, this time unopposed, and once again in 1885, defeating Brodie of Brodie who stood for the Conservatives, and C. H. Anderson who stood as an independent Liberal. In the home-rule crisis of 1885 he refused to follow W. E. Gladstone, and in the 1886 election moved to the Unionists, losing his seat by 119 votes to C. H. Anderson, who now stood as a home-ruler. In local politics he was convener of the county of Banff from 1868 to 1881, when he resigned because of the pressure of his parliamentary duties. Following his departure from Westminster he was re-elected to the position of Banffshire convener in 1887, finally retiring in 1896. He also held, until his death, the position of convener of the Banffshire Commissioners of Supply. He was appointed deputy lieutenant of Banffshire in 1860, of Inverness-shire in 1861, and of Morayshire in 1866. He was also a director of the Highland Railway Company from 1877 to 1903, and its chairman from 1897. As a central figure in the local community Macpherson-Grant also sat on parochial and other local boards, but it was his work in agriculture that was his greatest interest. Besides his national work as a livestock breeder, at the local level he devoted much of his time to assisting his tenants during the depression years from 1873 to 1896 and supporting the Spey, Aven and Fiddichside Farmers' Club, of which he was president.

In November 1907 Macpherson-Grant travelled south to Edinburgh, intending to winter in the south of England. While in Edinburgh he caught a chill, and remaining there a fortnight, died of heart failure on 5 December 1907. His body was returned to Ballindalloch Castle for the funeral, which took place on Tuesday 10 December. The numerous tenants and estate workers who turned out for the public funeral procession to the church at Inveravon were testimony not only to the high professional reputation he had earned by his work on the Ballindalloch herd but also to the great personal regard in which he was held locally as a considerate and caring landlord. There was no hearse, but a lorry, draped in the Grant tartan, drawn by two brown horses and flanked by gamekeepers, the piper piping 'Glengarry's Lament'. He was interred in the family vault in Inveravon churchyard, and was survived by Lady Macpherson-Grant, three sons, and a daughter. He was succeeded by Sir John Macpherson-Grant. There was still a herd of Aberdeen Angus cattle at Ballindalloch a century after his death.

RICHARD PERREN and ANDREW MASON

Sources J. R. Barclay and A. Keith, *The Aberdeen-Angus breed: a history* (1958) · *The Times* (6 Dec 1907) · *The Scotsman* (6 Dec 1907) · *Banff Journal* (17 Dec 1907) · W. M'Combie, *Cattle and cattle-breeders*, 4th edn (1886)
Archives NRA Scotland, 0771, NRA 17173 Macpherson
Likenesses W. Lehmann, oils, 1882 · photograph, repro. in *Banff Journal* (10 Dec 1907), 5 [supplement] · photograph, repro. in Barclay and Keith, *Aberdeen-Angus breed*, 33

Grant, George Monro (1835–1902), Presbyterian minister and educationist, was born on 22 December 1835 at Albion Mines, Pictou county, Nova Scotia. He was the third child of James Grant, farmer and district schoolmaster, who had emigrated from Banffshire in 1826, and Mary Grant of Inverness, formerly Mary Monro.

Owing to the accident of losing his right hand at the age of seven, Grant was brought up to be a scholar. At Pictou Academy he gained in 1853 a bursary tenable at either Glasgow or Edinburgh University. He chose Glasgow, and seven years later, on the completion of a distinguished course, he received his *testamur* in theology, and was ordained (December 1860) by the presbytery of Glasgow as a missionary for Nova Scotia.

After occupying various mission fields in his native province and in Prince Edward Island, Grant accepted a call in 1863 to the pulpit of St Matthew's Church, the leading Church of Scotland church in Halifax. He saw the need for a native-trained ministry for the established Presbyterian church in Nova Scotia, and struggled without success to establish a theological hall at Halifax, by way of supplement to Dalhousie College, which largely through his

efforts was reorganized as a non-sectarian institution in 1863. Meanwhile he directed his efforts to the union of the Presbyterian church throughout Canada. The federation of the provinces in 1867, which he eagerly supported, gave an impulse to the spirit of union, and 15 June 1875 saw the first general assembly of the united church.

On 7 May 1867 Grant married Jessie Lawson, the eldest daughter of William Lawson of Halifax, Nova Scotia. She died on 1 January 1901. Their only surviving child, William Lawson Grant (1872–1935), became principal of Upper Canada College, Toronto.

In 1877 Grant, who had for some years identified himself with educational reform, became principal of Queen's University, Kingston, Ontario, a Presbyterian foundation. He received the honorary degree of DD from Glasgow University in the same year. Queen's University was at the time in financial difficulties, and he undertook two strenuous campaigns in 1878 and 1887 to obtain increased endowment from private sources. The immediate financial situation saved, he concentrated his energies upon securing adequate recognition and aid from the provincial legislature; but he was faced by a prejudice against state-aided denominational colleges, which was encouraged by the claim of the University of Toronto to be the only properly constituted provincial university. In 1885 Queen's University rejected federation with Toronto. However, Grant's political influence steadily grew, and he secured for his university in 1893 a state-endowed school of mines, which subsequently became the faculty of practical science in the university. In 1898 he sought to sever the tie between the Presbyterian church and the arts faculty of Queen's. In 1900 he forced his views upon the church assembly, but he died two years later, and the assembly of 1903 reversed his policy, which was not enforced until June 1911. His powerful influence in education led to an invitation from Sir Oliver Mowat in 1883 to resign his principalship and accept the portfolio of education in his cabinet; Grant refused, believing that the education administration in the province should be wholly withdrawn from politics.

Grant acquired an intimate knowledge of Canada, having twice traversed the continent. In 1872 he accompanied Sandford Fleming on his preliminary survey of a route for the Canadian Pacific Railway, and in 1883, again with Fleming, he examined a route through the mountains. The first journey he recorded in *Ocean to Ocean* (1873), and the impressions of both journeys are merged in four articles contributed to *Scribner's Magazine* in 1880, and in *Picturesque Canada*, which he edited in 1884.

To the press and to periodicals Grant frequently communicated his views on public questions. His political comments in the *Queen's University Quarterly* were widely read. He powerfully supported the new imperialism, and urged on Canada her imperial responsibilities. He became president of the Imperial Federation League, Ontario, in 1889. To religious literature he contributed one book of importance, *Religions of the World* (1894). This was translated into many European languages and into Japanese.

To restore his health, which had been impaired by his

endowment campaign of 1887, Grant made a tour of the world in 1888. In 1889 he was elected moderator of the general assembly of the Presbyterian church in Canada, and became LLD of Dalhousie University in 1892. In 1891 he was elected president of the Royal Society of Canada. He was president of the St Andrew's Society, Kingston, from 1894 to 1896. From 1897 he actively opposed the temperance party, which aimed at the total prohibition of the liquor traffic. In 1901 he was created CMG. Grant died from a kidney disorder in Kingston on 10 May 1902. He was buried in Cataraqui cemetery in the same town.

PELHAM EDGAR, *rev.* C. A. CREFFIELD

Sources W. L. Grant and F. Hamilton, *Principal Grant* (1904) • *DCB*, vol. 13
Likenesses R. Harris, oils, 1889, Queen's University, Kingston, Ontario • H. McCarthy, bust, 1891, Queen's University, Kingston, Ontario

Grant, George Smith (1845–1911). *See under* Smith family (*per.* 1824–1975).

Grant, Sir (Alfred) Hamilton, twelfth baronet (1872–1937), administrator in India, was born in Edinburgh on 12 June 1872, the fifth and youngest son of Sir Alexander *Grant of Dalvey, tenth baronet (1826–1884), principal of Edinburgh University, and his wife, Susan (d. 1895), second daughter of James Frederick *Ferrier, professor of moral philosophy and political economy at St Andrews. He was educated at Fettes College, Edinburgh, from 1885 to 1890, and then at Balliol College, Oxford, where he was a rugby blue and graduated with third-class honours in classics in 1894, in which year he also passed the Indian Civil Service examinations. He was assigned to the Punjab commission and on 28 November 1896, while posted to Sialkot, married Mabel Bessie (d. 1910), fifth daughter of Thomas Heaton Lovett of Belmont, Shropshire, with whom he was to have a son and a daughter before Mabel's early death in 1910. In 1901, when Lord Curzon established the North-West Frontier Province as a separate unit, Grant was transferred to the government of India's foreign and political department which was responsible for administering the new province. He served as secretary to Sir Harold Arthur Deane, the first chief commissioner of the province, and also to Sir George Roos-Keppel, who succeeded Deane on his death in 1908. In 1904–5 he accompanied Sir Louis Dane on his mission to Kabul, and in 1908 he was appointed CIE. As he was still a young officer, the decoration was an indication that promotion lay ahead, and in 1912 he was made deputy secretary of the foreign department, with elevation to secretary following in 1914. He remained in this post throughout the war, serving under two Liberal viceroys in succession, lords Hardinge (1910–16) and Chelmsford (1916–21), with both of whom his own political views were largely in accord. He was appointed CSI in 1915 and KCIE in 1918.

Grant's most critical time as foreign secretary came in April 1919, when King Amanullah of Afghanistan launched an unprovoked attack upon India, precipitating the short-lived Third Afghan War. The British were never in serious military danger, but, wary of the Bolsheviks'

overtures to Amanullah and the passions the fighting had roused among the North-West Frontier Province tribes, the government of India was anxious to resume friendly relations with Afghanistan as soon as possible and therefore sought a solution which would save face on all sides. Grant, who was at the forefront of the negotiations, was distressed at the punishment Britain seemed intent on inflicting on Germany and her wartime allies, and he saw the Afghan talks as an occasion for showing to the world that Britain could be lenient and forgiving with repentant aggressors. Backed by Chelmsford, but largely on his own initiative, he negotiated an agreement at Rawalpindi in August 1919 whereby Britain agreed to surrender her old control of Afghanistan's foreign affairs. This concession was eventually incorporated in the treaty concluded in November 1921, but not before Lord Curzon and other imperial die-hards in London had poured scorn on Grant for imperilling British prestige.

In September 1919 Grant succeeded Roos-Keppel as chief commissioner of the North-West Frontier Province, but after several years of unremitting labour he was tired and in poor health. Moreover, although he claimed to be more amused than hurt by the home government's ungracious attitude towards his Afghanistan policy, his faith in Britain's political wisdom had been damaged. His letters to Chelmsford were increasingly gloomy, and he required constant reassurance that he was not seen as a weak administrator. This was a sore point with him, and in July 1920 he complained to Chelmsford that: 'We are always so afraid of appearing weak that we lose our opportunities of profitable generosity' (Grant to Chelmsford, 20 July 1920, BL OIOC, MS Eur. D. 660/25, fol. 57).

After a short and overdue period of leave Grant retired from the service in 1922 with the rank of KCIE, belated recognition of the success of his efforts to restore good relations with Afghanistan. On his return to Britain he became a director of the Northern Rhodesia Company, the General Co-operative Investment Trust, and several companies concerned with silver and oil production in Canada. He wrote occasionally for *The Times* on Indian matters and in November 1922 unsuccessfully stood as the Liberal candidate for Roxburghshire and Selkirkshire, the district which was home to the family of his second wife, Margaret Lucia (b. 1892/3), youngest daughter of Lieutenant Alexander Cochran RN, of Ashkirk, whom he had married at Calcutta on 12 March 1914.

Grant, known to his friends as Tony, was a familiar and popular figure on the golf courses of England and Scotland and also at White's Club, where he shone as a bridge player (the Rajah) and raconteur. He was a keen theatregoer and in the 1920s Lady Grant, under her maiden name of Miss Margaret Cochran, took to the London stage as the star performer in *The Good Old Days* at the Gaiety Theatre.

Grant died of a heart attack at his London home, 59 Onslow Square, on 23 January 1937. He had in the previous year succeeded to the baronetcy after the death of his only surviving brother, Sir Ludovic Grant, professor of public law at Edinburgh University, and the baronetcy now passed to his grandson, Duncan Alexander Grant (b. 1928), the son of his elder son, Alexander Lovett Grant (1901–1935), who had predeceased him. He was survived by his second wife, their son, Patrick, and daughters Esther and Guinevere—the latter of whom served as second officer with the WRNS during the Second World War—and his daughter with his first wife, Audrey Elizabeth Ferrier Grant.   KATHERINE PRIOR

Sources BL OIOC, Hamilton Grant MSS, MS Eur. D. 660 · *The Times* (25 Jan 1937), 1, 14 · Burke, *Peerage* (1959) · L. B. Poullada, *Reform and rebellion in Afghanistan, 1919–1929* (1973) · ecclesiastical records, BL OIOC · *The Fettes College list, 1870–1966* (1966) · *The historical register of the University of Oxford … to the end of Trinity term 1900* (1900) · *DNB*
Archives BL OIOC, corresp. and papers, Eur. MS D. 660 | BL OIOC, Chelmsford MSS · BL OIOC, Roos-Keppel MSS · CUL, corresp. with Lord Hardinge
Likenesses oils, *c.*1920, Government House, Peshawar, Pakistan · W. Stoneman, photograph, 1930, NPG · G. Glen, portrait, priv. coll.
Wealth at death £20,068 14s. 7d.: probate, 31 March 1937, CGPLA Eng. & Wales

Grant, Isabel Frances [Elsie] (**1887–1983**), promoter of Scottish Gaelic culture and writer, was born on 21 July 1887 at 34 Melville Street, Edinburgh, the eldest of the six children of Colonel Hugh Gough Grant CB (1845–1922), of the 78th and Seaforth Highlanders, and his wife, Isabel Mackintosh (1864–1960) of Balnespick. Isabel Grant, known familiarly from childhood as Elsie, was brought up in London and in the north of Scotland, particularly at Muchalls in Kincardineshire, details of which she was to recall in later writings. Her parents went to India when she was young, leaving her in London in the care of her grandfather Field Marshal Sir Patrick Grant, governor of Chelsea Hospital and gold stick-in-waiting to Queen Victoria, and with an unmarried aunt, Frances Gough Grant.

While living in London, Elsie Grant was educated privately with governesses; in the course of her education she frequently visited the British Museum, where she was inspired by the Elgin marbles and Greek and Roman sculpture. Although these were her earliest memories of museums, they were not her most formative ones. A visit to Stockholm and Oslo took her to the pioneering museum projects of Skansen in Sweden's Nordiska Museum and Norway's Sandvig collection at Lillehammer. Here the formal and conventional display of museum collections was combined with open-air collections of buildings and their contents, often moved from dispersed locations and re-erected on the site. The folk museum movement in Europe had grown in the 1870s out of the ideas and inspiration of the Swede Artur Hazelius, whose example had not been followed in Britain but whose work Elsie Grant admired. A visit to the Rijksmuseum in Amsterdam in 1912 showed her how the staff of a European national museum studied and presented 'peasant culture', methods particularly exemplified in the costume gallery.

From these experiences Elsie Grant developed her vision of a museum for the highlands of Scotland which would preserve a fast disappearing material culture and its Gaelic traditions and values. While adopting these examples, she nevertheless maintained that the concept of a folk culture of peasant communities was inappropriate to the Scottish highlands; she argued that the Gaelic way of life should be seen as the survival of an ancient and aristocratic culture rather than of the primitive and unsophisticated. The springboard for her highland folk museum was the Highland Exhibition held in Inverness in 1930, after which some of the 2100 exhibits were retained or acquired for a 'national folk museum'. This initiative failed to develop as envisaged but was carried forward by Elsie Grant personally when she used a legacy to purchase a building in Iona in which her folk museum was established in 1935. The collections soon outgrew this island site and the museum was moved to another property at Kingussie in Inverness-shire, where the museum, named Am Fasgadh ('The Shelter'), opened in 1944. It contained a unique wealth of highland and Hebridean artefacts, including domestic material and furniture, and the tools and implements of crofting and farming, demonstrating the distinctive identity of the material culture of highland history and also the rich variety evident between the regions and localities of a relatively small country. In addition she reconstructed four buildings on the site. The Highland Folk Museum was acquired for the four Scottish universities in 1954, when Elsie Grant decided to retire.

Elsie Grant was awarded the honorary degree of LLD by the University of Edinburgh in 1948 and the MBE in 1959. She was the author of more than a dozen books and a selection of articles, having developed her scholarly and critical faculties when working as a research assistant to J. M. Keynes during the First World War. This output included: her first and favourite work, *Everyday Life on an Old Highland Farm, 1769–1782* (1922), which analysed the farm accounts of a highland tacksman, a vilified class whom she persuasively defended; her seminal *The Social and Economic Development of Scotland before 1603* (1930); and the intriguing *The Lordship of the Isles* (1935). All are major works which still hold their place on university reading lists.

Elsie Grant was a tall and commanding figure whose temperament and determination matched the impression of a large physique. When she retired to Edinburgh, her hospitable flat in Heriot Row became a convivial meeting-place for the many Scottish scholars, young and old, invited to her often challenging soirées. She died, unmarried, at her home, Viewpoint, 22 Lennox Row, Edinburgh, on 19 September 1983, and her ashes were interred at Dalarossie, Strath Spey, on 25 September.

HUGH CHEAPE

Sources H. Cheape, 'Dr I. F. Grant (1887–1983): the Highland Folk Museum and a bibliography of her written works', *Review of Scottish Culture*, 2 (1986), 113–25 · I. F. Grant, *Along a highland road* (1980) · I. F. Grant, *The Highland Exhibition* (1930) · Edinburgh central library, I. F. Grant collection · *CCI* (1983) · private information (2004) · personal knowledge (2004) · *WWW*
Archives Edinburgh Central Reference Library · Highland Folk Museum, Kingussie · Mitchell L., Glas., corresp. mainly with Louie Ross and papers relating to Am Fasgadh
Wealth at death £165,010.73—in Scotland: confirmation, 1 Nov 1983, CCI

Grant, James, of Freuchie (1485?–1553). *See under* Grant family of Freuchie (*per.* 1485–1622).

Grant, James (1706–1778), vicar apostolic of the lowland district, was born at Wester Boggs, in the Enzie, Banff-shire, in July 1706, the son of Peter Grant and Anne Reid. He attended Scalan Seminary and was admitted into the Scots College at Rome on 16 January 1726; he was ordained priest in 1733. On his return to Scotland in 1735 he was appointed to the mission at Brae-Lochaber, to assist the Revd John Macdonald. In 1736 he was removed to the Isle of Barra. In 1746 ships landed soldiers there who threat-ened to desolate the island if the priest were not delivered up to them. Grant surrendered himself and was imprisoned in Mingarry Castle, on the west coast, where he was detained for some weeks. He was then moved to the prison at Inverness, and for several weeks was chained by the leg to another Jacobite sympathizer also held cap-tive. In 1747 he was released on bail, and from 1748 to 1759 he was stationed at Rathven, Banffshire.

Grant was nominated coadjutor to Bishop Alexander Smith, vicar apostolic of the lowland district, on 21 Febru-ary 1755, and papal briefs nominating him bishop of Sin-itis *in partibus* were issued on that date. He did not want the appointment, and at first opposed it, so that he was conse-crated in secret at Edinburgh only on 13 November in that year, retaining his charge of Rathven until 1759. On the death of Bishop Smith in 1767 he became, by right of suc-cession, vicar apostolic of the lowland district. He died on 3 December 1778 at Aberdeen, where he was buried at Snow churchyard.

THOMPSON COOPER, *rev.* ALEXANDER DU TOIT

Sources J. Darragh, *The Catholic hierarchy of Scotland: a biographical list, 1653–1985* (1986) · W. J. Anderson, ed., 'The college for the low-land district of Scotland at Scalan and Aquhorties: registers and documents', *Innes Review*, 14 (1963), 89–212 · P. J. Anderson, ed., *Records of the Scots colleges at Douai, Rome, Madrid, Valladolid and Ratis-bon*, New Spalding Club, 30 (1906) · J. F. S. Gordon, *Ecclesiastical chronicle for Scotland*, 4 vols. (1867) · C. Eubel and others, eds., *Hierarchia Catholica medii et recentioris aevi*, 8 vols. (Münster and Passau, 1913–78); repr. (Münster, 1960–82) · 'Vicars-apostolic of Scotland', *London and Dublin Orthodox Journal*, 4 (1837), 82–5 · N. M. Brady, *The espiscopal succession in England, Scotland and Ireland, 1400–1875*, 3 vols. (1877) · W. Forbes-Leith, ed., *Memoirs of Scottish Catholics*, 2 vols. (1909)

Archives Scottish Catholic Archives, Edinburgh

Grant, James, of Ballindalloch (1720–1806), army officer and colonial governor, was born in Ballindalloch Castle, Banffshire, Scotland, and baptized on 11 November 1720. He was the fifth of six children of Colonel William Grant (*d.* 1733), laird of Ballindalloch, and his wife, Ann (*d.* 1726), daughter of Ludovick *Grant of Grant. Both William and his eldest surviving son, Alexander, served the Hanover-ians as military officers. James, the younger son, became a relentless patronage hunter with a sometimes comical determination to 'have an Estate before I die' (Nelson, 10). He loved high living and died obese. Yet he was able, loyal, intelligent, charming, surprisingly idealistic, and brave. In 1731 he went to school in Edinburgh, and from 1736 read law at the university. But in September 1741 he aban-doned law for an ensign's commission in the Royal Scots.

James Grant of Ballindalloch (1720–1806), attrib. Allan Ramsay

He became a lieutenant in May 1742 and a captain in 1744. In 1745 he fought at Fontenoy before becoming aide-de-camp to General James St Clair; and in October 1746 he took part in the raid on Quiberon. In 1747–8 he accompan-ied St Clair on a mission to Vienna. From 1752 until 1755 he was tutor to St Clair's nephew, a student in Göttingen.

In 1757 Grant became major in Archibald Montgomery's highland battalion, which, after garrison duty in South Carolina, joined John Forbes's expedition of 1758 against Fort Duquesne. Grant quickly became Forbes's intimate and key adviser. But, sent to reconnoitre in force, he pro-voked a battle which ended with his defeat and capture. Exchanged, in 1760 he returned with Montgomery to South Carolina, now at war with the Cherokees. Both men sympathized with the Indians and, though they burnt the Lower Towns, they left the crops standing. After waiting for weeks for a peace delegation, they invaded the Middle Towns; but after a single battle near Etchoe, they took advantage of Amherst's orders to hurry back to New York.

In 1761 Grant (now a lieutenant-colonel with a local col-onelcy by brevet) reappeared in Charles Town with firm orders to crush the Cherokees. He moved slowly and only reluctantly destroyed the Middle Towns in the summer of 1761. In September he forced a conciliatory peace upon South Carolina, before joining the West Indies offensive in December. In 1763 Grant lost his colonelcy; but he did obtain the governorship of East Florida, reaching St Augustine in 1764. The colony attracted few settlers before his departure in 1771, although by then indigo had become a significant export, and Grant acquired for him-self a large plantation. Grant's most significant task was to reassure the Creeks, who were alarmed by the British conquests, by applying the imperial boundary policy of 1763. With John Stuart, superintendent of Indian affairs in the southern colonies, he negotiated a line calculated 'to Let our Creek Friends Breath a little' (Nelson, 56).

In 1770, when his nephew William died childless, Grant inherited Ballindalloch. The next year he went home on leave, but, once settled into the convivial life of a laird, he was not anxious to return to Florida. Besides, he was beginning a political career which might lead to a better government or to a prestigious military command. In April 1773 he was elected MP for Tain burghs and almost immediately resigned his governorship. In parliament Grant consistently supported the North ministry, but only partly because of his hopes of patronage. Convinced that most colonists were prisoners of a violent, republican minority, he preferred a blockade of America to reconquest. In 1775 Grant was recalled to active service, and on 30 July he arrived in Boston with the local rank of brigadier-general. On 11 December he received the long coveted colonelcy (in the 55th regiment), and two days later he became a major-general. He had lost none of his ingratiating charm, and was rumoured to have considerable influence over Howe. Grant's tactical sense was sound, if not always inspired or successful. It is true that in December 1776 he was surprised by Washington's thrust across the Delaware; and that in May 1778 he let Lafayette escape across the Schuykill. But he performed well at Brooklyn, Brandywine, and Germantown; and at Monmouth court house his division saved Clinton's baggage. The difficult West Indies campaign of 1778–9, an independent command, showed Grant to be an able strategist. But after falling ill, he left the Americas for the last time on 1 August.

In Britain, Grant divided his year between Ballindalloch and a house in Sackville Street, London. Though defeated in the 1780 election, he became a lieutenant-general and governor of Dumbarton Castle in 1782, and won another seat in 1787. He was re-elected in 1790, 1796, and 1801, retiring from parliament the following year at the age of eighty-one. Fidelity to Dundas and Pitt was rewarded with the command of Stirling Castle and of the king's troops in Scotland (1789) and promotion to general (1796). He voted only once against Pitt's wishes, on the Slave Trade Bill of 1791; Grant's liberal feelings about free Native Americans did not extend to black slaves. When in 1783 East Florida had been returned to Spain, Grant had sold his slaves and later obtained £3327 15s. compensation from the government. Though attached to his talented black cook Baptiste (whom he freed), he defended slavery to the last. In 1793 Grant was given command of the defence of northeastern England. But his age was too much for him and he retired from active service in 1796. He died at Ballindalloch Castle on 13 April 1806, and was buried in the castle grounds above the River Spey.

JOHN OLIPHANT

Sources P. D. Nelson, *General James Grant: Scottish soldier and royal governor of East Florida* (1993) • J. Oliphant, *Peace and war on the Anglo-Cherokee frontier, 1756–1763* (2000) • Ballindalloch Castle, Banffshire, Ballindalloch MSS • PRO, Amherst MSS, WO 34/47, 48 • E. Haden-Guest, 'Grant, James, of Ballindalloch, Banff', HoP, *Commons, 1754–90* • D. G. Henry and D. R. Fisher, 'Grant, James', HoP, *Commons, 1790–1820*

Archives BL, family MSS, Add. MSS 25905–25915 • NRA Scotland priv. coll., corresp. and MSS | Ballindalloch Castle, Banffshire, Ballindalloch MSS • BL, letters to Haldimand, etc. • BL, Add. MSS 38199, 38200, 38304, 38306, 38718, 33056, 36133, 41580, 24322 • NA Scot., letters to Sir Archibald Grant • NL Scot., legal corresp. with John Mackenzie • PRO, Amherst MSS, WO 34/47, 48 • PRO NIre., letters to G. V. Hart • U. Mich., corresp. with Thomas Gage • U. Mich., letters to J. Wemyss and W. Wemyss

Likenesses W. Staveley, oils, c.1785, priv. coll. • W. Staveley, oils, 1797, Scot. NPG • J. Kay, caricature, etching, 1798, NPG • attrib. A. Ramsay, oils, Dunrobin Castle, Sutherland [*see illus.*] • M. Rosenthal, caricature, engraving (after J. Kay), Hist. Soc. Penn. • attrib. W. Staveley, portrait, Scot. NPG • attrib. A. Waitt (as a child), Scot. NPG

Grant, Sir James, of Grant, eighth baronet (1738–1811), agricultural improver and politician, was born on 19 May 1738, the only son of Sir Ludovick Grant of Grant, seventh baronet (1707–1773), landowner, and his second wife, Lady Margaret Ogilvie, eldest daughter of James, fifth earl of Findlater and second earl of Seafield. Having been educated initially at Westminster School, he enrolled in February 1756 at Christ's College, Cambridge, and obtained his MA degree a year later. In 1758 he left the college in order to continue his education on the continent. Grant spent the latter months of 1758 until the middle of 1760 travelling to Geneva, Genoa, and Naples, as well as some time in Rome, where he met with Abbé Peter Grant of the Blairfindy Grants. Thereafter the abbé was to supply and indeed commission much of the art work that Grant continued to request from the continent until the mid-1760s.

After his marriage at Bath on 4 January 1763 to Jane Duff (d. 1805), only daughter and heir of Alexander Duff of Hatton, Aberdeenshire, Grant spent increasing amounts of time at Castle Grant, where, from 1765, he effectively managed the family's Inverness and Moray estates. Although he did not succeed his father until 18 March 1773, Grant was none the less the driving force behind the establishment of the planned villages of Grantown in 1765–6 and Lewiston in Urquhart in 1769. Much of the impetus to develop the estate commercially came about as a result of dire finances. By 1774, while income from the entire estate totalled £6650, the family's heritable debts stood at £130,000. The result was that between 1774 and 1785 sections of the estate to the value of over £52,500 were sold to near relations like the seventh earl of Findlater and Seafield, as well as kinsmen returning from successful careers in the East and West Indies.

Greater specialization in cattle grazing, as well as farm enclosure and consolidation, also ensured that from the early 1770s until 1804 the estate rental for Strathspey and Urquhart increased from £4284 to £9630. The result was that substantial emigration from these areas had emerged by the mid-1770s. Fearful for his farms' productivity, Grant opposed emigration outright and was to remain deeply suspicious of its social consequences throughout his life. Indeed he used all his political influence in an effort to persuade the government to intervene with legislation. On 19 April 1775, in a memorial to Henry Dundas, he argued:

> The state of the Highlands as to emigration really deserves the attention of government, notwithstanding the troubles in America that spirit is daily gaining ground. It is with regret, that I observe that government amongst the other regulations in regard to America has not proclaimed that no vessels loaded with emigrants are to be allowed to sail.   (NA Scot., GD 248/244/4/2)

Grant's linking of highland depopulation to political and military turmoil in the North American colonies not only was successful in that Dundas subsequently banned emigration, it also revealed just how astutely the region's landed class was able to participate within the arena of imperial politics.

More generally, Sir James was a prominent political force in the counties of Inverness-shire and Moray. He served as MP for Elginshire (Moray) (1761–8) and represented Banffshire (1790–95), and resigned the latter seat upon his appointment as general cashier of the excise for Scotland. Although he was a component element in Dundas's plans to balance the various electoral interests in the north-east of Scotland, Grant was noticeably independent. He became involved, for instance, in attempts to reform Scotland's voting system. By 1781 he had joined the Yorkshire Association, though by the early 1790s events in France had ended his espousal of limited political reform. Nothing better illustrates Grant's commitment to, and eagerness to defend, Britain's *ancien régime* than his recruiting record. On 1 March 1793 he was commissioned to raise a regiment of fencible infantry, with over 440 of the 740 men of the 1st battalion eventually being raised

from the counties of Inverness-shire and Moray. Less successfully, however, Grant also raised a line regiment, the 97th Strathspey Highlanders, in 1794. A year later, as the army rationalized its regimental structure, the unit was broken and drafted into older established regiments.

Yet, arguably, it was Grant's appointment in June 1794 as lord lieutenant of Inverness-shire that revealed his truly innovative and astute attitude towards Britain's mass military mobilization. While aware of their possible use as a defence mechanism, he quite deliberately used his authority to ensure that volunteer units operated as a bulwark against social disruption and emigration. When, in September 1801, these local units were threatened with disbandment on purely military grounds, Grant defended them as instruments of social stability. Volunteering, he admitted:

> augments the expence of government, yet very great advantages are derived from it in a political light. It keeps up a universal spirit of loyalty and good order. It is a great support to the people in bad seasons and is the most effectual check without appearance to that infatuated spirit of emigration which begun last year to prevail.   (NA Scot., GD 248/1530, pp. 104–6)

Indeed, such was Grant's faith in the influence of part-time military employment that, in October 1803, at a time when many offers of additional volunteers were being refused, he persuaded the government to allow a new battalion for the island of Skye, where, he argued, 600 people had been prevented from emigrating as a result of the Passenger Act legislation.

The death of his wife on 15 February 1805 hastened Grant's withdrawal from public life. In 1809 he resigned as lord lieutenant, though he retained something of his

Sir James Grant of Grant, eighth baronet (1738–1811), by Nathaniel Dance, *c.*1760 [left, with (left to right) John Mytton, the Hon. Thomas Robinson (later second Baron Grantham), and Thomas Wynne (later Baron Newborough)]

paternalistic influence on highland affairs through institutions such as the Highland Society of Edinburgh, of which he had been a founding member in 1784. Sir James died on 18 February 1811 at Castle Grant and was buried at Duthil. His eldest son, Sir Lewis-Alexander Grant, succeeded him to the lairdship of Grant before, on 5 October 1811, also becoming the fifth earl of Seafield.

ANDREW MACKILLOP

Sources D. J. Brown, 'Henry Dundas and the government of Scotland', PhD diss., U. Edin., 1989 · Scots peerage, vols. 4, 7 · W. Fraser, ed., The chiefs of Grant, 1 (1883) · minute book of the Highland Society of Edinburgh, NA Scot., RH1/188/1 · memorial on Sir James Grant of Grant's affairs, 1774, NA Scot., Seafield MSS, GD 248/26/2 · letter book of Sir James Grant, 1781–84, NA Scot., Seafield MSS, GD 248/533/1, GD 248/1540 · list of recruits of 1st fencible (Grant) regiment, NA Scot., Seafield MSS, GD 248/464 · NA Scot., GD 248/27/4, GD 248/49/4/20, GD 248/67/1/6, GD 248/248/66, GD 248/2894 and 2900, GD 248/244/4/2, GD 248/247/6/4, GD 248/227/1/58, GD 248/1530 · E. Haden-Guest, 'Grant, James', HoP, Commons, 1754–90, 2.531–2

Archives NA Scot., corresp., diary, papers

Likenesses N. Dance, group portrait, oils, c.1760, Yale U. CBA, Paul Mellon collection [see illus.] · W. Staveley, oils, 1797, Scot. NPG · J. Kay, caricature, etching, 1798, NPG

Grant, James, of Corrimony (1743–1835), advocate, was born on 13 April 1743 at his great-aunt's house of Rothiemurchus, Inverness-shire, the eldest of twelve children of Alexander Grant of Corrimony (1715/16–1797) and his wife, Jean Ogilvie. His father fought and was severely wounded at Culloden but otherwise escaped further penalty for his Jacobitism. James was educated at the parish school of Petty and at Edinburgh University before being apprenticed to John Syme, writer to the signet, on 24 June 1761. He opted for the bar and was admitted advocate on 24 February 1767.

Grant established a considerable practice, though his opposition to the government of the day blighted any chance of an official position. Among his friends were numbered Henry Erskine, Sir James Mackintosh, Francis Jeffrey, and Leonard Horner. He married, first, in 1779, Elizabeth Robertson, with whom he had two sons and two daughters. He married, second, Katherine Baillie Mackay (d. 1846), with whom he had a further six sons and four daughters.

An accomplished scholar as well as a talented musician, Grant's works included *Essays on the origin of society, language, property, government, jurisdiction, contracts, and marriage: interspersed with illustrations from the Greek and Gaelic languages* (1785), in which he drew on many classical texts as well as more contemporary accounts where European travellers had come into contact with indigenous peoples. He published *Thoughts on the Origin and Descent of the Gael* (1813) and provided the account of the parish of Urquhart and Glenmoriston for Sir John Sinclair's *Statistical Account of Scotland.*

Grant ran into financial difficulties that required him to put his estate in the hands of trustees in 1829. Four years earlier he had sold other property, at which time the barony of Corrimony passed out of family possession. He died, at the age of ninety-two, on 12 September 1835 at Lakefield, Glen Urquhart, Inverness-shire, and was buried

in the burial-ground of Claodh Churidan, Corrimony, on 15 September. An obelisk raised by public subscription bore an inscription by Lord Cockburn which described Grant as:

> Literary, amiable and independent, he was one of the very few of his class who, in his day, promoted those principles of political liberty which have since triumphed. He lived to be the oldest member of the Scottish Bar. He died the last of a race that for more than 350 years had inherited this glen. (Grant, *The Grants of Corrimony*, 27)

LIONEL ALEXANDER RITCHIE

Sources F. J. Grant, The Grants of Corrimony (1895), 21–32 · GM, 2nd ser., 4 (1835), 558–9 · F. J. Grant, ed., The Faculty of Advocates in Scotland, 1532–1943, Scottish RS, 145 (1944), 88 · Burke, Gen. GB (1952) · private information (1890) · DNB

Grant, James (1750–1808), East India Company servant and author, was born on 30 May 1750 at Shewglie, Glen Urquhart, Inverness-shire, the son of the laird of Shewglie. In 1768 he gained, via his uncle Alexander Grant, an appointment in Bengal with the East India Company. He arrived the following year but, because he did not get a regular position, his early years are difficult to trace in the company's records, which seem at times to confuse him with another James Grant then in Bengal. According to his own account, although not officially employed, he became involved in the Dacca district with collecting the revenue during the great famine that devastated Bengal in 1770. He returned to Great Britain in 1774, but went back to India, where he had a number of relatives; one of these, Charles *Grant, later became a dominant figure in the East India Company in London. He was sent to Masulipatam, in the territory known as the Northern Circars, which had been ceded to the company by the nizam of Hyderabad.

In 1781 Grant was appointed assistant to the company's resident at the nizam's court in Hyderabad, a position that required, according to Grant, getting the nizam to pay the company money that he had promised and convincing him that the British had no sinister designs on his territory (BL OIOC, Home miscellaneous series, 219.5). In the following year he became the resident, but remained in Masulipatam until his appointment ended in 1784, claiming ill health as an excuse for not going to Hyderabad. He spent his time in gathering information on the revenue system of the Northern Circars and of the neighbouring rulers, arguing that, while he had not been asked to do this, it was essential for the company to know the true value of its possessions. He had gained, he said, 'priceless knowledge of political arithmetic' that would become the foundation of a kind of empire that was 'perfectly new in the political history of the world' (Firminger, 2.164, 3.3). He continued his researches on the much larger and more important area of Bengal. These were first sent to the governor-general as a memorandum, part of which was later published in England as *An Inquiry into the Nature of the Zamindery Tenures in the Landed Property of Bengal* (1791).

The great question that the British had to answer as they took over rule in Bengal and elsewhere in India was, Grant said, 'Who owns the land?' He argued that in India, throughout recorded history, the sovereign was the sole and universal proprietor of the land. Private ownership of land in the European sense was unknown, and the peasants who worked the land paid, either directly to the sovereign or through intermediary officials known as *zamindars*, a part of the produce as rent for usage. As the central authority declined, these officials claimed to be the actual owners of the land, but were in fact, he insisted, only tax-collectors. His arguments had immediate practical significance, because, if true, the East India Company, which had replaced the Mughal emperor as sovereign, owned the land. Furthermore, he showed through a minute examination of land records that the Bengal territories were capable of providing far more revenue, as they had been under-assessed since the British took over, and, moreover, the *zamindars* were 'ignorant, merciless despots', who had stolen vast sums that should have gone to the company.

Grant's work was central to the ongoing debate over how Bengal should be governed, what the revenue assessment should be, and how the revenue should be collected. This involved him with the leading figures in the company's administration, including Warren Hastings and Philip Francis. His views were strenuously opposed by John Shore, adviser to the governor-general, Lord Cornwallis, who argued that while Grant had done an astonishing amount of work, it was based on a misreading of the record. In practical terms, what mattered was that the company had neither the personnel nor the knowledge to do without the *zamindars*. Shore therefore insisted that a revenue settlement should be made with them as *de facto* owners of the land. Grant's knowledge of the details of revenue collection was recognized by his appointment in 1785 to the office of *sheristadar*, or keeper of accounts, to prevent fraud on the part of the local accountants. There is not much evidence that he had the administrative skills or the power, despite his vast knowledge, to bring about any real changes. Nevertheless, as a critic of his work has put it, students of the history of Bengal and Bihar must turn to his researches when they undertake 'to recover the past history of any given district within these provinces' (Firminger, 2.xviii). In addition to his study of zamindary tenures Grant also published *A Political Survey of Northern Circars* (1784) and historical and comparative analyses of the finances and revenues of Bengal (1786 and 1788).

When under John Shore's influence the office of *sheristadar* was abolished in 1789, Grant was offered a post as collector, or chief official of a revenue district. This, however, he refused and returned to Scotland. He purchased the Redcastle estate in Ross-shire, styling himself 'Grant of Redcastle'. He proposed marriage to Maria Grant, the daughter of his cousin Charles Grant, who had also returned from Bengal a wealthy man, but she refused him, perhaps because she was thirty years younger, but also because James did not share the intense evangelical religious views of her father. Charles Grant had once commented, after James had visited him in Bengal, that, while his knowledge of Indian revenue systems 'must set him before all that have yet treated of them', he was 'filled with this world and regardless of another' (Morris, 83). Maria remained on good terms with him, however, and she was with him when he died, unmarried, on 22 October 1808, at Ruxley Lodge, near Esher in Surrey. His cousin Colonel Alexander Grant inherited Redcastle, but he left legacies to Maria and her sisters. AINSLIE T. EMBREE

Sources personal records, BL OIOC, O/6, appointments, 1; biographical sketches, 1; memos, xix, xx; writers' petitions, J/1/4 · BL OIOC, Home misc., 211.6, 219.2, 5, 79.359-63 · W. K. Firminger, ed., *The fifth report from the select committee of the House of Commons on the affairs of the East India Company, dated 28th July, 1812*, 3 vols. (1917-18) · H. Morris, *The life of Charles Grant* (1904) · F. D. Ascoli, *Early revenue history of Bengal* (1917) · R. Guha, *A rule of property for Bengal: an essay on the idea of permanent settlement* (Paris, 1963) · *GM*, 1st ser., 78 (1808), 1042 · correspondence of Warren Hastings, BL, Add. MS 29150 · *Memoirs of William Hickey*, ed. R. Hudson (1995)
Archives BL OIOC, India Office records

Grant, James (1802–1879), newspaper editor and historian, was born in Elgin, Morayshire. He was possibly a baker originally, but entered journalism at the age of nineteen as a contributor to *The Statesman* and other newspapers. In 1827 he helped to launch the *Elgin Courier* and was editor until 1833. He then left for London, but still kept an interest in the *Courier*. His first job in London was as a reporter under Stanley Lees Giffard on the newly launched *Standard*. From there he moved to the *Morning Chronicle* and later the *Morning Advertiser*, the organ of the Licensed Victuallers' Association. A peripatetic journalist during this period, he also found time to edit and launch other publications, including the *London Saturday Journal* (1839) and *Grant's London Journal* (1840).

For many years Grant was a gallery reporter, and his *Random Recollections of the Houses of Lords and Commons* (1836) was widely read. In 1850 he was appointed editor of the *Morning Advertiser*, and was to hold that position until 1871. During his editorship, in 1858, he had been the prime mover to accept Reuters telegrams free for a fortnight on trial, and then at a cost of £30 per month for a full service—£10 less than he was paying another party—leading to the newsagency's long association with national newspapers.

According to one account Grant was 'a right good fellow' and 'by no means over-exacting' towards his subordinates. But he was none the less 'an excellent reporter and a capable editor' (*Life and Adventures of George Augustus Sala*, 2.28). He was also a devout Calvinist, and in 1872 became editor of the *Christian Standard*. Despite his full-time journalism over many years he still found time to write almost forty books—very many of them touching on theological subjects—but these are now mainly forgotten. The one exception, however, despite being marred by inaccuracies, *The Newspaper Press; its Origins, Progress and Present Position* (3 vols., 1871-2), is rightly regarded as a classic. His other publications included biographical works, including a *Life of Mary Queen of Scots* (1828), several books on life in London, and accounts of Ireland, Paris, and a journey across the continent. He died at 35 Cornwall Road, Bayswater, London, on 23 May 1879, leaving at least one child, John Miller Grant, a stock- and sharebroker.

D. M. GRIFFITHS

Sources *The Times* (26 May 1879) · *N&Q*, 4th ser., 10 (1872), 55 · *N&Q*, 11 (1855), 451 · *N&Q*, 6th ser., 2 (1880), 15 · *Catalogue of the Advocates' Library* · catalogue [BM] · D. Griffiths, ed., *The encyclopedia of the British press, 1422–1992* (1992) · *The life and adventures of George Augustus Sala*, 2 (1895), 27–30 · G. L. M. Strauss, *Reminiscences of an old bohemian*, 2 vols. (1882)
Archives Boston PL, letters and papers
Likenesses photograph, priv. coll. · portrait, repro. in R. Boston, *The essential Fleet Street* (1990), 94 · wood-engraving, NPG; repro. in *ILN* (14 June 1879)
Wealth at death under £9000: probate, 2 July 1879, *CGPLA Eng. & Wales*

Grant, James (1822–1887), novelist and writer on history, was born on 1 August 1822 at Edinburgh, the eldest son of John Grant, captain in the Gordon Highlanders, and his wife, eldest daughter of Captain Andrew Watson. His paternal grandfather was James *Grant of Corrimony (1743–1835), advocate and Jacobite sympathizer. Through his mother, who died in 1833 (when he was a child), he was related to Sir Walter Scott and other eminent families.

Grant's father had served with distinction throughout the Peninsular War, and after his wife's death he obtained a command in Newfoundland; he sailed there in 1833, taking with him his three sons. After spending six years in North American barracks James returned home with his father, who had resigned his command. In 1840 James was appointed ensign in the 62nd foot regiment, based at Chatham; he was soon afterwards appointed commander of the depot, but in 1843 he resigned his commission and entered an architect's office in Edinburgh. He became a skilled draughtsman, but at this time he began to show a literary bent, and devoted himself to novel writing.

Grant's first novel was his four-volume *Romance of War* (1845), describing adventures of the Gordon Highlanders in the Peninsula, based on anecdotes related to him by his father. It enjoyed enormous sales, but produced only £20 for its author. In 1846 he published a sequel, *The Highlanders in Belgium*. *The Adventures of an Aide-de-Camp* (1848) equalled the popularity of his first novel. It was followed by *Jane Seton* (1853) and *The Yellow Frigate* (1855), and from this point on Grant produced at least one novel per year, including a number based on Scottish history. Their appeal was based on a quick succession of incident, vivacity of style, and convincing dialogue. Grant married Christian Macdonald, the eldest daughter of James Browne, and had two sons: James (who predeceased him) and Roderick. In 1852 he founded and acted as secretary to the National Association for the Vindication of Scottish Rights, upholding its principles in spite of the mockery of *Punch* and other English newspapers. He was an energetic supporter of the volunteer movement, and was one of the first to join its ranks. He was consulted frequently by the War Office as an authority on military matters, and many of his suggestions were adopted. In 1875 he converted to Roman Catholicism, his son Roderick having become a Roman Catholic priest.

In addition to fifty-six novels, Grant wrote widely on history, including *Memoirs of Montrose* (1851), *British Battles on Land and Sea* (1873), an *Illustrated History of India* (1876), and *Old and New Edinburgh* (1880). His last works of fiction were *Playing with Fire* (1887), a topical novel based on the war in the Sudan, and *Love's Labour Won* (1888), set in Burma. By the 1880s his popularity had declined, and he died in relative poverty on 5 May 1887 at his home, 25 Tavistock Road, Westbourne Park, London. He was survived by his wife.

M. G. WATKINS, *rev.* DOUGLAS BROWN

Sources Boase, *Mod. Eng. biog.* · Irving, *Scots.* · Allibone, *Dict.* · L. C. Sanders, *Celebrities of the century: being a dictionary of men and women of the nineteenth century* (1887) · J. F. Waller, ed., *The imperial dictionary of universal biography*, 3 vols. (1857–63) · W. D. Adams, *Dictionary of English literature*, rev. edn [1879–80] · J. Sutherland, *The Longman companion to Victorian fiction* (1988) · *CGPLA Eng. & Wales* (1887)
Archives NL Scot., corresp. and papers, MSS 8876–8885 | BL, letters as sponsor of the Royal Literary Fund, loan no. 96 · NL Scot., letters to William Blackwood & Sons
Wealth at death £490 3s. 6d.: administration, 8 June 1887, *CGPLA Eng. & Wales*

Grant, James (1840–1885), antiquary, born in Glen Urquhart, Inverness-shire, was educated at Aberdeen University, where he took the degree of MA. He obtained the Grant bursary, and studied law at Edinburgh with a view to the Scottish bar; but his grotesque dwarfish figure and his odd voice making success in this well-nigh unattainable, he devoted himself to studies connected with Scottish antiquities.

For a number of years Grant acted as assistant to Professor Cosmo Innes (whose books owe a good deal to him), and did much work under John Hill Burton and David Masson in preparing for publication the Scots privy council records. The work by which Grant deserves to be remembered, however, is his *History of the Burgh and Parish Schools of Scotland* of which only the first volume was published (1876), though the second was nearly finished. Based largely on unpublished sources, the book is a quarry for Scottish educational and social history. Grant also wrote a 'History of the University of Edinburgh' (unpublished). He was elected an FSA (Scotland), and enjoyed the friendship and esteem of David Laing and other distinguished Scottish scholars. He died at his brother's house, 114 Bell Terrace, Newcastle upon Tyne, on 9 August 1885, and was buried on 13 August in Glen Urquhart.

FRANCIS WATT, *rev.* H. C. G. MATTHEW

Sources *The Scotsman* (10 Aug 1885) · *The Scotsman* (14 Aug 1885) · *Inverness Courier* (13 Aug 1885) · K. Burton, *Memoir of Cosmo Innes* (1874)
Wealth at death £1482 15s. 8d.: confirmation, 1 Dec 1885, *CCI*

Grant, James Augustus (1827–1892), explorer in Africa, was born at Nairn, Scotland, on 11 April 1827, the fifth child and fourth son of James Grant (1790–1853), Church of Scotland minister at Nairn since 1815, and his wife, Christian, daughter of John Mackintosh. He was educated by private tutors and then successively at Nairn Academy and Aberdeen grammar school, and went on to Marischal College in Aberdeen in 1841 as a 'private' (that is, a nongraduating) student. For two years he attended lectures in natural philosophy, chemistry, and mathematics, as well

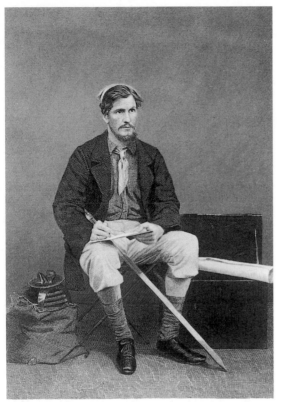

James Augustus Grant (1827–1892), by Samuel Hollyer (after Urquhart)

as classes that were to have considerable importance for him later on—those with Professor MacGillivray on natural history and with Dr Mathews Duncan on botany. During the two summers of his time at the college, he took further semi-official classes which were also to prove a significant influence upon him: these were in drawing and perspective with Patrick Auld, a Scottish artist of some note.

James Augustus Grant of Viewfield, a kinsman, after whom Grant was named, helped to secure the young man a commission in the 8th native Bengal infantry and he sailed for India in 1846. He was soon involved in the Second Anglo-Sikh War and other campaigns before being appointed adjutant of his regiment in 1853. When, with many others, his regiment mutinied in 1857, Grant was attached to the 78th highlanders. At the relief of Lucknow, he lost his right thumb and forefinger and was soon afterwards returned home on sick leave.

In 1852 Grant had spent some time shooting tigers with his friend and fellow Indian army officer, John Hanning Speke, who in 1859 invited his companion to join the Royal Geographical Society Nile expedition. Speke hoped to prove his contention that Lake Victoria, which he had discovered in 1858, was the source of the Nile. The two explorers and their porters now embarked on the 'long walk' on which Palmerston was later to remark and so provide Grant with the title of his book, *A Walk across Africa* (1864). It took them inland from the east African coast to Tabora and then northwards around the western shores of Lake Victoria to the kingdom of Buganda and ultimately down the Nile valley to Egypt. Grant himself had been delayed by a badly ulcerated leg in Karagwe for some months and did not reach Buganda until May 1862. There had been other delays and separations of the travellers, for they had been moving through a region much disturbed by the effects of demands from the outside world for its products—principally ivory and slaves. Arab and Swahili traders, petty or great African rulers, all vied with one another in trying to take advantage of the situation and the explorers' caravan inevitably became caught up in the intrigues and hostilities. For most of the time they were strong enough not to be completely at the mercy of those they met, but they were rarely strong enough to dominate any situation. Obtaining porters was always difficult and Grant, who was in independent command of sections of the expedition on several occasions, learned patience and tact.

Despite all the difficulties Grant pursued his researches into natural history, collected plants, and created a visual record of the journey. About twenty-five photographs had been taken in Zanzibar and these form an important record; but Grant found the dark tent and the other equipment too difficult to use and to have carried on the march and so soon reverted to making drawings and watercolours. No fewer than 147 of these works survive and are bound into two large portfolios; there are also further unmounted pictures. Some limited use of these drawings was made in Speke's (but, oddly, not in Grant's own) book, but they were refashioned and 'improved' by engravers and it was not until the whole collection came into the possession of the National Library of Scotland in 1982 that their full worth as the first visual record of a vast tract of eastern Africa became apparent. As well as sketching, Grant recorded his impressions in great detail in a large journal, 320 pages of which are filled with notes in minuscule handwriting. This ranks as one of the most remarkable extant firsthand records of the great nineteenth-century African exploratory expeditions.

Mutesa, the kabaka of Buganda, and his well-ordered and sophisticated yet brutal kingdom made a great impression on Grant. His visual record of the people and buildings is particularly important. When Mutesa finally allowed the two men to depart in July 1862, a guide took them too far north and it was Speke alone who made a 'flying march' back to what he named the Ripon Falls where the Nile debouches from Lake Victoria. Although he denied it in his published work after the tragic death of Speke, and loyally continued to deny it for the rest of his own life, there are some indications that Grant was disappointed and even somewhat resentful that he was not able to share in the glory of identifying the source of the Nile. Partly because there was no second testimony, it was possible for Speke's finding to be doubted for another dozen years. Immediately after Speke's discovery, the two men had rejoined each other and visited another considerable kingdom, Bunyoro, before proceeding down the Nile valley to Egypt.

Grant shared in the fame which resulted from the expedition, receiving the Royal Geographical Society's gold medal in 1864. *A Walk across Africa* (1864), his own account of the journey, is slightly disappointing; besides there being no illustrations, it reflected relatively little of the richness of observation available in the journal. On 25 July 1865 he married Margaret Thompson Laurie, who was the daughter of Andrew Laurie, and grandniece to a lord mayor of London and the heir to considerable riches; it was apparently a happy marriage. Somewhat tardily, Grant was appointed CB in the following year. Despite the fame and the material comfort available to them, the couple went to India when Grant elected to continue his career in the Indian army and was attached to the 4th Gurkha regiment. Then Sir Robert Napier decided to draw on Grant's African experience by appointing him second-in-command of intelligence when the great expedition to Ethiopia to destroy the emperor Theodore's power was mounted in 1867. Grant organized transport services in preparation for the final assault on Magdala and was awarded the Star of India. After this he retired from the army with the rank of lieutenant-colonel in 1868.

The rest of Grant's life was divided between Nairn and London. In Nairnshire he became a JP and deputy lieutenant for the county and he purchased a local property, Househill. His old university, now Aberdeen, gave him an honorary degree in 1890. In London he took a leading part in the activities of various societies, especially the Royal Geographical, serving on its council for the best part of twenty years. He became one of a small group of people influential in matters to do with Africa, for example advising the Church Missionary Society on its proposed work in Uganda. In 1876 King Léopold invited him to attend the Brussels Geographical Conference which was to have such important consequences for the future of Africa.

In the early 1870s Grant published a series of scientific papers on the results of the Nile expedition. A ninety-nine page article for the RGS *Journal* (1872) was followed by three contributions to the Linnean Society's *Proceedings* (1873–5), which included details of the 113 previously unknown species of plants that he had brought home. His other important publications were *Potato Diseases* (1873), and *Khartoom as I Saw it in 1863* (1885).

Grant was a tall and imposing figure. Yet he was rather shy and self-effacing. He was apparently well liked by most of his contemporaries. As a man of his time, he had little doubt about the benefits that would accrue to Africa if it were taken under European tutelage and ultimately colonial rule and in his later life he was working towards this end. If in this sense he was an imperialist, he was also one who thought in terms of responsibilities and duties rather than rewards. His two sons became involved in African schemes. Grant died at Househill on 11 February 1892, survived by his wife, and his coffin was borne to the grave in Nairn cemetery by men of the 78th highlanders, the regiment with whom he had served at Lucknow. He was somewhat underrated, perhaps because, although a member of the successful Nile expedition of 1860–63, he did not himself visit the actual source of the river. Yet his

scientific approach, his remarkable written and visual records of east Africa, and his later career mark him out as a considerable figure.   ROY BRIDGES

Sources [J. A. Grant], *Memoranda: J. A. Grant* (privately printed, [1886]) [a record of his life; copy in Aberdeen University Library] · R. C. Bridges, 'James Augustus Grant's visual record of east Africa', *Hakluyt Society Annual Report for 1993* [1994], 12–24 · J. A. Casada, 'James A. Grant and the Royal Geographical Society', *GJ*, 140 (1974), 245–53 · *Blackwood*, 151 (1892), 573–81 · R. C. Bridges, 'John Hanning Speke: negotiating a way to the Nile', *Africa and its explorers*, ed. R. I. Rotberg (1970), 95–137 · *DNB*
Archives NL Scot., corresp. and papers · RBG Kew, botanical notes · RGS, letters to Royal Geographical Society
Likenesses S. Hollyer, stipple (after photograph by Urquhart), NPG [*see illus.*] · C. Smith, oils, Nairn County Buildings · Watts, portrait; formerly in possession of Mrs Grant · commemorative window, U. Aberdeen, Mitchell Hall, Marischal College · memorial plaque, St Paul's Cathedral, London · photographs, RGS · portrait, repro. in *ILN* (4 July 1863) · stipple, NPG
Wealth at death £14,466 9s. 10d.: probate, 2 July 1892, *CGPLA Eng. & Wales*

Grant, Sir James Hope (1808–1875), army officer, was born on 22 July 1808 at Kilgraston House, Bridge of Earn, Perthshire, the youngest son of Francis Grant (d. 1819), of Kilgraston House, Perthshire, and his wife. His eldest brother was Sir Francis *Grant, the artist and president of the Royal Academy. Grant was educated at Edinburgh high school, and at Hofwyl, near Bern in Switzerland. In February 1847 he married, at Agra, Elizabeth Helen (d. 1891), daughter of Benjamin Tayler of the Bengal civil service.

Grant was gazetted into the 9th lancers as a cornet in 1826 and served with them for the next fourteen years in various garrisons in the United Kingdom. He was promoted lieutenant in 1828, captain in May 1835, and briefly acted as aide-de-camp to Major-General Lord Greenock during 1837. As well as displaying considerable ability as a soldier, Grant was an enthusiastic sportsman and musician. He was appointed in 1841 brigade major to Major-General Lord Saltoun, who had been ordered to assist Sir Hugh Gough during the First Anglo-Chinese War, on the recommendation of Sir David Baird, largely because of his ability to entertain senior officers by playing the violoncello during the lengthy outward voyage. On 13 December 1841 Grant embarked on HMS *Belleisle* and landed in China in June 1842. He served in the First Anglo-Chinese War and was present at the attack and capture of Chinkiang (Zhenjiang) and at the landing before Nanking (Nanjing). On 22 April 1842 he was promoted major. Following the signing of a peace treaty the British force embarked on 15 September 1842 for Hong Kong. For his services in China, Grant was made a CB in 1843. He remained under Saltoun's command at Hong Kong and was appointed assistant adjutant-general, a post he held until February 1844.

Grant landed at Calcutta, India, in March 1844 and rejoined the 9th lancers, who were then stationed at Cawnpore. He briefly commanded them, then served in the Sutlej campaign during the First Anglo-Sikh War (1845–6). He was present at the bitterly contested battle of Sobraon (10 February 1846), where the 9th lancers were chiefly employed protecting the horse artillery deployed on the left flank of Sir Harry Smith's division. Following the battle Grant seriously endangered his own career when he accused his commanding officer of being drunk on duty during the battle. Grant was promptly arrested for insubordination, but a court of inquiry that assembled six weeks later awarded an open verdict and he returned to his regiment. Owing to the absence of senior officers, Grant led the 9th lancers during the Second Anglo-Sikh War, in which it was engaged at the passage of the Chenab River at Ramnagar, and at the decisive battles of Chilianwala (13 January 1849) and Gujrat (21 February 1849). For his services he received the brevet of lieutenant-colonel.

The 9th lancers garrisoned Wazirabad following the Second Anglo-Sikh War and after the death of two senior officers in 1849 Grant was promoted lieutenant-colonel and given command of the regiment. His health deteriorated, however, and in February 1851 he returned to Britain on sick leave. In March 1854 he and his wife returned to India, and on 28 November of that year Grant was promoted full colonel. He was stationed at Ambala when the Indian mutiny broke out in May 1857. He was appointed brigadier of the cavalry which marched from Ambala to relieve Delhi, and on 8 June fought in the engagement at Badli-ki-sarai. Grant was made responsible for the security of the encampment on the ridge during the four-month siege of Delhi. He led his vastly outnumbered cavalry squadrons on numerous occasions in hand-to-hand fighting with rebel horsemen, and displayed considerable skill in organizing the outposts surrounding the encampment. On one occasion he narrowly escaped death when his horse was killed under him and he had to be dragged from the mêlée by his orderly in order to escape pursuing rebels. He led the cavalry brigade—moving in support of Major Reid's column—during the final assault on the city (14 September), where it suffered heavy losses from rebel artillery fire. Following the capture of Delhi, on 24 October, at Agra, Grant took command of a mobile column which soon after fought a successful engagement at Kali Nadi. The column then moved to Cawnpore where it formed the main part of the force assembling to relieve the beleaguered British garrison holding out at the Alambagh and the residency in Lucknow. Grant advanced across the Ganges on 30 October, but the following day he was ordered to halt to await the arrival of the commander-in-chief from Cawnpore. When Sir Colin Campbell arrived at Bunthira on 9 November Grant was promoted brigadier-general and allowed to retain command of the relieving force, with Campbell exercising only general supervision of the operations.

The British force first seized the Martinière on the outskirts of the city, and then on 16 November fought their way towards the residency by way of the *sikandarabagh*, the Shah Najafmosque, and the mess house. When the Moti Mahal was secured Grant was one of the first to greet Sir Henry Havelock after the defenders of the residency made contact with the relief column. The city was evacuated on 22–3 November, and all the non-combatants were escorted across the Ganges to Cawnpore, from where they were sent to safety at Allahabad. Under the overall command of Sir Colin Campbell, Grant and his command defeated a large force led by Tantia Topi which had threatened the town in early December during the third battle of Cawnpore. Grant led a flying column in pursuit of the rebels which brought them to battle at Serai Ghat and then at Goorsaigunj, with the support of the Cawnpore force which had joined him earlier at Chabepore.

After Sir Colin Campbell went to Allahabad, Grant took command at Unao, on 8 February 1858, of all the British troops concentrated between Cawnpore and Bunni. On 20 February he was appointed major-general (for 'distinguished service') and general of the cavalry, as well as being awarded a distinguished service pension of £200 per annum. When Campbell returned, Grant led a small expedition to Fatehpur Churassie, in pursuit of Nana Sahib; they camped overnight outside the town of Bungurmow, and Grant, a strict disciplinarian, ordered the flogging of twelve men of the 53rd regiment who had been caught looting the town while supposedly on guard duty. On 23 February his troops captured the town of Meangunj, held in strength by the rebels, before being ordered by Campbell to return. Grant rejoined the main body of British troops at Bunthira, in Oudh, from where the advance on Lucknow resumed. Following the capture of the city after heavy fighting later that month, Grant was once again placed in overall command of several mobile columns pursuing the remaining organized bodies of rebels in Oudh; they successfully engaged the enemy at Koorsie, on the Baree Road, and at Sirsi, Nawabgunj, and Sultanpur. Finally Grant commanded the trans-Gogra force during the last stages of the suppression of the uprising, running to earth the last remaining bodies of rebels and preventing their escape across the border into Nepal. It was during these operations that he first made the acquaintance of Garnet Wolseley, whose skill as a staff officer so impressed Grant that he helped advance his later career. For his services during the uprising Grant was made a KCB in 1858, although his promotion to major-general had been at considerable personal cost as he forfeited the value of his commission amounting to £12,000.

In 1860 Grant was nominated to command, with the local rank of lieutenant-general, a joint Anglo-French expedition sent to China. He sailed in February from Calcutta to Hong Kong, which formed the main base of operations. The combined force landed on 1 August near the town of Pehtang (Beitang), and successfully attacked the village of Sinho. However, there followed a serious disagreement between Grant and the French commander, Lieutenant-General Cousin de Montauban, about how to capture the Taku (Dagu) forts, mounting over 600 guns, which blocked the Peiho (Beihe). On 21 August Major-General Sir Robert Napier's 2nd division, supported by all the available artillery, followed Grant's plan and led the assault on the north Taku Fort on the left bank of the Peiho, resulting in its capture and the surrender of the remaining forts without any further resistance. The

Anglo-French force routed the Chinese at Palichiao (Baliqiao) on 21 September, and then advanced on Peking (Beijing). When the Summer Palace outside the city was looted by French troops on 7 October, Grant secured a small portion of the booty for his own army, resigned his share of the proceeds, and following an auction distributed the proceeds to his men without reference to London. This rather irregular decision, given the circumstances, won Queen Victoria's approval. Following the construction of breaching batteries outside the Anting (Anding) gate, Peking finally surrendered and a new peace treaty was signed. Grant returned to Shanghai and, following a short visit to Japan, went on leave to Europe, where he was briefly entertained in Paris by Emperor Napoleon III who made him a grand officer of the Légion d'honneur. In recognition of his services during his widely recognized and highly successful campaign in China, Grant was created a GCB by Queen Victoria.

When he returned to India, on 26 December 1861, Grant was appointed commander-in-chief of the Madras army. He held this post for three years, during which he oversaw a reduction in the number of regiments stationed in the presidency and, despite being opposed to the measure, the introduction of the irregular system in the remainder. In July 1865 he returned to Britain where he was made colonel of the 9th lancers, and began work as quartermaster-general at the Horse Guards four months later. In 1870 he succeeded Lieutenant-General Sir James Scarlett in the prestigious post of commander at Aldershot. Despite opposition from senior officers Grant introduced the realistic Prussian system of training in which bodies of troops were manoeuvred as two opposing forces during large exercises held each autumn; the system worked with great success. He also helped reform the entire system of outpost duty in use by the British army about which he had gained such wide experience in India, introduced the war game and military lectures, inaugurated a soldiers' industrial exhibition, and was a warm supporter of institutions for the social and religious welfare of the men under his command. A devout Christian throughout his life, Grant also organized a series of meetings to inculcate temperance, thrift, and biblical precepts among the troops. He was promoted general in 1872. During the autumn manoeuvres in 1874, however, he was clearly unwell and despite a leave of absence his health did not improve. He died on 7 March 1875 at 32 Grosvenor Gardens, Eaton Square, London, at the age of sixty-six, of an internal illness which had been exacerbated by his lengthy service in the tropics. He was buried with full military honours in Grange cemetery, Edinburgh.

T. R. Moreman

Sources *Life of General Sir Hope Grant, with selections from his correspondence*, ed. H. Knollys, 2 vols. (1894) · H. Knollys, ed., *Incidents in the China War of 1860 compiled from the private journals of Sir Hope Grant* (1875) · H. Knollys, ed., *Incidents in the Sepoy War, 1857–58, compiled from the private journals of Sir Hope Grant* (1873) · C. R. Low, *Soldiers of the Victorian age* (1880) · C. Hibbert, *The great mutiny, India, 1857* (1978) · S. N. Sen, *Eighteen fifty-seven* (Delhi, 1958) · G. Wolseley, 'Memoir of Sir Hope Grant', *United Service Magazine*, 3rd ser., 7 (1893), 751–91 · *DNB* · *CGPLA Eng. & Wales* (1875)

Archives BL, letter-book as commander in China, autobiographical fragment, Add. MSS 52414–52415 | NL Scot., letters to Sir Thomas Cochrane

Likenesses F. Grant, oils, 1853, Scot. NPG · photograph, c.1858–1861, BL OIOC, Photo 165 (3), 353, and 458 (10) · T. J. Barker, group portrait, oils, 1859 (*The relief of Lucknow, 1857*; after sketches by E. Lundgren), Corporation of Glasgow · H. H. Crealock, watercolour drawing, 1860, NAM · F. Grant, oils, c.1861, NPG · F. Grant, oils, c.1861, Crown Commissioners · engraving, pubd 1862, Coll. of the 9th/12th Royal Lancers, Market Harborough · C. G. Lewis, group portrait, engraving, pubd 1864 (*Intellect and valour of Great Britain*; after T. J. Barker), NPG · F. Grant, oils, 1865, Lawrence Asylum, Madras · J. Noble, Parian-ware bust, Royal Collection · photograph, NPG · photographs, Collection of the 9th/12th Royal Lancers, Market Harborough · photographs, repro. in Knollys, ed., *Life of General Sir Hope Grant*, frontispiece to vols. 1 and 2

Wealth at death under £3000: probate, 20 Oct 1875, *CGPLA Eng. & Wales*

Grant, James Macpherson (1822–1885), politician and land reformer in Australia, was born at Alvie, Inverness-shire, son of Louis Grant and his wife, Isabella, *née* McBean. He was educated at Kingdenie. The family emigrated to Sydney, New South Wales, in 1836, where James was articled to Chambers and Thurlow, a firm of solicitors. He went to New Zealand in 1844 and fought in the war against Honi Heki. After returning to Sydney, he qualified in 1847 as an attorney and solicitor and became Thurlow's partner. Unwilling to settle down, he sailed to San Francisco in 1850 with a cargo of supplies for gold-mines.

On his return to Australia, Grant and his brother went to Bendigo, where they were among the successful diggers on the newly discovered goldfields. In 1854 he married Mary, daughter of Francis Gaunson, a Sydney grocer and tea dealer; they had three daughters and a son. In the same year, Grant began practice in Melbourne; in December the miners' riots took place at the Eureka Stockade at Ballarat and he publicly took the miners' part. At the trial of the miners he acted as their attorney without a fee and played a prominent part in their acquittal. He was elected as representative of the Bendigo miners to the legislative council of Victoria in November 1855.

In the following year, with the introduction of responsible government, Grant was elected a member for the Sandhurst Boroughs in the newly created legislative assembly. In 1859 he was returned for Avoca which he continued to represent for the rest of his life. He soon established himself as a radical and a republican, views which damaged his legal practice but helped him politically. He first took office in Richard Heales's ministry as vice-president of the board of land and works, and commissioner of public works in February 1861, and served until the government fell in November that year. Grant again became vice-president of the board of land and works and commissioner of railways and roads in James McCulloch's ministry in June 1863, and in September 1864 he became president of the board and commissioner of crown lands and survey. His 1865 Land Bill was compromised by the legislative council, but clause 42 of the act authorized small-holding licences near goldfields at ministerial discretion. Grant used these powers ruthlessly so that, despite much criticism, he issued licences for up to 160 acres as far as 30 miles from any goldfield, allowing thousands to begin farming. Grant's 1869 Land Act extended free selection before survey to 320 acre lots and provided firm foundations for the rapid expansion of agriculture throughout Victoria. During the 1870s and early 1880s Grant briefly held various ministerial offices in the rapidly changing administrations of this politically turbulent period.

A Presbyterian, a fierce hater of the squatters, and a lover of strong drink, the tough, uncompromising Grant suffered a stroke and died on 1 April 1885 in Melbourne, a relatively poor man; parliament voted £4000 to his widow. He was buried in Melbourne general cemetery.

G. C. BOASE, rev. TONY DINGLE

Sources The Argus [Melbourne] (2 April 1885) · The Age [Melbourne] (2 April 1885) · The Times (4 April 1885) · The Leader [Melbourne] (4 April 1885) · J. M. Powell, The public lands of Australia Felix: settlement and land appraisal in Victoria, 1834–91, with special reference to the western plains (1970) · M. L. Kiddle, Men of yesterday (1961) · AusDB

Likenesses E. Gilks, lithograph and pen-and-ink drawings, 1874 · E. Gilks, pen-and-ink sketch, 1874, State Library of Victoria, Melbourne, La Trobe picture collection · cartoons, repro. in Melbourne Punch (29 Nov–13 Dec 1866)

Grant, James William (1788–1865), astronomer, was born at Wester Elchies in Morayshire on 12 August 1788, the son of Robert Grant and his wife, Isabel, formerly Campbell. His father made a fortune abroad and about 1783 bought the Elchies estate, hereditary in a branch of his family, to which he later added the lands of Knockando and Ballintomb. James William Grant entered the East India Company's service as a writer on 22 July 1805, and filled appointments of increasing importance in Bengal until his retirement in 1849. He married Margaret (d. 1855), the daughter of the Revd Thomas Wilson of Gamrie in Banffshire; their eight sons and four daughters were all born in India.

Grant employed his leisure in scientific pursuits, and with an excellent 5 foot achromatic he detected, on 23 July 1844, the companion of Antares, two years before it was identified as a double star. He had, however, failed to publish his discovery, which became known only through Professor Piazzi Smyth's examination of his observing papers.

On his elder brother's death, in 1828, Grant inherited the family estates. He returned from India to Scotland in 1849, taking with him a few Tibetan sheep; these did not thrive in the damp climate, but when crossed with local stock produced animals with fine wool and excellent meat. Grant erected at Elchies a fine observatory in granite, the entrance guarded by sphinxes. It housed the large refracting telescope which he had commissioned in 1849 and which had been exhibited by its maker, Andrew Ross, in the Great Exhibition of 1851. Its object-glass, 11 inches in diameter, was obtained from Munich, and the mount was constructed by Ransome and May. At the time, it was

the largest refractor in Scotland. Grant's use of it was hampered by the climate and growing ill health, but Smyth found its performance excellent in a set of observations on double stars made at Elchies in the autumn of 1862. It was sold in 1864 to a Mr Aytoun of Glenfarg, Perthshire.

Grant was elected a fellow of the Royal Astronomical Society on 13 January 1854. His sole publication was a letter, On the Influence of Climate upon the Telescopic Appearance of a Celestial Body, accompanying two sketches of Mars, made respectively at Calcutta and Elchies. He was an accomplished microscopist whose slides evoked the admiration of native and foreign experts, and he also cultivated botany, natural history, and painting. He died at Wester Elchies of gout on 17 September 1865, and was buried in Knockando churchyard. Grant was good-natured and of excellent character, and his death was regretted by his friends, his tenants, and those to whom he had been a benefactor.

A. M. CLERKE, rev. ANITA McCONNELL

Sources R. Grant, 'Letter to the editor', Monthly Notices of the Royal Astronomical Society, 23 (1862–3), 1–2 · C. Piazzi Smyth, 'Experiences with the Elchies equatoreally mounted refractor of 11 inches aperture, in September 1862', Monthly Notices of the Royal Astronomical Society, 23 (1862–3), 2–13 · C. Piazzi Smyth, 'On the great refracting telescope at Elchies in Morayshire and its powers in sidereal observation', Transactions of the Royal Society of Edinburgh, 23 (1864), 371–418 · The new statistical account of Scotland, 13 (1845), 61 · Banffshire Journal (19 Sept 1865) · L. Shaw and J. F. Gordon, The history of the province of Moray, 1 (1882), 112, 117 · A. Jervise, Epitaphs and inscriptions from burial grounds and old buildings in the north-east of Scotland, 1 (1875), 299 · Dodwell [E. Dodwell] and Miles [J. S. Miles], eds., Alphabetical list of the Honourable East India Company's Bengal civil servants, from the year 1780 to the year 1838 (1839)

Wealth at death £1371 18s. 6d.: confirmation, 6 Feb 1866, CCI

Grant, John, of Freuchie (d. 1528). See under Grant family of Freuchie (per. 1485–1622).

Grant, John, of Freuchie (d. 1585). See under Grant family of Freuchie (per. 1485–1622).

Grant, John, of Freuchie (1568?–1622). See under Grant family of Freuchie (per. 1485–1622).

Grant, John (1782?–1842), army officer and spy, was born at Elgin, Moray. He began his military career as an ensign on 2 November 1797 (lieutenant, 31 May 1798) in the Royal Glamorgan militia, with which he served in Ireland in 1799. In the same year he volunteered to the line from the embodied militia, and was appointed a lieutenant in the 4th foot, but was placed on half pay at the peace of Amiens. Before the renewal of the war he was appointed lieutenant in the Ross militia on 24 February 1803, and was promoted captain on 25 October 1803. He served as a major and later a lieutenant-colonel under Sir Robert Thomas Wilson on the Portuguese frontier in 1808–9 with the irregular force known as the Loyal Lusitanian Legion, and was wounded in an engagement with Marshal Victor at the Puente Romano of Alcántara on 14 May 1809. When Wilson was defeated by Marshal Ney in the Puerto de Baños (12 August 1809) and left Portugal, Grant remained with the legion, which he commanded at the battle of

Busaco (27 September 1810). In May 1811 the legion was absorbed into the regular Portuguese army under Marshal William Carr Beresford, Grant retaining his colonel's rank and also being given a commission in the British army as cornet in the 3rd dragoon guards (lieutenant, 24 July 1811).

Grant was employed extensively as a partisan leader and spy, in which capacity he assumed a variety of disguises, and experienced the most extraordinary adventures. In January 1810 he succeeded in intercepting Napoleon's private letters to his brother, King Joseph, and on another occasion he spent a night in Marmont's headquarters. There is much confusion by historians of his exploits with those of Major Colquhoun Grant (1780–1829), 11th foot, a scouting officer. However, the peasants differentiated them: Colquhoun as 'Granto el Bueno' and John as 'Granto el Malo'. John Grant commanded the *ordenanças* (levy *en masse* of the peasantry) of Lower Beira, and in this capacity inflicted severe losses on General Foy at Foz Giraldo on 1 February 1811. Wellington wrote to Beresford on 19 February 1811 in reference to this event, stating that Grant was apparently doing good work, and asking Beresford to tell him how much gratified Wellington had been at reading the accounts of his operations. In September 1811 Grant was severely wounded and captured by the French near Plasencia, but was released the following month by a guerrilla band under Temprano outside Talavera. At the end of the Peninsular War, Grant was appointed lieutenant in the 2nd Royal Veteran battalion (24 September 1814), and was retired on full pay when the veteran battalions were abolished on 24 May 1816. He married his second wife, Sarah Sophia Moore (c.1784–1848), at Marylebone on 24 July 1820, and they had two children. He had previously been married, probably in Spain or Portugal.

Grant became involved in radical politics and acted as secretary to the committee formed in London by the earl of Durham, Lord William Bentinck, and others in 1820, when Marshal Beresford was dismissed from his Portuguese command by the constitutional government. In 1823, at the time of the invasion of Spain by the French troops under the duc d'Angoulême, Grant's committee dispatched Sir Robert Thomas Wilson on a fruitless mission to the Peninsula. The promised volume of Wilson's memoirs dealing with the Lusitanian legion episode of 1808–9 and the Spanish mission of 1823 was never published (see introduction to *Life of Sir R. T. Wilson*, ed. H. Randolph, 1862), and Grant's share in these transactions has never been treated in detail. On 24 March 1829 Grant was appointed paymaster of the 56th foot; he transferred to the 80th foot on 1 June 1833 and to the 16th foot on 20 October 1837. He finally retired on full pay in 1839.

Grant died, in penury, of lung disease, after a long and painful illness, at the age of sixty, at 2 Church Street, Kensington, London, on 14 July 1842. He was buried at St Mary Abbot's, Kensington. His appeals for assistance were left unanswered until after his death, when Sir Robert Peel, the prime minister, authorized a grant of £100, which paid off the medical expenses of his final illness, and a lieutenant's widow's pension of £40 a year to his widow, who died at Chelsea on 26 May 1848.

H. M. CHICHESTER, rev. D. G. HALLIDAY

Sources PRO, officers' widows' pension papers, WO 42/19 239 · PRO, half-pay officers' service records, WO 25/760 · Naval and Military Gazette (4 March 1843), 137 · Naval and Military Gazette (1 July 1848), 429 [appeal for daughter] · W. Mayne, Narrative of the campaigns of the loyal Lusitanian legion (1812) · C. Oman, Studies in the Napoleonic wars (1929), 415 · C. W. C. Oman, A history of the Peninsular War, 3 (1908), 546, appx X · Fortescue, Brit. army, 7.415 · B. D'Urban, Peninsular journals, ed. I. J. Rousseau (1988), 181 · J. Rathbone, Wellington's war (1984), 176 [Wellington's dispatch 30/10/1811] · W. F. P. Napier, History of the war in the Peninsula and in the south of France, 11 (1882), 71 · W. F. P. Napier, History of the war in the Peninsula and in the south of France, 16 (1882), 145 · M. Girod de l'Ain, Vie Militaire du Général Foy (1900), 127 · Officer's statement of services, 1829, PRO, WO/796 · Army List (1830–43) · d. cert. · parish register, St Mary Abbot's, Kensington, 21 July 1842

Grant, Sir John Peter, of Rothiemurchus (1774–1848), politician and judge, was born on 21 September 1774, the only son of William *Grant, MD (d. 1786), of Lyme Street, London, and afterwards of the Doune of Rothiemurchus, Inverness-shire—descended from the sixteenth-century chief of clan Grant, James Grant, laird of Rothiemurchus—and his wife, Elizabeth (d. 1778), daughter and heir of John Raper of Twyford House, Essex, and Thorley Hall, Hertfordshire, from an old Buckinghamshire family which claimed Norman descent. Grant was educated privately by tutors, at Edinburgh high school, and at Edinburgh University from 1790, but he did not graduate.

Following the death on 17 May 1790 of his uncle Patrick Grant, laird of Rothiemurchus, called the White Laird, Grant succeeded to the entailed highland estate of Rothiemurchus. On 2 August 1796 at Houghton-le-Spring, co. Durham, he married Jane (b. 1775), aged just under twenty-one, daughter of the Revd William Ironside, rector of Houghton-le-Spring; they had two sons and three daughters. Through his wife Grant inherited estates in England. He introduced improvements on his Scottish and English estates. During the French wars and invasion scares he was captain-commandant of the Rothiemurchus Volunteers (1797), major-commandant (1801), and lieutenant-colonel-commandant of the Strathspey Volunteers (1808)—'a kilted regiment … with their plumed bonnets' (*Highland Lady*, ed. Strachey, 82)—and according to his eldest daughter, practised manoeuvres with wooden model soldiers. His eldest daughter described him as 'a little sallow brisk man without any remarkable feature' and claimed 'there was a charm in his manner I have never known any one of any age or station capable of resisting' (*Highland Lady*, ed. Tod, 1.10, 11).

Grant enjoyed a substantial income from his estates, including his Scottish timber, and could have lived comfortably as a highland laird. However, he was ambitious for a legal and political career. He studied law at Edinburgh and was admitted advocate in 1796. He was admitted at Lincoln's Inn on 1 May 1793 and called to the bar on 1 February 1802. He practised on the northern circuit without notable success. His eldest daughter later suggested that he had pretended to Inverness-shire in 1802, and was bought off by Charles Grant with 'unlimited Indian appointments ... the secret of my father's Indian patronage' (*Highland Lady*, ed. Tod, 1.71). From a whig family, he negotiated with the chief of his clan, Sir James Grant, for a Scottish parliamentary seat, but at the 1807 election was thwarted in Elginshire and withdrew disappointed. He then attempted to gain a seat at the 'thoroughly rotten borough' (*Highland Lady*, ed. Strachey, 153) of Great Grimsby, Lincolnshire, which had a resident freeman franchise and rival factions, the reds and the blues. Grant sold his Hertfordshire property for his election expenses, bought property in Grimsby, procured the election of an ally as town clerk, and gained support among the reds. Following heavy expenditure he was elected in October 1812. His eldest daughter later wrote, 'Great Grimsby was gained—at what cost the ruin of a family could certify' (*Highland Lady*, ed. Tod, 1.213). In parliament he supported the whigs and opposed the government. According to his eldest daughter, 'he made no figure. He spoke seldom, said little when he did speak, and never in any way made himself of consequence' (*Highland Lady*, ed. Strachey, 301). He had published *Essays Towards Illustrating Some Elementary Principles Relating to Wealth and Currency* (1812) and he considered himself an expert on currency, advocating a silver standard. He supported Roman Catholic relief. Unlike most whigs he supported the 1815 corn law, for which his Edinburgh house was attacked by a mob which broke his windows before being dispersed by dragoons. He opposed the slave trade and the treatment of the Glasgow radicals, and supported retrenchment and repeal of the Septennial Act. In June 1818 he was defeated at Grimsby by a richer candidate who reportedly spent about £5500; moreover, Grant's agents seem to have mismanaged his campaign. His affairs in disarray, he could no longer afford to contest Grimsby. The whig duke of Bedford appointed him to the family pocket borough of Tavistock, Devon, until the duke's heir came of age. Grant was elected by the obedient freeholders in March 1819 and sat for two parliaments, until in 1826 the duke replaced him by Lord William Russell. Grant opposed state lotteries and repressive legislation, advocated retrenchment, and criticized indirect taxation as oppressing the poor.

Grant, according to his eldest daughter, had had 'too many irons in the fire' (*Highland Lady*, ed. Strachey, 213). His ambition outran his ability and his income. Heavily in debt—according to his eldest daughter he owed upwards of £60,000—he was saved from financial ruin by appointment to an Indian judgeship, which he obtained, according to his eldest daughter, as a reward from the chamberlain Lord Conyngham for supplying George IV with Glenlivet whisky and ptarmigan on his visit to Scotland in 1822. In 1827 Grant was appointed puisne judge at Bombay, and was knighted on 30 June.

Fleeing from his creditors, Grant left for India in September 1827. In Bombay, under his active supervision, the Fever Hospital committee made several reports and many recommendations, but these produced no immediate practical results. In 1829 Grant quarrelled with Sir John Malcolm, the Scottish governor of Bombay, over what Grant saw as government interference in a judicial matter, whereas Malcolm and his government were concerned at judges' encroachments and usurpation of governmental authority. Lord Ellenborough, president of the Board of Control, wrote of Grant that two colleagues should be appointed to sit with him to 'keep him in check like a wild elephant between two tame ones' (Cotton, 170). In 1829 Grant, 'thoroughly out of temper' (*Highland Lady*, ed. Strachey, 439), closed the court. According to his eldest daughter, it was only because of Lord Brougham that he was not required to resign. However, he resigned in September 1830, went to Calcutta, and practised at the bar for three years until appointed puisne judge there in 1833. He resigned in 1848. His publications included pamphlets and speeches. On his voyage home he died at sea on 17 May 1848, and he was buried in the Dean cemetery, Edinburgh.

Ambitious and energetic, a man of the *ancien régime* and its Old Corruption, Grant was unreliable, evasive, and sometimes dishonest. *The Times* described him as 'wayward, extravagant and, though not without shining parts, impracticable and unsuccessful in life' (*Highland Lady*, ed. Tod, x). *Blackwood's Magazine* claimed he was 'one of those brilliant men who are not born to succeed' (ibid.).

Grant's second son was Sir John Peter *Grant (1807–1893), lieutenant-governor of Bengal and governor of Jamaica. Grant's eldest child was Elizabeth Grant [see Smith, Elizabeth (1797–1885)]. For her family she wrote her memoirs; edited and abridged by her niece Jane Marcia, Lady Strachey (daughter of Sir J. P. Grant junior), they were published as *Memoirs of a Highland Lady* (1898)—a fuller, unexpurgated edition edited by Andrew Tod was published in 1988—and contained information on her parents.   ROGER T. STEARN

Sources *Memoirs of a highland lady: Elizabeth Grant of Rothiemurchus*, ed. A. Tod, 2 vols. (1988) · *Memoirs of a highland lady: the autobiography of Elizabeth Grant of Rothiemurchus*, ed. J. M. Strachey (1898) · HoP, *Commons* · GM, 2nd ser., 30 (1848), 335 · Burke, *Gen. GB* (1937) · W. P. Baildon, ed., *The records of the Honorable Society of Lincoln's Inn: admissions*, 1 (1896) · D. Laing, ed., *A catalogue of the graduates ... of the University of Edinburgh*, Bannatyne Club, 106 (1858) · H. E. A. Cotton, *Calcutta old and new: a historical and descriptive handbook to the city* (1907) · J. W. Kaye, *The life and correspondence of Major-General Sir John Malcolm, G.C.B.*, 2 (1856) · W. S. Seton-Karr, *Grant of Rothiemurchus: a memoir of the services of Sir John Peter Grant, G.C.M.G., K.C.B.* (1899) · DNB

Archives NRA Scotland, priv. coll., corresp. and papers | BL OIOC, letters to his daughter-in-law Henrietta Grant, MS Eur. F 127

Grant, Sir John Peter (1807–1893), administrator in India and colonial governor, was born in London on 28 November 1807, the younger son of John Peter Grant of Rothiemurchus, Inverness-shire, and his wife, Jane, third daughter of William Ironside of Houghton-le-Spring, co. Durham. He entered Eton College in 1819, and East India College, Haileybury, in 1827, after a session at Edinburgh University. In 1828 he joined the Bengal civil service and in the following May, after a few months' study at Fort William College, Calcutta, was appointed assistant to the magistrate at Bareilly. He was not a natural district officer, however, and in 1832 he readily returned to Calcutta as head assistant of the *Sadr* board of revenue and once there set his sights on more senior posts in the secretariat. In the next nine years he served in various secretarial capacities, including that of secretary to the Indian law commission, of which T. B. Macaulay was president. On 16 February 1835, in Calcutta Cathedral, Grant married Henrietta Isabella Phillippa (*b.* 1817), daughter of Trevor Chichele Plowden, of the Bengal civil service. They had five sons and three daughters, including Jane Maria *Strachey, Lady Strachey [*see under* Strachey, Sir Richard].

In 1844, on his return from three years' furlough in Britain, Grant became something of a roving trouble-shooter, prized for his cogency, level-headedness, and tact. In the autumn of 1844 the government of India dispatched him to settle the debts of the maharaja of Mysore. In 1847 he was appointed to report on the agency established to suppress human sacrifice by the Gonds, a Dravidian population in the hill tracts of Orissa who, in resisting the agency's heavy-handed mission to civilize them, had generated unexpected political controversy about the agency's methods.

In October 1848 Grant was appointed officiating (subsequently confirmed) secretary to the government of Bengal. As the governor-general, Lord Dalhousie, was on tour up-country for almost four years, and as his deputy was a military man, by this appointment Grant became the virtual ruler of the lower provinces of Bengal, an opportunity which he grasped to streamline and expedite the cumbrous machinery of the judicial, revenue and police departments. During 1853–4 he officiated first as foreign and then as home secretary to the government of India. In May 1854 he became a member of the supreme council, an office which he held until 1859. For almost twenty years Grant had been producing able minutes on controversial topics but now, as a council member, his talent for logical and dispassionate argument gained wider recognition. He was not a dogmatic man and if in doubt about the wisdom of a particular course of action he preferred not to act, but once committed to a policy no threat of political unpopularity would deter him. His minute on the maladministration of Oudh persuaded the court of directors and the cabinet to proceed with the full annexation of Oudh, a measure which even Dalhousie had shied away from. He was also an ardent advocate of the right of Hindu widows to remarry, and regarded his controversial Hindoo Widow Remarriage Act (1856) as one of his most worthy achievements.

In the uprising of 1857 Grant served as the lieutenant-governor of the Central Provinces, a temporary post created when the spread of fighting to the provincial capital of Agra ruptured the chain of command between Calcutta and the central districts of Benares and Allahabad. The job was an ill-defined one, requiring tact rather than political showmanship, and it was Grant's significant if unspectacular achievement during these irregular times to have harmonized the workings of the military and the civilian arms of the administration and to have ensured a steady flow of men, stores and information up the Grand Trunk Road to the hot-spots of the rising. He shared with Lord Canning a desire to avoid indiscriminate revenge and, like Canning, was derided at home for exacting insufficient retribution. In October 1857 *The Times* ran a story stating that Grant had ordered the release of 150 of the 'Cawnpore massacre' rebels seized by General Neill, and had punished with death English soldiers who had assaulted them. Grant's official denial had little impact on the rumour and for a time he enjoyed in England a reputation only marginally better than that of the rebels themselves.

On 1 May 1859 Grant was appointed lieutenant-governor of Bengal. His administration was dominated by the 'blue mutiny', in which peasants who had endured years of enforced and unprofitable contract-growing of indigo began to revolt against the planters. In spite of the obloquy heaped upon him by planting interests in both India and England, Grant refused to accede to planters' demands that breach of contracts be made a criminal offence, and indeed encouraged the cultivators to resist new contracts, in effect dealing a death blow to a system which had threatened to engulf tracts of Bengal in peasant rebellion. Anglo-Indian opposition to Grant was intense but, harrowed still by the memories of 1857, both Canning and the home authorities considered his action sound. On 14 March 1862 he was made KCB, and in April he retired from the service and left India.

Grant's retirement was short-lived. In August 1866 he returned to colonial office as the governor of Jamaica, appointed in the wake of Edward John Eyre's draconian reaction to the rising of 1865. After his handling of the indigo crisis in Bengal, Grant was seen as a safe pair of hands, sufficiently distant from the plantation mentality to assess dispassionately the colony's need for reform. Within two months of taking office he had abolished the existing representative assembly and replaced it with a legislative council consisting of the governor and six official and three non-official members. He turned the government's finances around. By 1868 his reforms had produced a surplus after years of government debt—the result of extra taxation, stricter policing of customs and, most controversially, reductions in government pensions. He disestablished the church and replaced the old parish-based militias with a professional constabulary, incorporating Indians and black people at the rank and file level. At the same time the European troop presence was trimmed to just five companies, effecting both a financial saving and a winning declaration of official confidence in the colony's stability. He imported new district judges from England in an attempt to free the lower levels of the judiciary from the influence of the planters, and generally strove to improve the access of the labourers and small traders to civil justice. With an eye to stabilizing the labour market and easing planter pressure on the island's free labourers, he re-introduced the regulated importation of indentured labour from India.

Grant's reforms, although not always successful, earned for him a reputation as one of Jamaica's most able colonial administrators. He returned to Britain in 1874 and was made GCMG in the same year. In retirement he served as a JP for Hertfordshire and Middlesex, and also for Inverness-shire. He died at Clifton Lodge, Farquhar Road, Upper Norwood, London, on 6 January 1893, and was buried in the family's new burial place in Rothiemurchus churchyard.

KATHERINE PRIOR

Sources W. S. Seton-Karr, *Grant of Rothiemurchus: a memoir of the services of Sir John Peter Grant, G.C.M.G., K.C.B.* (1899) · *Jamaica and its governor during the last six years by a fellow of the Royal Geographical Society* (1871) · C. E. Buckland, *Bengal under the lieutenant-governors*, 2 vols. (1904) · BL OIOC, Strachey MSS, MS Eur. F 127 [incl. Grant's private papers] · BL OIOC, Haileybury MSS · *The Spectator* (21 Jan 1893), 70–71 · *The Pioneer* (12 Jan 1893) [Allahabad] · F. C. Danvers and others, *Memorials of old Haileybury College* (1894) · *The Times* (12 Jan 1893) · *Memoirs of a highland lady: the autobiography of Elizabeth Grant of Rothiemurchus*, ed. J. M. Strachey (1898) · *DNB* · *CCI* (1893)
Archives BL, corresp., Add. MSS 60632–60634 · BL OIOC, corresp. and papers, Eur. MSS F 127 · priv. coll., NRA, corresp. and papers | Bodl. Oxf., corresp. with Lord Kimberley · W. Yorks. AS, Leeds, letters to Lord Canning
Likenesses G. F. Watts, oils, after 1873, NPG; repro. in Seton-Karr, *Grant of Rothiemurchus*
Wealth at death £7040 5s. 7d.: confirmation, 6 June 1893, *CCI*

Grant, John Peter, of Rothiemurchus (1885–1963), promoter of highland bagpiping, was born at 20 India Street, Edinburgh, on 24 June 1885, son of John Peter Grant of Rothiemurchus (1860–1927), advocate, and his wife, Edith Mary, *née* Brewster-Macpherson (d. 1922). He was to achieve distinction in three separate spheres but dominating his life was an abiding love of the Scottish highlands and their culture.

Like so many of his contemporaries, Grant's education was largely in England. In 1899 he went from Cargilfield, his Scottish preparatory school, to Winchester College, where he was in the shooting eight, and thence, in 1904, to Magdalen College, Oxford. Between reading history and gaining a half blue for fencing he began to fulfil a long-cherished ambition to learn the highland bagpipe, the music of which was later to become the principal interest of his life. In 1908 he went to Edinburgh University to read law and was called to the Scots bar in 1913. On 10 April of the same year he married Gertrude Margaret Truell (1883–1967).

On the outbreak of the First World War Grant joined the Lovat scouts and had a distinguished war record. He saw service in Gallipoli, Macedonia, Egypt, and France. He was awarded the MC, and was mentioned in dispatches on three occasions. After the war he continued his connection with the scouts and was commanding officer from 1928 to 1932. He was in the Home Guard in the Second World War and was later a prominent figure in the Territorial Army Association from which he retired in 1947, being created CB in 1948.

In 1922 Grant was appointed sheriff of Shetland. In 1927, on the death of his father, he was appointed sheriff of Inverness, the only occasion on which a son has immediately succeeded his father on the same bench. For the next twenty-seven years he was a greatly respected and influential figure in the highlands. His knowledge of Gaelic and his deep understanding of highland culture gave him an authority which was reflected in the fact that none of his

judgments was ever overturned on appeal. He would often act as interpreter when elderly witnesses had difficulty with the English language and was adept at putting such people at their ease. He also put his knowledge of Gaelic to good use while serving in France, invariably writing in it to his wife, who was equally fluent, in order to best the censors. Rothiemurchus's relationship with the legal profession in Inverness was extremely cordial and his retirement from the bench was marked by a dinner attended by many prominent legal figures. His court room was deliberately kept informal. He himself always wore a kilt and latterly dispensed with wig and gown, except for jury trials, without ever compromising the dignity of the court.

It is, however, as a student of the great highland bagpipe that Rothiemurchus will be best remembered. He himself recalled that his love of pipe music dated from a visit to the Kingussie games at the age of six when, on being taken by his nanny for a walk round the ground to alleviate the tedium of sitting in the stand, he heard a piper playing a pibroch and at that moment the die was cast. Efforts to learn at school came to nothing and it was only when he arrived at Oxford that a fellow Scot, Alan Don, later dean of Westminster and a piper, encouraged him. Over the next few years he had tuition variously from Pipe-Major William Ross of the Scots Guards, Pipe-Major James Sutherland of the Seaforths, and John MacDonald of Inverness. It was about this time that the Piobaireachd Society was founded, largely as a result of the publication of Charles Thomason's great work *Ceol Mor* (1897), a collection of nearly 300 tunes which prompted a tremendous revival in pibroch playing. The society arranged competitions for which it set stated tunes and did all it could to generate interest. However, some of the older professional pipers, many of whom could not read music, found it hard to learn unfamiliar tunes and resented what they regarded as interference in their ways. Matters got worse until the society was virtually refounded under the presidency of Lord Lovat in 1907. A music committee was formed later with Rothiemurchus as the first secretary, charged with setting tunes and regulating all musical details. Under his guidance it soon established itself as the recognized authority and its reputation was further enhanced by the next secretary, Archibald Campbell of Kilberry. Neither Rothiemurchus nor Kilberry would have claimed to be pipers of great ability. A certain amount of what they stated as fact has not been supported by more recent research and at the time some of the greatest players were unhappy at being required to play as the society directed. However, without the enormous enthusiasm of Rothiemurchus, Kilberry, and Thomason, it is entirely possible that the resurgence of pibroch playing in the twentieth century might not have taken place. John Peter Grant of Rothiemurchus died at his residence, Corrour House, Rothiemurchus, Aviemore, on 23 August 1963, and was buried in Rothiemurchus old churchyard.

JAMES BURNET

Sources private information (2004) [S. M. Grant] · personal knowledge (2004) · *Inverness Courier* (27 Aug 1963) · priv. coll., Grant

MSS · b. cert. · d. cert. · Burke, *Gen. GB* (1939) · NA Scot., SC 29/44/147/360
Archives priv. coll.
Likenesses photographs, Royal Scottish Pipers' Society, Edinburgh
Wealth at death £28,349 9s. 1d.: confirmation, 9 Oct 1963, NA Scot., SC 29/44/147/360

Grant, Johnson (1773–1844), Church of England clergyman, was born in Edinburgh, the son of Dr Gregory Grant, a physician, and his wife, Mary, daughter of Sir Archibald Grant of Monymusk (son of Francis Grant, Lord Cullen). He matriculated from St John's College, Oxford, in October 1795, aged twenty-one, graduating BA in 1799 and MA in 1805. After being ordained by Henry Majendie, bishop of Chester, he served as curate to Edward Owen (1728–1807), rector of Warrington. In 1803 he was appointed perpetual curate of the chapel of ease at Latchford, near Warrington, in succession to James Glazebrook. He was identified as an evangelical and reinvigorated the Sunday school at Latchford, using his *Manual of Religious Knowledge for the Use of Sunday Schools*, which he had first published in 1800 (3rd edn, 1810).

Grant left Latchford in 1809 and lived in Edgware Road, London, holding curacies at Hornsey and St Pancras. Through the influence of Bishop Majendie he was presented to the rectory of Binbrooke St Mary, Lincolnshire, in 1818, a living in the gift of Lord Eldon, the lord chancellor, to which he added the vicarage of Binbrooke St Gabriel in 1836. In 1822 James Moore, vicar of St Pancras, appointed him to the perpetual curacy of Kentish Town, which he held in conjunction with his Lincolnshire livings until his death.

Despite his pluralism Grant was known as a hardworking clergyman in London, publishing his series of Lent lectures as *The Crucifixion* (1821) and *The Last Things* (1828), *Six Lectures on Liberality and Expediency* (1830), and *A Course of Lectures for the Year* (2 vols., 1833–5). His considerable literary output included *A Summary of the History of the English Church* (4 vols., 1811–26), a memoir (1827) of a girl parishioner, Frances Augusta Bell, who died in 1825, and occasional poetry, notably *Arabia* (2nd edn, 1815), inspired by travels to the Holy Land. He was married and had a son, Johnson Grant, who matriculated from St John's College, Oxford, in 1838 aged seventeen. Grant died in Kentish Town, London, on 4 December 1844.

M. C. CURTHOYS

Sources GM, 2nd ser., 23 (1845), 444 · Foster, *Alum. Oxon.* · W. Beamont, *A history of Latchford* (1889) · D. M. Lewis, ed., *The Blackwell dictionary of evangelical biography, 1730–1860*, 2 vols. (1995)
Archives Bodl. Oxf., corresp. with Thomas Burgess

Grant, Joseph (1805–1835), poet, was born on 26 May 1805 at his father's farm of Affrusk in Kincardineshire. As a child he was employed on the farm in the summer, and during the winter he picked up what learning he could at a village school. When only fourteen he began to write verses. In 1831 he was engaged as assistant to a shopkeeper at Stonehaven, and afterwards he was employed as a clerk at Dundee, first in the office of *The Guardian* newspaper, and then in that of a writer to the signet. In Dundee he made the acquaintance of several literary figures. He became ill, however, and died on 14 April 1835 at Affrusk.

Grant's poems—often like his prose tales of much merit—were written mainly in Scots, but some are in English. He contributed tales and sketches to *Chambers's Journal* between 1830 and 1835, and published *Juvenile Lays* (1828) and *Kincardineshire Traditions* (1830). At the time of his death he was preparing *Tales of the Glens: with Ballads and Songs*. This collection was published in 1836.

C. L. KINGSFORD, rev. JAMES HOW

Sources W. Norrie, *Dundee celebrities of the nineteenth century* (1873) · R. Nicoll, 'A memoir of the author', in J. Grant, *Tales of the glens: with ballads and songs* (1869), 1–9 · Anderson, *Scot. nat.* · Irving, *Scots.*

Grant [*née* Murray], **Lilias** (d. 1643/4), letter writer, was probably born at Tullibardine in Perthshire, the daughter of John Murray of Tullibardine, first earl of Tullibardine (d. 1613), and his wife, Catherine Drummond, who married before 17 November 1576. Nothing is known about her until her marriage (contract dated at Gask on 15 April 1591) to John *Grant of Freuchie (1568?–1622) [see under Grant family of Freuchie]. James VI and Queen Anne were present at the wedding. The marriage produced a son and four daughters.

While her husband was active in the king's service, Lilias seems to have stayed mostly at Ballachastell or Castle Grant, the seat of the Grants of Freuchie. She appears to have been fond of devotional literature, and nearly all of the twenty-eight books belonging to her were religious, including the works of St Augustine and Thomas à Kempis. She may also have written poetry: two long poems in her handwriting were among the Grant papers, but it is unknown whether these were original or copies of works written by others. John Taylor the water poet, who visited Ballachastell in 1618, wrote admiringly of her but did not suggest that she was a poet.

Lilias's husband died on 20 September 1622, and her son, John, became laird of Freuchie. He frequently consulted his mother about his affairs, even over questions like the raising of men for military service in France. His extravagance, however, soon began to affect the Grant estates, and he became known as Sir John Sell-the-Land. Owing to his extravagance Lilias had to renounce to him lands in Cromdale which her husband had left for her maintenance. She also had to allow him to raise money using the barony of Lethen as security, although Lethen, like the Cromdale lands, had been specifically bestowed on her by her husband to provide for her during widowhood.

Lilias outlived her son, who died in 1637. Her grandson James, the seventh laird, and other members of the family, evidently regarded her as something of a family matriarch, and frequently wrote to her about family and business affairs. Judging by their letters to her and to each other, they held her in high regard. Her correspondence, among the Grant papers (Fraser, 2.53–8), shows that she took a lively interest in the important issues of the day, including the controversy over Charles I's service book. This book was deeply resented by Scottish presbyterians when he attempted to impose it on Scottish worship, and ultimately led to the national covenant and rebellion. Like her husband, Lilias appears to have been royalist in sentiment, but her grandson James showed signs of sympathy for the presbyterian cause. This alarmed Lilias's brother, Patrick Murray, third earl of Tullibardine (d. 1644), who urged her by letter in 1638 to use her influence to keep her grandson loyal to the king.

Lilias drew up her will on 30 December 1643, leaving £100 Scots to her daughter Lilias, wife of Sir Walter Innes of Balvenie. She died within the next twelve months, and was buried in the Grant burial-ground at Duthil church, Morayshire.   ALEXANDER DU TOIT

Sources W. Fraser, *The chiefs of Grant*, 3 vols. (1883), 1.159, 192–6, 209–10, 267; 2.53–8, 429; 3.221, 236 · W. Shaw, *The history of the province of Moray*, 3 vols. (1882), 1.92, 101 · GEC, *Peerage*, new edn, 12.62–3 · *The works of John Taylor, the water poet*, ed. C. Hendley (1872) · 'Grant, John (1568?–1622)', *DNB*

Wealth at death £100 Scots bequeathed to daughter: will, 1643, Fraser, *Chiefs of Grant*

Grant, Ludovick, of that ilk (1650?–1716), politician and army officer, was the eldest son of James Grant (1616–1663), laird of Freuchie, and his wife, Lady Mary (d. 1662), only daughter of James Stewart, second earl of Murray (d. 1638). He was educated at St Andrews University. At the time of the death of his father in 1663, he was still under age and for a short period came under the guardianship of his uncle Lieutenant-Colonel Patrick Grant. On 23 May 1665 he was retoured heir to his father. In December 1671 (by contract dated 20 December) Grant married at Ballachastell his first wife, Janet, only child and heir of Alexander Brodie of Lethen; they had six sons and five daughters. Following Janet's death in 1697, he married, by contract dated 1 March 1701, Jean (d. 1734), daughter of Sir Patrick Houston and successively widow of Walter Dundas, second son of Walter Dundas, younger of that ilk, and then Richard Lockhart of Lee.

Grant was active in public affairs throughout his adult life. He served as a commissioner of supply in 1667, 1685, 1689, 1690, and 1704. He was summoned with his clan to provide assistance for the government during the 1679 covenanter rising, but his wife and the Brodies were prime suspects of actively participating in conventicles in the north-eastern highlands. He was commissioned at Michaelmas 1680 to sit as an MP for Inverness-shire in the 1681 parliament, but when it commenced on 28 July he actually represented Elginshire, alongside Thomas Dunbar of Grange. On 31 August Grant protested with Andrew Fletcher of Saltoun, one of the MPs for Haddingtonshire, against a clause in the Test Act which required its application to the electors of the commissioners of the shires, an act which angered James, duke of York, high commissioner to the parliament. However, Grant remained loyal to James's regime in Scotland and on 9 August 1682 he was appointed as a commissioner of justiciary for the highlands, a position he was also to hold in 1693, 1697, and 1701.

During the torture of a Mr William Carstairs, son of Mr John Carstairs, former minister in Glasgow, before a secret committee of the privy council on 5 and 6 September 1684, Grant was one of those named as having plotted for over ten years, in tandem with associates in England, to prevent the duke of York from succeeding to the Scottish and English crowns. Nothing appears to have come from this accusation and Sir John Lauder of Fountainhall, one of the senators of the college of justice, stated that Grant had in fact been one of those who were 'wrongously also named' (*Historical Notices*, 2.555–6). On 31 December 1684 a privy council proclamation for the levying of forces to resist the invasion of the earl of Argyll included instructions for Grant to raise 200 men. Nevertheless, throughout January and February 1685 Grant was brought to the attention of the privy council due to his wife's activities in conventicles. On 6 February both husband and wife were examined by commissioners appointed by the privy council, who accused them of harbouring an unlicensed minister, Alexander Fraser, and his family, and allowing him to pray and preach. Grant admitted to hearing unlicensed ministers preach and pray at his in-laws, the Brodies of Lethen, and at the same examination swore that he had no knowledge or involvement in plans for Argyll's invasion of Scotland. His wife, however, admitted to involvement in conventicles and on 11 February Grant was fined £42,500 Scots. Brodie of Lethen was also fined £40,000 Scots and to secure his safety Grant was obliged to pay 75 per cent of Brodie's fine. Ordered on 11 May by the privy council to raise 300 men on foot from his own kinsmen and vassals to help put down the Argyll rebellion, he obeyed.

Grant supported the cause of William of Orange during the revolution of 1688 and was an MP for the shire of Inverness in the 1689 Convention Parliament, serving on the committee for securing the peace of the kingdom (16 March) and the committee to meet and consider the condition of the highlands (18 March), both of which were concerned with strategic security. He signed the act declaring the convention to be a lawful meeting of the estates (16 March) and he was a member of the committee for settling the government (27 March), the committee which drew up the Scottish claim of right and articles of grievance, as well as being appointed as one of the Scottish commissioners nominated on 23 April to treat for a union of the two kingdoms with English commissioners. Grant was instructed by the convention on 19 April to oversee new elections of magistrates in the burgh of Inverness and on 23 April he was appointed sheriff of Inverness (he was to hold this office again in 1708).

Grant's support for the Williamite regime in Scotland was military as well as political. On 25 April 1689 he was instructed by the convention to import 600 stand of arms for the public service and on 3 July he was excused absence from parliamentary attendance because of military commitments for William. Grant volunteered to raise and equip a regiment of 600 men and on 22 April he was appointed colonel of a regiment of foot. His estates suffered heavy losses during the Jacobite rising of 1689–90 and the final military conflict, the battle of Cromdale (1 May 1690), took place on his lands and the surrounding area of Ballachastell. He petitioned the 1695 parliament for compensation for damages inflicted and loss of rent. Parliament recognized losses of £150,486 13s. 10d. Scots, including £30,000 for five years' loss of rent in the barony of Urquhart, but it appears that Grant was never fully compensated for his losses.

Grant was appointed a privy councillor in 1689, 1690, 1692, 1696, and 1698, and was often proactive in dealing with highland affairs. For example, on 14 November 1689 he brought forward petitions against four ministers in his area for refusing to read the proclamation of the estates of 13 April and for refusing to request consideration of proposals for suppressing robberies in the highlands. He was appointed a commissioner for the poll tax in 1693. In the parliament of 1689–1702, in which he was again MP for Inverness-shire, he was a commissioner for the visitation of universities, colleges, and schools (1690), and for the plantation of kirks and valuation of teinds (1690), and also served on important standing committees such as the committee for drawing up an answer to the king's letter to parliament on opening sessions (1693, 1696, 1700). He was one of the three members of the 1695 parliament instructed to draw up an address of condolence to King William following the death of Queen Mary. He was also a member of the committee for the security of the kingdom in 1696 and 1700. In the 1701 parliament (14 January) he voted in favour of an act, as opposed to an address, concerning the legality of the Darien project, and he later dissented from the address to the king (17 January) which had been secured by 108 to 84 votes. In the same session, on 28 January, he also voted against the supply and maintenance of the armed forces of 3000 men being continued to December 1702, and on 31 January he voted against a further 1100 men being supplied for four months.

Grant continued to represent Inverness-shire in the parliament of 1703–7. During the debate over the Act of Security, Grant was one of the forty-three shire members subscribing to the protest of Robert Dundas of Arniston (Edinburgh) on 30 July 1703 that the government for a twenty-day period should be invested in the members of parliament present in Edinburgh at the time of the death of the monarch, as opposed to the privy council. He also joined in the protest against the Wine Act on 13 September 1703 and in the Atholl protestation of 1 September 1705 which stated that no act for a treaty with England should be passed until the English Aliens Act had been repealed. However, he ultimately voted in favour of the Union in the last session of the Scottish parliament (1706–7).

Grant added to and consolidated his estate throughout his lifetime. He acquired the lands of Achmonie from Gillies Mackay about 1670, and Pitcherrell Croy and Auchatemrach from John Grant of Corriemony, in exchange for Carnoch and others, in 1674. In 1677 he purchased Pluscardine estate in Elgin for £5000 Scots, money which was provided by his father-in-law. Brodie stipulated that these lands should form the inheritance of his daughter's second son. On 28 February 1694 Grant received a crown charter erecting the barony of Freuchie into the

regality of Grant. His castle, formerly known as Ballachastell, became Castle Grant, and the town, previously known as Castletown of Freuchie, became the town and burgh of Grant. His own designation thereafter changed from laird of Freuchie to laird of Grant. In 1696 he acquired more land from John Grant of Glenmoriston. In 1699 he passed over his possessions in the district of Loch Ness to his eldest surviving son, Alexander *Grant (1674x9–1719), on the latter's marriage to Elizabeth Stewart. Following Alexander's second marriage, in 1709, Grant resigned his lands over to his son in 1710, but retained an annuity of £300 sterling for himself and his second wife, Jean. He also formally resigned the chiefship of his clan over to his son at the end of that year, with the whole clan assembled at Ballintomb in full dress. Grant died in Edinburgh in November 1716. He was buried alongside his father in the abbey church of Holyrood on 19 November 1716. His widow, with whom he had had no children, died on 31 January 1734.   JOHN R. YOUNG

Sources *Scots peerage* · *APS, 1670–1707* · *Reg. PCS*, 3rd ser., vols. 7, 10–11, 14–16 · *The diary of Alexander Brodie of Brodie … and of his son James Brodie*, ed. D. Laing, Spalding Club, 33 (1863) · *Historical notices of Scottish affairs, selected from the manuscripts of Sir John Lauder of Fountainhall*, ed. D. Laing, 2 vols., Bannatyne Club, 87 (1848) · M. D. Young, ed., *The parliaments of Scotland: burgh and shire commissioners*, 2 vols. (1992–3) · W. Fraser, ed., *The chiefs of Grant*, 3 vols. (1883) · D. Warrand, ed., *More Culloden papers*, 5 vols. (1923–30), vol. 1 · H. Mackay, *Memoirs of the war carried on in Scotland and Ireland*, ed. J. M. Hog and others, Bannatyne Club, 45 (1833) · *DNB*
Archives Hunt. L., letters to earl of London
Wealth at death see *Scots peerage*

Grant, Malcolm (1762–1831), army officer in the East India Company, was appointed to an infantry cadetship on the Bombay establishment in 1776, left England in January 1777, and was made ensign on 20 November. In 1779 he served in the war in support of Raghunath Rao against the Marathas. He became lieutenant on 1 May 1780, and in 1780–81 served at the siege of Bassein and elsewhere with the Bengal force under General Thomas Goddard. He was afterwards employed in the neighbouring districts, and subsequently in Malabar under General Macleod until 1788, when he went home on furlough. He became captain on 2 January 1789.

Grant returned to India in 1790, and was again employed in Malabar. When operations were begun against Tipu Sultan, during the Fourth Anglo-Mysore War, he commanded the Bombay native grenadier battalion in the force sent under Colonel Little to act against the Marathas. This force was obliged to retire, and Grant's corps embarked at Jaigarh and proceeded by sea to Cannanore, and from there reached Siddapur on the Cauvery before the fall of Seringapatam. After the capture of Mysore, Grant, in command of the 1st battalion 3rd Bombay native infantry, was employed with the troops under General James Stuart at Mangalore and in Kanara, and at the capture of the fortress of Chikmagalur. On 8 January 1796 he was promoted major, and on 6 March 1800 he became lieutenant-colonel of the 8th Bombay native infantry, with which he served for several years in Malabar, then in open rebellion. In 1804 he succeeded Colonel Montresor as commander-in-chief in Malabar and Kanara. The same year he effected the reduction of the fortress of Savana-drug, held by Huri Belal, for which he received the thanks of the Indian government and of the peshwa.

In 1807 Grant returned to England in extreme ill health. He was appointed lieutenant-colonel commandant on 1 October 1809, and on 25 July 1810 colonel of the 9th Bombay native infantry. He became a major-general on 4 June 1813 and lieutenant-general on 27 May 1825. He died at his residence in Upper Wimpole Street, London, on 28 September 1831.   H. M. CHICHESTER, *rev.* ALEX MAY

Sources *Indian Army List* · D. Forrest, *Tiger of Mysore: the life and death of Tipu Sultan* (1970) · M. Edwardes, *Glorious sahibs: the romantic as empire-builder* (1968) · *GM*, 1st ser., 101/2 (1831), 468

Grant, Patrick, Lord Elchies (**1690–1754**), judge, was the only son of Captain John Grant (1660–1715) of Easter Elchies, Knockando, Moray, where he was born. His mother was Elizabeth (*d.* 1729), daughter of John Grant of Ballindalloch. He was a student at Marischal College, Aberdeen (1701–5), and from November 1710 to 1712 studied under the most notable jurists at the University of Leiden, without taking a degree. He returned to Scotland and was admitted an advocate on 12 February 1712.

Upon Grant's marriage on 10 June 1713 to Margaret (1693–1746), daughter of Sir Robert Dickson, bt, of Carberry, his father settled on him the baronies of Easter Elchies, Edinvillie, and Rothes. The couple had at least nine children, of whom several predeceased Grant; their eldest son, John, became an advocate and a baron of exchequer in Scotland, and died in 1775 in Grenada where he had extensive sugar estates.

On 3 November 1732 Grant was raised to the bench in succession to Sir John Maxwell of Pollock, taking the title Lord Elchies. On 3 March 1737 he succeeded Walter Pringle of Newhall as a lord of justiciary, retaining both offices until his death. He earned a reputation as the best reporter of Scottish decisions; he collected the decisions from more than 1600 cases heard at the court of session which were subsequently published as *Decisions of the Court of Session from the Year 1733 to the Year 1754 Collected and Digested into the Form of a Dictionary* (1813). He was also credited with the anonymous *Annotations on Lord Stair's Institutions* (1828). John Ramsay of Auchtertyre, who observed him on numerous occasions, found Elchies to be hot-tempered, intolerant of being contradicted, and exerting himself 'with indecent fervour' to get defendants convicted. 'In signing the sentence of death there appeared a malignant smile on his face which shocked the spectators' (Allardyce, 1.92).

Known as a staunch Hanoverian, Elchies suffered the ransacking of his house at Easter Elchies by Jacobites. After his wife died he moved to Carberry, the seat of his brother-in-law, where he lived until it was sold in 1752. Having presumably mellowed with age, he was remembered there as 'in all respects a most regular and exemplary parishioner, bringing his family to church every Sunday … agreeable and good tempered although he was held to be of a severe character' (*Scots Magazine*, 16, 1754,

237). He died at his home, Inch House, near Edinburgh, on 27 July 1754, and was buried in Greyfriars churchyard, Edinburgh.   J. A. HAMILTON, *rev.* ANITA MCCONNELL

Sources *Scotland and Scotsmen in the eighteenth century: from the MSS of John Ramsay, esq., of Ochtertyre*, ed. A. Allardyce, 1 (1888), 90–94 · G. Brunton and D. Haig, *An historical account of the senators of the college of justice, from its institution in MDXXXII* (1832), 503–4 · J. Kay, *A series of original portraits and caricature etchings … with biographical sketches and illustrative anecdotes*, ed. [H. Paton and others], new edn [3rd edn], 2 vols. in 4 (1877) · D. M. Walker, *The Scottish jurists* (1985), 296 · H. D. Macwilliam, *Letters of Patrick Grant, Lord Elchies, with memoir* (1927) · *Scots Magazine*, 16 (1754), 357 · A. F. Tytler, *Memoirs of the life and writings of the Honourable Henry Home of Kames*, 2 vols. (1807), vol. 1, pp. 39–40 · Anderson, *Scot. nat.* · F. J. Grant, ed., *The Faculty of Advocates in Scotland, 1532–1943*, Scottish RS, 145 (1944)
Archives NL Scot., session papers and notes on cases
Likenesses A. Ramsay, oils, 1749, Scot. NPG

Grant, Sir Patrick (**1804–1895**), army officer in the East India Company, was born on 11 September 1804 at Auchterblair, Inverness-shire, the second son of Major John Grant, 97th foot, and his wife, Anna Trapaud Grant. On 16 July 1820 Grant was commissioned an ensign in the 11th Bengal native infantry, in the East India Company service. He arrived in India on 6 January 1821 and served with several native infantry regiments during the early nineteenth century, rising steadily through the ranks. He was promoted lieutenant on 11 July 1823 and captain on 14 May 1832. In 1832 he married Jane Anne, daughter of William Fraser Tytler of Aldourie, Inverness-shire, and Sanquhar, Morayshire, with whom he had two sons. Their elder son, Alexander Charles, joined the army and rose to the rank of colonel; their younger son, Aldourie Patrick, was killed during the Indian mutiny in 1857 while serving as a lieutenant in the 71st Bengal native infantry. Grant's first wife died in 1838 and on 17 September 1844 he married Frances Maria (*d.* 1892), daughter of Field Marshal Gough, with whom he had five sons.

Grant was appointed a brigade major in Oudh in 1834, and in August 1836 was selected to raise the Hariana light infantry. In recognition of the efficiency of this new corps he was posted by the commander-in-chief, Sir Henry Fane, on 22 February 1838, as second assistant in the adjutant-general's department. He was employed under the command of Major-General Lumley, the adjutant-general, in 1841, organizing the force for service on the north-west frontier, and on 9 November 1842 was appointed first assistant. On 27 October 1843 he was made deputy adjutant-general with the temporary rank of major. He served as deputy assistant adjutant under Sir Hugh Gough during the Gwalior campaign, and participated in the battle of Maharajpur on 29 December 1843. For his services he was mentioned in dispatches, and received the bronze star and a brevet majority on 30 April 1844. In the Sutlej campaign during the First Anglo-Sikh War Grant acted for Sir James Lumley, the adjutant-general, who was sick, at the battle of Mudki, on 18 December 1845. He was twice severely wounded during this engagement and had his horse shot under him 'whilst urging on the infantry to the final and decisive attack of the enemy's batteries'. He was present on 21 and 22 December at the battle of Ferozesh-ahr, although his wounds prevented him from taking any active part in the fighting. Although still suffering from his injuries at the battle of Sobraon (10 February 1846), Gough remarked in his dispatch that 'nothing could sur-pass' Grant's activity and intelligence in the discharge of his duties, 'ever laborious, and during this campaign over-whelming'. For his services Grant received the campaign medal with three clasps, was promoted to a brevet lieutenant-colonelcy, and was made a CB on 3 April 1846.

Grant was appointed adjutant-general of the Bengal army on 28 March 1846, and as such served under Gough throughout the Punjab campaign of the Second Anglo-Sikh War. He participated in the battles of Chilianwala (13 January 1849) and Gujrat (21 February 1849). For his ser-vices he was warmly thanked in dispatches, received the campaign medal and two clasps, was promoted colonel in the army on 2 August 1850, and was made aide-de-camp to Queen Victoria. During the spring of 1850 Grant served under Sir Charles James Napier, the new commander-in-chief in India, during operations against the trans-border Pathan tribes in the Kohat district, and later received the medal and clasp.

On 25 January 1856 Grant was appointed commander-in-chief of the Madras army, with the temporary rank of lieutenant-general, and on 2 January 1857 was made a KCB. Following the outbreak of the Indian mutiny and the death from cholera of General George Anson, commander-in-chief in India, on 27 May 1857, Grant was summoned to Calcutta by Lord Canning, the governor-general. He arrived there on 17 June, and was appointed, provisionally, commander-in-chief, the first East India Company officer ever to hold this office, bringing with him Major-General Henry Havelock who had just returned to Madras following the Persian campaign. Grant was immediately employed organizing the dis-patch of a force under Havelock's command to Allahabad for the relief of the beleaguered British garrisons at Cawn-pore and Lucknow. Although Canning recommended to the authorities in London that Grant should be confirmed as commander-in-chief in India, Sir Colin Campbell had already been nominated for the post. When Campbell arrived at Calcutta on 13 August 1857 Grant resumed com-mand at Madras, and held this post until 27 January 1861. His services during the uprising were richly praised in a dispatch by the governor-general in council which was fully endorsed by the secretary of state for India. Grant returned to Britain, and was made a GCB on 28 February 1861, and promoted lieutenant-general on 24 October 1862.

On 15 May 1867 Grant was appointed governor and commander-in-chief of Malta, and early the following year was made GCMG. He was promoted general on 19 November 1870, and in 1872 relinquished his post at Malta. On 20 February 1874 he succeeded Lieutenant-General Sir Sydney Cotton as governor of the Royal Hos-pital, Chelsea, and was promoted to the rank of field mar-shal. He was also made colonel Royal Horse Guards and gold-stick-in-waiting to Queen Victoria. Grant died at the

Royal Hospital, Chelsea, on 28 March 1895. He was buried with full military honours at Brompton cemetery, Lon-don, on 2 April.　　　　　　　R. H. VETCH, rev. T. R. MOREMAN

Sources　The Times (29 March 1895) • T. A. Heathcote, The military in British India: the development of British land forces in south Asia, 1600–1947 (1995) • C. Hibbert, The great mutiny, India, 1857 (1978) • J. W. Kaye, A history of the Sepoy War in India, 1857–1858, 3 vols. (1864–76) • J. H. Archer, Commentaries on the Punjab campaign, 1848–49 (1878) • E. J. Thackwell, Narrative of the Second Seikh War, in 1848–49 (1851)
Archives　BL OIOC, corresp. with Sir George Russell Clerk • Bodl. Oxf., corresp. with Lord Kimberley • N. Yorks. CRO, Havelock MSS
Likenesses　C. Martin, watercolour drawing, c.1856–1861, NPG • E. J. Turner, oils, 1883 (after photograph by Maull & Fox, after 1883), NPG • M. Fraser-Tytler, oils, 1887, Royal Horse Guards, London • G. Wade, statue, Royal Hospital, Chelsea
Wealth at death　£73,518 3s. 9d.: probate, 20 May 1895, CGPLA Eng. & Wales

Grant, Peter (1708–1784), Roman Catholic priest and agent, was born on 15 August 1708 in Glenlivet, the son of John Grant of Blairfindy. He first studied at the seminary at Scalan, then entered the Scots College, Rome, in 1726, where he was ordained before returning to Scotland in 1735. A Gaelic speaker, he was sent to Glengarry, Inverness-shire, where he worked as a priest until his appointment as Roman agent in 1737. As such, he was the essential link between the Scottish mission and the con-gregation of propaganda fide. Bishop Hay frowned upon the agent's busy social life, which in his opinion led Grant to neglect the interests of the mission. While his younger brother, Robert, had become the first secular rector of the Scots College, Douai, Peter refused the rectorship of the Scots College, Rome, which he was offered when the Jesu-its were suppressed in 1773. Pope Clement XIV was very fond of him and might have created him a cardinal had the pope lived longer. Hardly any British traveller, whether Catholic or protestant, visited Rome without let-ters of introduction to Abbé Grant, who would be their guide there. His diligence in getting private audiences with the pope for British gentry on the grand tour earned him the nickname 'l'Introduttore' and he received praise for the assiduousness and courtesy of his service. He also introduced British travellers to the artists he knew, including Angelica Kauffman and Gavin Hamilton. In 1783 he decided to return to Britain and embarked on a 'Grand Tour in reverse' (Skinner), which took him to the homes of those visitors to Italy he had formerly helped. He was in London at the time of his brother's death there in March 1784. He died at Rome on 1 September 1784 and was buried in the city's parish church in the piazza Navona.

CLOTILDE PRUNIER

Sources　W. J. Anderson, 'Abbé Peter Grant, Roman agent for the Scottish Catholic mission, 1738–1783', St Peter's College Magazine, 23 (June 1957), 4–8 • J. F. S. Gordon, ed., History of the Catholic Church in Scotland since the Reformation (1874) • B. Skinner, 'Abbé Grant, the arch-conductor of the grand tour', Glasgow Herald (17 June 1961) • M. Dilworth, 'Grant, Peter (Abbé)', DSCHT
Archives　NL Scot., letters to Sir Archibald Grant • Scottish Cath-olic Archives, Edinburgh, Blairs letters
Likenesses　A. Kauffman, portrait, c.1763; on loan to Scot. NPG, 1961; commissioned by James Moray of Abercairney • M. Tibaldi, miniature, 1763, repro. in Anderson, 'Abbé Peter Grant …'; for-merly in the coll. of the countess of Seafield, 1957 • marble effigy

on monument, 1784?, Sant'Andrea degli Scozzesi, Rome · portraits, repro. in Anderson, 'Abbé Peter Grant …'
Wealth at death a gold snuff box: Gordon, ed., *History of the Catholic church*

Grant, Peter [Pàdraig Grannd nan Òran] (**1783–1867**), Baptist minister and Gaelic evangelical poet, was born on 30 January 1783 at Ballintua, Strathspey, Scotland, the youngest of the five children of Donald Grant (*d.* 1806), a farmer, and his wife, Janet Stuart. Peter was converted through the preaching of Lachlan Mackintosh, a Haldane-supported missionary who became founder and first pastor of the Baptist church at Grantown-on-Spey, and became an itinerant missionary. On Mackintosh's departure from Grantown in 1826, he succeeded him as pastor, being ordained in 1829, and continued in that position until his death. During his ministry, in which he was assisted by his son William (one of eight children from his first marriage, to Ann Mackintosh (*d.* 1836)), the church achieved a membership of almost 300.

A skilled fiddle player, Grant wrote a number of Gaelic hymns (Grant's Gaelic name means 'Peter Grant of the songs') which explore the Christian's pilgrimage, extol the efficacy of Christ's blood, and anticipate the inevitability of death and the joy of the heavenly home. Set to well-known tunes, they remained extremely popular in the highlands at the end of the twentieth century. They were published in an edition by H. MacDougall in 1926 as *Spiritual Songs by Rev. Peter Grant*.

Grant, who married his second wife, Janet, in 1852, and was outlived by her, died at Grantown-on-Spey on 14 December 1867. DONALD E. MEEK

Sources P. Grant, *Dain Spioradail le Padruig Grannd…Fo laimh Eachainn Mhic Dhùghaill (Spiritual songs…Biographical sketch of the author by Annie G. Robinson and J. A. Grant Robinson)*, ed. E. Macdhùghaill, A. G. Robinson, and J. A. Grant Robinson (1926) · D. E. Meek, 'The Independent and Baptist churches of highland Perthshire and Strathspey', *Transactions of the Gaelic Society of Inverness*, 56 (1989–90), 269–343 · D. E. Meek, 'Images of the natural world in the hymns of Dugald Buchanan and Peter Grant', *Scottish Gaelic Studies*, 17 (1996), 263–77 · d. cert.
Archives Baptist church, Grantown-on-Spey
Likenesses A. D. Birnie, portrait, repro. in Grant, *Spiritual songs*; formerly priv. coll., 1926 · oils (in later years); exh. Grantown, July 1983

Grant, Peter (**1935–1995**), rock group manager, was born on 5 April 1935 in Birdhurst Road, Croydon, Surrey, the son of Dorothy Louise Grant, a private secretary, of South Norwood, Surrey. The name of his father is not recorded. He left school at thirteen and his height and weight—he was 6 feet 5 inches tall and weighed 18½ stone—led to his taking work as a bouncer, a stand-in for the actor Robert Morley, and a wrestler (under the name of Count Bruno Alassio of Milan). In the late fifties Grant worked at the Two Is coffee bar in Soho, a popular venue on the London pop circuit, where he met Don Arden, the 'Al Capone of Pop', who offered him a job as a tour manager. Grant's business skills were sharpened by this association; it was when he toured America with the UK rock group the Animals in 1964 that he spotted the potential of the US market, where he later made his fortune.

By the mid-sixties Grant had taken over the management of the Yardbirds, a UK rock band. He saw it as his duty to do his best for his artists by making sure that they were fully paid. In pursuing this policy, he became known for his often brutal dealings with promoters; he was not shy of using his intimidating physique to ensure payment.

When the Yardbirds split up in 1968 the band's guitarist Jimmy Page invited Grant to become the manager of his new band, Led Zeppelin. Page saw him as the manager who could ensure that the band kept control of their assets. While Page developed the band musically, Grant's marketing strategies and fearsome management techniques launched it into the stratosphere of the global rock business. He was regarded as the band's fifth member and took a 20 per cent share of the proceeds.

Grant's reputation as one of rock's shrewdest brains was evident in his negotiations with Atlantic Records when Led Zeppelin became the first rock band to appear on this prestigious rhythm and blues label. They received an astonishing $200,000 advance and the highest royalty rate hitherto negotiated by a group for their first album. The subsequent tremendous success of their albums can be ascribed to the band's musicianship and to Grant's albums-only policy. This strategy meant that the US FM radio stations, which were playing to Led Zeppelin's targeted 'underground rock' audience, would play the whole side of a Zeppelin album, rather than just singles lifted from the record. Eventually Atlantic allowed them to establish their own label, Swansong, which Grant ran until 1983.

However, Grant's notoriety as one of the toughest operators in rock history (aided and abetted by tour manager Richard Cole) was also made during the band's relentless touring of the US throughout the early to mid-seventies. Along with legendary tales of grotesque indulgence and debauchery, Grant's Svengali-like influence saw Led Zeppelin fill cavernous venues and negotiate with promoters up front a deal ensuring the band an extraordinary 90 per cent of the profits. In 1973 Zeppelin played to 56,800 people at Tampa Stadium, Florida, and grossed $309,000, thereby breaking the previous US box office record, set by a Beatles concert at Shea Stadium.

In many respects Grant's intimidating physical presence had produced this success. However, his and Coles's tendency to violence (most especially directed against bootleggers and other non-sanctioned merchandisers) eventually caught up with them. On the 1977 tour of the US they were arrested, along with the drummer John Bonham and security chief John Bindon, for assaulting one of promoter Bill Graham's security guards in Oakland, California, after he had manhandled Grant's son Warren. In many respects this disaster was the culmination of the major misfortunes that affected the band in the mid-seventies. Grant himself was divorced from his wife Gloria after fourteen years of marriage in 1976, the singer Robert Plant and his family had suffered an almost fatal car crash, and Plant's son Karac had died.

These problems stopped Led Zeppelin touring and the

band became ridiculed in some quarters as rock dinosaurs. Events took an even more tragic turn just before Zeppelin were to undertake a new American tour in 1980, when the drummer John Bonham died from alcohol abuse. Bonham's death led to Zeppelin's demise and Grant went into a near-terminal decline, locking himself away in his moated Sussex mansion and existing largely on cocaine—which he referred to as 'Peruvian marching powder'—and Marks & Spencer sandwiches and trifle.

When a slimmed-down Grant returned to public view in the late eighties, he had become an avuncular figure. He was by then a grandfather and was living in Eastbourne, enjoying his collections of classic cars, antique lamps, and furniture. He had no desire to return to a changed music business, although he did attend industry seminars where he entertained audiences with his tales from the past. On 21 November 1995 Grant died of a heart attack while returning to his Eastbourne home. At his funeral on 4 December his old associate Alan Callan commented that 'If you were his friend, then to you he would give his all' (Channel 4 television website). Grant's lasting significance was perhaps best summed up by Phil Everly of the Everly Brothers, who paid tribute to him as the first manager 'to make sure the artist came first and that we got paid and paid properly' (*The Guardian*, 24 Nov 1995).

MARK WHEELER

Sources 'Mr Rock and Roll', www.channelfour.com/nextstep/mr_rock_and_roll, 1999 · R. Cole and R. Trubo, *Stairway to heaven: Led Zeppelin uncensored* (1992) · S. Davis, *Hammer of the gods: Led Zeppelin unauthorised*, 2nd edn (1995) · *The Times* (24 Nov 1995) · *The Independent* (24 Nov 1995) · *The Guardian* (24 Nov 1995) · *Daily Telegraph* (24 Nov 1995) · A. Sweeting, 'We'll manage', *The Guardian* (3 Sept 1999) · b. cert. · d. cert. · C. Welch, *Peter Grant: the man who Led Zeppelin* (2001) **Archives** FILM Channel 4, 'Mr Rock and Roll', documentary, screened *c*.1999 **Likenesses** photograph, repro. in *The Times* · photograph, repro. in *The Independent* **Wealth at death** £509,600: administration, 27 June 1996, CGPLA Eng. & Wales

Grant, Richard [called Richard le Grand, Richard Magnus] (*d*. 1231), archbishop of Canterbury, was apparently a native of Nazeing in Essex. He had a brother and a sister, Walter and Agnes of Nazeing, to whom when he was archbishop he made an annual allowance of £10 from the archiepiscopal manor of Otford. His career is obscure until his first appearance as chancellor and head of the schools of Lincoln Cathedral on 16 December 1220, an office he held until his appointment to Canterbury on 19 January 1229, in succession to Stephen Langton. On that occasion he was recommended to Pope Gregory IX by Alexander Stavensby, bishop of Coventry and Lichfield, and Henry Sandford, bishop of Rochester, who had known him in the schools; their testimonial suggests that he was a man of eminent learning and that he had studied and taught at Paris. He was provided to Canterbury in his absence, and without reference to the chapter, by the pope who had, at the request of Henry III, quashed the election of Walter of Eynsham, the candidate chosen by Walter's fellow monks of Canterbury. Richard le Grand

(the sobriquet apparently referred to his tall stature, which was commented upon by Matthew Paris) was the choice of the suffragans of the Canterbury province, whose claims to a voice in the election of their archbishop were represented at the papal curia by Stavensby and Sandford. Pope Gregory's letter announcing the appointment refers to Richard's reputation for learning and his zeal for souls and for the liberties of the church. The king's assent was signified and the royal bailiffs were ordered to surrender the temporalities on 24 March 1229. Grant was consecrated at Canterbury by Henry Sandford on 10 June. He celebrated his receipt of the pallium from Rome in Canterbury Cathedral on 23 November in the presence of the king and the suffragans of the Canterbury province.

As a schoolman–bishop concerned for ecclesiastical reform, the eradication of abuses, and the freedom of the church from secular domination, Richard Grant was in the Langton tradition. The *acta* that survive from his brief episcopate show, in fact, that his administrative *familia* included a core of learned men who had served Langton, such as Master Thomas of Freckenham, who had been Langton's official, Elias of Dereham, Langton's steward, and Grant's own official, Master Richard of Wallingford. Like his great predecessor, Grant displayed boldness and determination in defending clerical immunities and the rights of his see. Early in 1230, when King Henry levied a scutage of 3 marks on baronial tenants of the crown to pay for his ill-considered expedition to Poitou, the archbishop incurred the king's anger by acting as spokesman for the prelates who opposed the levy. He argued that an assembly of lay barons that had approved the tax had no power to bind the clergy in such a matter. In thus questioning the right of the secular power to tax the clergy he raised an issue that was to become a major source of conflict between the crown and the papacy later in the century. At the same time he found himself in conflict with the all-powerful justiciar, Hubert de Burgh, over the territorial rights of his see. Following the death of Gilbert de Clare, earl of Gloucester, de Burgh had been assigned wardship of the Clare estates which included Tonbridge Castle and its adjacent area, in respect of which the earl had been a military tenant of the archbishopric. Archbishop Richard claimed that the wardship of Tonbridge belonged as of right to his see, but the justiciar refused to disgorge it, and his refusal was upheld by the king, who claimed the prerogative wardship of all the earl's military fees. Having failed to get redress, Grant excommunicated all those involved saving only the person of the king. According to Roger of Wendover, this invasion of the property of his see was one of the grievances he laid before the pope when he reached the curia in the summer of 1231.

Archbishop Grant's decision to make an *ad limina* visit to Rome was evidently prompted by his desire to secure papal support for the reform of the English church. One of the abuses he sought to remedy was the involvement of clergy in secular government and the work of the royal courts, with a corresponding neglect of their pastoral responsibilities; another was pluralism, of which the most conspicuous practitioners were royal clerks and which was facilitated by the readiness of the papacy to grant dispensations. He set out for Rome in the spring of 1231; his last recorded act on English soil was a charter confirming a gift of land in Kent to the Cistercian abbey of Dunes, which is dated 9 March 1231. He was sympathetically received at the curia and, according to Matthew Paris, the pope acceded to all his requests, despite objections by proctors representing the king. But Grant's plans for reform were frustrated by his death on the homeward journey. He died, possibly of malaria, at San Gémini in Umbria on 3 August 1231 and was buried there in the house of the Friars Minor. None of his theological *quaestiones* or commentaries has been traced, though a sermon under his name is preserved in a collection of Paris University sermons of the early thirteenth century. It does not appear that Grant had time to visit his province. The synodal statutes attributed to him in Lyndwood's *Provinciale* are those of Richard of Dover, archbishop of Canterbury (1173–84). There appears to be no contemporary evidence for Grant's use of the name Wethershed which has sometimes been attributed to him, and which appears to rest solely upon a late fourteenth-century interpolation in the *Polychronicon* of Ranulf Higden. Nevertheless the suggestion has been made, based on this name, that Richard Grant was identical with the theologian Richard of *Wetheringsett, author of the *summa*, *Qui bene presunt*. No conclusive evidence has been advanced in support of this theory, which must therefore be regarded as unproven.

C. H. LAWRENCE

Sources Archbishop Warham's register, LPL · dean and chapter muniments, chartae antiquae, Canterbury · *A descriptive catalogue of ancient deeds in the Public Record Office*, 6 vols. (1890–1915) · A. W. Gibbons, ed., *Liber antiquus de ordinationibus vicariarum tempore Hugonis Wells, Lincolniensis episcopi, 1209–1235* (1888) · C. W. Foster and K. Major, eds., *The registrum antiquissimum of the cathedral church of Lincoln*, 3–4, Lincoln RS, 29, 32 (1935–7) · W. P. W. Phillimore, ed., *Rotuli Hugonis de Welles, episcopi Lincolniensis*, CYS, 1 (1907) · *Rogeri de Wendover liber qui dicitur flores historiarum*, ed. H. G. Hewlett, 3 vols., Rolls Series, [84] (1886–9) · Paris, *Chron.* · *Ann. mon.* · Chancery records · *Les registres de Grégoire IX*, ed. L. Auvray, 1 (Paris, 1896) · M. Gibbs and J. Lang, *Bishops and reform, 1215–1272* (1934)

Archives BL, sermon, Royal MS 8 C.v, fol. 5

Grant, Sir Robert (1780–1838), administrator in India, was born on 15 January 1780 at Kidderpore, Bengal, the younger son of Charles *Grant, East India Company chairman and evangelical philanthropist, and his wife, Jane, daughter of Thomas Fraser of Balnain, Inverness. Charles *Grant, Lord Glenelg, was his elder brother.

Robert and Charles went to England in 1790 and were educated privately by the clergymen John Venn, of Clapham Sect fame, and Henry Jowett, before going up to Magdalene College, Cambridge, in 1795. Robert graduated BA in 1801 as third wrangler and second chancellor's medallist. In 1802 he was elected a fellow of Magdalene and in 1804 took the degree of MA. He was called to the bar at Lincoln's Inn in 1807 and practised chiefly on the western circuit before being appointed a commissioner of bankrupts in 1814. In 1813 he published a defence of the East India

Company's trading monopoly and a history of the company's development up to 1773.

In 1818, through the influence of Francis Grant, acting chief of the clan, Grant was elected member of parliament for Elgin burghs, which seat he held until 1820. Thereafter he was elected for Inverness burghs in 1826, for Norwich in 1830 and 1831 (in which year he was also sworn a privy councillor), and for the newly constituted borough of Finsbury in 1832. He was king's serjeant in the duchy court of Lancaster from 1827 until 1830, whereupon his brother's appointment as president of the Board of Control opened up a place for him as one of the board's commissioners. In 1832 he became judge advocate-general. He married in 1829 Margaret (d. 1885), only daughter of Sir David Davidson of Cantray, Nairnshire, with whom he had two sons, including Sir Robert *Grant, army officer, and two daughters.

As a member of parliament Grant championed the movement for repealing the civil disabilities of the Jews. In 1833, aided by Macaulay, Hume, and O'Connell, his bill for Jewish emancipation passed through the Commons, only to be rejected by the Lords. His bill of 1834 met the same fate. Although the Lords withstood a settlement of the question until 1858, long after Grant's death, Jewish leaders in London often acknowledged Grant's persistent advocacy of their rights.

In June 1834, after lobbying by his influential brother, Grant was appointed governor of Bombay, and in the following August was made a knight of the Royal Guelphic Order (GCH). As governor Grant attempted to improve the communications and commerce of his vast province. He promoted regular steam navigation with Europe, created a separate department for the construction of roads, called for the abolition of inland duties, and established experimental agricultural gardens. He extended public recognition to the fledgeling Bombay chamber of commerce, and encouraged both English and vernacular schools. He saw himself as an improving governor and repeatedly complained that the Anglo-Indian press, whose freedom of speech he regarded as an unhelpful anachronism in an unfree country, malignly misrepresented his best measures and purest motives. After a short illness he died unexpectedly on 9 July 1838 at the governor's residence at Dalpoorie and was buried the next day at St Mary's Church in Poona. Grant Medical College at Bombay was founded in his memory.

An active member of the Bible Society and a lover of music, Grant was remembered by the British public principally as a composer of hymns, most notably his version of Psalm 104, 'O worship the king all glorious above'. A selection of his compositions, entitled *Sacred Poems*, was published posthumously by his brother Charles in 1839 and reissued in 1844 and 1868.

E. J. RAPSON, *rev.* KATHERINE PRIOR

Sources HoP, *Commons, 1790–1820*, vol. 5 · H. Morris, *The life of Charles Grant* (1904) · BL OIOC, Grant MSS · *Bombay Gazette* (20 July 1838) · *Revised list of tombs and monuments of historical or archaeological interest in Bombay*, Government of Bombay [1912] · ecclesiastical records, BL OIOC · *WWBMP*, vol. 1

Archives BL, collection of poems, Eg. 1966 · BL OIOC, official and personal corresp. and papers, MS Eur. E 308 · NA Scot. · NL Wales, personal and family papers | BL, Broughton MSS · BL OIOC, Broughton MSS · NA Scot., letters to James Grant · NL Wales, Pitchford MSS
Likenesses G. Hayter, group portrait, oils (*The House of Commons, 1833*), NPG · F. C. Lewis, stipple (after J. Slater), BM

Grant, Robert (1814–1892), astronomer, was born on 17 June 1814 at Grantown-on-Spey, Morayshire, the son of Robert Grant, a tradesman, and his wife, Marjory. He attended a local school endowed by the earl of Seafield and showed promise in the classics, but was struck by a severe illness between his thirteenth and nineteenth years; after recovering he worked diligently to master Latin, Greek, modern languages, mathematics, and astronomy. He observed Halley's comet in 1835 and the annular solar eclipse of 1836. He attended King's College, Aberdeen, for the session 1839–40, then worked for four years in London as a bookkeeper in an elder brother's counting-house, meanwhile continuing his studies and laying plans for a history of astronomy.

In 1845 Grant took up a two-year residence in Paris, where he attended lectures by Arago at the observatory and by Leverrier at the Sorbonne, made use of the library of the Institut de France, and supported himself by teaching. During the next five years in London he continued his researches, having gained access to the library of the Royal Astronomical Society. He was introduced to Robert Baldwin, the enterprising publisher of a series of popular works under the title the Library of Useful Knowledge, and it was arranged to print his history in separate parts commencing in September 1848. After the issue of the ninth part this style of publication was abandoned, and the entire work appeared in 1852 as a single volume, *History of Physical Astronomy from the Earliest Ages to the Middle of the Nineteenth Century*. Grant had become a fellow of the Royal Astronomical Society in 1850. Augustus De Morgan and other members were immediately impressed by his *History* and expressed their approbation in the annual report of the council in February 1853. It earned him the gold medal in 1856, when the president called particular attention to his analysis of the controversial discovery of Neptune. Grant served on the council of the society from 1853 to 1860 and was editor of *Monthly Notices* from 1852 to 1860. He introduced for the first time abstracts of astronomical intelligence from *Comptes Rendus*, *Astronomische Nachrichten*, and other scientific periodicals, and he translated works by Arago under the titles *Biographies of Distinguished Men* (1854), *Popular Treatise on Comets* (1861), and, with William Henry Smyth, *Popular Astronomy* (2 vols., 1855–8).

In 1858 Grant undertook a course of instruction in observing techniques at Greenwich, a timely exercise, as in November 1859 he was offered the chair of practical astronomy in the University of Glasgow, on the recommendation of James David Forbes and John Couch Adams. He took up the appointment in May 1860, but immediately went to Spain for the total eclipse of 18 July and proved to his own satisfaction, as his *History* suggested,

Robert Grant (1814–1892), by unknown photographer

that the solar prominences and chromosphere originated in the sun. At Glasgow observatory Grant was faced with a cloudy and increasingly polluted atmosphere. He inherited some inferior instruments and the great Ertel transit circle of 6 French inches' aperture, set up but barely used by his wayward predecessor John Pringle Nichol, but through the liberality of friends and Glasgow citizens he was able to procure by 1863 a magnificent 9 inch Cooke refractor and a small transit telescope from the private observatory of the late Sir William Keith Murray, bt, at Ochtertyre in Perthshire. In 1861 he inaugurated a time service for the city and port, and in 1865 collaborated with the astronomer royal, George Biddell Airy, to ascertain accurately the difference in longitude between the Glasgow and Greenwich observatories by electrical signals. After testing the transit circle he commenced a series of observations on planets, asteroids, and a selection of stars from the British Association catalogue. He then embarked on a long series of stellar places from 1860 to 1881, with slender funding and a succession of temporary assistants, published in 1883 at government expense as *A Catalogue of 6415 Stars for the Epoch 1870*, with an introductory discussion on the proper motions of ninety-nine stars. A supplementary *Catalogue of 2156 Stars* appeared a few weeks after his death. Both were considered valuable at the time.

On 3 September 1874 Grant married Elizabeth Emma

Davison of Newcastle, New South Wales, and co. Monaghan, Ireland; they had one son and three daughters. He found time to make and publish in *Monthly Notices* and *Astronomische Nachrichten* observations of comets, meteors, double stars, and the transit of Venus of 1882, and to demonstrate in a letter to *The Times* of 20 September 1867 the forgery of certain papers attributed to Pascal. He was the first Glasgow professor to teach rigorous courses in astronomy for the new science degrees. He was awarded an honorary MA by King's College in 1854 and LLD by the united University of Aberdeen in 1865, the same year he was elected fellow of the Royal Society. He served as president of the Philosophical Society of Glasgow for three years and contributed to its *Proceedings*. During 1892 his health deteriorated; he returned to Grantown to recuperate, but died there, at Lethendry Lodge, on 24 October.

A. M. CLERKE, rev. DAVID GAVINE

Sources *Monthly Notices of the Royal Astronomical Society*, 53 (1892–3), 210–18 · *Nature*, 47 (1892–3), 36–7 · *Encyclopaedia Britannica*, 11th edn (1910–11) · *The Times* (2 Nov 1892) · E. J. S., *PRS*, 57 (1894–5), i-iii · *Glasgow Herald* (26 Oct 1892) · *The Scotsman* (26 Oct 1892) · *Men and women of the time* (1891)

Archives U. Glas. | NMM, Greenwich, Royal Observatory, Airy MSS · RAS, letters to RAS

Likenesses photograph, repro. in *The University of Glasgow old and new* (1891), 68 · photograph, RAS [*see illus.*]

Grant, Sir Robert (1837–1904), army officer, born at Malabar Hill, Bombay, on 10 August 1837, was younger son of Sir Robert *Grant (1780–1838), governor of Bombay, and was nephew of Charles *Grant, Baron Glenelg. His mother was Margaret (*d.* 1885), only daughter of Sir David Davidson of Cantray, Nairnshire, Scotland, who married as her second husband Lord Josceline William Percy MP, second son of George, fifth duke of Northumberland.

Robert was educated at Harrow School with his elder brother Charles [*see below*]. When he was seventeen he passed first in a public competitive examination for vacancies in the Royal Artillery and the Royal Engineers caused by the Crimean War, and was commissioned second lieutenant in the Royal Engineers on 23 October 1854, becoming first lieutenant on 13 December 1854. He served in Scotland, Jamaica, and British Honduras.

Grant passed first in the examination for the Staff College, just established, but after a few months there (January–May 1859) he became aide-de-camp to Lieutenant General Sir William Fenwick Williams, the commander of the forces in North America for six years. On 8 August 1860 he was promoted second captain. He was at home for the final examination at the Staff College, in which he easily passed first, despite his absence from the classes.

Grant returned from Canada in 1865, and from then until 1883 served in various appointments in England. He was promoted first captain in July 1867, major in July 1872, lieutenant-colonel in July 1878, and colonel in the army on 1 July 1882, and a year later was placed on half pay. On 5 May 1884, he was given the Royal Engineers' command in Scotland, with the rank of colonel on the staff.

Grant married in London, on 24 November 1875, Victoria Alexandrina, daughter of John Cotes of Woodcote

Hall, Shropshire, and widow of T. Owen of Condover Hall in the same county. She survived him. They had three children: a daughter who died young and twin sons, both in the army, of whom the younger, Robert Josceline, was killed at Spion Kop on 24 January 1900.

On 20 March 1885 Grant left Edinburgh suddenly for Egypt to join Lord Wolseley, who had telegraphed for his services, as colonel on the staff and commanding royal engineer with the Nile expeditionary force. He served with the headquarters staff and afterwards in command of the Abu Fatmeh district during the evacuation, but became seriously ill with fever and was invalided home in August. He was mentioned in dispatches. Not expecting so short a campaign, the authorities had filled his appointment in Scotland and he had to wait nearly a year on half pay.

On 1 July 1886 Grant was appointed deputy adjutant-general for Royal Engineers at the War Office. On 25 May 1889 he was created CB, military division, and on 23 October made a temporary major-general. Before he had quite completed his five years as deputy adjutant-general he was appointed to the important post of inspector-general of fortifications (18 April 1891), with the temporary rank of lieutenant-general, dated 29 April 1891. He succeeded to the establishment of major-generals on 9 May 1891, and became lieutenant-general on 4 June 1897. As inspector-general of fortifications Grant was an *ex officio* member of the joint naval and military committee on defence, and president of the colonial defence committee. During his term important works of defence and of barrack construction were carried out, under the loan for defences and military works. His services were so highly valued that they were retained for two years beyond the usual term. He was made KCB on 20 May 1896, and left the War Office in April 1898. He was created GCB on 26 June 1902, and retired on 28 March 1903. Always cool and self-contained, Grant was gifted with a sure judgement and a retentive memory. His health declined, and he died on 8 January 1904 at his residence, 14 Granville Place, Portman Square, London, and was buried in Kensal Green cemetery.

Sir Charles Grant (1836–1903), elder brother of Sir Robert Grant, was born in Bombay on 22 February 1836, and educated at Harrow School, at Trinity College, Cambridge, and at the East India College, Haileybury. He entered the Bengal civil service in 1858, was appointed a commissioner of the central provinces in 1870, and acting chief commissioner in 1879, when he became an additional member of the governor-general's council. He married in 1872 Ellen (*d.* 1885), daughter of the Rt Hon. Henry Baillie of Redcastle, Scotland. In 1880 he was acting secretary to the government of India for the home, revenue, and agricultural departments, and in 1881 was appointed foreign secretary to the government of India. He was created CSI in 1881, and in 1885 KCSI on retirement. He married on 15 October 1890 Lady Florence Lucia (*d.* 1909), daughter of Admiral Sir Edward Alfred John Harris and sister of the fourth earl of Malmesbury; they had children. He died suddenly at his residence, 5 Marble Arch, London, on 10 April 1903.

R. H. VETCH, rev. JAMES FALKNER

Sources war office records, PRO [WO ser.] · Royal Engineers Institution, Chatham, Royal Engineers records · *The Times* (13 April 1903) · *The Times* (9 Jan 1904) · *The Times* (10 Jan 1904) · *Army List* · *Hart's Army List* · *Royal Engineers Journal* (Feb 1904) · *LondG* (25 Aug 1885) · Venn, *Alum. Cant.*
Archives King's Lond., Liddell Hart C., corresp. and papers
Likenesses Henty, oils, 1887; formerly in possession of Lady Grant, 1912 · C. Lutyens, oils, 1897, Royal Engineers, Aldershot; replica, formerly in possession of Lady Grant, 1912
Wealth at death £35,038 16s. 9d.: probate, 13 Feb 1904, *CGPLA Eng. & Wales*

Grant, Robert Edmond (1793–1874), comparative anatomist and transmutationist, was born in Edinburgh on 11 November 1793. He was the seventh son in the family of twelve sons and two daughters of Alexander Grant (*d.* 1808), a wealthy writer to the signet, and Jane Edmond. Robert was the only son to stay in Britain, the others mostly joining the navy or the East India Company. After Edinburgh high school (1803–8), he used his inheritance—his father died in 1808—to study and travel for two decades.

Edinburgh University At Edinburgh University, Grant studied classics (1808), then medicine (1809–14). He was president of the Medico-Chirurgical Society in 1812. Inducted into the Royal Medical Society by Marshall Hall in 1811, he became its president in 1814. Of his four papers there, one, 'On the comparative anatomy of the brain in the class Mammalia' in 1814, twitted his mentor John Gordon for his anti-mechanist orthodoxy and attacks on Franz Gall. Grant was already diverging from his presbyterian teachers in a period of growing regency radicalism. Another paper, on the circulation of the blood in the foetus (which cited Erasmus Darwin), became his MD thesis in 1814.

In 1815 Grant left Edinburgh to attend Henri de Blainville's course in Paris, and then to study in Rome, Florence, and Germany. An inveterate walker, he had crossed the Alps seven times by foot before he arrived back in Scotland in 1820. A licentiate (1825) and fellow (1827) of the Royal College of Physicians of Edinburgh, he practised medicine for a while. He attended Robert Jameson's natural history course in 1823 and lectured on invertebrate anatomy in John Barclay's school in 1824, although he was unsympathetic to Barclay's anti-reductionism; in the same year he was elected to the Royal Society of Edinburgh. He witnessed James Hall's experiments on the artificial formation of rocks by heat, which stimulated Grant's cooling-earth explanation of fossil development.

Grant, who was a Francophile, specialized, like Lamarck, in the 'lower' invertebrates, and followed Jean Lamaroux's studies on the little-known colonial 'zoophytes' (Hydrozoa and Gorgonia), particularly the 'moss animals' (Bryozoa), corals, and sponges. He published twenty papers on invertebrates in 1825–7, most in the *Edinburgh Philosophical Journal* and *Edinburgh Journal of Science* (which he conducted temporarily). He described six new Scottish sponges and introduced the word 'Porifera'. He delineated the sponges' canal structure, establishing

Robert Edmond Grant (1793–1874), by Thomas Herbert Maguire, 1852

that they generated a water current and had separate entrance and raised exit pores. A serial progressionist like Lamarck and Blainville, he linked the sponges into a graduated sequence, which he believed reflected their ancestry. Demonstrating that the freshwater *Spongilla friabilis* (which he was first to section) had unraised faecal orifices, he considered it 'more ancient than the marine sponges, and most probably their original parent' (Grant, 270). Where Lamarck ranked sponges below the colonial polyp *Alcyonium*, Grant interposed his new Scottish intermediate, *Cliona*, which had canals and polyps. He sorted the sponges' spiculae into primitive and advanced designs, and suggested that *Spongilla*'s want of protective spiculae reflected the lack of predators in the primeval oceans. Such palaeo-environmental and transformist conclusions characterized his biology.

Like Friedrich Tiedemann, Grant traced animals and plants to a common monadic starting point. He showed that bryozoans and colonial hydroids produced free-swimming ciliated 'ova' (larvae). These were analogous to unicellular 'animalcules' and to the 'globules' (cells) common to animals and plants. Since algae also reproduced by animalcule-like ova, these ova lay at the junction of the two kingdoms. He believed that these free 'monads' could be spontaneously generated and that they were the earth's original inhabitants. Plants and animals were therefore to be understood by the same physico-chemical laws, and simple zoophytes were essential to comprehending 'higher' life forms.

In 1826 Charles Darwin came under Grant's wing and was encouraged to study the Firth of Forth invertebrates. Grant helped Darwin think in terms of generation, both of individuals and species, and introduced him to continental thinking on the relevance of embryological anatomy to the laws of life. Darwin always remembered Grant's admiration of Lamarck and examined Grant's monadism in his own transmutation notebooks of 1836–7.

Grant was a councillor of the university's Wernerian Natural History Society in 1825–6. Of his fifteen papers here, on topics ranging from zoophytes to mummified cats, 'The existence of a pancreas in certain species of cephalopods' shows Grant's acceptance of Étienne Geoffroy St Hilaire's unity of composition, which presumed that homologous organs persisted throughout the animal series. In 1826 he was secretary of the Plinian Society, whose milieu, with its student debates on human–animal mental continuity, was congenial to his biological reductionism.

Grant was initially encouraged by John Fleming (who erected the sponge genus *Grantia* in 1828). Fleming's evangelical presbyterianism, which underlay his quasi-actualistic geology (he saw no geological evidence for a catastrophic flood), perhaps explains Grant's own predisposition towards extreme gradualism. David Brewster, another patron, commissioned Grant's 'Zoophytology' for the *Edinburgh Encyclopaedia* (1830), while Brewster's own belief in an elastic energy allowing organisms to slide between niches provided a further telling backdrop to Grant's Lamarckism. Grant, however, stretched and deconsecrated these enabling presbyterian ideas into a deterministic evolutionism.

London University Grant was appointed professor of zoology (1827–74) at the new London University, and added the chair of comparative anatomy (the first in Britain) after J. F. Meckel proved too expensive to recruit. His announcement that he would investigate 'the origin and duration of entire species, and the causes which operate towards their increase ... and the changes they undergo by the influence of climate, domestication, and other external circumstances' (*An Essay on the Study of the Animal Kingdom*, 1828, 6) indicated how far he was departing from the taxonomic norms of contemporary zoologists. He built a zoology museum from scratch and instituted a gold medal at his own expense. He began a fossil zoology summer course in 1831 or 1832.

Although he attended Georges Cuvier's soirées in Paris and wrote 'On the life and writings of Baron Cuvier' (*Foreign Review*, 1830), Grant never adopted Cuvier's functionalism and four *embranchements*, but promoted Geoffroy's rival philosophical anatomy. His nature was a continuum from monad to man. This series exhibited a unity of composition; it was recapitulated during ontogeny and reflected the course of the 'metamorphoses' (evolution) of fossil life. Since the earliest known fossils—crinoids and crustaceans—were not the simplest, Grant argued that heat had effaced the fossil infusoria in the ancient rocks. His statements on squid-fish homologies showed his alignment with Geoffroy in his Académie clash with Cuvier in 1830. Grant Anglicized Geoffroy's nomenclature for the homologous bones, and like Geoffroy identified the fish's opercular plates with the mammalian ear ossicles. By 1836 Geoffroy himself was hailing Grant as the leading British savant.

With Charles Bell's resignation from the university in 1830, Grant's philosophical anatomy predominated. It met the Benthamites' needs for an academic approach based on nature's laws to replace craft practices. Published by *The Lancet* in 1833–4, Grant's sixty-lecture course became widely accessible. He delivered ten Friday lectures on philosophical anatomy at the Royal Institution in 1833–41, and in 1837–40 served as Fullerian professor of physiology. His domination of comparative anatomy in the early 1830s boosted the shift away from 'design' arguments and influenced a stream of pupils, including William Benjamin Carpenter, William Farr, Thomas Laycock, William Henry Flower, and Henry Charlton Bastian.

Grant's classification—summarized in his 'Animal kingdom' (1836 in R. B. Todd's *Cyclopaedia of Anatomy and Physiology*, which Grant initially helped to edit)—began, Lamarckian fashion, with the simplest invertebrates, but uniquely rested on nervous criteria: radiates were 'Cyclo-neura', articulates 'Diplo-neura', molluscs 'Cyclo-gangliata', and vertebrates 'Spini-cerebrata'. This nervous theme encouraged the hunt for links between groups. It also stimulated the search for nerves in lower animals, and in 1835 Grant announced his discovery of a nerve ring in the comb jelly *Beroë*.

Grant's finances teetered after the college's guaranteed £300 per annum expired in 1831. His courses were not compulsory for first-degree medical students, nor would he use theatrics to draw the crowds. Reliant on fees, he was forced to deliver 200 lectures a year (and in forty-six years apparently never missed one). Additional revenue came from lecturing at the Aldersgate Street school of medicine, Windmill Street School, and Marshall Hall's Sydenham College, but he remained unworldly about money and undercharged for his talks.

Grant was a radical who derided the 'monastic ignorance' (Grant to L. Horner, 5 Nov 1830, UCL, College Corres. P130) of Oxford and Cambridge. His speech on opening the medical session in 1833 (*On the Study of Medicine*, 1833) lambasted the Royal College of Physicians' Oxbridge Anglican fellowship restriction: he wanted its class privileges abolished and posts to be opened to merit. His naturalistic morphology, anti-vitalism, and Lamarckian self-development became a resource for London's dissenters and anti-Anglicans. They were seeking to replace Oxbridge's tinkering Paleyite deity (the mainstay of the undemocratic oligarchies running the Royal College of Physicians and Royal College of Surgeons) with a dispassionate divine legislator. Grant was puffed by Thomas Wakley's radical *Lancet* and the dissenters' *London Medical and Surgical Journal* as the 'English Cuvier'. The private anatomy schools proclaimed his science an essential tool for the new reforming general practitioner, enabling him to transcend the wealthy surgeon's lore. Nonconformists also realized that, by tracing the growth of homologous organs in the animal series, they could explain their human counterparts without recourse to vivisection. This all served to give Grant's science its partisan ring.

Grant was secretary of the faculty of medicine at London University from 1830 until 1831 or 1832, and its dean in 1847–9. He was also a councillor from 1837 and vice-president in 1839 of the militant GPs' union, the British Medical Association. His BMA address in 1841, on the state of the medical profession in England, demanded that the home secretary democratize the royal colleges and assume their licensing functions. Uncompromising, Grant, who was licensed in Edinburgh, refused to sit the Royal College of Physicians' own exam; thus he was prevented from practising medicine in London, which led *The Lancet* to proclaim him 'the most self-sacrificing … man in the profession' (*The Lancet*, 1, 1846, 418).

As the leading radical witness before Benjamin Hawes's select committee on the British Museum, Grant infuriated the church-and-king commissioners by indicting the pocket-borough control of the museum by aristocratic trustees. Championing the career zoologists, he advocated a Parisian type of salaried management and a display philosophy that would draw forth our own 'Lamarcks, our Latreilles, our Cuviers, and our Geoffroys' (*Report from the Select Committee on British Museum*, 1836, 127).

Nominated by the medical radicals and their allies, Grant became a fellow of the Royal Society in 1836. However, in his *Animal and Vegetable Physiology* (1834), Peter Mark Roget, the society's secretary, reproduced some of Grant's lectures, causing recriminations. When George Newport (a poor student for whom Grant had waived all fees) apparently plagiarized Grant's discovery of the motor function of the abdominal nerve in articulates and won the society's royal medal, Grant refused to take any part in Royal Society management. His radicalism also led to slipping footholds elsewhere. He started well, joining the councils of the Linnean Society (1829) and Zoological Society (1833). He gave forty Geoffroyan lectures at the Zoological in 1833 and his fossil course in 1834, and submitted eleven papers to the society's journals, including one on *Beroë*'s nerves and another on new species of the cephalopods *Loligopsis* and *Sepiola*. But Grant's careerists in the zoological museum, demanding democracy to increase the professionals' power, were opposed by the aristocratic game managers in the society's Regent's Park Gardens. Grant was removed from the council amid turbulent proceedings in 1835 and distanced himself from the society. He lost its exotic resources, which passed to the aristocrats' favourite, the anti-Lamarckian Richard Owen.

This rejection was paralleled at the Geological Society. Grant joined the council in 1832 (just as Charles Lyell published the anti-Lamarckian volume of *Principles of Geology*). Grant, having made transformism a palaeontological issue, taught that the Jurassic Stonesfield 'opossum', too early to have been a mammal, was a reptile, a point repeated in 'General view of the characters and the distribution of extinct animals' (*British Annual*, 1839). He similarly rediagnosed the *Cheirotherium* footprints as belonging to Triassic teleosaurs, not mammals. Owen's rivalry

was growing, exacerbated by the onslaughts on his College of Surgeons, and at the Geological Society he undermined Grant's '"progressive" theory' (*Athenaeum*, 570, 1838, 731), by arguing that the fossil 'opossum' was a true mammal. In 1842 Grant's 200-page memoir on mastodons was rejected by the society, which published only an abstract. He could no longer publicize his science in the way that Owen now could.

Later decline Grant's was a lonely life and poverty increased his frugality, but it honed his sarcasm, which was usually aimed at scripture or Platonic mysticism. In addition to these irreligious materialistic taints, Grant was probably seen to have breached contemporary mores (he never married and was rumoured to have been homosexual), which accelerated his decline in an increasingly puritanical society. Poverty, lecturing load, declining patronage and resources, and loss of ideological support with the collapse of the radical medical schools in the 1840s, explain why he 'did nothing more in science' (*Autobiography of Charles Darwin*, 49). Grant's *Outlines of Comparative Anatomy* (7 pts., 1835–41) was never completed, even if its 656 pages 'constitutes an era in the history of anatomy' (*Medico-Chirurgical Review*, 23, 1835, 376). Of his sixty articles, books, and letters, fifty were published in 1825–36.

Melancholic and living in a 'slum', he explained that the world was 'chiefly composed of knaves and harlots, and I would as lief live among the one as the other' (Beddoe, 32–3). He was laughed at for his eccentricities and frayed formal attire, and dismissed as a 'shadow of a reputation' (E. Forbes to T. H. Huxley, 16 Nov 1852, Huxley MSS, ICL). In 1850 University College finally granted him £100 per annum, while a public collection bought him a £50 annuity in 1853. He was refused a state pension in 1854. His inheritance of Indian government securities on the death in 1852 of his sole surviving brother, Francis, made life easier and allowed him to indulge his passion for opera. Fluent in many European languages—he was a founding member of the Philological Society in 1842—he increasingly spent his summers in Belgium, the Netherlands, Denmark, and Germany, and in 1852 was made a corresponding member of the Société Royale des Sciences of Liège.

In his sixtieth year Grant stood 'in the midst of the Philistines' (Grant to P. B. Ayres, 11 May 1852, Wellcome L.) as British Museum Swiney lecturer. His dry 'Palaeozoology' course (1853–7) combated Lyell's anti-progressionism and related the natural birth of higher forms—the replacement, say, of cold-blooded reptiles by warm-blooded mammals—to planetary cooling. He developed a unique classification, based on life's stages of self-development. 'Protozoic' covered the period until the air-breathing invertebrates; 'Mesozoic' to the emergence of fishes; 'Cainozoic' from fishes to the future extinction of life. It was a non-homocentric history of self-empowered ascent to challenge the don's stratigraphic terminology. Grant misanthropically labelled the lifeless ice-death era the 'Metazoic'. And just as cynically he taxed students on the forces responsible for 'originating and effacing the temporary organic film on our planet' (Zoology Examination

Papers, 1857–8, 'Grant on zoological subjects', UCL). His *Tabular View of the Primary Divisions of the Animal Kingdom* (1861), while praising Darwin's *Origin of Species*, proffered a distinct infrastructure, with multiple evolutionary trees, each from spontaneously generated stock. To the end he accepted the 'potentialities' of matter to produce life at the present day.

Grant's first achievement was the elucidation of sponges—in 1864 J. S. Bowerbank dedicated his *Monograph of the British Spongiadae* to him, and the family Grantiidae was named in his honour; his second was the introduction of academic comparative anatomy to Britain. However, by the 1860s his swallow-tail suit matched his archaic views. For thirty years he had delivered the same lectures in near-identical words. Rejected by the divines before Darwin, when a design-orientated zoology obeyed classificatory and creationist canons, he was no less relegated afterwards. Although as late as 1873 the 79-year-old was attending the 'Sunday Lecture Society' with T. H. Huxley and W. K. Clifford, an unsympathetic Huxley, doyen of respectable Darwinians, commented that Grant's advocacy of evolution 'was not calculated to advance the cause' (Huxley, 188). His denigration as a failed Darwinian precursor capped Grant's historiographic fate. Only from the 1980s did historians begin to re-evaluate his Lamarckian zoology, show its relations to Darwin's early views, and reveal Grant's Geoffroyan anatomy as the key moment for a radical generation.

In 1874 the deaf octogenarian was still delivering five lectures a week. Ill from dysentery in August 1874, and recognizing no close relatives, Grant adopted William Sharpey's suggestion and bequeathed his library, instruments, and money to University College. He died on 23 August 1874 at his home, 2 Euston Grove, Euston Square, London. E. A. Schäfer removed Grant's brain for weighing, and his body was buried in the unconsecrated north-east corner of Highgate cemetery.   ADRIAN DESMOND

Sources 'Biographical sketch of Robert Edmond Grant', *The Lancet* (21 Dec 1850), 686–95 · [W. Sharpey], *PRS*, 23 (1874), vi–x · G. V. Poore, 'Robert Edmond Grant', *University College Gazette*, 2 (1901), 190–91 · E. A. Schäfer, 'William Sharpey', *University College Gazette*, 2 (1901), 215 · 'Testimonial to Dr. Grant', *The Lancet* (5 Feb 1853), 140–42 · A. Desmond, *The politics of evolution: morphology, medicine and reform in radical London* (1989) [incl. bibliography] · A. Desmond, 'Robert E. Grant: the social predicament of a pre-Darwinian transmutationist', *Journal of the History of Biology*, 17 (1984), 189–223 · A. Desmond, 'Robert E. Grant's later views on organic development: the Swiney lectures on "Palaeozoology", 1853–1857', *Archives of Natural History*, 11 (1982–4), 395–413 · A. Desmond, 'The making of institutional zoology in London, 1822–1836', *History of Science*, 23 (1985), 153–85, 223–50 · P. R. Sloan, 'Darwin's invertebrate program, 1826–1836: preconditions for transformism', *The Darwinian heritage*, ed. D. Kohn (1985), 71–120 · J. A. Secord, 'Edinburgh Lamarckians: Robert Jameson and Robert E. Grant', *Journal of the History of Biology*, 24 (1991), 1–18 · *London Medical Directory* (1847), 63 · J. F. Clarke, *Medical Times and Gazette* (5 Sept 1874), 277–8 · J. Russell, letter, *Medical Times and Gazette* (14 Nov 1874), 563–4 · J. Beddoe, *Memories of eighty years* (1910) · *The autobiography of Charles Darwin, 1809–1882*, ed. N. Barlow, another edn (1969) · P. H. Jesperson, 'Charles Darwin and Dr. Grant', *Lychnos* (1848–9), 159–69 · T. H. Huxley, 'On the reception of the *Origin of species*', in *The life and letters of Charles Darwin*, ed. F. Darwin, 3rd edn, 2 (1887), 179–204 · R. E. Grant, 'On the structure and nature of the *Spongilla friabilis*', *Edinburgh Philosophical Journal*, 14 (1826), 270–84

Archives BL, lecture notes, Add. MS 31197 · UCL, corresp. and papers · UCL, lecture notes

Likenesses engraving, *c*.1837–1840, UCL · T. H. Maguire, lithograph, 1852, BM, NPG; repro. in T. H. Maguire, *Portraits of honorary members of the Ipswich Museum* (1852) [*see illus.*] · T. H. Maguire, lithograph, 1852 (after his earlier work), NPG · engraving, NHM · photograph (in old age), NHM

Wealth at death under £1500: administration with will, 24 Nov 1874, *CGPLA Eng. & Wales*

Grant, Roger (*d.* 1724), oculist, whose origins are unknown, enlisted as a soldier in the German emperor's service, in which he lost an eye. This misfortune he considered to qualify him to treat others with defective sight. He set up in London as an oculist, in Mouse Alley, Wapping (later he lived in St Christopher's Alley or Court, off Threadneedle Street), advertising twice a week in the *British Apollo* and sporadically in other journals.

The public was alerted to Grant's devious ways in 1709 when Timothy Childe exposed his methods in a pamphlet entitled *Account of a miraculous cure of a young man in Newington, that was born blind, and was brought to perfect sight by Roger Grant, oculist*. Grant, who was known as a Baptist preacher, had urged Annabella Jones, mother of the young man, to compel the minister of St Mary, Newington, to certify this

Roger Grant (*d.* 1724), by unknown engraver

'miraculous cure'. When the minister refused, saying that Jones was not previously blind but had defective sight which Grant's treatment had not improved, his signature was forged. This 'cure', along with many others, figured in a broadsheet published about 1712, in which Grant claimed to have improved the sight of some 2000 persons, identifying a dozen by name, in regions as far afield as Durham and Somerset. This self-advertisement paid off; for though illiterate and untrained, Grant, 'having cured great numbers in Her Majesty's service … [was] sworn Oculist and Operator in Extraordinary to Her Majesty' (*Gazette*, 28 Sept 1710). After the death of Sir William Reid in 1715 he held the same appointment under George I.

What little is known of Grant's private life comes from the brief will he made a few days before his death, when he was already ill. Describing himself as of St Dunstan-in-the-East, Grant bequeathed his property to his wife, Hannah, and his daughters Priscilla and Mary Jeffries. In 1784 there died at Tenbury, Worcestershire, Mary Jeffries, aged 106, a midwife, born in London in October 1678 and said to be the daughter of Roger Grant, oculist. Grant himself died on 7 April 1724.

G. T. Bettany, rev. Anita McConnell

Sources W. Wadd, *Nugae chirurgicae, or, A biographical miscellany* (1824), 72 • *Account of a miraculous cure of a young man in Newington, that was born blind* (1709) • *The Spectator* (30 July 1712), 61 • *The Spectator* (1 Sept 1712), 173 • R. R. James, ed., *Studies in the history of ophthalmology in England prior to the year 1800* (1933) • 'Chronological diary', *The historical register*, 9 (1724), 20 • *GM*, 1st ser., 54 (1784), 956 • will, commissary court, 1724, GL

Likenesses engraving, AM Oxf. [*see illus.*] • line engraving, Wellcome L.

Wealth at death see will, 1724, London Commissary Court

Grant, Thomas (1816–1870), Roman Catholic bishop of Southwark, was born at Ligny-les-Aires in the diocese of Arras, France, on 25 November 1816, the second son of Bernard Grant and his wife, Anne McGowan. Bernard Grant had changed his name from Garraghty to Grant on going to Scotland from Ireland to join the 71st highlanders division of the British army. This change of name was necessary for Irish Catholics who wished to make a full-time career in the British army. Bernard fought at the battle of Waterloo as a sergeant and later obtained a commission as a captain. After moving with the regiment to France, Malta, and Canada, the family settled in Chester in 1825. Thomas Grant lodged with the priest in charge of the mission there, John Briggs, later bishop of Beverley, who taught him Latin. He was sent to St Cuthbert's College, Ushaw, co. Durham, entering on 1 January 1829. Marked out early on as a student of great ability he was sent to the English College in Rome, which he entered on 1 December 1836; he graduated DD in August 1841 and the theses he defended were published in Rome in 1844. He was ordained priest in Rome on 28 November 1841.

Shortly after his ordination Grant became secretary to Cardinal Acton and continued his studies, particularly in civil and canon law. He was appointed rector of the English College on 13 October 1844, in succession to Charles Baggs. Soon afterwards he became the agent for the English vicars apostolic in Rome and assisted in the plans for the restoration of the Roman Catholic hierarchy in England. He had to translate many documents into Latin or Italian and furnished Mgr Palma with materials for the historical preface to the apostolic decree of 1850 by the hierarchy which was re-established. The following year he was nominated by Pope Pius IX as bishop of the new see of Southwark, being consecrated in Rome on 6 July 1851.

As the new cardinal, Nicholas Wiseman, was *persona non grata* with the British government, Grant conducted most of the negotiations that were required with government bodies. Regrettably he did not enjoy good relations with Wiseman, who refused to allocate to Southwark a large element of the funds of the old London district. These funds should have been distributed almost equally between the two dioceses which now comprised the area of the old district. In particular Wiseman refused to settle any of the mensal fund intended for the upkeep of the bishop and his household. Grant appealed to Rome in 1854 and his appeal was upheld in 1861. Wiseman, however, refused to do anything and it was left to the next archbishop, Henry Manning, to settle the matter.

In the 1850s, in collaboration with Manning, Grant arranged for chaplains to be sent to the Crimea and to India during the mutiny of 1857. He conducted negotiations with Sir Benjamin Hawes, which led to the act of parliament establishing the status and role of army chaplains. He was concerned in all religious matters regarding the British colonies and negotiated with Colonel Joshua Jebb to improve the access to prisoners for Catholic chaplains.

At the same time Grant also had to administer his vast diocese, which included the Channel Islands. During his episcopate the diocese grew rapidly. The number of priests increased from 66 to 159 and the number of churches from 58 to 144. The bishop encouraged the foundation of houses by different religious orders and was able to provide schools for 35,000 children, leaving only 3000 Catholic children in non-Catholic schools by the time of his death. Well known for his simplicity of life and practice of self-denial, from 1862 he suffered greatly from stomach problems, possibly ulcers (earlier writers suggested cancer, but this does not seem likely). Although in ill health he was appointed Latinist to the First Vatican Council; but after 14 February 1870 he was unable to take any further active role and he died in Rome at the English College on 1 June 1870. Pope Pius IX is reported to have said, on hearing of his death, 'Another Saint in heaven.' He was buried in the cemetery attached to the convent orphanage at Norwood in Surrey.

Grant was one of the most influential of the bishops of the restored English hierarchy, but he was so self-effacing that this hardly showed at the time. His workload was phenomenal and necessitated staying up often until 5 a.m. to finish writing letters. He was regarded as a saint even by those who disagreed with his strict views. Indeed, it is perhaps surprising that the cause of his canonization was not taken up soon after his death.

Michael Clifton

Sources *The Tablet* (11 June 1870), 741; (25 June 1870), 815 • *Weekly Register and Catholic Standard* (4 June 1870) • K. O'Meara, *Thomas*

Grant, first bishop of Southwark, 2nd edn (1878) · G. Albion, 'The bishops of Southwark: Thomas Grant, 1851–1870', *Southwark Record*, 18 (1939), 70–5 · M. Clifton, *The quiet negotiator* (1990) · Gillow, *Lit. biog. hist.* · private information (2004)

Archives English College, Rome, corresp. and papers · St George's Catholic Cathedral, Southwark, Southwark Roman Catholic diocesan archives, corresp. and papers | CUL, letters to Lord Acton · Westm. DA, letters to Wiseman

Likenesses oils, *c*.1844, Venerable English College, Rome, Italy · photographs, *c*.1864–1869, repro. in Ramsey, *Thomas Grant* · portrait, *c*.1865, Archbishop's House, Southwark, London · memorial bust, St George's Cathedral, Southwark, London; destroyed in Second World War

Wealth at death under £1500: probate, 25 June 1870, *CGPLA Eng. & Wales*

Grant, Sir Thomas Tassell (*bap.* 1795, *d.* 1859), inventor, was baptized at St Mary's, Portsea, Hampshire, on 27 March 1795. He was the third, and eldest surviving, son in a family of five sons and one daughter of Thomas Grant and his wife, Ann, *née* Sumpter, of Soberton, near Portsmouth. In 1812 he became a technical civil servant in the Admiralty. His abilities won him steady if slow promotion, and in 1828 he was appointed storekeeper at the Royal Clarence victualling yard, Gosport. About this time he married his wife, Emma; they had three sons and a daughter.

At Gosport, Grant began his noteworthy career as an inventor. In 1829 he devised machinery for making ship's biscuits; this was installed in the victualling yard three years later under the direction of Sir John Rennie. Most notably, the biscuits were docked, and stamped into hexagonal shapes, thereby ensuring that there was no waste. This mechanization speeded up the production process and substantially reduced its costs (from 7½*d*. to 2*d*. a hundredweight). Other government departments took up the invention, the annual saving to the British taxpayer being computed at £30,000. As recompense, parliament awarded Grant £2000. He also received a medal from the French king, Louis Philippe, and a gold medal from the Society of Arts in London. In 1834 he invented a desalination plant which distilled fresh water at sea; this was adopted by the naval authorities fourteen years later, and has been described as 'the greatest benefit ever conferred on the sailor, materially advancing the sanitary and moral condition of the navy' (*The Times*, 19 Oct 1859).

Around 1839 Grant devised a patent naval fuel, which bore his name, and in the 1840s a steam kitchen, given its first trials in the warship HMS *Illustrious*. He also constructed a new type of lifebuoy, and a feathering paddle wheel. He was elected a fellow of the Royal Society in 1840, and in 1850 he was promoted to the comptrollership of the Admiralty's victualling and transport service.

The outbreak of the Crimean War in 1854 tested to the limit Grant's administrative and improvisatory skills, his inventions helping to offset the widely condemned shortcomings of the war-time supply arrangements for the forces. Victualling yards at home worked day and night turning out machine-made biscuits for the army and navy, while Grant's distilling apparatus provided fresh and clean water on the spot. Over a period of three months, eleven ships of the Black Sea Fleet distilled over 4700 tons of water. The supply vessel, the *Wye*, was specially fitted up, and produced over 45 tons a day.

All these pressures and preoccupations caused Grant's health to give way, and early in 1858 he had to retire prematurely. His public services were recognized with the appointment as KCB, and Queen Victoria presented him with a gold and silver vase. He died of cancer on 15 October 1859 at his home, 20 Chester Terrace, Regent's Park, London, survived by his wife. Despite the marked improvements they bestowed on the quality of the beneficiaries' lives, Grant's inventions were perhaps too homely to receive the mention they deserved in histories of technology.   T. A. B. CORLEY

Sources *The Times* (19 Oct 1859) · *GM*, 3rd ser., 7 (1859), 534–5 · T. T. Grant, 'Apparatus for making ship's biscuits', *Transactions of the Society of Arts*, 50 (1836), 97–106 · Boase, *Mod. Eng. biog.* · T. A. B. Corley, *Quaker enterprise in biscuits: Huntley and Palmer of Reading, 1822–1972* (1972), 45–55 · *IGI* · d. cert.

Wealth at death under £4000: probate, 5 Nov 1859, *CGPLA Eng. & Wales*

Grant, William, Lord Prestongrange (1700/01–1764), judge, was baptized on 4 May 1701, the second of six children born to Francis *Grant, Lord Cullen (1658x63–1726), and his first wife, Jean Meldrum, daughter of the Revd William Meldrum of Meldrum, Aberdeenshire. His mother died when he was a small boy. Following his father in a law career, he was admitted to the Middle Temple on 7 February 1721 and the Faculty of Advocates on 24 February 1722. The date of his marriage to Grizel Miller (1708–1792), daughter of the Revd John Miller, has not been traced. They had four daughters: Janet (who married John Carmichael of Castlecraig, later fourth earl of Hyndford), Agnes (who married Sir George Suttie, bt, of Balgone), Jean (who married Robert Dundas of Arniston, later lord president of session), and Christian, who died in 1761 aged sixteen.

On 13 May 1731 Grant was appointed procurator (legal adviser) for the Church of Scotland and principal clerk to its general assembly. Church interests led to his writing *Remarks on the state of the Church of Scotland with respect to patronages, and with reference to a bill now depending before parliament* (1736). This closely argued pamphlet was not as partisan in favour of the rights of the kirk as those church leaders whom he describes as the 'warm men' would have wished. He was concerned for the rights of elders and presbytery but equally for the rights of local landowners, which had been eroded by the concentration of patronage in the hands of the state and those with multiple superiorities. He held his church posts until 1747. In the meantime he was appointed solicitor-general (20 June 1737), but was dismissed in 1742 when Lord Ilay, Sir Robert Walpole's minister for Scotland, was replaced.

Grant's appointment by the Pelham faction as lord advocate on 26 February 1746 came at a critical point in Scotland's history, coinciding with the defeat of the Jacobite rising of 1745. Grant is said to have authored a pseudonymous pamphlet—the *Scots Magazine* (26, 1764, 291) claimed it had 'undoubted evidence that he was the author'—entitled *The occasional writer: containing an answer*

William Grant, Lord Prestongrange (1700/01–1764), by Allan Ramsay, 1751

to the second manifesto of the Pretender's eldest son (1745). It displays a mastery of polemic and rhetoric not evident in his pamphlet on church patronage; its position, the standard Scots whig defence of the Hanoverians, is one he wholeheartedly supported. It speaks of the people's 'right to some redress or Atonement' (Britannicus, 10) if a king miscarry, and staunchly defends the forty-year-old Union as being to the 'common Benefit of both the British Nations' (ibid., 6), on both accounts echoing sentiments expressed in publications of his father.

Given the lack of a secretary of state for Scotland—the post was a casualty of the rising—the lord advocate's role was as much political as legal, and Grant supplemented his position by election to parliament as member for the Elgin burghs (at a by-election in February 1747, with re-election in July 1747 and May 1754). In his two roles he took a major part in drafting and steering through parliament a series of statutes that shaped the establishment's attitude towards the Scottish highlands for at least the next century. Blows were struck at traditional culture: symbolically in the banning of the wearing of highland dress, more practically in the prohibition against carrying arms (1746), in the ending of heritable jurisdictions of clan chiefs and other magnates (1747) and the same year the abolition of ward holding (tenures held on condition of military service rendered to the superior), and, in 1752, in annexing to the crown inalienably the estates forfeited by Jacobites in the previous uprising. Prosecution of the leading rebels took place in England, partly because it was felt that Scottish juries would fail to convict, as Grant found to his cost in the prosecution of Lord Provost Stewart of Edinburgh, who had appeared lukewarm in his efforts to defend the city against the Young Pretender. He was more successful in getting compensation for Glasgow council for burdens imposed on it by Charles for their more spirited opposition, and he achieved this in the face of considerable anti-Scottish sentiment in the government.

These were the sticks. Carrots were provided by bodies such as the commissioners and trustees for improving fisheries and manufactures in Scotland, to whose number Grant had been appointed on 28 August 1738, and the commissioners for the annexed estates (to which he was appointed in 1755). These commissioners planned to use the annexed estates for, as the Act of Annexing (1752) put it, 'civilizing the Inhabitants upon said Estates, and other Parts of the Highlands & Islands of Scotland, the promoting amongst them the protestant Religion, good Government, Industry & Manufactures, and the Principles of Duty and Loyalty to his Majesty'. Of the twenty-eight (and later thirty-five) commissioners Grant was one of few who conscientiously attended meetings and made outstanding contributions. On his own estate (he bought Prestongrange in Haddingtonshire in 1746) he carried out a few improvements on the house (being too mean to do more, went the gossip) and encouraged industrial activity, widening the local harbour and granting leases for the development of pottery. His elder brother, Archibald *Grant, who inherited the estate their father had bought at Monymusk in 1713, was one of the foremost agricultural improvers of the day.

An apparent attack on government policy towards the highlands and the annexed estate commissioners' work came with the murder in May 1752 of Colin Campbell of Glenure, one of the factors charged with evicting the old-style tenants. The Appin murder, as it came to be known, was attributed to a Jacobite deserter Alan Breck Stewart, whose romanticized story forms the subject of Robert Louis Stevenson's Kidnapped and Catriona. Alan Breck escaped immediately after the murder, but the government was determined to make an example of James Stewart of Ardshiel, a Stewart kinsman, bringing him to trial on the charge of being art and part (accessory), on somewhat flimsy evidence. Aspects of his treatment have been considered irregular—he was detained in solitary confinement to prevent the possibility of legal manoeuvres which could have ensured the trial was held in Edinburgh; eleven of the fifteen jurors bore the name Campbell (that of the Stewarts' traditional enemies); the trial judge was the Campbell chief, the earl of Argyll, in his capacity as lord justice general; and Grant himself took the unaccustomed step for a lord advocate of appearing for the prosecution in person. As he justified it himself:

> I resolved … to attend at the trial … and to do all that in me lay, consistently with law and justice, to convince the disaffected part of the Highlands of Scotland, that they must submit to this government, which they have several times in vain endeavoured to subvert. (Mackay, 109)

Opinions on Grant's conduct have varied. He claimed at the trial to be 'truly ignorant of the particular facts' surrounding Stewart's treatment, and there is evidence from a Stewart apologia written after the trial under the sobriquet A Bystander that Grant had stepped in to help the defence obtain the services of first-rate advocates. But his conviction that the 'barbarous' highlands were in 'need of being better civilised' and his fury at the ingratitude towards the government after clemency had been granted to many of the rebels of the forty-five (Stewart among them) blinded him to the unsatisfactory nature of many aspects of the trial. One irregularity in the trial was the admission as evidence of statements taken from Stewart's wife and children, but there was probably no jury rigging, as a majority of freeholders in the county were Campbells. Grant proposed that an account of the trial be published to show that the law had been upheld: *The Trial of James Stewart* went on sale in February 1753.

In August 1754, probably as a result of ill health, Grant was declared to have vacated by absence the office of lord advocate, which he had borne, in the words of John Ramsay of Ochtertyre, 'with less obloquy and ill-will than could have been expected' (*Scotland and Scotsmen*, 121), considering the sensitivity of his task. He resigned his parliamentary seat at the same time and was appointed on 14 November 1754 as an ordinary lord of session and lord of justiciary in the Scottish courts, taking the legal title Lord Prestongrange. He 'lost no fame by becoming a judge, being better suited to the bench than the bar' (ibid., 124); his stiff awkwardness and 'a chaining in his tones when he pled' had disgusted 'nice judges' (ibid., 124). He matriculated arms (that is, he registered his coat of arms with the lord Lyon's office) on 24 August 1759. He died at Bath, whither he had gone for the waters, on 23 May 1764; the death of his daughter Christian in 1761, according to Ramsay, had broken him physically and mentally. He was buried in the aisle of Prestonpans church, Haddingtonshire, on 7 June. A plaque to his memory erected on the outside of the church later became illegible, but the text is recorded.

Robert Dundas's verdict was that Grant loved his money better than public business, and Ramsay agrees that he was 'intent upon making a fortune for his family' (*Scotland and Scotsmen*, 125)—in stark contrast to his elder brother, who lost a fortune and was expelled from the House of Commons. He got this same brother appointed to the sinecure of keeper of the register of Hornings in 1749 after a failed attempt to get him back into parliament; his other brother, Francis, got a post of inspector with the annexed estates commission. Grant had had to be virtually prised from his lucrative church posts after his appointment as lord advocate. Ramsay illustrates his stinginess with a tale of his giving a beggar a gold coin and dispatching (unsuccessfully) a servant to get it back when his mistake was pointed out. However, Alexander Carlyle, whose father was minister in Prestonpans, where Grant was the patron, talks of his 'generosity to my mother, by giving her a grant of the glebe ... and a considerable part of the vacant stipend, to which she was not entitled' (*Autobiography*, ed. Burton, 487).

Grant was not a man who liked to be thwarted. He considered that he had been unjustly passed over for the lord advocate's post in 1742 and told the new incumbent so, though he did add his congratulations. In Haddingtonshire he fell out badly with the road trustees over concessions at turnpikes for his coal and salt. Contemporaries found him a dull dog—no circuit parties, no eloquence except that of common sense (though he was praised by Horace Walpole for speaking excessively well in the heritable jurisdictions debate), no quick and brilliant parts, but sobriety, shyness, and dignity. Carlyle says only that he was in good habits with him (and turns to more colourful neighbours). Ramsay says that as a criminal judge Grant was amiable, enlightened, and upright, and another (also inclined to sing a fellow lawyer's praises in public) highlights the 'universal approbation for his judgement in settling the claims on the forfeited estates' (Tytler, 40). Tytler talks also of his 'rectitude of moral feeling', 'virtuous integrity', and a 'winning gentleness of manners ... the pure offspring of a warm and benevolent heart ... In the prosecution of criminals, if at any time he allowed his passions to influence his conduct, it was ever on the side of mercy and humanity' (ibid.). Portraits by Allan Ramsay and a painter of the Scottish school catch a mixture of kindness, reserve, and a certain haughtiness. A youthful portrait by John Smibert, in fanciful armour, suggests a romantic streak. Stevenson, who admitted to not studying the facts, presented in *Catriona* an intriguing Jekyll and Hyde—warm and kind in domestic life, cold and ruthless in public.

DAVID MOODY

Sources G. W. T. Omond, *The lord advocates of Scotland from the close of the fifteenth century to the passing of the Reform Bill*, 2 vols. (1883) · G. Brunton and D. Haig, *An historical account of the senators of the college of justice, from its institution in MDXXXII* (1832) · D. N. Mackay, ed., *The trial of James Stewart (the Appin murder)* (1907) · *Scotland and Scotsmen in the eighteenth century: from the MSS of John Ramsay, esq., of Ochtertyre*, ed. A. Allardyce, 2 vols. (1888) · *Scots Magazine*, 8 (1746), 245–6 · *Scots Magazine*, 11 (1749), 303 · *Scots Magazine*, 17 (1755), 212 · *Scots Magazine*, 26 (1764), 291 · S. Carney, *The Appin murder: the killing of the red fox* (1994) · R. R. Sedgwick, 'Grant, William', HoP, *Commons*, 1715–54 · F. J. Grant, ed., *The Faculty of Advocates in Scotland, 1532–1943*, Scottish RS, 145 (1944) · *Report on the Laing manuscripts*, 2, HMC, 72 (1925) · A. F. Tytler, *Memoirs of the life and writings of the Honourable Henry Home of Kames*, 2 vols. (1807) · V. Wills, ed., *Reports on the annexed estates, 1755–1769* (1973) · 'Grant, Sir Frances, Lord Cullen', *DNB* · Britannicus [W. Grant], *The occasional writer: containing an answer to the second manifesto of the Pretender's eldest son* (1745) · *The autobiography of Dr Alexander Carlyle of Inveresk, 1722–1805*, ed. J. H. Burton (1910) · State trials · register of testaments, NA Scot., CC 8/8/119/2, CC 8/8/129/1 · register of sasines, NA Scot., RS 131–151, RS 132–176 · register house plans, NA Scot., RHP 41329 · road trustees minutes, NA Scot., CO 7/2/1/1 · gifts and deposits, NA Scot., GD 1/402/77, GD 1/402/78 · J. Shirlaw, 'Potters at Morrison's Haven, c1750–1833, and the Gordons at Bankfoot', *Transactions of East Lothian Antiquarian and Field Naturalists Society*, 24 (2000) · W. Grant, *Remarks on the state of the Church of Scotland with respect to patronages* (1841) · C. Rogers, *Monuments and monumental inscriptions in Scotland*, 2 vols. (1871–2) · R. L. Stevenson, *'Kidnapped' and 'Catriona'*, ed. E. Letley (1986) · *Fasti Scot.* · *Lothian, except Edinburgh*, Pevsner (1978) · W. F. Gray and J. H. Jamieson, *East Lothian biographies* (1941) · J. Foster, *Members of parliament, Scotland ... 1357–1882*, 2nd edn (privately printed, London, 1882)

Archives NL Scot., legal papers · NL Scot., memoirs and account book | BL, corresp. with Lord Hardwicke, Add. MSS 35446–35449, *passim* · NA Scot., minute books and letter books of the commissioners for the annexed estate, E 721, E726 · NA Scot., letters to Sir

Archibald Grant • NL Scot., letters to Erskine family • NL Scot., corresp. with the first and second marquesses of Tweeddale
Likenesses J. Smibert, portrait, c.1718–1722, priv. coll.; registered with Scot. NPG • A. Ramsay, oils, 1751, Scot. NPG [*see illus.*] • Scottish school, portrait, after 1754, priv. coll.; registered with Scot. NPG • J. McArdell, engraving (after Ramsay), Scot. NPG; versions, Scot. NPG • mezzotint (after Ramsay), repro. in *Autobiography of Dr Alexander Carlyle*
Wealth at death shareholdings in British Linen Company and Bank of Scotland: NA Scot., CC 8/8/119/2

Grant, William (d. 1786), physician and medical writer, a native of Scotland, graduated MD at Marischal College, Aberdeen, in 1755, and became licentiate of the London College of Physicians in 1763. He practised in the city of London with success, and was physician to the Misericordia Hospital, an institution for the treatment of venereal disease then located in Goodman's Fields. Grant married Elizabeth (d. 1778), daughter and heir of John Raper of Twyford House, Essex, and Thorley Hall, Hertfordshire, with whom he had one son, Sir John Peter *Grant. He died in Edinburgh on 30 December 1786.

Grant wrote mostly on the subject of fevers. *An Enquiry into … the Fevers most Common in London* (1771) and *An Essay on the … Fever … Commonly called Jail … Fever* (1775) underwent translation into other European languages. Interestingly, he does not appear to have written on the venereal diseases he encountered at the Misericordia Hospital; his only publication concerning a subject other than fevers was *Observations on the Atrabilious Temperament and Gout* (1799).   G. T. BETTANY, rev. RICHARD HANKINS

Sources Munk, *Roll*
Archives NRA Scotland, priv. coll., corresp. and papers

Grant, Sir William (1752–1832), judge, was born at Elchies, Moray, on the banks of the Spey on 13 October 1752, the eldest son of James and Christina Grant. His father was apparently a tenant farmer who later became collector of the customs in the Isle of Man. On the death of his parents Grant was taken care of by his uncle, Robert Grant, a wealthy London merchant whose firm had prospered in the Canadian fur trade. He was educated at the grammar school at Elgin, and at King's College, Aberdeen, and was admitted a student of Lincoln's Inn on 30 January 1769. He was called to the bar on 3 February 1774, and in the following year went to Canada, where he commanded a body of volunteers during the siege of Quebec. He was appointed attorney-general of Canada on 10 May 1776.

Upon his return to Britain, Grant first joined the western and afterwards the home circuit, but obtained so little success that he contemplated returning to Canada. On the advice of Lord Thurlow he abandoned the common law bar for the equity courts. In an interview with Pitt, who was then preparing a bill for the regulation of Canada, Grant made a good impression on the prime minister, who encouraged his parliamentary ambitions; and at the general election in June 1790 he successfully contested Shaftesbury. He soon drew attention to himself as a powerful orator. His first major speech was in opposition to the resolutions condemning the armament against Russia on 15 April 1791. On 11 May 1791 he spoke on the

Quebec Government Bill, giving a lucid explanation of the Canadian law, and in the same year was appointed a commissioner to report on the laws of Jersey. In February 1793 he received a patent of precedence, and in the same year became a bencher of Lincoln's Inn and was appointed joint justice of the Carmarthen great sessions. The acceptance of this office obliged him to stand for re-election, but he could not be sure of success at Shaftesbury, and it was not until February 1794 that he was returned on the court interest for New Windsor after a sharp contest with a local man. The following month he was appointed solicitor-general to the queen. He secured his reputation as a talented speaker with his defence of the Seditious Meetings Bill on 25 November 1795.

At the general election in June 1796 Grant was returned with government support for Banffshire, which county he continued to represent until his retirement from parliamentary life at the dissolution in September 1812. In 1798 he was promoted to be chief justice of Chester, and in July 1799 was appointed solicitor-general, and duly knighted. He left office with Pitt in February 1801, but four months later accepted from Addington, the new prime minister, the mastership of the rolls. He was sworn of the privy council on 21 May 1801. Now financially secure, he assisted the ministry in debate, particularly on major issues, as he did Pitt's second administration. His prominent role in the defence of Lord Melville in 1805 may have cost him an offer of the lord chancellorship on the formation of the Grenville ministry, to which he was essentially hostile. He declined the duke of Portland's offer of the Irish chancellorship in March 1807, but supported his ministry and that of his successor Perceval. Had Lord Wellesley formed a government in June 1812, Grant would have become lord chancellor.

Grant was one of the few lawyers who have made a great reputation in the House of Commons. Brougham, although critical of his tory prejudices, conceded that he was 'unquestionably to be classed with speakers of the first order. … No speaker was more easily listened to; none so difficult to answer' (Brougham, 138–9). Horner, who heard Grant's masterly speech in support of Pitt's ministry during the debate on the Spanish papers on 12 February 1805, described it as an

> extraordinary oration … quite a masterpiece of his peculiar and miraculous manner: conceive an hour and a half of syllogisms strung together in the closest tissue, so artfully clear that you think every successive inference unavoidable: so rapid that you have no leisure to reflect where you have been brought from, or to see where you are to be carried, and so dry of ornament or illustration or refreshment that the attention is stretched—stretched—racked. All this done without a single note. (Horner, 1.285)

At the same time, Horner criticized Grant's style on the grounds that it 'does not appear to me of a parliamentary cast, nor suited to the discussions of a political assembly' (ibid., 1.286). Grant's most important speeches, apart from those already mentioned, were made in the debates on Whitworth's motion respecting the armament against Russia (29 February 1792), Fox's motion for sending a minister to Paris (15 December 1792), the message relative to a union with Ireland (7 February 1799), the address of thanks (2 February 1801), the definitive peace treaty (14 May 1802), Whitbread's motion for the impeachment of Lord Melville (11 June 1805), the American Intercourse Bill (8 July 1806), the orders in council (5 February 1808), the conduct of the duke of York (13 March 1809), and the resolutions respecting the Regency (2 January 1811). His speech in defence of the treaty of Amiens won high praise from Bentham, who reckoned him to be 'an animal *sui generis* amongst lawyers, and indeed amongst parliamentary men', and added that 'the notions of the master about colonies approach nearer to what I call reason, than those of almost anybody else I have met with' (*The Correspondence of Jeremy Bentham*, ed. J. R. Dinwiddy, vol. 7, 1988, 57).

Grant retired from the rolls in 1817, but for a few years thereafter sat in the cockpit and assisted in the hearing of appeals. Although he had acquired a far greater reputation as a parliamentary orator than as a leader of the chancery bar, his success as a judge was conspicuous. The Catholic barrister Charles Butler declared that Grant possessed 'the most perfect model of judicial eloquence' to have come under his observation:

> His exposition of facts, and of the consequences deducible from them, his discussion of former decisions, and showing their legitimate weight and authority, and their real bearings upon the point in question, were above praise; but the whole was done with such admirable ease and simplicity that, while real judges felt its supreme excellence, the herd of hearers believed that they should have done the same. (Butler, 1.134–5)

Romilly, whose reform of the criminal law he supported, observed on Grant's retirement, 'His eminent qualities as a judge, his patience, his impartiality, his courtesy to the bar, his despatch, and the masterly style in which his judgments were pronounced, would at any time have entitled him to the highest praise' (S. Romilly, *Memoirs*, 1840, 3.324–5).

Grant, who acted as treasurer of Lincoln's Inn in 1798 and became major-commandant of the Lincoln's Inn corps in 1802, was elected lord rector of Aberdeen University in 1809 and was created a DCL by Oxford University on 14 June 1820. He was unmarried. The speaker of the House of Commons, Charles Abbot, commented that 'in private life he is the coldest and most reserved man I ever knew' (Colchester, 1.23), but Horner found him 'silent but very good-natured' in private (Horner, 1.220). Glenbervie pithily described him as 'a *fagot de bois sec* in society. Great on the bench, an oracle in Parliament, but like Mrs Siddons a preposterous body in a drawing room' (*Diaries*, 2.129). Grant died on 25 May 1832 at Barton House, Dawlish, the home of his sister, the widow of Admiral John Schank, and was buried at Dawlish.   D. R. FISHER

Sources D. R. Fisher, 'Grant, William', HoP, *Commons, 1790–1820* · Foss, *Judges*, 8.295–300 · H. Brougham, *Historical sketches of statesmen who flourished in the time of George III* (1839), 135–41 · *GM*, 1st ser., 102/1 (1832), 561–2 · *Scottish Notes and Queries*, 3rd ser., 6 (1928), 173–4 · W. S. Wallace, 'Strathspey in the Canadian fur-trade', *Essays in Canadian history*, ed. R. Flenley (1939), 278–95 · *Memoirs and correspondence of Francis Horner, MP*, ed. L. Horner, 2nd edn, 2 vols. (1853), vol. 1, pp. 220, 285–6 · *The diary and correspondence of Charles Abbot, Lord Colchester*, ed. Charles, Lord Colchester, 1 (1861), 22–3 · *The diaries of Sylvester Douglas (Lord Glenbervie)*, ed. F. Bickley, 2 (1928), 129 · *The journal of the Hon. Henry Edward Fox*, ed. earl of Ilchester [G. S. Holland Fox-Strangways] (1923), 29 · C. Butler, *Reminiscences*, 4th edn, 1 (1824), 134–5 · Cobbett, *Parl. hist.* · Hansard 1 · DNB · PRO, IR 26/1288/370

Archives Duke U., Perkins L., corresp.

Likenesses J. R. Smith, stipple, pubd 1793 (after J. Barry), BM, NPG · T. Lawrence, oils, exh. RA 1802, Graves Art Gallery, Sheffield · T. Lawrence, oils, 1817, NPG · G. H. Harlow, oils, Lincoln's Inn, London · W. H. Mote, engraving (after G. H. Harlow), repro. in Brougham, *Historical sketches*, 135 · S. W. Reynolds, mezzotint (after G. H. Harlow), BM, NPG

Wealth at death under £60,000: PRO, death duty registers, IR 26/1288/370

Grant, William (1839–1923), distiller, was born on 19 December 1839 in Conval Street, Dufftown, the son of William Grant, master tailor (known as Old Waterloo), and his second wife, Elizabeth, *née* Reid. At the age of seven, Grant was receiving payment as a cattle herder, and combined his work with attendance at the village school at Mortlach, near Dufftown. He was then apprenticed to a shoemaker and, aged twenty, married Elizabeth, daughter of John Duncan, a cattle dealer in Dufftown, and his wife, Margaret, *née* Grant, a labourer. After a period as a clerk to the Tininver lime works at Crachie, Grant in September 1866 became bookkeeper at Mortlach distillery near Dufftown. An active volunteer and freemason, and precentor in the Dufftown Free Church, Grant became a person of standing in the locality. For thirty years he saved to start his own distillery, which he eventually began building in 1886 at Glenfiddich, near Dufftown, using water from Dubh's Well. Initially, old equipment was used, cheaply bought from the nearby Cardow distillery, and labour was mainly provided by Grant's wife and their eight children. The temporary destruction (by fire) of the nearby Glenlivet distillery gave Grant the break he needed. He soon built a second distillery at Balvenie. In north-east Scotland, Glenfiddich was widely sold as a five-year-old whisky. Grant took advantage of the bankruptcy in 1898 of the Pattison family (the largest whisky wholesalers) to establish a base in Glasgow, sending his son Charles and his son-in-law Charles Gordon to sell a rapidly expanding number of blends (including Grant's Standfast).

In 1900 Grant suffered a severe stroke; in 1907 he began to lose his sight, and soon he was blind—his unmarried daughter, Meta, acting as his amanuensis. In 1903 he established the limited liability company of William Grant & Sons. With the Glasgow office showing a loss, Grant decided to export. His son John opened the Canadian business; Lord Strathcona, the governor-general and a distant relative, assisted with letters of introduction. By 1914 the company was trading in most countries of the British empire, and in Japan, the Philippines, and the USA, with over sixty agencies in thirty countries. From 1964 Glenfiddich was sold in its famous triangular bottle—the archetype of modern single-malt whiskies. Grant died from senile decay on 5 January 1923 at Balvenie House, Mortlach, and was buried in Mortlach churchyard.   H. C. G. MATTHEW

Sources F. Collinson, *The life and times of William Grant* (1979) · M. S. Moss and J. R. Hume, *The making of Scotch whisky* (1981) · m. cert. · d. cert.
Likenesses photographs, repro. in Collinson, *Life and times*
Wealth at death £65,153 4s. 4d.: confirmation, 19 March 1923, *CCI*

Grant, William Henry Smith (1896–1975). *See under* Smith family (*per.* 1824–1975).

Grant, William James (1829–1866),

history painter, was born at Hackney, the son of William James Grant. He showed considerable early talent for drawing, and at the age of ten he walked from home to see the Elgin marbles, by which he was much impressed. He studied drawing regularly, attended Benjamin Robert Haydon's lectures, and obtained two prizes from the Society of Arts, before becoming a student of the Royal Academy Schools in 1844. In 1847, while still a student, he exhibited his first picture there, *Boys with Rabbits*. In the following year he was more ambitious, with *Edward the Black Prince Entertaining the French King after the Battle of Poitiers*. During the next few years he painted chiefly sacred subjects, such as *Christ Casting out the Devils at Gadara* (1850) and *Samson and Delilah* (1852). In 1853, though, he reverted to historical subjects, which were executed with great attention to the detail of dress and historical context. He always made large charcoal preparatory studies for his paintings, and executed numerous drawings in red and black chalk, chiefly illustrations to poetry. Among his later pictures were *Scene from the Early Life of Queen Elizabeth* (1857), *Eugène Beauharnais Refusing to Give up the Sword of his Father* (1858), *The Eve of Monmouth's Rebellion* (1859), *The Morning of the Duel* (1860), and *The Last Relics of Lady Jane Grey* (1861). In 1866 he exhibited *The Lady and the Wasp* and *Reconciliation*, but he died, at Burford House, Upper Clapton, Middlesex, on 2 June in that year, at the early age of thirty-seven; he was survived by his father. Two years before his death the *Art Journal* singled him out as 'one of the most promising painters' of the day (*Art Journal*, Aug 1864, 233–5).

L. H. CUST, rev. MARK POTTLE

Sources Redgrave, *Artists* · *Art Journal*, 26 (1864) · *Art Journal*, new ser., 6 (1886) · Graves, *Artists* · *The exhibition of the Royal Academy* (1847–66) [exhibition catalogues] · *CGPLA Eng. & Wales* (1866)
Wealth at death under £300: administration, 21 June 1866, *CGPLA Eng. & Wales*

Grant, Sir William Keir [*formerly* William Keir] (1771–1852),

army officer, was the son of Archibald Keir HEICS and his wife, whose maiden name was Bruce, of Kinloch. On 30 May 1792 he was gazetted a cornet in the 15th King's light dragoons (later the 15th hussars), under the name of William Keir. He was promoted lieutenant in 1793, and accompanied part of his regiment to Flanders, where he fought at Famars, Valenciennes, and elsewhere in the campaigns of 1793–4. He distinguished himself on 17 April 1794, when a squadron of his regiment saved the prince of Schwartzenberg from the enemy's hussars during a reconnaissance; and he was also present at Villers-en-Cauchies on 24 April 1794 when two squadrons of the 15th and two of the Austrian Leopold hussars, although unexpectedly without supports, defeated a much larger force of French cavalry, pursued them through the French infantry, and captured three guns—an action which saved Francis II of the Holy Roman empire (later Francis I of Austria), who was on his way to Koblenz, from capture by the French.

Keir was promoted to a troop in the 6th dragoon guards (Carabiniers), with which he served in Germany in 1795 and Ireland in 1798. In the latter year Keir received permission from George III to wear the large gold medal given by the emperor in commemoration of the action at Villers-en-Cauchies. Only nine of these medals were struck, one being given to each of the eight British officers present, and the ninth placed in the Imperial Museum, Vienna. These officers were also made knights of the military order of Maria Theresa, which, as with other foreign orders of chivalry before 1814, carried the rank of a knight-bachelor in England and other countries. It also gave the wearer the rank of baron in Austria.

Keir joined the Russian and Austrian armies in Italy early in 1799, and served in the campaigns of 1799–1801. He was present at the battles of Novi, Rivoli, Mondovi, and Sanliano; he served in the gunboats at the siege of Genoa, in which he was frequently engaged, and in several actions in the mountains of Genoa, when the Austrians and Russians lost nearly 33,000 men; and he was also at the battle of Marengo and the sieges of Alessandria, Sanaval, Tortona, Cunio, and Savona.

On 3 December 1800 Keir was appointed lieutenant-colonel in the 22nd light dragoons, with whom he landed in Egypt after the end of hostilities in 1801. The regiment was disbanded on the peace of Amiens, and Keir was placed on half pay. For a short time he was aide-de-camp to the prince of Wales, and after acting as first aide-de-camp to Lord Moira who was commanding in north Britain from December 1804 to May 1806, he was appointed adjutant-general of the king's troops in Bengal. He commanded the advance of Major-General St Leger's force on the Sutlej in 1810. In 1811 he married a daughter of Captain Jackson RN. And in 1814, while on the Bengal staff, Keir, who had become a colonel in 1810 and a major-general in 1813, was appointed to command a small force of cavalry and grenadiers sent against Amir Khan (a noted Pathan freebooter, afterwards nawab of Tonk).

In 1815 Keir was made commander-in-chief and second member of council in the island of Java, a position he held until the island was restored to the Dutch after the peace. In 1817 he was appointed to the Bombay staff and commanded the Gujarat field force, part of the army of the Deccan, in the operations against the Pindaris. In February 1819 he was in command of a force assembled on the frontier of the Savantvadi state. The latter proving intractable, the troops entered the country, carried the strong hill fort of Rairi by storm, and marched to the capital, where a treaty meeting the full approval of the governor-general was signed with the regency. In March the same year he commanded a force sent against the raja of Cutch, which, after defeating the enemy and capturing the hill fortress of Bhuj, received the submission of that province.

In October 1819 Grant-Keir, as he was then called, was

dispatched by the Bombay government with a strong armament for the suppression of piracy in the Persian Gulf. The attack was specially directed against the Qasimi, a tribe of seafaring Arabs of the sect of Wahhabis, followers of the Arab religious reformer Ibn Abdul Wahhab (bestower of blessings), whose pirate craft had long been the terror of the coasts of western India. Ras al-Khaimah, their stronghold, had been destroyed by a small force from Bombay in 1809, but their power was again in the ascendant. Ras al-Khaimah was captured with small loss on 9 December 1819, and on 8 January 1820 Grant-Keir signed a general treaty of peace on behalf of the British government with the chiefs of the tribes of seafaring Arabs of the Persian Gulf, by whom it was subsequently signed at different times and places. It provided for the entire suppression of piracy in the gulf. For his services Grant-Keir received the thanks of the governor-general in council and the Persian decoration of the Lion and Sun. He returned home on the expiration of his staff service, and assumed later the surname Keir Grant. He was made KCB in 1822, lieutenant-general in 1825, GCH in 1835, colonel of the 2nd Royal North British Dragoons (Scots Greys) in 1839, and general on 23 November 1841.

He died at his residence, 20 Chapel Street, Belgrave Square, London, on 7 May 1852, aged eighty.

H. M. CHICHESTER, *rev.* JAMES LUNT

Sources PRO, War Office Records · *Dod's Peerage* · J. Philippart, ed., *The royal military calendar*, 3rd edn, 3 (1820), 267–9 · H. T. Prinsep, *History of the political and military transactions in India*, 2 vols. (1825) · H. H. Wilson, *The history of British India*, 4th edn, 8 (1848) · C. R. Low, *History of the Indian navy, 1613–1863*, 2 vols. (1877) · *GM*, 2nd ser., 37 (1852), 619 · P. Cadell, *History of the Bombay army* (1938) · C. E. Buckland, *Dictionary of Indian biography* (1906) · Boase, *Mod. Eng. biog.* · R. Cannon, ed., *Historical record of the fifteenth, or king's regiment of light dragoons, hussars* (1841) · *Life of General Sir Robert Wilson*, ed. H. Randolph, 2 vols. (1862) · J. B. Kelly, *Britain and the Persian Gulf, 1795–1880* (1968) [indexed under Keir]

Archives BL OIOC, letters to Lord Tweeddale, MS Eur. F 96 · U. Hull, Brynmor Jones L., letters and MSS relating to expedition to the Persian Gulf, PP 8ff

Grantham. For this title name *see* Robinson, Thomas, first Baron Grantham (1695-1770); Robinson, Thomas, second Baron Grantham (1738-1786); Robinson, Mary Jemima, Lady Grantham (1757-1830) [*see under* Yorke, Jemima, Marchioness Grey (1722-1797)].

Grantham, Sir Alexander William George Herder (1899-1978), colonial governor, was born on 15 March 1899 at Chippenham, The Avenue, Surbiton, the son of Frederick William Grantham, barrister, and his wife, Alexandra Ethelred Marie Sylvie Emilie von Herder. He was educated at Wellington College, the Royal Military College, Sandhurst, and Pembroke College, Cambridge. He served in the First World War after being commissioned to the 18th hussars in 1917.

Grantham joined the colonial administrative service as a Hong Kong cadet in 1922, learned Cantonese, and served mainly in the colonial secretariat for about ten years. Ambitious and determined to rise to a colonial governorship, he requested a transfer in 1934 in order to advance his promotion prospect, accepting in the process a drop of

Sir Alexander William George Herder Grantham (1899–1978), by Elliott & Fry, 1947

about one-third in salary. In that year he attended the Imperial Defence College and was called to the bar at the Inner Temple. He subsequently served as colonial secretary in Bermuda from 1935 to 1938 and in Jamaica from 1938 to 1941, and as chief secretary in Nigeria from 1941 to 1944, before being appointed governor of Fiji and high commissioner for the Western Pacific in 1945. He was knighted in that year. He assumed the governorship of Hong Kong on 25 July 1947 and retired on 31 December 1957, having been the colony's longest serving governor. Tall, handsome, charming, and intelligent, he was well liked by his subordinates and the non-official leaders of Hong Kong.

When the Second World War began Grantham was colonial secretary in Jamaica where his main contribution was to promote Anglo-American co-operation, as Jamaica was one of the colonies whose facilities Britain made available to the United States Navy in exchange for fifty old destroyers. He became more involved with the war after he became chief secretary in Nigeria, which was one of the four west African colonies that raised two divisions for operations in south-east Asia and an important source for groundnut oil, rubber, and tin. At the end of the war he was promoted to his first governorship: from 1945 to 1947 he presided over the rehabilitation of Fiji and played a positive role in establishing organs of international co-operation for the development and welfare of the south Pacific.

It was, however, during his final decade in Hong Kong

that Grantham made his most decisive contribution as a colonial governor. When he assumed the governorship Hong Kong was already on its way to economic recovery but it faced the danger of the spilling over of the Chinese civil war (between the Kuomintang and the Chinese Communist Party) into the colony. The threat from China to Hong Kong's survival as a British colony appeared to have reached a near crisis point when the communists won control of the Chinese mainland and marched towards the Sino-British border in 1949. Grantham took the lead in working out a policy to defuse the threat from communist China. He rightly assessed that the communists would not invade Hong Kong provided the latter acknowledged its existence as a borrowed place on borrowed time, and made itself valuable to China.

At the same time Grantham took the lead to devise a policy of non-provocative firmness in dealing with Hong Kong's communist neighbour and in maintaining strict neutrality in the as yet unfinished Chinese civil war, which turned into a stalemate across the Taiwan Strait after the United States Navy started to patrol the straits when the Korean War broke out in 1950. By a combination of pragmatism, realism, and the ability to remain firm against any unreasonable demands, he played a crucial role in establishing a *modus operandi* between the governments in Hong Kong and Beijing, which allowed the latter to sidetrack domestic irredentist pressure. It was under his governorship that the Chinese government's demand, raised since 1942, for the return of the leased part of Hong Kong, was put aside. This continued for over three decades and allowed Hong Kong to transform itself from a colonial outpost into a cosmopolitan modern metropolis.

Grantham played an even more important, indeed a pivotal, role in the shelving of democratic reforms which were strongly advocated by his predecessor, Sir Mark Young. Although both men related the issue of democratization to the future of Hong Kong, Grantham, unlike Young, believed Hong Kong had no other future apart from being either a British colony or part of China's Guangdong (Kwangtung) province, given that 90 per cent of its territories were leased from China until 30 June 1997. Confident in his knowledge of the Chinese people and their politics, Grantham thought Young was misguided in attempting to turn Hong Kong's Chinese residents into loyal British subjects. He did not believe the Chinese of Hong Kong could become either loyal British subjects or good democrats. He was convinced that giving them the vote could only lead to their voting to end British colonial rule and to rejoin mother China, even though they actually preferred the stability and good order offered by the colonial government. Hence, he delayed the implementation of Young's reform plan for almost two years, and then substituted it with a set of more conservative proposals when the Chinese civil war was reaching its climax and distracting public attention in 1949. He remained sceptical about the wisdom of democratic changes in Hong Kong, and did not push hard for his proposals when various officials in the Colonial Office doubted the wisdom of his alternative. After Hong Kong

started to suffer from its first recession, which threatened the livelihood of the overwhelming majority of its people and diverted their attention from the reform issue, Grantham adroitly manoeuvred to abandon democratization in 1952 on the ground that it would be 'inopportune', and skilfully sidetracked all subsequent demands to reopen the issue during the remainder of his governorship.

Grantham was married twice. His first marriage, to Maurine Samson (d. 1970) of San Francisco, took place in Hong Kong in 1925. After her death he married on 21 November 1972 Mrs Margaret Eileen Lumley (b. 1921/2), daughter of Charles S. Wright, a corn merchant. They had no children. He was appointed CMG in 1941, KCMG in 1945, and GCMG in 1951. In retirement Grantham lived in London, where he kept an interest in the welfare of Hong Kong and spoke and wrote occasionally to discourage others from 'rocking the boat'. He also wrote an autobiography of his colonial service, *Via ports: from Hong Kong to Hong Kong*, which was published by the Hong Kong University Press in 1965. It was his second wife who nursed him through illness before he died on 4 October 1978.

STEVE TSANG

Sources S. Y. S. Tsang, *Democracy shelved: Great Britain, China, and attempts at constitutional reform in Hong Kong, 1945–1952* (1988) · S. Tsang, 'Strategy for survival: the cold war and Hong Kong's policy towards Kuomintang and Chinese communist activities in the 1950s', *Journal of Imperial and Commonwealth History*, 25 (1997), 294–317 · S. Tsang, *Hong Kong: appointment with China* (1997) · A. Grantham, *Via ports: from Hong Kong to Hong Kong* (1965) · PRO, CO 537, 882/31, 1030, and FO 371 · G. B. Endacott, *A history of Hong Kong* (1964) · F. Welsh, *A history of Hong Kong* (1993) · *The Times* (9 Oct 1978) · interview with A. Grantham, Bodl. RH, MS Brit. Emp.s.288 · m. cert. · b. cert. · *CGPLA Eng. & Wales* (1979)

Archives Bodl. RH | Bodl. RH, Arthur Cruch-Jones MSS | FILM Hong Kong PRO | SOUND Hong Kong PRO

Likenesses Elliott & Fry, photograph, 1947, NPG [*see illus.*]

Wealth at death £320,097: probate, 9 Feb 1979, *CGPLA Eng. & Wales*

Grantham, Sir Guy (1900–1992), naval officer, was born on 9 January 1900 at Roman Bank, Skegness, Lincolnshire, the only son of Charles Fred Grantham, landowner and farmer, and his wife, Jane Marian, *née* Hildred. He was educated at Rugby School (1914–18) before joining the navy as a special entry cadet at the Royal Naval College, Osborne, in June 1918. He first served as a midshipman in the battleship *Monarch*, and then as a sub-lieutenant in the royal yacht *Victoria and Albert* and the cruiser *New Zealand*, flagship of the admiral of the fleet, Lord Jellicoe. He joined the Submarine Service in 1923, his first boat being the giant *M.1*, which was armed with a 12 inch gun. He returned to general service in the battle cruiser *Hood* in 1927, before going to the Royal Naval College, Dartmouth, in 1931, as river officer in charge of sailing. He returned to submarines in 1933 and commanded *L.56* and *Regent*. After early promotion to captain in 1937, he joined the staff of Admiral Sir Dudley Pound, the commander-in-chief Mediterranean, and when Pound became first sea lord in 1939 Grantham went to the Admiralty as his naval assistant. Meanwhile, in 1934 he had married Beryl Marjorie (d. 1991), daughter of T. C. B. Mackintosh-Walker, of Geddes, Nairn, Scotland. They had two daughters.

In 1940 Grantham commissioned the new light cruiser *Phoebe*, serving in the Home Fleet and then in the Mediterranean, where she took off thousands of soldiers in the evacuation of the army from Greece in April 1941 and then from Crete in May. Grantham was awarded the DSO for *Phoebe*'s part in the evacuation from Nauplia in Greece on 24 April. In August *Phoebe* was hit by an aerial torpedo on a run to Tobruk and was so badly damaged she was sent to America for repairs. Grantham was then sent by Admiral Sir Andrew Cunningham to be naval liaison officer to his brother, General Sir Alan Cunningham, commanding the Eighth Army, and was mentioned in dispatches for his services in the western desert.

In January 1942 Grantham took command of the light cruiser *Naiad*, and was flag captain and chief of staff to Rear-Admiral Sir Philip Vian, commanding the 15th cruiser squadron. On 11 March, as *Naiad* was returning to Alexandria, she was torpedoed off the harbour entrance by *U.565* and sank in twenty minutes. Grantham had no lifebelt, having been preoccupied with his attempts to save the ship. Vian and Grantham were picked up half an hour later by destroyers, both of them cold and oily, Grantham at the end of his tether and quite exhausted. However, there was no question of survivors' leave. Three days later Vian hoisted his flag in the newly arrived *Cleopatra*, and took Grantham with him as his flag captain. On 22 March 1942 *Cleopatra* took part in one of the most celebrated naval actions of the war, known as the second battle of Sirte, when light cruisers and destroyers under Vian defended a convoy to Malta against a much stronger Italian force including heavy cruisers and the battleship *Littorio*. Not at all abashed by their much larger and heavier gunned opponents, Vian's ships made skilful use of the weather gauge (as in Nelson's day), laying smokescreens, through which they advanced to attack with guns and torpedoes. At the height of the action *Cleopatra*'s bridge was hit by a 6 inch shell which Grantham saw coming straight for him. It struck the opposite corner of the bridge, where Vian normally stood, but luckily he had just gone to the chart house. Grantham escaped, but one officer and fourteen men were killed. Some ships besides *Cleopatra* were damaged, but they held the enemy off until nightfall, when the convoy made good its escape. Grantham was appointed CB.

In December 1942 Grantham took command of the carrier *Indomitable* and went out again to the Mediterranean, to provide air cover for operation Husky, the invasion of Sicily in July 1943. After *Indomitable* was damaged by an aerial torpedo Grantham transferred to the cruiser *Euryalus* to serve once again with Vian as his chief of staff for operation Avalanche, the Salerno landing in September, after which Grantham was mentioned in dispatches for the second time. In 1944 Grantham went to the Admiralty as director of plans and attended the conferences at Quebec, Yalta, and Potsdam, on the staff of Cunningham, who had succeeded Pound as first sea lord. He was appointed CBE in 1946.

From 1946 to 1948 Grantham was chief of staff to the commander-in-chief Mediterranean with the rank of commodore. Promoted rear-admiral in July 1947, he was flag officer (submarines) from 1948 to 1950. Early in 1950 he was appointed flag officer (air) and second-in-command Mediterranean Fleet, and promoted vice-admiral. In 1951 he went back to the Admiralty as vice chief of the naval staff. Following the change of government in October 1951 Duncan Sandys was put in charge of defence, and the navy's finances and traditional role came under fierce attack. It fell to Grantham to fight the navy's corner—with only partial success, although probably no one could have done better. He was appointed KCB in 1952, promoted admiral in 1953, and went out to the Mediterranean once more in 1954 to relieve Lord Mountbatten as commander-in-chief Mediterranean and commander-in-chief allied forces Mediterranean. Grantham could have been first sea lord in 1955 but the senior admirals believed that the navy was then battling for its very existence, and the higher-profile Mountbatten was chosen instead. Grantham was appointed GCB in 1956. In July that year President Nasser of Egypt nationalized the Suez Canal. Had Britain and France taken immediate military action, world opinion might have been on their side. But it took time to assemble the necessary forces, the plan of attack was changed, and it was not until October that operation Musketeer, the assault on Port Said, was launched. It was a military success, but a political disaster. In May 1957 Grantham became commander-in-chief Portsmouth, hoisting his flag for the first time on the periscope standard of a submarine at Gosport. The next year, when Mountbatten was due to become chief of the defence staff, Grantham could again have been first sea lord. Again the post went elsewhere—to Admiral Sir Charles Lambe, a friend and confidant of Mountbatten's. Grantham never showed or expressed any disappointment.

Grantham retired in 1959 to become governor of Malta—the first naval officer to hold the office since Sir Alexander Ball in 1800. He arrived in the middle of a political crisis. Dom Mintoff, the Labour prime minister, had just resigned over a British proposal for the island's future. Grantham had to govern in fact as well as in name until 1962 when Borg Olivier's Nationalist Party won the general election. He was principal naval aide-de-camp to the queen from 1958 to 1959; vice-chairman of the Commonwealth War Graves Commission from 1963 to 1970; governor of the Corps of Commissionaires from 1964 to 1992; and a lay canon of Portsmouth Cathedral.

'It is difficult to write, without being fulsome, a description which would do Grantham justice,' Vian wrote in his memoirs. 'He is, and always has been, a very perfect knight, without fear and without reproach' (Vian, 81). Yet Guy Grantham had a remarkably non-heroic, unassuming, somewhat schoolmasterly manner, indeed he was sometimes known as Granny Grantham. One admiral's daughter said of him: 'Guy is family. You can see him in his wellington boots calling at the back door on Sunday morning with vegetables he has dug up for lunch' (private information). He was a fair horseman and was one of the five admirals who rode, with differing degrees of skill, in the coronation procession of 1953. He died of a heart attack at North Lodge, Syston Park, Barkston, Lincolnshire, on 8 September 1992. He was survived by his two daughters; his wife had died in December 1991. JOHN WINTON

Sources *Daily Telegraph* (10 Sept 1992) · *The Times* (12 Sept 1992) · *The Times* (16 Sept 1992) · *The Times* (18 Sept 1992) · *The Times* (24 Sept 1992) · *The Independent* (17 Sept 1992) · *WWW*, 1991–5 · b. cert. · d. cert. · P. Vian, *Action this day: a war memoir* (1960) · private information (2004)
Likenesses photograph, repro. in *Daily Telegraph* · photograph, repro. in *The Times* · photograph, repro. in *The Independent*
Wealth at death £82,386: probate, 1 Feb 1993, *CGPLA Eng. & Wales*

Grantham [Granthan]**, Henry** (*fl.* 1566–1587), translator, made his living teaching Italian to the children of the English nobility, according to the eighteenth-century bibliographer Thomas Tanner. Nothing else is known about him. Tanner ascribed to him a translation of Boccaccio's *Filocolo* with the title *A Pleasaunt Disport of Divers Noble Personages. Entituled Philocopo* (1567), republished in 1571 and 1587 as *Thirtene most Pleasant and Delectable Questions*, a lively piece of English bringing over the energy of the Italian. 'Philocopo' seems to be a slip. The translation seems to have been done without reference to any of the French and Spanish versions then available. Tanner's ascription of this version to Grantham was disputed by Hazlitt, who proffered Henry Gifford on the unsound grounds that an experienced teacher of Italian would not have made the elementary mistakes in the English text. However, H. G. Wright argues from a comparison of the dedicatory epistles of these two works that Grantham did indeed do both versions: few translators avoid even the most elementary errors, and this English Boccaccio could indeed have been a successful beginner's exercise.

Tanner also ascribed to Grantham *An Italian grammar written in Latin by Scipio Lentulo, a Neapolitane, and turned into English by H. G.* (1575), which played a major role in the spread of Italian culture in sixteenth-century England, and seems to have been used well into the seventeenth century. Writing grammars of culturally important vernacular languages in Latin was not unusual at the time. The original was important enough to be translated several times into French, Italian, and German. Grantham dedicated his version to Mary and Frances, the daughters of Lord Henry Berkeley. The dedication is dated from Berkeley Castle in Gloucestershire. Like the medieval and humanist Latin grammars, Lentulo's grammar is patterned on Donatus's fourth-century grammar of Latin. It begins from the sounds of Italian and progresses to sentence structure by way of an assembly of grammar rules and Italian paradigms. Grammar and accidence were meant to be memorized *in toto* by the pupil in the usual Renaissance style. Grantham does not attempt to make his version less forbidding than the original. The British Library copy of the 1587 edition seems to have been in use until the 1660s. It is bound with a large number of blank pages, which carry notes by somebody who was obviously learning Italian overseas, including long paradigms of irregular verbs, and draft letters which look like the correspondence of a dutiful son overseas to an indulgent father.

Grantham may also have done the plain and uninteresting version of Girolamo Cataneo's military treatise published as *Most briefe tables to know redily howe manye ranckes of footemen … go to the making of a just battayle* (1574 and 1588). Apart from these translations, whose authorship is unsure, he seems to have left no other traces behind him. L. G. KELLY

Sources H. G. Wright, 'The Elizabethan translation of the *Questioni d'amore* in the *Filocolo*', *Modern Language Review*, 36 (1941), 281–303 · H. Grantham, *Thirteene most pleasaunte questiones translated out of Boccace's Philocopo*, ed. E. Hutton (1927) · R. C. Simonini, 'English–Italian language books', *Romanic Review*, 42 (1951), 241–4 · Tanner, *Bibl. Brit.-Hib.*, 339 · H. G. Wright, *Boccaccio in England* (1957)

Grantham, Thomas (*c.*1610–1664), schoolmaster and author, was a native of Lincolnshire and a nephew of Sir Thomas Grantham of Radcliffe, Nottinghamshire; his parents' names are unknown. He entered Hart Hall, Oxford, in 1626 and graduated BA in 1630. Two years later he entered Peterhouse, Cambridge, and in 1634 proceeded MA and was ordained. A man of vigour and wit (both intentional and unintentional), he might fairly be called diverting rather than distinguished, though his drollery was not without a serious, liberal, and constructive side. He appears as curate of High Barnet in 1641 and of Easton Neston, Northamptonshire, in the following year. By this time he had evidently begun his career as a teacher since his first known publication, which pre-dates this period, was an attack on what he described as Camden's 'false, obscure and imperfect' *Greek Grammar* (Collier, 197). He further condemned masters who used corporal punishment to force boys to learn grammar by rote. His taste for the absurd was shown by his *A Marriage Sermon … Called a Wife Mistaken* (1641), a celebrated piece of nonsense based on Genesis 29: 25. In a short treatise against imprisonment for debt, *A Motion Against Imprisonment* (1642), however, he used arguments of pure sense.

From at least the early 1640s Grantham held private schools at different locations in central London and his competitive streak led to a forceful insistence on the superiority of his own methods of instruction. In advertising tracts, including *A Discourse in Derision of the Teaching in Free Schools* (1644) and *Brainbreakers-Breaker* (1644 and 1650), he derided his competitors and challenged them to examine their boys against his own. As 'Professor of a speedy way of teaching' (Collier, 194) he claimed that under his tuition and kindly regime boys became proficient in Latin, Greek, and Hebrew in only two months. This was the more remarkable since his boys were allowed to play as much as they worked: he was, however, an early advocate of small-class teaching.

From 1646 Grantham held the rectorship of Waddington in Lincolnshire, from which he was ejected in 1656 to his own loud protestations of ill-treatment and illegality, voiced in *A Complaint to the Lord Protector* of that year. He had inherited the rectory of Waddington (along with The

Reindeer inn in Lincoln) from his uncle, but as rector he was apparently inactive. Immediately after the Restoration he published a translation in heroic couplets of the first three books of Homer's *Iliad* (1660). This lamentable production ranks with the very worst attempts at verse but was carried off with its author's customary arrogance and verve. The loyal verses to Charles II and others which accompany the translation are as poetry similarly awful. He further expressed his loyalty in a pamphlet—*Charles the Second, Second to None* (1661). He died in the parish of St Ann Blackfriars in March 1664. By his will, dated 3 March and proved 5 March, he left his property in Waddington and Lincoln to his London landlord, John Tring of Little Old Bailey, schoolmaster, and Tring's wife, Mary, who was the executor.

W. R. MEYER

Sources Wood, *Ath. Oxon.*, new edn, 4.165–7 · J. P. Collier, ed., *A bibliographical and critical account of the rarest books in the English language*, 2 (1865), 193–7 · T. Grantham, *Mnēmophthoropaiktēs: The brainbreakers-breaker, or, The apologie of Thomas Grantham for his method of teaching* (1644) · will, PRO, PROB 11/313, fol. 232r–v · *Walker rev.*, 250 · T. A. Walker, ed., *Admissions to Peterhouse or St Peter's College in the University of Cambridge* (1912), 47–8 · Foster, *Alum. Oxon.*

Wealth at death rectory of Waddington, Lincolnshire; Reindeer Inn, Lincoln: will, PRO, PROB 11/313, fol. 232r–v

Grantham, Thomas (1633/4–1692), General Baptist minister, was probably born in the village of Halton, near Spilsby, Lincolnshire. Since he died aged fifty-eight on 17 January 1692, he must have been born in 1633 or the first few days of 1634. While there are several Thomas Granthams born in Lincolnshire about that time, a likely match is the one baptized in the parish of Spilsby on 15 April 1633, the son of Ralf Grantam. A Ralf Grantham had married Elyzabeth Hunsworth in that parish on 11 April 1630. Grantham described himself as related to 'the ancient family of the Granthams, in the County of Lincoln' with relatives 'being persons of quality', but he was from their 'poor kindred' and 'one of the lowest in my Fathers House' (Grantham, *Christianismus primitivus*, 1.sig. b). His parents were said to have suffered 'much loss for the King' during the civil war. As a result, Grantham was apprenticed to a tailor, noting that 'in my youth I used the Imployment of my Father, who was both a Farmer and a Taylor' (Grantham, *Infants Advocate*, 8), but upon completing his service 'he gave himself to study and, became a great Proficient in Learning' (Firmin, sig. A2v–A3r).

About 1652 Grantham, aged about nineteen, underwent adult baptism and joined the Baptist church at Boston, Lincolnshire. The church dated back to at least 1644 and by 1651 the vast majority of its members favoured baptism by sprinkling, with only four people favouring the method of immersion. Grantham helped the latter group secure ministers to preach for them publicly while he 'exercised his own gifts among them privately' (Crosby, 3.77). In 1656, aged only twenty-two, Grantham was chosen as the pastor of this congregation, which gradually grew in size and was eventually granted Northolme chapel near Wainfleet. However, even during the interregnum, Baptists failed to escape

> the unkind usage ... of persecuting priests ... For in the time of Cromwell's usurpation, they did then hale us before the

judgment seats, because we could not worship God, after the will of their Lord Protector ... And we had then our goods taken away, and never restored. (Crosby, 3.85–6)

In July 1660 Grantham was a signatory to the reprinted Baptist publication *A Brief Confession or Declaration of Faith*, which he and a fellow Baptist presented to Charles II. Primarily a statement of Christian doctrine with a General Baptist emphasis, the pamphlet stressed the peaceful beliefs and practices of the sect and their respect for the civil magistrate. When in January 1661 the Lincolnshire Baptists sought to affirm their support for the king at the time of Venner's rising, Grantham's name headed the list of signatories to their *Second Humble Addresse*. Presumably the tract had little effect, however, as in the following month Grantham was the first of eight subscribers to *The Third Addres* who petitioned the king for their liberty from Lincoln gaol.

Grantham had regained his liberty by the time he was arrested at a Baptist meeting-house in Boston, Lincolnshire, in 1662. On this occasion he was gaoled in Lincoln for fifteen months. During his imprisonment he wrote *The Prisoner Against the Prelate* (1662?), which included a poetic version of *A Brief Confession*, and *The Baptist Against the Papist* (1663), which explicitly denied the rumour that he was a Roman Catholic. After the 1664 Conventicle Act took effect, soldiers arrested Grantham and several other Baptists who were forced to 'run along like *lacqueys* by their horses' (Crosby, 3.81). They were imprisoned at Louth, Lincolnshire, for six months. Soon after his release Grantham was sued for £100 by a man whose wife he had baptized, but the case was thrown out of court as a malicious prosecution. In 1666 Grantham was 'elected, by the consent of many congregations, and ordained to the office of messenger by those who were in the same office before me' (Taylor, 1.203). In part a messenger continued the work of an apostle in the primitive church, being a travelling minister responsible beyond his local congregation for creating and assisting churches in their ministry and ordinations.

As a messenger Grantham involved himself in many controversies. About 1670 he wrote a challenge (which was not accepted) to Robert Wright, a former Baptist and then Anglican priest, to debate infant baptism. He successfully engaged in public disputations within Lincolnshire with William Fort and the Quaker John Whitehead. Grantham also had 'a very Christian conference at London', with Dr William Lloyd, bishop of Asaph, 'which ended with much friendship' (Taylor, 1.311), and published controversies with Henry Danvers, John Horne, Samuel Petto, Giles Firmin, Martin Finch, and Joseph Whiston. Grantham was both courteous and at times abrasive in his pamphlet disputes with opponents. While he strongly urged all Baptists to use the laying-on of hands after baptism, he understood that others could not accept the ceremony, but nevertheless lamented the divisions between General, Particular, and Seventh Day Baptists.

When dissenters were offered government licences to preach under the terms of the 1672 declaration of indulgence Grantham was registered for Raiston (or Rouston) near Rolleston, Leicestershire. This sets him apart from the vast majority of Baptists who 'declined to take out licences on the ground that the state had no more right to give, than to take away, religious liberty' (M. Watts, *The Dissenters: from the Reformation to the French Revolution*, 1978, repr. 1985, 248).

Grantham's *Christianismus primitivus* (1678) is by far his largest book, at over 600 pages. Although it included several of his earlier works, new sections were written at the urging and encouragement of the Baptized churches in Lincolnshire, emphasizing, as the title suggests, that Christians should imitate the organization and simplicity of worship of the primitive church. The book gave instruction on a number of topics including doctrine, church organization, marriage, and divorce. Aware that women preachers were prominent among Quakers, Grantham insisted that females should be silent in the church. However, he thought women may exercise gifts of 'Edification … in a private way, and more especially among their own Sex' and be 'assistant in the Ministry, as some were in the Apostles Days; so that their Gifts are not given in vain' (*Christianismus primitivus*, 3.45, 48). Among Grantham's other notable works were *A Friendly Epistle* (1680), in which he appealed for better relations with the Church of England so that Baptist ministers might officiate in the established church.

About 1686 Grantham moved to Norwich, where he founded a General Baptist church. He was also responsible for the creation of churches elsewhere in Norfolk, at Yarmouth about 1686, King's Lynn (where he returned to preach occasionally) in 1689 or 1690, and finally at Smallburgh. Though based in Norwich, Grantham also worked in other counties. In September 1687 at the General Baptist church 'meeting in Bourn, Hackonby, Spalding and the Park [parts] adjacent, in Lincolnshire' he, with the consent of the church, ordained its new pastor, Joseph Hooke (F. J. Mason, 'The old minute book of Bourne Baptist church', *Baptist Quarterly*, 15, 1953–4, 226). Grantham appears to have had a continuing relationship with this church for as messenger he headed a list of its officers in August 1688. At Warboys, Huntingdonshire, in the same year he received two members into a General Baptist church by prayer and laying-on of hands. Grantham also presented sample marriage documents as some priests refused to marry Baptists who objected to 'the ceremonies of the ring, and kneeling to the alter' (Grantham, *Truth and Peace*, 74–5). He also attended the 1689 General Baptist assembly in London, where he took down the minutes.

In the late 1680s Grantham referred to his wife and family, while noting that some of his children had died in their infancy. He may have been married for some time, however. Grantham was a trustee of the 1679 will of John Tailor of Northolme; legatees include Abner and Mary Grantham, both under the age of twenty-one, and possibly two of Grantham's children. Writing in 1690 he noted that his 'Employ for many Years to get my Bread, has been farming' (Grantham, *Infants Advocate*, 8). In the following year John Willet, an Anglican priest, falsely accused Grantham of having stolen seven sheep. The falsity was soon realized and a confession written, but Willet lacked the 10s. to secure his release. Grantham took pity on him and provided the money so that his accuser might be set at liberty.

Grantham seems to have acquired much literary capacity through self-education, as his writings reveal an acquaintance with classical scholarship. He might possibly have had during his time in Norwich access to a manuscript copy of Michael Servetus's *Christianismi restitutio*, as Grantham's *A Dialogue between the Baptist and the Presbyterian* (1691) mentions Servetus. Servetus, a sixteenth-century anti-Trinitarian writer, presumably interested him as an early opponent of infant baptism. In 1691 Grantham engaged in a lengthy exchange of letters, especially on the subject of infant baptism, with the Revd John Connould of St Stephen's, Norwich. Grantham died on 17 January 1692, probably in Norwich, and Connould conducted the burial service that same year. A memorial to Grantham was later erected in the church he founded in Norwich: 'to prevent the indecencies threatened to his corpse [he] was interred … in the middle ai[s]le of St. Stephen's Church' (Richard, 117). Connould requested that his own burial should be beside Grantham, which was done in May 1703. Grantham's *Dying Words* were published in 1692; among the eight witnesses to them was Ann Grantham.

By his efforts over thirty years Grantham had helped establish a number of General Baptist congregations throughout East Anglia. Though in his latter years his theology seemed heavily influenced by the Quaker doctrine of the inner light, he remained a firm believer in the laying-on of hands. He is also noteworthy for his verses on Servetus which are among the first references to him in English.

OSCAR C. BURDICK

Sources T. Crosby, *The history of the English Baptists, from the Reformation to the beginning of the reign of King George I*, 4 vols. (1738–40), vol. 3 • W. R[ichard], 'Biography … of Thomas Grantham', *Universal Theological Magazine* (Jan–April 1805), 1–10, 57–68, 109–17, 165–71 • W. T. Whitley, ed., *Minutes of the general assembly of the General Baptist churches in England*, 1: 1654–1728 (1909) • A. Taylor, *The history of the English General Baptists*, 1: *The English General Baptists of the seventeenth century* (1818) • C. B. Jewson, *The Baptists in Norfolk* (1957) • *The Lyn persecution* (1692/3) • J. Browne, *A history of Congregationalism and memorials of the churches in Norfolk and Suffolk* (1877) • *CSP dom.*, 1672–3 • G. L. Turner, ed., *Original records of early nonconformity under persecution and indulgence*, 3 vols. (1911–14), vols. 1–2 • W. Kennett, *A register and chronicle ecclesiastical and civil* (1728) • *DNB* • T. Grantham, *The infants advocate: the second part* (1690) • G. Firmin, *Scripture-warrant* (1688) • T. Grantham, *Christianismus primitivus, or, The ancient Christian religion*, 4 pts in 1 (1678) • T. Grantham, *Truth and peace* (1691) • R. R. Kershaw, 'Baptised believers: Lincolnshire Baptists in times of persecution, revolution and toleration, 1600–1700', MA diss., U. Nott., 1995 • parish register, Spilsby and bishop's transcripts, 15 April 1633, Lincs. Arch. [baptism]

Grantham, Sir Thomas (*bap.* 1641, *d.* 1718), tobacco trader and naval officer, was baptized on 23 December 1641, the first of three children of Thomas Grantham (*d.* 1643 or 1645) of Bicester, Oxfordshire. In 1664 Grantham was acting as a merchant, shipping woollen goods to Virginia. In 1672 he informed Charles II that Virginia lacked arms and ammunition for self-defence and volunteered his services.

Upon his arrival in Virginia with a shipment of leather goods and a letter of recommendation from the duke of York, the governor, Sir William Berkeley, received him 'with several marks of friendship and esteem' (Grantham, 7) and appointed him admiral of a flotilla of twenty-five ships which he convoyed back to England in the summer of 1673. In 1674 as commander of the *Barnaby* he escorted the London tobacco fleet to Virginia. He became a prominent tobacco trader, as well as 'a master of Virginia's waters and an expert on their defenses' (Webb, 114).

When Grantham arrived in Virginia in September 1676 in command of the *Concord* (32 guns) Berkeley asked him to act as intermediary with the rebels led by Nathaniel Bacon. Grantham arranged a surrender by one group on 2 January 1677 by promising a pardon for all, and breaking out a barrel of brandy to calm everyone's nerves. He then persuaded another garrison to surrender, using similar tactics. Charles II awarded him £200 for his services.

On his next voyage to Virginia in 1678 Grantham beat off an attack by a large Algerine corsair, for which action Charles II recommended him to the East India Company. The company appropriately granted him a commission for a ship named the *Charles II*, and he was knighted by the king at the launch on 8 February 1683. He sailed in the summer with instructions to enforce the company's claims against the shah of Persia for half the revenues of Gombroon, a port at the entrance to the Persian Gulf, and to recapture Bantam, where the company had been expelled by the king's son and the Dutch forces. Grantham reached Bantam in June 1684, but by then a settlement had been reached in London. He proceeded to Gombroon, but found the Dutch already in possession; unable to carry out his mission, he sailed to Surat, where he received orders from John Child, president of the East India Company council, to suppress a mutiny at Bombay, where Captain Richard Keigwin had seized power. By diplomatic handling of the affair Keigwin and his supporters were won over, and Grantham returned to England in 1685.

In April 1689 Grantham was appointed gentleman of the privy chamber and esquire of the body to William and Mary, offices he retained under Queen Anne. In 1690 he bought the manor of Kempton, Sunbury, Middlesex, where he built Batavia House in 1697. He obtained a grant of arms in 1711, and died, probably in Sunbury, in January 1718. In his will Grantham asked to be buried at Bicester, specifically in the middle aisle of Bicester parish church 'where I received my Christianity and where my mother and father lyeth buried … and near that place to set up a marble monument of no less value than 200 Guineas with my name and age on it' (will, PRO, PROB 11/574, fol. 62v). He was buried there on 22 January and the monument was duly erected by his nephew Andrew Grantham.

[ANON.], rev. PETER LE FEVRE

Sources T. Grantham, *An historical account of some memorable actions, particularly in Virginia … perform'd … by Sr. T. G.* (1716), repr. with introduction by R. A. Brock (1882) · P. W. Coldham, *The complete book of emigrants, 1661–1699* (1990) · S. S. Webb, *The end of American independence* (1984), 103, 111–24 · W. E. Washburn, *The governor and the rebel* (1957) · J. Sutton, *Lords of the east: the East India Company and its ships* (1981) · sentence for Sir Thomas Grantham of Sunbury, 26 June 1719, PRO, PROB 11/571, fols. 404v–405r · will, PRO, PROB 11/574, fols. 62–3 · PRO, LC 3/31, pp. 19, 34 · private information (2004) [J. D. Davies] · parish register, Bicester, Oxfordshire Archives [baptism, burial]

Grantham, Sir William (1835–1911), judge, was born at Lewes on 23 October 1835, the second son of George Grantham of Barcombe Place, Lewes, Sussex, and his wife, Sarah, daughter of William Verrall of Southower Manor, Lewes. He was educated at King's College School, London, and was entered a student of the Inner Temple in 1860. A pupil in the chambers of James Hannen, he was called to the bar in 1863.

Choosing the home circuit Grantham was helped initially by his good local connection in Sussex. His pleasant manner, combined with pertinacity and great industry, soon secured him a steady practice. He obtained the reputation of being 'a very useful junior in an action on a builder's account, in a running-down case, in a compensation case, and especially in disputes in which a combined knowledge of law and horseflesh was desirable'. In 1865 he married Emma, eldest daughter of Richard Wilson of Chiddingly, Sussex. They had two sons and five daughters.

Grantham took silk in 1877, and was made a bencher of his inn on 30 April 1880, serving the office of treasurer in 1904. As a leader he achieved considerable success on circuit, but in London he failed to make any conspicuous mark.

Grantham's real and absorbing interest was in politics. A Conservative of the most orthodox school, gifted with an excellent platform manner and considerable rhetorical power, Grantham took a prominent part in promoting popular toryism in London and the home counties. At the general election of February 1874 he was returned together for East Surrey by a large majority, which he substantially increased in April 1880. After the redistribution of seats in 1885 he was selected to contest the borough of Croydon, carved out of his old constituency, and although the seat was regarded by the local Conservatives as marginal, he defeated his Liberal opponent comfortably.

On the death of his elder brother, George, in 1880 Grantham became squire of Barcombe and lord of the manor of Camois Court, a position which gave him additional prestige in 'the country party'. He became deputy chairman and eventually chairman of the east Sussex quarter sessions. In parliament he was a fairly frequent speaker, who saw himself as having a special mission to unmask and defeat the machinations of Gladstone; he was conspicuous among the militant spirits on the Conservative benches.

In January 1886, before he had the opportunity of taking his seat on his re-election for Croydon, Grantham was made a judge of the Queen's Bench Division, in succession to Sir Henry Lopes, and was knighted. It was Lord Halsbury's first judicial appointment. Halsbury was the last of a long line of lord chancellors who believed the

High Court bench was an appropriate reward for the politically deserving or, as Halsbury would have put it, that political experience helped make a man a better judge. Yet there were many conflicting claims among Conservative lawyers. It had been assumed that Sir John Gorst, then solicitor-general, would be chosen. Gorst, however, had the misfortune both of supporting Lord Randolph Churchill and of having a slim majority.

On the bench Grantham showed himself indefatigable and painstaking, and he never failed to clear his list on circuit. He was shrewd in his judgement of character, had a varied assortment of general knowledge, and his direct style made a favourable impression on juries. He had a competent knowledge of law for the ordinary work of *nisi prius*, and his industry and energy made a strong contrast to the methods of some of his colleagues. He lacked the breadth of mind and the grasp of intellect necessary for trying complicated issues, however, and he was an unsatisfactory judge in commercial cases. Among his failings was an inability to refrain from perpetual comment; his 'obiter dicta' brought him into collision at one time or another with nearly every class of the community—deans, publicans, chairmen of quarter sessions, the council of the bar, the Durham pitmen, his brother judges. His love of talking was not conducive to the dignity of the bench, and towards the close of his career he was given strong hints in the press that the public interest would be best served by his retirement.

Grantham's name would not have been known to posterity had he not in the spring of 1906 found himself on the rota of judges appointed to try election petitions. It was a task for which his strong and somewhat intemperate political views rendered him peculiarly unsuited. His decisions at Bodmin, at Maidstone, and at Great Yarmouth, all of which favoured the Conservative claims to the seats, caused much dissatisfaction. On 6 July 1906 a motion to take into consideration his proceedings at Yarmouth was introduced into the House of Commons by Swift MacNeill, nationalist MP for South Donegal. Grantham was severely criticized and as strongly defended. At the suggestion of the prime minister, Sir Henry Campbell-Bannerman, the house declined 'to take the first step in a course which must lead to nothing less than the removal of the judge from the bench' (*Hansard 4*, 160, 1906). His would have been the first successful removal of a High Court judge under the procedure provided by the Act of Settlement.

Grantham felt the stigma deeply, but was unwise enough to revive the memory of the debate, some five years later, by an indiscreet speech to the grand jury at Liverpool (7 February 1911), which brought him a severe rebuke in the House of Commons from the prime minister, H. H. Asquith, one of the severest ever dealt to an English judge by a minister of the crown (*Hansard 5*, 22, 1911, 366). Yet, despite dicta to the contrary, Grantham was no doubt sincere in his belief that in the discharge of his office he was uninfluenced by political partiality. As Arthur Balfour put it in the course of the 1906 debate: 'a

more transparently natural candid man than Mr. Justice Grantham never exercised judicial functions'.

Regarded as a fine model of the English country gentleman, a liberal landlord, always ready to champion the cause of his poorer neighbours, Grantham was devoted to all outdoor sports; he was a notable critic of horseflesh, was one of the founders of the Pegasus Club, and used to act as judge at the bar point-to-point races. An enthusiastic volunteer, he would sometimes appear at the inns of court dinners in an ancestor's scarlet coat from the old Bloomsbury Association or 'Devil's Own'. Although Grantham sat on the bench for upwards of a quarter of a century, and was for some years the senior puisne, his physical powers showed no sign of decay until he succumbed to a sharp attack of pneumonia, dying at his house, 100 Eaton Square, London, on 30 November 1911. He was buried at Barcombe, survived by his wife.

J. B. ATLAY, *rev.* ROBERT STEVENS

Sources *The Times* (1 Dec 1911) • J. Foster, *Men-at-the-bar: a biographical hand-list of the members of the various inns of court*, 2nd edn (1885) • E. Graham, *Fifty years of famous judges* [1930] • R. F. V. Heuston, *Lives of the lord chancellors, 1885–1940* (1964) • CGPLA Eng. & Wales (1912)
Archives E. Sussex RO, diaries and notebooks
Likenesses B. Lucas, oils, priv. coll. • Spy [L. Ward], chromolithograph caricature, NPG; repro. in *VF* (15 March 1890) • A. Stuart-Wortley, portrait, Barcombe Place, Sussex
Wealth at death £227,651 6s. 9d.: probate, 18 Jan 1912, CGPLA Eng. & Wales

Grantley. For this title name *see* Norton, Fletcher, first Baron Grantley (1716–1789).

Granton. For this title name *see* Hope, Charles, Lord Granton (1763–1851).

Granville. For this title name *see* Carteret, John, second Earl Granville (1690–1763); Gower, Granville Leveson-, first Earl Granville (1773–1846); Gower, Henrietta Elizabeth Leveson-, Countess Granville (1785–1862); Gower, Granville George Leveson-, second Earl Granville (1815–1891).

Granville, Augustus Bozzi (1783–1872), physician and Italian patriot, was born in Milan on 7 October 1783, the third son of Carlo Bozzi (1742/3–1826), postmaster-general of the Lombardo-Venetian kingdom, and his wife, Maria Antonietta Rapazzini. His father's family was connected to the Bonapartes in Corsica, while his maternal grandmother, Rosa Granville, was the daughter of Bevil Granville, a Cornishman who had settled in Italy on account of political problems in Britain. After a varied education in his native town, in 1799 Bozzi entered the University of Pavia to study medicine. He described himself as being at the time 'rather tall, with hair cut *à la Brutus*, affecting republican dress' (Granville, 34). An ardent republican, he was imprisoned for giving public addresses and writing lampoons in a daily sheet, the *Giornale senza Titolo*. On his release from prison he resumed his studies and in 1802 he graduated MD.

Bozzi next set out to travel around the Mediterranean.

In Corfu in 1803 he made the acquaintance of W. R. Hamilton, then private secretary to Lord Elgin at Constantinople, and travelled with him in Greece. When Hamilton returned home Bozzi became second physician to the Turkish fleet. On leaving the Turkish service, he sailed on a trading enterprise to Malaga, and practised medicine in Spain. Bozzi's mother died about 1805 and, in accordance with her deathbed wish, he took the name of Granville. In 1806 he arrived in Lisbon, where he obtained an appointment as assistant surgeon to the British navy; he subsequently became full surgeon in the service, a position he filled with much credit until 1813.

Granville served on a number of ships, but was invalided at Deal. He converted to Anglicanism about 1809, the year in which he married a Miss Kerr (*d*. 1861); they were to have four sons and one daughter. Also in 1809 he was appointed to the *Arachne* for the West Indian station, but in 1811 he was declared unfit for that station and was instead commissioned to deliver documents from General Bolívar to the colonial secretary in London. Granville became intimate with the chemist John Dalton during a short visit to Manchester, and published his first English writings. In 1813 Granville was sent to England to give evidence at a court martial and he settled in London on half pay as tutor to the sons of his old friend Hamilton.

Granville decided to enter general practice and, after studying with Sir Anthony Carlisle at the Westminster Hospital, and attending the lectures of George Tuthill, Mr Taunton, and Joshua Brookes, he became MRCS in 1813. In 1814 he brought to London the earliest specimen of iodine, then recently isolated by J. L. Gay-Lussac, and during 1814–15 he lectured on chemistry at the Great Windmill Street school of medicine, permanently losing his sense of smell as a result of an accident with chlorine gas. Throughout this time, the political vicissitudes of his homeland were never far from his thoughts. In 1813 he translated bulletins for distribution in Italy to excite a rising against the French, and he republished them in *L'Italico*, a journal he managed in London. In 1814 he went with Hamilton to the Paris congress, travelled through Italy promoting the movement for independence, and was arrested and then released by the Austrians; he returned to London with a warning, neglected by the government, of Napoleon's probable escape from Elba. In 1815 he introduced to the duke of Sussex a deputation from the provisional government at Milan, offering him the Italian crown. In the same year he materially assisted Antonio Canova in his mission to Paris to secure the restitution of Italian art treasures.

Granville soon abandoned the idea of becoming a general practitioner in favour of the specialities of obstetrics and children's diseases. On the advice of Sir Walter Farquhar, he spent most of 1816–17 in Paris, at La Maternité, in order to qualify as an accoucheur, and despite a gruelling schedule he found time to prepare an unpublished manuscript on the history of science in France during the revolution. On his return to London in 1817, Granville took the LRCP examination and was also elected FRS. In 1818 he settled in practice in Savile Row and became physician accoucheur to the Westminster General Dispensary, a position he filled until his retirement. Soon after he established a dispensary for sick children in the West End of London, while his private practice, favoured by his charming and winning manner, rapidly grew in extent and quality. He was active in 1825 in promoting the requirement of a knowledge of midwifery from candidates for the medical diplomas. In 1826–7 he was a candidate for the professorship of midwifery at the new University of London, but his testimonials were apparently suppressed by Lord Brougham in the interests of Lady Brougham's physician. As president of the Westminster Medical Society in 1829, he chaired the famous discussion of the Gardner peerage case.

From 1832 to 1852 Granville was secretary to the visitors of the Royal Institution, and introduced important reforms in its management. He criticized the constitution of the Royal Society in two controversial pamphlets (1830 and 1836), and helped to secure reforms in the mode of electing fellows and publishing papers. He was also an active member and vice-president of the British Medical Association. A close friend of the former king Joseph from 1832 to his death, he was present at some historic interviews between Joseph and his nephew Louis, afterwards emperor.

Granville was of average height, square-faced, with a high forehead, keen-looking, and firm. He was charming, a lively conversationalist, a versatile physician, and a prolific writer, whose interests spanned the sciences, history, politics, and the arts. He spoke his adoptive language with ease and elegance, and would perhaps have attained even greater fame if he had focused his considerable energies more narrowly. He published several books on various European spas and sea-bathing resorts, of which *The Spas of Germany* (2 vols., 1837) and *The Spas of England, and Principal Sea-Bathing Places* (3 vols., 1841) were the most famous. He wrote two works on obstetrical subjects in 1818 and 1833, popularized the use of prussic acid in pulmonary and cardiac diseases in 1819 and 1820, and wrote a book on the principles and practice of counter-irritation (1838). He also edited for a while the *Medical Intelligencer* and the *London Medical and Physical Journal*.

Granville took a keen interest in some of the most pressing sanitary problems of his day. In 1819 he gave important evidence in support of the quarantine laws before two parliamentary committees. In 1836–7 he advocated the adoption of a plan for purifying the River Thames, and he collected information in many parts of Europe on the disposal of sewage. His *Catechism of health, or, Simple rules for the preservation of health and the attainment of long life* (1832), a work aimed at the prevention of cholera, went through four editions in one month. Other works included an essay on Egyptian mummies (1825), a journal of his travels to St Petersburg (2 vols., 1828; 2nd edn, 1829), a history of the Royal Society in the nineteenth century (1836), and monographs on sudden death (1854) and on the use of sumbul-root in epilepsy (1850). He advocated the cause of Italian unity in two letters addressed to Lord Palmerston (1848).

After his wife's death in 1861 Granville gradually gave up practice in London, but he continued to practise at Kissingen, a German spa town he had been in the habit of visiting every year since 1840, and which he had done much to bring into popularity. On his retirement from practice in 1868, he devoted most of his time to writing his autobiography, which was published posthumously in 1874. He died at 20 Folkestone Road, Hougham, Dover, on 3 March 1872, his last words being 'light, all light' (Granville, 418). He was survived by his children. A catalogue of the contents of his library is held in the Bodleian Library, Oxford. ORNELLA MOSCUCCI

Sources A. B. Granville, *Autobiography of A. B. Granville*, ed. P. B. Granville, 2 vols. (1874) • *The Lancet* (6 April 1872), 490–91 • *DNB* • d. cert. • Munk, *Roll*
Archives LPL, corresp. with A. C. Tait
Likenesses engraving, repro. in Granville, *Autobiography*

Granville [Grenville], **Sir Bevil** (1665–1706), army officer and colonial governor, was born on 3 May 1665 at St Martin-in-the-Fields, Middlesex, the eldest son of Bernard Granville (1631–1701) and his wife, Anne (d. 1701), daughter and heir of Cuthbert Morley of Hawnby, Yorkshire. He was the grandson of the royalist commander Sir Bevil *Grenville (1596–1643), and his father was a prominent royalist who served as an MP and groom of the bedchamber to Charles II. Admitted as a nobleman to Trinity College, Cambridge, in 1677, he graduated MA in 1679 and attended academies in Paris in 1682–5.

In 1685 Granville obtained a commission as captain in the regiment of foot nominally commanded by his uncle John Grenville, first earl of Bath (1628–1701). In the same year he was returned as MP for Fowey in Cornwall on his uncle's interest. Although he was elected as the member for Lostwithiel in 1690 and returned for Fowey in both 1695 and 1698, Granville was primarily a military figure. He was knighted by James II at Hounslow Heath in 1686, and two years later was dispatched to Jersey to secure the garrison's support for William of Orange. Having been promoted to major in 1687, he then served for a number of years in the Low Countries before returning to England. In December 1693 he met William III, of whom it appears that he was a favourite, in order that he might provide the king with a first-hand account of the political and military affairs of Flanders. In January 1693 he was promoted to the colonelcy of Bath's regiment upon his uncle's resignation, and returned to Flanders to join his troops. In June 1695 he quarrelled violently with the marquess de Rada, a colonel of foot in the regiment, and fought a duel with him, shortly after which de Rada died of his wounds. The following year, in England, Granville 'kist the King's hand for the government of Pendennis Castle' in Cornwall (Luttrell, 4.33), but soon returned to Flanders, where he was court-martialled, having been 'accused by several officers for illegal practices on his regiment', but was acquitted of all charges (ibid., 5.254).

Granville's regiment was sent to serve in Ireland in 1698, and in 1702 Granville was offered and accepted the governorship of Barbados, at a salary of £2000 per year. He did not sail for Barbados until March 1703, and upon his arrival was much troubled by ill health. Shortly after he settled there he was accused by several leading Barbadian planters of extortion and tyrannical behaviour; although the privy council acquitted him after a full hearing, it recalled him to England in 1706. Before departing, Granville granted wider civil rights to the Jewish population of Barbados in exchange for a grant of £200 from the island's Jews. He died at sea of a fever during the voyage to England on 15 September 1706. As he was unmarried and childless at the time of his death, his will, dated 16 January 1702 and proved at London on 6 November 1706, bequeathed his entire estate to his younger brother, George *Granville (Grenville), poet, and later Lord Lansdowne. NATALIE ZACEK

Sources *DNB* • S. Johnson, *The works of the English poets, with prefaces, biographical and critical, by Samuel Johnson*, 70 vols. (1779–81) • Evelyn, *Diary* • N. Luttrell, *A brief historical relation of state affairs from September 1678 to April 1714*, 6 vols. (1857) • Venn, *Alum. Cant.* • J. S. Crossette, 'Granville, Bevil', HoP, *Commons, 1660–90*, 2.433 • *Calendar of the manuscripts of the marquis of Bath preserved at Longleat, Wiltshire*, 5 vols., HMC, 58 (1904–80), vol. 1
Archives Hunt. L., army accounts • PRO, entry book, 30/26/90

Granville, Christine. *See* Gizycka, Countess Krystyna (1915–1952).

Granville [*formerly* Grenville], **Denis** (1637–1703), dean of Durham and nonjuring Church of England clergyman, was born on 13 February 1637 at Kilkhampton, Cornwall, where he was baptized thirteen days later. He was the third surviving son of Sir Bevil *Grenville (1596–1643), who was killed fighting for the king at the battle of Lansdowne in July 1643, and his wife, Grace (d. 1647), daughter of Sir George Smith of Heavitree, Exeter. Though he was born with the name Grenville, both Denis and his kin came to prefer the spelling Granville. The evidence for his practice is not entirely consistent, but the predominant form which Denis chose for his name seems to have changed from Grenville to Granville in the course of 1685.

Grenville was educated probably at a local grammar school and possibly also at Eton. He was admitted to Exeter College, Oxford, in September 1657, where he matriculated on 6 August 1658. He was created MA on 28 September 1660 and DD in 1670. Robert Sanderson, bishop of Lincoln, ordained him deacon on 31 January 1661 at 'a convenient place in London' (Lincs. Arch., Lincoln episcopal register, 32, Sanderson, fol. 5). In July of that year he was presented to the family living of Kilkhampton, which he held until 1664 but where, however, he seems to have been totally non-resident. His elder brother, Sir John *Grenville, by now earl of Bath, sought a fellowship at Eton for him, but despite several royal mandates for his appointment it was never granted.

Grenville's circumstances soon changed dramatically, and preferments followed apace. In September 1662 John Cosin, the new bishop of Durham, presented him, then only twenty-five years of age, to the archdeaconry of Durham, the annexed rectory of Easington, and the first prebendal stall in Durham Cathedral. A few days earlier for good measure Grenville had also married, on 16 September, the bishop's youngest daughter, Anne (d. 1691), at Auckland St Andrew. In 1664 Cosin additionally preferred him to the rectory of Elwick, which in 1667, again on Cosin's presentation, he exchanged for the wealthier living of Sedgefield. Concurrently in April 1668 he was advanced from the first prebend to the wealthy second or 'golden' stall. This could be construed as blatant nepotism, though it seems unlikely; the marriage may, in fact, have been the result rather than the source of his preferments. A conscientious, efficient administrator and liturgist, Cosin had in 1660 set himself the colossal task of regenerating the diocese from its parlous post-interregnum state. Desperately needing energetic, efficient, like-minded key assistants he was the least likely of all prelates to select unsuitable, untrustworthy men simply on the grounds of family connection. Reportedly he had known Grenville earlier as an Oxford undergraduate of 'pious and devout temper' (Wheeler to Beaumont, 19 Aug 1693, Zouch, 2.unpaginated) and clearly considered him competent and dynamic enough to implement Anglican conformity.

This Grenville soon proved. The 1662 visitation articles for his archdeaconry were as strict as Cosin's own, and his critique of slovenly cathedral practices was positive and thorough. With evident sincerity, both as archdeacon and rector, he insisted, in his *Directions* (1669), on close observance of rubrics and on good relations between his curates and parishioners. In particular, he forbade uncanonical puritan pulpit prayers in place of the formal bidding prayer at sermon time, he enforced daily morning and evening prayer in parish churches, and pressed for the revival of weekly eucharists in the cathedral, 'this long sleeping rubric' (Ornsby, 1.xxxiii). As a priest of evident spirituality he further recommended clergy to use George Herbert's *Country Parson* as their model. Later, in 1683, Grenville reported that he had had 'a hard game to play these twenty years … in maintaining the exact order which bishop Cosin set on foot here' (*Life … of Sir William Dugdale*, 430).

Despite all this Grenville's life was seriously flawed. By December 1670 Cosin grew concerned about his personal extravagance and prolonged absences in the south—in Oxford where he and his curate were obtaining their DDs, and at Whitehall where his second brother, Bernard, was groom of the bedchamber. Improvidence was, however, the more serious problem. Despite his acknowledged talents and dedication in his different roles Grenville was undoubtedly plagued all his life, even as an Oxford undergraduate, by thriftlessness, and therefore debt. His tenure of wealthy Durham preferments when he was merely twenty-five years old only served to inflame his extravagance, and, aware of the problem, Cosin withheld his promised £1000 marriage dowry. Despite subsequent angry correspondence the bishop still promoted him to Sedgefield (1667), perhaps to alleviate his debts. Disgrace, however, followed in 1674, two years after Cosin's death. Still in surplice and hood at the end of a prestigious funeral with more than 200 gentry present Grenville was publicly arrested in the cathedral cloisters, and imprisoned immediately, despite claiming privilege as king's chaplain; he was, however, freed after appeal before the king at Hampton Court, and the offending officials were punished. The humiliation of this 'odious arrest' (Ornsby, 1.xx) not only haunted him all his life, but he sadly realized his shortcomings only too well, commenting in 1678, 'I cannot manage nor mind these money affairs' (ibid., 1.xxiii). Shortly afterwards, encouraged even by the king, he retired for a spell with his sister to Tour d'Aigues in Provence, where he lived more simply. Nor was this his only problem. His marriage was unhappy. His wife was reportedly a poor creature, weak in mind and prone to 'tipling … with the strong water bottles' (ibid., 1.242), so much so that even her father commented that Grenville had been 'led to marry a distracted wife' (Kitchin, 209–10).

Nevertheless, further preferment was on the horizon. Grenville's debts fuelled his passion for promotion, encouraging him to seek the deanery of Durham. William Sancroft, archbishop of Canterbury, who had known him there earlier, objected that 'Grenville was not worthy of the least stall in Durham church' (Ornsby, 1.187n.), to which Nathaniel Crewe, bishop since 1672, replied 'he would rather choose a gentleman than a silly fellow who knew nothing but books' (ibid.). Thus he was installed by proxy on 9 December 1684. Though resigning his 'golden' prebend, he still retained his other livings, in Lord Macaulay's words 'the richest deanery, the richest archdeaconry and one of the richest livings in England' (Kitchin, 221). Once dean he worked energetically, first fulfilling his aim of reintroducing a weekly eucharist; he then restored sermons on Wednesdays and Fridays in Advent and Lent, he himself, a competent preacher, preaching the first in December 1685. He tried, as dean, to make the cathedral a noteworthy seminary for the diocese, enticing academically able young men as minor canons with right of succession to chapter livings. To develop their regular collegiate life he planned construction of special lodgings for them. Nevertheless, personal finances still bulked large; his increased income as dean did nothing to alleviate his plight, and, despite his rich preferments, worth over £2308 a year, his debts in 1687 at £5717 remained huge.

Staunch Anglican though he was, Granville was unswervingly loyal to James II throughout the crises of the king's reign. Commanded to read the declaration of indulgence he unhesitatingly did so, commenting 'If the king goes beyond his commission, he must answer for it to God, but I'll not deface one line thereof' (Ornsby, 1.xxxvi). With William of Orange's landing imminent he became even more fiercely dedicated, raising £700 for James from the Durham chapter, £50 from each prebendary, and £100 from himself, and cajoling the clergy of his archdeaconry and his parishioners to remain loyal. He failed, however, so to persuade the magistrates, and with his letter of loyalty to the king intercepted, he realized the die was cast. On 9 December 1688, with William's followers nearby, he courageously preached 'a seasonable loyall sermon' (ibid., 1.xxxviii) in the cathedral, only to find himself restricted to his deanery. At midnight on 11 December he fled to Carlisle. Captured and robbed a few days later while hastening to Scotland, he eventually escaped by way of Edinburgh to France, and after landing at Honfleur on 19 March 1689, he stayed in Rouen with a loyal merchant, Thomas Hackett. Back at home the Durham chapter granted his wife, now destitute, a quarterly allowance of £20, while to cover his debts the sheriff distrained his possessions; he was, nevertheless, allowed to keep his preferments until finally deprived as a nonjuror on 1 February 1691. Apart from two hazardous visits to England in February 1690 and April 1695 he stayed in France.

Though the leading Anglican cleric with James II in exile at St Germain, Granville was denied the use of the Anglican liturgy, while James's priests so insulted him that he had to leave the court and retire to Rouen and then to Corbeil, where he claimed family connections. In 1691, as a seemingly cruel, empty gesture, James even nominated him to the archbishopric of York, newly vacant on Thomas Lamplugh's death. Tempting though full acceptance into James's court would have been, he unequivocally refused every attempt to convert him to Rome. James's queen, Mary of Modena, whom he came to style 'Mother', however, showed him warm friendship, adding cash gifts that she could ill afford to those sent riskily by relatives in England. Despite James's callous treatment of him, he remained fiercely, even naïvely, loyal, calling him 'Father', and grieving at his death (1701). In poverty and rejected by the Jacobite court he fell ill on 12 April 1703 and was taken to Paris, where he died, in Fossée St Victoire, on 18 April. He was buried privately at night that evening or the next in Holy Innocents' churchyard, the cost being borne by Mary of Modena. His wife had died on 12 October 1691, and was buried in Durham Cathedral on 14 October. There were no children.

In the 1680s Grenville published *The Compleat Conformist* (1682) on the frequency of the holy communion, and a sermon, *On the Revival of Sermons on Wednesdays and Fridays in the Cathedral* (1686), but more importantly in Rouen in 1689 he published an apologia for his position which included *Two Farewell Sermons* (of 1688), *A Farewell Speech to the Clergy of the Archdeaconry of Durham*, and a series of letters, *The Reasons for his Withdrawal to France*. 'A high-spirited man with a strong dash of the cavalier' (Surtees, 12n.), his life was seriously flawed by persistent improvidence. Once described as a 'truly pious and devout good man' (Ornsby, 1.xxiii), he was also a talented, energetic administrator and a cleric of integrity of conscience and evident inner spirituality. His greatest characteristic was his unhesitating loyalty, loyalty to his church and loyalty to his king, an incompatibility that finally and tragically proved his undoing. He had abandoned all to follow James; 'so good a servant deserved a better sovereign' (Noble, 1.119). In place of his earlier gregarious, lavish, and productive life, he ended his days in isolation and destitution.   WILLIAM MARSHALL

Sources P. Mussett, *Lists of deans and major canons of Durham, 1541–1900* (1974) · Durham episcopal register (Cosin), U. Durham, DDR/EA/ACT/1/4 · Durham Cathedral dean and chapter muniments, U. Durham L., archives and special collections, installation book 1 · 'The remains of Denis Granville, DD, dean and archdeacon of Durham', ed. [G. Ornsby], *Miscellanea*, SurtS, 37 (1861) · *The remains of Denis Granville … being a further selection from his correspondence, diaries, and other papers*, ed. [G. Ornsby], SurtS, 47 (1865) · D. Granville, *The resigned & resolved Christian and faithful & undaunted Royalist, in two … farewell sermons & a … farewell-visitation-sermon* (1689) · R. Granville, *The life of … Dennis Granville, dean and archdeacon of Durham* (1902) · G. W. Kitchin, *Seven sages of Durham* (1911) · Lincoln episcopal register, Lincs. Arch., 32 (Sanderson), fol. 5 · episcopal register of Gauden, Exeter, Devon RO, MS Chanter 24, fol. 17 · Foster, *Alum. Oxon.* · *Fasti Angl.* (Hardy), vol. 1 · *A biographical history of England, from the revolution to the end of George I's reign: being a continuation of the Rev. J. Granger's work*, ed. M. Noble, 1 (1806) · parish register, Auckland, St Andrew, Durham RO, EP/Au.SA 2, fol. 102 · *The genuine works, in verse and prose, of … George Granville, Lord Lansdowne*, another edn, 2 (1736) · R. Surtees, *The history and antiquities of the county palatine of Durham*, 1 (1816) · *The works of the Rev Thomas Zouch*, ed. F. Wrangham, 1 (1820) · *The life, diary, and correspondence of Sir William Dugdale*, ed. W. Hamper (1827) · H. C. Maxwell Lyte, *A history of Eton College, 1440–1910*, 4th edn (1911) · W. Sterry, ed., *The Eton College register, 1441–1698* (1943) · Eton, MSS ECR 60/5/1/5–7 and 60/5/8/1 · caution book, Exeter College, Oxford, MS A.I.22, fol. 171 · C. W. Boase, ed., *Registrum Collegii Exoniensis*, new edn, OHS, 27 (1894) · N. Luttrell, *A brief historical relation of state affairs from September 1678 to April 1714*, 4–5 (1857) · *Fasti Angl., 1541–1857*, [York] · York institution act books, Borth. Inst. · York Minster archive, chapter file, Borth. Inst.

Archives Bodl. Oxf., corresp. with John Locke · Durham Cath. CL, letters and papers

Likenesses G. Edelinck, engraving, 1691 (after portrait by Beaupoille, 1691), repro. in *'Farewell sermons'*; now lost · G. Edelinck, line engraving, 1691 (after Beaupoille), BM, NPG; repro. in Granville, *Resigned*

Wealth at death no probate exists; after deprivation in 1691 all goods in England were distrained to settle considerable debts; lived in France on cash gifts 1689–1703

Granville, George, Baron Lansdowne and Jacobite duke of Albemarle (1666–1735), politician and writer, was born on 9 March 1666 in Birdcage Walk, Westminster, the second son of Bernard Granville (1631–1701) (son of Sir Bevil *Grenville of Stowe in Cornwall, the royalist commander) and his wife, Anne (d. 1701), daughter of Cuthbert Morley, of Hornby, Yorkshire. His father's elder brother was John Granville, earl of Bath, General Monck's cousin and the greatest magnate in the west. He was ever conscious of his family's loyalty to the Stuarts and these notions were reinforced by his tutor and kinsman William Ellis, a proponent of the doctrine of divine hereditary right, with whom he travelled abroad in 1676–7 and who was later treasurer at the Stuart court at St Germain-en-Laye. Granville was admitted to Trinity College, Cambridge, in 1677 and when Mary of Modena, then duchess of York, visited the university, he composed English verses in her honour at the early age of twelve, and conceived a lifelong admiration for her. He attended academies in Paris from 1682 to 1687, learning mathematics and military science, as well as social accomplishments. In October 1688 he asked his father's permission, which was refused, to fight for James II, and in May 1690 he appears to have visited St Germain, where his uncle Denis *Granville was Anglican chaplain. During the reign of William III he lived in retirement at Marr near Doncaster in Yorkshire.

Literary career Granville's first play, written when he was fifteen, was *The She Gallants*, a comedy from the school of Etherege, involving cross-dressing and mistaken identities, which was first staged anonymously in 1695, but was not well received. His second venture, produced in 1697, was *Heroick Love: a Tragedy*, based on book 1 of Homer's *Iliad*, but developing from this: the chief heroine, Chruseis, a female captive of Agamemnon, is merely alluded to in Homer. Granville's blank verse tragedy owes much to Dryden and to a retrospective eye may be thought to place itself between *All for Love* (1678) and Dryden's own translation of book 1 of the *Iliad* which appeared in his *Fables* (1700). Like Antony in *All for Love* Granville's hero, Agamemnon, finally puts love before politics and war. As in Dryden's version of book 1 of the *Iliad*, the conflict between Agamemnon as leader of the league of princes and Achilles as a military champion and a single sovereign prince is well developed. Further, the sensational image of ravishing and rape, so commonly applied by each side to the political events of 1688–9, is here widely deployed, first in regard to the two female captives Chruseis and Briseis, but with an apparently widening political import. This is of course primarily a tragedy of love, but politics and war are also essential to its plot. It is also possible that it influenced Dryden's approach to book 1 of the *Iliad* with its developed motif of slavery.

Dryden also encouraged Granville to follow in his footsteps in the modern adaptation of Shakespeare. Granville's *The Jew of Venice* (acted in 1701) was, like his two previous plays, performed by the company of the great Thomas Betterton at Lincoln's Inn Fields. Granville here tried to address himself to features in Shakespeare's play which had troubled some parts of Shakespeare's perennial audience as well as impressing others. After a prologue consisting of a dialogue between Shakespeare and the recently dead Dryden, Granville's drama tries to build up Antonio (played by Verbruggen), develop Bassanio (played by Betterton himself), and reduce the dominance of Shylock. Shylock was here played by the noted comic actor Doggett. A new scene in which Shylock banquets with Christians must have given a wonderful opportunity to the players of Betterton's Company. Opinion is bound to be divided about Granville's adaptation, but it held the stage for forty years.

Five years later Granville had spectacular success with a musical play he had written much earlier. This was *The British Enchanters*, clearly in the mode of Dryden's play *King Arthur* (1691). The text of the youthful Granville need have been no masterpiece to have become a triumph, augmented by all the scenic and musical resources commanded by Betterton's Company, now at their new theatre in the Haymarket. The plot derives ultimately from Tasso through the French opera of *Armide*. Granville here writes in heroic couplets, save in the songs where he follows Dryden very closely indeed. In the revised version Granville produced for the revival of 1707 a final scene displayed Queen Anne as Oriana enthroned and able, at least in this action, to give peace to the world. *The British Enchanters* thus anticipated the many treaty of Utrecht poems when the tory peace was finally achieved.

Granville had throughout the late 1680s and the 1690s been writing non-dramatic verse more or less on the model of Edmund Waller, who composed lines in his praise. Not at all attracted to the satirical muse of his friend Dryden, Granville produced poetry of compliment and courtship to a fictional lady, Myra, based originally on Mary of Modena but later perhaps on the countess of Newburgh. His longest poem in this mode, 'The Progress of Beauty', also celebrated the chivalry of the Order of the Garter. It was perhaps written about 1700 and includes compliments to Mary of Modena and James II. When it was printed in Granville's *Poems on Several Occasions* (1712) it was much admired, though Samuel Johnson, some seventy years later, saw Granville the poet as a slavish imitator of Waller.

One who praised Granville's verse at this time was the young Alexander Pope, who had good reason to feel grateful. Granville had not only been one of that illustrious circle of men of letters among whom Pope's *Pastorals* had circulated in manuscript, but had written with enthusiasm about the new unknown poet to Henry St John: 'his name is Pope; he is not above Seventeen or Eighteen Years of Age, and promises Miracles' (Handasyde, 90–91). In his turn Pope praised 'Granville's moving Lays' in his first *Pastoral* ('Spring', 1.46) and with the encouragement of the older man, now statesman as well as poet, dedicated to him his *Windsor Forest* (1713) which shares with *The British Enchanters* a final vision of Queen Anne as peace bringer. Here too Granville is explicitly lauded by Pope and the chivalric cast of his vision recognized in a comparison with Henry Howard, earl of Surrey (1517?–1547): 'Surrey, the *Granville* of a former Age' (1.292). In his Epistle *To Arbuthnot* (1735) Pope paid tribute to a number of gentlemen and noblemen—whig and tory, but those with the most striking careers were tories—who had encouraged him to become a publishing poet. Granville, who had returned to England from Jacobite exile in France in 1729, headed the list:

> But why then publish? *Granville*, the Polite,
> And knowing *Walsh*, would tell me I could write …
> Ev'n mitred *Rochester* would nod the head,
> And *St John's* self (great *Dryden's* friends before)
> With open arms receiv'd one Poet more.
> (II.135–42)

Granville probably saw Pope's tribute in manuscript (at least a manuscript version of Pope's poem which included it had been drafted in 1732, M. Mack, *The Last and Greatest Art*, 1984, 419, 424), but he also lived to see it printed, dying at the end of the month in which Pope's poem was printed.

Political career With an established literary fame, Granville became a major tory politician in the reign of Queen Anne. His financial situation was transformed in 1701 (the last year of William III's life) by the death of his parents and that of his uncle the earl of Bath, who left him a pension of £100 a year and a pension of £3000 a year secured on the duchy of Cornwall. On the accession of Queen

Anne in 1702 his cousin John Granville (Lord Bath's son), government manager for the Cornish boroughs, secured his election for Fowey on the recommendation of St John, and in 1703 Granville became governor of Pendennis Castle in Cornwall. Handsome, 'illustrious by birth, elegant in manners and generally loved' (Johnson, 2.294), he was successful at court. Like St John he attached himself to Robert Harley, but he failed to secure a tellership of the exchequer, a very profitable office. Lobbied by Harley to vote for the 'tack' in 1704 (to tack the bill against occasional conformity to a money bill so that the Lords could not reject it), he absented himself from the division.

Again elected for Fowey in 1705, Granville appealed to Harley to be given office in return for his zeal 'for the Queen's and the public service' (Granville to Harley, 10 May 1705, BL, Add. MS 70165). He became a more reliable government supporter, voting for the court candidate as speaker on 25 October and supporting the court on the Regency Bill proceedings in February 1706. Lord Treasurer Godolphin considered him briefly for a diplomatic post, but gave him nothing. On the death of his cousin Lord Granville in 1707, George Granville became the leader of the Granville interest in Cornwall during the minority of the third earl of Bath. Granville campaigned vigorously on behalf of the tories at the 1708 general election and Harley used him as a 'whip' to get MPs from the south-west in for the beginning of the session. Thereafter, he advocated a reconstruction of the tory party on a high-church basis and often acted as an intermediary to prevent a breach between Harley and St John, with whom he frequently stayed at Bucklebury. Naturally he opposed the impeachment of Dr Sacheverell in February–March 1710.

After the fall of the Marlborough–Godolphin administration in 1710, Granville was in line for high office, possibly the treasuryship of the navy, the most lucrative office in the government. Instead, he was appointed secretary at war. With forty-one seats, only one fewer than the whole of Scotland, Cornish elections were vital to any government. Granville could not become warden of the stannaries, the usual manager of Cornish elections, an office given for life to Godolphin's nephew Hugh Boscawen. However, he had the advantage of being related in blood to nearly all Cornish county families, of rising high in the pro-Sacheverell tide, and with the help of the new lord lieutenant, Rochester, he had spectacular successes in these elections, on which he spent £4000, £1500 of which was never repaid. He scored a personal success by defeating Boscawen as knight of the shire. In 1711 he was one of the original members of the 'Brothers Club' founded by St John, but was threatened with expulsion for doing Harley's bidding. In the spring he prepared the army estimates and piloted through the Commons two important pieces of legislation: the recruitment and the mutiny bills. High tory inquiries into the mismanagement of the last administration and accusations of false musters at the time of the battle of Almanza in 1707, however, were awkward for him as St John had been secretary at war at the time.

On the death of the third earl of Bath without male heirs in May 1711, Granville took possession of Stowe, the Cornish family seat, and other estates worth between £6000 and £8000 a year as he believed the first earl of Bath had intended to leave him his title and estates as the male heir, but this was contested at law by Lord Bath's two daughters. He appealed to Harley to get him a peerage without which he could 'no longer appear at the head of that interest which I have been collecting with so much pains and expense in the west' and he petitioned the queen to revive 'the honours of my family in myself', so that he could enjoy 'the estates of my family' without trouble from other claimants (Portland MSS, 4.690, 696; BL, Add. MS 70312, petition of George Granville). In the autumn he was ill, probably of a mild stroke, which delayed his marriage on 15 December 1711, with a jointure of £12,000 a year, to Lady Mary Villiers (d. 1735), daughter of the first earl of Jersey and widow of Thomas Thynne, with whom she had had a son. The Granvilles had four daughters but no male heir. She was young, handsome, but with extravagant tastes and a love of lavish entertainments.

The political crisis caused by the whig majority in the Lords led to the creation of twelve new tory peers on 1 January 1712, one of whom was Granville, who became Baron Lansdowne. The Examiner praised Lansdowne's virtues but denounced bribery and corruption in the war office, which damaged his reputation. In June he was removed and became comptroller of the household until 1713 when he became treasurer of the household. Before the general election of 1713 he appealed to Harley, now earl of Oxford, for financial help in managing the Cornish elections:

> I have appropriated every penny of my own rents in that county for services of this kind, being attacked in every corporation. It is not to be imagined what efforts have been made and what money has been lavished upon this occasion. (Portland MSS, 5.229)

Although governments usually contributed the major part of election expenses in Cornwall and Lansdowne obtained a majority of ten to one for the tories, Oxford gave him nothing in return. In March 1714 he had to abandon his quest for the Granville inheritance and most of the estates of the first earl of Bath went to Bath's daughters.

Lansdowne lost all his offices after the accession of George I and retired to Longleat, the magnificent seat of his stepson, the young Viscount Weymouth. He was corresponding with Sir Thomas Higgons, his cousin and secretary of state to James III (James Francis Edward Stuart). D'Iberville, the French envoy, reported in 1714 that Lansdowne was totally devoted to James (Archives étrangères, correspondance politique Angleterre, Quai d'Orsay, 252 fol. 34). Lansdowne thought, however, there would be no hope of success for the 1715 rising without French military help. In September 1715 he was arrested on charges of high treason, was kept in the Tower until February 1717, but was never brought to trial. In December 1718 he spoke in the Lords against the repeal of the Occasional Conformity and Schism Acts attacking Gibson, the bishop of London, as the successor of Bradshaw, rather than that of Laud. During the South Sea Bubble he purchased £20,000 worth of South Sea stock, losing £10,000 when the Bubble burst.

Paris, 1720–1725, and final years In the summer of 1720 Lansdowne went with his wife to Paris where, with Lord Mar and General Dillon, he became one of the triumvirate directing James's affairs in France during the Atterbury plot. Lansdowne's polished manners and fluent French made him invaluable in attempts to persuade the regent to look favourably on a Stuart restoration (Royal Archives, Stuart papers, 49/38, Dillon to James, 7 Oct 1720). In March 1721 leading Jacobites in England were keen to have Lansdowne in Rome as James's secretary of state to balance the influence of the Scots at the Stuart court (ibid., 52/141, Sir Henry Goring to Dillon, 21 March 1721). Lansdowne was appointed general in Cornwall in the proposed Jacobite rising planned to take place during the 1722 general election on a signal to be sent by Atterbury. James sent a patent dated 6 October 1721 creating him earl of Bath with the seals as secretary of state, to take effect only if he landed with the expedition to England or if he went to Rome as secretary of state (ibid., 54/99, James to Lord Mar, 11 Aug 1721; ibid., 54/70, 19 Sept 1721). Lansdowne, however, was reluctant to go to Rome as it would mean forfeiture of his estates and financial ruin for his family (ibid., 55/19, James to Lord Mar, 4 Oct 1721; ibid., 56/31 Lord Mar to James, 8 Dec 1721). By a patent dated 3 November 1721 (Ruvigny, 3) in a separate creation he was made duke of Albemarle, a title Charles II was said to have promised to the first earl of Bath, should General Monck's issue fail, as it did in 1688 and which the Granvilles had claimed ever since. He was very influential in James's affairs when the Jacobites hoped to effect a restoration either through a free parliament procured with the help of Lord Sunderland, or through an English rising with the assistance of Irish troops in French and Spanish service. Lansdowne (as he continued to be called in the Jacobite correspondence) either wrote or directed most of the Jacobite propaganda produced in France at this time and he was the author of *A Letter from a Nobleman Abroad to his Friends in England* (1722), one of the most stirring of the Jacobite pamphlets published at this time: 'At this critical juncture when the Rumour of a new Parliament sounds like the last Trumpet to awaken the Genius of Old *England* and raise departed Liberty to Life, it would be a Crime to be silent' (p. 144).

Lord and Lady Lansdowne were intimate with Sir Robert Sutton (a cousin of the Jacobite Lord Lexington) the British ambassador at Paris. Handasyde thought this was indiscreet and that Lady Lansdowne had an amorous affair with Sutton's nephew, but the circumstances were very different. Destouches, the French envoy in London, reported on 16 January 1722 that Sutton was 'partial to the Pretender' and provided a safe channel for letters from James to Lansdowne and Lansdowne's replies, which Lady Lansdowne carried over to Sutton. This was detected by the English government and Sutton was recalled (*Archives étrangères, correspondance politique Angleterre*, 340 fols. 15–22). Plagued by his wife's financial extravagance and his mounting debts, Lansdowne grew desperate and, to avoid public

scandal, Mar and Dillon advanced him 15,000 livres out of James's funds, which he promised to repay within three months. James was told afterwards and sanctioned the loan (Royal Archives, Stuart papers, 59/89, Lord Mar to James, 9 May 1722).

After the death of Lord Sunderland, Robert Walpole discovered the plot and Atterbury's part in it, betrayed, according to Atterbury, by Lord Mar. Lansdowne refused to believe in Mar's guilt and was thus sidelined in Jacobite affairs. He informed Atterbury in 1725 that he was seeking a reconciliation with the Hanoverian government. Preceding him, Lady Lansdowne paid court to Queen Caroline. He was allowed to return to England soon after and he was presented to George II in 1729. In 1732 he dedicated a new edition of his *Works*, which still contained eulogies of James II and Mary of Modena, to Queen Caroline. He died in London on 29 January 1735, his wife having predeceased him by a few days, and he was buried, as she was, in St Clement Danes on 3 February 1735.

EVELINE CRUICKSHANKS

Sources E. Handasyde, *Granville the polite* (1953) · 'Granville, George', HoP, *Commons, 1690–1715* [draft] · private information (2004) [Howard Erskine-Hill] · *The manuscripts of his grace the duke of Portland*, 10 vols., HMC, 29 (1891–1931) · Royal Arch., Stuart papers · S. Johnson, *Lives of the English poets*, ed. G. B. Hill, [new edn], 3 vols. (1905) · E. Cruickshanks, 'Lord North, Christopher Layer and the Atterbury plot: 1720–23', *The Jacobite challenge*, ed. E. Cruickshanks and J. Black (1988), 95 · G. V. Bennett, *The tory crisis in church and state, 1688–1739* (1975) · marquis de Ruvigny, *The Jacobite peerage* (1904)

Archives BL, corresp. under Jacobite pseudonyms, Stowe MS 250 [copies] · PRO, letters, SP 34/5, 13–20 | BL, letters to Robert Harley, Add. MS 70288 · BL, letters to Robert Harley, loan 29 · BL, letters to duke of Marlborough, with related papers, Add. MSS 61134, 61296 · Bodl. Oxf., corresp. with sixth Baron North · NA Scot., letters to Lord Leven · Newport Central Library, Wales, letters, mostly to Mary Delaney · Royal Arch., Stuart MSS, letters · Trinity Cam., letters to Grace Granville

Likenesses G. Kneller, portrait · attrib. J. Richardson, oils, Longleat House, Wiltshire · Vandergucht, line engraving (after G. Kneller), BM, NPG; repro. in G. Granville, *Poems* (1726) · G. Vertue, line engraving (after G. Kneller), BM, NPG; repro. in G. Granville, *Works* (1732) · line engraving (after C. D'Agar), BM · oils, Bowood, Wiltshire

Wealth at death estates originally worth £8000 a year in trust (could not sell them); encumbered with debts, lost possession of Stowe to Lord Bath's daughters

Granville, Sir Keith [*formerly* Keith Granville Solomon] (1910–1990), airline executive, was born on 1 November 1910 in Faversham, Kent, the youngest of four children (all sons) of Albert James Solomon, sales representative, and his wife, Ada Miriam Chambers. He was educated at Tonbridge School. After he left he dropped the surname Solomon and used his second forename as his new surname. He joined Imperial Airways at Croydon airport in 1929 as one of two original commercial trainees, and was paid 10s. a week. His potential was immediately spotted, and he was one of the first trainees selected before the Second World War for service on overseas routes. During the 1930s he was successively station manager in Brindisi (Italy), Tanganyika, Southern and Northern Rhodesia, Egypt, and India, which were mainly Imperial Airways flying-boat bases. In 1933 he married Patricia Capstick; they had one daughter. The marriage was dissolved in 1945 and in 1946 he married Gertrude (Truda), daughter of Howard Belliss, gentleman farmer. They had one son and four daughters.

By the end of the war Granville had made his mark in the airline, by then renamed the British Overseas Airways Corporation (BOAC), and in 1947 was appointed manager, Africa and the Middle East. In 1948 he returned to London as general manager, mails, traffic, and catering, and he was promoted to sales director for all BOAC's overseas services in 1951. Further recognition followed in 1954 when he became commercial director. With the opening of Atlantic services, new routes to South America with Lockheed and Boeing aircraft, and the early jets of the 1950s and 1960s, he laid the foundation in BOAC of air travel marketing on a broad and popular scale. This was to be further developed through the arrival in service of the Boeing 747 (the 'jumbo jet') which, with its large passenger-carrying capacity, brought a completely new concept to long-haul travel. In 1958 Granville became managing director under Basil Smallpiece and was made CBE. He joined the board of BOAC in 1959 and in 1960 was appointed chairman of the airline's associated companies, becoming deputy chairman under Sir Giles Guthrie in 1964. In 1969 he was named managing director to the new chairman, Charles Hardie, retaining his post as deputy chairman. On 1 January 1971 he achieved the distinction of being the first member of the airline staff to become chairman. His was a popular appointment because he was respected and admired by his colleagues as an able administrator with a keen sense of humour, who made a significant contribution to the fortunes of BOAC.

Granville demonstrated sound judgement, was assertive, and liked to speak plainly. But his bluff, avuncular manner made him approachable, and he was ever ready to help with problems and complaints. His wide experience and abundant common sense was equally well regarded by many other senior executives throughout the international airline community. He also helped guide the airline through difficult times, facing problems involving operating rights, industrial relations, government pressure in the choice and number of aircraft orders, and investment restrictions. He was pioneering, creative, and innovative. Granville made a unique contribution to British civil aviation history when, in August 1972, he signed an order for five Concorde airliners, the world's first supersonic passenger aircraft. The order, later increased to seven aircraft, marked the culmination of more than ten years of close collaboration with the British and French manufacturers. When Concorde went into service to Bahrain for the first time in January 1976 it became the flagship of the British Airways fleet and the best known and most readily recognized aircraft in the world.

On the formation of the British Airways group in 1972 Granville became the first deputy chairman, and in September the same year he took up office as the president of the International Air Transport Association at its annual meeting in London. His international aviation career had thus come full circle, for he had represented his airline at the association's first traffic conference in Rio de Janeiro, Brazil, just after the war. He also became president of the Institute of Transport in 1963–4 and chairman of International Aeradio from 1965 to 1971. He was made an honorary fellow of the Royal Aeronautical Society in 1977 and was knighted in June 1973. He spanned a period of forty-five years during which civil aviation developed from biplanes and flying boats to jet aircraft and supersonic air travel.

Granville was portly, about 5 feet 10 inches tall, with smiling eyes and a firm, decisive nature. On his retirement in March 1974 he went to live in Château d'Oex, Switzerland, where he named his house Speedbird. He died in Lausanne, Switzerland, on 7 April 1990.

COLIN MARSHALL, *rev.*

Sources WWW · *The Times* (9 April 1990) · personal knowledge (1996) · private information (1996)
Likenesses photographs, 1990–01, Hult. Arch.

Granville, Mary. *See* Delany, Mary (1700–1788).

Grascome, Samuel (1641–1708), nonjuring Church of England clergyman and religious controversialist, was baptized on 21 February 1641 at Holy Trinity Church, Coventry, the son of John Grascome, and was educated at Coventry grammar school. He was admitted as a sizar at Magdalene College, Cambridge, on 1 June 1661, in his twentieth year. He graduated BA in 1665, and proceeded MA in 1674. He was ordained deacon at Peterborough on 30 July 1664 and priest on 21 May 1665. On 10 December 1680 he was appointed rector of Stourmouth, Kent, where he remained until his deprivation in July 1690 after refusing the oaths to William and Mary. He also served as curate to Bishop John Dolben at Bromley, Kent, in 1681–2. Dolben performed the marriage of Grascome and Elizabeth Watkins at Westminster Abbey on 19 January 1682. Grascome's first publication, *A letter to a friend in answer to a letter written against Mr. Lowth in defence of Dr. Stillingfleet*, licensed in December 1687, revealed Grascome's championship of high-church ecclesiology, comprising a stout defence of Simon Lowth, a 'downright Church of *England*-Man' (p. 31), and sought to expose the allegedly mendacious account of Lowth's ideas presented by Robert Grove, a well-connected prebendary of St Paul's. The inclusion of a postscript, in which Grascome revealed that he had recently received intelligence of his opponent's identity, occasioned the daring justification that 'he that will leave his Station, and make himself a Buffoon, may thank himself, if he be treated accordingly' (ibid.), an anticipation of the frank and foolhardy irreverence of his later polemics.

In the winter of 1688–9 Grascome was engaged in feverish activity, as a busy contributor to the unfolding series of debates on allegiance which followed the Dutch invasion. He published a letter he had sent to the latitudinarian Dr William Payne arguing the incompatibility of the new oaths with those sworn to King James. The publication of new state prayers for William and Mary prompted *Resolution of a case of conscience ... whether as matters now stand, it be lawful to frequent our parish-churches for communion in divine worship*. Here Grascome condemned the popular practice of subscribing oaths or attending worship with some form of reservation, explicit or otherwise, arguing that 'A man may as lawfully take the *Oaths* with a Declaration; [as] communicate with a Protestation: both are *contra factum* ... because the nature of Communion requires that it be entire' (p. 4), a principle to which he returned in his writings against occasional conformity in the reign of Queen Anne. A passage acknowledging the spiritual privations which would follow a withdrawal from communion offers a remarkable insight into the self-fashioning of the suspended clergymen, in a striking identification with the sufferings experienced by the early church: 'When God's people by the bloody *Heathen* Persecutors, were driven into Wildernesses, Dens, Caves ... you cannot thing [*sic*] ... there was much Communion in such places, and yet there were never better Christians then in those times'. It reached its climax no less dramatically: 'Suppose some of us should be cut off; yet the fall of those may prove the rise of more, for Martyrs' blood is rich and fruitful' (p. 8).

Following suspension Grascome was in due course deprived, and his writings from this time give vehement expression to the pitiful condition of the ejected clergy, as exemplified in his unflattering comparison of their lot with that of their forebears after the civil war: 'not so much being left to keep them from starving, as was allowed by their sworn Enemies, the *Rump* ... so much a *Dutch* Mercy exceeds an *English* Rebel's!' (*Two Letters Written to the Author of a Pamphlet, Entitled, 'Solomon and Abiathar'*, 1692, 8). He was thus dependent on the charity of well-wishers and found a patron in Sir Thomas Fanshaw, a supporter of anti-Catholic polemic, to whose generosity he paid moving acknowledgement:

I and Mine had perished long since, had not a gracious and merciful God stirred up the Hearts of pious charitable Christians, who had been mostly meer Strangers to us ... You have sent once and again to my Necessity, when I was personally unknown to You. (*An Answer to a Book Entitled 'A Short and Plain Way to the Faith and Church'*, 1702, A6r)

About this time Grascome ministered to a congregation at Scroop's Court in the parish of St Andrew, Holborn, a circumstance which perhaps informs his vivid account of the harassment of such assemblies:

when all others have their Liberty, they alone are not suffered to serve God; but if they do meet together, the Hell-Hounds which are set to hunt them, seize the Persons ... and the Minister [is] committed to *Newgate* or some filthy Prison for high Misdemeanour. (*Two Letters*, 8)

In the immediate aftermath of his deprivation Grascome wrote with vigour against the clerical apologists for deprivation, who constellated around Edward Stillingfleet. A principal argument of the nonjurors was that the provenance of such arguments was deeply Erastian; that is, that they underestimated the proper spiritual authority of the church, surrendering up vital elements of its rightful jurisdiction to the civil powers. In an acute and satirical exegesis, Grascome ridiculed Stillingfleet's

dependence on constitutional history: 'To secure the Law on his side he cites *Glanvil* and *Bracton*, but forgets what St. Paul and St. *Peter* said; let him take his share with the Lawyers; I will venture my Soul with the Apostles' (*A Brief Answer to a Late Discourse Concerning the Unreasonableness of a New Separation*, 1691, 12). Grascome was equally active on a second and related front: demolishing the case made by an Oxford scholar, Humphrey Hody, who, chancing upon a Byzantine document in the Bodleian Library, alleged that it provided an apposite precedent for the crown's deprivation of members of the episcopate. Grascome was in the vanguard of the counter-attack, demonstrating the scholarly inadequacy of the 'swaggering Wadhamite' (*Considerations upon the Second Canon*, 1693, 32) and the dishonest suppression of an inconvenient appendix, which contradicted his reading. A measure of Grascome's success is suggested by the response of the administration, which endeavoured to suppress his work. From the same period date *The Sseparation of the Church of Rome from the Church of England, Founded upon a Selfish Interest* (1691) and *An Historical Account of the Antiquity and Unity of the Britanick Churches* (1692), both of which asserted the historical antecedence and independence of the English church from the see of Rome and its jurisdiction.

Like many nonjurors, Grascome did not confine his writings to the scholarly and theological but extended them to the dangerous and fugitive world of Jacobite pamphleteering. He may have been the author of *The Loyal Martyr Vindicated* (1691), an apology for John Ashton, the Jacobite intrigant executed in 1691, and certainly wrote *An Appeal of Murther* (1693), critique of the conduct of the trial of the printer William Anderton, executed in 1693. Grascome ministered to him at his death and:

after he had particularly embraced Mr. Anderton, fervently recommended his soul to God, and taking his last farewell of him, went down out of the cart. The sheriffs civilly commanded a way to be made, and were readily obeyed, he passing through the crowd, not only with ease, but respect. (*State trials*, 12.1264–5)

New Court Contrivances, an anonymous pamphlet published in the same year, which detected the government's hand in the fabrication of sham Jacobite plots, was widely attributed to Grascome. The inflammatory *Considerations upon the Second Canon* (1693), which proclaimed 'all those excommunicated who do not own the King's Authority' (p. 4), a position that many nonjurors could not endorse, has been variously attributed to Grascome and his fellow polemicist, Abednego Sellar. Suspicions of his involvement in these publications probably account for the warrant issued for Grascome's arrest for treasonable practices in 1694. This obscure episode was followed by a *succès de scandale* of far greater magnitude which excited the administration's wrath: the publication of the anonymous *An Account of the Proceedings in the House of Commons, in Relation to the Recoining the Clipp'd Money* (1696). Widespread anxieties as to effects of devaluation had led to panic hoarding and consequently a widespread shortage of specie, and meanwhile 'the distress of the common people was severe' (Lord Macaulay, *Works*, 1866, 8 vols., 4.249). The pamphlet claimed that these moneys were 'ready to cross the Seas to their Fellows and become *Denizens of another Country*' and clearly breached parliamentary privilege in publishing the division list on the controversial recoinage bill, so that electors might 'be fully enabled to judge uprightly of this Matter ... and, according to the English Proverb, *To lay the Saddle on the Right Horse*' (*An Account of the Proceedings in the House of Commons*, 2, 5). The House of Commons declared it a 'false and seditious libel' and ordered it to be burnt. A proclamation of 10 December offered a reward of £500 'for the apprehension of Grascomb, who ... brought the manuscript ... to be printed' (*CSP dom.*, *1696*, 460). The following 'nineteen months, to the great detriment of his health and Family' were spent as a fugitive, but Grascome appears to have eventually made some accommodation with the government: a letter in his hand, which defended his flight on the grounds of 'being aged, infirm, poor ... exceedingly troubled with the Stone [and] fearing a Prison, which he apprehended would quickly kill him', included his offer to give himself up, on the assumption 'that Parliament being now dissolved ... all proceedings may cease upon that account'. The letter denied Grascome's authorship or any other part in the pamphlet's writing (Bodl. Oxf., MS Rawl. D. 890, fol. 174*r*). It seems likelier that he was its courier, a circumstance alleged in the warrant, rather than the writer, and that the author of this, and also *An Appeal to True Englishmen, or, A Cry for Bread* (1699), often ascribed to Grascome, was in fact the nonjuror Thomas Wagstaffe.

Grascome took up his pen again in the more congenial circumstance of the reign of Queen Anne, with a series of pamphlets against protestant and Roman Catholic dissenters, each of which bore either his initials or that favoured appellation of the nonjuror, 'presbyter of the Church of England'. The first of these, *An Answer to ... 'A Short and Plain Way to the Faith and Church'* (1702), was written in response to the Benedictine John Huddleston, nephew of Richard Huddleston, who had republished his uncle's proselytizing tract. Further dissuasives followed with the publication of *Certamen religiosum* (1704) and *Concordia discors* (1705). Grascome's debate with the nonconformists was prompted by the writings of the Welsh dissenter James Owen, whose *Moderation a Virtue* had been answered by the nonjuror William Higden in *Occasional Conformity a Most Unjustifiable Practice*, a pamphlet often erroneously attributed to Grascome. The appearance of Owen's rejoinder *Moderation Still a Virtue*, prompted Grascome's plangent *The Mask of Moderation Pull'd off the Foul Face of Occasional Conformity* (1704). Owen's co-pastor at Shrewsbury, the veteran presbyterian Francis Tallents, now entered the fray, challenging Grascome's assertion 'That all who are guilty of Schism live in a Course of Sin ... and are in a State of Damnation' (Tallents, *A Short History of Schism*, 1705). Grascome retorted robustly, averring, 'Occasional Conformity is either a Mask for Hypocrisie, or proceeds from a Coldness, Indifference, and Looseness, with respect to Religion' (*Moderation in Fashion, or, An Answer to ... 'A Short History of Schism'*, 1705, 238). Tallents's rejoinder

occasioned the compendious *Schism Triumphant* (1707), a careful dissection of his adversary's arguments and an impassioned defence of the theological foundations of the Church of England's intolerance. This was apparently the last tract published before his death, which occurred, probably in the City of London, between 3 August 1708, when he wrote his will, and 13 October 1708, when the will was proved by his wife, Elizabeth. The will describes him as of the City of London, mentions one son, James, and states that he held the lease of half of the income of the rectory at Newbourne, Northumberland, from the bishop of Carlisle. Grascome no doubt continued a nonjuror until his death; as late as 1706 he corresponded with Richard Johnson, endeavouring to persuade him of the legitimacy of the birth of the prince of Wales and the consequent sinfulness of swearing allegiance to Anne.

Comparatively few of Grascome's works were published under his name or even initials, leaving a large body of anonymous tracts which, with varying degrees of plausibility, have been attributed to him. Grascome offered an instructive reminder of the need for caution, noting how Tallents had accounted him the author of an anonymous tract written by Henry Gandy, on the slender basis that it appeared in the bookseller's list advertised after his work. The substantial collection of Grascome's papers in the Bodleian Library is an invaluable source in establishing a canon for the theological and casuistic tracts but, unremarkably, it can offer no assistance in tracing his hand in the more fugitive Jacobite pamphlets with which his name has been associated. Many of these attributions, first published by Francis Lee in his *Memoirs of the Life of Mr. John Kettlewell* (1718), must remain doubtful, and some are certainly wrong. Moreover, Lee's motives are suspect, having been coloured by his judgment that such reckless pamphleteering encouraged successive hardships in that 'what was done by One or Two came to be laid upon the whole Body of the Non-complyers' (Lee, 329). Macaulay's magisterial denunciation of Grascome offers little more than a sonorous reprise of Lee's judgment.

D. A. BRUNTON

Sources Grascome's writings, Bodl. Oxf., MSS Rawl. D. 373, 843, 846, 848, 851, 890 · *State trials*, vols. 12, 22 · T. Lathbury, *A history of the nonjurors* (1845) · [F. Lee], *Memoirs of the life of Mr. John Kettlewell* (1718) · J. C. Findon, 'The nonjurors and the Church of England, 1689–1716', DPhil diss., U. Oxf., 1978 · M. A. Goldie, 'The nonjurors, episcopacy, and the origins of the convocation controversy', *Ideology and conspiracy: aspects of Jacobitism, 1689–1759*, ed. E. V. Cruickshanks (1982), 15–35 · *CSP dom.*, *1696* · Venn, *Alum. Cant.* · *IGI* · will, PRO, PROB 11/504, sig. 237 · J. L. Chester, ed., *The marriage, baptismal, and burial registers of the collegiate church or abbey of St Peter, Westminster*, Harleian Society, 10 (1876)
Archives Bodl. Oxf., MSS Rawl., papers

Gratianus (*fl.* 340). *See under* Roman officials (*act.* AD 43–410).

Grattan, Henry (*bap.* 1746, *d.* 1820), politician, was baptized at St John's Church, Fishamble Street, Dublin, on 3 July 1746, the first son of James Grattan (*c.*1708–1766) of

Henry Grattan (*bap.* 1746, *d.* 1820), by Alexander Pope, in or before 1814

Belcamp, co. Dublin, recorder of Dublin and MP for Dublin city (1760–66), and Mary Marlay (*d.* 1768), the daughter of Lord Chief Justice Thomas Marlay of Marlay Abbey, co. Dublin.

Early years Grattan was educated in Dublin city. Sent initially to Mr Ball's day school in Great Ship Street, he withdrew from the school after a contretemps with a teacher, following which he attended Mr Young's day school in Abbey Street. This was more to his liking, and he proceeded from there to Trinity College, Dublin, where he was admitted on 1 November 1763. His interest in literature as a student displeased his father, with whom his relations were difficult. Grattan père thought his son should pursue a career in the law. Henry was less than excited by this prospect, but his options narrowed when, following his father's death in 1766, he learned that he was not to succeed to the family seat at Belcamp. This seems to have been unanticipated, though Grattan ought not, perhaps, to have been surprised since his father was choleric and disinclined to forgive those who had differed with him, as had Henry on several personal and political matters. The death of James Grattan certainly strained the family's precarious finances. Grattan's family was so reduced in circumstances by the death of his father that the lord mayor

and aldermen of Dublin petitioned the lord lieutenant to make some provision for his mother. It is not clear if the response was positive, but financial problems can only have contributed to Grattan's melancholic disposition at this time. The deaths of his sister Catherine in 1767 and mother the following year were also factors, but, despite this, Grattan graduated BA from Trinity College in spring 1767 and was admitted to the Middle Temple in the same year to read law.

Grattan found London both exciting and challenging at first, but once he and Robert Day, who was a year his senior at Trinity, decided to share quarters he settled in well. He attended the Robin Hood Club, which was a popular debating forum, and was pleased that his contributions were favourably received. At the same time he was acutely conscious that he had much to learn, and so rather than immerse himself in law books he devoted much of his time to reading history and politics and attending the gallery of the House of Commons. He spent many hours listening to debates and studying oratorical technique, which he practised assiduously.

While still in his teens Grattan was drawn to the politics of patriotism. Indeed, it was a major cause of difficulty with his father, who was strongly opposed to the reformist faction within Dublin corporation headed by Charles Lucas. Grattan, by contrast, was attracted by the patriots' claim that they were guided in their actions by their wish to sustain a virtuous constitution and to eradicate corruption from the body politic. To this end he supported the campaign to limit the duration of parliament in the mid-1760s and, as a result of the marriage of his sister Mary to the Kilkenny landowner and active patriot Gervaise Parker Bushe in autumn 1768, he found congenial company in a circle of patriot politicians that, as well as Bushe, included Henry Flood and Hercules Langrishe. Grattan visited them in Kilkenny on his trips home from England, and it was there that he learned at first hand of their disapproval of the lord lieutenant, Lord Townshend, and, specifically, of their unease at his attempts to enhance the power of the Irish executive *vis-à-vis* the Irish parliament. He was already familiar with the whig argument that George III's political master plan was to augment the power of the crown at the expense of parliament from the controversy generated at Westminster by the Wilkes affair and the evolving crisis in British America, and so he had no difficulty in embracing the Irish patriots' analysis that Townshend was embarked on the same despotic course. Indeed, he was anxious to contribute to their cause in whatever way he could, and with this in mind he penned several essays for publication in the *Freeman's Journal* as part of the influential opposition propaganda series that achieved renown as *Baratariana*. The fact that he wrote the dedication to Lord Townshend in the collected version that went to three pamphlet editions between 1772 and 1777 emphasizes both his involvement and commitment. His other contributions were presented under the pen-names Posthumous and Pericles; the most notable was a hagiographical account of William Pitt, earl of Chatham, appended as a note to the 'Ballad on the rejection of the Altered Money Bill'.

Patriot politician, 1775–1782 Though his friendship with Bushe, Flood, and Langrishe may have encouraged his hopes, Grattan's prospects of a career in politics in the early 1770s were slim since he possessed neither the wherewithal to purchase a seat nor a patron prepared to nominate him. In truth, few patrons were prepared to allow their nominees the liberty of political choice he desired. Given his dependence on a small family inheritance, Grattan's priority in the early 1770s was with making a living. With few options, he sought entry to the Irish bar and, following his admission in 1772, he endeavoured, without much success, to develop a legal practice. He went on circuit but, as he conceded to his friend Billy Broome, he had neither the temperament nor the eye for detail necessary for a successful career in the law. He sustained his political involvement during this time through his membership of bodies such as the patriot club, the Society of Granby Row, but a fringe role might have been his destiny had fate not taken a hand. The accidental death of Francis Caulfeild, MP for Charlemont, in November 1775 created a representational vacancy that his brother Lord Charlemont nominated Grattan to fill. He was admitted to the House of Commons on 11 December and he made his maiden speech four days later against the provision of an increased allowance to the vice-treasurers. He was on the losing side, but one Dublin newspaper observed presciently on the basis of this contribution that if he continued in this manner he would 'be a valuable weight in the scale of patriotism' (Webb, 224).

Grattan entered the Irish House of Commons at an opportune moment for the recently listless patriot connection. The outbreak of war in Britain's American colonies in the summer of 1775 provided its members with a series of major issues on which they could focus, as the demands of fighting a war made it necessary to impose a series of embargoes that inhibited commercial opportunity and to deploy to America troops normally on the Irish army establishment. As a junior MP Grattan was obliged to cede to more senior patriots such as Barry Yelverton and Hussey Burgh as he contrived to identify his own policy niche. At the same time he made it clear that he was not content simply to be a supporting player when, on 19 February 1776, he described the redoubtable Henry Flood's defence of the imposition of an embargo on Irish exports to America as a 'necessary action' as 'the tyrant's plea', and deemed the embargo to be illegal (Almon, 36). Grattan's proclivity for 'violent' (Gilbert MS 93, fol. 375) expression elicited disapproving comment from Dublin Castle sympathizers, but it endeared him to both his fellow patriots and the politicized public.

Returned to represent Charlemont for a second time at the general election held in 1776, Grattan repaid the confidence his patron vested in him by increasing the frequency and import of his contributions during the 1777–8 session. Having established fiscal matters as his primary focus in 1775–6, he concentrated on the state of the country's finances and, in particular, on the failure of successive administrations to balance the budget, which he ascribed pointedly to the refusal of the British government to allow them to curtail the pension list and to reduce military expenditure. These were well-established patriot targets and, encouraged by the response to his contributions to date, Grattan proposed on 6 February 1778 that the House of Commons should address the king on the need for retrenchment. The motion was lost by a large margin because a majority of MPs deemed it inappropriate in the context of an impending Franco-American *rapprochement*. However, rather than drop the issue, Grattan was provoked by the British parliament's refusal in 1778 to approve the anticipated generous extension in Ireland's rights to trade within the empire, and he criticized MPs for being unwilling to demand government intervention to redress the kingdom's mounting economic problems. This prompted allegations that he was seeking to foment a rebellion; these were palpably unjustified, but they did his reputation little harm with an increasingly politicized public that identified with and applauded his remarks.

This is not to say that Grattan perceived himself as the mouthpiece of public opinion. Like all but the most active proponents of parliamentary reform, Grattan believed that legislators should be guided in their actions by principle and that their role was to make law for the public good rather than to answer to public demand. It just so happened in the late 1770s and early 1780s that his vision of what was legislatively necessary corresponded closely to what the politicized public sought. Significantly, he articulated no reservations about the volunteers as they increased exponentially in number in 1778–9. Quite the contrary: convinced more than ever of the need for 'free trade', he was one of the first patriot politicians to appreciate that the volunteers' support could facilitate its achievement. This realization, combined with his exceptional rhetorical talent and commitment, further boosted Grattan's profile, as emphasized by his membership of the influential patriot club known colloquially as the Monks of the Screw. More importantly, he was active among the small cabal of patriots who were determined in the run-up to the opening of the 1779–80 session to commit the Irish parliament on exacting the right to free trade from the British government. Once the session commenced, Grattan played a powerful and active part in pursuing this cause. It was he, for example, who moved an amendment to the address on 12 October declaring that the only effectual remedy for the Irish economy was 'to open its ports for exportation of all its manufactures'. This wording was replaced by a tighter statement that simply requested 'free trade' but so commanding was Grattan's performance that Henry Grattan jun. described the debate as 'the real commencement of Mr Grattan's career' (Grattan, *Memoirs*, 1.387). It is a contestable claim, but there is little doubt that it signalled his arrival as one of the leading patriot MPs. This was underlined six weeks later when the approval of his motion of 24 November that 'at this time it would be inexpedient to grant new taxes' (O'Connell, 186) compelled ministers to concede the right to trade within the empire on the equal terms Grattan deemed were Ireland's by right.

Having hastened the abolition of the mercantilist restrictions that had long been perceived by many Irish MPs as a galling index of their dependence, Grattan vowed to seek the amelioration of the even more contentious problem of the constitutional bonds limiting the legislative authority of the Irish parliament. It was his intention, he informed the Dublin Guild of Merchants in January 1780, to 'strain every nerve to effectuate a modification of the Law of Poynings ... [and] to secure this country against the illegal claims of the British parliament' (H. Grattan, *Miscellaneous Works*, 1822, 143). With this in mind, he undertook to press for a 'declaration of the rights of Ireland' and, on 19 April, he made a long and powerful speech in support of his contention 'that the king's most excellent majesty, lords and commons of Ireland are the only powers competent to make laws to bind this kingdom' (Callen, 2.149). It did not progress, but this did not reflect badly on Grattan. He was now commonly identified as the most electrifying set-piece patriot orator in the House of Commons. The challenge was how to marry his capacity to move MPs with the support forthcoming from an expectant public to secure the requisite legislative changes.

In the course of a relatively uneventful inter-sessional interval, Grattan defined his priorities for the 1781–2 session as an annual mutiny bill and legislative independence, as he indicated in the pamphlet *Observations on the mutiny bill, with some strictures on Lord Buckinghamshire's administration in Ireland*, published in the autumn of 1781. However, despite the efforts of the volunteers to rally public opinion before the session began, he was unable to make an impression in the division lobbies in the House of Commons. Indeed, it was the administration rather than the patriots who grasped the political initiative: in an absence of agreement about whether the patriot cause would be better served by pursuing Henry Flood's assertive, or Barry Yelverton's moderate, definition of what constituted legislative independence, Grattan seemed unsure how best to proceed. He was rescued from this dilemma by the intervention of the Ulster Volunteers, who determined to convene a delegate assembly at Dungannon on 15 February 1782. Eager to shape the outcome according to their own design, Grattan and Henry Flood met with Lord Charlemont to draft two resolutions, identifying the constitutional changes they desired, for communication to the delegates. In addition, Grattan privately prepared a further resolution urging the further 'relaxation of the Penal Laws against our Roman Catholic fellow subjects' (Grattan, *Memoirs*, 2.207). This reflected his startling conclusion that it was now possible to forge a more embracing and inclusive concept of 'the Irish nation' than that exclusively protestant definition of the nation that had prevailed since the 1690s, consistent with principles and constitutional values enshrined in the revolution of 1688. All three resolutions were submitted to and were approved enthusiastically by the delegate convention. Encouraged by this and by the impressive manifestations of public support, Grattan made several unsuccessful efforts, notably on 22 February, to get the Irish parliament to endorse motions calling for legislative independence. It took the fall of Lord North's ministry in March to create the circumstances that made it possible.

'Grattan's parliament' The whig ministry headed by Lord Rockingham that took power in spring 1782 was willing to concede that the legislative authority of the Irish parliament should be enhanced, but it wished to do so in such a way as to reserve to Britain the final authority in matters of imperial concern. This was an important test for Grattan and Charlemont, who were identified by the whigs as the Irish patriots with whom they wished to deal. It was logical that the whigs should seek to proceed thus since Grattan and Charlemont were personally friendly with and ideologically well disposed to Charles James Fox and Rockingham respectively. Indeed, Grattan was offered and might have taken office at this time had he not concluded that this would conflict with his commitment to serve Ireland. He was likewise disinclined to compromise in any way on what he and Charlemont were agreed were 'our rights', and with this in view they politely declined all overtures to discuss key constitutional points with ministers and officials before the Irish parliament was afforded an opportunity to state its position. With political and public opinion strongly supporting unconditional concession, Grattan knew he was in a strong position and, overcoming the illness that diminished his political effectiveness during much of 1782, he moved a third time for a declaration of rights in the House of Commons on 16 April 1782. Even by Grattan's high standards his performance on the day was exceptional for its skill in capturing the mood of the moment. His motion to amend the anodyne address favoured by the administration was approved unanimously. This greatly reinforced his contention that the government must accede unconditionally to his demands for the repeal of the Declaratory Act, the amendment of Poynings' law, an annual mutiny bill, and the enhancement of the independence of the judiciary. In return, Grattan emphasized his commitment and that of Irish protestants generally to maintain a close connection with Britain. 'The Crown of Ireland', he observed, was

> an imperial crown inseparably annexed to the crown of Great Britain ... and ... the people of this kingdom have never expressed a desire to share the freedom of England without declaring a determination to share her fate likewise with the British nation. (*Parliamentary Register*, 1.339)

Such expressions, reinforced by his suggestion that the Irish parliament should provide funds to allow the recruitment of 20,000 men by the British navy, increased Grattan's fame across the political spectrum in Ireland in 1782. By way of reciprocation, the Irish House of Commons took the highly unusual step on 31 May of awarding him £50,000 'in testimony of the gratitude of this nation for his eminent and unequalled services to this kingdom' (ibid., 1.383). This enabled Grattan to purchase a house at Tinnehinch, co. Wicklow, and an estate at Moyanna in Queen's county. It also meant effectively that he was free of money worries for the rest of his life, and it is not just a coincidence that he married Henrietta Fitzgerald, the second daughter of Nicholas and Margaret Fitzgerald of Greensborough, co. Kilkenny, in December that year.

Unhappily from Grattan's viewpoint, by this time his reputation with the public was already in decline. This was because he refused to support Henry Flood's controversial contention that the 'simple repeal' of the Declaratory Act did not constitute an absolute renunciation by the British parliament of its claim to make law for Ireland. No less importantly, his popular reputation to date derived from his efforts to promote commercial and constitutional reforms, and their attainment in 1780 and 1782 necessitated that he rethink his position. His refusal to take office on the appointment of Lord Northington, a whig, as lord lieutenant of Ireland in 1783 seemed to suggest that his preference was to pursue the opposition role with which he was familiar. But this option was closed off by his stand on renunciation and by his unwillingness to endorse the campaign for parliamentary reform spearheaded by the Ulster Volunteers in 1783, though he favoured some reform of the representative system. Instead, his preparedness to work with Lord Northington meant that he became what one contemporary described as a 'minister … without any employment' (BL, Add. MS 33100, fols. 358–9). He was ill-suited to the role. He accepted a nomination to the Irish privy council in September and voted with the administration in the Commons, but he did not favour their inflexible opposition to parliamentary reform, and he was alarmed by Northington's appointment to high office of figures such as John Fitzgibbon whom he found ideologically uncongenial. He might, had he been possessed of a more penetrating mind, advantageously have cut his ties with the administration at this point, but, as his premeditated and carefully prepared verbal attack on Henry Flood on 28 October attested, he still felt bitter about being upstaged. Flood, moreover, was not one to leave abuse unanswered, and his description of Grattan as a 'mendicant patriot' (Parliamentary Register, 2.42) hurt all the more because it reflected what many were saying in private. It might have been worse had the two men not been bound over before they could exchange shots in a duel, but the whole episode reflected badly on Grattan.

Given these circumstances, Grattan could only continue to co-operate with Dublin Castle, his reservations notwithstanding. His opposition to the popular campaign for protecting duties in 1783–4, and his belief that the volunteers, whom he memorably disparaged as 'armed beggary' (Parliamentary Register, 4.41) in 1785, should disband, contributed further to diminish his popular appeal and to his unexplained breach with Lord Charlemont, though he continued to represent the borough of the same name, to which he had been returned for a third time in 1783. He occupied himself meanwhile with fiscal reform, but it

won him little applause with either government or opposition and produced no beneficial changes. To be sure, his relationship with Dublin Castle was not entirely without advantage, as he demonstrated in February 1785 by securing significant modifications to the financial terms of William Pitt's proposal for a commercial union. Subsequent additions that were deemed incompatible with the legislative authority of the Irish parliament and effective campaigning by the Foxite whigs obliged him to take a more public stand, despite intense government lobbying. His speech against the arrangement on 12 August 1785 was a typical tour de force, as even his critics conceded, and it contributed in no small way to its failure to advance. It also signalled Grattan's return to the politics of opposition.

In the absence of Henry Flood, whose primary focus in the late 1780s was Westminster, Grattan was free to resume his place as the leading opposition spokesman in the Commons. He worked closely during these years and in the early 1790s with John Forbes, the MP for Drogheda, in seeking reform of the pension list, but without success. More controversially, he took up the issue of tithe reform, following an outbreak of sustained resistance by the peasantry of Munster to its payment. Having visited Munster 'to obtain every possible information' (Dublin Evening Post, 6 Sept 1787), he proposed that parliament agree to exempt barren lands and inaugurate a scheme of commutation, but neither was acceptable to the vigorous conservative lobby that gathered to defend the existing establishment in church and state. Grattan's energetic efforts to advance tithe reform suggested that he was eager for political power. George III's unexpected incapacity in winter 1788–9 certainly encouraged such hopes: it appeared to opposition whigs in both Britain and Ireland that if they could ensure that George, prince of Wales, became regent he would pave their way to power. Excited by this prospect and encouraged by his whig colleagues in England, Grattan was to the fore in persuading the Irish parliament to request the prince to exercise full royal authority while the king was indisposed. When the lord lieutenant refused to transmit an address to this effect, Grattan moved a series of resolutions on 20 February appointing a deputation, of which he was to be a member, to present the address to the prince, asserting the rights of the House of Commons and censuring the lord lieutenant. It was a defiant act that rebounded badly when George III recovered in time to avert the need for a regency. Grattan's reputation with the public was enhanced none the less and, eager to capitalize on this, he joined with Lord Charlemont and John Forbes in founding an Irish Whig Club in June 1789 whose objects were to promote political reform and sustain the constitution achieved in 1782.

The foundation of the Whig Club, as Grattan had hoped, gave greater direction and coherence to the parliamentary opposition in the early 1790s. Grattan's priority was patronage reform. Though none of his initiatives aimed at curtailing the administration's resort to patronage in 1790, 1791, and 1792 was successful, his efforts enabled him to sustain a high public profile; they also helped secure his election, along with Lord Henry Fitzgerald, to represent Dublin city in 1790. It was the first time Grattan had stood for election in a 'popular' constituency, marking the start of a formal political relationship with Dublin's electorate that extended over most of the rest of his political life.

The most controversial political question Grattan had to address in the early 1790s was Catholic enfranchisement. Despite supporting Catholic relief in 1782, as the representative for a city many of whose voters espoused 'protestant ascendancy', Grattan had to tread warily. With this in mind, he sought to steer a path between his sense of obligation to Catholics and his wish not to antagonize his constituents; so he promised to support relief 'only in as much as' it was 'consistent with' protestant ascendancy (H. Grattan, *Miscellaneous Works*, 1822, 289). He did not, as it happened, believe that the Catholic demands posed any 'hazard [to] the constitution in church and state' (Minto MS 12927, fol. 6). And despite allegations that he 'encouraged claims injurious to the Protestant ascendancy', he cleverly subverted such reactionary rhetoric by arguing that 'the Protestant ascendancy should be strengthened by enlarging its base, and uniting the Roman Catholic under a Protestant head' (ibid., fol. 18). This seemed to suggest that Grattan favoured Catholic enfranchisement, though it was not at issue in 1792; this was confirmed a year later when his mounting alarm at the direction of events in France persuaded him that Catholic enfranchisement was essential. Convinced that the 'decree of the French constitution generally expressed against all crowned heads' amounted to 'a declaration against the King of Great Britain and Ireland and ... a declaration of war against these nations', Grattan spoke strongly in January 1793 in favour of Catholic relief 'as essential for allaying discontents' (ibid., fol. 44) and diminishing the appeal of 'doctrines pernicious to freedom' (Grattan, *Memoirs*, 4.87) emanating from France. As a political moderate convinced of 'the necessity of the [British] connexion' (Minto MS 12927, fol. 44), Grattan believed that the most effective response to the challenge posed by the French Revolution was to embark on a programme of reform. Thus while he publicly announced his support for the war with France at the opening of the parliamentary session in 1794, he was also sharply critical of the Irish administration's decision in 1793 to seek parliamentary approval for a ban on delegate conventions and of their refusal to agree to proposals to reform the Irish legislature in 1793 and 1794. The former, he alleged, diminished the subject's constitutional right to petition effectively and, by implication, condemned all previous delegate meetings that had performed this function.

Measures were enacted in 1793 to limit the pension list, and together with a place and responsibility bill, a barren lands bill, and the Catholic enfranchisement legislation these indicated that Grattan's efforts were not without legislative impact. None the less he was acutely aware that the prevailing trend of government was towards reaction. Grattan's dissatisfaction with this was eased unexpectedly in the late summer of 1794 when he learned that the liberal whig Earl Fitzwilliam was to be appointed lord lieutenant. Informed by Fitzwilliam that the goal of his administration was 'to purify ... the principles of government, in the hopes of thereby restoring to it that tone and spirit which so happily prevailed formerly' (Grattan, *Memoirs*, 4.173–4), Grattan set out without delay for England to consult personally with the new lord lieutenant. Convinced that political harmony in Ireland and the harmony of the Anglo-Irish connection depended on the 'repeal of all disqualifications against Catholics' (Fitzwilliam (Grattan) MS T3649/8), he contrived to generate a powerful public call for precisely such changes by encouraging Catholics to reanimate their demand for relief when the British government was unforthcoming. This was a highly problematic action by someone who was expected to take a leading role on behalf of the new administration in the House of Commons. Grattan, however, did not conceive of himself as a Castle loyalist in the traditional sense, as witness his refusal to accept an offer of office. His priority was to promote and advance a programme of liberal reforms that would enable government in Ireland to escape the worst effects of the polarization and confrontation that was currently taking place. Grattan had concluded that the reactionary government provided by the so-called 'Irish cabinet' assembled by Fitzwilliam's predecessor, Lord Westmorland, had contributed in no small way to this unfortunate situation, so he was content that one of Fitzwilliam's first actions should be to dismiss those conservatives who held office in the gift of the crown. This created a vacuum at the head of the Irish executive that Grattan contrived to fill. He was the administration's leading voice in the Commons, where he performed energetically on its behalf on a variety of issues including defence, the Dublin police, and parliamentary reform. He also moved, fatally for the administration, for leave on 12 February 1795 to introduce a bill for the further relief of Catholics. This was going further than ministers were prepared to countenance; fearing for their ability to control Ireland in the future, they determined that Fitzwilliam should be recalled.

Though there is no evidence to suggest that Grattan believed that he had behaved other than properly, he must share the blame for the Fitzwilliam administration's politically incautious manner since he was among the lord lieutenant's most trusted advisers. He endeavoured to press ahead regardless with his proposal to admit Catholics to sit in parliament, but with the conservatives back in power it was a forlorn hope: his bill was rejected by a large margin, 155 to 84, on 5 May. The ratification of legislation providing for the establishment of a Catholic seminary at Maynooth, a police act, and a responsibility act indicated that the session of 1795 was not a complete write-off as far as Grattan's reform agenda was concerned, but this did little to dilute his disappointment. He was permanently embittered, as is suggested by his infamous allegation, in his reply to an address from the Catholics of Dublin, that the conservative-dominated establishment was motivated by 'tyranny, ... rapacity and ... malice' (Grattan, *Memoirs*, 4.219).

The years 1796 and 1797 were among the most depressing in Grattan's political life as his efforts to resist the reactionary policies promoted by Dublin Castle and favoured by a large majority of MPs fell increasingly on deaf ears. Grattan had spent the latter part of 1795 attempting unsuccessfully to encourage Catholics to continue to press for the amelioration of their grievances. Their disinclination reflected the general disillusionment of liberals and radicals, with the result that he spoke from largely empty benches and in vain when he sought in 1796 and 1797 both to resist the repressive policies of the administration and to promote his own reform programme. Thus his attempts on 17 October 1796 to advance Catholic emancipation were defeated by 149 to 12 and 143 to 19 while his cautions against the suspension of habeas corpus and the Insurrection Act were ignored. On 20 March 1797 he protested, again without result, against General Lake's proclamation whereby the whole of the province of Ulster was placed under martial law. Marginalized in the House of Commons, he was demoralized by the refusal of those in power to accept his analysis that reform was a more appropriate response to the country's problems than repression, and that the policies being pursued must culminate in 'a military government, a perfect despotism … a union … [or] a separation' (Grattan, *Speeches*, 3.342–3); so he withdrew with the other Irish whigs from the House of Commons in May 1797.

Despite the depth of his disenchantment with the Irish House of Commons, Grattan did not despair sufficiently of parliamentary government to embrace revolutionary radicalism. In a letter to the citizens of Dublin in 1797 he explained why he did not offer himself for re-election; he would, he said, adhere to this position 'so long as the present state of representation in the Commons' continued (H. Grattan, *Miscellaneous Works*, 1822, 40). In keeping with this, he did not respond to the attempts by members of the United Irishmen to enlist him in their cause. He was, however, familiar with some of their number, and his preparedness to travel to Maidstone to give evidence at the trial of Arthur O'Connor led to the groundless accusation that he was a sworn member of the society. This perception was reinforced when he published further critiques of government, which elicited a host of critical responses disparaging his analysis and his person. Indeed, he was regarded with such suspicion in conservative circles by 1798 that he wisely stayed in England for the duration of the rebellion. It did not secure his family and home from the unfriendly attentions of local loyalists or prevent his removal from the Irish privy council and other marks of public disfavour. As a consequence, when it emerged in the early winter of 1798 that the administration had it in mind to unite the parliaments of Great Britain and Ireland, the low esteem in which he was held by much of the protestant public meant he was poorly positioned to resist it.

Because he was no longer a member of parliament, Grattan could do little other than observe with relief when the Irish House of Commons determined in January 1799 not to admit the question of a legislative union to be formally presented. Illness obliged him to spend most of the year recuperating in England, and ensured that he made no contribution also to the rather desultory opposition campaign of summer 1799. Determined, however, to play his part when parliament resumed in 1800, he purchased a parliamentary seat for the borough of Wicklow and made a dramatic entrance to the Commons chamber on the morning of 16 January dressed in a volunteer uniform. His health was still poor, but on being given leave to speak from a sitting position he spoke eloquently for over two hours on the value of liberty and how it was incompatible with a legislative union. It was to no avail. Dublin Castle had the votes to ensure that they won the division that followed and every division that mattered thereafter. Some Castle observers maintained that Grattan's presence on the opposition benches weakened the anti-union cause because of the continuing suspicion with which he was regarded by conservative opponents of a union, but this is belied by the efforts they made to neutralize his contributions. This climaxed on 14 February 1800, when Isaac Corry's personalized attack prompted a duel between the two men in which Corry was slightly wounded. Grattan also clashed verbally with Lord Castlereagh, and felt obliged to publish a response to Lord Clare's pointed criticisms entitled *An Answer to a Pamphlet Entitled the Speech of the Earl of Clare*. It was effort in vain because it did not prevent the Act of Union becoming law. With it passed the phase of Irish parliamentary history launched in 1782 which nineteenth-century nationalists personalized as 'Grattan's parliament'. This particular term is a fine example of how later generations can isolate and give precedence to one aspect of an event or to one person from an earlier generation for their own purposes. Despite the critical role he played in ensuring that 'legislative independence' was brought about, Grattan's influence on the legislative decisions of the Irish parliament during the eighteen years that followed was modest, and his impact on its deliberations fitful. He was, at the same time, faithful to the liberal vision that caused him to pursue this goal in the first place, as his futile if symbolically significant opposition to its abolition emphasizes.

Catholic relief, 1800–1820 In the aftermath of the Union Grattan devoted his life to study and estate matters. Disapproving of both the conservative and radical agenda for Irish politics, he was reinforced in his convictions by the 'stupidity' and 'barbarity' (Grattan, *Memoirs*, 5.223–4) of Robert Emmet's disastrous attempt at rebellion in 1803; the best way forward for Ireland, he thought, was to extend the civil rights of Catholics. This meant allowing them to sit in parliament at Westminster, and it was this issue that tempted him back into politics in 1805. Having previously declined a nomination in 1801, he accepted the offer of Earl Fitzwilliam to represent the borough of Malton for the specific purpose of promoting the cause of Catholic emancipation. He made his maiden speech on 13 May in support of Charles James Fox's motion that a petition submitted by Irish Catholics seeking concessions should be referred to a committee. It was not an unqualified success. Grattan's brand of declamatory oratory and idiosyncratic actions was received with less favour at Westminster than earlier at College Green, though 'his great, but singular ... talent' (*Diary and Correspondence*, 2.2) won over most sceptics. His success was facilitated by his gregarious personality; he made friends easily, which ensured him a warm reception in the salons of many grandees. As a result, Grattan negotiated the transition to the imperial stage well—though, at fifty-nine, he was approaching old age when he took his seat. Favoured by the whigs who had overseen his re-entry to parliament and with whom he was ideologically aligned, his political rehabilitation was completed in 1806 when he was restored to the privy council and he declined the offer to become chancellor of the Irish exchequer. His election to represent the city of Dublin in November of the same year was a further personal triumph. Encouraged by this, Grattan redoubled his efforts to advance Catholic emancipation.

Though Grattan did not consciously avoid speaking on other Irish issues (he supported an insurrection bill in 1807 as 'necessary' to curb the influence of the 'French party', for example), he made the admittance of Catholics to sit in parliament the primary focus of the last fifteen years of his political life. Acutely conscious of the strength of opposition at Westminster to this eventuality, he concluded that progress would be made only if Catholics acceded to some compromise that allayed the fears of the strong 'no popery' interest in the Commons. The most obvious option was the acceptance of a state veto on Catholic episcopal appointments, since the Irish bishops had agreed in principle to the suggestion at the time of the Union. The problem was that Irish opinion generally, and episcopal opinion in particular, was less accepting of the idea in 1808 when Grattan made it a central feature of his speech in support of the admission of a Catholic petition. The ensuing fall-out persuaded Grattan not to press the question again until 1810, and he was unsuccessful then and again in 1811 and 1812. In February 1813, by contrast, he obtained Commons approval to introduce a relief bill to allow Catholics to hold all but the highest offices of state, with appropriate securities to safeguard the protestant succession and the Church of England. The inclusion of a provision to reject the nomination to the Catholic episcopacy of anyone whose loyalty was questionable was resented in Ireland, but it was the intervention of the speaker, Charles Abbot, with a motion excluding Catholics from sitting in parliament, that killed the measure. The episode hastened a split in Catholic ranks in Ireland and increased the reserve with which Grattan was regarded in Catholic circles, but there was nobody of equivalent stature to take his place. He presented several petitions in 1814 but did not speak on them, and his pronouncement in 1815 that Catholics could not hope for relief unless they 'offered securities ... in deference to the feeling of their Protestant countrymen' (*Diary and Correspondence*, 2.546) did little to ease friction. As a result, such efforts as were made to advance emancipation in 1816 and 1817 were stillborn. This did not damage Grattan electorally as he was returned to represent Dublin city for the last

time in 1818 with the help of Robert Peel, then Irish chief secretary, who refused to oppose his candidature. The O'Connellite, anti-veto wing of Catholic opinion was not best pleased, but Grattan showed no outward resentment, and he co-operated with Henry Parnell in raising the matter again in 1819 when he spoke in parliament for the last time. Despite ill health, he determined to raise the question of Catholic emancipation once more in 1820 and he rejected his doctor's advice and travelled to London for this purpose in May. However, his health, never robust, gave way and he died in Portman Square, Baker Street, London, on 4 June. He was buried on 16 June, at the request of the whigs, in Westminster Abbey, close to the spot where Fox and Chatham lay. He was survived by his wife and his two sons—James, who, after a career in the army, was MP for co. Wicklow between 1821 and 1841, and Henry, his biographer, who was also an MP—and two daughters, Mary Anne and Harriet.

Grattan's interment at Westminster Abbey was symbolic of the successful transition he made from Irish politics at College Green to imperial politics at Westminster. His failure to endorse the efforts of his son Henry to support an anti-union campaign in 1810 suggests, moreover, that he was content by that date that the Act of Union should continue, though he made no explicit statement to that effect. This is not surprising. Always sensitive when his reputation was concerned, as his duelling record evinces, both Grattan and his son Henry jun. were determined that his memory would be a positive one. With this in mind Grattan devoted much effort in his later years to ensuring that posterity would hold him in the high esteem he believed he was due. His most notable achievement was a four-volume edition of his political speeches, the earlier of which he subtly recast to emphasize his prescience and insight. His son subsequently reinforced the positive image provided by this work, and by a volume devoted to miscellaneous works which was also published in 1822, by producing a five-volume life that has never been equalled in scale or reverence. It was, and remains, an important source of information on Grattan and his times, and it has amply fulfilled the purpose for which it was written: more than any other work it has contributed to creating the overwhelmingly positive image Grattan enjoys in Irish popular consciousness to the present day. This is most easily demonstrated by reference to the continued use of the term 'Grattan's parliament' to describe the phase of Irish parliamentary history that extends from 1782 to 1800; by the presence on College Green of a statue in his honour; and by the naming of bridges, roads, and even public houses after him. In many respects Grattan's reputation is larger than his achievements warrant. He was a superb orator and a determined advocate of constitutional and political rights. However, he was less effective when he sought to master complex detail, and such attempts as he made to promote tithe and commercial reform in the 1780s were frequently found wanting for that reason. He was, in short, first and foremost an outstanding opposition politician who had few peers when faced with the challenge of making a vigorous speech in which emotion took precedence over logic and rhetoric prevailed over substance. This rhetorical style was not without its limitations, but Grattan's energetic, hyperbolic, and high-flowing oratory was warmly received in Ireland. There he was popularly perceived as the finest exponent of the ostentatious style of public speaking that flourished in late eighteenth-century Ireland. An orator rather than a debater, Grattan carefully prepared the set-piece statements upon which his fame rests. He regarded every major speech as a performance, and learned his lines as an actor might. This helped create an illusion that he was speaking extempore when it was seldom the case. His speeches derive their particular quality primarily from his penchant for vivid language and extravagant rhetorical devices. His predisposition for arresting images, strained metaphors, and forced antitheses may sound artificial today, but they impressed contemporaries. They were further impressed by his ability to rescue mediocre performances and banal speeches with sustained bursts of eloquence that drew the admiration even of his critics. Grattan's vocal impact was reinforced by his unique body movement. Though his bearing was described by some who observed him as 'grotesque' (*Diary and Correspondence*, 2.2) and by others as bizarre, it served in a curious way to reinforce his words. He was aided, of course, by the fact that personally he was an agreeable man who, while he liked being the source of attention, made others feel at ease in his company. However, it is for his role in achieving legislative independence that he continues to be best remembered, as is borne out by the fact that nineteenth-century nationalists chose to name after him the parliament that resulted. No other Irish politician has achieved such an accolade, and it is likely for that reason that his name will continue to echo strongly. Modern historians are more prone to draw attention to his personal and political limitations, and to be less susceptible to what has been called 'the Grattan mystique'.

JAMES KELLY

Sources H. Grattan, *Memoirs of the life and times of the Rt Hon. Henry Grattan*, 5 vols. (1839–46) • H. Grattan, *The speeches of the Right Honourable Henry Grattan*, ed. H. Grattan, 4 vols. (1822) • J. Porter, P. Byrne, and W. Porter, eds., *The parliamentary register, or, History of the proceedings and debates of the House of Commons of Ireland, 1781–1797*, 17 vols. (1784–1801) • [H. Grattan and others], *Baratariana: a select collection of fugitive political pieces*, ed. [Rev. Simpson] (1772) • *An edition of the Cavendish Irish parliamentary diary, 1776–1778*, ed. A. R. Black, 3 vols. (Delavan, WI, 1984–5) • J. Almon, *Narrative of proceedings in the parliament of Ireland* (1777) • G. O'Brien, 'The Grattan mystique', *Eighteenth-Century Ireland*, 1 (1986), 177–84 • J. Kelly, *Prelude to Union: Anglo-Irish politics in the 1780s* (1992) • J. Kelly, *That damn'd thing called honour: duelling in Ireland, 1570–1860* (1995) • J. Kelly, *Henry Grattan* (1994) • J. Kelly, *Henry Flood: patriots and politics in eighteenth-century Ireland* (1998) • M. R. O'Connell, *Irish politics and social conflict in the age of the American revolution* (1965) • PRO NIre., Fitzwilliam (Grattan) MSS, T3649/8 • Dublin Public Library, Gilbert MS 93 • Fitzwilliam papers, Sheff. Arch., Wentworth Woodhouse muniments, F. 30 • BL, Pelham papers, Add. MS 33100 • NL Scot., Minto MS 12927 • *The diary and correspondence of Charles Abbot, Lord Colchester*, ed. Charles, Lord Colchester, 3 vols. (1861) • T. M. O'Connor, 'The conflict between Flood and Grattan, 1782–3', *Essays in British and Irish history*, ed. H. A. Cronne and others (1949) • A. B. Tyrell, 'Homage to Grattan', *Dublin Historical Record*, 37/1 (1983–4), 31–43 • R. Koebner, 'The early speeches of Henry Grattan', *BIHR*, 30 (1957), 102–14 • *Annual Register* (1820), 1174–86 • Burke, *Gen. Ire.* (1976) • R. Mahony, 'The pamphlet campaign against Henry Grattan in 1797–99', *Eighteenth-Century Ireland*, 2 (1987), 149–66 • P. J. Jupp, 'Grattan, Henry', HoP, *Commons, 1790–1820* • A. J. Webb, *A compendium of Irish biography* (1878) • R. V. Callen, 'Cavendish's diary of the Irish parliament, October 12, 1779 to September 2, 1780', PhD diss., Notre Dame University, 1973

Archives NL Ire., family and other corresp., accounts, and notes • TCD, draft speeches and notes • U. Hull, Brynmor Jones L., political and other corresp. | NL Ire., letters to John Forbes • Sheff. Arch., corresp. with Edmund Burke; corresp. with Earl Fitzwilliam

Likenesses N. Kenny, oils, 1782, TCD • F. Wheatley, oils, 1782, NPG • M. A. Shee, oils, 1788, NG Ire. • P. Turnerelli, plaster bust, 1812, NPG • A. Pope, drawing, in or before 1814, priv. coll. [*see illus.*] • F. Chantrey, bronze statue, exh. RA 1826, City Hall, Dublin • J. E. Carew, statue, 1844, St Stephen's Hall, Westminster, London • T. A. Jones, oils (after J. Ramsay), NG Ire. • F. C. Lewis, engraving (after N. Kenny), repro. in Grattan, *Memoirs*, 1, frontispiece • A. Pope, watercolour, BM • T. Scott, ink drawing (after A. Pope), NG Ire. • G. Stuart, oils, NG Ire. • F. Wheatley, group portrait, oils (*The Irish House of Commons, 1780*), Leeds City Art Galleries, Lotherton Hall, West Yorkshire • statue, College Green, Dublin

Grattan, Thomas Colley (1791–1864), journalist and novelist, was born in Dublin, a younger son of Colley Grattan (1754–*c*.1815), a Dublin solicitor, later coroner of Kildare, and his wife, Elizabeth Warren. His father was a second cousin both of the Irish parliamentary leader Henry Grattan and, through his mother, Hannah Colley, of Arthur Wellesley, later duke of Wellington. The family soon moved to Clayton Lodge in co. Kildare, destroyed in 1798, and then to Athy where Grattan was educated by the Revd Henry Bristow. He was sent to Dublin to study law, which he soon abandoned. The country was at war and he wanted to serve in the army. Two of his brothers were already on active service, but one was killed in Java and the other wounded at Badajos, so his father opposed the idea until the war was over. Grattan had to content himself with a commission in the Louth militia. He planned to fight with Bolívar in South America in 1817, but on his way to Bordeaux to join a French vessel bound for Venezuela he met Eliza Sarah (d. 1870), daughter of John O'Donnel MD, married her, and settled near Bordeaux. His eldest son, Edmund Arnaut, was born in 1818, soon followed by Henry Colley (b. 1819), Albert (b. 1821), and Emma Jane, so he turned to writing to make a living.

Philibert: a Poetical Romance (1819), loosely based on the case of the false Martin Guerre, was an attempt at verse-narrative in the manner of Scott's *Marmion*, but poetry was not Grattan's medium. He moved to Paris to work as a journalist, contributing frequently to Henry Colburn's *New Monthly Magazine* and launching his own *Paris Monthly Review of British and Continental Literature* (1822–3). Sociable and professionally ambitious, he assiduously cultivated literary contacts: he was one of the first to tell English readers about contemporary French poets such as his friends Lamartine and Béranger. Already well travelled and a natural story-teller, he began writing sketches and curious anecdotes not unlike those in the *Sketchbook* of Washington Irving, then in Paris. Irving privately found Grattan 'an arrant literary tradesman' and 'a bore' (Irving,

Thomas Colley Grattan (1791–1864), by unknown engraver, pubd 1853

Journal, 17 Feb and 17 Nov 1824). But he generously read his work and helped him find a publisher for a collection of his stories which eventually appeared in 1823 under the title *Highways and Byways, or, Tales of the Roadside*, dedicated to Irving. This made his name and remained his best-known work. French translations soon followed and there were further series in 1825 and 1827. *Traits of Travel* (1828), in the same vein, was also successful. Before Grattan left Ireland he had met Edmund Kean on tour and he persuaded him to produce and act in his tragedy *Ben Nazir, the Saracen* at Drury Lane in 1827. But Kean's great days were over and he broke down completely on the first night, which killed the play.

Obliged to move to Brussels after financial losses, Grattan turned increasingly to the writing of history and historical novels. His *History of the Netherlands* was first published in 1830 and was later incorporated into Lardner's *Cyclopedia* (1838). His novel *The Heiress of Bruges* (1830) was translated into French the following year. The *New Monthly Magazine* (July 1831) tried to promote him as 'the Flemish Sir Walter' and Grattan opportunistically sent Scott a copy, together with *Jacqueline of Holland* (1831). These are probably his best novels, rambling romances solidly based on unfamiliar historical sources. The Belgian revolution of 1830 again disrupted his household. He moved to Antwerp and then to The Hague where he became interested in the long-running boundary dispute between Canada and the United States, which the king of the Netherlands

had been asked to arbitrate. Eventually returning to Brussels, he was well received by Leopold, the new king of the Belgians, and soon emerged as a sympathetic commentator on Belgian affairs at a difficult time, acting as a Brussels correspondent for *The Times* from 1834. Leopold helped him to obtain an appointment as British consul in Massachusetts in 1839, where his previous knowledge of the boundary dispute made him very useful to both parties when Lord Ashburton was sent out to negotiate the matter with Daniel Webster in 1842. Allowed to resign his consular appointment in favour of his eldest son in 1846, when he returned to London, he retained his interest in American affairs, publishing *Civilized America* in 1851 and the timely *England and the Disrupted States of America* in 1861. The autobiographical *Beaten Paths; and those who Trod them* appeared in 1862. Grattan died at his home at 117 Jermyn Street, London, on 4 July 1864.

Unsympathetic to O'Connell and the politics of repeal, Grattan wrote little about Irish affairs and could be a severe critic of his fellow countrymen. Prolific as a journalist, novelist, and popular historian, he was a versatile and competent literary journeyman rather than a great writer. His historical novels and travel writings are now justly forgotten, but he cultivated a wide acquaintance and lived in interesting times and places, so his rather diffuse published recollections of people and events are still useful to biographers and historians.

G. C. BOASE, *rev.* NORMAN VANCE

Sources T. C. Grattan, *Beaten paths; and those who trod them* (1862) · 'Our portrait gallery, no. LXXI: Thomas Colley Grattan, esq.', *Dublin University Magazine*, 42 (1853), 658–65 · *DNB* · Burke, *Gen. Ire.* (1976) · W. Irving, *Journals and Notebooks, 1819–1827*, ed. W. A. Reichardt (1970) · *GM*, 3rd ser., 17 (1864), 252–3 · 'Living literary characters, No. VII', *New Monthly Magazine*, new ser., 32 (1831), 77–80 · *Wellesley index* · M. G. Baxter, *One and inseparable: Daniel Webster and the union* (1984) · *The journal of Thomas Moore*, ed. W. S. Dowden, 6 vols. (1983–91) · *The letters of Sir Walter Scott*, ed. H. J. C. Grierson and others, centenary edn, 12 vols. (1932–79) · *BL cat.* · *CGPLA Eng. & Wales* (1864)

Archives BL, corresp. with Lord Aberdeen, Add. MS 43123 · BL, corresp. with Sir Robert Peel, Add. MS 40411, fol. 66; Add. MS 40535 fols. 13–25 · NL Scot., corresp. with George Combe · U. Southampton L., corresp. with Lord Palmerston · UCL, corresp. with the Society for the Diffusion of Useful Knowledge

Likenesses lithograph, pubd 1853, NPG; repro. in *Dublin University Magazine*, facing p. 658 [*see illus.*] · J. Thomson, stipple (after drawing by F. W. Say), BM, NPG; repro. in *New Monthly Magazine*, facing p. 77

Wealth at death under £4000: administration with will, 9 Aug 1864, *CGPLA Eng. & Wales*

Gratton, John (1642/3–1712), Quaker preacher and writer, was born at Bonsall, Derbyshire, the son of a yeoman or farmer. As a boy Gratton tended his father's sheep, and subsequently went to Chesterfield as an apprentice to his grandfather. Fond of card playing, shooting, and bell-ringing, he was also spiritually sensitive, making an effort in the 1650s to hear noted preachers. Although he belonged to a presbyterian church, the doctrine of predestination troubled him, causing him to fear he was reprobate. Following the Ejection in August 1662 he attended

Anglican services, but found the liturgy barren and life-less. For a time he worshipped in a mixed congregation of presbyterians, Independents, and Baptists, but he quickly tired of their internal disputes and began attending services at an Independent church in Chesterfield, whose theology he deemed Arminian. Dismayed by their efforts to avoid persecution, he explored the teachings of John Reeve and Lodowick Muggleton, finally concluding the latter was a false prophet. After moving to Monyash, Derbyshire, about 1668, he found a Baptist congregation to be 'nearest the Scriptures of any I had yet tried' (Gratton, 25); occasionally it met in his house. He became disillusioned when his sister received adult baptism and he saw no manifestation of the Spirit, leading him to conclude that baptism was a lifeless rite. On 24 June 1669 he married a woman identified only as Anne (d. 1707); they had four children, John (b. 4 April 1670), Joseph (b. 30 Oct 1671), Phoebe (b. 16 July 1675), and Josiah (b. 10 Sept 1676). Gratton refused Anne's requests that they worship in the established church.

About 1671, as Gratton rode alone to Sheldon, he had a Pauline experience in which he sensed the Spirit's light shining within him. God, he averred, now revealed that the Quakers were his people. Having never attended a Quaker meeting, he visited one at 'Exton' (possibly Eyam), where he found the assurance for which he had long sought; he was now twenty-eight. Several days later he held a meeting at Tideswell, where he spoke for four hours. One of his first converts was a Muggletonian woman, whose irate spouse persuaded Muggleton to curse Gratton. Among his other early converts were many relatives, his wife, and Baptists in Cheshire. Meanwhile, he held meetings in Yorkshire, Lincolnshire, Nottinghamshire, Staffordshire, and Derbyshire, and in 1674 participated in his first London yearly meeting. While in London, he visited Muggleton with Robert Barclay and two other Friends, but neither side yielded. The same year he published his first book, *John Baptist's Decreasing*, defending the Quaker doctrine of Spirit baptism. For attending a conventicle, magistrates distrained his goods, but no one at Monyash would purchase them. At the earl and countess of Devonshire's behest, Sir Henry Every JP intervened on Gratton's behalf, as he subsequently did on several occasions, saving him from financial penalties. Gratton associated with Quaker leaders, especially at the London yearly meetings; George Fox visited him in 1678, and he corresponded with William Penn, who thought highly of him.

On 16 August 1680 Gratton was arrested at Bakewell on a writ *de excommunicato capiendo* for failing to appear in an ecclesiastical court on charges of recusancy. He was imprisoned at Derby, and efforts of his friends to obtain his release on a writ of habeas corpus failed. His incarceration was not unduly harsh, for he could hold meetings in the prison and occasionally leave for brief periods, as when his son died. He sometimes preached through his window, on one occasion converting the gaoler's son. With the father's permission, he took the young man to London and established him as a trading partner with another Friend. In *To All Persecutors* (1682) and *The Prisoners*

Vindication (1683) he lashed out against those who punished Quakers; God, he warned in the latter tract, would soon empower Friends to trample Satan underfoot. An epistle to the London yearly meeting, dated 22 May 1683, indicates that he handled his imprisonment well. He was in London during one of his temporary respites when Charles II died. With hundreds of others, Gratton was liberated by James II on 23 March 1686, the efforts of his enemies to block Gratton's release having been thwarted by Every. For nearly a decade Gratton travelled throughout England, Scotland, and Wales preaching the Quaker message. From 23 July to 8 November 1695 he visited meetings throughout Ireland, and he returned in September 1696 for the Munster provincial meeting. When Gratton, George Whitehead, and others defended the Quakers from an attack by William Lancaster, they were in turn castigated by George Keith in *Gross Error and Hypocrisie Detected* (1695). The same year, Gratton published an exposition of the Quaker doctrine of spiritual ordinances, *A Treatise Concerning Baptism, and the Lord's Supper*. His final work, *The Clergy-Man's Pretence of Divine Right to Tythes* (1703), rejected the professional clergy's claim to tithes.

When Gratton's wife's health declined, the couple sold their house at Monyash and settled first with their son Joseph and shortly thereafter with their daughter, Phoebe Bateman, at Farnsfield, Nottinghamshire. Following Anne's death on 4 December 1707, Gratton travelled in southern England, but his own health began to fail. After a month's painful illness, he died at Farnsfield on 9 March 1712, aged sixty-nine, and was buried two days later beside his wife at Farnsfield. A 'solid and serious' man whose 'discourse tended much to edification', according to his contemporary, Josiah Langdale (Gratton, vi), Gratton earned respect beyond Quaker circles from such people as the earl and countess of Devonshire, Sir John Every, and Sir John Rodes, helping the Friends gradually attain social acceptance.   RICHARD L. GREAVES

Sources J. Gratton, *A journal of the life of that ancient servant of Christ John Gratton*, ed. J. Whiting (1795) • J. Smith, ed., *A descriptive catalogue of Friends' books*, 2 vols. (1867); suppl. (1893) • W. C. Braithwaite, *The second period of Quakerism*, ed. H. J. Cadbury, 2nd edn (1961) • *The short journal and itinerary journals of George Fox*, ed. N. Penney (1925) • *The papers of William Penn*, ed. M. M. Dunn, R. S. Dunn, and others, 1 (1981) • 'Record of Friends travelling in Ireland, 1656–1765 [pt 1]', *Journal of the Friends' Historical Society*, 10 (1913), 157–80, esp. 164 • C. W. Horle, *The Quakers and the English legal system, 1660–1688* (1988) • S. F. Locker-Lampson, ed., *A Quaker post-bag: letters to Sir John Rodes of Barlbrough Hall, in the county of Derby, baronet, and to John Gratton of Monyash, 1693–1742* (1910) • 'Dictionary of Quaker biography', RS Friends, Lond. [card index] • E. Manners, *John Gratton: a Derbyshire 'Quaker' preacher and prophet* (1922)
Archives RS Friends, Lond., Monyash monthly meeting minute book

Graunt, John (1620–1674), statistician, was born on 24 April 1620 at the sign of the Seven Stars in Birchin Lane, London, the eldest of the seven or eight children of Henry Graunt, a Hampshire man by birth who became a collar maker in London, and his wife, Mary. After his education (of which details are not known), Graunt was apprenticed at the age of sixteen to his father, by then described as a haberdasher of small wares, and was admitted to the free-dom of the Drapers' Company five years later. In February 1641 he married Mary Scott, of the parish of St Botolph without Bishopsgate (who was possibly from an Essex family); they had four children. After his marriage he apparently worked in his father's shop until the latter's death in March 1662. Graunt's friend Aubrey said: 'He was a very ingenious and studious person, and generally beloved, and rose early in the morning to his study before shop-time. He understood Latin and French. He was a pleasant facetious companion, and very hospitable' (*Brief Lives*, 114). Aubrey also reported that he was brought up as a puritan, wrote shorthand dexterously, was often chosen for his prudence and justness to be an arbitrator, was a great peacemaker, had an excellent working head, and was very fluent in his conversation.

Graunt was an influential figure in the City. In 1650 he was able to obtain for his friend William Petty a post as professor of music at Gresham College. He served in vari-ous ward offices in Cornhill ward, becoming a common councilman about 1669–71. He was captain, and later major, of the trained band, was warden of the Drapers' Company in 1671 and a member of the court of assistants in 1671–3, and was a member of the New River Company from 25 September 1666. In March 1657 he leased a house on the west side of Birchin Lane. In April 1663 Pepys went there and was most impressed with his collection of prints of houses, churches, and antiquities in Italy and France.

Graunt's place in the history of statistical enquiry is based upon his *Natural and Political Observations … upon the Bills of Mortality*, published in 1662. It was an instant suc-cess, running into five editions by 1676. The bills of mor-tality were printed statements of the numbers of people who died each week, classified according to the apparent cause of death, whose purpose was to warn of plague epi-demics so that wealthy people could move to the sup-posedly healthier countryside. Graunt investigated these bills for a long series of past years, recognizing their scien-tific potential. One of the book's achievements was the publication of the first known life table to be based, in part, on real mortality data. Although the bills did not record the age at death, Graunt observed that about one-third of all deaths occurred from childish ailments and guessed that some of the other illnesses also caused deaths among children. From this he estimated that about 36 per cent of all deaths related to children under six years old. Hence he argued that, of every 100 children con-ceived, only sixty-four would reach the age of six. He then used a mathematical projection to obtain the numbers of the original 100 who would reach ages sixteen, twenty-six, thirty-six, and so on.

Another of Graunt's main purposes was to estimate the London population, which common talk often asserted ran into millions. He approached the question in several different ways and produced an estimate of 384,000 people, which twentieth-century demographers con-sidered reasonably accurate. His book was a starting point for both statistics and demography. He was the first per-son to analyse a considerable body of social data carefully, considering possible recording inaccuracies, checking from other sources where possible, and drawing conclu-sions directly from the data. His work on the life table was of fundamental importance for the development of actu-arial science. He succeeded in identifying regularities in the patterns of life and death in groups of people.

There has been great controversy over whether Graunt's book was written largely by his friend Petty. Graunt would almost certainly have consulted Petty—a doctor of medicine—about the ambitious and novel pro-ject he was undertaking, if only to get a better understand-ing of medical terms. It would have been natural for some-one of such a lively mind as Petty to suggest ideas and per-haps a methodology. Aubrey wrote, 'I believe, and partly know, that he had his hint from his intimate and familiar friend Sir William Petty' (*Brief Lives*, 115) and similar sug-gestions were made by other contemporary writers (Eve-lyn, Halley, Burnet, Houghton, and Southwell). However, even if one admits Petty's likely help, it is clear that most of the work, and particularly the painstaking data collec-tion and analysis, was carried out by Graunt himself. The Royal Society was sufficiently convinced of the value of his work to elect him a member later in 1662, with endorsement from the king. The question is discussed in depth by D. V. Glass (*PRS*, 159B, 1963), although he perhaps understates Petty's probable involvement when he con-cludes that the book was in all essential respects Graunt's work.

Graunt was quite active in the Royal Society, as appears from its minutes, providing information on the multipli-cation of carp in a pond, communicating with Petty about the latter's experimental ship, supplying a box of Macas-sar poison for analysis, and helping to control the society's finances. He was chosen as a member of the council in November 1664 and represented the society at various meetings. However, his society activities seem to have ceased in October 1667. His house was destroyed in the 1666 fire, and he had to rebuild it. This may well have aggravated the money troubles he experienced in later years, which culminated in bankruptcy. On 21 March 1668 he wrote from Salisbury to Sir Robert Harley: 'I am engaged in a very unfortunate business of the hearth money for the County of Wilts that I fear it will be my half undoing' (Graunt to Harley). Apparently Graunt's partner as a collector of this tax had absconded with £500, and Graunt was worried that he might have to pay it himself.

In his later years Graunt became interested in Socinian doctrines and later, much to Petty's disgust, went in the opposite direction and converted to Roman Catholicism. One of Graunt's daughters had entered a Belgian nunnery in 1667. He was accused of recusancy and appeared in court twice in 1674. However, before the adjourned case was heard he died of jaundice, on 18 April 1674 at his home, which by then was in Bolt Court, London. He was buried in the church of St Dunstan-in-the-West four days later.

C. G. LEWIN

Sources D. V. Glass, 'John Graunt and his *Natural and political observations*', *PRS*, 159B (1963), 2–37 · T. Birch, *The history of the Royal Society of London*, 4 vols. (1756–7) · *Aubrey's Brief lives*, ed. O. L. Dick (1949) · C. H. Hull, *The economic writings of Sir William Petty* (1899) · *The Petty papers: some unpublished writings of Sir William Petty*, ed. marquis of Lansdowne [H. W. E. Petty-Fitzmaurice], 2 vols. (1927), 273–84 · K. Pearson, *The history of statistics in the 17th and 18th centuries* (1978) · letter, J. Graunt to Sir Robert Harley, 21 March 1668, BL, Add. MS 70011 · A. Hald, *A history of probability and statistics and their applications before 1750* (1990) · J. Graunt and G. King, *The earliest classics* (1973) [facs. edn with introduction by P. Laslett] · *The Petty–Southwell correspondence, 1676–1687*, ed. marquis of Lansdowne [H. E. W. Petty-Fitzmaurice] (1928) · Pepys, *Diary* · *DSB* · C. G. Lewin, '1848 and all that', *Fiasco* [Institute of Actuaries Students' Society], nos. 110–11 (Dec 1988–Jan 1989) · *The diary of Robert Hooke … 1672–1680*, ed. H. W. Robinson and W. Adams (1935)

Archives BL, Petty MSS · BL, Portland MSS

Wealth at death see *Diary of Robert Hooke*, 100

Gravelet, Jean-François Émile [*performing names* Blondin, Charles Blondin] (1824–1897), tightrope walker, was born on 28 February 1824 at Hesdin, near St Omer in France, the son of André Gravelet (*c*.1789–1832/3), himself a tightrope walker and a soldier in Napoleon's grande armée, the holder of the cross of the Légion d'honneur. His mother was Eulalie Merlet (*c*.1794–1833/4). In 1829 a troupe of travelling entertainers came to the neighbourhood and Jean-François was fascinated by them. He tried out tightrope walking between two chairs with disastrous but salutary results. He was then and there convinced of the necessity of being almost obsessively well prepared for any dangerous acts he proposed to carry out. A local former sailor skilled in climbing rigging took an interest in the boy's ambitions and helped him to practise in a wood nearby. When the parents were convinced of their son's prowess and single-mindedness they enrolled him at the age of five as a residential pupil in the famous École de Gymnase in Lyon, the foremost training ground for acrobats of all kinds. He appeared professionally as the Little Wonder some six months later, and within two years was in Turin at the royal command of the king of Sardinia.

After leaving the school Gravelet, who was orphaned by the age of ten, joined circus troupes and appeared all over the continent for about eighteen years. In 1851 he became a member of the famous Ravel Family of French acrobats, which included one with the name Blondin, from whom some authorities say the pseudonym may have derived; others assert that he adopted a nickname first applied to his father. With the troupe he went to America under a contract from Phineas T. Barnum. In the course of the journey across the Atlantic, Blondin rescued a young nobleman who was swept overboard in a storm, and who was later to show his gratitude in a material way. With the Ravels he appeared at Niblo's Gardens in New York, and in Boston and Philadelphia. In the spring of 1858 Blondin visited Niagara Falls and conceived his plan of making a crossing on a rope. With his usual attention to detail, it took him nearly a year to work out a possible line of approach. About 1858 he married Charlotte Sophia Lawrence (*d*. 1888), who was said in the dedication of a pamphlet by G. L. Banks in 1862 to be 'the high-minded and exemplary wife of a brave and devoted husband'. They had three daughters and two sons. Blondin was described at this time as of medium height (5 feet 5 inches), stocky, weighing 10 stone, with a broad chest and muscular arms, light grey close-set eyes, fair (though not blond) hair to his shoulders, and a small imperial beard. He was a teetotaller.

Blondin had no capital to fund his venture and approached the editors of the *Niagara Falls Daily Gazette*, obtaining their support when he convinced them that he was in earnest. His agent, Harry Colcord, also took some persuading that the apparently mad plan was feasible. All sorts of problems were presented: General Porter, the owner of Goat Island, near the falls, where Blondin had calculated he should make the crossing, would not give permission and he had to go further downstream; the 3-inch-wide rope would cost $1300; and while the owners of local hotels and tourist venues were not slow to see the attraction of the 'show', they would not provide much finance. But Blondin doggedly went ahead, and crowds variously estimated at between 10,000 and 25,000 were brought in by extra trains and steamers.

Blondin stepped out onto the wide rope (by his standards) at five o'clock on a sunny day, 30 June 1859, with his 30 foot balancing-pole weighing 40 lb. He completed the crossing from the American to the Canadian side in seventeen and a half minutes, having stopped on the way to lie down to rest and to pull up a bottle of refreshing drink from the deck of the steamer *Maid of the mist*, moored in midstream. Bands played on both sides and were packing up when Blondin announced that he would make the return journey, and did so in seven minutes. Accounts of the feats he performed differ fairly widely, but it is certain that various other 'stunt' crossings were organized in the next few weeks. On 14 September 1860 the prince of Wales, then on a tour of Canada and America, witnessed a performance. Blondin offered to take the prince across on his back but this was vetoed by the duke of Newcastle, who was in charge of the party. The prince none the less much enjoyed the spectacle, which included a crossing on stilts, and sent a cheque in appreciation. This must have been welcome, as no great financial success attended the venture. Jones' Wood in New York was his next venue, and there he met again the young nobleman, 'Comte A', whom he had rescued at sea; he urged Blondin to give up his dangerous profession and, when unsuccessful in his plea, presented him with a diamond ring.

Henry Coleman, Blondin's new manager, sailed for England and arranged an appearance at the Crystal Palace in London in June 1861, which was accompanied by the band of the Coldstream Guards. The crowds applauded, but Dickens and *Punch* were scathing, the latter publishing a skit interview between Boswell and Johnson on Blondin. The Crystal Palace Company made £10,000 profit from seats at half a crown and 5*s*. (pre-booked), from which Blondin received only £1200, out of which he had to pay all his expenses. A provincial tour followed, during which a lion was pushed across the rope strapped into a wheelbarrow. Further years at the Crystal Palace earned more money, and Blondin bought a house in London's Finchley

Road, which he named Niagara Villa, with a carriage and pair and servants to ease Madame Blondin's domestic life. After a farewell performance in February 1863, the Blondin family set off on a tour of France, Spain, Russia, Portugal, and Italy, and in 1864 he went to South America for two years. India, Australia, and New Zealand followed, with another tour of South America. He became a naturalized British subject on 4 June 1868. In 1879 some unrecorded financial disaster struck, the house and trappings were sold, and another, more modest one, in Ealing, was purchased. So the performances had to continue: Europe and even Ceylon, then London again, and off to New York. Madame Blondin died on 19 December 1888. Another residence, Niagara House, was built in Northfield Lane, Ealing, where Blondin, though never fully retired, kept domestic animals and made small handicraft objects.

At the age of seventy Blondin again performed at the Crystal Palace, refusing a net, and in 1895 at Blackpool he injured his back. He married the nurse who looked after him, Katherine, *née* James (1864/5–1901), at Brentford register office on 29 November 1895, and lived another two years with her. His final performance was at Belfast in 1896. He died at Niagara House of diabetes on 22 February 1897 and was buried beside his first wife in Kensal Green cemetery. Phrenological examination, which was popular at the time, showed him to be careful, prudent, jealous of his own self-respect, and conscious of his obligations to his family and society.   J. GILLILAND

Sources K. Wilson, *Everybody's heard of Blondin* (1990) · P. Larousse, ed., *Grand dictionnaire universel du XIXe siècle*, 17 vols. (Paris, 1866–90) · S. D'Amico, ed., *Enciclopedia dello spettacolo*, 11 vols. (Rome, 1954–68) · G. L. Banks, ed., *Blondin, his life and performances* (1862) · *The Times* · H. Le Roux, *Acrobats and mountebanks* (1890) · *Encyclopaedia Britannica*, 14th edn (1961) · H. Demoriane, *The tightrope walker* (1989) · Wilson, *The life of Blondin: the ascentionist at the Crystal Palace* (1869) · *Dean's new moveable book of Leotard, Blondin as the ape, female Blondin, etc.* [1862] · m. cert. · d. cert.
Likenesses Barber of Birmingham, working effigy · J. Provost, photographs · E. de Silhouette, cut outs · engravings, Harvard TC · prints, repro. in Banks, ed., *Blondin*, frontispiece
Wealth at death £1832 16s. od.: probate, 22 March 1897, *CGPLA Eng. & Wales*

Gravelot [*formerly* Bourguignon], **Hubert-François** (1699–1773), book illustrator and engraver, was born on 26 March 1699 at St Germain l'Auxerrois, Paris, the younger of the two sons of Hubert Bourguignon, a master tailor, and his wife, Charlotte Vaugon. He took the name Gravelot as a young man, apparently from his godfather. Gravelot was probably the greatest single influence on the development of book illustration in eighteenth-century England, and he is also recognized as a major protagonist in the introduction of the rococo style to English art.

Gravelot was educated at the Collège des Quatre Nations in Paris, alongside his brother, the geographer Jean-Baptiste Bourguignon d'Anville. He then travelled to Lyons to work for the ambassador to Rome, Louis d'Aubusson, duc de la Feuillade, although he never got to Rome, having allegedly wasted the money he had been given to make the journey. On his return to Paris his father sent him to Santo Domingo with the governor-general of

Hubert-François Gravelot (1699–1773), by Jean Massard (after Maurice-Quentin de La Tour)

the island, the chevalier de la Rochelard. There Gravelot made a map of the island, but apparently little else. The loss of a ship containing merchandise sent by his father left him penniless, and he returned to Paris in 1729.

In Paris Gravelot trained in the studios of Jean Restout the younger and François Boucher, where he presumably developed his flowing, graceful style. By 1733 he was in London, having been invited by Claude du Bosc to work on a new edition of Bernard Picart's *The Ceremonies and Religious Customs of the Various Nations of the World* (Amsterdam, 1725–43). Gravelot helped to re-engrave the plates for the English edition (1733–7) and also added twenty-two new headpieces. During the twelve years that he spent in London his obvious technical ability, and what George Vertue called his 'great and fruitful genius for designs' (Hammelmann, 38), made him a favourite among booksellers. Over this period he produced work for more than fifty publications, ranging from ornamental surrounds for the portrait of Handel for the published score of *Alexander's Feast, an Opera*, in 1738, to major commissions, such as twenty-seven plates for John Dryden's *Works* (1735) and sixteen plates for John Gay's *Fables* of 1738 (drawings in the British Museum).

Vertue later described Gravelot as a 'designer and etcher of history' (Hammelmann, 38), and he was a leading illustrator of the British past. His ornamental surrounds for Jacobus Houbraken's portraits of illustrious figures, first for the third edition of Rapin's *History of England* (1743–7) and then for Thomas Birch's *Heads of Illustrious Persons of Great Britain* (1743–51), added key visual detail and dramatic effect to the representation of history, as in the putti mourning over the severed head of Thomas Howard, duke of Norfolk, the original drawing for which is in the Tate collection. Gravelot also produced designs for John Pine's *Tapestry Hangings of the House of Lords*, showing portraits of the central figures involved in the Anglo-Spanish battles of 1588 (thirty-one original designs are in the Victoria and Albert Museum, London), and worked with Vertue on engravings of ancient monuments, such as the *View of the Monument of Henry VII* (1735; impression in the Guildhall collection, London). However, he is probably better remembered for his elegant theatrical illustrations, especially his thirty-six plates for the second edition of Theobald's *Works of Shakespeare* (1740, reprinted 1752, 1772, and 1773). Scenes such as *Othello Murdering Desdemona* (original drawing in the Huntington Library) show a relatively early attempt to represent a Shakespearian scene by rehashing earlier scenes from non-Shakespearian French prints and placing the action in an anachronistically contemporary interior. These works nevertheless reveal Gravelot's flowing, sketchy draughtsmanship and his mastery of gesture. Also, inadvertently, they show his precise eye for the contemporary interior. His other musical and theatrical illustrations include *The Adieu to the Spring Gardens*, for George Bickham's *The Musical Entertainer* (1737–8; impression in the Guildhall collection) and *Songs in the Opera of Flora* (1737). His illustrations for Samuel Richardson's *Pamela* (1742; drawings in the British Museum and the Ashmolean Museum, Oxford) helped to popularize the novel genre.

In London Gravelot was an important figure in the artistic community. He lived at the Golden Cup in King Street, Covent Garden, and later in James Street, Covent Garden. He appears to have taught at the St Martin's Lane Academy and to have been a regular drinking companion of Francis Hayman, with whom he collaborated on the designs for Thomas Hamner's *Works of Shakespeare* (1743–4). He was also a lifelong friend of the actor David Garrick and seems to have collaborated with L. F. Roubiliac on his design for the monument to the duke of Argyll in Westminster Abbey. Another drinking companion was William Hogarth, with whom Gravelot shared a taste for satire: he could often be heard holding forth at Slaughter's Coffee House 'with considerable violence and freedom for or against whom he pleases' (Vertue, *Note books*, 3.91). His political caricatures, such as *The State Packhorse* (original drawing in the Tate collection), are, however, too allegorical and customarily elegant to match the savagery of his companion's productions.

Gravelot's output in London was varied and extensive. His gracious rococo designs may be found on trade cards, bookplates, fans, badges, and invitation cards (examples are in the Victoria and Albert Museum and the British Museum). He is said to have designed for furniture makers and upholsterers, while designs survive for gold boxes, watches, and watchcases. Long after his return to France his designs were being reproduced on Bow and Chelsea

porcelain. Gravelot was a skilled engraver of his own and other's designs, and during his stay in England he produced several oil paintings of genre scenes, including *Le lecteur* (priv. coll.) and *Building Card Houses* (National Gallery of British Sports and Pastimes, London).

Gravelot returned to Paris in October 1745, apparently tired of accusations, in the hostile climate after the battle of Fontenoy, that he was a French spy. He is said to have taken home £10,000 in savings. Twenty years after his departure he was still receiving commissions from English booksellers. V. Salomons, who valued Gravelot's French work more, considered England to have stultified the engraver's natural artistic passion, which returned in full on his return to his homeland. He was as popular in France as in England, and produced illustrations for Boccaccio's *Decameron* (1757–61), Rousseau's *La nouvelle Héloïse* (1761), Voltaire's *Théatre de Pierre Corneille* (1764) and *Œuvres* (1768–74), the *Almanach iconologique* (1765–79), Ovid's *Metamorphoses* (1767–71), and Tasso's *Gerusalemme liberata* (1771).

Many years after the death of his first wife, Marie-Anne Luneau (1710–1759), he married, in November 1770, Jeanne Ménétier (*b.* 1736/7), who was nearly thirty years his junior. Apparently he failed to inform his family on the occasion of both his marriages; both were childless. On 20 April 1773, after an eight-day illness, Gravelot died at the Oratoire in St Germain l'Auxerrois, Paris. He was buried in the church of St Germain l'Auxerrois.

Gravelot is said once to have remarked that 'De English may be very clever in deir own opinions, but dey do not draw de draw' (Hammelmann, 39), and subsequent commentators have all agreed that Gravelot left British art more sophisticated than he found it. Brian Allen has discerned the influence of Gravelot on Francis Hayman's group portraits, which exhibit the relaxed informality of the Frenchman's work. Gravelot taught Thomas Gainsborough, whom he employed on his ornamental work for Rapin's *History of England*, and he is thought to have been a great influence on Gainsborough's formal and stylistic development. Thomas Major and Charles Grignion were also pupils. Echoes of his swirling engraved frames and theatrical interiors could still be discerned years after his departure in the work of Samuel Wale and Thomas Stothard.　　　　　　　　　　　　　　　M. G. SULLIVAN

Sources H. Hammelmann, *Book illustrators in eighteenth-century England*, ed. T. S. R. Boase (1975), 38–46 • E. Goncourt and J. Goncourt, *L'art du XVIIIme siècle* (1882) • V. Salomons, *Gravelot* (1911) • M. Snodin and E. Moncrieff, eds., *Rococo: art and design in Hogarth's England* (1984) [exhibition catalogue, V&A, 16 May – 30 Sept 1984] • K. Rorschach, 'Gravelot [Bourguignon, Hubert-Francois]', *The dictionary of art*, ed. J. Turner (1996) • Redgrave, *Artists* • M. Baker, 'Roubiliac's Argyll monument and the interpretation of eighteenth-century sculptor's designs', *Burlington Magazine*, 134 (1992), 785–97 • *DNB* • Vertue, *Note books* • B. Allen, *Francis Hayman* (1987) • S. Foister, R. Jones, and O. Meslay, *Young Gainsborough* (1997) [exhibition catalogue, National Gallery, London, 29 Jan – 31 March 1997, The Castle Museum, Norwich, 19 April – 15 June 1997, and The Laing Art Gallery, Newcastle, 21 June – 17 Aug 1997]
Likenesses Henriques, engraving, 1770 (after H. F. Gravelot) • C. E. Gaucher, line engraving, BM • H. F. Gravelot, self-portrait,

repro. in Salomons, *Gravelot* · J. Massard, line engraving (after M. Q. de La Tour), BM, NPG [*see illus.*]

Wealth at death surprisingly little: Salomons, *Gravelot*

Graves family (*per. c.*1812–1892), engravers, printsellers, and writers on art, came to prominence with **Robert Graves** (1798–1873), line engraver, who was born in Tottenham Court Road, London, on 7 May 1798 (some secondary sources give the month of his birth as November). His family originated from Yorkshire, although his father and grandfather became notable printsellers in London. The family business had been established in 1752 by his grandfather Robert Graves (*d.* 1802) in Catherine Street, Strand, and was continued in Pall Mall by his father, also Robert Graves (*d.* 1825), who was reputedly the best connoisseur of rare prints in his day, and who succeeded in getting all eight of his sons apprenticed in business connected with art.

The training of the third Robert Graves started in 1812, when he attended a life school in Ship Yard, Temple Bar, and became a pupil of John Romney, a line engraver. At an early date he received commissions to produce both facsimiles in pen and ink of rare engravings by masters such as Wenceslaus Hollar and William Faithorne (a technique in which his grandfather had also excelled) and bookplates. Some of his early work as an engraver was the reproduction of artists' work as book illustrations. His engraved portraits appeared, for instance, in James Caulfield's *Portraits, Memoirs and Characters of Remarkable Persons from the Revolution to the End of the Reign of George II* (1819–20), John Preston Neale's *History and Antiquities of the Abbey Church of St Peter's, Westminster* (1818–23), and Gilbert Burnet's *History of the Reformation* (1838). Interestingly, the last plate he completed was a portrait of Dickens after William P. Frith, which was used in John Forster's *The Life of Charles Dickens* (3 vols., 1872–4). Graves also engraved the illustrations for several celebrated pieces of prose and poetry, including a vignette by Richard Westall illustrating *Paradise Lost* for John Milton's *Poetical Works* (1835), and several illustrations such as *Ivanhoe* after William Boxall and *Anne of Geierstein* after William Mulready for an edition of Sir Walter Scott's Waverley novels in 1842. For more popular ephemera, such as the *Literary Souvenir*, *The Iris*, *Forget-me-Not*, and *The Amulet*, Graves produced engravings on steel plates after paintings by Murillo, Sir David Wilkie, Sir Thomas Lawrence, and other artists.

Once Graves started to exhibit his work, he tended to reproduce paintings as single large engravings rather than as book illustrations, even though some of them were reproduced in books. The first engraving he exhibited was a medallion portrait of Sir Mark Masterman Sykes which was shown at the launching exhibition of the Society of British Artists in 1824; it also adorned the sale catalogue of Sykes's notable print collection. Graves continued to exhibit at Suffolk Street until 1830, from various addresses: 40 Frederick Place (1824), 43 Seymour Street, Euston Square (1827), and Mornington Place, Hampstead Road (1829). On 15 February 1832 Graves married at St Pancras Old Church, Lucy Matilda Percy, with whom he had two sons. In 1836 he was elected an associate engraver of

the Royal Academy after the death of James Fittler, and from then on exhibited solely at the academy. He presented as his diploma picture *Lord Byron* after Thomas Phillips's half-length portrait of 1813. Further addresses for Graves are recorded in the Royal Academy's catalogues: 19 Grove Terrace (1837), Fitzroy Cottage (1846), and 20 Grove Terrace (1855), all in Kentish Town.

Although a few of Graves's exhibited engravings were after the work of old masters, such as Murillo's *Good Shepherd* (1863), the same artist's *Madonna* (1865), and Raphael's *Via dolorosa* (1869), most of his work reproduced paintings by contemporary British artists. He engraved several of Sir George Harvey's pictures, including *The Examination of Shakespeare* (1839) and *A Castaway* (1841) (both for the Association for the Promotion of the Fine Arts in Scotland), and several after Sir Edwin Landseer, including *The Highland Whisky-Still* (1842), which he engraved on steel and which was published by both the Art Union of London and Graves and Walmsley. It is arguably his best piece of work.

A number of Graves's plates were reproduced in the *Art Journal*, starting with his engraving after Charles Locke Eastlake's *Haidee, a Greek Girl* in 1850, and including three engravings of royal princesses after Sir Thomas Lawrence, Franz Winterhalter, and John S. Copley (in 1855, 1857, and 1860, respectively). A later venture to promote British painting was Graves's reproduction of a series of portraits by Thomas Gainsborough and Sir Joshua Reynolds, which were published by his brother Henry Graves [*see below*]. This scheme was launched with an engraving after Gainsborough's *The Hon. Mrs Graham* (exh. RA, 1866); it included a reproduction of Reynolds's *Mrs Lloyd* (1868), and was interrupted by Graves's death, so that his plate after Gainsborough's *Lady Bowater* had to be completed by James Stephenson.

Of Robert Graves's engravings, a contemporary wrote that they were 'characterised more by their refinement and delicacy—and in these qualities they [could] scarcely be surpassed—than by any remarkable vigour of line' (*Art Journal*). He trained only one pupil, John R. Jackson, from 1836, who took to working in mezzotint, producing a portrait of his master in this manner. Another portrait of Graves was engraved by one of his sons, Frederick Percy, who went on to become a landscape artist; his other son, Robert Edmund, worked at the British Library. Robert Graves died on 28 February 1873, at his home, 20 Grove Terrace, Highgate Road, Kentish Town, London, and was buried on 6 March in Highgate cemetery, in the vault of his brother Henry. His wife survived him. Proof impressions of his engravings are in the British Museum and the Victoria and Albert Museum, London.

Robert Graves's younger brother **Henry Graves** (1806–1892), printseller and fine art publisher, was born on 16 July 1806. At sixteen he was employed by the art dealer Samuel Woodburn at 112 St Martin's Lane, and later became manager of the print department of Messrs Hurst, Robinson & Co., the successors of John Boydell, at 90 Cheapside, then at 6 Pall Mall. When this firm failed in 1826, Henry Graves purchased much of its print stock jointly with Francis Graham Moon and Thomas Boys. This new partnership became one of the three leading London printsellers, alongside Thomas McLean and Thomas Agnew, and by 1829 it was able to issue a substantial catalogue of engravings. Many of the partnership's engravings were printed from steel plates. On 6 January 1831 Henry Graves married at St James's, Westminster, Mary Squire (d. 1871), with whom he had two sons, Boydell and Algernon *Graves (1845–1922), who was a compiler of dictionaries of artists.

When both Moon and Boys pulled out of the publishing venture, in 1833 and 1835 respectively, Henry Graves remained at Pall Mall. He found a new partner in Richard Hodgson between 1834 and 1841. Together they published *A Catalogue of Engravings after the Finest Pictures of the Schools of Europe* in May 1836, and advertised their prints regularly in the *Art Union* (a journal which was founded partly on capital laid down by Hodgson). This partnership achieved some success, for it could afford to buy the old stock of the printseller Martin Colnaghi in February 1839, and was appointed that same year to be 'Her Majesty's printsellers and publishers in Ordinary'.

After Hodgson moved away, Graves joined forces for a time with a Mr Warmsley. Together they advertised sixty-seven 'recently published' works in the *Art Union* of June 1843. By 1844, however, Graves was trading alone, using the name Henry Graves & Co. He received assistance from 1838 from his brother Francis (b. 25 Dec 1802, d. 15 Oct 1859), who had served an apprenticeship with A. Molteno of Pall Mall from 1815 and gained experience at Colnaghis of Cockspur Street (1826).

At the height of his career Henry Graves was recognized as the pre-eminent London printseller, and was responsible for publishing many fine engravings after the work of famous painters. As one of Graves's contemporaries put it, he was not so much 'a discoverer of new talent' as someone who was good at 'knowing what would take the public taste, and of sparing neither money nor pains in bringing such work before the public' (*The Times*). For instance, about 1845 he published lithographs of sketches after artists including Sir Augustus Wall Callcott, Samuel Prout, Sir David Wilkie, and Clarkson Stanfield. Additionally, between 1860 and 1880 he issued important library editions of prints after Sir Joshua Reynolds, Thomas Gainsborough, and Sir Thomas Lawrence, among others. Another artist whose work he helped to popularize was Sir Edwin Landseer. He organized in 1873/4 an exhibition of engravings of Landseer's work in Piccadilly (the catalogue was compiled by his son Algernon), and then arranged for twenty engravings of the artist's paintings of Queen Victoria's pet dogs to be engraved by Thomas Landseer, Charles Lewis, and others. Hunnisett recorded: 'It was said that Landseer received over £500,000 from Graves for the engraving of his pictures' (Hunnisett, 149).

Henry Graves became masterful at protecting his interests as a publisher, often appearing in court to do so. In 1855, for instance, he summoned the engraver Charles Lewis before a magistrate for having failed to produce a plate of a picture after Landseer within the set time of two years, and was awarded damages. Only once did he lose a great deal of money, when a fire broke out on 6 December 1867 in his premises and destroyed several galleries full of paintings and engravings. While he lost much property and was not fully insured (which may explain why the surviving pictures from his gallery were auctioned off at Christies on 7 March 1868), other people suffered too. Dixon, the printer, for instance, who had sent about a hundred plates of portraits to Graves for safe-keeping, learned that they had all been irrevocably damaged by fire and water, and that their defacing had been made complete by Algernon Graves with a penknife!

Aside from making his name in business, Henry Graves became known as an active figure in public life. He was a member of both the Printsellers' Association and the Artists' General Benevolent Institution. He also had links with the Pattenmakers' and Cutlers' companies, being elected master to both guilds on several occasions during the 1860s and 1870s, and lending many paintings to an exhibition of general, surgical, and sword cutlery at the Cutlers' Company in May 1879. Furthermore, he was a governor of the Shakespeare Memorial Theatre at Stratford, and bequeathed to this institution ten paintings and 100 prints. To the National Portrait Gallery he bequeathed portraits of the engravers John Boydell and John Burnett, as well as a portrait of himself by William M. Tweedie. He died in his house at 6 Pall Mall, London, on 23 August 1892, and was buried in Highgate cemetery; his first wife, Mary Squire, had predeceased him by some twenty-one years, while his second, Annie, outlived him. A deceased daughter, Emily Jane, is mentioned in his will.

SUSANNA AVERY-QUASH

Sources *Art Journal*, new ser., 12 (1873), 125 [Robert Graves (1798–1873)] · *ILN* (8–15 March 1873) [Robert Graves] · *The Athenaeum* (3 Sept 1892) [Henry Graves 11309] · *The Times* (24 Aug 1892) [Henry Graves] · G. W. Friend, *Index of painters and engravers with the titles of their work declared at the office of the Printsellers' Association, London* (1894) · *Engraved Brit. ports.* · Graves, *RA exhibitors* · W. Sandby, *The history of the Royal Academy of Arts*, 2 (1862), 222–3 · J. H. Slater, *Engravings and their value*, 6th edn (1929), 353 · *DNB* [Robert Graves] · *DNB* [Henry Graves] · R. K. Engen, *Dictionary of Victorian engravers, print publishers and their works* (1979) · F. Lugt, *Les marques de collections de dessins et d'estampes* (Amsterdam, 1921); repr. (The Hague, 1956) · Redgrave, *Artists* · Bryan, *Painters* (1903–5) · Thieme & Becker, *Allgemeines Lexikon* · B. Hunnisett, *Steel engraved book illustration in England* (1980), 39, 104, 174, 211, 214 · B. Hunnisett, *Engraved on steel: the history of picture production using steel plates* (1998), 91, 99, 102–3, 145, 147–50 · B. Hunnisett, *An illustrated dictionary of British steel engravers*, new edn (1989) · Boase, *Mod. Eng. biog.* · J. Johnson, ed., *Works exhibited at the Royal Society of British Artists, 1824–1893, and the New English Art Club, 1888–1917*, 2 vols. (1975) · *IGI* [Henry Graves 11309] · *CGPLA Eng. & Wales* (1873) [Robert Graves] · *CGPLA Eng. & Wales* (1893) [Henry Graves]

Archives V&A

Likenesses T. L. Atkinson, engraving (Henry Graves; after W. M. Tweedie), BM, NPG · J. J. Chant, engraving (Henry Graves; after W. M. Tweedie), BM, NPG · R. Graves, engraving (Henry Graves; after W. M. Tweedie), BM, NPG · F. Hull, engraving (Henry Graves; after W. M. Tweedie), BM, NPG · H. S. Mendelssohn, photograph (Henry Graves), NPG · C. Mottram, engraving (Henry Graves; after W. M. Tweedie), BM, NPG · R. B. Parkes, engraving (Henry Graves; after W. M. Tweedie), BM, NPG · G. Sanders, engraving (Henry Graves; after W. M. Tweedie), BM, NPG · F. Sandys, chalk drawing

(Henry Graves), NPG · J. Scott, engraving (Henry Graves; after W. M. Tweedie), BM, NPG · W. H. Simmons, engraving (Henry Graves; after W. M. Tweedie), BM, NPG · E. A. Smith, engraving (Henry Graves; after W. M. Tweedie), BM, NPG · J. Stephenson, engraving (Henry Graves; after W. M. Tweedie), BM, NPG · J. Watkins, photograph (Robert Graves), repro. in Hunnisett, *Illustrated dictionary*, 42 · G. Zobel, engraving (Henry Graves; after W. M. Tweedie), BM, NPG

Wealth at death under £1000—Robert Graves: probate, 30 July 1873, *CGPLA Eng. & Wales* · £4448 17s. od.—Henry Graves: probate, 18 Jan 1893, *CGPLA Eng. & Wales*

Graves, Alfred Perceval (1846–1931), poet and educationist, was born on 22 July 1846 at 12 Fitzwilliam Square, Dublin, second of the eight children of Charles *Graves (1812–1899), bishop of Limerick from 1866, and his wife, Selina, eldest daughter of John *Cheyne (1777–1836), physician-general to the forces in Ireland. The Graves family had for several generations contributed with distinction to scholarship and to the learned professions in Ireland, notably in the persons of Alfred's great-great-uncle Richard *Graves, the dean of Ardagh (1763–1829); his first cousin twice removed the physician Robert James *Graves (1796–1853); his uncle the biographer and vice-warden of Alexandra College, Dublin, Robert Perceval Graves (1810–1893); and his father, a fellow of the Royal Society and professor of mathematics and fellow of Trinity College, Dublin. From 1856 Alfred was educated at Windermere College; but when in 1860 his father was appointed dean of the Chapel Royal, he was privately tutored at their home in Dublin Castle. In 1864 he went up to Trinity College, Dublin, where he later won a university scholarship in classics; but in 1867 he joined the English civil service before completing his degree course.

In London this mustachioed young man with regular features, blue eyes, flaming red hair, and a sensitive expression, combined the duties of a clerkship in the Home Office with literary work, and contributed lively poems to *Punch*, the *Gentleman's Magazine*, and other periodicals. Graves's first book of poems, *Songs of Killarney* (1873) was well received, especially by *The Spectator*, to which he became a regular contributor. On 29 December 1874 he married Jane Cooper (d. 1886), eldest daughter of James Cooper of Cooper's Hill, near Limerick, of a family whose members were renowned for their beauty.

In 1875 Graves (often known as APG) became an inspector of schools. While an assistant inspector in Manchester, he collaborated with his colleague Rice-Wiggin on *The Elementary School Manager* (1879), which became the standard work in this field. In 1880, promoted to full inspector, he took charge of the West Riding district of Yorkshire. Encouraged by Tennyson to regard poetry as his principal calling, he published *Irish Songs and Ballads* (1880). Two years later, his wife seriously ill with tuberculosis, he moved to Taunton, from where he ran the west Somerset district, and published his *Songs of Old Ireland* (1882), in collaboration with his boyhood companion C. V. Stanford. Graves, who wrote the words and adapted them to old Irish folk tunes chiefly derived from George Petrie's collection, parted outright with fifty songs for £80. He

therefore made only £1 12s. from 'Father O'Flynn', which (originally published in *The Spectator* back in 1875), became world-famous after being sung by Charles Santley at a concert in the early eighties.

In 1886 Graves was left a widower with three sons (one of whom, Philip, later became a notable foreign correspondent for *The Times*) and two daughters. The family remained at Taunton; and in 1888–9 Graves and his brothers Arnold and Charles Larcom Graves of *Punch* published (under Charles's name) two volumes of satirical verse on the Irish home rule question: *The Blarney Ballads* and *The Green above the Red*. On 30 December 1891 Graves married Amalie (Amy) Elizabeth Sophie (1857–1951), eldest daughter of Heinrich Ritter von Ranke (1830–1909), professor of paediatrics at Munich University, and great-niece of the historian Leopold von Ranke, who had married Graves's aunt Clarissa many years previously. In 1893 Graves was appointed to the metropolitan district of Southwark. He moved to Wimbledon, where his eighth and Amy's third child, Robert von Ranke *Graves, later to become famous as a poet and novelist, was born on 24 July 1895.

Graves was the founder of educational councils in Southwark, in Battersea, and in numerous other boroughs, chiefly in London, but some as far afield as Taunton and Norwich. The councils did especially good work in providing playgrounds and playing fields, an enterprise dear to Graves's heart. In June 1904 his article advocating organized games in primary schools appeared in the *Contemporary Review*; and in due course his proposals were adopted both in New Zealand and in Great Britain, where they passed into law in 1906. After his retirement in 1910 Graves promoted the educational use of the cinema, and was active as chairman of the representative managers of the London county council schools (1911–19).

Graves (a devout protestant, who was reputed never to have made an enemy) had presided in 1891 over the inaugural meeting of the Irish Literary Society of London, of which he was twice president. He also helped to establish the Welsh Folk Song Society; and (as author, editor, anthologist, and songwriter) made an enormous contribution in over thirty publications to the dissemination of Irish and Welsh culture, not least in Stanford's *National Song Book* (1906), a standard work in the British classroom for forty years. In 1912 Graves was installed as a Welsh bard under the name Canwr Cilarne (singer of Killarney); and in 1919 he retired to Erinfa, his holiday home at Harlech in north Wales. There he organized and wrote the greater part of the books for the historical pageants of 1920, 1922, and 1927, and his autobiography, *To Return to All That* (1930), the title and penultimate chapter of which were in reply to his son Robert's *Goodbye to All That* (1929).

Graves died peacefully of heart failure at Erinfa on 27 December 1931, and was buried on the 31st in Harlech churchyard beneath a Celtic cross. He was survived by Amy and by his ten children.

RICHARD PERCEVAL GRAVES

Sources A. P. Graves, *To return to all that* (1930) · R. P. Graves, *Robert Graves: the assault heroic, 1895–1926* (1986) · R. P. Graves, *Robert Graves:*

the years with Laura Riding, 1926–1940 (1990) • R. von R. Graves, *Goodbye to all that* (1929) • Graves family Bible, priv. coll. • personal knowledge (2004) **Archives** NL Ire., corresp. • NL Wales, letters • TCD, corresp. and literary papers | BL, corresp. with Society of Authors, Add. MSS 56715, 63254 • NL Wales, letters to T. Gwynn Jones • NYPL, Berg collection, includes diaries 1911–31 • Royal Society of Literature, London, letters to the Royal Society of Literature • U. Leeds, Brotherton L., letters to Clement Shorter • University College, Dublin, letters to D. J. O'Donoghue **Likenesses** photograph, repro. in Graves, *Robert Graves: the years with Laura* • photographs, priv. coll. • portrait, repro. in Graves, *To return to all that*, frontispiece • six photographs, repro. in Graves, *Robert Graves: the assault heroic* **Wealth at death** £7391 0s. 6d.: probate, 1 April 1932, CGPLA Eng. & Wales

Graves, Algernon (1845–1922), writer on art, was born on 24 February 1845 at 6 Pall Mall, London, the second son of Henry *Graves (1806–1892) [see under Graves family], print publisher, and his first wife, Mary Squire (d. 1871). He trained at the family firm of Henry Graves & Co. and ran the business after his father's death. In his spare time Graves undertook research for catalogues of the work of the celebrated English painters, Sir Edwin Landseer (1875), Samuel Cousins (c.1887) and Sir Joshua Reynolds (with W. V. Cronin; 4 vols., 1899–1901). Graves also supplied engravings for a book about the exhibited and engraved works of Sir Thomas Lawrence (1900) and another to accompany an exhibition of sixty of Lawrence's drawings (1913) held at the Edward Gallery, 26 King Street, St James's, London. These publications reproduce numerous engravings by his uncle, Robert *Graves (1798–1873) [see under Graves family].

Graves's best-known and most innovative publications are lists enumerating works of art exhibited in various London venues. Graves later recorded how, when convalescing after a fall on his twenty-eighth birthday, 'the idea suddenly occurred to [him] that to arrange the painters alphabetically would be a valuable work'. Since his handwritten lists proved 'at once … of great importance in [his] father's business, as well as being constantly referred to by [his] friends outside', he decided to publish a summary of them (Graves, *RA exhibitors*, vii–viii). The result was *A Dictionary of Artists who have Exhibited Works in the Principal London Exhibitions from 1760 to 1880* (1884), revised and enlarged (to include more venues and exhibitions up to 1893) in 1895 and 1901. Graves also used his fifty manuscript volumes to generate publications about individual institutions, each comprising a more detailed list of contributors and their work than had been possible in his earliest dictionary. An eight-volume work, *The Royal Academy of Arts: a Complete Dictionary of Contributors and their Work from its Foundation in 1769 to 1904*, was the first to be published in 1905–6. This was followed by similar volumes for the Society of Artists of Great Britain, 1760–1791, the Free Society of Artists, 1761–1783 (1907) and the British Institution, 1806–1867 (1908). Finally, Graves compiled the five-volume *A Century of Loan Exhibitions, 1813–1912* (1913–15). Taking his compilation work yet further, Graves published a *Summary of and Index to Waagen* (1912), comprising indexes of the paintings and owners mentioned chiefly in

Gustav Waagen's *Treasures of Art in Great Britain*, 4 vols. (1854–7). Finally he produced a three-volume list, *Art Sales from Early in the Eighteenth Century to Early in the Twentieth Century* (1918–21).

Attractively produced—many were printed by the Chiswick Press—Graves's publications were also notable for the new information they contained. In *The Royal Academy of Arts*, for example, Graves thanked the earl of Rosebery for permission to study his set of catalogues annotated by Horace Walpole, and in his *A History of the Works of Sir Joshua Reynolds, P. R. A.* (1899–1901) Graves stated that he was the first to utilize information from the artist's payment ledgers (which he owned) and from private sources, including Reynolds's descendants. Graves's Reynolds catalogue was widely admired, and continued to be regarded as highly authoritative for many years after his death. Though it was subject to criticism in the twentieth century, not least from the influential art historian Ellis Waterhouse, its usefulness to scholars has once again been recognized by David Mannings in his own *catalogue raisonné* (*Sir Joshua Reynolds: a Complete Catalogue of his Paintings*, 2000, 2.20).

The contemporary response to Graves's publishing initiatives was positive. Both Queen Victoria and Edward VII allowed Graves to dedicate several publications to them, while the list of subscribers to his reference work on Waagen includes the names of many leading art galleries, printsellers, and noblemen. Graves was made a fellow of the Society of Arts, a title he first used in his book on Reynolds.

Graves resided at various London addresses. He was twice married. Little is known of his first marriage, though he had several sons; the youngest, Herbert Seymour, who helped to compile the later editions of *A Dictionary of Artists*, died in 1898. He was outlived by his second wife, Madeline Lilian (Sophia) Wakeling, née Walker (b. 1871/2) whom he married on 2 July 1919 at the register office, St Marylebone; she was also widowed, with two daughters, Dorothy and Gladys. Graves died on 5 February 1922 at his home, 77 New Cavendish Street, Marylebone, and was buried three days later at Brompton cemetery.

SUSANNA AVERY-QUASH

Sources *The Times* (7 Feb 1922), 1 • preface, Graves, *RA exhibitors* • preface, Graves, *Artists*, all edns • preface, Graves, *Soc. Artists* • preface, Graves, *Brit. Inst.* • preface, A. Graves, *Summary of and index to Waagen* (1912) • 'list of subscribers', A. Graves, *Summary of and index to Waagen* (1912) • A. Graves and W. V. Cronin, introduction, *A history of the works of Sir Joshua Reynolds*, 4 vols. (1899–1901) • b. cert. • m. cert. **Archives** V&A NAL, MSS for subsequently published dictionaries **Likenesses** R. Corder, oils, 1878, repro. in A. Graves, *Art sales from early in the eighteenth century to early in the twentieth century*, 1 (1918) • A. Zeitlin, plaster bust, 1901, NPG **Wealth at death** £2355 12s. 5d.: probate, 24 March 1922, CGPLA Eng. & Wales

Graves, Charles (1812–1899), bishop of Limerick and mathematician, was born in Dublin on 6 November 1812. He was the youngest son of John Crosbie Graves, chief police magistrate of Dublin, and of Helena, daughter of the Revd Charles Perceval of Templehouse, co. Sligo. He went to a private school near Bristol and then, in 1829, entered Trinity College, Dublin, where he was elected to a foundation scholarship in 1832, a distinction then given only to those proficient in classics. Intended originally for the army, he became an expert swordsman and rider, played cricket for his university, and later in life did much boating and fly-fishing. In 1835 he graduated as the first senior moderator and gold medallist in mathematics and mathematical physics. In 1836 he obtained the rare distinction of election to a fellowship on a first candidature. In 1840 he married Selina (d. 1873), daughter of Dr John Cheyne; they had five sons, including the poet and educationist Alfred Perceval *Graves, and four daughters.

In 1841 Graves made an important mathematical contribution when he published *On the General Properties of Cones of the Second Degree and of Spherical Conics*, translated from the work by Chasles. In the copious notes appended to this translation he gave a number of new theorems of much interest, which he arrived at principally by Chasles's methods. The most remarkable of these was his extension of the construction of an ellipse, as traced by a pencil which strains a thread passing over two fixed points, by substituting for the points a given ellipse, with which he showed that the locus is confocal. This he deduced from the more general theorem in spherical conics that if two spherical conics have the same cyclic arcs, then any arc touching the inner curve will cut off from the outer a segment of constant area. Bertrand's famous treatise on integral calculus (1864) attributed Graves's theorem to Chasles, who arrived at it later by an independent investigation. In a long appendix to the volume Graves gave a method of treating curves on a sphere corresponding to the Cartesian method on the plane, arcs of great circles taking the place of right lines. This work was greatly admired by Sylvester and other distinguished mathematicians, but their high expectations of its usefulness were never fulfilled.

This was Graves's only published mathematical work. His other pieces of original research were either embedded in his lectures as professor or in papers read before, and published by, the Royal Irish Academy. During this period Sir William Hamilton, McCullagh, and Humphry Lloyd were also members, and the meetings were often used to announce the results of scientific investigation and research undertaken at the University of Dublin.

While Hamilton was explaining in a series of communications his new calculus of quaternions, several contemporary mathematicians simultaneously came up with more or less analogous systems which also involved new imaginaries. Graves proposed a system of algebraic triplets of this kind, but it never had the importance of his work on quaternions, being a mathematical curiosity rather than a valuable working method.

Other papers by Graves, published by the Royal Irish Academy, related to the theory of differential equations, to the equation of Laplace's functions, and to curves traced on surfaces of the second degree. He also gave some important applications of the calculus of operations to the calculus of variations, and arrived at an elegant and simple demonstration, by the operational method, of Jacobi's celebrated theorem for distinguishing between maxima and minima values in the application of the calculus of variations.

Graves's scholarly interests were linguistic as well as mathematical, and he became particularly interested by the ogham inscriptions, an alphabet of twenty characters used in ancient Britain and Ireland. He made a project out of applying to them the accepted methods for the decipherment of writings, known or presumed to be alphabetical, and thus gave readings and renderings of a number of the inscriptions on cromlechs and other stone monuments. He also published some *Suggestions* on the Brehon laws in 1851, which brought before the government the importance of having these old Irish laws edited and translated by competent scholars. Graves was appointed to the Historic Manuscripts Commission, which helped bring this into effect.

In 1843 Graves was chosen professor of mathematics in the University of Dublin in succession to James McCullagh. He was made dean of the Chapel Royal, Dublin, in 1860 and dean of Clonfert in 1864. He was elevated to the bishopric of Limerick, Ardfert, and Aghadoe in 1866, being one of the last bishops appointed before the disestablishment of the Irish church. He held that office for thirty-three years until his death.

In 1837, having been elected a member of the Royal Irish Academy, Graves successively filled the offices of secretary of the council and secretary of the academy, and served as president from 1861 to 1866. He was elected a fellow of the Royal Society in 1880, and was given the honorary degree of DCL by the University of Oxford in 1881. He died at Portobello House, Dublin, on 17 July 1899, and was buried in Limerick Cathedral churchyard. A monument to his memory was placed in the cathedral bearing a Latin inscription translated into English and Irish.

Graves's work was characterized by symmetry and elegance, of both method and results, which matched his literary and artistic tastes. His breadth of learning meant that he was as comfortable with mathematical theories as he was with ecclesiastical affairs. He was the last of the great antiquarian scholar–bishops. His broadmindedness, dignity, and personal charm made him an agreeable companion. His friends included Wordsworth, Mendelssohn, Huxley, Froude, and Matthew Arnold. However, he was not a great preacher, and as he grew older the diocesan business was increasingly devolved to other clergy. Nevertheless, his moderate approach to church affairs and his long experience made him a highly valued member of the house of bishops. Yet it is his mathematical and antiquarian endeavours which probably provide his most important legacy.

BENJAMIN WILLIAMSON, rev. DAVID HUDDLESTON

Sources *The Times* (18 July 1899), 10 · *WW* (1898) · J. B. Leslie, *Ardfert and Aghadoe clergy and parishes* (1940) · H. Cotton, *Fasti ecclesiae Hibernicae*, 6 (1878) · J. B. Leslie, ed., *Clergy of Connor: from Patrician*

times to the present day (1993) • H. E. Patton, *Fifty years of disestablishment* (1922) • R. B. McDowell, *The Church of Ireland, 1869–1969* (1975) • *CGPLA Ire.* (1899)
Archives Representative Church Body Library, Dublin, corresp. and papers • Royal Irish Acad., papers relating to Irish antiquities • TCD, corresp. and papers | Bodl. Oxf., corresp. with Lord Kimberley • Limerick University Library, letters to Lord Dunraven • NL Ire., letters to Lord Emly • NL Ire., Monsell MSS • PRO NIre., Wyndham-Quin MSS • TCD, corresp. with Sir W. R. Hamilton
Likenesses J. H. Foley, marble relief, NG Ire. • Lafayette, photograph, repro. in *ILN* (29 July 1899) • S. Purser, portrait, Royal Irish Acad.
Wealth at death £45,402 16s. 5d.: resworn probate, Feb 1900, *CGPLA Eng. & Wales* (1899) • £4388 15s. 0d.: probate, 7 Nov 1899, *CGPLA Ire.*

Graves, George Windsor (1873–1949), comedian, was born at 13 Mare Street, Hackney, London, on 2 January 1873, the youngest child of Thomas Graves, a publican, and his second wife, Martha Alice, daughter of John Mulvey, a compositor. From early childhood it was his desire to be an actor although he had no theatrical ancestry. He left Margate College at the age of ten when his father died, and at fourteen entered a solicitor's office, but found it little to his liking. There followed a series of dead-end jobs, most of which he lost through practical joking. In 1896 he had his first professional engagement on the stage and toured the country; he went on to tour the world, and appeared in Russia in 1899 in the George Edwardes productions of *A Runaway Girl*, *The Shop Girl*, and *The Geisha*.

Graves's first appearance in pantomime—and he became a great pantomime comedian—was at the Prince's Theatre, Manchester, in 1900, as the Emperor of China in *Aladdin*. His first London success was at the Prince of Wales's Theatre, on 9 May 1903, as General Marchmont in *The School Girl*, a musical comedy. He had then been on the stage for only seven years, but he presented something quite new in the way of comic elderly men. From that success he never looked back. He had a clear-cut, incisive style, a number of curious mannerisms, and a most distinctive voice. He developed a wonderful propensity for 'gagging'—he was in that respect second only to Arthur Roberts, and convulsed not only the audience but his fellow players by jokes invented on the spur of the moment. Modern commentators, indeed, regard him as a highly popular but often destructive comedian, 'inclined to give his own stand-up performance regardless of the show' (Gänzl, 577).

Graves had a long and distinguished career as a comedian in the very front rank of musical comedy, playing comedy lead in no fewer than seven Drury Lane pantomimes between 1909 and 1915. He was also well known on the music-halls, where he appeared in sketches, notably 'Koffo of Bond Street' and 'The key of the flat'. He was just as popular in revue. Perhaps his greatest success was as Baron Popoff in *The Merry Widow* at Daly's Theatre in 1907. His amazing discourses on the adventures of 'Hetty the Hen' were never forgotten by those who heard them. Nor had his performance of General Des Ifs in *The Little Michus* at the same theatre in 1905 been far behind in brilliance.

In that he invented a strange little creature called 'the Gazeka' which became 'all the rage'.

On 23 February 1901 Graves married Lillian Josephine, daughter of an actor, Thomas Finnellan Doyle. The couple had a daughter, but later divorced. On 19 September 1918 he married the actress Madge Compton, daughter of George Mussared. This marriage was also dissolved and in 1927 Graves married Flora Emily Sarah, daughter of the late Foster Richard Courtenay, an actor.

However much Graves clowned and gagged, he always remained in character and in the general picture, for he was an excellent actor apart from his amazing gifts of comedy, and possessed a fine stage sense. One of his last big successes was in the long-running musical show *Me and my Girl*, first produced at the Victoria Palace in 1937, in which he gave a memorable performance of a rich and fruity county gentleman of title, Sir John Tremayne. He had success in films as well and was one of the best-known men of his time, almost a household word. His dressing-room was full of surprising gadgets, such as chairs which collapsed when sat upon, glasses which dripped all over their users, or cigars which blew up. He could never resist a joke, practical or otherwise. This did not always endear him to his colleagues. He was a member of the Savage Club, a follower of sport, a regular attendant at race meetings and big fights, and a keen card player. One of the last great gagsters and individualists of the actor–manager period, he died on 2 April 1949 at Nuffield House, Guy's Hospital, London, active to the very last.

W. J. Macqueen-Pope, *rev.*

Sources K. Gänzl, *The encyclopedia of the musical theatre*, 2 vols. (1994) • G. W. Graves, *Gaieties and gravities: the autobiography of a comedian* (1931) • personal knowledge (1959) • *The picturegoer's who's who and encyclopaedia* (1933) • J. Parker, ed., *The green room book, or, Who's who on the stage* (1907) • *The Times* (5 April 1949) • *CGPLA Eng. & Wales* (1949) • b. cert. • m. cert. [Lillian Doyle] • m. cert. [Madge Mussared] • d. cert.
Archives FILM BFI NFTVA, peformance footage | SOUND BL NSA, performance recording
Likenesses E. Kapp, drawing, 1919, Barber Institute of Fine Arts, Birmingham • C. Buchel and Hassall, lithograph, NPG
Wealth at death £38,550 18s. 1d.: probate, 28 June 1949, *CGPLA Eng. & Wales*

Graves, Henry (1806–1892). *See under* Graves family (*per. c.*1812–1892).

Graves, James (1815–1886), archaeologist, eldest son of the Revd Richard Graves, was born in the town of Kilkenny on 11 October 1815. He was educated by his father, who ran a classical school. He graduated BA at Trinity College, Dublin, in 1839 and became a clergyman of the protestant Episcopalian church in the diocese of Ossory. He was curate of Skeirke, Queen's county (1846–54); rector of Maine (1854–60); vicar of Kilsheelan, Clonmel, co. Tipperary (1860–63); and rector of Inisnag, near Kilkenny (1863–86).

Through the influence of a relative, J. G. A. Prim, editor and subsequently proprietor of the *Kilkenny Moderator*, Graves became interested in archaeology and wrote articles on his findings for the newspaper. Research by Graves and Prim on the ancient topography of Kilkenny was included in a volume of annals of Ireland edited by the Revd Richard Butler (1849).

In May 1849 Graves and Prim helped to establish the Kilkenny Archaeological Society for the preservation, examination, and illustration of ancient monuments of Irish history, manners, customs, and arts, especially as connected with the county and city of Kilkenny. The first edition of its journal appeared in 1850. In 1857 Graves and Prim published on the history, architecture, and antiquities of the cathedral church of St Canice, Kilkenny. Its illustrations were taken from measured drawings by Graves. This was part of a projected work on the history of the diocese of Ossory, which was never completed. In 1869 the Kilkenny Archaeological Society became the Royal Historical and Archaeological Association of Ireland, and Graves became editor of its journal. He was aided by Prim, who died in 1875. Graves was awarded a government pension of £100 in 1878 for his services to literature. He is known to have been married. He died at home at Inisnag rectory on 20 March 1886.

As well as his work with Prim, Graves wrote a life of Ormond and edited a number of manuscripts for publication. His obituary in the *Irish Times* spoke of him as a leader of a new race of Irish scholars.

J. T. GILBERT, *rev.* MARIE-LOUISE LEGG

Sources *Journal of the Royal Historical and Archaeological Association of Ireland*, 4th ser., 7 (1885–6), 467–9 · *The Times* (29 March 1886) · *CGPLA Ire.* (1886) · *CGPLA Eng. & Wales* (1886)
Archives NL Ire., MS account of Raths and Duns in Ireland · NL Ire., papers and transcripts relating to Irish history · PRO NIre., papers relating to history of diocese of Ossory · Representative Church Body Library, Dublin, collection relating to history of diocese of Ossory
Wealth at death £1135 15s. effects in England: probate, 7 June 1886, *CGPLA Eng. & Wales* · £4208 4s. 10d.: probate, 7 June 1886, *CGPLA Ire.*

Graves, John James (1832–1903), schoolmaster and advocate of teachers' associations, was born on 15 January 1832 at Chesterton, near Cambridge, the son of John and Sarah Graves. He was the eldest of eight children, six of whom survived childhood. His father was a shoemaker who in 1835 moved to Cambridge, where John James attended the national school. In 1844 the family moved to Meppershall, Bedfordshire, where his father took charge of the village school, with his two oldest sons acting as monitors. In 1846 John James (now aged fourteen) went to London, where he attended the central school of the National Society at Westminster before becoming an assistant at St Anne's Anglican charity school in Soho. In 1847 he became an assistant at St Paul's School, Cambridge, and in 1848 was appointed master of the school at Saleby in Lincolnshire.

On 3 March 1851 Graves married Elizabeth Ann Lister of Saleby and in the same year he and his wife were appointed to take joint charge of the school at Hanging Houghton, near Lamport, Northamptonshire. Graves had attended a teachers' mutual improvement society at Cambridge in 1847–8 and, on moving to Lamport, joined the Northampton Church Teachers' Association which had

been founded in 1846 with clergy support to hold monthly lectures and demonstration lessons. He also attended the first meeting of the Associated Body of Church Schoolmasters (ABCS) held in London in 1853, and in 1855, as secretary of the Northampton association, put before the ABCS a resolution in favour of admitting Anglican clergymen to membership. This was defeated by a large majority but, despite this defeat and his relative youthfulness, Graves was elected secretary of the ABCS in 1857. While remaining a firm supporter of the church system of education, he became a champion of teaching as a profession in its own right. He vigorously defended the teachers against the criticisms made in the Newcastle report (1861) but the imposition of the revised code in 1862 seemed to demonstrate the futility of the teachers' associations and Graves resigned as secretary of the ABCS in 1863. He was, however, re-elected three years later and re-formed the local associations into a General Association of Church Teachers, which played a key role in the movement towards a united profession.

The extension of the franchise in 1867 stimulated discussion of the need for universal, compulsory elementary education and in 1868 the church schoolmasters formed a London association to bring their views before parliament. In April 1870 a joint conference was held with the nonconformist teachers' associations which agreed to support a general system of Bible teaching, with a conscience clause similar to that adopted in the Education Act of that year. In June a meeting representing teachers of all denominations agreed to establish a National Union of Elementary Teachers and elected Graves as its first president. His presidential address in September 1870 combined good sense and idealism in equal proportions. The union dropped the word 'Elementary' from its title in 1889 and Graves continued to serve on the executive of the union until 1900. In that year he was able to claim that many improvements had taken place in the status and position of the teacher, including better salaries, pensions on retirement, modifications in the code, and the abolition of payment by results.

Graves was chairman of the Schoolmistress Newspaper Company, one of the founders of the Church Teachers' Benevolent Institution, and several times president of the Northampton and District Teachers' Association. He was, however, content to remain as the village schoolmaster and choirmaster at Lamport. His wife Elizabeth died in 1882 and on 21 May 1885 he married Georgiana Perkins (d. 1919), schoolteacher at nearby Maidwell, when he was fifty-three and she thirty-three. With his first wife he had two sons, but the eldest died in 1874 and the second in infancy; there were no children of his second marriage. In the 1880s Graves was secretary of the Brixworth Conservative Association and in the 1890s served on the Brixworth Board of Guardians. He retired from the mastership of Lamport school in 1901 and died at Scaldwell, Northamptonshire, on 31 January 1903, of pernicious anaemia. He was buried at Lamport, where a memorial plaque was installed in the church by his fellow teachers. He was a man of firm convictions but without strong personal ambition, and it was said of him that 'he worked simply for teachers'. MALCOLM SEABORNE

Sources M. Seaborne and G. Isham, *A Victorian schoolmaster: John James Graves* (1967) · *Northampton Mercury* (6 Feb 1903) · *The Northampton Herald* (7 Feb 1903) · *The Schoolmaster* (7 Feb 1903) · *The Schoolmaster* (14 Feb 1903) · M. Seaborne and G. Isham, 'A Victorian schoolmaster: John James Graves, 1832–1903', *Northamptonshire Past and Present*, 4 (1966–72), 3–12, 107–19 · G. Isham, 'J. J. Graves's first wife', *Northamptonshire Past and Present*, 4 (1966–72), 389 · D. de Cogan, 'More light on John James Graves of Lamport', *Northamptonshire Past and Present*, 7 (1983–8), 101–5 · A. Tropp, *The school teachers* (1957)
Archives Northants. RO, Lamport and Hanging Houghton charities collection
Likenesses photograph, NUT, Hamilton House, London
Wealth at death £1547 5s. 10d.: probate, 16 March 1903, CGPLA Eng. & Wales

Graves, John Thomas (1806–1870), jurist and mathematician, born in Dublin on 4 December 1806, was the eldest son of John Crosbie Graves, barrister, grandnephew of Richard Graves DD and cousin of Robert James Graves MD. After attending a school run by the Revd Samuel Field at Westbury-on-Trym, Gloucestershire, he entered Trinity College, Dublin, in 1823. There he distinguished himself in both science and classics, was a fellow student and friend of Sir William Rowan Hamilton, and graduated BA in 1827. He then moved to Oxford and became an incorporated member of Oriel College on 11 November 1830. He proceeded MA at Oxford in 1831, and at Dublin in 1832. Graves was called to the English bar in 1831 as a member of the Inner Temple, having previously (1830) entered the King's Inns, Dublin. He practised for a short time until 1839, when he was appointed professor of jurisprudence at University College, London, in succession to John Austin, who had retired in 1835. Soon after he was also elected an examiner in laws for the University of London.

With two of his professorial colleagues, the classicist Henry Malden and the mathematician Augustus De Morgan, Graves established enduring friendships, serving with the latter on the committee of the Society for the Diffusion of Useful Knowledge. He was elected a fellow of the Royal Society in 1839, and subsequently sat upon its council. He was also a member of the Philological Society and of the Royal Society of Literature. In 1846 Graves was appointed an assistant poor-law commissioner, and in the next year, under the new Poor Law Act, one of the poor-law inspectors of England and Wales. He married Amelia, a daughter of the politician William *Tooke, on 24 March 1846. They had no children.

Graves's principal works as a jurist are twelve lectures on the law of nations, reported in the *Law Times*, commencing 25 April 1845, and two elaborate articles contributed to the *Encyclopaedia metropolitana* on Roman law and canon law. He was also a contributor to Smith's *Dictionary of Greek and Roman Biography*, his articles including very full lives of the jurists Cato, Crassus, Drusus, and Gaius, and one on the legislation of Justinian.

Graves also had a high reputation among his contemporaries as a mathematician. In 1826, aged only nineteen, he began research into exponential functions. The results were published in the *Philosophical Transactions* for 1829 under the title 'An attempt to rectify the inaccuracy of some logarithmic formulae'. His principal discovery was the existence of two arbitrary and independent integers in the complete expression of an imaginary logarithm. He thus considered that he had elucidated the subject of the logarithms of negative and imaginary quantities, which at different periods had caused disagreements between mathematicians such as Leibniz and Johann Bernoulli, Euler, and D'Alembert.

However, Graves's conclusions also occasioned some initial controversy since they were not at first unanimously accepted by the British mathematical community, the most prominent objectors being George Peacock and Sir John Herschel. Graves accordingly communicated to the British Association for the Advancement of Science a defence and explanation of his discovery, which was printed in its *Report* for 1834. The same report contained a paper by Hamilton, in which he fully confirmed his friend's conclusions. Hamilton explicitly acknowledged that it was 'in reflecting on the important symbolical results of Mr. Graves respecting imaginary logarithms, and in attempting to explain to himself the theoretical meaning of those remarkable symbolisms' that he was drawn to 'the theory of conjugate functions, which, leading on to a theory of triplets and sets of moments, steps, and numbers' (*Notes and Abstracts of … the British Association for the Advancement of Science*, 1834, section 2) was to be the foundation of his future remarkable contributions to algebra, culminating in the discovery of quaternions. When this occurred in 1843, it was to Graves that Hamilton made his first written communication, on 17 October. Further acknowledgements of his obligation to Graves for stimulus and suggestion can be found in Hamilton's preface to his *Lectures on Quaternions* and in a prefatory letter to a communication in the *Philosophical Magazine* for December 1844. Graves modestly disclaimed the credit of suggestion.

For many years Graves had been Hamilton's sympathetic friend and mathematical confidant, and the two men maintained an active correspondence, in which they competed with each other in their attempts to produce a full and coherent interpretation of imaginaries. Graves worked at perfecting algebraic language; Hamilton had the higher object of arriving at the meaning of the science and its operations.

Soon after Hamilton's discovery of quaternions Graves concentrated on extending to eight squares Euler's theorem that the sum of four squares multiplied by the sum of four squares gives a product which is also the sum of four squares. He went on to conceive a theory of octaves analogous to Hamilton's theory of quaternions, introducing four imaginaries, additional to Hamilton's i, j, k, and conforming to 'the law of the modulus'. This was of great interest to Hamilton, but turned out to be less effective than quaternions as a practical algebraic system. Further mathematical papers followed, principally on complex numbers and the theory of equations, but these were largely of less significance than his earlier output and declined in number after the mid-1840s, owing to increasing pressure of work.

For many years Graves's principal recreational interest was mathematical bibliography, and his collection of mathematical works of all ages and countries was generally described as one of the most complete and valuable private libraries of the kind ever formed. It was bequeathed in his will to University College, London, in remembrance of their former association. Comprising over ten thousand books, 4577 pamphlets, and a considerable number of manuscripts, covering all aspects of the mathematical sciences over a period of five centuries, the current value of the Graves Library is inestimable, many of the items being exceedingly rare, some probably unique.

Three days after making this bequest, on 29 March 1870, Graves died at Thirlestaine Lodge, his home in Cheltenham. He was buried beside his mother in the graveyard of Swindon church, near Cheltenham. His wife survived him.   ADRIAN RICE

Sources *University College Gazette*, 1 (1886–7), 189–90 · *PRS*, 19 (1870–71), xxvii–xxviii · R. P. Graves, *Life of Sir William Rowan Hamilton*, 3 vols. (1882–9) · A. R. Dorling, 'The Graves mathematical collection in University College London', *Annals of Science*, 33 (1976), 307–9 · University College London, *Proceedings at the Annual General Meeting of the Members of the College* (1870–71), 19 · University College London, *Catalogue of books in the general library and in the south library at University College London*, 1 (1879), iii · *CGPLA Eng. & Wales* (1870)
Archives TCD, corresp. and papers · UCL, collections, lecture notes | BL, letters to Charles Babbage, Add. MSS 37189–37200, *passim* · Bodl. Oxf., corresp. with Sir Thomas Phillipps · TCD, letters to Sir W. R. Hamilton · UCL, letters to Society for the Diffusion of Useful Knowledge
Likenesses photograph (after portrait), UCL
Wealth at death under £25,000: probate, 26 April 1870, *CGPLA Eng. & Wales*

Graves, Margaret Ethel [Peggy; *pseud.* Jane Gordon] (1901–1962), journalist, was born at 41 Montpelier Square, London, on 24 January 1901, the only daughter of the Hon. Rowland Charles Frederick Leigh, a barrister, and his wife, Mabel, *née* Gordon. She worked as a nurse in Paddington Green Children's Hospital even while carrying on a successful career as a journalist and author, and in the 1920s she was a mannequin for Reveilles of London, an occupation to which her tall, slim figure and good looks suited her. Her initial foray into journalism was as a writer on the woman's page of the *Daily Express*, where as Jane Gordon, she reported on the seasonal Paris fashions. As fashion and beauty expert for the *Daily Telegraph*, and with the successful publication of *Home Beauty Treatments* (1934), she embarked on a series of popular beauty self-help books, reflecting the trend for health and fitness that had entered women's beauty culture in the 1930s. Her books and newspaper columns, which appeared variously in the *News Chronicle*, *Bystander*, and the *New York Times*, were so popular that by the 1950s she was receiving up to 4000 letters weekly. Her books included *Techniques for Beauty* (1940), *Slimming* (1951), *Jane Gordon's Beauty Book* (1953), and *Household Knowledge* (1955) and stated her belief that beauty 'problems' could be best solved by a combination of diet

and exercise rather than consulting expensive professionals. In 1950 she wrote her autobiography, which chronicled her life as a member of London's café society and her friendships with figures such as the film star Marlene Dietrich and the American heiress Barbara Hutton. It is rather tellingly entitled *Married to Charles* (1950), for, although an author in her own right, she regarded her greatest achievement as marrying the renowned columnist and author Charles Patrick Ranke Graves (1899–1971), at St Margaret's, Westminster, on 17 December 1929. Margaret Graves died at her home, 102 Gloucester Place, London, on 29 August 1962.   CAROLINE COX

Sources J. Gordon [M. E. Graves], *Married to Charles* (1950) · C. L. White, *Women's magazines, 1693–1968* (1970) · J. Winship, *Inside women's magazines* (1987) · N. A. Walker, ed., *Women's magazines, 1940–1960* (1998) · b. cert. · m. cert. · d. cert.
Likenesses photograph, repro. in Gordon, *Married to Charles*
Wealth at death £2845 4s. 0d.: probate, 21 Feb 1963, *CGPLA Eng. & Wales*

Graves, (Frances) Marjorie (1884–1961), politician, was born at Dowsefield, Allerton, Liverpool, on 17 September 1884, the daughter of William Samuel Graves (*b.* 1850), shipowner, who later settled in Horsham, Sussex, and his wife, Fanny Charlotte, *née* Neilson. Her grandfather Samuel Robert Graves (1818–1873) had been Conservative MP for Liverpool. She was educated privately and at Château de Dieudonne, Bornel, France. Graves undertook research in the Bibliothèque Nationale and the Archives Nationales in Paris and published studies of Louis I, duke of Orléans (1913), a revised edition of *The Private Life of Marie Antoinette* (1917), and an edition of medieval estate inventories of the house of Orléans (1926). During the First World War she worked for the Foreign Office and she was present at the Paris peace conference in 1919. She was afterwards seconded to the intelligence department of the Home Office (1919–20).

Graves was a Conservative member on Holborn borough council (1928–34). At the general election in October 1931 she was elected for Hackney South, after defeating the Labour incumbent, Herbert Morrison, with a comfortable majority of 3093. Of the new women members of parliament, Graves was one of only two who had pursued a professional career, and her experience of international affairs informed her major contributions to debates. Her maiden speech, in July 1932, was on the Lausanne conference on the settlement of war debts, when she loyally defended the agreement reached at Lausanne as 'the foundation stone of a good edifice to come' (*Hansard 5C*, 268, 1932, 1191). But while she applauded this example of European co-operation, she warned against the reduction of British naval power throughout the empire, and appealed for twenty-five years of British leadership in Europe: 'The spirit of Palmerston is the spirit which should inspire British foreign policy at this hour' (ibid., 1193).

In subsequent debates on foreign policy Graves supported collective security through the League of Nations as 'the only solution for the future' (*Hansard 5C*, 301, 640).

Her view that British policy should be even-handed survived a visit to Germany early in 1935. Faced with Hitler's repudiation of disarmament and reintroduction of conscription, she argued: 'We have to face the German point of view … We have to accept Germany' (ibid.).

Graves applied the same spirit of compromise to Italian colonial expansion in Abyssinia. Her proposal in July 1935 that Abyssinian lands bordering Eritrea and Italian Somaliland should be made an Italian mandate under the League of Nations was criticized by Eleanor Rathbone as rewarding Italy for a flagrant violation of the covenant of the league. Graves remained convinced that the league mandate, albeit administered by Italy, would afford better protection of Abyssinian rights than could be gained by any form of sanctions (*Hansard 5C*, 304, 1935, 593).

At the general election held in November 1935 Graves was a casualty of the modest swing to the left that unseated five of the Conservative women elected in 1931. She continued to be active in local government and became the first woman to serve as chairman of the metropolitan area of the National Union of Conservative and Unionist Associations, 1936–7, representing London on the national executive. She was also a British government delegate at the seventeenth assembly of the League of Nations in Geneva. Latterly she lived at Cocknowle, Wareham, Dorset, where she was a member of the county council. She died, unmarried, at Cocknowle on 17 November 1961.   MARK POTTLE

Sources *The Times* (20 Nov 1961) · WWBMP · WWW · *Hansard 5C*, 268.1190–94; 70.607–8; 301.638–42; 304.592–5 · P. Brookes, *Women at Westminster: an account of women in the British parliament, 1918–1966* (1967) · M. Phillips, *The divided house: women at Westminster* (1980) · F. W. S. Craig, *British parliamentary election results, 1918–1949*, rev. edn (1977) · C. Rallings and M. Thrasher, *British electoral facts, 1832–1999* (2000) · b. cert. · d. cert. · Walford, *County families* (1875) [William Samuel Graves]

Wealth at death £213,044 17s. 1d.: probate, 16 March 1962, *CGPLA Eng. & Wales*

Graves, Richard (1677–1729), antiquary, was born on 22 April 1677 at Mickleton Manor, Gloucestershire, the eldest son of the nine children of Samuel Graves (1649–1708) and his wife, Susanna Dandlo Swann, daughter of Captain Richard Swann of the Royal Navy. After attending Campden grammar school under Robert Morse and also Stratford upon Avon grammar school, he went to Pembroke College, Oxford, where he matriculated on 30 June 1693. On 21 October of the same year he was admitted to Lincoln's Inn, following in the footsteps of his father and grandfather, also Richard Graves (1610–1669). In 1697 he acquired a chamber in Chancery Lane Row in Gatehouse Court but did not proceed to be called to the bar and disposed of the chamber on 7 May 1700. In 1699 he was awarded his BA of Oxford University. Thereafter he spent most of his life at Mickleton. He married Elizabeth Morgan (d. 1723), daughter and coheir of Thomas Morgan, and they had four sons and two daughters. The second son, the Revd Richard *Graves (1715–1804), is said to have given an impression of his father in the character of Mr Townsend in his novel *The Spiritual Quixote* (1773).

Richard Graves (1677–1729), attrib. James Maubert

Much of Graves's life at Mickleton was spent as an enthusiastic researcher into antiquities and genealogy and he developed a friendship with Thomas Hearne, with whom he exchanged information on antiquarian subjects and for whom he gathered material from 1715 onwards. His protégé George Ballard, also from Mickleton, whom he encouraged in research, admired him as a 'complete master of the Greek, Latin, and Saxon tongues; … admirably well read and skilled in the Roman and British antiquities; … and a most curious Historian, Antiquary, and Medalist' (Nash, 1.199). Besides drawing up an elaborate historical pedigree of his own family, he made large collections of material about the history of the hundred of Kiftsgate adjoining Mickleton, gathering information from Domesday Book and from manuscripts and records in the Tower, Cottonian, and Bodleian libraries. He also planned a history of the antiquities of Evesham. He built up a collection of 500 coins, chiefly Greek and Roman, gathered in Gloucestershire, Wiltshire, and Worcestershire. Painstaking and conscientious, he was concerned for historical accuracy and, sceptical about his family's right to use the Grave arms, he gathered sufficient fresh information to be granted a coat of arms by the College of Arms on 4 July 1728.

Graves died suddenly at Mickleton Manor on 17 September 1729 and was buried on 22 September in the north aisle of Mickleton church. Hearne remembered him not only as an excellent scholar but also as a modest and sweet-tempered man, kind to his tenants and to the poor. His papers were purchased by James West, who composed the epitaph for his monument in Mickleton church, and on West's death in 1773 they passed to the earl of Shelburne. His books were purchased by Mr Harding, clerk of the House of Commons, and his collection of coins by his antiquarian friend Roger Gale.

GORDON GOODWIN, rev. F. D. A. BURNS

Sources parish register (baptism), Mickleton, 4 May 1677 · parish register (burial), Mickleton, 22 Sept 1729 · Hockaday abstracts of parish registers, Gloucester Library, Gloucester, Hockaday MSS, 281 · Foster, *Alum. Oxon.* · W. P. Baildon, ed., *The records of the Honorable Society of Lincoln's Inn: admissions*, 1 (1896), 347 · Red Book, Lincoln's Inn, London, vols. 2, 36, 57 · *Remarks and collections of Thomas Hearne*, ed. C. E. Doble and others, 11 vols., OHS, 2, 7, 13, 34, 42–3, 48, 50, 65, 67, 72 (1885–1921), vol. 5, p. 88; vol. 6, p. 96; vol. 7, pp. 23, 29, 33, 57, 82, 101, 127, 179, 182, 199, 249, 334, 348, 365, 378, 381, 397; vol. 8, pp. 3, 9, 11, 19, 24, 46, 47, 57, 59, 82, 92, 110–13, 117, 128, 143, 159, 170, 172, 174, 210, 221, 278, 329, 331, 347, 349, 351; vol. 9, pp. 39, 42, 44, 66, 74, 106, 113, 182, 213, 214, 227, 229, 276, 304, 305, 352, 391; vol. 10, pp. 19, 92, 99, 102, 111, 162, 184, 299, 320, 446; vol. 11, pp. 11, 13, 36, 50, 57, 70, 217, 223, 337 · T. Nash, *Collections for the history of Worcestershire*, 1 (1781), 198–9 · Nichols, *Lit. anecdotes*, 2.466–70 · F. A. Bates, *Graves' memoirs of the civil war* (1927), 258–73 · C. Tracy, *A portrait of Richard Graves* (1987), 6–11, 16, 19, 31 · J. Maclean, 'The family of Graves', *The Genealogist*, 4 (1880), 103–6 · D. Macleane, *A history of Pembroke College, Oxford*, OHS, 33 (1897), 376 · C. J. Hill, *The literary career of Richard Graves* [1935], 2 · Glos. RO, Graves Hamilton MSS

Archives Bodl. Oxf., Hearne MSS · Glos. RO, Graves Hamilton MSS

Likenesses attrib. J. Maubert, portrait; Sothebys, 2 March 1983, lot 14 [*see illus.*] · G. Vertue, line engraving, BM, NPG; repro. in Nash, *Collections*, facing p. 189 · copper printing plate, Glos. RO, Graves Hamilton MSS

Wealth at death estate value £800 p.a.; son able to raise £3100 on mortgage, Dec 1729: Hearne, *Remarks and collections*, vol. 10, p. 184; Harrowby Manuscript Trust, Sandon Hall, Staffordshire, Harrowby MS 905/199/68, quoted in Tracy, *Portrait*, 11

Graves, Richard (1715–1804), writer and translator, was born at Mickleton Manor, Mickleton, Gloucestershire, on 4 May 1715, the second son of Richard *Graves (1677–1729), antiquary, and his wife, Elizabeth Morgan (d. 1723), a Welshwoman, daughter of Thomas Morgan. Educated at the school run by the local curate, William Smith, he read Hesiod and Homer at the age of twelve. From the age of thirteen he attended Roysse's Grammar School in Abingdon, Berkshire, winning a scholarship to Pembroke College, Oxford, and 'the character of a tolerable Grecian' (Graves, 13). He matriculated on 7 November 1732.

A bookish enthusiast eager for well-born society, Graves joined a set of students who drank water while reading obscure Greek authors. '[S]educed from this mortified symposium' by west country ale drinkers, rescued in turn by some countrymen—'politer votaries of Bacchus' who objected to 'those sons of Comus' for drinking ale instead of port, punch, and claret (Graves, 13–18)—Graves finally joined William Shenstone and Anthony Whistler in a congenial 'triumvirate' who balanced study with literary play. According to the extempore 'Character' Shenstone wrote at Oxford in 1735, Graves combined supreme elegance with extreme diffidence (Shenstone, 1765, 2.41–3). They remained close friends all their lives, and after Shenstone's death in 1763 Graves worked anonymously with Robert Dodsley to edit his works; his preface introduces the third volume, containing letters (1769). After graduating BA on 25 June 1736, Graves became a fellow of All

Richard Graves (1715–1804), by James Northcote, 1799

Souls, Oxford, in November. His friends included William Blackstone—'A few trifling anecdotes' of whom he included in *The Triflers*—and members of the Holy Club, the gathering of Oxford Christians from which the Methodist movement emerged. On 10 October 1737 Charles Wesley discussed the apparent madness of Graves's brother Charles Caspar Graves with him; explaining 'the nature of true religion', he called it 'no other than what you [Graves] once laboured after, till the gentleman swallowed up the Christian' (*Journal of the Rev. Charles Wesley*, 1.77).

Recoiling from religious fervour, Graves attended Frank Nicholls's lectures on anatomy in London during 1738 and 1739 but abandoned physic after a prolonged nervous fever. He took his MA in October 1740 and was ordained on 24 May 1741. As curate of Tissington, near Ashbourne, Derbyshire, and family chaplain to William Fitzherbert, who had attended the Inner Temple with Graves's elder brother, Morgan, Graves enjoyed the lively good society and local travel, leaving only to move closer to Oxford. Supported by Morgan and a relation, Samuel Knight, archdeacon of Berkshire, he became curate of Aldworth in 1744, and held various posts at All Souls between 1744 and 1748.

Graves had earlier jilted his childhood tutor's daughter, the dauntingly literate Utrecia Smith; he erected a monument to her in Mickleton churchyard after she died on 5 March 1743 and commemorated her as Ophelia in his novel *The Spiritual Quixote*. In late 1746 or early 1747 he eloped to London with Lucy Bartholomew (*bap.* 1730, *d.* 1777), the daughter of the Aldworth farmer with whom he boarded. After the Revd George Walker promised him the curacy of Whitchurch, Oxfordshire, worth £50 a year, he married her secretly in the Fleet on 2 August 1747; Richard, their first child, was baptized in St Giles, Bloomsbury, on 22 October 1747. Lucy briefly attended boarding-school in London in 1748, apparently to acquire social polish, Graves commemorating their separation in a poem, 'The Parting' (reprinted, Tracy, 72–3). Their second child, Morgan, was baptized at Whitchurch on 25 January 1749; Graves and Lucy had two more sons and a daughter, remaining together until Lucy's death on 1 May 1777. Graves wrote to Dodsley on 26 October 1754: 'I left a Fellowship of All-Souls Coll. for a handsome Wife—& shou'd take some pleasure in letting my Friends see that I was not disappointed in my expectation of happiness' (*Correspondence*, 180). Marriage violated the terms of Graves's fellowship at All Souls: it ceased in January 1749, when he could no longer conceal his marriage. By marrying beneath his station he also permanently offended his brother Morgan, closing other avenues of preferment.

Recommended by Sir Thomas Head of Langley, a schoolfellow, in June 1749 Graves accepted the rectory of Claverton, near Bath, from William Skrine, fulfilling the position without a month's consecutive absence until he died in 1804. Through Ralph Allen, a hospitable parishioner and friend, he became vicar of Kilmarsden from 1763 until 1794, employing a curate, and private chaplain to Lady Chatham. In 1767 he purchased the advowson of Claverton parish; in 1802 he accepted the living of Croscombe to keep it warm for a friend. A conscientious clergyman who disliked preaching, Graves outlined his position in *A Letter from a Father to his Son at the University* (1787), a pamphlet included with only ten sermons in *Sermons* (1799). To augment his income, for forty years he ran a school which eventually housed forty boys on a storey of the local manor, rented from Allen. His patron's son, Henry Skrine, William Warburton's son Ralph, and Thomas Robert Malthus were pupils; Thomas Bowdler and Graves's friend Prince Hoare, the dramatist, artist, and essayist, may have been pupils. Graves walked almost daily into Bath, where his friends included Lady Miller, for whose circle at Bath Easton he wrote many poems, and the bluestocking writers Elizabeth Montagu and Catharine Macaulay. According to the *Dictionary of National Biography* Graves was 'short and slender, and he was eccentric in both dress and gait, but his features were expressive and his conversation was marked by a sportive gaiety'. He was a whig in politics. Now a friend, Malthus attended him in his last illness and administered the last rites of the church shortly before Graves died, at Claverton rectory, on 23 November 1804; he was buried on 1 December in his own church, where a mural tablet was placed to his memory. After his wife's death in 1777 Graves had placed an urn in the chancel of the church.

A versatile writer who presented his verse and lighter prose as a genteel and sociable accomplishment, Graves frequently collected items published, even collected, before (see Tracy, 157–61). Encouraged by Shenstone, he contributed eight poems to Robert Dodsley's *Collection of Poems* (1755–8) and three fables to his *Select Fables* (1761). He contributed poems to various journals and to such collections as *Poetical Amusements at a Villa Near Bath* (1775–81) and *Six Odes Presented to … Mrs. Catharine Macaulay, on her Birthday* (1777). *The Festoon: a Collection of Epigrams, Ancient and Modern … with an Essay on that Species of Composition* (1765, dated 1766) appeared under different titles in Dublin (1767, 1784). *Euphrosyne, or, Amusements on the Road of Life* (1776) absorbed much of it, adding *The Love of Order: a Poetical Essay* (1773) and *The Progress of Gallantry: a Poetical Essay* (1774); the second edition (1780) added a second volume that included Graves's opera, *Echo and Narcissus* (2nd edn in *The Coalition, or, The Opera Rehears'd: a Comedy*, 1794), and in 1783 gatherings of poems written for Lady Miller. 'Werter to Charlotte' and 'On Suicide' appeared with an anonymous translation from Goethe, *The Sorrows of Werther*, that Dodsley published in 1784; they were collected in *Lucubrations: Consisting of Essays, Reveries, &c., in Prose and Verse*, 'by the late Peter of Pontefract' (1786). Other notable poems include his epilogue, written with his friends Shenstone and Dodsley, for Dodsley's play *Cleone* (1758), and his elegy, inscribed to Sir Joshua Reynolds, on the death of Samuel Johnson (1785; reprinted in Hill, 117–18). *The Reveries of Solitude: Consisting of Essays in Prose, a New Translation of the Muscipula, and Original Pieces in Verse* (1793) suggests his variety; *Senilities, or, Solitary Amusements in Prose and Verse* (1801), his self-deprecation. *The Invalid: with the Obvious Means of Enjoying Health and a Long Life* (1804) includes an account of his nervous fever. *The Triflers: Consisting of Trifling Essays, Trifling Anecdotes, and a Few Poetical Trifles* (1805) incorporated both a new edition of his satirical poem, *The Rout, or, A Sketch of Modern Life* (1789), and *The Farmer's Son: a Moral Tale* (1795), a poem dedicated to Hannah More.

Graves won fame for his prose. His collections often identify the anonymous author as the 'editor' of his popular first novel, *The Spiritual Quixote, or, The Summer's Ramble of Mr. Geoffry Wildgoose: a Comic Romance* (3 vols., 1773; German trans., 1773; Dutch trans., 1798–9; ed. C. Tracy, 1967). Strongly influenced by Henry Fielding, this episodic novel views an impressive range of society with gentlemanly amusement. His head turned by reading the religious polemics in his family library, Wildgoose becomes an itinerant preacher, abandoning his estate and worthy mother in the company of the hearty cobbler Jerry Tugwell (Sancho Panza to this spiritual Quixote). His attempts to preach usually lead to farce, satirizing the ignorance and ill breeding that the irrational enthusiast encourages. A blow to the temple from a flung decanter finally precipitates Wildgoose's return to his senses, allowing him to resume his proper station and to woo successfully the beautiful Miss Townsend. Graves especially satirizes Whitfield. This servitor (not fellow) of Pembroke College, Graves snobbishly insists, did not originate Methodism (Tracy edn, 31); the dignified stranger who opposes Wildgoose's doctrinal extremes is no follower of Wesley but John Wesley himself (ibid., 326)! In this playful but deeply personal novel, Graves explored and disciplined the enthusiasm he shared with his mad brother. In a substantial inset tale, 'Mr. Rivers's Story', he described his own enthusiastic courtship. He also portrayed many friends, including the Fitzherbert household and Shenstone at The Leasowes, where Wildgoose drains the famous cascade and overturns the statue of a faun.

In *Columella, or, The Distressed Anchoret: a Colloquial Tale* (1779) Graves disparages idle solitude—his view of Shenstone's retirement. This novel was admired by the Bath poet Christopher Anstey, by Elizabeth Montagu, and later (to judge from a cheery allusion in *Sense and Sensibility*) by Jane Austen. *Columella* prompted Montagu's suggestion that Graves translate François Fénelon's ode on solitude, the nucleus of *Fleurettes* (1784), his slim volume of verse translations from French. Montagu encouraged his reply to Samuel Johnson's account of Shenstone in *Lives of the Poets* (1781): the resulting anecdotal memoir, *Recollection of some Particulars in the Life of the Late William Shenstone, Esq.* (1788), is Graves's best and most personal work after *The Spiritual Quixote*. Bluestocking influence shapes the reformed rural felicity of *Eugenius, or, Anecdotes of the Golden Vale: an Embellished Narrative of Real Facts* (2 vols., 1785), a novel that uneasily defends modern times. Its gentle hero wins the rustic heroine from a scheming city rival; his patron Ralph Allen notwithstanding, its plot was therefore closer to his heart than the worth-versus-birth pretext of his last novel, *Plexippus, or, The Aspiring Plebeian* (2 vols., 1790; German trans., 1793).

Graves's translations reveal a teacher committed to scholarship, didacticism, contemporary application, and stylistic ease. Possibly working from a Latin version, he paraphrased Giovanni de la Casa's *Galateo* under the title *Galateo, or, A Treatise on Politeness and Delicacy of Manners … from the Italian of Monsig. Giovanni De La Casa* (1774). His versions of classical Greek were long reprinted: *The Heir Apparent, or, The Life of Commodus, the Son and Heir of the Good M. Aurelius Antoninus, Emperor of Rome: from the Greek of Herodian* (1789); *The Meditations of the Emperor Marcus Aurelius Antoninus* (1792); and *Hiero; on the Condition of Royalty: a Conversation from the Greek of Xenophon* (1793). Contrary to his usual practice, Graves allowed *Meditations* to appear over his name. He thereby angered James Dodsley, his publisher, who had declined it; he never again published with Dodsley.

In the disciplines and duties of the established church, Graves satisfied his religious ardour, his craving for activity, and his devotion to traditional forms. Although he married a farmer's daughter out of passion, he disliked the blurring of social distinctions. Graves criticized the ambiguous position, at once gentlemen and servants, of servitors at Oxford, and of sizars at Cambridge (Graves, 27–30). He offers ambivalent praise for bluestocking patronage of Anne Yearsley, 'the ingenious and virtuous Bristol milkwoman; whom they have nobly … left … in a situation to court the muses at her leisure':

> But as 'Apollo himself does not always string his bow',—and as verse, in this tasteless age, is not always a marketable commodity, it would not be amiss, if Mrs. Yearsly … were instructed to make cheese-cakes and custards with her milk, as well as to make verses; in which case, any productions of her muse, which lay upon her hands, might be usefully

employed in protecting the more lucrative productions of her oven. (Graves, *Eugenius*, Dublin edn, 1786, 1.116–17n.)

Graves sounds like a thorough curmudgeon, yet he spoke as a gentleman who wrote (and taught) indefatigably for money, a fellow poet who knew from experience that verse does not pay. An enthusiast, Graves admired the Methodists' ardour but resented their defiance of established forms. When he wrote he playfully adopted literary forms to temper self-revelation with decorum, sympathy with pride of rank, passion with humour.

DAVID OAKLEAF

Sources C. Tracy, *A portrait of Richard Graves* (1987) • C. J. Hill, *The literary career of Richard Graves* [1935] • [R. Graves], *Recollection of some particulars in the life of the late William Shenstone, esq., in a series of letters from an intimate friend of his to —, esq., F. R. S.* (1788) • *The correspondence of Robert Dodsley, 1733–1764*, ed. J. E. Tierney (1988) • *The journal of the Rev. Charles Wesley*, ed. T. Jackson, 2 vols. [1849] • W. Shenstone, *The works in verse and prose*, and edn, 2 vols. (1765); 3 (1769) • *The letters of William Shenstone*, ed. M. Williams (1939)
Archives Bath Central Library, letters • Som. ARS, letters • Yale U., MSS | PRO, letters to first earl of Chatham, PRO 30/8 • Som. ARS, Phillipps MS 13851
Likenesses T. Gainsborough, crayon drawing, 1760–69, Morgan L.; repro. in Tracy, *Portrait* • J. Skinner, coloured drawing, *c.*1797, BL, diary, Add. MS 33635 • J. Northcote, oils, 1799, NPG [*see illus.*] • mezzotint, 1799 (after J. Northcote), Victoria Art Gallery, Bath; repro. in Tracy, *Portrait of Richard Graves* • S. Reynolds, mezzotint, pubd 1800 (after J. Northcote), BM, NPG • J. Basire, line engraving, 1812 (after T. Gainsborough), BM; repro. in Nichols, *Lit. anecdotes* • caricature, line engraving, NPG • study, repro. in *Public Characters of 1799–1800* (1799)
Wealth at death £2000–£3000—total legacies: Tracy, *Portrait*, 101; Hill, *Literary career of Richard Graves*, 11

Graves, Richard (1763–1829), dean of Ardagh and theologian, was born at Kilfinnane, co. Limerick, on 1 October 1763. He was the fifth and youngest child of the Revd James Graves, vicar of Kilfinnane and Darragh, co. Limerick, and his wife, Jane, daughter of the Revd Thomas Ryder, rector of Mitchelstown, co. Cork. He was descended from Colonel Graves, who commanded a cavalry regiment in the parliamentary army and volunteered for service in Ireland in 1647. Having been tutored at home by his father and his elder brother Thomas (afterwards dean of Connor), he entered Trinity College, Dublin, on 5 June 1780, under the tutorship of the Revd William Day. He did well at university, being elected a scholar in 1782, taking part in the College Historical Society, and graduating BA in 1784, MA in 1787, BD in 1794, and DD in 1799.

On 12 June 1786 Graves was a successful candidate for a fellowship on his first trial, and he was admitted to deacon's and priest's orders in 1787. In the same year he married Elizabeth Mary (1766/7–1827), the daughter of the Revd James Drought, regius professor of divinity at the University of Dublin from 1790 to 1819. They had at least three sons and one daughter. The eldest, Richard Hastings *Graves, published his father's collected works; a younger son, Robert James *Graves, became an eminent doctor. In 1797, and again in 1801, he was elected Donnellan lecturer, his subject being 'The divine origin of the Jewish religion, proved from the internal evidence of the last four books of the Pentateuch'. These were later published and helped to establish his literary career. In July 1799 he was co-opted to a senior fellowship of his college, and in 1801 was presented to the prebend of St Michael's, Dublin. He soon became widely known as a preacher. In 1799 he was professor of oratory, in 1810 regius professor of Greek, and in 1806 and 1807 he held the office of university librarian.

In 1809 Graves was presented to the rectory of Raheny, co. Dublin, and in 1813 he also received from the crown the offer of the deanery of Ardagh, which he hesitated to accept, since the appointment would have involved the resignation of his fellowship. On being appointed deputy professor of divinity in 1814, however, he resigned his fellowship to become dean and in 1819 succeeded to the professorship of divinity. In 1823 he resigned the prebend of St Michael's, and became rector of St Mary's, Dublin, a benefice which he held until his death. He succeeded in making considerable improvements to the methods and examinations used in the divinity school over which he presided, and he was a conscientious parochial minister. Graves was the author of several influential works, including *An Essay on the Character of the Apostles and Evangelists* (1798), *Lectures on the Four Last Books of the Pentateuch* (1807), and *Calvinistic Predestination Repugnant to the General Tenor of Scripture; in a Series of Discourses* (1825). He died at Harcourt Street, Dublin, from a paralytic stroke on 31 March 1829, two years after the death of his wife, and was buried on 3 April, in a family plot, in the old churchyard of Donnybrook, near Dublin.

B. H. BLACKER, rev. DAVID HUDDLESTON

Sources *The whole works of Richard Graves*, ed. R. H. Graves, 4 vols. (1840) · 'Life and writings of Dean Graves', *Dublin University Magazine*, 17 (1841), 634–45 · 'Our portrait gallery, no. XXVII, Robert James Graves, with an etching', *Dublin University Magazine*, 19 (1842), 260–73 · J. Wills, *Lives of illustrious and distinguished Irishmen*, 6 (1847), 442–5 · H. Cotton, *Fasti ecclesiae Hibernicae*, 2 (1848), 70 · H. Cotton, *Fasti ecclesiae Hibernicae*, 3 (1849), 189–91 · B. H. Blacker, *Brief sketches of the parishes of Booterstown and Donnybrook*, [new edn] (1874), 39–40 · [J. H. Todd], ed., *A catalogue of graduates who have proceeded to degrees in the University of Dublin, from the earliest recorded commencements to … December 16, 1868* (1869), 232 · Burtchaell & Sadleir, *Alum. Dubl.*, 2nd edn · A. J. Webb, *A compendium of Irish biography* (1878), 234
Archives TCD
Likenesses R. Graves, line engraving, repro. in Graves, *Whole works of Richard Graves*

Graves, Richard Hastings (1791–1877), Church of Ireland clergyman and theological writer, was the eldest son of Richard *Graves (1763–1829), dean of Ardagh, and his wife, Elizabeth Mary Drought. Robert James *Graves was his brother. He was born in co. Dublin. He entered Trinity College, Dublin, in 1807 and graduated BA in 1812, MA in 1815, and BD and DD in 1828. He was ordained deacon in 1814 and was vicar of Kildrum from 1817 to 1823. He was then appointed vicar of Ballymoyer in the diocese of Armagh from 1823 to 1830. Graves became rector of Brigown in the diocese of Cloyne, being collated to a prebendal stall in 1832, and served as prebendary until 1875. In 1840 he published a complete edition of his father's works with a memoir of his life. He also published a number of

theological and controversial works, including *The Arguments for Predestination and Necessity Contrasted with the Established Principles of Philosophical Inquiry* (1829), *Apostolical Succession Overthrown and Evangelical Succession Established* (1854), *The Terminal Synchronism of Daniel's Two Principal Periods* (1858), and *The Church of Ireland: English menace answered and inthralment of the state averted by declining a charter* (1870). Graves never married. He died at his home, 31 Raglan Road, Dublin, on 25 December 1877.

DAVID HUDDLESTON

Sources *The whole works of Richard Graves*, ed. R. H. Graves, 4 vols. (1840) · J. B. Leslie, *Armagh clergy and parishes* (1911) · W. M. Brady, *Clerical and parochial records of Cork, Cloyne, and Ross*, 3 vols. (1863–4) · H. Cotton, *Fasti ecclesiae Hibernicae*, 1 (1845) · H. Cotton, *Fasti ecclesiae Hibernicae*, 6 (1878) · CGPLA Ire. (1878) · Irish calendar of wills, 1878, 269
Archives TCD
Wealth at death under £9000: probate, 31 Jan 1878, CGPLA Ire.

Graves, Robert (1798–1873). *See under* Graves family (*per.* c.1812–1892).

Graves, Robert James (1796–1853), physician, was born on 28 March 1796 in Holles Street, Dublin, the seventh of ten children of Richard *Graves (1763–1829), and his wife, Elizabeth, *née* Drought. He received his early education in the diocesan school at Downpatrick, co. Down, and later from a Dr Leney in Blackrock, co. Dublin. Graves entered Trinity College, Dublin, at the age of fifteen in 1811, having obtained first place in the entrance examination. He graduated BA in 1815 and MB in 1818. Graves subsequently travelled to Britain and Europe to gain postgraduate experience, and studied in London, Göttingen, Berlin, and Edinburgh. He also visited medical schools in Denmark, France, and Italy. During his travels Graves was arrested in Austria on suspicion of being a spy and imprisoned for ten days in Vienna. When crossing the Alps into Italy in autumn 1819 he met the artist John Mallard Turner. The two men struck up a friendship and travelled together through Italy to Rome. Graves was one of the few people in whose company Turner worked.

In 1821 Graves was appointed physician to the Meath Hospital, Dublin. The work he undertook in the hospital along with his colleague William Stokes, who was appointed physician in 1826, brought the Meath Hospital international renown. In 1827 the two men published *Clinical Reports of the Medical Cases in the Meath Hospital*; it was primarily intended as a textbook for their students but it received a much wider readership. This work, along with the articles Graves regularly contributed to the *Dublin Journal of Medical Science*, the *London Medical and Surgical Journal*, and the *London Medical Gazette*, had a major influence on the development of clinical practice in the English-speaking world.

Graves laid out his philosophy of medical education in the first lecture he gave to students in 1821, and introduced the practice of bedside teaching, which he had first encountered while studying in Berlin. He also allowed his students to take a more active role in the treatment of patients than had hitherto been the case. His approach to clinical teaching was subsequently embraced and

Robert James Graves (1796–1853), by John Kirkwood, pubd 1842 (after Charles Grey)

adopted by his colleagues in Ireland, Britain, and North America. Graves stressed to his students the importance of careful observation of the patient's condition and symptoms. In 1830 he published a paper on pulse counting in the *Dublin Hospital Reports*, emphasizing the significance of relating the changes in pulse rate to changes in the clinical condition of the patient. Along with his colleague Stokes he also introduced the stethoscope to Dublin medicine; indeed Stokes had written the first work in English on the subject when a student in Edinburgh in 1825. Graves's reputation quickly grew to such an extent that his clinical lectures became the best attended in Dublin. His ground breaking work with Stokes led to a steady stream of doctors from around the world visiting the Meath Hospital. With a number of colleagues Graves founded the Park Street medical school in 1824. The syllabus of the school differed from others in the city in its emphasis on the practical experience gained by the students.

Fever, primarily typhus, was rife in Dublin in the 1820s and the Meath Hospital treated many sufferers in huts erected in the hospital grounds in a rudimentary effort at isolation. Graves had treated victims of an outbreak of typhus fever in Galway in 1822, an experience which stimulated his interest in the treatment of the disease. Fever patients were generally given very little in the way of food and drink. Graves, however, believed that patients needed the strength gained from a full and healthy diet to fight the fever they were suffering. In the Meath Hospital fever patients were nourished by generous meals, which replaced the meagre rations previously allocated. In a memoir of his colleague Stokes recollected that Graves's students once asked him what he would like as his epitaph. He suggested that it should record that 'he fed fevers'.

In 1835 Graves published an article entitled 'Newly observed affection of the thyroid gland in females', in the *London Medical and Surgical Journal*. In it he presented a description of a form of goitre which became known as Graves's disease in his honour. Graves published his greatest work, *A System of Clinical Medicine*, in 1843. Full of brilliant and original clinical observations, this work was translated into French, German, and Italian and was also published in North America. Graves resigned from the Meath Hospital in 1843 to concentrate on his Dublin private practice in Merrion Square. His reputation was such that he received many patients from abroad. He was elected president of the King and Queen's College of Physicians in Ireland in 1843 and held the position again in the following year.

Graves was a critic of the government's handling of the great famine (1845–9). He attacked the policies which led to overcrowding in workhouses and large congregations of people at food depots, and stressed the contagious nature of diseases such as cholera and typhus. His views brought him into disagreement with other members of the Irish medical establishment such as Dominic Corrigan (physician to Jervis Street Hospital, Dublin), who attributed the cause of fever to starvation rather than contagion. He also attacked the meagre payments offered by the central board of health to the doctors who treated fever victims. In 1848 he clashed with the board of health in Dublin over a circular they issued in response to the threat of an epidemic of cholera in the city. The board stated that the disease was not contagious, a view with which Graves vehemently disagreed. Such was Graves's standing among his peers that many followed his advice rather than that of the board of health when the disease arrived in Dublin in 1849.

A committed monarchist, Graves held the evangelical beliefs of his father, Richard Graves, dean of Ardagh, who had been regius professor of divinity and Greek at Trinity College, Dublin, and was recognized as one of the best preachers in the city. Coakley, one of Robert Graves's biographers, noted that very little was known of Graves's personal life and that early biographers appeared reticent to give any details. Graves married three times. His first wife, Matilda Jane Eustace, whom he married in December 1821, died in 1825, and his second wife, Sarah Jane Brinkley, died in 1827, the year following their wedding. With his third wife, Anna Grogan, whom he married in 1830, he had five children. Graves died on 20 March 1853 of a painful disease of the liver at Cloghan Castle, Banagher, King's county, the family residence he had purchased a year earlier.   KARL MAGEE

Sources D. Coakley, *Robert Graves, evangelist of clinical medicine* (1996) · J. D. H. Widdess, *A history of the Royal College of Physicians of Ireland, 1654–1963* (1963) · L. H. Ormsby, *Medical history of the Meath Hospital and County Infirmary*, 2nd edn (1892) · S. Taylor, *Robert Graves: the golden years of Irish medicine* (1989) · D. Coakley, *Irish masters of medicine* (1992) · P. Gatenby, *Dublin's Meath Hospital* (1996) · W. Stokes, 'The life and labours of Graves', in R. Graves, *Studies in physiology and medicine* (1863) · R. Graves and W. Stokes, *Clinical reports of the medical cases in the Meath Hospital* (1827) · R. Graves, 'Newly observed affection of the thyroid gland in females', *London Medical and Surgical Journal*, 7 (1835) · R. Graves, 'Letter relative to the proceedings of the central board of health of Ireland', *Dublin Journal of Medical Science*, 4 (1847), 513–44
Archives Adelaide and Meath Hospital, Dublin, Meath Hospital archives · Royal College of Physicians of Ireland, Dublin, Kirkpatrick archive
Likenesses C. Grey, ink drawing, 1842, NG Ire. · J. Kirkwood, etching, pubd 1842 (after ink drawing by C. Grey), NG Ire., NPG [*see illus.*] · J. H. Lynch, lithograph, pubd 1853 (after L. Gluckman), NG Ire. · J. Hogan, marble bust, 1854, Royal College of Physicians of Ireland, Dublin · A. B. Joy, statue, 1877, Royal College of Physicians of Ireland, Dublin

Graves, Robert von Ranke (1895–1985), poet and novelist, was born on 24 July 1895 at Red Branch House, Lauriston Road, Wimbledon, Surrey, the third of the five children of Alfred Perceval *Graves (1846–1931), poet and educationist, and his second wife, Amalie Elizabeth Sophie (Amy; 1857–1951), eldest daughter of Heinrich Ranke, professor of medicine at Munich University, and his wife, Luise. With his indefatigable Irish father famous as the author of the popular song 'Father O'Flynn', and his saintly but moralistic German mother proud to be the great-niece of the historian Leopold von Ranke, Graves was brought up within a literary family in which it was taken for granted that artistic achievements were of the greatest importance. After being educated first at a dame-school and then at several preparatory schools, including most notably Copthorne School (1908–9), Graves went to Charterhouse (1909–14), where from 1911 his poems appeared regularly in *The Carthusian*, and poetry became his ruling passion. Graves's earliest Carthusian verse, though technically imperfect, is highly forceful, reflecting as it does the desperately overwrought condition into which he had been plunged by the assiduous bullying of those who resented him, chiefly because he was trying to live up to the high moral standards of his home. Under the protective tutelage of George Mallory, with whom he went rock-climbing, poetry became not merely an escape, but a positive pleasure. This pleasure was heightened by Graves's close friendship with a much younger boy, G. H. (Peter) Johnstone, which made writing poetry a celebration of the kind of highly charged idealistic relationship which Graves would later describe as pseudo-homosexual.

On leaving Charterhouse in the summer of 1914, this large man with thick dark curly hair and blue eyes, whose otherwise regular features were disturbed by a nose which had been broken in a game of rugger and a slightly

Robert von Ranke Graves (1895–1985), by John Aldridge, 1968

twisted mouth, was on his way to take up a classical exhibition at St John's College, Oxford, when he was caught up in the First World War. Although a convinced pacifist, Graves was so shocked by the German violation of Belgian neutrality that joining up seemed the only honourable course of action. The fact that at the time he was staying at Erinfa, Harlech, north Wales (the holiday home where he had spent many of his happiest hours) led to his being commissioned into the Royal Welch Fusiliers, a regiment for which he retained a lifelong affection.

Graves was sustained during the terrible trench warfare which followed by his Christian faith, and by his friendship both with Johnstone and with his brother officer and fellow poet Siegfried Sassoon, with whom he planned to live and work after the war. The stresses of Graves's wartime experiences—during the battle of the Somme in 1916 he was so badly wounded in the lung that he was left for dead and was later able to read his own obituary in *The Times*—had a major impact upon his poetry, especially when combined with the thoroughgoing criticism which he had received from Edward Marsh, the editor of successive volumes of *Georgian Poetry*. In 1916 an impressive first volume of Graves's poems appeared, entitled *Over the Brazier*.

In June 1917 Graves was hospitalized with shell-shock; and while recovering (and preparing *Fairies and Fusiliers*, 1917), he underwent a major change of emotional direction. The first sign of this, a sickbed attraction for a pretty nurse, was followed shortly afterwards by a revulsion from Peter Johnstone, who had been convicted of making homosexual advances. A few months later, Graves was in love with the young, stylish, and artistic but also fiercely dogmatic Annie Mary Pryde (Nancy Nicholson; 1899–1977), daughter of the artist William Newzam Prior Nicholson, and sister of the artist Ben Nicholson. They were married on 23 January 1918; and in 1919 (after Graves's demobilization) they moved into Dingle Cottage in John Masefield's garden on Boars Hill near Oxford, and Graves began reading English at St John's.

Graves's hopes for popular success as a poet faded after the poor reception given in 1920 to *Country Sentiment*, his third volume of poems; while in 1921 Nancy's efforts to earn money by running a shop on Boars Hill also ended in failure. In addition, between 1919 and 1924 Nancy gave birth to four children in under five years; while Graves (now an atheist like his wife) suffered from recurring bouts of shell-shock. For a while, their retreat in 1921 to the World's End, Islip, gave them renewed hope; but Graves had been compelled by the poor state of his nerves to abandon his undergraduate work (although, unusually for a non-graduate, he gained a BLitt degree in 1925, after writing a thesis, 'Poetic unreason'). For several years he and Nancy were depressingly dependent upon familial hand-outs and assistance from friends, among whom he numbered T. E. Lawrence and Edmund Blunden. His relationship with Nancy, who was also ill with worry, began to deteriorate, and by 1925, when he was appointed professor of English literature at Cairo University, Graves feared that his own personality was on the verge of disintegration.

Fortunately for him, Graves set sail for Egypt in January 1926 not only with his wife and family but also with the young American poet Laura Riding (1901–1991), the daughter of Nathan S. Reichenthal, a tailor, and his second wife, Sadie. The former wife of Louis Gottschalk, a lecturer in history at Cornell University, Riding was a woman of forceful intellect and magnetic sexuality, and she had agreed to be Graves's collaborator; together they would write the ground-breaking *Survey of Modernist Poetry* (1927). Not long after their return to England in July 1926, she also became his mistress and his muse. He had soon come to depend upon her not only as lover, companion, critic, and mentor—she helped him to prepare his *Poems, 1914–1926* (1927)—but also as a unique source of ultimate wisdom.

After a bizarre period during which the *ménage à trois* between Robert Graves, Nancy, and Laura became a *ménage à quatre* with the Irish poet Geoffrey Phibbs (a period which ended only when Laura attempted suicide by hurling herself from the window of 35A St Peter's Square, London), Laura rescued Graves both from his failing marriage and from the moral censure of his wider family. She also acted as intellectual and spiritual midwife both to a kind of personal rebirth, and to Graves's writing *Good-bye to All that* (1929), the war-period autobiography which made him famous. In its original form, this is a searing work of genius in which Graves offers up a heavily rewritten version of his past life upon the altar of his present love.

Later that year Graves and Laura decamped to Deyá, Majorca, where they lived and worked together, and where the quality of Robert's literary work was dramatically improved by Laura's detailed criticisms. They also collaborated on a novel, *No Decency Left* (1932), published under the pseudonym Barbara Rich. As well as producing a steady stream of poetry, and being at the centre of a circle which at various times included James Reeves, John Aldridge, and Jacob Bronowski, Graves published his best-selling historical novel *I, Claudius* (1934), winner of the Hawthornden and James Tait Black memorial prizes, and made into a critically acclaimed television miniseries starring Derek Jacobi in 1976. Graves also published *Claudius the God and his Wife Messalina* in 1935, and his most original novel (later to become Philip Larkin's favourite) *'Antigua, Penny, Puce'*, in 1936. The outbreak of the Spanish Civil War in 1936 sent Graves, Laura, and a few of their most loyal followers wandering through Europe, with Graves finding time to write *Count Belisarius* (1938), and to prepare his *Collected Poems* (1938). However, Laura had long been sexually disenchanted with Graves, and when they went to America in 1939, she left him for her admirer Schuyler Jackson, after some nightmarish episodes during which she deliberately caused Schuyler's wife much mental distress.

Graves returned to England alone, and was saved from a breakdown only by the advent of Beryl (b. 1915), the youngest child of the solicitor Harry Pritchard and his wife Amy, and the wife (since January 1938) of Alan Hodge. Beryl, who had long admired Robert, became his new muse and mistress; from 1940 (the year of Graves's *Sergeant Lamb of the Ninth*) they set up house in Devon, where they stayed during the Second World War. These years, although clouded by the death in action of Robert's eldest son, David, also saw the birth of two more sons and a daughter, the writing of some fine love poetry, and the publication of Graves's social history (with Alan Hodge, who had remained a friend) *The Long Weekend* (1941). At this time his novel *Wife to Mr Milton* (1941) also appeared, and formed an attack upon Milton so ferocious as virtually to reveal the dark side of Graves's own soul.

In 1946, the year in which Graves published his *King Jesus*, he returned with Beryl and their three children to Canellun, Deyá. There he completed *The White Goddess* (1948, rev. 1952, 1966), perhaps his most durable and certainly his most original prose work. Subtitled 'a historical grammar of poetic myth', it gives Graves's explanation of what it is to be a romantic poet, and identifies the white goddess of Pelion with the triple muse, whom Graves now believed to be the only source of true poetic inspiration. In 1950, six months after Nancy Nicholson granted him a divorce, Graves married Beryl; their fourth child was born in 1953.

During his second period in Majorca, Graves published several notable works: *The Nazarene Gospel Restored* (1953), *The Greek Myths* (1955), and his novel *Homer's Daughter* (1955), while as a poet his reputation soared. In 1954 he was asked to give the prestigious Clark lectures at Cambridge, where he entertained the undergraduates with iconoclastic attacks upon Dryden, Pope, Yeats, Pound, Eliot, Auden, and Dylan Thomas, among others. In 1957 he began a lucrative series of lecture tours and poetry readings in the United States; in 1959 his *Collected Poems* was published; and in 1960 he was awarded the gold medal of the National Poetry Society of America. From 1961 to 1966 he was professor of poetry at Oxford, and in 1968 one of his poems was awarded an Olympic gold medal at the games in Mexico City. Later that year the queen presented him with her gold medal for poetry. Finally, in 1971, St John's College, Oxford, made him an honorary fellow.

Private life was less easy for this large and eccentric man, with his broad-brimmed hats and his straw baskets, who looked as he aged increasingly like one of the Roman emperors about whom he had written. Graves's devotion to his ideal of the poetic muse (necessarily the enemy of domesticity) led him and his family into some extraordinarily difficult situations. The beautiful artist Judith Bledsoe (*b.* 1934), who acted as Graves's muse from 1950 to 1952, and Margot Callas (*b.* 1934), her equally beautiful successor from 1960 to 1963, proved no serious threat to Beryl (though Graves had a brief affair with Margot), and both became her friends. The highly sexed Aemilia (Cindy) Lee, *née* Laraçuen (*b.* 1926), who followed from 1963 to 1966, was more dangerous; when in 1965 Graves accompanied her to Mexico it was uncertain whether he would return. The ballet dancer Julia (Juli) Simon (*b.* 1949), from 1966 onwards Graves's final muse, enjoyed a platonic relationship with him and became Beryl's friend.

During the early 1970s Graves began to suffer from increasingly severe memory loss, and by his eightieth birthday in 1975 he had come to the end of his working life. By this time he had published more than 135 books, including his novels *The Golden Fleece* (1944) and *Seven Days in New Crete* (1949); his critical works *The Crowning Privilege* (1956) and *Oxford Addresses on Poetry* (1964); and his *Collected Poems* of 1975. He survived for ten more years in an increasingly dependent condition until he died from heart failure on 7 December 1985. He was buried the next morning in the churchyard at Deyá, on the site of a shrine which (fittingly enough) had once been sacred to the white goddess of Pelion. RICHARD PERCEVAL GRAVES

Sources R. P. Graves, *Robert Graves: the assault heroic, 1895–1926* (1986) · R. P. Graves, *Robert Graves: the years with Laura Riding, 1926–1940* (1990) · R. P. Graves, *Robert Graves and the white goddess, 1940–1985* (1995) · personal knowledge (2004) · private information (2004)
Archives Southern Illinois University, Carbondale, Illinois, corresp. and papers · State University of New York, Buffalo · U. Lpool L., papers · University of San Francisco, corresp., literary MSS, and papers · University of Victoria, British Columbia, corresp., diaries, and literary MSS | Bodl. Oxf., letters to Alexander Pugh; letters to E. J. Thompson · Indiana University, Bloomington, Lilly Library, corresp. with Kenneth Charles Gay · King's Lond., Liddell Hart C., corresp. with Basil Liddell Hart · NL Scot., letters to W. S. Henry; letters to C. K. Scott Moncrief · NL Wales, letters to Alun Lewis and Gweno Lewis · NYPL, letters and MSS to Edward Marsh · University of Iowa, Iowa City, corresp. with Edmund Blunden · University of San Francisco Library, letters to James Reeves
Likenesses E. Kennington, pastel drawing, 1918, NMG Wales · B. Brandt, photograph, 1941, NPG · D. Simmons, sculpture, *c.*1941–1942, State University of New York, Buffalo, Lockwood Memorial

Library · J. Ulbricht, oils, 1966, State University of New York, Buffalo, Lockwood Memorial Library · J. Aldridge, oils, 1968, NPG [*see illus.*] · P. Stark, photographs, 1970–79, NPG · M. Stern, photographs, 1972, NPG · M. Fitzgibbon, bronze bust, Royal Dublin Society, Library · Ramsey & Muspratt, bromide print, NPG · F. Topolski, portrait, NPG
Wealth at death £70,240 in England and Wales: probate, 25 April 1986, *CGPLA Eng. & Wales*

Graves, Samuel (1713–1787), naval officer, was born on 17 April 1713, fourth son of Samuel Graves and his wife, whose maiden name was Moore. The family originated in Yorkshire but came to have many ramifications. He entered the navy in the *Exeter* (Captain Robert Trevor) on 21 November 1732, and in March 1733 he moved to the *Swallow*, in which he spent two and a half years, first under Captain Trevor, and then with his uncle, Thomas Graves; after this he served in several other ships for short periods, until he passed for lieutenant on 6 October 1739. He was appointed lieutenant of the fireship *Aetna* on 3 March 1740, but was shortly afterwards moved into the *Norfolk*, with his uncle again, in which ship he distinguished himself at the capture of the batteries at Cartagena. After being for a time in the *Cumberland* he was promoted by Sir Chaloner Ogle to the command of the sloop *Bonetta* on 5 December 1743, still in the West Indies. On 11 September 1744 he was promoted captain into the *Rippon's Prize*, and in 1747–8 he commanded the *Enterprise* in the West Indies. In the early part of the Seven Years' War he commanded several line-of-battle ships—the *Duke*, *St Albans*, *Princess Amelia*, and the *Barfleur*—in which he was in the Rochefort expedition in 1757 and with the main fleet in 1758. Again in the *Duke*, he fought at Quiberon Bay and continued in her until promoted rear-admiral in 1762. Up to this time his career was creditable, but with little sign of exceptional ability. A long period of unemployment was to follow.

On 28 March 1774 Graves, a vice-admiral since October 1770, was appointed by Lord Sandwich to the command of the North American squadron, and proceeded to his station in the *Preston*. His task was daunting. Boston, one of the squadron's main centres, was the focal point of the increasing difficulties with the North American colonies. Moreover, his squadron was small (nineteen ships and vessels), and by long practice they were dispersed, with one at each of the colonies, a situation which in the existing circumstances was difficult to alter. Parliament had passed the Boston Port Act, prohibiting the landing, loading, or shipping of goods to or from that port, and the only addition to the usual orders for the station, which normally enjoined the commander-in-chief to assist the governors and local magistrates, was the order to enforce this act. John Montagu, his predecessor, had declared a blockade of Boston, but this proved difficult to carry out owing to the many channels of entry, even by concentrating nine vessels on the task. Moreover the rest of the coast was left clear, and smuggling, one of the normal problems of the station, therefore increased. Further orders came to prohibit the import of gunpowder, arms, and ammunition, another wishful hope in view of the great length and indented nature of the coast and the wide oceanic approaches. From the outset Graves requested more ships, but he received only third-rates, too large and clumsy for the task. There were loopholes in the Port Act which made captures difficult to uphold, and the constant sea time wore out the ships and predisposed their crews, probably unhappy at their duties, to desertion—and seamen could not be replaced, especially as attempts to press infuriated the colonists.

Events worsened Graves's problems. Although he used his ships' boats to transport troops for the expedition to Lexington and Concord, Graves, in deference to the views of Thomas Gage, the governor and army commander, would only act when attack was imminent. There was constant harassment by the colonists' small craft in and near Boston, which was difficult to stop and wore out the crews. Supplies of provisions for the army dried up, as producers were hostile or intimidated. Graves, however, would not, without authority, authorize his ships to fire unless actually attacked, a policy perhaps creditable enough at first but which became increasingly unrealistic. He received authority to seize American vessels only in September 1775. Although more ships were sent out later that year the needs were also becoming greater.

Meanwhile discontent with Graves's performance and lack of vigour was growing in London among the advocates of strong measures, and Lord Sandwich, who always supported him, urged attacks on coastal towns, but the only one—on Falmouth, Massachusetts, on 18 October 1775—merely aroused more colonist fury. Sandwich's efforts to justify Graves failed in the face of George III's personal call for his dismissal. Sandwich was thus obliged to appoint Molyneux Shuldham, originally as a second-in-command, but soon as a successor, and Graves handed over on 27 January 1776, and returned home. While Graves was faced with an impossible situation, he does not appear to have been the man to meet it. Moreover, rumours spread of bad blood between him and the army commander, General Gage, although Burgoyne's criticism of him for not supplying the army with sheep and oxen gives the navy tasks it did not have. One critic even termed him 'a corrupt admiral without any shadow of capacity'.

Graves was not blamed for his actions, and Sandwich continued to favour him, especially in advancing his several nephews, and then by offering him another command. This episode became complicated, but does illustrate Graves's weaknesses. Originally the offer was for the Mediterranean, but other factors intervened, including a lack of confidence in him among ministers, and it had to be amended to the Plymouth command. Graves angrily declined, though stating that he was ready for any active command. He did not seem to recognize that Sandwich was trying to make some amends, and continued an indignant correspondence. He then signed a memorial critical of the Admiralty board in 1779, but even afterwards still sought another command, but without success.

Graves rose in the usual course to admiral of the blue and then admiral of the white. He was twice married, first to Elizabeth Sedgwick of Staindrop, co. Durham, and secondly to Margaret (d. in or after 1787), daughter of Elmes Spinckes of Aldwincle, Northamptonshire, but he had no children. He held property in Devon, Durham, Northampton, Huntingdon, and Middlesex, as well as in Ireland and Nova Scotia, which in his will he went to great lengths to preserve in the family. He died at his home, Hembury Fort, near Honiton, Devon, on 8 March 1787 of a haemorrhage of the bladder, and was probably buried at Buckerell church, Devon. His obituary stated that he would be a great loss to the neighbourhood for his Christian and charitable virtues. A. W. H. PEARSALL

Sources DNB · The private papers of John, earl of Sandwich, ed. G. R. Barnes and J. H. Owen, 1–2, Navy RS, 69, 71 (1932–3) · P. Mackesy, The war for America, 1775–1783 (1964) · N. A. M. Rodger, The insatiable earl: a life of John Montagu, fourth earl of Sandwich (1993) · J. A. Tilley, The British navy and the American revolution (1987) · A. Valentine, Lord George Germain (1962) · D. A. Yerxa, 'Vice Admiral Samuel Graves and the North American squadron, 1774–76', Mariner's Mirror, 62 (1976), 371–85 · GM, 1st ser., 57 (1787), 277 · J. Charnock, ed., Biographia navalis, 5 (1797), 301 · PRO, ADM 1/485, 578 [letters] · PRO, ADM 107/3, 351 [passing certificate] · PRO, ADM 36/372 Bonetta, 1044 Enterprise, 1059 Exeter, 3465 Swallow [muster bks] · D. A. Baugh, 'The politics of British naval failure, 1775–1777', American Neptune, 52 (1992), 221–46 · D. Syrett, The Royal Navy in American waters, 1775–1783 (1989) · N. R. Stout, The Royal Navy in America, 1760–1775 (1973) · will, PRO, PROB 11/1151, fols. 182r–188r
Archives NMM, corresp. with Lord Sandwich · U. Mich., Clements L., corresp. with Thomas Gage
Wealth at death considerable property; total bequests almost £2500 besides main estate: will, PRO, PROB 11/1151, fols. 182r–188r

Graves, Thomas, first Baron Graves (1725–1802), naval officer, was born at Thanckes, Cornwall, on 23 October 1725, the second son of Rear-Admiral Thomas Graves (d. 1755), and his second wife, Elizabeth Budgell. On 22 June 1771 he married Elizabeth (d. 1827), daughter of William Peere-Williams of Chudleigh in Devon; they had one son, Thomas North, second baron (1775–1835), and three daughters.

Early career Graves entered the navy in the care of Commodore Henry Medley and was later present with his father in the Norfolk in the unsuccessful expedition against Cartagena in 1741. From the West Indies the Norfolk was sent to the Mediterranean. On 25 June 1743 Graves was promoted lieutenant in the Romney (50 guns) and on 11 February 1744 he was present in her in the action off Toulon in which Admiral Thomas Mathews commanded. In 1746 he was lieutenant in the Princessa with Admiral Richard Lestock in the expedition against Lorient, and on the admiral's death he was appointed to the Monmouth with Captain Harrison. In her he was present at the first and second battles of Cape Finisterre on 3 May and 14 October 1747. In 1751 he went to the coast of Africa as first lieutenant of the Assistance with Commodore Buckle and later with Commodore Stepney. On his return in 1754 he was promoted to the command of the sloop Hazard and on 8 July 1755 he was promoted captain in the frigate Sheerness (20 guns) in which he continued to be employed in the channel.

In the Sheerness, on 14 December 1756 off Ushant, Graves discovered six ships to windward of him and he sailed down to them and tacked across the squadron several times in order to ascertain their exact strength and destination. The precise detail he sent to the Admiralty was warmly approved by the board. The warmth of this approbation was diminished when, on the night of 26 December 1756, Graves saw another vessel which he judged also to be a French ship of the line, possibly separated from those seen earlier; because of the disparity in size he did not attempt to engage her. An Admiralty inquiry, deciding the ship was a French East-Indiaman and that Graves should have engaged, ordered his court martial. He was sentenced under article 36 to be publicly reprimanded for an error of judgement. His immediate career did not appear to suffer from this reprimand.

In January 1758 Graves was appointed to the *Unicorn* (28 guns), attached to the Grand Fleet under Anson, and in the following year to the squadron under Rear-Admiral George Rodney with whom he was at the bombardment of Le Havre. From September 1760 to May 1761 he had temporary command of the *Oxford* and then on 15 May 1761 he was appointed to the *Antelope* (50 guns) to carry out instructions given to the late Captain Webb to proceed to Newfoundland as governor and commander-in-chief. Arriving there on 5 July he learnt of the presence of the French Admiral de Ternay's squadron in St John's. Too weak to tackle the French head on, he made for Placentia, anchored in the bay, and put men ashore to strengthen the garrison. At the same time he sent urgent requests for reinforcements to Rear-Admiral Lord Colvill and General Amherst in Halifax. Colvill arrived on 14 August and noted that Graves had been 'employed in repairing the ruined fortifications of this Place and putting everything in a posture of Defence with all possible diligence …' (ADM 1/482). Colvill's presence caused the departure of de Ternay and the general expressed himself happy to leave Newfoundland's government to Governor Graves 'who is well qualified for such an office' (ibid.).

Graves left Newfoundland on 21 November 1762 and in November 1764 was appointed captain of the *Téméraire*, guardship in Plymouth; from her he was sent on special service to the coast of Africa in January 1765 with a broad pennant in the *Edgar*. On his return in August he resumed the command of the *Téméraire* which he held for the two following years. During the dispute with Spain in 1770 over the Falkland Islands he was appointed to the *Cambridge* (80 guns). In 1773 he had command of the *Raisonnable* in the channel and in 1776 of the *Nonsuch*. In 1777 he moved into the *Conqueror*, one of the squadron which went with Vice-Admiral John Byron to North America and afterwards to the West Indies. Graves was recalled on his promotion on 19 March 1779 to rear-admiral of the blue. On his return to England he hoisted his flag on the *London* in the Channel Fleet under the command of Sir Charles Hardy. While in the Channel Fleet he joined with Richard Kempenfelt in experiments to devise a more flexible manner of signalling and command.

War with America In March 1780 he was ordered to prepare a squadron to reinforce the North American station and in late April he sailed from Plymouth, having first resolved a mutiny in his squadron brought about by the failure to pay the sailors what was due to them. The king wrote to Sandwich, 'The conduct of the Rear-admiral on this occasion shows that he is both a man of sense and resolution' (*Private Papers of … Sandwich*, 3.243). Graves joined Admiral Mariot Arbuthnot in New York on 13 July 1780 and was with him at the action off the mouth of the Chesapeake on 16 March 1781. On 4 July 1781 Graves assumed command of the North American station in place of the ailing Arbuthnot whose tenure had left the station in need of considerable reform and re-equipment. From the outset Graves was faced with a number of serious problems: internally he had to bring back to fighting readiness ships damaged by storm and in action; he had to re-establish personal relationships riven by quarrels between Arbuthnot, Rodney, and Sir Henry Clinton. The French squadron of de Barras was at Rhode Island and externally there was the likely threat of a powerful French reinforcement coming to his zone of command from the West Indies.

Graves was well informed of this danger by a letter from the Admiralty dated 5 April 1781 and confirmed by a letter from Rodney in the West Indies which announced the arrival of a very considerable French squadron on 29 April. Graves wrote immediately to Rodney and stressed the importance of 'the early intelligence and detachment upon the first movement of the enemy' (*Graves Papers*, 18). In the event this was the only positive information Graves received before the arrival of the French in North America yet, in less than eight weeks into his command, he found himself in an action which was to prove critical in the outcome of the American War of Independence.

Graves was distracted from concentrating his squadron at New York by compelling but false intelligence from London of a French convoy which would provide the rebels 'with the only possible means of carrying on the war' (ADM 2/1339). No admiral could ignore such a threat but the sole outcome of Graves's cruise towards Boston to seek the convoy was storm damage to his squadron which reduced his effective force to five ships of the line.

Sir Samuel Hood arrived off New York on 28 August from the West Indies with fourteen ships of the line and news of the departure from the West Indies of Admiral de Grasse. On the same day Graves received intelligence that de Barras had sailed from Rhode Island, destination unknown. He sought out the French as soon as the wind came free, sailing from New York with Hood on 31 August with a combined force of nineteen ships of the line. The squadron made a swift and stormy passage to the Chesapeake. On passage Graves discovered that many of Hood's squadron 'were but shadows of ships' (*Private Papers of … Sandwich*, 4.183). Landfall was made early on 5 September and by 10 a.m. up to twenty-six sail of large ships could be picked out within the river. Only now was it clear that Graves was faced with a more formidable force than that of de Barras. Graves immediately ordered a line of battle and, with a favourable wind, ran towards the Chesapeake. By 1 p.m. the fleet was rapidly approaching the shoal water of the Middle Ground and soon after 2 p.m. the squadron veered, ship by ship, until sailing seawards on a west/east line in reverse order of divisions. The French were less well placed because of foul wind and tide but by noon the first ships were struggling to weather the capes and heading to sea on a line parallel to that of the British. Graves continued to order his line, signalling the rear (Hood's) division to make more sail to get closer to the enemy as the rear was sagging to leeward while the van and centre was close and parallel. It was not until shortly after 4 p.m. that the van and centre divisions began their engagement.

From the centre to the van of each line the action was spirited, French ships were forced out of the line and significant casualties and damage were sustained. The rear was unscathed. By evening the French appeared to be breaking off the engagement which ended soon after sunset. For the next few days the fleets manoeuvred in sight of each other without renewing the engagement and at this time Graves ordered the *Terrible* to be sunk. Contact was lost on the night of 9/10 September and Graves steered for the Chesapeake on 11 September to discover that de Grasse, joined by de Barras, was once more at anchor within the capes, now with thirty-six line ships. Graves, with only eighteen, had no alternative but to return to New York which he reached on 20 September. Lord Cornwallis's position in Yorktown was critical and at once Graves and Clinton prepared a relief expedition of 7000 soldiers which sailed on 19 October, arriving off the Chesapeake on 24 October with an augmented naval force now increased to twenty-five line and two 50-gun ships as a result of the arrival from England of Rear-Admiral Robert Digby with three ships and the tardy arrival of two ships from the West Indies. When it was discovered that Cornwallis had surrendered on the day that Graves had left New York and that de Grasse and de Barras had combined their forces and were anchored within the capes, the relief force, no longer with an attainable objective, returned to New York. Graves handed over his command to his successor, Rear-Admiral Digby, and sailed in the *London* to the West Indies on 10 November.

Career and reputation after the loss of Yorktown The initial reaction in London had been that a modestly successful action had been fought. Swiftly following the arrival of Graves's dispatches, though, had come the news of Cornwallis's surrender combined with critical and bitter letters from Sir Samuel Hood condemning the whole conduct of Graves in the battle. Hood appeared to have better access to public opinion than Graves and the biased descriptions and assessment of the Chesapeake which are still repeated by reputable historians are to be found directly in the dispatches and letters of Samuel Hood. Graves found himself unjustifiably the principal candidate for naval failure and George Germain even proposed he should be court martialled, a course which Lord Sandwich refused to countenance. The reality was that Graves went to the capes with a force made inadequate by wrong decisions in the West Indies and that in the battle half of Graves's squadron, Hood's division, did not get into action.

Graves's posting to the West Indies predated the Chesapeake battle by some months but he was sensitive to the opportunities this move would give to his critics, enabling them to suggest that his move from the command in North America indicated a lack of confidence in him at the Admiralty. Accordingly he requested permission to return to England to rebut the mounting criticism in press and parliament of his conduct of the battle. His request was granted but it did not break this period of misfortune. His return was to include the task of escorting a convoy of merchantmen with a squadron of warships that were largely unfit for sea. His squadron ran foul of an Atlantic storm of unusual severity and he had the misfortune to lose many ships of the convoy. His flagship, the *Ramillies*, was one of the vessels which foundered but only after a feat of superb seamanship enabled Graves to save his whole crew. Graves got on board the *Belle* merchant ship in which he reached Cork on 10 October 1782, having lost many of his personal papers left behind in the *Ramillies*.

Graves returned to an England of furious charge and counter-charge for the loss of Yorktown. Public opinion was stirred against him by the letters of Hood from America, by Rodney's speeches in the House of Commons, and by his letter from Bath which reveals either a faulty recollection of events or a deliberate distortion of the instructions he claims to have given. Yet the criticisms levelled by Hood, Rodney, and their followers were demonstrably false. It would not have been possible for Graves to reach the Middle Ground or enter the river before the French could get out of the Chesapeake, and it would have been strategically unsound for Graves to enter the Chesapeake after the action and risk being shut in the river by the French, inevitably losing command of the sea with the dire consequences to New York that would have followed.

Graves's reputation was damaged by the criticisms initiated by Hood yet he had been caught in the pincers of other people's incompetence. Rodney and Hood had dealt no significant blow to de Grasse in the four months that they had faced him in the West Indies. They had made significant errors of judgement in their appraisals of de Grasse's possible moves to North America and, as a consequence, they had failed to send adequate advance information or reinforcements to Graves. Hood and Rodney, it could be argued, were anxious, sometimes by distorting the facts, to divert attention from their own shortcomings. The failure to impose naval superiority at the Chesapeake had far-reaching consequences for the war with America and for the government at home leading, as it did, to a demand for a parliamentary inquiry into the conduct of the war. In the longer term Graves emerged from this period of criticism with continued employment and promotion and ended his career honoured and praised for his part in the battle of 1 June 1794.

On 24 September 1787 Graves was promoted vice-admiral of the blue and in 1788 became commander-in-chief at Plymouth. On the outbreak of war with France in 1793 he was appointed second in command of the Channel Fleet under Lord Howe. He became admiral of the blue on 12 April 1794 and, aboard his flagship the *Royal Sovereign*, played an important part in the success of 1 June 1794, for which he was raised to the Irish peerage as Baron Graves, and received the gold medal and chain and a pension of £1000 per annum. This action marked the end of his active career, however, as he was badly wounded in the right arm and was obliged to resign his command. He had no further service and died at Thanckes, Cornwall, on 9 February 1802. He was buried at Thanckes. Graves was survived by his wife who died in 1827, before April.

Graves's naval career may be judged by the praise with which it was frequently marked by his contemporaries and superiors, from the commendation he received early in his career for his work in Newfoundland to the final honours awarded to him for his support as second in command to Lord Howe in 1794. Earlier, while in the Channel Fleet in 1779–80, he was a convinced supporter of the experiments and innovations in signalling undertaken by Richard Kempenfelt and took many of these ideas with him to North America. As Captain Sir John Jervis wrote to Clinton on Graves's appointment to America in 1780, 'He is very knowing in his profession, distinct and clear in his understanding' ('Letters', 7.101).   KENNETH BREEN

Sources PRO, ADM 1 · PRO, ADM 2 · PRO, ADM 8 · PRO, ADM 11 · NMM, Montagu MSS · *The private papers of John, earl of Sandwich*, ed. G. R. Barnes and J. H. Owen, 4 vols., Navy RS, 69, 71, 75, 78 (1932–8) · *Letters written by Sir Samuel Hood*, ed. D. Hannay, Navy RS, 3 (1895) · *GM*, 1st ser., 50 (1780), 249 · *GM*, 1st ser., 51 (1781), 487, 539 · *GM*, 1st ser., 52 (1782), 501 · *Annual Register* (1781) · *Graves papers relating to naval operations of Yorktown campaign*, ed. F. Chadwick (1916) · *Sir Henry Clinton's narrative of his campaigns*, ed. W. Willcox (1954) · G. B. Mundy, *The life and correspondence of the late Admiral Lord Rodney*, 2 vols. (1830) · K. Breen, 'The navy in the Yorktown campaign, the battle of the Chesapeake, 1781', MPhil. diss., U. Lond., 1971 · K. Breen, 'Graves and Hood at the Chesapeake', *Mariner's Mirror*, 66 (1980), 53–64 · K. Breen, 'Divided command: the West Indies and North America, 1780–1781', *The British navy and the use of naval power in the eighteenth century*, ed. J. Black and P. Woodfine (1988), 191–206 · 'Letters of Captain John Jervis to Sir Henry Clinton, 1774–1782', ed. M. M. Hatch, *American Neptune*, 7 (1947), 87–106
Archives NMM, logbooks, letter-books, and papers | NMM, corresp. with Lord Sandwich
Likenesses Bartolozzi, Landseer, Ryder, and Stow, group portrait, line engraving, pubd 1803 (*Commemoration of the victory of June 1st 1794*; after *Naval victories* by R. Smirke), BM, NPG · F. Bartolozzi, mezzotint (after J. Northcote), BM, NPG
Wealth at death estate, house, and all buildings and fields adjacent; annuity to wife of £900, then to son: will, PRO, PROB 11/1378

Graves, Sir Thomas (*c*.1747–1814), naval officer, was the third son of the Revd John Graves of Castledawson, co. Londonderry. He was nephew of Admiral Samuel *Graves, and first cousin of Admiral Thomas *Graves. His three brothers all served as captains in the navy, becoming admirals on the superannuated list. Thomas entered the navy at a very early age, and served during the Seven Years' War with his uncle Samuel on board the *Scorpion*, *Duke*, and *Venus*. After the peace he was appointed to the *Antelope* with his cousin Thomas, whom he followed to the *Edgar*, and by whom, in 1765, while on the coast of Africa, he was promoted to be lieutenant of the *Shannon*. In 1770 he was lieutenant of the *Arethusa*, and in 1773 he was

appointed to the *Racehorse* with Captain Constantine Phipps for the voyage of discovery in the Arctic seas.

In the following year Graves went out to North America with his uncle Samuel, and was appointed by him to command the *Diana*, one of the small schooners employed for the prevention of smuggling. She had thirty men, with an armament of four 2-pounders. On 27 May 1775, *en route* from Boston into the Charles River, the *Diana* was attacked by a large force of rebels, whose numbers swelled until they reached upward of two thousand men, with two field guns. It fell calm, and towards midnight, as the tide ebbed, the *Diana* grounded and lay over on her side. The colonial forces succeeded in setting her on fire, and the small crew, after a gallant defence, were compelled to abandon her, Graves having been first severely burnt. After this, he continued in command of other tenders in the neighbourhood of Boston and Rhode Island until, on the recall of his uncle, he rejoined the *Preston* and returned to England. He was again sent out to North America in the same ship, commanded by Commodore Hotham.

In 1779 Graves was promoted to the command of the *Savage* sloop on the West Indian and North American stations, and in May 1781 he was advanced to post rank. In the temporary absence of Commodore Edmund Affleck he commanded the *Bedford* in the action of 5 September, off the Chesapeake, and continuing afterwards in the *Bedford*, as Affleck's flag captain, was present in the engagement at St Kitts on 26 January 1782, and in the actions to leeward of Dominica on 9 and 12 April.

In the following autumn Graves was appointed to the *Magicienne* frigate, in which, on 2 January 1783, he fought a severe action with the French *Sybille*, a frigate of superior force, but encumbered with a second ship's company which she was carrying to the Chesapeake. Both frigates were reduced to wrecks and so parted. The *Magicienne* reached Jamaica a fortnight later; the *Sybille* was captured on 22 January by the *Hussar*. During the peace Graves spent much of his time in France, and was unemployed during the early years of the revolutionary war. It was not until October 1800 that he was appointed to command the *Cumberland* (74 guns) in the Channel Fleet, under the orders of Lord St Vincent.

On 1 January 1801, as part of the general promotion to celebrate the union of Britain and Ireland, Graves was promoted to be rear-admiral of the white. In March he hoisted his flag aboard the *Defiance* as third in command of the fleet going to the Baltic under Sir Hyde Parker. He fought in her at the battle of Copenhagen on 2 April. He received the thanks of parliament and the appointment as KCB for his part in the battle. Despite poor health, he shifted his flag to the *Polyphemus* and then to the *Monarch*, remaining aboard her until January 1802. From January 1804 to November 1805 he was third in command of the Brest blockade, usually flying his flag in the *Foudroyant* and commanding the inshore squadron. He faced some criticism for taking his fleet to Quiberon Bay to water in January 1805, thereby allowing Missiessy's Rochefort squadron to slip out and beginning the chain of events that led to the battle of Trafalgar. His promotion to vice-admiral on 9 November 1805 was a double-edged sword, for it led to his removal from command (due to the number of vice-admirals chasing places): Graves wrote to William Cornwallis, explaining that 'a severe cold and inflammation in my eyes' prevented him expressing in person his 'surprise ... disappointment, and mortification of being removed in so extraordinary a manner' (BL, Add. MS 40668, fol. 105). He retired to Woodbine Hill, Honiton, Devon, a property he had owned since at least the 1790s, was promoted admiral on 2 August 1812, and died at Woodbine Hill on 29 March 1814. The administration of his will refers to a wife, Susanna (apparently his second wife), and a daughter, Mary. J. K. LAUGHTON, *rev.* J. D. DAVIES

Sources Graves's letter-book and order book, 1801–5, BL, Add. MSS 40667–40668 · J. Leyland, ed., *Despatches and letters relating to the blockade of Brest*, 2 vols., Navy Records Society (1899–1902) · *Naval Chronicle*, 8 (1802), 353–72 · *Naval Chronicle*, 31 (1814), 352 · miscellaneous papers relating to Graves, NMM, MS RUSI/NM/86 · papers of Alexander Davison, NMM, MS DAV/1 · will, PRO, PROB 6/191, fol. 204v · *Letters and papers of Charles, Lord Barham*, ed. J. K. Laughton, 3, Navy RS, 39 (1911) · *Letters of admiral of the fleet, the earl of St Vincent: whilst the first lord of the admiralty, 1801–1804*, ed. D. Bonner-Smith, 2 vols., Navy RS, 55, 61 (1921–7)
Archives BL, letter-book and order book, Add. MSS 40667–40668 · NMM, corresp. and papers | PRO, Admiralty MSS
Likenesses J. Northcote, oils, 1802, NMM

Gravesend, Richard of (d. 1279), bishop of Lincoln, was a member of a Kentish family from Milton near Gravesend. Like so many of Henry III's bishops, he probably studied at Oxford and was *magister* by 1248. Treasurer of Hereford Cathedral before 1239 and archdeacon of Oxford by 1250, he has been conjecturally identified as the unnamed archdeacon who, according to Matthew Paris, accompanied Robert Grosseteste abroad in that year. In 1254 he occurs as chaplain to John, cardinal of San Lorenzo in Lucina, and in August of that year he is named dean and later prebendary of Langford Manor in Lincoln Cathedral. The following year he was appointed executor of a papal mandate for the excommunication of contraveners of Magna Carta. As a papal delegate he was engaged in 1258 in assessing the validity of Osney Abbey's claim to the chapel of St George-in-the-Castle, Oxford. Gravesend was elected to the see of Lincoln on 21 or 23 September 1258. Royal assent followed on 13 October and the temporalities were restored four days later. He was consecrated on 3 November at Canterbury by Archbishop Boniface. Shortly afterwards he left for France with Walter de Cantilupe, bishop of Worcester, and the earls of Leicester and Gloucester—Simon de Montfort and Richard de Clare—an indication of his political sympathies. After abortive initial negotiations at Cambrai in May 1259 the treaty of Paris was concluded, followed on 4 December by Henry III's performance of homage to Louis IX for his French possessions. Possibly Gravesend was present, since he spent Christmas with the court and witnessed royal charters. In 1261–2 he made a further journey abroad, to Viterbo, perhaps to take his oath of allegiance to the pope.

In the early 1260s, Gravesend became increasingly involved in the conflict between Montfort and the king. On 4 July 1263 he was appointed a commissioner, together with the bishops of London and of Coventry and Lichfield, to mediate between the parties. But the agreement to submit to Louis's arbitration resulted in the mise of Amiens (23 January 1264), which was unfavourable to the barons, and civil war ensued. A fine of 500 marks was levied against Gravesend for failure to place the episcopal castles of Newark and Sleaford at Henry's disposition. He attended the London parliament which assembled in June 1264 for the pacification of the realm following Montfort's victory at Lewes and the king's capture. In the autumn he was in attendance on Henry at Canterbury. With two other bishops he was deputed to examine the plundering of church property during the recent disturbances and attended the parliament of January 1265 which was concerned to implement the pro-baronial mise of Lewes. Reversal of the political situation came with the Lord Edward's victory at Evesham in August 1265, and following the arrival of the papal legate Ottobuono, Gravesend was one of four bishops suspended for aiding the king's enemies. He seems to have been more leniently treated than the others, and having made his peace with the king left for the curia in December 1266 to secure absolution from excommunication. On his return in October of the following year he resumed his diocesan duties, although he was absent from England on unknown business between December 1270 and March 1272.

Gravesend's itinerary points to his having been at the reforming legatine council summoned by Ottobuono to St Paul's, London, in 1268. In October 1269 he is named first among the bishops attending a clerical council at the New Temple, where objections were raised to a royal subsidy and an appeal was launched to the apostolic see. Although he was not a member of the English delegation to the Council of Lyons in 1274, some manuscripts indicate that he did attend Archbishop Pecham's council at Reading (1279) at which many of its provisions were promulgated. He was one of those who sealed Pecham's letter of 31 July 1279 for the protection of the liberties of Oxford University. It would appear that Gravesend misinterpreted Pecham's intentions, as expressed in the Reading legislation, and he was severely reproved by the archbishop for over-zealous action against pluralists.

In 1275 Pecham insisted on appointing a coadjutor on the grounds of Gravesend's infirmity, but this seems to have been only temporary. From 1272 until his death he devoted his time to his diocese. Nine rolls detailing his *acta* are preserved at Lincoln, mainly recording institutions. He was diligent in ordaining vicarages for appropriated churches, including the prebendal churches attached to the canonries of his cathedral. Frequently he made provision for the maintenance of chaplains in hamlets remote from the parish church. His practice was to hold two ordination ceremonies every Lent, and he endeavoured to carry out a triennial circuit of his extensive diocese. He was apparently on good terms with his chapter; an undated ordinance provides an endowment, house, and *magister* for the twelve choristers previously boarded on the residentiary canons. Gravesend gave plate, vestments, a processional cross, and a Lenten veil to his cathedral church. To Rochester Cathedral priory he left a book, possibly two—now Royal MSS 3B.xiii and 2F.xii in the British Library. During his time as dean and bishop the magnificent angel choir of Lincoln was under construction, and must have been nearing completion when he died at his manor of Stow on 18 December 1279. He was buried in the south-east transept of his cathedral, close to the tomb of Grosseteste.

ROY MARTIN HAINES

Sources F. N. Davis and others, eds., *Rotuli Ricardi Gravesend*, Lincoln RS, 20 (1925) · C. W. Foster and K. Major, eds., *The registrum antiquissimum of the cathedral church of Lincoln*, 10 vols. in 12, Lincoln RS, 27–9, 32, 34, 41–2, 46, 51, 62, 67–8 (1931–73) · H. E. Reynolds, ed., *Consuetudinarium ecclesiae Lincolniensis tempore Ricardi de Gravesend* (1885) [notes by C. Wordsworth] · M. Richter, ed., *Canterbury professions*, CYS, 67 (1973) · *Chancery records* · *List of ancient correspondence of the chancery and exchequer* (1902) · F. M. Powicke and C. R. Cheney, eds., *Councils and synods with other documents relating to the English church, 1205–1313*, 2 vols. (1964) · *The historical works of Gervase of Canterbury*, ed. W. Stubbs, 2: *The minor works comprising the Gesta regum with its continuation, the Actus pontificum and the Mappa mundi*, Rolls Series, 73 (1880) · Paris, *Chron.*, vol. 5 · *Ann. mon.*, vol. 1 · J. S. Brewer, ed., *Monumenta Franciscana*, 1, Rolls Series, 4 (1858) · M. Gibbs and J. Lang, *Bishops and reform, 1215–1272* (1934) · F. M. Powicke, *King Henry III and the Lord Edward: the community of the realm in the thirteenth century*, 2 vols. (1947) · W. Stubbs, *The constitutional history of England in its origin and development*, 2 (1875) · D. M. Smith, *Guide to bishops' registers of England and Wales: a survey from the middle ages to the abolition of the episcopacy in 1646*, Royal Historical Society Guides and Handbooks, 11 (1981) · *Fasti Angl., 1066–1300*, [Lincoln] · Emden, *Oxf.*

Archives Lincs. Arch., rotuli Ricardi Gravesend

Gravesend, Richard of (*d.* 1303), bishop of London, was born into a Kentish family, which took its name from the town of Gravesend, where it held the manor of Parrocks in Milton by Gravesend. His parents' names and the date and place of his birth are unknown, but he did have at least one brother, Stephen, who was over forty in 1303, when he was named in Richard's will as his heir. Richard was also certainly related to Richard of Gravesend, bishop of Lincoln from 1258 to 1279, from whom he received his early preferment. The younger Richard of Gravesend first appears in the diocese of Lincoln, as a canon of the cathedral and prebendary of Leighton Ecclesia, in 1262–3, by when he was also a university graduate, since he is described as *magister*, although where he obtained his degree is unclear. In 1263–4 he additionally obtained the rectorship of Ecclesborough in Buckinghamshire. After this reference he disappears from the records until the 1270s, when he is found in the diocese of London. He owed his preferment here, as he later made clear in his will, to Henry of Sandwich, bishop of London from 1263 to 1273, 'meus promotus', who had served in Lincoln diocese as archdeacon of Oxford during the episcopate of Richard's kinsman. In January 1271 or 1272 Richard of Gravesend was archdeacon of Essex, but obtained the archdeaconry of Northampton by 5 November 1273. At the time of his election to the bishopric of London he was still a canon of St Paul's. He had retained his links with the diocese of Lincoln, however, being granted the prebend of Sutton-cum-Buckingham some time before November 1276.

In 1280, on or by 7 May, Gravesend was elected bishop of

London, following the resignation of Fulk Lovel. Royal assent to the election was granted on 9 May, and he received the temporalities of the see on 17 May. He was consecrated on 11 August of that year by Archbishop John Pecham (*d.* 1292) in the cathedral at Coventry. Little is known about his administration of the diocese; the episcopal register, a vital source for the work of a bishop within his see from the late thirteenth century, which he is known to have kept, has been lost. But probably before 1290 he reissued the synodal statutes of Bishop Fulk Basset (*d.* 1259), with eight additional clauses, and he attended some of the provincial councils summoned by archbishops Pecham and Winchelsey. It is clear, moreover, that he was concerned for the education of his cathedral clergy. Bishop Gravesend had himself an extensive library, numbering over eighty volumes at his death, and he insisted that the chancellor should be qualified as a doctor, or at least a bachelor, of theology, and that he should lecture upon this subject in the church. He was also responsible for establishing the office of subdean at St Paul's. Outside his see, however, he was involved in the politics of his day. He had intervened in the case of Amaury de Montfort, Simon's son, captured and imprisoned by Edward I when on his way to Wales in 1275: an extant letter from Gravesend to Pecham reveals that he had asked the king for Montfort's release, but his request had been refused. However he also served the king abroad, attending Edward in Gascony in 1289–90, and going on embassies to France in 1293 and to the Low Countries in 1294 and 1296, while at home he was one of the councillors of Prince Edward during the king's absence in 1297.

Richard of Gravesend died at Fulham on 9 December 1303. In death he did not forget those whose spiritual well-being had been in his care, for from his estate of £3000 he not only founded a chantry at St Paul's, and left money for the maintenance of the cathedral, but also made bequests to the poor of London. He was buried on 12 December 1303, as he had requested, in St Paul's near the tomb of the man to whom he felt he owed so much, Henry of Sandwich.

PHILIPPA HOSKIN

Sources *Fasti Angl., 1066–1300*, [St Paul's, London] · *Fasti Angl., 1066–1300*, [Lincoln] · F. N. Davis and others, eds., *Rotuli Ricardi Gravesend, diocesis Lincolniensis*, CYS, 31 (1925) · W. H. Hale and H. T. Ellacombe, eds., *Account of the executors of Richard, bishop of London, 1303, and of the executors of Thomas, bishop of Exeter, 1310*, CS, new ser., 10 (1874) · D. L. Douie, *Archbishop Pecham* (1952) · *Registrum epistolarum fratris Johannis Peckham, archiepiscopi Cantuariensis*, ed. C. T. Martin, 3 vols., Rolls Series, 77 (1882–5) · Emden, *Oxf.* · F. M. Powicke and C. R. Cheney, eds., *Councils and synods with other documents relating to the English church, 1205–1313*, 1 (1964), 633

Wealth at death £3000: Hale and Ellacombe, eds., *Account of the executors*

Gravesend, Stephen (*c.*1260–1338), bishop of London, may have been a son of Stephen Gravesend, knight, although in 1303 the latter is stated to have been only 'forty or more'. Richard Grene of Gravesend, treasurer of St Paul's, was possibly his brother, more likely his cousin. The Grene family held Parrocks manor in Milton by

Gravesend, which was in Bishop Stephen Gravesend's possession at his death. Richard of Gravesend, bishop of London (d. 1303), was his uncle. His earlier studies were probably at Oxford, but although Merton College inherited the bulk of his library there is no evidence that he went there. He was subdeacon when he became rector of Stoke Hammond (Lincoln diocese) on 22 June 1278. Entitled *magister*, he occurs *c.*1291 as prebendary of Chamberlainwood in St Paul's, and in 1306 was licensed to absent himself for three years from his benefice of Stepney, Middlesex, in order to study at Paris.

Gravesend was elected bishop of London on 11 September 1318, a choice agreeable to Edward II, who restored the temporalities on 6 November. Consecrated on 14 January 1319 at Canterbury by Archbishop Walter Reynolds (d. 1327), he was enthroned on 30 September. He had already had some altercation with Reynolds, and in 1320 unsuccessfully opposed his metropolitical visitation. At the Westminster parliament of October 1320 he was delegated, with Rigaud d'Assier (d. 1323), to approach Thomas of Lancaster. The envoys carried papal bulls for peace with Robert I, and for the reconciliation of Lancaster and the king. But having helped to consecrate Assier as bishop of Winchester at St Albans on 16 November, Gravesend fell ill at Northampton, and not until 6 February 1321 did he return to Westminster, his mission unsuccessful.

The summer of 1321 Gravesend spent as mediator between the king and his opponents encamped outside London. But an agreement reached in mid-August broke down when Queen Isabella was refused entry to Leeds Castle in Kent in October. Gravesend joined Reynolds and the earl of Pembroke in urging Edward to raise the ensuing siege, but Leeds soon fell. His sympathies remained with Edward, for he was among the four bishops who joined Archbishop Reynolds at the convocation of December 1321 summoned to secure approval for the Despensers' recall.

Following the battle of Boroughbridge (16 March 1322) and Lancaster's death Edward complained about the devotion paid to a representation of the earl on a tablet in St Paul's. Bishop Gravesend and his chapter suffered harassment in the courts on that account. Despite this, on Isabella's invasion in 1326, Gravesend joined his colleagues Reynolds and John Stratford, bishop of Winchester, in publishing at St Paul's an amended version of a papal bull originally issued in 1320 against the Scots. After the king's flight from London he joined other bishops at Lambeth, and is said to have urged the sending of a delegation to the queen. As dean of the province he summoned a convocation to St Paul's for 16 January 1327 to raise a subsidy for the pope against the emperor. This project was overtaken by events in parliament, where Gravesend refused to assent to Edward's deposition, and subsequently declined to subscribe to the Guildhall oath (13 January) which called for this. None the less he did take part in Edward III's coronation on 1 February.

When opposition to the regime of Isabella and Mortimer erupted during 1328, Gravesend accompanied John Stratford on an unsuccessful mission from the October parliament at Salisbury to persuade Henry of Lancaster, the leader of that opposition, who was then at Winchester, to attend. Just before Christmas he joined Archbishop Simon Mepham, Stratford, and members of the baronage in devising articles critical of the government. Lancaster arrived in London in January 1329 and his force moved into the midlands. But Gravesend and Mepham now sought to compromise with Mortimer and Isabella, and this precipitated the collapse of the Lancastrian *chevauchée* at Bedford in mid-January. Subsequently Mortimer's *agents provocateurs* spread a rumour that Edward II remained alive. Gravesend was among those implicated in this 'treason', for which the gullible earl of Kent was beheaded at Winchester in March 1330. Following Edward III's assumption of power in 1330 Gravesend was one of those deputed to preside over royal councils in London on 24 August 1335 and 3 January 1337.

Gravesend's episcopal register is fragmentary but his activity as dean of the province can be partly recovered from other registers. He executed numerous papal bulls, many relating to political affairs, and was a principal collector of the papal tenths of 1319 and 1322. As papal mandatory on 16 July 1329 he published a bull at Paul's Cross excommunicating the emperor, Lewis IV (r. 1314–47), and the antipope, Nicholas V. Gravesend died on 8 April 1338 at Bishop's Stortford rectory in Hertfordshire and his funeral, on the 27th, was conducted by Archbishop Stratford, for whom he had acted as vicar-general in 1334–5. This was attended by the king and two cardinals, among many others. He had requested burial in his cathedral next to the tomb of his uncle, and had founded a chantry there with two priests to pray for the souls of the king, of himself, and of his uncle. His substantial library, which he bequeathed to three Oxford colleges, contained numerous texts by Aristotle, and other works of logic, theology, and natural philosophy. A courageous man, he remained loyal to Edward II and his memory.

ROY MARTIN HAINES

Sources BL, Cotton MSS, Faustina B. V [Historia Roffensis] · letters of Gravesend, PRO, SC 1 · will dated 19/2/1337, GL, St Paul's Cath. MS.66 A. 27 [Stephen de Gravesend] · composite episcopal register, GL, St Paul's Cath. MS 9531/1 · R. C. Fowler, ed., *Registrum Radulphi Baldock, Gilberti Segrave, Ricardi Newport, et Stephani Gravesend*, CYS, 7 (1911) · F. N. Davis and others, eds., *Rotuli Ricardi Gravesend, diocesis Lincolniensis*, CYS, 31 (1925) · W. H. Hale and H. T. Ellacombe, eds., *Account of the executors of Richard, bishop of London, 1303, and of the executors of Thomas, bishop of Exeter, 1310*, CS, new ser., 10 (1874) · *Chancery records* · Rymer, *Foedera* · *RotP* · A. H. Thomas and P. E. Jones, eds., *Calendar of plea and memoranda rolls preserved among the archives of the corporation of the City of London at the Guildhall*, 1 (1926) · *CIPM*, vol. 8 · *John Lydford's book*, ed. D. M. Owen, Devon and Cornwall RS, new ser., 20 (1974) · W. Stubbs, ed., *Chronicles of the reigns of Edward I and Edward II*, 2 vols., Rolls Series, 76 (1882–3) · *Adae Murimuth continuatio chronicarum. Robertus de Avesbury de gestis mirabilibus regis Edwardi tertii*, ed. E. M. Thompson, Rolls Series, 93 (1889) · *Chronicon Galfridi le Baker de Swynebroke*, ed. E. M. Thompson (1889) · 'Chronica Guillielmi Thorne', *Historiae Anglicanae scriptores X*, ed. R. Twysden (1652) · *Thomae Walsingham, quondam monachi S. Albani, historia Anglicana*, ed. H. T. Riley, 2 vols., pt 1 of *Chronica monasterii S. Albani*, Rolls Series, 28 (1863–4), vol. 1 · K. Edwards, 'The political importance of the English bishops during the reign of Edward II', *EngHR*, 59 (1944), 311–47 · R. M. Haines,

The church and politics in fourteenth-century England: the career of Adam Orleton, c. 1275–1345, Cambridge Studies in Medieval Life and Thought, 3rd ser., 10 (1978) · W. E. L. Smith, *Episcopal appointments and patronage in the reign of Edward II*, SCH, 3 (1938) · *Fasti Angl., 1300–1541*, [St Paul's, London] · *Fasti Angl., 1300–1541*, [Introduction] · Emden, *Oxf.*

Archives GL, St Paul's Cathedral MS 9531/1 · PRO, ancient corresp., letters, SC 1

Wealth at death see will, 1337, GL, St Paul's MS 66.A.27

Gravet, William (*d.* 1599), Church of England clergyman, was a native of Buckinghamshire. Having matriculated as a pensioner at Peterhouse, Cambridge, at Michaelmas 1554, he graduated BA in 1557/8 and in 1558 was made a fellow of Pembroke College, where he proceeded MA in 1561 and BTh in 1569. On 8 October 1566, on presentation of the queen, he was instituted vicar of St Sepulchre, London, and in the same year he was presented by John Collyer to the rectory of Little Laver, Essex. Gravet held both these benefices until his death. On 27 July 1567 he was collated to the prebend of Wilsden in St Paul's Cathedral, and he is said by Cooper to have held the rectory of Bradfield, Berkshire as well. In 1568 he ministered at the deathbed of the famous scholar Roger Ascham, who lived in St Sepulchre's parish. In 1582 Gravet was one of twenty-six divines recommended to confer with recently apprehended Jesuits and seminary priests. On 25 June 1587 he preached at Paul's Cross, a sermon later published. In the Marprelate tracts, however, he appears as Parson Gravat, a drinking companion of 'dumb John' (Whitgift), who, it was proposed, should employ both 'drunken Gravate' and Richard Bancroft as 'the yeomen of his cellar' (*Hay any Work for Cooper*, 33; *The Just Censure and Reproofe*, sig. Ciiv). The author's hostility to Bancroft doubtless stems from his role in unearthing radical opponents of the church, and the gibes against Gravet must likewise have owed something to his appointment as a press censor in 1588. In the 1590s he employed two clerical assistants at St Sepulchre's, and though it is possible that this unusual departure stemmed from Gravet's non-residence, the parish was very large. In 1597 he was sued for having allegedly slandered one John Rogers as a sorcerer. Gravet died before 5 March 1599, when his successor was collated to his prebend.   STEPHEN WRIGHT

Sources Venn, *Alum. Cant.* · Cooper, *Ath. Cantab.*, 2.268 · J. Strype, *The life and acts of John Whitgift*, new edn, 3 vols. (1822), vol. 1 · H. G. Owen, 'The London parish clergy in the reign of Elizabeth I', PhD diss., U. Lond., 1957 · *Fasti Angl., 1541–1857*, [St Paul's, London] · R. Newcourt, *Repertorium ecclesiasticum parochiale Londinense*, 1 (1708) · *The Marprelate tracts, 1588–1589*, ed. W. Pierce (1911) · H. G. Owen, 'Parochial curates in Elizabethan London', *Journal of Ecclesiastical History*, 10 (1959), 66–73

Gray. *See also* Grey.

Gray, Sir Alexander (1882–1968), economist and poet, was born on 6 January 1882 at Marshall Street, Lochee, Dundee, the third son of John Young Gray and his wife, Mary Young. His father was then art teacher at Dundee high school, and to this school Gray went before going on to the University of Edinburgh, where in 1902 he took first-class honours in mathematics and was awarded a gold medal.

Sir Alexander Gray (1882–1968), by Walter Stoneman, 1947

In 1905, after study at the universities of Edinburgh, Göttingen, and Paris, he took a second degree, again with first-class honours, in economic science, and was awarded the Gladstone memorial prize. At Edinburgh one of his fellow students was John Anderson, with whom he formed a lifelong friendship. Anderson and he were placed first and second in the civil service examination in 1905, and were assigned to the Colonial Office and the Local Government Board respectively. It is said that Gray went to congratulate Anderson on being placed first in the examination: when asked how he could possibly know what had not yet been announced, he explained that he had been told officially he was second and only one man could be ahead of him.

Gray spent sixteen years in the civil service before his appointment in 1921 to the Jaffrey chair of political economy in Aberdeen. During that time he was mainly occupied with problems of social insurance. After four years with the Local Government Board, and three with the Colonial Office, he was transferred together with Anderson to the National Health Insurance Commission in 1912; he left it in 1919 to go to the insurance department of the newly formed Ministry of Health. These years as an administrator stood him in good stead later, both as a teacher of economics and as a member of innumerable public bodies, giving to his handling of classes and committees alike a sense of the realities of government.

Meanwhile Gray's first book, *The Scottish Staple at Veere*, had appeared in 1909. Although based on notes left by Professor John Davidson this involved Gray in extensive research, and developed into a full-scale study of the early organization of Scottish foreign trade. It drew also on Gray's powers as a linguist, since much of the material was in Dutch. Gray was one of the few British economists able to speak the Dutch language, and he had an almost complete monopoly in reviewing the works of Dutch economists for the *Economic Journal*.

In 1911, a few years after joining the civil service, Gray submitted the winning essay for a prize of 100 guineas given by Dr J. Peddie Steele on the occasion of the quincentenary celebrations of the University of St Andrews, a distinction of which he was specially proud.

Gray's published work as an economist is largely on the development of economic thought. It is marked by simplicity, clarity, and above all humour and readability. His *Development of Economic Doctrine* (1931) took many years in the writing and eventually delighted a generation of undergraduates, who found other textbooks dull by comparison. In the same vein but aimed at a wider audience was his *Socialist Tradition, Moses to Lenin* (1946), completed in wartime after an even longer period of gestation. Gray disarmingly confessed his dislikes—singling out Marx, Lassalle, and Rousseau—as well as naming those like Fourier whom he felt to be kindred spirits. Although never doctrinaire or partisan, he expressed his own views with candour and forthrightness in the form of critical comments on the ideas of others.

Apart from these two volumes, Gray published little in economics, putting teaching in front of publication. A lecture, published as *Some Aspects of National Health Insurance*, appeared in 1923, and a later lecture on family allowances was expanded into a book, *Family Endowment* (1927), which took a critical and rather hostile view of the campaign then in progress, arguing that the wage bargaining process would be transformed by payments of allowances out of general taxation, so that strikes, for example, might be much longer and more successful.

Gray's emphasis was on political economy rather than on the more quantitive and scientific aspects of the subject. He warned his audience against unwarranted precision resting on inappropriate assumptions, and underlined the limitations of mathematical techniques in the formulation of economic policy. He was very much alive to the complexity of economic problems and their involvement in wider human motives and interests.

Gray had a lively and vigorous prose style, which showed to particular advantage in his prefaces and addresses: for example, the prefaces to his successive volumes of translations of songs and ballads from German, Dutch, and Danish, and his entertaining presidential address to the economics section of the British Association in 1949. He was also a poet of distinction whose work is represented in most anthologies of modern Scottish verse. His interest in verse translation originated in the preparation in 1915 of an English version of *J'accuse!*—a work in German in which were scattered passages of verse. His success in handling the translation of these passages encouraged him to tackle, for his own amusement, German songs and ballads and, later, songs by Heine, and he discovered that much of it went better into Scots than English. Although begun with no thought of Schumann or of the *Dichterliebe* cycle, the translations fit perfectly the Schumann settings and are among his best work. His first translations (*Songs and Ballads Chiefly from Heine*, 1920) were followed by a volume of German ballads, *Arrows* (1932); *Sir Halewyn* (1949), translations mainly from Dutch originals; and *Four and Forty* (1954). The last of these, which appeared when he was already over seventy, is an outstanding rendering into Scots verse of forty-four Danish ballads, undertaken to while away overnight railway journeys to London.

In addition to his translations, Gray published several volumes of his own verse, some in English, some in the Scottish dialect. Most of these are included in his *Any Man's Life* (1924) and *Gossip* (1928); a selection from his poems edited by Maurice Lindsay appeared in 1948. These were all short lyrics, predominantly in English, and are more introspective and nostalgic than one might expect. They also give expression to deeper and more personal responses to the human situation than his other writings, and many of the best of them show his characteristic deftness and wit.

Gray was very much a Scot and strongly rooted, with a profound understanding of his country. In his last work, *A Timorous Civility* (1966), published only in a very limited edition, he brought together a number of his essays and addresses in which he ranged over Scottish literature, history, and character with authority, insight, humanity, and wit. But he was also a European and had no sympathy for a narrow nationalism, or for what he took to be attempts to revive artificially the use of Lallans.

It was above all as a teacher that Gray excelled. It was his deeply felt belief that the first duty of a professor was to lay down a clear conspectus of the subject to his first-year class. Those who took his classes at Aberdeen, where he was particularly happy, or at Edinburgh, to which he moved in 1935, looked back always with pleasure on his lectures on political economy. In the days after the war, when a class of 400 first-year students would gather to hear him in the Pollock Hall in Edinburgh, he would sit playing the organ until the appointed hour and then turn and begin his discourse. He spoke with authority, humour, and a ready command of language, and addressed himself to the imagination as much as to the intelligence of his students. He was equally concerned for their educational attainments and general welfare.

In the twenties, and even more in the thirties, Gray was kept busy on a series of government committees, at first dealing mainly with national health insurance but later with issues relating to pay and employment, labour disputes, unemployment assistance, and so on. He was a member of the royal commission on national health insurance (1924–6) and of the white fish commission (1938), and was chairman of a number of courts of inquiry under the Industrial Courts Act. He was also chairman, during and after the Second World War, of many of the appeal tribunals set up by the Ministry of Labour, retaining the trust of all parties in this work. Later he served as chairman of the Scottish Schools' Broadcasting Council and was a member of the Fulbright commission. He found time also to act as chairman of the executive committee of the Youth Hostels Association in its early years (1931–5), and he was president of the Scottish Economic Society (1960–63) and a vice-president of the Royal Economic Society from 1955 until his death.

Among other distinctions Gray was appointed CBE in 1939 and knighted in 1947. He held honorary degrees from four universities, including the two in which he taught for thirty-five years. After his retirement in 1956 he was invited to stand as rector of Edinburgh University, but declined.

Gray's conversation, enriched by a slight burr, was an assured and steady flow of comment on the world's affairs. He was a most witty and entertaining speaker, without contrivance or show, and with a ready fund of quotations and modern instances to draw upon. But there was also a good deal of the preacher in him and it was at the moral rather than the technical level that what he had to say made the deepest impression.

Gray was short, with a ruddy complexion, and an out-of-doors farming appearance. He led a full and happy family life, having married in 1909 Alice (d. 1967), daughter of William Gunn, solicitor in Edinburgh; they had one son and three daughters. He died in Edinburgh on 17 February 1968, shortly after the death of his wife.

ALEC CAIRNCROSS, rev.

Sources personal knowledge (2004) · private information (2004) · b. cert. · WWW · CGPLA Eng. & Wales (1968)
Archives BLPES, corresp. with Eduard Rosenbaum · NL Scot., letters to Nan Shepherd
Likenesses W. Stoneman, photograph, 1947, NPG [see illus.]
Wealth at death £46,768 8s. od.: confirmation, 29 March 1968, NA Scot., SC 70/1/1750/164–8

Gray, Andrew, first Lord Gray (b. c.1390, d. in or before 1470), administrator and landowner, was the son and heir of Sir Andrew Gray of Broxmouth in Roxburghshire (d. before 17 July 1445) and his first wife, Janet, daughter of Sir Roger Mortimer of Fowlis in Angus; the union did much to enhance the wealth and status of the Grays.

First recorded in 1424 as a hostage for the release of James I from captivity in England, Gray (whose father's lands were then valued at 600 merks annually) was exchanged on 9 November 1427 for Malcolm Fleming the younger of Cumbernauld, and thenceforward benefited from royal service. In 1436, probably as a knight, he was one of 1200 Scots who accompanied James I's daughter Margaret to France for her marriage to the dauphin, Louis, but it was probably as a supporter from 1444 of William, eighth earl of Douglas (d. 1452) and his brothers during the minority of James II that his advancement was principally hastened. He had been created Lord Gray of Fowlis by 1 July 1445. In August 1445 Gray and Thomas Spens (d. 1480), archdeacon of Moray, accompanied James II's sisters Eleanor and Joanna to France for their marriages; Gray went from there to the court of the duke of Brittany on behalf of James II, who was still a minor and dominated by a faction led by the Douglases and Livingstons. On 7 October 1449 Gray had a royal charter for lands at Littletoun in Angus, and in the same year he served as ambassador to England and conservator of an Anglo-Scottish truce, roles he repeated in 1451. From 3 January 1450 he was a regular royal council member and parliamentarian.

If Gray had been a Douglas supporter, he traded this for the rewards of serving the crown once James II had asserted his independent authority in 1449–50. The contemporary Auchinleck chronicle names Gray and his eldest son and heir, Patrick, among the seven courtiers who dispatched the eighth earl of Douglas after James II stabbed him (despite a safe conduct) at Stirling Castle on 22 February 1452. Sir Robert Lindsay of Pitscottie's unsubstantiated sixteenth-century tale that Douglas had executed MacLellan, tutor of Bombie (nephew of Patrick, master of Gray), may have some basis in fact as a motivation for Gray's actions. By 12 April 1452 Andrew was master of the king's household and Patrick had received disputed Perthshire lands at Cluny—reasons enough to betray Douglas, perhaps; the other assassins were similarly favoured by the crown.

As one of James II's leading lay supporters in the political crisis following the murder, Gray was envoy to England in June 1452, and after 26 August that year received a royal licence allowing him to erect Huntly Castle in Longforgan in the carse of Gowrie. On 9 June 1455 he sat on the parliamentary assize which finally forfeited the Black Douglases. He served as march warden (1459) and lord auditor (1464), and on 5 March 1465 accompanied James III to Berwick to ratify a fifteen-year truce with England.

Gray had died by 20 January 1470. He had married, by contract dated 31 August 1418, Elizabeth, daughter of Sir John Wemyss of Rires, Fife, who survived him; they had two sons and one daughter. Patrick, Gray's heir, married Margaret, daughter of Sir Malcolm Fleming of Cumbernauld (contract dated 7 February 1440), and then (c.1445) Anabella, daughter of Alexander, first Lord Forbes (d. 1448). He and Anabella had three daughters and a son, **Andrew Gray** (d. 1514), who was served heir to his dead father in the lands and castle of Cluny on 5 November 1464 and succeeded his grandfather as second Lord Gray, probably as a minor.

In looking to regain the local and court status of his grandfather, lost during his minority, Gray became a committed opponent of James III and of the king's favoured subject David Lindsay, fifth earl of Crawford (d. 1495), Gray's rival in Angus. Gray consequently played a prominent part in the rebellions of 1482 and 1488. In August 1482, with Crawford, he surrendered the town of Berwick to the English army of Richard, duke of Gloucester, which had accompanied James III's exiled brother, Alexander Stewart, duke of Albany, to Edinburgh, ostensibly to enable Albany to usurp the Scottish throne as Alexander IV. Gray is named in sixteenth-century histories as one of the nobles responsible for seizing James III at Lauder on 17 July 1482 and imprisoning him in Edinburgh Castle. By

January 1483 Gray had joined Albany's supporters at Dunbar in attacking the newly liberated James III. On 11 February 1483 Gray, Archibald Douglas, fifth earl of Angus (d. 1514), and James Liddale of Halkerstoun, now in England, renounced their Scottish allegiance and became liegemen of Edward IV, promising to break the Franco-Scottish alliance and help Albany to depose James III.

Gray, however, was forced to re-enter James III's peace later in 1483; at the same time Crawford was made master of the king's household, an office formerly held by the first Lord Gray. But in 1488 (with Crawford, created duke of Montrose in May) Gray joined those rebels supporting Prince James against the king. Pitscottie and George Buchanan, both writing in the following century, speculate respectively that either a 'lordis grayis servandis' or Gray's son Patrick was responsible for James III's death at Sauchieburn.

As a member of James IV's royal council, Gray had on 29 October 1488 letters to grant remission to Crawford once he had given Gray the sheriffdom of Forfar. Gray was named by the rebels of 1489–90 as being among the 'parciale personis' of the post-Sauchieburn government, who were exploiting royal patronage, finances, and justice to the detriment of their local rivals. In June 1489 Gray was awarded the lands of Lundie in Angus, and the office of justice-general of the north, forfeited by Robert, second Lord Lyle (d. 1497). He continued to receive royal favour after the political compromise of 1490, obtaining several grants of Forfar lands from James IV as well as the office of justice-general of the south before 24 May 1505.

Gray and his first wife, Janet, daughter of William Keith, first Earl Marischal (d. 1483), had one son and two daughters: Patrick, who married Janet, daughter of George Gordon, second earl of Huntly (d. 1502) (and widow of Alexander, master of Crawford, whom she was accused of smothering), about 1493; Isobel, who married Alexander Stratoun of Lauriston; and Elizabeth, who married John, fourth Lord Glamis (1487), Alexander Gordon, third earl of Huntly (1511), and George Leslie, fourth earl of Rothes (1525). Gray married his second wife, Elizabeth, third daughter of John Stewart, first earl of Atholl, before 1483; they had four sons and two daughters. Gray and his third wife, Margaret Houston (widow of his nephew Robert, second Lord Lyle), whom he married after 1497, had no children. Gray died in February 1514 and was buried near his grandfather in the collegiate church of Fowlis Easter, founded by the latter about 1453.

MICHAEL A. PENMAN

Sources J. M. Thomson and others, eds., Registrum magni sigilli regum Scotorum / The register of the great seal of Scotland, 11 vols. (1882–1914), vol. 2 · P. Gray, The descent and kinship of Patrick, master of Gray (1903) · G. Burnett and others, eds., The exchequer rolls of Scotland, 5–13 (1882–91) · T. Dickson and J. B. Paul, eds., Compota thesaurariorum regum Scotorum / Accounts of the lord high treasurer of Scotland, 1–4 (1877–1902) · [T. Thomson] and others, eds., The acts of the lords of council in civil causes, 1478–1503, 3 vols. (1839–1993) · [T. Thomson], ed., The acts of the lords auditors of causes and complaints, AD 1466–AD 1494, RC, 40 (1839) · APS, 1424–1567 · Scots peerage · C. McGladdery, James II (1990) [incl. repr. of Auchinleck chronicle, pp. 160–73] · The historie and cronicles of Scotland ... by Robert Lindesay of Pitscottie, ed. A. J. G. Mackay, 3 vols., STS, 42–3, 60 (1899–1911) · J. Lesley, The history of Scotland, ed. T. Thomson, Bannatyne Club, 38 (1830) · D. McRoberts, 'The fifteenth-century altarpiece of Fowlis Easter Church', From the Stone Age to the 'forty five, ed. A. O'Connor and D. V. Clarke (1983), 384–98

Gray, Andrew, second Lord Gray (d. 1514). See under Gray, Andrew, first Lord Gray (b. c.1390, d. in or before 1470).

Gray, Andrew, seventh Lord Gray (d. 1663), royalist nobleman, was the eldest son of Patrick *Gray, sixth Lord Gray (d. 1611), and his second wife, Lady Mary, daughter of Robert Stewart, earl of Orkney. The only clues as to his date of birth are that his parents married in 1585, and he himself was married, by a contract of 3 December 1608, to Anne, widow of James Douglas, earl of Buchan (d. 1601), and daughter of Walter Ogilvy, Lord Ogilvy of Deskford. He succeeded his father as Lord Gray on 4 September 1611, and in 1624 he became lieutenant of the Scots gens d'armes in France when the unit was revived by George Gordon, earl of Enzie. On the outbreak of war between France and England in 1627 he moved to England. His first wife having died, in February 1628 he married Mary (d. 1631), daughter of John Guldeford of Kent and the widow of Sir John Sydenham. The contemporary report that she was eighty and he twenty-four was wrong, at least as to the groom's age. In 1629 both Gray and his wife were convicted as Roman Catholic recusants, and most of her estates were seized by the crown. In the same year action was taken to ensure that sons of Scottish Catholic noblemen received protestant educations. Gray's son by his first marriage was sent to the University of Edinburgh but he and the earl of Angus's son behaved 'verie scandalouslie in that colledge; they refuse to go to church ... spends Sundays in suspect places and companies ... corrupts other youths' (Reg. PCS, 1629–30, 156). Gray ignored an order to attend the privy council to answer for his son's conduct, but at about this time he agreed to surrender his hereditary sheriffship of Forfarshire in return for 50,000 merks (about £2800 sterling), which was evidently never paid. His second wife had died in 1631, and by 1639 he was married to Catherine Cadell.

In December 1638 Charles I granted Gray permission to levy a regiment of 1000 men in Scotland for the French service, but by that time the country was largely under the control of the covenanters, who had rebelled against the king's religious policies. After a visit to Scotland, Gray reported in April 1639 to Charles I in York on the military preparations being made by the covenanters, and on 29 May 1639 he was granted a pass to return to the French king's service, for clearly there was no chance of recruiting men for France while the covenanters were raising an army. Gray was back in England later in 1639, but his activities in the next few years are obscure. Late in 1643 he was in Edinburgh—again recruiting for his French regiment and again it was a bad time to choose, for the covenanters were raising an army for a new invasion of England. Gray sought to encourage the king's supporters in Scotland, but there is no evidence of his taking any part in the marquess of Montrose's campaign in 1644–5. None the less, after Montrose was defeated at Philiphaugh in September

1645 Gray was taken prisoner and, on the advice of Lieutenant-General David Leslie, the committee of estates on 30 October ordered that he be banished from Britain, under threat of being put to death if he returned during the 'troubles'. Clearly it was suspected that he was deep in royalist plots, and this is confirmed by a French diplomat's comment in August 1647 that Gray 'has been detained in Scotland for some years in the service of the King of Great Britain' (Fotheringham, 2.218).

Gray's banishment was not enforced, however, perhaps because the covenanters wished to avoid offending the French, for whom he continued to seek troops. The church, in June and December 1646, expressed its 'great offence' at his continued presence, but the report that he was excommunicated in 1649 is unconfirmed. After the English conquest of 1654 Gray, who had returned to the continent, was penalized as a royalist, being fined £1500 sterling by the 1654 Act of Grace and Pardon, though this was reduced to £500 in 1655. At the request of the exiled Charles II, he resigned his lieutenancy of the Scots *gens d'armes* at some point in the 1650s. He returned to Scotland after the restoration of monarchy in 1660 and died in 1663. DAVID STEVENSON

Sources *DNB* · *GEC, Peerage* · *Scots peerage* · *Reg. PCS*, 1st ser. · *Reg. PCS*, 2nd ser. · *CSP dom.*, 1628–41 · J. G. Fotheringham, ed., *The diplomatic correspondence of Jean de Montereul and the brothers de Bellièvre: French ambassadors in England and Scotland, 1645–1648*, 2 vols., Scottish History Society, 29–30 (1898–9) · D. Stevenson, ed., *The government of Scotland under the covenanters*, Scottish History Society, 4th ser., 18 (1982) · A. F. Mitchell and J. Christie, eds., *The records of the commissions of the general assemblies of the Church of Scotland*, 3 vols., Scottish History Society, 11, 25, 58 (1892–1909)

Gray, Andrew (1633–1656), Church of Scotland minister, was born in a house on the northern side of the Lawnmarket, Edinburgh, in 1633 and baptized on 23 August, the fourth son of Sir William Gray of Pittendrum, a merchant and fervent royalist, and Egidia Smith, the sister of Sir John Grothill, one time provost of Edinburgh. Little is known about his upbringing and early education although an encounter with a beggar whom he discovered engaged in earnest prayer in a field adjacent to Leith during his boyhood led to his conversion and had a profound impact on his future vocation as a preacher and pastor. He graduated MA from the University of St Andrews in 1651 and was licensed by the presbytery of Hamilton to preach the gospel in 1653.

Having greatly impressed Patrick Gillespie, the principal of the University of Glasgow and a leading remonstrant or protester, and others within the jurisdictional area of the presbytery of Glasgow, Gray was called to the Outer High Kirk, Glasgow, and ordained minister of that charge on 3 November 1653 by the protester party within the Church of Scotland, who held firmly to the covenant and declined to compromise with Charles II. However, his appointment initially met with opposition from the town council and others. Robert Baillie, a prominent resolutioner on the opposite wing, registered his dissent at Gray's licence to preach and subsequent ordination on the grounds that he was too young, inexperienced, relatively untried, and unknown within the church. He further suggested that Gray's voice was too weak to make him an effective preacher and that he had:

> the new guyse of preaching, which Mr Hugh Binning and Mr Robert Leighton began in contemning the ordinarie way of exponing and dividing the text, of raising doctrines and uses, bot runs out in a discourse on some common head, in a high, romancing, unscriptural style, tickling the ear for the present, and moving the affections of some, but leaving, as he confesses, little or nought to the memorie and understanding.   (*Letters and Journals of Robert Baillie*, 3.258–9)

The popular appeal of his experiential preaching and the success of his short ministry, however, would suggest that Baillie's expostulations were coloured by political considerations. James Durham, Gray's illustrious colleague in the ministry in Glasgow, once remarked that in preaching he 'could make men's hair stand on end', while another contemporary, George Hutchison, himself a resolutioner, referred to him as 'a spark from heaven' (Wodrow, 3.54; *Works*, ii). It was testimony to Gray's great attraction as a preacher that many of his sermons and communion addresses were taken down in shorthand by his hearers for private meditation.

On 31 March 1654 Gray married Rachel, daughter of George Baillie of Jerviswood and Margaret Johnston, with whom he had a son Robert, who was baptized on 12 June 1656 but died in childhood, and a daughter, Rachel, who was formally declared his heir on 26 June 1669. Gray died on 8 February 1656 after contracting 'purple' fever. The day before his death, having been confined to bed for a week and significantly weakened through sleep deprivation and 'sad and grievous torment' (*Works*, 499) caused by the ravages of his illness, he had a friend, whose name went undisclosed, record his dying thoughts to his wife's uncle Archibald Johnston, Lord Wariston. He sorely lamented Scotland's backsliding and apostasy, most notably in relation to its failure to uphold the national covenant. His body was interred in Blackadder's or St Fergus's aisle within Glasgow Cathedral. His widow later married George Hutchison, minister at Irvine.

Gray's sermons were first collected, revised, and published for posterity under the editorial auspices of Robert Trail and John Stirling. Thereafter his works have been repeatedly published and republished down to the present. Among the best known are: *The Mystery of Faith Opened up: the Great Salvation and Sermons on Death* (Glasgow, 1659; London, 1660), both editions of which included a dedication to Lord Wariston and which was later censored by the Restoration regime; *Great and Precious Promises* (1669); *Directions and Instigations to the Duty of Prayer* (1669); *The Spiritual Warfare* (Edinburgh, 1671; London, 1673), the London edition of which notably carried a preface by the illustrious puritan Thomas Manton; and *Eleven Communion Sermons*, which was dedicated to John Clerk of Penicuik and included the letter to Wariston that Gray had composed on his deathbed (1716). These were first collected into a single volume entitled *The Works of the Reverend and Pious Mr Andrew Gray, Late Minister of the Gospel in Glasgow* (1762). The definitive edition was published in Aberdeen in 1839 and republished in 1992. Gray's published works have brought his name and ministry to the attention of a relatively wide and varied readership, not only in Great Britain but also in North America and protestant Europe, particularly the Netherlands, where his extant works were translated into Dutch. His lengthy treatise on sanctification titled *A door opening into everlasting life: an essay tending to advance gospel holiness, and to establish the hearts of true believers against their many doubts and fears*, which was excluded from his *Works*, was similarly republished as recently as 1989.   A. S. WAYNE PEARCE

Sources *The works of Andrew Gray*, ed. J. R. Beeke (1992) · *Fasti Scot.*, new edn, 3.465 · *DNB* · *DSCHT*, 378 · *The letters and journals of Robert Baillie*, ed. D. Laing, 3 (1842) · *The diary of Alexander Brodie of Brodie*, ed. D. Laing (1863) · R. Wodrow, *Analecta*, ed. M. L. [M. Leishman], 4 vols. (1842–3), vol. 3

Gray, Andrew (*d.* 1728), Presbyterian minister and Church of England clergyman, is said to have come from Scotland but nothing further is known of his origins. He was the first minister of the nonconformist meeting established at Tintwistle in the parish of Mottram in Longdendale, Cheshire, when a barn belonging to John Didesbury was registered under the Toleration Act in October 1692. A Calvinist and for some time a rigid nonconformist, Gray is said to have often preached vehemently against church ceremonies and to have repeatedly abused the surplice. To the great surprise of his congregation he suddenly conformed to the Church of England and succeeded William Coulborn, who had died in June 1697, as vicar of Mottram. The first time that he appeared in his parish church his former congregation 'went in great numbers to hear him, being rather curious to know with what face he would receive them' and how he would present himself in the surplice he had so often derided. Nor were they disappointed, 'being not a little amused by his confused countenance and awkward deportment upon the occasion' ('Statistical view'). He was the author of *A Door Opening into Everlasting Life* (1706), 'an excellent, practical, experiential volume stressing the necessity of a godly walk of life' (Gray, v). This work has been incorrectly attributed to the more famous Scottish divine of the same name, Andrew Gray (1633–1656). It was republished in 1810 by the Revd Matthew Olerenshaw, vicar of Mellor, Derbyshire, and again, in 1989, in America. The 1706 edition could not be obtained in 1880 and may no longer exist. Gray was also the author of *The Mystery of Faith*, for which no details are available. He and his wife, Dorothy, had at least three sons and three daughters. Gray left Mottram about 1716 and died at Anglezark, near Rivington, Lancashire, where he had probably been curate, early in 1728.

DAVID L. WYKES

Sources J. P. Earwaker, *East Cheshire: past and present, or, A history of the hundred of Macclesfield*, 2 (1880), 131–2, 170–71 · 'Statistical view of dissenters in England and Wales: Cheshire', *London Christian Instructor, or, Congregational Magazine*, 4 (1821), 102 · Cheshire quarter session records, Ches. & Chester ALSS, QDR 7, s.v. 11 Oct 1692 [enrolments, registrations, and depositions (religion)] · W. Urwick, ed., *Historical sketches of nonconformity in the county palatine of Cheshire, by various ministers and laymen* (1864), 355–6 · A. Gordon, ed., *Freedom after ejection: a review (1690–1692) of presbyterian and congregational nonconformity in England and Wales* (1917), 15–17 · A. Gray, *A door opening into everlasting life: an essay tending to advance gospel holiness, and to establish the hearts of true believers against their many doubts and fears* (1989)

Gray, Andrew (1805–1861), Free Church of Scotland minister, was born at Aberdeen on 2 November 1805, the eldest child of William Gray, stocking maker, and his wife, Ann Taylor. He attended schools kept by Gilbert, father of Forbes Falconer, and John Paterson, before entering Marischal College, where he graduated AM in 1824, and passed through the theological course (1824–8). He was licensed to preach by the Aberdeen presbytery on 25 June 1829, and became minister of a chapel of ease at Woodside, near Aberdeen, on 1 September 1831. Here he remained until he was inducted to the West Church, Perth, on 14 July 1836. On 23 July 1834 he married Barbara, daughter of Alexander Cooper; they had no children. Gray was an orthodox evangelical and a vigorous controversialist. He was active in the agitation for the Chapels Act of 1834 (by which chapels of ease were fully incorporated into the structure of the Church of Scotland), in opposition to Catholic emancipation, and especially in the disputes over patronage which resulted in the Disruption of 1843 and the foundation of the Free Church of Scotland. A pamphlet by him, *The Present Conflict between Civil and Ecclesiastical Courts Examined* (1839) had a wide circulation and great influence, being commended by Thomas Chalmers, Hugh Miller, and Robert Candlish. On his secession from the Church of Scotland, nearly all his congregation followed him; his new church was opened on 28 October 1843.

In 1845 Gray drew up, at the request of the Free Church leaders, *A Catechism of the Principles of the Free Church* (1845–8), which involved him in a controversy with the duke of Argyll. Later in 1845 Gray visited the continent and travelled as far as Constantinople. The reason for his journey was partly ill health but he was also commissioned to visit Switzerland to investigate the dispute which had taken place in the church of the canton of Vaud. His report led to active support from the Free Church for dissenting protestant churches in France. In 1855 he was appointed convener of the Glasgow evangelization committee, and he was always active in home missions and in educational projects. Failing health made another long continental tour necessary in 1859; he died at his home, 3 Atholl Place, Perth, on 10 March 1861. Gray left numerous publications, mainly of a controversial nature. A collection of nineteen sermons representative of his ministry was published in 1862 under the title *Gospel Contrasts and Parallels*, with a memoir by Robert Candlish and a portrait.

[ANON.], *rev.* R. H. CAMPBELL

Sources R. S. Candlish, 'Memoir of Rev. Andrew Gray', in A. Gray, *Gospel contrasts and parallels* (1862) · *Disruption worthies: a memorial of 1843* (1876), 143–5 · *Fasti Scot.* · J. Smith, *Our Scottish clergy*, 3rd ser. (1851), 281–8 · T. Brown, *Annals of the Disruption*, new edn (1893) · NA Scot., SC 49/31/71/792

Likenesses D. O. Hill and R. Adamson, photograph, NPG · engravings, repro. in Candlish, 'Memoir' · engravings, repro. in *Disruption worthies*

Wealth at death £1577 17*s*. 8*d*.: inventory, 6 May 1861, NA Scot., SC 49/31/71/792

Gray, Andrew (1847–1925), physicist, was born in the parish of Auchterderran, Fife, on 2 July 1847, the eldest son of John Gray, labourer, then farmer, of Lochgelly, Fife, and his wife, Margaret Wilson. He was educated at the local village school and later studied with private teachers in Edinburgh. His talent for mathematics was recognized and he was encouraged to enter the University of Glasgow in 1872 at the comparatively advanced age of twenty-five. He graduated MA with honours in mathematics and physics in 1876, winning prizes in natural philosophy (1874–5) and mathematics (1875–6). He was appointed, in 1874, private assistant and secretary to Sir William Thomson (later Lord Kelvin), professor of natural philosophy at Glasgow, and in 1880 he was made official assistant. He was Eglinton fellow in mathematics, 1876. In 1870 he married Ann Gordon; they had four sons and four daughters.

Gray became the foundation professor of physics in the University College of North Wales, Bangor, in 1884, and succeeded Kelvin as professor of natural philosophy at Glasgow in 1899, winning the chair against competition which included the young C. T. R. Wilson, and ushering in a period of undistinguished research in physics that lasted nearly fifty years. It would not be unfair to say that Gray dotted Kelvin's *i*s and crossed his *t*s, and did little that was original. The splendid, but now lost, lecture theatre in Gray's 1907 Natural Philosophy Institute building (later the Kelvin building) was designed with Kelvin's expansive style in mind. Gray's major publications (*Absolute Measurements in Electricity and Magnetism*, 1883; *Theory and Practice of Absolute Measurements in Electricity and Magnetism*, vol. 1, 1888, vol. 2, 1893, new edn, 1921; and *Dynamics and Properties of Matter*, 1901) reflect Kelvin's interests of a decade or so earlier. The story may not be untrue that just after the Second World War a drawer in the natural philosophy department was found to contain shards of glass along with a note saying 'Glass broken by Lord Kelvin'. He published *The Scientific Work of Lord Kelvin* in 1908, the year following Kelvin's death, and organized the first of the historical collections of Kelvin apparatus and instruments to be preserved in the department. Yet his *Absolute Measurements in Electricity and Magnetism*, expanded in 1888, 'did much to make experimental electricity an exact science' (*Proceedings of the Royal Society of Edinburgh*, 375), and was very helpful to physicists in national laboratories when determining electrical standards. Another of Gray's notable contributions to the physical literature was his massive *Treatise on Gyrostatics and Rotational Motion* (1919). In this difficult subject he was reputed to have attained Dirac's ideal of understanding: he could say what would happen without actually solving the equations.

Gray's principal achievements were as an indefatigable teacher, including extension teaching, and university administrator. Where Kelvin might easily have fallen foul of modern teaching quality assessments, Gray's attention to detail, his advice and guidance to students, kindness, and pastoral care would have seen him through with flying colours. As a result the number of students taking the various natural philosophy classes in the university increased enormously, though few of them were inspired to greatness as many were by Kelvin's exciting but, for the ordinary student, execrable lectures. Gray reorganized the obsolete department he inherited at Glasgow, and founded the Natural Philosophy Institute in 1906, the largest building devoted to physics in Britain; by 1923 more than 600 students a year took laboratory courses there.

Gray was elected FRS (Edinburgh) in 1883 and served as a member of council (1903–6) and vice-president (1906–9); in 1896 he became FRS (London) and was awarded an honorary LLD by the University of Glasgow. He played a full part in the life of the university, serving as senate assessor on the university court (1904–12), and in the intellectual life of the city. He was president of the mathematical and physical section of the then extremely active Royal Philosophy Society of Glasgow in 1902–3 and was for some years a member of its council.

His organizational exertions on numerous committees during the First World War, the death of a son in 1915, and the demands of vastly increased student numbers after the war undermined Gray's already uncertain health and he resigned his chair in 1923. He died on 10 October 1925 at 15 Victoria Circus, Glasgow. He was survived by his wife. It was a source of satisfaction to him that James Gordon Gray, his second son, had renounced the engineering profession for physics and been appointed professor of applied physics at Glasgow.   R. R. WHITEHEAD

Sources prize lists, matriculation records, U. Glas., Archives and Business Records Centre · *Proceedings of the Royal Society of Edinburgh*, 45 (1924–5), 373–7 · *Proceedings of the Royal Philosophical Society of Glasgow*, 54 (1925–6), 119 · A. R., *PRS*, 110A (1926), xvi–xix · election certificate, RS · b. cert. · d. cert. · *CGPLA Eng. & Wales* (1926)
Archives U. Glas. L., letters | CUL, corresp. with Lord Kelvin
Wealth at death £2781 6s. 7d.: confirmation, 11 Jan 1926, *CCI*

Gray, Sir Archibald Montague Henry (1880–1967), dermatologist, was born on 1 February 1880 at Ottery St Mary, Devon, the son of Frederick Archibald Gray, a general practitioner, and his wife, Louisa Frances Waterworth; he was the only son and the eldest of four children. He was educated at Cheltenham College and University College and Hospital, London, and later at the University of Bern. In 1903 he qualified MRCS LRCP and obtained his London MB with honours; in 1904 he gained his BS with honours in obstetrics. For the next five years he held resident and junior appointments at University College Hospital and the Hospital for Women, Soho Square. He proceeded MD in 1905 in midwifery and diseases of women and was awarded the university medal. He was admitted MRCP (1907) and FRCS in 1908 when he was elected a fellow of University College, London. He decided to specialize in obstetrics and gynaecology and became the first obstetric registrar at University College Hospital, where he performed the first caesarean Wertheim operation in England.

In 1909, however, the post of physician for diseases of the skin at University College Hospital was offered to Gray who, after six months' study under J. Jadassohn at Bern, took up this appointment, which he was to hold until 1946. His career was interrupted by the First World War, during which he was attached to the general staff at the

Sir Archibald Montague Henry Gray (1880–1967), by Rodrigo Moynihan, 1956

War Office with the rank of lieutenant-colonel in the Royal Army Medical Corps. In 1917 Gray married Elsie, daughter of F. Bernard Cooper, solicitor, of Newcastle under Lyme. They had one daughter and a son, John Archibald Browne Gray, who became professor of physiology at University College, London, and later secretary of the Medical Research Council. From 1918 to 1919 Gray was consulting dermatologist with the army in France; he was mentioned in dispatches and appointed CBE. After the war he was for many years honorary consulting dermatologist to the Royal Air Force; in 1931–3 he was a member of the government committee on the medical services of the navy, army, and air force.

At University College Hospital Gray secured for his department a good allocation of beds and rooms in the medical school. The latter facilitated the installing of Dr W. Freudenthal from Jadassohn's clinic at Breslau in the early Nazi period, and the eventual establishment of a readership in cutaneous histology. From 1920 to 1934 Gray was also in charge of the skin department of the Hospital for Sick Children, Great Ormond Street. There he made important observations on the rare disease *sclerema neonatorum*, which he reported in 1926 to the American Dermatological Association. His work in paediatric dermatology was extended by his appointment by the London County Council as consulting dermatologist (1935–51) to Goldie Leigh Hospital.

From 1916 to 1929 Gray was editor of the *British Journal of Dermatology*. It was partly for the purpose of financially supporting and controlling this journal that he suggested the formation of the British Association of Dermatology,

which came into being in 1921. He was president in 1938–9 and its treasurer from 1940 to 1960 during which time he quintupled its funds. From these, on Gray's inspiration, the association in 1957 contributed towards the new building for the Royal College of Physicians in Regent's Park on condition that a room be named after Robert Willan, one of the founders of dermatology.

From 1935 Gray represented London University on the governing body of the postgraduate medical school at Hammersmith. With Sir Francis Fraser he planned the expansion of the school into a federation of specialist institutes which materialized in 1947 as the British Postgraduate Medical Federation. Gray was a member of its governing body until 1960. During the same period he was first chairman of the committee of management of the Institute of Dermatology which had taken over the affairs of the London School of Dermatology, of which he was also chairman. In the urgent task of finding adequate in-patient accommodation he was helped by his experience in carrying out, with Dr Andrew Topping, the survey of London hospitals for the Ministry of Health, the report of which was published in 1945. It was not, however, until 1959, the year before Gray retired from the chairmanship, that the institute was officially recognized as a member of the British Postgraduate Medical Federation.

In 1913 Gray was editor and one of the secretaries of the dermatological section of the 17th International Congress of Medicine in London. This may well have been the mainspring of his subsequent enthusiastic encouragement of international contacts. He was vice-president of the 8th International Congress of Dermatology at Copenhagen in 1930, and president of the 10th International Congress in London in 1952. His reputation abroad was shown by his election as honorary member of twelve foreign societies.

Gray contributed to sections on skin diseases for the official medical history of the First World War and for *Nomenclature of Diseases*, Royal College of Physicians (1931), and he wrote the skin diseases section for eight editions of Price's *Textbook of the Practice of Medicine*. He was the first dermatologist to give the Harveian oration to the Royal College of Physicians (1951), his subject being the history of dermatology from the time of Harvey.

Gray was honorary secretary of the Royal Society of Medicine (1919–24), treasurer (1926–32), president (1940–42), and was president of its section of dermatology (1931–3). He served on the Goodenough committee on the organization of medical schools (1942–4) and in 1948–62 he was adviser in dermatology to the Ministry of Health. University College Hospital and medical school were naturally primary recipients of his services and influence. From 1926 to 1935 he was both dean of the medical school and chairman of the medical committee of the hospital. In 1948 he became chairman of the medical school council and a member of the board of governors of the hospital, holding the former post for four years and the latter for five. His work for the University of London as a whole was even more important: member of the senate (1929–50); dean of the faculty of medicine (1932–6); chairman of the professoriate committee (1941–50); member of the commission which visited Trinidad to investigate the practicability of starting a medical school there; member of the court (1947–58); member of the General Medical Council representing the university (1950–52); chairman of the board of management of the London School of Hygiene and Tropical Medicine (1951–61); and vice-chairman of the council of the School of Pharmacy (1949–64). In 1958 the university conferred on him an honorary LLD. He was knighted in 1946 and appointed KCVO in 1959. In the following year he gave up his private practice.

Gray's physical appearance was unimpressive. He was small and drably dressed. His voice, however, was clear and strong, and his speaking and writing were lucid and cogent. Of his dermatological prowess he was unduly modest, but in administrative work he was more sure of his talents and he enjoyed holding the reins of government. He held his opinions so strongly that he was at times impatient with those who disagreed. But he was essentially friendly, of liberal outlook, and kind and helpful to younger men and women, especially those hampered by prejudices against their race, sex, or religion. He had few avocations and lived simply, with a touch of disdain for aesthetic pleasures. Gray died at his home, 7 Alvanley Gardens, Hampstead, London, on 13 October 1967.   W. N. GOLDSMITH, rev. ANITA McCONNELL

Sources BMJ (21 Oct 1967), 178; (11 Nov 1967), 365 · The Times (14 Oct 1967) · British Journal of Dermatology (Dec 1967) · G. B. Dowling, 'The British Association of Dermatology, 1920–70', British Journal of Dermatology (1970) [special jubilee issue] · A. P. Bewley, 'Sir Archibald Gray KCVO, CBE, MD, FRCP, FRCS, LLD, dermatologist', International Journal of Dermatology, 36 (1967), 552–5 · M. L. Rosenhaim, The annual address delivered to the Royal College of Physicians of London (1968) · O. Goms, Hautarzt, 18 (1967) · personal knowledge (1981) · private information (1981) · CGPLA Eng. & Wales (1968)

Likenesses R. Moynihan, portrait, 1956, RCP Lond. [see illus.] · double portrait, photograph, 1964 (with Sir Henry Hallett Dale), Wellcome L.

Wealth at death £61,594: probate, 7 March 1968, CGPLA Eng. & Wales

Gray, Basil (1904–1989), museum curator, was born on 21 July 1904 at 13 Elvaston Place, South Kensington, London, the younger son (there were no daughters) of Surgeon-Major Charles Gray of the Royal Army Medical Corps, a passionate traveller, and his wife, Florence Elworthy, daughter of the Revd Henry von der Heyde Cowell. He was educated at Bradfield College and at New College, Oxford, where he gained a third class in literae humaniores (1926) and a second in modern history (1927). On going down from Oxford, in 1928 he worked for a season on the excavations at the great palace of the Byzantine emperors in Constantinople, where, however, his interests firmly turned to eastern rather than classical art, and then, for three months, in Vienna under Josef Strzygowski.

Gray entered the British Museum late in 1928. There being no vacancy in the antiquities departments, he spent an interim year in the department of printed books. In 1930 he transferred to the subdepartment of oriental prints and drawings, then still a division of the department of prints and drawings, under R. Laurence Binyon,

the poet and distinguished orientalist whom he joined, with J. V. S. Wilkinson, to write the standard work Persian Miniature Painting (1933). In 1933 he married Nicolete Mary (1911–1997) [see Gray, Nicolete], daughter of Laurence Binyon, herself a distinguished medievalist, designer of inscriptions, and historian of lettering. They had two sons and three daughters. Their eldest daughter, Camilla (d. 1971), the historian of the Russian avant-garde, married the son of the composer Sergey Prokofiev.

When the department of oriental antiquities was created in 1933, Gray was given the task of redisplaying the collection of Indian sculpture. The Chinese exhibition of 1935 then directed his attention to the Far East. By the outbreak of the Second World War his writings covered the whole field of eastern art, Islam, India, China, and Japan. His later work, however, dealt with the close relations between the arts of China and Persia, following the Mongol invasion and under the successors of Tamerlane—for example, in his important contributions, as editor and joint author, to The Arts of the Book in Central Asia, 1307–1506 (1979), which definitively establish the prime role of princely patronage in the painting of eastern Islamic cultures.

Gray was placed in charge of the oriental collections in 1938, though, on account of his youth, he was appointed deputy keeper only in 1940 and keeper of oriental antiquities in 1946. Under his long keepership (until 1969) the immensely important collection of orientalia in the British Museum was complemented by a department of carefully chosen distinguished younger specialists. Gray was the friend and trusted adviser of many great collectors, stimulating their interest and moulding their taste. His confidence in their public-spiritedness was more than justified by their generosity to the British Museum.

Gray's outstanding career at the British Museum was recognized when he was made CBE in 1957 and CB in 1969, and by his appointment as acting director and principal librarian in 1968. In 1966 he was elected a fellow of the British Academy, and was closely associated with the British institutes of Persian and of Afghan (later South Asian) studies. His chairmanship of exhibitions of Islamic art in Cairo (1969) and Beirut (1974) culminated in the exhibition 'The arts of Islam', at the Hayward Gallery, London (1976), the most important of its kind since the Munich exhibition of 1910. His particular contribution to the study of Persian art was marked by his election as president of the Societas Iranologica Europaea, a post he held from 1983 to 1987.

After his retirement in 1969 Gray continued to travel, lecture, write, and advise official committees, one of his few recreations being the Savile Club, of which he was a member for sixty years. He was a committed member of the Church of England and was churchwarden both in London at St George's, Bloomsbury, and in Oxfordshire at Long Wittenham, where he lived for the last twenty years of his life. He was elegantly neat in physique, with austere features offset by humorous eyes and bushy eyebrows. His suits and shirts were always tailor-made even when he was not well off. His colleagues remember him as forthright and rather autocratic in his earlier years. To his younger colleagues, however, he was a remarkable teacher, by precept and example, and his works reveal his patience and his eagle eye for decorative detail. Gray died in the John Radcliffe Hospital, Oxford, on 10 June 1989 and was buried in Long Wittenham parish churchyard.

J. M. ROGERS, rev.

Sources J. M. Rogers, 'Basil Gray', *Iran*, xvii (1979) [with a bibliography] · D. Sutton, 'Basil Gray', *Apollo* (Jan 1989) · D. Scarisbrick, interview with Basil Gray, *Apollo*, 129 (1989), 40–44 · M. Medley, 'Basil Gray CBE', *Transactions of the Oriental Ceramic Society 1988–89* (1990) · personal knowledge (1996) · private information (1996) [Edmund Gray, son] · *CGPLA Eng. & Wales* (1989)

Wealth at death £180,711: probate, 3 Oct 1989, *CGPLA Eng. & Wales*

Gray, Benjamin (1676/7–1764). *See under* Vulliamy family (*per. c.*1730–1886).

Gray, Benjamin Kirkman (1862–1907), historian of philanthropy and social policy, was born on 11 August 1862 at Blandford, Dorset, the eldest son of Benjamin Gray (*d.* 1905), Congregational minister, and his wife, Emma Jane (*d.* 1904), daughter of George Buchanan Kirkman. George Buchanan *Gray was his younger brother. A voracious young reader, he was educated by his father before being sent to work in a London warehouse at the age of fourteen. He continued to read widely in his spare time and taught in a Sunday school, but this life proved distasteful to his mystic and at times fiery temperament. At one time inclined to emigrate, he returned instead to Dorset in 1882, after which he formed a strong bond with his mother and taught in local schools.

A growing concern with social questions, and a belief that their solution lay through religion, led Gray to train for the Congregational ministry at New College, London. But he failed to secure a 'pulpit', seemingly unfitted by his distaste for preaching and his growing theological doubts. But he developed a strong interest in economics, attending University College, London (1888–90), and winning in 1890–91 the Ricardo scholarship, with an income of £20 for three years. After a further spell of teaching, he moved to Leeds, taking on social work and evening-class teaching as assistant to the Revd R. Westrope of Belgrave Chapel between September 1892 and March 1893. But Gray's increasing heterodoxy led him towards the Unitarians, whose minister he became at Warwick in 1894.

In common with many contemporaries, Gray found that his fading interest in religious dogma was matched by a growing attraction to social reform. He moved decisively in this direction, when having met his future wife, Sarah Eleanor Stone (*b.* 1864/5), the daughter of Henry Stone, a manufacturer, on his first visit to the continent in 1897, he resigned his ministry and returned to London. He now took up social work at the Bell Street Mission, Marylebone, supported by his wife after their marriage at Rosslyn Hill Chapel, Hampstead, on 9 May 1898. Infused by a strong idealism, he sought to combine a transcendental vision of the universe with an increasingly collectivist approach to the state. His experience of the life of the poor and his belief that only the state could humanize their condition led him naturally towards the labour movement. But a nervous breakdown in 1902 ended his active social work.

Gray moved to Hampstead, and now took up a detailed study of social questions, publishing in 1905 *A History of English Philanthropy*, a work combining pioneering and impressive empirical research with a bold social vision. Although very much a solitary scholar, Gray received helpful support from Sidney Webb and had outlined his ideas in lectures at the London School of Economics. He also at this time joined the Independent Labour Party, visited Germany (1905–6), and took part in a number of early social work ventures, such as the National Conference Union of Social Service and the British Institute of Social Service. He occasionally spoke at Quaker meetings, while writing frequently for the Unitarian *Inquirer*. A strong sympathizer with the garden city ideal, he moved to Letchworth, Hertfordshire, shortly before his death. He died at his home there, White Cottage, Norton Way, on 23 June 1907; he was cremated in Letchworth, and his remains were interred there. His wife survived him.

Gray's posthumous *Philanthropy and the State, or, Social Politics* (1908), in many ways a sociological complement to A. V. Dicey's *Law and Opinion* published in the same year, set out clearly his analysis of the transition from individualism to collectivism, together with his appreciation of the intermediate part for philanthropy and voluntarism. His life and *œuvre* provide an excellent illustration of the intellectual background to the rise of the welfare state. They also exemplify the turn-of-the-century progressive mind, struggling to reconcile religion and socialism, individualism and the state, ethics and modern urban life.

A. C. HOWE

Sources *A modern humanist: miscellaneous papers of B. Kirkman Gray*, ed. H. B. Binns (1910) · *DNB* · Belgrave Congregational Chapel records, W. Yorks. AS, Leeds · *Annual Report* [British Institute of Social Service], 3 (1907) · m. cert. · *CGPLA Eng. & Wales* (1907)

Likenesses photograph, repro. in Binns, ed., *Modern humanist*, frontispiece

Wealth at death £174 6s. 3d.: administration with will, 8 Nov 1907, *CGPLA Eng. & Wales*

Gray, Charles (*bap.* 1696, *d.* 1782), lawyer, politician, and antiquary, was born in Church Street, Colchester, and baptized on 20 September 1696 at St Nicholas's, Colchester, the only son and elder child of George Gray (1677/8–1747), a glazier, and his wife, Elizabeth (*d.* 1727). His father owned substantial property in the town, and was a member of the borough corporation. Charles was educated at Colchester grammar school, to which he was admitted in June 1702, and entered Gray's Inn in 1724. He may have spent some of the intervening time at Cambridge University, though he did not matriculate there. He was called to the bar in 1729 and became a bencher in 1737. He was elected a fellow of the Royal Society in 1754.

Gray was a man of several talents: he was a respectable classical scholar and Hebraist, a lawyer with an extensive practice, and an antiquary and early numismatist. His fortunes were most literally made, however, by his marriage in 1726 to Sarah Creffield, *née* Webster (1688–1751), the widow of Ralph Creffield. In the eighteenth century the cloth trade was in evident decline in Colchester, but in the past the principal manufacturers of the new draperies had made substantial profits there. The Creffields, with the Flemish dynasty of the Tayspills behind them, were a conduit through which much of that accumulated wealth was distributed to the town's leading families in the following generations. Sarah Creffield lived in a handsome new house, Hollytrees, on the edge of the castle grounds in Colchester. Her mother, Mary Webster (d. 1755), herself the widow of a substantial London merchant, gave Gray the castle as a wedding present, and the huge Norman keep, with its surrounding earthworks, was perhaps the most prized of his many possessions.

Charles Gray's father, George, was a whig and a leading member of Colchester corporation; he became an alderman in 1719 and served as chamberlain of the borough until 1725. When Charles Gray began to practise in 1729 he was made an honorary freeman of the town, and in 1734 an alderman, but he declared himself a tory. In doing so he took on the tradition of the Creffields. In 1744 he was mentioned by a French observer as a potential Jacobite, but he inclined to the group associated with the prince of Wales; Lord Egmont, in one of his surveys, reckoned him a tory 'of tolerable sense' (HoP, *Commons*), though given to reform. Gray's schemes included a measure of electoral reform as a means of inhibiting corruption, and a more effective administration of the poor law. His only known publication is a pamphlet entitled *Considerations on Several Proposals Lately Made for the Better Maintenance of the Poor* (1751), which was reprinted twice and appeared again in 1752 with the draft of a bill. He had more success as a champion of the British Museum, of which he became a foundation trustee.

Gray was first returned as a member for Colchester in 1742, when he and Samuel Savill unseated two candidates of Sir Robert Walpole's on petition. He subsequently represented the town in four more parliaments, three times with Isaac Martin Rebow; on the last occasion, in 1768, at the age of seventy-two, he headed the poll.

In 1739 Gray's father was convicted of sodomy, a capital offence, but he was pardoned in 1740 on the grounds that he was the victim of a conspiracy. In October of that year he confronted the corporation with a mandamus for the restitution of his aldermanry. The mayor's refusal to accept it fired a dispute which resulted in 1741 in the remaining officers renouncing their powers in king's bench and the corporation falling into abeyance. Faction in the borough prolonged the interregnum for twenty years, and it was not until 1763 that Charles Gray and his fellow member, Rebow, brought a new charter home in triumph. By that time Gray's father was dead. Charles, who was already recorder of Ipswich, became an alderman of the new corporation and a justice of the peace.

Gray was a conventional benefactor to Colchester, but his principal service there was as a promoter of civic culture. He gave support and encouragement to his friend Philip Morant, the learned historian of the county of Essex and of parliament. His local circle also included Samuel Parr, then master of the grammar school, and John Abbot, rector of All Saints', Colchester, and father of Charles Abbot, first Baron Colchester. He rescued the castle keep from ruin, roofing its southern chamber and landscaping the grounds. In 1755 he furnished the first floor of the keep to accommodate the library bequeathed to the town by Archbishop Samuel Harsnett, which Morant had tended and listed, and added books of his own and curios to establish what became the castle library and, later, a town museum.

Gray enhanced both his professional and his antiquarian expertise by a wide practice in manorial stewardships, but he regarded his fortune as something of a family trust. His wife, Sarah, died on 30 June 1751, and their daughters, Mary (1727–1749) and Charlotte Rachel (1729–1743), both died young. In 1755 Gray married Mary (d. 1795), the daughter of Randle Wilbraham MP, of Chester. He died in December 1782, and was buried in All Saints', Colchester, on 20 December. Beyond annuities to his wife and to his sister, Jemima Price, and a niece, he left the bulk of his estate in Essex, including Hollytrees, and property in London to James Round of Little Birch and his wife, Tamar, who was the daughter and heir of Gray's stepson, Peter Creffield (1719–1748). Later members of that family include the historian John Horace Round.

G. H. MARTIN

Sources L. C. Sier, 'Charles Gray, MP, of Colchester', *Essex Review*, 57 (1948), 17–21 · L. C. Sier, 'The ancestry of Charles Gray', *Essex Review*, 61 (1952), 92–6 · J. Bensusanbutt, 'A friend to his country: William Mayhew and the recovery of the Colchester charter, 1763', *Essex Archaeology and History* (1987), 63–74 · G. H. Martin, *The story of Colchester* (1959) · S. D'Cruze, 'The middling sort in provincial England: politics and social relations in Colchester, 1730–1800', PhD diss., University of Essex, 1990 · E. Cruickshanks, 'Gray, Charles', HoP, *Commons* · Borough of Colchester, assembly book, 1712–41, Essex RO, Colchester, D/B5 Gb7 · Register of the Royal Society · J. H. Round, ed., *Register of the scholars admitted to Colchester School, 1637–1740* (1897)

Archives Essex RO, Chelmsford, MSS · Essex RO, Colchester, corresp. and papers | BL, corresp. with Philip Morant, Add. MS 37222 · Essex RO, Chelmsford, corresp. with Philip Morant · Essex RO, Chelmsford, Birch Hall estate MSS

Wealth at death extensive property in Essex; property in London: will, summarized, Sier, 'Charles Gray'

Gray, Charles (1782–1851), marine officer and songwriter, was born at Anstruther Wester, Fife, on 10 March 1782, the son of Charles Gray and his wife, Margaret Raker. His education and early training fitted him for the sea, and in 1805, through the influence of a maternal uncle, Major-General Bush, he received a commission in the Woolwich division of the Royal Marines. He spent thirty-six years in the service, much of it in the Mediterranean, and retired on a captain's full pay, settling in Edinburgh in 1841.

Gray was a schoolfriend of William Tennant and Thomas Chalmers, and pursued an interest in poetry throughout his life. He was on friendly terms with many literary people, including Robert Chambers, Patrick Maxwell, and David Vedder. He published *Poems* in 1811, which went into a second edition in 1814 as *Poems and Songs*. In 1813, on a visit to Anstruther, he helped form a

'Musomanik Society', to which members presented new songs. In 1817 he married Jessy Carstairs, sister of the Revd Dr Carstairs of Anstruther. He published *Lays and Lyrics* in 1841, including several pieces set to music by Peter M'Leod. One of them—'When autumn has laid her sickle by'—which Gray himself liked to sing, makes almost the only allusion to his life at sea. He contributed to Wood's *Book of Scottish Song*, and to *Whistle-Binkie*. Besides his original verse, about 1845 Gray contributed criticism to the *Glasgow Citizen* under the title 'Cursory remarks on Scottish song'.

Gray died in Edinburgh after a long illness on 13 April 1851, having been predeceased by his wife and one of their two sons; the remaining son was a lieutenant in the Royal Marines. T. W. BAYNE, rev. SARAH COUPER

Sources M. F. Conolly, *Biographical dictionary of eminent men of Fife* (1866) · Anderson, *Scot. nat.* · J. G. Wilson, ed., *The poets and poetry of Scotland*, 2 (1877) · *Whistle-binkie, or, The piper of the party: being a collection of songs for the social circle*, new edn, 1 (1878) · Boase, *Mod. Eng. biog.* · m. reg. Scot. · IGI

Gray, Christopher (1694–1764), nurseryman, was probably the second son of William Gray senior, and his wife, Sarah, of Fulham, Middlesex. William Gray junior, the older son, had a nursery garden in Fulham, at Parson's Lane, later Peterborough Road; but the better-known Fulham garden of the period was the one established before 1700 by the elder William Gray and later taken over by Christopher. It occupied nearly 30 acres between Hurlingham Road and the (New) King's Road, with some land on the other side of the King's Road added by the middle of the eighteenth century.

Early in his career, soon after the death in 1713 of Henry Compton, bishop of London, Christopher Gray was one of the nurserymen who bought plants from the bishop's collections in the gardens of Fulham Palace. These included many plants from North America, and their introduction may have prompted Gray to specialize in them. Gray was also one of the twenty nurserymen in the Society of Gardeners, which was led by Philip Miller and which met frequently in an attempt to standardize the names of the plants they were growing. The first part of their *Catalogus plantarum*, the only section published, appeared in 1730 as a joint catalogue of trees and shrubs, many of them recent introductions and several from North America.

In the preface to his *Hortus Britanno-Americanus* (written in 1749 but not published until 1763) Mark Catesby, the pioneer naturalist of the south-eastern states of America, said that

> Mr Gray at Fulham has for many years made it his business to raise and cultivate the plants of America (from whence he has annually fresh supplies) in order to furnish the curious with what they want … Through his industry and skill, a greater variety of American forest-trees and shrubs may be seen in his gardens, than in any other place in England. (Willson, 19)

About 1737 Gray published a broadsheet catalogue in French and English, its alphabetical list of 'American Trees and Shrubs that will endure the Climate of England' framing a *Magnolia grandiflora* which also appeared in the second volume of Catesby's *The Natural History of Carolina* (2 vols., 1729–47); the engraving was after a drawing by G. D. Ehret of a magnolia in flower in the garden of Sir Charles Wager in Parson's Green in 1737. The one in Gray's own garden, planted before 1719, survived until 1810. Several American oaks, maples, dogwoods, walnuts, the tulip tree, the tupelo, the amelanchier, and other trees now established in Europe were also in this catalogue, along with the occasional less welcome import, such as poison ivy.

A later catalogue of 1755 listed more of Gray's stock, 'a greater Variety of Trees, Shrubs, Plants and Flowers … than can perhaps be found in any other Garden, for Sale, not only in England, but also in any other part of Europe' (Harvey, 79). One of Gray's customers was Horace Walpole of Strawberry Hill, who described some of his purchases from 'the nurseryman at Fulham' in a letter of 8 November 1755 to George Montagu:

> I mention cedars [of Lebanon] first, because they are the most beautiful of the evergreen race, and because they are the dearest; half a guinea apiece in baskets … Gray … sells cypresses in pots at half a crown apiece; you turn them out of the pot with all their mould, and they never fail. (ibid., 79)

Gray was buried in Fulham on 15 November 1764. His wife, Hannah, lived on until 24 February 1778. Most of his property was left to her in a will containing no mention of any children. The nursery was taken over by William Burchell, whose family kept the land until it was sold for building in 1882. SANDRA RAPHAEL, rev.

Sources J. Harvey, *Early nurserymen* (1974), 78–9 · B. Henrey, *British botanical and horticultural literature before 1800*, 2 (1975), 348–50 · E. J. Willson, *West London nursery gardens* (1982), 16–20

Gray, David (1838–1861), poet, was born on 29 January 1838 at Duntiblae-on-Banks of Luggie, Kirkintilloch, Dunbartonshire, the eldest of the eight children of David Gray, hand-loom weaver, and his wife, Ann, née Cloggie. In his childhood the family moved to the neighbouring hamlet of Merkland. Having left the parish school at Kirkintilloch he was a pupil teacher in Glasgow and managed to give himself a university career. His parents hoped that he would become a Free Church minister but he began to contribute to the 'Poet's corner' of the *Glasgow Citizen* and resolved to devote himself to literature. He made various metrical experiments—some of them in the manner of Keats and one after the dramatic method of Shakespeare—and then settled to the composition of his idyllic poem 'The Luggie'. At the same time Gray was writing numerous letters to literary celebrities, asking for advice and assistance. R. Monckton Milnes replied to one such letter that on no account was Gray to come to London but his letter had precisely the opposite effect. On Gray's arrival in May 1860 Milnes strongly urged his return to Scotland and to his profession but, finding Gray resolved on staying, he gave him some light literary work. Abandoning a temporary lodging Gray moved into what he called the 'ghastly bankrupt garret' (Buchanan, 64), in Blackfriars, with his friend Robert Buchanan. Soon Gray's health became troublesome, and tuberculosis (perhaps contracted in Hyde Park, where he spent his first London night) was diagnosed. After revisiting Scotland he went south again for the milder climate, staying first at Richmond and then (through the intervention of Milnes) in Torquay, where he refused to enter the sanatorium after being met by 'a nurse of death' (Stuart, 2). Finding his health no better and becoming hysterically nervous, he determined on going home at all costs and he returned finally to Merkland in January 1861.

Lingering through that year Gray wrote a series of sonnets with the general title 'In the Shadows'. He died, aged twenty-three and unmarried, in Merkland, on 3 December 1861, having the previous day been gladdened by seeing a proof of a page of 'The Luggie', which was at last being printed. Buchanan worthily embalms their friendship in 'Poet Andrew' and 'To David in Heaven'. Another friend with whom Gray corresponded much and whose exertions led to the publication of his poems was Sydney Dobell. *The Luggie and other Poems* first appeared in 1862. The title poem, with its sense of natural beauty and its promise of didactic and descriptive power, constitutes Gray's chief claim as a poet, although his sonnets have twice been reprinted, in 1920 and 1991, as *In the Shadows*. Milnes's interest in Gray was generous and practical to the last, and he wrote the epitaph for his monument, erected by friends in 1865 over his grave in Kirkintilloch churchyard.   T. W. BAYNE, *rev.* JAMES HOW

Sources A. V. Stuart, *David Gray, the poet of the Luggie: a centenary booklet* (1961) · R. Buchanan, 'David Gray: a memoir', *A poet's sketch book* (1883), 35–90 · J. Heath-Stubbs, 'Introduction', in D. Gray, *In the shadows* (1991), v–vi · J. Hedderwick, 'Memoir of the author', in D. Gray, *The Luggie and other poems* (1862), xv–xlviii · R. M. Milnes, 'Introductory notice', in D. Gray, *The Luggie and other poems* (1862), vii–xiv · J. Ferguson, 'In the shadows', *The Scottish Bankers' Magazine*, 9 (1917), 213–19 · J. Kilpatrick, *Literary landmarks of Glasgow* (1898) · L. C. Sanders, *Celebrities of the century: being a dictionary of men and women of the nineteenth century*, new and rev. edn (1890) · H. F., 'David Gray', *N&Q*, 174 (1938), 77 · Irving, *Scots.* · *IGI* · d. cert.

Archives NL Scot., corresp. and MSS | Trinity Cam., letters to Lord Houghton

Likenesses pencil or ink?, repro. in R. Buchanan, *David Gray and other essays* (1868) · portrait (after pencil or ink portrait), repro. in Kilpatrick, *Literary landmarks*

Gray, Edmund Dwyer (1845–1888), newspaper proprietor and politician, second son of the Irish nationalist Sir John *Gray (1816–1875) and Anna, daughter of James Dwyer, was born in Dublin on 29 December 1845. After his education Gray joined in the management of his father's newspaper, the *Freeman's Journal*, becoming proprietor on his father's death in 1875. Sir John Gray had become co-proprietor of the newspaper in 1841 and then sole owner in 1850. During the younger Gray's stewardship, the family owned other periodicals, including the *Belfast Morning News*, and he expanded the family financial involvement in other enterprises. In 1866 young Gray saved five persons from drowning in Dublin Bay, for which he was awarded the Tayleur medal, the highest honour of the Royal Humane Society. A witness to his bravery, Caroline Agnes, daughter of Caroline *Chisholm, author of *The Emigrant's Friend*, became his wife in 1869. Although he was descended from a protestant family, Gray converted to his wife's faith, Catholicism,

Edmund Dwyer Gray (1845–1888), by James Russell & Sons, 1887

and the *Freeman's Journal* became a mouthpiece of the Irish Catholic hierarchy. The Grays had one son who survived Gray and played a major role in the management of the newspaper.

As the son of an MP who owned the most influential Liberal-nationalist newspaper in Ireland, Gray's involvement in public life was natural. In 1875 he was a member of the O'Connell monument committee and also entered the corporation. Following in the footsteps of his father, who was knighted for his efforts to bring the water supply to Dublin, the son interested himself in public health problems, and chaired a corporation committee investigating the subject which led to the speedy revolution of the municipal health system. On 28 April 1875 Gray unsuccessfully contested the parliamentary by-election in Kilkenny that resulted from his father's death. He was returned to the House of Commons at the Tipperary by-election on 15 May 1877. Though sometimes supporting Charles Stewart Parnell's campaign of parliamentary 'obstruction', Gray never dissociated himself from the leadership of Isaac Butt. During the 1870s he established contacts with a number of Liberals, including particularly Joseph Chamberlain and Sir Charles Dilke. His relations with Parnell were cool and the two men had a famous dispute in 1879 when the latter referred to him as a 'papist rat' (Lyons, 93). Parnell denied using the phrase and the two men were reconciled by Archbishop Thomas Croke, although they never became close. Gray was lord mayor of Dublin in 1880 and in this capacity he chaired the Mansion House committee formed on 2 January 1880 to raise funds for the relief of distressed peasants. This committee, which ultimately raised around £180,000, was denounced by Parnell during his tour of North America, which added to the distance between the two men. At the general election in April 1880 Gray captured Carlow and chaired the meeting of home-rule MPs on 17 May that elected Parnell sessional chairman of the party. Gray personally did not take an active part in the land war, though he and his newspapers supported the claims of Ireland's tenants. In May 1881 Gray and his newspaper were critical of the party leader's insistence that nationalist MPs abstain on the second reading of the Land Bill. Deprived of effective newspaper support, Parnell and sympathizers purchased the titles owned by Richard Pigott, and converted them into a weekly newspaper, *United Ireland*. Thereafter, whenever Gray's journals showed signs of straying from the Parnellite line, the threat of turning *United Ireland* into a daily newspaper kept them up to the mark. In 1881 Gray retired from the Dublin corporation when it declined to confer the distinction of honorary burgesses on Parnell and John Dillon. When nationalists captured a majority of the council seats in November 1881 and granted them this title, he re-entered the corporation. In 1882, when Gray was high sheriff of Dublin, the *Freeman's Journal* criticized the jurors in the trial of Francis Hynes, who was convicted of murder and executed. As proprietor, Gray was held in contempt of court, fined £500, and sentenced to three months' imprisonment, although he spent only six weeks behind Richmond's walls. A public subscription was raised to pay the fine. His connection with the corporation ceased in the following year. From mid-1882 Parnell's moderation was more in tune with Gray's own predilections, and the two men had few political differences. Gray's concern for public health issues persisted, and in 1884–5 he was a member of the royal commission on the housing of the working classes. He continued to have an active concern in this question. Also, he promoted the interests of Dublin commerce, and used his considerable social and political contacts in 1885 to prevent the transfer of mail contracts from the City of Dublin Steam Packet Company to an English firm. Even during the period of bitter political hostility in the early 1880s Gray had remained on good personal terms with leading Liberals and, though a nationalist in Irish affairs, he would have considered himself generally a supporter of Gladstone. At the general election of 1885 Gray was returned for both Carlow and the St Stephen's Green division of Dublin, but chose to sit for the latter. At the Galway by-election in February 1886 he used the influence of the *Freeman's Journal* to help to quell the revolt against Parnell's choice for the vacancy, Captain William O'Shea, husband of his mistress. Gray was one of the few Parnellites to welcome those portions of the first Home Rule Bill in 1886, proposing an upper order intended to protect capital.

In 1887 the Grays' newspaper interests were converted into a limited liability company, enabling Gray to realize a large capital sum, amounting to £125,000. He continued to run the journal but he suffered from asthma and his health was not robust. Following a brief illness, he died in Dublin on 27 March 1888. His funeral and interment on 31 March in Glasnevin cemetery in Dublin attracted huge crowds but Parnell was not present. Gray was a considerable political figure, though he did not pretend to oratorical brilliance. His forte was the patient use of behind-the-scenes influence, and he derived immense authority from close contacts with the Irish bishops. He was one of the few leading nationalists primarily interested in urban rather than rural issues.

G. B. SMITH, *rev.* ALAN O'DAY

Sources *Freeman's Journal* [Dublin] (28 March 1888) · *Freeman's Journal* [Dublin] (29 March 1888) · *Freeman's Journal* [Dublin] (2 April 1888) · *Irish Times* (28 March 1888) · H. Boylan, *A dictionary of Irish biography*, 2nd edn (1988) · WWBMP · B. M. Walker, ed., *Parliamentary election results in Ireland, 1801–1922* (1978) · *Dod's Parliamentary Companion* · C. C. O'Brien, *Parnell and his party, 1880–90* (1957) · A. O'Day, *The English face of Irish nationalism* (1977) · A. O'Day, *Parnell and the first home rule episode* (1986) · F. S. L. Lyons, *Charles Stewart Parnell* (1977) · C. H. D. Howard, ed., *Joseph Chamberlain* (1953) · *The Red Earl: the papers of the fifth Earl Spencer, 1835–1910*, ed. P. Gordon, 2 vols., Northamptonshire RS, 31, 34 (1981–6)

Archives BL, corresp. with Lord Carnarvon and W. E. Gladstone, Add. MS 60821 · TCD, corresp. with John Dillon · U. Birm. L., Joseph Chamberlain MSS

Likenesses J. Russell & Sons, photograph, 1887, NPG [*see illus.*] · M. Redmond-Dunne, marble bust (after marble bust, 1889), NG Ire. · wood-engraving (after photograph by LaFayette of Dublin), NPG; repro. in *ILN* (14 April 1888)

Wealth at death £89,611 15s. 3d.: probate, 11 May 1888, CGPLA Ire.

Gray, Edward Earl [Eddie] (1898–1969), comedian and juggler, was born on 10 June 1898 at 2 Carey Place, Pimlico, London, one of nine children of Edward Earl Gray, a Pimlico general dealer, and his wife, Rebecca Daniels. With his brother Danny, Gray was apprenticed to a juggling troupe at the age of nine. In his youth he toured extensively in Europe, the United States, the Middle East, and the Far East. He first came to notice as a technically accomplished and innovative straight juggler and only gradually incorporated into his act the laconic, idiosyncratic humour for which he would be renowned. From 1919 he worked often with the double act of Jimmy Nervo and Teddy Knox (having first met Nervo when both were child performers in 1912) and appeared with them in their innovative revues of 1925, *Young Bloods of Variety* and *Blue Bloods of Variety*, and in *Chelsea Follies* in 1930. In counterpoint to their anarchic, practical-joking comedic style Gray developed a droll, slightly seedy stage persona, accompanying his juggling feats with an ironic, self-deprecating commentary. He toured extensively throughout the twenties, including a spell with Harry Lauder's company touring Australia and South Africa. He married Marie Cecilia Loftus (d. 1994), a variety performer, in 1931. She was known professionally as Patti Loftus and she came from a dynasty of female entertainers, being the niece of Marie Loftus, a well-known 'principal boy'.

In November 1931 Gray appeared, with the double acts of Nervo and Knox, Charlie Naughton and Jimmy Gold, and Billy Caryll and Hilda Mundy in what was billed as a 'crazy week' at the London Palladium. The great success of this event led directly to the formation of the *Crazy Gang, with whom Gray would continue to be associated. He appeared more or less continuously with the gang in a series of spectacularly popular variety shows and revues at the Palladium until 1940. It was during this time that he perfected the persona of the Monsewer, a droll grotesque with steel frame glasses and preposterous curly moustache, juggling and performing card tricks in an idiosyncratic comic patois of cockney and cod French: 'Now, ce soir—that's foreign for this afternoon—moi's gonna travailler la packet of cards—*une* packet of cards, not deux, *une*.' Veering in a deadpan manner between technical brilliance and apparent ineptitude, at one moment a polished performer eating apples as he juggled with them, the next a hilariously incompetent dog trainer, Gray developed an eccentric, inscrutable comic manner that made him a favourite among other comedians.

When the Crazy Gang split up in the early years of the war, Gray, like the other members of the group, toured in variety (including a run in *Hi-de-hi* at the Palace Theatre with Flanagan and Allen in 1943) and worked with the Entertainments National Service Association, touring in Europe and the Middle East. After the war Gray pursued a successful solo career in variety. He joined the re-formed Crazy Gang for a royal variety performance on 1 November 1948, but didn't fully rejoin until the revue *These Foolish Kings* at the Victoria Palace in December 1956. He subsequently appeared in all the gang's shows, and after their final show, *Young in Heart* in May 1962, continued to enjoy success as a solo act and as a performer in *A Funny Thing Happened on the Way to the Forum* with Frankie Howerd.

Gray was much loved for his idiosyncratic humour, both on and off stage. Paul Jennings, in *The Times*, called him 'the funniest man in the world' and he was renowned as the favourite comedian of the poet laureate John Betjeman. There are many fond accounts in show-business reminiscences of his penchant for hoaxing and practical jokes; the most often repeated among these concerns his trick of persuading passers-by that a postman had become trapped inside a letter box. Although he was a founding member of the Crazy Gang and had helped define its characteristic, anarchic comedic style he always remained a semi-detached member of the group—a kind of eccentric cog in its deranged mechanism. He famously refused to sign contracts with managements throughout his career and so tended to be paid less than his talents were worth, leading him to quip frequently about his lack of 'remooneration'. He continued to work until the end of his life, and died on 15 September 1969 at Southlands Hospital in Shoreham by Sea, Sussex, three days after making an impromptu guest appearance with Elsie and Doris Waters (Gert and Daisy) at the Hippodrome, Eastbourne.

DAVID GOLDIE

Sources M. Owen, *The Crazy Gang: a personal reminiscence* (1986) · J. Fisher, *Funny way to be a hero* (1973) · R. Wilmut, *Kindly leave the stage!* (1985) · *The Times* (16 Sept 1969) · R. Hudd, *Roy Hudd's cavalcade of variety acts* (1997) · R. Busby, *British music hall: an illustrated who's who from 1850 to the present day* (1976) · I. Bevan, *Top of the bill* (1952) · B. Green, ed., *The last empires: a music hall companion* (1986) · *CGPLA Eng. & Wales* (1969) · b. cert. · d. cert. · private information [Mrs Wendi Lynch, first cousin, once removed]

Archives SOUND BL NSA, documentary recording

Likenesses group photograph, 1956, Hult. Arch. · group photograph, 1959, Hult. Arch.

Wealth at death £6733: administration, 13 Nov 1969, *CGPLA Eng. & Wales*

Gray, Edward Whitaker (1748–1806), physician and museum curator, was born on 21 March 1748, probably in London, the second son of Samuel *Gray (*bap.* 1693?, *d.* 1766), seedsman, and his wife, Juliana, *née* Kelly (*d.* 1774). A younger brother, Samuel Frederick Gray, went into the

Edward Whitaker Gray (1748–1806), by Sir Augustus Wall Callcott [detail]

family business. Gray attended the anatomical school of Dr William Hunter in London and in 1771 was admitted member of the Royal College of Physicians, where he was employed for two years as librarian and beadle. Having secured a licence, he departed in late 1773 or early 1774 for Portugal, where he spent four years at the hospital attached to the English wine merchants' factory house at Oporto. He married in Oporto Elizabeth Bazeley; two daughters, Juliana (1775–1837) and Elizabeth (*b.* 1777), were born there, and two sons, Francis Edward (1784–1810) and William Herman (*d.* 1794), were born after the Grays returned to England.

After sending a quantity of plants to Sir Joseph Banks in 1777, Gray returned in 1778 with a varied natural history collection, particularly amphibia. Back in London he was elected fellow of the Royal Society in 1779, took up the post of secretary and treasurer to the Society for the Improvement of Medical Knowledge, and joined a philosophical society; the last two were of a social nature. He was appointed in 1788 to a humble position within the British Museum, where he rose within nine years to become keeper of the natural history collections. At the Royal Society he delivered the Croonian lectures on a medical theme in 1785–6, and in 1797 was elected senior secretary. In 1802 he was appointed a trustee of the new Hunterian Museum of the Royal College of Physicians. His wife and family lived at Blackheath while Gray himself, as keeper, occupied rooms at the British Museum.

At the British Museum Gray earned additional emoluments by arranging the bird collection according to the Linnaean system, which took him two years and brought him £100. He then cleaned, classed, and labelled the specimens in the insect room, which brought him £200, and dealt with two major acquisitions, the Hatchett minerals and the Cracherode shells. However, under reforms imposed by the new librarian, Joseph Planta, Gray's empire was judged wanting, its catalogues and documentation defective, its objects neglected. Gray resigned as secretary to the board before the trustees met in 1806 to discuss these findings, though he retained his keepership for another year. He died in his apartments at the museum on 27 December 1806 and was buried on 3 January at St George's, Bloomsbury. ANITA McCONNELL

Sources A. E. Gunther, 'Edward Whitaker Gray, 1748–1806, keeper of natural curiosities at the British Museum', *Bulletin of the British Museum (Natural History)* [Historical Series], 5 (1976–7), 193–210 · A. E. Gunther, *The founders of science at the British Museum, 1753–1900* (1980) · Munk, *Roll* · *GM*, 1st ser., 77 (1807), 90 · parish register (burial), London, St George's, Bloomsbury Way, 3 Jan 1807
Likenesses A. W. Callcott, oils, RS [*see illus.*]

Gray [*formerly* Smith], **(Kathleen) Eileen Moray** (1878–1976), designer and architect, was born on 9 August 1878 at Brownswood, the family estate in Enniscorthy, co. Wexford. She was the third of three daughters and youngest of five children of James Maclaren Smith (1832–1900), an amateur painter, and Eveleen (1841–1919), daughter of Captain Jeremiah Londsdale Pounden, of Brownswood, and his wife, Lady Jane Stewart, daughter of the tenth earl of Moray. In 1893 Eveleen Smith inherited the title Baroness Gray, and two years later her husband changed his name to Smith-Gray, by royal licence. From then on the children took the surname Gray.

Eileen Gray's education was erratic. She spent most of her childhood with her mother at Brownswood or in London, sometimes travelling with her artist father in Switzerland and Italy. She retained a strong feeling for nature. In 1901 she persuaded her mother to allow her to enrol at the Slade School in London, where her teachers were Henry Tonks, P. Wilson Steer, and Frederick Brown.

Gray was already showing signs of obsession with technique. She first learned lacquer making in the workshops of D. Charles in Dean Street, Soho. In Paris she worked with the Japanese craftsman Sugawara on the lacquered screens and furniture that established her reputation. In 1902 she moved to Paris permanently, taking the flat at 21 rue Bonaparte which was to be her base for the next seventy years.

Gray's career developed in two distinct phases. For the first twenty years she was a fashionable Paris decorator, protégée of Paul Poiret and Jacques Doucet, working in a style related to art deco. In 1913 she first exhibited in public in the Salon de la Société des Artistes Décorateurs. In 1922 she opened a furniture gallery—Jean Désert— in the rue du Faubourg St Honoré. She began designing highly original abstract rugs and carpets, forming a close partnership with the English weaver Evelyn Wyld. Although she was never a sociable person Gray was on the fringes of the lesbian subculture, forming a glamorous liaison with Damia (Marie-Louise Damien), the gravel-voiced *chanteuse*.

In the mid-1920s Gray turned to modernism, influenced by the Dutch architecture of De Stijl and by her chief publicist, collaborator and, for some years, lover, Jean Badovici, Romanian modernist architect and critic, editor of *L'Architecture Vivante*. For Badovici, Gray designed E-1027 at Roquebrune in the south of France, a house that became a modernist icon. Gray was furious when Le Corbusier, a friend of Badovici's, painted eight lascivious murals on the walls of her fastidious interiors. It was from the rocks below E-1027 that Le Corbusier later swam out to his death.

Between 1932 and 1934 Gray built her own house, Tempe à Pailla, nearby at Castellar. This building shows her mastery at integrating furnishings and architecture and her new-found fascination with industrial components. The house was later acquired by Graham Sutherland. From the mid-1930s her reputation lapsed. Her failure to build on a large scale can be ascribed as much to her own diffidence, combined with a certain aristocratic bloody-mindedness, as to prejudice against a British woman architect, though there is evidence that Gray was cold-shouldered by the European male modernist clique. In the war she was interned in France as an alien. It was not until the 1970s that the true nature of her perfectionist talent was recognized, with retrospectives at the RIBA in London in 1971, the Victoria and Albert Museum, and, in 1980, the Museum of Modern Art, New York. In 1972, at the age of ninety-four, she was appointed a royal designer for industry. Prices in the salerooms for Gray's original pieces, especially the lacquer work of her early period, rose spectacularly. New editions of her modernist furniture of the 1920s and early 1930s were put into production in the 1970s. There are examples of Eileen Gray's furniture in the collections of the Victoria and Albert Museum and the Musée des Arts Décoratifs, Paris, and drawings and models in the collection of the RIBA in London.

Eileen Gray was not so much a theoretic innovator, not perhaps even a major design influence, but she was a practitioner with a unique breadth of vision, encompassing both luxuriance and purism, a designer of consummate judgement and finesse. By the mid-1990s the intuitive qualities she brought to architecture gained her new admirers among critics who distrusted the doctrinaire formalism of Le Corbusier and his disciples. In his important study *The Other Tradition of Modern Architecture* (1995), Professor Colin St John Wilson includes Gray—with Alvar Aalto, Hugo Haering, and Hans Scharoun—in an alternative, more flexible, humane tradition of European modernism, commenting that 'Gray had a unique gift for turning the practical into the poetic' with her intense 'perceptions of habitability'. She was the implacable enemy of cosiness. In appearance she was as stylish and *soignée* as one of her own interiors. She was witty, in an Irish way, and childlike in her zest for new experience. Her character, however, had its areas of elusiveness. She veered away from domesticity in her love affairs, female and male. In later years her chief emotional dependence was upon her niece, the painter Prunella Clough. She died in hospital in

Paris, after a fall in her studio, on 30 October 1976. Her ashes were deposited on 5 November in the Père Lachaise cemetery.   FIONA MACCARTHY

Sources P. Adam, *Eileen Gray: architect designer* (1987) [incl. catalogue raisonné] · S. Johnson, *Eileen Gray: designer, 1879–1976* (1979) · J. Rykwert, 'Eileen Gray: pioneer of design', *ArchR*, 152 (1972), 357–61 · *The Times* (3 Nov 1976) · *DNB* · b. cert. · *WWW* · C. St J. Wilson, *The other tradition of modern architecture* (1995) · D. Walker, '"L'art de vivre": the designs of Eileen Gray (1878–1976)', *Irish Arts Review Yearbook*, 15 (1999)
Archives Musée des Arts Décoratifs, Paris · RIBA · RSA, Archive of Faculty of Royal Designers · V&A, corresp.; notes; photographs
Likenesses B. Abbott, photographs, 1926, RSA, archive of faculty of royal designers

Gray [*née* Anderson], **Elizabeth** (1831–1924), fossil collector, was born on 21 February 1831 at the Burns Arms inn, Alloway, near Ayr, the second child of Thomas Anderson, innkeeper, and his wife, Mary Hamilton Young. She began her education at a small private school in Girvan, after her father moved to Enoch to become a farmer. At the age of fifteen, she was sent to a boarding-school in Glasgow for a year, before returning home in order to help look after her six younger brothers. Her father, a keen naturalist and collector known to Scottish geologists, encouraged her interest in the local Girvan fossils.

At the age of twenty-four Elizabeth met Robert *Gray (1825–1887), a Glasgow bank inspector, on an ornithological visit to the Ayrshire coast. They were married on 8 April 1856, and continued to make excursions to Girvan each summer, recording the results in the journals of the Natural History Society of Glasgow. Collecting the rich Ayrshire Palaeozoic assemblages became an absorbing family pursuit that was continued every year despite the growing number of children. In 1874 the family moved to Edinburgh when Robert Gray accepted a new post, and Elizabeth Gray then began her co-operation with the many palaeontologists who described her Ordovician fossils.

Throughout her life Elizabeth Gray preferred to devote her energies to discovering fossils and later her objective became the extension of faunal lists. She trained all her family in the practical methods of collecting and documenting specimens. Her successive collections were acquired by the Hunterian Museum, Glasgow (1866); the Royal Scottish Museum (1889); the Geological Survey (c.1890); the Sedgwick Museum (1907–10); and the British Museum (Natural History), London; together they form a unique resource of Palaeozoic fossils.

In 1900 Elizabeth Gray was made an honorary member of the Geological Society of Glasgow for the contribution her collections had made to geological literature. The Murchison geological fund was awarded to her in 1903 in recognition of her skilful services to geological science. A woman of considerable character, determination, and resourcefulness, with a phenomenally retentive memory, she was renowned for her extensive collecting in the Girvan district, which she carried on until the autumn of 1923. She died of heart failure at 59 George Street, her Edinburgh home, on 11 February 1924, after packing a batch of fossils the previous day. An obituarist, J. Horne, described her as 'one of the most successful fossil collectors in Scottish geology'.   R. J. CLEEVELY

Sources R. J. Cleevely, R. P. Tripp, and Y. Howells, 'Mrs Elizabeth Gray, 1831–1924: a passion for fossils', *Bulletin of the British Museum (Natural History)* [Historical Series], 17 (1989), 167–258 · A. Gray and Robert Gray jun., *Mrs Robert Gray and family*, biographical notes, 1938, NHM, palaeontology library archives · *Proceedings of the Geological Society of London*, no. 1502 (1953), cxliii–cxlv · P. Macnair and F. Mort, eds., *History of the Geological Society of Glasgow, 1858–1908* (1908), 122 · R. J. Cleevely, *World palaeontological collections* (1983), 134 · A. S. Alexander, *Across watersheds* (1939), 53–6 · J. Horne, *Transactions of the Geological Society of Edinburgh*, 11 (1925), 392 · *The Scotsman* (12 Feb 1924) · private information (2004) · bap. reg. Scot., AYR 578/10/261 · m. reg. Scot. · d. cert.
Archives NHM, corresp. and papers | NHM, Thomas Davidson notebooks
Likenesses photograph, 1905, NHM, palaeontology library, Mrs Gray archive · photographs, 1920–23, NHM, palaeontology library, Mrs Gray archive; repro. in Cleevely, Tripp, and Howells, 'Mrs Elizabeth Gray'
Wealth at death £605 15s. 3d.: confirmation, 17 April 1924, *CCI*

Gray, Ellington. *See* Jacob, Naomi Eleanor Clare (1884–1964).

Gray [*née* Hopwood], **Faith** (1751–1826), diarist, was born on 31 January 1751 in Goodramgate, York, the eldest of the seven children of Jonathan Hopwood (1718–1784), tradesman, and his wife, Margaret (1720–1787), daughter of William Batty of Ouston, Tadcaster, and his second wife, Jane. Faith began her diaries at the age of fourteen, initially with sporadic records concerned with social visits but gradually recording comments on religious interests and lectures attended. No formal education was mentioned, but she commented on a religious and moral upbringing, particularly influenced by her father, and on being taught to read 'at a very early age'. On the death of her mother, in 1787, Faith recalled the happiness of their early family life:

> The days were occupied in active employment and the evenings in a way calculated to improve and gratify the mind. My brothers were engaged in the study of languages, in reading History, learning geography, or in music. My mother, sisters and myself were sewing or reading. (Gray, 76)

On 9 October 1777 Faith married William Gray (1761–1845), a weaver's son, who was articled to a solicitor and became a partner in a York firm. Always diligent, William was obliged to work particularly hard during the early years of their marriage in order to save the business, and thus his family, from bankruptcy occasioned by the extravagance and misconduct of his partner's profligate nephew. The Grays were strongly influenced by the evangelical movement, to the distress of Faith's parents who feared that they would become Methodists, and were friends of William Wilberforce and the Revd Joseph Milner of Hull, an evangelical divine. They were also close friends of the Revd W. Richardson, Dr Thomas Withers, and the Revd John Graham, with whom William Gray helped found Sunday schools in York, the local association of the Church Missionary Society, the York Dispensary, and York County Hospital.

Despite the demands of her growing family Faith Gray was deeply committed to charitable pursuits. In 1782 the first of these endeavours, in association with her friend Catherine Cappe, involved arranging for the children and girls employed by a local hemp manufacturer to learn reading at night and to attend church on Sundays. Three years later the ladies founded their spinning school, followed later by a knitting school for younger children, in order to 'excite a spirit of virtuous industry among the children of the poor' (C. Cappe, *An Account of Two Charity Schools for the Education of Girls, and of a Female Friendly Society in York*, 1799, unpaginated). The schools were entirely directed and run by a group of like-minded women who taught the girls, kept the accounts, and organized church attendance and Sunday visiting to homes of the poor. At the school girls were taught basic literacy and learned to spin, for which they were rewarded with clothing and a quarter of their earnings in money—to help encourage the co-operation of the parents. Garments were issued in fixed proportion to the quantity of wool that was spun, and the possession of decent clothing, which the girls themselves were taught how to make, was considered particularly valuable in effecting a change in morals, manners, and bearing. On leaving, the girls were helped to find places of employment and were therefore able to avoid the poverty and vice endemic in their backgrounds.

Following the success of the spinning school, Faith Gray was approached for advice on the reform of the local Grey Coat Charity School for Girls. After investigations at the school, tactfully phrased papers were sent to the monthly Gentlemen Governors meetings, which finally resulted in Gray and her group taking over the direction and day-to-day administration, the previous master having been found 'unfit' and his wife in a 'deranged state'. In 1788 they also established the York Female Friendly Society, membership open to all who had attended the Spinning or Grey Coat schools, with the object of 'contributing in health towards the support of members in sickness' (Gray, 67).

In 1788 Faith Gray noted in her diary the move into the house in Minster Yard, thereafter called Gray's Court. Although after this date the diaries are increasingly dominated by details of Gray's growing family, they also chart the continued involvement of the Grays in the increasingly assertive and influential evangelical movement. In August 1796 Gray arranged for the circulation of Hannah More's *Cheap Repository Tracts* in York and its environs; she later visited More at least twice, in 1799 and 1809. In keeping with her anxiety to promote moral reform and with her hostility to revolutionary France, a tour of southern England in September and October 1796 included a pilgrimage to Windsor, where she attended prayers at St George's Chapel in the presence of George III and Queen Charlotte. William Wilberforce was an occasional guest, staying with Gray when campaigning for election as member for Yorkshire in 1796, 1803, and 1806. Gray continued to advise on the establishment of female friendly societies around Yorkshire, often in association with Catherine Cappe. On 3 February 1813 she resigned from the board of

the Grey Coat School, but she continued to attend quarterly meetings.

The diaries are not only of interest for their details of the schools, but are also of particular value for their depiction of the developing middle-class religion, culture, and attitudes. They record the lives of a hard-working, rather pious couple, closely involved with their children, their extended family, and a wide circle of friends and acquaintances. They also show that Faith Gray remained steadfast in her religious beliefs despite her many losses, including two younger brothers, two of her seven children in infancy, and her adored second daughter Lucy in 1813 at the age of twenty-five. Gray finally ceased keeping a diary when her health started to deteriorate, following the death of her much loved firstborn daughter and her first granddaughter, both named Margaret, in her house on the same day, 31 January 1826. She died at home in Gray's Court on 20 December 1826 and, greatly mourned, was buried early in January 1827 in St Maurice's churchyard, York.   POLLY HAMILTON

Sources Mrs E. Gray, *Papers and diaries of a York family, 1764–1839* (1927) · H. Blodgett, *Centuries of female days: Englishwomen's private diaries* (1989) · M. R. Hunt, *The middling sort: commerce, gender, and the family in England, 1680–1780* (1996)
Archives York City Archives, family MSS
Likenesses Wright, pastel drawing, repro. in Gray, *Papers and diaries of a York family*

Gray, Frances Ralph (1861–1935), headmistress, was born on 9 July 1861 at Roscrea, co. Tipperary, the daughter of James Gray, clerk to Roscrea board of guardians, and his wife, Sarah Meredith. In her autobiography, *And Gladly Wolde he Lerne and Gladly Teche* (1931), Frances Gray makes little of her own formal education before the age of sixteen, when she moved to Plymouth high school: 'I had hitherto learned of school subjects chiefly what I pleased' (Gray, 4), and she is dismissive of the small day school she attended until the age of twelve, run by two elderly sisters: Gray describes their educational methods as being 'exclusively of their own' (ibid., 3). After this point she attended no educational establishment and instead ascribed the most important influence to her father, and in particular the daily walks she and her sister Sarah (later a doctor) had with him. An obituarist claimed, however, that 'during her girlhood she had been in contact with well-arranged successful educational centres, first at Dunheved College, Launceston, then at the Plymouth High School' (*Hermes*, 42–3). This might better explain her success at Plymouth, where she took a first class with distinction in three groups of the Cambridge higher local examination, namely English history and literature, Latin and Greek, and political economy and constitutional history.

On the strength of this Frances Gray proceeded to Newnham College, Cambridge, in 1880. Her academic performance here was, however, rather less successful. In 1883 she obtained a third in part one of the classical tripos. In her autobiography, Gray refers obliquely to problems with religious beliefs she experienced at the time. Born a member of the Wesleyan Methodists in Ireland, while at

Cambridge she had become an evangelical Anglican. Constance Maynard, recommending her to the council of Westfield College, the evangelical college for women in London, referred to this 'difficult position', which she had nevertheless overcome and had hence 'won the respect of all her companions during the time of her residing there' (Westfield council minutes, 1.77). Gray was appointed a classics lecturer at Westfield in 1883.

Constance Louisa *Maynard (1849–1935), founder and first mistress of Westfield, had learned of Gray through a mutual friend, Anne Richardson, who was also at Newnham. Richardson also joined the staff of Westfield and for ten years a very intense triangular relationship evolved between the three women. In her unpublished personal diaries, Maynard monitored in precise detail the turbulent nature of her liaison with Gray, to whom she referred as Ralph. It is significant that only parts of this record remain; in 1935, a few months before her own death, Gray saw it fit, as executor of Maynard's will, to destroy significant parts of this account. In spite of this, however, evidence of their intimacy remains. For 2 December 1883 Maynard records, for example: 'I stepped into her little dark room, and in a moment more was welcomed into her strong, warm arms'. Whether Gray was as committed to the relationship as Maynard is uncertain; indeed Maynard always felt she had 'failed' with her. The emotional strain on Gray, however, seems to have contributed to her resignation as resident lecturer in 1885. In 1891 she returned to live at Westfield, but three years later applied for the post of headmistress of St Katharine's, a preparatory school in St Andrews. Maynard described writing Gray's reference as 'writing an epitaph on a tomb'. Some of the quarrels recorded by Maynard throw light on Gray's views on education, and also, perhaps, her academic insecurities. In charge of the library, Gray was of the opinion that the students should be exposed to books that would 'really educate', books that were currently the subject of public debate, such as Arnold's *Culture and Anarchy* and Eliot's *Adam Bede*. Maynard, by contrast, was much more proscriptive in her choice, wanting simply books that they '*ought* to read'. On another occasion, Gray violently accused Constance of failing to respect her academically; the endless correction of elementary Latin had apparently eroded her self-respect.

The networks which existed between female educationists in the late nineteenth century probably account for Gray's appointment to St Katharine's, a job for which there were over a hundred applicants. When teaching at St Leonard's (to which St Katharine's was a preparatory school), Maynard had had a similarly intimate relationship with Louisa Lumsden, the headmistress. The influence undoubtedly helped in gaining a position to which, Gray herself admitted, she was very ill-prepared. Little is known of her headship of St Katharine's which she held from 1894 until 1903; apart from a discussion of her introduction of bookbinding onto the curriculum, Gray is vague about her time there.

In 1903 Gray was appointed out of sixty-seven applicants to the position of headmistress (high mistress from 1909) of St Paul's Girls' School, founded in that year by the Mercers' Company. The early governors' minutes show how tenaciously Gray fought for the school and her ideas. She was keen to establish a boarding-house, a swimming pool, and a pension scheme for her staff, all of which she achieved within a few years. On some matters of policy, she was, however, rather less successful. In her autobiography Gray made much of her belief that the best form of teacher training was achieved through practice in schools, and not through the study of theory: 'instinctively I shrank from the notion of being told how to do anything … I had come to believe in the apprenticeship system as that which promised best for the training of a teacher' (Gray, 34). Within a few months of the school opening, in her report to the governors, Gray asked that the school might apply to the Board of Education to be registered as a training school. She was asked to withdraw her proposals. A reason is not given but the fact that the boys' school did not offer similar opportunities might be the explanation. Gray never abandoned these beliefs, however. At the meeting of the Association of Head Mistresses on 12 July 1912, for example, she strongly supported opening schools for the training of teachers.

Although unmarried and herself dependent on a profession, Gray was unambiguous in her conviction that the principal aim of female education was to prepare her students as 'future home-makers'. Bemoaning the fact that many middle-class girls were needlessly going out to work, she made her motto *Back to the home!* (Gray, 89). Writing in *Paulina* in 1922, she commented: 'Every woman that is born into the world is given by God the duty of being a home maker' (*Paulina*, 1922). Linked to this was her criticism of the competitive examination system. She warned of the dangers of overwork and also hoped for the day when children were not 'ground under the heel of the Matriculation Tyrant' (Gray, 222). Instead she advocated a system of continual assessment by teachers which would be justified through regular and close inspection of schools. The tension between providing a rigorous education while preparing her students for a more traditional role is aptly shown in a letter to Sir John Watney, a mercer, in 1925:

> I should like the parents to realise that while we shall certainly send many of our girls to University and equip them in various ways for earning a living, they need not be afraid to trust us to give them the refinements of life. (St Paul's Girls' School correspondence, Mercers' misc. MSS 16.6)

This was not to be achieved by making subjects attractive, however, and she was often keen to demonstrate her aversion to 'the theory that the happiness of the child must be secured in all the activities of the school' (Gray, 254). She expected absolute obedience. In a paper given to the National Union of Women Workers in 1913, she is reported as having recommended that 'now and then, not often, as a reward, the reason for a command might be given. But if the reason was given beforehand, all the virtue of the obedience was lost' (*Sheffield Telegraph*, 8 Oct 1913).

Gray was clearly a formidable figure. Just as she developed a hold over Constance Maynard, so also students and colleagues were impressed by her physical presence. A letter to Ethel Strudwick (her successor as high mistress) from the president of the Association of Head Mistresses on Gray's death commented on her 'noble presence and beautiful voice'. Girls likewise remember her 'commanding and grand manner'. Dame Evelyn Sharp, one of the first female permanent secretaries in the civil service, remembered that a punishment for a misdemeanour included being told to kneel down in Gray's office to pray for forgiveness.

Frances Gray retired from St Paul's in 1927, by which time she had established it as one of the leading girls' schools in Britain. She was the president of the Association of Head Mistresses in 1923–5 and the president of the University Association of Women Teachers in 1921–2. She was secretary of the Women's University Settlement committee at Southwark in the early days of its work, and had led the development of Dame Colet House in Stepney. In 1920 she was made a JP for London and worked closely with the juvenile court. She was awarded an MA from Trinity College, Dublin, and an OBE in 1926. She was in favour of women's suffrage, particularly for single women and widows. In 1893 she contributed passionately to a debate on the subject at Westfield. As high mistress she was one of 223 signatories to a petition advocating women's suffrage submitted by the Association of Head Mistresses to Asquith in 1909 and in 1910 chaired a debate on the subject at St Paul's. Frances Gray died at her home, Church Side, Grayshott, near Hindhead, Hampshire, on 10 November 1935.   ELIZABETH COUTTS

Sources F. R. Gray, *And gladly wolde he lerne and gladly teche* (1931) · C. L. Maynard, diaries and unfinished autobiography, Queen Mary College, London, Queen Mary and Westfield College Archives · Westfield council minutes, vols. 1–4, Queen Mary College, London, Westfield College Archives · *The Times* (Nov 1935) · *Hermes* [magazine of Westfield College] (Dec 1935) · *Paulina* [magazine of St Paul's Girls' School] (1905–35) · M. Vicinus, *Independent women: work and community for single women, 1850–1920* (1985) · J. Sondheimer, *Castle Adamant in Hampstead: a history of Westfield College, 1882–1982* (1983) · St Paul's Girls' School, minutes and correspondence, Mercers' Hall, London · [A. B. White and others], eds., *Newnham College register, 1871–1971*, 2nd edn, 1 (1979), 70

Archives Mercers' Company, London, archives · Queen Mary College, London, Westfield College Archives

Likenesses S. W. Hodgkinson, photograph, repro. in Gray, *And gladly wolde he lerne*, frontispiece

Wealth at death £1450 3s. 8d.: probate, 5 March 1936, CGPLA Eng. & Wales

Gray, Francis James [Frank] (**1880–1935**), politician, was born in Oxford on 31 August 1880, the only son of Alderman Sir Walter Gray and his wife, Emily Alice Savage. **Sir Walter Gray** (**1848–1918**), property speculator and local politician, was born in Weston, Hertfordshire, and educated at Stevenage grammar school. He joined the Great Northern Railway Company and became stationmaster at Waddington, Lincolnshire, where John Shaw-Stewart, a member of Keble College's council, was a regular passenger. On Shaw-Stewart's recommendation, Gray was brought to Oxford in 1870 as steward to the newly established college. He stayed in the post for thirteen years, and began a series of property speculations in north Oxford and elsewhere that made his fortune. He was elected a Conservative councillor for the city's north ward in 1881 and, following the collapse of the Liberal-dominated Oxford Building and Investment Company in 1883, he achieved a political coup by becoming the company's official liquidator. He was elected alderman on the new county borough council in 1889 and was for many years the recognized leader of the Conservatives on the council. He was mayor of Oxford four times between 1888 and 1901 and was knighted in 1902. In 1917 Gray was passed over as the Conservative parliamentary candidate for the Oxford city constituency in favour of the historian J. A. R. Marriott. This snub is sometimes said to have converted his son to the Liberal cause, but Frank had already become an enemy of class privilege by that time. Walter Gray died at Rothbury, Northumberland, on 17 March 1918.

Frank Gray was educated at Rugby School and at F. B. Harvey's crammer in Woodstock before being articled as a solicitor's clerk to Dr Harry Galpin, the Oxford City solicitor, in 1898. His articles were transferred to the Hon. Robert Lyttelton in London in 1902, and after passing his final law exams he remained with Lyttelton until 1906. On returning to Oxford, he set up as a solicitor in partnership with Andrew Walsh and, with influential local contacts, soon built up a successful local practice. He achieved local celebrity in 1913–14 when he and William Richard Morris roused public opinion in a battle to bring motor buses to Oxford. On 11 July 1914 he married Eveline Reine Panton, with whom he had one daughter; the couple separated in the early 1930s.

Gray's friendships with a chimney sweep, a bookmaker, and other dubious local characters demonstrated his unconventional nature and, despite exemption from conscription, he enlisted in the army on 13 February 1917. Refusing a commission, he served as a private until the armistice, seeing action at Passchendaele before securing a staff appointment. His wartime experiences encouraged him to stand for parliament, but he was defeated as the Liberal candidate for Watford in March 1918. He retired as a solicitor in 1919 and campaigned on behalf of farm workers before unsuccessfully trying to get a job as a miner in Warwickshire in order to expose working conditions in the pits.

In 1920 Gray was adopted as the Liberal candidate for Oxford City and in November 1922 his populist style won him a majority of 3806 in a seat which the Conservatives had held since 1885. An active MP at Westminster, Gray nursed his constituency by holding regular surgeries and by his involvement with many local institutions. He defended the seat in November 1923 when his support for free trade led to a bitter dispute with his former friend W. R. Morris. He was re-elected with a reduced majority of 2693 and was rewarded with the post of junior whip, but he was soon found to have exceeded his election expenses. A petition was filed in February 1924 and Gray's inexperienced agent was found guilty of corrupt practices; Gray himself escaped censure but his election was declared void. He stood for parliament again at Central Portsmouth in October 1924, but was heavily defeated. He blamed the disappointing result on the effects of the Zinoviev letter.

Freed from parliamentary commitments, Gray served on the Oxfordshire county council and Ploughley rural district council, but he found local government frustrating and concentrated his energies elsewhere. A long-term interest in tramps encouraged him to disguise himself as a vagrant and see for himself the conditions in local workhouses. After the repeal of the poor law in 1929, he established Frank Gray House in the former Bicester workhouse to help reclaim young vagrants; he also welcomed many tramps at his home in Shipton Manor, Shipton-on-Cherwell, and tried to find useful work for them. In 1926 he flirted with exploration, using two standard Jowett cars to drive across Africa from Lagos to the Red Sea. In 1928 he helped to establish the *Oxford Mail*, the city's first evening newspaper, and then threw himself into a scheme to develop a zoo, pleasure garden, and associated housing at Kidlington as a gateway to Oxford.

Frank Gray was a smallish man who typically wore a black tie and black coat with checked trousers and a grey Homburg hat. A colourful and restless personality, he enlivened one quiet evening by racing a guest to London, ramming the other man's car when he looked like losing; in August 1923, he courted publicity by challenging a fellow MP to a walking race from Banbury to Oxford in full infantry kit. After a period of illness, Gray went to South Africa to recuperate, but had a stroke on the return journey and died at sea on 3 March 1935. His coffin was carried on a flower-bedecked fire engine from Shipton Manor and he was buried at Wolvercote cemetery, Oxford, on 6 March 1935.   MALCOLM GRAHAM

Sources C. Fenby, *The other Oxford* (1970) • F. Gray, *The confessions of a private* (1920) • F. Gray, *The confessions of a candidate* (1925) • F. Gray, *The tramp: his meaning and being* (1931) • *Oxford Mail* (4–7 March 1935) • *Oxford Mail* (3 May 1976) • *Oxford Journal Illustrated* (19 May 1915) • *Oxford Journal Illustrated* (20 March 1918) • *Oxford Journal Illustrated* (17 April 1918) • *Oxford Times* (18 July 1914) • *Oxford Times* (23 March 1918) • *Oxford Times* (8 March 1935) • *The Times* (4–5 March 1935) • *The Times* (22 June 1935) • parish registers, St Giles, Oxford • Oxfordshire county electoral registers, Oxon. RO • Kelly, *Handbk* (1928) • *Oxford Chronicle and Berks and Bucks Gazette* (27 Oct 1922)
Archives U. Warwick Mod. RC, writings, incl. chapters of autobiography
Likenesses photographs, repro. in Fenby, *The other Oxford*, facing pp. 65, 80, 81
Wealth at death £30,160 0s. 11d.: probate, 15 June 1935, CGPLA Eng. & Wales

Gray, Sir George, third baronet (*c.*1710–1773). *See under* Gray, Sir James, second baronet (*c.*1708–1773).

Gray, George (1758–1819), painter, born at Newcastle upon Tyne, was the eldest of the three sons of Gilbert Gray (1709–1794), a bookbinder and well-known Quaker of that town, and his second wife, whose maiden name was Spence. He was educated at the Royal Free Grammar School in the Spital, Newcastle, and was apprenticed to a fruit painter named Jones, with whom he lived and worked in York. Besides painting, Gray studied chemistry,

mineralogy, and botany, developing an extensive knowledge of natural history. In 1787 he left Whitehaven to go on a botanical expedition to the Americas. In 1791 he was sent on an expedition to investigate the geology of Poland. In 1794 Gray settled in Pudding Chare, Newcastle and kept a shop in Dean Street from which he sold portraits and paintings of fruit and undertook sign-painting. He was also employed as a drawing master at a school for young ladies. In 1811 he exhibited a fruit painting at the Royal Academy. He devised numerous ingenious inventions, such as making bread from roots and weaving stockings from nettles. Gray's humour and originality made him popular. He was a close friend of Thomas Bewick and an oil on paper portrait of Bewick, by Gray, *c.*1780, is in the Laing Art Gallery, Newcastle. Another of John Bewick (*c.*1780) by Gray is in the Museum of the Natural History Society, Newcastle. Late in life Gray married the widow of a shoemaker, Mrs Dobie, whom he survived. He died at his house in Pudding Chare on 9 December 1819, and was buried on 12 December in St John's churchyard, Newcastle.

L. H. CUST, rev. HEATHER M. MACLENNAN

Sources B. Stewart and M. Cutten, *The dictionary of portrait painters in Britain up to 1920* (1997) • M. Hall, *The artists of Northumbria*, 2nd edn (1982) • R. Robinson, *Thomas Bewick: his life and times* (1887); repr. (1972) • R. Walker, *National Portrait Gallery: Regency portraits*, 2 vols. (1985) • Graves, *RA exhibitors* • *A memoir of Thomas Bewick, written by himself*, ed. I. Bain (1975) • Waterhouse, *18c painters* • I. Bain, *The watercolours and drawings of Thomas Bewick and his workshop apprentices* (1989) • T. Fawcett, *The rise of English provincial art: artist, patron and institution outside London, 1800–1830* (1974) • R. Welford, *Men of mark 'twixt Tyne and Tweed*, 3 vols. (1895) • Graves, *Soc. Artists*
Likenesses W. Nicholson, portrait • H. P. Parker, portrait • sketch, repro. in Welford, *Men of mark*

Gray, George Buchanan (1865–1922), Congregational minister and Hebrew scholar, was born at Blandford, Dorset, on 13 January 1865, the second son of the Revd Benjamin Gray, Congregational minister at Blandford, and his wife, Emma Jane, daughter of George Buchanan Kirkman. He was educated at private schools at Blandford and Exeter. Subsequently, he acted as a schoolmaster at Blandford for several years, during which he studied for matriculation at London University, passing the examination in 1882. He continued to teach while studying for his degree at New College, Hampstead, and University College, London, where he read Greek and Latin and began working at Hebrew. He took the degree of BA in 1886, and began working for his MA, but left London before finishing the course in order to study at Oxford. Here, as a non-collegiate student, he studied Semitic languages at Mansfield College, and obtained a first class in the school of oriental studies in 1891. He also won the Pusey and Ellerton Hebrew scholarship (1889), the junior Hall-Houghton Septuagint prize (1890), and the junior (1891) and senior (1893) Kennicott Hebrew scholarships. He completed his studies at the University of Marburg.

On taking his Oxford degree in 1891 Gray was appointed a tutor at Mansfield College, and in 1893 was ordained to the Congregational ministry. In 1900 he was promoted to be professor of Hebrew and the exegesis of the Old Testament at Mansfield College, where he remained for the rest of his life. On 29 March of the same year he married Frances Lilian (*b.* 1870/71), only daughter of Alfred *Williams (1832–1905), the alpine landscape artist, and his wife, Eliza Walker. They had one son and one daughter.

Gray was both a teacher and an original researcher. As a teacher, he successfully encouraged a succession of students, both inside and outside his own college, to pursue Hebrew studies, winning their affection and respect with his mixture of scholarship and humanity. Calm, critical, and emotionally reticent, he sought to guide his students towards objective and well-founded interpretation of the Bible. His research produced many original articles on Semitic and biblical subjects in learned and religious publications, and several books. Among the most significant of these are *Studies in Hebrew Proper Names* (1896), in which he showed that the Hebrews tended to employ different types of personal names at different periods of their history and that these may therefore be of importance in the critical examination of the documentary sources of the Old Testament; the *Forms of Hebrew Poetry* (1915); a *Commentary on Numbers* (1903); a *Commentary on Isaiah I–XXVII* (1912) in the International Critical Commentaries, and the *Commentary on Job* (1921) in which he completed the work of Samuel Rolles Driver. The very high standard of his commentaries was the more remarkable since this type of work was not congenial to him, forcing him to deal with some matters in which he was not necessarily interested. His posthumous *Sacrifice in the Old Testament* (1925) discussed exhaustively everything connected with the altar and sacrifice, the festal calendar, and the priesthood, and indicated why some regarded him as the foremost Old Testament scholar of his day.

Gray is often described as having continued the school of biblical criticism represented in England by Driver; but he was an independent thinker, and in his work on Hebrew names and sacrifice he stood closer to W. Robertson Smith than to Driver. Deeply moved by the Old Testament scriptures, he nevertheless remained shrewd and cautious in his critical judgement. At the same time he regarded it as part of his mission to spread modern knowledge about the Bible beyond the academic and clerical worlds, lecturing freely to schools and meetings, to societies of the Friends, and to ministerial gatherings. His preaching, generally based on texts from the Old Testament, revealed how deeply he was permeated by its devotional spirit.

Apart from his biblical studies, Gray was much interested in problems of social welfare; he frequently visited the Mansfield College settlement in Canning Town and for many years was an active member of its committee. His political and ecclesiastical opinions were liberal: he was a convinced free churchman and an old-fashioned independent, keenly interested in the men and affairs of country chapels, among whom he had been brought up. He was a loyal and devoted friend and colleague, who carried his learning lightly, was generous in controversy, and indulged a strong sense of humour. In his younger days he had been an alpine climber, and in later life he took to lawn tennis and to bicycling both in France and in England.

Gray paid a visit to Palestine and Syria for purposes of study in 1904 and served for many years on the committee of the Palestine Exploration Fund. He also made two journeys to the United States of America, the first at the request of the council of Mansfield College on a tour of inquiry concerning a possible successor to Dr A. M. Fairbairn as principal of the college (1908), and the second to give a course of lectures at the University of Chicago (1919). Among the honours which he received were the honorary degree of DD of Aberdeen University (1903) and the degree of DLitt of Oxford University (1905). At Oxford he held also the offices of Speaker's lecturer in biblical studies (1914–19) and Grinfield lecturer on the Septuagint (1919–21). He was president of the Society for Old Testament Study for 1922. He died suddenly at a meeting of the board of theological studies in the Clarendon Building, Oxford, on 2 November 1922, on the afternoon of the day on which he was expected in the evening to deliver his inaugural address as president of the Society of Historical Theology. He was survived by his wife.

G. R. DRIVER, *rev.* J. W. ROGERSON

Sources A. S. Peake, 'G. Buchanan Gray', *Holborn Review* (1923) [repr. in Peake, *Recollections and appreciations* (1938), 81–6] • *The Times* (3 Nov 1922) • *WWW*, 1916–28 • private information (1937) • m. cert. • *CGPLA Eng. & Wales* (1922)

Wealth at death £4257 17s. 10d.: probate, 12 Dec 1922, *CGPLA Eng. & Wales*

Gray, George Edward Kruger (1880–1943), designer, was born on 25 December 1880 at 126 Kensington Park Road, London, the son of Edwin Charles Kruger, merchant, of St Helier, Jersey, and his wife, Frances Hester, daughter of John Dafter Harris, of Bath. He did not add the surname Gray until his marriage on 4 June 1918 to Frances Audrey Gordon, daughter of the Revd John Henry Gray, who was at one time archdeacon of Hong Kong.

Kruger Gray was educated at the Merchant Taylors' School, Great Crosby, and afterwards at the Bath School of Art. While studying there he won a scholarship at the Royal College of Art, where he worked under W. R. Lethaby and took his diploma in design. He exhibited watercolours at the Royal Academy from 1905; the earliest of these were landscapes, flower studies, and portraits, and it was not until after the First World War in which he served with the Artists' Rifles and the camouflage section of the Royal Engineers that he began to achieve positive success in the types of designing for which he became known. In 1923 a group exhibit of coinage at the Royal Academy included casts from original models of the half-crown, florin, and farthing pieces which Kruger Gray executed for the Union of South Africa; thereafter he was much employed as a designer of coinage, being later responsible for the George V and George VI silver coinage, and for the George V jubilee crown piece. He also designed the great seal of George VI, the reverse of the great seal of Ulster, the great seal of the dominion of Canada (1939), and many other seals and medals.

Kruger Gray also designed and executed a large number

of stained-glass windows. His series of windows for Eltham Palace (1936) and for the chapel of King's School, Canterbury (1939–40), are among his most important figure-subjects; he was equally prominent for his heraldic designs, which he executed for Sheffield city hall (1930), for Exeter University College (1936), and also for public buildings in Manchester, Leeds, Taunton, and Chelmsford. In much of this public work Kruger Gray was associated with the architect E. Vincent Harris.

Kruger Gray's career encompassed a range of other work, including book illustration, poster design, and cartoons for *Vanity Fair*. Among his more miscellaneous commissions were the two maces he designed for the Ulster parliament, a series of panels in memory of distinguished Harrovians which he designed and painted for Harrow School, and his work on the historical costumes and heraldry for the Aldershot military tattoo between 1935 and 1939.

Kruger Gray's success as a designer was securely based on his knowledge of heraldry and of the materials for which he worked. He seldom gave his designs to others to execute, but normally carried them through to their final form himself. The result was that he was able to maintain a high standard of excellence throughout, and during the last twenty years of his life his work was much in demand.

Kruger Gray was appointed CBE in 1938. He died at St Richard's Hospital, Chichester, on 2 May 1943, survived by his wife and the one son of their marriage.

JAMES LAVER, rev. CHRISTOPHER MARSDEN

Sources *The Times* (4 May 1943) · *WWW*, 1941–50 · private information (1959) · *CGPLA Eng. & Wales* (1943) · b. cert. · m. cert. · d. cert.
Wealth at death £8755 1s. 8d.: probate, 16 Sept 1943, *CGPLA Eng. & Wales*

Gray, George Robert (1808–1872), zoologist, was born on 8 July 1808 in Little Chelsea, London, the third of the four children of Samuel Frederick *Gray (1766–1828), naturalist and pharmacologist, and his wife, Elizabeth, *née* Forfeit (1777–1852). His older brother was John Edward *Gray (1800–1875). He was educated at Merchant Taylors' School, London, in 1820–24, and at an early age used to help John George Children (1777–1852) in arranging his insect collections.

In 1830 Gray was given the opportunity to work for Children at the British Museum (his brother John had worked there since 1824). Gray's first year was unpaid and during 1831 he was paid on a daily rate; in 1832 he became a member of the permanent staff. Initially he worked on the insect collection, but moved on to be responsible for the bird collection. On 28 July 1869 he was appointed senior assistant keeper of zoology, a post he held until his death.

Gray was a prolific writer. He published his first book, *The Entomology of Australia, Part I*, in 1833. Dedicating it to the duke of Sussex (then president of the Royal Society), Gray funded the work by subscription. He was one of several contributors to Agassiz' *Nomenclator zoologicus* (1842) and contributed to the translation by Griffith (1827–35) of

Cuvier's *Règne animal distribué d'après son organisation*. However, Gray's greatest achievement was his three-volume work *The Genera of Birds* (1844–9), the subscribers for which included Queen Victoria and Prince Bonaparte, prince of Canino. The work described over 2400 genera. Thomas Bell of Selborne wrote in a letter in 1869 that 'it was considered by all naturalists the standard work in the subject and evinced the deepest research combined with great accuracy in the arrangement' (letter from T. Bell, July 1869, NHM). For each genus he gave a description which included physical characteristics, habits, and a list of references. Gray took immense care to find the best available illustrator and chose David William Mitchell (1813–1859), but, owing to his demanding post of secretary to the Zoological Society of London, Mitchell felt that he could not illustrate the third volume; as a result, it was illustrated by J. Wolf of Koblenz. Gray also wrote numerous accounts of the British Museum's collections, of which the *Handlist of Genera and Species of Birds* (3 vols., 1869–71) is probably the most widely known. He was known to resent having to put out specimens of birds for students, as he did not like to be interrupted, and by some was considered unwelcoming.

Gray was elected a fellow of the Royal Society in 1865, and was a fellow of the Linnean and Zoological societies. He was a member of the Imperiale e Reale Accademia Economico-Agraria dei Georgofili di Firenze. He died on 6 May 1872 at his home, 60 Adelaide Road, Haverstock Hill, London. He was survived by his wife, Anne, daughter of John Bolton Hodgson MRCS; they had no children.

CATHARINE M. C. HAINES

Sources correspondence, 1833–72, NHM, Gray G. MSS, BRN 115299 · general index of printed minutes, Jan 1866–Dec 1872, BM · *The Athenaeum* (11 May 1872), 593 · general index of printed minutes, –Dec 1847, BM, C3612–7409 · A. E. Gunther, *A century of zoology at the British Museum through the lives of two keepers, 1815–1914* (1975) · C. J. Robinson, ed., *A register of the scholars admitted into Merchant Taylors' School, from AD 1562 to 1874*, 2 (1883) · Mrs E. P. Hart, ed., *Merchant Taylors' School register, 1561–1934*, 2 vols. (1936) · *Annals of Natural History*, 4th ser., 9 (1872), 480 · d. cert. · *CGPLA Eng. & Wales* (1872)
Archives BL, corresp., Egerton MS 2348 · U. Cam., department of zoology, ornithological papers | NL Aus., Mathews collection, ornithological papers
Likenesses Moore, lithograph (after B. Smith), BM
Wealth at death under £800: probate, 28 May 1872, *CGPLA Eng. & Wales*

Gray, Gilbert (d. 1614), college head, belonged to a prominent burgess family in Aberdeen, where he was born probably in the early 1570s. His mother was a sister of Alexander Rutherford, provost of Aberdeen. Gray is said to have studied at King's College, Aberdeen, but he completed his arts curriculum in Edinburgh as a pupil of Robert Rollock (first principal of that university and a notable biblical commentator) and graduated MA in 1592. Gray is also said to have studied at Heidelberg; this is not confirmed by any matriculation record, but he may have travelled abroad in the mid-1590s. By the end of 1597 he was back in Aberdeen and married to Marjorie Menzies, daughter of another important family in the city. They had seven children (two died young) baptized in Aberdeen between 1602 and 1614.

In 1598 Gray succeeded Robert Howie as principal of

Mariscal College, which had been founded in 1593; he held this office until his death. His *Oratio de illustribus Scotiae scriptoribus* (written 1611; printed in 1623) drew on the dubious resources of Hector Boece's 1527 *Scotorum historiae*; but it also paid tribute to Rollock and other contemporary scholars (the text is known only from its reprinting by George Mackenzie in the early eighteenth century). Gray's only other known work (Edinburgh, 1614) was a funeral oration on the noted scientist Duncan Liddel (1561–1613), whom he must have known after Liddel's return from Germany to Aberdeen in 1607 and who was a posthumous benefactor of Mariscal College. Gray himself probably died in Aberdeen in December 1614, and was buried in St Nicholas's Church on the 29th of the month.

J. H. BURNS

Sources P. J. Anderson and J. F. K. Johnstone, eds., *Fasti academiae Mariscallanae Aberdonensis: selections from the records of the Mariscal College and University, MDXCIII–MDCCCLX*, 3 vols., New Spalding Club, 4, 18–19 (1889–98) · old parish registers, Aberdeen, NA Scot. · J. P. Edmond, *The Aberdeen printers: Edward Raban to James Nicol, 1620–1736* (1886) · J. F. Kellas Johnstone and A. W. Robertson, *Bibliographia Aberdonensis*, ed. W. D. Simpson, Third Spalding Club, 1 (1929) · G. Mackenzie, *The lives and characters of the most eminent writers of the Scots nation*, 1 (1708), xxi–xxxiv · A. M. Munro, ed., 'Register of burgesses of guild and trade of the burgh of Aberdeen, 1399–1631', *The miscellany of the New Spalding Club*, 1, New Spalding Club, 6 (1890), 1–162 · J. M. Thomson and others, eds., *Registrum magni sigilli regum Scotorum / The register of the great seal of Scotland*, 11 vols. (1882–1914), vol. 6, no. 636

Gray, Gordon Joseph (1910–1993), cardinal and Roman Catholic archbishop of St Andrews and Edinburgh, was born on 10 August 1910 at 143 Leith Walk, Leith, the second son and third of the four children of Francis William Gray (1870–1950), mechanical engineer, and his wife, Angela Jane, *née* Oddy (1882/3–1970), teacher. His father, born in Banffshire, had come to Edinburgh in 1887, was apprenticed to an engineering firm and rose to be managing director. His mother, educated by Ursuline sisters in Edinburgh, taught in a Catholic primary school in the city. Gray was educated at Holy Cross Academy, near his home. Religious influences on him came from home and school and from his uncle, John Allan Gray, a priest in the diocese. Gray decided to be a priest but it was diocesan policy not to accept relatives of a priest already serving. Accordingly he entered St Joseph's junior seminary at Mark Cross, Sussex, in September 1927 and progressed two years later into the senior seminary, St John's College, Wonersh, near Guildford, where he remained for six years. Then, being accepted by the new archbishop of St Andrews and Edinburgh, he was ordained priest in Edinburgh Cathedral on 15 June 1935.

Gray's first appointment was to assist his uncle, parish priest at St Andrews; while there he studied for a degree at the university. Four years later he graduated with honours in English language and literature. His archbishop wished him to acquire an educational qualification but the outbreak of war in September 1939 thwarted the plan. Instead he continued to work in the parish. In August 1941 he was appointed parish priest of Hawick. Pastoral work was complicated by wartime conditions and he also served German and Italian prisoner of war camps. He was appointed dean of the borders, served on Roxburgh education committee, and in 1944 published a booklet for the parish centenary.

In 1947 the Scottish bishops appointed Gray rector of the national junior seminary, St Mary's College, Blairs, near Aberdeen. He was also headmaster and procurator, with an estate and two farms under his care, but his main concern was to feed 200 growing boys despite post-war shortages. Although he considered the college regime less spartan than at Mark Cross, he wondered later if he should have been more liberal. In June 1951, aged just forty, he was appointed archbishop of St Andrews and Edinburgh, one of the youngest archbishops in the whole Roman Catholic church.

Gray received episcopal ordination in Edinburgh Cathedral on 21 September 1951. The tasks confronting him were enormous, for it was a far-flung diocese and, owing to the late archbishop's illness, there was an enormous backlog of confirmations due. At that time, too, people were being moved out from overcrowded city centres to housing estates on the outskirts, necessitating the establishment of new parishes. He worked flat out, until after eighteen months he suffered a complete breakdown, from which his recovery was slow. Two notable achievements marked his first years as archbishop. In 1953 he established a diocesan senior seminary at Drygrange, near Melrose, and he was one of the first bishops in the world to send priests to Africa in response to the papal appeal in *Fidei donum* (1957). This led eventually, in 1964, to his assuming responsibility for staffing and financing the church in Bauchi province, Nigeria. His responsibilities in Scotland also grew: in 1963–4 he was apostolic administrator of Aberdeen diocese and from 1963 he was president of the Scottish bishops' conference.

The Second Vatican Council took place in 1962–5. Gray sent in suggestions for the agenda but was unwilling to make any spoken intervention, as it had to be in Latin. Indeed he was very critical of this regulation, for it disadvantaged the 'pastoral' bishops and often prevented them from speaking. Extra difficulty was caused when at weekends he had to fly home to Edinburgh and Aberdeen.

Right from its first meeting in October 1963, Gray was much involved in the International Commission for English in the Liturgy (ICEL). In 1965–71 he was its chairman and thereafter remained on its episcopal board. Not surprisingly, given his initiative in Bauchi, in late 1968 he became a member of the Sacred Congregation for the Evangelization of Peoples. Already his long membership had begun on the Consilium (later upgraded to be the Sacred Congregation) for Divine Worship.

Gray was severely critical of the Vatican's poor record in dealing with the media. He had assisted in setting up the National Catholic Radio and Television Centre at Hatch End, London, in 1955 and for many years sat on the Central Religious Advisory Council for the BBC. In 1970 he agreed to chair the Pontifical Commission for Social Communication, but only after it was agreed to install simultaneous translation for meetings; then as chairman he overruled the formal regulations and allowed free debate. The first agenda was to finalize the pastoral instruction on communications, which appeared in 1971 simultaneously with readable versions in the main languages.

In April 1969 Gray was created a cardinal—technically cardinal-priest of the title Santa Chiara a Vigna Clara—which was perhaps unexpected but not surprising, given his work on the ICEL and Vatican bodies. He was also a personal friend of the pope, Paul VI. His elevation was welcomed almost unanimously by the media and the churches in Scotland. At Rome over 400 Scots attended the ceremonies, at one of which Pope Paul presented him with a relic of St Andrew. His duties as cardinal were to include taking part in the conclaves which elected John Paul I and John Paul II and accompanying the latter to Poland, France, and Ireland. Honours were bestowed on him in Scotland too: honorary degrees from St Andrews in 1967 and Heriot-Watt in 1981, and an honorary fellowship of the Educational Institute of Scotland in 1970.

The highlight of Gray's career was undoubtedly the visit of Pope John Paul II to Scotland in June 1982. The visit was an unqualified success and not only because of the enthusiastic youth rally and the papal mass before 300,000 people. It was also an outstanding ecumenical success, with leaders of other churches taking part and crowds lining the streets wherever the pope went. The culmination was the pope and the moderator of the general assembly of the Church of Scotland shaking hands beneath the statue of John Knox: formal perhaps, but of enormous significance.

In the early 1980s, as his health deteriorated, Gray offered to resign and finally retired in May 1985. He himself admitted that he found it hard to say 'No' or to delegate, which increased his workload. From his early youth he had worked with his hands; in fact he was skilled at woodwork and a very competent gardener. In his later years he rather unwisely continued to do heavy work in his garden despite trouble with his back, until increasingly he was confined to a wheelchair through arthritis and other ailments. Taken to Edinburgh Royal Infirmary with a failing heart, he died there on 19 July 1993 and was buried on 23 July in the crypt of his cathedral.

Gray was essentially a simple man with simple tastes, kindly and hospitable, shrewd but cautious. Physically he was big, with craggy features and a natural dignified bearing. His voice, strong, deep, and warm, was an asset and his Scots accent never varied, perhaps because he was a very poor linguist. He was almost the epitome of a Scotsman and proud of his traditionally Catholic Banffshire ancestry. The combination of these qualities made him a sort of father figure, known for his gardening, his dog, and his pipe, rather than as a prince of the church.

Great changes marked Gray's long episcopate. He was naturally cautious and, being a traditional Catholic, conservative as regards doctrinal and moral questions. Friendly by nature, he enjoyed increasingly warm relations with other churches, accepted invitations to speak or preach and sat on inter-church bodies. In 1966 he gave the imprimatur for the Catholic edition of the Revised Standard Version Bible, but theologically he went no further than stressing what Catholics and others held in common. His attitude to Rome was similar, combining veneration for the papacy as an institution with disapproval of some features of papal government. He twice protested strongly and successfully against what he considered interference in a diocesan matter by a Roman curial body. He appreciated the new vision of the Second Vatican Council and implemented the required changes, but with caution and in some matters with a certain scepticism.

Gray established thirty new parishes and built thirty-seven churches, while the number of priests increased, reached a peak in 1965, and then declined, making it necessary to unite parishes. He was greatly distressed by men leaving the priesthood and, after his retirement, by the closure of Blairs College and his diocesan seminary. But along with this decline went a rise in prestige. The papal visit in 1982—or perhaps, rather, the reaction of Catholics and others to it—showed that the Roman Catholic church was no longer on the sidelines but in the mainstream of Scottish life. Gray, the first resident Scottish cardinal since the Reformation, played an important part in this change.

MARK DILWORTH

Sources M. T. R. B. Turnbull, *Cardinal Gordon Joseph Gray: a biography* (1994) • I. Stewart, 'Gordon Joseph Gray: Scottish cardinal', *Innes Review*, 44 (1993), 168–80 • J. Darragh, *The Catholic hierarchy of Scotland: a biographical list, 1653–1985* (1986) • *Catholic Directory for Scotland* (1994) • *The Times* (20 July 1993) • *The Independent* (20 July 1993) • Scottish Catholic Archives, Edinburgh • personal knowledge (2004) • WWW

Archives Scottish Catholic Archives, Edinburgh | SOUND BL NSA, current affairs recording

Likenesses bust, Edinburgh Cathedral • photograph, repro. in *The Times* • photograph, repro. in *The Independent* • photographs, repro. in Turnbull, *Cardinal Gordon Joseph Gray* • portrait, Cathedral House, Edinburgh • two portraits, archbishop's house, Edinburgh

Wealth at death £11,107.10: confirmation, 25 Nov 1993, NA Scot., SC/CO 712/13

Gray, Henry (1826/7–1861), anatomist and author, about whose family, childhood, and early education little is known except that his father was private messenger to George IV and William IV, and that he had one sister and two brothers, entered St George's Hospital, London, as a perpetual student in May 1845. There he showed early signs of his intense interest in anatomy and was described by his contemporaries as diligent, painstaking, and methodical. In 1848 he became MRCS (and soon became a fellow by examination) and in the following year was awarded the college's triennial prize for an essay on the nerves of the eye. He won the Astley Cooper prize in 1853.

In 1850, as a newly appointed house surgeon to St George's Hospital (where he later became lecturer in anatomy), Gray presented a paper to the Royal Society 'On the development of the optic and auditory nerves'. This earned him the unusual distinction of being elected to a fellowship of the society at the age of twenty-five (1852). In 1854 he published *On the Structure and Use of the Spleen*, a substantial work of 380 pages, based on original observations. His famous *Anatomy, Descriptive and Surgical* (1858) was published by John W. Parker in England, and by Blanchard and Lea in the United States in 1859. No medical text has ever been so widely used by successive generations of medical students and doctors. By the time of its centenary, there had been twenty-six new editions by eight successive editors in Britain and eleven in the United States.

The success of the book was not due to an absence of rivals. There were already several texts on anatomy, the most famous being *Elements of Descriptive and Practical Anatomy* (1828) by James Quain. Gray's *Anatomy*, however, eclipsed all others, partly for its meticulous detail, partly for its emphasis on surgical anatomy, but most of all perhaps for the excellence of the illustrations, based on drawings by H. V. Carter, who assisted Gray with the dissections, and engraved by Messrs Butterworth and Heath with remarkable skill. The design of the book, and the skill with which the illustrations were interpolated in the text, could hardly have been improved. For a man in his early thirties it was a remarkable achievement. The book was well received by *The Lancet* and the *British Medical Journal*, but was savagely attacked by an anonymous reviewer in the *Medical Times and Gazette* of 1859, who dismissed it, in a ridiculous review for which the most likely reason was personal animosity or jealousy, as 'a book which is not wanted [and] is not even up to the mark of the existing vade-mecums. A more unphilosophical amalgam of anatomical detail and crude surgery we have never met with'.

Gray was already working on the second edition when he caught smallpox from his nephew, developed the confluent form of the disease, and died at his residence, 8 Wilton Street, Belgrave Square, London, on 12 June 1861, aged thirty-four. It is a measure of Gray's single-minded devotion to anatomy and authorship that Gray's *Anatomy* continued to be not only an important book of reference but virtually a household phrase.　　　　IRVINE LOUDON, *rev.*

Sources C. Goss, *A brief account of Henry Gray, FRS, and his anatomy, descriptive and surgical* (1959) · *PRS*, 12 (1862–3), xi · *The Lancet* (15 June 1861), 600 · review, *Medical Times and Gazette*, 18 (5 March 1859), 241–4 · W. Brockbank, 'The centenary of false prophecy: a warning to reviewers', *Medical History*, 2 (1958), 67–8 · d. cert.
Wealth at death under £1000: resworn administration, Feb 1868, *CGPLA Eng. & Wales* (1861)

Gray, Herbert Branston (1851–1929), headmaster, was born at Putney on 22 April 1851, the second son of Thomas Gray, of St Peter's, Isle of Thanet, a businessman in the City of London, and his wife, Emily Mary (*d.* 1857), daughter of William Heath, of Pennsylvania Castle, Isle of Portland. In 1865 he went to Winchester College where, in the following year, he gained an exhibition. He proceeded in 1870 with a classical scholarship to Queen's College, Oxford, and obtained a first class in classical moderations in 1872 and a second class in *literae humaniores* in 1874 (BA in 1875, MA in 1878, and BD and DD in 1892).

In 1875 Gray joined the staff of Westminster School, where he came under the influence of A. P. Stanley, whose liberal churchmanship he shared. Gray was ordained deacon in 1877 and priest in 1878 and, while retaining his mastership at Westminster, gained some parochial experience in London. In 1878 he was appointed headmaster of Louth grammar school, and went there in 1879. Gray raised the numbers and developed the school, but when, in 1880, he was offered the headmastership of St Andrew's College at Bradfield in Berkshire, he decided to accept a position which, however unpromising at the time, seemed to him to offer more scope for his abilities. Shortly after taking the Bradfield post he married, in 1882, Selina, youngest daughter of the Revd Wharton Booth *Marriott, assistant master at Eton College, and a cousin of the Revd Charles Marriott. They had two sons.

The rebuilding of Bradfield proved to be the main work of Gray's life. The expectations formed at the time of the foundation of the school in 1850 had not been realized. During the first ten years the numbers had risen to 120, but decline followed, and when Gray came, the boys numbered barely 50, only a few were paying fees, and the closure of the school seemed likely. When he retired thirty years later, the number of boys was nearly 300. In 1880 Bradfield needed rebuilding, in two senses. Gray supplied the necessary skill and enthusiasm. A new constitution replaced the patriarchal rule of Thomas Stevens, the founder, rector of Bradfield and lord of the manor; and new buildings were added from time to time, paid for largely out of Gray's own pocket, to supplement an old country house.

Gray's energy, mental and physical, was exceptional, and it had full scope. Though short in stature, he was very muscular; he played fives with picked boys and beat them, until quite late in life. His lawn tennis was of a quality not often seen at that time, and he rarely seemed to be walking at less than 5 miles an hour. When he retired, Bradfield was fully equipped in the many areas which were later considered necessary for a leading public school. He also instituted a rifle corps, a school mission, and a navy class, and established engineering workshops at a time when the value of practical work was little recognized. Outside Bradfield, he was best known as the founder of the Bradfield Greek play, and of the open-air theatre near the school, built in 1890, partly by the boys themselves, on the model of the Greek theatre at Epidaurus. Gray himself several times acted as the *coryphaeus* in the triennial performances.

The height of Gray's success was in the 1890s. Thereafter his wider interests reduced his contact with the school, and turned him into a somewhat remote figure. Discipline suffered, and numbers declined after 1904. Imperial questions became his leading interest, and his vision of linking the public schools with the dominions led to his establishment in 1909 of a ranch at Calgary, Canada, where boys leaving Bradfield could learn local conditions of agriculture. He personally funded the venture, which, though acknowledged to be pioneering, was not a success and was wound up. The strain led to a breakdown in his health, and forced his resignation in 1910.

After leaving Bradfield Gray travelled widely, living in

Canada in 1910–12, where he acted as secretary to the commission on taxation in British Columbia. He returned to England to publish *The Public Schools and Empire* (1913), a wide-ranging critique of English education, which alleged the inadequacy of public schools to meet imperial needs and called for reform by state action. In collaboration with Sir Samuel Turner (1878–1955), he added *Eclipse or Empire?* (1916) to the body of literature predicting dire consequences from the unscientific character of English schooling. He had been a member of Alfred Mosely's educational commission to North America in 1903, and a further visit in 1917 resulted in an enthusiastic account of the priority given to education in the USA, *America at School and at Work* (1918). His mission to Bucharest in 1920 at the invitation of the Romanian government to advise on the establishment of schools on the English public-school model, proved abortive. From 1916 he was an active member of the committee of the Shaftesbury Homes and *Arethusa* training ship.

In 1918 Gray became vicar of St Mary's Church, Bury St Edmunds, and in 1926 rector of Lynton, Devon. He died at the Hulse Road Nursing Home, Southampton, on 5 April 1929. G. S. FREEMAN, *rev.* M. C. CURTHOYS

Sources *The Times* (6 April 1929) · *The Times* (8 April 1929) · *The Times* (9 April 1929) · *The Times* (11 April 1929) · S. Gray, *Gray of Bradfield* (1937) · J. Blackie, *Bradfield, 1850–1975* (1976) · *CGPLA Eng. & Wales* (1929)
Likenesses Lady Harris, medallion, 1905; formerly in possession of Mrs Gray, 1937 · J. Pettie, drawing; formerly in possession of Mrs Gray, 1937
Wealth at death £6426 17s. 9d.: probate, 1 June 1929, *CGPLA Eng. & Wales*

Gray, Hugh (d. 1604), theologian, matriculated sizar from Trinity College, Cambridge, at Easter 1574. He was elected scholar and graduated BA in 1578/9; after taking up a fellowship in 1581, he was awarded an MA in 1582 and the doctorate in theology in 1595. It is clear that he was a critic of the English church. On 8 January 1587 in a sermon at Great St Mary's he complained of its fondness for 'Jewish music', and lamented that too many of its ministers could not preach and that Christmas was celebrated superstitiously, 'as ethnics, atheists, and epicures'. It was reported that he also 'insinuated that some in the university sent news to Rome and Rheims' (Cooper, *Ath. Cantab.*, 2.392). For this sermon Gray was brought before the vice-chancellor and heads of colleges, though he later claimed that his words had been misrepresented. In December 1589 he was a signatory of a petition in favour of the imprisoned future separatist Francis Johnson, of Christ's College, Cambridge. The following year he argued that, like the Jews, whose pretended fear of being accounted rebels was used as an excuse not to build the temple, 'so do we in these times pretend the same excuse why we proceed not in the building of the spiritual Temple' (Porter, 145); and he expressed before the vice-chancellor himself his disappointment at the slow pace of reform in religion.

In 1596 Gray stood for election as Lady Margaret professor of the university but was defeated, by twenty-eight votes to twelve, by Thomas Playfere. Collated on 9 April 1600 to the Lincoln Cathedral prebend of Milton Manor, he was installed on 12 December. He was also rector of Meonstoke, Hampshire. Not earlier than 1598 he was appointed the second Gresham professor of divinity in succession to Andrew Wotton. Nothing is certainly known about his tenure: Gray entrusted to a minister, William Jackson, the lectures he had given at Gresham College, but these were not printed and have not survived. Gray died between 20 May 1604, when his will was signed, and 5 July, when his successor was collated to Milton Manor. The following day letters were received by the aldermen of London recommending William Dakins as his successor at Gresham College. Gray remained single but six of his brothers and one sister were still living at the time of his death. He may have remained a radical in religion, for two of the ministers remembered in his will, Brian Lister and Josias Horne, were soon afterwards deprived for nonconformity. He bequeathed a piece of plate worth £5 to Gresham College, and also left money to the poor of Meonstoke, and to Trinity College, Cambridge, to build a pulpit. STEPHEN WRIGHT

Sources Venn, *Alum. Cant.* · Cooper, *Ath. Cantab.* · J. Ward, *The lives of the professors of Gresham College* (1740) · PRO, PROB 11/104, sig. 70 · H. C. Porter, *Reformation and reaction in Tudor Cambridge* (1958)
Wealth at death modest: will, PRO, PROB 11/104, sig. 70

Gray, Sir James, second baronet (c.1708–1773), diplomatist and antiquary, was the elder son of James Gray (d. 1722), a courtier, who was created first baronet on 5 March 1707 by Queen Anne, and his wife, Hester Dodd (c.1684–1781). The snobbish Horace Walpole commented that 'his father was first a box-keeper and then footman to James II' (Walpole, *Corr.*, 20.409). After succeeding as second baronet in 1722, he entered Clare College, Cambridge, and received the degree of MA in 1729. From 1731 to 1733 he travelled to France, Italy, Malta, and Portugal with Joseph Alston (1703–1733). His younger brother, **Sir George Gray** (c.1710–1773), entered the army and became colonel of the 61st foot (1759) and of the 37th foot (1768) and then lieutenant-general of the 61st (1770). The two brothers were founder members of the Society of Dilettanti in 1738 and George acted as secretary and treasurer to the society from 1738 until his death. George was known in aristocratic circles as a keen amateur architect and in the 1750s Lord Spencer employed him to advise on John Vardy's Palladian designs for Spencer House in London.

James Gray entered the diplomatic service in June 1744 when he was appointed secretary to Robert D'Arcy, fourth earl of Holdernesse, on his mission to Venice. Promoted to resident in March 1746, he remained in Venice until August 1752 apart from a few months' absence on leave in 1749. In 1750 he met James Stuart and Nicholas Revett, then about to start for Athens, and arranged for their election to the Society of Dilettanti. In October 1753 he was appointed envoy-extraordinary to the court of Naples, where he arrived from Genoa in December. He was quickly on good terms with the young king, Charles VII (later Charles III of Spain), and offered architectural advice about the king's new palace at Caserta. He took a close interest in the archaeological discoveries at Portici and Herculaneum and commissioned Antonio Joli to paint the Doric ruins at Paestum. As young grand tourists passed through Naples, Gray recommended them for membership of the Society of Dilettanti. In spring 1755 he undertook a mission to Rome concerning the Pretender but otherwise his diplomatic duties seem to have been routine. He was made a knight of the Bath in 1759. During his time in Naples he fathered two illegitimate children, James and Catherine Gray, but nothing is known of their mother.

Gray left Naples on leave in April 1763, leaving his secretary Philip Changuion in charge, and did not return. His final posting was Madrid; this was an unpopular diplomatic destination and since no peer could be found to fill the position, Gray was appointed ambassador, a rare honour for a commoner, in June 1767. He arrived in Madrid in the autumn but stayed for less than two years and left on 2 August 1769. He was sworn of the privy council in 1769. He died of an apoplexy at court in London on 9 January 1773 and was buried in Kensington on 19 January. His brother, George, succeeded as third baronet but died only a few weeks later on 14 February 1773 and was buried in Kensington on 17 February. Their mother survived both her sons and died on 24 October 1781, aged about ninety-seven; she was buried with her sons, as was George's widow, Charlotte, who died on 1 June 1788.

L. H. CUST, rev. S. J. SKEDD

Sources GEC, *Baronetage* · D. B. Horn, *British diplomatic representatives, 1689–1789* (1932) · L. Cust, *History of the Society of Dilettanti* (1914) · J. Ingamells, ed., *A dictionary of British and Irish travellers in Italy, 1701–1800* (1997) · D. B. Horn, *The British diplomatic service, 1689–1789* (1961) · Colvin, *Archs.* · Venn, *Alum. Cant.* · Walpole, *Corr.*
Archives BL, corresp. with Lord Holdernesse, Egerton MSS 3419, 3464 · BL, letters to duke of Newcastle, etc., Add. MSS 32702–32896 · BL, letters to Thomas Robinson, Add. MSS 23818–23828 · Hunt. L., corresp. with duke of Bedford and Lord Holdernesse · NRA, priv. coll., letters to Thomas Steavens · PRO, letters to Lord Chatham, PRO 30/8
Likenesses G. Knapton, oils, 1741, Brooks's Club, London, Society of Dilettanti · G. Knapton, portrait, 1744 (George Gray), Brooks's Club, London, Society of Dilettanti

Gray, James (1770?–1830), schoolmaster, Church of England clergyman, and writer, was born, probably in 1770 (his baptism is not recorded in the parish register, but his age is given as sixty on his death certificate), in Duns, Berwickshire. His father, Thomas Gray (*b.* 1750?, *d.* before 1823), 'a shoemaker, latterly, by courtesy, a leather merchant' (Steven, appx, 103), was an elder in the Anti-Burgher congregation in the town; his wife, and James's mother, was probably Sarah (*b.* 1747), daughter of Robert Norrie. There appear to have been five children (two boys and three girls) born after James. On leaving the parish school he was, against his inclinations, apprenticed to his father, before attending classes in arts at Edinburgh University (1787–93?), although without graduating. He is also said to have studied for the ministry of the Church of Scotland.

After a period as an usher at Duns grammar school, Gray was in April 1794 appointed rector of the grammar school in Dumfries. Among his pupils there were Robert Burns's children, and he came to know the poet well. It was at Dumfries, on 30 November 1795, that he married Mary (1773–1806), daughter of Peter Phillips, tenant farmer, of Longbridgemoor, Annandale, Dumfriesshire. They had five sons and three daughters. In September 1801 he moved to Edinburgh as a classics master in the high school.

Despite his nervous, even febrile manner in the classroom, Gray was a popular and conscientious teacher. His dislike of corporal punishment (his own schoolmaster at Duns had been a notorious flogger) attracted him to the new Lancasterian or monitorial system, which, with his colleague James Pillans, he was among the first to introduce on a large scale in any school. A letter by Gray on the subject to Edward Wakefield was published as an appendix to Jeremy Bentham's *Chrestomathia* (1815), and he knew and corresponded with Francis Place and his family.

But Gray's chief enthusiasm was always poetry, and his intelligence, high spirits, and sociability took him to the heart of the literary life of the Scottish capital. Among the many friends who met at his house, none was closer than James Hogg, who was later to marry a sister of Gray's first wife; Hogg depicted Gray as the fifteenth bard in *The Queen's Wake* (1813), and Gray contributed to Hogg's short-lived journal *The Spy* (1810–11). More famously, in two published letters to Alexander Peterkin (1815) and Gilbert Burns (1820), Gray vigorously—perhaps too vigorously—rebutted allegations of habitual drunkenness made against Robert Burns by his first editor, James Currie: the most he would concede, even in private, was that Burns had been led into 'one awful night' by 'a few scoundrels of Englishmen' (*The Works of Robert Burns*, ed. the Ettrick Shepherd [J. Hogg] and W. Motherwell, 5 vols., 1834–6, 5.5). William Wordsworth's *Letter to a Friend of Robert Burns* (1816) was addressed to Gray, who had urged its composition. In addition to contributions to magazines (many of them pseudonymous and still unidentified), his own publications comprised two textbooks on classical subjects, an edition of the poems of Robert Fergusson (1821), and two volumes of poetry, *Cona, or, The Vale of Clwyd, and other Poems* (1814)—the publication of which was facilitated by Hogg—and *A Sabbath among the Mountains* (1823). Later poems on 'A Sabbath at Sea' and 'India' remained unpublished.

In many of his activities Gray was closely partnered by his second wife, Mary (1767–1829), daughter of Alexander Peacock, architect, of Edinburgh, whom he had married there on 25 October 1808. Mary, herself a poet and a frequent contributor to *The Spy*, had been a confidante of Agnes McLehose, Burns's 'Clarinda', and is often mentioned in her friend's correspondence with the poet. Her marriage with Gray was childless.

Gray's contemporaries affectionately admired his loyalty, generosity, and warm-heartedness, while despairing of the rashness and impulsiveness which made him an easy prey of the unscrupulous, especially if they claimed to be poets: 'nobody ever joined so much integrity with so much imprudence' (*Memoirs and Correspondence of Mrs.*

Grant of Laggan, ed. J. P. Grant, 3 vols., 1844, 3.199). He was slightly but wirily built, with black hair and deep-set, piercing eyes; his bustling and unsettled demeanour left an impression of restless activity barely kept in check.

Disheartened by repeated professional disappointments—he was considered, but rejected, as founding editor of *Blackwood's Magazine*, and in 1820 applied unsuccessfully for the rectorship of the high school and the chair of Greek at St Andrews—Gray left Scotland in December 1822 to be principal of Belfast Academy. He was ill-suited to this situation, as his impractical and unbusinesslike nature caused a gradual descent into serious financial difficulties, although these were only partly of his own making. His ordination to the Anglican priesthood in 1824 provided a means of escape, for late in 1825 he unexpectedly left Belfast to apply for a chaplaincy in the East India Company, formally resigning the principalship in February 1826.

Shortly after Gray's arrival in India—loyally accompanied by his wife, although she already knew herself to be terminally ill—he was in 1827 appointed chaplain at Bhuj, Cutch (Kachchh). He opened a school and a library, and was appointed tutor to the young rao, Desal II. He also began a translation of the gospels into Cutchee; his version of Matthew was to appear in 1834. But this task was cut short by his death at Bhuj, on 25 September 1830, from 'water in the chest' (Steven, appx, 106). He was buried beside his wife at Bhuj, where a monument was later raised to his memory by his royal pupil.

PETER JACKSON

Sources J. T. Mowbray, *Sketch of the life of the Rev. James Gray, M.A.* (1859) • W. Steven, *The history of the high school of Edinburgh* (1849) • A. T. Q. Stewart, *Belfast Royal Academy: the first century, 1785–1885* (1985) • J. Hogg, 'Memoir of the author's life' and 'Familiar anecdotes of Sir Walter Scott', ed. D. S. Mack (1972) • R. P. Gillies, *Memoirs of a literary veteran*, 3 vols. (1851) • J. Hogg, *The spy*, ed. G. Hughes (2000), 562–4 • P. Jackson, 'William Wordsworth, James Gray, and the *Letter to a friend of Robert Burns*: some unpublished correspondence', *N&Q*, 248 (2003) • parish registers, Duns, Mousewald, Dumfries, Edinburgh • m. reg. Scot., 1808 • matriculation records, U. Edin. L., special collections division, university archives • BL OIOC • N. Parr, *James Hogg at home: being the domestic life and letters of the Ettrick Shepherd* (1980) • *Certificates in favour of James Gray, senior master of the high school* [n.d., 1820?] • S. J. McNally, 'The chaplains of the East India Company', unpublished typescript, 1976, BL OIOC • *Scots Magazine and Edinburgh Literary Miscellany*, 68 (1806), 967 • *Belfast News-Letter* (15 June 1824) • U. Reading, Longman archives, pt 1, item 98 [information from Dr Gillian Hughes] • *Edinburgh Evening Post* (2 April 1831); repr. in *Belfast Commercial Chronicle* (19 April 1831) and *Guardian and Constitutional Advocate* [Belfast] (12 April 1831)

Archives BL, corresp. • Dove Cottage and the Wordsworth Museum, Cumbria, corresp. • Liverpool City Libraries, corresp. • NL Scot., corresp. with William Roscoe • PRO NIre., corresp. • U. Edin. L., corresp.

Likenesses W. Y. (or W. J.), pencil and wash drawing, 1816, Belfast Royal Academy; repro. in Stewart, *Belfast Royal Academy*

Wealth at death see list of payments to the East India Company from estate, BL OIOC

Gray, Sir James (1891–1975), zoologist, was born in Wood Green, London on 14 October 1891, the only son and younger child of James Gray, an accountant, and later chairman and managing director of the Electrical Construction Company in London, and his wife, Jessie Taylor. Both his parents were Scottish; his father was originally from Coatbridge. Gray was educated at Merchant Taylors' School from 1905 to 1909, and then at King's College, Cambridge, where he was a foundation scholar. He obtained first classes in both parts of the natural sciences tripos (1911 and 1913). He did further study in Naples and was elected to a King's fellowship in 1914. Almost immediately, however, he joined the Queen's Royal West Surrey regiment, where he served with distinction in France and Palestine, attaining the rank of captain. He was awarded the Military Cross (1918) and the Croix de Guerre avec palme, the latter presented to him in the field by Marshal Ferdinand Foch.

Gray returned to Cambridge in 1919, resumed his fellowship at King's, and soon took on a number of college posts. In 1921 he married Norah Christine, daughter of Ernest Carter King, director of the Cannon Brewery in Hampstead. They later adopted two children, a boy and a girl.

In 1924 Gray was made a university demonstrator, and in 1926 a university lecturer. At this stage he gave up his college commitments and turned to research in the department of zoology. In 1929 he was elected FRS, and in 1931 he became reader in experimental zoology. Though he was not to be made professor of zoology until 1937, it was in large measure Gray who provided the impetus, and raised the money, to build the new department of zoology which was completed in 1934. He reigned over it with authority for twenty-two years. He was also Fullerian professor of physiology at the Royal Institution in 1943–7.

Gray was an impressive teacher, with an austere manner lightened by an occasional impish sense of humour. But his greatest contribution was without doubt his research and its influence on others. When Gray was a young man zoology was mostly a descriptive science, only just beginning to spread out into genetics. Significantly, one of his teachers at Cambridge was Leonard Doncaster, a cytologist and embryologist, with whom he wrote his first paper in 1911. It had an experimental approach, and Gray's classic *Text-Book of Experimental Cytology* (1931) stemmed from this early collaboration and established a wholly new branch of biology.

Perhaps more significant than Gray's own research, however, was the influence he had on others, an influence that grew when he was appointed head of what was to become a very large department. In the 1930s and for a time after the war, it was pre-eminent in Europe. At one point no fewer than nine members of his staff were fellows of the Royal Society, and many of his pupils gained distinction in Cambridge and elsewhere.

In the early 1930s, however, Gray switched completely his line of research. For the rest of his active career he worked on animal locomotion, believing, rightly, that new techniques and ideas were needed before a study of the cell could be much further advanced. The work on animal locomotion was meticulous and scholarly, but was not seminal. One of his junior colleagues, working in the field of experimental cytology, recalls Gray asking to be told 'when my work becomes boring', and it has to be said that his later work was never as significant as his earlier.

Gray was for many years editor of the leading *Journal of Experimental Biology*, his control of it, in the words of one observer, being 'that of a wise and beneficent autocrat'. And among many other things he was chairman of the advisory committee on fishery research (1945–65), president of the Marine Biological Association (1945–55), and president of the British Association (1959). He received honorary degrees from Aberdeen, Edinburgh, Durham, Manchester, and Wales. He was appointed CBE in 1946 and was knighted in 1954.

Gray was tall and distinguished in appearance. In manner, as a close friend put it, he was 'reserved and quite shy, a formidable fighter for things he wanted, austere, kind-hearted and hospitable, with a lot of personal things to say but with great difficulty in doing so'. He died at his home, King's Field, West Road, Cambridge, on 14 December 1975. He was survived by his wife.   MICHAEL SWANN, rev.

Sources H. W. Lissmann, *Memoirs FRS*, 24 (1978), 55–70 · A. Hardy, *Journal of the Marine Biological Association of the United Kingdom*, 56 (1976) · *Annual Report of the Council* [King's College, Cambridge] (1976) · personal knowledge (1986) · *CGPLA Eng. & Wales* (1976)
Archives CUL, scientific papers and autobiographical material | CAC Cam., corresp. with A. V. Hill · ICL, corresp. with J. W. Munro · Rice University, Houston, Texas, Woodson Research Center, corresp. with Sir Julian Huxley
Likenesses W. Stoneman, photograph, 1931–9, NPG · J. Epstein, bust, U. Cam., department of zoology · R. Lutyens, portrait, King's Cam.
Wealth at death £43,533: probate, 8 March 1976, *CGPLA Eng. & Wales*

Gray, John de (d. 1214), administrator and bishop of Norwich, has been claimed as a native of Norfolk, but he is more likely to have been one of the Grays descended from Ansketel de Grai who held land in Rotherfield, Oxfordshire, at the time of Domesday. He was uncle of Walter de Gray, bishop of Worcester and subsequently archbishop of York. By 8 February 1198 he was in the service of Count John, then on the continent. On John's accession Gray crossed to England, and as a senior chancery clerk he sealed royal charters there and in France between 1199 and 1200. In the first year of the new reign, he secured the archdeaconries of Cleveland and Gloucester and he was elected to the see of Norwich by 3 September 1200, being consecrated on the 24th by Archbishop Hubert Walter in St Katherine's Chapel, Westminster. About three months later his name reappears in the charter rolls, where it occurs with varying frequency until his death. In 1203 he accompanied Archbishop Walter, then chancellor, on an abortive mission to Philippe Augustus. At that time he held the king's regalia in pawn and on other occasions lent John money. He also acted as a royal justice and he headed the northern eyre circuit of 1202.

With the death of Hubert Walter in 1205 Gray was influential in securing the chancellorship for his own nephew, Walter de Gray. At Canterbury the chapter elected the subprior, Reginald, to be the new archbishop, but both the king, who had disliked Hubert Walter, and the bishops of

the province attempted to influence the choice of candidate. On 11 December 1205, in the king's presence, the monks were forced to elect John de Gray. Pope Innocent III had quashed the election before 30 March 1206 but Gray continued to use the style 'archbishop-elect' until 29 May. The pope, having rejected both candidates, consecrated Stephen Langton on 17 June 1207. In the ensuing conflict King John expelled the Canterbury monks and confiscated episcopal baronies, while the pope imposed an interdict (1208) and excommunicated John (1209). Gray and Peter des Roches of Winchester alone among the bishops remained loyal to the king.

Gray was then sent to Ireland, perhaps late in 1208, where he succeeded Meiler fitz Henry as justiciar. He remodelled the Irish coinage on the English pattern, and he has been credited with implementing the royal policy of introducing English judicial practices and restructuring local government. The king was in Ireland between June and August 1210 for a projected attack on Hugh de Lacy. Afterwards Gray was left with the task of building castles in Connacht, and he led an army into Athlone. However, in 1212 he was defeated in Fircal, Offaly, by Cormac O'Melaghlin with the loss of his baggage train. Nevertheless in the autumn he was commanded to bring forces to Chester for an expedition against the Welsh. Gray was still justiciar in 1213 when, according to Matthew Paris, he brought a force of knights from Ireland to Barham Down in Kent to repulse the threatened invasion by Philippe Augustus. In July of that year he accompanied William (I) Longespée on a mission to the emperor Otto IV, but the resulting coalition against Philippe Augustus was defeated at Bouvines in 1214.

Gray was one of two members of the episcopate—the other being the archbishop of Dublin—who attested John's charter of 15 May 1213 whereby the king surrendered his kingdom to the papacy and received it back as a fief. Thereafter he played a prominent role in negotiating the king's settlement with the church, acting as surety for the good treatment of Langton and of the English bishops forced into exile. He travelled abroad to facilitate the bishops' return, and with Peter des Roches and some secular lords went to Rome to negotiate terms of compensation for the damage they had sustained. With des Roches he negotiated postponement of the payment of the sum promised by the king. While at the curia he received papal absolution for the sentences he had incurred, having been himself excluded from the general pardon. His diplomacy did much to modify Innocent's attitude towards John. The see of Durham had been vacant since 1208. The monks now elected Richard Poor, dean of Salisbury, only to have the election quashed by the pope. Meanwhile a fresh *congé d'élire* had been issued (26 January 1214) and at the direction of the papal legate Gray was postulated on 20 February, as John would have wished. But the bishop-elect died at St Jean d'Angély on 18 October on his return journey and was buried in Norwich Cathedral. His monument is no longer extant.

Although Gray enjoyed the full confidence of the king, and was throughout his life involved in secular business which entailed lengthy absences, he was not oblivious to the needs of his diocese, where he appropriated a number of churches to the cathedral priory and others to St Paul's Hospital in Norwich. He secured a royal charter with a grant of a weekly market and two annual fairs for Bishop's Lynn, as it was called before its alienation to the crown in Henry VIII's reign. At nearby Gaywood he built a sumptuous palace. Allegedly a learned and pleasant companion, he is supposed by Blomefield to have written a defence of Geoffrey of Monmouth against the criticism of William of Newburgh. Matthew Paris dubbed him an 'evil counsellor' and understandably regarded his election to Canterbury as the origin of all the subsequent discord. Perhaps King John's partial rehabilitation will lead to a similar reassessment of his undoubtedly astute minister.

ROY MARTIN HAINES

Sources Chancery records · H. S. Sweetman and G. F. Handcock, eds., Calendar of documents relating to Ireland, 5 vols., PRO (1875–86), vol. 1 · Rymer, Foedera · Bartholomaei de Cotton … Historia Anglicana, ed. H. R. Luard, Rolls Series, 16 (1859) · Historiae Dunelmensis scriptores tres: Gaufridus de Coldingham, Robertus de Graystanes, et Willielmus de Chambre, ed. J. Raine, SurtS, 9 (1839) · Paris, Chron. · Selected letters of Pope Innocent III concerning England, 1198–1216, ed. C. R. Cheney and W. H. Semple (1953) · H. G. Richardson and G. O. Sayles, The administration of Ireland, 1172–1377 (1963) · S. Painter, The reign of King John (1949) · J. Weever, Ancient funerall monuments (1631) · Fasti Angl., 1066–1300 · F. Blomefield and C. Parkin, An essay towards a topographical history of the county of Norfolk, [2nd edn], 11 vols. (1805–10); with J. N. Chadwick, Index nominum (1862)

Gray, John (c.1799–1883), socialist and writer on economics, was by his own account educated between the ages of nine and thirteen at Repton School, Derbyshire, where he 'learned little else than to catch fish, to play at marbles and to climb trees' (Gray, 338). Subsequently, at the age of fourteen, he was employed in a manufacturing and wholesale house in Cheapside. It was from this time on, he informs us, that he concerned himself with the reform of the social system.

Having penned an abortive tract on the subject, entitled 'The national commercial system', Gray, at the instigation of his brother James, took an interest in the ideas of Robert Owen and heard him speak at the London tavern debates of August 1817. However, it was some years before Gray once again committed his ideas to paper; his first published work was A Lecture on Human Happiness, published in January 1825. Gray claimed that he had arrived at the central ideas of this book independently of Owen, but it certainly reflects many of the central concerns of Owenite socialism. It is, in essence, an indictment of competitive capitalism, which in Gray's view (substantiated by reference to Patrick Colquhoun's Treatise on the Population, Wealth, Power and Resources of the British Empire, 1814), had produced a distribution of wealth skewed in favour of the unproductive part of the nation and detrimental to those whose labour was its source. This distribution was effected by means of unequal exchanges which in a competitive context favoured the owners of capital and land, who were able to exact interest and rent from those with only their labour to sell. Gray argued further that these evils could be eliminated by the formation of co-operative communities where the business of competitive exchange would have no place.

This preoccupation with co-operative communities led Gray to take an interest in that established by Abram Combe and Archibald Hamilton at Orbiston near Motherwell in 1825. He visited it in that year but his reaction, as expressed in A Word of Advice to the Orbistonians (1826), was highly critical. In 1825 too he began publishing a 'gratis' newspaper given over entirely to advertisements, the Edinburgh and Leith Advertiser. This was converted into a regular newspaper but failed after fifty-three numbers, to be replaced by the Edinburgh, Leith, Glasgow and North British Commercial and Literary Advertiser (later the North British Advertiser), which proved commercially successful. In 1830 he sought to establish a printers' hall in Edinburgh which would enable several firms to share modern machinery in common premises. This proved a disaster and led to a short period of imprisonment for debt, but the business of newspaper publishing was ultimately to make Gray's fortune: at the peak of its success some 19,000 copies of the North British Advertiser (merged with another of Gray's papers, the Ladies' Own Journal, in 1874) were being distributed in Scotland and the north of England.

Yet in the 1830s and 1840s Gray continued to stress the need for a change in existing economic and social arrangements. Specifically, in The Social System: a Treatise on the Principle of Exchange (1831) he abandoned his earlier communitarianism and argued for a technocratically run and centrally planned economy. This could be effected through a national chamber of commerce that comprised 'eminent merchants, bankers, brokers etc', a single 'controlling and directing power' which 'having the means of ascertaining, at all times, the actual stock of any kinds of goods in hand, would always be able to say at once where production should proceed more rapidly, where at its own pace and where also it should be retarded' (Gray, 45). The power to do this would be derived from its control of the means of production (a control to be voluntarily given to it by the owners of land and capital) and would be exercised in particular to ensure that aggregate demand expanded pari passu with aggregate supply, so eliminating the general economic depressions which had bedevilled Britain in the post-Napoleonic wars period. Here we have one of the first examples of an attempt to articulate a political economy of central planning.

The salient themes of The Social System were to be reiterated in An Efficient Remedy for the Distress of Nations (1842). However, by 1848 and the publication of his Lectures on the Nature and Use of Money Gray had abandoned the idea of central planning and his antipathy to competition and had come to believe that a full and efficient utilization of resources could be secured by a fundamental reform of the monetary system. As he put it, 'a few salutary monetary laws are all that are wanted'.

Little is known about Gray's private life, in particular the years after 1850. The death on 30 January 1831 of his first wife, Caroline Mordaunt, is recorded on a monument in St Cuthbert's parish churchyard in Edinburgh, and there is mention here too of a second wife, Jane Renny, by whom, together with a married daughter, he was survived. It is also known that, after residing at Faldonside, Galashiels, in the 1840s, he purchased an estate of 26 acres, Bonaly Tower, near Edinburgh, in October 1854. This was sold in 1866, Gray having previously moved to Church Road in Upper Norwood, a part of London which in the 1880s was, as one commentator has put it, 'the home of people who thought they were no small beer'. It was here that he died on 26 April 1883, leaving a personal estate of £14,831.   NOEL THOMPSON

Sources J. Kimball, *The economic doctrines of John Gray, 1799–1883* (1948) • D. Martin, 'Gray, John', *DLB*, vol. 6 • J. B. Paul, ed., *Monumental inscriptions in St Cuthbert's churchyard, Edinburgh* (1919) • G. Claeys, *Machinery, money and the millennium: from moral economy to socialism, 1815–60* (1987) • H. S. Foxwell, 'Introduction', in A. Menger, *The right to the whole produce of labour* (1899) • G. D. H. Cole, *Socialist thought: the forerunners, 1789–1850* (1959) • A. Gray, *The socialist tradition, Moses to Lenin* (1946) • J. Gray, *The social system, a treatise on the principle of exchange* (1831) [autobiographical app.] • N. Norrie, *Edinburgh papers, past and present* (1891) • J. F. C. Harrison, *Robert Owen and the Owenites in Britain and America: the quest for the new moral world* (1969) • E. Lowenthal, *The Ricardian socialists* (1911) • N. Thompson, *The market and its critics: socialist political economy in nineteenth century Britain* (1988)

Archives Co-operative Union, Manchester, Owen corresp.

Wealth at death £14,831 15s. 11d.: probate, 28 May 1883, *CGPLA Eng. & Wales*

Gray, John (1807–1875), legal writer and lawyer and public official, was born in Aberdeen, the seventh son of George Gray. He was educated at Gordon's Hospital in Aberdeen, before entering the office of Messrs White and Whitmore, solicitors, in London. He was admitted to the Middle Temple in January 1834 and called to the bar in January 1838, joining the Oxford circuit. Appointed QC in 1863, he became solicitor to the Treasury in March 1871 and in 1873 during his tenure of the office took part in the celebrated prosecution of Arthur Orton, the claimant to the title and estates of Roger Tichborne. Gray published two works on the subject of legal practice, which at the time were considered valuable textbooks and passed through several editions. He was also the author of a work on costs. Gray died at 16 Gloucester Road, Regent's Park, London, on 22 January 1875, leaving a son and a daughter.

[ANON.], rev. CATHERINE PEASE-WATKIN

Sources Boase, *Mod. Eng. biog.* • J. Hutchinson, ed., *A catalogue of notable Middle Templars: with brief biographical notices* (1902) • private information (1890) • *CGPLA Eng. & Wales* (1875)

Wealth at death under £12,000: probate, 26 Feb 1875, *CGPLA Eng. & Wales*

Gray, Sir John (1816–1875), newspaper proprietor and politician, was the third son of John Gray, of Claremorris, co. Mayo. He was born in Claremorris, graduated MD and master in surgery at Glasgow University in 1839, and practised medicine in Dublin. In the same year, he married Mary Anna Dwyer of Limerick; they had five children, three sons and two daughters.

Drawn to politics and journalism, Gray became joint owner of the Dublin *Freeman's Journal* in 1841, and its political editor. A protestant supporter of Daniel O'Connell, he was charged in October 1843, beside O'Connell and others, with conspiracy against British rule. Sentenced to nine months' imprisonment the following February, Gray was released on appeal in September. He was careful thereafter to distance himself from the advocacy of violence in the national cause. Sympathetic to Young Ireland, he was not involved in its attempt at rebellion in 1848. The growing influence of the *Freeman's Journal*, of which he was sole proprietor from 1850, and his prominence in Dublin municipal politics, made him a significant figure in the deceptively quiet period of Irish politics between the famine and the resurgence of nationalism in the 1860s. He was one of the provisional secretaries who helped to organize the Tenant League's founding conference in 1850, and unsuccessfully contested county Monaghan with the league's backing in the 1852 election.

In the same year Gray became a Dublin councillor. His work to give the city an improved water supply from the Vartry Reservoir was the ostensible reason for the knighthood conferred upon him in 1863. The Liberal government of the day was also anxious to conciliate an influential representative of the moderate nationalists who then supported British Liberalism in the absence of an organized movement that would resume O'Connell's constitutional agitation. Gray and his newspaper exploited this shift in British policy in alliance with Paul Cullen (1803–1878), the Catholic archbishop of Dublin, a man devoted to O'Connell's memory. It was an unlikely partnership, given Cullen's reservations about protestants, but it underpinned the archbishop's creation, the National Association of Ireland, established in 1864 and intended to provide a moderate alternative to the revolutionary nationalism of the Fenians. The *Freeman's Journal* made the National Association's aims its own: disestablishment of the Anglican church in Ireland, land reform, and the educational aspirations of Irish Catholicism. Elected for Kilkenny city in 1865, a seat held until his death, Gray campaigned effectively at Westminster and in Ireland for these aims: his newspaper's inquiry into the anomalous wealth of the established church in the midst of a predominantly Catholic population was a notable contribution to the agitation that ended in W. E. Gladstone's Irish Church Act of 1869.

The Gladstonian programme of Irish reform needed to be sustained by proof that Irish demands were not to be satisfied by anything less than radical legislation. Gray again helped to furnish this proof when the 1870 Land Bill was being fought over inside the government. Like others, he asked for fixity of tenure, thus enabling Gladstone to persuade reluctant colleagues that they must concede compensation for disturbance and recognize customs of tenant-right. The bill's initial reception in Ireland, Gladstone was told, turned on the verdict of the *Freeman's Journal* (Ramm, 1.79). The qualified failure of the Land Act, the accompanying coercion, and disappointment with Gladstone's handling of the university question and national education finally took Gray into the home-rule majority returned in 1874. His defection from the Liberals was confirmation of their lasting decline in Ireland. Gray was widely mistrusted: the British thought him a rogue, and the Fenians dismissed him as a whig (ibid.; Thornley, 89).

Nevertheless, a statue was erected to him in Dublin, on O'Connell Street, in 1879. He died at Bath on 9 April 1875, survived by his widow and children, and was buried in Glasnevin cemetery, Dublin. His second son, Edmund Dwyer *Gray, took over the *Freeman's Journal*.

DAVID STEELE

Sources *Freeman's Journal* [Dublin] (10 April 1875) · A. D. Macintyre, *The Liberator: Daniel O'Connell and the Irish party, 1830–1847* (1965) · T. W. Moody and others, eds., *A new history of Ireland*, 5: *Ireland under the Union, 1801–1870* (1989) · J. H. Whyte, *The independent Irish party, 1850–59* (1958) · E. Larkin, *The making of the Roman Catholic church in Ireland, 1850–1860* (1980) · E. Larkin, *The consolidation of the Roman Catholic church in Ireland, 1860–1870* (1987) · E. R. Norman, *The Catholic church and Ireland in the age of rebellion, 1859–1873* (1965) · *The political correspondence of Mr Gladstone and Lord Granville, 1868–1876*, ed. A. Ramm, 2 vols., CS, 3rd ser., 81–2 (1952) · E. D. Steele, *Irish land and British politics: tenant-right and nationality, 1865–1870* (1974) · E. D. Steele, 'Cardinal Cullen and Irish nationality', *Irish Historical Studies*, 19 (1974–5), 239–60 · D. Thornley, *Isaac Butt and home rule* (1964) · *CGPLA Ire.* (1876)

Archives BL, corresp. with W. E. Gladstone, Add. MSS 44413–44428, *passim* · Roman Catholic Diocesan Archives, Dublin, Cullen MSS

Likenesses T. Farrell, marble statue, 1879, O'Connell Street, Dublin · S. C. Smith jun., oils, NG Ire.

Wealth at death under £20,000: probate, 4 Dec 1876, *CGPLA Eng. & Wales*

John Edward Gray (1800–1875), by Maull & Polyblank, 1855

Gray, John Edward (1800–1875), zoologist and museum curator, was born at Walsall, Staffordshire, on 12 February 1800, the second son of Samuel Frederick *Gray (1766–1828), naturalist and pharmacologist, and his wife, Elizabeth Forfeit (1777–1852), the daughter of a picture dealer in Covent Garden. His father obtained employment with the metallurgist Charles Hatchett (1765–1847) that year and the family moved back to London. Gray's younger brother was the zoologist George Robert *Gray (1808–1872).

Gray had no formal education, but was taught to read and write by his parents and instructed himself through reading the *Encyclopaedia Britannica*. He assisted in his father's Wapping pharmacy (*c*.1812–15) and, after that failed, he helped a general practitioner in Shoreditch before working in the laboratory of a wholesale chemist. Although he was a weak child (for many years he was unable to eat meat) his health improved in adolescence; Gray attributed this to weekend excursions into the countryside during which he was befriended by the entomologist J. F. Stephens (1792–1852).

Despite family links with horticulture Gray was encouraged by his father to enter the medical profession. During the 1820s, he attended lectures at St Bartholomew's and Middlesex hospitals and the City Dispensary, and classes held by John Taunton and William Salisbury elsewhere in London. However, a constitutional revulsion to surgery (and an unsuccessful application for an assistantship at the British Museum) probably contributed to Gray's suffering a nervous breakdown in 1822 and he left the medical profession with only a certificate of attendance at the lectures given by C. J. Cusack in 1823. Gray's recovery was much helped by Maria Emma *Gray (*née* Smith) (1787–1876), the widow of his cousin Francis Edward Gray (1775–

1814), and her circle of acquaintances. In 1826 he married Maria Gray and she later became active in science herself, etching plates for *Figures of Molluscous Animals* (1859) and arranging the algae in the herbaria at Kew and the British Museum. The union was long and happy and Gray acknowledged 'my wife has been my companion and helper in all my studies … and my cares' (Gunther, *Century*, 183).

About 1816 Gray was introduced to Dr W. E. Leach (1790–1836), of the British Museum; Gray subsequently spent all his spare time naming and arranging the zoological collections at Montagu House. Through Leach he gained access to the Banksian Library and met other naturalists, whose encouragement prompted him to switch from botany to zoology. Following Leach's retirement in 1821, Gray failed to obtain a position as assistant at the museum, and, other posts he had at that period, such as editing the *Mechanics Weekly Journal* or a work on shells with James Sowerby, proved only temporary.

Gray had earlier provided material for his father's *Supplement to the Pharmacopoeia* (1818). In 1821, at Gray's suggestion, his father issued the contentious *A Natural Arrangement of British Plants* that criticized the Linnaean system and adopted other European methods of classification. Gray himself was responsible for the larger synoptical portion of that work, and it marked the first expression of his urge to use a catalogue as a means of conveying progress in natural history. The adverse reaction to the book had considerable influence on Gray's life, increasing his determination to succeed in science and 'thus [he] acquired the combative habit' (*Annals and Magazine of Natural History*, 282). Publication of *A Natural Arrangement*, and a failure to mention Sir J. E. Smith when referring to *English Botany* were alleged to be the reasons that he was black-balled when seeking election to the Linnean Society in 1822 (he was finally elected in 1857).

After assisting J. G. Children (1777–1851), keeper of the zoological department at the British Museum, with the shell collection, Gray was offered a temporary position to compile a *Catalogue of Reptiles* in December 1824 at 15s. per day. He began by completing Children's catalogue of shells—also publishing thirty papers that year. Over the next fifty years he endeavoured to make the museum's collections 'the most extensive, the best known, the best exhibited, the most freely available and only catalogued exhibition of its kind' (Gunther, 'Note', 66) as he later outlined to the select committee on the British Museum in 1836. His significant evidence to the committee brought several changes, notably the separation of the zoological and mineralogical departments and his own appointment as assistant keeper from 27 May 1837 (he became keeper on Children's retirement in March 1840). In the same year he initiated the first register of accessions and soon after through his keen interest in systematics increased the series of publications on the collections.

Many of the lists and catalogues on mammals Gray wrote himself, including those on seals, whales, monkeys, lemurs, fruit-eating bats, and the carnivores, pachyderms, edentates, and ruminants. He produced others on the lizards and shield reptiles, while his *List of the Specimens of British Animals in the British Museum* (1845) provided an updated faunal list. For other catalogues Gray used outside specialists whenever necessary, but avoided any increase in expenditure that might displease the trustees. Other significant publications were the *Illustrations of Indian Zoology* with General Hardwicke (1832–4) and the privately printed *Gleanings from the Menagerie and Aviary at Knowsley* (1846).

Gray's successors at the museum acknowledged that the growth of the collections was wholly due to Gray's efforts despite opposition from the administration and lack of finance. Gray attributed success in fulfilling his objectives to a catholic taste in dealing with all groups of animals. Among the many reference collections he shrewdly acquired for his department were Gilbertson's collection of fossils (in 1836) and the skins and skeletons of Indian animals amassed by B. H. Hodgson (in 1845). Both acquisitions contradicted museum policy and thwarted his colleagues, in addition to upsetting Richard Owen, who wanted the osteological specimens for the Royal College of Surgeons. Inevitably, with Owen's appointment as superintendent of the natural history departments in 1856, the pair had further differences on both museum and zoological subjects.

All Gray's contemporaries remarked on his indefatigable energy and enthusiasm and attributed the mistakes he made to his trying to do too much with insufficient material, time, or help. One concluded that 'it would have been better, both for zoology and his own future fame, if the outcome … had been represented by half, or even a quarter of the literature under Dr. Gray's name' (Allman,

xlvi). Gray's lack of field knowledge led to 'the needless number of genera and species he introduced' which was 'thought to be detrimental to science' (*DNB*). His depreciatory criticism of the Cuming collection of shells reflects haste and a lack of use of that collection, which was exacerbated by Mrs Gray's mishandling of it when relabelling specimens according to museum policy.

Gray's interests were not confined to zoology, or even natural history for, apart from his tremendous output of more than 1100 papers, his radical upbringing led him to tackle many social matters, among them prison discipline, imprisonment for debt, the treatment of lunatics, the rescue and treatment of drowned victims, and sanitary reform. He continually sought improvements in museum exhibits and for free access, also advocating this for other public institutions. On moving to Blackheath he became involved with the mechanics' institutes, lecturing in that at Greenwich. He claimed to have proposed a system of prepaid postage by stamps in 1834 and published a *Hand-Catalogue of Postage-Stamps* in 1862. He also published numerous articles in 1854–7 on the proposed adoption of the decimal system for coinage, weights, and measures in Britain. In later life he renewed his interest in botany and published a *Handbook of British Waterweeds or Algae* in 1864. He also fulfilled obligations to his earlier benefactors by publishing *A Synopsis of the Mollusca of Great Britain* (1852), prepared by Leach, and then in 1866 *The Genera of Plants*—an early experiment in natural classification by his tutor R. A. Salisbury.

Gray was elected a fellow of the Royal Society in 1832. He was a founder member of the Zoological Society in 1826 (vice-president in 1865–74), of the Royal Geographical Society in 1830, of the Entomological Society in 1833 (president, 1858–9), of the Botanical Society of London in 1836 (president, 1836–57), and of the Palaeontographical Society in 1847. In 1854 the University of Munich conferred on him the honorary degree of *doctor philosophiae* in recognition of his having formed the largest zoological collection in Europe.

From the age of sixty Gray was plagued by ill health; he suffered several mild strokes and recurring periods of near-blindness and was immobile in his later years. He never fully recovered from a paralytic stroke in May 1869, but continued in post until December 1874, when his retirement was arranged for the following summer. He died, in his official apartment at the British Museum, on 7 March 1875, and was buried six days later in the churchyard of St Mary's, Lewisham.

Gunther has asserted that Gray marked his place by the 'formulation of the concept of the British Museum as a comprehensive national institution for natural history' (Gunther, *Century*, 85) and then helped to make it one of the foremost museums in the world. His approach to natural history was that of a collector and an organizer of knowledge. Gray realized the limitations of his preoccupation with the external form of animals and neglect of internal structures, having earlier even pointed out the problems this had caused when describing molluscs. In an obituary he was described as 'a warm-hearted, judicious, kind, and firm friend' to those that knew him, someone who was 'always ready … to give advice and assistance to earnest students' (*Annals and Magazine of Natural History*, 285) but whose shrewdness in discerning hidden motives and an acquired causticity of manner, often raised prejudices against him. Gray himself felt that he had two very opposite qualities: 'First I am fearless and very obstinate in doing what I think justified' but also 'genuinely affectionate to those in distress and wanting my assistance' (Gray, autobiographical journal, NHM, 110).

R. J. CLEEVELY

Sources A. E. Gunther, 'A note on the autobiographical manuscripts of John Edward Gray (1800–1875)', *Journal of the Society of the Bibliography of Natural History*, 7 (1974–6), 35–76 · A. E. Gunther, *A century of zoology at the British Museum through the lives of two keepers, 1815–1914* (1975), 17–209, 476–95 · A. E. Gunther, 'The miscellaneous autobiographical manuscripts of John Edward Gray (1800–1875)', *Bulletin of the British Museum (Natural History)* [Historical Series], 6 (1977–80), 199–244 · A. E. Gunther, *The founders of science at the British Museum, 1753–1900* (1980), 65–98, 121–8 · A. E. Gunther, 'John George Children, FRS (1777–1852), of the British Museum: mineralogist and reluctant keeper of zoology', *Bulletin of the British Museum (Natural History)* [Historical Series], 6 (1977–80), 75–108 · *DNB* · *The history of the collections contained in the natural history departments of the British Museum*, British Museum, 2 (1912) · A. Günther, appendix, *The history of the collections contained in the natural history departments of the British Museum*, British Museum, 2 (1912) · G. J. Allman, *Proceedings of the Linnean Society of London* (1874–5), xliii–xlvii · *Gardeners' Chronicle*, new ser., 3 (1875), 334–5 · E. Newman, *Zoologist*, 10, 4466–8 · E. Newman, *The Entomologist*, 8 (1875), 93–6 · J. E. Gray, 'Gray the naturalist', *The Athenaeum* (19 Sept 1863), 368 · A. T. Gage, *A history of the Linnean Society of London* (1938) · J. C. Thackray, *A catalogue of manuscripts and drawings in the general library of the Natural History Museum, London* (1995), 29–31 · G. D. R. Bridson, V. C. Phillips, and A. P. Harvey, *Natural history manuscript resources in the British Isles* (1980) · D. E. Allen, *The naturalist in Britain: a social history* (1976) · *Annals and Magazine of Natural History*, 4th ser., 15 (1875), 281–5 · J. E. Gray's autobiographical journal, NHM

Archives American Philosophical Society, Philadelphia, corresp. and papers · BL, corresp. and papers, Add. MSS 29533, 29717, 40140–40141 · Linn. Soc., letters and reports · NHM, department of zoology, accession reports; album; autobiographical journal; collection catalogues; collection of shells; corresp. and papers · RS, letters · U. Cam., department of plant sciences, collection of algae · U. Cam., department of zoology, letters | Auckland Public Library, letters to Sir George Grey · Elgin Museum, Elgin, letters to George Gordon · Linn. Soc., letters to William Swainson · Maison d'Auguste Comte, Paris, letters to Henri Ducrotay de Blainville · Museum of Scotland, Edinburgh, letters to William Jardine · NHM, letter to Cuvier · NHM, notes and MSS on John Edward Gray by A. E. Gunther · NHM, letter to T. H. Huxley · NHM, corresp. with Richard Owen and William Clift · NHM, letters to members of the Sowerby family · RBG Kew, letters to William Hooker · Sheff. Arch., letters to Margaret Gatty · U. Newcastle, Robinson L., letters to Walter Trevelyan

Likenesses A. Archer, group portrait, 1819, BM · H. Phillips, oils, 1830, RBG Kew · B. Smith, etching, 1835, repro. in Gunther, 'A note on the autobiographical manuscripts', fig. 2 · R. Westmacott jun., bust, 1845, NHM · M. S. Carpenter, oils, 1846, RS · T. H. Maguire, lithograph, 1851, BM, NPG; repro. in T. H. Maguire, *Portraits of honorary members of the Ipswich Museum* (1852) · Maull & Polyblank, albumen print, 1855, NPG [*see illus.*] · drawing, 1855, repro. in Gunther, *Century of zoology*, 67 · G. G. Adams, bronze medal, 1863, NPG · Caldesi, Blanford & Co., photograph, 1863, repro. in Gunther, 'A note on the autobiographical manuscripts', fig. 4. · London School of Photography, double portrait, carte-de-visite, 1864 (with his wife), NPG · Maull & Polyblank, photograph, c.1868, Linn. Soc. · photograph, 1872 · T. Bridgford, lithograph (after drawing, c.1846) · Caldesi, Blanford & Co., carte-de-visite, NPG · E. Edwards, photograph, NPG; repro. in E. Edwards, *Portraits of men of eminence in literature, science and the arts, with biographical memoirs*, ed. L. Reeve and E. Walford, 1 (1863) · bust, NHM · photograph (after H. Phillips), NHM

Wealth at death under £5000: resworn probate, Jan 1876, CGPLA Eng. & Wales

Gray, John Henry (1866–1934), author and Roman Catholic priest, was born at 2 Vivian Road, Bethnal Green, a working-class suburb of London, on 10 March 1866. He was the eldest of the nine children of John Gray (1843–1892), of Scottish ancestry though born in Kent, a carpenter and wheelwright employed in the Royal Arsenal, Woolwich, and his wife, Hannah Mary Williamson (1845–1903). In 1893 John Henry Gray's mother converted to Roman Catholicism and raised her three youngest children in the faith. (Beforehand the family was nonconformist, probably Methodist.)

At the age of thirteen Gray's formal school ended when his father arranged for his apprenticeship as a metal turner at the Royal Arsenal. Three years later he entered the civil service as a clerk, eventually moving to the Foreign Office library in 1893. From 1888 he began associating with artists and writers, the result of his friendship with the artists Charles Ricketts and Charles Shannon, editors of *The Dial*, to which he contributed prose and verse.

In 1889, after Gray met Oscar Wilde, a relationship developed, the precise nature of which remains unknown, though Gray adopted Wilde's dandiacal mannerisms and appearance. He signed himself Dorian in letters to Wilde and, in Richard Ellmann's view, Wilde's naming of the hero of his novel *The Picture of Dorian Gray* 'was a form of courtship' (Ellmann, 290). From 1890 Gray attended (as a guest) meetings of the Rhymers' Club and also moved in Parisian avant-garde literary circles; as a result he translated (or 'imitated', he said) poems of Baudelaire, Verlaine, Mallarmé, and Rimbaud for his first volume of verse, *Silverpoints* (1893).

In late 1892 Gray (a convert to Roman Catholicism since 1890) suddenly suffered a mental collapse, apparently precipitated by a spiritual crisis at the time of his relationship with Wilde, his recovery resulting in translations of devotional verse, later published in *Spiritual Poems* (1896). In early 1893 the wealthy Russian-Jewish émigré and poet André Raffalovich rescued Gray with financial and emotional support. A homosexual and, in 1896, a convert to Catholicism, the devoted Raffalovich moved to Edinburgh in 1907 after Gray was assigned to a parish there following his ordination in 1901 as a priest while studying at Scots College, Rome.

During the years that Father (later Canon) Gray served at St Peter's Church in Edinburgh, built through Raffalovich's generosity, he continued his literary career: in addition to many essays and poems, he edited *The Last Letters of Aubrey Beardsley* (1904) and wrote *Park: a Fantastic Story* (1932), an experimental novel. On 14 June 1934 he died of heart failure in Edinburgh following an operation for an abscessed lung, just four months after Raffalovich died in his sleep. Both were buried in Mount Vernon cemetery outside Edinburgh, Gray, on 19 June, in the section reserved for clergy.   KARL BECKSON

Sources J. H. McCormack, *John Gray: poet, dandy and priest* (1991) · B. Sewell, *In the Dorian mode: a life of John Gray* (1983) · B. Sewell, *Footnote to the nineties: a memoir of John Gray and André Raffalovich* (1968) · B. Sewell, ed., *Two friends: John Gray and André Raffalovich* (1963) · P. J. Vernon, 'The letters of John Gray', PhD diss., U. Lond., 1976 · R. Ellmann, *Oscar Wilde* (1987) · b. cert.
Archives Dominican Chaplaincy, Edinburgh · JRL · NL Scot. | JRL, letters to his niece and Francis Langdale · NL Scot., corresp. with André Raffalovich · NYPL, Berg collection · Princeton University, New Jersey, O'Connell collection
Likenesses C. H. Shannon, lithograph, 1896, Carlisle City Art Gallery · R. Savage, lithograph, NPG · photographs, repro. in McCormack, *John Gray*
Wealth at death £64,722 14s. 3d.: confirmation, 26 Jan 1935, CCI

Gray, John Miller (1850–1894), writer on art and curator, was born on 19 July 1850 at 2 Craigie Terrace, Edinburgh, his mother, Jane, *née* Miller, dying at his birth. His father, John Gray (d. 1871), had retired from business as a shawl manufacturer but was ruined by the failure of the Western Bank of Scotland in 1857. Consequently Gray, having left Mr Munro's school, in Middleby Street, Newington, Edinburgh, joined the Bank of Scotland as an apprentice clerk in 1866 rather than continuing his education. Though he found the work 'utterly repugnant and irksome' (*Memoirs*, 1.7) he remained at the bank for nearly eighteen years, devoting his leisure time to the study of literature and art.

Gray gradually made a beginning as a critic, writing exhibition notices and book reviews, principally for the *Edinburgh Courant* and *The Academy*; occasionally longer articles of his appeared in the *People's Friend*, the *Art Journal*, *Blackwood's Magazine*, and the *Magazine of Art*. In 1880 he published a monograph on the wood-engraver and painter George Manson. His circle of acquaintance included like-minded writers and artists, particularly in Edinburgh, where he counted among his friends Dr John Brown and William Bell Scott (his biography of the latter's brother David Scott was published in 1884). When the Board of Manufactures, responsible for establishing the Scottish National Portrait Gallery, sought (at the prompting of the project's donor, John Ritchie Findlay) their first curator, Gray was the obvious choice. He was appointed in February 1884 and his first task was to organize the loan exhibition of historical portraits of important Scots held in the Royal Scottish Academy National Galleries, Edinburgh. In addition to presenting displays in the temporary premises used between 1885 and 1888, he sought out and assessed potential acquisitions. When Sir Robert Rowand Anderson's great Gothic palace, built to house the Scottish National Portrait Gallery, opened on 15 July 1889 Gray's arrangement of the embryonic national collection of portraits, augmented by many loans, was widely praised. His qualities as a professional curator won him the admiration of Sir George Scharf, director of the National Portrait Gallery, London.

Gray continued to produce reviews for journals and magazines; he was the main art critic for the *Scottish Leader* from its inauguration in 1887, but his writing now reflected his curatorial preoccupations. He wrote the first handbook to the Scottish National Portrait Gallery, guides to several private Scottish collections, a series of articles on the iconography of Robert Burns for *The Scotsman* in 1893, and, in the year of his death, a study of the life and work of the portrait medallists James and William Tassie. His interests became increasingly antiquarian and historical; he was the originator of the Edinburgh Heraldic Exhibition (1891), and he edited Sir John Clerk of Penicuik's journals for the Scottish History Society in 1892.

Reserved in character and delicate in appearance, Gray lived in Edinburgh all his life and never married. He died, following a brain haemorrhage, on 22 March 1894 at his home, 28 Gayfield Square. He was buried on 27 March at Echobank cemetery, Edinburgh. He left practically all that he possessed to form a fund for the purchase of portraits for the Scottish National Portrait Gallery.

J. L. CAW, rev. NICOLA KALINSKY

Sources *John Miller Gray: memoirs and remains*, ed. J. Balfour Paul and W. R. Macdonald, 2 vols. (1895) · *The Scotsman* (23 March 1894) · *The Scotsman* (28 March 1894) · *The Academy*, 45 (31 March 1894) · *Scottish Leader* (24 March 1894) · *The Athenaeum* (16 June 1894) · *Magazine of Art* (April 1894) · Scot. NPG committee, minute books, 1883–6, NA Scot., NG7/1/1 (MS) · Board of Manufactures, minutes, 1881–4, NA Scot., NG1/1/47 (MS) · Board of Manufactures, letter box, 1882–6, NA Scot., NG1/3/38 (MS) · Board of Manufactures, press cuttings, 1873–93, NA Scot., NG 1/68/1 · Board of Manufactures, press cuttings, 1893–1905, NA Scot., NG1/68/2 · Bank of Scotland, salary books, nos. 3–4, Bank of Scotland Archives, 1/277/3, 1/277/4 (MS) · bap. reg. Scot. · d. cert. · *CGPLA Eng. & Wales* (1894) · *CGPLA Eng. & Wales* (1895) · will, SC70/4/276, pp. 833–43
Archives Scot. NPG, notebooks
Likenesses G. R. Halkett, watercolour caricature, 1881, Scot. NPG · P. W. Adam, oils, 1885, Scot. NPG · C. Matthew, bronze medallion, 1886, Scot. NPG · C. Matthew, pencil drawing, 1888, Scot. NPG · W. G. Burn Murdoch, pencil drawing, 1889, Scot. NPG · photograph, repro. in *John Miller Gray*, ed. Balfour Paul and Macdonald, vol. 1, frontispiece
Wealth at death £1707 4s. 3d.: confirmation, 6 July 1894, CCI · £295 14s. 5d.: additional estate, 21 Nov 1895, CCI

Gray, Louis Harold (1905–1965), physicist and radiobiologist, was born in London on 10 November 1905, the only child of Harry Gray, civil servant, of Barnes, Surrey, and his wife, Amy Bowen. He was educated at Latymer School and then as a scholar at Christ's Hospital, whence in December 1923 he won an exhibition to Trinity College, Cambridge. Cambridge and Trinity profoundly influenced Gray, both broadening his outlook and consolidating his dedication to science. Cambridge was at that time a most exciting place for physics. The Cavendish Laboratory, headed by Sir Ernest Rutherford, was producing both excellent work and a number of future Nobel prize winning scientists. After gaining good firsts in the natural sciences tripos, parts one and two (1926 and 1927), and achieving a senior scholarship in the process, Gray was honoured by admission to the Cavendish in 1928. His postgraduate work there on the interaction of radiation with matter led to the degree of PhD and a prize fellowship at Trinity in 1930.

Meanwhile Gray (known as Hal) had become engaged to,

and in 1932 married Frieda Marjorie, daughter of William John Picot, procureur du roi of Alderney in the Channel Islands. She was the first blind woman to be admitted to Cambridge University, reading English and theology at Girton and subsequently Newnham College. She studied from braille books with the help of readers (among them Gray, who was thus introduced to English literature as a relaxation and became dedicated to pacifist Christian ideals). They had two sons.

Feeling perhaps that there was more to life than nuclear physics, Gray was attracted by an invitation in 1933 to establish a physics laboratory to measure radiation in the treatment of cancer at Mount Vernon Hospital, Northwood, Middlesex, recently converted from a tuberculosis sanatorium. There he went in 1934 as senior physicist and Prophit scholar of the Royal College of Surgeons. Those were challenging days, for treatment by X-rays and the gamma rays of radium was in transition from an empirical art to scientific measurement. St Bartholomew's and the Middlesex (teaching) hospitals had professorial departments of medical physics and the Cancer Hospital, Fulham Road, had W. V. Mayneord developing methods of dosimetry. Gray, fired by the opportunities offered by Mount Vernon's director, Sir Cuthbert Wallace, and the pathologist J. C. Mottram, had accepted the post, even at a financial loss, provided he was able to spend most of his time on research. In his fellowship thesis Gray had formulated a theory—now known as the Bragg–Gray principle [see Bragg, Sir William Henry]—for deducing the energy absorbed by a material exposed to gamma rays from the ionization within a small gas-filled cavity in the material. At Mount Vernon he was able to apply his theory to X-rays and, later, in suitably adapted form to the new radiation, neutrons.

So began a new commitment: the improvement of survival of sufferers from cancer. A new science, biology, had to be learned from the ground roots and appropriately Mottram introduced Gray to the broad bean, the root growth of which could be measured reliably, cheaply, and statistically to reveal the dynamics of growth and give relations of dose (radiation) versus effect. The biological effects of the new neutron radiation had to be compared with those of the well-known alpha, beta, and gamma radiations from radium and with X-rays. Gray, now supported by John Read, planned and built, with support from the British Empire Cancer Campaign, a 400 kV neutron generator. This inexpensive but efficient machine yielded the first quantitative results demonstrating the increased biological effectiveness for cellular damage of neutrons compared with X-rays. In this work Gray and Read expressed their neutron dose values in energy units—foreshadowing the adoption by the International Commission on Radiological Units some fifteen years later (1953) of the unit 'rad' for measuring all types of ionizing radiation. (In 1975 the commission, through the International System of Units, redefined the physical unit of dose as the Gray (=100 rad) in resolution 9 of the fifteenth Conférence Générale Poids et Mesures.

Gray, a conscientious objector, remained throughout the Second World War at Mount Vernon. After the war, in 1946, he was recruited by the secretary of the Medical Research Council, Sir Edward Mellanby, to head the laboratory side of the radiotherapeutic unit in the Hammersmith Hospital, which had been expanded to encompass the advances made possible by nuclear fission. Gray collected about him a team which in five years made dramatic discoveries in the basic science of radiobiology; but differences of opinion on the strategy of the research between him and his medical director (and the Medical Research Council) led to his resignation in 1953. To Gray, who was emotionally wholly committed to the relief of cancer by radiotherapy and, now from his own theoretical deductions and limited observations, to fuller investigation of the role of oxygen in radiobiological effect, this was a grievous time. However, within a few months the British Empire Cancer Campaign established for Gray, as director, their own research unit in radiobiology at Mount Vernon Hospital. Time had been lost, but Gray, as able as a theoretician as with his hands, competent administratively and universally respected, reorganized his life and work. In due course he collected around him many of his former colleagues and a succession of new ones to found a school of international repute. Unhappily for science, within ten years he suffered a severe stroke which left him physically disabled. Gray, undismayed, returned to work, but perhaps did too much, for within two years he had a second stroke and died at his home, 5 St Mary's Avenue, Northwood, on 9 July 1965. His ashes were taken to the family vault in Alderney, an island where he was proud to have roots and to which he returned each year. One of his favourite methods of relaxation was to lie on his back in the water and look up at the colours of the cliffs in Telegraph Bay, which he thought the most beautiful place in the world. He was survived by his wife.

Many awards and honours were conferred on Gray. He was elected a fellow of the Royal Society in 1961 and made an honorary DSc of Leeds University in 1962 and an honorary member of the American Radium Society. He received the Barclay medal of the British Institute of Radiology in 1960, and the Bertner award in 1964. In 1953 he was Silvanus Thompson memorial lecturer at the British Institute of Radiology. He is commemorated by periodic L. H. Gray memorial conferences. Nothing could be more apt, for Gray above all loved people and scientific discussion. His enthusiasm was as infectious as his laughter, and his contacts were worldwide. Himself always sincere and never bigoted, he remained to the end at times naïve and unworldly. In the two decades between 1945 and 1965 he was a member of numerous national and international committees, and president of the International Congress of Radiation Research, 1962. Perhaps he was even more at home in learned societies, great and small—the Royal Society, the British Institute of Radiology (of which he was president in 1950), the Hospital Physicists' Association (of which he was chairman, 1946–7), and the multidisciplinary Association for Radiation Research, of which he was the founder and first chairman (1959–60).

J. F. LOUTIT, rev.

Sources J. F. Loutit and O. C. A. Scott, *Memoirs FRS*, 12 (1966), 195–217 · *International Journal of Radiation Biology*, 9 (1965), 509–11 · *British Journal of Radiology*, 38 (1965), 706–7 · personal knowledge (1981) · private information (1981) · *WWW* · *The Times* (13 July 1965) · d. cert. · *CGPLA Eng. & Wales* (1965)
Archives Bodl. Oxf., corresp. with C. A. Coulson and draft of Coulson's memorial tribute to Gray
Wealth at death £7737: probate, 1 Oct 1965, *CGPLA Eng. & Wales*

Maria Emma Gray (1787–1876), by George J. Stodart (after John Ayling)

Gray, Maria Emma (1787–1876), conchologist and algologist, was born at the Royal Naval Hospital, Greenwich, Kent, the daughter of Lieutenant Henry Smith RN, who was then resident there. In 1812 she married Francis Edward Gray, who died two years later; they had two daughters. In 1826 she married her late husband's second cousin, John Edward *Gray (1800–1875), a zoologist at the British Museum.

Mrs Gray greatly assisted her husband in his scientific work, especially by her drawings. Between 1842 and 1874 she published privately five volumes of etchings, entitled *Figures of Molluscan Animals for the Use of Students*, and she mounted and arranged most of the Cuming collection of shells in the British Museum. She also undertook the study of algae, and arranged many sets for presentation to schools throughout the country so as to encourage the pursuit of this subject. Her own collection was bequeathed to the Cambridge University Museum, and her assistance in this branch of his studies was commemorated by her husband in 1866 in the genus *Grayemma*. He also had a bronze medallion struck in 1863, bearing both their portraits. Mrs Gray survived her husband by a year, and died at her home, 43 Russell Square, London, on 9 December 1876.   G. S. BOULGER, *rev.* P. E. KELL

Sources J. E. Gray, 'On anadyomene and microdictyon', *Journal of Botany, British and Foreign*, 4 (1866), 41–51, esp. 45 · 'Botanical news', *Journal of Botany*, 6 (1877), 32 · S. O. Gray, *British sea-weeds* (1867), viii–ix · *Gardeners' Chronicle*, new ser., 6 (1876), 789 · A. Crawford and others, eds., *The Europa biographical dictionary of British women* (1983), 176 · *The Athenaeum* (16 Dec 1876), 804–5
Archives U. Cam., herbarium, algae collection
Likenesses G. G. Adams, bronze medallion, 1863, Linn. Soc., NPG · G. J. Stodart, stipple (after J. Ayling), BM, NPG [*see illus.*]
Wealth at death under £7000: probate, 22 Dec 1876, *CGPLA Eng. & Wales*

Gray, Maurice Charles Harrison- (1899–1968), bridge player and writer, was born Maurice Charles Gray on 13 November 1899 at Ingatestone, Essex, the son of Oswald Harrison Gray, maltster and fellmonger, and his wife, Gloria Gladwin, *née* Terry. He later adopted the surname Harrison-Gray. After attending Haileybury College (1914–18) he joined his family's brewing business in East Anglia and when this was taken over he turned to writing short stories. He also began writing about bridge and this proved so successful that it became his full-time occupation. On 1 January 1938 he married Stella Sonia Soltz; there were no children. During the Second World War he served as a flight lieutenant in the Royal Air Force.

Maurice Harrison-Gray, or Gray as he was known by all, including his wife, was widely regarded as the finest all-round bridge player of his day. Yet it was only a series of sporting accidents—his youth was dominated by participation in dangerous pursuits such as motor cycle scrambling—that led him to the card table, relatively late, in his early thirties. Within three years he had graduated from the sixpenny game at a Kensington club to become perhaps the dominant player in Britain. Reflecting on Harrison-Gray's long career, Victor Mollo observed: 'If it was true then that no novice had matured so quickly, it is no less true today that no veteran has stayed young so long' (Mollo, 79). Indeed, he enjoyed some of his greatest successes when in his sixties.

Harrison-Gray was a founder member of the famous Acol team, which gave its name to the main bridge bidding system still in use nearly seventy years after its conception. Acol was invented in the 1930s by Gray and his compatriots Jack 'Grandfather' Marx and S. J. 'Skid' Simon, among others. It was a response to the dominance over the game of the American bidding system, although Acol itself is not so much a system, more a way of life. As fellow 'Acolyte' Iain Macleod wrote in his classic *Bridge is an Easy Game*: 'It is infinitely flexible, and a hopeless system for the unimaginative' (Macleod, 11–12). To Victor Mollo the essence of Acol was to 'think a move ahead and do "what comes naturally"', and in his opinion nobody did as much 'to develop and to perfect it, and to popularize it' as Harrison-Gray (Mollo, 80).

Harrison-Gray was renowned for being a bridge machine, totally dependable and steady, a strategist, a natural leader. He captained the Acol team to unprecedented success in British bridge and he was the first player to reach the rank of life master in England. Arguably his greatest success was as the playing captain of the Great Britain team that won the European championships three years in a row—in 1948, 1949, and 1950. He was also a member of the winning team in 1963 and competed in the championships of 1939, 1958, and 1966. He represented Great Britain in the world championships in 1950 and 1965, and in the pairs Olympiad in 1962 and the team Olympiad in 1964. Gray's basic philosophy at the bridge table was to avoid mistakes—to play 'par bridge'. As Paul Stern put it: 'To win an international tournament, you do not need four bridge-players; you need four oxes who can sit there all day and just play cards which are not horse-cards' (Ramsey, 44).

To see Gray at the table was to see a tall, upright body, flushed cheeks under deep-set eyes, spotless, heavy hands meticulously flipping card after card from between two fingers, the bald head, crammed with bridge lore, gleaming. But Gray was a nervous man, especially before a big match, when he was like an actor before a performance. And he did not react well when his performance was criticized: he needed at least a night's sleep before he would admit his folly. Gray's nervous disposition rendered pre-match sleep hard to come by. He had been told that watching tropical fish aided sleep, so he invested in some tropical moths, and then proceeded to breed and rear them with such an enthusiasm that it almost rivalled his passion for bridge. Moths and bridge players are both nocturnal creatures, but he never mixed the two lives. And since neither entomology nor bridge playing created order, it fell to Stella, Gray's Russian wife, to pick up the pieces. Small and pale, with an Egyptian profile, she was totally loyal to Gray and his eccentric friends, and their Hampstead cottage was regularly the venue for lunch at 2.45 in the afternoon, or supper at two in the morning.

Gray derived his income principally from his bridge writing, and it is for this that he is remembered. He was the bridge correspondent of the *Evening Standard* and contributed also to the *European Bridge Review* and *Bridge World*, but it was for a weekly column in *Country Life* that he was most famous. After his death Jack Marx explained why this column enjoyed such enduring popularity: 'He concerned himself with the human aspects of the game as well as its technicalities and had a flair for weaving a thread of instruction into the articles' (Brock, 184). Gray wrote with humour and elegance and caught exactly the character of friends such as 'Skid' Simon, about whom he wrote a moving obituary:

> He crossed the busiest street, nose buried in a book. He dismounted from buses travelling at full speed, nose still buried in a book. Dishevelled, but with an exotic taste in ties and sportswear; disgraceful, but with a world of grace in the turn of phrase … he was the greatest character to adorn the bridge world. (ibid., 183)

The same could be said of Gray, who died of heart failure at his home, 14a Lancaster Grove, Hampstead, on 24 November 1968. His untimely death deprived British bridge of one of its great figures. He served as a delegate on the council of the English bridge union for many years and was a member of the selection committee. And he won the gold cup of British bridge in 1937, 1947, 1949, and 1962, before crowning a remarkable career with three successive wins in 1966, 1967, and 1968. At the time of his death he was entered for the trials to choose the British team for 1969. He often partnered the younger players at the trials and was 'outstanding in the help and encouragement' he gave to those starting in the game (*The Times*, 25 Nov 1968).   ANDREW ROBSON

Sources *The Times* (25 Nov 1968) • V. Mollo, *The bridge immortals* (1967) • *Haileybury and Imperial Service College Register, 1862–1994*, The Haileybury Society, 2 (1996) • G. Ramsey, *Aces all* (1955) • I. Macleod, *Bridge is an easy game* (1980) • R. Brock, *The best of Gray: the Country Life book of bridge revisited* (1999) • b. cert. • d. cert. • m. cert.

Gray, Milner Connorton (1899–1997), artist and designer, was born on 8 October 1899 in Blackheath, London, the second son and the second of the five children of Archibald Campbell Gray (d. 1944?), a member of the Baltic exchange, and of his wife, Katherine May, *née* Hart, of Eynsford, Kent.

Gray was educated privately and at Colfe's Grammar School, Lewisham, but his frequent absences from school, caused by the weak health that he always claimed to enjoy, resulted in a lack of formal educational qualifications. In 1916 he began studying painting and design at Goldsmiths' College, London University, but his studies were interrupted the following year when he was called up to the 19th London regiment. Saved by his health from a posting to France, he was sent instead to the Royal Engineers' School of Camouflage.

Gray returned to Goldsmiths' in 1919 for two years. On leaving, he established—with fellow students Charles Bassett and his brother Henry—the Bassett–Gray Group of Artists and Writers, effectively the first British multidisciplinary design consultancy. The group's complement of freelance creators included Gray's lifelong friend Graham Sutherland and, later, Misha Black. Commissions, particularly for exhibition work, came initially from advertising agencies; Gray himself began designing textiles, china, and packaging.

During this period Gray began work on what he came to regard as his lifetime's achievement: the formation of a representative association aimed at raising the designer's status to that of a recognized profession. The Society of Industrial Artists (SIA) was formally established in 1930, with Gray as its honorary secretary from 1932 to 1940.

In 1935 the Bassett–Gray Group was reorganized as the Industrial Design Partnership, with Misha Black a partner. Gray's work included mural designs and decorative features for Kardomah Cafes (1936–40) and exhibits in the Modern Architectural Research (MARS) Group show of modern architecture (London, 1938) and the British pavilion at the New York World Fair (1939). At the same time he taught at Goldsmiths' College; Chelsea School of Art; and the Reimann School of Art and Design. From 1937 to 1940 he was principal of the Sir John Cass School of Arts and Crafts and on the visiting staff of the Royal College of Art from 1939 to 1940.

On 12 July 1934 Gray married Gnade Grace Osborne-Pratt (b. 1913). They lived first at Meadow Cottage, Eynsford (close to the Sutherlands), but soon moved to Hampstead as Gray's teaching and voluntary SIA activities required increasing evening work. In 1939 they purchased 8 Holly Mount, London NW3, which became their principal London residence for the next fifty-four years. In 1953 they also acquired Felix Hall, Kelvedon, the ruins of an imposing Palladian mansion in Essex which they converted into a comfortable country home. There were no children of the marriage.

Gray's growing professional stature was recognized in 1938 by his election as a royal designer for industry (RDI).

However, on the outbreak of the Second World War the Industrial Design Partnership was disbanded. Gray himself was chosen by Frank Pick, director-general, to head the Ministry of Information's exhibitions branch. Here, between 1940 and 1944, he was able to use his pre-war experience to recruit a team of talented artists and craftsmen to work on a series of information and propaganda exhibitions. Many of these used innovative techniques to present such government messages as 'London pride', 'Dig for victory', and 'America marches', attracting large numbers of visitors. One of Gray's tasks was to draw the royal coat of arms for the ministry's displays, the first of several similar commissions.

As peace approached, Gray's thoughts turned to the opportunities for designers in the post-war world and in 1945 he became a founder partner in the Design Research Unit (DRU), the aim of which was to present 'a service so complete that it could undertake any design case which might confront the State, Municipal Authorities, Industry or Commerce' (Blake, 32). Among early projects were two influential exhibitions, including 'Britain Can Make It' at the Victoria and Albert Museum, London, 1946, but the practice soon began its ground-breaking work in a field which became a dominating factor in commerce over the next four decades: corporate identity.

This involved establishing a co-ordinated visual style across the full range of items, from printed material to vehicles, by which a company presented itself to the world. Beginning in 1946 with the Rolex Watch Company and with Ilford Ltd (where the connection lasted for twenty years), DRU built up a reputation for high standards and a client list of prestigious British companies. The most influential, in both the design and commercial fields, was probably the company's work for British Rail (1963). From 1957 to 1960 Gray was also responsible for co-ordinating the design of the public areas in the P. & O. Orient liner *Oriana*.

The Festival of Britain (1951) provided many opportunities for Britain's designers. Gray was jointly responsible, with Robin Day, for the South Bank signposting; he also designed the royal coat of arms engraved on the glass screen at the entrance to the royal box in the Royal Festival Hall. He was subsequently invited to render the royal arms, crown, and cipher for the queen's coronation decorations and souvenirs (1952–3) for the Council of Industrial Design, which led to a long association with the council. He joined the Royal Mint advisory committee in 1952 and in 1961 was appointed design consultant to the mint for coin inscriptions and coin and medal packaging. In the heraldic field Gray produced armorial bearings for the Post Office in 1970; a badge for the Balmoral Estate Ranger Service in 1972; and, in 1976, the official emblem (for street decorations and souvenirs) for the queen's silver jubilee, receiving the queen's silver jubilee medal in 1977.

From its foundation, Gray was continuously involved in the development of the SIA. He was president from 1943 to 1949 and, for forty years after the war, served on a variety of committees to formulate policy for the society (which became the Society of Industrial Artists and Designers in 1963) in the fields of education and professional practice. He was elected president for the second time in 1966–7, and from 1973 to 1976 supervised the work that led to the society's receiving a royal charter. Gray had been the first recipient of the society's medal, in 1955, and in the royal charter year (1976) the society's annual design oration was renamed the Milner Gray lecture. In 1979, to honour Gray's contribution to his profession, and to mark his eightieth birthday, the society presented him with his portrait painted by Graham Sutherland (subsequently donated by his widow to the National Portrait Gallery, London).

Gray also found time for other professional associations: he was master of the Faculty of Royal Designers for Industry and vice-president of the Royal Society of Arts in 1955–7; master of the Artworkers' Guild in 1963; and British president of the Alliance Graphique Internationale from 1963 to 1971. He published numerous articles on various aspects of design; his books include *Package Design* (1955) and (jointly with Ronald Armstrong) *Lettering for Architects and Designers* (1962). His achievements were recognized publicly by his appointment as CBE in 1963. In 1979 he was awarded an honorary doctorate by the Royal College of Art.

In his professional life Gray did much to set the standards for designers for most of the twentieth century. His own designs—which embraced, from the early 1930s, bottles, cookware, table china, furniture, and even the Ascot gold cup, as well as graphics, exhibition design, and packaging—were always immaculate, combining craftsmanship and deep respect for materials. In a field of generally ephemeral work, he was probably right to claim the establishment of the SIA (now the Chartered Society of Designers) as his most lasting achievement. On a personal level he was a delightful companion, with an irreverent wit, and a formidable mimic. His sense of fun made him an immensely popular member of the Arts Club, unfailingly courteous and always a generous host.

Gray continued to 'enjoy weak health' until he died, aged ninety-seven, at Felix Hall on 29 September 1997. At his own wish, he was cremated (a week later on 6 October, at Colchester) without ceremony or witnesses, apart from his wife who had been his unfailing support in life and work for sixty-three years.   GEOFFREY V. ADAMS

Sources A. Blake, *Milner Gray* (1986) · J. Blake and A. Blake, *The practical idealists* (1969) · R. Negus, *The Independent* (8 Oct 1997) · J. Holland, *Minerva at fifty* (1980) · personal knowledge (2004) · *CGPLA Eng. & Wales* (1997) · private information (2004) [Gnade Grace Gray, wife]
Archives Chartered Society of Designers, London, MSS, papers and printed materials · V&A NAL, artworks, MSS, and papers | RSA, Faculty of Royal Designers for Industry records | SOUND Chartered Society of Designers, London, collection of taped interviews with leading members
Likenesses photograph, 1930, Chartered Society of Designers, collection of past presidents · photographs, 1930–79, repro. in Blake, *Milner Gray* · G. Sutherland, oils, 1979, NPG
Wealth at death £661,222: probate, 13 Nov 1997, *CGPLA Eng. & Wales*

Gray [*née* Binyon], **Nicolete Mary** (1911–1997), historian of lettering, letter carver, and art critic, was born on 20 July 1911 at Stevenage, Hertfordshire, the last of three children of Laurence *Binyon (1869–1943), poet, art critic, and scholar, and his wife, Cicely Margaret (1876–1962), daughter of Henry Pryor Powell, a banker of Ockley, Surrey. Quakers and bankers featured among the ancestors of both Nicolete's parents, although neither brought to the marriage any major inheritance. Their chief wealth was intellectual: both wrote and translated, Laurence Binyon publishing his first book of poems while an undergraduate at Oxford and becoming renowned as 'the scholar poet of the British Museum', where he worked as the head of oriental prints, drawings, and paintings and where the family had an official residence. Through him Nicolete, whose godfather was Sir Henry Newbolt, met many leading writers, artists, and scholars of the period. At fourteen she began studying the Italian and German drawings in the British Museum print room, her father making lists of what she should see. She also accompanied him on visits to art galleries, in this way becoming familiar with a learned, historical, and aesthetic approach to artefacts. Her intelligence gained her a scholarship to St Paul's Girls' School, London, and another to Lady Margaret Hall, Oxford, where between 1929 and 1932 she read history, specializing in the medieval period, with St Augustine as her special subject. Drawn to the Roman Catholic faith, she chose Father D'Arcy as her mentor, and placed herself under his instruction. At her parents' request she waited a year before entering the Catholic church but never doubted that it was the most important event in her life— one which, as she once said, 'has coloured and conditioned everything that has happened since' (Gray, 8).

After leaving Oxford Nicolete Binyon went on a scholarship to the British School at Rome, and travelled Italy, studying medieval inscriptions. In 1948 she published 'Paleography of Latin inscriptions in the eighth, ninth and tenth centuries in Italy' in *Papers of the British School at Rome*. The reason for its delay was her marriage, in 1933, to Basil *Gray (1904–1989), followed by the birth of five children— two sons and three daughters—between 1934 and 1943. Having first worked in the same department as Nicolete's father, Basil Gray was made head of the department of oriental antiquities, in which post he remained for more than thirty years. In 1961 he and his family moved into the official museum residence, where Nicolete had passed her childhood. Throughout this period family life left her unable to consider full-time employment, yet anxious to make use of her education and abilities.

A solution was initially found in writing art criticism for *Life and Letters*. Nicolete Gray's interest in art went back to her schooldays. She had not only siphoned off money from her dress allowance to buy a Paul Nash watercolour, an Eric Gill drawing, and some prints but had also founded an art society that made visits to the Tate Gallery. There, while certain of her friends laughed aloud at the work of Van Gogh, she did not. She already possessed a drawing by Barbara Hepworth, given to her by George

Nicolete Mary Gray (1911–1997), by Colin Hardie, *c*.1940

Hill, keeper of coins at the British Museum, who persuaded Laurence Binyon to engage Hepworth's husband, John Skeaping, to carve Nicolete's portrait. Her familiarity with art was further enriched by her father's pioneering articles and books on English art, while his interest in Chinese, Japanese, Indian, and Persian art helped to free her from the conventional artistic prejudices of the day. It was, however, her friendship with Helen Sutherland that fostered her incipient interest in contemporary art. She first visited Helen at her home, Rock Hall, in Northumberland, in the summer of 1929, shortly before she went up to Oxford.

Helen Sutherland's 'family' of artists had developed in the wake of her failed marriage and an absence of children, aided in part by her inherited wealth. She received encouragement from Freddy Mayor, of the Mayor Gallery, London, and initially began buying a wide array of work; but after an introduction to Ben and Winifred Nicholson, in November 1925, rapidly developed into a warm friendship she acquired work mostly by artists whom she knew. Her aesthetic interests closely paralleled those of H. S. (Jim) Ede, the Tate curator and, later, the creator of Kettle's Yard, Cambridge, with whom she corresponded and who introduced her to David Jones, another of her key artists. Like Ede she merged her passion for art and literature with her religious beliefs into a way of life—high-minded, spiritual, and slightly austere—first at Rock Hall and later at Cockley Moor, Cumberland, where she offered creative refuge to her artist and writer friends during the summer months. Nicolete Gray's understanding, scholarship, religious outlook, and enthusiasm for contemporary art made a strong bond between the two women, and in time she inherited the greater part of her friend's collection. Helen Sutherland's example lies behind Nicolete Gray's remark, in an essay on bringing up children for Elizabeth Pakenham's *Catholic Approaches* (1955), on the need 'to make some sort of rhythm out of our day, and to make the material things which surround us echo spiritual things by their order and beauty' (p. 126).

In the mid-1930s, though England began to emerge from a period of blinkered parochialism and became more open to art from abroad, most avant-garde painters and sculptors had difficulty in making a living—even Hepworth at one point had to expend her energies on making masks for Elizabeth Arden's beauty salon. Nicolete Gray devised a scheme whereby artists lent her work so that in her own home, at 12 York Gate, Regent's Park, she could promote an up-to-date selection of contemporary art. In 1935 she wrote about abstract art in *Oxford Outlook*; then, aged twenty-five, she went on to mount the exhibition 'Abstract and concrete' in 1936. It was the first international showing of non-representational art in Britain, containing work by sixteen different artists from nine different countries. Nicolete Gray was convinced of two things: that the abstract movement crossed national boundaries and that it was the most significant art movement in modern Europe. Yet when an evaluation of the exhibits was sought Christies was prepared to testify, for the purposes of customs and insurance, that they were almost worthless in monetary terms. Two paintings by Mondrian were sold, each for about £50, Helen Sutherland acquiring one (now in the Tate collection) and Nicolete Gray the other. The show opened in Oxford (at the Oxford Art Club in St Giles'), went on tour to London, Liverpool, and Cambridge, and received a mixed press, the *Daily Mail* dismissing it as 'a jolly leg pull'.

In the following year Basil Gray published *The English Print*, a book which, as he privately acknowledged, had been partly written by his wife. For the chapter on nineteenth-century commercial print Nicolete Gray had gone to the St Bride Printing Library, where she found specimen books of type arranged chronologically by each founder. They showed the advent of numerous and often delightfully fantastic designs, and prompted her groundbreaking study, *XIXth Century Ornamented Types and Titles* (1938), later revised and enlarged under the title *Nineteenth Century Ornamented Typefaces* (1976). She praised their robustness and ingenuity, and in this way obliged calligraphers, typographers, and designers to reassess their views on many aspects of Roman letterforms. The richness of nineteenth-century display types had already caught the attention of John Betjeman, John Piper, and John Harling as a form of popular art but Nicolete Gray was the first to make a serious study of them. Thus at the same time that she was extolling high modernism she was also at work on a pioneering study of Victoriana. It is thought that the subsequent revival of nineteenth-century typefaces at the Festival of Britain in 1951 owed much to her advocacy.

Evacuated to Oxford during the first part of the war, Nicolete Gray shouldered responsibilities for the Ministry of Food until 1943, when the family returned to London. However, the strain of looking after five children under ten, with limited help, contributed to her physical breakdown in 1947. Nevertheless she had found the energy, in 1944, to write a short study, *Dante, Rossetti and ourselves*, (published in 1947), which blended her thinking on contemporary art and literature with her knowledge of the middle ages and the Victorian period. Her need to share and communicate her interests led her to take up parttime teaching in the late 1940s at convent schools in London, and to compile *Jacob's Ladder*, in which illustrations chosen from Anglo-Saxon and later medieval manuscripts were combined with scriptural narratives to create a Bible picture book for children. Later it became the basis for a series of filmstrips to be used in schools as an aid to the teaching of religion.

It was not until 1952 that Nicolete Gray was able to undertake a major project. She accepted an invitation to write a series of articles for the *Architectural Review*, which she later published as *Lettering on Buildings* (1960). It opened up the subject of architectural lettering by arguing that the design, shape, and spacing should be in sympathy with their architectural setting. Subsequently lettering became her main interest. She joined the staff at the Central School of Arts and Crafts (from 1966 to 1989 the Central School of Art and Design; now Central St Martin's College of Art and Design), where she taught part-time between 1964 and 1981, producing a handbook for students, *Lettering as Drawing* (1970). She also assisted her colleague Nicholas Biddulph in creating the Central Lettering Record; mainly a photographic archive, this is held at Central St Martin's College of Art and Design. On trips with her husband around Britain and abroad, including Islamic and Eastern trips, she took many photographs for the record of lettering in streets, museums, churches, and mosques. She also organized lettering exhibitions, acted as external examiner in typography and graphic design at Reading University, and lobbied persistently against shoddy, ill-formed lettering. She was, however, opposed to slavish use of the pattern book, and in the 1960s and 1970s favoured a modern joined-up cursive script that she argued well suited the biro. She was pleased to be elected the first woman member of the Double Crown Club, the inner circle of typographers, and she became an active member of the Association Typographique Internationale. She also practised what she preached: from the 1950s onwards, after taking a short course in Hammersmith, she regularly undertook lettering commissions. Her carvings include Agatha Christie's tombstone and a relief, in five different woods, that fills an entire wall at the Shakespeare Centre at Stratford with the names of Shakespeare and his contemporary playwrights, the style and size of the lettering adjusted to convey the character and stature of each author. She also undertook three inscriptions for Westminster Cathedral, the boldest and most imaginative of which is executed in mosaic and fills the arch over the north-west door.

After Basil Gray's retirement he and Nicolete moved to Long Wittenham, in Berkshire, where Helen Sutherland's pictures mingled with their own. Here Nicolete Gray wrote her last three books. She returned to the contemporary art of her youth by writing two books on her lifelong friend David Jones: one on his inscriptions (1981), celebrating his free interpretation of letter forms ('midway between poetry and painting') and the other on his paintings (1988), which, in addition to a personal appreciation, gave a succinct analysis of his development and the influence of his religious, literary, and historical interests on his subject matter. Her last lettering book was *A History of Lettering* (1986), which upheld her earlier conclusion that the dominance of Trajan's column as a source for imperial Roman capitals had detracted from other viable models. It also reflects her great love of medieval lettering, to which she devoted six of the fourteen chapters, and contains many original insights into this period. She encouraged her daughter Camilla to write her landmark study of twentieth-century Russian art, *The Great Experiment*. Of all her children she was closest to Camilla, whose untimely death in 1971 brought out in Nicolete an acceptance inspired by her faith. A similar approach governed her attitude to her last years, when she was undermined by a progressive loss of memory and disorientation. She died in the Westminster Hospital, Chelsea, on 8 June 1997 and was buried in Long Wittenham church.

In the course of her life Nicolete Gray wrote extensively on art, lettering, and religion in articles and reviews, and also lectured fairly widely. She regretted the element of kitsch that had infiltrated the devotional images used by the Catholic church, arguing that this was in direct contrast with its artistic achievement in the past and with its teaching that one should offer one's best to God. She herself had arrived at an aesthetic creed at the early age of twenty-four while promoting her scheme to find patrons for avant-garde artists. 'I am interested', she wrote in an open letter to the principal of Lady Margaret Hall, 'in everything that seems to me to be a true expression of a real feeling or a true statement of a real thing' (copy of letter, Tate collection, archives). This search for integrity and truth, which began as a youthful ideal, remained the directive behind her entire life.   FRANCES SPALDING

Sources M. Twyman, 'Nicolete Gray: a personal view of her contribution to the study of letterforms', *Typography Papers*, 3 (1998), 87–102 • F. Spalding, '"A true statement of a real thing": Nicolete Gray's promotion of modern art', *Typography Papers*, 3 (1998), 103–14 • priv. coll., Edmund Gray collection • N. Gray, 'Lettering became my subject', *Brown Book* (1987) • *CGPLA Eng. & Wales* (1998) • private information (2004) [Edmund Gray, son]
Archives Tate collection
Likenesses C. Hardie, photograph, *c*.1940, priv. coll. [*see illus.*] • photograph, repro. in *The Times* (13 June 1997) • photograph, repro. in *Daily Telegraph* (16 June 1997)
Wealth at death £6,070,701: probate, 2 Jan 1998, *CGPLA Eng. & Wales*

Gray, Norah Neilson (1882–1931). *See under* Glasgow Girls (*act.* 1880–1920).

Gray, Patrick, **fourth Lord Gray** (1515×20–1584), nobleman, was the eldest son of Gilbert Gray of Buttergask (*d.* 1541), and his wife, Egidia, daughter of Sir Laurence Mercer of Aldie. He came of a family which claimed kinship with the Grey family of Chillingham in Northumberland. Settled at Broxmouth, Roxburghshire, in the early fourteenth century, the Scottish Grays afterwards had their principal seat at Castle Huntly, Forfarshire (Angus), and it was there that the third Lord Gray died in April 1541, leaving no son to succeed him. In 1524, however, the estate had been entailed in favour of his half-brother Gilbert Gray of Buttergask (the father of both men was Andrew Gray, second Lord Gray). This grant had become null under James V's act of revocation of 1537, and it was only in 1542, after negotiation and delay, and following a promise to pay 10,000 merks to the treasurer, that Patrick Gray of Buttergask received charter to the Gray estates as heir of tailzie to the third lord. Further, he received the hereditary office of sheriff of Forfar, an annual rent out of the customs of Dundee, and custody of Broughty Castle. By the terms of a contract dated 21 September 1537 Gray had married Marione, daughter of James Ogilvie, fourth Lord Ogilvie of Airlie. They had fifteen children, six sons and nine daughters. Their eldest son and two of their daughters married or contracted to marry members of the Ruthven family, presumably as part of efforts to settle differences between their father and the Ruthvens.

In November 1542 Gray accompanied the Scottish army to Solway Moss, where he was taken prisoner. He was sent to Newcastle under the guardianship of Walter Strickland, but was back in Carlisle in January 1544 awaiting a pledge for his release. He received the gift of £100 from Henry VIII for his assurance, and upon payment of a ransom of £500 he was sent home on the understanding that he would dedicate himself to Henry VIII's cause. Gray attended the parliament of March 1543 which approved the vernacular Bible and the marriage treaty between Prince Edward of England and Queen Mary of Scotland.

Shortly after the governor Arran's reversal of this policy in September of 1543, Gray (along with others who were thought to have favoured protestantism and who opposed Cardinal Beaton) was arrested by the cardinal and imprisoned in Blackness. With the arrival of the earl of Hertford's army in Scotland in May 1544, however, he was released and was brought over to support of the cardinal's party and policies, being inveigled into a plan to wrest the town of Perth from the control of Lord Ruthven, a supporter of the queen mother, Mary of Guise. To counteract Ruthven's influence Beaton planned to intrude his own candidate as provost of Perth. To provide the required coercion, Gray was induced to take part in a raid on the town, where his small force was trapped by the master of Ruthven and the townsmen, and suffered considerable loss of life.

Despite the failure of the raid, Beaton continued to court Gray's support with a grant of part of the lands of Rescobie, Forfarshire, but Gray 'only hoped to benefit personally' (Sanderson, 192) by helping the cardinal, and after one or two appearances on the privy council towards the end of 1546 he turned his attention to the more generous largesse of the English king. In March 1547 he signed special and separate articles promising to do all he could to promote the marriage of Prince Edward to the Scottish queen. In the following month Gray further pledged himself to the English cause, promising to turn over his castle at Broughty Crag to the English. On the arrival of the English fleet in the Firth of Tay in September 1547, Broughty Castle was delivered to the English, Gray receiving a gift of money in exchange for its surrender.

Gray was subsequently employed by the English, becoming 'an active agent in the policy of Somerset' (A. I. Cameron, 277n.), and being given responsibility for attempts to bribe the earl of Argyll into joining the English cause. Gray did arrange a conference between English agents and Argyll at Coupar Angus Abbey, but it brought him trouble with the English when Argyll cast doubt on Gray's taking English money and forced him to defend himself to his paymasters.

Argyll was not in fact far off the mark. Gray did indeed offer his services to Mary of Guise at this same time. She wrote to thank him for his band of service and to send a small pension, pending something more substantial. Gray remained in the role of 'double agent' until November 1548. In the following month he received a summons for treason and a demand for the delivery of his house at Castle Huntly, which probably lay behind his request for English protection for his property, friends, and servants, all of whom, so he claimed in a letter to Sir John Lutterall at Broughty Castle, had been made the object of spoliation and harassment. Eventually he was arrested in Edinburgh where the French advisers of Mary of Guise sought his execution. However, the Scots lords would not hear of such an act. Gray was granted a precept of remission in August 1549, but despite this was handed over to the French ambassadors and was warded once more in the castle at Blackness. His wife Marione wrote to Mary of Guise seeking Gray's release in November 1550, but no response is recorded. Gray was still in Blackness in July 1552 but according to a treasurer's account was at large again in June 1554.

Gray was once more taken prisoner by the English in the raid of Swinton in 1558 but was free on bond by December 1559, and had joined the reforming lords showing 'all the signs of attachment to the Reformation' (Donaldson, 44). Yet in May 1560 he received a letter from the queen regent, thanking him for his pledge of support to herself and her daughter, and in the following October he received a similar missive from Queen Mary herself, urging his continued loyalty and good service. Meanwhile he attended the parliament of August 1560, giving his assent to the various articles but leaving without signing the contract with England.

In April 1561 Gray was called to make entry into ward in England for payment of his ransom as negotiated in 1558 or 1559, and it was only with the help of a letter and intervention by Queen Mary in July 1562 that a suitable bond was negotiated.

Gray did not take any prominent part in the Darnley and Bothwell episodes of Queen Mary's reign, but he did join the other lords to seek revenge for Darnley's murder. He sat on the privy council with some regularity between 1565 and 1575 and attended the first parliament of the regent Moray after the queen's abdication. He voted for the queen's divorce from Bothwell in 1569. Latterly he came round to support Queen Mary and in 1570 signed a letter asking for help from Queen Elizabeth.

When the estates met for the election of a regent after the death of the earl of Mar on 28 October 1572, Gray joined the earl of Atholl in sending a letter asking that the election be delayed, but no attention was paid to their request. Gray gave in his submission to Morton after the pacification of Perth (23 February 1573), but in his later years he came into conflict with the authorities over the administration of his estates. When Morton resigned the regency in 1578, Gray was by then a staunch supporter of King James, and was one of the council-extraordinary chosen to assist the king. By this time, however, his son, the master of Gray, was taking his father's place at council meetings. The latter's testament is dated 18 August 1581, and in 1583 the fourth lord was described as being 'an aged man … of no great power or frendes' (*Bannatyne Miscellany*, 1/1, 64)—a sad comment, but probably a truthful one, on the fruits of a life of exceptional improbity and double-dealing. He died in the following year, probably of old age, and was succeeded by his eldest son Patrick, who became fifth Lord Gray. MARY BLACK VERSCHUUR

Sources *CSP Scot., 1547–63* • J. Bain, ed., *The Hamilton papers: letters and papers illustrating the political relations of England and Scotland in the XVIth century*, 2, Scottish RO, 12 (1892) • *LP Henry VIII*, vols. 17–18 • *CSP for., 1561–2* • *The Scottish correspondence of Mary of Lorraine*, ed. A. I. Cameron, Scottish History Society, 3rd ser., 10 (1927) • J. M. Thomson and others, eds., *Registrum magni sigilli regum Scotorum / The register of the great seal of Scotland*, 11 vols. (1882–1914), vols. 3–4 • *Reg. PCS*, 1st ser., vol. 1 • *Scots peerage*, 4.280–81 • J. Cameron, *James V: the personal rule, 1528–1542*, ed. N. Macdougall (1998) • M. H. B. Sanderson, *Cardinal of Scotland: David Beaton, c.1494–1546* (1986) • G. Donaldson, *All the queen's men* (1983) • 'An opinion of the present state, faction, religion, and power of the nobility of Scotland, 1583', *The Bannatyne miscellany*, ed. W. Scott and D. Laing, 1/1, Bannatyne Club, 19 (1827), 64 • *DNB* [references to the Gray inventory and Perth retours, now in NA Scot.] • NA Scot., Gray inventory, 2.443, 513

Gray, Patrick, sixth Lord Gray (*c*.1558–1611), nobleman and courtier, was the eldest son of Patrick Gray, fifth Lord Gray (1538–1608), and Barbara (*d*. in or after 1594), daughter of William Ruthven, Lord Ruthven; Patrick *Gray, fourth Lord Gray (1515x20–1584), was his grandfather. He was educated at St Andrews University, where he allegedly 'professed the true religion and communicated with the faithful at the table of the Lord' (Calderwood, 4.253). By contract dated 18 May 1575 he married Elizabeth (*d*. in or after 1587), second daughter of John *Lyon, eighth Lord Glamis (*c*.1544–1578). Shortly afterwards they separated and Gray left Scotland for France. In Paris, despite his previous orthodoxy, he was soon associating with various Marians, notably Mary's ambassador James Beaton, former archbishop of Glasgow. Gray's enthusiasm for the queen impressed not only Beaton but also the Guise family and the Spanish ambassador, who was subsequently to reward him for his services with 'a cupboard of plate worth five or six thousand crowns' (*Gray Papers*, 3).

From time to time Gray returned to Scotland. One visit probably occurred in the summer of 1581 after the Lennox–Arran faction had overthrown the earl of Morton. On this occasion his religious credentials were challenged by members of a kirk sufficiently powerful to pressurize not just him but, as the negative confession shows, much bigger targets such as Esmé Stewart, first duke of Lennox, and even the king himself. However, the day before he was due 'to renounce papistrie and embrace the true Christian religion' (Calderwood, 4.253), Gray apparently left for France. He probably remained abroad until summer 1583, when James VI escaped from the control of the Ruthven raiders. Certainly in November that year Gray was entrusted with the task of bringing to Scotland from France Ludovick Stuart, who had succeeded his father as second duke of Lennox.

It was at this juncture that Gray's career really took off. The king had already revealed his weakness for good-looking young men and Gray by all accounts was handsome. One modern historian has acutely observed that Gray possessed 'a Lucifer-like beauty' combined with 'all the mingled potentialities of talent and treachery of the former archangel' (Fraser, 540). Over the next few years Gray was amply to justify this assessment of his character. On three separate occasions between 1584 and 1587 he played a significant role in Anglo-Scottish affairs. He participated in the negotiations which ultimately resulted in the alliance being signed between the two countries; then, shortly afterwards, he was implicated in the English attempts at destabilizing the regime of James Stewart, earl of Arran, and finally, in the aftermath of the Babington plot, he was involved in the discussions about Mary's fate.

In 1584 two figures dominated James VI's government: Arran and John Maitland of Thirlestane. Both favoured closer ties with England. In October, in pursuance of this objective, Gray, recently appointed master of the royal wardrobe and commendator of Dunfermline Abbey, was sent to England as a royal ambassador. In London his previous allegiance to the Marian cause would appear to have been conveniently forgotten. Consequently, requests from Mary while he was there that he should petition Elizabeth for Mary's restoration as joint sovereign with her son, the constitutional arrangement known as the association, were completely ignored by her former agent. Instead Gray proposed to Sir Francis Walsingham and the others an alliance between the two countries wherein James VI would actually repudiate any interest in the association. In May 1585 the initial steps towards an Anglo-Scottish treaty (eventually signed in 1586) were taken when the king received his first financial subsidy from England. The same month Gray's estranged wife divorced him for adultery, and shortly before 22 July he married Lady Mary Stewart, eldest daughter of Robert

*Stewart, first earl of Orkney (1533–1593), the king's uncle.

Although he still retained the friendship of James VI, Arran was unpopular within the country, especially with the ultra protestant faction, who were suspicious, like the English government, of his religious leanings and his attitude towards France. Gray, whose personal ambition, as one English official at the time commented, 'burnt in his stomach' (Fraser, 542), clearly saw an opportunity to encompass Arran's downfall. His efforts at achieving this even by his own standards were exceedingly tortuous. In July 1585 Arran briefly fell out of favour with the king as a result of a border incident in which one of his associates, Ker of Fernihurst, killed Sir Francis Russell, son of the earl of Bedford, and cast a temporary cloud over Anglo-Scottish relations. However, on this occasion Gray apparently used his influence with the king on Arran's behalf. Seemingly, money had talked and Arran had bribed Gray in order to enlist his support. Yet within a month Gray had become an agent of the English government and was conspiring against Arran. He contacted Wotton, their ambassador, and suggested that Archibald Douglas, eighth earl of Angus, the Hamilton brothers, and various other opponents of Arran whom earlier in the year he had persuaded the English to expel from the borders, should be encouraged to return and re-enter the kingdom. Elizabeth's release of these exiles in November ensured the collapse of Arran's administration and a successful outcome for Gray's machinations.

In November 1586, following the revelations of Queen Mary's complicity in the Babington affair, the English parliament sought her execution. With the threat of another crisis imminent, the Scottish government sent Gray and Sir James Melville to England. Both commissioners strongly opposed any suggestion of the death penalty for Mary. In fact, before he left for London, Gray, in a letter to Walsingham, warned him that James VI's reaction was likely to be highly unfavourable. A similar stance was taken by the two envoys at the subsequent discussions, accompanied by the request that James VI's right of succession to the English throne should be acknowledged. But other forces were also at work. Angus's kinsman Archibald Douglas, an individual with a chequered career which stretched back to involvement in the Riccio and Darnley murders, was at Westminster as well. In contrast to Gray and Melville, Douglas secretly informed the English that his master was prepared to accept his mother's execution. Moreover, provided the question of his right of succession was satisfactorily resolved, there would be no danger of Scottish retaliation. On his return to Scotland Gray found that his position was, as he had feared, seriously undermined. Mary's death provoked outrage in the country, and it was the royal favourite who became the principal scapegoat. In May Gray was accused of a number of grave offences including consenting to the queen's execution in return for English money. Found guilty, he was sentenced to death, only for John, Lord Hamilton, doubtless grateful for Gray's assistance in 1585, to take the lead in interceding on his behalf. James VI commuted his sentence to banishment, and the next month Gray departed for France. Here he lived by serving as a mercenary soldier, but, as he later recounted, he was aware that in the long term this would undermine his honour.

However, Gray's heyday was not quite over as in April 1589, apparently at Walsingham's intervention, he was allowed to return to Scotland. Shortly afterwards he was restored to the privy council and to his former appointment as master of the royal wardrobe. But there was to be no resumption of his previous influence at the royal court. Instead, by 1592 he had become an ally of the outlawed Francis Stewart, earl of Bothwell, and was supporting the latter's challenge to the king's authority. The association may well have stemmed from the antipathy which they shared for Maitland of Thirlestane, now James VI's leading minister. Such feelings were prevalent among numerous noblemen, jealous of Maitland's rise to power. One of the charges against Gray in 1587 had actually been plotting the assassination of the royal chancellor. In June 1592 Gray joined forces with Bothwell and was one of those who that month made an unsuccessful attempt to seize the king at Falkland Palace.

Gray's subsequent behaviour did him little credit. Bothwell had been outspoken in his criticism of James VI's leniency towards the mainly Catholic magnates known as the Catholic earls, and for this reason some of the clergy looked favourably on him. Gray, possibly conceiving an opportunity to win over the king, now accused Robert Bruce, one of the most prominent ministers in the kingdom, of being implicated in the abortive coup at Falkland. At the same time he promised Bothwell he would help to restore him to royal favour provided he backed his allegations against Bruce. But the earl, suspicious of Gray's motives, refused to co-operate, leaving the latter in a humiliating position as his case against the minister collapsed.

Thereafter Gray's career was more humdrum. An offer of his services to Elizabeth's chief minister, Robert Cecil, before James VI succeeded to the English throne, was rejected. None the less, the king appears to have retained some affection for him since in 1606 he gave instructions that the sum of nearly £20,000 Scots owing to Gray by the crown, presumably during his time as master of the wardrobe, should be paid to him. The same year Gray, in his capacity as hereditary sheriff of Angus, helped Dundee town council suppress a serious disturbance among the craftsmen in the town. The last entry of any note concerning Gray in the minutes of the privy council, which he attended fairly regularly, relates to a family dispute. He had taken control of family finances, doubtless on account of his father's age, but on 2 April 1607 his father complained that the master had brought his wife and family into his house 'consuming thairby all that mean portion that he had reserved for his ain maintenance' (*Reg. PCS*, 8.46). The privy council supported his father, but Lord Gray died shortly before 10 March 1608. Gray finally came into his inheritance, but could not enjoy it for long. He died on 4 September 1611, and was succeeded as seventh

Lord Gray by his son Andrew *Gray (d. 1663) from his second marriage. His first wife had married William Ker in 1587.   G. R. HEWITT

Sources D. Calderwood, *The history of the Kirk of Scotland*, ed. T. Thomson and D. Laing, 8 vols., Wodrow Society, 7 (1842–9), vols. 3–7 · *CSP Scot., 1571–88* · *Reg. PCS*, 1st ser., vols. 2–8 · *Scots peerage*, vol. 4 · *Memoirs of his own life by Sir James Melville of Halhill*, ed. T. Thomson, Bannatyne Club, 18 (1827) · *Gray papers*, Bannatyne Club (1835) · *DNB* · A. Fraser, *Mary queen of Scots* (1968) · G. Donaldson, *Scotland: James V–James VII* (1965) · D. H. Willson, *James VI and I* (1956) · GEC, *Peerage* · K. M. Brown, *Noble society in Scotland: wealth, family and culture from Reformation to revolution* (2000)
Archives Glos. RO, Trustees of the Berkeley Castle Muniments, letters to Sir George Carey

Gray, Peter (1807/8–1887), actuary and mathematician, was born at Aberdeen. Little is known about his origins, but he was educated at Gordon's Hospital (subsequently Gordon's College) and at Aberdeen University for two years. He developed a passion for mathematics and, in order to assist the work of a friend, took a special interest in the study of life contingencies. This led to honorary membership of the Institute of Actuaries, and numerous contributions to its journal. In 1851 he undertook the task of organizing and preparing for publication, together with Henry Ambrose Smith and William Orchard, assurance and annuity tables issued by the Institute of Actuaries: these used demographic data from the Carlisle bills of mortality, 1778–88, compiled by Dr John Heysham. Gray also constructed an extensive table of values of log 10 for students of the institute. In 1865 he published further tables dealing with the formulation of logarithms and antilogarithms.

A fellow of the Royal Astronomical and Royal Microscopical societies, Gray was also distinguished for his knowledge of optics and applied mechanics. He apparently never married. He died at 53 Fairmead Road, Holloway, London, on 17 January 1887, survived by his sister, Susannah Nash Gray.   ROBERT BROWN

Sources *Journal of the Institute of Actuaries*, 26/1 (1887), 301–2, 406 · *Monthly Notices of the Royal Astronomical Society*, 48 (1887–8), 163–5 · C. Walford, *The insurance cyclopaedia*, 6 vols. (1871–80) · Boase, *Mod. Eng. biog.* · *The life of John Heysham … and his correspondence with Mr Joshua Milne relative to the Carlisle bills of mortality*, ed. H. Lonsdale (1870)
Archives Institute of Actuaries, London, MSS
Wealth at death £2216 15s. 5d.: probate, 16 Feb 1887, *CGPLA Eng. & Wales*

Gray, Robert (1762–1834), bishop of Bristol, born on 11 March 1762 in London, was the son of Robert Gray, a London silversmith. He was educated at Eton College and St Mary Hall, Oxford, where he graduated BA in 1784, before proceeding MA (1787), BD (1799), and DD (1802). In 1790 he published *A Key to the Old Testament and Apocrypha*, in which he analysed the individual books, as well as discussing their historical context. This was well received, and became a textbook at both universities. He continued to publish throughout the next thirty years, including his Bampton lecture sermons (1796). In 1791–2 he undertook a grand tour in the company of Sir Thomas Clarges, the nephew of Shute Barrington, bishop of Durham. He was presented to the vicarage of Faringdon, Berkshire, in 1794, and in the same year he married Elizabeth, daughter of the Revd John Camplin, precentor of Bristol Cathedral, with whom he had a large family.

Gray became a prebend of Chichester Cathedral in 1797, and in 1800 Bishop Barrington promoted him to the rectory of Crayke, Yorkshire, and he resigned Faringdon. In 1804 he was appointed by Barrington to the seventh stall in Durham Cathedral, and in the following year to the rectory of Bishopwearmouth, when he resigned Crayke. He was also a magistrate of the town of Sunderland. He remained at Bishopwearmouth (in which he had succeeded William Paley) until his elevation, in 1827, to the bishopric of Bristol. He was allowed to keep the stall at Durham, although Lord Liverpool expected him to vacate Bishopwearmouth. This accommodation was probably thought necessary, despite the moves to reduce instances of pluralism in the church, as Bristol was not a valuable see, with an income of about £1700, whereas Bishopwearmouth was reputed to be worth in excess of £3000 p.a. The Durham stall was valued at over £1700 in 1805.

Gray was noted for holding firmly to his principles, and for his courage, kindness, and concern for his parishioners. At Bishopwearmouth he established several schools and helped to raise money for the building of a local infirmary and dispensary. He also encouraged Sir Humphry Davy in his work on the safety lamp. As bishop, he instigated programmes of church building and of poor relief, and strongly promoted residency among his clergy. He often spoke in the House of Lords on church matters, showing concern for the welfare of the established church. He was a firm opponent of Catholic emancipation, giving voice to the beliefs of petitioners from Bristol that the 'ruinous condition of Ireland' in 1829 was 'owing to the prevalence in that country, of the Catholic religion' (Hansard, 2nd ser., 20, 1829, 376–7). He subsequently spoke in the debates on educational provision and church reform in Ireland.

Gray was opposed to parliamentary reform, and voted against it in both 1831 and April 1832. In the long and acrimonious debate of 17 May 1832 on the plan to create enough new peers to push through the Reform Bill, Gray maintained it was an unconstitutional exercise of the royal prerogative to 'swamp the independence' of the House of Lords in this way, and that it was the duty of opposition peers to continue to amend the bill to make it 'more serviceable and more palatable to the country' (Hansard, 3rd ser., 12, 1832, 1071). In the Bristol riots which followed the failure of the Reform Bill in October 1831, Gray's palace was set alight, although the crowd's anger was mainly directed at the staunch anti-reform recorder of Bristol, Sir Charles Wetherall. Despite calls to postpone divine service during the riots, Gray refused to do so, maintaining that it was his duty to be at his post. The service was held as usual, and he was himself the preacher. During the turmoil his palace was burnt to the ground, a library of 6000 volumes stolen or destroyed, and his wine cellars plundered. The losses he sustained (besides that of his papers) were estimated at £10,000.

Gray died at home at Rodney House, Clifton, on 28 September 1834, having suffered ill health for over a year. He was buried with great ceremony, on 6 October, in the graveyard attached to Bristol Cathedral, and a marble monument by Edward H. Bayly RA was erected in the cathedral by the clergy and laity of the city. His wife survived him. His son Robert *Gray (1809–1872) became bishop of Cape Town and metropolitan of Africa.

B. H. BLACKER, rev. M. E. CLAYTON

Sources Annual Biography and Obituary, 19 (1835), 258–64 · BL, Add. MS 38302, fols. 207–9 · Hansard 1 (1819), 19.118 · Hansard 2 (1829), 20.376, 1303 · Hansard 3 (1832) [12.1071]; (1833), 13.1; (1838), 18.811, 1292 · W. B. Maynard, 'Pluralism and non-residence in the archdeaconry of Durham, 1774–1856: the bishop and chapter as patrons', Northern History, 26 (1990), 103–30 · G. Amey, City under fire (1979), 66–70 · GM, 2nd ser., 2 (1834), 645 · Annual Register (1834), 242 · A catalogue of all graduates … in the University of Oxford, between … 1659 and … 1850 (1851) · G. M. Evans, 'Robert Gray, bishop of Bristol', Essays in cathedral history, ed. E. Ralph and J. Rogan (1991), 72–7 · W. Jerdan, National portrait gallery of illustrious and eminent personages of the nineteenth century, with memoires, 5 vols. (1830–34) · H. J. Rose, A new general biographical dictionary, ed. H. J. Rose and T. Wright, 12 vols. (1853)

Archives Beds. & Luton ARS, volume containing transcripts of letters | JRL, letters to Hester Piozzi

Likenesses J. Jenkins, stipple, 1831 (in episcopal robes; after J. W. Wright), BM, NPG; repro. in Jerdan, National portrait gallery (1831) · E. H. Bayly, medallion on marble monument, after 1834, Bristol Cathedral · memorial window, after 1834; in Almondsbury church, south Gloucestershire, in 1890 · Evans, oils, University College, Durham

Gray, Robert (1809–1872), bishop of Cape Town, the son of Robert *Gray (1762–1834), bishop of Bristol, and Elizabeth, née Camplin, was born on 3 October 1809 at Bishopwearmouth, co. Durham. He entered as a commoner at University College, Oxford, in 1827, and took his BA degree in 1831, gaining an honorary fourth class after having originally presented himself for a pass degree. Soon after taking his degree he visited the continent, and travelled in France, Switzerland, Italy, and Sicily. In 1833 he was ordained deacon by his father, and in the following year priest by the bishop of Bath and Wells. He first held the small living of Whitworth, Durham, and afterwards that of Stockton, to which he was presented in 1845. On 6 September 1835 he had married Sophia Wharton Myddleton, whose family owned Grinkle Park, Easington, Yorkshire, and who until her death in April 1871 was his constant help and companion.

Archbishop Howley soon afterwards pressed Gray to accept the bishopric of Cape Town, and he sacrificed his own inclinations to what he recognized as a call of duty. He was consecrated on 29 June 1847. He arrived at his diocese at the beginning of the following year. He found it in a most neglected condition, other denominations of Christians having done more for the propagation of their religion than Anglicans. But his presence was felt immediately, and in about six years he succeeded in dividing his unwieldy diocese into three parts, two new bishoprics being erected at Grahamstown and Natal. After he had been twelve years bishop of Cape Town, the island of St Helena was erected into a separate bishopric (1859). It was

Robert Gray (1809–1872), by Henry Hering, 1860s

chiefly owing to his determination that the universities' mission to central Africa was set on foot, and a bishop consecrated to superintend it on 1 January 1861.

Until November 1853 Gray had been simply bishop of Cape Town and a suffragan of Canterbury; but in this month he formally resigned his see, so that it could be divided and Cape Town be made a metropolitical see, with jurisdiction over Grahamstown and Natal, to which the new bishops were consecrated on 30 November 1853 by virtue of letters patent issued by the crown in the same month. Gray was reappointed bishop of a reduced diocese of Cape Town, and metropolitan by letters patent issued on 8 December of the same year.

Gray's contemporaries seem for the most part to have respected him for a firmness which was coupled with a very gentle manner. All things seemed to have gone on smoothly until 1856, when, upon his resolving to hold a synod of his diocese, he issued summonses to the clergy and certain delegates of the laity. Mr Long, one of his clergy, refused to attend, and repeated the refusal in 1860, when a second synod was proposed to be held. It was alleged that Gray had no authority either from the crown or the local legislature to hold any such synod; and on 8 January 1861 the offending clergyman was suspended by Gray from the cure of souls, and in March following he was deprived by the withdrawal of his licence. In an action

brought by the clergyman and his churchwardens before the supreme court of the colony the judges decided in favour of Gray, on the ground that though no coercive jurisdiction could be claimed by virtue of the letters patent of 1853, when he was constituted metropolitan, because they were issued after a constitutional government had been established at the Cape, yet the clergyman was bound by his own voluntary submission to acquiesce in the decision of the bishop since he had taken an oath of canonical obedience on receiving the bishop's licence. From this judgment Long appealed to the judicial committee of the privy council, who on 24 June 1863 reversed the findings of the colonial court, the judicial committee agreeing with the inferior court that the letters patent of 1847 and those of 1853 were ineffectual to create any jurisdiction. The dispute between Gray and Long was therefore to be treated, if treated at all, as a suit between members of a religious body not established by law. And Long could not be compelled to recognize the authority of an ecclesiastical tribunal created by the very synod against whose existence he had protested. It was further held that Long had not been guilty of any offence which by the laws of the Church of England would have warranted his deprivation. Accordingly he was restored to his former status.

In the same year (1863) Gray was engaged in another lawsuit. One of his suffragans, John William *Colenso, bishop of Natal, was presented to him by the dean of Cape Town and the archdeacons of George and Grahamstown, on the charge of heresy. Bishop Colenso protested against the jurisdiction of his metropolitan, and offered no defence of his opinions, but admitted that he had published the works from which passages had been quoted, and alleged that they were no offence against the laws of the established church. Accordingly on 16 December 1863 Gray pronounced the deposition of the bishop of Natal, to take effect from 16 April following, if the bishop should not before that time make a full retraction in writing of the charges brought against him. This judgment, however, was reversed, on appeal to the judicial committee of the privy council, on the ground that the crown had exceeded its powers in issuing letters patent purporting to convey coercive jurisdiction to a bishop in any colony having its own legislative institutions. Nor did Colenso's oath of canonical obedience to Gray give the metropolitan any authority to depose him, for the letters patent were held, in spite of their invalidity, to have created ecclesiastical persons who could not be unmade except by the crown. And because the letters patent could not confer jurisdiction Colenso ought not to have taken an oath of obedience to a metropolitan who had no legal authority to demand it.

It is a remarkable fact that the judge who presided at the pronouncement of this judgment, Lord Chancellor Westbury, was the very person who, as attorney-general, had drawn the letters patent which he now pronounced to be null and void in law. The result of the whole litigation was that Colenso continued to hold religious services in his cathedral, while the dean (who recognized Gray's authority as metropolitan) also held other services at a different hour, and this state of things continued until the death of the deprived bishop of Natal in 1883. Meanwhile Gray made his appeal to the bishops of the English church to give him their countenance and support, as a bishop of a free and independent province. His anxious desire was that the Church of England, through her bishops and convocations, should sanction his proceedings and concur with him in appointing a new bishop for the see, after passing the sentence of excommunication on Colenso. On the whole the upper as well as the lower house of convocation of Canterbury agreed in supporting Gray in his project of consecrating a new bishop for the diocese, though with a different name and title. In 1867 the matter was also brought before the first Lambeth conference of 1867, which all the bishops in communion with the Anglican church had been invited to attend. Here, owing to the attitude of the American bishops, Gray carried his point, 'that this conference accepts and adopts the wise decision of the convocation of Canterbury as to the appointment of another bishop to Natal'. This was carried with three dissentients only, although only two days before, on 25 September, the archbishop had refused to put a resolution approving the excommunication and deposition of Colenso. Gray, in deference to the archbishop of Canterbury, had acquiesced in his decision; but after the conference was over fifty-five bishops joined in the following declaration: 'We the undersigned bishops declare our acceptance of the sentence pronounced upon Dr. Colenso by the metropolitan of South Africa, with his suffragans, as being spiritually a valid sentence'.

Gray's next step was to find a person willing to accept the bishopric, and who would be acceptable to all parties concerned. The see to which he was to be appointed was designated that of Maritzburg. After many refusals the Revd W. K. Macrorie in January 1868 accepted the post, and the next difficulty that arose was as to the place of consecration, it being found that there were legal difficulties as to a consecration taking place without the queen's mandate in any place where the Act of Uniformity was in force. The new bishop was finally consecrated at Cape Town on 25 January 1869 by Gray, assisted by the bishops of Grahamstown, St Helena, and the Free State.

The incessant work in which Gray had been engaged was now beginning to tell upon him, and his anxieties were increased by domestic afflictions. In 1870 he lost a daughter, and in the spring of the following year his wife died. He also very obviously felt the loss of Bishop Cotterill of Grahamstown, who in the same year became coadjutor-bishop (afterwards diocesan bishop) of Edinburgh. The bishopric of Grahamstown being thus vacant, Gray had the satisfaction of consecrating for the see his old and tried friend Archdeacon Nathaniel James Merriman.

Gray had never been physically strong, having suffered a breakdown in health on several occasions through overwork and exhaustion. He had nevertheless been engaged in incessant travelling throughout his very extensive diocese, visiting every part of it, often in areas where there were no roads and where there were mountain ranges and rivers to be crossed. His most remarkable characteristic, his admirers thought, was his tenacity of purpose in carrying out to the end what he judged to be his duty. At the very end of his life his doctors came to the conclusion that he was diabetic and that his condition had been exacerbated by a fall from a horse and the onset of a fever, all these factors together causing his death. He died in Cape Town on 1 September 1872, and is commemorated on that day in the calendar of the South African Anglican church.

Gray published, besides many pamphlets and some charges, journals of visitations held in 1848 and 1850 (1852), in 1855 (1856), in 1864 (1864), and in 1865 (1866).

NICHOLAS POCOCK, *rev.* PETER HINCHLIFF

Sources [H. L. Farrer], *Life of Robert Gray, bishop of Cape Town and metropolitan of Africa*, ed. C. Gray, 2 vols. (1876) · A. E. M. Anderson-Morshead, *Pioneer and founder* (1905) · A. Brooke, *Robert Gray, first bishop of Cape Town* (1947) · P. B. Hinchliff, *The Anglican church in South Africa* (1963) · *DSAB* · C. Lewis and G. E. Edwards, *Historical records of the church of the province of South Africa* (1934), 31–112, 146–74 · P. B. Hinchliff, *John William Colenso* (1964), 85–166 · J. Guy, *The heretic: a study of the life of John William Colenso* (1983), 95–160 · T. E. Yates, *Venn and Victorian bishops abroad: the missionary policies of Henry Venn and their repercussions upon the Anglican episcopate of the colonial period, 1841–1872* (1978), 92–176, 192–4 · R. T. Davidson, *The Lambeth conferences of 1867, 1878, and 1888* (1896)

Archives Bishops Court, Cape Town · Diocesan Archives, Cape Town · University of the Witwatersrand, Johannesburg, Church of the Province of South Africa Central Record Library, corresp. and papers incl. notebooks and diaries | Auckland Public Library, letters to Sir George Grey · BL, corresp. with Lord Carnarvon · Bodl. Oxf., corresp. with Samuel Wilberforce · Keble College, Oxford, letters to John Keble · LPL, corresp. with Lady Burdett-Coutts · LPL, letters to Charles Longley · LPL, corresp. with A. C. Tait · LPL, letters to Christopher Wordsworth · National Library of South Africa, letters to Sir George Grey · Pusey Oxf., letters to Edward Pusey

Likenesses J. Thomas, stipple, pubd 1848 (after G. Richmond), BM · H. Hering, photograph, 1860–69, NPG [*see illus.*] · H. N. King, carte-de-visite, NPG · C. W. Sharpe, lithograph (after G. Richmond, 1847), Diocesan Library, Cape Town, South Africa

Wealth at death under £9000: administration with will, 17 Jan 1873, *CGPLA Eng. & Wales*

Gray, Robert (1825–1887), ornithologist and bank official, was born at Dunbar, East Lothian, on 15 August 1825, the son of Archibald Gray, a merchant, and his wife, Agnes Hendre. He was educated at the parish school and at the age of fifteen became an apprentice at the British Linen Company Bank. In 1843 he joined the local branch of the City of Glasgow Bank. He moved to its head office in 1845, eventually becoming a branch inspector and then an agent of the St Vincent Street branch in 1871. In March 1874 he obtained a post with the Bank of Scotland in Edinburgh as superintendent of branches, and in 1882 became cashier. His departure from the City of Glasgow Bank was timely; the bank ceased business in October 1878 and, after a trial, its directors and officers were imprisoned for theft.

Gray became interested in natural history as a youth and ultimately specialized in ornithology. The frequent opportunities for travel as a branch inspector enabled him to study the bird life of Scotland. His notebooks and their illustrations formed the basis for his book, *Birds of the West of Scotland, Including the Outer Hebrides* (1871), which provided the first genuine account of the birds of the Clyde area (some 200 species). Its accurate observations have made it a minor classic to which modern ornithologists are indebted and now it is regarded as 'one of the masterly bird books of all time' (J. A. Gibson, *Regional Checklist of Clyde Birds*, 1981, 71).

In 1856, on one of his trips to Ayrshire, Gray met Elizabeth Anderson (1831–1924) [see Gray, Elizabeth], the daughter of Thomas Anderson, a recognized naturalist and collector. They were married on 8 April 1856 and lived first in Glasgow, but moved to Partick in 1859. In spite of having a growing family both Robert Gray and his wife managed to continue their joint natural-history activities by returning to Girvan each summer. In a paper published with his father-in-law in 1869 (the precursor of Gray's own book on the birds of the region), they advocated the protection of all birds of prey and argued that similar protection for all birds was 'a paramount duty', if the diminution in their numbers was to be prevented and the 'nicely-balanced harmony' in Nature was to be maintained (R. Gray and R. Anderson, 'On the birds of Ayrshire and Wigtownshire', *Proceedings of the Glasgow Natural History Society*, 1, 1869, 322–3). Robert Gray was also responsible for the initial contact made with the various palaeontologists who described material from his wife's fossil collection.

Throughout his life Gray was involved with local natural history societies. In 1851 he had been one of the founders of the Natural History Society of Glasgow, and he frequently contributed articles to its *Proceedings*. He served as treasurer in 1854–6 and was elected its secretary in 1858, holding the post until 1871 when his promotion in the City of Glasgow Bank caused him to resign. After moving to Edinburgh he was elected a fellow of the Royal Society of Edinburgh in 1875, elected to serve on its council in 1878/9, 1879/80, and 1886/7, and was vice-president for the sessions of 1882/3–1885/6. However, his most significant influence was to resurrect the Royal Physical Society—one of the oldest scientific bodies in Edinburgh—then in 'one of its periodic fits of depression'. In 1877 Gray accepted its secretaryship and his energy, courtesy, and charm, together with his business sense and organizational powers, introduced the necessary reforms that encouraged new members and activated existing ones, thereby ensuring its continued existence.

Gray died of a cerebral haemorrhage at the age of sixty-one, on 18 February 1887, two days after being found unconscious at Bank of Scotland House, his home in The Mound, Edinburgh. At the time of his death he was engaged with William Evans on a work dealing with the birds of the east of Scotland, but this was never published. Gray made his own particular contribution to natural history through his two publications on birds. All subsequent 'Clyde ornithologists' regard Robert Gray as the pioneer of their tradition and as 'a genuine true-hearted Lowland Scotsman' (Traquair, xx). R. J. CLEEVELY

Sources R. H. Traquair, *Proceedings of the Royal Society of Edinburgh*, 15 (1887–8), xvi–xx · R. J. Cleevely, R. P. Tripp, and Y. Howells, 'Mrs Elizabeth Gray, 1831–1924: a passion for fossils', *Bulletin of the British Museum (Natural History)* [Historical Series], 17 (1989), 167–258 · A. Gray and R. Gray jun., Mrs Robert Gray and family, biographical notes, 1938, NHM, palaeontology library archives · *DNB* · *Glasgow Naturalist*, 4 (1912), 65–6 · parish register (marriage), 8 April 1856, Girvan · d. cert. · private information (2004) [J. A. Gibson]

Archives NHM, department of geology · NHM, department of palaeontology, archives

Likenesses photograph, repro. in Cleevely, Tripp, and Howells, 'Mrs Elizabeth Gray', 72

Wealth at death £3240: confirmation, 24 Nov 1887, CCI

Gray, Samuel (*bap.* 1693?, *d.* 1766), seedsman, may have been the Samuel Gray baptized on 28 January 1693 at St Giles Cripplegate, London, but A. E. Gunther, in *A Century of Zoology at the British Museum* gives his birth date as 1694. Very little is known of Gray's life other than his success in running the family-owned seed business at the Black Boy in Pall Mall, London. He inherited the company from his father, also Samuel Gray, but seems to have been the more active in developing business. He bought a garden at Tettlefields, Westminster, and lived there, bequeathing it in turn to his eldest son, along with the Black Boy premises and business concerns, at his death in 1766. The house at Tettlefields was pulled down in 1828 when Carlton House was built. The company traded extensively with the Netherlands and at some point Gray expanded his interests to include a mill on the River Ravensbourne, near Deptford, later called Armoury Mill, where he introduced the commercial novelty of ground mustard (mustard flour). Before then, mustard seeds were crushed with a pestle and mortar. His firm subsequently achieved something of a mustard monopoly. The mill also produced cut glass for domestic and decorative use.

On 6 December 1730 at Aspeden, Hertfordshire, Gray married Juliana Kelly, who outlived him, dying in 1774. Their first child was Juliana (1734–1811), who remained unmarried, then came Samuel and Edward Whitaker *Gray, both of whom became distinguished naturalists. **Samuel Gray** (1739–1771), seedsman and botanical writer, worked in the family firm and carried on the business after his father's death. In 1760 he translated parts of Linnaeus's *Philosophica botanica*, which was published as *An Introduction to Botany* under James Lee's name. On 7 May 1761 at St James, Westminster, he married Frances Wade (1738–1801), whose father was a picture dealer in Maiden Lane, Covent Garden. The couple had four children in quick succession, only one of whom survived, a sickly boy called Samuel Frederick *Gray (1766–1828). Samuel Gray died unexpectedly in 1771, leaving all the family property to his younger brother, who was then in Portugal but afterwards became keeper of natural history at the British Museum at Montague House from 1787. Gray's wife, Frances, was consequently left with very little money on which to bring up their son. JANET BROWNE

Sources A. E. Gunther, 'The miscellaneous autobiographical manuscripts of John Edward Gray (1800–1875)', *Bulletin of the British Museum (Natural History)* [Historical Series], 6 (1977–80), 199–244, esp. 204 · A. E. Gunther, *A century of zoology at the British Museum through the lives of two keepers, 1815–1914* (1975) · *IGI*

Gray, Samuel (1739–1771). *See under* Gray, Samuel (*bap.* 1693?, *d.* 1766).

Gray, Samuel Frederick (1766–1828), naturalist and pharmacologist, was born on 10 December 1766 at Westminster, the only surviving child of Samuel *Gray (1739–1771) [*see under* Gray, Samuel (*bap.* 1693?, *d.* 1766)], seedsman at the Black Boy, Pall Mall, London, and his wife, Frances Wade (1738–1801). His grandfather, Samuel *Gray (*bap.* 1693?, *d.* 1766) was also a seedsman. When his father died unexpectedly, Gray had no patrimony other than that which his uncle Edward Whitaker Gray supplied. Some accounts mix up the generations and incorrectly claim that Gray was born after the death of his father and that this was the cause of the financial oversight. (Gunther, 'Miscellaneous autobiographical manuscripts', 206). What is certain is that Samuel Frederick Gray was both poor and extremely sickly as a child, nearly dumb, and was taught energetically by his mother. By the time he was ten or eleven years old he had learned to read and speak, but with a considerable impediment.

Gray was studious, well taught in Latin and Greek, and attempted to qualify for medicine in London. Apparently breaking down in the attempt, he turned to medical and botanical writing and for some years assisted Nares on the *British Critic*. About this time he fell in love with Elizabeth Forfeit (1777–1852) but was dismayed to discover that his uncle strongly disapproved of a marriage and was prepared to disown him. Notwithstanding this Gray married her in 1794 and moved to Walsall, in Staffordshire, where he used his knowledge of chemistry to start an assay office, also coming to know Joseph Black and Joseph Priestley, whom he assisted with experiments. Two sons were born in Walsall.

Gray spent some time in the midlands before returning to London in 1800, where he lived first in Devonshire Street, Queen Square. A *rapprochement* between uncle and nephew greatly helped Gray's studies in natural history. He also acted as a private accountant to Charles Hatchett FRS. After his uncle's death in 1806, Gray moved his family to Chelsea where another son and a daughter were born. Here he lectured on scientific subjects, assisted William Curtis and William Salisbury of the Physic Garden, and contributed unsigned articles on botany to the *Monthly Magazine* (1807–1815). Gray, who still felt unsettled in his career, then initiated plans to go into business as a bookseller in the Strand, but this failed.

In 1812 or 1813 Gray moved to Wapping, where he purchased an apothecary's business; he intended that his son, Samuel Forfeit Gray, should join him, but took a younger son, John Edward *Gray, instead when the older boy went to the Society of Apothecaries. On the failure of this business about 1816, the family moved to Hatton Garden. From then to the time of his death, Gray wrote many botanical articles, some in collaboration with his son John Edward, edited the *London Medical Repository* (1819–21), and published a useful *Supplement to the Pharmacopoeia*, which ran to five editions (1818–31, rev. by Redwood in 1847). Though not much noted at the time, it was the first work in English to use Jussieu's natural system for the classification of plants. Gray expanded the project in *A Natural Arrangement of British Plants* (1821), and lectured on Jussieu's system, partly in conjunction with John Edward, at the Sloane Street Botanical Garden and at Mr Taunton's Medical School in Hatton Garden. The younger Gray later contested authorship of the book, claiming he did all the work, especially in consulting sources in Sir Joseph Banks's library, and it was sneered at by Linnaean botanists of the day, allegedly for referring to 'Sowerby's' *English Botany* instead of 'James Edward Smith's'. It was deliberately ignored in Lindley's *Synopsis*, a strongly Linnaean work of 1829. The family disagreement about authorship continued into the next generation, when Samuel Octavius Gray (1828–1902), a grandson, defended Samuel Frederick Gray's claim when presenting a portrait of him to Kew Gardens in 1894 ('Portrait of S. F. Gray').

Towards the end of his life Gray suffered constant illness. He further published *Elements of Pharmacy* (1823) and *The Operative Chemist* (1828), practical works of high merit. He died, a few weeks before publication of the latter, on 12 April 1828, and was buried in New Chelsea Church. His two middle sons, John Edward and George Robert *Gray, were naturalists at the British Museum; his oldest son, Samuel Forfeit Gray (1798–1872), a capable botanist and pharmacist, was elected fellow of the Linnean Society in 1825; and his daughter, Charlotte Frances (1811–1885), married Samuel Birch, keeper of oriental antiquities, British Museum, in 1839.   JANET BROWNE

Sources J. Britten, 'Bibliographical notes', *Journal of Botany, British and Foreign*, 59 (1921), 176–8 · 'Portrait of S. F. Gray', *Bulletin of Miscellaneous Information* [RBG Kew] (1894), 76–8 · A. E. Gunther, 'The miscellaneous autobiographical manuscripts of John Edward Gray (1800–1875)', *Bulletin of the British Museum (Natural History)* [Historical Series], 6 (1977–80), 199–244 · A. E. Gunther, *A century of zoology at the British Museum through the lives of two keepers, 1815–1914* (1975)
Archives NHM, lectures on plants and insects
Likenesses oils, presented in 1894, RBG Kew

Gray, Stephen (*bap.* 1666, *d.* 1736), experimental philosopher, was baptized on 26 December 1666 at All Saints' Church, Canterbury, the fifth of the seven children of Matthias Gray (or Graye), a dyer, and Anne Tilman. He came from a family of rapidly rising artisans who lived in Canterbury for several generations. His great-grandfather bought the freedom of the city to trade as a blacksmith in 1599 and his grandfather was a blacksmith too, but his father established a family dyeing business. Gray entered the business and was granted the freedom of the city to trade as a dyer in 1692. Definitive information concerning his formal education is lacking, but it is likely that he received a useful primary education, probably at St Mary of the Poor Priests, one of the two schools in Canterbury that provided basic education for sons of local tradesmen.

During the 1690s Gray began to show a growing interest in natural curiosities. The acquisition of amateur knowledge of nature was considered a definite step into polite society, and was closely associated with social and economic ascent, giving a 'man of polite imagination … a kind of Property in every thing he sees' (*The Spectator*, 21 June 1712, 411). Through his brother Matthias, a grocer who became the mayor of Canterbury in 1692 and who was an amateur naturalist himself, Gray established links with two major centres of learning, the Royal Society of London and the Royal Greenwich Observatory. His connection with Henry Hunt, a minor official at the Royal Society from near Canterbury, earned him his first copies of the society's official journal, the *Philosophical Transactions*. His early experimental work was inspired by the articles he read in the journal. He studied insects in longstanding water, and systematically investigated small organisms in a variety of fluids readily available to him, such as 'wine, Brandie, vinegar, beer, spittle, urine, etc.' ('A letter from Stephen Gray', *PTRS*, 19, 1696, 284). During the course of these studies he developed a special interest in designing observational equipment, such as a water microscope, which used a water droplet inserted in a tiny hole in a brass plate, and a method for improving the barometer so as to make the mercury level more accurately determinable. Moreover, like many other naturalists of his time, he developed an interest in palaeobiology. He carefully recorded his observations and studies in letters to Hans Sloane, the secretary of the Royal Society. Several of these records were published in the *Philosophical Transactions*.

From 1696 Gray was in regular contact with the astronomer royal, John Flamsteed. His astronomical reports primarily dealt with solar and lunar eclipses, the revolutions of Jupiter's satellites, and sunspots. He also devised a new technique for drawing a meridian line using the pole star, and explained how his observational arrangement could be used to confirm 'the truth of the Earth's motion' ('A letter from Stephen Gray', *PTRS*, 22, 1701, 818). His reports suggest that he used several telescopes of different sizes, and it is possible that he constructed his own instruments, with lenses he ground himself.

Gray's letters to Flamsteed show a modest, loyal man, devoted to patient research. He worked determinedly, despite his poor health caused by years of hard labour as an artisan. Unlike wealthier naturalists he lacked the money to purchase books and instruments, which were made available to him by Flamsteed. Yet it was typical of the patronage system within which Gray pursued his scientific interests that his services to Flamsteed were not confined to astronomical observations. He was rewarded with an unusual commission in 1705: to investigate a ghost story, which excited Canterbury as well as London, relating the apparition of a dead woman, Mrs Veal. Gray responded to Flamsteed's request with a meticulous and sober account of the affair (which was also the topic of a successful short story written by Defoe).

However, it was through his electrical studies that Gray gained fame, by inaugurating a new approach to the phenomenon of electricity and interweaving philosophical learning with public entertainment. Writing to Hans Sloane in 1708, he reported his admiration of the 'Luciferous Experiments and Noble Discoveries' (Chipman, 'An unpublished letter of Stephen Gray', 34) in

electrical phenomena that the curator of experiments at the Royal Society, Francis Hauksbee the elder, had published in the *Philosophical Transactions* over the previous three years. Emulating Hauksbee, Gray forwarded his own electrical experiments to Sloane. At the time of this letter Gray was staying at Trinity College, Cambridge, to assist the new Lucasian professor, Roger Cotes, in his attempts to establish an observatory there. He subsequently returned to Canterbury. In 1716 he moved to London and became an assistant to J. T. Desaguliers, Hauksbee's successor at the Royal Society.

In their attempts to systematize the experimental production of electrical effects, Hauksbee and Desaguliers had reaffirmed the traditional assumption associating electrical effects with the material properties of the amber-like bodies known as electrics. However, Gray's early reports challenged this basic assumption. He noted that attraction and repulsion were not systematically related to the electric, since very light objects in its vicinity attracted and repelled one another as well. In an article dated 1720, Gray introduced a new concept by which he attributed electrical effects to the 'communication' of the electrical 'virtue', rather than to the electric itself (*PTRS*, 31, 1720, 140–48). This concept of electrical conductivity provided the crucial means for a breakthrough in electrical research: it created the opportunity to recognize, investigate, and reproduce new phenomena that were no longer confined to the behaviour of electrics.

Gray was admitted to the Charterhouse as a pensioner in 1720. Towards the end of the 1720s his innovative work began to be publicly appreciated, as he embarked upon a new experimental project, which consisted in the development of techniques for the 'communication' of electricity. The new trials were held in his residence at the Charterhouse and at the estates of John Godfrey, an amateur astronomer, and Granvil Wheler, a fellow of the Royal Society. His experimental reports show his determination to transmit electricity as far as possible, using a variety of materials as 'lines of communication'. From 1731 until his death in 1736, his audience included members of the Royal Society, who rewarded him with a fellowship in 1733 and the first Copley medal for scientific achievement, as well as companies of ladies and gentlemen who witnessed his performances at the Charterhouse. He held his audience by exciting sparks from water, turning Charterhouse schoolboys into electrical conductors, and condensing the electric vertue in various materials over a period of weeks. The communicated electrical vertue rapidly conquered the market of polite culture. The new effects were soon exhibited as 'philosophical fireworks' which, along with other conjuring tricks, popularized experimental natural philosophy.

In the poetic imagery of his assistant at the Charterhouse, Anna Williams, who was a daughter of one of the pensioners, Gray's experimental virtuosity was the emblematic key 'to break the sleep of elemental fire: To rouse the pow'rs that actuate Nature's frame' (Williams, 42). In the eyes of William Stukeley, a contemporary fellow of the Royal Society, the spectacular identification of the new principle of communication singled Gray out as 'the father, at least first propagator, of electricity' (*Family Memoirs*, 378). For experimental philosophers in Britain and on the continent, Gray's work comprised the conceptual basis for the distinction between conductors and non-conductors and the recognition that all material bodies fall into these categories, and it paved the path for the invention of the Leyden jar.

Gray's last contribution to science was an electrical simulation of pendulum motion to explain planetary motion—an endeavour to link his astronomical experience with his achievements as an electrician. Shortly before his death, as he was lying ill at the Charterhouse, he communicated an outline of the new project to the secretary of the Royal Society in person. Gray died the next day, 17 February 1736.   MICHAEL BEN-CHAIM

Sources D. H. Clark and L. Murdin, 'The enigma of Stephen Gray, astronomer and scientist, 1666–1736', *Vistas in Astronomy*, 23 (1979), 351–404 · M. Ben-Chaim, 'Social mobility and scientific change: Stephen Gray's contribution to electrical research', *British Journal for the History of Science*, 23 (1990), 3–24 · R. A. Chipman, 'An unpublished letter of Stephen Gray on electrical experiments, 1707–1708', *Isis*, 45 (1954), 33–40 · J. L. Heilbron, *Electricity in the 17th and 18th centuries: a study of early modern physics* (1979) · S. Schaffer, 'Natural philosophy and public spectacle in the eighteenth century', *History of Science*, 21 (1983), 1–43 · S. Schaffer, 'Self evidence', *Critical Inquiry*, 18 (1992), 327–62 · R. A. Chipman, 'The manuscript letters of Stephen Gray, FRS, 1666/7–1736', *Isis*, 49 (1958), 414–33 · I. B. Cohen, 'Neglected sources for the life of Stephen Gray', *Isis*, 45 (1954), 41–50 · J. T. Desaguliers, *A course of experimental philosophy*, 2 vols. (1734–44) · F. Hauksbee, *Physico-mechanical experiments on various subjects*, 2nd edn (1719) · J. Priestley, *The history and present state of electricity*, 3rd edn, 1 (1775) · A. Williams, 'On the death of Stephen Gray', *Miscellanies in prose and verse* (1766), 42 · *The family memoirs of the Rev. William Stukeley*, ed. W. C. Lukis, 2, SurtS, 76 (1883), 378 · parish register (baptism), 26/12/1666, Canterbury, All Saints' Church · 'A letter from Granvile Wheler esq., to Dr Mortimer … containing some remarks on the late Stephen Gray FRS his electrical circular experiment', *PTRS*, 41 (1739–41), 118–25

Archives NMM, Greenwich, Royal Observatory | BL, Sloane MSS · RS, letters to Royal Society

Wealth at death received Charterhouse pension

Gray, Sylvia Mary (1909–1991), businesswoman and women's institute leader, was born on 3 July 1909 at 44 Clifton Road, Rugby, Warwickshire, the daughter of Henry Bunting Gray, a racquet maker, members of whose family had been rackets coaches at Rugby School since 1867, and his wife, Elizabeth Mary Frost. She was educated at Wroxall Abbey.

Sylvia Gray joined her local women's institute (WI) in 1929 and served as chairman of the Oxfordshire Federation of Women's Institutes from 1951 to 1954. A rural organization, based in the villages, the WI had a democratic structure, with committees elected at each of the three levels—village, county, and national—and Sylvia Gray was one of many members who went on to other things after gaining confidence on a WI committee. In 1935 she bought the Bay Tree Hotel, an old coaching inn in Burford, Oxfordshire, and after the war she bought a second hotel, in Moreton-on-Marsh, another Cotswold town, and formed Bay Tree Hotels Ltd. She remained chairman of the company until 1983. At the Bay Tree Hotel she

employed only female staff and trained women for careers in hotel management. At the same time she began to participate in local affairs, and was a member of Witney rural district council from 1943 to 1954, the last four of these years as vice-chairman. She also chaired the board of governors of Burford grammar school. She was appointed MBE in 1952 for her services to local government.

After serving on the executive committee of the National Federation of Women's Institutes (NFWI), to which all the county organizations were affiliated, Sylvia Gray was elected chairman of the NFWI in 1969, the first chairman who was also a professional woman. She presided over a fundamental change in the constitution of the WI, a change she believed was the most important thing that happened during her chairmanship. Enshrined in the constitution was the rule that 'the character of the movement is non-sectarian and non-party political', but a resolution passed at the 1971 annual conference redefined the rule to make it clear that this should not be interpreted as preventing the village women's institutes from concerning themselves with political or religious issues, 'provided the movement is never used for party-political or sectarian propaganda'. While some feared that the WI was becoming apathetic, there were others who knew that, with the government intruding more and more in people's lives, many WIs were already discussing what the government was doing. The conference was reminded that in times of stress Lady Denman, first chairman of the NFWI, had always said 'trust the institutes'. Sylvia Gray anticipated that the debate on the resolution would be heated, but she knew that the WI must move with the times, sensing that 'the time seemed just right to rely on the common sense of the members not to allow themselves to be used for party political purposes' (Goodenough, 53). This change paved the way for the WI to comment more publicly on government legislation affecting women, especially those in the countryside, although the WI officially remained non-political.

At the beginning of her chairmanship, a national appeal, launched in 1965, had just reached its target of £500,000, and Sylvia Gray made sure that the NFWI became aware of the need for sound financial management. In 1970 the appeal fund helped to finance the building of new accommodation and teaching blocks at Denman College, the WI adult education college, opened in 1948. She was also responsible for bringing in management consultants to advise on improvements to the administrative structure of the organization, and she created a public relations position. After the success of *The Brilliant and the Dark*, composed for the WI by Malcolm Williamson, and performed in the Royal Albert Hall in 1969 by a choir of a thousand people selected from the village WI choirs, plans were laid for a permanent WI national choir, and, with the encouragement of the conductor Anthony Hopkins, Sylvia Gray started the WI Music Society. She also inaugurated the NFWI/Green Shield Stamps tennis championship. When she retired as chairman in 1974 the membership of the WI had grown to nearly half a million.

Sylvia Gray was also on the executive committee of the Keep Britain Tidy Group from 1969 to 1978, chairman of the south midlands regional committee of the National Trust from 1975 to 1981, and a member of the National Consumer Council from 1975 to 1977 and of the Redundant Churches Committee from 1976 to 1984. She was appointed CBE in 1975. She died, unmarried, on 27 April 1991 at her home, St Winnow, High Street, Burford. A memorial service was held at the church of St John the Baptist, Burford, on 21 May.   ANNE PIMLOTT BAKER

Sources S. Goodenough, *Jam and Jerusalem* (1977) · *The Independent* (4 May 1991) · b. cert. · *The Times* (22 May 1991) · d. cert.
Likenesses photograph, repro. in Goodenough, *Jam and Jerusalem*, 51 · photograph, repro. in *The Independent*
Wealth at death £1,180,989: probate, 29 Aug 1991, CGPLA Eng. & Wales

Gray [Grey], **Sir Thomas** (*d.* 1369), chronicler, was a member of the old Northumberland family of Grey of Heaton. His father, also called Thomas, was a knight who took part in the Scottish campaigns of Edward I and Edward II from *c.*1297 and was captured at Bannockburn in 1314. Constable of Norham Castle from 1319 to 1331, he resisted two sieges by the Scots. In 1319 he was granted lands in Howick, near Alnwick, which had been confiscated from John Maitland, a partisan of the Scots, and in 1323 he was appointed sheriff of Norham and Islandshire. His wife was a certain Agnes, whose surname was perhaps Beyle; their son, the chronicler, was already a knight by the time his father died, shortly before 12 March 1344.

In 1338 Thomas Gray the chronicler received letters of protection to go to Flanders in the retinue of William de Montagu, earl of Salisbury. On 10 April 1345 he did homage to the bishop of Durham and had livery of his family's manor of Heaton, while on 8 January 1346 he was appointed constable and sheriff of Norham, like his father. The king thanked him for his part in the battle of Nevilles Cross in 1346. Two years later he was commissioned to guarantee the truce of Calais in the borders, while in October 1353 he was directed to levy men from Northumberland. In 1355, however, following a sally from Norham Castle, he was captured by the Scots and imprisoned in Edinburgh Castle. There, to while away his time, he undertook the compilation of the *Scalacronica* in Anglo-Norman French. His captivity ended in the second half of 1357 when he was appointed guardian to one of King David's hostages. In 1359 he received letters of protection to go to France in the company of Edward, the Black Prince. In 1361 he was appointed a warden of the marches, and in 1367 he was granted the fourth part of the manor of Upsettlington West, on the Scottish side of the Tweed. He died shortly before 22 October 1369, leaving a son, Thomas, aged ten years, whose mother was Margaret, daughter and heir of William Pressen of Presson, near Wark in Northumberland. This Thomas also became a knight and (in 1390) constable of Norham Castle, as his father and grandfather had been. He was to marry Joan, daughter of John (III) Mowbray, Lord Mowbray (*d.* 1368),

and from him were descended in the male line the barons Grey of Powis, the barons Grey of Howick, and the earls Grey.

The prologue of the *Scalacronica* relates Gray's dream, in which a Franciscan master in divinity, Thomas of Otterbourne, held a five-runged ladder; a sibyl explained this ladder and its five stages, the first four of which were inhabited by ancient historians who would inspire his own work: Walter of Oxford for the first book devoted to Britons; Bede for the second, Saxon, era; Ranulf Higden, author of the *Polychronicon*, for the third book and the unification of England; and John Tynemouth, author of the *Historia aurea*, source of the fourth book which spreads from 1066 to 1362. The fifth rung gave access to the future. Possibly a laicization of the mystic ladders evoked by Bonaventure of Siena, by John Gobi, and by Walter Hilton, this ladder, or *scala*, gave the title of Gray's chronicle; as a family motif, it is still part of the family crest of the Greys of Howick and may come from a pun, *gre* meaning 'stair' in Middle English and Old French. In spite of the plan set out in the prologue, the *Scalacronica* is not merely a history of Britain, but resembles more a universal chronicle, starting from the creation of the world and giving a summary of the histories of Israel, Troy, and Rome. Within each period, several countries are taken into account, mostly England, then Scotland, but also Rome, Germany, France, and Spain.

Gray's ideal of knighthood is embodied in his father, who is one of the heroes of the chronicle. Left for dead in 1297 at Lanark and in 1304 at Stirling Castle, he survived. He strongly despised unnecessary rashness motivated only by the code of courtesy. Through his father's recollections, Gray was able to produce reliable reports of the wars preceding his own birth. His account of the battle of Bannockburn was written twenty years before that of John Barbour. He is a valuable source for Edward III's continental wars, especially after the victory at Poitiers; probably he gathered information from eyewitnesses. For the period 1359–60, when he was fighting in France, he used his own observation. He is the main authority for the English expedition from Calais to Rheims in the winter of 1359. He gives details on riots in Paris and on the rivalry between the provost of the merchants and the dauphin.

Only one medieval manuscript of the *Scalacronica* is presently known. It has been kept in Corpus Christi College, Cambridge, from *c.*1575 (MS 133), as part of the bequest of Matthew Parker, former master of this college and first Anglican archbishop of Canterbury. This manuscript was often collated. Under Henry VIII, John Leland inserted into his *Collectanea* an abstract which is still useful, as in its present state the Corpus Christi manuscript is lacking part of the annals for 1339 and 1356 and all the annals from 1340 to 1355. Some time before 1567, Nicholas Wotton, dean of Canterbury, wrote out numerous extracts which are now in a British Library manuscript (Harley 902). A printed edition of the authentic text was published at Edinburgh in 1836 by Joseph Stevenson, but only from the conquest onwards.   J. C. THIOLIER

Sources *Scalacronica, by Sir Thomas Gray of Heton, knight: a chronical of England and Scotland from* AD MLXVI *to* AD MCCCLXII, ed. J. Stevenson, Maitland Club, 40 (1836) · *Scalacronica: the reigns of Edward I, Edward II and Edward III as recorded by Sir Thomas Gray*, trans. H. Maxwell (1907) · A. Gransden, *Historical writing in England*, 2 (1982), 57, 59–60, 93–6, 196, 208, 459–60, 465, 478 · J. Taylor, *English historical literature in the fourteenth century* (1987), 5, 15, 21, 104, 163–4, 171–4 · J. C. Thiolier, 'La *Scalacronica*: première approche (MS 133)', *Les manuscrits français de la Bibliothèque Parker, Actes du Colloque 24–27 mars 1993* (1993), 121–55 · *Joannis Lelandi antiquarii de rebus Britannicis collectanea*, ed. T. Hearne, [3rd edn], 6 vols. (1774), vol. 1, pp. 206–9; vol. 2, pp. 509–79 · N. Wilkins, *Catalogue des manuscrits français de la Bibliothèque Parker* (Cambridge, 1993), 52–3, 55–9 · GEC, *Peerage*, new edn, 6.119–23, 136–7 · C. Moor, ed., *Knights of Edward I*, 2, Harleian Society, 81 (1929), 155 · *A catalogue of the Harleian manuscripts in the British Museum*, 1 (1808), 470 · M. L. Meneghetti, *I fatti de Bretagna. Cronache genealogiche anglo-normanne dal XII al XIV secolo* (1979), lix–lxii, 49–51, 67–71 · *Debrett's Peerage* (1990), 542–4
Archives BL, Harley MS 902 · BL, Cotton MS Faust. A.vi · CCC Cam., MSS 119, 133
Wealth at death Gray, *Scalacronica*, ed. Stevenson, lvii–lxiii · custody of manor of Middlemast-Middleton in 1344: Gray, *Scalacronica*, ed. Stevenson, xix · ' … a heavier ransom demanded from him than he was able to pay' (1355): *RotS*, vol. 1, p. 798; Rymer, *Foedera*, vol. 3, p. 343 · moiety of Felkington and Allerdean in Norhamshire in 1359: R. Surtees, *The history and antiquities of the county palatine of Durham* · fourth part of the manor of Upsettlington-West, with the appurtenances (1366): Letterbook of the prior of Durham, BL, Cotton MS Faust. A. vi, fol. 45b

Thomas Gray (1716–1771), by John Giles Eccardt, 1747–8

Gray, Thomas (1716–1771), poet and literary scholar, was born on 26 December 1716, the son of Philip Gray (1676–1741), scrivener, and Dorothy Antrobus (1685–1753), in his father's house in Cornhill (later numbered 41), close to the Royal Exchange in the City of London. Philip Gray, described in his obituary notice as 'an Exchange Broker of Reputation and Fortune' (*Daily News*), took to speculative building in his later years. His wife, the daughter of a prosperous scrivener whose sons had entered the learned professions, was co-proprietor with her sister Mary of a millinery business. Philip Gray made a pre-nuptial agreement with Dorothy that Mary should continue to conduct the business, all the profits from Dorothy's share in it being paid to Dorothy for her personal use. After the marriage took place, about 1709, Mary ran the business, with some assistance from Dorothy, in a shop on the ground floor of Philip Gray's house in Cornhill. In that house Thomas was born, the fifth of twelve children, and the only one to survive infancy. That he lived was owing to the courage of his mother, who, finding him in a fit, opened a vein with her scissors and relieved the paroxysm.

Early life and education In 1725 Gray was sent to Eton College, where two of his mother's brothers, Robert (1679–1730) and William (1688–1742), were then assistant masters. His mother supported him with her income from her sister's business, and it seems likely that it was her project to save her son from the counting-house and ensure his future in a socially respectable profession. Before his death in 1730 Robert initiated his nephew into the study of botany, which was to be a lifelong interest. Gray did not, as his uncle had hoped, become a physician. Instead he found himself beginning to 'take pleasure in reading Virgil for his own amusement, & not in school-hours, or as a

task' (*Correspondence*, 3.1290). He began to acquire a reputation as a writer of Latin verse; many years later his Eton contemporary, the scholar Jacob Bryant, could recall a line and a half from one of his school exercises.

At Eton Gray was one of four friends, self-styled the 'quadruple alliance'. The others were Thomas Ashton (1716–1775), the son of a schoolmaster; Horace Walpole (1717–1797), youngest son of Sir Robert Walpole, then prime minister; and Richard West (1716–1742), only son of Richard West (*d.* 1726), sometime lord chancellor of Ireland. They gave each other nicknames of a literary sort: Ashton was Almanzor from John Dryden's *Conquest of Granada*; Walpole was Celadon from D'Urfé's *Astrée*; West was Favonius or Zephyrus from Latin names for west winds; and Gray was Orosmades from Nathaniel Lee's *The Rival Queens*. The origins of these names indicate their shared interest in the theatre and French literature. Gray, who once admitted to imagining a paradise in which he could 'read eternal new romances of Marivaux and Crebillon' (*Correspondence*, 1.192), was likewise an enthusiastic theatregoer whenever he was in London.

In 1734 the four friends left Eton, West proceeding to Oxford, the others to Cambridge. Gray, who had been entered at Peterhouse, where his uncle Robert had been a fellow, was admitted on 4 July and took up residence on 9 October; a week later he was awarded the Cosin scholarship, which required him 'to wear a Square Cap, to make 6 [Latin] verses upon the Epistle or Gospel every Sunday morning, to chant very loud in Chappel, to wear a clean Surplice, &c: &c:' (*Correspondence*, 1.4). College records suggest that Gray lived frugally in his first year. Supported only by his scholarships and the earnings of the millinery business, he had no choice. He was supposed to be preparing for a career as a barrister, and on 22 November 1735 was admitted to the Inner Temple. It may have been the cost of supporting her son at Cambridge that brought long-standing differences between Dorothy and Philip Gray to a head, impelling her early in 1736 to seek legal advice on the possibility of separating from her husband, who was threatening to force Mary Antrobus and her shop out of the ground floor of his house. Philip Gray's refusal to contribute to the cost of his son's education, his irrational jealousy of his sister-in-law, and his brutal physical abuse of his wife, won her the sympathy of her adviser, John Audley of Doctors' Commons, but provided insufficient evidence of cruelty to support a plea for judicial separation. Mrs Gray was advised to try to compose matters. Perhaps because of her *démarche*, the domestic crisis seems to have passed; the shop continued in operation at its accustomed location, and Dorothy Gray remained in her husband's house. A few days after Dr Audley had issued his learned opinion, her son Thomas inherited the estate of his father's sister, Sarah Gray, who died on 12 February 1736. His possession of a small independent income relieved some of the financial pressures. He returned to Cambridge, to do nothing, as he claimed; but nothing included translating part of Statius's *Thebaid* into English, and taking lessons in Italian. He also contributed a poem in Latin to a collection by members of the university congratulating the prince of Wales on his marriage that spring.

In October 1736, beginning a new academic year after a summer holiday spent with his mother's sister Anne and her husband Jonathan Rogers at Burnham, Buckinghamshire, and in London, Gray decided not to take the BA degree, which was not required if he were to read law at the Inner Temple. His ability in Latin verse was recognized by the invitation to compose the 'Tripos-verses' for public circulation in March 1737 ('Luna habitabilis'). By the spring of 1737 he had progressed sufficiently in his Italian studies to read Dante and Petrarch, and render a few stanzas of Tasso into English couplets.

Gray left Cambridge in September 1738. He and West, both under family pressure to become barristers, planned to reside in the Temple together to pursue their legal studies, alleviating by companionship a prospect attractive to neither. Gray in fact spent the autumn and winter at his father's house in London, while West remained at his mother's house in Epsom. Early in 1739 Walpole, about to embark on a tour of Europe, suggested that Gray should accompany him. Seeing Europe in the company of the prime minister's son was not only an attractive prospect in itself, but an unimpeachable excuse for deferring a career at the bar for several more years. Gray accepted the invitation, and on 18 March 1739 the two friends took passage from Dover for Calais.

The continental tour, 1739–1741 Walpole and Gray stayed for two months in Paris. They visited churches, attended operas and plays, and made two visits to Versailles. On 1 June Gray and Walpole travelled to Rheims, where they intended to improve their command of French. After a dull three months they journeyed to Dijon and Lyons, whence they made a short visit to Geneva, calling at the monastery of the Grande Chartreuse on the way. They set out for Italy on 31 October. Crossing the Alps as winter came on was a difficult and dangerous journey; a wolf carried off Walpole's pet spaniel in broad daylight, and the travellers had to be carried over the pass in chairs on poles. Gray read Livy's account of Hannibal's crossing the Alps, and Silius Italicus's poetical rendition of the same. Passing through Turin, Genoa, Piacenza, Parma, Reggio, and Modena to Bologna, they reached Florence on 16 December. Here they passed the winter, introduced to Florentine society and art collections by the British resident, Horace Mann. In March 1740, following the death of Pope Clement XII, Gray and Walpole went to Rome, hoping to observe a papal election. The papal conclave was slow-moving, and the friends made a tour to the south. While in Naples they explored the recent excavations at Herculaneum: 'As you walk you see parts of an amphitheatre, many houses adorned with marble columns, and incrusted with the same; the front of a temple, several arched vaults of rooms painted in fresco' (*Correspondence*, 1.164). They returned to Florence on 8 July, staying with Mann in an apartment overlooking the Arno. As the prospect of a general European war loomed larger, the two travellers settled down to a second winter in Florence, adding to their circle John Chute (1701–1776), and his cousin Francis Whithed (1719–1751). Gray embarked on a philosophical poem in Latin hexameters entitled 'De principiis cogitandi', dedicating it to West. Gray's self-deprecating characterizations of this project, as 'an absurdity' or 'Master Tommy Lucretius' (ibid., 1.183, 225), should not obscure its importance for his later poetry. Gray understood the challenge which Lockean epistemology presented to traditional poetics, and undertook 'De principiis' to reconcile philosophy and creativity. He could abandon it after completing only the first book because he had achieved all he needed to sustain his future artistic development.

Gray and Walpole finally departed from Florence on 24 April 1741, heading for Venice (the first important stop on a return route through Austria, Germany, and the Low Countries). On the way, at Reggio on about 3 May, they quarrelled. However the angry words came about (there is reason to think that Ashton had relayed to Walpole some expressions of Gray's), the wealthy son of the prime minister outraged the sensitive pride of the impecunious scrivener's son. Travelling separately, both proceeded to Venice. War with France did not break out that year, and Gray, after three uncomfortable weeks in which he and Walpole stayed in the same house, made his way home through northern Italy, crossing the Alps by way of the Grande Chartreuse. Memories of his earlier visit inspired the ode in Latin alcaics, 'O tu, severi religio loci', which he inscribed in the monastery album (21 August). Ten days later he was back in England.

Two deaths, and return to Cambridge, 1741–1742 Continental travel had deferred Gray's reading for the bar for more than two years. In his absence West had gone to reside in the Temple in the autumn of 1739 and left it in the following June, claiming that he could read law books just as well somewhere else. Now deeply distressed by his widowed mother's relationship with his father's former secretary, and suffering from the consumption that was to kill him, West can hardly have done much to whet Gray's long-blunted purpose. Then Gray's father died, on 6 November 1741. Philip Gray had invested in properties around London, and had recently built a country house in Essex at considerable expense. His family inherited assets which were not immediately realizable; his son slowly disposed of the properties over time, retaining at his death only the house in Cornhill. Gray spent the winter in London, enjoying West's company until his friend's weakening health forced him to retire to a relative's country house. Gray was beginning a blank verse tragedy, 'Agrippina', modelled on Racine's *Britannicus*, for the English stage; only the opening scene and a fragment of the second were written. During the spring of 1742 Gray and West continued to share their literary interests by letter, discussing Tacitus as eagerly as Henry Fielding's recently published *Joseph Andrews*. West addressed a poem on the spring to Gray, and Gray responded with his first English poem of consequence, the 'Ode on the Spring'. West never saw it; he died on 1 June 1742, and Gray's letter containing the poem was returned unopened. The first anguish of the grief that inspired his poetry for a decade Gray expressed in Latin, in verses fittingly appended to 'De principiis'.

Gray's uncle and aunt Rogers were now living in the Buckinghamshire village of Stoke Poges, not far from Windsor, and here Gray spent part of the summer of 1742. From their house he could look across the Thames towards Eton, and in August he composed the 'Ode on a Distant Prospect of Eton College', the distance being both physical and temporal, as he contrasts carefree youth with suffering maturity. In the same month he wrote his sonnet on the death of West and the 'Ode to Adversity'. West's death, coming as it did when the death of Philip Gray had imposed responsibility for his mother and aunt on Gray's shoulders, brought home to the 25-year-old poet the fragility of human life and its moral requirements; 'Teach me to love and to forgive', he asks at the end of the 'Ode to Adversity', 'What others are to feel, and know myself a man.'

While West lived, Gray was committed to a shared preparation for a career in the common law courts. His friend's death freed him from this obligation, and in the summer of 1742 he decided that practice as a proctor in the more rarefied atmosphere of Doctors' Commons would suit him better. To study for the requisite qualification of a doctorate in civil law, he returned to Cambridge in the autumn of 1742. The opinion, frequently repeated in his letters of the 1730s, that the university was a dull, lazy, and boorish institution, found expression at this time in the fragment of a 'Hymn to Ignorance', plainly influenced by the recent publication of Alexander Pope's *New Dunciad*. But Cambridge had two powerful attractions; there he could live as a gentleman on a limited income, and

indulge his passion for learning. To Cambridge he went, and there, with one extended absence, he made his home for the rest of his life.

Reconciliation with Walpole and the *Elegy*, 1742–1751 Trinity Hall was the Cambridge college pre-eminent for the study of civil law, and Gray, in a letter to John Chute, names it as his destination. In the event he returned to Peterhouse, this time as a fellow-commoner; that is, he lived as a fellow without the responsibilities of a fellow. Late in 1742 his mother and her sister Mary gave up the millinery business, let the house in Cornhill, and retired to Stoke Poges to live with their sister Anne, whose husband, Jonathan Rogers, had died in October. That they were able to do this suggests that a year after Philip Gray's death his troubled affairs had been brought under control, and that his properties were producing enough income to support his heirs. For the remainder of his mother's life Gray spent the summers at Stoke.

Though resident in Peterhouse, Gray looked across Trumpington Street to Pembroke College for company. A number of friends from his undergraduate days were in residence there in 1742, including his contemporary Thomas Wharton, a fellow since 1739, and the somewhat older James Brown, a fellow active in college business. Gray borrowed from the Pembroke library, and interested himself in Pembroke politics, sympathizing with the fellows in their periodic tussles with the elderly master, Roger Long. By the time Gray had fulfilled the requirements for the bachelor of laws degree (16 December 1743), financial and parental pressures to qualify himself for the legal profession had abated. No longer constrained to prepare himself to earn an income, Gray ceased to attend law lectures, abandoned thoughts of the doctorate, and devoted himself entirely to his intellectual interests. In the mid-1740s these included classical antiquities and Greek philosophy, both contributing to a chronology of ancient Greece; travel literature, ancient and modern; and scientific, especially medical, writings of the later seventeenth century. He continued to read, as he had since his schooldays, the Greek and Latin poets. His method was to read through authorities systematically, gathering notable passages, and arranging them under topics; details relevant to dating were entered in the appropriate places in the chronology. As a scholar Gray was primarily a collector. He read critically, ever alert to confusion or contradiction on the part of his authors; he summarized their views and commented on them; but he did not publish, having 'a certain degree of pride, which led him … to despise the idea of being an author professed' (Mason, 335). The scrivener's son would not toil for money or fame: 'though without birth or fortune, or station, his desire was to be looked upon as a private independent gentleman, who read for his amusement' (Temple).

In November 1745 Gray and Walpole were reconciled. Walpole wrote offering a meeting, and Gray went up to London, to be kissed on both cheeks; after a dinner (the occasion of a reconciliation with Ashton also) and a break-fast together, Gray parted from Walpole 'far better satisfied, than I had been hitherto' (*Correspondence*, 1.227). Ashton was no longer a person of significance in Gray's eyes, but with Walpole he maintained a lifelong friendship, of particular importance in that it was the means of bringing his poetry into print. A year after the reconciliation Gray was showing Walpole the poems he had written in 1742. Stimulated by his friend's appreciative interest, he began to write poetry again. Walpole later recalled seeing the opening lines of the *Elegy* about this time. The 'Ode on the Death of a Favourite Cat', a graciously indirect compliment to Walpole by way of moralizing a domestic accident, was composed in February 1747; in the same month Walpole was proposing to publish a memorial collection of West's poems. This project came to nothing, but Walpole did arrange the anonymous publication of Gray's Eton College ode (folio; price 6*d*.) by Robert Dodsley on 30 May 1747. Seven months later (15 January 1748), this poem, with 'Ode on the Spring' and 'Ode on the Death of a Favourite Cat', appeared in the first edition of Dodsley's three-volume *Collection of Poems*. Again, Gray's name was not given.

Dodsley's *Collection* included an ode by a recent acquaintance of Gray's: William Mason, a young graduate of St John's College with literary ambitions, whose nomination in 1747 to a fellowship at Pembroke Gray was instrumental in arranging. Mason thus joined two other candidates for fellowships whom the fellows of Pembroke were determined to see elected. The equally determined master resisted them until March 1749. Another younger man who became a friend in the mid-1740s was Richard Stonhewer of Peterhouse. A better poet than Mason, Christopher Smart, fellow of Pembroke since 1745, was already succumbing to the wine and extravagance that terminated his once promising career at the university. Gray and others tried to help him, but without much success.

On 25 March 1748 a fire started in a wig maker's house in Exchange Alley off Cornhill and burned for ten hours, destroying or seriously damaging buildings between Cornhill and Lombard Street, including the Grays' house in Cornhill. The house was insured for £500, but cost £650 to rebuild. After a 3 per cent reduction for reasons unknown, the Grays received £485 from the insurers; Gray, taking advantage of a rising stock market, was able to augment this to £525; his aunt Mrs Rogers added £100, but even so he had to raise the possibility of borrowing from his friend Wharton to reach the total—an interesting demonstration of the narrow financial margins of his life at this point.

While he wrestled with these business affairs Gray returned to the challenge of a philosophical poem, this time in English pentameter couplets. 'The Alliance of Education and Government' reached only 107 lines before being abandoned in the spring of 1749, when a reading of Montesquieu's *De l'esprit des lois* convinced Gray that the French writer had anticipated him. The poem would have drawn on Gray's study of civic virtue in Plato's *Republic* and the orations of Isocrates. Echoes of these themes can be found in the *Elegy*, the final text of which Gray sent to Walpole from Stoke on 12 June 1750, as recently completed. Walpole, recognizing in the *Elegy* a poem of no common quality, encouraged the making and circulation of copies, which rapidly penetrated good society. Early in September 1750 two ladies called on Gray on a flimsy pretext; their real purpose was to provoke a return visit to the manor house of Stoke Poges so that the lady of the manor, Lady Cobham, might meet the author of the poem she had so much admired. Gray paid the visit, and soon found himself on friendly terms with Lady Cobham and the two ladies. One of them, Lady Cobham's niece Henrietta Speed (1728–1783), who lived with her aunt, turned out to be a lively companion. A decade later, when Gray and Miss Speed had attended Lady Cobham during her final illness, and Miss Speed had inherited a fortune from her aunt, Gray joked about a rumour that he would marry her. (She married the son of the Sardinian minister at London in 1761.) More immediately, her high spirits inspired Gray to write a comic ballad, 'A Long Story', commemorating the opening of their acquaintance; it began to circulate in manuscript through the ranks of fashionable society.

The *Elegy* did not remain exclusively with the fashionable, however, and on 10 February 1751 Gray received a letter intimating that the editors of the monthly *Magazine of Magazines* had received a copy of his poem entitled 'Reflections in a Country-Churchyard' which they intended to print. Gray wrote to Walpole, asking him to have Dodsley immediately print the poem from the manuscript in Walpole's possession, with the new title 'Elegy, Wrote in a Country Church-Yard' and a note claiming that the poem, author still unnamed, came into the bookseller's hands by accident. Walpole complied, and the *Elegy* was published in a quarto pamphlet on 15 February 1751. Gray's efforts to maintain his anonymity were defeated by the advertisements of the shameless *Magazine of Magazines*. The poem was an instant success, Dodsley's quarto going through five editions by the end of the year. It was printed in five magazines within three months, and soon became the most admired and imitated poem of the century.

Growing literary reputation and the *Odes*, 1751–1757 The secret of Gray's authorship now revealed, Walpole planned a new publication: a collection of Gray's published poems with illustrations by his friend Richard Bentley. In October 1751 Gray sent to Walpole the unpublished 'Ode to Adversity' of 1742 for inclusion. Bentley took some time to complete the extensive pictorial component of the volume. Gray insisted that the title give primacy to Bentley, and was appalled to discover at the last moment that Walpole intended to include a frontispiece portrait of the poet, based on a portrait painted by Giles Eccardt in 1747 for Walpole's house, Strawberry Hill. His protest was heeded, and the splendid folio *Designs by Mr. Bentley, for Six Poems by Mr. T. Gray* was issued by Dodsley on 29 March 1753. Gray's thoughts were otherwise occupied. Two weeks earlier, on 11 March, his mother had died. She was buried at Stoke Poges in the grave of her sister and former business partner Mary, who had died in 1749. Her grieving son placed a sorrowful inscription on the tomb.

As a poet Gray had always written with his predecessors in mind; he told Norton Nicholls that he 'never sat down to compose poetry without reading Spencer for a considerable time previously' (*Correspondence*, 3.1290). In 1752 he began a systematic study of the history of English poetry from the earliest times, encouraged by a copy of Pope's outline for such a history, which Mason had obtained from William Warburton, Pope's literary executor. Mason was eager that he and Gray should prepare such a history for publication, and Gray seems at first to have agreed, spending much of the next five years in studying early English, Welsh, and Scandinavian poetry to ascertain the history of rhyme. At the same time he pursued a different kind of historical argument in the first of his Pindaric odes, 'The Progress of Poesy', begun probably in 1751 and completed in 1754, which traces the spirit of liberty and poetry from ancient Greece to medieval Italy to modern England. As he studied the origins of rhyme, Gray was led to the study of Welsh poetry. This research enriched the composition of the companion ode, 'The Bard'; it was begun in 1755, laid aside in 1756, and completed in May 1757, when a visit to Cambridge by the blind Welsh harper John Parry 'set all this learned body a'dancing' (ibid., 2.502). No longer seeking anonymity, Gray sold the copyright in the odes to Dodsley for 40 guineas, reserving the right to reprint them in one collected edition of his poems. Walpole then intervened to secure the printing of the edition of 2000 copies at his newly installed press at Strawberry Hill. After inevitable delays, *Odes, by Mr. Gray, Printed at Strawberry Hill*, appeared on 8 August 1757. Some readers were enthusiastic, but many had difficulty with unfamiliar historical references and literary allusions. Gray was disappointed. Yet it can hardly have been true that 'all people of condition are agreed not to admire, nor even to understand' (ibid., 2.519) for in December the lord chamberlain, unsolicited, offered him the poet laureateship, apparently with assurances that the traditional new year's and birthday odes would not be required. Gray refused; to succeed Colley Cibber was a distinction he could very well forgo.

Migration to Pembroke College and other changes, 1756–1762
Gray had a lifelong dread of fire, and had installed outside his bedroom window at Peterhouse a bar, still in place, to accommodate a rope ladder. Early in March 1756 some undergraduates, probably not for the first time, gave a false alarm of fire with the intention of embarrassing the poet. The master of Peterhouse refusing to treat the matter with sufficient seriousness, Gray moved to Pembroke College, where he was admitted as a fellow-commoner on 6 March 1756. This episode, Gray wrote, 'may be look'd upon as a sort of Æra in a life so barren of events as mine' (*Correspondence*, 2.458), but in various ways the late 1750s were a period of transition in Gray's intellectual and personal life. After the publication of the odes in 1757 he wrote no more lyric poetry, and about this time ceased studying classical literature, ancient and oriental history, and geography. The history of English poetry was laid aside in favour of the study of medieval buildings in England, with particular attention to the Gothic architecture

of the cathedrals, and, concomitantly, to English history and the archival sources on which it should be based. The death of his mother's sister Anne (Mrs Jonathan Rogers) in September 1758 broke his family connection with Stoke Poges, although he continued to spend time each summer with Lady Cobham and her circle until 1760, the year of Lady Cobham's death. From this time he could afford to keep a manservant.

In July 1759 Gray took up residence in London, in lodgings formerly occupied by his friend Wharton in Southampton Row. For the next two years his principal occupation was historical research in the manuscript holdings of the recently opened British Museum, some of it by way of assisting Walpole in his historical projects. In November 1761, having read enough at the museum, Gray returned to his rooms at Pembroke. In February 1762 an undergraduate, Norton Nicholls, caught his attention by quoting Dante; the friendship thus begun was one of the warmest of Gray's later years.

Since the death of his mother Gray had been in the habit of travelling in England during the summer: to Durham in 1753, the midlands in 1754, Hampshire in 1755. In the six succeeding years his tours were less extensive, being mostly around Cambridge or in the home counties. In 1762 he travelled to Yorkshire at the beginning of July; after a short stay with Mason in York, he spent four months at Old Park with Wharton and his young family. Returning to London on 18 November, he discovered that Shallet Turner, regius professor of modern history at Cambridge, had died five days earlier. Encouraged by friends, Gray applied to Lord Bute, the prime minister, who responded with a civil denial. Gray's eye had been on this professorship for some time; a false report of Turner's death in 1747 had elicited his opinion that he was as well qualified for the position as anyone at Cambridge. Sounded out by a colleague in 1759, when Turner appeared likely to die, he had replied that he would not apply, not choosing to be refused. Now he had applied and been refused, the chair going to Lawrence Brockett, fellow of Trinity College, who had been tutor to Bute's nephew.

Natural history and tours, 1763–1768 Gray's interest in English history was fading. The acquisition of a copy of the tenth edition of Linnaeus's *Systema naturae* in 1759 signalled the rekindling of his youthful interest in natural history. He began to collect specimens of insects and plants, and to record observations on weather, the progress of the seasons, and anything which might differentiate English flora and fauna from the Swedish on which Linnaeus had based his work.

In 1764 Gray's outrage at the willingness of preferment-hungry Cambridge divines to support the candidacy of a notorious libertine, the earl of Sandwich, for high steward of the university was expressed in 'The Candidate', perhaps the most successful of his satirical poems. In the summer of 1765 he returned to Yorkshire to stay with Mason and Wharton; then in mid-August he set off for Glamis Castle in Perthshire as the guest of the ninth earl of Strathmore, who had been enrolled at Pembroke a decade earlier. There he met James Beattie of the Marischal

College, Aberdeen, who came especially to meet him. Gray went on a tour into the highlands, after which he wrote: 'in short since I saw the Alps, I have seen nothing sublime till now' (*Correspondence*, 2.894). This journey marks a shift in Gray's interests when travelling, from antiquities to natural scenery. The letters recording his observations, published by Mason in 1775, made him an influential pioneer of scenic tourism in Britain. In the summer of 1766 Gray travelled to Kent; in 1767, to Yorkshire to see Mason and Wharton, making tours into Derbyshire and the Lake District.

The original plates for the 1753 edition having become worn after two reprintings, Dodsley in 1767 proposed to have Bentley's illustrations re-engraved in a smaller format. Gray made it clear that he would prefer his poems to appear without illustrations, and without 'A Long Story', which had been included only to explain Bentley's designs. In its place Gray supplied two translations from Old Norse, 'The Fatal Sisters' and 'The Descent of Odin', and one from Welsh, 'The Triumphs of Owen', all probably dating from 1761, when his enthusiasm for James Macpherson's Ossianic productions temporarily revived his interest in the prehistory of English poetry. He also provided notes explaining some of the obscurities of the 1757 odes. About the same time Beattie proposed a collected edition, to be printed by the Foulis brothers of Glasgow. With Dodsley's approval, Gray consented, and on 1 February 1768 sent to Beattie the same instructions and the same new material that he had supplied to Dodsley. The London edition appeared on 12 March 1768, the Glasgow edition on 4 May. While visiting Kent in June, Gray wrote the satirical lines 'On Lord Holland's Seat near Margate', deftly adapting some lines by the peer himself.

Professor of modern history, 1768–1771 On 24 July 1768 Brockett fell off his horse and died, and the chair of modern history once again became vacant. Three days later the prime minister, the duke of Grafton, acting on the advice of his secretary, Gray's friend Stonhewer, wrote to Gray, offering him the appointment. Gray accepted immediately, and kissed hands at court on 28 July. The duties of the chair, worth £400 a year, were to deliver public lectures on modern history and to pay the salaries of instructors in French and Italian. Gray drafted an outline of an inaugural lecture, but never delivered it. His predecessors had, like most professors in eighteenth-century Cambridge, refrained from lecturing; Gray followed suit, but his conscience was troubled by this dereliction. He prepared plans for lecturing to selected undergraduates, but these were not acted upon, at least in part because of Gray's declining health. The only public function he undertook was to compose an 'Ode for Music' for the installation, on 1 July 1769, of the duke of Grafton as chancellor of Cambridge University.

Later that summer Gray travelled to Yorkshire to visit Mason and Wharton, making a fortnight's tour of the Lake District at the beginning of October. In December 1769, while visiting London, he met a young Swiss,

Charles Victor de Bonstetten (1745–1832), son of the treasurer of Bern, who was making an extended stay in England to learn English and make the acquaintance of people in good society. Bonstetten had met Norton Nicholls at Bath, and Nicholls gave him a letter of introduction to Gray, who was immediately drawn to this handsome young admirer of his poetry. A few days later Bonstetten eagerly accompanied Gray to Cambridge, where he took lodgings near Pembroke; he may subsequently have occupied rooms in the college. He spent his days and evenings with Gray, who read Milton and Shakespeare with him, introduced him to distinguished members of the university, and arranged for his instruction in Linnaean botany by the curator of the physic garden. Bonstetten, though emotionally volatile, was a young man of genuine intellectual eagerness who, despite his wondering contempt for the monkish society of Cambridge, was happy to be instructed by so eminent a figure as Gray. For his part, Gray made Bonstetten his protégé, moved by his beauty and idealizing him as a young man of unusual talents, remarkably untouched by aristocratic vices or the fashionable infidelity of France. When Bonstetten's father ordered him to return to the continent late in March 1770, Gray was distraught, as his letters to Nicholls clearly show.

In the summer of 1770 Gray, after spending the first two weeks of June with Mason in Yorkshire, devoted July to a tour of south-western England with Nicholls, being particularly impressed by the valley of the Wye from Ross to Chepstow. Also touring in these parts was William Gilpin, whose notes of his journey Gray later read. It was Gray's encouragement which led Gilpin ultimately to publish these observations, the first of a series of books that stimulated late eighteenth-century interest in the picturesque.

Gray's health was giving cause for concern. On 2 July 1770, before setting out on his tour, he made his will. He and Nicholls were planning a journey to Switzerland in the summer of 1771 to visit Bonstetten, but in May of that year Gray, though eager to see Bonstetten again, had to withdraw, citing 'bodily indisposition' (*Correspondence*, 3.1188). He was suffering from pain and recurrent fevers—symptoms, it is now believed, of progressive failure of the kidneys. A deepening depression was aggravated by irrational guilt over his failure to perform his professorial duties. His early summer visit to London was prolonged when he became too ill to travel. He returned to Pembroke on 22 July, intending to travel on to Yorkshire, but collapsed in hall two days later. The Cambridge physicians could not alleviate the 'Gout in the Stomach' that they diagnosed. Gray began to suffer convulsions and loss of consciousness, and finally lapsed into a coma. He died at 11 p.m. on 30 July 1771 in his rooms at Pembroke. His old friend James Brown, now master of Pembroke, and his cousin Mary Antrobus, the Cambridge postmistress, accompanied his corpse to Stoke Poges where, in accordance with his wishes, he was buried in his mother's grave early in the morning of 6 August. His name was not added to the inscription he had composed for his mother; the famous son was content to be lost in the memorial to his beloved parent.

The privacy which Gray had preserved in life was first invaded after his death by his friend and literary executor William Mason, who in *The Poems of Mr. Gray, to which are Prefixed Memoirs of his Life and Writings* (1775) added poems Gray had chosen not to print, and constructed the memoirs from selected letters, linked where necessary with brief passages of narrative. This method was adopted by numerous subsequent biographers, notably James Boswell, who expressly modelled his life of Johnson on Mason's memoirs of Gray. There is some irony here, since Gray's relatively early death qualified him for inclusion in the collection of the 'most eminent English Poets' for which Johnson wrote the much reprinted 'Prefaces biographical and critical'. In his preface to Gray's poems, usually known as the *Life of Gray* (1781), Johnson, drawing on Mason's *Memoirs*, censured Gray's life as finical and unproductive, and his poetry as pretentious. Whereas Johnson's hostile treatment of Milton provoked a considerable number of defences and even new biographies of Milton, his assault on Gray aroused some indignation but no substantial printed rebuttal. Twenty years later, in a moment of national emergency, Wordsworth, rejecting Johnson, wrote: 'Milton! thou shouldst be living at this hour'. Gray he had invoked on a less heroic occasion, in his preface to *Lyrical Ballads* (1800), in Johnsonian manner illustrating his strictures on the vicious poetic diction of his predecessors with a strikingly impercipient reading of the sonnet on the death of West. Matthew Arnold's essay (1880) accepts Johnson's conclusion, but justifies it by turning Gray into a historical phenomenon, a 'born poet' who 'fell upon an age of prose'. Arnold's suave assurance that Gray was not to blame for his birth date does not mean that Arnold diverged from Johnson's view that Gray was a failed poet; sterility may be more a dignified diagnosis than costiveness, but both explain an absence.

The antidote to these enormously influential interpretations of Gray has proved to be more extensive acquaintance with Gray as he is revealed in his letters. Unhappily, Mason falsified many of the letters he printed, and subsequently destroyed many of the originals, but the great edition of Toynbee and Whibley (1935; 1971) presents more than 600 letters. These show Gray clearly to have been a man of his age, more precisely a gentleman of his age, who numbered among his private accomplishments the occasional composition of poetry, who wished to share with others only those poems which met his own standards of excellence, and who, except for the two Pindaric odes, was reluctant to see any of them appear in print. Among these was one, perhaps the richest in self-revelation, the one which Johnson excepted from his censures, a poem which through many changes of taste has retained its popularity and defined the literary rank of its author. Gray's *Elegy* is one of the great poems of the English language; to many readers, learned and otherwise, it has stood almost for the idea of poetry itself.

JOHN D. BAIRD

Sources *Correspondence of Thomas Gray*, ed. P. Toynbee and L. Whibley, 3 vols. (1971), with additions and corrections by H. W. Starr · R. W. Ketton-Cremer, *Thomas Gray: a biography* (1955) · W. P. Jones, *Thomas Gray, scholar: the true tragedy of an eighteenth-century gentleman* (1937) · *The poems of Gray, Collins, and Goldsmith*, ed. R. Lonsdale (1969) · Walpole, *Corr.* · R. Martin, *Chronologie de la vie et de l'œuvre de Thomas Gray* (1931) · W. Mason, *The poems of Mr. Gray, to which are prefixed memoirs of his life and writings by W. Mason, M. A.*, 2nd edn (1775) · *Daily News* (7 Nov 1741) · [W. J. Temple], 'A sketch of the character of the celebrated *Mr. Gray*, author of the *Elegy in a country church-yard*', *London Magazine*, 41 (1772), 140 · *The complete poems of Thomas Gray*, ed. H. W. Starr and J. R. Hendrickson (1966); repr. (1972) · *Cambridge Chronicle and Journal* (1763–71) · *GM*, 1st ser., 41 (1771), 375 · S. H. Clark, '"Pendet homo incertus": Gray's response to Locke', *Eighteenth-Century Studies*, 24 (1990–91), 273–92, 484–503 · R. Lonsdale, 'Gray and Johnson: the biographical problem', *Fearful joy*, ed. J. Downey and B. Jones (1974), 66–84 · R. L. Mack, *Thomas Gray: a life* (2000)

Archives BL, corresp., notes, and papers, Add. MSS 5821, 5832, 36817–36818, 36359, 37683, 38511 · Harvard U., Houghton L., notes and papers · Hunt. L., letters and literary MSS · Pembroke Cam., notebooks and letters · Yale U., Farmington, Lewis Walpole Library, letters, notes, and poems · York Minster Library, notebooks | BL, corresp. with W. T. How, Add. MS 26889 · BL, letters to Thomas Wharton, Egerton MS 2400 · Hants. RO, letters to John Chute · Morgan L. · NYPL, Berg collection · U. Aberdeen L., corresp. with James Beattie · Yale U., Beinecke L., letters to Norton Nicholls

Likenesses A. Pond? (J. Richardson?), oils, c.1730, FM Cam. · J. G. Eccardt, oils, 1747–8, NPG [*see illus.*] · F. Mapletoft, silhouette, c.1760, Pembroke Cam. · oils, c.1771, York Minster library · B. Wilson, oils, 1774, Pembroke Cam. · J. Bacon senior, medallion on monument, 1778, Westminster Abbey · W. Doughty, etching, 1778 (after W. Mason), BM, NPG; repro. in T. Gray, *Poems* (1778) · J. Basire, pencil drawing (after W. Mason, c.1771), BM; repro. in T. Gray, *Poems* (1778) · J. Chapman, stipple (after B. Wilson), BM; repro. in T. Gray, *Poems* (1799) · W. Henshaw, etching (after W. Mason), NPG · W. Mason, pencil drawing, Pembroke Cam. · etchings (after W. Mason), NPG · plaster bust, NPG

Wealth at death approx. £7000; bequeathed amounts of stock nominally valued at £500 to two relatives on father's side, and to Stonhewer and Wharton; and amounts of nominal value £600 to two Antrobus cousins, who also inherited furniture and personal goods; house at 41 Cornhill to cousin; £50 in stock and his clothing and linen to servant, Stephen Hempsted; books and papers went to William Mason, to be preserved or destroyed at his discretion: will, *Correspondence*, ed. Toynbee and Whibley, vol. 3, pp. 1283–6, 1277, and n. 4

Gray, Thomas (1787–1848), promoter of railways, the son of Robert Gray, engineer, was born in Leeds, and afterwards lived in Nottingham. As a boy he had seen John Blenkinsop's pioneering steam locomotive at work on the Middleton colliery cogged railroad. He was staying in Brussels in 1816, when the project of a canal from Charleroi for the purpose of connecting Holland with the mining districts of Belgium was under discussion. In connection with John, son of William Cockerill, he advocated the superior advantages of a railway. He became obsessed with the preparation of a revolutionary treatise which was intended to give force to his argument. In 1820 he published the result of his labours as *Observations on a general iron railway, with plates and map illustrative of the plan; showing its great superiority … over all the present methods of conveyance.* In this work he envisaged that horses would be entirely superseded by steam traction. He also suggested the desirability of making a railway between Liverpool and Manchester. The treatise went through four editions in two years. In 1822 he added a diagram showing a number of suggested lines of railway connecting the principal towns of England, and another suggesting links between the leading Irish centres.

Gray pressed his pet scheme for 'a general iron road' upon leading public figures of the day. He sent memorials to Lord Sidmouth in 1820, and to the lord mayor and corporation of London a year later. In 1822 he addressed the earl of Liverpool and Sir Robert Peel. He petitioned the government in 1823. By that time his Nottingham acquaintances were declaring him 'cracked', while a contemporary, William Howitt, who frequently came in contact with him, stated: 'With Thomas Gray, begin where you would, on whatever subject, it would not be many minutes before you would be enveloped in steam, and listening to a harangue on the practicability and the advantages to the nation of a general iron railway'. In 1829, in the midst of the Rainhill trials, when there was heated public discussion concerning the most effective form of locomotive power to be deployed on smooth-edge rails, Gray advocated his by now outdated plan for a greased railway employing cog transmission. He ultimately fell into poverty, and sold glass and lead on commission. He died, allegedly broken-hearted, on 15 October 1848, at 1 Austwick Terrace, St Thomas, in Exeter.

JAMES BURNLEY, rev. M. W. KIRBY

Sources W. W. Tomlinson, *The North Eastern railway: its rise and development* [1915]; repr. with new introduction by K. Hode (1967) · S. Smiles, *Lives of the engineers*, 3 (1862) · *GM*, 2nd ser., 30 (1848) · R. V. Taylor, ed., *The biographia Leodiensis, or, Biographical sketches of the worthies of Leeds* (1865) · d. cert.

Likenesses R. A. Clack, oils, 1848, Royal Albert Memorial Museum, Exeter, Devon

Gray, Walter de (*d.* 1255), archbishop of York, was the younger son of John de Gray of Rotherfield Greys, Oxfordshire, and his wife, Hawisia. His uncle, another John de Gray, was bishop of Norwich (1200–14), and a favourite of King John. In the event Walter became the most important member of an influential clerical family. His nephews, the brothers Henry and Walter de Gray, were to be promoted by him to canonries of York, and a third nephew, William de Langton of Rotherfield Greys became first dean of York from about 1260 to 1279, and then archbishop-elect, though papal opposition deprived him of the see. Walter was also connected to the Giffards of Boyton, Wiltshire, one of whom, Walter Giffard, brother of Godfrey, bishop of Worcester, became bishop of Bath and Wells (1265–6) and subsequently archbishop of York (1266–79).

Education, election to York, and support of King John At Oxford—to which university he was to bequeath Black Hall, worth £5 a year—Gray heard the lectures of Edmund of Abingdon, a future chancellor of York and archbishop of Canterbury, who was teaching arts in the early 1200s, and for whom Gray later offered to provide a glossed Vulgate. His period of residence at the university is unknown, but he did not incept.

In October 1205, at an unusually early age, Gray became King John's chancellor, an office for which he paid 5000 marks. This appears to have been somewhat of a business venture, since he was little concerned with the relevant duties. He surrendered the seal temporarily in October 1213 during his absence in Flanders, resuming it in the following January, and retained it until October 1214. One of the firmest and most consistent of John's supporters, he was among those instrumental in delaying publication of the papal bull of excommunication (1209). This earned him the king's gratitude, and hence support for his ecclesiastical advancement. His election by the Lichfield chapter to the see of Coventry was quashed by the papal legate Pandulf. Elected a second time in 1213, he was equally unsuccessful. However, thanks to royal efforts he became bishop of Worcester in the following year. The rare conjuncture of pressure from the king and the wishes of Innocent III secured his translation to the primatial see of York in 1215. His candidature was opposed by the dean and chapter who wished to appoint Simon Langton, brother of Stephen Langton, the Canterbury metropolitan. They stigmatized Gray as illiterate, but under threat of an independent papal appointment they reluctantly nominated him, commending such quality as they could discern—his chastity. Pope Innocent was assured that his nominee had been a virgin from the day he left his mother's womb. Such exemplary virtue ensured confirmation of his election. At the time Gray was attending the Fourth Lateran Council at Rome, where he secured the pallium and was alleged by the unsympathetic chronicler Wendover to have paid £10,000 to the curia.

Gray was at Dover on 15 May 1213 when King John, admitting that he had offended God and the church, surrendered his realms to the pope. Although Gray did not witness the charter then issued, the story that he refused to append the chancellor's seal is unfounded. As chancellor he attested John's repetition of his act of submission, 3 October 1213, which was incorporated in Innocent's confirmation of 21 April 1214. After his promotion to Worcester he accompanied the king abroad, and deferred his consecration as bishop until 5 October 1214. Present at Runnymede in 1215, he is named among the bishops in the preamble to Magna Carta. Subsequently he was abroad raising mercenaries to fight the barons. After John's death, on the night of 18–19 October 1216, Gray supported the legate Guala Bicchieri in his excommunication of the opponents of the young Henry III; Henry did not assume personal rule until 1227. During Henry's minority Gray acted against the rebellious William de Forz, count of Aumale (*d.* 1241), in and around Lincolnshire, in 1221, and fostered opposition among the vassals of Louis IX in Brittany, Normandy, and Poitou.

Gray's closeness to King John has not endeared him to modern historians. He never incurred the king's disapproval, but remained in his service throughout the interdict, even acting as guarantor of John's good faith. However, as ruler of the northern archbishopric he bears an excellent reputation. Following a lengthy vacancy he came as an outsider uncontaminated by local factionalism. His co-operation with the chapter was fruitful, and he brought order into both diocesan and metropolitan administration. After the first decade of his episcopate his *acta* are recorded in two rolls of unequal length—the earliest records of the kind at York, conceivably a consequence of the Fourth Lateran Council and perhaps influenced by the practice of the English chancery.

Activities as archbishop Gray attended the reforming council held at St Paul's in 1237 by the legate Otto di Monteferrato, and is thought to have been responsible for a series of York synodal statutes which have been dated between 1241 and 1255. He insisted upon clerical celibacy, and was concerned to ensure the suitability of those presented to benefices. He combated hereditary succession to livings, saw to the endowment of vicarages, ensured the appointment of vicars in accordance with the legislation of the Lateran Council, and consolidated churches which had been divided. He conducted visitations of monasteries and assisted a number of them with financial or disciplinary problems. Among other assistance to the cathedral chapter—annexing Newthorpe and Acomb to the treasurership and appropriating a number of churches—he established the subdeanery, and attached to it the church of Preston in Holderness. To this dignity, perhaps from its inception, the office of penitentiary was attached.

Gray's gifts to York Minster included a golden chalice and paten, set with precious stones, a costly mitre, and thirty-two copes. The south transept of his cathedral was completed by 1241. Within it he founded a chantry with an altar dedicated to St Michael and All Angels, where two chaplains and a clerk were to intercede for the souls of the archbishops, the canons, and all Christians. But although he encouraged extensive rebuilding of the minster, particularly of the transepts, no evidence has survived to suggest that he undertook financial responsibility for any part of the fabric. By means of indulgences he promoted the building of the west front of Ripon collegiate church, where he translated the remains of St Wilfrid to a new shrine, and endowed an additional prebend, that of Stanwick. Other indulgences assisted the building of the choirs of the collegiate churches of Beverley and Southwell. Legend has it that he was responsible for the building in the early English style of Skelton church near York. What is certain is that in 1247 he confirmed a donation to the church by the treasurer of the minster.

Against Archbishop Stephen Langton, Gray was a doughty defender of his right to have his metropolitan cross borne erect before him in the southern province. However, Honorius III by a bull of 6 February 1218 forbade Gray to carry his cross within Canterbury province. Gray's response was to absent himself from Henry III's second coronation in May 1220, seemingly with the intention of avoiding a disturbance. Two years later the primates faced each other in the neighbourhood of Lincoln, within the confines of their respective jurisdictions, but were unable to agree on a compromise. On the grounds of seniority of consecration Gray formally claimed the right to sit on the legate Otto's right hand at the council of 1237, but the latter diplomatically pointed out that although saints Paul and Peter were depicted on the papal *bulla* respectively to the right and left of the central cross, they were held in

equal honour. Within his province, Gray's consecration of Nicholas of Farnham as bishop of Durham in 1241, and his receiving a profession of obedience from him, set a precedent which was to cause considerable friction in the time of archbishops William de Wickwane and John Romanus. He also attempted to exert metropolitan authority over the Scottish see of Whithorn. He increased the dignity of his own see in a number of other ways. For example, he purchased the village of Thorpe St Andrew (now Bishopthorpe) and built a manor house there. This was conveyed in trust to the dean and chapter for the use of the archbishop for the time being. At Westminster he purchased a house from the Dominicans in 1244 and established a residence there—the later York Place—which was to be converted into Whitehall Palace by Henry VIII.

Gray's part in public life, his death, and reputation In the sphere of public affairs, Gray officiated in 1221 at the marriage of Alexander II, king of Scots, to Henry III's sister Joan. He also took part in the festivities which accompanied Henry's Christmas visit to York in 1228, and did so again in 1230 when Henry returned with the Scottish king. But the most spectacular of these events in the minster occurred in 1252, when Henry III and his queen arrived with the Scottish royal family for the marriage of Alexander III to Henry's daughter Margaret. More than a thousand knights were present for the ceremony and the banquet which followed is said to have cost the archbishop some 4000 marks. In 1238 Gray was summoned to London to protect the legate, who had fled from Oxford following an affray between his followers and the scholars. Subsequently he was instrumental in securing a pardon for the university.

During Henry III's absence abroad between May 1242 and September 1243 Gray acted as regent, but he was reluctant to accept the position a second time in May 1254, when Queen Eleanor left England to join her husband. Royal policy and behaviour, coupled with the problems of raising money, increasingly disillusioned the ageing prelate. Matthew Paris suggests that Gray made advancing age and remoteness an excuse to avoid attending royal councils. When Henry III sought to extract a crusading tenth from the bishops in 1252, this was rejected in the absence of both Gray and the archbishop of Canterbury. Gray was not at the 1254 parliament, and the king's overbearing behaviour in that of 1255 is said to have hastened the archbishop's death. He arrived in London in April of that year, but died at Fulham on 1 May. He was interred on Whitsun eve, 15 May 1255, in the south transept at York, where his effigy rests on a tomb chest in what is considered to be the earliest canopied tomb in England. A temporary painted effigy was discovered on the lid of the coffin when it was opened in 1968. The chalice, paten, ring, and crozier recovered from the body are on permanent exhibition at the minster. Despite the fact that he owed his ecclesiastical eminence to a king notorious for his disregard of the English church, Gray's reputation both as an administrator and as metropolitan of the northern province has stood the test of time. On a personal level, however, both

Roger of Wendover—admittedly partisan—and Matthew Paris retail a story of his exceptional avarice in dealings with underlings.   ROY MARTIN HAINES

Sources Borth. Inst., MS B1, Register 1, A Rotulus major, B Rotulus minor · J. Raine, ed., *The register or rolls of Walter Gray, lord archbishop of York*, SurtS, 56 (1872) · *Chancery records* · Paris, *Chron.*, vols. 2, 5 · *Rogeri de Wendover liber qui dicitur flores historiarum*, ed. H. G. Hewlett, 3 vols., Rolls Series, [84] (1886–9), vols. 2–3 · *Ann. mon.* · [J. T. Fowler], ed., *Memorials of the church of SS Peter and Wilfrid, Ripon*, 1, SurtS, 74 (1882) · J. C. Holt, *King John* (1964) · J. C. Holt, *Magna Carta* (1965) · S. Painter, *The reign of King John* (1949) · W. L. Warren, *King John* (1961); repr. (1964) · C. R. Cheney, 'The alleged deposition of King John', *Studies in medieval history presented to Frederick Maurice Powicke*, ed. R. W. Hunt and others (1948), 100–16 · W. H. Dixon, *Fasti Eboracenses: lives of the archbishops of York*, ed. J. Raine (1863) · J. Solloway, *Walter de Gray*, York Minster Historical Tracts, 11 (1927) · H. G. Ramm and others, 'The tombs of archbishops Walter de Gray (1216–55), and Geoffrey de Ludham (1258–65) in York Minster and their contents', *Archaeologia*, 103 (1971), 101–47 · *Selected letters of Pope Innocent III concerning England, 1198–1216*, ed. C. R. Cheney and W. H. Semple (1953) · F. M. Powicke and C. R. Cheney, eds., *Councils and synods with other documents relating to the English church, 1205–1313*, 2 vols. (1964) · R. M. Haines, 'Canterbury versus York: fluctuating fortunes in a perennial conflict', *Ecclesia Anglicana: studies in the English church of the later middle ages* (1989), 69–105 · Emden, *Oxf.*

Archives Borth. Inst., MS B1, register 1, A Rotulus major, B Rotulus minor

Likenesses painting on coffin lid, York Minster · tomb effigy, York Minster

Gray, Sir Walter (1848–1918). *See under* Gray, Francis James (1880–1935).

Gray, William (*bap.* 1601, *d.* 1674), chorographer and merchant, was baptized at St Nicholas's Church, Newcastle upon Tyne, on 21 September 1601, the eldest of the eleven children of Cuthbert Gray (*d.* 1623), merchant, and his wife, Elizabeth Huntley (*fl.* 1600–1644). He was almost certainly educated at Queen Elizabeth's Free Grammar School in St Mary's Hospital, Newcastle, under the school's first headmaster, Robert Fowberry, and was admitted to the Drapers' Company, probably as a freeman's son, in 1624. After his father's death Gray joined his mother, who was still living in 1644, in the management of the family's many prosperous businesses. He is, however, best known not for his work as a merchant but for a single, slim volume, his *Chorographia, or, A Survey of Newcastle upon Tine* (1649), the first historical and topographical account of his native city and its surrounding region. Gray presents his book, which provided the starting point for such eighteenth-century successors as Henry Bourne and John Brand, as a continuation on the local level of the national chorographies of William Camden and John Speed. But he had a more immediate motivation as well. He wrote, as he says, 'that those Monuments which these late Warrs have obliterated and ruin'd, may be left to Posterity' (preface).

Twice occupied by the Scots, first in 1640 to 1641 and again between 1644 and 1647, Newcastle suffered greatly for its adherence to the royalist cause. Both the suffering and the adherence find expression in Gray's book. He laments in particular that, after so many centuries of serving as a bulwark against the Scots, Newcastle, through the perfidy of the English parliamentarians, 'was stormed,

our Churches and Houses defaced, the ornaments of both plundered, and carried away, the *Crowne* of our Heads is fallen'—a clear allusion to the execution a few months earlier of Charles I—'woe now unto us, for we have sinned' (p. 27). And he remarks wryly on the perils of publishing 'in an Age, that Mechanicks will presume to Step into Moses Chaire, and become Politians to contradict and controle whatsoever is acted and done according to the Laws Divine and Humane' (preface).

Though Gray's business ventures were no doubt severely hurt, as was the commerce of Newcastle generally, by the exactions and disruptions of the 1640s, he still owned extensive property, including at least seven tenements, in and around Newcastle when he made his will in 1656. He was then living in one of his two tenements in a street called The Side with his principal heirs, his sister Elizabeth and her husband, Robert Ellison, merchant and MP for Newcastle in the Long Parliament, and he seems to have continued living with them for the rest of his life. Among his occupations during the decade that followed the publication of his *Chorographia* was the accumulation, in view of a possible second edition, of further notes on the history and topography of Newcastle. These notes survive in the margins and on added leaves in Gray's own copy of *Chorographia*, which remained in his family until the 1880s but which eventually reached the Huntington Library in San Marino, California. Joseph Crawhill and Andrew Reid published many of the notes in their 1884 edition of *Chorographia*, one of four eighteenth- and nineteenth-century reprintings of Gray's book. Gray died, probably unmarried, in Newcastle and was buried on 7 February 1674 in St Nicholas's Church.

                                        RICHARD HELGERSON

Sources R. Welford, 'Cuthbert Gray, merchant', *Archaeologia Aeliana*, new ser., 11 (1886), 65–81 · R. Welford, *Men of mark 'twixt Tyne and Tweed*, 3 vols. (1895) · M. H. Dodds, *Register of freemen of Newcastle upon Tyne* (1923) · J. Brand, *The history and antiquities of the town and county of the town of Newcastle upon Tyne*, 2 vols. (1789)

Archives Hunt. L., Gray's annotated copy of his *Chorographia*

Wealth at death £30—goods and chattels; lands and tenements perhaps conveyed to heirs before death: will and inventory, printed in Welford, 'Cuthbert Gray', 77–81

Gray, (Edward) William (1786–1860), banker and topographer, was born in Newbury, Berkshire, on 28 October 1786, the youngest son and ninth child in the family of eight sons and four daughters of Joseph Gray (1745–1805), cheesemonger and mealman, who was mayor of Newbury in 1779, and Ruth, *née* Tinsley (1744–1834). After leaving school William Gray joined two of his brothers in a provision business at Alton, Hampshire. In 1806 Henry Austen, an army agent who that year became senior partner of a London bank, established a bank in Alton, in which Gray subsequently became a partner. Three years later Henry's mother and two sisters, one being the novelist Jane Austen, went to live in Chawton, near Alton. Letters to and from these family members were included in the bank parcel which the London mail coach regularly delivered and collected at The Swan inn, Alton. Jane Austen's letters included several which she inscribed 'By favour of Mr Gray'.

Henry Austen withdrew from his partnership at the Alton bank in October 1815. Gray's remaining partner was William Vincent of Newbury, a second cousin by marriage. With the collapse of the wartime agricultural boom in 1815, the bank encountered cash problems, as a high proportion of its assets were private and unsecured loans. In November 1815, when the failure of the Alton bank was imminent, Gray informed his grocer brother Frederick, who in turn tipped off his father-in-law, the Alton attorney Thomas Clement. On the day before its closure, by means of accomplices, the three withdrew all but 16s. of the bank's cash holdings.

Early in December, Gray was declared bankrupt and assignees were appointed. These were Frederick Gray and two of his cronies, nominated after they had hoodwinked the other creditors as to the correct hour of the meeting. The aggrieved creditors brought a case before the lord chancellor, John Scott, Baron Eldon, who angrily ordered the replacement of the assignees. In July 1817 the new assignees recovered more than £500 from the Grays and Clement at the Hampshire assizes.

Gray already owed more than £6500 to the Austen bank in London, which closed its doors a few months later, in March 1816. Henry Austen subsequently claimed that his crash was directly due to Gray's defalcation, which cost the bank £10,000 that was never repaid. Released from bankruptcy in July 1817 Gray returned to Newbury, where he took over the family cheesemongering business. He became a councillor in 1835 and mayor four years later. His many public interests included local charities, the revival of the moribund grammar school, administration of the Newbury Poor Law Union, the Literary and Scientific Institute, and the local cattle show.

In 1839, as the main contributor, Gray published anonymously *The History and Antiquities of Newbury and its Environs*. He was helped by fellow members of the institute, while others compiled the appended catalogue of plants found in the neighbourhood. It had been his original intention to publish the book in instalments, but he abandoned it after the appearance of the first in 1831. In 1855 he published *Notes and Observations* gained during a seven-week trip through northern England and Ireland.

Gray, who never married, died at his Newbury home on 19 June 1860; he had arranged for his funeral, at Enborne, near Newbury, on 26 June, to be conducted very privately at 8 a.m. His estate was valued at under £800, and he had directed that all personal effects should be divided equally among five nephews and nieces, a scheme, in his words, adopted in preference to 'gratifying public curiosity by an exposure of my property to visitation'. Secretive to the last, he merits a brief note as one who indirectly helped, through financial recklessness and dishonesty, to darken the final year and a half of Jane Austen's life.

T. A. B. CORLEY

Sources R. Honan, *The Gray matter* (1987) · H. Purvis, 'Newbury's first historian', *Transactions of Newbury District Field Club*, 14/1 (1991), 28–30 · case before lord chancellor, 23 Aug 1816, PRO, B1/134, 253– 7 · *Hampshire Chronicle* (21 July 1817), 3 · *Jane Austen's letters*, ed. D. Le Faye, 3rd edn (1995) · W. Money, *The history of the ancient town and borough of Newbury in the county of Berks.* (1887) · *Reading Mercury* (23 June 1860) · *Reading Mercury* (30 June 1860) · *N&Q*, 4th ser., 3 (1869), 554, 607 · T. A. B. Corley, 'Jane Austen and her brother Henry's bank failure, 1815–1816', *Jane Austen Society Report for 1998* (1999) · *DNB* · *CGPLA Eng. & Wales* (1860)

Wealth at death under £800: probate, 10 July 1860, *CGPLA Eng. & Wales*

Gray, William (1801–1835), writer, was born in the parish of Kirkcudbright on 10 January 1801, the only son of James Gray of Kirkcudbright and Agnes Walker. He matriculated as a gentleman commoner of St Alban Hall, Oxford, on 30 October 1824 but migrated to Magdalen College in 1825 when the principal of St Alban Hall died. As an undergraduate he showed literary promise. In his first year at Magdalen he wrote for the *Oxford Herald* an obituary account of Peter Elmsley as principal of St Alban Hall, among other contributions: this was reprinted in the *Gentleman's Magazine* in April 1825. He edited a beautifully produced volume, published by the university press, *Miscellaneous Works of Sir Philip Sidney, with a Life of the Author and Illustrative Notes* (1829), which includes the whole of the 'Astrophel and Stella' sequence, and *The Defence of Poetry*. The volume was reprinted in Boston, USA, in 1860. In the same year he founded an *Oxford Literary Gazette*, of which six numbers appeared. He graduated BA on 25 June 1829 and MA on 2 June 1831. Eight days later he was called to the bar by the Society of the Inner Temple, but ill health prevented him from practising. In his last months he saw through the press an interesting short book, his *Historical sketch of the origin of English prose literature, and of its progress till the reign of James 1* (1835). In 100 pages of his own fine Augustan prose he tells the story of the nation's literature from the time of the druids, with their rich tradition of encyclopaedic verse. Gray gives proper emphasis to Alfred and his literary descendants, arguing for the centrality of a Saxon tradition. He gives passing notice to William Tyndale, ignoring the significance of his Bible translations, but seeing him as one of several who wrote well for the nation against 'the unscrupulous despotism of the holy see' (p. 71). He contrasts 'the correct and idiomatic Swift' with 'the sonorous and Latinized Johnson' (p. 15). His last five lines consummate the tradition in his own homeland, seeing 'the great magician of the north advancing with the mastery of a conqueror over the whole empire of fancy'—Scott, of course. Gray died at Dumfries on 29 November 1835.

DAVID DANIELL

Sources *GM*, 2nd ser., 5 (1836), 326–7 · bap. reg. Scot. · Allibone, *Dict.* · Foster, *Alum. Oxon.* · *DNB*

Gray, Sir William (1823–1898), shipbuilder and shipowner, was born on 18 January 1823 in Blyth, Northumberland, one of five children of Matthew Gray and his wife, Ann Jane Bryham. His father was a draper and shipowner. He received his schooling at Bruce's academy, Newcastle upon Tyne, before he learned the drapery business under his father. He also spent several years in London before, in 1844, he set up on his own account in Hartlepool. On 15

May 1849 he married Dorothy (d. 1906), daughter of Captain John Hall RN. Although at that time they were living at Lewisham, Kent, the Hall family had strong connections with north-east England. The couple had five daughters, including the politician and philanthropist Julia *McMordie, and two sons.

Gray invested his spare capital in ships, building his fortune 'in shop and by ship' as his father had done. In 1863, having withdrawn from the drapery business, he formed a partnership with John Punshon Denton, an established builder of wooden ships, in Hartlepool, to build iron vessels at Denton's Middleton yard. Gray was initially the junior partner in the firm of Denton, Gray & Co., but in practice there was equality between the two men. With the demise of Pile, Spence & Co., a larger yard in West Hartlepool became available and the business was transferred there in 1869. Denton died at the end of 1871 and a disagreement between Gray and Denton's sons over the terms of the partnership went to litigation. The dispute was finally resolved in 1874 and the business that emerged was William Gray & Co. Gray took his son Matthew into partnership in 1877.

The yard prospered and in 1878 it achieved the distinction of launching the largest tonnage of any shipyard in the world, a feat to be repeated on a number of occasions. The ships were largely medium-size cargo steamers of the well-decked type built in the Hartlepools. These ships were viewed with suspicion by the Board of Trade and Gray initiated an insurance club with the specific goal of fostering public confidence in them. He had already set up, with George Pyman, the East Coast Iron Steamship Association in 1868. Specialization in cargo steamers was part of the reason for the company's success. However, as demand for oil tankers developed the firm secured a share of that market, building the *Bakuin* (1886), the first tanker for a British owner, and the *Murex* (1892), the first tanker to navigate the Suez Canal. The latter vessel was the first of a number built for Marcus Samuel, founder of Shell Transport and Trading. Another factor in the yard's success was Gray's willingness to offer extended credit to shipowners, or to take an interest in vessels himself.

In 1884 Gray moved away from dependence on other builders of marine engines, with the opening of the Central Marine Engineering Works. Three years later the demand for larger ships led to the opening of the Central shipyard, with three berths capable of allowing ships up to 450 ft to be built. Repair facilities had always existed and were further developed. The undertaking became a private limited liability company in December 1888.

Gray was active in public affairs, serving the Hartlepool port and harbour commission for many years, latterly as chairman. He was mayor of Hartlepool in 1861 and was re-elected the following year. On the incorporation of West Hartlepool in 1887, he was its first mayor; later he became the first person to receive its honorary freedom. He was knighted in 1890 and made president of the chamber of shipping in the following year. He also served on the parliamentary load-line committee and was a director of the North Eastern Railway. He was denied the opportunity to represent Hartlepool as its MP when, standing as a Liberal Unionist in 1891, he was narrowly defeated by Sir Christopher Furness. He served as a JP for many years and in 1892 was made high sheriff of the county of Durham. Gray was also a considerable philanthropist. A staunch Presbyterian, he largely cleared the debts of the churches in the presbytery of Darlington, as well as of all the nonconformist places of worship in the Hartlepools.

On the death of his son Matthew, in 1896, Gray took over the rolling mills of the West Hartlepool Steel and Iron Company. By now his own health was failing and he died of a paralytic stroke at his home, The Cottage, Greatham, West Hartlepool, on 12 September 1898. He was buried at West Hartlepool on 15 September. His surviving son, William Cresswell Gray (1867–1924), continued the family involvement in the business, becoming chairman of the company. He was created a baronet in 1917.

Like many businessmen of his era, there seems to have been little to distinguish Gray's public life from his private one, so involved was he in business, civic, and religious matters. The esteem in which he was held was evidenced by the erection of a bronze statue in West Hartlepool, of whose development he had been the principal agent. His worldly success was attested to by his personal fortune, which exceeded £1.5 million.

LIONEL ALEXANDER RITCHIE

Sources R. Craig, 'William Gray and Company: a West Hartlepool shipbuilding enterprise', *Shipping, trade and commerce: essays in memory of Ralph Davis*, ed. P. L. Cottrell and D. H. Aldcroft (1981) · R. Craig, 'Gray, Sir William', *DBB* · R. Wood, *West Hartlepool: the rise and development of a Victorian new town* (1967) · R. Martin, *Historical notes and personal recollections of West Hartlepool and its founder* (1924) · B. Spaldin, *Shipbuilders of the Hartlepools* (1986) · *South Durham and Cleveland Mercury* (16 Sept 1898) · *Northern Daily Mail* (13 Sept 1898) · *Northern Guardian* (13 Sept 1898) · *The Times* (14 Sept 1898) · *The Engineer* (16 Sept 1898) · *Engineering* (16 Sept 1898) · *ILN* (24 Sept 1898) · *Shipping World* (25 Nov 1936), 545–7 · *Biograph and Review*, 6 (1881), 106–8 · *Transactions of the North-East Coast Institution of Engineers and Shipbuilders*, 15 (1898–9), 263–5 · *WWW* · Burke, *Peerage* · *CGPLA Eng. & Wales* (1899)
Archives Hartlepool Maritime Museum and Hartlepool District Library, William Gray & Co. Ltd records
Likenesses W. D. Keyworth, bronze statue, 1898, Church Square, West Hartlepool · photograph, repro. in *ILN*, 439
Wealth at death £1,500,422 14s. 2d.: probate, 10 Feb 1899, *CGPLA Eng. & Wales*

Gray, William John St Clair Anstruther-, Baron Kilmany (1905–1985), politician, was born on 5 March 1905 in Kilmany, Cupar, Fife, Scotland, the only son of two children of Colonel William Anstruther-Gray (1859–1938), army officer and Unionist MP for St Andrews district (1906–10, 1910–19), and his wife, Clayre Tennant CBE. The Anstruther family had adopted the name of Gray on succeeding to the Carntyne estate in 1904. He was educated at Eton College and at Christ Church, Oxford, where he took a fourth in modern history in 1926. Considered to be a man of 'perfect manners' (Ball, 277), Anstruther-Gray was commissioned into the Coldstream Guards in 1926, and served until 1930, with a period (1927–8) attached to the Shanghai defence force. He entered parliament in 1931, taking the seat of North Lanark from the sitting Labour

MP, Jennie Lee, by overturning a 4204 majority. In 1934 he married Monica Helen, only child of Geoffrey Lambton and granddaughter of the fourth earl of Durham. They had two daughters. Against his own expectations he retained his parliamentary seat in 1935, managing to increase his own majority to 5034. From November 1935 to September 1939 he acted as parliamentary private secretary to John Colville, who was Scottish secretary from 1938 to 1940.

During the 1930s Anstruther-Gray championed the cause of the army in the rearmament debate. With the outbreak of war in September 1939 he became a member of the members' service committee, having rejoined the Coldstream Guards, and voted against the Chamberlain government in the Norway division of May 1940. He saw active service in north Africa, France, and Germany with the guards' armoured division and the Lothians and Border horse. He was awarded the Military Cross in 1943. His military experiences led him to make a highly critical speech during a secret session of the House of Commons in 1944, blaming the Churchill coalition government for its 'slackness and dilatory methods of production, [and] of antique models' in the sphere of tanks and their production. The considered opinion of a fellow MP was that this was a 'damaging onslaught … He shook the Government to its very foundations, and had there been a division HMG would certainly have fallen' (*Chips*, ed. James, 390).

Although military service interrupted his political career, Anstruther-Gray finished his tenure at the colours in May 1945 with the observation: 'I'm going back to be a pot-bellied politician. We shall get kicked out, but we'll be back' (Hennessy, 85). He served briefly in Churchill's 1945 caretaker government as assistant postmaster-general before his and the Conservative Party's anticipated defeat in the June 1945 general election. Although he unsuccessfully contested Berwick and East Lothian in 1950, he was returned to parliament in 1951 and successfully defended the seat in 1955, 1959, and 1964 by the narrowest of margins before defeat in 1966 led to elevation to the House of Lords as the life peer Baron Kilmany. The claim that the Conservative Party's uniqueness rested with its ability 'to push the ship of State uphill' was attributed to him (Shepherd, 101).

Situated to the centre-right of the conservative political spectrum, Anstruther-Gray was sympathetic to the cause (although never a member) of the Suez group, a ginger group of Conservative back-benchers who advocated a hard-line approach in British Middle East policy and, specifically, towards Egypt. He was created a baronet in July 1956. Between 1962 and 1966 he acted as deputy speaker to the House of Commons. With Harold Macmillan's abrupt resignation as Conservative leader in 1963, he was one of the so-called 'magic circle' who encouraged and engineered Alec Douglas-Home's elevation to the party leadership. From the general election of 1964 until 1966 he was chairman of the Conservative back-benchers' 1922 committee. As a result he joined the party committee chaired by Home, from November 1964, that decided to introduce an electoral mechanism for selecting future party leaders.

Outside politics he maintained an interest in the turf: he served as a member of the National Hunt committee in 1948 and the Horserace Betting Levy Board from 1966 to 1974. Between 1974 and 1980 he served as lord lieutenant of Fife. On 22 July 1985 he collapsed in the chamber of the House of Lords and was taken to the Westminster Hospital. He died on 6 August 1985.   N. J. CROWSON

Sources *The Times* (23 July 1985) · *The Times* (8 Aug 1985) · *Parliament and politics in the age of Baldwin and MacDonald: the Headlam diaries, 1923–1935*, ed. S. Ball (1992) · *'Chips': the diaries of Sir Henry Channon*, ed. R. R. James (1967) · F. W. S. Craig, *British parliamentary election results, 1918–1949* (1969) · J. Ramsden, *The age of Churchill and Eden, 1940–1957* (1995) · R. Shepherd, *The power brokers: the tory party and its leaders* (1991) · S. Onslow, *Backbench debate within the conservative party and its influence on foreign policy* (1997) · N. J. Crowson, *Facing fascism: the conservative party and the European dictators, 1935–1940* (1997) · P. Hennessy, *Never again: Britain, 1945–1951* (1992)

Archives NL Scot., corresp. and papers · NRA Scotland, priv. coll., diaries and family MSS | Bodl. Oxf., conservative party archive, 1922 Committee

Likenesses photograph, repro. in *Dod's Parliamentary Companion* (1985), 156

Wealth at death £830,445.41: confirmation, 3 Feb 1986, *CCI*

Graydon, John (*d.* 1726), naval officer, served in the navy from at least 1680, when he was a volunteer in the *Hampshire*. In June 1685 he was appointed lieutenant of the galley *Charles*, in May 1688 he became first lieutenant of the *Mary*, and in September he was advanced to the command of the *Saudadoes*. In her he took part in the action of Bantry Bay on 1 May 1689, and he was shortly afterwards promoted to the *Defiance*, which he commanded in the battle off Beachy Head (30 June 1690). He commanded the *Hampton Court* in the battle off Cape Barfleur in 1692, and with the Grand Fleet until March 1695. From 1695 to 1697 he commanded the *Vanguard*, also with the Grand Fleet.

In April 1697 he was accused by his chaplain and lieutenants of drunkenness, irreligious behaviour, mocking his superiors, and talking up the French; although he was originally acquitted at a court martial, new evidence emerged, and he was dismissed in October. Restored to service as captain of the *Assistance*, he went to Newfoundland in April 1701 in command of the convoy and as governor, and he produced a detailed report on the fishery for the Board of Trade and Plantations. After seeing the Newfoundland trade into the Mediterranean he was back in England by the spring of 1702. In June, while in command of the *Triumph* at Portsmouth, he was promoted rear-admiral of the blue, and ordered out to join Sir George Rooke on the coast of Spain. He was with him in the attempt on Cadiz, and in the destruction of the enemy's ships at Vigo. With his flag in the *Lancaster*, he returned home in company with Sir Cloudesley Shovell in charge of the prizes, and on 24 December he married Mary Gregory.

In January 1703 Graydon was promoted vice-admiral of the white, and appointed commander-in-chief of a squadron sent to the West Indies. He sailed with special orders to make the best of his way out, to collect such force, both of ships and troops, as might be available, and going north to reduce the French settlement of Placentia. A few days after he sailed, on 18 March, he fell in with a squadron of four French ships of force clearly inferior to the five with him. Graydon, however, considered that he was bound by his instructions to avoid all chances of delay; he allowed them to pass him unhindered, and did not pursue. He arrived at Barbados on 12 May, and at Jamaica on 4 June.

The necessity of refitting; the poor condition of several of the ships, some of which had been long on the station; the lack of stores; and the ill feeling which sprang up between Graydon and 'some of the chief persons of Jamaica' all combined to delay the expedition, so that it did not reach Newfoundland until the beginning of August. From that time for thirty days it was enveloped in a dense fog; it was 3 September before the fleet was again assembled, and then a council of war, considering the lateness of the season, the bad condition of the ships, the sickly state of the men, the want of provisions, and the strength of the enemy at Placentia, decided that the attack ought not to be made. On 24 September the fleet accordingly sailed for England; in bad weather the ships were scattered, and singly and in much distress reached home in October.

The failure both to engage the French ships on the outward voyage, and then of the expedition as a whole, led to Graydon's examination before the privy council in November 1703 and a House of Lords committee in April 1704. By then complaints had arrived from Jamaica of his pressing householders and slaves and whipping masters of merchant ships, and that 'his carriage was generally very haughty and affrontive to the whole country, saying one time in a public manner that there were none but brutes lived there' (*House of Lords MSS*, new ser., 5.500). Graydon's unsatisfactory responses, and the evidence of his previous dismissal, led to the committee's recommendation that he should not be employed again. This was upheld, despite the lack of a trial or any other due process. His pension was stopped, and he seems to have retired to the life of a farmer at Fordwich, Kent. He died, probably in Fordwich, on 12 March 1726, and was survived by his wife, four sons, and one daughter. To one contemporary, he was 'a vain blustering bold fellow, but makes more noise than brave men generally do' (*Memoirs of the Secret Services*, 110).

J. K. LAUGHTON, rev. J. D. DAVIES

Sources PRO, Admiralty MSS, ADM 1, ADM 6/424, ADM 3, ADM 8 · *The manuscripts of the House of Lords*, new ser., 12 vols. (1900–77), vol. 5, pp. 463–9, 490–510 · will, PRO, PROB 11/615, fol. 173 · NMM, Sergison MSS, SER/136 · *Memoirs of the secret services of John Macky*, ed. A. R. (1733) · *The journal of Sir George Rooke ... 1700–1702*, ed. O. Browning, Navy RS, 9 (1897) · N. Luttrell, *A brief historical relation of state affairs from September 1678 to April 1714*, 6 vols. (1857) · M. Godfrey, 'Graydon, John', *DCB*, vol. 2 · parish register, Hoo, St Werburgh, Medway Archives and Local Studies Centre, Rochester, Kent, 24 Dec 1702 [marriage] · J. Burchett, *A complete history of the most remarkable transactions at sea* (1720)

Archives PRO, Admiralty MSS

Likenesses G. Kneller, oils, *c.*1703, NMM

Wealth at death lands in Fordwich and West Beer, Kent to wife: will, PRO, PROB 11/615, fol. 173

Grayle [Graile], **John** (1613/14–1651/2), Church of England clergyman, was born at Stone, Gloucestershire, the elder surviving son of John Grayle (*bap.* 1579, *d.* 1636), vicar of

Stone, and his wife, Alice Bingham (*d.* 1648); the poet and physician Edmund *Graile (1575/6–1643) was his uncle. He matriculated from Magdalen Hall, Oxford, on 11 May 1632, aged eighteen, and graduated BA on 24 October 1634. On his father's death he inherited various parcels of land in the parish of North Nibley, Gloucestershire; some years later, he bought land in Stone from his brother, Josias Grayle. After proceeding MA on 15 June 1637 he taught for a while in a private school in Buckinghamshire. The following year, at his mother's instance, he became chaplain to John Stephens of Upper Lypiatt, Gloucestershire, a landowner sympathetic to nonconformists.

By 1645 Grayle was working as an assistant to the ailing Thomas Gataker, rector of Rotherhithe, Surrey, a wellknown puritan minister. At the end of that year he married Bridget, daughter of Henry *Scudder (*d.* 1652), rector of Collingbourne Ducis, Wiltshire. Grayle was living there in 1646, and may have ministered to the parish during his father-in-law's absence in London. About 1647 he became rector of North Tidworth, Wiltshire, where (according to Anthony Wood) 'he was much followed by the precise and godly party'. Wood describes him as 'a presbyterian, yet tinged with arminianism' (Wood, *Ath. Oxon.*, 3.363). The latter characterization was something Grayle took pains to deny in *A modest vindication of the doctrine of conditions in the covenant of grace, and the defenders thereof, from the aspersions of Arminianism & popery, which Mr. W. E. cast on them* (1655). His adversary was William Eyre, minister of St Edmund's, Salisbury, a schismatic who was silenced for his nonconformity after the Restoration. *A modest vindication* was published posthumously, although a note in the text states that the book had been delivered to Mr Eyre in Grayle's lifetime.

In his funeral sermon for Grayle, Humphrey Chambers, rector of Pewsey, Wiltshire, recounts how the minister when already ill insisted on taking his turn to preach 'at a place somewhat remote from his own habitation ... under the weight of which labour of love, his weak body did apparently sink in the time and place of that publick service' (Chambers, 124). After returning home he declined steadily until his death, which occurred some time between Christmas 1651 and May 1652. The many who attended his funeral heard Chambers emphasize Grayle's great learning, conscientious character, and opposition to superstitious ceremonies. He was survived by his wife, two sons, and two daughters. His elder son, John Grayle (1648/9–1732), followed him into the ministry, became rector of Blickling, Norfolk, and was grandfather of the Norfolk historian and antiquary Antony Norris (1711–1786).

P. L. DICKINSON

Sources Wood, *Ath. Oxon.*, new edn, 3.362–3, 610–11, 885–6; 4.501 · J. Graile, *A modest vindication of the doctrine of conditions in the covenant of grace, and the defenders thereof, from the aspersions of Arminianism & popery, which Mr. W. E. cast on them* (1655) · H. Chambers, 'Pauls sad farewell to his Ephesians ... opened in a sermon at the funeral of Mr John Graile', in J. Graile, *A modest vindication of the doctrine of conditions in the covenant of grace, and the defenders thereof from the aspersions of Arminianism & popery* (1655) · *Gloucestershire inquisitions post mortem, Charles I*, pt 2, British RS, 13 (1895), 86–7 · PRO,

C9/5/79 · will, PRO, PROB 11/222, sig. 110 · Foster, *Alum. Oxon.* · wills, Glos. RO, 1636/49 · J. Smyth, *A description of the hundred of Berkeley*, ed. J. Maclean, *The Berkeley manuscripts*, 3 (1885) · parish registers, Stone, Glos. RO · R. Bigland, *Historical, monumental and genealogical collections, relative to the county of Gloucester*, ed. B. Frith, 3 (1992), 1174 · will, Norfolk RO, Norwich consistory court wills, 1732 (69 Bransby) · B. Brook, *The lives of the puritans*, 3 (1813), 229–30 · F. Blomefield and C. Parkin, *An essay towards a topographical history of the county of Norfolk*, 5 vols. (1739–75), vol. 3, p. 642 [memorial inscription]

Wealth at death bequeathed several different items of silverware to his children and others, and legacies of £150 to his daughters; also left land in North Nibley, Gloucestershire, to his son and referred to land he owned in Stone, Gloucestershire: will, PRO, PROB 11/222

Grayson, Cecil (1920–1998), Italian scholar, was born on 5 February 1920 at 1 Court 6, Taylor Street, Batley, Yorkshire, the second son of John Grayson (d. 1926), boiler maker, and his wife, Dora, née Hartley (d. c.1980), a seamstress. Educated at Batley grammar school and St Edmund Hall, Oxford, he obtained first-class honours in modern languages in 1947, his academic work interrupted by war service in India (1940–46). In 1947 he married Margaret Parry Jordan (1922–1999), with whom he had three daughters and a son. In 1948 he began teaching as university lecturer in Italian at Oxford; in 1958 he was elected to Oxford's Serena chair. At one time his pupils filled nearly half the Italian university teaching posts in Britain, and a goodly proportion of Commonwealth and American university teachers of Italian also counted him as their mentor.

When Professor Grayson was elected president of the Modern Humanities Research Association in 1987, his presidential address discussed the advantages and disadvantages of a literary life: the allusion to the *De commodis litterarum atque incommodis* of Leon Battista Alberti (1404–1472) was clear to Renaissance specialists. It was the first of Alberti's writings on which he worked, a cautionary introduction which warns against expecting too many material rewards from academic life. His research was closely identified with the development of the so-called *nuova filologia* ('new philology') as practised by scholars such as Michele Barbi, Vittorio Cian, and Carlo Dionisotti. Professor Grayson's was a similarly rigorous critical approach; he had little patience with the cavils of post-war literary criticism; his method, which depended upon verifiable literary and historical evidence, concentrated on detailed textual analysis.

In 1949 Grayson produced with Carlo Dionisotti an edition with commentary of *Early Italian Texts*. The *Opuscoli inediti di Leon Battista Alberti* (1954) firmly established his scholarly reputation, providing him with his first major edition and a breakthrough into the Italian academic hierarchy. For a quarter of a century after his election to the chair he was a vigorous co-editor of the journal *Italian Studies*. He became a natural choice as one of Britain's vice-presidents of the International Association of Italianists (AISLLI), which he served for forty years.

Professor Grayson's strong interest in Alberti continued with a brief but elaborate edition of an unpublished letter to Matteo de' Pasti, subtitled *Alberti and the Tempio Malatestiano*, published in 1957. And shortly afterwards he discovered and edited manuscripts of Vincenzo Colli ('Il Calmeta'), hardly known to scholarship before Grayson showed that here were the first pages of modern literary criticism; these he published as *Prose e lettere edite e inedite* in 1959. In 1960 his inaugural lecture appeared: *A Renaissance Controversy: Latin or Italian*. What began as an objective examination of the Italian *questione della lingua* provoked ideas which rumbled on for a decade, though Grayson treated it as a casual sideline; the argument reached its apogee in 1971 when his essay 'Machiavelli and Dante' initiated further international debate. During that same period Professor Grayson had been engaged on his edition of the works of Alberti (*Opere volgari*), published in three ample volumes in 1960, 1966, and 1973. He also began editing Alberti's vernacular grammar, which he published in 1964 as *Leon Battista Alberti e la prima grammatica della lingua volgare*. In 1972 he edited Alberti's *On Painting and on Sculpture: the Latin Texts of De pictura and De statua*. His final Alberti edition was the text of *De pictura* (1980), though he published an English version in 1991.

Apart from his work on the Renaissance, Professor Grayson's essays on Dante's language and style, particularly in his *Cinque saggi su Dante* of 1972 and on the development of pre-Renaissance vernacular literature, became minor classics. He gave regular lectures on Dante and for a quarter of a century was president–secretary of the Oxford Dante Society, whose essays he edited for Oxford University Press in *The World of Dante* in 1980; he celebrated the tenth anniversary of his own retirement by giving Oxford's Paget Toynbee Dante lectures. In 1965 he edited for Oxford University Press a selection from Francesco Guicciardini, translated by his wife, Margaret. He also translated three of the historical biographies of Roberto Ridolfi (Savonarola, Machiavelli, and Guicciardini), items he considered part of his relaxation.

Cecil Grayson had an imposing international reputation beyond Europe. In the United States he enjoyed many fellowships or visiting professorships: fellow in residence at Chicago's Newberry Library in 1965; and visiting professor at Yale (1966), Berkeley (1969 and 1973), UCLA (1980, 1984, 1987, and 1994), and New York University, where he taught for the whole of the academic year 1995–6 when already seventy-six years of age. He undertook long stints as visiting professor at Cape Town (1980 and 1983) and Perth (1973 and 1980), and was a frequent visitor to South Africa and the Antipodes.

Professor Grayson was elected to Italy's most prestigious academies: the Lincei, the Crusca, Arcadia, the Istituto Veneto, and Bologna's Commissione per i Testi di Lingua and Accademia delle Scienze; in 1974 he was given the international Galileo prize, and in 1976 the British Academy's Serena gold medal, three years before his election to the Academy itself. His CBE in 1992 was anticipated by Italy seventeen years earlier with the title of Commendatore dell'ordine al merito. The honorary fellowship awarded him in 1986 at his old college, St Edmund Hall, gave him particular pleasure. At his retirement dinner he was presented with the nearest that Oxford approaches to a Festschrift: *The Languages of Literature in Renaissance Italy* (1988), edited by his Oxford colleagues; in 1997 another Oxford University Press volume, *Dante and Governance*, was dedicated to him, marking the anniversary of his retirement. He lived in Oxford from 1947 to 1998, principally at 11 Norham Road, though he enjoyed much time at his cottage in Pembrokeshire acquired in 1960. In 1998 the city council of Mantua nominated him for honorary citizenship; he was preparing to attend the ceremony when he was taken into the John Radcliffe Hospital, where he died of coronary thrombosis on 29 April 1998. He was cremated in Oxford.   J. R. WOODHOUSE

Sources *WW* (1997) · *The Times* (27 May 1998) · *The Independent* (2 June 1998) · J. G. Woodhouse, 'Cecil Grayson, 1920–1998', 105, 461–70 · private information (2004) [Robin Grayson; Celia McDonald] · personal knowledge (2004) · b. cert. · d. cert.
Likenesses photograph, British Academy, London · photograph, repro. in *The Independent* · photographs, Magd. Oxf. · photographs, priv. coll.

Grayson, (Albert) Victor (*b*. 1881), politician, generally known as Victor Grayson, was registered as having been born at 8 Taliesin Street, Liverpool on 5 September 1881. His father was given as William Grayson, a carpenter, and his mother as Elizabeth, *née* Craig (*d*. 1929). The circumstances of his birth remain disputed. Some sources (for example Clark, *Labour's Lost Leader*, 156–7) refer to rumours that these were not his natural parents, and that his father was an aristocrat.

Grayson's formal education was at St Mathew's Church of England School on Liverpool's Scotland Road; he then served an apprenticeship as a turner at the Bank Hall engine works. His mother was deeply religious; at the age of eighteen he began to attend the undenominational Bethel mission, and he later moved to the Hamilton Road mission. A talent for oratory became evident during his activities first as a Sunday school teacher, and then as an outdoor speaker. In the autumn of 1904 he entered the Home Missionary College in Manchester to train for the Unitarian ministry, and also attended classes at the University of Manchester. Increasingly involved in socialist activities, he joined the Manchester central branch of the Independent Labour Party (ILP). Unemployment was high in Manchester during 1905 and Grayson emerged as a popular and effective speaker at demonstrations. His passion for socialism replaced his religious commitment, and in July 1906 he withdrew from his course.

Grayson's subsequent political rise was meteoric. In significant respects his experience of the labour movement was narrow. He preferred the emotions of the platform to the humdrum tasks of political organization. He had no experience of trade unionism and could be critical of what he considered its narrowness of vision. But in the circumstances of 1906–7, his revivalist socialism struck a telling chord among many activists of the ILP.

The general election of 1906 had produced a Parliamentary Labour Party of thirty members, several of whom identified themselves as socialists. ILP membership was

increasing, and many new recruits were unhappy about the constraints intrinsic to the ILP's alliance with the trade unions. These enthusiasts wished to attack Liberal seats in by-elections. In the context of these sentiments the Mancunian roots of Grayson's politics were perhaps significant. The conurbation's socialists included many who were critical of the Labour Party's caution and wished for an alternative socialist alliance of the ILP and the Social Democratic Federation (Social Democratic Party from 1908).

During 1906 Grayson became a frequent and enthusiastically received speaker in the Colne Valley, a safe Liberal seat to the south-west of Huddersfield. A West Riding constituency of mill villages, nonconformist chapels, and moorland, it included the well-established Colne Valley Labour League. This was essentially a network of ILP branches and clubs; local trade unionism was sparse. When a by-election was called in June 1907 Grayson was adopted as the league's candidate. He was not endorsed by the national Labour Party. Formally this resulted from the lack of a local Labour Representation Committee, itself symptomatic of trade union weakness, but there appear also to have been doubts about Grayson's suitability not least on grounds of his inexperience.

Grayson's campaign combined orthodox Labour politics with revivalist oratory. His victory by 153 votes in a three-cornered contest held on 18 July 1907 led him to a contrasting verdict—'this epoch making victory has been won for pure revolutionary socialism' (Thompson, 22). Many activists felt that Grayson's victory demonstrated the feasibility of a radical alternative to established Labour politics, and he became symbolic of this discontent. His oratory expressed at socialist meetings could seem threatening to other Labour politicians. Attempts to negotiate his inclusion within the Parliamentary Labour Party failed. The gulf was revealed dramatically on successive days in October 1908 when he twice flouted parliamentary procedure to demand a debate on unemployment. Prior to his first removal from the chamber, he castigated Labour members—'you are traitors to your class' (*Hansard 4*, vol. 194, col. 497, 15 Oct 1908). His use of the parliamentary 'scene' brought approval from George Bernard Shaw, but provoked predictable hostility from Labour members. Some responded by spreading rumours about Grayson's liking for alcohol and his enjoyment of luxuries. The ILP conference in 1909 revealed the limits of his influence. Many critics of the Labour Party leadership nevertheless remained committed to the basic strategy of an ILP–trade union alliance. Grayson clearly was not; his journalism firstly for A. P. Orage's *New Age* and subsequently for Robert Blatchford's *Clarion* demonstrated a commitment to a socialist alternative. A book, *The Problem of Parliament* (1909), written with G. R. S. Taylor, presented parliament not as an instrument for reform but as a socialist platform.

Grayson's brief parliamentary career ended with the general election of January 1910. Even in Colne Valley his politics divided socialists, and in an election dominated by the Liberal issues of House of Lords reform and the people's budget, his socialist rhetoric could seem less compelling. His vote fell by 499 and he finished third. In the second 1910 election he stood for Kennington, south London, as a socialist, but polled only 408 votes. Throughout 1911 he campaigned for a new socialist party through his column in *The Clarion*. The Salford Unity Conference at the end of September elected him to the steering committee charged with the task of devising a party constitution. Yet his hopes for the consequential British Socialist Party (BSP) proved brief. The Social Democratic Party under H. M. Hyndman moved into the BSP en bloc and soon marginalized the ILP dissidents and *Clarion* readers that represented Grayson's support. By the spring of 1912 he had retired from the organization. His combination of passionate platform oratory and high living was lubricated increasingly by alcohol; his status within the socialist movement declined further.

On 7 November 1912 at Chelsea register office, describing his occupation as 'journalist', he married Ruth Nightingale (1886/7–1918), an actress with the stage name of Ruth Norrey; she was the daughter of John Webster Nightingale, banker. The fragility of Grayson's health and the unpredictability of his wife's earnings meant poverty. During 1913 donations from political sympathizers allowed them to travel abroad in the hope of Grayson's recovery. After visiting Italy and, for a longer period, New York, they returned to Britain at the end of the year. A daughter was born in April 1914.

Grayson strongly supported Britain's entry into the war in August 1914. The influence of Robert Blatchford might have been significant; the result was to separate Grayson further from many of his sympathizers. In the spring of 1915 the Graysons left for Australia. Ruth had obtained a theatrical engagement and Victor spoke at meetings and wrote for political journals. Initially his pro-war views harmonized with those of the Australian labour party leadership, but the growth of anti-conscription feeling produced criticism. Similar problems confronted him when he arrived in New Zealand in 1916. Not only did his pro-conscription views prove unpopular, but his speeches could be marred by alcohol, and there were allegations of financial deception. In November 1916 he enlisted in the New Zealand expeditionary force, and he arrived in France in the following September. On 12 October 1917 he was wounded, and subsequently discharged, probably suffering from shell-shock. Early in 1918 he featured as a pro-war orator in alliance with the seamen's leader Havelock Wilson; the campaign was interrupted by his wife's death during childbirth in February.

This reappearance on public platforms was brief. Grayson subsequently lived in apparent affluence—a contrast with his recent poverty—in a West End flat. His associates included Maundy Gregory, the man at the heart of the post-war honours scandal. The significance of this relationship and the source of Grayson's income remain unknown; and then, probably in September 1920, began a greater mystery. Grayson disappeared. Subsequent sightings proved inconclusive; no death certificate was ever issued. Speculations have included murder at the hands of Gregory or his associates, a breakdown, or the construction of a new identity.

Beyond the unresolved mysteries stands the power of Grayson's spellbinding oratory. Often charming, and attractive to both men and women, his politics lacked depth. For his sympathizers he represented the hope of a better world that owed more to moral conversion than to legislation; for his detractors he represented the irrational, the destabilizing, and the potentially violent both as pre-war socialist and as wartime patriot. From one standpoint he is the flawed socialist hero; but his distinctive trajectory also illuminates specific and important themes within the Edwardian left. A character in a morality play, he was nevertheless very much a man of his time and place.   DAVID HOWELL

Sources D. Clark, *Labour's lost leader: Victor Grayson* (1985) · D. Clark, *Colne Valley: radicalism to socialism* (1981) · D. Morris, 'Labour or socialism? Opposition and dissent within the ILP with special reference to Lancashire', PhD diss., University of Manchester, 1982 · D. Tanner, 'Ideological debate in Edwardian labour politics: radicalism, revisionism and socialism', *Currents of radicalism*, ed. E. Biagini and A. Reid (1991) · S. Pierson, *British socialists: the journey from fantasy to politics* (Cambridge, Mass., 1979) · K. Laybourn and J. Reynolds, *Liberalism and the rise of labour, 1890–1918* (1984) · R. Graves, *The mystery of Victor Grayson* (1946) · W. Thompson, *The life of Victor Grayson* (1910) · D. Marquand, *Ramsay MacDonald* (1977) · P. Snowden, *Autobiography*, 1 (1934) · independent labour party conference report, 1908–9, JRL · b. cert. · m. cert. · *Hansard 4* (1908), 194.495–7, 631–4 [Grayson's 'scenes'] · H. Pelling, 'Two by-elections: Jarrow and Colne Valley, 1907', *Popular politics and society in late Victorian Britain* (1968), 130–146

Archives Labour History Archive and Study Centre, Manchester, papers | BLPES, corresp. with independent labour party · BLPES, independent labour party national administrative council minutes · BLPES, Francis Johnson corresp. · JRL, Ramsay MacDonald MSS · Man. CL, Independent Labour Party Manchester central branch minutes · People's History Museum, Manchester, labour party corresp. · PRO, Ramsay MacDonald MSS · U. Lpool, Bruce Glasier corresp. and diaries · University of Huddersfield, Colne Valley Labour League minutes

Likenesses photographs, repro. in Clark, *Labour's lost leader*

Graystanes, Robert. *See* Greystones, Robert (*b*. before 1290, *d*. 1334).

Greame, Philip Lloyd-. *See* Lister, Philip Cunliffe-, first earl of Swinton (1884–1972).

Greathead, Henry (1757–1816?), reported inventor of the lifeboat, was the younger of twin children, born at Richmond, Yorkshire, on 27 January 1757. His father, John Greathead, an officer of salt duties, following promotion removed to Shields in 1763. Greathead was at first apprenticed to a boat builder and subsequently went to sea as a ship's carpenter. In 1785 he returned to South Shields and set up in business on his own account as a boat builder, marrying in the following year. The ship *Adventure*, of Newcastle, was stranded in March 1789 on the Herd Sands, a shoal off Tynemouth haven, not far from Greathead's home. The crew were all lost in sight of many spectators, and Greathead resolved to construct a lifeboat. Lionel Lukin (1742–1834), a coach-builder of Longacre, London, had written a pamphlet upon 'unimmergible boats', and

Henry Greathead (1757–1816?), by William Ridley, pubd 1804

took out a patent in 1785. William Wouldhave (1751–1821), parish clerk of South Shields, had also studied the subject. A public subscription was now got up to offer a reward for the best lifeboat. Greathead won it against the competition of Wouldhave and many others. Greathead's completed boat was 28 ft 6 in. long by 9 ft 6 in. in width, and 3 ft 2 in. deep amidships. The whole construction much resembled a Greenland whale boat, lined inside and out with cork, the latter weighing some 7 cwt. Greathead's was a ten-oared boat, and although of shallow draught it could carry twenty people. It succeeded admirably and Greathead made a second lifeboat for the duke of Northumberland, who presented it to North Shields. Numerous learned societies awarded honours to Greathead, and voted him money grants. The Royal Humane Society gave him 50 guineas and a gold medal, Trinity House of London gave him 100 guineas, and Lloyds of London a further 100 guineas. Following a parliamentary petition the government awarded him, in June 1802, £1200 in consideration of the value of his invention to the nation. Dr Trotter, physician to the fleet, wrote an adulatory ode. Greathead published *The report of evidence and other proceedings in parliament respecting the invention of the lifeboat. Also other documents illustrating the origin of the lifeboat, with practical directions for the management of lifeboats* (1804). He probably died in London in 1816 after leaving Shields; his wife died in London in March 1814 as reported in the *Newcastle Courant* of 19 March 1814. There is an inscription to his memory in the parish church of St Hilda, South Shields.

JAMES BURNLEY, rev. ARTHUR G. CREDLAND

Sources L. Lukin, *The invention, principles of construction and uses of unimmergible boats* (1806) • F. Robus, *Lionel Lukin of Dunmow, the inventor of the lifeboat* (1925) • W. A. Hails, *An enquiry concerning the invention of the lifeboats etc.* (1806) • *Public characters of 1806* (1806), 181–206 • A. G. Osler, *Mr Greathead's lifeboat* (Tyne and Wear Museum Service, 1990) • *Tyne Mercury* (29 Nov 1803) • 'Account of Mr Henry Greathead's lifeboat', *European Magazine and London Review*, 43 (1803), 325–8 • J. Burnley, *The romance of life preservation* (1888) • *Newcastle Courant* (19 March 1814) • 'Mr Henry Greathead of South Shields', *European Magazine and London Review*, 46 (1804), 3–7

Likenesses W. Ridley, stipple, BM, NPG; repro. in 'Mr Henry Greathead of South Shields', 2–3 [*see illus.*] • oils, NMM

Greathead, James Henry (1844–1896), civil engineer, was born in Grahamstown, Cape Colony, on 6 August 1844, the son of James Henry Greathead of Grahamstown, a member of the legislative council of Cape Colony 1859–60. He was educated at St Andrew's College, Grahamstown. He went to England in 1859 to complete his education at Westbourne Collegiate School, London.

In 1864 Greathead began a three-year pupillage with P. W. Barlow, followed by a year on the construction of the Midland Railway extension from Bedford to London, under W. H. Barlow and C. B. Baker. At about this time Peter Barlow was promoting the idea of a network of underground railways as the solution to London's street-traffic problems. It was agreed that a pedestrian tunnel, the Tower subway, should be driven under the Thames 'as a sample of the system', but the memory of the extreme difficulties of Isambard K. Brunel in completing the Thames Tunnel resulted in none of the contractors approached by Barlow being willing to tender for the work. In 1868, however, Greathead made an offer to build the tunnel for the sum of £9400 and Barlow accepted. Work began the following year, using a shield which, though similar to one patented by Barlow in 1868, was designed by Greathead; it was forced forward by powerful screw-jacks as excavation proceeded, and the 1350 ft long tunnel was completed in less than a year.

Greathead set up his own practice as a consulting engineer in 1870 and continued to devise improvements to his tunnelling shield while being employed mainly on surface railway schemes. In 1886, however, work began on the long-delayed City and Southwark subway, the beginning of a line that became the City and South London Railway, the world's first underground electric railway. For the excavation of the twin tunnels through water-bearing strata, compressed air had to be used in conjunction with a much-improved design of the Greathead shield, which enabled the first of the tunnels under the Thames to be completed in only fifteen weeks.

Greathead was involved in the early 1890s with several other deep tunnel railway schemes, including the Blackwall Tunnel under the Thames, and as a complete contrast he was also associated with Sir Douglas Fox in the construction of the Liverpool overhead electric railway, opened in 1893. He was much sought after as an expert witness in arbitrations and parliamentary inquiries, where his engineering expertise and powers of logical exposition carried much weight.

Greathead was elected a member of the Institution of Mechanical Engineers in 1879, and the Institution of Civil Engineers in 1881, serving as a member of the council of the latter in 1894. He retained close connections with

South Africa as consulting engineer to the Durban tramways.

In 1884 Greathead married Blanche Emily Caldecott, daughter of Selby Coryndon of Kimberley. They had one son and two daughters. He died suddenly at his house, Ravenscraig, Leigham Court Road, Streatham, on 21 October 1896. He was survived by his wife. The many underground railway schemes on which he was engaged at the time of his death had to be completed by others, but the Greathead shield was his lasting memorial.

RONALD M. BIRSE, *rev.*

Sources PICE, 127 (1896–7), 365–9 · DBB · C. E. Lee, 'The Tower subway: the first tube tunnel in the world', *Transactions* [Newcomen Society], 43 (1970–71), 41–51 · A. A. Jackson and D. F. Croome, *Rails through the clay: a history of London's tube railways* (1962) · *DSAB*, vol. 3
Wealth at death £18,874 15s. 8d.: probate, 29 Dec 1896, CGPLA Eng. & Wales

Greathed, William Wilberforce Harris (1826–1878), army officer, was born on 21 December 1826 in Paris, the youngest son in the family of five sons and three daughters of Edward Greathed (d. 1840) of Uddens, Dorset, and his wife, Mary-Elizabeth, daughter of Sir Richard Carr-Clynn. Greathed entered Addiscombe College in February 1843, and received a commission as second-lieutenant in the Bengal Engineers on 9 December 1844. He arrived in India in 1846, and was attached to the Bengal Sappers and Miners at Meerut. The following year he was appointed to the irrigation department of the North-Western Provinces, but on the outbreak of the Second Anglo-Sikh War in 1848 he joined the field force before Multan. He took part in the siege, and at the assault of the town, on 2 January 1849, he was the first officer through the breach. After the capture of Multan he joined Lord Gough, and was present at the battle of Gujrat on 21 February 1849. This concluded the campaign, and he at once resumed his work in the irrigation department. He was promoted first-lieutenant on 14 May 1852, and took a furlough to England for two years. On his return to India in 1854 Greathed was appointed executive engineer in the public works department at Barrackpore, and in 1855 he was sent to Allahabad as government consulting engineer in connection with the extension of the East India Railway to the upper provinces. He was at Allahabad when the mutiny broke out at Meerut, followed by the seizure of Delhi in May 1857.

As soon as news of the catastrophe at Delhi reached him, the lieutenant-governor of the North-Western Provinces, John Russell Colvin, who had formed a very high opinion of Greathed, summoned him to Agra, attached him to his staff, and employed him to carry dispatches to Meerut and to civil officers on the way. Greathed succeeded not only in reaching Meerut (the first European to have done so from 'down country' since the mutiny broke out) but also in returning to Agra. He was then dispatched in command of a body of British volunteer cavalry to release some beleaguered British in the Doab, the region between the Ganges and Jumna rivers. A month later he was again sent off with dispatches from Colvin and Lord Canning to the general commanding the force which was moving against Delhi. A second time he ran the gauntlet and reached Meerut in safety. From there he made his way across country and joined Sir Henry Barnard beyond the Jumna.

Appointed to Barnard's staff, Greathed took part in the action at Badli-ki-sarai on 8 June, which gave the Delhi field force the position on the ridge it held so long. When the siege began, Greathed was appointed director of the left attack. He greatly distinguished himself on 9 July against a sortie in force from Delhi, when he and Burnside of the 8th regiment were with their party in a serai surrounded by mutineers. They resolved on a sudden rush, and, killing the men immediately in front, put the enemy to flight. Greathed had two brothers with him at Delhi, Hervey, the civil commissioner attached to the force, and Edward, colonel of the 8th regiment. During the assault of 14 September he was senior engineer of the column commanded by his brother Edward. As they approached the edge of the ditch he fell, severely wounded through the arm and lower part of the chest.

On recovering from his wounds Greathed joined, in December, as field engineer, the column under Colonel Thomas Seaton, which marched down the Doab. He took part in the engagements at Gangari, Patiali, and Mainpuri. He then served as directing engineer of the attack on Lucknow, under Colonel Robert Napier, where he again distinguished himself. His services in the mutiny were rewarded by a brevet majority (28 August 1858) and a CB (18 May 1860).

In 1860 Greathed accompanied Napier to China as extra aide-de-camp; he was present at the battle of Senho (Xinhe) and at the capture of the Taku (Dagu) forts on the Peiho (Beihe), and took part in the campaign until the capture of Peking (Beijing), when he was made the bearer of dispatches home. He arrived in England at the end of 1860, and was made a brevet lieutenant-colonel on 15 February 1861 for his services in China.

In March 1861 Greathed was appointed to succeed his friend Lieutenant-Colonel Henry Norman as assistant military secretary at the Horse Guards. In 1863 he married Alice, daughter of the Revd Archer Clive of Whitfield, near Hereford.

After serving from 1865 to 1867 at Plymouth and on the Severn defences, Greathed returned to India, and was appointed head of the irrigation department in the North-Western Provinces and joint secretary to the government irrigation branch, with the rank of lieutenant-colonel (1 July 1867). The Agra Canal from the Jumna and the Lower Ganges Canal were among his major works. He was made brevet colonel on 7 July 1868, commanded the Royal Engineers assembled at Delhi at the reception of the prince of Wales in December 1875 and January 1876, and was promoted full colonel on 30 March 1876.

Greathed had been increasingly ill from overwork, and he left India in July 1876 with a good service pension. He lived as an invalid over two years longer, during which he was promoted major-general on 1 October 1877. He died on 29 December 1878 at 30 Upper Grosvenor Street, London, and was buried on 4 January 1879 at Hampreston church, Dorset. R. H. VETCH, rev. ALEX MAY

Sources Army List · Indian Army List · private information (1890) · E. J. Thackwell, *Narrative of the Second Seikh War, in 1848–49* (1851) · F. R. Maunsell, *The siege of Delhi* (1912) · A. Llewellyn, *The siege of Delhi* (1977) · J. W. Kaye, *A history of the Sepoy War in India, 1857–1858*, 9th edn, 3 vols. (1880) · G. B. Malleson, *History of the Indian mutiny, 1857–1858: commencing from the close of the second volume of Sir John Kaye's History of the Sepoy War*, 3 vols. (1878–80) · C. Hibbert, *The great mutiny, India, 1857* (1978) · H. M. Vibart, *Addiscombe: its heroes and men of note* (1894) · Boase, *Mod. Eng. biog.* · *CGPLA Eng. & Wales* (1879)
Archives Merseyside County Museum, Liverpool · NAM, letter-books and papers
Likenesses T. J. Barker, oils, 1859 (*The relief of Lucknow*), NPG
Wealth at death under £16,000: probate, 25 Jan 1879, *CGPLA Eng. & Wales*

Greatheed, Bertie (1759–1826), poet and playwright, was born on 19 October 1759, the son of Samuel Greatheed (1710–1765) of Guy's Cliffe, near Warwick, and his wife, Lady Mary Bertie, daughter of Peregrine, second duke of Ancaster. Orphaned at fourteen, Greatheed was placed with his brother Peregrine under the partial guardianship of an uncle by marriage, General Edward Mathew, an equerry to George III. According to Greatheed himself, it was at the suggestion of the king that he was sent to the university at Göttingen in 1775 (Greatheed, xi). He married his first cousin Ann Bertie on 31 July 1780, and they travelled in France, Switzerland, and Italy between 1782 and 1786 (ibid.).

While residing in Florence, Greatheed became part of a coterie known as *gli Oziosi* ('the Idlers') and contributed to their privately printed collection of fugitive pieces entitled *The Arno Miscellany* (Florence, 1784). The following year, he was one of the group of literary dilettanti and sympathizers with the cause of Italian nationalism who put together *The Florence Miscellany* (Florence, 1785). Contributing poets included Hester Lynch Piozzi, William Parsons, and the soon-to-be-notorious Robert Merry, whose pseudonym, Della Crusca, was retrospectively applied to the productions of the whole group. Back in England in 1788, Greatheed intruded on the amatory poetic correspondence of Della Crusca and 'Anna Matilda' in *The World* with a poem to the lady signed 'Reuben', and, as William Gifford gleefully asserts, 'rouzed the jealousy of Della Crusca' (Gifford, 106 n. 5). Whether this was the true cause of Greatheed's rift with Merry (*Thraliana*, 2.716), Gifford's savage attacks in the *Baviad, and Maeviad* (1797) certainly heralded the end of Greatheed's poetic career. His one attempt at the drama had fared no better. A blank-verse tragedy in a studied Shakespearian style, *The Regent* was brought out at Drury Lane Theatre on 1 April 1788. It ran for only nine nights despite featuring an epilogue by Mrs Piozzi and having both John Kemble and Mrs Siddons among its cast. The latter, a former attendant on Greatheed's mother and frequent guest at Guy's Cliffe, withdrew on the second night owing to illness. On her reappearance the play's title, and its portrayal of a tyrannical regent, proved too great a risk for theatre managers

in the current climate of anxiety over the king's health (ibid., 2.725; Greatheed, xii).

Greatheed's radical sympathies endured, eventually prompting him to remove his only son, Bertie, from Eton College and educate him at home and on the continent, where he proved an amateur artist of some talent. While on a visit to Paris in 1803 to view the collection in the Louvre, the Greatheed family were taken prisoners of war on the resumption of hostilities. Shortly after their release, Bertie the younger became ill and died in Vicenza, Italy, on 8 October 1804, aged twenty-three. He left a wife and one daughter, who married, on 20 March 1823, Lord Charles Percy, son of the earl of Beverly. Greatheed the elder returned to Guy's Cliffe, where he died on 16 January 1826, aged sixty-six. CORINNA RUSSELL

Sources *An Englishman in Paris, 1803: the journal of Bertie Greatheed*, ed. J. P. T. Bury and J. C. Barry (1953) · *Thraliana: the diary of Mrs. Hester Lynch Thrale (later Mrs. Piozzi), 1776–1809*, ed. K. C. Balderston, 2nd edn, 2 (1951) · *GM*, 1st ser., 29 (1759), 497 · *GM*, 1st ser., 96/1 (1826), 367–8 · *GM*, 1st ser., 74 (1804), 1073, 1236 · W. Gifford, *The Baviad, and Maeviad*, new edn (1797) · Genest, *Eng. stage*, 6.477–8 · D. E. Baker, *Biographia dramatica, or, A companion to the playhouse*, rev. I. Reed, new edn, rev. S. Jones, 1 (1812), 296; 3 (1812), 197 · W. N. Hargreaves-Mawdsley, *The English Della Cruscans and their times* (1967)
Archives Warks. CRO, items for commonplace books and papers · Yale U., Beinecke L., corresp. and papers
Likenesses B. Greatheed, oils, repro. in Bury and Barry, eds., *An Englishman in Paris*

Greatorex, Ralph (*c*.1625–1675), maker of scientific instruments, whose parentage and date of birth are unknown, was bound an apprentice clockmaker for nine years from 25 March 1639, when he was about fourteen. His masters were Thomas Dawson and then Elias Allen, who had premises in the Strand, London. Although Greatorex's apprenticeship expired in 1648, he did not take his freedom until 25 November 1653, after Allen's death. In 1650, Greatorex acquired his own premises in the Strand, known the following year as the Sign of Adam and Eve. His first apprentice, Henry Wynne, was bound in 1654; he later became an instrument maker of repute. At least three others followed. The date and place of Greatorex's marriage to his wife, Anne, are unknown; she outlived him.

During the 1650s and 1660s, Greatorex made mathematical instruments: these included sundials (from 1651), Christopher Wren's perspectograph and a surveying instrument (by 1653), a 'sphere of wire' (probably an armillary sphere) by 1660, and a ruler for Samuel Pepys with special engravings (possibly a sector) in 1663. He was also among the first professional makers of mechanical and philosophical instruments. Thus Samuel Hartlib referred to Greatorex's diving apparatus from 1653, a new kind of brewing vessel in 1655, and water-lifting and fire engines in 1656 (the latter praised by John Evelyn). Robert Boyle commissioned an air-pump about 1658, and Pepys a thermometer in 1663. Greatorex had other interests: he made implements for sowing corn and cutting tobacco, and in 1657 took a garden in Arundel House for experimental growing of exotic herbs. His chemical interests included inventing a new metal for coinage, corresponding with Robert Boyle on practical matters (1655–6), and demonstrating a new varnish (1663). Astronomy was another interest and in 1658 Greatorex advised on the terminology of scientific instruments to Edward Phillips, lexicographer. As a surveyor, he was employed by the crown in Hampshire (1664), at Woolwich (1668–9), in Whitehall (1670), and in Cambridgeshire (1674). He surveyed the town and castle at Windsor in 1672.

Greatorex had many other contacts within the scientific community. The mathematician William Oughtred, a client of Elias Allen, was an early acquaintance and correspondent. In the 1650s, Greatorex had links with the Oxford experimentalists. He attended early meetings of the Royal Society from 1660; a concern was the construction of defences at Tangier—Greatorex's diving bell was tested with a view to using it there, and he helped with a device for lifting stones. In 1665 he was expected to go there himself; he came back to England during April or early May 1666 and intended to return after 2 July. Tangier brought Greatorex into contact again with Jonas Moore, who had lodged with Allen in the 1640s, during Greatorex's apprenticeship. With Moore, Greatorex surveyed part of London devastated by the fire of September 1666.

Greatorex's last year in the Strand was 1663; by 1665, he had moved to the east side of the south end of St James Street. He resisted attempts to be drawn more closely into the Clockmakers' Company in 1666; in 1668 he was finally elected an assistant but never sworn into office, and by 1671 was not paying his company dues. In 1673, he took an Ordnance office commission as captain of miners and pioneers in the expedition of the third Dutch war.

Greatorex was described by Hartlib as having 'a most piercing and profound witt' and by Sir Hugh Cholmley in a letter of 22 July 1665 as 'a very ingenious person but ... to much subject to ... good Fellowshipp and to spend his time and money idelly ... hee is not ... to bee trusted with money' (N. Yorks. CRO, zcg, v/1/1/1, fol. 183). He probably died in April 1675, for a man with this surname was buried at St Martin-in-the-Fields on 28 April 1675. In his will of 26 October 1674, proved on 4 May 1675, Greatorex left 1s. to his son Ralph and the remainder of his estate to his wife, Anne, sole executor.   SARAH BENDALL

Sources A. V. Simcock, 'An equinoctial ring dial by Ralph Greatorex', *Making instruments count*, ed. R. G. W. Anderson, J. A. Bennett, and W. F. Ryan (1993), 201–15 • F. H. Willmoth, *Sir Jonas Moore: practical mathematics and Restoration science* (1993) • Sheffield University, Hartlib MSS • Pepys, *Diary* • F. W. Steer and others, *Dictionary of land surveyors and local map-makers of Great Britain and Ireland, 1530–1850*, ed. P. Eden, 2nd edn, ed. S. Bendall, 2 vols. (1997) • E. G. R. Taylor, *The mathematical practitioners of Tudor and Stuart England* (1954) • S. Thurley, *The Whitehall Palace plans of 1670* (1998) • GL, Clockmakers' Company MSS • parish records, St Clement Danes and St Martin-in-the-Fields, City Westm. AC, 28 April 1675 [burial] • N. Yorks. CRO, Cholmley papers • will, PRO, PROB 11/347, sig. 46 • T. Birch, *The history of the Royal Society of London*, 4 vols. (1756–7) • *The diary of Robert Hooke ... 1672–1680*, ed. H. W. Robinson and W. Adams (1935); repr. (1968)

Greatorex, Thomas (1758–1831), organist and conductor, was born at North Wingfield, near Chesterfield, Derbyshire, on 5 October 1758. The pedigree compiled by Hayman in *The Reliquary* (4.220) shows his descent from Anthony Greatrakes of Callow, of a family that has flourished for over five centuries in the neighbourhood of Wirksworth, Derbyshire. Greatorex's father, Anthony (1730–1814), by trade a nailer, was a self-taught musician, and became an organist. Further details of his mother, Ann, are unknown. The doubtful story that the elder Greatorex constructed an organ with his own hands after he was seventy may refer to that built by John Strong, the blind weaver, and bequeathed to the elder Greatorex (Gardiner, 10–11). Martha, the eldest daughter, was thirteen when chosen the first organist of St Martin's, Leicester. She pursued her calling with considerable success, becoming 'a performer of eminence' (ibid., 1.9), and her earnings bought her a small estate at Burton upon Trent.

The family moved to Leicester when Thomas was eight years old and already 'remarkable for his grave and studious turn; his mind had a strong bias to mathematical pursuits, but, living in a musical family, his ear was imperceptibly drawn to the study of musical sounds' (Gardiner, 1.9). Greatorex studied music under Dr Benjamin Cooke, organist of Westminster Abbey, in 1772; two years later, after meeting the earl of Sandwich and Joah Bates, he was enabled to increase his knowledge of church music and the music of Handel particularly by attending the oratorio performances (in 1774–6) at Hinchinbrook, the country seat of the earl of Sandwich. Afterwards he became an inmate of the earl's household in town and country, and for a short time succeeded Bates as Sandwich's musical director. Greatorex sang in the Concerts of Ancient Music, established in 1776, but his poor health obliged him to seek a northern climate, and he accepted the post of organist of Carlisle Cathedral in 1780. In his leisure hours he studied science and music, and two evenings in each week he enjoyed philosophical discussions with Dr Thomas Percy, Dr Charles Law, Archdeacon Paley, and others. Greatorex left Carlisle for Newcastle in 1784. In 1786 he travelled abroad, provided with introductions, and was kindly received by English residents; among them the Jacobite pretender, Prince Charles Edward Stuart, who bequeathed to him several volumes of manuscript music. While in Rome Greatorex had singing lessons from Santarelli, and at Strasbourg he was taught by Pleyel.

At the end of 1788 Greatorex settled in London, and made large sums from teaching as many as eighty-four singing lessons in a week at a guinea each. Much of this lucrative business had to be renounced when in 1793 he accepted the conductorship of the Ancient Concerts in succession to Bates. Following the death of George Williams in 1819, Greatorex was appointed organist of Westminster Abbey, and in 1822 he was on the board of the Royal Academy of Music on its establishment, and the chief professor there of the organ and pianoforte. In 1801 he joined William Knyvett, Harrison, and Bartleman in reviving the Vocal Concerts, and he was also a professional member of the Madrigal Society, the Catch Club (from 1789 to 1798), and of the Royal Society of Musicians (from 1791). No important oratorio performance in town or country was thought complete without his co-operation as conductor or organist, and he frequently conducted the triennial music festivals at Birmingham, as well as those at York and Derby. His work at these provincial musical festivals in his later years, when suffering from gout, hastened his death. His last public appearance as a conductor was at his own benefit concert at the Hanover Square rooms on 20 June 1831 and was attended by Queen Adelaide, 'no less a proof of the Queen's discrimination than of the high character of him who was the object of such exalted patronage' (*The Harmonicon*, 1831, 179). After three years of illness, a cold caught while fishing was the immediate cause of his death at Hampton on 18 July 1831. He was buried near Benjamin Cooke in the cloisters of Westminster Abbey on 25 July; Croft's burial service and Greene's 'Lord let me know mine end' were sung during the ceremony, which was attended by a vast concourse of people. Greatorex was survived by his widow, six sons, and one daughter.

Greatorex's organ playing was masterly. 'His style was massive', writes Gardiner; 'he was like Briareus with a hundred hands, grasping so many keys at once that surges of sound rolled from his instrument in awful grandeur' (Gardiner, 2.641). The same writer also remarks: 'Although Mr. Greatorex was a sound musician and a great performer, he never appeared to me to have a musical mind; he was more a matter-of-fact man than one endowed with imagination' (ibid., 2.523). As a teacher he was widely admired, and when conducting his thorough knowledge of his art, his cool head, and sound judgement secured careful performances. During the thirty-eight years that Greatorex held the post of conductor of the Ancient Concerts, it is said that he never once was absent from his duty, or five minutes late for any rehearsal, performance, or meeting of the directors. Little but Handel's music was heard at these concerts, in accordance with the taste of George III and other patrons. Greatorex, too, had conservative ideas in artistic matters. He remarked of Haydn's *Creation* that 'it never will be much performed; it is so difficult, and its lightness of style will never suit the English taste' (ibid., 3.109). Although he could harmonize and adapt with great ease, he did not attempt original work. A few songs and ballads were converted by him into glees, and were popular at the Vocal Concerts; 'Faithless Emma' was one of these pieces. At various meetings his orchestral parts to Marcello's psalm 'With songs I'll celebrate' and to Croft's 'Cry aloud' were used. Of his published works, *Parochial Psalmody*, containing a number of old psalm tunes newly harmonized for congregational singing, appeared in 1825; his *Twelve Glees from English, Irish, and Scotch Melodies* was not printed until about 1833, after his death.

In 1817 Greatorex discovered a new method of measuring the altitude of mountains, which gained him the fellowship of the Royal Society; he was also a fellow of the Linnean Society. He was keenly interested in chemistry, astronomy, and mathematics, and was a connoisseur of paintings and of architecture. After his death his library and telescopes were sold; the Handel bookcase and contents (the works of the master in the handwriting of J. C. Smith) fetched 115 guineas. Warren's manuscript collection of glees, which fetched £20, included a manuscript note in Greatorex's hand, commenting on the manners of earlier times, illustrated by the grossness of the poetry then habitually chosen for musical setting. Greatorex's town house was 70 Upper Norton Street, Portland Place; in the country he had a beautifully situated house at Burton upon Trent on the banks of the river.

NICHOLAS SALWEY

Sources 'Memoir of Thomas Greatorex', *The Harmonicon*, 9 (1831), 231–3 · W. Gardiner, *Music and friends, or, Pleasant recollections of a dilettante*, 3 vols. (1838–53) · J. Cradock, *Literary and miscellaneous memoirs*, 2 vols. (1826) · *The Harmonicon*, 9 (1831), 179 · *Quarterly Musical Magazine and Review*, 6 (1824) · C. F. Pohl, *Haydn in London* (1867) · *New Grove* · *IGI*
Wealth at death Handel works and bookcase fetched 115 guineas; collection of glees fetched £20: *DNB*

Greatrakes, Valentine [nicknamed the Stroker] (1629–1683), faith healer, was born on 14 February 1629 at Affane, co. Waterford, Ireland, the eldest son of William Greatrakes (1573–c.1643), landowner, and his wife, Mary (d. c.1656), daughter of Sir Edward Harris (1575–1636) of Devon, who was chief justice of Munster in the early part of the seventeenth century. The Greatrakes family first became established in Ireland under Valentine's grandfather, also William (c.1540–1628), who accompanied Sir Walter Ralegh to Munster in the late sixteenth century. The family clearly prospered, making good marriages, and, critically, fell under the patronage of Richard Boyle, first earl of Cork, whose residence at Lismore was just a few miles from Affane and whose political, social, and economic dominance in this part of southern Ireland was complete.

Educated initially at the free school of Lismore, a Boyle foundation, Greatrakes fled with his mother to England soon after the outbreak of rebellion in Ireland in 1641. Originally intending to pursue his academic studies at Trinity College, Dublin, he now became domiciled at the home of his maternal uncle, Edmund Harris, in Cornworthy, Devon. On the latter's death he was placed under the tutelage of John Daniel Getsius, parson of nearby Stoke Gabriel, Devon, a protestant émigré from the wars of religion in Germany. Some time in 1647–8, and following the death of his father in Ireland, Greatrakes returned to his place of birth determined to make his fortune and reclaim the family estates which had been temporarily alienated. According to the autobiographical account appended as a preface to his published defence of his cures in 1666, Greatrakes at this time led a solitary, hermit-like existence, withdrawing into semi-retirement and a life of contemplation at the fortress of Cappoquin, a few miles from Affane (Greatrakes, *A Brief Account*, 17–18). Documentary evidence, however, strongly suggests that this may represent a somewhat distorted picture of Greatrakes's actual

'adventurers') and the new settlers (usually ex-soldiers) who saw in Cromwellian Ireland an ideal opportunity to acquire land and new roots in the wake of the great dispossession. Greatrakes's success in this respect, however, was tempered by the troubled relationship which he experienced throughout the 1650s and 1660s with his landlord, Richard Boyle, second earl of Cork, a religious and political conservative, whose frequent confrontations with Greatrakes over property entitlements were often coloured by wider political concerns. At the restoration in 1660 Greatrakes was temporarily deprived of his offices, but once pardoned by Charles II (almost certainly through the intercession of his patron, Roger Boyle, now earl of Orrery) he resumed his active role in Munster society. In 1661, for example, he appeared as an expert witness in the trial of a Youghal woman for witchcraft, and in 1663 he served as sheriff for the county of Waterford and acted as collector of the hearth tax.

It was at about this time (c.1662) that Greatrakes first began to practise among his neighbours his new-found gift of healing by touch, or 'stroking'. Initially reluctant to publicize his successful cures, within a few years his fame had spread to such an extent that his home at Affane was besieged with sufferers, many of them travelling across the Irish Sea from England to seek relief at Greatrakes's hands. An account of one such hopeful patient is provided in the case of the young John Flamsteed, future astronomer royal, who later claimed, in line with many others, that Greatrakes possessed 'a kind of majestical, yet affable, presence, a lusty body, and a composed carriage' (F. Baily, ed., *An Account of the Revd John Flamsteed*, 1835, 12, 16, 21). Not surprisingly Greatrakes's cures soon aroused disquiet in official circles, particularly as he professed a particular skill in the cure of the king's evil, or scrofula, the cure of which disease was widely held to be the special preserve of monarchs. Greatrakes was accordingly summoned to Dublin in the summer of 1665 to face the hostile interrogations of the clerical hierarchy. But despite official disfavour and further admonitions to cease his 'stroking', Greatrakes continued to exercise his gift of healing, and in the same year he was invited by Viscount Conway to Ragley Hall in Warwickshire, where it was hoped he might effect the cure of his celebrated wife, Anne, who suffered from debilitating headaches. At first reluctant to comply, Greatrakes eventually embarked for England in January 1666, there to achieve fame and notoriety in equal measure in that momentous year.

Though Greatrakes ultimately failed to cure Lady Conway, he did appear to meet with much greater success in the neighbouring towns and villages. In February 1666 he was invited to Worcester, where he continued to exhibit his peculiar skills, and it was while resident there that he received a summons from the king, via the secretary of state Lord Arlington, to perform his cures at court. Greatrakes failed to impress Charles, whose own ability to cure the king's evil was seen by many as persuasive evidence of the recently restored monarch's right to his throne. But in London itself he achieved enormous acclaim and was

Valentine Greatrakes (1629–1683), by William Faithorne the elder, pubd 1666

activities at this troubled and confusing period in the history of Ireland. In September 1649, for example, he petitioned the royalist duke of Ormond for the return of the family estates at Affane, then in the possession of one Colonel Hennessey. Just a few months later, however, he played a leading role in the surrender of Cappoquin, an important garrison town, to the forces of the invader, Cromwell, a volte-face which, not surprisingly, Greatrakes wished to obscure in his published memoirs. Thereafter, having opted to support the Cromwellian regime in Ireland, Greatrakes saw active service in the army, serving as lieutenant in the regiment of a close friend, Colonel Robert Phaire, the regicide, under the command of Roger Boyle, Lord Broghill.

In 1656, following the disbandment of the army in Ireland, Greatrakes finally returned to civilian life and his restored estates at Affane. From there he continued to serve the Cromwellian regime in various guises—for example, as a local JP and a clerk of the peace for the county of Cork. He was also appointed as registrar for the transplantation of the native Irish Catholics to Connaught, a post which he undoubtedly exploited in his new career as a land speculator. At this time Greatrakes began to invest heavily in the buoyant Irish land market, often acting as a middleman between English investors (or widely held by many in authority, including bishops, MPs, and magistrates, to possess a real gift of healing. Pamphlets both for and against Greatrakes soon appeared, and shortly before his departure for Ireland in May 1666, 'the stroker' completed the draft of his own defence, *A Brief Account*, in which he sought to vindicate his divine gift, both through a personal memoir of his unblemished and loyal life and character, and through a series of signed testimonials of specific cures which he had performed in London and elsewhere. Among the signatories were Robert Boyle, Andrew Marvell, Ralph Cudworth, John Wilkins, Benjamin Whichcote, Simon Patrick, and Sir Edmund Berry Godfrey, many of whom testified not only to the veracity of Greatrakes's cures, but also, most tellingly, to the pious and loyal nature of the charismatic Irishman.

As to the manner of the cures, numerous observers agreed that Greatrakes worked largely through the application of his hands to those sick or enfeebled parts of the body, the 'morbifick matter' being driven out by strong rubbing into some extreme part of the body, usually the fingers or toes. On occasion, however, he did employ basic surgical operations. Moreover, he did not claim to be infallible and he frequently refused to attempt the cure of some patients whose physical defects were beyond repair, as in the case of blindness and the illnesses of old age. Like the majority of his supporters, including the eminent scientist Robert Boyle, brother of Greatrakes's patron, he rejected a miraculous rationale for his methods and success, though he did aver that 'there was something in it of an extraordinary gift of God' (Greatrakes, 34). Some, such as the controversialist Henry Stubbe, used the occasion of Greatrakes's cures as an opportunity to spread heterodox religious opinions, though there is no evidence to suggest that this was orchestrated by Greatrakes or the majority of his closest supporters. As for Greatrakes himself, it may be significant that, on a number of occasions, he was inclined to ascribe a thaumaturgical element to his practice, as, for example, when he compared his actions to those of a skilled exorcist. Frequently accused by his opponents and others of consorting with demons and dabbling in the black arts, he was clearly fascinated by witchcraft and supernatural phenomena, and he claimed on numerous occasions to possess a particular expertise in such matters.

Both contemporaries and historians have tended to ascribe an ulterior motive to Greatrakes's healing claims, most notably in respect of the potentially subversive religious and political significance implicit in his public performances. Certainly a radical spirit is suggested by his service to the Cromwellian republic in Ireland in the 1650s, alongside his lifelong friendship with prominent religious radicals such as Colonel Robert Phaire and his less well-documented acquaintance with Lodowick Muggleton in the 1670s. However, this view of Greatrakes needs to be balanced against the deep-seated royalism of the family of his first wife, Ruth (1633–1678), daughter of Sir William Godolphin, whom he probably married some

time between 1656 and 1663, and that of her kinsman, Sir Ames Meredith (c.1616–1668), who acted as both business partner and confidant to Greatrakes throughout much of the 1650s and 1660s. If there was any common religious and political denominator in the support which Greatrakes received in the 1660s for his celebrated cures it is probably most manifest in the profound desire of so many of his followers for an end to the policies of religious and political exclusion which were threatening to divide once and for all the political nation in England and Ireland. Significantly, the vast majority of those who openly pledged support for his cures, or were themselves the beneficiaries of his 'stroking', had, like Greatrakes, served, or benefited under, the Cromwellian regime. What they now sought, above all else, was reconciliation with the restored regime and reintegration into a body politic which many perceived by the mid-1660s to be on the verge of irredeemable disintegration. Accordingly, Greatrakes's cures might best be understood not as covert acts of sedition, but rather as a means of chastising the monarch—Greatrakes's moderation and unblemished piety being offered as a model for emulation rather than implying disparagement.

On his return to Ireland in late May 1666, Greatrakes resumed the life of a country gentleman, all the while continuing in close contact with a number of his former London acquaintances and supporters. Foremost among these was Sir Edmund Berry Godfrey, whose surviving correspondence with 'the stroker' between 1666 and 1671 attests to Greatrakes's continuing interest in the financial, religious, and political affairs of the capital in these years. Greatrakes was a frequent visitor to England in the years after 1666 and he continued to practise his gift of healing, though with far less publicity than previously. In 1668, for example, he returned to old haunts in London, Ragley, and the west country, recounting details of the continuing success of his cures in a letter to Robert Boyle. He was also in London in 1672 and 1675; on the latter occasion, he was acting as an intermediary between the Irish Muggletonians and their charismatic, London-based leader, Lodowick Muggleton. The vast majority of his time, however, as befitted a country gentleman, seems to have been taken up with business matters related to his considerable property interests in both south-west Ireland and Devon. The survival of one of his books of accounts for the 1660s, as well as the letters of various creditors such as Sir Robert Southwell and William Petty, underlines the precarious nature of Greatrakes's financial position in these years, a situation only partly redeemed by the confirmation of his Irish estates under the Act of Settlement in the 1660s.

Valentine and Ruth Greatrakes had two sons, William and Edmund. William (1663–1686) was educated at Trinity College, Dublin, and shortly before his death, in 1685, he was abroad in Spain in the company of his maternal uncle, the diplomat and Catholic convert, Sir William Godolphin (1635–1696); he married Mary Wheeler, the granddaughter of Dr Jonah Wheeler, bishop of Ossory.

Edmund (d. 1690), named after Greatrakes's close friend and correspondent, Sir Edmund Berry Godfrey, married Anne, the daughter of Thomas Willcocks, a wealthy merchant of Bristol. Greatrakes's first wife, Ruth, died in 1678, and he subsequently married Alice (née Tilson), widow of Mr Rotherham of Camolin, co. Wexford; 'the stroker' died at Affane on 28 November 1683, survived by his wife Alice. He requested in his will that he be buried in Lismore Cathedral; his wishes were not followed and he was buried next to his father in Affane. PETER ELMER

Sources V. Greatrakes, A brief account of Mr Valentine Greatrak's (1666) • S. Hayman, 'Notes on the family of Greatrakes', The Reliquary, 4 (1863), 81–96, 220–36; 5 (1864), 94–104 • MSS of Richard Boyle, second earl of Cork, Chatsworth House, Derbyshire, Lismore MSS 29 and 30 • The Conway letters: the correspondence of Anne, Viscountess Conway, Henry More, and their friends, 1642–1684, ed. M. H. Nicolson (1930), 246ff. • The works of the Honourable Robert Boyle, ed. T. Birch, new edn, 1 (1772), lxxv–lxxxv; 6 (1772), 195, 199, 221, 390 • J. Glanvill, Saducismus triumphatus, or, Full and plain evidence concerning witches and apparitions, trans. A. Horneck, 2 pts (1681), 90–94, 180–81, 183, 189, 247–50 • H. Stubbe, The miraculous conformist (1666) • [D. Lloyd], Wonders no miracles (1666) • CSP Ire., 1660–62, 318 • MSS of the duke of Ormond, Bodl. Oxf., MSS Carte 66, fols. 249r–255r; 156, fols. 15–16; 165, fols. 55v, 145 • letters to V. Greatrakes from Sir E. B. Godfrey and others, 1666–71, NL Ire., MS 4728 • abstract of V. Greatrakes's will, Representative Church Body Library, Dublin, MS 80/B2/2, p. 285 • DNB

Archives BL, account and memorandum book, Add. MS 25692 | Bodl. Oxf., Radcliffe Science Library, Boyle letters, nos. 3, 21
Likenesses three line engravings, 1794, Wellcome L. • W. Faithorne the elder, line engraving, BM, NPG; repro. in Greatrakes, Brief account [see illus.]
Wealth at death income of £1000 p.a. towards end of life

Greatrakes, William (c.1723–1781), barrister and supposed author of the Letters of Junius, born in Waterford, was the eldest son of Alan Greatrakes of Mount Lahan, near Killeagh, co. Cork, and his wife, Frances Supple, of the neighbouring village of Aghadoe. He entered Trinity College, Dublin, as a pensioner on 9 July 1740, and became a scholar in 1744, but did not take a degree. He may have served for a few years in the army. On 19 March 1751 he was admitted as a student at the Middle Temple, and was called to the Irish bar in the Easter term of 1761. He does not appear to have practised very much, nor to have had a residence in Dublin; and he had formally retired from the bar before 1776. He is thought to have lived for some time at Castlemartyr, co. Cork. He died, unmarried, at The Bear inn, Hungerford, Berkshire, on 2 August 1781, while travelling from Bristol to London, and was buried in Hungerford churchyard. His tombstone was inscribed 'stat nominis umbra' ('the shadow of the name remains', or 'the legacy of the reputation remains').

Greatrakes acquired some posthumous importance from his supposed connection with the authorship of the Letters of Junius (1769–72), as expounded by Sir Nathaniel Wraxall and others. The evidence remains extremely flimsy, and was taken from a series of late eighteenth- and early nineteenth-century periodicals. These suggestions were fuelled by a supposed correlation between the wording on Greatrakes's tombstone and the motto prefixed to the Letters, and by family members who circulated spurious 'proofs' of the original text. John Britton's The Authorship of the 'Letters of Junius' Elucidated (1848) reproduced these and other examples as fact. Sir Philip Francis is now considered to be the most likely author.

GORDON GOODWIN, rev. M. E. CLAYTON

Sources The letters of Junius, ed. J. Cannon (1978), 540–72 • admissions register, Middle Temple, 1.343 • GM, 1st ser., 83/2 (1813), 547 • The historical and the posthumous memoirs of Sir Nathaniel William Wraxall, 1772–1784, ed. H. B. Wheatley, 5 vols. (1884)

Greaves, Sir Edward, baronet (bap. 1613, d. 1680), physician, the son of John Greaves (1579–1617) and his wife, Sara (d. 1640), was baptized at Colmore, Hampshire, where his father was rector. Thomas *Greaves and John *Greaves were his brothers. Edward studied at Oxford and was elected a probationer fellow of All Souls College in 1634. After this he studied medicine at Padua, where in 1636 he wrote some complimentary Latin verses to Sir George Ent on his graduation, and after returning to Oxford graduated BM on 18 July 1640, and DM on 8 July 1641. In 1642 he continued his medical studies at the University of Leiden, and on his return practised physic at Oxford, where, on 14 November 1643, he was appointed Linacre superior reader of physic. In the same year he published Morbus epidemicus anni 1643, or, The New Disease with the Signes, Causes, Remedies, an account of a mild form of typhus fever which was epidemic at Oxford in that year, especially in the houses where sick and wounded soldiers were quartered. Charles I is supposed to have created him a baronet on 4 May 1645. Of this creation, the first of a physician to that rank, no record exists, but Le Neve did not doubt the fact, and explained the absence of enrolment (letter of Le Neve in T. Smith, Clarissimi ac doctissimi viri Joannis Gravii … vita, 1699). With his friend Walter Charleton, Greaves became travelling physician to Charles II, but settled in London in 1653, although sometimes practising in Bath, and was admitted a fellow of the College of Physicians on 18 October 1657. He delivered the Harveian oration at the College of Physicians on 25 July 1661 (published in 1667), of which the original manuscript is in the British Library (Sloane MS 302). It contains few facts and many conceits, but some of these are happy. He says that before Harvey the source of the circulation was as unknown as that of the Nile, and compares England to a heart, whence the knowledge of the circulation was driven forth to other lands. He became physician-in-ordinary to Charles II, lived in Covent Garden, died there on 11 November 1680, and was buried in the church of St Paul's, Covent Garden. In his will Greaves left his house in Bath and other bequests to his wife, Anna, with provision for her unborn child if she should prove to be pregnant. To his daughter Mary Greaves, his executor, he left properties in Kent, Surrey, Sussex, Oxfordshire, and Hampshire, as well as his house in Henrietta Street, Covent Garden. To his daughter Elizabeth Greaves he left £2000, and to his daughter Margaret he left 20s.

NORMAN MOORE, rev. MICHAEL BEVAN

Sources Munk, *Roll* · Wood, *Ath. Oxon.*, new edn · BL, Sloane MSS 51 and 302 · IGI · *Hist. U. Oxf.* 4: *17th-cent. Oxf.*, 516, 522, 527, 712, 718, 720 · PRO, PROB 11/364, fols. 180r–180v
Wealth at death wealthy; left house in Bath; properties in Kent, Sussex, Oxfordshire, and Hampshire; house in Henrietta Street, Covent Garden, London; plus sums of £2000 and 20s.: will, PRO, PROB 11/364, fols. 180r–180v

Greaves, Sir George Richards (1831–1922), army officer, was born on 9 November 1831 at Briery Close, Lowwood, Windermere, Westmorland, one of the eight children of George Greaves, a retired captain in the 60th rifles. Greaves's mother had poor health and the family went abroad in 1838, eventually settling at Grätz, with the result that three of his brothers subsequently joined the Austrian services. Greaves himself attended a number of continental day schools but, intended by his father for the Royal Artillery, returned to Quartman's preparatory school, Woolwich. The unexpected death of Greaves's sponsor left him without nomination to the Royal Military Academy, but an uncle secured nomination to the Royal Military College, Sandhurst, on 13 October 1846, and Greaves was commissioned as ensign without purchase in the 70th foot on 30 November 1849.

Greaves joined the 70th in India in October 1850, being promoted lieutenant on 16 January 1852. The routine of regimental service was alleviated by a spell as deputy assistant adjutant-general during the Usofzai expedition on the north-west frontier in 1857–8, Greaves's regiment remaining on the frontier throughout the mutiny. After becoming regimental adjutant in May 1858, Greaves married Ellen, the daughter of Brigadier-General Hutchison, on 9 July 1859. Promoted captain on 11 October 1859, Greaves next accompanied his regiment to New Zealand in January 1861, becoming deputy assistant quartermaster-general on the staff and surveying the Waikato River country. He was present at actions against the Maori at Mangatawhiri, the Gate Pa, and Weraroa Pa. Promoted to both a brevet majority and a lieutenant-colonelcy as a result of his services on 1 March 1864 and 21 March 1865 respectively, he brought part of the 70th home and, having turned down the offer of an appointment in Ceylon, became brigade major at Dover in April 1867. Greaves was then appointed deputy assistant adjutant-general at the Horse Guards on 1 June 1870, sharing an office with Garnet Wolseley.

Greaves's particular passion in India had been sport; introduced to a form of callisthenics by a fellow officer, he had developed a powerful physique. Wolseley laid particular store on physical strength and later described Greaves as 'a good sportsman, strong and healthy in body and resolute in mind' (Wolseley, *Story of a Soldier's Life*, 2.280). However, Wolseley also added that Greaves was 'with strong opinions—I might even add prejudices' and, in many respects, this was to become Greaves's defining characteristic to the ultimate detriment of his career. One officer wrote that Greaves was a 'short, sharp-featured individual, with a pompous and rather disagreeable manner, a loud voice, a quick temper, and a sense of his own importance which defied everything' (E. G. Parry, *Suakin*, 1885,

120). Another recalled Greaves as having 'an old-fashioned vocabulary of exceptional virulence and potency' (Younghusband, 95). Yet, he also had a roguish charm. His first wife died in 1880, but Greaves had already made the acquaintance of Julia Rose Venour, daughter of the Revd E. Morris and wife of W. Venour, the doctor of the 15th hussars. Mrs Venour was certainly Greaves's mistress by 1884, but he then took up with Mrs Rochfort-Boyd (Lady Wolseley to Wolseley, 27 Nov and 25 Dec 1884, Hove, LW/P 10/28 and 30). He married the widowed Mrs Venour in 1908; she survived him.

Wolseley wanted Greaves as chief of staff on his Asante expedition in 1873, but the commander-in-chief, the duke of Cambridge, feared criticism if two of his staff secured the principal appointments while also claiming Greaves was too young, despite being older than Wolseley. However, the wounding of John McNeill led to Greaves, who had received a brevet colonelcy on 12 September 1872, being sent in December 1873, receiving the CB for his services. Greaves then returned to the Horse Guards as assistant adjutant-general in April 1874, serving on the Stanley committee in 1877. In July 1878 Greaves again accompanied Wolseley as chief of staff to Cyprus, succeeding him as administrator in May 1879. However, Greaves believed the island insufficiently healthy for a major British base, offending government by the forthright public expression of his views. As Wolseley was to remark, Greaves 'has yet to learn that it does not do to insert the whole truth in official correspondence' (Wolseley to Lady Wolseley, 8–13 Aug, 1879, Hove, W/P 8/19). Indeed, Greaves did not secure the KCMG for which Wolseley had recommended him until May 1881.

Greaves escaped Cyprus in July 1879 on appointment, at Wolseley's suggestion, as adjutant-general in India, the Second Anglo-Afghan War having broken out. Cambridge had favoured T. D. Baker, but he was private secretary to the viceroy, Lord Lytton, and the commander-in-chief in India, Sir Frederick Haines, advised against any impression that the new incumbent was Lytton's nominee. Greaves, who took up his post on 30 October 1879, suggested in his memoirs that he acted as chief of staff to Haines at Lytton's request, at the same time loyally supporting Haines in his frequent clashes with Lytton. In reality, as Lytton complained, Greaves's 'incessant endeavour' was to 'get the entire control of military operations, little by little, through the CinC, into his own hands' (Lytton to Roberts, 20–21 March 1880, Roberts MSS 7101-23-37/84). Moreover, Greaves urged himself on Haines as chief of staff directing field operations while simultaneously endeavouring to prevent Haines from taking the field personally by communicating Haines's intentions to Lytton through his fellow Wolseley protégé Henry Brackenbury.

Having been promoted major-general on 25 October 1882, Greaves completed his term in India on 31 October 1884, being chosen almost immediately for the expedition to Suakin in February 1885. Wolseley had urged the appointment of either McNeill or Greaves to command, but Cambridge refused on the grounds that both were junior to the commander at Suakin, Major-General A. J. Lyon-

Fremantle. The unhappy compromise was Sir Gerald Graham in command, with Greaves as chief of staff and McNeill and Fremantle each commanding a brigade. Even before they left England, Greaves was referring to Graham as a 'fiddle headed fool' (Lady Wolseley to Wolseley, 11 Feb 1885, Hove, LW/P 11/7). Sent to report on the situation after the near-disastrous action at Tofrek in March, Wolseley concluded that 'every one seemed to desire to play his own hand and to think solely of himself whilst he hated and ridiculed his neighbour' (Wolseley to Lady Wolseley, 20–27 May 1885, Hove, W/P 14/13). Indeed, Wolseley now believed Greaves could not be entrusted with more than a divisional command in future. Greaves briefly commanded at Suakin after the main expedition's withdrawal and was rewarded with the KCB in August 1885 before returning to India to command the Meerut division in November.

Greaves was made commander-in-chief in Bombay on 14 March 1890, receiving promotion to lieutenant-general on 11 October 1890. His tenure was marked by improvements to the hospitals and barrack accommodation of Indian troops as well as the establishment of Deolali as a convalescence camp for British troops. Greaves also improved musketry standards and marked the young Douglas Haig as suitable for Staff College training. Greaves expected to succeed Roberts as commander-in-chief in India in October 1892, blaming his subsequent passing over by the much junior Sir George White on the accession of the Liberal government at home and the machinations of Roberts. However, as Brackenbury noted, Greaves's defects of character had ruled him out of consideration from the beginning: 'He is very quarrelsome & rude—jealousy being always the cause of his rudeness' (H. Brackenbury to R. Buller, 19 July 1892, Buller MSS 2065M/SS4/27). Greaves promptly resigned his command and left India two years early on 31 March 1893.

Greaves was promoted full general and created GCB upon his retirement in 1896, becoming honorary colonel of the East Surrey regiment in 1898 to add to that of the Bengal-Nagpur Railway volunteer rifle corps, which he had assumed in India. He settled at Netherwood, Saundersfoot, Pembrokeshire, where he died on 11 April 1922.

IAN F. W. BECKETT

Sources G. R. Greaves, *Memoirs* (1924) · Hove Central Library, Wolseley MSS · *Roberts in India: the military papers of Field Marshal Lord Roberts, 1876–1893*, ed. B. Robson (1993) · B. Robson, *Fuzzy-wuzzy: the campaigns in the eastern Sudan, 1884–85* (1993) · *In relief of Gordon: Lord Wolseley's campaign journal of the Khartoum relief expedition, 1884–1885*, ed. A. Preston (1967) · Viscount Wolseley [G. Wolseley], *The story of a soldier's life*, 2 vols. (1903) · J. H. Lehmann, *All Sir Garnet: a biography of Field-Marshal Lord Wolseley* (1964) · G. Younghusband, *A soldier's memories* (1917) · H. Brackenbury, *The Ashanti war*, 2 vols. (1874) · WWW

Archives Devon RO, Buller MSS · Hove Central Library, Wolseley MSS · NAM, Roberts MSS · NAM, letters to Sir Frederick Haines · Royal Arch.

Likenesses photographs, repro. in Greaves, *Memoirs*

Wealth at death £9,948 4s. 8d.: probate, 8 July 1922, CGPLA Eng. & Wales

Greaves, James Pierrepont (1777–1842), mystic, was born on 1 February 1777, the eldest surviving child of Charles Greaves (1740–1800), a City linen draper, and his wife, Ann, *née* Pierrepont (1752–1805). Greaves, like his brothers and sisters, was an evangelical churchman; he entered the family business but lost his fortune owing to trading difficulties in the Napoleonic wars, and in 1810 was declared bankrupt. In 1817 he underwent 'some strong interior visitations' (*The Dial*, 3, 1842–3, 423), a mystical experience which changed his life, and he left England, spending three years with the educationist Pestalozzi in Switzerland, where he absorbed the lesson that education was the process of releasing the innate goodness in the child. After teaching briefly at the Basel Mission Institute, he went to Tübingen where, to the disapproval of the authorities, he gathered an unofficial group of students around him. It was probably in Germany that he came to reject empiricism, finding in idealism a more congenial philosophy; he also became a devotee of Jakob Boehme, whose works he later offered to lend Thomas Carlyle.

On his return to England in 1825 Greaves was briefly secretary of the Infant School Society, but though he is credited with founding infant education in Britain, the society was already in the hands of the evangelicals and Henry Brougham. Greaves, who was fiercely celibate, had adopted a diet eschewing all stimulants, and eventually lived solely on fruit and vegetables, preferably uncooked; he was also indifferent to dress. In 1832 with his sister he set up a scheme to relieve rural poverty in the village of Randwick, Gloucestershire, by providing work in return for metal tokens which could be exchanged for bibles, prayer books, clothes, or household goods. This venture showed him that society could not be reformed by external actions, and he became convinced that man needed to transform himself: hence he called himself a sacred socialist, in contrast to the materialist Robert Owen. Surprisingly, the Owenite Alexander Campbell was converted by Greaves's prolix letters, which he published, with a benign portrait, after Greaves's death. However, John (Zion) Ward resisted recruitment as did Emma Martin, the Owenite lecturer.

Back in London, Greaves gathered a group of disciples into an 'aesthetic institution' at his home in Burton Street. They included literary men like F. F. Barham, who notoriously described Greaves as 'essentially a superior man to Coleridge' (Barham, 8), and J. A. Heraud, whose *Monthly Magazine* the American transcendentalist A. Bronson Alcott excitedly read in the Boston Athenaeum to bring himself into touch with Greaves's circle. There were also disciples from Greaves's own mercantile background; these men ran his ideal community at Alcott House, Ham Common, Surrey, among them Charles Lane, who wrote for Emerson's *Dial*.

Greaves seems to have been a truly good man, giving his life to God in an attempt to renew the world, beginning at Ham Common. All descriptions stress his remarkable presence with his 'singularly bright' eyes which were 'as well inlets as outlets to the soul' (Lane, 285). Greaves summed up his beliefs in the aphorism 'As Being is before knowing and doing I affirm that Education can never repair the defects of Birth' (engraved in his own hand on his portrait), a dispiriting stance for an educator. Despite this, Greaves founded the community and school at Alcott House (1838–48) as an embodiment of his principles and as a tribute to the American transcendentalist whose teaching he so admired and who visited the community in 1842. It was funded by Sophia Chichester, a well-connected widow, who gave him £100 a year and paid for the posthumous publication of his works. Suffering from a painful hernia, Greaves moved early in 1842 to take the cold water cure at Alcott House, the first hydropathic establishment in England. He died there on 11 March 1842 and was buried five days later at St Andrew's, the Ham parish church.   J. E. M. LATHAM

Sources R. W. Emerson, 'English reformers', *The Dial: a Magazine of Literature, Philosophy and Religion*, 3 (1843), 227–47 · C. Lane, 'James Pierrepont Greaves', *The Dial: a Magazine of Literature, Philosophy and Religion*, 3 (1843), 247–55, 281–96 · F. F. Barham, *A: an odd medley of literary curiosities, original and selected*, 2 (privately printed, London, 1845) [memoir of J. P. Greaves] · *Letters and extracts from the MS writings of James Pierrepont Greaves*, ed. A. Campbell, 2 vols. (1843–5) · J. Myerson, 'William Harry Harland's "Bronson Alcott's English friends"', *Resources for American Literary Study*, 8 (1978), 24–60 [Harland's careful article is based on primary sources now lost] · *Zion's works: new light on the Bible from the coming of Shiloh, the spirit of truth, 1828–1837*, ed. C. B. Holinsworth, 16 vols. (1899–1904), vols. 5–7, 15–16 · J. E. M. Latham, *Search for a new Eden. James Pierrepont Greaves (1777–1842): the sacred socialist and his followers* (1999) · parish register (burials), 16 March 1842, Ham, Surrey, St Andrew's

Archives Basel Mission Institute, Switzerland | LUL, Wilderspin papers · Som. ARS, Strachey MSS, collections of aphorisms · Staats- und Universitätsbibliothek Hamburg Carl von Ossietzky, Germany, N. L. Wurm papers

Likenesses engraving, repro. in Campbell, ed., *Letters and extracts*, frontispiece · stipple, NPG

Greaves, John (1602–1652), astronomer and orientalist, was probably born at Alresford, Hampshire, the eldest of the four sons of John Greaves (1579–1616), rector of Colmer, a noted schoolmaster, and his wife, Sara (*d.* 1640). His three brothers also achieved distinction: Nicholas became a fellow of All Souls College, Oxford, and dean of Dromore in Ireland; Thomas *Greaves deputized for Thomas Pococke as professor of Arabic at Oxford University; and Edward *Greaves became a physician to Charles I.

Greaves was said to have been educated by his father, he entered Balliol College, Oxford, in 1617, graduated in 1623, and was elected a fellow at Merton College, Oxford, in 1624. About this time he studied Greek, Arabic, and Persian astronomical texts; his publications suggest that he became more familiar with Persian than Arabic, but who taught him either language is unknown. In February 1631, with the support of John Bainbridge and Peter Turner, he succeeded Turner as professor of geometry at Gresham College, London, retaining his fellowship at Merton College. After visits to Paris, Venice, Padua, and Leiden, Greaves planned a journey to the Levant, one of the first scientific expeditions, in order to acquire Arabic and other oriental books and coins for Archbishop Laud, and to make astronomical observations.

Among texts Greaves was keen to acquire was the *zij*

John Greaves (1602–1652), by Edward Mascall, 1650

(astronomical tables) prepared by eminent Islamic astronomers at the observatory of Samarkand under the patronage of the prince, Uluğ Beg (1394–1449). In seeking these tables, the last important *zij* of many produced through the centuries at Islamic observatories, he was concerned, not with the history of astronomy, but with the possible use of the supposedly most accurate tables available, better than those of Ptolemy. For his astronomical observations he recognized that for accuracy he had to have large instruments, some of which were produced for him by Elias Allen; the degree arcs of the large brass sextant and quadrant were divided with transversals, and a cross-staff was 10 feet long with 10,000 divisions. (Several of the instruments are now in the Museum of the History of Science at Oxford University.)

Accompanied by Edward Pococke, Greaves set out from England in 1637, to Constantinople, where he found no teachers of Arabic. Despite great difficulties in acquiring manuscripts, he expected to bring back copies of most of the Greek mathematicians transcribed into Arabic. He obtained a fine *Almagest* stolen from the royal library in the Seraglio, measured Santa Sophia, observed the Turkish army, and noted the Greek use of egg yolk mixed with colours for religious pictures. While at Constantinople, he tried to organize observations of a lunar eclipse at Baghdad, Constantinople, Smyrna, and Alexandria, and his own observations included magnetic observations and sunspots. After leaving Constantinople for Alexandria he put in at Rhodes, where he measured the latitude, faulting Ptolemy (but his own calculations were also in error).

During two visits to Cairo, Greaves's curiosity was roused by several matters, especially by the chicken hatcheries, artificial incubators which had fascinated other European travellers. An artificial incubator was among the lesser secrets communicated to Elias Ashmole; Johann Vesling, of the universities of Venice and Padua, like Greaves, knew William Harvey, and the interest in the incubators may have influenced the history of embryology. Greaves's account of the hatcheries was published posthumously by Ent in 1678 in the *Philosophical Transactions of the Royal Society* (no. 137). Greaves made a detailed metrological study of the pyramids, and his measurements, published in *Pyramidographia* (1650) were used by Isaac Newton. From Alexandria, he went to Florence, Rome, and Naples where he made astronomical and magnetic observations. At Florence he met Sir Robert Dudley, the naval commander and designer of astronomical instruments. Greaves returned to England early in 1640. On the death of Bainbridge he became Savilian professor of astronomy at Oxford in 1643, but in November 1648 he was banished from Oxford by the parliamentary visitors and was succeeded in the professorship by his friend Seth Ward. He went to London and stayed in Kent with John Marsham, writer on chronology and Egyptologist.

Greaves's first published work was an edition of Bainbridge's *Canicularia* (1648). His additions include the positions of important stars from the observations of Uluğ Beg. With Pococke's *Notae*, it was the first book published at Oxford to use Arabic type; the Arabic in a lecture by Pasor was presented in Hebrew type; that in a lecture by Thomas Greaves had been written in by hand. More material from Uluğ Beg appeared in Greaves's *Astronomica quadam ex traditione Shah Cholgii Persae* [Mahmud Shah Khalji] *una cum hypothesibus planetarium* (1650), which includes *Binae tabulae, una Nassir Eddini Persae* [Nasir ad-din at-Tusi] *altera Ulug Beigi Tartari* (1648). This was dedicated to Marsham. Greaves wrote in Latin the first Persian grammar to appear in England, *Elementa linguae Persicae* (1649). He found Uluğ Beg's work useful for his interest in chronology and this resulted in *Epochae celebriores … ex traditione Ulug Beigi* (1650), from various cultures. He also wrote on navigation, calendar reform, the Roman foot, and the *denarius*. Greaves's catalogue of Archbishop Laud's coins has not been found.

In the autumn of 1651 Greaves married Elizabeth Gibbon of Bishopstone, Kent, who survived him; he died on 8 October 1652, and was buried in St Benet Sherehog, London.   FRANCIS MADDISON

Sources T. Smith, *Clarissimi ac doctissimi viri, Joannis Gravii … vita* (1699) • J. Ward, *The lives of the professors of Gresham College* (1740), 135–53, 337–8 • T. Birch, 'An historical and critical account of the life and writings of Mr John Greaves', in *Miscellaneous works of Mr John Greaves*, ed. T. Birch, 1 (1737), i–lxxii • R. Mercier, 'English orientalists and mathematical astronomy', *The 'Arabick' interest of the natural philosophers in seventeenth-century England*, ed. G. A. Russell (1994), 158–214 • R. T. Gunther, 'The first observatory instruments of the Savilian professors at Oxford', *The Observatory*, 60 (1937), 190–97 • R. T. Gunther, 'The first Savilian instruments at Oxford', *The Observatory*, 61 (1938), 135–6 [letter] • E. Bernard, 'Instrumenta astronomica Musei Saviliani', *Catalogi librorum manuscriptorum Angliae et Hibernicae*, ed. E. Bernard, 2 vols. in 1 (1697), pt 1, p. 302 • Wood, *Ath. Oxon.* • W. Pope, *The life of the right reverend father in God, Seth, lord bishop of Salisbury* (1697), 18–21 • T. Hervey, *History of Colmer and Priors Dean* (1896), 74–81

Archives BL, biographical collections concerning Greaves, Add. MS 4243 • Bodl. Oxf., commonplace book; corresp. and papers | BL, letters to Edward Pococke, Add. MS 6193

Likenesses E. Mascall, copper engraving, 1650 (after painting?), BM, NPG [*see illus.*]

Greaves, Thomas (*fl.* 1604), composer and lutenist, was in the service of Sir Henry Pierrepoint, whose seat was at Holme in Nottinghamshire, and to whom Greaves dedicated his *Songs of Sundry Kinds*, published in 1604. This volume is the only evidence of the composer's existence, its dedicatory poems indicating that he was now elderly. Sir Henry's wife, Frances, was a cousin of the composer Michael Cavendish, who in 1598 had published a volume containing three differing groups of pieces: solo lute airs, lute airs in four-voice arrangements, and madrigals; six years later this pattern was followed by Greaves in his volume, except that the four-voice lute airs were replaced by a group of viol-accompanied (consort) songs. These two collections are the only ones from the period to contain both madrigals and lute songs.

Greaves was a limited composer, his work at times rough in technique and melodically pallid. Three of his six madrigals (all for five voices) were obviously very recent: 'England, receive the rightful king' hailed the accession of James I only the previous year, and the madrigal pair 'Sweet nymphs that trip along' and 'Long have the shepherds' would seem to have been a greeting to James's queen, Anne of Denmark. By far the best of the madrigals is the exuberant 'Come away, sweet love'. In contrast, the six consort songs, described as 'songs of sadness' (probably after the final group of songs—originally also viol-accompanied—in William Byrd's *Psalms, Sonnets and Songs of Sadness and Piety*, 1588), represent an older tradition. Notable for their religious or moralizing texts, unbroken viol textures, and restrained expression, they contain little that could not have been composed half a century earlier. Greaves's nine lute songs are simple tuneful airs, and they make up the most attractive group in the volume.

DAVID BROWN

Sources 'Greaves, Thomas', *New Grove*, 2nd edn • E. H. Fellowes, *The English madrigal composers*, 2nd edn (1950)

Greaves, Thomas (1611–1676), oriental scholar, was born at Colmer, Hampshire, the third of four sons of John Greaves (1579–1617), rector of Colmer and a famous schoolmaster, and his wife, Sara (d. 1640), and younger brother of John *Greaves (1602–1652) and elder brother of Edward *Greaves (*bap.* 1613, d. 1680). He entered Charterhouse School as a scholar on 28 June 1619, and matriculated as a scholar of Corpus Christi College, Oxford, on 15 March 1628. He graduated BA on 19 February 1631, proceeded MA on 18 March 1634, and became fellow of his college in 1636. His chamber-fellow, a great friend of his brother John, was Edward Pococke, who instructed Thomas in oriental languages, especially Arabic. For the duration of Pococke's absence in Constantinople from 19 July 1637 to 1641, Greaves was appointed his deputy in reading the Arabic lecture, through the influence of John Greaves with the chancellor, Archbishop Laud. He published his inaugural lecture, *De linguae Arabicae utilitate & praestantia* (1639), a trite rehearsal of traditional themes advocating the study of Arabic. Greaves was appointed rector of Dunsby, Lincolnshire, in 1638, and of Minton in the same county in 1642, but continued to reside at Oxford (where he proceeded BD on 22 October 1641), until shortly before he was expelled from his fellowship and from the university on 14 July 1648, for failing to submit to the parliamentary visitors. His deposition supporting John Greaves's attempts to avoid expulsion undoubtedly also harmed him.

On 18 October 1648 Greaves married Dorothy Besouth at Stoke Hammond, Buckinghamshire; their eldest son, John, was baptized at Dunsby on 9 August 1649. Greaves lamented his exile from books in the marshes of Lincolnshire in a poem appealing to John Selden to help him escape, but was forced to remain there until the Restoration. In 1652 he inherited the collection of choice Arabic and Persian manuscripts assembled by his brother John, but soon sold most of them to Selden. In the same year he was named by Brian Walton as one of the participants in the projected edition of the polyglot Bible. His contribution is confined to notes in volume six on the Persian versions of the Pentateuch and gospels. Greaves refused to collaborate with Edmund Castell in his heptaglot lexicon, and published nothing further apart from the pamphlet *A Brief Summe of Christian Religion* (1656), written for his Dunsby parishioners. However, in a letter to Richard Baxter of 5 August 1656, he claimed to have composed a polemical treatise against Islam, which Archbishop Ussher had advised him to publish. This does not survive, but parts may have been incorporated in Greaves's translation of and commentary on the Koran, which he left, very incomplete, in manuscript (BL, Add. MS 21901). Despite this work and his association with three of the foremost oriental scholars of his time—Pococke, his own brother John, and Samuel Clarke, and the encouragement of Selden and Ussher—Greaves was neither a profound nor an assiduous student of Arabic and Persian.

At the Restoration Greaves was rewarded by Charles II for his loyalty on 10 December 1660 with appointment as rector of North Church Berkhamsted, Hertfordshire and on 10 October 1661 with a doctorate from Oxford. In 1664 he became rector of Benefield, Northamptonshire, and in October 1666 was granted a prebend at Peterborough Cathedral. He remained rector of Benefield for the rest of his life, apparently having lost his earlier scholarly interests, but at some time after 1670, prevented from performing his duties by an impediment in his speech, he retired to his property in nearby Weldon. He died there on 22 May 1676, and was buried in the chancel of Weldon church. He was survived by his wife (who died on 22 January 1686), two sons, and four daughters. His manuscripts (which included some writings of Richard James, his friend and likewise a fellow of Corpus) were sold to the Bodleian Library by his son in 1678. **G. J. TOOMER**

Sources Wood, *Ath. Oxon.*, new edn, 3.1061–2 · Wood, *Ath. Oxon.*: *Fasti* (1815), 454; (1820), 3, 259 · G. J. Toomer, *Eastern wisedome and learning: the study of Arabic in seventeenth-century England* (1996), 130–34, 176–8, 207–9 · *Miscellaneous works of Mr John Greaves*, ed. T. Birch, 1 (1737), lxii–lxx · PRO, PROB 11/351, fols. 78v–79v · H. J. Todd, *Life of Brian Walton*, 1 (1821), 49, 225–30 · B. Marsh and F. A. Crisp, eds., *Alumni Carthusiani: a record of the foundation scholars of Charterhouse, 1614–1872* (1913), 4 · letter of Greaves to Laud, PRO, SP 16/432, fol. 19r · *The works of the most reverend father in God, William Laud*, 5/1, ed. J. Bliss (1853), 176–7, 237 · T. Hervey, ed., *The parish registers of Priors Dean and Colmer* (1886), 12, 102–4, 123 · W. D. Macray, *Annals of the Bodleian Library, Oxford*, 2nd edn (1890), 147–8 · M. Burrows, ed., *The register of the visitors of the University of Oxford, from AD 1647 to AD 1658*, CS, new ser., 29 (1881), 163 · Bodl. Oxf., letter to Selden, MS Selden supra 108, fol. 54 · L. Twells and S. Burdy, *The lives of Dr Edward Pocock … Dr Zachary Pearce … Dr Thomas Newton … and of the Rev Philip Skelton*, 1 (1816), 14–15, 35, 51, 190, 211–12, 255, 297–8 · T. Greaves, letter to Edward Bernard, Bodl. Oxf., MS Smith 45, p. 81 · Edmund Castell to Greaves, BL, Add. MS 4162, fol. 63 · J. Selden, letter to Greaves, Bodl. Oxf., MS dd Dashwood (Bucks) I 1/1/1 · Foster, *Alum. Oxon.* · *Fasti Angl., 1541–1857*, [Bristol], 131 · parish register, Stoke Hammond, Bucks. RLSS, 18 Oct 1648 [marriage] · J. Bridges, *The history and antiquities of Northamptonshire*, ed. P. Whalley, 2 (1791), 357, 446–7

Archives BL, partial translation of Koran, Add. MS 21901 · Bodl. Oxf., corresp., collections, and MSS | Bodl. Oxf., letter to Edward Bernard, MS Smith 45, p. 81 · Bodl. Oxf., letter to Selden, MS Selden supra 108, fol. 54

Wealth at death bequeathed approx. £4000; incl. *c*.£2000 in money, two leases of manors, and 10 acres of land value £6 p.a.; plus household property and more land; also books and MSS max. £100: will, PRO, PROB 11/351, fols. 78v–79v

Greaves, Walter (1846–1930), boat builder and painter, the son of Charles William Greaves, a Chelsea boat builder and waterman, and his wife, Elizabeth Greenway, was born on 4 July 1846 at 31 Cheyne Walk, Chelsea, London. He was living at 10 Lindsey Row in Chelsea when in 1863 the young James Abbott McNeill Whistler and his mother moved into 7 Lindsey Row. Whistler became friends with Greaves and his brother Henry, two years his senior; the brothers took Whistler rowing on the Thames—as their father had rowed J. M. W. Turner—and the American painter later used such expeditions for inspiration when painting his 'nocturne' views of the river at night. 'He taught us to paint', Walter Greaves said, 'and we taught him the waterman's jerk' (E. R. Pennell and J. Pennell, *Life of James McNeill Whistler*, 76), the Thames rowing stroke. The brothers, both amateur artists who drew detailed Chelsea scenes, became Whistler's studio assistants and he taught them to paint in an impressionistic style. Their styles diverged somewhat from their master's: Walter Greaves explained matter-of-factly, 'To Mr. Whistler, a boat was always a tone, to us it was always a boat' (Brinton, 62).

Walter Greaves's own work—in oils, watercolour, pastel, pen and ink, pencil, and etching—was varied, the best retaining the high quality of his topographical draughtsmanship and that in Whistlerian style showing marked individuality of touch. The most celebrated and mysterious of his paintings is *Hammersmith Bridge on Boat-Race Day*, a naïve masterpiece, which he claimed to have painted when he was aged sixteen; however, since he was unreliable over dates, its history has never been settled. The Greaves brothers accompanied Whistler to life class and Walter tried portraiture, some of his most successful being of their neighbour Thomas Carlyle, whom Whistler also painted. Greaves also drew and painted Whistler, sometimes in caricature, in Chelsea settings and in characteristic moods. In 1876 the brothers helped Whistler decorate the Peacock Room (now in the Freer Gallery of

Art, Washington, DC), for the shipowner Frederick Leyland.

Two years later Whistler left Lindsey Row, moving to the smarter Tite Street, and the Greaves brothers were gradually discarded, the break becoming final on Whistler's marriage a decade later. Having abandoned boat building, the brothers tried to live as artists but, despite a commission to paint murals of riverside scenes in Streatham town hall, they were reduced to hawking drawings of Chelsea in pubs and at tradesmen's entrances. Greaves's attempts at a reconciliation with Whistler failed and he was turned away from the house in which his former patron was dying in 1903. Henry Greaves died a year later, in 1904, and Walter fell deeper into penury.

In 1911 a large number of Greaves's paintings were discovered in a second-hand bookshop; William Marchant, the dealer, recognized their quality and exhibited them at the Goupil Galleries in London. The exhibition was a sensation, the newspapers making much of Greaves's friendship with Whistler and the latter's cavalier treatment of his friend. When a critic suggested that it was Greaves who had inspired Whistler, and not vice versa, the latter's American friends Joseph and Elizabeth Pennell fiercely defended his reputation. They claimed that the paintings were unfinished works by Whistler, which Greaves had stolen from his studio, touched up, and signed himself. Unjust as this was, it so damaged Greaves's reputation that the exhibition closed and he returned to near destitution. He moved to 525 Fulham Road in 1897 and to 33 Lillie Road, Fulham, in 1919. Yet he still haunted the Chelsea riverside in his battered top hat, with his grey moustache and hair darkened with bootblack, selling his drawings for trifling sums or bartering them for food or coal.

Finally, in 1921, several prominent artists—Augustus John, William Nicholson, and William Rothenstein among them—rescued both Greaves and his reputation. Another exhibition was arranged, he was elected an honorary member of the Chelsea Arts Club, and in 1922 a place of retirement was found for him at the Charterhouse in the City of London. Greaves died, unmarried, of pneumonia in West London Hospital, Hammersmith, on 23 November 1930. He was buried in the Charterhouse graveyard at Little Hallingbury in Essex. Two self-portraits by Greaves are in the Tate collection, which also owns other examples of his work, including *Hammersmith Bridge on Boat-Race Day*; another large painting in oils, *The Last Chelsea Regatta*, is in Manchester City Galleries and another major work in oils, *The Boating Pond, Battersea Park*, was rediscovered in 1992 and is now in a private collection. Exhibitions have been held by the royal borough of Kensington and Chelsea (1968) and by the Parkin Gallery, London (1980 and 1984).   TOM POCOCK

Sources T. Pocock, *Chelsea reach: the brutal friendship of Whistler and Walter Greaves* (1970) · J. Rothenstein, *Artists of the 1890s* (1928) · C. Brinton, *Walter Greaves (pupil of Whistler)* (1912) · E. Robins Pennell and J. Pennell, *The life of James McNeill Whistler*, 2 vols. (1908); 5th edn in 1 vol. (1911) · E. R. Pennell and J. Pennell, *The Whistler journal* (1921) · W. Marchant, *A reply to an attack* (1911) · *Annual Report* [Chelsea Society] (1928–92) · J. Yeoman, *The Greaves brothers and Victorian Chelsea* (1968) [exhibition catalogue, Royal Borough of Kensington

and Chelsea, London] · W. Greaves, preface, in W. Marchant, *Mr Walter Greaves, pupil of Whistler* (1911) [exhibition catalogue, Goupil Gallery, London, 1911] · W. Greaves, 'Notes on Old Chelsea', in W. Marchant, *Walter and H. Greaves, pupils of Whistler* (1922) [exhibition catalogue, Goupil Gallery, London, 1922] · M. Parkin, *Walter Greaves, a pupil of Whistler* (1980) [exhibition catalogue, Parkin Gallery, London] · M. Parkin, *Walter Greaves, 1846–1930, and the Goupil Gallery: paintings, drawings and etchings* (1984) [exhibition catalogue, Parkin Gallery, London] · *The Times* (29 Nov 1930)

Archives Chelsea Library, Old Town Hall, Chelsea, MSS · Tate collection

Likenesses W. Greaves, self-portrait, c.1870, priv. coll. · W. Greaves, self-portrait, oils, 1880–90 (with his sister Alice), Tate collection · W. Greaves, self-portrait, oil on paper, c.1910, Tate collection · photograph, 1911, Chelsea Library · photograph, 1911, priv. coll. · photograph, 1911, Michael Parkin Gallery, London · W. Nicholson, oils, c.1912, Man. City Gall. · W. Rothenstein, pencil, 1915, NPG · P. Evans, pen-and-ink drawing, c.1928, NPG · photograph, 1930, priv. coll.; repro. in Pocock, *Chelsea reach*

Wealth at death £412 12s. 6d.: administration, 26 May 1931, *CGPLA Eng. & Wales*

Greaves, William Michael Herbert (1897–1955), astronomer, was born in Barbados, West Indies, on 10 September 1897, the only son of Eustace C. Greaves, a medical practitioner and graduate of the University of Edinburgh. From Codrington College, Barbados, he won a scholarship to St John's College, Cambridge, where he was a wrangler of the mathematical tripos of 1919 and was awarded the Tyson gold medal for astronomy. In 1921 he won a Smith's prize, became the Isaac Newton student, and was elected a fellow of his college. At St John's he came under the influence of H. F. Baker, Lowndean professor of astronomy and geometry, who induced him to take up problems in the field of celestial mechanics. As an Isaac Newton scholar Greaves was expected to spend a period at the Royal Greenwich Observatory to familiarize himself with problems of practical astronomy. Having worked there for some months he was offered the post of chief assistant early in 1924. He married in 1926 Caroline Grace Kitto (1900–1978), a sister of the Greek scholar H. D. F. Kitto; another sister was the wife of L. J. Comrie, one-time superintendent of the *Nautical Almanac* office. The Greaves's only son, George, became a mathematician.

Greaves's principal interest, and that which established his reputation, now became the use of photography for the study of the continuous spectra of stars. In 1926, in co-operation with C. R. Davidson, he started a major programme of spectroscopic observations of stars which were to be employed as spectrophotometric standards. Using first the 30 inch and later the 36 inch telescopes of the Greenwich observatory, they succeeded in measuring the 'gradients' or colour temperatures of some 250 stars. The work required making comparisons with a light source of known temperature mounted on the roof of the observatory's octagon room. It also involved painstaking studies of the behaviour of photographic emulsions and the influence of numerous irksome factors such as atmospheric absorption. Also at Greenwich, in collaboration with H. W. Newton, Greaves reanalysed the magnetic records kept there, interpreting them in terms of major and recurrent solar disturbances.

In 1938 Greaves succeeded R. A. Sampson as astronomer

royal for Scotland and professor of astronomy at the University of Edinburgh. He found at the Royal Observatory on Blackford Hill a 36 inch reflector similar to that at Greenwich and a Hilger prism spectrograph. He embarked on a new programme to be devoted to the photometry not of the continuous but of the line spectra of stars. The programme made a promising start, but following the outbreak of the Second World War observational work had to be curtailed and eventually suspended. However, a new and important field of activity now emerged. In the autumn of 1940, when the country became the target of severe air raids, the astronomer royal, Sir Harold Spencer Jones, recommended that the Edinburgh observatory be equipped to provide an independent national time service in case of emergency. Greaves took up this task with enthusiasm, and by the end of the year he managed to complete the installation of the necessary equipment. In January 1941, when the Greenwich time service was disrupted by enemy action, he operated the broadcast time signals, and he kept this service operating until 1946. As a by-product of this work he and L. S. T. Symms of Greenwich compared the performance of the Edinburgh and Greenwich free pendulum Shortt clocks with that of the quartz crystal clocks newly installed by the Post Office. They demonstrated the latter's superiority both as long-term standards and for the day-to-day control of time signals.

After the end of the war the spectrophotometric programme was resumed. It covered about a hundred blue stars of O and B type down to magnitude 5. Their spectra were photographed and the spectrograms calibrated in a separate multiple slit spectrograph. For the reduction of the spectra, Greaves introduced a novel method of measurement designed to reduce the effect of photographic plate grain and of random and systematic errors. All spectrograms of stars of each particular type were measured at up to 1500 individual wavelengths and the measurements numerically superimposed. This was carried out by means of a manually operated microphotometer designed and constructed by Greaves's ingenious chief assistant E. A. Baker. Such a method led to appreciably greater accuracy than conventional procedures and was capable of discovering very faint spectral features, including previously unknown interstellar bands. With computerized techniques still in the future, it was, however, inordinately laborious and time-consuming. The spectrophotometric programme dominated the observatory's activities for many years and was ultimately to result in seven major publications, the second, in 1955, being Greaves's last. The programme was completed after Greaves's death by his collaborators.

In his later years Greaves, who in 1943 was elected to the Royal Society, became very much an elder statesman whose advice was sought in many quarters, especially in the Royal Astronomical Society (whose meetings in London he never missed, and of which he was president in 1947–9). He was a prominent member of the International Astronomical Union and was president of its commission of stellar photometry. When the post-war needs of British astronomy came up for discussion Greaves was one of the few astronomers who came out in full support of the new field of radio astronomy, strongly advocating Sir Bernard Lovell's ambitious proposal for a steerable radio telescope at Jodrell Bank. He served on the advisory committee of the Jodrell Bank experimental station and on the board of visitors of the Greenwich observatory. Scrupulous in all his duties and a formidable critic, Greaves was the most helpful of colleagues and the kindest of friends. He died suddenly of heart failure at his home at the Edinburgh observatory on Christmas eve 1955, and his remains were cremated on 28 January 1956 at Warriston crematorium, Edinburgh. HERMANN A. BRÜCK

Sources H. A. Brück, *The story of astronomy in Edinburgh* (1983), 80–89 · J. Jackson, *Monthly Notices of the Royal Astronomical Society*, 116 (1956), 145–51 · R. d'E. Atkinson, *Nature*, 177 (1956), 209–10 · H. M. Smith and G. B. Wellgate, 'Quartz crystal clocks', *Vistas in Astronomy*, 1 (1955), 438 · *Publications of the Royal Observatory, Edinburgh*, 1–2 (1939–61) · *WW* · *The Scotsman* [burial notice?]
Archives Royal Observatory, Edinburgh
Likenesses photograph, *c.*1947, Royal Observatory Library, Edinburgh; repro. in Brück, *Story of astronomy*; copy, RAS
Wealth at death £4976 2s. od.: probate, 12 March 1956, *CGPLA Eng. & Wales*

Grebill, Agnes (d. 1511). *See under* Lollard women (*act. c.*1390–*c.*1520).

Green, Aaron Levy (1821–1883), rabbi, was born in Middlesex Street (popularly known as Petticoat Lane), Aldgate, London, in August 1821, the youngest of the eight children of Levy Ephraim Green (1784–1858), a local tradesman, and his wife, Amelia Hyams (1779–1854). He was educated at the Talmud Torah section of the Jews' Free School in Bell Lane, Spitalfields. He became a leading member of the generation of English-born preachers who transformed the profession of a Jewish minister from that of a mere servant of the congregation and reader of services, spoken entirely in Hebrew, to that of a leader of the congregation, whose sabbath sermons in English became an integral part of public worship.

A precocious pupil, Green had a fine voice, and at the age of fourteen was permitted to conduct a service in the Great Synagogue, Duke's Place, London. In May 1838, three months before his seventeenth birthday, he was appointed minister to the Bristol community. On 31 July 1844 he married Phoebe Levy, a native of Bristol, who cried throughout the ceremony—occasioned, it was later discovered, not by emotion but by an oncoming attack of measles. They had seven sons and five daughters, all of whom survived him. Though a great success at Bristol, he felt that his talent required greater scope, and in 1851 applied for and secured the post of second reader at the Great Synagogue, Duke's Place. He remained there until his appointment in June 1854 to the prestigious post of reader and preacher at the newly established West End branch of the Great Synagogue in Great Portland Street, where he served for the remainder of his life. It was a wealthy congregation, and there was scarcely a communal institution, charitable or educational, whose honorary officers did not belong to the synagogue, and he acted as almoner for many of their charitable donations.

In addition to his ministerial duties Green threw himself wholeheartedly into the work of communal institutions involved in education, religious culture, and the state of the Jewish poor. A supporter of the establishment of Jews' College, he served as its honorary secretary from 1859 until his death. His library of about 6000 books, his most cherished possession, was donated to the college after his death and formed the nucleus around which the library expanded. He was an instigator of the industrial department and visitation committee of the Jewish Board of Guardians, a founder of the Jewish Association for the Diffusion of Religious Knowledge, a member of the council of the Anglo-Jewish Association, and was on the committee of the Mansion House Relief Fund. His firm friendship with Professor David Marks of the Reform synagogue smoothed away many of the differences that divided the Orthodox from the Reformers.

A brilliant columnist, Green's impressive contributions to the *Jewish Chronicle* under the pseudonym Nemo were widely discussed and particularly influential. Though he could be impatient with those slower of thought, and particularly those slower of action, and sometimes showed it, by 1870 he had established himself as a figure of outstanding authority in the community. Though his formal education ended before he was seventeen, he never ceased to be a student. He devoted his nights mostly to the study of Jewish learning, and once a month stayed up all night to review his studies of the previous four weeks.

Green died unexpectedly on 11 March 1883 at St Bartholomew's Hospital, London, and was buried three days later at Willesden Jewish cemetery in a grave adjacent to the one he had consecrated on the morning of his death.

GERRY BLACK

Sources A. M. Jacob, 'Aaron Levy Green, 1821–1883', *Transactions of the Jewish Historical Society of England*, 25 (1973–5), 87–106 · *Jewish Chronicle* (16 March 1883) · A. M. Jacob, 'No ordinary tradesmen: the Green family in nineteenth-century Whitechapel', *Jewish Historical Studies*, 33 (1992–4), 163–73 · V. D. Lipman, *A century of social service, 1859–1959: the Jewish Board of Guardians* (1959) · A. Newman, *The United Synagogue, 1870–1970* (1976) · I. Finestein, *Jewish society in Victorian England* (1993) · D. Cesarani, *The Jewish Chronicle and Anglo-Jewry, 1841–1991* (1994) · G. Black, *JFS: the history of the Jews' Free School, London, since 1732* (1998) · Boase, *Mod. Eng. biog.* · *CGPLA Eng. & Wales* (1883)
Archives Jewish Museum, London, sermons and lectures
Likenesses S. A. Hart, oils, exh. RA 1858 · B. S. Marks, portrait, *c.*1878 · photograph (after B. S. Marks), repro. in *Transactions of the Jewish Historical Society of England*
Wealth at death £3102 6s. 0d.: resworn probate, July 1888, *CGPLA Eng. & Wales* (1883)

Green, Alexander Henry (1832–1896), geologist and mathematician, was born at Maidstone on 10 October 1832, son of the Revd Thomas Sheldon Green, headmaster of the grammar school, Ashby-de-la-Zouch, and his wife, whose maiden name was probably Derington. He was educated at his father's school where, influenced by one of his teachers, the Revd William Coleman (*c.*1816–1863), he early developed an interest in the local geology. He entered Gonville and Caius College, Cambridge, in 1851 to read mathematics and graduated sixth wrangler in 1855. Elected a fellow of his college the same year, Green taught mathematics and attended the lectures of the Woodwardian professor of geology, Adam Sedgwick (1785–1873). In 1861 he was appointed to the geological survey with whom he mapped extensive tracts of the Carboniferous and Mesozoic rocks of the midlands and north of England and became a leading authority on coal-bearing strata and coal-mining geology. His geological survey memoir, *Geology of the Yorkshire Coalfield* (1878), long remained a classic. While working for the survey Green married, in 1866, Mary Marsden (*d.* 1882), with whom he had two sons and a daughter.

In 1874 Green left the survey to become the first professor of geology at the newly founded Yorkshire College at Leeds. Here he had a disappointing time, with so few students that he later assumed additionally the chair of mathematics, but he continued to research steadily and was elected FRS in 1886. Two years later he was appointed to succeed Sir Joseph Prestwich (1812–1896) as professor of geology at Oxford, where he had more students, as geology had recently been accepted as a subject for honours in the school of natural science. His teaching at Oxford stressed rigorous scientific method, with emphasis on proper instruction in the field.

Photographs of Green show a gentle figure, adorned by a long grey beard. He was vigorous and hard-working, always believing that the best geology was done in the field. Apart from his survey memoirs he was not a prolific writer but his contributions represent scientific writing at its best, characterized by a logical precision stemming in part from his mathematical background. His *Manual of Physical Geology* (1876; 3rd edn, 1883) became well known for its lucid presentation and practical outlook. Green was widely respected in the geological community. He was a modest man of simple tastes, warm and genial in manner, sincere and straightforward. He served on the councils of both Royal and Geological societies, and was a vice-president of the latter, which also awarded him the Murchison medal in 1892. Following the death of his first wife he married, on 27 December 1883, Wilhelmina Maria Armstrong (*b.* 1845/6), who survived him. There was one son and one daughter of the marriage. Green, who had been in poor health for some time, died of a stroke at Oxford on 19 August 1896 and was buried at Wolvercote cemetery.

E. A. VINCENT

Sources C. L., *PRS*, 62 (1897–8), v–ix · A. Harker, 'Alexander Henry Green', *The Naturalist* (April 1897), 111–14 [with portrait] · *DNB* · E. A. Vincent, *Geology and mineralogy at Oxford, 1860–1986* (1994) · *Kelly's directory of Oxford* · m. cert. [Wilhelmina Armstrong]
Archives MHS Oxf., corresp.; drawings; lecture diagrams · U. Birm., Lapworth Museum of Geology, notebooks · U. Leeds, Brotherton L., drawings | MHS Oxf., letters to Sir E. B. Poulton
Likenesses photograph, repro. in *The Naturalist* · two photographs, Oxf. U. Mus. NH, Geological Collections
Wealth at death £7437 2s. 0d.: probate, 17 Oct 1896, *CGPLA Eng. & Wales*

Green [*née* Stopford], **Alice Sophia Amelia** [*known as* Alice Stopford Green] (1847–1929), historian and Irish nationalist, was born on 31 May 1847 at Kells, co. Meath, the seventh of the nine children of the Revd Edward Adderley Stopford (1810?–1874), archdeacon of Meath, and Anne Catherine Duke of co. Sligo. The Stopford family had played a prominent role in Irish academic and ecclesiastical circles since the early eighteenth century. Edward Adderley Stopford upheld the family tradition by combining his pastoral duties with scholastic pursuits, publishing on a number of questions, most notably on ecclesiastical law. He also involved himself in the political side of church affairs by conferring with Gladstone on the Irish Church Bill of 1869. Although he disapproved strongly of the disestablishment of the Church of Ireland, he lent his expertise to the debate in the interest of producing a fair settlement. His wife was a fervid evangelical who led her children in family prayers every morning and presided over a disciplined and orderly household. Strict religious observance featured strongly in the lives of the Stopford children, but Alice Stopford became increasingly disenchanted with evangelicalism and gradually subscribed to a broader form of Christianity.

Stopford and her three sisters were educated by a succession of governesses at the family home. An eager student, she was given the run of her father's library and struggled to teach herself Greek, German, and metaphysics. Her studies were interrupted, however, by eye trouble which led to near blindness at the age of sixteen. She was forced to spend a year in a darkened room and was unable to read until an operation in 1871 restored her sight. The family left co. Meath and moved to Dublin while she was recovering. She took advantage of both her improved health and the intellectual opportunities available in Dublin by seeking permission to attend lectures at the college of science. To the amazement of male students, she and a female companion attended physics lectures at the college. The death of her father forced another move, this time to England, where she settled with her mother and sister at Chester in 1875. This arrangement was by no means agreeable to Stopford, who found her mother's evangelicalism and her disapproval of female intellectuals stifling. By the time she moved to Chester, Stopford was in her late twenties, and resigned to becoming what she described as an 'old maid'. Despite this, she developed a fondness for debate, fun, and lively company. Travels throughout Ireland and further afield to Scotland and the continent had broken the monotony of life in co. Meath, and Stopford's Chester home provided a useful base from which to visit English friends and relations. In particular, she enjoyed the literary environment at the London home of her cousin Stopford Brooke. A literary and liberal man, Brooke entertained a number of intellectuals at his Manchester Square home and it was there that Stopford met her future husband, John Richard Green (b. 1837), to whom she became engaged in 1876, and whom she married on 14 June 1877.

A former curate in the East End, Green had established a reputation as a journalist and historian by the time he met Alice Stopford. Although Green had been educated at Oxford and was more widely read than his haphazardly educated wife, the couple enjoyed a stimulating and mutually beneficial intellectual rapport. J. R. Green directed his wife's reading while she acted as his research assistant and intellectual confidante. The marriage was by all accounts a happy one. As well as pursuing their mutual and individual intellectual interests, the couple enjoyed an active social life, visiting and entertaining friends. Their happiness was, however, clouded at regular intervals by Green's poor health. He had a weak chest and was susceptible to colds and influenza; he suffered a haemorrhage a month after his marriage and winters were subsequently spent in Italy or in the south of France. Green was often so weak that he was forced to dictate his work to his wife, and together they produced *A Short Geography of the British Islands* in 1879. After a last painful attempt to return to his work, he died on 7 March 1883.

Although she was devastated by the loss of her husband, Alice Stopford Green was committed to establishing herself in her own career. In 1884 she applied for the post of mistress of Girton College, Cambridge, but despite the support of Florence Nightingale, her application was unsuccessful. She turned instead to history, initially because of her connection with her husband, but eventually on her own terms. She completed one of her husband's books (*The Conquest of England*, 1884), and produced a new edition of his most famous work, the *Short History of the English People* (1888); she was also approached by John Morley to contribute a short life of Henry II for the Twelve English Statesmen series (1888). Her next project, a history of urban life in fifteenth-century England, was far more ambitious. This two-volume study (*Town Life in the Fifteenth Century*, 1894) contributed greatly to her growing fame as a historian and as an intellectual in her own right. Her husband's death had left her with an annual income of about £1800, more than enough to allow her to give away a third of her income each year and to entertain regularly at her Kensington Square home. She moved to Grosvenor Road in 1903, and her reputation as a lively and generous hostess who provided a good table grew. Red-haired, vivacious, and allegedly fonder of the company of men than women, she attracted a diverse collection of guests to her home, entertaining statesmen, writers, journalists, and civil servants among others. She became deeply interested in colonial affairs, most particularly those relating to Africa, and after visiting prisoner-of-war camps on the island of St Helena during the Second South African War in 1900 she publicized and urged the need for their reform. In 1901 she co-founded the African Society (Royal African Society from 1935), became its vice-president and edited its journal. Her main interest was in discussing African conditions and she objected to what she saw as the politicization and commercialization of the society. Despite this, in 1905 she helped to finance the *African Mail*, and through her connection with this publication she joined the Congo Reform Association. Her interest in the Congo brought her into contact with Roger Casement, an Irish diplomat who had published a damning report on labour conditions in the Congo Free State. Their common nationality and interest in both Irish and African affairs led to a strong friendship and a combined effort to gain support for the association from Irish nationalist leaders.

From around the turn of the twentieth century Stopford Green became increasingly interested in Irish issues. She was enthused by the Gaelic revival, which boosted interest in the Irish language and in Irish history. Although she never mastered the Irish language, she strongly supported its teaching and in 1903 she helped to set up the School of Irish Studies in Dublin. She became increasingly interested in Irish history, disapproving of the way in which historians had tended to focus on the Anglo-Irish at the expense of Gaelic tradition, history, and culture. She consequently published in 1908 *The Making of Ireland and its Undoing, 1200–1600*, a book which concentrated strongly on Celtic civilization. Its nationalist tone offended some sections of Unionist opinion and it was banned by the Royal Dublin Society. Stopford Green went on to publish a number of books on Irish history, each of which exhibited a distinctly nationalist outlook. Her interest in the subject strongly informed her developing political beliefs. As a Liberal, she had supported Irish home rule in a passive sense since the late nineteenth century, but her politics became increasingly practical as she formed close friendships with Irish economic and political reformers in the early twentieth century. She lent her support to a number of causes, including the publication in 1905 of an anti-army recruitment pamphlet and the establishment of a non-denominational Irish university. A constitutional nationalist, Stopford Green was greatly enthused by the Home Rule Bill of 1912 and dismayed by Ulster Unionist threats to resist its implementation. She consequently endorsed the foundation of the Irish Volunteers, an organization established in 1914 to defend the Home Rule Bill. She became chair of the London Committee, an illegal organization which raised funds and co-ordinated the purchase of arms for the Irish Volunteers. She contributed personally a large proportion of the £1500 raised; this money was subsequently used to secure German arms.

This dramatic episode was overshadowed by the outbreak of the First World War, which split nationalist opinion. While Casement abhorred the involvement of Irish soldiers in the British army and attempted to involve Stopford Green in his anti-British campaign, she supported the decision of Irish party leader John Redmond to pledge Irish support to the British war effort. As an advocate of the attainment of Irish self-government by constitutional means, she was profoundly shocked by and disapproved of the 1916 Easter rising in Dublin. Despite her condemnation of Casement's role in the rebellion, she intervened after his arrest, writing letters about his treatment, visiting him in prison, and organizing a defence fund to which she contributed generously. After Casement was tried and sentenced to death, she worked towards securing a reprieve, drafting petitions, speaking with MPs, and even making an appeal to Buckingham Palace. Her efforts were in vain, but Casement's execution and the dramatic shifts in Irish politics after 1916 absorbed her almost completely

and led to her decision to leave London, at the age of seventy, and to take up residence in St Stephen's Green, Dublin.

Stopford Green remained a constitutionalist, but she acknowledged that simple home rule would no longer satisfy Irish demands and advocated dominion status instead. She published widely on Irish issues, expounding her nationalist views in a number of pamphlets between 1917 and 1918, and maintaining that the strongest obstacle to Irish self-rule of any form was Ulster Unionism, with which she had little sympathy despite her own protestant and Unionist upbringing. Although she disapproved of violence and strongly condemned offences committed by crown forces and republican rebels, she admired some young members of Sinn Féin, and received many of them—including Michael Collins—at her home while they were on the run from British authorities. Her home was raided and searched by crown forces on several occasions. When the end of the conflict between British forces and Irish rebels initiated another war—this time between supporters and opponents of the Anglo-Irish treaty of 1921—Stopford Green supported the treaty strongly. As a defender of the Commonwealth, she distributed pro-treaty leaflets and joined Cumann na Saoirse (the 'league of freedom'), a women's pro-treaty organization. She was appointed in 1922 to a seat in the senate of the Irish Free State, an honour which carried certain risks and which necessitated the instalment of a military guard outside her house.

The end of the Irish Civil War saw Stopford Green once more engrossed in her favoured pursuits: history, Gaelic culture, and entertaining. Her Dublin home became a centre of intellectual debate which attracted numerous guests, both Irish and foreign, who were prominent in the arts, politics, and academe. She helped to found the Irish Book Shop, which became an informal centre of literary Dublin, produced a number of short books on Irish history for schools, and became an active member of a senate, to which she presented in 1924 a casket of silver and bronze which was decorated with Celtic motifs. Her health began to fail as she approached her eightieth birthday. Her hearing deteriorated and she suffered a heart attack in 1925, but continued to preside over convivial dinner parties. After a short illness, she died at St Stephen's Green on 28 May 1929.

S. Pašeta

Sources R. B. McDowell, *Alice Stopford Green: a passionate historian* (1967) · L. Ó Broin, *Protestant nationalists in revolutionary Ireland: the Stopford connection* (1985) · *CGPLA Eng. & Wales* (1929) · *DNB*
Archives NL Ire., corresp. and MSS · NL Scot., corresp. | BL, corresp. with Macmillans, Add. MSS 55059–55061 · BLPES, corresp. with E. D. Morel · CUL, letters to Lord Acton · Jesus College, Oxford, corresp. and papers relating to John Richard Green · NL Scot., corresp. with Lord Haldane · Plunkett Foundation, Long Hanborough, Oxfordshire, corresp. with Sir Horace Plunkett · TCD, corresp. with Mary Childers
Likenesses W. Rothenstein, portrait; known to be at the Dublin Municipal Gallery of Modern Art in 1967
Wealth at death £22,639 0s. 2d.: resworn probate, 7 Sept 1929, *CGPLA Eng. & Wales*

Green, Amos (1735–1807), fruit and landscape painter, was born in Halesowen, Shropshire, into a family that had 'want of fame and fortune' (Green, 78). Green had a poor education, followed by an apprenticeship with the Birmingham printer John Baskerville, for whom he decorated trays and boxes. His speciality lay in fruit and flower pieces in imitation of still lifes by J. B. Monnoyer and J. van Huysum. He came to move in polite and educated circles through residence with the wealthy Deane family of Hagley, Birmingham.

By 1757 Green had worked for Lord Lyttelton and was acquainted with William Shenstone, who spoke highly of his abilities 'in fruit pieces &c.' (GM, 16). Both lived locally, although his reputation had spread to Oxford. Green moved with Anthony Deane to Bergholt, Suffolk, then to Clifton, near Bristol, and then to Bath, where they 'resided during many years' (GM, 124). He was particularly noted for successfully imitating the landscapes of Claude Lorrain, and exhibited at the Society of Artists, from Birmingham, between 1760 and 1765. His landscapes are generally of woods, waterfalls, and lakes, in browns, greens, and yellows. Their effect is described by Mallalieu as 'a little woolly' (Mallalieu, Watercolour artists, 116). He was also noted to be a good landscape gardener. About 1789 Green, at the request of Andrew Harrison, altered the landscapes in two of George Stubbs's paintings, which were then engraved by Henry Birche and published in 1790. Joseph Farington thought the alterations 'very unworthy' of the paintings (Farington, Diary, 28 Feb 1814, 13.4458). He contributed illustrations to The History and Antiquities of Doncaster and its Vicinity (1804).

At Bath in the summer of 1793 Green met Harriett Lister (1750/51–1821) of York, who was aged forty-two, 'a lady of large fortune … whose skill in drawing was almost equal to his own' (GM, 124). They married on 8 September 1796 in Bridlington, and lived in York, but had no children. In 1799 they moved to a house in Castle Hill, York, which was decorated by Green's 'pure and elegant taste and masterly pencil' (Green, 133). Amos and Harriett travelled frequently in summertime, sketching and visiting around the country. Memoirs and records of conversation in educated circles reveal a taste strongly influenced by theories of the picturesque, and of James Thomson's Seasons in particular. In 1806 they purchased a second property in Ambleside, where Green opened an exhibition that Farington visited with the sole remark that the 1s. entrance fee made £400 per annum (Farington, Diary).

Green died at his York home on 10 June 1807. At his death he was worth something near £3500. He left 'drawings paintings and all … my moveable property … house grounds [and] carriage' to Harriett, and £1800 to nephews and nieces (will). Green suffered from considerable hearing deficiencies and the gout. His contemporaries saw him as humble, generous, and even-tempered, and his wife loved him enough to write a lengthy posthumous memoir, which extols his virtues as a Christian and a husband, besides his artistic talents. He was buried at Fulford and a monument to his memory was placed in Castlegate church, York. His portrait, engraved by W. T. Fry after a drawing by Robert Hancock, provides the frontispiece to Harriett's Memoir. Three of Green's watercolours are in the British Museum, the Victoria and Albert Museum, London, and Cartwright Hall, Bradford, Yorkshire. Some of his watercolours were engraved, notably his Partridges in mezzotint by Richard Earlom.

Of Green's two brothers, Benjamin *Green (bap. 1739, d. 1798), mezzotint engraver, is noticed separately; **John Green** (fl. 1758), engraver and drawing master at Oxford, was probably a pupil of James Basire. He engraved plates from William Borlase's drawings for The Natural History of Cornwall (1758) and also views for the Oxford Almanack, besides some portraits including one of Dr Shaw, principal of St Edmund Hall, Oxford.

L. H. CUST, rev. NICHOLAS GRINDLE

Sources GM, 1st ser., 93/1 (1823), 16, 124, 290 • H. Green, Memoir of Amos Green, esq., written by his late widow (1823) • will, PROB 11/1464, fol. 576 • Family Record Centre, London, IR26/125/137 • Farington, Diary • George Stubbs, 1724–1806 (1984) [exhibition catalogue, Tate Gallery, London, 17 Oct 1984 – 6 Jan 1985, and Yale U. CBA, 13 Feb – 7 April 1985] • 'Christies sales, 1820–1844', manuscript, Courtauld Inst. • Mallalieu, Watercolour artists • GM, 1st ser., 77 (1807)
Archives Birm. CL, letters to Boulton family
Likenesses W. T. Fry, engraving (after drawing by R. Hancock), repro. in Green, Memoir of Amos Green, frontispiece • W. T. Fry, stipple (after R. Hancock), NPG
Wealth at death approx. £3500: PRO, death duty registers, IR 26/125/137

Green, Bartholomew [Bartlet] (1529/30–1556), protestant martyr, was born in the parish of St Michael Bassishaw, in the city of London. Bartholomew, or Bartlet, Green attended Oxford, where he proceeded BA in 1547. He was converted to protestantism at Oxford, where he attended Peter Martyr's lectures on theology. Green went on to study at the Inner Temple, and although he would later bemoan his gluttony and pride during this period, he remained a zealous evangelical. At Easter 1554, along with Christopher Goodman and Michael Renniger, Green received communion according to the Edwardian rite in the private rooms of John Pullain, the rector of St Peter Cornhill, who performed the service. At the next Easter, with Goodman and Renniger now in exile, Green again attended Pullain's covert communion service, and throughout Mary's reign he refused to attend mass or make confession.

If Green had confined his resistance to religious matters, he might have survived into the next reign. But in 1555 a bill denouncing Philip and Mary and advocating Elizabeth's claim to the throne was smuggled from Danzig into London; evidence suggests that Green was behind its circulation. Green's role in this came to be suspected when a letter he wrote to Goodman was intercepted. (Goodman had been a friend of Green in Oxford and, while in exile, would be a guest of their old teacher, Peter Martyr.) In the letter Green reported on the circulation of a bill (Goodman may well have had a hand in smuggling it into England) and also reported to Goodman that 'The queen is not yet dead' (Foxe, 1459). Green was imprisoned in the Fleet and later transferred to the Tower. The charge of treason against him broke down, but while he was in prison he incautiously denied the real presence in the mass. On 10 November 1555 the privy council ordered that Green be sent to Edmund Bonner, bishop of London, to be examined for heresy. He was at first treated well by Bonner, being detained in the bishop's London palace, where he shared a room with John Dee, who was also in Bonner's custody. As a result of this lenient treatment, rumours spread that Green had recanted and John Philpot wrote a letter to Green rebuking him for backsliding. Green responded, in a letter printed by Foxe, indignantly denying this, and reproving Philpot for believing 'slanders' made against him.

Green remained firm in his determination not to submit although, in addition to Bonner's efforts, Green's grandfather is said by Foxe to have offered his grandson large sums of money to renounce protestantism. Green was formally examined by Bonner on 27 November 1555, and several other examinations followed. Finally on 15 January 1556 he was brought back before Bonner and, after fruitless and protracted debate with John Feckenham, abbot of Westminster, and other leading theologians, he was condemned to death and taken to Newgate. Foxe reports—from third- or fourth-hand sources—that Bonner had Green scourged, but this is unbelievable, and merely reflects the odium which Green's conviction attracted. Green was popular and friends from the Temple—including future MPs such as Thomas Hussey and William Fleetwood—visited him in prison; Green also wrote to them in his final days, urging them to pay the debts of, and otherwise aid, individual prisoners he met in Newgate. It was probably due to Green's popularity, as well as previous demonstrations in support of protestant martyrs at their executions, that a curfew was placed on servants and young people on the morning of his burning.

The date of Green's execution has been disputed; the London diarist Henry Machyn, usually quite reliable about dates, states that it took place between 7 and 8 a.m. on 22 January 1556. But the chronicler Charles Wriothesley and John Foxe both give the date as 27 January 1556, and the issue is settled by the fact that a letter Green wrote just before his execution is still extant and is dated 27 January (Emmanuel College, Cambridge, MS 260, fols. 63r–64r). On that day Green was burnt at Smithfield along with six other people.   THOMAS S. FREEMAN

Sources J. Foxe, *Actes and monuments* (1563), 1458–66 · Emmanuel College, Cambridge, MS 260, fols. 63r–64r [letter by Green to friends in the Temple; first printed in Foxe, *Actes*, 1465–6] · BL, Add. MS 19400, fol. 56r–v [letter from Green to Elizabeth Clarke; first printed in *Certain most godly, fruitful and comfortable letters*, ed. H. Bull (1564), pp. 555–7] · Emmanuel College, Cambridge, MS 260, fol. 141r · P. M. Took, 'The government and the printing trade, 1540–1560', PhD diss., U. Lond., 1978, 279–81 · *The diary of Henry Machyn, citizen and merchant-taylor of London, from AD 1550 to AD 1563*, ed. J. G. Nichols, CS, 42 (1848) · Wood, *Ath. Oxon.*, new edn, 1.125 · Foster, *Alum. Oxon.*, 1500–1714 [Bartholomew Green] · APC, 1554–6, 191
Likenesses woodcut (of his execution), repro. in *Actes and monuments*

Green, Benjamin (*bap.* **1739**, *d.* **1798**), drawing master and engraver, was the ninth and youngest child of William Green (1696–1754) and his wife, Sarah (1696/7–1788); he

was baptized at Halesowen parish church, Shropshire, on 5 April 1739. His career as an artist was probably founded on a family connection with William Green (*fl.* 1732–1752) and his son John (*fl.* 1776), who were established artists at Oxford. Benjamin's elder brother James (1729–1759) engraved his first university almanac after William Green's design in 1752. In 1756 and 1757 respectively James Green succeeded George Vertue as engraver to the University of Oxford and to the Society of Antiquaries. Benjamin Green was established at Oxford by 1759 and took over the engraving of the university almanac from his brother, producing the plates for 1760, 1761, 1762, and 1766 after designs by Samuel Wale. The brothers worked together on Robert Dodsley's *London and its Environs Described* (1761), for which James engraved fifteen plates and Benjamin twenty-five, also after drawings by Samuel Wale, the university draughtsman. In 1762 Benjamin Green was appointed assistant drawing master to Christ's Hospital in the City of London, where another elder brother, Charles, had been wardrobe keeper and assistant clerk since 1758. Green moved to London, living near the Strand and then in Little Britain. In 1766 he was elected drawing master, with a salary of £50. The following year he was allocated one of Christ's Hospital's houses, and in 1772 he was granted a house rent-free, having taken an additional ten pupils. He had married Ann (*d.* 1829) by 1766. His eldest daughter, Sarah, was born in 1767, Ann in 1769, and a son, Charles, in 1771.

Benjamin Green was elected a fellow of the Incorporated Society of Artists in 1765 and a director in 1771. He exhibited seven mezzotints and two drawings with the society between 1765 and 1774. The earliest of these were mezzotints of flowers after paintings by his brother Amos *Green; the later mezzotints reproduced paintings by George Stubbs. Green was Stubbs's earliest and most important professional interpreter, and the nine large mezzotints that Green engraved after him contributed greatly to the animal painter's fame in England and abroad. After 1771, however, most of Green's effort went into plates for drawing books. He was a gifted draughtsman and was good at imitating the style of other artists. Many of his prints reproduce drawings by contemporaries such as Jean Pillement, Thomas Worlidge, Philippe Jacques de Loutherbourg, Thomas Gainsborough, and George Stubbs. He also etched a large number of his own landscape drawings. He worked in every printmaking medium and was technically innovative, improvising methods to copy the appearance of drawings. Green was one of the first English artists to use soft-ground etching, his earliest work in that medium being dated 1771. 178 plates were sold after his death but many more were already in the hands of other publishers. In 1788 he published a book of aquatints after Salvator Rosa with some by his eldest daughter, Sarah.

Green died in May 1798 at Christ's Hospital, having suffered for several years from a 'very severe and expensive illness' (Bell, 45), and was buried at St Botolph, Aldersgate. His will reveals that he had been a keen angler, a passion shared with his friend William Wilcox and his son,

Charles. The British Museum, the Victoria and Albert Museum, and Christ's Hospital hold examples of Green's work. TIMOTHY CLAYTON

Sources H. Philips, *Catalogue of the genuine collection of drawings, prints and copper-plates, the property of the late Mr. Benjamin Green, drawing master to Christ's Hospital* (1798) · J. Bell, *1951 festival exhibition of pictures by the eighteenth century Halesowen artists James, Amos and Benjamin Green* (1951) [exhibition catalogue, Council House, Halesowen, 13 – 20 Oct 1951] · C. Lennox-Boyd, R. Dixon, and T. Clayton, *George Stubbs: the complete engraved works* (1989) · will, PRO, PROB 11/1309, sig. 478 · A. M. Hind, 'Notes on the history of soft-ground etching and aquatint', *Print Collector's Quarterly*, 8 (1921), 377–405 · J. Hayes, *Gainsborough as printmaker* (1971) · H. Petter, *The Oxford almanacks* (1974) · Graves, *Soc. Artists*, 103 · J. C. Smith, *British mezzotinto portraits*, 2 (1879), 529–31 · Christ's Hospital court minutes, 1790–1812, GL, MS 12806, fol. 259

Green, Benjamin (*bap.* 1813, *d.* 1858), architect, was baptized on 15 February 1813 in Horsley, Northumberland, younger son of John *Green (1787–1852) of Newcastle upon Tyne, architect and civil engineer, and his wife, Jane Stobart. A pupil of Augustus Charles Pugin, in the mid-1830s he became a partner of his father. Thereafter they practised together until the latter's death in 1852, and it is not always possible to distinguish the work of one from that of the other. The somewhat undistinguished Gothic-style churches in Northumberland and Durham, which formed a substantial element in the firm's output, for example, are in general simply ascribed to 'John and Benjamin Green', and the same applies to their best-known work, the monument to John Lambton, first earl of Durham, at Penshaw Hill, co. Durham (1844), in the form of a Greek Doric temple. However, the normal pattern appears to have been that the father concentrated on the civil engineering works and the son on the more purely architectural.

The Greens were active as railway architects, and the stations on the main line between Newcastle and Berwick upon Tweed, commissioned by George Hudson in 1846—'Fine, handsome buildings ... more like the villas raised by retired tradesmen than residences for railway officers' (Welford, 2.330)—are said to have been by Benjamin Green. More important, the Theatre Royal (1836–7) and the Grey Column (1837–8) in Newcastle, stately neoclassical structures which were key elements in the heroic replanning of the city centre by Richard Grainger, were evidently also his conceptions, and suggest that he might have become a more significant figure in his own right had he not died relatively young, surviving his father by a mere six years.

In contrast to his father, Green was 'an artistic, dashing sort of a fellow' whose style was 'ornamental, florid and costly' (Welford, 2.330). He died in a mental home at Dinsdale Park, co. Durham, on 14 November 1858.

PETER LEACH, *rev.*

Sources Colvin, *Archs.* · R. Welford, *Men of mark 'twixt Tyne and Tweed*, 3 vols. (1895) · *CGPLA Eng. & Wales* (1859) · IGI
Wealth at death under £450: administration, 2 May 1859, *CGPLA Eng. & Wales*

Green, Benjamin Richard (1807/8–1876), watercolour painter and author, was born in London, the only son of James *Green (1771–1834), a portrait painter, and his wife, Mary Byrne (1776–1845), a well-known miniature painter and the daughter of William *Byrne (1743–1805) [*see under* Byrne family], an engraver. He was admitted to the Royal Academy Schools on 1 April 1826, at the age of nineteen. Between 1837 and 1858 he exhibited forty portraits, many of them miniatures, at the Royal Academy. His sitters included MPs, university professors, clergymen, and other public figures. He also showed thirty-eight works at the Society of British Artists galleries in Suffolk Street, London, between 1832 and 1862, and exhibited at the New Watercolour Society.

As well as painting, teaching, and lecturing, Green also published *A Numismatic Atlas of Ancient History* (1829), *A Series of Heads after the Antique* (1863), *A Guide to Pictorial Perspective* (1851), and *The Grammar of Form: a Series of Examples for Students in Drawings* (1855). He was secretary of the Artists' Annuity Fund for many years. Green died on 6 October 1876 at his home, 5 Bayhill Villas, Downs Park Road, Clapton, London. He was survived by his wife, Anne, and at least one daughter. Three of his paintings are in the Victoria and Albert Museum, London.

ANNE PIMLOTT BAKER

Sources D. Foskett, *Miniatures: dictionary and guide* (1987), 550 · Mallalieu, *Watercolour artists*, vols. 1–2 · S. C. Hutchison, 'The Royal Academy Schools, 1768–1830', *Walpole Society*, 38 (1960–62), 123–91 · Graves, *RA exhibitors* · L. Lambourne and J. Hamilton, eds., *British watercolours in the Victoria and Albert Museum* (1980) · R. Ormond, *Early Victorian portraits*, 2 vols. (1973) · d. cert. · *CGPLA Eng. & Wales* (1876)
Wealth at death under £1500: resworn probate, Nov 1877, *CGPLA Eng. & Wales*

Green, Bernard [Benny] (1927–1998), jazz saxophonist, writer, and broadcaster, was born at 260 Meanwood Road, Leeds, on 9 December 1927. His father, David Green, was a tailor and saxophonist and had met his mother, Fanny Fryer, while he was playing with a band in Leeds. They were married in London in 1926 and lived with David's father, an immigrant Russian-Jewish tailor, at 1 Greenwell Street in the Tottenham Court Road area of London, a chaotic family home where music and gambling were endemic. Benny Green was born in Leeds because his mother preferred to be looked after by her own family at this crucial time, but the family were soon back in London to live round the corner from Greenwell Street, in a basement flat in Cleveland Street. Here he grew into the streetwise but sentimental cockney-Jewish character who eventually became a well-loved radio figure, spoilt by doting aunts and on his way to fulfilling a casual prophecy that he would not do a day's paid work until he was twenty-one. He was first educated at Clipstone junior mixed school 'on the slummy edge of Marylebone' and then, as he put it, 'uneducated' at Marylebone grammar school (*The Times*, 24 June 1998). After leaving without scholastic distinction in 1941, he continued a sporadic education at the North London emergency secondary school, mainly educating himself, with great success as it turned out, by a thorough indulgence in whatever enthusiasms he happened to discover. These did not include national service, which he

Bernard Green (1927–1998), by Doug McKenzie, *c*.1990

endured for 167 days in 1946–7 before contriving his release.

Benny Green's own writings and a sensitive, amusing, and perceptive book, *Benny Green: Words and Music* (2000), by his son Dominic Green see his life as falling into two distinct parts—the early days as a footloose saxophonist, and then, after a complete change in the late 1950s, a second career as a highly professional and wide-ranging writer and broadcaster. Encouraged by his father, he took up the saxophone in 1941, and he started to play professionally in 1943 along with his boyhood friends Ronnie Scott and Harry Klein. He earned a modest living as a jazz musician, achieving the distinction of being voted 'most promising new jazz musician' in a *Melody Maker* poll in 1953. There had been a brief period of study at the Royal College of Music and a period with the band led by the pianist Ralph Sharon, and in 1953 he joined Ronnie Scott's nine-piece band (which was later expanded). A high point was two days in the ranks of the visiting Stan Kenton orchestra. In 1957 Green played in the Dizzy Reece quintet, but, although an accomplished jazzman and an often outstanding soloist, he decided that he was not destined to make his true mark as a musician. A battery of letters offering his qualifications and qualities as a writer was sent around; one to the Decca Record Company resulted in a commission to write a chapter on jazz saxophone in *The Decca Book of Jazz* (1958)—a competent and discerning piece that was one of the best in the book—followed by a number of record sleeve notes. Green began to write a weekly column for the *New Musical Express*, and in 1958 took over from Kingsley Amis as jazz columnist for *The Observer*. His experience as a playing musician, a rare asset among the critics of the time, made him a particularly perceptive jazz critic; his book *The Reluctant Art* (1962) is still one of the best British books on the subject. He also wrote a jazz-slanted novel, *Blame it on my Youth* (1964), followed by *Fifty-Eight Minutes to London* (1969), which captured the night life of Brighton, always his favourite town after London. Soon after joining *The Observer* he became a regular jazz record reviewer for the BBC Third Programme and from then on was rarely absent from radio, notably presenting a Sunday afternoon record programme on Radio 2 during the last twenty or so years of his life. He was always astonished that such a fleeting medium as radio brought a celebrity to his life that years of professional playing and writing had failed to do. He was a natural talker and teller of anecdotes, and his broadcasts were enjoyed by so many because of the bonus of wit and humour that was added to the fund of knowledge and wisdom they contained.

Once set on his course as a writer and broadcaster, Green laid down the saxophone and thereafter made only brief returns to playing. On 4 January 1962 he married the actress (Ray) Antoinette Franklin, professionally known as Toni Kanal (*b*. 1941/2), and they eventually settled in a large house beyond Watford on the A41 and had five children. Beyond jazz he had a great width and depth of other interests. He was film critic for *Punch* from 1972, and this work overlapped with a period as literary critic for *The Spectator*. His literary interests embraced H. G. Wells; George Bernard Shaw—resulting in one of his best books, *Shaw's Champions* (1978), on Shaw's interest in prize-fighting; P. G. Wodehouse—leading to *P. G. Wodehouse: a Literary Biography* (1981), which dwelt on his theatre writings; and Jerome K. Jerome—giving rise to a well-annotated edition of *Three Men in a Boat* (1982). He published an anthology of poems, *London* (1984), and a short, well-rounded book entitled *Fred Astaire* (1979). This last item reflected his wide interest in popular music that took in music-hall, on which subject he made one of his best broadcasts, *Maxie and a Lost Empire* (on Max Miller), and compiled an anthology, *The Last Empires: a Music Hall Companion* (1986). His own theatre writings included a revised libretto for *Showboat* (1972), two Cole Porter compilations staged at the Mermaid, *Cole* (1974) and *Oh, Mr Porter* (1977), *The Quality of Mercer*, written with Helen Shapiro, and an anthology, *Words and Music*, given at the Ambassador's Theatre in 1984. Three musicals based on the writings of Shaw were less successful.

Throughout Green was a prolific journalist and wrote over 2000 scripts for radio, contributed to numerous magazines, wrote record sleeve notes and introductions to archival photographic books, read prolifically, and talked incessantly. His other great passion was cricket. He claimed that one of his great experiences was watching Denis Compton score 167 at Lord's in 1947. From this love came such compilations as *The Cricket Addict's Archive*, four volumes of *The Wisden Anthology* (1979–83), *The Lord's Companion* (1987), *The Wisden Papers* (3 vols., 1989–91), *The Concise Wisden* (1990), and *A History of Cricket* (1988). 'Since I retired as a saxophonist', he contentedly wrote, 'I've never gone to work. I just pursue my hobbies' (*Daily Telegraph*).

It was ironic that, not having smoked until he was twenty-six, Green then succumbed through the sheer boredom of sitting in a touring band's coach. It was seventeen years before he gave up the habit, and by then it had induced the cancer that ended his career. He died in the Royal Marsden Hospital, Chelsea, on 22 June 1998. At the time he was working on books on Gilbert and Sullivan and Ronnie Scott. PETER GAMMOND

Sources D. Green, *Benny Green: words and music* (2000) · personal knowledge (2004) · *Daily Telegraph* (24 June 1998) · *The Times* (24 June 1998) · *The Times* (30 June 1998) · *The Guardian* (24 June 1998) · *The Independent* (24 June 1998) · b. cert. · m. cert. · d. cert.
Likenesses D. McKenzie, photograph, *c.*1990, Hult. Arch. [*see illus.*]
Wealth at death £337,544—gross; £336,537—net: probate, 3 Nov 1998, *CGPLA Eng. & Wales*

Green, Charles (*bap.* 1734, *d.* 1771), astronomer, was baptized in Wentworth, near Rotherham, Yorkshire, on 26 December 1734, the youngest son of Joshua Green, a farmer of Swinton. He obtained most of his education from his eldest brother, the Revd John Green, who was master of a school at Denmark Street, Westminster, where Charles later worked as an assistant teacher. In 1760 he became assistant to the astronomer royal, James Bradley, at the Royal Greenwich Observatory, succeeding Charles Mason, who went to the Cape of Good Hope to observe the transit of Venus. Green himself observed the transit with Bradley at Greenwich on 6 June 1761.

When Bradley died in July 1762, Green remained at Greenwich as assistant to his successor, Nathaniel Bliss, who was in precarious health and spent much of his time in Oxford, with the result that most of the observational work at Greenwich fell to Green. In August 1763 the board of longitude asked Green to go to Barbados with Nevil Maskelyne to make observations in connection with the trial of the fourth timekeeper of John Harrison. Bliss agreed that a temporary assistant should be provided at Greenwich until his return.

Green and Maskelyne embarked in the *Princess Louisa* (60 guns) at Spithead on 9 September 1763 and reached Barbados on 7 November, when they set up an observatory ashore and began observations to settle the longitude of the island. William Harrison (John Harrison's son) and the timekeeper arrived on 13 May 1764, the necessary observations were made, and Green sailed for home on 4 June, reaching Greenwich in July.

Bliss died in September 1764, and Green took charge of the observatory until the arrival of the new astronomer royal, Maskelyne, in March 1765. His Greenwich observations were published at the end of the second volume of Bradley's *Observations* (1805). On 5 September 1765 Green's youngest sister, Mary, married the astronomer and mathematician William Wales at Greenwich.

Despite past disagreements, Maskelyne recommended that Green should go with James Cook to observe the 1769 transit of Venus in the Pacific, which Green, then serving as purser in the frigate *Aurora*, agreed to do for 200 guineas. On 8 March 1768 he married Elizabeth Long in London, and on 26 August the *Endeavour* sailed from Plymouth. Green and Cook successfully observed the transit together in Tahiti on 3 June 1769. During the subsequent exploration of New Zealand and Australia, Green was, in Cook's words,

indefatigable in making and calculating these observations [for latitude and longitude] which otherwise must have taken up a great deal of my time … Not only this, but by his instructions several of the petty officers can make and calculate these observations almost as well as himself. (*Journals*, 392)

Before the *Endeavour* arrived in Batavia in October 1770 (whence the records of his Venus observations were dispatched to England), Green had been sick with scurvy and dysentery. He died at sea of fever on 29 January 1771.

He had long been in a bad state of health, which he took no care to repair but on the contrary lived in such a manner as greatly promoted the disorders he had had long upon him, this brought on the Flux which put a period to his life. (*Journals*, 448)

DEREK HOWSE

Sources private information (1997) · A. Kippis, *The life of Captain James Cook* (1788), 176–8 · *The journals of Captain James Cook*, ed. J. C. Beaglehole, 1, Hakluyt Society, 34a (1955) · C. Green and J. Cook, 'Observations made at King George's Island', *PTRS*, 61 (1771), 397–421 · council minutes, 1767, RS · Central Library, Rotherham
Archives CUL · PRO, admiralty records

Green, Charles (1785–1870), balloonist, son of Thomas Green, fruiterer, of Willow Walk, Goswell Street, London, who died in May 1850, aged eighty-eight, was born at 92 Goswell Road, London, on 31 January 1785. He may have been the Charles Green, son of Thomas Green and his wife, Anne, baptized in the local church, St Luke's, Old Street, on 1 February 1786. On leaving school he was taken into his father's business. At some point in or before 1807 he married Martha Morrell, who died at North Hill, Highgate, Middlesex.

Green's first aeronautical ascent was from the Green Park, London, on 19 July 1821, by order of the government, at the coronation of George IV, in a balloon filled with carburetted hydrogen (coal gas): he was the first person to ascend with a balloon so inflated. Supposedly, he had first become interested in gas for the purpose of shop lighting. After this he made over 500 ascents, with passengers, solo, or on the back of a pony. In 1836 he constructed the *Royal Vauxhall* balloon for Gye and Hughes, proprietors of Vauxhall Gardens, from whom he purchased it in 1840 for £500. In the autumn of 1836 he made six ascents with it from Vauxhall, including the celebrated continental voyage, undertaken at the expense of Robert Hollond, MP for Hastings, who, with Thomas Monck Mason, accompanied him. The three men left Vauxhall Gardens at 1.30 p.m. on 7 November 1836 and, after crossing the English Channel from Dover the same evening, descended the next day, at 7 a.m., at Weilburg in Nassau, Germany, having travelled altogether about 500 miles in eighteen hours—a record that stood until 1907. The *Great Nassau* (as the *Royal Vauxhall* was now renamed) again ascended from Vauxhall Gardens on 24 July 1837, with Green accompanied by Edward Spencer and Robert Cocking. At a height of 5000 feet

Charles Green (1785–1870), by Hilaire Ledru, 1835

Cocking freed himself from the balloon and, descending in a parachute of his own construction into a field on Burnt Ash Farm, Lee, was unfortunately killed. The balloon (after a frightening rise out of control owing to the loss of weight) came down the same evening near Malling, Kent, and it was not until the next day that Green heard of the death of his companion.

In 1838 Green made two experimental ascents from Vauxhall Gardens at the expense of George Rush of Elsenham Hall, Essex. The first took place on 4 September, with Rush and Edward Spencer accompanying him. They attained the height of 19,335 feet, and descended at Thaxted in Essex. The second experiment was made on 10 September, for the purpose of ascertaining the greatest altitude that could be attained with the *Great Nassau* balloon inflated with coal gas and carrying two people only. Green ascended with Rush for his companion, and they reached an elevation variously calculated as between 20,000 and 27,000 feet, depending on the degree of credence that is placed on the readings of a barometer of Rush's own invention. On several occasions the balloon was carried by the upper currents at between 80 and 100 m.p.h. On 31 March 1841 Green ascended from Hastings, accompanied by Charles Frederick William, duke of Brunswick, and in five hours descended at Neufchâtel, about 10 miles southwest of Boulogne. His final public ascent took place from Vauxhall Gardens on Monday 13 September 1852. He did plan to come out of retirement in 1859 as balloonist to James Glaisher, but by then the *Great Nassau* had become too decrepit, and Henry Coxwell (Green's successor in reputation) took his place.

During his career Green had many dangerous experiences. In 1822, when ascending from Cheltenham, accompanied by a Mr Griffith, some malicious person partly severed the ropes which attached the car to the balloon, so that in starting the car broke away from the balloon; its occupants had to take refuge on the hoop of the balloon, in which position they had a perilous journey and were both injured on landing in a tree. Green also landed in a tree near Henley the following year, and twice ended up in the sea. In 1827 Green made his sixty-ninth ascent, from Newbury, accompanied by Mr H. Simmons of Reading, who was deaf and mute, when a violent thunderstorm threatened the safety of the balloon. On 17 August 1841, on going up from Cremorne with Mr Macdonnell, a jerk of the grappling-iron upset the car and went near to throwing out the balloonist and his companion.

Green was

> certainly the greatest English aeronaut and one of the most skilful and successful balloon pilots that the world has ever seen … a bluff, massively built man with a heavy, rubicund face … genial and talkative on the ground, he became a taciturn martinet in the air. (Rolt, 118–20)

Ultimately, however, he seemed to find the pressure towards mere showmanship a disappointment, having failed in the hope attributed to him 'to have placed aerial navigation in its proper place, and raised it from the inferior position in which he found it' (Glaisher, 30). Most ambitiously, in 1840 (when laid up after a hard landing in Essex) he conceived a project to cross the Atlantic by balloon, scooping up sea water with a special device. Alas, this ended merely as the subject of jokes, cartoons, and hoaxes, such as Edgar Allan Poe's announcement in 1844 that Green's former passenger Monck Mason had actually made the crossing.

Green was the first to demonstrate, in 1821, that coal gas was applicable to the inflation of balloons. Before his time pure hydrogen gas was used, a volatile and very expensive substance, which was so slow to generate that two days were required to fill a large balloon. He was also the inventor of the 'guide-rope', a rope trailing from the car, which could be lowered or raised by means of a windlass and used to regulate the ascent and descent of the balloon. After living in retirement for many years he died suddenly of heart disease at his home, Ariel Villa, 51 Tufnell Park Road, Holloway, on 26 March 1870. He was survived by his second wife, Jane. His son from his first marriage George Green, who had made eighty-three ascents with the *Nassau* balloon, died at Belgrave Villa, Holloway, on 10 February 1864, aged fifty-seven.

G. C. BOASE, *rev.* JULIAN LOCK

Sources J. E. Hodgson, *The history of aeronautics in Great Britain, from the earliest times to the latter half of the nineteenth century* (1924), chap. 8 · L. T. C. Rolt, *The aeronauts: a history of ballooning, 1783–1903* (1966) · L. A. T. Ege, *Balloons and airships, 1783–1973*, ed. K. Munson, trans. E. Hildesheim (1973) · D. D. Jackson, *The aeronauts* (1981) · Boase, *Mod. Eng. biog.* · *The Times* (30 March 1870), 10 · *The Times* (25–7 July 1837) [reports of Cocking inquest] · *ILN* (4 Sept 1852), 192 · *ILN* (18 Sept 1852), 224 · *ILN* (11 Sept 1852), 199 · *ILN* (16 April 1870), 401–2 · C. H. Turnor, *Astra castra: experiments and adventures in the atmosphere* (1865) · J. Glaisher and others, *Travels in the air*, ed. J. Glaisher (1871) · *CGPLA Eng. & Wales* (1870) · *IGI*

Likenesses H. Ledru, oils, 1835, NPG [*see illus.*] · G. T. Payne, mezzotint, pubd 1838 (after J. Hollins), BM, NPG · G. P. Harding, lithograph, pubd 1839, BM, NPG · wood-engraving, 1852 (after daguerreotype by J. E. Mayall), NPG; repro. in *ILN* (4 Sept 1852) · J. Hollins, group portrait, oils (*A consultation prior to the aerial voyage to Weilburg, 1836*), NPG · J. E. Mayall, group portrait, daguerreotype (*Scientific balloon ascent from Vauxhall Gardens*), repro. in *ILN* (4 Sept 1852), 192 · J. H. Robinson, group portrait, engraving (*Consultations prior to the aerial voyage to Weilburg, Nov. 7, 1836*; after J. Hollins), repro. in Hodgson, *History of aeronautics*, 250 · medal, repro. in Hodgson, *History of aeronautics*, 130 · portraits, repro. in Hodgson, *History of aeronautics* · wood-engraving (after photograph by J. E. Mayall), NPG; repro. in *ILN* (16 April 1870)

Wealth at death under £2000: probate, 9 April 1870, *CGPLA Eng. & Wales*

Green, Charles Alfred Howell (1864–1944), archbishop of Wales, was born on 19 August 1864 in Llanelli, Wales, the eldest of the family of six sons and two daughters of the Revd Alfred John Morgan Green (1833–1911), then curate of Llanelli, and his wife, Elizabeth Bond (c.1842–1924), daughter of Richard Thomas Howell, merchant, also of Llanelli. The family moved to St David's in 1867 for his father to become master at the small cathedral school. Green was educated there until he won scholarships successively to Charterhouse (1878–83), and Keble College, Oxford (BA, 1887; MA, 1892). He became librarian and afterwards president of the Oxford Union. He was placed in the second class of the honours list in *literae humaniores* in 1887, was ordained deacon in 1888 and priest in 1889. He proceeded BD (1907) and DD (1911) at Oxford. The first twenty-six years of his ministry were spent at Aberdâr, where he was curate for five years and vicar for twenty-one years. Green spent a good deal of his time at Aberdâr on scholarly pursuits, and also on organizational issues. He left his successors 'detailed arrangements of precise administration' for running the parish business (Edwards, 41). He consistently stated his belief that the church should stay strictly out of social and political issues, in the context of his coal dominated parish being rent by desperate industrial disputes in 1893 and later. But he was himself attacked for supporting the Conservatives and 'acting as a political agent to a Tory candidate' in one general election (Edwards, 42).

On 18 January 1899 Green married Katherine Mary (c.1864–1950), daughter of Sir William Thomas *Lewis who was subsequently created Baron Merthyr. They had no children. From 1914 until 1921 he was archdeacon of Monmouth and canon residentiary of Llandaff Cathedral. Green's advice as a scholar of canon law was extensively sought by church leaders in the drawing up of the constitution of the Church in Wales in preparation for disestablishment in 1920. Walker suggests that this was his 'greatest contribution to the life of the Church' (Walker, 175). When the new diocese of Monmouth was formed, Green was the obvious choice for its first bishop, and he was duly consecrated on 21 December 1921. As bishop, he demanded a respectful and dignified manner from his clergy, seeing them only by appointment and monitoring their standards of dress. He was not a unifying figure. His 'advancement was welcomed by his friends as successes for their own brand of churchmanship' (Walker, 174). A

high-churchman, in 1922 he had occasion to defend himself against the charge made by Bishop Hensley Henson that the ceremonial which had been used at an ordination did not comply with the constitution of the Church in Wales.

In 1928 Green was elected to the see of Bangor, and in November 1934 he was elected archbishop of Wales. Green rose in the church because he was, as Edwards says, the 'ecclesiastical administrative genius that the Church of Wales needed' to cope with the 'upheavals of disestablishment' (Edwards, 108). But having seen through the earlier years of stress, his years in the highest position saw little new development. He was elected a proctor in convocation (1913), a member of the court of governors of the University College of South Wales (1914), a member of the theological board of the University of Wales (1915), a member of the council and court of governors of the University College of North Wales (1933), of the National Museum of Wales (1935), and the National Library of Wales (1936). He proceeded to BCL and DCL when he was seventy-four years old, his book *The Setting of the Constitution of the Church in Wales* (1937) being accepted as a thesis for these degrees. He was a select preacher at Cambridge (1923) and Oxford (1927–9), and was elected an honorary fellow of Keble College in 1935.

Green was shy and retiring, sometimes considered unapproachable, but in reality warm-hearted. He died at Bishopcourt, Bangor, on 7 May 1944 and was buried in the cemetery of Llandaff Cathedral on 11 May.

FREDERIC HOOD, *rev.* MARC BRODIE

Sources A. J. Edwards, *Archbishop Green: his life and opinions* (1986) · *The Times* (8 May 1944) · *The Times* (12 May 1944) · D. Walker, 'Disestablishment and independence', *A history of the Church in Wales*, ed. D. Walker (1976) · Burke, *Gen. GB* · Burke, *Peerage* [Merthyr] · J. Foster, *Oxford men, 1880–1892: with a record of their schools, honours, and degrees* (1893)

Archives NL Wales, diaries, addresses, and sermons · St Deiniol's Library, Hawarden, corresp. and MSS

Likenesses photograph, NPG

Wealth at death £5114 11s.: probate, 3 July 1944, *CGPLA Eng. & Wales*

Green [*née* Symonds], **Charlotte Byron** (1842–1929), promoter of women's education, was born on 12 August 1842 at Berkeley Square, Bristol, the youngest of four surviving children of Dr John Addington *Symonds (1807–1871), author and physician, and his wife, Harriet, eldest daughter of James Sykes. Harriet Symonds died of scarlet fever in 1844 and the children were cared for by their maternal aunt, Mary Ann Sykes.

Charlotte Green was educated at home. The atmosphere there was highly cultured, and her development was furthered by her close relationships with her father and her brother, John Addington *Symonds the younger. Through them she met Benjamin Jowett, master of Balliol College, Oxford. On 1 July 1871 she married Thomas Hill *Green (1836–1882), tutor in philosophy at Balliol and an undergraduate contemporary of her brother. The marriage was childless. She became an influential figure at the college.

Charlotte Green was among the early generation of dons' wives who organized lectures for women in Oxford, succeeding Mary Ward (Mrs Humphry Ward) and Louise Creighton (Mrs Mandell Creighton) in 1873 as secretary to the lectures committee. She was a founding member and the first woman secretary of the Association for Promoting the Education of Women in Oxford, established in 1878 to co-ordinate the teaching of women students. She resigned her secretaryship in 1883 but remained a member of the association's council until its dissolution in 1920.

The Greens were strong supporters of Somerville Hall (later College) which opened in 1879 as a non-denominational hall of residence for women. She arranged tuition for the first students and for many years acted as a chaperone, knitting throughout the mixed lectures to which she accompanied them. She became a member of Somerville council in 1884 and served as vice-president from 1908 to 1926, when she was made a life member. A Greats tutorship established in 1929 was named in her honour. She was great-aunt of a future principal of the college, Janet Vaughan. She also became a member of the first committee of the Society of Home Students (forerunner of St Anne's College) in Oxford, founded in 1893, and continued to serve on the governing body of the society until 1921. She was an intimate friend of its principal, Bertha Johnson. With Elizabeth Wordsworth she received the degree of MA *honoris causa* in October 1921, the year after Oxford opened its degrees to women.

Devastated by the premature death of her husband in March 1882, Charlotte Green was urged by Jowett to remain in Oxford 'where you are so greatly respected and beloved' (E. Abbott and L. Campbell, *Life and Letters of Benjamin Jowett*, 2, 1897, 194). She was spoken of as a possible principal of both Somerville and Girton colleges, but instead took up nursing in her widowhood, training at the Radcliffe Infirmary, Oxford, for eighteen months and then for six months at the London Hospital. She became a district nurse in Oxford. Jowett was among her patients: she nursed him through his final illness and was reputed to have saved his life in an earlier illness. Much of her work was with the poor and at the Radcliffe Infirmary where her cousin, Horatio Symonds, was a surgeon. In 1893 she was elected to the infirmary's committee of management.

By 1887 Charlotte Green felt that she had been able to do 'what my Husband wanted me to do—to make friends with working people and help them if I could that way' (C. Green to R. L. Nettleship, 24 Dec 1887, R. C. Whiting, ed., *Oxford*, 1993, 47 n.). Her civic activities included involvement with local schools and membership of the education committee of Oxford city council. She had a particularly close association with the Central School for Girls, and promoted the teaching of domestic science and the care of children regarded as 'backward'. She was a member of the Women's Local Government Society and, sharing her husband's temperance views, a committee member of the British Women's Temperance Association. Although she had been a signatory in 1889 to Mrs Humphry Ward's protest against women's suffrage, by 1912 she appeared on a suffragist platform and was involved with the National Union of Women Workers.

Charlotte Green died on 4 September 1929 at her home, 56 Woodstock Road, Oxford, and was buried in St Giles's churchyard on 7 September. Her sharp intellect and her continuing interest in higher education made her a popular figure at Somerville College to the end of her life. In her portrait, 'the small, firm mouth and keen grey eyes in the beautiful serene face testify to the capacity for caustic utterance which occasionally varied her tranquil kindness' (V. Brittain, *The Women at Oxford*, 1960, 42).

C. A. CREFFIELD

Sources *The Times* (5 Sept 1929) · *The Times* (9 Sept 1929) · *Oxford Times* (6 Sept 1929) · *Oxford Magazine* (7 Nov 1929) · T. H. Green, 'Service of commemoration and thanksgiving', in H. Darbishire, *Somerville College chapel addresses and other papers* (1962), chap. 4 [19 June 1941] · P. Adams, *Somerville for women: an Oxford college, 1879–1993* (1996) · M. Richter, *The politics of conscience: T. H. Green and his age* (1964) · P. Grosskurth, *John Addington Symonds: a biography* (1964) · R. Butler and M. H. Prichard, eds., *The Society of Oxford Home Students: retrospects and recollections* (1930) · V. Farnell, *A Somervillian looks back* (1948) · J. A. Symonds, *Miscellanies*, ed. J. A. Symonds (1871) · M. St. C. Byrne and C. H. Mansfield, *Somerville College, 1879–1921* [1922] · *Dear Miss Nightingale: a selection of Benjamin Jowett's letters to Florence Nightingale, 1860–1893*, ed. V. Quinn and J. Prest (1987) · *The memoirs of John Addington Symonds*, ed. P. Grosskurth (1984) · b. cert. · d. cert.

Archives Balliol Oxf., Jowett MSS · Somerville College, Oxford, archives · St Anne's College, Oxford, B. Johnson MSS

Likenesses H. Rivière, oils, 1914, Somerville College, Oxford · photograph, repro. in Adams, *Somerville for women* · photographs, repro. in Grosskurth, *John Addington Symonds*

Wealth at death £18,298 3s. 9d.: probate, 16 Nov 1929, CGPLA Eng. & Wales

Green, David John (1912–1998). *See under* Tayler, Herbert (1912–2000).

Green, Eliza S. Craven (1802/3–1866), poet, was born in Leeds. Her major publication was a collection of verse entitled *Sea Weeds and Heath Flowers, or, Memories of Mona* (1858). This volume reprinted *A Legend of Mona*, first published under Green's maiden name, Eliza S. Craven, in 1825. She spent several years in the Isle of Man during her youth, and her subject matter is much influenced by its scenery and legends. She lived for some time in Manchester, then returned to Leeds, where she became a regular contributor of verse to the *Leeds Intelligencer* (which had first published her work when she was about thirteen) and other periodicals, including *Hogg's Instructor*, *Chambers's Edinburgh Journal*, and *Le Follet*. On 13 May 1828 she married James Green, a comedian, in Wakefield, Yorkshire. Little more is known of her private life. She is described by the *Leeds Intelligencer* as moving in 'a comparatively humble sphere of life, and was little known in literary circles' (17 March 1866).

Green also wrote prose, chiefly tales and sketches, reportedly under assumed names. She edited (1862) *Flowers from the Glen: the Poetical Remains of James Waddington*. Some degree of popularity in her own lifetime is evident from the warm reception *Sea Weeds and Heath Flowers* received in 1858, and it went into a second edition shortly before her death in 1866, published in London and Liverpool. She received a grateful note of acknowledgement from Florence Nightingale for a poem of 1856 heralding her return to Britain, a piece which displayed Green's tendency to respond to current events, as did another poem on Queen Victoria planting an oak in Windsor Great Park. Her work was brought to the attention of the queen, who made her a gift from the privy purse.

Green's verse is fluent, descriptive, and direct, and she was regarded by Charles Forshaw, author of *Yorkshire Poets Past and Present* (1888), as being of 'a very charitable and amiable disposition'. She died of chronic heart disease and bronchitis on 11 March 1866 at her home, 80 Meanwood Street, Little London, Leeds.   ROSEMARY SCOTT

Sources W. Andrews, *Modern Yorkshire poets* (1885) · Boase, *Mod. Eng. biog.* · *Leeds Intelligencer* (17 March 1866) · C. F. Forshaw, *Yorkshire poets past and present* (1888) · R. V. Taylor, ed., *Supplement of the Biographia Leodiensis, or, Biographical sketches of the worthies of Leeds* (1867), 610–11 · d. cert. · *IGI*

Green, Evelyn Ward Everett- (1856–1932), writer, was born on 17 November 1856 at 7 Upper Gower Street, London, the second of the three surviving daughters of George Pycock Green (*c*.1811–1893), portrait and landscape artist, and his wife, Mary Anne Everett *Green, née Wood (1818–1895), historian; she had also one older brother. She was baptized at Great Queen Street Wesleyan Methodist Chapel on 22 February 1857 as Eveline; later she adopted the spelling Evelyn and, like the rest of her family, the additional surname Everett. She was educated at home until the age of twelve, then for three years attended Mrs Bolton's Gower Street preparatory school. From her earliest childhood she invented stories to tell her sisters, and while at school wrote a historical tale about Lady Jane Grey. In 1872–3 she went to Bedford College, London, with a Reid scholarship, but found the curriculum undemanding, and, released from her mother's earlier restrictions on her reading, fell into the delights of fiction as supplied by Mudie's circulating library. She also had time to write her first novel, which failed to find a publisher. After her year at Bedford she studied at the London Academy of Music, and in addition to practising several hours a day, continued to write. At this time she hoped to go to India to keep house for her brother, an engineer, but his death in 1876 ended that scheme and she threw herself instead into 'good works'—district visiting, Sunday and night school teaching, and eventually hospital nursing, possibly at St George's Hospital.

In 1880 Everett-Green's first book, *Tom Tempest's Victory*, was published under the pseudonym H. F. E., and in the following two years four other books appeared. Finding time to write amid the pressures of home life was difficult, and London winters did not suit her health, but a friend, Catherine Mainwaring Sladen (1845–1943), whose family home had recently been broken up, suggested that she come to live with her in the country. From 1883 the two lived together, possibly initially in Somerset, and from the early 1890s in Surrey, at Albury near Guildford (first at Vale Cottage and later at Albury House). In 1911 they went abroad, eventually settling on Madeira, though during the

First World War they lived at Battramsley House near Lymington, Hampshire. Everett-Green came to England every year, visiting her sister Gertrude, wife of James Gow, and doing business with her publishers.

Everett-Green's works are more remarkable for their number—about 350—and their variety than their content. At first she wrote principally for children and boys, dispensing the piety inculcated by her Methodist upbringing, but she soon turned to the books for slightly older girls for which she is now best remembered, typically taking a houseful of girls and reviewing their development from the schoolroom to adulthood. Careers are mentioned without disapproval, but marriage was the inevitable ending. Between 1890 and 1909 she produced some fifty historical tales, occasionally making use of her mother's work and ranging widely through medieval and modern history. After two early three-volume novels she left adult fiction alone for nearly twenty years, returning to it shortly before her move abroad; after that romantic fiction gradually became her sole genre. In 1909 she adopted the pseudonym Cecil Adair for some of her fiction, and these books, remarkable for their chaste sensationalism, enjoyed a certain success. She had earlier sometimes used the pseudonyms E. (or Evelyn) Ward, and Evelyn Dare, and occasionally collaborated with Louisa Bedford and Emma and Beatrice Marshall.

Everett-Green died at her home, Quinta Pico de São João, Funchal, Madeira, on 23 April 1932. Although her books were sufficiently popular in their own day to bring her in an adequate income, they lack real distinction, and are now read, if at all, solely for the light they cast on their social background. That she wrote no series or sequels also told against her continuing popularity, and even before her death her girls' books had become the victims of changing times.   HILARY CLARE

Sources *WWW*, 1929–40 · D. L. Kirkpatrick, ed., *Twentieth-century children's writers* (1978) · E. Everett-Green, 'When I was a girl', *Silver Link*, pt 25 (Jan 1894) · H. F. E. [E. Everett-Green], *Little Freddie* (1882) · B. Doyle, *The who's who of children's literature* (1968) · *DNB* · private information (2004) · *The Times* (25 April 1932) · *The Times* (26 April 1932) · b. cert. · register (baptism), 22 Feb 1857, London, Great Queen Street Wesleyan Methodist Chapel · *WW* (1914–16) · d. cert.

Wealth at death £6046 11s. 11d.: resworn probate, 8 Oct 1932, *CGPLA Eng. & Wales*

Green, Frederick William Edridge- (1863–1953), physician and expert on colour perception, was born at 29 Stock Orchard Crescent, Holloway, London, on 14 December 1863, the son of Thomas Allen Green, whose family were makers of Crown Staffordshire ware, and his wife, Maria, née Smith. After studying at St Bartholomew's Hospital and at the University of Durham he qualified LRCP in 1887 and in the same year obtained the MB (Durham) with first-class honours. He was awarded the MD with gold medal two years later for a thesis which dealt with colour vision and contained his first criticism of the Holmgren wool test, then used to assess defective colour vision. He became FRCS by examination in 1892. On 26 April 1893, by which date he was using the name Edridge-Green, he married Minnie Jane (1869/70–1901), daughter of Henry Hicks, physician. There were two sons, one of whom died in childhood, and the other shortly after the end of the First World War.

After serving as resident surgical assistant at Newcastle upon Tyne Infirmary, Edridge-Green became assistant medical officer of Northumberland House Asylum, and subsequently medical superintendent of Hendon Grove Asylum. The two dominant interests of his life thus asserted themselves early in his career.

Edridge-Green's professional work in mental disease in the earlier part of his life is reflected in his studies on memory, on which he wrote while still a student and more extensively in a substantial volume, *Memory* (1888). *Memory and its Cultivation* appeared in the International Scientific Series in 1897. Phenomena of vision were, however, his main interest: his *Colour-Blindness and Colour Perception* was first published in 1891 and had a second edition in 1909. His contention that the Holmgren wool test, based on matching coloured wools, ignored the factor of saturation and in practice did not pick up the dangerously colour-blind, attracted immediate attention but little support, even after he was appointed a member of the International Code of Signallers' committee. In 1892 a committee of the Royal Society unanimously recommended the continued use of the Holmgren test on railways and ships, but over the years an increasing number of observers, such as Doyne and Gotch at Oxford, recognized the validity of Edridge-Green's work. In his test for colour-blindness the examinee had to recognize and name a range of colours seen in normal conditions of lighting and through filters which produced anomalous conditions simulating low illumination, mist, or fog. After much controversy, and only after questions were asked in parliament, the inadequate wool test was finally abandoned in 1915 by the Board of Trade and a lantern test, based on Edridge-Green's principles, adopted for testing pilots and other personnel. He was appointed ophthalmic adviser to the board in 1920, the year in which he was appointed CBE and published his *Physiology of Vision*, which summarized in considerable detail his theoretical work on colour vision and other visual phenomena. His mature views on colour vision were expressed in his article for the *Encyclopaedia Britannica* (1922). In his booklet *Science and Pseudo-Science* (1933) Edridge-Green was critical of those who had opposed his work, yet had never bothered to test it for themselves, and who had therefore held back the improvements in safety which he was trying to bring about. In later years he devoted himself exclusively to ophthalmology, acting as adviser to the London pensions board and the Ministry of Transport as well as the Board of Trade. In the First World War he had been chairman of the ophthalmic board of the central London recruiting boards for national service.

Edridge-Green's colour perception lantern remained widely used by the Royal Navy and British Railways among others, and his bead test by the national service boards. His practical tests eliminated the dangerously colour-blind from occupations where good colour vision was essential. They stimulated much work on the theoretical aspects of colour vision but his own academic contributions were unremarkable, being based less on laboratory investigations than on a pseudo-evolutionary theory of colour vision.

Rather slight in build, Edridge-Green found relaxation in travelling, golfing, chess, and bridge; he was a member of the Savage Club. He died at 40 Mill Road, Worthing, on 17 April 1953. A named memorial lecture at the Royal College of Surgeons was established under his bequest and is devoted to the physiology of vision.

ARNOLD SORSBY, *rev.*

Sources *BMJ* (2 May 1953), 998 · *The Lancet* (25 April 1953), 856–7 · personal knowledge (1971) · *The Times* (18 April 1953), 8d · F. W. Edridge-Green, *Science and pseudo-science* (1933) · *WWW* · *Who's who in science* (1968), 509 · W. J. O'Connor, *British physiologists, 1885–1914* (1991), 153–4 · b. cert. · m. cert. · d. cert.
Likenesses G. Belcher, charcoal caricature, 1895, RCS Eng. · F. Walenn, oils, 1895, RCS Eng.
Wealth at death £15,451 13s. 6d.: probate, 8 Aug 1953, *CGPLA Eng. & Wales*

Green, George (1793–1841), mathematical physicist and miller, was born on 14 July 1793, probably at Wheatsheaf Yard, Nottingham, the eldest child and only son of George Green (1758–1829), miller, and his wife, Sarah (1770–1826), *née* Butler. After study for four terms at an 'academy' in Nottingham run by Robert Goodacre, George had to work in his father's bakery from the age of nine, and later at the corn mill which his father constructed at Sneinton, then a village outside Nottingham. By the 1820s he seems to have been the mill manager, but he was teaching himself mathematics and perhaps contemplating research topics; the Nottingham Subscription Library contained a respectable stock of scientific publications, including even some foreign material, and, since the mill was apparently prosperous, Green may have been able also to buy some of this literature. He probably also knew John Toplis, a Cambridge graduate mathematician, then headmaster of Nottingham Free Grammar School, who was unusually sensitive to the superiority of continental mathematics.

Whatever the motivations and means of access, Green made himself familiar with the current state of mathematical analysis and mathematical physics, especially French work, and made a most remarkable contribution in an *Essay on the Mathematical Analysis of Electricity and Magnetism* (1828). At that time these branches of physics were gaining considerable attention, from both experimental and mathematical points of view. In particular, the French mathematician S. D. Poisson (1781–1840) had published papers in 1826 in which he treated a magnetic body 'M' as composed of separate dipoles and analysed mathematically the strength of its attraction to internal and to external monopoles. In the first paper he found a theorem which converted triple integrals over the volume of M to double integrals over its surface. An English translation of a summary of the paper appeared in the *Quarterly Journal of Science* in 1824 and, while the mathematical details were not given, it could have excited Green's curiosity. When the full paper appeared, he must have been inspired by the above theorem, which was novel at the time and of which Poisson himself was not fully appreciative, entitling it merely a 'simplification' of certain formulae, reducing triple integrals to double integrals. Green realized that it had the far more profound consequence of relating properties inside a body to properties on its surface and vice versa. Whatever the motive, in his book he produced a similar theorem (the version now called 'symmetric', using two functions over M). Such theorems are rightly named after him, for he was the first to stress their physical interpretation.

In a feature of the book that was without precedent, Green sought the function which satisfied the basic differential equation representing the physical situation which also took given values on the surface of M and vanished to zero at an infinite distance from M. He called it 'the potential function' (later known as 'Green's function'), and in the rest of his book he sought particular cases for electrostatic and magnetic situations.

Another important result has become known as Green's 'reciprocity theorem', relating the electrostatic charges and the attendant potentials of a collection of conductors in two different states of equilibrium. He also studied the total charge of Leyden jars arranged in series. In a long final section he found expressions for the potentials of magnetic bodies of various kinds, such as solids and shells, and compared his predictions with experimental data published by C. Coulomb and J. B. Biot.

As a piece of research and development, Green's book is of the highest calibre, extraordinary for an autodidact; but his sales and marketing were lamentable. He published it in Nottingham at his own expense with the help of a local subscription list—still a common manner of publication then but hopeless for a book of this kind. The recent revival in mathematics in Britain meant that he might have had a chance with a publisher, and he certainly could have summarized his main result in a paper in, say, the *Quarterly Journal* or the *Philosophical Magazine*. He did none of these things, and probably never thought of them. However, the book did find one informed reader among the subscribers: Edward ff. Bromhead (1789–1855), also a Cambridge graduate and a member of the Analytical Society there which had helped to rejuvenate British mathematics in the 1810s. In correspondence during the 1830s he encouraged Green's formal education and further researches.

In the meantime, in 1829, Green's father had died, leaving him and his sister to inherit the mill and various properties. He was now financially established to pursue his mathematical researches, but one residue of the past remained: about 1824 he had commenced a liaison with a lace-dresser, Jane Smith (1802–1877), and seven children were born to them between 1824 and 1840. They never married, seemingly because of his father's disapproval of the loss of status entailed, and perhaps also because Green had set his sights on a Cambridge career where fellowship would require celibacy.

Bromhead helped Green to secure entry into his own old college, Gonville and Caius, in 1833, as a very mature student. Green graduated four years later, but only as fourth wrangler in the competitive ranking system then in operation. A fellow student, J. J. Sylvester, was ranked second, and colleagues at Caius included the mathematicians Robert Murphy (who knew of his book) and Matthew O'Brien. Green was appointed to a Perse fellowship (worth £10 a year) in 1839, which he held until his death two years later, but he spent some time at the mill, with his family living nearby.

During this Cambridge decade Green produced nine papers on various aspects of mathematical physics. The majority of them appeared with the Cambridge Philosophical Society, of which Bromhead was already a member and which Green himself joined in 1837. A few notable features are noted here, largely in chronological order of publication.

Typically for a mathematical physicist of that time, Green exploited analogies between types of phenomena and theories. His first paper (1835) investigated 'the equilibrium of fluid analogous to the electric fluid', expressing potentials in terms of Legendre functions without any specific interpretation. A paper of the same year on 'attractions of ellipsoids of variable densities' was more novel, for he formed the equation by optimizing the value of a volume integral by a principle to which the name of his German contemporary J. P. G. Dirichlet has become attached, and which became a major technique in 'potential theory' (as the subject came to be called). He solved the equation by a special method now known as 'WKB', the initials of the surnames of three independent rediscoverers in 1926.

In an analysis of 'the vibration of pendulums in fluid media' (1836) Green treated the effect of the surrounding air on the motion of the pendulum. Taking it to be ellipsoidal in shape so as to draw upon work by P. S. Laplace, he investigated its motion in the directions of its three principal axes; then he could state its motion as a combination of these three, in a clever use of superposition of special solutions (another well-known technique of the time).

A paper of 1838 dealt with 'the reflection and refraction of sound', giving the first detailed study of total internal reflection. Reflection and refraction were properties more closely associated with light, which Green examined in two papers. Following A. L. Cauchy and A. J. Fresnel, he assumed that the ether was an elastic solid and that optical phenomena were caused by activity within it. In 1838 he analysed them at the intersection of two noncrystalline media (that is, media with no special properties); he worked out the conservation of potential energy when the media were placed under strain. Four years later he applied similar methods to the propagation of light in general in crystalline media, setting up two different models based upon certain assumptions about the stress properties of the ether and the types of vibration possible within it; in one model he obtained a version of one of Cauchy's models.

Green died on 31 May 1841 at Jane Smith's house, 3 Notintone Place, Sneinton, and was buried on 4 June in St Stephen's churchyard, Sneinton, near the mill. Green's papers entered in the general mass of writing on mathematical physics, though they did not gain all the attention that they deserved, but his book remained unknown; two rather passing mentions in those papers had not given his public much chance. However, while at Cambridge he had given some copies to the mathematical coach William Hopkins (1793–1866), who in turn gave one in 1845 to a bright young student, William Thomson (1824–1907). At last Green had his first active reader; Thomson told his friends in both Britain and France, and arranged for the book to be reprinted in three parts in a leading German mathematical journal between 1850 and 1854. He also profited from its contents, for example to invent his 'method of images' to calculate potentials in various contexts.

Thanks to this publicity and use of its ideas, Green's importance was recognized in the later development of potential theory; his theorem and functions were central tools, and his name was attached to both. An edition of his works appeared in 1879: it included the book, which itself was reprinted and translated into German late in the century, and the edition was reprinted in 1903, in Paris. His ideas, especially the theorem and the function, were to receive fresh boosts later in the twentieth century, in some parts of engineering and above all the development of quantum mechanics (the contributions of 'W', 'K', and 'B' belonged to this movement).

However, scholarly work on Green came too late to save the manuscripts which he seemed to have left but which were destroyed after the death of his last child in 1919. Thus there is no access to his other thoughts, and not even a known likeness. Only in the mid-1970s was a major effort launched, centred on the reconstruction of the mill, which had fallen into desuetude; it was opened in 1985 both as a working mill and as a science centre for educational purposes. This county recognition was enhanced to the national level in 1993, the bicentenary of Green's birth, when a plaque bearing a depiction of the mill was unveiled in the section for scientists of Westminster Abbey, near to the tomb of Isaac Newton and next to plaques of Thomson (as Lord Kelvin), James Clerk Maxwell, and Michael Faraday. A fine biography by Mary Cannell also appeared in that year, making Green appreciable as a historical figure at last.

I. GRATTAN-GUINNESS

Sources H. G. Green, 'A biography of George Green', *Studies and essays in the history of science and learning in honor of George Sarton*, ed. A. Montagu (1946), 545–94 · R. M. Bowley and others, *George Green, miller, Sneinton*, 2nd edn (1980) · D. M. Cannell, *George Green: miller and mathematician, 1793-1841* (1988) · D. M. Cannell, *George Green: mathematician and physicist, 1793–1841* (1993); 2nd edn (2000) · I. Todhunter, *A history of the mathematical theories of attraction and the figure of the earth*, 2 vols. (1873) · P. M. Harman, ed., *Wranglers and physicists: studies on Cambridge physics in the nineteenth century* (1985) · I. Grattan-Guinness, 'Why did George Green write his essay of 1828 on electricity and magnetism?', *American Mathematical Monthly*, 102 (1995), 387–96 · G. J. Whitrow, 'George Green, 1793–1841', *Armali dell' Istituto di Storia della Scienza di Firenze*, 9 (1984), 45–68 · G. Green, *Mathematical papers*, ed. N. Ferrers (1871) · E. T. Whittaker, *History of the theories of aether and electricity* (1951) · D. M. Cannell, 'George Green: an enigmatic mathematician', *American Mathematical Monthly*, 106 (1999), 136–51
Archives U. Nott. L., George Green Library, archives
Wealth at death various houses and monies: Green, 'Biography'

Green, George Frederick (1911–1977), writer, was born on 12 April 1911 at Oakbank, Old Whittington, near Chesterfield in Derbyshire, the youngest of the three sons of Arthur Green (1878–1958), iron-founder, and Isabella White (1880–1963), whose parents came from Carlisle and who died when she was very young.

Dick, as he was always known, was educated at the Wells House preparatory school, Malvern, and subsequently at Repton School and at Magdalene College, Cambridge, where he took an English degree. After leaving Cambridge in 1932 he became for a brief period tutor to the young son of Jonathan Cape, the publisher. He had always aimed to be a writer, and now he began to work on short stories which were set in the Derbyshire mining country that he had known so well in his childhood. They took as their theme the relationship, or lack of it, between men and youths of different social or cultural background. With his fine ear for the local voice and an elegant, pared-down style, these stories examine betrayal and tragedy in a desolate world. 'A Skilled Hand' appeared in *New Stories* (1935), 'A Death in the Family' in the *London Mercury* and the *Best Short Stories of 1936*, 'A Wedding' in *The Spectator* and the *Best Short Stories of 1938*, and 'Room Wanted' in *Horizon* and the *Best Short Stories of 1940*. His work, with its deceptively simple-seeming prose style, was much praised at the time by Elizabeth Bowen, Stephen Spender, John Lehmann, Christopher Isherwood, and others.

After the outbreak of the Second World War Green was called up (1940) and served first as a private in the 3rd Suffolk infantry regiment. After passing out from an officer cadets training unit he joined the Border regiment as a second lieutenant. Later he was posted to Ceylon, where he shortly became aide-de-camp to the brigadier. He transferred to the public relations department of the commander-in-chief in Colombo, where he edited and produced *Veera Lanka*, a magazine which appeared in two languages, Sinhalese and Tamil. In gathering material for the magazine he travelled all over the island and found it utterly enchanting. An added advantage was that it took him away from army life and the officers' mess, which he loathed. A homosexual, he was attracted to the Sinhalese youths, and this, together with his heavy drinking, was his undoing. For when drunk he blatantly courted disaster. It came in 1944 when he was caught *in flagrante* with a Sinhalese rickshaw-puller; he was court-martialled and sentenced to two years' imprisonment. The first months of his sentence were spent in military detention in a Ceylon gaol, during which time he kept a diary. This he was later to use in an article entitled 'Military detention' by Lieutenant Z, which was published in 1947 in Penguin New Writing no. 31.

Back in England, Green served the rest of his time with stoicism in Wakefield prison in Yorkshire. He was released in March 1946 in a sadly disoriented state, from which he was rescued by Dr Charlotte Wolff, a psychiatrist who helped him towards rediscovering his identity. But still he could not settle anywhere, nor could he resist alcohol. Even so, he kept writing and was greatly encouraged when his early stories were published in a single volume under the title *Land without Heroes* (1948). This was reissued in 1963 in paperback by Four Square Books, with an introduction by Alan Sillitoe. In 1950 Faber and Faber published *First View*, an anthology of stories about children; Dick made the selection, and provided a foreword in which he developed his ideas of the child's view of the world. From this followed naturally his novel *In the Making* (1952), which drew upon his own memories of childhood and prep school, and was highly praised by E. M. Forster.

Aware that he was destroying himself with drinking, Green suddenly forswore alcohol altogether. In 1957, when he inherited money from his uncle, he bought a large, run-down, mainly eighteenth-century house in a Somerset village, where he lived for the rest of his life. Its garden, which sloped down to a brook, was almost derelict, and during the following years he and his friends recreated it in the Italian style to the design of an architect friend. They constructed fountains, pools, and a grotto; they built stone arches, balustrades, and parterres; there were formally clipped yew hedges and a hornbeam walk. It was a fascinating and continuing project which Dick found absorbing. Notwithstanding this he was also working on his novel *The Power of Sergeant Streater* (1972), in reality three linked novellas, the central one of which, *The Last of the Snow*, has a lyrical quality as well as a bleakness which rank it among the finest of his works. About his work he would say that words could not be spared merely to create character or plot 'because they are used—strictly as in a symbolist poem—as furtherance to the pattern of events'. He looked upon his writing as 'poetry with a sort of astringent lyricism' in which the poetry resided in the pattern. He went on to write a series of stories set in Ceylon, but he was always a slow and meticulous worker, and they did not achieve publication until after his death. He was already ill with terminal lung cancer, brought about no doubt by his heavy smoking. No treatment was possible, so, rather than linger on while his faculties deteriorated, he chose his own moment of going. He died at his home, Rockwells House, Batcombe, Shepton Mallet, Somerset, on 13 August 1977, and his remains were cremated at Yeovil crematorium, Somerset, on 17 August.

The five Ceylon stories were published posthumously in a memorial volume entitled *A Skilled Hand* (1980). They were interspersed with various friends' recollections of him. All spoke of the warmth and generosity of his nature, his eccentricities, his honesty in exploring human relationships, and his infectious laughter and sense of the ridiculous. Although he so often wrote about the lack of love between people, everyone who knew him seemed to love him and feel the pleasure of his companionship.

CHLOË GREEN

Sources *A skilled hand*, ed. C. Green and A. D. Maclean (1980) · A. Sillitoe, introduction, in G. F. Green, *Land without heroes* (1948) · G. F. Green, *First view* (1950), foreword · G. F. Green, prison journal, priv. coll. · G. F. Green, letters to brother, John Green, priv. coll. · G. F. Green, letters to sister-in-law, Chloë Green, priv. coll. · V. Cox, *The Times* (15 Aug 1977); repr. in *Daily Telegraph* (16 Aug 1977) · personal knowledge (2004) · private information (2004) · d. cert.
Archives priv. coll. | priv. coll.
Likenesses R. Buhler, oils, *c*.1930 · photograph
Wealth at death £30,000: probate, 26 Oct 1977, *CGPLA Eng. & Wales*

Green, George Smith (*d.* 1762), writer, of whose early life nothing is known, worked in Leicester, Cirencester, and Ross, before establishing himself as a watchmaker in Oxford, first in his shop opposite All Souls College, and from 1760 in Magdalen parish, opposite the 'Grand Spicery' (Davies, 60, 215d). He was admitted to Oxford University as a privileged tradesman on 8 January 1756. He published under the pseudonym of A Gentleman of Oxford, in 1745, *The state of innocence and fall of man, described in Milton's 'Paradise Lost', rendered into prose, with notes, from the French of Raymond* [Nicholas François Dupré] *de St. Maur*. Isaac D'Israeli called it 'one of the singular literary follies practised on Milton, and that Green's new version has utterly ruined the harmony of Milton's Cadences' (*N&Q*, 48). In 1750 Green published in his own name a picaresque novel, *The Life of John Van ... being a Series of many Extraordinary Events and Vicissitudes*. His publications include the *Parson's Parlour*, a poem (1756), *The Image of the Ancients, Particularly those in the University of Oxford* (1758), and two unacted plays, *Oliver Cromwell* (1752), a ponderous five-act play, and *A Nice Lady* (1762).

Green was also something of an eccentric. In 1756 he put up a notice threatening 'to defend This property with Artillery' against those who defaced his curiously worded signboard (Davies, 56, 135b). Three years later he was obliged to publish a denial in the local press that he sold mixed metal for silver, and shortly before his death he lost his privileged tradesman status with the university when he was publicly discommoned, members of the university being forbidden to have dealings with him. He died in Oxford on 28 April 1762, leaving a wife, Sarah, who was formerly the wife of John Andrews of Peterborough.

JAMES BURNLEY, *rev.* MICHAEL BEVAN

Sources *N&Q*, 3rd ser., 10 (1866), 47–8 · E. C. Davies, *A chronological synopsis and index to Oxfordshire items in 'Jackson's Oxford Journal', 1753–1780* (1967) · *Jackson's Oxford Journal* (20 Feb 1762) · *Jackson's Oxford Journal* (1 May 1762) · Foster, *Alum. Oxon.* · will, 1762, PRO, PROB 11/878, sig. 399, fols. 361v–363r
Wealth at death estate near Peterborough: will, 1762, PRO, PROB 11/878, sig. 399

Green, Gustavus (1865–1964), aero-engine designer, was born in Hounslow, Middlesex, on 11 March 1865. He subsequently took the surname of his stepfather, Samuel Green. At the age of about sixteen he moved to Hastings where he was in turn a jeweller and a hairdresser; in 1897 he moved to Bexhill where he established a cycle business. He became interested in the internal combustion engine, taking out his first patent in 1900, but it was not until 1904 and 1905 that he patented the method of cylinder construction which was to form the basis of his subsequent designs. The Green Motor Patents Syndicate was formed to exploit his patents, his principal partners being Henry Francis Pelham-Clinton-Hope (later eighth duke of Newcastle) and Joseph Miller, dental surgeon. The syndicate became a private limited liability company in 1906. It manufactured small stationary engines and motor cycles until the First World War, but in 1906 produced two cars, one of which was exhibited in March at Cordingley's automobile exhibition at the Royal Agricultural Hall, London. Colonel J. E. Capper, superintendent of the balloon factory at Farnborough, was attracted by the lightweight construction of the engine and invited Green to design an 80 hp airship engine. This water-cooled V8 engine was the first designed by Green to use a single overhead camshaft (patented in 1908) which, with his patented cylinder construction, was to be a characteristic feature of all his subsequent aero- and marine engines. Intended for the *Nulli Secundus*, it was not used until 1910, in the airship *Gamma*.

A 35 hp four-cylinder engine appeared in 1908 followed by a 60 hp version the following year. The latter, in an aeroplane built by Oswald Short and his brothers, enabled J. T. C. Moore-Brabazon (later Lord Brabazon of Tara) to win in 1909 the *Daily Mail* £1000 prize for the first circular flight of 1 mile by a British pilot in an all-British aeroplane. For the five years before the First World War Green engines were the most successful British aero-engines, powering seven Michelin Trophy winners. In 1910 Patrick Y. Alexander sponsored a competition to encourage the design and construction of British aero-engines. Although the 35 hp Green engine was the only one to complete the tests, it produced slightly less power than required and so no prize was awarded. The following year the competition was opened to foreign engines and a 60 hp Green engine gained the first prize of £1000. In 1913 the Sopwith Batboat, powered by a 100 hp six-cylinder Green engine won the £500 Mortimer Singer prize for seaplanes and in 1914 a 120 hp six-cylinder Green engine won the £5000 prize offered by the War Office in the naval and military aeroplane engine competition.

Marine versions of all these engines were produced and in 1912 Fred May, an exponent of racing motor boats, acquired the assets of the syndicate to form the Green Engine Company Ltd, with Green as technical director and a minority shareholder. The company acquired new premises at Edwin Road, Twickenham, in 1914. During the war Green was asked to build engines for Thornycroft Coastal Motor Boats, for which Thornycroft were unable to provide sufficient engines. Twelve-cylinder 300 hp and eighteen-cylinder 450 hp engines were produced, followed by a 24-cylinder 1000 hp engine in 1920 of which only a prototype was made. After the war the company continued to produce marine versions of its pre-war aero-engines until it was wound up in 1930.

Green was a gifted mechanic rather than a trained engineer. Although in 1908 his patented features allowed the construction of light and powerful engines for that period, he made little subsequent technical progress. The engines produced in the 1920s were virtually identical to those produced in 1908 and he had been left behind by the scientific and technical advances in engine design which had taken place during the war, though he continued to file patents until his retirement. Green had little interest in production engineering or sustained development programmes and the company for the most part only built prototype engines. The production of the smaller engines was carried out by the Aster Engineering Company of Wembley and the large wartime marine engines by Peter Brotherhood Ltd, of Peterborough.

In February 1893 Green married Joanna Beatrice, daughter of James Easton, a carpenter; they had one son and three daughters. He retired in 1925 and devoted the rest of his life to the hobby of clockmaking. In 1958 it was brought to the attention of the Royal Aeronautical Society that Green was still alive and on 15 January 1959 he was made an honorary companion of the society in recognition of his contribution to early British aviation. He still retained the alert, distinguished appearance which had characterized him throughout his life. He died at the age of ninety-nine on 29 December 1964 at his house, 97 Strawberry Vale, in Twickenham.　　P. R. MANN, *rev.*

Sources Autocar (3 March 1906), 396–7 · Engineering (1910–20) · Flight (1909–22) · (The Motor Ship and) Motor Boat (1914–23) · Aeroplane (18 April 1917), 971–2 · H. F. Cowley, Gustavus Green (privately circulated, 1958) · patents, 1900–24 · PRO, BT31/11579/89387; BT31/20790/123108; BT31/14161/130990 · private information (1981) [G. C. Parry, granddaughter; H. de B. Saunders] · The Times (30 Dec 1964), 10e · d. cert. · m. cert.
Likenesses photograph, 1958, Sci. Mus., Science and Society Picture Library; [SCM/PER B580467A]
Wealth at death £26,221: probate, 30 March 1965, CGPLA Eng. & Wales

Green, Sir Henry (*d.* 1369), justice, apparently came from Northamptonshire. His parents are unknown. He is first recorded in a legal context in April 1331, when he witnessed an indenture in the company of such distinguished lawyers as William Shareshull, Robert Sadington, and Roger Hillary. By Michaelmas term 1337 he was appearing as counsel in the bench, and he was created serjeant-at-law in 1342. In spite of a youthful brashness which in Hilary term 1345 brought him a sharp snub from Chief Justice Stonor—'I am amazed that Grene makes himself out to know everything in the world, and he is only a young man' (Pike, 1905, 446–8)—he became a king's serjeant later that same year. He also appears to have served Queen Isabella, who in 1346 gave him the lease for life of the manor of Brigstock, Northamptonshire, and he became a member of the council of Edward, the Black Prince, receiving an annual payment for his pains 'on the prince's business when matters of law are on hand' (Tout, *Admin. hist.*, 5.385). In February 1354 he was appointed a justice of the bench and knighted; the grant of 80 marks per annum on top of his yearly salary of 40 marks may have been meant to act as a safeguard against corruption. Frequently employed as a commissioner of oyer and terminer and justice of assize and gaol delivery, above all in the midlands, Green's involvement in the violent dispute between Bishop Thomas Lisle of Ely and Blanche, Lady Wake, led to his being excommunicated by the pope in 1357. This did him no harm in the king's eyes, for on 24 May 1361 he was appointed to succeed Shareshull as chief justice of king's bench, and in that capacity made the opening speech in the parliament of Michaelmas 1362. A trier of petitions at that parliament, and again at Michaelmas 1363 and Hilary 1365, Green also presided over sessions of his court in Yorkshire in 1363 and the eastern counties (where it sat for three successive sessions) in 1364.

But Green's career was to be shattered when at its height, for in 1365 he and Sir William Skipwith, the chief baron of the exchequer, were arrested for what the chronicler Henry Knighton called his 'enormous derelictions' (*Knighton's Chronicle*, 193), and on 30 October Green was ordered to hand over to John Knyvet all the records associated with his office of chief justice. Knighton offers no other explanation for the king's action against the justices, and adds only that they redeemed themselves by a fine. Corruption is certainly a possible cause. Green built up a substantial estate, with properties in Yorkshire, Nottinghamshire, Northamptonshire, Hertfordshire, Bedfordshire, Buckinghamshire, and London, and did not always obtain royal licence for dealings in land where the strict letter of the law required this; he also invested in the wardships and marriages of heirs. By 1359 he was rich enough to lend the king £100 and forgo repayment. Personal enmities may also have played their part. In February 1364 Sir Peter Malory and his son were reported to have been convicted in the mayor of London's court of forcible trespass against Green; an award of £300 in damages suggests that the offence was regarded as serious. But as no record of any fine by the dismissed justices has been discovered, it is just as likely that the king's motives were essentially political. Skipwith was later able to resume his judicial career, but Green, although he was remembered in the following reign as a learned judge, was never again employed in the courts. Nevertheless he suffered no diminution of his estate, which at his death in Northamptonshire, on 6 August 1369, descended to his sons Thomas and Henry, as their father had arranged some years earlier. The younger Henry Green was to be notorious as a counsellor to Richard II in the last years of that king's reign, and was executed in 1399. Sir Henry Green the elder, who had married Katherine, daughter of Sir John Drayton of Drayton, was buried in Boughton church in Northamptonshire, as he had directed in his will, drawn up on 20 July 1369. It is a measure of his wealth that he died possessed of cash amounting to £460. As well as making bequests to the bailiff of each of his manors, and to all his farm workers (*Famuli*), he left £40 to the fabric of Boughton church, where his effigy long represented him 'in a short goune that should show hym a lawyer, having also a serjeant's coyfe' (Baker, *Serjeants*, 70).

HENRY SUMMERSON

Sources Chancery records · G. O. Sayles, ed., *Select cases in the court of king's bench*, 7 vols., SeldS, 55, 57–8, 74, 76, 82, 88 (1936–71), vol. 6 · B. H. Putnam, ed., *Proceedings before the justices of the peace in the fourteenth and fifteenth centuries* (1938) · *Knighton's chronicle, 1337–1396*, ed. and trans. G. H. Martin, OMT (1995) [Lat. orig., *Chronica de eventibus Angliae a tempore regis Edgari usque mortem regis Ricardi Secundi*, with parallel Eng. text] · A. J. Horwood, ed. and trans., *Year books of the reign of King Edward the Third*, 1, Rolls Series, 31b (1883) · *Year books of the reign of King Edward the Third*, 8, ed. and trans. L. O. Pike, Rolls Series, 31b (1900) · A. J. Horwood and L. O. Pike, eds. and trans., *Year books of the reign of King Edward the Third*, 15 vols., Rolls Series, 31b (1883–1911), vols. 10–12 · Baker, *Serjeants* · *RotP*, vol. 2 · Tout, *Admin. hist.*, vol. 5 · HoP, *Commons, 1386–1421*, 3.225–8 · B. H. Putnam, *The place in legal history of Sir William Shareshull* (1950) · *CIPM*, 12, no. 355 · A. Gibbons, ed., *Early Lincoln wills* (1888)
Likenesses tomb effigy; now lost
Wealth at death cash valued at £460; also estates: Gibbons, *Early Lincoln wills*, 47; PRO, C 12/355

Green, Henry (1801–1873), Unitarian minister and author, was born near Penshurst, Kent, on 23 June 1801. His father, a successful paper-maker, expected him to enter his own business, but the influence of the Unitarian minister George Harris, under whose care he was placed, led him to train for the ministry. He entered Glasgow University in November 1822, and gained seven prizes, including the university prize for translation into English of Plato's *Phaedo*. He took his MA degree in April 1825, and then served as a supply minister at Hanley, Staffordshire and Diss, Norfolk. In January 1827 he became minister of the Unitarian Brook Street Chapel, Knutsford, Cheshire, which he held until his resignation in June 1872.

During part of his pastorate Green conducted a large private school and published several handbooks to Euclid, which provided a useful additional source of income. He was also closely involved in various educational projects, including the Allostock chapel school, Cheshire, of which he was the founder in 1847 and manager until 1858. Green was a close friend and colleague of the Revd William Gaskell and his wife, the novelist Elizabeth Gaskell, and was a very highly regarded and conscientious pastor.

Green's main interest was, however, the history of dissent and Unitarianism in northern England—and Cheshire in particular—and he wrote a series of articles on the subject in the *Unitarian Herald*. He compiled a series of notebooks, now in the Cheshire Record Office (Ches. & Chester ALSS), giving extensive transcripts of early documentary sources and including numerous short biographies of seventeenth- and early eighteenth-century ministers. His *Knutsford and its traditions and history, with reminiscences, anecdotes, and notices of the neighbourhood* (1859) is short but competent. Green edited six volumes of the Holbein Society's facsimile reprints in the years 1869–71, and also published several works on emblems and emblem books.

Green married Mary (d. 1871), daughter of John Brandreth, about 1827. He died on 9 August 1873 at his home, Heathfield, Knutsford, and was buried in Brook Street Chapel yard on 13 August. Five of his six children survived him; his only son, Philip Henry (d. 1883), after a distinguished career at the bar, was appointed to an Indian judgeship.   ALBERT NICHOLSON, *rev.* ALAN G. CROSBY

Sources Ches. & Chester ALSS, Green papers · W. R. Strachan, ed., 'Non-parochial registers of Brook Street chapel, Knutsford, and Allostock chapel, Allostock, Cheshire', unpub. typescript, 1982, Ches. & Chester ALSS · *Unitarian Herald* (22 Aug 1873), 269 · *CGPLA Eng. & Wales* (1873)
Archives Brook Street Chapel, Knutsford · Ches. & Chester ALSS · Hunt. L., papers relating to Andrea Alciati

Wealth at death under £4000: probate, 26 Sept 1873, *CGPLA Eng. & Wales*

Green, Henry. *See* Yorke, Henry Vincent (1905–1973).

Green, Hugh (*c*.1585–1642), Roman Catholic priest, was born in London, the son of John Green, a goldsmith in the parish of St Giles-in-the-Fields. Both his parents were protestants and he was educated from 1601 at Peterhouse, Cambridge, where he graduated BA in 1606 and MA in 1609. Subsequently he travelled on the continent and became a Roman Catholic. He entered the English College at Douai in 1609, and on 7 July 1610 he took the college oath and was admitted an alumnus. He was confirmed at Cambrai on 25 September 1611, advanced to minor orders, and ordained subdeacon at Arras on the following 17 December, deacon on 18 March, and priest on 14 June 1612. He left the college and tried his vocation with the order of Capuchins, but left for the English mission on 6 August 1612. For nearly thirty years he exercised his ministry in Staffordshire and various places under the name of Ferdinand Brooks. When Charles I, in 1642, issued the proclamation commanding all priests to depart the realm within a stated time, Green, who was then at Chideock Castle, Dorset, as chaplain to Lady Arundell, decided to leave for the continent. Lady Arundell begged him to stay at Chideock, pointing out that the day fixed in the proclamation had already passed. Green, however, thinking there was still time, went to Lyme, and was boarding a vessel for France when he was seized by a custom-house officer, was carried before a justice of the peace, and by him was committed to Dorchester gaol. On 17 August 1642, after five months' close confinement, he was tried and sentenced to death by Justice Robert Foster. He was executed on a hill outside Dorchester on 19 August 1642, being hanged, drawn, and quartered before an angry and vindictive mob. He was buried that day, near to the gallows. Mrs Elizabeth Willoughby, who attended him at the scaffold, wrote a minute narrative of his death, published in Jean Chifflet's *Palmae cleri Anglicani*, at Brussels, in 1645. He was beatified by Pius XI on 15 December 1929.

GORDON GOODWIN, rev. G. BRADLEY

Sources G. Anstruther, *The seminary priests*, 2 (1975), 137 · R. Challoner, *Memoirs of missionary priests*, ed. J. H. Pollen, rev. edn (1924), 421 · Gillow, *Lit. biog. hist.*, 3.18–24 · J. Chifflet, *Palmae cleri Anglicani* (1645) · P. Caraman, ed., *The years of siege: Catholic life from James I to Cromwell* (1966), 77 · E. H. Burton and T. L. Williams, eds., *The Douay College diaries, third, fourth and fifth, 1598–1654*, 2, Catholic RS, 11 (1911), 103, 115, 447 · Venn, *Alum. Cant.* · D. Underdown, *Fire from heaven: the life of an English town in the seventeenth century* (1992), 197–9

Likenesses miniature, St Mawgan's Carmelite Convent, Lanherne, Newquay, Cornwall

Green, Hugh Hughes [Hughie] (1920–1997), entertainer, was born at 8 Weymouth Court, 1 Weymouth Street, St Marylebone, London, on 2 February 1920, the son of Hugh Aitchison Green, fish broker and former major in the Canadian militia, and his wife, Violet Elenore, *née* Price. His parents had lived in Canada between 1907 and 1917, and retained strong Canadian connections thereafter: one of Green's godfathers was Sir Sam Hughes, the Canadian

Hugh Hughes Green (1920–1997), by unknown photographer, 1971

minister of militia during the First World War. His Scottish father had been dubbed Canada's Fishmonger General, and his Irish mother sang as an amateur soprano. Green's early years were steeped in show business, as his father invited the stars from the local variety theatres round for Saturday night singsongs. Evelyn Laye sang, Jack Buchanan tap-danced, and Harry Tate, the walrus-whiskered comedian, became Green's other godfather. When he was seven he made his stage début as the unseen engine cranking the propeller of Tate's comedy aeroplane at the London Coliseum. And so were born the twin loves of his life, the stage and flying. After a trip to Canada at the age of seven, when Green sang in the ship's concert and absorbed the twang that gave him that popular accent known as 'mid-atlantic', the family returned to Golders Green, Middlesex, where four years later Green staged his own show at the Hoop Lane Hall, and raised £4 3s. 0d. to help the Royal National Hospital towards its target of £50,000. Meanwhile, he was educated, first at a preparatory school in St John's Wood, then at a boarding-school in Bromley.

Green's first professional engagement came in 1931 at the Garrick Theatre. In an old time music-hall show he put on one of Harry Tate's ginger moustaches and sang 'Gilbert the Filbert', finishing off with Tate's classic catchphrase, 'Goodbye-eee!' Two years later Bryan Michie, talent spotter for BBC radio, got Green and his 'Gang' of youngsters an audition which resulted in a short series of shows. His signature tune was 'The Wearing o' the Green'; and among his youthful cast were Lauri Lupino Lane and Connie Wood, who later attained fame as songstress Kathy Kay.

The year of Green's big break was 1934. First he and his Gang entered 'cine-variety', touring the Paramount cinema circuit; then he was filmed by the Pathetone Weekly playing office boy to Harry Tate; and finally Gaumont-British cast him in the feature *Little Friend* supporting their child star Nova Pilbeam. In the following year he played the title role in the film of Marryat's famous novel *Midshipman Easy*. Carol Reed directed, Green saved Margaret Lockwood from bandits, and the mate was played by Harry Tate. More films followed. Green was a guest star in *Radio Pirates* (1937), doing a selection of his impressions, an act he repeated in *Music Hall Parade* (1939). His repertoire included Jack Buchanan, Claude Dampier ('the professional idiot'), Charles Laughton as Captain Bligh, Robertson Hare, Vic Oliver, Nellie Wallace, and, of course, Harry Tate. He saved Margaret Lockwood from the Crystal Palace fire in *Melody and Romance* (1937) and starred with his stage Gang in *Down our Alley* (1939).

Green's other career, flying, took off when he was nineteen. He flew solo in June 1939. When the Second World War began he volunteered for the Royal Air Force. Rejected, he went to Canada, joined the Royal Canadian Air Force, and soon became sergeant instructor for Link trainer aircraft. After Pearl Harbor he transferred to Ferry Command and spent his war flying Catalinas from California to Russia. After the war he found himself forgotten by show business, no longer a talented teenager. He tried Canadian radio in 1945 without much success, played a small part in the Hollywood film *If Winter Comes* (1947), and returned to England the next year for a supporting role in *Paper Orchid*.

In 1949 Green put up the idea of a new type of amateur talent show, and the BBC radio producer Dennis Main Wilson took it on. *Opportunity Knocks*, with Green billed as 'Your master of opportunities', was a swift success, with its unusual idea of big-name talent spotters. The film star Sheila Sim was the first, and discovered talent included Jean Bayliss and Louise Traill. Later came Louise Gainsborough, the Gaunt brothers, the Kordites, and a trumpet impersonator named Spike Milligan. Embarrassingly, Green's rejects included Alma Cogan and Tony Hancock. By the end of the first series Green had travelled 20,000 miles, auditioned 4000 acts, and broadcast 165 of them. Meanwhile Green had been trying, unsuccessfully, to persuade the BBC to show the programme on television. After the programme was dropped, in 1950, he brought a court action against the BBC, claiming that, for corrupt reasons, they were 'conspiring to prevent the show being screened' in favour of Carroll Levis's *Discoveries* (*Daily Telegraph*, 5 May 1997). Despite Lord Hailsham's taking up his case, Green lost, and was bankrupted. Undaunted, he returned to his alternative career as a pilot, ferrying planes and working as a Hollywood stuntman. Nevertheless he retained his European and broadcasting connections, transferring *Opportunity Knocks* to Radio Luxemburg (where it was sponsored by Horlicks malted milk) in 1950, and in 1954 devising a new show for Radio Luxemburg. This was *Double your Money*, a cash quiz show. The first winners were newly-weds Mr and Mrs Smith, who answered a series of six questions and won the top prize of £32. The new sponsor was Lucozade.

Independent Television (ITV) came to England in 1955, and the smiling face of Hughie Green beamed out of the monochrome screen for the first time. The visual version of *Double your Money* was an immediate hit. The top prize was still £32, but a new addition was the Treasure Trail which came to a head at £1024, an unheard of sum at the time. In the following year Green brought his *Opportunity Knocks* to ITV, with a top prize of £400. Green introduced his new device, the 'Clapometer', which measured audience applause. Many new stars were born, including Russ Abbot, Frank Carson, Les Dawson, Freddie Davis, known as Parrotface Davis, Mary Hopkin, Bonnie Langford, Little and Large, Tom O'Connor, and Lena Zavaroni. *Double your Money* ran until 1968, when it was replaced by a similar show, *The Sky's the Limit*, again with Green as presenter, which ran until 1974. *Opportunity Knocks* was taken off the air in 1978. Green blamed the broadcasting executives and critics, who had criticized his populist approach and his frequent (and increasingly bizarre) expressions of right-wing political views:

> TV's been taken over by anti-patriots. The Reds aren't under the beds, they're right in there running programming. Why else did they stop me praising our heritage, and giving viewers good old rousing patriotic stuff to get this country back on our feet? (*Daily Telegraph*, 5 May 1997)

Following his departure from television, Green pursued a variety of business interests, while continuing to criticize the major television companies for their 'anti-patriotic' broadcasters. He was a staunch supporter of Mary Whitehouse, for being 'prepared to speak up for clean boots and short hair' (*The Times*, 5 May 1997). He returned briefly to the BBC in 1987, as a consultant for a new series of *Opportunity Knocks*, but resigned over the choice of presenter. In 1989 he unsuccessfully sued the New Zealand Broadcasting Corporation for pirating his *Opportunity Knocks* format (including the 'Clapometer'), spending £250,000 on legal fees in the process.

Green married his childhood sweetheart, Claire Wilson, in 1942, and they had a son (Christopher) and a daughter (Linda). The marriage was dissolved in 1975. He died in London on 3 May 1997. At his memorial service Noel Botham, a friend, revealed that Green was the father of Paula Yates (1959–2000), a television personality, and daughter of Heller Thornton. This came as a shock to Miss Yates, who thought her father was Green's colleague, the television producer Jess Yates, and to Green's children. However, in December 1997 DNA tests proved that Green was indeed the father.　DENIS GIFFORD

Sources H. Green, *Opportunity knocked* (1995) · *The Times* (5 May 1997) · *The Independent* (5 May 1997) · *Daily Telegraph* (5 May 1997) · *The Observer* (14 Dec 1997) · b. cert. · *CGPLA Eng. & Wales* (1997)

Archives BL NSA, oral history interview | SOUND BL NSA, oral history interview

Likenesses photographs, 1930–75, Hult. Arch. · photograph, 1971, Hult. Arch. [*see illus.*] · photograph, repro. in *The Times* · photograph, repro. in *The Independent* · photograph, repro. in *Daily Telegraph*

Wealth at death £287,869: probate, 25 July 1997, *CGPLA Eng. & Wales*

Green, James (*bap.* 1692), music compiler, was baptized at Darfield, Yorkshire, on 5 May 1692, and was the younger brother of John Green (*bap.* 1677). The two collaborated on *A Book of Psalm Tunes*, of which the earliest edition extant is the second, in 1713; on the title-page they are described as being 'of Wombwell, in the parish of Darfield' in the East Riding of Yorkshire. The Greens provided a preface with instructions. A third edition, *A Collection of Choice Psalm Tunes*, appeared in 1715, published in Nottingham, Sheffield, and London. From the fourth edition in 1718, *A Collection of Psalm Tunes*, James Green's name appeared alone.

The Greens took their music largely from Henry Playford's *The Divine Companion* (1701) and John Bishop's *A Sett of New Psalm Tunes* (1710). Most of the tunes were abridged, reducing the number of voice parts to move them within the range of country congregations. They also added music used in provincial churches that in some cases reflected conventions regarded as outdated in cathedral music. Their audience seems to have been mainly in Yorkshire and the east midlands; the fifth edition of 1724, *A Book of Psalmody*, was published in London but 'sold by the booksellers at Hull, Lincoln, Louth and Gainsborough'. It reached its eleventh edition in 1751.

There are no certain biographical details about James Green, but later compilers relied on his work; in that context it is not surprising that traditions gathered around his name. He was at one time believed to have been an organist in Hull, but there is no record of him holding the position at either of its eighteenth-century churches. He may also have been confused with Henry Green, a blind London organist who died in 1741. A hymn for two voices, 'When All thy Mercies', published about 1790, was ascribed to him, as were four entries in Joseph Warren's *A Selection of Cathedral Chants by the Old English Masters* (1840). William Hayman Cummings stated that Green 'lived in London in later life, and was a great bell-ringer, having a belfry of his own at the top of his house' (Cummings) but left the statement unsourced.   MATTHEW KILBURN

Sources N. Temperley, *The music of the English parish church*, 2 vols. (1979) · M. Frost, ed., *Historical companion to 'Hymns ancient and modern'* (1962) · G. H. Smith, *A history of Hull organs and organists* (c.1910) · N. Temperley, 'Green [Greene], James', *New Grove*, 2nd edn · W. H. Cummings, 'Greene, James', Grove, *Dict. mus.* (1927) · *DNB* · C. F. Pohl, *Mozart und Haydn in London*, 2 vols. (Vienna, 1867), 21, 36 · D. Baptie, *A handbook of musical biography* (1883), 86 · J. D. Brown, *Biographical dictionary of musicians: with a bibliography of English writings on music* (1886), 288

Green, James (1771–1834), portrait painter, was born at Leytonstone in Essex on 13 March 1771, the son of John Green, builder, and his wife, Sarah. He was apprenticed to Thomas Martyn, a draughtsman of natural history, who resided at 10 Great Marlborough Street, London. When his apprenticeship expired, he entered the Royal Academy Schools in 1791, where he attracted the notice of Sir Joshua Reynolds, and copied many of his pictures. In 1793 he exhibited at the Royal Academy several views of Tunbridge Wells, and some portraits. On 13 February 1805 Green married at St Marylebone, Marylebone Road, Marylebone, Middlesex, Mary Byrne [**Mary Green** (1776–1845)], second daughter of William *Byrne (1743–1805) [*see under* Byrne family (*per.* 1765–1849)], the landscape engraver. She was a pupil of (L. A.?) Arlaud, and was a well-known miniature painter, exhibiting at the Royal Academy, the British Institution, and the Society of British Artists from 1795 to 1845. She was a member of the Associated Artists in Water-Colours from 1807 to 1810, and letters by her relating to this society are in the Victoria and Albert Museum, London. Her large miniature of Queen Adelaide, signed 'My Green', is in the Royal Collection. Foskett noted that 'she was a good artist who painted with freedom and placed her sitters well' (Foskett, 550).

Green gradually attained a good reputation for his portraits in watercolour. In 1804 he had belonged for four years to an informal sketching club that included the patron and landscape painter Sir George Beaumont, Samuel Shelley the miniature painter, 'Nattes and Hills drawing Masters and Pyne, a designer, who met weekly in each others' houses during the winter months to sketch and converse on art' (Farington, *Diary*, 6.2271). His execution was more elegant than powerful, but his portraits do not lack dignity. Many of them have been engraved, including those of Benjamin West, president of the Royal Academy (original painting in the Metropolitan Museum of Art, New York) and Sir R. Birnie, both engraved in mezzotint by W. Say; George Cook, the actor, as Iago (Garrick Club, London), engraved in mezzotint by James Ward; and Joseph Charles Horsley ('the stolen child'), engraved by R. Cooper. In the National Portrait Gallery, London, there are portraits by him of Thomas Stothard RA, William Say, Peter Nicholson, and Sir John Ross, the latter being Green's last work. The portrait of Stothard was sold at Samuel Rogers's sale in May 1856, as by George Henry Harlow, whose works Green's portraiture resembled at times although it is signed 'James Green, 1830'. It was engraved by E. Scriven for the *Library of the Fine Arts* (April 1833). Green also painted large subject pictures in oil, including *Zadig and Astarte* (exh. RA, 1826, of which an engraving was reproduced in the *Literary Souvenir*, 1828); *Bearnaise Woman and Canary*, engraved, and reproduced in the *Literary Souvenir* (1827); and *Belinda*. His picture *The Loves Conducted by the Graces to the Temple of Hymen* was painted in watercolour. Green also was a frequent exhibitor from 1806 to 1832 at the British Institution, where he showed mainly genre and subject pictures, and in 1808 was awarded a premium of £60. He was a member of the Associated Artists in Water-Colours. Many of his pictures were commissions, notably from Francis Chaplin of Riseholme, Lincolnshire. He resided for many years at Rathbone Place, London, and subsequently at 8 South Crescent, Bedford Square, London. He died at Bath on 27 March 1834. He was buried in Walcot church. On her husband's death Mary Green retired from her profession, though she continued to exhibit; she died on 22 October 1845, and was buried at Kensal Green, Middlesex. Her copies after Reynolds and Gainsborough were much valued. James and Mary Green had two children, Benjamin Richard *Green and a daughter.   L. H. CUST, *rev.* JOHN SUNDERLAND

Sources Graves, *RA exhibitors* · Mallalieu, *Watercolour artists*, vol. 1 · *IGI* · Farington, *Diary* · administration, PRO, PROB 6/210, fol. 226r · D. Foskett, *Miniatures: dictionary and guide* (1987)
Likenesses A. E. Chalon, group portrait, pen, ink, and watercolour drawing (*Study at the British Institution, 1805*), BM
Wealth at death £600: administration, PRO, PROB 6/210, fol. 266r

Green, John (1706–1779), bishop of Lincoln, was born at Beverley, Yorkshire, son of John Green, tax collector, and received his early education there. He was then admitted as a sizar at St John's College, Cambridge, on 10 June 1724 from which he graduated with a BA (1728), an MA (1731), a BD (1739), and a DD (1749). He was also awarded a fellowship in 1730 which he held until 1750. In 1729 he served as an usher at the Lichfield grammar school before being ordained priest by the bishop of Lincoln in 1731 and taking up the position of vicar of Hinxton, Cambridgeshire, in the same year.

Further preferment followed after Green became domestic chaplain to Charles, duke of Somerset, the chancellor of the University of Cambridge, in 1744. In 1747 the duke presented him to the rectory of Borough Green near Newmarket and in 1749 Green also obtained the living of Barrow in Suffolk by right of being the senior fellow in orders at St John's College. Green's career then became closely linked to that of the great master of ecclesiastical patronage, the duke of Newcastle, who in 1748 became chancellor of the University of Cambridge following the death of the duke of Somerset. In the same year, thanks to Newcastle, Green was appointed to the university's most senior chair, the regius professorship of divinity. In this he was also assisted by his friendship with Philip Yorke, later second earl of Hardwicke, to whose whiggish-inclined *Athenian Letters* (first published 1741–3) Green made a number of contributions. Green later reciprocated by playing an active part in ensuring Hardwicke's election as high steward of the university in 1764. From 1753 to 1756 Green served as a royal chaplain.

Green's loyalty to the house of Hanover was spelt out in a commencement sermon at the university before the duke of Newcastle in July 1749: 'Pure and reformed religion', he urged, '… can only be perpetuated to us by the … settlement of the crown in his [George II's] royal and illustrious house' (*A Sermon Preached at St Mary's*, 16). Green was further rewarded in the following year when he became master of Corpus Christi College, Cambridge, despite having no connection with the college. Green's reputation as a client of Newcastle was further strengthened by his vigorous defence of the disciplinary reforms which the chancellor introduced into the university in 1750 in the face of considerable controversy. In 1756 Green was promoted to the deanery of Lincoln and resigned the professorship of divinity. However, he continued his connection with the university by serving as vice-chancellor in 1756–7.

Through the patronage of Newcastle, Green became bishop of Lincoln in 1761—a promotion which led him to resign his other ecclesiastical positions though he retained the mastership of Corpus until 1764. Consistent with his whig principles Green was a strong believer in the civic function of religion in ensuring social and political order, a view predicated on the assumption that Christianity, like the Hanoverian state, was in accord with reason. He therefore regarded the rise of more 'enthusiastic' forms of Christianity with dismay—hence about the same year that he was elevated to the bench he published two pamphlets attacking the Methodists. In the first of these (addressed to John Berridge in 1760) he deplored the tendency 'to abandon the guidance' of reason. Green also regarded too much emphasis on faith rather than works as socially unsettling, being 'greatly liable to be misapplied by the common people, and likely to lead them into mistakes of a very mischievous nature' (*The Principles and Practices of the Methodists Considered*, 6, 62). Similarly, in his subsequent pamphlet addressed to Whitefield in 1761, Green again expressed his concern at 'some degrading expressions, which you and your associates occasionally throw out about human reason, as well as learning' (*The Principles and Practices of the Methodists Further Considered*, 11). So great was Green's alarm at the spread of such unsettling conceptions of Christianity that he planned a third anti-Methodist pamphlet but was persuaded by Archbishop Secker not to publish, as the archbishop 'looked upon the Methodists to be a well-meaning set of people' (*GM*, 51.624).

Green's position as bishop of Lincoln brought with it a house in London which became a centre of literary and scientific discussion, being the site of the *conversaziones* of the Royal Society from 1765. In the early part of George III's reign he remained in good standing at court: in 1771, for example, he was granted a residentiary canonry at St Paul's to supplement the income from his see which he regarded as insufficient. But Green was true to his whig principles both in and out of season and the fact that he was the only bishop to vote in favour of the bill for the relief of protestant dissenters in 1772 led to a waning of royal favour. George III reportedly responded by saying 'Green, Green, he shall never be translated' (Wordsworth, 625). This indeed proved to be the case, for Green died at Bath in 1779 with no further promotion. He never married. JOHN GASCOIGNE

Sources 'Memoirs of the life of the late bishop of Lincoln', *GM*, 1st ser., 49 (1779), 234–6 · *GM*, 1st ser., 51 (1781), 624 · E. Pyle, *Memoirs of a royal chaplain, 1729–1763*, ed. A. Hartshorne (1905) · Nichols, *Illustrations*, 6.794 · BL, Newcastle correspondence, Add. MS 32717, fols. 463–547 · C. Wordsworth, *Social life at the English universities in the eighteenth century* (1874) · P. Yorke and others, *Athenian letters, or, The epistolary correspondence of an agent of the king of Persia, residing at Athens during the Peloponnesian War*, ed. T. Birch, 4 vols. (1741–3), vol. 3; new edn, 2 vols. (1798) · Venn, *Alum. Cant.*
Archives Cambs. AS, poems and letters in verse, Latin and English | BL, letters to earls of Hardwicke, etc., Add. MSS 35359–35658, *passim* · BL, corresp. with duke of Newcastle, Add. MSS 32714–33090, *passim* · Representative Church Body Library, Dublin, letters to Lord Townshend

Green, John (*fl.* 1758). *See under* Green, Amos (1735–1807).

Green, John (1787–1852), architect and civil engineer, was born on 20 June 1787 at Newton Fell House, Nafferton, Northumberland, the son of John Green, builder, carpenter, and agricultural implement-maker, and his wife, Ann.

After attending a local school he evidently gained a practical education by working in his father's business, and soon after he came of age he was taken into partnership. The firm then moved to the larger town of Corbridge, and here they expanded their activities into general building work, with the son turning his attention to the architectural side of the business. About 1820 he moved to Newcastle upon Tyne, from where he established his extensive professional practice in the area of Northumberland and co. Durham.

Green's early works as an architect included the Newcastle Literary and Philosophical Society's building (1822–5) and the beginnings of a lengthy sequence of somewhat undistinguished Gothic-style churches. He also developed a reputation as a designer of farmhouses: he was employed in this capacity on the Beaufront estate near Hexham (1824), and by Hugh Percy, second duke of Northumberland. Green's principal contribution, however, was in the field of civil engineering, as a builder of road and railway bridges. In 1829–31 he built two wrought-iron suspension bridges, at Scotswood across the Tyne (dem. 1967) and at Whorlton across the Tees, the latter of which survives as the oldest bridge of its type in the country still supported unaided by its original chains. He also built several handsome examples in masonry; and, most important, at the Ouseburn and Willington Dene bridges (1836–9; dem.) on the Newcastle and North Shields Railway and in a number of subsequent examples he successfully employed a system of laminated timber arches, which, for a short time, was widely imitated in railway bridge construction. In 1840 Green was elected to the Institution of Civil Engineers and the following year he was awarded the institution's Telford medal for his work on laminated arch design.

Green was said to have been a 'plain practical shrewd man of business' whose style was 'plain, severe and economical' (Welford, 330). In 1805 he married Jane Stobart; they had two sons, John and Benjamin *Green, both of whom became architects. The latter in the mid-1830s became a partner of his father, and it is not always possible to distinguish the work of the father from that of the son. The monument to John Lambton, first earl of Durham, at Penshaw Hill, co. Durham (1844), in the form of a Greek Doric temple, for example, is simply ascribed to 'John and Benjamin Green'. In general, however, the father appears to have concentrated on the civil engineering works and the son, who was a pupil of Augustus Charles Pugin, on the more purely architectural. John Green died in Newcastle on 30 September 1852. Drawings by John and Benjamin Green are in the Laing Art Gallery, Newcastle upon Tyne.　　　　　　　　PETER LEACH, rev.

Sources Colvin, *Archs.* • H. Hagger, 'The bridges of John Green', *Northern Architect*, 8 (April 1976), 25–31 • R. Welford, *Men of mark 'twixt Tyne and Tweed*, 3 vols. (1895) • IGI

Likenesses T. M. Richardson, watercolour drawings (repro. as lithographs; after his watercolour drawings), Laing Art Gallery, Newcastle

Green, John (1801–1874). *See under* Townsend, George Henry (d. 1869).

Green, John Alfred (1867–1922), educationist, was born on 15 October 1867 in Langset Road, Nether Hallam, near Sheffield, one of the three sons of Walter Green, a grocer and provision dealer, and his wife, Sarah Jane Wild. He attended the elementary school near his home in Parson Cross and then Burton Street council school, where he became a pupil teacher; he went to evening classes at Firth College in Sheffield from 1882 until 1886. He gained further experience at the Borough Road Training College, was appointed a junior tutor there, and was awarded his BA degree in London.

In 1894 Green was appointed lecturer in education at the University College of North Wales, Bangor, and in 1900 he became professor. He was responsible for the day training department of the college, and helped to promote the training of secondary teachers and also that of kindergarten teachers. Outside Bangor he was involved in several educational organizations, including the British Association, and he studied the educational institutions of several continental countries, including Germany. He married Adeliza Norman Johnston, a colleague in the department and the daughter of a Manchester councillor; they had five sons and one daughter.

In 1906 Green returned to his native Sheffield as professor of education at the newly constituted university with an annual salary of £550. He was responsible for the training of secondary teachers and for instruction in advanced psychology and education, and took charge of the newly created department of education. He was awarded the MA degree by the university in 1908. Active in the administration of the new university, he served as dean of the faculty of arts from 1916 to 1919, and was prominent in helping to develop a close relationship between the university and its local community. Some regarded his best work as being in connection with the Sheffield Workers' Educational Association, in which he was a leading figure. In his public roles he was an engaging and direct speaker. From 1917 he was also a member of the Sheffield education committee, where he quickly gained a controversial reputation for his outspoken views as a champion of the principle of free secondary education for all. His other involvements included work with the Froebel Society, the Handwork Association, the Teachers' Registration Council, and the Training College Association. He was regarded as a moderate Liberal in his politics; he was not identified with any religious denomination.

Green's early research was in educational theory and history, especially the ideas of the continental educational reformer J. H. Pestalozzi. His interests turned increasingly to the new developments in educational psychology on the continent after the turn of the century. He became a prominent member of the British Psychological Society and was editor of the *Journal of Experimental Pedagogy* for many years. He was one of the earliest supporters in Britain of the Binet–Simon scheme of psychological tests. His published work included a number of books on Pestalozzi, notably *The Educational Ideas of Pestalozzi* (1907), an edited collection *Pestalozzi's Educational Writings* (1912), and a *Life and Work of Pestalozzi* (1913); he also wrote on psychology and teaching practice (*An Introduction to Psychology: More Especially for Teachers*, with T. Loveday, 1912, and *A Primer of Teaching Practice*, with C. Birchenough, 1914). He was an outstanding teacher with a wide range of audiences and interests, and a strong administrator who helped to establish the study of education at the university level. He was a prominent figure in educational debates at the time of his sudden and early death, from appendicitis, at 64 Clarkegrove Road, Sheffield, on 12 March 1922. He was buried on 15 March at City Road cemetery, Sheffield. His widow, Adeliza Norman Green, became lecturer in education at University College, Southampton. GARY McCULLOCH

Sources *Sheffield Daily Telegraph* (28 Feb 1907) · *Sheffield Daily Telegraph* (27 Sept 1917) · *Sheffield Daily Telegraph* (14 March 1922) · *Sheffield Daily Telegraph* (16 March 1922) · *Sheffield Daily Telegraph* (20 March 1922) · *Sheffield Independent* (14–15 March 1922) · A. W. Chapman, *The story of a modern university: a history of the University of Sheffield* (1955) · *Times Educational Supplement* (18 March 1922) · b. cert. · d. cert.
Archives University of Sheffield
Wealth at death £5648 3s. 1d.: administration with will, 24 April 1922, *CGPLA Eng. & Wales*

Green, John Richard (1837–1883), historian, was born on 12 December 1837 at 5 St John's Street, Oxford, the second of the four children of Richard Green (1799–1852), maker of silk gowns for fellows, and his wife, Rachel Hurdis Green (1801–1881).

Childhood and education, 1837–1860 Green grew up in straitened circumstances in a strongly tory and Anglican household. His small size and delicate health deprived him of the normal boyhood activities, but he displayed an early passion for books and history. In 1852 he suffered the loss of both his father and his beloved elder sister, Adelaide. Placed under the domination of an ultra-conservative uncle who demanded constant gratitude and deference, Green rebelled by adopting outspokenly liberal viewpoints, evidenced in a school history essay sharply criticizing Charles I. This act of defiance resulted in his expulsion in 1854 from Magdalen College School, Oxford, by the headmaster, Dr James Ellison Millard. His preparation for university was completed under the tutelage of James Ridgway (1854) and, more successfully, Charles Duke Yonge (1855), later a professor of English at the University of Belfast.

Green managed to secure a scholarship to Jesus College, Oxford, then perhaps the least distinguished college in a university barely stirring from its pre-reform torpor. After beginning his studies there in 1856, he quickly became disillusioned, read widely on his own, wrote scathing satires of dons and fellow students, and contented himself with a pass degree in 1859. Immediately afterward, he was commissioned by the editors of the *Oxford Chronicle* to write a series of articles on eighteenth-century Oxford life. These vivid pieces, which were published as *Oxford during the Last Century* in 1859, display both Green's considerable narrative gifts and his love of local history and the spirit of municipal liberty. While they were, as Green himself came to recognize, rather too colourfully written,

John Richard Green (1837–1883), by Frederick Sandys, 1882

they were an impressive beginning to his career as a historian. He was, however, deflected from this course by his sudden decision to become a clergyman.

From clergyman to historian, 1860–1874 During his final year at Jesus College, Green had fallen under the spell of A. P. Stanley whose doctrine of ennobling Christian service propelled him into the Anglican priesthood. He was ordained as a deacon on Christmas day 1860 and as a priest exactly a year later—on both occasions by A. C. Tait, bishop of London. With Stanley's friendly encouragement, as well as the active support of Bishop Tait, Green might well have forged an impressive clerical career. Yet, at his own insistence, he spent the next decade working in the most impoverished and demanding parishes of east London, aggravating the tubercular condition that would cause his early death. He served as curate at St Barnabas, Finsbury (1861–3), Holy Trinity, Hoxton (1863–4), and St Peter's, Stepney (1864–5); in 1865 he was appointed incumbent of St Peter's. In addition to his religious duties, Green undertook a gruelling regimen of social work among his parishioners, including the district's many prostitutes. He was also an early developer, together with Edward Denison, of the settlement house idea, and served as a poor-law guardian, a duty he took quite seriously.

Thanks in part to his close friendship with the geologist William Boyd Dawkins, Green had become a disciple of Charles Darwin and was present at the famous 1860 debate between T. H. Huxley and Bishop Samuel Wilberforce. During the years of his east London ministry he took a leading part in the movement to liberalize the

Church of England, including unsuccessful efforts to establish a church liberal association. He ardently defended the views of Anglican critics such as Bishop J. W. Colenso of Natal and the authors of the controversial *Essays and Reviews* (1860). Green strove to bring Church of England doctrines into line with modern science and historical criticism, but the Church's muzzling of dissidents, as well as his own waning faith and physical exhaustion, led him finally to resign his East End living in 1869. He did, however, gratefully accept from Tait, now archbishop of Canterbury, the librarianship of Lambeth Palace, a position he held from 1869 to 1877.

Ensconced at Lambeth and sustained partly by the donations of friends, Green was able to turn his attention wholeheartedly to the writing of history, an ambition he had never abandoned even during the most committed years of his east London ministry. Knowing that his worsening health was likely to cut his life short, he was determined to leave behind him at least one significant historical work. He had presented a paper on Dunstan before the Somerset Archaeological Society in 1862, an occasion important for leading to his reacquaintance with Edward Augustus Freeman, whom he had first met while a pupil at Magdalen College School. The two became close friends. At about the same time Green formed a close and enduring friendship with William Stubbs, whose Teutonist interpretation of English history (that modern concepts of liberty and structures of representative government originated among the Angles, Saxons, and other early Germanic peoples) was, like Freeman's, to have a powerful impact on his views. At Freeman's urging, Green began writing articles and reviews for the *Saturday Review* in 1867. While many of these were light-hearted character sketches and social satire (such as 'Children by the sea' and 'Pretty women'), quite a few were serious historical essays and reviews of the latest historical scholarship. In the latter, Green displayed an often sharp and independent critical judgement, not sparing the works even of friends such as Stanley, Freeman, or Stubbs: his review of Stanley's *Historical Memorials of Westminster Abbey* (1868) was particularly harsh. Freeman looked upon Green as his protégé, and was disappointed that Green refused to take up a project on England under the Angevins, which Freeman saw as a sequel to his own work on the Norman Conquest.

The 'Short History' and its aftermath, 1874–1877 Green had already begun to develop the outline for his *Short History of the English People*, a work that was a natural outgrowth of his increasingly radical political and religious opinions. Nothing short of a general history, which took seriously the 'people' in the title, would serve as a forum for his ardently held beliefs. In his earlier historical essays he had already shown a marked preference for social and cultural history over more traditional political and military accounts. He was encouraged in his new undertaking by the publisher Alexander Macmillan, who provided a handsome advance for what both he and Green thought would be a moderately successful school primer. Both

men were astonished at the enormous popularity of the book after it was published in November 1874. Thirty-two thousand copies were sold in the first year alone, half a million during the ensuing decades, making it second only to T. B. Macaulay's *History of England from the Accession of James II* (1855–61) in its appeal to the reading public. Macmillan generously tore up the original agreement, which had assigned the copyright to him, substituting for it a royalty contract that provided Green with a comfortable income for the rest of his life.

Green's reputation rests almost entirely on the *Short History of the English People*, a book that was extremely influential in the United States as well as throughout the British empire. It also quickly began to supplant the *Student's Hume* as a school manual. Green's vivid story telling powers, as well as his facility in evoking places and characters, made his radical methodology and views palatable to his readers. Informed by a disdain for traditional political and military narratives and a reverence for the common people, the *Short History* was an important milestone in the development of social and cultural history. While monarchs and political leaders are by no means neglected, considerable attention is paid to major literary figures and intellectuals. Town life, and the aspirations and struggles of the lower orders, are treated with particular sympathy. The book does exhibit a reverential tone for the supposedly freedom-loving Anglo-Saxons common to other 'whig' historians of the period, but Green never made the 'germ' theory of modern institutions central to his history. Rather, he depicted a recurring tendency to the formation of oppressive oligarchic structures from which, periodically, ordinary Englishmen had to liberate themselves. He devoted the most space and accorded the greatest significance to the constitutional struggles of the seventeenth century, with an extremely negative view of royalist policies and a corresponding adulation of parliamentary leaders. Similarly, the *Short History* was strongly favourable toward the American War of Independence, and George III had not been as vilified by any historian since Catharine Macaulay.

Aside from some complaints of numerous small errors of fact (corrected in later editions), Green was attacked by conservative critics for denigrating the country's hereditary institutions and proud military traditions. Even supporters such as Freeman, who otherwise praised the *Short History*, found its rejection of monarchical reigns as the organizing principle and its shift of focus away from élites disturbingly unorthodox. Green's politically charged defence of his approach was 'I *won't* divide by Kings, a system whereby History is made Tory unawares and infants are made to hate history' (Brundage, 105). In following years the book came in for increasing criticism from the new class of professional historical writers, for it appeared just as history was being transformed from a branch of literature written by amateurs and antiquaries to a professional, university-based discipline. Green's literary flair, popular tone, and neglect of archival sources made him suspect to the emerging professionals, among whom, increasingly, the currency of academic respectability was the production of heavily documented monographs intended for fellow specialists.

Capitalizing on Green's newly won fame, Macmillan engaged him in a wide range of writing and editorial projects, including the editing of several series of primers (among which was W. E. Gladstone's *Homer* of 1878). Green's reputation also made him a powerful voice in popular Liberal politics. His opinions were quite sympathetic to republicanism, and he considered himself a partisan of Joseph Chamberlain during the latter's most radical phase. Of all the issues of the decade, the Bulgarian atrocities campaign drew him in most deeply. He took his place alongside most of the other major historians of the day in condemning the Disraeli government's support of Turkey. An active member of the Eastern Question Association, he worked alongside James Bryce, William Morris, and Stopford Brooke in writing the association's 1877 manifesto denouncing British policy in the Balkans. Green was strongly opposed to traditional power politics and imperialism, and became an early advocate of Irish home rule. The advanced Liberal positions which he held on the contentious issues of the 1870s clearly reflected the political and social values expressed in the *Short History*.

Marriage and friendships, 1877–1881 The majority of Green's books were published after 1877, the year he married Alice Sophia Amelia Stopford (1847–1929) [*see* Green, Alice Sophia Amelia]. This was no coincidence, for she was a major force in encouraging him in his work and materially assisting in research, editing, and correspondence. Alice, the daughter of Edward Adderley Stopford, archdeacon of Kells, and his wife, Anne Catherine Duke, met Green through her cousin Stopford Augustus Brooke. The marriage took place on 14 June 1877 and proved an extremely happy, though childless, union. With Alice's help, Green produced a four-volume *History of the English People* (1877–80), an expanded version of the *Short History*. The couple co-authored a *Short Geography of the British Islands* (1879), in which Green's characteristic insistence on the importance of geography for history was emphasized. He also edited *Readings from English History* (1879) and *Essays of Joseph Addison* (1880).

With the steady income from his numerous publications, John and Alice Green were able in 1880 to acquire a comfortable Georgian house at 14 Kensington Square, London, where many of the major intellectual figures of the day were frequent visitors. Such friends as Freeman, Stubbs, Bryce, W. E. H. Lecky, Sir Henry Maine, and Mary Ward (Mrs Humphry Ward) were drawn to the house, for Green's conversational powers were of the highest order. His small, wasted frame was animated by a thin, angular face remarkable for its expressiveness, the black eyes reflecting the intense and often irreverent play of his mind on the subject at hand. Both his ardour for life and his sense of humour were highly infectious.

Last years, last works, and death, 1881–1883 Despite his financial and social success, Green still felt the sting of being dismissed as a popularizer and 'picturesque compiler', and was determined to write more scholarly works. His tubercular condition worsened in 1881 and obliged the couple to spend a substantial part of each year in Italy, which had been an annual destination for him since 1870. For the last two years of Green's life, they spent much of their time in a small villa in Mentone. Physicians' warnings of his impending death served as a powerful goad to undertake the more narrowly focused scholarly work he thought necessary to secure his reputation as a serious historian. It was decided to treat the period from the Anglo-Saxon migrations to the completion of the Norman conquest, and Alice suggested splitting the project in two, so that it might be possible to produce at least one book should death cut short his labours. *The Making of England*, published in 1882, was considerably more scholarly than the *Short History*, without sacrificing any of the clarity and power of Green's earlier work. The book also made extensive use of both geography and archaeology, substantial innovations for the time.

With his physical condition deteriorating rapidly, Green and his wife undertook the companion volume, carrying the history forward from the Danish invasions. Green called on the last vestiges of his strength and extraordinary will, dictating chapters to his wife, and even making major revisions after an early version of the book had gone to press. *The Conquest of England* had to be completed by Alice from Green's rough notes, for he died at the Villa St Nicholas, Mentone, Italy (now Menton, France) on 7 March 1883. He was interred in the campo Santo above the town, and on his gravestone was the epitaph he had created for himself years earlier: 'John Richard Green, the historian of the English people. He died learning'.

Influence, achievement, and reputation While Green's final two books failed to achieve for him the scholarly eminence he sought, his popular reputation remained firm for the next half-century. *The Short History* continued to be available in cheap editions, as well as the sumptuous, illustrated four-volume edition (1892–4) prepared by Alice Green and published by Macmillan. The book was frequently on the reading list of the Workers' Education Association, and early Labour MPs cited him as one of the historians who had the most profound impact on their views. *The Letters of John Richard Green*, edited by Leslie Stephen and published in 1901, brought to public attention those qualities of mind and character which his friends found so compelling: his intensity, quickness, nimble mind, wide sympathies, insatiable curiosity, generosity, irreverence, and sense of fun.

Methodologically, Green was going against the grain of the emerging historical profession by his neglect of archival sources. While this was due in part to the delicacy of his health, there were more compelling reasons. He believed that the sudden proliferation of archival materials encouraged 'dryasdust' scholarship. As he put it in an 1868 article in the *Saturday Review*: 'So prodigious has been the store of original documents, charters, rolls, dispatches, which have of late been disinterred from the archives of the past, that history has retrograded into annals'. He viewed the chroniclers, on the other hand, as direct links to the mental climate of the past, as pioneers of a vibrant secular literature, and as voices of the people. However remiss Green may have been in his disdain for archival sources, his use of archaeological evidence and close attention to geography were certainly innovations. In other ways, too, he aspired to infuse historical writing with greater professional rigour. This is evident in his plans for an Oxford historical society, which reflected both his intense local pride and abiding interest in urban history. It can also be seen in his striving to establish a journal of history as a vehicle for new scholarship and criticism. Characteristically, however, he wanted the publication to be a popular shilling monthly instead of the quarterly preferred by James Bryce, the model adopted with the launching of the *English Historical Review* in 1886.

The historians most immediately influenced by Green's approach were his wife, Alice Stopford Green, and Kate Norgate. The former's *Town Life in the Fifteenth Century* (1894) drew heavily on her husband's treatment of the tension between artisans and urban oligarchies, while her *The Making of Ireland and its Undoing* (1908) celebrated the achievements of the Irish people in a manner reminiscent of the *Short History*. Norgate dedicated her *England under the Angevin Kings* (1887) to 'the memory of my dear and honoured master John Richard Green'. This book may be considered the treatment of the Angevin period that Green had long been urged by Freeman to write as a sequel to his own work on the Norman conquest. Some of the other historians affected by Green's work were J. A. R. Marriott, A. F. Pollard, A. P. Newton, and, in the United States, Charles Beard. His wider influence in the historical profession was more diffuse, often unacknowledged, and frequently misunderstood. Attempts to cluster him with Freeman, Stubbs, and other 'whig' historians miss the distinctiveness of his approach to the past. Green was clearly a crucial figure in the transition to forms of history writing that shifted the focus from politics and warfare to society and culture.   ANTHONY BRUNDAGE

Sources *The letters of John Richard Green*, ed. L. Stephen (1901) · A. Brundage, *The people's historian: John Richard Green and the writing of history in Victorian England* (1994) · R. Jann, *The art and science of Victorian history* (1985) · J. W. Burrow, *A liberal descent: Victorian historians and the English past* (1981) · R. L. Schuyler, 'John Richard Green and his short history', *Political Science Quarterly*, 64 (1949), 321–54 · P. B. M. Blaas, *Continuity and anachronism* (1978) · R. B. McDowell, *Alice Stopford Green: a passionate historian* (1967) · W. G. Addison, *J. R. Green* (1946)
Archives BL, Macmillan archives · BL, notebooks, Add. MSS 40169–40172 · Jesus College, Oxford, corresp. and papers · LPL, corresp., MSS 1725 · LPL, historical notes and draft | BL, corresp. with Macmillans, Add. MS 55058 · Bodl. Oxf., Bryce MSS · Jesus College, Oxford, letters to Sir William Boyd Dawkins · NL Ire., Alice Stopford Green papers
Likenesses Alinari brothers, photograph, 1869, repro. in Stephen, ed., *Letters of John Richard Green*, frontispiece · F. Sandys, watercolour drawing, 1882, Macmillan Publishers [*see illus.*] · Alinari brothers, photographs, Jesus College, Oxford, Green MSS · G. J. Stodart, stipple (after F. Sandys), BM, NPG · engraving (after pencil sketch by F. Sandys), repro. in J. R. Green, *The conquest of England* (1883)

Wealth at death £3339 16s. 11d.: probate, 3 April 1883, CGPLA Eng. & Wales

Green, Jonathan (1787/8–1864), surgeon, was probably born in or near Brosely, Shropshire, from where he acquired provincial membership of the Royal College of Surgeons on 7 December 1810, at the age of twenty-two. Following several years as a surgeon in the Royal Navy, he settled in London and set up practice in 1822 with a suite of 'fumigating baths' at 5 Bury Street, St James's, London.

The study of skin diseases and their treatment through various types of bathing (hot, warm, or cold) was then an expanding surgical specialism pioneered by London surgeon Robert Willan, who produced a systematic classification of cutaneous diseases. Green records that Willan and others set up an Institute for the Treatment of Cutaneous Diseases in Marlborough Street, which included a suite of fumigating or vapour baths. Having, as Green explained, seen 'a near relative of mine … receive such immediate and permanent relief, from the use of Fumigating Baths as to occasion me much satisfaction, and also a great desire to investigate them more minutely' (Green, *Fumigating Baths*, iii), he went to Paris for a year to study the installations of Drs Gales and d'Arcet in French government hospitals. His account of the visit, *The utility and importance of fumigating baths illustrated, or, A series of facts and remarks, shewing the origin, progress and final establishment (by order of the French government) of the practise of fumigations for the cure of various diseases*, was published in 1823.

Green's Bury Street practice provided baths for the 'higher ranks of society … not exempt from this tormenting class of diseases' (Green, *Fumigating Baths*, iii), who could not be accepted at the institute, which was a charity for the poor. Like any spa doctor Green treated not only chronic muscular conditions which responded to heat, such as palsy, gout, or rheumatism, but also the surgeon's staples such as psoriasis, leprosy, and syphilis. The fumigating bath was a steam bath of hot vapour mixed with aromatic herbs, or mineral salts of sulphur, chlorine, or mercury. The patient had a waxed cloth hung round him to the neck and with vapours rising from below, sweated for 5 to 12 minutes before the final drying treatments. Sulphur fumigations, which caused the top layer of skin to peel off 'as in a fever' were considered to be particularly effective.

Green also patented a successful domestic or portable vapour bath, and in 1825 moved to a larger suite at 40 Great Marlborough Street, London. The peak of his career, in the 1830s, was marked by the publication of *Some Observations on the Utility of Fumigating and other Baths* (1831, 2nd edn 1835). He obtained an MD from Heidelberg in 1834, and in 1835 was elected a fellow of the Royal Medical and Surgical Society. He worked closely with the London hospitals, treating patients from St George's, the Middlesex, and several other hospitals and infirmaries, where he was also asked to set up fumigating suites of baths. His last work, *An Improved Method of Employing Mercury* (1852) indicates an increasing reliance on syphilis patients, probably to the detriment of his practice. Mercury baths, he claimed, were not only 'more pleasant and cleaner' but the patient could 'proceed with his cure in secret, that is, without the knowledge or exposure to servants, observing friends, or talking washerwomen, as in cases when we influence the system by rubbing in blue ointment' (Green, *An Improved Method of Employing Mercury*, 16).

For whatever reason, between 1852 and 1864 Green's practice failed, and he finally entered Charterhouse, London (a foundation for destitute but worthy old gentlemen and ex-members of the armed services), presumably without any family to support him. He died there on 23 February 1864 at the age of seventy-six.   VIRGINIA SMITH

Sources J. Green, *The utility and importance of fumigating baths illustrated* (1823) · J. Green, *An improved method of employing mercury* (1852) · *GM*, 3rd ser., 16 (1864), 537 · *A general list of the members of the Royal College of Surgeons London* (1812) · Boase, *Mod. Eng. biog.*
Wealth at death died destitute: *GM*

Green, Joseph Frederick (1855–1932), peace campaigner and politician, was born on 5 July 1855 at 12A Myddelton Square, Clerkenwell, London, the son of Joseph Edwin Green JP (*c*.1830–*c*.1900), merchant and member of Lloyds, and his wife, Hannah Rosa, formerly How. He was descended from John Green, MP for Essex and speaker of the House of Commons in 1461. On 31 December 1898 he married Eliza Emma Claydon from Norwich (*b*. 1866); they had no children.

Green was educated at Islington proprietary school, St Mary Hall, Oxford, and King's College, London. He was ordained in 1880 and was curate of St Mary's, Tothill Fields, London, from 1880 to 1886, but 'abandoned the clerical profession in the latter year' (*WWW*), devoted himself to politics, and became an influential figure in a number of overlapping radical circles. Like others he was also involved in the search for doctrines of ethics and morality based on rationalism, which, for him, led to positivism. He was chairman of the English Positivist Committee from 1923 to 1931.

Green's two most important roles were in the International Arbitration and Peace Association, of which he was honorary secretary (1886–1917) and editor of its journal *Concord* (1905–14), and the Society of Friends of Russian Freedom, whose monthly journal, *Free Russia*, he co-edited for twenty years.

Green was never a pacifist in the strict sense, and he shared the positivist dislike of Cobden's doctrine of 'no foreign politics'. He was strongly internationalist, was frequently a delegate at international peace and socialist conferences, and was in favour of the establishment of international institutions, such as the court at The Hague, to settle international disputes by arbitration. He was anti-imperialist and favoured the democratic control of foreign policy but supported defensive war when all else failed. Despotic Russia was a threat to peace; only a democratic regime could bring a peaceful approach to international relations and liberate the talents of its people.

For a time Green was on the executive committee of the Fabian Society (but resigned over its support for the Second South African War), was treasurer of the Social Democratic Federation (later the Social Democratic Party), which he left in 1911, and was secretary of the British

national committee of the Second International (1905–8). He was on the committee of the Humanitarian League and was prospective socialist candidate for Rossendale, Lancashire (1907), and Bristol (1908).

Green described himself in his first appearance in *Who's Who* in 1907 as 'an active socialist propagandist and frequent lecturer on socialist and humanitarian subjects'. S. G. Hobson (p. 124) described him as:

> one of the most interesting of the minor personalities of the Socialist movement … He was bald as a billiard ball, clean shaven, his profile circumstantial evidence of the Darwinian hypothesis. With a small private income, a large fund of good stories in four or five languages, a broad sense of humour with an equally broad grin … to Green's house, or, as his guests, at the National Liberal Club, came the malcontents of Europe … Malatesta of Italy, Ferrer the Spanish educationalist … and many others including Bernstein … He died at an outrageous age and looked about fifty.

Green became a principled supporter of the First World War in 1914 over what he saw as Germany's sudden and brutal attack on Belgium and France but moved to the right and became more enthusiastic as time passed; the *Who's Who* of 1919 records him as 'a strong supporter of the war'. He joined the Socialist National Defence Committee, set up to counter Independent Labour Party opposition to the war, and was chairman of the executive committee of the National Democratic Party, founded in 1918 to bring together supporters of the Lloyd George coalition government within the labour movement.

In the 1918 general election Green defeated Ramsay MacDonald at Leicester West on a National Democratic and coalition ticket by 20,570 votes to 6347, but he was defeated in 1922. He was a conscientious parliamentarian. In the short 1919 session, for example, he asked nineteen parliamentary questions on national and international matters, and in the next session he made twenty-two interventions on the Operation of Profiteering Bill. He was parliamentary private secretary to the Conservative transport minister Sir Eric Geddes from 1920 to 1921. After 1922 he joined the Conservative Party, worked in Conservative central office, and spent time on good works and a range of artistic and literary matters. He died of kidney failure at his home, 32 Upper Mall, Hammersmith, on 1 May 1932, and was survived by his wife.

ROBERT GOMME

Sources *WWBMP*, vol. 3 · *WW* (1907–32) · P. Laity, 'The British peace movement, 1896–1916: ideas and dilemmas', DPhil diss., U. Oxf., 1995 · B. Hollingsworth, 'The Society of Friends of Russian Freedom: English liberals and Russian socialists, 1890–1917', *Oxford Slavonic Papers*, new ser., 3 (1970), 45–64 · A. J. A. Morris, *Radicalism against war, 1906–14* (1972) · R. Grant, 'The Society of Friends of Russian Freedom (1890–1917): a case study in internationalism', *Journal of the Scottish Labour History Society*, 3 (Nov 1970), 1–23, esp. 15 · *Concord* [International Arbitration and Peace Association] · *Free Russia* · *Positivist Review* · S. G. Hobson, *Pilgrim to the left: memoirs of a modern revolutionist* (1938), 123–37 · D. J. Newton, *British labour, European socialism, and the struggle for peace, 1889–1914* (1985) · S. Cooper, *Patriotic pacifism: waging war on war in Europe, 1815–1914* (1991) · *The Times* (3 May 1932) · P. Laity, *The British peace movement, 1870–1914* (2001) · M. Ceadel, *Semi-detached idealists: the British peace* *movement and international relations, 1854–1945* (2000) • b. cert. • m. cert. • d. cert. • *WWW* • *CGPLA Eng. & Wales* (1932)

Archives People's History Museum, Manchester, corresp. relating to international affairs | BLPES, National Peace Council records • BLPES, peace yearbooks

Likenesses portrait, repro. in *XVII Universal Peace Conference, London, 1908: official report* (1909) • portrait, repro. in *The Times*

Wealth at death £9247 14s.: probate, 25 June 1932, *CGPLA Eng. & Wales*

Green, Joseph Henry (1791–1863), surgeon and natural philosopher, was born on 1 November 1791 at the family home, 11 London Wall, London, and was baptized on 12 December 1791 at St Alfege, London Wall. He was the only child of Joseph Green (1765?–1834), a successful London merchant who later headed the shipping firm of Green and Ross on St Martin's Lane, off Cannon Street, and Frances Cline, sister of the prominent London surgeon Henry *Cline (1750–1827).

Green's biographer, John Simon, the public health official, reports that after a sickly childhood his primary education was conducted at schools in Ramsgate and Hammersmith. All biographies have recorded, without documentation, that he then travelled with his mother to the German states, principally Hanover (some sources state Berlin), from 1806 to the end of 1809, where they were occasionally joined by his father. The decision of a British family to travel to these regions of Europe at a time of considerable political uncertainty (the French invasion of Prussia and other German territories had commenced on 7 October 1806, with the capture of Berlin on October 26) must be considered unusual. Green is not listed as a matriculated student at the University of Göttingen, Hanover, a popular location for foreign medical study by British students in the late eighteenth and early nineteenth century, where medical theorist Johann Blumenbach was regularly lecturing. Green's awareness of Blumenbach's medical theories is, however, evident in his early surgical lectures (see *The Lancet*, 8 Oct 1825).

Upon his return to England Green began a surgical apprenticeship at St Thomas's Hospital under his uncle Henry Cline. Following the retirement of the senior Cline in 1812 he continued as an apprentice of his cousin Henry Cline jun., who assumed his father's surgeonship. During this period he met Anne Eliza Hammond (*fl.* 1790–1870), sister of his fellow apprentice William Hammond, and they were married on 25 May 1813. They lived at 6 Martin Lane until 1816. Green received his surgeon's licence from the Royal College of Surgeons on 1 December 1815, and the couple moved in 1816 to 22 Lincoln's Inn Fields. They moved to 46 Lincoln's Inn Fields in the 1820s and remained there until moving to an estate, The Mount, at Hadley, near Barnet, north of London in Middlesex in 1836, where they spent their remaining years.

Green delivered his initial surgical lectures as demonstrator of anatomy at St Thomas's along with Henry Cline the younger and the eminent Astley Cooper. Socialized into the community of Hunterian surgical medicine, Green established a growing reputation as an expert surgeon, with particular skill in ophthalmology and lithotomy.

Joseph Henry Green (1791–1863), by Thomas Phillips, exh. RA 1829

Green's deeper engagement with German thought in the spring and summer of 1817 reflected in part the growing appreciation of German intellectual and cultural life in Britain that followed the end of the Napoleonic wars and the stimulation given to the study of German culture in England by Germaine De Stael's immensely popular *On Germany*, published first in French in London in the autumn of 1814, quickly followed by an English translation in early 1815. This Germanophilia had been further encouraged by the publication of Coleridge's *Biographia literaria* in the summer of 1817. Green's serious study of German philosophical literature can be dated specifically from his contact with a group of London Germanophiles on 13 June 1817 when he met the visiting German scholar Johann Ludwig Tieck, who had come to England to do literary research. Green's acquaintance with Samuel Taylor Coleridge can be definitively dated from this time as well. As a result of these conversations with Tieck, Green and his wife travelled to Berlin in October of that year to undertake a private tutorial in philosophy with Tieck's close friend Karl Wilhelm Ferdinand Solger, of the University of Berlin, a disciple of Schelling and a philosopher of aesthetics. They remained in Prussia until late in the year.

The content of Green's study with Solger has been impossible to determine, but his subsequent work suggests that he was most likely engaged in a systematic study either of the synthetic and dynamic *Naturphilosophie* of Schelling or the works of Kant. The sale catalogue of Green's private library listed none of Solger's works, but it did list the primary works on *Naturphilosophie* by Schelling and several works of Kant, some of which were bequeathed by Green to Derwent Coleridge, later to form part of the Coleridge collection at the British Library. Many of these works contain annotations by Coleridge. Whatever the nature of the study of German philosophy in these years, Green's subsequent writings display a familiarity with the efforts of Kant and his successors to attain a unity of natural science, aesthetics, and theology in a form that bears little relation to contemporary British philosophical traditions.

Upon his return to London, Green began attending Coleridge's Shakespeare lectures at a hall in Fleur-de-Luce Court that commenced on 27 January 1818, and in April he initiated weekly private tutorials with Coleridge that continued until the poet's death on 25 July 1834. Surviving correspondence and manuscript materials demonstrate that the interactions of Green and Coleridge were deep and substantial. By December of 1817 they were corresponding on Kant's philosophy and the deficiencies of Schelling's system. Green began in 1818 to take the dictation of Coleridge's philosophical thoughts that were to appear later publicly in such of Coleridge's works as his *Confessions of an Inquiring Spirit* (1849), and he took down the dictation comprising the manuscript of his unpublished 'Opus maximum' and several of his other philosophical treatises. Green's more disciplined, medical, and anatomical perspective, and his deeper knowledge of the scientific materials can be measured against Coleridge's imaginative philosophical speculations, deeply indebted to German sources, that fill his unpublished philosophical manuscripts. Green's mature scientific and medical thought also owes a great debt to these interactions with Coleridge, with some evidence that Coleridge may have even supplied material for Green's surgical lectures. Green was also able to discipline the views of his mentor and apply his insights, along with those of other German philosophical writers he had studied, systematically to concrete issues in the life sciences. It is reported that Green's portrait hung over the fireplace in Coleridge's home in Highgate.

Green's importance as a biological theorist with a powerful synthetic vision of the life sciences was first displayed to the public in his position as the prestigious Hunterian professor of comparative anatomy at the Royal College of Surgeons in Lincoln's Inn Fields, a post to which he was appointed in July 1823, succeeding Benjamin Collins Brodie sen. His lectures began on 30 March 1824, and over a course of five years Green surveyed the comparative anatomy of the invertebrates (1824), the fishes (1825), reptiles (1826), birds (1827), and mammals (1828). These lectures presented his illustrious audience of surgeons, physicians, and London dignitaries with a comprehensive course in philosophical comparative anatomy of remarkable scope.

Organizing these lectures was a theoretical framework, transported largely from German sources, and refracted through Coleridge, that conceived of nature both as process and product, with the connection between these two aspects achieved by appeal to Blumenbach's notion of the formative force (*Bildungstrieb*). Through this dynamic model Green sought to reconcile George Cuvier's static and descriptive analysis of the animal kingdom as a series of discrete and discontinuous groups with the new historical and genetic view of animal relationship expounded by Jean Baptiste Lamarck. This relationship he conceived as best represented through the metaphor of a branching tree. In 1825 he was elected to the Royal Society of London.

Green's studies of the German authors and his tutorials with Coleridge also seem to have been fundamental in the extension of his teaching and research into the realm of art and aesthetics. In 1825 he was appointed to the position of anatomist to the Royal Academy of Art, a position that he held until 1852. In these lectures he expounded both on the fundamentals of anatomy and on the philosophy of aesthetics (as in, for example, *The Athenaeum*, 23 Dec 1843, 2, 16).

Green's growing prominence in British medical circles resulted in his appointment as the first professor of surgery at the new King's College, London, in 1830, at which time he resigned his professorship at St Thomas's Hospital. At King's he joined an illustrious faculty that included, by 1831, Charles Lyell, whose first series of geology lectures Green attended in the spring of 1832. Beginning in 1831 Green commenced a series of public discourses that were to develop his ideal of a unified approach to surgical education that would connect the profession of surgery with liberal learning, advancing 'surgery from a mechanical art to the rank of a liberal profession' (J. H. Green, *Distinction without Separation*, 1831, 13).

In his inaugural lecture of 1 October 1832 ('An address delivered in King's College, London', 1832), Green expanded on his synthetic approach to learning and culture. Reflecting the importance of Coleridge's conception of national leadership by an élite 'clerisy', Green further sought to relate medicine and surgery to liberal education, theology, and the concept of interrelated professions. He also opposed in this address utilitarian and craft conceptions of medical training.

Green's growing importance as a public medical figure was confirmed early on by his being called to testify to the royal commission on the evils of the factory system in 1832, and through his appointment to a series of medical offices. In 1835 he was made a councillor to the Royal College of Surgeons, in 1846 he was appointed to the board of medical examiners, and in 1849 and 1858 served as its president. In 1853 he was made an honorary doctor of civil law at Oxford.

Upon Coleridge's death Green and Henry Nelson Coleridge assumed the task of co-editing Coleridge's literary remains, with Green's primary responsibility the philosophical writings. An inheritance received on his father's death in 1834 enabled him to resign his professorship at King's in 1836 and he and Anne moved to Hadley. Except for his infrequent lectures at the Academy of Art, his teaching career ended in 1836, but Green continued to serve London medicine in many official capacities until his death.

Green's developing systematic philosophical views, drawn in part from his work on the Coleridge materials, were expressed publicly in two important Hunterian orations: one, 'Vital dynamics' (February 1840), presented his philosophy of science and his theory of vital forces; the second, 'Mental dynamics' (February 1847), treated issues of psychology and theory of instinct from a Coleridgean perspective. Reactions of contemporary reviewers, however, suggest that his hearers no longer related to his synthesis of Coleridge and German philosophy.

Green and H. N. Coleridge jointly brought to press Coleridge's *Confessions of an Inquiring Spirit* in 1849, with a 53-page introduction by Green. Delays in the publication of Coleridge's remaining manuscript works resulted in charges by C. Mansfield Ingleby that Green was illegitimately hoarding a large body of important manuscripts. He responded with the claim that all relevant Coleridge manuscripts had been published, and the main remaining manuscripts contained 'a philosophical *Cosmogony*, which I fear is scarcely adapted for scientific readers, or corresponds to the requirements of modern science' (Green, 544). However, he announced at this time his plan to present his own exposition of Coleridge's philosophical views. Green's original introduction to this work was published only in 1995. A philosophical synthesis of Coleridge's philosophy, the two-volume *Spiritual Philosophy*, was left in manuscript form at his death and was seen to press by his biographer and disciple John Simon in 1865. The first volume of this work expounded Coleridge's epistemological principles, the relation of reason to experience, his theory of induction, and his dialectical logic. The second volume developed Coleridge's theology. Unfortunately, by 1865 Coleridge's views had long since lost their broad appeal, and the work essentially fell stillborn from the press, compared unfavourably to the writings of John Stuart Mill (*Fortnightly Review*, 3, 1866, 384).

Green died of congestive heart failure at his home, The Mount, Hadley, on 13 December 1863 and was buried at Highgate cemetery. At the time of death he was president of the Council of Medical Education and Registration, a member of the council of the Royal College of Surgeons, a member of the board of examiners in dentistry, and chairman of the Medical and Clerical Life Assurance Company. His wife, Anne, survived him. There were no children. No sizeable body of Green's manuscripts has been uncovered. Copies of several of his lectures on comparative anatomy in William Clift's hand were deposited in the library of the Royal College of Surgeons, London. Several letters and Coleridge manuscripts in Green's hand are in the Coleridge archives at Victoria College at the University of Toronto. The Egerton Coleridge manuscripts at the British Library include Coleridge's comments on Green's surgical lectures. A Sothebys sale catalogue of his library was published in 1880.   PHILLIP R. SLOAN

Sources J. Simon, 'Memoir of the author's life', in J. H. Green, *Spiritual philosophy: founded on the teaching of the late Samuel Taylor*

Coleridge, ed. J. Simon, 2 vols. (1865), i–lxi · H. J. Jackson, 'Coleridge's collaborator, Joseph Henry Green', *Studies in Romanticism*, 21 (1982), 161–79 · V. G. Plarr, *Plarr's Lives of the fellows of the Royal College of Surgeons of England*, rev. D'A. Power, 2 vols. (1930) · *Medical Times and Gazette* (19 Dec 1863), 650–52 · R. L. Kilpatrick, 'Nature's schools: the Hunterian revolution in London hospital medicine, 1780–1825', PhD diss., U. Cam., 1986 · P. R. Sloan, introduction, in *Richard Owen's Hunterian lectures in comparative anatomy: May–June 1837* (1992), 3–72 · S. T. Coleridge, *Shorter works and fragments*, ed. H. J. Jackson and J. R. de J. Jackson, 2 vols. (1995) · *Sale catalogue of the library of the late Joseph Henry Green* (1880) [Sothebys] · *The manuscript papers of British scientists, 1600–1940* (1982) · R. M. MacLeod and J. R. Friday, *Archives of British men of science* (1972) [microfiche] · *Henry Crabb Robinson on books and their writers*, ed. E. J. Morley, 3 vols. (1938) · J. D. Campbell, *Samuel Taylor Coleridge: a narrative of the events of his life*, 2nd edn (1896) · J. Winsor, 'Notes on Cline's lectures taken by James Winsor, surgeon, Liverpool', National Library of Medicine, Bethesda, Maryland, MS #A B 59 C1HMO/MS · G. H. Lewes, 'Review of *Spiritual philosophy*', *Fortnightly Review*, 3 (1866), 383–4 · C. M. Ingleby, 'Coleridge's unpublished MSS', *N&Q*, 8 (1853), 43 · C. M. Ingleby, 'Coleridge's unpublished MSS', *N&Q*, 9 (1854), 496–7 · J. H. Green, 'Coleridge's unpublished manuscripts', *N&Q*, 9 (1854), 543–4 · R. Lambert, *Sir John Simon, 1816–1904, and English social administration* (1963) · A. Desmond, *The politics of evolution: morphology, medicine and reform in radical London* (1989) · private information (2004) [research archivist, Dr Haenel, Georg-August-Universität Göttingen; Professor Heather Jackson, Victoria College, University of Toronto] · Z. Cope, *The Royal College of Surgeons of England: a history* (1959) · microfilm of St Alfege parish register general, 1732–1812 · R. Holmes, *Coleridge: darker reflections* (1998)

Archives National Library of Medicine, Bethesda, Maryland, archives · RCS Eng., lecture notes · St Thomas's Hospital, London, hospital archives | BL, Egerton MSS, Coleridge MSS · University of Toronto, Victoria University, Coleridge MSS

Likenesses T. Phillips, oils, exh. RA 1829, RCS Eng. [see illus.] · Beynon & Co., colour lithograph, Wellcome L. · G. H. Lynch, lithograph (after G. F. Teniswood), BM, Wellcome L. · H. Weekes, marble busts, RA, RCS Eng. · marble statue, St Thomas's Hospital, London

Wealth at death under £45,000: probate, 19 Feb 1864, *CGPLA Eng. & Wales*

Green, Sir Justly Watson, second baronet (1755–1826). *See under* Green, Sir William, first baronet (1725–1811).

Green, Mary (1776–1845). *See under* Green, James (1771–1834).

Green [*née* Wood], **Mary Anne Everett** (1818–1895), historian, was born on 19 July 1818 in Sheffield, the second of six children of the Revd Robert Wood (1787–1851), Wesleyan Methodist minister, and his wife, Sarah, *née* Bateson (1795–1866). The Woods descended from the Dulverton branch of the Sydenham family, according to Green's own research, published with the Revd Frederick Brown as *Extracts from Pedigrees of the Sydenham Family* (1884). Her grandfather James Wood was twice president of the Wesleyan conference and author of a *Dictionary of the Bible* (1804). During her childhood her father served Methodist congregations in various towns, including Sheffield (1818–23), Bristol (1823–8), York (1828–9), and Salford, Manchester (1829–40). Her linguistic and historical skills were developed early in her life by her father, whose engaging educational methods she described in a *Memorial of the Rev. Robert Wood, Wesleyan Minister* (privately printed in 1854),

Mary Anne Everett Green (1818–1895), by George Pycock Green

and through contact with her father's friends, including James Montgomery and James Everett, after whom she was named. In 1841 her father was assigned to a congregation in Islington and the family moved to 7 Upper Gower Street, London (later 100 Gower Street), where she lived for the rest of her life. In the British Museum reading-room and other London libraries and archives she began the research that led to her first published works. Though the composition of *Lives of the Princesses* began as early as 1843, her publisher, Coburn, delayed its publication (1849–55) until the completion of Agnes Strickland's *Lives of the Queens of England* in 1848. This delay proved propitious. On 27 September 1845 she married the artist George Pycock Green (1811–1893) and six months later published *Letters of Royal and Illustrious Ladies* (2 vols., 1846) under her maiden name Mary Anne Everett Wood. Her husband's artistic study took her to Paris and Antwerp, where she substantially revised her *Lives of the Princesses*, drawing on materials in continental archives. Covering the period from the Norman conquest to the daughters of Charles I, *Lives of the Princesses* garnered Green praise for her archival research and scholarly method. Her acknowledgements in the first volume are a veritable who's who of antiquaries, archivists, and librarians in Britain and Paris, including Dawson Turner (to whom the work was dedicated), Sir Thomas Phillipps, M. Guizot, and Sir Francis Palgrave (then of the Record Commission), suggesting not only the extent of Green's researches but also her entry into the field of historical scholarship. In 1851 Green added her name to those of Dickens, Carlyle, Macaulay, Agnes Strickland, Ainsworth, and S. R. Maitland, who were petitioning for free access to the public records for literary researchers.

Sir Francis Palgrave was highly impressed with Green when she conducted research in the archives of the Record Commission and on 17 May 1845 sent his father-in-law, Dawson Turner, the young historian's autograph, writing 'her knowledge of ancient records etc. is truly wonderful' (Cantwell, 170–71). As the first deputy keeper of the Public Record Office, Palgrave recommended Green to the master of the rolls, John Romilly, who in 1854 appointed her the first of four external editors of calendars of state papers. Shortly thereafter Romilly also appointed the Revd John Brewer, John Bruce, and Markham John Thorpe. Over the next forty years Green became the most prolific and among the most highly respected of the editors involved in this monumental government project.

When she was approached for the calendars editorship, Green, then aged thirty-six, was editing the diary of John Rous, which was eventually published in 1856. She accepted the appointment, noting her husband's approval, and began work in 1855 at the state paper office. Despite giving birth to a daughter in November 1856, and being assisted in her calendaring work only by her sister Esther Wood, when other editors were provided with staff assistants, Green proved to be the most efficient compiler of calendars, and in 1857 the first volume of *Calendar of State Papers, Domestic, James I* appeared, with its editor identified as Mary Anne Everett Green, 'author of the *Lives of the Princesses of England*'. In the same year she published the *Life and Letters of Henrietta Maria*. She continued at the pace of more than a calendar volume a year for the next thirty-eight years (she edited forty-one volumes in total), while bringing up four children: Robert (1847–1876), Gertrude (b. 1856), Eveline (b. 1857), and Constance (b. 1859). Green became a fixture at the Public Record Office, remembered for her indefatigable work habits as well as for feeding pigeons on the steps of the officers' chambers (Cantwell, 343).

Green edited (in order of publication) the *Calendar of State Papers, Domestic* of James I (4 vols., 1857–9), Charles II (vols. 1–7, 1860–66), and Elizabeth I (vols. 3–8 and 12, 1867–72), of the Interregnum (13 vols., 1875–85), the *Proceedings of the Committee for the Advance of Money* (3 parts, 1888), the *Proceedings of the Committee for Compounding with Delinquents* (5 parts, 1889–92), and the *Calendar of State Papers, Domestic* of Charles II (vols. 8–10, 1893–5). From the outset reviewers praised not only Green's scholarship, but also her ability to bring documents to life. It was in the reviews of the volumes of *Calendar of State Papers, Domestic* of Elizabeth (which she took over after the death of Robert Lemon), however, that Green's more detailed, comprehensive, and accurate methods of abstracting documents were promoted as the standard for calendaring. So definitive did Green's practice become that when C. S. Knighton came to re-edit Lemon's calendars in 1992, he denied to the very person who had defined 'calendar' that designation for his own work: 'it is far from being a calendar as that term has come to be understood and would now be known as a descriptive list' (*Calendar of State Papers, Domestic, Edward VI*, 1992, vii). Conversely, Knighton explained that his new calendar did not include descriptions of Edwardine documents in the *Calendar of State Papers, Domestic, Addenda Edward VI to James I*, 'as they were well and fully described by M. A. E. Green in the *Calendar of State Papers, Domestic Series, 1601–1609; with Addenda, 1547–1565* (London, 1870)' (ibid.).

Throughout this distinguished and prolific career as a calendarer, Green struggled with a succession of deputy keepers and masters of the rolls over matters of editorial practice and her own payment, which she argued lagged behind that of her male colleagues. Perhaps her most important victory was her first: in accepting Romilly's invitation to undertake the editorship of state papers, Green offered to write historical prefaces to each volume, which Romilly initially rejected. After some negotiation he relented, and the prefaces by Green and other editors became an integral part of the calendars—and of reviewers' responses to them. Ultimately, Green wrote over 700 pages of prefaces for her forty-one volumes, treating with vivid detail and careful judgement subjects ranging from the restoration of the monarchy and great fire to petitions from royalists' widows. Even her indexes to the Interregnum volumes, astonishingly listing every participant in committee activities, could be animated. Of them David Masson wrote that:

> the labour of Mrs. Green in these Calendars is nothing less than that of driving a whole population of the defunct before her from month to month, knowing all the chief of them familiarly by head-mark, and accurately noting the casual appearances and disappearances of the less well known. (*The Academy*, 20 May 1876)

Green's work on the state papers prevented her from completing research she had begun for a biography of the electress Sophia and for lives of the queens of the house of Hanover. Her notes for the latter project she turned over to her friend A. W. Ward shortly before her death. Green's son had died in 1876, and her husband in 1893. Green died on 1 November 1895 at her home in Gower Street, London, while attempting to finish the project begun by her colleague John Bruce almost forty years earlier: calendaring the state papers of Charles I. This volume was completed by her niece Sophia Crawford Lomas, whom she had trained. Green had survived not only Bruce but all the major figures who had been involved from the early stages with the calendaring of state papers: Brewer, Thorpe, Romilly, and Palgrave, as well as T. D. Hardy, who followed Palgrave as deputy keeper. At Green's death in 1895 Lomas succeeded her aunt at the Public Record Office but, as John Cantwell notes, 'with the exception of the part-time cleaners and the ladies' attendant [Lomas] was the only female on the strength' (Cantwell, 351).

Of Green's daughters, Evelyn Ward Everett *Green became a prolific novelist, Gertrude married Dr James

Gow, headmaster of Westminster School, and Constance, unmarried at her mother's death, was the chief beneficiary of Green's will. Green was buried in Highgate cemetery on 6 November 1895.   CHRISTINE L. KRUEGER

Sources M. A. E. Green, *Memorial of the Rev. Robert Wood* (1854) • J. D. Cantwell, *The Public Record Office, 1838–1958* (1991) • R. A. Mitchell, '"The busy daughters of Clio": women writers of history from 1820–1880', *Women's Historical Review*, 7/1 (1998), 107–34 • P. Levine, *The amateur and the professional: antiquarians, historians and archaeologists in Victorian England* (1986) • correspondence, PRO, PRO 1/19 • S. R. Gardiner and J. B. Mullinger, *Introduction to the study of English history*, 2nd edn (1882) • *DNB* • F. Brown and M. A. E. Green, *Extracts from pedigrees of the Sydenham family* (1884) • W. Odom, *Hallamshire worthies* (1926) • *Men of the times: a dictionary of … biographical notices … of both sexes* (1875) • will • R. A. Mitchell, *Picturing the past: English history in text and image, 1830–1870* (2000) • m. cert.
Archives BL, letters and notes • Bodl. Oxf., papers relating to history of Hanoverian queens • CUL, extracts, mainly from corresp., and historical notes | Bodl. Oxf., corresp. with Sir Thomas Phillipps • PRO, Phillipps-Robinson MSS, 1/19 • U. Edin., letters to David Laing
Likenesses G. P. Green, chalk drawing, NPG [*see illus.*]
Wealth at death £782: probate, 14 Nov 1895, *CGPLA Eng. & Wales*

Green, Matthew (1696–1737), poet, is said to have been born into a dissenting family in London, but the puritanical strictness of the sect wearied him, so that he took up 'some free notions on religious subjects' (*European Magazine*). He held a post in the custom house, where he discharged his duty diligently; and died, aged forty-one, in 1737, at a lodging in Nag's Head Court, Gracechurch Street, London.

A few anecdotes are recorded in the *European Magazine* to show that he was a witty and pleasant companion. When an allowance for supplying the custom house cats with milk was threatened by the authorities he wrote a successful petition in their name. When a waterman insulted a Quaker friend as he was bathing, the friend wondered how his sect could be detected when he had no clothes. Green immediately replied that the waterman detected him by his swimming against the stream. His poem 'On Barclay's Apology for the Quakers' (1735) implies that he admired the Quakers, but lacked the independence of means needed to follow them.

Green's wit is shown more decisively by *The Spleen*. The poem appeared posthumously in 1737, with a preface by his friend Richard Glover. It is a light-hearted poem in octosyllabic couplets, giving Green's recipes for avoiding ill humour and expressing a wish for a tranquil, retired life. His wit and graceful ease of versification derive from the tradition of such poems as Matthew Prior's *Alma*. Johnson objected that *The Spleen* was 'not poetry', but its conversational informality has appealed to others (Boswell, *Life*, 3.38). A poem called *The Grotto* (on Queen Caroline's grotto at Richmond) was privately printed in 1732. Green's use of the pseudonym Peter Drake, a Fisherman of Brentford, is a comic allusion to Stephen Duck, the thresher poet, whom Queen Caroline installed in the grotto as resident hermit. These and four previously unpublished short poems were published in Robert Dodsley's *A Collection of*

Poems (1748–58). They afterwards appeared in Johnson's, Chalmers's, and Anderson's collections. Green's small output of poetry is now little known, but its charm remains appealing for admirers of light verse.

LESLIE STEPHEN, rev. W. B. HUTCHINGS

Sources R. Dodsley, ed., *A collection of poems … by several hands*, 3 vols. (1748) [new edn] G. Pearch, ed., 4 vols. (1783) • *European Magazine and London Review*, 8 (1785), 27–8 • Boswell, *Life* • D. F. Foxon, ed., *English verse, 1701–1750: a catalogue of separately printed poems with notes on contemporary collected editions*, 2 vols. (1975)

Green, (James) Maurice Spurgeon (1906–1987), journalist, was born at Padiham in Lancashire on 8 December 1906, one of the two sons of Lieutenant-Colonel James Edward Green, and his wife, Constance Ingraham-Johnson. He was educated at Rugby School where he was a scholar and at University College, Oxford, where he won a double first-class degree in Greats and was counted among the most brilliant of his generation.

Brendan Bracken, who had a sharp eye for able young men, gave him his first job on the *Financial News*. Green quickly made his mark, first on market reports and then as a leader writer. He was among the small group of young men in the 1930s who helped to lay the foundations of modern financial journalism. At the age of only twenty-eight he became editor and stayed in that post for five years. Together with Otto Clarke, his chief leader writer and head of the 'Lex' column, he devised the Financial News 30-share index which eventually became the Financial Times ordinary share index. He married first, on 15 January 1930, Pearl Oko of Cincinnati, Ohio, who died in 1934. On 14 October 1936 he married Janet Grace Norie, daughter of Major-General C. E. M. Norie. They had two sons. Green moved to *The Times* in 1938 and had a year there as financial and industrial editor before the Second World War broke out. Green had joined the Territorial Army and for the next five years served with the Royal Artillery, finishing his military career as a major on the staff of the 3rd anti-aircraft group at Bristol. He was made an MBE (military) for his wartime service.

Reckoned to be too old to serve overseas, Green was released from the army in 1944 and rejoined *The Times*, where his value was seen to lie in judgement rather than drive. There he became assistant editor in 1953. After eighteen years with *The Times*, he moved to the *Daily Telegraph* as deputy editor in 1961, and in 1964 was appointed editor there in succession to Sir Colin Coote. The period of his editorship, 1964–74, was politically divided between six years of Harold Wilson and four years of Edward Heath. Both prime ministers were made to feel the weight of Green's economic philosophy and influence. Always more interested in economics than politics, he held firmly to the doctrine of the free market before it became more fashionable a decade later. Thus throughout Green's tenure as editor the *Daily Telegraph*'s leader writers were given the clearest economic guide posts. Many of the editorials were written by Green himself. His writing was exact rather than exciting. There was no embroidery. He applied the somewhat austere disciplines he imposed on the work of colleagues to all his own writing.

From 1971 onwards Green's relations with Edward Heath became increasingly strained; mainly because he profoundly disagreed with the prime minister's economic policy. Green's economic beliefs led him to see virtue in the line being taken by Margaret Thatcher and her friends, and he was among her early supporters. He encouraged her to stand for the Tory leadership when her chances of gaining it looked slim.

As an editor Green was admired and respected for his intellect, but he also exercised a gentle, persuasive art of his own. With his slightly donnish stoop, he would approach his specialists for guidance with endearing modesty. Rooted in clear principles, particularly in the economic sphere, he did not have to raise his voice to make his point. At the *Daily Telegraph* 135 Fleet Street specialists and leader writers worked in separate rooms. Green rarely summoned anyone to his room; he preferred to visit them in theirs. Economics apart, Green's editorial policies were generously described by *The Times* as 'marked by civilised, humane ideals' (*The Times*, 21 July 1987). It was an apt comment. His apparent air of detachment concealed a firm hold on the principles by which he felt the affairs of the *Daily Telegraph* should be conducted. He often thought for what seemed an unnervingly long interval before giving his answer to some question or request. But when it arrived, the answer was usually hard to gainsay.

For some years after he retired as editor, Green remained a contributor to the *Daily Telegraph* on economic subjects. He attended the annual budget statement and would turn out a long leader on the subject within ninety minutes of returning to the office. In 1976–7 he was president of the Institute of Journalists. It was a time when trade unions exercised considerable power in Fleet Street, as they had done throughout his tenure as editor. Strenuously opposed to the single-union closed shop, Green used his position to utter repeated warnings to his profession against its dangers. His interests and his recreations lay in many fields. Foremost among them was fly fishing which he practised principally on the River Itchen. He was a keen shot. When the *Sunday Telegraph* was founded in 1961, Green, then deputy editor of the *Daily Telegraph*, asked not to be considered because it would deprive him of Saturday shooting. He played the piano, collected porcelain and watercolours, won a half-blue at Oxford for chess, and was an authority on wine. Early in his life he was an enthusiastic collector of wild fungus. In the early post-war years he went on bicycling tours of Europe with his wife. Green died on 19 July 1987 at Winchester, Hampshire.

DEEDES

Sources private information (2004) [M. J. Green; A. Green, son] • *Financial Times* (22 July 1987) • *The Times* (21 July 1987) • R. Fry, *The Economist* (26 Dec 1987) • WWW • D. Hart-Davis, *The house the Berrys built: inside the 'Telegraph', 1928–1986* (1990) • CGPLA Eng. & Wales (1987)
Wealth at death £364,030: probate, 7 Oct 1987, CGPLA Eng. & Wales

Green [*alias* Harris], **Paul** (*b.* 1573?, *d.* in or after 1642), Roman Catholic priest, was born in Derbyshire and studied for the priesthood at the English College of St Gregory, Seville, where he was ordained in 1602. In 1603 he called at the English College at Douai en route for England. At Rome in 1609 he was appointed chaplain to the diplomat Robert Shirley, known as Lord Shirley, then about to travel to Spain. About 1613 Green settled in Dublin, where he went under the name of Paul Harris, by which he is better known, and for a time he was chaplain at Luttrellstown Castle. In the 1620s he engaged in controversy with William Bedell, the provost of Trinity College, and with Archbishop Ussher, whose Wanstead sermon of 1624 he challenged in *A Briefe Confutation* (1627), written under the pseudonym Paulus Veridicus. Later he became the leading polemicist on behalf of the Irish secular clergy in their dispute with the regulars, and published a series of acrimonious attacks on the Irish Franciscans and on Thomas Fleming, the Franciscan archbishop of Dublin, whom he accused of furthering the ambitions of his order. He compiled the list of eleven allegedly heretical propositions attributed to the Irish Franciscans which were published at Paris by his colleague Patrick Cahill and condemned by the Sorbonne in January 1631. A riposte written by Francis Matthews OFM, under the pseudonym Edmundus Ursulanus, was answered by Harris in his hard hitting *Arktomastix* ('A scourge for the bear'), published at Dublin in 1633. In this controversy he had the co-operation of the English Gallican theologian Henry Mailer, a leading supporter at Paris of Richard Smith, titular bishop of Chalcedon, in his dispute with the English regular clergy. Both Mailer and Smith had been his contemporaries at the English College in Seville, where Smith was briefly a lecturer.

In his trenchant *Fratres, sobrii estote* (1634) Harris continued his denunciation of the Franciscans, whom he charged with resisting reform and promoting superstition and heresy. In 1634 Archbishop Fleming, aided at Rome by his fellow Franciscan Luke Wadding, obtained authorization from Rome for suspending Harris and expelling him from the diocese. In his last published work, *Exile Exiled* (1634), Harris appealed over the heads of his ecclesiastical superiors to the civil authorities. The dispute served their interests in widening the division between the loyalist old English secular clergy and the more numerous regulars whose political allegiance was to Spain; Archbishop Fleming believed Harris to have government protection. In July 1642 he was reported to have been among the Catholic priests banished from Dublin and recently landed at La Rochelle, and in October he was reported in residence at the Irish College, Paris. His later career is unknown.   G. MARTIN MURPHY

Sources M. Murphy, *St Gregory's College, Seville, 1592–1767*, Catholic RS, 73 (1992), 16, 70 · D. Gaffney, 'The practice of religious controversy in Dublin, 1600–1641', *The churches, Ireland, and the Irish*, ed. W. J. Sheils and D. Ward, SCH, 25 (1989), 145–58 · C. McNeill, ed., *The Tanner letters*, IMC (1943) · B. Jennings, ed., *Wadding papers, 1614–38*, IMC (1953) · A. F. Allison and D. M. Rogers, eds., *The contemporary printed literature of the English Counter-Reformation between 1558 and 1640*, 2 (1994) · A. F. Allison, 'Richard Smith's Gallican backers and Jesuit opponents [pt 1]', *Recusant History*, 18 (1986–7), 329–401, esp. 367–8 · E. H. Burton and T. L. Williams, eds., *The Douay College diaries, third, fourth and fifth, 1598–1654*, 1, Catholic RS, 10 (1911) · *Report on Franciscan manuscripts preserved at the convent, Merchants' Quay, Dublin*, HMC, 65 (1906) · B. Millett, ed., 'Catalogue of Irish material in vols. 132–139 of the *Scritture originale riferite nelle congregazione generali* in Propaganda archives', *Collectanea Hibernica*, 12 (1969), 7–44

Archives NL Ire., MS 16250

Green, Sir Peter James Frederick (1924–1996), insurance underwriter, was born at 1 Priory Grove, Kensington, London, on 28 July 1924, the elder son of John Everard Green (1899–1966), a prominent marine insurer at Lloyds who later changed his second forename to Edward, but was universally known as Toby, and his wife, Margaret Blanche Holford. The Green family had been actively involved in shipping and shipbuilding since the eighteenth century, and until 1921 were owners of the Orient Line.

Green was educated at Harrow School and Christ Church, Oxford, and from 1943 onwards served as a seagoing junior naval officer on Russian convoys and in the Mediterranean. After demobilization he joined his father in the Janson Green agency at Lloyds. On 19 April 1950 he married Aileen Pamela (1916–1985), the only daughter of Sir Gerald Ellis Ryan, bt. Already an experienced yachtsman, Green crewed the Lloyds boat, the *Lutine*, in the Bermuda race of 1952 and five years later helped to found the admiral's cup. He was commodore of the Royal Ocean Racing Club from 1961 to 1964; he also shot and fished. A second-generation freemason, he was grand master of one of the three Lloyds lodges. On his father's death in 1966 he became chairman of Janson Green, and in 1974 he was elected a committee member of Lloyds.

Stocky and with a mischievous sense of humour, but at times a martinet and even given to bullying, Green was a predictable choice in 1979 for the chairmanship of Lloyds. After some earlier damaging in-house disputes, the lawyer Sir Henry Fisher had conducted an inquiry into Lloyds system of regulation, and had recommended (among other provisions) the establishment of a ruling council with stronger powers and new disciplinary procedures. Green used his drive and chairman's authority to push through these reforms. At a mass meeting in the Albert Hall, London, he secured an overwhelming vote of confidence for a private parliamentary bill to be drafted. The Lloyds Act of 1982 duly imposed the first substantive changes for over a century to that body's management.

Green also strengthened the financial base of Lloyds by sharply increasing, to £250,000, the sum that applicants had to guarantee before being accepted as non-underwriting members, or 'names'. He drove home the implications of unlimited liability by requiring his syndicate's new members to sign a blank cheque, which he pocketed. As most Lloyds underwriters had scant professional knowledge of management or the law, he organized seminars for their benefit. His achievements were rewarded with a knighthood in 1982 and a Lloyds gold medal a year later.

However, by 1983 Lloyds was beset by recurring crises.

Insurance risks had escalated with the arrival of super-tankers, jumbo jets, nuclear plants, asbestosis, and environmental pollution, together with increasingly costly natural disasters such as hurricanes and floods. Exemplary qualities of leadership were therefore needed to enforce maximum transparency and fairness, as well as the most rigorous investigation and punishment of any breach of the rules. Here Green failed to root out the clubby and cliquish culture in Lloyds, where some underwriters were widely believed to be creaming off the most lucrative business and leaving the residue to names. Worse still, Green himself was found to have been guilty of favouritism by investigating on his own an erring underwriter, who happened to have worked in his father's syndicate, and finding him innocent of any dishonesty. Inspectors at the Department of Trade and Industry took a less accommodating view, and the underwriter had to pay back $400,000 and move abroad. In 1983 the Bank of England was alarmed enough to compel Lloyds to appoint its first chief executive, the outside accountant Ian Hay Davison.

Within a year Green was forced out of the chairmanship by revelations that he had made a fortune out of reinsuring business on the quiet with an overseas company (which he partly owned) in a tax haven. Following a lengthy inquiry by the Inland Revenue and Green's resignation from active underwriting, the Lloyds disciplinary committee in 1987 judged that his underhand dealings with the tax-haven company, and submission to itself of inaccurate and misleading information, represented both serious and gross negligence and discreditable conduct. He was fined (with costs) more than £70,000, a note of censure being posted at Lloyds. On appeal, a tribunal upheld these findings.

Green's wife had died in 1985, and on 23 September 1986 he married Jennifer Mary Whitehead (b. 1935), the widowed daughter of Guy Alderson-Smith, a naval officer. There were no children of either marriage. Green remained as chairman of Janson Green until 1988, occasionally appearing in the United States as an expert witness in insurance litigation. Early in 1996 four names began a High Court action against Green and two other former chairmen of Lloyds. However, he died of cancer at his home, Stutton Mill House, near Ipswich, on 27 July of that year, survived by his second wife, leaving an estate valued at over £2.5 million. He was regarded by some as a tragic figure, flawed by an inability to grasp that his self-seeking conduct was a dereliction of duty to the entire Lloyds community in a very dark hour.

T. A. B. CORLEY

Sources G. Hodgson, *Lloyd's of London* (1984) · I. H. Davison, *Lloyd's: a view of the room* (1987) · D. Kynaston, *The City of London*, 4 (2001) · *The Times* (30 July 1996) · *Daily Telegraph* (30 July 1996) · *The Independent* (31 July 1996) · *Financial Times* (31 July 1996) · J. Mantle, *For whom the bell tolls: the lesson of Lloyd's of London* (1992) · R. Macre, *A survey of Lloyd's syndicate accounts* (1986) · M. Lehmann-Brune, *Lloyd's of London* (1988) · C. Gunn, *Nightmare on Lime Street: whatever happened to Lloyd's of London* (1992) · D. McClintick, 'The decline and fall of Lloyd's of London', *Time Europe*, 155 (21 Feb 2000) · Burke, *Gen. GB* (1952) · b. cert. · m. certs. · d. cert. · *CGPLA Eng. & Wales* (1996)

Likenesses photograph, 1980, repro. in Mantle, *For whom the bell tolls* · photograph, *c.*1985, repro. in *The Independent* · photograph, repro. in *The Times*
Wealth at death £2,696,975: probate, 16 Sept 1996, *CGPLA Eng. & Wales*

Green, Richard (1803–1863), shipowner and philanthropist, was born on 5 December 1803, probably in the family house in Blackwall Yard, Poplar, London, the fourth child, and third son, of George Green (1767–1849), shipbuilder, and his first wife, Sarah Perry (1774–1805), daughter of John Perry and his wife, Elizabeth. The shipyard at Blackwall, one of the principal yards in the kingdom, was founded in 1612, and had been managed by the Perry family since 1708. In 1810 the Perrys retired, and George Green inherited their half-share of the yard, the remainder being in the hands of the Wigram family.

Richard Green was the only child of Sarah Perry to live to maturity. He was educated at Dr Cogan's school at Higham Hall, Walthamstow, and studied at Edinburgh University, but he does not appear to have taken a degree. In 1829, after working in the shipyard for a time, he was admitted as a partner.

The yard had always been much concerned with building the ships of the East India Company, but the company's trading days were to end in 1834, and a new source of business was essential. The firm already had shares in ships it had built, but the Greens and the Wigrams separately resolved to enter the field of shipowning more actively, to supply the place of the East India ships. At first they made only a few voyages each year, and also entered the South Sea whaling trade. However, after 1834, more ships were built for the Indian trade. Richard, with two brothers from his father's second marriage, Henry (1808–1879) and Frederick (1814–1876), shared the direction. Richard managed the ships, Henry, who had served an apprenticeship in the yard, supervised the shipyard, which built most of their ships, while Frederick in 1836 took charge of F. Green & Co., which dealt with passengers and cargo. The venture succeeded, and George Green felt able to retire in 1838, to concentrate on his charitable activities.

The state of British shipping was arousing much anxiety in the 1830s, the East India Company having been the only shipowner which required qualifications in its officers; its ships were the largest, and the best run, for their passengers were important and influential, and their cargoes valuable. The Greens set out to preserve the fine traditions of the East India service in a more commercial world. Their ships, if at first rather smaller, were well found and well victualled, with officers from the company's service, and they attracted and retained good seamen for their crews. A high standard of discipline and of navigation was expected, and the ships sailed at the date advertised and consistent passages were sought. Despite the competition which soon arose from the P. & O. steam contract mail service to India, the business prospered, so that from 1837 until 1862 one or more ships were built each year for the firm's service; they lost only four ships in that period. In the late 1840s some sailings were made to Australia, and after the discovery of gold there in 1852 these were increased to a monthly service. The Wigrams and some other owners followed a similar course; the smartness of the ships led to their being familiarly called 'Blackwall frigates'. Green, however, had the largest firm, with thirty ships about 1860.

Although head of a great business and widely respected in shipping circles, Green did not seek the limelight. Nevertheless, he gave evidence to several commissions and committees on shipping matters, and was a member of the royal commission on manning the navy in 1858–9. His views were then influential in the foundation of the Royal Naval Reserve. His actions, however, spoke for themselves. He took the lead in founding and became chairman of the *Worcester*, the Thames training ship for merchant officers. With his father, he set up a seamen's home in Poplar for his crews; he arranged courses in navigation, and liberal standards were observed in his ships. He was an important benefactor to the Merchant Seamen's Orphan Asylum and the Dreadnought Seamen's Hospital. To be in his service was a credit; he was described as a 'model shipowner', and did much to raise the standard of merchant shipping.

Father and son also gave generously to Poplar charities. Poplar Hospital owed its existence to them, as did several schools, and Green supplied food for the poor in bad winters. The family also had a connection with Deal and Walmer in Kent. George Green was a low-churchman for many years, but after a dispute, he turned to the Congregationalists, building for them, in Poplar, a new chapel, Trinity Chapel, at which the family henceforth worshipped, and where both George and Richard were buried.

Of medium height and average physique, Green was handsome, with a dreamy expression. He had, however, powers of quick decision as well as good judgement. He once said he had no time to hesitate. Living in the shipyard house, he and Henry, both with good practical experience, were in close touch with their business. Nevertheless he found time to walk round Poplar, with the capacious pockets of his waistcoat filled with sixpences and sweets, which he dispensed generously. Green never married.

Richard Green's health was never very good; early in 1863 it deteriorated, and he was moved to his sister's house, 7 Hanover Terrace, Regent's Park, to be nearer the doctors. His death there on 17 January 1863 was described as little less than a public calamity. His funeral was attended by great crowds, as was the unveiling of a statue by E. W. Wyon, paid for by public subscription, which still stood near Poplar church in the East India Dock Road at the end of the twentieth century. He was buried on 24 January in Trinity Chapel, Poplar.

JAMES BURNLEY, *rev.* A. W. H. PEARSALL

Sources H. Green and R. Wigram, *Chronicles of Blackwall Yard* (1881) • F. C. Bowen, 'The Greens and London River', *Journal of Commerce* (13 Oct 1932) • D. Laing, ed., *A catalogue of the graduates … of the University of Edinburgh*, Bannatyne Club, 106 (1858) • *ILN* (31 Jan 1863) • *East End News* (24 Jan 1863) • *Mitchell's Maritime Register* (24 Jan 1863) • B. Lubbock, *The Blackwall frigates*, 2nd edn (1950) • S. Porter, ed., *Poplar, Blackwall and the Isle of Dogs: the parish of All Saints*, 2 vols.,</td>

Survey of London, 43–4 (1994) • NMM, Green MSS, GRN/1–25 • private information (2004) • parish register (births), St Dunstan, Stepney, London, 5 Dec 1803 • parish register (baptism), St Dunstan, Stepney, London, 31 Dec 1803 • *DNB* • *CGPLA Eng. & Wales* (1863)
Archives NMM, Green MSS, GRN/1–25
Likenesses E. W. Wyon, statue, 1865–6 (after death mask), East India Dock Road, London • E. W. Wyon, bust • wood-engraving (after photograph), NPG; repro. in *ILN*
Wealth at death under £350,000: double probate, May 1863, *CGPLA Eng. & Wales*

Green, Roger Gilbert Lancelyn (1918–1987), writer, was born on 2 November 1918 at Swanington Hall, Norwich, Norfolk, the eldest of the four children of Gilbert Arthur Lancelyn Green (1887–1947), major, Royal Field Artillery, and his wife, Helena Mary Phyllis, *née* Sealy (1885–1972). The history of the family's 900 year-long association with the manors of Poulton-Lancelyn and Bebington is recorded in Roger Lancelyn Green's *Poulton-Lancelyn: the Story of an Ancestral Home* (1948). Although he claims his account is of 'an undistinguished country family' (Green, *Poulton-Lancelyn*), it is evident that Poulton Hall, its history and its famous Queen Anne library with the Revd Thomas Green's collection (4496 volumes), furnished the inner landscape of his life and work. Childhood illness interrupted his schooling at Dane Court, Pyrford, Surrey, and Liverpool College, but his father enjoyed reading aloud to his children the books of an earlier generation of writers: Lewis Carroll, Rudyard Kipling, Andrew Lang, H. Rider Haggard, Harrison Ainsworth, Jeffery Farnol, and others. This upbringing left his son with impressions of childhood as a golden age suffused with literary romance and adventure, which he kept intact throughout a lifetime in a period of great social change.

At Merton College, Oxford (1937–40), Green's interest in romantic fantasy was encouraged by his tutor, C. S. Lewis, whose friend, J. R. R. Tolkien, was writing *The Lord of the Rings*. Tolkien's 1939 lecture 'On fairy stories' about the 'secondary world' of the imagination confirmed Green's scholarly preferences for traditional fairy- and folk-tales, classical myths and legends, the Arthurian cycle, medieval romances, Norse sagas, the Old Testament, and Egyptian history, all of which would form the sources of his later writings. After taking his degree (1940) he had short spells as an actor in Oxford and London (Pirate Noodler in *Peter Pan*), a schoolmaster, and an antiquarian bookseller before returning to Oxford to take his MA degree and, tutored by Tolkien, to write his BLitt thesis on Andrew Lang (1944). He became deputy librarian of his college (1945–50), had many friends, and pursued a literary career of individual connoisseurship. On 31 March 1948 he married June Burdett (*b.* 1926), actress and speech and drama examiner; they had two sons and one daughter.

Green will be remembered for *Tellers of Tales*, (1946), a landmark and early example of serious consideration given to children's books as a distinctive literature. In his clear, urbane, man-of-letters style, he presents biographical descriptions of his favourite childhood authors, mostly those who lived between 1850 and 1920. Green's erudition and his acceptance of writing for children as an important literary activity made his book a great success as a source of reference, especially with teachers and librarians. Later editions (1953; 1965) addressed adults more directly, although by 1969, in the last edition, a number of his subjects had become topics of antiquarian interest for specialist readers. The Bodley Head monographs on *Lewis Carroll* (1960), *J. M. Barrie* (1960), *Mrs Molesworth* (1961), *Andrew Lang* (1962), all members of his pantheon, and of his tutor and friend *C. S. Lewis* (1963, revised 1969) show Green at his most characteristic. About his distinction as a writer there is no doubt. What he knew best he revisited on behalf of a wide range of readers. *The Story of Lewis Carroll* (1950) is for the young; their elders have his edition of Carroll's *Diaries* (1953), *The Lewis Carroll handbook: being a new version of a handbook of the literature of the Rev. C. L. Dodgson* (1962, rev. edn 1970), and *The Work of Lewis Carroll*, edited by John Tenniel (1965). Other editorial tributes include *The Readers' Guide to Rudyard Kipling's Work* (1961), *Kipling: the Critical Heritage* (1971), and *Plays and Stories of J. M. Barrie* (1962). Green's attachment to creators of 'secondary worlds' is also clear in the somewhat hagiologic biography of C. S. Lewis that he wrote with Walter Hooper (1974).

As a critic, Green accepted literary values as self-evident. His biographical approach to children's books continued to influence other writings about them for at least twenty-five years after his essay 'The golden age of children's literature' (1962, 59–73). Later, Peter Hunt argued that Green was 'committed to books in a way that few of us could hope to be' (*Signal*, 56, 1988, 146) and 'the arcadia from which Green wrote is only available to us if we reject the world as it is' (ibid., 147). Nevertheless, Hunt admits that Green was 'one of the first to take children's literature into the more hallowed academic halls' (ibid., 148). Rarely committing himself to forthright opinions on the works of his contemporaries, Green brought to his own a distinctive kind of scholarly strength. Having tried his hand at writing conventional stories for children, he ruefully acknowledged that their settings in country houses were '"out of date" and not sufficiently "period" to satisfy the critics' (Hammond, 335).

Green's continuing reputation rests on his retellings of tales he loved as a child and came to know intrinsically as a scholar. His anthologies owe much to his passion for collecting, as described in *Tellers of Tales*. But, rather than a simple bringing-together of distinctive genres, each book is a recreative enterprise. During the 1960s and 1970s this work included, for Dent: *Tales of Make-Believe* (1960), *Ten Tales of Detection* (1967), *Thirteen Uncanny Tales* (1970), *Tales of Terror and Fantasy* (from Edgar Allan Poe; 1971); and for Hamish Hamilton: *The Hamish Hamilton Book of Dragons* (1970), *Magicians* (1973), and *Other Worlds* (1976). In retelling heroic legends Green stays as close as he can to his reading of the originals; in prefaces he lets his readers know about his sources in a way that engages them as fellow scholars. *King Arthur and his Knights of the Round Table* (1953) has brought at least two generations of young readers as near to Malory as they are likely to get. The book has been continuously in print; a new edition was printed in 1994, and as a Puffin Classic it is also an audiobook (1998). Green's

dignified, austere language is spell-binding for a more demotic age. The same effect is noticeable in *Heroes of Greece and Troy* and *The Tale of Israel* (1969). In *Mystery at Mycenae* (1959) and *The Luck of Troy* (1961), devotion to the world of Homer brought him the success in writing fiction and the attention of an audience that had eluded him earlier.

Green died of cancer at his home, Poulton Hall, Poulton Lancelyn, Bebington, Cheshire, on 8 October 1987, and was buried at St Andrew's Church, Bebington. By dint of his prolific exertions during his life as a country gentleman, he enhanced writing for children with his scholarship and won for himself a unique reputation. His academic distinctions included the William Noble research fellowship in English at the University of Liverpool (1950–52), where he was later a member of council (1964–70) and from which he was awarded an honorary degree of DLitt (1981). At the University of St Andrews (Scotland) he was the Andrew Lang lecturer in 1968. He edited the *Kipling Journal* from 1957 to 1975. His obituary in the *Times Educational Supplement* (23 October 1987) recorded that children's literature had 'lost a pioneering researcher and an eloquent advocate'. MARGARET MEEK

Sources works of R. L. Green, BL, prefaces · G. Hammond, 'Roger Lancelyn Green', *Twentieth-century children's writers*, ed. T. Chevalier, 3rd edn, 334–6 [full bibliography] · R. L. Green, *Poulton-Lancelyn: the story of an ancestral home* (1948) · R. L. Green, 'The golden age of children's books', *Essays and Studies by Members of the English Association*, new ser., 15 (1962), 59–73 · P. Hunt, 'Second impression: "Tellers of Tales" by Roger Lancelyn Green', *Signal*, 56 (1988), 142–9 · M. Fisher, *Intent upon reading* (1961) · V. Watson, 'Roger Lancelyn Green', *The Cambridge guide to children's books in English*, ed. V. Watson (2001) · P. Hollindale, *Choosing books for children* (1974) · E. Cook, *The ordinary and the fabulous: an introduction to myths, legends and fairy tales*, 2nd edn (1976) · W. Hooper, *C. S. Lewis: a companion and guide* (1996) · R. L. Green and W. Hooper, *C. S. Lewis: a biography* (1974) · J. R. R. Tolkien, 'On fairy stories', *Tree and leaf* (1965) [first pubd in *Essays presented to Charles Williams* (1947)] · private information (2004)
Archives NRA, priv. coll., MSS
Wealth at death £1,637,886: probate, 6 Jan 1988, *CGPLA Eng. & Wales*

Green, Rupert (1767/8–1804). *See under* Green, Valentine (1739–1813).

Green, Samuel (*bap.* 1740, *d.* 1796), organ builder, was baptized at Cuddesdon, Oxfordshire, on 21 September 1740, the son of Henry Green, a distiller, and his wife, Mary Juggins. He was apprenticed to organist and clock builder George Pyke in 1754; he may also have learned from the second John Byfield, Richard Bridge, and the younger Abraham Jordan, as well as John Snetzler. From 1768 he was in partnership with the third John Byfield. In 1772 he married Sarah, the daughter of the clockmaker Eardley Norton, and set up his own business on Red Lion Street, Holborn, as a freeman of the Clockmakers' Company. He later moved his premises to Islington, and in 1789 to Isleworth.

Green took the lead in the movement towards 'delicacy' in organs, muffling mechanical noise with leather and tapped wires, and changing the sound of the organ by, among other measures, reducing the size of the pipe foot and increasing the number of indentations (nicks) on the pipes. He is usually credited with having followed Snetzler by echoing trends in furniture design rather than architectural woodwork, particularly in his use of the Gothic style and preference for mahogany; but 'it can be shown … that most, if not all, of Green's gothic cases were applied to organs that were built under the supervision of advisers' (Wickens). The nineteenth-century organ historian Sir John Sutton deplored the changes that Green had wrought: 'One would suppose that Green was anxious in his instruments to emulate the tone of a musical snuff box, rather than that of an Organ' (Sutton, 82). Despite Sutton's criticisms, Green's innovations, which also included a swell using Venetian shutters and a horizontal rise instead of the traditional diagonal bellows, became the standard in the nineteenth century, known in French as the 'mécanique anglaise' (Bicknell, 187).

About 1780 Green was commissioned by George III to build a new organ for St George's Chapel, Windsor. Further major commissions followed, including an organ for Canterbury Cathedral, which was temporarily housed in Westminster Abbey for the Handel commemoration of 1784. Its keyboard could be detached from the organ to enable the organist to sit with the orchestra. George III also commissioned an organ from Green for Salisbury Cathedral in 1792; it was moved to St Thomas's, Salisbury in 1876.

Green died on 14 September 1796 in Isleworth, Middlesex. Although the *Dictionary of National Biography* says he 'died in something like poverty' he had constructed a large number of organs for cathedrals, churches, and country houses across the country. He left the business to his widow, Sarah, probably including works in progress such as the organ erected in 1800 for Down Cathedral, Downpatrick, co. Down. Her foreman, Benjamin Blyth, carried on Green's tradition in the early nineteenth century.   MATTHEW KILBURN

Sources S. Bicknell, *The history of the English organ* (1996) · J. Sutton, *A short account of organs built in England from the reign of King Charles the Second to the present time* (1847) · D. C. Wickens, 'Green, Samuel', *New Grove*, 2nd edn · M. Gillingham, 'Green, Samuel', *New Grove* · C. Clutton and A. Niland, *The British organ*, 2nd edn (1982) · *DNB* · *IGI*

Green, Samuel Gosnell

Green, Samuel Gosnell (1822–1905), Baptist minister, was born on 20 December 1822 at Falmouth, the eldest son of Samuel Green, a Baptist minister, and his wife, Eliza, daughter of Benjamin Lepard. He had four brothers and four sisters. When the family moved from Thrapston in Northamptonshire to Walworth in 1834 he was sent to a private school at Camberwell, where his literary tastes were encouraged. After leaving school he worked until the age of nineteen in the printing office of John Haddon in Finsbury, and then acted as a tutor in private schools at Cambridge and Saffron Walden.

In 1840 Green entered Stepney College (later Regent's Park College) to prepare for the Baptist ministry, and graduated BA at the University of London in 1843. After holding ministerial posts at High Wycombe in 1844 and at Taunton in 1847, he became in 1851 classics and mathematics tutor at Horton Academy, Bradford, moving with it to Leeds in 1859, when it became known as Rawdon College. Green acted as president from 1863 to 1876. He impressed his students as a scholar of broad sympathies and a stimulating teacher.

As a preacher, Green proved a special favourite with children. He had married Elizabeth Leader (d. 1905), eldest daughter of James Collier, in October 1848, and they had three sons and a daughter of their own. Long connected with the Sunday School Union, he succeeded his father as editor of the monthly 'Notes on the Scripture lessons' and was elected a vice-president of the union in 1894. His addresses and lectures to children on the Bible and his contributions to the *Union Magazine* were separately published under various titles. As the first Ridley lecturer at Regent's Park College in 1883, Green delivered the substance of his *Christian Ministry to the Young* (published the same year).

In 1876 Green went to London to serve as editor, and in 1881 as editorial secretary, of the Religious Tract Society. Thenceforth his main energies were devoted to literary work. His most important work was the *Handbook to the Grammar of the Greek Testament* (1870), which ran to four revised editions; it was followed in 1894 by a primer, which also had a wide circulation. A companion volume on the Hebrew of the Old Testament appeared in 1901. In 1898 he published his Angus lecture, *The Christian Creed and the Creeds of Christendom*; in 1903 *A Handbook of Church History* appeared, a compact and comprehensive manual, and in 1904 a revised edition of Dr Angus's *Bible Handbook*. In a revised edition of the English Bible (1877), designed by Joseph Gurney, Green, together with George Andrew Jacob, headmaster of Christ's Hospital, was responsible for the New Testament. He also contributed to the Religious Tract Society's series, Pen and Pencil Sketches. Green wrote widely on religious and educational subjects, producing a history of the Religious Tract Society in 1899.

Green was elected president of the Baptist Union of Great Britain and Ireland for 1885–6. He maintained a great interest in hymns, contributing a paper, 'Hymnody in our churches', to the Baptist Union meeting in 1895. For the Manchester manufacturer John Rylands (1801–1888) he printed for private circulation an anthology, *Hymns of the Church Universal* (1885), and he was chairman of the editorial committee of the *Baptist Hymnal*.

An appreciative and widely read critic of secular literature, Green advised John Rylands's widow, Enriqueta, on various literary and benevolent schemes. He published a memoir of Rylands and, with his third son, J. Arnold Green (1860–1907), assisted the widow in the collection of the John Rylands Library, Manchester, which opened in 1899. Retaining his vitality to the last, Green died at Northcourt, Mount Ephraim Road, Streatham, on 15 September 1905, some four months after his wife. He was buried in Norwood cemetery. His eldest son, Samuel W. Green, taught at Regent's Park College between 1878 and 1925, and his daughter, Lily Watson, wrote a number of children's stories.   CHARLES WELCH, *rev.* L. E. LAUER

Sources E. C. Starr, ed., *A Baptist bibliography*, 9 (1964), 132–7 · J. S., 'Memoirs of deceased ministers and missionaries', *Baptist Hand-Book* (1906), 439–42 · J. Stuart, *Watford Observer* (30 Sept 1905) [memoir] · *Christian World* (21 Sept 1905), 3 · *The Athenaeum* (23 Sept 1905), 403 · private information (1912) · *CGPLA Eng. & Wales* (1905)
Likenesses H. A. Oliver, oils, *c.*1900; given to Rawdon College, Bradford by Green in 1905
Wealth at death £10,614 15s. 2d.: probate, 14 Oct 1905, *CGPLA Eng. & Wales*

Green, Sarah (*fl.* **1790–1825**), novelist, was, according to *A Biographical Dictionary of the Living Authors of Great Britain and Ireland*, 'a native of Ireland'. Latterly her address was 18 Dartmouth Street, Westminster, near St James's Park. *Charles Henly, or, The Fugitive Restored*, published by the Minerva Press in 1790, is sometimes ascribed to her on the evidence of a Minerva Library catalogue of 1814 assigning the novel to 'Mrs Green'. Several of her works were printed by the Minerva Press, including the treatise *Mental Improvement for a Young Lady* (1793), 'addressed to a favourite niece'; its praise of Fanny Burney perhaps suggests novelistic ambition. In 1795 she defended the sanity of the visionary Richard Brothers (1757–1824) in *A Letter to the Publisher of Brothers's Prophecies*; the glimpses of somewhat fervent spiritual life afforded there seem at odds with the conservatism of her other work.

In 1799 Green embarked on a productive career as a novelist, with the first work of fiction that can be attributed to her with any certainty, *Court Intrigue, or, The Victim of Constancy*. Over the next twenty-six years she produced a further sixteen substantial novels, usually under pseudonyms (a Cockney) or partially concealed authorship (S. G****). Much of her work was professedly satirical in character; in *Romance Readers and Romance Writers* (1810) and *Scotch Novel Reading, or, Modern Quackery* (1824) particularly, she addressed the issues of her profession in a highly self-conscious way. She also wrote historical romances, and in *The Carthusian Friar* (1814) produced a successful imitation of Radcliffean Gothic. There were also a number of tales of marriage in contemporary settings. Her novels were fairly expensive—*The Royal Exile* (1811) was priced at £1—and most of them were reviewed in the standard journals. Comment was initially rather supercilious. *The Private History of the Court of England* (1808), a characteristic mix of history and invention, was loftily dismissed by the *Monthly Review* as a 'clumsy fiction' of scurrilous intent because of its recasting of the prince of Wales's amours into a fifteenth-century setting (58, January–April 1809, 101). *The Reformist!!!* (1810), a satire on Methodism, was thought to be 'good-humouredly written' but improper in its venturing onto religious controversy (*Monthly Magazine*, 30, supplement, 31 January 1811, 676), while the *Monthly Review* found it too slavish in its adherence to government policy (64, February 1811, 216–17). The latter article also questioned the gender of the writer:

> we cannot be such dupes of the preface as to believe that the experience of a lady could have furnished all the scenes which are here delineated; and much less would we attribute to a female pen the great illiberality which occasionally displays itself.

The view was reiterated in the same journal's review of *Good Men of Modern Date* (1811), though it was also noted that the work contained 'some grammatical errors that savour not of a classical education' (*Monthly Review*, 68, May–August 1812, 109). None the less, guarded praise of the characterization and humour in the novels began to emerge, and the *British Critic* four times declared Green 'well qualified for much better undertakings' (35, January–June 1810, 299; 36, July–December 1810, 407; 37, January–June 1811, 414; and 39, March 1812, 311). The last dated work ascribed to her is *Parents and Wives, or, Inconsistency and Mistakes* (1825).

PAUL BAINES

Sources Blain, Clements & Grundy, *Feminist comp.*, 457–8 · D. Blakey, *The Minerva Press, 1790–1820* (1939), 149, 163, 177, 188, 232–3, 256 · [J. Watkins and F. Shoberl], *A biographical dictionary of the living authors of Great Britain and Ireland* (1816) · E. Copeland, *Women writing about money: women's fiction in England, 1790–1820* (1995), 11, 18–19, 76–84, 172–5, 182, 190 · W. S. Ward, *Literary reviews in British periodicals, 1798–1820: a bibliography*, 1 (1972), 288–9 · *Monthly Review*, new ser., 58 (1809), 101 · *Monthly Review*, new ser., 64 (1811), 216–17 · *Monthly Review*, new ser., 68 (1812), 109 · *British Critic*, 35 (1810), 299 · *British Critic*, 36 (1810), 407 · *British Critic*, 37 (1811), 414 · *British Critic*, 39 (1812), 311 · *Monthly Magazine*, 30 (31 Jan 1811), 676 [suppl.] · M. Summers, *A Gothic bibliography* (1940), 51–2, 262, 272, 286, 292, 323–4, 333, 342, 345, 359, 457, 461, 469, 472, 476, 484, 489, 528 · M. B. Tymn, ed., *Horror literature: a core collection and reference guide* (1981), 75 · W. S. Ward, *Literary reviews in British periodicals, 1821–1826: a bibliography* (1977), 104 · catalogue, JRL · *The new Cambridge bibliography of English literature*, [2nd edn], 3, ed. G. Watson (1969), col. 729

Green, Thomas (*bap.* **1658**, *d.* **1738**), bishop of Ely, was baptized on 12 December 1658 at St Peter Mancroft in Norwich, the son of Thomas and Sarah Green of Norwich. He was educated at the free school there and was admitted to Corpus Christi College, Cambridge, on 28 July 1674, graduating BA in 1679. He was made a fellow of Corpus Christi in 1680 and at some point became a tutor. He proceeded MA in 1682 and was created DB in 1690 and DD in 1695. Contemporaries described Green as 'a very worthy, good man' and according to Cole he was 'very nice and somewhat finical'. He was 'thinly made' with feminine features which earned him the nickname Miss Green from his peers at Cambridge University (*DNB*).

Early on in his career Green enjoyed the patronage of Thomas Tenison, who became archbishop of Canterbury in 1695. The nonjuror Thomas Hearne, who did not have a high opinion of Green, related that 'By his Sneaking and Cringing (for nobody knew of any other Merits that he had) he [Green] insinuated himself mightily into the favour of the Archbp' (*Remarks*, 1.217). It may have been through Tenison's influence that Green became the domestic chaplain of Sir Stephen Fox. Tenison then employed Green as his own chaplain, and on 2 April 1695, through the influence of the primate, Green was appointed to the vicarage of Minster in the Isle of Thanet, upon which he resigned his fellowship. On 26 May 1698, again through the patronage of Tenison, Green became master of Corpus Christi College, a position he was to hold until 1716. Hearne claimed that this appointment was 'to the Regret of all men of learning and Probity in that University' (ibid., 1.218). Notwithstanding Hearne's judgement, Green made a number of reforms as master of the college

Thomas Green (*bap.* **1658**, *d.* **1738**), by unknown artist, *c.*1730

and made its government more effective. According to Robert Masters, the historian of Corpus Christi, Green introduced the practice of holding public prayers in chapel after locking up the college gate, in order to know 'what scholars were abroad' at night (Lamb, 268).

In 1699 Green was elected vice-chancellor of Cambridge University, a position he held again in 1713. In May 1702 Tenison installed him as a prebendary of Canterbury, and on 28 October 1708 collated him to the rectory of Adisham-cum-Staple in Kent. The following month Green was installed as archdeacon of Canterbury, upon which he resigned from the vicarage of Minster. It was also in 1708 that, as master of Corpus Christi, Green became involved in a controversy with Robert Moss, who had been a member of the college and who had recently been given the Tuesday lectureship at St Lawrence Jewry, London. Moss was in possession of a Norfolk fellowship but with his new position his preferments gave him a total annual income of £240. Consequently Green requested that Moss should resign his fellowship. Moss refused and, despite Green's attempts and the support of two lawyers, retained his fellowship until 1714.

It would appear from the patronage which Green received from Tenison and the animosity which Hearne exhibited that Green was a religious moderate or was whiggish in political outlook. This is substantiated by Robert Masters who claims that 'The zeal which he shewed for the House of Hanover on the death of Queen Ann, and his prudent conduct at this juncture, laid the foundation of his fortunes' (Lamb, 210). It may have been as a result of this zeal that Green was made a royal chaplain of George I

in 1715. In the same year he supported the crown against the Jacobite rising, preaching and publishing two sermons in which he condemned the Jacobites and offered thanks for their subsequent defeat. At some point Green married Catherine Trimnell (*c.*1682–1770), the sister of the whig and low-church Bishop Charles Trimnell, a union which Hearne cynically saw as a move 'to strengthen his interest among the whiggs'. Through this marriage Green had two sons, Thomas and Charles, and seven daughters, Catherine, Anne, Margaret, Elizabeth, Catherine, Sarah, and Mary. According to the *Dictionary of National Biography* his sons were responsible for adding the final 'e' to their surname.

In 1715 his patron Tenison died and Green was made one of the trustees of Tenison's will. Through the disposal of the late primate's options, Green became vicar of St Martin-in-the-Fields, Westminster, which he held *in commendam*. Following this appointment he resigned his mastership of Corpus Christi and in February 1716 he was also made vicar of Adisham. He was consecrated bishop of Norwich on 8 October 1721, and was translated to the bishopric of Ely on 24 September 1723. During his time as bishop Green continued his support of the government, voting consistently with the ministry in the House of Lords.

As bishop of Ely, Green was drawn into a controversy with Richard Bentley, master of Trinity College, Cambridge, over the visitation rights to that college. Bentley had attracted the criticism of many of the fellows for maladministration, and they pressed Green to make a visitation and look into the matter. On 1 April 1729 Bentley, who had already disputed the visitation rights of the bishops of Ely in the past, was ordered by Green to go to Ely House on 5 May to answer the charges laid against him by the fellows. However, on 3 May Bentley appealed against Green's actions to the court of king's bench, which upheld his objections. Green then sent Bentley a list of the charges against him and requested that Bentley should inform him of any objection that he had to the allegations. Bentley appeared at Ely House on 10 June and expressed his objections to the charges, but Green overruled them. Bentley again applied for a prohibition from the king's bench which was granted on 10 November 1729. On 31 March 1730 Green lodged an objection against the prohibition and in November of that year Bentley's prohibition was lifted, but in the Trinity term of 1731 the court reversed its decision. The following year Green applied to the House of Lords to consider the case and on 6 May the Lords reversed the prohibition by a majority of twenty-eight peers to sixteen. Green was now free to proceed with a trial of Bentley at Ely House, which took place on 13 June 1733. On 27 April 1734 Green found Bentley guilty of dilapidating the goods of his college and violating its statutes and ruled that he should be deprived of his mastership. Green did not take further action against him.

While bishop of Ely, Green preached before the Society for the Propagation of the Gospel in Foreign Parts and the

Society for the Reformation of Manners. Both of these sermons he subsequently published. He also published theological works on the principles of religion, the sacrament, and death. He died at Ely House, Holborn, on 18 May 1738 and was buried on the south side of Ely Cathedral.

Green's son **Thomas Greene** (d. 1780), like his father a Church of England clergyman, matriculated at Corpus Christi College, Cambridge, in 1727, graduating BA three years later. He was made a fellow of Corpus Christi in 1732 and proceeded MA in 1734. Two years later he resigned his fellowship and instead became a fellow of Jesus College, a position he held until 1738. He was ordained deacon at Ely on 30 July 1737 and became rector of Cottenham in Cambridgeshire. Also in 1737 Greene was made a prebendary of Ely, a position he continued to hold until his death. According to Cole, Greene was 'thin and very delicate' like his father and while at Ely Cathedral he stopped the practice of using incense during festivals because it gave him headaches (BL, Add. MS 5873, fol. 82). In 1749 Greene was created DD and became chancellor of the diocese of Lichfield. Also in that year he was appointed chaplain to George II, a position he retained until 1757. In 1756 he was installed as a canon of Westminster; he held that post until he was made dean of Salisbury the following year. He died on 23 March 1780, in Gerard Street, London, and was buried in St Martin-in-the-Fields.

REBECCA LOUISE WARNER

Sources Masters' History of the college of Corpus Christi and the Blessed Virgin Mary in the University of Cambridge, ed. J. Lamb (1831) · Venn, Alum. Cant., 1/1–3 · J. Bentham, The history and antiquities of the conventual and cathedral church of Ely (1771) · J. Britton, The history and antiquities of the see and cathedral church of Norwich (1816) · J. H. Monk, The life of Richard Bentley, DD, 2nd edn, 2 vols. (1833) · Remarks and collections of Thomas Hearne, ed. C. E. Doble and others, 11 vols., OHS, 2, 7, 13, 34, 42–3, 48, 50, 65, 67, 72 (1885–1921), vols. 1, 7 · DNB · Fasti Angl., 1541–1857, [Ely] · Fasti Angl., 1541–1857, [Salisbury] · BL, Add. MS 5873 (Cole MSS) · will, PRO, PROB 11/690, fols. 59v–61r
Archives Berks. RO, letters to Charles Greene [Thomas Greene] · U. Nott. L., letters to third Duke of Portland [Thomas Greene]
Likenesses portrait, c.1730, Bishop's Palace, Ely [see illus.] · oils, St Martin-in-the-Fields, London · oils, CCC Cam.
Wealth at death legacies totalling £23,403, excluding landed property: will · substantial; bequeathed leasehold estate of Hemingford Gray Rectory, Huntingdon, plus £1200 to son Thomas; two farms in Huntingdon plus £1200 to son Charles; £2000 each to four daughters

Green, Thomas (1679/80–1705), seaman and pirate, of unknown parentage, was brother to John Green, a London attorney. In 1701, when his age was said to be twenty-one, Captain Green, commanding the frigate-built Worcester, chartered by Thomas Bowrey, weighed anchor for India to obtain a cargo of cowries, pepper, turmeric, and saltpetre. This was a Separate Stock (non-East India Company) voyage and Green and others, to their later detriment, were instructed by Bowrey to communicate using a simple cipher. All was not smooth sailing; bad weather detained the Worcester in the Downs until 8 March 1702, while Bowrey wrote to his supercargo:

> Wee have some reason to think that Captain Green may have some directions or design of bringing from India, either for himselfe or some others, some sorts of Druggs or other

goods prohibitted by us. Wee doe therefore order you to put Captain Green in mind of his charter party. (Temple, 101)

The Worcester proceeded by way of Madeira, the Canaries, and Delagoa Bay on the east African coast—where the crew allegedly saw a mermaid—before arriving on the Malabar coast in mid-November. It is clear that there were disputes with the locals in disposing of the Worcester's goods, which included arms and ammunition. Captain Alexander Hamilton later remarked that Green came aboard his ship at Calicut 'very much overtaken with drink' and confessed to having disposed of arms to the pirates at St Mary's and having transported pirates from the Mascarene Islands thence (Temple, 127). When Hamilton was visited by Green's chief mate

> [h]e burst out in tears and told me he was afraid that he was undone … they had acted such things in their voyage that would certainly bring them to shame and punishment if they should come to light; and he was assured that such a company of drunkards as their crew was composed of could keep no secret tho' the discovery would prove their own ruin. (ibid., 128)

At about this time the Worcester's sloop, Dellagoa, was armed against local pirates and sent on several coastal trading journeys before running ashore at Carnople and being lost. In late April, while still on the Malabar coast, the Worcester sprung a leak and proceeded to Bengal for repairs; from Calcutta she headed home, arriving at the Cape of Good Hope on 21 February 1704 and sailing from there with a Dutch convoy to avoid French privateers. Delayed by another leak the Worcester sailed to the west coast of Ireland rounding the north coast of Scotland to avoid enemy cruisers. From Fraserburgh the Worcester moved on to Edinburgh to await convoy south, making Leith on 31 July.

On 12 August, after a spate of rumours and while Green was ashore recovering his health, the Worcester was seized by the Darien Company in reprisal for the London arrest of the Scottish East Indiaman Annandale. It was found that the goods on board were not stowed but in great confusion in the hold: furthermore the master, John Madder, produced an African company seal, which he could not have obtained lawfully. Green subsequently demanded that his vessel be returned. He was not allowed on board and appealed to the secretary of state, the chancellor, and the queen's advocate. While it became clear that the Worcester had no legal connection with the East India Company, in proceedings which were probably not unrelated to the seizure Green and his crew were charged with piracy on 5 March 1705. The vessel pirated was generally believed to be the Speedy Return (Captain Drummond), which other sources suggest was seized by Captain John Bowen at St Mary's, Madagascar, in 1701–2. The charge was based in part on the construction given certain remarks by the crew, but was reinforced by testimony of the ship's cook who claimed to have heard of the matter after he joined the vessel in Bengal. Matters were not helped by Bowrey's decision to economize in his captain's defence:

> Wee have hitherto used all our indeavour's to justifie your innocency of the crimes laid to your charge, and wee esteeme your imprisonment to be a trick to gett the ship

unladen, and are informed that the Scots cannot find sufficiente proofe against you. This matter has already cost us a great deal of money, and as wee hope it cannot affect your lives, we are unwilling to be at such large expenses. (Temple, 224–5)

In the course of the trial it was alleged that Green's crew had killed the men on the pirated vessel and thrown the bodies overboard. Testimony was also given by two Indians, Antonio Ferdinando and Antonio Francisco (the captain's servant, who, at the time of the alleged piracy, was 'chained and nailed to the Floor of the Fore-Castle'; *Tryal*, 42).

On 16 March by a plurality of the votes cast, the Scots jury found Green and most of his crew guilty of piracy. On the 21st those convicted were sentenced 'to be taken to the sands of Leith within flood mark, betwixt the hours of eleven o'clock in the forenoon and four o'clock in the afternoon, and there to be hanged upon a gibbet till they be dead' (Temple, 246). The conviction was followed by confessions from several of the crew, probably in the hope of a pardon, a raft of rumours (alleging bribery of witnesses and the poisoning of Ferdinando when he desired to recant), and information forwarded from England concerning the true fate of the *Speedy Return*. Green's date of execution was originally scheduled as 3 April, but this was postponed a week by the privy council at the request of Queen Anne. The case became embroiled in Anglo-Scottish union politics, with unionists supporting Green's innocence and nationalists his guilt. Secretary Johnstone noted that '[t]his business of Green, etc. is the deil and all. It has spoiled all business … the Whigs make a National Jacobitish business of it, and it will be trumped up at all the elections' (ibid., 276). On 10 April 1705 the privy council declined to further postpone Green's reprieve and on the 11th, amid Edinburgh mob violence, Green, his mate, and gunner were transported to Leith for execution (the rest of the crew were reprieved and later quietly released). Green in a (retouched) dying declaration noted

> We are condemned as Pirates and Murderers on a Coast far distant from this place. Is there any of you who want either a friend whom we have murdered? Or whose goods have we taken? …
>
> I went not a roving out of the road of our trade and commerce, … I never had occasion to shoot powder or draw weapon in wrath during the voyage. And I would have the considering world examine if ever a master of ship went a pirating for owners or freighters and returned to Europe or to the port from whence he came. (Temple, 284–6)

Henry Smith, quoting the commander of the guards at the execution, states

> [h]e sayd there was at least 80,000 armed men, that one might have walked on their heads from Edinburgh to Leith sands; for the country fifty mile round came in, being exasperated by a ballad Roderick Mackenzie had caused to be made, printed, and cryed about the streets, wherein was mentioned Captain Green and his bloody crew had beheaded Drummond and throwne his seamen into the sea, tyed back to back. (Temple, 292)

Daniel Defoe in his *History of the Union* (1709), speaking of Captain Green's trial, notes:

the world is divided on the subject. Some will have Green and his crew to be guilty of all that is charged on them; others say the [Darien] Company carried all against them that they might have a good pretence for confiscating the ship.

He concluded 'these things left a corroded mass of ill-blood in the minds of the people on either side, and is improved by the malicious fomenters of each party' (Temple, 430–33).   SAMUEL PYEATT MENEFEE

Sources R. Temple, *New light on the mysterious tragedy of the 'Worcester': 1704–1705* (1930) • *The tryal of Capt. Thomas Green and his crew: for piracy, robbery and murder* (1705), with MS • *The case of Capt. Thomas Green, commander of the ship Worcester, and his crew, tried and condemned for pyracy and murther in the high court of admiralty of Scotland* (1705) • *Remarks upon the tryal of Capt. Thomas Green and his crew* (1705) • *A letter from Scotland to a friend in London: containing a particular narrative of the proceedings against the Worcester and her crew* (1705) • *Some cursory remarks on a late printed paper called 'The last speeches and dying words of Captain T. G., commander of the ship Worcester'* (1705) • *Observations in the tryal of Captain Green and the speech at his death* (1705) • *An English ointment for the Scotch mange, or, A short memorandum of the Scots cruelty to Captain Thomas Green* (1705) • *Last speech and dying words of Captain Thomas Green, commander of the ship The Worcester* (1705) • J. H. Burton, *Narratives from criminal trials in Scotland*, 2 vols. (1852) • will, PRO, PROB 11/496, sig. 205

Green, Thomas (*bap.* 1719, *d.* 1791), musician and tuner of musical instruments, was born in Cheshunt, Hertfordshire, where he was baptized on 14 January 1719, the second son of Hannibal Green (*d.* 1757), glazier. His elder brother, John, was also a glazier, and he had a sister, identified in his will as 'my sister Cross'. It is likely that the family moved to Cheshunt not long before Thomas was born.

In 1738 Green was appointed organist of the parish church in Cheshunt. In August 1744, he was appointed to the more prestigious post of organist at All Saints' Church, Hertford, which he held to the end of his life. As the leading church in Hertfordshire's county town All Saints' was an important social as well as an ecclesiastical and musical focus, supporting a fashionable choir of charity school children as well as an organ. For his first few years at All Saints', Green continued to live in Cheshunt and he travelled nearly 10 miles to and from Hertford to perform his duties as organist. In June 1748 he moved to Hertford to live in West Street with Charles Bridgeman (*d.* 1798), nurseryman and gardener, his wife, Jenny (*d.* 1800), and their young family. He remained there for the rest of his life, apparently regarding himself as part of the large and extended Bridgeman family. Almost all his property—including a house in Cheshunt inherited from his father—was left in his will to members of the family, and his successors as organist at All Saints' were two of Charles Bridgeman's grandchildren; Charles Bridgeman the younger (1778–1873) held the post for eighty-one years.

Despite describing himself in official documents as 'organist', a post for which he received £23 per annum, Green's major occupation and main source of income was in tuning musical instruments, but he was also a teacher, of drawing as well as of music, both privately and in schools, and his chief significance lies in the detailed accounts he maintained of his professional and personal activities covering the period 1742 to 1791. These offer valuable source material on the nature and range of musical activity in eighteenth-century Hertfordshire, the history of individual musical instruments, and the life of an eighteenth-century professional man.

Green tuned musical instruments for a wide range of clients, ranging from the nobility, such as the second Earl Cowper, to tradespeople, such as Mrs Binyon, a milliner. He had professional contacts with over 400 families, predominantly with women, who were the chief participants in amateur music-making at this period. His accounts record clients' names and addresses and describe both the specification and the manufacturer's inscription for many instruments. He tuned mainly harpsichords and spinets but also pianofortes, which were growing in popularity from the mid-1750s, and other instruments, such as guitars and harps. His teaching and tuning work involved much travel, mainly within an 8 mile radius of Hertford, although his work did occasionally take him further, to London, Essex, and Bedfordshire. He usually travelled on horseback and hired horses for the day, although in 1773 he bought himself a grey horse, called George. He often travelled to London for pleasure, attending concerts and visiting the fashionable Vauxhall Gardens. He also promoted, with Charles Bridgeman, several series of subscription concerts, held from 1753 to 1767 in a specially built concert room attached to Bridgeman's house in Hertford.

Although Green's interests and activities were mainly musical he took an interest in other fashionable pursuits of the day, dabbling in scientific investigation and writing extensive verse, including 'On Hertford and its environs' (1775, Hertford Archives and Local Studies, D/EHx/F56), a description of the town of Hertford and its surrounding countryside and stately homes. He also took an interest in his clothes and appearance; in 1774 he described to a friend the ridicule he received when, at the age of fifty-five, he adopted the new fashion of wearing a wig with a pigtail.

Green continued tuning musical instruments until 1786 and teaching until 1790. He died in West Street, Hertford, on 8 August 1791, aged seventy-two, and was buried three days later in the churchyard of All Saints'.

GILLIAN SHELDRICK

Sources G. Sheldrick, *The accounts of Thomas Green, 1742–1790* (1992) • G. Sheldrick, *Three centuries of music at All Saints' Church, Hertford* (1987) • R. T. Andrews, *Amongst the tombs* (1884)
Archives Herts. ALS, papers, incl. accounts, D/EHx/F48–F58 | Herts. ALS, Gordon Moodey collection, D/EGm/61B; D/EGm/62
Wealth at death under £2000—goods, chattels, and credits, incl. real estate in Cheshunt; also musical instruments, paintings, furniture, and personal property; also £850 in annuities and 25 guineas in cash: will, PRO, PROB 10/3184, PFF/4895

Green, Thomas (1722–1794), political writer, was the son of Thomas Green, a former soapboiler of Wilby, Suffolk, and his wife, Jane Mould. The background of his parents remains obscure and Green's early years are equally elusive, yet it is known that he received a good education. He acquired a taste for literature from an early age and developed over the years as a talented writer. By 1769 Green had moved from Wilby to Ipswich and was married by this time to Frances Martin. In that year Green's only child was born, also named Thomas *Green (1769–1825) and known as a poet and man of letters who made a significant contribution as a loyalist pamphleteer to the political debate of the 1790s. He was known for his admiration of the British constitution and 'his political creed was firm and consistent' throughout his life, reflected as it was in his political writings which earned him the respect of his loyalist colleagues and the acknowledgement that he possessed 'united literary attainments of the highest order, and an intimate acquaintance with the fine arts, in the knowledge and relish of which he had not many superiors' (*GM*, 85). He seems to have acquired his writing abilities and conservative political interests from his father. The first display of the elder Green's literary talents came in 1769 when he edited a periodical published at Ipswich called *Euphrasy*. Offering articles which supported the Church of England against dissenters and which took a conservative stance against the burgeoning reform movement, *Euphrasy* was in large part written by Green himself and ran for twelve numbers.

As a pamphleteer Green was not prolific, but in the turbulent years between the American War of Independence and the outbreak of the French Revolution he made a profound contribution with *A Prospect of the Consequences of the Present Conduct of Great Britain towards America* (1776); *A discourse on the imprisoning of mariners, wherein Judge Foster's argument is considered and answered* (1777); *A letter to Dr James Butler of Ireland, occasioned by his late publication entitled 'A justification of the tenets of the Roman Catholic religion'* (1787); and *Strictures on the Letter of the Rt Hon. Mr Burke, and the Revolution in France* (1791). Green died on 6 October 1794. While the precise value of his estate and possessions is not known, he had amassed a considerable fortune during his lifetime such as to bequeath significant amounts to his wife, to several friends, and for the poor parishioners of Wilby. His son also inherited a sizeable fortune which allowed him to devote the remainder of his life to travel and research. Green was buried in his home town of Wilby.

MICHAEL T. DAVIS

Sources DNB • will, PRO, PROB 11/1250 • GM, 1st ser., 95/1 (1825), 85–6 [obit. of Thomas Green, son]
Wealth at death see will, PRO, PROB 11/1250

Green, Thomas, the younger (1769–1825), writer, was born at Monmouth on 12 September 1769, the son of Frances Martin and Thomas *Green the elder (1722–1794), a political writer and former soap-boiler of Wilby, Suffolk. Related on his paternal side to Dr Thomas Green, bishop of Ely, and on his maternal to Archbishop Sancroft, Green was educated partly at the free grammar school in Ipswich, and then privately under a Mr Jervis of Ipswich. He was admitted to the Inner Temple on 7 July 1785, and in 1786 he was admitted to Gonville and Caius College, Cambridge, but was prevented by illness from taking up residence and going to the university. He was called to the bar, and for a few years went the Norfolk circuit. On coming into his property on his father's death in 1794, he gave up his profession and devoted himself to a literary life. He lived at Ipswich, visiting Europe and different parts of England from time to time. In October 1795 he married Catharine, daughter of Lieutenant-Colonel (afterwards General) Hartcup; they had one son, Thomas.

Green's claim to remembrance is his *Diary of a Lover of Literature*, extracts from which he published in 1810. In this he discusses and criticizes the books he read from day to day, sometimes giving lengthy arguments on the authors' subjects, in particular on metaphysical points, to which he had given considerable attention. It is varied by vivid descriptions of scenery in the Isle of Wight and Wales. The extracts are drawn only from the diary for the years 1796 to 1800. Green continued it throughout his life, however, and his friend J. Mitford of Benhall printed a large additional portion from January 1834 to June 1843 in the *Gentleman's Magazine*, of which he was then editor, concluding with a sketch of Green's character.

Besides the extracts from the diary, Green published numerous pamphlets on diverse subjects including *Gibbon's Critical Observations on the 6th Book of the Aeneid* (1794), *An examination of the leading principles of the new system of morals … in Godwin's enquiry concerning political justice* (1798; 2nd edn, 1799), and Reveley's *Notices illustrative of the drawings and sketches of some of the most distinguished masters in all the principal schools of design*, the last of which he revised for the press in 1820. He also contributed to the *Gentleman's Magazine* and the *European Magazine*, and some poems by him were published in *The Chaplet* (1807) and *The Suffolk Garland* (1818). Green died at Ipswich on 6 January 1825, soon after his return from a trip to Europe, and was buried at Wilby, Suffolk. He was survived by his son.

H. R. LUARD, *rev.* REBECCA MILLS

Sources Venn, *Alum. Cant.* · *GM*, 2nd ser., 1–20 (1834–43) · Watt, *Bibl. Brit.*, 1.437 · *IGI* · I. F. [J. Ford], *A memoir of Thomas Green of Ipswich, with a critique on his writings and an account of his family and connections* (privately printed, Ipswich, 1825)
Archives Yale U., letters to John Mitford
Likenesses W. H. Worthington, line print (after W. M. Bennett), NPG · portrait, repro. in Ford, *Memoir of Thomas Green of Ipswich*, frontispiece

Green, Thomas Hill (1836–1882), philosopher, was born on 7 April 1836 at Birkin, near Ferrybridge, Yorkshire. He was the second son and youngest of four children of the Revd Valentine Green, rector of Birkin, and his wife, Anna Barbara Vaughan, the eldest daughter of Edward Thomas Vaughan, vicar of St Martin and All Saints, Leicester. Thomas's mother died when he was one year old. He was educated by his father up to the age of fourteen and in 1850 he was sent to Rugby School, which had recently been reformed by Dr Thomas Arnold. His headmaster was Dr E. M. Goulburn.

In October 1855 Green matriculated from Balliol College, Oxford. While at Balliol he was a pupil of Benjamin Jowett. He took a second in classical moderations in 1857, a first in Greats (*literae humaniores*), and a third in law and

Thomas Hill Green (1836–1882), by Charles William Sherborn

modern history. He graduated BA in 1859. He was president of the Oxford Union Society and was closely associated with a debating group called the Old Mortality Society, where he was friendly with A. V. Dicey, James Bryce, and Algernon Swinburne. His religious views made him unwilling to enter the Church of England as a curate, but he considered becoming a dissenting preacher and also considered a teaching position in Owens College, Manchester. After some vacillation he signed the Thirty-Nine Articles, a prerequisite for receiving his MA in Oxford. In 1860 he was appointed lecturer in ancient and modern history at Balliol, during the absence of W. L. Newman, and in November of that year he was elected a fellow. Shortly after his marriage in 1871 he was re-elected, in April 1872. At his first election he was one of the earliest lay fellows in Oxford. In 1862 he was awarded the chancellor's prize at Oxford for his essay 'The value and influence of works of fiction'. In 1863 he refused, on Jowett's advice, an offer of the editorship of the *Times of India*.

In 1864 Green was an unsuccessful candidate for the chair in moral philosophy at the University of St Andrews. In December 1864 he was appointed an assistant commissioner in the midlands to the schools inquiry commission chaired by Lord Taunton. His main responsibility, until 1866, was to inspect the endowed schools of Warwickshire and Staffordshire and later Buckingham, Leicester, and Northampton. The final report of the commission, with his contribution, was published in 1868. The Endowed Schools Act of 1869, however, nowhere lived up to his hopes for the reconstitution of society through education. After his commission work, Green was elected as a teachers' representative on the governing body of King Edward's School in Birmingham (a school on which he had reported to the royal commission). In the spring of 1866 he briefly considered standing for a professorship at Owens College, Manchester. However, in September 1866 he was appointed to the teaching staff of Balliol as tutor, on the death of James Riddell, and in the same year was made senior dean. He examined *literae humaniores* in 1870–71 and from 1875 to 1877. On Jowett's election as master of Balliol in 1870 Green took over the subordinate management of the college. He believed strongly in extending access to higher education to poorer students and working men. With the support of Jowett, Balliol Hall—an annex to the main college—was provided for students with financial difficulties. Green presided over the hall and its outstudents. Both he and Jowett were also supporters of the university extension movement which began in the 1870s. He also campaigned for the admission of women to Oxford University. In 1867 he stood for the Wayneflete professorship of moral and metaphysical philosophy, but was defeated by Henry Chandler. In 1878 he was elected to the Whyte's professorship of moral philosophy.

Green, following John Bright, was an enthusiastic supporter of the extension of the franchise. He was a member of the Oxford Reform League which backed the national franchise campaigns before the 1867 Reform Bill. He also worked in his local Liberal Party organization and in 1875 was elected as a Liberal member to Oxford town council. He was on the delegacy of the Oxford local examinations and from 1874 was a member of the Oxford school board. In addition, he provided £200 towards the building of a grammar school in Oxford and founded a scholarship, of £12 a year, for children from the elementary schools of Oxford.

Green was closely associated with the temperance movement: he joined the United Kingdom Alliance in 1872 and publicly committed himself to teetotalism. He was made a vice-president in 1878. Also president of the Oxford Temperance Alliance, and treasurer to the Oxford diocesan branch of the Church of England Temperance Society, he was president of the Oxfordshire Band of Hope and Temperance Union from 1876. His personal interest in this issue included setting up a coffee tavern in St Clement's, Oxford, in 1875. His brother suffered from alcoholism, and, even after the 1874 Licensing Act, child and adult drunkenness was rife in industrial and agricultural areas of Britain. Green saw intemperance as part of a connected pattern of inequality and poverty, characteristic of a policy of *laissez-faire*. His views on temperance were consistent with his more general political philosophy. Alcohol was yet another impediment to the citizen's moral development. The state had a duty to contain such obstacles. Green favoured the 'local option' policy, which entailed local control on the sale of alcohol. In 1873 he came into direct and open dispute with the Liberal chancellor of the exchequer, Sir William Harcourt, over the latter's opposition to tighter regulation on drink.

Green's wife, whom he married on 1 July 1871, Charlotte Byron *Green, was the daughter of John Addington *Symonds (1807–1871) and his wife, Harriet, and sister of John Addington *Symonds (1840–1893), an old friend of Green's from the 1850s. There were no children from the marriage. Charlotte's father gave the couple £10,000 as a marriage settlement, no small amount at the time. Green's appearance, from photographs, gives the impression of a very stolid and serious demeanour. He had a large head, pale skin, thick black hair, and heavy dark eyebrows. According to contemporaries, his more regular facial expression was one of slight fatigue. His dress was reticent, and some have described it as careless. W. L. Newman described his clothes as always black and grey, and as 'true to his character'—'sober-suited and steady-going' (*Works*, 3.lxii). Green was a deep admirer of the plainness and seriousness of the puritans of the English Commonwealth and nonconformists of his own time. He said that he was always attracted by ordinary people of the lower and middle classes. His voice retained a soft northern accent. He was not, however, at ease as a communicator in either lectures or personal discussion. Yet his austere appearance and demeanour seem to have obscured a basic generosity as well as occasional lightness of spirit and slightly caustic wit, especially likely to be observed by friends and students. Nettleship reported, at the close of his 'Memoir', that Charlotte Green thought of her husband as Sir Bors in Tennyson's *Holy Grail*:

A square set man and honest; and his eyes,
An out-door sign of all the warmth within
Smiled with his lips—a smile beneath a cloud.

One of the more imaginative representations of Green—and one of the more dynamic accounts of his religious and moral influence on his pupils—is contained in *Robert Elsmere* (1888), the novel by Mary Augusta (Mrs Humphry) *Ward. The book is dedicated to Green and follows the fortunes of a young Elsmere, going to a thinly disguised Balliol in the 1870s. The novel contains a character—Professor Grey—directly modelled on Green. Elsmere comes under the influence of Grey and after taking orders in the Church of England (against Grey's advice), experiences a crisis of faith. With the approval of Professor Grey he resigns his living and goes to work with the poor in the East End of London, where he eventually founds a church, 'The New Brotherhood of Christ', not dependent on miracles or dogmas; this echoed Green's theology and was disapproved of by W. E. Gladstone in his review of the novel. The novel also contains a graphic and dramatized account of Green's *Lay Sermons* in Balliol, which generated such enthusiasm and devotion in his pupils. J. H. Muirhead, for example, thought the lay sermons contained Green's whole philosophy in condensed form, expressed with 'singular clearness and with a telling application' (*John Henry Muirhead*, 42).

Although not an easy writer or dynamic speaker, Green had a significant effect on generations of students, including many who were to become academics, churchmen, politicians, and public servants: for example, Herbert Henry Asquith, Edward Grey, Alfred Milner, Arthur Acland, A. C. Bradley, Arnold Toynbee, Bernard Bosanquet, R. L. Nettleship, J. H. Muirhead, Charles Gore, and Henry Scott Holland. As R. G. Collingwood noted in his *Autobiography*, in 1910 Green's major effect was to send into public life:

> a stream of ex-pupils who carried with them the conviction that philosophy … was an important thing, and their vocation was to put it into practice … Through this effect on the minds of its pupils, the philosophy of Green's school might be found, from 1880 to about 1910, penetrating and fertilizing every part of the national life. (Collingwood, 15–17)

After his death in 1882, Green left a powerful legacy of achievement and a degree of mythology, which carried through to the twentieth century. His philosophy, which blended metaphysical, religious, and epistemological concerns with a theory of ethics and politics, set a standard of academic rigour which helped change the character of British philosophy from the early twentieth century. His educational ideas on a 'ladder of learning' for all citizens directly influenced both R. B. Haldane and H. A. L. Fisher and, indirectly, early twentieth-century education policy. The influence of his ideas was not only felt in the sphere of education. In politics, before 1914, his philosophy precipitated, in many minds, a reassessment of some of the key values of liberalism. He did not suggest a wholesale revision of liberalism, more a bringing to fruition of some of its latent tendencies for social reform. His ethical and political philosophy, which many contemporaries saw exemplified within his own life, was seen by some to provide a cogent rationale for a more statist and welfarist liberalism, enabling it to meet, more humanely, the problems of an increasingly complex industrial society.

Social work was another area of Green's impact on early twentieth-century society, particularly through the burgeoning university settlements, such as Toynbee Hall (founded in 1884 by Green's pupil and admirer Arnold Toynbee, or 'Apostle Arnold', as he was known to his friends) or the Passmore Edwards Settlement, founded by Mrs Humphry Ward in 1896. It is no exaggeration to say that the majority of those who worked on and supported the early twentieth-century welfare state reforms, for example W. H. Beveridge, R. B. Morant, Llewellyn Smith, Ernest Aves, W. J. Braithwaite, J. A. Spender, Max Beer, R. H. Tawney, and Clement Attlee, all had university settlement experience—most at Toynbee Hall—and were influenced by its culture of civic idealism and social duty. Thus, if there is one important intellectual bequest from Green, it is a strong communitarian and ethical theory of citizenship and the state, devoted to the promotion of a worthwhile life for all its citizens. Despite a definite decline of interest in his work between the 1930s and 1970s, there has been some revival since the 1980s.

Green's major published works were: a comprehensive introduction to an edition of *The Philosophical Works of David Hume* (1874–5), with T. H. Grose as joint editor; the *Prolegomena to Ethics* (ed. A. C. Bradley, 1883), which was largely compiled from his Oxford professorial lecture notes and articles in *Mind* in January, April, and July 1882; *'The Witness of God' and 'Faith': Two Lay Sermons* (ed. Arnold Toynbee, 1883), which contains the famous lay sermons delivered at Balliol; *The Works of Thomas Hill Green* (3 vols., ed. R. L. Nettleship, 1885–8); and *Lectures on the Principles of Political Obligation* (repr. from vol. 2 of the *Works*, 1895). A revised edition of the latter work, with previously unpublished essays, appeared in 1986. Green also translated some of H. Lotze's *Metaphysic*, under the editorship of Bernard Bosanquet (1884). Apart from the Hume introduction, all Green's major works were edited and published after his death by former pupils. His general contribution can be summarized under three headings: religion, philosophy, and politics.

Religion Most of Green's religious writings were not prepared for publication. Apart from two early Ellerton prize essays, the only fully worked out piece is a lay sermon 'On faith'. The gist of Green's views on religion, and the substance of his influential *Lay Sermons*, is that he wanted to return the Christian religion to a more pristine condition, based upon the ordinary experience of humanity. The incarnation, life, death, and resurrection of Christ must inform the ordinary day-to-day lives of humanity. The individual cannot rely on miracles or historical events: God becomes immanent in everyday duties. He thus wanted to change a religion based upon dogma into one that was coincidental with the moral life of the ordinary citizen. The 'Christed self' of the ordinary citizen is at the same moment an expression of the common good and the principle of moral agency. Green took this to be the essential message of St Paul's writings. 'Christ the dogma' must become 'Christ the idea of morality'. In this indwelling God, symbolized in Christ, he thought he had found a bridge between the religious and secular worlds. Christ is what all humans are in potentiality. Religion was thus giving expression to God in the moral life. Until each individual denied the immediate self through the daily round of moral and civic duties, the true common good could not be realized. This was a heady brew for those keen to pursue the duties of citizenship. The impetus for these ideas was derived from a combination of sources—primarily Hegel and the later Hegelian theologian, and doyen of the Tübingen school of theology, Friedrich Christian Baur. In fact, Green started, but did not complete, a translation of Baur's *Geschichte der christlichen Kirche*. Christianity, for Baur, was not a finished product, but rather a developing process. Christ was viewed as the eternal act of God perpetually re-enacted in man. F. D. Maurice and Jowett also played an influential background role in the development of Green's religious ideas.

The role of religion in Green's thought is still vigorously contested. In his own time there was some controversy as to whether he could even be considered a Christian. In the twentieth century scholarly arguments claiming that Green's philosophy was essentially a surrogate religion for an age of declining faith have probably had the most profound effect. However, other commentators have contended that the religious perspective has been given too much prominence and that the social and political aspect of his thought is far more significant. It has also been argued that Green produced a philosophy of religion and not a religious philosophy and that his philosophy should be seen as distinct from his direct religious and even his political interests. Alternatively, others have argued for a more integral view, where the religious ideas of the *Lay Sermons* particularly might be said to be superseded by their expression in philosophy, but philosophy still embodies and rearticulates the core religious theme.

Apart from the *Lux mundi* essays, published not long after Green's death by theologians influenced by his perspective, Green's theological views might be said to have contributed to the general tone of liberal theology in the twentieth century. The emphasis placed upon the socially responsible church, by figures such as Bishop Gore and Archbishop William Temple (both Balliol products and influenced by idealism—directly by Green in the case of Gore and by Edward Caird in the case of Temple), shows the definite lineaments of Green's religious concerns.

Philosophy With Bernard Bosanquet and F. H. Bradley, Green was a leading figure among idealist philosophers. He made notable contributions to metaphysics, the history of philosophy, ethics, and political philosophy. As an idealist, he was a critic of empiricism and naturalism. His characteristic philosophical approach was to argue that knowledge of the world and nature does not explain the nature of knowledge, since knowledge presupposes a knower and is characterized by that presupposition. Knowledge of the world exists for the self-conscious agent. For Green, empiricism and naturalism committed the fallacy of trying to identify the real outside of thought.

In Green's own day Oxford was still dominated by classical studies and, in philosophy, by Aristotelianism. The Oxford examination statute of 1850 contained no mention of Kant or Hegel, or of J. S. Mill for that matter. It was not until 1875 that the first questions on Kant and Hegel appeared, owing largely to Green's influence. There is still a debate over the precise influence on him of both German and Greek philosophy. The consensus is that, of the Greeks, Aristotle was more significant than Plato. He made uncompleted attempts to translate two of Aristotle's works. The jury is still out, however, over the influence of Kant and Hegel.

Green's philosophical status was for a time central. Every important philosopher in Britain between 1880 and 1914 responded in some way to his work. This influence was not confined to Britain. His work was considered seriously in the USA, Italy, and more particularly in Japan, where he had a consistent body of admirers throughout the twentieth century. In addition, he made a pivotal contribution to the professionalization of philosophy in Oxford, encouraging a much more rigorous research-orientated approach to the discipline and widening its sphere of operation to include continental philosophy.

In German thought Green was primarily interested in the philosophies of Kant and Hegel, although it is ironic that he was one of the first to advocate the serious academic study of David Hume in Britain. He saw most of the defects of empiricism (including Hume's) and naturalism through Kantian eyes. The most important philosophical question for him was Kantian, namely, 'How is knowledge possible?' For Green, the self-conscious agent is the precondition of knowledge. The problem, as he saw it was Kant's doctrine of the manifold independent of the agent. Kant wanted to retain the idea of a world independent of consciousness which cannot be known in itself. Following Hegel, Green argued that Kant had fallen into an unnecessary dualism. There was no need to postulate a world independent of the determinations of judgement. The 'thing-in-itself' did not exist for Green. He took a similar line in his work on Aristotle, arguing that Aristotle's theory of knowledge and his account of matter would have been improved immeasurably if he had realized that knowledge of things implies judgement and in every judgement the self-conscious subject is implied.

It was the Kantian agent that also formed the starting point for Green's cryptic Hegelianism. The major theme that he developed from Hegel was the idea that Reason or the eternal consciousness was the unity implicit in the world and human history. The aim of the philosopher was to articulate the Reason of the world. If Green read Aristotle through Kantian eyes, he often read Kant through Hegelian eyes. The self-conscious agent presupposed, via a transcendental argument, an eternal consciousness or unifying Spirit, equivalent to Hegel's notion of *Geist*. The eternal consciousness was the presupposition of the unity of knowledge of individual self-conscious agents. A central ambiguity, at this point, was that if the eternal consciousness reproduced itself through individual agents, then was the separate human agent merely an imperfect form of the eternal consciousness? This particular point became a bone of contention between absolute and personal idealists in Britain up to the early 1920s.

However, Green was not credulous of Hegel. It is often reported by commentators that Green felt that Hegel's work must all be done over again. Green repudiated the idea that Hegel had discovered some fundamental secret of the universe and he rejected the dialectical development in Hegel's writings. In fact, he often turned the tables, to read Hegel with Kantian eyes, reaffirming the central epistemological and moral role of the self-conscious agent.

The self-conscious agent thus contained a problematic legacy. It formed the central element of his reaction to empiricism and a focus for his ethics and politics. Yet the logic of this agent in metaphysics led Green to the eternal consciousness, sometimes identified, in an ontological manner, with philosophical thought. This was a thesis that even Green had doubts about and critics certainly found problematic. It is possibly this unease with Hegel that led him to his interest in Lotze. The uncertainty over the status of the metaphysics has led some twentieth-century commentators to down-play the metaphysics and to concentrate on the moral or political philosophy.

The most complete statement of Green's ethics is to be found in the *Prolegomena to Ethics*. Some scholars, influenced by the dogmas of post-1945 analytic philosophy particularly, see his ethics as the most philosophically challenging aspect of his thought. The central ethical concept is character. Moral action is the expression of character, which is a quality of the self implied in action. Green's ethics is also a doctrine of self-realization. The self is identified with latent capacities and powers of the person. Humans distinguish themselves from animals by their ability to think about desires. The conceived desire is a motive. The self posits an object which will satisfy the conceived desire. The capacity to choose an object is the will. In all action an individual is positing an object which will satisfy the conceived desires. The satisfaction is described as a good. However, the 'true good' is that object which provides complete satisfaction, which is the full realization of the potentialities of the self. Such a realization cannot be identified with pleasure. Pleasure or happiness may be a by-product of moral action, but cannot be the end of it. The self cannot be identified with discrete sensations, since the self is the presupposition to any sensations. This is a basic point in his rejection of utilitarian ethics, although some twentieth-century commentators have argued that he is, despite appearances, more sympathetic to utilitarianism and consequentialism than is often supposed.

Politics The central category of Green's political philosophy was citizenship. Citizenship implied a consciousness of the ends of human life as embodied within the institutional structures of the state, in other words, a consciousness of the common good. The state was the organized body within which this consciousness functioned. For Green, society and its institutional structures were the means to individual self-realization. Therefore, social institutions or legal practices were justified only to the extent that they furthered the self-realization of individuals. The citizen, for Green, was not simply the passive recipient of rights, but rather an active self-realizing being. He viewed all political concepts from this standpoint. Rights, obligations, property, or freedom were devices to allow individuals to realize their powers and abilities. These, and other themes, are explored in his *Lectures on the Principles of Political Obligation*. The nub of his vision of politics was the provision of an ethical 'enabling and educative state'.

Green's essay 'Liberal legislation and freedom of contract' is important for understanding his conception of liberalism. The essay was written to reassure the Liberal Party over the changing character of its legislative programme. He constructed a historical picture of liberal concerns. First, liberalism had struggled for political freedoms against aristocratic privileges. Second, it had struggled for economic freedoms against protectionism. However, liberalism was moving into a third phase, characterized by social freedoms. For liberals concerned about freedom of contract, Green asked, 'What is freedom?' He answered that freedom was a 'positive power of doing or enjoying something worth doing or enjoying' ('Liberal legislation', *Works*, 3, 1888, 371). Positive freedom was identified with rational and moral action, a reconciliation of the objects of will and the objects of reason, that is, willing the common good. It was coincidental with self-realization, character, and genuine citizenship. The progress of society was measured by the growth of this freedom. Simply being left alone—negative freedom—was what Green called the primitive sense of the term and was of little or no assistance to a citizen's moral development. Thus, when liberals spoke of freedom of contract it was not just freedom from restraint, but the maximum power of all members of a community to make the best of themselves. State involvement in the regulation of drink, housing conditions, land ownership, employment conditions, and education was justifiable on the above grounds. Interference should at all times be directed to removing barriers and providing the conditions for the realization of citizens' powers.

There is still scholarly debate over exactly what Green's political philosophy entailed. Some scholars have pointed out that he was very much a man of the late Victorian period, obsessed with issues such as character and temperance. Further, being committed to a liberal market order, his notions of economic and political reform were limited. For example, although deeply worried about poverty and urban decay, he did not seriously suggest revolutionizing the economic order or property relations. Despite these reservations, others have maintained that there is evidence to the effect that his writings, among others, and personal influence had a quite definite impact in preparing the basic political and ethical groundwork for the twentieth-century welfare state in Britain before 1914.

Green's character was sometimes described by contemporaries as indolent, although a glance at his life's work must moderate this judgement. Contemporary commentators noted that he suffered from heart disease, the symptoms of which had gradually developed from 1878. He was taken ill on 15 March 1882 and died, at nearly forty-six years of age, on 26 March 1882 at 35 Beaumont Street, Oxford. His death certificate records ulcerated tonsils and then pyaemia as the causes of death. He was buried in St Sepulchre's cemetery in Oxford. Among his legacies to be paid after the death of his wife (which she in fact paid immediately) were £1000 to the University of Oxford for a prize essay on moral philosophy, £1000 for a scholarship to Oxford high school, and £3500 for Balliol College to promote education in large industrial towns.

ANDREW VINCENT

Sources *Works of Thomas Hill Green*, ed. R. L. Nettleship, 3 vols. (1885–8) [incl. 'Memoir' by R. L. Nettleship (vol. 3), the earliest full account of Green's life] • Balliol Oxf., archives • M. Richter, *The politics of conscience: T. H. Green and his age* (1964) • A. Vincent, ed., *The philosophy of T. H. Green* (1986) • A. Vincent and R. Plant, *Philosophy, politics and citizenship: the life and thought of the British idealists* (1984) • G. Thomas, *The moral philosophy of T. H. Green* (1987) [incl. list of archival papers and MSS] • H. Ward, *Robert Elsmere* (1888) • I. M. Greengarten, *Thomas Hill Green and the development of liberal democratic thought* (1983) • B. Wempe, *Beyond equality: a study of T. H. Green's positive freedom* (1986) • P. P. Nicholson, *The political philosophy of the British idealists: selected studies* (1990) • A. R. Cacuollous, *Thomas*

Hill Green: philosopher of rights (1974) • A. J. M. Milne, *The social philosophy of English idealism* (1962) • *The memoirs of John Addington Symonds*, ed. P. Grosskurth (1984) • C. Gore, ed., *Lux mundi* (1889) • R. G. Collingwood, *An autobiography* (1939) • *John Henry Muirhead: reflections by a journeyman in philosophy on the movements of thought and practice in his time*, ed. J. W. Harvey (1942) • H. S. Holland, *Memoir and letters*, ed. S. Paget (1921) • J. Prest, 'The death and funeral of T. H. Green', *Balliol College Record 1998* (1998), 23–6 • T. H. Green, *The collected works of T. H. Green*, ed. P. P. Nicholson, 5 vols. (1997) • M. G. Brock and M. C. Curthoys, eds., *Nineteenth-century Oxford, Part 2* (2000), vol. 7 of History of the University of Oxford

Archives Balliol Oxf., papers • Bodl. Oxf.

Likenesses C. W. Sherborn, etching, BM, NPG [*see illus.*] • photograph (with Old Mortality Society), Bodl. Oxf. • photographs, repro. in Richter, *Politics of conscience* • photographs, repro. in Nettleship, ed., *Works of T. H. Green*, vol. 3, frontispiece

Wealth at death £15,205 1s. 2d.: probate, 24 July 1882, CGPLA Eng. & Wales

Green, Thomas William (1894–1975), athlete, the son of Tom Chatwin Green and his wife, Flora Nettle, was born on 30 March 1894 in the police station at Fareham, Hampshire, where his father was the local constable. He overcame a remarkable series of misfortunes before being crowned an Olympic champion in 1932. Because of rickets he was unable to walk until he was five years old. In 1906 he falsified his age in order to join the army but he was invalided out four years later as a result of injuries sustained when a horse fell on him. He then worked in a butcher's shop before being recalled to the colours in 1914. While serving in France with the King's Own hussars he was wounded three times and badly gassed.

After the war Green held a variety of jobs before finding permanent employment in the wheel shop at Eastleigh railway works. On the advice of a doctor he took up sprinting and amateur boxing to counteract the damage to his lungs caused by gas during the war. In 1926, at the age of thirty-two, he first realized his potential as a walker after helping a war-blinded friend train for the St Dunstan's London to Brighton walk and decided to try his luck in the 12 mile Worthing to Brighton race. To his surprise he was the winner and, encouraged by a victory in his first race, he joined Belgrave Harriers, which was then one of the leading walking clubs in England. He went on to win virtually every road race of importance. He won the London to Brighton walk four times (1929–31; 1934), the Manchester to Blackpool race for six consecutive years (1929–1934), and he was the Road Walking Association champion over 50 kilometres in 1930. The only major title that eluded him was the Road Walking Association 20 mile championship, although he was twice placed second. Other major successes included the classic Milan 100 kilometres in 1930, but Green's greatest triumph came in the 50 kilometre road walk at the 1932 Olympic games in Los Angeles. At the age of thirty-eight he overcame exceptional heat to finish more than a half-mile ahead of his nearest rival; and after the 1996 games he was still the oldest ever winner of the event. He narrowly failed to make the Olympic team for a second time in 1936 but continued walking for many years and eventually finished his career in appropriate style by winning the Poole to Wareham event in 1948. Green was aged fifty-four at the time and

many of those who followed him home in his final race were less than half his age.

In 1934 Green left the railway works to become the landlord of the Meadowbank Hotel in Eastleigh, and in 1953 he moved to the Crown Hotel; he retired seven years later. He was married and had a son. A prominent freemason and a leading figure in local sporting circles he died at the Western Hospital, Southampton, on 29 March 1975.

IAN BUCHANAN

Sources *Eastleigh Weekly News* (3 April 1975) • *Athletics Weekly* (10 May 1975) • b. cert. • d. cert.

Wealth at death £8000: administration with will, 15 Aug 1975, CGPLA Eng. & Wales

Green, Valentine (1739–1813), engraver and publisher, was the son of a dancing master. He was born on 3 October 1739 at Salford Priors, Warwickshire, near Evesham, Worcestershire. He spent two years training as a lawyer under William Phillips, town clerk of Evesham, but then apprenticed himself to Robert Hancock, who designed and engraved for the Worcester porcelain manufactory. Before leaving Hancock in 1765 Green wrote *A Survey of the City of Worcester* (1764) illustrated with plates by Hancock after Green's own drawings. Green then moved to London and, starting in 1766, began to exhibit with the Incorporated Society of Artists. In recognition of the quality of his work he was elected a fellow in 1767 and a director in 1771. Between 1768 and 1772 he exhibited a series of important mezzotints, most of which were published by John Boydell. These included prints of Benjamin West's first striking history paintings, and such famous subjects as Joseph Wright of Derby's *A Philosopher Showing an Experiment on the Air Pump* and *Mr Garrick with Shakespeare's Bust* by Thomas Gainsborough. His exhibits culminated in *Regulus's Return to Carthage* after a painting by West that had been commissioned by the king. In 1773, for this and its companion, *Hannibal Swears Eternal Enmity to the Romans*, both huge and complex mezzotints, Green was appointed mezzotint engraver to the king. He was then persuaded to switch his allegiance away from the Society of Artists to the Royal Academy and in 1774 was elected an associate engraver. He became a fellow of the Society of Antiquaries the following year.

After this remarkable and rapid rise to fame and royal favour, Green was established as the preferred engraver of Benjamin West, the royal favourite, and he had another powerful ally in the publisher John Boydell. A portrait of Green's first wife, Mary (d. 1789), and their son Rupert [*see below*] was published in 1770 as a companion to one of Elizabeth West and her son Raphael. In that year Green moved to Salisbury Street off the Strand and began to publish on his own account. He took John Dean as an apprentice in 1769 and James Walker in 1773 and later added several other pupils, some from abroad. The foreign dimension to his business seems to date from the tour through Flanders and Holland to the Rhineland that he undertook in 1775 ostensibly, perhaps, in order to make a drawing of Pompeo Batoni's portrait of the elector palatine Carl

Valentine Green (1739–1813), by Lemuel Francis Abbott, 1788

Theodor for the engraving that Green published in 1777. At Mannheim he was appointed engraver to the elector and professor of the academy at Düsseldorf. In the latter town a deal was struck whereby the printseller Johann Gottfried Huck would import Green's prints.

Green continued to engrave important mezzotints, sometimes for Boydell and sometimes on his own account, notably after Joshua Reynolds, Benjamin West, and West's fellow Americans John Singleton Copley, Charles Wilson Peale, and John Trumbull. The American subjects included a portrait of George Washington (1781). As well as portraits and history prints in mezzotint he published a number of large aquatints by himself and Francis Jukes of picturesque castles and cathedrals. John Young told Joseph Farington that while he was a pupil of Green (about 1780) he was one of five assistants and that Green was making £2000 a year out of his business. A series of full-length portraits after Reynolds, *Beauties of the Present Age*, was launched as a speculative publication in 1780. Prestigious commissions included portraits of Queen Charlotte (1778) and of all the royal children and, for the Royal Academy, portraits of Reynolds and Sir William Chambers (1780). Green exhibited with the academy every year until 1784. In 1782, at the height of his prosperity, he visited Paris and on his return published *A review of the polite arts in France, at the time of their establishment under Louis XIVth, compared with their present state in England*. This was highly critical of the British attitude to art as an unnecessary luxury and of existing patterns of patronage in England. Before leaving, Green insured the contents of his house at 29 Newman Street for £3000, a figure raised to £4000 in 1786. At this date Green owned about 130 plates

and a stock of impressions of his prints for other publishers. He lived in Newman Street a few doors away from Benjamin West. Foreign visitors such as the German aristocrat Sophie von la Roche would visit both studios in one trip. On 13 September 1786 she 'finished up the morning at Mr Green's the famous and wealthy engraver, at whose place we witnessed one of the most complete collections of works in this art' (von la Roche, 154).

In 1785 Green took his son into partnership and their projects became increasingly ambitious. A *History of the Queens of England* (1786) after drawings by his German pupil Johann Gerhard Huck proceeded under the patronage of Queen Charlotte and of other European queens. On 3 June 1789 the Greens were awarded the privilege 'to Engrave and Publish Prints from all, or any of the Pictures in the Gallery at Düsseldorf to their own use and benefit at their own risk and expence' (*A Descriptive Catalogue*, 9). Green was now employing engravers to work for him and commissioning reproductive drawings and even original paintings. Acquaintances provided capital to support his enterprises. At first the Düsseldorf Gallery went well. Seventy-two drawings of the paintings had been made by March 1793 as models for engravings and they were exhibited at Spring Gardens. The French declaration of war on England provided further opportunities. When Valenciennes fell to the duke of York the Greens and Chrétien de Mêchel of Basel commissioned Philippe Jacques de Loutherbourg to paint the siege and James Gillray to sketch portraits of the participants. Rupert Green accompanied the two artists to the Low Countries. Later a painting of Lord Howe's victory was commissioned as a companion. Green paid £500 for each painting, £1200 for each engraving, and £200 per annum for a room to exhibit the paintings in.

But the death of Green's wife, Mary, on 31 December 1789 proved the first in a series of setbacks. French victories in Europe hindered the international trade upon which Green's fortune depended. According to Joseph Farington's hostile account of 1797 Green had 'retired to Warren Street on an annuity of £200 and lives there with a widow' subsequently identified as Mrs Charlton (c.1745–1831). He was already 'cunning and circumventing' (Farington, *Diary*, 896). Then disaster struck. In 1798 the French bombardment of Düsseldorf 'laid the castle, and the gallery which adjoins it, in ruins, destroyed, together with a very considerable property belonging to Mr. Green and his colleagues' (*Monthly Mirror*, 1809, 2.7). The Greens were declared bankrupt on 31 July 1798, and their goods were auctioned on 31 October with 'few but brokers present' (Farington, *Diary*, 1078). James Ross, a friend and backer and 'too much a sufferer to speak with impartiality' (*GM*, 1813, 446), blamed Green's overweening ambition and pride for the disasters.

Green continued to live with the widow in seriously reduced circumstances. Young told Farington, 'They pass as married people; but it is believed that no act of marriage has taken place, as by that £150 a year which she possesses would have been forfeited to his creditors' (Farington, *Diary*, 2502). Nevertheless, he was a frequent guest at artistic dinners attended by Joseph Farington and in 1805 Green was appointed keeper of the British Institution, a responsible and influential role. His younger stepdaughter married Sir James Innes Ker, soon after fifth duke of Roxburghe. Green visited her in 1812 in her new estate near Melrose Abbey. He died of old age in St Albans Street on 29 June 1813 and was buried in London. The British Museum and Victoria and Albert Museum, London, and the Bibliothèque Nationale, Paris, hold collections of his prints.

Rupert Green (1767/8–1804) was the son of Valentine and Mary Green. He was taken into partnership by his father as a young man in 1785 to help him run his burgeoning international print-publishing business. About 1790 he married 'a daughter of Mr Slade Haberdasher, in the Borough', described by Joseph Farington as 'weak, proud & dressy' (Farington, *Diary*, 896) but heir to a fortune of some £40,000. Unfortunately her father was another victim of the turbulent 1790s and failed in 1796. After the Greens' own bankruptcy two years later Rupert Green moved with his wife and six children to a house near Chelsea. He tried to earn some money through miniature painting but on 16 November 1804 he died aged thirty-six, survived by his wife, and was buried in Hampstead churchyard.   TIMOTHY CLAYTON

Sources *Monthly Mirror*, 1 (1809), 323 · *Monthly Mirror*, 2 (1809), 7 · letter from Valentine Green, *Monthly Mirror*, 2 (1809), 135 · *GM*, 1st ser., 83/1 (1813), 666 · letter from James Ross, *GM*, 1st ser., 83/2 (1813), 446 · A. Whitman, *Valentine Green* (1902) · Farington, *Diary* · *A descriptive catalogue of pictures from the Dusseldorf Gallery exhibited at the Great Room, Spring Gardens, London, by Messrs. V. and R. Green* (1793) [exhibition catalogue, Dusseldorf Gallery, London, 1793] · J. C. Smith, *British mezzotinto portraits*, 2 (1879), 532–99 · S. von la Roche, *Sophie in London 1786, being the diary of Sophie v. la Roche*, trans. C. Williams (1933) · D. Hill, *Mr Gillray the caricaturist* (1965) · T. Clayton, *The English print, 1688–1802* (1997) · Graves, *Soc. Artists* · *DNB*
Archives RSA, letters to the Society of Arts
Likenesses L. F. Abbott, oils, 1788, NPG [*see illus.*] · V. Green, mezzotint, 1788 (after L. F. Abbott), BM · group portrait, line engraving, pubd 1798 (after P. Sandby), BM · A. E. Chalon, group portrait, pen, ink, and watercolour (*Study at the British Institution, 1805*), BM · P. Sandby, drawing, Royal Collection

Green, William (1713/14–1794), Hebraist, was born in Newark, Nottinghamshire. He was admitted to Clare College, Cambridge, as a sizar on 16 March 1734, and matriculated in 1735. He was admitted a scholar on Mr Wilson's foundation on 20 January 1736, then as a scholar on Mr Freeman's foundation on 19 January 1737. In 1738 he graduated BA, was ordained deacon on 24 September, and was appointed fellow of Lord Exeter's foundation on 11 December. On 19 February 1739 he was elected a fellow of Mr Diggon's foundation. In June 1740 Green was ordained as a priest in Norwich; he received his MA in 1741, and on 2 November 1743 succeeded to a fellowship of the old foundation. In 1759 the master and fellows of Clare College presented him with the rectory of Hardingham, Norfolk, worth £400 per annum; he remained there until his death. Between 1790 and 1794 he was rector of Barnham Broom.

Green was a dedicated scholar and insightful translator of the scriptures. Many eminent divines and theologians sought his opinion on academic issues, and were grateful for his advice and approval, as his correspondence with fellow Hebraists, such as Thomas Secker, Richard Grey, William Newcome, Benjamin Blayney, Thomas Newton, and Alexander Geddes, reveals. Some contemporary reviews suggest that Green was renowned primarily for his perceptive comments on the biblical texts he translated, whereas his poetic skills were occasionally found to be weak. At a time when many poets wrote with the genteel reader in mind, it is unsurprising that not all critics took to Green's deliberate use of unadorned language, with the explicit aim of making the scriptures accessible to 'every order of men, … the unlearned as well as the learned' (Green, preface, *The Song of Deborah*, 1753, v). In doing so he aimed first to rescue the text from 'the palpable blunders of transcribers' (Green, preface, *A New Translation … of the Prayer of Habakkuk*, 1755, vi); second, to do away with the previous translators' convoluted style that obscured meaning, and restore the text to its 'primitive perfection' (*Song of Deborah*, v). Besides *The Song of Deborah* and *A New Translation … of the Prayer of Habakkuk*, Green's other works include a metrical translation of *David's Lamentation*, a version of *The Prayer of Moses*, and versions of Psalms 139 and 110 (all 1755), as well as *A New Translation of the Psalms* (1762). His version of the *Poetical Parts of the Old Testament* (1781) was apparently translated into Dutch in 1786.

Green died at Hardingham on 31 October 1794, aged eighty. His wife, Mary, died on 21 June 1791, aged seventy-five.   ARTEMIS GAUSE-STAMBOULOPOULOU

Sources *GM*, 1st ser., 64 (1794), 1060 · *GM*, 1st ser., 89/2 (1819), 3–4, 100–02, 212–14, 320–22, 414–19, 503–4 · *GM*, 1st ser., 92/1 (1822), 125–8 · Nichols, *Lit. anecdotes*, 9.716 · Watt, *Bibl. Brit.*, 1.437 · Venn, *Alum. Cant.*, 1/2.259 · S. A. Allibone, *A critical dictionary of English literature and British and American authors*, [another edn], 1 (1877) · H. J. Rose, *A new general biographical dictionary*, ed. H. J. Rose and T. Wright, 12 vols. (1848), vol. 8, p. 99 · *DNB*

Green, Sir William, **first baronet** (1725–1811), military engineer and army officer, was born on 4 April 1725 in St Martin-in-the-Fields, Westminster, and baptized in the parish church on 11 April. He was the eldest son of Farbridge Green, and his wife, Helen Smith. His father came from Ireland and had married his mother in Aberdeen. Farbridge Green settled in Durham, but his son William was educated in Aberdeen by his mother's sisters. On 1 January 1737 Green joined the Royal Military Academy at the Woolwich warren as a cadet gunner and on 12 March 1744 was appointed practitioner engineer and stationed at Portsmouth. Early in 1745 he joined the engineer brigade in Flanders, taking part in all the operations of the campaign and being present at the battle of Fontenoy. He embarked with the expedition to Brittany in 1746 led by General James Sinclair, and was present at the siege of Lorient and the attack on Quiberon. On 2 January 1748 Green was promoted to sub-engineer and sent into operations at Flanders, having the local rank of engineer-in-ordinary. He was present in the military action at Sandberg and the battle of Val where he was wounded and taken prisoner. He was also present at the siege of Bergen-op-Zoom from mid-July to mid-September 1751; the four

Sir William Green, first baronet (1725–1811), by unknown artist

plans he drew of this fortress, dated 1751, are now retained in the British Library. When the army withdrew from Flanders he remained with other engineers and together they made a survey of the Austrian Netherlands. With a brother officer he made plans of the area between 's-Hertogenbosch and Geertruidenberg, marking inundation and also showing drawings of the galleries and mines of the fortress of Luxembourg; all these drawings are in the British Library.

On 1 January 1749 Green was appointed engineer-extraordinary and was recalled from the Netherlands and sent to Portsmouth to urge forward the fortification of the dockyards. He remained at Portsmouth until the summer of 1750 when he was sent to Landguard Fort to work under Sub-Director Justly Watson.

In 1752 he was ordered to Newfoundland, where he completed a survey and made a report on the defences. On 26 February 1754, Green married Miriam (d. 1782), Watson's daughter. They had two sons and five daughters. Miriam was with her husband in the theatre of war in Canada and later in much of the siege of Gibraltar. The year 1755 saw him posted as chief engineer at Newfoundland where he had the task of making a reconnaissance of Louisbourg and sending a plan of the town and harbour to George II. When the engineers were granted military rank on 14 May 1757 Green became captain-lieutenant. That month he joined the expedition commanded by John Campbell, fourth earl of Loudoun, at Halifax, Nova Scotia. For a time he instructed the forces at Halifax in military engineering. He then joined the fleet and reconnoitred Cape Breton

and Louisbourg, later being present at the landing on the former and at the successful siege and capture of the latter under Loudoun's replacement, Major-General James Abercromby. He was next sent to the Lake Country where Abercromby detached him to build a fort at the Oneida station. He was promoted captain on 4 January 1758.

In the campaign of 1759 Green was attached to General James Wolfe's force and was present at the repulse of Montmorenci on 31 July during the siege of Quebec. On 10 September 1759 Green was advanced to the ranks of sub-director and major. In the battle on the Plains of Abraham in the September, Green was wounded in the forehead by a shell splinter. He was also engaged in the final subjugation of Canada and in particular the capture of Montreal. The year 1760 saw him at the battle of Sillery on 28 April and, later, involved in the defence of Quebec during the French siege.

At the end of the Canadian campaign Green returned to England and was stationed in Plymouth, whence he was dispatched to Gibraltar at the end of 1760 as senior engineer. On 8 February 1762 he was made lieutenant-colonel. He returned to England in 1769 to describe to the Board of Ordnance his notions for improving the defence of Gibraltar. In 1770 Green returned to Gibraltar, wrote his report on the defence works and made his proposals for rendering the rock of Gibraltar impregnable, an estimate of the cost being £50,000; this report is in the British Library. George III sanctioned the proposed expenditure on the advice of the chief engineer of Great Britain, Lieutenant-General William Skinner. Green's services were rewarded in November 1770 when he was awarded an extra daily payment of 30 shillings to be drawn from Gibraltar's revenues. In 1771 he designed Gibraltar's general hospital.

Green's experience during the reconstruction of the defences of Gibraltar convinced him that the best workmen for military engineering tasks came not from among civilian hired labour but from mechanics in army regiments, particularly the artillery. He proposed, through Governor Edward Cornwallis, that a corps of military artificers should be formed to work exclusively on engineering tasks. The royal warrant for the soldier–artificer company, as it was called, was issued on 6 March 1772; the new company, headed by Green, evolved into the Royal Sappers and Miners (1815) who in 1856 were incorporated into the non-commissioned ranks of the Royal Engineers.

Green was highly regarded by Cornwallis's successor, George Eliott. On 28 August 1777 he was promoted colonel, and soon afterwards was sent by Eliott to London to seek additional resources for the perfection of Gibraltar's fortifications. Green had several personal interviews with George III and returned to Gibraltar in May 1778 empowered to proceed with the proposed works, which included a new, superior battery above the existing posts on the north face of the rock, later renamed Green's Lodge. December 1778 saw Green promoted to the engineer rank of director, equivalent to his army rank of lieutenant-colonel.

Green's additional work at Gibraltar was undertaken against the background of deteriorating relations with

Spain, which entered into a secret alliance with France in April 1779, thus joining the American War of Independence in the hope of reducing the British presence in the Mediterranean and the West Indies. By 18 June 1779 Gibraltar was under close blockade by land and sea; open hostilities with Spanish forces began on 12 September 1779, when the British garrison opened fire on the Spanish lines. Green, one of only eight officers commanding approximately 4800 troops, lived in Gibraltar with his wife and their youngest daughter, Charlotte, at a house he had built, Mount Pleasant, as well as in the chief engineer's official residence. Miriam Green kept a diary of the siege from 1779 until her health collapsed in 1781, which is useful as a record of the privations suffered by the non-military inhabitants. Green himself suffered from poor health for much of the siege but none the less displayed consistent leadership. In August 1780, following a verbal assault in front of their regiment, the 39th foot, by Colonel Charles Ross on the deputy governor, Lieutenant-General Robert Boyd, Green presided at the court martial that sentenced Ross to twelve months' suspension and discharged him from the regiment, a sentence immediately mitigated by Eliott. In September that year, perhaps seeking to improve fellow feeling among the senior ranks, Green formed the American Club, consisting of officers who had served in North America with Wolfe.

The engineer's residence was destroyed by bombardment in April 1781; Green's family survived in a shelter but Mrs Green's health, already frail, gave way altogether. She and Charlotte departed for England in June 1781, where Mrs Green died on 21 June 1782. Green was promoted brigadier in April 1781, and major-general in October, but his request to return home in February 1782 was denied. Green supervised the continual reconstruction of the batteries on the north face and from May 1782 supervised the construction of the famous subterranean galleries there, although the concept and execution of the galleries was the work of his sergeant-major, Henry Ince.

On 13 September 1782 Green was conspicuous in his exertions against the combined attack of the enemy's land forces and fleets. The uninterrupted firing of hot shot throughout the day and night, from his kilns, ending in the destruction of the enemy's line of bombarding ships, contributed especially to the garrison's success. The enemy on one occasion opened a cave on the precipitous side of the rock which Green had closed up before the siege and, although then aged fifty-seven, he caused himself to be lowered down the face of the rock for several hundred feet to ensure that it was being competently dealt with. The famous Orange bastion on the sea face—a heavy piece of masonry—was also rebuilt during the continuous cannonade. By this time peace talks were advanced; hostilities ended on 2 February 1783.

On 7 June 1783, after more than twenty-two years of service at Gibraltar, Green returned to London, had an audience with George III, and received the thanks of both houses of parliament. He was appointed a member of the board supervising fortifications of Plymouth and Portsmouth in 1784. On 27 June 1786 he was created a baronet

and on 15 November the same year, chief engineer after the death of Major-General James Bramham. In 1787 he extended the artificer companies and was appointed commandant of the corps. He was made president of the defence committee in 1788, a position he held until 1797. On 12 October 1793 he was promoted lieutenant-general, and finally, on 1 January 1798, he attained the rank of full general. Sir William retired on pension in 1802 and lived at Brambleberry House, Plumstead, Kent. He died on 11 January 1811 at Bifrons House, near Canterbury, Kent, the home of his eldest daughter, Miriam, and her husband, Major Oliver Nicholls. He was buried at Plumstead.

Green's son, **Sir Justly Watson Green**, second baronet (1755–1826), was born in Newfoundland on 8 October 1755. He also followed a military career, becoming an officer in the 1st Royals. By 1783 he had attained the rank of captain, when, on 12 September, he was appointed 'instructor in Mathematicks and other branches of military knowledge' (*Later Correspondence of George III*, 6.4301) by George III to the king's fourth son, Edward, later duke of Kent. Green travelled with Prince Edward on the continent, probably until the prince's unauthorized return home in 1790. From Gibraltar on 24 January 1791 Edward recommended Green for promotion, as someone 'equally respectable as a man and as an officer' (*Later Correspondence of George III*, 1.650). Green later became a colonel. He succeeded his father in 1811, but never married, and died at Chichester, Sussex, between 12 November and 15 December 1826, when the baronetcy became extinct.

R. H. VETCH, *rev.* W. JOHNSON

Sources T. H. McGuffie, *The siege of Gibraltar, 1779–1783* (1965) · J. Russell, *Gibraltar besieged, 1779–1783* (1965) · W. Johnson, 'The siege of Gibraltar: mostly relating to the shooting of hot shot and setting fire to a besieging fleet', *International Journal of Impact Engineering*, 6 (1987), 175–210 · W. Porter, *History of the corps of royal engineers*, 1 (1889) · R. F. Edwards, ed., *Roll of officers of the corps of royal engineers from 1660 to 1898* (1898) · [M. Green], 'A lady's experiences in the great siege of Gibraltar', *Royal Engineers Journal*, new ser., 15 (1912), 37–44, 107–18, 163–82, 245–62, 309–26, 383–400 · [M. Green], 'A lady's experiences in the great siege of Gibraltar', *Royal Engineers Journal*, new ser., 16 (1912), 31–50 · J. Drinkwater, *A history of the late siege of Gibraltar* (1785) · S. Ancell, *A circumstantial journal of the long and tedious blockade and siege of Gibraltar*, 2nd edn (1785) · J. Heriot, *An historical sketch of Gibraltar, with an account of the siege which that fortress stood against the combined forces of France and Spain* (1792) · J. Spilsbury, *A journal of the siege of Gibraltar*, ed. B. H. T. Frere (1908) · D. Chandler and I. Beckett, eds., *The Oxford illustrated history of the British army* (1994) · *The later correspondence of George III*, ed. A. Aspinall, 5 vols. (1962–70) · GEC, *Baronetage*, 5.253 · *GM*, 1st ser., 81/1 (1811), 188 · J. Burke and J. B. Burke, *A genealogical and heraldic history of the extinct and dormant baronetcies of England, Ireland and Scotland*, 2nd edn (1841); repr. (1844)

Archives NAM, report on the fortifications of Gibraltar · PRO, MSS relating to defences at Gravesend, etc., PRO 30/11

Likenesses J. S. Copley, group portrait, oils (*The defeat of the floating batteries at Gibraltar*), Guildhall Art Gallery · oils, Royal Engineers, Brompton barracks, Chatham, Kent [*see illus.*]

Green, William (1760–1823), landscape painter and etcher, was born on 25 August 1760, at 3 Windmill Street, Lad Lane, Deansgate, Manchester, the son of Joshua Green (*b.* 1725), schoolmaster, and his wife, Catherine Simpson (1734–1760). Initially his father's pupil, he later attended

Dr Henry Clarke's Mathematical School at Salford and in 1776–7 trained with a surveyor and planner, Christopher Woodroofe. First engaged as assistant to the surveyor William Yates employed in mapping in north Lancashire, he was encouraged to become an artist by Benjamin West. He returned to Manchester and became a drawing-teacher, producing an important plan of Manchester (1787–92, Manchester Museum).

Green was primarily a watercolourist and etcher, but he occasionally painted in oils. He published engravings of Derwent Water in the Lake District (some of which are now in the British Museum, London) and then in 1795 a series of forty-eight etchings, *Picturesque Views of the North of England and Wales*. In the late 1790s he moved to London where he furthered his education. He etched W. H. Watts's illustrations of Thomas Garnett's *Tour of the Highlands and Western Isles* (1800) on fifty-two oval plates; in 1800 he also etched thirty-six *Views of Kent* after drawings by J. Wood. On 29 April 1800 he married Anne Bamford (1784–1833), a barmaid, and with his bride settled in Ambleside and devoted himself to drawing the scenery of the Lake District; the couple had ten children. Green's patrons were both locals and visitors; purchasers from further afield included George IV and even European royalty. At his best he produced many important watercolours of the area, but he also had a flourishing—if less accomplished—line for the tourists.

In 1804 Green published a series of sixty aquatints of the district. At this time he was supplementing his income by intensive teaching courses, for which some of his drawings were done as examples to copy: seventy-eight of these *Studies from Nature*, in the form of large soft- and hard-ground etchings of Westmorland and Cumberland, were published in 1809. In 1810 another sixty, larger, *Studies from Nature*, mostly views of lakes and mountains and all soft-ground etchings, were published together with a small book of text to explain the prints. He produced his book of sixty small prints in 1814 with an accompanying explanatory text, and in 1815 he made a further series of sixty aquatints of the mountains and lakes. At the same time he began preparing guidebooks. In 1819 he published the *Tourist's New Guide* in two volumes, illustrated with a variety of etchings and aquatints of the Lake District. It was sold in two formats of either 1 or 2 guineas, the latter supplied complete with a set of his own paints with which to colour his illustrations. (Hence copies of the *Guide* can still be found where his precise, unfaded palette may still be seen.) In 1819 too Green had brought out a set of thirty-six etchings of buildings in and around Ambleside; there followed in 1821 a series of forty etched *Views of Keswick and Ambleside*. These last two editions show a high standard of technical draughtsmanship and in 1820 his twelve large aquatinted *Views of the Lakes* appeared, which were probably his finest aquatints. According to 'fliers' inserted in his publications, he planned to publish similar volumes with views of buildings and scenery in the north of England, but these do not seem to have been completed.

Although when he came to Ambleside in 1800 Green deplored the modernization of houses in the village,

when he wrote his tourist's guide he included a detailed plan for a 'garden city' above Keswick and also suggested the building of a canal from Newby Bridge to the coast to help the tourist trade. His artistic and mental vigour were matched by his astounding physical energy in climbing throughout the district in order to select his ideal view points. Despite his attachment to the locality he was by no means a commonplace topographical artist. He admired and learned from the works of landscape painters as diverse and eminent as Claude Lorrain and Salvator Rosa, and was particularly remarkable for his depiction of cloudy skies. Among British artists he admired the landscape painter J. C. Ibbetson, whose influence has been seen in his treatment of trees. Green's careful diligence was particularly apparent in his engravings and etchings: his aquatints were often hand-coloured, and he frequently heightened his etchings in his own hand with indian ink. Throughout his life at Ambleside, he made a considerable number of large pencil drawings of outstanding quality.

William Green died on 29 April 1823 at Ambleside, and was buried in Grasmere parish churchyard; his wife survived him and died on 15 January 1833. William Wordsworth, who wrote his epitaph, celebrated there his 'skill and industry as an artist' and praised his 'faithful representations of the country and lasting memorials of its more perishable features'. The Romantic visualization of the Lake District certainly owed much to his paintings; his works are in local collections such as the Abbot Hall Art Gallery in Kendal and Dove Cottage in Grasmere, as well as in national collections such as the Victoria and Albert Museum and the British Museum, London.

MARY E. BURKETT

Sources C. Roeder, *William Green, the Lakes artist (1760–1823): a biographical sketch* (1897) [repr. from *Transactions of the Lancashire and Cheshire Antiquarian Society*, vol. 14] • 1802–21, Abbot Hall Art Gallery, Kendal, William Green MSS • M. E. Burkett and J. D. G. Sloss, *William Green of Ambleside: a Lake District artist (1760–1823)* (1984) • *Harrop's Mercury* (1787–95) • *Miss Weeton's journal of a governess*, ed. E. Hall, 1 (1936); repr. with an introduction by J. J. Bagley (1969) • tombstone, churchyard, parish church, Grasmere, Westmorland
Archives Abbot Hall Art Gallery, Kendal
Likenesses pencil and chalk sketch, repro. in H. D. Rawnsley, *By fell and dale at the English lakes* (1911)

Green, William Curtis (1875–1960), architect, was born at Alton, Hampshire, on 16 July 1875, the second son of Frederic Green, barrister, and his wife, Maria Heath Curtis. Educated at Newton College, Devon, he studied engineering at West Bromwich Technical School and architecture at Birmingham School of Art. He moved to London where he was articled to John Belcher and trained at the Royal Academy Schools under R. Phené Spiers. There his superb architectural draughtsmanship became apparent, and his illustrations regularly featured in the architectural periodicals of the time. He joined the staff of *The Builder* for a brief period in 1897, and he travelled widely at home and abroad to develop his skills. Much later, the results of these and other journeys were embodied in a book, published in 1949.

Curtis Green commenced practice in 1898 and was soon

William Curtis Green (1875–1960), by Elliott & Fry, 1942

character. The sometimes austere, but finely detailed, masonry of his banks and insurance offices is combined with a use of the classical orders that could be a little overdone. This was often relieved, however, by the rich flow of his beautifully designed wrought ironwork, in grilles and balconies, and by the scarlet, gold, and black of his colour schemes, particularly in the interior of Wolseley House. In one of his later works, the charming little Barclays Bank at 161 New Bond Street, he adopted a cheerful and inventive chinoiserie. During the last years of his career, when he was associated with his son-in-law and son, his work exhibited a quiet maturity and eliminated the orders. The new building for Scotland Yard on the Embankment (1935–40) and the exterior of the Equity and Law Life Assurance Society, in Lincoln's Inn Fields (1936–7), have serene Portland stone elevations, with fine fenestration and a sense of scale that is urbane and satisfying.

The Dorchester Hotel in Park Lane is perhaps Green's best-known building. It is not his happiest creation, but he came to design it in unusual and difficult circumstances. Sir Owen Williams and three architects in succession had worked on the scheme and brought it up to ground level. The sponsors then asked Curtis Green to take it on. His hand was tied by the existing foundations and predetermined outline, but with energy and skill he tackled this complex problem. The hotel was opened on the advertised date in 1930, thirteen months later, owing largely to Green's careful supervision of every aspect of the project, including the architectural design, intricate plan requirements, complex construction, décor, and furnishing. The Queen's Hotel at Leeds, in collaboration with his partners and W. H. Hamlyn, likewise shows his skill in hotel planning.

Among Green's many domestic buildings, most of which were small in scale, Stockgrove Park near Leighton Buzzard, Bedfordshire, is remarkable. It was one of the largest houses built between the two wars and, in addition to the mansion on its commanding site, with covered swimming bath, rackets court, and gardens, there is a detached stable court, with a water tower, a guest house, an agent's house, entrance lodges, gates, and cottages, and a delightful thatched boathouse on the lake. The main house is planned round a forecourt, and expressed a sumptuous way of life soon to pass. Completed in 1939, it is a fine example of resurgent Georgian architecture, humane, English, and well-proportioned, with its multicoloured brickwork, its white sash windows, its green shutters, and its tiled roofs. Stanmore village, Winchester, and Hardwick Garden Village, Chepstow, in collaboration with William Dunn, further demonstrate Curtis Green's skill in planning layout and designing the small house. He twice built houses in Surrey for himself: Langdown, Frensham, and Goodmans Furze, Headley (1932).

Green's churches—the Good Shepherd, Dockenfield, Surrey; St Christopher's, Cove; St George's, Waddon; St Francis's, Rough Close, Stoke-on-Trent; and All Saints', Shirley, Croydon—are quiet and pleasing examples of ecclesiastic architecture. Curtis Green should be judged by the standards of his generation; and by that standard of

busy with domestic and other buildings. Among his first important buildings were two fine generating stations for electric tramway companies, at Bristol (1899) and Chiswick (1904), and the Painswick Institute (1907). He was joint author with Galsworthy Davie of *Old Cottages and Farmhouses in Surrey* in 1908. He was elected fellow of the Royal Institute of British Architects (RIBA) in 1909. When Edwin Lutyens first went to New Delhi, he asked Green to take charge of his office while he was away. This greatly influenced him and enlarged his understanding of monumental work in the grand manner. A further opportunity came to him in 1910, when he was taken into partnership by Dunn and Watson who had a large city practice: soon he was left in sole charge. From 1919 to 1927 he practised on his own and then he established a partnership with his son, Christopher, and his son-in-law Antony Lloyd. They continued the practice after his death at the firm of Green, Lloyd, and Adams.

In London, Curtis Green made a lasting mark in Piccadilly. His first large building, Wolseley House (1922–3), originally a motor showroom and later a bank, made a great impact in its day and received the first RIBA medal for the best building of the preceding three years. This was followed by the Westminster Bank (1926–7) on the other side of Piccadilly, and later Stratton House (1929), next to Devonshire House. 6 King Street, adjacent to Piccadilly, and the London Life Association building in King William Street belong to the same group of buildings of similar scholarly, personal design, fine building, and good craftsmanship he stands high. In his long working life his enthusiasm and integrity produced a large output, and he was equally happy in town and country. From his days as a student at the schools, Curtis Green was a staunch supporter of the Royal Academy, to which he was elected as an associate in 1923, becoming a full academician ten years later. He was a royal gold medallist of RIBA in 1942 and was chairman of its board of architectural education. He was president of the Architectural Association, a member of the Royal Fine Arts Commission, and an officer of the Académie Française. For thirty-eight years he gave devoted service to the Artists' General Benevolent Institution.

Curtis Green was twice married: first, on 19 October 1899, to Cicely Dillworth (1872/3–1934), daughter of Francis Henry Lloyd; and second, on 2 August 1935, to Laura Gwenllian James (1874/5–1952), widow of the third Lord Northbourne and daughter of Admiral Sir Ernest Rice. From his first marriage he had one son and four daughters. He died at his house in London, 16/17 Pall Mall, on 26 March 1960. He shared his interest in traditional craftsmanship with his brother, Arthur Romney Green (1872–1945), a craftsman and furniture designer. Romney Green had been a mathematician at Cambridge but abandoned academic life to concentrate on his enthusiasm for furniture and woodworking at his workshop in Christchurch, Hampshire. His work combines underlying geometric principles with the traditional practices associated with the work of Ernest Gimson and the Barnsley brothers, but he was also indebted to Georgian prototypes. He was the author of *Woodwork in Principle and Practice* (1918).

HUBERT WORTHINGTON, *rev.* CATHERINE GORDON

Sources *The Times* (28 March 1960) · *RIBA Journal*, 67 (1959–60), 307 · A. S. Gray, *Edwardian architecture: a biographical dictionary* (1985), 199–200 · *The Builder*, 198 (1 April 1960), 642 · *AA Journal*, 75/842 (May 1960), 229 · [Green, Lloyd, and Adams], *W. Curtis Green R. A.* (1978) [exhibition catalogue, RIBA Heinz Gallery] · *The drawings of W. Curtis Green R. A.* (1949) · C. H. Reilly, *Representative British architects of the present day* (1931), 99–110 · M. Comino, *Gimson and the Barnsleys* (1980), 173, 179, 190–91 · m. certs. · d. cert. · *CGPLA Eng. & Wales* (1960) · private information (1971) · personal knowledge (1971)
Archives Architectural Association, London, administration papers · priv. coll., MSS · RIBA, nomination papers, etc.
Likenesses W. Stoneman, photographs, 1933, NPG · Elliott & Fry, photograph, 1942, NPG [*see illus.*]
Wealth at death £93,921 9s. 4d.: probate, 24 May 1960, *CGPLA Eng. & Wales*

Green, Sir William Kirby Mackenzie (1836–1891), diplomatist, born in 1836 at Nauplia in Greece, was the son of Sir John Green (d. 18 Sept 1877), consul-general at Bucharest from 1867 to 1874, and his wife, Margaret, daughter of George Suter. He was educated abroad and entered the consular service at the age of seventeen. In 1856 he became private secretary to the consul-general for Egypt, and in 1859 became secretary to John Drummond Hay, remaining in the public service in Morocco for several years. He was vice-consul at Tetuan and acting consul at Tangier, and was engaged on special missions in the court of Morocco at various times during the next ten years. In

1863 he married Mary, daughter of Colonel Sir Thomas Radle, agent and consul-general in Tunis. They had children, including two sons, one of whom, John Arthur, was a clerk in the consulate in Tangier, in 1891.

In 1869 Green was transferred to Tunis as acting agent and consul-general, and thence was moved to Damascus in 1871 and to Beirut in 1873. In 1876 he was promoted to be consul at Scutari, and on 6 January 1879 he became consul-general for Montenegro and the vilayet of Scutari. He consistently maintained the view that the Turkish government, though in urgent need of reform, was not beyond hope, and that the Christian subjects of the Porte were not faultless. He was frequently consulted by government, his opinions appeared in many blue books, and he was freely attacked by the anti-Turkish party in England. In 1881 he was created CMG in recognition of his services, and on 21 June 1887 KCMG.

On 1 July 1886 Green succeeded Sir John Drummond Hay as envoy to Morocco and consul-general at Tangier. In Tangier his excellent knowledge of oriental languages, together with his diplomatic ability, enabled him to obtain several important concessions from Mawlay Hassan, among others the running of a telegraph cable between Tangier and Gibraltar, which the sultan had consistently refused in the previous twelve years. It is not clear whether this cable was in fact run: certainly it would have presented technical difficulties.

On 10 December 1890 Green started on a special mission to Morocco to obtain from the sultan compensation for the destruction of the factories of the North-West Africa Company by a party of Bedouin Arabs. He was successful in his mission, but died suddenly in the city of Morocco on 24 February 1891. He was buried at Tangier on 8 March.

E. I. CARLYLE, *rev.* ELIZABETH BAIGENT

Sources Burke, *Peerage* (1891) · Burke, *Peerage* (1907) · *FO List* (1891) · *The Times* (3 March 1891) · *The Times* (4 March 1891) · *The Times* (9 March 1891) · *The Times* (10 March 1891) · *The Times* (14 March 1891) · K. R. Haigh, *Cableships and submarine cables* (1968) · consular records, Registrar General Office · *CGPLA Eng. & Wales* (1891)
Archives BL, corresp. with Sir Austen Layard, Add. MSS 39012–39034, 39134, *passim* · Bodl. Oxf., letters to Sir Edmund Monson
Likenesses wood-engraving (after photograph by Elliott & Fry), NPG; repro. in *ILN* (14 March 1891)
Wealth at death £922 16s. 4d.: resworn administration with will, May 1893, *CGPLA Eng. & Wales* (1891)

Green, William Pringle (1785–1846), naval officer and mechanical engineer, was born apparently at Halifax, Nova Scotia, the eldest son of Benjamin Green (d. 1794), treasurer of the province of Nova Scotia, a member of the house of assembly, and a justice of the court of common pleas. Green entered the *Cleopatra* as a midshipman in 1797, then served for three and a half years in the West Indies in *La Topaze*. He was afterwards in the *Circe* and the *Sanspareil*. After the peace of Amiens was signed he served in the *Trent*, and later the *Conqueror*, in which he took part in the capture of the *Bucentaure* during the battle of Trafalgar. He was promoted lieutenant for his services on 8 January 1806, and appointed to the *Formidable*. He afterwards served on the American coast as first lieutenant of the

Eurydice; it was during this period that he communicated to Sir John Borlase Warren, the squadron commander, his plans for bringing British ships up to the same gunpower as those of the Americans. In 1811 he commanded the brig *Resolute*, and carried out his plans for training the crew to the satisfaction of the Admiralty. The *Resolute* was paid off in 1815, and Green devoted his time to inventions, until he was appointed in 1829 to a Falmouth packet. After nearly three years' service she was paid off, and Green was then on half pay until 1842, when he was appointed lieutenant of the *Victory*. He fell into financial difficulties, however, and had to resign a year later.

Green was an officer of great mechanical ingenuity. In spite of constant discouragement he devoted the greater part of his life to the promotion of inventions and improvements connected with the service, many of which were introduced throughout the navy. The Society of Arts in 1823 presented him with a silver medal for his improvements in rigging ships, as they subsequently did for his 'tiller for a disabled rudder' and his 'gun-carriage and jointed ramrod for naval use'. In 1836, and again in 1837, he took out patents for improvements in capstans (no. 7193), and in machinery employed in raising, lowering, and moving heavy objects (no. 7400). He had previously, in 1833, published *Fragments from remarks of twenty-five years in every quarter of the globe on electricity, magnetism, aerolites, and various other phenomena of nature*. He died at Landport, Portsmouth, on 18 October 1846, leaving his widow and ten children with a pension of just £50 a year.

Despite his inventive turn of mind and the early patronage of the duke of Kent, Green lacked the political support necessary for a successful naval career, and gained no tangible benefit from his work in an era when intellectual property rights could only be upheld with powerful financial backing. JAMES BURNLEY, rev. ANDREW LAMBERT

Sources O'Byrne, *Naval biog. dict.* · *GM*, 2nd ser., 27 (1847), 209
Likenesses portrait, repro. in W. P. Green, *Fragments… on electricity, magnetism, aerolites, and various other phenomena of nature* (1833)
Wealth at death pension of £50 p.a.: *DNB*

Greenacre, James [called the Edgware Road Murderer] (1785–1837), murderer, was born at West Winch, Norfolk. He was the son of a farmer, and by his own account, went to London as a young man and started a grocery and tea business in the parish of St George's, Woolwich. He had three wives all of whom died, but not in suspicious circumstances. The first was the daughter of Charles Weer (or Ware) who kept the Crown and Anchor in Woolwich, whom he married in 1803 or 1804; she died of 'a putrid sore throat'. The second was the daughter of John Romford of Essex, with whom he had three children and who died of brain fever. The third was a Miss Simmonds of Bermondsey, with whom he had seven children, only two of whom lived for any length of time. Greenacre was considered a respectable citizen into whose charge many well-connected apprentices were given, despite his reputation for violent political opinions. He acquired three cottages in Jane Place, Old Kent Road, and eight more in Bowyer Lane, Camberwell; by 1830 he had opened a large grocery shop in the Kent Road in which he displayed political

pamphlets, and he was elected parish overseer on Easter Tuesday 1832. He made orations at the White Lion Radical Committee room and was associated with Arthur Thistlewood and his co-conspirators, and narrowly escaped arrest for complicity in the Cato Street conspiracy.

In May 1833 a seizure of sloe leaves, an illegal additive to tea, was made on Greenacre's premises, to which he riposted by writing a pamphlet on the adulteration of tea. He could not pay the fine of £150 and departed for America with one of his sons, leaving his third wife behind to deal with his affairs. She, however, died three weeks later of cholera, and all the property was claimed by her relatives. Greenacre was married yet again in America, to the daughter of a London coach proprietor who had been sent out to live with a rich female relative. He became a carpenter and showed remarkable ingenuity in inventing a washing machine. He returned to London without his wife and son in 1835 to try to recoup his affairs. Rumours began to circulate about him at this time, and on 31 May 1836 he took out a warrant against a Mr and Mrs Gild of Camberwell who had accused him of having murdered an illegitimate child which had disappeared, but the case foundered. He was also accused of drugging a woman in order to procure an abortion, but this charge was withdrawn for lack of evidence.

About September 1836, when living at 6 Carpenter's Buildings, Camberwell, Greenacre advertised in *The Times* for a partner to provide £300 for the commercial exploitation of his washing machine; it was answered by a washerwoman named Hannah Brown. She was the widow of a shoemaker, Thomas Brown, who had met his death at sea when he left her to go to America. She stated that she had just the sum of money Greenacre was looking for, and a marriage between them was arranged for Christmas day 1836 in St Giles, Camberwell. On 24 December, when she joined him at his house, he murdered her. He cut up the body and disposed of the pieces in various localities round London, where they began to be found later in December, the head, for example, in the Regent's Canal at Stepney. Inspector Feltham was put in charge of the case and on 24 March 1837 arrested Greenacre, who was preparing to sail for America, at St Alban's Place, Kennington Road. With him was also arrested his mistress, Sarah Gale: Hannah Brown's earrings were found in Gale's possession. Greenacre, who was by now aged fifty-one or fifty-two, of middle height and stout build, was visited in prison by members of parliament and noblemen.

The trial at the central criminal court, at which Greenacre appeared clad in a blue coat, a fancy waistcoat, and a black stock, lasted two days, 10 and 11 April 1837, and both defendants were convicted and sentenced to death. Greenacre insisted that Gale had not known about the murder, to which he ultimately admitted, and her sentence was commuted to transportation for life to Australia, where she died in 1888. Greenacre tried to hang himself in his cell, and spent his time writing many letters and explanatory documents. He was hanged on 2 May 1837 in front of Newgate, the execution being witnessed by at least 20,000 persons who gathered over two days; a fairground atmosphere prevailed, with prize-fighters sparring under the gallows to keep the crowd amused. Greenacre showed great self-possession and strength of nerve on the scaffold, where he asked, 'Don't leave me too long in the concourse and make the rope tight'. Back in Newgate, Greenacre's head was shaved for examination by phrenologists before he was buried in the prison. He was survived by four of his children. Plays based on the Edgware Road murder were given in the penny theatres and an effigy of Greenacre was made for Madame Tussaud's waxwork exhibition. Greenacre's death mask, made on 4 May 1837 by J. Miller of Theobald's Road, later became an exhibit in New Scotland Yard's Black Museum, along with handwritten notes which he passed to his counsel during the trial.   GORDON GOODWIN, *rev.* J. GILLILAND

Sources R. D. Altick, *Victorian studies in scarlet* (1972) · *The Times* (26 March 1837) [*et seq.*] · *Life and career of J. G. etc.* (1837) · 'The Paddington tragedy', *Oddities* (1837) · C. J. Williams, *Greenacre, or, The Edgware-Road murder* [n.d., *c.*1837] · C. Pelham, *The chronicles of crime*, [another edn], 2 vols. (1886) · B. Waddell, *The Black Museum: New Scotland Yard* (1995) · P. Chapman, *Madame Tussaud's* (1984) · T. Ingoldsby [R. H. Barham], *The Ingoldsby legends, or, Mirth and marvels*, ed. D. C. Browning, 3 vols. (1960) · J. Greenacre, *The osier bed at Camberwell* (1837)
Archives New Scotland Yard, London, Black Museum
Likenesses E. Evans, portrait, repro. in *Catalogue of English portraits* (1853), no. 16514 · death mask, New Scotland Yard, London, Black Museum · effigy, Madame Tussaud's · eight portraits, repro. in *Weekly Chronicle* (1837)

Greenall, Peter (1796–1845), brewer, was born on 25 April 1796 at Wilderspool, Warrington, the second son of Edward Greenall (1758–1835), brewer, and his wife, Betty (*d.* 1835), daughter of John Pratt of Liverpool. His grandfather, Thomas Greenall (1733–1805), taking advantage of the opening up of the south Lancashire coalfield by canal in 1757, set up as common brewer four years later in Hardshaw. Over the course of the next century this hamlet developed into the town of St Helens. Before his death Thomas Greenall had bought 350 acres of land in the neighbourhood as well as 14 public houses and other properties. In 1786 he became associated with others in the brewery at Wilderspool, which his son Edward managed from 1792. Edward in his turn acquired all the business interests of his brothers Peter (*d.* 1815) and William (*d.* 1817). In 1818 Edward sent his son Peter, not yet twenty-two years old, to take charge of the brewery at St Helens and the considerable family possessions there. On 6 March 1821 Peter Greenall married Eleanor Pilkington (1798–1846), who brought a dowry of £1000. Eleanor was sister of Richard and William Pilkington, already partners with their father in the little town's flourishing wine and spirit business. The couple had two daughters.

Peter Greenall accepted his responsibilities as leading local resident in an industrial district which by then numbered ten thousand people, of whom about four thousand lived in the town itself. Pipes were laid from the brewery's ponds to supply water to those inhabitants who could afford to pay for it. The first (terminating) building society in the area was formed at his instigation and helped to put up houses, many of them on his land. By 1830 Greenall's rents in the area totalled nearly £2500 a year. He headed the local Oddfellows lodge, Manchester Unity, when it was opened in 1825; when St Helens was raised to district status he became its grand master. His signature appeared on share certificates of the local Gas Light Company, formed in 1832, and, more importantly, he took the lead in the creation of the St Helens and Runcorn Gap Railway in 1830. This provided transport down to the River Mersey, from November 1832, in competition with the canal. In the longer run, however, it was Greenall's involvement in what was to become Pilkington Brothers glassworks which was to be of much greater significance. Greenall held only three of the eleven shares in the partnership—his two brothers-in-law, who had reluctantly forsaken the prosperous wine and spirit business, held the rest. Nevertheless, it was undoubtedly his influence at the Warrington bank of Parr, Lyon, and Greenall that saved the struggling firm from going under before it had grown strong enough to survive unaided; by 1842, at the depth of the worst depression of the century, the overdraft had reached £20,000, when all eleven shares were valued at only £22,600.

Greenall, a confirmed tory, contested one of the Wigan borough seats unsuccessfully in 1837, but he was returned in 1841. He then used his influence as an MP to get the St Helens Waterworks Bill through parliament in 1844 and, in 1845, the St Helens Improvement Bill, which gave the town's population, then just under 12,000, its first effective local government. Greenall died soon afterwards, on 18 September 1845, at his own house in St Helens, of 'apoplexy—first attack of five minutes duration', according to the death certificate. The shops half-closed their shutters. On the day of the funeral six days later at the parish church, the shops closed altogether. Many people flocked into the town to pay their last respects to the man who had so dominated the town's early growth and had died so unexpectedly, before his fiftieth birthday. His great reputation, however, was entirely local: the very brief notice in *The Times* merely drew attention to a tory vacancy in the Commons.   THEO BARKER

Sources T. C. Barker and J. R. Harris, *A Merseyside town in the industrial revolution: St Helens, 1750–1900* (1954); repr. with corrections (1993) · T. C. Barker, *Pilkington Brothers and the glass industry* (1960) · *Liverpool Mercury* (19 Sept 1845) · *Manchester Guardian* (20 Sept 1845) · *Manchester Courier* (20 Sept 1845) · *The Times* (22 Sept 1845), 56 · *Liverpool Mercury* (26 Sept 1845) · *Annual Register* (1845), 296–7 · Burke, *Peerage* · d. cert. · will of Peter Greenall, proved Chester, 2 March 1846 · parish register (burials), St Helens, Lancashire, 24 Sept 1845 · private information (2004) · Greenall brewery, St Helens, Lancashire, Greenall MSS
Likenesses Spindler, portrait, St Helens town hall, Lancashire
Wealth at death under £35,000: will, proved, 2 March 1846

Greenaway, Catherine [Kate] (1846–1901), illustrator, was born on 17 March 1846 at 21 Cavendish Street, Hoxton, London, the second child of John Greenaway (1816–1890) and his wife, Elizabeth Jones (1813–1894).

Childhood and education Greenaway's father was a wood-engraver; and the irregularity of his income led her mother to open a successful milliner's shop in Islington in

Catherine Greenaway (1846–1901), by Elliott & Fry, 1870s

1851. It was here that most of Kate Greenaway's childhood was spent, often in the care of her elder sister, as her sternly respectable and somewhat humourless mother worked long hours. She was fascinated by the shops and entertainments of London, but was still more happy when on holiday with relatives in Rolleston in Nottinghamshire: many of her early watercolours depict the scenes and people of this quiet village. Shy yet temperamental, she was unhappy at the dame-schools to which her mother sent her and was largely educated by private tutors. Her favourite childhood activities reflected her vivid and emphatically visual imagination: she built up a large collection of dolls, around which she wove fantasies, and enjoyed looking at the illustrations of the leading periodicals and attending the theatre.

At the age of twelve Greenaway was enrolled as a full-time student at the Finsbury School of Art, where she had already taken evening classes. Here she studied for six years, completing the national course of art instruction initiated by Henry Cole to train designer craftsmen: the course's emphasis on linear design and geometry clearly influenced the patterned effect of her later illustrations. In 1865 she moved on to the National Art Training School in South Kensington, where she spent at least six years. Her shyness meant that she made few friends there, but among them was the painter Elizabeth Thompson, afterwards Lady Butler. She later attended the Heatherley School of Fine Art and enrolled at the Slade School of Fine

Art: both institutions advocated a less rigid approach to drawing and painting than Cole's school, but Greenaway found it difficult to modify her detailed and imitative style.

Early career as a book illustrator In 1867 Kate Greenaway's first book illustration—the frontispiece to *Infant Amusements, or, How to Make a Nursery Happy*—was published, clearly influenced by the style of John Leech and John Gilbert, book illustrators who worked within the picturesque and caricaturist style of the 1830s and 1840s. In the following year she exhibited drawings publicly for the first time, at the Dudley Gallery. In 1869 she received an important commission to produce six watercolours to illustrate *Diamonds and Toads*, a children's book published by Frederick Warne. By 1870 she had earned over £70 through book illustration, and her career was launched, with commissions secured for her by her early patron, William Loftie, and her father. She had also started designing cards for Marcus Ward & Co., her images ranging from delicate images of fairies and goblins to Pre-Raphaelite-inspired lovers.

In 1877 Greenaway broke with Ward & Co., who were using her card designs in books without consulting her; she was also driven by the desire to write the letterpress for her own illustrations (Ward had rejected the poems she had submitted with some of her designs). Her father approached Edmund Evans, with whom he had formerly worked in Ebenezer Landells's workshop and who now owned and ran a very successful colour-printing firm, producing many children's books. Evans liked her odd nonsense verses and their accompanying designs, and agreed to publish a book, *Under the Window* (1879). She became a close friend of the Evans family and a frequent visitor to their home at Witley in Surrey. Through Evans she was introduced to Randolph Caldecott, a fellow illustrator of children's books, and the society poet Frederick Locker, who was asked to amend some of her verses.

By 1879 Greenaway's income was large enough to allow her to pool resources with her father and buy a new house, 11 Pemberton Gardens, Holloway, for the family. She began illustrations for Charlotte Yonge's *The Heir of Redclyffe* and *Heartsease*: although she succeeded in capturing the sweetly insipid character of Violet, the heroine of *Heartsease*, these illustrations are among her worst, and they rightly confirmed her in her preference for illustrating her own text. She never completed this commission from Macmillan, but the runaway success of *Under the Window*—sales of which reached 100,000 copies in Greenaway's lifetime—had ensured her career. Her delicate and economical designs, her genius for the use of blank spaces, and her ability to dovetail her images to her text are all apparent in this book, which attracted artistic attention to her work. The Royal Academician Henry Stacey Marks offered well-meaning criticism of her treatment of feet, and Walter Crane—who described her book as 'old world atmosphere tinted with modern aestheticism' (Engen, 1981, 61)—was alarmed by the popularity of his new rival's work.

Relationship with Ruskin Through Marks, Greenaway was introduced to the ageing Ruskin, who found that her images of young girls ministered to his obsession for Rosa La Touche. He wrote her an extraordinarily impertinent letter on 6 January 1880, to which she responded warmly. She was swiftly adopted as one of his circle of female art protégées (E. E. Kellett later recalled how Ruskin brought fifty of her pictures to one of his Slade lectures and passed them round), and their correspondence continued for some twenty years, the lion's share falling to Kate. She was becoming an artistic celebrity and lost much of her erstwhile shyness: in the 1880s she became friends with Anna Thackeray Ritchie, the Tennyson family, and other literary lions.

In the autumn of 1880 Greenaway published *Kate Greenaway's Birthday Book*, a collection of illustrations which was an instant success. *Mother Goose, or, The Old Nursery Rhymes*, F. Locker-Lampson's *London Lyrics*, and *A Day in a Child's Life* followed in 1881, and the first of her illustrated almanacs appeared in 1883; 1884 saw the publication of a new edition of an old classic, William Mavor's *The English Spelling Book*, with Greenaway's illustrations, and an illustrated book of verses, *Marigold Garden*. Strongly influenced by eighteenth-century art, particularly the paintings of Gainsborough, and her most expensive book to date, this last was rather poorly received.

In the same year Greenaway spent a fortnight with Ruskin at Brantwood, and their friendship deepened. His lecture of that year, 'In fairyland', praised Greenaway and Helen Allingham for revitalizing the essential Greek spirit of fancy through their work. Nevertheless, he constantly advised her to undertake close studies of nature and to improve her grasp of anatomy, to adopt a more naturalistic yet neo-classical approach to her art. In one year her Christmas card to Ruskin of a wide-eyed girl led the critic to comment, 'To my mind it is a greater thing than Raphael's St Cecilia' (Engen, 1981, 76), an apparent absurdity which illustrates his intention to make Greenaway elevate her art. She took his advice very seriously, spending a week in Scarborough drawing after he had advised her to go to a seaside town to learn how to draw children's naked feet. Her work also occasionally showed the influence of the academic neo-classicists, such as Lord Leighton and Sir Edward Poynter; the frontispiece to *A Day in a Child's Life*, for instance, is reminiscent of Albert Moore.

By late 1883 Ruskin was alarmed by the degree of Greenaway's personal devotion—although still transfixed by the streams of drawings of young girls she sent to him (always clothed and often behatted, to his disappointment). He put off her visits to Brantwood, ignored her when he took tea at her house (concentrating all his attention on one of her models, Mary), and was a severe critic of *The Language of Flowers* (1884), an illustrated book on flower symbolism which she had produced under his influence.

1880s: Hampstead days In 1883 Greenaway moved to Hampstead, and in 1885 she bought 39 Frognal, a house which was designed for her by Norman Shaw, the leading architect in the Queen Anne style. The house contained an extensive studio, which she decorated in an aesthetic mode, and a garden, which she planted informally with traditional cottage flowers. She began to consider the possibility of abandoning book illustration in favour of painting—a course which seemed particularly tempting in view of the growing number of Greenaway imitators and the influence of Ruskin—but was still not prosperous enough to break her connection with Evans. Buoyed up by the high spirits which normally preceded a return of his periodic insanity, Ruskin collaborated with her to produce the decidedly undistinguished *Dame Wiggins of Lee* (1885), a revamped version of an early nineteenth-century children's story in verse. In July of that year she visited Brantwood, but departed as Ruskin's illness advanced.

The next few years proved bleak, with Ruskin either suffering fits of madness or absorbed in writing his autobiography, *Praeterita*. Greenaway's reputation was in decline in Britain (although sales of her work in America were buoyant). She continued to produce her almanacs and also illustrated Bret Harte's *The Queen of the Pirate Isle* (1886) for Chatto and Windus, a rare departure from her connection with Evans. In 1887 she illustrated Robert Browning's *Pied Piper of Hamelin* (1888) in a Pre-Raphaelite style. It is possibly her best work. The frontispiece is an accomplished and complex design with a beautifully rendered cherry tree at its heart, suggestive of Japanese influence as well as Greenaway's delight in English springs. The illustrations inside, meanwhile, are handsomely married to the text; the statuesque townsfolk, the Dantesque piper, the mastery of perspective (Ruskin's influence is apparent) and picturesque architectural settings, and the limited autumnal range of Greenaway's palette—all olive greens, pale teal blues, russets, browns, and salmon pink—contribute to make it one of the best illustrated children's books of the Victorian period.

Greenaway—as well as Ruskin—was unwell in the later 1880s, and she called in the physician Elizabeth Garrett Anderson to treat the first of a continuing series of colds, influenza, and rheumatic pains. Rather more cheeringly, in 1888 she spent much time with Helen Allingham at Witley, and was influenced by both her artistic ambitions and her robust attitude to Ruskin. In 1889 she turned down an invitation to Brantwood to embark on a series of watercolours for exhibition, inspired by Allingham's success and often joining her new companion on painting trips to the countryside. She sent thirteen of her original book illustrations to the Paris Universal Exhibition, where they met with considerable success, and she was elected to the Royal Institute of Painters in Water Colours. Her correspondence with Ruskin—often intermittent on his part—now ceased, and she turned to his cousin and companion Joan Severn for friendship and news.

Photographs of the younger Kate Greenaway show that she was always a rather plain woman—even the kindly Caldecott conceded that she was 'not beautiful' (*Yours Pictorially: Illustrated Letters of Randolph Caldecott*, ed. M. Hutchins, 1976, 38)—and in middle age she became stout. But, despite her stumpy nose, her deep-set dark eyes had—according to her early patron, William Loftie—'a certain impressive expression' (Engen, 1981, 46), which must have been all the more striking as, with advancing age, her eyebrows became increasingly marked.

The 1890s: new directions Greenaway's publications of 1889—*The Royal Progress of King Pepito* and *Kate Greenaway's Book of Games*—were not commercially successful, and she was obliged to sell an earlier picture, *Bubbles* (version, V&A), to the soap manufacturer Pears to be used as an advertisement. In 1890 her father died, leaving his family in some financial distress. Greenaway rose to the occasion, arranging a joint exhibition (with Hugh Thomson) of her old paintings and drawings at the Fine Art Society in 1891: sales of her work raised £964. But her health was declining, and enjoyable holidays in Bournemouth and Cromer with friends (the Ponsonbys and the Locker-Lampsons) failed to restore it. She continued to work towards another exhibition of her work at the Fine Art Society in early 1894. As at the previous exhibitions, both critics and buyers continued to prefer her earlier work to the larger and more ambitious watercolours which were now the staple of her output. Her mother's death in February 1894 caused her to stop working altogether for a couple of months, but she began to recover later in the year, paying visits to the invalid Ruskin in 1894 and 1895 and visiting London galleries, where she was equally, though differently, alarmed by Aubrey Beardsley and the impressionists. She viewed her own work now as a solitary attempt to maintain the artistic standards of the high Victorian Renaissance.

In 1895 Greenaway met and began a close (but probably not lesbian) relationship with Violet Dickinson, better known as the lover of Virginia Woolf. A robust personality, she ensured that Greenaway turned out for social occasions and cultural events and introduced some colour into her sober and shabby style of dress. During the late 1890s Greenaway continued to exhibit her watercolours, without much critical success. An exhibition at the Fine Art Society in 1898 was decidedly low-key, and Greenaway became increasingly reliant on wealthy patrons who were often also friends, such as Lady Dorothy Neville. She experimented with portraits of children in oils, began an autobiography which was never finished, resumed writing soothing letters to Ruskin, and planned to return to book illustration. She illustrated one last book: Elizabeth von Arnim's *The April Baby's Book of Tunes* (1900). In that year Ruskin died, a devastating blow for Greenaway. She was already suffering from breast cancer, a condition which she concealed from friends and family. In July 1900 she had an operation, but the cancer had now spread to her chest. She died at her home, 39 Frognal, Hampstead, on 6 November 1901; her body was cremated at Woking on 12 November, and on the following day her ashes were placed in the family plot in Hampstead cemetery.

Reputation and achievement A posthumous exhibition of Greenaway's work was held at the Fine Art Society in 1902, a biography by Marion Spielmann and G. S. Layard appeared in 1905, and a Greenaway memorial fund was established. Her reputation flourished on the continent and in America, but it was not until the 1920s that it

revived in Britain as collectors began to buy her work. The centenary of her birth led to a spate of new articles and books, and in 1955 the Kate Greenaway medal was established as an annual award for an outstanding illustrator of children's books. Reprints of some of her books have continued into the twenty-first century, her images have appeared on greetings cards, and her original drawings and first editions of her books have continued to fetch high prices in salerooms.

Despite all Greenaway's attempts to pursue the Ruskinian path of high art, both her popularity and her achievement really rest on her work as one of the three great illustrators of children's books in the mid-Victorian period. Her work clearly owes a debt, as contemporaries suggested, to the delicate engravings of Thomas Stothard. The illustrators of her own age with whom she is often compared are Walter Crane and Randolph Caldecott: with them, she promoted the Queen Anne style, a major facet of the aesthetic movement in the 1870s and 1880s. In her idyllic and profoundly nostalgic depictions of vaguely eighteenth-century and slightly stilted children, Greenaway combined strong outlines and a keen ability to arrange and pattern space with the use of a palette of soft, silvery pastel colours (it was not her fault that printers occasionally rendered these colours too crudely). Undoubtedly her range of subjects was narrow, and her illustrations lack both the sophistication of Crane's elaborate images and the visual wit and talent for characterization apparent in Caldecott's work. Nevertheless, as Percy Muir has put it, 'she created a small world of her own, a dream-world, a never-never-land' (Muir, 170) which appealed as much to adults as to children. It was a world that continued to be popular: the work of Hugh Thomson and the Macmillan 'Cranford' school adhered to the Greenaway tradition in the age of Beardsley. Mark Girouard nicely captures the modern commentator's ambiguous reaction to her illustrations: 'Many people, when looking through her books, must find revulsion from so much sweetness and quaintness fighting with admiration for her extraordinary skill'. But, he concludes, 'she is a minor master' (Girouard, 146).

ROSEMARY MITCHELL

Sources R. Engen, *Kate Greenaway* (1981) · M. Spielmann and G. S. Layard, *Kate Greenaway* (1905) · M. Girouard, *Sweetness and light: the Queen Anne movement, 1860–1900* (1977) · DNB · I. Taylor, *The art of Kate Greenaway: a nostalgic picture of childhood* (1991) · W. Ruddick, *Kate Greenaway, 1846–1901* (1976) [exhibition catalogue, Bolton Art Gallery, 1976] · *The reminiscences of Edmund Evans*, ed. R. McLean (1967) · T. E. Schuster and R. Engen, *Printed Kate Greenaway: a catalogue raisonné* (1986) · R. Engen, *Kate Greenaway* (1976) · P. Muir, *Victorian illustrated books* (1985) · J. I. Whalley and T. R. Chester, *A history of children's book illustration* (1988) · M. Hardie, *English coloured books* (1906) · b. cert. · CGPLA Eng. & Wales (1901) · E. E. Kellett, *As I remember* (1936)

Archives Boston PL, letters · Keats House, Hampstead, London, original drawings, proofs, Christmas cards, and books · Morgan L.

Likenesses photograph, 1867, repro. in Engen, *Kate Greenaway* · Elliott & Fry, photograph, 1870–79, NPG [*see illus.*] · watercolour, 1883 (after self-portrait by K. Greenaway), repro. in Engen, *Kate Greenaway* · photograph, c.1895, repro. in Engen, *Kate Greenaway*

Wealth at death £6281 16s. 1d.: administration, 20 Dec 1901, *CGPLA Eng. & Wales*

Greenbaum, Salman Mendel [Sidney] (1929–1996), grammarian, was born on 31 December 1929 at Underwood Street, Stepney, London, the younger of the two sons of Lewis Greenbaum (d. 1944/5), a tailor, and Nellie Bernkopf. Greenbaum was thus brought up in the heart of the 'Jewish' East End of London, and in a thoroughly practising Orthodox Jewish household, suffused with learning and a love of books.

Greenbaum won a place at the Grocers' Company's School, Hackney, but had to leave at fifteen following the death of his father. He earned a living of sorts through teaching Jewish religion classes in east London and officiating in synagogue ceremonial. His knowledge of Hebrew and the Hebrew scriptures was sufficient to gain him admission to Jews' College, the religious training seminary, which had an affiliation with the University of London. In 1951 he was awarded, through the college, a BA degree from the university, with honours, in Hebrew and Aramaic. Two years later he gained his MA, and meanwhile obtained, from the college, the diploma qualifying him as a Jewish minister of religion. In 1954 he was awarded a postgraduate certificate in education, and became a primary school teacher.

These qualifications enabled Greenbaum to obtain employment as a 'supply teacher' with the London county council. From 1957 until 1964 he taught full-time at the Hasmonean grammar school, Hendon, under its formidable founder and principal, Rabbi Dr Solomon Schonfield. But Greenbaum's interests had already turned from the study of the sacred texts of Judaism to that of the English language. In 1951 he had enrolled at Birkbeck College to study for the University of London's BA in English, which he obtained in 1954. A decade later, following a series of confrontations with Schonfield over matters of management, he resigned from the Hasmonean. In the following year, while continuing to teach evening classes at Goldsmiths' College, Greenbaum obtained employment as a research assistant working for Randolph (later Lord) Quirk in the survey of English usage at University College, London. Thus began Greenbaum's lifetime professional association with Quirk, under whose supervision he obtained his PhD in 1967.

Greenbaum's earliest monograph was *Studies in English Adverbial Usage* (1969). He was subsequently appointed first as visiting professor in English language at the University of Oregon, Eugene, then as associate professor at the University of Wisconsin, Milwaukee. He had embarked on a punishing schedule of teaching, research, and publication. *Verb-Intensifier Collocations in English* and *Elicitation Experiments in English* (written with Quirk) were both published in 1970. Greenbaum was one of the 'gang of four' authors (the others were Quirk, Geoffrey Leech, and Jan Svartvik) who together wrote *The Grammar of Contemporary English* (1972) and the *Comprehensive Grammar of the English Language* (1985); these volumes remained standard works of reference with worldwide currency into the twenty-first century. Greenbaum's *University Grammar of English* (also written jointly with Quirk) was published in 1973. Having spent 1972–3 as visiting professor at the Hebrew University of Jerusalem, Greenbaum returned to Milwaukee in 1973 to take the chair in English language. He also edited several books on the English language, among them *Acceptability in Language* (1977) and, with Leech and Svartvik, *Studies in English Linguistics: for Randolph Quirk* (1980). In addition to publishing widely in scholarly journals, Greenbaum was also interested in language pedagogy, specifically composition.

In 1983 Greenbaum succeeded to the post of Quain professor of English language and literature and director of the survey of English usage, which Quirk had vacated at University College, London (UCL), following his appointment as vice-chancellor of the University of London. Greenbaum's book *The English Language Today* was published in 1985 and from 1986 to 1988 he served as dean of the faculty of arts at UCL. While undertaking a range of administrative duties, Greenbaum also found time to dabble in the larger politics of the federal university, in which he became a senator. He did not agree with the majority of his academic colleagues at University College, who yearned for the breakup of the federation and the independence of the college, out of which the university had grown. In 1989 his support was crucial to the election as chairman of the university's academic council of Professor Geoffrey Alderman, an out-and-out 'federalist'. Greenbaum had taught Alderman at a London county council primary school in 1954. The two became close friends and allies in what became an epic and ultimately successful struggle during the early 1990s to save the 'federation' from its many enemies in academia and government. The University of Wisconsin at Milwaukee awarded Greenbaum an honorary doctorate in 1989 and in 1990 he was made research professor and director of the survey of English usage. A *Student's Grammar of English*, written with Quirk, appeared in 1990.

In the early 1990s, building on his early pioneering experimental techniques investigating English grammar and usage, Greenbaum founded the International Corpus of English (ICE), a major research project based at the survey of English usage. The aim of the ICE was to establish identically constructed corpora in different countries of the English-speaking world. He described the project in an edited volume, *Comparing English Worldwide: the International Corpus of English* (1996). The British component of ICE (ICE–GB) was the first corpus to be completed and become fully searchable, using dedicated state-of-the-art software whose early development Greenbaum supervised. In an age when computers were still the prerogative of the scientific community, Greenbaum was tenacious in advocating computing for the humanities; as dean of arts at University College he was the first academic to insist on adequate funding of humanities computing and on the provision of professional training in computing for humanities teachers and researchers.

One of Greenbaum's last publications was *The Oxford English Grammar* (1996). This work was innovative because it was based on real-language data taken from the International Corpus of English. Widely reviewed in the British press, it was both praised and criticized for its intolerance of non-standard usage. Greenbaum wrote that:

> good English is sometimes equated with correct English, but the two concepts should be differentiated. Correct English is conformity to the norms of the standard language. Good English is good use of the resources available in the language. In that sense we can use non-standard dialect well and we can use standard language badly.   (*The Oxford English Grammar*, 17)

On his return to England from the USA Greenbaum had re-established his links with London's Jewish communities and with Jews' College. He assisted Dr Immanuel Jakobovits, the United Synagogue's chief rabbi, in the English translation of the centenary edition of the *Singer's Prayer Book* (1990), the standard book of prayer used by Orthodox Jews throughout the British Commonwealth. He was a member of a number of Jewish organizations including the Jewish Historical Society, the Society for Jewish Studies, the Sternberg Centre for Judaism, and the Maccabeans. He was also a member of the Reform Club. Yet Greenbaum was a very private, intensely lonely, and in some respects tragic person, generous to his friends but awkward in female company and quite lacking in social graces. Unusually for an Orthodox Jew, he never married. He was at his best when entertaining family and colleagues. While drinking a glass of whisky and smoking a cigar he would sit in his favourite chair, talking to his guests. Towards the end of his life he suffered increasingly from ill health.

In 1990 Greenbaum resigned the Quain chair at University College on personal grounds but was able to continue directing the survey of English usage. On 28 May 1996, while delivering a lecture at Moscow University, he died of heart failure. His body was brought back to London by a colleague and by friends and was buried on 3 June 1996 at the Federation Jewish cemetery, Edmonton.

BAS AARTS and GEOFFREY ALDERMAN

Sources *Who's who in the world*, 13th edn (1996) · *The Guardian* (31 May 1996) · *The Independent* (31 May 1996) · *Jewish Chronicle* (14 June 1996) · *The Times* (5 June 1996) · files of the survey of English usage, UCL
Wealth at death £344,895: probate, 23 Sept 1996, *CGPLA Eng. & Wales*

Greenberg, Leopold Jacob (1861–1931), newspaper editor and Zionist, was born at 26 Frederic Street, Birmingham, on 6 September 1861, the second of three sons (there were also two daughters) of Simeon Greenberg, jewellery manufacturer, and his wife, Matilda Samson. His parents were Orthodox Jews. He was sent to London for his education, first at Northwick College, Maida Vale, a Jewish private academy conducted by the Revd Abraham Pereira Mendes (1825–1893), and subsequently at University College School. While retaining strong links to his native city, he settled in the capital. A political radical in his youth, he forged links to Birmingham statesman Joseph Chamberlain, and remained a lifelong Liberal. He worked initially on two Liberal papers, the *Pall Mall Gazette* and the *Daily News*, and in 1883 set up his own business, Messrs Greenberg & Co., publishers and advertising agents. A proud and assertive Jew, possessing a deep and abiding love for Jewish culture in all its aspects and a knowledgeable interest in Jewish music, he played a key part in 1886 in saving London's oldest surviving synagogue, Bevis Marks, from demolition, and in 1906 he became president of the Birmingham Young Men's Association, to which since its foundation in 1879 he had given steady support. In 1896 he began publication of the *Jewish Year Book*, which remains the authoritative chronicle of record for Anglo-Jewry. The following year, with the Australian-born historian and folklorist Joseph Jacobs (1854–1916) he launched *Young Israel*, a monthly periodical which aimed to instil Judaic values into Jewish youth. Struggling financially, it folded in 1906.

Greenberg was a member of the executives of the Jewish Board of Guardians, of the Jewish Health Organization of Great Britain, and of the Jewish Hospital, Stepney Green. He sat for some time on the board of the (Orthodox) Hampstead Synagogue, which he represented on the council of the United Synagogue organization; while championing moderate reforms in the Orthodox ritual he was to prove an inveterate critic of the Liberal Judaism which developed in Britain from 1902. He became personally associated with the much less radically progressive Reform Judaism, having married on 28 November 1888 at the West London Synagogue, Upper Berkeley Square, Britain's leading Reform congregation, Marion (c.1861–1918), daughter of a non-Jew of independent means, Robert Gates. She had converted to Judaism in preparation for the marriage. They had three sons, one of whom died in infancy, and one daughter. His first wife died on 7 July 1918; and he married second, on 6 May 1920, also at the West London Synagogue, Florence, daughter of Alexander Oppenheimer, merchant. This second marriage produced a daughter.

An early recruit to political Zionism following publication in 1896 of Theodor Herzl's *Der Judenstaat*, Greenberg saw in the cause of Jewish nationalism not only a necessary liberation movement for the oppressed but a means of countering assimilation among the more fortunate. He became foundation honorary secretary of the English Zionist Federation (formed in January 1899) and in 1900 served as that body's sessional chairman, undertaking a lecture tour of provincial communities to promote Zionism. He had the previous year briefed colonial secretary Joseph Chamberlain and first lord of the Treasury Arthur Balfour on the subject, with encouraging results. He attended several Zionist congresses abroad, and was vice-president of the one held at The Hague in 1907. His capacity and zeal impressed Herzl, who called him 'the most able of all my helpers'. In 1902, through Chamberlain's good offices, Greenberg arranged Herzl's appearance before the royal commission on alien immigration; in 1903 he testified before it himself. In 1902 he represented the World Zionist Organization (WZO) in the negotiations regarding the acquisition of land for Jewish settlement at al-ʿArish in the Sinai peninsula, a project supported by

Chamberlain but stymied by the viceroy of Egypt, Lord Cromer. In 1903 Greenberg served as the intermediary through whom Chamberlain offered Herzl territory in British East Africa, the Zionist movement's rejection of which (following Herzl's death) prompted the creation in 1905 of the Jewish Territorialist Organization by dissidents led by Israel Zangwill. From 1905 to 1907 Greenberg was a member of the WZO's executive. In 1906 he became a director of the Jewish National Fund (established 1901) and resigned the secretaryship of the English Zionist Federation, but in 1909 accepted that body's London vice-presidency.

Learning, at the end of 1906, that the well-respected London-based weekly *Jewish Chronicle* (published but for a brief interlude since 1841) was for sale, and that the pro-Territorialist consortium which owned the rival *Jewish World* aimed to purchase it, Greenberg enthusiastically proposed to his associates in the high echelons of the WZO that it should be acquired in the Zionist interest. This was speedily done, but a factional dispute then erupted, and the Jewish Colonial Trust pulled out of its substantial financial commitment to the venture. Greenberg rescued matters by forming a company to provide the required capital. He was principal shareholder and director for life as well as controlling editor of the paper, which from 1907 until his death served as the vehicle for his own robust and unyielding Zionism. Early in 1917 he introduced Mark Sykes of the Foreign Office to Chaim Weizmann, setting in motion the intensive talks that led to the Balfour declaration issued on 2 November in that same year. He was unhappy with the vague wording of the declaration, and in his forthright editorials as well as in the column which he wrote under the pen-name Mentor he inveighed against what he saw as Britain's reneging, in white papers and elsewhere, on its commitment to that document. He also, both publicly and privately, continually excoriated Weizmann for failing to insist that 'Palestine must be politically Jewish' and for the problems which he regarded as stemming from that failure. Greenberg campaigned vigorously against the Aliens Act of 1905, which restricted immigration into Britain, and strenuously opposed the even tougher Aliens Act of 1919. His uncompromising stance on these issues brought him into conflict with the traditional, low-key, upper-class, non-Zionist, and ostentatiously patriotic Anglo-Jewish leadership centring on the League of British Jews, which from 1919 to 1931 issued a newspaper of its own, the *Jewish Guardian*, in direct competition to Greenberg's paper. That enterprise deflected lucrative advertising revenue away from the *Jewish Chronicle*, but since its readership scarcely extended beyond the very limited membership of the league, it otherwise did the *Chronicle* little harm. Nor did Greenberg's paper suffer unduly from competition posed by other short-lived journals started by Jewish communal figures disgruntled by his approach.

By 1913 Greenberg, through astute improvements in its style, coverage, and format, had doubled his paper's circulation. That year he acquired the ailing *Jewish World*, recasting it as a journal of opinion. By contrast, he broadened the *Jewish Chronicle*'s reportage of Jewish organizational news and of provincial communities, and cultivated its appeal to the Yiddish-speaking, working-class Jews of London's East End as well as to the growing numbers of Jewish middle-class suburbanites. Accordingly, the paper justified its masthead slogan: 'The organ of Anglo-Jewry'. During the First World War Greenberg introduced and constantly paraded the motto 'England has been all she could be to the Jews; the Jews will be all they can be to England'. He felt it politic to suspend a regular supplement detailing antisemitism in Russia, then an allied nation, but in 1915 was censured by the press bureau for apparently breaching the Defence of the Realm Act by detailing the tsarist regime's military order requiring the brutal expulsion of Jews from the war zone on the eastern front.

As editor of Britain's pre-eminent Jewish newspaper Greenberg stood in a powerful opinion-moulding position, and he impressed his personal stamp upon every issue. During the final five years of his life he became increasingly arthritic and pain-wracked. He died on 15 November 1931 at his London residence, 8 Aylestone Avenue, Brondesbury Park, of myocardial degeneration and rheumatoid arthritis. In his will, made two days earlier, he directed that his remains should 'be cremated without any religious service' so long as that was acceptable to the West London Synagogue. The funeral took place on 17 November at Golders Green crematorium, conducted by the rabbi of that synagogue, where a memorial service was held several days later. In accordance with Greenberg's wishes his ashes were conveyed to Palestine, to be 'buried without any religious ceremony on Mount Scopus near Jerusalem'. But the Orthodox rabbinate in Palestine, insisting that cremation contravened Jewish law, refused to allow the ashes to be interred in consecrated ground. An unseemly wrangle ensued, during which Greenberg's ashes remained in the customs hall at Haifa; they were eventually laid to rest in 1932 at Kibbutz Deganya, by the shore of Lake Galilee.

Among his intimates Greenberg was known for his engaging jollity. His son Ivan (1896–1966), who had been assistant editor of the *Jewish Chronicle* since 1925, was thwarted in his ambition to succeed him as editor; following a boardroom tussle he held that post from 1936 to 1946, and as a staunch supporter of Vladimir Jabotinsky he proved a trenchant critic of British policy in Palestine.

HILARY L. RUBINSTEIN

Sources D. Cesarani, *The Jewish Chronicle and Anglo-Jewry, 1841–1991* (1994) · *Jewish Chronicle* (20–27 Nov 1931) · *The Jewish Chronicle, 1841–1941: a century of newspaper history*, Jewish Chronicle (1949) · private information (2004) [family] · will, Principal Registry of the Family Division, London, 13 Nov 1931 · *Birmingham Jewry 1870 and 1929* (1929) · S. A. Cohen, *English Zionists and British Jews: the communal politics of Anglo-Jewry, 1895–1920* (1982) · Z. Joseph, ed., *Birmingham Jewry, 1740–1930* (1984) · G. Kressel, 'Greenberg, L. J.', *Encyclopaedia Judaica*, ed. C. Roth, 7 (Jerusalem, 1971), 905 · L. Stein, *The Balfour declaration* (1961) · C. Dresner and B. Litvinoff, eds., *January 1905 – December 1906* (London, New Brunswick, NJ, and Jerusalem, 1973), vol. 4 of *The letters and papers of Chaim Weizmann, series A: letters*, ed. M. W. Weisgal (1968–80) · b. cert. · d. cert. · *CGPLA Eng. & Wales* (1932)

Archives Central Zionist Archives, Jerusalem, CZA A18, 364; CZA A121/108, 109, 147, 151 · Woburn House, London, Board of Deputies of British Jews | U. Southampton L., corresp. with J. H. Hertz **Wealth at death** £1446 2s. 4d.: probate, 23 Feb 1932, CGPLA Eng. & Wales

Greenbury, Richard (b. before 1600?, d. 1670), painter, sometimes known, wrongly, as Robert Greenbury, was perhaps the son of Richard Greenbury (d. by 1613) of the parish of St John, Walbrook, London. He was employed by the crown in 1623 and called painter to the queen in 1631. It is possible that he obtained royal patronage through an introduction by Sir Theodore Mayerne, court physician who held a high opinion of Greenbury's painting. A payment dated 30 January 1623 for £30 to Greenbury for a portrait is entered in the privy council register, and the exchequer of receipt files for 1630–31 contain payment to the same for, among other items, a portrait of Queen Anne, a copy after *Venus and Mercury* by Correggio, staining, painting, and gilding of frames, and glass painting in enamel. Thomas Howard, second earl of Arundel, also commissioned him to make copies, including copies of Charles I's two paintings by Dürer: his self-portrait and the portrait of his father (latter, National Gallery, London). Greenbury's copies are listed in van der Doort's catalogue of Charles I's collection, made in 1639; and from that of Dürer the elder, now at Syon House, London, the etching by Hollar of 1644 was taken. Greenbury was sufficiently admired by the court physician and connoisseur Sir Theodore Mayerne to be associated by him with Rubens and Van Dyck.

In 1625 Greenbury was also commissioned by the East India Company to paint a large picture giving details of the cruelties inflicted on the English by the Dutch at Amboyna in 1623. From 1626 to 1638 he was employed in Oxford, painting the portrait of William Waynflete, the founder of Magdalen College, which still hangs in the college. Evelyn mentions in his diary entry of 24 October 1664 a further painting on blue cloth by Greenbury of *The Last Supper*, which was hanging in the college's chapel at that time. It is probable that this was put up between 1629 and 1635, when Greenbury was designing the stained glass for the chapel, but it was removed in 1745. That he was a Roman Catholic is indicated by the fact that in December 1628 he was summoned before the Westminster justices as a recusant in St Martin's parish, where he was a householder. In 1636 he patented (no. 99) a process for painting in oils on different types of cloth. He was last documented as painting a portrait of Sir Charles Scarburgh, physician to Charles II, James II, and Mary II, and his assistant Edward Arris for the Barber–Surgeons' Hall in 1651. An engraving after the portrait by J. Brown is in the British Museum. Although no further works by Greenbury are recorded after this date, Mrs Poole records that 'it is supposed that Greenbury's death occurred in 1670' (Poole, 2, xxi). L. H. CUST, *rev.* SARAH HERRING

Sources E. K. Waterhouse, *The dictionary of British 16th and 17th century painters* (1988), 111 · Mrs R. Lane Poole, ed., *Catalogue of portraits in the possession of the university, colleges, city and county of Oxford*, 3 vols. (1912–25), vol. 1, pp. xvii, xxviii; vol. 2, pp. xv–xxiii, 107, 141, 149, 153, 172, 209 bis, 217, 219; vol. 3, pp. 11–12 · 'Abraham van der Doort's catalogue of the collections of Charles I', ed. O. Millar, *Walpole Society*, 37 (1958–60), 11 · Evelyn, *Diary*, 3.386, n. 3 · C. C. Stopes, 'Gleanings from the records of the reigns of James I and Charles I', *Burlington Magazine*, 22 (1913), 276–82 · C. H. Collins Baker, 'Notes on Syon House pictures, Part II', *Connoisseur*, 62 (1920), 191–8 · C. J. Holmes, 'The history of our new Dürer', *Burlington Magazine*, 5 (1904), 431–8 · C. Dodgson, 'The portrait of Dürer the elder', *The Athenaeum* (6 Feb 1904), 185
Archives City Westm. AC | BL, Sloane MS 2052 · Exchequer of Receipt files · PRO, state papers domestic, Charles I, 123, no. 12 · PRO, Privy Council Register, vd.xxxi, p. 278

Greene family (*per.* 1801–1920), brewers, came to prominence with **Benjamin Greene** (1780–1860), born on 5 April 1780 in Oundle, the youngest child (there were thirteen by two marriages) of Benjamin Greene (1732–1782), draper, and his second wife, Rebecca Ashton (1739–1830). The family throughout the eighteenth century were engaged in the woollen drapery business of the south midlands and possessed impeccable dissenting credentials through their long association with the Howard Congregational Chapel in Bedford. There is no evidence of Benjamin Greene's education beyond his apprenticeship in the late 1790s with the leading London brewing firm of Whitbread. He appears to have settled in Bury St Edmunds in 1801 on forming a partnership with John Clark, brewer, in Guildhall Street. By 1804 the partnership was in difficulties, and early in 1806 Greene entered a new partnership with William Buck (a one-time yarn merchant, leading Suffolk dissenter, and the father-in-law of Thomas Clarkson, the great anti-slavery campaigner) to brew beer in the town's historic Westgate Brewery.

Sales of beer in land-locked, backward Bury were unlikely to take off dramatically before the railways, and output during Greene's management of the brewery (1806–36) probably never exceeded that he declared in 1831—5000 barrels of strong and 2000 of small beer. But Greene was an energetic and unconventional brewer whose abilities and ambitions were never realized in running a small country brewery. By good fortune Greene's neighbour across the brewery yard was a relatively impoverished, rackety, and, most significantly, childless owner of a West Indian plantation, Sir Patrick Blake, second baronet (d. 1818). Greene became one of his executors, obtained the management of his Suffolk and St Kitts estates, and on his widow's death in 1823 was left her Nicola Town plantation on the island. Greene had become a proprietor in the West Indies himself. In addition to the Blake properties he managed those of a south Norfolk landowning family (Molyneaux), and there were three more he acquired on his own account. In 1829 his eldest son, the immensely capable Benjamin Buck *Greene (1808–1902) was sent out to St Kitts to run all these properties and consolidate the family's good fortune. On his return to England in 1836 he was managing and modernizing no fewer than eighteen estates (together producing one third of the island's sugar exports in the mid-1830s) and enjoying the greatest reputation as a planter.

Meanwhile Benjamin Greene had thrown himself with enormous vigour into representing the interests of the West Indian slave proprietors at a critical juncture of their affairs. To effect this he acquired the *Bury and Suffolk Herald* in 1828. For six years he ran this ultra-tory provincial newspaper during the heady period surrounding the Reform Act and the abolition of slavery amid mounting controversy, involving himself in no fewer than three libel cases. Utter reaction to these key pieces of legislation was a strange position for a one-time prominent dissenter to occupy and the third case heaped such obloquy upon him that he left Bury in 1836 to found a sugar importing and shipowning firm at 11 Mincing Lane, London. He died at Russell Square on 26 November 1860, was buried in Highgate cemetery, and left an estate sworn under £80,000.

Benjamin Greene was twice married: in 1803, to Mary, third daughter of Abraham Maling, yarn merchant of Bury St Edmunds, and in October 1805, a year after Mary's death, to Catherine (1783–1855), daughter of the Revd Thomas Smith (1749–1801), minister of the Howard Chapel in Bedford, and his wife, Elizabeth (1750–1792), only daughter and heir of Zachariah Carleton of London, banker. The second marriage produced seven sons (two dying in infancy) and six daughters. Four of the five sons, all of whom were educated at Bury's renowned Edward VI Grammar School, inherited their father's ability. Besides the eldest, Benjamin Buck Greene (later governor of the Bank of England), John (1810–1867) was a solicitor, prominent in the affairs of Bury and west Suffolk and twice mayor of the town in 1841 and 1852. The career of the third son, Edward, brewer and MP, is discussed below. Charles (1821–1840) succeeded his eldest brother in the management of the St Kitts estates at the tender age of sixteen. It was, however, neither the burdens of his task nor his father's expectations, formidable as both were, which killed him three years later, but fun (he supposedly fathered thirteen illegitimate children) and yellow fever, the traditional toll upon the longevity of West Indian planters. Only the youngest, William (1824–1881), failed in all the tests his father set him, being completely unable to establish himself in any settled occupation. His nine children included Sir William Graham *Greene, permanent secretary to the Admiralty and Ministry of Munitions, 1911–18, and Charles Henry Greene (1865–1942), headmaster of Berkhamsted School between 1910 and 1927, the father of Graham *Greene (1904–1991), the novelist, and Sir Hugh Carleton *Greene (1910–1987).

Edward Greene (1815–1891), Benjamin's third son, was born at the Westgate Brewery House in 1815. Trained in his father's brewery, he completely transformed the business between 1840 and 1870. His success, achieved entirely in the free trade before 1865, was based upon a system of agents and travellers working across East Anglia. Doubtlessly he was aided by the railways after 1845 and rising beer consumption even in agricultural districts between 1830 and 1880. At first producing the traditional heavy, vatted, strong Suffolk ales, after the 1850s he successfully brewed a Burton-type pale ale (the in-vogue beer of Victorian Britain) which he sold cheaply. By the 1870s the output of the Westgate Brewery had increased to more than 40,000 barrels a year, realizing its proprietor in some

years an income in excess of £10,000 a year. In 1887, in the wake of Guinness's spectacular capitalization, Edward Greene merged his brewery with that of his pushy neighbour, Frederick William King. The new company, Greene King, was generously valued at £555,000. Ownership was almost entirely confined to eight individuals in the Greene and King families with Edward becoming the first chairman of the new company. His (and F. W. King's) policy of acquiring tied public houses, which went back to the late 1860s, was pursued with an increased vigour. Owning and leasing about 200 on the merger of the two firms, the company possessed no fewer than 460 in 1919.

Edward Greene's interests were predictable enough for a member of his class and calling. He became MP in the Conservative interest for Bury St Edmunds in 1865, representing the town for twenty years before transferring to the Stowmarket division of Suffolk, 1886–91. He was also an active justice of the peace and deputy lieutenant of the county. In parliament, where he spoke quite often at the outset of his career, he was an authority on agriculture (especially horses—he was master of the Suffolk hunt, 1871–5) and housing. A well-built man of middle height, his speeches were delivered in a harsh Suffolk accent. Invariably they possessed a loud evangelical directness. Disraeli reckoned him to be 'the fiercest Protestant in the House' (*The Letters of Disraeli to Lady Bradford and Lady Chesterfield*, 1928, 2.62). Clearly a figure of some fun among metropolitan parliamentarians he was for thirty years an extremely popular speaker in Suffolk on the themes of farming, progress, the work ethic, and paternalism. All were couched in homely terms and larded with examples taken from his own experiences of business and landowning. He was at this level an effective communicator, appealing across the broadest spectrum of political opinion from Lord Bristol to the humblest agricultural worker. He never lost the common touch in a patently straightforward approach to life.

Agriculture was Edward Greene's other great pursuit after the mid-1850s. In 1865 he set the seal on his election to parliament by renting the Ixworth Abbey estate where he farmed on an extensive scale. Nine years later he bought Nether Hall, Pakenham (which he rebuilt), with 850 acres. He was a bold innovator in experiments with the application of steam-driven ploughs in the 1860s and was a county representative to the national chamber of agriculture after 1867. In 1870 he founded the Ixworth Farmers' Club, which for a generation was the liveliest talking shop for agriculture affairs in East Anglia. He was also chairman of the Bury and Thetford Railway Company, 1865–76. With his experience in business, farming, and parliament there was no greater recognized authority on rural issues in west Suffolk in the 1865–90 period.

In private life Edward Greene's agenda was that of the typically successful brewer. Both his marriages were into families rather better connected than his own. His first wife, Emily Smythies (1820–1848), whom he married in 1840, was the daughter of a Huntingdonshire parson and magistrate, the Revd H. Y. Smythies; his second, Dorothea (1827–1912), daughter of C. Prideaux-Brune, belonged to a

Cornish landowning family and was the widow of Rear-Admiral Sir William Hoste, bt (*d.* 1868). Greene and his first wife had a son and four daughters; his marriage to Lady Hoste, whom he married in 1870 and who retained her title, produced one daughter. When he died on 15 April 1891 at Nether Hall, Pakenham, it was generally reckoned that Edward Greene was among the most successful country brewers of his generation, and his fortune (£360,000) revealed the prosperity enjoyed by Victorian brewers. He was buried in the churchyard at Pakenham.

Greene's only son, **Sir (Edward) Walter Greene**, first baronet (1842–1920), was born at the Westgate Brewery on 14 March 1842. Educated at Rugby School he then travelled on the continent before becoming a brewery pupil at Tamplin's in Brighton. Just before he became of age he was given a partnership in his father's firm. Two years later he married Anne Elizabeth Royds (1842/3–1912), the daughter of a Lichfield prebendary, the Revd C. Smith Royds, and they had two sons and three daughters. Good looking and the apple of his father's eye, Walter had three great (and expensive) interests in life: hunting (he hunted packs of harriers and fox and stag hounds in Suffolk and Worcestershire), driving carriages four-in-hand, and his succession of ever bigger steam yachts. The running of the brewery was, in effect, left to his steely, independent, highly competent first cousin, E. W. Lake (1852–1922). Lake was prominent in Suffolk affairs, mayor of Bury no fewer than six times, and under his guidance for almost half a century the brewery went from strength to strength. By 1920 it owned 460 public houses in East Anglia and was reckoned to be one of the best managed and most profitable breweries in England. The success was largely Edward Lake's.

After his father's death Walter Greene, chairman of Greene King from 1891 to 1920, did no more than attend a weekly directors' meeting, if he was in Suffolk. He drew an income from the brewery not far short of £20,000 in some years before 1914. In 1897 he served office as high sheriff of Suffolk and three years later he was rewarded with the baronetcy his father had been promised shortly before his death. Although nowhere near as effective on the hustings as Edward Greene (Sir Walter's speeches lacked gravity and substance) he was Conservative MP for Bury St Edmunds in the parliament of 1900–06. Indeed in that parliament there were two other Greene members besides Sir Walter: his elder son, Raymond Greene (1869–1947), and his first cousin Henry Greene QC (1843–1915), the third son of Benjamin Buck Greene.

Sir Walter was characteristic of many third generation British businessmen. The Bible and Surtees formed the limits of his reading matter; sport and practical jokes were his favourite pursuits. Although dutiful—an avid churchman, colonel of militia, and JP—his convivial life was a prolonged pursuit of pleasure. He was fortunate that Edward Lake was one of the shrewdest brewers of his generation. Sir Walter Greene died at Nether Hall on 27 February 1920 and was buried at Thurston church, Suffolk.

After the Greene–Lake regime at Greene King came to an end in 1922 the brewery was run by Edward Lake's eldest son, Major E. L. D. Lake (1881–1946), one of the best-known country brewers of the 1920–45 period. Lacking his father's capacities he nevertheless ran the company well on somewhat military lines and effectively sidelined the next two Eton- and Oxford-educated Greene baronets, Sir Raymond Greene and Sir Edward Greene (1882–1966), although both served (Raymond very briefly) as chairmen of Greene King. Sir Raymond initially had a promising career as MP (for West Cambridgeshire, 1895–1906; North Hackney, 1910–23), as member of London County Council, and as a distinguished soldier in the First World War. But he lacked ambition and, like so many of his generation, his health never fully recovered from the war. When Sir Walter died in 1920 both brothers showed provincial Suffolk a clean pair of heels. Enjoying society, they lived principally in London. On Sir Edward's death in 1966 the baronetcy became extinct. The Greene connection with the brewery was maintained by Sir Hugh Carleton Greene, who, on the strength of his high profile at the BBC, became a director in 1964 (he was chairman, 1971–8); his son, Graham C. Greene, publisher and chairman of the British Museum trustees, has continued the Greene interest since 1979. Like his schoolmaster father and troubled grandfather, Sir Hugh, a great-grandson of the firm's founder, had had nothing to do with brewing. But he and his brother Graham had a long held interest in sampling the beers of different breweries during their holidays. Possessing a deep respect for the industry's traditions Hugh brought a breath of the outside world to the board, although Benjamin and Edward Greene must have shifted uneasily in their graves at the prospect of William Greene's grandson heading their brewery.

The Greenes provide a classic illustration of the upward mobility of countless families engaged in industry and commerce in the century before 1914, a microcosm of a significant slice of our social history in these years. Benjamin Greene and his sons, Edward and Benjamin Buck, were men of ability and achievement bent on establishing their families at the pinnacle of Victorian society. Plantation owning, sugar trading, banking, and, above all, brewing, provided all the mammon-based trappings of nineteenth-century social arrival—country and London houses, steam yachts, expensive educations, membership of the House of Commons, eventually a title. With these advances came a diminution in business application. But the Greene family has a greater interest than this typically British plutocratic evolution of those supremely successful in business, for no brewing dynasty possesses more celebrated literary connections since Graham Greene and Christopher *Isherwood were both direct descendants of the founder of Greene King, Benjamin Greene.

R. G. WILSON

Sources R. G. Wilson, *Greene King: a business and family history* (1983) · private information (2004) [private family MSS, Greene, Blake, and Molineux-Montgomerie families] · *Bury and Norwich Post* (1828–34) · *Bury and Norwich Post* (17 April 1875) · *Bury and Norwich Post* (21 April 1891) · *Licensed Victuallers' Gazette and Hotel Courier* (March 1875) · R. G. Wilson, 'Greene, Edward', *DBB*, vol. 2, pp. 634–8 · Burke, *Gen. GB* (1965) [Greene formerly of Harston House] ·

Greene King and Sons PLC, Westgate Brewery, Bury St Edmunds · R. G. Wilson and T. R. Gourvish, 'The profitability of the British brewing industry, 1880–1914', *Business History*, 27 (1985), 146–65 · *Bury and Suffolk Herald* (1828–34) · *WWW*, 1916–28 · d. cert. [Anne Elizabeth Greene] · Greene pedigree, Coll. Arms · Burke, *Peerage*
Archives　Greene King & Sons plc, Bury St Edmunds · Suffolk RO, Bury St Edmunds, hunting diaries of Sir Edward Walter Greene
Likenesses　photograph, *c.*1875 (Edward Greene), repro. in Wilson, *Greene King*, pl. 3 · photograph, *c.*1910 (Edward Walter Greene), repro. in Wilson, *Greene King*, pl. 12 · oils (Benjamin Greene), Greene King & Sons plc, Bury St Edmunds; repro. in Wilson, *Greene King*, pl. 1 · oils (Edward Walter Greene), Greene King & Sons plc, Bury St Edmunds
Wealth at death　under £80,000—Benjamin Greene: family MSS of late Raymond Greene · £356,945 14s. 6d.—Edward Greene: probate, 9 July 1891, *CGPLA Eng. & Wales* · £350,000—Edward Walter Greene: probate, 1920, *CGPLA Eng. & Wales*

Greene, Anne (*c.*1628–1659), survivor of execution, was born at Steeple Barton, Oxfordshire, the daughter of William Greene and his wife. At the age of about twenty-two, in 1650, she was a servant in the household of Sir Thomas Read of Duns Tew, sometime sheriff of Oxfordshire, where, according to her own later petition, she was 'led … into the foul and fearful sin of fornication' by her master's grandson, Jeffrey Read, who was about sixteen or seventeen (BL, Add. MS 72892, fol. 9).

Greene became pregnant and miscarried at about eighteen weeks: while working hard at turning malt one day she felt very ill and went to the privy, where she was delivered of a stillborn foetus and then, terrified, hid it in a corner of the privy covered with dust and ashes. However, her employers discovered the matter and she was accused of infanticide and imprisoned. Under the 1624 statute (21 James I c. 27) single women who concealed their infants' deaths could be presumed guilty of infanticide, although many judges were chary of enforcing the act's strictest provisions. Greene claimed, as did many women accused of infanticide, that she was not sure that she was pregnant and that she did not know what had happened to her; midwives later testified that the foetus was extremely premature. However, the secrecy of her pregnancy and Sir Thomas Read's determination as prosecutor seem to have been sufficient to secure a conviction at the Oxford assizes in December 1650, and she was sentenced to hang.

The execution took place in the courtyard of Oxford Castle on 14 December. Greene bequeathed her clothes to her mother and her last words from the scaffold, according to a contemporary pamphlet, were of the 'lewdness of the family wherein she lately lived' (Watkins, 2). As she was hanged her friends pulled on her body to hasten death. The body was being prepared for dissection when she was observed to breathe and she was brought back to consciousness through the efforts of four physicians (William Petty, professor of anatomy, Thomas Willis, Ralph Bathurst, and Henry Clerke) and the unnamed woman who was appointed to lie in bed with her 'rubbing her lower parts gently' (BL, Add. MS 72892, fol. 2). After her recovery she went to recuperate with her friends in the country, taking the coffin she had been laid in as a souvenir; her father took a collection from the many visitors, which paid her apothecaries' bills and enabled her to sue for a free pardon, which was granted.

Greene's miraculous recovery inspired several pamphlets, celebrating divine intervention as the evidence of her innocence. A petition in her name survives, detailing her experiences, requesting a pardon and demanding compensation from Sir Thomas Read. However, Read died three days after her pardon was granted (suggesting to some commentators her innocence and his complicity in her trials). Forty-one scholars, including Christopher Wren, wrote poems on the miracle of her recovery, appended to Richard Watkins's *Newes from the dead, or, A true and exact narration of the miraculous deliverance of Anne Greene* (1651), which is based on Petty's detailed notes on the case history. Anthony Wood recorded the story in his memoir. The case contributed to contemporary unease with the harshness of the infanticide statutes, as well as with the use of bodies for anatomical investigation.

Greene married and had three children. She died in 1659.　　　　　　　　　　　　　LAURA GOWING

Sources　[R. Watkins], *Newes from the dead, or, A true and exact narration of the miraculous deliverance of Anne Greene*, 2 editions (1651) [second edition has expanded number of poems] · Petty papers, BL, Add. MS 72892, fols. 2–9 · *A wonder of wonders* (1651) · *A declaration from Oxford, of Ann Green* (1651) · *The life and times of Anthony Wood*, ed. A. Clark, 1, OHS, 19 (1891), 169–70 · R. Plot, *The natural history of Oxfordshire* (1677), 199
Likenesses　woodcut, repro. in *Wonder of wonders*

Greene, Benjamin (1780–1860). *See under* Greene family (*per.* 1801–1920).

Greene, Benjamin Buck (1808–1902), merchant, was born at Bury St Edmunds, Suffolk, the eldest of seven sons and six daughters of Benjamin *Greene (1780–1860) [*see under* Greene family], brewer, and his second wife, Catherine (1783–1855), daughter of the Revd Thomas Smith of Bedford. He was educated at Bury's King Edward VI Grammar School.

Greene's father, with William Buck, in 1806 acquired a Bury brewery and in 1823 considerably extended his business interests when he inherited an interest in St Kitts' sugar estates from his neighbour, Lady Blake, widow of Sir Patrick, a local landowner for whom he had acted as trustee and adviser. He also managed other Blake estates in the West Indies and Suffolk. Greene was dispatched to St Kitts in 1829 to care for his father's interests, introducing new methods of cultivation and processing, winning 'the greatest reputation as a planter' (Wilson, *Greene King*, 45) and, unlike many of his contemporaries, making large profits. The Greenes also owned ships carrying sugar exports.

In 1836, Greene's father placed his brewery under management of his third son and moved to London. With Greene, who returned to Britain in 1837, he established Benjamin Greene & Son, West India merchants and shipowners, at 11 Mincing Lane. In 1837 Greene married Isabella Elizabeth (*d.* 1888), only daughter of Thomas Blyth of Limehouse, London, a wealthy ship chandler whose sons, James and Henry, controlled much of the external trade and sugar production of Mauritius. They had three sons and three daughters.

In 1846, when his father retired, Greene built on his wife's connections by forming a partnership with James and Henry Blyth, as Blyths and Greene, merchants and shipowners, although his old firm continued until about 1848. The merged business grew to form one of London's largest colonial merchants and shipowners, importing sugar from Mauritius, the East and West Indies, India and France, and exporting British manufactures to Mauritius.

The firm worked closely with the Mauritius house of Blyth Brothers, in which Greene was also a partner. In 1860 he went to Mauritius to investigate and bring order to its affairs, earning a reputation for being 'ruthlessly efficient', 'judicious', and for 'possessing the utmost probity' (Wilson, 56). Henry Blyth died in 1864, James in 1873, and in 1874 the firm's style was changed to Blyth, Greene, Jourdain & Co. Greene, now almost seventy, appears to have taken a lesser role at this time, but was joined in the business by his son Frederick.

Greene's high standing resulted in his election as a Bank of England director (1850–1900), culminating in his deputy governorship (1871–3) and his governorship (1873–5). His careful management left London relatively untouched by the 1873 financial crisis which swept continental Europe and North America, an achievement seemingly without precedent. With H. H. Gibbs, he gave important new direction to the bank's monetary policy, using bank rate to protect reserves through the attraction of gold from abroad—the so-called Greene&Gibbs policy. During the 1890 Baring crisis, with Bertram Currie he was selected by the Bank of England—although not its first choice—to investigate and confirm the solvency of Barings as justification for the bank's rescue through a loan secured by a £17 million guarantee provided by the banking community. His own £10,000 contribution was somewhat modest. He was also a director of the Atlas Assurance Company (1856–1902), a member of the important royal commission inquiring into the stock exchange (1877–8), a public works loan commissioner, deputy lieutenant for the City, and a seemingly unlikely Paraguayan consul in London (1850s–1870s).

In 1856 Greene purchased Midgham House and 1300 acres near Woolhampton, Berkshire, improving the estate, its church and school. His home, on returning from the West Indies, was 52 Woburn Place, London, from where he moved to 25 Kensington Palace Gardens about 1853. He died at Midgham on 3 April 1902, four years after his wife, leaving unsettled estate of £470,000, most of which passed to his children.

Greene emerged from relatively modest circumstances to become an important West Indies sugar planter and, later, one of London's leading colonial merchants. This led him to a directorship of the Bank of England, where he proved to be one of the ablest governors of his generation. On his death the bank referred to his 'eminently high character' and 'unvarying kindness and courtesy', while his old school reckoned that he 'left behind ... a good

report as a pattern of what an English merchant should be' and 'had nothing in common with the modern millionaire' (Wilson, 57). JOHN ORBELL

Sources R. G. Wilson, *Greene King: a business and family history* (1983) · A. Muir, *Blyth, Greene, Jourdain & Co. Ltd, 1810–1960* (1961) · L. S. Pressnell, 'Gold reserves, banking reserves and the Baring crisis of 1890', *Essays in money and banking*, ed. C. R. Whittlesey and J. S. G. Wilson (1968) · CGPLA Eng. & Wales (1902)

Likenesses engraving, repro. in Muir, *Blyth, Greene, Jourdain & Co. Ltd*

Wealth at death £466,171 14s. 10d.: resworn probate, Dec 1902, *CGPLA Eng. & Wales*

Greene, Edward (1815–1891). *See under* Greene family (*per.* 1801–1920).

Greene, Edward Burnaby [*formerly* Edward Burnaby] (*d.* 1788), poet and translator, was the eldest son of Edward Burnaby (*d.* 1759), one of the chief clerks of the Treasury, and his wife, Elizabeth Greene (*d.* 1754), daughter of Thomas Greene (*d.* 1740), a wealthy brewer of St Margaret's, Westminster, London. Edward Burnaby inherited his grandfather's fortune of £4000 per annum as well as his business. An act of parliament enabled him to take the name of Greene in addition to his own. He entered Corpus Christi College, Cambridge, on 22 October 1755, under the tuition of the Revd Dr Sharpe, but did not take a degree.

Greene married a Miss Cartwright of Kensington, 'a lady of merit and fortune' (*GM*, 1788) on 12 February 1761. They had three children, Anne, Pitt, and Emma. For a time he enjoyed great prosperity, living in Northlands near Kensington, but he had not been brought up to the brewing business and his poor management eventually plunged him into debt. In 1779 his property was sold and he was forced to retire to a lodging. His valuable library was sold by Christies.

In addition to a handful of original poems, Greene made numerous translations from Latin and Greek authors. These include 'Hero and Leander', *a Poem from the Greek of Musaeus* (1773), *The works of Anacreon and Sappho, with pieces from ancient authors* (Bion, Moschus, Virgil, Horace), and *occasional essays* (1768), *The Pythian, Nemean, and Isthmian Odes of Pindar, Translated into English Verse with Remarks* (1788), and *The Satires of Juvenal Paraphrastically Imitated, and Adapted to the Times* (1779). Greene accommodates Juvenal to eighteenth-century tastes; he tones down the 'shameless' portrayal of 'immodest ideas' (p. xii) and gives the satires a modern gloss:

> If music fires her, the delighted fair
> Will rummage Oswald's with fantastic care;
> And while great Handel's in the corner plac'd
> Purchase Arne's friperies to shew her taste;
> Or, if she still more modishly would die,
> A set of Glasses will from Schuman buy.
> (p. 76)

Greene's works were lambasted by more than one critic. D. H. was particularly severe on his *'Argonautic Expedition', Translated from the Greek with Notes* (1780).

> Mr Greene seems ambitious of forming a corps diplomatique of every Greek poem *made* into English, and tagged with notes more unintelligible and superfluous than those of the Dutch commentator. I should be sorry to reflect on any man

for his misfortunes, either as a trader or a translator; but really Mr E. B. G. as the Scotch say, is very *misfortunate*. (*GM*, 1782, 395)

A footnote in the same magazine remarks of Greene's versions of Pindar, Anacreon, and Juvenal that they may all be seen 'at Mr Brich's Pastryshop (late Horton's) opposite the Royal Exchange, and at all the principal Cheesemongers in London and Westminster' (ibid., 253).

Although Greene was not a talented poet, his prefaces demonstrate a lively interest in the processes of translation, an interest which is reflected in the wide range of verse forms he employs, adapting his style to suit different authors. *Hero and Leander*, for example, is written in blank verse:

Oh! Love, thou honey'd anguish, Hero's soul
Feels thy sharp voice enamor'd, thrilling fires
Throb in each vein tumultuous, to the ground
Her eye declining bows; Leander hangs
Gazing her charms intranc'd, he cannot quit
The fascinating object; the warm blush
Melts on her cheek, as dew-drops on the rose,
While bursts the silver note from Hero's tongue.

Greene's other works include *Strictures upon a Pamphlet* (1782), in which he argues that Chatterton was not the author of the Rowley poems, and *Critical Essays* (1770), a volume containing observations on Longinus and Virgil's *Aeneid*. Greene died on 12 March 1788, following a severe illness.   SARAH ANNES BROWN

Sources *GM*, 1st ser., 24 (1754), 530 · *GM*, 1st ser., 29 (1759), 497 · *GM*, 1st ser., 31 (1761), 94 · *GM*, 1st ser., 52 (1782), 253, 395 · *GM*, 1st ser., 58 (1788), 276 · Venn, *Alum. Cant.*, 1/2.455 · Nichols, *Lit. anecdotes*, 8.148–9, 9.670 · E. B. Greene, *The satires of Juvenal paraphrastically imitated and adapted to the times* (1779) · *DNB*

Greene, George (*b.* 1747/8, *d.* in or after 1816), traveller, was born in 1747 or 1748 of unknown parentage. In 1787 a decree in the court of chancery deprived him of the greater part of his fortune. Unable to find employment at home, he became at Easter 1790, on the recommendation of Lord Adam Gordon, land steward to the prince of Monaco on his estate at Torigny in Lower Normandy. From 14 October 1793 until 24 January 1795 he was imprisoned by the revolutionary leaders, with his wife Isabella and their five children, in the castle at Torigny. The duke of Valentinois, the son and successor of the prince of Monaco, after being restored to his castle and such part of his estates as remained unsold, appointed Greene his land steward in February 1796. The *coup d'état* of 4 September 1797 again threw Greene out of employment. In 1798 he went to Paris, and tried in vain to obtain passports for England. He returned to Torigny, where he was again arrested on 14 July 1798, and he was imprisoned in the citadel of St Lo until December 1799. In February 1800 he was allowed to return to England. To relieve his financial distress he published by subscription *A relation of several circumstances which occurred in … Lower Normandy … 1789 … to 1800* (1802). Greene afterwards lived for many years in Russia, and wrote a *Journey from London to St Petersburg by Way of Sweden*

(1813) which contained topographical descriptions and information for travellers. He was described as still alive in the *Biographical Dictionary of Living Authors* (1816).
            GORDON GOODWIN, *rev.* ELIZABETH BAIGENT

Sources [J. Watkins and F. Shoberl], *A biographical dictionary of the living authors of Great Britain and Ireland* (1816) · Watt, *Bibl. Brit.* **Wealth at death** financially distressed in 1802: *DNB*

Greene, (Henry) Graham (1904–1991), author, was born on 2 October 1904 at St John's, Berkhamsted, Hertfordshire, the fourth of six children of Charles Henry Greene (1865–1942), teacher, and his wife and cousin, Marion Raymond (1872–1959), eldest daughter of the Revd Carleton Greene, and a distant relative of Robert Louis Stevenson.

Early years and education Graham Greene spent his first sixteen years at Berkhamsted School, where his father, a shy man of modest talents but high moral standards, was headmaster. His tall and regal mother was a powerful force in the boy's life, but she was emotionally reserved and showed more interest in Graham's sisters, Molly and Elizabeth, than in him and his brothers—Herbert, Raymond, and Hugh (who became director-general of the BBC). A troubled child, Greene felt uncomfortable on both sides of the green baize door that divided the main schoolroom from the family quarters. The need to satisfy his father as both a pupil and a son proved overwhelming, and caused the boy so much distress that he tried to kill himself. He developed a particular fascination for Russian roulette and, in later years, gave various accounts of a period in his teens when he supposedly played the deadly game with a revolver borrowed from an older brother.

Until he was thirteen Greene lived with his parents, and thus was spared the communal struggle of dormitory existence. When he finally joined one of the boarders' houses at his father's school, he found the experience traumatizing. He was bullied ruthlessly, partly because he was the headmaster's son, and partly because he was an awkward, bony youth with an introverted personality and little aptitude for games. His fellow boarders mocked him to his face, played cruel jokes on him, jabbed him with sharp objects, twisted his arm, and punched him. He grew desperate and tried running away.

Alarmed by his inability to cope with life as a boarder, Greene's parents took a step that was radical by the standards of their class and generation. They sent him away for psychiatric treatment in London. He was only sixteen when he was placed in the care of an amiable amateur psychoanalyst called Kenneth Richmond. After six peaceful and relatively pleasant months living with Richmond and his wife, Greene returned to Berkhamsted, where he was allowed to live in the family quarters as a day boy while finishing his final year at the school.

In 1922 Greene went up to Balliol College, Oxford, where he kept largely to himself, developed a fondness for writing verses, and was influenced by T. S. Eliot's early works. Though he found Oxford more to his liking than Berkhamsted, he continued to suffer from periodic bouts of depression and was often bored with his studies. In the memoirs of his famous contemporaries, he is rarely more

(Henry) **Graham Greene** (1904–1991), by Bassano, 1939

than a vague presence among the 'Brideshead set'. Evelyn Waugh observed that 'Graham Greene looked down on us (and perhaps all undergraduates) as childish and ostentatious. He certainly shared in none of our revelry' (Shelden, 86). It was only after they were both established novelists that Waugh and Greene became friends. Cyril Connolly summed up Greene's social life at Balliol by saying 'he was of us, but not with us' (Connolly, 10).

Greene spent much of his time and energy on poetry, which he contributed to the student magazine *Oxford Outlook* and to the *Weekly Westminster Gazette*. His verse also appeared in three successive volumes of the prestigious annual *Oxford Poetry*. In 1925, his last year at university, Basil Blackwell published his short collection *Babbling April*. The book attracted so many bad notices, however, that a disappointed Greene abruptly surrendered his ambition to be a poet. After coming down from Oxford with a second-class degree in history, he spent several months looking for work and finally decided to make his living as a journalist, starting as an unpaid assistant at the *Nottingham Journal*.

Marriage, religion, and early novels While at Oxford Greene fell in love with Vivienne (later Vivien) Dayrell-Browning (*b.* 1905), an apprentice assistant to Basil Blackwell, and the daughter of Sidney and Muriel Dayrell-Browning. A sentimental, dreamy young woman, she shared Greene's love of poetry and wrote one book of verse. In later years she won renown as an authority on antique dolls' houses and wrote a history of the subject, *English Dolls' Houses of the Eighteenth and Nineteenth Centuries* (1955). On 15 October

1927 Greene and Vivienne were married at St Mary's, a small Catholic church in Hampstead. They had two children, Lucy Caroline and Francis, born in 1933 and 1936 respectively.

A convert to Catholicism before her marriage, Vivienne encouraged her future husband to take an interest in her religion. While working in Nottingham he met Father George Trollope, of Nottingham Cathedral, and received religious instruction from him. In February 1926 Father Trollope baptized Greene in a simple ceremony with no friends or family present. Though Greene later objected to being called a 'Catholic novelist', he became celebrated for employing religious themes in his works, praised by Catholic critics during his lifetime for the powerful way in which his novels explore the subjects of sin, damnation, evil, and divine forgiveness. But Greene's relationship with the church was never easy, and he was often critical of the religion. In his last years he began referring to himself as a 'Catholic atheist' (Shelden, 6).

Greene and his wife made their first home in London, where in 1926 he had been appointed a sub-editor at *The Times*. In his spare time he wrote his first novel, *The Man Within*, which enjoyed widespread critical and commercial success when Charles Evans, the managing director at William Heinemann, published it in June 1929. The novel sold 13,000 hardback copies, an amazing feat for a first novel by an unknown author who was only twenty-five. Emboldened, Greene negotiated a generous financial arrangement with his publisher and was able to leave his job at *The Times*.

In many ways, however, *The Man Within* was a false start for Greene. A rousing historical romance about the smuggling trade on the Sussex coast in the early 1800s, the novel is an apprentice effort set in a time and place that Greene did not know well. But the book's success made him think that his future lay in writing more tales of the same kind, and he quickly produced another two novels of romantic adventure, *The Name of Action* (1930) and *Rumour at Nightfall* (1931), neither of which enjoyed the popularity of his first book. By 1931 he was in debt to his publishers and was worried that his income would soon dry up. In an effort to save money, and to revive his literary fortunes, he moved to a thatched cottage in the Cotswolds, on the outskirts of Chipping Campden, and began work on a new fictional work set on the Orient Express.

Major novels and 'entertainments', 1932–1950 As Greene later admitted, *Stamboul Train* (1932) was a calculated effort to win back a large readership and to keep him in business as a full-time writer. In particular, he wanted to please Hollywood, believing that his story was perfect for a lucrative screen adaptation. Long before the appearance of such films as *The Thirty-Nine Steps* and *The Lady Vanishes*, he was able to see the cinematic potential of a drama unfolding on an express train crossing vast expanses. He had briefly visited Constantinople in 1930, while on a cruise, but his only experience of the Orient Express was limited to its run from Ostend to Cologne. Relying mostly on his imagination, he created a narrative involving a vivid cast of exotic characters caught up in political intrigue, spying, and crime. During the first eight months of 1932 he stayed in the Cotswolds and wrote his book, exercising the rigid discipline that became a familiar feature of his career: he began a steady habit of writing a certain number of words (usually 500) each day and then stopping until the next day.

Stamboul Train was a considerable success, selling 21,000 copies in its first year and earning £1500 in film rights from Twentieth Century Fox. The book became the first of Greene's so-called 'entertainments', a term that was meant not only to attract readers of popular fiction, but also to disarm highbrow critics. It was a convenient way of telling the reviewers that he had more serious ambitions in mind, and that writing thrillers was simply a kind of hobby, albeit a profitable one. In any event, his thrillers helped him to move to more spacious quarters, first to an expensive modern flat in Woodstock Close, Oxford, and then to a large, elegant house in London at 14 North Side, Clapham Common. The house was built in 1720 and had once been the home of Zachary Macaulay, the historian's father. Greene and his family occupied the house from 1935 until 1940, when bomb damage during the blitz made it uninhabitable.

Greene once explained that his entertainments were 'exciting' stories 'with just enough character to give interest in the action', but that 'in the novels I hope one is primarily interested in the character and the action takes a minor part' (Pryce-Jones, 62). *Stamboul Train* saved his career; but its designation as an 'entertainment' created a false impression of his talent, for his entertainments have much in common with his supposedly 'serious' works, and are not mere trifles to be tasted once and thrown aside. All the powerful obsessions that fill the pages of his masterpieces—*Brighton Rock* (1938), *The Power and the Glory* (1940), *The Heart of the Matter* (1948)—are also present in *Stamboul Train*, *A Gun for Sale* (1936), *The Ministry of Fear* (1943), and other entertainments. It is also not the case that the 'minor' works lack fully developed characters. Two of Greene's most compelling creations are the assassin Raven in *A Gun for Sale* and the petty racketeer Harry Lime in *The Third Man* (1950). Even Greene was occasionally uncertain of the dividing line between his entertainments and his other work. When it was first published, *Brighton Rock* was called an entertainment in the American edition, but not in the British edition. After the 1950s the author stopped trying to label his works of fiction, but the impression remains among some readers that the thrillers are potboilers that do not deserve serious consideration. If this were true Greene would never have bothered to create, for example, the complexity of Arthur Rowe's nightmare world of private and public war in *The Ministry of Fear*, or the intricate duel between good and evil in *The Confidential Agent* (1939). Until much later the artist in Greene was never far behind the entertainer.

In his entertainments Greene was not imitating a tried-and-true commercial formula, but was creating a new form of fiction—one that stands somewhere between the traditional art of the novel and the new art of the cinema.

He tried to reproduce on paper the experience of watching a well made film. Nowhere is this more apparent than in *A Gun for Sale*. Many of its scenes are placed in short sections that seem ready to go before the camera. The opening section arrests the reader's attention with a no-nonsense, almost wordless scene in which two people are swiftly and brutally murdered by a mysterious gunman. Even the killer looks at the murder scene as though it is something his eyes have filmed. When he enters the house where his victims are working, he looks slowly round the room, like a cameraman executing a careful panning shot, taking notice of every detail.

Greene was a self-taught student of the cinema. At Oxford he was an avid filmgoer and contributed his first film review to the *Oxford Outlook*. In the 1930s he spent four and a half years writing film reviews for *The Spectator*, commenting on over 400 productions. He was also film critic for the short-lived *Night and Day* magazine which he helped to start. (It folded after Greene lost a libel suit brought against him by the representatives of the nine-year-old Shirley Temple in 1938 for suggesting that she exploited male sexual desire.) The works he liked best were those that filled the screen with evocative images. The 'poetry' of the cinema spoke to his concerns as a novelist, giving him new ideas for literary imagery. He was especially fond of lingering close-ups. Reviewing *Anna Karenina* in 1935, he was impressed by the shots of Greta Garbo leaning over a croquet ball and of her face emerging from a cloud of locomotive steam. What he learned from such a film was a way to make images carry more of the meaning in his own fiction. Memorable images such as Raven's harelip in *A Gun for Sale*, the gulls swooping over the pier in *Brighton Rock*, the yellow-fanged *mestizo* in *The Power and the Glory* (1940), all seem to have sprung from the darkness of the cinema.

Until he went to work as a screenwriter for the movie mogul Alexander Korda in the 1940s, Greene was not fully aware that what he had been creating in his works of the 1930s were very sophisticated, highly polished versions of a 'screen treatment'. Under Korda's guidance, and with the help of a true genius of the cinema, British director Carol Reed, Greene became so adept at the art of the screenplay that he never produced one without first writing a complete treatment of the story, and some of these works eventually emerged as books. The short novel *The Third Man* is simply the screen treatment that Greene created as a first step in the production of the film version, which appeared in 1949 and which won first prize at the Cannes film festival.

In large measure, speed and intense concentration were the secrets of Greene's success as a writer of entertainments. His steady method of working meant that he could finish a book in less than a year, and this focus of attention allowed him to achieve the unity of vision that works so well on film. In a few cases his pace became almost feverish, as though he were trying to live through each frame of the story as he wrote it. *The Confidential Agent* was written in only six weeks, *The Third Man* in eight.

Brighton Rock is his most successful attempt to create a

work that is as fast-paced as a thriller and as complex as a more leisurely character study. It deals with the racecourse gangs who created havoc in Brighton during the 1930s and is an exciting story of murder and duplicity in the underworld. More important, it offers the unforgettable portrait of Pinkie Brown, a bloodthirsty young gangster who courts damnation with the zeal of a saint seeking salvation. Partly inspired by a gruesome murder in Brighton in 1934, the novel provides a deeply disturbing insight into the cruel heart of a killer who cannot decide whether he is God's child or Satan's. He uses religion to enhance the pleasure of doing evil, and then dares God to save him as a perverse test of divine mercy.

Each of Greene's three masterpieces is overflowing with what his friend Douglas Jerrold called 'emotion recollected in hostility' (*Picture Post*). Vague, festering grievances lie at the heart of each story, and the main characters wrestle with the question of whether it is best to lash out at an unjust world or to destroy themselves in a private war against God. In *The Power and the Glory* the unnamed whisky priest finds that he is the last representative of the Catholic church in a rebel Mexican state that recognizes neither the power nor the glory of the church. He decides to stay in the dangerous land not because he is faithful to his religion, but because he wants to live outside the rules of both God and man. He revels in his own condition as an outcast in a lawless world and seeks power and glory in personal independence.

Disloyalty, betrayal, and the grim satisfactions of self-destruction also infect the heart of the colonial policeman Major Scobie, in *The Heart of the Matter*, who is tormented by a loveless marriage that he cannot escape and a guilt-ridden affair with a vulnerable younger woman. Like the whisky priest, he is a traditional figure of authority who finds that he cannot keep order in his own life. Suicide appeals to him as a desirable way out of his troubles. He thinks that the only escape is to embrace defeat and to take pride in suffering the fate of a defiant loner unfettered by loyalty to anyone or anything.

Not long before he died, George Orwell reviewed *The Heart of the Matter* and harshly condemned it. From his perspective as a moral critic, he could not approve of Greene's fascination with sin, suicide, and damnation. A straightforward thinker who had once been a colonial policeman himself, Orwell found no evidence in the novel of the 'ordinary human decency' that he valued so much in life and literature. Indeed, he detected a certain snobbishness in Greene on the question of hell: 'He appears to share the idea, which has been floating around ever since Baudelaire, that there is something rather *distingué* in being damned; Hell is a sort of high-class nightclub, entry to which is reserved for Catholics only' (*New Yorker*).

Most contemporary readers, however, did not share Orwell's reservations. *The Heart of the Matter* was enormously popular, selling more than 300,000 copies in Britain. It was also a main selection of the Book-of-the-Month Club in America. Though Greene considered the book his most serious work to date, it brought him more money

than all his previous entertainments combined. (*The Ministry of Fear*, for example, sold a 'mere' 18,000 copies five years earlier.) From 1948 until his death Greene continued to enjoy large sales, widespread critical respect, and largely favourable publicity in the mainstream press, both at home and abroad. After nineteen years of hard work—in which he brought out a new book almost every year—he was established for life.

War years and espionage   *The Heart of the Matter* is set in wartime Sierra Leone, where Greene worked as an intelligence officer for fourteen months between 1941 and 1943. After the Second World War broke out his first government job was at the Ministry of Information in London, where he commissioned and edited various works of propaganda. At night he served as an air raid warden. But he soon grew weary of the bureaucratic dullness at the Ministry of Information, and sought more adventurous work with the Secret Intelligence Service (MI6). He officially joined the service in July 1941 and became officer 59200, the same code number given to Wormold's immediate superior in Greene's later parody of the espionage world, *Our Man in Havana* (1958). He held a position in section V, the unit responsible for counter-espionage. After receiving his training in England, he went to west Africa and spied on the Vichy French colonies and on neutral ships that docked at his home base in Freetown. As a cover, he was placed in the police service of the Colonial Office.

When he returned to Britain, Greene took a job in the Iberian department of the service, which kept track of intelligence operations in Gibraltar, Lisbon, Madrid, and Tangier, all of which were hotbeds of espionage activity. His immediate superior was Kim Philby, who later achieved notoriety when he was exposed as a secret agent for the Soviet Union. Greene worked closely with Philby and liked him, but if he somehow discovered that his friend was a double agent, he never betrayed him. Instead, he abruptly submitted his resignation from service less than a month before the D-day invasion in 1944 and kept his distance from Philby, who continued to rise in the Secret Intelligence Service hierarchy until the 1950s. After the spy defected to the Soviet Union in 1963 Greene wrote a sympathetic introduction to Philby's autobiography, *My Silent War* (1968), revealing a certain degree of admiration for the skill with which his former boss had managed such a long and intricate scheme of deception and betrayal. He sometimes spoke of Philby as though he were a character in one of his own novels and may have used the spy as a model for Harry Lime in *The Third Man*. As Greene was aware, Philby had been involved in an underground socialist movement in Vienna in 1934 and, like Harry Lime, had used the city's extensive network of sewers as a hide-out.

Greene's own fondness for secrecy and deception is evident in his willingness to continue serving the Secret Intelligence Service unofficially for many years. As late as the 1980s he was still providing help to his contacts, giving assistance during his many foreign trips. From the 1950s to the 1970s one of his closest contacts in the service was

Maurice Oldfield, who became director-general in 1973. In exchange for expenses he gave his help to the organization in many places—most notably Vietnam, Poland, Russia, and China. On a trip to Warsaw in 1955, for example, he spied on the Catholic Pax movement, which was a Soviet-sponsored group. During several visits to Vietnam in the 1950s, he actively spied on both the French colonial army and the communist insurgents, and worked closely with Trevor Wilson, the British consul in Hanoi, who was also the local Secret Intelligence Service station chief and a wartime colleague of Greene's in section V. In 1957 alone, Greene's foreign journeys covered, by his own estimate, 44,000 miles, and much of this travel was paid for by the service. The thrill of spying and the opportunity for constant travel helped to ease the burdens of writing, and allowed him to keep at bay the depression and boredom that plagued him for much of his life. In the words of his official biographer Greene 'was the perfect spy … an intensely secretive man' (Sherry, 2.xiv).

As his literary fame grew in the 1950s and 1960s Greene took pains to make public declarations of his sympathy for international socialism and his suspicion of American capitalism and military expansion. But friends who knew of his work for the Secret Intelligence Service did not take such public comments seriously. In 1960 Evelyn Waugh confided to a friend that he was not fooled by Greene's occasional efforts to praise the Soviet Union, explaining that Greene 'is a secret agent on our side and all his buttering up of the Russians is "cover"' (Waugh, *Letters*, 548). Waugh knew that his fellow novelist had previously shown little interest in the left and had, in fact, been closely associated in the past with men who favoured the right, such as the tory MP Victor Cazalet (who backed *Night and Day* in 1937) and the apologist for Franco Douglas Jerrold (who employed Greene as his deputy at the publishing house of Eyre and Spottiswoode in the mid-1940s). In any event Greene was not averse to wealth and privilege. With his literary earnings he acquired a villa on Capri, apartments in Antibes and Paris, and, towards the end of his life, an apartment overlooking Lake Geneva. To reduce his taxes he decided in the 1960s to end his status as a permanent resident of England and to move to the continent. Afterwards, whenever he made brief visits to London, he invariably stayed at the Ritz.

The last of Greeneland After the war Greene separated informally from his middle-class wife and began a passionate affair with the rich American-born beauty Catherine Walston (1916–1978), who was married to Henry Walston, later Lord Walston, the Labour peer. Greene never divorced his wife, but did not live with her after 1946. Instead, he spent as much time as possible with Catherine Walston, visiting her at her homes in Cambridgeshire and travelling with her to Capri for long holidays. She was the great love of his life and the inspiration for his powerful novel about the pains and pleasures of adultery, *The End of the Affair* (1951). A highly unconventional society hostess, she liked to shock guests at her dinner parties by wearing jeans and doing cartwheels across the floor. Her playful,

mischievous manner prompted one of her friends to call her 'a Marie-Antoinette in elegant jeans' (Shelden, 359).

Greene became obsessed with her and demanded that she spend all her time with him. But she had other lovers, as well as a husband and five children, and was unable to give Greene the attention he craved. Inevitably, they quarrelled and began to drift apart because she would not leave her husband. The intense dynamics of this three-way relationship are vividly portrayed in *The End of the Affair* (1951), and the narrator's heart-rending comments on his turbulent affair are some of the most compelling passages in Greene's work. He dedicated the book to 'C' in the British edition and to 'Catherine' in the American. The real affair survived the novel's publication, but the acute tension between the lovers gradually decreased in the 1950s, and their tumultuous romance ended in the early 1960s.

The End of the Affair is not a conventional love story: the protagonist and narrator, Maurice Bendrix, says in the opening chapter that he will provide the reader with a record of hate. The story of this affair with a married woman becomes a harrowing tale of spiritual torture because sin and guilt stimulate the couple more than love. What gives the novel its special power, however, is Greene's ability to show the many complex ways in which love and hate can become confused. In life and art he was fascinated by borderlines and liked exploring the ambiguities that attend them. His best novels portray destabilized worlds in which all the borders collapse, and this in turn forces individual characters to chart their own course in a 'journey without maps' (this was the title of a travel book about Africa that Greene published in 1936).

For many critics 'Greeneland' has become a convenient term for describing the murky territory of shifting boundaries inhabited by Greene's characters. The first critic to use the term was Arthur Calder-Marshall in 1940, but the novelist himself suggested the pun four years earlier in *A Gun for Sale*. In the minds of some readers Greeneland is associated with rugged landscapes in dangerous parts of Latin America or Africa or Asia. But until the 1950s the novelist set most of his works of fiction in Europe. *The Power and the Glory* and *The Heart of the Matter* are the notable exceptions. It is only after *The End of the Affair* that Greene shifts his focus almost entirely to regions outside Europe. Indeed, Greeneland has two different sets of cast and scenery. One is an urban, lower-middle-class world of sordid European streets haunted by lonely killers, desperate lovers, and assorted lost souls; the other occupies desolate backwaters of wretchedly poor Third World countries where tortured Europeans find their lives halted at a dead end. This second version is evident in *The Quiet American*; *Our Man in Havana* (1958); *A Burnt-Out Case* (1961), set in Africa; *The Comedians* (1966), set in Haiti; and *The Honorary Consul* (1972), set in South America.

By writing about such places as Haiti, the Congo, Cuba, and Vietnam, Greene was able to establish a reputation for himself in the cold war era as a writer with a strong social conscience and a keen interest in other cultures. But that reputation was misleading. Though he altered the landscape of his fiction, the major themes in his work changed very little from the 1930s, and have only slight connections to political, social, or cultural ideology. Whether the backdrop is Brighton or Haiti, Greene always places his greatest focus on the torments that distinguish an individual character's private hell. In *The Quiet American*, for example, the political references and exotic details help to disguise the fact that the story is essentially the same as that in Greene's third novel—*Rumour at Nightfall*, an almost forgotten work—which is set against the background of the Carlist wars, in the 1870s. In both books a tough-minded journalist covering a controversial war betrays an idealistic friend partly out of jealousy. The wartime atmosphere in the later novel is brilliantly conveyed, but its treatment of political matters is as superficial as that in the earlier book. Though the British journalist Fowler in *The Quiet American* has complete contempt for imperial adventurism, he is not 'committed' to anything in Vietnam besides his opium pipe.

Despite his extensive travels in the cold war era, Greene rarely stayed in one place for very long, except when he was at home in Britain, France, or Italy. The portrait of Papa Doc Duvalier's Haiti in *The Comedians* is based on a visit in 1963 that lasted only a fortnight. Greene visited Latin America often, but never bothered to learn Spanish and spent much of his time cultivating the goodwill of such undemocratic regimes as Fidel Castro's in Cuba and General Omar Torrijos's in Panama. In the 1970s and 1980s he visited Panama frequently and made so many friends among the members of Torrijos's military entourage that the general once paid for his flight home on Concorde. He had a personal obsession with Torrijos, as is clear in his non-fiction work *Getting to Know the General* (1985). Fifty years earlier, when he was fascinated by the Carlist wars, he developed a special liking for the doomed figure of a Spanish general called Torrijos. He thought fate had brought him together with Panama's leader of the same name. But none of the Panamanians seems to have known that their fondness for him was compromised by his continuing contacts with his old friends in the British intelligence community.

Greene's last major novel was his most explicit treatment of the world of espionage. *The Human Factor* (1978) is set in the 1970s, but the writer drew his material primarily from his wartime memories of office life at Philby's section V headquarters in central London. After a quarter of a century of avoiding London as a setting in his fiction, he returned to it with great success, bringing vividly to life a part of town that he knew better than any other place in the world. In the novel the old red bricks of St James's Palace glow in the winter afternoon, the night porter scrubs the steps of the Albany (where Greene once kept a set of chambers), a young woman giggles into a telephone at Piccadilly Circus station, and prostitutes lurk in the doorways of Soho. Sure of himself and intimately knowledgeable about his subject and his primary setting, Greene produced a novel that ranks just below his masterpieces written before the cold war. It also enjoyed the greatest commercial success of any of his works, selling especially well in the United States, where it stayed on the *New York Times* best-seller list for six months.

Final years After his relationship with Catherine Walston ended, Greene began an affair with another married woman who soon became his principal companion, and who remained as such until his death. In 1959 he met Yvonne Cloetta (1930?–2001), the wife of a French businessman, and moved to Antibes in the 1960s partly because he wanted to be near her home in Juan les Pins. Though she never left her husband, Jacques, she was almost always at Greene's side when he was in Antibes, and would usually spend holidays with him on Capri. He had a comfortable life with Mme Cloetta, who made few demands on him, and he was reasonably content in Antibes, where the local people left him alone and the authorities treated him with respect. In 1969 the French government appointed him chevalier of the Légion d'honneur. In the early 1980s, however, his life in Antibes became difficult after he made angry charges of corruption against the mayor of Nice in a pamphlet he called *J'Accuse: the Dark Side of Nice* (1982). Threats were made against his life, and he was successfully sued for libel in a Paris court by one of the men he charged with corruption.

Greene finally left France in 1990 and spent the last year of his life at the village of Corseaux, outside Vevey, Switzerland, sharing an apartment with Mme Cloetta. Suffering from a mysterious blood disease, he sought treatment at Vevey's Hôpital de la Providence, where he was given transfusions every fortnight. The new blood helped and, for a while, it seemed that he would recover. But late in March 1991 he became seriously ill and was rushed by ambulance to the Hôpital de la Providence, where he died just before noon on 3 April 1991. His last words were 'Why must it take so long to come?' He was buried on 8 April in the small cemetery at Corseaux.

Subsequent reputation In most studies of twentieth-century British fiction Greene's considerable body of work ranks high. In the period between the great depression and the beginning of the cold war the three indispensable novelists are Greene, George Orwell, and Evelyn Waugh. Of the three, Greene is the one whose career was the longest and most diverse. He left behind more than two dozen novels, several plays, many essays and short stories, three travel books, two volumes of autobiography, a history of British drama, and a literary biography of the Restoration poet Lord Rochester (1974), which he had begun in his twenties (Rochester's rebelliousness, passionate nature, and ambiguous relationship with sin appealed to Greene, but publishers had found the sexual content too explicit in the 1930s). He wrote the screenplay for one of the most highly regarded British films of the twentieth century—*The Third Man*—and since his death his fictional works have continued to attract film-makers. All his major novels have been filmed—*The End of the Affair* twice (1955, 2000)—and *Travels with my Aunt* (1969) has been adapted for both the screen and the stage.

Greene had a rare ability to capture the confusion and

terror of the twentieth century. His sharp narrative voice misses nothing. In arresting detail it reveals the cracks waiting to open up, the towers beginning to lean. The monstrous Pinkie of *Brighton Rock* forever slouches towards the bright lights of the resort town with nothing but destruction in mind. The charmingly ruthless Harry Lime perpetually prowls the ruined streets and labyrinthine sewers of post-war Vienna like a refugee from hell. Both Pinkie and Harry are iconic figures of the twentieth century whose hearts of darkness reflect the worst fears of the age. In his talent for plumbing the depths of that darkness, Greene stands without rival among the writers of his time.　　　　MICHAEL SHELDEN

Sources M. Shelden, *Graham Greene: the man within* (1994) · N. Sherry, *The life of Graham Greene*, 2 vols. (1989–94) · D. Pryce-Jones, *Graham Greene* (1963) · E. Waugh, *The letters of Evelyn Waugh* (1980) · G. Orwell, review of *The heart of the matter*, New Yorker (17 July 1948) · E. Waugh, *A little learning* (1964) · D. Jerrold, 'Pleasure-hater', *Picture Post* (15 March 1952) · C. Connolly, *The evening colonnade* (1973)

Archives Boston College, Massachusetts, John J. Burns Library, residual library and archives · Georgetown University, Washington, DC, Lauinger Library, corresp. and papers · NRA, corresp. and literary papers · Ransom HRC | BFI, corresp. with Joseph Losey · Bodl. Oxf., letters to Jack Lambert, with Lambert's interview notes · Morgan L., letters to Herbert Greene · NL Wales, corresp. with Emyr Humphreys · U. Reading, letters to Bodley Head Ltd · U. Sussex, corresp. with *New Statesman* magazine

Likenesses Bassano, photograph, 1939, NPG [*see illus.*] · B. Brandt, photograph, 1950, National Gallery, London · I. Penn, vintage gelatine silver print, 1950, NPG · F. Topolski, pencil on paper, *c*.1950–1955, NPG · Y. Karsh, photograph, 1960–69, Camera Press Ltd · Y. Karsh, bromide print, 1964, NPG · M. Boxer, ink, *c*.1970–1979, NPG · Snowdon, photograph, 1980–89, Camera Press Ltd · A. Palliser, oils, 1981–3, NPG · A. Springs, bromide print, 1988, NPG · B. Levine, pencil drawing, NPG · P. Stackpole, photograph, repro. in *Life Magazine* (1957) · photographs, Hult. Arch.

Greene, Harry Plunket (1865–1936), singer, was born at Old Connaught House, Bray, co. Wicklow, on 24 June 1865, the son of Richard Jonas Greene, barrister, of Dublin, and his wife, Louisa Lilias, fourth daughter of William Conyngham *Plunket, first Lord Plunket, lord chancellor of Ireland. After his education at Henry Tilney Basset's school, Dublin, and later at Clifton College, Bristol (1877–1881), he travelled abroad in 1883 to study first with Hromada in Stuttgart and later, unhappily (since he never favoured Italian bel canto), with Vannuccini in Florence. After returning to London he initially continued his studies for six months with some dissatisfaction under J. B. Welsh, after which (at Charles Stanford's recommendation) he went to Alfred Blume, who until Blume's death remained his mentor. He made his public début as a bass-baritone at the People's Palace, Stepney, on 21 January 1888 in Handel's *Messiah*, an appearance so successful that he was rapidly engaged at all of London's most important concert venues. In 1890 he performed at Covent Garden as the Commendatore in *Don Giovanni* and as the Duke of Verona in Charles Gounod's *Roméo et Juliette*, but he gravitated more naturally to oratorio and to the solo song repertory, in which he became a specialist. In the autumn of 1890 Plunket Greene appeared for the first time at the Three Choirs festival in Worcester, but it was two years later at

Gloucester, as Job in Hubert Parry's eponymous oratorio (a role he made his own) that he achieved national renown. Thereafter he became closely associated with Parry's large-scale festival works, a connection further cemented by his marriage to Gwendolen Maud (1878–1959), Parry's younger daughter, on 20 July 1899. He was also an exponent of Edward Elgar's oratorios, undertaking the part of the Priest and Angel of the Agony in *The Dream of Gerontius*, which he sang on numerous occasions (including the first disastrous performance at Birmingham in 1900), and the role of Judas in *The Apostles*, while Stanford's two popular collections of sea songs, *Songs of the Sea* (1904) and *Songs of the Fleet* (1910) (written for and dedicated to him), and numerous orchestral song arrangements enhanced his fame yet further.

Eschewing the royalty ballad and the mixed entertainment of the 'miscellaneous concert', Plunket Greene and the pianist Leonard Borwick pioneered the solo song recital in London, giving their first performance at St James's Hall in December 1893. This duo, later joined by the accompanist Samuel Liddle, lasted ten years, during which time they developed a reputation as exponents of German lieder and in particular of the work of Schumann (whose *Dichterliebe* cycle they gave complete for the first time in London on 11 January 1895) and Brahms. They were, moreover, keen promoters and interpreters of English song, and Plunket Greene was frequently the preferred executant (and in many cases dedicatee) of new works, notably Stanford's Irish song cycles and collections (including *An Irish Idyll* op. 77 and *Cushendall* op. 118, which he often sang), Parry's *scena The Soldier's Tent*, Arthur Somervell's fine cycle *Maud*, Elgar's *Two Songs* op. 31, Walford Davies's *The Long Journey* op. 25, Ralph Vaughan Williams's *Songs of Travel*, and works by Roger Quilter, Norman O'Neill, and Herbert Howells.

In later years Plunket Greene devoted his time more to teaching, as a professor at the Royal Academy of Music (1911–19) and the Royal College of Music (1912–19), and formulated his thoughts on solo song in his treatise *Interpretation in Song*, published in 1912. This book was, to all intents and purposes, Plunket Greene's artistic testimony, enshrining those facets of his powers as a singer—clarity of diction, a wide interpretative palette, and carefully planned programmes, as well as a compelling presence as a performer—which made him hugely popular with audiences in Britain and in the USA (where he was a regular visitor). In 1916 he published *Pilot and other Stories*, but it was not until after his retirement from his teaching positions in 1919 that he turned his hand more seriously to writing, producing many articles for *Music and Letters* (some of which found their way into his book *From Blue Danube to Shannon*, published in 1934), a book on his lifelong passion, fishing (*Where Bright Waters Meet*, 1924), and a biography of Charles Villiers Stanford (1935). He also did much adjudicating in Britain and visited Canada on two occasions, first in 1923 with Granville Bantock and later in 1932 with Harold Samuel and Maurice Jacobson. He was president of the Incorporated Society of Musicians in 1933 and, as a cricket lover, a member of the MCC.

An Irish tory, Plunket Greene had a politically reactionary disposition similar to that of his fellow countryman Stanford. His Conservative views (which led him to oppose women's suffrage and Irish home rule) brought him into conflict with the more radical views of his father-in-law, and the relationship between the two men was uncomfortably turbulent. Furthermore, his marriage to Gwendolen, which produced two sons and a daughter, proved unhappy, and separation took place in 1920. He died in St George's Hospital, London, on 19 August 1936 and was buried close to his Hampshire home at Hurstbourne Priors three days later.　　　JEREMY DIBBLE

Sources J. A. Fuller-Maitland, 'Greene, Harry Plunket', Grove, *Dict. mus.* (1927), rev. (1998) · J. Dibble, *C. Hubert H. Parry: his life and music* (1992); pbk edn (1998) · H. Plunket Greene, *From blue Danube to Shannon* (1934) · H. Plunket Greene, *Charles Villiers Stanford* (1935) · A. Boden, *Three Choirs: a history of the festival* (1992) · J. N. Moore, *Edward Elgar: a creative life* (1984) · H. Plunket Greene, *Interpretation in song* (1912) · M. Ritchie, 'Plunket Greene as a teacher', *Recorded Sound*, 32 (1968), 328 [with discography] · *The Times* (20 Aug 1936) · *DNB* · *CGPLA Eng. & Wales* (1936) · m. cert. · d. cert. · R. A. Jones, *Arthur Ponsonby: the politics of life* (1989), 131–2
Archives BL, corresp. with Society of Authors, Add. MS 56716 · BL, corresp. with Macmillans, Add. MS 55240 · Bodl. Oxf., letters to Lord Ponsonby · U. Leeds, Brotherton L., letters to Herbert Thompson | SOUND BL NSA, performance recordings
Likenesses photograph, 1899, Shulbrede Priory · E. Millar, photograph, 1935, NPG · J. Gunn, portrait, 1936 · Bacon, photograph, Royal College of Music, London · Elliott & Fry, photograph, Royal College of Music, London · Ellis & Walery, photograph, Royal College of Music, London · photographs, Royal College of Music, London
Wealth at death £365 9s. 0d.: probate, 2 Nov 1936, *CGPLA Eng. & Wales*

Greene, Sir Hugh Carleton (1910–1987), journalist and broadcaster, was born on 15 November 1910 at St John's, Chesham Road, Berkhamsted, the youngest of four sons and the fifth among the six children of Charles Henry Greene, headmaster of Berkhamsted School, and his wife, Marion Raymond (a cousin), the daughter of the Revd Carleton Greene, vicar of Great Barford. The novelist Graham *Greene was his brother. He was educated at Berkhamsted School and at Merton College, Oxford, where he obtained a second class in both classical moderations (1931) and English (1933).

Early career Having spent some time in Germany before entering Merton, Greene returned there on leaving Oxford in 1933. From working as a stringer for the *Daily Herald* and the *New Statesman* in Munich, he joined the Berlin office of the *Daily Telegraph*, becoming its chief correspondent in 1938. However, he was expelled from Germany in May 1939 in reprisal for the expulsion from London of a German correspondent. The rise of the Nazis, witnessed at first hand, deeply influenced him for the rest of his life, teaching him to hate intolerance and the degradation of character to which the loss of freedom led. The experience confirmed him in his career as a journalist. He was to say in 1969 that he had never considered himself an ex-journalist at any time after.

Greene's next posting, to Warsaw, was short-lived. Within a week of the German invasion, on 1 September 1939, he was forced to leave Poland. Equipped only with a bottle of beer and a gas mask, he travelled first to Romania, but, as the war spread, moved on to report from a number of other European countries. He finally returned to Britain in June 1940, escaping from Brussels and then Paris just ahead of the German army.

At the BBC After a brief spell in the Royal Air Force as a pilot officer in intelligence, a series of delicate negotiations secured Greene's release to join the German service of the British Broadcasting Corporation in October 1940. For its commitment to impartial and accurate reporting and its avoidance of propaganda, the service, of which Greene became the news editor, was known as 'white' in contrast to the non-BBC service of 'black' programmes. Dedicated to undermining the faith of German listeners in their own domestic broadcasts, the latter proclaimed its motto as 'Never lie accidentally, only deliberately.'

At considerable personal danger, and with hardly less physical discomfort for his large frame, Greene was flown to Sweden in 1942 to discover how badly intensive jamming by the Germans was affecting reception of the BBC's programmes. He reported on his return that, provided the broadcaster's speech was kept clear, measured, and simple, the results were not discouraging. While some of the changes he introduced on his return, including an increase in news broadcasts and a reduction in feature programmes, may have reflected a personal preference, they greatly increased the impact of the BBC's output on German audiences. Eventually those audiences numbered many million, many of whom regularly endangered their lives to listen.

The BBC's commitment to the pursuit of truth in wartime was to serve as a model in the reconstruction of German broadcasting when the war was over. Seconded as controller of broadcasting in the British zone of Germany from 1946 to 1948, Greene himself made an important personal contribution to the rebuilding process. He imbued a spirit of independence in his staff and, characteristically, tried to limit party-political interference in appointments, but in that, less characteristically, he was not entirely successful.

Following his return to Britain in 1948, Greene was appointed head of the BBC's eastern European service. Two years later he was seconded again: to the Colonial Office and the emergency information service in Malaya. There he oversaw the conduct of psychological warfare against the communist insurgents. Two senior appointments in external broadcasting followed: the first in 1952, as assistant controller, overseas services, and then, in 1955, as controller. Appointed to be director of administration in 1956, he was temporarily distanced from a direct involvement with programmes. However, it was recognized that Sir Ian Jacob, then director-general, was now identifying Greene as his successor.

Director, news and current affairs After another two years, as an even clearer signal of preferment, Greene was appointed director, news and current affairs. It was a new post, created, in the BBC's own words, 'to secure overall co-ordination and editorial direction of topical output' in both radio and television. More directly, its purpose was to close the deep rift which existed between a highly conservative news division, which regarded the new medium as little more than an appendix to sound radio, and a television service eager to explore in news the full range of possibilities it was developing in other kinds of output. Greene came almost immediately into conflict with Tahu Hole, head of the news division. The two men differed profoundly in temperament and in their attitudes to broadcast journalism. Since the launch of Independent Television News in 1955, the BBC had been competing unsuccessfully in both innovation and audience numbers. Inside the BBC, Greene was not alone in attributing the poor performance of BBC television news to Hole's leadership. To resolve the hostility between the two men, Jacob accepted Greene's suggestion that Hole should be transferred into the now vacant post of director of administration, a prelude to his early retirement from the BBC on Greene's promotion as director-general in 1960.

Soon after taking over as director of news and current affairs, Greene instituted a review by three senior television programme makers of the shortcomings of BBC television news and of how it might be transformed into a service worthy of the BBC's traditions. Two of the three belonged to the television talks department, which, from beyond the reach of Hole's news division, had established an independent reputation for its treatment of current affairs, including levels of political discussion news division had not achieved. The group made a series of radical criticisms, and their report found a receptive response. Although Greene considered the criticisms more valuable than the proposed remedies, the report led to profound changes in both management structures and style—fresh evidence of the dynamism of Greene's attitude towards programme making.

Director-general Formal confirmation of Greene's appointment as Jacob's successor in 1960 was received with general delight among the corporation's staff. Particular pleasure was felt at the appointment of a director-general, the first in the BBC's history, who had made his career very largely within the corporation. To programme makers Greene's transformation of news and current affairs in both television and radio had clearly demonstrated his belief in them as the BBC's foremost asset. Jacob, as a long-serving military man, had been said to treat them as if they were junior officers to be assigned the duties devised by their superiors.

On taking office Greene abolished the post of director of news and current affairs, retaining for himself the functions of editor-in-chief. He remained a working journalist capable, when the need arose, of dealing expeditiously with those editorial issues that were referred to him. To do so, however, meant keeping closely in touch, as his instinct already was, with the thinking of producers and editors, for whose ideas he retained a ready ear and much imaginative sympathy.

Greene's appointment was rapidly followed by the creation of a committee of inquiry into broadcasting, chaired by W. H. Pilkington. Greene's approach to the committee was combative, reflecting techniques learned in psychological warfare during and after the Second World War. Objectives once defined were frequently restated, enemies rattled, and friends rallied. A 'black book' recording the interests outside television of the commercial franchise holders was intended to show that they had loyalties conflicting with their public service obligations. In a report which came embarrassingly close to overpraising the BBC, the Pilkington committee recommended that the BBC should be given a second television channel and an opportunity to develop local radio stations. For its part, Independent Television was rewarded with swingeing criticisms of undemanding programme standards and a call for a more forceful assertion of its responsibilities by its regulator, the Independents Television Authority.

Developments in television During the two years taken by the Pilkington committee to complete its report, the BBC's hand had been greatly strengthened by an upturn in the fortunes of its television service. Greene had inherited a situation in which BBC programmes were viewed by barely 25 per cent of all viewers (a fact which weakened the effect among some politicians of the committee's strictures on Independent Television). Shortly after the report was published, however, the BBC could point, for the first time since 1955, to a quarter in which it had a majority of the audience. Its revitalized television schedules had wide popular appeal. A variety of light entertainment and drama series, documentaries, and current affairs programmes attracted audiences from across the whole of society. Many of the single plays were written by contemporary writers and, while dismissed as 'kitchensink drama' by their critics, often dealt with characters and themes neglected in the commercial theatre. A surefootedness, owing much to Greene's support, was discernible almost everywhere in the output, not least in areas where Independent Television had been expected to dominate. In a benign economic climate, with a less deferential mood among the generation then reaching maturity, and, at least until the mid-1960s, a tolerant government, the challenges Greene encouraged to many of the orthodoxies of British society could count on favourable responses.

Inevitably, however, the new spirit which Greene had set at large within the BBC met opposition, especially, but not exclusively, over television programmes. Strong language in comedies, supposedly overexplicit portrayals of sexual activity in single plays, the undermining of authority figures in Z Cars, a long-running series about northern policemen, and ridicule directed at politicians and the church all stirred up intense controversies, short-lived in themselves, but contributing, despite the praise which the same programmes drew from other sections of the audience, to a persistent current of unease about the direction in which its director-general might be leading the BBC.

However, despite differences with some members of

the board and influential critics outside the BBC, Greene maintained a strong defence of the corporation's duty to deal responsibly, but vigorously, with major issues in society. He held that provocation could be socially imperative, though outrage was not. By the time he resigned as director-general in 1969, after twenty-nine years of serving the BBC, he was acknowledged by both admirers and critics to have been the most influential director-general since John Reith a generation earlier. For his admirers, he was the champion of liberal values and a great liberator of talent. He himself wished to be remembered as the man who had turned down the central heating at the BBC and opened the windows. For his critics, not all politically on the right, he had been one of the principal agents in what they regarded as the widespread destruction of traditional values throughout the 1960s.

Retirement In 1967 Lord Hill, then chairman of the Independent Television Authority, was appointed chairman of the BBC. In those days of still aggressive competition between the two sets of broadcasters, his transfer was compared in the BBC to the appointment of the German general Rommel to the command of Britain's Eighth Army at the height of the desert war. Greene himself felt affronted, believing, rightly or wrongly, that the appointment was intended as a warning shot across the BBC's bows. As a result, he never settled into an easy relationship with his new chairman. In 1968 Greene, facing his second divorce, proposed that, after more than eight years in office, it was time for him to move on. To make clear that the board had not forced the director-general's hand, Hill suggested that, after a short break, Greene should become a governor. The offer was accepted, and Greene left office on 31 March 1969, flattered at the honour of becoming the first member of staff to reach the board.

His short period as a governor was personally unsatisfactory. Although the tensions in his relationship with the chairman had eased during his final months on the staff, he was conscious of his waning influence in a BBC that was changing as society changed and of a growing awareness that his presence inevitably complicated the life of his successor. Before two more years had passed he had left the board.

In retirement Greene made some programmes for the BBC and for Independent Television, the latter arousing criticism from some BBC contemporaries opposed to the idea of so senior a BBC figure working for its competitors. He wrote several books on the rivals of Sherlock Holmes and became chairman of Bodley Head, the publishing house of his brother Graham Greene. Recognizing the totalitarian character of the colonels' regime in Greece, he became active in the opposition being organized against it.

Honours and assessment Greene was appointed OBE in 1950 and KCMG in 1964. He was given an honorary DCL by East Anglia (1969) and a DUniv by York (1973). In 1973 he also received a DUniv from the Open University, in whose establishment he had played a considerable part, despite opposition among some BBC staff who feared that educational interests might exercise an undue influence on programmes. Germany honoured him with the grand cross of the Order of Merit (1977).

At 6 feet 6 inches tall, Greene resembled his predecessor Lord Reith, but there, with the exception of a mutual commitment to the BBC's independence and the licence fee as the means of securing it, resemblance ended. Reith was an upholder of the establishment, frustrated that, after leaving the BBC, the establishment had not taken him at his own valuation. Greene, however, was anti-establishment. He could be cavalier towards critics, sometimes displaying an impatience which lacked his usual political acuity. A strong element of mischief in his make-up encouraged him to mock the pompous and the pretentious. It was a characteristic which his features could sometimes give away. Ruskin Spear caught the mood so triumphantly in his official portrait of Greene that, on its unveiling in the council chamber in Broadcasting House, the painting drew a gasp of delighted recognition. When necessary, he could be incisive to the point of ruthlessness. An aloof personality, attributed by some to shyness, brought him few close friends and may partly explain the failure of his first two marriages. His first wife (whom he married on 24 October 1934) was Helga Mary (b. 1915/16), the daughter of Samuel Guinness, a banker, of London. They had two sons, but were divorced in 1948. Three years later, on 24 September 1951, he married Elaine Shaplen (b. 1920/21), the daughter of Louis Gilbert, an accountant, of New York, and the former wife of Robert Shaplen. Two more sons were born, but the marriage was ended in 1969. On 11 May 1970 Greene married Else Neumann (1909/10–1981) (the German actress Tatjana Sais, with whom he had lived in the late 1940s), the daughter of Martin Hofler of Frankfurt am Main, Germany. She died in 1981, and on 19 December 1984 he married Sarah Mary Manning Grahame (b. 1940/41), a script supervisor and the daughter of David Grahame, a concert manager of Brisbane, Australia. Greene, who should not be confused with his near-contemporary, the entertainer Hugh Hughes ('Hughie') *Green, died from cancer in the King Edward VII Hospital, London, on 19 February 1987.   COLIN SHAW

Sources A. Briggs, *The history of broadcasting in the United Kingdom*, 3 (1970); 5 (1995) · H. Greene, *The third floor front* (1969) · G. Mansell, *Let truth be told* (1982) · L. Miall, *Inside the BBC* (1994) · G. Wyndham Goldie, *Facing the nation* (1971) · M. Tracey, *A variety of lives* (1983) · personal knowledge (2004) · private information (2004) · b. cert. · m. certs. · d. cert. · *The Times* (21 Feb 1987)

Archives Bodl. Oxf., corresp. and papers; papers

Likenesses photograph, 1967, Hult. Arch. · R. Spear, portrait, Broadcasting House, London · photograph, repro. in *The Times* (20 Feb 1987) · photograph, repro. in *The Times* (21 Feb 1987)

Wealth at death £404,287: probate, 8 May 1987, *CGPLA Eng. & Wales*

Greene, John (1578–1653), serjeant-at-law, was the eldest son of Thomas Greene, a haberdasher on London Bridge and of Bois Hall, Navestock, Ongar, Essex, and of his wife, Margaret, daughter of Lawrence Greene of London. John probably matriculated from St John's College, Cambridge, taking his BA in 1599 and his MA in 1602, before entering

Lincoln's Inn on 4 May 1605. It is most likely after his call to the bar on 16 June 1612 that Greene married Anne Blanchard (d. 1641), the daughter of a citizen draper of London. Greene served as pensioner in the year before his call to the bench on 4 November 1628, and delivered his reading in August 1631. On that occasion he took considerable advantage of a reader's traditional privilege, admitting to the house no fewer than nineteen new members, mostly Londoners, including his eldest son, John *Greene, the clergyman Jonathan Browne DCL, rector of St Faith's, London, and the city's two sheriffs. Appointed treasurer for Lincoln's Inn's contribution to the masque jointly staged by the four inns of court at Whitehall early in 1634, Greene shortly afterwards reported a budgetary shortfall of over £200.

Although named fee'd counsel to the city of Chester in 1628 at the request of a kinsman, the Welsh judge Sir John Bridgeman, Greene's career was otherwise firmly centred on Westminster Hall and the City of London, where in 1634 he became judge of the sheriff's court. He appeared (as 'John Greene of London': Essex RO, D/Eb 17) among those proposed to Charles I by the judges in 1637 as fit persons to be made serjeants-at-law, although Greene—like some others listed—was denied this promotion until 1640. Among those then named as patrons at his call were Edward Sackville, fourth earl of Dorset, and the former chief justice Henry Montagu, earl of Manchester. At this time Greene was living in Coleman Street, London, and classed as one of the ward's wealthiest inhabitants.

During the civil war years Greene remained in London, where he was assessed to pay a weekly contribution of 10s. in 1644, and continued his legal practice. His acceptance in June 1650 of the title serjeant of the Commonwealth of England, borne by very few lawyers, may or may not indicate the depth of his commitment to the new republican regime. Greene also served regularly as an assize judge from 1646, being commissioned on the northern, midland, and home circuits almost every year until his death at home in Fleet Street, London, on 17 May 1653. His will combines a conventional Calvinist statement of assurance with an assertion of Trinitarian orthodoxy. Following his stated wish, he was buried in the parish church of Navestock, Essex, 'neare to my late loveing wife Anne' (PRO, PROB 11/239, fol. 333); a memorial inscription notes that their two sons and four daughters ('besides some few that died young') produced a total of twenty-two surviving grandchildren (Le Neve, 2.20). Greene indeed founded a legal dynasty. The bulk of the substantial landed estate in Essex and London 'wherewith God of his great mercy hath blessed me' (PRO, PROB 11/239, fol. 333) was inherited by his diarist son John, who, having married the eldest daughter of Philip Jermyn, justice of king's bench from 1648, succeeded his father as judge of the sheriff's court and became recorder of London shortly before his early death in 1659, while *his* son (also John) served as serjeant-at-law from 1700 to 1725.   WILFRID PREST

Sources W. R. Prest, *The rise of the barristers: a social history of the English bar, 1590–1640*, 2nd edn (1991) • W. C. Metcalfe, ed., *The visitations of Essex*, 2, Harleian Society, 14 (1879) • *The visitation of London, anno Domini 1633, 1634, and 1635, made by Sir Henry St George*, 1, ed. J. J. Howard and J. L. Chester, Harleian Society, 15 (1880) • W. P. Baildon, ed., *The records of the Honorable Society of Lincoln's Inn: admissions*, 1 (1896) • W. P. Baildon, ed., *The records of the Honorable Society of Lincoln's Inn: the black books*, 2 (1898) • J. S. Cockburn, *A history of English assizes, 1558–1714* (1972) • Baker, *Serjeants* • will, PRO, PROB 11/239, sig. 344 • M. J. Groombridge, ed., *Calendar of Chester city council minutes, 1603–1642*, Lancashire and Cheshire RS, 106 (1956) • J. Le Neve, *Monumenta Anglicana*, 2: 1650–1679 (1718) • E. M. Symonds, 'The diary of John Greene (1635–57)', *EngHR*, 43 (1928), 385–94, 598–604; 44 (1929), 106–17 • *The obituary of Richard Smyth … being a catalogue of all such persons as he knew in their life*, ed. H. Ellis, CS, 44 (1849) • Venn, *Alum. Cant.*, 1/2.255

Wealth at death substantial; estate in Essex and London property inherited from father; manor of Dunmow Parva, Essex, and other lands at Navestock and Stamford Rivers; lease of house in Lombard Street, London, bought for £1300, plus various other London properties: will, PRO, PROB 11/239, fols. 333–333v

Greene, John (1616–1659), lawyer and diarist, was born in Middlesex on 28 October 1616, the third of seven children of John *Greene (1578–1653), barrister, and Anne (d. 1641), daughter of Thomas Blanchard, citizen and draper of London. His father was appointed judge of one of the London sheriff's courts in 1634 and made serjeant-at-law in 1640. John Greene went to school at Brentwood in Essex. He was admitted to St John's College, Cambridge, in 1632, but does not seem to have graduated. He had already been admitted to Lincoln's Inn in August 1631. He was called to the bar in 1639. On 24 April 1643 he married Mary Jermyn (1627–1659), daughter of Philip Jermyn (c.1588–1655), subsequently justice of the king's bench. Greene lived in his father's house in the City of London during the law terms, first in the Old Jewry and subsequently in Fleet Street. In the vacations they lived at Blois Hall in Essex, where his father owned the manor. Greene succeeded his father as judge in the sheriff's court in 1653. On 18 March 1659 he was elected recorder of London in preference to, among others, Greene's friend the future lord chancellor Heneage Finch. Greene died on 1 November 1659; his wife died four weeks later in childbirth. Eight of their children survived infancy, five sons and three daughters.

Greene inherited property in London and Essex from his father. He probably received a substantial portion from his father-in-law. He seems to have had a successful legal practice, at one stage successfully defending the astrologer William Lilly. Greene purchased further properties in Essex and London and also did a certain amount of moneylending. Nevertheless, when he came to write his will, shortly before his death, he was clearly concerned about the ability of his estate to pay his debts and provide portions for his children, and gave instructions for various properties to be sold to make up the deficit.

Greene's diary is written in the pages of almanacs published by astrologers. Eleven volumes survive and it is likely that there were others which are now lost. The first is from 1635, when he was studying at Lincoln's Inn. The next volumes cover the years 1643 to 1649; there is then a gap until the final three volumes, which cover the years 1653, 1654, and 1657. Except in the first and last volumes Greene wrote a summary of public affairs at the beginning of each year, which provide a useful indication of how the dramatic political events of this period were perceived. The diary also provides many details of London society in this period, including some indication of the impact of the religious changes of the 1640s and also material on legal affairs. There are few indications of his own religious and political affiliations, but his father-in-law was undoubtedly a puritan and parliamentarian; he served the Commonwealth as a judge in the upper bench, as king's bench was known in the interregnum. Greene's own father was sufficiently trusted by the parliamentarians to be appointed an assize judge in the late 1640s. Extracts from the diary were published by E. M. Symonds in the *English Historical Review* in 1928 and 1929. The original is in the possession of Greene's descendants.

BEN COATES

Sources E. M. Symonds, 'The diary of John Greene (1635–57)', *EngHR*, 43 (1928), 385–94, 598–604; 44 (1929), 106–17 · will, PRO, PROB 11/300, fols. 185–186v · will, PRO, PROB 11/239, fols. 333–333v [John Greene, father] · will, PRO, PROB 11/234, fols. 258v–259v [Phillip Jermyn] · repertories of the court of aldermen, CLRO, 62, 66–7 · W. P. Baildon, ed., *The records of the Honorable Society of Lincoln's Inn: the black books*, 4 (1902); 5, ed. R. Roxburgh (1968) · W. P. Baildon, ed., *The records of the Honorable Society of Lincoln's Inn: admissions*, 2 vols. (1896) · Venn, *Alum. Cant.* · GL, MSS 22, 1107, Add. MS 765 · W. R. Prest, *The rise of the barristers: a social history of the English bar, 1590–1640* (1986) · W. R. Prest, *The inns of court under Elizabeth I and the early Stuarts, 1590–1640* (1972) · *The obituary of Richard Smyth … being a catalogue of all such persons as he knew in their life*, ed. H. Ellis, CS, 44 (1849)

Archives priv. coll., diaries

Greene, Maurice (1696–1755), organist and composer, was born in London on 12 August 1696, the youngest of the seven children of the Revd Dr Thomas Greene (1648–1720) and his wife, Mary, *née* Shelton (*d.* 1722). Claiming descent from the medieval Greenes of Green's Norton in Northamptonshire, the Essex branch of the family to which Maurice belonged had held estates in Navestock since the end of the sixteenth century, and, over the years, had produced several figures of some consequence in the law. Maurice's grandfather, for instance, had been recorder of the City of London at the time of his death (in 1659), and an uncle, sometime attorney of the lord mayor's court, was to become a serjeant-at-law in 1700. The Revd Thomas Greene was vicar of the united parishes of St Olave Jewry and St Martin Pomeroy, Ironmonger Lane, in the City of London; he was also a chaplain of the Chapel Royal and a canon of Salisbury Cathedral. As the youngest child—and showing some early talent for music, it may be supposed—Maurice was brought up as a chorister of St Paul's Cathedral under Jeremiah Clarke and Charles King. On the breaking of his voice he was articled to Richard Brind, who, on Clarke's death in December 1707, had succeeded him as organist.

Still in his teens Greene gained his first professional appointment as organist of St Dunstan-in-the-West, Fleet Street, in March 1714. In February 1718 he moved on to a similar but rather more prestigious post (previously held by Daniel Purcell) at St Andrew's, Holborn. No sooner was he installed, however, than Brind died, and Greene was straight away chosen to succeed him. Though there was

Maurice Greene (1696–1755), by unknown artist

then no such post as assistant organist of the cathedral, Greene had clearly been acting as such for the previous four or five years, and it was during this period that he first came into contact with Handel, who had a particular liking for the St Paul's organ and would sometimes turn up after evensong to play it (with Greene pumping the bellows), in the course of which the two became friends. Some years later, however, they fell out, so disastrously, it seems, that Handel is said never again to have spoken of Greene 'without some injurious epithet' (Burney, *Hist. mus.*, 2.489). The reason generally given (though it can hardly represent the whole truth of the matter) is that Greene was discovered to have been courting the attention of Handel's rival, Giovanni Bononcini (who arrived in London in October 1720).

On 20 March 1718 Greene was sworn in as a vicar-choral of St Paul's, and as such he then became eligible for appointment as cathedral organist. Shortly afterwards he married Mary Dillingham (*bap.* 1699, *d.* 1767), a cousin of Jeremiah Clarke, and the first of their five children, a son, was born in May of the following year. Educated at Eton College, he died while still a student at Cambridge in 1737. Of the other four, only one survived infancy. There was evidently some congenital defect in the male line, and Maurice himself, like several of his late seventeenth-century forebears, was not only short but suffered from a spinal deformity (though there is no sign of this in any of the surviving portraits). In 1722 the family settled in Beaufort Buildings, just off the Strand, and there no doubt they took in the first of Greene's articled pupils: John Travers, William Boyce, the blind John Stanley, and Martin Smith.

As organist of St Paul's Greene found himself responsible not only for the daily round of services but also for the annual Sons of the Clergy festival, which, by virtue of the large number of vocal and instrumental performers involved, was then considered to be a major event in the musical life of the metropolis. It also provided him with a useful platform for some of his own large-scale orchestrally accompanied anthems and Te Deum settings in particular. One such piece was performed at court in July 1721, and such was Greene's growing reputation in the world of church music generally that he was the obvious person to become organist and composer of the Chapel Royal when, in August 1727, William Croft died. Greene did not preside at the coronation of George II, however, for Handel already held a Chapel Royal appointment (as composer); thus, whenever the interests of the royal family itself were involved, it was Handel, not Greene, who was called upon to hymn the event. In January 1735 (and not yet forty), Greene succeeded John Eccles as master of the king's musick, in which capacity he had the unenviable task of setting to music the feebly eulogistic texts of Colley Cibber, then poet laureate, for the twice-yearly court odes. Of thirty-five works so produced, only thirteen are still extant.

But Greene was also much involved in the secular musical life of the capital. With Talbot Young, he was a founder member (c.1724) of the Castle Society, and also (in January 1726) of the Academy of Vocal (later Ancient) Music, at which some of his own music was performed. After a celebrated incident involving Bononcini on a charge of plagiarism (and in which he himself was implicated), Greene evidently left the academy in disgust and formed his own splinter group, the Apollo Society, which met at the Devil tavern in Fleet Street and was apparently concerned mainly with the music of Greene, Boyce, and Festing. The latter, a close friend and professional associate over many years, was the leading English violinist of the period, and his son was later (in 1750) to marry Greene's daughter and only surviving child. Greene was also an original subscriber to the 'Fund for the Support of Decay'd Musicians or their Families' set up by Festing in April 1738. Festing had also, almost certainly, been one of those several well-known London musicians who, in July 1730, accompanied Greene to Cambridge for the first performance at the official opening of the new Senate House of his ode for St Cecilia's day with a text specially revised for the occasion by Alexander Pope. The work, which doubled as an exercise for a doctorate in music, was evidently so well received that Greene, in compliment to his performance, was very shortly afterwards elected professor of music. The post itself, vacant since the death of Thomas Tudway in 1726, was purely honorary, and did not require residence, still less any obligation either to teach or to examine.

As a composer Greene is now remembered chiefly for his church music, and in particular his *Forty Select Anthems* published by subscription in 1743. But there are a further sixty-odd anthems (including all those with orchestral accompaniment) which never made it into print in his lifetime. On the secular front there are many songs and cantatas, mostly published except for those to Italian texts, and a great deal of keyboard music (though no chamber music curiously enough). His contribution to the orchestral repertory is limited to a single set of *Six Overtures* (1745), but there are also three oratorios (one lost), two operas, and a masque, the latter no longer extant. On the death of a bastard cousin (natural son of the aforementioned serjeant-at-law) in January 1752, Greene inherited the ancestral Essex estates (apparently worth £700 p. a.) and, almost immediately, set about the editing for publication of a historical anthology of English church music, one copy of which he intended to present to every cathedral and collegiate foundation in the land. Sadly he died before the project could be completed, and it was left to another good friend and former pupil, William Boyce, to bring it to fruition. Greene himself died at his home in Beaufort Buildings on 1 December 1755 and was buried in St Olave Jewry on 10 December. On the demolition of that church in 1888 his remains were transferred to St Paul's Cathedral, where they now share a grave with those of Boyce.   H. DIACK JOHNSTONE

Sources Burney, *Hist. mus.*, new edn · J. Hawkins, *A general history of the science and practice of music*, new edn, 3 vols. (1853); repr. in 2 vols. (1963) · 'The life of Doctor Greene', *A new and elegant edition of … forty select anthems* (c.1792) · 'Memoir of Maurice Greene', *The Harmonicon*, 7 (1829), 71–2 · H. D. Johnstone, 'The life and work of Maurice Greene (1696–1755)', DPhil diss., U. Oxf., 1967 · H. D. Johnstone, 'A Cambridge musical event: the public commencement of 1730', *Cambridge Review* (22 Nov 1974), 51–3 · H. D. Johnstone, 'The genesis of Boyce's "Cathedral music"', *Music and Letters*, 56 (1975), 26–40 · H. Burnett, 'The sacred music of Maurice Greene (1696–1755)', PhD diss., City University of New York, 1978 · D. Burrows, 'Handel and the English Chapel Royal during the reigns of Queen Anne and King George I', PhD diss., Open University, 1981 · P. Daub, 'Music at the court of George II (r. 1727–1760)', PhD diss., Cornell University, 1985 · H. W. Shaw, *The succession of organists of the Chapel Royal and the cathedrals of England and Wales from c.1538* (1991) · H. D. Johnstone, 'Handel and his bellows-blower (Maurice Greene)', *Göttinger Händel-Beiträge*, 7 (1998), 208–17 · F. G. E. [F. G. Edwards], 'Dr Maurice Greene (1696?–1755)', *MT*, 44 (1903), 89–93 · E. Walker, 'The Bodleian manuscripts of Maurice Greene', *Musical Antiquary*, 1 (1909–10), 149–65, 203–14 · E. Cole, 'The bellows blower', *RCM Magazine*, 51/3 (1955), 62–6 · E. Janifer, 'The English church music of Maurice Greene and his contemporaries', PhD diss., U. Lond., 1959 · C. Dearnley, *English church music, 1650–1750* (1970) · R. McGuinness, *English court odes, 1660–1820* (1971) · D. Dawe, *Organists of the City of London, 1660–1850* (1983)
Archives priv. coll., papers
Likenesses J. Highmore, oils, c.1735, priv. coll. · oils, c.1735, NPG · F. Hayman, double portrait, oils, 1747 (with J. Hoadly), NPG · portrait, priv. coll. [*see illus.*]
Wealth at death considerable; estates in Essex £700 p.a.; musical appointments £500 p.a.

Greene, Nathanael (1742–1786), revolutionary army officer in America, was born on 27 July 1742 in Warwick, Rhode Island, the son of Nathanael Greene senior, co-owner of an ironworks, and Mary, *née* Mott. Greene's father, a man of some means, did not believe in extensive formal education. So at a relatively early age Greene joined the family business, which included several uncles. Somehow Greene, highly intelligent with an inquiring mind, discovered literature and history. It is ironic that he

Nathanael Greene (1742–1786), by Charles Willson Peale, 1783

developed a particular taste for books on war and military theory and training, because he came from a devout Quaker family. Greene's involvement in the American War of Independence resulted in his being read out of the Society of Friends.

A military mystery of the war is how Greene emerged in 1775 with an appointment as brigadier-general of the Rhode Island army of observation and, a brief time later that year, as general of the same rank in the American congress's continental army. Handsome and somewhat stocky, Greene was 5 feet 10 inches tall and only thirty-two years old; a year before he had been a private in the Rhode Island forces. Yet such remarkable advancement is hardly unknown in wartime, especially during revolutions. Napoleon said that many a private carried a marshal's baton in his knapsack. Greene was bright and well informed, and struck contemporaries as a man of presence with leadership qualities. His visibility among Rhode Island leaders of the resistance increased because he served actively on a committee of the colonial legislature responsible for the defence of the province.

General George Washington, commander-in-chief of the continental army, also found Greene impressive for his military knowledge and grasp of problems facing the revolutionary forces. But Greene's role the first year of the war (1775–6) hardly appears remarkable, though he gained major-general's rank. Illness forced him to miss the battle of Long Island in 1776 and, when Washington evacuated New York city, Greene unwisely prevailed among the American generals in advocating that Fort Washington, on the northern part of Manhattan Island, be held. The fort proved more vulnerable than Greene

realized. It soon surrendered to the British, with the loss of valuable artillery and 3000 men.

Yet Greene's career continued to advance. Colonel Henry Knox, chief of American artillery, said that within a year or so Greene became equal, if not superior, to all Washington's generals in ability. Beginning with the Christmas season of 1776, Greene's fortunes vastly improved. He performed well in the Trenton–Princeton campaign in New Jersey that spilled over into 1777. At Brandywine Creek in Pennsylvania, Greene's division moved rapidly, 4 miles in forty-five minutes, to cover the collapsed American right wing, and then helped bring order to Washington's retreating army. About two weeks later, at Germantown, outside Philadelphia, the British and American armies again clashed. The outcome was indecisive, though technically it was an American defeat since Washington's forces gave up the field; but Greene, his division engulfed in a dense fog that may well have deprived the Americans of victory, kept his composure and fought his way to safety.

From 1778 to 1780 Greene left the field and became an administrator, heading the commissary department. This was a difficult and thankless task, and Greene accepted the post only reluctantly, at Washington's urging. The vast department of 3000 employees taxed his managerial skills. He faced complaints of profiteering on the part of his staff, and he himself and his two principal subordinates eventually faced similar accusations. Whatever the truth as to the unproved charges against him, he created a good measure of order and efficiency in a department previously noted for its chaotic condition.

All the while, Greene missed field command. In fact Washington twice returned him to temporary active duty. He provided valuable leadership at the battles of Monmouth and Springfield in New Jersey. He escaped the quartermaster job in October 1780 when (at Washington's request) congress selected him to head the southern department. Greene encountered another daunting assignment, since the British general Charles, Lord Cornwallis, controlled Georgia and almost all of South Carolina. In the south Greene displayed diplomatic skills in dealing with local politicians and militia leaders. This explains much of the success of the Rhode Islander, who had never before set foot in the region below the Potomac. He gathered around him able subordinates such as General Daniel Morgan, and he encouraged South Carolina guerrilla chieftains to co-ordinate their efforts with his. He urged southern state governors to collect supplies and boats at key locations to be used when needed.

Greatly outnumbered, Greene turned to partisan or guerrilla warfare, which he had never tried before. In mid-December 1780 he split his small army, sending Morgan into western South Carolina while he crossed into the eastern part of that state. Cornwallis dispatched Tarleton's legion after Morgan, who literally destroyed the legion at the Cowpens. With Cornwallis's main army on Morgan's heels, Greene reunited his own army in North Carolina. After wearing Cornwallis to a frazzle and adding reinforcements, he turned around and fought the

British in the indecisive battle of Guilford court house in March 1781. Cornwallis's battered and ill-supplied force now limped to the North Carolina coast and moved up into Virginia, where Washington and a French fleet compelled its surrender. Continuing the game of cat and mouse, Greene returned to South Carolina, picking off Cornwallis's interior posts in that state. The result was that by late 1781 Greene had brilliantly rid the state of Cornwallis's army, and confined his remaining units in the lower south to Charles Town and Savannah, Georgia, where they remained until the end of the war. British desires to solidify existing gains and pacify the countryside in the south before attempting new conquests were never really tested, owing to Greene's tempting Cornwallis to play the American general's game. Having left his South Carolina bases unprotected and then stayed only briefly in North Carolina, Cornwallis all but destroyed the British presence in both states, and left a weakened force vulnerable at Yorktown in Virginia.

There is another, lesser known, side of Greene's service in the south. He had a better opportunity than any other American general of the revolution, with the possible exception of Washington, to make a solid contribution in the area of civil government and domestic tranquillity. Greene worked to end the violent mistreatment of the tories, to restore the judicial processes, and to re-establish viable state governments in a land that had been ravaged by friend and foe alike from 1779 to 1782. All things considered, he could have hardly accomplished more.

Greene's post-war years were at best a mixed blessing. He returned temporarily to his native Rhode Island and was proclaimed a conquering hero. Having recognized him as a military statesman second only to Washington, a superb strategist in the south, the states of Georgia and South Carolina rewarded Greene with estates. But he suffered from additional charges—probably unfounded—of profiteering, and the bankruptcy of a business partner left him with thousands of dollars of debt. Greene died suddenly on 19 June 1786, in his forty-fourth year, at Mulberry Grove, in Georgia, and was buried the following day at Savannah. He was survived by his wife, Catherine, née Littlefield (1753–1814), whom he had married on 20 July 1774, and five children under the age of eleven. Catherine, who was noted for her warmth and charm, continued to live at Mulberry Grove. In later years Eli Whitney visited her plantation and gained ideas there for inventing the cotton gin. Washington said that Greene's passing was too painful to discuss. Thomas Jefferson put him in the highest rank of American leaders of his day. His premature death may well have ended a life destined for other realms of public service, as was true of the subsequent careers of various other American generals of the revolution.

DON HIGGINBOTHAM

Sources The papers of General Nathanael Greene, ed. R. K. Showman, D. M. Conrad, and others, [11 vols.] (1976–) · T. Thayer, Nathanael Greene (1960) · M. F. Treacy, Prelude to Yorktown (1963) · J. S. Pancake, This destructive war: the British campaign in the Carolinas, 1780–1782 (1985)

Archives Duke U., MSS · Rhode Island Historical Society, Providence, MSS · U. Mich., MSS
Likenesses C. W. Peale, portrait, 1783, Independence National Historical Park, Philadelphia [see illus.] · R. Peale, portrait, Rhode Island Historical Society, Providence · T. Sully, portrait, priv. coll.

Greene, Richard (1716–1793), antiquary and museum proprietor, was born at Lichfield and may have been educated at its grammar school; there is no record of his attendance at university. His brother, the Revd Joseph Greene (1712–1790), was headmaster of Stratford upon Avon grammar school; his only other known relative was Samuel Johnson, although the precise relationship is not known. His friend Mark Noble, the prolific if inelegant biographer, wrote of him: 'A Scottish university, without any solicitation of his own, sent him the degree of M.D. He was gratified by it; but never assumed the title of Doctor' (Nichols, Illustrations, 6.320). Though he refused to be called Doctor he was in fact an apothecary. Among his patients were Johnson and the bishop of Sodor and Man, whom he treated for gout. He appears to have run a busy practice, for he wrote to John Nichols that 'If ever again you visit Staffordshire, I hope my patients will continue to be free from ailments, or excuse my frequent visits, that I may enjoy more of your company' (Sherbo, 3). Greene's life centred around Lichfield, which he seldom left; he served as sheriff in 1758, as alderman, and as bailiff in 1785 and 1790. He married first, at St Mary's, Lichfield, on 12 May 1741, Mary Dawson, with whom he had a daughter. His second wife was Theodosia Webb (d. 1793), of Croxall, Derbyshire; they had one son, Thomas, a lieutenant and surgeon in the Stafford militia.

Greene was an avid collector and put his myriad objects on display in the old register office of the Lichfield diocese. Boswell described the museum in some detail following his visit with Johnson on 23 March 1776:

> It was, truly, a wonderful collection, both of antiquities and natural curiosities, and ingenious works of art. He had all the articles accurately arranged, with their names upon labels, printed at his own little press; and on the staircase leading to it was a board, with the names of contributors marked in gold letters. A printed catalogue of the collection was to be had at a bookseller's. (Boswell, Life, 709)

In a handbill of 22 January 1782 Greene gave a fuller description of the museum's contents. He listed the various categories, with the contents of each, as 'Animals, Shells, Stones, Woods, Roman (and other Coins, Casts, and Metals), Dresses (and Ornaments of the Natives of Otaheite), English and Foreign Weapons, Remains of Antiquity, Roman Missals, and An uncommon Musical Altar Clock: Model of Lichfield Cathedral, &' (Sherbo, 14–15).

Greene was also a respected antiquary with a wide acquaintanceship in the antiquarian world, being on terms of some intimacy with Samuel Pegge, Sir Ashton Lever, John Nichols, Francis Grose, and others. He also numbered Thomas Pennant among his friends, and was of assistance to Bishop Percy. His antiquarian contributions came in the form of some thirty letters to the Gentleman's Magazine from September 1751 to December 1792. Many of

Richard Greene (1716–1793), by unknown engraver

his antiquarian finds were in and around Lichfield, a number of his letters being accompanied by drawings by Edward Stringer, 'a very ingenious painter' of Lichfield (Nichols, *Illustrations*, 6.324); others relate to the collections in his museum.

Greene would be less well remembered had it not been for his relationship with Johnson. It was to Greene that Johnson turned, in a letter of 2 December 1784, eleven days before his death, requesting that he undertake to see that epitaphs for his father, mother, and brother, written by himself, be 'engraved on the large size, and laid in the Middle Aisle in St. Michael's Church [in Lichfield]', adding 'I beg that all possible hast [*sic*] may be made, for I wish to have it done while I am yet alive' (*Letters of Samuel Johnson*, 4.443). Greene was Johnson's intermediary to Lucy Porter, Greene's stepdaughter, and to his friend Mrs Elizabeth Aston. He may have been a man of few words, for when he visited Johnson in London in 1775 Johnson wrote to Mrs Thrale that he had 'paid a visit from Lichfield, and having nothing to say, said nothing and went away' (ibid., 2.244). Johnson 'lent Mr. Greene the axe and lance' for his museum, commenting 'Sir, I should as soon have thought of building a man of war, as of collecting such a museum' (ibid., 11).

Greene died in Lichfield on 4 June 1793, his widow on 1 August. Mark Noble wrote of him: 'He was religious, strictly just, diligent in business, and very moderate to his charges [as apothecary and surgeon] … As a husband, father, neighbour, and master he was most estimable; I think he could not have had an enemy in the world' (Nichols, *Illustrations*, 6.320). A few years after his death Greene's collection was broken up and sold to a number of

collectors. Sir John St Aubyn bought the fossils and minerals; the arms and armour, purchased by William Bullock, found their way into the Tower of London after several changes of ownership; the remaining curiosities were bought by Walter Honeywood Yates, of Bromsberrow Place, Gloucestershire, for £600.

ARTHUR SHERBO

Sources *The letters of Samuel Johnson*, ed. B. Redford, 5 vols. (1992–4) · A. Sherbo, *Letters to Mr Urban of the Gentleman's Magazine, 1751–1811* (1997) · Nichols, *Illustrations* · Nichols, *Lit. anecdotes* · Boswell, *Life* · *DNB* · *GM*, 1st ser., 55 (1785), 497 · *The correspondence of the Reverend Joseph Greene: parson, schoolmaster and antiquary (1712–1790)*, Dugdale Society, 8 (1965) · J. Boswell, *Life of Johnson*, ed. R. W. Chapman, rev. J. D. Fleeman, rev. edn (1980) · *IGI*

Archives FM Cam., corresp. · Shakespeare Birthplace Trust RO, Stratford upon Avon, corresp. and papers · Staffs. RO, commonplace book

Likenesses etching, BM, NPG [*see illus.*] · portrait, repro. in S. Shaw, *History of Staffordshire* (1798), vol. 1, p. 30 · woodcut, repro. in *GM* (1746), 465

Greene, Richard Marius Joseph (1918–1985), actor, was born on 25 August 1918 at 12 Windsor Place, Plymouth, Devon, the son of Richard Abraham Greene and Kathleen Marie Josephine Davidson (*née* Gerrard), both stage actors who were on tour there at the time. He came from a long line of actors, and his grandfather was William Friese-*Greene, the pioneer of cinematography. He was soon placed with a nursemaid while his parents returned to the stage. He was educated at Cardinal Vaughan School in Kensington, London, before making his acting début in 1933 as a spear carrier in *Julius Caesar* at the Old Vic. He also modelled, to make ends meet, and got a small role in a revival of *Journey's End* and a bit part in the Gracie Fields film *Sing as you Go* (1934), but it was edited out. He toured Britain for a year, learning his craft with the Brandon Thomas repertory company. Back in London, another bit part, in a short run of *Antony and Cleopatra*, was followed by the juvenile lead in the big hit *French without Tears*. Interest from film studios followed: Korda in Britain, Selznick International and MGM in Hollywood. But it was Twentieth Century Fox with whom he signed. Almost immediately he was starring in John Ford's *Four Men and a Prayer* (1938) as one of the four sons, opposite Loretta Young. There was a positive reaction to his début and Twentieth Century Fox built him up as a major competitor to their star actor Tyrone Power, although his films were mixed. He did, however, star again for Ford, in *Submarine Patrol*, and again with Young in *Kentucky* (both 1938), and with Shirley Temple in *The Little Princess* (1939). He played Sir Henry Baskerville in the fine version of *The Hound of the Baskervilles*, and supported Spencer Tracy and Cedric Hardwicke in *Stanley and Livingstone* (both 1939).

Released from his contract to return to England, Greene joined the Royal Armoured Corps of the 27th lancers in September 1940, serving in France, Holland, and Belgium. He was commissioned lieutenant in the following May, was granted leave later in the year to make the propaganda film *Unpublished Story* (1942), and on 24 December 1941 married British actress Patricia (Paz Maria) Medina (*b.* 1920). A leg injury in May 1943 led to a staff liaison role as captain. On leave again, he starred in another propaganda film, the Wilcox–Neagle production *The Yellow Canary* (1943), and in *Don't Take it to Heart* (1944) with Medina. In December 1944 he received his military discharge.

After the war Medina was invited to Hollywood and Greene resumed his career there, but perhaps thanks to the costume epic *Forever Amber* (1947) he found himself for some years stuck chiefly in other costume dramas: *The Fighting O'Flynn* (again with Medina) and *The Fan*, based on Wilde's *Lady Windermere's Fan* (both 1949), *The Desert Hawk* (1950), *Lorna Doone* (1951), *Rogue's March* and *The Black Castle* (both 1952), and *The Bandits of Corsica* and *Captain Scarlett* (both 1953). He had appeared in an American television version of *Coriolanus* in 1951, the year that he and Medina divorced, but was probably no longer seen by Hollywood as a serious actor; he was there either to provide the love interest or show his flair for swashbuckling. By the mid-1950s his career was in decline. He had lost money on a play, *The Secret Tent*, which did not reach the West End, and was now best known for advertising a haircream. But it was commercial television which rescued him. He played the eponymous hero in over 140 episodes of the series *The Adventures of Robin Hood* (1955–60), 'fast-moving, uncomplicated stories of good and evil' (*The Times*, 3 June 1985), a part with which he was thereafter identified. It revived his acting standing and his financial situation (he bought a 15 foot sloop to indulge his passion for sailing) and it made him a household name. He reprised the role in the film *The Sword of Sherwood Forest* (1961), shot in Ireland, which he also co-produced.

Having married again in 1960—his second wife was Beatrice Summers—Greene bought an estate in co. Wexford, Ireland, and virtually retired to breed horses, which he did with great success. He made a family film, *Island of the Lost* (1967), for the Ivan Tors studio and twice played Nayland Smith, nemesis of evil Fu Manchu (played by Christopher Lee) in *The Blood of Fu Manchu* (1969) and *The Castle of Fu Manchu* (1970). He also featured in one of the stories in *Tales from the Crypt* (1972) and made occasional television and stage appearances through the 1970s, including at the Chichester Festival. In 1982 Greene collapsed and underwent an operation on a brain tumour. He died following a fall in his home, 1 Hall Cottages, Kelling Hall, Kelling, Norfolk, on 1 June 1985, survived by his Brazilian third wife, Beatriz, whom he had married in 1973.

ROBERT SHARP

Sources *The Times* (3 June 1985) · www.uk.imdb.com, 29 Sept 2001 · J. R. Parish and W. T. Leonard, *Hollywood players: the thirties* (1976) · b. cert. · m. cert. [Patricia Medina] · d. cert.
Likenesses photographs, 1938–49, Hult. Arch.
Wealth at death £58,435: probate, 11 Nov 1985, *CGPLA Eng. & Wales*

Greene, Robert (*bap.* 1558, *d.* 1592), writer and playwright, was probably the Robert Greene, son of Robert Greene, baptized on 11 July 1558 at St George's, Tombland, Norwich. Greene later described himself as from Norwich on his title-pages, and the year is appropriate for the Robert Greene who matriculated at St John's College, Cambridge, as a sizar on 26 November 1575. The author's father was probably one of two Robert Greenes found later in parish records: either a saddler who lived modestly in the parish until 1599, or a cordwainer who kept an inn in Norwich from the late 1570s until his death in 1591. The saddler appeals to biographers who attribute the writer's later low-life sympathies to a humble birth; the innkeeper, a more prosperous man possibly related to landowners, interests scholars who note the social ambitions of Greene's early works. However, in his will proved in 1591, the innkeeper did not mention a son Robert, although he may have disinherited that son (as the writer implied in one autobiographical statement; (see *Complete Works*, 12.103)).

Education and early life The young Greene probably attended the free grammar school at Norwich for some time, although enrolment documents for this period are lost. Since Corpus Christi College, Cambridge, offered closed scholarships for students from the school, Greene's matriculation at St John's has been seen as anomalous. In retrospect Greene certainly appears more in step with the disorderly brilliance of St John's than with the sectarian fervour of Corpus Christi, as the headmaster, Stephen Limbert, a St John's man, might have known. St John's was also a college favoured by the gentry of south Yorkshire, a group that yielded several of the otherwise obscure dedicatees of Greene's first books, and to which the innkeeping Robert Greene may have been connected: he had resided in Snaith, West Riding of Yorkshire, from about 1571 to 1577 (Richardson, 171). Greene held a rather undistinguished place in the intellectually distinguished St John's: on 22 January 1580 he graduated 38 out of 41 at St John's, or 115 out of 205 university-wide. He apparently transferred to Clare College for his 1583 MA, a rather better 5 out of 12 in college, 29 of 129 at the university. After he was granted a 1588 MA from Oxford, almost certainly a courtesy degree, he identified himself on some of his title-pages as 'Utruisq. Academiae in Artibus Magister'—master of arts in both universities. His works evince an inexhaustible linguistic facility, grounded in wide (if not painstaking) reading in the classics, and extra-curricular reading in the modern continental languages. At some time after graduation he moved to London, and became one of the patronless, proto-bohemian writers later dubbed the university wits. Other events of his youth must be derived from autobiographical remarks that may not be reliable. The claim that he married a wealthy gentlewoman called Doll, spent her fortune, and then sent her with a child back to her Lincolnshire family is all too plausible; the story that he travelled in Italy and Spain where he 'sawe and practizde such villainie as is abhominable to mention' (*Complete Works*, 12.172) is less so, since his writings reveal no direct knowledge of those countries.

Prose romances The first of Greene's many publications, *Mamillia*, was listed in the Stationers' register on 3 October 1580, within nine months of his BA (the earliest surviving dated edition is from 1583). Over the next twelve years Greene published some twenty-five prose titles, in genres ranging from courtly romance to crime exposé (the 'coney-catching' pamphlets) and deathbed confession. He also wrote some half-dozen stage plays, probably between 1587 and 1592, some highly successful but none published in his lifetime. Walter Davis has divided Greene's many prose works into four stages: experiments in the euphuistic mode (1580–84); collections of short tales (1585–8); pastoral romances strongly influenced by Greek romance (1588–9); and pamphlets of repentance and roguery, in the main non-fictional (1590–92) (Davis, 139). The chronology of his production is not actually so neat, although Davis's schema does point to the four genres in which Greene's work was most influential. Through the 1580s, while Sir Philip Sidney's *Arcadia* was still confined to a coterie audience, Greene was the foremost romance-writer in England, his fiction leading the field not just in number, but also in range and inventiveness. Within a year of taking his BA, he conceived a romance in imitation of John Lyly's *Euphues: the Anatomy of Wit* (1578) and its sequel *Euphues and his England* (1580), sensations at court, in the city, and in the universities. Crucially, Greene seized on Lyly's strategy of fanning expectations for a sequel at the end of the first part of his romance. That sequel, *Mamillia: the Triumph of Pallas*, was entered and published in 1583 by the young William Ponsonby, launching his career as a publisher of literary ambitions. Both parts of *Mamillia* aspired to convey social and intellectual exclusivity, prominently mentioning the author's Cambridge association on their title-pages. The first part has an epistle dedicatory to Lord Darcy, and commendatory verse by 'Roger Portington Esquier'. The second part has three dedicatory letters and two verse epistles, one in Latin, and is signed 'Robert Greene. From my Studie in Clarehall the vii. Of Julie', the very date in 1583 on which Greene graduated MA from Clare College. Both parts of *Mamillia* also adopted the fashionable strategy of appealing to male courtiers by addressing readers as gentlewomen. While Lyly had confined the strategy to one epistle in his continuation, Greene addressed women readers more prominently. *Mamillia's* first part was subtitled 'a mirrour or looking-glasse for the ladies of Englande', and it was the first English prose romance whose title named only a woman character. Part 2 added a goddess in its subtitle, and its long title describes its purpose as a defence of women, by implication against the attacks in Lyly's romances 'Wherein with perpetual fame the constancie of gentlewomen is canonised, and the unjust blasphemies of womens supposed fickleness (breathed out by diverse injurious persons) by manifest examples clearly infringed' (*Complete Works*, 2.139).

Greene's next fiction works after *Mamillia* opened up courtly forms: his single romances became less euphuistic and more pastoral, often with inset verse; his novella collections explored characteristic themes of masculine prodigality, feminine steadfastness, and reversals of fortune. The romances continue to address female readers with a regularity beyond convention. Thomas Nashe described him acerbically in 1588 as 'the *Homer* of women' (*Works of Thomas Nashe*, 1.12). Many works included a 'feminine' subtitle, a dedication to a prospective female patron,

or a verse addressed to 'ladies', but these are always counterpoised by a letter 'to the gentlemen readers' or 'to the gentle readers' (addressed as males). (Greene never dedicated a book to women as a group.) Even in the frame-tales that take female virtues as their primary topics, the effect of this dual address is voyeuristic. For instance, *Penelopes Web … a Christall Myrror of Faeminine Perfection* (1587) illustrates the 'three especiall vertues' of women: 'Obedience, Chastitie, and Sylence' (title-page). However, its epistle tells gentlemen readers that '*Mars* will sometime bee prying into *Venus* papers, and gentlemen desirous to hear the parlie of Ladies' (*Complete Works*, 5.144–5).

In 1584 Greene produced three euphuistic romances whose titles echo Lyly's title, combining a protagonist's name with an abstract theme: *Gwydonius: the Carde of Fancie*; *Arbasto: the Anatomie of Fortune*; *Morando: the tritameron of love*. These three romances were as successful as they were quick; all were placed with publishers of note and proceeded to a second edition in three to five years. Although the first extant edition of *Pandosto: the Triumph of Time* dates from 1588, a surviving inventory suggests that the work may have been printed by 1585. From its title it would seem to belong to this series; however, in *Pandosto* Greene turned from euphuism to new continental and classical models: pastoral modes from Longus's *Daphnis and Chloe*, and the dramatic plot twists and devices of Heliodorus's *Aethiopica*. Neither of these appeared in English translation until 1587. It has been assumed that *Arcadia* was the model for the generic mix of *Pandosto*, but the earlier date would suggest that Greene independently synthesized the same models as Sidney had. *Pandosto's* other distinction is its remarkably long appeal to general audiences. It was the only one of Greene's fashionable romances republished in 1592, and the only Greene romance in print after 1640. After that, as the love story of *Dorastus and Fawnia*, it was continuously reprinted in full text through the seventeenth century, and as a chapbook adaptation into the 1840s. It figures as a cheap-print favourite in Samuel Richardson's *Clarissa* (1747) and Isaac Bickerstaff's *Love in a Village* (1762). It apparently held audiences quite apart from its role as the source for Shakespeare's *Winter's Tale*.

By 1588, Greene's titles relied not on Lylyesque patterns but on his own well-known name, and romantic fiction began to be displaced by personal repentance. The first such title, *Grene his Farewell to Folly* (1587), ironically echoes *Riche his farewell to the military profession* (1581); it says farewell to exactly the love themes that Barnaby Rich's collection embraced. Next, five titles coined generic labels, now branded with Greene's name: *Alcida: Greenes metamorphosis* (1588), *Greenes orpharion* (1590), *Greenes Never too Late*, *Greenes Mourning Garment* (1590), and *Greenes farewell to folly* (1591). The titles shift from classicized romance (*Metamorphosis*) to vernacular repentance (*Farewell to Folly*). *Greenes Mourning Garment* promises 'the reformation of a second Ovid'; this time, Greene insists, he is not just 'changing the titles of my Pamphlets' but showing the genuine 'inward metamorphosis of my minde' (*Complete Works*, 9.121, 122).

Rejecting his earlier claims that his romances were didactic, he now renounced them as erotic, pronouncing in *Greenes Never too Late*, 'I have done with frivolous toyes' (ibid., 8.8). The posthumously published *Greenes Vision* stages a debate between Chaucer and Gower, deciding whether Greene had 'done well or ill in setting forth such amorous trifles' (ibid., 12.213–14).

Even late in his career Greene continued to publish romances whose primary appeals were courtly and scholarly. In 1589 Greek and Latin verses accompanied *Ciceronis amor*, a love-story improbably starring Cicero, the hero of rhetoric; and the young Nashe contributed a cocky 'Preface to the Gentlemen Students of both Universities' to *Menaphon*. These would be the romances most reprinted for Jacobean readers. *Menaphon* is still favoured by critics for its unalloyed pastoral mood and its fluid style. In its audacious plot, the disguised heroine Sephestia is wooed unknowingly by her husband, father, and son. Its verses, plangent or parodic, have been widely anthologized. *Menaphon* too has been linked to Sidney, and taken to evince Greene's access to the *Old Arcadia* in manuscript. But Greene probably knew Sidney's romance only indirectly: the only specific resemblances are character names and the Arcadian setting, and Greene adapts the pastoral mode to his own distinctive theme of class disparity between lovers. This half-reference to Sidney contrasts with the unmistakable and unabashed allusion to *The Countess of Pembrokes Arcadia* in the title of Greene's otherwise unSidneian last romance, *Philomela: the Lady Fitzwaters Nightingale* (1592). Indeed, later, posthumous editions of *Menaphon* replace the Lylyesque subtitle 'Camillas alarum to slumbering Euphues', with the Sidneyesque 'Greenes Arcadia'.

Authorial persona Greene was England's first celebrity author, a role that he invented and others elaborated for him. By the late 1580s he and his contemporaries agreed that his had become a household name, a fact that Gabriel Harvey in his much-quoted invective in *Foure Letters* (1592) was to turn against Greene:

> Who in London hath not heard of his dissolute, and licentious living; his fonde disguising of a Master of Arte with ruffianly haire, unseemely apparell, and more unseemelye Company ... his fine coosening of Juglers, and finer juggling with cooseners, ... [his] impudent pamphletting, phantasticall interluding, and desperate libelling. (Harvey, 19–20)

Greene, although a 'Master of Arte', has fallen to 'pamphletting' and 'coosening' in the 'unseemlye Company' of criminals and popular entertainers. Harvey saw commercial publication as akin to a crime. Greene's main worry was that it was humiliating. Late pamphlets such as *Greenes Vision* express regret at the damage overpublication has done to his name:

> I foresee that I am likely to sustaine the shame of many follies ... when I am shrowded in my winding sheete ... I crave pardon of you all, if I have offended any of you with lacivious Pamphleting ... In seeking to salve private wantes, I have made my selfe a publique laughing stock. Hee that commeth in Print, setteth himselfe up as a common marke for every one to shoote at. (*Complete Works*, 12.195–6)

What is 'lacivious' about pamphlets is not their content, but the conditions of their publication. Having 'made [him]selfe ... publique' by 'com[ing] in Print', Greene has become 'common', 'marke[d]' as wanton, mercenary, and shameful. Only recently has Greene's commercialism been understood less as a personal failing than as a new kind of career being improvised jointly by Greene, the stationers, preface-writers, commentators, and the eager reading public. But Greene could not rest secure in this popular authorship, which in the end was less profitable to him than to the publishers and fellow writers who were to capitalize on his inglorious demise.

Greene himself built his persona around a myth of prodigal decline that cannot be taken at face value. Like many other university-trained humanists of his generation who wrote for publication, Greene was deeply attracted to the prodigal-son narrative, which pervades his works and unites their otherwise disparate subjects. Even the ballad (not extant) entered in the Stationers' register for 1581 as 'by Greene' was a call for youth to repent (Arber, *Regs. Stationers*, 2.391). His first known romances replicate the prodigal course of John Lyly's protagonist in *Euphues*. As Greene reiterated the prodigal convention over the next decade, he began to link his repentant rakes and whores to self-representations in his framing texts, making this Elizabethan narrative commonplace a narration of himself *as* fiction writer. But if he claimed publishing 'pamphlets' as his defining sin, each published account of repentance proved that repentance false. Puzzled critics have tried to pinpoint whether Greene sincerely repented in 1590, when the promises came thickest, or, as the *Repentance* claims, briefly after hearing a fiery sermon at St Andrew's Church in Norwich, and again on his deathbed. Greene claimed his recidivism so often that he seemed to honour repentance more in the breach than the observance. The works ultimately express more faith in the arbitrariness of Fortune than in the judgment of God. On the other hand, to view Greene's habitual non-repentance as a marketing ploy is to underestimate his final desperation.

Coney-catching pamphlets Once, Greene had apologized for publishing *Pandosto* as an 'imperfect pamphlet'; in his last works he and his publishers fully exploited the topicality, brevity, and formlessness that earned pamphlets the reputation for imperfection. Inevitably, publishers' eagerness to market his works encouraged Greene to find new ways to use his famous name. His writings were some of their publishers' most valuable copies, according to his own boast. The most famous confirmation is Nashe's qualified defence in *Strange News* (1592): 'in a night & a day would he have yarkt up a Pamphlet as well as in seaven yeare, and glad was that Printer that might bee so blest to pay him deare for the very dregs of his wit' (*Works of Thomas Nashe*, 1.287). There is also the nettled testimony of Thomas Bowes, who had graduated with Greene from St John's: 'this fellow in his life time and in the middest of his greatest ruffe, had the Presse at commaundement to publish his lascivsous [*sic*] Pamphlets' (Crupi, 150–51). More objectively, during Greene's own lifetime, the sheer number of titles he produced, and the number of stationers involved, confirm that 'Printers' were indeed 'glad' enough of his works to fight over them. However, Greene's success in marketing his books to publishers must be set against his evident failure to secure regular patronage. Greene's works of the 1580s beg patrons to shroud his efforts with their names; later works drop such attempts.

Interestingly, when Greene began publishing his coney-catching pamphlets in 1591, he kept his name out of his titles. Only *A Disputation betweene a hee Conny-Catcher, and a shee Conny-Catcher* (1592) gives his initials on the title-page; the earlier coney-catching pamphlets confine his initials to prefatorial signatures. Of course those prefaces tap Greene's reputation boldly: it is as a famously sinful writer that he now promises to benefit the commonwealth by exposing crime. In the *Disputation* and the less certainly attributed *Defence of Conny Catching*, the author becomes a subject in the texts themselves, as disputers vow revenge on 'R. G.' should his promised black book reveal their criminal secrets. Of course, Greene was greatly exaggerating the newsworthiness of his allegations, many of which were taken from previous works, particularly Gilbert Walker's *Manifest Detection of Diceplay* (1552), were repeated from one Greene pamphlet to the next, and thence borrowed by later coney-catching writers. There was a wide gap between public fantasies about rogue confederacies and the desperate conditions of the criminal poor in a nation where vagabondage was a felony. Greene may have been keeping his own professional desperation at bay by publishing these pamphlets, but their linguistic energy and clever self-reflexivity do not betray this concern.

The coney-catching pamphlets further elaborated the stationer–author strategy of proliferating sequels: perhaps Greene had learned that dividing his work into short, almost-simultaneous pieces was the best way a professional author could survive in a market place where stationers, not authors, owned the works. Both *A Notable Discovery of Cosenage* and *The Second Parte of Connye Katching* were entered, to different sets of stationers, on 13 December 1591. A year later, two of these stationers reissued the second part as 'The Second and Last Part', while a 'Thirde and Last Part' was entered to yet another stationer. While the rivalry for the 'Last Part' suggests just how desirable a commodity Greene's series had become, the simultaneous registration of the first two parts suggests that stationers and author were conspiring to their mutual benefit. Certainly someone co-ordinated the matching woodcuts of humanized rabbits (coneys) found on these pamphlets' title-pages.

Greene's most-reprinted pamphlet was the topical *Quip for an Upstart Courtier*, which saw an astonishing six editions in 1592 alone. In this debate on social values, Cloth Breeches and Velvet Breeches argue their relative value to the commonwealth; the jury finds for the homespun tradition of Cloth Breeches. The first state of the first edition included an attack on the Harvey family, which Greene, destitute as he was, paid the printer to remove under stop-press conditions; this attack apparently motivated Harvey's diatribes against Greene.

Drama At the end of Greene's life, the prose writer was also familiar as a playwright. In an epistle to *The Repentance*, publisher Cuthbert Burby claimed that Greene's 'pen in his lifetime pleased you as well on the Stage, as in the Stationers Shops' (*Complete Works*, 12.155). Within the *Repentance*, Greene claimed to have despised dramatic writing most of all (ibid., 12.177). None of his plays was entered or published until after his death, but his name and motto did mark some editions from the 1590s. The plays can be dated approximately by tracing their evolution from Marlovian imitation to a more individual style. Presumably earliest are two plays with blank-verse bombast and transgressive heroes competing directly with the two *Tamburlaine* plays of 1588–9: *The Comicall Historie of Alphonsus, King of Aragon* (printed 1599) almost parodies Marlowe; *The Tragical Raigne of Selimus* (printed 1594) portrays the Ottoman tyrant Selim I (1512–20) as a Tamburlaine-like atheist, and even promises a sequel. (The authorship of *Selimus* is disputed, but lines from the play are attributed to Greene in *England's Parnassus* of 1600.) *A Looking-Glasse for London and England* (printed 1594), written collaboratively with Thomas Lodge, adapts the loose form and didacticism of homiletic drama to secular comedy. The best, presumably latest, plays build a new multiplot form of romantic comedy that contrasts overweening courtly ambition to forgiving rural love. In *The Historie of Orlando Furioso* (1589?, printed 1594), the villain Sacrepant drives Orlando to jealous madness, while the princess Angelica remains loyal in pastoral retreat. In *The Honorable Historie of Frier Bacon and Frier Bongay* (1589, printed 1594), ingeniously staged magical devices link the rival magicians to the rival wooers of Margaret, daughter of the Keeper of Fressingfield. Academia is satirized in the episode of the brazen head, which speaks oracular truths while Friar Bacon sleeps and his foolish subsizar Miles dozes. *The Scottish Historie of James the Fourth* (1590?, printed 1598) makes even freer use of known historical figures, as the king's villainy fails to dislodge Ida's modest love for her social equal. Although *Selimus* and *Frier Bacon* are named on early title-pages as Queen's Men's plays, the latter was also performed by Lord Strange's Men and Sussex's Men during the 1590s. *Frier Bacon* probably remained longest in repertory; the 1630 edition claims a recent performance.

Greene advanced English stage comedy by importing techniques he had developed as a romance writer: thematic parallels that link plots, sympathetic characterizations of women and historical personages, and a light handling of the reversals of fortune. Unfortunately, in theatre history, the merits of Greene's plays have been overshadowed by the passage from the posthumous *Greenes Groats-Worth of Witte* that is the first contemporary reference to Shakespeare:

there is an upstart Crow, beautified with our feathers, that with his *Tygers heart wrapt in a Players hide*, supposes he is as well able to bumbast out a blanke verse as the best of you: and being an

absolute Johannes fac totum, is in his owne conceit the onely
Shake-scene in a countrie.　(*Complete Works*, 12.144)

Especially in the nineteenth century, blame for this attack
on Shakespeare as an autodidact (and conceivably as a pla-
giarist) threw a bar between the two playwrights. However, Greene's work in comic and chronicle forms clearly
carried over into Shakespeare's. Both writers may have
contributed (not necessarily at the same time) to the *Henry
VI* plays or *Titus Andronicus*. Certainly Shakespeare drew
affectionately on *Pandosto* and the coney-catching pamphlets in *The Winter's Tale* (1610–11), and Autolycus, his ballad-
selling rogue, may memorialize Greene himself.

Death and posthumous reputation　The multiple accounts of
Greene's death are surprisingly consistent. Greene was
residing in the garret of a shoemaker's house in Dowgate
when he contracted his fatal fever. He died there on 3 September 1592. These details and other seamy allegations
appeared in a series of pamphlets about his death, an
unprecedented free-for-all in authorial notoriety. Three
posthumous pamphlets claimed to be autobiographical,
raising complex questions about dating, attribution, and
reliability. *Greenes Vision*, representing itself as a deathbed
confession, was probably actually composed in 1590. *The
Repentance of Robert Greene, Master of Arts* (entered in the Stationers' register on 6 October 1592), long regarded as
doubtful, now appears to be legitimate (see Jowett).
Entered on 20 September 1592, *Greenes Groats-Worth of
Witte* is the work for which Greene is best-known, but
quantitative attribution studies suggest that it was largely
an opportunistic forgery by its 'editor', stationer Henry
Chettle. Later, in the preface to *Kind-Hartes Dreame*
(entered on 8 December 1592), Chettle justified his role in
publishing *Groats-Worth*. Greene, he calmly explained,
had died 'leaving many papers in sundry Booke sellers
hands'. All Chettle had done was 'writ it over, and as neare
as I could' for 'Greenes hand was none of the best, [but]
licensd it must be' (G. B. Harrison, ed., *Henrie Chettle, 'Kind-
Hartes Dream'*, 1923, 5–6). Of course Chettle's burden in the
preface was to deny having interpolated the controversial
passage to the playwrights—or having assembled the
whole work, which is probably what he did. Although
such misattributions were not unheard of in the period,
this instance had particularly far-reaching implications
for Greene's reputation.

　The 'Manner of the death and last end of *Robert Greene
master of artes*', appended to the *Repentance*, agrees with
Harvey's account of his death in his *Foure Letters* and that
Greene wrote to his wife on the back of a bond for £10, asking her to redeem that debt to his landlord. The two
sources give variant texts of this pathetic letter, with only
the *Repentance* reporting that it renounced sin. Greene was
buried on 4 September 'in the New-churchyard neere Bed-
lam', Harvey reported with grim satisfaction (Harvey, 22).
He also averred that Greene had taken up with a prostitute, sister to the criminal Cutting Ball, and fathered an
illegitimate son named Infortunatus. In fact historians
have uncovered a Fortunatus Greene (buried at Shoreditch on 12 August 1593) whose folk-tale name might lie
behind Harvey's jest. Finally, Harvey claimed that the

dead writer had been crowned with bay by the shoemaker's wife, Mrs Isam. Despite Greene's long efforts to
control his own name, it was these grotesque details that
finally, posthumously, forged his reputation as wastrel
writer.

　Greene's name remained to be appropriated as an
authorial ghost by imitators and speculators. When Nashe
heard of his friend's death, he quickly added a new feature
to *Pierce Penniless* (1592), as it went into its second edition
within months. The conceit of this facetiously titled 'private Epistle of the Author to *the Printer*' was to list other
items that Nashe's expansion did *not* add:

> Had you not beene so forward in the republishing of it, you
> shold have had certayne Epistles to Orators and Poets, to
> insert; As namely, to the Ghost of *Machiavill*, of *Tully*, of *Ovid*
> … and lastly, to the Ghost of *Robert Greene*, telling him, what
> a coyle there is with pamphleting on him after his death.
> (*Works of Thomas Nashe*, 1.153)

Nashe did not actually supply this item, but several other
authors entered the coil of pamphleting. Writing as or
about Greene's ghost, they joined a game that had started
with the ghosts of Chaucer and Gower appearing in
Greenes Vision. Chettle's *Kind-Hartes Dreame* put Greene's
ghost in dialogue with ghosts of four other popular Elizabethan entertainers. B. R. (Barnaby Rich) brought out
Greenes Newes both from Heaven and Hell (1593), of which the
best part was the rest of the title: 'Prohibited the first for
writing of bookes, and banished out of the last for displaying of *conny-catchers*'. In Rich's pamphlet, Greene's ghost
explains to the *Quip* characters Cloth Breeches and Velvet
Breeches, as they all travel reluctantly towards St Peter,
that reviewing his books might have prevented their
errors. In John Dickenson's *Greene in Conceipt* (1598),
Greene's ghost dictates a story of domestic virtue. A
delightful title-page woodcut illustrates Greene, 'suted in
deaths livery', writing the tale at a desk full of scholarly
accoutrements. Regrettably, the shrouded figure lacks the
features Nashe had vividly attributed to Greene: flamboyant dress, long hair, and a 'jolly long red' beard 'which he
cherisht continually without cutting, whereat a man
might hange a Jewell' (*Works of Thomas Nashe*, 1.287).

　Greene's sordid final year, and its exploitation by Nashe,
Harvey, Chettle, and the other ghost writers, did not
entirely discredit Greene's work in romance. In *Greenes
Funeralls*, a set of sonnets by 'R. B.' (perhaps Richard Barn-
fielde), a verse catalogue of Greene's works lists sixteen
items, half of his non-dramatic output. The list is heavily
weighted towards the courtly romances, *Mamillia*,
Gwydonius, *Ciceronis amor*, *Philomela*, and *Arbasto*; but the set
is rounded out with his topical pamphlets on the Spanish
and on coney-catchers, and even with those sensational
autobiographies, *Never Too Late* and the *Repentance*. At least
for R. B., tastes for Greene's romances and for his pamphlets could coexist.

　As late as the 1690s Anthony Wood could remember that
diverse appeal: Greene, he wrote, was the 'author of several things which were pleasing to men and women of his
time. They made much sport, and were valued among

scholars, but since have been mostly sold on ballad-mongers stalls' (Wood, *Ath. Oxon.*, 3rd edn, 1.245–6). Later descriptions of Greene, shaped by his notorious description of Shakespeare in *Groats-Worth*, have tended to identify him more specifically with the commercialism of the Elizabethan stage. The repellent 'Nick Greene' recurs as a figure of literary greed throughout Virginia Woolf's *Orlando* (1928), and is the actor–manager who seduces Shakespeare's sister, Judith, in *A Room of One's Own* (1929). On the other hand, in John Madden's film *Shakespeare in Love* (1998), young Will Shakespeare proves his cleverness by selling one play to two different playing companies, a trick that one coney-catching pamphlet credits to Greene himself (*Complete Works*, 11.75). With renewed interest in Elizabethan authorship and popular culture, Greene's critical fortunes are beginning to rise again.

The trajectory of Greene's prose from longer, polished works in conventional genres to shorter, more ephemeral and sensational topics has been treated as a decline in literary quality, a slide into commercial exploitation, and a fall into perdition. Judgements of literary decline fail to register that his last works, the coney-catching and repentance pamphlets, immediately fascinated readers with their lively topicality, and are still rising in critical estimation. Greene should be credited as a wide-ranging innovator who moved prose romances towards originality and grace, pamphlets towards freedom of form and voice, and stage comedy towards thematic unity. Even more remarkable than this range is the fact that Greene's authorial career is no retrospective construction but a myth shaped during his lifetime. The authorial persona he built throughout his works, particularly in their titles and prefaces, may be his most lasting achievement.

L. H. NEWCOMB

Sources A. F. Allison, *Robert Greene: a bibliographical catalogue of the early editions in English* (1975) • C. W. Crupi, *Robert Greene* (1986) • W. R. Davis, *Idea and act in Elizabethan fiction* (1969) • *The plays and poems of Robert Greene*, ed. J. Churton Collins, 2 vols. (1905) • *The life and complete works in prose and verse of Robert Greene*, ed. A. B. Grosart, 12 vols. (1881–3) • G. Harvey, *Foure letters*, ed. G. B. Harrison (1923) • R. Helgerson, *The Elizabethan prodigals* (1976) • J. C. Jordan, *Robert Greene* (1915) • J. Jowett, 'Johannes Factotum: Henry Chettle and Greene's groatsworth of wit', *Papers of the Bibliographical Society of America*, 87 (1993), 453–85 • A. F. Kinney, *Humanist poetics: thought, rhetoric, and fiction in sixteenth-century England* (Amherst, Mass., 1986) • *The works of Thomas Nashe*, ed. R. B. McKerrow, 5 vols. (1904–10); repr. with corrections and notes by F. P. Wilson (1958) • L. H. Newcomb, *Reading popular romance in early modern England* (New York, 2002) • R. Pruvost, *Robert Greene et ses romans* (1938) • B. Richardson, 'Robert Greene's Yorkshire connexions: a new hypothesis', *Review of English Studies*, 10 (1980), 160–80 • J. Raymond, *Pamphlets and pamphleteers: print, politics, and polemic in early modern Britain* (2002) • P. Salzman, *English prose fiction, 1558–1700* (1985) • D. J. Vitkus, ed., *Three Turk plays from early modern England* (New York, 2000) • L. Woodbridge, *Vagrancy, homelessness, and English Renaissance literature* (Urbana, Ill., 2001) • A. Rodger, 'Roger Ward's Shrewsbury stock: an inventory of 1585', *The Library*, 5th ser., 13 (1958), 247–68
Likenesses woodcut (of Greene's ghost), repro. in J. Dickenson, *Greene in conceipt* (1598)
Wealth at death £10 in debt; 3s. in clothing: *Repentance* (1592); Harvey, *Foure letters*

Greene, Robert (*c.*1678–1730), natural philosopher, the son of Robert Greene, a mercer of Tamworth, Staffordshire, and his wife, Mary Pretty of Fazeley, was educated at Clare College, Cambridge, to which he was admitted as a sizar on 8 October 1694. He graduated BA in 1700, MA in 1703, and DD in 1728. Having been awarded a fellowship by the college in 1703 and ordained in London in 1705, Greene thereafter devoted his life to teaching and writing in defence of the Christian religion and of what he considered a form of natural philosophy that was not antagonistic to true religion. His conscientiousness, if not his effectiveness, as a tutor is evident in the formidable curriculum outlined in his pamphlet *Encyclopaedia, or, A Method of Instructing Pupils* (1707).

Though a student of Richard Laughton, the famed pro-Newtonian 'pupil-monger', Greene adopted very different political, scientific, and religious views from the whig, latitudinarian Laughton. At a time when the university was deeply divided in its response to the changes wrought by the revolution of 1688, Greene sided with the tories. Such a political stance is evident in his fulsome dedication of *The Principles of Natural Philosophy* (1712) to Robert Harley as one 'Rais'd by the Providence of Almighty God for the Support and Patronage of our most Holy Faith'. Greene's theological position was consistent with his political attachment to the tory party as a protector of the established church: the goal of this work, as of its predecessor, *A Demonstration of the Truth and Divinity of the Christian Religion* (1711), was to undermine the claims of those theologians who down-played the role of the church as an interpreter of revelation by focusing on forms of natural religion that could be arrived at through the use of reason. As he wrote in *A Demonstration*, 'Reason has usurp'd by its Artifice and Cunning, and its subtle and plausible insinuations, an unwarrantable Power and Authority' (p. 188). Similarly in the preface to *The Principles* he decried the influence of 'those Divines in our present Age, who are too fond of what they call Rational, who put too great a stress upon their reasonings from Nature'.

For Greene the defence of revealed religion involved the developing of an alternative system of natural philosophy to put in the place of the dominant mechanical philosophy, which he viewed as promoting materialism. Though respectful of Isaac Newton personally, he feared that his work, too, could lend aid to the rationalists and materialists. For, as he wrote in the preface to his third and most encyclopaedic major work, *The Principles of the Philosophy of the Expansive and Contractive Forces* (1727), the Newtonian system was 'much the same [as the Cartesian] as to the Principles of a Similar and Homogeneous Matter'. Hence Greene sought to replace it with what he termed a 'truly English, a Cantabrigian, and a Clarensian one … I shall venture to call the Greenian' (p. iv). As its title suggests, the aim of this work was to argue that matter could be resolved into a range of forces, thus reinforcing Greene's basic contention that matter was neither passive nor homogeneous as the mechanists and materialists maintained. Greene carried further the intent of his previous book 'wherein', as Roger Cotes reported to Newton before it was published, 'I am informed he undertakes to overthrow the Principles of your Philosophy' (Turnbull, 5.166). However, along with Newton, Greene dismissed John Locke, arguing that his empiricist theory of the mind favoured the materialists and reduced mankind to 'no Degree above an Oyster, unless that he has more senses' (*Philosophy of … Forces*, 628).

Greene served as vicar of Everton, Bedfordshire, and Tetworth, Huntingdonshire, from 1723, but his central focus remained the university, where he served as proctor in 1727. He died on 16 August 1730 while on a visit to his birthplace. He left an elaborate will, the provisions of which confirmed his reputation for eccentricity—among its more bizarre stipulations was that his body should be dissected and the skeleton hung in the library of King's College, Cambridge. Greene also wanted monuments to his memory to be placed in the chapels of Clare College and King's College, in the university church, and at Tamworth. It appears that none of his wishes was complied with and ultimately, most of his estate went to Clare College.   JOHN GASCOIGNE

Sources will of Robert Greene, Clare College, Cambridge, Archives · will, Notts. Arch. · *GM*, 1st ser., 53 (1783), 657 [will] · *GM*, 1st ser., 61 (1791), 725 · [M. D. Forbes], ed., *Clare College, 1326–1926*, 2 vols. (1928–30) · *The correspondence of Isaac Newton*, ed. H. W. Turnbull and others, 7 vols. (1959–77) · C. Middleton, letter to Harley, 6 Sept 1730, BL, Loan 29/167 · Venn, *Alum. Cant.* · *DNB*

Wealth at death house at Tamworth plus £200 bank stock to Clare College: will, Notts. Arch.; Clare College, Cambridge

Greene, Thomas (*bap.* 1573, *d.* 1612), actor, said on 16 June 1607 that he was thirty-four years old, that he was born at Romford, Essex, and that he had lived in Whitechapel for three years and, before that, in the Tower of London for six. He must therefore be the Thomas Grene, son of John Grene, who was baptized at Romford on 13 September 1573. He had a sister, Elizabeth Barrett, and brothers, John and Jeffrey Greene, alive in 1612, and he may be the Thomas Greene who wrote *A Poets Vision* (1603) and a commendatory poem for Drayton's *Barons Wars* (1605). On 15 March 1604, during the great plague of 1603–4, he appears next to last in a list of Queen Anne's Men, having succeeded, apparently, the company's famous clown Will Kemp (*fl.* 1585–1602). About the same time he married Susan (1577/8–1648), the widow of Robert Browne, an actor who held a lease on the Boar's Head playhouse in Whitechapel, where Queen Anne's (then called Worcester's) Men had recently played. Browne had died of plague in mid-October 1603, and Susan Browne acquired his property on 9 January 1604. She was about twenty-five years old and the mother of five infants.

While the plague continued, the company tried unsuccessfully to legitimate themselves by promoting a patent that gives Greene's name first among the members and provides that the company play 'Aswell w^th^in there now usuall Howsen, Called the Curtayne, And the Bores head, … as in any other play howse not used by others, by the said Thomas Greene, elected, or by hym hereafter to be builte' (Berry, 73). Evidently he owed sudden prominence to his wife and to access to capital. On 1 July 1611 he held,

Thomas Greene (*bap.* 1573, *d.* 1612), by unknown engraver, pubd 1614 [as Bubble the city gallant in *Greene's Tu quoque* by John Cooke]

or had lately held, leases on the Curtain playhouse and other properties nearby.

Greene was 'one of the principall and chief persons of the said Companie' until his death (Greenstreet, 499). They were at the Boar's Head in the winter of 1606–7, then at the Red Bull playhouse in Clerkenwell. He is first among Queen Anne's Men in their patent of 1609 and received payments for their performances at court from 1609 to 1612. He lived in Clerkenwell from at least May 1608.

Greene once played a baboon, and in 1611 in John Cooke's play *Greene's Tu quoque* he played Bubble, an amiable ass whose tag line suitable for all occasions is 'Tu quoque'. Bubble apparently represented Greene's usual stage persona. When characters propose to go to a play, Bubble does not care 'whither, so the Clowne have a part: For I fayth I am no body without a Foole'. 'Why then', says another, 'wee'le goe to the Red Bull; they say Green's a good Clowne'. Bubble replies 'Greene? Greene's an Asse', and, when asked why, adds, 'Indeed I ha' no reason: for they say, hee is as like mee as ever he can looke' (Cooke, sig. G2*v*). A woodcut in all three early editions of the play shows a man, who should be Greene, saying 'Tu quoque, To you Sir'; and the frontispiece of Francis Kirkman's *The Wits* (1673) shows a man saying 'Tue quo que' as he comes through curtains to join bits of old plays being performed on a stage.

Greene's will, dated 25 July 1612, provides for Browne's children as well as Greene's daughter, Honor, baptized in Clerkenwell on 17 April 1609. He was a man of means, for he left bequests of £344, plus a residue (including his share in Queen Anne's Men) to provide for his widow. He was buried at St James's, Clerkenwell, on 7 August 1612. One of five admiring epigrams suggests that he had been overseas just before he died. Thomas Heywood, the company's playwright, wrote 'without flattery' that 'there was not an Actor of his nature in his time of better ability in performance of what he undertooke; more applaudent by the Audience, of greater grace at the Court, or of more general love in the Citty' (Cooke, sig. A2). Browne's son, William, asked in 1634 to be buried as near as possible 'to my father Greene' (Bentley, 2.636).

In June 1613 Greene's widow married James Baskervile, who fled to Ireland in 1617 charged with debts and bigamy. She had protracted financial dealings with Queen Anne's Men that led to lawsuits in 1617 and from 1623 to 1626, when she prevailed. She also acquired an interest in the Fortune playhouse. She died in January 1648 and was buried at St James's, Clerkenwell.   HERBERT BERRY

Sources E. K. Chambers, *The Elizabethan stage*, 4 vols. (1923) · H. Berry, *The Boar's Head playhouse* (1986) · M. Eccles, 'Elizabethan actors, II: E–J', *N&Q*, 236 (1991), 454–61 · LMA, DL/C/217, (photo R1098), pp. 214–17 · PRO, C54/2075/17 · *Malone Society Collections*, 1/1 (1907), 265, 270 · J. Greenstreet, 'Documents relating to the players at the Red Bull, Clerkenwell, and the Cockpit in Drury Lane in the times of James I', *New Shakespere Society's Transactions* (1880–86), 489–508 · G. E. Bentley, *The Jacobean and Caroline stage*, 7 vols. (1941–68) · R. Hovenden, ed., *A true register of all the christenings, mariages, and burialles in the parishe of St James, Clerkenwell, from … 1551 (to 1754)*, 6 vols., Harleian Society, register section, 9–10, 13, 17, 19–20 (1884–94) · J. Cooke, *Greenes Tu quoque, or, The cittie gallant* (1614) · J. Cooke, *Greenes Tu quoque, or, The cittie gallant*, new edn (1622) · J. Cooke, *Greenes Tu quoque, or, The cittie gallant*, new edn (1628) · J. Cooke, *Greene's Tu quoque, or, The cittie gallant*, ed. A. J. Berman (1984) · R. Brathwaite, *Remains after death* (1618) · F. Kirkman, *The wits* (1673) · E. A. J. Honigmann and S. Brock, eds., *Playhouse wills, 1558–1642: an edition of wills by Shakespeare and his contemporaries in the London theatre* (1993) · parish register, Romford, Essex RO, Chelmsford, MS D/P 346/1/1

Likenesses engraving, pubd 1614, BL [*see illus.*] · woodcut, repro. in Cooke, *Greenes* (1614)

Wealth at death £344—bequests; plus residue to provide for widow: will, LMA, DL/C/360/129; Honigmann and Brock, eds., *Playhouse wills*

Greene, Thomas (*d.* 1780). *See under* Green, Thomas (*bap.* 1658, *d.* 1738).

Greene, Sir (Edward) Walter, first baronet (1842–1920). *See under* Greene family (*per.* 1801–1920).

Greene, Wilfrid Arthur, Baron Greene (1883–1952), judge, was born at 8 Fox Grove Road, Beckenham, Kent, on 30 December 1883, the son of Arthur Weguelin Greene, a solicitor, and his wife, Kathleen Agnes, daughter of Octavius Fooke. Although a Roman Catholic, he was educated at Westminster School and Christ Church, Oxford, where he was a scholar. He won the Craven scholarship in 1903 and the Hertford scholarship in 1904. In the same year he took a first in classical moderations. He won the chancellor's prize for Latin verse in 1905, taking as his subject

Wilfrid Arthur Greene, Baron Greene (1883–1952), by Gluck, 1949

Artes magicae. He took a first in *literae humaniores* in 1906 and was elected a fellow of All Souls in 1907. He won the Vinerian scholarship in 1908. He was called to the bar by the Inner Temple in 1908, winning a studentship in the same year, and he went into the chambers of Philip Stokes, one of the busiest and most esteemed equity practitioners. On 28 May 1909 he married Nancy, eldest daughter of Francis Wright, secretary, of Allerton, Yorkshire; there were no children.

In 1910 Greene moved to the chambers of F. H. Maugham. He had already created a profound impression as a junior when war broke out in 1914. Within six weeks he was gazetted a second lieutenant in the Oxfordshire and Buckinghamshire light infantry, in which he rose to be captain. He served in France, Flanders, and Italy, and with the rank of major was successively employed as GSO 3 on the staff of the Fifth Army, GSO 3 on the general headquarters staff in Italy, and GSO 2 on the British supreme war council. His services were recognized by appointment as an OBE, and the award of the MC, the Croix de Guerre of France, and the order of the Crown of Italy.

In 1919 Greene returned to the bar, taking silk in 1922, and in 1925 became a bencher of his inn. Patrick Devlin records in his memoirs how he was instructed as Greene's junior to whom, as was Greene's wont, he dictated his opinion. Devlin records 'He was a charming man and it was all done in the most delightful way in consultation'. Greene prepared his cases with meticulous care and his advocacy combined the results of the painstaking application of an outstanding intellect with a charm and humour such as had not previously characterized the advocacy of the leading Chancery practitioners. While at the bar, Greene commissioned the building for himself of a unique country house, Joldwynds at Leith Hill, which was modelled on a ship. He and his wife entertained generously both there and at their London house.

While carrying on one of the largest Chancery practices of his day, Greene found time to perform a great deal of unpaid public work. In 1925 he was chairman of the committee on company law, which laid the foundation of the Companies Act of 1929. In 1930 he became chairman of the committee on trade practices. In 1931 he was chairman of the advisory committee to inquire into the position of Imperial and International Communications Ltd, in connection with a cable merger. In 1934 he was chairman of the committee on the beet sugar industry. Towards the end of his career at the bar he confined himself to appearing in the House of Lords and the judicial committee of the privy council but, even so, by 1935 he was utterly exhausted by a practice of legendary proportions and, after arguing a case in the judicial committee in July, he confessed that he was 'really done'. Though he had extraordinary mental stamina, his small, slight build did not suggest a robust constitution.

The time had come for him to leave the bar and in October 1935, when Maugham became a lord of appeal in ordinary, Greene succeeded him in the Court of Appeal, was knighted, and sworn of the privy council. He later recalled that he was

> sitting quietly at Monte Carlo with a glass of champagne in my hand, ready to relax at last after being appellant in the last five cases in the Privy Council, when I got a telegram. It asked me to go direct to the Court of Appeal. I couldn't refuse, could I? But I don't know how many years it's going to take me to sort out my income tax and surtax. They really ought to give you some warning. (N. Faulks, *A Law unto Myself*, 1978, 114)

In moving direct to the Court of Appeal rather than being appointed in the first instance to the High Court bench, Greene was unusual (though the same was true of Donald Somervell a decade later, and Cyril Radcliffe was elevated from the bar direct to the House of Lords and Richard Wilberforce from the High Court bench direct to the House of Lords—all four having been more or less contemporaneous fellows of All Souls).

In 1937 Greene, by reason of his towering ability and although one of the more junior members of the Court of Appeal, was appointed master of the rolls. He was created Baron Greene, of Holmbury St Mary, Surrey (a hereditary peerage) in 1941. By virtue of his new office Greene also became keeper of public records and to the duties which this imposed he devoted much energy. He was chairman of the Royal Commission on Historical Manuscripts and president of the British Records Association from 1937. During the war his zealous initiative saved from destruction innumerable documents of historic importance, especially local records. He worked with enthusiasm and energy as chairman of the National Buildings Record (1941–5), formed at the start of the war in 1939 to preserve by drawings and photographs the details of buildings imperilled by the hostilities. In June 1942 Greene also served as chairman of the board of investigation of the coalminers' wages claim.

In 1943 Greene recorded, with prescience, that 'unless steps are taken to place the Judicial Committee in a position of authority which will be accepted by the Dominions, the disappearance of its jurisdiction in Appeals from the Dominions in a comparatively short time is inevitable' (Stevens, 151), a result that he believed would be regrettable but which successive governments neglected to avoid.

The tenure of the office of master of the rolls for any considerable time is notoriously exhausting. Greene held it for twelve years and at the end he was visibly worn out. The burden was exacerbated after 1945 because of the extensive use made by the Labour government of judges, including members of the Court of Appeal, to chair royal commissions and departmental committees, which in 1948 led Greene to urge the lord chancellor, Lord Jowitt, to procure the release of two members of the Court of Appeal from such duties. When, in 1949, he was appointed a lord of appeal in ordinary it was hoped that less exacting duties would restore him, but the hope was vain and in May the following year he resigned on the ground of ill health. On 16 April 1952 he died at the Garth Nursing Home, Dorking, Surrey. His home had been for many years at Holmbury St Mary, near Guildford.

Greene was a man of singular charm, sensitiveness, and modesty who brought to the practice of the law the mind of a scholar, as well as the highest sense of honour, exemplified by the fact that, when master of the rolls, he felt strongly that he could not accept the use of a government-owned car to drive him between the law courts and Waterloo Station 'because it would be a present from the Executive, offered without Parliamentary authority' (Stevens, 123). To a natural lucidity of thought, he joined felicity and elegance of expression and, on occasion, a whimsical wit, which lent his arguments at the bar a quality all their own. He received a number of honorary degrees including the DCL of Oxford, of which he was standing counsel from 1926 to 1935. He was an honorary student of Christ Church, an honorary FRIBA, a trustee of the Pilgrim Trust, the British Museum, and the Chantrey Bequest, and principal, from 1936 to 1944, of the Working Men's College, St Pancras.

Half a century after Greene's death his judicial reputation stood fully as high as it did in his lifetime, with his judgments cited daily in the courts. As particularly important among those judgments, mention may be made of those in *Associated Provincial Picture Houses* v. *Wednesbury Corporation* (1947), a landmark case in the field of judicial review of administrative action, *Re Diplock* (1948), a leading case on restitutionary remedies in which the Court of Appeal's decision was affirmed by the House of Lords, where Greene's eighty-nine page review of the earlier authorities was unqualifiedly endorsed, and *Young* v. *Bristol Aeroplane Company Ltd* (1944), which modified the application of the doctrine of precedent. Although, when at the bar, Greene had not been much concerned with revenue work, his technical virtuosity in making coherent sense of legally troublesome wartime fiscal legislation was universally admired.   JEREMY LEVER

Sources *Law Times* (25 April 1952) • *Law Journal* (25 April 1952) • *The Times* (18 April 1952) • *The Times* (1 May 1952) • R. Stevens, *The independence of the judiciary: the view from the lord chancellor's office* (1993) • D. Pannick, *Judges* (1987) • P. Devlin, *Taken at the flood* (1996) • private information (2004) • b. cert. • m. cert. • d. cert.
Archives Bodl. Oxf., letters to A. L. Goodhart, MS Eng. c. 2886
Likenesses Gluck, oils, 1939, Inner Temple, London [*see illus.*] • photograph, All Souls Oxf. • photograph, repro. in *The Times* (18 April 1952)
Wealth at death £44,541 18s. 10d.: probate, 10 June 1952, CGPLA Eng. & Wales

Greene, William (1696–1758), colonial governor, was born on 16 March 1696 in Warwick, Rhode Island, the eldest of the five children of Samuel Greene (1671–1720), farmer and local office-holder, and his wife, Mary (1673–1732), daughter of Benjamin Gorton of Warwick and his wife, Sarah. The Greene family was prominent in Rhode Island and was associated with the founding of both Providence and Warwick, two of the first four towns in the colony. William's grandfather John Greene was deputy governor of Rhode Island from 1690 to 1700, and his father was a frequent deputy to the general assembly from Warwick in the first two decades of the eighteenth century. On 30 December 1719 William married his second cousin Catharine Greene (1698–1777), and one of their six children, William *Greene (1731–1809), also served as Rhode Island's governor, from 1778 to 1786.

Rhode Island, the smallest of the New England colonies, had a population that approximated one-half of New Hampshire's, one-fourth of Connecticut's, and one-sixth of Massachusetts's for most of the eighteenth century. But what Rhode Island lacked in numbers it made up for in political noise. Connecticut, Massachusetts, and New Hampshire politics could be disputatious, but a shared puritan ethos in these colonies mitigated some of the conflict. Founded on the principles of 'fat mutton and liberty of conscience' (Bridenbaugh), colonial Rhode Island enshrined a spirit of economic and intellectual individualism that would become a characteristic of nineteenth-century America. Called 'Rogues Island' (Daniels, *Fragmentation*, 107) by its puritan neighbours, the tiny colony seemed perpetually convulsed by acrimonious political battle. In the eighteenth century yearly elections for governor, deputy governor, the governor's council, and the general assembly degenerated into organized campaigns of mud-slinging, in which rival factions came very close to meeting the definition of modern political parties.

Greene's unusual career as a colonial governor is largely explained by this partisan strife. Over the fourteen years between his first election in 1743 and his last in 1757 he was defeated three times, only to return victorious one or two years later. Thus, Greene's eleven-term governorship was broken into four periods, from 1743 to 1745, from 1746 to 1747, from 1748 to 1755, and from 1757 until his death in 1758.

Greene entered public life in 1732, when he was elected one of Warwick's four deputies to the lower house of the general assembly. He served five more terms as deputy in the decade, and in 1734 was chosen speaker of the house. A trained surveyor, Greene was named by the assembly to help negotiate Rhode Island's disputed western border with Connecticut, which he did to most Rhode Islanders' satisfaction. Some time during that period he became an ally of Richard Ward of Newport, the secretary of Rhode Island. In the 1730s the two main rival factions were organized around the Ward and Wanton families, both of Newport, Rhode Island's largest town. Each of the two families sought alliances in other towns. The Wards formed a partnership with the Greenes of Warwick, and the Wantons formed one with the Browns of Providence. Although they never committed their election plans to writing or put them in any legal document, the Ward and Wanton factions devised informal slates of candidates to contest the annual colony-wide elections. In 1740, when Richard Ward became governor, Greene was elected deputy governor on the Ward faction ticket. Three years later, when his patron, Ward, declined to run for re-election for personal reasons, Greene succeeded him as governor and as leader of the Ward faction. Always embattled and occasionally battered at the polls or in the general assembly, Greene nevertheless dominated Rhode Island politics for the next fifteen years until his death.

Greene had many successes in his four tenures as governor. When Governor William Shirley of Massachusetts and Admiral Peter Warren complained that Rhode Island was deficient in supplying military aid during King George's War, Greene refuted the charges and maintained the colony's control over its militia. Remarkably, he won a protracted border dispute with Massachusetts, which resulted in the transfer of five towns—Cumberland, Warren, Bristol, Little Compton, and Tiverton—from long-defunct Plymouth Colony to Rhode Island's jurisdiction. In nasty battles over currency emissions which bedevilled Rhode Island (and several other colonies) for most of the 1740s and 1750s, Greene fought less successfully on the side of hard-money advocates trying to preserve the value of Rhode Island's currency.

Greene was defeated for re-election in 1745 and 1747 by Gideon Wanton, and then again in 1755 by Stephen Hopkins, a Providence resident who assumed the leadership of the Wanton faction. Having intended to retire after his third defeat, Greene was prevailed upon to run yet again in 1757, after charges were levelled that Hopkins had corruptly enriched himself at the taxpayers' expense. This final term came to an end with Greene's death at Warwick on 22 February 1758. He was replaced by Hopkins, who, along with his friends in Providence, became so dominant in politics as to assume the mantle once held by the Wanton faction. Samuel Ward, son of Richard, now took over leadership of the rival Ward group.

Little of Greene's personality can be gleaned from his surviving correspondence. One should resist the natural temptation to infer from his fiercely partisan political career that he necessarily was a combative person who loved a good fight. Equally plausibly, Greene may have been simply a talented leader who practised politics the Rhode Island way.   BRUCE C. DANIELS

Sources S. V. James, *Colonial Rhode Island: a history* (1975) • D. S. Lovejoy, *Rhode Island politics and the American revolution, 1760–1776*

(1958) • B. C. Daniels, *Dissent and conformity on Narragansett Bay: the colonial Rhode Island town* (1983) • C. Bridenbaugh, *Fat mutton and liberty of conscience: society in colonial Rhode Island, 1630–1690* (1976) • J. N. Arnold, ed., *Vital record of Warwick, Rhode Island* (1983) • J. Bartlett, ed., *Rhode Island colony records*, 5, 6 (1860–61) • B. C. Daniels, *The fragmentation of New England: comparative perspectives on economic, political, and social divisions in the eighteenth century* (1988) • I. B. Richman, 'Greene, William', *DAB* • C. H. Greene, *Ebenezer Greene and his descendants* (1951)

Likenesses oils, Rhode Island Historical Society Library, Providence

Wealth at death see Warwick probate, Rhode Island genealogical records, 6.219

Greene, William (1731–1809), revolutionary politician in America, was born on 16 August 1731 at Coweset Farm, Warwick, Rhode Island, the third son of William *Greene (1696–1758), farmer and governor of the colony of Rhode Island and Providence Plantations (1743–58), and Catharine (1698–1777), daughter of Captain Benjamin Greene, also of Warwick, Rhode Island, and his wife, Susanna Holden. On 30 September 1758 William Greene married his second cousin, Catharine (1731–1794), daughter of Simon Ray and Deborah Greene of New Shoreham, Block Island. Catharine was also the great-great-granddaughter of Roger *Williams, the founder of the colony of Rhode Island. They had five children, Ray, Phebe, Celia, Samuel Ward, and Anne. Like his father, William was a surveyor and farmer, and spent much of his life in public office.

Greene's first foray into public life was as a deputy from Warwick to the Rhode Island general assembly. First elected in 1773, he was re-elected in 1774, 1776, and 1777. An early supporter of the American independence movement, in 1776 he was appointed by the general assembly to committees to import salt into Rhode Island, to raise hard currency to finance American military operations in Canada, and to 'visit' a person suspected of treasonable activities and inspect his papers. In August 1776 he was chosen first associate justice in the Rhode Island superior court and in December, after the British had taken control of Newport and Aquidneck (Rhode) Island, he was named to the state's council of war. In May 1777 he was elected speaker of the house of deputies and in October of that year he was re-appointed to the council of war. In February 1778 he was chosen chief justice of the superior court and in May he was elected governor of the state, defeating the sitting lieutenant-governor, William Bradford.

As governor Greene was noted for his integrity and his simple lifestyle. When the assembly met in Providence, for example, Greene often walked the 10 miles from his home in Warwick to attend the meetings. This intelligent, if uneducated, man had little chance to dominate the state's politics. In Rhode Island the legislature was supreme, exercising great power in the executive and judicial operations of the state. The governor's influence derived from his position as the state's leading official and from his personal importance as a political leader. He had no appointive power. Despite these restrictions on his power, Greene, a leader of the 'mercantile party', was an active governor, particularly in matters relating to the war

(Polishook, 124). This activity was particularly evident during the campaign to recapture Aquidneck (Rhode) Island from the British in 1778. With the state's council of war Greene helped co-ordinate military affairs with the American military commander, John Sullivan, mobilized the state's militia, and pushed neighbouring states to provide men and provisions for the effort. He served as governor from 1778 to 1786 through difficult and troubled times, yet, as he noted in his valedictory address, was re-elected repeatedly 'with scarse a dissenting vote' (Staples, 549). In 1786 Greene lost the governorship to John Collins, because of his opposition to a new emission of bills of credit designed to help the state's debtors. After his defeat Greene retired to his farm. Several times he attempted a return to politics. He ran for congress in 1796, and in 1802 he ran for governor as the federalist candidate. Both times he was defeated. He died on 29 November 1809 at Warwick. Ray Greene, the eldest of his children, was a United States senator from 1797 to 1801.

DENNIS M. CONRAD

Sources L. B. Clarke, *The Greenes of Rhode Island, with historical records of English ancestry, 1534–1902* (1903) • I. H. Polishook, *Rhode Island and the union, 1774–1795* (1969) • J. R. Bartlett, ed., *Records of the colony of Rhode Island and Providence plantations, in New England*, 10 vols. (1856–65), vols. 7–10 • W. R. Staples, *Rhode Island in the continental congress, 1765–1790* (1870) • P. F. Dearden, *The Rhode Island campaign of 1778: inauspicious dawn of alliance* (1980) • *The papers of General Nathanael Greene*, ed. R. K. Showman and others, 1–3 (1976–83) • R. S. Mohr, *Governors for three hundred years, 1638–1959: Rhode Island and Providence Plantations* (1959) • I. B. Richman, 'Greene, William', *DAB*

Greene, William Friese- (1855–1921), developer of moving pictures and photographer, was born as William Edward Green on 7 September 1855 at 68 College Street, Bristol, one of seven children of James Green (*b.* 1816), a metalworker and goldsmith, and his wife, Elizabeth Sage (*b.* 1816). He entered Queen Elizabeth's Hospital school, Brandon Hill, Bristol, at the age of ten, leaving on his fourteenth birthday. He was apprenticed to a local photographer, Maurice Guttenberg, and developed a special skill for portrait photography. At the age of eighteen, in 1874, he left to run his own studio. That same year he married Victoria Mariana Helena Friese (*d.* 1895)—a Swiss woman whose name he joined to his own. Two years later they had their only child, Ethel Adelaide. Friese-Greene enjoyed a high reputation as a photographer, opening two shops in Bristol, one in Plymouth and two in Bath—the family's new home.

It was in Bath that Friese-Greene met John Arthur Roebuck Rudge (1837–1903), an instrument maker and inventor who had devised several adaptations of the magic lantern which created an illusion of movement by showing a number of photographic plates in quick succession. Friese-Greene assisted him in this work and demonstrated the machines. It undoubtedly inspired him to try to develop more fluid moving pictures. In 1885 he moved to London where he opened six studios and had a laboratory. He subsequently studied science at the Regent Street Polytechnic and joined a number of learned societies.

By early 1888 Friese-Greene had designed his first camera for taking a series of photographs on a flexible base,

William Friese-Greene (1855–1921), self-portrait, c.1890 [series of facial expressions adopted for an experiment to analyse motion]

which at that time was paper film. Friese-Greene then had a second camera built with two lenses for stereoscopic filming. He next teamed up with Mortimer Evans, a civil engineer, to improve on these designs. They claimed their patent 10,131 (provisionally registered on 21 June 1889 and accepted in May 1890) could take ten pictures a second, but the speed is likely to have been slower. It did, however, incorporate many of the mechanical essentials for a moving picture camera. The first film successfully taken and projected with the new apparatus was supposedly of a scene at Hyde Park Corner in October 1889; it was first publicly exhibited at Chester town hall in July 1890 (*DNB*). However, some film historians now dispute this testimony, arguing that such projection would not have been possible.

A few months later Eastman celluloid film became available in this country and Friese-Greene immediately used it for filming. With Frederick Varley he further improved on the camera designs and demonstrated these new models at photographic societies. Meanwhile, Friese-Greene was trying various means of showing these images. A number of his contemporaries have testified to seeing him project films off a strip of transparencies about 1890.

Friese-Greene spent the considerable profits from his studios on inventing and in the process neglected his business affairs to such an extent that he was sued for debt and imprisoned in 1891. The following year he was declared bankrupt. None the less, he made some money from his patents for high-speed printing of photographs for cigarette cards and publications.

By 1895 the beginnings of commercial moving pictures were happening in Europe, but they were led by Thomas Edison, Auguste and Louis Lumière, and Robert Paul rather than Friese-Greene, who had been largely forgotten. He nevertheless persisted with his printing ideas, and

registered a patent for photographic typesetting and a system for printing without ink. His wife had been of poor health for some time and died that year. He remarried in 1897. His second wife was Edith Harrison (d. 1921); they had six sons, one of whom died in infancy.

From the late 1890s Friese-Greene started to focus on creating moving pictures in colour. By 1905 he had a working system in which successive images were taken through alternating filters (for example, red and blue-green), with the printed frames then being dyed these colours. If projected at sufficient speed, they created an impression of colour. By this time he and his family were living in Brighton.

In the first decade of the twentieth century, Friese-Greene's patented ideas included the electrical transmission of images (inspired by a meeting with Guglielmo Marconi), a chemically driven engine, and a gyroscopically controlled airship (which according to his sons was sold to the German government). By 1910 Friese-Greene was bankrupt again, but ironically he was called to New York to testify to his prior invention in a case which broke the Edison monopoly on film production and distribution. On returning he found himself in a prolonged court battle with Charles Urban over their rival colour processes. Friese-Greene won, but it was Urban's Kinemacolor that made all the money.

The onset of the First World War stopped all colour developments. Friese-Greene and his family were by this time in such a state of poverty that a friend organized a collection for them from the film industry. It was too much for his wife, who left him in 1917. Friese-Greene worked for the government during the war and afterwards returned with vigour to his ideas for colour cinematography. New companies were formed that successfully exploited his patents, though without benefit to him. On 5 May 1921 Friese-Greene attended a major meeting of film distributors, at the Connaught Rooms, 61–3 Great Queen Street, London, where he stood up and made a speech in which he wondered what a film of his life might be like and whether it would tell the truth. He died a few minutes later. In his purse was 1s. 10d.—apparently all the money he had. His wife survived him, but died later the same year.

The film industry gave Friese-Greene a big funeral and commissioned a monument by Sir Edwin Lutyens for his grave in Highgate cemetery, where he was buried on 13 May 1921. His tombstone was inscribed with the words 'the inventor of Kinematography', as well as patent number 10,131. A film about his life was produced by the film industry for the Festival of Britain: this was *The Magic Box* (1951), directed by John Boulting, and was a fitting tribute. He was one of the few to point the way ahead for the film industry, and he inspired Edison's workers in their crucial research. As an inventor he was often ahead of his time.

PETER CARPENTER

Sources R. Allister [M. Forth], *Friese-Greene, close up of an inventor* (1948) • B. Coe, 'William Friese-Greene and the origins of cinematography', *Screen*, 10/2 (March–April 1969), 25–41 • B. Coe, 'William Friese-Greene and the origins of cinematography', *Screen*, 10/3

(May–June 1969), 72–83 · B. Coe, 'William Friese-Greene and the origins of cinematography', *Screen*, 10/4 (July–Oct 1969), 129–47 · W. Friese-Greene, *Moving Picture News*, 3/49 (3 Dec 1910) [court affidavit] · private information (2004) · G. H. Friese-Greene, 'William Friese-Greene: the beginnings of cinematography', *The Elizabethan* [magazine of Queen Elizabeth's School, Bristol] (July 1947) · E. Rudge, 'John Arthur Roebuck Rudge', *The Bath Critic* (Jan 1953) · W. E. L. Day, *Twenty-five thousand years to trap a shadow*, unpublished MS, Cinémathèque Française, Paris [chapters on Friese-Greene and Rudge] · B. R. Davis, 'William Friese-Greene', *The Elizabethan* [magazine of Queen Elizabeth's School, Bristol] (March 1947) · G. Hendricks, *The Edison motion picture myth* (1961), 173–180 · H. V. Hopwood, *Living pictures: their history, photo-production, and practical working* (1899); repr. (New York, 1970) · *DNB* · b. cert. · d. cert. · m. cert.

Archives Cinémathèque Française, Paris, France, Will Day MSS · National Museum of Photography, Film, and Television, Bradford, Yorkshire | FILM BFI NFTVA · Cinémathèque Française, Paris, France

Likenesses W. Friese-Greene, self-portrait, photograph, *c.*1890, National Museum of Photography, Film and Television, Bradford [*see illus.*]

Greene, Sir William Graham (1857–1950), civil servant, was born at Takeley, Essex, on 16 January 1857, the eldest son of William Greene, who later resided at East Lodge, Bedford, and his wife, Charlotte, daughter of William Smith, of Wrawby, Lincolnshire. He was educated at Cheltenham College and in Germany. Between 1875 and 1879 he worked for some time at Bury St Edmunds in a brewery which belonged to his family, and then trained in engineering at Bedford; but having given this up through ill health, he studied for the civil service examination for the higher division, and in July 1879 was appointed assistant surveyor of taxes under the Board of Inland Revenue. From the outset he wanted to work at the Admiralty; in June 1881 he was transferred to the department of the accountant-general of the navy, and in April 1884 he was moved to the Admiralty secretariat as a junior clerk. Here he was soon selected for special duty in the military, political, and secret branch, and was chosen to be secretary of the foreign intelligence committee (the forerunner of the naval intelligence department). In January 1887 Lord George Hamilton appointed him his assistant private secretary. This post he retained for fifteen years under successive first lords, from Hamilton to Selborne.

As assistant private secretary and head of the first lord's private office, Greene gradually built up a position unique in the public service. On behalf of the first lord and subject to his approval he controlled the nomination and entry of naval cadets and assistant clerks (the junior rank of the paymaster branch), the arrangements for all ceremonial functions, and correspondence with the court on matters requiring the sovereign's approval. He also advised the first lord on all official business not requiring the professional view of the naval private secretary.

In 1899 Greene was appointed CB, and in December 1902 he was promoted principal clerk and placed in charge of the personnel branch of the secretariat; he was thus mainly responsible for putting into effect the scheme of educational reform promoted by Sir John Fisher and promulgated by Lord Selborne at Christmas in that year. In 1907 he became assistant secretary of the Admiralty and in 1911 was promoted KCB and appointed permanent secretary. On the outbreak of war in 1914 Winston Churchill made him one of the war staff group which settled all important matters. He enjoyed the confidence of Churchill's successors, Arthur Balfour and Carson. Greene was noted for his vast experience and great capacity for work, sometimes staying at the Admiralty until 2 a.m. Ironically, this mastery of administrative detail identified him with all the perceived faults of the Admiralty and there were some who thought he lacked the flexibility for the unprecedented demands of the war. Beatty—probably unfairly—labelled him 'one of those half dead men' (Marder, 4.215), and Keyes referred to him as 'that creature' leading 'a lot of cunning and unscrupulous civilians' (*Keyes Papers*, 367). A civilian working at the Admiralty described him as 'a dry old stick, a bachelor, devoted to the office, experienced, prudent and precise' (Marder, 4.215). Hankey, the secretary of the war cabinet, regarded him as dragging his feet over implementing the reforms recommended by the war cabinet as a result of the submarine crisis of April 1917, notably the development of a statistical department. Greene was also reluctant to co-operate with the shipping controller concerning the alteration of convoy routes, on the grounds that this was a purely naval matter. Hankey complained to Lloyd George, and when Sir Edward Carson was replaced by Sir Eric Geddes, Lloyd George, who had never seen Greene, insisted upon his immediate retirement. Greene left the Admiralty in August 1917. Churchill, however, who at the same time became minister of munitions, welcomed the opportunity of securing his services as secretary of the ministry, an office which he held until the ministry was disbanded after the war.

In 1920 Greene began work not requiring constant attendance in London, which he continued for twenty years, on a number of sub-committees of the committee of imperial defence, dealing with statistics and such subjects as the history of the Ministry of Munitions, and the use of national manpower. He also wrote a number of unpublished memoranda containing acute observations of leading men with whom he had worked. In retirement he lived mainly at his home, Harston House, Harston, near Cambridge, and soon became fully engaged in local activities. He was a justice of the peace of London and Cambridgeshire, and of the latter also county councillor and, in 1942, alderman. He was until 1948 treasurer of the Navy Records Society which he had helped to found in 1893.

Greene was an active man all his life, fond of hunting and shooting in younger days, and a keen gardener at his country home until the end. He was one of the ablest civil servants of his generation. A man of slight physique, he was a tireless worker with a single-minded devotion to his official duty, part of which he conceived to be the maintenance of the authority of the minister at the head of the department. He died, unmarried, at Harston House on 10 September 1950, and was buried on the 12th, probably in Harston churchyard.

V. W. BADDELEY, *rev.* PAUL G. HALPERN

Sources PRO, Admiralty records · private information (1959) · personal knowledge (1959) · S. W. Roskill, *Hankey, man of secrets*, 1 (1970) · A. J. Marder, *From the Dreadnought to Scapa Flow: the Royal Navy in the Fisher era, 1904–1919*, 5 vols. (1961–70) · *The Keyes papers*, ed. P. G. Halpern, 1, Navy RS, 117 (1972) · N. A. M. Rodger, *The admiralty* (1979) · M. Gilbert, *Winston S. Churchill*, 3: *1914–1916* (1971) · Burke, *Peerage* · *The Times* (11 Sept 1950) · *CGPLA Eng. & Wales* (1951) **Archives** Bodl. Oxf., corresp. · NMM, corresp. and papers · PRO, Admiralty records, MSS as secretary of the Admiralty | CAC Cam., letters to Lord Fisher, ref. FISR · NL Aus., letters to Alfred Deakin, ref. 3296A **Likenesses** W. Stoneman, two photographs, 1917–33, NPG · R. E. Fuller-Maitland, oils, *c*.1921, Admiralty House, London **Wealth at death** £28,051 10*s*. 11*d*.: probate, 20 Jan 1951, *CGPLA Eng. & Wales*

Greenfield, William (*c*.1255–1315), administrator and archbishop of York, was probably born in the mid-1250s. Arrangements made in 1314 for a chantry chapel within the York archiepiscopal manor of Ripon suggest that his parents were Clement and Edith de Grenefeld. Possibly the family originated in Gloucestershire, where the name survives in the village of Compton Greenfield within the bishop of Worcester's hundred of Henbury. He was well connected, being a kinsman of Walter Giffard, archbishop of York (d. 1279), and hence of the latter's brother, Godfrey Giffard, bishop of Worcester (d. 1302), as well as of John Giffard of Brimpsfield, Gloucestershire, who was executed after the rebellion against Edward II at Boroughbridge in 1322. William had a brother Robert—he died early in 1314—whose son, Gillemyn, served his uncle the archbishop.

Godfrey Giffard made William Greenfield a canon of Westbury-on-Trym and collated him to the rectory of Blockley on 10 December 1291, while from Archbishop Giffard he secured canonries at Southwell (1269), Ripon (1272), and York (1278), and received money towards his expenses for as long as he was at Oxford University after he came into residence about 1269. He studied for a while in Paris (perhaps during 1271), became a doctor of civil law by 1287, and of canon law by about 1300. An undated petition to the papal curia by Amadeus (V), count of Savoy, who acted as a councillor and diplomatic agent for Edward I, reveals that following his regency in canon law Greenfield planned to pursue theology for five years. Archbishop Robert Winchelsey (d. 1313) during his metropolitan visitation in 1299—although expressing a desire not to disturb Greenfield's course of lectures at Oxford—cited him for non-residence in the deanery of Chichester, to which he had recently been worthily promoted (the precise date of this promotion is not recorded).

A royal clerk from 1290, Greenfield was summoned as a councillor to parliament between 1295 and 1302. On 6 December 1302, thanks to a petition by Edward I, he received papal licence to be absent from his benefices while in royal service, and to enjoy the fruits of his deanery for seven years. He had earlier embarked on a diplomatic career, having been engaged during 1289 and 1291 in negotiations with the kings of Naples and Aragon. At the curia in 1290 he secured a crusading tenth for Edward I. Together with the Dominican provincial, William

Hothum (d. 1298) he was among those who were canvassed for their opinions as to the respective rights of Bruce and Balliol in the Great Cause (1292), but illness forced him to give his response in writing. In 1296 he was at Cambrai as a commissioner for the truce concluded with Philippe IV of France (r. 1285–1314) under the aegis of cardinals sent by Pope Boniface VIII (r. 1294–1303). About 1299 he was made a papal chaplain, presumably as a consequence of his strenuous efforts in the cause of peace. With Amadeus of Savoy, among others, he was appointed on 25 April 1302 to secure a permanent peace between the French and English kings. His manifold services were rewarded on 30 September of that year with his appointment as chancellor, although further diplomatic activity abroad compelled him to surrender the great seal to Adam Osgodby (d. 1316) a month later.

The York chapter elected Greenfield archbishop on 4 December 1304. Royal assent followed on the 24th and five days later, having resigned the chancellorship, he sought permission to journey to Rome to be consecrated and receive the pallium. Because of the delay in electing a successor to Benedict XI (r. 1303–4), Greenfield's consecration by Clement V (r. 1305–14) at Lyons did not take place until 30 January 1306. The protracted stay abroad, coupled with the customary papal *servicia*, left the new archbishop seriously in debt. He was constrained to borrow from the Ballardi of Lucca, and from monastic and secular clergy throughout the north of England. The temporalities of his see were restored on 31 March. Summoned to the Westminster parliament of May 1306, in June of that year Greenfield was made regent of the kingdom jointly with the treasurer, Walter Langton (d. 1321). At Edward I's last parliament at Carlisle (January–March 1307) Greenfield proclaimed the peace concluded between England and France, a peace cemented by the marriage of Edward, prince of Wales, and Isabella of France. With the accession of Edward II, Clement V—since the exiled Winchelsey was under sentence of suspension—thought that Greenfield would crown the new monarch. However, Winchelsey became reconciled to the king, and authorized the bishop of Winchester to officiate in his absence.

Greenfield's tenure of York was bedevilled by the time-honoured feud with Canterbury over the claim of each metropolitan to raise his primatial cross within the jurisdiction of the other. Trouble was anticipated following a wrangle between Greenfield's immediate predecessor, Thomas Corbridge (d. 1304), and Winchelsey. Edward I, in a letter to the pope, had insisted that the elect of York should on his return be permitted to move freely to parliaments and other royal business in the southern province without Canterbury's interference—the question of the right of the archbishop of York to raise his cross throughout England being still *sub judice* at the curia. Although the king issued a safe conduct for Greenfield on 10 February 1306, Winchelsey instructed his vicar-general Henry Eastry, prior of Canterbury (d. 1331), to issue a warning to Greenfield against raising his cross in the southern province. Should he do so, the places involved were to be placed under interdict, and any acknowledgement of

York's blessing was to incur excommunication. According to the annals of St Paul's, thanks to Edward I's intervention Greenfield on his return was able to ignore the threats and to have his cross carried before him in London. One of the statutes thought to have been issued—or possibly reissued—by him at Ripon in 1306 upheld York's independent primacy, and forbade tuitory appeal (that is, for protection) to the court of Canterbury. Greenfield's title 'primate of England' is entered on the parliamentary roll for 1307. Both archbishops planned to attend the parliament of April 1309 in London, but Winchelsey declined to come if the northern metropolitan were to elevate his cross. In the event, the chroniclers report, conflict was avoided when Greenfield, who had taken up residence in his Westminster house, was forced by the king to leave London because of his insistence on having his cross carried before him. Nevertheless, his register points to Greenfield's having been in London in May.

In 1309 Greenfield and his suffragan, Antony (I) Bek, bishop of Durham and patriarch of Jerusalem (d. 1311), were named principal commissioners for inquiry into the alleged misdeeds of the templars. The archbishop informed Clement V that the conflict of jurisdictions would prevent his acting within the southern province, while the bishops of Lincoln and Chichester, who had been associated with him, could not act within that of York. It would seem that he was reluctant to conduct this unsavoury business at all, but in pursuance of the papal commission he summoned a council to meet at York on 20 May 1310. Nothing much was accomplished, but another council was convoked in the following year. This assembled in May, and again in July when, on the first of the month, the archbishop opened the proceedings. Subsequent sessions were presided over by Master Robert Pickering, the council continuing its deliberations until 30 July. Twenty-four templars submitted to public reconciliation and had penances imposed upon them. In August 1311 the archbishop travelled by way of Dover—not without some harassment because his cross was raised—to the general council at Vienne, where, with Chancellor Walter Reynolds (d. 1327), he appears to have been a principal representative of the king. At Vienne the order of the Temple was suppressed, the decision being incorporated in the bull Vox in excelso, which (perhaps significantly) finds no place in Greenfield's register. On his return, following further molestation, he authorized members of the York chapter to raise at the curia the matter of his right to have his primatial cross elevated within Canterbury province.

After Winchelsey's death in 1313 the dispute continued acrimoniously with the latter's successor, Walter Reynolds. The situation was further complicated by the fact that campaigns against the Scots necessitated migrations of the English court to the north, a practice that also served to enhance the importance of the northern archbishopric. After his defeat at Bannockburn (1314) Edward II was entertained by Greenfield at York. Reynolds, however, allegedly supported by the king with the aid of the earls of Lancaster and Warenne, is recorded not only as having had his cross carried before him when attending the York parliament of 1314, but even as celebrating mass at the high altar of the minster. The following year Greenfield in his turn provocatively visited the York peculiar of Churchdown in Gloucestershire, a visitation of which he had conducted as recently as 1309. Reynolds ordered the bishop of Worcester, Walter Maidstone, to threaten him with excommunication. Following pronouncement of that sentence Greenfield, who had been strongly supported by John Giffard of Brimpsfield and other local knights, launched yet another appeal to the apostolic see.

Archbishop Greenfield was diligent in both diocese and province. His primary visitation of his extensive diocese, begun in 1306, was not completed until four years later. A further visitation was undertaken in 1313. While the see of Durham was vacant in 1311 he carried out a visitation of the diocese, despite resistance by the prior and convent, who claimed the right to administer the spiritualities during vacancies. As the north of England came increasingly under pressure from Scottish raids, the archbishop twice in 1315 summoned assemblies of clergy and magnates to co-ordinate the defence of the realm and of the church. He was rigorous in his attitude to appropriation, and made careful inquiry into the claims of religious houses to hold the greater tithes of parish churches. For his consistory court he issued a series of statutes, and appended constitutions to earlier diocesan legislation at York. His register leaves the impression of a prelate who from his first entry into his diocese was diligent about his ecclesiastical duties.

Already exhibiting signs of ageing on his return from Vienne in 1312 Greenfield was forced to call upon the services of some Irish bishops and of his suffragans at Carlisle and Durham. He died at Cawood Castle in Yorkshire, one of his principal residences, on 6 December 1315, and was buried in the chapel of St Nicholas in the north transept of York Minster. The monumental brass on his tomb is much damaged, the lower part of the effigy having been stolen in 1829.   ROY MARTIN HAINES

Sources register of Walter de Maidstone, Worcs. RO · *The register of William Greenfield, lord archbishop of York, 1306–1315*, ed. W. Brown and A. H. Thompson, 5 vols., SurtS, 145, 149, 151–3 (1931–40) · *The register of William Giffard, lord archbishop of York, 1266–1279*, ed. W. Brown, SurtS, 109 (1904) · *The register of John le Romeyn … 1286–1296*, ed. W. Brown, 1, SurtS, 123 (1913) · *Registrum Roberti Winchelsey, Cantuariensis archiepiscopi, AD 1294–1313*, ed. R. Graham, 2 vols., CYS, 51–2 (1952–6) · *Chancery records* · W. Stubbs, ed., 'Annales Paulini', *Chronicles of the reigns of Edward I and Edward II*, 1, Rolls Series, 76 (1882), 253–370 · *Johannis de Trokelowe et Henrici de Blaneforde … chronica et annales*, ed. H. T. Riley, pt 3 of *Chronica monasterii S. Albani*, Rolls Series, 28 (1866) · J. Raine, ed., *The historians of the church of York and its archbishops*, 2, Rolls Series, 71 (1886) · W. H. Dixon, *Fasti Eboracenses: lives of the archbishops of York*, ed. J. Raine (1863) · T. Stubbs, 'Life of Greenfield', *Decem Scriptores*, ed. R. Twysden (1652) · W. D. Peckham, ed., *The chartulary of the high church of Chichester*, Sussex RS, 46 (1946) · T. Madox, *The history and antiquities of the exchequer of the kings of England*, 2nd edn, 2 vols. (1769); repr. (1969) · F. M. Powicke and C. R. Cheney, eds., *Councils and synods with other documents relating to the English church, 1205–1313*, 2 vols. (1964) · P. Chaplais, ed., *Treaty rolls preserved in the Public Record Office*, 1 (1955) · J. R. Maddicott, *Thomas of Lancaster, 1307–1322: a study in the reign of Edward II* (1970) · R. M. Haines, *Ecclesia Anglicana: studies in the*

English church of the later middle ages (1989) · M. Stephenson, *A list of monumental brasses in the British Isles*, [new edn] (1964) · D. M. Smith, *Guide to bishops' registers of England and Wales: a survey from the middle ages to the abolition of the episcopacy in 1646*, Royal Historical Society Guides and Handbooks, 11 (1981) · *Fasti Angl., 1300–1541*, [St Paul's, London] · *Fasti Angl., 1300–1541*, [York] · *Fasti Angl., 1300–1541*, [Chichester] · Emden, *Oxf.*

Archives Borth. Inst., register, Regs 7–8, 5A, 8A, 8B
Likenesses effigy, York Minster; repro. in T. Gent, *The antient and modern history of the loyal town of Rippon* (1733), 115; lower half stolen, 1829

Greenfield, William (1755–1827), Church of Scotland minister and university professor, was born on 2 February 1755, the son of Captain John Greenfield and his wife, Grisel Cockburn, and was baptized at Dalkeith a week later. He married Janet Bervie (d. 1827) on 22 November 1782, and they had three sons and three daughters.

Greenfield was awarded an MA degree by the University of Edinburgh on 7 April 1778, and was ordained to West Wemyss parish church, Fife, on 6 September 1781. He was translated to become the first minister of St Andrew's, the first parish of the New Town of Edinburgh, on 25 November 1784; and again on 1 April 1787, to the High Church or St Giles. Greenfield was appointed almoner to the king in March 1789, was awarded the degree of DD by the University of Edinburgh on 31 March 1789, and was elected moderator of the general assembly of the Church of Scotland on 19 May 1796. Two sermons from this period are extant: his *Address delivered to the congregation of the High Church of Edinburgh, on Thursday 9th March 1797* and his sermon to the general assembly as retiring moderator in May 1797.

Greenfield's academic accomplishments also won him plaudits. He was nominated for, but not awarded, the chair of mathematics at Marischal College, Aberdeen, immediately after his graduation MA in 1778, and he was elected a fellow of the Royal Society of Edinburgh on 3 November 1783 (the year of its foundation). He presented a paper, 'On the use of negative quantities in the solution of problems by algebraic equations', which was published in the first volume of its *Transactions* in 1788. He held both his Edinburgh charges concurrently with the regius chair of rhetoric and *belles-lettres* at the University of Edinburgh, as joint professor with and successor to Hugh Blair, who retired from active university duties in 1784, and who was also his colleague at the High Church. Greenfield was considerably influenced by Blair, and even named his first son Hugh Blair Greenfield. The poet Robert Burns nevertheless thought Greenfield superior to Blair in literary ability and in preaching, particularly admiring his taste in sentimental writing.

This flourishing career was cut short when scandalous rumours circulating in Edinburgh caused Greenfield to resign his position in the church on 20 December 1798 and to flee to England. On receiving his letter of resignation, and taking his flight as a tacit admission of guilt, the presbytery of Edinburgh deposed him as a minister of the gospel and excommunicated him from the church. The university senate likewise swiftly removed him from the position of professor and withdrew his degrees of MA and DD. Neither body thought it appropriate to record the

crime of which Greenfield was accused, but his flight into subsequent anonymity, an expression of shock by Adam Ferguson that Greenfield had 'exposed himself to the gallows for what he did' (Ferguson to Carlyle, 25 Dec 1798), and one or two later broadsides, suggest that it was of a homosexual nature. Greenfield and his wife were separated by his flight; she and their children subsequently changed their family name to Rutherford. From his exile in England Greenfield continued to write, publishing (anonymously) in London an edition of his university lectures in London entitled *Essays on the Sources of the Pleasures Received from Literary Compositions* in 1809, and also contributing anonymously to the *Quarterly Review*. He was even rumoured to be the author of the Waverley novels. William Greenfield died on 28 April 1827, probably somewhere in the north of England.

EMMA VINCENT MACLEOD

Sources *Fasti Scot.*, new edn, 1.60–61, 88; 5.121 · bap. reg. Scot. · University of Edinburgh senate minutes, 31 Dec 1798, U. Edin., mic. dup. 436 · D. Cook, 'Murray's mysterious contributor: unpublished letters of Sir Walter Scott', *Nineteenth Century and After*, 101 (1927), 605–13 · M. Moonie, 'William Greenfield: gender and the transmission of literary culture', *The Scottish invention of English literature*, ed. R. Crawford (1998), 103–15 · A. Ferguson, letter to A. Carlyle, 25 Dec 1798, U. Edin. L., MS Dc.4.41.58 · A. Grant, *The story of the University of Edinburgh during its first three hundred years*, 2 (1884) · R. B. Sher, *Church and university in the Scottish Enlightenment: the moderate literati of Edinburgh* (1985) · S. Sloane, 'Professor William Greenfield, sad successor to Professor Hugh Blair: a study of the second regius professor of rhetoric and *belles lettres* at the University of Edinburgh, 1784–1798', *Scottish rhetoric and its influences*, ed. L. L. Gaillet (1998), 95–109 · R. B. Sher, 'Literature and the Church of Scotland', *The history of Scottish literature*, ed. C. Craig, 2: *1660–1800*, ed. A. Hook (1987), 259–69 · *The life and works of Robert Burns*, ed. R. Chambers, rev. W. Wallace, [new edn], 4 vols. (1896), vol. 2

Greenfield, William (1799–1831), philologist, was born in London on 1 April 1799. His father, William Greenfield, a native of Haddington, attended Wells Street Chapel, London, then under the ministry of Alexander *Waugh (1754–1827), the Scottish Congregationalist. He joined a missionary voyage in the ship *Duff*, and was accidentally drowned when his son was two years old. In the spring of 1802 Greenfield was taken by his mother to Jedburgh. In the summer of 1810 they returned to London, and Greenfield lived for some time with his two maternal uncles, who gave him instruction; they were men of business who studied languages in order to understand learned quotations, and they taught him. In October 1812 Greenfield was apprenticed to a bookbinder named Rennie. A Jewish employee in his master's house, and a reader of the law in the synagogue, taught him Hebrew for no charge.

At sixteen Greenfield began to teach in the Fitzroy Sabbath School, of which his master was a conductor. At seventeen he became a member of Wells Street Chapel, and a close friend of the minister, Dr Waugh. In 1824 he left business to devote himself to languages and biblical criticism. In 1827 he published *The Comprehensive Bible … with … a General Introduction … Notes*. The book, though fiercely attacked as heterodox by *The Record* and a Dr Henderson, became very popular, especially among unitarians. An abridgement was afterwards published as *The*

Pillar of Divine Truth Immoveably Fixed on the Foundation of the Apostles and Prophets. Greenfield's *Defence of the Serampore Mahratta version of the New Testament* (in reply to the *Asiatic Journal* for September 1829), published in 1830, attracted the attention of the British and Foreign Bible Society, by whom he was engaged about April of that year as superintendent of the editorial department. He had no previous knowledge of the Maratha and other languages referred to in the pamphlet, which, it is said, was written within five weeks of his taking up the subject. He followed it up with *A Defence of the Surinam Negro-English Version of the New Testament* (1830).

During his nineteen months in the society's service Greenfield wrote on twelve European, five Asiatic, one African, and three American languages, and acquired considerable knowledge of Peruvian, African-English, Chippeway, and Berber. His last undertaking for the society was the revision of the *Modern Greek Psalter* as it went through the press. He published several books on New Testament Greek and on Hebrew. He also projected a grammar in thirty languages, but in the midst of this remarkable surge of philological inquiry, he was struck down by brain fever, and died at Islington, London, on 5 November 1831. He left a widow and five children, on whose behalf a subscription was opened.

GORDON GOODWIN, *rev.* H. C. G. MATTHEW

Sources T. Wood, funeral sermon, *British preacher*, 3 (1832) • *GM*, 1st ser., 101/2 (1831), 473 • *GM*, 1st ser., 102/1 (1832), 89–90
Likenesses W. Holl, stipple, pubd 1834 (after G. Hayter), BM, NPG

Greenhalgh, John (1588/9–1651), royalist army officer, was probably born at Brandlesome, Lancashire, the only son of Thomas Greenhalgh (*d.* 1591) of Brandlesome and Mary, daughter of Robert Holt of Ashworth, Lancashire; he was aged two at the time of his father's death in September 1591, and he appears to have been brought up in the household of Sir Richard Assheton of Middleton, Lancashire, whom his mother married before 22 September 1599. In 1609 Greenhalgh married Alice Massie (*d.* 1620), daughter of William Massie, rector of Wilmslow, Cheshire; they had three sons and three daughters. In December 1620, not long after his first wife's death, he married Mary Assheton (*b.* 1589), daughter of William Assheton of Clegg Hall, Lancashire, and they had a daughter. After Mary's death he married Alice Holt, a widow and the daughter of George Chadderton of Lees Hall, Lancashire.

Greenhalgh succeeded his grandfather of the same name in part of the Brandlesome and other estates in Lancashire in 1615. Although little else is known of his early life, Greenhalgh's family had been in the service of the Stanleys, earls of Derby, and he seems to have continued this tradition. He served as a captain of the county militia in the 1630s and in 1640 was appointed governor of the Isle of Man by the Stanleys. In 1645 James, seventh earl of Derby acknowledged Greenhalgh's special military role by appointing him lieutenant-general of the island. His adherence to the royalist Stanleys inevitably led to the sequestration of his estates by parliament and cost him

his place on the Lancashire county bench, membership of which he claimed to have enjoyed for 'thirty years together' (*Liber scaccarii*, 1649, 51 [2]) before he was removed by parliament on 24 October 1642 as a 'notorious malignant' (*JHC*, 2.821). He was one of two of the earl's servants dispatched to negotiate on Derby's behalf with parliament's representative, Sir John Meldrum, in Lancashire in the autumn of 1644. Otherwise he was active in the administration and military organization of the island throughout the 1640s. Contrary to the tradition that he was present and even died on the battlefield of Worcester, there is clear evidence that Greenhalgh remained on the island after the earl of Derby departed to join the army of Charles II in August 1651 (*Liber scaccarii*, 1651, inter 41–2 [1]). He died on 16 September, probably in Castletown, Isle of Man, and was buried three days later at the parish church of Malew.

J. R. DICKINSON

Sources *VCH Lancashire*, 5.133–4 • Libri Scaccarii, 1640–51, Manx Museum Library • inquisition post mortem of Thomas Greenhalgh, 22 Sept 1599, PRO, DL7/17/61 • *The journal of Nicholas Assheton*, ed. F. R. Raines, Chetham Society, 14 (1848), 4 (n. 1), 70 (n. 1) • J. H. Stanning and J. Brownbill, eds., *The royalist composition papers*, 2, ed. J. H. Stanning, Lancashire and Cheshire RS, 26 (1892), 107–115 • *JHC*, 2 (1640–42), 821 • W. Dugdale, *The visitation of the county palatine of Lancaster, made in the year 1664–5*, ed. F. R. Raines, 2, Chetham Society, 85 (1872), 124–6 • Malew parish registers (burial), 1651, Manx Museum Library, microfilm PR 19 • *The registers of the parish church of Bury in the county of Lancaster: christenings, burials and weddings*, 1: 1590–1616, ed. W. J. Lowenberg and H. Brierley (1898), Lancashire Parish Register Society, 1 (1898) • *The registers of Middleton, 1541–1663*, ed. G. Shaw, Lancashire Parish Register Society, 12 (1902) • *The registers of the parish church of Bury in the county of Lancaster: christenings, burials and weddings*, 2: 1617–1646, ed. W. J. Lowenberg and H. Brierley, Lancashire Parish Register Society, 10 (1901) • B. G. Blackwood, *The Lancashire gentry and the great rebellion, 1640–60*, Chetham Society, 3rd ser., 25 (1978), 39
Likenesses G. E. Madeley, lithograph (after oil painting), BM, NPG • oils, Bury Library and Museum
Wealth at death estate divided in general and minor bequests: will

Greenham, Peter George (1909–1992), painter, was born on 9 September 1909 at 11 Conyers Road, Streatham, London, the second son of George Frederick Greenham (1874–1950), telephone engineer, and his wife, Isabel, *née* Duckworth (1878–1961). He was educated at Streatham and Dulwich College. From there he gained a demyship at Magdalen College, Oxford, to read history, but later changed to English. At Oxford, where C. S. Lewis was his tutor, he was not happy, and he later said that he would have much preferred to go to Cambridge and be taught by F. R. Leavis. After graduating with a fourth-class degree in 1931 he became a schoolmaster, first at Thame and later at Marylebone grammar schools. However, he had always wanted to be a painter and at the age of twenty-six he became an art student at the Byam Shaw School of Drawing and Painting, run by F. E. Jackson, a great teacher of drawing. Jackson's teaching, in which a classical approach to form was realized through a searching and sensitive touch, was exactly suited to Greenham, as was the free but dedicated atmosphere of the school. Greenham became a fine draughtsman who ever afterwards acknowledged the influence of Jackson.

When the Second World War came the Byam Shaw closed, and Greenham had to take to teaching again, this time at Magdalen College School, Oxford. By now he was exhibiting landscapes and portraits at the Royal Academy and other venues. His reputation grew quickly and in 1951 he was elected an associate of the Royal Academy. He became a full academician in 1960. In 1964 he was made keeper and took over the running of the Royal Academy Schools. Until the end of his life he was closely involved with the Royal Academy, an institution he valued as much for its personalities and eccentricities as for its history. He had for some time been teaching drawing, both at the reopened Byam Shaw and at the Royal Academy Schools, and he now had full scope for his beliefs about art teaching—unassertive, yet deeply convinced of the paramount importance of drawing. Though sympathetic to his students of whatever leaning, he insisted that they should all spend time in the life room. Such were his good relations with them that he was able to do this at a period of turmoil in art education. His attitude to teaching was very typical of the way his apparently easy-going manner was based on strong conviction; in his painting, too, his beautiful touch had nothing merely sensitive or vague about it, but was always a means towards greater precision of structure.

On 21 August 1964, the year he took over the schools, Greenham married a fellow painter, Irene Mary (Jane) Dowling (b. 1925), daughter of Geoffrey Barrow Dowling, physician. The years that followed were particularly fulfilling, with his happy marriage, many commissions, a daughter, Mary, and a son, David, and a move to the Oxfordshire village of Charlton-on-Otmoor. His portraits during these years included ambitious full lengths, but he was most truly himself in the more intimate studies in which his qualities of sympathy and sensitivity of observation came out. Two of the most memorable were those of Lady Bonham Carter, a tender evocation of old age, and of F. R. Leavis. To be painted by Greenham was to accept that sittings might go on a long time, sometimes indeed for years; but his sitters seem to have enjoyed the experience, and he once said that he grew very fond of them all—except a certain general. But it would be a mistake to think of Greenham as primarily a portrait painter. His landscapes were equally important to him, and the late seascapes and beach scenes, with their pearly, iridescent colour, are very beautiful.

Greenham had a comfortable presence, his clothes well worn, his manner sympathetic. He had a warm and humorous sociability, his humour often self-deprecatory; but under this easy-going manner was always an incisive and watchful mind. He loved music, and the English language, which he wrote with style and relish. He only published one book, *Velasquez* (1969), but his short articles, even the annual Royal Academy keeper's report, were composed and polished with equal care. He was appointed CBE in 1978. He died of prostatic cancer in Oxford on 11

July 1992, having been converted *in extremis* to the Roman Catholic church, and was buried at Charlton-on-Otmoor on 15 July. He was survived by his wife and two children.

BERNARD DUNSTAN

Sources The Times (16 July 1992) · The Times (21 July 1992) · The Times (1 Aug 1992) · The Independent (13 July 1992) · The Independent (15 July 1992) · The Independent (24 July 1992) · The Independent (27 July 1992) · WWW, 1991–5 · m. cert. · personal knowledge (2004) · private information (2004) [Jane Greenham, wife; Mary Rose Greenham, daughter]

Likenesses L. H. Rosoman, group portrait, acrylics, 1979–84 (The meeting, Royal Academy of Arts), NPG · photograph, repro. in The Times (16 July 1992) · photograph, repro. in The Times (21 July 1992) · photograph, repro. in The Times (1 Aug 1992)

Wealth at death £697,805: probate, 6 Jan 1993, CGPLA Eng. & Wales

Greenham, Richard (early 1540s–1594), Church of England clergyman, was probably born in the early to mid-1540s, as can be inferred from his own statement that he was 'a child in Q Maries daies' (JRL, English MS 524, fol. 16v) and his matriculation as sizar of Pembroke College, Cambridge, on 27 May 1559. Samuel Clarke, who has almost every date wrong in his biography, assumes that Greenham was about sixty when he died. This has led historians to believe mistakenly that he was born in the 1530s and that he delayed matriculation out of conscientious objection to the Marian church. Nothing is known of his geographical origins, parents, or early years. He graduated BA in 1564 and proceeded MA in 1567, becoming a fellow of Pembroke College also in 1567. Matthew Hutton, master of Pembroke since 1562, probably brought Greenham to the attention of John Hutton, a Cambridgeshire gentleman of godly inclinations who may have been a kinsman of the master. John Hutton offered Greenham the lucrative living of Dry Drayton, a rural parish of about thirty households located 5 miles from Cambridge, in the summer of 1570. In August 1573 he married Katherine Bownd (d. 1612), widow of the physician Robert Bownd, mother of the puritan writer Nicholas Bownd and of John Dod's wife, Ann, and sister-in-law of John Hutton. They had no children.

In the year of his marriage Greenham was threatened with suspension for refusing to subscribe to a statement that the prayer book was 'such as conteynethe nothing in yt repugnynge or contrarie to the word of God', that the surplice and square cap were 'not wicked but tollerable', and that the articles of religion contained 'most godlye and holsome doctryne' (Ely diocesan records, B/2/6, 198). In defending himself to Bishop Richard Cox he argued that although he could not subscribe in good conscience, he did not agitate his parish over ceremonies or surplices but occupied himself only 'in preaching Christ crucified' (A Parte of a Register, 86–93). While Greenham did sign two letters supporting Thomas Cartwright in 1570, George Downame remembered him rebuking students from Great St Mary's pulpit for being drawn into debates that threatened the church's peace. Greenham saw the Devil's hand in efforts to divide the church, and his refusal to 'break the peace of the church' over 'a meer outward thing' (JRL, English MS 524, fols. 54v–55r) was a consistent theme of his ministry. Cox was persuaded that Greenham was no schismatic, and rather than removing him employed him to confer with recusants and members of the Family of Love. Greenham played a central role in the 1580 anti-familist campaign, devising the articles to which suspects would subscribe, and through personal conversation returning some to orthodoxy. He vigorously attacked the separatists represented by Martin Marprelate, leading to whining about his 'shril pipes' (M. Some Laid Open in his Coulers, 122).

In addition to routine pastoral activities in his parish, Greenham presided over the first known household seminary, a major advance in clerical education much imitated in the next century. While he devised a scheme to have one 'toward schollar' at a time as his assistant 'to bee framed … fit for the work of the lord' (JRL, English MS 524, fols. 57v–58r), he seems to have had many students, whose university education offered no practical preparation for ministry, attending him at any time. Some, like Arthur Hildersham and Henry Smith, became major figures. These disciples took extensive notes of his actions and advice, notes which were copied and circulated widely. One collection was owned by a minister as far away as Halifax. Greenham published only one sermon during his lifetime and his most important work, a treatise on the sabbath, had not been completed to his satisfaction when he died. In 1599 Henry Holland published these materials, meditations on some scriptural passages, and an incomplete catechism that were found among Greenham's papers, along with an edited version of a manuscript collection of his sayings, letters of spiritual advice revealing the nature of his ministry to afflicted persons (something for which he was famous), and notes of some of his sermons. All these were sent to Holland by others; additional sermons, letters, and collections of sayings were incorporated into later editions. After Holland's death in 1603 Stephen Egerton took over editorial duties, and in 1612 produced a fifth and final edition, more rationally organized and with a superb index. Greenham's work on the sabbath was regarded by contemporaries as profoundly influential. In it he was an early advocate of strict sabbath observance as a moral obligation on all Christians, rejecting the notion that it interfered with Christian spiritual liberty.

In 1591 Greenham moved to London, where he became lecturer at Christ Church Greyfriars. Thomas Fuller's father reported that Greenham's successor at Dry Drayton told him in 1616 that Greenham felt there had been 'noe good wrought by my ministerie on any but one familie' (Warren, 366) and Clarke asserted that Greenham's departure was due to 'the untractableness and unteachableness' of his flock, in spite of his 'exceeding great pains' (Clarke, 15). Historians have used these reports to argue that if such a devoted pastor as Greenham 'could not make committed Protestants of more than a tiny handful of his parishioners, then nobody could and the task was impossible' (Haigh, 213). However, careful study of Elizabethan Dry Drayton has shown that, pace Fuller and Clarke, Greenham's ministry was by many standards quite successful. Moreover, Greenham consistently rejected the notion that 'for some trobles' a minister might 'depart from his calling', since he would then 'bee out of any calling, for-as-much as every calling hath his lets and impediments' (JRL, English MS 524, fol. 3) and he seems to have had a finely developed sense of delayed gratification (ibid., fol. 7v).

In fact Greenham relocated because influential Londoners, led by Thomas Fanshawe, persuaded him that a suitable replacement to serve Dry Drayton could easily be found while the needs of the London godly were such that only Greenham could meet them. He became part of the 'steady influx of mature nonconformists from the provinces' in the 1590s that saved London nonconformists, under pressure from Bishop Aylmer and Archbishop Whitgift, 'from impotent silence' (Seaver, 218–19). In February 1592 Aylmer granted Greenham a preaching licence only when Fanshawe made special assurances that Greenham 'would neither stir up nor spread any innovations or disputes' (LMA, DL/C/335, fol. 60v). In April 1593, apparently at Aylmer's behest, he joined two other divines in visiting the imprisoned John Penry, who rejected their 'intermeddling'.

During the virulent outbreak of plague of 1593, Greenham preached a series of well-attended fast sermons. Although that exposed him to danger, the plague did not claim his life. He had been troubled by a number of health problems—including severe toothaches, a fistula, and stomach problems—for at least a decade. He died late in April 1594, of unknown causes, and was buried on 25 April within Christ Church; no details of his funeral survive. He left no will; Katherine was granted the administration of his goods on 30 April.

Greenham's death was regarded, according to Henry Holland, as 'no small wrack to the Church and people of God' (Workes, 1599, A2v) since 'for practicall divinity he was inferiour to few or none in his time' (ibid., 1605, 724). Most especially he was remembered as 'that excellent Physitian of the Soule' (Gamon, 31). For Fuller, 'his masterpiece was in comforting wounded consciences' and 'many, who came to him with weeping eyes, went from him with cheerful souls' (Fuller, 219–20). His writings were often quoted in print by such writers as Robert Bolton; diaries and inventories show that his Works were widely owned and read.

ERIC JOSEF CARLSON

Sources K. L. Parker and E. J. Carlson, 'Practical divinity': the works and life of Revd Richard Greenham (1998) • E. J. Carlson, '"Practical divinity": Richard Greenham's ministry in Elizabethan England', Religion and the English people, 1500–1640, ed. E. J. Carlson (1998), 147–98 • JRL, English MS 524 • T. Fuller, The church-history of Britain, 11 pts in 1 (1655) • S. Clarke, The lives of thirty two English divines, in A general martyrologie, 3rd edn (1677) • GL, MS 9163 • liber vicarii generalis, 1590–95, LMA, DL/C/335 • The workes of … Richard Greenham, ed. H. Holland (1599); 2nd edn (1599); 3rd edn (1601); 4th edn, ed. S. Egerton (1605); 5th edn, ed. R. Hill (1612) • A parte of a register [1593] • Gon. & Caius Cam., MS 53/30 • Ely diocesan records, B/2/6; D/2/10H • H. Gamon, Praise of a godly woman (1627) • G. Downame, Two sermons (1608) • M. Some laid open in his coulers (1589) • J. Waddington, John Penry (1852) • C. F. S. Warren, N&Q, 6th ser., 7 (1883), 366 • P. S. Seaver, The puritan lectureships: the politics of religious dissent, 1560–1662 (1970) • C. Haigh, The reign of Elizabeth (1984)

Archives JRL, English MS 524

Greenhill, Sir Alfred George (1847–1927), mathematician, was born on 29 November 1847 at Montpelier Row, Twickenham, the third son of Thomas Greenhill, an engineer, and his wife, Louisa, daughter of Thomas Tagg, a gardener in Oxford. In April 1856 he was admitted from St Pancras, London, as a pupil at Christ's Hospital; at that time his father had seven other children and an annual income of less than £250. He was presented to the school by the parish of Twickenham, which had been left money by John and Frances West, who were related to Greenhill, to endow a scholarship there. At school he showed considerable mathematical talent and when, in 1866, he went up to read mathematics at St John's College, Cambridge, he was successively Pitt Club exhibitioner, Somerset exhibitioner, and foundation scholar. Simultaneously he held a Whitworth engineering scholarship and a university scholarship at the University of London where he registered in 1868. In 1870 he was second wrangler in the Cambridge tripos, tied with the first wrangler for the Smith's prize and was elected to a fellowship at St John's; the following year he completed his London BA.

In 1872 Greenhill was appointed professor of applied mathematics at the newly founded Royal Indian Civil Engineering College at Cooper's Hill, but the next year he returned to Cambridge as fellow and lecturer at Emmanuel College. Three years later, in 1876, he became professor of mathematics to the advanced class of the Royal Artillery officers at Woolwich; he remained in that post until his retirement in 1907. Greenhill was elected FRS in 1888 and knighted in 1908. The De Morgan medal of the London Mathematical Society was among the numerous honours he received from British and foreign learned societies. He was greatly admired by many of his contemporary mathematicians, although some considered that he did not sufficiently appreciate the developments in mathematics and physics of his own time.

Greenhill's interests lay principally in applied mathematics; his work in pure mathematics grew out of a need to discover new tools to solve practical problems. He wrote many textbooks, was a prolific researcher, and examined in the tripos. In all these activities, and in his teaching, he insisted that mathematical problems and their solutions must correspond closely to the nature of the problems met with in engineering and everyday reality. He considered that numerical answers were an integral part of any solution—a view not commonly held at that time. His greatest successes were achieved in the context of dynamics, hydrodynamics, and elasticity. He made extensive use of elliptic functions and wrote a textbook on their application in 1892; he directed the preparation of a table of these functions for the Smithsonian collection in 1922.

Greenhill's text-book *Differential and Integral Calculus* (1885) broke new ground by developing the differential and the integral calculus side by side, a practice which later became standard. His *Treatise on Hydrostatics* (1894) was also an innovation; in order to write it, he hunted through the scientific and engineering literature for realistic problems in shipbuilding, aeronautics, and hot-air ballooning (among others) with which to introduce the principles of hydrostatics. Mathematics was only brought in when absolutely essential. He worked with Woolwich colleagues on ballistic and gunnery problems and derived particularly valuable results on the rifling of heavy breech-loading ordnance.

In retirement Greenhill, who did not marry, lived in London, first at New Inn and then at 1 Staple Inn, Holborn, working in seclusion on mathematical and historical research. Despite his kindliness and light-heartedness, his idiosyncratic behaviour and opinions added to his long-standing reputation for eccentricity. He enjoyed the social life of the combination room of St John's, the Savile Club, the Athenaeum, and the tearoom of the Royal Society. He died at 19 Queen Adelaide Road, Penge, London, on 10 February 1927, partly from the effects of a fall from a bus the previous year. He was buried at Lewisham cemetery on 16 February. MARGARET E. RAYNER

Sources *The Times* (14 Feb 1927) · *Nature*, 119 (1927), 323–5 · *PRS*, 119A (1928), i–iv · *Proceedings of the London Mathematical Society*, 3 (1928), 27–32 · *The Eagle*, 45 (1927–9), 46–8 · *Emmanuel College Magazine*, 25 (1926–7), 68 · Venn, *Alum. Cant.* · Christ's Hospital presentation papers, GL, GL MS 12, 818A/30, no. 19 · University of London registration book, LUL · b. cert. · d. cert. · *CGPLA Eng. & Wales* (1927)

Archives CUL, Sir G. Larmon MSS

Likenesses J. W. Hicks, photograph, 1916, repro. in *PRS*, facing p. i · photograph, repro. in *The Times*, p. 16

Wealth at death £13,225 17s. 5d.: probate, 25 March 1927, *CGPLA Eng. & Wales*

Greenhill, Denis Arthur, Baron Greenhill of Harrow (1913–2000), diplomatist, was born at 17 Eastwood Road, Woodford, Essex, on 7 November 1913, the son of James Greenhill, a bank clerk and later bank manager, and his wife, Susie Beatrice, *née* Matthews. His family were of staunchly nonconformist stock. He was brought up in the London suburb of Woodford and won a scholarship to Bishop's Stortford College, where his contemporaries included Dick White, later head of MI5 and MI6. He went on to Christ Church, Oxford, where he read history under J. C. Masterman and was tutored by Patrick Gordon Walker, under whom he later worked briefly but closely when the latter was foreign secretary. During vacations from Oxford he travelled in Germany and Italy and saw something of the rise of fascism. He graduated with a second-class degree in 1935.

After Oxford Greenhill joined the London North Eastern Railway as a graduate trainee and in the period immediately before the Second World War saw at first hand the effects of the industrial recession in north-east England, which left a lasting impression on him. His railway duties included co-ordinating the movement of evacuees after the Munich crisis. At the outbreak of war he volunteered for service in the army and—in view of his experience—was appointed to the Royal Engineers. With them he served during the next six years in Egypt, Italy, and southeast Asia, being promoted to colonel and appointed a military OBE and twice mentioned in dispatches. During the war he married, in 1941, Angela McCulloch, whom he had met in Cairo where she was working for British intelligence. It was a long-lasting and happy marriage which resulted in the birth of two sons, Nigel (*b*. 1942) and Robin (1945–1986).

After the war, with the railways nationalized, Greenhill was persuaded by a wartime acquaintance, Edwin Chapman-Andrews, who had become head of personnel at the Foreign Office, to take the diplomatic service entry competition. He was employed in the Foreign Office from November 1945, and was appointed a member of the foreign service and first secretary on 1 January 1946. As a new entrant he gained early experience of working with ministers when he accompanied Ernest Bevin in 1946 to talks with the Egyptians about the future of military bases on the Suez Canal. His first proper foreign posting was to Bulgaria as first secretary, in December 1947, where his wife helped him to recover after he narrowly escaped death as a result of incompetent medical treatment. At this period the communist government of Bulgaria was deeply involved in fomenting guerrilla activity within Greece, and at a staged trial connected with this and with the arrest of a number of Bulgarian protestant pastors Greenhill was accused of obtaining military secrets and was declared *persona non grata*. It was an inauspicious start to a diplomatic career.

However, Greenhill's next posting, in August 1949, was as first secretary in Washington, where his Bulgarian adventure was not held against him. It was for him the start of a long and significant relationship with the United States. He learned much from his ambassador, the celebrated Oliver Franks, under whom he was responsible for the Middle East desk in the chancery at the time of the hostile nationalization of the Anglo-Iranian oil company. Washington was followed by a further spell in the Foreign Office, from September 1952 to January 1954, again dealing with Middle Eastern affairs, and a year at the Imperial Defence College, from January to December 1954. He was then posted to Paris as head of chancery at the UK delegation to NATO during the period of the Suez crisis. Already a strong flavour of defence and intelligence, as well as Anglo-American relations, was beginning to characterize his career.

A posting in December 1956 to Singapore, an area he had known during the war, enabled Greenhill to travel widely in south-east Asia and get a broader view of British diplomatic missions—invaluable to him when he later became head of the service. After returning to London in January 1959 he handled liaison between the Foreign Office and the intelligence services, and then in October 1959 he was again posted to Washington, this time as counsellor and head of chancery. His five-year period in Washington was by any standard eventful. He attended the meeting at Key West in 1961 at which the prime minister, Harold Macmillan, established a useful working relationship with the much younger President Kennedy. He was also present during the Cuban missile crisis. His contribution to the work of the mission was recognized by his

being made CMG in 1960 and by an unusual promotion *sur place* from counsellor to minister.

In 1964 Greenhill returned to London as an assistant under-secretary in the Foreign Office. He was again promoted *sur place*, in 1966, to deputy under-secretary of state. Once again his responsibilities included defence and intelligence matters. He was made KCMG in 1967. He had always been considered good at dealing with ministers: powerful in argument, but skilful in avoiding giving offence. His most testing experience in this regard came at this stage of his career, when George Brown became foreign secretary and took a strong aversion to many whom he considered patronizing 'mandarins'. Partly because of Greenhill's easy manner and professionalism, and partly (according to Richard Crossman) because Brown mistakenly believed that Greenhill's father had been an engine driver, Brown found he could work well with Greenhill. He first offered him the job of head of one of the intelligence organizations, and then in 1968—much to the surprise of many more senior colleagues—nominated him to succeed Sir Paul Gore-Booth as permanent under-secretary of state at the Foreign Office. The appointment was the more surprising as Greenhill had never been an ambassador anywhere. Despite raised eyebrows in the cabinet, Harold Wilson confirmed the appointment.

In October 1968 the Foreign and Commonwealth departments were amalgamated and in February 1969 Greenhill succeeded Gore-Booth as head of the combined Foreign and Commonwealth Office with the title of head of the diplomatic service. Problems were not long in emerging, the 'Soames affair' (in which President de Gaulle accused the British of leaking the report of a private conversation between himself and Christopher Soames, the British ambassador in Paris) being among the first to require his tactful handling. Rhodesian unilateral independence was also a pressing problem, and Greenhill accompanied Harold Wilson to his fruitless talks with Ian Smith on HMS *Fearless*.

When the Conservative government led by Edward Heath came into office in June 1970, Greenhill found he could get on easily and well with Sir Alec Douglas-Home, the new foreign secretary. He worked hard and successfully to achieve Britain's acceptance into the European Community. But as always it was defence and intelligence questions that took up much of his time and effort. He went to Moscow to urge Gromeko to reduce the number and change the character of Soviet officials at their embassy in London, and when his representations fell on deaf ears he masterminded in 1971 the expulsion of 105 suspected Soviet spies from the embassy, thus dealing a body blow to communist intelligence-gathering in the UK, and provoking what he described as the Soviet Union's 'general beastliness' (*The Guardian*, 11 Nov 2000). While thus engaged in matters of state, he also managed to find the time and goodwill to preside benignly over the amalgamated departments of state, and he handled as benevolently as he could the necessary declaration of thirty senior diplomats as redundant—something that had never happened before. He was advanced to GCMG in 1972 and retired in November 1973. In the following year he was created a life peer as Baron Greenhill of Harrow and took his seat on the cross-benches in the upper house.

After his retirement Greenhill took on a wide variety of paid and unpaid jobs. He became, from 1973 to 1978, one of the two government nominees to the board of British Petroleum, a task made the more difficult by allegations that BP was disregarding the oil embargo on Ian Smith's Rhodesia. He was also a director of British American Tobacco, the merchant banking firm of S. G. Warburg, the Clerical Medical and General Life Assurance Company, the Wellcome Foundation, the Hawker Siddeley Group, and Leyland International. He was a governor of the BBC (1973–8) and a member of the security commission (1973–82). On all these boards and committees his wide experience of both the public and the private sectors, and his robust good sense and lively good humour, made him a valued contributor to debate and to decisions.

Along with all these activities Greenhill managed to find time to be active in the House of Lords, where he was on several select committees, mostly concerned with the EC. He also found time to write an autobiographical work—*More by Accident* (1992)—a mixture of commentary on the diplomatic history of his time and more light-hearted anecdotes. He wrote regularly to the press on matters that caused him concern, and on which, while in government service, he had had to remain silent. He looked increasingly frail during the last year or two of his life, and he died in London on 8 November 2000, survived by his wife Angela and the elder of their two sons. The premature death of their younger son some years before had been a source of deep grief.

Greenhill never sought to be a high-profile public servant, and in many respects his influence on policy and the management of the diplomatic service of which he became the head were far greater than was appreciated by those outside Westminster and Whitehall. A lugubrious exterior belied a jocular spirit. His appointment to the top post in the Foreign and Commonwealth Office was unexpected on a number of grounds: not only had he no ambassadorial experience, but there were many colleagues ahead of him in seniority and fame, and many with more distinguished social backgrounds and more brilliant academic achievements. It was a measure of the man that his preferment was never resented in a service where critical assessment of contemporaries was a well-developed professional pastime.   JOHN URE

Sources Lord Greenhill, *More by accident* (1992) · *The Guardian* (11 Nov 2000) · *The Times* (13 Nov 2000) · *The Independent* (15 Nov 2000) · Burke, *Peerage* · *WWW* · *FO List* (1960) · private information (2004) · personal knowledge (2004) · b. cert.

Archives PRO, Foreign Office files, FO 371, etc.

Likenesses photograph, repro. in *The Guardian* · photograph, repro. in *The Times* · photograph, repro. in *The Independent*

Wealth at death £754,515—gross; £754,515—net: probate, 25 May 2001, *CGPLA Eng. & Wales*

Greenhill, Henry (1646–1708). *See under* Greenhill, John (1644–1676).

Greenhill, John (1644–1676), portrait painter, was born in Salisbury, the eldest son of John Greenhill, a merchant and later registrar to the diocese of Salisbury, and Penelope Champreys of Orchardleigh, Somerset. His grandfather was Henry Greenhill of Steeple Ashton, Wiltshire. The Greenhills had been a prosperous family through East Indies trade and the English wool trade, but at the time of John Greenhill junior's birth, the family was not as prosperous as formerly. Greenhill's artistic training is unknown, but his first work was reputedly a portrait of his paternal uncle, James Abbot of Salisbury. The date he left Salisbury for London is also unknown, but a letter home dated 7 October 1662 shows that he was already a member of the Covent Garden studio and household of Peter Lely, Charles II's principal painter. Talented, by all accounts very hard working and considered to be 'the most excellent of Lely's disciples' (Vertue, *Note books*, 2.148), he was not surprisingly influenced by Lely's style of painting, although showing greater directness than Lely, as well as the earlier work of Van Dyck. According to Vertue, his copy after Van Dyck's *Killigrew with a Dog* was so skilful it was impossible to distinguish from the original. At some point soon after this he left Lely's studio—Vertue claimed that Lely had become jealous of his pupil's skill and reputation—and established his own independent practice. Although he painted a wide variety of sitters, such as James, duke of York (Dulwich Picture Gallery, London) and John Locke, a close friend of his brother-in-law, and his fellow west countrymen Bishop Seth Ward (Salisbury town hall) and Anthony Ashley, earl of Shaftesbury, both on a number of occasions, many of his sitters were actors and playwrights. He was a close friend of Thomas Betterton, considered by many to be the Restoration theatre's greatest actor, and five of Greenhill's portraits were listed in the 1710 sale catalogue of Betterton's collection, including a chalk drawing of Betterton as Solyman in Davenant's *Siege of Rhodes* (Kingston Lacy, Dorset). This and a similar drawing produced the following year in 1664, of fellow actor Henry Harris as Wolsey in *Henry VIII* (Magdalen College, Oxford), are among the earliest representations of actors in costume. Greenhill may well have been introduced to the new vogue for producing portraits in chalk while in Lely's studio, but in contrast to Lely's more monochromatic works, Greenhill's are closer in style to the more coloured studies of Edmund Ashfield and Edward Luttrell. According to the artist Thomas Gibson, these 'Heads done in Crayons' and other examples such as *Sir Thomas and Lady Twisden* (print room, BM), were done 'with great skill and perfection' and 'equal to any master whatever' (Vertue, *Note books*, 4.86). Three pastel drawings, now lost, were displayed in glass and belonged to the theatre manager William Cartwright, who also owned, as part of an album, other drawings by Greenhill and six oil paintings (all still part of the collection of Dulwich Picture Gallery) including a *Self-Portrait* (c.1665) based on Van Dyck's *Self-Portrait with a Sunflower* (priv. coll.); a three-quarter-length portrait of William Cartwright with his dog, again based on a Van Dyck, this time his portrait of Killigrew which, as noted above, Greenhill had famously

John Greenhill (1644–1676), self-portrait, before 1665?

copied; a *Portrait of a Lady with a Sheep* (called 'The First Mrs Cartwright' which is impossible as she died in May 1652); and *Mrs Cartwright in a Painted Oval*. Their characteristic directness and sometimes awkward placing of hands gave way to a more continental baroque style in the next decade, although Lely's sense of design is still clearly seen in works of this later period, for example *Thomas Herbert, Later 8th Earl of Pembroke* (NPG), of which there is also a version at Wilton House, Wiltshire. Many of his portraits were engraved, for example the earl of Shaftesbury by Abraham Blooteling; John Locke, who praised Greenhill in verse, by Pieter van Gunst; and mezzotints by Francis Place were produced after his chalk drawings of Philip Woolrich (print room, BM) and the actor Henry Harris. His portrait of Sir William Davenant, manager of the Duke's Company, is now known only through Faithorne's engraving which formed the frontispiece to Davenant's *Works* of 1672. Greenhill himself experimented with printmaking; in 1667 he made an etching of his brother Henry (print room, BM), impressions of which were probably given as private gifts to family and friends rather than made as a commercial venture.

At the beginning of his career Greenhill was reputedly very ambitious and his *Self-Portrait* mentioned above shows a serious young man gazing steadily at the viewer. Contemporaries remarked on how an increasingly dissolute lifestyle affected his artistic output and damaged his reputation, but in April 1676, just one month from his early death, he was still considered one of the country's leading portrait painters. On that occasion the Painter–Stainers' Company commissioned him to paint the second duchess of York, with the commissions to paint the

other members of the royal family, the king, the queen, and the duke of York, given to Lely, Huysmans, and Wright respectively. Greenhill's commission was never realized as on 19 May 1676, returning home drunk from the Vine tavern, he fell into a gutter in Long Acre and died shortly afterwards at his lodgings in Lincoln's Inn Fields, the house of the artist and dealer Parry Walton. He left a widow, to whom Lely paid an annuity, and a young family. He was buried at St Giles-in-the-Fields, described in an epitaph written by his friend the writer Aphra Behn as 'The famous Greenhill'. Another writer, Bainbrigg Buckeridge, wrote in his 'Essay towards an English school' of 1706 that:

> had he not died young, the Effect of his too free Living, England might have boasted a Painter who according to his Beginnings, could not have been much inferior to the very best of Foreigners … whom we have always so much encourag'd in the Portrait way. (Buckeridge, 426)

Henry Greenhill (1646–1708), younger brother of John Greenhill, born at Salisbury on 21 June 1646, distinguished himself in the merchant service in the West Indies, and was rewarded by the admiralty. He was appointed by the Royal African Company governor of the Gold Coast. In 1685 he was elected an elder brother of Trinity House, in 1689 commissioner of the transport office, and in 1691 one of the principal commissioners of the navy. The building of Plymouth Dockyard was completed under his direction. He received a mourning ring under Samuel Pepys's will. He died on 24 May 1708, and was buried at Stockton, Wiltshire, where there is a monument to his memory.

DIANA DETHLOFF

Sources Vertue, *Note books*, 2.148; 4.86 · M. Whinney and O. Millar, *English art, 1625–1714* (1957) · [B. Buckeridge], 'An essay towards an English school of painters', in R. de Piles, *The art of painting, and the lives of the painters* (1706), 398–480, esp. 426 · L. Stainton and C. White, *Drawing in England from Hilliard to Hogarth* (1987) [exhibition catalogue, BM] · A. Griffiths and R. A. Gerard, *The print in Stuart Britain, 1603–1689* (1998) [exhibition catalogue, BM, 8 May – 20 Sept 1998] · *Mr Cartwright's pictures: a seventeenth century collection* [1987] [exhibition catalogue, Dulwich Picture Gallery, London, 25 Nov 1987–28 Feb 1988] · R. Jeffree, 'Greenhill, John', *The dictionary of art*, ed. J. Turner (1996)

Likenesses J. Greenhill, self-portrait, oils, probably before 1665, Dulwich Picture Gallery, London [*see illus.*] · J. Greenhill, chalk drawing, BM · P. Lely, pastel drawing, BM

Greenhill, Joseph (1704–1788), Church of England clergyman and religious controversialist, was born at Abbots Langley, Hertfordshire, in February 1704 and baptized there on 21 February, the son of William Greenhill, counsellor-at-law (one of a family of thirty-nine children by the same father and mother), and his wife, Mary. He was educated at Westminster School from April 1718 and entered Sidney Sussex College, Cambridge, on 12 February 1723, where he graduated BA in 1726–7 and was admitted MA in 1731. He was ordained and appointed rector of East Horsley in 1727, and of East Clandon—also in Surrey—in 1732, both small livings in terms of number of parishioners and financial rewards. He resided for the rest of his life at East Horsley.

The public events of the 1750s provoked Greenhill to disturb the leisured style of a country life 'alloted by him to be spent in a Manner agreeable' (Greenhill, *Essay*, v). He was distressed in turn by the Jewish Naturalization Act; the Marriage Act; the spread of the practice of inoculation; the outbreak of the Seven Years' War; and the Militia Act. He responded to the 'important Situation of Public Affairs' (Greenhill, *Sermon*, 3) with a succession of published sermons and essays. The first of these, *An Essay on the Prophecies* (1755), attacked the idea that the millennium and the rule of Christ's saints on earth was still to come, suggesting instead that it lay in the past and that current events were 'Tokens of some signal Judgment of God drawing near' (ibid., 2). In the course of his exegetical argument he aimed attacks at Bishop Benjamin Hoadly; Samuel Clarke; the regicides; those who thought that there might be millenarian justification for the readmission of the Jews to England; and those who defended clandestine marriage. The *Essay* had gone through eight editions, with frequent enlargements, by 1778. The second edition was dedicated to Greenhill's patron, Peter King, third Baron King, and the eighth to 'that Most Reformed Church', the Church of England. In later editions he widened his attacks to take in the Quakers, and continued to assert the need for meetings of convocation. He appended *A Sermon on the Millennium*, which had five editions by 1774, to the *Essay*. In 1756 he published *A Sermon: Inoculation a Presumptuous Practice Destructive to Man* (which was reprinted at Canterbury in 1777), and he continued to combat this 'destructive Piece of Quackery' and its proponents, especially the members of the Sutton family, in *Occasional Letters on the Practice of Inoculation* ([1767]; p. 5). Greenhill deplored the idea of a standing army and asserted the importance of restoring the health of the Church of England to enable it to play the role of the militant church of Christ at the end of days. By the late 1760s, however, he began to express exasperation at the ridicule that his work excited and to display frustration at the failure of newspapers to take up his crusades. He published a *Sermon on Christian Duty in Patiently and Chearfully Waiting at All Times for Salvation* in 1773. He died at East Horsley on 10 March 1788, having given instructions that he should be buried in the churchyard there.   SCOTT MANDELBROTE

Sources J. Greenhill, *An essay on the prophecies of the New Testament* (1755); 2nd edn (1759); 8th edn (1778) · J. Greenhill, *A sermon preached on the Sunday preceding the fast-day, February 11, 1757* (1757) · [J. Greenhill], *Occasional letters on the practice of inoculation* [1767] · will, PRO, PROB 11/1164, fols. 336v–337r · Venn, *Alum. Cant.*, 1/2.260 · O. Manning and W. Bray, *The history and antiquities of the county of Surrey*, 3 (1814), 35 · *Old Westminsters*, 1.397 · *IGI* · *DNB*
Wealth at death over £300 in bequests; estates in Norfolk: will, PRO, PROB 11/1164, fols. 336v–337r

Greenhill, Thomas (*fl.* 1698–1732), surgeon and author, was the son of William Greenhill (*d.* 1681) of Greenhill, in Harrow, Middlesex, counsellor-at-law and secretary to General Monck, and Elizabeth, daughter of John Jones, of London. Most of the basic details of his life are a matter for conjecture. Essential parish papers have been mutilated, so his birth date remains obscure, but he was probably not born in 1681 as has been suggested. Papers concerning his

family shed no direct light on his education, practice, family, or death. He lived in London, in King Street, Bloomsbury and there is evidence of his son Thomas's being apprenticed to him in 1732. The fecundity of Greenhill's mother has been one source of his reputation. She apparently had, with Greenhill's father, thirty-nine children, all born alive and baptized, and all single births except one. In 1698, Greenhill, as the thirty-ninth child, applied to the College of Arms for an addition to be made to the arms of the family, in commemoration of this extraordinary case. His application was successful.

Greenhill's reputation as an author is entirely based upon his *Nekrokēdeia, or, The art of embalming; wherein is shewn the right of burial, and funeral ceremonies, especially that of preserving bodies after the Egyptian method* (1705). Two small articles in the *Philosophical Transactions* of 1700 and 1705 on medical curiosities are insignificant by comparison. Greenhill's central purpose was to reverse the decline of embalming by advocating its restoration within aristocratic burial practices, and by making it the exclusive preserve of surgeons, rather than undertakers and quacks. He proceeded as an antiquary, making his theological, historical, and anthropological arguments with extensive reference to classical texts, patristics, and the scriptures. The work is dedicated to Thomas, eighth earl of Pembroke, who was the dedicatee of John Locke's *An Essay Concerning Human Understanding* (1690). Paid for by subscription, the essay enjoyed the patronage of notable dignitaries, including the archbishop of Canterbury, Thomas Tenison. London's medical men also gave the project crucial support; from 217 subscribers, 34 were surgeons, 18 physicians, and 12 apothecaries. The book is divided into three letters. The first is addressed to Charles Bernard, serjeant surgeon to Queen Anne, on the rites of burial and funeral customs. The second, which is addressed to John Lawson, a former president of the Royal College of Physicians and accomplished orientalist, discusses Egyptian embalming techniques within a rich cultural and geographical account of the country. The last letter, addressed to Hans Sloane, a leading physician and secretary to the Royal Society, is 'a succinct Account of the *Pyramids*, Subterranean Vaults and Lamps of the Egyptians' (Greenhill, 308).

The book was abstracted in the *Philosophical Transactions* of 1705. It is prefaced by introductory poems that champion Greenhill's achievement. Yet posterity has not been kind to him. Occasional antiquarian interest aside, embalming continued to decline profoundly despite Greenhill's efforts; no other book was published explicitly on the subject in English during the eighteenth century. Greenhill himself had recognized that the practice had become deeply unpopular. Aristocrats were favouring night-time funerals which avoided embalming, probably from a mixture of religious concerns, fears of live dissection, and, in the case of women, scruples about erotic impropriety. Although *Nekrokēdeia* is mentioned in the article on embalming in the *Encyclopédie* (1755), Greenhill's efforts were implicitly dismissed as useless by William Hunter, a founding father of modern embalming. When the *Gentleman's Magazine* requested information on Greenhill in 1805, there was no reply. Historians have largely reinforced Greenhill's anonymity. Yet, *Nekrokēdeia* is a lovely object, the illustrations are fine, and Greenhill's scholarship is impressive. It offers rich evidence on attitudes to death, of early eighteenth-century antiquarianism and Egyptology, and the medical politics of the day, in an accessible and interesting blend.

L. A. F. DAVIDSON

Sources T. Greenhill, *Nekrokēdeia, or, The art of embalming* (1705) · G. Grazebrook, 'A heraldic and physiological curiosity', *Miscellanea Genealogica et Heraldica*, 3rd ser., 5 (1902–3), 296–9 · C. Gittings, *Death, burial and the individual in early modern England* (1984) · J. Litten, *The English way of death: the common funeral since 1450* (1991) · *N&Q*, 5th ser., 9 (1878), 468, 512 · *GM*, 1st ser., 75 (1805), 405 · Le chevalier de Jaucourt, 'Embaumeurs', *Encyclopédie, ou, Dictionnaire raisonné des sciences, des arts et des métiers*, 5 (Paris, 1755), 552–5 · P. Ariès, *The hour of our death* (1981), 363 · W. Hunter, 'The art of embalming dead bodies', in Lectures on anatomy, Royal College of Surgeons MSS 526–544 · GL, Greenhill family of London, MS 16905–23 · P. J. Wallis and R. V. Wallis, *Eighteenth century medics*, 2nd edn (1988) · *DNB*

Archives GL

Likenesses Nutting, engraving (after T. Murray), Wellcome L.; repro. in Greenhill, *Nekrokēdeia*, frontispiece

Greenhill, William (1597/8–1671), Independent minister, was probably the son of John Greenhill, husbandman, of Harrow on the Hill, Middlesex. After studying at Harlington School, Middlesex, Greenhill was admitted at age seventeen to Gonville and Caius College, Cambridge, on 26 June 1615. He graduated BA in 1619 and proceeded MA in 1622, having attained facility in Hebrew, Greek, Latin, classical history, and theology. Ordained at Lincoln on 21 December 1628, he became rector of Oakley, Suffolk, on 20 February 1629. In the 1620s, with his friend Jeremiah Burroughs, who had been at Emmanuel College while he was at Caius, Greenhill visited London to hear noted preachers. His puritan convictions were probably shaped by John Preston, whom he would have known at Cambridge and with whom he corresponded until the latter's death in 1628. To his patron, Jane, Lady Bacon, he complained about the king's orders in December 1629 that catechism classes should replace afternoon sermons and that lecturers should use the Book of Common Prayer and wear the surplice. With Burroughs, Thomas Young, John Symonds, and Robert Stansby he participated in a combination lecture at Mendlesham, Suffolk, in the 1630s, and with Burroughs, William Bridge, and Robert Peck in the lectureship at St George's Tombland, Norwich. Matthew Wren, bishop of Norwich, deprived Greenhill in 1636 for refusing to read the Book of Sports.

Greenhill and Burroughs then went to Rotterdam, where they worshipped in the Independent church with Bridge, Sydrach Simpson, and others. Disguised as soldiers, Greenhill and Burroughs returned to England in the autumn of 1637, landing at Great Yarmouth with several barrels full of seditious books, including John Bastwick's *Letany*. Miles Corbett, the future regicide, gave them shelter.

By 1641 Greenhill had settled in London. On 6 September of that year the House of Commons approved a petition from Stepney residents to employ lecturers at their own expense. The petition was presented by Sir Gilbert Gerard, brother-in-law of Sir Thomas Barrington, with whose mother, Joan, Lady Barrington, Greenhill corresponded; the first appointees were Greenhill and Burroughs. Greenhill preached at St Pancras, Soper Lane, the next year, as did William Carter. Also in 1642 Greenhill, Burroughs, and Hugh Peter supported the 'additional sea adventure', whose architects, including the earl of Warwick, Lord Brooke, and Viscount Saye and Sele, sent a military expedition to Ireland in an attempt to quell the rebellion; they planned to recompense financial backers with 2.5 million acres of Irish land. When civil war erupted in England, Greenhill supported parliament. His first parliamentary fast sermon, preached to the Commons on 26 April 1643 and published as *The Axe at the Root* (1643), took as its text Matthew 3: 10 and warned that the axe of divine judgement had been wielded because of idolatry, profaning the sabbath, injustice, and immorality. Greenhill urged parliament to enforce justice, implement reforms, and defend Magna Carta, the petition of right, and parliamentary privileges. 'You are a free Parliament, preserve your freedome, our Laws and Liberties are in your hands' (*The Axe at the Root*, 38). Greenhill subsequently preached a fast sermon to the Lords on 31 December 1645 and a thanksgiving sermon to the Commons on 29 August 1649.

The breakdown of royal authority facilitated the expansion of separatist congregations, discomfiting both presbyterians and Independents. Greenhill joined presbyterians such as Stephen Marshall and William Twisse and Independents such as Bridge, Burroughs, Simpson, Thomas Goodwin, Philip Nye, and Joseph Caryl in issuing *Certaine Considerations to Diswade Men from Further Gathering of Churches in this Present Juncture of Time* (1643), yet the following year he accepted the pastorate of a gathered congregation. Drawn from both within and outside Stepney, it included such prominent radicals as the merchant Maurice Thompson and Colonel John Okey; Anna Traphel was a well-known associate. However, meeting in the parish church, they were denounced by the sectary Katherine Chidley for worshipping in a building where idolatrous services had been conducted. As Greenhill emerged as one of the prominent London Independent leaders he worked closely with other Independent divines in the city, as in the conferences they convened when Henry Jessey embraced Baptist tenets in June 1645. Such co-operation was also manifest by his work in the Westminster assembly, where he was affiliated to the Dissenting Brethren, though, unlike Burroughs, Goodwin, Bridge, Nye, and Simpson, he was not a signatory of the 'Apologeticall narration'. With this group and William Carter, Greenhill submitted on 12 December 1644 the reasons for their opposition to presbyterian polity, but the following year they published *A Copy of a Remonstrance Lately Delivered in to the Assembly*, in which they explained why they would not provide an alternative model of congregational church government. Not only had parliament by this time already implemented a form of presbyterian polity, but the remonstrants also felt the assembly had not seriously considered their previous reports.

While serving in the Westminster assembly, Greenhill, a gifted exegete as well as a popular preacher, began his *magnum opus*, a learned commentary on Ezekiel, the first volume of which, *An Exposition of the Five First Chapters of the Prophet Ezekiel*, was published in 1645 with a dedication to Elizabeth, queen of Bohemia, reflecting an interest in her perhaps stemming from the influence of Preston, who had visited her about 1621 at The Hague. Four subsequent volumes appeared between 1649 and 1662. Discerning readers could find much of relevance to current events. In the first volume Greenhill pointedly noted that in Ezekiel's day 'a Malignant party' led by priests and false prophets had opposed the work of reformation and acted seditiously (*An Exposition*, 1.17). Now, he reflected, a similar party despised the prophets and scorned the saints. Like the ancient Jews, the people of England lived in a state of captivity, with their lives, liberties, estates, and religion in jeopardy. For their injustice, immorality, idolatrous practices, and abuse of the prophets, God would overthrow kings, councils, nobility, and gentry.

Clearly, Greenhill's views were evolving in the two decades following his ordination, for he was part of a coalition of Independents and Baptists that supported the House of Commons after it condemned the Levellers' *Agreement of the People* on 9 November 1647. The same month sixteen Independents and Baptists, including Greenhill, Jessey, Thomas Brooks, John Simpson, Christopher Feake, Hanserd Knollys, and William Kiffin, anonymously published *A declaration by congregational societies in and about the City of London, as well of those commonly called Anabaptists, as others*; an alternative title-page omitted the reference to Anabaptists. The authors defended religious liberty—indeed Greenhill was a consistent advocate of toleration—but denounced polygamy, community of property, and social levelling, positions the Levellers did not actually espouse, as William Walwyn rightly insisted.

Like John Owen, Greenhill subsequently supported Charles's execution, after which he served as chaplain to the royal children. In the ensuing years he aided the republic by recommending godly mariners for positions as naval officers—many leading officers worshipped in his Stepney congregation in the late 1640s and 1650s. In 1651 the coalition of sixteen issued another statement, *A declaration of divers elders and brethren of congregationall societies in and about the City of London*, this time including their names. In it they opposed a government based solely on the gathered churches but supported a franchise that excluded libertines, opponents of private property, and royalists. Although Greenhill and his fellow Independents were working closely with Baptists at this point, he, Nye, Caryl, William Strong, and John Dury unsuccessfully sought leniency for the presbyterian minister Christopher Love after he was found guilty of conspiring to restore the monarchy. Greenhill's network of ministerial contacts was extensive. In addition to those already noted

are those reflected in the commendatory epistles he wrote for books by Jeremiah Burroughs, William Bridge, Thomas Shepherd, Thomas Allen, Simon Moor, Samuel Eaton, and John Robotham. Such volumes had great value for Greenhill; books, he noted in his preface to Burroughs's *The Excellency of a Gracious Spirit* (1657), 'are more needful then Arms; the one defends the body, the other the soul'. Apparently his literary tastes included astrology as well as theology.

Greenhill's activities were wide ranging in the 1650s. Early in 1652 he and nine others, including Owen, Nye, Bridge, Strong, Sydrach Simpson, and George Griffith, met with a parliamentary committee to draft a statement condemning the Racovian catechism, a Socinian document. Responding to a request from the committee for the propagation of the gospel in Wales, Greenhill, Bridge, Strong, and others issued *The Humble Proposals of Mr Owen, Mr Tho Goodwin, Mr Nye and other Ministers* (1652) in which they called for two commissions to oversee the established church. While local committees examined and approved clergy, a national commission would eject unfit ministers and teachers. Greenhill's interest in Wales is reflected in the certificate he signed with Burroughs, Nye, and others commending Vavasor Powell's activities.

Greenhill also supported missionary work with Native Americans. With Marshall, Goodwin, Sydrach Simpson, Simeon Ashe, and others he had addressed a letter to parliament in 1647 endorsing such endeavours; it was subsequently published as the preface to *The Day-Breaking, if not the Sun Rising of the Gospel with the Indians in New England*. Henry Whitefield's collection of letters from New England about the conversion of Native Americans, *Strengthe out of Weaknesse* (1652), included a commendatory epistle by Greenhill, Owen, Griffith, Goodwin, and seven other Independents. Such was Greenhill's stature that Richard Baxter recommended him to Dury in May 1652 as one of four or five men from each religious group that should be convened to draft a statement on the issues that separated and united them. Greenhill in turn encouraged Dury's ecumenical endeavours.

Serving the interregnum governments brought rewards. Greenhill became vicar of Stepney on 6 October 1652, with admission under the great seal following on 2 June 1654. From 1653 to 1657 he also served as governor of Harrow School. When the nominated assembly proposed to appoint national commissioners to present and eject clergy, Greenhill was among the twenty-one who would have served. He was one of thirty-eight members of the committee for the approbation of public preachers (triers) established in March 1654, and on 24 October 1657 he was named an assistant to the Middlesex commission, which ejected unfit clergy and teachers. With Owen, Goodwin, Nye, Caryl, and Bridge he drafted a declaration of faith and order for the Savoy conference, which approved the document on 12 October 1658. After the army dissolved the restored Rump in October 1659, Greenhill and other leading Independents, concerned about George Monck's intentions, sent a delegation to Scotland to confer with him. On 13 December, Greenhill, Owen, Nye, Bridge,

Caryl, and others wrote to Monck, urging him to reach an agreement with John Lambert, but to no avail.

In 1660 Greenhill was ejected from his vicarage. Although following the Fifth Monarchist insurrection of Thomas Venner in January 1661, Greenhill and twenty-four other congregationalists denounced the rebels in *A Renuntiation and Declaration*, on 12 June cautious magistrates required Greenhill and Matthew Meade, a fellow congregationalist, to post bonds of £300 each, and the following month Greenhill's name was included on a list of dissidents with Dutch contacts compiled by Sir George Downing's clerk. But Greenhill was no threat to the government, taking no part in political activity against it, and he managed to continue ministering to his gathered congregation in Stepney, sometimes meeting in his house adjacent to the parish church, sometimes in a concealed attic. In time his flock numbered nearly 500, and in 1669 he and his assistant (and his successor in 1671) Meade, were also preaching to a conventicle of 300 in Meeting-house Alley, Wapping.

Greenhill had a low opinion of the court, as reflected in his epistle to Increase Mather's *The Mystery of Israel's Salvation* (1669), where he denounced potentates who indulged their lusts, abused their power, persecuted the good, and oppressed the poor. For the most part, Greenhill's sermons and lectures focused on strictly spiritual concerns; his lecture 'What must, and can, persons do towards their own conversion' is typical, as are the sermons in *The Sound-Hearted Christian* (1670). Obeying the second Conventicle Act (1670), he 'kept out [of his meetinghouse] and resolv'd not to offend' (PRO, SP 29/277/3). Throughout this period Greenhill worked with congregationalists in the London area, twice writing to the governor of Massachusetts in 1669, urging him to cease persecuting Baptists. On 21 August 1671 a group of magistrates and ministers in Massachusetts wrote to Greenhill and eighteen others requesting help for Harvard College.

It is not known whether Greenhill ever married. In his will, dated 23 September 1671, the principal legatees were his sister Audrey Lindsey, 'now living with me in Stepney', her son Joseph Lindsey, and a cousin, Zacharie Bourne, who received 'my library of books' in order 'to encourage [him] … to learning and to the study of divinity'. Lands in four East Anglian parishes also sustained bequests of £100 to needy ejected ministers, £30 to the poor, and small sums to a number of 'marriners', brewers, and other friends and relatives. Greenhill died four days later on 27 September and was buried on 2 October. The books he loved were auctioned on 18 February 1678.

RICHARD L. GREAVES

Sources CSP dom., 1652–3, 74; 1655–6, 37; 1655, 295; 1657–8, 108; 1659–60, 464; 1660–61, 471; 1670, 310 · Calamy rev. · Venn, Alum. Cant. · K. W. Shipps, 'Lay patronage of East Anglian puritan clerics in pre-revolutionary England', PhD diss., Yale U., 1971 · F. J. Bremer, Congregational communion: clerical friendship in the Anglo-American puritan community, 1610–1692 (1994) · R. Brenner, Merchants and revolution: commercial change, political conflict, and London's overseas traders, 1550–1653 (1993) · G. L. Turner, ed., Original records of early nonconformity under persecution and indulgence, 3 vols. (1911–14) · Essex RO, MS D/DBy C24, fol. 19 · Calendar of the Clarendon state papers preserved in the Bodleian Library, 5: 1660–1726, ed. F. J. Routledge (1970) · The correspondence of John Owen (1616–1683), ed. P. Toon (1970) · T. Webster, Godly clergy in early Stuart England: the Caroline puritan movement, c.1620–1643 (1997) · R. S. Paul, The assembly of the Lord: politics and religion in the Westminster assembly and the 'Grand debate' (1985) · PRO, PROB 11/337, fols. 241–2

Archives Essex RO, Chelmsford, letters, MS D/DBy/C24 | Bodl. Oxf., Tanner MS 68 · DWL, Baxter MSS · Worcester College, Oxford, Clarke MSS

Wealth at death land in East Anglia; left £100 to ejected ministers and £30 to the poor; many other small bequests: Calamy rev.; will, PRO, PROB 11/337, fols. 241–2

Greenhill, William Alexander (1814–1894), physician and sanitary reformer, was born at Stationers' Hall, London, on 1 January 1814, the youngest of the three sons of George Greenhill (1766–1850), secretary to the Stationers' Company, and his wife, Sarah Ann. The Greenhill family had a long-standing association with the Stationers' Company: William Alexander's grandfather Thomas had been master in 1787–8, and his father was treasurer for fifty-two years and was succeeded in that post by his brother, George. William Greenhill was educated at a private school at Edmonton and at Rugby School, which he entered in 1828, the year that Thomas Arnold became headmaster. At Rugby his chief friends were A. C. Clough, W. C. Lake, A. P. Stanley and C. J. Vaughan, all of whom, like Greenhill were deeply influenced by Arnold. He was the anonymous 'old pupil', whose letter from Arnold is printed in Dean Stanley's *Life* (1.372, 2.54, 116). In 1832 he left Rugby with an exhibition but, failing to gain a scholarship at Trinity College, Oxford, matriculated there as a commoner on 9 June 1832.

At first Greenhill enjoyed Oxford less than Rugby but the renewal of his friendship with A. P. Stanley, two years his junior, helped him to settle more comfortably into the academic and social life of the university. In 1837 he befriended the young Benjamin Jowett, giving him a gift of £20 for extra coaching. This was the foundation of a lifelong friendship. Greenhill later helped Jowett with his translation of the *Timaeus* and Jowett became godfather to Greenhill's second daughter, Catherine.

Greenhill was already resolved on a medical career, and although he passed the required examinations he took no degree in arts. He studied at the Radcliffe Infirmary, Oxford, and in 1836–7 visited Paris to gain knowledge of the hospital practice there. Not greatly impressed by the experience, he none the less gained a good knowledge in French. He graduated BM and was appointed physician to the Radcliffe in 1839; in 1840 he became DM and also married Laura (1815–1882), daughter of John Ward, collector of customs at West Cowes and Arnold's niece. They had three sons and two daughters; their eldest daughter Mary died young of pulmonary consumption, and a son died following a surgical operation while a student at Oxford.

A devout churchman with an interest in theology, Greenhill was a member of the Theological Society, founded by E. B. Pusey in 1835. Greenhill's memories of a meeting on 3 November 1837 at which John Henry Newman read a paper are recorded in H. P. Liddon's *Life of Pusey*

(1.337). Greenhill's house at 91 High Street, Oxford, was a gathering place for the society's religious and academic discussions, and he numbered among his close friends Tractarian sympathizers such as W. J. Copeland, Charles Marriott, J. B. Morris, and J. B. Mozley. Greenhill was additionally acquainted with Newman through being a parishioner of St Mary's; Newman appointed him churchwarden, an office he held at the time of Newman's resignation as vicar in 1843. Greenhill always held Newman in admiration and affection, and despite Newman's conversion they continued to correspond from time to time. However, Greenhill was never drawn into the Oxford Movement in a partisan way, and somewhat regretted later Tractarianism. In old age Dean Lake recalled that he was regarded in Oxford as having maintained an 'armed neutrality' among religious parties (Lake, 307).

Essentially an independent thinker Greenhill retained something of Arnold's theological liberalism. With Stanley, Jowett and Donkin he was one of 'the younger liberals', as Dean Church called them (p. 61); they gave moral support to the proctors to exercise their power of veto when the condemnation of Tract 90 was proposed in 1845, since they feared such a move would lead to a new test in regard to subscription to the Thirty-Nine Articles. Greenhill worked enthusiastically to elect W. E. Gladstone as a member of parliament for the university in 1847, acting as a member of his election committee. He remained a Liberal in politics throughout his life, but felt unable to support the party at the election of 1885 for fear of disestablishment and in 1886 when, as a Liberal Unionist, he could not endorse Gladstone's home-rule proposals.

By temperament a historian, Greenhill had in the 1840s turned his attention to the study of Arabic and Greek medical writers. He published a Greek and Latin edition of *The Physiology of Theophilus* (1842), an English translation from the Arabic of Rhazes, entitled *Treatise on the Small Pox and Measles* (1847), and wrote numerous articles on Greek and Roman physicians and medicine for Sir William Smith's *Dictionary of Greek and Roman Biography and Mythology* (1844–9). He also published for the Sydenham Society *Thomae Sydenham opera omnia* (2 vols., 1844 and 1846), and lives of Sir James Stonehouse (1844) and Thomas Harrison Burder MD (1845). Although a fastidious scholar his writing lacked a popular touch.

Greenhill's interest in sanitary matters began in 1849 when there was an outbreak of cholera in Oxford, and he drew up a series of important reports on public health in the city for the Ashmolean Society which included mortality tables that were copied elsewhere. In 1851 he left the Radcliffe and moved from Oxford to Hastings, chiefly on account of his health, though it is suggested in Sir B. W. Richardson's memoir that Greenhill had become weary of religious controversy in Oxford. For the next forty-three years he led a quiet though busy life in Hastings, becoming a well-known and respected citizen. He took over the practice of James Mackness and became one of the physicians at the local infirmary, and he also took an active part in the work of various local charities.

In 1855 Greenhill published 'Observations on the death-rate of Hastings' in the first volume of the *Journal of Public Health*, a subject he pursued later in the *Sussex Archaeological Collections* (vol. 14, 1862). This showed how insanitary many artisan dwellings were and what an injurious effect this had on the town, which was increasingly becoming a popular resort. To ameliorate the housing conditions in the poorer parts of Hastings, Greenhill founded the Hastings Cottage Improvement Society in 1857 and remained its secretary until 1891. A commercial venture, the society bought up, repaired, and improved old and insanitary dwellings and built new houses on modern lines. The venture was so successful that with some of the original shareholders Greenhill started a similar organization, the London Labourers' Dwelling Society (also, despite its name, based in Hastings); he was its secretary from 1862 to 1876. He also founded the Albert House Institution for Domestic Servants at St Leonards, Sussex, and helped to found the local Mendicity Society for wayfarers. In 1881, on Gladstone's recommendation, he was granted a civil-list pension of £60.

Greenhill devoted his spare time to the study of the writings of Sir Thomas Browne, and published Browne's 'Religio medici', 'Christian morals', and 'A letter to a friend' in Macmillan's Golden Treasury series in 1881. This was not superseded as regards its annotation until the 1960s. At the time of his death Greenhill was engaged in an edition of Browne's 'Hydriotaphia' and his 'Garden of Cyrus', which was completed by his friend E. H. Marshall and issued in the Golden Treasury series in 1896. Greenhill was also a member of the editorial staff of the *British Medical Journal* and a frequent contributor.

Greenhill was a handsome man with a peculiarly pleasant voice. He had a deep but restrained piety and an intense sense of duty. He could be candid in controversy and somewhat severe in manner, but was widely respected for his philanthropic endeavour and genuine humility. He died suddenly at his residence, The Croft, Hastings, from syncope, on 19 September 1894, and was buried in the borough cemetery on 22 September. A memorial tablet in St Clement's, his parish church, refers to a surviving son and daughter. PERRY BUTLER

Sources B. W. Richardson, 'Memoirs', *The Asclepiad*, 2nd ser., 11 (1894), 165–89 · *The Athenaeum* (29 Sept 1894), 421–2 · *The Guardian* (26 Sept 1984), 1451 · *The Lancet* (29 Sept 1894), 748 · *BMJ* (29 Sept 1894), 734 · A. P. Stanley, *The life and correspondence of Thomas Arnold ... of Rugby School*, 2 vols. (1844) · H. P. Liddon, *The life of Edward Bouverie Pusey*, ed. J. O. Johnston and others, 4 vols. (1893–7), vol. 1 · K. Lake, ed., *Memorials of William Charles Lake, dean of Durham, 1869–1894* (1901) · *Life and letters of Dean Church*, ed. M. C. Church (1895) · *Hastings and St Leonards Times* (22 Sept 1894) · *Hastings and St Leonards News* (21 Sept 1894), 5 · *DNB* · census returns, 1851

Archives Bodl. Oxf., corresp. · RCP Lond., corresp. and papers · Trinity College, Oxford, corresp. | Oriel College, Oxford, letters to J. H. Newman and others · Pusey Oxf., letters to Pusey · U. Leeds, Brotherton L., letters to Thomas Arnold · UCL, SDUK MSS, letters to SDUK

Likenesses A. E. L. Rosti, bust, Trinity College, Oxford · autotype (after photograph), repro. in Richardson, *Memoirs*, 165

Greenhow, Edward Headlam (1814–1888), epidemiologist and physician, was born in North Shields, Northumberland, the son of Edward Greenhow, physician, of

North Shields, and nephew of T. M. Greenhow MD FRCS (1791–1881), surgeon for many years to the Newcastle Infirmary, a notable operator and sanitary reformer (*BMJ*, 1881, 799). After attending schools in North Shields he studied medicine at Edinburgh and Montpellier universities, and then practised for eighteen years in partnership with his father in North Shields and Tynemouth. On 24 October 1842 he married Elizabeth (*d.* 1857), daughter of John Weston, a sailor, and widow of William Barnard; their son, Edward, was later ordained. In 1852 Greenhow graduated MD at Aberdeen, and in 1853 settled in London. After Elizabeth's death, in 1862 he married Eliza Burnley, daughter of Joseph *Hume MP; she died in 1878, their two daughters surviving her.

In 1856 Greenhow was appointed lecturer on public health at St Thomas's Hospital, and he joined the medical school of the Middlesex Hospital as assistant physician and joint lecturer on medical jurisprudence in 1861. He became full physician to the Middlesex in 1870 and lecturer on medicine in 1871. He was an enthusiastic supporter of the medical school, acting as dean in 1868, and treasurer in 1870. In 1875 he delivered the Croonian lectures at the Royal College of Physicians, on Addison's disease. The Clinical Society was founded in 1867, mainly by his exertions; he was its treasurer from its foundation until 1879, when he became president. He was a zealous and successful teacher and researcher, and an excellent and thoroughgoing man of business.

Greenhow's later career fell into two phases: the years 1856–61, when his principal interest was in public health; and 1861–81, following his appointment to the Middlesex, when he was an active consulting physician. From 1856 he reported frequently on epidemics and questions of public health to the Board of Health and to the privy council, and he served on several royal commissions. Recruited into government service by John Simon in 1857, he also undertook pioneering epidemiological studies which established the pattern of much of the health department's later work. In particular his inquiry into the different proportions of deaths produced by certain diseases in different districts of England marked a new approach to public health problems by attempting systematically to collate and compare statistical information on mortality. Not only did this report lead to further such studies under Simon's direction, but it also led to the compilation and publication by the General Register Office of its series of decennial reports. Greenhow also contributed important studies on diphtheria, diarrhoeal diseases, infant mortality, and the incidence of respiratory disease in English industrial districts. As a clinician Greenhow was distinguished both for his work on Addison's disease and for his continued research into pulmonary disease among factory workers. He published many papers on a variety of subjects, notably on diphtheria and on chronic bronchitis.

Greenhow was a clubbable character but also a man of great energy and determination. He was widely respected for a methodical, disciplined approach in all his undertakings. Twice widowed he retired in 1881 to Reigate, Surrey.

Greenhow died suddenly from heart disease in the waiting room at Charing Cross Station on 22 November 1888, on his return from a meeting of the pension commutation board, to which he was medical officer.

G. T. Bettany, *rev.* Anne Hardy

Sources *The Lancet* (1 Dec 1888), 1104–6 • C. F. Brockington, 'Public health at the privy council', *Medical Officer*, 101 (1959), 212–13 • *BMJ* (1 Dec 1888), 1249–50 • Munk, *Roll* • *The Lancet* (21 Nov 1857), 536 • m. cert. • d. cert.
Wealth at death £6262 7s.: probate, 22 Dec 1888, *CGPLA Eng. & Wales*

Greenidge, Abel Hendy Jones (1865–1906), ancient historian, second son of Nathaniel Heath Greenidge and his wife, Elizabeth Cragg Kellman, was born on 22 December 1865 at Belle Farm estate, Barbados, in which island his father's family had been settled since 1635. His father, for many years vicar of Boscobel parish, was afterwards headmaster of various schools, and enjoyed a high reputation as a teacher.

Greenidge was educated at Harrison College, Barbados, winning in 1884 the Barbados scholarship, and in the same year (on 15 October) matriculating at Balliol College, Oxford. Elected to an exhibition in the following year, he was placed in the first class both in classical moderations in 1886 and in the final classical school in 1888. He graduated BA in the same year, and proceeded MA in 1891 and DLitt in 1904.

On 5 December 1889 Greenidge was elected, after examination, fellow of Hertford College. He became lecturer there in 1892 and tutor in 1902, and he retained these offices until his death. He was also lecturer in ancient history at Brasenose College from 1892 to 1905. He married on 29 June 1895 Edith Elizabeth, youngest daughter of William Lucy of Oxford, and they had two sons. Hertford's fellowships remained closed to married men, and he was obliged to vacate his fellowship. It was to be ten years before he secured another. In the meantime he faced considerable financial hardship, the worry of which took a severe toll of his health.

George Beardoe Grundy, tutor in ancient history at Brasenose College, 1904–17, thought Greenidge 'one of the best and most conscientious men' he had ever known and wondered why, given the excellence of Greenidge's teaching, he was not given a fellowship at Brasenose. Grundy could only surmise that members of the governing body there were opposed to any who showed 'a disposition to fill in their leisure time with research', and that Greenidge was suspected 'of a tendency that way' (Grundy, 80). An obituary notice observed that Greenidge had 'a zeal for research, which occupied in his life most of the time and enthusiasm which the majority of men feel compelled to bestow upon a variety of interests' (*Oxford Magazine*, 24/16, 287). He had a remarkably wide range of contacts with German, French, and Italian scholars. His 'extraordinary unselfishness' (ibid.) was eventually recognized when he was elected, with Henry Pelham's support, to an official fellowship at St John's College, on 29 June 1905. This, however, came too late to be of any real benefit to him. He died suddenly from a heart attack at his home,

4 Blackhall Road, Oxford, on 11 March 1906, and was buried in Holywell cemetery. On 28 March 1907 a civil-list pension of £75 was granted to his widow 'in consideration of his services to the study of Roman law and history'. Edith Greenidge, though, had shared fully the anxiety and trials of her husband's later years, and she died 'broken-hearted' (ibid.) on 9 July 1907.

In spite of his early death, and his diligently undertaking all the ancient history work of two colleges, Greenidge's literary work was notable for its quality and quantity. Shortly after graduating he contributed numerous articles to a new edition of *Smith's Dictionary of Antiquities* (1890–91). His first book, *Infamia, its Place in Roman Public and Private Law*, was published at Oxford in 1894. There followed *A Handbook of Greek Constitutional History* (1896); *Roman Public Life* (1901); and *The Legal Procedure of Cicero's Time* (1901), which was the most important of Greenidge's completed works. He also revised Sir William Smith's *History of Rome* (1897), and the first part (down to the death of Justinian) of the *Student's Gibbon* (1899). In 1903, in co-operation with Agnes Muriel Clay, a tutor at Lady Margaret Hall, he produced *Sources for Roman History, B.C. 133–70* designed to prepare the way for a new *History of Rome*. In 1904 he contributed a historical introduction to the fourth edition of Poste's *Gaius*. In the same year appeared the first volume of *A History of Rome during the Later Republic and Early Principate*, covering the years 133 to 104 BC. This work was designed to extend to the accession of Vespasian and to fill six volumes, but no second volume was issued. Much of Greenidge's most interesting work was in scattered articles, more particularly in the *Classical Review*. His merit as a historian lay in his accurate accumulation of detail, combined with critical insight and power of exposition, which were not unmixed with occasional paradox.

R. W. LEE, *rev.* MARK POTTLE

Sources private information (1912) · *Journal of Comparative Legislation*, new ser., 7/1, 282 · *Oxford Magazine* (14 March 1906) · *Oxford Magazine* (25 April 1906) · *The Times* (12 March 1906) · G. B. Grundy, *Fifty-five years at Oxford: an unconventional autobiography* (1945) · O. Murray, 'The beginnings of Greats, 1800–1872: ancient history', *Hist. U. Oxf.* 6: *19th-cent. Oxf.*, 520–42 · *CGPLA Eng. & Wales* (1906)
Likenesses oils, Harrison College, Barbados
Wealth at death £3762 4s. 1d.: probate, 28 April 1906, *CGPLA Eng. & Wales*

Greening, Edward Owen (1836–1923), co-operative movement activist and social reformer, was born on 17 August 1836 at Warrington, Lancashire. His father owned a small wire-drawing factory, and the family moved to Manchester in Edward's early years. There he attended the Quaker school in Mount Street and remained influenced by Quaker teachings all his life, although for most of his adult years he seems to have belonged to the Unitarian church.

Greening left school at thirteen and was apprenticed to the wire-working trade. In his middle teens he moved into office work, began to attend evening classes to remedy the deficiencies in his formal education, and at seventeen became involved in the Anti-Slavery Society, a Manchester organization which collected funds for the abolitionist

movement in America. He also joined the temperance movement and later served on the executive committee of the United Kingdom Alliance.

Manchester was a major centre of support for the Northern cause in the American Civil War and it marked an important stage in Greening's intellectual and political development. He was a founder member of the Union and Emancipation Society, and served as one of its two honorary secretaries. He lectured in many parts of the country in support of the north and was a prolific correspondent and writer in the local and regional press, and, to a lesser extent, in national papers such as the *Daily News*. His own political views moved steadily to the radical wing of the Liberal Party, and he helped to establish the Manchester and Salford Manhood League, a regional section of the Reform League, remaining closely involved in the suffrage agitation until the passing of the 1867 Reform Act. He was also becoming involved in the growing co-operative movement, and was working with the leading personalities at the national level, including G. J. Holyoake, E. T. Craig, Lloyd Jones, and Thomas Hughes.

Greening's only direct intervention in politics was in 1868, when he was invited to stand for Halifax by a group of local radicals in the general election. Halifax was a two-member constituency, and one of the sitting MPs was a local industrialist, a conservative whig much disliked by the radicals. Greening joined forces with the other candidate, James Stansfeld, a friend of Mazzini and Garibaldi, and although unsuccessful he gained 2802 votes.

For the rest of his long life Greening worked within the various organizations of the co-operative movement. In 1868 he founded the Agricultural and Horticultural Association, popularly known as the One and All. He became its managing director and, as it was established in London, Greening left Manchester to live in the south. The object of the new association was to supply agricultural requirements—tools, seeds, manure—on co-operative principles, and in its early years it prospered. Greening also edited its main publications, including a widely circulated *One and All Gardening Annual*. His energy was remarkable and his involvement wide-ranging: in May 1869 he had taken a central part in the organization of the first national Co-operative Congress; he was a prime mover in the annual National Co-operative Festival held at the Crystal Palace between 1886 and 1910; and he was closely involved, with G. J. Holyoake and E. V. Neale, in the formation of the International Co-operative Alliance in 1895. He was a prolific writer on co-operative affairs, a lively and much sought-after speaker, and he travelled widely at home and abroad, as he recorded in *The Co-Operative Traveller Abroad* (1888).

The co-operative movement, as it grew steadily during the third quarter of the nineteenth century, developed a range of ideas about its role and future development. In the 1870s there arose a vigorous debate on the 'bonus to labour' schemes whereby co-operative enterprises, especially those in manufacturing, should pay supplementary bonuses parallel to the dividend on purchases of the retail societies. Greening belonged to the group which favoured radical ideas for co-operative production, but they were in a minority, and with falling prices and economic depression after 1872 they were easily defeated by their more conservative opponents.

While Greening remained quite radical towards the co-operative movement, he was becoming steadily more conservative in his political ideas as the end of the century approached. The emergence of socialist ideas in the 1880s and the increasing demand for independent labour representation at Westminster met with his vigorous opposition and his continued adherence to the Liberal Party. Until the beginning of the First World War Co-operative Congresses rejected the calls for independent representation, although the minority views were growing steadily. The war years radically altered the position. At the 1917 Swansea congress a motion to seek 'direct representation in Parliament and on all local bodies' was agreed by an overwhelming majority. Greening and Fred Madison had moved a dismissive amendment which received only 201 votes against 1979 for the substantive resolution.

Greening's own business collapsed in 1870 and thenceforth his income came from work in and about the co-operative movement. In his last years he was in some financial difficulties and these were in part met by at least two testimonial appeals. He had first married in 1860 Emily Hepworth, and they had several children, of whom at least one, E. W. Greening, shared his father's interest in the co-operative movement. His second wife survived him. Greening died at his home at Oak Lawn, Belmont Grove, Lee, Lewisham, on 5 March 1923, and he was buried in Hither Green cemetery.   JOHN SAVILLE

Sources T. Crimes, *Edward Owen Greening: a maker of co-operation* (1923) • G. D. H. Cole, *A century of co-operation* (1945) • *DLB* • B. Jones, *Co-operative production* (1894) • S. Pollard, 'Nineteenth-century co-operation: from community building to shopkeeping', *Essays in labour history in memory of G. D. H. Cole, 25 September 1889 – 14 January 1959*, ed. A. Briggs and J. Saville (1960), 74–112 • S. Pollard, 'The foundation of the Co-operative Party', *Essays in labour history, 1886–1923*, ed. A. Briggs and J. Saville (1971), 185–210 • P. Redfern, *The story of the C.W.S.* (1913) • *Co-operative News* (10 March 1923) • *The Times* (10 March 1923) • *Kentish Mercury* (16 March 1923) • *Report of the Annual Co-operative Congress* [Co-operative Union] (1923)
Archives Co-operative Union, Manchester, Co-operative Union archive, corresp. and papers
Wealth at death £555 12s. 8d.: probate, 12 May 1923, *CGPLA Eng. & Wales*

Greenly, Edward (1861–1951), geologist, was born in Bristol on 3 December 1861, the only child of Charles Hickes Greenly (1804–1895), medical practitioner, and his wife, Harriett, née Dowling (1818–1892). He was educated at Clifton College, Bristol, and in 1883 became for three years an articled clerk to a London solicitor. His real interests, however, increasingly came to lie in science and, probably from 1886, his father paid for him to attend University College, London, where he studied chemistry. He was mainly self-taught as a geologist, and in his spare time he began an interest in geological mapping. Quite by chance he met Professor A. H. Green (1832–1896) of Leeds, to whom he showed his maps. Green recommended Greenly to the director of the Geological Survey to which he was appointed

in July 1889. He went to the northern highlands of Scotland, where he learned geological field techniques from the experienced surveyors B. N. Peach and C. T. Clough, and developed a lifelong fascination with Precambrian metamorphic rocks. On 26 September 1891 he married Annie, the fourth of the five daughters of John Barnard, dispensing chemist, of Bath, who often accompanied him on his geological work. They had no children.

Greenly resigned from the official survey in the spring of 1895 because of his wife's health. A man of modest but independent means, he spent the next fifteen years mapping the Isle of Anglesey. His meticulously accurate map and report of these mainly Precambrian rocks were 'adopted' by the Geological Survey, published in 1919 and earned him an honorary doctorate (1919) from the University of Wales, and in 1920 the Lyell medal of the Geological Society of London (of which he was a senior fellow and later vice-president).

About 1917 Greenly moved to Clevedon, Somerset, where he made valuable contributions to Precambrian, Palaeozoic, and Quaternary geology. After June 1919 he lived in Bangor, and mapped in the Arvon district, a natural extension of his studies of Anglesey and which became his final geological work. He continued his researches with vigour, having learned to drive a car at the age of seventy-five and despite the amputation of a leg three years later. He led his last field excursion to Anglesey at the age of eighty-six.

Greenly, in addition to his Anglesey memoir, was the author of over fifty geological papers, several being conceptually far ahead of their time. He also co-authored (with Howel Williams) the invaluable *Methods in Geological Surveying* (1930), and other books for the general reader.

Greenly has been aptly described as 'a gentleman of the old school, kindly, courteous and cultured'. He was a connoisseur of music, especially Beethoven's piano works, poetry, and literature (in several languages). All the field sketches and watercolours illustrating his geological work were his own. He was also a lover of animals, cats especially, and a vegetarian. His exquisite prose is perhaps most evident in his unusual book *A Hand through Time* (1938), which he had originally intended should not be published until after his death. This meditative and philosophical work, written after the death of his beloved wife in March 1927, is largely composed of memories of her; their relationship was unusually close and mutually inspiring. It also includes descriptions of his early days on the survey and pen portraits of the great geologists of those times. Greenly was religious in a pantheistic, nondoctrinal sense, and had a serene assurance of an immortal reunion with his wife. Greenly died at his residence at Aethwy Ridge, Bangor after a brief illness on 4 March 1951. After cremation, his ashes were interred at Llangristiolus, Anglesey.   E. N. K. CLARKSON

Sources E. Greenly, *A hand through time*, 2 vols. (1938) • D. W., *Quarterly Journal of the Geological Society of London*, 106 (1951), lxiii–lxv • *CGPLA Eng. & Wales* (1951)
Archives BGS, letters to Finlay Kitchin; letters to Herbert Thomas; notes on Anglesey

Wealth at death £23,993 14s. 6d.: probate, 31 May 1951, *CGPLA Eng. & Wales*

Greenly, Henry (1876–1947), railway engineer and writer, was born on 3 June 1876 at 20 Priory Street, Birkenhead, the first of three sons and two daughters of Edwin Greenly, railway guard, and his wife, Sophia, daughter of John Howard, the owner of a wood-turning factory in Newington Butts, south London. Henry started his education at a boarding-school in Birkenhead but in the spring of 1887 the family moved to the Queen's Park district of west London, where he continued his education at Beethoven Street School in Kilburn Lane until 1890, when he left to work in the jewellery workshops of William Whiteley of Bayswater. His stay was short and was followed by employment at the Commercial Travellers Institute and then Smith, Fawdon, and Law, solicitors.

In 1894 Greenly was awarded a London county council scholarship with distinctions, which took him to the Kenmont Gardens Science School (1894–7) and in 1896 he was awarded an evening exhibition to the Regent Street Polytechnic. The turning point in what became a distinguished career came on 22 February 1897, when he started work in the drawing-office of the Metropolitan Railway Company at Neasden works, where he pursued both mechanics and architecture, being ultimately appointed as assistant to the chief surveyor and architect.

As early as 1895 Greenly was a regular contributor to the *Engineer* and *Engineering*, taking the great engineers of the day to task over technical issues, and he soon became well known. As a result, on 15 October 1896, he was appointed to a subcommittee at the Science Museum alongside twenty-five other distinguished engineers, with the objective of establishing a permanent railway museum. With the introduction of the *Model Engineer and Amateur Electrician* magazine in 1898 he became a regular contributor and was a founder member of the Society of Model Engineers.

He published numerous books throughout his career, such as *Model Electric Locomotives and Railways* (1921), which became the 'bible' for the model railway world. The *Model Railways and Locomotives* magazine was founded by him in 1908 and became a platform from which he could share his knowledge and expertise with others. His association with Bassett-Lowke Ltd of Northampton, the world-famous model engineering company, as design consultant led to a remarkable career in the early development of miniature passenger-carrying railways.

Apart from many ventures, such as the Rhyl Miniature Railway and the Ravenglass and Eskdale Railway, Greenly's most notable success was his involvement with the Romney, Hythe, and Dymchurch Railway in Kent (1925–9). In 1915 he joined the design staff of the Royal Aircraft Factory in Farnborough, where he invented the 'flash eliminator' for machine-guns and in 1937 patented an inductor relay for lift control and automatic train control.

On 28 September 1901, at the church of St Bartholomew, Gray's Inn Road, London, Greenly had married Lilly Maria, daughter of Henry Richardson, a London businessman.

They had a daughter and two sons. By 1942 Greenly was in ill health but still carried on the family model engineering business. He died at his home, 66 Heston Road, Heston, Isleworth, on 4 March 1947 and was buried at Heston parish church. He was survived by his wife, who when she died in 1967 was buried beside him.

W. J. MILNER, *rev.*

Sources E. A. Steel and E. H. Steel, *The miniature world of Henry Greenly* (1973) · private information (1993) [Eleanora H. Steel, daughter] · b. cert. · d. cert.
Wealth at death £844 19s. 2d.: probate, 29 Aug 1947, *CGPLA Eng. & Wales*

Greenock. For this title name *see* Cathcart, Charles Murray, second Earl Cathcart [*formerly* Lord Greenock] (1783–1859).

Greenough, George Bellas (1778–1855), geologist, was born George Bellas on 18 January 1778 in the parish of St Gregory by Paul, London. He was the only surviving child of George Bellas (d. 1784), a proctor in Doctors' Commons, and his wife, Sarah (1750–1784), daughter of the wealthy apothecary and chemist Thomas Greenough. Both parents died when he was six and he was adopted by his maternal grandfather. His grandfather died in 1794, but his will provided George with substantial independent means, and in 1795 he took his grandfather's surname as his own.

George Bellas was frequently unwell in childhood; he began his schooling at Mr Cotton's school in Salthill, and then went to Eton College, from which he was removed after only a year to attend Dr Thomson's school in Kensington. He then progressed to Pembroke College, Cambridge. Because he was a dissenter, he left after nine terms without taking a degree and, intending to study law, enrolled at the University of Göttingen in 1798. It was while he was a student at Göttingen that his lifelong interest in geology was awakened by the teaching of the natural historian Professor Blumenbach. The Harz Mountains' mines gave opportunities for geological enquiry and the beginning of Greenough's considerable collection of minerals. His broader interests in literature and art were extended by close friendships with fellow students Samuel Taylor Coleridge (1772–1834) and Clement Carlyon (1777–1864).

On his return to England in 1801 Greenough pursued geological and mineralogical exploration in Cornwall, Ireland, and Scotland. He met Humphry Davy (1778–1832) in Penzance, and the two men formed a lasting scientific relationship. Excursions with both artistic and scientific aims were pursued in France, Switzerland, and Italy during the cessation of hostilities in 1802, and, after Waterloo, in 1816 (when he met Goethe, Werner, and Raumer).

Greenough's importance in the development of British geology was more as an organizer than as a discoverer, theoretician, or classifier. His first major technical feat was to organize the production of a geological map of England and Wales. The first such map had been constructed by William Smith (1760–1839), but Greenough's map of

1820, with a second edition in 1840 and a third, posthumously, in 1865, is also recognized as a major step towards the national geological survey. His one book, *A Critical Examination of the First Principles of Geology*, published in 1819, is a manual of guidance for newcomers to geology. Greenough has been classified as a stern empiricist; certainly he did not spring into acceptance of new hypotheses. He can be judged as one of those who prepared the stage for the next generation of geologists.

In 1807 Greenough was a founder member of the club which was to become the Geological Society of London. Greenough was its first president until 1813 and was re-elected from 1818 to 1820 and from 1833 to 1835. He was valued in linking his colleague fellows with French and German geologists. In his later years his major practical achievement was co-ordinating the publication of a geological map of the Indian subcontinent. Greenough was also promoter of geography, being president of the Royal Geographical Society in 1839 and 1840 and encouraging African exploration.

Greenough cultivated a wide range of interests in the arts as well as in science. He was elected a fellow of the Royal Society as early as 1807 and was twice a vice-president. He was proud of being a member of thirty-seven learned societies, in fields as diverse as ethnology, botany, linguistics, and archaeology. From about 1822 his main home was in Grove Lodge, Regent's Park, where he personally supervised the planting of a large garden. His friend Decimus Burton (1800–1881) designed the house and he and Greenough were involved in the development of Hastings–St Leonards.

Greenough was a supporter of the Society for the Diffusion of Useful Knowledge and a founder member of the British Association for the Advancement of Science. He was one of the proprietors of the company which established University College, London, and personally drew up plans for laboratories and chaired a select committee to inquire into the state of the university during a critical period. In his early years he was involved in politics, linked with the utilitarians and the liberal party, and from 1807 to 1812 he was member of parliament for the pocket borough of Gatton. A crucial event in his political life was his public denunciation of the Peterloo massacre, by resigning his commission in the light horse volunteers.

Greenough never married. He appears to have been regarded by his contemporaries as a genial chairman, capable of handling difficult meetings, and as a patient encourager of aspiring geologists. An engraved portrait of him shows a bright-eyed and humorous expression in an almost Pickwickian face. In 1855, while *en route* for the Middle East, he was taken ill at Naples with a recurrence of dropsy and died there on 2 April. He was buried at Kensal Green cemetery.   JOHN WYATT

Sources M. J. S. Rudwick, 'Hutton and Werner compared: George Greenough's geological tour of Scotland in 1805', *British Journal for the History of Science*, 1 (1962–3), 117–35 · J. Goulden, *A list of the papers and correspondence of George Bellas Greenough* (1981) · J. F. Wyatt, 'George Bellas Greenough: a romantic geologist', *Archives of Natural History*, 22 (1995), 61–71 · R. Laudan, *From mineralogy to geology: the foundations of a science* (1987) · R. Porter, *The making of geology: earth science in Britain, 1660–1815* (1977) · A. Saunders, *Regent's Park: a study of the development of the area from 1086 to the present day* (1969) · *Literary Gazette* (14 April 1855) · *The Athenaeum* (21 April 1855), 462–3 · *Journal of the Royal Geographical Society*, 25 (1855), lxxxviii · UCL, Greenough MSS

Archives BGSL, papers · DWL · GS Lond., geological papers · RGS, report · UCL, corresp. and papers; notebooks | NL NZ, letters to Gideon Algernon Mantell · NL Scot., letters to James Skene · UCL, letters to Society for the Diffusion of Useful Knowledge

Likenesses R. Westmacott, bust, 1843, GS Lond. · M. Gauci, lithograph (after E. U. Eddis), BM, NPG · engraving, GS Lond.

Wealth at death £54,000—bequests in money

Greenshields, James (*b.* 1668/9, *d.* in or before 1741), Scottish Episcopal clergyman, was the son of Luke Greenshields (*c.*1639–1725), later minister of Ardrossan, Ayrshire, and his wife, Elizabeth Hamilton, widow of the Revd Robert Row. He matriculated at Edinburgh University in 1683 and graduated MA at Glasgow University in 1687. While studying divinity at Glasgow in 1689 he helped defend an Episcopalian minister against a revolutionary mob. Ordained presbyter by the deprived bishop of Ross in 1694, he soon followed his father in obtaining an Irish curacy, in Down and Connor, and in 1697 that of Tynan, co. Armagh. About 1694 he married Elizabeth Paterson; they had eight children. He visited Scotland about February 1709 to obtain recommendations for preferment. Having been dismissed by his new rector in Tynan, he was invited to hold services in Edinburgh for English officials and other Episcopalians. He used the Book of Common Prayer and, untypically for a Scottish Episcopalian, prayed for the queen. In August an act of the commission of the general assembly of the Church of Scotland against innovations in worship was aimed at the increasing use of the liturgy by Episcopalians, including Greenshields, who was regarded by Presbyterians as a Jacobite agent. Following the successive closures of his meeting-houses by the magistrates, on 7 September 1709 the presbytery of Edinburgh prohibited him from ministering again, but he rejected their authority. For defying the magistrates' similar ban of 10 September he was gaoled five days later. His patrons probably already included his distant kinsmen Lord Balmerino and Harry Maule, Jacobite sympathizers who aimed at toleration and crown support of loyal Episcopalians, and took advantage of his religious zeal and political naïvety. Greenshields immediately sought Anglican help, and appealed to the court of session, which in December refused his argument that there was no law against his ministry, on the grounds of his allegedly invalid orders. His next appeal was to the House of Lords in February 1710, but it was delayed by Henry Sacheverell's case and the dissolution of parliament. He was released from prison in April. Jacobite Episcopalians lobbied hard for support from English bishops and peers, the nonjuring clergy ambivalently so. Bishop Nicolson of Carlisle, a chief supporter along with Archbishop Sharp, judged him to be of 'great modesty and humility' (Nicolson to Wake, letters to Archbishop William Wake, vol. 17, fol. 264). On 1 March 1711 the Lords overturned the magistrates' decision, undermining the kirk's claims to jurisdiction over Episcopal clergy who took the oaths of allegiance and abjuration. The Scottish nonjurors shared the Presbyterians' fear of enforced oaths, but relished the blow against the kirk. During the ensuing year of ecclesiastical conflict, Greenshields was lauded by many Anglicans as the persecuted apologist for the English liturgy, received honorary degrees at Oxford and Cambridge, and continued to be used as the stalking-horse of Jacobite MPs, such as George Lockhart, who plotted the overthrow of Presbyterianism. Resulting from tory political strength, the Toleration Act of 1712, which permitted loyal Episcopalians using the English liturgy to worship free of kirk hindrance, was the logical outcome and main significance of Greenshields's case. To avoid inflaming Scottish opinion further, the earl of Oxford contrived to keep Greenshields in London, dangling hopes of resuming his ministry in Scotland or of preferment elsewhere. Despite being abandoned by some supporters, Greenshields remained active in the Episcopalian cause. From 1711 until 1714 he helped to raise funds from Anglican sympathizers and to organize the distribution of 19,000 prayer books and devotional works in Scotland. He became the rector and vicar of the parish of Finnoe, in Killaloe, Ireland, on 6 October 1715. Arrears of his royal pension worsened his debts, which in 1725 forced him to sell a military chaplaincy while in debtors' prison in Dublin. The duke of Chandos generously assisted him. He probably died in his parish before 23 January 1741, when his son William succeeded him.   TRISTRAM CLARKE

Sources *The manuscripts of the House of Lords*, new ser., 12 vols. (1900–77), vol. 8, pp. 356–9 • G. Grub, *An ecclesiastical history of Scotland*, 4 vols. (1861), vol. 3, pp. 361–3 • D. Szechi, 'The politics of "persecution": Scots Episcopalian toleration and the Harley ministry, 1710–12', *Persecution and toleration*, ed. W. J. Sheils, SCH, 21 (1984), 275–87 • T. Clarke, 'Politics and prayer books: the Book of Common Prayer in Scotland, c.1705–1714', *Edinburgh Bibliographical Society Transactions*, 6/2 (1990–2002), 57–70 • *The London diaries of William Nicolson, bishop of Carlisle, 1702–1718*, ed. C. Jones and G. Holmes (1985) • J. Greenshields, letters to Dr Arthur Charlett, 1711–15, Bodl. Oxf., MS Ballard 36 • letters to W. Wake, 1709–25, Christ Church Oxf. • papers of Archbishop Sharp, Glos. RO, Lloyd–Baker–Sharp MSS, D3549 • 'Genealogy of the family of Maule of Panmure', c.1708, NL Scot., Acc. 5321 • Killaloe diocesan succession list, Representative Church Body Library, Dublin, MS 61/2/10 • R. S. Tompson, 'James Greenshields and the House of Lords: a reappraisal', *Legal history in the making*, ed. W. W. Gordon and T. D. Fergus (1991), 109–24 • D. Robertson, *Reports of cases on appeal from Scotland, decided in the House of Peers*, vol. 1: 1707–1727 (1807) • *The case of Mr Greenshields fully stated and discuss'd in a letter from a commoner of north Britain to an English peer* (1711) • *Fasti Scot.*, new edn, 3.78 • matriculation rolls, U. Edin. L., special collections division, university archives, vol. 1, 1623–1774 • C. Innes, ed., *Munimenta alme Universitatis Glasguensis / Records of the University of Glasgow from its foundation till 1727*, 3, Maitland Club, 72 (1854), 142

Archives Bodl. Oxf., Ballard MSS • Christ Church Oxf., Wake MSS • Glos. RO, Lloyd–Baker–Sharp MSS • NA Scot., Panmure papers; episcopal chest

Greenstreet, Sydney Hughes (1879–1954), actor, was born on 27 December 1879 at The Butts, Sandwich, Kent, the son of John Jack Greenstreet, tanner, and his wife, Ann Baker. Educated at Dane Hill preparatory school, Margate, from 1887 to 1897, he worked as a tea planter in Ceylon between 1899 and 1901, memorizing Shakespeare to ameliorate the tedium. He was serving as agency manager for the Watney, Coombes, and Reed Brewery in Harrow (1901–2) when he joined the Ben Greet School of Acting and made his stage début as killer Jim Creigen in *Sherlock Holmes* by Sir Arthur Conan Doyle and William Gillette (1902) at the Marine Theatre, Ramsgate. Two years later he toured the United States with Greet's ensemble, making his Broadway bow in the morality play *Everyman* (1904). Settling in America (he became a citizen in 1925), he appeared in everything from *Twelfth Night* (1905) to popular farces such as *Excuse me* (1912), and he honed his craft with the Harry Davis Stock Company (1909–10) and the Henry W. Savage Company (1910–12). Although Greenstreet claimed to have spent much of this period 'sailing like a small blimp through bedroom farces' (Sennett, 9), he was also an accomplished Shakespearian clown, prompting Sir Herbert Beerbohm Tree, after his 1916 performance in *The Merry Wives of Windsor*, to describe him as 'the greatest unstarred star of the English stage' (ibid.). However, it was his Duke in *As You Like It* at Bryn Mawr, Pennsylvania, that stood out; as the stage collapsed beneath him, he emerged from the rubble to deliver the line, 'True it is, we have seen better days' (Miller, 85).

In 1918 Greenstreet married Dorothy Marie Ogden, with whom he had a son, John Ogden Greenstreet. Meanwhile, his reputation for diverse characterization was continuing to burgeon in such plays as *The Rainbow Girl* (1918); *The Humble* (1925), a reworking of *Crime and Punishment*; *Much Ado about Nothing* (1928); Karel Capek's *R. U. R.* (1930); and *Roberta* by Jerome Kern and Otto Harbach (1933), in which he sang opposite Bob Hope. He also unearthed a talent for dastardly as Dr Grundt in *Berlin* (1931), with the *New York Times* declaring him 'a rip-snorting and delightfully malign villain' (Sennett, 11). However, his greatest stage successes came with the Broadway productions of the Theatre Guild (1935–41), alongside Alfred Lunt and Lynn Fontanne. In addition to headlining Ben Jonson's *Volpone* (1930), he was acclaimed as Baptista in *The Taming of the Shrew* (1935), as Dr Waldersee in Robert E. Sherwood's *Idiot's Delight* (1936), and as Sorin in Anton Chekhov's *The Seagull* (1938). Yet it was Robert E. Sherwood's *There Shall be No Night* (1940) that transformed his career, for film director John Huston consequently cast him as Kasper Gutman in Warner Brothers' *The Maltese Falcon* (1941). Having rejected countless other Hollywood overtures, the 61-year-old débutant made an immediate impression in this prototype *film noir*, landing a best supporting Oscar nomination. He also began a ten-film partnership with Peter Lorre—their combination of jovial infamy and weaselly grasping earning them the nickname 'the Laurel and Hardy of crime' (Sennett, 2). In the majority of these pictures Greenstreet essayed sophisticated, corrupt villains, who chucklingly delighted in their malevolent ingenuity. He was invariably filmed from below, so that his imposing bulk could dominate the screen (his weight was usually about 285 lbs, but he could balloon to 325 lbs); he also had a genius for injecting black comedy into the most menacing dialogue. Having played Japanese collaborator Dr Lorenz in *Across the Pacific* (1942), he excelled as

Señor Ferrari in *Casablanca* (1942). But, in reteaming with Lorre and Humphrey Bogart in one of the glories of the studio era, he had the misfortune to get stuck in an on-set telephone box, which had to be dismantled to release him.

A consummate professional who tolerated any amount of improvisation, providing he was fed his scripted cues, Greenstreet enlivened several mediocre movies with his inveterate scene-stealing. Warners demanded devilry and Greenstreet delivered: he was Nazi spy Colonel Robinson in *Background to Danger* (1943), the vengeful Mr Peters in *The Mask of Dimitrios* (1944), duplicitous solicitor Jerome K. Arbutny in *Three Strangers* (1946), disgraced police inspector George Grodman in *The Verdict* (1946), Count Fosco in *The Woman in White* (1948) and, perhaps his most malicious performance, Sheriff Titus Semple in *Flamingo Road* (1949). Greenstreet was considerably less effective in benign roles, such as the celestial interrogator in *Between Two Worlds* (1944) and the amateur sleuth in *Conflict* (1945), but he hankered after comedies, complaining that 'you'd hardly expect a musician to stick to one string on his violin' (Sennett, 197). Conveniently ignoring his unremarkable work in *Pillow to Post* and *Christmas in Connecticut* (both 1945), he retired in 1952, lamenting

> I was a character comedian on the stage for forty-one years, but not one single comedy role has come my way in Hollywood. So I'll keep turning down the sinister parts and take it easy until something worthwhile comes along, but it will have to be good. (ibid., 148)

Having devoted himself to painting, sculpting, and collecting antiques, Greenstreet died in Los Angeles, California, from a combination of diabetes and Bright's disease, on 18 January 1954. He was buried in Forest Lawn memorial parks, Glendale, California.   DAVID PARKINSON

Sources T. Sennett, *Masters of menace* (1979) · *The international dictionary of films and filmmakers*, 2nd edn, 3: *Actors and actresses*, ed. N. Thomas (1992) · D. Thomson, *A biographical dictionary of film*, 3rd edn (1994) · F. Miller, '*Casablanca': as time goes by …* (1992) · D. Shipman, *The great movie stars: the international years*, rev. edn (1980) · E. G. Jarvis, *Final curtain* (1993) · b. cert.
Likenesses photographs, Kobal collection · photographs, Huntley archive · photographs, Ronald Grant archive

Greenway, Charles, first Baron Greenway (1857–1934), oil industrialist and merchant, was born in Taunton on 13 June 1857, the only son of the three children of John David Greenway, a draper, and his wife, Lucy Emily Wiffen, of Essex. He was educated at Taunton, and after working for a London cotton trader, in 1876 he joined the London branch of a Calcutta-based mercantile company headed by (Charles) William Wallace.

In 1883 Greenway married Mabel Tower of Caterham, a solicitor's daughter; they had a son and two daughters. Two years later, he moved to India to take a post with the merchants Ralli Brothers. Then in 1893 Wallace, back in Britain, invited Greenway to join the Calcutta office of what had become Shaw, Wallace & Co. Since 1891 Shaw Wallace had been marketing agent in the subcontinent for the kerosene of the Burmah Oil Company, and when Greenway joined them he immersed himself mainly in the oil side of this prosperous firm; later he became senior

Charles Greenway, first Baron Greenway (1857–1934), by Walter Stoneman, 1927

partner. Thanks to his energy and commercial acumen, Greenway rapidly built up Burmah Oil's trade throughout India, the largest single market in the eastern hemisphere outside Europe. This success aroused very determined opposition from larger rivals, especially Royal Dutch–Shell's marketing subsidiary in the East, the Asiatic Petroleum Company. After a prolonged price war, in 1905 Burmah Oil reached a market-sharing agreement with Asiatic; yet by the time Greenway left India three years later, Burmah Oil was supplying nearly half the kerosene marketed there.

Wallace called Greenway home for a far more demanding assignment. In May 1908, extensive oil deposits had been discovered in Persia. Under the shah's original concession, granted in 1901 to William Knox D'Arcy and later taken over by a syndicate including Burmah Oil, a separate company had to be set up. As the only executive director of Burmah Oil in London, Wallace bore the main burden of launching that company, and needed Greenway's immediate help. Greenway proved to be resourceful over large and small matters alike, even borrowing furniture from Wallace's firm for the new offices. In April 1909 the Anglo-Persian Oil Company (from 1954 the British Petroleum Company) was floated in London, to considerable popular interest. With the great imperial figure of Donald Smith, Baron Strathcona and Mount Royal, as part-time chairman, Wallace took charge as managing director, and Greenway became his executive assistant with a seat on the board. In 1910 Wallace handed over the managing directorship to Greenway, who thus had the major responsibility (as vice-chairman under Wallace) for technical and financial matters. Two years later John Cargill, the chairman of Burmah Oil (which was Anglo-Persian's largest shareholder) became alarmed at Greenway's resolve to bid for a concession in neighbouring Mesopotamia (later Iraq), because there were already problems over pipeline-laying and refining in Persia, and the marketing of refined products. Cargill therefore refused to authorize further funds for Anglo-Persian and Greenway at once turned for assistance to the British government. The subsequent period, during which he carried out many arduous negotiations in Whitehall, took Greenway to the brink of exhaustion, but it ended successfully in two agreements signed in May 1914. The first lord of the Admiralty, Winston Churchill, was anxious to obtain a secure source of fuel oil for the navy at a time when there were no substantial oil deposits in the British empire, except in remote Burma. The Treasury thus acquired a 51 per cent stake in Anglo-Persian, while the Admiralty signed a contract to purchase large quantities of fuel oil over the next twenty years.

Greenway became chairman of Anglo-Persian in 1914 but continued as managing director until 1919. It was very largely his initiatives that converted the company from merely a producer in Persia into a vertically integrated oil major, capable of taking its place in the world league. Between 1914 and 1918 he planned systematically to this end. Most importantly, he laid the foundations of a fully-fledged selling organization by acquiring in 1917 the British Petroleum Company, the marketing subsidiary of a recently expropriated German company. He also placed orders with British shipyards for a fleet of tankers, to escape from Shell's domination of the tanker-chartering market. Longer-term plans included the building of a refinery in Britain, at Llandarcy, near Swansea; this was completed in 1921.

Greenway received a baronetcy in recognition of his public services in 1919, and thereafter he continued to extend Anglo-Persian's activities world-wide. He set in motion exploration projects in many parts of the world, and established oil-bunkering stations on the principal sea routes as well as marketing organizations in most European countries. Recognizing that future developments required the expertise of scientifically trained top management, in 1921 he recruited as technical adviser Sir John Cadman, a distinguished professor and government scientific adviser, who had been chairman of the petroleum executive and of the inter-allied petroleum conference during the First World War. Cadman later became deputy chairman of Anglo-Persian, and was chairman designate when Greenway retired in 1927. In recognition of his signal achievements, a barony, named for Stanbridge Earls, Greenway's Hampshire country home, was bestowed on him in that year. In retirement Greenway took no part in public affairs but enthusiastically pursued a range of leisure activities. He enjoyed entertaining on a generous scale. As well as riding and shooting, he played golf on his private course and fished in the River Test.

Greenway's most marked attribute was an exuberance of spirit, which invigorated not only himself but also those aides striving with him for the latest objective. He set himself practical goals, which more often than not he achieved through persistence. He never flinched from the company's tussles with commercial rivals, and particularly with Shell, which, quite as pertinaciously, had striven to clip the wings of the fledgeling Anglo-Persian. Greenway was a past master at playing the patriotic card and whenever public figures accused Shell of being unpatriotic and mercenary, that company suspected his malign influence. Since Greenway had no scruples about denigrating rivals in Whitehall circles, those rivals not unexpectedly denigrated him before a wider world. Henri Deterding of Royal Dutch–Shell declared that Greenway would never have got anywhere near the top of a major corporation but for the backing of the British government.

The American radical author Upton Sinclair, in *Oil!* (1927), characterized Greenway as 'Old Spats and Monocle'; yet in essence he was a tough merchant adventurer. Indeed, no establishment figure could have matched Greenway's almost single-handed achievements in preserving the independence of the Anglo-Persian Oil Company and transforming it into a corporation that dominated oil production in the Middle East until the end of the Second World War. Greenway died on 17 December 1934 at Stanbridge Earls. T. A. B. CORLEY

Sources *The Times* (18 Dec 1934) · R. W. Ferrier, 'Greenway, Charles', *DBB* · R. W. Ferrier, *The history of the British Petroleum Company*, 1: *The developing years, 1901–1932* (1982) · J. H. Bamberg, *The history of the British Petroleum Company*, 2: *The Anglo-Iranian years, 1928–1954* (1994) · T. A. B. Corley, *A history of the Burmah Oil Company*, 2 vols. (1983–8) · H. Townend, *A history of Shaw Wallace & Co. and Shaw Wallace & Co. Ltd* (1965) · GEC, *Peerage* · *WWW* · G. Jones, *The state and the emergence of the British oil industry* (1981) · d. cert.
Archives Burmah Castrol Archives, Swindon · U. Warwick Mod. RC, BP archives | CUL, corresp. with Lord Hardinge
Likenesses W. Stoneman, photograph, 1927, NPG [*see illus.*] · photographs, Burmah Castrol archives, Swindon · photographs, U. Warwick Mod. RC, BP archives
Wealth at death £298,953 12s. 11d.: probate, 12 April 1935, *CGPLA Eng. & Wales*

Greenway, Francis Howard (1777–1837), architect, was born on 20 November 1777 in Mangotsfield, Gloucestershire, the youngest of the three sons of Francis Greenway or Grinway, mason of Mangotsfield, and his wife, Ann Webb. He became a pupil in London of John Nash, and it was presumably through Nash's connection with south Wales that in 1801 he was employed to design a small public building in Carmarthen. The story of his subsequent career is an unusually dramatic one. About 1805 he and his brothers Olive and John Tripp Greenway established themselves in Bristol at 7 Limekiln Lane, as 'stonemasons, architects, builders etc.', with Francis the architect member of the partnership (Colvin, *Archs.*, 430). In 1806 he designed the hotel and assembly rooms in the suburb of Clifton, which the firm contracted to build; but at the same time the brothers were speculating by buying unfinished houses in Clifton which they completed and sold, and in 1809 they were overtaken by bankruptcy. Then, some time later, Francis Greenway was accused of forgery in connection with a building contract made shortly before the business failure. He was tried at Bristol assizes on 23 March 1812, pleaded guilty, and was sentenced to transportation for life.

After arriving in Australia in February 1814, however, Greenway quickly resumed his profession and became the virtual father of Australian architecture. Within months of his arrival he established a practice at 84 George Street, Sydney, and found a patron in Governor Lachlan Macquarie of New South Wales, who had ambitious plans for public works in the colony; and in 1816 he was appointed civil architect. He received his emancipation in the following year, and his wife, Mary (d. 1832), whom he had married in 1804, rejoined him in Australia with their three children. In 1822, following Macquarie's departure, Greenway was dismissed from the post, but during his short period of office he had carried out or initiated a remarkable number of substantial building projects in Sydney and its neighbourhood, the most important of which were the Macquarie lighthouse (c.1816–18; dem.), the churches of St Matthew, Windsor (c.1817), St Luke, Liverpool (1818–24), and St James's Sydney (c.1820), the stables at Government House (1817), Fort Macquarie at Benelong Point (c.1817; dem.), and the Hyde Park convict barracks (1817; now the district courts), which last project earned Greenway absolute pardon in 1819. The stables and the fort were in a conventional castellated style, but most of his work is in a bold and simple classical idiom of considerable originality and merit.

Greenway is said to have been self-confident, 'temperamental and quick to take offence' (Herman, 43). After his dismissal in 1822 he continued in private practice in a small way for some years, evidently living in somewhat reduced circumstances. In 1837 he retired from Sydney to his government land-grant property on the Hunter River, where he died in September of that year. He was buried on 26 September 1837 in East Maitland cemetery, New South Wales. His views on Australian architecture were published in an essay in the *Australian Almanac* (1835). His wife had opened a small school for girls in Sydney, and of their five sons and three daughters, one son, Charles, became an archdeacon and canon at Grafton Cathedral.

PETER LEACH, *rev.*

Sources Colvin, *Archs.* · M. E. Herman, *The early Australian architects and their work*, 2nd edn (1970) · W. Ison, *The Georgian buildings of Bristol* (1952) · M. H. Ellis, *Francis Greenway: his life and times* (1949) · *AusDB*

Archives Mitchell L., NSW

Likenesses F. H. Greenway, self-portrait, repro. in Ellis, *Francis Greenway*, inside cover; priv. coll.

Wealth at death living in reduced circumstances at time of death: Ellis, *Francis Greenway*

Greenway [Greneway, Grenewey], **Richard** (*fl.* 1598), translator, was born in an unknown year; his ancestry and parentage are similarly obscure. He may have been a relative of the Richard Grenewey who was a member of Henry VIII's chamber and accompanied the king to France in 1544; this Grenewey appears in the patent rolls through much of Elizabeth's reign and appears to have had Buckinghamshire connections. The translator is more likely to have been the Richard Greneway who was among five residential commoners living in Oxford in 1565 and having tutors at Corpus Christi College, though not appearing in the college records and not having matriculated. Another, somewhat less likely possibility is that he was the Robert Greneway (the first name perhaps an error) of Gloucester Hall who was in trouble with authorities for concupiscence in September 1568. Richard is the given name used to sign the printed dedication of Greenway's translation of Tacitus in 1598. Either of these latter identifications would fit someone who was a close contemporary of the classical scholar and fellow Tacitean translator Sir Henry Savile, who was a student at Brasenose College from 1561 and fellow of Merton College from 1565. If the Corpus Christi identification is correct, then Greenway was probably of the same Basingstoke family that sent several of its progeny to Corpus over the years, and which produced the college's fifth president (1562–8), Thomas Greneway. A Richard Grenewey was resident in Paris in 1581 and corresponded, as a familiar, with Humphrey Ely, the Catholic exile who had also been at both Brasenose and St John's College in Oxford in the 1560s. This Oxford connection suggests this Grenewey to have been the future translator, though the association with Ely does not establish his own religious beliefs with any reliability.

Greenway is known to posterity almost exclusively from the translation he published in 1598 of two works by the Roman historian Tacitus, the *Germania* and the *Annales*, as *The Annales of Cornelius Tacitus. The Description of Germanie*. These were adjoined to a re-edition of Savile's translation of Tacitus's two other major works, the *Histories* and *Agricola*, which Savile had first published, with a dedication to the queen, in 1591. Greenway's is widely regarded as the inferior of the two translations, though this distinction appears to rest more on his personal obscurity in comparison with Savile's much greater prominence. Greenway's translation is accurate but lacks the lively quality of Savile's own prose; nor does he appear to have intruded his own political views into the translation as Savile is now known to have done. In combination, their collective edition of Tacitus's works was a major publication of the 1590s. This was the decade in which Tacitus came into particular vogue in England, both for his epigrammatic and terse style (in contrast with the more florid rhetoric of Livy) and for his political acumen. Tacitus's political wisdom, linked to the contemporaneous advent of neo-Stoicism in European authors such as Justus Lipius, was alternatively regarded as providing a safer advice for rulers than offered by the maligned Machiavelli, and also as offering counsel on how to survive and endure under a tyrant.

Both Savile and Greenway were connected to the circle of Robert Devereux, second earl of Essex, in Savile's case through the earl's secretary, Henry Cuffe, who was executed with the earl following the ill-fated rebellion of 1601. The precise nature of Greenway's connection to Essex is less clear, but he dedicated the *Annales* and *Germania* to the earl, declaring his wish that it serve 'as a glasse' that would reflect not only ancient times but 'your L. owne honourable vertues' (sig. ¶3). Given Essex's own known interest in Tacitus and in history more generally, it is possible that Greenway was simply retained by Savile, perhaps at Essex's instigation, to provide English versions of the two Tacitean works Savile himself had not translated in order to make up a complete edition. Savile himself was by 1596 already busy as provost of Eton College, while simultaneously serving as warden of Merton; intellectually, he was by then engaged on an edition of medieval chronicles and had left Tacitus behind.

Greenway's translations were republished several times in the early seventeenth century. It is not known when he died, or whether he had any heirs, though a Richard Greenway appears as an author of religious works in the 1660s. **D. R. WOOLF**

Sources *Hist. U. Oxf.* 3: *Colleg. univ.*, 690 • *CSP dom.*, 1547–90 • *CPR*, 1560–63; 1572–8 • *LP Henry VIII*, 19/1.275 • P. E. J. Hammer, *The polarization of Elizabethan politics* (1999) • F. J. Levy, *Tudor historical thought* (1967) • D. Womersley, 'Sir Henry Savile's translation of Tacitus and the political interpretation of Elizabethan texts', *Review of English Studies*, new ser., 42 (1991), 313–42 • M. Smuts, 'Court-centred politics and the uses of Roman historians, 1590–1630', *Culture and politics in early Stuart England*, ed. K. Sharpe and P. Lake (Stanford, 1993), 21–43 • D. R. Woolf, *The idea of history in early Stuart England* (1990) • A. T. Bradford, 'Stuart absolutism and the 'Utility' of Tacitus', *Huntington Library Quarterly*, 45 (1983), 127–55 • J. H. M. Salmon, 'Stoicism and Roman example: Seneca and Tacitus in Jacobean England', *Journal of the History of Ideas*, 50 (1989), 199–225

Greenwell, Dorothy [Dora] (1821–1882), poet and essayist, was born on 6 December 1821 at Greenwell Ford, Lanchester, co. Durham, the only daughter of the five children of William Thomas Greenwell (1777–1854), a magistrate and deputy lieutenant, and his wife, Dorothy Smales (1789–1871). She was educated at home, and taught herself five languages while reading widely on philosophy, theology, and political economy.

In 1847 William Greenwell was declared bankrupt, and he and his family were forced to sell their home and move in with the clergyman son, William *Greenwell, at Ovingham, Northumberland. In Northumberland Greenwell published her first volume of poems, in 1848. It was well received and was followed by another volume in 1850, *Stories that Might be True, with Other Poems*.

During 1850 Greenwell moved with her parents to Lancashire, where she found work as a schoolmistress, and met Josephine Butler and Christina Rossetti, with whom she formed lasting and influential friendships. In 1854 her father died, and she returned to Durham with her mother. She became involved in local philanthropy, working with the poor in Durham workhouse and prison, and campaigning on behalf of the antivivisection and women's suffrage movements. Her principal prose work, *The Patience of Hope* (1860), a collection of theological

essays, was dedicated to Josephine Butler and demonstrates the religious fervour that characterizes much of her work. In a different vein, however, was 'Our Single Women', published in the *North British Review* in February 1862, in which she rejected the conservative ideal of gender-determined 'separate spheres' and pleaded for the extension of educated women's work. Another essay, 'On the education of the imbecile', published in the *North British Review* in 1869, provoked much speculation on its authorship, the president of the British Medical Association remarking that 'It must have been written by some very able physician' (Dorling, 93). During 1869 Greenwell also published *Carmina crucis*, a volume of devotional poetry which became her best-known work.

In 1871 Greenwell's mother died, and she moved to London, where she produced *Colloquia crucis*, following up the success of its companion volume of 1869. She also wrote a memoir of the Quaker John Woolman (1871) and *Liber humanitatis: Essays on Spiritual and Social Life* (1875). Her final collection of poems, *Camera obscura* (1876), was well received, *The Athenaeum* noting that 'her productions are calculated to afford constant delight to educated and sympathetic readers'.

Declining health impaired Greenwell's writing career and her social work, and towards the end of her life she became addicted to opium. A near-fatal accident in 1881 led to her eventual death on 29 March 1882 at her home, 7 Oakfield Road, Clifton, Bristol. Her *Selected Poems* was issued in 1889, and Constance Louisa Maynard prepared another edition in 1904. **KATHERINE MULLIN**

Sources Blain, Clements & Grundy, *Feminist comp.* • C. Devonshire, 'Greenwell, Dora', *Dictionary of British women writers*, ed. J. Todd (1989) • J. Shattock, *The Oxford guide to British women writers* (1993), 190–1 • 'Greenwell, Dora', *Bloomsbury guide to women's literature*, ed. C. Buck (1992), 598 • W. Dorling, *Memoirs of Dora Greenwell* [1885] • H. Bett, *Dora Greenwell* (1950) • C. L. Maynard, *Dora Greenwell* (1925) • *The Athenaeum* (12 Aug 1876), 202–3 • J. Gray, 'Dora Greenwell's commonplace book', *Princeton University Library Chronicle*, 57/1 (1995), 47–74 • *DNB* • *CGPLA Eng. & Wales* (1882)
Archives Beds. & Luton ARS
Wealth at death £3576 4s. 1d.: probate, 16 Aug 1882, *CGPLA Eng. & Wales*

Greenwell, Sir Leonard (1781–1844), army officer, was the third son of Joshua Greenwell of Kibblesworth, of the family of Greenwell of Greenwell Ford, co. Durham, and his wife, Mary. He entered the army by purchase as ensign in the 45th regiment in 1801, becoming lieutenant in 1802 and captain in 1804. In 1806 he embarked with his regiment in the secret expedition under General Crauford, which ultimately was sent to La Plata as a reinforcement, and was wounded in the operations against Buenos Aires. He landed with the regiment in Portugal on 1 August 1808, and was present with it throughout the Peninsular campaigns from Roliça to Toulouse, during which he was wounded. He was in temporary command of the regiment during Massena's retreat from Torres Vedras, at the battle of Fuentes d'Oñoro, and at the final siege and fall of Badajoz, where he was among the first officers to scale the walls. He became regimental major after Busaco, and received a brevet lieutenant-colonelcy after the battle of

Salamanca; he led the light troops of Picton's division at Orthez, and succeeded to the command of his regiment on the fall of Colonel Forbes at Toulouse. In 1819 Greenwell took his regiment to Ceylon, and commanded it there for six years, until compelled to return home through ill health. Appointed colonel and aide-de-camp to the king in 1825, he retired on half pay in 1827; in 1831 he was appointed commandant at Chatham, a post he held until promotion to major-general on 10 January 1837. He had purchased all but one of his commissions.

Greenwell was made a KCH (1832) and KCB (1838), and held the gold medal and clasps for Badajoz, Fuentes d'Oñoro, and Orthez. He died, unmarried, in Harley Street, Cavendish Square, London, on 11 November 1844, and was buried in St Nicholas's Church, Newcastle.

H. M. Chichester, *rev.* James Falkner

Sources *Army List* · J. Philippart, ed., *The royal military calendar*, 3rd edn, 4 (1820) · *Hart's Army List* · *GM*, 2nd ser., 23 (1845), 98 · H. C. Wylly, *History of the 1st and 2nd battalions, the Sherwood Foresters, Nottinghamshire and Derbyshire regiment, 1740–1914*, 2 vols. (1929) · *Sherwood Foresters Annual Journal* (1928)
Likenesses Lawrence, oils, 1835, repro. in *Sherwood Foresters Annual Journal*; sold at Phillips, 8 March 1876

Greenwell, William (1820–1918), archaeologist, was born on 23 March 1820 at Greenwell Ford, Lanchester, co. Durham, the family seat for over three hundred years. The eldest of four sons of William Thomas Greenwell (1777–1854), deputy lieutenant of the county, and his wife, Dorothy (1789–1871), daughter of Francis Smales, a Durham solicitor, he was the elder brother of Dora *Greenwell, the evangelical poet. His education commenced under the Revd George Newby at Witton-le-Wear, continuing at Durham grammar school. He matriculated at University College, Durham, in October 1836, graduating BA in 1839. He entered the Middle Temple, but owing to ill health returned to University College in 1841, obtaining his LTh in 1842 and MA in 1843. Ordained deacon (1844) and priest (1846) on the Pemberton fellowship, which he held 1844–54, he was bursar (1844–6) and chaplain (1846–7) of University College, and sub-librarian of the university (1844–7); in 1882 the university elected him an honorary DCL.

Greenwell held the perpetual curacy of Ovingham with Mickley from 1847 to 1850, when a kinsman of the patron replaced him. He then briefly served Robert Isaac Wilberforce as curate at Burton Agnes, Yorkshire, before becoming assistant to William George Henderson, principal of Hatfield Hall, Durham. In 1852 he was appointed principal of Neville Hall, a hostel for students at Newcastle College of Medicine, with whom he worked among the town's cholera victims in 1853. Greenwell resigned in 1854 when he became a minor canon of Durham Cathedral and assumed the post of chaplain and censor of Bishop Cosin's Hall, Durham, which he held for some ten years. From 1863 to 1908 Greenwell was librarian of Durham Cathedral, where he continued the work of cataloguing the holdings begun by Joseph Stevenson. In 1865 he was appointed to the living of St Mary-the-Less in Durham. He was appointed a JP in 1870, later chairing the Durham ward petty sessions, and was elected an alderman in 1904.

He resigned his minor canonry in 1908. He died, unmarried, at North Bailey, Durham, on 27 January 1918, and was buried at Lanchester.

In 1852 Greenwell edited the *Boldon Buke* for the Surtees Society (of which he was vice-president 1890–1918), and went on to edit other texts, including the *Feodarium prioratus Dunelmensis* (1872), in which he demonstrated the foundation charters of the Benedictine convent at Durham to be fraudulent. Greenwell's main claim to fame lies, however, in his activity as an archaeologist and collector. Greenwell excavated some 295 burial mounds. His first dig was at Chollerton in 1847, and from 1862 he undertook intensive fieldwork. He reported his finds in *British Barrows* (1877), produced in collaboration with George Rolleston. Greenwell rarely recorded the structure of the mounds he examined in detail, and was criticized by his rival J. R. Mortimer for hasty excavation. He nevertheless took justified pride in the serious scholarly purpose of his archaeology: among those he influenced was A. H. L. F. Pitt-Rivers, who worked with him in 1867. The artefacts he sold or presented to the British Museum between 1879 and 1907 form one of the foundation collections of British prehistory. In 1909 Greenwell also gave the museum a leaf of one of the three pandects commissioned by Abbot Ceolfrid of Jarrow (d. 716), discovered in a Newcastle shop (BL, Add. MS 37777). Among Greenwell's other collections, his Greek coins were sold for £11,000 in 1901; some seventy examples of Anglo-Saxon stonework ('obtained by gift, by purchase and by felony') remain in Durham Cathedral Library; and his collection of skulls was presented to the University Museum, Oxford. Greenwell was president of the Architectural and Archaeological Society of Durham from 1865 to his death, vice-president of the Society of Antiquaries of Newcastle (1890–1918), and a member of the London Society of Antiquaries and the Ethnological Society; he was elected fellow of the Royal Society (1878) and honorary fellow of the Society of Antiquaries of Scotland (1879).

The 'Canon', as he was known, was bluff and plain-spoken: Sir John Evans remembered him as 'eminently unclerical in his manners and manner of thinking, and a very sensible man'. Greenwell was a Liberal in politics, and in religion a Tractarian who in later life retreated to more conservative high-churchmanship. He remained a keen angler to his ninety-eighth year, and in 1854 created the 'Greenwell's glory', the most famous of British trout flies.

Arthur Burns

Sources J. C. Hodgson, 'Memoirs of the Rev. William Greenwell', *Archaeologia Aeliana*, 3rd ser., 15 (1918), 1–21 · J. T. Fowler, *Durham University: earlier foundations and present colleges* (1904) · H. Bett, *Dora Greenwell* (1950) · B. M. Marsden, *The early barrow diggers* (1974), chap. 12 · I. A. Kinnes and I. H. Longworth, *Catalogue of the excavated prehistoric and Romano-British material in the Greenwell collection* (1985) [incl. calendar of excavations] · H. D. Hughes, *A history of Durham Cathedral Library* (1925) · J. Roberts, *The new illustrated dictionary of trout flies* (1988) · I. H. Longworth, interview, 1994, BM · J. Evans, *Time and chance: the story of Arthur Evans and his forebears* (1943) · private information (2004) · BL, Add. MS 37777
Archives Durham Cath. CL, corresp. | CUL, letters to S. G. Perceval · Salisbury and South Wiltshire Museum, letters to A. H. L. F.

Pitt-Rivers • U. Newcastle, Robinson L., letters to Sir Walter Trevelyan • W. Yorks. AS, Leeds, Yorkshire Archaeological Society, letters to William Hornsby [copies] **Likenesses** A. S. Cope, oils, 1898, Durham Cath. CL • J. T. Fowler, photograph, 10 June 1915, repro. in Hodgson, 'Memoirs' • J. W. Gordon, portrait, Tweed Valley Hotel, Walkerburn **Wealth at death** £3925 15s. 2d.: probate, 25 Feb 1918, CGPLA Eng. & Wales

Greenwich. For this title name see Campbell, John, second duke of Argyll and duke of Greenwich (1680–1743); Townshend, Caroline, suo jure Baroness Greenwich (1717–1794).

Greenwood, Alice Drayton (1862–1935), historian, was born on 18 November 1862 at 15 Lime Grove, Chorlton, Lancashire, the eldest child of Dr Joseph Gouge *Greenwood (1821–1894) and his first wife, Elizabeth (Eliza) Taylor, daughter of the Revd John Taylor, a well-known Unitarian minister. Her mother died after the birth of a second daughter, and her father remarried in 1871. The family lived thereafter in Fallowfield, Manchester, where Dr Greenwood was first tutor, then professor of classics and history, and finally principal at Owens College (1857–89). From 1880 to 1886 he was vice-chancellor of Victoria University of Manchester. Brought up in an academic environment, Alice Greenwood was educated at Cheltenham Ladies' College (1875?–82), and on returning home attended lectures and classes at Victoria University, taking advantage of the fact that, although women were not admitted to the building, the teaching was conducted in separate premises in Brunswick Street. The friendship and encouragement of teachers at the college, notably Adolphus William Ward, then professor of English language and history, and later master of Peterhouse, Cambridge, of Augustus Samuel Wilkins, professor of classics, and Dr Herman Hager, a specialist in German literature, gave direction to her interests, while her father can be credited with a general, rather than a particular, influence. She developed a fine taste in reading, exact standards of scholarly accuracy, a strong sense of public duty, and an unobtrusive but strong attachment to the Church of England.

Alice Greenwood entered Somerville Hall, Oxford, in 1886, and obtained a first-class honours degree in 1888 along with one other woman, Gertrude Bell of Lady Margaret Hall, and nine men, though the two women's names did not appear in the published list. She was remembered at Oxford for her vivacity and leadership in debate, and won a money prize for a historical essay offered by Mary (Mrs Humphry) Ward to the Association for Promoting the Education of Women in Oxford. In 1888 she was appointed assistant mistress at Clifton High School for Girls, Manchester, greatly enjoying the teaching but expressing even then a dislike for the idea of becoming a headmistress, wholly engaged in administration. When a colleague at the school was appointed headmistress of the North Manchester High School for Girls in 1892, she moved there with her. Meanwhile Adolphus Ward succeeded her father as principal of Owens College, and under his auspices the independent Withington Girls School was founded in 1891. Alice Greenwood became its

second headmistress in 1896, when the first moved to a larger school. She was a vigorous and successful holder of the post until 1900, when she resigned. Her first book, *Europe and Papacy in the Middle Ages*, for schools, had been published in 1892 (2nd edn, 1896), and the steady flow after 1900 of deeply researched work on literature and history, some of which served, or responded to, requests from Adolphus Ward, probably explains her decision at thirty-eight years of age to leave teaching for writing.

Under Sir Adolphus Ward's editorship of the *Cambridge Modern History* (1901–12) and co-editorship of the *Cambridge History of English Literature* (1907–16) Alice Greenwood wrote three chapters in volume 2 of the latter on the later middle ages, showing fastidious care in the study of variant texts and sensitivity in appraising literary style, language, and early grammar. Both for the *Cambridge History of English Literature* and for the *Cambridge Modern History* she did innumerable grinding chores, compiling genealogies, chronological tables, and indexes. Her two most notable, independently written, books dealt with eighteenth-century England. One was a two-volume study, *Lives of the Hanoverian Queens of England* (1909, 1911), demonstrating her thorough reading of manifold documents. She resisted the temptation, when evidence about the women was thin, to write more freely about the men, but following the conventions of her age cultivated a certain reserve which is tantalizing to the modern reader; her style is in contrast with the 'brazen candour' of her sources. But some constraints were self-imposed, inasmuch as she deemed biography different from history, and strove to see circumstances 'as they probably appeared to the actors themselves' (A. Greenwood, *Hanoverian Queens*, 1911, 2.x). Her study *Horace Walpole's World: a Sketch of Whig Society under George III* (1913) better displayed her skill in depicting an age in succinct, arresting phrases. Other works included school textbooks on English and European history, tales from Richard Hakluyt, and a selection from the Paston letters. She always matched her style to her readership: her school textbooks were written in a friendly, informal way, yet summarized in sharply discerning sentences the most significant long-term trends. Her original scholarly research investigated fresh sources and private letters with impressive thoroughness. Above all she was concerned to place people at the centre of the stage and to achieve a sense of actuality that made the past live before her readers' eyes. She probed character and personality in order to arrive at portraits that went beyond the mere public image. Her judgements were shrewd and often memorable, especially in her opening sentences. She cared nothing for fame, but wished to 'hand on the torch of honest study and true patriotism'. A pupil described her as 'a splendid and powerful woman' (Wilson, 9).

Alice Greenwood moved to Oxford some time before 1910 and was associated with St Hugh's College, becoming a member of council (1910–16) and honorary secretary (1914–16). In 1916 she moved with a former colleague, Helen M. Turing, to Wandsworth Common, London, and then to Somerset, first to an old house and then to a new one in Williton, looking towards the Quantock hills.

There she much enjoyed country walks, her large garden, and birds. She did not give up writing until 1934 and died at Shercroft, Catwell, Williton, on 27 April 1935. Her grave is in Wolvercote cemetery, Oxford, next to her sister who died in 1912.   JOAN THIRSK

Sources E. C. W. [E. C. Wilson], *Alice Drayton Greenwood … a memorial sketch* (privately printed, [Oxford], [1935]) · Registers of Cheltenham Ladies' College, Cheltenham Ladies' College · b. cert. · d. cert.
Wealth at death £6938 16s. 7d.: probate, 17 June 1935, *CGPLA Eng. & Wales*

Greenwood, Arthur (1880–1954), politician, was born on 8 February 1880 at 13 Carey Street, Hunslet, Leeds, the eldest son of William Greenwood (d. 1940), a painter and decorator, and his wife, Margaret Nunns, of Dewsbury. From St Jude's board school he won a scholarship to Bewerley Street School in 1893, and from 1895 became a pupil teacher as a way of continuing his education. As a schoolboy he read the socialist paper *The Clarion* and bought Labour pamphlets from the Leeds market. In 1899 he entered the Yorkshire College in Leeds on one of the queen's scholarships available to teachers. The highlight of an otherwise undistinguished BSc ordinary degree (second division) awarded in 1902 was a prize certificate for exceptional work in education, and he also gained his teacher's qualification at the same time. His degree was translated into a BSc from Leeds in 1905 to mark the Yorkshire College's transformation into university status.

Greenwood stayed on as an associate of the college during 1902–3 for further study in history and economics. He did well in the latter, taking lectures from J. H. Clapham, then the head of department. Under the terms of his scholarship he had to return to schoolteaching, but he went on to become head of economics at Huddersfield Technical College. On 28 December 1904 he married Catherine Ainsworth, the daughter of John James Brown, a bookkeeper, of Leeds. They had one daughter and one son. In 1913 he moved to the economics department at Leeds University, where his most public act was to join Professor D. H. MacGregor and Henry Clay in criticizing Sir Michael Sadler, the vice-chancellor, for offering students as volunteers to keep local services running during a strike by municipal workers.

Greenwood's experience in pre-war Yorkshire was clearly fruitful. He had heard Philip Snowden's famous lecture to socialists 'The Christ that is to be' and seen the effects of industrial work on the adolescents he had met as a schoolteacher. In Greenwood's mind, 'book learning' was not the basis of real political commitment; living a working-class life, rather than observing it, was the key. Yet in lectures at Huddersfield on 'principles and methods of social advance' he emphasized the importance of the investigation and correct diagnosis of social problems, and it was in this period that his contribution to the intellectual side of the labour movement began to emerge in a spate of articles about education. In journals such as *The Child*, *The Crusade*, and *Highway*, and perhaps more notably the *Economic Journal*, the *Journal of the Royal Statistical Society*,

Arthur Greenwood (1880–1954), by Karl Pollak, 1948

and the *Political Quarterly*, he put across two essential points. First was the damaging effect of employment on the health and therefore the educational capacity of the adolescent. The ill effects of half-time working and the often negligible impact of teaching which had to be fitted in around the working day through evening and continuation schools had been borne out by his own experience and confirmed by observation of how the effect of educational reforms in Bradford (including an open-air school) had been weakened by industrial work. His second major theme was the need for a general rather than a narrowly vocational education for working-class children. Like most socialists of his time he felt that the crime of capitalism was to stress material worth and utility above the more human values of co-operation and public spirit. The most substantial item in his output at this time was a pamphlet, *The Health and Physique of Schoolchildren* (1913), which set out his own views about the incompatibility of education and employment for young adolescents. But it also illustrated the elevated circles in which Greenwood was beginning to move, because it was published by the Ratan Tata Foundation at the London School of Economics, and its director, R. H. Tawney, provided the introduction. Greenwood also worked with Tawney in the Workers' Educational Association. He had set up the northern district, for which he was to act as chairman down to 1945, and lectured on housing, industrial relations, and the poor law.

Labour Party research department Greenwood left Leeds in 1914 for London, where he again showed his ability to move in the right circles. He went as secretary to the Council for the Study of International Relations, for which he contributed study guides and to a book with R. W. Seton-Watson and Alfred Zimmern, *The War and Democracy* (1914). He appeared at a Ruskin conference with A. C. Pigou and Sidney Webb, which led to a pamphlet, *The Reorganisation of Industry* (1916). Later, in 1926, he contributed an article to William Temple's journal of Christian politics and religion, *The Pilgrim*. Having edited a labour paper in Leeds before 1914 and also *The Athenaeum* during the war, a career in journalism appeared likely, but Greenwood's most substantial work was as a civil servant in the Ministry of Reconstruction, where he worked closely with Christopher Addison and Arthur Henderson. He also served on committees examining trusts and profiteering. He produced a report on adult education with Tawney and played a large part in setting up the Whitley councils. At the same time he was involved in discussions about Labour's policy with the Webbs and G. D. H. Cole, and showed good judgement by keeping loyal to the Webbs when disenchantment with Cole set in. He had now established himself within Labour's intellectual circles, and was appointed secretary of the joint Labour Party–TUC research department. In 1920 he was appointed secretary to the party's advisory committees and in 1927 head of the research department, a post which he held until 1943.

In addition to his earlier interest in education Greenwood had now become involved in the more politically central questions of industrial organization. His thought and activities ran down two channels. As a matter of socialist politics he believed that employer autocracy was an anomaly in an increasingly democratic society, and he saw scope for the state, the trade unions, and voluntary organization to give workers a greater say in the running of enterprises. The Whitley councils which he had helped establish were intended to regulate conditions in trades where workers were relatively powerless. But he also saw that new interest in industrial psychology and the practical improvements in working conditions—lighting, ventilation, and so forth—was worth pursuing; he sat on the council of the National Institute for Industrial Psychology as well as acting as honorary treasurer of the British section of the International Association for Labour Legislation.

Minister of health and deputy Labour leader Greenwood had already shown interest in a parliamentary career by standing unsuccessfully for Southport in the 1918 general election. In 1922 he was returned for Nelson and Colne, which he represented until 1931. He had also taken a more prominent role in party affairs by drafting a report on unemployment for a special conference in 1921 and being a member of the party's commission on Ireland. He was also secretary to the joint Labour Party–TUC committee on the cost of living, which published three reports in 1921. In the 1924 Labour government he was parliamentary secretary to the minister of health, John Wheatley, whose housing legislation was one of the high points of

that government. At this point Greenwood had established himself within the new generation of Labour politicians who were expected to provide leadership in the future. But now the drink problem emerged. At a dinner in 1925 Beatrice Webb, one of Greenwood's supporters, noted that Ben Spoor was smelling of whisky and 'Arthur Greenwood looked as if he was going the same way' (*Diary*, 4.58). This did not prevent Greenwood from being one of the more successful members of the ill-fated 1929–31 administration. As minister of health he improved widows' pensions in 1929, and the Housing Act of 1930 permitted slum clearance and rebuilding in the 1930s. As importantly for his place in the Labour Party of the 1930s, he came out early, in January 1931, against cuts in social services as a means of balancing the budget, a line he maintained through the summer crisis. He lost his seat in 1931, but came back in 1932 as MP for Wakefield, which he represented until his death.

There was considerable scope for rethinking policy and rebuilding morale after 1931, and Greenwood played a full part in this, including the drafting of the 1935 election manifesto. Following the general election Greenwood stood, with Bevin's backing, against Attlee and Morrison in the party leadership election. He finished last on the first ballot, and his supporters ensured Attlee's victory. Because Morrison refused to take the deputy leadership, it became Greenwood's. His regular drunkenness had now become firmly established, and many of his afternoons must have been unproductive. An NEC enquiry into the research department which he ran found that it was 'not, either administratively or psychologically, in a happy condition' (report as an appendix to the NEC minutes of 22 June 1938). The upshot was that supervision of detailed work went to Greenwood's assistant, and he was left with liaison between the department and the parliamentary party. But the report still went out of its way to emphasize the debt the party owed to Greenwood, and he became known as the Human Bluebook for his mastery of policy detail.

The context for his most notable public act was the declining confidence in the foreign policy of the Chamberlain government from 1938 onwards. With Attlee ill in 1939, it fell to Greenwood to demand a more resolute stand against Hitler. Although up to that point he was not known as a speaker for the big issue, being more at home with the specialized talk to an informed audience, his speech on Saturday 2 September was widely remembered as the high point of his career. The British government's response to Germany's invasion of Poland had been muted on the Friday, and in the house on the Saturday Chamberlain seemed to be wavering; there were fears that he was considering further approaches to Hitler. With Amery's urging to 'Speak for England', Greenwood provided a firmer line: 'I wonder how long we are prepared to vacillate at a time when Britain and all that Britain stands for, and human civilisation, are in peril. We must march with the French' (*Hansard 5C*, 351, 1939, cols. 282–3). In the months that followed Greenwood played a central part in Labour's strategy of supporting the war effort but refusing full co-operation with Chamberlain. This was a remarkable and isolated period in Greenwood's career when his actions and Attlee's own weakness suggested the deputy as a possible replacement for his leader. As Hugh Dalton remarked to Ellen Wilkinson in 1942:

> Greenwood had done extremely well at the outbreak of the war, never before or since had he reached the same high standard and it seemed to me that *any* substitution would have been better than none. But this was a phase which had passed. (*War Diary of Hugh Dalton*, 510)

War cabinet and the Attlee government In the coalition government formed by Churchill in May 1940 Greenwood had a place in the war cabinet and was given charge of the production council and the economic policy committee. But he was an ineffectual figure and Churchill disbanded both committees in January 1941. Greenwood was switched to reconstruction policy but was eventually sacked in February 1942. In his publicizing of Beveridge's committee on social insurance he still showed his eye for social policy, which had popular attraction, although his performance in the parliamentary debate where Labour became distinctively associated with the speedy implementation of Beveridge's report was uncertain. Greenwood was now in decline, and his successful candidature for the party treasurership in 1943 owed something to animosity towards his rival, Morrison, and to a sense that he had been brutally treated by Churchill. Even so, Dalton wondered whether the standing of the party would be helped by its endorsement of such an apparently hapless figure. None the less, Greenwood survived to play a part in the 1945–50 government as lord privy seal and from July 1946 to March 1947 as paymaster-general. According to the historian of the Attlee period Greenwood was a major architect of the National Health Service and the national insurance scheme through his chairmanship of the cabinet social services committee. This did not prevent his dismissal from office in September 1947 on the spurious grounds of the need to bring in younger men. But he retained his position in the party, winning posts which depended upon seniority, regard, and a certain distance from key factions. He was elected chairman of the national executive in 1952 and retained the treasurership in 1953, even though he was then, according to Dalton, 'quite gaga' (*Political Diary*, 615). Morrison was again the loser, since by withdrawing his candidature he lost any backing he might have had for the treasurership in the future, with the result that Gaitskell was elected Greenwood's successor.

Although those who worked closely with Greenwood sometimes felt they might be damaged by his reputation, he was universally liked for his genuinely friendly and unassuming manner. But was there a more substantial career destroyed by its character's own failings, principally through drink? Greenwood had certainly shown good judgement at various points, as in 1931 and 1939, and his ability to see what was politically promising in the continuing discussions about social policy was valuable for the party. He was also, early in his career, able to win the trust of key figures and so place himself in the right circles. He therefore displayed real political flair and at his death was recognized as one of the key figures in the party's early history. But he lacked some of the unpleasant virtues required for achieving the highest ranks. He was never able or willing to turn his well-known sociability to aggressive effect. He formed no faction which might have pushed him further, even when Attlee's leadership drove the party to despair. Attlee was able to defend himself by knowing everything that was going on in the intrigues and machinations which occasionally swirled around him; Greenwood also had reserves of defence and resilience but largely because everyone liked him. If lives in the Labour Party are sometimes explained by faction, they can also be accounted for by loyalty, and Greenwood's was probably one of these. What to a serious-minded outsider might seem to have been an improbably long career was, when viewed from within, more intelligible.

Greenwood was sworn of the privy council in 1929, made a freeman of the city of Leeds and an honorary doctor of laws of the university in 1930, and created a Companion of Honour in 1945. He refused a viscountancy in 1947. His appearance did not bear the stamp of a working-class background. He was tall and lithe, with well-defined features, and was able to beat off a knife-carrying assailant outside the Commons late one night in July 1942. His father had owned a number of houses in working-class districts of Leeds, and, although his inheritance on his father's death in October 1940 was complicated by the difficult behaviour of his brother Willie, he enjoyed a small rental income. His wife also owned several properties in London, and together the rents from these properties increased his earnings when out of government by about one-third. But in 1948 he was seriously and expensively ill with throat trouble and had financial problems, with tax payments overdue and difficulty paying the rent on his Dolphin Square flat. In 1954 he was ill with pleurisy before he died at his home, 8 Gainsborough Gardens, Hampstead, on 9 June 1954. He was cremated at Golders Green crematorium on 14 June. His son, Arthur William James (Anthony) *Greenwood, also made a career in the Labour Party.

R. C. WHITING

Sources Bodl. Oxf., MSS Greenwood · People's History Museum, Manchester, Labour Party archives · U. Leeds · *The political diary of Hugh Dalton, 1918–1940, 1945–1960*, ed. B. Pimlott (1986) · *The Second World War diary of Hugh Dalton, 1940–1945*, ed. B. Pimlott (1986) · *The diary of Beatrice Webb*, ed. N. MacKenzie and J. MacKenzie, 4 vols. (1982–5), vols. 3–4 · B. Pimlott, *Labour and the left in the 1930s* (1977) · B. Pimlott, *Hugh Dalton* (1985) · P. Addison, *The road to 1945* (1975) · K. O. Morgan, *Labour in power, 1945–1951* (1984) · P. Williamson, *National crisis and national government: British politics, the economy and empire, 1926–1932* (1992) · b. cert. · m. cert.

Archives Bodl. Oxf., corresp. and papers; draft memoirs; press cuttings · JRL, *Manchester Guardian* archives, letters to the *Manchester Guardian* · PRO, corresp. and papers as lord privy seal, CAB 118/29, 40 · U. Leeds, archives, press cuttings; national executive committee; university career | People's History Museum, Manchester, labour party archive, corresp. with J. S. Middleton | FILM BFI NFTVA, documentary footage · BFI NFTVA, news footage · BFI NFTVA, party political footage · IWM FVA, actuality footage

Likenesses W. Stoneman, three photographs, 1924–41, NPG · photographs, 1929–47, Hult. Arch. · I. Opffer, sanguine, 1930, NPG · H. Coster, photographs, 1930–39, NPG · Lenare, three photographs, 1939, NPG · F. Man, photograph, 1939, NPG · photograph, 1940 (with Attlee), Bodl. Oxf. · K. Pollak, photograph, 1948, NPG [*see illus.*] · T. Cottrell, print, NPG · photographs, Bodl. Oxf., Greenwood MSS, MS photographs c.85

Wealth at death £7591 14*s*. 3*d*.: probate, 27 July 1954, *CGPLA Eng. & Wales*

Greenwood, Arthur William James [Anthony], **Baron Greenwood of Rossendale** (1911–1982), politician, was born at Leeds on 14 September 1911, the only son and younger child of Arthur *Greenwood (1880–1954) MP, and his wife, Catherine Ainsworth, daughter of John James Brown, clerk, of Leeds; he was later known as Anthony or Tony (perhaps to distinguish him from his father whose forename he shared). He was educated at Merchant Taylors' School, London, and Balliol College, Oxford. He became president of the Oxford Union and took part in the famous 'king and country' debate (8 February 1933); he also gained third-class honours in politics, philosophy, and economics. After going down from Oxford, he drifted somewhat for a time. He went on a debating tour of India but was then unemployed for a period, during which he contemplated going to fight for the republicans in the Spanish Civil War. However, in 1938–9 he worked for the National Fitness Council. In 1940 he married Gillian Crawshay Williams, an artist, daughter of Leslie Crawshay Williams, an engineer and inventor of Bridgend, and a descendant of Thomas Henry Huxley. They had two daughters. At the outbreak of the Second World War he joined the Ministry of Information, and from 1942 served in the RAF as an intelligence officer. He worked with the Allied Reparations Committee and attended the conference at Potsdam in 1945.

Not surprisingly for one whose father became a cabinet minister and deputy leader of the Labour Party, Greenwood developed strong political interests early on. He joined the Labour Party at the age of fourteen, attended socialist gatherings at Easton Lodge, and showed a strong interest in the movements for Indian independence, Zionism, and resistance to fascism. Before the war he became prospective candidate for Colchester, and he led the Labour group on Hampstead borough council from 1945 to 1949. In a by-election in February 1946 he was elected for Heywood and Radcliffe. After redistribution, he moved to become member for Rossendale in 1950 and held the seat for the next twenty years. Latterly he was sponsored by the transport workers' union. He served as parliamentary private secretary to the postmaster-general in 1949 and became vice-chairman of the Parliamentary Labour Party in 1950–51. Among his early interests was the campaign against blood sports, and he was a sponsor of Seymour Cock's anti-hunting bill 1949.

It was, however, after 1951 that Greenwood became a major political figure. A factor here may have been the death in 1954 of his father, who had somewhat overshadowed him even though they had never been especially close. Greenwood was a strong supporter of Aneurin

Bevan in the internal Labour Party disputes of the fifties, and backed up Bevan in resisting the 1951 rearmament programme and charges on the health service. In 1954 he was elected to the party national executive committee (NEC) as part of the left-wing tide at that period. He served on the NEC until 1970. He shortly entered the shadow cabinet, where he served successively as spokesman on Home Office affairs and education. He also became a very popular platform speaker and television performer on the programme *In the News*. When the Campaign for Nuclear Disarmament was founded, Greenwood was a staunch supporter and took part in the first Aldermaston march in 1958. He challenged Hugh Gaitskell vigorously on defence policy, and on 13 October 1960 he resigned from the shadow cabinet in protest at Gaitskell's resistance to the unilateralist vote at the party conference. He backed Harold Wilson against Gaitskell for the party leadership later that month. In November 1961 he stood himself for the leadership but was defeated by Gaitskell (by 171 votes to 59), as his father had been by Attlee back in 1935.

Greenwood's career gained a lift in February 1963 when Wilson succeeded Gaitskell as leader, following the latter's unexpected death. Indeed, Wilson owed him a good deal for not standing himself and splitting the left-wing vote. Greenwood also served as party chairman in 1963–4. He was assured of cabinet office in a future Labour government, and duly became colonial secretary under Wilson in October 1964.

There was much for Greenwood to do at the Colonial Office. He visited the Caribbean, Aden, and Mauritius. He took a close interest in the affairs of Belize, which gained its independence in 1964, and helped create a unitary state in southern Arabia. In December 1965 a cabinet reshuffle saw him moved to the Ministry of Overseas Development. Following Labour's handsome election victory, he became minister of housing and local government in August 1966. His private ambitions were for the Home Office, but housing was an area in which he had long had a specialist interest. In 1966–7 house construction went on rapidly, with over 400,000 houses—a record—completed in 1967. However, his reputation suffered from the draconian cuts in the housing budget imposed in 1968 in the aftermath of the devaluation of the pound. Although he passed a Countryside Act and a notable Housing Act in 1969, he was attacked by the left for not resisting cuts in public expenditure more vigorously. Richard Crossman was a particularly savage critic. He was also widely felt to be insufficiently assertive as a departmental minister. The home secretary, James Callaghan, brushed him aside to take charge in 1968 after the flats at Ronan Point had collapsed. In October 1969 his housing ministry was placed under the expanded department of local government and regional planning headed by Anthony Crosland. Greenwood's being dropped from the cabinet was another sign of waning fortunes.

Greenwood suffered another blow in July 1968 when, after being persuaded to stand for the general secretaryship of the Labour Party, he was unexpectedly opposed on the NEC by right-wing trade unionists, supported by Callaghan and George Brown. Greenwood was defeated 14–12 by Harry Nicholas of the transport workers. Basically, he lost because he was felt to be Wilson's creature, but he took his defeat with considerable dignity. A final set-back came in 1970 when he was offered the chairmanship of the Commonwealth Development Corporation by Wilson. However, Labour lost the election and the new Conservative prime minister, Edward Heath, rescinded the appointment. Greenwood, who had resigned his seat in anticipation of his new post, was out of parliament and in serious financial straits as well. The marriage of a daughter at this time brought some financial embarrassment. A life peerage was scant consolation.

However, after 1970 Greenwood showed much resilience in developing a new career. His finances were repaired by business directorships in the Britannia Building Society and the Municipal Mutual Insurance Company. He was also very active in a host of social and charitable causes, including the Greenwood Development Housing Company to build Greenwood Homes, the UK Housing Trust, the Cremation Society, and the Piccadilly Advice Centre for the homeless. He was also much involved in the British Council for the Rehabilitation of the Disabled, the National Society for the Abolition of Cruel Sports, the Pure Rivers Society, and the movement for Christian Responsibility in Public Affairs (this last although he was never a regular churchgoer). From his new home in East Mersea, he was active in the affairs of rural Essex, including preserving its rivers and wildlife. He was deputy lieutenant of Essex in 1974 and also pro-chancellor of the University of Lancaster. He became a privy councillor in 1964, an honorary LLD of the University of Lancaster in 1979, and from 1950 had been a JP.

Tony Greenwood was an attractive politician: tall, handsome, and elegantly dressed. He cut a fine figure on the platform and was a most effective public speaker. He was well-liked on all sides of the Labour Party. It may have been a lack of ruthlessness that prevented his rising to the highest offices. His later years were marked by numerous set-backs. But they never soured him, while he played a notable part in the revival of the British left down to 1964. Unlike many sons of famous men, he carved a notable career of his own. He died suddenly of a heart attack on 12 April 1982, at his home in Essex, Old Ship Cottage, East Mersea (he had had health problems since 1970), and was cremated at East Mersea. He was survived by his wife.

KENNETH O. MORGAN

Sources Bodl. Oxf., MSS Anthony Greenwood · Bodl. Oxf., MSS Arthur Greenwood · Museum of Labour History, Manchester, labour party archives · *The Times* (14 April 1982) · *The backbench diaries of Richard Crossman*, ed. J. Morgan (1981) · R. H. S. Crossman, *The diaries of a cabinet minister*, 3 vols. (1975–7) · *The Castle diaries, 1964–1970* (1984) · private information (2004) [Gillian, Lady Greenwood] · *Tribune* · *New Statesman* · *Hansard 5C* (1964–70) · A. Benn, *Diaries, 1940–62* (1994) · A. Benn, *Diaries, 1963–7* (1987) · A. Benn, *Diaries, 1968–72* (1988)

Archives Bodl. Oxf., papers | Bodl. Oxf., corresp. with Attlee · Bodl. Oxf., corresp. with Lord Monckton · Bodl. RH, corresp. mainly relating to Mauritius · PRO, cabinet office MSS, corresp. with Sir William Jowitt, CAB 127/159, 163 | FILM BFI NFTVA, documentary footage | SOUND BBC WAC

Likenesses photograph, 1970, Hult. Arch. · G. Greenwood, portrait, Greenwood Homes head office, Northampton

Wealth at death £116,944: probate, 22 June 1982, *CGPLA Eng. & Wales*

Greenwood, Christopher (1786–1855), land surveyor and map maker, was born on 21 May 1786 at Coverdale in Gisburn parish, Yorkshire, the third of the ten children of John Greenwood, grazier, and his wife, Ellen (*née* Bullock). The family had been long established in the district. After learning his trade, and presumably practising locally for some years, he set up in Dewsbury in 1815. Soon afterwards he settled in Wakefield, where he married Maria Elizabeth, the daughter of William Fowler, a local wool stapler, at St John's Church, on 5 June 1816. In 1814 or 1815 he had embarked on the survey of Yorkshire which launched the career in county map making which was to occupy the rest of his professional life; it was published in Wakefield between May 1817 and August 1818. Trained to survey small estates and farms, Greenwood learned the techniques of triangulation and the use of instruments needed to survey areas the size of counties from the engineer and surveyor, Francis Giles, who supervised his local triangulation of Yorkshire.

Following the death of his mother in July 1818 Greenwood moved to London. With only the Yorkshire map in print, he had determined to map the whole of the rest of England at one inch to one mile, and Wales at three-quarters of an inch to one mile. In 1822, with eleven counties already on sale, he advertised the complete scheme in detail: a set of forty-two maps comprising 184 sheets to cost 135 guineas. Greenwood was not the first private surveyor to embark on such a risky enterprise—as it turned out, six English counties and most of Wales were never surveyed—but he came far closer than any other map maker since his fellow Yorkshireman, Christopher Saxton, in the 1570s, to surveying all the English counties. His assistant in all his county maps was his younger brother **John Greenwood** (1791–1867), who had been working for him since before he left Gisburn. In fifteen years (1815–30) the brothers surveyed thirty-three English and four Welsh counties; the result is thirty-five maps at a scale of one inch to one mile or thereabouts (Yorkshire and south-east Wales at three-quarters of an inch to one mile, and Middlesex at 2 inches). Even allowing for the use of the major triangulation of the Ordnance Survey, and possibly some help from existing surveys, it was an astonishing achievement for a private surveyor in so short a time. The majority of these surveys anticipated publication of the sheets of the Ordnance Survey. Even in the south of England and in Lincolnshire, where the Ordnance Survey published their maps first, Greenwood did not slavishly copy the work, but offered a distinctive style and some additional information; not least of the attractions of his maps was the high standard of the engraving.

For a wider market an *Atlas of the Counties of England* appeared in parts between 1829 and 1834. The enduring popularity of its plates came partly from the beautifully engraved vignettes of cathedrals, castles, or town views that graced each one. The Greenwoods' only venture outside county or regional map making was their map of London (1827) at eight inches to one mile, engraved to high standards by James and Josiah Neele, who probably printed most of Greenwood's maps.

Although Greenwood can rightly be regarded as an important and successful map maker, by concentrating on the publication of original surveys—rather than on popular atlases and derivative maps—he was taking risks. He relied on the patronage of the aristocracy, but also depended heavily on his business partners. On his arrival in London he established himself at 50 Leicester Square. In 1820 the firm moved to 70 Queen Street, Cheapside—the premises of George Pringle, a solicitor, and George Pringle junior, who had become his new partners by 1819. His father-in-law was already a financial partner, and in 1821 or 1822 John Greenwood also became a partner. The firm secured its first unshared premises in 1824, at 13 Lower Regent Street, a fashionable address where the business had its most successful years. Each map was dedicated to 'the nobility, clergy, and gentry' of the county concerned. But Greenwood was not unusual in failing to find long-term security in making county maps—he faced increasing competition (reflected in acrimonious exchanges in local newspapers) from other private surveyors, notably Andrew Bryant. In the longer term it was the Ordnance Survey which overwhelmed him: by 1834, when the business was already foundering, southern and midland counties, as well as south Wales, were covered by the Ordnance Survey.

In 1828 George Pringle junior left. Thereafter the publication of maps tailed off and some plates were sold to other publishers who printed from them with little or no revision. By late 1830 Greenwood had left Regent Street and within four years, after struggling on in Covent Garden and Paternoster Row, the business appears to have collapsed. The Greenwoods had published three county topographies in 1822–3, and, after seeing his cartographic business prematurely collapse, Christopher turned, unsuccessfully, to publishing county historical guides from an office in Hart Street, Bloomsbury.

John Greenwood had returned to Yorkshire by 1835 and made estate, enclosure, and tithe maps until at least 1850. He died on 1 October 1867, aged seventy-six, and was buried in Gisburn. Christopher Greenwood's stock-in-trade was sold at Sothebys on 18 June 1840. He died in obscurity on 25 March 1855 at 2 Sarah Place, on Kingsland Road, Dalston, Hackney, London. PAUL LAXTON

Sources J. B. Harley, *Christopher Greenwood county map-maker and his Worcestershire map of 1822* (1962) · J. B. Harley and R. W. Dunning, 'Introduction', *Somerset maps: Day and Masters, 1782 Greenwood, 1822*, Somerset RS, 76 (1981) · J. B. Harley and G. Walters, 'English map collecting, 1790–1840: a pilot survey of the evidence in Sotheby sale catalogues', *Imago Mundi*, 30 (1978), 31–55 · advertisements and letters in local newspapers and prospectuses, priv. coll. · A. E. Long, ed., *The parish register of Gisburne: part two, 1745–1812* (1952) · d. cert. · *CGPLA Eng. & Wales* (1867) [John Greenwood]

Wealth at death under £100—John Greenwood: probate, 1867, *CGPLA Eng. & Wales*

Greenwood, Frederick (1830–1909), author and newspaper editor, born in Kensington, London, on 25 March 1830, was the eldest of the eleven children of James Caer Greenwood, a coach builder, and his wife, Mary Fish. He was educated privately at home before being apprenticed, aged fifteen, to a firm of publishers and printers. Within a year his indentures were cancelled and he was engaged as a reader. Thereafter he supported himself entirely by writing for newspapers and a variety of journals, although he would have preferred to make his reputation as a man of letters, not as a journalist. In 1853 he contributed a *Life of Louis Napoleon* to a series, The Napoleon Dynasty. This was republished as a book in 1855. A year earlier he had published *The Loves of an Apothecary*. A contribution to *Tait's Edinburgh Magazine* was republished, lavishly illustrated, as *The Path of the Roses* (1859). Greenwood's brother, James, was also a journalist and a prolific story writer. Together they wrote *Under a Cloud*, which first appeared in the *Welcome Guest* and then, in 1860, as a three-volume novel. Since its foundation in 1855 Greenwood had been a constant contributor to Henry Vizetelly's *Illustrated Times*. Occasionally he undertook some of the journal's editorial supervision. In September 1861 he was appointed editor of a new illustrated paper, *The Queen*, but when it was combined with the *Lady's Newspaper* in July 1863 he severed all connection. Meanwhile, he had established close relations with George Murray Smith, proprietor of the *Cornhill Magazine*. Two contributions in particular that Greenwood wrote for the *Cornhill*—'An essay without end' (1860) and 'Margaret Denzil's history' (1863)—convinced Smith of Greenwood's abilities. When Thackeray resigned as editor in 1862, Smith appointed Greenwood, together with George Henry Lewes, to direct the *Cornhill* under his supervision. When Lewes withdrew in 1864 Greenwood became sole editor. For some time Greenwood had nurtured an idea for an independent daily paper modelled on Canning's *Anti-Jacobin*. He had discussed this scheme with Johnny Parker, owner and publisher of *Fraser's Magazine*, and had considered, with Thomas Carlyle, possible candidates as editor. His father's death forced Parker to withdraw from the enterprise, but George Smith, who had been contemplating a similar scheme, was pleased to take Parker's place. On 7 February 1865 the first edition of the *Pall Mall Gazette* appeared, with Greenwood as editor.

In his role as editor Greenwood exercised an exceptional personal influence. E. A. Freeman was not alone in supposing Greenwood to be 'the perfect editor'; certainly he showed considerable acumen in finding and attracting new writing talent. He was a sound judge of contributors, and possessed those qualities of temperament and character that, for the most part, earned in turn the contributors' loyalty and affection. He wrote well himself and encouraged his contributors to develop a more natural, idiomatic style, rather than the somewhat stilted, mannered prose fashionably affected by journalists. Leslie Stephen, a regular contributor, called the paper 'Greenwood's incarnation' (F. W. Hirst, *Early Life and Letters of John Morley*, 2, 1927, 91). Editorial dominance was particularly evident in the political comment. At different times Greenwood

Frederick Greenwood (1830–1909), by unknown engraver, pubd 1892

described his politics as 'sceptical tory' and 'independent conservative', but as time went on he swung his paper further and further into the tory camp. This increasing partisanship mirrored club opinion. He took a particular interest in foreign affairs, profoundly distrusting every Liberal move and championing each tory initiative. In Europe he admired no one more than Bismarck, although he resisted a personal proposal from the Iron Chancellor that the *Pall Mall Gazette* be given preferential treatment in return for small favours. Special treatment was expected from Conservative foreign ministers, and, like William Mudford of *The Standard*, Greenwood was later bitterly resentful of the favours exclusively given to G. E. Buckle and *The Times*. Early in November 1875 the khedive of Egypt, Isma'il Pasha, ruined by the Turkish sultan's bankruptcy, entered into secret negotiations with two French syndicates for the sale of his Suez Canal shares. Greenwood learned of the negotiations from the financier Henry Oppenheim and immediately told Lord Derby. The foreign secretary was not impressed by Greenwood's insistence that it was a vital British interest that the canal should not be wholly French-owned. Derby's view was shared by most of the cabinet, but Disraeli persuaded them otherwise. Disraeli was obliged to turn to the Rothschilds to finance the coup, and their involvement rather overshadowed Greenwood's earlier contribution of intelligence. For the rest of his life Greenwood nursed a grievance that his part in the Suez purchase had been insufficiently recognized by Disraeli.

Convinced that to maintain Turkish integrity was vital to British interests, Greenwood vehemently attacked Gladstone's Bulgarian crusade as sentimental. He turned the *Pall Mall Gazette* into the most relentlessly anti-Gladstonian, thoroughly jingoistic newspaper. Then, in April 1880, the proprietor, Smith, presented the newspaper to his son-in-law, Henry Yates Thompson, who declared his intention to turn the *Pall Mall Gazette* into a Liberal organ. Greenwood and his staff chose to leave Northumberland Street. Their exodus was made the more unpalatable by Yates Thompson publicly acknowledging Greenwood's 'untiring assiduity and unflinching independence' (Mills, 47) as editor, and shamelessly publishing articles earlier accumulated by Greenwood. The immediate riposte was the publication of the *St James's*

Gazette. To all intents and purposes, this new *Gazette* was the old *Pall Mall* in everything but name—a platform for Greenwood to continue his campaign against all manner and conditions of Liberals and Irish nationalists, not excluding the frequent ambuscade of tory men and measures that had earned his displeasure. As an evening, clubland paper offering commentary and initiating public discussion on issues of the day, the *St James's Gazette*, for all its small circulation, enjoyed a measure of influence. But the paper was not without defects, which became increasingly conspicuous as Greenwood indulged his many political peccadilloes. Its appeal to the general body of tories decreased, and George Meredith, who looked kindly upon Greenwood as his literary mentor, admitted the *St James's Gazette* was spoiled by incessant carping and barking. Lord Salisbury, for one, found Greenwood's hard-line Conservatism sour and unprofitable. In 1885 Greenwood effectively offered Randolph Churchill the *St James's Gazette* as 'your own organ at your own disposal' (Koss, 274) but Churchill, despite an insatiable appetite for publicity, refused the offer. As Greenwood's judgement and tone grew increasingly wayward, circulation declined. The proprietor of the *St James's Gazette*, Henry Hucks Gibbs, grew ever more disillusioned at having to keep afloat a sinking property that brought neither financial nor political reward. Gibbs sold out to Edward Steinkopff, who was not inclined to give Greenwood the editorial freedom he thought was his due. Within a year Greenwood angrily resigned. Soon after he simultaneously announced that he had given up daily journalism and brought out the first edition of a weekly, *The Anti-Jacobin*, on 31 January 1891. It proved a commercial and journalistic flop, folding within a year. Greenwood continued to write for a number of magazines, including the *Saturday Review* and *Blackwood's Edinburgh Magazine*. He published two further books: *The Lover's Lexicon* (1893) and *Imagination in Dreams* (1894). When *Blackwood's* gave its editorial support to the war in South Africa, Greenwood ceased writing the series of articles he had begun in 1898 under the general title of the 'Looker on'. He had never had a good opinion of Joseph Chamberlain and distrusted the radical Unionists. Thus, on South Africa, the incorrigible jingo found himself, somewhat incongruously, sharing the camp of the pro-Boers.

In 1850 Greenwood had married Katherine Darby, who came from a Quaker family; she died in 1900. Of their five children, a son and two daughters survived him. Greenwood failed in his pleas for a civil-list pension, but his daughters were granted pensions of £100 a year on his death. He died at his home, 6 Border Crescent, Sydenham, on 14 December 1909. When editor of the *Pall Mall Gazette*, Greenwood had supposed that he enjoyed 'a place of power equal to half a dozen seats in parliament' (F. Greenwood, 'Press and government', *Nineteenth Century*, 28, 1890, 109). Editors of papers that specialized in views rather than news not uncommonly entertained exaggerated notions of their political importance. As a political commentator, especially in the latter half of the 1880s at the *St James's Gazette*, Greenwood's snapping and snarling gave some substance to Labouchere's dismissal of him as no more than 'a clever ass' (Labouchere to T. H. S. Escott, 1885, BL, Escott MSS). Greenwood did not seek to cultivate politicians with sweet words or, like Delane, by dining out and socializing. But at his best, in his *Pall Mall* days, as John Morley testified, Greenwood 'fought the battle of public life as honourably and uprightly as that battle can be fought'. Gladstone acknowledged what an 'effective supporter Lord Beaconsfield had in Mr Greenwood' (Scott, *Life and Death*, 63). As a literary editor few excelled Greenwood in his ability to detect and encourage young authors. There, instinct and skill combined with a perfect sincerity and absolute disinterestedness.   A. J. A. MORRIS

Sources J. W. Robertson Scott, *The story of the Pall Mall Gazette* (1950) · J. W. R. Scott, *The life and death of a newspaper* (1952) · S. E. Koss, *The rise and fall of the political press in Britain*, 1 (1981) · *DNB* · J. S. Mills, *Sir Edward Cook KBE: a biography* (1921)
Archives BL, corresp. with Lord Carnarvon, Add. MS 60778 · NL Scot., corresp. with Blackwoods · UCL, letters to David Hannay
Likenesses Ape [C. Pellegrini], caricature, watercolour study, NPG; repro. in *VF* (19 June 1880) · wood-engraving, NPG; repro. in *ILN* (14 May 1892) [*see illus.*]
Wealth at death £6552 13s. 9d.: probate, 12 Jan 1910, *CGPLA Eng. & Wales*

Greenwood, Sir Granville George (1850–1928), politician and animal welfare reformer, was born in London on 3 January 1850, the second son of John Greenwood QC (1800–1871) of the western circuit (solicitor to the Treasury, 1866–71) and his wife, Fanny H. Welch, daughter of William Collyns of Starcross, Devon. He was educated at Eton College (1862–9) and at Trinity College, Cambridge, where he matriculated in 1869, was a foundation scholar 1871, and gained a first class in classics in 1873. He was admitted to the Middle Temple in 1872, called to the bar in 1876, and joined the western circuit. He was assistant commissioner for charities (1884). On 11 April 1878 he married Laurentia Trent, daughter of Laurence Trent Cumberbatch MD of 25 Cadogan Place, London; they had one son and three daughters; his wife survived him. He was an original member of the Eighty Club and, from 1879, of the United University Club. He unsuccessfully contested Peterborough for the Liberals in 1886 and Central Hull in 1900. With the financial and political support of Herbert Gladstone he was elected Liberal MP for Peterborough in 1906, and sat until defeated in 1918. He was knighted in 1916.

As a Liberal MP, Greenwood advocated reforms concerning land, education, the House of Lords, poor and labour laws, pensions, death certification, women's suffrage, national health insurance, proportional representation, handling of police complaints, rights of colonial natives, and, between 1914 and 1918, the condition of British troops abroad and the quality of the army's medical services. He was critical of capital punishment and strongly opposed the flogging of schoolchildren and colonial natives. His main concern, however, was the protection of animals, especially as regards vivisection, abattoirs, zoos, live exports, the treatment of horses, the sale of deer, field sports, the transport of poultry, plumage imports, and the condition of pit ponies. He was a council member of the Royal Society for the Prevention of Cruelty to Animals

from 1908 to 1927. His greatest achievement politically was to steer through parliament the Protection of Animals Act (1911), where his polite, businesslike, and practical approach proved successful. This consolidating act remained the basic law protecting animals from cruelty throughout the twentieth century.

Greenwood's main literary interest was in Shakespeare, on whose works he was considered expert. From his *The Shakespeare Problem Restated* (1908) to *Shakespeare's Handwriting and the Northumberland Manuscript* and *The Stratford Bust and the Droeshout Engraving* (both 1925) Greenwood published about a dozen pieces arguing that William Shakespere (*sic*) of Stratford was not the author of Shakespeare's works. Not a Baconian but an agnostic, Greenwood made negative attacks on Shakespearian orthodoxy with 'a curious mixture of suavity and abuse' (Schoenbaum, 427), and argued the plays were the work of a talented lawyer. The *Encyclopaedia Britannica* and others have rated his contribution to this long controversy as 'scholarly' and 'rational'. His other writings included attacks on field sports, steel traps, vivisection, the Church of England, the death certification procedure, and the government of Turkey. He also published two philosophical works.

Intelligent and humane, Greenwood described himself in an enclosure with a letter to Sir Henry Campbell-Bannerman as 'not a churchman' but 'a strong advocate of impartial justice to all' (letter to Sir H. Campbell-Bannerman, 3 June 1907, BL, Add. MS 41239). His motive for entering politics was, he said, his urgent desire for reform of the House of Lords—a cause he had championed for many years. He might well have been in government but he did not enter parliament until his fifty-seventh year—'too late and long after I had left ambition in the rear' (Greenwood, letter to Lord Gladstone, 22 Dec 1909, BL, Add. MS 46068). In his *The Faith of an Agnostic* (2nd edn, 1919; under the pseudonym George Forrester), Greenwood sided with T. H. Huxley against clericalism and in support of science and agnostic rationalism, advocating that 'the sacred feeling of compassion should be extended so as to embrace all sentient beings' (p. 17). Greenwood lived at several London addresses including 53 Chester Square and, later, at 33 Linden Gardens. He died at the latter on 27 October 1928.   RICHARD D. RYDER

Sources WWBMP, vol. 2 · Hansard 5C (1906–18) · WWW, 1916–28 · G. G. Greenwood, *The faith of an agnostic*, 2nd edn (1919) · S. Schoenbaum, *Shakespeare's lives*, new edn (1991); pbk edn (1993) · G. G. Greenwood, *The Shakespeare problem restated* (1908) · G. G. Greenwood, letters, BL · E. S. Turner, *All heaven in a rage* (1992) · R. D. Ryder, *Animal revolution: changing attitudes towards speciesism* (1989) · Venn, *Alum. Cant.* · Boase, *Mod. Eng. biog.* · *The Eton register*, 3 (privately printed, Eton, 1906) · Burke, *Peerage* (1924)
Archives L. Cong., manuscript division, corresp. with Harrington Putman · Ransom HRC, corresp. with John Lane relating to his work on Shakespeare
Wealth at death £14,446 14s. 8d.: probate, 4 Dec 1928, *CGPLA Eng. & Wales*

Greenwood, Hamar, first Viscount Greenwood (1870–1948), politician and businessman, was born on 7 February 1870 at Whitby, near Toronto, Ontario, Canada. He was the eldest son in the family of two sons and six daughters of John Hamar Greenwood (1829–1903), a lawyer who as a youth had emigrated from Llanbister, Radnorshire, Wales to Canada. His mother was Charlotte Churchill Hubbard (*d.* 1903), daughter of Thomas C. Hubbard; she was from a United Empire loyalist family, one of whose ancestors had emigrated to Canada after the American War of Independence. At birth, his forenames were first registered as Thomas Hubbard, but he always used the name Hamar. He attended Whitby high school and the University of Toronto, taking his BA degree in 1895. He worked in the Ontario department of agriculture, and for seven years was an officer in the Canadian militia.

In 1895 Greenwood emigrated to England, where he read for the bar. In 1906 he was called to the bar at Gray's Inn, and became a bencher in 1917 and a KC in 1919. His work in helping to raise a regiment of British subjects from overseas, the King's Colonials (later King Edward's Horse), in 1902, indicated the strength of his imperial loyalties. His belief in temperance—he never drank alcohol—drew him initially to the Liberal Party. At the 1906 general election he was elected Liberal MP for York. For four years he was parliamentary private secretary to Winston Churchill. His speeches in the Commons on imperial defence were more in line with the Conservatives than the Liberals. He lost his seat in January 1910 but returned to parliament in December that year as the Liberal member for Sunderland. As a leader of Canadian society in London he argued that England needed 'Canadianising', publishing in 1913 *Canada as an Imperial Factor*, 'a description of his mother country more enthusiastic than critical' (*DNB*). He married on 23 May 1911 Margery, daughter of Walter Spencer of Fownhope Court, Herefordshire. They had two sons and two daughters.

In August 1914 Greenwood's connection with L. S. Amery, his sister's husband, brought him into the recruiting department at the War Office, a position where he developed his ability for making quick decisions. He himself raised the 10th battalion, South Wales Borderers, and commanded it on the western front in France. Created a baronet in February 1915, he was transferred by Lord Derby to London the next year for additional recruiting work. In August 1916 he returned again to politics, becoming a Coalition Liberal supporter of Lloyd George. In January 1919 he was made under-secretary for home affairs and in July took charge of overseas trade. In April 1920 he joined the cabinet as the last chief secretary for Ireland, the principal minister responsible for Irish affairs.

The Anglo-Irish War had been under way for more than a year, but Greenwood actually knew little about Ireland. He shared Lloyd George's view that the Irish people were terrorized by the IRA, a 'murder gang'. Determined to reassert British authority at Dublin Castle by force, the government reinforced the army. But since the cabinet was not yet prepared to declare a state of martial law, the main responsibility for order fell to the greatly undermanned Royal Irish Constabulary (RIC). RIC recruits were hastily brought to Ireland, most of them recently demobilized British war veterans. Their surplus khaki uniforms

and black belts earned them the label Black and Tans after the name of Limerick's famous pack of hounds. This appellation was at times mistakenly given to the new 1500 man auxiliary division, RIC, an auxiliary police comprised mainly of former British officers. Undisciplined and inappropriately trained for police work, the Black and Tans and auxiliaries were ignorant of the Irish countryside and its people. This left them ill equipped to deal with the violent methods of the IRA, which they replicated in retaliation for the attacks made upon them.

In parliament the chief secretary's role was to defend both reprisals and the Lloyd George government's policy toward Ireland. Since Greenwood and the government believed that reprisals were beneficial, they made only a token effort to eliminate them. He quickly became known for his denials and evasions in the House of Commons, and his performance was accurately caricatured by the phrases 'to tell a Greenwood' and 'there is no such thing as reprisals, but they have done a great deal of good' (Seedorf, 'The Lloyd George government', 114). As the competition in violence increased, 'unauthorized reprisals' became the greatest obstacle to implementing Lloyd George's policy of force, or of limited 'police war'. The actions of crown forces, culminating in 'bloody Sunday' (21 November 1920), when auxiliaries machine-gunned spectators after a Gaelic football match at Croke Park, Dublin, defeated their own purpose and caused a revulsion of the British conscience as it awakened to the state of affairs in Ireland.

Newspapers and editorials in Ireland condemned the government's failure to investigate and to end reprisals. In addition, Irish opinion became ever more supportive of the IRA, making prolonged guerrilla warfare possible despite Michael Collins's assertion that the Irish never numbered as many as 3000 armed men at any given moment. The Irish hated the British and were willing to bear any amount of suffering to see them go. Lloyd George comprehended this before Greenwood, but despite this kept Greenwood in his cabinet. While privately constraining Greenwood, Lloyd George defended him in public.

By April 1921 circumstances were changing. Lloyd George had already coupled appeasement with his policy of force, and was exploring the chances for negotiation with the Irish republican leaders. After George V's visit to Belfast on 22 June 1921 Lloyd George directly communicated with the Irish leader, Eamon De Valera, and the truce of 11 July was arranged over Greenwood's head. Greenwood was present at the Anglo-Irish conference in London in October, and signed the Anglo-Irish treaty of 6 December 1921, but he took little active part in the deliberations. When the Irish Free State was set up in January 1922 he remained chief secretary in order to work for the pension rights of the Royal Irish Constabulary, which the free state at once disbanded. When Lloyd George fell from power in October 1922 Greenwood resigned as chief secretary. In the general election of November 1922 he lost his seat at Sunderland, and failed to regain it the following year.

Like other coalitionists, Greenwood moved to the right and was returned to parliament as an 'anti-Socialist' for East Walthamstow in 1924. No office was offered then, but in August 1929 he was elevated to the peerage as first Baron Greenwood of Llanbister, his father's original home in Radnorshire. Between 1933 and 1938 he also served as honorary treasurer of the Conservative Party, securing substantial moneys for the party from his many business friends, and in February 1937 he advanced to a viscountcy. Lady Greenwood was herself appointed CBE in 1920 and DBE in 1922 for her services in Ireland.

Essentially an administrator and executive, Greenwood had the ability to take charge of meetings, which was valuable in business where simultaneously he was chairman of eight of the sixteen company boards of which he sat. These included Dorman, Long & Co., and the Aerated Bread Company. He was also president of the Iron and Steel Federation in 1938. He had a talent for after-dinner speaking; as president of the Pilgrims Society he took charge of the placing of the Franklin Roosevelt statue in Grosvenor Square. He died soon after in London on 10 September 1948. His wife survived him and his elder son, David Henry Hamar Greenwood (b. 1914), succeeded to the titles.   MARTIN F. SEEDORF

Sources DNB · *The Times* (11 Sept 1948) · *The Times* (21 Sept 1948) · Burke, *Peerage* · L. S. Amery, *My political life*, 2: *War and peace* (1954) · M. F. Seedorf, 'Defending reprisals: Sir Hamar Greenwood and the "troubles", 1920–21', *Éire–Ireland*, 25/4 (1990), 77–92 · D. G. Boyce, *Englishmen and Irish troubles* (1972) · C. Townshend, *The British campaign in Ireland, 1919–1921* (1975) · J. McColgan, *British policy and the Irish administration, 1920–22* (1983) · T. Jones, *Whitehall diary*, ed. K. Middlemas, 3 (1971) · S. Lawlor, *Britain and Ireland 1914–1923* (1983) · J. W. Wheeler-Bennett, *John Anderson, Viscount Waverley* (1967) · F. Pakenham, *Peace by ordeal* (1935) · M. F. Seedorf, 'The Lloyd George government and the Anglo-Irish War, 1919–1921', PhD diss., University of Washington, Seattle, 1974 · K. O. Morgan, *Consensus and disunity: the Lloyd George coalition government, 1918–1922* (1979) · CGPLA Eng. & Wales (1948)
Archives PRO, cabinet records | HLRO, corresp. with Viscount Davidson and Andrew Bonar Law · HLRO, corresp. with David Lloyd George · Lpool RO, Stanley MSS, corresp. with seventeenth earl of Derby · NA Scot., corresp. with Philip Kerr · NL Ire., letters to John Redmond, MS 15192 · PRO, corresp. with Lord Midleton, PRO 30/67 · Wilts. & Swindon RO, corresp. with Viscount Long
Likenesses W. Stoneman, photograph, 1918, NPG
Wealth at death £44,823 8s. 5d.: probate, 22 Nov 1948, CGPLA Eng. & Wales

Greenwood, (Peter) Humphry (1927–1995), ichthyologist, was born on 21 April 1927 in Redruth, Cornwall, the only child of Percy Ashworth Greenwood (1896–1963), mining engineer, and his wife, Joyce May, née Wilton (1893–1957). His father (a Lancastrian, who had met his Cornish wife while studying at the Camborne School of Mines) was at that time working in South Africa, but his mother returned to Cornwall for his birth. Greenwood attended Passmore Edwards School in Redruth (1934) but most of his early years were spent in South Africa, where he attended St John's College, Johannesburg (1934–9), and Michaelhouse, Balgowan, Natal (1939–41). He spent six months at the 'General Botha' Training School of the

South African naval forces (1942), and attended Krugersdorp high school, Krugersdorp from 1942 to 1944. He enlisted in the South African navy in August 1944 and served in the Indian Ocean in HMS *Ceylon*. Having been demobilized in February 1946, he entered the University of the Witwatersrand, Johannesburg, in March, and obtained an honours degree in zoology in 1950. In January that year he married Marjorie George, a demonstrator in the zoology department at 'Wits'. They had four daughters.

On graduating Greenwood obtained a colonial fisheries research studentship, the first seven months of which were to be under the supervision of Dr Ethelwynn Trewavas at the British Museum (natural history), London. There he began work on the haplochromine cichlid fishes of Lake Victoria that were to remain a dominant interest throughout his career. Between 500 and 1000 species of these remarkable fishes have evolved in that lake, to which all are unique. Field studies began early in 1951 at the East African Fisheries Research Organization, Jinja, Uganda, where he remained until July 1957. He returned to the museum in London on a civil service commission fellowship before becoming a member of staff, and remained there until his retirement in 1989 with the rank of deputy chief scientific officer; subsequently he became a visiting research fellow.

When Greenwood began to study the haplochromine cichlids of Lake Victoria, some sixty species were already known, but the real wealth of species was unsuspected. One objective was to discover, describe, and name the entire fauna. This proved to be a major undertaking, beyond the capabilities of a single individual. Nevertheless Greenwood made substantial progress and set new standards in the descriptions of the fifty or so new species that he discovered. This, and the painstaking re-description of previously described species, laid the foundations for an understanding of the relationships of these fishes one with another, and of how they might have evolved. His descriptions, republished as a collected volume in 1981, *The Haplochromine Fishes of the East African Lakes*, stand as a monument to his skill, industry, and patience.

Of wider interest was Greenwood's attempt in 1974 to explain the biology and evolution of this remarkable species flock. He concluded that it was monophyletic: that is, its constituents were derived from a single ancestral species. However, as a result of applying rigorous aspects of that method of classification and the recognition of affinities known as cladistics, he later became dissatisfied with this conclusion, and in 1980 he repudiated it. For technical reasons this was a mistake, and when the development of molecular methods enabled an independent approach to be made, this showed that his original conclusion was correct. Although it has been said that the problems he 'was unable to settle after thirty years of morphology are now more likely to be resolved in a few months by a graduate student and a sequencer' (Patterson, 207) this overlooks the fact that, without his groundwork, such an approach would be impossible as the species involved could not even be identified. Furthermore such investigations tell one nothing about the structure and habits of these fishes, an understanding of these being necessary before meaningful evolutionary changes can be deduced. Here Greenwood's morphological work was of permanent value. However, the discovery of further species led to taxonomic problems that proved contentious, and the extermination of many of these fishes by the introduced Nile perch and other destructive human interference with the lake inevitably caused these studies to end on a note of disappointment.

Greenwood's other published African work embraced descriptions of new fishes, the breeding habits of a catfish and a lungfish, various matters relating to both living and fossil fishes, and a semi-popular book on the fishes of Uganda. For several years in the 1960s and 1970s he was chairman of a team that studied the productivity of Lake George, Uganda. He also made substantial contributions to the higher level systematics of teleost (modern bony) fishes. Particularly significant was a paper with D. E. Rosen, S. H. Weitzman, and G. S. Myers, published in the *Bulletin of the American Museum of Natural History* in 1966, that proposed a classification fundamentally different from its predecessors in certain respects. Other work included studies on the Weberian apparatus, skulls, swim bladder, hyoid and gill-arch musculature, and on the interrelationships of various groups. He also took an interest in marine coelacanths.

Greenwood had an impish sense of humour, reflected in his physiognomy; he was an excellent mimic, and always an entertaining companion. He was elected a fellow of the Royal Society in 1985, and received the scientific medal of the Zoological Society of London (1963), the Linnaeus medal of the Linnean Society of Sweden (1978), and the Linnean medal of the Linnean Society of London (1982), having been president of the last-named society from 1976 to 1979. He became a foreign member (class VII) of the Swedish Royal Academy of Science in 1984.

Following his retirement from the British Museum in 1989, Greenwood returned to South Africa, where he had been an honorary research associate at the J. L. B. Smith Institute of Ichthyology, Rhodes University, since 1977, and lived in Grahamstown. On a brief stopover in London, *en route* for the University of Bergen, Norway, to teach a course in fish anatomy, he collapsed from a stroke in the museum in which he formerly worked. He died two days later, on 3 March 1995, at the Chelsea and Westminster Hospital, London, and he was cremated at Putney Vale. He was survived by his wife, from whom he separated about 1989, and four daughters. A celebration of his life was held at the Linnean Society of London on 21 April 1995.

GEOFFREY FRYER

Sources C. Patterson, *Memoirs FRS*, 43 (1997), 193–213 · P. H. Greenwood, *The haplochromine fishes of the east African lakes: collected papers on their taxonomy, biology and evolution* (1981) · *The Independent* (11 March 1995) · *The Times* (1 May 1995) · *WWW* · d. cert. · personal knowledge (2004) · private information (2004) · *CGPLA Eng. & Wales* (1996)

Likenesses Godfrey Argent Studios, photograph, repro. in *Memoirs FRS*, 194
Wealth at death £95,119: South African probate sealed in London, 25 April 1996, *CGPLA Eng. & Wales*

Greenwood, James (1683?–1737), grammarian, is of unknown parentage. He may have entered Merchant Taylors' School, London, in 1696. At some time he married Susan, or Susannah, who was to outlive him. He became usher to Benjamin Morland at a private school in Hackney, Middlesex, but about 1711 he opened a boarding-school at Woodford in Essex. This school may have taken girls as well as boys. In 1721 he was appointed surmaster at St Paul's School, London, probably on the recommendation of Morland, who had become high master earlier in the year. He retained this post until his death.

Greenwood's earliest published work was *The London Vocabulary, English and Latin* (1711?; 3rd edn, 1713). This was in the style of Comenius's *Orbis pictus* and enjoyed great popularity, being reprinted until at least 1828. Greenwood became best known, however, for *An Essay towards a Practical English Grammar* (1711), which was reprinted five times up to 1753. He also compiled an anthology of English verse, *The Virgin Muse* (1717), which was dedicated to nine young ladies, probably pupils, past or present, of his school at Woodford. The selection of pieces is clearly intended to appeal to girls as much as, if not more than, to boys, and includes a fair number of poems by women. Moreover, this compilation, which includes annotations and a large index explaining the meaning of 'hard words', was the first attempt to teach appreciation of literature for its own sake rather than as a means of illustrating some aspect of the language.

Greenwood's last work, *The Royal English Grammar* (1737), was an abridgement of his *Essay* of 1711 and was dedicated to the princess of Wales. It continued in print up to 1780. Greenwood, who was an advocate of education for women, wrote in the preface

> I have likewise endeavoured to make every Thing Easy and Familiar to the *Fair Sex*, whose Education, perhaps, is too much neglected in the Particular … It is therefore worth the while of Persons of both sexes to take some Pains in the Study of this useful and necessary Art. (Greenwood, *Royal English Grammar*, 1737, vii)

As a grammarian Greenwood was conventional rather than innovative. The *Essay*, as its title indicates, was practical and did not make philosophical claims or propound new theories. It was eclectic, drawing upon the work of previous grammarians, including John Wilkins, George Hickes, and, notably, John Wallis, the preface to whose *Grammatica linguae Anglicanae* Greenwood largely incorporated. He also acknowledged his debt to Locke: 'in two or three Places I have made use of Mr *Lock's* Expressions, because I lik'd them better than my own' (Greenwood, *Essay*, 1711, sig. A4r). This does less than justice to his use of Locke, whom he quotes extensively throughout the grammar without further reference. Like Wallis, Greenwood advocated the teaching of English before Latin and essentially avoided imposing Latin categories on English grammar. In spite of its modest pretensions, Greenwood's grammar was very influential and was used in their work by a number of later grammarians, among them William Loughton. Greenwood died at St Paul's School on 12 September 1737.   FRANCES AUSTIN

Sources R. C. Alston, *A bibliography of the English language from the invention of printing to the year 1800*, 10 vols. in 1 [1965–73]; repr. with corrections (1974) • I. Michael, *The teaching of English from the sixteenth century to 1870* (1987) • I. Michael, *English grammatical categories and the tradition to 1800* (1970) • E. Vorlat, *The development of English grammatical theory, 1586–1737: with special reference to the parts of speech* (1975) • M. McDonnell, *The annals of St Paul's School* (privately printed, Cambridge, 1959) • M. McDonnell, ed., *The registers of St Paul's School, 1509–1748* (privately printed, London, 1977) • *GM*, 1st ser., 7 (1737), 574 • *DNB*

Greenwood, Joan Mary Waller (1921–1987), actress, was born on 4 March 1921 at 122 Fulham Road, Chelsea, London, the only child of Sydney Earnshaw Greenwood, artist, and his wife, Ida Waller. The name Mary does not appear on her birth certificate. She was educated at St Catherine's School in Bramley, Surrey, and at the Royal Academy of Dramatic Art. She first appeared on stage in 1939, when she was seventeen, in a small part in *The Robust Invalid*, a translation of Molière's *Le malade imaginaire* at the Apollo Theatre, London, and two years later in an unimportant film, *John Smith Wakes Up*.

Thereafter Joan Greenwood was much in demand on both stage and screen, in every sort of production. Her first major film was *The Gentle Sex* in 1943, directed by Leslie Howard, as one of a group of conscripts in the ATS (Auxiliary Training Service). Her first leading part was in a comedy of 1946 called *A Girl in a Million*, playing opposite Hugh Williams. It took her longer to make her mark in the theatre. During the war she took over from Deborah Kerr in *Heartbreak House*, toured with ENSA (the Entertainments National Service Association), did a season with Worthing Repertory Company, and toured with the company run by Donald Wolfit, playing Ophelia in *Hamlet* and Celia in *Volpone*. For several years after the war she concentrated on the cinema, becoming well known to the general public when she had roles in a number of Ealing films. *Saraband for Dead Lovers* (1948) was a historical romance with Stewart Granger, then at the height of his popularity. Her light touch as a comedian was particularly suitable for the gentle Ealing comedies of the day and she appeared in three of the best: *Whisky Galore!* (1948), *The Man in the White Suit* (1951), and, above all, *Kind Hearts and Coronets* (1949). In 1952 she was a piquant Gwendoline in the elegant film of *The Importance of being Earnest*, directed by Anthony Asquith.

In the United States, Joan Greenwood appeared in New York and made two disappointing films in Hollywood, where she disliked the lifestyle. On her return to London, after taking over from Lilli Palmer in *Bell, Book and Candle* at the Phoenix Theatre in 1955, she scored two critical successes with *Lysistrata* at the Royal Court Theatre in 1957, later transferred to the West End, and *Hedda Gabler* at the Oxford Playhouse in 1960, which was repeated in the West End in 1964. When appearing in *Hedda Gabler* at Oxford, at the age of thirty-nine, she surprised everyone by eloping to Jamaica and secretly marrying an older fellow member

Joan Mary Waller Greenwood (1921–1987), by Dorothy Wilding, 1954

of the cast, André Cecil Morrell (d. 1978), son of André Mesritz Morrell. They had one son.

Joan Greenwood appeared at the Chichester festival of 1962 in *The Broken Heart*, and the following year in the film *Tom Jones*, Tony Richardson's rip-roaring adaptation from the novel by Henry Fielding. This, however, was the last big film in which she had a role of any importance. She appeared in a few minor productions, the last being a partly animated Anglo-Polish version of *The Water Babies* which, despite a wonderful cast, was disappointingly flat. She later returned to the screen in 1987, the year of her death, for a small cameo part in the distinguished film *Little Dorrit*. On the stage she gave a fine performance in *The Chalk Garden* in 1971 but, like her film career, her stage career virtually ended when she was in her mid-fifties, although she did appear in several television series later than this. She also returned to the stage later to take over the part in *The Understanding* played by Dame Celia Johnson, when the latter died in 1982.

A versatile actress and a talented comedian, Joan Greenwood appeared in everything from sophisticated comedy, romance, and adventure to classical drama and even revue. Only 5 feet tall, slight, and with dazzling blonde hair, she was both sophisticated and elfin, quizzical and mocking, with her full pouting mouth and lingering glance. Her distinctive voice and almost exaggerated diction have been described as 'gargling with champagne', husky, purring, deliciously seductive. Her work as an intelligent and witty comedian endeared her to a discriminating minority, and her films, especially the Ealing comedies, brought her a wider public. However, both on stage and screen her career seems to have been strangely uneven. Perhaps the very distinctiveness of her style limited the opportunities offered to her. The strength and emotional power of her Lysistrata and even more her Hedda Gabler suggest possibilities not realized in the rest of her career. Joan Greenwood died of acute bronchitis and asthma on 27 February 1987, at her home, 27 Slaidburn Street, Chelsea, London.   RACHAEL LOW, *rev.*

Sources *The Times* (3 March 1987) · *The Independent* (4 March 1987) · I. Herbert, ed., *Who's who in the theatre*, 17th edn, 2 vols. (1981) · J. Walker, ed., *Halliwell's film guide*, 8th edn (1991) · b. cert. · m. cert. · d. cert.
Likenesses photographs, 1942–71, Hult. Arch. · D. Wilding, bromide print, 1954, NPG [*see illus.*] · portrait, BFI NFTVA
Wealth at death £590,797: probate, 2 July 1987, *CGPLA Eng. & Wales*

Greenwood, John (*c.*1539–1609), schoolmaster, was probably a native of Yorkshire. He entered St John's College, Cambridge, as a pensioner on 27 May 1558 or at Easter 1559. He apparently transferred to St Catharine's College, where he proceeded BA in 1562 and MA in 1565. He was given letters dimissory from Archbishop Parker on 7 September 1565 and was ordained priest at Ely on 23 March 1567.

On 23 November 1570 Greenwood was appointed headmaster of Brentwood School in Essex. His learning apparently served the community in other ways. In 1573, for example, he acted as attorney for one Thomas Cowper, yeoman, in the surrendering of a lease. In 1590 his only book, *Syntaxis et prosodia versiculis compositae*, was printed by John Legate at Cambridge. Dedicated to Sir John Petre (1549–1613), the book consists of a 44-page Latin grammar, including a short section on syntactical figures, and a 28-page section on verse writing in Latin. The illustrations are drawn mainly from Ovid, Horace, and Virgil, but also from Christopher Ocland, author of *Anglorum praelia* (1558). In 1595 Greenwood and ten other clergy were appointed deputies of the archdeacon of Essex. In the same year Greenwood was presented by the townspeople for enclosing a footpath near the schoolhouse.

Two of Greenwood's sons converted to Catholicism: Christopher (1585–1651) and Henry (1586–1645). After spending some time at Cambridge, Christopher entered the English College in Valladolid, Spain, in 1602 and later became a Jesuit priest. Henry entered Valladolid in 1604 and became a Benedictine monk in 1612. Several of Greenwood's students were also Catholics. In his application for admission to Valladolid, Joseph Haynes claimed that Greenwood was responsible for his conversion to Roman Catholicism. When applying for admission to the English College in Rome, Robert Rookwood told school officials that his teacher, John Greenwood, had died a Catholic. However, he also revealed that his Brentwood schoolmaster had sometimes beaten him for not attending Church of England services. Greenwood's most famous pupil was John Clarke (1582–1653), who was later president of the College of Physicians.

On 29 September 1608 Greenwood resigned his position at Brentwood School. He died at Brentwood; his will, dated 1 March 1609, was proved by his son Henry on 6 October. He left his house in Brentwood to Henry and money to Christopher, Henry, Joseph Haynes's father, and his cousin Christabell Wadell. His will also mentions a third son, Edward, who 'was indebted when he dyed'.

EDWARD A. MALONE

Sources R. R. Lewis, *The history of Brentwood School* (1981) · D. Shanahan, 'Brentwood School and the Greenwood family, 1570–1645', *Essex Recusant*, 5 (1963), 4–11 · R. R. Lewis, 'An Elizabethan school book', *Transactions of the Essex Archaeological Society*, new ser., 24 (1951), 160–61 · A. Kenny, ed., *The responsa scholarum of the English College, Rome*, 1, Catholic RS, 54 (1962) · E. Henson, ed., *The registers of the English College at Valladolid, 1589–1862*, Catholic RS, 30 (1930) · T. M. McCoog, *English and Welsh Jesuits, 1555–1650*, 2 vols., Catholic RS, 74–5 (1994–5) · J. McCann and H. Connolly, eds., *Memorials of Father Augustine Baker and other documents relating to the English Benedictines*, Catholic RS, 33 (1933) · Venn, *Alum. Cant.* · Cooper, *Ath. Cantab.* · Wood, *Ath. Oxon.*, new edn · W. Pressey, 'State of the church in Essex in 1563', *Essex Review*, 46 (1937), 144–57 · catalogue of Brentwood School, Essex RO, D/DBg 1/9 · quarter sessions typescript, Essex RO, 130/19 and 21 · PRO, PROB 11/114, fol. 287*v*
Archives Essex RO
Wealth at death £200 or less; also house in Brentwood: will, PRO, PROB 11/114, fol. 287*v*

Greenwood, John (*c.*1560–1593), religious controversialist, was of unknown origins. He is first recorded on 18 March 1578, when he matriculated as a sizar of Corpus Christi College, Cambridge; he graduated BA in 1581. He does not seem to have taken another degree, although he is sometimes styled MA.

Greenwood was ordained deacon by John Aylmer, bishop of London, in 1581, and priest by Thomas Cooper, bishop of Lincoln, on 8 August 1582. He served as rector of Wyam, Lincolnshire, from about 1581 to 1582, and as a curate in Norfolk, perhaps at Rackheath, until about September 1585, when he resigned, turned to separatism, and travelled to London. The circumstances of his conversion are not known. He later denied any connection with the separatist leader Robert Browne, commenting only that 'I disgraded my self through God's mercy by repentance' (Carlson, *Writings of John Greenwood*, 22).

In London, Greenwood attended conventicles with remnants of previous separatist groups and others. Eventually, he was one of a group of twenty-two who were arrested on 8 October 1587 at the house of one Henry Martin in St Andrew by the Wardrobe. He was examined the same day and committed to the Clink prison. On 19 November following, Henry Barrow—a friend who was destined to become the greatest of the Elizabethan separatists—visited Greenwood. After they had been together about fifteen minutes, the keeper of the prison arrested Barrow on the orders of Archbishop Whitgift.

Greenwood and Barrow were confined in the Clink until May 1588, when they were brought to Newgate sessions. Indicted as recusants under 23 Eliz. c. 1, they were convicted, fined £260 each, and transferred to the Fleet prison. Despite the miserable and unhealthy conditions of his captivity Greenwood wrote several separatist works. He also collaborated closely with Barrow on a steady stream of printed letters, treatises, petitions, and examination transcripts. Collectively, Barrow's and Greenwood's writings constitute the most comprehensive and consistent statement of Elizabethan separatist beliefs and principles.

All these works were written under difficult circumstances before being smuggled out of prison by friends and sympathizers and printed abroad. The constant, repetitive themes of this literature were the necessity of immediate separation from the false and 'anti-Christian' established church, and the formation of gathered and covenanted congregations that adhered faithfully to the primitive Christian pattern set forth in the New Testament.

Greenwood was clearly the junior partner in this literary relationship. Barrow assumed the principal task of denouncing the established church, defending separation, explaining the ideas and practices of the primitive church, and justifying separatist purposes. Meanwhile, in a lengthy controversy with George Gifford, vicar of Malden, Essex, Greenwood focused more narrowly on explaining separatist attitudes towards true worship, denouncing read prayer, and rejecting stinted liturgies. He also sought to disprove Gifford's charge that the separatists were merely Donatists, who were creating a schism within the true church of God. Rather, Greenwood contended that the separatists were leaving a false church and establishing a true one.

Although Greenwood's own writings are not numerous, they form a sound basis for identifying his personal views. In his first recorded examination, about 24 March 1589, he again rejected the use of read, or stinted, prayer in church services, and included the Lord's prayer in this prohibition. He also denounced the Church of England as anti-Christian, branded its sacraments and government as false, and refused to acknowledge the queen's position as supreme governor of the church.

During March and April 1590 Greenwood elaborated on his views during a series of 'conferences' ordered by the ecclesiastical authorities. In these polemical debates with several puritan ministers and other clerics, he contended that the English parish congregations were confused gatherings of 'profane people' who had been received into the church at Queen Elizabeth's coronation 'without conversion of life by faith and repentance', and he claimed that they had remained 'a church of idolators and atheists ever since'. 'God call forth his elect from this fellowship', he concluded (Carlson, *Writings of John Greenwood*, 129–30, 140).

In other verbal exchanges Greenwood helped Barrow to expose the illogicality of the puritans' positions. The puritans were vulnerable to this criticism because, although they frequently denied the authority of the bishops and struggled for further reformation, they still maintained that the Church of England was a true church. These conferences were unfruitful and frustrating for Barrow and Greenwood, as well as for their opponents.

In July 1592 Greenwood was one of several separatists released from the Fleet into the custody of responsible citizens. Two months later a newly organized London separatist congregation elected him its 'teacher', or 'doctor',

and Francis Johnson its pastor. But Greenwood's period of freedom came to an end on the night of 5–6 December 1592, when he and Johnson were arrested at the home of another separatist, Edward Boyes, in Fleet Street. Within a day or two, he was back in the Fleet.

Now, as part of its vindictive reaction to the separatist and puritan agitation of the previous five and a half years, the government decided to prosecute Greenwood, Barrow, and others. On 11 and 20 March Greenwood was examined by Sir John Popham, lord chief justice of the queen's bench, and Sir Edmund Anderson, lord chief justice of the common pleas. Greenwood readily admitted his part in writing and publishing several works attributed to him and Barrow jointly, among them *A Collection of Certaine Sclaunderous Articles Gyven out by the Bisshops* (1590) and *A collection of certain letters and conferences lately passed betwixt certaine preachers and two prisoners in the Fleet* (1590). Material from these books furnished the basis for an indictment, part of which survives.

The trial began on 21 March 1593. The prosecution alleged, among other things, that Greenwood had disavowed the Book of Common Prayer, proved the congregation of the Church of England profane, and said that it had no true ministry. It also maintained that Greenwood held that all the established church's laws were false and anti-Christian, and that its assemblies were not governed by scripture but rather by superstitious canons of popes and councils.

On 23 March, Greenwood, Barrow, and three other separatists tried at the same time under similar charges were convicted of felony and sentenced to death under the statute 23 Eliz. c. 2, s. 4, which forbade anyone to 'devyse and wrighte, print or set forth, any manner of booke … letter or writing conteyning any false, sedicious and slaunderous matter to the defamacion of the Queene's Majestie' (Carlson, *Writings of Greenwood and Barrow*, 272–3 n. 1).

The next day, the jailers struck the prison irons off both men, loaded them into a tumbril, and took them to Tyburn, where they were reprieved. On 31 March they were again reprieved, but only after the noose had been placed around their necks and they had almost finished uttering their last words. Finally, this lethal game of cat and mouse came to an end. Under circumstances of dubious legality, they were returned to Tyburn and hanged early on the morning of 6 April. Contemporary sources state that they were executed at the instigation of Whitgift.

Greenwood remained steadfast to his beliefs in the face of trials, tribulations, and long imprisonment. He died bravely, and, along with Barrow, became one of the emerging separatist movement's most celebrated martyrs. He is also still revered as a founder of modern Congregationalism.

Greenwood's own writings, as well as those which he co-authored with Barrow, were published by Leland Carlson in editions printed in the Elizabethan Nonconformist Texts Series in 1962 and 1970. The satirical diatribe *Master Some Laid Open in his Coulers* (1589), which has in the past been attributed to Greenwood, is now generally accepted as the work of Job Throckmorton.

Greenwood was married, but his wife's name is unknown. They had at least one child, a son named Abel, who was born in the autumn of 1587 and was still unbaptized on 24 March 1589.   MICHAEL E. MOODY

Sources *The writings of John Greenwood, 1587–1590*, ed. L. H. Carlson (1962) · *The writings of Henry Barrow, 1587–1590*, ed. L. H. Carlson (1962) · *The writings of Henry Barrow, 1590–1591*, ed. L. H. Carlson (1966) · *The writings of John Greenwood and Henry Barrow, 1591–1593*, ed. L. H. Carlson (1970) · P. Collinson, 'Separation in and out of the church: the consistency of Barrow and Greenwood', *Journal of the United Reformed Church History Society*, 5 (1992–7), 239–58 · L. H. Carlson, *Martin Marprelate, gentleman: Master Job Throkmorton laid open in his colors* (1981), 132–57 · F. Powicke, *Henry Barrow, separatist (1550?–1593) and the exiled church of Amsterdam (1593–1622)* (1900)

Greenwood, John (1727–1792), portrait painter and auctioneer, was born on 7 December 1727 in Boston, Massachusetts, and baptized on 10 December in the Old North Church, Boston, the son of Samuel Greenwood (1690–1742), a Harvard graduate (1709) and merchant, and his second wife, Mary Charnock. He was a nephew of Professor Isaac Greenwood of Harvard College. In 1742, just after his father's death, he was apprenticed to Thomas Johnston, water colourist, heraldic painter, engraver, and japanner. His earliest surviving work is *Jersey Nanny* (1748; Museum of Fine Art, Boston), a mezzotint which is unusual for its depiction of a servant. The following year he drew *Prospect of Yale College*, engraved by Thomas Johnston. Beginning in 1749 Greenwood turned his attention exclusively to painting portraits, capitalizing on the opportunity created in Boston by the retirement of John Smibert. He remained in Boston for the next four years but fewer than fifty portraits from his stay there are known. *Benjamin Pickman* (1749; Peabody Essex Museum, Salem) is typical of his work, but his confident nature led him to paint the large group portrait *The Greenwood-Lee Family* (*c*.1750; Museum of Fine Art, Boston), which includes a self-portrait. His portrait of the Revd Thomas Prince was engraved in 1750 by Peter Pelham, stepfather of John Singleton Copley the elder.

Greenwood's considerable ambition and sense of adventure precipitated his move late in 1752 to the Dutch colony of Surinam, where he remained for over five years, executing in that time 113 portraits, which brought him 8025 guilders. He visited plantations, made notes about the country, and collected or sketched its fauna, plants, and natural curiosities, all of which he recorded, along with his portrait commissions, in a notebook (MS, New York Historical Society). The only painting to survive from his stay in South America is *Sea Captains Carousing in Surinam* (*c*.1758; St Louis Art Museum), a tavern-scene conversation piece which is his most important and best-known work and very probably inspired by a print after William Hogarth's *A Midnight Modern Conversation* (Yale U. CBA). Desiring to perfect himself in the art of mezzotinting, Greenwood left Surinam, and arrived in May 1758 at Amsterdam. He soon acquired many friends, and was instrumental in the re-establishment there of the Academy of Art. At Amsterdam he finished a number of portraits, studied under Michiel Elgersma, and issued several subjects in mezzotint, some of which were heightened by etching. He entered into partnership with P. Foquet as a dealer in paintings. In August 1763 he visited Paris, where he purchased a number of paintings for resale on the London art market. About the middle of September Greenwood reached London, and permanently settled there a year later.

Over the next twenty years Greenwood became one of the city's most prominent auctioneers. A small half-length mezzotint portrait by W. Pether depicts Greenwood bearing an auctioneer's mallet, along with an artist's palette and brushes. By 1770 Greenwood also claimed to Copley that he had brought over 1500 paintings to London (Burroughs, 51). He was invited by the London artists to their annual dinner at the Turk's Head on St Luke's day, 18 October 1763, and at their fifth exhibition at Spring Gardens, Charing Cross, in the following spring displayed two paintings, *A View of Boston, N. E.*, and *A Portrait of a Gentleman*. Early in 1765 a charter passed the great seal founding the Incorporated Society of Artists of Great Britain, and Greenwood became a member of the society.

In 1768 Greenwood exhibited his mezzotint *Frans von Mieris and Wife*, after the original self-portrait by that artist in the Hague Gallery; in 1773 *A Gipsey Fortune-Teller* in crayon; in 1774 a painting, *Palemon and Lavinia*, from Thomson's poem *The Seasons*, and in 1790 *Seven Sisters*, a large landscape and figures representing a circular clump of elms at Tottenham, embracing a view of the artist's summer cottage, with himself on horseback and his wife and children (National Art Gallery, Wellington, New Zealand). His attention, however, was for some years principally directed to mezzotints, including portraits and general subjects after his own designs, and pictures of the Dutch school of which his *Rembrandt's Father* (1764), *Happy Family*, after Willem Van Herp, and *Old Age*, after Albert Eckhout, both finished for Boydell in 1770, are good examples, and *Amelia Hone*, a young lady with a teacup (1771), probably the best.

Greenwood was married on 17 December 1769 at St George's Church, Hanover Square, London, to Frances Stevens (1744–1808) of that parish. She was born on 18 January 1744, the eldest daughter of William and Frances (*née* Scrivens) Stevens of Northampton, England. In the marriage licence he is described as 'of St James, Westminster'.

The Royal Academy was founded by dissentient members of the Incorporated Society of Artists in December 1768. Greenwood, then a director of the latter society, tried in vain to persuade his friend and countryman, John Singleton Copley, to adhere to his society, but Copley joined the Academy.

At the request of the earl of Bute Greenwood made a journey, in July 1771, into the Netherlands and France purchasing paintings; he afterwards visited the continent, buying up the collections of Count Van Schulembourg and Baron Steinberg. In 1776 he was occupying Ford's

Rooms in the Haymarket, London, as an art auctioneer. In this business he continued to the end of his life, moving in 1783 to Leicester Square, where he built a commodious room adjoining his dwelling-house, and communicating with Whitcomb Street.

Greenwood died while on a visit at Margate, on 16 September 1792, and was buried there on 20 September. His wife, who survived him fifteen years, was buried at Chiswick, Middlesex, close to the tomb of Hogarth.

Greenwood was not, as has been said elsewhere, the father of Thomas Greenwood, the scene-painter at Drury Lane Theatre, who died on 17 October 1797. His eldest son, Charnock-Gladwin, died an officer in the army at Grenada, West Indies; the second, John, succeeded him in business; James returned to Boston; and the youngest, Captain Samuel Adam Greenwood, senior assistant at the residency of Baroda, India, died at Cambay in 1810.

[ANON.], *rev.* RICHARD H. SAUNDERS

Sources A. Burroughs, *John Greenwood in America, 1745–1752* (1943) [exhibition catalogue, Addison Gallery of American Art, Andover, MA] · I. J. Greenwood, *The Greenwood family of Norwich, England, in America* (privately printed, Concord, New Hampshire, 1934) · R. H. Saunders and E. G. Miles, *American colonial portraits, 1700–1776* (1987), 170–5 [exhibition catalogue, National Portrait Gallery, Washington, 9 Oct 1987 – 10 Jan 1988] · D. Sutton, 'The Dundas pictures', *Apollo*, 86 (1967), 204–13 · F. W. Kampf, 'John Greenwood: an American-born artist in eighteenth-century Europe', *Bulletin of the New York Public Library*, 31 (1927), 623–34 · C. White, D. Alexander, and E. D'Oench, *Rembrandt in eighteenth century England* (1983), 58, 128–9 [exhibition catalogue, Yale U. CBA]

Likenesses mezzotint, *c*.1758–1763, Gemeentelijke Archiefdienst, Amsterdam · W. Pether, mezzotint, *c*.1792, repro. in Greenwood, *Greenwood family* · W. Pether, mezzotint, BM

Greenwood, John (1791–1867). *See under* Greenwood, Christopher (1786–1855).

Greenwood, Joseph Gouge (1821–1894), university administrator, born at Petersfield, Hampshire, was the son of the Revd Joseph Greenwood (*d.* 1839), a Congregational minister and his wife, Maria Gouge. At the age of fourteen he was sent to University College School, London, of which Thomas Hewitt Key and Henry Malden had recently been appointed joint headmasters. Thence he proceeded to University College, London. In 1840 he graduated BA in the University of London, with honours in both classics and mathematics, gaining the university scholarship in the former subject.

A year before this Greenwood's father had died, leaving the young student responsible for a family of six younger children. For several years he supported himself and others by private tuition, and after a time as an assistant master in his old school; during an interval he acted as substitute for Henry Malden in the Greek chair at University College. In his day he had few superiors in London as a private tutor in the classical languages and literature. One of his earliest pupils was Edward A. Leatham, who dedicated to him his striking *Tale of the Great Athenian Revolution: Charmione* (1859). Greenwood had no time himself for the luxuries of authorship; but to this period of his life must have belonged his translation of the *Pneumatics of Hero of Alexandria*, edited by Bennet Woodcroft (1851), and the first

Joseph Gouge Greenwood (1821–1894), by John H. E. Partington, 1883

plan at least of his *Elements of Greek Grammar* (1857), an attempt to supplement Hewitt Key's application of the 'crude-form system' to Latin grammar by completing Malden's fragmentary Greek grammar designed on the same principles.

In 1850 Greenwood accepted the offer of the chair of classics and history in the newly founded Owens College at Manchester. At first the college had failed to establish a hold upon Manchester and its district, and in July 1857, when its fortunes were almost at their lowest ebb, he was appointed to the principalship on the resignation of this post by Alexander John Scott. Greenwood continued to lecture, but soon after his appointment as professor the subject of history had been detached from his chair and assigned to Richard Copley Christie. Latin and classical Greek were later transferred to separate professors and during the last few years Greenwood retained only the teaching of Greek Testament criticism. His teaching of this subject (afterwards commemorated by the endowment of a Greenwood Greek Testament lectureship in the college) was, in keeping with the non-denominational system of the college, as well as with his own disposition as a teacher, essentially confined to textual criticism. He had joined the Church of England at some time before his appointment at Owens College; his private opinions were those of an orthodox but liberal churchman.

In the earlier years of the college Greenwood advocated much change in the system of college teaching, to make it more attractive to Manchester businessmen. In 1853 he took an active part in opening classes for the schoolmasters of primary schools. In 1858 he became honorary secretary of a working men's college run on the same lines as that of the London college that had opened a few years earlier under the influence of Frederick Denison Maurice. Greenwood was instrumental in bringing about its amalgamation, in 1861, with Owens College, of which for a long time to come it formed an important department.

The recovery in the fortunes of Owens College by the early 1860s owed much to Greenwood's energy and perseverance. A highly successful administrator, who relished committee work, he helped to bring to fruition the proposals of Sir Henry Roscoe that the college should develop as a centre for applied and experimental science. In collaboration with Roscoe, Alderman Alfred Neild (who presided over the governing body of the college during the greater part of Greenwood's principalship), and Thomas Ashton (1818–1898), a Manchester cotton spinner, he took a leading part in the movement inaugurated in 1867 to raise Owens College to the level of a university institution. He did much of the detailed preparatory work for the acts of parliament of 1870 and 1871 which reconstituted Owens College as the Owens Extension College. In the absence of government funding, the rebuilding of the college on a new site had to be financed from private sources. A site was purchased in 1868 and sufficient money had by that year been raised for construction of the new buildings to commence. Although the college developed extensive scientific facilities, Greenwood was anxious to balance traditional and newer branches of university study, delivering on the opening of the new college buildings in 1873 an address 'On some relations of culture to practical life'. In 1872 the Manchester medical school was incorporated with the Owens College, after negotiations in which Greenwood showed much tact; and two years later the new medical buildings of the college were opened.

Greenwood took a chief part in the negotiations which in 1880 ended in the grant of a charter on federal principles to the Victoria University of which Owens College was, until 1884, the only constituent college. He became its first vice-chancellor, holding the office until 1886. He took a particular interest in arranging the courses of study in the new university. In these questions many of his colleagues regarded him as a somewhat conservative figure at odds with more progressive policies. Later, he was recognized as a successful defender of the interests of Owens College in relation to Leeds and Liverpool, the other members of the federation.

The most controversial question in which Greenwood became involved during the later years of his principalship concerned the admission of women students into the college, which had been permitted by the 1870 act. Greenwood, who was deeply committed to the belief that emotional and intellectual differences between the sexes demanded their education in separate institutions, opposed moves, dating from 1875, to carry this permission into effect, and was instrumental in delaying full co-education at Manchester. Although the Victoria University charter opened its degrees to all comers without

distinction of sex, women were not immediately admitted, and they continued to be taught in a separate institution, the Manchester and Salford College for Women, which was established in 1877. Restrictions remained even after women were finally admitted in 1883 and Greenwood continued to express his opposition to women's receiving the same type of education as men. True to his aversion to mixed teaching, he duplicated his Greek Testament criticism class for the women students.

Towards the close of 1889, owing to failure of health, Greenwood resigned the principalship, which he had held for thirty-seven years. He received honorary degrees from Cambridge University (1873), whose chancellor, the seventh duke of Devonshire, was president of the Owens College, and Edinburgh (1884). In retirement he settled at Eastbourne, Sussex, where he occupied himself with literary pursuits, including a revision of the text of Wordsworth, his favourite author through life. Greenwood was twice married: first, in 1863, to Elizabeth (Eliza), the daughter of John Taylor, a Unitarian minister in Manchester, with whom he had two daughters including the historian Alice Drayton *Greenwood, who survived him; and second, in 1871, to Katharine Elizabeth, daughter of William *Langton, the Manchester banker and antiquary. He died at his home, 34 Furness Road, Eastbourne, on 25 September 1894. A. W. WARD, rev. M. C. CURTHOYS

Sources Manchester Guardian (26 Sept 1894) · The Times (27 Sept 1894) · E. Fiddes, Chapters in the history of Owens College and of Manchester University, 1851–1914 (1937) · M. Tylecote, The education of women at Manchester University, 1883–1933 (1941) · W. H. Chaloner, The movement for the extension of Owens College, Manchester, 1863–73 (1973) · CGPLA Eng. & Wales (1894)

Likenesses J. H. E. Partington, portrait, 1883, Man. City Gall. [see illus.] · photograph, repro. in H. B. Charlton, Portrait of a university (1851)

Wealth at death £4695 17s. 11d.: probate, 13 Nov 1894, CGPLA Eng. & Wales

Greenwood, Major (1880–1949), epidemiologist and medical statistician, was born in Shoreditch, east London, on 9 August 1880, the eldest son and only surviving child of Major Greenwood (1854–1917), general practitioner, and his wife, Annie (1858–1904), daughter of P. C. Burchell MB. Greenwood's two younger siblings both died of tuberculosis in infancy; his mother died of the same disease shortly after he had qualified in medicine. During Greenwood's childhood and youth, his father and grandfather, both of whom also bore the first name of Major, together ran the family general practice in Hackney. Greenwood himself was expected to qualify in medicine and eventually take over the practice; but at Merchant Taylors' School, which he attended from 1889 to 1896, he developed a strong interest in history and Latin, which never left him. His father, however, insisted on a medical education, and young Greenwood bowed to parental pressure.

With an entrance scholarship to the London Hospital, Greenwood went on to qualify in 1904. He then struck out on his own, greatly influenced by two of the country's outstanding scientists at the turn of the century: Leonard Hill, in whose physiology department at the London Hospital medical college Greenwood became a demonstrator;

and Karl Pearson, whose courses in the rapidly developing science of mathematical statistics he followed at University College, London. In Hill's laboratories Greenwood was schooled in the realities of a scientific approach to medical research, becoming at the same time an early medical convert to Pearson's biometry. Throughout his career, he unified and extended the intellectual legacy of his two mentors; he developed medical statistics and helped to make its methods acceptable to an initially reluctant medical profession, and he added good clinical judgement to the rigorous mathematics which characterized Pearson's work. In 1908 Greenwood married Rosa (1880–1945), daughter of Andreas Baur, in her home town of Baden, Germany. There were two sons of the marriage, one of whom became a professional statistician.

In 1909 Greenwood brought his biometrical convictions to bear on the existing debate, between bacteriologists and clinicians, which surrounded Almroth Wright's research on the so-called 'opsonic index'. His criticism of Wright's data was based on a technical distinction between 'functional' errors of technique and 'mathematical' inferential errors. His arguments drew the attention of C. J. Martin, director of the Lister Institute, who then created for Greenwood a new post, the first of its kind in Britain, as resident statistician at the institute. Here Greenwood conducted statistical investigations into tuberculosis, infant mortality, and hospital fatality rates. At the same time he was involved in interpreting data from the institute's ongoing major epidemiological study of bubonic plague in India. From this start Greenwood never looked back; he had found his professional feet.

During the First World War Greenwood served in the sanitary service of the Royal Army Medical Corps. In 1916 he was seconded to the health and welfare section of the Ministry of Munitions, for statistical work. When the new Ministry of Health was created in 1919, Greenwood moved there from the Lister Institute, becoming the ministry's first senior statistical officer, working closely with George Newman, its chief medical officer. Based at the Medical Research Council's National Institute for Medical Research in Hampstead, rather than in Whitehall, he was once again alongside his old 'chief', Leonard Hill, by then head of the MRC's division of applied physiology.

Greenwood's statistical ideas had now evolved from the early insistence on the adaptation of Karl Pearson's rigorous mathematics and 'measurement as an end in itself' to a more humanely biological approach, reflecting the clinical influence of his medical training. During and after his term at the Lister Institute, it was the humanizing aspect of his pioneering work on large-scale trials, designed to evaluate prophylactic and therapeutic measures, which gradually began to break down the medical profession's resistance to statistical analysis. By then Greenwood's mind was increasingly focused on the application of statistics to experimental epidemiology, and in the early 1920s he became associated with W. W. C. Topley. Topley needed the co-operation of a statistician in the studies he had initiated in 'experimental epidemiology', using controlled populations of laboratory mice. For both men these studies centred on attempts to simplify experimental conditions by limiting the number of variable factors to manageable proportions and by magnifying the time-scale of observations by using short-lived animals.

Greenwood's studies were carried out under the auspices of the MRC and continued, with various co-workers, until the mid-1930s. By then Topley and Greenwood had been colleagues, since 1927, as professors of bacteriology and of epidemiology and vital statistics respectively, at the London School of Hygiene and Tropical Medicine (created as successor to the London School of Tropical Medicine). There Greenwood built up a new department, where teaching was an important duty for himself and his staff, most of whom followed him from the MRC and continued in dual positions within the school and the MRC. In 1935 Greenwood's lectures were published in book form as *Epidemics and Crowd Diseases*. His books and papers published in his lifetime on statistical, biometric, epidemiological, and historical subjects, numbered well over a hundred.

Greenwood had a complex personality; he could appear remote, even cynical and censorious on occasion, but he never wavered in his intellectual integrity nor in his total loyalty to those admitted to his limited circle of friends. Millais Culpin, a former colleague of Greenwood, considered that some

> thought that he selected statistics as his life's work because this branch of medicine was most remote from the emotional. Perhaps they were right; he was a sensitive soul and often found refuge in doing sums, though the human meaning might still intrude. (*BMJ*, 15 Oct 1949, 878)

Greenwood became a member of the Royal College of Physicians in 1919 and a fellow in 1924; in 1928 he was elected to fellowship of the Royal Society. He was a founder member, in 1930, of the Socialist Medical Association. He was also active in the Voluntary Euthanasia Society; a few weeks before his death he was chosen to put its case in a broadcast debate arranged by the BBC. He retired in 1945 and died in London, suddenly, during a meeting on cancer research, on 5 October 1949.   LISE WILKINSON

Sources L. Hogben, *Obits. FRS*, 7 (1950–51), 139–54 · autobiographical fragment (1880–1926), American Philosophical Society, Philadelphia, Pearl MSS, 1–8 · A. Bradford Hill, 'Introduction', in M. Greenwood, *The medical dictator* (1986) · *The Lancet* (15 Oct 1949), 721 · *The Lancet* (2 June 1917), 853 · *BMJ* (15 Oct 1949), 877–9 · *BMJ* (5 Nov 1949), 1055 · *BMJ* (26 May 1917), 703 · J. R. Matthews, 'The British biometric school and bacteriology: the creation of Major Greenwood as a medical statistician', *Quantification and the quest for medical certainty* (1995) · M. Greenwood, *Epidemics and crowd diseases* (1935) · M. Greenwood, *Some British pioneers of social medicine* (1948) [dedication] · M. Greenwood, *Medical statistics from Graunt to Farr* (1948) · WWW

Archives King's AC Cam. · UCL, notes and MSS | American Philosophical Society, Philadelphia, Pearl MSS · Bodl. Oxf., corresp. relating to Society for the Protection of Science and Learning · CAC Cam., corresp. with A. V. Hill · UCL, letters to Karl Pearson

Likenesses photograph, RS · photograph, London School of Hygiene and Tropical Medicine

Wealth at death £18,104 9s.: probate, 3 Dec 1949, *CGPLA Eng. & Wales*

Greenwood, Marion. *See* Bidder, Marion Greenwood (1862–1932).

Greenwood, Thomas (*bap.* **1752?**, *d.* **1797**), scene-painter, is believed to be the son of the engraver John Greenwood (1729–1768), who may have come to London from Yorkshire where there was a thriving branch of the family. Thomas Greenwood was not, however, related to the American-born painter John Greenwood (1727–1792) who settled in England in 1763, and exhibited at the Society of Artists. His parents may have been John Greenwood and Elizabeth Holroyd, who married in St George's Chapel, Hyde Park, London, on 1 July 1750. If so, it is likely that he was the Thomas Greenwood whose baptism was recorded in London at St Andrew, Holborn, on 23 February 1752, and that he was nineteen in November 1771 when we have the earliest definite evidence of his career, from an account book for the Theatre Royal Drury Lane, London, which records a payment to him, possibly for work on the spectacular masque *The Institute of the Garter*. Greenwood worked at Drury Lane from 1771 until his death in 1797, becoming chief scene-painter there in 1776 after the death of John French, who had held the post since 1765. On 13 August 1774 he married, at St Leonard's, Shoreditch, Elizabeth Meaburn, with whom he had several children, including a son Thomas, baptized at St Andrew, Holburn, on 4 April 1779.

Greenwood did not work exclusively at Drury Lane, since he also worked for the 1777–8 season at the Theatre Royal, Covent Garden, and for Sadler's Wells Theatre from 1778 to 1797; he was the first scene-painter to be associated with that theatre. Other work included repainting the interior of Drury Lane with William Capon (1757–1827), before the opening of the 1782–3 season; painting scenery for Privy Garden, the duke of Richmond's private theatre, in 1788; for theatrical entertainments at Blenheim Palace, in 1778; for the King's Theatre, in 1791–4, when the Drury Lane Company were playing there, and in 1795 for the new Theatre Royal, Birmingham, which opened the following year.

Greenwood started working at Drury Lane at a time of great change and innovation in scene design on the British stage, when David Garrick's improvements there in lighting and the mechanics of mounting scenery on stage made scene design more exciting and creative than was formerly possible. He may have begun working at Drury Lane Theatre as a pupil of French (just as Andrew Roberts later became Greenwood's pupil at Sadler's Wells), but probably most influential for his work was that of the innovative scene designer Philippe Jacques de Loutherbourg (1740–1812), whom David Garrick employed at Drury Lane from 1772 as scenic director. De Loutherbourg, noted for his creation of spectacular stage effects, had taken the unusual step of stipulating that Garrick employ him solely as a scene designer, with overall authority to supervise the execution of his ideas, and hence Greenwood's early work for Drury Lane entailed realizing many of de Loutherbourg's designs, including *Maid of the Oaks* (1774) and *Queen Mab* (1775). Generally in the eighteenth-

century theatre artists who designed scenery painted it themselves, and by 1778 Greenwood was realizing his own designs and his name was credited in playbills accordingly.

Greenwood excelled at landscape and topographical work, and the two anonymous watercolour designs credited to him in the Victoria and Albert Museum (believed to be scenes for Covent Garden Theatre, 1777), reveal his mastery of architectural detail and perspective, and an appreciation of the dramatic effect of monumental backdrops. Much of Greenwood's work was for opera and pantomime, which demanded a wide variety of settings, especially at the rebuilt Drury Lane Theatre of the 1790s, where audiences loved spectacular presentations on the enlarged stage. Thomas Greenwood died in October or November 1797 at his home in Charles Street, Covent Garden, London, and was described in the *Gentleman's Magazine* as 'an artist of great eminence, and conductor of the painting department of Drury Lane theatre' (*GM*, 984). His last work there was for *The Castle Spectre*, which opened at Drury Lane in December 1797, and for which his son, Thomas Greenwood (1779–1832), completed his work, with Charles Pugh. Greenwood was succeeded at Drury Lane by his son, who designed much of the scenery for Edmund Kean's performances at Drury Lane in 1814–15. Thomas junior's son was the theatrical manager and writer Thomas Longdon Greenwood (1808–1879). Elizabeth Ann Greenwood was executrix and sole beneficiary of her father's will, proved on 11 November 1797.

CATHERINE HAILL

Sources Highfill, Burnim & Langhans, *BDA* · S. Rosenfeld, *Georgian scene painters and scene painting* (1981) · S. Rosenfeld and E. Croft-Murray, 'A checklist of scene painters working in Great Britain and Ireland in the 18th century [4 pts]', *Theatre Notebook*, 19 (1964–5), 6–20, 49–64, 102–13, 133–45 · S. Rosenfeld, 'Scene painters at the London theatres in the 18th century', *Theatre Notebook*, 20 (1965–6), 113–18 · S. Allen, 'Notes and Queries', *Theatre Notebook*, 18 (1963–4) [article on the scene designs attributed to Thomas Greenwood in the V&A] · S. Rosenfeld, 'A transparency by Thomas Greenwood the elder', *Theatre Notebook*, 19 (1964–5) · A. Oliver and J. Saunders, 'De Loutherbourg and Pizarro, 1779', *Theatre Notebook*, 20 (1965–6) · S. Rosenfeld, 'A Sadler's Wells scene book', *Theatre Notebook*, 15 (1960–61) · S. D'Amico, ed., *Enciclopedia dello spettacolo*, 11 vols. (Rome, 1954–68) · C. Baugh, *Garrick and Loutherbourg* (1990) · S. Rosenfeld, *A short history of scene design in Great Britain* (1973) · *GM*, 1st ser., 67 (1797), 984 · R. C. Kern, 'Two designs by Thomas Greenwood the elder', *Theatre Notebook*, 15 (1960–61) · *Who was who in American art, 1564–1975* (Sound View Press, 1999) · two designs attributed to Thomas Greenwood, V&A, department of prints and drawings, E.718-1939, E.719-1939 · *IGI* · apprentice binding register, Painters & Stainers' Company, 1666–1795, GL · will, PRO, PROB 11/1298, sig. 691

Wealth at death owed considerable amount by Richard Brinsley Sheridan: Highfill, Burnim & Langhans, *BDA*; will, PRO, PROB 11/1298, sig. 691

Greenwood, Thomas (1790–1871), historian, was the second son of Thomas Greenwood, a London merchant. He was educated at St John's College, Cambridge, graduating BA in 1815 and MA in 1831. He entered Gray's Inn on 14 March 1809, and was called to the bar on 24 June 1817. He was appointed fellow and reader in history and polite literature in the University of Durham, and in 1836 he published *The First Book of the History of the Germans: Barbaric Period*, covering the period to AD 772. In the preface of this large and detailed work, Greenwood declares: 'the fact that the Teutonic race has evinced itself the master-family of mankind, cannot now be disputed'. The work did not gain a wide readership.

In 1837 Greenwood was chosen as a bencher of Gray's Inn, and from 1841 to 1842 he filled the office of treasurer. His research into the history of the Roman patriarchate led to *Cathedra Petri: a Political History of the Great Latin Patriarchate* (5 vols., 1856–65), in which he described the history of the papacy up to the close of the pontificate of Innocent III. The work was considered learned, but was overshadowed by H. H. Milman's highly acclaimed history of Latin Christianity (1855). The *Cathedra Petri*, and Greenwood's earlier pamphlet, *Position and Prospects of the Protestant Churches of Great Britain and Ireland* (1851), show Greenwood's antipathy to the establishment of the Roman Catholic hierarchy in England and his preoccupation with the political effects of Roman Catholicism.

Greenwood died, apparently unmarried, at 14 Westbourne Terrace, Hyde Park, London, on 1 November 1871.

E. I. CARLYLE, *rev.* MYFANWY LLOYD

Sources Boase, *Mod. Eng. biog.* · *Saturday Review*, 9 (1860), 404–5 · Venn, *Alum. Cant.* · J. Foster, *The register of admissions to Gray's Inn, 1521–1889, together with the register of marriages in Gray's Inn chapel, 1695–1754* (privately printed, London, 1889)
Archives Man. CL, Manchester Archives and Local Studies, corresp. and papers
Wealth at death under £14,000: probate, 14 Dec 1871, *CGPLA Eng. & Wales*

Greenwood, Thomas (1851–1908), promoter of public libraries and publisher, son of William and Nanny Greenwood, was born on 9 May 1851 at Mount Pleasant, Woodley, Cheshire. His father, a yeoman farmer turned millworker and an active Chartist, died when Thomas was just five months. From the age of three he attended St Mark's national school, Bredbury, and later the school of the Primitive Methodist chapel in Woodley, which he left aged eleven for casual employment at the W. H. Smith bookstall in Stockport Station, followed by clerical positions in London Road Station, Manchester, and in Ward's hat factory, Hatherlow, Cheshire. Meanwhile, he continued his education informally under the extra-mural supervision of the Revd William Urwick, pastor of Hatherlow old school. Greenwood joined the school's mutual improvement society and Sunday school, and became treasurer of the latter. On 2 April 1874 he married Marianne Pettet, with whom he had a son and two daughters.

Aged nineteen, Greenwood became a commercial traveller for a hardware firm in Sheffield. While 'on the road' he invariably sought out the local public library, for personal reading and noting organization and procedure. This in part qualified him at the age of twenty-two to become branch librarian of the Upperthorpe Public Library, Sheffield, a post which he resigned after eighteen months to return to travelling, this time for the technical journal *The Ironmonger*, of which he became business manager in London shortly afterwards. In 1877, with W. Hoseason Smith, he founded his own technical journal, the *Hatter's Gazette*, followed by the *Pottery Gazette* (1878), the *Oil and Colourman's Journal* (1879), and the *Decorator's, Plumber's and Gas Fitter's Gazette* (1882), acting as chief editor for each. Greenwood also published technical books. These ventures provided the basis of a large fortune, out of which he was to finance his crusade in support of public libraries.

Greenwood's *Free Public Libraries* (later *Public Libraries*) was published in 1886 and ran to several editions. Dealing with the development, use, and management of free libraries, this book became highly influential in the work of the public library movement. Greenwood became a leading advocate of municipal free libraries, encouraging local councils to place them higher on their agenda of active interests. Drawing on the experience of advertising and promotion he had gained as a commercial traveller, Greenwood launched his own propaganda campaign in support of public libraries. His expertise in publicity was in great demand in towns considering the adoption of the public libraries acts. In numerous public meetings and in his writings Greenwood praised the virtues of public library provision and use that he himself had experienced as a young and enthusiastic reader in the Manchester Free Public Library and elsewhere. He became known as the 'apostle of the library movement', as he sought to reinvigorate the public library ideal after the initial burst of activity generated by the permissive Public Libraries Act (1850) had subsided.

The increased equality of opportunity which public libraries were meant to provide was mirrored in Greenwood's attachment to nonconformity and Liberal politics. His support of the self-help ethic, as well as of public libraries, induced him to restore the reputation of one of the pioneers of public libraries, the self-made Edward Edwards (1812–1886), chief witness to the select committee on public libraries (1849) and the Manchester Free Public Library's first librarian. Greenwood wrote Edwards's biography (1902), arranged for a monument for his unmarked grave, and presented to Manchester Public Libraries his collection of Edwards's books, personal belongings, and notebooks. Mindful of Edwards's plea that librarianship achieve a professional status, Greenwood assembled as a training tool a library for librarians, comprising bibliographies, library catalogues, book-sale catalogues, rare book specimens of early printing and binding, and texts on historical bibliography and library economy. The library, of about 10,000 volumes, was presented to Manchester Public Libraries in 1904, and Greenwood left £5000 in his will for further purchases.

Greenwood travelled abroad extensively, and on a visit to Japan in 1907 he contracted blood poisoning, which undermined his constitution and contributed to his death at his home, Frith Knowl, Elstree, Hertfordshire, on 9 November 1908. His remains after cremation at Golders Green were interred in the family vault of the Congregational church at Hatherlow. ALISTAIR BLACK

Sources G. Carlton, *Spade-work: the story of Thomas Greenwood* (1949) • S. Horrocks, 'Thomas Greenwood and his library', *Manchester Review*, 8 (1959), 269–77 • A. Sparke, 'Thomas Greenwood', *Library Association Record*, 52 (1950), 383–4 • 'Books of local interest: Thomas Greenwood', *Manchester Review*, 6 (1949), 232–5 • R. J. Prichard, *Thomas Greenwood: public library enthusiast* (1981) • G. Carlton, *Biographical notes on Sir Ernest Baker and Thomas Greenwood* (1950) • *CGPLA Eng. & Wales* (1908)
Archives Man. CL, G920/4/G38
Wealth at death £40,734 3s. 9d.: probate, 15 Dec 1908, *CGPLA Eng. & Wales*

Greenwood, Walter (1903–1974), novelist and playwright, was born on 17 December 1903 in Salford, Lancashire, the elder child and only son of Tom Greenwood (d. 1912/13), master hairdresser, and his wife, Elizabeth Matilda Walter. He was educated locally at the Langworthy Road council school until he was thirteen, having worked as a pawnbroker's clerk outside school hours for the previous twelve months. He inherited the family tradition of determined radicalism, enthusiasm for books, and love of music, which fostered his ambition to escape from the life of the industrial slum. His father had died of alcoholism when he was nine and his mother supported them by working as a waitress. The family experience was typical of many in the area at the time, long stretches of unemployment alternating with brief periods of ill-paid and usually manual work. By the age of thirty Greenwood had been a clerk, a stable-boy, a packing-case maker, a signwriter, a driver, a warehouseman, and a salesman, and he had never earned more than 35s. a week. He had also started to record his impressions of working-class life in south Lancashire, drawing on what he himself knew of subsistence in the slums and the emotional escape from them in books and music, as well as physical release in cheap-day excursions to the Pennine hills and the Peak District. These were the materials he used in his first and best-known work, *Love on the Dole*, published in 1933.

The strength of *Love on the Dole* as a novel lies not in its descriptions or its narrative but in the honesty with which it tells its story of urban poverty and in the richness and accuracy of its dialogue. It is occasionally comic, it ends in tragedy, and it is essentially an account of courage in desperately universal circumstances. It became a subject for questions in parliament and, although written in prose, it can be seen as successor to the idiomatic plays of W. S. Houghton and Harold Brighouse, dramatists of the Manchester school a generation earlier, and to the verse of Samuel Laycock which came half a century before. *Love on the Dole* was itself redrafted for the stage by its author in collaboration with Ronald Gow in 1934, subsequently filmed (1941), and eventually resurrected as a musical in 1970. But it became a landmark in its original form because it vividly told recognizable truths when the country was suffering them in the slump. It was expected that Greenwood's success would enable him to marry his long-term fiancée Alice Miles, who had formed the basis for Sally Hardcastle, the heroine of his novel. He changed his mind, however, and she sued for breach of promise in January 1936, obliging him to settle out of court. On 23 September 1937 he married Pearl Alice Osgood (b. 1911/12),

an American actress, the daughter of Charles Edward Osgood, and they moved from Salford to London.

Greenwood produced nine other novels and a book of short stories, all written with the same unaffected directness, and among them *Only Mugs Work* (1938) was also turned into a play. As he mastered the techniques of drama, he looked more and more to the stage for his successes, and *My Son my Son* (1935), *The Cure for Love* (1951), and *Saturday Night at The Crown* (1953) were highly applauded for their vigour, their humour, and their characterization, while always remaining within a strictly conventional view of the theatre. A secondary career in writing film scripts began in 1935, when he wrote *No Limit* for the comedian George Formby, and during the war he wrote the screenplay for a documentary about the merchant navy, and *Six Men of Dorset* (1944), a dramatization of the career of the Tolpuddle Martyrs. He found yet another outlet for his talents in the growth of television, producing many scripts for the BBC, notably the serial *The Secret Kingdom* in 1960. Much more adaptable than most writers of his period, he was fundamentally a story-teller of primitive gifts which were never in danger of being obscured by literary finesse. His autobiography, *There was a Time* (1967), was written to read like a novel and betrayed his uneasiness with writing outside his chosen forms. It was dramatized in 1970 as *Hanky Park*, the name he gave to the archetypal Salford slum.

Greenwood remained throughout his life a man of the people from whom he came, affable but guarded. In 1971 he was made an honorary DLitt at Salford University. He died on 10 or 11 September 1974 (he was found on the 11th) after suffering heart failure at his home in Douglas, Isle of Man, where he had lived for many years.

GEOFFREY MOORHOUSE, *rev.*

Sources *The Times* (16 Sept 1974) • W. Greenwood, *There was a time* (1967) • *Who's who in the theatre* • R. Webster, '*Love on the dole* and the aesthetics of contradiction', *The British working class novel in the twentieth century*, ed. J. Hawthorn (1984) • S. J. Kunitz and H. Haycraft, eds., *Twentieth century authors: a biographical dictionary of modern literature* (1942) • P. Parker and F. Kermode, eds., *The reader's companion to twentieth-century writers* (1995) • *Wilson Library Bulletin*, 11/2 (1936), 78 • m. cert.
Archives Man. CL, Manchester Archives and Local Studies, MSS • U. Reading L., corresp. and literary papers • University of Salford Library, corresp., literary MSS, and inscribed editions | JRL, corresp. with Robert Donat • NL Scot., letters to Naomi Mitchison
Likenesses photograph, repro. in *The Times*

Greer, (Frederick) Arthur, Baron Fairfield (1863–1945), judge, was born in Liverpool on 6 October 1863, the eldest of the fourteen children of Arthur Greer, a Manxman, and his wife, Mary Hatfield Moore. His father, a metal merchant living mostly in the Isle of Man, bought the famous steamboat *Great Eastern* when she was due for breaking up. After some preliminary education at Ormskirk grammar school, Greer was sent to the Old Aberdeen grammar school, and he went on to the University of Aberdeen, where after a brilliant academic career he graduated with first-class honours in mental philosophy and won the Fullerton scholarship (1883). Family circumstances compelled him to start work in his profession without delay and he proceeded to London. Called to the bar by Gray's Inn in 1886 after winning the Bacon and Arden scholarships, he joined the northern circuit. Success did not come quickly, and for some years he had to supplement his income by writing for the *Liverpool Daily Post* and the *Liverpool Courier*. At one moment hope almost failed him and he resolved to abandon the bar and take to journalism. He applied to Sir Edward Richard Russell, the famous editor of the *Liverpool Daily Post*, for a place on the staff of the paper. Russell advised him to reconsider, and Greer continued his struggle at the bar and his writing for the newspapers. On 17 August 1901 he married Katherine (*d.* 1937), daughter of Emanuel van Noorden, of Orangeburg, South Carolina; they had a daughter.

In 1902 the turn of the tide for Greer's legal career came in a civil action at the Liverpool assizes which aroused much local interest. Greer appeared for the plaintiff. His conduct of the case attracted the attention of solicitors in Liverpool and his practice on the circuit grew steadily. He also lectured on law at the University of Liverpool for three years. In 1907, twenty years after his call and while still a junior, he moved to London and practised both there and at the Liverpool assizes. Work at those assizes together with appeals to courts in London made up the largest part of his substantial practice. In 1910 the persuasion of his friends at length overcame his modesty and he applied for silk, which was immediately granted. In 1911 he appeared for the defendants in the famous case of *Lloyd v. Grace, Smith & Co.* (1911), a case of the liability of a principal for the fraudulent act of a servant, where the decision of Mr Justice Scrutton at Liverpool in favour of the plaintiff was reversed in the Court of Appeal and restored in the House of Lords. For some time after he took silk Greer's work continued to be mainly on the northern circuit, but he eventually established an excellent practice in London, mainly in the commercial court and in the higher courts. In the First World War he was engaged in several of the more important cases in the prize court. Those who knew him about that time remembered the tall figure, the piercing blue eyes, the bent shoulders, the keen, intellectual face, and also the lines of pain which chronic attacks of arthritis had already begun to trace upon his features.

In 1919 Greer was appointed a judge of the King's Bench Division by Lord Chancellor Birkenhead, receiving the customary knighthood, and he sat frequently in the commercial court. The most famous criminal case over which he presided was the trial of Frederick Rothwell Holt for the murder of Mrs Breaks, which aroused great interest at the Manchester assizes in 1920. His discharge of his judicial duties created a general expectation that he would be promoted and in 1927 he was appointed a lord justice of appeal and sworn of the privy council. He sat in the Court of Appeal until his retirement in 1938.

Greer was admirably equipped in both mind and temper for the work of a judge. He was patient and free from any tendency to rush to a conclusion. He had a wide knowledge of the principles of law and especially of the common law, of which he was a learned authority. When a number of decisions bearing on a principle of law had to be scrutinized and assessed he accomplished the task with accuracy and subtlety. He had a marked aversion to any obscurity in thought or in expression. One of his most notable characteristics was a strong independence of mind, and, despite his modesty, if he was unable to agree with his colleagues in the Court of Appeal he never shrank from the responsibility of expressing his dissent. On several occasions his dissenting judgments were afterwards approved in the House of Lords. When an action for breach of promise was still possible his dissenting opinion in the Court of Appeal that a promise to marry made between decree nisi and decree absolute was valid was upheld by the House of Lords, Greer's view being that the dissolving marriage had by then become a mere shell (*Fender* v. *St John Mildmay*, 1938). He made a significant contribution to the development of banking, commercial, and shipping law. Usually on appeal his judgments were affirmed: *Banco de Portugal* v. *Waterlow* (1932), measure of damages for putting bogus banknotes into circulation; *Midland Bank* v. *Reckitt* (1933) and *Greenwood* v. *Martins Bank* (1933), liability of customer and of bank for forged cheques; *Arcos* v. *Ronaasen* (1933), liability of seller of commercial goods by description; *Stage Line* v. *Foscolo Mango* (1932), liability for deviation by a ship; *Drefus* v. *Tempus Shipping* (1931), general average; and *Ellerman Lines* v. *Murray* (1931), wages due to a shipwrecked sailor. In a few cases his view was not upheld: the effect of mistake in a commercial contract, *Bell* v. *Lever Brothers* (1931); the right to recover the cost of hiring a substitute vessel following loss of a vessel, *Liesbosch* (1933); and contributory negligence, *Swadling* v. *Cooper* (1931).

Greer's judgments were well arranged and free from digression and from obscurity or artifice in language. They reveal admirably the vigour and the lucidity of his mind. If need arose he was always ready to ease and smooth the path of forensic controversy. He was courteous to all who appeared before him, in whatever capacity, and beneath a shy and reserved demeanour he hid a real kindliness of heart. He greatly admired Lord Justice Scrutton and Lord Atkin, his contemporary masters of the commercial law, and to some extent modelled himself upon them.

Greer received the honorary degree of LLD from the University of Aberdeen in 1926 and from Liverpool in 1930. He became a member of the Council of Legal Education in 1917 and served as chairman from 1934 to 1936. He collaborated with his son-in-law, Ronw Moelwyn Hughes, in the article on bills of exchange, promissory notes, and negotiable instruments which appeared in the second edition of Halsbury's *Laws of England*. In the early 1930s he collaborated with Lord Maugham in an attempt to reform the law of civil evidence. In 1932 he was one of the British representatives at the International Congress of Comparative Law at The Hague.

In 1939 Greer was raised to the peerage as Baron Fairfield of Caldy, in the county palatine of Cheshire. In the same year, his first wife having died two years previously, he married Mabel, daughter of William John Fraser, civil engineer, of London, and widow of Charles Woodward

Neele, chief electrical engineer of the Great Central Railway. He died at his home, Fairfield House, Croft Drive, East Caldy, on 4 February 1945, and his peerage became extinct.   C. T. LE QUESNE, *rev.* ALEC SAMUELS

Sources personal knowledge (1959) · private information (1959) · *WWW* · Burke, *Peerage* (1939) · *CGPLA Eng. & Wales* (1945)
Likenesses L. Greer, oils, Gray's Inn, London · portrait, priv. coll.
Wealth at death £25,830 8s.: probate, 28 May 1945, *CGPLA Eng. & Wales*

Greer, Samuel Macurdy (1809–1880), politician, eldest son of the Revd Thomas Greer, Presbyterian minister of Dunboe, co. Londonderry, and his wife, Elizabeth Caldwell, was born at Spring Vale in that county. Educated at Coleraine and Glasgow University, where he took an MA degree in 1828, he was called to the Irish bar in 1835. In 1845 he married Marion Fletcher, the daughter of James McCrone of Rockville, Isle of Man.

Never sympathetic to Irish nationalism, even in its mildest guise, Greer acquired a provincial rather than a national reputation, beginning as a spokesman for the essentially moderate agrarian politics of protestant Ulster. The harsh economic conditions of the later 1840s incited usually prosperous tenant farmers to demand statutory protection for Ulster custom, the most developed form of tenant-right found all over Ireland. Their representatives made common cause with those of other provinces in the Tenant League established in 1850. Greer, who had published a series of letters on the tenant-right that he knew, was one of the provisional secretaries who organized the founding conference (Whyte, 11). But his inability to accept the historic demand for the three Fs (fair rent, fixity of tenure, and free sale of occupancy-right) led to an immediate and final breach with the movement (Duffy, 36–7). Greer's political base was in his native county, where he stood for a reviving Presbyterian radicalism combined with the agrarian causes he had championed. Between 1852 and 1865 he contested the county three times, and the city of Londonderry twice, against the dominant landed interest. He was successful only once, and sat for the county in 1857–9. At Westminster he adopted a generally radical stance on other issues besides Irish land.

His persistence in keeping up the fight in Londonderry helped to create the plebeian Liberalism that became a political force in late nineteenth-century Ulster until overshadowed by the confrontation between unionists and nationalists from the mid-1880s. Greer eventually gave up active politics to concentrate upon the law: he was recorder of Londonderry in 1870 and county court judge of Cavan and Leitrim from 1878 until his death, which took place at his home, 3 Gardiner's Place, Dublin, on 23 November 1880; he was buried at Spring Vale. Gladstone's legislation on Irish land and the ballot of 1870 and 1872 conceded as much as he had tried to obtain from previous governments. Historians have accorded Greer only passing mention, but the progress of his career can be followed in the newspapers of the province.

THOMAS GREER, *rev.* DAVID STEELE

Sources J. H. Whyte, *The independent Irish party, 1850–59* (1958) · C. G. Duffy, *The league of north and south* (1886) · *Hansard 3* (1857–9) · T. W. Moody and others, eds., *A new history of Ireland*, 5: *Ireland under the Union, 1801–1870* (1989) · *WWBMP* · *Dod's Parliamentary Companion* · *Freeman's Journal* [Dublin] · *Belfast News-Letter*
Wealth at death under £3000: probate, 18 Feb 1881, *CGPLA Ire.*

Greer, William Derrick Lindsay (1902–1972), bishop of Manchester, was born on 28 February 1902 at St Matthew's rectory, Belfast, the younger son and second of the four children of the Revd Richard Ussher Greer, of Rhone Hill, co. Tyrone, and his wife, Elizabeth Lindsay Greer (his second cousin), daughter of Frederick Greer RN of Tullylagan, co. Tyrone. Greer's home background in Ulster gave him a lively awareness of the interaction of religion and politics, the needs of the socially deprived, and the virtue of tolerance. He was educated first at Campbell College, Belfast, and from 1915 to 1920 at St Columba's College, Rathfarnham, Dublin, where his deep love of literature was first kindled. In 1920 he won a scholarship to Trinity College, Dublin, and in 1924 graduated senior moderator in mental and moral philosophy.

Although Greer was deeply involved in the Student Christian Movement at Trinity College, his decision to offer himself for ordination was not made until after he had joined the Northern Ireland civil service, in which from 1925 to 1929 he served as assistant principal in the ministry of home affairs.

In 1929, after spending three terms training for the ministry of the Church of England at Westcott House, Cambridge, Greer was ordained to a curacy at St Luke the Evangelist, Newcastle upon Tyne, where, contrary to the established convention, he succeeded his vicar three years later. In 1935 he left Tyneside for London to become the general secretary of the Student Christian Movement. Although he was temperamentally more at home in the university world than in parish life, five of his nine years in this influential and congenial office were made exceptionally difficult by wartime conditions. The letters he wrote to students on active service were much appreciated and have been compared to those written in Germany by Dietrich Bonhoeffer. The ecumenical character of the Student Christian Movement entirely accorded with his own convictions. He was involved in the formation of the World Council of Churches and spoke out explicitly for the reunion of the Anglican and Methodist churches.

In 1944 Greer was appointed to the principalship of his old theological college, Westcott House, with the formidable task of following Canon B. K. Cunningham, whose eccentric and endearing personality had dominated the college since its foundation in 1919. Greer's knowledge of the world, his quiet sagacity, and his keen sense of the incongruous were just the qualities needed for dealing with the problems of former servicemen returning to begin their training for the ministry. His devotion to the comprehensiveness of the Church of England and to the decent order enshrined in the Book of Common Prayer inspired confidence that the distinctive tradition of Westcott House was secure for many years to come.

In 1947, however, to the surprise and dismay of many of his friends, Greer was taken from Cambridge to become bishop of Manchester. He was consecrated in York Minster on 29 September. The diocese presented him with almost insuperable post-war problems, especially those of repairing bomb damage and finding clergy to serve in its 372 parishes. Despite these burdens, he promoted ambitious programmes of adult education and threw his energies into his chairmanship of the BBC's Central Religious Advisory Council. His principal aim was always to integrate the life of the church with the life of society at large and he was singularly successful in establishing close relations with the Manchester business community. He himself was an enthusiastic president of the Manchester and Salford Savings Bank. At the same time he pursued his lifelong concern for the underprivileged. He played a leading part in founding (in 1963) William House at Withington, a hostel for discharged prisoners, and (in 1971) St Ann's Hospice in Cheadle for terminal cancer patients. It was well known that the bishop held firm convictions on disarmament and, despite his extreme caution, he publicly advocated the unilateral renunciation by Britain of atomic weapons.

In 1946 Greer married Marigold Hilda Katharine, the daughter of Edgar Stogdon, vicar of Harrow on the Hill. They had one son, Richard Edgar, and two daughters, Elizabeth Louise and (Martha) Lindsay Dundas. In the early 1960s his health began to fail and only a strong sense of duty enabled him to persevere until his retirement in April 1970. Twenty-three years in so conservative and demanding a diocese was far too long for anybody and especially so for a man of his shy intelligence.

Although Greer's personal distinction was recognized by honorary doctorates from Trinity College, Dublin (1947), and the universities of Edinburgh (1951) and Manchester (1971), Greer was not (like some bishops of his generation) a frustrated academic. He wrote only one book, and that was the biography of an Irish friend who died when still a curate: *John Bainbridge Gregg* (1931). On his retirement he sought seclusion at the Old Rectory, Woodland, Broughton in Furness, his rural retreat near Coniston, but he was already too ill to enjoy his favourite pastimes of walking and gardening. He died there on 30 October 1972.   E. W. HEATON, *rev.*

Sources *The Times* (1 Nov 1972) · private information (1986) · personal knowledge (1986) · *CGPLA Eng. & Wales* (1973)
Wealth at death £40,018: probate, 29 Jan 1973, *CGPLA Eng. & Wales*

Greet, Sir Philip Barling Ben (1857–1936), actor and theatre manager, was born on 24 September 1857 on board the *Crocodile* (a recruiting ship which his father commanded) lying off the Tower of London, the younger son of Captain William Greet and his wife, Sarah *née* Barling. Educated at the Royal Naval School, New Cross, he was intended by his parents for a career in either the navy or holy orders, but instead he chose schoolmastering at a private establishment at Worthing, which perhaps accounts for his dedication to the educative value of drama in

Sir Philip Barling Ben Greet (1857–1936), by Paul Coe, *c.*1921

general and Shakespeare in particular on the minds of the young.

Greet made his professional stage début in J. W. Gordon's stock company at Southampton on 1 November 1879. He then joined Sarah Thorne at the Theatre Royal, Margate, where he remained for three years, gaining the thorough grounding in his profession for which Miss Thorne's management was noted. On 28 March 1883 he made his London début, as Caius Lucius in *Cymbeline* with Ellen Wallis at the Gaiety Theatre. After engagements with Minnie Palmer (as the comic 'dude' Dudley Harcourt in *My Sweetheart*) and Lawrence Barrett, he secured the role of the Apothecary in Mary Anderson's 1884–5 revival of *Romeo and Juliet* at the Lyceum Theatre, because, he maintained in old age, he was the twelfth candidate and thirteen was regarded as unlucky. Greet and Mary Anderson became and remained firm friends.

An engagement with Beerbohm Tree in Charles Young's *Jim the Penman* at the Haymarket (25 March 1886) followed, but Greet now entered into his principal life's work: theatrical management, albeit of a very different kind from Tree's in the fashionable West End. Open-air performances were the forte of Greet's companies. It was in one such, at Downing College, Cambridge, in June 1904, that Sybil Thorndike made her professional début. Well-to-do, respectable, non-theatrical families such as the Thorndikes entrusted their stage-struck offspring to Greet, reassured that, though he paid little or nothing in wages, he ran a highly respectable outfit. Thus H. B. Irving, Dorothea Baird, Robert Loraine, and Mrs Patrick Campbell, among many others, entered the profession through Greet. His personal supervision—surveillance—could not be guaranteed, however, for he regularly had ten to fifteen companies on the road, and at one time he had twenty-three. The fare ranged from *The Sign of the Cross* and *The Little Minister* to *Diplomacy* and *The Belle of New York*.

A committed high-church Anglican, Greet became one of the leaders of the Church and Stage Guild, which was founded in May 1879 by the Christian socialist Stewart Headlam to further better understanding and closer links between the two institutions. Aptly, therefore, Greet's greatest success was the medieval morality play *Everyman*, originally revived in 1901 by William Poel, in association with whom Greet staged it at the Imperial Theatre, London, in 1902. For the next twelve years he played *Everyman* in countless theatres, churches, halls, and open spaces on both sides of the Atlantic, and became personally increasingly identified with the American stage. Indeed his future might have lain in the United States had not the two irresistible forces of patriotism and Lilian Baylis summoned him to his destiny at the Old Vic in 1914.

Undaunted by wartime shortages, Greet persevered in his mission of bringing Shakespeare, twenty-four of whose plays he produced, to all sorts and conditions of men. He rarely promoted himself as an actor, though his Shylock and Malvolio were well-justified exceptions, but he made a virtue of necessity by casting women as male characters, most notably Sybil Thorndike as Prince Hal. One of his most successful wartime innovations at the Old Vic was the introduction of schools' matinées, as a consequence of which in 1918 he formed a company to perform Shakespeare's plays in London county council schools and other educational centres. In four years the performances were attended by more than four million children. Further afield, he was associated with W. E. Stirling in the presentation of English plays in Paris, for which he was awarded the diploma and gold medal at the exhibition of 1926. Each autumn from 1929 to 1932 Greet toured in America, while devoting the spring and summer to his seasons of pastoral plays, principally for schools, in England. The knighthood which he received in 1929 was for services to 'drama and education'. In the same year his own profession marked its golden jubilee with a complimentary dinner.

The foundation by Robert Atkins in 1933 of the Open Air Theatre in Regent's Park clearly owed much to the tradition of open-air performances which Greet had sustained and developed. Greet was actively involved in the first three seasons between 1933 and 1935. He performed character parts, such as Touchstone and Friar Lawrence, which were well suited to his years, physique (increasing bulk and white hair), and talents, but he took special pride in the office of master of the greensward, in which capacity he appeared before each play to welcome the audience and comment on the weather.

In April 1935, at the Criterion Restaurant, Greet was accorded a further complimentary dinner to mark his fifty-five years on the stage, and in March he appeared as the Messenger in *Everyman* at the Ambassadors Theatre. He was summoned to his own reckoning on 17 May 1936 at St Thomas's Nursing Home, Lambeth, on admission to which he said: 'Give me a nurse who can read Shakespeare' (*The Stage*). He was buried in Charlton cemetery, Greenwich, on 20 May.

Too modest a man to harbour claims to great eminence as an actor, Greet acquitted himself creditably in character parts. As a producer, he was patient, painstaking, and practical; the roll-call of actors whose early careers he fostered is its own testament. As a manager, he owed much to the ideas of others, especially William Poel, but he pursued them with enthusiasm into a new era. Greater than the sum of his parts, at home and abroad Greet was a quintessentially English figure who, like the master of greensward, embodied the durability and idiosyncrasy of his country's vernacular theatre.   RICHARD FOULKES

Sources W. F. E. C. Isaac, *Ben Greet and the Old Vic: a biography of Sir Philip Ben Greet* (1964) · J. Parker, ed., *Who's who in the theatre*, 8th edn (1936) · B. Hunt, ed., *The green room book, or, Who's who on the stage* (1906) · *The Stage* (21 May 1936) · *The Times* (18 May 1936) · C. Hamilton and L. Baylis, *The Old Vic* (1926) · R. Thorndike, *Sybil Thorndike* [1929] · S. Thorndike and R. Thorndike, *Lilian Baylis* (1938) · E. J. Dent, *A theatre for everybody* (1945) · G. Powell, *The Old Vic theatre: a history* (1993) · *Robert Atkins: an unfinished autobiography*, ed. G. Rowell (1994) · d. cert.
Archives NYPL, corresp. · Theatre Museum, London | University of Toronto, Canada, letters to James Mavor
Likenesses P. Coe, photograph, c.1921, NPG [*see illus.*] · portraits, repro. in Isaac, *Ben Greet and the Old Vic*
Wealth at death £127 16s. 2d.: probate, 5 Aug 1936, CGPLA Eng. & Wales

Greeting, Thomas (*d.* 1682), musician, is of unknown origins. Nothing of his life is known before December 1662, when he was appointed 'Musitian in ordinary without Fee' to Charles II. In 1664 he and his wife, Joyce, were resident in the Drury Lane area of Westminster, but three years before, in August 1661, their daughter Joyce had been baptized at St Clement Danes. She was presumably short-lived, for in 1671 another daughter of the same name was baptized at St Martin-in-the-Fields. A daughter Elizabeth was baptized at the latter church on 24 September 1673 and buried a year later. A daughter Catherine was baptized on 12 May 1676.

In April 1668 Greeting was listed among the twenty-four violins of the court, as a deputy for either John or Robert Strong. In October 1673 he was paid £12 'for a violin bought by him for his Majesty's service', the bill for this substantial sum being signed by Louis Grabu. In March 1674 he became a royal violinist and sackbut player in the Chapel Royal; this was his first salaried court position. Payment was generous, consisting of £16 2s. 6d. yearly livery plus a 1s. a day, and an extra 5s. per day if required to attend at Windsor, which often gained him an extra £11 or more annually. Greeting was also employed from 1673 to 1682 in the household of the duke of York as music tutor to his daughters (the future queens Mary and Anne).

When the flageolet, a new type of small fipple-flute, became a popular instrument, taking over from the recorder, Greeting wrote a book of instruction for it which was published by John Playford, *The Pleasant Companion, or, New Lessons and Instructions for the Flagelet*. It went into at least seven editions, of which the earliest to survive is dated 1672. Samuel Pepys bought a copy on 16 April 1668, but Ashbee and Lasocki suggest that this may have been in manuscript. Pepys owned a flageolet which could come apart in three pieces and be conveniently carried in his pocket. In February 1667 he paid Greeting the sum of £4 to teach Mrs Pepys flageolet playing, calling it 'an art that would be easy and pleasant for her'. The agreement was that instruction should continue until she could 'take out any lesson', but Mrs Pepys did not practise, and Pepys generously concluded that this was a 'bad bargain' for Greeting, whom he paid a further 20s. a month to continue calling at the house and teach him the flageolet. Pepys bought two 'great Ivory pipes' from Greeting for 32s. In 1668 Greeting, with two other musicians, played at Pepys's house during a dinner party, and he later arranged for the duke of Buckingham's musicians to play dance music there. Greeting thus earned a very comfortable living as player, teacher, and entrepreneur. He was skilful in taking advantage of fashion: *The Pleasant Companion* contains fifty-four pages of tunes, but Greeting is not really regarded as a composer.

Greeting took part in the introduction of opera to England. In July 1674 the marriage of the duke of York was celebrated with an opera by Robert Cambert, newly brought over from the court of Louis XIV, and Greeting was among the twelve violinists for this and a masque given the following January. In 1674 Greeting and a fellow court musician, John Banister, played the flageolet in Matthew Locke's *Psyche*, an opera with spoken dialogue based on Thomas Shadwell's play. Banister and Greeting may have helped Locke to write for this innovatory instrument. In 1675 the twenty-four violins were ordered to 'practice Mons. Grabu's musicke'.

Greeting was among those drowned when the frigate *Gloucester*, taking the duke of York to Scotland, was wrecked off the Norfolk coast on 6 May 1682. When the duke succeeded to the throne as James II in 1685, he gave Greeting's son Edward a place in the Private Musick in compensation for his loss, and granted a pension to Greeting's widow, Joyce, which was apparently paid out of secret service funds. Whether this latter indicates that Greeting had another string to his bow as well as his musical career must remain uncertain.

JULIA GASPER

Sources *New Grove*, 2nd edn · G. Abraham, ed., *New Oxford history of music* (1968), repr. (1998), vol. 4, p. 752 · D. Arnold, ed., *New Oxford companion to music* (1983) · P. Holman, *Four and twenty fiddlers: the violin at the English court, 1540–1690* (1993) · I. Spink, ed., *The Blackwell history of music in Britain*, vol. 3: *The seventeenth century*, 416 · A. Ashbee, ed., *Records of English court music*, 1 (1986) · A. Ashbee and D. Lasocki, eds., *A biographical dictionary of English court musicians, 1485–1714*, 1 (1998) · Pepys, *Diary*

Greg, Henry Philips (1865–1936), industrialist, was born at Lode Hill, Styal, near Wilmslow, Cheshire, on 13 August 1865, the only son (there were also five daughters) of Henry Russell Greg (1832–1894) and his wife Emily *née* Gair. His childhood was spent at Lode Hill, and he was educated first at Rugby School and later at Trinity College, Cambridge. In 1898 he married Jane Emily, daughter of Frederick Lewis Diblee, a civil engineer. They had one son and four daughters. He was a Unitarian, and was treasurer of Manchester College, Oxford and a trustee of the *Hibbert Journal*.

Greg began work in 1887 at Albert Mill, Reddish, near Stockport, a mill built in 1847 by his grandfather, Robert Hyde *Greg, for spinning and doubling cotton. In 1856 Robert Hyde Greg was joined in partnership by his third son, Henry Russell Greg. On Robert Hyde Greg's death, in 1875, H. R. Greg took control, in partnership with Charles Sharpe Parker. On Henry Russell Greg's death, in 1894, Henry Philips Greg became sole partner in R. Greg & Co. of Reddish. He expanded and modernized the mill, shifting production towards fancy yarns used in upholstery, and replaced flyer throstles and mule spindles with ring spindles. These moves later ensured the mill's competitive success in the 1920s and 1930s.

A Liberal in politics Greg was a committed free-trader who, for many years, was treasurer of the Knutsford Division Liberal Association, and an active member of the North Western Free Trade Union. He disliked government intervention of all kinds, and was especially opposed to any idea of state intervention to alleviate the problems of over-capacity and obsolescence, which beset the cotton industry in the inter-war period. It fixed internal minimum prices, established the Cotton Industry Board as the means of control, and as the institution for orchestrating change in the industry. Deploring any measures that would restrict competition, Greg believed instead that the way forward lay in the fundamental modernization of the industry.

Greg was, therefore, in the vanguard of technological innovation in the cotton industry at the beginning of the twentieth century. In 1904, on behalf of Ashton Brothers Ltd of which he became chairman in 1907, he visited the United States and arranged for 500 automatic looms to be imported. As a result of this initiative the British Northrop Loom Company was established, and Greg became its chairman. Keen to enhance the competitiveness of the British cotton industry by improving the quality of research and development, he was instrumental in establishing the British Cotton Industry Research Association. In addition he was involved in setting up the research laboratories at the Shirley Institute at Didsbury in south Manchester. In an article in the *Journal of the Textile Institute*, co-authored with W. Morton and entitled 'The cotton textile industry in the United States', he outlined what he saw as the virtues of the 'American System' of manufacturing as it applied to the cotton industry. He traced the organizational, managerial, and technological features of cotton manufacturing in the United States and pointed to the productivity advantages which this brought.

Greg believed that business efficiency depended on both technological superiority and human capital investment. In line with family tradition, he was a paternalist in his labour and community relations. In Styal he fulfilled the role of the local squire and, at the time, when Quarry Bank Mill (his cousin Edward Hyde Greg's mill) was being run down, and when morale in the village was low, he tried to revitalize the community by setting up the Village Club. This was intended to provide an alternative source of entertainment to the local public house, The Ship inn, which he had inherited from his father—somewhat to his embarrassment—as he saw excessive drink as the major social curse. Accordingly, he limited all customers to two glasses of beer, using the profits to fund the club, where villagers could read, play games, attend debates and classes, and give concerts. He valued the Styal community, and allowed no speculative building. As a consequence, somewhat ironically for one so keen on modernization, he bitterly opposed the building of the new Ringway airport, which after the Second World War was to become Manchester airport, and which involved the compulsory purchase of some of his land. At Reddish, for his own workforce, he developed a range of welfare schemes, adding playing fields and a recreation room, and appointed a welfare secretary in 1915. He died at his home, Lode Hill, Styal, on 3 June 1936, and was buried at Dean Row Chapel in Styal. MARY B. ROSE

Sources M. B. Rose, *The Gregs of Quarry Bank Mill: the rise and decline of the family firm, 1750–1914* (1986) · Burke, *Gen. GB* · R. Greg & Co. Ltd, obituary, Quarry Bank Mill, Wilmslow [held by Quarry Bank Mill] · M. B. Rose, 'Greg, Henry Philips', *DBB* · A. Fowler, 'Trade unions and technical change: the automatic loom strike, 1908', *North West Labour History Society Bulletin*, 6 (1979–80), 43–55 · W. Morton and H. Greg, 'The cotton textile industry in the United States', *Journal of the Textile Institute*, 17 (1926), 147–52 · d. cert.
Archives Man. CL
Likenesses photograph, repro. in obituary of Henry Philips Greg
Wealth at death £113,472 0s. 5d.: probate, 1 Feb 1937, *CGPLA Eng. & Wales*

Greg, Percy (1836–1889), journalist and novelist, son of the writer William Rathbone *Greg (1809–1881) and his wife, Lucy (d. 1873), the daughter of William Henry, was born at Bury St Edmunds. He was a journalist for most of his life, contributing regularly to the *Manchester Guardian*, *The Standard*, and *Saturday Review*; he also gained a distinguished reputation as a political writer and, later, as a novelist and historical writer. Between 1859 and 1888 he contributed articles to *Blackwood's Magazine*, *Macmillan's Magazine*, the *Quarterly Review*, the *Fortnightly Review*, *Fraser's Magazine*, and the *National Review*, among other well-known journals of the day.

In his youth Greg became known as a secularist, in middle age as a spiritualist, and in his later years as a champion of feudalism and absolutism. His violent opposition to the Unionist side in the American Civil War was made public in his *History of the United States to the Reconstruction of the Union* (1887) and earned him the reputation of political hard-hitter on the *Penny Press*. His more eccentric political and religious convictions were forcefully urged in two collections of his essays, *The Devil's Advocate* (1878), and *Without God: Negative Science and Natural Ethics* (1883), as well as in imaginative novels like his *Across the Zodiac* (1880), *Errant*

(1880), *Ivy Cousin and Bride* (1881), *Sanguelac* (1883), and *The Verge of Night* (1885). He also published poetry under the pseudonym Lionel H. Holdreth, and published one volume of verses, *Interleaves* (1875), under his own name. Greg died at his home, 16 Tedworth Square, Chelsea, London, on 24 December 1889, leaving a widow, Emma.

RICHARD GARNETT, rev. JOANNE POTIER

Sources Boase, *Mod. Eng. biog.* · W. E. A. Axon, *The Academy* (18 Jan 1890), 45 · *Wellesley index* · T. H. S. Escott, *Masters of English journalism* (1911); repr. (1970) · *Manchester Guardian* (30 Dec 1889) · *CGPLA Eng. & Wales* (1890)
Archives Co-operative Union, Holyoake House, Manchester, letters to G. J. Holyoake · NL Scot., letters to William Blackwood & Sons · U. Durham L., letters to Earl Grey
Wealth at death £1083 16s. 2d.: probate, 28 March 1890, *CGPLA Eng. & Wales*

Greg, Robert Hyde (1795–1875), cotton manufacturer and economist, born at 35 King Street, Manchester, on 24 September 1795, was son of Samuel *Greg (1758–1834), founder of the Quarry Bank Mill, Styal, Cheshire, and brother of William Rathbone *Greg and Samuel *Greg [*see under* Greg, Samuel]. His mother was Hannah (1766–1828), daughter and coheir of Adam Lightbody, a Liverpool merchant, and a descendant of Philip *Henry, the nonconformist. He probably attended Lant Carpenter's Unitarian school at Bristol before proceeding to Edinburgh University and then joining his father in business as a cotton merchant and manufacturer. He travelled in Spain, Italy, and the East. In 1817 he entered the Literary and Philosophical Society of Manchester, and afterwards contributed papers to its *Memoirs* on antiquarian subjects arising from his travels, including the site of Troy (1823) and the round towers of Ireland (1823). He married on 14 June 1824 Mary, eldest daughter of Robert Philips of the Park, Manchester; they had four sons and two daughters.

Greg took a leading part in public work in Manchester, aiding in the foundation of the Royal Institution and the Mechanics' Institution, and in the affairs of the chamber of commerce, of which for a time he was president. He was an ardent Liberal politician, and an enthusiastic supporter of both parliamentary reform and the repeal of the corn laws. He was a founder member of the Anti-Corn Law Association, which soon gave way to the Anti-Corn Law League. He was elected MP for Manchester, as the league candidate, in September 1839, during his absence from Britain. He took the seat against his will and he retired in July 1841. In the meantime he published a speech on the corn laws, which he had delivered in the House of Commons in April 1840, and a letter to Henry Labouchere, afterwards Lord Taunton, *On the pressure of the corn laws and sliding scale, more especially upon the manufacturing interests and productive classes* (1841; 2nd edn, 1842).

In 1837 Greg expressed his opposition to factory legislation and his contempt for the Ten Hours Movement in a pamphlet entitled *The Factory Question and the Ten Hours Bill*. His suspicion of organized labour and of protective legislation for mill workers continued into later life and in 1855, as chairman of the National Association of Factory Occupiers, he spearheaded opposition to the compulsory fencing of shafting in factories. He was also much interested in horticulture and in practical and experimental farming, which he carried on at his estates at Norcliffe, Cheshire, and Coles Park, Hertfordshire. He wrote three pamphlets on agricultural subjects, *Scottish Farming in the Lothians* (1842), *Scottish Farming in England* (1842), and *Improvements in Agriculture* (1844).

Greg died at his home, Norcliffe Hall, Styal, Cheshire, on 21 February 1875, and was buried four days later at the Unitarian chapel, Dean Row, Wilmslow, Cheshire.

C. W. SUTTON, *rev.* MARY B. ROSE

Sources M. B. Rose, *The Gregs of Quarry Bank Mill: the rise and decline of the family firm, 1750–1914* (1986) · M. B. Rose, 'The Gregs of Styal, 1750–1914', PhD diss., University of Manchester, 1977 · R. P. Greg, 'The genealogical history and traditions of the family of Greg', Man. CL · Burke, *Gen. GB* · *Manchester Guardian* (23 Feb 1875) · *Manchester Examiner* (27 Feb 1875) · *Proceedings of the Literary and Philosophical Society of Manchester*, 14 (1875), 135 · *Manchester Guardian* (27 Feb 1875)

Archives Herts. ALS · Man. CL | Derby Central Library, Pares MSS · Liverpool Central Library, Melly MSS · Man. CL, Anti-Corn Law League MSS, Manchester chamber of commerce, Wilson · U. Lpool, Rathbone MSS · UCL, corresp. with E. Chadwick

Likenesses photographs (after portraits at the ages of thirty and seventy), Quarry Bank Mill, Styal, Cheshire

Wealth at death under £60,000: probate, 15 March 1875, *CGPLA Eng. & Wales*

Greg, Samuel (1758–1834), cotton manufacturer, was born on 26 March 1758 in Belfast, the second surviving son of Thomas Greg, a wealthy Belfast merchant and shipowner, and his wife Elizabeth, daughter of Samuel Hyde, a Lancashire merchant and landowner. In 1766, at the age of eight, he went to live with his childless uncle Robert Hyde of Ardwick Hall, near Manchester. Robert Hyde, a substantial Manchester linen merchant in partnership with his brother Nathaniel, was trading with both Europe and the American colonies, and to secure succession in the business, he effectively adopted Samuel. Samuel Greg completed his formal education at Harrow School under Dr Parr; in 1778 he began learning the textile trade at Hyde & Co., becoming a partner in the firm in 1780. Robert Hyde died in 1782 and, since his uncle Nathaniel was by then a confirmed alcoholic, Samuel Greg inherited the firm. As heir to £10,000 from Robert Hyde and to the stock and goodwill of one of Manchester's largest merchant manufacturers, he became a wealthy young man. On 3 November 1789 he married Hannah (1766–1828), third daughter of Adam Lightbody, a prominent Liverpool merchant, and his wife Elizabeth. They had six boys and seven girls, though one son died as a child. They lived first at 35 King Street, Manchester, retaining it as a town house for a number of years. In 1796 Greg built Quarry Bank House adjacent to his cotton mill at Styal near Wilmslow in Cheshire. Raised in a Scottish Presbyterian family, Greg married into a prominent Unitarian family. His children were brought up as Unitarian, but his own religious affiliation remains uncertain. However, he became part of the 'charmed circle' of nonconformist families which dominated Manchester's commerce and society in the late eighteenth and early nineteenth centuries and he was a member of the Manchester Literary and Philosophical Society.

Greg was one of the pioneers of the industrial revolution, and his achievements were entirely as a cotton factory owner and a merchant. His first cotton-spinning mill, Quarry Bank Mill, began operation in 1784, and was the foundation of what became, by his retirement in 1832, the largest coarse spinning and weaving concern in the country. The firm grew slowly during the Napoleonic wars, allowing Greg to divert some of his wealth into a small estate in Styal and land at Reddish, near Stockport in Cheshire, adding to real estate he owned in Manchester, North America, and the West Indies. However, to secure his sons' futures, he built or purchased four other cotton mills during the 1820s—at Caton near Lancaster, Lancaster, Bury, and Bollington, near Macclesfield. At the same time he expanded spinning capacity at Quarry Bank and undertook extensive community development in the adjacent village of Styal. Unlike his son Samuel [*see below*], Greg was not a philanthropist, but viewed his factory colony as an essential adjunct to rural factory ownership. However, his labour policies and some of the institutions that developed in the village, such as the Female Society, reflected the strong influence of his free-thinking wife Hannah. Her interest in religion and education also had a lasting impact on her younger sons, especially Samuel, and William, and she provided a calming influence on the increasingly difficult relationship between Greg and his sons. After Hannah's death, on 4 February 1828, Greg remained in good health until 1832 when, at seventy-four, he was attacked by a tame stag in the grounds of Quarry Bank House and his injuries forced his retirement. His four younger sons, Robert, John, Samuel, and William Rathbone Greg, took control of Samuel Greg & Co., with Robert becoming the senior partner. Greg never fully recovered from his accident and died at Quarry Bank House on 4 June 1834.

The fourth surviving son, **Samuel Greg** (1804–1876), mill owner and philanthropist was born on 6 September 1804 at Quarry Bank House, Styal. From 1811 to 1819 he attended the Unitarian school of the Revd J. J. Taylor of Nottingham, followed by two years at Dr Lant Carpenter's school in Bristol. His years at Bristol were to have a profound effect on him since it was during this time that his scientific and literary tastes were formed. Two years spent gaining experience in the family business were followed, in 1823, by a winter of study at the University of Edinburgh. He became a partner in Samuel Greg & Co. in 1827 and, like his brothers, travelled in Europe prior to starting full-time work. On his father's retirement in 1832 he became responsible for Lowerhouse Mill at Bollington. He married Mary Priscilla Needham of Lenton, near Nottingham, in June 1838 and they had six girls and two boys, one of whom died in infancy.

Unlike his father and elder brother Robert, for whom business success was a driving force, the younger Samuel Greg saw mill ownership as an opportunity for social experiment. Passionately committed to improving the educational opportunities of working people, in 1830 and 1831 he gave a series of scientific lectures to his father's workers at Styal. His move to Bollington gave him ample opportunities for more wide-ranging social experimentation and the creation of a model village. He outlined his plans and objectives for his community in *Two Letters to Leonard Horner on the Capabilities of the Factory System* (1840). He established a Sunday school, a gymnasium, drawing and singing classes, baths and libraries, and founded the order of the Silver Cross in 1836 as a reward for good conduct for young women. In 1847 he introduced new machinery for stretching cloth, a move which proved so unpopular that his workforce came out on strike, devastating him and precipitating a nervous breakdown. This led him to retire from business, though he continued to live at The Mount, Bollington. His philanthropic interests were transferred to Macclesfield, where, in the 1850s and 1860s, he gave evening classes and scientific lectures to working people and became president of the Society for the Diffusion of Useful Knowledge. He died at The Mount on 14 May 1876, after a long illness, survived by his wife. Prefaced by a brief memoir by Dean Stanley, *A Layman's Legacy* (1877), which contains a selection of his writing, was published to celebrate his life.   MARY B. ROSE

Sources M. B. Rose, *The Gregs of Quarry Bank Mill: the rise and decline of the family firm, 1750–1914* (1986) · R. P. Greg, 'The genealogical history and traditions of the family of Greg', Man. CL · *Manchester Guardian* (9 Feb 1828) · *Manchester Guardian* (7 June 1834) · Man. CL, Greg MSS · will, proved, 22 July 1834, Ches. & Chester ALSS [Samuel Greg (1758–1834)] · *CGPLA Eng. & Wales* (1876) [Samuel Greg] · *Manchester Guardian* (30 June 1838) · A. P. Stanley, memoir, in S. Greg, *A layman's legacy in prose and verse: selections from the papers of Samuel Greg* (1877) [Samuel Greg (1804–1876)]

Archives Man. CL, MSS | U. Lpool, Rathbone MSS

Likenesses two photographs, Quarry Bank Mill, Styal, Cheshire

Wealth at death under £20,000: will, 1834, Ches. & Chester ALSS · under £9,000—Samuel Greg (1804–1876): will, 1876

Greg, Samuel (1804–1876). *See under* Greg, Samuel (1758–1834).

Greg, Sir Walter Wilson (1875–1959), literary scholar and bibliographer, was born on 9 July 1875 at Park Lodge, Wimbledon Common, the only son of William Rathbone *Greg (1809–1881), a social and political commentator, and his second wife, Julia, second daughter of James *Wilson (1805–1860). He was named after his grandfather and after Walter Bagehot, who married Wilson's eldest daughter. *The Economist*, founded by Wilson and brilliantly edited by Bagehot, was a family paper, and from childhood Greg was intended some day to be its editor. His father died in 1881, and with his mother he spent some years travelling in Europe, acquiring a knowledge of French and German and a passion for mountains and mountaineering. He did not distinguish himself at Harrow School (1889–93), and at Trinity College, Cambridge, his work for the modern and medieval languages tripos was so desultory that he gained only a pass degree (1897). But at Trinity he met Ronald Brunlees McKerrow (1872–1940), who was the most formative influence on his life. All thoughts of a career in financial journalism were soon abandoned: when he should have been writing essays on monetary theory he was collecting material for a bibliography of the English drama and discussing with McKerrow projects for editing Elizabethan drama and the textual methods to be used. In

1898 he joined the Bibliographical Society, and began a forty years' friendship with its secretary, A. W. Pollard (1859–1944). His first publication of importance was a finding-list (1900) of English plays written before 1643 and published before 1700. It was the beginning of that descriptive bibliography of the English drama of which the first volume was published in 1939 and the fourth and last in 1959. He had been, in his own words, 'sixty years on the job'.

Greg was fortunate in being able to pursue his research without having to earn a living: at the time of his death he was the largest individual shareholder in *The Economist*, to which he was also an occasional contributor. From his Wimbledon home he was a constant visitor to the British Museum and in almost daily touch with Pollard and McKerrow. Near by was the publishing house of A. H. Bullen, who suggested and published McKerrow's great edition of the sixteenth-century author Thomas Nash, and Greg's edition of the Henslowe *Diary* and *Papers* (1904–8). Greg's work on this three-volume edition laid the foundations of his expert knowledge of Elizabethan theatrical companies and Elizabethan handwriting. Bullen also published his one book on literary history, *Pastoral Poetry and Pastoral Drama* (1906), an important survey of the subject down to 1650. At the same time, in numerous articles he was establishing new standards of bibliographical and textual criticism in relation to Elizabethan texts. Almost as influential as his books and articles in raising the standards of English scholarship were his reviews, of which he wrote more than 200. He could be extremely severe, as in his review in the *Modern Language Review* for April 1906 of the edition of Robert Greene by Churton Collins, but he was constructive while being destructive. His most brilliant work in these early years, and one which drew widespread attention to the value of the bibliographical tools which he and Pollard and McKerrow were using, was the proof that ten early quartos of Shakespearian interest purporting to be published at varying dates from 1600 to 1619 were all printed by William Jaggard in 1619.

From 1907 until his resignation on his marriage (on 20 June 1913) to his cousin Elizabeth Gaskell (1885–1969), youngest daughter of Walter Greg of Lee Hall, Prestbury, Cheshire, Greg was librarian of Trinity College, Cambridge, his one salaried academic post. The treasures of that library might have led him to become a medievalist, and he published much work on medieval manuscripts of dramatic interest: his Sandars lectures on the miracle cycles in 1913 were the prelude to editions of plays from the N-Town (1915) and Chester (1935) cycles. But he was already committed to his dramatic bibliography and to the Malone Society. Of this society, founded at Pollard's suggestion for the exact reproduction of English plays and dramatic documents before 1640, Greg was general editor from 1906 to 1939 and president from 1939 to 1959. There were few of its hundred-odd volumes which did not profit from his scrutiny, and for many he was solely responsible. Pollard had insisted that the bibliographer must have continually in his or her mind's eye the actual material manuscript from which the compositor was working, and both

Greg and McKerrow realized that before this was possible they must know much more than was known to earlier scholars. Greg made available evidence relating to the relations between publishers, printers, and booksellers, the practices of Elizabethan printers in matters such as casting-off and proof correction, dramatic companies and their relations with dramatists and censors, the different types of dramatic manuscripts, and the handwritings of dramatists and playhouse scribes. His editions and studies of *The Merry Wives of Windsor* (1910), Robert Greene's *Orlando Furioso* and George Peele's *The Battle of Alcazar* (published in one volume, 1923), texts marred by memorial transmission, put the problem of the origins of 'bad' quartos in a new light: he returned to the subject in his work on Marlowe's *Doctor Faustus* (1950). His gifts as a textual critic and palaeographer found scope in his editions of manuscript plays, of which the most famous was *Sir Thomas More* (1911), three pages of which are believed to be in Shakespeare's hand. Other valuable works are his *Dramatic Documents from the Elizabethan Playhouses* (1931) with facsimiles and discussion of surviving theatrical and dramatic documents and *English Literary Autographs, 1550–1650* (1925–32), which gives facsimiles and transcriptions with comments on the hands of dramatists and other writers. Thanks in part to these works, attempts to identify hands of dramatists and playhouse scribes have met with some success. In *The Variants in the First Quarto of 'King Lear'* (1940) he demonstrated the importance of examining the corrected and uncorrected forms of a book.

On the function of bibliography and its relations to textual criticism Greg had much to say, and although he hardly ever produced an edition with established text and commentary he profoundly altered editorial procedure. Like McKerrow, he maintained that bibliography is the study of books, irrespective of their contents, with the purpose of ascertaining the exact circumstances and conditions in which they were produced; but unlike McKerrow he extended its boundaries by insisting that manuscripts and the investigation of textual transmission fell within its province. The duty of the editor of a printed text was not only to establish the relationship between the different editions of a work but to attempt to discover what sort of copy a printer worked from and how far he may have departed from his copy-text. The boundary between bibliography and textual criticism may have appeared a little obscure sometimes, but, thanks mainly to Greg's writings, it came to be recognized that analytical bibliography was an essential preliminary to textual criticism. A corollary of his view was that no emendation ought to be considered *in vacuo* without reference to the known history of the text, although he never supposed that textual criticism could be reduced to a set of mechanical rules. His essay *The Calculus of Variants* (1927), which grew out of his work on the miracle cycles, met with little scholarly success, but 'The rationale of copy-text' (1950) has been widely influential in the editing of literary works. The finest practical example of his doctrine is his parallel-text edition of *Marlowe's 'Doctor Faustus', 1604–1616* (1950), a work of minute scholarship.

After the outbreak of war in 1939 Greg sold his Wimbledon house and settled at River in Sussex. There he spent the happiest and most fruitful years of his life, seeing his great bibliography and his *Doctor Faustus* through the press. *The Editorial Problem in Shakespeare* (3rd edn, 1954) and *The Shakespeare First Folio: its Bibliographical and Textual History* (1955) were landmark publications and his reconstruction of Jonson's *Masque of Gipsies* (1952) from three different versions exhibited his characteristic daring. In his Lyell lectures on *Some Aspects and Problems of London Publishing, 1550–1650* (1956) he returned to a subject he had already touched on in 1930 in his edition (with Eleanor Boswell) of *Records of the Court of the Stationers' Company, 1576 to 1602* and to which the posthumously published *Licensers for the Press, &c. to 1640* (1962) and *A Companion to Arber* (1967) contributed more. His *Collected Papers*, edited by J. C. Maxwell, was published in 1966.

In youth Greg was unusually handsome and in old age he remained an impressive figure. Redoubtable in print, he was sometimes so in person, if angered by pretence or arrogance or slipshod writing. But he was friendly and accessible to younger scholars, and always a punctual correspondent. His admirably exact and lucid books were written in a neat and elegant hand: he did not use a typewriter. He loved the theatre, both live and on radio. His religious views were undogmatic.

Greg and his wife had two sons and one daughter. His many honours included the honorary degrees of DLitt from Oxford University (1932) and LLD from Edinburgh (1945), a fellowship of the British Academy (1928), and foreign membership of the American Philosophical Society (1945). He became gold medallist of the Bibliographical Society in 1935 and honorary fellow of Trinity in 1941. In 1950 he was knighted 'for services to the study of English literature'. He died at River on 4 March 1959. His body was cremated, and his ashes were scattered at Bishop's Ring on the south downs, Sussex.

F. P. WILSON, *rev.* H. R. WOUDHUYSEN

Sources W. W. Greg, *Biographical notes, 1877–1947* (1960) · F. P. Wilson, 'Sir Walter Wilson Greg, 1875–1959', *PBA*, 45 (1959), 307–34 · personal knowledge (1971)

Archives Bodl. Oxf., papers · Folger, corresp. · U. Southampton L., corresp. and papers relating to English drama | Bodl. Oxf., Chambers MSS · NL Scot., letters to D. N. Smith; corresp. with John Dover Wilson

Likenesses W. Stoneman, photograph, 1930, NPG

Wealth at death £47,716 7s. 8d.: probate, 21 May 1959, *CGPLA Eng. & Wales*

Greg, William Rathbone (1809–1881), industrialist and writer, was born at Quarry Bank House, Styal, Cheshire, the youngest son of Samuel *Greg (1758–1834) and his wife, Hannah (1766–1828), daughter of Adam Lightbody of Liverpool and his wife, Elizabeth. His elder brothers included Robert Hyde *Greg (1795–1875) and Samuel *Greg (1804–1876) [*see under* Greg, Samuel (1758–1834)]. His childhood was spent at Quarry Bank House in the Bollin valley. He was educated by Dr Lant Carpenter at his Unitarian school in Bristol, and in 1826 attended courses at Edinburgh University, where he was a contemporary of Charles Darwin. He became a prominent member of the

Plinian Society, which challenged orthodox religious beliefs. His other enthusiasms, shared by his elder brother Samuel, included phrenology and mesmerism.

In 1827 his father purchased Hudcar Mill, Bury, which William was to manage by way of apprenticeship to the family partnership. After a period travelling through France, Switzerland, Italy, Sicily, and Greece—his experiences are recorded in a pamphlet entitled *Sketches in Greece and Turkey* (1853)—he became a partner in Samuel Greg & Co. in 1830, taking sole responsibility for Hudcar Mill on his father's retirement in 1832. He married Lucy, the daughter of William Henry, a Manchester physician, in 1835. They had two sons and two daughters; one of the sons, Percy *Greg, became a journalist. Lucy's physical and mental health was poor, and in 1842 the family moved to The Craig, below Wansfell, near Ambleside in Westmorland. It was a move which severely reduced the attention William could give his mill. This, combined with efforts to salvage his brother Samuel's mill following his nervous breakdown in 1847, meant that Hudcar Mill was eventually sold in 1850, on the verge of bankruptcy. Although diligent, William lacked any real talent for business, and throughout the 1830s and 1840s he showed an increasingly active, and often radical, interest in the major political and social questions of the day. In 1837 he was an unsuccessful parliamentary candidate for the borough of Lancaster.

Greg emerged as a leading essayist, reviewer, and political and social commentator. In 1831 he wrote *An enquiry into the state of the manufacturing population and the causes and cures of the evils therein existing*, and during the 1840s he published three pieces on the corn laws, including his essay *Agriculture and the Corn Laws* (1843), which won a prize offered by the Anti-Corn Law League. For six years after the sale of his mill he supported himself entirely by writing and published forty-six reviews and articles, mainly in the *North British Review*, the *Westminster Review*, and the *Edinburgh Review*. In the 1850s he was also a regular leader columnist in *The Economist* and for a while was its manager. His writing was not confined to periodicals, however, and his reputation as religious sceptic was confirmed in this period by the publication of the *Creed of Christendom* in 1851. However, the need for a secure and regular income became increasingly pressing and in 1856 he accepted, with some reluctance, Sir George Cornewall Lewis's offer of a post in the board of customs and moved from Westmorland to Park Lodge, Wimbledon. The rest of his working life was spent as a civil servant and, from 1864 until he retired in 1877, he was comptroller of the Stationery Office. However, he remained an energetic contributor to the periodical press and published a number of social and political commentaries, including *Political Problems for our Age and Country* (1870), *Enigmas of Life* (1872), *Rocks Ahead, or, The Warnings of Cassandra* (1874), and *Mistaken Aims and Attainable Ideals of the Working Classes* (1876). A radical and often sceptical thinker, Greg supported both the 1832 Reform Act and the repeal of the corn laws in 1846. However, he became increasingly anti-democratic as he aged,

doubting the benefits of later reforms of the franchise and any increase in populism in politics.

In 1873 Greg's first wife, Lucy, who had been insane for many years, died, and the following year he married Julia, the daughter of his closest friend, James *Wilson, the founder and editor of *The Economist*. Their marriage was the culmination of a profound friendship which spanned nearly a quarter of a century. Their only son, the scholar Walter Wilson *Greg, was born in 1875. William Rathbone Greg died at his home, Park Lodge, Wimbledon, Surrey, on 15 November 1881.   MARY B. ROSE

Sources M. B. Rose, *The Gregs of Quarry Bank Mill: the rise and decline of the family firm, 1750–1914* (1986) · R. P. Greg, 'The genealogical history and traditions of the family of Greg', Man. CL · J. Morley, *Critical miscellanies*, 3 (1886) · R. D. Edwards, *The pursuit of reason: The Economist, 1843–1993* (1993) · Burke, *Gen. GB* · *Wellesley index*

Archives BL, journals and papers, Add. MSS 44882–44884 · Man. CL | BL, corresp. with W. E. Gladstone, Add. MSS 44363–44785, *passim* · Man. CL, Anti-Corn Law League letter-books · NL Scot., letters to Alexander Campbell Fraser · NL Wales, letters to Sir George Cornewall Lewis · priv. coll., Eliza Wilson Bagehot's diaries · U. Durham L., archives and special collections, corresp. with Earl Grey

Likenesses photograph, 1860–1869?, Quarry Bank Mill, Styal, Cheshire · portrait, repro. in Edwards, *Pursuit of reason*

Wealth at death £5,347 16s. 3d.: probate, 6 Jan 1882, *CGPLA Eng. & Wales*

Gregan, John Edgar (1813–1855), architect, was born at Dumfries, Scotland, on 18 December 1813. Of his parents nothing is known. He studied architecture first under Walter Newall and afterwards at Manchester under Thomas Witlam Atkinson. He began independent practice in 1840 and became a fellow of the Royal Institute of British Architects in 1849. In his brief career he specialized in ecclesiastical and commercial building in Manchester and Lancashire. His church of St John, Longsight (1845–6), follows Pugin's principles, while St John's, Miles Platting (1855), is Romanesque. He employed Italian Renaissance palazzo forms for the warehouses of Robert Barbour (dem.) and Thomas Ashton, Sir Benjamin Heywood's bank of 1848 (William Deacon's Bank) in St Ann's Street, and the new mechanics' institution of 1855 (now the Museum of Labour History) in David Street (now Princess Street). He also built a Puginesque chancel at St John's, Salford (1846), and erected St Peter's, Inskip (1848), St Peter's, Belmont (1849–50), and Rossall School chapel (1850; now a library).

Gregan's zeal for art and education led him to take much interest in various local institutions, no doubt encouraged by his patron Sir Benjamin Heywood. He was honorary secretary of the Royal Institution, promoted the local school of art, and sat on the committee which founded the Manchester Free Library. When the British Archaeological Association visited Manchester, he read 'Notes on Humphrey Chetham and his foundation', published in the association's journal for 1851. He died at home at York Place, Manchester, on 29 April 1855, aged forty-one, and was buried in St Michael's churchyard, Dumfries.   C. W. SUTTON, *rev.* VALERIE SCOTT

Sources *A compendium of Pevsner's Buildings of England*, ed. M. Good (1995) [CD-ROM] • *Dir. Brit. archs.* • J. Beesley and P. de Figueiredo, *Victorian Manchester and Salford* (1988)
Archives RIBA BAL, RIBA nomination papers

Gregg, Hilda Caroline [*pseud.* Sydney C. Grier] (1867/8–1933), novelist and short-story writer, was born in North Cerney, Gloucestershire, in 1868, the eldest of the two daughters of Sarah Caroline Frances French (*d.* 1913) and the Revd John Robert G. Gregg (*d.* 1882). Hilda Gregg was brought up in a family with strong religious convictions and Irish protestant connections. Her father, descended from a long line of Ulster clergymen, was described by Gregg's cousin Winifred Peck in her autobiography, *A Little Learning*, as 'an Irish clergyman of, I imagine, the strictest sect of Ulster Old Testament Protestants'. Her brother John became archbishop of Armagh, while her sister, Katherine, one of the first women doctors to qualify in Britain, undertook medical missionary work in Japan and India. Hilda Gregg was educated privately, her only academic distinction being an honorary MA from London University. Her first story was published in the *Bristol Times* in 1886, the year in which she moved to 27 St Anne's Road, Eastbourne, to look after her widowed mother. She began writing for a living, spurred on by financial need as well as by a subsequent success in a short-story competition run by *Cassell's Family Magazine*. Over the next three decades her short fiction and novels featured in a variety of genteel literary periodicals, including *Cassell's*, *Argosy*, the *Lady's Realm*, and the *Girl's Own Paper*. In 1894 Gregg sent her first novel, *In Furthest Ind*, a fictional memoir of a seventeenth-century Englishman's adventures in India, on speculation to the Edinburgh firm of William Blackwood, who published it in 1895 under the pseudonym of Sydney C. Grier. Blackwood remained her publisher throughout her writing career. *In Furthest Ind*, praised for its seemingly first-hand knowledge of locale and its skilful dialogue, set the tone and style for Gregg's subsequent works, which she produced at a rate of one a year until 1925. Gregg followed *In Furthest Ind* with *His Excellency's English Governess* (1896), a historical romance set in Baghdad, and then with *An Uncrowned King*, serialized in *Blackwood's Magazine* between December 1895 and September 1896, and *A Crowned Queen* (1898), both historical romances set in the Balkans. Other locales featured in her thirty-three novels included Ethiopia (*Peace with Honour*, 1897), Bengal (*Like another Helen*, 1899), Afghanistan (*The Wardens of the Marches*, 1901), and Sicily (*One Crowded Hour*, 1912). Gregg died on 22 June 1933 at 48 St Leonards Road, Eastbourne, her home since 1926, leaving an estate valued at slightly over £4200.   DAVID FINKELSTEIN

Sources G. F. Seaver, *John Allen Fitzgerald Gregg, archbishop* (1963) • W. Peck, *A little learning* (1952) • NL Scot., Blackwood MSS • Blain, Clements & Grundy, *Feminist comp.*
Archives E. Sussex RO | NL Scot., Blackwood MSS
Likenesses photograph, repro. in *The Bookman* (Oct 1898), 22
Wealth at death £4222 6s. 4d.: probate, 9 Sept 1933, *CGPLA Eng. & Wales*

Gregg, John (1798–1878), Church of Ireland bishop of Cork, Cloyne, and Ross, was born on 4 August 1798 at Cappa, near Ennis, co. Clare, the fifth son of Richard Gregg and his wife, Barbara, daughter of William Fitzgerald of Ashgrove, co. Clare. After attending a classical school in Ennis, he entered Trinity College, Dublin, in 1819, where he was a scholar and won many prizes. He graduated BA in 1825. A sermon which he heard by the Revd B. W. Matthias in Bethesda Chapel decided him to enter the church, and in 1826 he was ordained in Ferns Cathedral. He became curate of the French church, Portarlington, in 1826. In 1828 he obtained the living of Killsallaghan, in the diocese of Dublin, and threw himself vigorously into the work of the parish. In 1830 he married Elizabeth Nicola, daughter of Robert Law of Dublin. They had six children, including Robert Samuel *Gregg, later archbishop of Armagh.

Gregg's reputation as an eloquent evangelical clergyman, who could preach with equal fluency in English and Irish, made him a natural choice as incumbent of the Bethesda Chapel, Dublin, where he took up his post in 1836. Trinity Church was built for him in 1839 and became under his care a chief centre of evangelical life in Dublin. After refusing various offers of preferment he accepted the archdeaconry of Kildare in 1857, still remaining incumbent of Trinity. In 1862 he was appointed by the lord lieutenant (the earl of Carlisle) bishop of the united dioceses of Cork, Cloyne, and Ross. During his episcopate the new cathedral of St Fin Barre was built at a cost of nearly £100,000. He died at the bishop's palace, Cork, on 26 May 1878 and was buried in Mount Jerome cemetery, Dublin, on 30 May. He was one of the most active and influential evangelical leaders of the Irish episcopal church. Gregg published *A Missionary Visit to Achill and Erris* (1850) and many other sermons, lectures, and tracts during his episcopate.

THOMAS HAMILTON, *rev.* DAVID HUDDLESTON

Sources R. S. Gregg, *Memorials of the life of John Gregg D.D.* (1879) • W. M. Brady, *Clerical and parochial records of Cork, Cloyne, and Ross*, 3 (1864), 89–90 • J. H. Cole, *Records of the united diocese of Cork, Cloyne and Ross* (1903) • D. Bowen, *The protestant crusade in Ireland, 1800–70* (1978) • H. E. Patton, *Fifty years of disestablishment* (1922) • *CGPLA Ire.* (1878) • *Irish calendar of wills, 1878*, 272
Archives Representative Church Body Library, Dublin, bound address, with signatures from laity of dioceses, supporting opposition to ritualism in the Church of Ireland
Likenesses Guy of Cork, photograph, 1870–78, repro. in Gregg, *Memorials* • wood-engraving, NPG; repro. in *ILN* (8 June 1878)
Wealth at death under £2000: probate, 19 June 1878, *CGPLA Ire.*

Gregg, Robert Samuel (1834–1896), Church of Ireland archbishop of Armagh, was the second son of John *Gregg (1798–1878) and his wife, Elizabeth Nicola (*née* Law) of Dublin. He was born at the rectory, Killsallaghan, co. Dublin, on 3 May 1834. He entered Trinity College, Dublin, on 2 July 1851 and graduated BA in 1857, proceeding to an MA in 1860. In the year of his graduation Gregg was ordained for the curacy of Rathcooney, co. Cork, and in 1859 was appointed incumbent of Christ Church, Belfast, an important inner city cure which brought him in touch with working-class people. In 1862 he returned to the diocese of Cork as rector of Frankfield and chaplain to his father, who had just been appointed bishop of Cork,

Cloyne, and Ross. On 3 June 1863 he married Elinor, daughter of John Hugh Bainbridge of Frankfield House, Cork. They had two children: John William, who later settled at Causestown House, Athboy, co. Meath, and Amy Elinor, who later married R. Walsh, archdeacon of Dublin.

In 1865 Gregg became rector of Carrigrohane and precentor of St Fin Barre's Cathedral, Cork. Here he quickly acquired a reputation for administrative ability, as well as for the qualities of sound judgement, moderation, and common sense. In the controversies which followed the disestablishment of the Church of Ireland, and particularly in disputes over the revision of the prayer book, Gregg took the conservative side, but was conciliatory in his approach. His principal achievement at this time was to restructure the finances of his own diocese of Cork so well that his plan was adopted by the disendowed Church of Ireland as a whole. In 1873 he was presented by the University of Dublin with the degrees of BD and DD, in recognition of his services to the Church of Ireland.

In 1874 Gregg was appointed dean of Cork and in the following year was selected by the Irish bishops to succeed Bishop O'Brien in the diocese of Ossory, Ferns, and Leighlin. Gregg, at forty-one years of age, thus became a member of the episcopal bench while his father was still bishop of Cork. On his father's death on 26 May 1878, the synods of Cork, Cloyne, and Ross at once selected Gregg to succeed him. As bishop of Cork, Gregg's most notable achievement was to see the cathedral of St Fin Barre, which had been rebuilt during his father's episcopate at a cost of over £100,000, to its completion. He also won a deserved reputation, not only for administrative efficiency, but also for a statesmanlike grasp of church problems. On the death in 1893 of Robert Bent Knox, Gregg was selected to succeed him to the highest office in the Irish church: that of archbishop of Armagh and primate of all Ireland.

Gregg was neither a great scholar nor an eloquent preacher. He had a quiet and thoughtful demeanour in marked contrast to the passionate eloquence of his father. But he possessed a sound grasp of administration and had a practical sense of church affairs. He exercised his authority quietly but effectively and became an influential figure within the general synod of the Church of Ireland. Gregg's wife, Elinor, died in 1893 and Gregg himself died at the bishop's palace, Armagh, on 10 January 1896, after only two years as primate. He was buried, as his wife had been, at Frankfield, co. Cork, on 17 January. A memorial window was placed in Armagh Cathedral and an inscribed marble tablet in St Fin Barre's Cathedral, Cork.

C. L. FALKINER, *rev.* DAVID HUDDLESTON

Sources J. B. Leslie, *Ossory clergy and parishes* (1933), 42–3 · W. M. Brady, *Clerical and parochial records of Cork, Cloyne, and Ross*, 3 (1864), 90 · J. R. Garstin, *Anglican archbishops of Armagh* (1900), 14–15 · *The Times* (13 Jan 1896) · *The Times* (16 Jan 1896), 7 · C. A. Webster, *The diocese of Cork* (1920), 360–64 · H. E. Patton, *Fifty years of disestablishment* (1922)

Archives Representative Church Body Library, Dublin, Limerick diocese MSS

Likenesses R. Ponsonby Staples, oils, 1896–1900, Palace, Armagh, Ireland · Paris studio of Cork, photograph, repro. in *ILN* (18 Jan 1896) · lithograph (after drawing by C. W. Walton), Palace, Kilkenny, Ireland · photograph, repro. in Patton, *Fifty years of disestablishment* · photograph, NPG

Wealth at death £12,113 16s. 1d.: probate, 6 March 1896, *CGPLA Ire.* · £4760 10s. 1d.: Irish probate sealed in London, 19 March 1896, *CGPLA Ire.*

Gregg, Tresham Dames (1800–1881), protestant religious controversialist, was born in the parish of St Michan, Dublin, on 11 August 1800, the eldest son of Hugh Gregg, a tradesman, and his wife, Martha Dames. According to tradition he was the grandson of Tresham Gregg, governor of Newgate prison, who served Robert Emmet his last breakfast in 1803. When his father died at an early age, Gregg's mother married a schoolmaster, Charles von Feinaiglian, who kept a Dublin institution of education. Under the tutelage of his stepfather, Gregg received an education of an advanced nature for his age. This enabled him to enter Trinity College, Dublin, in 1821. He graduated BA in 1826, MA in 1830, and BD and DD in 1853. In the university Gregg was acknowledged as a profound scholar of Hebrew, and an able mathematician.

For two years Gregg taught in his stepfather's institution, but his deepening evangelical convictions from his days at Trinity College, Dublin, were to determine his career development. He was convinced that Daniel O'Connell's political campaigns were a direct threat to protestantism, as Roman Catholicism played its part in the movements both for Catholic emancipation and repeal of the union. He sought ordination in the Church of Ireland, and was ordained deacon in the diocese of Ossory in 1828. Then he moved to England to be ordained priest in the archdiocese of York. He was perpetual curate of Earlsheaton, Dewsbury, Yorkshire, for three years, then in 1833 he became curate-assistant at St George's, Sheffield. It was at this time that he encountered the appalling poverty of Irish immigrants, which he attributed to the state of ignorance in which they had long been held by Rome. In 1832 he married Sarah, daughter of Samuel Pearson of Pannel Hall, Knaresborough, with whom he had three children.

Gregg returned to Ireland in 1837, his family following him three years later. He immediately identified himself with militant churchmen who strongly opposed Roman Catholicism. In 1840 he was chosen to be chaplain of Swift's Alley Church, one of the evangelical proprietary chapels in Dublin, and his skill at controversial preaching soon brought him a strong working-class following. It also brought him the censure of Richard Whately, the archbishop of Dublin, who wished to avoid sectarian tensions with Roman Catholicism. From 1842 Gregg was inhibited from preaching in the archdiocese.

Gregg's fame after his apparent victory in 1838 over the Roman Catholic controversialist Thomas Maguire was such, however, that protestant parishioners used an ancient prerogative to elect Gregg as chaplain of the chantry of St Mary, in the parish of St Nicholas Within, Dublin. He was to hold this position, which gave him an adequate income from ancient leases, until his death in 1881. The

Tresham Dames Gregg (1800–1881), by unknown engraver

the fire: the celebrated prophecy of Isaiah (1852) • T. D. Gregg, *Triumph of Christ and his truth, the perdition of Antichrist and his idol: an oracle for the times on Daniel's prophecy of the seventy weeks* (1853) • T. D. Gregg, *Evangelical doctrine and apostolic order: sermons in proof … of the evangelical doctrines of the Church*, 2nd edn (1850) • T. D. Gregg, *An appeal to public opinion upon a case of injury and wrong … in the case of a question of prerogative that arose between his grace the archbishop of Dublin and the author* (1860) • T. D. Gregg, *Report of the arguments of counsel and judgment of the court in the case of the archbishop of Dublin against the Rev. T. D. Gregg* (1848) • T. D. Gregg, *Address and instrument of ministerial testimony to the clergy of the United Church of England and Ireland assembled at the Rotunda, Dublin, for the April meetings* (1867) • T. D. Gregg, *Crown of the ascendancy of truth replaced by the award of God himself and forever on the brow of the Irish church* (1869) • institution act book, 1821–31, Borth. Inst., Inst. AB 19/20 • Burtchaell & Sadleir, *Alum. Dubl.* • J. B. Leslie, 'Biographical succession list of clergy of Dublin archdiocese', RCB Library, Dublin • parish register (marriages), Sheffield, Yorkshire, 1832 • d. cert.

Archives Representative Church Body Library, Dublin | BL, corresp. with Sir Robert Peel, Add. MSS 40516, 40566 • Bodl. Oxf., letters to Disraeli

Likenesses engraving, NPG [*see illus.*] • etching, repro. in T. D. Gregg, *Covenant of eternal life* (1975), frontispiece

chantry had been free of episcopal jurisdiction since the reign of Edward IV.

From the security of this chaplaincy Gregg carried on a campaign of religious controversy, much to the annoyance of Dublin's English prelate, who was not popular with the protestant working class. Gregg organized the Protestant Operatives Association, which strongly contested O'Connell's repeal agitation; he travelled widely in his controversial preaching tours, and was known popularly as 'Trash'em' Gregg because of his prowess in the pulpit. He helped to keep himself before the public eye by a celebrated public quarrel with a Roman Catholic abbess, which earned him a week's stay in the Bridewell in 1841. He was a voluminous writer, but in his later years he had strange ideas about the rule of the Antichrist, and his own personal immortality. His attacks on Richard Whately ensured that he never received preferment and he died in obscurity at 55 Strand Road, Sandymount, Dublin, on 28 October 1881. He was survived by his wife and children.

Desmond Bowen

Sources J. Crawford, 'In the hopes of the latter day: a biography of Tresham Dames Gregg, 1800–1881', Representative Church Body Library, Dublin • *Authenticated report of the discussion between the Rev. T. D. Gregg and the Rev. Thomas Maguire from 29 May to 2 June, 1838* (1839) • D. Bowen, *The protestant crusade in Ireland, 1800–70* (1978) • T. D. Gregg, *Protestant ascendancy vindicated and national regeneration through the instrumentality of national religion urged in a series of letters to the corporation of Dublin* (1840) • T. D. Gregg, *Authenticated report of the extraordinary case of the Rev. T. D. Gregg, chaplain of St. Nicholas Within, Dublin, and his committal to Bridewell for refusing to give his recognizance: letters to the protestant public in recognition of himself* (1841) • T. D. Gregg, *Free thoughts on protestant matters in one volume* (1846) • T. D. Gregg, *Battle of the warrior, and the burnings of the fuel of*

Gregg, William (*bap.* **1673**, *d.* **1708**), conspirator, was baptized at Montrose, Scotland, on 4 June 1673, the eldest of fourteen children of William Greige (*d.* 1701), a shipmaster of Montrose engaged primarily in the Baltic commerce, and his wife, Margaret Marshall. Gregg received his early training in merchandising during the later 1690s in the household of the London merchant Thomas Couttes, but in 1698 his father secured for him a position as private secretary to a distant kinsman, Hugh Greg, secretary to, and subsequently resident minister of, the British embassy at Copenhagen. This action was taken to curb the younger Gregg's financial recklessness and impetuous behaviour in London, character traits which would plague him throughout his short life and bring him to the scaffold. The death of his employer in December 1701 placed Gregg temporarily in charge of the conduct of affairs, and in April 1702 he was reappointed as secretary to James Vernon junior, the new envoy-extraordinary. He was dismissed in the autumn of 1704 for being, in Gilbert Burnet's subsequent biased phrase, 'a vicious and a necessitous person' (*Bishop Burnet's History*, 5.342). Certainly, Gregg's correspondence in this period revealed a developed sense of his own capacities, over-reaching ambition, and arrogance, combined with living beyond his means. Back in London and in search of employment, Gregg began in January 1705 a sustained campaign to acquire a governmental position under secretary of state Robert Harley. Harley eventually sent Gregg to Edinburgh in a private capacity to report on the session of the Scottish parliament between June and September 1705, and, following constant importuning, appointed him to a junior clerkship in his office on 16 April 1706.

Dissatisfied with his humble duties as a copying clerk—work he termed 'a perfect drudgery' (*JHL*, 18.518)—and repulsed when he attempted to increase his responsibilities or change employment, Gregg's immature idealization of Harley turned to disillusionment. Overcome by indebtedness, Gregg initiated in October 1707 treasonous correspondence with Michael de Chamillart, the French minister of war. At first he merely passed on public knowledge, but on 28 November in an unsuccessful attempt to secure Chamillart's confidence, he began copying confidential papers in the secretary of state's office. Gregg's treason was detected almost simultaneously at Brussels and Rotterdam by postmasters in the pay of the British administration. Interrogated before the committee of the privy council on 31 December, Gregg was committed to Newgate. Tried at the Old Bailey on 19 January for correspondence with France, he pleaded guilty, was sentenced to death, and executed at Tyburn on 28 April 1708.

As a conspirator, Gregg was inconsequential; as a pawn in the political manoeuvring between the whig junto and Harley he acquired lasting significance. His genuine assertions that no religious or political motivation existed for his crimes were disbelieved, his actions were erroneously linked to the espionage of more important French agents detected at this time, and Gregg was vilified in the popular press as an arch-traitor. Secretary of state Charles Spencer, earl of Sunderland, exploited this climate of suspicion in his effort to drive Harley from office, but ultimately he found better, more serviceable evidence elsewhere. There is no reason to believe that the committee of the House of Lords (the infamous Seven Lords: the dukes of Somerset, Devonshire, and Bolton, the earl of Wharton, Viscount Townshend, and lords Halifax and Somers) who repeatedly questioned Gregg behaved improperly, although this belief became effective Harleyite propaganda in the 1709–11 period. Harley, who had nothing to hide except a carelessly organized office routine, developed a compulsive interest in the Gregg affair, and attempted to purchase the prisoner's loyalty by payments to a woman whom Gregg called his companion and strumpet but who in 1710 identified herself as the deceased's widow and mother of his son. Ultimately, through the writings of Jonathan Swift and others, Gregg proved far more serviceable to Harley in death than in life.   J. D. ALSOP

Sources BL, Add. MSS 7076, 28910–28915, 61498, 61607, 61618, 70024–70025, 70325, 70338, 70340, 70352–70357 · PRO, SP 34/9, 44/77, 146 · JHL, 18 (1705–9), 516–42 · State trials, 14.1371–94 · The manuscripts of his grace the duke of Portland, 10 vols., HMC, 29 (1891–1931), vol. 4 · W. Scott, ed., A collection of scarce and valuable tracts … Lord Somers, 2nd edn, 13 vols. (1809–15) · The prose works of Jonathan Swift, 3: The Examiner and other pieces written in 1710–11, ed. H. Davis (1941) · F. H. Ellis, Swift vs Mainwaring: The Examiner and The Medley (1985) · A true copy of the paper left by Mr. William Gregg (1708) · Bishop Burnet's History of his own time: with the suppressed passages of the first volume, ed. M. J. Routh, 6 vols. (1823) · county of Forfar, Montrose sessions records, General Register Office for Scotland, Edinburgh, OPR, fols. 8v, 11, 72 · dispatches to Hugh Greg and William Gregg, PRO, SP 75/23H, 24H, SP 104/4 · will of William Greige, 15 Oct 1701, NA Scot., CO 3/3/8 [Commissariat of Brechin] · IGI
Archives BL, corresp. and papers, Add. MSS 70352–70357
Wealth at death heavily in debt: BL, Add. MS 70357

Grego, Joseph (1843–1908), writer on art, was born on 23 September 1843 at 23 Granville Square, Clerkenwell, London, the elder son of Joseph Grego (1817–1881), a looking-glass manufacturer, and his wife, Louisa Emelia Dawley.

His grandfather, Antonio Grego, a native of Como, Italy, settled in London before 1821 as a looking-glass manufacturer, the firm becoming Susan Grego & Sons in 1839, and Charles and Joseph Grego in 1845.

After education at private schools Grego was for a time with Lloyds, the underwriters. Having inherited an interest in collecting from his father he too turned to that pursuit and combined it with dealing and writing on art. He specialized as writer and collector in the work of James Gillray, Thomas Rowlandson, George Morland, and George Cruikshank, and was an acknowledged authority on all of them. He was chiefly responsible for an edition of James Gillray's works, The Works of J. G. the Caricaturist, with the History of his Life and Times (1873), edited by Thomas Wright for which he himself wrote the history, and he edited Rowlandson the Caricaturist (2 vols., 1880). Both books, which illustrate Grego's comprehensive and thorough method of work, became standard books of reference.

Grego collected much material for a life of Morland, which he did not complete. In 1874 he compiled Thackerayana (1875), a volume based on books with marginal and other sketches from Thackeray's sale; owing to copyright difficulties it was immediately suppressed, but was reissued in 1898. A frequent writer on art in periodicals and the press, and editor of Pears Pictorial (1893–6), Grego also wrote History of Parliamentary Elections in the Old Days, from the Time of the Stuarts to Victoria (1886; new edn, 1892). He also edited R. H. Gronow's Reminiscences, with twenty illustrations 'made up' from contemporary prints (1889); Gaston Vuillier's History of Dancing, to which he contributed a sketch of dancing in England (1898); Pictorial Pickwickiana: Charles Dickens and his Illustrators (2 vols., 1899); and Oliver Goldsmith's Vicar of Wakefield, including John Forster's essay on the story (1903). In 1904 he published Cruikshank's Water Colours, with an introduction and colour reproductions.

Grego, who was always ready to lend prints and drawings for public exhibitions, occupied much of his time in organizing exhibitions—such as the Royal Naval Exhibition, for which he published an illustrated souvenir with historical notes in 1891, and 'English Humorists in Art'. He was himself adept with his pencil, doing much work as a designer of theatrical costumes and etching the designs of others. He invented a system of reproducing eighteenth-century colour prints in such exact facsimile that they have often been mistaken for originals. From 1897 to 1899 he was secretary of the Kernoozer's Club, formed to promote 'friendly intercourse between Gentlemen who study or collect Ancient Armour and Arms' (minutes, BL, Add. MSS 40678–40681). He was a director of Carl Hentschel, Ltd, photo-engravers, from 1899 to 1908 and a substantial shareholder in the firm of Kegan Paul & Co. (of which he was a director from January 1903 until his death) and of the Graphic Company.

Grego died, unmarried, on 24 January 1908 at 23 Granville Square, where he was born and where he lived all his life. His vast accumulations of prints, drawings, and books were dispersed on his death—at Christies on 28 April and 4 June 1908, and at Puttick and Simpsons in April, June, and July 1908.

WILLIAM ROBERTS, *rev.* ANNETTE PEACH

Sources WWW, 1897–1915 · CGPLA Eng. & Wales (1908)
Archives BL, corresp. with John Brown, Add. MS 42713 · BL, corresp. with Montague John Guest, Add. MSS 57934–57941 · BL, minute books of Kernoozer's Club, Add. MSS 40678–40681 · RA, collection on Royal Academy
Likenesses J. Bastien-Lepage, pen and ink, c.1880–1881 · photograph, repro. in *The Graphic* (1 Feb 1908)
Wealth at death £8891 6s. 5d.: probate, 15 May 1908, CGPLA Eng. & Wales

Gregor, Walter (1825–1897), folklorist, was born on 23 October 1825 at Forgieside, in the parish of Keith, in Banffshire, the son of James Gregor, tenant farmer, and Janet Leslie. He was educated at the school in Keith, a successful parochial school of the old style, gaining a bursary in 1845 to pursue a distinguished undergraduate career at King's College, the older of Aberdeen's two universities. He graduated with an honours MA in 1849 and shortly afterwards was appointed master of the Macduff parish school in the Moray Firth fishing village of Gamrie, in Banffshire. He spent ten successful years in this post, during which time—as was not uncommon—he underwent a course in divinity and was licensed to preach by the presbytery of Turriff in 1857 at the late age of thirty-two. A popular and well-respected man, he was ordained to Macduff parish church two years later, before being presented by Queen Victoria in 1863 to the parish of Pitsligo in the farming countryside of Aberdeenshire. Here he spent the rest of his working life.

Gregor had many ups and downs during his professional life, especially in his relationship with his presbytery: he held that his manse was insanitary and refused to live in it until it was eventually remodelled. He was nevertheless held in high regard by his parishioners, especially for the courage shown in his single-handedly ministering to the sick during a severe cholera epidemic. On 24 December 1862 he married Margaret Avon, *née* Gardiner (1836/7–1906), of Greenskares, Gamrie, Banffshire. They had two children, Alexander, who went on to practise in England, and a daughter, Janet Leslie, a teacher, who worked for some years in Germany.

A cheerful, humorous man, Gregor was a perpetual student and combined the life of a parish minister with that of a prolific scholar. He rapidly gained an international reputation as an archaeologist and folklorist, as well as a natural historian and expert in Scottish history, literature, language, balladry, and general antiquities, drawing on Banffshire and Aberdeenshire for much of his findings. While a schoolmaster he provided the Natural History Museum of Marischal College (Aberdeen's other university until its fusion with King's College in 1860 to form the University of Aberdeen) with many valuable specimens. He was proficient in several languages, including Hebrew and French, having attended Renan's courses in Hebrew at Paris, and was even considered for the chair of Hebrew

at Aberdeen University in the 1870s. He was granted an honorary LLD by the university in 1885.

Gregor was a member and president of the Buchan Field Club, an active research society, and convenor of the archaeology committee of the New Spalding Club, a prestigious historical publishing society which was later to initiate the Greig-Duncan Folk Song Collection. He was also a member of the Society of Antiquities of Scotland and of the ethnographical committee of the British Association. He helped found the Scottish Text Society, and acted as its enthusiastic secretary and text editor for many notable years.

Gregor's research output—ten books and editions, together with over sixty-five papers and pamphlets—was both prodigious and catholic, and his works were published in both English and French (with translations from the Spanish) in British and continental journals. He made his name with a superb *Dialect of Banffshire with a Glossary of Words not in Jamieson's Scottish Dictionary* (1866), his *Echo of Olden Times from the North of Scotland* (1881), and *Notes on the Folk-Lore of the North-East of Scotland* for the Folk-Lore Society (1881), which continued to be used throughout the twentieth century. For the Scottish Text Society he edited crucial texts such as *Ane Treatise Callit The Court of Venus be Iohne Rolland* (1884), *The Poems of William Dunbar* (1884–93), and *The Gude and Godlie Ballatis* (1897). He was a member of the Société des Traditions Populaires and his name is on the first list of members of the Folk-Lore Society. In 1895 Gregor retired to Bonnyrigg, Midlothian, where he died at his home, Lauder Villa, on 4 February 1897 after a short illness. He was buried in Lasswade churchyard in Bonnyrigg. On 8 July 1906 his widow, Margaret, died, aged sixty-nine.

Gregor is best remembered for his pioneering work in folklore and dialect, especially of Scotland. His obituary in *Folklore* described him as having 'in fullest measure that prime essential of a successful collector of folklore—a gracious and genial nature. All who came into contact with him felt his charm, and none could help yielding to his influence'. In many ways he was a man far ahead of his day, especially in his own country (and a hundred years afterwards folklore studies struggle to achieve any academic recognition in the United Kingdom); his remarkable work, moreover, has stood the test of time.

IAN A. OLSON

Sources Fasti Scot. · D. Buchan and I. A. Olson, 'Walter Gregor: a life and provisional bibliography', *Folklore*, 108 (1997), 115–17 · 'Death of Walter Gregor', *Aberdeen Journal* (6 Feb 1897) · 'Walter Gregor', *Transactions of the Buchan Field Club*, 9 (1906–8), 268–70 · *Folklore*, 8 (1897), 188
Archives Warburg Institute, London, Folklore Society, James E. Crombie MSS
Wealth at death £597 4s. 10d.: confirmation, 23 April 1897, CCI

Gregor, William (1761–1817), mineralogist and Church of England clergyman, was born on 25 December 1761 at Trewarthenick, Cornelly, Cornwall, the younger son of Francis Gregor, a military man and member of an old Cornish family, and his wife, Mary, sister of Sir Joseph Copley, baronet. He went to Bristol grammar school, where he developed a taste for chemistry, and then spent two years with a private tutor in Walthamstow before entering St John's College, Cambridge, from where he graduated BA in 1784. A prize won for Latin prose gained him a Platt fellowship at his college; he proceeded MA in 1787 but resigned his fellowship and moved to the rectory of Diptford, near Totnes, which his father had purchased for him. In 1790 he married Charlotte Anne (d. 1819), only daughter of David Gwatkin and his wife, Anne Lovell; they had one daughter.

Dr John Ross, bishop of Exeter, to whom his wife was related, presented him in 1793 to the rectory of Bratton Clovelly, Devon, which in the same year he exchanged for the rectory of Creed in Cornwall, where he remained for the rest of his life. In this remote setting, with little apparatus, Gregor began to undertake original and, for the time, remarkably accurate analyses of Cornish minerals. His most important discovery, that of the metal titanium, was the outcome of his examination of a local mineral occurring in a stream in the Menaccan valley. Gregor correctly identified this mineral, now known to be a variety of ilmenite, as a compound of iron, with traces of manganese and the calx of an unknown metal which he proposed to call menaccine. His account of this mineral, named by him menaccanite (the place name and the minerals derived from it are variously spelt), was published in 1791 in French and German journals, and read to the Royal Society.

No further notice was taken of the mineral until 1795 when Martin Heinrich Klaproth published his analysis of rutile, showing that it was composed of the oxide of a new metal to which he gave the name titanium. Two years later the same chemist analysed a sample of menaccanite, and on finding that it contained the same metal, acknowledged Gregor's prior claim to the discovery of titanium; Gregor's name for the metal was, however, dropped as being too similar to that of the mineral. Gregor subsequently found titanium in corundum from Tibet and in black tourmaline from a Cornish tin mine. He was also the first to describe wavellite. His results were published in 1805, the name being later applied by Humphry Davy whose specimens had been provided by Dr W. Wavell of Barnstaple. Gregor and Davy both recognized it as a hydrate of alumina but Gregor detected traces of phosphoric acid and fluorine, which Davy missed.

An erudite, kindly, and modest man, and known to his parishioners as a devoted parson, Gregor was painstaking in his work but never let his love of science interfere with his parochial duties. He was an original member of the Royal Geological Society of Cornwall on its foundation in 1814. He was distinguished as a painter of landscapes, an etcher, and a musician. He was one of the first to introduce vaccine inoculation in Cornwall, overcoming local prejudice. In his latter years he became increasingly incapacitated by tuberculosis, from which he died at his home, the rectory, Creed, on 11 June 1817 (not 11 July, as given in *DNB*). He was buried at Creed. His wife died in 1819 at Exeter.   G. C. BOASE, *rev.* ANITA MCCONNELL

Sources A. Russell, 'The Rev. William Gregor, 1761–1817, discoverer of titanium', *Mineralogical Magazine*, 30 (1953–5), 617–24 · J. A. Paris, *A memoir of the life and scientific labours of the late Rev. W. Gregor* (1818) · 'Biographical notice of the Rev. William Gregor', *Annals of Philosophy*, 11 (1818), 112–14 · M. E. Weeks and H. M. Leicester, *Discovery of the elements*, 7th edn (1968), 520–23 · R. J. Cleevely, 'The contributions of a trio of Cornish geologists to the development of 18th century mineralogy', *Transactions of the Royal Geological Society of Cornwall*, 22 (2000), 89–120 · *Flindell's Western Luminary and Family Newspaper* (17 June 1817), 3 [death notice]

Archives Cornwall RO, letters to Rashleigh and Hawkins · NHM, corresp. with Sowerby, letters to Hawkins · Royal Institution of Cornwall, Truro, Courtney Library, letters to Rashleigh · W. Sussex RO, Hawkins

Gregorie [Gregory], **David** (1625–1720), physician and inventor of a cannon, son of the Revd John Gregorie, minister of Drumoak in Aberdeenshire, and elder brother of James *Gregory (1638–1675), was born on 20 December 1625. His early education was probably undertaken by his mother, Janet, daughter of David Anderson, from whom much of the mathematical and medical genius of the Gregorie family is thought to have been inherited. He was apprenticed (probably unwillingly) by his father to a mercantile house in the Netherlands, possibly dealing in herrings and stockings—the principal Aberdeen exports of the time. He returned to Aberdeen in 1655, gave up all forms of trading, and devoted himself to literary and scientific studies. He held the post of librarian of Marischal College Library (1663–9) where he had access to many books of interest to him. He also corresponded with scientific contemporaries in Britain and abroad. On the death of his elder brother, Alexander, in 1664 he inherited Kinnairdy in Banffshire, where he lived for many years. He married Jean Walker on 8 February 1655 and they had fifteen children. Jean died in childbirth in 1671. He married Isabel Gordon on 15 February 1672 and they had fourteen children. Nine of his twenty-nine children died in infancy. He had the distinction of seeing three of his sons, David *Gregory (1659–1708), James (1666–1742), and Charles (1681–1754), all professors of mathematics in British universities at the same time. His daughter Margaret was the mother of Thomas *Reid, metaphysician, who recorded much of what is known of his grandfather's career.

Gregorie was ridiculed by his neighbours at Kinnairdy for his ignorance of farming, but although entirely self-taught, he acted as local doctor to rich and poor and was greatly admired for it. He never charged for his services. His practice occupied a great deal of his day, so he used to retire to bed early, rise about 2 a.m. to study his books and instruments, then return to bed for a further hour before breakfast. He was the first person in the area to possess a barometer, and it was said that his forecasts of weather nearly led to his prosecution for witchcraft, when he was the only landowner in the district to harvest his crops before the onset of an autumn storm.

In 1690 Gregorie settled the estate on his son David and moved to Aberdeen where, during the wars of Queen Anne, he turned his attention to the subject of gunnery. With the help of an Aberdeen watchmaker he constructed a model of an improved cannon, and prepared to take it to Flanders. Meanwhile he forwarded his model to his son David who showed it to Isaac Newton. According to Reid,

Newton advocated the suppression of the invention as being destructive of the human species. As the model was never found it must be assumed that Newton's advice was followed. During the Jacobite rebellion of 1715 Gregorie took his family to the Netherlands, returning to Aberdeen when the trouble had subsided. He appears to have been discouraged from further invention, and devoted the later years of his long life to the compilation of a history of his time and country that was never published. He died in 1720. **JAMES BURNLEY, rev. PAUL LAWRENCE**

Sources P. D. Lawrence, 'The Gregory family: a biographical and bibliographical study', PhD diss., U. Aberdeen, 1971 · U. Aberdeen, Gregory MSS
Archives U. Aberdeen

Gregory [Gregory of Huntingdon] (*fl. c.*1300), prior of Ramsey and book collector, held the priorate of the Benedictine abbey at Ramsey some time before the mid-fourteenth, and probably in the late thirteenth, century. He appears as a donor of books in his abbey's surviving catalogue, compiled in the second quarter of the fourteenth century. Copies of this are extant in two fragments (LPL, MS 585, pp. 661–2 and 663–4, and BL, Cotton MS Rolls II.16), which list at least sixteen volumes (the relationship between the entries for Gregory's donations in each is not entirely clear). Prominent among these books are works in Greek and Hebrew. In a story that he probably gleaned from the former monk of Ramsey whom he cites as Johannes Infantius (John Young), the bibliographer John Leland (*d.* 1552) recounts that Prior Gregory bought the Hebrew books when the Jews to whom they belonged auctioned them at Stamford, Lincolnshire, on the point of their expulsion from England in 1290. According to Leland, Lawrence Holbeck, a monk of Ramsey in the early fifteenth century, put these books to good use by producing a Hebrew dictionary, which at the time of the dissolution was in the hands of Robert Wakefield (*d.* 1537/8).

John Bale (*d.* 1563) credited Gregory with the authorship of a number of works, giving the titles and incipits of eleven in his *Index Britanniae scriptorum*. The first incipit, however, would appear to refer to *De constructione*, by the sixth-century Roman grammarian Priscian, and the title of the work echoes that of one of the volumes that Gregory gave to Ramsey. The remaining works that Bale credited to Gregory were almost certainly among the other contents of this volume. These include the *Imago mundi* of the twelfth-century theologian Honorius Augustodunensis. It is therefore very unlikely that Gregory was the author of any of these works. There is no evidence earlier than that of Bale that Gregory was from Huntingdon. **MARIOS COSTAMBEYS**

Sources R. Sharpe, *A handlist of the Latin writers of Great Britain and Ireland before 1540* (1997) [incl. details of Lambeth and BL MSS] · R. Sharpe and others, eds., *English Benedictine libraries: the shorter catalogues* (1996) · Bale, *Index*

Gregory of Caergwent. *See* Caer-went, Gregory of (*fl.* 1237).

Gregory the Great. *See* Giric son of Dúngal (*d. c.*890).

Gregory, Alice Sophia (1867–1946), midwife, was born on 22 November 1867 at St Mary's Parsonage, Princes Road, Lambeth, the youngest of three daughters of Robert *Gregory (1819–1911), Church of England clergyman, later dean of St Paul's, and his second wife, Charlotte Anne, daughter of Admiral Sir Robert Stopford. Alice was educated at home by a governess and was very close to her sister Christiana, who was nearest to her in age. Alice led an uneventful life, sketching, making visits at home and abroad, attending lectures on cooking and health, until, at the age of twenty-six, she began to train as a general nurse at the Cottage Hospital, Paulton, Somerset, where Mrs Lelia Parnell, a widow, was matron. In 1895 Alice became a pupil at the Clapham School of Midwifery, where she studied under Dr Annie McCall (1859–1949), and after attending eighty confinements she obtained her diploma as a trained midwife from the London Obstetrical Society. Alice then returned to Somerset where she worked as a district midwife for eight years. She supported herself from fees, amounting to 8*s.* for a confinement, and an allowance of £50 from her father. In 1899 she met Maud Cashmore, seven years her junior, who accompanied Alice on her district rounds before studying obstetrics at the Clapham Maternity Hospital and qualifying as a midwife. Lelia, Alice, and Maud became close friends and remained inseparable companions for the rest of their lives. As Marks observed:

> Much of their work stemmed from a strong belief both that women could achieve independence through a professional career such as midwifery, and that women should be given the best possible maternity care. Their views and actions were also inspired by a deep sense of Christian morality and the need to help the poor, as well as a strong feminist orientation. (Marks, 73–4)

Alice Gregory and her friends were typical of a small number of middle-class women who took examinations in midwifery at a time when there was no requirement that midwives should be trained. However, there was growing pressure in the 1890s to raise the status of midwifery, which culminated in the Midwives Act of 1902. Thereafter no woman could use the title of midwife unless she was registered. Hence there was now a new emphasis on the need for training. Alice Gregory, along with Lelia Parnell and Maud Cashmore, began to develop a training scheme for midwives which would involve a year's training in general nursing and then six months' specialized midwifery training. The Midwives' Institute, which represented the interests of qualified midwives, thought that the plan was unrealistic and that training should increase by degrees. Undaunted, Alice Gregory acted on her own initiative. With the help of Charles Escreet, a clergyman who was chairman of the local board of guardians and the Charity Organization Society, she established a Home for Mothers and Babies in Woolwich in order to train educated women to work among the poor. The hospital was opened in May 1905 with six beds which quickly increased to twelve. Lelia Parnell was matron, Maud Cashmore head midwife, and Alice Gregory secretary and district nurse supervisor. Alice also founded the Council for Promoting the Higher Training of Midwives.

In 1915 the mothers' and babies' home was amalgamated with the lying-in hospital for married women in Long Acre and the name was changed to the British Hospital for Mothers and Babies. Further expansion was made possible when Alice Gregory was successful in gaining funding from the Ministry of Health to build a new hospital which was opened by Queen Mary on 22 May 1922. Lelia Parnell again acted as matron until her death in 1931 when Maud Cashmore took her place. By the 1930s the hospital had become so large that it passed out of the hands of the original founders into those of a hospital committee.

Alice Gregory made a significant contribution to the development of the training of midwives at a time of transition in the profession and this was recognized when she was made CBE in 1929. Many of her pupils found her to be an inspiring and supportive teacher, but she was also a controversial figure in the profession. She was a member of the council of the Midwives' Institute and was often at odds with the officers, in particular over her forthright criticisms of untrained 'handywomen' and her assertion during the First World War that the majority of midwives were uninterested in antenatal care. None the less, in 1911 she was asked to represent the institute on the advisory committee for the National Insurance Bill.

Alice Gregory continued to work in the Woolwich hospital throughout the Second World War, when there was extensive damage to the building from air raids, and was instrumental in ensuring that a new wing was opened by the princess royal in 1944. In January of the next year she reported a troublesome cough and then hurt her back in a fall. In March she was diagnosed as having an enlarged heart and a congested lung which led to her resignation from the hospital in June. She retired with Maud Cashmore to The Sanctuary, a cottage on the south Downs, overlooking Alfriston, Sussex, which had been built for her by her father so that she could take short breaks in the countryside. It was here that she died on 8 November 1946 as a result of a cerebral haemorrhage.

JUNE HANNAM

Sources R. Morland, *Alice and the stork* (1951) · 'Famous nurses: Alice Gregory', *Nursing Mirror* (26 April 1979), 37 · Midwives' Institute, annual general meetings reports, Royal College of Midwives, London · L. V. Marks, *Metropolitan maternity: maternal and infant welfare services in early twentieth century London* (1996) · b. cert. · d. cert. · 'Gregory, Robert (1819–1911)', *DNB*
Likenesses photograph, repro. in J. Towler and J. Braman, *Midwives in history and society* (1986) · photograph, repro. in N. Leap and B. Hunter, *The midwife's tale: an oral history from handy woman to professional midwife* (1983) · photographs, repro. in Morland, *Alice and the stork*
Wealth at death £10,630 7s. 2d.: probate, 11 March 1947, *CGPLA Eng. & Wales*

Gregory, Arthur John Peter Michael Maundy (1877–1941), honours broker, was born on 1 July 1877 at 9 Portland Terrace, Southampton, second of three sons of Francis Maundy Gregory (1849–1899), clergyman, and his wife, Elizabeth Ursula Wynell, *née* Mayow (1847–1936), cousin of third Baron Lyveden. After attending Banister Court School for the sons of merchant marine officers, where he was nicknamed Bum Cheeks, he passed the Oxford University entrance examination and went into residence there as a non-collegiate student in 1895. Intended for holy orders, he left Oxford shortly before his finals and began appearing professionally as a drawing-room entertainer. During 1900 he acted in the theatrical company of Ben Greet; his first sizeable role was as a comic butler in a tour of *The Brixton Burglary* (1902). He became manager of Frank Benson's company (1903) but was dismissed for fraud (1906). In 1908 he made his earliest known attempt at blackmail. Harold Davidson, afterwards notorious as the vicar of Stiffkey, who had been his boyhood friend, induced Lord Howard de Walden and other rich men to finance Maundy-Gregory (as he then called himself) in the Combine Attractions Syndicate which crashed in 1909. Gregory next edited a gossip sheet, *Mayfair* (1910–14). As a sideline he ran a detective agency specializing in credit rating based on information supplied by hoteliers and restaurateurs. Gregory claimed that after *Mayfair* folded he was engaged in espionage. Conscripted in July 1917, he became a private in the Irish Guards.

In 1918 Lord Murray of Elibank introduced Gregory to his successor as Liberal chief whip, Frederick Guest, as a potential intermediary between rich men who wanted honours and the Lloyd George coalition which needed money. Guest and his successor, Charles McCurdy, together with Lloyd George's press agent Sir William Sutherland, used Gregory as a tout to build up the Lloyd George political fund by the sale of honours. Between £1 million and £2 million were raised by this device in 1919–22 (with Gregory receiving commission of perhaps £30,000 a year). Knighthoods cost about £10,000 and baronetcies £40,000. Gregory occupied resplendent headquarters in Parliament Street replete with dispatch boxes and autographed photographs of royalty. As an accessory to this business Gregory in August 1919 founded the *Westminster Gazette and St James's Review*, which masqueraded as a government publication and was circulated gratis on a mailing list of 1000; Gregory duped foreign embassies into paying for special supplements in the belief that they would be influential and also wrote puffing profiles of prominent men for a fee. His editorial policy was reactionary and antisemitic. He financed White Russian intrigues through his Anglo-Ukrainian Council and believed that his life was threatened by Comintern agents. However the outcry at the flagitiously corrupt birthday honours of 1922 precipitated the fall of the Lloyd George coalition. The Honours (Prevention of Abuses) Act (1925) checked but did not stop Gregory's fouling of the fount of honour. J. C. C. Davidson, on becoming chairman of the Unionist Party in 1927, determined to break Gregory by excluding from all honours lists anyone known to have been a client of Gregory's. This slowly wrecked Gregory's credibility as an honours broker.

In 1927 Gregory acquired the Ambassador Club at 26 Conduit Street in London's Mayfair, where, with ingratiating flamboyance, he entertained prospective clients, collected gossip, and planted stories. He displayed a gold cigarette case given him by the duke of York, afterwards George VI, at whose wedding he was a steward. In 1929 Gregory bought *Burke's Landed Gentry*. In 1931 he leased Deepdene Hotel near Dorking, which became a favourite assignation for rich Londoners desiring a dirty weekend. As his traffic in British honours petered out, he diversified into the less profitable market of foreign decorations, and after being received into the Roman Catholic church in 1932 did brisk business in papal honours.

Gregory was confronted by the necessity in 1932–3 to repay to the executors of Sir George Watson £30,000 advanced for a barony never received. For a decade he had lived platonically with a tipsy retired musical actress, Mrs Edith Marion Rosse. She died mysteriously (14 September 1932) bequeathing £18,000 to Gregory, who ensured her burial in an unsealed coffin only a few inches below the surface of a water-sodden cemetery on the banks of the Thames. Still desperate for funds Gregory rashly sought £10,000 from Commander E. W. Billyard-Leake in return for procuring a knighthood. Following Billyard-Leake's complaint to the authorities, Gregory was arrested (4 February 1933). He initially pleaded not guilty, and political party organizers feared that he would air his activities together with the names of those implicated (half of the proceeds of Lloyd George's political fund had reached the Conservative Party). J. C. C. Davidson's organization accordingly approached him, warned that he could not avoid conviction, but undertook that if he kept silent the authorities would be lenient. After a discreet trial he changed his plea on 21 February and received the lightest possible sentence of two months and a fine of £50. On his release from Wormwood Scrubs (12 April) he was met at the prison gates by a friend of Davidson who took him to France, gave him a down payment, and promised him an annual pension of £2000. Rosse's corpse was exhumed (28 April 1933), but it was impossible to ascertain the cause of her death. Gregory did not return from France for her inquest, but was suspected of murder by some policemen.

Gregory was short, paunchy, bald, rubicund, monocled, and epicene. He wore ostentatious jewellery, including a green scarab ring he claimed had been Wilde's, and used to fidget with a rose-coloured diamond carried in his waistcoat pocket which supposedly had belonged to Catherine the Great. His manner was grandiose, mysterious, watchful, and confidential. Lord Birkenhead, whom he exploited in the late 1920s, interested him in rare books. His passion for collecting bronze, porcelain, and terracotta statues of the beautiful boy Narcissus indicates his sexual preferences. Arrested by the Germans in November 1940, Gregory was confined in their camp at Drancy, where his health deteriorated without the whisky upon which he depended. He died of cardiac failure, aggravated by a swollen liver, on 3 October (possibly 28 September) 1941, at Val de Grâce Hospital, Paris. He was buried in Ivry-Paris new cemetery, but five years later his bones were removed to an ossuary. RICHARD DAVENPORT-HINES

Sources T. Cullen, *Maundy Gregory, purveyor of honours* (1974) · G. Macmillan, *Honours for sale: the strange story of Maundy Gregory* (1955) · A. J. A. Symons, *The quest for Corvo* (1935) · *Memoirs of a Conservative: J. C. C. Davidson's memoirs and papers, 1910–37*, ed. R. R. James (1969) · G. R. Searle, *Corruption in British politics, 1895–1930* (1987) · R. Aldington, *Frauds* (1957) · C. Coote, 'Scandals of the century', *Daily Telegraph Magazine Supplement* (27 Feb 1970) · *National Review*, 79 (1922), 817–24, 940–48 · D. Marquand, *Ramsay MacDonald* (1977) · Lord Vansittart [R. G. Vansittart], *The mist procession: the autobiography of Lord Vansittart* (1958)
Archives HLRO, Bonar Law, Davidson, and Lloyd George MSS
Likenesses photographs, c.1920–c.1930, repro. in Cullen, *Maundy Gregory* (1974)
Wealth at death supposedly vast: Cullen, *Maundy Gregory*, 246 · however, he lived his last years as a remittance man and probably died in reduced circumstances

Gregory [*née* Persse], **(Isabella) Augusta**, **Lady Gregory** (1852–1932), playwright, folklorist, and literary patron, was born on 15 March 1852, at Roxborough House, near Loughrea, co. Galway, Ireland, the twelfth of sixteen children of Dudley Persse (1802–1878), and his second wife, Frances, *née* Barry (c.1816–1896). The Persses came to Ireland as English settlers around 1602, founding Roxborough in the late seventeenth century. The estate, eventually more than 6000 acres, was the main seat for an extended family of considerable influence in co. Galway, but neither Dudley Persse, known as a harsh landlord, nor Frances Persse, a proselytizing evangelical protestant, was liked by their tenantry, and Lady Gregory would later characterize Roxborough to Yeats as almost feudal in its exercise of ascendancy rule. As the youngest and plainest daughter in a resolutely male-centred household, Augusta Persse was little encouraged, receiving only sporadic home-schooling, and her memoirs tellingly refer to her family rarely and without warmth. Though displaying an independence and desire for learning from an early age in reaction to the limitations of her background, she none the less internalized much of the Roxborough insistence on female self-abnegation, and devoted her early adult life to local philanthropy and caring for a sick brother.

Marriage, Coole Park, and early writing On 4 March 1880, at the age of twenty-eight, when it had seemed she would remain a spinster, Augusta Persse married Sir William Henry *Gregory (1816–1892) of neighbouring Coole Park. Gregory, thirty-five years her senior, had recently retired as governor of Ceylon, and enjoyed a high reputation in Irish and English political and social circles for his personality and cultivation, counting figures such as Robert Browning, Tennyson, and Henry James among his friends. Despondent since the death of his first wife in 1873, Gregory seems to have remarried primarily in search of an intelligent companion for his old age, but he soon recognized and encouraged the potential Augusta Persse displayed. The marriage transformed her life, introducing her to prominent literary and political society in London where they lived part of each year, to progressive social and religious views, and to extensive foreign travel, and she flourished in her new milieu, quickly earning a reputation as a hostess, conversationalist, and thinker. Yet if the twelve years of her marriage were, as she acknowledged, a 'liberal education' (draft memoirs, Berg MSS), they were also confiningly conventional in

(Isabella) Augusta Gregory, Lady Gregory (1852–1932), by Sir William Orpen

many respects, and she was expected to follow Gregory's interests dutifully and to endure repeated separations from their one child, Robert, born in 1881, to satisfy her husband's penchant for travel. Though she would wear mourning black for the forty years of her widowhood, her diaries and autobiographical writings suggest some disappointment at the marriage's limitations, a disappointment registered also in her brief clandestine affair with poet and anti-imperialist Wilfrid Scawen Blunt (1840–1922) in 1882–3. Her shared enthusiasm with Blunt for the Egyptian nationalist leader Arabi Pasha inspired her first significant publication, 'Arabi and his household', an essay printed in *The Times* in 1882 and subsequently as a pamphlet. The Irish land war of the early 1880s compounded this first political awakening, and in 'An emigrant's notebook', a series of unpublished autobiographical sketches written in 1883, she began to reflect sustainedly on Irish culture, ascendancy rule, and her own identity. The challenge to landlord power posed by the 1886 Home Rule Bill and the rise of Parnell further heightened her self-consciousness of her uneasy position as a landlord. Short stories written around 1890 show her negotiating the tensions between her staunchly protestant, ascendancy views and her love of the Irish country people. Drawing closely on her personal experiences, they use the distinctive Clare–Galway idiom of her tenants for literary purposes well before her development of 'Kiltartan' speech under the influence of Hyde and Synge a decade later. The promise of such early writings, though, was not fully realized during the marriage, during which wifely and maternal duties took priority. Paradoxically, while marriage was the essential step into a world of intellect and social standing without which her subsequent achievement would not have been possible, it was only Sir William's death in 1892 and the demands of widowhood that brought her to the independence necessary for a distinctive creative voice.

Left £800 a year in estate income, but anticipating land reform and with Coole already encumbered, Lady Gregory retrenched by selling their London house and living in Ireland. There, her desire to write and her need to reassess her personal situation began to coincide more productively. *A Phantom's Pilgrimage*, an attack on Gladstone's 1893 Home Rule Bill, displays and explores a significant tension between her self-interest as a Unionist and her recognition of the needs of Catholics, nationalists, and the Irish peasant class. Its underlying debate as to where her cultural loyalties should lie continued and developed as she edited her husband's autobiography (published 1894), and then *Mr Gregory's Letter-Box* (published 1898), the political papers of his grandfather, under-secretary of Ireland, 1813–31, both of which projects involved sustained reflection on the course of nineteenth-century Irish politics. When a 'tendency to Home Rule' was noted in her commentaries in the latter volume, she declared that it was impossible to study Irish history 'without getting a dislike and distrust of England' (Gregory, *Our Irish Theatre*, 41). She was also becoming progressively more aware of the growing literary movement in Ireland, having read and admired Yeats's *The Celtic Twilight* prior to first meeting him briefly in 1894, and having begun, under its influence, to investigate folklore herself.

Yeats, Irish nationalism, and folklore When Yeats came to stay as a guest of her neighbour Edward Martyn in August 1896, Lady Gregory was thus well advanced on the road to Irish nationalism, and, as she later wrote, her 'energy was [already] turning to' literature (*Seventy Years*, 390). Seeking Yeats out, she immediately asked if he could set her to some work in the literary movement. The friendship was cemented when they next met in spring 1897 in London, where she hosted him at a series of dinners, introduced him to influential friends, and gave him the folklore she had gathered that winter. Yeats, at a low point financially and emotionally, and, as his father had observed in 1896, never able to 'work alone' or without the 'sympathy' of a friend (Murphy, 192), was disarmed by and receptive to her energetic and determined wish to manage and nurture him. She in turn was ready to lionize and support the young poet, acknowledging later that 'the achievement of a writer' was the one for which she had long had 'most admiration' (draft memoir, Berg MSS). But she was also shrewdly conscious of the specific benefits such a friendship might confer, both in furthering her connection with the world of nationalism, and in providing an outlet for her creative energies. She was, moreover, herself disposed towards working in partnership rather than alone. Throughout her life she would remain caught in a tension between the need to assert herself creatively and the ingrained imperatives of womanly self-sacrifice Roxborough had encouraged, a tension heightened by the widespread antipathy to female enterprise in the Ireland of her time. Prior to meeting Yeats, she had defined her few creative initiatives in terms of service to her family, to her husband, and briefly to Wilfrid Blunt, roles which certainly protected her from seeing herself or being seen as transgressively ambitious, but which also severely limited her opportunities for individual achievement. Working with, for, and through Yeats, however, provided her with a role in which self-fulfilment and duty were also not in apparent conflict, but which offered her real creative scope. For the remainder of her literary career she would define her efforts in terms of service to Yeats, to Ireland, to the Abbey Theatre, or to the country people of Galway, thereby downplaying, at least publicly, the force of her underlying determination.

In July 1897 Yeats came to Coole for the first of twenty consecutive long summer stays, and Lady Gregory at once helped to make his long-harboured ideas of founding an Irish dramatic movement a reality by offering the first monetary guarantee for the Irish Literary Theatre and persuading friends to underwrite most of the remainder needed. Short seasons of plays were produced in Dublin in 1899, 1900, and 1901, paving the way for the founding of the Abbey Theatre in 1904, of which Lady Gregory became patentee and co-director. They also began to gather folklore together, resulting in a series of long articles and a revised and extended edition of *The Celtic Twilight* (1902), in which her hand and influence are manifest. Her independent work developed in tandem with her efforts for Yeats, and between 1897 and 1901 she published some three dozen short articles, essays, and letters, mainly on folklore. She also quickly demonstrated her considerable abilities as an organizer promoting literary and nationalist causes, and as a hostess, making Coole both a retreat for Yeats and recognized as a creative centre for most of the prominent Irish literary figures of the time, including George Moore, J. M. Synge, Douglas Hyde, and, later, George Bernard Shaw and Sean O'Casey, most of whom engaged in significant creative, and often collaborative, work while there. From around late 1897 she began to support Yeats with cash and gifts of furniture, clothing, and food, thereby allowing him to do less journalism for money and focus instead on his creative work. Her patronage was substantial for several years, and Yeats eventually repaid her £500 in 1914. By 1898 the friendship had become crucial to both writers emotionally as well as artistically and practically, and although an element of formality always lingered between them—signalling their shared sense that creative responsibilities must always take priority—for the next two decades they were each other's closest counsel, with Yeats memorably articulating the complex bonds between them in 1909 when he wrote 'She has been to me mother, friend, sister and brother. I cannot realize the world without her' (Yeats, *Memoirs*, 160–61).

From around 1901 on Lady Gregory began to pursue her own creative opportunities even more energetically. Her redaction of the *Táin bó Cúailnge*, published in 'Kiltartan' English as *Cuchulain of Muirthemne* (1902), was fulsomely praised by Yeats as the best Irish book of his time, and became a vital source of legendary and imaginative material for him, as did her *Gods and Fighting Men* (1904), a retelling of the Fianna legends. In seeking popular readership for these books, she suppressed or modified violent and sexual elements in the source tales, while also emphasizing their heroic and ideal elements as part of her avowed aim to bring 'dignity' to Ireland. These translations became her best-selling prose works, though their 'Kiltartan' idiom is now usually regarded as stylistically limited.

The Abbey and writing for the theatre More surprising was Lady Gregory's sudden emergence, at the age of fifty, as a dramatist. Having assisted Yeats secretarially on his plays, she gradually assumed ever greater direct responsibility in his work, co-authoring *Cathleen ni Houlihan* with him in 1901, and *Where there is Nothing* in 1902, and then contributing substantially to all his other non-verse plays of that decade. Yeats had initially sought her help merely to supply peasant dialogue and realist folk details to offset his own tendency to symbolism, but their creative exchanges quickly developed into a more complex stylistic, ideological, and imaginative interdependence. Claiming that more plays, and particularly comedies, 'were needed' for the theatre movement (Gregory, *Our Irish Theatre*, 53), she wrote some three dozen works of her own between 1902 and 1927, displaying particular skill with tightly constructed one-act dramas. Comedies such as *Spreading the News* (published 1905), *Hyacinth Halvey* (1906), and *The Jackdaw* (1909) became staples at the Abbey as short companion pieces for works of peasant realism or tragedy, but her most powerful one-act plays are typically those in which a political component animates the action, such as *The Rising of the Moon* (1904), *The Workhouse Ward* (1909), and *The Gaol Gate* (1909). As in her folklore volumes *Poets and Dreamers* (1903) and *The Kiltartan History Book* (1909, expanded 1926), her focus in these 'political' plays is on the beliefs and rituals which sustain community and which allow individuals to assert themselves in the face of oppression or poverty. In longer plays she explored Irish history more directly, but here too her creativity seems to have been most animated in dealing with legendary figures who displayed some exemplary form of strength of character—notably, female figures, in *Dervorgilla* (1908) and *Grania* (1912)—than in treating conventionally pivotal moments in Irish history such as in *Kincora* (1905). Her later work is progressively more invested in myth-making functions, with plays like *The Image* (1910) which centred on the transformative power of a hidden 'heart secret'.

Styled 'the greatest living Irishwoman' and 'the charwoman of the Abbey' by Bernard Shaw (Laurence and Grene, xxv, 66), Lady Gregory became the most tenacious champion of the theatre she had helped Yeats found, campaigning for funds, touring with and promoting the Abbey company in England and America, and encouraging younger writers (though also earning the resentment of others who felt their merits had been ignored). Sean O'Casey credited her encouragement and advice as crucial to his emergence as a writer in the 1920s, though their close friendship was permanently damaged by the Abbey's rejection of *The Silver Tassie* in 1928. Her 1913 history, *Our Irish Theatre*, a somewhat self-serving and partisan account of the inception and development of the

Abbey, powerfully conveys her tactical shrewdness, determination, and excitement in defending the theatre during crises such as the controversies over Synge's *Playboy of the Western World* (1907) and Shaw's *Shewing-up of Blanco Posnet* (1910). She openly acknowledged that Yeats's interests always came first for her at the Abbey, thereby generating resentment in Synge and others, but she was also often charged with using her directorial position to promote her own work. In the theatre's first two decades, her plays were indeed the most frequently performed of any author's, but they were also, particularly in the early years, the most consistently successful at the box office.

Losses and later life At her peak of influence just prior to the start of the First World War, Lady Gregory thereafter suffered a succession of sapping blows. The death of her nephew Sir Hugh Lane on the *Lusitania* in 1915 began the long legal controversy over paintings he left to Ireland in an unsigned codicil to his will, and she spent much of her energy for the remainder of her life fighting an ultimately unsuccessful battle to win Ireland's claim. Robert's enlistment in 1915 left her constantly anxious, and his death in 1918 as an airman on the Italian front was a loss from which she never recovered. Her later 'wonder' plays such as *The Golden Apple* (1916) and *The Dragon* (1920) take on fantastic and otherworldly mythic structures as their subject matter, as if following her own observation that peasant lore typically became richer in proportion to the poverty or difficulty from which it emerged. A mystical and religious element becomes more pronounced in plays such as *The Story Brought by Brigit* (1924) and *Dave* (1928). Yeats's marriage in 1917 also inevitably reduced her long-held position of primacy in his life. His time spent at Coole diminished, although their friendship was left unshaken, and *Visions and Beliefs in the West of Ireland*, the folklore project they had begun together in the 1890s, appeared in 1920. She worked sporadically on an autobiography from late 1914 until the early 1920s, but withheld it from publication as unsatisfactory, and its narrative symptomatically closes with distraught chapters on the war, the 1916 rising, and Robert's death. Her final draft, *Seventy Years*, was eventually published in 1974.

During the Anglo-Irish War and the civil war which followed the Anglo-Irish treaty (1922) Lady Gregory was a horrified but perceptive spectator at Coole, recording events in her substantial *Journals* (published 1978 and 1987). Her expanded *Kiltartan History Book* (1926), a significant pioneering work in the field now termed contemporary folklore, embodies country people's responses to the recent conflicts, and reflects her own increasingly controlled response to the cultural shifts taking place and to her own losses. Although increasingly republican in her sympathies, she was aware that her position was marginal within the new Irish state for which she had worked so long, and when nominated for a senate seat in 1925 she declined to campaign and fell well short of election. Unlike so many ascendancy houses, Coole survived the troubles, but land reform had by the 1920s reduced the estate's viability, and her right to life tenure there under

the terms of her husband's will had in any case become ambiguous after Robert's widow assumed ownership in 1918. Following several smaller sales, the remainder of the estate was sold to the Irish ministry of lands, and maintained by the forestry department, with Lady Gregory remaining as a tenant in the house (which was demolished in 1942). Determined not to risk a fall-off in the quality of her work, she published her *Last Plays* in 1928, reserving her final energies for *Coole* (1931), an elegy for the Gregory family, Coole Park, and her own part in its final flowering. Recognizing her decline, Yeats, who spent much of her last year with her at Coole, responded by contributing 'Coole Park' (later 'Coole Park, 1929') as the opening poem for the volume, and then writing 'Coole and Ballylee, 1931', his most elaborate celebrations of their long partnership, her formidable character, and powerful influence. Operations for breast cancer in 1923, 1926, and 1929 were only temporarily successful, but she declined further surgery, enduring increasing pain and disability over her last two years of life, and refusing to the end to take any pain-killing drugs that might affect her mind. Lady Gregory died at Coole on 22 May 1932, and was buried at Bohermore cemetery in Galway city.

JAMES L. PETHICA

Sources letters, diaries, draft memoirs, and other materials, NYPL, Humanities and Social Sciences Library, Berg collection · unpublished letters, diaries, draft memoirs, and other materials, Emory University, special collections · unpublished letters, diaries, draft memoirs, and other materials, NL Ire., Gregory MSS · unpublished letters, diaries, draft memoirs, and other materials, priv. coll. · *Lady Gregory, seventy years, 1852–1922: being the autobiography of Lady Gregory*, ed. C. Smythe (1974) · *Lady Gregory's journals*, ed. D. Murphy, 2 vols. (1978–87) · *Lady Gregory's diaries, 1892–1902*, ed. J. Pethica (1996) · Lady Gregory [I. A. Gregory], *Coole* (1971) · Lady Gregory [I. A. Gregory], *Our Irish theatre* (1972) · *Lady Gregory: fifty years after*, ed. A. Saddlemyer and C. Smythe (1987) · E. Coxhead, *Lady Gregory: a literary portrait* (1967) · Burke, *Gen. Ire.* (1976) · Lady Gregory [I. A. Gregory], *Sir Hugh Lane: his life and legacy* (1974) · W. B. Yeats, *Memoirs*, ed. D. Donoghue (1972) · W. B. Yeats, *Autobiographies* (1955) · D. H. Laurence and N. Grene, eds., *Shaw, Lady Gregory and the Abbey* (1993) · W. M. Murphy, *Prodigal father: the life of John Butler Yeats* (1978) · *CGPLA Éire* (1932) · personal knowledge (2004)

Archives Emory University, Atlanta, Georgia, papers · Ransom HRC, papers | BL, corresp. with the Society of Authors, Add. MS 56717 · BL, corresp. with George Bernard Shaw, Add. MS 50534 · FM Cam., letters incl. MS poems to Wilfrid Scawen Blunt · NYPL, Berg collection, corresp. and literary MSS · NYPL, Quinn collection, papers · Sligo County Library, Sligo, corresp. with Sara Allgood · Southern Illinois University, corresp. with Lennox Robinson · TCD, corresp. with Thomas Bodkin · TCD, corresp. with Mary Childers · TCD, corresp. with J. M. Synge · U. Glas., special collections department, letters to D. S. MacColl

Likenesses J. B. Yeats, oils, 1903, NG Ire. · W. Orpen, group portrait, pen-and-ink caricature, 1907, NPG · A. Mancini, 1908, Hugh Lane Gallery of Modern Art, Dublin · J. Epstein, bronze bust, 1910, Hugh Lane Gallery of Modern Art, Dublin · F. Lion, lithograph, 1913, NPG · G. Kelly, oils, c.1914, Abbey Theatre, Dublin · W. Orpen, oils, NG Ire. [*see illus.*] · G. Russell, drawing, Abbey Theatre, Dublin · T. Spicer-Simson, bronze medallion (after his plasticine medallion), NG Ire. · T. Spicer-Simson, plasticine medallion, NG Ire. · J. B. Yeats, drawing, Abbey Theatre, Dublin · J. B. Yeats, pencil sketch, repro. in *Samhain* (Dec 1904); copy, NYPL · photograph, repro. in *Seventy years*, ed. Smythe, cover; priv. coll. · photograph, repro. in

Murphy, ed., *Lady Gregory's journals*, 2, cover; priv. coll. • photographs, priv. coll.

Wealth at death £4809 3*s.* effects in England: probate, 21 Nov 1932, *CGPLA Eng. & Wales* • £746 19*s.* 3*d.*: probate, 16 Sept 1932, *CGPLA Ire.*

Gregory, Sir Augustus Charles (1819–1905), explorer and surveyor in Australia, born on 1 August 1819 at Farnsfield, Nottinghamshire, was the second of the five sons of Joshua Gregory (1790/1792–1838), an army officer from an old Nottinghamshire family, and his wife, Frances (1794–1859), the sister of Charles Blissett Churchman of London. His father retired after having been wounded in action, and received in lieu of pension a grant of land in the Swan river settlement in Western Australia; he arrived there with his wife and family on 6 October 1829.

After being privately educated in England and Australia, Gregory worked from 1841 to 1854 in the survey department of Western Australia. He proved a skilful surveyor and organizer, and an alert observer of the bush. In 1846, having obtained leave of absence, he began exploring the interior of the continent, starting on 7 August from Bolgart Spring, 60 miles north-east of Perth, accompanied by his brothers Francis [*see below*] and Henry Churchman. Their progress eastwards was soon stopped by an immense salt lake. This compelled them to turn northwest, where, after travelling 950 miles in forty-seven days, they discovered some good grazing land and a coal seam at the headwaters of the River Irwin east of Geraldton. In September 1848 Gregory led a party northward. He revealed the pastoral wealth of the Murchison and Champion Bay (Geraldton) districts and discovered a lode of galena in the bed of the Murchison River, 350 miles north of Perth; the journey of 1500 miles had taken ten weeks.

After seven years of routine surveying, in 1855–6 Gregory undertook an expedition under the auspices of the imperial government, via the Royal Geographical Society, to explore the unknown interior of the northern territory and search for traces of the lost explorer Ludwig Leichhardt. The party, which included the distinguished botanist Ferdinand von Müller and the artist Thomas Baines, ascended the Victoria River in the Northern Territory from its mouth to its source, found that the south-flowing Sturt Creek ended in desert, and then made its way to the Gulf of Carpentaria and thence across the northern peninsula and down the east coast to Rockhampton. The expedition shed much light on the drainage of the region, discovered the watershed formed by the Newcastle and Gregory ranges at the northern end of the Great Dividing Range, and charted 5000 miles of hitherto unknown territory. No certain traces of Leichhardt were found and the natural resources discovered were disappointing, but for this expedition Gregory was in 1857 awarded the founder's medal of the Royal Geographical Society. His report of 1857 stimulated considerable pastoral settlement but did not establish him as a heroic explorer, as he understated his role as an inventive and thorough organizer.

In 1858 Gregory was sent by the New South Wales government to renew the search for Leichhardt. He started from Sydney on 12 January and reached the Barcoo River

in April. At latitude 24° 25′ S and longitude 145° E, he found a tree marked L and some stumps of others which had been felled with an axe. In May he reached the Thomson River, and followed it upstream until it ran out. He then pushed down Cooper Creek, which he found to be the lower reaches of the Barcoo River and then on south to Adelaide. He had solved the problem of the north-east inland river system and found that south-west Queensland had pastoral possibilities, but the fate of Leichhardt was as much in doubt as ever.

Gregory was then employed in defining the southern boundary of Queensland. From 1859 to 1863 he was the colony's first commissioner of crown lands, and from 1859 to 1875 he was its surveyor-general. Charged with allocating the new colony's lands, its greatest resource, he favoured large-scale squatters over smallholders, and in 1867 he handed over much of the Darling downs to pastoralists. In 1875 he was appointed Queensland's geological surveyor. In 1882 he was nominated to the legislative council, where he was prominent in debate, his intimate knowledge of the country and its resources and his fund of scientific information securing him a hearing even from those whose opinions differed from his. He always sat with the opposition in order to be free to criticize government measures, and generally allied himself with reactionary squatter interest.

Gregory was one of the first members of the Toowong shire council, and in 1902 became its first mayor. He was a trustee of the Queensland Museum from 1876 to 1899, and from 1876 to 1883 sat on the commission to inquire into the condition of the Aborigines. In 1895 he was president at Brisbane of the Australian Association for the Advancement of Science, and devoted his opening address to a sketch of the geological and geographical history of Australia. He was created CMG in 1874 and KCMG on 9 November 1903. He was an active freemason for fifty years and was a devoted member of the Church of England. He died unmarried, of pneumonia, on 25 June 1905 at his home, Rainsworth, Rosalie, Brisbane, and was buried after a masonic funeral in Toowong cemetery.

Gregory was one of Australia's foremost explorers, but in person and in his writings lacked the panache of the pioneer, and his reputation suffered as a result. In 1884 the Queensland government published *Collected Journals of Australian Exploration*, his collected papers and those of his brother **Francis Thomas Gregory** (1821–1888). The latter was employed in the survey office of Western Australia from 1841 to 1860 and took up land in the Avon district. He accompanied Augustus in his first expedition in 1846, and led two expeditions himself in 1858 and 1861, when he traced a number of rivers from the Shark Bay and Nickol Bay areas, some 400 and 800 miles north of Perth respectively. On the latter journey he discovered the Hamersley ranges, and was awarded the gold medal of the Royal Geographical Society in 1863. After going to Queensland in 1862, he was appointed commissioner of crown lands, and on 11 May 1865 he married Marion (*b.* 1841), the daughter of Alexander Hume. He was nominated to the legislative council in 1874, and was briefly postmaster-general in the first McIlwraith ministry in 1883. He died on 23 October 1888. ELIZABETH BAIGENT

Sources D. B. Waterson, 'Gregory, Sir Augustus Charles', *AusDB*, vol. 4 • *Brisbane Courier* (26 June 1905) • A. C. Gregory and F. T. Gregory, *Collected journals of Australian exploration* (1884) • E. Favenc, *History of Australian exploration*, 1 (1888) • E. Favenc, *Explorers of Australia* (1908) • R. Erickson, ed., *Dictionary of Western Australians, 1829–1914*, 5 vols. (1979–86), vol. 2 • C. R. Markham, *The fifty years' work of the Royal Geographical Society* (1881) • H. R. Mill, *The record of the Royal Geographical Society, 1830–1930* (1930)

Likenesses U. Canburn, portrait, 1891, Masonic museum, Brisbane, Australia

Gregory, Barnard (1796–1852), newspaper proprietor, was the son of a grocer. He was a schoolmaster, an itinerant preacher, and a druggist before he turned to journalism. He came to public notice as editor and proprietor of a London weekly paper, first issued on 10 April 1831, called *The Satirist, or, The Censor of the Times*. It was printed by James Thompson at 119 Fleet Street, published at 11 Crane Court, London, cost 7*d*., and had a circulation of 10,000. The motto on the first page was: 'Satire's my weapon. I was born a critic and a satirist; and my nurse remarked that I hissed as soon as I saw light'. The paper was ferociously anti-tory, a scandal sheet with a strong element of blackmail. The libels were often sent in manuscript to the persons concerned, threatening publication unless a price were paid for suppression. The weak yielded and were plundered, the strong resisted and were libelled, when, owing to the uncertain state of the law and the expenses attending a trial, it was not easy to obtain any redress.

During a period of eighteen years Gregory was almost continually engaged in litigation, and several times was convicted and imprisoned. In September 1832 John Deas, an attorney, recovered £300 damages and costs from Gregory for a libel. On 11 February 1833 the proprietor was convicted of accusing a gentleman called Digby, of Brighton, of cheating at cards (Barnewall and Adolphus 4.821–6). In November 1838 an action was brought for a libel printed on 15 July 1838, which attacked the characters of the marquess of Blandford and his son the earl of Sunderland (*The Times*, 23 Nov 1838, 6), in which Lord Denman described Gregory as 'a trafficker in character'. In the same year Gregory libelled J. Last, the printer of *Town*. Here, however, he made a mistake in his policy, for Renton Nicholson, the editor of that paper, replied in a series of articles that thoroughly exposed Gregory's character and his proceedings (*Town*, 28 July 1838, 484ff.). On 14 February 1839 Gregory was convicted in the court of queen's bench for a libel on the wife of James Weir Hogg, MP for Beverley, and imprisoned for three months. Charles, duke of Brunswick-Lüneburg, who after his flight from his dukedom in September 1830 lived for many years in England, was a frequent target of the *Satirist*. On 14 November 1841 it libelled the duke and his attorney, Mr Vallance; proceedings were taken, and on 2 December 1843 Gregory was sentenced to six months' imprisonment in Newgate. He appealed, and, with considerable legal agility, kept the case in the courts until 13 June 1850, when the judgement was affirmed. On 25 February 1843 he was again found guilty in a case in the court of exchequer, *McGregor* v. *Gregory*, for a libel published 11 October 1842, in which the plaintiff was called, among other things, a black sheep and the associate of blacklegs. In the same year Gregory was imprisoned for six months for another series of libels on the duke of Brunswick, in which he charged him with being the assassin of Eliza Grimwood, a prostitute murdered in her room in Wellington Terrace, Lambeth, on 26 May 1838. The duke brought a third action against Crowle, the printer of the *Satirist*, in 1848, and was awarded damages, which, however, he never succeeded in obtaining.

Gregory was a good actor and held his own on the professional stage. However, when he was playing Hamlet at Covent Garden on 13 February 1843, the duke of Brunswick led a mob which broke up the performance. Gregory brought an action for conspiracy against Brunswick, whose defence was that Gregory's libels against him and others made the journalist a person unfit to be allowed to appear on the stage. The jury on 21 June 1843 found for Brunswick. In August 1846, at the Haymarket, his Hamlet again led to co-ordinated rioting. Gregory's Richard III in September 1846 was his last appearance on the stage. He wrote four unpublished plays, two of which were successfully performed. A changing public mood and Brunswick's persistence led to the final issue of the *Satirist*, no. 924, on 15 December 1849; it had lasted longer than might have been expected.

In March 1847 Gregory married Margaret, *née* Thompson, niece of John Thompson of Frognal Priory, Hampstead. Thompson died just before the marriage, and Gregory inherited his money; Gregory's compulsion to denounce may have been correspondingly diminished. After three years of illness from a lung disease, Gregory died at The Priory, 22 Aberdeen Place, St John's Wood, London, on 24 November 1852. His will, dated 17 November 1852, was proved on 22 April 1853. In it he mentions a daughter by a first wife who had greatly offended him, and he refers in bitter terms to his 'enemy', the duke of Brunswick. G. C. BOASE, *rev.* H. C. G. MATTHEW

Sources *The Era* (19 Feb 1843) • D. Cook, 'An amateur actor', *The Theatre*, new ser., 1 (1878–9), 117–21 • I. McCalman, *Radical underworld: prophets, revolutionaries, and pornographers in London, 1795–1840* (1988); pbk edn (1993) • R. V. Barnewall and J. L. Adolphus, *Reports of cases argued … in the court of the king's bench*, 5 vols. (1831–5) • Boase, *Mod. Eng. biog.*

Gregory, David. *See* Gregorie, David (1625–1720).

Gregory, David (1659–1708), mathematician and astronomer, was born in Upper Kirkgate, Aberdeen, on 3 June 1659, the fourth of fifteen children of David *Gregorie (1625–1720), medical practitioner of Kinnairdy in Banffshire, and his first wife, Jean (*d.* 1671), daughter of Patrick Walker of Orchiston. The younger David Gregory adopted the Anglicized spelling of his surname when he moved to England. In 1664 his father inherited Kinnairdy and the family moved there from Aberdeen. Little is known of Gregory's early life or education, but he probably studied at Aberdeen grammar school. He entered Marischal College, Aberdeen, in 1671, aged twelve, and left four years

David Gregory (1659–1708), by William Townesend, 1708

friend and correspondent the mathematician John Collins. Gregory returned home in the summer of 1681 and spent most of the next two years there in close study of his uncle's papers.

Gregory may have met Pitcairne in Paris in 1680, or they may have met in Edinburgh between 1681 and 1683, or at an unknown earlier time. It seems probable that they had met by March 1683, when Pitcairne issued a public challenge to John Young, who had taught mathematics (without the title of professor) at the University of Edinburgh since James Gregorie's death. Young's unsatisfactory responses to Pitcairne led to his replacement by David Gregory, who was elected to his uncle's chair in October 1683. He was granted an MA degree by the university in the next month, and shortly thereafter delivered his inaugural address, 'De analyseos geometricae progressu et incrementis', a history of the progress of mathematics.

Gregory's first publication, *Exercitatio geometrica de dimensione figurarum*, appeared in 1684. It was based on his uncle's work on infinite series, and was reviewed by John Wallis in the Royal Society's *Philosophical Transactions*. Gregory sent a copy to Newton, acknowledging the latter's work on the calculus. This prompted Newton to begin to write up his own work. In 1685 Gregory and Pitcairne met the Scot John Craige, who soon after moved to Cambridge. Through Craige they learned more of Newton's work.

Gregory and Pitcairne were sharing lodgings in 1687 when Gregory received his copy of Newton's *Principia*. He wrote an effusive letter of praise to Newton, correctly calculating that Newton would prove to be a useful patron in the future. Gregory began a commentary, known as *Notae in Isaaci Newtoni 'Principia'*, which he worked on intermittently for the rest of his life. Copies of the *Notae* circulated in manuscript, but it remained unpublished. The mathematician William Whiston (1667–1752) claimed that Gregory was the first to lecture publicly on the Newtonian philosophy (*Biographia Britannica*, 2366). However, very little Newtonian science appeared in Gregory's Edinburgh lecture course, though he did introduce a few students to Newtonian ideas, as evidenced by their essays.

The revolution of 1688 disrupted Gregory's life. As an Episcopalian and an associate of Pitcairne, a known Jacobite, Gregory was under suspicion, even though his personal politics seemed to be strictly pragmatic and his personal religion notable mainly for its lack of conviction. In 1690 the Scottish parliament empowered a university commission to enforce loyalty to the new regime by means of oaths. The commissioners had the power to eject unfit masters. Although Gregory refused the oaths, he was not ejected, probably because he had powerful patrons; it is unlikely that, as some sources have claimed, his reputation as a Newtonian had much influence on the commission. However, his position remained precarious, and when the Savilian professorship of astronomy at Oxford fell vacant in 1691, he mounted a campaign to attain it.

Gregory travelled to England in the summer of 1691, where he met Newton, Flamsteed, and Halley. He

later, probably without taking a degree. He appears then to have returned to Kinnairdy.

Between 1675 and 1683 Gregory became a proficient mathematician and gained the friendship of the Edinburgh physician Archibald Pitcairne, a major influence in his life. Unfortunately, the chronology of Gregory's life in this critical period remains somewhat obscure. He came from a long line of mathematicians and medical men, and he combined the interests of his forebears in his own work. His uncle the mathematician James Gregorie died in October 1675, leaving his books and papers to his brother. Gregory began to study these in the 1670s.

In 1679 Gregory was sent abroad to complete his education. He matriculated as a medical student at the University of Leiden in September and remained there for several months. He then embarked on a typical peregrination through Europe, with stops at Rotterdam, Paris, and finally London, where he spent the spring of 1681. While in the Netherlands and France, Gregory continued his studies, gaining a knowledge of the mathematics of Descartes, Hudde, and Fermat. He also indulged his growing interests in natural philosophy: in Paris between August and December 1680, for example, he visited the observatory and sketched several of the instruments there. In London he was invited to a meeting of the Royal Society, and he made notes on Boyle's air-pump and Newton's reflecting telescope. He undoubtedly visited his uncle's obtained the support of Newton and Flamsteed for the chair. Halley, his main rival, was passed over because of rumours of his irreligion; a later anecdote describes a Scot who travelled to London to meet Halley, the only man 'that has less religion than Dr Gregory' (Bodl. Oxf., MS Rawl. J).

Gregory was elected to the chair in December 1691 and took the degrees of MA and MD at Oxford in February 1692, when he was admitted a fellow of Balliol College. His degree theses, on optics, were drawn from his Edinburgh lectures on that topic. In his 'Tres lectiones cursoriae' he contrasted Galen's qualitative optics with his own, based on 'true mathematical principles' (Aberdeen University Library, MS 2206/8, fol. 1), and described the optic nerve in terms Newton had recently disclosed to Pitcairne. Gregory was very interested in medicine, as his papers and correspondence with Pitcairne indicate. A manuscript notebook survives (BL, Add. MS 29243) detailing his medical practice, which was confined to his friends and family but was more sophisticated than the usual lay medicine. He was elected an honorary fellow of the Edinburgh College of Physicians in 1705.

Gregory's inaugural lecture for the Savilian chair summarized the necessary relationship between astronomy and geometry, and heaped praise on English achievements in this area. As this lecture indicated, he gladly left troubled Scotland behind, though he continued to be interested and involved in Scottish politics. His father signed Kinnairdy over to him in 1690, and Gregory visited nearly every summer. Most of his family continued to reside in Scotland, and in 1695 he married Elizabeth Oliphant, of the Oliphants of Langtoun. Her brother Charles was an Edinburgh physician and one-time protégé of Pitcairne. The Gregorys had nine children, only two of whom—their eldest son, David *Gregory (1695/6–1767), and third son, Charles—reached adulthood.

Gregory was elected a fellow of the Royal Society in 1692 and published several mathematical papers in the *Philosophical Transactions*. His *Catoptricae et dioptricae sphaericae elementa*, an edited version of his Edinburgh lectures on optics from the 1680s, appeared in 1695 (2nd edn, 1713; English trans., 1715; 2nd edn, ed. J. T. Desaguliers, 1735). It is notable for an appended remark that suggested the possibility of constructing an achromatic compound lens by employing lenses of different media, on the model of the crystalline and vitreous humours of the eye.

Gregory lectured conscientiously at Oxford, though less often than the Savilian statutes demanded. As in Edinburgh, his lectures emphasized fairly basic knowledge and seldom mentioned Newton's work. He was interested in the reform of mathematics teaching and drew up several papers on this topic, none of them published. He suggested that teaching be in English rather than Latin, and emphasized practical knowledge. He was a well-liked teacher and strongly influenced several of his students, including James and John Keill and John Freind. His work on practical geometry, composed in Edinburgh, was published by Colin Maclaurin in 1745 as *A Treatise of Practical Geometry* and remained a popular textbook, reaching a ninth edition in 1780.

Like many of his contemporaries, Gregory sought the prestige of an appointment at the royal court. With the support of Newton and Bishop Gilbert Burnet (a friend of his late uncle), he was named mathematics tutor in 1699 to the young duke of Gloucester, son of Princess Anne. Flamsteed also tried for the post; his disappointment caused his relationship with Gregory, already made difficult by the latter's closeness to Newton, to deteriorate further.

The death of the young duke in 1700 severed this promising tie to the court, but Gregory nevertheless moved to London about 1704, and lived at St John's Street, Long Ditch, Westminster. Newton obtained for him an appointment as overseer of the Scottish mint in 1707, following the union of parliaments. Gregory, a supporter of the union, supervised the reminting of Scottish coins to bring them up to the English standard, spending several months in Edinburgh. He helped to calculate the Equivalent, a payment to the Scottish Treasury to offset the expected loss in Scottish customs duties resulting from the Union.

In 1702 Gregory published his major work, *Astronomiae physicae et geometricae elementa*, the first textbook on astronomy to integrate Newton's gravitational theory with standard findings. It was dedicated to Prince George of Denmark. Newton contributed to the book the first publication of his lunar theory and a preface that asserted the antiquity of the concept of universal gravitation, known, he said, to the *prisca sapientia*. Gregory's work was an influential textbook, and was translated into English in 1715 (second editions of both Latin and English texts appeared in 1726). His predecessor in the Savilian chair, Edward Bernard, had initiated a project of new editions of ancient mathematical works, and Gregory edited a folio volume of Euclid's works in Greek and Latin (*Euclidis quae supersunt omnia*, 1703). He worked with Halley on an edition of Apollonius, but died before its completion.

Gregory's health was not strong in his later years, and he may have suffered from tuberculosis. In the autumn of 1708 he was encouraged to go to Bath to seek relief, 'a ridiculous advyse', according to his friend Pitcairne (*Best of Our Owne*, 54). Upon learning that his only daughter was ill with smallpox, he hastened to return to London after less than a week in Bath, but being ill himself was forced to stop at Maidenhead, where he sent for his friend Dr John Arbuthnot to attend him. Gregory died, soon after Arbuthnot's arrival, on 10 October 1708 at The Greyhound inn in Maidenhead. His daughter had meanwhile died of smallpox, and three of his sons were also ill. Gregory was buried in the churchyard at Maidenhead, and his widow later had a marble monument erected to his memory in St Mary's Church, Oxford. The monument incorrectly gave Gregory's date of birth as 1661 and of death as 1710.

Gregory was not a notable observational astronomer: he made only one recorded observation, and Flamsteed characterized him as a 'closet astronomer' (*DNB*). He was a skilled but not brilliant mathematician. In character he was ambitious but well liked by his friends, who included Arthur Charlett, Halley, Wallis, Aldrich, and Arbuthnot. His importance lay rather in his considerable talents as a correspondent, communicator, and teacher, particularly of Newtonian natural philosophy.   ANITA GUERRINI

Sources C. M. Eagles, 'The mathematical work of David Gregory, 1659–1708', PhD diss., U. Edin., 1977 · A. G. Stewart, *The academic Gregories* (1901), 52–76 · P. D. Lawrence and A. D. Molland, 'David Gregory's inaugural lecture', *Notes and Records of the Royal Society*, 25 (1970), 143–78 · *David Gregory, Isaac Newton, and their circle*, ed. W. G. Hiscock (1937) · R. S. Westfall, *Never at rest: a biography of Isaac Newton* (1980) · *The best of our owne: letters of Archibald Pitcairne, 1652–1713*, ed. W. T. Johnston (1979) · A. Guerrini, 'The tory Newtonians: Gregory, Pitcairne, and their circle', *Journal of British Studies*, 25 (1986), 288–311 · *The correspondence of Isaac Newton*, ed. H. G. Turnbull and others, 1–4 (1959–67) · A. Charlett, correspondence, Bodl. Oxf., MS Ballard 14 · *Biographia Britannica, or, The lives of the most eminent persons who have flourished in Great Britain and Ireland*, 4 (1757), 2365–72 · U. Aberdeen, MS 2206/8, MS 2206/46 B1 · Bodl. Oxf., MS Rawl. J · *DNB*

Archives BL, medical notebook, Add. MS 29243 · Christ Church Oxf., notes and tables · RS, corresp. and papers · U. Aberdeen L. · U. Edin. L., corresp. and papers · U. St Andr. L., treatises and lecture notes · University of Toronto | BL, Sloane MSS, letters mainly to Sir Hans Sloane · CUL, letters to Sir Isaac Newton

Likenesses W. Townesend, monument, 1708, St Mary's Church, Oxford [*see illus.*]

Wealth at death £50 p.a. to wife for life; £330 each to four younger sons; £500 to daughter; remainder, incl. family possessions in Scotland, to eldest son: will, PRO, PROB 11/504, sig. 249

Gregory, David (1695/6–1767), dean of Christ Church, Oxford, and philanthropist, was one of nine children of Dr David *Gregory (1659–1708), Savilian professor of astronomy at Oxford University, and his wife, Elizabeth Oliphant (*d.* in or after 1708). Two years after his father's death Gregory was admitted a queen's scholar of Westminster School and in 1714 he matriculated from Christ Church, Oxford. He graduated BA on 8 May 1718 and proceeded MA (1721), BD (1732), and DD (1732). The fact that he travelled abroad in his youth and was fluent in a number of modern languages, together with his stout adherence to whig principles, undoubtedly secured his appointment on 18 April 1724 as the first regius professor of modern history. The chair, together with one in Cambridge, was instituted by George I in order to encourage whig loyalties in both universities and to train a future generation of diplomatists. Gregory certainly intended to use his new position to reform Oxford's curriculum and announced:

> the measures of education in our universities have been in some measure defective, since we are obliged to adhere so much to the rules laid down by our forefathers ... the old scholastic learning had been for some time despised, but not altogether exploded, because nothing else has been substituted in its place. (Ward, 132)

Gregory initiated some modest changes by encouraging several foreign tutors to teach in the university but otherwise made little impact as professor. He resigned the chair in 1736 on his appointment to a canonry in Christ Church Cathedral. Having taken holy orders, he had been presented to the rectory of Semley, Wiltshire, in 1735.

Gregory's usefulness to the whigs was best served by his tireless promotion of their interests in the university and by his daily correspondence with the first duke of Newcastle, in which he reported the party politics for the best part of thirty years. His influence in the university was strengthened with his promotion to the deanery of Christ Church, where he was installed on 18 May 1756. His court connections doubtless owed much to his marriage to Lady Mary Grey (1719/20–1762), daughter of Henry *Grey, first duke of Kent (*bap.* 1671, *d.* 1740), courtier and politician, and his first wife, Jemima Crew (*d.* 1728); they had several children.

Gregory took his college duties seriously and endeavoured to reform the curriculum by outlining a four-year programme of studies that incorporated classics, poetry, history, logic, mathematics, philosophy, and divinity. Furthermore he instituted examinations each term, encouraged weekly declamations in English on historical subjects, and founded four annual prizes. Considerable improvements were made to the fabric of Christ Church under his direction: the hall and Tom Quad were restored and he contributed towards George Clarke's building of the library (1717–38). He occupied his spare time in writing Latin verse, and marked the accessions of both George II and George III with congratulatory and loyal verses.

On 15 September 1759 Gregory was appointed master of Sherborne Hospital in Durham, where he generously funded a new building to house some of the brethren. Gregory died aged seventy-one on 16 September 1767 and was buried under a plain slab in Christ Church Cathedral.

E. T. BRADLEY, *rev.* S. J. SKEDD

Sources *An essay on the life of David Gregory, D.D., late dean of Christ Church, Oxford* (1769) · Foster, *Alum. Oxon.* · *Old Westminsters* · H. L. Thompson, *Christ Church* (1900) · W. R. Ward, *Georgian Oxford* (1958)

Archives BL, letters to the duke of Newcastle, etc., Add. MSS 32689–33064

Likenesses portrait, Christ Church Oxf.

Gregory, Donald (1803–1836), antiquary, was one of the five surviving sons of James *Gregory (1753–1821), professor of medicine at the University of Edinburgh, and his wife, a McLeod. He was the twin brother of William *Gregory (1803–1858) and the elder brother of Duncan Farquharson *Gregory (1813–1844). Educated for the legal profession, his preference for literary pursuits led him to a different career. Holding a keen interest in his highland ancestors, he applied himself to historical research. In 1829 he was elected secretary to the Antiquarian Society of Scotland, a position he held until his death. Much of the energy and zeal of the society at that time was attributed to his enthusiasm and energy. He was also secretary to the Iona Club, and an honorary member of the Ossianic Society of Glasgow and of the Newcastle upon Tyne Society of Antiquaries, and a member of the Royal Society of Antiquaries of the North at Copenhagen.

Following extensive investigation into the genealogy and history of the clan Gregor, Gregory read his findings to the Society of Antiquaries of Scotland on 22 March 1830. This was later published in the fourth volume of the *Archaeologia Scotica* in 1831, under the title 'Historical notices of the clan Gregor: inquiry into the earlier history of the clan Gregor with a view to ascertain the causes which led to their proscription in 1603'.

Gregory is best remembered as the author of *History of the Western Highlands, and Isles of Scotland, from A.D. 1493 to A.D. 1625*, published shortly before his death in 1836. The work was of great interest, as the subject had hitherto been much overlooked by historians. His detailed research drew upon Scottish manuscripts in the British Museum, state papers, and private documents, such as those from the charter chest of Kilravock and ancient charters of the Gigha family. Acknowledging the shortcomings of his work, Gregory stated that the purpose of his *History* was not to draw general conclusions, but to act as a pioneering work for future historians of the highlands. A contemporary review of the book in *The Athenaeum*, aimed at a predominantly English readership, considered it to be dry, somewhat local, and limited in scope. However, it was thought to provide useful information and to be invaluable to the future historian. Gregory had intended to add a dissertation on the manners, customs, and laws of the highlanders, and contemporary opinion suggested that this topic might have excited a wider interest. However, this plan was postponed, as lack of space forced Gregory to omit this from the book. Preparation of the material for a further volume was under way when his premature death adjourned his work altogether. Donald Gregory died on 21 October 1836, following a short illness, at his home, 31 Ainslie Place, Edinburgh.

CHRISTINE LODGE

Sources *The Scotsman* (2 Nov 1836) • *Inverness Journal* (11 Nov 1836) • *The Athenaeum* (18 March 1837), 188–90 • *The Athenaeum* (1 April 1837), 232–3 • *GM*, 2nd ser., 6 (1836), 688 • *The letters of Sir Walter Scott*, ed. H. J. C. Grierson and others, centenary edn, 12 vols. (1932–79)
Archives NA Scot., bundle of copies of and extracts from various documents relating to the highlands • NL Scot., collection on highland and Hebridean history | NL Scot., letters to Sir William Forbes
Wealth at death £1206 19s. 3d. • £569 3s. 1d.

Gregory [*married name* Alison], **Dorothea** (*bap.* 1754, *d.* 1830), companion of Elizabeth Montagu, was baptized on 4 June 1754 at St Nicholas's Church, Aberdeen, the elder of the two daughters of John *Gregory (1724–1773), professor of medicine at Edinburgh University, and his wife, Elizabeth (*d.* 1761), daughter of Sir William Forbes and his wife, Dorothy Dale. Her mother died when she was still a child. In 1766 her father took her and her sister on a visit to the Northumberland estate of the wealthy Montagu family. Elizabeth Montagu, literary hostess and 'queen' of the bluestockings, childless since the death of her only son in 1744, was captivated by both girls. They became her 'dear dear little friends' (Rizzo, 114), and after touring Scotland with them during that summer, she invited them to stay in Northumberland after their father returned home. Montagu described how Dorothea and her sister had been educated 'in a philosophical simplicity' (Hunt. L., Montagu MSS, MO 3183, 9 Sept 1766) by their father, who asked her to draw up a plan of education for the two girls. Grateful for her advice, Gregory assured

Montagu that he would try 'to procure to them as many funds of entertainment within themselves as possible, & in every respect to make them as independent of my own worthless sex as lies in my Power' (ibid., MO 1072, 12 Feb 1767).

In 1770 there was another long visit during which Montagu offered to take Dorothea Gregory into the household and to make a companion of her. By 1772 Dorothea had left her family. She was intelligent, self-reliant, and capable, and Montagu quickly came to depend on her for practical tasks—above all, driving the carriage on long excursions—and emotional support. The death of John Gregory in 1773 cemented the arrangement. His book *A Father's Legacy to his Daughters* (published a year after his death), was a popular conduct guide which advised girls to behave in the submissive and helpful manner of the ideal companion, which Dorothea evidently was. She went everywhere with Montagu, who treated her as a daughter, and she earned the respect and approval of all. Fanny Burney found her 'far more agreeable than I believed she could have been … frank, open, shrewd, and sensible' (Rizzo, 116). This happy state of affairs lasted for ten years, marred only (and ominously) by Montagu's refusal to countenance a lover for Dorothea. Nor did she show any sign of wanting to settle an independence on her. Rather, she seems to have decided that marriage between her nephew and heir, Matthew Robinson, a malleable young man then barely twenty, and the older Dorothea would best suit everybody's purposes. In summer 1782 the two were often thrown together, but while Matthew developed a 'fondness', Dorothea did not. Instead, having obtained permission from Montagu to visit her family in Edinburgh that autumn, she fell in love with a friend of her brother's, Archibald *Alison (1757–1839), an impecunious curate. Montagu was furious, and an eighteen-month-long battle ensued, marked by 'very disagreeable altercations' (Rizzo, 136) and fainting fits on both sides.

On 19 June 1784 Gregory married Alison, thus giving up the prospect of a massive inheritance, and entering upon a new life as a clergyman's wife with modest means at her disposal. The rift with Montagu was slow to heal, though Dorothea did name her first daughter after her. Five more children followed, among them William Pulteney *Alison and Sir Archibald *Alison, baronet. The marriage appears to have been extremely happy, and the family was comfortably off by the time Archibald Alison published his well-received book *Essays on the Nature and Principles of Taste* in 1790, the same year that he was given a living in Shropshire. Literary friends whom Dorothea had known during her time with Montagu stayed in touch and occasionally visited, a sign that she had been well liked on her own account. The picture of a parsonage childhood recalled by Sir Archibald suggests an affectionate family life, bookish, full of nature observation, politics, poetry, and watercolour sketching. In 1800 they moved to Edinburgh where they were welcomed into literary circles. The family was struck by typhus fever in 1812 when one daughter died; a second daughter, nursed for six weeks by Dorothea—who hid her own distress and kept Eliza's death secret—survived. Her son's judgement that she was 'a remarkable woman' of 'strong good sense' and 'a determined will' seems appropriate (Alison, 1.292). She died in her sleep at Edinburgh, on 7 July 1830, and was buried in the city's St John's churchyard.   NORMA CLARKE

Sources B. Rizzo, *Companions without vows: relationships among eighteenth-century British women* (1994) · A. Alison, *Some account of my life and writings* (1883) · IGI
Archives Hunt. L., Montagu collection, letters

Gregory, Duncan Farquharson (1813–1844), mathematician, was born on 14 April 1813 in Edinburgh, the youngest of the ten children of James *Gregory (1753–1821), professor of medicine at the University of Edinburgh, and his wife, Isabella McLeod. Gregory came from a family with a long tradition in science: one direct ancestor was the mathematician James Gregory (1638–1675), an associate of Isaac Newton. As a child he did not show any predilection for mathematics, and found amusement in astronomy and in inventing mechanical devices. His father died when he was seven, and until the age of ten he was educated entirely by his mother. Afterwards he was also attended by a private tutor.

In 1824 Gregory went to Edinburgh Academy for three years, and then spent a winter at a private academy in Geneva, where his mathematical talent became apparent. In 1828 he began studying at Edinburgh University, where he became a favourite pupil of William Wallace (1768–1843), under whose tuition he made significant progress in higher mathematics. He was also interested in chemistry, especially in experiments on polarized light. In 1833 he matriculated at Trinity College, Cambridge, graduating as fifth wrangler in 1837. During the first years of his residence at Cambridge he acted as assistant to the professor of chemistry. He was one of the founders of the Chemical Society in Cambridge, and occasionally lectured in its rooms. He also studied botany, astronomy, and natural philosophy, but on graduating devoted himself exclusively to the study of mathematics. In 1837, together with R. L. Ellis, he founded the *Cambridge Mathematical Journal*, which had an important role in the revival of the subject in Cambridge. Gregory acted as its chief editor until a few months before his death.

In 1838 Gregory was an unsuccessful candidate for the chair of mathematics at Edinburgh University. He was elected a fellow of Trinity College in 1840, and, on receiving his MA in 1841, he was offered a position at the University of Toronto. This he declined on the grounds of poor health, and he remained at Cambridge, serving as an assistant tutor (1840–43), and as a moderator of the tripos (1842).

Gregory's special field of study was the algebra of differential operators, which originated in the work of J. L. Lagrange, and had been particularly developed by the Alsatians L. F. A. Arbogast and F. J. Servois. Perceiving the utility of operator methods, he sought to establish them upon rigorous foundations and to deploy them successfully for the solution of linear differential equations with constant coefficients. He published more than twenty

Duncan Farquharson Gregory (1813–1844), by unknown artist

papers, covering a wide range of applications, in the first two volumes of the *Cambridge Mathematical Journal*. These were collected and edited after his death by his friend William Walton as *The Mathematical Writings of D. F. Gregory* (1865). Efforts by a recent biographer to attribute many other *Cambridge Mathematical Journal* articles to Gregory are, however, unconvincing. In particular, the signature S. S. G. refers to Samuel Stephenson Greatheed (1813–1887), who was a mathematician in his own right, though he is best known for his church music. It is not a pseudonym for Gregory.

Gregory's elaboration of differential operator methods formed the basis of his textbook, *Examples of the Processes of the Differential and Integral Calculus* (1841). Especially noteworthy was his treatment of partial differential equations and definite integrals largely connected with Fourier's theory of heat. A notable successor to the volume published by Babbage, Herschel, and Peacock in 1820, this was the first English treatise to make constant and well-founded use of the method of separation of symbols. Gregory's study of commutative operations led to Boole's work on non-commutative operations, thus furnishing the grounds for further research on the calculus of operations until the 1860s.

Gregory's other mathematical concern was with developing the system of solid geometry solely by means of symmetrical equations. In 1842 he commenced the writing of *A Treatise on the Applications of Analysis to Solid Geometry*, which was completed and published after his death by Walton in 1845. Gregory's novel development of analytic geometry largely superseded J. Hymers's earlier approach. On the whole, his work reveals a vast acquaintance with continental mathematics, and is often enlivened with historical remarks. The quality of his mathematical advances was indeed unusual for one who never held a senior position in the university. Of an amiable disposition and an active disinterested kindness, he unfailingly shared with others the extent and variety of his information, and his experience as an editor. On realizing the potential of the young and self-taught George Boole he helped him establish his reputation, by offering significant advice for his first contributions to his journal. Just as Gregory paid tribute to his mentor Wallace by saving from oblivion some of his unpublished discoveries, so too Boole would later acknowledge the value of his friendship with Gregory, in his 1859 treatise on differential equations.

Gregory died unmarried, in his thirty-first year, at his father's house, Canaan Lodge, Edinburgh, on 23 February 1844, having suffered from continuous ill health for the previous two years.　　　H. R. LUARD, rev. MARIA PANTEKI

Sources R. L. Ellis, 'Biographical memoir', *The mathematical writings of D. F. Gregory*, ed. W. Walton (1865), xi–xxiv · M. Panteki, 'Relationships between algebra, logic and differential equations in England, 1800–1860', PhD diss., CNAA, 1992, esp. 'The development of the calculus of operations from Murphy to Boole: 1837–1845', 253–314 · R. Harley, 'George Boole FRS', *British Quarterly Review*, 44 (1866), 141–81 · *DSB* · private information (2004) · b. cert.
Archives CUL, corresp. with Lord Kelvin, Add. MS 7342 · Trinity Cam., letters to Greatheed, Add. MS c.1.136–141
Likenesses drawing, repro. in Ellis, 'Biographical memoir', frontispiece [*see illus.*]

Gregory, Edmund (*b.* **1615/16**), author, was the son of Henry Gregory, rector from 1609 to 1630 of Sherrington, near Salisbury, Wiltshire, a benefactor of the poor of that parish. He matriculated from Trinity College, Oxford, on 10 October 1634 aged eighteen, and graduated BA on 5 May 1636; he is not to be identified with the Edmund Gregory of Cuxham, Oxfordshire, who attended Merton College, Oxford. Gregory of Trinity was the author of *An historical anatomy of Christian melancholy, sympathetically set forth, in a threefold state of the soul* (1646), to which is prefixed his portrait, aged thirty, engraved by W. Marshall. This does not represent him in clerical dress, and may suggest that Anthony Wood was wrong to assert that he was ordained. Nothing further is known of him.　　　STEPHEN WRIGHT

Sources Foster, *Alum. Oxon.* · Wood, *Ath. Oxon.*, new edn, vol. 3 · *VCH Wiltshire*, vol. 15 · E. Gregory, *An historical anatomy of Christian melancholy, sympathetically set forth, in a threefold state of the soul* (1646) [Thomason tract E 1145(1)]
Likenesses W. Marshall, line engraving, repro. in Gregory, *An historical anatomy*

Gregory, Edward John (1850–1909), painter in oils and watercolours, was born in Southampton on 19 April 1850, the eldest of three sons and five daughters of Edward Gregory and his wife, Mary Ann Taylor. Gregory's grandfather was an engineer on Sir John Franklin's last Arctic expedition; his father was also a ship's engineer and on leaving Dr Cruikshank's school at fifteen the young Gregory entered the drawing office of the P. & O. Steamship Company. However, he showed a natural talent for art; at

life classes in Southampton he met Hubert Herkomer, a lifelong friend, and together they went to London where they attended the South Kensington Art School. Herkomer recorded in his *Autobiography* that when Gregory's mother put the question of her son's career to him he replied, 'He has more talent than any of us'. Subsequently Gregory studied at the Royal Academy Schools before being employed to help with the decorations at the new South Kensington (later Victoria and Albert) Museum.

From 1871 to 1875 Gregory produced illustrations for *The Graphic*; his work for the magazine included covering the Prussian side in the Franco-Prussian War. In 1871 Gregory and Herkomer were both elected to the New Watercolour Society (subsequently the Royal Institute of Painters in Water Colours) but Gregory was never a prolific artist and, although an active member of the institute for the rest of his life, exhibited with them only fifty-five times. He first showed at the Royal Academy in 1875 and was elected an associate four years later in 1879; here again, however, he showed only thirty-four pictures, more than half of which were portraits. At the Deschamps Gallery in 1879 Gregory exhibited *Dawn*, his first major oil painting; a portrait of two figures caught in 'flirtations's most violent phase' (*Magazine of Art*, 1884, 354); it was subsequently owned by John Singer Sargent. Gregory was elected an Academician in 1898 following the exhibition of his most celebrated picture, *Boulter's Lock, Sunday Afternoon* (Lady Lever Art Gallery, Port Sunlight). At the time there was a craze for boating and the work depicted a busy river scene near Maidenhead; it took some ten years to complete, and there were many preparatory studies. The *Art Journal* said of the painting: 'It is the kind of picture which foreign critics recognise as national; it is in fact the three-volume novel in art, the guide-book and encyclopedia of the manners and customs of the English people' (*Art Journal*, 1897, 179–180). *Boulters Lock* was one of seventy-seven pictures by Gregory collected by Charles Galloway, a Manchester businessman, and sold for £808 10s. in June 1905 after Galloway's death, when his pictures were dispersed at Christies. However, Galloway's near monopolization of Gregory's output inevitably limited his reputation.

Gregory's work is invariably confident and technically able, and his watercolours—such as *Marooning* (exh. RA, 1887; Tate collection)—are particularly fluent and attractive. His obituarist in *The Times* admired them for 'combining Meissonier-like finish with a cheerful modern sentiment of youth and the open air' (*The Times*, 23 June 1909). In 1882 Gregory visited Italy and produced a series of Venetian pictures, and in later years he won gold medals at exhibitions in Paris, Brussels, and Munich. His work can also be found in the Ashmolean Museum in Oxford, the British Museum, London, and the City Art Gallery, Manchester.

On 13 December 1876 Gregory married Mary Ann Joiner (*b.* 1856/7), the daughter of Joseph Joiner, a broker; there were no children. Catalogues give addresses for him in Maida Vale and, from 1890 to 1897, in Cookham Dene in Berkshire. From 1898 until his death, Gregory served as president of the Royal Institute of Painters in Water

Colours; although handicapped by a pronounced stammer, he was a popular and successful administrator. He was also said to be among the best-read men in London. Portraits of Gregory depict him as short and stout, with a round face and full beard. In a memoir written in 1926 the artist Thomas Rooke recalled him as a man:

> of a joyous sturdy old English sort of temperament, absolutely without an ambition beyond the realising of his ideal that the true object of life is to enjoy living, [but] in attaining to it [he] produced an insufficient mass of concentrated work to impress a wide public or to perpetuate the fame his ability deserved   (Rooke, memoir)

Edward John Gregory died after a short illness on 22 June 1909 at his home, Brompton House, Great Marlow, Buckinghamshire, and was buried in Great Marlow churchyard. He was survived by his wife. A studio sale of remaining works and artists' props in 117 lots was held by Christie, Manson, and Woods on 31 January 1910 and realized £640 17s.   SIMON FENWICK

Sources DNB · The Times (23 June 1909) · T. Rooke, MS memoir of Gregory, 1926, Royal Watercolour Society Archives, London, MS X 34 · E. Morris, *Victorian and Edwardian paintings in the Lady Lever Art Gallery* (1994), 41–5 · F. Wedmore, *Magazine of Art*, 7 (1884), 353–9 · *Art Journal*, new ser., 17 (1897), 179–80 · H. Herkomer, *Autobiography* (1890), 36 · m. cert. · *The exhibition of the Royal Academy* (1875–1908) [exhibition catalogues] · CGPLA Eng. & Wales (1909)
Likenesses E. J. Gregory, self-portrait, watercolour, 1879, NPG · E. J. Gregory, self-portrait, oils, 1883, Aberdeen Art Gallery · E. J. Gregory, self-portrait, watercolour, 1884, repro. in *Magazine of Art* · R. W. Robinson, photograph, 1891, NPG · W. H. Bartlett, group portrait, oils (*Saturday Night at the Savage Club*), Savage Club, London · Elliott & Fry, photograph, NPG · E. J. Gregory, self-portrait, oils, Lady Lever Art Gallery; repro. in *Boulter's Lock* (1897) · J. Parker, portrait; Sotheby's, 13 May 1980 · group portrait, woodcut (after *The graphic artists* by T. B. Wirgman), BM
Wealth at death £776 1s. 2d.: probate, 1 Sept 1909, CGPLA Eng. & Wales

Gregory, Elizabeth. *See* Fitzhenry, Elizabeth (d. 1790).

Gregory, Francis (1623–1707), Church of England clergyman and writer, was born on 23 June 1623 at Woodstock, Oxfordshire, the son of Francis Gregory and his wife, Ann (d. 1675). He attended Westminster School and was elected to a scholarship at Trinity College, Cambridge, in 1641, graduating BA in 1644–5 and proceeding MA in 1648. During the interregnum he first served as usher at Westminster School under the famous Dr Richard Busby, and then, in 1654, became master of the free school at Woodstock. His teaching success led to his publishing two scholarly works—the popular *Onomastikon brachu, sive, Nomenclatura brevis Anglo-Latino-Graeca in usum scholae Westmonasteriensis*, a glossary with English, Latin, and Greek in parallel columns (1651), which had gone through twenty editions by 1695, and *Etymologikon mikron, sive, Etymologicum parvum*, a Greek–Latin dictionary (1654, 1670). By about 1659 he had married his first wife, Catherine (d. 1678), with whom he had a daughter, Mary (d. 1672), and two sons, John (d. 1714) and Edmund (d. 1682), who entered Trinity College, Oxford, early in 1676 aged sixteen.

The Restoration inspired Gregory's royalism (and he may have published an elegy on Charles I in 1649). In 1660 he penned *Teares and Bloud, or, A Discourse of the Persecution of Ministers*, a celebratory collection of his poems and those of his scholars (*Votivum Carolo, a Welcome to his most Sacred Majesty from Woodstock School*), and a thanksgiving sermon preached at St Mary's, Oxford, on 27 May, *David's Return from Banishment*, as well as the anonymous *The Last Counsel of a Martyred King*. He was incorporated DD at Oxford, from St Mary Hall, on 12 September 1661.

Some time after 1660 Gregory became master of the free school at Witney, Oxfordshire, but he turned from teaching to preaching in the 1670s. He may have served as rector of Wick Rissington, Gloucestershire, in 1670. In July 1671 Earl Rivers presented him to the rectory of Hambleden, in Buckinghamshire. His outspoken royalism perhaps brought him to the attention of Charles II, for he also became one of his chaplains-in-ordinary in 1672. He became a popular preacher of occasional sermons, among which were published: a visitation sermon (1673); *The Gregorian Account* (preached before Londoners surnamed Gregory, 1673); a sermon before his 'country-men' 'at the Oxfordshire Feast … at Drapers-Hall' (*Agaipé*, 1675); and a sermon preached before London's mayor on the Gunpowder Plot anniversary (1679). He also published at least two anti-Roman Catholic works—a series of sermons 'to confirm my own Parishioners in their present Faith' (*The Trial of Religions*, 1674, sig. A2) and *The Grand Presumption of the Roman Church in Equalling their own Traditions to the Written Word of God*, dedicated to his friend Thomas Barlow, bishop of Lincoln (1675). Catherine Gregory was buried at Hambleden on 12 August 1678, and Gregory married on 28 October 1679, at St Katharine by the Tower, London, Mary Wallis (d. 1732). They had five children—Francis (1680/81–1720), Mary (1682–1743), Penelope (b. 1684, d. after 1733), Charles (1685–1703), and Henry (1688–1728), later of Christ Church, Oxford, and then vicar of Steverton, Northamptonshire. Like Gregory himself, his brothers were also clergy and teachers. John Gregory (d. 1678) was rector of Hemstead, Gloucestershire, and author of works on the sabbath and the Greek New Testament. Abraham Gregory (d. 1690) was a vicar and rector in Gloucestershire and spent some time in prison for disaffection to William III.

Gregory continued to live and preach in Hambleden. He wrote a defence of the Trinity (1695), an attack on the Socinian 'Apron Schoolman' John Smith (1696), a thanksgiving sermon on the deliverance of William III from the assassination plot (1696) and another upon the treaty of Ryswick (1697), *A Modest Plea for a due Regulation of the Press* (1698), and *Impartial Thoughts upon the Nature of Humane Soul, and Some Passages … in the Writings of Mr. Hobs, and Mr. Collier* (1704). Gregory died on 26 June 1707 and was buried at Hambleden church, where a tablet was erected to his memory. His widow, Mary, was living in Oxford when she died but was also buried in Hambleden, on 20 September 1732.   NEWTON E. KEY

Sources Wood, *Ath. Oxon.: Fasti*, new edn · Foster, *Alum. Oxon.* · J. Welch, *The list of the queen's scholars of St Peter's College, Westminster,*

ed. [C. B. Phillimore], new edn (1852) • F. Gregory, *The trial of religions: with cautions to the members of the reformed church against defection to the Roman* (1674) • F. Gregory, *Agaipé, or, The Feast of Love: a sermon at the Oxfordshire Feast, kept on Thursday Nov. 25. 1675. at Drapers-Hall in London* (1675) • private information (2004) [A. S. Gordon]
Archives probably BL, Cole MSS, vol. 45, fol. 265

Gregory, Francis Thomas (1821–1888). *See under* Gregory, Sir Augustus Charles (1819–1905).

Gregory, Frederick Gugenheim [*formerly* Fritz Gugenheim] (1893–1961), plant physiologist, was born at 236 Tufnell Park Road, Upper Holloway, London, on 22 December 1893. Fritz was the fourth of the eight children of Carl Gugenheim, a manufacturing jeweller, and Laura Maison. His father was a Jewish expatriate from Germany who was said to be morose and melancholic (although a great lover of the visual arts). His mother was the daughter of a haberdasher, a vivacious and optimistic lover of the opera, and an ardent suffragette. By the time his parents married in 1889 his father had ceased to be a practising Jew and Fritz was brought up as an agnostic. Music was important in the family, and the many German expatriates teaching the arts in London who visited the Gugenheims' house instilled in Fritz a taste for the visual and literary arts. His extensive involvement with the German community and attachment to German culture (which entailed always speaking German at home and learning English only at school) was bitterly resented during the First World War, when some of Fritz's colleagues at the Cheshunt Experimental Station destroyed his laboratory notebooks. This led Fritz, in 1916, to change his name by deed poll from Fritz Gugenheim to Frederick Gugenheim Gregory.

Carl Gugenheim was a very strict father, and it seems that Fritz Gugenheim's famous impatience and rebelliousness was a result. This temperament, however, was combined with intellectual brilliance from the earliest days at Owen's School, London. While inheriting from his father artistic skills, Fritz Gugenheim was convinced by the science master, G. H. Armitage, to pursue a scientific career. He was top of the class, winner of a number of prizes, and in 1912 passed the intermediate examination of London University in mathematics, mechanics, chemistry, and physics. Gugenheim's most important diversions from these scientific studies were music and reading. Musically, although he admired Hindemith and Britten, he was most devoted to the romantic composers, especially Mahler and Bruckner, and his enthusiasm for them was so intense that he never developed an independent style in his own compositions for the pianoforte and wind instruments. He was equally engrossed by the literary styles of Meredith, Dostoyevsky, and Proust, and the philosophical writings of Whitehead and Santayana. Gugenheim also greatly loved the countryside, enjoying long walking tours throughout the south of England. Not surprisingly, therefore, he has been described as a romantic, a passionate and imaginative attitude which informed his lifelong work in plant physiology.

In 1912 Gugenheim went to Imperial College, where he spent the rest of his career. His intention had been to study chemistry, but he became so excited by J. B. Farmer's

Frederick Gugenheim Gregory (1893–1961), by Elliott & Fry, 1958

lectures on botany that he changed his mind and graduated ARCS in 1914 and BSc (London) in 1915, both with first-class honours in botany, and was awarded the Forbes prize. He was also awarded the DIC in 1917, the MSc in 1920, and the DSc in 1921. Having been exempted on medical grounds from military service in the First World War, following his graduation, and with a scholarship from the board of agriculture, Gregory, as Gugenheim had now become, joined the Research Institute in Plant Physiology established in the college by V. H. Blackman. He began work on the physiology of greenhouse crops at the research institute's Cheshunt Experimental Station. In the course of this work he was struck by the profound differences in the growth of plants under constant temperature but at different times of the year. Aware of Blackman's ideas about expressing life histories in mathematical terms, Gregory suggested that photosynthetic efficiency could be expressed by a quantity he termed the net assimilation rate, calculated by dividing the plant's dry weight by its leaf area and the number of hours of light. Some of the very speculative assumptions behind this were challenged by G. E. Briggs and there ensued a lively controversy between them. This brought Gregory into prominence at a very early age, and in 1918 he returned to Imperial College to work in the research institute proper.

After his return Gregory spent a short time measuring the effects of small electric currents on plant growth as part of Blackman's own investigations. However, his overriding interest remained the analysis of growth, and thus in 1919 he began a long series of studies at the Rothamsted Experimental Station on the growth of barley. Using statistical correlations and regressions, he sought to define equations that would describe the growth of the plant and allow inferences about the effects of particular climatic factors. This statistical approach brought him into contact with R. A. Fisher, who was also at the time working at Rothamsted. Gregory soon applied Fisher's recently introduced factorial techniques to study the effects on growth of plant nutrients. When summing up the ten years he dedicated to these researches, in a paper published in 1937, he attempted very broad generalizations. It is said by even those close to Gregory that he was too impatient to be a good experimentalist, and in fact with relatively little direct evidence he linked together the several aspects of metabolism which he and his students had studied into a scheme of chemical reactions which attracted great, if sometimes critical attention.

By 1928 the importance of Gregory's contributions to plant physiology resulted in his invitation to advise the Empire Cotton Growing Corporation on the irrigation of cotton in Sudan. He quickly set up statistical studies in Gezira, which were so insightful that his final report was widely used for the further development of agronomy in Sudan, and on his return to Britain he became a member of the corporation's scientific advisory committee. The following year, following Blackman's promotion to head of the biological laboratories at Imperial College, Gregory was appointed assistant professor of plant physiology and assistant director of the research institute. He now had to give lectures on plant physiology for the first time, and in the succeeding decade his interests diversified in keeping with this new responsibility. His laboratory became known for publications concerned with vernalization and photoperiodism, in which Gregory himself played a major role, and on transpiration, stomatal behaviour, and carbohydrate metabolism. He was always in demand for advice both at the college and at the several research stations where staff of the research institute were working. In fact, Gregory's mind exuded ideas, derived from his fertile imagination and wide-ranging reading. He entered passionately into all these activities and his strongly expressed opinions and speculations evoked responses ranging from awe and respect to outright hostility. This vivid personality attracted to him numerous visitors from across the world, and those closest to him believe that this power to inspire others was his greatest contribution to plant physiology. On Blackman's retirement in 1937 there was little doubt that Gregory should be appointed his successor.

The Second World War disrupted work at Imperial College, and the staff of the research institute were dispersed to experimental stations outside London. In 1947 Gregory was appointed director of the research institute, and he directed his energies into rebuilding laboratories, research, and teaching in London. His appointment to the governing body of the Glasshouse Research Station further marked his increasing involvement in administrative aspects of research. These years also marked the increasing formal recognition of Gregory's scientific stature. He was elected fellow of the Royal Society in 1940, serving on its council from 1949 to 1951, and receiving its royal medal in 1957. At about the same time that he was so honoured by the Royal Society many of the Indian students who had enjoyed his teaching at Imperial College succeeded in electing him to the membership of the newly established Indian Society of Plant Physiologists. He received as well the rare distinction of being elected foreign associate member of the United States National Academy of Science.

Notwithstanding all this international recognition Gregory became increasingly depressed. The threat of nuclear war weighed heavily upon him and he felt very strongly that scientists had a responsibility to make their voice heard. Thus he was actively involved in 1952 in the organization of Science for Peace, acting as its first chairman, but his increasingly deteriorating health forced him to withdraw two years later. In 1955 his much loved sister and companion Mollie died, and within the next two years so did another sister and his equally beloved nanny and lifelong housekeeper, Josephine Mengele. Gregory found it increasingly difficult to fulfil his many duties. Therefore he retired as soon as he reached his sixty-fifth birthday in December 1958. Yet he had never married, and his sudden loneliness proved even more burdensome. Gregory died in Hampstead General Hospital on 27 November 1961.

H. K. PORTER, rev. PAOLO PALLADINO

Sources H. K. Porter and F. J. Richards, *Memoirs FRS*, 9 (1963), 131–53 · A. D. Krikorian, 'Gregory, Frederick Gugenheim', *DSB*, 5.523–4 · *The Times* (30 Nov 1961) · b. cert. · d. cert. · CGPLA Eng. & Wales (1962)
Archives ICL, notebooks, drawings, and MSS
Likenesses W. Stoneman, photograph, 1940, NPG · Elliott & Fry, photograph, 1958, NPG [*see illus.*] · E. Kohler, oils, ICL
Wealth at death £12,690 14s. 3d.: probate, 3 July 1962, CGPLA Eng. & Wales

Gregory, George (1754–1808), Church of England clergyman and writer, son of an Irish clergyman, was educated at Liverpool for the counting-house. For several years he was clerk to Alderman Charles Gore, merchant of Liverpool, but took more interest in literature and the drama than in his employment, and was director of a small private theatre, for which he wrote several farces and plays. He married a Miss Nunes, daughter of a Liverpool merchant. Resolving to give up business, he studied at the University of Edinburgh, and was ordained in the established church. He graduated DD in 1792.

Gregory settled in London in 1782, and became evening preacher at the Foundling Hospital. In the next year he began his varied writing career with *Essays Historical and Moral*. This was followed by poetry, printed in *Elegant Extracts* (1785), edited by Vicesimus Knox; a volume of sermons with 'Thoughts on the composition and delivery of a sermon' (2nd edn, 1789); *The Elements of Polite Education*, a selection of Lord Chesterfield's letters (1800); and *Letters on*

Literature, Taste and Composition (1808). Works of philosophy and history included *The Economy of Nature Explained* (1796) and a *History of the Christian Church* (1790). He also published *A Translation of Bishop Lowth's Lectures on the Poetry of the Hebrews* (1787) and a revised edition of John Hawkesworth's translation of Fénelon's *Les aventures de Télémaque* (1795).

Gregory's life of Thomas Chatterton was published in 1789 as a reprint of his article in Andrew Kippis's *Biographia Britannica*. On Kippis's death in 1795 Gregory was appointed editor of the *Biographia* but made little progress with the work, and the sixth volume, to which he had contributed a preface, was burnt in the warehouse of Nichols & Son on 8 February 1808. He was also for some years editor of the *New Annual Register*, a publication started in 1780 by Kippis as a rival to the *Annual Register*. During his editorship Gregory changed the publication's politics from whig to tory at the time of Henry Addington's administration (1801–4).

In 1802 Gregory was presented to the living of West Ham, Essex, a preferment said to have been given him by Addington for his support. He became prebendary of St Paul's Cathedral in 1806, and at the time of his death was also chaplain to the bishop of Llandaff. Gregory was a hard-working parish priest, and an energetic member of the Royal Humane Society. He died on 12 March 1808 and was buried on 21 March at West Ham.

L. C. SANDERS, *rev.* PHILIP CARTER

Sources GM, 1st ser., 78 (1808), 277, 386 · N&Q, 13th ser., 1 (1923), 296 · D. E. Baker, *Biographia dramatica, or, A companion to the playhouse*, rev. I. Reed, new edn, rev. S. Jones, 3 vols. in 4 (1812)

Gregory, George (1790–1853), physician and vaccinator, was born on 16 August 1790 in the precincts of Canterbury Cathedral, second son of the Revd William Gregory, one of the six preachers there, and his wife, Catharine Sayer. Gregory received his early education at the King's School in the city. On the death of his father in 1803 he moved to Edinburgh to live with his paternal uncle James Gregory, professor of medicine at the university medical school. He studied arts at Edinburgh University before following in the footsteps of his uncle and his grandfather John Gregory by studying medicine. Gregory received the best possible education of the day. From 1806 he attended courses at the Edinburgh medical school. In 1809 he moved to London where his studies were supervised by Matthew Baillie, the distinguished anatomist and a close friend of James Gregory. There Gregory attended lectures in anatomy by Benjamin Brodie at the Windmill Street School and in chemistry by William Brande. In 1811 he returned to Edinburgh and obtained his MD with a thesis on pulmonary tuberculosis. In 1812 Gregory became a member of the Royal College of Surgeons and entered the Army Medical Service. The following year he was sent to the Mediterranean. In 1816 he returned to London, became a member of the Royal College of Physicians, and set up in practice. From 1817 he served as physician and later consulting physician to the St George's and St James's Dispensary.

Gregory's reputation among his contemporaries rested on his teaching and textbooks. From 1818 he gave a course of lectures on the practice of medicine at the Windmill Street School, which he published as *Elements of the Theory and Practice of Physic* (1820). The structure of the text was traditional, drawing on the works of William Cullen, the great Scottish practitioner, but it incorporated much new material on recently identified diseases, the novel ideas of the French pathological anatomists, and the tissue theory of Xavier Bichat. The work was widely praised and it went through several editions in Britain and the United States. In 1842 Gregory was appointed lecturer in skin diseases at St Thomas's Hospital and again produced a textbook. His *Lectures on the Eruptive Fevers* (1843), describing the character and treatment of the most common exanthemata, particularly smallpox, was less well received. Gregory was applauded for the clarity and directness of his lectures, but his abrupt manner served him less well in his practice.

Gregory also published a large amount of original material, much of it on smallpox and vaccination—as physician to the Smallpox and Vaccination Hospital, a post he held from 1824 until his death, he had access to a unique amount of clinical material. His most significant and controversial finding, published in *Observations on Vaccination and Smallpox* (1841), was that the severity of smallpox suffered by previously vaccinated patients bore no relationship to the degree of scarring left by the original vaccination. At the time most practitioners believed that levels of immunity were reflected in the size and form of the vaccine cicatrix. Gregory served on the Provincial Medical and Surgical Association's vaccination committee, investigating the permanence of immunity conferred by the procedure, though he disagreed publicly with the final report penned by its chairman, John Baron. He also joined the debate on the relationship of cowpox—the complaint from which vaccine was derived—to smallpox and related diseases. Gregory was a prolific contributor to medical journals: one biographer reported that he had produced no fewer than 212 papers.

Gregory was an active member of the profession. In addition to holding membership in the Provincial Medical and Surgical Association, he was a founder member of the Westminster Medical Society and in 1821 he became a fellow of the Medico-Chirurgical Society. In 1839 he was made a fellow of the Royal College of Physicians and he was also a fellow of the Royal Society. In late 1851 Gregory began to display symptoms of heart disease. He died at his home at 6 Camden Square, London, on 25 January 1853, and was buried in Kensal Green cemetery.

DEBORAH BRUNTON

Sources *Medical Times and Gazette* (19 March 1853), 295–6 · BMJ (1853), 114 · Munk, *Roll*, 3.152–3 · *The Lancet* (29 Jan 1853), 124 · GM, 2nd ser., 39 (1853), 444–5 · DNB

Gregory, Henry (*fl.* 1660–1692). *See under* Gregory, William (d. 1663).

Gregory, James (1638–1675), mathematician, was born at the manse of Drumoak, near Aberdeen, in November 1638, the youngest son of John and Janet Gregory. His

James Gregory (1638–1675), by unknown artist

father, minister of Drumoak, was fined, deposed, and imprisoned by the covenanters. Somewhat sickly as a child, Gregory received his early education (including an introduction to geometry) from his mother, who belonged to the scholarly Anderson family. His older brother David, an enthusiastic amateur mathematician, sent him to Aberdeen, first to a grammar school and later to Marischal College. After graduating there, Gregory moved to London in 1662 where he published his first work, *Optica promota* (1663). In the epilogue Gregory describes the revolutionary design of a telescope based not on lenses but on mirrors, the idea that Newton developed later; Newton's design, however, is different and easier to construct. In 1663 the London optician Richard Reeve was commissioned by Gregory to construct a telescope according to his design, but failed to polish its mirrors correctly, so Newton's telescope was the first reflector actually built. The first Gregorian telescope was presented to the Royal Society by Robert Hooke in 1674.

During his stay in London, Gregory established a friendship with the influential Robert Moray. In order to improve his mathematical education he moved to Italy in 1664, where in Padua he studied under Stefano degli Angeli, a pupil of Evangelista Torricelli. During his four years in Italy Gregory came into contact with the discoveries and methods of the Galileian school. These methods are generally labelled as pre-calculus techniques. The Italians were interested in problems of quadratures, rectification of curves, finding tangents, and so on, problems which were later dealt with in much more general terms in the calculi invented by Newton and Leibniz. Recent

research shows that Gregory in his manuscripts and letters had anticipated many calculus concepts and methods.

The fruits of the Italian period were the *Vera circuli et hyperbolae quadratura* (1667) and the *Geometriae pars universalis* (1668). In the first work Gregory tried to prove that it is impossible to achieve an algebraic quadrature of the general conic sector—and of the whole circle in particular. His demonstration was attacked by Huygens and a controversy ensued. Some themes of the controversy were dealt with in *Exerciationes geometricae* (1668), where Gregory studied the quadrature of the cissoid and the conchoid and gave a geometrical demonstration of Nicolas Mercator's quadrature of the hyperbola. The *Geometriae pars universalis* is an anthology of contemporary methods in tangent, quadrature, cubature, and rectification problems. Gregory maintains the interesting idea that, in order to solve these problems, general methods of 'transmuting' the properties defining a curve are needed. These methods allow the reduction of the problem to the quadrature of a curve which is already known. Similar techniques of 'transmutation' later played a prominent role in Leibniz's invention of the calculus.

About Easter 1668 Gregory returned to London where, backed by John Collins's reviews of the two treatises written in Italy, he was elected to the Royal Society on 11 June. In late 1668, probably through Moray's recommendation, he was elected to the chair of mathematics in St Andrews. One year later he married Mary, daughter of George Jameson the painter and widow of Peter Burnet. They had two daughters and a son, James, afterwards professor of physics in King's College, Aberdeen. Much of Gregory's time was spent teaching elementary mathematics. His scientific production continued, however, as is evident from his letters to John Collins and from his manuscripts. About 1670, upon reading Mercator's *Logarithmotechnia* (1668), he became interested in series expansions. Through Collins he became aware of recent results achieved by mathematicians such as Barrow, Huygens, and Newton. Early in 1671 Moray tried unsuccessfully to secure for Gregory a post as *pensionnaire* at the French Académie des Sciences.

In his letters to Collins, Gregory demonstrated his advanced knowledge on series expansions; they also show that he discovered the binomial theorem independently of Newton. In February 1671 he communicated to Collins without proof several trigonometric series. The printing of Gregory's manuscripts in 1939 made it clear that he obtained these series by the method now known as the Taylor expansion of a function.

A manuscript entitled *Geometriae propositiones quaedam generales*, published in 1996 by A. Malet, shows furthermore that Gregory was interested in the foundational aspects of his quadrature techniques. He came very close to the theory of prime and ultimate ratios, presented in the first section of Newton's *Philosophiae naturalis principia mathematica* (1687). Thus the analogies with Newton's work relate not only to the binomial theorem (which Newton found about 1665) and the Taylor expansion (which

Newton stated in the 1690s), but also to the conceptual foundations of the new techniques of approximation. Newton was indeed disturbed by some similarities between his and Gregory's mathematical work. In 1684, David Gregory, James's nephew, published (without due acknowledgement to James) many of his uncle's results on series in a work entitled *Exercitatio geometrica*. Upon reading this work, Newton was induced, in order to establish his priority over the Gregories, to initiate a mathematical treatise entitled *Matheseos universalis specimina*. James Gregory, trained in pre-calculus techniques, is one of the mathematicians who, before Newton and Leibniz, came close to the discovery of calculus.

Gregory's scientific achievements were not restricted to the telescope and to pure mathematics. In an appendix to a book on hydrostatics, *Great and New Art of Weighing Vanity* (1672), written in collaboration with William Sanders, under the pseudonym Patrick Mathers, Arch-Bedal to the University of St Andrews, in order to disprove the theories maintained by the Glasgow professor George Sinclair, he contributed an important result in dynamics, deducing the infinite series which expresses the time of vibration in a circular pendulum for a small arc of swing. Gregory also contributed to astronomy: in a letter to Oldenburg of 8 June 1675 he suggested the differential method of stellar parallaxes; elsewhere he pointed out the use of transits of Venus and Mercury for determining the distance of the sun, and originated the photometric method of estimating the distances of the stars. The photometric method was utilized by Newton in *The System of the World* (1728), another sign of Newton's debt to Gregory.

In 1673 Gregory travelled to London to purchase telescopes and other instruments and to consult Flamsteed on this topic. During his absence the students at St Andrews had rebelled against the antiquated curriculum. Gregory's attempts to introduce science in the university were now seen as a threat to the old system, and he met with many difficulties at St Andrews—even his salary was not paid. In 1674 he was invited by Edinburgh University to take the newly established chair of mathematics. In October 1675, a few months after his arrival in Edinburgh, a paralysing stroke blinded him while he was showing Jupiter's satellites to his students. He died of apoplexy a few days later.   NICCOLÒ GUICCIARDINI

Sources D. T. Whiteside, 'Gregory, James', *DSB* · *Biographia Britannica, or, The lives of the most eminent persons who have flourished in Great Britain and Ireland*, 4 (1757), 2355–65 · H. W. Turnbull, ed., *James Gregory tercentenary memorial volume* (1939) · A. Malet, *From indivisibles to infinitesimals: studies on seventeenth-century mathematizations of infinitely small quantities* (1996) · A. Malet, 'Studies on James Gregorie, 1638–1675', PhD diss., Princeton University, 1989 · G. A. Gibson, 'James Gregory's mathematical work', *Proceedings of the Edinburgh Mathematical Society*, 1st ser., 41 (1923), 2–25 · P. D. Lawrence, 'The Gregory family: a biographical and bibliographical study', PhD diss., U. Aberdeen, 1971
Archives BL, papers, Sloane MS 3208 · U. Edin. L., papers | NRA, priv. coll., corresp. with John Collins · RS, corresp. with John Collins, etc. · U. St Andr. L., corresp. with John Collins
Likenesses eleventh earl of Buchan, chalk drawing (after unknown artist), Scot. NPG · eleventh earl of Buchan, pencil and chalk drawing (after John Scougall), Scot. NPG · W. Holl, stipple, BM, NPG; repro. in Chambers, *Scots.* · portrait; at Marischal College, U. Aberdeen, in 1890 · portrait, Fyvie Castle, Aberdeenshire [*see illus.*]

Gregory, James (1753–1821), physician, son of John *Gregory (1724–1773), and his wife, Elizabeth (*d.* 1761), daughter of Sir William Forbes, was born at Aberdeen in January 1753 and baptized on the 9th of that month. His sister, Dorothea *Gregory, was a companion of Elizabeth Montagu and wife of the writer on aesthetics Archibald Alison. James Gregory was educated at Aberdeen grammar school, briefly at King's College, Aberdeen, and Edinburgh University, where he did an arts course. He spent a year (1766–7) at Christ Church, Oxford, where his cousin David *Gregory (1695/6–1767) was dean. In 1767 Gregory returned to Edinburgh to study medicine under such teachers as William Cullen, Alexander Monro secundus, Joseph Black, and John Hope, as well as his own father, who died in the middle of his course. James suggested that he should complete his father's lectures, so, while still a student, he became temporary professor. He graduated MD at Edinburgh in June 1774, and then spent two years studying medicine in Leiden, Paris, and in Italy.

In June 1776 Gregory was elected professor of the institutes of medicine in Edinburgh, a vacancy arising because of the transfer of Cullen to the chair of the practice of physic on the death of John Gregory. This was the beginning of a lifelong connection between James Gregory and the University of Edinburgh. The university had an excellent reputation in medicine, and Gregory was effectively chief of the medical faculty. He took a leading part in the teaching and examination work at the medical school and at the same time gradually established himself in practice in the city. As a result of his teaching he came to feel the need for a new book on the theory of medicine, and in 1788 he published *Conspectus medicinae theoreticae*. For many years this was a leading textbook, and was also the standard work for examination in medical Latin. Because of the elegance of its writing it was also sometimes used as a Latin text.

By 1790 Gregory had so well established his reputation that he was appointed joint professor of the practice of physic, with the right to survivorship, on Cullen's retirement. After Cullen's death he remained the sole occupant of this chair for the rest of his life. In November 1818, because of the increase in his practice, he employed his nephew William Pulteney *Alison to assist with the lectures.

Gregory was noted as a superb lecturer, his explanations covered all aspects of medicine. Sir Robert Christison said of him: 'in fluency as in choice of language, he surpassed all lecturers I have ever heard before. His doctrines were set forth with great clearness and simplicity, in the form of a commentary on Cullen's *First Lines of the Practice of Physic*' (*Life*, 78–9). As an examiner Gregory was known to be thorough and fair. He considered that the best physician was one who could distinguish what he could do from what he could not do. According to Christison, Gregory

James Gregory (1753–1821), by Sir Henry Raeburn, c.1798

anticipated sundry pathological and therapeutic principles … In treating of blood-letting in fever, which was about to break out as a mania with our profession, he briefly but emphatically cautioned us that it does not answer at all in some types of epidemic fever … In his notice of acute rheumatism, he condemned the common notion of his day … I could quote other similar proofs of his acuteness as an observer. (*Life*, 81)

Gregory's ideas on bloodletting were soon superseded. But his name lived on in homes throughout the country well into the twentieth century in connection with the celebrated Gregory's powder or Gregory's mixture. Composed of powdered rhubarb, ginger, and magnesium oxide, it acted as an antacid, stomachic, and cathartic.

Gregory spent a great deal of his creative talents in feuds with his contemporaries, both individual and institutional, as witnessed by the long list of pamphlets, mostly sizeable books, among his published works. One such feud in 1793 involved James Hamilton, professor of midwifery at Edinburgh University. A quarrel ended with Gregory beating Hamilton with his cane. For this he was taken to court and fined £100, which Gregory, when paying, offered to double for another opportunity. It was the practice of the members of the colleges of physicians and surgeons to attend the Edinburgh Infirmary by a monthly rotation, so that the patients could never be sure which physician would treat them. The public in general, and Gregory in particular, took exception to this and Gregory attacked this system in *Memorial to the Managers of the Royal Infirmary* (1800). With public support Gregory eventually persuaded the managers of the infirmary to appoint medical officers on a permanent basis. Gregory's public feuds,

often sarcastic and very personal, were often humorous. Although considered by many to be a waste of his talents they were often a source of entertainment and were never conducted for selfish ends. He usually had the best both of the argument and of the clever writing. As a result of one of his publications, *Review of the Proceedings of the Royal College of Physicians in Edinburgh* (1804), he was charged by the college with violation of his oath not to divulge its proceedings. Eventually Gregory was pronounced guilty by the college and in May 1809, having refused to apologize, was suspended from the rights and privileges of the fellowship of the college.

Gregory was described as a large man of striking appearance, a great talker and lecturer, and noted Latin scholar. He was also very popular with his students, and showed great kindness and understanding towards them. In spite of his feuding he was a very popular doctor, and his advice was sought by practitioners and patients throughout Europe. Because of the time spent on his writings Gregory's contribution to medical literature was limited to his *Conspectus*. He had wide interests and in 1792 published a work on metaphysics entitled *Philosophical and Literary Essays*, parts of which were read before the Royal Society of Edinburgh in 1784 and 1785. His essay 'The theory of the moods of verbs' was published in the *Transactions of the Royal Society of Edinburgh* in 1790. From about 1780 he wrote nearly all the Latin epitaphs and dedications which were required in Edinburgh and district. His many friends included Robert Burns, who sent him poems to criticize and considered him the last of the Scottish Latinists.

When Gregory first returned to Edinburgh in 1776 he lived in his father's old house in St John Street. It was here that he brought his first wife, Mary Ross, whom he married in 1781. This marriage ended with Mary's death in April 1784. They had no children. By 1796 he had moved to St Andrews Square, and also bought Canaan Lodge, a few miles out of the city. It was in the garden of Canaan Lodge that Gregory grew the Turkestan rhubarb whose roots provided one of the main constituents of his famous powder. Descendants of these plants were still growing in the garden in fairly recent times. On 19 October 1796 James Gregory married Isabella (*c.*1772–1847), daughter of Donald Macleod of Geanies, Ross-shire, sheriff of Ross-shire. They had eleven children: John (1797–1869); Hugh (1799–1811); James Craufurd (1801–1832); William *Gregory (1803–1858) and twin Donald *Gregory (1803–1836); Jane Macleod (1805–1813); Elizabeth Forbes (1808–1811); Margaret Craufurd (1809–1849), who married her first cousin, William Pulteney Alison; Georgina (1811–1877); Duncan Farquharson *Gregory (1813–1844); and Isabella (1816–1818).

During his lifetime Gregory was an honorary member of numerous literary and scientific societies, and received the freedom of several towns and cities. He was a fellow of the Royal Society of Edinburgh, occasionally serving as an officer of the society. In 1799 he was appointed first physician to the king in Scotland—this commission being renewed on 18 May 1820 by George IV. In 1818 Gregory had a serious carriage accident, and during 1820 had attacks of difficulty in breathing, being unable to lecture after Christmas of that year. He died in Edinburgh of hydrothorax on 2 April 1821. Given a public funeral by the corporation of Edinburgh, he was buried in the Canongate churchyard. His wife outlived him and died in June 1847.

PAUL LAWRENCE

Sources P. S. Gregory, 'Records of the family Gregory', 1887, U. Aberdeen, 60–68, and appx, 40–43 · P. D. Lawrence, 'The Gregory family: a biographical and bibliographical study', PhD diss., U. Aberdeen, 1971 · A. G. Stewart, *The academic Gregories* (1901), 125–140 · Anderson, *Scot. nat.*, 2.379–81 · Chambers, *Scots.* (1835), 2.177–8 · *DNB* · *The life of Sir Robert Christison*, 2 vols. (1885–6)
Archives McGill University, Montreal, Osler Library, lecture notes · NL Scot., lecture notes · RCP Lond., case notes · Royal College of Physicians of Edinburgh, corresp. and lecture notes · U. Aberdeen, MSS · U. Edin. L., special collections division, corresp. and papers · University of British Columbia, Woodward Biomedical Library, lecture notes · University of Dundee, archives, lecture notes · University of Toronto, lecture notes · Wellcome L., lectures and notes; notes on cases treated at Edinburgh Royal Infirmary
Likenesses J. Tassie, paste medallion, 1791, Scot. NPG · J. Kay, caricature, etching, 1795, BM, NPG, Wellcome L. · H. Raeburn, oils, *c.*1798, priv. coll. [*see illus.*] · G. Dawe, mezzotint, pubd 1805 (after H. Raeburn), BM, Wellcome L. · S. Joseph, plaster bust, 1821, Scot. NPG · J. Kay, caricature, etching (*The Craft in Danger*), NPG · H. Raeburn, oils; copy, Royal College of Physicians of Edinburgh

Gregory, John (1607–1646), orientalist, was born at Amersham, Buckinghamshire, on 10 November 1607, the eldest son of John Gregory. His family was poor, and when he was about fifteen he was sent to wait on Sir William Drake of Amersham. He accompanied Drake to Christ Church, Oxford, which he entered as a servitor in 1624 and was placed under the tuition of George Morley, at the time a member of the Great Tew circle and later the bishop of Worcester and Winchester. Shortly after he waited on Sir Robert Croke. His industry at Christ Church, where he spent sixteen hours a day studying, amazed his contemporaries. Due to rank as one of the best Hebraists of his day, Gregory is said to have learned the language during a single vacation spent with the nonconformist minister John Dod at his benefice of Fawsley in Northamptonshire. Gregory was famed for the 'learned elegance' of his style in English, Latin, and Greek, and soon learned numerous other languages, modern and ancient, including Syriac, Arabic, Ethiopic, Samaritan, and Saxon. In 1635 he was studying Armenian.

Gregory graduated BA on 11 October 1628 and proceeded MA on 22 June 1631. From 1628 to 1630 he acted as college librarian. He was subsequently ordained and appointed chaplain to Christ Church Cathedral by Brian Duppa, who had been nominated dean of Christ Church in 1629. When Duppa was made bishop of Chichester in 1638 Gregory, who had been presented by his college to the living of St Mary Magdalen in Oxford in 1635, became the new bishop's domestic chaplain and remained so after his translation to Salisbury in 1641.

Gregory was a versatile scholar, described by his friend, editor, and biographer John Gurgany, the future chaplain of Merton College, as 'the Miracle of his Age' (Gregory, pt 2, sig. A3v). Proficient in astronomy, geometry, and arithmetics, he wrote on globes and cartography, church

music, ancient history, and chronology. He had hoped to edit the chronicle of John of Antioch (Malalas), but completed only the notes (Bodl. Oxf., MS Rawl. D. 1083). His first publication was the 1634 edition of Thomas Ridley's *View of the Civile and Ecclesiasticall Law*, to which he provided annotations displaying his knowledge of Saxon documents. He also left an unpublished treatise on the custom of praying towards the east, 'Al-Kibla' (Bodl. Oxf., MS Tanner 7).

Gregory's most important contributions were in the field of biblical scholarship. Working in the humanist tradition of scriptural studies—philological and historical—associated with Lorenzo Valla and Erasmus, he compared as many recensions of the scriptures as he could find, in the many languages he knew. His conclusions were often well ahead of his time. He was one of the first serious scholars to realize that most of the Old Testament Apocrypha had originally been written in Hebrew or Aramaic, and in the course of his research in the Bodleian he discovered an Arabic manuscript of the apocryphal 2 Esdras which revolutionized the study of the book.

In his *Notes and Observations upon some Passages of Scripture* (1646) Gregory discussed themes ranging from the upper chamber of the temple and the separation of milk and flesh to amulets, silver shrines, and the mark of Cain. He proved remarkably conversant with Hebrew sources. Besides the standard rabbinic commentaries he was acquainted with texts little known among Christians, such as Isaac ben Arama's commentary on the Pentateuch, and with various Kabbalistic works from which he derived an unusual familiarity with Jewish mysticism. He also exhibited a wide reading in Arabic, which led him to make some curious comparisons between the textual tradition of the Koran and that of the Bible.

Gregory's writings had the success they deserved, confirming his international reputation. They were reissued repeatedly for over fifty years after his death, always with Gurgany's biographical sketch and in different combinations. *Posthuma* (1649) contained the brief tracts on various subjects. *Opuscula* (1650), of which John Evelyn had his copy magnificently bound, was entitled *Works* from 1665 and included the tracts and 'Notes and observations'. 'Notes and observations' was also reprinted independently several times from 1650. In Richard Stokes's Latin translation, it was inserted in the 1660 and 1698 editions of John Pearson's *Critici sacri*.

Besides his learning Gregory was known for his courtesy and humility—he thanked John Selden for his 'free disposition towards a pretender to schollarship, for soe I can but account my selfe' (Bodl. Oxf., MS Selden supra 108, fol. 74)—and was renowned for his generosity to other students, 'not disdaining', wrote Gurgany, 'the meanest Scholars, nor proud of his victorious Discourses with the best Learned' (Gregory, pt 2, sig. A1v).

Because of the breadth of his interests and the high reputation he soon acquired as a scholar, Gregory had masters, friends, and patrons of every religious and political persuasion. According to Gurgany he was in touch with Jews and Jesuits abroad. He had learned Hebrew from a puritan; he was in correspondence with the independently minded John Selden and, in 1642, made transcriptions for him at the Bodleian; and he was later protected by Sir Edward Bysshe, the antiquary and expert on heraldry who served parliament as Garter and Clarenceux king of arms. In 1665, under his own name and with no acknowledgement, Bysshe published Gregory's translation from Greek into Latin of three tracts on the Brahmans which had been transmitted to him by Gregory's friend and fellow chaplain of Christ Church Edmund Chilmead. But the majority of Gregory's admirers and supporters were Arminians. Besides Duppa, these included William Laud, Richard Montagu, and Augustine Lindsell, bishop of Hereford, whom he assisted in editing Theophylactus's commentaries on the Pauline epistles (1636). And Gregory, who was at one point even suspected of Roman Catholicism, undoubtedly shared the high-church beliefs of the Laudians.

In 1643, during the royalist occupation of Oxford, Gregory hoped to avoid the military activities of the civil war. He forfeited his Oxford living by withdrawing to the nearby village of Kidlington, where he lodged in an alehouse belonging to one Sutton, whose son attended him. He had long suffered from gout and died, unmarried, at his lodgings on 13 March 1646. His friends arranged for his body to be transported to Oxford and he was buried in Christ Church Cathedral on the following day. His younger brother Henry, who had matriculated at Christ Church in 1633 and proceeded MA in 1637, 'became afterwards eminent for his learning' (Wood, *Ath. Oxon.: Fasti*, 1.497).
ALASTAIR HAMILTON

Sources M. Feingold, 'Oriental studies', *Hist. U. Oxf.* 4: 17th-cent. *Oxf.*, 449–503 · G. J. Toomer, *Eastern wisedome and learning: the study of Arabic in seventeenth-century England* (1996) · A. Hamilton, *The apocryphal apocalypse: the reception of the second book of Esdras (4 Ezra) from the Renaissance to the Enlightenment* (1999) · J. Gregory, *Works*, 2 pts (1665) [incl. biographical sketch] · Wood, *Ath. Oxon.*, new edn, 3.205–8 · Wood, *Ath. Oxon.: Fasti* (1815), 497 · DNB · Bodl. Oxf., MS Top. Oxon. c. 916 [Christ Church Cathedral Registers, burials]

Archives Bodl. Oxf., 'Al-Kibla', Tanner MS 7 · Bodl. Oxf., notes to Malalas, Rawlinson MS D.1083 · Bodl. Oxf., letters to Selden, Selden MS supra 108, fols. 52, 74, 243

Gregory [Gregorie], **John** (1724–1773), physician and writer, the youngest son of James Gregorie (1674–1733), professor of medicine at King's College, Aberdeen, and the grandson of James *Gregory (1638–1675), was born on 3 June 1724 in Aberdeen. His mother, Anna Chalmers (d. 1770), was his father's second wife. When he was only eight John's father died and his grandfather, Principal Chalmers, and his half-brother James, by then professor of medicine at Aberdeen, took care of his education. His studies were also greatly influenced by his cousin Thomas Reid, the moral philosopher. Having been educated at Aberdeen grammar school and King's College, Aberdeen, in 1742 Gregory moved with his mother to Edinburgh, where he studied medicine at the university under Alexander Monro, primus, Andrew Sinclair, and John Rutherford. During his time in Edinburgh Gregory joined the Edinburgh Medical Society and became a close friend of the physician and poet Mark Akenside.

Following his medical course in Edinburgh, Gregory went to Leiden in 1745 and studied under Gaubius, Albinus, and others. While there he received the degree of MD in 1746 from King's College, Aberdeen. He soon returned to Aberdeen and, in June 1746, was elected regent (professor) of philosophy at King's College, lecturing in mathematics and moral and natural philosophy. At the same time he started to practise medicine in Aberdeen, and in September 1749 he resigned his regentship to concentrate on his practice. On 2 April 1752 he married Elizabeth (c.1728–1761), the younger daughter of William Forbes, thirteenth Lord Forbes (d. 1730), and his wife, Dorothy (d. 1777?). His wife's 'great beauty and engaging manners, joined a very superior understanding, and uncommon share of wit' (McCullough, 57). They had three sons, including the physician James *Gregory (1753–1821), and three daughters. As medical practice in Aberdeen was mostly in the hands of his brother James, Gregory moved to London in 1754. Knowing John Wilkes and Charles Townshend from his time in Leiden, he now became acquainted with George Lyttelton, as well as Edward Montague and his wife, Elizabeth. It was during this period in London that he changed the spelling of his name from Gregorie to Gregory. In November 1755 Gregory was elected 'mediciner' at Aberdeen on the death of his brother, and the following year he was elected a fellow of the Royal Society.

Gregory tried to establish permanent medical lectures in Aberdeen, but failed because of the limited number of medical students. He did, however, become a member of the Aberdeen Philosophical Society, where he read many essays; these were later collected, modified, and published anonymously under the title *A Comparative View of the State and Faculties of Man, with those of the Animal World* (1765). Gregory considered human nature to be a uniform non-variant, whose principles and function can be discovered through experiment. The two principles of mind are reason ('a weak principle') and instinct (which guides morality). Gregory wrote that 'The task of improving our nature, of improving man's estate, involves the proper development and exercise of the social principle and the other principle of instinct, with reason subordinate to instinct and serving as a corrective on it' (McCullough, 150). The study of nature is then, according to Gregory, the best means of cultivating taste ('a good taste and a good Heart commonly go together') and religious understanding, the aim being to produce morally well-formed individuals (ibid., 154).

After the death of his wife, on 29 September 1761, Gregory wrote *A Father's Legacy to his Daughters* to relieve his loneliness and to record her opinions about the education of their two surviving daughters, the eldest of whom was Dorothea *Gregory (bap. 1754, d. 1830). He may have incorporated the advice given him by his friend and celebrated bluestocking Elizabeth Montagu, who approved his pattern of educating the girls 'in a philosophical simplicity' (Hunt. L., Montagu MSS, MO 3183, Elizabeth Montagu to Elizabeth Carter, 9 September 1766). This little work was not intended for publication, but was to be given to his daughters after his death. However, it was published by his son James in 1774 and was an immediate success, running into many editions and translations. The work contains advice on religion and moral conduct, female friendship, and behaviour towards the opposite sex, principally regarding love and marriage. Deploring the forwardness and freedom of contemporary female manners, Gregory argued that modesty, delicacy, and elegance would better secure men's respect and admiration. His concern for his daughters' reputations in the world led him to advocate caution and prudence; thus he advised them to conceal their learning and wit, advice that was scornfully dismissed as a system of dissimulation by Mary Wollstonecraft in *Vindication of the Rights of Woman*. His wife's death also spurred Gregory to write: all his works post-date the event.

In 1764 Gregory took his children to Edinburgh, where his practice grew quickly, and he became a celebrity on the publication of *A Comparative View*. On 5 March 1765 the Royal College of Physicians of Edinburgh granted him a licence to practise, and on 6 August 1765 he was admitted as a fellow of the college.

In 1766 Gregory was elected professor of the practice of physic at Edinburgh University, and only then was he required to resign his Aberdeen chair. This election was the cause of ill feeling. Rutherford resigned on condition that Gregory, known to be an excellent teacher, was elected in his place, rather than the students' preference, William Cullen, then professor of chemistry. Accordingly Gregory was given an interim appointment and, on 12 February that year, was granted the freedom of the city of Edinburgh. In that same year the chair of the institutes (or theory) of medicine at the university became vacant. Students petitioned that Gregory be transferred to this chair and Cullen be appointed to the chair of the practice of physic. This was refused, and Cullen was appointed to the chair of the institutes of medicine. In May 1766 Gregory was appointed first physician in Scotland to George III. Between 1767 and 1769 Gregory lectured on the practice of medicine, then in 1769 permission was granted for Cullen and Gregory to give alternate courses on the practice and theory. This unprecedented arrangement continued until Gregory's death. In 1767 Gregory began lecturing on medical ethics. When he heard that a copy of his lectures had been offered to a bookseller, he published a corrected version, entitled *Observations on the Duties and Offices of a Physician and on the Method of Prosecuting Enquiries in Philosophy* (1770); it was issued two years later in a revised edition as *Lectures on the Duties and Qualifications of a Physician*. These writings have been called 'the first philosophical, secular medical ethics in the English language' (McCullough, 6).

Gregory's *Elements of the Practice of Physic* (1772) dealt with the nosology of diseases and the diseases of infants and children. In this book Gregory defines medicine as 'an active and practical art, the exercises of wc can be acquired by … extensive practice only'. It was not a 'speculative science, to be acquired by reading' (McCullough, 168). This approach harked back to a view of medicine

which Gregory had expounded in *A Comparative View*, when he stressed the importance of experiment and observation, praised Sydenham and Boerhaave, and railed against 'useless theories and voluminous explanations and commentaries on those theories' (ibid., 157).

Gregory is described as a large man, somewhat stooped, and heavy featured. In conversation he was very animated and warm, his whole face lighting up and showing great interest. He was kind towards his patients and students and was noted as an excellent teacher. He had a keen interest in music and was a regular attender at the Aberdeen Musical Society. Gregory died in Edinburgh on 9 February 1773. Elizabeth Montagu remembered him fondly:

> The hours I passed in his company were amongst the most delightful in my life. He was instructive and amusing, but was much more; one loved Dr Gregory for the sake of virtue and virtue (one might almost say) for the sake of Dr Gregory. (McCullough, 171)

PAUL LAWRENCE

Sources L. B. McCullough, *John Gregory and the invention of professional medical ethics and the profession of medicine* (1998) · P. S. Gregory, 'Records of the family Gregory', unpublished, 1887, 48–60 · P. D. Lawrence, 'The Gregory family: a biographical and bibliographical study', PhD diss., U. Aberdeen, 1971 · W. Smellie, *Literary and characteristical lives of John Gregory and others* (1800), 1–118 · A. G. Stewart, *The academic Gregories* (1901), 100–24 · Anderson, *Scot. nat.* · Chambers, *Scots.* (1835) · *DNB* · D. Brewster, *Edinburgh encyclopaedia* (1830), vol. 10, pp. 510–11 · *Encyclopaedia Britannica* · S. Skedd, 'The education of women in Hanoverian Britain, c.1760–1820', DPhil diss., U. Oxf., 1997

Archives McGill University, Montreal, Osler Library of the History of Medicine, lecture notes · NL Scot., lecture notes · Royal College of Physicians of Edinburgh, lecture notes · U. Aberdeen, family MSS · U. Edin. L., accounts and MSS · U. Edin. L., lectures on the practice of physic · University of British Columbia, Woodward Biomedical Library, lecture notes · University of Kansas, Lawrence, Clendening History of Medicine Library and Museum, lecture notes · Wellcome L., lectures on the Institutes of Medicine | Hunt. L., letters to Elizabeth Montagu · NA Scot., letters to Sir Archibald Grant · NL Scot., letters to Sir William Forbes

Likenesses R. Earlom, mezzotint, pubd 1774 (after G. Chalmers), BM, Wellcome L. · W. Ridley, stipple, 1804 (after F. Coates, 1764), Wellcome L. · J. Horsburgh, line engraving, 1825 (after F. Coates, 1764), Wellcome L. · J. Beugo, stipple (aged forty; after F. Coates), BM, Wellcome L.; repro. in J. Gregory, *A father's legacy to his daughters* (1788) · Cook, line engraving (after G. Chalmers, 1787), Wellcome L. · W. Howison, stipple (after G. Chalmers), Wellcome L. · portrait (as a young man), repro. in Anderson, *Scot. nat.*, vol. 2 · portrait (later in life), repro. in Chambers, *Scots*, vol. 2

Gregory, John Walter (1864–1932), geologist and explorer, was born at 18 Gainsborough Road, Mile End Old Town, London, on 27 January 1864, the son of John James Gregory, wool merchant, and his wife, Jane, née Lewis (there were also at least two daughters). He was educated at Stepney grammar school before becoming, at the age of fifteen, a wool sales clerk in London. Despite the demands of this position, Gregory continued his education, taking night classes in the natural sciences and matriculating at Birkbeck College in January 1886. The following year he became assistant in the geological department of the British Museum (Natural History), under Robert Etheridge sen. and Henry Woodward. While working at the museum, Gregory also studied at Birkbeck College, graduating BSc in 1891. He was awarded a DSc in 1893 for studies largely concerned with palaeontology (polyzoa, corals, and echinoids).

By the early 1890s Gregory had been gripped by the urge to visit the more remote regions of the earth. In 1891 he travelled to the Rocky Mountains and Great Basin of North America. The following year he was seconded to a proposed expedition to British East Africa. When the original plan failed Gregory set out with forty Africans. In five months he made a spectacular series of scientific observations on structural and glacial geology, anthropology, and parasitology. In particular, he recognized the essential character of the region, recorded in his first classic book *The Great Rift Valley* (1896). That same year he joined Sir Martin Conway in the first crossing of Spitsbergen and in 1899 went to the West Indies with his wife, Audrey (*née* Chaplin), whom he had married on 6 June 1895.

Gregory was appointed to the chair of geology and mineralogy at the University of Melbourne in December 1899 and began work there in February 1900. From November 1901 he was also director of the geological survey of Victoria. During his time in Australia he carried out a wide range of studies concerning mining and the landscape. He also gained fame for a rapid summer traverse of Lake Eyre in central Australia, accompanied by a group of senior students. His record of the journey was subsequently published as *The Dead Heart of Australia* (1906), a book compiled from his newspaper reports of the expedition. However, his inclination to rush to conclusions on scientific matters (particularly the origin of Australia's artesian water) did not win Gregory universal praise. Nor was he always easy to get along with; despite initially accepting the directorship of the civilian scientific staff of Robert Scott's national Antarctic expedition (1901–4), he resigned because he and Scott could not get on.

Frustration with the lack of funding and equipment at Melbourne University, combined with his wife's ill-health, led Gregory to accept the newly established chair of geology at the University of Glasgow in 1904, a position he held until his retirement in 1929. There he formed a strong department. However, he continued to travel, reporting *inter alia* on the Cyrenaica region in 1908 and on Angola in 1912, as sites for possible Jewish colonization. In 1922 he undertook a 1500 mile walk (with his son Christopher) from Burma to south-west China and Tibet, a journey that became the subject of another classic book.

In all, Gregory published twenty books and more than 300 papers on a wide range of scientific topics, though largely in geology and physical geography. His *Geography, Structural, Physical, and Comparative* (1908), based on the ideas of Eduard Suess, was particularly influential. He received many awards and honours including honorary degrees from the universities of Liverpool, Glasgow, and Lima, and he was elected FRS in 1901. He was president of the Geological Society of London (1928–30) and of several sections of the British Association (C in 1907 and E in 1924).

Small of stature, Gregory, a keen skier, was a wiry, energetic character, well liked for his enthusiasm and good nature, and admired for his immense knowledge on a wide range of subjects. Active until the end, Gregory died while leading an expedition in Peru, three years after his retirement. He was drowned on 2 June 1932 when his canoe overturned on the Urubamba River, on the banks of which he was subsequently buried.   D. F. Branagan

Sources P. G. H. B. [P. G. H. Boswell], *Obits. FRS*, 1 (1932–5), 53–9 · *The Times* (14 June 1932), 16 · G. W. Tyrrell, *Quarterly Journal of the Geological Society of London*, 89 (1933), xci–xciv · 'How Professor Gregory died: report from expedition', *The Argus* [Melbourne] (7 Sept 1932), 6 · B. Willis, 'J. W. Gregory', *Nature*, 130 (1932), 310–11 · D. F. Branagan and E. Lim, 'J. W. Gregory and the dead heart', *Records of Australian Science*, 6 (1985), 71–84 · C. J. Gregory, *J. W. Gregory: a sketch* (privately printed, Chelmsford, 1977) · 'A geologist's death: Professor Gregory's last expedition', *The Times* (2 May 1933), 9 · J. W. Gregory, 'Contributions to the geology of Cyrenaica', *Quarterly Journal of the Geological Society*, 67 (1911), 577 · *Alma Mater* [University of Melbourne], 5 (April 1900), 8 · *Alma Mater* [University of Melbourne], 5 (May 1900), 57 · *The Argus* [Melbourne] (15 June 1932), 7 · *The Argus* [Melbourne] (14 June 1904), 5 · *The Times* (16 June 1932), 13 · *The Times* (18 June 1932), 14 · *The Times* (20 June 1932), 15 · *CGPLA Eng. & Wales* (1932) · b. cert. · m. cert. · LUL

Archives Bodl. Oxf., corresp. · NHM, report on Caribbean · RGS, corresp. and papers · Scott Polar RI, corresp. · U. Glas., Archives and Business Records Centre, notes and plans relating to Africa | Palestine Exploration Fund, London, corresp. with Palestine Exploration Fund

Likenesses photograph, 1899–1900, repro. in 'Professor Gregory', *Alma Mater* (May 1900), 57 · photograph, *c*.1910, repro. in *Argus* (15 June 1932), 7 · W. Stoneman, photograph, 1920, NPG · photograph, 1920?–1929, repro. in *Obits. FRS*, 52

Wealth at death £15,031 1s. 5d.: probate, 20 Aug 1932, *CGPLA Eng. & Wales*

Gregory, Olinthus Gilbert (1774–1841), mathematician, was born on 29 January 1774 at Yaxley, Huntingdonshire, of unknown parentage. For more than ten years he studied intensively at the local boarding-school of the Leicester botanist and mathematician Richard Weston. At nineteen he secured the advice of patron John Joshua Proby, earl of Carysfort, before publishing *Lessons, Astronomical and Philosophical … Interspersed with Moral Reflections* (1793, revised 6th edn 1824), a work of natural theology for children. In 1794 Weston introduced Gregory as a mathematical problem solver to the annual *Ladies' Diary*. An unpublished treatise on the sliding rule, composed when he was twenty, brought him to the attention of Charles Hutton.

In 1794 or 1795 Gregory's friendship with J. S. Copley and other distinguished Cambridge students encouraged thoughts of a college career. These aspirations subsided when he absorbed William Frend's arguments and briefly adopted Socinianism. Thereafter, wary of religious hubris, he returned to the gospels for spiritual guidance; following Hartley he opposed subscription to articles of religion, and also matriculation. About 1798 he nevertheless settled in Cambridge where he worked for a few months as sub-editor of the *Cambridge Intelligencer* under Benjamin Flower. He abandoned journalism, began to teach mathematics in the town and university, and for about a year kept a bookshop.

A Treatise on Astronomy (1802), hastily written in the

Olinthus Gilbert Gregory (1774–1841), by Thomson, pubd 1823 (after Derby)

spring of 1801 and dedicated to Hutton, brought him into public notice. With the death of Charles Wildbore the Stationers' Company employed him to edit the *Gentleman's Diary* (1802–19) and one of their almanacs. From 1818 he edited the companion *Ladies' Diary*, managed White's *Ephemeris*, and, replacing Hutton, undertook the general superintendence of all the Stationers' almanacs and their astronomical calculations. Like his predecessor, Gregory used this key position to foster provincial mathematical talent. Hutton ensured that Gregory filled the new post of second mathematical master (December 1802) at the Royal Military Academy, then expanding with the growth of the Royal Artillery after the union with Ireland. From Woolwich Gregory marketed the *Astronomy*, his comprehensive, copiously illustrated, and highly successful *Treatise of Mechanics* (3 vols., 1806), and his annotated work, dedicated to Carysfort, *An Elementary Treatise on Natural Philosophy* (2 vols., 1807), from the French original by René Just Haüy, as together forming a complete course of natural philosophy; the *Mechanics* was used as a class book at West Point during the 1830s. Marischal College, Aberdeen, awarded him an honorary AM (1806) and an LLD (1808). The doctorate was a response to Gregory's gift of the opening volume of a vastly ambitious survey of human genius, learning, and industry, the *Pantologia* (12 vols., 1808–13).

As a versatile mathematical practitioner, Gregory advised technical publishers, negotiated with the Surrey Institution to give lectures on the mechanical part of experimental philosophy (1812), revised and extended Hutton's works (the famous *Course of Mathematics* of 1811 and other mathematical textbooks, dictionaries, and tables), composed a trigonometry primer (1816), and prepared a topical dissertation on weights and measures

(1816). Although looking back to Newton and Desaguliers in his early writings, Gregory was well aware of the French theoretical engineering of Monge, Hachette, and Navier. Thus, in 1803 and 1804, he translated papers for Hutton's voluminous abridgement of the early *Philosophical Transactions*, while in the first volumes of the *Retrospect of Philosophical, Mechanical, Chemical, and Agricultural Discoveries* (8 vols., 1806–15), he reviewed critically the most recent British and foreign papers and inventions.

Woolwich offered Gregory facilities for large-scale collaborative investigations, and a stronghold from which to snipe at the Royal Society. His dissertations on the trigonometrical survey (1815) doubled as a defence of Thomas Colby and the academy's Lieutenant-Governor William Mudge from Royal Society criticism. At Woolwich Gregory and Mudge responded to the select committee of artillery officers by measuring the velocity of projectiles using a vast ballistic pendulum (1815–17); an excursion to the Shetlands with Colby to determine the shape of the earth by means of astronomical observations and pendulum experiments (1817) ended acrimoniously when Gregory quarrelled with his French collaborator Biot. Experimenting again with mortars, guns, and muskets, Gregory accurately determined the velocity of sound (1823).

Gregory was an active institutional actor. He was a lecturer on ballistics, a vice-president (to Carysfort's president), and an anniversary orator (1817) for the short-lived Philosophical Society of London. After that society's collapse, he published, anonymously, a scathing exposé of the Royal Society presidency of Hutton's *bête noir*, Sir Joseph Banks (1820). Thus irrevocably allied to British scientific reformers, he worked alongside Babbage, Herschel, and Millington as a founder (1820), secretary (1824–8), and vice-president (1829–30) of the Astronomical Society. As an honorary member of the Institution of Civil Engineers (1824) he heeded Henry Brougham's call and compiled a commonplace book of *Mathematics for Practical Men* (1825, 4th revised edn 1862) designed for the institution's younger members. He was recruited as an honorary member to literary, philosophical, statistical, and antiquarian societies in Newcastle, Bristol, Cambridge, Dijon, Paris, and New York. His last public address (1839) was to the Woolwich Institution, of which he had been elected president on its formation.

From the age of seven Gregory had scoured works of mathematics, universal grammar, and ancient and modern philosophy for rational solutions to profound metaphysical questions (the abstract nature of eternity, and of simple duration considered as an attribute of the Deity). In adulthood he toyed with Unitarianism, then regained his belief in the Trinity, only to abandon thoughts of becoming a minister when he concluded that both the discipline of the Episcopal church and the democratic government of the orthodox dissenting churches deviated greatly from the primitive pattern. His *Letters to a Friend on the Evidences, Doctrines, and Duties of the Christian Religion* (2 vols., 1811), written at the height of the evangelical revival, went through numerous editions, were abridged for the Religious Tract Society (1841), attracted heated debate in several languages, and won Gregory the patronage of William Wilberforce. The *Letters* were written, in part, for the religious instruction of his children, the offspring of his first marriage, on 20 December 1809, to Miss Beddome. One daughter became an ardent Unitarian; a son, Charles Hutton Gregory, became an eminent engineer; a second son was drowned in the Thames shortly before Gregory's death. The identity of his second wife is unknown.

Gregory was active in the formation (1812) of the Blackheath Auxiliary Bible Society and twice addressed its annual meetings (1815, 1816). As John Bonnycastle's successor in the Woolwich mathematics chair (May 1821), and as a prominent dissenter, he was one of the projectors of the non-sectarian London University. His name was inscribed on the foundation stone laid in Gower Street on 30 April 1827. Gregory was a frequent contributor to contemporary reviews and magazines. He composed biographical memoirs of his mentor, Hutton (1823), of the preacher and polymathic co-editor of the *Pantologia*, John Mason Good (1828), and of his Cambridge friend, the distinguished Baptist theologian Robert Hall, whose works he also edited (1832).

Gregory retired from his chair in June 1838, after a decade of debilitating illness. A farewell address on the acquisition of knowledge (1838) and a collection of hints for teachers of elementary mathematics (1840) distilled the pedagogic wisdom of forty years. The Stationers had allotted him a substantial annual pension. He died at his home on Woolwich Common on 2 February 1841. He was survived by his second wife. Capel Molyneux saw in Gregory's life 'a conclusive and valuable testimony … that true philosophy [science] and true religion are not incompatible' (Molyneux, 17).

ALEXANDER GORDON, *rev.* BEN MARSDEN

Sources 'Memoir of Olinthus Gregory … professor of mathematics, Royal Military Academy, Woolwich', *Imperial Magazine*, 5 (1823), 777–92 · *The Times* (6 Feb 1841) · *GM*, 2nd ser., 15 (1841), 438–9 · *Monthly Notices of the Astronomical Society of London*, 5 (1839–43), 81–2 · C. Molyneux, *A sermon occasioned by the death of Olinthus Gregory* (1841) · D. P. Miller, 'Between hostile camps: Sir Humphry Davy's presidency of the Royal Society of London, 1820–1827', *British Journal for the History of Science*, 16 (1983), 1–47 · [J. Watkins and F. Shoberl], *A biographical dictionary of the living authors of Great Britain and Ireland* (1816) · Watt, *Bibl. Brit.* · W. Jerdan, *National portrait gallery of illustrious and eminent personages of the nineteenth century, with memoires*, 5 vols. (1830–34) · W. C. Taylor, *The national portrait gallery of illustrious and eminent personages, chiefly of the nineteenth century: with memoirs*, 4 vols. in 2 (1846–8) · F. K. Brown, *Fathers of the Victorians: the age of Wilberforce* (1961) · D. P. Miller, 'The revival of the physical sciences in Britain, 1815–1840', *Osiris*, 2nd ser., 2 (1986), 107–34 · Gregory to unnamed correspondent, 7 April 1812, Wellcome L., WMS/ALS, Olinthus Gregory dossier · private information (1890) · private information (2004) · d. cert.

Archives RAS, RAS letters · Royal Artillery Institution, Woolwich, London, papers | BL, Babbage MSS, Add. MSS 16947, fol. 42, 34536, fol. 13 · BL, Charles Blacker Vignoles MSS, Add. MS 40210, fol. 405 · Bodl. Oxf., Wilberforce MSS · Inst. CE, membership records · Portsmouth Central Library, Charles Blacker Vignoles MSS · RAS, William Herschel MSS, 13.G.21 [microfilm] · RS, J. F. W. Herschel MSS · RS, John Lubbock MSS · Smithsonian Institution, Washington, DC, Dibner Library of the History of Science and Technology, Dibner collection · Wellcome L., Pettigrew MSS

Likenesses Thomson, stipple, pubd 1823 (after Derby), NPG [*see illus.*] · H. Robinson, stipple, 1834 (after R. Evans), BM, NPG; repro. in W. Jerdan, *National portrait gallery*

Gregory, Sir Richard Arman, baronet (1864–1952), writer on science, was born on 29 January 1864 in Bristol, the son of John Gregory, cobbler and poet, and his wife, Ann, daughter of Richard Arman, farm overseer of Chiseldon, Wiltshire. He first attended the Wesleyan day school at Baptist Mills, Bristol, until 1874, then Queen Elizabeth's Hospital school until 1875, and finally an elementary school in Bristol until 1876. He left school at the age of twelve and moved through a number of jobs. In 1879 he was apprenticed to a shoemaker, but decided to spend his spare time at evening classes at the Bristol Trade and Mining Schools (later the Merchant Venturers' College). This led to a meeting with J. M. Wilson, the headmaster of Clifton College, who offered him the post of laboratory assistant there. The work included looking after a small astronomical observatory. In 1885 he won a student teacher scholarship to the Normal School of Science, South Kensington, and moved to London in the following year.

Gregory came from a strongly Methodist background. His grandfather had been a well-known preacher in north Devon, but his father's main concern was with social reform. By the time Gregory moved to London his father had become one of the leaders of local labour politics in Bristol, influencing among others the trade unionist Ernest Bevin. Gregory was more concerned with science than politics, but he struck up a lifelong friendship at South Kensington with a fellow student, H. G. Wells, which entailed a continuing discussion of both.

Gregory was soon drawn into the experiments that C. V. Boys was doing on fine wires and fibres. This led to his first publication—a joint paper with a fellow student on the tenacity of spun glass, which Boys communicated to the Physical Society. In 1887, having obtained first-class marks in astronomy and physics, Gregory took up a teaching post at Portsmouth Dockyard school. In 1888 he married Kate Florence, daughter of Charles Napier Pearn, an accountant at Portsmouth Dockyard. She was the widow of Frederick George Dugan of the Royal Marines, and already had two children. They had two further children together—a boy and a girl.

In 1889 he returned to South Kensington as assistant to J. N. Lockyer in his solar physics work. The solar measurements Gregory was expected to make were routine in character, but contact with Lockyer opened up a wider prospect of science. In particular it led Gregory into the world of science journalism. Lockyer was founder editor of the journal *Nature*, published by Macmillans. He recruited Gregory to write articles and reviews for the journal on astronomy and related topics. At the same time Gregory became an extension lecturer for Oxford University. These two activities increased his interest in disseminating scientific knowledge, and he now moved entirely into this field. He immediately wrote a series of textbooks on the basis of his extension lectures: they appeared from 1891 onwards. (One devoted to physiography was jointly

Sir Richard Arman Gregory, baronet (1864–1952), by Henry Raeburn Dobson, 1929

authored with H. G. Wells.) In 1893 Lockyer appointed him assistant editor of *Nature*. This brought him into close contact with Macmillans. They were soon publishing his books, and in 1905 they made him their scientific editor, a post which he held for thirty-four years, during which time he was instrumental in commissioning many of their most successful textbooks.

Gregory used the pages of *Nature* to promote both technical education and extramural lectures. In 1897 he was offered the chair of astronomy at Queen's College, London, and used this as an opportunity to provide lectures for the general public. The following year he helped establish the *School World*, a monthly journal for teachers (with a special emphasis on science teaching). This was incorporated into the *Journal of Education* after the First World War; Gregory remained joint editor throughout the inter-war years. In the latter years of the nineteenth century Gregory also became increasingly involved in the activities of the British Association. Along with H. E. Armstrong he helped get agreement in 1901 to the formation of a new section of the association, section L, which was devoted to education. Gregory was successively secretary, recorder, and in 1922 president of the section.

Gregory's advocacy of the importance of science and of a scientific education led in 1916 to his best-known book, *Discovery, or, The Spirit and Service of Science*. This ran through several editions, finally appearing after the Second World War in a revised version for Penguin Books, and gave its name—*Discovery*—to a well-known science periodical. Discussion of the need for more science teaching also led in 1916 to the formation of the neglect of science committee,

of which Gregory was a member. Though there were, inevitably, disputes with teachers of the humanities on the time to be devoted to science in the school curriculum, this, and other groups with which Gregory worked, prepared the way for a greater role for science in post-war education.

Gregory continued to be concerned not only with science in the formal education system, but with its wider communication and its impact on public affairs. In 1903 Lockyer, then president of the British Association, had taken as the theme for his presidential address the need for Britain to devote much more attention to science. He hoped to stir up the British Association to new activity in promoting scientific input to policy and planning. In 1905, after the association had failed to respond fervently enough, Lockyer formed the British Science Guild, whose task was to emphasize the importance of applying scientific method to public affairs. At the end of the First World War Gregory took over the running of the guild. He decided this was a good opportunity to capitalize on the increased interest in science that the war had brought about, and, via the guild, he organized an exhibit of British scientific products in London. In the exhibition catalogue he hammered home the theme that pre-war neglect of science in Britain had allowed Germany to take over industrial leadership, and that this must not be allowed to happen again. A successful exhibition in 1918 was followed by another in 1919. In that year Gregory's contributions, not least in terms of organizing these exhibitions, were recognized by a knighthood.

In 1919 Gregory also took over from Lockyer as editor of *Nature*. More and more work had fallen on him as assistant editor for several years past, but his new appointment gave him much more opportunity to introduce his own ideas. *Nature* increasingly became the channel for the rapid announcement of new and important developments in scientific research. Gregory's wide interests ensured both that the journal took an international viewpoint, and that it emphasized, particularly via his own editorials, the importance of science for national and international policy. These wider concerns led to his involvement in other scientific information activities. He published an important *Catalogue of British Scientific and Technical Books* in 1921, supported the formation of the Association of Special Libraries and Information Bureaux (ASLIB), and in 1924 inaugurated a science news service run by the British Science Guild. After the death of Gregory's first wife—who had become increasingly an invalid and suffered greatly from arthritis—in 1926, in 1931 he married Dorothy Mary Page, daughter of the historian William *Page. There were no children from this marriage.

In the immediate post-war period Gregory attempted to interest organized labour in the importance of science for policy questions. He was in contact with both the Trades Union Congress and the Labour Party, the latter via his friend from Bristol days, Ramsay MacDonald. MacDonald supported his idea for a major conference on science and labour in 1924, but the outcome proved less fruitful than

Gregory had hoped. He returned to stimulating concern for policy among the scientists themselves. As part of this he developed closer links with the Association of Scientific Workers. In 1933 the association joined forces with the British Science Guild to establish a new pressure group, the parliament and science committee. At the same time he continued his efforts to increase interest in science and public affairs at the British Association, with sufficient success that in 1936 the British Science Guild was amalgamated with the British Association. Gregory's wide-ranging efforts received appropriate recognition. He was awarded a baronetcy in 1931, and became a fellow of the Royal Society in 1933 under the statute which permits the election of people who have rendered conspicuous service to the cause of science.

After the amalgamation of the British Science Guild with the British Association Gregory pressed for a clear lead by the association regarding the policy matters that had concerned the guild. This led in 1938 to the formation of a division for the social and international relations of science with Gregory as chairman. In the following year he was elected president of the British Association for the meeting in Dundee. The imminence of war brought an abrupt ending to the meeting, and Gregory's presidential address was not delivered until 1946. Wartime curtailment of the activities of scientific societies also meant that it fell to Gregory to maintain the British Association as a going concern during the war years. His most important contribution was to help organize four major conferences on science and post-war problems between 1940 and 1943. His wide range of scientific and political contacts ensured that these deliberations contributed to the post-war consensus on the importance of science in affairs of state.

By the end of the Second World War, Gregory was over eighty years old. Though he continued to correspond extensively his activities became increasingly curtailed. He died on 15 September 1952 at his home, the Manor House, Middleton-on-Sea, Sussex. He was survived by his second wife. His two children predeceased him, and the baronetcy became extinct on his death.

A. J. MEADOWS

Sources W. H. G. Armytage, *Sir Richard Gregory: his life and work* (1957) · F. J. M. Stratton, *Obits. FRS*, 8 (1952–3), 411–17 · *Nature*, 170 (1952), 520–22 · *CGPLA Eng. & Wales* (1953)
Archives Bodl. Oxf., corresp. relating to the Society for the Protection of Science and Learning · U. Sussex, professional and family papers | BL, corresp. with Marie Stopes, Add. MS 58473 · CAC Cam., corresp. with A. V. Hill · ICL, corresp. with Herbert Dingle · Rice University, Houston, Texas, Woodson Research Center, corresp. with Julian Huxley
Likenesses H. R. Dobson, oils, 1929, NPG [*see illus.*] · W. Stoneman, photograph, 1936, NPG · H. R. Dobson, portrait; known to be in family possession in 1971 · photograph, repro. in Armytage, *Sir Richard Gregory* · two photographs, RS
Wealth at death £14,300 14s. 6d.: probate, 21 Jan 1953, *CGPLA Eng. & Wales*

Gregory, Robert (1729?–1810), director of the East India Company and politician, was born in co. Galway, Ireland. Little is known of his background other than that he was the son of Henry Gregory of Galway and his wife, Mary, daughter of Robert Shaw of Newford, also in Galway. His family, who had been established in Ireland under Cromwell, had sufficient influence to obtain for him a licence from the East India Company to trade as an independent, or 'free', merchant in India, and he arrived in Bengal about 1747. After a long and successful career in India he was described by Robert Clive, then governor of Bengal, as a 'great Merchant having acquired a Fortune of one hundred thousand Pounds sterling in Trade in the most Honourable Manner, his Integrity & Abilities are unquestionable & his Character a very respectable one' (Clive to J. Walsh, 5 Feb 1766, BL OIOC, MS Eur D546/1, fol. 131).

Gregory returned from India in 1766. He acquired Coole Park in his native Galway and Valence in Kent, and it was at the latter that he settled. Seeking election to parliament, he approached Lord Rockingham, leader of the main opposition party. He made a good impression on Rockingham who described him as a 'gentleman of good fortune … and whose character and abilities I think well of' (Rockingham to Newcastle, 4 March 1768, BL, Add. MS 32989, fols. 29–30). Gregory sought Rockingham's help in finding a seat but was concerned that 'where he stood it might be with the countenance of the neighbouring gentlemen and some old and known interest, as thinking that ground was better and freer from the accusation of coming as an adventurer' (ibid.). With Rockingham's help he stood for Maidstone on the interest of Lord Aylesford and was elected comfortably. In parliament Gregory voted consistently with the opposition, but built a reputation for independence of party in Indian matters. During debates in 1773 on Lord North's bill to regulate the company's Indian administration, he declared that:

> most of the gentlemen now in India are my particular friends, but I am willing to do all I can for the ease of the inhabitants of India. A place without law can never be happy. I prefer the happiness of seventeen million of souls to the emoluments of my friends. (HoP, *Commons, 1754–90*)

Gregory was elected to the company's court of directors in 1769 and here too he professed to put the interest of the company before his own. He became closely involved in the company's campaign to defeat North's East India Regulating Bill and continued to act in this with Lord Rockingham who retained the 'Highest opinion' of his integrity and knowledge in Indian matters (Rockingham to Edmund Burke, *post* 13 Dec 1773, quoted in Sutherland, 2.497). But Gregory did have more personal interests in Indian affairs, particularly through longstanding business connections with Maharaja Nandakumar. Nandakumar had once enjoyed power and influence at the court of the nawab of Bengal, a puppet of the company by the 1760s, but had been removed during the governorship of Robert Clive. Gregory had taken Nandakumar's case to Clive, and later, when a company director, acted as his London agent (Khan, 290, 300–01; 'Letters of Richard Barwell', 107). When Laurence Sulivan, Clive's powerful rival for control of the company, was re-elected to the court of directors in 1771, Gregory supported him in ordering the dismissal of Clive's allies in the company's Bengal administration who stood in the way of Nandakumar's return to power. There seems little doubt that Nandakumar's involvement in the political intrigues in Bengal against the governor-general, Warren Hastings, in the 1770s influenced Gregory's own views of Hastings's governorship. Hastings was told by a friend, Francis Sykes: 'I dined yesterday with Gregory … and others and find that Nundcomar writes them everything wch happens and something more, by every ship. This is a fact for I found they had everything from him' (Khan, 300–01). Nandakumar was brought to trial in Bengal for his intrigues, and executed, and Gregory joined the growing party at East India House calling for Hastings's recall.

Gregory lost his parliamentary seat in the 1774 election but was returned after a contest at Rochester. He opposed the American war and voted against the North government on all but Indian issues, where he committed himself to vote with the government in any legislation that represented the mutual interests of the public and the company. When Edmund Burke pledged himself, Gregory, and the opposition to support the government in any such measure, Gregory refused to be bound by such a pledge, saying that he 'stood connected with no party, nor with the honourable Member … he would give his opinion freely, and his support where he thought it due … being as independent in his principles and his seat as any man in the House' (HoP, *Commons, 1754–90*).

Following a ballot in the House of Commons for membership of a committee of inquiry into the war in the Indian Carnatic, Gregory's reputation and stature ensured that he came top of the poll, receiving support from both sides of the house. In the following year he was elected chairman of the East India Company. Although professedly more sympathetic now to Hastings's governorship after the committee of inquiry's findings, Gregory found it difficult to take the company's line in defence of Warren Hastings when the Pitt government tried to have him removed. He was described to Hastings by a friend as 'your shifting friend (the backward way) … upon the whole against You, altho pretends a great deal of candour' (J. Woodman to Hastings, 24 June 1782, BL, Add. MS 29154, fol. 479).

In 1782 Gregory had a serious illness and resigned his chairmanship of the company. Such was his reputation that he was still named as one of the commissioners for Indian affairs in Fox's East India Bill in 1783. His last parliamentary speech was in support of the bill later that year. He did not stand in the 1784 general election. With his wife, Maria, *née* Nimmo, the daughter of an East India merchant, Gregory had a daughter and three sons, the youngest of whom, William *Gregory (1762–1840), was under-secretary to the lord lieutenant of Ireland. Three children of Robert Gregory were baptized at Calcutta on 3 February 1766; their mother's name is given as Johanna in the official records, possibly a clerical error. Gregory died in Berners Street, London, on 1 September 1810, aged eighty-one.　　　　　　　　　　　　　J. G. PARKER

Sources J. G. Parker, 'The directors of the East India Company, 1754–1790', PhD diss., U. Edin., 1977 • HoP, *Commons, 1754–90*, 3.536–7 • L. S. Sutherland, *The East India Company in eighteenth century politics*, 2nd edn (1962) • BL, Hastings MSS, Add. MSS 29132–29173 • BL, Newcastle MSS, Add. MSS 32699–33070 • BL OIOC, Ormathwaite MSS, MS Eur. D546 • [E. Burke], *The correspondence of Edmund Burke*, 2, ed. L. S. Sutherland (1960) • A. M. Khan, *The transition in Bengal, 1756–1775: a study of Saiyid Muhammad Reza Khan* (1969) • 'The letters of Richard Barwell [pt 10]', *Bengal Past and Present*, 13 (1916), 74–124, esp. 107 • *GM*, 1st ser., 80 (1810), 291 • Burke, *Gen. GB* (1937) • BL OIOC, N/1/2/F135
Wealth at death accumulated substantial fortune in India

Gregory, Robert (1819–1911), dean of St Paul's, born at Nottingham on 9 February 1819, was the eldest son of Robert Gregory, merchant, of Nottingham and his wife, Anne Sophia, daughter of Alderman Oldknow, grocer, Nottingham. His parents were Methodists; both died in 1824. Educated privately, Gregory entered a Liverpool shipping office in 1835. At the age of twenty-one, influenced by the *Tracts for the Times*, he resolved to be ordained. He was admitted a gentleman commoner of Corpus Christi College, Oxford, on 2 April 1840; graduated BA in 1843, proceeding MA in 1846, and DD in 1891; was Denyer theological prizeman in 1850; and was ordained deacon in 1843 and priest in 1844 by the bishop of Gloucester and Bristol. After serving the curacies of Bisley, Gloucestershire (1843–7), Panton and Wragby, Lincolnshire (1847–51), and Lambeth parish church in London (1851–3), Gregory was from 1853 to 1873 vicar of St Mary-the-Less, Lambeth. A zealous incumbent, he improved the church, built schools, founded a school of art, and closely identified himself with church work in elementary education. In 1867 he was select preacher at Oxford, and served on the royal commission on ritual.

Gregory was twice married: first, in 1844 to Mary Frances (*d.* 1851), daughter of William Stewart of Dublin, with whom he had two sons, who survived him; and second, in 1861 to Charlotte Anne, daughter of Admiral Sir Robert Stopford, with whom he had four daughters, of whom three survived him. The youngest daughter was the pioneering midwife Alice *Gregory (1867–1946).

In 1868 Gregory was appointed canon of St Paul's, but for five years still held his Lambeth living. With H. P. Liddon and R. W. Church Gregory worked to attain Church's purpose, 'to set St Paul's in order, as the great English cathedral, before the eyes of the country' (*Life and Letters*, 200). As treasurer of the cathedral he negotiated with the ecclesiastical commission the arrangement of the cathedral finances which helped to make reform possible. The changes made were not universally welcomed, but Gregory was unmoved by criticism. Church described him as 'of cast iron' (*Life and Letters*, 235). Four lectures contrasting the social conditions of England in 1688 and 1871, delivered by Gregory in St Paul's in November 1871, drew on him the accusation of misusing the cathedral. The advance in the cathedral ritual and the decoration of the fabric led to hostility, which resulted in litigation in 1888–9 over the reredos.

For forty-three years Gregory was a member of the lower house of the convocation of Canterbury. He entered it as proctor for the archdeaconry of Surrey in 1868, and became proctor for the dean and chapter in 1874. His influence was immediately felt, more especially on educational questions and in defence of higher Anglican policy. W. C. Magee in 1881 wrote of him as 'the Cleon of the lower house' (Macdonnell, 2, 1896, 154); J. W. Burgon, in a published letter of the same year, said, 'In the lower house of convocation you … obtain very much your own way'. On the delivery of the Purchas judgment [see Purchas, John], Gregory joined Liddon on 2 March 1871 in telling John Jackson, bishop of London, that they would not obey it. In 1873 he was forward in defence of the Athanasian creed; in 1874 he presented to convocation a petition in favour of retaining the impugned 'ornaments' of the church; in 1880, during the Burials Bill controversy, he favoured abandoning the graveside service, if this was also accepted by the nonconformists. In 1881 he supported the memorial for the toleration of ritual, and in convocation presented a *gravamen* and *reformandum* to the same effect.

He was an interesting mixture of high-churchmanship and ritualism. An ardent supporter of church schools and long treasurer of the National Society for Promoting the Education of the Poor, Gregory was elected a member of the London school board in 1873, but did not seek re-election when his three years' term ended. He was also a member of the education commission in 1886, and of the City parochial charities commission in 1888.

Appointed dean of St Paul's on the death of Church in 1890, and installed on 5 February 1891, Gregory continued his predecessor's policy, carried out in the face of some criticism, of the decoration of the cathedral with mosaics by W. B. Richmond. He resigned on 1 May 1911, died at the deanery on 2 August, and was buried in the crypt of St Paul's.   A. R. BUCKLAND, rev. H. C. G. MATTHEW

Sources *The Times* (3 Aug 1911) · *The Times* (7 Aug 1911) · *The Guardian* (4 Aug 1911) · *The Guardian* (11 Aug 1911) · *The autobiography of Robert Gregory*, ed. W. H. Hutton (1912) · J. Hannah, *A tribute of affection to the memory of friendship, with memoirs of Robert and Anne Sophia Gregory* (1824) · *Life and letters of Dean Church*, ed. M. C. Church (1895) · J. W. Burgon, *Canon Robert Gregory: a letter of friendly remonstrance* (1881) · J. J. Hannah, *The lighter side of a great churchman's character* (1912) · J. C. Macdonnell, *The life and correspondence of William Connor Magee: archbishop of York, bishop of Peterborough*, 2 vols. (1896) · B. A. Smith, *Dean Church: the Anglican response to Newman* (1958)
Archives Lancing College, West Sussex, letters to Nathaniel Woodward · LPL, letters to E. W. Benson; A. C. Tait MSS; letters to Frederick Temple
Likenesses W. Richmond, oils, exh. RA 1899; formerly at the deanery, St Paul's Cathedral, London, 1912 · Lock & Whitfield, woodburytype photograph, NPG; repro. in T. Cooper, *Men of mark: a gallery of contemporary portraits* (1877) · wood-engraving (after photograph by S. A. Walker), NPG; repro. in *ILN* (3 Jan 1891)
Wealth at death £17,297 16s. 7d.: probate, 10 Oct 1911, CGPLA Eng. & Wales

Gregory, Roderic Alfred (1913–1990), physiologist, was born on 29 December 1913 at 63 Braemar Road, Plaistow, London, the only child of Alfred Gregory (1884–1938), motor mechanic, and his wife, Alice Jane, *née* Greaves (1889–1978). He was educated at George Green's School, London, and from there he went to University College,

London (UCL), to read physiology (1931–4). He graduated with first-class honours and was then Bayliss and Starling memorial scholar (1935) and Sharpey scholar (1936–9) at UCL; he was awarded an MSc in biochemistry (1938) and the medical degree MRCP, LRCS (1939). At George Green's School he had met his wife-to-be, Alice Emma Watts (b. 1915), only child of J. D. Watts. They were married on 29 July 1939 and had one daughter. Earlier that year Gregory had been awarded a Rockefeller travelling medical fellowship, which he then took up at Northwestern University, Chicago, where he gained a PhD (1941), and at the Mayo Clinic, Rochester, Minnesota. In 1941 he returned to UCL, where he did wartime research on the properties of mustard gas. He was appointed to the academic staff of the physiological laboratory of the University of Liverpool in 1945, first as senior lecturer and from 1948 to his retirement in 1981 as George Holt professor and head of department.

Gregory ('Rod', or to some contemporaries 'Greg') 'determined to become a physiologist' when, as a sixth-former, he read William Bayliss's *Principles of General Physiology*, and was fascinated by the revelation that physics and chemistry could be used to understand biological problems (Grossman, 543–5). The idea dominated the rest of his professional life. His interest in gastrointestinal physiology arose from the suggestion by his mentor Charles Lovatt Evans that he should gain experience in this field in the laboratory of Andrew Ivy, who was then at the height of his powers, in Chicago. It was a wise choice. Gregory made seminal discoveries that showed how the complex processes of digestion were controlled at a molecular level, and in particular, how the release of acid by the stomach was regulated. He is best known for his characterization of the acid-stimulating hormone gastrin.

Virtually all of Gregory's work on gastrin was done together with Hilda Tracy. Between 1958 and 1962 they developed methods to obtain gastrin in a pure form. Their starting material was the pyloric antral part of the stomach from pigs killed at a local abattoir; the work required heroic efforts. At one stage many hundreds of pig stomachs were processed in the laboratory each week. The final success came on Christmas day 1962, when gastrin was purified as two distinct peptides. The structure of the resulting material was determined by George Kenner and his group in the chemistry department of the University of Liverpool: the two peptides were shown to possess seventeen amino-acid residues and to differ in the presence or absence of a sulphate ester on a solitary tyrosine. In the next few years Gregory and Tracy defined the spectrum of biological activities of the gastrins and, together with Kenner and Jack Morley, made the then surprising discovery that just four of the seventeen amino acids were necessary and sufficient to stimulate acid secretion. Gregory and Tracy recognized that the increased acid secretion and intractable peptic ulceration that was associated with the human condition known as the Zollinger-Ellison syndrome might be due to over-production of gastrin in the pancreatic tumours found in such patients. The hypothesis was convincingly verified with the subsequent chemical characterization of gastrin from these tumours, providing an early and clear indication of the importance of molecular physiology for clinical gastroenterology. As well as many papers for learned journals, Gregory wrote *Secretory Mechanisms of the Gastro-Intestinal Tract* (1962).

Gregory was a popular and influential teacher, and an effective and respected scientific adviser (member of the Medical Research Council, 1967–71; vice-president of the Royal Society, 1971–3). But these activities were secondary to his lifelong enthusiasm for the practice of research at the laboratory bench, where he executed experimental manoeuvres with panache and self-evident skill. He carried his distinction lightly, and had a well-developed sense of humour. Physically, he was wiry and energetic; he had been a University of London boxing champion at featherweight, and remained very active until he developed carcinoma of the oesophagus, which led to his death at his home, Ashburnham, 7 Knowsley Road, Cressington Park, Liverpool, on 5 September 1990. He was cremated at Liverpool crematorium on 12 September. Gregory received many academic distinctions and was elected FRS (1965), appointed CBE (1971), and awarded a royal medal of the Royal Society (1978). GRAHAM J. DOCKRAY

Sources personal knowledge (2004) · private information (2004) · M. I. Grossman, 'Presentation of the first Beaumont prize', *Gastroenterology*, 71 (1976) · *WWW* · m. cert. · b. cert.
Archives SOUND priv. coll.
Likenesses photograph, 1974, repro. in *Journal of Physiology*, 241 (1974), frontispiece
Wealth at death £6506: probate, 1991, *CGPLA Eng. & Wales*

Gregory, William (d. 1467), chronicler, was the son of Roger Gregory of Mildenhall, Suffolk. William married three times—to Johanne, Julian, and Johanne—and had two daughters, one of whom, Margaret, married John Croke, alderman and skinner. Gregory himself trained in London as a skinner, and his main interest was in the preparation and sale of furs. He sold ermine, marten, and squirrel furs to the royal household, and even as an old man had men and apprentices in his service. He probably served as master of the Skinners' Company, since he was active on the company's business as early as 1427, and left bequests to both fraternities and to the company's priest in his will.

Gregory lived in the parish of St Mary Aldermary, and was alderman of Cordwainer ward from October 1435 to March 1461, sheriff in 1436–7, and mayor in 1451–2. During his mayoralty he attempted to check the growth of bureaucracy in the city by restricting the number of officials sheriffs could maintain.

John Stow and his successors attributed the foundation of a chantry in the church of St Anne and St Agnes, Aldersgate, set up under the will of William Gregory senior (enrolled 5 October 1467), to the mayor, and consequently a plate was put up there in 1840. Another William Gregory, 'myddell', citizen and skinner (d. 1461), was also active at this time and there may have been some kinship between the various Gregorys.

A single reference, to a papal indulgence issued in 1455, associates Gregory personally with the chronicle attributed to him but the extent of his authorship is uncertain. The chronicle, which covers the period 1189–1470, begins with an often abbreviated account of the years up to 1439–40, which has much in common with other fifteenth-century London chronicles. Gregory very probably compiled that part dealing with the years 1440–52, a brief but independent account which contributes little of importance except for the detailed account of Cade's revolt of 1450. The writer clearly witnessed such stirring events as the battle for control of London Bridge, when for two days 'they were fighting upon London Bridge, and many a man was slain and cast in Thames, harness, body and all' (*Historical Collections*, 193). Nothing is known of the writer who acquired the manuscript and continued the narrative until 1469–70, some years after Gregory's death. This is in fact the more interesting and lively section of the chronicle, based on personal knowledge. Recent research (McLaren, *London Chronicles*) does not support the assumption that Gregory was the author.

William Gregory the alderman died in January 1467 in the parish of St Mary Aldermary and was buried in that church. Probate was granted by the prerogative court of Canterbury on 23 January 1467 for the will dealing with his moveables, which is dated 6 November 1465; parts of his will dealing with London properties which he held or which had been entrusted to him were enrolled before the court of husting on 2 March 1467, 3 December 1470, 9 March 1473, and 12 December 1474. ELSPETH VEALE

Sources 'William Gregory's chronicle of London', *The historical collections of a citizen of London in the fifteenth century*, ed. J. Gairdner, CS, new ser., 17 (1876), 55–239 · A. H. Thomas and I. D. Thornley, eds., *The great chronicle of London* (1938) · E. M. Veale, *The English fur trade in the later middle ages* (1966) · exchequer, king's remembrancer, accounts various, PRO, E 101/409/2, 6, 12 · Calendar of records, 1965, The Worshipful Company of Skinners, London · Roll of the Fraternity of Corpus Christi, The Worshipful Company of Skinners, London · Roll of the Fraternity of Our Lady's Assumption, The Worshipful Company of Skinners, London · R. R. Sharpe, ed., *Calendar of letter-books preserved in the archives of the corporation of the City of London*, [12 vols.] (1899–1912), vol. K · R. R. Sharpe, ed., *Calendar of wills proved and enrolled in the court of husting, London, AD 1258– AD 1688*, 2 vols. (1889–90) · W. McMurray, ed., *Records of two city parishes* (1925) · A. B. Beaven, ed., *The aldermen of the City of London, temp. Henry III–[1912]*, 2 vols. (1908–13) · A. Gransden, *Historical writing in England*, 2 (1982) · C. L. Kingsford, *English historical literature in the fifteenth century* (1913), 96–8 · M.-R. McLaren, 'The textual transmission of the London chronicles', *English Manuscript Studies, 1100–1700*, 3 (1992), 39–72 · M.-R. McLaren, *The London chronicles of the fifteenth century: a revolution in English writing* (2002)
Wealth at death probably wealthy; made extensive charitable bequests (twenty-one institutions noted) although some later thoughts led him to reduce the £10 to be given to one of the Skinners' Company's fraternities to his 'six best silver dishes': Gairdner, *Historical collections*

Gregory, William (fl. 1495–1537), prior of Albi and religious author, was Scottish by birth; he is first recorded in 1495 as a bachelor of arts in Paris, lodging at the Collège de Montaigu, where his patron was Queen Marie, wife of Louis XII and sister of Henry VIII. In July 1499 he joined a group of students from the college who, in response to an appeal from Louis d'Amboise, bishop of Albi, volunteered to be the nucleus of a reformed Carmelite community there. After living for a month in the episcopal palace, being instructed in the religious life, they were clothed in the habit on 10 August. On the following day, with the connivance of the Carmelite provincial, the bishop entertained the local community to a dinner in his palace; meanwhile, the student group was installed in the friary, and the local community, on its return, was confronted with the choice of either joining the reform or transferring elsewhere.

Gregory was ordained in 1501 and celebrated his first mass on 25 March. Some time later he was appointed prior of Melun, south of Paris, the second community to join the reform. He then returned to Paris to continue his studies, and received his doctorate on 19 December 1516. He was elected vicar-general of the expanding congregation of Albi in 1518 and held office until May 1520. On 20 February 1519 Gregory signed an agreement on behalf of the congregation with the prior-general to resolve some difficulties which had arisen over the direction of the Carmelite house of studies in Paris, which had been entrusted to the congregation. It is claimed that Gregory was, at times, confessor to François I. In 1520 Gregory was appointed prior of Toulouse, which had just accepted the reform. In 1527 John Bale spent some weeks there, during a tour of France, and he describes Gregory as: 'very learned, a brilliant scholar and writer, perceptive in argument and a famed preacher, whose life and behaviour were exemplary, a humble and kind man but of mediocre stature' (BL, Harley MS 3838, fol. 246). Apparently, Gregory assured Bale of a doctorate from Toulouse University if he would remain for a year. Gregory was re-elected vicar-general in 1531 and held office until May 1534, when he was appointed prior in Albi. The last record is of his presiding at a chapter there in 1537.

Bale lists the titles of sixteen lost works written by Gregory. One work, *Funerale et processionale*, according to the Carmelite rite, was printed in Toulouse in 1518. Others included *De duplici potestate*, which was dedicated to Louis d'Amboise, an address to a Franciscan provincial chapter, and a theological vocabulary. RICHARD COPSEY

Sources L. van Wijmen, *La congregation d'Albi, 1499–1602* (1971), 25–6, 73 n, 82 n, 87 n, 88 n, 92, 109, 111, 113, 115, 207, 214 · BL, Harleian MS 1819, fols. 117v, 123v [Bale's notebook of his visit to France] · BL, Harleian MS 3838, fols. 246–246v [Bale's 'Viri preclari'] · Bale, *Cat.*, 2.221–2 · B. Zimmerman, ed., *Monumenta historica Carmelitana* (1907), 418 · I. Johnson, 'Scots Carmelites and the French reform', *Innes Review*, 5 (1954), 141–3 · Tanner, *Bibl. Brit.-Hib.*, 343

Gregory, William (d. 1663), flautist, was appointed as flautist at the English court by warrant of 20 February 1626, following the death of James Harden; he was paid from Christmas 1625. Gregory served in the wind group until it was disbanded in 1642. He is named among members of the Corporation of Musick of Westminster in their charter of 15 July 1635. At the Restoration he was restored to his place and from Christmas 1661 was one of four wind players given responsibility for training boys 'especially on the flutes and cornetts'. He died on 6 September 1663

William Gregory (d. 1663), by unknown artist

and was buried 'a poore man' at St Martin-in-the-Fields on 12 September; he left a widow, Mary.

Gregory's son **Henry Gregory** (fl. 1660–1692), flautist, was appointed with his father and two other wind players (John Mason and Thomas Mell) by warrant of 3 February 1662 to train boys on flutes and cornets; eventually he was the sole survivor in the post. By the time of the Restoration his father was old, and a warrant of 13 March 1662 appointed Henry as assistant to him without fee; he gained the full place on 10 September 1663. Gregory was active in the Corporation of Musick of Westminster, being chosen as assistant on 23 July 1674 and serving as warden in 1675–6 and 1678–9. His last appearance at court was at the coronation of James II on 23 April 1685, but evidently he lived on, for payments of arrears to him are recorded until 23 February 1692.

William Gregory (bap. 1624?, d. 1691), violist and composer, may have been a son or near relation of William Gregory (d. 1663): a William, son of William Gregory, was baptized at St Margaret's, Westminster, in December 1624. He is first noted among teachers of 'Voyce or Viole' in John Playford's *A Musicall Banquet* (1651), and he became one of Oliver Cromwell's musicians about 1654. He was 'eminently skilful at the Lyra Viole', taught Susanna Perwich of Hackney (d. 3 July 1661), and was doubtless the Mr Gregory, 'an able and sober man', whom Pepys appointed to teach his wife on the viol on 20 November 1666. Gregory was appointed as violist at court in 1660 and from 1662 also played the bass viol in the Chapel Royal. He succeeded his colleague Thomas Bates in the place of instructor to the royal children at midsummer 1679, but was not reappointed after the death of Charles II in 1685.

Gregory's compositions are slight, though they show some imagination in expression and design; many of the fourteen extant airs for solo lyra viol, fourteen suites in two and three parts, and seventeen songs were published by John Playford; two keyboard suites are in Matthew Locke's *Melothesia* (1673). Hawkins also mentions two anthems: 'Out of the deep' and 'O Lord, thou hast cast us out', which are in partbooks at York Minster. Gregory was buried at St Clement Danes on 15 January 1691.

A Thomas Gregory, composer of eighty-one extant works for lyra viol, was active by the 1630s, but is not known to be related to William. Nor is Prince Gregory, gentleman of the Chapel Royal (1740–55), who was perhaps the son of Richard and Sarah baptized at St Martin-in-the-Fields on 10 November 1695.

ANDREW ASHBEE

Sources J. Batchiler, *The virgin's pattern* (1661) · J. Hawkins, *A general history of the science and practice of music*, new edn, 3 vols. (1853) · R. Poole, 'The Oxford music school and the collection of portraits formerly preserved there', *Musical Antiquary*, 4 (1912–13), 143–59 · C. L. Day and E. B. Murrie, *English song-books, 1651–1702: a bibliography with a first-line index of songs* (1940) · J. Riley, 'The identity of William Gregory', *Music and Letters*, 48 (1967), 236–46 · Pepys, *Diary*, vol. 7 · I. Spink, *English song: Dowland to Purcell* (1974) · A. Ashbee, ed., *Records of English court music*, 1 (1986) · A. Ashbee, ed., *Records of English court music*, 2 (1987) · A. Ashbee, ed., *Records of English court music*, 3 (1988) · A. Ashbee, ed., *Records of English court music*, 5 (1991) · A. Ashbee, ed., *Records of English court music*, 8 (1995) · G. Dodd, *Thematic index of music for viols* (1980–) · A. Ashbee and D. Lasocki, eds., *A biographical dictionary of English court musicians, 1485–1714*, 2 vols. (1998) · will, PRO, PROB 11/312, sig. 114 · will of William Gregory, d. 1691, PRO, PROB 11/403, sig. 24
Likenesses oils, U. Oxf., faculty of music [*see illus.*]
Wealth at death £80—specified bequests; William Gregory: will, PRO, PROB 11/403, sig. 24

Gregory, William (*bap.* 1624?, *d.* 1691). *See under* Gregory, William (*d.* 1663).

Gregory, Sir William (1625–1696), judge and speaker of the House of Commons, the second but eldest surviving son of Robert Gregory (*d.* 1643) and his wife, Anne, daughter of John Harvey of Broadestone, Gloucestershire, was born at his father's vicarage, possibly called Cattys Court, Fownhope, near Hereford, on 1 March 1625. His father, vicar of Fownhope and rector of Sutton St Nicholas, also in Herefordshire, descended from an ancient Warwickshire gentry family of which a branch had settled at Fownhope since the sixteenth century. Gregory was educated at Hereford Cathedral school and in 1640 was admitted to Gray's Inn. Although he matriculated at All Souls College, Oxford, on 9 April 1644, he may have had to earn a living earlier than he had expected, as in a later account he noted how his father's death in 1643 had left him impoverished. He served as clerk to the Herefordshire county committee in 1644 and was called to the bar about 1650 and established as a barrister at Gray's Inn. Gregory built an extensive practice and was steward for several manor courts in Herefordshire and agent for the marchioness of Hertford and for the Scudamores of Ballingham and Holme Lacy. His stewardship of Lady Hertford's estates helped fund his future purchases in Herefordshire. In 1653 he married Katharine (*d.* 1700), daughter and heir of James Smith of Tillington and widow first of John Carpenter of The Homme, Dilwyn, also in Herefordshire, and second of Humphrey Tomkyns, merchant, of London. During the interregnum Gregory assisted both former royalists and parliamentarians. In 1653 he became deputy steward for Hereford city and in 1656 he protested when the radical sheriff ignored voices for Presbyterian candidates in the borough's election.

By 1660 Gregory was among Herefordshire's ruling gentry. He was a stalwart JP, being placed on the county commissions of 1660, 1662, and 1680, and he was active virtually continuously at quarter sessions between 1665 and 1679. He was acting *custos rotulorum* on the Herefordshire bench in 1671, 1678, and 1679. He purchased further property at Fownhope in 1660 and in 1677 he acquired the manor and estate of How Caple as well as lands in Woolhope, Fownhope, and Sellershope. He purchased Fownhope manor outright in 1681. Gregory moved his country seat to How Caple, although he resided mainly in London.

Gregory's legal stature grew during the 1670s. He was a bencher by 1673 and in 1675 he was elected autumn reader at Gray's Inn. He also had an extensive practice in the Oxford circuit. In 1672 he became recorder at Gloucester and in 1677 he received the dignity of the coif and became serjeant-at-law. Gregory regularly trimmed his politics, working both with presbyterians and with arch-Anglicans. He nevertheless remained strongly antipapist throughout his career. He made plans to seek a seat in parliament as a country candidate when the member for Weobley died at the end of December 1674. By March 1675 he planned to stand against court candidate Sir Thomas Williams. Gregory, however, feared 'nothing so much as foul play from the sheriff, who appears very much my Sir Thomas Williams his friend' (Longleat, Thynne MS 20, fol. 225). Indeed on 22 April 1675 the sheriff secured Sir Thomas's return after allowing dubious votes. By the end of the year a future tory fumed how the opposition 'close designing party' had 'cantoned out' county and borough seats, including a Hereford city seat for Gregory (*CSP dom.*, 1675–6, 460–61). But Gregory did not give up on Weobley. In February 1678 the Commons accepted his petition (U. Nott. L., Pw2 Hy 196) and declared Williams's election void. Gregory waged a vigorous by-election campaign by proxy, sending letters to Weobley and using his son to canvass nearby gentry; no opposition appeared on election day. Although parliament met for only two more brief sessions that year Gregory was an active member, serving on thirty committees and making five speeches. He was especially active in regard to the Popish Plot and was fearful of the presence of Roman Catholic officers in the army.

Gregory was re-elected at Weobley to the first Exclusion Parliament. During wrangling between king and Commons over the former exercising veto on choice of speaker, Lord Russell proposed Gregory. On 17 March 1679 Gregory was led to the chair. Although he was a quiet and unforceful speaker of the house, parliament did pass the

Habeas Corpus Act during his tenure. Roger North indicated that Gregory worked closely with the court party by claiming that, as speaker, Gregory once carried a bill up to the Lords upon motion before the opposition could say anything and before it was brought to a question. However, Gregory was seeking to expedite the disbandment of the army rather than help the court. Although authorities differ on the assessment of Gregory's term as Speaker—the *Dictionary of National Biography* echoes Manning's boilerplate that he was 'firm, temperate, and impartial' whereas Knights asserts that Gregory was 'inept in controlling the House' (Knights, 123)—such assessments are based on his brief two-month tenure during which period increasing political polarity caused Gregory's moderate position to be marginalized. On the day parliament was dissolved, 14 July 1679, Gregory was elevated to fill a vacancy on the judicial bench as a baron of the exchequer and was knighted within a week. In 1681 he and Sir William Dolben judged the high-treason trial of Sir Miles Stapleton (they left the case fairly to the jury, who acquitted). Gregory, although no longer eligible for the Commons, remained important in Herefordshire politics.

Although Gregory had been an anti-court candidate during the 1670s, and although Shaftesbury marked him 'doubly worthy' (1678) or 'worthy' (1679) on his lists (HoP, *Commons, 1660–90*), Gregory did not vote on the first Exclusion Bill, and in 1682 he claimed to support those 'entirely well principled towards the government both of Church and State' (Longleat, Thynne MS 21, fol. 366). He may have assisted in the surrender of Hereford's charter. In February 1682 Gregory and two other local squires went to Whitehall to present to the king 'the Humble Address of Hereford', which rejected Shaftesbury's 'Rebellious Association' (*London Gazette*, 13–16 Feb 1682). Whigs objected, claiming that Gregory's position as judge should place him above such partisan addresses. It was rumoured that he attended 'for fear he should be remov'd, of which there has been a strong report' (Luttrell, 1.165–6). Gregory remained a baron for four more years, though he was replaced as deputy steward of Hereford in 1682. On 10 February 1686 he was removed from the exchequer bench for giving opinion against James II's dispensing power. The next year the king deprived him of the recordership at Gloucester.

On the eve of the revolution of 1688 Gregory prepared to re-enter politics. In October 1688 Robert Harley thought Paul Foley and Gregory would be returned at Hereford City, notwithstanding 'the people have a particular "pique" against' the latter, doubtless for his action in the surrender of their charter (Rowlands, 49). In December he subscribed £30 for the prince of Orange. The next month Gregory was returned to the convention for Hereford, but vacated the seat when elected as a judge of the common pleas in April. Two months later, on 8 May 1689, he was elevated to become judge of the king's bench, which position he retained until his death. In June the Commons investigated Gregory, along with other Stuart judges. Gregory's only recorded comment was that the king had

approached him with a paper and Gregory had spoken against the dispensing power.

Gregory suffered with stone at least from late 1694. During this period he refurbished the parish church at How Caple. Gregory was predeceased by his two children, a daughter who died as an infant and James (1654–1691), a bencher of Gray's Inn. Gregory himself died in London on 28 May 1696. He was survived by his wife, Katharine, his daughter-in-law, Elizabeth (d. 1716), and five grandchildren. Gregory was buried at How Caple church, where a monument is inscribed to his memory and to which he left funds to finish the chancel and tower.

NEWTON E. KEY

Sources HoP, *Commons, 1660–90* · Foss, *Judges* · J. A. Manning, *The lives of the speakers of the House of Commons*, 2nd edn (1851) · J. Duncumb and others, *Collections towards the history and antiquities of the county of Hereford*, 3 (1882) · T. Rowlands, '"As black as Hell to my own people": James II's reputation in Herefordshire', *Midland History*, 14 (1989), 43–52 · J. Hillaby, 'The parliamentary borough of Weobley, 1628–1708', *Transactions of the Woolhope Naturalists' Field Club*, 39 (1967–9), 104–51 · N. Luttrell, *A brief historical relation of state affairs from September 1678 to April 1714*, 1 (1857); repr. (1969) · BL, Add. MS 70114 · *The manuscripts of his grace the duke of Portland*, 10 vols., HMC, 29 (1891–1931), vol. 3 · Bodl. Oxf., MS Tanner 147 · Herefordshire, Pevsner (1963) · Herefs. RO, Q/SO/1; Q/SO/2 · Herefs. RO, L38/22 · *An inventory of the historical monuments in Herefordshire*, Royal Commission on Historical Monuments (England), 2 (1932) · *A letter from a person of quality to his friend, about abhorrers and addressors, &c.* (1682) · Cobbett, *Parl. hist.*, vol. 5, 14 June 1689 · M. Knights, *Politics and opinion in crisis, 1678–1681* (1994) · Longleat House, Wiltshire, Thynne MS 20, fol. 225 · U. Nott. L., Pw2 Hy 196

Archives Longleat House, Wiltshire, Thynne MSS, 20, fols. 217–386; 21, fol. 366; 22, fol. 353 · PRO, SP 29/316, nos. 26–II

Likenesses oils, Palace of Westminster, London

Gregory, William (1762–1840), politician, was the youngest of three sons of Robert *Gregory (1729?–1810), an East India merchant of Anglo-Irish birth, and his wife, Maria Nimmo. William was born in India in February 1762, but went to Britain in 1766 and was educated at Harrow School (c.1775) and Trinity College, Cambridge, where he obtained a BA in 1783 and an MA in 1787. On 16 May 1781 he was admitted as a student at the Inner Temple; he was called to the bar in 1788 but never practised. He married in 1789 Lady Anne Trench (d. 1833), daughter of the first earl of Clancarty; they had one daughter, Anne, and two sons, Robert (d. 1847), father of Sir William Henry Gregory, and William, rector of Fiddown. He inherited his father's estate at Coole Park, co. Galway, in 1810.

Gregory sat in the Irish parliament (1798–1800) as MP for Portarlington (a borough under the influence of the Trench family of co. Galway) and vigorously supported the Act of Union. He served as a captain of militia in co. Galway in 1798 and as high sheriff of that county the following year. In 1799–1806 he was a commissioner examining the claims of loyalists who had suffered during the 1798 rebellion. In 1800 he was made secretary to the Irish board of inland navigation, and, having acquired a reputation as an able administrator, was promoted to the revenue commission in 1810. Gregory was appointed in October 1812 civil under-secretary to the lord lieutenant of Ireland, with a salary of £2500 and a residence in Phoenix Park, of which he held the additional post of ranger. In 1819 the offices of civil and military under-secretary were merged, with Gregory holding the united position until 1830. As under-secretary he enjoyed great authority as the confidential adviser and close friend of successive viceroys and chief secretaries, and soon became the linchpin of the machine of Irish government. He was credited by O'Connell and other hostile critics with being the real ruler of Ireland. Gregory was intimate with Robert Peel during his chief secretaryship (1812–18) and remained his chief adviser on Irish affairs until Peel's conversion on the question of Catholic emancipation. Despite his disagreements with the pro-Catholic viceroy, Lord Wellesley, after 1821, Gregory's position remained secure until the formation of Canning's ministry in 1827. The new viceroy, Lord Anglesey, sought and obtained Gregory's resignation, but the death of Canning and the collapse of the short-lived Goderich ministry ensured Gregory's survival. He was finally removed from office in December 1830 following the accession of Lord Grey's reforming government and the return to Ireland of Lord Anglesey. Gregory died at his residence in Phoenix Park, Dublin, on 13 April 1840. His brief obituary in the *Gentleman's Magazine* coldly noticed that 'a pension of £445 devolves to the civil list by his death' (*GM*, 668).

Like his father William Gregory was 'originally a man of liberal opinions' (Jenkins, *Sir William Gregory*, 11), and he retained an interest in promoting the social welfare of the Irish population despite his preference for harsh repression of social unrest and political opposition. His intense political Conservatism as under-secretary owed much to his connection with the Trench family of co. Galway, who were both leading tories and proponents of the evangelical campaign in Ireland known as the Second Reformation (Archbishop Trench of Tuam was Gregory's brother-in-law). Gregory's own evangelicalism was well known; he was a member of the Philanthropic Society and believed that the advance of protestant proselytism would resolve many of the problems of the country. Like many of his generation he was deeply alarmed by the 1798 rebellion and resolved thereafter to oppose any further concessions to Catholic agitation, which he was convinced sought the destruction of the established church, the protestant ascendancy, and eventually the union itself. He expressed both despair and a sense of personal betrayal when Peel and Wellington finally acceded to Catholic emancipation in 1829.

Opinions were polarized over Gregory's character. To O'Connell he was 'the very demon of Orangeism at the Castle' (*Correspondence of Daniel O'Connell*, 4.177–8) while Anglesey thought him an '*Arch* Jobber. A man who has the Press at his command—a determined intriguer. False as hell. A violent Anti-Catholic—a furious Tory—and quite ready to betray the secrets of any one whose confidence he obtains' (Anglesey to William Lamb, 17 Sept 1827, Anglesey MSS). However, his devoted grandson, William Henry *Gregory, claimed that 'few people have been more

popular in Ireland during so long a period of great power, and though he was a tory of the tories, he was not disliked by those who differed with him in politics' (*Sir William Gregory*, ed. Gregory, 9). A selection from his correspondence was edited by his grandson's widow, Augusta, Lady Gregory, for publication as *Mr Gregory's Letter-Box* (1898).

PETER GRAY

Sources B. Jenkins, *Sir William Gregory of Coole* (1986) · *Mr Gregory's letter-box, 1813–30*, ed. I. A. Gregory (1898) · *Sir William Gregory*, ed. I. A. Gregory (1894) · B. Jenkins, *Era of emancipation: British government of Ireland, 1812–1830* (1988) · J. Brooke, 'Gregory, Robert', HoP, *Commons* · *GM*, 2nd ser., 13 (1840), 668 · *DNB* · *The correspondence of Daniel O'Connell*, ed. M. R. O'Connell, 4, IMC (1977) · PRO NIre., Anglesey MSS
Archives Emory University, Atlanta, Georgia, Robert W. Woodruff Library | BL, letters to Sir Robert Peel, Add. MSS 40195–40205, 40334, *passim* · NL Ire., Richmond MSS · PRO NIre., corresp. with second Earl Talbot · Staffs. RO, corresp. with second Earl Talbot, D240/J/5 · Surrey HC, letters to Henry Goulburn, acc. 319
Likenesses bust, repro. in Gregory, ed., *Mr Gregory's letter-box*

Gregory, William (1803–1858), chemist and psychic investigator, was born at St Andrew's Square, Edinburgh, on 25 December 1803, the fourth son of James *Gregory (1753–1821), professor of medicine in the University of Edinburgh, and his second wife, Miss McLeod. He was descended from a long line of 'academic Gregories'. After a medical education he graduated at Edinburgh in 1828, but he had already shown a strong bent towards pharmaceutical and organic chemistry, and he soon made these areas his speciality. In 1831 he devised a procedure for making pure morphine from opium ('Gregory's salt'), as a result of which Edinburgh became an important centre for the commercial preparation and sale of alkaloid drugs. After further studies on the continent, including a semester with Justus Liebig at the University of Giessen in 1835, he established himself as an extramural lecturer on chemistry at Edinburgh, where he published methods for preparing nitrogen sulphide and potassium permanganate. After further short spells as chemistry lecturer at Anderson's University, Glasgow, in 1837, and at the Dublin medical school in 1838, in 1839 he was appointed professor of medicine and chemistry at King's College, Aberdeen. In 1842, after further studies with Liebig on uric acid derivatives the previous year, he appealed to the British government to fund new chemical laboratories for chemical teaching and research. The appeal was a factor in the establishment of the Royal College of Chemistry in London in 1845. In 1844 he was elected to the chair of chemistry at Edinburgh in succession to his former teacher, Thomas Charles Hope. There, in 1849, he developed a valuable method for purifying chloroform, which had been recently introduced as an anaesthetic.

Gregory was a successful expository lecturer and accomplished textbook writer, especially on the subject of organic chemistry. He published three chemistry textbooks and collaborated with Liebig on an extensive revision of Edward Turner's *Elements of Chemistry* in 1842. He served on the council of the London Chemical Society

(1843–6). Never robust, and dogged by weakness occasioned by an attack of rheumatic fever in 1826, in the 1850s he virtually abandoned chemistry for the more sedentary subject of microscopy. He published a number of excellent descriptive papers on diatoms.

In July 1839 Gregory married Lisett Barbara Scott, who was part-German and had been born at Bensdorff near Koblenz. They named their only son, James Liebig, in honour of Gregory's revered teacher. Gregory's skills in French and German enabled him to keep abreast of continental chemical developments. As a personal friend of Liebig's, Gregory did much to introduce his researches on agriculture, physiology, and nutrition to British audiences by translating, editing, and extolling his work. He translated seven of Liebig's books into English and conducted a regular correspondence with him in German. More controversially, in the 1840s, Gregory became interested in George Combe's system of phrenology and its hypnotic variant, phreno-magnetism, upon which he published in *The Zoist* and in a treatise on mesmerism in 1851. The latter volume proved popular and went through three editions. These investigations at the margins of rational science led Gregory to study the curious work of Karl Reichenbach, a Viennese industrial chemist, who was investigating the ability of 'sensitive' individuals to detect electricity, magnetism, heat, light, and crystals under conditions in which normally they could not be experienced. Gregory accepted Reichenbach's findings and their interpretation in terms of an all-pervading 'odylic' force which he also saw as an explanation of the mesmeric trance. By translating Reichenbach's works in 1850, Gregory incurred ridicule among many of his academic colleagues for what they perceived as his credulous beliefs in animal magnetism, clairvoyance, telepathy, and spiritualism.

Gregory died in Princes Street, Edinburgh, on 24 April 1858 and was buried in the family vault in Canongate churchyard following a civic funeral. His widow, known as Mrs Makdougal Gregory, became active in spiritualist circles, holding fashionable séances at her Mayfair home during the 1870s. She was described as the 'high priestess of spiritualism' (Oppenheim, 75). W. H. BROCK

Sources *Quarterly Journal of the Chemical Society*, 12 (1860), 172–5 · G. C. Green, 'William Gregory', *Nature*, 157 (1946), 465–9 · D. P. Jones, 'Gregory, William', *DSB* · W. H. Brock and S. Stark, 'Gregory and the British Association', *Ambix*, 37 (1990), 134–46 · W. Gregory, *Letter to the right honourable George, earl of Aberdeen … on the state of the schools of chemistry in the United Kingdom* (1842) · W. Gregory, *Letters … on animal magnetism* (1851) · A. G. Stewart, *The academic Gregories* (1901) · A. Findlay, *The teaching of chemistry in the universities of Aberdeen* (1935) · J. Oppenheim, *The other world: spiritualism and psychical research in England, 1850–1914* (1985) · Boase, *Mod. Eng. biog.* · *DNB* · private information (2004) · NA Scot., SC 70/1/99/92–97

Archives NHM, slides and notebooks · NL Scot., corresp. mainly with George Combe · Staatsbibliothek, Munich, Liebigiana, corresp. with Liebig · U. Newcastle, Robinson L., letters to Sir Walter Trevelyan

Likenesses C. Cook, stipple and line print, NPG · F. Schenck, lithograph (after W. Stewart), NPG · engraving, repro. in J. S. Muspratt, *Chemistry, theoretical, practical and analytical as applied and relating to the arts and manufactures*, 12 vols. (1853–61) · portrait, repro. in J. D. Comrie, *History of Scottish medicine*, 2 (1932), 624

Wealth at death £789 9s. 11d.: probate, 17 Nov 1858, NA Scot., SC 70/1/99/92–7

Gregory, Sir William Henry (1816–1892), politician and colonial governor, was the son of Robert Gregory of Coole Park, co. Galway, and Elizabeth O'Hara of Raheen in the same county. He was born on 13 July 1816 at the under-secretary's lodge, Phoenix Park, Dublin, the residence of his grandfather William *Gregory.

Gregory was educated first (1827–30) at Mr Ward's school at Iver, Buckinghamshire, and afterwards at Harrow School, which he entered in 1831 under Charles Thomas Longley, who considered him the cleverest boy he ever taught. Gregory was head of the school before leaving for Oxford. At Harrow he began a lifelong friendship with Anthony Trollope, who was later a frequent visitor in Ireland. Gregory matriculated at Christ Church on 6 June 1835, but was less successful there, running second for the Craven scholarship in two successive years. Deeply disappointed by this failure, and increasingly distracted by an interest in horse-racing, he left Oxford without a degree. In 1840 Gregory travelled abroad with his parents for some time. He had up to this time taken no serious interest in politics; but in January 1842 he was induced to stand at a by-election as the Conservative candidate for Dublin, and was returned against the whig-Liberal Viscount Morpeth. The election cost £9000, of which the chief item was a 'gratification for 1500 freemen at £3 a head'. The gross electoral irregularities surrounding this contest became a spur for the passage of the Irish Polling Places Act of 1846. Gregory's election was dependent on the support of the popular ultra-protestant party in Dublin led by the charismatic Revd Tresham Gregg, and he therefore found it expedient to declare himself 'a firm and uncompromising supporter of our Protestant institutions both in church and state' (*Dublin Evangelical*, 14 Jan 1842). He was subsequently embarrassed by this, and by his equally firm pledge to uphold the corn laws.

Gregory was soon regarded as being among the promising young men of his day in the House of Commons. He was popular with all parties and attracted the attention and regard of men as different as Peel, Disraeli, and O'Connell, the latter in the vain hope that Gregory would become a 'conservative repealer'. It was Peel, however, who came to exercise a paramount influence over Gregory, and who weaned him away from the political and religious intolerance he had inherited from his grandfather. In his first major speech, in February 1844, Gregory followed the prime minister in combining a robust defence of limited coercion with the advocacy of practical remedial measures to allay Irish unrest. Under pressure from his Orangeist constituents, he felt obliged to oppose the Maynooth grant in 1845, but was careful not to alienate himself from Peel. In early 1846 he offered firm support to Peel's corn-law policy. Shortly before Peel's loss of office Gregory was offered the Irish lordship of the Treasury, with the conduct of Irish business in the House of Commons, in the temporary absence of Lord Lincoln, who was then chief secretary, from parliament. Gregory was persuaded by his friends, who feared the charge of unprincipled office-seeking, to refuse this offer, a decision he always deeply regretted.

After Peel's overthrow Gregory remained in nominal opposition to the ministry of Lord John Russell. His main concern in the following years was to protect the Irish landed interest from the upheavals brought about by the potato famine. He took an active part in 1847 in the discussion of the Poor Law Extension Act, designed by the Russell ministry to 'make Irish property support Irish poverty'. He was the author of the 'Gregory clause', which disentitled the possessor of more than a quarter of an acre of land, and his family, to relief. He declared in parliament on 29 March 1847 that the smallholding class was 'no longer an object of pity'. He also procured the insertion of provisions for assisting emigration. Gregory inherited his father's Galway estates in spring 1847, and soon acquired a reputation as a humane and improving landlord. However, he found it difficult to dissociate his name from the 'Gregory exterminator clause', which was widely employed by less conscientious landowners to clear their estates, and which appears to have added significantly to the total of famine mortality.

At the general election of August 1847 Gregory found that his Peelite tendencies had alienated many of his old supporters, and he failed to secure re-election. He was then nominated for county Galway, but, having insufficient support, he withdrew his candidature, as he was again obliged to do in 1852. In 1850 he was appointed high sheriff of Galway, and became active in local affairs.

Gregory's already considerably encumbered estates were pushed further into debt by his famine expenditure. His financial embarrassments were compounded by his passion for the turf, where he made heavy losses in the early 1850s. His association with a series of racing, financial, and political controversies did little to help his standing, and from 1857 he was obliged to sell more than half his estate in the encumbered estates court. After this financial breakdown Gregory finally quitted the turf, but he retained his interest in racing matters to the end of his life.

At the general election of April 1857 Gregory was returned as a Liberal-Conservative and supporter of Lord Palmerston for county Galway. He was re-elected for the same constituency at three successive general elections, and continued to represent it until 1871. His electoral success was due to his astute balancing of opposed electoral interests, including the whig Clanricarde and the tory Clancarty families (with both of which he had connections), and the local Catholic hierarchy, whom he sought to conciliate, and whose interests he advocated.

During this second period of his active political life Gregory acquired a distinguished position in the House of Commons. He became a leading spokesman for the Confederate cause during the American Civil War. Until 1865 he ranked as a Liberal-Conservative, but after the death of Lord Palmerston he formally joined the Liberal Party. On Earl Russell's accession to the premiership in 1866 he was

offered a lordship of the Admiralty, but he declined this minor position under a man he disliked. He was opposed to the wide extension of the franchise, and became associated with the so-called 'cave of Adullam' in opposition to Russell's Reform Bill of 1866.

In 1868 Gregory was disappointed when Gladstone ignored his desire to become Irish chief secretary and to introduce a programme of constructive reforms, but he subsequently supported Gladstone in his Irish church disestablishment measure and in his Land Act of 1870. Gregory held pronounced views on the subject of Irish agrarian legislation, and in 1866 introduced a measure which anticipated in some of its clauses the provisions of the later Land Acts. By 1870 political expediency had converted Gregory to the cause of 'full tenant right', and he was unhappy about the limitations of Gladstone's act.

Gregory became best known in parliament for his promotion of state funding for the arts. In 1860 he chaired a House of Commons inquiry into the British Museum, and he subsequently had much to do with the arrangement and development of the South Kensington collections. He was an ardent supporter of the opening of public museums on Sundays and took a keen interest in popularizing the study of the arts. In 1867 he was appointed by Disraeli a trustee of the National Gallery, and he took the keenest interest in the enlargement of the national collection. Shortly before his death he presented the best of his private collection to the National Gallery.

Early in 1871 Gregory was sworn of the Irish privy council, and later that year he was appointed, on the recommendation of Lord Granville, governor of Ceylon. In January 1872 he sailed for that colony, in which he remained for over five years. In this position Gregory exhibited high administrative qualities, and his tenure of the governorship was one of considerable success, and popularity. He spent more money on transport and irrigation works than any other governor, doing much to stimulate the cultivation of coffee and tea, and to improve the harbours of the island. His efforts at social reform and attempts to end the commercial monoculture of coffee were more circumspect and of limited success. He also took a great interest in the culture and antiquities of Ceylon, and established a museum at Colombo. In 1875 he received the prince of Wales in Colombo and was knighted. Increasingly bored by administrative routine, irritated by the criticisms made of him by the plantation interest, and having clashed with the Conservative colonial secretary over the privileges of the Anglican church in the colony, Gregory decided to resign in 1876. After a visit to Australia in January 1877, he returned to Ireland.

Thenceforward Gregory took no active part in public affairs, though his interest in them remained keen. As an Irish landlord he was deeply alarmed by the land war, and he vehemently criticized Gladstone's Land Act of 1881. In 1882 he had a sharp confrontation with his tenants over rent levels, and relations were subsequently strained on the Coole estate. He was strongly opposed to the home-rule movement, and in 1881 he printed privately a 'confidential letter', attacking what he took to be the separatist aims of Parnell and his followers. From 1886 Gregory considered himself a Liberal Unionist, ready to support coercion against agrarian agitation, but looking increasingly to tenant purchase as the solution to the land question.

Gregory had a strong interest in the Middle East; he visited Egypt and north Africa in 1855–6, and published an account of his travels privately in 1859. In 1882 he advocated the cause of Arabi Pasha, the Egyptian nationalist leader, in letters to *The Times*. Subsequently to his retirement from the Ceylon government he paid three visits to that island. He contributed to *The Racing Life of Lord George Bentinck* by John Kent and Francis Lawley (1892) and in 1889 he published an article on Daniel O'Connell in the *Nineteenth Century*.

Gregory was twice married: first, on 11 January 1872, to Elizabeth, daughter of Sir William Clay and widow of James Temple Bowdoin, a lady of considerable private fortune, who died in 1873; second, on 4 March 1880, to Isabella Augusta (1852–1932), youngest daughter of Dudley Persse of Roxborough, co. Galway [*see* Gregory, (Isabella) Augusta, Lady Gregory]. She survived him with one son, William Robert Gregory, and both published Gregory's posthumous autobiography and turned Coole Park into the centre of the Irish literary renaissance. After 1890 Gregory's health gradually failed, and he died at his London home, 3 St George's Place, on 6 March 1892.

C. L. FALKINER, *rev.* PETER GRAY

Sources B. Jenkins, *Sir William Gregory of Coole* (1986) · *Sir William Gregory, KCMG, formerly member of parliament and sometime governor of Ceylon: an autobiography*, ed. Lady Gregory (1894) · B. Bastiampillai, 'The administration of Sir William Gregory, governor of Ceylon 1872–7', *Ceylon Historical Journal*, 12 (1968), 1–188 · *The Times* (8 March 1892)

Archives Emory University, Atlanta, corresp. and papers · NL Ire. · priv. coll. | BL, letters to Lord Carnarvon, Add. MS 60858 · BL, corresp. with Sir Austen Layard, Add. MSS 38949–39103, *passim* · BL, letters to Lord Stanmore, Add. MS 49207 · Bodl. Oxf., letters to Lord Kimberley · NL Ire., letters to E. O'Flaherty · NYPL, Berg MSS · PRO, Colonial Office, Ceylon corresp. · W. Yorks. AS, Leeds, Clanricarde MSS

Likenesses S. Wagner, lithograph, 1844, repro. in Jenkins, *Sir William Gregory* · J. E. Boehm, statue, 1879, Museum, Colombo, Sri Lanka · Ape [C. Pellegrini], chromolithograph caricature, NPG; repro. in *VF* (30 Dec 1871) · W. Roffe, stipple (after A. Clay, Grillion's Club series), BM, NPG · Walker & Boutall, photogravure (after F. Hollyer), NPG · engraving, repro. in *ILN* (15 Jan 1876) · engraving, repro. in *ILN* (13 March 1892) · photograph, repro. in Gregory, *Autobiography*

Wealth at death £17,464 18s. 6d.: resworn probate, Nov 1894, *CGPLA Eng. & Wales* (1892) · £3431 10s. 7d.: probate, 17 Nov 1893, *CGPLA Ire.*

Gregson, Matthew (1748/9–1824), antiquary, one of thirteen children of Thomas Gregson, shipbuilder, of Liverpool, previously of Whalley, Lancashire, was baptized in St George's, Castle Street, Liverpool, on 24 August 1749. He was many years in business as an upholsterer and interior decorator in the firm of Urmson and Gregson in Castle Street and later in Preeson's Row; the firm was then known as Gregson and Bullen. When he retired in 1812 he owned an estate in Wavertree and a dozen warehouses in Liverpool, and also held the lordship of the manor of Overton in Cheshire. On 1 May 1785 he married Jane Foster

at St Helens, Lancashire. They had five children, all of whom were born between 1786 and 1792 in Liverpool. He later married Anne Rimmer (*d.* 1826) of Warrington, with whom he had two sons and several daughters.

Although of deficient education Gregson took a deep interest in literature and science, and especially devoted attention to collecting documentary and pictorial illustrations of the history of Lancashire. These he used in compiling his *Portfolio of Fragments Relative to the History and Antiquities of the County Palatine and Duchy of Lancaster*, which he brought out in 1817 in three folio parts. It contained 800 engravings, mostly by local artists, whom Gregson employed; one of these, William Hughes, was appointed engraver in wood to the prince regent on the recommendation of Gregson. The second and enlarged edition is dated 1824 and, although he lost money on the project, the third, edited and indexed by John Harland, came out in 1867. This work led to his election as a fellow of the Society of Antiquaries, and to his honorary membership of the Newcastle upon Tyne Society of Antiquaries. He was offered a knighthood by the prince regent on presenting a copy of the book, but declined the honour, to the amazement of those who felt that he was a snob of the first order. The *Portfolio of Fragments* remains a standard work of reference for local history and genealogy; the Baines family of historians, both Edward Baines (1774–1848) and his son Thomas (1806–1881), as well as Dr William Fairbairn, owed a considerable debt to Gregson's work in writing their *History of the County Palatine of Lancaster* (1824–5) and *Lancashire and Cheshire Past and Present* (1867). Gregson also wrote often on antiquarian subjects and on industrial design in the *Gentleman's Magazine*.

Gregson played an energetic part in developing the public institutions of his native town, especially the school for blind people, the Blue Coat Hospital (where he served as a treasurer), the Liverpool Library, the Royal Institution, botanic gardens, and academy of art. However, he annoyed the leading radicals in Liverpool by his support of the slave trade. He also introduced the art of lithography into Liverpool and encouraged gifted amateurs such as Rosamund White: he included her portraits of her father and grandfather in his *Fragments*.

Gregson was elected in 1801 a member of the Society of Arts, and in 1803 received the gold medal of that society 'for his very great attention to render useful the articles remaining after public fires'. He had shown that paint, varnish, and printers' ink could be produced from burnt grain and sugar (*Transactions of the Society of Arts*, 22.185).

Adorned by his large family, Gregson was a most charitable and hospitable man, a Conservative in politics, and his house at 38 St Anne's Street was ever open to his acquaintances and clients, many of whom he advised on the purchase of prints and books for their families. His home acquired the title of 'Gregson's Hotel'. He died there on 25 September 1824, aged seventy-five, after a fall from a ladder in his library. He was buried in St Nicholas's Church. A monument to his memory was afterwards placed in St John's churchyard, Liverpool.

C. W. SUTTON, *rev.* D. BEN REES

Sources J. A. Picton, *Memorials of Liverpool*, rev. edn, 2 vols. (1903) · J. R. B. Muir, *A history of Liverpool* (1907) · G. Chandler, *Liverpool* (1957) · H. A. Taylor, 'Matthew Gregson and the pursuit of taste', *Transactions of the Historic Society of Lancashire and Cheshire*, 110 (1958), 157–76 · H. C. Marillier, *The Liverpool school of painters: an account of the Liverpool Academy from 1810 to 1867, with memoirs of the principal artists* (1904) · IGI · GM, 1st ser., 94/2 (1824), 378
Archives BL, Staffordshire and Lancashire pedigrees, Add. MS 24457 · Lpool RO, corresp., notes, accounts, etc., and valuation notebook; MSS collection and printed materials (started by J. Holt) for history of Liverpool · U. Lpool, corresp. and papers relating to Liverpool Royal Institution
Likenesses W. Bigg, portrait, repro. in Taylor, 'Matthew Gregson', 158 · M. Gauci, lithograph (after W. Bigg), NPG; repro. in M. Gregson, *Portfolio of fragments, relative to the history and antiquities of the county palatine and the duchy of Lancaster*, 2nd edn (1824)
Wealth at death wealthy: Taylor, 'Matthew Gregson', 160

Gregson, Samuel (1793–1865), merchant and politician, was born on 23 July 1793 in Lancaster, the eldest of the four sons and two daughters of Samuel Gregson (1762–1846), manager of the Lancaster Canal Company, and his wife, Bella (1771–1841). He was educated at the grammar school, Lancaster, but left before 1808, and went to work in the counting-house of an unspecified enterprise in Liverpool. He later went to India where, residing in Calcutta as a 'free merchant' between 1821 and 1823, he founded the partnership of Gregson, Melville, and Knight, East India agents, which had a base in London by 1825, operating firstly from Old South-Sea-House, Old Broad Street, then by 1827 from 14 Austin Friars. The firm's designation had changed to Gregson, Melville & Co. by 1836, but following 1839 it was referred to simply as Gregson & Co.

Gregson's marriage to Ellen (d. 1857), daughter of his father's cousin, Matthew Gregson of Overton Hall, Malpas, Cheshire, on 2 March 1826, produced a daughter, Elizabeth. They were living at 11 Upper Harley Street, London, by 1837; Gregson later resided at 32 Upper Harley Street. In 1839 he was elected to a committee set up by the London East India and China Association, a political pressure group promoting China trade interests and entrusted to treat with the government. By 1847 he had become its deputy chairman and on 15 April he was able to demonstrate his technical mastery of the tea trade when examined by the select committee on commercial relations with China. By the mid-1850s he was acting as the association's chairman.

Gregson was elected as MP for Lancaster in 1847, but was unseated in early 1848 following allegations of corrupt electoral practices. He was re-elected in 1852, 1857, and 1859. His political creed as an 'advanced liberal' was reported in the *Lancaster Guardian* of 5 June 1847: 'Gentlemen, I appear before you as the friend of civil, religious and commercial freedom, and as the friend of all I see around me. My sole desire is to promote the interests of all classes.' Such sentiments were, however, not fully borne out by his future parliamentary activity. True, he was an industrious chairman of the private petitions committee in 1858–65—a thankless post—and he had dutifully registered his vote in favour of the ballot in 1853 and against

church rates in 1855. Yet he rarely deviated from his primary focus on the China trade in which Lancaster had only a partial interest. In his espousal of free trade there was a heavy underlay of self-interest. His motivation in advocating a reduction in the tea duty, achieved in the budgets of 1863 and 1865, arguably sprang more from a vision of increasing mercantile wealth than from a sense of justice towards China. He even advocated an imperial self-sufficiency based on supplies of raw materials from India in response to shortages experienced during the Crimean War. Nevertheless, Gregson's demands in support of the China trade were consistent: to hold the Chinese to their obligations under the treaties of Nanking (Nanjing) (1842) and Peking (1860) which, in concluding the first and second opium wars, had conferred commercial advantage on British merchants. After the Chinese seizure of the *Arrow* in 1856 he recommended a British diplomatic presence in Peking and in 1862 he was anxious to warn the Commons of the piratical character of the Taiping insurgents.

Outside parliament, Gregson's appointments included a directorship of the East and West India Dock Company, where he helped to found the Dock Provident Society, and the London Assurance. His political and business links were reinforced by his membership of the Reform, Oriental, and City clubs. He died from a heart attack following influenza at his home, 32 Upper Harley Street, on 8 February 1865, and was buried at Byfleet, Surrey. Lancaster had benefited from the generosity of this slightly built but senatorial figure: Christ Church was constructed and endowed in 1855–7 and in 1863 he donated public baths.

A recipient of effusive praise from both Palmerston and Gladstone, Gregson had been, for the most part, a diligent foot soldier in the cause of liberal reform, exhibiting its representative characteristics and internal contradictions. Nevertheless, against the background of the East India Company's decline and the ending of its monopoly of the China trade in 1834, Gregson was a forceful proponent of the expansion of free trade, and he did, for a period, shine as the principal spokesman of British merchants in the Far East, particularly between 1856 and 1859, when public attention was firmly fixed on the dramatic events unfolding in China.   PHILIP K. LAW

Sources *Lancaster Guardian* (1847–65) [various entries] · Hansard 3 (1852–65) · *The Post Office London directory* (1825–65) · *East-India Register and Directory* (1821–3) · *Correspondence, returns … and other papers respecting the opium war and opium trade in China*, 31 (1971) [repr. from Parl. papers (1840–85)] · *Correspondence, memorials, orders in council … respecting the Taiping rebellion in China*, 32 (1971) [repr. from Parl. papers (1852–64)] · 'Select committee on commercial relations with China', Parl. papers (1847), vol. 5, no. 654; repr. in *Report of the Select Committee on Commercial Relations with China*, 38 (1971) · C. Hibbert, *The dragon wakes: China and the West, 1793–1911* (1970) · D. Hurd, *The arrow war: an Anglo-Chinese confusion* (1967) · W. C. Costin, *Great Britain and China, 1833–1860* (1937) · J. K. Fairbank, *Trade and diplomacy on the China coast: the opening of the treaty ports, 1842–1854*, 2 vols. (1953) · *The Times* (1852–65) · A. Murray, ed., *A biographical register of the Royal Grammar School, Lancaster* (privately printed, Lancaster, c.1955) · parish register (birth), Lancaster, 23 July 1793 · parish register (baptism), Lancaster, St John, 16 Aug 1793 · *The Times* (9 Feb 1865)

Likenesses J. Bradley, photograph, 1856–9, Lancaster Public Library
Wealth at death under £250,000: PRO

Greiffenhagen, Maurice William (1862–1931), painter, was born on 15 December 1862 in London, the third and youngest son of August Greiffenhagen and his wife, Helen Cundell. The family was of Danish origin, though the artist's grandparents had left Denmark and settled in England before his father was born. After completing his general education at University College School, London, Greiffenhagen began his artistic training at the age of fourteen with visits to the British Museum to study the Elgin marbles. At sixteen he was admitted to the Royal Academy Schools where he won numerous awards, including the cartoon medal and the Armitage prize. During the early part of his career he was a prolific illustrator, and his work for magazines such as the *Illustrated London News*, the *Ladies' Pictorial*, and *Punch* established his reputation as a vivid recorder of modern life. He also produced illustrations for numerous contemporary novels, including *She* (1887) and *Montezuma's Daughter* (1894) by Rider Haggard, whose portrait he painted (exh. RA, 1921) and with whom he developed a close personal friendship.

In 1906 Greiffenhagen was invited by Francis H. Newbery, the headmaster of Glasgow School of Art, to become head of the life school, a post he held until 1929. During this period he maintained his residence in London, spending six months of each year in Glasgow. In addition to teaching, his chief output as a creative artist was in subject pictures and portraits in oils, which he executed in a robust, colourful style, with vigorous brushwork similar to the contemporary work of the Scottish colourists. His most distinctive achievement, however, was in the field of allegorical mural painting, for which he developed a more decorative, linear idiom reminiscent of the Celtic revival work of John Duncan and Phoebe Traquair. He produced ambitious, multi-panel interior schemes for Langside Library and the café at Pettigrew and Stephens, in Glasgow, and contributed historical panels for the British exhibition pavilions at Paris and Dunedin (1925) and Antwerp (1930). He also worked for various transport companies, providing murals for ocean liners such as SS *Empress of Britain*, and designing the poster 'Carlisle—the gateway to Scotland' for the London, Midland, and Scottish Railway. A frequent exhibitor at the Royal Academy since 1884, he was elected an associate in 1916 and Royal Academician in 1922. He also exhibited regularly at the Glasgow (later Royal Glasgow) Institute of the Fine Arts as well as at many major international art exhibitions in cities such as Munich, Venice, and Pittsburgh. He was a founder member of the New English Art Club, and received the honorary degree of LLD from Glasgow University in 1926.

A sociable and much liked man, Greiffenhagen married Beatrice Mary, daughter of John Latham, in 1889; they had two sons, the elder of whom was killed in naval service in the First World War. Though apparently in excellent health, Greiffenhagen died suddenly of angina pectoris on 26 December 1931 in London; he was survived by his wife. In 1933 the Royal Academy celebrated his achievement by the inclusion of fifty-six of his paintings in the winter exhibition. Examples of his work are to be found in the Walker Art Gallery, Liverpool (including his masterpiece of 1891, *The Idyll*), the Tate collection, and many art galleries and museums throughout the world.

JAMES LAVER, *rev.* RAY MCKENZIE

Sources *Memorial exhibition: works by the late Maurice Greiffenhagen* (1935) [exhibition catalogue, Glasgow School of Art, 1935] · *Classic panels by Maurice Greiffenhagen* (*c.*1925) [Pettigrew and Stephens Ltd] · *Maurice Greiffenhagen* (1990) [exhibition catalogue, Bourne Fine Art, London, 1990] · *The Times* (28 Dec 1931) · Thieme & Becker, *Allgemeines Lexikon* · private information (1949) · CGPLA Eng. & Wales (1932)
Likenesses M. Greiffenhagen, self-portrait, oils, 1925; formerly in family possession, 1949 · M. Greiffenhagen, self-portrait, oils, NPG · M. Greiffenhagen, self-portrait, oils, Marylebone Public Library
Wealth at death £3793 10s. 8d.: administration, 12 March 1932, CGPLA Eng. & Wales

Greig, Alexis Samuilovich (1775–1845), naval officer in the Russian service, son of Sir Samuel *Greig (1735–1788), was born at Kronstadt on 18 September 1775. As a reward for his father's services, he was enrolled at his birth as a midshipman in the Russian navy. He first distinguished himself in 1807, during the Russo-Turkish War of 1806–12, when a rear-admiral. After the defeat of the Turks off Lemnos in 1807, he was sent by Admiral Senyavin in pursuit of some ships which had escaped to the Gulf of Monte Santo; Greig blockaded the Turkish capitan pasha so closely that he was compelled to burn his vessels and retreat overland.

Greig greatly distinguished himself in the next Russo-Turkish War (1828–9). While Field Marshal Wittgenstein invaded Ottoman territory by land, Greig was entrusted with the task of attacking the fortresses on the coast of Bulgaria and Rumelia, and the eastern shore of the Black Sea. He appeared off Anapa on 14 May; on 24 June it surrendered, and Greig was promoted full admiral. In conjunction with the Russian land forces he laid siege to Varna, but the place was not taken until two and a half months had elapsed (11 October). During the operations Tsar Nicholas visited the fleet and stayed on board the *Paris*, the admiral's ship.

After the war was concluded (by the peace of Adrianople, 14 September 1829), Greig devoted himself to the improvement of the Russian navy. To him the Russians were largely indebted for the formation and development of their Black Sea Fleet. He was created admiral in attendance on the tsar and made a member of the imperial council and a knight of the order of St George of the second class; he also received other decorations. He died on 30 January 1845 at St Petersburg, and was buried in the Smolensk cemetery there; a monument was erected to his memory at Nikolayev. One of his sons greatly distinguished himself at the siege of Sevastopol.

W. R. MORFILL, *rev.* ROGER MORRISS

Sources *Morskoi Sbornik* [Naval miscellany] (1801), no. 12 · *Morskoi Sbornik* [Naval miscellany] (1873), no. 3 · *Morskoi Sbornik* [Naval miscellany] (1882), nos. 11–12 · V. Bronevskii, *Zapiski morskago ofitzera*

(St Petersburg, 1836) [Memoirs of a naval officer] · N. G. Ustrialov, *Russkaya istoria*, 2 [Russ. history] · H. Seton-Watson, *The Russian Empire, 1801–1917* (1967) · R. H. Davison, *Turkey* (1968)

Greig, Gavin (1856–1914), folksong collector and teacher, was born on 10 February 1856 in the North Lodge, Parkhill estate, near Dyce in Aberdeenshire, the fourth of five children of Gavin Greig (1822–1881), forester and land steward, and his wife, Mary (1815–1893), daughter of Robert Moir, box maker, and his wife, Margaret Stiven. He was educated at Dyce parish school and Old Aberdeen grammar school, and then entered Aberdeen University in 1872 as fourth bursar in the fiercely contested bursary competition (having turned down the thirty-third bursary in 1871). He graduated MA in 1876, having studied English and logic under Alexander Bain and gained the second competition bursary to study divinity for four years at the Aberdeen Free Church College. On 2 September 1878 he married his childhood friend Isabella Burgess (1856–1918), and their first child was born seven days later (they had a family of two sons and seven daughters eventually). These circumstances no doubt influenced Greig's decision to abandon his studies in favour of teaching, despite an excellent class record.

In 1879 Greig gained the position of schoolmaster at Whitehill School, New Deer, Aberdeenshire, against fierce competition (the Dick bequest had virtually doubled the salaries of regularly examined holders of Aberdeenshire posts, which were therefore sought by good-quality graduates). He set to and transformed a run-down school into one of the best in the region, and he introduced music and singing to the curriculum. Thereafter he threw himself into the musical life of the community, conducting choirs and brass bands, playing the piano and church organ, and writing and composing songs, hymns, plays, operettas, and musicals. In addition he wrote poetry, articles, and novels (serialized in the local newspapers); he lectured extensively on the glories of Scottish song as exemplified by the works of Burns, James Hogg, Lady Nairne, and others.

In 1902 Greig was asked by the New Spalding Club (an Aberdeen historical publishing society whose patron was Edward VII) to examine the feasibility of rescuing whatever still remained of the traditional music and song of the north-east of Scotland—vocal or instrumental, popular, secular, or religious—in order, perhaps, to fill a small volume. Greig was initially doubtful (during his lifetime in the region he had only come across a couple of examples of traditional song), but nevertheless started out collecting with his usual thoroughness and enthusiasm in late 1903. A very tall, outgoing, and popular man who put local folk at ease by speaking their native Scots, he was both surprised and delighted to find within a matter of months a considerable body of songs, well beyond his expectations, within a few miles' radius of his house.

Greig soon realized that he had hit upon a hitherto unsuspected treasure chest of traditional music and song—and that the task of collecting it was more than one person could manage. Furthermore, in 1905 the Folk Song Society in England (which Greig had joined in 1904) published in its *Journal* a number of songs collected by Cecil Sharp, edited to the highest modern standards, together with a list of sources (costing more than Greig's annual salary), which were deemed essential for a modern collector. Greig applied to the Carnegie trust for the universities of Scotland, and gained the first of five large research grants; he also recruited his old friend the Revd James Bruce Duncan as collaborator.

James Bruce Duncan (1848–1917), folksong collector and minister of the United Free Church of Scotland, was born on 13 February 1848 in the croft of Weetingshill, Whitehill, New Deer, Aberdeenshire (near to Greig's school), the fifth of eleven children of William Duncan (1814–1895), a millwright and carpenter, and his wife, Elizabeth Birnie. He was educated at Whitehill School, and (from 1862) Aberdeen grammar school before entering Aberdeen University in 1865 as fourteenth bursar at the age of seventeen. Unusually for the time, he graduated MA with honours (second class: philosophy) in 1869, and thereafter studied divinity at the United Presbyterian Divinity Hall, Edinburgh, and Leipzig University. An academic high-flyer, he was assistant to Bain (and taught Greig) at Aberdeen University before being ordained to the United Presbyterian (later the United Free) Church at Lynturk, Alford, in 1876; for the rest of his life he remained there, a hard-working and devoted pastor. On 10 August 1876 he married Maggie Anderson (1845/6–1893). A dark, reserved man, with a good sense of humour, he was not only an excellent musicologist but also came from a noted singing family, and had a considerable store of folk-song available to him, especially from his brother George and sister Margaret (later Mrs Gillespie).

In the decade before the First World War, Greig and Duncan collaborated in collecting a large and unique body of traditional music and song, mainly from the north-east of Scotland. Personal fieldwork was supplemented by correspondence stimulated by lectures and concerts and by a weekly folk-song column written by Greig for the *Buchan Observer* between 1907 and 1911, later published as *Folk-Song of the North-East* (1914). As the years passed, the compilation of a 'small volume' rapidly transformed into an overwhelming task of editing some 3500 texts and 3100 tunes (later published in eight volumes as *The Greig–Duncan Folk Song Collection*, 1981–2002). Greig suggested they should initially bring out a 'popular' edition, but Duncan objected on the grounds that this would necessitate bowdlerization; they therefore made a start on a volume of the great 'classical' ballads (as categorized by Francis Child of Harvard in his *English and Scottish Popular Ballads*, 1882–98) that they had found, and for which the region was already noted. But even this was incomplete when Greig died of heart failure on 31 August 1914 at the schoolhouse in Whitehill, where he lived, and Duncan died, as the result of a stroke some months earlier, on 30 September 1917 at his home, the manse at Lynturk. Greig was buried in Culsh cemetery, New Deer, on 4 September 1914; Duncan was buried at Alford, Aberdeenshire, on 3 October 1917.

Greig had drawn attention to their work by publishing

and circulating widely *Folk-Song in Buchan* in 1906 (a greatly expanded version of his presidential address to the Buchan Field Club in 1905), a ground-breaking survey and analysis that brought recognition from as far away as Berlin. It was not significantly altered by any of their later writings or addresses, but these were relatively few, and regrettably neither collector managed to publish any final analysis or conclusions. The collection is significant for its size, quality, and comprehensiveness; it was also a major compilation using modern techniques by collectors who were themselves native to the region, and thus familiar with the language and culture. They were surprised to find that their informants eschewed what was then (and still is) regarded as Scottish national song—'we may say that Scottish book-songs [of Burns, Hogg, etc.] have never been the songs of the mass of the Scottish people' (Greig, *Folk-Song of the North-East*, 1914, ix)—but any hopes that they might rewrite Scottish song (as Sharp had done for England) were dashed when they realized that their songs belonged to a corpus that transcended regional, national (Scottish and British), and even international boundaries.

Their deaths, the First World War, and the demise of the New Spalding Club in 1926, brought the project to an end and the papers were handed to Aberdeen University for safe keeping. In 1925 their attempted volume of Child ballads (some 13 per cent of the whole) was completed by Alexander Keith (1895–1978) under the direction of the elderly William Walker (1840–1931), who chose the unnecessarily elegiac title (the north-east song tradition was, and still is, thriving) of *Last Leaves of Traditional Ballads and Ballad Airs*, published by the Buchan [Field] Club. Although the editorial introduction was mainly devoted to employing the findings of Greig and Duncan to defend the disputed integrity of an earlier collector, Peter Buchan, and is unreliable in biographical and local details, the book was both widely circulated and influential. It was not until 1964 that Paul Duncan (a grandson) persuaded the English Folk Dance and Song Society to provide an editor for a joint publication of the entire collection by the University of Aberdeen and the School of Scottish Studies, Edinburgh; the first volume of this unique, important, and revolutionary eight-volume collection appeared in 1981. IAN A. OLSON

Sources *Buchan Observer* (1 Sept 1914) · P. N. Shuldham-Shaw, ed., *Folk songs of Aberdeenshire collected by the Rev. James B. Duncan* (1967) · P. N. Shuldham-Shaw and E. B. Lyle, 'Folk song in the north-east: J. B. Duncan's lecture to the Aberdeen Wagner Society, 1908', *Scottish Studies*, 18 (1974), 1–37 · I. A. Olson, 'The Greig–Duncan collection and the New Spalding Club', *Aberdeen University Review*, 50 (1983–4), 203–28 · I. A. Olson, 'Greig–Duncan provisional bibliography', *Folklore*, 95 (1984), 204–9 · I. A. Olson, 'The Greig–Duncan folk song collection and the Carnegie trust for the universities of Scotland', *Aberdeen University Review*, 51 (1985–6), 37–73 · I. A. Olson, 'The influence of the Folk Song Society on the Greig–Duncan folk song collection: methodology', *Folk Music Journal*, 5 (1985–9), 176–201 · I. A. Olson, 'Gavin Greig's lecture to the Scottish National Song Society, November 1909: a failure of nerve?', *Northern Scotland*, 7 (1986–7), 151–8 · I. A. Olson, 'Scottish traditional song and the Greig–Duncan collection: last leaves or last rites?', *The history of Scottish literature*, 4: *Twentieth century*, ed. C. Craig (1987), 37–48 · I. A. Olson, 'The Greig–Duncan folk song collection: last leaves of local culture?', *Review of Scottish Culture*, 5 (1989), 79–85 · I. A. Olson, 'The influence of nineteenth century migrant workers on the Greig–Duncan folk song collection', *Review of Scottish Culture*, 9 (1995–6), 113–27 · I. A. Olson, 'Gavin Greig', *The Greig–Duncan Folk Song Collection*, 8 (2002), 531–9 · I. A. Olson, 'James Bruce Duncan', *The Greig–Duncan Folk Song Collection*, 8 (2002), 541–6 · b. cert. · m. cert. · d. cert. · General Register Office

Archives Aberdeen Central Library · U. Aberdeen L. | English Folk Dance and Song Society, London, Lucy Broadwood and Cecil Sharp MSS · Surrey HC, Lucy Broadwood MSS · U. Aberdeen, letters to James Duncan and papers · U. Aberdeen, Alexander Keith MSS · U. Aberdeen, William Walker MSS · University of Florida, Gainsville, William Walker MSS

Likenesses photographs, U. Edin., School of Scottish Studies

Wealth at death £361 14s. 11d.: confirmation, 6 Feb 1915, *CCI* · £427 11s. 4d.—James Bruce Duncan: inventory, 26 Jan 1918, *CCI*

Greig, John (1758/9–1819), writer on arithmetic and astronomy, was a graduate of Aberdeen. By 1800 he was a private teacher of writing, geography, and mathematics in London, and he is mentioned as teaching at Chelsea during the period 1809–16. He is known as the author of six texts on arithmetic and astronomy. The most popular, *The Young Lady's Guide to Arithmetic*, had sixteen editions from 1798 to 1864; a sixth edition of his *Globes* (1st edn, 1805) was advertised in 1816. Greig died at Somers Town, London, on 19 January 1819, aged sixty. RUTH WALLIS

Sources GM, 1st ser., 89/1 (1819), 184 · E. G. R. Taylor, *The mathematical practitioners of Hanoverian England, 1714–1840* (1966), 313

Greig, Sir Louis Leisler (1880–1953), courtier, was born in Glasgow on 17 November 1880, the ninth of eleven children. His father, (Robert) David Greig (1838–1900), was a prosperous merchant; his mother, Jessie, *née* Thomson (1844–1915), also from middle-class stock, was a woman of formidable energy and rectitude. Greig was educated at Glasgow Academy, Merchiston Castle School, Edinburgh, and Glasgow University, where he studied medicine. He shone academically and, still more, athletically—captaining Scotland at rugby and playing first-class tennis. After graduating and working as a junior doctor in the Gorbals, he joined the navy in 1906 and won the gold medal at Haslar, the naval hospital training school.

In 1909 Greig joined the Royal Naval College, Osborne, and met Prince Albert, the future duke of York and King George VI. The prince was gauche, stammering, and ill-equipped for this hearty and exclusively male society; Greig was ambitious enough to realize how the royal cadet could further his career but also genuinely liked him and appreciated his potential. The prince, for his part, hero-worshipped his stalwart and self-confident mentor. Prince Albert's father encouraged the relationship and ensured that they served together in HMS *Cumberland*, where Greig was ship's surgeon.

In 1914 Greig was transferred to the marines. He took part in the defence of Antwerp and spent eight months as a German prisoner before being exchanged. On 16 February 1916 he married Phyllis Scrimgeour (1885–1973), with whom he had a son and two daughters. In June 1917 he joined HMS *Malaya*, in which Prince Albert was serving, and he was largely responsible for his protégé's recovery from debilitating stomach ulcers. For the next seven years the two men were virtually inseparable. In 1918 Greig was appointed equerry, and the following year he and the prince joined the fledgeling Royal Air Force. It was during these years that the association attracted public attention when they were partners at Wimbledon (being heavily defeated in the first round).

As well as accompanying Prince Albert to Cambridge and on trips abroad, Greig nurtured his social life. He encouraged the prince's wooing of Lady Elizabeth Bowes-Lyon and thus put a term to his own position in the royal household. The duchess of York never quarrelled with Greig, but there was not room in the duke's life for two such intimate associations. Greig was gradually frozen out and resigned in pique when omitted from a royal tour of the Balkans.

The rest of Greig's life was an anticlimax. He worked successfully for a firm of stockbrokers and became close to Ramsay MacDonald, playing a small but useful role in the formation of the National Government. It was Mac-Donald who pressed Greig to accept a knighthood in 1932. In the same year he was created deputy ranger of Richmond Park. His close association with the throne went into abeyance under Edward VIII, who disliked and distrusted him, but revived after the abdication when George VI reappointed him, as a gentleman usher. In the same year he was elected chairman of Wimbledon. He rejoined the RAF in 1939 and served in the Air Ministry in an ill-defined but valuable liaison role. In 1952 cancer was diagnosed. An operation seemed temporarily successful, but Sir Louis Greig died on 1 March 1953, and was buried two days later at St Andrew's Church, Ham, Surrey.

PHILIP ZIEGLER

Sources G. Greig, *Louis and the prince* (1999) · J. H. Wheeler-Bennett, *King George VI: his life and reign* (1958) · S. Bradford, *King George VI* (1989) · R. Rhodes James, *Spirit undaunted: the political role of George VI* (1998)
Archives priv. coll., papers | PRO, Ramsay MacDonald MSS · Royal Arch., George VI MSS
Likenesses J. Oppenheimer, oils, 1935, priv. coll. · H. A. Stermann, plaster life mask, NPG
Wealth at death £41,564 9s. 10d.: probate, 28 May 1953, CGPLA Eng. & Wales

Greig, Sir Samuel (1735–1788), naval officer in the Russian service, was the son of Charles Greig, shipowner and naval officer of Inverkeithing in Fife, Scotland, and his wife, Jean, daughter of Revd Samuel Charters of Inverkeithing. Greig was born in Inverkeithing on 30 November 1735, where he attended parochial school before his family moved to Edinburgh and later to Burntisland, Fife. He went to sea on merchant vessels, then joined the navy and quickly rose to master's mate. Greig took part in the reduction of Goree in 1758 aboard the *Firedrake* and afterwards served on Admiral Edward Hawkes's flagship, the *Royal George*, during the blockade of Brest and at the battle at Quiberon Bay. In 1761 he was acting lieutenant in the *Albemarle* and on 25 January 1762 he passed his examination, but at the war's end he remained a master's mate. With his career stalled, he accepted a commission in the Russian navy which promised swift promotion. He married Sarah (1752–1793), daughter of Alexander Cook of St Petersburg, on 1 September 1768, and they had at least five children.

Greig made his mark quickly with innovative methods for arming warships and with suggestions on ship construction. In 1769 he advanced from captain to commodore and was placed in charge of a division of the new Mediterranean squadron under Vice-Admiral Spiridov. Greig avoided the acrimonious squabbles between Spiridov and his rear-admiral, John Elphinston, and became the adviser to the inexperienced fleet commander, Admiral Aleksey Orlov.

On 5–6 July 1770 the Turks and Russians met in fierce combat at Chesma in the Mediterranean. Elphinston and Spiridov argued over tactics and Orlov supported Spiridov, who led the attack and lost his flagship immediately. Then Elphinston employed his ships and forced the Turks to retreat inside the bay. In the morning Greig, commanding Orlov's flagship, brought four ships of the line, three frigates, a bomb-ketch, and four fire ships into action. The crowded Turkish vessels were set ablaze and the enemy fleet was nearly destroyed.

The flag officers then fought for laurels, which has created a lasting historical argument that Elphinston was denied credit, while Orlov was immortalized. Orlov acknowledged Greig's contribution, confiding to Empress Catherine 'that he knew nothing about sea affairs; that even at Tchesmin he had done nothing himself; that Greig had done everything'. Greig won promotion to rear-admiral and remained attached to Orlov until the final victory. Spiridov's reputation was damaged and Elphinston was set aside and left Russia in 1775. As A. G. Cross has noted, 'Greig proved himself not only courageous and capable, but loyal and discreet, and his career prospered accordingly' (Cross, 255).

Greig returned to Kronstadt in 1775, but on the voyage home he became embroiled in the affair of the adventuress Princess Tarakanova. It seems that Orlov placed the notorious pretender on Greig's ship in Leghorn in order to deliver her to St Petersburg. Greig has been accused of assisting in the entrapment of the unfortunate Tarakanova, who paid dearly for her challenge to Catherine's legitimacy. In 1775 Greig was promoted vice-admiral, made a knight of the orders of St George and St Anna, and named commander at Kronstadt. The empress later reviewed the fleet and dined on Greig's flagship where she bestowed the order of Alexander Nevsky upon him.

An efficient administrator, Greig devoted himself to the improvement of Kronstadt, enlarging the sea walls and upgrading the dry docks and harbour facilities. He added significantly to the barracks, built hospitals, and improved the cadet college and the admiralty, and attended to the fitting and armament of ships. Greig employed foreign engineers and imported foreign technology, frequently from his native Scotland, which caused complaints in some quarters of the expense and of foreign influence. British officers in the Russian navy regarded Greig as their patron and in 1788 pressured him to sign a petition to deny John Paul Jones the rank of rear-admiral. He signed but then convinced the disgruntled officers to drop the matter. When sailors at Kronstadt rioted to protest the watering of vodka, he strode among the malcontents and then redressed their grievances. Greig took an active part in freemasonry and was senior warden at the foundation of the 'Neptune' chapter of the Swedish order, and later master. He regarded masonry as a mechanism for bonding Russian and foreign officers around the principles of idealism, simplicity, and service.

When the Swedes declared war on Russia in 1788 Greig deployed the fleet to block them in the Gulf of Finland. Although an engagement off Högland Island on 17 July was indecisive, it prevented a descent on St Petersburg. The admiral disciplined seventeen captains who did not join the battle and sent them to hard labour for life. Afterwards the Russians had success in the blockade of Sveaborg, in other engagements, and in the capture of Högland. The pleased empress rewarded her admiral by making him a knight of the orders of St Vladimir and St Andrew.

Greig died of fever on his flagship in Reval harbour on 26 October 1788. He was buried at the Lutheran cathedral in Reval and his life was commemorated in masonic lodges and churches in the Russian capital.

Greig's eldest son, Alexis Samuilovich *Greig, rose to the rank of admiral in the Russian service. Another son, Samuel, was the father of the barrister Woronzow *Greig.   RICHARD H. WARNER

Sources A. G. Cross, 'Samuel Greig, Catherine the Great's Scottish admiral', *Mariner's Mirror*, 60 (1974), 251–6 · V. A. Chistiakov, 'Den *Sisoia Velikogo*' [The day of Sisoia the Great], *Morskoi Sbornik* (July 1988), 78–83 · R. C. Anderson, 'British and American officers in the Russian navy', *Mariner's Mirror*, 33 (1947), 17–27 · R. C. Anderson, 'Great Britain and the rise of the Russian fleet in the eighteenth century', *Mariner's Mirror*, 42 (1956), 132–46 · R. C. Anderson, *Naval wars in the Levant, 1559–1853* (1952) · R. C. Anderson, *Naval wars in the Baltic during the sailing-ship epoch, 1522–1850* (1910); repr. as *Naval wars in the Baltic, 1522–1850* (1969) · *Obshchii morskoi spisok* [General naval list] (1885–1907) · V. N. Berkh, *Zhizneopisaniia pervikh rosisskikh admiralov* [Descriptions of the lives of the first Russian admirals] (St Petersburg, 1843) · F. F. Veselago, *Kratkaia istoriia russkogo flota* [A short history of the Russian fleet] (1939) · V. A. Divin and others, eds., *Boevaia letopis' russkogo flota* [Chronicle of the battles of the Russian fleet] (Moscow, 1948) · E. V. Tarle, 'Chesmenskii boi i pervaia ekspeditsiia v arkhipelag' [The battle of Chesme and the first expedition to the archipelago], *Tri ekspeditsii russkogo flota* [Three expeditions of the Russian fleet] (Moscow, 1956) · *DNB*

Archives Bodl. Oxf., family corresp. and papers

Likenesses J. Walker, mezzotint, pubd 1788 (after D. Levitsky), NPG · I. P. Argunov, oils, Inverkeithing, Fife

Greig, Teresa Mary Billington- (1876–1964), suffragette and political theorist, was born at 197 Friargate, Preston, Lancashire, on 15 October 1876, the second daughter of William Billington, variously described as an engineer, shopkeeper, and shipping clerk, and his wife, Helen (or Ellen) Wilson. She was educated until the age of thirteen at the Convent of Notre Dame, Blackburn. At seventeen she ran away from home, escaping the burdens of domestic and waged labour. Her uncle took her in at Manchester, where she trained as a pupil teacher at St Edmund's and studied, organized, and debated at the Ancoats University settlement. In 1903 she became a teacher in a Manchester

Teresa Mary Billington-Greig (1876–1964), by unknown photographer

elementary school. She rejected Roman Catholicism in favour of militant socialist agnosticism and was transferred to a Jewish school, with the help of Emmeline Pankhurst, to prevent her being sacked for refusing to give prescribed religious teaching.

In April 1904 Billington helped to organize the Manchester teachers' equal pay league, having joined the Women's Social and Political Union (WSPU) as a major speaker shortly before. She had started a career in political activism very young because she had exceptional oratorical and administrative skills, reinforced by self-confidence. In 1905 she became a paid organizer for the Independent Labour Party. Sylvia Pankhurst described her as 'a large, powerfully built woman, with a round pleasant face', who 'sought to be considered unconventional'. Others more charitable noted her green eyes and inspiring vigour (Pankhurst, 187). In May 1906 she helped to organize a major suffrage deputation from the East End of London to parliament, and participated in the militant campaign of disrupting cabinet members' public appearances. She horsewhipped the stewards who ejected her from Asquith's meeting in Northampton. She spent some periods in Holloway prison, always protesting against the illegitimacy of a man-made legal system. She has been described as the non-violent militant but she was fined in

July 1906 for dealing a return blow with her fist to a police-man in Cavendish Square, crying 'You shall not strike our women!' (ibid., 210, 212–13). She was among those arrested and imprisoned after creating a disturbance at the open-ing of parliament in October 1906 in protest against the government's refusal to include women's suffrage in its legislative programme. A character sketch of her by Fred-erick Pethick-Lawrence singled out her moral courage, and J. J. Mallon suggested that she had intransigence and passion too: 'There will be quick loves but equally quick repulsions' (*Non-Violent Militant*, 7).

In autumn 1906 Billington went to Scotland to organize WSPU branches. She took part in the by-election cam-paign at Aberdeen South in February 1907, when the WSPU pursued its line of opposing all Liberal candidates, regardless of their views on women's suffrage. During this hectic period she married in Glasgow, on 8 February 1907, a socialist businessman, Frederick Lewis Greig (1875/6–1961), who worked as a manager for a billiard table manu-facturer. He was the son of Frederick Murray Greig, a sad-dler. Their two names were united in a nuptial agreement which ensured equal rights in marriage.

Billington-Greig's theory was refined during 1906–7 in a series of articles, pamphlets, and speeches for which her notes survive. She developed a distinctive demand for full sexual equality, rejecting bad tactics even for good ends and attacking misogyny in social relations. She rejected the psychological disability which society created in women as well, seeking 'emancipation from all shackles of law and custom, from all chains of sentiment and superstition, from all outer imposed disabilities and cher-ished inner bondages which unite to shut off liberty from the human soul borne in her body' (*Non-Violent Militant*, 137). In December 1907 she debated with Margaret Bond-field (a leading Labour Party activist and trade unionist) about whether women formed a sex class: 'The quicker you give women the power to care for women's interests, the quicker all women will have redress' (*Sex Equality versus Adult Suffrage*, Manchester Women's Freedom League, 1908; Holton, 58).

Throughout her life Billington-Greig found it difficult to work collaboratively, and she fell out with the Pankhurst leaders of the WSPU in 1907. With Edith How-Martyn and Charlotte Despard she formed the Women's Freedom League, which continued to protest against the 'man-made laws' that oppressed women. A particularly imaginative strategy was the refusal to participate in the census of 1911, and generally their tactics stressed non-co-operation rather than aggressive demonstration or court-ing arrest. In her 'The militant suffrage movement' (first published in *The New Age*) she rejected the emphasis on the vote, in 'Feminism and politics' in favour of a feminism which would 'remake society, would set up new stand-ards, would destroy old customs, would establish a new morality' (*Non-Violent Militant*, 227).

In December 1910 Billington-Greig left the Women's Freedom League and retired from direct action, becoming a critic and historian of the suffrage agitation. She retained a belief in the efficacy of passive resistance, as a superior tactic which could include women of all classes, over demonstration, hunger striking, and arson. She spent the next three years as a freelance journalist and speaker. In 1913 she wrote against the 1912 White Slave Act and feminist emphases on social purity for women; in 1914 she demonstrated yet further estrangement from the mainstream of suffragism by writing in favour of birth control. After a brief marital separation in winter 1913–14 she returned to Glasgow and gave birth to her daughter Fiona in December 1915. During the war and again in 1923 she spent some time substituting for her husband at the billiard works, an interest which was later to lead her to create the Women's Billiards Association and the sports fellowship which would enable poor girls to take part in athletics. Feminism remained important to her, and she managed to earn money briefly as paid organizer for the Business and Professional Women's Club in 1936.

In 1937 Billington-Greig re-entered the Women's Free-dom League and turned it into Women for Westminster in 1945; she carried out a merger with the National Women Citizens' Association in 1948, representing women's organizations on various official bodies. She clearly now believed that political participation could bring about the systematic cultural change for which she yearned. She believed herself a failure when in later life she could not find a publisher for a life of Charlotte Despard, leader of the Women's Freedom League, and had little writing pub-lished after 1911. Her draft autobiography was never com-pleted. Her husband died in 1961, and she died of cancer at the South London Hospital for Women on 21 October 1964. She had retained her feminist principles throughout. While believing that the unity of all women through their womanly activities, above all as consumers, was the way forward, she never ceased to believe in the power of women through independent organization to make cul-tural change. Her collected writings might have been bet-ter described as the title of her last major publication, in 1912, *The Consumer in Revolt*, and she herself as in her own critique of direct action, 'a feminist, a suffragist, and a rebel'. Despite her own sense of frustration and failure, she has inspired substantial critical commentary.

D. THOM

Sources *The non-violent militant: selected writings of Teresa Billington-Greig*, ed. C. McPhee and A. Fitzgerald (1987) · B. Harrison, *Prudent revolutionaries: portraits of British feminists between the wars* (1987), chap. 2 · E. S. Pankhurst, *The suffragette movement: an intimate account of persons and ideals* (1931) · S. S. Holton, *Feminism and democracy: women's suffrage and reform politics in Britain, 1900–1918* (1986) · M. Mulvihill, *Charlotte Despard: a biography* (1989) · C. Eustance, '"Daring to be free": the evolution of women's political identities in the Women's Freedom League, 1906–1930', DPhil diss., Univer-sity of York, 1993 · L. Leneman, *A guid cause: the women's suffrage movement in Scotland* (1995) · O. Banks, *The biographical dictionary of British feminists*, 1 (1985) · b. cert. · m. cert. · *CGPLA Eng. & Wales* (1964)

Archives London Metropolitan University, MSS incl. notes for articles and biography of Charlotte Despard | Women's Library, London, Billington-Greig MSS

Likenesses photograph, Women's Library, London [*see illus.*]

Wealth at death £5147: probate, 8 Dec 1964, *CGPLA Eng. & Wales*

Greig, Woronzow (1805–1865), barrister, the elder son of Samuel Samuilovich Greig (1777/8–1807) and Mary Fairfax, later Mary *Somerville (1780–1872), the scientific expositor, was born at Great Russell Street, Bloomsbury, London, on 29 May 1805. He was named after Count Semyon Vorontsov, Russian ambassador to London, whose daughter Catherine was Greig's godmother; she married the eleventh earl of Pembroke in 1807. Samuel Greig, son of Samuel *Greig, admiral of the Russian Baltic fleet and governor of Kronstadt, had married his cousin Mary, daughter of Vice-Admiral Sir William George *Fairfax, at Burntisland, Fife, in June 1804. He was a captain and became Russian naval commissioner in London; through Vorontsov's influence he was appointed consul-general in November 1806, but he died on 26 September 1807, aged twenty-nine. His widow returned with Woronzow and her younger son, William George (1807–1814), to her parents' home at Burntisland. She developed a keen interest in higher mathematics and physical astronomy, and cultivated the company of leading Scottish intellectuals. In May 1812 she married her cousin William Somerville MD, and they moved to Edinburgh in 1813 when he was nominated head of the army medical department in Scotland.

Greig received private tuition from the young naturalist George Finlayson, and attended Edinburgh high school. On his stepfather's appointment to the army medical board in 1816 the family transferred to London, where Greig studied at Charterhouse School. He matriculated at Trinity College, Cambridge, on 9 January 1823, graduated BA in 1827, and proceeded MA in 1830. From June 1827 until the beginning of 1829 he travelled through much of Europe, for some time in Charles Babbage's company, spending several months in Naples, Sicily, and Malta. In June 1828 he shipped to England a 'perfect collection of volcanic minerals' (W. Greig to Mary Somerville, 20 June 1828, Bodl. Oxf., MSS Somerville, dep. c. 364) from mounts Vesuvius and Etna, which was to be called for at the Athenaeum (to which he had been elected in May 1826). After his return to England he petitioned Tsar Nicholas, on 12 October 1829, against a Russian government claim on an alleged debt due from his father that had resulted in two-thirds of his inheritance being detained 'under the Protection of the English Court of Chancery' (Bodl. Oxf., MSS Somerville, dep. c. 375). It was not until May 1833 that his mother congratulated him on his 'escape from the hug of the bear' (Mary Somerville to W. Greig, 6 May 1833, Bodl. Oxf., MSS Somerville, dep. c. 361)—the withdrawal of the Russian claim on his property.

Greig was admitted a barrister at the Inner Temple on 14 May 1830. He declined an invitation three years later to become chief justice of Mauritius, because he hoped to obtain a seat in parliament. He was appointed a perpetual revising barrister of voters' lists for the northern circuit, comprising Yorkshire's East Riding and some surrounding areas, in 1836, and then for the North Riding in 1838. He married Agnes Graham (*bap.* 1808, *d.* 1874), daughter of George Graham and Marion Somerville, at East Kilbride on 27 October 1837, and they moved into Lower Belgrave Street, off Eaton Square, London, in 1838. They had no children.

Greig was elected a fellow of the Royal Society on 7 February 1833: his certificate, recommending him as 'well acquainted with various branches of Science', was endorsed by seventeen signatories, including his stepfather and several of his mother's close scientific associates, Brewster, Chantrey, Lyell, and Murchison. In May 1833 Greig and Mary Somerville were instrumental in obtaining for the society a bust of Laplace from his widow. In September 1832 and March 1834 Mary Somerville wrote two letters in which she offered Tsar Nicholas a copy of *The Mechanism of the Heavens* (1832), her scientific exposition of Laplace's *Mécanique céleste*, and emphasized her family's long-standing connections with Russia.

On 3 May 1834 Greig became a member of the newly founded Statistical Society. He was the society's honorary secretary (1834–9), and, after visiting Ireland to investigate the subject during August and September, contributed a cogent paper to its *Proceedings* (vol. 1, 1834–5), 'On the character and present condition of the Irish labourer'. In his capacity as secretary he attended a dinner held at Newcastle in June 1838 by the British Association for the Advancement of Science to honour Sir John Herschel.

Greig's seven letters to Babbage (1832–47, BL, Add. MSS 37187–37193) cover electioneering, the Royal Astronomical Society, his mother's researches, the patenting of inventions, and Babbage's calculating machine. In September 1836 Greig introduced Babbage to his uncle Alexis Greig, a naval friend of William IV and admiral of the Black Sea Fleet; like his father, Admiral Samuel Greig, Alexis Greig was an honorary member of the Russian Academy of Sciences. Much of Woronzow Greig's correspondence with Herschel between 1845 and 1863 reflects their promotion of Mary Somerville's papers and publications. A letter from Herschel in June 1846, together with two fragments of his letters from 1847, suggests that Greig was editing a so far unidentified work on English photography. In general his largely untapped but catalogued correspondence in the Somerville collection is a unique source of information about his wide associations and interests.

In August 1842 Greig and his mother wrote to ask Peel, the prime minister, to support his application for the post of judge under the County Courts Bill then before parliament, enclosing a letter from Peel's predecessor Lord Melbourne, who as home secretary had promised Greig the position if a similar bill had succeeded in 1831 (BL, Add. MS 40513, fols. 150–52). Nothing came of their request, but in 1849 Greig was appointed clerk of the peace for Surrey County, and occupied Surrey Lodge, 1 North Street, Lambeth, London, as his official residence. As custodian of the records of the court of quarter sessions, he was responsible for judicial and local government affairs. There is evidence that he may also have been legal adviser to two archbishops of Canterbury at nearby Lambeth Palace. Three well-preserved photographs of Greig by Robert Jefferson Bingham, author of the *Photogenic Manipulator* (1848), portray him holding a book, probably alluding to his writing activities. Greig died, suddenly, of heart congestion on 20 October 1865, at Surrey Lodge. He left notebooks of conversations with his mother and incomplete biographies of his grandfathers, Admiral Samuel Greig, and Vice-Admiral Sir William George Fairfax, and of Ada Byron, Lady Lovelace, whose early mathematical studies had been supervised by Mary Somerville at the request of Lady Byron, the poet's widow. JOHN H. APPLEBY

Sources J. H. Appleby, 'Woronzow Greig (1805–1865), FRS, and his scientific interests', *Notes and Records of the Royal Society*, 53 (1999), 95–106 · Bodl. Oxf., MSS Somerville dep 358–359, 363–364, 375; dep b 205–208, 233; dep c 361–368 · E. C. Patterson, catalogue of the Somerville collection, 1969–82, Bodl. Oxf. · R. Greig, letter, *The Scotsman* (30 June 1941) · *DSB* · E. C. Patterson, *Mary Somerville and the cultivation of science, 1815–1840* (1983) · A. L. Fullerton, *Descendants of John Cook (1679–1780)* (1998) · Papers of Counts Alexander and Simon Romanovich Vorontsov, Moscow, Vorontsov MSS, 19, 1881 · *Parl. papers* (1840), vol. 29 · *Parl. papers* (1841), vol. 13 · *The Athenaeum* (16 June 1838), 423 · *GM*, 1st ser., 75 (1805), 581 · *GM*, 1st ser., 77 (1807), 600 · Venn, *Alum. Cant.* · *IGI* · d. cert. · BL, Add. MSS 37187–37193; 40513, fols. 150–52
Archives BL, Add. MSS 37187–37193 | Bodl. Oxf., MSS Somerville, dep 358–359, 363–364, 375; dep b 205–208, 233; dep c 361–368
Likenesses S. Durant, marble bust, 1866, RS; on loan · R. J. Bingham, three photographs, Somerville College, Oxford; repro. in Appleby, 'Woronzow, Greig' · Jackson, portrait, Bodl. Oxf., MSS Somerville dep c 363
Wealth at death under £4000: administration with will, 5 March 1866

Grein, Jacob Thomas [Jack] (**1862–1935**), drama critic and impresario, was born on 11 October 1862 in Amsterdam, the elder son of Jacob Herman Grein (*fl.* 1840–1888), merchant, and his wife, Frances (*d.* 1920), daughter of Dr Thomas Davids of Amsterdam and his wife, Louisa.

Educated in Dutch and German schools, and a Bremen commercial college, Grein then worked in business for two uncles. By 1882 he was drama critic for Amsterdam's leading newspaper, *Algemeen Handelsblad*. When Grein moved to London in 1885 he remained in commerce but continued writing for continental journals. Subsequently he was drama critic for *Life* (1888–91), the *Sunday Special* (1897–1918), and *Ladies Field* (1911–14). His final assignment was with the *Illustrated London News* (1920–35), where he wrote alongside his wife, Alice Augusta Greeven (pseudonym Michael Orme; 1874–1944), whom he had married on 14 July 1904. His assessments of some of the 12,000 plays he claimed to have witnessed were published in *Dramatic Criticism* (5 vols., 1898–1903).

Grein's major achievement was establishing the Independent Theatre in London in 1891. Modelled after André Antoine's Théâtre Libre, Grein adopted many of Antoine's principles but eschewed what he termed the immorality and slovenliness of Antoine's work. Grein endeavoured to stage plays of high literary and artistic value rejected by the commercial theatre or suppressed by the censor (whom the Independent Theatre circumvented by being a subscription society). Its first production was Ibsen's *Ghosts* (1891), regarded as cutting-edge drama and already censored. More than 3000 people applied for tickets, and the production became a *cause célèbre*: Ibsen was vilified by traditionalist critic Clement Scott, but defended by William Archer. The subsequent repertoire proved less radical and sensational although it included the 1892 production of *Widower's Houses*, the first of Shaw's plays to be performed. Since there were only 175 regular subscribers Grein subsidized the organization until it became a limited company in 1895 (the year of his naturalization). The Independent Theatre ceased operations in 1897. Grein was involved with similar ventures, such as the Stage Society (1899 onwards), the London German Theatre (1901–7), the French Players (1917), and the People's Theatre (1923). He began the People's National Theatre (1930) with actress Nancy Price, but her domineering personality and Grein's ill health forced him to withdraw within a year. He died of a heart attack at his London home, 4 Cambridge Place, Victoria Road, on 22 June 1935.

Rather short and stocky, with a round, moustached face, Grein was genial and incurably enthusiastic. As a critic he was cosmopolitan but undiscriminating; he lacked the trenchant, scintillating style of Bernard Shaw or Max Beerbohm. However, Grein's dedicated organizational abilities nurtured serious drama and he planted the seeds of the alternative theatre movement, an achievement recognized by numerous honours. J. P. WEARING

Sources N. Schoonderwoerd, *J. T. Grein: ambassador of the theatre, 1862–1935* (1963) · M. Orme [A. A. Greeven], *J. T. Grein: the story of a pioneer, 1862–1935* (1936) · *Who was who in the theatre, 1912–1976*, 4 vols. (1978) · *The Times* (24 June 1935) · J. Woodfield, *English theatre in transition, 1881–1914* (1984) · J. P. Wearing, 'Nancy Price and the People's National Theatre', *Theatre History Studies*, 16 (1996), 71–89 · m. cert.
Archives BL · priv. coll. · Theatre Museum, London
Likenesses Bassano, portrait, repro. in Orme, *J. T. Grein* · Elliott & Fry, portrait, repro. in Orme, *J. T. Grein* · Karsh, photograph, repro. in Orme, *J. T. Grein* · photograph, repro. in J. Parker, ed., *The green room book, or, Who's who on the stage* (1907) · photograph, repro. in *ILN* (29 June 1935), 1155
Wealth at death £2200: resworn administration, 1935, *CGPLA Eng. & Wales*

Greisley, Henry (**1613–1678**), translator, was born at Shrewsbury on 9 November 1613, the son of John Gresley, Gresly (which spellings are also used of the son, the latter on his gravestone), or Greisley, and Joan, daughter of Jasper More of Larden, Shropshire. He was educated at Westminster School, and then elected a student of Christ Church, Oxford; he matriculated on 1 September 1634. Having proceeded BA on 11 April 1638 and MA on 8 July 1641, Greisley was expelled from the university in 1648 by the parliamentary visitors; in 1651 he was incorporated at Cambridge. Greisley travelled in France, was instituted to the rectory of Severn-Stoke, Worcestershire, on 28 September 1661, and was installed a prebendary of Worcester on 19 April 1672. He married first Mary, daughter of Edward Allye of Hatfield, Worcestershire, on 5 June 1655, and second Eleanor, daughter of Gervase Buck of Kempsey in the same county, on 16 April 1667.

The Prince (1648), a thick duodecimo, is translated from the French of Jean Louis Guez de Balzac, of whose works, especially his letters, several translations were made into

English at the time. While Balzac presents a flattering portrait of Louis XIII, Greisley's blandishment is clearly directed to Charles I, though he mentions the name of neither king; his dedicatee is Gervase Holles, a colonel under Charles. Although the translation tries to be lively, it does not always live up to the elegant stylization of the original. Greisley also translated from Senault's French *The Christian Man, or, The Reparation of Nature by Grace* (1650), a lengthy treatise on Christian virtues and the nature of the church. A disclaimer in the 'Advertisement' at the start of the book points out that the original author is a Roman Catholic who 'expresseth himself too grossly' concerning transubstantiation, although these passages have been left in 'for the reader's censure, so as not to render the translation guilty of incivility to the author'.

As well as some intelligent and moving, if occasionally overblown, English verse in *Death Repeal'd*, the Christ Church collection on the death of Paul, Viscount Bayning of Sudbury, in June 1638 (pp. 14–15), Greisley has seventeen Latin hexameters on the birth of Prince Henry in *Horti Carolini rosa altera* (1640) that demonstrate some facility in the form. Greisley died on 8 June 1678 at Severn-Stoke, and was buried there, where his second wife (*d.* 17 January 1703, aged sixty-four) and their son, John (*d.* 15 April 1718, aged forty-nine), were also interred.

ROSS KENNEDY

Sources Wood, *Ath. Oxon.*, new edn, 2.1167–8 · J. Walker, *An attempt towards recovering an account of the numbers and sufferings of the clergy of the Church of England*, pt 2 (1714), 108 · *Old Westminsters*, 1.399 · Foster, *Alum. Oxon.* · T. Nash, *Collections for the history of Worcestershire*, 2 (1782), 345–7 · Wood, *Ath. Oxon.: Fasti* (1815), 468, 500; (1820), 3 · D. K. Money, 'A diff'rent sounding lyre: Oxford commemorative verse in English, 1613–1834', *Bodleian Library Record*, 16 (1997–9), 42–92 · IGI

Greive [*formerly* Grieve], **George** (1748–1809), political reformer and persecutor of Madame Du Barry, was born at Felton, Northumberland, the son of Richard Grieve (*bap.* 1682, *d.* 1765), an attorney, of Alnwick, and his second wife, Elizabeth Davidson (1679/80–1764). Both George's father and his grandfather, Ralph Grieve (*d.* 1715), a merchant, had been prominent at Alnwick in political contests, and George's elder brother, Davidson Richard (1741–1793), was high sheriff of Northumberland in 1788. As a young man Grieve was apprenticed to the London merchant Peter Thellusson, inherited a share of family property in Alnwick (a local source mentions a fortune of £20,000), and lived on the family estate at Swansfield, near Felton. On coming of age he had to go to law with the corporation to take up his freedom, their plea being that his father, who had died in 1765 at the age of eighty-four, had been temporarily disenfranchised at the time of George's birth. Twice, in 1772 and in 1778, he led the freemen of Alnwick in forcible efforts to restore to the town moorland granted away by the close corporation.

From the beginning of the Wilkite movement Grieve was an advocate of the 'popular cause' in Northumberland, London, and Newcastle upon Tyne. He was one of those who called for a county petition to dissolve parliament after Wilkes's expulsion, and in 1774 he took an active part in defeating the duke of Northumberland's attempt to nominate both of the members for the county. Soon afterwards he headed a grand jury that attacked decisions made by the county justices.

In London Grieve was an early member of the Society of the Supporters of the Bill of Rights and a frequent dining companion of Wilkes. In 1774 he stood unsuccessfully for sheriff, an effort that earned him the thanks of the society. In the early months of the association movement, Grieve was again in London, possibly connected with John Almon's *London Courier and Westminster Chronicle*. At the meeting of Middlesex freeholders in January 1780 he argued successfully against an amendment which would have broken step with the Yorkshire petitioners in their bid for parliamentary and economical reforms. Subsequently he was an active member of the Westminster Committee and attended the London meetings (as a representative of Newcastle upon Tyne) to discuss Wyvill's plan for a national association.

Grieve had become associated with pro-Wilkes freemen in Newcastle as early as 1771. He was an organizer of the Constitutional Club of Durham, Northumberland, and Newcastle, which supported parliamentary reform and subsequently the American cause. In the dispute between freemen and the corporation over the Newcastle town moor, a conflict linked closely to Wilkite sympathies in the town, Grieve secured the services of Serjeant John Glynn, radical recorder of London and member of parliament for Middlesex, for the freemen; he was rewarded with the freedom of many of the companies of the town. In 1775 he opened a meeting of Newcastle freemen that thanked Wilkes and Lord Effingham for their conduct regarding America, and approved instructions calling for peace and parliamentary reform to be sent to the town's representatives in parliament. In 1777 Grieve acted as agent for Andrew Robinson Bowes, the candidate of the local opposition in the Newcastle parliamentary by-election, and was involved in the legal challenge to Bowes's narrow defeat.

Three years later, possibly in the second half of 1780, Grieve, perhaps concerned about a threat of legal prosecution for libel, left England for the continent, where he apparently had travelled often in the previous decade and where he had met the American representatives Silas Deane and Benjamin Franklin a few years earlier. After taking an oath of allegiance to America, Grieve sailed for his adopted land with letters of introduction from Deane and Franklin to George Washington and Thomas Jefferson. He journeyed extensively in America and then returned to France in 1783. He was the anonymous translator of the first English edition (1787) of the marquis de Chastellux's *Voyages de M. le marquis de Chastellux dans l'Amérique septentrionale dans les années 1780, 1781 et 1782*, to which he added substantial notes based on his own observations. Grieve may also have been the translator into English of other works of travel and into French of the political writings of Richard Price and Joseph Priestley. Both in America and in France he seems to have pursued business interests which are not clearly identified in surviving references.

During the French Revolution Grieve became a member of the Jacobin Club, an associate of Marat, a revolutionary activist in the Seine et Oise, and the chief persecutor of Madame Du Barry, the former mistress of Louis XV. In the winter of 1792, during Du Barry's visit to London in search of her stolen diamonds, he won over two of her servants to the side of the revolution, held a club in her house, and procured an order for seals to be placed on her papers and valuables. On her return in March 1793 he drew up a list of 'suspects' for arrest, her name being the first, and on 1 July he escorted the municipality to the bar of the convention, where authority to apprehend her was obtained. A petition from the villagers of Louveciennes having effected her release, he published on 31 July a virulent pamphlet entitled *L'égalité controuvée ou Petite histoire … de la Du Barry*. He signed himself 'Greive, defendeur officieux des braves sans-culottes de Louveciennes, ami de Franklin et de Marat, factieux et anarchiste de premier ordre, et desorganisateur du despotisme dans les deux hemispheres depuis vingt ans'. In September he obtained a fresh order for her arrest and escorted her part of the way to Paris, but a petition again secured her release. In November she was once more apprehended. Greive superintended the successful search for her jewels, got up the case against her, and was himself one of the witnesses in her fatal trial. Some months after Robespierre's fall Greive was arrested at Corbie in Picardy and taken to Versailles, where twenty-two depositions were lodged against him, but the prosecution was dropped. During his imprisonment he reviewed his services to mankind in a 'Mémoire pour Georges Greive citoyen des Etats Unis d'Amérique aux représentants du peuple composant le comité de sûreté générale de la Convention nationale'. Living on an inheritance from his older brother, Davidson Richard, who had died in 1793, Greive eventually settled at Brussels, where he died on 22 February 1809, the register describing him as a native of 'Newcastel, Amerique'.

THOMAS R. KNOX

Sources G. Tate, *The history of the borough, castle and barony of Alnwick*, 2 vols. (1866–9) · T. R. Knox, 'Popular politics and provincial radicalism: Newcastle upon Tyne, 1769–1785', *Albion*, 11 (1979), 224–41 · T. R. Knox, 'Wilkism and the Newcastle election of 1774', *Durham University Journal*, 72 (1979–80), 23–37 · T. R. Knox, '"Bowes and liberty": the Newcastle by-election of 1777', *Durham University Journal*, 77 (1984–5), 149–64 · F. -J. marquis de Chastellux, *Travels in North America in the years 1780, 1781 and 1782*, ed. and trans. H. C. Rice, 2 vols. (1963) · C. Vatel, *Histoire de Madame Du Barry*, 3 vols. (1883) · J. G. Alger, 'English actors in the French Revolution', *EdinR*, 166 (1887), 445–64 · J. G. Alger, *Englishmen in the French Revolution* (1889) · G. Lenotre, ed., *Paris révolutionnaire: vieilles maisons, vieux papiers*, 6 vols., 2nd ser. (1920–30) · municipal records, Brussels · *A history of Northumberland*, Northumberland County History Committee, 15 vols. (1893–1940), vol. 7
Archives Archives Nationales, Paris, Mémoire pour Georges Greive

Greive, James (*bap.* 1729, *d.* 1773). *See under* Grieve, James (*bap.* 1708, *d.* 1763).

Grellán of Cráeb Grelláin (*fl.* 5th–6th cent.). *See under* Connacht, saints of (*act. c.*400–*c.*800).

Grene, Christopher (1629–1697), Jesuit, was born in the diocese of Kilkenny, one of the family of four sons and three daughters of George Grene and his wife, Jane Tempest; his parents, though English, had gone to live in Ireland because of the persecution in England. After Grene's early studies in Ireland he was sent in 1642 either to the English Jesuit college at St Omer or to the English Jesuit college at Liège. In 1647 he went to the English College in Rome to study for the priesthood. After his ordination in September 1653 he was sent to Ghent in Flanders to be the spiritual director at the convent of English Benedictine nuns there. He entered the Society of Jesus on 7 September 1658 following in this his elder brother Martin *Grene (1616/17–1667). Two years later he was on the English mission in the college or district of the Holy Apostles (East Anglia and Cambridge). From there in 1663 he went to Rome, where he remained for the rest of his life. About 1674 he became the English penitentiary, a priest appointed to hear the confessions of English pilgrims, first at the shrine at Loreto near Ancona and from 1686 to 1692 at St Peter's in Rome. Then, until his death, he was spiritual director at the English College and managed the business of the vineyard at Monte Porzio near Rome, which then belonged to the English Jesuits.

Grene rendered great service to historians by collecting the scattered records of the English and Welsh Catholic martyrs and by preserving other materials relevant to the history of Catholics in England. An account of those portions of his manuscript collections that are preserved in the Stonyhurst 'Anglia' manuscripts, at Oscott, in the archives of the archdiocese of Westminster, and in the English College at Rome was given in volume 3 of John Morris's *Troubles of our Catholic Forefathers* (3 vols., 1872–7). Grene died at the English College in Rome on 11 November 1697. THOMPSON COOPER, *rev.* GEOFFREY HOLT

Sources H. Foley, ed., *Records of the English province of the Society of Jesus*, 3 (1878), 499–500; 6 (1880), 369; 7/1 (1882), 317; 7/2 (1883), 1387–8 · G. Holt, *The English Jesuits, 1650–1829: a biographical dictionary*, Catholic RS, 70 (1984), 106 · W. Kelly, ed., *Liber ruber venerabilis collegii Anglorum de urbe*, 2, Catholic RS, 40 (1943), 39 · A. Kenny, ed., *The responsa scholarum of the English College, Rome*, 2, Catholic RS, 55 (1963), 502 · B. Basset, *The English Jesuits, from Campion to Martindale* (1967), 6–7 · records and catalogues, British province of the Society of Jesus, 114 Mount Street, London · J. Morris, ed., *The troubles of our Catholic forefathers related by themselves*, 3 (1877), 3–7 · G. Oliver, *Collections towards illustrating the biography of the Scotch, English and Irish members, SJ* (1838), 91 · Gillow, *Lit. biog. hist.*, 3.48–9 · records, English College, Rome
Archives Archives of the British Province of the Society of Jesus, London, Stonyhurst MSS, collectanea · English College, Rome, archives · Oscott College, Birmingham · Westm. DA

Grene, Martin (1616/17–1667), Jesuit, son of George Grene and Jane Tempest, was born in Ireland in either 1616 or 1617. Two early Jesuit catalogues list Kent as his birthplace but this is most likely a scribal error for Kilkenny, where his two brothers, Thomas (*b.* 1615) and the Jesuit Christopher *Grene (1629–1697), were born. Their parents were English, perhaps from Yorkshire, who retired to Ireland for religious reasons. Both Thomas and Christopher were educated in Ireland until the age of thirteen or fourteen; most likely Martin followed the same programme. By 1637 he was a student at the English College at St Omer.

In 1638 Grene entered the Jesuit noviciate then at Ghent because of the Thirty Years' War. The noviciate returned to Watten in 1639. From 1640 to 1644 he studied philosophy and theology at the English College in Liège. A rapid deterioration of finances brought on by the civil war in England and the Thirty Years' War on the continent nearly bankrupted the English Jesuits. Forced to economize the provincial sent some Jesuits to other provinces: Grene completed his theological studies in Pont-à-Mousson, where he was most likely ordained about 1646, and in 1647 he taught at the Jesuit college in Rheims. He returned to the English province in 1648 as minister and consultor at the noviciate in Watten. By 1653 he had been assigned to England, to the Residence of St Mary, in Oxfordshire. He was professed of the four vows in London on 23 November 1654. From information provided in letters to his brother Christopher we know that he was in Sherborne, Dorset, for at least part of 1664-6.

In September 1664 Grene exhorted his brother to persuade the Italian Jesuit historian Daniello Bartoli to proceed with his proposed history of the society's work in England, which was published in 1667:

> It is a story that requires a good pen, which I want, and much leisure and convenience of books, which I have not. Yet I will do what I can to collect together the matter, which I shall be glad to send Father Bartoli, and serve in what I can in so pious a design.   (Foley, 3.497)

Despite his protest that he 'wanted' a pen, Grene's literary achievements should not be underestimated.

Grene was assigned the unenviable task of preparing a reply to the English translation of Pascal's *Les provinciales, or, The Mysterie of Jesuitisme*, four editions of which were published in England before 1659. His *An Answer to the Provinciall Letters* (Paris, 1659) was more than a mere translation: he improved the original and added a preface on the history of Jansenism.

In 1661 the English government investigated the possibility of rescinding or modifying the penal laws. Some secular clergy were willing to sacrifice Jesuits, whose political machinations were, of course, the reason why Catholic loyalty was suspect, and the laws were passed, in return for the repeal of all penal laws. Grene defended the society against such accusations with *An Account of the Jesuites Life and Doctrine* (1661), the first English refutation of the popular image of the 'evil Jesuit' responsible for every mishap and disaster. Attacking stories about Jesuit wealth, disloyalty, and doctrines—for example, regicide—Grene stressed that most Jesuits pursued humble tasks such as teaching, administering sacraments, and working in hospitals and prisons. Regardless of what doctrines Jesuits had taught forty or fifty years ago, English Jesuits had demonstrated their loyalty by adhering to the royalist cause throughout the civil war and interregnum.

By March 1666 Grene had returned to Watten as rector and novice master. There he died on 6 October 1667. His

Account so impressed James, duke of York, who had been given a copy in 1680 by James Forbes, superior of Jesuits in Scotland, that he wanted it reprinted for circulation during the hysteria associated with the Popish Plot. It was not reprinted, but sections were reissued and rebutted in *Autokatakritoi, or, The Jesuits Condemned* (London, 1679).

THOMAS M. MCCOOG

Sources T. M. McCoog, *English and Welsh Jesuits, 1555-1650*, 2 vols., Catholic RS, 74-5 (1994-5) · T. M. McCoog, ed., *Monumenta Angliae*, 1-2 (1992) · H. Foley, ed., *Records of the English province of the Society of Jesus*, 7 vols. in 8 (1875-83) · G. Holt, *St Omers and Bruges colleges, 1593-1773: a biographical dictionary*, Catholic RS, 69 (1979) · T. H. Clancy, *A literary history of the English Jesuits: a century of books, 1615-1714* (1996) · T. H. Clancy, *English Catholic books, 1641-1700: a bibliography*, rev. edn (1996) · A. Kenny, ed., *The responsa scholarum of the English College, Rome*, 2, Catholic RS, 55 (1963)
Archives Archives of the British Province of the Society of Jesus, London · Archivum Romanum Societatis Iesu, Rome

Grenfell family (*per. c.*1785-1879), copper smelters, were influential merchants from St Just in Cornwall, but came to national prominence through **Pascoe Grenfell** (*bap.* 1761, *d.* 1838), industrialist and politician, and through the marriage of members of the family to leading figures of the time. Pascoe Grenfell was born in Marazion, Cornwall, and baptized at St Hilary's Church on 24 September 1761, the son of Pascoe Grenfell of Marazion, merchant and consul to the states of Holland, and his wife, Mary, third child of William Tremenheere, attorney, of Penzance. Educated at Truro grammar school, the younger Pascoe Grenfell was sent, through his father's connections, to learn banking with the firm of Hope Brothers of Amsterdam. He returned to London, entering into business with his father and uncle as merchants and dealers in tin and copper ores. He later became involved with the copper magnate Thomas Williams, acting as his agent on a sales trip to France.

A close association developed from this involvement with Williams. Grenfell became a shareholder in several of Williams's enterprises, and by the late 1780s he was running Williams's newly established office in London. Their business relationship was further extended in 1794 when Grenfell went into partnership with Williams's son Owen to buy Cornish ores, primarily to supply Williams's Middle and Upper Bank smelting works in Swansea. Following Thomas Williams's death in 1802 Grenfell and Owen Williams took over these works. Owen Williams withdrew his interest in 1825, which led to the establishment of the family firm of Pascoe Grenfell & Sons, which remained a major copper producer for most of the nineteenth century.

Grenfell's association with Thomas Williams extended into politics. Having purchased Taplow House, Grenfell succeeded Williams as MP for Great Marlow, Buckinghamshire, from 14 December 1802 until 29 February 1820. He subsequently served as MP for Penryn in his native Cornwall from 9 March 1820 to 2 June 1826. In the Commons Grenfell associated himself with the Grenville party and his strong evangelical faith and friendship with William Wilberforce led him to speak against the slave trade. Recognized as an expert on financial matters Grenfell was instrumental in the introduction of the periodical publication of accounts by the Bank of England, of which he was a vigilant observer. He was also governor of the Royal Exchange Insurance Company and a commissioner of the lieutenancy for London.

Grenfell married twice. His first wife, his cousin Charlotte Granville, died in 1790. They had two sons, the eldest of whom, George Granville Grenfell (1789–1853), became MP for Buckingham. The younger, **Charles Pascoe Grenfell** (1790–1867), was born in London on 4 April 1790. He was educated at Harrow School and at Christ Church, Oxford, and married Lady Georgiana Molyneux, eldest daughter of the second earl of Sefton. The couple had four children, including Henry Riversdale *Grenfell. Charles Pascoe Grenfell served as MP for Preston in 1847–52, and also again in 1857–65. Between 1846 and 1848 he was chairman of the London and Brighton Railway Company. Listed in directories as a copper master of Upper Thames Street, Charles was, for many years, senior partner in Pascoe Grenfell & Sons. He died at Taplow Court, Taplow, Buckinghamshire, on 21 March 1867.

The second wife of Pascoe Grenfell, whom he married on 15 January 1798, was Georgiana St Leger, seventh and youngest daughter of St Leger St Leger (formerly St Leger Aldworth), first Viscount Doneraile of the second creation. They had two sons, **Pascoe St Leger Grenfell** (1798–1879) and **Riversdale William Grenfell** (1807–1871), both of whom were closely involved in Pascoe Grenfell & Sons and became prominent figures in Swansea. Pascoe and Georgiana Grenfell also had eleven daughters of whom Fanny [see Kingsley, Frances Eliza (1814–1891)] married Charles Kingsley, Charlotte married James Anthony Froude, and Marianne married George Carr *Glyn. Pascoe Grenfell died at 38 Belgrave Square, London, on 23 January 1838. He was predeceased by his second wife, who had died on 12 May 1818.

The first member of the family to be resident in Swansea was Riversdale William Grenfell, who moved to the town in the 1830s to look after the family's industrial interests. He had one son and two daughters, the elder of whom married the oriental scholar Max Müller. The Grenfell family's involvement in smelting, however, continued principally through the Eton educated Pascoe St Leger Grenfell, who not only took over the management of the smelting works following his arrival in Swansea in the 1840s, but became closely involved in local affairs.

Both Riversdale and Pascoe St Leger Grenfell were, like their father, devout evangelical churchmen, and they enhanced the family's reputation for being particularly concerned with the welfare of their workers. Unlike other smelters, Pascoe St Leger Grenfell built his home, Maesteg House, in close proximity to his workers and downwind of the noxious copper smoke produced by the smelting works. The family, together with the Freemans of the White Rock copper smelting works, established schools in Kilvey as early as 1806. This collaboration continued when the Grenfells built All Saints' Church, Kilvey, in 1842 on land donated by Freeman & Co. The family also built the Foxhole music hall in 1853, and their church involvement

also included becoming patrons of the living of St Thomas.

Pascoe St Leger Grenfell's personal commitment to church and community was considerable. He taught a Bible class in a Sunday school for over thirty years, was involved with the British and Foreign Bible Society and the London Missionary Society, and in 1868 became the first chairman of the Released Prisoners' Aid Society. He was chairman of the Swansea Harbour Trust from 1850 to 1859, remaining chairman of its finance committee for many years afterwards. He was chairman of the Swansea Vale Railway Company, a member of the Swansea corporation, a justice of the peace, a feoffee of Swansea grammar school, and was deputy lieutenant for Glamorgan. In 1859 he founded the 6th Glamorgan rifle corps, which he commanded as its lieutenant-colonel.

Pascoe St Leger Grenfell married twice. His first marriage, in 1824, was to Catherine Anne Du Pré, daughter of James Du Pré of Wilton Park, Buckinghamshire, and cousin of Henry Labouchere, the Victorian radical. They had five sons and four daughters. Catherine died in 1845 while giving birth. His second marriage, on 30 September 1847, was to Penelope Frances Madan (d. 1868), the daughter of Spencer Madan, dean of Chichester. Of the nine children from the first marriage, two rose to prominence in very different ways. Elizabeth Mary (1836–1894), known as Mary, was deeply religious and devoted much time and energy to the family's philanthropic works in Swansea, and was particularly involved with the temperance movement. The youngest son, Francis Wallace *Grenfell (1841–1925), had a distinguished military career, rising to become Field Marshal Lord Grenfell.

Pascoe St Leger Grenfell died at the Rope Walk, Standard Hill, Nottingham, on 28 March 1879. His brother predeceased him, dying at Elibank, near Taplow, Buckinghamshire, on 1 June 1871. Their deaths removed the two most influential figures from the family smelting business. After the death of Pascoe St Leger Grenfell *The Cambrian* noted that the works fell:

> into the hands of the fourth generation of the copper smelting Grenfells … [who] … chiefly comprised of young men under the age of 30, have decided to sever themselves, and such others of the family as are now in it, from the manufacture of copper and yellow metal. (Roberts, 55)

However, the family maintained a strong financial interest in the firm, even after it became a limited company in 1890. It has been suggested that this apparent lack of interest was at least partly responsible for the decline of the firm, although all British copper smelters were under severe pressure from adverse market conditions by the end of the nineteenth century. The firm went into voluntary liquidation in October 1892 and was taken over by Williams, Foster & Co. to form Williams, Foster, and Pascoe Grenfell, with the Grenfells having just one seat on the board.   EDMUND NEWELL

Sources M. E. Chamberlain, 'The Grenfells of Kilvey', *Glamorgan Historian*, 60 (1973), 123–42 • J. R. Harris, *The copper king: a biography of Thomas Williams of Llanidan* (1964) • R. O. Roberts, 'Enterprise and capital for non-ferrous metal smelting in Glamorgan, 1694–1924', *Morgannwg*, 23 (1979), 48–82 • Boase, *Mod. Eng. biog.* • *The Cambrian*

(9 June 1871) · *The Cambrian* (28 March 1879) · *The Cambrian* (1 April 1879) · *CGPLA Eng. & Wales* (1871) · *CGPLA Eng. & Wales* (1879) · m. cert. [Pascoe St Leger Grenfell and Penelope Frances Madan] · d. cert. [Pascoe St Leger Grenfell] · d. cert. [Charles Pascoe Grenfell] · d. cert. [Riversdale William Grenfell] · *DNB*

Archives Bucks. RLSS, corresp. and MSS; journal, ledgers, corresp., and papers | Birm. CL, corresp. with Boulton family · BL, letters to Lord Grenville, Add. MS 58977 · BL, corresp. with Lord Grenville; papers relating to the Bank of England, Add. MS 69082 · U. Wales, Bangor, Mona Mine MSS

Likenesses portrait (*The Grenfells*), Swansea Museum?, Lower Swansea fact sheet 9, 34

Wealth at death under £45,000—Riversdale William Grenfell: probate, 19 June 1871, *CGPLA Eng. & Wales* · under £30,000—Pascoe St Leger Grenfell: probate, 2 May 1879, *CGPLA Eng. & Wales*

Grenfell, Alice (1842–1917). *See under* Grenfell, Bernard Pyne (1869–1926).

Grenfell, Bernard Pyne (1869–1926), papyrologist, was born on 16 December 1869 in Birmingham, the eldest and only surviving son of John Granville Grenfell FGS (*d.* 1897), a master at King Edward's School, Birmingham, and previously (1861–6) assistant in the department of Greek and Roman antiquities at the British Museum. His mother was **Alice Grenfell** (1842–1917), the second of six daughters of Henry Pyne (1809–1885), assistant commissioner of tithes, and his wife, Harriet James. She supported the women's suffrage movement in Bristol and London, and sat on the Bristol school board for three years.

Grenfell's parents married in 1869, and in 1870 his father was appointed a housemaster at Clifton College, Bristol, where the family remained until 1889. As a child Grenfell was delicate and was given special treatment at Clifton College, where he was a pupil from 1878 to 1888, but his health improved at the Queen's College, Oxford, where he obtained a scholarship in 1888. After graduating with a double first in classics in 1892, he decided to spend a fifth year at Oxford studying economics, but he soon changed to the new subject of Greek papyri, and successfully applied in 1893 for the university's Craven travelling fellowship. In the winter of 1893–4 he went for the first time to Egypt, to learn excavation techniques under W. M. Flinders Petrie at Qift (Coptos). Petrie bought a long Greek papyrus roll which he asked Grenfell to edit. Grenfell's first publication, however, was of three seventh-century contracts from Apollonopolis Magna (*Journal of Philology*, 22, 1894). In 1894 he was elected a research fellow of Queen's. During the winter of 1894–5 he spent a second season in Upper Egypt with Petrie, and had the good fortune to acquire a second roll containing the remainder of Petrie's text, which consisted of fiscal enactments of Ptolemy II (*r.* 285–246 BC). In 1896 he published the whole as *The Revenue Laws of Ptolemy Philadelphus*. Although he consulted other scholars the work was essentially Grenfell's own and gave convincing proof of his exceptional gifts as decipherer and commentator.

During 1895 the Egypt Exploration Fund (afterwards Society) decided to embrace in its scope the Graeco-Roman period; and in the winter of 1895–6 Grenfell and David George Hogarth (1862–1927), joined in January by Arthur Surridge Hunt (1871–1934), a friend of Grenfell's

from Queen's, were sent to the Faiyûm in order to examine likely sites and determine whether excavating for papyri would be cheaper than buying them from dealers. Excavations at Kom Aushim (Karanis) and Umm al-Asl (Bacchias) were fruitful enough to justify the experiment, and enabled Grenfell to study the conditions in which papyri were preserved in mummy cases and rubbish mounds. He developed a system of searching for them using trained workers, which Grenfell and Hunt applied the next winter at Bahnasa (Oxyrhynchus) in middle Egypt, with unprecedented success. They discovered works of Christian literature, among them the 'Sayings of Jesus' (now known to be from the apocryphal 'Gospel of Thomas'), many classical fragments, including part of a new Nereid ode by Sappho, and important documents of the Roman and Byzantine periods. The interest these aroused led to the formation of the Graeco-Roman branch of the Egypt Exploration Fund in 1897. From then on almost all Grenfell's work was performed in collaboration with Hunt.

After his father's death abroad in 1897, Grenfell's mother came to live with him in Oxford. She began to learn hieroglyphs, and became an authority on Egyptian amuletic scarabs, contributing articles to academic journals; these included a catalogue of the Queen's College scarab collection (1915).

After further excavations in the Faiyûm (1898–1902), some at Umm al-Breigat (Tebtunis) for the University of California, operations were transferred in March 1902 to al-Hiba, until the first part of the next season, when Grenfell and Hunt returned to Bahnasa. Successive campaigns brought to light vast quantities of papyri, which were published in the annual volumes of the fund: *The Oxyrhynchus Papyri* (more or less annually from 1898), *Fayûm Towns and their Papyri* (1900), and *The Hibeh Papyri* (pt 1, 1906); together with *The Tebtunis Papyri* (pt 1, 1902; pt 2, 1907), published by the University of California. They also catalogued important material already in collections: *The Amherst Papyri* (2 pts, 1900–01) and the *Greek Papyri* volume (1903) of the Cairo Museum catalogue.

Unfortunately Grenfell's health began to deteriorate. His first nervous breakdown occurred in the 1906–7 season in Egypt, although he recovered before returning to Oxford. In 1908 Oxford University created the world's first chair of papyrology for him, but a second and more serious attack in the autumn of that year incapacitated him for over four years, during which his professorship lapsed. His mother was able to nurse him back to full health by the spring of 1913. Although Hunt was appointed to the vacant chair in 1913, Grenfell became honorary professor in 1916 and joint professor in 1919. During most of the First World War, when Hunt was on military service, Grenfell worked single-handed preparing parts 12–15 of *The Oxyrhynchus Papyri* for press, besides working on volume 3 of *The Tebtunis Papyri* and collecting materials for a comprehensive study of the geography of Egypt. Early in 1920 he visited Cairo in order to collate the texts of certain papyri intended for part 16 of *The Oxyrhynchus Papyri*. He returned in April, apparently in good health and spirits, but the old symptoms soon afterwards reappeared, and it eventually became necessary for him to go first to a sanatorium near St Andrews and thence to Murray's Royal Mental Hospital, at Eley, near Perth. This time he lacked the care of his mother, who had died in Oxford on 8 August 1917. Despite occasional rallies he never really recovered, and he remained in hospital until he died, of a heart attack, on 18 May 1926. His funeral was held in Queen's College chapel, and he was buried with his mother in Holywell cemetery, Oxford, on 22 May. He never married.

Grenfell's contribution to the infant discipline of papyrology was enormous. The techniques he developed for excavating papyri became standard, and the volumes he and Hunt edited remain the basic reference works of the subject. Although they had to be prepared in the time available between field seasons, in the accuracy of their texts and the quality of their commentary, evading no difficulty but free from superfluity, they have never been surpassed, and their methods served as a model to other editors. Grenfell's interests were primarily historical rather than literary, and although a good decipherer he was not a palaeographer as such. He was peculiarly gifted for his life's work. To excellent eyesight and a gift for the marshalling and lucid exposition of a complex mass of evidence he united energy, enthusiasm, and a brain at once imaginative and critical. A very rapid worker, he spared no pains to correct first impressions by later revision. His work was recognized by an honorary LittD from Trinity College, Dublin, in 1900, the same year in which he became the first ever recipient of the Oxford DLitt; he was elected FBA in 1905. He had a singularly attractive personality. Ardent, generous, affectionate, and given to hospitality, he made friends easily and retained them when made. He was said to have won the trust, affection, and respect of his Egyptian workmen.

H. I. BELL, *rev.* R. S. SIMPSON

Sources DNB · A. S. Hunt, 'B. P. Grenfell, 1869–1926', *PBA*, 12 (1926), 357–64 · *Journal of Egyptian Archaeology*, 12 (1926), 285–6 · *The Times* (19 May 1926), 21 · *The Times* (22 May 1926), 8 · W. R. Dawson and E. P. Uphill, *Who was who in Egyptology*, 3rd edn, rev. M. L. Bierbrier (1995), 178–9 · *WWW, 1916–28* · *The Clifton College register 1860–1897*, ed. E. M. Oakeley (1897) · *The Times* (17 Aug 1917), 9 [Alice Grenfell] · *Journal of Egyptian Archaeology*, 4 (1917), 280 [Alice Grenfell] · A. S. Hunt, *Aegyptus*, 8 (1927), 114–16 · Boase, *Mod. Eng. biog.*
Archives AM Oxf., corresp. · Bodl. Oxf., corresp. | BL, corresp. with Idris Bell, Add. MS 59511 · Egypt Exploration Society, London, corresp. with the Egypt Exploration Society
Likenesses W. Stoneman, photograph, 1917, NPG · Elliott & Fry, photograph, repro. in A. S. Hunt, ed., *The Oxyrhynchus Papyri*, 17 (1927), frontispiece

Grenfell, Charles Pascoe (1790–1867). *See under* Grenfell family (*per. c.*1785–1879).

Grenfell, Edward Charles, first Baron St Just (1870–1941), merchant banker and politician, was born on 29 May 1870 in Pimlico, London, the only son of Henry Riversdale *Grenfell (1824–1902), of Taplow, and his wife,

Alethea Louisa, daughter of Henry John Adeane of Babraham, Cambridgeshire, MP for Cambridgeshire. His father was MP for Stoke and a director, and from 1881 to 1883 governor, of the Bank of England. Edward was educated at Harrow School and at Trinity College, Cambridge, where he won the Greaves essay prize in 1891 and took a second in history in 1892.

Edward Grenfell's family connections drew him to banking. He joined Brown, Shipley & Co., the London branch of the Anglo-American firm Brown Brothers (which also employed Montagu Norman, future governor of the Bank of England), and he moved in 1894 to Smith Ellison's Bank at Lincoln; he eventually became manager of the Grimsby branch. Grenfell's family and banking connections soon lured him back to the City of London, however: well known to Walter Hayes Burns and John (Jack) Pierpont Morgan, partners in the Anglo-American bank J. S. Morgan & Co., he was invited to join the bank in April 1900. His main duty was to oversee the firm's internal operations and thereby enable the general partners to concentrate on developing business. Grenfell soon made himself indispensable, being equally effective with office routine and clients. He was made a general partner in January 1904 with a 4 per cent share of the profits (his portion amounted to £5113 that year); in 1909 the provisions of J. P. Morgan's will resulted in the bank being renamed Morgan, Grenfell & Co., and Grenfell remained the senior partner until his death.

As the London end of the house of Morgan, Morgan Grenfell was fully involved in financing foreign trade and, in particular, issuing loans on behalf of foreign governments and utilities. Grenfell was the partner who dealt with governments, home and abroad, and with their bankers. During the First World War his position was of acute importance: the American house, J. P. Morgan & Co., became the purchasing agent in the USA for the British War Office and Admiralty and the financial agent for the Treasury, and Grenfell was largely responsible for relations with the cabinet and Treasury. This importance extended into the 1920s, when the house of Morgan was the leading bank involved in raising capital for the reconstruction of Europe. Morgan Grenfell led on most of the associated bonds issued in London for European governments and other institutions. Grenfell himself conducted most of the London negotiations, such as those for the currency-stabilization loans for Belgium and Italy.

Grenfell continued the family tradition of quiet involvement in politics: both his father and maternal grandfather had been MPs, and a by-election victory with a majority of 3936 in May 1922 made him the Conservative MP for the City of London; he was returned unopposed in 1922 and 1923, and he served in the House of Commons until he was awarded a barony in 1935. He concentrated on financial and international questions, speaking against the Anglo-Soviet treaty in August 1924 and against the French war debt agreement in July 1926, betraying some suspicion of both countries. His interventions during debates on finance bills were always on the side of caution, though after 1927 he seldom spoke in the house at all, preferring to work behind the scenes. During the 1931 financial crisis, which led to the fall of the Labour government, Grenfell acted as liaison between the prime minister, Ramsay MacDonald, and the American bankers whom the British government had asked for a loan.

Grenfell was a director of the Bank of England from 1905 to 1940, a position of some tension during the First World War. The governor, Walter Cunliffe, was of a dictatorial frame of mind and fought the Treasury over external financial policy; Grenfell was Cunliffe's cousin and was often, he claimed, the only man who could speak with him. Other City positions included a seat on the board of the Sun Assurance Group and directorships of the White Star Line and of Shaw, Saville & Co. He was also a lieutenant of the City of London and, from 1922 until his death, a governor of Harrow School, a position which gave him great satisfaction.

Grenfell was a man of great formality and reserve whose wife, a keen devotee of the ballet, strove to loosen him up: he arrived home one evening, for example, to find dancers from the Diaghalev company dancing on his tables. She was Florence Henderson, elder daughter of George William Henderson, a merchant importer; Grenfell married her in 1913. Their only child, Peter George (1922–1984), who was born in 1922, elected to follow her cultural interests rather than the banking enterprises of his father.

Lord St Just was a banker's banker. Hard-working, loyal, sound, sometimes acerbic, and a man of his word, he was in his prime one of the half-dozen leading merchant bankers in London. This was partly because of his own qualities but partly also because he was the link with the most powerful investment bank in the world, J. P. Morgan & Co. His closest friend was probably Jack Morgan, son of the famous Pierpont Morgan and head of the house of Morgan from 1913 until his own death in 1943. The two of them bestrode the world of international finance, and their deaths, within two years of each other, signalled the end of an era of overwhelming Anglo-American financial dominance.

Lord St Just died on 26 November 1941 at Bacres, Henley-on-Thames, after a long illness. He was survived by his wife. KATHLEEN BURK

Sources GL, Morgan Grenfell MSS · Morgan Grenfell Group, London, Morgan Grenfell MSS · K. Burk, *Morgan Grenfell, 1838–1988: the biography of a merchant bank* (1989) · K. Burk, 'The treasury: from impotence to power', *War and the state: the transformation of British government, 1914–1919*, ed. K. Burk (1982), 84–107 · *The Times* (28 Nov 1941) · WWW · WW · *Debrett's Peerage* · *CGPLA Eng. & Wales* (1941) **Archives** GL, Morgan Grenfell MSS · Morgan Grenfell Group, London, Morgan Grenfell MSS **Likenesses** F. May, caricature, gouache, NPG · photographs, Morgan Grenfell, 23 Great Winchester Street, London · photographs, repro. in Burk, *Morgan Grenfell* · portrait, Morgan Grenfell, 23 Great Winchester Street, London **Wealth at death** £880,331 15s. 2d.: probate, 22 May 1942, CGPLA Eng. & Wales

Grenfell [née Fane], **Ethel Anne Priscilla** [Ettie], **Lady Desborough** (1867–1952), hostess, was born on 27 June 1867, the daughter and only surviving child of Julian *Fane (1827–1870), diplomatist, and fourth son of John *Fane,

Ethel Anne Priscilla Grenfell, Lady Desborough (1867–1952), by Bassano, c.1913

eleventh earl of Westmorland (1784–1859), and his wife, Lady Adine (d. 1868), daughter of the sixth Earl Cowper. Both her parents died before she was three, and she used to say that until she was five she never wore anything but black. She was brought up at Panshanger, Hertfordshire, and was heir to that estate of 30,000 acres and a fine collection of pictures. She grew up to be outstandingly pretty, and had numerous admirers, but she chose solid worth in the shape of William Henry (Willy) *Grenfell (1855–1945) of Taplow Court, Buckinghamshire, athlete and public servant, whom she married on 17 February 1887; he was created Baron Desborough in 1905. She was an extra woman of the bedchamber to Queen Mary from 1912.

Ettie Grenfell was notable in three different roles: as a mother, as a brilliant hostess, and as mistress (perhaps platonic) to a series of devoted men. She had five much-loved children (Julian, Billy, Monica, Ivo, and Imogen), in whose lives she played a big part. As a young man Julian *Grenfell, who was an uncomfortable mixture of athlete and poet, rebelled against her worldly lifestyle, but he still wrote to her: 'I don't want to see you again ever because everyone after you is like flat soda water' (Desborough, 186).

Ettie Grenfell was a leading member of the group of politically minded intellectuals known as the Souls, whom she entertained at her famous Saturday to Monday parties at Taplow Court. Arthur Balfour, the central figure, was one of her greatest friends. Osbert Sitwell called her the last of the great whig hostesses and certainly, descended as she was from Lady Melbourne and Lady Palmerston, she was bred for the part; she also looked the part, like a Gainsborough picture, and she talked in the Holland House drawl. She had an insatiable interest in human beings: Sitwell described how every guest when he left Taplow believed he was the only person she had wished to talk to, and not only that, but also that his presence had been the very making of the party. Lord David Cecil described how, seated between the prime minister and a fifteen-year-old schoolboy—himself—she lavished her attention and charm equally on both. Max Beerbohm in his skit on Taplow in *The Seven Men* added a barb: 'exclusive she was but not of publicity. Next to Windsor Castle [Taplow] was the most advertised house in England' (M. Beerbohm, *The Seven Men*, 1919, 62).

Perhaps due to her traumatic childhood with its many bereavements, Ettie Grenfell had a hunger for admiration, and, not satisfied with the dog-like devotion of her husband—whom she loved none the less—she embarked on a series of long-drawn-out love affairs. The first was with George *Wyndham (1863–1913); he was succeeded by Evan Charteris (1864–1940) and by John *Baring, later second Baron Revelstoke (1863–1929), who was hers for life. Maurice Baring, the novelist, was also enamoured of her and portrays her as Leila, the vamp in *C* (1924). As she grew older she favoured younger men such as Archie Gordon, who was engaged to Violet Asquith. He was killed in a car crash in 1909. 'Ettie is an ox', commented Margot Asquith, 'she will be made into Bovril when she dies' (Desborough, 185).

Lady Desborough was soon to need all her toughness. From the outbreak of the 1914 war her two elder sons, Julian and Billy, fought gallantly in France, but in 1915 both of them were killed. To staunch her grief, and as a memorial to her sons, she told the story of their lives, mainly from their letters, in *Pages from a Family Journal*, published privately in 1916. It is a touching yet unsentimental work. Her elder daughter, Monica, also served in the war, as a Red Cross nurse in France. Her youngest son, Ivo, died in a car accident in 1926.

Between the wars the Desboroughs continued to live in their two great houses, Taplow and Panshanger, giving weekend parties for Arthur Balfour and the thinning ranks of the Souls. Willy died in 1945; an old friend described Ettie in her last years as 'a lady of great age, lying half paralysed in a huge empty house and saying with the heart rending ghost of a gay smile: "we did have fun didn't we?"' (*The Times*, 30 May 1952). She died at Panshanger on 28 May 1952; the funeral was at Hertingfordbury and the burial at Taplow on 1 June.

JANE RIDLEY and CLAYRE PERCY

Sources Lady Desborough [E. A. P. Grenfell], *Pages from a family journal, 1888–1915* (privately printed, Eton, 1916) • N. Mosley, *Julian Grenfell* (1976) • D. Cecil, *The Times* (3 June 1952), 8 • O. Sitwell, *The Times* (9 June 1952), 8 • M. Asquith, *The autobiography of Margot Asquith*, 2 vols. (1920–22) • A. Lambert, *Unquiet Souls: the Indian summer of the British aristocracy, 1880–1918* (1984) • Burke, *Peerage* • *The Times* (29 May 1952)

Archives Herts. ALS, corresp., diaries, and papers | CAC Cam., letters to Duff Cooper • Herts. ALS, MS relating to the life of Julian Fane and corresp. • PRO NIre., Stewart MSS, letters to Lord Londonderry
Likenesses J. S. Sargent, black chalk drawing, 1909 • Bassano, photograph, *c.*1913, NPG [*see illus.*] • R. Whistler, three caricatures, *c.*1940 • Bassano, photographs, NPG • photographs, repro. in Lambert, *Unquiet souls*
Wealth at death £406,685 4s. 6d.: probate, 8 July 1952, CGPLA Eng. & Wales

Grenfell, Francis Wallace, first Baron Grenfell (1841–1925), army officer, the fourth son of Pascoe St Leger *Grenfell (1798–1879) [*see under* Grenfell family], of Maesteg House, Swansea, Glamorgan, and his first wife, Catherine Anne, daughter of James Du Pré MP, of Wilton Park, Beaconsfield, Buckinghamshire, was born at Maesteg House on 29 April 1841. The Grenfells were a Buckinghamshire and City banking family.

Grenfell was educated at Milton Abbas School, Dorset, but left school early, and after passing the army entrance examination, purchased his commission into the 3rd battalion of the 60th rifles on 5 August 1859. His early service was uneventful; he purchased his commission as captain on 27 October 1871 in the last gazette in which purchase was allowed. In 1874 he decided to leave the army, but he was unexpectedly invited to become aide-de-camp to General Sir Arthur Cunynghame in South Africa. In 1875 he took part in the Diamond Fields expedition in Griqualand West, and in 1878 he acted as staff officer during the last Cape frontier wars. A successful expedition was undertaken against the Galeka tribe during which Grenfell was present at the action of Quintana Mountain; this was followed by a march against the rebellious Gaika tribe, in the north-east of Cape Colony, which ended with their rout in the Gwili Gwili Mountains. For his services Grenfell received a brevet majority. During the Anglo-Zulu War Grenfell served on the headquarters staff, and took part in the battle of Ulundi. He was next appointed brigade major at Shorncliffe, receiving a brevet lieutenant-colonelcy for his war services. In 1881, when the First South African War broke out, he returned to Natal to act as deputy assistant quartermaster-general, but peace was made soon after his arrival.

In 1882 Grenfell was assistant adjutant-general to Sir Garnet Wolseley on the Egyptian expedition, and was present at the battle of Tell al-Kebir. After the campaign he remained in Egypt as assistant adjutant-general to the permanent garrison, and was promoted brevet colonel and aide-de-camp to Queen Victoria. He accepted the appointment under Sir Evelyn Wood of second in command of the Egyptian forces, then under British control. During the Gordon relief expedition in 1884, he commanded at Aswan the Egyptian troops on the Nile and the communications of the whole expedition. After its failure in 1885 Grenfell remained at Aswan in command of the Egyptian detachments.

Grenfell was appointed sirdar of the Egyptian army in April 1885. He had an important role in operations defending the frontier against the Mahdists. He commanded a division of the Anglo-Egyptian forces at the battle of

Francis Wallace Grenfell, first Baron Grenfell (1841–1925), by Barraud, pubd 1889

Giniss on 30 December 1885, for which he received the CB and the grand cordon of the Mejidiye, and in 1886 he was created a KCB and promoted major-general. He commanded the Egyptian forces which repulsed Osman Digna's attack on Suakin at Gamaiza (20 December 1888), and defeated the amir of Kordofan at Toski (3 August 1889). In 1891 he consolidated the Egyptian hold on Suakin. On the death of the Khedive Tawfiq, in the spring of 1892, Grenfell reluctantly resigned the sirdarship. His tenure of office was notable for the reorganization of the Egyptian forces, which were to prove valuable during Kitchener's reconquest of the Sudan. Without ever giving proof of any outstanding gifts of generalship, Grenfell had effectively completed his task in Egypt.

In 1887 Grenfell married Evelyn, daughter of Major-General Robert Blucher Wood. They had no children and she died in 1899.

After being rewarded with the GCMG, Grenfell was appointed deputy adjutant-general for reserve forces at the War Office, and in 1894 he was appointed inspector-general. In 1897 he was appointed to command the British garrison in Egypt. This position was not easy, since Kitchener was in command of the expedition which had been advancing up the Nile since spring 1896. Grenfell self-effacingly refrained from any act that might hinder Kitchener, and, although he was the latter's senior in rank—having been promoted lieutenant-general in 1898—he generously subordinated his own authority to that of the sirdar.

In January 1899 Grenfell was appointed governor of Malta, where he showed much interest in the antiquities and methods of cultivation. In 1902 he was made Baron Grenfell of Kilvey, co. Glamorgan. He married, in 1903, the Hon. Margaret (d. 1911), daughter of Lewis Asshunt Majendie MP, of Hedingham, Essex; they had two sons and a daughter. Also in 1903 he was selected for the command of the newly created 4th army corps and, on promotion to full general in 1904, was appointed commander-in-chief in Ireland, a post which he held until 1908, when he was promoted field marshal. During the remainder of his life he devoted himself to the Church Lads' Brigade, the Royal Horticultural Society, of which he was president, and to various other voluntary services. He was also a keen Egyptologist and antiquary. He received many honours: military, academic, and civic. Grenfell died at Windlesham, Surrey, on 27 January 1925. He was succeeded as second baron by his elder son, Pascoe Christian Victor (b. 1905).

H. DE WATTEVILLE, rev. JAMES FALKNER

Sources The Times (28 Jan 1925) · Memoirs of Field-Marshal Lord Grenfell (1925) · Army List · Hart's Army List · Burke, Peerage
Archives priv. coll., diaries, corresp., and papers | NA Scot., letters to J. A. Hope · NRA Scotland, priv. coll., corresp. with Sir John Ewart · PRO, corresp. with Lord Cromer · U. Durham, corresp. with Sir Reginald Wingate | FILM BFI NFTVA, news footage
Likenesses W. Stoneman, photograph, 1919, NPG · photograph, 1919 (after F. Dicksee), NPG · H. Leslie, silhouette, 1925, NPG · Barraud, photograph, NPG; repro. in Men and Women of the Day, 2 (1889) [see illus.] · Spy [L. Ward], chromolithograph caricature, NPG; repro. in VF (19 Oct 1889) · photograph, repro. in Kings Royal Rifle Corps Chronicle (1924), frontispiece · photograph, repro. in Kings Royal Rifle Corps Chronicle (1905), 50 · photograph, repro. in Navy and Army Illustrated (27 Nov 1896), 293 · prints, NAM
Wealth at death £46,778 17s. 4d.: probate, 15 June 1925, CGPLA Eng. & Wales

Grenfell, George (1849–1906), Baptist missionary and explorer in Africa, was born at Ennis Cottage, Trannack Mill, Sancreed, near Penzance, Cornwall, on 21 August 1849, the son of George Grenfell of Trannack Mill, afterwards of Birmingham, and his wife, Joanna, daughter of Michael and Catherine Rowe of Botree, Sancreed. Educated at a branch of King Edward VI Grammar School, Birmingham, Grenfell was apprenticed to Messrs Scholefield and Goodman, a hardware and machinery firm in Birmingham. The loss of an eye in early life in no way impaired his energy.

Though Grenfell's parents were Anglicans he soon joined Heneage Street Baptist Church, where he was baptized, and admitted to church membership on 7 November 1864. Influenced by the lives of David Livingstone and Alfred Saker (1814–1800), Grenfell, in September 1873, entered Bristol Baptist college, and on 10 November 1874 the Baptist Missionary Society (BMS) accepted him for work in the Cameroons under Alfred Saker. Grenfell and the veteran missionary arrived there in January 1875.

Grenfell's earliest work consisted in following the Yabiang River up to Abo and in discovering the lower course of the Sanaga River as far as Edea. On 11 February 1876, while back in England, he married at Heneage Street

George Grenfell (1849–1906), by William Coles

Baptist Church Mary Hawkes, of Birmingham, whose brother, Joseph, was an old friend.

Shortly afterwards Grenfell returned to the Cameroons, where, on 10 January 1877, Mary died, following the premature delivery of a dead child. Grenfell continued to explore the rivers inland, especially the Wuri, and in 1878 made an ascent of the Mongo ma Loba Mountain. On 5 January 1878 he received instructions to undertake pioneer work with T. J. Comber up the lower Congo. After the discoveries in 1877 of Sir Henry Morton Stanley, Robert Arthington (1823–1900), the Leeds recluse and philanthropist, had offered £1000 to the Baptist Missionary Society for such work. A brief preliminary expedition, with the help of the (Dutch) Afrikaansche Handels-Vereeniging, was followed by a second and longer expedition, which led Grenfell and Comber to São Salvador on 8 August 1878. Received there by the king of the Kongo, Dom Pedro V or Ntolela, they pushed on to the Makuta country, but at Tungwa the chief forbade their proceeding towards the upper Congo.

Grenfell and Comber returned to São Salvador, where on 20 August Grenfell resigned from the missionary society. His Jamaican housekeeper, Patience Rose Edgerley (d. 1927), was pregnant by him, and he returned to Victoria to marry her. They married that year. Their first daughter, Patience, was educated in England and Brussels. She later returned to the Congo as a mission teacher, but died of haematuric fever at Yakusu on 18 March 1899. The Grenfells had eight children in all, of whom four survived infancy: Patience, Caroline, Gertrude, and Grace. For two years after his resignation from the BMS Grenfell worked for a commercial concern in the Cameroons. However, on 23 April 1880 the BMS committee agreed to re-engage Grenfell as superintendent of a supply depot at the mouth of the Congo. Before long, he was removed from this limited role to become the spearhead of a new missionary policy of advance up the Congo River.

On 28 January 1884, in a small steel 'tender' 26 feet long, Grenfell set out to survey the Congo up to the equator at a point long. 18° E, passing the mouth of the Kwa River and visiting Bolobo, Lukolela, and Irebu, and inspecting the confluence of the Ubangi and the Congo. He now made his headquarters at Arthington, near Leopoldville, and on 13 June 1884 he successfully launched at Stanley Pool the *Peace*, a river steamer, with seven watertight compartments of Bessemer steel, which was built by Messrs Thornycroft, at Chiswick, at Arthington's cost, and under Grenfell's supervision, in 1882. It was constructed to draw only 18 inches when carrying 6 tons of cargo, and to be dismantled at the cataracts.

On 7 July 1884 the *Peace* started on her first voyage of discovery, taking Grenfell and Comber along the Kwa, Kwango, and Kasai rivers. On the second *Peace* expedition (13 October 1884) he journeyed 130 miles up the Ubangi River, thereby establishing its independence of the Congo. He also discovered the Ruki or Black River; navigated the Ikelemba; found himself in contact with cannibals in the Bangala region; ascended the Itimbiri or Rubi River up to lat. 2° 50′ N; visited the Swahili Arab slave dealer, Tippu Tib (Tipu-Tipu) at Stanley Falls on 24 December 1884; and in February 1885 followed the Ubangi for 200 miles as far as the Zongo rapids at lat. 4° 40′ N. This was by far the most northerly point reached by any European in the exploration of the Congo basin.

On the third voyage of the *Peace* (2 August 1885) Grenfell was accompanied by his wife, their daughter Patience, and by Von François, a German explorer, and eight children from the Baptist mission schools. This time his object was to explore the affluents of the Congo from the east and the south—the Lulonga, the Maringa, and the Busira or Ishuapa, on whose banks he found pygmy peoples (the Batwa).

Grenfell's fourth journey (24 February 1886), in company with Baron von Nimptsch of the Congo Free State, and Hermann von Wissmann the German explorer, took him up the main stream of the Kasai, thence up the Sankuru, the Luebo, and the Lulua (careful notes being taken of the Bakuba and Bakete people), and so back to the Congo and on to Stanley Falls. On the fifth voyage (30 September 1886) he passed up the Kwa and the Fimi to Lake Leopold II and on the sixth (December 1886), with William Holman Bentley, he explored the Kwango up to the Kingunji rapids. In all these journeys he made exact observations, which were published in 1886 by the Royal Geographical Society, and together with his chart of the Congo basin gained for him the founder's medal of the society in 1887.

During his furlough he was received by Leopold II at Brussels in July 1887. Hearing in August of the death of

Comber, he returned at once to the Congo and was busily occupied on the *Peace* in supplying the needs of the mission stations. But in September 1890 the Congo Free State, in spite of Grenfell's protests, impounded the vessel for operations against the Arabs. Grenfell came home and after long negotiations the *Peace* was restored, an indemnity being declined. A second steamer, the *Goodwill*, also made by Messrs Thornycroft, was launched on the upper Congo in December 1893.

On 13 August 1891 Grenfell, whom Leopold had invested with the insignia of chevalier of the order of Leopold, was invited to represent the Congo Free State in negotiating a settlement with Portugal of the frontier of the Lunda, and was allowed by the Baptist Missionary Society to accept the offer. At Kasongo Lunda he met Senhor Sarmento, the Portuguese plenipotentiary, and after inspecting the rivers of the Lunda district the party eventually reached Luanda (partly by railway) on 16 June 1893, the delimitation being agreed upon during July. For his services Grenfell was made commander of the Belgian order of the Lion and received the order of Christ from the king of Portugal.

From 1893 to 1900 Grenfell remained chiefly at Bolobo on the Congo, where a strong mission station was established. After a visit to England in 1900 he started for a systematic exploration of the Aruwimi River, and by November 1902 had reached Mawambi, about 80 miles from the western extreme of the Uganda protectorate. Between 1903 and 1906 he was busy with a new station at Yalemba, 15 miles east of the confluence of the Aruwimi with the Congo. Meanwhile he found increasing difficulty in obtaining building sites for new mission stations from the Congo Free State, which accorded them freely to Roman Catholic missions. Grenfell was, moreover, no longer so confident of the morally beneficent character of the free state, in which he had previously had full confidence. As evidence proliferated of atrocities committed by state agents in the conduct of the rubber trade, Leopold set up in 1896 a commission for the protection of the natives, and appointed Grenfell as a member. Grenfell, by now admitting the existence of abuses, but still persuaded of Leopold's personal good intentions, regarded the commission as little more than a farce. When the full extent of the rubber atrocities was proved in 1903 by the publication of a report by Roger Casement, the British consul at Boma, Grenfell resigned from the commission, bitterly disillusioned with the moral failure of Leopold's rule and his continuing opposition to protestant expansion on the upper Congo.

After a bad attack of blackwater fever Grenfell died on 1 July 1906, at Basoko, where he was buried. He was an observant explorer and an efficient student of African languages. He promoted industrial training, and deserves to be remembered as one of the most significant strategists of missionary expansion in Africa in the Victorian age.

E. H. PEARCE, *rev.* BRIAN STANLEY

Sources H. H. Johnston, *George Grenfell and the Congo*, 2 vols. (1908) • G. Hawker, *The life of George Grenfell* (1909) • B. Stanley, *The history of the Baptist Missionary Society, 1792–1992* (1992) • R. M. Slade, *English-speaking missions in the Congo Independent State, 1878–1908* (1959) • D. Lagergren, *Mission and state in the Congo* (1970) • B. Stanley, 'Author's reply', *International Bulletin of Missionary Research*, 22/4 (Oct 1968), 160

Archives Regent's Park College, Oxford, Angus Library, corresp. and papers | RGS, corresp. with RGS • SOAS, letters to Walter Stapleton

Likenesses W. Coles, photogravure, unknown collection; copyprint, NPG [*see illus.*]

Grenfell, Henry Riversdale (1824–1902), merchant banker, was born on 5 April 1824, the younger son (in a family of four) of Charles Pascoe *Grenfell (1790–1867) [*see under* Grenfell family], copper merchant, and later Liberal MP, and his wife, Lady Georgiana Molyneux, eldest daughter of the second earl of Sefton. The Grenfell family, originally from Cornwall, had risen to prominence and wealth as the London partners of various copper enterprises during the early industrial revolution, particularly under Grenfell's grandfather, Pascoe *Grenfell [*see under* Grenfell family].

Grenfell, like his father and brother, was educated at Harrow School (1836–8) and at Christ Church, Oxford (matriculated 1842). A prompt start in the City of the 1840s ended in family disagreements, and Grenfell, under the wing of his Christ Church friend, Chichester Fortescue, entered more fully the world of politics and London society. Among his friends he was nicknamed Wigs. He acted as private secretary to Lord Panmure at the War Office, and to Sir Charles Wood at the India Office. He also became an intimate of the 'Nuneham set' of Lady Waldegrave, whose notice he wrote for the *Dictionary of National Biography*. He entered parliament, for Stoke, in 1862, but by then his career had veered back towards the City after the untimely death of his brother, Charles, in 1861. Edged out as Liberal candidate at Stoke in 1868, he contested South-West Lancashire with W. E. Gladstone—the first of a series of failures to re-enter parliament. He was for the most part a Liberal of the *juste milieu*, friend of Italy (see his *Italy*, 1863), foe to Governor Eyre. But by 1886 he was a Liberal Unionist, acting in the forefront of City opposition to home rule.

Within the City Grenfell slipped easily into the hereditary world of the Bank of England, succeeding his father as a director in 1865 (part of an almost continuous tradition of family service between 1830 and 1940). He took his turn as deputy governor (1879–81) and as governor (1881–3), and remained a director until his death. He played an active part in defending the bank from its critics, and in urging (in vain) a consolidating banking act to tidy up the loose ends left by Peel's Bank Charter Act of 1844. His growing enthusiasm for monetary issues led to his joining the Political Economy Club in 1876 (he served as its treasurer from 1882 to 1900). Most importantly, he became after 1880, with his fellow bank director Henry Hucks Gibbs, an inexhaustible advocate of the bimetallic standard, which he defended in several pamphlets published in 1886, and various subsequent writings and articles, especially in *The Bimetallist*, 1895–1901. Although influenced in this by French and American theorists, he claimed that his views arose from his practical experience as a bank director. Yet this crusade commanded little support within the bank despite Grenfell's (even while governor) forcefully propagating his views through the International Monetary Standard Association, and, in a more populist vein, the Bimetallic League. He gave evidence to the royal commission on precious metals in 1887, served as vice-president of the International Monetary Congress at Paris in 1889, and did much to keep the issue firmly in the public mind. This represented a significant attempt to formulate an economic policy to remedy falling prices during the 'great depression', while in several ways anticipating twentieth-century international monetary diplomacy and perceptions of a damaging conflict of interests between the 'City' and 'industry' in the British economy.

Outside the bank parlour, Grenfell took on the crop of directorships and responsibilities appropriate for 'one of the City's most eminent personages' (*The Times*, 26 Nov 1887). He sat on the royal commission investigating the Metropolitan Board of Works in 1888–9, and chaired, *inter alia*, the National Mortgage and Agency Co., New Zealand, the Royal Sardinian Railway, and the Buenos Aires Water Co. But in 1887 his association with the more dubious Harney Park Dacotah Tin Mining Co. led to his losing a suit for slander brought by the founder of the *Financial News*, Harry Marks. In 1892 the family firm itself was wound up, with Grenfell falling into comparative poverty by City standards (leaving some £38,000 at death).

On 25 July 1867 Grenfell married Alethea, daughter of H. J. Adeane, MP for Cambridgeshire from 1857 to 1865. Their only child, Edward Charles *Grenfell prospered with J. S. Morgan & Co. (later Morgan Grenfell), and became Baron St Just. Grenfell himself died of pneumonia at his country home, Bacres, Hambleden, Buckinghamshire, on 11 September 1902.   A. C. HOWE

Sources A. C. Howe, 'Bimetallism, *c*.1880–1898: a controversy re-opened?', *EngHR*, 105 (1990), 377–92 · E. H. H. Green, 'Rentiers versus producers? The political economy of the bimetallic controversy, *c*.1880–1898', *EngHR*, 103 (1988), 588–612 · *... and Mr Fortescue: a selection from the diaries of Chichester Fortescue, Lord Carlingford*, ed. O. W. Hewett (1958) · Y. Cassis, *Les banquiers de la City à l'époque Edouardienne (1890–1914)* (1984) · *The Times* (26 Nov 1887) · *The Times* (23 Aug 1892) · *The Times* (12 Sept 1902) · *City Press* (13 Sept 1902) · *Hansard 3* (1862–8) · D. Kynaston, *The City of London*, 1 (1994) · B. Mallet, *Thomas George, earl of Northbrook* (1908) · Burke, *Peerage* · *WWW* · *CGPLA Eng. & Wales* (1902)
Archives Bucks. RLSS | Balliol Oxf., Mallet MSS · Bank of England Archive, London · Bucks. RLSS, corresp. with Charles Venables and election papers · CAC Cam., letters to W. T. Stead · GL, Gibbs MSS · Herts. ALS, corresp. with his nephew, Lord Desborough · priv. coll. · Som. ARS, Strachie MSS · U. Durham L., letters to third Earl Grey
Likenesses photograph, Bank of England, Museums section
Wealth at death £37,898 0s. 9d.: resworn probate, May 1903, *CGPLA Eng. & Wales* (1902)

Grenfell, Hubert Henry (1845–1906), naval officer and expert on gunnery, born at Rugby, Warwickshire, on 12 June 1845, was the son of Algernon Grenfell, a clerk, and his wife, Maria Guerin Price.

Joining the navy as a cadet on 13 December 1859, at the age of fourteen, Grenfell passed out first from the *Britannia*, and gained as sub-lieutenant the Beaumont testimonial in 1865. He qualified as gunnery lieutenant in 1867, and was appointed first lieutenant on HMS *Excellent* on 22 September 1869. While holding this appointment he worked out, with Naval Engineer Newman, what are claimed to have been the first designs of hydraulic mountings for heavy naval ordnance. He also contributed technical articles to *Engineering* and service journals. On 11 September 1872 he married Eleanor Kate Cunningham at Alverstoke, Hampshire.

On 31 December 1876 Grenfell was made commander, and on 1 May 1877 was appointed, on account of his linguistic abilities, second naval attaché to the maritime courts of Europe. He also acted as naval adviser to the British representatives at the Berlin Congress of 1878. On 22 September 1882 the sloop *Phoenix*, under his command, foundered off Prince Edward Island. No lives, however, were lost. Grenfell retired with the rank of captain on 2 December 1887.

Grenfell was afterwards for many years associated with the experimental work of the engineering firm of Armstrong, Whitworth & Co. He was the first to direct the Admiralty's attention to the night-sighting of guns; and about 1891, on the introduction of the incandescent electric lamp, he invented his 'self-illuminating night sights for naval ordnance'. The invention was for fifteen years attached to all heavy guns in the British navy, and was adopted by some foreign navies. Grenfell was also one of the first to suggest the use of sight-scales marked in large plain figures for naval guns, and advocated, though without success, the adoption of a telescopic light for day use. He also worked out the arrangement subsequently adopted for quick-firing field artillery, by which the changes of angle between the line of sight and the axis of the bore which were required when firing at a moving target could be effected without altering the line of sight.

In April 1877 Grenfell advocated, before the Institution of Naval Architects, the trial of Grüson's chilled cast-iron armour in England, and in 1887 published *Grüson's Chilled Cast-Iron Armour* (translated from the German of Julius von Schutz). He helped to form the Navy League, and served at one time on its executive committee. He died at his home, 5 Anglesey Crescent, Crescent Road, Alverstoke, Hampshire, on 13 September 1906, survived by his wife.

S. E. FRYER, *rev.* IAN ST JOHN

Sources *The Times* (26 Sept 1906) · *Engineering* (28 Sept 1906) · H. Garbett, *Naval gunnery* (1897) · C. O. Brown, *Armour and its attacks by artillery* (1893) · W. L. Clowes, *The Royal Navy: a history from the earliest times to the present*, 7 vols. (1897–1903), vol. 7 · *Navy List* (Jan 1888)
Wealth at death £76 1s. 6d.: administration with will, 24 Dec 1906, *CGPLA Eng. & Wales*

Grenfell, John Pascoe (1800–1869), naval officer in the Brazilian service, born at Battersea on 20 September 1800, was a son of John G. Grenfell of the City of London, and nephew of Pascoe Grenfell. In 1811, when eleven years old, he entered the service of the East India Company; but, after having made several voyages to India, in 1819 he joined the service of the young Chilean republic under

Lord Cochrane, was made a lieutenant, and took part in most of Cochrane's exploits during the Chilean War of Independence (1819–23), most notably in the cutting out of the *Esmeralda*, when he was severely wounded. In 1823 he accompanied Cochrane to Brazil, with the rank of commander, and served under him in the Brazilian War of Independence (1823), specially distinguishing himself in the capture of Pará. Afterwards, under Commodore Norton, he lost his right arm in the action off Buenos Aires on 29 July 1826. He went to England to convalesce, returning to Brazil in 1828. In 1835–6 he commanded the squadron on the lakes of the province of Rio Grande do Sul against the rebel flotillas, which he captured or destroyed, thus compelling the rebel army to surrender. In 1841 he was promoted rear-admiral.

In 1846 Grenfell was appointed Brazilian consul-general in England, to reside in Liverpool. In August 1848, while superintending the trial of the *Alfonzo*, a warship built at Liverpool for the Brazilian government, he assisted in saving the lives of the passengers and crew of the emigrant ship *Ocean Monarch*, burnt off the mouth of the Mersey. For his exertions he received the thanks of the corporation and the gold medal of the Liverpool Shipwreck Society. In 1851, on the outbreak of war between Brazil and Argentina, he returned to take command of the Brazilian navy, and in December, after a sharp conflict, forced the passage of the Paraná. After the peace he was promoted vice-admiral, and then admiral; but in 1852 he returned to Liverpool and resumed his functions as consul-general. He held the office until his death.

Grenfell married, at Montevideo in 1829, María Dolores Masini. One of their children, Harry Tremenheere Grenfell, became a captain in the Royal Navy; on 13 February 1882, while shooting in the neighbourhood of Artaki, in the Sea of Marmara, he was severely wounded when attacked by local shepherds and narrowly escaped with his life. (His companion, Commander Selby, was killed.) An elder son, John Granville Grenfell, became commissioner of crown lands in New South Wales, and was killed defending the mail against bushrangers on 7 December 1866. Grenfell himself died at Prince's Park, Liverpool, on 20 March 1869.   J. K. LAUGHTON, rev. ROGER MORRISS

Sources *The Times* (22 March 1869) · *ILN* (4 Dec 1852), 492–3 · M. G. Mulhall, *The English in South America* (1878) · J. Armitage, *History of Brazil, 1808–31* (1836) · private information (1890) · *Sydney Morning Herald* (21 Dec 1866) · Boase, *Mod. Eng. biog.* · J. Lynch, *The Spanish American revolutions, 1808–1826* (1973) · R. J. Barman, *Brazil: the forging of a nation, 1798–1852* (1988)
Archives U. Lpool L., Sydney Jones Library, corresp., logbooks, and papers
Likenesses engraving, repro. in *ILN*
Wealth at death under £4000: probate, 5 May 1869, *CGPLA Eng. & Wales*

Grenfell [*née* Phipps], **Joyce Irene** (1910–1979), actress and broadcaster, was born in London on 10 February 1910, the elder child and only daughter of Paul Phipps (1880–1953), an architect and a fellow of the Royal Institute of British Architects, and his wife, Nora Langhorne (1890–1955) from Virginia, USA, who was the sister of Nancy Astor, the

Joyce Irene Grenfell (1910–1979), by Anthony Buckley, 1962

first woman to sit in the House of Commons. She was educated at Francis Holland School, London, and the Christian Science school Clear View in South Norwood, and at a finishing school in Paris. She said later that she had 'been stage-struck since I'd first been taken to the theatre, aged seven' ('Chelsea childhood', 34); she entered the Royal Academy of Dramatic Art but only lasted there one term, and considered that that 'was the finish of my dreams of becoming an actress' (*Joyce Grenfell Requests*, 112). On 12 December 1929 she married Reginald Pascoe Grenfell (1903–1993), a chartered accountant, and elder son of financier Arthur Morton Grenfell and his wife, Lady Victoria Grey, daughter of the fourth Earl Grey of Howick. They had no children. After her marriage, Joyce earned a little as a poster and card artist, and also had some verse published in *Punch*.

In 1936 Joyce Grenfell met J. L. Garvin, editor of *The Observer*, at a lunch held by Nancy Astor at Cliveden, and discussed with him her enthusiasm for listening to radio broadcasts. Some months later he offered her the new position of weekly radio critic for the paper. In 1939 she met Herbert Farjeon, theatre critic of *The Tatler* and author of a current revue, *Nine Sharp*, at a party given by Stephen Potter (with whom she was later, in 1943, to broadcast the popular *How* programmes). Joyce was persuaded to entertain the company with a rendering of a talk she had heard at a Women's Institute meeting. It was called 'Useful and acceptable gifts', and was the foundation-stone upon which her stage career was built. Farjeon was so amused by it that he invited her to give this talk in his coming revue, *The Little Revue*, which was to open in March 1939.

Feeling she had nothing to lose, and being of a fearless disposition, Joyce accepted, and was received with warm reviews. Like the characters and material she devised throughout her career, it was 'a sympathetically amused insight into the quirks and oddities of English feminine character' (*The Times*, 1 Dec 1979), although very much of a particular class and time.

Thus began Joyce Grenfell's long and successful career as an entertainer. Not only did she write a large number of monologues, many of which, notably the *Nursery School* series (with their refrain of 'George dear—don't do that'), became classics, but lyrics as well, the music for which was for the most part composed by Richard Addinsell. Her monologue characters, ranging through every stratum of society, catching the tones and manners of, among others, a chair of a north country ladies' choral society, a wife of an Oxbridge university vice-chancellor, a foreign visitor at a cocktail party, a country cottager, an American mother, and a cockney girlfriend, were keen and often hilarious pieces of social observation. Along with her songs, sung in a small but pretty and perfectly tuned voice, they provided evenings of rare entertainment.

Joyce Grenfell had an instantaneous success. There were two more Farjeon revues, *Diversion* and *Light and Shade*, and then during the Second World War she went on two long tours abroad for the Entertainments National Service Association, visiting hospitals and isolated units in fourteen countries. She was appointed OBE in 1946. In 1945 she appeared in the revue *Sigh No More* by Noël Coward, in 1947 *Tuppence Coloured*, and in 1951 *Penny Plain*. She also took part in a radio discussion programme, *We Beg to Differ*, in 1949, and over the years appeared in a variety of films: *Genevieve* (1953), *The Happiest Days of your Life* (1950), *The Million Pound Note* (1953), *The Yellow Rolls-Royce* (1964), to name the better known, and the St Trinian's series, in which her interpretation of a much badgered, gawky, toothy, and gauche games mistress brought her increased fame.

In 1954 Joyce Grenfell had her own show at the Fortune Theatre, *Joyce Grenfell Requests the Pleasure*, which led eventually to her handling a two-hour programme solo and touring the world with it. She played in Canada, the USA, Australia, New Zealand, Hong Kong, and Switzerland (but not South Africa) many times, and in every part of Britain. After nearly forty years she retired from the stage in 1973, her final performance of songs and monologues being given before the queen and her guests at the Waterloo dinner in Windsor Castle. She continued to appear on television, contributing regularly to the musical quiz programme *Face the Music* and giving a memorable interview to Michael Parkinson in September 1976.

Through the years Joyce Grenfell was committed to projects unconnected with show business. In 1957 she became president of the Society of Women Writers and Journalists; from 1960 to 1962 she served on the committee concerned with the 'future of the broadcasting services in the UK', chaired by Sir W. H. Pilkington; and in 1972 she was appointed a member of the council of the Winston Churchill Memorial Fellowship Trust. A lifelong Christian Scientist she was deeply interested in metaphysics, and on a number of occasions spoke in the 'dialogues' initiated by the Revd Joseph McCulloch from the two pulpits in St Mary-le-Bow Church in London. She also spoke in Truro Cathedral and Westminster Abbey (where in 1980 a memorial service was held for her). She lectured on 'communication' to all sorts of groups in universities, colleges, and technical institutes, was made an honorary fellow of Lucy Cavendish College, Cambridge, and Manchester Polytechnic, and often contributed to the BBC morning programme *Thought for the Day*. During her partial retirement from public life she wrote her autobiography in two volumes, *Joyce Grenfell Requests the Pleasure*, a bestseller published in 1976, and *In Pleasant Places* (1979).

Joyce Grenfell's enjoyment of life was the keynote to her character. She had a genuine love of goodness and sought it in all things, in music, literature, nature, and above all people. Her talent was unique in that although she caricatured her subjects and pin-pointed their idiosyncrasies, there was never a hint of censure. Although she became a true professional she retained one attractive element of the amateur, in that she seemed to be doing it all for fun, and her manifest zest for living coupled with her artistry, kind-heartedness, and sense of humour had a cherishing effect upon her audiences. They loved her. On the stage, television, and radio she had a huge following and at her death from cancer, at her home, 34 Elm Park Gardens, Chelsea, London, on 30 November 1979, she had become in the nature of an institution. She was cremated in London. She was to have been appointed DBE in the 1980 new year honours list.   VIRGINIA GRAHAM, *rev.*

Sources J. Grenfell, *Joyce Grenfell requests the pleasure* (1976) · J. Grenfell, *In pleasant places* (1979) · *Joyce and Ginnie: the letters of Joyce Grenfell and Virginia Graham*, ed. J. Hampton (1997) · J. Grenfell, 'A Chelsea childhood', *Joyce: by herself and her friends*, ed. R. Grenfell and R. Garnett (1980) · J. Grenfell, *Darling Ma: letters to her mother, 1932–1944*, ed. J. Roose-Evans (1988) · R. Baker, *The Observer* (2 Dec 1979) · *The Times* (1 Dec 1979) · Burke, *Peerage* · WWW · J. Halliwell, *Filmgoer's companion*, 5th edn (1976)
Archives Lucy Cavendish College, Cambridge, corresp., diaries, and papers · NRA, corresp., etc. · University of Bristol, Theatre collection, scripts, broadcasts, books, recordings, sketches | NL Wales, corresp. with Thomas Jones | FILM BFI NFTVA, *Heroes of comedy*, Channel 4, 20 Oct 1995 · BFI NFTVA, home footage · BFI NFTVA, performance footage | SOUND BL NSA, oral history interviews · BL NSA, performance recordings · BL NSA, *Talking about music*, 113, 1LPO152935 S1 BD3 BBC TRANSC · BL NSA, *Talking about music*, 136, 1LPO153645 S2 BD3 BBC TRANSC
Likenesses photographs, 1928–70, Hult. Arch. · A. Buckley, photograph, 1962, NPG [*see illus.*]
Wealth at death £196,358: probate, 8 Feb 1980, *CGPLA Eng. & Wales*

Grenfell, Julian Henry Francis (1888–1915), army officer and poet, was born at 4 St James's Square, London, on 30 March 1888. He was the eldest son of William Henry *Grenfell, first Baron Desborough (1855–1945), and his wife, Ethel Anne Priscilla *Grenfell (1867–1952), the daughter of Julian Henry Charles *Fane and his wife, Lady Adine Cowper. Grenfell's parents were notable figures in late Victorian society, members of the select group of friends known as 'the souls'. In 1898–1901 Julian attended

Julian Henry Francis Grenfell (1888–1915), by Maull & Fox

Summerfields, Oxford, and in 1901 he went to Eton College, where his achievements were sporting and literary rather than academic. He had not been entered for a scholarship to the school, and later failed in an attempt to gain one to Balliol. He had, nevertheless, an intelligent and original mind: when editor of the *Eton College Chronicle* he helped to found *The Outsider*, a short-lived but popular and parodying rival. When he arrived at Oxford in the autumn of 1906 he was 'a splendid figure of a man, over six feet high, with two greyhounds, a famous Australian stockwhip, and an immense enjoyment of life' (*Balliol College War Memorial Book*, 1.196).

At Balliol Grenfell's 'animal high spirits' descended into rowdyism and bullying. He took as 'a sincere compliment' his nickname of 'Rough Man' or 'Roughers', and used his stock-whip on disfavoured contemporaries, notably Philip Sassoon. Grenfell disapproved of the latter's 'Oriental and cushioned "digs"', and would drive him from Balliol quad by 'cracking the prodigious lash within inches of Sassoon's sleek head' (Jones, 53–4). Such malpractices went unchecked, though not unseen, by the authorities. When one victim, A. B. Keith, determined on legal action he was warned by the master that if he persisted he would have to leave the college (Hist. Univ. Oxf. 7: 19th-cent. Oxf. pt 2).

Like his father, also a Balliol man, Grenfell was renowned for his athletic and sporting prowess. He boxed middleweight for the university, rowed at Henley, and won college steeple-chases. But his greatest passion was for hunting with his favourite dog, 'Slogbottom', the subject of his poem 'To a Black Greyhound' (*c*.1912). This solitary pursuit epitomized Grenfell's deliberate detachment from society. He regarded friendship as 'approximating to brotherhood' and kept to a close circle, mostly comprising Etonians (*Balliol College War Memorial Book*, 1.197). Some of these saw 'a gentle, and in some ways a very humble disposition', which contrasted with Grenfell's habitual air of self-sufficiency (Jones, 53). In fact there was an intensely sensitive side to his character, evident in his depressed reaction to frequent disputes with his mother. Ettie Grenfell was a woman of great social distinction, and it was in rebellion against the conventional values that he believed she represented that Julian wrote, in the summer of 1909, 'a series of slashing essays on … the outward forms and manners of modern society' (*End of an Era*, 62). They were poorly received by family and friends, and were never published. The impotency of this protest probably contributed to the breakdown that Grenfell experienced that December, and from which he emerged shaken next spring. He made peace with his mother, and that summer fell in love with Pamela Lytton, wife of the second earl of Lytton. Their relationship was curtailed when Grenfell joined the Royal Dragoons: he was sent to India at the end of 1910, and to South Africa the following year.

Though he was apparently well suited to the army, Grenfell found aspects of the life stultifying, and he planned to leave. Events, however, overtook him. At the outbreak of war in August 1914 the Royal Dragoons were sent to France, and he soon tasted battle. He wrote home early in November: 'It is all *the* best fun. I have never never felt so well, or so happy, or enjoyed anything so much …. The fighting–excitement vitalizes everything, every sight and word and action. One loves one's fellow man so much more when one is bent on killing him' (*Pages from a Family Journal*, 479–80). A fortnight later he shot three Germans during sorties on the enemy lines, employing stalking skills learned on Scottish moors to crawl in daylight to within feet of their trenches. He entered in his game book, directly after '105 partridges', early in October: 'November 16th. One Pomeranian. November 17th. Two Pomeranians' (Mosley, 243). During the latter expedition Grenfell spotted signs of an imminent German attack, and for alerting his side to this danger he was awarded the DSO.

A trench diary, begun in the new year, offers glimpses of a different kind of war, and soldier. An entry in February records: '… heard noise of bomb dropping on top of dugout. Petrified. Lost self-control—lay still, clenching my hands, for 20 secs. Asked what it was. "Rum jar thrown away"' (Desborough MSS). Nevertheless the love of combat survived and late in April 1915, during the second battle of Ypres, Grenfell wrote the poem 'Into Battle', for which he is most known. It is a statement of the credo by which he lived and died: that combat is intrinsic to life, and the fighting man closest to nature. It enjoyed immediate success and remains one of the most anthologized poems of the First World War. But as an idealized response to the conflict, glorifying death, it contrasts with much that was later written, most obviously by Wilfred Owen and Siegfried Sassoon.

On 13 May 1915 Grenfell volunteered to run messages during a heavy bombardment, and that afternoon he was seriously wounded by a shell splinter to the head. He died in the military hospital in Boulogne on 26 May. The next day 'Into Battle' was published in *The Times*, on the eve of the author's burial in the military cemetery above Boulogne. The following month Billy Grenfell, Julian's younger brother, was killed in action in France. The pair were given a sentimental literary memorial by their mother, the privately printed *Pages from a Family Journal*. Commenting on it for Margot Asquith, Wilfrid Scawen Blunt on 10 November 1916 wrote that he found neither Julian nor Billy sympathetic characters once they left Eton. Had Julian lived he would have become 'the Club bore, telling tiger and buffalo stories'. This harsh judgement, though, misses the complexity of Julian's character. He was both a poet and a boxing blue, combining aesthetic sensibilities with primitive instincts in a manner alien, and even alarming, to later generations.

MARK POTTLE

Sources Lady Desborough [E. A. P. Grenfell], *Pages from a family journal, 1888–1915* (privately printed, Eton, 1916) · E. Hilliard, ed., *The Balliol College register, 1832–1914* (privately printed, Oxford, 1914) · *Balliol College war memorial book, 1914–1919*, 1 (1924) · L. E. Jones, *An Edwardian youth* (1956) · N. Mosley, *Julian Grenfell: his life and the times of his death, 1888–1915* (1976) · W. S. Blunt to Margot Asquith, 10 Nov 1916, priv. coll., Lady Asquith MSS · *End of an era: letters and journals of Sir Alan Lascelles, 1887–1920*, ed. D. Hart-Davis (1986) · R. Bridges, *The spirit of man* (1916) · E. B. Osborn, *The muse in arms* (1917) · M. Baring, *Poems: 1914–19* (1920) · *Hist. U. Oxf.* 7: *19th-cent. Oxf.* pt 2 · Herts. ALS, Desborough MSS

Archives Herts. ALS, corresp. and family MSS; corresp.; journals; photographs; TS poems; sketches [Grenfell family deposit]

Likenesses Duchess of Rutland, drawing, 1909, repro. in A. Lambert, *Unquiet souls: the Indian summer of the British aristocracy, 1880–1918* (1984) · photograph, 1910, repro. in Desborough, *Pages from a family journal* · photograph, 1915, Weidenfeld and Nicolson Archives · Maull & Fox, sepia photogravure, NPG [*see illus.*]

Grenfell, Pascoe (*bap.* **1761**, *d.* **1838**). *See under* Grenfell family (*per. c.*1785–1879).

Grenfell, Pascoe St Leger (**1798–1879**). *See under* Grenfell family (*per. c.*1785–1879).

Grenfell, Riversdale William (**1807–1871**). *See under* Grenfell family (*per. c.*1785–1879).

Grenfell, Sir Wilfred Thomason (**1865–1940**), medical missionary and social reformer, was born at Parkgate, Cheshire, on 28 February 1865, the second of the four sons of the Revd Algernon Sidney Grenfell (1836–1887), headmaster and proprietor of Mostyn House School, Parkgate, and later chaplain of the London Hospital, and his wife, Jane Georgina (1832–1921), daughter of Colonel John Hutchison, an engineer with the Indian army, and his wife, Elizabeth Thomason. Grenfell was educated at Mostyn House School and then at Marlborough College, before entering the London Hospital medical college in 1883. A rugged, energetic athlete, he played rugby for the

Sir Wilfred Thomason Grenfell (1865–1940), by Walter Stoneman, 1928

hospital and for Richmond. Encouraged by his surgical lecturer, Frederick Treves, he gave his spare time to practical good works, running a summer camp for working boys and opening up a Sunday school and a boxing club in his house in Hackney. Having attained the conjoint diploma LRCP MRCS in 1888, he failed the MB examination at the University of London. Later that year he resided at Queen's College, Oxford, for the Michaelmas term, winning blues for rowing and rugby and a half-blue for athletics.

While still a medical student Grenfell was moved to action by the American evangelists Dwight Moody and Ira Sankey and decided to devote his life to practical Christianity. Through the influence of Treves, he outfitted the first hospital ship of the Mission to Deep Sea Fishermen. He then embarked as ship's doctor and spent considerable time among the fishing fleets. In 1892, as superintendent of the mission, he inaugurated a floating medical service for the fishing communities of northern Newfoundland, coastal Labrador, and the Quebec north shore. Then, with the aid of supporting associations that he subsequently organized throughout Canada, the United States, Britain, and Ireland (later named the International Grenfell Association, which he founded in 1913), he built a wooden hospital in St Anthony and a network of smaller hospitals and nursing stations in coastal communities.

Not content merely to treat illness Grenfell also concentrated on the social deficiencies of the region. He provided schools, orphanages, co-operatives, cottage industries, agricultural initiatives, and other ventures (including the King George V Seamen's Institute in St John's) and earned recognition throughout the world for his benevolence and self-sacrifice. Such a wide range of activity amounted to cultural intervention in the colony, however, and it brought Grenfell into conflict with the elected authorities, particularly when he revealed, through his many books, articles, and public lectures, the poverty and starvation that prevailed among fishermen. But the Grenfell mission, as it came to be known, continued to attract international support and in 1981 it was transformed into a provincial medical service of the government of Newfoundland, known as Grenfell Regional Health Services.

In 1908, after surviving a night adrift on a floating pan of ice, Grenfell acquired a heroic reputation which was enhanced by his widely read survival narrative *Adrift on an Icepan* (1909). By now regarded as one of the chief benefactors of the colony, he built a house near the hospital at St Anthony and brought there his wife, whom he married in 1909, Anne Elizabeth Caldwell MacClanahan (1886–1938), of Lake Forest, Illinois, daughter of the Chicago lawyer Edmund Burke MacClanahan, formerly of Madison county, Tennessee, and Rosamond Hill, of Burlington, Vermont. The Grenfells took up residence in St Anthony, and two sons were born: Wilfred Thomason jun. (*b.* 1910), and Kinloch Pascoe (*b.* 1912). In 1916 Grenfell served for six months in France as a volunteer surgeon with the Harvard Surgical Unit. A daughter, Rosamond Loveday, was born in 1917.

Following the First World War, Grenfell continued full time as a lecturer, writer, and publicist, aided in large measure by his wife. His autobiography, *A Labrador Doctor* (1919), and his absorbing lectures on life in the north brought him a host of fresh admirers and volunteers. In 1927 he opened a modern hospital of concrete construction in St Anthony and that year was created a knight in the Order of St Michael and St George. From this point the running of the Grenfell mission passed to younger hands, notably those of Harry Paddon in North West River, Labrador, and Charles Curtis in St Anthony. Grenfell resigned from the direct management of the mission in 1936 but remained active as a lecturer, writer, and fundraiser, dividing his time between his residence at Kinloch House, near Charlotte, Vermont, and the southern United States, where he journeyed to recuperate from chronically debilitating heart problems. Grenfell died of a coronary thrombosis at Kinloch House on 9 October 1940, and his ashes were brought to St Anthony, where they were placed inside a rock face overlooking the harbour, near those of his wife and close colleagues.

Grenfell received considerable attention from journalists and biographers throughout his lifetime. He was the subject of at least a dozen biographical works and figured prominently in the numerous memoirs of former colleagues and volunteers. He was also awarded numerous honorary degrees, medals, prizes, and awards in Great Britain, the United States, and Canada. He was made CMG in 1906, and awarded the first honorary MD by Oxford University in 1907. He was given both the Murchison bequest by the Royal Geographical Society (1911) and the Livingston gold medal of the Royal Scottish Geographical Society (1930). In 1928 he was elected lord rector of the University of St Andrews. He was elected both an honorary fellow of the College of Surgeons of America (1915) and a fellow of the Royal College of Surgeons, London (1920) and was awarded gold medals by both the National Academy of Social Sciences of America (1920) and the Royal Empire Society (1935).

As an author Grenfell possessed a direct, ingenuous literary style and a gift for sentimental narrative. He published over thirty books, including personal memoirs, religious reflections, and *sententiae* as well as short fiction and essays about Labrador. His huge journalistic output, consisting of reports of mission activities, religious reflections, and promotions of Labrador as a separate region, is scattered through newspapers and journals in Britain and North America, notably in the Grenfell mission magazine, *Among the Deep Sea Fishers*.

RONALD ROMPKEY

Sources Yale U., Sterling Memorial Library, Grenfell papers · Mostyn House School, Parkgate, Cheshire, Mostyn House MSS · Provincial Archives of Newfoundland and Labrador, St John's, Newfoundland, International Grenfell Association MSS · mission records, Royal National Mission to Deep Sea Fishermen, London · R. Rompkey, *Grenfell of Labrador: a biography* (1991) · W. T. Grenfell, *Adrift on an icepan* (1909) · W. T. Grenfell, *A Labrador doctor: the autobiography of Wilfred Thomason Grenfell, M.D. (Oxon.), C.M.G.* (1919) · *WWW* · parish register (birth and baptism), 28 Feb 1865 and 28 April 1865, Neston, St Mary and St Helen · d. cert.

Archives Grenfell Historical Society, St Anthony, Newfoundland · Marine Biological Association of the United Kingdom, Plymouth, notebook relating to North Sea tow-netting · Mostyn House School, Parkgate, Cheshire · Royal National Mission to Deep Sea Fishermen, London · Tower Hamlets Health Authority Archives, London, London Hospital records · Yale U., Beinecke L., papers relating to Labrador | FILM Grenfell Historical Society, St Anthony, Newfoundland | SOUND BBC

Likenesses W. Stoneman, photograph, 1928, NPG [*see illus.*] · commemorative stamp, 1942, Newfoundland · stamp, 1965, Canada · H. Melis, bronze statue, 1970, Confederation Building, St John's, Newfoundland · H. Melis, bronze statue, 1976, Charles S. Curtis Memorial Hospital, St Anthony, Newfoundland · gargoyle, Washington National Cathedral · stained-glass window, St Mary's Anglican Church, St Anthony, Newfoundland · window, Washington National Cathedral

Wealth at death 64 acres of land at Charlotte, Vermont, with dwelling house (known as Kinloch House), farmer's cottage, study, and boys' camp buildings: will, 13 Oct 1939, Vermont

Grenfell, William Henry, Baron Desborough (1855–1945), sportsman and politician, was born in London on 30 October 1855, the eldest son of Charles William Grenfell MP (1823–1861) of Taplow Court, Buckinghamshire, and Georgiana Caroline Lascelles (*d.* 1911), daughter of William Saunders Sebright Lascelles MP, and granddaughter of Henry Lascelles, second earl of Harewood. Though a well-known athlete and a noted public servant both nationally and locally, Grenfell is better known to posterity as the father of the war poet Julian Henry Francis *Grenfell and his younger brother, Gerald William (*b.*

William Henry Grenfell, Baron Desborough (1855–1945), by John Singer Sargent, 1912

1890), known as Billy, both killed in action in 1915. Their twin cousins Francis and Riversdale were also both killed in the war: Francis Grenfell had the distinction of winning the war's first Victoria Cross.

The family had been established in Buckinghamshire since 1790, and Grenfell's great-grandfather Pascoe *Grenfell had been MP for Great Marlow in the pre-reform parliament in the whig interest. Willy Grenfell was educated at a school in Malvern Wells, at Harrow School (1868–74), and at Balliol College, Oxford, from which he graduated in 1879: he was elected an honorary fellow of Balliol in 1928 and received an honorary DCL from the university ten years later. On coming down Grenfell was immediately invited to stand as Liberal candidate at Salisbury, and secured election in 1880. Appointed a parliamentary groom-in-waiting in 1882, he lost the by-election then necessary for office-holders, but was returned in 1885. Grenfell was private secretary to the chancellor of the exchequer, Sir William Harcourt, but lost his seat again in 1886. After a spell as special correspondent of the *Daily Telegraph* at Suakin in the Sudan in 1888, he contested Windsor unsuccessfully in an 1890 by-election, but was returned as a Gladstonian Liberal for Hereford City in 1892. Grenfell, however, could not support Irish home rule and resigned his seat in 1893. Subsequently, in 1900, he won the Wycombe division of Buckinghamshire for the Unionists, a constituency which included Marlow. In 1905 he was raised to the peerage as Baron Desborough of Taplow: the title derived from the Desborough hundred, one of the three 'Chiltern Hundreds'.

Desborough did not achieve great political office and he declined the offer of governor-general of Canada in 1921 on family grounds, but he was indefatigable in undertaking other public offices. He filled a variety of appointments in both Berkshire (he was twice elected mayor of Maidenhead) and Buckinghamshire (of which he was a justice of the peace and deputy lieutenant and served a term as high sheriff). His public appointments were enormously varied and included the chairmanship of the Thames Conservancy Board, which he held for thirty-two years, the presidency of the London chamber of commerce and of the British imperial council of commerce, the chairmanship of the Home Office committee on police for England, Scotland, and Wales, the presidency of the international navigation congress (1923), and the presidency of the Royal Agricultural Society (1925). It was said that, at one point, he was serving on 115 committees simultaneously. His most prominent public service, however, was during the First World War. A long-serving officer of the Buckinghamshire rifle volunteers, in August 1914 Desborough became president of an interim committee supporting the raising of new volunteer bodies as a defence against possible German invasion. As a result of pressure from Desborough and Percy Harris, a Liberal member of the London county council, on 27 September the War Office authorized the creation of the Volunteer Training Corps. The interim committee was translated into a central organization of Volunteer Training Corps and received official recognition as the Central Association of Volunteer Training Corps on 19 November 1914. Desborough became president of the association. Subsequently, with his fellow Buckinghamshire magnate the marquess of Lincolnshire, who also lost his son in the war, Grenfell initiated new volunteer legislation in the Lords in 1915, which was eventually passed in 1916. Conceivably over 1 million men served in the Volunteer Training Corps at one time or another, the majority of whom were either over-age for military service or in protected occupations. In practical terms they released trained troops from static guards, assisted in bringing in the harvest, worked in dockyards and munitions factories, and helped staff anti-aircraft defences around London. Desborough also represented the minister of munitions on a trip to France in 1915 to select skilled men to be returned to industry from the army, administered a naval hospital at Southend, and turned Taplow Court into a nurses' rest home. He was appointed CVO in 1907, KCVO in 1908, and GCVO in 1925. He was admitted to the Garter in 1928 and was captain of the yeomen of the guard from 1924 to 1929.

For all his public duties, Grenfell was probably best-known by contemporaries for his sporting prowess. He had represented Harrow at cricket and Oxford in fencing, athletics, and rowing. He made two appearances in the university boat race in 1877 and 1878: the first was a dead heat and the second a victory for Oxford. He won the

Thames punting championships for three successive years (1888–90), stroked an eight across the channel, sculled the London–Oxford stretch of the Thames in a crew of three in twenty-two consecutive hours, and rowed for the Leander club in the Grand Challenge Cup at Henley while an MP. Having won foils at both Harrow and Oxford, Grenfell also represented Britain, and became founding president of the Amateur Fencing Association. He twice swam Niagara, crossing the pool just below the falls, and he ascended the Matterhorn by three different routes. In one eight day period he ascended the Matterhorn, the little Matterhorn, Monte Rosa, the Rothorn, and the Weisshorn. On one occasion he was lost for three days in the Rocky Mountains. He was also a keen horseman, hunter, and fisherman. He went big-game shooting in India, Africa, and British Columbia, and caught tarpon off Florida. He had been master of the draghounds at Oxford and maintained his own harriers at Taplow Court, which had formerly been hunted by King Edward VII as prince of Wales. An excellent whip, he was president of the Coaching Club and the Four-in-Hand Club. One of the conservators of the Thames, he was the founding chairman of the Thames Salmon Association. Three times acting president of the Life Saving Society, he was also president and chairman of the Bath Club from 1894 to 1942. At various times Desborough was also president of both the Marylebone Cricket Club and the Lawn Tennis Association as well as being president of the Olympics held in London in 1908. He was chairman of the Pilgrims of Great Britain from 1919 to 1929 and president of the Amateur Athletics Association from 1930 to 1936.

A genial and popular man, with a wide circle of acquaintances, Grenfell married on 17 February 1887 Ethel Anne Priscilla Fane (1867–1952) [see Grenfell, Ethel Anne Priscilla]. Together they made Taplow Court, whose grounds skirted Boulter's Lock on the Thames, a highly fashionable society venue: in 1901, for example, they entertained all the colonial premiers visiting London for the coronation. Edward VII was a frequent visitor, as was Field Marshal Lord Kitchener, whom Grenfell had first met in 1885. Kitchener, indeed, became very attached to his sons and was much affected by their deaths. Of their three sons and two daughters the Desboroughs suffered not only the loss of the two eldest sons in the war, but the third, who was unmarried, was killed in a motor-car accident in 1926. As a result, the peerage became extinct when Desborough died at Panshanger, Hertfordshire, on 9 January 1945. He was buried at St Nicholas's Church, Taplow. His wife survived him.   IAN F. W. BECKETT

Sources C. A. M. Press, Buckinghamshire leaders (1905) • V. Meynell, Julian Grenfell (1917) • N. Mosley, Julian Grenfell (1976) • Memoirs of Field-Marshal Lord Grenfell (1925) • R. W. Davis, Political change and continuity, 1760–1885: a Buckinghamshire study (1972) • J. Buchan, Francis and Riversdale Grenfell: a memoir, 3rd edn (1920) • I. F. W. Beckett, 'Aspects of a nation in arms: Britain's volunteer training corps in the Great War', Revue Internationale d'Histoire Militaire, 63 (1985), 27–39 • J. M. Osborne, 'Defining their own patriotism: British volunteer training corps in the First World War', Journal of Contemporary History, 23 (1988), 59–75 • Burke, Peerage (1924) • DNB

Archives Bucks. RLSS, D86/31 | BLPES, letters to Tariff Commission • Bucks. RLSS, travel diaries, D86/1–11 • Herefordshire Archives and Local Studies, Hereford, corresp. and papers, D/ERV • Nuffield Oxf., corresp. with Lord Cherwell | FILM BFI NFTVA, propaganda footage (Hepworth Manufacturing Company)
Likenesses W. Roffe, line engraving, pubd 1890 (after photograph by Marsh), NPG • J. S. Sargent, drawing, 1912, priv. coll. [see illus.] • A. S. Cope, oils, 1918, Firle Place, East Sussex • W. Stoneman, photograph, 1933, NPG • O. Edis, photograph, NPG • E. Roberts, portrait; known to be in family possession, 1959 • J. S. Sargent, drawing; known to be in family possession, 1959 • Spy [L. Ward], caricature, chromolithograph, NPG; repro. in VF (20 Dec 1890) • group portrait, wood-engraving (with crew of boat race), NPG; repro. in ILN (24 March 1877) • photograph, repro. in Press, Buckinghamshire leaders
Wealth at death £104,882 14s. 4d.: probate, save and except settled land, 1 May 1945, CGPLA Eng. & Wales • £30,000: probate, limited to settled land, 19 Sept 1945, CGPLA Eng. & Wales

Grenville [Grenvile], **Sir Bevil** [Bevill] (**1596–1643**), royalist army officer, was born on 23 March 1596 at Brinn in St Withiel, Cornwall, the son and heir of Sir Bernard Grenvile (1567–1636) of Stow, Cornwall, and his wife, Elizabeth (d. after 1607), daughter and sole heir of Philip Bevill of Killigrath, Cornwall, and the grandson of Sir Richard *Grenville of the Revenge. The royalist army officer Sir Richard *Grenville was a younger brother. Grenville's own spelling of his name was Bevill Grenvile.

Grenville was admitted to Exeter College, Oxford, in 1611 and graduated BA in 1614, but later regretted his overindulgence in the 'sweet delights' of poetry and history, to the exclusion of other subjects, which had left him 'greatly defective', particularly in the management of weighty affairs (V&A, Forster collection, Grenville to his son Richard, 12 Jan 1639). After Oxford he spent some time at court, where his father had an interest and connection with Endymion Porter. He had left London by 18 November 1618, when he married Grace (d. 1647), daughter of Sir George Smith of Madford, Heavitree, Exeter. They settled at Tremeer in Lanteglos by Fowey, Cornwall, where their first son, Richard, was born in March 1621; they had a further six sons and five daughters (among them John *Grenville, the third but eldest surviving son, and Denis *Granville). In March 1622 Grenville's grandmother, Elizabeth Bevill of Killigarth, died, leaving him the residue of her estate and 'all my manors etc in Cornwall, Devon, Somerset'. Three years later Grenville, Grace, and Sir Bernard resettled the family estates on Grenville's promise to pay his father's debts of £15,000. The main Grenville manors of Kilkhampton and Stow, with other land, were settled on Grenville and his wife for life (so providing Grace with a jointure), with remainder to their eldest son Richard in tail. Other lands including Bideford, Lundy island, and Killigarth were to be held by Sir Bernard for life, with remainder to Grenville absolutely.

Grenville entered parliament in 1621 as knight of the shire for Cornwall, and was again returned for the county in 1624; in 1625 he changed seats to Launceston, which he also represented in the parliaments of 1626 and 1628–9. Throughout this period Grenville was a close friend of Sir John Eliot, working with him and other members of his faction in opposition to the duke of Buckingham and to arbitrary government policies. On 18 May 1626 Grenville wrote to his wife that 'the King hath lately sent [Eliot] to the tower, for some wordes spoken in the Parl[ia]m[en]t. But we are all resolved to have him out againe, or will proceed in noe business' (Granville, 161). In 1627 Grenville was one of five Cornish loan commissioners who refused to pay but, unlike the others, he was neither summoned by the privy council nor punished, possibly as a favour to his father, a supporter of Buckingham. His letter of 23 August to his friends Eliot and William Coryton during their imprisonment for loan refusal reveals his frustration:

whence it growes that I am thus long left at home, when now of late also more of the honest knot are fetch'd away, drives me into wonder and amazement, no man hath with more bouldness declar'd his resolution in this perticular then my selfe, which nor fire nor torture can divert me from, while in myn owne heart I am satisfied that it belonges unto the duty of an honest Englishman so to do.   (ibid., 163)

At the county election of March 1628, when Eliot and Coryton stood against the government candidates, Grenville was one of their most active supporters. The second signatory on their election indenture, he canvassed the most influential voters in the county by letter, and, with John Arundell of Trerice and Charles Trevanion of Caerhayes, arrived at the election, each with 500 men 'at their heels'. During Eliot's imprisonment, between the dissolution of parliament in 1629 and his death in 1632, he and Grenville corresponded regularly and affectionately. But Grenville never forgave Coryton for his submission to the king and desertion of Eliot, promising Eliot in January 1632 that, if rumours of a new parliament were true, he could be sure of the first knight's place, but that he would certainly not have his 'old partner' Coryton (Granville, 182). Shortly afterwards, deeply concerned for Eliot's health, Grenville urged him to reconsider his position:

I beseech you be not nice, but pursue y[ou]r libertie if it may be had on honourable termes. I will not desire you to abandon a good cause, but if a little bending may prevent a breaking yeald a little unto it, it may render you the stronger to serve y[ou]r cuntry hereafter.   (Granville, 183–4)

After Eliot's death Grenville withdrew from politics and county affairs, telling his father of his 'resolution not to intermeddle with the affairs of the commonwealth' and of 'the disproportion between my disposition and the course of the time'. Bevil and Sir Bernard had been on poor terms for a decade, not least because of their opposing political affiliations, but they became reconciled in 1635. After Sir Bernard's death on 16 June 1636 Bevil regretted that their reconciliation had been so short, since 'I have taken more comfort in his late loving expressions to me then ever I did in any thing in my life' (Granville, 137). On his deathbed Sir Bernard had pressed Grenville to take on his deputy lieutenancy of Cornwall and to assume command of his regiment

w[hi]ch I had often before refus[e]d … He added for reason likewise, that seeing those places had ever been in the hands of my Ancestors ever since the first institution of them, and that the Reg[imen]t lyes about my habitation, and in the heart of my estate, it were unfitt for me to suffer a stranger to come in.   (Granville, 192)

Sir Bernard's persistence, and his appeal to family honour and duty, persuaded Grenville to accept.

By 1638 Grenville had become an ardent royalist, raising a troop of horse and joining the king's army in the first bishops' war. In Scotland he was attached to the earl of Pembroke's royal bodyguard troop, and he was knighted for his service in July 1639. Resisting advice from Sir John Trelawny to consider his wife and children, Grenville proclaimed:

but S[i]r for my journey it is fixt. I canot contain myself w[i]thin my doors when the K[in]g of En[glan]ds Standard waves in the field upon so just occasion, the cause being such as must make all those that dye in it little inferiour to Martyrs. And for myne owne p[ar]t I desire to acquire an honest name or an hon[oura]ble grave. I never loved my life or ease so much as to shunn such an occasion w[hi]ch if I should I were unworthy of the profession I have held, or to succede those Ances[tors] of mine, who have so many of them in several ages sacrificed their lives for their country. (Granville, 213)

In April 1640 Grenville again represented Launceston, while in October he was returned unopposed for the county: there is no record of his activity in either parliament. In summer 1642 Sir Bevil was one of the most active Cornish commissioners of array, and took a lead in promoting the array and suppressing the militia ordinance at the Launceston assizes on 5 August. On 8 August the Lords summoned him as a delinquent; not appearing, on 19 September, he was disabled from sitting in parliament. A week later Grenville marched west to Truro with Sir Ralph Hopton's royalist army, determined 'to fetch those traitors out of their nest at Launceston, or fire them in it' (V&A, Forster Collection, Bevil Grenville to Grace Grenville, October 1642). The *posse comitatus* was raised, Launceston was occupied, and the parliamentarian forces were driven from the county. Hopton could not legally take the posse out of the county, so the royalist leaders decided to raise an army of volunteers. Grenville, described by Clarendon as 'the generally most loved man' in Cornwall (Clarendon, *Hist. rebellion*, 2.452), raised his own foot regiment, maintaining them at his own expense.

On 19 January 1643 Hopton's army was victorious against Colonel Ruthin's parliamentarian force at the battle of Braddock Down, near Liskeard. When Hopton launched the attack, deciding to 'leave all to the mercy of god & valour of our side', Grenville led his servants and tenants in a charge so wild that they 'strook a terror' in the enemy (Bevil Grenville to Grace Grenvile, 19 Jan 1643, Granville, 249–50). In May the earl of Stamford's parliamentarian army entered Cornwall, occupying what is now known as Stamford Hill, near Stratton in north Cornwall. On 16 May Hopton's army attacked, advancing uphill in four sections, Grenville and Sir John Berkeley taking the south-west, but was constantly driven back. At 3 o'clock in the afternoon, concealing a shortage of powder from their men, Hopton and Grenville ordered a final charge uphill with swords and pikes, 'without making any more shot till they reached the top of the hill, and so might be upon even ground with the enemy' (Clarendon, *Hist. rebellion*, 3.70). By the time the royalists regrouped at the top, 300 parliamentarians were slain and 1700 captured, with thirteen cannon and all their baggage. Hopton and Grenville celebrated this 'seasonable victory' with 'public prayers upon the place and a solemn thanksgiving to Almighty God for their deliverance' (Clarendon, *Hist. rebellion*, 3.71).

The next major engagement for the Cornish army, now united with that of Prince Maurice and the marquess of Hertford, was at the battle of Lansdown, near Bath, on 5 July 1643. Again Grenville led a charge uphill, towards Sir William Waller's parliamentarian army, but, gaining the brow of the hill, they still faced the enemy on the plateau. The Cornish army suffered terrible losses and, in the third charge of the parliamentarian horse on the ridge, Grenville was struck on the head with a pole-axe and seriously wounded. Shortly afterwards the royalists seized the victory, but Grenville died the next day at Cold Ashton parsonage. He was buried at Kilkhampton, north Cornwall, on 26 July, and succeeded by his third son, John (1628–1701), later first earl of Bath.

Clarendon said that Grenville's death, which 'would have clouded any victory' (Clarendon, *Hist. rebellion*, 3.92), was

> to the universal grief of the army, and, indeed, of all who knew him. He was a gallant and a sprightly gentleman, of the greatest reputation and interest in Cornwall, and had most contributed to all the service that had been done there. (ibid., 3.82)

Sir John Trelawny shared this great grief, writing to Lady Grace on 20 July 1643:

> Seeing it hath pleased God to take him from your Ladyship, yet this may something appease y[ou]r greate flux of tears, that he died an Honourable Death, w[hi]ch all Enemies will Envy, fighting with Invincible Valour, and Loyalty ye Battle of his God, his King, and his Country. A greater honour then this, no man living can enjoy. But God hath called him unto himselfe, to Crowne him with Imortall Glory for his noble Constancye in this Blessed Cause.   (Granville, 269)

ANNE DUFFIN

Sources A. Duffin, *Faction and faith: politics and religion of the Cornish gentry before the civil war* (1996) • M. Coate, *Cornwall in the great civil war and interregnum, 1642–1660* (1933) • *DNB* • R. Granville, *History of the Granville family* (Exeter, 1895) • B. Grenville, letters, V&A NAL, Forster Library • Clarendon, *Hist. rebellion* • *Bellum civile: Hopton's narrative of his campaign in the West, 1642–1644*, ed. C. E. H. Chadwyck Healey, Somerset RS, 18 (1902) • J. Derriman, *Killigarth: three centuries of a Cornish manor* (1994), privately printed • J. Forster, *Sir John Eliot: a biography*, 2 vols. (1864) • J. L. Vivian, ed., *The visitations of Cornwall, comprising the herald's visitations of 1530, 1573, and 1620* (1887) • Keeler, *Long Parliament* • J. Stucley, *Sir Bevill Grenile and his times, 1596–1643* (1983)

Archives Hunt. L., letters • V&A NAL, letters to family

Likenesses R. Cooper, stipple and line print, NPG • W. Faithorne, line engraving, BM, NPG; repro. in *Verses by the University of Oxford on his death* (1684) • R. Grenville, stipple, NPG • school of A. Van Dyck, oils, Petworth House, Sussex • G. Vertue, double portrait, line engraving (with Lord Hopton), BM • portrait, priv. coll.

Wealth at death appears to have been land rich and money poor: Granville, *History* • by 1638 affairs in Cornwall had already been settled; mortgaging some of holdings for £20,000 and others within next three years for perhaps £7000 more, preparing to devote himself to king's cause

Grenville, Denis. *See* Granville, Denis (1637–1703).

Grenville, George (1712–1770), prime minister, was born at Wotton, Buckinghamshire, on 14 October 1712, the second of the six sons of Richard Grenville (1678–1727), landowner and whig MP, and his wife, Hester (1684–1752), the second daughter of Sir Richard Temple, third baronet, of Stowe, Buckinghamshire. Grenville was often spelt Greenville by contemporaries, and that may have been the pronunciation.

Education and family Grenville was educated at Eton College from 1725 and entered Christ Church, Oxford, in 1730, but did not graduate. As the landless younger son of a squire, he was evidently destined for a legal career. In 1729 he entered at the Inner Temple, whence he was called to the bar in 1735, and he retained chambers there until 1744. He handled the family's legal business, but it is unclear how far he engaged in general practice before politics engrossed his attention.

Grenville owed his political career to his mother's brother, Richard Temple, first Viscount Cobham of Stowe, who at the general election of 1741 brought him into parliament for his borough of Buckingham, a seat Grenville held until his death. He joined his uncle's youthful opposition group of Cobham's Cubs, among whom William Pitt was the rising star. The prime minister, Sir Robert Walpole, dubbed them the Boy Patriots. When Walpole resigned in 1742 the Cubs remained in opposition to the Carteret ministry, but they joined the Pelham administration in the ministerial reshuffle of 1744. Grenville, having earned his spurs by some notable speeches, was appointed to the Admiralty board. He acted as Admiralty spokesman in the Commons, and also busied himself with wartime administrative duties. Three years later, with a salary rise from £1000 to £1400, he moved to the Treasury board, where for the next seven years he acquired his formidable mastery of the national budget.

Grenville meanwhile put his own finances in order. He was later to claim that he added each year's official salary to his capital, living off only the interest, until he became prime minister. The thrifty Grenville acquired capital from family sources, inheriting £3000 from his father in 1727, £7562 of Bank of England stock from his deceased younger brother Thomas in 1747, and £5000 in 1749 from Lord Cobham. By 1750 he had £15,358 of stock. After he married he claimed only the interest and not the capital of his wife's dowry of £10,000, which was still owed to his estate at his death. His bride on 16 May 1749 was Elizabeth (1719/20–1769), the second daughter of the former tory leader Sir William *Wyndham and Lady Catherine Seymour, the daughter of the sixth duke of Somerset. The bride's grandfather snobbishly disapproved of the match and bequeathed her only an insulting annuity of £100. Both her parents were long since deceased, but her brother Charles, who became second earl of Egremont in 1750, was to be a friend and political ally of her husband. Lady Bolingbroke unkindly remarked that the new Mrs Grenville looked forty-nine at her marriage age of twenty-nine, for her face had been scarred by smallpox. George had made a fortunate marriage to a devoted wife, who took such a keen interest in her husband's political career

George Grenville (1712–1770), by Sir Joshua Reynolds, 1764

that she kept a diary of it, long attributed to Grenville himself. 'She was the first prize in the marriage lottery of our century', wrote Grenville's friend Lord Buckinghamshire in 1765 (Lawson, 56). The happy couple had four sons and five daughters: the second son, George Nugent-Temple-*Grenville, succeeded to Stowe in 1779 and was created marquess of Buckingham in 1784; the fourth son, William Wyndham *Grenville, became Lord Grenville in 1790 and prime minister in 1806. Stowe had been bequeathed in 1749 to George's mother, who was created Countess Temple. In 1752 it passed, on her death, to his elder brother, Richard, who as second Earl Temple often behaved as if his rank and wealth gave him political equality with William Pitt, who had replaced Cobham as leader of their political faction. From 1752 Lord Temple, for an annual rent of a mere £10, leased the Grenville family home of Wotton to George, who also depended on his brother for his Buckingham parliamentary seat.

The 'Brotherhood' The meagre parliamentary records of the Pelham era reveal little about Grenville's debating role, but a creditable performance is implied by Pitt's comment to Lord Chancellor Hardwicke in 1754—'Mr Grenville is … one of the very best Parliament men in the House'—mentioning particularly his understanding of Commons procedure (*Correspondence of William Pitt*, 1.406). Pitt was expressing pleasure at the promotion of Grenville to be treasurer of the navy, with a salary of £2000, in the ministerial reshuffle consequent on the death of the prime minister, Henry Pelham, on 6 March. Grenville,

who was also sworn of the privy council on 21 June, was by then deemed second to Pitt in their Commons faction. When on 16 November 1754 Pitt married Hester Grenville, the only sister of George and Lord Temple, a close political bond seemed to be forged of the 'Brotherhood'. Twelve months later, in November 1755, Pitt and Grenville were dismissed from office for criticizing the duke of Newcastle's foreign policy as too Europe-orientated. After a year in open opposition Pitt formed a short-lived ministry with the duke of Devonshire when Newcastle abdicated responsibility for the disastrous start to the Seven Years' War, and Grenville returned to his old post of treasurer of the navy. He had hoped for the more lucrative pay office, and the sense of injury was deepened when he often had to deputize for the unwell Pitt as leader of the Commons.

The administration was dismissed in April 1757, and during subsequent negotiations with Newcastle to form a coalition Pitt's demand that Grenville be made chancellor of the exchequer, a post he had coveted for some years, proved to be an obstacle until Grenville himself suggested that it be dropped. For the third time he took the office of treasurer of the navy. There he was instrumental in passing the Navy Act of 1758 that speeded up the payment of seamen's wages: this was not merely to improve naval recruitment but also for humanitarian motives, to alleviate distress for naval families. The same sense of fairness had caused him to oppose the execution of Admiral Byng in 1757. Grenville maintained a low profile during the Pitt–Newcastle ministry, although as a competent administrator he shared background responsibility for Britain's naval success in the war. But he was quietly nursing his resentment that his relatives Pitt and Lord Temple, both of whom were in the cabinet, were not pushing him for promotion. Personal and political ties between them and Grenville were weakening during these years. Grenville was critical of Pitt's cavalier attitude to the cost of the war, and was maintaining his own links with the Leicester House court of the young prince of Wales that had begun when both groups were in opposition in the mid-1750s. The ground was being prepared for Grenville's political volte-face after the prince became king in October 1760.

Changing allegiances Grenville then hoped to become chancellor of the exchequer at last, since the current incumbent, Henry Legge, had given offence to the king and his favourite Lord Bute: but when Legge was removed in March 1761 he was replaced by Lord Barrington. Once again Pitt had failed to push Grenville's cause, and the breach between them widened. Grenville's ambitions now centred on the speaker's chair, which was being vacated by Arthur Onslow. It was a post for which his parliamentary expertise well suited him. But the king and Bute were anxious to reserve Grenville for high political office, and the opportunity arose later in the year. The cabinet was split over Pitt's demand for a pre-emptive naval strike against Spain, which was preparing to side with France in the war. When Pitt was outvoted on this, he and Lord Temple resigned in October, but Grenville did not follow them out of office. At the instigation of Lord Bute he had left London for Wotton during the political crisis, so as to avoid the emotional pressure of his family. He was then summoned back, to receive the offer of Pitt's post as secretary of state for the southern department. This Grenville refused, both from personal delicacy and from fear of a Commons confrontation with an irate Pitt. George III accepted Grenville's suggestion that Lord Egremont should succeed Pitt, but did not allow him the safe haven of the speakership. Grenville was needed on the government front bench, and when Newcastle vetoed his appointment as chancellor of the exchequer he became leader of the house, with a seat in the cabinet, while still remaining only treasurer of the navy.

A family quarrel was the inevitable consequence, with Lord Temple and Pitt bitter about Grenville's apostasy. He also was apprehensive about his parliamentary role, commenting to Newcastle, 'What figure shall I make? … I have no friends', meaning no following of his own (Lawson, 142). But when the Commons met in November Pitt did not launch the onslaught Grenville dreaded, while Grenville's reservations about an expensive European war struck a popular note among MPs. Grenville was able to rebuff Pitt's demand for information on the Spanish negotiations by the contention that diplomacy was the prerogative of the crown. Nor did Pitt exploit the onset of the Spanish war in January 1762, a development that enabled Grenville to press for a reduction of expenditure in the German campaigns. He was instrumental in forcing the resignation of the duke of Newcastle from the Treasury on 7 May 1762, after the cabinet had decided to end the annual subsidy to Britain's ally Frederick II of Prussia.

Secretary of state Bute now took the Treasury and formed a ministry, but Grenville refused to accept the post of chancellor of the exchequer assigned to him. Instead he insisted on the northern secretaryship being vacated by Bute. The king thought Grenville presumptuous, and added the further objection that his brother-in-law Lord Egremont was already southern secretary. Grenville proved adamant, and obtained the post on 28 May. His spell as northern secretary was an unhappy one. A conventional explanation has long been that his talents were not suited to international diplomacy. But the true reason was that Grenville differed from George III and Bute over the conduct of the peace negotiations. He opposed many concessions that Bute was willing to make in his desire for peace. A whole series of disputes over Martinique, St Lucia, and Cuba culminated in October in the replacement of Grenville by Henry Fox as Commons leader, for fear Grenville would not push through a peace of which he disapproved. He was also compelled to exchange offices with the first lord of the Admiralty, Lord Halifax. His Admiralty salary was about £2500, less than a third of the emoluments of a secretary of state. Although Grenville remained in the cabinet, he was excluded from the final phase of the peace negotiations and took little part in Commons debates during the session of 1762–3. In March 1763 he suffered a public humiliation at Pitt's hands in a discussion of a new cider tax. Infuriated by Pitt's populist criticism, he challenged his brother-in-law to suggest where he could find an alternative tax. Pitt mocked him

by murmuring the popular ditty 'Gentle Shepherd, tell me where', and thereafter 'the Gentle Shepherd' was often a sobriquet for Grenville in the contemporary press.

The sorry record of Grenville during the Bute ministry was the precursor to his appointment as prime minister. He seemed to have lost all chance of such high office, George III commenting to Bute on 14 March 1763 that 'Grenville has thrown away the game he had two years ago' (Lawson, 149). Bute had always intended to resign after the achievement of peace, and when Henry Fox declined to succeed him, preferring political retirement in the House of Lords, it became apparent that there was no other choice than either the appointment of Grenville or surrender to Newcastle and Pitt, for the other members of the Bute cabinet patently lacked the calibre for the post. Grenville received the offer on 25 March, and his appointment, as both first lord of the Treasury and chancellor of the exchequer, was made public on 6 April. The political world thought Grenville would be a dummy minister, with Bute the power behind the throne. But in the negotiations of March 1763 Grenville showed his mettle and secured some key concessions. He insisted on full control of Treasury patronage, contrary to George III's inclinations; he killed a plan to replace his brother-in-law Egremont as southern secretary by Bute's young protégé Lord Shelburne; and he obtained the acceptance of several of his recommendations for vacancies at the Treasury and Admiralty boards. He also secured the promise of a pension of £3000 for when he left office. Newcastle knew little of this, but shrewdly perceived that Bute had chosen the wrong man if he wanted a puppet minister.

Prime minister, 1763–1765 Bute's intention to retire was genuine, and it was publicly given out that the new ministry was a 'triumvirate' of Grenville and the two secretaries Egremont and Halifax. But George III disliked his ministers, and for the next few months insisted on consulting Bute on public business. At the beginning of August the ministry gave the king an ultimatum to choose between full support of his cabinet or forming another administration. George III essayed the latter option, but Pitt pitched his terms so high that the king turned again to Grenville, accepting his condition that Bute should take no further part in politics; he also promised to back Grenville against his cabinet colleagues, for Grenville's ally Egremont had died on 21 August, and the reshuffled administration chiefly comprised adherents of the duke of Bedford. George III assured Grenville that 'he meant to put his government solely into his hands' (*Grenville Papers*, 2.212). Grenville was now 'first minister', his own designation of his status.

Mastery of the House of Commons was, however, thrown into doubt by the first case involving the MP John Wilkes, arrested for a libel of the king in his paper the *North Briton* under a general warrant that did not name who was to be seized. That was a tactical blunder by the secretaries of state, for the implication of a widespread threat to individual liberty raised the political temperature: some fifty persons altogether, printers and others, had been arrested. Few doubted that there had been a libel, and Grenville was on safe ground when he made that issue a vote of confidence. The Commons condemned the libel and expelled Wilkes by large majorities. But the parliamentary opposition so exploited the general warrants issue as to bring on in February 1764 one of the great Commons confrontations of the century. Grenville won by majorities of ten and fourteen against the oratory of William Pitt and the canvassing of Newcastle. Many independent MPs were uneasy about the legality of general warrants, and Grenville in debate did not seek to defend it, simply arguing that it was a matter to be decided not by the House of Commons but by the law courts, which indeed soon condemned the practice. Despite the hopes of his opponents, and the opinions of some historians, Grenville's tenure of the Treasury was not at stake. He had not seen the question as one on which he should resign if defeated, and neither had the king, for many MPs voted against him only over that one issue. After the excitement died down Grenville turned his attention to the matter for which he is best known, the taxation of America.

The American colonies The decision to tax America, to finance the army stationed in that continent, had been made in principle by the Bute cabinet, of which Grenville had been a member. He himself was particularly concerned from his Admiralty days about enforcing the customs laws, and the first proposal to raise a colonial revenue was one to halve an existing duty of 6d. a gallon on foreign molasses, the basis of rum, entering North America, but to enforce it. That was introduced in Grenville's first budget speech on 9 March 1764. He also then announced a plan to impose stamp duties on the colonies, and a draft American Stamp Bill had been in preparation since September 1763. When objection was made that the colonies should be consulted, Grenville postponed the tax for a year: he meant to invite other ideas on parliamentary taxation, but not to allow colonies to tax themselves; that old error of some contemporaries and historians has been corrected by recently discovered evidence.

Unsurprisingly, not one colony suggested how it might be taxed by parliament. Instead there was a flood of protests. This colonial reaction led the ministry to proceed with the Stamp Act in order to establish parliament's right to tax the colonies as well as to obtain money. No MP objected to the principle, but fifty voted against the expediency of the tax when Grenville introduced the measure in a well-prepared speech on 6 February 1765, in which he systematically demonstrated the constitutional right of parliament to impose the tax, and then the equity and propriety of doing so. The stamp duty was payable on newspapers, many legal documents, shipping cargo lists, and numerous sundry items. Britain had had such duties for nearly a century, and the common assumption was that they would be accepted in America, albeit under protest. Taxation was only part of the colonial policy of the Grenville ministry, and other measures owed little to his initiative: he himself opposed the creation of reservations for Native Americans west of the settlement colonies, but was outvoted on that point in cabinet on 16 September 1763. But while the concept of a 'Grenville programme'

for America is a misnomer, only such a conscientious and industrious prime minister could have achieved so much in so short a time. A man so concerned with finance and legal right must have been shocked at the disorder and defiance of authority in the colonies. Hence the obviously retrospective comment attributed to an unknown official: 'Mr Grenville lost America because he read the American despatches, which his predecessors had never done' (Thomas, *British Politics*, 113).

Concern for efficiency and economy in government was the Grenville hallmark. He raised official morale by prompt payment of salaries, and he curbed needless expenditure: contemporary cartoons mocked him as saving candle ends. Foreign policy had to be cheap, and so expensive European alliances were avoided. But Grenville defended Britain's imperial interests. He played his part in sending Lord Clive back to Bengal in 1764 to secure British control there, and what has anachronistically been described as his 'gunboat diplomacy' deterred French and Spanish encroachments on British settlements in Honduras, Turk's Island, and the Gambia: in each instance the mere threat of a naval squadron sufficed.

Dismissal Before the consequences of his American policy became known, Grenville was out of office. George III got rid of Grenville because he was insolent in attitude and tedious in behaviour: insolent because Grenville, paranoid about Bute's influence after his return to London in 1764, tried to insist on making all recommendations to official appointments; tedious because of his verbosity and tendency to lecture the king on his constitutional role. 'When he has wearied me for two hours', complained George III, 'he looks at his watch, to see if he may not tire me for an hour more' (Thomas, 'George Grenville', 123). Grenville had that effect on almost everybody. His cousin Thomas Pitt recalled that 'he was diffuse and argumentative, and never had done with a subject after he had convinced your judgment till he wearied your attention. The foreign ministers complained of his prolixity, which they called amongst each other, being *Grenvilise*' (Namier, 539).

The relationship between Grenville and the king had already deteriorated beyond redemption before the Regency Bill episode of spring 1765, which many then and later erroneously thought the cause of his removal from office: discord with George III over that matter arose briefly from a ministerial misapprehension that the king intended to name his mother and not his wife as prospective regent, the objection being her close friendship with Bute. By then George III had already decided to change his ministry, but his uncle the duke of Cumberland, not Bute, was the royal intermediary. A first attempt in May ended in a public fiasco when Pitt refused office, and the Grenville cabinet thought itself safely entrenched in power when the same month saw a personal and political reconciliation of Grenville with his brother Lord Temple, for Pitt always then made Temple's support a condition of office. But George III, determined to rid himself of Grenville, persuaded the Newcastle group to form a ministry under Lord Rockingham in July 1765. Grenville's formal dismissal came on 10 July, when the king made it clear that he was being dismissed because of his attitude, not his policies or incompetence. Grenville, who became prime minister without a party, left office with one, estimated at some seventy MPs, but in opposition it soon dwindled to less than half that size.

Opposition, 1765–1770 George III was said to have declared that he would henceforth rather see the Devil in his closet than George Grenville. Aware of this royal antipathy, Grenville behaved as a man free to declare his opinions regardless of consequences. He earned respect for his forthright and honest behaviour, but a return to office never now seemed likely. His attitude in the Stamp Act crisis of 1765–6, one of alarm and anger at American defiance, led him into blunders. As early as a Commons debate of 17 December 1765 he absurdly denounced the colonial resistance to his taxation as rebellion, comparable to the Jacobite rising of 1745. On 7 February 1766, after some tactical successes in earlier debates, he overplayed his hand by a Commons motion that in effect demanded enforcement of the Stamp Act, a proposal likely to lead to bloodshed. The majority of 274 to 134 against him that day destroyed his attempt to prevent repeal, which the ministry subsequently carried by large majorities. The courtier Gilbert Elliot commented that 'Mr Grenville and his friends are like to have leisure enough to repent of their headstrong and ill-advised conduct', and John Walsh, another MP not without sympathy for Grenville, wrote on 19 February that he did 'not possess in any eminent degree opposition talents' (Lawson, 226). It was not a role Grenville was accustomed to playing, but one he faced for the indefinite future when George III in July 1766 successfully turned to Pitt, now created earl of Chatham, to replace the Rockingham ministry. There began a steady haemorrhage of Grenville's parliamentary support as his followers faced a bleak future.

When parliament resumed in November 1766 Grenville launched almost alone a campaign against the legality of a royal proclamation of 24 September forbidding the export of grain. Constitutionally he was correct, as it breached the Bill of Rights. But tactically he was wrong, because most MPs realized that the government had thereby averted a food scarcity and consequent rioting. Later that session Grenville did enjoy a parliamentary triumph, the defeat of the ministry on 27 February 1767 on an opposition motion to reduce the land tax from 4s. to 3s. The three opposition parties of Rockingham, Bedford, and Grenville had found a popular topic, and although Grenville did not make the amendment he received most credit, as his wife noted in her diary: 'All the country gentlemen coming round Mr Grenville, shaking him by the hand, and testifying the greatest satisfaction' (*Grenville Papers*, 4.212). Mistaken euphoria led the opposition leaders to discuss an alliance, but the idea foundered on the impasse that both Rockingham and Grenville wanted the Treasury in any new ministry. In negotiations of July, when Rockingham for a while thought he had been asked to form a ministry, Grenville disdained any idea of taking

part, perhaps because he was suspicious of the administration initiative. Certainly it did divide the opposition. The Bedford group decided to go their own way, and Rockingham's personal and political resentment at Grenville boiled over into an indiscreet statement at a Newmarket race meeting that he would never serve in government with him. Grenville responded by a savage attack on the Rockinghamite party in the opening debate of the new parliamentary session, on 24 November 1767. Bedford in rage and despair opened successful negotiations to join the ministry. Grenville, upset at this desertion by his long-term ally, found further ground for pessimism when his Commons party was reduced to thirty-one MPs after the general election of early 1768.

But that same election saw the return of John Wilkes for Middlesex, an event precipitating a major political controversy that gave renewed spirit to the opposition and eventually led to the fall of the ministry, led by the duke of Grafton after the unwell Chatham resigned in October 1768. Grenville himself encountered some embarrassment in this second Wilkes case, for some of the issues from the first one of the *North Briton*, when he had been the premier acting against Wilkes, arose again; however, on the central point of the ministry's determination to expel Wilkes he entertained no doubts that it was unconstitutional. On the motion of 3 February 1769 for expulsion Grenville made what his brother Lord Temple said was 'universally deemed the best speech he ever made' against the proposal: it was later printed as a pamphlet (*Correspondence of William Pitt*, 3.349). The case led him into co-operation with Rockingham, and during the summer recess of 1769 the return of Chatham to health and to the political arena increased the threat to the ministry, for he condemned the Middlesex election decision and allied with his brothers-in-law Grenville and Temple to form another triumvirate. Grafton resigned in January 1770 as his Commons majority crumbled, but Lord North stepped into the breach and robbed the opposition of victory. Grenville, however, enjoyed the satisfaction later that session of carrying his Election Act of 1770, which transferred the decision of election petitions from the House of Commons to a small committee of fifteen MPs chosen by lot. An obvious attempt to secure fairness, in the light of the Middlesex election case, it was a personal triumph, carried against ministerial wishes by the support of independent MPs. Contemporaries knew it as the Grenville Act.

Death and reputation Grenville became ill early in the summer of 1770, and died on 13 November at his London home in Bolton Street, Piccadilly; he was buried at Wotton. A post-mortem revealed widespread bone corrosion, particularly of the ribs and skull. He was a professional politician in a sense that few men of his time were. His cousin Thomas Pitt wrote:

> he was a man born to public business, which was his luxury and amusement. An Act of Parliament was in itself entertaining to him, as was proved when he stole a turnpike bill out of somebody's pocket at a concert and read it in a

corner in despite of all the efforts of the finest singers to attract his attention.   (Namier, 539)

The House of Commons was his natural habitat, but the same verbosity that alienated George III:

> rendered him an unpleasant speaker. Yet though his eloquence charmed nobody, his argument converted … The abundance of his matter, his experience of the forms and practice of the House … and above all the purity of his character … gave him … weight … He never took notes; he never quitted his seat for refreshment in the longest debates, and generally spoke the last.   (ibid., 539)

The hostile Horace Walpole conceded that 'Mr Grenville was confessedly, the ablest man of business in the House of Commons, and though not popular, of great authority there from his spirit, knowledge, and gravity of character' (Lawson, 287–8). Edmund Burke, in his famous speech of 19 April 1774 on American taxation, agreed that

> Mr Grenville was a first-rate figure in this country. With a masculine understanding, and a stout and resolute heart, he had an application undissipated and unwearied. He took public business, not as a duty which he was to fulfil, but as a pleasure he was to enjoy; and he seemed to have no delight out of this House, except in such things as in some way related to the business that was to be done within it.
> (Writings and Speeches, 2.431)

When parliament was not sitting, Grenville usually retired to his native Buckinghamshire, enjoying a countryside life and his family circle: all his seven surviving children were still under age at his death. He improved Wotton, and made nineteen property purchases in the county between 1754 and 1769, when his wife died, on 5 December, which was a grievous blow. Grenville so husbanded his finances that he left £154,674 in trust for his children. But Grenville is remembered by posterity not as a family man or even as a parliamentarian. He is recalled as the man whose taxation started the American War of Independence. Grenville never doubted that America should contribute to Britain's budget. He was scornful of the Rockingham ministry policy of 1766 that claimed the right of taxation but did not seek to enforce it, deeming such equivocation as more reprehensible than Pitt's open denial of parliamentary right. It was Grenville's pressure in the Commons on 26 January 1767 that extracted a premature promise from the chancellor of the exchequer, Charles Townshend, of renewed colonial taxation: and when, on 5 March 1770, he was confronted with a choice between the partial repeal of Townshend's taxes by the North ministry and an opposition amendment for their complete abolition, Grenville simply led his followers out of the house.

Grenville was a man who saw issues in black and white, and said and did what he thought was right. If he was obstinate in character, he was tactless in behaviour. His cousin Thomas Pitt recalled that 'he had nothing seducing in his manners. His countenance had rather the expression of peevishness and austerity' (Namier, 539). Lord Egmont, who held the Admiralty in the Grenville cabinet, wrote in 1768 that 'Mr Grenville is a most disagreeable man to do business with'. But he added, 'he is nevertheless

the fittest person to be at the head of this country' (*Correspondence of William Pitt*, 3.334n.). Grenville may have made more enemies than friends, but he commanded respect from everybody.

J. V. BECKETT and PETER D. G. THOMAS

Sources P. Lawson, *George Grenville: a political life* (1984) · A. S. Johnson, *A prologue to revolution: the political career of George Grenville, 1712–1770* (Lanham, MD, 1997) · P. D. G. Thomas, *British politics and the Stamp Act crisis: the first phase of the American revolution, 1763–1767* (1975) · L. M. Wiggin, *A faction of cousins: a political account of the Grenvilles, 1733–1763* (1958) · P. D. G. Thomas, 'George Grenville', *The prime ministers*, ed. D. H. van Thal (1974), 1.116–25 · J. L. Bollion, *A great and necessary measure: George Grenville and the genesis of the Stamp Act, 1763–1765* (Princeton, NJ, 1982) · L. B. Namier, 'Grenville, George', HoP, *Commons, 1754–90* · J. V. Beckett, 'George Grenville, prime minister, 1763–1765: career politician or country gentleman', *Parliamentary History*, 14 (1995), 139–48 · N. Tracy, *Navies, deterrence, and American independence* (Vancouver, 1988) · *The Grenville papers: being the correspondence of Richard Grenville … and … George Grenville*, ed. W. J. Smith, 4 vols. (1852–3) · P. D. G. Thomas, *John Wilkes: a friend to liberty* (1996) · *Correspondence of William Pitt, earl of Chatham*, ed. W. S. Taylor and J. H. Pringle, 4 vols. (1838–40) · *The writings and speeches of Edmund Burke*, ed. P. Langford, vol. 2: *Party, parliament and the American crisis, 1766–1774* (1981)

Archives BL, political and family corresp. and papers, Add. MSS 42083–42088, 57804–57837 · Bodl. Oxf., corresp. · Bucks. RLSS, Stowe MSS, family papers · Coutts Bank, London, bank account · Duke U., Perkins L., corresp. · Hunt. L., corresp. and papers · Northants. RO, Stowe MSS, family papers · U. Mich., William L. Clements Library, corresp. · Yale U., Farmington, Lewis Walpole Library, corresp. and papers | BL, letters to Robert Clive, William Pitt, and Lord Temple [microfilm] · BL, corresp. with first Lord Hardwicke and R. Keith, Add. MSS 34585, 35589–35597 · BL, letters to Charles Jenkinson, loan 72 · BL, corresp. with first Earl Liverpool, Add. MSS 38191, 38304–38305 · BL, Newcastle MSS · Norfolk RO, corresp. with earl of Buckinghamshire · NRA, priv. coll., letters to J. Oswald · PRO, letters to William Pitt, first Earl Chatham, and Lady Chatham · Suffolk RO, Bury St Edmunds, corresp. with third earl of Bristol · U. Mich., Clements L., corresp. with William Knox · Yale U., Farmington, Lewis Walpole Library, letters to E. Weston

Likenesses F. G. Aliamet, line engraving, pubd 1757 (after W. Hoare), NPG · W. Hoare, oils, 1764, Christ Church Oxf. · J. Reynolds, portrait, 1764, Col. U. [*see illus.*] · W. Hoare, portrait, Mansell Collection; repro. in Thomas, 'George Grenville' · J. Reynolds, oils, Courtauld Inst.; repro. in Johnson, *Prologue to revolution* · J. Reynolds, oils, John Bass Museum, Miami, Florida; version, Petworth House, West Sussex · G. Walker, line engraving (after J. Reynolds), BM, NPG

Wealth at death £154,674—in trust

Grenville, George Neville (1789–1854). *See under* Griffin, Richard, second Baron Braybrooke (1750–1825).

Grenville, George Nugent-Temple-, **first marquess of Buckingham** (1753–1813), politician, was born George Grenville on 17 June 1753 in London, the eldest surviving son of George *Grenville (1712–1770), prime minister, and his wife, Elizabeth Wyndham (d. 1769), daughter of Sir William Wyndham. He was educated at Eton College from 1764 to 1770 and matriculated at Christ Church, Oxford, on 20 April 1770. He left without taking a degree, succeeding in the same year to Wotton and other properties in Buckinghamshire on his father's death. In 1774 he made the grand tour with Lord Bulkeley, travelling mainly in Italy and Austria. In the same year he was elected to one of the seats for Buckinghamshire. His father, besides making

George Nugent-Temple-Grenville, first marquess of Buckingham (1753–1813), by unknown artist, c.1787–9

other provisions, had endowed him with the spoils of politics, and at the tender age of eleven he had become a teller to the exchequer, a highly lucrative place.

On 16 April 1775 Grenville married Lady Mary Elizabeth Nugent, *suo jure* Baroness Nugent (*d.* 1812), eldest daughter and coheir of Robert *Nugent, first Earl Nugent (1709–1788), politician, and his third wife, Elizabeth Berkeley, dowager countess of Berkeley, at St Margaret's, Westminster. It was an advantageous marriage, bringing with it large landed properties in Ireland and England; one seat for the borough of St Mawes in Cornwall (Grenville would later acquire the second); and through his brother-in-law, the earl of Berkeley, the start of extended family connections in the House of Lords. As a builder of the family fortunes, Grenville was a worthy successor to his father and his uncle, Richard Grenville, second Earl Temple.

During his time in the House of Commons, Grenville, though somewhat embarrassed by his father's famous Stamp Act, generally played a loyal part in upholding the Pitt–Temple line of opposition to the American War of Independence. In September 1779 he succeeded his uncle as third Earl Temple. Shortly afterward he prefixed by royal licence the names Nugent-Temple to his surname.

As a peer, he continued to espouse the positions he had championed in the lower house. His maiden speech in February 1780 was in support of Shelburne's motion for an inquiry into public expenditure, which the opposition held to be wantonly wasted on a long-lost cause.

On the fall of North and the accession of Rockingham's government, Temple received his first reward in being made lord lieutenant of Buckinghamshire on 30 March 1782. In July he became lord lieutenant of Ireland. In that office he presided over the granting of Irish legislative independence. Lord Charlemont said of him at the time that 'He knows a great deal, but is too fond of communicating that knowledge, and too verbose and minute. … He is proud and too apt to undervalue his equals; passionate and sometimes imprudent' (GEC, *Peerage*, 2.407 n.). Though this was an accurate enough characterization of Temple, then and later, it did not prevent him from doing a passable job. Initially opposed to the renunciation of English legislative supremacy, he ultimately promoted it; it was hardly a solution, but none the less a necessary measure at the time. More to his taste, in 1783 he presided as grand master over the institution of the new Order of St Patrick.

The resignation of Shelburne from office late in February 1783 was quickly followed by Temple's own, though because of the delay in finding a successor, he did not return to England until early in June. He was soon advising the king about his schemes to get rid of the unwanted Fox–North coalition, which he roundly abused in the debate on the address at the opening of parliament in November. Thereafter he became George III's chosen champion, denouncing the introduction of the ministry's 'infamous' India Bill, and receiving the king's express permission to declare that anyone who voted for it was not only not a friend of the king, but his enemy; or, indeed, to use any language, even stronger, that might be to the purpose. Although highly controversial, his strategy proved effective, and the bill was defeated by nineteen votes in the Lords. In his cousin William Pitt's government, which followed the dismissal of the coalition, Temple was named home secretary. On 22 December, only three days after his appointment, in a manifestation of those traits of pride, passion, and imprudence noted by Charlemont, he resigned after a dispute with Pitt over whether or not there should be an immediate dissolution of parliament.

The negotiations which followed about how Temple was to be rewarded for his services to the king once again reflected the less pleasant traits of his character. He thought he deserved nothing less than a dukedom and the Garter. The king ruled out the former and did not seem forthcoming about the latter, but was willing to offer a marquessate. Temple was about to turn down the offer in a fit of ill humour, but was dissuaded by his youngest brother, William Wyndham *Grenville, the future Lord Grenville, whose tactful mediation elicited not only the offer of the title, but coupled with it the promise of a Garter when more pressing demands allowed. This proposal Temple was willing to accept. He became marquess of

Buckingham in December 1784 and was finally installed as a knight of the Garter in 1801.

After several years out of office Buckingham was once more appointed lord lieutenant of Ireland in November 1787. This placed him in Ireland just before the king's first extended bout of mental derangement precipitated the regency crisis in the following year. In Ireland the crisis culminated in an address of the two houses of parliament in February 1789 requesting the prince of Wales to assume the government of the kingdom during his father's illness. Buckingham dealt with the crisis simply by refusing to transmit the address, brazenly persisting until the king's recovery the next month. Then, defied by placemen in the parliament, who had entered into a pact never to accept office again if any of their number was punished, he responded by offering amnesty to those who forsook opposition and speedy ejection to those who did not. The opposition promptly melted. Buckingham had shown spirit and pluck in defusing what might have become a highly embarrassing situation for Pitt's government. After resigning the lieutenancy the following October, Buckingham returned home to claim his reward. His success this time was no greater. The king was adamant in his refusal of a dukedom, and nothing less would satisfy Buckingham. He was desolate and thought himself 'the most disgraced *public man* if no mark of favour or approbation is given to me' (Beckett, 73). He recovered sufficiently by 1794, however, to request an Irish barony for his wife with remainder to his second son, George Nugent *Grenville. This was finally granted in 1800, and George became second Lord Nugent on his mother's death in 1812.

Buckingham was never to hold office again after 1789, and as a politician he can scarcely be said to have been a striking success. He continued, however, to exercise influence behind the scenes, and the results continued to be mixed. As a former lord lieutenant, he was listened to with respect on Irish affairs. He was capable of statesman-like vision, being one of the first to champion Catholic emancipation, which he pressed upon the government from 1791. The government listened but the king did not, and union with Ireland in 1801 was not accompanied by Catholic relief. This question was to become the main domestic issue for the separate Grenville party which emerged shortly thereafter and which included some of the ablest advocates of the cause, including his brother Lord Grenville and his own son, Lord Nugent. Unfortunately, however, in Irish affairs, as in others, Buckingham all too often fell victim to his own pettiness and self-importance. In 1798, the year of the Vinegar Hill rising and the abortive French invasion, he did his best to sour relations between the viceroy and the home government, simply because the former had refused to let him lead his Buckinghamshire militiamen into battle against the French. In the meantime, made privy by Lord Grenville to the government's decision to go forward with union, the marquess was so pleased by this mark of confidence that he could not restrain himself from talking about it.

Yet Buckingham would not have been in Ireland but for a highly constructive action that set a precedent and greatly enhanced Britain's defence capabilities. Lord lieutenants, including the marquess, had blocked government attempts to draw units selectively from county militia regiments. Early in 1798, however, Buckingham got around the problem by the simple device of volunteering his whole regiment for service in Ireland. Militia regiments thus became available for service far removed from their home areas, bringing into play a large hitherto unexploited source of manpower. His advice and assistance in military matters continued to be much valued by governments. In 1808, in the course of a series of reforms of the volunteer system, Robert Jenkinson, the future Lord Liverpool, wrote that

> your proposed arrangement has met with the most entire approbation of His Majesty and of his government, and that your letter and its enclosures have been of great service in enabling us and facilitating arrangements of a similar nature in other counties. (BL, Add. MS 38320, fol. 72)

While doubtless gratifying to the marquess, such recognition cannot have been much comfort to someone of his once vaulting ambition. Nor would it give him much claim to the attention of posterity.

Few politicians can have equalled Buckingham in providing a solid—one might even have thought well-nigh impregnable—basis for a great political family. He was fortunate in his inheritance from his father and uncle, but what he built upon it would have made them giddy. Marriage was perhaps his greatest instrument, not only his own to the coheir of Earl Nugent, but also that of his elder son, Richard Grenville, to Anna Eliza Brydges, the sole heir of the last duke of Chandos. He consolidated and built on his accumulated acquisitions with great intelligence and success, politically as well as financially. He kept the county seat he had won in 1774 in the family thereafter. In 1779 he inherited the two seats at Buckingham as well as the earldom from his uncle. He acquired the second seat at St Mawes in 1785. As a result of over a quarter of a century of judicious purchases and other more ephemeral expenditures he managed by 1806 to establish control of one of the Aylesbury seats. He failed only at Saltash. Nor were six seats in the Commons his only parliamentary influence. During the premiership of his brother Lord Grenville in 1806–7, Buckingham's careful marriage policy had added further useful connections—his wife's half-brother Lord Berkeley, and the husbands of all three of his sisters, lords Braybrooke, Fortescue, and Carysfort. His daughter's marriage in 1811 to the heir of Lord Arundel of Wardour could for more than one reason bear political fruit only in the future, since the Arundels were Roman Catholics.

At the time the marriage was something of an embarrassment to Lord Grenville, as both Lady Buckingham and Lady Mary were already Catholic converts, which suggested to some that the Grenvilles' motive for Catholic emancipation was self-interest. Buckingham's tellership of the exchequer was also proving an embarrassment in a period preoccupied with economy and rooting out political corruption, though no more of an embarrassment than Grenville's own auditorship of the exchequer. But, while Buckingham and his family could embarrass the premier and party leader, his loyalty to his brother in the years of Grenville's greatest success and influence was quite remarkable. Grenville led the party, and whatever his other problems he did not need to look over his shoulder in fear of a stab in the back. The vaunted Grenville family affection kept him secure. This situation would not outlast Buckingham's death, and in the next generation family affection would become a source of weakness, not strength.

Although a careful manager, Buckingham did not shun expense in what he considered good, or useful, causes. He was generous to family and friends, and, in common with his contemporaries, he believed that a great family demanded great houses. He commissioned John Soane to rebuild two houses in Pall Mall as one, Buckingham House, and he largely completed the magnificent renovation of Stowe begun by his uncle.

Buckingham may have shrunk from the limelight in his later years, but he did not manage to avoid it completely. One problem was the tellership, which in the first decade of the new century was worth the immense sum of between £20,000 and £25,000 a year. Not until the last year of his life did he seriously attempt to deal with the unfortunate impression which such a sum left on the public mind, and even then he agreed to return only a third of his income from the office. The result was to keep him in the spotlight, like a pig at the public trough, and it was as a pig that Gillray loved to caricature him. Unfortunately, even the most flattering portraits never managed to present Buckingham as anything less than plump, and in his last years it is clear that he was a good deal more than that. Add to this that he wore dark-rimmed round spectacles, and his irresistibility to a caricaturist is evident. Scantily clothed, with a great round bespectacled face and an enormous belly protruding over a precariously receding drapery, the marquess appeared in the windows of print shops as often as his friends who at least had the pleasure of office in 1806–7.

Besides making him an object of ridicule, Buckingham's obesity probably also shortened his life. Lady Buckingham's death in March 1812 hit him hard, but it was diabetes that actually killed him. He died at Stowe on 11 February 1813, a few months before his sixtieth birthday. He was buried with his wife in the family tomb at Wotton.

R. W. DAVIS

Sources J. V. Beckett, *The rise and fall of the Grenvilles: dukes of Buckingham and Chandos, 1710 to 1921* (1994) · J. J. Sack, *The Grenvillites, 1801–1829* (1979) · R. W. Davis, *Political change and continuity, 1760–1885: a Buckinghamshire study* (1972) · GEC, *Peerage* · DNB · J. Cannon, *The Fox–North coalition: crisis of the constitution, 1782–4* (1969) · HoP, *Commons, 1754–90* · D. Hill, *Mr. Gillray, the caricaturist* (1965) · T. Bartlett, *The fall and rise of the Irish nation: the Catholic question, 1690–1830* (1992) · G. C. Bolton, *The passing of the Irish Act of Union* (1966) · J. Ehrman, *The younger Pitt, 3: The consuming struggle* (1996) · J. Ingamells, ed., *A dictionary of British and Irish travellers in Italy, 1701–1800* (1997), 153–4, 428

Archives BL, Buckingham letter-books; corresp. relating to lace trade, Add. MS 59302 · BL, corresp. relating to Ireland, Add. MSS 40177–40180, 40733 · BL, general corresp., Add. MS 57828 · CKS, political corresp. · Hunt. L., corresp. and papers relating to Ireland · NL Ire., corresp. and papers | BL, corresp. with Lord and Lady Camelford, Add. MS 69043 · BL, corresp. with Lord Grenville, Add. MSS 58874–58879 · BL, corresp. with Thomas Grenville, Add. MSS 41851, 42058 · BL, letters to second Earl Spencer · BL, letters to Lord Wellesley, Add. MSS 37284, 37308–37310 · BL, corresp. with William Windham, Add. MSS 37875–37884, *passim* · Bucks. RLSS, corresp. with Scrope Bernard · Bucks. RLSS, corresp. with Sir William Henry Fremantle · Bucks. RLSS, letters to Thomas Grenville · Bucks. RLSS, corresp. with Lord Hobart · CKS, letters to James Cornwallis · CKS, letters to Henry Grenville · priv. coll., letters to Lord Lansdowne · PRO, letters to William Pitt, PRO 30/8 · Royal Military College, Sandhurst, letters to J. G. Le Marchant · Sheff. Arch., corresp. with second marquess of Rockingham · Croome Estate Trust, letters to the Coventry family

Likenesses J. Reynolds, group portrait, oils, 1780–82 (*George Grenville, Marquess of Buckingham, and his family*), NG Ire.; repro. in Beckett, *Rise and fall*, facing p. 85 · E. Smyth, stone statue, 1783, St Patrick's Cathedral, Dublin, Ireland · T. Gainsborough, 1787, Hughenden Manor, Buckinghamshire · oils, *c.*1787–1789, NPG [*see illus.*] · J. K. Sherwin, line engraving, pubd 1788 (after T. Gainsborough), BM, NG Ire., NPG · J. K. Sherwin, five group portraits, line engravings, pubd 1803 (*The installation banquet of the knights of St Patrick in the Great Hall, Dublin Castle, 17th March 1783*), NG Ire. · J. K. Sherwin, group portrait, line engraving, pubd 1803 (*Installation dinner of the order of St. Patrick, 1783*), BM · R. Dighton, caricature, coloured etching, pubd 1811, V&A · Gillray, caricatures · J. Jackson, oils, Christ Church Oxf. · J. C. Lochée, Wedgwood medallion (after V. Waldré, 1788), Wedgwood Museum, Barlaston, Staffordshire · W. Sadler, mezzotint (after R. Hunter, *c.*1783), NG Ire. · J. Sayers, three caricatures, etchings, NPG · J. K. Sherwin, group portrait, sketch (*The installation banquet of the knights of St Patrick, 1783*), NG Ire. · portrait (after T. Gainsborough), Hughenden Manor, Buckinghamshire

Grenville, George Nugent, second Baron Nugent of Carlanstown (1788–1850), politician and writer, younger son of George Nugent-Temple-*Grenville, first marquess of Buckingham (1753–1813), and his wife, Lady Mary Elizabeth Nugent (1758/9–1812), only acknowledged daughter and coheir of Robert *Nugent, Earl Nugent, was born on 30 December 1788 at Kilmainham, Dublin. A sickly child, he was brought up and educated with his sister Mary amid the palatial splendours of Stowe, and matriculated in April 1804 at Brasenose College, Oxford, where he pursued a brilliant academic career. The degree of honorary DCL was conferred upon him in July 1810 following the installation of William Wyndham Grenville as chancellor of Oxford University. The Irish barony of Nugent having been revived in his mother's favour in December 1800, he succeeded by special remainder on her death (16 March 1812); in September 1813 he married his childhood sweetheart Anne Lucy (1790–1848), second daughter of General the Hon. Vere Poulett.

Despite a preference for military life (cornet, 2nd Bucks yeomanry, 1803; lieutenant-colonel, 1813), at his father's insistence Grenville entered parliament in January 1810 to represent Buckingham, the Grenville pocket borough, and, from October 1812, Aylesbury. Disinclination and ill health restricted his parliamentary appearances, however, and he made little mark until the sessions of 1815–16. Thereafter he closely identified himself with financial retrenchment and civil liberties (cf. *Substance of speeches spoken by Lord Nugent in the House of Commons on the treaty of peace, army establishments and income tax*, 1816) and split

George Nugent Grenville, second Baron Nugent of Carlanstown (1788–1850), by Sir Thomas Lawrence, begun 1813

from his family in 1817; when the Grenvilles led by his brother (Richard Temple-Nugent-Brydges-Chandos-*Grenville, first duke of Buckingham and Chandos) broke with the whigs, Nugent remained conspicuously with the opposition, and at the general election of 1818 he made clear his commitment to parliamentary reform (*Jackson's Oxford Journal*, 11 June 1818). His growing radicalism seriously damaging his brother's local influence, he made repeated offers to resign his seat, but the duke resolved for the sake of family unity to leave him in undisturbed possession.

An assiduous supporter of Queen Caroline and a diligent member of both the London Spanish and Greek committees—his mission to Cadiz on behalf of the former in the summer of 1823 occasioned George Canning's famous speech (*Hansard* 2 10.1275) on that 'most enormous breach of neutrality', which had the house roaring with delighted laughter—Nugent was prominent both nationally and locally in the cause of anti-slavery, parliamentary reform, and religious liberty (for example *A Letter to the Electors of Aylesbury on the Catholick Question*, 1820; *A Plain Statement in Support of the Political Claims of the Catholics*, 1826; *Bucks. Chronicle*, 2 June 1827). On the formation of Lord Grey's

reform ministry in November 1830, he was appointed a lord of the Treasury, but in July 1832, in serious financial difficulties and finding that his hopes of further preferment were not to be realized, he accepted the vacant position of lord high commissioner of the Ionian Islands. He was appointed GCMG in August 1832.

With his political reputation and philhellenic sympathies, Nugent was a popular if somewhat exuberant governor, promoting education, fiscal reform, and an agricultural loan scheme, which paved the way for the establishment of the Ionian Bank; his brief administration (December 1832–February 1835), conspicuous for its liberal spirit, ensured that there could be no easy return to the more restrictive system of his predecessors. He resigned in December 1834 in consequence of the sudden fall of the whig ministry, and returned home to find his proceedings viciously attacked in the press (such as *The Courier*, 26 November 1835; 24 and 26 September 1836), and himself but tardily supported by government. He stood for Aylesbury in 1837 but, committed as he was to free trade, lost the election, and suffered a humiliating defeat when he again offered himself in 1839. After failing to secure the nomination for Marylebone and losing at Southampton in 1842, he was finally returned for Aylesbury at the general election in 1847, when he warmly advocated penal reform, Roman Catholic relief, the amelioration of the condition of the rural poor, and the Hungarian uprising. In the interval he had been active in the cause of popular education, a frequent contributor to *The Examiner*, and an eager pamphleteer: on the ballot (1837), the abolition of capital punishment (1840), and free trade (1842).

Nugent inherited the Grenville aptitude for literary and scholarly pursuits. His earliest composition, *An Essay on Duelling* (1807), was followed by *Portugal, a Poem, in Two Parts* (1812), the fruit of a visit to the Peninsula in the autumn of 1810, which was poorly received by the critics (for example, Thomas Moore's reference to 'patriotic monsters from Spain' in Letter V of the collection *The Twopenny Post Bag*, 3rd edn, 1813); although his later, more ephemeral poetic efforts were by no means contemptible. Nugent was also a competent classicist and historian: he became an FSA in 1825, and his long-contemplated and ardently sympathetic *Some Memorials of John Hampden, his Party and his Times* (1831), the standard exposition of civil-war parliamentary propaganda, had still not been superseded over a century and a half later. The work was widely and favourably reviewed, although Robert Southey's strictures (*Quarterly Review*, 47, July 1832) provoked an acrimonious correspondence. His residence, Lilies, near Aylesbury, became a popular venue for literary men and politicians; he published with Lady Nugent *Legends of the Library at Lilies* (1832). Other publications included *Lands Classical and Sacred* (1845), the consequence of a visit to Greece and the Levant, and an agreeable fictional persiflage, *Tract entitled true and faithful relation of a worthy discourse between Colonel John Hampden and Colonel Oliver Cromwell* (1847), purporting to be by William Spurstowe.

Nugent died at Lilies on 26 November 1850, after a

lengthy illness. There being no surviving issue from his marriage, the barony accordingly became extinct. While greatly respected for his honesty, consistency, and high principles, and one of the most polished and agreeable men of his day, it is clear he lacked any real political weight in Westminster; his influence was limited to that of moulding and leading local opinion in his county. Reputedly of an amorous disposition, he possessed in ample measure the Grenville tendency to corpulence and financial ineptitude. A. A. D. SEYMOUR

Sources J. Forster, 'Memoir', in G. Grenville, *Some memorials of John Hampden, his party and his times*, 3rd edn (1854) · R. W. Davis, *Political change and continuity, 1760–1885: a Buckinghamshire study* (1972) · J. J. Sack, *The Grenvillites, 1801–1829* (1979) · J. V. Beckett, *The rise and fall of the Grenvilles: dukes of Buckingham and Chandos, 1710 to 1921* (1994) · M. Aspioti, 'O lordos Nioutzeut stēn Kerkyra', *Deltion tēs Anagnōstikēs Hetairias Kerkyras*, 11 (1974), 93–144 · *The Examiner* (30 Nov 1850) · *The Bucks. Advertiser and Aylesbury News* (30 Nov 1850) · *Annual Register* (1850), 283 · *GM*, 2nd ser., 35 (1851), 91–2 · Nugent/ Henry Karslake, 14 Jan 1849, Hunt. L., Stowe MSS, STG 224/12

Archives BL, letters on family, political, and literary topics, Add. MS 58900 · Hunt. L., corresp. and papers | BL, Broughton (John Cam Hobhouse) MSS, letters on political affairs, Spain, etc., Add. MS 36460–36466, *passim* · BL, letters to Lord Grenville, Add. MS 58900 · Devon RO, Fortescue MSS, letters on political and family affairs · Hunt. L., Stowe MSS, letters on family, financial, and political topics · Lincs. Arch., Tennyson d'Eyncourt MSS, letters on political and general topics, Ionian Islands, etc. · Lpool RO, fourteenth earl of Derby MSS, letters on Ionian Islands and political topics · NA Scot., G. W. Hope MSS, corresp. · U. Durham, third Earl Grey MSS, letters on political topics · UCL, Brougham MSS, letters on political affairs · V&A, corresp. with John Forster on literary topics, etc.

Likenesses R. Dighton, coloured etching, pubd 1808 (*A noble student of Oxford*), BM, NPG · T. Lawrence, oils, begun 1813; Christies, New York, 11 Jan 1995, lot 127 [*see illus.*] · R. Dighton, coloured etching, pubd 1822 (*A view of Nugent*), V&A · W. Ward, mezzotint, pubd 1822 (after T. Lawrence), BM · J. Doyle, pen and pencil caricature, 1830 (*Auction extraordinary*), BM · B. P. Gibbon, line engraving, pubd 1830 (after S. J. Rochard), BM, NPG · B. R. Haydon, painting (Guildhall banquet to celebrate the passing of the Reform Bill) · probably P. Prossalendis or I. Kalosgouros, bronze bust, Palace of St Michael and St George, Corfu · S. J. Rochard, oils, repro. in *Catalogue of engraved portraits*

Wealth at death very heavily in debt: Stowe MSS, STG 224/12, Nugent/Henry Karslake, 14 Jan 1849

Grenville, John, first earl of Bath (1628–1701), nobleman, was born on 29 August 1628 at his family's estate at Stowe, Kilkhampton, Cornwall, the third but eldest surviving son of Sir Bevil *Grenville (1596–1643) and his wife, Grace (d. 1647), daughter of Sir George Smythe of Madford, Devon. By the time he was thirteen his two older brothers had died, leaving him heir to the family's considerable property in Cornwall and Devon. His early education was at home, which his grandson later described as 'a kind of academy for all young men of family in the country' (Stucley, 56). There is a tradition that Grenville matriculated at Gloucester Hall, Oxford; although an elder brother did study there, no documents survive proving John's admission. If he did go to Oxford, his education was disrupted by the outbreak of the civil war.

By November 1642 Grenville had joined the royalist army, holding a commission in his father's regiment. At first his service was not continuous; in February 1643 he

was in Cornwall being tutored at home. At Sir Bevil's death in the battle of Lansdown on 5 July 1643 John, now just under fifteen, became head of the family. He received a melancholy recognition of his father's sacrifice and his own service when on 3 August he was knighted in Bristol following the city's capture. On 27 October that year he was seriously wounded at the second battle of Newbury, and in 1645 he became a gentleman of the bedchamber to the prince of Wales, the beginning of an association which would continue until the prince's death forty years later.

After the defeat of the royalist armies in England, Grenville assumed command of the Isles of Scilly in the king's name. While there he presided over an effective privateering campaign against parliamentarian shipping. In 1650–51 royalist privateers attacked both English and Dutch vessels, raising prize money for the exiled court. A Dutch plan to assault the islands under the leadership of Admiral Maarten Tromp was only forestalled when an English fleet commanded by Robert Blake forced Grenville's surrender after a spirited defence. The capitulation terms, which came into effect on 2 June 1651, were generous. The defenders were allowed to leave the Scillies for Scotland or Ireland, and their commander was only briefly held as a prisoner in Plymouth. Though the surrender gave him liberty to join Charles Stuart on the continent, Grenville remained in England.

Grenville became an important clandestine supporter of the king's cause throughout the 1650s. He strengthened his royalist connections as well as his own estate when about October 1652 he married Jane Wyche (d. 1692), daughter of Sir Peter Wyche, a wealthy London merchant and former comptroller of the royal household. Although Clarendon reported that Grenville was 'often restrained' by a revolutionary government suspicious of his movements, this seems to have had little effect upon his busy royalist plotting (Clarendon, *Hist. rebellion*, 6.193–4). For most of the decade he supplied the king with money and carried messages on his behalf to a variety of royalist conspirators such as the earls of Northampton and Middlesex. His most important contribution, however, was probably his service as a middleman between the king and General George Monck. Related to Monck through his mother, Grenville cultivated him through his clerical brother Nicholas, whom Grenville named to the living at Kilkhampton. In October 1658, soon after the death of Lord Protector Cromwell, Grenville approached the king for permission to sound out Monck. Charles agreed and a secret negotiation ensued, with Grenville playing a key role during 1659 and early 1660. In August 1659 the council of state ordered his arrest but he was released soon after. In March 1660 he secretly met Monck in St James's Palace, and carried a message from the general to the king, then in Brussels. On 1 May 1660 Grenville delivered Charles II's letters from Breda to Monck and the parliament, a service for which parliament voted him a gift of £500. More significant than this, however, were the rewards that would come from the restored king. In April 1660 Grenville was agitating for the place of groom of the stole and an earldom, and although he had to wait until 20 April 1661 for his earldom, the king demonstrated his favour soon after his return. In 1660 Grenville became groom of the stole, keeper of St James's Palace, and, in recognition of his west country roots, steward of the duchy of Cornwall and its castles, steward of the borough of Bradninch, and the rider and master of Dartmoor. In 1663 he was added to the privy council and from April to July 1665 he was lord lieutenant of Ireland, though he never took up the post. More importantly, in 1660 Charles II also named him warden of the stannaries and lord lieutenant of Cornwall, and in 1661 he received the key post of governor of Plymouth. In 1680 he added the governorship of Pendennis to his offices. Thanks to this formidable array of power, Grenville, created earl of Bath on 20 April 1661, began a thirty-five year career as the crown's most important servant in the west. He jailed former republicans within his lieutenancy, remodelled Cornish corporations, and ensured the loyalty of Cornish JPs. A staunch anti-exclusionist, he acted vigorously in support of the duke of York's succession. From 1682 to 1685 he led the campaign to recharter Cornwall and Devon's many corporate boroughs, overseeing the surrender of thirty of thirty-two charters. His service to Charles continued to the end; he and the earl of Feversham were the only peers present at the king's deathbed conversion to Catholicism in February 1685.

Bath's relationship with James II was not as close as with Charles II. Upon his accession James replaced Bath as groom of the stole, appointing his close friend and co-religionist the earl of Peterborough to the post. Nevertheless, this blow seems not to have affected Bath's devotion to the crown. James compensated him with command of the 10th regiment of foot, and he served faithfully against the duke of Monmouth's failed rising. He campaigned tirelessly in the west for tory candidates in the election of 1685, earning the scorn of Gilbert Burnet, who accused him of corruptly influencing contests. In February 1688 he travelled from London to the west to put pressure on local gentlemen to fall in line behind the king's plan for religious toleration. James relied upon his support and in October 1688 hastened him to Plymouth to prepare for the prince of Orange's invasion. While the king received reassuring news about Bath's activity on his behalf, the earl was privately considering his options. He had been in touch with William of Orange through an intermediary, Henry Sidney, and when the invasion came on 5 November 1688 Bath was prepared. He temporized with James, writing that Exeter was indefensible and that he feared the militia was unreliable—and therefore that he would not attempt to assemble it. On 19 November, after William occupied Exeter without resistance, Bath openly abandoned James, offering to surrender Plymouth to the prince. On 4 December he presided over a meeting of Cornish magistrates, where he presented them with William's declaration, and formally joined his cause.

Bath's timely change of allegiance ensured that he would survive the transition from James to William. He kept his offices and added to them the lord lieutenancy of

Devon and the governorship of the Isles of Scilly—returning to the scene of his notable services of forty years before. But William's gratitude for Bath's aid did not prevent him, in 1694, from pressing the earl to retire from several of his offices. Bath laid down his regiment and the governorship of Plymouth, and in 1696 was pressured to resign as lord lieutenant of Cornwall and Devon. His disillusionment with William was complete when in 1697 the king ennobled his favourite, Joost Keppel, as earl of Albemarle—Bath had, since the death of the second duke of Albemarle in 1688, claimed that title for himself, based upon his mother's connection to the Monck family.

Bath's final years were embittered by his legal struggle over the Albemarle estate. From 1691 he waged an expensive legal campaign against the second duke's heirs. The lawsuits, in which the earl was said to have spent 'vast summes of money' (Luttrell, 4.443) ultimately failed amid charges of fraud and perjury. The profits of his many offices had been considerable, and were bolstered by a £3000 pension (which was, however, often in arrears), but his estate was weakened by the legal expenses he incurred, as well as the huge cost of rebuilding the family house at Stow from 1679. Maintaining his position as a western grandee was also very expensive, and when he died in St James's, London, on 22 August 1701 he was struggling to remain solvent. His son and heir, Charles, committed suicide only two weeks later, allegedly overwhelmed by the burden of debts his father left behind. Father and son were buried on the same day, 22 September 1701, in the family vault at Kilkhampton.

VICTOR STATER

Sources GEC, *Peerage* · *Calendar of the Clarendon state papers preserved in the Bodleian Library*, 5: 1660–1726, ed. F. J. Routledge (1970), 2, 4 · Clarendon, *Hist. rebellion*, vols. 3–4, 6 · J. Stucley, *Sir Bevill Grenville and his times, 1596–1643* (1983) · N. Luttrell, *A brief historical relation of state affairs from September 1678 to April 1714*, 1–4 (1857) · *CSP dom.*, 1651; 1659–62; 1664–7; 1684–8 · W. A. Shaw, *Calendar of treasury books*, 1–2, PRO (1904–5) · V. Stater, *Noble government: the Stuart lord lieutenants and the transformation of English politics* (1994), 97, 126, 153, 157, 177–8 · R. Hainsworth, *The swordsmen in power* (1997), 51–3, 268 · H. Horwitz, *Parliament, policy and politics in the reign of William III* (1977), 57, 116, 117, 172, 179, 325 · will, PRO, PROB 11/462
Archives Cornwall RO, lieutenancy papers; letters as lord-lieutenant of Cornwall and Devon | Surrey HC, Somers MSS, MSS regarding Albemarle claim
Likenesses oils, *c*.1637, priv. coll. · J. M. Wright, oils, Dunrobin Castle, Scotland
Wealth at death heavily indebted: will, PRO, PROB 11/462

Grenville, Sir Richard (1542–1591), naval commander, was born in May or June 1542, the son of a sea captain, Roger Grenville (*d.* 1545) of Stowe, Cornwall, and Thomasine, daughter of Thomas Cole.

Origins and early life The Grenvilles were a substantial gentry family, with lands in both Devon and Cornwall. His grandfather Richard (*d.* 1550) had been knight marshal of Calais when Arthur Plantagenet, Viscount Lisle (whose wife was a Grenville), had been lord deputy, and his estate was valued at £237 p.a. The younger Richard's father was master of the *Mary Rose*, and drowned when she capsized in the Solent in July 1545. Shortly after this disaster Richard's mother married Thomas Arundell of Clifton,

Sir Richard Grenville (1542–1591), by unknown artist, 17th cent. [original, 1571]

Devon, and his wardship was granted to one Nicholas Wadham, who relinquished it on 21 November 1550 to Sir Hugh Paulet. Paulet appears to have managed his ward's lands at Bideford and Buckland, Devon, and Stowe, Cornwall, but had no recorded influence as a guardian. Instead Grenville seems to have been brought up by his mother and stepfather at Clifton, but virtually nothing is known about the circumstances; he was probably educated at home by private tutor.

In Michaelmas term 1559 Grenville enrolled as a student at the Inner Temple. He remained in London for at least three years. On 19 November 1562 Grenville became involved in a brawl somewhere in the parish of St Clement Danes, in the course of which he stabbed one Robert Bannester to death. For this offence he was indicted; he fled, and was outlawed. Family influence or mitigating circumstances obtained his pardon in 1563, and in June he was licensed to enter upon his estates. Late in 1564 or early in 1565 he married Mary, the daughter of Sir John St Leger of Annery. Their first child, Roger, died in early infancy and was buried at Kilkhampton, Cornwall, on 10 December 1565. Three further sons and three daughters were born of the union.

Ireland and Cornwall Grenville's whereabouts between 1565 and 1568 are uncertain, although there is a tradition that he served with a band of Cornish volunteers in one of the emperor Maximilian's campaigns in Hungary. In 1568

he accompanied his kinsman Warham St Leger to Ireland and was subsequently appointed sheriff of Cork. He remained in Munster for about eighteen months, contributing 106 followers to a small English settlement near Cork, and was actively involved in the suppression of serious disorders. His wife accompanied him, and was for a time besieged in Cork while Grenville sought further support from England. In 1570, following the northern uprising, it was required that all justices of the peace and other officers should take the oath of supremacy already required of clergy. Grenville was sworn on 28 April at Bodmin, although there is no evidence that he was then on the commission of the peace; his earliest appearance in that capacity was in 1573. Nothing is known of the religious affiliation of his stepfather, Thomas Arundell, but Grenville never showed any affection for the 'old religion', and is always counted as one of Elizabeth's protestant 'sea dogs'.

Grenville first became interested in maritime adventures about 1569, probably as an investor rather than a practitioner, because he was heavily committed in Ireland at that time. How he obtained his seafaring experience is not clear, but it was probably through business connections with John Hawkins. In 1574 he purchased the 200 ton *Castle of Comfort* jointly with Hawkins, the intention being to send her on a piratical voyage to the Carribbean, under the pretext of seeking 'terra australis incognita'. Elizabeth, however, had been at great pains to rebuild her relations with Philip II after the tensions of 1568–71, and the patent for the voyage, although originally granted, was revoked. Instead the *Castle of Comfort* was used as a privateer under licence from the prince de Condé, but what share of the profit came to Grenville is not apparent.

Grenville sat as knight of the shire for Cornwall in the brief parliament of April–May 1571, and a Mr Greenfield, who may or may not have been Richard, served on a number of committees, including that for religion. At some point between 1574 and 1576 he was knighted, and he served as sheriff of Cornwall in 1576–7, so his absence from the parliament of 1572–84 does not seem to have been occasioned by any loss of favour. It may rather be attributed to a growing preoccupation with business which took him out of the country.

America In or soon after 1578 Grenville became interested in Sir Humphrey Gilbert's plans for planting a colony in the New World, and for seeking the north-west passage. Gilbert made two voyages, in 1578 and 1583, in which Grenville was probably an investor, although he does not seem to have sailed on either of them. Gilbert was lost at sea in the latter year, but his plans were immediately picked up by his cousin, Sir Walter Ralegh, and in these plans Grenville's involvement was practical and immediate. By 1585 war with Spain was imminent, and the council evolved a strategic plan for seizing the initiative in the Atlantic. In April Grenville departed to plant an English colony on the mainland of North America, within reach of the Spanish treasure route; in June Bernard Drake was sent to Newfoundland; and in September Sir Francis

Drake sailed for the West Indies, in what was the first official act of the war. The choice of Grenville to convey Ralph Lane and his colonists to Virginia is significant, because it was a task requiring a seaman of status, skill, and experience, and there is no evidence of how Grenville acquired the latter two qualities.

After leaving Lane and his colonists at Roanoke, Grenville went privateering and took a number of prizes. One, taken off Bermuda, yielded a cargo that he himself estimated at £12,000–15,000; other evidence suggests it may have been worth as much as £50,000. The discrepancy between these figures is significant, because the former represents the declared value, against which the shareholders would have been paid. The latter, if true, demonstrates the profit that the captain (and to a lesser extent the crew) would have derived, and helps to explain the enthusiasm for such ventures. Virginia seems to have been intended, not so much as a colony, but rather as a privateering base, since it was required to pay for itself from the beginning. Lane's decision to abandon the project in the following year, 1586, was due not so much to faintheartedness or shortage of food as to the inability of the settlers to find a deep-water harbour out of which to operate. Both Ralegh and Grenville intended to keep the Virginia base supplied, and Grenville actually returned to Roanoke with a small fleet only weeks after Lane and his men had left. Frustrated of a part of his purpose Grenville then turned again to privateering, and took enough prizes to cover the costs of his voyage. He seems to have planned a further voyage with three ships in the summer of 1587, but it was almost certainly abandoned, since Grenville was assembling ships and men for another voyage by the end of the year. On that occasion he was overtaken by events, because the council had good warning of the preparations being made in Spain, and prohibited any ships from leaving England on private expeditions. Grenville was instructed to hand all his ships over to Drake, and did so, with the exception of two pinnaces, which made an unsuccessful voyage and probably cost their owner a fair slice of his earlier profit.

The last fight of the *Revenge* Rather surprisingly, although he contributed three ships to the fleet that sailed against the Armada in 1588, Grenville seems not to have been at sea himself. This may have been because of his local status and responsibilities in Devon and Cornwall. He had been a vice-admiral under Lord Thomas Howard since 1571, and a commissioner for musters since before 1577. In the parliament of 1584–6 he again sat as knight of the shire for Cornwall, and in 1587 had been appointed a deputy lieutenant, which would have meant a front-line command in the home defence forces during the Armada crisis. In 1589, while Drake and Sir John Norris were making fools of themselves at Lisbon, Sir Richard was at sea again, raiding the Azores, but without any very conspicuous success. In 1591 he was back on the same station, this time as vice-admiral under his old superior, Lord Thomas Howard, and in command of the queen's ship *Revenge*, a 500 ton galleon of modern design. Howard's intention was to intercept the treasure fleet from America, but the Spaniards (as

usual) were well aware of his presence in the Azores, and sent out a powerful fleet of about fifty ships to see the precious silver through this blockade. Howard received intelligence of the Spanish fleet on 31 August, while at anchor on the north side of the island of Flores. Himself commanding only about sixteen ships, and having no necessity to confront such odds, he decided to retreat. Many of his men were sick, and many were ashore when warning of the Spanish approach was received, but he succeeded in putting most of his fleet to sea, and was able to stand off, well out of reach of interception. The *Revenge*, however, remained behind.

There are many accounts of what followed, several of them contemporary, and although Walter Ralegh did his best to justify his kinsman's action, the consensus of opinion is that Grenville acted ridiculously. There was no reason why it should have taken him any longer than it took the other captains to get his men aboard, but he made no attempt to follow his admiral, in spite of being expressly ordered to do so. Either he did not receive the order, or he thought the approaching squadron was the anticipated treasure fleet. For whatever reason, he apparently decided to sail straight through the middle of the enemy. This was not because he lacked the skill to take evasive action, and he seems to have taken his decision in a spirit of passionate and angry determination. Grenville was a knowledgeable seaman, but he had no experience of serious fighting at sea, and he may have felt a contempt for his opponents that a more seasoned campaigner would not have shared. The inevitable happened. Although in fact only about twenty of the Spaniards were fighting ships, and Howard's decision to withdraw may have been premature, they were more than enough to destroy the *Revenge*, which became trapped among them and so was unable to exploit her superior sailing qualities. Grenville was mortally wounded, most of his crew killed, and his ship reduced to matchwood. Whether the Spaniards were more impressed by his reckless courage or amazed by his folly is not apparent; he had taken one of their ships and a fair number of their men with him. Sir Richard Grenville's last fight quickly became the stuff of legend, but his actions have never been satisfactorily explained. 'Wilful and obstinate' he was called by Sir William Monson a generation later, and it seems that the same defect of character that had caused him to kill a man in a street brawl in 1562 was his eventual undoing. Both Ralph Lane, who knew him well, and Jan Van Linschoten, who was in the Azores at the time of the battle, made adverse comments on Grenville's character. He was, Lane told Sir Francis Walsingham, a man of intolerable pride and insatiable ambition, while Linschoten described him as being so fierce and hard that his own men hated him, although his courage was greatly respected, even by his enemies. Perhaps he was deliberately seeking death, but there is no suggestion that he saw himself as a martyr.

Richard Grenville died at sea of his wounds on 2 September 1591. His son Bernard did not receive the administration of his estate until February 1593; there may have been some difficulty about verifying his death, or a dispute over his inheritance. Bernard died in 1636, and at the end of the nineteenth century there were four Cornish families claiming descent from him. Sir Richard Grenville and the last fight of the *Revenge* were together immortalized by Alfred, Lord Tennyson, in his poem 'The *Revenge*: a ballad of the fleet', published in *Ballads and other Poems* (1880).

DAVID LOADES

Sources A. L. Rowse, *Sir Richard Grenville of the Revenge, an Elizabethan hero* (1937) · HoP, *Commons, 1558–1603* · J. L. Vivian and H. H. Drake, eds., *The visitation of the county of Cornwall in the year 1620*, Harleian Society, 9 (1874) · CPR, 1563 · R. Hakluyt, *The principall navigations, voiages and discoveries of the English nation* (1589) · *The naval tracts of Sir William Monson*, ed. M. Oppenheim, 5 vols., Navy RS, 22–3, 43, 45, 47 (1902–14) · K. R. Andrews, *Elizabethan privateering: English privateering during the Spanish war, 1585–1603* (1964) · JHC, 1 (1547–1628) · S. D'Ewes, ed., *The journals of all the parliaments during the reign of Queen Elizabeth, both of the House of Lords and House of Commons* (1682) · *The most honourable tragedie of Sir Richard Grenvile* (1595) · administration act book, 1593, PRO, PROB 6/5, fol. 45r · S. G. Ellis, *Ireland in the age of the Tudors* (1998)
Likenesses oils, 17th cent. (after original, 1571), NPG [*see illus.*] · W. and M. van de Passe, line engraving, BM, NPG; repro. in H. H. [H. Holland], *Heröologia Anglica* (Arnhem, 1620)
Wealth at death wealthy; owned lands

Grenville, Sir Richard, baronet (*bap.* 1600, *d.* 1659), royalist army officer, was the second son of Sir Bernard Grenville (*d.* 1636) and his wife, Elizabeth Bevill of Bryn, a Cornish heiress. He was the grandson (and namesake) of Sir Richard *Grenville, the Elizabethan hero of the *Revenge*. The Grenville seat was Stowe Hall, near Kilkhampton in north Cornwall, close to the Devon border. He was baptized there on 26 June 1600.

Early military service and marriage Grenville may, like his elder brother, Bevil *Grenville, have attended Exeter College, Oxford, though no record exists of his enrolment. Like his grandfather, and unlike his father, he was adventurous and energetic, and took the first opportunity offered to follow a military vocation overseas. He joined the expedition sent from England to assist the palatinate in 1620 and served under Maurice of Nassau; he took part in the attack on Cadiz in 1625; and was with the forces commanded by the duke of Buckingham which briefly occupied the Île de Ré in 1627. A narrative of the latter service has been, probably incorrectly, attributed to him. He was knighted, as a follower of the duke, at Portsmouth on 20 June 1627. He was given command of a regiment of foot for the La Rochelle expedition, which was noticed in Devon in spring 1628. But when it sailed Grenville was left behind. He had apparently returned to Portsmouth from the west country too late to catch the boat.

With the backing of his powerful patron, Grenville obtained a Cornish seat (Fowey) in the parliament of 1628. He spoke in defence of his father, too elderly and disabled to attend, in a disputed election case, accusing others of malice. He was censured, but excused on the grounds that as a soldier he was politically inexperienced. He also acquired a rich wife. He married in November 1628 Mary (1596–1671), daughter and heir of Sir John Fitz of Fitzford, Devon, and the widow of Sir Charles Howard. This lady

was four years older than Sir Richard, had previously been married three times to aristocratic suitors—a Percy and a Darcy before Howard—and so was well connected to some of the leading political families in England. Grenville was granted a baronetcy on 9 April 1630, which set the seal on his enhanced importance and wealth. A son, Richard, was baptized on 16 May 1630, and a daughter, Elizabeth, was born in the following year.

But with his marriage Grenville entered on a sea of troubles. Mary came with considerable baggage. She may have had a child by her steward, who remained active in her service. The relatives of her late husband, the Howard clan headed by her brother-in-law Theophilus *Howard, second earl of Suffolk, were grasping and powerful. Grenville was politically naïve, and his main protector, Buckingham, had been assassinated. He found himself embroiled in litigation over his wife's inheritance. For her part Mary claimed that Richard had treated her with great barbarity, and Suffolk that he had called him 'a base lord'. Star Chamber, chancery, and the court of high commission found against Grenville, and the fines imposed and damages awarded were enough to ruin him. '[I was] necessitated to sell away mine own estate', he wrote later, 'and to impawn my goods, which by it were quite lost' (*Genuine Works*, 1.515, 547). He was committed to the Fleet for nonpayment, but after sixteen months' incarceration succeeded in escaping in October 1633. If Grenville had faults of character before this experience, lacking as he did the social skills of his popular and celebrated elder brother, he was even more embittered thereafter.

Grenville fled to the continent. He enrolled for a time as a student of mathematics at Leiden University, and advanced his military career by serving in the Swedish forces in Germany, and under Robert Sidney, earl of Leicester, a remote kinsman, in the Anglo-Dutch brigade. The outbreak of the bishops' wars at home gave him—as it did several other exiled outlaws—the opportunity to return and offer his services to the crown. He attempted to make use of the Long Parliament's attack on Star Chamber to reverse the judgments against him, but failed. He was given a command of the horse in both campaigns. A subordinate in 1640 was Philip Sidney, Lord Lisle, the eldest son of Leicester, and when the Irish uprising broke out in the following year Grenville was well placed to gain a post in the army, commanded by Leicester, to be sent to quell it.

Ireland and defection Grenville landed in Ireland with a force of 400 horse in February 1642, along with the foot regiment of his cousin George *Monck. He immediately showed drive and skill at the battle of Kilrush, and in the storming of Trim, where it was said that he 'had the principal share' in taking the town. He was appointed governor. Raiding over a wide area, he brought fire and sword to the local population. While he gained prestige with the victory of Rathconnell in January 1643, the conduct of his horse was criticized in another action and he was known as a ruthless commander. The term 'Trim law' became shorthand for a style of warfare that rode roughshod over the civilian population.

With the political divisions in England, and the parliamentarian blockade of Ireland, the government troops found it increasingly difficult to subsist, and Grenville and other commanders grew disillusioned. He and Monck seem also to have fallen out with the crown's representative, the marquess of Ormond, and when the king ordered the cessation of arms (September 1643) both returned to England. While Monck immediately joined the king, Grenville's choice of sides was uncertain. His support for parliament was equivocal; he found himself arrested by the roundhead governor of Liverpool, and sent under armed guard to London. His political skills had apparently much improved, for he was able to persuade the Commons of his loyalty, to the extent that he was granted large sums to raise forces, made lieutenant-general to Sir William Waller, and invited to join their councils of war (January 1644).

But it was all a deception, probably designed to hasten the payment of his arrears: Grenville was still in desperate need of money. Very publicly, *en route* to join the forces besieging Basing House, he defected; on 8 March 1644 he appeared at Oxford in a coach and six, with his officers, cavalry mounts, £600, and parliament's most secret plans for the coming campaign. The royalist high command immediately dispatched him to the west country, where the Grenville name and his known experience would do most good for the cause.

Parliament was outraged. The Commons voted Grenville 'traitor, rogue, villain, and skellum', and set up two gibbets in London to which their denunciation (in three languages, according to his earliest biographer) was fixed, to do duty until the man himself would be placed there. He became, in roundhead propaganda, a notorious hate figure: the term 'skellum' (Dutch for rascal) associated him with the cruelties practised by foreign mercenaries in the continental and Irish wars. Until he retired from service in 1646 London newsbooks gave maximum publicity to the many atrocity stories relating to his conduct in the west country (Rushworth, 5.380, 384–5; Lloyd, 474).

For his part Grenville defended his move by asserting that he had no thought of changing sides when he returned to England, but had been rapidly disillusioned with the parliamentarian cause after only a short time in London. He claimed its forces were unpaid, its propaganda demonstrably false, and that religion was merely 'a cloak for rebellion'. In any case orthodox belief in the capital was being undermined by the sects (Rushworth, 5.385).

The king's general Grenville was immediately commissioned by the king to assist in the siege of Plymouth and raise more forces in Cornwall; fortuitously, the local general, Sir John Digby, was wounded, and Grenville assumed full command. He made his estranged wife's house at Fitzford his headquarters and, using his new authority (he was also sheriff of Devon), began to rebuild his fortune in Cornwall and west Devon. However, the march of Essex to the south-west interrupted proceedings, and with exceptional skill he shadowed the invaders, husbanding his resources until the arrival of the main royalist army. His small force played an important part in the trapping of Essex's foot at Lostwithiel in August–September 1644. When the king left the west he ordered Grenville to stay behind to complete the taking of Plymouth, which he promised could be quickly accomplished.

In fact Grenville was denuded of supplies, and could not prevent the reinforcement of the town by sea. But he was as active and ruthless as he had been at Trim. The estates of Lord Robartes, the Drake family, and the earl of Bedford were seized and their tenants exploited, and the usual military taxation, the county contribution, levied in full. He rebuilt his army by every means possible, summoning the trained bands and assembling the 'power of the county' (the sheriff's posse), to guard Plymouth, while raising a new infantry force of four Cornish regiments, which has been styled his 'new Cornish tertia' (Stoyle, 'New Cornish tertia', 26–44). He took pleasure in settling old scores. He hanged his wife's former solicitor on a trumped up charge, and imprisoned her steward/lover. In the drive to get his troops promptly paid it was said that he executed a dozen constables, and massacred prisoners of war at the taking of Saltash. He was accused of starving other captives in the gaol at Lydford. Some of his actions were perhaps reprisals. A young Captain Grenville, captured and executed as a spy in Plymouth, may have been his bastard son.

But Grenville cared most about his soldiers' welfare, declaring that 'he neither would nor could command men who were not paid' (Clarendon, *Hist. rebellion*, 4.61). His experience on the continent and in Ireland had taught him that discipline and morale could not be maintained without 'constant pay' (ibid.). He did not permit the taking of free quarter, as Lord Hopton did, and was notoriously severe on soldiers who robbed or plundered, unlike Lord Goring or Prince Maurice. The paradox of Grenville's military government was that he was popular with his men, especially the Cornish, so long as they remained obedient, and with ordinary farmers and townsmen, so long as they paid their taxes, but feared and hated by landlords and other wealthy men, local officials, and rival commanders.

Royalist divisions When the king set up a mixed government of 'swordsmen and gownmen', under the nominal command of his fifteen-year-old son, the prince of Wales, to bring order to the fragmented war effort in the south-west, trouble would quickly ensue. The civilian politicians, including Hyde and Culpepper, were appalled at Grenville's behaviour. It did not help that the president of the council was the ineffective earl of Berkshire, a leading member of the Howard family with which Grenville had long feuded. Bombarded by the bitter complaints of county and parish office-holders, important landowners, and rival governors—especially Sir John Berkeley at Exeter and later Lord Goring, nominally commander-in-chief in the west—the prince's council attempted in vain to gain his co-operation. This coloured the account of the war in the west which Hyde, a close friend of Berkeley, wrote in the following year, and incorporated in his *History*. It has been well said that Grenville is the villain of the piece (Stoyle, 'Last refuge', 31). Modern historians have allowed Goring also a share of the blame.

Grenville was reluctant to send his forces to assist Goring at the siege of Taunton until it was too late (March 1645). While inspecting Wellington House (home of the Pophams, and fortified by the local parliamentarians), he was severely wounded in the groin, and was forced to hand over his command to his great rival Sir John Berkeley. The subsequent desertion of many Cornishmen loyal to Grenville, and the disobedience of those who remained, impeded the operations of Goring's army.

Remarkably Grenville made a speed recovery and was offered overall command of the western forces by the prince's council in April, with the title of field marshal general. But this army did not exist, and his rivals retained their independence: the king actually enhanced Goring's status with a new commission, and made Grenville subordinate. His frustration increased when in June the arrival of the victorious New Model Army brought his siege of Lyme Regis to an end. Without warning, he resigned his command to the prince's council. In a face-to-face interview with the young prince at Liskeard on 25 July 1645 he was publicly rebuked.

Grenville retired to one of the houses he had seized in Cornwall, where he still enjoyed local support. A reconciliation with Goring was brokered and, as a sceptical Hyde reported, Grenville 'promised wonders' (*CSP dom.*, 1645–7, 46–7). One of the factors in his favour was the backing of the Oxford high command. After Goring's crushing defeat at Langport (10 July) those about the king wanted Grenville promoted, Rupert declaring that he was 'the only souldier in the West' (*Diary of John Evelyn*, ed. H. Wheatley, 4 vols., 1879, 4.165). But royalist-held territory was shrinking fast. The New Model Army took Bristol in September 1645, and the prince's council retreated before its advance. Goring abandoned the fight, leaving behind a 'dissolute and odious army' at the mercy of both the enemy and a furious local populace (Clarendon, *Hist. rebellion*, 4.100).

Concentrating his remaining forces west of the Tamar, Grenville proposed desperate measures to the council, now based at Truro. A strong defensive line should be constructed along the river, to preserve Cornwall and west Devon from the incursions of the enemy and Goring's disorderly cavalry. Behind it the prince, who was duke of Cornwall and possessed his own revenues from the sale of tin, could, if guided by a Grenville, make a successful appeal to Cornish pride. A semi-independent and self-sufficient Cornwall would be strong enough to negotiate a separate peace with parliament.

Nothing was likely to come of these proposals. Instead the council appointed Hopton, one of its members, commander-in-chief (15 January 1646), with Grenville as general of the foot. At first he accepted this post. But within three days he had resigned, and was immediately arrested for insubordination, at Launceston. For two months he lay in prison at St Michael's Mount, until, with the general collapse of the cause and the flight of the prince and his councillors, he took ship for France, arriving in Brest in early March 1646.

Exile and death Immediately the major participants in the quarrels that had so damaged the royal cause in the west took up their pens to continue the fight, blame their opponents, and justify their actions. Grenville learnt that Hyde was preparing a narrative (most of book 9 of his *History*), and had asked Hopton for his account of the campaign. He responded by writing a memoir of these events, from his point of view, as soon as he reached France. This memoir, 'A narrative of the affairs of the west', was published the following year. It was reprinted later in Carte's *Original Letters and Papers* (Carte, 1.96–109).

Grenville and his sixteen-year-old son then spent a year travelling in Italy, and also made a secret and dangerous trip to England, in disguise, possibly to preserve some of his goods from the sequestrators. It was reported that his son was hanged much later as a highwayman. Grenville had suffered grave losses at the end of the war, but, on his return to Brittany, had enough credit to assist the royalists holding out in the Channel Islands (1650) and to invest in privateering ventures. He appears to have kept in regular contact with conspirators in Ireland, and in Cornwall, where he remained popular. But, attending the new king, Charles II, in France and the Low Countries (1650–52), he found any further progress in the royal service blocked by his old enemies at court.

Grenville particularly blamed Hyde, and in spring 1653, with other dissidents, he plotted his downfall. 'So fatte a Hide ought to be well tanned', he wrote to his fellow conspirators (Lister, 3.72). He alleged that Hyde had committed treason by visiting Cromwell. The charges were serious enough to be investigated by the king and council, before being dismissed in 1654 as 'a malicious calumny'. Grenville was banished from the court, and despite several attempts on his part, never regained the confidence of the king.

An embittered and even pitiable figure, Grenville spent the remainder of his life in the Netherlands. He justified his conduct, listed his grievances, and provided some more autobiographical details in a final short account, entitled *Defence Against All Aspersions of Malignant Persons*, published in the Netherlands in January 1654. It struck a valedictory note, expressing no higher hope than that 'free from any kind of worldly affairs' he might 'find a quiet dying place in my native land' (Miller, 154). But he still had enough energy to renew his quarrel with the Howard family, with the predictable result that he and his daughter Elizabeth, who had joined him, found themselves entangled in costly lawsuits. In 1657, ill and impoverished, he suffered imprisonment in Brussels, no doubt for debt.

Grenville died in Ghent on 21 October 1659. No record of

his burial, nor any memorial, exists, but it was later asserted that a stone on his grave carried the legend: 'Sir Richard Grenville, the King's General in the West' (Miller, 162). No will survives. His daughter was granted administration of his estate after the Restoration, which was, however, not large enough to prevent her being dependent on charity for the rest of her life. His estranged wife, Mary, Lady Howard, died in 1671.

An undated portrait of Grenville as a young man (still in family possession) shows him to advantage, his regular features and lively expression topped by a mass of auburn hair: to his opponents he was 'the red fox'. A younger son, he carved out a remarkable career for himself, distinctively different from his much admired and wealthier older brother Bevil. Vigorous, combative, and resilient, 'a man of honour and courage', he became an excellent soldier, and brought to the English wars the experience and skills he had acquired on the continent and in Ireland. He showed himself a resourceful and active commander in the west, respected by his followers and the local populace alike for his strict discipline. But his character contained a self-destructive element, which, combined with his political insensitivity, brought little but disaster. The villain depicted in the black propaganda of the London press, and—in smoother, more magisterial terms—by Clarendon, had a basis in fact. He was, or could be, cruel and vindictive. He quarrelled constantly with those in authority, both military and civilian, and pursued personal vendettas. An able tactician, he was unable to ground his strategic thinking in the political and military realities facing him. His last years, in exile, were deeply troubled, the result of further self-inflicted wounds.

Later members of his family attempted to combat Clarendon's unfavourable verdict; in particular the tory Jacobite peer and playwright George *Granville, Lord Lansdowne, who wrote a vindication and reprinted some of Grenville's narratives. His career inspired the excellent historical novel by Dame Daphne du Maurier, *The King's General* (1946).   IAN ROY

Sources *The genuine works, in verse and prose, of … George Granville, Lord Lansdowne*, 2 vols. (1732) · A. Miller, *Sir Richard Grenville of the civil war* (1979) · *Calendar of the Clarendon state papers preserved in the Bodleian Library*, 1: *To Jan 1649*, ed. O. Ogle and W. H. Bliss (1872); 2: *1649–1654*, ed. W. D. Macray (1869), vols. 1 and 2 · *A collection of original letters and papers, concerning the affairs of England from the year 1641 to 1660. Found among the duke of Ormonde's papers*, ed. T. Carte, 2 vols. (1739) · Clarendon, *Hist. rebellion* · M. Coate, *Cornwall in the great civil war and interregnum, 1642–1660* (1933) · T. H. Lister, *The life and administration of Edward earl of Clarendon, with original correspondence and authentic papers never before published*, 3 vols. (1837–8) · D. Lloyd, *Memoires of the lives … of those … personages that suffered … for the protestant religion* (1668) · J. Rushworth, *Historical collections*, 5 pts in 8 vols. (1659–1701) · M. J. Stoyle, 'The last refuge of a scoundrel: Sir Richard Grenville and Cornish particularism, 1644–6', *Historical Research*, 71 (1998), 31–51 · M. J. Stoyle, '"Sir Richard Grenville's creatures": the new Cornish tertia, 1644–46', *Cornish Studies*, 4 (1996), 26–44 · G. H. Radford, 'Lady Howard of Fitzford', *Report and Transactions of the Devonshire Association*, 22 (1890), 66–110 · J. L. Vivian and H. H. Drake, eds., *The visitation of the county of Cornwall in the year 1620*, Harleian Society, 9 (1874) · GEC, *Baronetage*
Archives Bodl. Oxf., Carte MSS, letters; Clarendon MSS, letters; Tanner MSS, letters · Cornwall RO, letters to Lewis Tremayne · Devon RO, letters to Edward Seymour; letters to Edward Tremayne
Likenesses portrait, repro. in Miller, *Sir Richard Grenville*
Wealth at death estate not significant enough to be sequestered or compounded for; daughter lived on charity after 1660

Grenville [*later* Grenville-Temple], **Richard**, **second Earl Temple** (1711–1779), politician, was born on 26 September 1711 in St James's parish, Westminster, the eldest of the six children of Richard Grenville (1678–1727), landowner, of Wotton Underwood, Buckinghamshire, and his wife, Hester (*bap.* 1684, *d.* 1752), the second daughter of Sir Richard *Temple, third baronet, of Stowe, and his wife, Mary Knapp, and the sister of Richard *Temple, Viscount Cobham. After receiving his education at Eton College (1725–8) he toured the continent with his tutor, M de Lizy, between 1728 and 1732, staying for extended periods in Switzerland, Italy, and France.

Early career and marriage For more than three decades Grenville played a prominent role in the political life of the realm. Following his return to England, in the election of 1734 he was chosen, through the influence of his uncle Lord Cobham, to represent the borough of Buckingham in parliament. In 1741 he successfully contested the county of Buckingham, but at the general election in 1747 he chose to return to the relatively inexpensive security of the borough. On the death of Cobham in September 1749, his mother, Hester Grenville, succeeded her brother as Viscountess Cobham in her own right, by a special remainder to herself and her sons, with Richard taking the additional surname of Temple. Later the Grenvilles obtained a patent granting her the title of Countess Temple, again with a remainder to the male heirs. Upon her death, on 6 October 1752 Richard Grenville succeeded to the peerage and entered the House of Lords as the second Earl Temple.

Grenville's political influence at Westminster and in Buckinghamshire essentially rested upon the wealth he derived from various properties in four counties, particularly the estates of Wotton and Stowe in Buckinghamshire, which he inherited respectively from his father in 1727 and from his uncle Cobham in 1749. On 9 May 1737 he married Anna *Chamber (1709?–1777), the daughter and coheir of Thomas Chamber of Hanworth, Middlesex, and his wife, Lady Mary Berkeley, the daughter of Charles, second Earl Berkeley. Their forty years of marriage, ended by Anna's death on 7 April 1777, proved to be an affectionate, as well as a mutually advantageous, union. The single great tragedy of their long relationship was the death of their only child, Elizabeth, in 1742 at four years of age. Anna's fortune, valued at over £50,000, enabled her husband to carry out, under his personal supervision, extensive agricultural improvements at Wotton and Stowe, which he converted by enclosure from arable farmland to pasturage, thus taking advantage of the growing national market in beef cattle. By the time of his death he had increased the total value of his rent rolls to more than £21,000 per annum. Among some contemporaries, he was

Richard Grenville, second Earl Temple (1711–1779), by Allan Ramsay, 1762

reputed to be the richest man in England—an exaggeration, but one which he cultivated with considerable pride and enterprise.

Pitt's steadfast supporter In his early political career Grenville attained notoriety as a member of the so-called patriot opposition to Walpole, particularly as one of Cobham's 'cubs'—that bright and impertinent young cohort of Walpole-baiters who, besides himself, included most prominently his brother George Grenville and their future brother-in-law William Pitt. Horace Walpole's biased assessment of Grenville as 'the absolute creature of Pitt, vehement in whatever faction he was engaged' (Walpole, 1.135–6) was only partially accurate. During more than four decades—with one brief exception—Grenville was Pitt's most steadfast and indispensable political ally and personal friend. Pitt not only relied upon the political influence and wealth that his noble ally brought to the partnership, he also depended upon the latter's advice and abilities in devising and executing the political strategies and tactics which led to power.

Grenville's admittedly volatile temperament and a tendency towards blunt arrogance when contradicted prevented him from attaining great distinction in the House of Commons. With his accession to the House of Lords,

however, he became the most prominent spokesman in the upper house for the Pittite party and their avowed patriot cause. During the course of the great mid-century struggle with Bourbon France, he particularly took the lead in the Lords in opposing what he and Pitt regarded as a foreign policy which favoured Hanoverian interests at the expense of the vital interests of Britain—above all the failure to defend and expand the overseas empire against their French rivals. His capacity for independent thought and action was singularly displayed in 1753 in his nearly solitary opposition in the Lords to the Pelham government's repeal of the Jewish Naturalization Act, an action which he denounced as a cowardly, illiberal concession to the bigoted 'clamor that has been raised among the very lowest of our people' (Cobbett, 15.95). Despite Walpole's characteristically cynical dismissal of his motives as arrogant partisanship, Temple's defiant assertion of principle drew considerable approval and admiration among several contemporaries, including Smollett, who, upon this occasion, described Temple as 'a nobleman of distinguished abilities … frank, liberal, humane and zealously attached to the interests and honor of his country' (Smollett, 3.169).

When Newcastle, after Pelham's death, dismissed Pitt and other members of his party from office in 1755, Temple enthusiastically renewed his opposition in the Lords to the government's 'Hanoverian' foreign policy. He assured Pitt, who had become his brother-in-law in November 1754, that the course of events would turn in their favour, and made up Pitt's loss of income from office-holding by providing him with £1000 per annum 'till better times'. After the outbreak of the Seven Years' War it was Temple who at first perceived that the French invasion of Minorca might provide an effective focus for a renewed assault, both in parliament and in the forum of public opinion, upon the Newcastle government's ill-fated and unpopular management of foreign policy and war making. Late in 1756, with the creation of the Pitt–Devonshire ministry, Temple, despite great misgivings, yielded to Pitt's urgings and took up the post of first lord of the Admiralty. The extraordinarily short duration of this administration gave him little opportunity to remedy his acknowledged lack of technical knowledge of naval business but none the less allowed him sufficient time, characteristically, to alienate the professional sailors of the Admiralty over control of naval patronage. In opposition he had aroused the animosity of George II for his parliamentary denunciations of Hanoverian influence over British foreign policy, and once in office he earned the implacable enmity of the king for what the monarch described as his 'impertinence' and 'insolence' in the closet, particularly in pressing him to pardon Admiral Byng, whom Pitt and Temple regarded as a scapegoat for the failures of the Newcastle administration. Not surprisingly, on 5 April 1757 Temple was the first major figure in the Pitt–Devonshire government to be dismissed from office at the behest of the king. Even after George found it impossible to obtain an administration that excluded the Pittite party and was forced to accept a coalition headed by

Pitt and Newcastle, he persisted in vetoing any appointment for Temple 'which required frequent attendance in the Closet' (*Memoirs and Speeches of … Waldegrave*, 205). At Pitt's insistence Temple was finally appointed lord privy seal—along with a vague hint of a Garter.

Lord privy seal In the new ministry Temple found himself increasingly redundant and isolated from the affairs of state; he was barred from cabinet by the king's ban and, worse still, largely ignored by Pitt as he planned the great war for empire against France. He loyally accepted Pitt's volte-face regarding continental engagements and in the Lords defended the administration's German subsidies, all at the cost of considerable derision for his apparent abandonment of patriot principles. Ever proud and ambitious, he grew increasingly frustrated with the king's manifest disfavour and Pitt's apparent indifference. He demanded the long anticipated Garter and, after nearly a year of being fobbed off by Newcastle's protests of the king's veto, in November 1759 he asked to be relieved of office. Pitt, now stung into a realization of his gratuitous neglect of his most loyal ally, and recognizing the danger of his own isolation in the administration should Temple be permitted to resign, made the award of the Garter to his brother-in-law a matter of personal confidence. Newcastle, thoroughly alarmed by Pitt's threat of resignation, wore down the resistance of the king, who, none the less, displayed his personal revulsion to Temple's Garter at the awards ceremony: 'muttering indistinctly, some expressions of dissatisfaction, [the king] threw it [the Riband] across him, and turned his back at the same instant, in the rudest manner' (Wraxall, 1.124). Temple resumed office and, at Newcastle's insistence, was admitted to cabinet meetings. He returned to the councils of state, however, only in time to take part in the disintegration of the Pitt–Newcastle regime, which arose out of conflict over issues of peace and war, precipitated by the accession of George III and Bute's admission into the administration. In cabinet, Temple vehemently supported Pitt's opposition to major concessions in peace negotiations with France and his demand for a pre-emptive declaration of war against Spain. Finally, in October 1761 he loyally joined Pitt in resigning from office when they found themselves isolated in cabinet deliberations.

Return to opposition Temple's fall from power brought about a bitter schism with his brother George, who chose to remain in office under Bute, the only member of the Grenville 'cousinhood' to do so. Temple, his injured pride doubly wounded by what he regarded as the desertion of his favourite brother and heir, publicly denounced George's betrayal and privately threatened to deprive him and his children of the succession to the family estates. As he settled into the familiar role of a leading voice in opposition, Temple found a formidable ally in an old political associate from Buckinghamshire, John Wilkes, whose *North Briton* not only attacked the person and policies of Bute but also caricatured George Grenville's perfidy. Temple originally revelled in Wilkes's assault upon the Bute

administration; however, the increasingly scurrilous content of the *North Briton* prompted him publicly and privately to disavow rumours of his patronage of the publication. Nevertheless, in 1763, when the government arrested Wilkes and seized his papers on a general warrant, Temple's whiggish sensibilities were aroused. As he later commented:

> The violations of liberty lately complained of, were not taken up as the cause of one man, but as the concern of the WHOLE … tending to undermine the very foundations of our liberty, and establish the most illegal, dangerous, and tyrannical power, in the officers of the crown.
> ([R. Grenville-Temple], *A Letter from Albemarle Street*, 1764, 9–10)

He personally contested the government's refusal to free Wilkes on a writ of habeas corpus, and he financed Wilkes's legal defence, as well as the successful court challenge against the legality of general warrants. In the Lords, he opposed the rescinding of Wilkes's immunity from arrest and his expulsion from parliament, even after Wilkes ignored his advice against republishing number 45 of the *North Briton*. As a consequence of his support of Wilkes, Temple was dismissed from the lord lieutenancy of Buckinghamshire.

On three occasions after 1761, Temple had the opportunity to return to power with Pitt: firstly following Bute's resignation; then at the time of George Grenville's dismissal; and finally at the formation of Chatham's administration. In the last two instances it was Temple who turned down the offer of the Treasury in an administration headed by Pitt. During Grenville's premiership he had found himself increasingly torn in loyalty and principle between his brother and brother-in-law, whose own bitter political rivalry had become notoriously public. Most significantly, Temple, who was an astute man of business in his private finances, grew more sympathetic towards his brother's efforts to deal with the enormous debt accruing from the profligate costs of Pitt's war policies. When America defied the Grenville administration's attempt to obtain colonial contributions towards imperial expenses, Temple's proud patriotism was turned against the colonies as he, in contradiction to Pitt, became convinced that they were bent upon independence. He initiated a conspicuous reconciliation with his brother in May 1765 and subsequently justified his refusal to join Pitt in power because he found his brother barred from office by the king, and also because he was unwilling to join any administration where he would be isolated among individuals whose principles and policies he had publicly opposed, particularly those regarding America. During Chatham's administration the breach among the brothers-in-law became complete, with Temple joining George Grenville in an active, if discomfited, opposition to his old ally. Chatham's resignation in October 1768 brought a full restoration of their friendship, and within a year the rejuvenated patriot cousinhood again found a common cause in the Wilkes Middlesex election controversy. With George Grenville and Chatham leading the attack in parliament against the expulsion of Wilkes and the seating of his defeated opponent in the Commons, Temple during the late summer of 1769 successfully roused the electors of Buckinghamshire to join in the petitioning campaign on behalf of Wilkes and the electors of Middlesex.

The Middlesex election crisis marked the last hurrah of Temple's political career. Within a year his brother was dead, while Chatham, increasingly debilitated by illness, proved to be a spent force in politics. After 1770 Temple largely abandoned the maelstrom of political life and devoted his attention, his talents, and much of his wealth to making Stowe a rival to the greatest houses of England. He completed William Kent's transformation of the gardens into a masterpiece of English informal landscape gardens, and he personally planned and supervised the rebuilding of the house into a magnificent neo-classical structure. Deprived of an heir of his own, he spent a great part of his later years assiduously enhancing and increasing his wealth and properties for the benefit of George Grenville's children, to whom he became a mentor and protector as well as a faithful trustee of their father's bequests. When he died at Stowe on 11 September 1779, as a result of head injuries he suffered upon being thrown from his phaeton in Stowe Park, his nephew George Nugent-Temple-*Grenville succeeded to the earldom and to his uncle's great legacy. Temple was buried at Stowe but was later reinterred, with his beloved wife, among his Grenville ancestors and siblings at Wotton parish church.

Character During his lifetime Temple was esteemed by his friends as an amiable, charming, and exciting companion; his conversation was considered animated, brilliant, and entertaining. Contemporary commentators, such as Horace Walpole and Lord Waldegrave, who opposed Temple politically, discounted his avowals of patriotism and summarily depicted him as a capricious curmudgeon whose ambitiousness and rapacity in pursuit of office and honours outstripped his abilities and achievements. Victorian historians, such as Macaulay and Lord Rosebery, seized upon such partisan calumnies to make Temple the scapegoat for the manifest failures of Pitt's later career, castigating Temple's uninhibited penchant for the characteristic rough-and-tumble of eighteenth-century politics as self-serving and demagogic—a characterization which has continued to influence more recent histories. Yet in his own day, among the larger political nation—the burghers of Buckingham, the gentry and freeholders of Buckinghamshire, and the popular electors of London and Middlesex—Temple's passionate commitment to the principles of patriotism and to 'Wilkes and Liberty' commanded ungrudging admiration and enthusiastic support. In this respect Temple seems to personify, on a grand scale, all those complex qualities of the eighteenth-century whig aristocracy whom David Cecil characterized as a 'club full of conflict and plain speaking, where people were expected to stand up for themselves and take and give hard knocks [who] believed in ordered liberty, low taxation and the enclosure of land [and] disbelieved in despotism and democracy' (Cecil, 18–19).

LELAND J. BELLOT

Sources *The Grenville papers: being the correspondence of Richard Grenville … and … George Grenville*, ed. W. J. Smith, 4 vols. (1852–3) · J. V. Beckett, *The rise and fall of the Grenvilles: dukes of Buckingham and Chandos, 1710 to 1921* (1994) · L. J. Bellot, 'Wild hares and red herrings', *Huntington Library Quarterly*, 56 (1993), 15–39 · J. C. D. Clark, *The dynamics of change: the crisis of the 1750s and English party systems* (1982) · P. D. G. Thomas, *John Wilkes: a friend to liberty* (1996) · H. Walpole, *Memoirs of the reign of King George the Second*, ed. Lord Holland, 2nd edn, 3 vols. (1847) · *The memoirs and speeches of James, 2nd Earl Waldegrave, 1742–1763*, ed. J. C. D. Clark (1988) · N. W. Wraxall, *Historical memoirs of my own time*, 2nd edn, 2 vols. (1815) · T. Smollett, *The history of England*, 5 vols. (1812) · J. M. Robinson, *Temples of delight: Stowe landscape gardens* (1990) · Cobbett, *Parl. hist.* · D. Cecil, *Melbourne: the young Melbourne and Lord M in one volume* [1955] · Hunt. L., Stowe Grenville MSS · Northants. RO, Stowe papers · BL, Grenville MSS · GEC, *Peerage* · IGI · J. Ingamells, ed., *A dictionary of British and Irish travellers in Italy, 1701–1800* (1997), 429 · DNB

Archives BL, corresp. and papers, Add. MSS 57809–57837, *passim* · Bucks. RLSS, letter-book relating to Buckinghamshire election · Hunt. L., corresp. and papers · Northants. RO | BL, corresp. with first and second earls of Hardwicke · BL, corresp. with duke of Newcastle, Add. MSS 32708–33069, *passim* · GL, corresp. with John Wilkes · PRO, letters to Lord and Lady Chatham, 30/8 · U. Nott. L., department of manuscripts and special collections, corresp. with duke of Newcastle · W. Sussex RO, letters to duchess of Gordon

Likenesses R. Carriera, pastel?, 1731, repro. in B. Sari, *Rosalba Carriera* (1988), no. 184 · P. Scheemakers, bust, 1740, Stowe School, Buckinghamshire · W. Hoare, oils, 1760, NPG · A. Ramsay, oils, 1762, National Gallery of Victoria, Melbourne [*see illus.*] · J. Reynolds, oils, 1776 · W. Dickinson, mezzotint, pubd 1778 (after J. Reynolds), BM, NPG · J. S. Copley, group portrait, oils (*The collapse of the earl of Chatham in the House of Lords, 7 July 1778*), Tate collection; on loan to NPG

Wealth at death estates and real property (London) valued at £21,000 p.a. rental; mansion houses at Wotton Underwood and Stowe, Buckinghamshire: Hunt. L., Stowe Grenville MSS; Stowe MSS, Northants. RO; Beckett, *Rise and fall of the Grenvilles* · art collection, books, etc.

Grenville, Richard Plantagenet Campbell Temple-Nugent-Brydges-Chandos-, third duke of Buckingham and Chandos (1823–1889), politician, the only son of Richard Plantagenet Temple-Nugent-Brydges-Chandos-*Grenville, second duke of Buckingham and Chandos (1797–1861), and Lady Mary Campbell (1795–1862), younger daughter of John Campbell, first marquess of Breadalbane, was born on 10 September 1823. He was styled Earl Temple until 1839, then marquess of Chandos until succeeding to the dukedom in July 1861. He was at Eton College from 1835 to 1841 when he went to Christ Church, Oxford for eighteen months. The university conferred on him an honorary DCL in 1852. He was twice married: first, on 2 October 1851, to Caroline (d. 28 Feb 1874), daughter of Robert Harvey of Langley Park, Buckinghamshire; second, on 17 February 1885, to Alice Anne, eldest daughter of Sir Graham Graham Montgomery, bt.

Chandos sat unopposed as Conservative member of parliament for the borough of Buckingham from 1846 to 1857. In the Derby ministry of 1852 he was a junior lord of the Treasury. Son and heir of a strong defender of the landed interest against commerce and industry, he became an early example of a member of the high aristocracy entering the world of business. He was chairman of the London and North-Western Railway from 1853 to 1861.

The continuing need to repair the family fortunes, devastated by his father's bankruptcy, meant that he did not stand in the general election of 1857 and refused office in the Derby ministry in 1858. When he opposed Gladstone for one of the Oxford University seats in the general election of 1859 he lost by 859 to 1050 votes.

On the return of the Conservatives to office in July 1866 Buckingham entered the cabinet as lord president of the council. When the fourth earl of Carnarvon, along with Lord Cranborne (later third marquess of Salisbury) and General Peel, resigned from the cabinet in March 1867 over the Reform Bill, Buckingham succeeded him as secretary of state for the colonies. He had to deal with the implementation of the British North America Act. His official involvement with the continuing controversy over Bishop Colenso of Natal attracted some criticism from high-churchmen. His period of ministerial office ended with the resignation of the government in December 1868.

Buckingham was governor of Madras from 1875 to 1880 and during the famine of 1876 and 1877 organized aid on a large scale. In 1876 839,000 people received help and 716,000 were daily employed on relief works. At his suggestion the lord mayor of London set up a relief fund, which collected £475,000. In May 1886 he succeeded Lord Redesdale as chairman of committees in the House of Lords. In spite of a brusque manner he was highly regarded. He was always a staunch Conservative supporter but made few political speeches. His efforts to pay off his father's debts commanded respect and earned praise from Disraeli, and he succeeded in settling the majority of the claims. In 1883 he again owned a total of 10,482 acres, including Stowe, with an annual value of £18,080. Buckingham held many positions appropriate to his social position: he was chairman of the executive committee of the royal commission for the Great Exhibition of 1862, lord lieutenant of Buckinghamshire, keeper of the privy seal to the prince of Wales from 1852 to 1859, a special deputy warden of the stannaries, and honorary colonel of the Buckinghamshire yeomanry and the 1st Middlesex artillery volunteers. Before the House of Lords in 1868 he established his right to the title of Lord Kinloss in the peerage of Scotland, which had been dormant (J. E. B. Bruce, *Remarks on Scottish Peerages, Particularly with Reference to the Barony of Bruce of Kinloss*, 1868; *The Times*, 17, 18, and 22 July 1868). Buckingham, who suffered from diabetes, died at his London home, Chandos House, Cavendish Square, on 26 March 1889 and was buried in Wotton church on 2 April, his dukedom becoming extinct.

E. J. Feuchtwanger

Sources Burke, *Peerage* · GEC, *Peerage* · J. E. Doyle, *The official baronetage of England*, 1 (1886), 265–6 · C. Brown, *An appreciature life of … the earl of Beaconsfield*, 2 (1881), 50 · R. Blake, *Disraeli* (1966) · 'Progress of the International Exhibition', *ILN* (1 March 1862), 225 · *ILN* (22 Feb 1862), 186 · 'The cabinet ministers', *ILN* (9 Feb 1867), 142 · *The Times* (28 March 1889), 7 · *The Times* (3 April 1889), 11 · J. V. Beckett, *The rise and fall of the Grenvilles: dukes of Buckingham and Chandos, 1710 to 1921* (1994) · DNB · *ILN* (6 April 1889), 450
Archives BL, personal and family corresp. and papers, Add. MSS 70956–70983, 70992–70997 · BL, corresp., Add. MSS 41860, 43742 · Bucks. RLSS, out-letter books · Bucks. RLSS, corresp. and papers · Hunt. L., corresp. and papers | BL, corresp. with W. E. Gladstone, Add. MSS 44373–44475, *passim* · BL, letters to Lord Ripon, Add. MS 43592 · Bodl. Oxf., Disraeli MSS; corresp. with Sir Charles Doyle; corresp. with Lord Kimberley · LPL, corresp. with A. C. Tait · Lpool RO, letters to fourteenth earl of Derby · State Library of New South Wales, Sydney, Dixson Library, corresp. relating to duke of York · Suffolk RO, Ipswich, letters to Lord Iddesleigh
Likenesses Ape [C. Pellegrini], chromolithograph caricature, NPG; repro. in *VF* (29 May 1875) · H. Gales, group portrait, watercolour (*The Derby cabinet of 1867*), NPG · M. Jackson, group portrait, engraving (*The commissioners of the International Exhibition of 1862*), repro. in *ILN*, 40 (1862), 215 · C. A. Tomkins, mezzotint (aged sixty-five; after A. Chandos and Buckingham), BM · engraving, repro. in *ILN*, 94 (1889), 443 · group portrait, engraving (*The new cabinet*), repro. in *ILN*, 50 (1867), 132 · portrait, repro. in *Graphic* (22 May 1875), 501 · portrait, repro. in *Graphic* (6 April 1889), 360 · two portraits, repro. in *Pictorial World* (4–11 April 1889)
Wealth at death £115,316 18s. 4d.: resworn probate, Dec 1890, *CGPLA Eng. & Wales* (1889) · £18,080 p.a.: GEC, *Peerage*

Grenville, Richard Plantagenet Temple-Nugent-Brydges-Chandos-, second duke of Buckingham and Chandos (1797–1861), politician and bankrupt aristocrat, was born at Stowe, Buckinghamshire, on 11 February 1797, the only child of Richard Temple-Nugent-Brydges-Chandos-*Grenville, first duke of Buckingham and Chandos (1776–1839), and his wife, Anna Eliza (1780?–1836), only child and sole heir of James Brydges, third and last duke of Chandos. Styled Lord Cobham from birth and then Earl Temple from 1813 to 1822, he was educated first at Eton College, where he reportedly kept low company, and then briefly in 1815–16 at Oriel College, Oxford, where he became entangled with a young lady, who was bought off by his father. As a result of the experience she spent the rest of her life in Bethlem Hospital while he was packed off on a grand tour. This failed to keep him out of mischief, however, since in Rome he fathered an illegitimate daughter who subsequently styled herself Countess Anna Ellen St George Chandos, and was supported by the Grenvilles until her death in 1887. He proclaimed himself a reformed character on returning to England in 1818 to become, under his father's influence, one of the MPs for Buckinghamshire, which he remained until his succession to the dukedom in 1839. But although he began to take politics seriously from 1825 the reformation of his character was barely skin-deep, a taste for womanizing and reckless overspending being ingrained.

His father's practice of infidelity and indebtedness was the only paternal example which Temple chose to follow, otherwise adopting a classic oppositional stance. When his father was advanced to the dukedom in 1822 in return for swinging the votes of the Grenville faction behind Lord Liverpool, he advanced to the courtesy title of marquess of Chandos. The duke, although religiously indifferent, was a supporter of Catholic emancipation since both his mother and his sister were Roman Catholics; from 1825 onwards Chandos, although also religiously indifferent, duly became one of the leading opponents of emancipation, his mother, the duchess, being a hardline protestant and his wife an active Scottish Presbyterian. A good-

Richard Plantagenet Temple-Nugent-Brydges-Chandos-Grenville, second duke of Buckingham and Chandos (1797–1861), by Samuel Freeman, pubd 1836 (after Anne Mee)

looking, dissolute charmer, in 1819 he married the upright, austere, and rather unaffectionate Mary Campbell (d. 1862), second daughter of the fourth earl (and later first marquess) of Breadalbane, no doubt hoping that the Grenville luck with marriages would hold good and eventually bring forth something more to his advantage than Mary's modest marriage portion.

In the event the marriage lured the grasping and financially embarrassed Chandos into a tangle of lawsuits after his father-in-law's death in 1834. He challenged the Breadalbane will in the hopes of laying his hands on a third of the personalty, at the price of further souring relations with his wife and her mother, relations already soured soon after the birth of their two children by Chandos's affairs, most publicly with Mrs Anne Wyndham in 1831. Chandos later recalled Mary 'striking and kicking' him and 'forcing me from her bed' (Beckett, 116). Mary, a duchess from 1839 on, more or less stayed with her duke until physically separating from him in 1848, and obtaining a legal separation in 1850 when the financially ruined duke conducted a ruinously public affair with Mrs Henrietta Parratt, wife of the clerk of the journals of the House of Lords. In the midst of his infidelities he continually professed his love, but Mary in the end learned that he was no more to be trusted with women than with money.

In the political sphere, however, Chandos's following remained devoted and never doubted his integrity. Following his success as a leading opponent of Catholic emancipation in 1828–9 Chandos gleefully became a moderate parliamentary reformer, to the intense irritation of his pocket borough-owning father, and earned constitutional immortality as the author of the Chandos clause in the 1832 Reform Act, which enfranchised £50 tenants-at-will (that is, tenant farmers with middling and above holdings) in the county constituencies, thus augmenting the 'legitimate' influence of landowners in the shires. This consolidated his claim to be the farmer's friend, and, as the future of the corn laws became an increasingly live issue, he and the fifth duke of Richmond were the foremost uncompromising protectionists in public life, and in the eyes of much of the farming community could do no wrong.

Buckingham, as he became on the death of his father in January 1839, was appointed lord privy seal in Peel's 1841 cabinet, but within four months resigned (January 1842) when Peel proposed to change the sliding-scale duties fixed in the 1828 corn law, a resignation which further strengthened his farm support. His departure from high politics coincided with the presentation to him by the Buckinghamshire gentry and farmers of the Chandos testimonial, a vast silver centrepiece standing 4 feet 6 inches high, commemorating his defence of the agricultural interest. He reappeared only briefly on the national political stage, in 1844–6, as vice-president, to Richmond's president, of the central association of the Agricultural Protection Society known as the Anti-League, but by that time he was heavily preoccupied with his self-inflicted financial wounds and was rapidly sliding into bankruptcy.

The second duke's notoriety rests on the humiliating spectacle of the great Stowe sale of August–September 1848, when over a period of forty days the entire contents of the house were auctioned. The duke was sold up 'like a bankrupt earthenware dealer' (The Economist, 938). The Times thundered in its best fashion at:

> the destroyer of his house, the man whose reckless course has thrown on the ground a pillar of the state, and struck a heavy blow at the whole order to which he unfortunately belongs … a man of the highest rank, and of a property not unequal to his title, has flung all away by extravagance and folly, and reduced his honours to the tinsel of a pauper and the bauble of a fool. (The Times, 14 Aug 1848)

The disaster, which as well as leaving Stowe an empty shell (only reoccupied, and partially refurnished, in 1861 by the third duke) led to the sale of well over 40,000 of the 55,000 acres which the second duke had inherited in 1839, was not entirely of his own making. His father was recklessly extravagant, spending huge sums on estate purchases to boost his status and his political influence, and indulging in old masters as well as mistresses, to the extent that his debts reached the level where he had to be sent abroad to economize while trustees managed the estates and attempted, fruitlessly as it turned out, some retrenchment.

The second duke thus inherited a heavily encumbered estate, but it was his own folly, extravagance, and breathtaking incompetence which turned a serious situation into a hopeless case of unprecedented disaster. Quite how Buckingham came to have debts of nearly £1.5 million by 1847, with annual interest payments of at least £66,000 and an annual income of at most £61,000, has never been completely clear. Much could be ascribed to his habit, while still Lord Chandos, of borrowing heavily on the security of his expectation of inheriting, always a most expensive ploy. Something was owing to his own estate purchases, mainly for political purposes, and to his lavish expenditure on electioneering; to his building and collecting activities, often of inferior and overpriced objects—as John Evelyn Denison commented after viewing the Stowe sale:

> Bad Taste reigns triumphant and lords it in every department. The Pictures are all copies down to a Stansfield—a copy of a living artist is carrying the copying trade very far. The marbles and busts all very bad … For a Man to have ruined himself for such things is a great aggravation of the offence.   (Thompson, 48)

The Buckinghamshire yeomanry, which he maintained at his own expense, was an expensive enthusiasm. Entertaining the queen and Prince Albert at Stowe in 1844 was by no means cheap—its expense exemplified by the queen's exclamation on seeing the carpet in her bedroom, 'O Prince Albert, I know this carpet I have seen it before,— it was offered to me, but I did not like to spend so much money on one carpet' (Beckett, 212). Perhaps Lord Stanley was near the mark when he commented on the duke's 'incredible mismanagement' that:

> he liked to have not less than £10,000 in ready money by him. To keep this fund he was compelled to borrow, and it cost in 8 or 9 years not less than £90,000 for which there was absolutely nothing to show.   (Vincent, 174–5)

In fact within a year or so of inheriting he was borrowing simply in order to meet the interest payments on previous debt, and insolvency was bound to follow.

What followed after the crash in 1848 was that the duke after long prevarication, many deceits, and harsh words with his wife and his son, was obliged to surrender the control of his estates and his financial affairs to Chandos, and to live at first in lodgings in Wilton Street, and towards the end of his life in the Great Western Hotel at Paddington. He lived on an allowance from his son, but never gave up his scrounging and borrowing habits, even touching Disraeli for £50 one evening in the Carlton in 1857. Totally blind to reality and impervious to his shattered reputation he brazenly asked Derby to make him governor-general of India in 1852. Denied that source of income, he sold some of the Grenville family papers, which ultimately came into the hands of the publisher John Murray, and an arrangement was made to publish the several volumes of letters under the title of *Memoirs of the Court and Cabinet* of George III, George IV, and Victoria which appeared in the 1850s and early 1860s as if they had been edited by the duke. Penniless to the last, on his deathbed Buckingham was reconciled with his son and daughter, though not with his wife, dying in the Great Western Hotel 'with dropsical symptoms' (Beckett, 266) on 29 July 1861. He was buried on 5 August at Wotton, Buckinghamshire, perhaps the favourite Grenville house,

with a good show of tenantry and yeomanry. He was succeeded by his only son, Richard Plantagenet Campbell Temple-Nugent-Brydges-Chandos-*Grenville, third and last duke of Buckingham; Mary, his duchess, lived at Hampton Court after their 1850 separation, surviving long enough to move back to Stowe when it was reopened in 1861, and dying there in June 1862. The duke's only legitimate daughter, Anne Eliza Mary [see Langton, Lady Anna Eliza Mary Gore-], married William Henry Powell Gore-Langton, of Newton Park, Somerset, and when the dukedom of Buckingham became extinct in 1889 her eldest son inherited the title of Earl Temple of Stowe (under the special remainder in its 1822 creation for the first duke) and the original Grenville seat of Wotton.

F. M. L. THOMPSON

Sources J. V. Beckett, *The rise and fall of the Grenvilles: dukes of Buckingham and Chandos, 1710 to 1921* (1994) · F. M. L. Thompson, 'The end of a great estate', *Economic History Review*, 2nd ser., 8 (1955–6), 36–52 · *DNB* · *The Times* (14 Aug 1848) · *The Times* (31 July 1861) · Burke, *Peerage* (1902) · GEC, *Peerage* · *The Economist* (19 Aug 1848) · *Disraeli, Derby and the conservative party: journals and memoirs of Edward Henry, Lord Stanley, 1849–1869*, ed. J. R. Vincent (1978)
Archives BL, personal and family corresp. and papers, Add. MSS 70956–70983, 70992–70997 · Bucks. RLSS, corresp. and papers · Hunt. L., corresp. and papers · NRA Scotland, priv. coll. | BL, corresp. with Sir Robert Peel, Add. MSS 40356–40605 · Bodl. Oxf., letters to Benjamin Disraeli · Bucks. RLSS, corresp. with Fremantle family · Durham RO, letters to Lord Londonderry · Hants. RO, Ashburton MSS · NL Wales, letters to Louisa Lloyd · W. Sussex RO, letters to duke of Richmond
Likenesses J. Jackson, oils, 1829, Stowe School, Buckinghamshire · G. Hayter, group portrait, oils, 1833 (*The House of Commons, 1833*), NPG · S. Freeman, stipple, pubd 1836 (after A. Mee), NPG [see illus.] · R. Cooper, stipple, BM · J. Doyle, drawings, BM
Wealth at death £200: probate, 13 Aug 1861, *CGPLA Eng. & Wales*

Grenville, Richard Temple-Nugent-Brydges-Chandos-, first duke of Buckingham and Chandos (1776–1839), politician, was born in London on 20 March 1776, the elder son of George Nugent-Temple-*Grenville, first marquess of Buckingham (1753–1813), and his wife, Lady Mary Elizabeth, *suo jure* Baroness Nugent (1759?–1812), only daughter and heir of Robert, first Earl Nugent. Known as Earl Temple from 1784 to 1813, he matriculated at Brasenose College, Oxford, in December 1791 and was still in Oxford in 1794. He grew immensely fat, and was known variously as 'Lord Grenville's fat nephew', the 'gros Marquis', and by Canning, as the 'Ph[at] D[uke]' (Beckett, 101; *Letters of George IV*, 3.133). He was elected MP for Buckinghamshire in June 1797, and sat for the county until he succeeded his father as second marquess of Buckingham in 1813. His contribution to public life was to give a sustained display of greed and ambition. When his uncle William Wyndham Grenville offered him a place at the Admiralty in May 1800 he turned it down as being beneath the dignity of his rank, and demanded a position at the Treasury; when that was not forthcoming he accepted the post of commissioner at the India board, which he held until March 1801. When his uncle became prime minister in 1806 he expected a major office, but had to be content with the vice-presidency of the Board of Trade and a joint paymaster-generalship of the land forces. On leaving office in March 1807 he created a stir by taking with him the official stationery, pens, and ink in a characteristic display of meanness. In 1825 he tried, in vain as it turned out, to blackmail Canning into making him governor-general of Bengal by threatening to withdraw the support of the Grenville faction, and in 1829 he hoped to become viceroy of Ireland. In 1830 he was briefly, from July to November, lord steward of the household, and in May 1832, when it looked as though Wellington would return to form a government, he angled for the Irish viceroyship or the first lordship of the Admiralty, causing Lord Ellenborough to remark: 'He is unfit for either, and so unpopular he would sink any Govnt. He should look after the King's dinners as he did before' (*Three Diaries*, 249).

Buckingham's one great achievement, from the point of view of his family, was to secure the dukedom in 1822 which had long been their cherished ambition, and which had been denied by the half promises and prevarication of George III. It was a straightforward 'old corruption' transaction in which Lord Liverpool purchased the support of the Grenville faction in the Commons, reckoned to be ten or eleven MPs, in return for a dukedom for Richard Grenville and places for his friends—Charles Watkin Williams Wynn in the cabinet as president of the Board of Control, Thomas Henry Fremantle (the go-between) and Joseph Phillimore as commissioners of the Board of Control, Henry Williams Wynn as minister to Switzerland, and Plunket as Irish attorney-general. While some imagined he had been made a duke as a token of friendship by George IV, insiders were well aware that he had been bought over from the whigs, with whom the Grenvillites had voted since 1806. Several registered contempt, at least in the privacy of their diaries. Lord Holland remarked that 'all articles are now to be had at low prices except Grenvilles' and said that the new duke was 'never satisfied but always asking for more'. Sir Charles Bagot, in slightly different vein, said:

> I am glad that the Grenvilles are taken into the Govt. and (for Grenvilles) they come tolerably cheap. I see no objection to a Dukedom in the head of the Grenville family, but I see many to giving it to the actual blubberhead who now reigns over them.

Mrs Arbuthnot joined in the chorus, recording that 'The Duke of Buckingham is odious and unpopular to the last degree … [and] utterly without talent or the respect of one human being' (GEC, *Peerage*, 2.408–09; Beckett, 108–10). Unsurprisingly the duke was firmly opposed to parliamentary reform, and Creevey recorded gleefully in 1831 that:

> I saw the stately Buckingham going down to the Lords just now. I wonder how he likes the boroughs of Buckingham and St Mawes being bowled out. He would never have been a duke without them, and can there be a better reason for their destruction? (Gore, 323)

By the ruling conventions the Grenville estates of more than 57,000 acres, with a gross rental of nearly £65,000, were amply sufficient to support the dignity of a dukedom, but it was not generally known that by 1822 Richard Grenville had already been living beyond his means for so

long that he was unable to sustain the extravagant and self-indulgent spending habits which he considered essential to a ducal style. A sizeable proportion of this estate, approaching one third, was the Chandos inheritance acquired through his marriage on 16 April 1796 to Lady Anna Eliza (1780–1836), the only surviving daughter and sole heir of James Brydges, third and last duke of Chandos, a marriage first discussed by the two sets of parents in 1786 when Anna Eliza was only six. In recognition of the Chandos inheritance he took the surname Temple-Nugent-Brydges-Chandos-Grenville in 1799. Anna Eliza matured into a strong and determined woman, a foil for her weak and incorrigible husband, who added one or two mistresses to his other indulgences. When it emerged that he had been selling parts of the Chandos inheritance in contravention of the marriage settlement and without her knowledge, she forced through a resettlement in 1828 on her own terms, forbidding any sales of Chandos lands to pay off ducal debts, thereby ensuring that some lands survived the eventual crash of the second duke, their son. By 1827 Buckingham was in serious difficulties. Anna Eliza went to live at Avington in Hampshire, the favourite Chandos house, Stowe was shut up, and the duke was packed off abroad in a move typical of supposed aristocratic economy. He conducted his exile in style, however, having a yacht specially built for the purpose, the *Anna Eliza*, which had extra wide gangways because of his great size and extra large cabins because he liked to sail with a grand piano. Once he reached Italy he proceeded to indulge his taste for collecting pictures and sundry artefacts, which so effectively defeated the object of the exercise that when he returned to England in 1830 his affairs were in greater confusion and his debts larger than when he had left. His travel diary, including several forays into poetry, was published as *The Private Diary of the Duke of Buckingham* (3 vols., 1862). The yacht came in handy during the Swing riots which swept southern England late that year, as Lord Ellenborough heard: 'The D. of Buckingham had had a fight and taken 31 prisoners', he recounted.

> He went down to Avington, sent for his yacht's guns, six of them, and all his yacht's men & other sailors; put his house in a state of defence with 40 well-armed people, & got together 150 more—farmers, labourers, gamekeepers, &c. Thinking his house might be injured by a siege he advanced and met the rioters, read the Riot Act & charged at once. (*Three Diaries*, 24)

By this time Stowe was reoccupied, and duke and duchess once more lived together, but the finances worsened further, with their son, Richard Plantagenet Temple-Nugent-Brydges-Chandos-*Grenville, the marquess of Chandos, more than equalling his father's capacity to run up debts. In 1833, in another standard move for deeply indebted aristocrats, the estates were put in the hands of trustees, but since the duke frequently ignored, misled, or cheated them they made no headway in reducing the debts and resigned in despair in 1836. At this point, with the duke becoming increasingly fat and immobile, his steward 'had invented a kind of machine to raise and lower the Duke from one floor to another; he [the steward] unfortunately fell through the aperture he had made and broke his neck' (Gibbs, 3.285). Anna Eliza died later in 1836, and the duke, gout-ridden and enfeebled, left matters to his son and a new set of more pliant trustees. He died on 17 January 1839 at Stowe, leaving his son to complete the ruin and humiliation of the proud Grenvilles. He was buried on 25 January at Stowe. Selections of his correspondence on public affairs were later published as *Memoirs of the Court of George IV* (1859) and *Memoirs of the Courts and Cabinets of William IV and Victoria* (1861).

F. M. L. THOMPSON

Sources J. V. Beckett, *The rise and fall of the Grenvilles: dukes of Buckingham and Chandos, 1710 to 1921* (1994) · *DNB* · A. Aspinall, ed., *Three early nineteenth-century diaries* (1952) [extracts from Le Marchant, E. J. Littleton, Baron Hatherton, and E. Law, earl of Ellenborough] · GEC, *Peerage* · *The later correspondence of George III*, ed. A. Aspinall, 5 vols. (1962–70) · *The letters of King George IV, 1812–1830*, ed. A. Aspinall, 3 vols. (1938) · [T. Creevey], *Creevey*, ed. J. Gore (1948) · R. Gibbs, *Buckinghamshire: a record of local occurrences and general events, chronologically arranged*, 4 vols. (1878–82)

Archives Hunt. L., corresp. and papers · U. Nott. L., corresp. | BL, letters to Lord Auckland, Add. MSS 34456–34459 · BL, corresp. with Lord and Lady Camelford, Add. MS 69043 · BL, corresp. with Lord Grenville, Add. MSS 58898–58899, 59044 · BL, letters to Thomas Grenville, Add. MSS 41854, 42058 · BL, corresp. with Sir Robert Peel, Add. MSS 40361–40418 · BL, letters to Lord Spencer, p 8 · BL, Stowe MSS · BL, letters to Lord Wellesley, Add. MSS 37284–37311 *passim* · Bucks. RLSS, corresp. with Scrope Bernard · Bucks. RLSS, letters to first Baron Cottesloe · Bucks. RLSS, corresp. with Admiral Fremantle and Sir W. H. Fremantle · Bucks. RLSS, letters to Thomas Grenville · Bucks. RLSS, Stowe MSS · Essex RO, Chelmsford, letters to Louisa Lloyd · Hants. RO, Ashburton MSS · Hunt. L., Stowe MSS · NA Scot., letters to Alexander Ross · NL Wales, letters to Louisa Lloyd · NL Wales, letters to William Lloyd · NL Wales, letters to Charles Watkin Williams Wynn · NMM, corresp. with Francis Lunn · NRA Scotland, letters to Alexander Ross · St Deiniol's Library, Hawarden, Flintshire, letters to Lady Mary Glynne

Likenesses J. Reynolds, group portrait, 1780–82 (with his father and family), NG Ire. · W. Beechey, oils, 1802–4, Stowe School, Stowe, Buckinghamshire · R. Cooper, stipple (after miniature by G. L. Saunders), BM, NPG · G. Hayter, group portrait, oils (*The trial of Queen Caroline, 1820*), NPG

Wealth at death under £250,000 estate: PRO, death duty registers, IR 26/1506, fol. 308 · capital value of estates est. £1,800,000; debts of approx. £300,000

Grenville, Thomas (1755–1846), politician and book collector, was born on 31 December 1755, the third son of George *Grenville (1712–1770), politician, and Elizabeth (*d.* 1769), daughter of Sir William Wyndham. He was educated at Eton College from 1764 until 1771, and then entered Christ Church, Oxford, as a gentleman commoner, matriculating on 9 December 1771. In 1778 he was appointed ensign in the 2nd foot guards, and in October 1779 was gazetted as lieutenant in the 86th regiment of foot. Denied further advancement by North's government, Grenville resigned his commissions in 1780. In 1779 he was elected member of parliament for Buckinghamshire. Called upon by Fox in the following session to describe to the house the ill treatment he had received when seeking promotion in the infantry, Grenville made a statement which was very damaging to the ministry, but

helpful to Fox, who was attacking the government for political bias in military appointments. Grenville joined Fox's party, and subsequently became his good friend. This placed him in opposition to the politics of his family, from whom he became estranged until the period of the French Revolution, although the strong family loyalty and affection so characteristic of the Grenvilles remained largely intact. Grenville was prepossessing in appearance and a good speaker. Pitt sought his support, and Fox's high opinion of his abilities was such that, according to one account, if the India Bill was passed he meant to appoint him governor-general (*GM*, 197).

In 1782 Grenville was entrusted by Fox with negotiating the terms of the treaty with the United States. He went to Paris and made some progress, but was suddenly recalled on the death of Lord Rockingham. He remained loyal to Fox, and supported the coalition ministry. After the dissolution of 1784 he lost his seat, but was returned for Aldeburgh in 1790. In 1791 he brought forward a motion against the increased naval force after the Ochakov crisis, but his resolution was defeated by 208 to 114. While member for Aldeburgh he joined the Portland whigs and gave general support to Pitt. In 1793 he supported the Aliens Bill and other government measures, and in the following year he was sent with Earl Spencer as minister-extraordinary to the court of Vienna. At the elections of 1796 he was returned for the family borough of Buckingham, which he continued to represent until 1810. In 1798 he was sworn of the privy council.

In 1799 Grenville accepted the post of ambassador to Berlin to propose an alliance against France. The ship carrying him was driven back by ice, and the *Proserpine*, to which he transferred, was wrecked off Newerke Island and several of the crew perished. Grenville escaped with difficulty, losing everything but his dispatches. The English ambassador's enforced delay had enabled the French directory to dispatch Sieyès to Berlin, thereby frustrating Grenville's purpose. The king of Prussia having been persuaded by the French to adhere to his neutrality, the British mission returned to England.

In 1800 Grenville received the sinecure office of chief justice on eyre south of Trent, with a salary of £2000. He was the last to be appointed to this office, which was abolished in 1817. He opposed the Addington administration and the treaty of Amiens, against which he voted in a small minority of twenty with William Windham. The Grenvilles and the Portland whigs came together in opposition with the Foxites in 1804, Grenville playing the role of go-between. In 1805 he voted for the prosecution of Lord Melville. Following the death of Pitt the recently allied parties took office together in the 'ministry of all the talents' in February 1806, but Grenville did not immediately take office, even though his brother, William Wyndham *Grenville, first Baron Grenville, was prime minister. In the following July he became president of the Board of Control on the appointment of Lord Minto as governor-general of Bengal. After the death of Fox he was appointed first lord of the Admiralty. On the fall of the 'talents' ministry at the end of March 1807 Grenville, whose ambition for office had never been strong, practically withdrew from public life. He voted on only three further occasions, in favour of Catholic emancipation, for the repeal of the income tax, and for his nephew Charles Watkin Williams Wynn in the speakership election of 1817. In 1813 he was again returned for a Buckinghamshire seat, to keep it warm for his young great-nephew, Richard Grenville, later second duke of Buckingham and Chandos. He duly retired from parliament in 1818, and from that time until his death he lived in the company of his friends and his books, and devoted himself to the formation of his splendid library.

When Lord Glastonbury died in 1825 he left Grenville, his cousin, all his landed and funded property for life, with a remainder to his nephew, the dean of Windsor. Grenville immediately gave up the landed property to the dean. His pursuit of book collecting began early in life, and he claimed that when in the guards he bid at a sale against a whole bench of bishops for a scarce edition of the Bible. He was appointed a trustee of the British Museum.

Grenville, who never married, died in London at Hamilton Place, Piccadilly, on 17 December 1846. His large benefactions became known after his death. He had originally bequeathed his library to his nephew the duke of Buckingham, but revoked this bequest in a codicil, stating that as his books had been in great part acquired from a sinecure office, he felt it right to leave them to the British Museum. He was doubtless also motivated by what might happen to his collection if the duke's precarious finances were to topple, as well as by his close friendship with Antonio Panizzi, the museum's librarian. The British Museum thus received upwards of 20,000 volumes, which were notable for their fine condition and were valued at more than £50,000. The collection consisted chiefly of printed books. The most valuable classes of the collection were the works of Homer, those of Aesop (of which there were also some manuscripts), works by Ariosto (early voyages and travels), works on Ireland, classics—both Greek and Latin—and old Italian and Spanish literature. Also included were a fine copy of the first folio of Shakespeare and other old English books. A catalogue of the library by H. J. Payne, H. Foss, and W. B. Rye was published in three volumes as *Bibliotheca Grenvilliana* between 1842 and 1848.

G. B. SMITH, *rev.* R. W. DAVIS

Sources *Annual Register* (1846) · *GM*, 2nd ser., 27 (1847), 197–201 · J. V. Beckett, *The rise and fall of the Grenvilles: dukes of Buckingham and Chandos, 1710 to 1921* (1994) · HoP, *Commons, 1790–1820* · M. M. Drummond, 'Grenville, George', HoP, *Commons, 1754–90* · *Hansard 1* · W. Y. Fletcher, *English book collectors* (1902)
Archives BL, corresp. and MSS, Add. MSS 34472, 41851–41859, 42058, 60487 · Duke U., Perkins L., letters · Hunt. L., corresp. and MSS | BL, letters to Philip Bliss, Add. MSS 34568–34578 · BL, corresp. with Lord Collingwood, Add. MS 40096 · BL, corresp. with Charles James Fox, Add. MSS 47563, 47569, 47601 · BL, letters to Mrs Gladstone, Add. MS 46227 · BL, corresp. with Lady Grenville, Add. MS 69044 · BL, corresp. with Lord Grenville, Add. MSS 58880–58890, 69040–69041 · BL, corresp. with Anthonio Panizzi, Add. MSS 36714–36715, 36726 · BL, letters to second Earl Spencer · Bucks. RLSS, corresp. with Sir William Fremantle · NL Scot., letters to Lord Minto · NL Wales, corresp. with C. W. W. Wynn · Sandon Hall, Staffordshire, letters to Lord Harrowby · U. Durham L., letters to second Earl Grey · Yale U., Beinecke L., letters to George Neville Grenville
Likenesses C. Turner, mezzotint, pubd 1805 (after J. Hoppner), BM, NPG · oils, 1807 (after J. Hoppner), Hughenden Manor, Buckinghamshire · W. Say, mezzotint, pubd 1808 (after J. Hoppner), BM, NPG · T. Phillips, oils, exh. RA 1810?, Althorp House, Northamptonshire · C. Manzini, miniature, 1841, NPG · J. B. Comelli, marble bust; on loan to Plymouth Museum · Dear, engraving (after portrait by J. Hoppner) · Lady Delamere, lithograph (aged eighty), BM · J. Posselwhite, stipple (aged ninety; after G. Richmond), BM · bust, BM

Grenville, Thomas Henry (1719–1747), naval officer, was born on 3 April 1719, the fifth and youngest son of Richard Grenville (1684–1727) of Wotton Hall, Buckinghamshire, and Hester Temple (*bap.* 1684, *d.* 1752), who became Viscountess Cobham in 1749 and Countess Temple in 1750. Richard *Grenville (later Grenville-Temple), second Earl Temple, and George *Grenville were his brothers.

From June 1734 to January 1737 Grenville attended the Royal Naval Academy at Portsmouth. Though approved for sea service he did not go directly to a ship but briefly attended Eton College, probably while waiting for the *Dursley Galley*, under Captain Thomas *Smith, a cousin, to come home. In the Mediterranean in 1740 he moved with Smith to the *Romney* (50 guns) and was promoted by Admiral Nicholas Haddock to be her lieutenant on 2 May. Later that year he became third lieutenant of the *Somerset*, Haddock's flagship, where he rose by succession to first lieutenant but was not promoted captain until 6 April 1742, when Smith resigned command of the *Romney* to create the vacancy. Citing the 'incredible' usefulness of Smith and 'the Obligations I am under to him', Grenville urged his eldest brother to muster all his friends and interest 'to get over any Difficulties he [Smith] may meet with at the Board' (Hunt. L., Stowe–Grenville papers, box 191 (16, 17)). Three of Grenville's brothers were members of parliament.

Admiral Thomas Mathews assigned the *Romney* to cruise off Cape St Vincent, a favourite station, where on 18 February 1743 a ship heading for Cadiz was sighted and chased. Despite her being warned and towed inshore by Portuguese fishing boats Grenville secured his prize, the *Santa Rosa*. She was a Spanish register ship (from Vera Cruz) and only the high court of Admiralty could condemn her, so Grenville got permission to shift to the *Guarland* to bring her home. Presuming that there would be various contentions and claims he begged, upon arrival in the Thames, that the captured 'Spanish' crew, all French, be confined (they would be hostile witnesses) until after the court made its decision, and this was done (PRO, Adm. 1/1829). The amount at stake was huge. Over £100,000 was netted by sale of silver and cochineal, one quarter of which went to Grenville.

Spring 1744 saw Grenville at Portsmouth, trying to get the *Falkland* (50 guns) fitted out and manned. At this time he bought an estate sufficient to qualify him for a seat in the House of Commons. He also loaned Captain Smith £6000 to buy an estate worth £300 p.a. and hence qualify to stand for parliament (Kent Archives Office, U 1590,

S2/013, pp. 1–2). The *Falkland*'s channel cruising was cut short in July by orders to go with Sir John Balchen's squadron. On the return voyage she was stationed ahead and got back safely before a fierce storm in early October shattered the squadron and sank the flagship *Victory* with no survivors. Ordered from Spithead to search for her, Grenville called at Guernsey, where he saw, washed ashore, masts and spars bearing the *Victory*'s markings.

In December Grenville's brother George was appointed to the Admiralty board. Shortly afterwards their elder sibling Richard told George: 'Give yourself no trouble about the parish officers, only take care of the naval ones, and provide a most excellent station for poor Tom, that if the public be not benefited by your administration, your family at least may' (*Grenville Papers*, 1.33–4). A month later the *Falkland* and two other ships had orders to cruise off Cape Clear, and by early May 'poor Tom' was back in Spithead, £2500 richer. The *Falkland* cruised in the channel during the remainder of 1745. Grenville craved command of a 70-gun ship, an idea that George disliked: 'rich as you are, you want money more than you do honour' (ibid., 1.35). George's efforts to provide orders for independent cruising were frustrated in 1746. After moving to the *Defiance* (60 guns) Thomas was under Charles Watson in the Bay of Biscay, and after mid-September with Lord Anson's western squadron. A November storm near Cape Finisterre forced him to replace a mast at Lisbon.

On 12 December 1746 Grenville was elected MP for Bridport in a closely contested by-election; the accomplishment stemmed from George Grenville's initiative, the duke of Bedford's patronage, and use of his own money. Meanwhile George was developing a plan for a golden cruise to the Canary Islands to intercept register ships. A second ship was required to overcome the strong Spanish escort, and the brother of another board member, Lord Sandwich, was selected. At the last moment the orders were suspended because Anson needed both ships for a squadron that he was hurriedly assembling to intercept a strongly escorted French convoy. George was so incensed at the postponement that he tried underhandedly to circumvent the decision, to the great annoyance of Bedford, the absent first lord. Anson personally assured George that he would quickly release the two ships and make no claim to a flag share of any prizes that they might take, but Thomas Grenville did not survive the victorious battle of 3 May 1747. He was struck by a large splinter, 'which shattered the bone of his left thigh in several pieces'; after an immediate amputation he 'lived near five hours, sensible most of the time, but very faint with the great loss of blood and excessive pain' (*Grenville Papers*, 1.58–63). He was the only captain killed. His body was brought back and buried at Wotton.

When reporting this first battle of Cape Finisterre to the duke of Newcastle, Anson commented: 'the King has lost an excellent Officer; there is no man in the whole fleet that was so generally esteemed' (PRO, SP 42/69, 11 May 1747)—posthumous exaggeration perhaps, yet there were many earlier indications that Grenville was not only esteemed but also, notwithstanding his being a 'favourite', well liked. His family hoped for fortune but he placed honour above it. A memorial column stands in the gardens at Stowe, Buckinghamshire.   DANIEL A. BAUGH

Sources DNB · *The Grenville papers: being the correspondence of Richard Grenville … and … George Grenville*, ed. W. J. Smith, 1 (1852) · Hunt. L., Stowe-Grenville papers, box 23 (58); boxes 191–2 · captain's letters, PRO, Adm. 1/1829–30 · N. A. M. Rodger, *The wooden world: an anatomy of the Georgian navy* (1986) · *Correspondence of John, fourth duke of Bedford*, ed. J. Russell, 1 (1842) · L. M. Wiggin, *The faction of cousins: a political account of the Grenvilles, 1733–1763* (New Haven, CT, 1958) · R. R. Sedgwick, 'Grenville, Thomas Henry', HoP, *Commons, 1715–54* · monument, Stowe, Buckinghamshire
Archives Hunt. L., Stowe-Grenville papers | PRO, letters to Lord and Lady Chatham, PRO 30/8
Wealth at death probably over £30,000

Grenville, William Wyndham, Baron Grenville (1759–1834)

Grenville, William Wyndham, Baron Grenville (1759–1834), prime minister, was born on 24 October 1759 at Wotton House, Buckinghamshire, the fifth of seven children and the youngest son of George *Grenville (1712–1770), prime minister, and Elizabeth Wyndham (1720–1769), daughter of Sir William *Wyndham, third baronet, politician.

Family, education, and political apprenticeship, 1759–1784

Grenville was born into a family that had risen from comparative obscurity in the seventeenth century to become, partly through marriage and partly through a combination of ambition, ability, and influence, one of the richest and most powerful in Britain. The head of the family was his uncle, second Earl Temple, the owner of Stowe and a major political figure in the 1750s and 1760s, who on his death in 1779 bequeathed to Grenville's eldest brother, George, the third earl, an annual rent roll of as much as £21,000 as well as six parliamentary seats. His father, although far less well off financially, was even more successful politically. He became prime minister in 1763 before being dismissed by George III in 1765 over the question of who controlled patronage—one of the first clashes between the king and the Grenvilles. Moreover, he had other influential family ties. His mother was the daughter of one of the leaders of the Hanoverian tories under the first two Georges, and, much more importantly, he was a cousin of his exact contemporary, the younger Pitt, as a result of the marriage between his aunt, Hester Grenville, and Pitt the elder. In fact the rise of the elder Pitt, Temple, and George Grenville to the forefront of politics in the 1750s and 1760s was so swift that they were referred to as the 'cousinhood'—a term of disparagement that the Grenvilles were never able to elude.

Grenville was educated successively at East Hill School in Wandsworth, Eton College (1770–76), Christ Church, Oxford (1776–80), and Lincoln's Inn (1780–82), but was never called to the bar. His parents died within a year of each other just at the point when he started at Eton and this tragedy was followed nine years later by the death of his guardian, Earl Temple, shortly before he finished at Christ Church. Although it is difficult to be certain, his parents' deaths probably meant that Eton and Oxford had much more influence on him than might otherwise have

William Wyndham Grenville, Baron Grenville (1759–1834), by John Hoppner, *c*.1800

been the case. He certainly became a considerable scholar in mathematics and the classics and in 1779 won the Oxford chancellor's prize for Latin verse with a composition entitled 'Vis electricita'. One of his tutors, Lewis Bagot, dean of Christ Church, was sufficiently impressed with his 'uncommon diligence' and his 'astonishing' progress in mathematics to predict 'more than common attainments' in the future (Jupp, 13). Moreover, Grenville also made a number of lifelong friends, some of whom were to be important in his political career.

The death of his guardian in 1779 made Grenville's brother George the head of the family. It came at a time when Grenville was considering his future. He was undoubtedly aware of his intellectual gifts but also knew that he was dependent to some degree on his brother for money and influence, his own resources as the youngest son being comparatively modest. In 1780 he wrote privately of his aversion to being dependent and of his hope of being able to overcome it by marriage or, more seriously, by diligence in a career. For most of that year and the next he studied law in London, and he became a member of Goosetree's, a club of young, newly elected or aspiring MPs which included the younger Pitt. Law failed to interest him, however, with the result that he agreed to be returned by his brother as MP for Buckingham in February 1782.

The two-year political crisis that followed the collapse of Lord North's government in February 1782 had a decisive impact on Grenville's career. Somewhat fortuitously it led to his first experience of office. On entering parliament he followed his brother Temple's lead and supported the

whig opposition against North on the grounds of the government's incompetent war policy and the excessive influence it was alleged to wield as a result of the support of the king and the patronage at its disposal. On the fall of the whig government that had succeeded North's in July 1782, Temple chose to accept office as lord lieutenant of Ireland in the new administration led by Lord Shelburne, and Grenville followed him once again, accepting the post of Irish chief secretary and membership of the Irish privy council, but only after considerable thought. Moreover, chance played its hand once again when Shelburne's government was defeated on its peace terms in February of the following year and was succeeded by the Fox–North coalition. Grenville, unlike Temple, was inclined to support the peace terms and certainly advised his brother to continue in office in the coalition. However, in deference to Temple's opinion, he declined to make his real views on the peace public, and when the king declared his hostility to the coalition, he was delighted that Temple decided to resign rather than to stay on board. This made the Grenvilles the king's 'friends' and led to Temple playing the crucial role in bringing about the overthrow of the coalition on its East India Bill and the elevation of himself and Pitt to the joint headship of a new administration. It was at this point that a decisive reversal in fortune took place. Temple was forced to resign in the face of allegations of the improper use of his influence with the king. Pitt therefore became sole head and Grenville was appointed paymaster of the forces and a member of the British privy council. The head of the Grenville interest had been cast into the wilderness, leaving Grenville, his charge, as the real beneficiary.

The crisis also gave Grenville valuable political experience. His most notable achievement was the negotiation of the Renunciation Act in his capacity as chief secretary. The point at issue was the demand by Irish politicians that Britain renounce its past and future ability to reject legislation passed by the Irish parliament; the Shelburne cabinet was keen not to tie the hands of future governments on this issue. Grenville's role was to negotiate directly with the cabinet and, in the face of considerable dithering, to persuade it to agree to what was an act of recognition rather than renunciation and which established the rights of legislative independence claimed by the Irish but which was silent about the future. His handling of the negotiation and his introduction of the measure in the Commons in his maiden speech earned him widespread praise, Lord Townshend commenting that he was much impressed by Grenville's 'great attention, clearness and precision' (Jupp, 28).

Grenville also strengthened or established connections with key political figures. One of these was Pitt. Although they had known each other as boys and had almost certainly met at Goosetree's, the evidence suggests only a formal acquaintance between them prior to 1783. They became personal friends, however, during January and February of that year, when Grenville was in London negotiating the Renunciation Act, and by April Grenville was committed to acting with his cousin in any attempt to bring down the coalition on the king's behalf. The other connection was with the king himself. In March and April he saw Grenville on four occasions to discuss his forthcoming 'enslavement' and was 'lavish in the praises', finding him 'truly amiable and right-headed'. Moreover, despite the reservations he must have had about the king as a result of the way he had treated his father twenty years earlier, Grenville found himself sympathizing with his feelings and espousing 'his resentments' warmly (Jupp, 33–4). The route was open for the descendants of the 'cousinhood' to reclaim the position their parents had lost in the 1760s.

Pitt's lieutenant, 1784–1791 Grenville's and Temple's roles in British politics for the next seventeen years were largely settled in the first months of Pitt's ministry. Although Temple headed a political group consisting of eleven MPs after the general election of 1784, eight of whom were in the Commons, his role in the overthrow of the Fox–North coalition made him unemployable until the dust had settled. Fuming at the 'sacrifice' he had made, he asked for a dukedom and was even more enraged when the king's decision to restrict the rank to the royal princes meant that he had to make do with the marquessate of Buckingham. The view that he had been treated harshly remained with him for the rest of his life and was inherited by his successor in 1813.

Buckingham's plight undoubtedly influenced the way Grenville thought about his own future. He owed his progress so far to his brother, a point reinforced when he was elected for one of the Buckinghamshire seats at the 1784 election with the full support of the family interest. Moreover, the other Grenville brother, Tom, was estranged both politically and personally from Buckingham by his attachment to Fox. A combination of loyalty, sympathy, and brotherly gratitude therefore encouraged Grenville to regard his own career as less important than Buckingham's, at least until 1789.

This, together with his respect for Pitt, led Grenville to set his sights at a relatively modest level. Pitt clearly believed that his cousin's aptitudes and experience—the clarity of his intellect, his negotiating skill, the knowledge that he had acquired of commercial and fiscal matters in his Irish post, and a pamphlet he had published on the East Indian question—qualified him for membership of the government's two engine-rooms of reform, the Board of Control and the Board of Trade. He also offered him the governor-generalship of India in the summer of 1784 but Grenville turned it down. What he wanted to do, he said, was to acquit himself in his current posts in such a way as would qualify him for his ultimate objective: a cabinet post without significant duties and a sinecure for life.

During the next seven years Grenville achieved more than his objective and became, with Henry Dundas, Pitt's principal adviser. This was accomplished partly by his conduct in the posts that he occupied: joint paymaster-general (March 1784 to September 1789); member, and from August 1786 vice-president, of the Board of Trade (March 1784 to August 1789); and commissioner, and from March 1790 president, of the Board of Control (September 1784 to June 1793). The critical posts were those on the two boards. Grenville was as fully committed as Pitt to the task of financial and commercial reconstruction following the loss of the American colonies and the removal of statutory control over Irish legislation. He therefore played an important part in all the principal measures that flowed from the boards and were adopted by the cabinet. These included the reform of the East India Company's finances (1784–6), after which Grenville's contribution to Indian policy declined; the framing of the ill-fated adjustment of commercial relations with Ireland (1784–5); the unsuccessful trade treaty with Portugal and the successful one with France (1785–7); and the establishment of the sinking fund in 1786. When writing his autobiography many years later Grenville singled out the sinking fund as the measure to which he had contributed most—'a larger share than I believe anybody knows' (Jupp, 57). How far he was right it is impossible to tell, but it is worth noting that when he published a pamphlet in 1828 arguing that its usefulness had come to an end contemporaries thought that his recantation spelt its death knell.

Grenville's growing influence was also due to various other contributions to the policies and the well-being of the government. These included his speeches in parliament. He was never in the same league as Pitt, but by dint of careful preparation and a short temper he gradually acquired a reputation as a speaker whose formal speeches, although tedious to listen to, were certainly worth reading, and as a debater who possessed formidable forensic skills. His qualities as a debater were widely praised when he took a leading part in steering the Anglo-French commercial treaty through the house in 1787, not least by Sir Gilbert Elliot, who thought that he had exceeded Pitt in that department. He later made a series of formal orations, including ones on Admiralty business and the regency, which were highly regarded. In fact his speech on the regency in January 1789 was the first of his to be published.

Other contributions were made as an adviser. Grenville's most notable official contribution in this capacity was when he went to The Hague and to Paris in 1787 to advise the cabinet on a conflict in the United Provinces between the Orange and patriot parties which threatened the European equilibrium. Despite going reluctantly as a result of a feeling of inadequacy, he did the job extremely well. His reports to the king and to the cabinet were well-informed, and in backing the Orangeists the government took the line that he had recommended. The recipients of his reports were impressed, most notably the professional diplomats such as Eden, Harris, and Carmarthen as well as the best-informed European specialist in British governing circles, the king. But he also played a significant role at a private and personal level. The most important example was his advice to Buckingham and Pitt during the regency crisis in 1788–9. Buckingham had been given an opportunity to re-establish himself politically by being appointed lord lieutenant for a second time in 1787. However, his pride and volatility soon got the better of him and these weaknesses were stretched to breaking point when the

Irish parliament seemed ready to vote the prince of Wales a regency in Ireland on terms that Pitt and Grenville were determined he would not obtain in Britain. Throughout Buckingham's spell as lord lieutenant, which came to an end in 1789, it was Grenville who kept his brother informed of relevant developments in Britain and who mediated between his demands and the requirements of policy in London. He was also largely responsible for persuading his brother not to take a number of actions against the pro-prince party in Ireland which, if they had been taken, would have made things infinitely worse. What he was unable to prevent, however, was Buckingham's leaving Ireland with his reputation in Britain tarnished even further and with his political career effectively at an end.

Grenville also worked closely with Pitt during the regency crisis but it was probably his readiness to support the prime minister in whatever way he could as much as the acuity of his advice that led him to become one of the triumvirate that governed policy, and, in the view of some, the second in command. His call to duty over the Dutch episode has already been noticed and he responded once again amid the regency crisis by agreeing to his election as speaker of the Commons as a result of the death of the incumbent. This was not a post he wanted nor one for which he was particularly qualified, but Pitt deemed it essential that one of his trusted colleagues occupy the chair in view of the uncertain outcome of the crisis.

Grenville occupied the post, creditably enough, for only six months, and essentially as a stopgap until the regency crisis had passed. What he wanted, as he had made clear earlier, was a relatively undemanding cabinet post and a sinecure. The promise of the latter had been secured when Buckingham was lord lieutenant and Pitt now obliged with the former. He had previously offered his cousin the Admiralty as a result of some useful interventions in debate but Grenville had declined it on the grounds that he had no practical experience of naval matters. In June 1789, however, Pitt offered him the Home Office, a cabinet post which was not then thought too demanding. Grenville therefore accepted it and consequently entered the cabinet ahead of Dundas, the other member of the triumvirate. A few weeks later he resigned the offices of joint paymaster-general and vice-president of the Board of Trade.

Despite the fact that Grenville had now achieved the objectives that he had set himself at the beginning of the ministry, further sacrifices were required on Pitt's behalf. Initially he found the duties of the Home Office far from onerous and predicted that the French Revolution would be short-lived and have little impact internationally. However, he did introduce some notable improvements in the working practices of the office and was responsible for one important measure—the Canada Act of 1791. In keeping with his growing pragmatism, it was based on the assumption that the colony would ultimately become independent and was therefore designed to delay that event as long as possible. The fact that its central provisions—the partitioning of Canada and the establishment

of hereditary councils and elected assemblies—did not encounter serious opposition until the 1820s is testimony to reasonable success.

However, there were reasons why Grenville did not make more of a mark as home secretary. One was that he soon took up additional duties. During the first half of 1790 he spoke on a range of issues not connected with Home Office business and gave the appearance to at least one observer that he had become Pitt's natural successor as 'the first servant of the Crown' in the Commons. Then, in November 1790, in the aftermath of the general election in which Grenville had been returned once again for Buckinghamshire and in response to a crisis in the management of the House of Lords, Pitt persuaded him to accept a peerage and to take on the onerous task of leadership there. Although Grenville, who was created Baron Grenville on 25 November 1790, was flattered with the dignity, he was not overjoyed at the considerable extra responsibilities and, perhaps, his removal from the Commons just at the moment when his stock had risen there.

The other reason was that his tenure at the Home Office was short. In March and April 1791 the government threatened and then backed away from a war with Russia in the Ochakov crisis. The hawkish foreign secretary, the duke of Leeds, resigned in protest and Pitt turned first to Dundas as a replacement and, when he refused, to Grenville. Once again Grenville hesitated, although this time it was perfectly understandable given the tensions that Ochakov created in the cabinet and the much more onerous duties of the Foreign Office. Yet once again, on 21 April 1791, he finally accepted Pitt's call to duty. Compensation came in the form of being appointed to the sinecure office of ranger and keeper of St James's and Hyde parks on 13 December 1791, a post he exchanged in February 1794 for the much more lucrative sinecure of auditor of the exchequer, although he did not take up its £4000 salary until he ceased to be foreign secretary in 1801.

Foreign secretary, 1791–1801 When Grenville became foreign secretary he was on the verge of his thirty-second birthday and had acquired an appearance and habits that changed little thereafter. By that stage he needed spectacles for reading and had acquired a disproportionately prominent head and posterior. These, together with his habit of always wearing the same type of nondescript clothes, gave him the ungainly and goblin-like appearance that earned him the nickname Bogey. His lack of interest in his appearance was complementary to his style of life, which was dominated by government business of a particularly arduous kind. The Commons and the Whitehall departments had been his principal habitat since 1783 with the result that, although he joined White's and maintained a close circle of friends, he rarely partook of the daily round of social events that accompanied the parliamentary season. Instead he repaired quietly to the house that he had rented in Wimbledon since June 1784, following his decision to give up occupancy of Temple's grander accommodation in Pall Mall.

It was about this time that two decisive changes took place in Grenville's private life. The first was a change in his relationship with Buckingham. For most of the 1780s Grenville had regarded his own political career as secondary to that of his brother and had treated him with suitable deference. However, Buckingham's political career effectively came to an end in 1789 and he was incensed when Grenville did less than he had expected to press his claims for a dukedom or an office in the royal household. From that moment Grenville himself became the figurehead of the family's political interest and the relationship with Buckingham, although always warm, was never quite the same.

The much more important change was Grenville's marriage to his cousin Anne Pitt (1772–1864), daughter of Thomas *Pitt, first Baron Camelford (1737–1793), and Anne Wilkinson (d. 1803), on 18 July 1792. To some extent the marriage was arranged and prudential. Grenville had known Anne since her birth in 1772 and both Buckingham and her father were keen that he should marry her, Buckingham and Grenville both being attracted by the promised dowry of £20,000. In the personal sense, however, it began and endured as a marriage of affection. During their three years of courtship they grew increasingly attached, Grenville finding himself completely smitten by a teenager who, although not a beauty, possessed considerable intelligence and, like his mother and himself, was a devout Anglican. It is possible that this was his first physical relationship with a woman and it was certainly his last.

Grenville's foreign secretaryship, which he combined with leadership of the House of Lords, lasted a few months short of ten years, one of the longest tenures of the office in British history. The fact that it coincided with the onset of the French wars also made it one of the most demanding. Although there is some debate about the government's foreign policy and Grenville's role in its formulation, historians are agreed that he ran the Foreign Office and managed government business in the Lords with great efficiency. In the case of the Foreign Office he presided over a number of changes in administrative procedures and staffing that were all designed to make the processing and recording of information more professional. He managed the House of Lords in a similar vein and also adapted his style of speaking to suit the needs of leadership, making his interventions less interrogatory and more rounded. Lord Auckland was one of a number of observers who thought he was an outstanding leader and later research has confirmed that judgement.

In the case of foreign and, subsequently, war policy, hostile appraisals by whig historians in the nineteenth century and by a descendant of Grenville, Sir John Fortescue, in 1911 have been overtaken by later studies designed to contextualize problems and decisions, most notably by John Ehrman in his study of the younger Pitt. Moreover, although the surviving evidence makes it difficult to tell exactly what part each member of the controlling triumvirate (Pitt, Grenville, and Dundas) played in the successive phases of policy, it is accepted that Grenville's part was substantial at all times. There is also a growing consensus that the French wars presented the government with a wholly novel combination of problems, among which the conflict between secular ideologies, the conscription of popular armies, the emergence of Russia as a major participant, and their longevity and huge cost were particularly important. The government therefore took some time to adjust to these problems with the result that its war policy passed through distinct phases.

During the first phase—from the outbreak of war between the German powers and France in April 1792 and the French declaration of war on Britain in February 1793—Grenville believed that the German armies would defeat an economically weakened France before an invasion of the Netherlands obliged Britain, her treaty partner, to take part. He therefore favoured, in the interim, a twin-track strategy of minimizing the growth of radicalism at home by means such as the official encouragement given to John Reeves's loyalist associations, and maintaining neutrality in the war—principally by trying to persuade the Netherlands to reject Austrian overtures to join the allied side and by rebuffing French overtures for a bilateral peace.

The diplomatic arm of this policy was based on false assumptions, however. The German armies were not as successful as Grenville expected and the French economy managed to survive on a tide of paper money. When the swift progress of the French forces towards the Netherlands and the issuing of the decree abolishing free access to the Scheldt in November 1792 convinced the government that war with France was inevitable, Grenville's diplomacy took a form which prompted the French declaration of war.

The detached and often hostile attitude towards the continental powers that Grenville exhibited in the period prior to Britain's entry—an attitude encapsulated in the sarcastic words of one of his officials, Bland Burges, as 'salt water intrenchment'—continued to be a feature of his thinking during the first phase of the war (Jupp, 146). Throughout this period from February 1793 to September 1795 he believed that the continental monarchies had sufficient reasons of their own to win the war against France without their having to call upon Britain for more than naval, and modest auxiliary, support in the field—the last chiefly in the form of subsidized troops from the smaller courts. From this perspective he thought one of his principal tasks was to ensure that foreign rulers knew where their real interests lay.

However, despite his distaste for Britain's erstwhile allies, Grenville devoted himself energetically to the construction of the first allied coalition. Its history, in summary, is as follows. The objectives were to be the restoration of the *status quo ante* with question marks left over the issues of indemnities (or territorial revision) and whether Britain would insist on the restoration of the Bourbons. The means, initially, was a coalition whose axis would be Britain and the German powers, the latter making the main drive to recover the Low Countries, and whose supporting parts would be as many of the other powers in the Baltic, Mediterranean, and Atlantic as could be gathered together. However, when Prussia began to look for the separate peace with France that materialized in April 1795, a different course was chosen. This led to an axis consisting of separate alliances between Britain and Russia and Britain and Austria and to a military strategy which envisaged allied operations combining with those of French royalists brought into play by British efforts. As it happened this coalition finally came into being in September 1795, just at the point when the military balance shifted decisively in France's favour. This led many in the government to regard a peace as a better option than war.

Grenville contributed a great deal to these events. In the case of war objectives and the hope of an alliance with the two German powers he combined caution with a particular distrust of Prussia. He disagreed with Pitt's readiness to commit the allies to the restoration of the Bourbons and indemnities, and was therefore responsible for the ambivalent posture the government struck on these issues. In addition, he was extremely hostile to the decision to subsidize Prussia's participation in the coalition. He disliked subsidies in general but opposed one to Prussia on the grounds that she was bound by treaty to fight for the recovery of the Netherlands and therefore had no right to require subsidies to do so, especially as she was likely to use the money to further her own objectives in eastern Europe. He fell out bitterly with Pitt on this issue and would have resigned had not a sudden twist in events stayed his hand. Although his hostility to the subsidy was probably not a major reason why Prussia decided to turn her back on the allies and make a separate peace, it certainly did not encourage her to continue with the war.

Grenville's contribution to other aspects of policy was more positive. He was particularly active in making agreements with the secondary powers such as Denmark, Sardinia, the two Sicilies, and much to his satisfaction, given his father's stamp tax, with the USA. In addition, it was he who was responsible for the negotiation of axis alliances with Russia and Austria. Moreover, he placed considerable faith in the success of a military strategy in which Austria liberated the Netherlands while French royalists took the fight to France, a cause which he took particularly to heart and which he did most to initiate.

How far Grenville was responsible for the failure of these plans it is difficult to say. He certainly overestimated the strength of royalism in France and consistently underestimated that of republicanism. In addition, he placed excessive confidence in the readiness of Austria to liberate the Netherlands, given that she was anxious to exchange Belgium for Bavaria at the first opportunity. On the other hand the evidence suggests that both German powers were concerned chiefly with their rivalry in central Europe and that in Austria's case no amount of blandishments would have persuaded her to give priority to allied operations.

In the two years between the summers of 1795 and 1797 the government's war policy passed through a further phase, the distinguishing features of which were to postpone any further operations on the continent, to explore the possibilities of a peace with France, and to take the offensive against enemy possessions in the West Indies. The underlying objective, if peace was unobtainable on acceptable terms to Britain and her allies, was to manoeuvre into a position to fight the war more effectively. Thus, in addition to the sending of an expeditionary force to the Caribbean, there were four separate negotiations with the Directory, culminating in a failure at Lille in July and August 1797.

Although Grenville participated fully in what was more Pitt's and Dundas's strategy, he viewed it with extreme caution. His own hopes remained focused on drawing Russia and Austria into effective operations with French royalists—a policy which received more support in the cabinet following the accession of the Portland whigs in July 1794. He was therefore unenthusiastic about the expedition to the West Indies. In addition, he was determined that the negotiations with France should be conducted in collaboration with the allies and should be based on the principal of indemnities for their and Britain's efforts as well as the restoration of the territorial *status quo ante* in Europe. He was therefore opposed to a unilateral peace that had the effect of trading French hegemony in Europe for British hegemony overseas.

Grenville's influence on events was at its strongest during the abortive Lille peace talks. Earlier he had fumed at the abandonment of the counter-revolutionary strategy in 1795 and had been frustrated in the following year when the successful negotiation of a subsidy treaty with Austria coincided with the emperor's being forced by military set-backs to negotiate a preliminary treaty with France. The result was that although he was now unable to insist that the Lille talks be conducted with Austria, he was determined not to allow Pitt to negotiate a peace on lower terms than he felt necessary. He therefore insisted successfully that indemnities rather than the *status quo ante* be the basis of any bargain in order to present France with a tough negotiating stance, and would probably have resigned had that not been agreed to. In the event, a change of leadership in the Directory brought the negotiations to an end, but Grenville's authority in the cabinet had increased and with it battle was joined between the continentalists and those who supported a blue water policy.

The last phase of the government's war policy for which Grenville shared responsibility lasted from August 1798 until February 1801. It began with a vigorous debate within the cabinet on whether to construct another European coalition or whether to place the emphasis upon overseas conquest. As a result of a number of encouraging developments on the continent, the former path was chosen and a second coalition was formed consisting of alliances between Britain and Russia and Russia and Austria. Its military strategy consisted of a two-pronged assault: one thrust through Switzerland by Russian and imperial forces and the other through the Netherlands by Russian and British forces which would be aided, it was hoped, by large numbers of downtrodden Orangeists. Both assaults, however, ended in defeat in October 1799, that through the Netherlands foundering on overstretched supply lines and the paucity of local support. The government therefore scaled down its hopes for a European offensive and turned to a policy of defending its overseas interests.

Grenville's influence during this phase was most strongly felt in the construction of the second coalition and in the planning of its military strategy. Indeed this was the period when his influence was at its height and when Pitt and Dundas seem to have been willing to give him his head. Grenville therefore initially tried to bring into being a project sponsored principally by the king: a four-power coalition between Britain, Russia, and the German powers which would have agreed aims and objectives and whose military operations would be conducted by a permanent council of ministers. However, although some of Grenville's personal contributions to this idea bore fruit later in the planning of the third and fourth coalitions, the scheme foundered on Prussia's decision to prolong her peace with France and on Grenville's refusal to compromise with Austria on the terms of a subsidy. The axis of the second coalition was therefore as limited and disjointed as the first, with Britain allied to Russia and Russia to Austria.

Grenville's investment in the military plan was even greater. He believed that his faith in a continental strategy based upon counter-revolution would be vindicated and that his reputation would be secured by a brilliant victory in the Low Countries. He was therefore cruelly disappointed when he discovered that he had overestimated the number of Russian troops that would be available and had placed far too high a premium on the strength of counter-revolutionary feeling in the Netherlands. The one major war policy that can be regarded as his and on which he 'founded my hopes of credit and success' failed to topple the enemy (Jupp, 230). Instead the only positive results were the capture of the Dutch fleet and the delaying of further French successes in Italy and central Europe.

Grenville refused to despair of a continental strategy, however. In the aftermath of the Dutch débâcle he pinned his hopes on further co-operation with Russia, but in the light of the tsar's withdrawal into what would eventually become a threatening 'armed neutrality' he reluctantly made an agreement with Austria designed to advance towards France along the Mediterranean riviera. When this also failed, leaving Austria to sue for peace, he reluctantly conceded the case for a defensive posture until such time as the continental monarchies were ready and willing to take to the field once more. The scaling down of the government's objectives led him to rethink his position on a peace. Hitherto one of his objections to a settlement had been the instability of French governments but by 1800 the consulate seemed likely to endure. Thus although he did not abandon a continental strategy—he was thinking of ways to challenge the 'armed neutrality' and to prepare Portugal to act, if required, with Spain—he did concede in November 1800 that there might be a case for discussions with Bonaparte.

Resignation, retirement, and the return to politics, February 1801 to January 1806 In February 1801 Grenville followed Pitt and the bulk of the government in resigning in the face of the king's refusal to allow Catholics to sit in parliament as an accompaniment to the union with Ireland. As was the case with the government's war strategy, Grenville had exercised a consistent influence on its Irish policies. Building on the experience he had gained in the 1780s, he played an important role in 1794–5 in ensuring that Earl Fitzwilliam was dismissed as lord lieutenant for siding with the Irish whigs, and between 1798 and 1800 he was a major contributor to the scheme of union. He was therefore responsible for the clauses dealing with the representation of the Irish peerage in the House of Lords and took a leading part at Pitt's side in devising the tactics on the Catholic question, his own view being that concessions were essential to prevent a second uprising. Above all he seems to have played a crucial role in the devising of a new relationship between the various religious institutions and the state in the two countries, part of which involved the state payment of Catholic and dissenting clergy. The king's hostility to Catholic relief put paid to the scheme but it is arguable that it laid the basis for a similar idea in a memorandum of 7 August 1828 sent to George IV and sponsored by Wellington, the brother of one of Grenville's closest friends, Lord Wellesley.

Following his resignation Grenville contemplated retirement from active politics. He sold his London house in Cleveland Row, which had been built following his marriage, and moved all his books and papers to Dropmore, a house and a small estate he had purchased in Buckinghamshire in 1792. It was there that he intended to devote himself to his wife and friends, to reading and writing, and to the landscaping of the demesne and to the planting of trees and gardens that were eventually to become famous. Three years later, in 1804, his proprietorial duties were increased when his wife inherited Camelford House in Oxford Street and Boconnoc in Cornwall, the latter being the cornerstone of estates in excess of 20,000 acres.

However, the prospect of very early retirement—Grenville was only forty-one when he resigned—never materialized. The principal reason was his opposition to the Addington government's treaty of Amiens, which, he argued, conceded two basic points never envisaged by its predecessor: the abandoning of means to renew the war in collaboration with allies, and the acceptance of a permanent increase in the power of France and a consequent decrease in that of Britain. Grenville felt so strongly on the issue that he wrote a stream of letters and made a major speech along these lines. The other reason was of a more personal kind. Thus in the course of 1801 Buckingham's personal followers and many of Grenville's own admirers emerged as the 'Grenvilles' or a 'new opposition' to the government, largely on the issue of Amiens. In addition, he learned that Pitt had had a hand in the negotiation of the treaty but had failed to take the first opportunity to tell him of his role.

These events led to one of the more extraordinary changes of course in modern political history, for Grenville was eventually drawn into becoming the joint head with Fox of a coalition between the 'new' and the 'old' oppositions, and into a political separation from Pitt. Grenville's purpose throughout this complex and intermittent process was the formation of a government that would be more capable than Addington's of confronting Bonaparte's hegemony—a purpose that became more determined following the renewal of the war in May 1803. In the aftermath of Amiens he initially acted separately from the 'Grenvilles' and looked to Pitt's resuming the lead of a Pittite–Addingtonian government in which he would play a part. On the eve of the renewal of war, however, when Pitt was negotiating with Addington to form such a government, he changed his mind and called for a union of parties that would include members of both the new and old oppositions. Pitt thought sufficiently highly of Grenville's abilities to add this to the hand he was playing but Addington called his bluff and the negotiations broke down, therefore delaying Pitt's return to office by more than a year.

Following the renewal of the war doubts about Addington's capacity to manage it grew with the result that Grenville, who was by now acting more like a leader of the new opposition, approached Pitt once again with the idea of a government of all the parties with his cousin at its head. Pitt rejected the proposition, however, so Grenville and his colleagues approached Fox, who agreed to act with them to bring the government down and to replace it with a union of parties. It was against this background that the decisive event in Grenville's political transformation took place. Thus in May 1804 Addington's government was forced to resign in the face of the opposition of the Pittites, the Grenvilles, and the Foxite whigs. The king called upon Pitt to form an administration which would exclude Fox and would not propose Catholic relief. Pitt then turned to Grenville but the latter declined to accept office on the grounds of Fox's exclusion—a reason that was strengthened considerably in his mind by Fox's declaring that he would not stand in his way. Grenville's objective of a national government under Pitt's leadership which would return to the policies of the 1790s had therefore been wrecked, partly by circumstances beyond his control, and partly by his alliance with, and sudden loyalty to, Fox—a politician whom the king would not accept in office and who was almost Grenville's opposite in character and political creed. Indeed the only views they shared were support for the abolition of the slave trade and for Catholic relief.

Grenville's course thereafter left his new colleagues frustrated. Having failed to bring about a national government he decided to refrain from the course of systematic opposition advocated by the Grenvilles and practised by the whigs. Thus, although he was one of the sponsors in 1805 of the first Catholic petition to the imperial parliament, he eschewed all thoughts of active party leadership. Moreover, during the winter of 1805–6, when the war was going badly for the third coalition, he and Fox were at loggerheads over policy, Grenville favouring a new allied concert and Fox calling for peace. It was at this point that Pitt died and the king, following the advice of the duke of Portland, the most senior member of the cabinet, asked Grenville to form a government that included Fox.

Prime minister, 1806–1807 Although Grenville had more experience of office than any of his colleagues and most of the outgoing government, he was in other respects unsuited to be prime minister. He feared the physical and mental burdens of the post and was unwilling to resign his more lucrative sinecure in order to occupy it. He therefore proposed that Earl Spencer become a sort of dummy prime minister while he took one of the secretaryships of state, and agreed to take the lead only when Fox agreed to arrange for trustees to manage the sinecure until Grenville's prime ministership came to an end. He was also poor at managing others. What mattered most to Grenville was policy and the reasoning that had led him to this or that position. The difficulties raised with others were nearly always a secondary consideration. He recognized this as a weakness and told Buckingham on one occasion that he was not competent in 'the management of men' and never had been (Jupp, 412). Moreover, he was in a comparatively weak political position. Thus, although he was the prime minister, Fox, the foreign secretary, was the leader of the strongest party in what had been the coalition of the new and old oppositions, and the Grenvilles were less numerous than two of the other political groupings, the Addingtonians (the followers of Lord Sidmouth) and the Pittites.

Despite all his misgivings Grenville proved to be a very hard-working prime minister with a distinctive style of management. In keeping with the professionalism he had encouraged in the home and foreign departments, he conducted business in a methodical and businesslike manner and developed a system in which he worked closely with Fox and the other party chiefs but in about equal measure with the other departmental heads. This was supplemented with regular cabinet meetings, at least once and sometimes twice a week. The result was a form of departmental government in which Grenville tried to supervise the whole without his colleagues feeling that they were being treated like ciphers.

The burdens of the office were compounded by Grenville's conviction that a national government was required to confront a French hegemony that was enlarged enormously by the military victories over the two German powers. In the government's initial form Grenville found places for four of the five principal parties—his own, the Foxites, the Addingtonians, and the followers of the prince of Wales—and made gestures to the fifth, the Pittites, which were sufficient to prevent them from going into systematic opposition. However, the tenacity with which Grenville held his convictions and his increasing nervousness about the government's vulnerability meant that he never believed this to be sufficient. He therefore spent a considerable amount of his time as prime minister trying to construct a national government, or a 'ministry of all the talents' as it was sarcastically referred to at the time. The two principal objects of his attention were the Pittites—particularly Canning, for whom he had great respect and affection—and the king, who had considerable influence over the independent MPs. In both cases his manoeuvres proved to be self-defeating. Thus in a series of unsuccessful attempts to recruit Canning he managed to antagonize both Lord Sidmouth and the Pittites, and even left Canning confused. Moreover, the king was not pleased when he was asked to agree to a general election in the autumn of 1806, ostensibly because of a government reshuffle following Fox's death in September but secretly because Grenville wanted to prove to the Pittites and the independents that his government had royal support. The king took the view that an election was unnecessary because the government had never lacked majorities in the existing house and gave his consent, but not his customary donation to election expenses, with extreme reluctance. The upshot was that Grenville increased his already substantial majority by twenty to thirty votes but at the cost of antagonizing the king and of stirring up party rivalries in the constituencies—the very reverse of what he wanted to achieve.

The general strategy of the government was also dominated by the continental débâcle which left Russia as Britain's only great-power ally. As far as foreign policy was concerned the widely anticipated falling-out between Grenville and Fox never materialized. Both agreed, albeit from different motives, on negotiations with France and Fox gave way to Grenville's insistence that these should lead to a multilateral, as opposed to a bilateral, peace in order to protect the interests of Britain's allies. It was on this point that negotiations broke down, although by the time they did Fox was dead.

The other feature of foreign policy was the setting in train of a number of military operations stretching from the Dardanelles to Buenos Aires. Initially an expedition was sent to Sicily to hold the island as a demonstration of good faith to the tsar, and plans were laid to assist Portugal in the event of a Franco-Spanish invasion. Later other expeditions were sent to the Dardanelles on behalf of the tsar, to Alexandria to prevent the French occupation of Egypt, and to the River Plate to consolidate the unauthorized capture of Buenos Aires and to initiate a campaign in South America that would deny the French the resources of the Spanish overseas empire. Although all these operations were designed to harass Bonaparte until such time as the great powers were ready to continue the war, they all failed. Further, when the great powers did show signs of renewing their activity in the wake of the devastating defeat of Prussia in October 1806, Grenville was too miserly to offer them anything near the subsidies they demanded. Overall the verdict of history has been that Grenville scattered too many resources too widely and to no good effect. A fairer assessment would be that although the underlying motive was sensible the end results were a failure.

With one exception, Grenville's domestic policy was dominated by what was perceived to be the necessity of preparing the country for a renewal of the war. The exception was the abolition of the slave trade—a cause to which Grenville had been committed since the 1780s. The government's first initiative was the 1806 Foreign Slave Trade Act, which gave legal force to an 1805 proclamation banning British subjects from importing slaves into captured colonies. Its second, which Grenville proposed and managed on the government's behalf, was the famous Slave Trade Abolition Act of 1807. Although history rightly credits William Wilberforce with the achievement of this measure on the basis of his leadership of the national anti-slavery movement, it is now accepted that it was Grenville who made the decisive move in its favour at the parliamentary level.

In other respects domestic policy was focused on achieving what Grenville referred to later as a 'defensive and *husbanding* system' (Grenville to Earl Fitzwilliam, 9 Jan 1809, BL, Add. MS 58955, fols. 98–100), the principal features of which were a reform of recruitment into the regular army, a new method of funding the war, and an even-handed policy in Ireland that would prevent conflict there being a threat to the war effort. Despite the fact that he had no direct departmental responsibility for any of these policies, Grenville's contribution to their formulation was considerable. In the case of the army reforms his influence was most strongly felt in the introduction of limited service for the regulars, his impact on other aspects being limited by his inability to control the mercurial conduct of William Windham, the war minister. Moreover, he was the principal author of 'the new plan of finance' unveiled in 1807, which was designed to finance a war for thirteen years without the need to increase taxes. However, the strains of producing these two measures—and the signs were visible by February 1807—were not rewarded. The army reforms failed to produce the anticipated recruits through the reserves, and the new plan was thought too complicated and inflexible to be a success.

Grenville's Irish policy was designed to conciliate each of the parties: the pro- and anti-union lobbies within the protestant élite by such measures as an even-handed distribution of patronage and plans to reinvigorate the Church of Ireland; and the Catholics by appointing a few of their number to offices and by acting as patron of the campaign to secure Catholic relief. Although its underlying objectives of maximizing Irish parliamentary support for the government and minimizing the potential of Irish issues to frustrate the government's war policy were met during 1806, the policy ran into the sand in 1807. The crux of the problem was the government's wish to dissuade Catholic leaders in Dublin from presenting a petition for Catholic relief to the new parliament on the grounds that many of its members, including Grenville, would be bound to support it and that the king would be equally bound to oppose it, thereby bringing about the government's demise. Grenville and his colleagues therefore decided to introduce a bill that would enable Catholics to serve in the army up to the rank of general in the hope that this would persuade the Catholic leaders to postpone their petition until a more propitious moment.

It was on this issue that the government fell. Grenville was tired and distracted by other problems besetting the government. He hoped that he could persuade the king that the bill simply replicated an Irish Act of 1793, to which the monarch had then given his assent, even though it actually went further. The king smelt a rat and refused his assent, demanding that his ministers pledge themselves not to raise the Catholic question with him again. Although Grenville and his Foxite colleagues agreed to drop the bill, they declined to take the pledge and, in the former's case, left office on 25 March 1807 with a huge sigh of relief.

Leader of the whig party, 1807–1817 Although Grenville followed the precedent of February 1801 and toyed with the idea of retirement, he soon adopted the role of leader of the whig party. The fundamental reasons were his colleagues' expectation that he should do so and his hostility to the Pittites for having taken the king's side during the crisis over the Catholic question. In his view their 'unconstitutional' actions meant that they no longer deserved to be known as Pittites and were best referred to as tories. However, it was not a position for which he was ideally suited. On the positive side, he had had much more experience of office than any other member of either the Grenvillite or Foxite partners in what was still a coalition party. In addition, he was widely admired for his intellectual qualities, particularly by some of the younger activists, and, partly for this reason, received wholehearted support from the party in his successful campaign to be elected chancellor of Oxford University in 1810. The negative features, however, were more weighty. He was the head of the minority partnership in the party and sat in the Lords at a time when the party was exceptionally strong in the Commons. Moreover, although he was always deferred to by Lord Grey, the leader of the Foxite wing, he was a stranger to the heartlands of Foxite politics—Brooks's Club and Holland House. Above all, there were serious differences between Grenville and the bulk of the Foxites on policy. Grenville's programme consisted of the continuation of a defensive war, Catholic emancipation with safeguards for the protestant establishment, opposition to economic and parliamentary reform, and an economic policy which included his new plan of finance, a return to the gold standard, and the advancement of free trade. The majority of the Foxites, however, favoured a peace rather than war, Catholic emancipation without safeguards, and progress with reform. The only subject on which they were not initially at loggerheads was economic policy, largely because it was not one in which many Foxites had an interest.

During 1807–12 the basic feature of Grenville's leadership was annual exchanges with the party leaders prior to the opening of parliamentary sessions which were designed to hammer out an agreed line of opposition. In his classic study, *The Whig Party, 1807–1812* (1939), Michael Roberts examined this from a predominantly Foxite perspective and underlined the constant wrangling not only between the two wings of the party but also between the moderates and the radicals in the Foxite wing. On the other hand, research suggests that Grenville's leadership

had succeeded by 1812 in establishing the following compromise policies: support for a defensive war or peace negotiations; a refusal to office without the royal assent to a Catholic relief bill but no specific commitments on the safeguards that might accompany it; the abolition of sinecures coupled with state pensions for retired ministers; and measures of parliamentary reform that stopped short of enfranchising large towns. There is consensus, however, that whatever success Grenville had in reconciling party leaders over policy, he botched one of four opportunities they had to take office in this period when they could have done so on their own terms. This occurred when the regency was established in February 1811. It was then that his concern to act consistently with his conduct in 1788–9 and his high-handed dealings with both his colleagues and the prince of Wales played a part in maintaining Spencer Perceval's government in office.

After 1812 Grenville's influence declined. This was due partly to the waning influence of the party chiefs in the Lords over the direction of policy, and partly to developments that made most of Grenville's compromise package redundant. One of these was the success of both the Peninsular campaign and the fourth coalition, which obviously put paid to the idea of a defensive war. Another was Lord Liverpool's establishing of the Catholic question as an open one for his government. And a third was the post-war surge in popular pressure for economic and parliamentary reform. Thus, although Grenville made a powerful case against the corn law (1815) and played an important part in persuading the whig party to accept many of the provisions of the 1815 peace settlement, he fell out with his colleagues on the restoration of the Bourbons and on the need for the re-enactment of Pitt's and his own measures of the 1790s to curb popular radicalism, both of which he supported. Indeed it was on this last issue that he retired from the leadership in 1817 and handed over to Lord Grey.

Retirement and death, 1817–1834 On this occasion Grenville's retirement from active politics was permanent. He therefore declined playing a part with the Grenville group which quickly re-entered the old Pittite fold in 1822. He chose instead to enjoy the company of family and friends at his estates at Dropmore and Boconnoc, and to restrict his political activities to correspondence and the occasional speech or pamphlet. In 1823 a minor stroke inhibited his movements, but his 1828 pamphlet in favour of abandoning the sinking fund was influential and he took particular pleasure in the passage of Catholic relief in 1829, writing that this convinced him that his life had not been 'in vain' (Jupp, 459). He died at Dropmore on 12 January 1834 and was buried in Burnham on 20 January.

Grenville had a considerable and sometimes critical influence on British political history for some thirty-five years, longer in fact than each of the more famous politicians with whom he was associated—Pitt, Fox, and Grey. Part of that influence arose from measures for which he was wholly or chiefly responsible, such as the Canada Act, but a much greater part stemmed from policies that he devised with others, most particularly war policy in the

1790s. On the other hand, his influence and his place in history could have been greater. One of the reasons for this was his family's appetite for public honours and public money—an appetite that was vilified by contemporaries and historians alike and which Grenville shared, albeit to a more modest and understandable degree than his immensely rich brother. The most important reason, however, was that he lacked the personal qualities that attracted affection and loyalty from all types of politicians. Grenville's strengths lay in a brilliant intellect, an ability to spot the connections between different spheres of policy, and reasoned arguments in favour of specific policies. Thus his one clear legacy to the whig party was the commitment of its economically literate members to free trade, a subject upon which he had lectured to them and, many years earlier, so he claimed, to the younger Pitt.   P. J. JUPP

Sources P. Jupp, *Lord Grenville, 1759–1834* (1985) · J. Ehrman, *The younger Pitt*, 3: *The consuming struggle* (1996) · M. Duffy, 'Pitt, Grenville and the control of British foreign policy in the 1790s', *Knights errant and true Englishmen: British foreign policy, 1660–1800*, ed. J. Black (1989), 151–77 · A. D. Harvey, *Lord Grenville, 1759–1834: a bibliography* (1989) · GEC, *Peerage*

Archives BL, corresp. and papers, Add. MSS 58855–59478, 69038–69411 · BL, papers supplementing the Dropmore papers, Add. MSS 71587–71596 · Duke U., Perkins L., letters · Hunt. L. · PRO, letterbook of dispatches from Berlin, PRO 30/8/338 | Balliol Oxf., letters to Richard Jenkyns · BL, corresp. with Lord Auckland, Add. MSS 34426–34460, *passim* · BL, corresp. with third Earl Bathurst, loan 57 · BL, corresp. with Lord Bute, Add. MSS 36808–36810 · BL, corresp. with Francis Drake, Add. MS 46822 · BL, letters to Henry Dundas, Add. MSS 40100–40102 · BL, corresp. with Sir William Fremantle, Add. MSS 58966–58967 · BL, letters to Sir Willoughby Gordon, Add. MS 49476 · BL, corresp. with Thomas Grenville, Add. MSS 41852–41853, 42058 · BL, corresp. with Sir William Hamilton, Add. MSS 41199–41200 · BL, letters to third earl of Hardwicke, Add. MSS 35349–36278, *passim* · BL, corresp. with Lord and Lady Holland, Add. MSS 51530–51531 · BL, corresp. with Sir Robert Murray Keith, Add. MSS 35543–35544 · BL, letters to duke of Leeds, Add. MSS 28060–28067, *passim* · BL, corresp. with earls of Liverpool, Add. MSS 38220–38331, 38472, 38570–38576 · BL, letters to earls of Liverpool, loan 72 · BL, letters to Lord Macartney, Add. MS 62665 · BL, corresp. with first Viscount Melville, Add. MS 40101 · BL, corresp. with Robert Peel, Add. MSS 40366–40401 · BL, corresp. with Lord Henry Spencer, Add. MSS 34470–34471 · BL, Spencer MSS, letters to second Earl Spencer · BL, letters to Count Starhemberg, Add. MSS 39841–39842 · BL, corresp. with Lord Wellesley, Add. MSS 37282–37297, *passim* 70927–70928 · BL, corresp. with William Windham, Add. MSS 37844–37910 · BLPES, letters to Francis Horner · Bodl. Oxf., corresp. with Patrick Craufurd Bruce; corresp. with Sir James Burgess; letters to Richard Herber; letters to Sir John Newport; corresp. with third Baron Talbot of Malahide · Broomhall, Dunfermline, corresp. with Lord Elgin · Bucks. RLSS, corresp. with Scrope Bernard; corresp. with Sir William Fremantle; letters to John Grenville; letters to Duke of Somerset · CKS, letters to William Pitt and bishop of Lincoln · Cumbria AS, Carlisle, corresp. with Lord Lowther · Devon RO, letters to Sir Thomas Dyke Acland; corresp. with Lord Simouth · Duke U., Perkins L., letters to Charles Moss; letters to Sir John Newport · Hants. RO, corresp. with William Wickham · Hunt. L., corresp. with marquess and duke of Buckingham; letters to Thomas Crawfurd; letters to Thomas Grenville; letters to Charles O'Conor · Morgan L., letters to Sir James Murray-Pulteney · NA Scot., corresp. with Lord Melville · NL Scot., corresp. with William Elliot; corresp. with Robert Liston; corresp. with Lord Minto; letters to John Ramsay · NL Wales, corresp. with C. W. W. Wynn; letters to H. W. W. Wynn ·

NMM, corresp. with Lord Carysfort [copies] · NRA Scotland, priv. coll., letters to William Adam · NRA, priv. coll., letters to Lord Ranfurly · Pembroke College, Oxford, letters mainly to G. W. Hall · priv. coll., corresp. with Spencer Perceval, etc. · priv. coll., letters to Francis Wilson · PRO, corresp. with Lord Hervey, FO528 · PRO, corresp. with William Pitt, PRO30/8 · PRO NIre., corresp. with Lord Castlereagh · Royal Arch., letters to George III · Sandon Hall, Staffordshire, Harrowby Manuscript Trust, corresp. with Lord Harrowby · Sheff. Arch., corresp. with Edmund Burke; corresp. with Earl Fitzwilliam · U. Durham L., corresp. with second Earl Grey · W. Yorks. AS, Leeds, letters to George Canning · Woburn Abbey, Bedfordshire, letters to sixth duke of Bedford; corresp. with Sir Morton Eden

Likenesses G. Romney, oils, 1781, Eton · G. Dupont, oils, 1792 · J. Hoppner, oils, *c.*1800, NPG [*see illus.*] · J. Hoppner, oils, *c.*1800, North Carolina Museum of Art, Raleigh, North Carolina · J. Sayers, caricature, etching, 1804, NPG · Argus [C. Williams], caricature, coloured etching, pubd 1806, V&A · J. Nollekens, marble bust, 1810, Royal Collection · Paul Pry [W. Heath], caricature, coloured etching, pubd 1810, V&A · T. Philips, oils, exh. RA 1810, RCS Eng. · W. Owen, oils, exh. RA 1812, Christ Church Oxf. · J. B. Comelli, bust, *c.*1820–1830; sold at Stowe sale, 1848 · J. Chapman, bust, after 1830 · J. S. Agar, engraving (after W. Owen) · T. A. Dean, stipple (after J. Jackson), BM, NPG; repro. in W. Jerdan, *National Portrait Gallery of illustrious and eminent personages of the nineteenth century, with memoires*, 5 vols. (1830–34) · J. Fittler, engraving (after portrait by T. Philips) · M. Gauci, lithograph (after C. Proby), BM, NPG · G. Hayter, group portrait, oils (*The trial of Queen Caroline, 1820*), NPG · G. Jones, group portrait, oils (*Reception of the prince regent in Oxford, June 1814*), Magd. Oxf. · H. Meyer, two engravings (after W. Owen) · E. Radclyffe, engraving (after J. Chapman), repro. in W. Dowling, *Poets and statesmen, their homes and haunts, in the neighbourhood of Eton and Windsor*, 2nd edn (1857) · S. W. Reynolds, engraving (after J. Hoppner) · E. Scriven, engraving (after J. Hoppner)

Gresham, Edward (1565–1613), astrologer, of Stainford, Yorkshire, was born on 14 April 1565, presumably in Stainford. He was probably connected to the London commercial and financial dynasty, perhaps through Sir Richard Gresham, who had acquired extensive monastic properties in Yorkshire at the dissolution. Gresham (or a namesake) matriculated at Trinity College, Cambridge, in 1584, proceeding MA in 1606. He divided his time between Stainford and London, where he lived next to Dyers' Hall at Thames Street.

Gresham held advanced ideas in astronomy. During the plague of 1603 rumours were fathered on him and John Dee to the effect that its future course depended on the imminent fall of a planet to earth. To dispel such idle notions he compiled a scholarly treatise on the planets, *Astrosteron*, in which he championed the Copernican system and denied the existence of solid planetary spheres, arguing that the heavenly bodies moved freely in space. For several years, between 1603 and 1607, he published astrological almanacs. The edition for 1605, no longer extant, was said to have foretold the Gunpowder Plot so accurately that it brought him under suspicion of complicity. Gresham himself, however, placed little reliance on 'vulgar astrologie', and was one of the earliest English champions of a reformed astrological science. A capable mathematician and astronomer, he compiled detailed planetary tables for astrological use. To refute charges of atheism he cited two religious treatises he had written, 'Sabbath-dayes exercises' and 'Positions in divinitie' (apparently unpublished and now lost). He also practised medicine and magic, and the latter brought him an unsavoury reputation.

In his last years Gresham's fame as a magician drew him into the sordid court intrigues surrounding the divorce of Robert Devereux, third earl of Essex. The countess of Essex had employed the magician Simon Forman to secure the love of Robert Carr (later earl of Somerset), the king's favourite, and to rid her of an unwanted husband. On Forman's death in 1611 she approached Gresham through her confidante Anne Turner, and he employed his skill in efforts to render the earl impotent and to win the queen's goodwill. Essex's alleged impotence was the central issue facing the royal commission set up in 1613, which duly ruled the marriage unconsummated and granted a divorce, freeing the countess to marry Carr. It seems that Gresham also employed his magical arts against Sir Thomas Overbury, an open critic of the proposed marriage, whom the countess was determined to remove. Richard Weston, an associate of Gresham's, was certainly involved in the plot against Overbury and was later hanged for his part in the murder.

Gresham himself did not live to see the outcome of any of these nefarious schemes. He died in London on 13 January 1613 and was buried the next day at All Saints-the-Less. Shortly before his death he had conveyed his magical paraphernalia (lead and wax images, crosses, and charms) to Richard Weston, directing them to be buried secretly. He left only a daughter, Jane, a lunatic. A near-contemporary judged that 'without all question he was a very skilfull man in the Mathematicks, and in his latter time in Witchcraft'. He was fortunate in dying before the Overbury scandal became public; a maidservant, less lucky, is said to have been hanged subsequently as a witch.　　BERNARD CAPP, rev.

Sources E. Gresham, 'Astrostereon', Bodl. Oxf., MS Ashmole 242 · [M. Sparke], *The narrative history of King James* (1651) · B. S. Capp, *Astrology and the popular press: English almanacs, 1500–1800* (1979) · probate, 1613, GL, Act books, Archdeaconry Court of London, Register 5, fol. 22v · Venn, *Alum. Cant.*

Gresham, James (*fl.* 1626), poet, is known only by his publication, in 1626, of *The Picture of Incest, Lively Portraicted in the Historie of Cinyras and Myrrha*. This rare poem, written in heroic couplets, is a translation from book x of Ovid's *Metamorphoses* and is a competent performance. Only two copies of the text are extant, owned by the British Library and by Yale University Library; the former was reprinted by A. B. Grosart in 1876.

The author may be identical with the James Gresham, gentleman, who married Elizabeth, the widow of Roger Hurst, a brewer, in 1631. In June 1636 he was forced by mounting pressure from his own creditors to petition the king for clemency over the repayment of Hurst's substantial debts. The council was instructed to assist Gresham, although his beleaguered financial position continued until as late as January 1637.

ALSAGER VIAN, rev. ELIZABETH HARESNAPE

Sources STC, 1475–1640 · BL cat. · CSP dom., 1636–7, 30, 414 · DNB

Gresham, Sir John (*c.*1495–1556). *See under* Gresham, Sir Richard (*c.*1485–1549).

Gresham, Sir Richard (*c.*1485–1549), mercer, merchant adventurer, and mayor of London, was born at Holt, Norfolk, about 1485, probably the third of the four surviving sons—William, Thomas, Richard, and **Sir John Gresham** (*c.*1495–1556)—of John Gresham and his wife, Alice, *née* Blythe, of Stratton. His father's family had since at least the late fourteenth century been resident in the Norfolk village which bore their name. His grandfather James Gresham set the family on the path to fame and fortune and by the mid-fifteenth century had adopted the well-known family crest of the grasshopper. At about that time he moved to Holt, some 3 miles distant from the ancestral home, where he built the imposing manor house located in the centre of the village in which Richard was born and spent his childhood. Richard Gresham was apprenticed to the eminent London mercer and stapler John Middleton (*d.* 1509). During his frequent sojourns in the great commercial city of Antwerp he formed a close friendship with one William Copeland. This was to stand him in good stead when he took his freedom in the Mercers' Company in 1507, and he and Copeland entered into a partnership.

Richard Gresham and William Copeland's partnership During the ensuing decade (*c.*1508–1517) the two young men prospered mightily. When during these years interest rates fell on the Antwerp bourse and English commerce expanded at the Brabant fairs (1505–9 and 1514–15), the partners engaged in the normal mercers' trade, buying silks such as velvet, satin, taffeta, and sarsenet which, together with fine woollen cloths and tapestries, commanded a ready market in London. Such business was transacted at the quarterly markets, known as the koud (winter), Pasche (Easter), Sinxen (Whitsun), and bamus (autumn) marts. They accumulated sufficient cash to buy their wares by exporting English cloth or by taking up money on the exchange from their fellow merchants to finance their operations. Their standing among that group at this time was reflected in the ½ per cent discount they could obtain on the rate they had to pay when obtaining such credits. These were balmy days for the young Gresham and his partner, when, availing themselves of the increasingly cheap commercial credits on the Antwerp bourse, they created a major trading house and established themselves among the élite members of the London mercantile community.

Nor was their position seriously threatened when Habsburg intervention on the Antwerp bourse (in 1509–13 and late 1515–17) resulted in a rise in interest rates and caused a recession in commercial activity at the Low Countries marts. Like their peers, they responded to the new and threatening situation by deploying their growing volume of commercial assets in new business ventures in order to ensure the stability of their trading house. During the first Antwerp crisis of 1509 to 1513 the scope for such diversification was limited to the founding of direct trades to France, the Baltic, and the Levant. Yet, limited as the opportunities were, London merchants responded readily. In 1511 and 1512 they freighted 'diverse ships of London' to sail to 'Sicily, Candy, Chios and sometimes to Cyprus, as also to Tripoli and Beirut and Syria'. More mundane perhaps, but quantitatively probably more significant, were the activities of those men who contributed a vessel to the small fleets of English ships which sailed in consort during each year of the first Antwerp crisis to Danzig or (save in 1512–13) to Bordeaux, in order to sell English goods and to acquire those wares which in more settled times had been obtained from Antwerp. These Londoners were the pioneers who ventured first into the new direct trades which were later to become permanent features of English commerce whenever crisis conditions beset Antwerp. In 1509–13 Gresham and Copeland participated only indirectly in these activities, hiring their ship—the *Anne of London*—to those who ventured their fortunes in northern seas.

By the time of the next crisis on the Antwerp bourse in late 1515 to 1517, when Venice was added to the list of destinations for English trading vessels, Gresham and Copeland were ready to join directly in the fray. In the autumn of 1515 they freighted a ship, the *Anne of Fowey*, in order to join those merchants who at the time of the bamus mart abandoned their Low Countries connections to trade at Bordeaux. Nor was this the only destination to which the partnership now dispatched ships as a new spirit of adventure permeated English mercantile circles. Having completed her voyage to Bordeaux, the *Anne of Fowey* was freighted for either Eastland or Prussia. In the same year they leased the heavily armed king's ship the *Mary George*, and, with Richard's elder brother William acting as factor, sent her on a voyage into the Mediterranean. As during the years 1509–13, diversification into direct trade was again the order of the day, but, although it might prove cheaper than trade via Antwerp, it carried its own costs. The rate of capital turnover decreased so that, even allowing for reductions in freights negotiated on carriage out and back, the costs involved in such enterprises were high. Only the more substantial members of the London merchant community possessed the means to support such risk-relieving business strategies, and clearly Richard and William Gresham and Copeland had become members of that élite group.

By about 1517 Richard Gresham felt sufficiently secure to marry Audrey (d. 1522), the daughter of William Lynne, of Southwick in Northamptonshire, with whom he had four children—John, Thomas *Gresham, Christiana, who married the wealthy Sir John Thynne of Longleat, and Elizabeth. While his young family was growing up he was not, however, without his own problems. Not least among these was the death of Copeland, which threatened the financial stability of his merchant house. Yet with a certain ingenuity he set all to rights by arranging the marriage of his elder brother William to Copeland's widow, Ellen. Thus the Copeland money was kept in the firm, which now underwent a further expansion to include Richard's younger brother, John, who on completing his

apprenticeship in 1517 had also become free of the Mercers' Company.

Richard and the 'House of Gresham', 1517–1547 The foundations of a great merchant house had been laid. Henceforth, through two generations, the Greshams, as they were known to their contemporaries, were a force to be reckoned with in international trade. Richard's role in the restructured concern remained much as before. Whenever normal trading conditions prevailed at Antwerp, as a mercer he continued to deal largely in fine cloths—Italian silks and Netherlands woollens and tapestries. His other speciality was the importation of armour and weaponry (designated as 'harness' in contemporary parlance). To pay for these wares he either put over the necessary moneys on the exchange or exported English woollen cloth, developing a trade of considerable dimensions in this product. He was actively engaged at the Brabant fairs in 1526, when the large cloth shipments owned by himself and his brothers William and John were seized by order of the emperor at Nieuport in retaliation for the arrest in England of the imperial ambassadors. By 1534–5, on his own account, he contributed more than a third of the company's combined trade in English woollens, which amounted to some 2278 cloths (that is, lengths of cloth), or almost 3 per cent of the total exports through London in that year. This was, however, the highest recorded level of his cloth exports. In 1546–7, two years before his death, he contributed less than 10 per cent of the Greshams' total exports of some 1325 cloths. Whenever circumstances allowed during the years between 1517 and 1547, therefore, Richard pursued the traditional trade of the mercer and merchant adventurer, his importance in this branch of commercial activity being recognized by both his contemporaries and the crown. He was elected warden of the Mercers' Company in 1524, served the office of master in 1533, 1539, and 1549, and acted as deputy governor in 1536 and governor in 1538. He was consulted by the crown during the acrimonious election of William Casteleyn to the post of governor and proffered advice to the privy council on all major legislation touching on the activities of the company.

Nor was Gresham's livelihood, or the trading house's stability, seriously threatened when crisis conditions prevailed on the Antwerp market in many of the succeeding years, disrupting trade there. He responded as before, developing those direct trading connections which he had pioneered in late 1515 to 1517. Initially this led to his involvement in the Baltic trades, where the Greshams developed close links with the great Augsburg house of Höchstetter. Indeed it was probably from the latter's factor in Danzig that Richard obtained in 1521 the four shiploads of wheat which he dispatched to England in anticipation of a scarcity, but which were seized *en route* by Margaret, duchess of Savoy, to relieve the contemporary Netherlands famine. Certainly in 1526 close relations existed between Richard and Joachim, the son and Antwerp factor of Ambrose Höchstetter, for it was through the latter's good offices that a safe conduct was obtained to secure Richard and his brothers' release after their arrest at Nieuport in that year. These favours were recalled during the years 1527–9, when crisis conditions at Antwerp and famine in England again elevated Richard's Baltic interest to the forefront of the Greshams' commercial activities. In 1527, with his brother John, he entered into an agreement with Höchstetter to deliver from Poland 11,000 quarters of grain to the port of London. Unfortunately again the grain failed to arrive, and the close friendship between the parties was somewhat strained by this turn of events. On being pressed in August to fulfil the terms of his contract, Höchstetter 'eloyned himself beyond the sea' (*LP Henry VIII*, 4 (2), no. 4662/2). The Greshams accordingly proceeded against his factor; Höchstetter complained to Cromwell and to Henry himself, alleging that the detention of the grain was by order of the authorities at Nieuport and that as a result of the Greshams' action his credit had been undermined on the continent, by which he had suffered a loss of £30,000. Accusation and counter-accusation were exchanged, but such were the bonds previously forged that before the end of the year the two parties were once more reconciled. In December 1527 and the early months of 1528 business relations with Höchstetter were resumed, Richard bargaining to supply kerseys and other kinds of cloth in exchange for cereals, quicksilver, and vermilion. Then, in the spring of 1528, amid the turmoil of the contemporary mining crisis, the Höchstetters went bankrupt. The house's involvement in an abortive attempt to create a world mercury monopoly had left them dangerously exposed, holding a large proportion of their assets in stocks of the overvalued metal. When the mining crisis broke they were soon in difficulties. At the end of March 1528 Wolf Tucher wrote to his father, Leinhard, from Lyon that 'there has been a complete loss of faith in the Höchstetter on the exchange, so that no-one will loan them money' (Ehrenberg, 1.216); (Klier, 92, 57n). Richard Gresham responded rapidly to the news of the emergent threat to the financial stability of his merchant house. In London he began purchasing cloth to ship on the small fleet of vessels which was to venture directly from the Thames that summer for the Baltic ports. In the process he was able not only to maintain the exports of his own mercantile house but also could reinforce by example his support in March for Wolsey's unpopular policies to alleviate unemployment in the clothing districts. His task of collecting debts in crisis-torn Antwerp proved more difficult. In the process, so Joachim Höchstetter later claimed, Richard was forced to 'declare him a bankrupt, which so defamed him that he was obliged to sell a mass of silver at five hundred pounds below its true value to recover his credit by paying ready money' (PRO, SP 1/50 fol. 34r). By such an act the finances of the Greshams might be saved but the damage to the old friendship with the Höchstetters became irreparable.

Changing interests, death of Audrey Gresham, and second marriage 1528 had thus been a painful year for Richard Gresham, as he was forced to court the hostility of his

peers for the support given to his old friend Wolsey, and to break with the Höchstetters in order to preserve the financial integrity of his family business. Certainly such actions seem to have affected him deeply. Henceforth he turned his back on his old Baltic interests. Nor could he be induced to show much enthusiasm for the other direct trading ventures which he had pioneered during 1516. Henceforth it was his brothers John and William who developed the company's expanding interest in the Levant trade; their (now lost) account books provided the basis for Hakluyt's famous description of this increasingly important branch of English commerce. Richard's interest in the more traditional trade to the Netherlands also waned. Slowly and methodically, from around 1535, he withdrew from active involvement in this branch of the company's trade, surrendering its management to his younger son, Thomas. While from 1528 to 1535 the House of Gresham continued to prosper, others now directed its course. These years marked the beginning of the end of Richard's career as a merchant.

They also witnessed increasing difficulties in Gresham's domestic life. Following the death on 28 December 1522 of his first wife, Audrey, who was buried at St Lawrence Jewry, Richard had remarried. On this occasion his choice was the wealthy widow Isabelle Taverson, *née* Worpfall (*d.* 1565), who, with her daughters, moved into the family home in Milk Lane. For many years their life together seems to have been untroubled, at least until the close of the disastrous year 1532, when his wife's eldest daughter died in October while his wife and one of his sons were lying very ill and close to death. Perhaps because of these events he now wished to eschew the peripatetic life of a merchant in order to spend more time with his family. If so, then his new choice of career as financier allowed him to pursue just such a course of action.

Financier and property speculator, c.1536–1547 Certainly the years 1532–3 marked a distinct change in Gresham's attitude towards his financial operations. Until that time his business in Lombard Street had involved him either in exchange dealings to finance his commercial activity or in the making of small loans to his political patrons. Thus Wolsey was the recipient of at least two loans, each amounting to around £250. Similarly in October 1525, when Gresham, by a timely advance of £50, saved Sir Robert Wingfield, deputy at Calais, from selling his plate, the money was again repaid by Wolsey. Then in 1532, short of money after his term in office as sheriff and deeply worried by domestic matters, Gresham began, not always tactfully, to call in his outstanding loans. The impact of these measures on his debtors was not always a pleasant one. On 6 October 1533 Archbishop Cranmer begged him for some respite in his repayments until his next audit at Lambeth. Sir Francis Bigod's lot was even worse for, as he explained, when begging Cromwell's help with his debts, he 'dare not come to London for fear of Mr Gresham and Mr Lodge' (*LP Henry VIII*, 7, no. 42). Yet relentlessly Gresham called in all his outstanding debts, and with additional funds diverted from his commercial activities established himself in that business he knew best—dealings on the exchange. Thereafter, from 1532–5 until his death in 1549, he occupied himself with putting out money on the exchanges, proving himself as successful in his new trade as in his old. As early as 1536 his paramount position in the Anglo-Netherlands exchange market was recognized when the crown made the Greshams its major agent for the transferral of funds to the continent. Thereafter Richard, and later John, not only undertook the transfer of the vast sums dispatched by Henry VIII and Edward VI to the continent but also became the major source of information to the crown on all matters concerning the exchange. To the world, the name of Gresham had become synonymous with expertise on the exchange, and it was this image that Sir Richard, who had been knighted on 18 October 1537, wished to enshrine when in 1537–8 he proposed to Cromwell the building of a bourse in Lombard Street.

Yet already by that date Gresham was making far more money from his speculations in monastic property than from his exchange dealings. Between 1538 and 1545 he poured tens of thousands of pounds into the purchase of monastic properties in Suffolk, Norfolk, Kent, Cheshire, Hertfordshire, Surrey, Lincolnshire, and Yorkshire, most of which he resold at a considerable profit, retaining only properties at Ringshall, Suffolk, at Inwood Hall, Norfolk, and at Orembery, Yorkshire. These, with his London houses, were valued at £800 when his will was proved in 1549. These transactions were accompanied by the wholesale asset-stripping of the properties concerned. Thus Sir Richard and his brother Sir John were both profitably involved, in a private and a public capacity, in the burgeoning trade in monastic lead. Indeed it was probably his involvement in the monastic property market which ensured Sir Richard a high income during his latter years.

Public office holder, death, and reputation Following that mid-life crisis, which during the years 1531–5 had made him aware of the fragility of domestic happiness and public esteem, Gresham had commenced on a new career as exchange dealer and property speculator. He also assumed the public responsibilities associated with his new role in society. On midsummer day 1531 he was elected sheriff of London and Middlesex, with Edward Altham. Public office, however, brought with it private costs, which in 1531–2, as he lamented, were great 'because of his office of sheriff'. Undeterred, on 22 May 1536 he became alderman for the ward of Walbrook, and on 9 October 1539 he was translated to Cheap ward, which he continued to represent until his death.

Gresham was elected lord mayor at Michaelmas 1537 and entered on a busy year. In his invitation to Cromwell to his 'feastful daye' he dwelt on his intention of dispensing the traditional hospitalities on a lavish scale. He asked Cromwell to move the king to give him 'of his Dooes' for the feast. Three weeks later, on 8 November, on the death of Jane Seymour, he caused 1200 masses to be said within the city, and proposed 'that ther shullde bee allsoo at

Powlles a sollem derige and masse' to be followed by a distribution of alms for the 'many poor people in the city' (*LP Henry VIII*, 12, (2), no. 1042). Within his first weeks in office he had thus revealed the style of his mayoralty, combining public duty with the traditional values of hospitality and charity. He continued in the same vein, petitioning the king as an act of charity to grant three hospitals and the new abbey of Tower Hill for the benefit of 'pore, sykk, blynde, aged and impotent persons … tyll they be holpen and cured of they diseases and syknes' (BL, Cotton MS Cleo. E.4, fol. 22r), and at the end of his mayoralty he acquired for the Mercers' Company the hospital of St Thomas of Acon. He displayed a sense of compassion in the performance of his public duties, as he revealed when dissolving the monastery of Walsingham and bringing its prior to submission, for while efficiently carrying out his task he entreated Cromwell to make the prior, who was impotent and lame but of good reputation, parson of Walsingham church. During his mayoralty, and afterwards, when between 1538 and 1547 he acted in the capacity of economic adviser to the crown, Gresham was, to use his own words, 'conformable in all things to his Highness's pleasure', but in implementing his sovereign's will he always acted with a sense of legal correctness and in a spirit of hospitality, charity, and compassion. He died at Bethnal Green, on London's eastern outskirts, on 21 February 1549, and was buried in the church of St Lawrence Jewry, close to Guildhall, in the heart of the city. Sir John Gresham died on 23 October 1556, 'of a malignant fever', and was buried in the church of St Michael Bassishaw, also within the city of London.

Sir Richard Gresham, whom successive biographers of Sir Thomas Gresham have reduced to little more than a cipher—the father of a great man—was thus very far from that. A successful merchant, exchange dealer, and property speculator, he could on occasion display a certain ruthlessness in his business dealings, while at the same time conforming in both his public and private life to the traditional values of domesticity, hospitality, charity, and compassion. He was also the creator of the 'Gresham myth', an ideal which his more famous son tried throughout his life to emulate.   IAN BLANCHARD

Sources *APC*, 1542–7 · *CSP dom.*, 1547–80 · *CSP for.*, 1547–58 · *LP Henry VIII* · *State papers published under … Henry VIII*, 11 vols. (1830–52), vol. 1, pts 1–2; vol. 2, pt 3 · H. Ellis, ed., *Original letters illustrative of English history*, 1st ser., 3 vols. (1824) · H. Ellis, ed., *Original letters illustrative of English history*, 2nd ser., 4 vols. (1827) · H. Ellis, ed., *Original letters illustrative of English history*, 3rd ser., 4 vols. (1846) · L. Lyell and F. D. Watney, eds., *Acts of court of the Mercers' Company, 1453–1527* (1936) · R. Hakluyt, *The principal navigations, voyages, traffiques and discoveries of the English nation*, 2nd edn, 3 vols. (1598–1600) · Götz, Freiherr von Polnitz, *Jakob Fugger*, 2 vols. (1955) · G. von Polnitz, *Anton Fugger*, 2 vols. (1958) · R. Klier, 'Der Konkurrenzkampf zwischen dem böhmischen und der idrianischen Quecksilber in der ersten Hälfte des 16 Jahrhunderts', *Bohemia*, 8 (1967) · R. Ehrenberg, *Das Zeitalter der Fugger, Geldkapital und Creditverkehr in 16 Jahrhundert*, 2 vols. (1896), 1.216 · J. W. Burgon, *The life and times of Sir Thomas Gresham, compiled chiefly from his correspondence preserved in her majesty's state-paper office: including notices of many of his contemporaries*, 2 vols. (1839) · will of Sir Richard Gresham, PRO, PROB 11/32, sig. 31 · will of Sir Thomas Gresham, PRO, PROB 11/38, sig. 28

Archives Birmingham Public Library, Muckelowe Account Book · CLRO, Repertories 1, 7, and 9–10 · PRO, Exchequer, Particular Customs Accounts, E122 82/17 · Rigsarkivet, København, Denmark, Sundtoldregudkab 1528 · Wojewódzkie Archiwum Państwowe, Gdańsk, Poland, Pfahlkammereschnung 3, 19/9–1 **Wealth at death** £800—real estate: Burgon, *Life and times*

Gresham, Sir Thomas (*c.*1518–1579), mercer, merchant adventurer, and founder of the Royal Exchange and Gresham College, the second of the two sons and two daughters of Sir Richard *Gresham (*c.*1485–1549) and his first wife, Audrey (*d.* 1522), the daughter of William Lynne, of Southwick in Northampton, was born in his father's house in Milk Lane, London, about 1518. Nothing is known of his childhood, save that his mother died when he was only three or four. He was later sent to Cambridge and admitted as a pensioner at Gonville Hall, and at the age of seventeen he was apprenticed to his uncle John Gresham. Some eight years later, in 1543, he took his freedom in the Mercers' Company. As he himself later explained, this was a somewhat unusual course of events, as

> I need not have bynne prentisse for that I was free by my Father's coppye: albeit my Father Sir Richard Gresham being a wyse man, although I was free by his coppye, it was to no purpos, except I was bound prentisse to the same; whereby to come by the experience and knowledge of all kinds of merchandise. (Burgon, 1.47)

Richard Gresham's own years of personal misfortune had made him only too aware of the fragility of domestic happiness and public esteem, and at this time he was not only plotting out a new career for himself but was also carefully grooming his sons for their future roles in life.

John Gresham Richard's eldest son and heir apparent, John Gresham (*d.* 1560), with his wife, Frances, the daughter and coheir of Sir Henry Thwaytes of Lownd in Yorkshire, benefited during the remainder of the 1540s from a peripheral contact with Richard's operations as a speculator in monastic property. In 1538 they obtained, probably through his good offices, leases from the crown for Wabourne Priory, Norfolk, with the rectories of Wabourne and East Beckham. They had by this date, however, abandoned their connections with the mercantile financial operations of the 'House of Gresham', preferring instead life as members of the lesser gentry. When required in 1544 to muster troops for Henry VIII's French expedition, John was able to provide his quota of seven men for the levy. When, as in 1545–6, he was called on to assume such minor public offices as the king's commissioner at Dover, he performed his duties unenthusiastically, but with sufficient diligence to ensure himself a knighthood, bestowed in 1547. Unlike his father, John cared little for either business or court life. His investments in Chancellor's ill-fated expedition to Russia in 1553 and in the Muscovy Company in 1555 were probably passive ones, and his office of assistant of the newly created company titular rather than active. The focus of his life lay far from London on his Norfolk estates. Here he lived a quiet rustic life, enlivened only by occasional visits to his metropolitan town house or attendances at the family gatherings which were hosted by Sir Richard and then

Sir Thomas Gresham (*c.*1518–1579), by unknown artist, 1544

Thomas Gresham at Inwood Hall. For most of their adult life Sir John and Frances were the London Greshams' rustic relatives. They were also their poor relations, and on his death in 1560 John left his widow in somewhat straitened circumstances. Yet such were the filial ties between the brothers that Thomas immediately came to the rescue, bestowing on Frances a handsome annuity of £133 6*s.* 8*d.*, which was to be her main financial support until her death in October 1580. If, as seems probable from his marriage into the gentry and his early involvement in Sir Richard's property dealings, John was being groomed by his father for a partnership in the family property business, then Sir Richard was going to be sadly disappointed. Such talents and connections as John possessed were deployed to a far more traditional end—a successful marriage for his only daughter and heir, Elizabeth. And in this at least he was successful, for she was matched with Sir Henry Neville of Billingbere, who had received from his grandfather considerable estates in Berkshire which were to descend in the family line for generations to come.

Thomas Gresham's apprenticeship and early career Sir Richard's moulding of his younger son's career was far more successful. During the years 1535–47, as he withdrew from the management of the Greshams' mercery trade at the Netherlands marts, he set about grooming Thomas to take his place. By apprenticing Thomas to his uncle John Gresham in 1535, Sir Richard hoped to give him the experience and knowledge of all kinds of merchandise which would fit him for the mercer's craft. Perhaps as a result of his disappointment at the course John's life had taken, Richard guided his younger son through the mysteries of exchange dealings, preparing him for a partnership in this branch of his father's business empire. He augmented his now favoured younger son's existing knowledge of classical languages with a pragmatic education in contemporary tongues—French and Flemish. By securing Thomas's admission to Gray's Inn he provided him with at least a cursory knowledge of law. Thomas made the most of the opportunities which his father opened up for him, proving a very adept pupil. Thus, having spent some time prior to the summer of 1538 in Paris, where he obtained both a knowledge of the intricacies of his uncle John's French trading connections and of the French tongue, Thomas was soon able to put his seemingly excellent French to practical use. After returning to London in June he was rapidly embroiled by his father in the lavish hospitality which the latter, in his capacity as lord mayor, had arranged for the lady of Montreuil and her train during their stay (22–8 August 1538) in the English capital. It was Thomas, by reason of his knowledge of the language, moreover, that he sent to accompany the ladies on their protracted five-day journey to Dover. He also saw fit to inform Cromwell of the fact and utilized the opportunity to bring the young man to his attention.

Thereafter the young apprentice mercer was employed by the crown on various small errands in the Netherlands. On 25 February 1540, for instance, he was said to be with a Mr Parker and Mr Blunt, collectively described as Henry's servants, in Brussels on the king's business. He departed via Calais for England before 29 March, and by 2 April Wyatt was writing as though he had by then returned to London and had probably already seen Cromwell. His work seems to have sufficiently impressed Cromwell for the latter to note that he should 'remember Mr Gresham'. Through his direct services for the crown the young Thomas was beginning to make his mark. Acting on his father's behalf in the latter's exchange dealings, he also seems to have attracted the attention of royal officials. Thus Wyatt, writing from Ghent to Cromwell at this time, not only asked the latter to thank Sir Richard Gresham for the letters of exchange he had dispatched but was also concerned that Cromwell should know of his treatment of Sir Richard's son Thomas, who, having delivered the bills of exchange, had now returned to London. 'I suppose his son [Thomas] will say I have done him some pleasure in these parts', he wrote; at the age of twenty-two Thomas was clearly marked out for further advancement in royal service.

Contemporaries also recognized Gresham's worth as a merchant. By the time of his admittance to the freedom of the Mercers' Company in 1543 he was already well on the way to becoming the *de facto* head of the Greshams' commercial operations. Before he could in 1546–7 assume the mantle fashioned for him by his father, however, he had one more obstacle to overcome. On 3 March 1545 Secretary Paget wrote from Brussels that Thomas, then trading in his own right, was one of the English merchants whose goods had been seized by order of Charles V. He also explained why the Greshams, because of their particular activities, were likely to survive this disastrous turn of events:

> Some in dede shall win by it [the seizure]; as William Lok, Sir Richarde Gressam and his sonne [Thomas], and William Gressem, with such other for the most parte that occupie sylkes, who owe more than they have here. But Mr Warren, Mr Hill, Chestre, and dyverse others a greate nombre, ar like to have a greate swoope by it; having muche here, and owing nothing or little. (Burgon, 49)

And so it was. Gresham, like those other mercers, had already taken delivery of these goods in time for the Easter mart, and, although their suppliers might dun them for payment, having no alternative customers for their wares, they were unlikely to follow such a drastic course of action, particularly as these mercers had nothing at Antwerp on which to distrain. The Italian silk dealers knew that the money needed to pay for their wares would be available only when merchants such as the Greshams had sold their cloths at Antwerp and others had been able to honour their bills of exchange from the proceeds of their own cloth sales. They had no alternative but to endure the delay. Gresham thus emerged out of the crisis virtually unscathed.

Mercer and merchant adventurer, 1543–1551 In three short years following his admission to the freedom of the Mercers' Company in 1543 Gresham had fulfilled every aspiration that his father had of him. During this period he was entrusted by the crown with increasingly delicate tasks on the continent. In 1546 he took charge of the Greshams' Netherlands commercial operations. This involved him, as it had his father, in the normal mercers' trade, buying silks such as velvet, satin, taffeta, and sarsenet, which together with fine woollen cloths and tapestries commanded a ready market in London. Also like his father, Gresham's other speciality was the importation of armour and weaponry, which was designated in his accounts as 'harness'. To pay for these wares he continued, moreover, to follow the time-honoured practice of either putting over the necessary moneys on the exchange or exporting English woollen cloth. Following the lifting of the restraint on the English merchants' goods at Antwerp on 6 April 1545 he was responsible for more than 90 per cent of the company's goods shipped from the mart: four chests and a pack containing fifty pieces of velvet (1117 yards) and twenty-two pieces of taffeta (873 yards), six sacks of cotton, and six vats of harness, officially valued at £1394. The transition to his effective headship of the company's Netherlands operations in 1546 was thus accomplished with considerable ease. In that year he was again solely responsible for the company's purchases of mercery and harness at the Netherlands marts and for the shipment of these wares to London. Most of the company's woollen cloth (1025 'cloths', that is, lengths of cloth, or 75 per cent of a total of 1375 cloths) dispatched from London to the Netherlands to provide cash for the purchase of this mercery were also registered in his name. The older generation of Greshams now contributed only diminutive quantities of textiles—Sir Richard and William 100 cloths each and Sir John 150 cloths—to the company's exports and received from Thomas's hands a correspondingly diminutive share in the company's mercery imports.

Commercial difficulties and changing priorities Yet Gresham's situation during the years 1546–51 was a very different one from that in which his father had found himself some twenty years earlier. Successive debasements of the English silver coinage by the profligate Henry VIII and his son had led to the emergence of a system of bimetallic premiums on the Anglo-Netherlands exchange which, in enhancing the cost of commercial credits, had resulted in the overpricing of English textiles at the Netherlands marts. In response to this phenomenon, Gresham, like many of his peers, varied the goods exported, replacing traditional long and short cloths with the lightweight, and cheap, kersey. In 1546–7 kerseys made up almost half (635 cloths, or 46 per cent) of the company's exports, only marginally ceding ground to the short cloths (661 cloths, or 48 per cent), which remained the staple of earlier trade, and completely displacing the luxurious longs (71 cloths, or 6 per cent). Yet, in spite of this initiative on his part, the company's woollen cloth exports during the years 1546–51 never exceeded 60 per cent of that achieved by the House of Gresham in 1535. Gresham accordingly had to resort to other means to generate the necessary cash flow for the purchase of mercery and harness at the Netherlands marts. Like other members of the family he dabbled in the monastic lead trade, the very low price of the base metal at this time ensuring its ready sale on continental European markets. Moreover, when in 1548–9 a consortium of bankers was able to monopolize Bohemian tin production and, with the support of King Ferdinand, to exclude Saxon and English competition, thereby raising tin prices to a level some 40 per cent higher than those prevailing on the free market, he responded rapidly to the new situation. His servant John Elliot stepped up his acquisition of Cornish tin, which was shipped to London for export to the continent, supporting a trade which for some eighteen months, before the collapse of the German consortium and resultant fall in tin prices, made a significant contribution to the company's coffers. He also performed during the years to 1549 small services for his father and his uncle John in their continuing operations for the crown on the Anglo-Netherlands exchange. By such means for some five years (1546–51) he secured for the House of Gresham a leading place in Anglo-Netherlands commerce. Then by his own account, on securing the post of royal agent in the Netherlands during the winter of 1551–2, Gresham closed the account book in which he had recorded all his business since 1546 and finally turned his back on his mercantile activities. Like so many other such statements, written by him in a spirit of self-advertisement, however, this was only a half-truth. With the exception of Robert Berney, the factors and agents who had served him well as a merchant remained in his service beyond that winter. When requested by their master to undertake some small commercial favour for his political patrons they were still able to fulfil his instructions with ease. Gresham did not sever his mercantile connections, for during July–November 1553 and March 1556–December 1557 when, possibly as a consequence of the intrigues of the lord treasurer, he lost his post as royal agent and was consigned to the political wilderness, he simply resumed his activities as a merchant. On 8 December 1551, when he received at London his last shipment of harness from the Netherlands, Gresham, as he himself declared, left 'my occupying and whole trade of living for the space of two years'; yet with his fall from grace in July 1553 he was able immediately to pick up his old trade, buying some 308 cloths that summer for the winter mart. His ability to resume, with such ease, the threads of his earlier life on this occasion belies the self-proclaimed discontinuity in his career associated with his assumption of the office of royal agent. Indeed, it would be wrong to categorize Gresham and his associates as solely merchants or financial agents at any given period: they were both. The House of Gresham did not close its doors in December 1551. It merely underwent a metamorphosis, as Gresham added a range of new activities to his old ones.

Domestic arrangements In 1544, at the age of twenty-six, with status and wealth already in prospect, Gresham married Anne Ferneley (d. 1596), the widow of the mercer William Read, who had two young sons from her first marriage. The Reads were already closely associated with the Greshams because Sir Richard was a trustee of Read's will. As was common at this time, Anne remarried very quickly after the death of her first husband. For a young man such as Gresham this well-endowed woman must have been a very attractive bride, for after their marriage he not only managed the estates which were held in trust for her sons but also amalgamated her late husband's business with his own and took over Read's apprentices and factors. When Gresham took control of the Netherlands operations the couple had been married eighteen months and had recently moved into a rented house in Basinghall Street, for the lease of which they paid £66 13s. 4d. In July 1548 he bought a house from the crown for £47 12s. 0d. It was a former chantry, by Cheapside, in the parish of St Lawrence Jewry. During the years 1543–63, when he continued to combine the roles of merchant and royal agent, he was frequently absent from home, travelling back and forth between London and Antwerp. He also travelled to Norfolk and Suffolk to check on the management of the Read estates and to visit Ringshall in Suffolk and Inwood Hall in Norfolk, where he regularly made his filial devotions until his father's death in 1549 and thereafter, having inherited these properties, entertained the Gresham clan.

The domestic arrangements over which his wife presided were determined largely by Gresham's business activities. In the years to 1548 the Basinghall Street household could consist of William, her young son, Thomas Bradshaw, her husband's apprentice, John Elliot, his factor, and personal and household servants and, from 1547, Edmund Hogan and William Bindlosse, who joined her husband's employ in that year. Anne's elder son, Richard, was away from home at this time, boarding with Ralph Ratcliffe, who was paid £10 a year for his tuition and keep. He went to London on visits from time to time but there is no indication that he enjoyed regular holidays with his mother or stepfather. In 1546, when Anne was pregnant and Gresham away, her father, William Ferneley, took up temporary residence at Basinghall Street. She gave birth to Richard, the only live child the couple seem to have had, in March 1547. The birth may have been a difficult one, for three separate payments were made in that month to different physicians. A nurse was found for the little boy and in May his father provided 3 yards of silk saye to be made up as clothing for him. Thanks to the generosity of William Ferneley, the Basinghall Street house was well furnished. During his temporary stay there Ferneley paid that year's rent for the property and bought a long list of furniture which was required for the new house.

Household expenses amounted to between £150 and £175 a year, including most of the food consumed, small purchases, and servants' wages. Some special foodstuffs and domestic items were bought or imported by Gresham for the household. Besides housing and feeding their dependants, the Greshams also clothed them, taking cloths from the stock in the shop to be made up, and enlisting the services of an embroiderer and shoemaker.

Other details of the couple's lives are recorded: minstrels were hired to play for them over Christmas 1547, and Thomas at least attended the celebrations when his uncle John became lord mayor that year. Thomas indulged in gaming, usually playing dice, but on occasion a game called bank notes, and advances of money for this purpose and the settling of debts are noted fairly frequently in his accounts. His wife's expenses show her most frequent amusement to have been attending the christenings of her friends' children.

Apart from being the head of a large household, Gresham was also a member of a prosperous and mutually supportive extended family. Many of his relatives received, by gift or sale, cloth and imported wares. When his sister Christiana married Sir John Thynne in 1548 he gave her a gold ring set with a ruby and valued at £13 6s. 8d. He supplied the Thynnes with a wide range of cloths and household goods such as coverlets, and irons, and silver plate in the form of eight bowls and a basin and ewer. Thynne apparently had expensive tastes, as the items mentioned above cost him £35 3s. 6d. and £24 18s. 9d. respectively, and on another occasion he bought a diamond for the large sum of £25. Gresham's stepmother, Isabelle, and sister Elizabeth received presents of cloth, as did his brother

John and sister-in-law Frances and their daughter Elizabeth—usually velvet or damask in varying lengths—and he frequently imported wine and sturgeon for his father and uncle John. William Ferneley frequently received payments from his son-in-law and, on his side, acted for Gresham when he was abroad. Anne's sister Jane married Nicholas Bacon, the lord keeper, thus providing Gresham with another patron at court, and the usual gifts of cloth were made to this couple. The relationship was later reinforced when Gresham's illegitimate daughter, Anne, who had probably been born abroad, married Nicholas Bacon, the son of Nicholas and Jane.

This lifestyle remained at the core of their domestic arrangements in spite of their frequent changes of address—Basinghall Street (1546–8), Cheapside (1548–51), and Lombard Street (c.1553–c.1563) in London and an unlocated property (1551–3) and house in the Lange Nieustrate in Antwerp (1559–67)—and in spite of the necessity of completely refurbishing their home when, as Thomas explained, 'my plate, household stuff and apparel of myself and my wife (which I sent and prepared unto Antwerp to serve me during my service there) by casualty of the weather coming from Antwerp' in July 1553 were 'all lost'. During the years 1544–63 Anne's domestic responsibilities expanded; in addition to her duties at her husband's metropolitan residences she also became in the course of time mistress of Inwood Hall in Norfolk, which Gresham had inherited from his father in 1549. Here with their children, Richard and Thomas's illegitimate daughter Anne, the couple entertained the Gresham clan and such royal officials as were in the neighbourhood. From here Thomas was also able to undertake the supervision of the administration of a rapidly growing country estate in Norfolk. In 1553 he acquired Walsingham and Westacre Priory, valued at about £260 and £150 per annum respectively. In 1556 to this was added the priory of Austin Canons at Massingham, with the manor and rectory at Langham and advowson of the vicarage, and the manors of Walsingham, Narford, Merston, and Combes, and the advowson of their respective rectories, which he later declared yielded him an annual income of £200.

From 1549 Gresham occasionally retired with his family to Inwood Hall, where he maintained the now old-fashioned style of hospitality practised by his father. The income to support Inwood and the maintenance of the property at Ringshall, also inherited from his father, which he used at this time when forced to stop over at Ipswich in the course of his duties as merchant and crown agent, however, now increasingly derived from revenues from his Norfolk estates, the rewards for his service as royal agent in the Netherlands, rather than than from the profits of his trading and exchange operations.

Royal agent in the Netherlands, 1551–1564 Gresham's appointment to the post of royal agent in the Netherlands in December 1551 came at a particularly critical juncture in the operations of the English crown on the Antwerp money market. Ever since that fateful instruction in May 1544 when, amid a myriad of fund-raising schemes, the English crown ordered the then royal agent, Stephen

Vaughan, to raise a loan on the Antwerp bourse, the indebtedness of the English crown to the great South German merchant-banking houses had increased. In 1548 it amounted to almost £240,000 sterling and in 1551 it increased to some £325,000. Thereafter it was steadily reduced in the years to 1564, when, in transformed conditions on the London market, the crown resumed its practice of borrowing in England. Even at its height, however, English royal indebtedness at Antwerp was minute in comparison with that of the Habsburgs, and accordingly successive royal agents were price-takers in a market dominated by the imperial authorities. Throughout the years 1544–64 the base-line rates of interest paid on loans raised for the English crown shadowed those paid by the agents of Charles V and Philip II. Such rates were also subject to marked fluctuations about this trend, largely brought about by the personalities of the negotiators managing the English royal debt on the continent.

Initially, under Vaughan's guidance during the years 1544–7, this mounting debt had been carefully managed. Secure in the support of the king's council, Vaughan's primary objective during 1544 had been to gain a knowledge of the labyrinthine tactics of the denizens of the Antwerp bourse—the South German merchant bankers, the brokers, and the underwriters—who, possibly under the orders of the emperor, for a year managed to manipulate the inexperienced agent, creating a major differential between the nominal and real interest rates on the loans he raised for the English crown. Vaughan was an apt pupil, however, and before leaving his post as royal agent in the Netherlands in 1547 he had been able to cut through this tangle of financial ploys, simplifying the basis for negotiations and establishing direct links with the Antwerp agents of the South German merchant bankers. Thereby he was able to reduce transactions costs and the real rate of interest paid by the English crown. By the accession of the boy king Edward VI, the English crown was able to borrow what it required at Antwerp at a discounted rate which shadowed that obtained by the Habsburgs on continental markets.

Neither of Vaughan's principal successors, William Dansall (1547–51) and Gresham (1551–64), enjoyed the same unreserved support from their political masters as he had done. Throughout their periods in office, political expediency and economic illiteracy on the part of council members combined to plague relations between the crown and its agents in the Netherlands which, at least until 1564, were reduced to a low ebb. Whenever money could be raised easily on the continent the agents were left to their own devices and the crown obtained loans at a discounted rate which shadowed that obtained by the Habsburgs. When rates rose, usually as a result of Habsburg intervention on these markets in 1549–52, 1554–5, and 1557–8, the members of the king's council panicked, displaced their agent, and either appointed others or took over direct negotiations with the bankers—with disastrous results.

For nearly the first three years of Dansell's term in office, from the winter marts of 1546–7 to 1549–50, annual interest rates on the Antwerp bourse fell from 12 per cent to an all-time low of 9 per cent. He was left, therefore, very much to his own devices, successfully rolling over a debt of about £240,000 sterling at a cost which was usually no more than 2 per cent above base interest rates. Then for two years, from the marts of 1549–50 to 1551–2, circumstances conspired against him. Habsburg intervention forced up the cost of finance on the Antwerp bourse at a time when the council was becoming very rate conscious as a result of the increasing cost of servicing royal debts arising from the contemporary crisis on the Anglo-Netherlands exchange. In this situation the council took the unwise step of displacing its agent and undertaking, at the autumn marts of 1550 and 1551, direct negotiations with the bankers. The terms obtained were disastrous, and, as the total debt of the English crown at Antwerp rose to an all-time high of £325,000 sterling, relations between the crown and its agent deteriorated as a welter of accusations and counter-accusations were exchanged, finally resulting in Dansell's dismissal on 29 December 1551 and the appointment of a new agent—Gresham.

The task facing Gresham, at this critical juncture in the operations of the English crown on the Antwerp money market, was a formidable one, but fortune now smiled on him. Interest rates on the bourse might continue to rise; they attained a level of 16 per cent a year at the Whitsun mart of 1552. Then a developing crisis in central European silver production lifted the price of that metal on Antwerp bullion markets, causing the exchange to rise. This increase in the value of sterling, from 16 to 22 Flemish shillings, for which Gresham fancifully claimed full credit, goes a long way towards explaining the success of his operations at this time. Deploying a part of the sterling balances reserved for scheduled payments at the lower exchange rate to the end of loan redemption, he managed, within a mere nine months of taking office, to reduce the level of royal indebtness to £108,000 sterling. These remaining debts, renegotiated at the winter and Whitsun marts of 1551–2, might carry nominal interest rates of 14 and 15½ per cent respectively but, at the enhanced exchange rate prevailing at Whitsun, the service charges amounted to only £16,500 sterling, or less than a third of the amount paid during the previous winter. As he had declared to Northumberland in the summer of 1552, Gresham fully intended to clear the king's debts entirely in one or two years.

In this course of action Gresham was thwarted, however, by the death of the young king and the accession of Mary in July 1553. Judged politically unreliable, he was removed from office, whereupon he resumed his old trade, buying some 308 cloths that summer for shipment to the Netherlands at the winter mart of 1553. For some four months the inexperienced Christopher Dawntsey acted in his stead—with catastrophic results. In spite of moneys being available for the English crown at the autumn mart at the 'normal' 2 per cent discount on the Habsburg rate of 12 per cent, the hapless Dawntsey took up on 10 November some 200,000 guilders (around £128,300 sterling) from Lazarus Tucher at a 'nominal' 13 per cent, which the latter turned into a 'real' 14 per cent by delaying delivery of the cash for a month. The council's response on receipt of the bond for this transaction was immediate. Letters were drafted removing Dawntsey from office and reappointing Gresham as royal agent in the Netherlands. Thus, with his arrival at Antwerp on 17 November 1553, Gresham resumed the work abandoned some four months earlier, but not before he had repaired the serious damage done to the English crown's credit in the interval. In conditions of acute monetary disorder and exchange instability, and with the remembrance of Dawntsey's extravagant terms still fresh in the bankers' minds, Gresham had to struggle long and hard during the winter mart of 1553–4 to conclude new loans at reasonable rates. By his efforts, however, he was able to re-establish the queen's credit and obtain moneys at rates (12 per cent) which were again discounted (by 2 per cent) in relation to those secured by the Habsburgs before he sailed homewards on 3 March 1554. The financial strategy for the remainder of the decade was now established. The £100,000 sterling raised by Gresham at 12 per cent was not, as he probably hoped, used to pay off Tucher as part of a debt conversion operation but rather was spent, raising royal indebtedness once again to c.£230,000 sterling. Nor was any serious attempt made to reduce these debts before 1560. Gresham's task henceforth was to roll over existing debts on the most favourable terms available—a commission not always easy to accomplish, as he was to find on his return to Antwerp on 12 May in time for the Whitsun mart of 1554.

As Gresham had already anticipated the previous November, by this time the market was in turmoil. Rates, already edging up at Easter, stood at 14⅛ per cent at the opening of the new fair, but before its close they had reached 18 per cent. The time had come to move on, and during the fortnight of his stay at Antwerp Gresham busied himself with putting together a deal, like the one first proposed to him by Genoese merchants the previous January, whereby he entered into contracts with Anton Fugger and nephews, Gaspar Schetz and brothers, John de Mantansa, John Lopez de Gallo, Antonio Spinola, and Octavian Lomellini which involved the delivery of bills of exchange to him for payments of 300,750 ducats (worth £97,878 15s. 0d. sterling) in Spain. Thus began the 'Spanish venture' which required him, from June 1554, to travel to Spain, collect the moneys, and ship them to England. By the end of the year this task had been accomplished, and then, prudently perhaps, Gresham disappeared, pursuing his commercial interests in Spain and leaving the job of rolling over the crown's Flemish debts to his cousin John and Nicholas Holbourne.

By the time of Gresham's return to duty at Antwerp, shortly before Whitsun 1555, however, the situation had eased considerably. Over the next two years he had little difficulty in securing prolongations of the queen's debts and, as interest rates fell from 14 to 12 per cent, of reducing them from the post-crisis level of 1,357,446 florins (around £226,245 sterling) in 1555 to 506,769 florins (around £98,785) in October 1556.

Gresham's further plans for English government debt redemption were thwarted, however, when during 1556–7, in conditions of rapidly rising interest rates, the Antwerp bourse was again thrown into turmoil as a result of the imperial state bankruptcy. Old tensions reappeared between the council and its financial agents in the Netherlands, and, possibly as a consequence of the intrigues of the lord treasurer, Gresham lost his post as agent between March 1556 and December 1557 and was consigned to the political wilderness. How those negotiating loans for Mary fared during these months is uncertain, but their legacy to the reinstated agent at the winter mart of 1557–8 is only too clear. To cover outstanding debts he had to negotiate in 1558 loans amounting, according to contemporary calculations, to £336,133 sterling. Mary's reign thus closed with the English crown's debts at Antwerp again hovering about the third of a million pounds sterling mark.

Only under her successor, Elizabeth, was Gresham again able to resume the task, which he had set himself some six years earlier, of reducing English royal indebtedness abroad. Under the tutelage of his friend Cecil, and secure in the confidence of both Elizabeth and her council, he now operated, largely free from constraint, on an Antwerp market which, in the aftermath of the imperial bankruptcy, had been transformed. Antwerp's financial prosperity was no longer subject to the depredations of the Habsburgs, who henceforth secured their funds from dealings on the Sevillian–Genoese financial axis. Its driving force was now the provision of commercial investments, and as trade boomed from 1559 to 1565 these could be funded at interest rates which fell rapidly from 12 to slightly more than 9 per cent. In these circumstances Gresham could hardly fail, and by deploying a part of the sterling balances reserved for scheduled payments at the higher interest rates to the end of loan redemption he henceforth reduced the level of royal indebtness to around £280,000 sterling in 1560, and to a mere £20,000 in 1565, some two years before he departed from Antwerp for the last time.

Public benefactor, 1564–1579 The years 1559–64 marked the high point of Gresham's career as a servant of the crown. He was knighted in December 1559, preparatory to taking up a temporary appointment as ambassador to the court of the duchess of Parma, regent of the Netherlands, and his career had thereafter gone from strength to strength. Having all but eliminated the English crown's debts to the Antwerp financiers, he stood high in Elizabeth's esteem and was increasingly involved by her in such wide-ranging schemes as the recoinage of 1560 and the reform of the London custom house in 1561–2. His successes in public office, moreover, brought with them public reward and, much to the delight of his socially ambitious wife, Anne, a complete change in lifestyle. He acquired new country houses, convenient to London, at Mayfield in Sussex and Osterley in Middlesex, whose opulence may perhaps be gauged by the valuation of the former property's furnishings at some £7550. In London he transformed his modest house in Lombard Street into business premises and took up occupancy in the grandiose Gresham House, which he had built a few years before 1566 in Bishopsgate and furnished at a cost of some £1128. Whether at Antwerp or his English properties, he dispensed, moreover, a lavish hospitality, of which all classes were glad to take advantage. Public recognition and esteem were also coupled at this time with domestic contentment. When in London he enjoyed the company of his now adult children and stepchildren and the companionship of his cousins Noel and Cecily; the latter, with her husband, German Coill, occupied the neighbouring Crosby Hall before Coill's bankruptcy in 1566. A son was fathered on his servant Anne Hurst, provision being made for the boy and a husband found for his mother. Gresham must have later remembered these as the good years.

Certainly from 1564 life was never to be the same again. He had been plagued since 1560 with a mis-set broken leg, the result of a riding accident, and his health thereafter, in spite of the efforts of the surgeons, steadily deteriorated until, writing to Walsingham in 1575, he declared himself as 'being 62 years of ayge and blinde and lame' (*CSP dom., 1547–80*, 505). He was in fact only fifty-seven, and, though weak of sight, not blind.

Far more significant in shaping Gresham's later life, however, was the psychological trauma occasioned by the death in 1564 of his only son, Richard. As in the case of his own father, some forty years earlier, domestic tragedy made Thomas only too aware of the fragility of familial happiness and public esteem and caused him to review his life. With his link to immortality through his son suddenly severed, he soon set about re-creating it—in stone. On 4 January 1565 he proposed to the court of aldermen of the City that a bourse or exchange should be built in London at his expense for the accommodation of merchants. Thus began a project which was to occupy both Gresham and his factor and friend Richard Clough fully for some three years. Initially, in March 1565 a subscription was opened which, before its termination in October 1566, raised the £3737 needed to buy properties on Cornhill and to pay for clearing the site where the bourse was to be built. Already by Christmas 1565 the necessary arrangements for the acquisition of the properties had been made and notice given to the tenants to vacate their dwellings. Such was the sense of urgency felt by Gresham, however, that within a fortnight of the last tenant's being evicted, on 10 April, while the site was still being cleared, he requested Cecil's permission to visit Norfolk to take order for the freestone needed for the foundations of the structure. On 7 June 1566 he personally laid its foundation stone. Clearly nothing was going to be allowed to interfere with his attempt to enshrine his own immortality in bricks and mortar, and over the next two and a half years Gresham employed the full resources of his estates and business to complete the project.

Yet even before the final touches were put to the edifice in December 1568, and commercial success ensured by Elizabeth's visit thereto in January 1571, Gresham continued energetically in his new role as public benefactor. Thus were built the eight almshouses behind his mansion in Bishopsgate. It was probably also at about this time that he first conceived the idea of making an educational endowment, his first choice of recipient seemingly being his old university of Cambridge. When it came to making the necessary dispositions in 1575, however, it was not Cambridge that benefited. Gresham ordained that Lady Gresham should enjoy his London house, as well as the rents from the Royal Exchange during her life, but that thereafter they would be vested in the hands of the corporation of London and the Mercers' Company, who would conjointly nominate seven professors to lecture there successively, one in each day of the week, on the seven sciences. And so, following the death of his widow in November 1596, Gresham College came into being. The first professors occupied their chambers in the Bishopsgate property during March 1597 and lectures commenced the Trinity term following.

Domestic difficulties, death, and reputation Gresham thus secured his place in history, but at a heavy cost. As she watched the family fortunes dissipated in her husband's self-glorificatory projects, relations between Anne and Thomas rapidly deteriorated, reaching a particularly low ebb during the period from June 1569 to April 1572, when their enforced and protracted entertainment of the Lady Mary Grey put intolerable strains on their marriage. How much Anne actually resented her husband's profligate course of action, however, was revealed only after his death, at Gresham House on 21 November 1579, when twice she tried to undo the complex arrangements surrounding his establishment of Gresham College. On both occasions her efforts were thwarted, but she perhaps had the last word, making arrangements so that she would be buried, with her husband in St Helen, Bishopsgate, on 14 December 1596, as she had always wanted to live, with great public display and heraldic pomp.

An energetic and competent man, albeit of limited abilities, who spent his life trying to live up to the Gresham myth created by his father, Thomas Gresham possessed one true talent, for self-advertisement, which ensured him a place in history. For 250 years he was remembered, as he himself had wished, as the founder of the Royal Exchange and Gresham College. Then in the early years of Victoria's reign he was 'rediscovered'. When the Royal Exchange was destroyed by fire in 1838 its founder was reinstated as a public figure, causing enough interest for Gresham College to be rebuilt and newly funded, for a street in the City to be named after him, and for the publication of a comprehensive biography of his life and career as a public servant for the Tudors. He even had the honour to have a law of economics wrongly attributed to him. The Victorians re-created him to accord with their own popular notion of a self-made man who rose to greatness, and it is perhaps this image which is the greatest testimony to the true talents of Thomas Gresham—the maker of myths.

IAN BLANCHARD

Sources J. W. Burgon, *The life and times of Sir Thomas Gresham compiled chiefly from his correspondence preserved in her majesty's state-paper office: including notices of many of his contemporaries*, 2 vols. (1839) · S. T. Bindoff, *The fame of Sir Thomas Gresham* (1973) · F. R. Salter, *Sir*

Thomas Gresham (1518–1579) (1925) • C. MacFarlane, *The life of Sir Thomas Gresham: founder of the Royal Exchange* (1845) • G. W. G. Leveson-Gower, *Genealogy of the family of Gresham* (1883) • J. Ward, *The lives of the professors of Gresham College* (1740) • J. Newman, 'Thomas Gresham: private person rather than public figure', *History Teaching Review: Year Book*, 7 (1993), 13–22 • R. A. De Roover, *Gresham on foreign exchange: an essay on early English mercantilism: with the text of Sir Thomas Gresham's memorandum for the understanding of the exchange* (1949) • APC, 1542–7, 1547–8, 1550–52, 1552–4, 1554–6, 1556–8, 1558–70, 1571–5, 1575–7, 1577–8, 1578–80, 1580–81 • *CSP dom.*, 1547–80; 1595–7 • *CSP for.*, 1547–58 • *CSP for.*, 1558–79 • *LP Henry VIII*, vols. 8–13/2, 14/1–21/2 • J. Stow and E. Howes, *The annales, or, Generall chronicle of England … unto the ende of the present yeere, 1614* (1615) • T. Tanner, *Notitia monastica* (1744) • T. S. Willan, *The early history of the Russia Company, 1553–1603* (1956) • T. S. Willan, *The Muscovy merchants of 1555* (1953) • H. Kellenbenz, 'Sächsiches und böhmisches Zinn auf dem europäischen Markt', *Historia Socialis et Oeconomica: Festschrift für Wolfgang Zorn zum 65. Geburtstag*, ed. H. Kellenbenz and H. Pohl (1987) • C. E. Challis, *The Tudor coinage* (1978) • W. R. Douthwaite, *Gray's Inn: notes illustrative of its history and antiquities* (1876) • H. Hall, *Society in the Elizabethan age* (1886) • will, PRO, PROB 11/61, sig. 47

Archives BL, state papers, letters • Bodl. Oxf., state papers, letters • Mercers' Company, London, daybook • PRO, state papers, letters, SP | BL, papers, Cotton MSS • Morgan L., letters, mainly to Nathaniel Bacon, and documents • PRO, Exchequer, Particular Customs Accounts, E 101, 347/16 • PRO, Exchequer, Particular Customs Accounts, E 122, 81/32A, 84/8–9, 12, 85/3, 7, 9, 11, 86/2, 6–7, 87/4, 167/1

Likenesses oils, 1544, Mercers' Hall, London [*see illus.*] • S. van der Meulen, oils, 1550–75 (after unknown artist), Audley End House and Garden [English Heritage], Essex • A. Moro, double portrait, oils, *c.*1560 (with Lady Anne Gresham), Rijksmuseum, Amsterdam • A. Moro, oils, *c.*1565 • oils, *c.*1565, NPG; version, Mercers' Hall, London • Thew, engraving, *c.*1792 (after oil painting by A. Moro, *c.*1560) • R. Woodman, engraving, 1839 (after unknown artist), repro. in Burgon, *Life and times of Sir Thomas Gresham* • F. Delaram, engraving (after oil painting by A. Moro, *c.*1565), NPG • oils, NG Can.

Gresley, Sir (Herbert) Nigel (1876–1941), railway engineer, was born in Edinburgh on 19 June 1876, the fourth and youngest son and youngest of five children of the Revd Nigel Gresley, rector of Netherseale, Leicestershire, and his wife, Joanna Beatrice, daughter of John Wilson, and grandson of Sir William Nigel Gresley, ninth baronet. He was educated at Marlborough College and began his engineering apprenticeship in 1893 under Francis Webb at the Crewe locomotive works of the London and North Western Railway. Subsequently he was a pupil of John Aspinall of the Lancashire and Yorkshire Railway at Horwich, near Bolton; he became an assistant manager at their carriage workshops at Newton Heath, Manchester, in 1901, and works manager in the following year. In 1901 Gresley married Ethel Frances (d. 1929), daughter of W. P. Fullager, solicitor, of St Anne's, Lancashire. They had two sons and two daughters. In 1904 he was appointed assistant carriage and wagon superintendent of the Lancashire and Yorkshire, and in 1905 transferred to the Great Northern Railway in Doncaster as carriage and wagon superintendent.

In 1911 Gresley succeeded Henry Ivatt as locomotive engineer. He introduced more powerful general-purpose main-line 2-6-0 and 2-8-0 freight locomotives, followed in 1922 by the prototype Pacific (4-6-2) type for heavy long-distance passenger trains. In 1920 he was appointed CBE for his direction of war material production at Doncaster works.

In 1923 Gresley became chief mechanical engineer of the London and North Eastern Railway (LNER), following the merger of independent companies into four railway groups. He was responsible for the maintenance and repair of over 7000 locomotives, 21,000 passenger coaches, and 300,000 goods wagons, as well as for new design and construction, with control of some 30,000 workshop and out-station staff. The task of integrating the individual railways into the LNER was not easy. Over the first five years he introduced new locomotive designs and continued the development of the main-line Pacific type, incorporating detailed improvements pioneered by George Jackson Churchward of the Great Western Railway (GWR), whose work he greatly admired. This was characteristic of Gresley, who ensured that he and his design team were fully informed on the latest developments abroad and adopted ideas pioneered elsewhere if they were proved relevant to his needs. Thus from 1928 onwards he collaborated closely with the French engineer André Chapelon, whose rebuilding of existing locomotives enabled their power and efficiency to be greatly increased. His great technical knowledge and ability were combined with thoroughness; all important engineering drawings were personally approved by him and all new features were tested on prototypes before being put into quantity production. While he was a commanding personality and very much the 'chief' in his department he consulted closely with, and was advised by, his engineers before taking technical decisions. He also circulated 'third copies' of all technical correspondence to his design staff to ensure that all were fully informed.

Gresley's earlier work on improved passenger coaches continued on the LNER and new trains were built with simple but attractive internal decoration and fittings. There were also new restaurant cars with all-electric cooking to reduce fire risks, improved sleeping-cars, and new types of high-capacity goods wagon. In 1934 the LNER investigated using high-speed diesel trains, as in Germany, for a London to Newcastle business service. However, tests showed that a faster schedule could be operated with a Pacific-hauled steam train of Gresley's comfortable coaches seating double the number of passengers. In 1935 the fully streamlined *Silver Jubilee* train, the first in Britain, went into service, averaging 71 m.p.h. between London and Darlington. In 1938 one of the streamlined Pacific locomotives, *Mallard*, attained a maximum speed of 126 m.p.h., a world record for steam traction. From 1936 184 heavy 2-6-2 mixed traffic locomotives were built and played a major part in main line operation.

While a strong advocate of improving the steam locomotive to the maximum degree possible, Gresley also tested diesel locomotives and railcars and realized that the future for main-line railway operation lay with electric traction when capital resources were available. In 1936 it was decided to electrify the severely graded cross-Pennine main line from Sheffield to Manchester and he was responsible for the design of electric locomotives for this service. From 1927, and later supported by his friend William Stanier of the London, Midland, and Scottish Railway (LMSR), he had advocated the building of a national locomotive testing station capable of handling the largest locomotives, and in 1937 work on the station was started at Rugby.

Gresley was involved actively for many years with the International Railway Congress Association as a member of its permanent commission and gave a comprehensive report on improvements in steam locomotives at the Madrid Congress in 1930. He was president of the Institution of Mechanical Engineers in 1936, the Institution of Locomotive Engineers in 1927 and 1934, and the Association of Railway Locomotive Engineers in 1926 and 1927. He served on a number of government committees, including those on automatic train control and on railway electrification. In 1936 he was knighted and awarded an honorary DSc by Manchester University. He enjoyed a simple life in the country best, being with his grandchildren and his dogs, shooting, and fishing. Gresley died at his home, Watton House, Watton-at-Stone, Hertford, on 5 April 1941, shortly before his intended retirement. He was buried at Netherseale, near Burton upon Trent.

GEORGE W. CARPENTER, rev.

Sources H. A. V. Bulleid, *Master builders of steam* (1963), 44–71 • E. Bannister, *Trained by Sir Nigel Gresley* (1984) • private information (1993) • J. Bellwood and D. Jenkinson, *Gresley and Stanier*, 2nd edn (1986) • *CGPLA Eng. & Wales* (1941)
Archives FILM Tua Films, 17 Kingsway, Leicester, short film of LNER centenary exhibition, Darlington, 1925
Likenesses portrait, 1936, Institution of Mechanical Engineers, London • photograph, repro. in Bellwood and Jenkinson, *Gresley and Stanier*
Wealth at death £27,317 6s. 10d.: probate, 30 June 1941, *CGPLA Eng. & Wales*

Gresley [Greisley], **Sir Roger, eighth baronet** (1799–1837), politician, born on 27 December 1799, was the son of Sir Nigel Bowyer Gresley, seventh baronet, of Drakelow Park, Burton upon Trent, and his second wife, Maria Eliza, daughter of Caleb Garway of Worcester. He succeeded his father in 1808 and entered Christ Church, Oxford, on 17 October 1817, where he remained until 1819, but took no degree. After an unsuccessful attempt to obtain a seat in parliament for Lichfield in 1826, he was returned for Durham City in 1830 and New Romney, Kent, in 1831. He failed in South Derbyshire in 1832, was elected there in 1835, but did not stand again. He was in most respects a moderate tory. In June 1821 he married Lady Sophia Catharine, youngest daughter of George William Coventry, seventh earl of Coventry; their one child, Editha, died an infant in 1823. He was groom of the bedchamber to the duke of Sussex, captain of the Staffordshire yeomanry cavalry, and FSA. Gresley, who often affected the name Greisley, published several pamphlets hostile to Catholic emancipation, a tale about the evils of contemporary Rome, *Sir Philip Gasteneys: a Minor* (1829), and an anti-papal essay, *Gregory the Seventh* (1832). He died on 12 October 1837 and was buried on 28 October at Church Gresley, Derbyshire.

W. F. WENTWORTH-SHIELDS, rev. H. C. G. MATTHEW

Sources *GM*, 2nd ser., 8 (1837), 649–50 • review of Gresley's *Sir Philip Gasteneys, a minor*, *The Athenaeum* (2 Sept 1829), 547–8 • review of Gresley's *Life and pontificate of Gregory the Seventh*, *The Athenaeum* (22 Sept 1832), 614–16
Archives Derbys. RO, corresp. • Derbys. RO, family corresp., papers, and MSS relating to his guardianship and education

Gresley, William (1801–1876), Church of England clergyman and author, was born on 16 March 1801 at Kenilworth, Warwickshire, the eldest son of Richard Gresley (1766–1850) of Stowe House, Lichfield, Staffordshire, bencher of the Middle Temple, a descendant of the ancient Gresley family which came to England at the time of the conquest and settled at Drakelow, Derbyshire, and his first wife, Caroline (d. 1817), youngest daughter of Andrew Grote, banker, of Blackheath, Kent. George Grote, historian of ancient Greece, was a first cousin of Gresley's on his mother's side. He entered Westminster School on 14 January 1811, and was awarded a king's scholarship in 1815. On 21 May 1819 he matriculated at Christ Church, Oxford, where he retained a studentship until his marriage in 1828. He took a second class in *literae humaniores* in 1822, graduating BA on 8 February 1823 and MA on 25 May 1825. Gresley was admitted to the Middle Temple in 1822, but problems with his eyesight, which troubled him throughout life, thwarted his original intention to follow his father and study for the bar. He was ordained deacon in 1825 and priest the following year. On 28 October 1828 he married Ann Wright Scott (bap. 5 Sept 1804), daughter and heir of John Barker Scott, banker, of Lichfield, and his wife, Betsey. They had nine children between 1830 and 1842, but most died in infancy or childhood, and Gresley survived all of them.

Curate briefly in 1828 at Drayton Bassett, near Tamworth, Staffordshire, Gresley then returned to Stowe House, and from 1830 to 1837 was assistant curate in the parish of St Chad's, Lichfield, where Stowe was situated. He served also as morning lecturer at St Mary's, Lichfield, for some of this period. On 27 November 1840 he was appointed by the bishop of Lichfield, James Bowstead, to the prebendal stall of Wolvey in Lichfield Cathedral, an honorary preferment.

Gresley's first publication was *Ecclesiastes Anglicanus* (1835), a treatise on the art of preaching in epistolary form. He came to much wider public notice, however, with the appearance of his first work of fiction, *Portrait of an English Churchman*, in 1838. The *Portrait* virtually founded the canon of religious and social tales by which Gresley and his fellow Tractarian and friend F. E. Paget endeavoured to popularize high-church principles. Its assertion of the catholicity of the Church of England firmly aligned him with the Tractarian movement, and it ran through numerous editions. In partnership with Edward Churton he then served as editor of The Englishman's Library, a series of similar church fables founded by the publisher James Burns early in 1839. Gresley wrote six of the thirty-one volumes which appeared under its aegis between 1839 and 1846, his undemanding and formulaic tales characterized by their vehement hostility to religious and political liberalism. *Clement Walton, or, The English*

William Gresley (1801–1876), by Richard Smith, pubd 1841 (after James Pardon)

Citizen (vol. 1) and *The Siege of Lichfield: a Tale Illustrative of the Great Rebellion* (vol. 13) both appeared in 1840, and *Charles Lever, or, The Man of the Nineteenth Century* (vol. 15) and *The Forest of Arden: a Tale Illustrative of the English Reformation* (vol. 19) in 1841. *Church-Clavering, or, The Schoolmaster* (vol. 24), which depicted his ideal of church education and drew on material published earlier in the *Englishman's Magazine*, appeared in 1843, and *Coniston Hall, or, The Jacobites: a Historical Tale* (vol. 31) in 1846. He also contributed two of the twenty-one tales published in The Juvenile Englishman's Library, edited successively by F. E. Paget and J. F. Russell. Other works for children are *Holyday Tales* (1842) and *Frank's First Trip to the Continent* (1845). If any of his stories is remembered, however, it is *Bernard Leslie, or, A Tale of the Last Ten Years* (1842), a semi-autobiographical novel written to portray 'the commencement and growing up' of the Oxford Movement. He published a second volume in 1859.

A belligerent controversialist, Gresley also published numerous books and pamphlets in defence of Tractarianism and hostile to evangelicalism. His *Evangelical Truth and Apostolical Order: a Dialogue* (1846) was followed in the same year by *The Real Danger of the Church of England*. This provoked various pamphlet ripostes, most notably from Francis Close, evangelical vicar of Cheltenham, with Gresley publishing second and third statements of *The Real Danger* in 1846 and 1847. Similar publications include *A Word of Remonstrance with the Evangelicals* (1850) and a supplement of 1851.

In the summer of 1851 Gresley began a spell as volunteer assistant priest at St Paul's, Brighton, which, though noted for its pastoral success, ensnared him in considerable controversy. He gained some reputation for preaching and district visiting, and in particular for his work among prostitutes. However, the publication of his *Ordinance of Confession* (1851), which exhorted the clergy to its greater use, drew attention to his activities as a confessor and provoked local opposition, manifested in the protests of the Brighton Protestant Defence Committee (1851–3). He was also plunged into prolonged dispute with the bishop of Chichester, Ashurst Turner Gilbert, who pronounced the *Ordinance* inconsistent with church teaching and warned that he would not license Gresley as an assistant curate.

Gresley returned to Lichfield, and in 1857 accepted the perpetual curacy of All Saints', Boyne Hill, near Maidenhead, Berkshire, where a church, parsonage house, and school were under construction out of the charity of three local women. Gresley superintended the completion of the project, and All Saints' was consecrated by the bishop of Oxford, Samuel Wilberforce, on 1 December 1857. A curate's house, almshouse, and infant school were built soon after, with a schoolmaster appointed in 1866 and the school further enlarged in 1872. Three of his children survived to accompany him to Boyne Hill but they all died, two of them in 1868, and in his later years Gresley was cared for by a widowed daughter-in-law. His health had been deteriorating for some time before declining sharply in early 1876. On 19 September, while opening the service at Boyne Hill, he suffered a serious attack from which he never recovered. He died two months later on the evening of 19 November 1876 at Boyne Hill, and is buried in the churchyard.

Gresley was a pugnacious champion of the Tractarian movement, but never belonged to its extreme wing. He remained unsympathetic to Roman Catholicism as well as to later ritualist developments, which induced his resignation as vice-president of the English Church Union in January 1867. His theological writings—of which *Remarks on the Necessity of Attempting a Restoration of the National Church* (1841), *Anglo-Catholicism* (1844), *A Short Treatise on the English Church* (1845), and *Distinctive Tenets of the Church of England* (1847) are all typical—are standard restatements of the Anglican *via media*. His later works are animated less by party spirit than by apprehension at the disbelief of the age. To this end he published such books as *Idealism Considered* (1860), *Sophron and Neologus, or, Common Sense Philosophy* (1861), *Priests and Philosophers* (1873), and *Thoughts on Religion and Philosophy* (1875), with extracts from the last two appearing posthumously, with a brief sketch of Gresley by his curate, as *The Scepticism of the Nineteenth Century* in 1879. A select preacher at Oxford in 1836, Gresley's sermons were also published throughout his life. Among his larger collections are *Sermons on some of the Social and Political Duties of a Christian* (1836), *Parochial Sermons* (1842), *Practical Sermons* (1848), and *Sermons Preached at Brighton* (1858).

S. A. SKINNER

Sources *The scepticism of the nineteenth century: selections from the latest works of the Rev. William Gresley … with a short account of the author,*

ed. S. C. Austen (1879) • *The Guardian* (22 Nov 1876), 1522 • *The Guardian* (29 Nov 1876), 1545 • *The Guardian* (6 Dec 1876), 1585–6 • *Church Times* (24 Nov 1876), p. 599, col. 2 • Burke, *Gen. GB* • J. Welch, *The list of the queen's scholars of St Peter's College, Westminster*, ed. [C. B. Philli-more], new edn (1852), 479, 485–6, 490, 508 • *Old Westminsters*, 1.399 • Foster, *Alum. Oxon.* • Crockford (1876) • *Fasti Angl.* (Hardy), 1.642 • J. Hutchinson, ed., *A catalogue of notable Middle Templars: with brief biographical notices* (1902), 105 • *IGI*
Archives Pusey Oxf., corresp. and papers relating to The Englishman's Library
Likenesses R. Smith, stipple, pubd 1841 (after stipple and line print by J. Pardon), NPG [*see illus.*]
Wealth at death under £25,000: resworn probate, Feb 1878, *CGPLA Eng. & Wales* (1877)

Gresse, John Alexander (1741–1794), painter and drawing master, was born in London. His father, Peter Gaspard Gresse (*d.* 1771), was a native of Rolle, on the Lake of Geneva, Switzerland, and owned a small property close to Oxford Street, London, on which Stephen Street and Gresse Street, Rathbone Place, were built about 1771. Gresse studied drawing under Gerard Scotin, the engraver, and was one of the first students to work in the gallery of casts founded by the duke of Richmond. He also studied at the St Martin's Lane Academy. In 1755 he obtained a premium at the Society of Arts for a drawing by a student under the age of fourteen years, and in 1759 he gained three premiums for drawings and studies from the human figure. He was successful again in 1761 and 1762, obtaining in all nine premiums before attaining the age of twenty-one. Having inherited a sufficient income from his father, Gresse was able to pursue an artistic career with few financial concerns. He was for a short time pupil of Thomas Major, the engraver, and worked for several years under Giovanni Battista Cipriani, profiting at the same time by the instruction of Francesco Zuccarelli. He was employed by the publisher John Boydell to make drawings. In 1763 he exhibited a landscape at the Free Society of Artists, and in 1764 two miniatures and a Madonna. In 1765 he became a member of the rival Incorporated Society of Artists, and exhibited with it for four years, chiefly miniatures. In 1768 he sent a stained drawing of the earl of Bessborough's seat at Roehampton. Gresse excelled in this branch of watercolour painting, and some of his views were engraved. He occasionally practised etching, and etched the plates for James Kennedy's *A New Description of the Pictures and Statues at the Earl of Pembroke's House at Wilton* (1769). He published a few other etchings, including one, *St. Jerome*, after Guido, and *A Satyr Sleeping* after N. Poussin. On 24 October 1771, at the Old Church, St Pancras, London, Gresse married Elizabeth Thornton (*d.* 1799). He became one of the most fashionable drawing masters of his day. In 1777 he was appointed drawing master to the daughters of George III, and was soon a favourite at court. The watercolourist Robert Hills was his pupil. His corpulence obtained for him the nickname Jack Grease. Gresse 'died suddenly on Thursday last' on 20 February 1794, and was buried in London at St Anne's, Soho (Farington, *Diary*, 1.166). He was a collector of works of art, which were sold by auction shortly after his death, the sale occupying six days. Mrs Gresse later eloped with the painter

Francis Wheatley to Dublin. She bequeathed to her executor, 'Joseph Lane Yeomans of King Street Southampton Row Bloomsbury [Wheatley's famous] painting of The Irish House of Commons' (PROB 11/1322, sig. 269, fol. 155*v*). This was noted to have been in her possession when she died (Farington, *Diary*, 4.1216).

L. H. CUST, *rev.* ANNETTE PEACH

Sources E. Edwards, *Anecdotes of painters* (1808); facs. edn (1970) • Redgrave, *Artists* • Dodd, 'Manuscript history of English engravers', BL, Add. MS 33401 • Mallalieu, *Watercolour artists* • D. Foskett, *Miniatures: dictionary and guide* (1987) • *IGI* • PRO, PROB 11/971, sig. 374 [Peter Gaspard Gresse] • PRO, PROB 11/1322, sig. 269, fols. 155*v*–157 [Elizabeth Gresse] • PRO, IR 26/30, fols. 86–7 [Elizabeth Gresse] • Farington, *Diary*, 1.666; 4.1216
Archives BL, exhibition catalogues, Add. MS 33401
Likenesses chalk drawing, *c.*1770, NPG

Gresswell, Dan (1819–1883), veterinary surgeon, the son of William Gresswell, a farmer, was born on 13 May 1819 at Kelsey Hall, Spilsby, Lincolnshire. He entered the Royal Veterinary College, London, in March 1839 and passed his examinations on 18 June 1840, the same year in which he was elected a fellow of the Veterinary Medical Association in recognition of an essay entitled 'Inflammation of the mammillary glands in the mare, cow and ewe'. On 18 December 1845 he married Anne (*b.* 1825/6), daughter of William Beastall, farmer of Reston, near Louth, in Lincolnshire; they had eight sons and seven daughters. Several of his sons also became veterinary surgeons.

Gresswell settled in Louth and became widely known as a veterinary surgeon. On 20 February 1877 he was elected fellow of the Royal College of Veterinary Surgeons as a reward for original research. He wrote many papers: for example, 'Paralysis in the horse', 'Excision of the uterus in the cow', 'Treatment and aetiology of splenic apoplexy or anthrax', 'Tetanus', 'Arsenical poisoning', and other works. He also held several professional appointments: he was examiner of prizes for proficiency of knowledge in cattle pathology for the Royal Agricultural Society; and examiner in cattle pathology for the Royal College of Veterinary Surgeons. He was also an inspector under the Contagious Diseases (Animals) Act for the Louth petty sessional division; and local consulting veterinary surgeon to the Royal Agricultural Society. After his death his sons published several works on veterinary science, partly embodying his manuscripts and verbal instructions.

Gresswell took an active part in local politics; he was a strong Conservative, and did much to improve the sanitary arrangements of Louth. He was elected to the town council on 1 November 1862 as a member for the south ward of Louth, with 296 votes; alderman in April 1871; and mayor on 9 November 1871. He continued to be an alderman until his death, at Mercer Row, Louth, on 13 March 1883. He was survived by his wife and children.

[ANON.], *rev.* LINDA WARDEN

Sources *The Veterinarian*, 56 (May 1883) • *The Louth and Lincolnshire Advertiser* (8 Nov 1862) • *The Louth and Lincolnshire Advertiser* (11 Nov 1871) • register of pupils, 1794–1907, Royal Veterinary College, London • private information (1890) • m. cert. • d. cert.

Wealth at death £1952 12*s.* 6*d.*: probate, 13 April 1883, *CGPLA Eng. & Wales*

Greswell, Edward (1797–1869), biblical scholar, was born in Denton, near Manchester, on 3 August 1797, one of the seven sons of the Revd William Parr *Greswell (*bap.* 1765, *d.* 1854), the bibliographer, and his wife, whose details are not known. Richard *Greswell, also an Oxford tutor, was his brother. Greswell was taught at home and then at Manchester grammar school. He matriculated at Brasenose College, Oxford, on 5 April 1815, where he was elected a scholar in the same year. In 1816 he won the scholarship at Corpus Christi College, Oxford, set aside for students from Lancashire; he graduated BA (1819), MA (1822), and BD (1830). He was ordained deacon in 1825 and priest in 1826, and he held the office of college tutor from 1822 to 1834. He was elected a fellow of Corpus Christi College in 1823 and remained a fellow until his death in 1869. He held the academic positions of Latin reader (1824), junior dean (1825), Greek reader (1827), college librarian (1830), and vice-president (1840 to 1869).

Greswell's early work on biblical chronology, published as *Dissertations upon the Principles and Arrangement of a Harmony of the Gospels* (1830) or *Harmonica evangelica*, became a set text at the University of Oxford, which defended the integrity of the four traditional gospels despite the challenges of biblical scholars elsewhere, and particularly in Germany. When a dispute broke out in 1836 over the appointment of Renn Dickson Hampden to the regius professorship of divinity at the University of Oxford, Greswell published his opinions on the case in a *Letter to his Grace the Duke of Wellington, Chancellor of the University* (1837), and he later criticized Bishop Colenso's work on the Pentateuch (1863). He declined the offer of the headship of the college in 1843 for fear that it would interfere with his studies. Greswell died in Oxford, at Corpus Christi, on 29 June 1869 and was buried in the college cloisters.

Greswell was a prolific writer and his works of biblical scholarship, though apparently ignorant of the findings of contemporary patristic scholars, helped ordinands at the University of Oxford to maintain traditional Anglican positions on the harmony of the four gospel accounts of the life and divinity of Jesus. Of historical interest for high-church Anglican theological thought and scholarship of the day, his works included *An Exposition of the Parables, and of other Parts of the Gospels* (6 vols., 1834–5), *Prolegomena ad harmoniam evangelicam* (1840), *Fasti temporis Catholici and origines kalendariae: History of the Primitive Calendar* (1852), and *The three witnesses and the threefold cord; being the testimony of the natural measures of time, of the primitive civil calendar, and of antediluvian and postdiluvian tradition, on the principal questions of fact in sacred and profane antiquity* (1862). Greswell also published *Joannis Miltoni fabulae* (1832) and *The Zulus and the Men of Science* (1865).

C. W. SUTTON, *rev.* SINÉAD AGNEW

Sources J. F. Smith, ed., *The admission register of the Manchester School, with some notes of the more distinguished scholars*, 3/1, Chetham Society, 93 (1874), 79 · Foster, *Alum. Oxon.* · W. R. Ward, *Victorian Oxford* (1965) · Boase, *Mod. Eng. biog.* · Ward, *Men of the reign*, 373 · Allibone, *Dict.*

Wealth at death under £4000: probate, 5 Aug 1869, *CGPLA Eng. & Wales*

Greswell, Richard (1800–1881), college teacher and promoter of church schools, born at Denton, Lancashire, on 22 July 1800, was the fourth son of a family of seven sons and two daughters of the Revd William Parr *Greswell (*d.* 1854) and his wife, Anne Hague (1766–1841). He was the younger brother of Edward *Greswell. Educated first by his father, he entered Worcester College, Oxford, where he held a scholarship from 1818 to 1824. In 1822, having gained firsts in both classics and mathematics, he was appointed assistant tutor of Worcester, and in the next year full tutor. He became fellow in June 1824. He graduated BA in 1822, MA in 1825, and BD in 1836, and was ordained in 1828, but never held a cure of souls. As a tutor he was learned and skilful, and his lectures were considered models in their way. For many years he devoted the proceeds of his tutorship to public and charitable objects, his personal expenses being defrayed from a modest fortune brought by his wife, Joana Julia, daughter of the Revd James Armetriding (or Armitriding), rector of Steeple Aston, whom he married on 5 April 1836. Although Greswell relinquished his fellowship on his marriage, he retained his college teaching position until 1853, making him one of the first instances of a married tutor. His interests spanned wide areas of knowledge: one of the earliest members of the Ashmolean Society and elected FRS in 1830, he had in the late 1820s supported the idea of a museum for natural history in Oxford, and began a subscription for that purpose in 1850. He also advocated in 1843 the establishment of university professorships in the theory of art, arguing that the study of art (and especially Christian art) should be an essential part of education, and that it was important to inculcate the principles of taste among future patrons. A supporter of the Tractarian movement, he acted as chairman of Gladstone's election committee for the Oxford University parliamentary seat from 1847 until Gladstone's defeat in 1865.

In 1843, following the defeat of the education clauses of Sir James Graham's Factory Bill, Greswell opened a subscription to re-endow the Anglican National Society, which ran church schools. Giving £1000 himself, Greswell, who had the support of the prime minister (Peel) and the archbishop of Canterbury (Howley), raised over £200,000, an initiative which helped to secure the dominance of the Church of England as a provider of elementary education. He was a great benefactor to his father's parish of Denton, and by his exertions a new church, Christ Church, was built and provided with parsonage, schools, and endowment (1853). He was also a supporter of the Universities' Mission to Central Africa. Many kindly and beneficent acts are related of Greswell, whose 'chief characteristics were great and varied learning, boundless benevolence, and a childlike simplicity' (Burgon, 2.118).

After the death of his wife in 1875 Greswell, who was increasingly infirm, was nursed by his two daughters, Joana Julia (*b.* 1838) and Helen Margaret (*b.* 1840). He had educated both, and the former, a considerable scholar of Greek and Hebrew, published a *Grammatical Analysis of the Hebrew Psalter* (1873). Greswell died at his home, 39 St Giles', Oxford, on 22 July 1881, and was buried at St Mary Magdalen, Oxford.

C. W. SUTTON, rev. M. C. CURTHOYS

Sources J. W. Burgon, *Lives of twelve good men*, [new edn], 2 (1889), 93–121 · Crockford · Foster, *Alum. Oxon.* · W. R. Ward, *Victorian Oxford* (1965) · J. Booker, 'A history of the ancient chapel of Denton, in Manchester parish', *Miscellanies, II*, Chetham Society (1855), 1–141
Archives Worcester College, Oxford | BL, corresp. with W. E. Gladstone, Add. MS 44181
Likenesses J. Bridges, oils, 1836, Worcester College, Oxford · T. W. Smith, print, c.1850, AM Oxf.
Wealth at death £21,275 8s. 3d.: probate, 4 Nov 1881, *CGPLA Eng. & Wales*

Greswell, William Parr (*bap.* 1765, *d.* 1854), Church of England clergyman and bibliographer, son of John Greswell of Chester, was baptized at Tarvin, Cheshire, on 23 June 1765. He was ordained on 20 September 1789 to the curacy of Blackley, near Manchester. While at Blackley he became acquainted with the first earl of Wilton, who appointed him tutor to his son. On 24 September 1791 the earl conferred on him the incumbency of Denton, also near Manchester. This living, which when he took it was worth only £100 a year, Greswell held for the long period of sixty-three years. To add to his income he opened a school.

Greswell married Anne Hague on 30 August 1794 and they had seven sons and two daughters. He educated his own sons, five of whom went to Oxford University and won high honours. They were: William (1796–1876), MA, fellow of Balliol College and author of works on ritual; Edward *Greswell (1797–1869), BD, fellow and tutor of Corpus Christi College; Richard *Greswell (1800–1881), BD, fellow and tutor of Worcester College; Francis Hague (*b.* 1803), MA, fellow of Brasenose College; and Clement (*b.* 1809), MA, fellow and tutor of Oriel College and rector of Tortworth, Gloucestershire. His other sons were Charles (*b.* 1802), a medical practitioner, and Thomas Heamer (*b.* 1795), master of Chetham's Hospital, Manchester.

In spite of his literary talent, Greswell's published works were unsuccessful. He wrote two works on the Parisian press which were said to be 'inexact' by Jacques Charles Brunet in *Manuel du libraire* (1835), while his Latin translations of the memoirs of Angelus Politianus and others were condemned in the *Retrospective Review* as careless and unmethodical (9/1, 1824, 64–5). Greswell resigned his incumbency of Denton in 1853, and died on 12 January 1854 at Denton, where he was buried. His large library was sold at Sothebys in February 1855.

C. W. SUTTON, rev. ZOË LAWSON

Sources J. Booker, 'A history of the ancient chapel of Denton, in Manchester parish', *Miscellanies, II*, Chetham Society (1855), 1–141, 109 · *GM*, 2nd ser., 41 (1854), 427 · J. F. Smith, ed., *The admission register of the Manchester School, with some notes of the more distinguished scholars*, 2, Chetham Society, 73 (1868), 77–8 · J. W. Burgon, *Lives of twelve good men*, [new edn], 2 vols. (1888–9)

Greswold, Edward (*bap.* 1594?, *d.* 1633), religious recluse, was probably baptized on 5 August 1594 at Tanworth, Warwickshire. He was the son of Thomas Greswold (*d.* 1598/9), landowner, and his wife, Elizabeth (*d.* 1645), daughter and heir of Benedict Shuckburgh of Cubbington, Warwickshire. His father, who owned significant property in and around Solihull, died when Greswold was a child and in July 1602 his mother married William Lisle of Evenley, Northamptonshire. Although a younger son, Greswold was apparently well provided for and lived at Cubbington, a manor owned by his mother's family, with his wife, Margaret. They had at least eight children.

Greswold's career provides an intriguing insight into the puritan community in early Stuart England, and the relationship between godly protestants within the established church and those who rejected this church entirely. It also offers a bizarre illustration of religious extremism before the civil war. His story was recorded by two contemporaries, the puritan minister Samuel Clarke, who found Greswold's actions repugnant, and the royalist gentleman Sir William Dugdale, who related Greswold's story as a curiosity and seemed more concerned with the rightful descent of the Greswold property. Clarke recalled that Greswold was a respected member of the godly community in Warwickshire during the 1620s. About 1629, however, he came into contact with the separatist preacher John Canne, who 'began to seduce him from his former opinions' (Clarke, 112). In later writings Canne published his arguments that Christians should be 'separated from the world, and the false worship and the ways thereof' (Canne). The majority of English puritans rejected this radical view, but it did appeal to a desire among godly protestants to create a church of true Christians untouched by the 'superstitious' habits of the wider world. It appears that Greswold took Canne's ideas about separation from the Church of England to their most extreme conclusion. He decided first that he could not attend the local church, second that he could not listen to any 'conformable minister' and from there 'fell to separation' (Clarke, 112). He eventually came to believe 'that all civil society with others, defiled him' (ibid.), locked himself and his family in his house, and instructed his servants to bring them food through the windows. Local ministers, including Clarke, came to remonstrate with him but were ignored. When one of his children died he placed the body in the next room and later ordered a servant to bring moss which he placed in the cracks between the rooms to stop the smell. This was only discovered when a justice of the peace 'sent some with command to break open his chamber door' (ibid., 113), and Greswold and his family were found 'with their haire, and nailes growne very long, [and] their clothes almost rotten on their backes' (ibid.).

When released neither Greswold nor his children, 'being so tutored by him' (Clarke, 113), would speak to anyone. His children were sent to friends and eventually recovered but Greswold never wavered from his beliefs. He took to his bed, ignoring all those who came to him and 'intreated, counselled, threatn'd, and prayed' (ibid., 114).

He turned his face to the wall and spoke not a word until his death 'which was not long after' (ibid.), in 1633. He was succeeded by his son John, who died in 1640.

D. J. OLDRIDGE

Sources S. Clarke, *A mirrour or looking glasse* (1646) • W. Dugdale, *The antiquities of Warwickshire illustrated* (1656) • J. Canne, *A necessitie of separation from the Church of England* (Amsterdam, 1634) • D. Oldridge, *Religion and society in early Stuart England* (1998) • J. F. Wilson, 'Another look at John Canne', *Church History*, 33 (1964) • C. Burrage, *The early English dissenters*, 2nd edn (1967) • A. Hughes, *Politics, society and civil war in Warwickshire, 1620–1660* (1987) • Greaves & Zaller, *BDBR* • *Warwick county records: quarter session's indictment book, 1631–1674*, ed. S. C. Ratcliffe and H. C. Johnson (1941) • *VCH Warwickshire*, vols. 4, 6 • *IGI* • J. Burman, *The story of Tanworth-in-Arden, Warwickshire* (1930) • J. Burman, *Old Warwickshire families* (1934)

Gretton, John, first Baron Gretton (1867–1947), brewer and politician, was born on 1 September 1867 at Bladen House, Winshill, Burton upon Trent, Staffordshire, the eldest of the three sons and five daughters of John Gretton (1833–1899), of Bladen House, Winshill, Staffordshire, and Grantham Lodge, Cowes, Isle of Wight, and his wife, Marianne Louisa (1847–1891), the daughter of Major John Richard Molineux (1817–1902). His father, who left an estate worth £2,883,640, was a director of England's leading brewery, Bass, Ratcliff and Gretton, of Burton upon Trent. Having leased Sudbury Hall, Derbyshire, from Lord Vernon in the late 1890s, Gretton inherited Stapleford Park, near Melton Mowbray, Leicestershire, the ancestral home of Lord Harborough bought by his father in 1894, and a great house in Knightsbridge, London.

After education at Harrow School, Gretton went to work in the brewery at the age of about twenty. In 1893 he joined the board, and was soon crucial in political resistance to the temperance movement. He was diligent rather than keenly entrepreneurial, and in 1909 he succeeded Michael Arthur Bass, first Baron Burton, as chairman of Bass, Ratcliff and Gretton. The brewery paid dividends of 30 per cent in 1896–7 and remained superbly profitable throughout Gretton's chairmanship: average annual dividends on ordinary shares typically exceeded 20 per cent throughout the period 1934–45. Gretton was too conservative and complacent about the excellence of his products to develop forward strategies, however, and competition from Worthington's bottled beers troubled the firm from about 1900. Antagonism existed at all levels between the two companies; nevertheless, in 1926 Gretton agreed a merger with Arthur Manners, his counterpart at Worthington. But the two companies were left unintegrated, so that the anticipated benefits of this huge merger were never achieved. Manners always proved more astute and ruthless in boardroom politics than Gretton, whose resignation as chairman he provoked in 1945.

Despite his Quaker descent, Gretton joined the Staffordshire volunteer regiment when young and maintained a lifelong devotion to soldiering. Known as 'Colonel' Gretton, he commanded the 6th battalion of the North Staffordshires (1900–07), and was their honorary colonel (1912–32). Military recruitment, training, and inspection consumed his energies in 1914–18.

Gretton was an archetype of the reactionary tory brewer. For forty-eight years he was a Conservative MP, representing successively South Derbyshire (1895–1906), Rutland (1907–18), and Burton upon Trent (1918–43). As a protectionist he testified to the tariff commission (1903); he was an implacable opponent of the Licensing Bill (1908) and of government restrictions on the wartime drinks trade. Lord Balniel characterized him in 1910:

> One of the best-hearted fellows one has ever met, kind, generous, self-effacing: ugly as possible, blinking at one through gold-rimmed spectacles: inarticulate, for it is almost impossible to hear a word he says, and his handwriting is simply deplorable. He has all the noble qualities of the mole. (Vincent, 169)

He hated the Lloyd George coalition, and resigned the tory whip (1921–2) in protest at its Irish settlement, foreign policy, and budget 'squandermania'. His inability to co-operate with Lord Salisbury, however, resulted in the leadership of the die-hard Unionists passing to Salisbury by the summer of 1922. Gretton, who sought the party chairmanship later in 1922, chaired the Unionist reconstruction committee (1920–21) and the National Union of Conservative and Unionist Associations (1920–29). He was a gloomy, stubborn, and suspicious politician but a sharp-eared gossip who often exasperated his party leaders by demanding 'reactionary policy that the country would not stand' (*Austen Chamberlain Diary*, 358).

After the Conservative defeat in 1929, Gretton mustered the die-hards against Baldwin, and as a leader of the India defence committee stood beside Churchill in a last-ditch fight against the Government of India Bill in 1931–5. Cuthbert Headlam wrote of him in 1934:

> He is a terrible cripple nowadays and getting very old—in the House he collapses into a heap snoring so loud that he almost disturbs a debate. It is odd that he has had so much influence in politics for he has no parliamentary ability— and is not even an average speaker: presumably he is a clever intriguer. I like him. (Ball, 297)

Gretton was a Derbyshire magistrate (1899), deputy lieutenant of Leicestershire (1929), a freeman of Burton upon Trent (1943), lord of the manor of Wymondham, and patron of five livings in Leicestershire, Rutland, and Staffordshire. He was created CBE in 1919, sworn of the privy council in 1926, and received a barony in 1944. In 1900 he married Maud Helen de Moleyns (1870–1934), the fourth daughter of the fourth Baron Ventry; they had a son and two daughters. He died of hemiplegia and a cerebral thrombosis on 2 June 1947 at Stapleford Park, and was buried at Stapleford on 6 June.

RICHARD DAVENPORT-HINES

Sources *The Times* (4 June 1947) • C. C. Owen, 'The greatest brewery in the world': a history of Bass, Ratcliff & Gretton, Derbyshire RS, 29 (1992) • T. R. Gourvish and R. G. Wilson, *The British brewing industry, 1830–1980* (1994) • *The Crawford papers: the journals of David Lindsay, twenty-seventh earl of Crawford … 1892–1940*, ed. J. Vincent (1984) • *Parliament and politics in the age of Baldwin and MacDonald: the Headlam diaries, 1923–1935*, ed. S. Ball (1992) • W. A. S. Hewins, *The apologia of an imperialist: forty years of empire policy*, 2 vols. (1929) • M. Gilbert, ed., *Winston S. Churchill*, companion vol. 5/2 (1981) • *The Austen Chamberlain diary letters: the correspondence of Sir Austen Chamberlain with his sisters Hilda and Ida, 1916–1937*, ed. R. C. Self, CS, 5th ser., 5 (1995) • Lord Croft, *My life of strife* (1949) • *ILN* (14 Oct 1899), 529 • *ILN* (23 Dec

1899), 924 · R. P. T. Davenport-Hines, 'Gretton, John', *DBB* · b. cert. · d. cert. · Burke, *Peerage*

Archives Bass Museum, Burton upon Trent, Bass, Ratcliff and Gretton MSS · BLPES, tariff commission MSS · Bodl. Oxf., J. S. Sandars MSS · CAC Cam., corresp. with Lord Croft · CUL, Baldwin MSS · HLRO, Bonar Law MSS · HLRO, Davidson MSS · HLRO, Lloyd George MSS · University of Sheffield, corresp. with W. A. S. Hewins · W. Sussex RO, Leo Maxse MSS

Likenesses photograph, *c.*1920, repro. in Hewins, *Apologia*, vol. 2, facing p. 248

Wealth at death £2,302,972 12*s.* 4*d.*: probate, 8 March 1949, *CGPLA Eng. & Wales*

Gretton, Sir Peter William (1912–1992), naval officer, was born on 27 August 1912 at Dalhousie, near Simla, India, the elder of the two sons of George Foster Gretton (1878–1950), a major in the Indian army who, after 1919, became an active joint partner of Lillywhites, Piccadilly, developing its range of ski goods, and his wife, Teresa Anne (1875–1947), the eldest of eleven children of William McEnery (1839–1919), medical practitioner. His younger brother, Richard John (Dick; *b.* 1915), was killed in action in north Africa in 1941. Four members in five generations were recognized by the Royal Humane Society: indeed Gretton also later became a vice-president. His mother, daughter of an Irish doctor, was a Catholic. So Gretton went initially to Ladycross, a Catholic preparatory school; and he sent his own three sons to Ampleforth, two under Basil Hume's housemastership. He himself went to Dartmouth and Greenwich Royal Naval colleges, where he was prone to overwork to exhaustion. In his examinations for the rank of lieutenant, he gained 'a full house of firsts in the Subs' course' (autobiography, 47), that is five certificates. In 1930 he was assigned to *Renown*, flagship of the battle-cruiser squadron. The following decade gave him a rich naval panorama—fleet assemblies at Gibraltar and Palma, a West Indies cruise, seatime in *Rodney*. He tried fleet flying, but found his pilot gifts wanting. His heart went to destroyers, where command responsibility came quickly; indeed he avoided specializing, preferring to remain a 'salthorse'. During the 1936 Arab uprising he was ashore at Haifa, protecting truck convoys by mounting a 2 pound ship's pompom on a hired lorry for night work. He later led a mixed platoon of seamen to help the local police fire-fighting and street-fighting, for which he was awarded a DSC, though on land. He spent his last two years of peace instructing at the Royal Naval College, Dartmouth. A timely anti-submarine course saw him into war no longer 'on the beach', but into east-coast convoys. He was just twenty-seven and an all-round athlete—horses had long featured in recreation.

In April 1940 Gretton became Captain Philip Vian's first lieutenant in the destroyer *Cossack*, in time for the second Narvik battle, where the battleship *Warspite* and her escort destroyer sank *U-64* and the eight survivors of the ten large German destroyers that reached port from the first Narvik battle. He was granted a mention in dispatches. The following year, commanding a destroyer kept at sea a year beyond its due life, he was appointed OBE for western approaches duties. One August night in 1942, commanding an escort destroyer, he rammed and sank an Italian submarine while screening a carrier, thus earning his first DSO.

Each of the services had cause to fight and win a crucial campaign: in 1940 the RAF over Britain; in 1942 the army in the desert; in 1943 the navy in the Atlantic. Each had its remarkable heroes. As to the Atlantic, two convoy escort commanders shone by their inventiveness and fierce efficiency. The first was Captain Johnny Walker (second escort group), who won the CB and four DSOs, dying of exhaustion in Liverpool in July 1944: he had persuaded his Catholic son to defer priestly training in Rome to become a submariner, as which he died at sea. The second was Gretton (B7 group), who won three DSOs and the OBE, coming through the war with strains that caused his premature retirement as fifth sea lord. Where Walker's forte was in beating U-boat tactics by team technique, Gretton's was in trained expectancy of his captains' independence. Both showed unrelenting vigour, communicated to their teams. Walker had been Gretton's Captain D in 1942. Churchill afterwards wrote: 'The Battle of the Atlantic was the dominant factor all through the War' (Gretton, *Convoy*, 181). Support groups were formed first in 1942, and were gradually joined by escort-carriers, and distant land-based air strikes. The 'crisis of crises' came in the first twenty days of March 1943: in 10 days 41 ships were lost, in 10 more days 56—all in convoys. The New World and the Old were all but isolated one from another. During April a hundred U-boats left the Bay of Biscay against convoys. Seemingly Britain was on the edge of surrender—leaving Europe without hope of liberation (for how might D-day have been launched from across the Atlantic?).

After the last nightmare month—March 1943—monthly shipping losses never again reached three figures, fast dipping away in the summer of 1943. The battle was specifically won during four successive convoy actions, three fought by Gretton's B7 group. Details were set out in his memoir, *Convoy Escort Commander* (1964) and the May 1968 issue of *Navy*. HX231 was a fast convoy of 61 ships sailing to the UK, attacked by a pack of 17 U-boats, which sank 6 ships at the cost of considerable damage to themselves. ONS5 was a slow convoy of 39 ships sailing to the USA, attacked by 4 packs of U-boats (16, 17, 24, and 16 successively) which sank a third of the convoy; B7 group sank 8 U-boats (2 collided), damaging several more. This proved the turning point. Gretton called it 'the fiercest convoy action of the War' (unpublished autobiography, 83); Stephen Roskill in *War at Sea* called it 'as decisive as Quiberon Bay or The Nile' (Gretton, *Convoy*, 147). SC130 was a slow convoy of 39 ships sailing to the UK, attacked by 4 packs each of 20 U-boats. Five of these were sunk, one of them carrying Admiral Dönitz's son, while others were damaged. The fourth such convoy was HX239. Dönitz later wrote that Germany had 'radically to increase the fighting power of the U-boats ... accordingly I withdrew the boats from the North Atlantic' (Gretton, *Convoy*, 161–2)—on 24 May, as SC130 reached home waters. In May alone, an intolerable forty-one U-boats had been sunk. In 1974, soon after full sources had been released, Gretton published his study of a single action, *Crisis Convoy: the Story of HX231*.

That convoy was the first to benefit from long-range air escort from Liberators based in Iceland and Northern Ireland, combined with new support groups. Air support became crucial: HX239 had with it the first escort-carriers.

On 29 May 1943 Gretton married Dorothy Nancy Gladys (Judy; b. 1920), daughter of James Eastwood Du Vivier and his wife, Caroline Vau de Venne, of Belgium. She was at that time serving as a WRNS officer. There were four children: Anne (b. 1944), Michael Peter (b. 1946), William Philip (b. 1948), and George Richard (b. 1953). Later in that auspicious year Gretton, to the delight of B7, was given the role of commanding the support group, reinforcing convoy escorts. During a three-week spell at sea he supported five convoys, his ship sharing the destruction of two U-boats. His leadership, seamanship, training capacity, and grasp of problems at sea earned him his third DSO. He finished his war by writing a new Admiralty convoy instruction, on which he lectured around the Home Fleet, causing wonder. He was finally posted to the Admiralty, next to Churchill's chiefs of staff headquarters for joint planning. He was shifting from stale sailor to studied scholar, crystallizing what he had lived. He was privy to the fruits of Ultra and occasionally present at meetings of the chiefs of staff. His team estimated what U-boat design was reaching: if such boats got into action 'a new Battle of the Atlantic would be fought' (autobiography, 90)—so Bomber Harris prevented production until too late. Gretton flew to Nuremberg to watch the war crimes trials: 'Admirals Raeder and Dönitz were most dignified' (ibid., 92).

Gretton reached the rank of captain early, aged thirty-six, in 1948. Until 1950 he was an observer at Washington's Naval War College, analysing S. E. Morison's new war history and arguing for large compact convoys professionally escorted. Against nuclear bombs, he advocated a full allied appreciation of Japan's collapsing economy in 1945. Until 1952 he was naval assistant to the first sea lord, Lord Fraser, who took him to allied co-ordinate meetings in Europe and the USA, showing him the nascent NATO (founded in 1949). In 1951 he represented Fraser at negotiations in Rome, finding himself overridden by the chief of the air staff. The Korean War loomed, US forces setting the pace. Churchill returned to power, overplaying his cards about Atlantic naval command. Gretton's meeting with him generated his 1968 book: *Former Naval Person: Churchill and the Navy*. Gretton then commanded the cruiser *Gambia*, largely in peaceable Malta. It assisted after a Greek earthquake, supplying by sea. Then in 1955 he became chief of staff to the admiral of the naval mission in Washington. Mountbatten became first sea lord and in November visited, essentially to co-ordinate upon nuclear submarines: 'He knew everyone from the President downwards' (autobiography, 131). Then in 1956–7 Gretton was commodore in command of the naval task group for the British atomic tests at Christmas Island. There was no harbour there, and the anchorage enjoyed heavy swells. The USA claimed ownership, despite Captain Cook's discovery; so Gretton flew to Washington again to 'sort it out with Arleigh Burke' (ibid., 134) of the US navy. Three H-bombs

were dropped on schedule. Then the scientists asked for more unscheduled tests, as Gretton's health broke. In 1958, losing health, he was promoted rear-admiral, and made senior naval member of the directing staff, the Imperial Defence College. He introduced a course on nuclear deterrent strategy. In 1960 he became flag officer, sea training; and was in 1961 promoted vice-admiral (his first son, Michael, following him in that rank). At Portland he trained thirty-three ships in fifteen months. In 1962 he became deputy chief of naval staff and fifth sea lord, being knighted KCB in 1963, when he retired because of his health. His legacy was to show all branches of the navy that their uncoordinated pipe dreams added up to massive financial unreality. Soon afterwards, defence budgets were hit by a wilting national economy.

After a restful but busy 1964, when he completed two books, his war memoir and a study of current defence problems, *Maritime Strategy* (1965), Gretton was appointed domestic bursar of University College, Oxford. There he brought high standards to the local administration. In his years there his college took in hand the creation of a science library, the erection of the Mitchell Building, the modernization of external student developments, and the refurbishing (with Judy) of college annexes. He was quickly elected a fellow, and on his retirement in 1971 a senior research fellow. His last book, initially published in Spanish, was a full-length study, *The Forgotten Factor: the Naval Aspect of the Spanish Civil War* (1984). An exceptionally handsome man, Gretton died in Oxford on 11 November 1992. He was survived by his wife and four children.

ALBERIC STACPOOLE

Sources autobiography to 1980, priv. coll. • P. W. Gretton, *Convoy escort commander* (1964) • P. W. Gretton, *Crisis convoy: the story of HX231* (1974) • P. W. Gretton, 'The Atlantic battle won', *Ampleforth Journal*, 73 (1968), 400–04 • S. W. Roskill, *The war at sea, 1939–1945*, 2 (1956) • R. Seth, *The fiercest battle* (1961) • K. Dönitz, *Memoirs: ten years and twenty days*, trans. R. H. Stevens and D. Woodward [1959] • *WWW, 1991–5* • Burke, *Peerage* • *The Independent* (12 Nov 1992) • *Daily Telegraph* (12 Nov 1992) • *The Times* (13 Nov 1992) • personal knowledge (2004)
Archives CAC Cam., autobiographical papers • NMM, papers | King's Lond., Liddell Hart C., corresp. with Sir B. H. Liddell Hart • University College, Oxford, reminiscences of life as domestic bursar of University College
Likenesses photograph, repro. in *The Independent* • photograph, repro. in *Daily Telegraph* • photograph, repro. in *The Times* • photographs, priv. coll.
Wealth at death £618,410: probate, 24 March 1993, *CGPLA Eng. & Wales*

Gretton, William (1736–1813), college head, was the son of John Gretton of Bond Street, London. Educated at St Paul's School he matriculated from Peterhouse, Cambridge, at Michaelmas 1754, as Pauline exhibitioner and scholar, and graduated BA in 1758; he proceeded MA in 1761 and DD in 1799. Having been ordained deacon in London on 24 December 1758 he was presented in 1761 to the rectory of Littlebury, in Essex, and in 1766 to the vicarage of neighbouring Saffron Walden. In 1784 Lord Howard of Walden appointed him his domestic chaplain. He was a JP for Essex, and was made archdeacon on 2 December 1795.

In 1797 Gretton was elected master of Magdalene College, Cambridge, and in 1800–01 was vice-chancellor of the university. His election brought to an abrupt end the evangelical character of Magdalene engendered by his predecessor, Peter Pickard. In its place falling admissions and 'a mounting academic and moral mediocrity, signalled by the collapse of discipline among the fellowship' typified his sixteen-year-long mastership (Duffy, 194). He died in Cambridge on 29 September 1813, aged seventy-eight, his wife, Henrietta, and daughter Jane having predeceased him.   J. M. RIGG, *rev.* S. J. SKEDD

Sources Venn, *Alum. Cant.* · *GM*, 1st ser., 36 (1766), 344; 54 (1784), 719; 65 (1795), 1062; 67 (1797), 1137; 70 (1800), 1118; 83 (1813), 405 · E. Duffy, 'Late eighteenth century to early nineteenth century', in P. Cunich and others, *A history of Magdalene College, Cambridge, 1428–1988* (1994), 133–99 · will, PRO, PROB 11/1550, sig. 596
Likenesses Dighton, caricature, coloured etching, pubd 1809 (*A view from Magdalen College, Cambridge*), NPG · oils, Magd. Cam.

Greville, Algernon Frederick (1798–1864), army officer and private secretary, was born on 29 January 1798, the second son of Charles Greville (1762–1832), fifth son of Fulke Greville of Wilbury, Wiltshire, and his wife, Lady Charlotte (*d.* 28 July 1862), eldest daughter of William Henry Cavendish, third duke of Portland. He was the brother of Charles Cavendish Fulke *Greville and Henry William *Greville. On 1 February 1814 he was commissioned ensign in the 1st (Grenadier) foot guards, and was present at Quatre Bras and at Waterloo; he was also at the attack and capture of Péronne. He was appointed shortly afterwards aide-de-camp to General Sir John Lambert, with whom he served in the army of occupation in France until he was appointed aide-de-camp to the duke of Wellington, on whose staff he served until the army returned to England in 1818, the year in which Wellington had a brief affair with Greville's mother. Greville was afterwards Wellington's aide-de-camp in the Ordnance office in January 1819. On Wellington's being appointed commander-in-chief in January 1827, he appointed Greville his private secretary, which post he held while Wellington was prime minister, secretary of state for foreign affairs, and commander-in-chief again in December 1842. Greville wrote the final copy of many of Wellington's letters, and in the 1840s repeatedly toned down Wellington's uncivil replies to requests for interviews. Greville was from 1830 until his death Bath king of arms, and during Wellington's lifetime was secretary for the Cinque Ports. He also held a pension, and the post of commissioner of the alienation office. Like those of others of his family, his emoluments were published in John Wade's *Extraordinary Black Book* (1832).

Greville married, on 7 April 1823, Charlotte Maria, daughter of Richard Henry Cox; she died on 10 April 1841. His eldest daughter, Frances Harriett, married, on 28 November 1843, Charles Lennox, sixth duke of Richmond and first duke of Gordon, and died on 8 March 1887. Greville died at Hillingdon, Middlesex, the seat of his brother-in-law, on 15 December 1864.

GORDON GOODWIN, *rev.* JAMES FALKNER

Sources *Army List* · *The Times* (20 Dec 1864) · *GM*, 3rd ser., 18 (1865), 125–6 · Burke, *Peerage* · F. W. Hamilton, *The origin and history of the first or grenadier guards*, 3 vols. (1874) · N. Thompson, *Wellington after Waterloo* (1986) · J. Wade, ed., *The extraordinary black book*, new edn (1832) · Boase, *Mod. Eng. biog.*
Archives BL, letters to Philip Bliss, Add. MSS 34574–34800, *passim* · NA Scot., corresp. relating to Cinque Ports · U. Nott. L., letters to the fifth duke of Portland · W. Sussex RO, letters to duke of Richmond
Likenesses T. Lawrence, drawing, *c.*1803, Goodwood House, West Sussex
Wealth at death under £60,000: resworn probate, Feb 1880, *CGPLA Eng. & Wales*

Greville, Charles Cavendish Fulke (1794–1865), political and social diarist, was born on 2 April 1794. His father, Charles Greville, MP for Petersfield and under-secretary of state in the Home department, was a grandson of the fifth Baron Brooke of Beauchamps Court. His mother, Lady Charlotte Cavendish Cavendish-Bentinck, was the eldest daughter of William Henry Cavendish Cavendish-*Bentinck, the third duke of Portland, twice prime minister; and it was in the duke's house, Bulstrode in Buckinghamshire, that Greville spent his earliest years. He was educated at Eton College and at Christ Church, Oxford, which he left without taking a degree to become private secretary to Lord Bathurst, secretary of state for war and the colonies in Lord Liverpool's administration. He had little work to do in this appointment and none at all in the secretaryship of Jamaica, a post obtained for him through the influence of his grandfather, the well-paid duties of which he left in the hands of a salaried deputy without once visiting the island. Also with the duke's help, Greville was appointed to a clerkship-in-ordinary to the privy council, a none-too-demanding employment which increased his already comfortable income by £2000 (rising to £2500) a year, enabling him to pay off all his debts and to lead the rest of his life in the midst of that fashionable society which so intrigued him.

This appointment also gave Greville an unrivalled opportunity to enter the most influential political circles of the day and, in the course of a long career, to enjoy the confidence of Wellington, Melbourne, Palmerston, Peel, Clarendon, the duke of Bedford, the earl of Aberdeen, Lord Holland, and Princess Lieven. From these, and from many others, he gleaned the materials for diaries which are not only an extremely important source for the history of British politics from the Regency to the Crimean War but a social document of wide range and the most acute observation. Carefully recording everything of interest that came under his own observation in London and in the many country houses in which he was a welcome guest, from Woburn and Petworth to Chatsworth, Stowe, and Belvoir, he also went out of his way to collect information from his numerous friends and acquaintances, believing, as he put it, that 'there is always something to be learned from everybody if you touch them on the points they know'. Yet, well aware that 'half the things one hears are untrue', he was constantly revising what he had written in the light of later intelligence or personal knowledge; and, whenever he was led to believe that one in the last few months—5 vols of Gibbon—St Simon—Marmontel's memoirs—Rousseau's confessions—Memoirs of Q. Eliz.—Lives of the Poets—Boswell's Life of Johnson' (*Greville Memoirs*, 1.68). He was also a frequent contributor of articles and anonymous letters to *The Times* and the author of three authoritative pamphlets: one on Irish affairs in 1845; another on Prince Albert's precedence; and a third, published in 1846, on Peel and the corn laws. He edited a volume of Thomas Moore's *Correspondence* and helped to edit the last two volumes of Thomas Raikes's *Journal*.

Greville had always intended that his own journals should be published. He let it be known that they would eventually be handed over to Sir George Cornewall Lewis, home secretary from 1859 to 1861 and a former editor of the *Edinburgh Review*; but Lewis died in 1863 and Greville decided to leave them in the care of Henry Reeve, a privy council colleague of his. Reeve published expurgated editions of the journals in three instalments in 1874, 1885, and 1887. In 1938 the diaries were published in their entirety in eight volumes, edited by Lytton Strachey and Roger Fulford; Strachey had become interested in Greville when researching his *Queen Victoria*. The twenty-nine volumes of manuscript are in the British Library, presented by Reeve's widow in 1895.

The appearance in print of the private diaries of a man who had known everyone of importance in public life for a generation, and who had not hesitated to set down what they had told him and his opinion of their characters and attainments, caused an uproar in society in 1874. Disraeli described their publication as 'a social outrage'; another of those men in public life who appeared in their pages observed, 'It is like Judas writing the lives of the apostles' (*Greville Memoirs*, 1.viii–ix); Gladstone reviewed them for the *English Historical Review* (April 1887).

Queen Victoria was '*horrified* and *indignant* at this dreadful and really scandalous book. Mr Greville's indiscretion, indelicacy, ingratitude, betrayal of confidence and shameful disloyalty towards his Sovereign make it *very important* that the book should be severely censored and discredited,' she wrote indignantly. 'The tone in which he speaks of royalty is unlike anything which one sees in history, even of people hundreds of years ago, and is most reprehensible … Of George IV he speaks in such shocking language, language not fit for any gentleman to use.' As for the editor, he was guilty of an act in 'DISGRACEFULLY *bad taste*' (Hibbert, *Queen Victoria*, 237–8; Hibbert, *Greville's England*, 7–8).

Greville's features, as depicted in T. C. Wilson's drawing of 1838 and in David Wilkie's painting of Queen Victoria's first council, are those of a man unlikely to have been too deeply disturbed by such strictures. Smooth and urbane, they are marked by a long, pointed chin and a prominent nose which earned him the nickname of 'Punch'. He was also known as 'the Gruncher', for he could be excessively grumpy, especially when troubled by one of his frequent attacks of gout or exasperated by the deafness with which he had been afflicted at an early age, and which became worse as he grew older. Indeed, Emily Eden described him

Charles Cavendish Fulke Greville (1794–1865), by Alfred, Count D'Orsay, 1840

of his frank and penetrating character sketches had been unjustly harsh, he would be at pains to correct or ameliorate what he had first written.

He was as well-informed about bloodstock and the turf as he was about politics and fashionable society. A leading member of the Jockey Club, he was for five years manager of the racing establishment of his friend the duke of York, 'the only one of the royal Princes who has the feelings of an English Gentleman', as Greville described him in a characteristically percipient sketch which emphasized the duke's amiable disposition, his delight in a life of gaiety and pleasure, his fondness for the society of scamps and for 'jokes full of coarseness and indelicacy' (*Greville Memoirs*, 1.56–60).

Greville was subsequently a partner of those other racing enthusiasts, his cousin Lord George Bentinck, and the reckless George Payne who, having lost a fortune gambling, proceeded to lose two more in the same way. Greville himself owned some fine horses, notably Orlando, Preserve, and, most celebrated of all, Alarm, which, but for an accident at the start, would have won the Derby in 1845. It was one of Greville's greatest disappointments in life that he never did win the Derby and won the St Leger only once.

His diaries are full of regrets that he wasted so much of his time at race meetings; he also blamed himself for not making the effort to read more, once recording his low spirits after a dinner at Holland House where his 'loose reading' had preventing him from taking proper part in the conversation. Yet he was, in fact, a conscientious reader. At the end of 1818 he wrote in his diary, 'I have read as being 'crosser than any pair of tongs'; and, as an elderly, crotchety man, he was once seen to weep with mortification when, at a dinner party, he was not given the particular piece of chicken he had had his eyes on. 'Certainly not,' he sharply retorted when asked by his hostess to take in a certain lady at another dinner party, 'I hardly know if I can take in myself' (*Greville Memoirs*, 1.xvii–xviii).

Yet, for all his occasional cantankerous outbursts and his frequently sardonic comments, Greville was a fundamentally sympathetic and generous man, a delightful companion, and a faithful friend, renowned, as his fellow observer of society Captain Gronow put it, for the 'bustling kindness' of the manner in which he concerned himself with the problems of other men's affairs (Hibbert, *Gronow*, 238–9). A 'friend of many', Sir Henry Taylor observed, he was 'always most a friend when friendship was most needed' (Taylor, 1.315). 'No power on earth would induce him to get out of an arm chair he had selected,' so it was also said of him. Yet 'he would go from London to Berwick to serve a friend' (*Greville Memoirs*, 1.xviii). Dressing with 'studied plainess and scrupulous cleanliness' he did not escape charges of vanity. Disraeli, who claimed to have known him 'intimately', declared, 'He was the vainest being—I don't limit myself to men— that ever existed: and I don't forget Cicero and I know Lord Lytton' (Hibbert, *Greville's England*, 7).

When not travelling on the continent or on one of his prolonged visits to friends in the country, Greville lived nearly all his adult life in London, at first in bachelor apartments in Hanover Square, then in Grosvenor Place, before moving, in 1849, to a ground-floor suite of rooms in Lord Granville's house, 16 Bruton Street, where he was known to the family as 'the Lodger'. It was here that he died of heart disease on 18 January 1865. He had never married but had had several love affairs, and one of his mistresses had borne him a son who died as a young man on his way home from India. His youngest brother, Henry William *Greville (1801–1872), also kept a diary of social and political events, two comparatively pedestrian selections from which were published in 1883–4 and 1905.

CHRISTOPHER HIBBERT

Sources H. Reeve, preface, in *The Greville memoirs*, ed. H. Reeve, 8 vols. in 3 pts (1874–87) · *The Greville memoirs, 1814–1860*, ed. L. Strachey and R. Fulford, 8 vols. (1938), vol. 1, pp. xiii–xix · [H. Taylor], *Autobiography of Henry Taylor*, 2 vols. (1885) · *Captain Gronow: his reminiscences of Regency and Victorian life*, ed. C. Hibbert (1991) · [J. R. Thursfield], 'Notes on the "Greville Memoirs"', *EngHR*, 1 (1886), 105–37 · W. E. Gladstone, 'The history of 1852–60, and Greville's latest journals', *EngHR*, 2 (1887), 281–302 · *Greville's England: selections from the diaries of Charles Greville, 1818–1860*, ed. C. Hibbert (1981) · C. Hibbert, *Queen Victoria in her letters and journals* (1984) · *Diaries and correspondence of James Harris, first earl of Malmesbury*, ed. third earl of Malmesbury [J. H. Harris], 4 vols. (1844)
Archives BL, MSS of memoirs · BL, political journal, Add. MSS 41095–41123 · Bodl. Oxf., journal [transcript, Reeve's clerk's copy of memoirs] · Harrowby Manuscript Trust, Sandon Hall, Staffordshire, corresp. and extracts from diary | BL, corresp. with Princess Lieven, Add. MSS 47377–47378 · BL, corresp. with Henry Reeve, Add. MSS 41184–41185 · BL, corresp. with C. A. Windham, Add. MS 41760 · Bodl. Oxf., letters to fourth earl of Clarendon · Hunt. L., corresp. with William Hamilton · Keele University Library, letters to Ralph Sneyd · PRO, letters to second Earl Granville · PRO, corresp. with Lord John Russell and the duke of Bedford, PRO 30/22 · U. Durham, archives and special collections, letters to second Earl Grey · U. Durham, archives and special collections, letters to third Earl Grey · U. Southampton L., letters to first duke of Wellington · W. Sussex RO, letters to the duke of Richmond · Woburn Abbey, letters to duke of Bedford
Likenesses D. Wilkie, group portrait, oils, 1837 (*The first council of Queen Victoria*), Royal Collection · T. C. Wilson, drawing, 1838, repro. in Hibbert, *Greville's England* · Count D'Orsay, chalk, 1840, NPG [*see illus.*] · J. Brown, stipple, pubd 1864 (after photograph by J. E. Mayall), NPG · T. C. Wilson, lithograph, BM, NPG; repro. in Wildrake [G. Tattersall], *The cracks of the day* (1841) · oils, Goodwood House, West Sussex
Wealth at death under £35,000: resworn probate, Aug 1865, CGPLA Eng. & Wales

Greville, Charles Francis (1749–1809), mineralogist and horticulturist, was born, probably at Warwick Castle, on 12 May 1749, the second son of Francis, eighth Baron Brooke and first earl of Warwick (1719–1773) and his wife, Elizabeth (1720/21–1800), daughter of Lord Archibald Hamilton. He was educated at Harrow School and Edinburgh University (although he seems not to have graduated), and was elected a fellow of the Royal Society in 1772. Later vice-president of the society, he contributed two papers to its *Philosophical Transactions*. He was MP for Warwick in 1774–90 and for Petersfield in 1795–6. On the Board of Trade from 1774 to 1780, he left to become a lord of the Admiralty. From 1794 to 1805 he was vice-chamberlain of the royal household.

Greville is most commonly remembered for his involvement with Emma Lyon (1765–1815) [see Hamilton, Emma, Lady Hamilton], later the wife of his uncle William *Hamilton (1731–1803) and subsequently the mistress of Horatio Nelson. They lived in Paddington Green, Middlesex, where Greville also indulged his passion for collecting minerals, plants, and works of art. Emma was his mistress for four years until, anxious to find a wealthy bride (a search which ultimately ended in failure), he sent her in 1786 to stay with his widowed uncle, then ambassador to Naples. At this time Greville was managing his uncle's Welsh estate in his absence, laying the foundation for Milford Haven's future development as a port.

Greville made lasting contributions to mineralogy and horticulture. It has been said that his appreciation of beauty eclipsed any truly scientific interest or understanding of these subjects, but this is perhaps unfair—he was a patron of science almost on a par with Joseph Banks. Greville's mineral collection, based on that of Ignaz von Born (1742–1791), was begun in 1773 and was strong in meteorites and gem minerals. By 1803 it was one of the finest in the world. He was the principal supporter of the comte de Bournon, mineralogist and refugee from the French Revolution, and much of the excellence of Greville's collection must be attributable to his influence. (Although not recognized by him at the time, the first specimen of the rare lead chloro-carbonate, phosgenite, was later found in his collection, among specimens acquired in Derbyshire about 1785.) Greville was a member of a panel convened in 1799 to assess the mineral collection of the British Museum: to improve the disappointing national collection it recommended the purchase of the collection of

Charles Hatchett (1765–1847) which was to lay the foundation for the museum's subsequent rise to international status. It was also Greville's recommendation that established Adolarius Forster as the first state mineralogist in New South Wales in 1803.

Greville is credited with the introduction to Britain of several species of lily, peony, camellia, and magnolia. He joined the Linnean Society in 1802 and in 1804 helped found the Royal Horticultural Society. He was one of the society's first vice-presidents and its treasurer from 1806 to his death. The genus *Grevillea* was named in his honour by Thomas Brown in 1808. Elected to the Society of Dilettanti in 1774, Greville became its 'very high steward' in 1778. He was a patron of the artist Paul Sandby (1730–1809) and has been credited with the introduction to England of aquatint engraving made popular by Sandby, though it is likely that Sandby acquired the method independently.

Greville died intestate at his home in Edgware Row, Paddington Green, on 23 April 1809 and was buried in the family vault at St Mary's Church, Warwick. His 14,800 mineral specimens were bought for the nation for £13,727. The 5200 faceted gems were sold separately. The acquisition raised the British Museum's mineral collection to the first rank but few of Greville's specimens can now be recognized within it.

MICHAEL P. COOPER

Sources A. Simmonds, 'The founders: the Rt. Hon. Charles Greville, FRS, FLS, 1749–1809', *Journal of the Royal Horticultural Society*, 67 (1942), 219–32 • F. Fraser, *Beloved Emma* (1986) • *The Hamilton and Nelson papers*, ed. A. Morrison, 2 vols. (privately printed, London, 1893–4) • L. Fletcher, 'The Department of Minerals', *The history of the collections contained in the natural history departments of the British Museum*, British Museum, 1 (1904), 343–442 • M. M. Drummond, 'Greville, Hon. Charles Francis', HoP, *Commons*, 1754–90, 550–51 • P. Edwards, 'Clubman, MP and botanist: Charles Francis Greville, 1749–1809', *Country Life*, 174 (1983), 1498–9 • P. S. Burr, 'Notes on the history of phosgenite and matlockite from Matlock, England', *Mineralogical Record*, 23 (1992), 377–86 • T. G. Vallance, 'The start of government science in Australia: A. W. H. Humphrey, his majesty's mineralogist in New South Wales, 1803–1812', *Proceedings of the Linnean Society of New South Wales*, 105 (1981), 107–46 • A. Valentine, *The British establishment, 1760–1784: an eighteenth-century biographical dictionary*, 2 vols. (1970) • A. Bruce, *American Mineralogical Journal*, 1 (1810), 55–6 • J. Ball, *Paul and Thomas Sandby, Royal Academicians: an Anglo-Danish saga of art, love and war in Georgian England* (1985) • W. E. Wilson, 'The history of mineral collecting, 1530–1799', *Mineralogical Record*, 25/6 (1994), 75–8 • E. L. Dellow, *Svedenstierna's tour in Great Britain, 1802–3: the travel diary of an industrial spy* (1973) • W. C. Smith, 'A history of the first hundred years of the mineral collections in the British Museum', *Bulletin of the British Museum (Natural History)* [Historical Series], 3 (1962–9), 237–59 • W. C. Smith, 'Early mineralogy in Great Britain and Ireland', *Bulletin of the British Museum (Natural History)* [Historical Series], 6 (1977–80), 49–74 • W. T. J. Gun, ed., *The Harrow School register, 1571–1800* (1934) • GEC, *Peerage*, new edn, vol. 2
Archives BL, corresp. and papers, Add. MSS 40715–40716, 42071–42076 • BL OIOC, corresp. and papers relating to India, MSS Eur E 309 • Warks. CRO, papers | Birm. CA, letters to Boulton family • BL, corresp. with Sir Joseph Banks, Add. MSS 33978–33992 • BL, corresp. with first earl of Liverpool, Add. MSS 38222–38231, 38309–38311, 38351 • Hunt. L., corresp. with Sir William Hamilton • NL Wales, letters and papers relating to Pembrokeshire estate • NMM, corresp. with Emma Hamilton
Likenesses J. Reynolds, group portrait, 1777 (with members of the Society of Dilettanti), V&A • G. Romney, portrait, 1781, Parham Park, Sussex • J. Zoffany, group portrait, 1781–3, Towneley Hall,

Burnley; *see illus. in* Townley, Charles (1737–1805) • H. Meyer, mezzotint, pubd 1810 (after G. Romney, 1781), BM, NPG, Royal Horticultural Society; repro. in Simmonds, 'The founders' • G. Romney, group portrait, sketch, NPG
Wealth at death mineral collection valued at £13,727

Greville [*née* Macartney], **Frances** (1727?–1789), poet, was probably born in Ireland, the fifth surviving child of James Macartney (1692–1770), MP in Ireland for Longford and Granard, and Catherine Coote (d. 1731). Her lawyer father, coheir of the earls of Longford, in 1713 inherited half of the Longford lands and by 1722 was in London, in the circle of the prince of Wales. Frances's close girlhood friends were the daughters of William Pulteney, Sir William Stanhope, and Charles Lennox, second duke of Richmond.

Frances Macartney was beautiful, spirited, and celebrated for her clever verses in the fast set revolving round Henry Fox, married in 1744 to Lady Caroline Lennox. In 1747 she met the haughty Fulke Greville (1717–1806), of Wilbury in Wiltshire, then the most accomplished and *tonish* young man in society; they eloped on 26 January 1748. Their daughter, Frances Anne, later the famous Frances Anne *Crewe, was christened on 28 November. In summer 1749 the family departed for Paris, then for Lorraine, where they remained until 1753 or 1754. Evidence connecting Greville to his Jacobite cousins the dukes of Beaumont suggests that he was their contact with Charles Stuart. Three sons were born abroad, Algernon (1750?), William Fulke (1751), and James (1753).

After her marriage Frances Greville confined her writing to satirical and occasional ephemera for the amusement of the fashionable world, but her growing fame piqued her husband, who had assigned her to 'the shade', and she hid her work from him with the exception of her famous poem, the *Ode to Indifference*, written either in 1756 or in 1757 in Italy where the Grevilles had retreated after the death of Algernon in May 1756. The ode, variously interpreted as a plea not to feel for others or not to please others and thus be hurt by them, escaped into print, became as celebrated as Thomas Gray's *Elegy*, and roused her husband's rancour.

Frances Greville's god-daughter Frances Burney described her as 'pedantic, sarcastic, and supercilious', affrighting 'the timid and braving the bold, to whom she allowed no quarter', of the utmost feminine beauty but with depth, soundness, and capacity of understanding, a croaking voice, and a manner of lounging 'completely at her ease, in such curves as she found most commodious, with her head alone upright'. But to the few who possessed her favour, 'she was a treasure of ideas and of variety' (D'Arblay, 1.56–7). In 1778 Burney found her godmother fit for a portrait by Spenser as 'a penetrating, puissant, and sarcastic fairy queen', famed, 'her Ode to Indifference having twined around her brow a garland of wide-spreading and unfading fragrance' (ibid., 2.103). In that year Hester Thrale wrote to Samuel Johnson that Mrs Greville had 'a commanding Manner & loud Voice'; 'she downs everybody' and 'is said to have formed her Manner upon yours' (*Letters of Samuel Johnson*, 2.262).

As her husband gambled away his fortune, Frances Greville produced three more sons, Robert (1758), Henry (1760), and Charles (1762), and used her friendships with Henry Fox and Georgiana, Lady Spencer, to keep her husband and family afloat. Fox sent Greville to Munich as Britain's envoy-extraordinary in 1766, but after Mrs Greville departed in ill health, the mysterious death of Robert in 1768 caused his father to return to England in a state of collapse. Ruin ensued in 1782, when Wilbury was sold, after which Greville pursued his wife's separate income, left her by her father, with threats of incarceration. She took refuge in Ireland to escape him, spending much of the period from 1783 to 1788 there under the protection of the Lennox daughters, the duchess of Leinster and Lady Louisa Connoly, and her cousins the Longfords of Pakenham (now Tullynally). By 1788 a legal separation was effected and she took a house in London in Sackville Street, where, worn out, she died on 30 July 1789, and was buried in the church at Petersham, near Richmond, Surrey.

Some speculation that Frances Greville was concealing poems equal in quality to the 'Ode' persisted for years, but her notebook of poems reveals that her adept verses were intentionally trivial. She also left an unfinished novel.

BETTY RIZZO

Sources Madame D'Arblay [F. Burney], *Memoirs of Doctor Burney*, 3 vols. (1832) · *Correspondence of Emily, duchess of Leinster (1731–1814)*, ed. B. Fitzgerald, 3 vols., IMC (1949–57) · *The letters of Samuel Johnson*, ed. R. W. Chapman, 2 (1952), 262 · *The political journal of George Bubb Dodington*, ed. J. Carswell and L. A. Dralle (1965) · Walpole, *Corr.* · private information (2004)
Archives BL, Add. MS 51527, fols. 30–43 · BL, Althorp papers · BL, letters to Lady Camelford, Add. MS 69307
Likenesses O. Humphry, chalk drawing, 1768, priv. coll.; copy, photograph, Courtauld Inst.
Wealth at death approx. £2000 bequeathed to youngest son; £800 p.a. inherited income passed to eldest son: will, PRO, PROB 11/1183/150; BL, Althorp papers, F66, 26 Aug

Greville, Frances Anne. *See* Crewe, Frances Anne, Lady Crewe (*bap.* 1748, *d.* 1818).

Greville [*née* Maynard], **Frances Evelyn** [Daisy], **countess of Warwick** (1861–1938), society beauty and socialist, was born at 27 Berkeley Square, London, on 10 December 1861, the elder of the two daughters of Colonel Charles Maynard (1814–1865), only son and heir of the third Viscount Maynard, and his second wife, Blanche Adeliza Fitzroy (*d.* 1933). Her father and grandfather both died in 1865 and Daisy Maynard inherited the bulk of the Maynard estates, worth some £20,000 a year in rents alone. They were centred on Easton Lodge, near Great Dunmow in Essex, and it was here that she spent most of her childhood, even after her mother married the fourth earl of Rosslyn in 1866, and produced five more children. As a great heiress Daisy would always have been sought after in marriage; she was also one of the great beauties of the age. Queen Victoria, seeking a suitable bride for her youngest son, Prince Leopold, duke of Albany, considered Daisy, but it was Leopold's aide-de-camp, Francis Richard Charles Guy Greville, Lord Brooke (1853–1924), heir to the earldom of Warwick, whom she married on 30 April 1881 in Westminster Abbey.

Young socialite: the Babbling Brooke After an early miscarriage, Lady Brooke produced a son and heir in September 1882, and threw herself into the extravagant social life of the aristocracy, entertaining in London and at Easton Lodge. This was the era of the great country-house party, whereat the principal amusements were hunting (which Daisy adored), shooting (which occupied her husband), and dalliance (for which she became notorious). She bore a daughter in 1884 and a short-lived son in 1885, and late in 1886 she began an affair with Lord Charles *Beresford. The affair cooling, she was enraged to discover that Lady Charles was pregnant, and in January 1889 wrote to Beresford in unrestrained terms. Lady Charles opened the letter, and a society scandal ensued, especially after Daisy brought the prince of Wales into the quarrel. By throwing herself on the mercy of the prince she not only ensured that she would not suffer social ostracism as a consequence of the exposure of her affair and imprudence but she also acquired the prince as her lover, supplanting Lily Langtry as *maîtresse en titre*. She was also implicated in the 1890 Tranby Croft baccarat scandal: although she was not present during the disputed card game, she was widely accused of having leaked the story, and acquired the sobriquet the 'Babbling Brooke'. The Beresford affair blew up again with renewed vigour in autumn 1891, when Lady Charles's sister Lucy Paget published a thinly disguised account of the business as *Lady Rivers*, which included the text of Daisy's indiscreet letter; the public scandal tarnished Daisy's reputation badly—although the prince of Wales stood by her—and even her generally complaisant husband was brought to consider divorce. The marriage survived (as it survived further infidelities), and in 1893 Brooke succeeded his father as fifth earl of Warwick.

Lady Warwick's life at this time was a curious mixture of philandering and philanthropy. Like most women of her class she took seriously her responsibilities towards the poor on her estates and gave generously in personal charity. But she could see the inadequacies of this kind of charity, and in 1890 set up the first of a series of institutions intended to address problems more structurally. This was a needlework school at Easton for girls and young women unable to go into domestic service. The school, and the London shop set up as an outlet for the work, were heavily subsidized from her own pocket, as were many of the enterprises that succeeded it, including Bigods School, near Dunmow in Essex, which she founded in 1897 to provide a co-educational agricultural and technical education for middle-class children. She was encouraged to think seriously about such matters by the professional moralizer W. T. Stead, whom she first met in 1892 and who hoped to use her as a channel to influence the prince of Wales to take his moral responsibilities seriously. Under Stead's influence she began to lecture the prince—her 'parishioner', as she and Stead called him (Blunden, 82)—on the needs of the poor and the injustices of society; his interest was limited, and in 1898 he replaced Daisy with the less troublesome Alice Keppel. The prince's relationship with Lady Warwick had caused some distress to his wife. When it ended in 1898 (shortly before the birth of the Warwicks' second son, Maynard, after a gap of thirteen years) Daisy was careful to mend her fences with the princess of Wales, as well as ensuring the prince's continued friendship. In letters that they exchanged, intended for Alexandra's eyes, they made clear that their relationship had been 'platonic for some years' (ibid., 126).

Early interest in socialism Lady Warwick was elected as a poor law guardian for Warwick in December 1894. She was troubled by the condition of society around her (especially for the rural poor) but as yet her efforts at relief were directed along more or less traditional lines. A spectacular fancy dress ball held at Warwick Castle in February 1895 provided work for many dressmakers, milliners, caterers, and other staff, and Lady Warwick was shocked and angered to see it described in Robert Blatchford's socialist paper, *The Clarion* (which she regularly read), as a 'mad rivalry of wanton dissipation' that displayed a 'callousness that mocks and laughs at misery' (16 Feb 1895). She took the next train to London and stormed into Blatchford's office, demanding an explanation. Blatchford gave her a lecture on the difference between productive and unproductive labour which she never forgot. The meeting was not a Damascene conversion, and Lady Warwick did not become a socialist overnight, but it marked out a new path for her. She became interested in trade unionism and entertained trade unionists at Warwick Castle and made public speeches in their support; in 1897 she found Joseph Arch living in Warwickshire and persuaded him to write his memoirs, which she edited; she pursued with vigour her plans for providing agricultural training for middle-class women. In 1898 she set up a hostel for women in Reading, which in 1903 moved to Studley Castle, in Warwickshire, where it became known as the Studley Agricultural College for Women. It was the only one of her enterprises that survived to become financially independent of her, receiving its first government grant in 1926. It continued in operation until 1969.

Increasing interest in socialism did not prevent Lady Warwick from becoming a vigorous supporter of Dr Jameson after the notorious raid of 1895, nor from using her friendship with Cecil Rhodes to secure the lucrative Tanganyika concession, a speculation in the Katanga copper mines that between 1904 and 1914 brought in some £5000 or £6000 a year. The income was a vital re-injection of capital into the Warwick finances, which had been haemorrhaging for twenty years; income from estates had been declining dramatically, while Lady Warwick's style of living and entertaining, and her various philanthropic projects, took no account of the financial realities. From the jingoism of the 1890s, Daisy Warwick had by 1900 become a convinced opponent of the Second South African War because it overshadowed the needs of the British poor: 'they had heard much of patriotism and our glorious Empire, but too many people had their sunshine shadowed by poverty and the workhouse' (Blunden, 149).

She expanded her interests in education; she employed the men from a Salvation Army colony to work on her redesigned gardens at Easton; she spoke from the platform for a variety of societies in which she was interested, especially trade unions and co-operatives, travelling widely throughout the country to speak on the plight of the workers and the poor. Dressed as flamboyantly and extravagantly as ever, she cut a dashing figure at the municipal halls in which she spoke and was a target for easy criticism and cheap laughs. By 1904 (following the birth of her second daughter and fourth child, at the age of forty-two) she was almost ready to announce her conversion to socialism.

Lady Warwick attended the International Congress of Socialists in Amsterdam in August 1904, where she met H. M. Hyndman, who succeeded Stead as her mentor. In November she joined the Social Democratic Federation; Hyndman celebrated his coup in gaining such a visible supporter and exploited her novelty value: 'There is of course a lot of snobbery in this, but what matters?' he wrote to his socialist colleague H. G. Wilshire; 'People would come to see and hear her who would never come to see or hear you or me' (Blunden, 176). The public adoption of the theory of class war by a countess (even a countess whose personal reputation had worn rather thin) aroused hostility in widely different circles. To some of her own class she was a traitor, although rather more considered her socialism an attention-seeking fad that would pass; to many in the working classes, and especially in the organized labour movement, she was a foolish woman bringing discredit to the genuine grievances and activities of the workers. Ramsay MacDonald (who later fell under the spell of 'Circe', Lady Londonderry) declined to meet her, expressing grave doubts 'as to the permanent good which can be done to a democratic movement by the exploitation of an aristocratic convert' (Marquand, 70). In many respects Lady Warwick was the original champagne socialist, mingling socialist theory and political campaigning with country-house parties and continued charitable work.

Author and Labour Party candidate Daisy Warwick continued to be generous beyond her means to the causes she took to heart. Planning a socialist magazine, she became mired in a relationship with a dishonest financier and found herself encumbered with even greater debts. She took to writing as a means of generating income, persuading her neighbour R. D. Blumenthal to give her a weekly column in the Conservative *Daily Express*. A number of books appeared under her name but most were ghost-written for her, several by Samuel Bensusan, who was one of the literary and radical political circle based around her Essex estates. Others of this circle included journalist John Robertson Scott, novelist H. G. Wells, and Conrad Noel, the socialist vicar of Thaxted (of which living Daisy was patron). Her first book, *Warwick Castle and its Earls* (1903), she seems to have written herself, basing it on research by Harvey Bloom, but later works, including her two unreliable volumes of memoirs—*Life's ebb and Flow* (1929) and *Afterthoughts* (1931)—were largely the work of other hands. Indeed she also largely handed over her newspaper column to Bensusan. She tried turning her hand to film script-writing, and in later years attempted a novel, *Branch Lines* (1932), described by her usually sympathetic biographer as 'one of the worst novels ever written' (Blunden, 315). It was her desperate financial situation that led her to take steps to raise funds by publishing her memoirs, including her intimate correspondence with Edward VII when prince of Wales. She confided in Arthur du Cros, apparently hoping that he would buy the letters himself to prevent damage to the royal family or that he would persuade them to pay for the letters. The duke of Wellington had famously responded to a similar attempt at extortion, 'Publish and be damned!'. George V took more vigorous action, taking out an injunction against publication of the letters and eventually securing their destruction.

On the outbreak of war in 1914 Lady Warwick became involved in Red Cross work but she followed the socialist line that the war was the product of unfettered capitalism. She resisted Germanophobia, bitterly opposed the effects of the war on the home front, and welcomed the Russian revolution. In February 1918 a large part of Easton Lodge was destroyed by fire, taking with it most of her papers. The war over, she was approaching sixty. Her enthusiasm for socialism was unabated, and she continued to host gatherings of socialists and trade unionists at Easton, where they were surrounded by her ever-increasing menagerie of animals—monkeys, peacocks, marmosets—and the decaying grandeur of an aristocratic estate run to seed. She withdrew from the Labour candidacy for the Walthamstow East constituency, after some months, in 1920 but in 1923 stood for the party in a by-election (which was merged into a general election) for Warwick and Leamington, where she was opposed by her son's brother-in-law, Anthony Eden, and came third in the poll after a gruelling campaign. Lord Warwick, who had been in poor health for years, died six weeks after the election. Earlier, in 1923, Lady Warwick had offered to hand over Easton Lodge to the Labour Party executive as a centre for conferences and residential study. They took it under a temporary arrangement but it was not renewed. She then offered it to the Independent Labour Party, who held summer schools there for a time, and subsequently approached the Trades Union Congress with a view to their forming a labour college there, but the general strike of 1926 put paid to the scheme.

The next decade saw no abatement of Lady Warwick's interest in socialism or her literary activities, and in 1930 a series of weekend conferences was held at Easton to revive socialism in the Labour Party. But the money was gone and she was reduced to borrowing money from old friends; in April 1937 she advertised for a paying guest. Burglars at Easton in January 1938 found little to steal. Daisy Warwick had become extremely stout in middle age, but a new acquaintance recognized the beauty that she had once been: 'her face had still the fixed pink-and-white attractions which one associates with the Lily Langtry era, and an "electric light" smile which was turned on

in a brilliant flash and gone again' (M. Cole, *Growing up into Revolution*, 1949, 146). She died at Easton Lodge on 26 July 1938, and was buried with her husband in the family vault at Warwick. She bequeathed property worth £37,000 to her surviving son, Maynard (a mere fraction of the wealth that she had inherited in 1865), and left 500 pet birds and 13 dogs to the housekeeper at Easton. She had hoped that the grounds at Easton would become a permanent wildlife refuge, but ironically they were destroyed to make an airfield during the war. In 1946 Easton Lodge suffered another serious fire and it was demolished in 1947.

Reputation Daisy Warwick has received a mixed press. Treated as a minor figure of fun by labour historians, she has been dismissed as 'ridiculous or hypocritical or both' (Cannadine, 538). Her earlier manifestation, as a society beauty and mistress of the prince of Wales, had by the late twentieth century become a glamorous tale of romance in high society rather than one of squalid adultery. She was the subject of a scholarly biography, published in 1967, which attempts to understand the entirety of her extraordinary career. Disorganized and contradictory, hazy about the truth, enthusiastic and passionate, she flitted from lecture platform to newspaper column, from cause to cause; but despite considerable pressure to conform she never wavered in her belief in the virtues and eventual triumph of socialism. In 1897 she wondered: 'When one has so many interests and does so many things how can one understand any one thing or do any one thing well?' (Blunden, 115). It was a perceptive question, and one to which she never found a satisfactory answer.

K. D. REYNOLDS

Sources M. Blunden, *The countess of Warwick* (1967) · Frances, countess of Warwick, *Life's ebb and flow* (1929) · Frances, countess of Warwick, *Afterthoughts* (1931) · C. Hibbert, *Edward VII* (1976) · A. Leslie, *Edwardians in love* (1972) · D. Cannadine, *The decline and fall of the British aristocracy* (1990) · D. Marquand, *Ramsay MacDonald* (1977) · H. M. Hyndman, *Further reminiscences* (1912) · Burke, *Peerage* (1939) · C. Zeepvat, *Prince Leopold* (1998)

Archives Warks. CRO, corresp. and papers | BL, corresp. with Society of Authors, Add. MS 56840 · Essex RO, Chelmsford, letters to Sir Joseph Laycock · HLRO, letters to Ralph Blumenfeld · University of Essex Library, letters to Samuel Levi Bensusan

Likenesses Barraud, photograph, c.1888, NPG · E. Roberts, oils, 1899, Warwick Castle, Warwickshire · J. S. Sargent, double portrait, oils, 1905 (with her son), Worcester Art Museum, Massachusetts · E. Boehm?, marble bust, St Mary's Church, Little Easton, Essex · Ellis & Walery, photograph, NPG · Walery, cabinet, NPG · photograph, NPG

Wealth at death £37,100: probate, 17 Aug 1938, CGPLA Eng. & Wales

Greville, Fulke, first Baron Brooke of Beauchamps Court (1554–1628), courtier and author, was born on 3 October 1554, the first of two children of Sir Fulke Greville (1536–1606) and Lady Anne (d. 1583), daughter of Ralph Neville, earl of Westmorland. He was probably born at Beauchamp's Court in Alcester, Warwickshire, the home of his paternal grandfather, Sir Fulke Greville (d. 1560), the second son of Sir Edward who married Elizabeth, one of three daughters and coheirs of Edward Willoughby, the only son of Robert, Lord Willoughby. As the sole heir of the Willoughby family Elizabeth—*de jure* Baroness Willoughby de Broke—brought to the younger branch of the Grevilles not only the right to a title but also thirty-two manors (including Beauchamp's Court) in eight counties. The youngest of the three Fulke Grevilles was thus a member of an influential landowning Warwickshire family with ties to the aristocratic families of Willoughby, Beauchamp, Neville, Ferrers, Grey, Talbot, Devereux, and Dudley.

Friend of Sir Philip Sidney (1554–1586) At ten Greville was sent, on 17 October 1564, to join Philip Sidney at the newly founded Shrewsbury School. Three years together at school cemented the friendship of the two boys, and Sidney's influence remained for the rest of Greville's life. The two boys were parted when Greville went to Jesus College, Cambridge (where he matriculated at Easter 1568), and Sidney to Christ Church, Oxford. Greville left Cambridge in 1571 or 1572 without taking a degree. Nothing is known of his activities during the period of Sidney's continental travels from 1572 to 1575.

On Sidney's return to England Greville joined him at court, imbued with the humanist notion of service to one's prince, and with a desire to establish his autonomy; it would be many years before he could expect to come into his inheritance. Greville attached himself to the radical or 'forward' protestant faction of Sidney's uncle, Robert Dudley, earl of Leicester. Like Sidney's, his political ambitions were frustrated by his failure to secure any significant office during these early years. What little he achieved he owed to his connection with the Sidneys. In February 1577, with the support of Sir Henry Sidney, Greville was granted the reversion of two sinecure Welsh offices: clerk of the council and clerk of the signet. (By 1583 he was granted the reversion of the office of secretary to the council of the marches. Within a few years, this monopoly of the Welsh administrative offices provided him with the major source of his public income.) Later in 1577, when Sidney was sent as ambassador to condole the death of the emperor, Maximilian II, Greville, along with Sir Edward Dyer, accompanied him. They had meetings with Don John of Austria in Louvain, John Casimir, count palatine, in Heidelberg, Emperor Rudolph II and his brother Ernest in Prague, Ludwig VI, the elector palatine, in Neustadt, and William of Orange in Gertruidenburg. In 1579 Greville escorted John Casimir and Sidney's friend Hubert Languet back to Germany, and on his return met William of Orange. A similar ceremonial duty was assigned to him in 1582, when he, Sidney, and Sir Walter Ralegh accompanied the duke of Anjou back to Antwerp at the end of the protracted French courtship of Elizabeth.

Greville's attempts at significant actions were met with frustration. In 1578, when he tried to join an expedition designed to discourage the Dutch from allying themselves with the French, he was expressly forbidden from doing so by the queen. Soon afterwards he accompanied Sir Francis Walsingham to the Low Countries without the queen's permission, and was reprimanded for his pains. In 1585 he and Sidney attempted to join Sir Francis Drake's expedition to the West Indies. But he and Sidney were recalled in disgrace, though not before the perspicacious Greville had detected Drake's disingenuous conduct of using Sidney's status to hasten the fitting out of the fleet. In the same year Sidney was allowed to accompany the earl of Leicester on the Low Countries expedition, but Greville was ordered to remain in England. In 1587 Greville departed without permission to witness the battle of Coutras (20 October) between the forces of Henri of Navarre and those of Henri III under the command of the duke of Joyeuse. On his return the queen kept him in disgrace, but gave out that he had been on a secret mission. When he did manage to engage in official military or naval actions these also met with frustration. In 1580, for example, he was appointed captain of one of three ships sent to protect the Irish coast. He spent five uneventful months at sea without seeing any action, and discovered on his return that the enemy fleet of four ships had eluded them.

The chronology of Greville's literary works is unclear, though it appears that he began writing in a spirit of collaborative emulation with Sidney and, to a lesser extent, with Sir Edward Dyer. The first seventy-six sonnets of Greville's sequence entitled *Caelica* appear to have been written after 1577, when the three friends were experimenting with verse forms. The nature of Sidney's and Greville's friendly rivalry is revealed by the name of the central female figure in each collection: Sidney's mistress is Stella (a single star), Greville addresses his poems to the entire sky (Caelica). Both sonnet sequences can be seen as responses to the challenge presented by the practice of Petrarchan love. While Sidney fails to resolve the conflicting demands of selfless adoration and physical desire in the lover, Greville turns from exploring the psychological consequences of the conflicting demands to a cynical rejection of ideal earthly love. For him, women are unfaithful and men are inevitably self-deceiving.

Servant to Queen Elizabeth, 1586–1603 The great crisis of Greville's life came with the death of Sir Philip Sidney on 17 October 1586, twenty-five days after being wounded at the battle of Zutphen. In many ways the remainder of Greville's life can be seen as an attempt to come to terms with his memory of Sidney. In this respect his first obligation was to prevent unauthorized publication of what is now known as Sidney's *Old Arcadia* in November 1586. Eventually, in 1590, he oversaw the publication of the significantly revised torso of the work, with his own chapter divisions, chapter summaries, and rearrangement of the eclogues. Three years later, under the auspices of Sidney's sister the countess of Pembroke, his act of homage was replaced by a hybrid edition consisting of two and a half books of revised text and a slightly modified text of the earlier version. Nevertheless, as late as 1615 Greville cherished plans for a double tomb with Sidney. Greville's bond with Sidney would have obliged him to maintain contact with the immediate members of his friend's family, but it is clear that the acrimony between the editors of the 1590 and 1593 editions of the *Arcadia* in some measure reflected the relationship between Greville and the countess of

Pembroke, who each saw themselves as custodians of Sidney's memory. Evidence for the breach between the two can be found in the fact that when Samuel Daniel lost the countess's patronage in the mid-1590s, he was immediately taken under Greville's wing.

During the next fifteen years Greville wrote few poems. In *Caelica*, sonnets 77–81, he had already turned from concerns with human love to political and religious questions which preoccupied the Senecan closet-dramas— *Mustapha*, *Alaham*, and *Antony and Cleopatra*—written between about 1595 and 1600. In these fundamentally pessimistic plays Greville was concerned with the dangers and evils of power and intrigue in an absolute monarchy, and with the corrupting effect of this on the individual. The works are modelled on ones by Robert Garnier, whose plays enjoyed a vogue among writers of the countess of Pembroke's circle in the 1590s: dramas not intended for stage performance provided a covert figuration of English political circumstances. The countess herself translated *Marc Antoine* and Samuel Daniel provided a sequel in *Cleopatra*. By 1601 Greville had probably also completed 'A Letter to an Honourable Lady'. This prose *consolatio* in the form of a Senecan epistle has much in common with the other works written in the 1590s, advocating patience in the face of the vicissitudes of life and trust in the consolation of Heaven. In it one can see Greville coming to terms with the main issue of his life and writings, the frustration at the lack of personal autonomy.

Greville found no way of advancing his political career in the years following Sidney's death, apart from representing Warwickshire in all the remaining parliaments of Elizabeth's reign, and continuing to hold the lucrative Welsh offices. He did, however, attach himself to Sidney's political heir, Robert Devereux, earl of Essex, who had inherited Sidney's sword and married his widow. In 1599, after many years of unwilling submission to the queen's restraints, Greville obtained, with Essex's support, the treasurership of the navy. He was also appointed a rear-admiral in expectation of the second armada. These were his first significant appointments, and he retained the treasurership despite his patron's disgrace and subsequent execution in 1601. Greville counselled Essex to avoid confrontation with Elizabeth, and ensured that he himself did not alienate Essex's great enemy, Sir Robert Cecil. He also took the further precaution of destroying all copies of his play *Antony and Cleopatra* to prevent it from being read in terms of current events. The queen, moreover, had taken the measure of Greville's independent actions and knew that his loyalties lay with her. For this reason Greville had some success in moderating proceedings against Essex and his immediate followers after the Essex uprising on 8 February 1601. In order to remove his influence from the queen Cecil arranged for Greville to be posted at Rochester until after Essex's execution on 25 February. Greville avoided the immediate retaliation of the ever-distrustful Cecil. He was made a knight of the Bath on James I's accession in 1603 and his position as secretary of the council of the Welsh marches was confirmed, but Cecil ensured that he surrendered his naval office because of the embarrassment he suffered when Greville refused to connive at the corruption of his fellow administrators. At the age of forty-nine Greville retired to Warwickshire, seemingly at the end of his career.

Councillor to King James, 1603–1625 Despite the loss of his naval office Greville was neither impoverished nor idle. Though he was financially independent, he did his best to ingratiate himself with Robert Cecil. With a substantial annual income he was able to occupy himself not only with the practical affairs of maintaining his six residences, but from 1604 with refurbishing at the enormous cost of £10,000 over several years his seventh residence, Warwick Castle. He was also at liberty to engage in his most productive period of authorship.

From 1603 the bulk of Greville's writing consisted of lengthy philosophical poems. 'A Treatise of Monarchy', completed by 1610, focuses on the problematic origin and nature of monarchy and on the practicalities of cautious but effective rule. Some time between 1610 and 1612 he completed the work for which he is best known, 'A Dedication to Sir Philip Sidney'. Greville intended it as a preface to his then completed philosophical poetry. The first part consisted of an account of Sidney as an ideal subject, and the second of an encomiastic account of Elizabeth's reign designed to reveal the shortcomings of James I. It is likely that the work was intended for the eyes of Prince Henry, since Greville lost interest in it after Henry's death in November 1612. The 'Dedication' is not found in the collection of manuscript fair copies of his works whose preparation Greville supervised. It was first published in 1652 as *The Life of the Renowned Sir Philip Sidney*, and as such became the major source of the Sidney hagiographic tradition.

In the second part of the 'Dedication' Greville attempts to write a form of the new civil history that was being pioneered by his friend and client William Camden. Greville claims that he had originally intended to write a history of Elizabeth, but had been denied access to state papers by Robert Cecil. For his material on the queen he simply translated passages from the Latin of Camden's manuscript 'Annals' (published in 1625). This collaboration with Camden should be seen as a continuation of the tradition of patronage which Greville and the countess of Pembroke inherited from Sidney. Through Greville, Camden was appointed Clarenceux king of arms in the herald's office, which freed him from schoolmastering to take up his historical researches. Others who benefited from Greville's patronage were John Coke (later secretary of state), John Speed, Bishop Joseph Hall, Lancelot Andrewes, John Overall, Samuel Daniel, William Davenant, and Martin Peerson, the musician.

Robert Cecil's death in May 1612 cleared the way for Greville's return to office, but Greville did not succeed Sir Julius Caesar as chancellor and under-treasurer of the exchequer until October 1614. During the period of waiting he wrote 'An Inquisition upon Fame and Honor', in which he proposes that virtue grounded in faith is the only possible alternative to the delusion of opinion ('fame') and worth ('honor'). Sonnets 85–105 of *Caelica* share the sense of religious disillusionment in this poem. Ronald Rebholz sees in the stern Calvinistic views of the 'Inquisition' evidence for a major religious conversion some time before 1614, but Greville's views were Calvinist throughout his life.

Greville owed his return to major office to the pro-Spanish Howard faction. His immediate superior was the lord treasurer, Thomas Howard, earl of Suffolk, whose incompetence and lack of probity doomed to failure any efforts by Greville to balance the king's ordinary income with his expenditures, let alone find new sources of revenue. In July 1618 Suffolk was expelled from office and was replaced by a treasury commission headed by Greville until the end of 1620. The efforts of the commission produced a slight surplus of revenues over expenditure, but were incapable of persuading the king to restrain his extravagance. In December 1620 Greville's hopes for the office of lord treasurer were dashed by the appointment of Henry Montague, Viscount Mandeville. During the course of the following year, in compensation for his disappointment, Greville was created Baron Brooke of Beauchamp's Court and granted all fines for licences of alienations in chancery for seven years. His claim to the barony of Willoughby de Broke was denied.

In October 1621 Greville lost his treasury office to Sir Richard Weston, a member of the pro-Spanish court party headed by George Villiers, duke of Buckingham, the new royal favourite. He retained his seat on the privy council and was made gentleman of the bedchamber, but because of his known protestant views he had to devote much time and energy ingratiating himself with Buckingham. Towards the end of 1623, with the failure of the Spanish marriage plans for Prince Charles, Buckingham's political views became more congenial to Greville, who was now faced with the dilemma of having to choose loyalty either to the ageing king or to Buckingham. Instead he opted for a strategy of evasion, while yet retaining the good will of both parties. On the accession of Charles I in March 1625 Greville was reinstated as a privy councillor, but his illness in the following autumn prevented him from contributing much to the management of public affairs.

Later writings and death   Following the loss of his treasury office in 1621, Greville once again turned to writing philosophical poems. 'A Treatise of Humane Learning', 'A Treatise of Wars', and 'A Treatise of Religion' probably date from this period. Between 1619 and 1625 he supervised the preparation of manuscript fair copies of his literary works, excluding the 'Dedication'. These are now known as the Warwick manuscripts in the British Library. He indicated in a note the order in which the poems were to be placed: '1. Religion. 2. Humane learning. 3. Fame and Honor. 4. War' (BL, Add. MS 54567, fol. 3). There is no mention of 'A Treatise of Monarchy'. This is because Greville probably realized that even if published posthumously a work which argued that monarchy is the product of human fallibility would be unacceptable. He had already run foul of the authorities over his attempt to establish a lectureship in history at Cambridge in 1627. The first appointee, Isaac Dorislaus, whose opinions on monarchy

were similar to Greville's, had been examined by Laud and others, and the lectures on Tacitus discontinued. (Greville attempted to make provision for the lectureship in his will, but failed to have the codicil witnessed.) When Greville's *Certaine Learned and Elegant Workes* was published in 1633 under the supervision of Sir John Coke and Sir Kenelm Digby a further poem was omitted. It would appear that 'A Treatise of Religion' was removed from all copies on the orders of Laud, who was then bishop of London, on account of the slur on episcopacy and criticism of the established church. The two potentially subversive poems had to wait until 1670, when they were published in a volume entitled *The Remains of Sir Fulke Greville*. 'A Dedication to Sir Philip Sidney' (retitled *The Life of the Renowned Sir Philip Sidney*) was not published until 1652, when its implicit criticism of Stuart monarchy and advocacy of an aggressive, anti-Catholic foreign policy would find a ready Commonwealth readership. In addition to the *editio princeps* derived from an unknown manuscript source it survived in four scribal copies, two of which represent a significantly earlier form of the work.

The 'Dedication' remains Greville's most influential work, largely because it is the only source for the anecdotes central to the development of the Sidney myth. In particular Greville provides the story of the water bottle which made Sidney the icon of self-sacrifice from the nineteenth century onwards. At the battle of Zutphen the severely wounded Sidney is reported to have forgone slaking his thirst in favour of a wounded common soldier with the words, 'Thy necessity is yet greater than mine' (*Prose Works*, 77). These words received an almost proverbial status. At the time of the supposed event Greville was in England. His source for the anecdote has not been traced.

As a poet Greville has always been admired for the difficulty of his writing, but his reputation was never higher than in the twentieth century, especially in the United States, where his standing as a poet of the plain style could be attributed to the writings of Yvor Winters and his followers. Winters regarded Greville as a poet who 'should be ranked with Jonson as one of the two great masters of the short poem in the Renaissance' (Winters, 44). This view has not met with general assent, but it has encouraged others to take Greville seriously for his own sake, especially those on either side of the Atlantic who regard themselves more as cultural, rather than simply literary, critics. The circumstances of Greville's life and career, the political and material conditions of his authorship, and the thematic concerns with the exercise of power and with the predicament of the individual in an absolute monarchy render them readily accessible to new historicists and cultural materialists, or to proponents of any other approaches concerned with matters of ideology and power. The spiritual or religious dimension of Greville's work is in consequence occluded.

The duke of Buckingham, the despised favourite of both James I and Charles I, was assassinated on 23 August 1628. Soon afterwards, on 1 September at Brooke House in Holborn, Greville was attacked by his servant Ralph Hayward, who acted it would seem not from political motives, but from dissatisfaction at the terms of Greville's will. Greville was stabbed in the stomach while Hayward was assisting him to fasten his breeches. Greville forbade anyone from pursuing Hayward. Immediately after the attack Hayward committed suicide. Greville died of gangrene on 30 September, physicians having replaced the depleted natural fatty membrane around their patient's intestines with animal fat. The bulk of his estate and his title went to his adopted heir, Robert Greville, the son of his cousin Fulke Greville (d. 1632) and Mary Copley. At the time of his death Greville's annual income from both lands and offices was probably about £7000, with ordinary expenses running between £2000 and £3000. He owned several properties, including Warwick Castle, Beauchamp's Court, and three London houses (at Austin Friars, Hackney, and Holborn). The title of Baron Willoughby de Broke eventually went to the descendants of Greville's sister Margaret (1561–1631/2), who married Sir Richard Verney.

Greville never married and it has been suggested that he was homosexual. There is no evidence for this. He was however given to close, almost possessive friendships: for example, with Sidney and Sir John Coke. By nature introverted, circumspect, even over-cautious—an observer rather than the man of action he admired so much in Sidney—he often failed to take assertive action in times of crisis. His instinct for self-preservation allowed him to maintain a remarkably extended career at court. His portrait presents him as sombrely dressed, aloof, and intelligently sensitive, with a long face and the thin hands of a mandarin. Sir Francis Bacon described him as an elegant speaker (Rebholz, 269).

Greville was buried in the family crypt in St Mary's Church, Warwick. Nearby, enclosed in a small room, is a tomb Greville prepared for himself. It bears the inscription: 'Fulke Greville, Servant to Queen Elizabeth, Councillor to King James, and Friend to Sir Philip Sidney. Trophaeum Peccati'. Greville often thought of himself as an adjective rather than a substantive, and the inscription emphasizes the sense of his derivative identity. The ambiguous awareness of the wages of sin underscores the complexity of his Calvinist attitude to life in general, and to public service in particular. The tomb, enclosed in a small room, emphasizes the dominant mode of his life: frustration.   JOHN GOUWS

Sources R. A. Rebholz, *The life of Fulke Greville, first Lord Brooke* (1971) · *The prose works of Fulke Greville, Lord Brooke*, ed. J. Gouws (1986) · G. A. Wilkes, 'The sequence of the writings of Fulke Greville, Lord Brooke', *Studies in Philology*, 56 (1959), 489–503 · W. H. Kelliher, 'The Warwick manuscripts of Fulke Greville', *British Museum Quarterly*, 34 (1969–70), 107–21 · D. Norbrook, *Poetry and politics in the English Renaissance* (1984), 157–74 · J. Gouws, 'Fulke Greville, first Lord Brooke', *Sixteenth-century British nondramatic writers: fourth series*, ed. D. A. Richardson, DLitB, 172 (1996), 105–15 · B. Worden, 'Friend to Sir Philip Sidney', *London Review of Books* (3 July 1986) · BL, Warwick Castle manuscripts, Add. MSS 54566–54571 · P. Bennet, 'Recent studies in Greville', *English Literary Renaissance*, 2 (1972), 376–82 · Y. Winters, 'Aspects of the short poem in the English Renaissance', *Forms of discovery: critical and historical studies on the forms of the short poem in English* (1967), 1–120 · J. Gouws, 'Fact and anecdote in Fulke Greville's account of Sidney's last days', *Sir Philip Sidney: 1586 and the creation of a legend*, ed. J. van

Oorsten and others (1986), 62–82 · J. Gouws, 'The nineteenth century development of the Sidney legend', *Sir Philip Sidney's achievements*, ed. M. J. B. Allen and others (1990), 251–60 · *DNB* · J. Dollimore, *Radical tragedy*, 2nd edn (1989), 120–33 · U. Aberdeen, MS 271

Archives BL, corresp. and papers as treasurer of navy, Add. MSS 64870–64897 · BL, Deptford housekeeping accounts, X 94 · BL, official papers and household and estate accounts, Add. MSS 69934–69935 · BL, papers, Add. MSS 69868–69935 · BL, Warwick Castle MSS · Warks. CRO, accounts as treasurer of marine causes · Warks. CRO, legal papers · Warks. CRO, letters | BL, Earl Cowper MSS · CKS, corresp. with Lionel Cranfield · Herts. ALS, MSS ACC2418 · Shrewsbury Public Library, MS 295 · Trinity Cam., MSS R.7.32, R.7.33

Likenesses oils, 1586, priv. coll.; copy, Warwick Castle · J. Jenkins, stipple, BM, NPG

Wealth at death substantial: Rebholz, *Life of Fulke Greville*, 185–92

Greville, Henry William (1801–1872), diarist, youngest son of Charles Greville, grandson of the fifth Baron Brooke of Beauchamps Court, and Lady Charlotte Cavendish Cavendish-Bentinck, eldest daughter of William Henry, third duke of Portland, was born on 28 October 1801. He was educated at Westminster School and Christ Church, Oxford, where he graduated BA on 4 June 1823. Much of his boyhood was spent on the continent, chiefly at Brussels, where his family resided. He thus learned to speak French and Italian with fluency. He was taken by the duke of Wellington to the celebrated ball given by the duchess of Richmond at Brussels on the night before the battle of Waterloo. He became private secretary to Lord Francis Egerton, afterwards earl of Ellesmere, when he was chief secretary for Ireland. From 1834 to 1844 he was attaché to the British embassy in Paris. He afterwards held the post of gentleman usher at court. He was fond of society, of music, and of the drama. Fanny (Frances Anne) Kemble knew him well, and describes his fine voice and handsome appearance in her *Records of a Girlhood*.

Like his brother, Charles Cavendish Fulke *Greville, Henry Greville long kept a diary of public and private events, portions of which were edited by his niece, Viscountess Enfield (afterwards countess of Strafford), under the title *Leaves from the Diary of Henry Greville* (4 vols., 1883–1905). The *Diary* derives some importance from the author's position at Paris between 1834 and 1844, but otherwise it is of no special value, and Greville lacked his brother's wit and malice. He died, unmarried, on 12 December 1872 at his house in Queen's Street, Mayfair, London.   J. M. RIGG, rev. H. C. G. MATTHEW

Sources Lady Enfield, memoir, in *Leaves from the diary of Henry Greville*, ed. A. H. F. Byng, countess of Strafford, 4 vols. (1883–1905), vol. 2 · F. A. Kemble, *Record of a girlhood*, 3 vols. (1878) · Burke, *Peerage*

Archives Keele University Library, letters to Ralph Sneyd

Likenesses two oils, 1844, Goodwood House, West Sussex · J. Jackson, oils, Hardwick Hall, Derbyshire

Wealth at death under £35,000: probate, 17 Jan 1873, *CGPLA Eng. & Wales*

Greville [née Anderson], **Dame Margaret Helen** (1863–1942), society hostess, had a difficult early life. She was born in London on 20 December 1863. Her mother, Helen (1835/6–1906), had married William Anderson, day porter

Dame Margaret
Helen Greville
(1863–1942), by
Emile Auguste
Carolus-Duran,
1891

estate of Polesden Lacey. The original Grecian villa built under the supervision of Thomas Cubitt in 1824 had recently been extended by Ambrose Poynter for Sir Clinton Dawkins. Its interior was sumptuously refitted for the Grevilles by Charles Frédéric Mewès and Arthur Davis, the architects of the Ritz Hotel, in a manner reviving the Windsor Castle style of the 1820s. Polesden Lacey is a consummate display of Edwardian opulence and eclecticism: the woodwork in the hall was made from the altarpiece of a Wren church in the City of London; 'the Drawing Room is a sumptuous mock-Louis-Quatorze confection in white, gold and red with wall mirrors, ornate pilasters, imported French Rococo fireplaces and Italian ceiling paintings' (Pevsner, 415). Maggie Greville inherited some good English pictures, and bought others herself. Although only 22 miles from London, the house was surrounded by sylvan gardens and commanded glorious views over the Dorking valley. Polesden Lacey's parvenu luxuries and spacious seclusion were mistaken for aristocratic elegance by middle-class politicians such as Sir Robert Horne.

The premature death of Ronnie Greville from throat cancer in 1908 required little adjustment in his widow's life. Early in her widowhood Maggie declined a proposal from Sir Evelyn Ruggles-Brise, and after hesitation she decided not to marry Sir John Simon in 1917. By the death of her father in 1913 she inherited an estimated £1.5 million including two-thirds of the voting shares in William McEwan's brewery, a private company which merged with William Younger to form Scottish Breweries Ltd in 1931. McEwan board meetings were held at Polesden Lacey, where she treated the directors with such autocratic harshness that they would leave her room trembling. She had a highly materialistic outlook, and was implacable in her pursuit of material gain. She also inherited M'Ewan's Mayfair home, which formerly had been the town house of the earls of Craven. Its upstairs drawing-room floor was fitted with priceless Louis XIV *boiserie* producing an effect 'of great beauty, very perfect in taste' (Repington, 2.482).

Maggie Greville was first cousin to George *Younger and Robert *Younger, who were both raised to the peerage in 1923, and as a rich brewer was herself created DBE during the former's chairmanship of the Unionist Party (1922). 'Appropriately she looked a rather blousy old barmaid', according to Sir Oswald Mosley (Mosley, 79). Kenneth Clark characterized her guests as 'stuffy members of the government and their mem-sahib wives, ambassadors and royalty' (Clark, 269). She shunned bohemians, and admitted only the most plutocratic Americans to her salon. Though Edward VIII ostracized her as a bore, her appetite for royalty remained insatiable. 'One uses up *so* many red carpets in a season', she declared (Pearson, 134); another boast was that in the course of one morning three kings sat on her bed. During a visit to India as the guest of the marquess of Reading in 1922 she chaperoned Edwina Ashley, who accepted a proposal from Lord Louis Mountbatten in Greville's sitting room in the viceregal lodge. The future George VI spent part of his honeymoon at Polesden Lacey in 1923.

at the Edinburgh brewery of William M'Ewan [see McEwan, William (1827–1913)]. M'Ewan supposedly put Anderson on night duty to facilitate his own access to Mrs Anderson, who was a cook. After the porter's death M'Ewan in 1885 married Helen Anderson and adopted her daughter, who was his presumptive only child. He was a plain, blunt man, and a domineering but indulgent father.

On 25 April 1891 Margaret Anderson married the Hon. Ronald Henry Fulke Greville (1864–1908), elder son and heir of the second Baron Greville. He was a suave and genial captain in the Life Guards, but she so disliked army society that after a few years she threatened to leave him unless he sent in his papers to enable her to launch her social career in London. Her husband complied, and became a reputable if unexciting Unionist free-trader MP for East Bradford (1896–1906). Their marriage was her grappling hook onto society, where her father's money and her own persistence secured her a permanent place. After 1901 she was one of the pretty young hostesses who entertained Edward VII. Her energetic worldliness proved well attuned to the temper of the court. 'I don't follow people to their bedrooms,' she told the marquess of Carisbrooke, 'it's what they do outside them that is important' (*Chips*, ed. James, 336). Her success with the old king provoked resentment: the diversions provided for him by Lord and Lady Savile at Rufford Abbey and by the Grevilles at Reigate Priory earned them the sobriquet of the Civils and Grovels.

M'Ewan in 1906 bought for the Grevilles the Surrey

In addition to cultivating monarchs Maggie Greville was assiduous in entertaining foreign ambassadors. This brought her one innocuous advantage: red carpets and special trains during her inveterate travels. There was a less innocent consequence of her attentions to diplomatists. Harold Nicolson complained in 1939:

> The harm which these silly selfish hostesses do is really immense. … They convey to foreign envoys the impression that policy is decided in their own drawing-rooms … They dine and wine our younger politicians and they create an atmosphere of authority and responsibility and grandeur, whereas the whole thing is a mere flatulence.   (Nicolson, 396–7)

After she had decried Churchill in 1942, the diplomat Charles Ritchie similarly deplored her 'trivial but not harmless gossip' (Ritchie, 145). Her waspishness was such that Lady Leslie exclaimed, 'Maggie Greville! I would sooner have an open sewer in my drawing-room' (Lees-Milne, 1.109). The earl of Crawford described her in 1933: 'Full of stories, and if with a spice of scandal so much the better; very anti-semitic—a real good sort; but I should love to see her in a temper' (Vincent, 551). 'There is no one on earth quite so skilfully malicious as old Maggie', Henry Channon wrote approvingly in 1939, 'she was vituperative about almost everyone' (Chips, ed. James, 208). Loyal in her friendships, she was unforgiving to her enemies, especially her rival Emerald Cunard. 'You mustn't think that I dislike little Lady Cunard, I'm always telling Queen Mary she isn't as bad as she's painted,' she catted to Carisbrooke (Chips, ed. James, 336). She found Hitler charming and Mussolini pompous.

During the blitz Greville shut her Mayfair house and lived mainly in Claridges and the Dorchester hotels. After a long period of disablement, during which she continued to entertain gamely, she died on 15 September 1942, at the Dorchester Hotel, and was buried on 18 September outside the walled rose garden at Polesden Lacey. In her will (for which the executors included lords Ilchester, Bruntisfield, and Dundonald) she left Marie Antoinette's necklace to Queen Elizabeth, £25,000 to the queen of Spain, £20,000 to Princess Margaret, and £10,000 to Osbert Sitwell. Polesden Lacey was bequeathed to the National Trust.

'She was so shrewd, so kind and so amusingly unkind, so sharp, such fun, so naughty', wrote Queen Elizabeth after Greville's death, 'altogether a real person, a character, utterly Mrs Ronald Greville' (Bradford, 111). Sir Cecil Beaton was less enamoured: 'Mrs Ronnie Greville was a galumphing, greedy, snobbish old toad who watered at her chops at the sight of royalty … and did nothing for anybody except the rich' (Buckle, 215–16).

RICHARD DAVENPORT-HINES

Sources K. Clark, *Another part of the wood* (1974) · C. Ritchie, *The siren years* (1974) · S. Bradford, *King George VI* (1989) · J. Lees-Milne, *Ancestral voices* (1975) · C. À Court Repington, *The First World War*, 2 vols. (1920) · H. Nicolson, *Diaries and letters*, ed. N. Nicolson, 1 (1966) · *'Chips': the diaries of Sir Henry Channon*, ed. R. R. James (1967) · R. Buckle, ed., *Self-portrait with friends: selected diaries of Cecil Beaton* (1979) · J. Pearson, *Façades: Edith, Osbert and Sacheverell Sitwell* (1978) · *The Crawford papers: the journals of David Lindsay, twenty-seventh earl of Crawford … 1892–1940*, ed. J. Vincent (1984) · R. Feddon, 'Polesden Lacey, Surrey I', *Country Life*, 103 (1948), 478–81 · R. Feddon, 'Polesden Lacey, Surrey II', *Country Life*, 103 (1948), 526–9 · O. Mosley, *My life* (1968) · B. Nichols, *All I could never be* (1949) · S. Keppel, *Edwardian daughter* (1958) · *Surrey*, Pevsner (1971) · earl of Portsmouth, *A knot of roots* (1965) · m. cert. · d. cert. · B. Masters, *Great hostesses* (1982) · P. Ziegler, *Osbert Sitwell* (1998) · National Trust, *Polesden Lacey* (1999), 56 · *The Times* (4 Sept 1906), 1a · *The Times* (19 Sept 1942)

Likenesses E. A. Carolus-Duran, oils, 1891, Polesden Lacey, Surrey [*see illus.*] · H. Schmiechen, oils, 1899, Polesden Lacey, Surrey

Wealth at death £1,623,191 17s. 0d.: resworn probate, 5 Jan 1943, CGPLA Eng. & Wales

Greville, Robert, second Baron Brooke of Beauchamps Court (1607–1643), parliamentarian army officer and religious writer, was born in May 1607, the son of Fulke Greville (1575–1632) of Thorpe Latimer, Lincolnshire, and his wife, Mary, daughter of Christopher Copley of Wadsworth, Yorkshire. Mary's first husband was another Yorkshire gentleman, Ralph Bosvile, and Godfrey—her son from this marriage—was to be closely associated with his half-brother in his colonial, political, and military endeavours of the 1630s and 1640s.

Inheritance and marriage Brooke's father was the first cousin of his namesake Fulke *Greville, first Baron Brooke of Beauchamps Court (1554–1628). Lord Brooke had no wish to marry and Robert was adopted early in life as his heir, and named as his successor in the patent granting the barony in January 1621. The Laudian polemicist Peter Heylyn, smarting from Robert Greville's attack on low-born bishops, claimed that the second lord's father had acted as the first lord's gamekeeper and had not been allowed to sit at table with him. The second lord's contemporary biographer was, conversely, concerned to stress he was 'no new man, or gentleman of the first head, but stockt in a long race of worthie Ancestors' (Spencer, 173). Robert Greville was given an intellectually demanding and cosmopolitan education supervised by the first lord, with a Dutch tutor and with three years' foreign travel between 1624 and 1627 which included attendance at the universities of Leiden and Paris and visits to Geneva and Venice.

The bulk of the first lord's extensive estates was settled on Robert Greville in February 1628 and through the Greville influence he sat as MP for Warwick borough in the first session of the 1628 parliament. After the first lord's murder in September he succeeded to the title and was thus in the Lords for the stormy session of 1629. He had inherited a landed income of more than £4000 p.a. with lands in twelve counties and London, and managed his fortune efficiently so that his widow and children enjoyed increased revenues in the 1650s despite the very large sums that he had expended in colonial enterprises and on raising forces for parliament. Brooke's marriage, about 1631, to Katherine Russell (c.1618–1676), daughter of Francis *Russell, fourth earl of Bedford, connected him with networks of puritan aristocratic critics of Charles I's personal rule. His wife was some ten years his junior and their first son, Francis, was not born until 1637. Four more sons came in rapid succession between 1638 and 1643. The youngest, Fulke, born posthumously, ultimately inherited the title.

Political dissent and colonial ventures, 1630–1640 Brooke was an active Warwickshire JP from 1631 but divided his time between his seat at Warwick Castle and his Holborn residence. He had uneasy relationships with Warwick borough and was regarded as an *arriviste* by some of the county gentry. Many shared the resentment of the first lord's close kin (such as his nephews the Verneys of Compton Verney) at the largesse shown to a more distant cousin. In 1640–41 Brooke had only limited success in obtaining parliamentary seats in Warwickshire for his political allies. His radical religious and political stance, as much as his ambiguous origins, however, distanced Brooke from mainstream provincial opinion. He worked most closely with ideologically committed figures from the minor local gentry and clergy, and with the national networks of godly opponents of Charles, such as John Pym, Oliver St John, Robert Rich, earl of Warwick, and especially William Fiennes, Lord Saye and Sele.

Brooke was heavily involved in godly colonial enterprises and made probably the largest financial commitment to the Providence Island Company, which established in 1630 a small volcanic island in the Caribbean as a base for puritan colonizing and anti-Spanish privateering. In 1632 Brooke, with Saye and Sele, Pym, Knightley, and others, acquired a patent to found a settlement at Saye-Brooke in Connecticut. Brooke's despair at developments in England led him, with Saye and Sele, to contemplate emigration. The two peers wrote to John Winthrop of Massachusetts late in 1635 to seek clarification on political and religious arrangements in New England. They sought a commonwealth with a two-house legislative assembly made up of a hereditary order of gentlemen and a second rank of freeholders. The answers from New England left them unsatisfied, but it seems that they were less alarmed by the lack of an aristocracy in New England, than about the theocratic requirement that political rights should be confined to full church members. Saye and Sele and Brooke feared the potential for religious tyranny in Massachusetts, and consistently rejected clerical involvement in civil affairs in both old and new England.

Brooke was none the less a consistent supporter of the New England colonies in their disputes with the crown in the 1630s and a zealous promoter of settlement in New England. Close associates from Warwickshire went to Connecticut including gentry like George Willis and clerics like Ephraim Huitt. Brooke owned the land on which John Davenport and others from St Stephen, Coleman Street, London, founded New Haven. Brooke's colonial activities forged contacts with city figures, notably Maurice Thompson, that were to be crucial to parliamentarian mobilization in the 1640s.

Besides his plans to emigrate Brooke's irreconcilable opposition to the king was paraded in his conspicuous absence from Warwick when Charles himself visited the town in August 1636. He was an early and predictable supporter of the Scots. In early 1639 he refused to attend the king against the Scots, 'unless it be adjudged he should by

parlyment' (PRO, SP 16/413/92). In April Brooke and Lord Saye and Sele—'twoe hereticall Lords', according to one newsletter; 'two popular men, and most undevoted to the Church, and in truth to the whole government' according to Clarendon (PRO, SP 16/418/30; Clarendon, *Hist. rebellion*, 1.154)—were briefly imprisoned at York for refusing to fight or swear loyalty to Charles. It is likely that Brooke was already in close, treasonable contact with the Scots, and a Scots preacher, probably Samuel Rutherford, was entertained at Warwick Castle in December 1639. After the failure of the Short Parliament Brooke was briefly arrested and among his papers seized by the authorities were found several petitions of grievances and 'discourses' on the liturgy—probably copies of the exchanges on church government between John Cotton and English clergy such as John Ball and Simeon Ashe. In August 1640 he was one of the twelve peers who petitioned the king to call a parliament, and he was one of the commissioners appointed to treat with the Scots at Ripon after their successful invasion.

Religious radical Richard Baxter claimed that Brooke (like Sir Henry Vane the younger) was a 'noted gross sectary' before the civil war (*Reliquiae Baxterianae*, ed. M. Sylvester, 1696, part 1, 63). Certainly Brooke's patronage of ministers, and his own published writings, reveal an extraordinarily open-minded intellectual and practical radicalism. 'A deare foster-father he was to manie Ministers and Schoole-Masters, allowing them yeerlie pensions or salaries', wrote the moderate puritan Warwickshire minister Thomas Spencer in his life of Brooke: 'Not only those that went his way, but also such as did conforme to the Church-government were his Beneficiaries' (Spencer, 173). By the early 1640s Brooke's main personal chaplain was the Independent Peter Sterry, whose interests in neo-Platonic and Behemist ideas were shared by his patron, but throughout the 1630s he supported men of a more mainstream stamp such as Simeon Ashe, Samuel Clarke, Thomas Dugard, and George Hughes. He also promoted the schemes of Samuel Hartlib and John Drury for educational reform and religious unity. At another extreme a notorious London separatist of the early 1640s, John Spencer, had been Brooke's coachman.

Brooke's 'way' extended to arguing for broad toleration of protestants and sympathy for radical separatists. Sterry's influence may be present in Brooke's first publication, *The Nature of Truth*, a platonic treatise written in the summer of 1640 and licensed for the press in November. It has affinities also with the views of the younger Sir Henry Vane, who had acted as an agent for Brooke and Saye and Sele in New England. For Brooke truth was conformity with God, but could take a variety of forms. Brooke argued for goodness within all existence: 'all things are but one emanation from the divine power' (Greville, *Nature of Truth*, 115) and concluded with millenarian hopes that humanity would come to comprehend the unity of truth and that 'wee might see how Christ is one with God, and wee one with Christ, so wee in Christ, one with God' (ibid., 170).

In this work Brooke denounced the 'cringings,

crouchings, all those ceremonies of will-worship' within the established church (Greville, *Nature of Truth*, 155). As truth took diverse forms, no-one should be compelled to worship against their conscience or reason. His second tract developed these views for a wider audience: *A Discourse Opening the Nature of that Episcopacie* was a vividly written contribution to the 'Smectymnuan' debate on episcopacy in 1641, more radical than most of the broadly presbyterian responses to Joseph Hall's defence of episcopacy. Brooke denied there was any basis in scripture or the practice of the early church for episcopacy as practised in England, where bishops had authority over many congregations and wielded secular power:

> There are three sorts of Bishops, as Beza saith. There are of God's Institution, and they are those who have a power over their proper flock, with the rest of the Church and no other. There are also of mans Institution and this ever overfloweth into the Neighbour Parish. And lastly, there is a demonicall Bishop, and this is he who challengeth the sword as well as the keyes. (Greville, *Episcopacie*, 68)

Brooke expected that God would free England from 'Tyrannicall Prelates' as Scotland had been freed (ibid., 87).

This second tract demonstrated an 'aristocratic constitutionalism' shared with Saye and Sele, arguing that lowborn bishops, desperate for money and office, were fawning buttresses of arbitrary power. A free, independent aristocracy, on the other hand, was a barrier to royal excesses. More startling was Brooke's matter-of-fact acceptance of religious diversity and error: 'Heresies must come', he wrote simply (Greville, *Episcopacie*, 86). The freedom of the United Provinces where religion flourished was to be preferred to the 'unity of Darknesse and Ignorance' found in Spain (ibid., 91). You could no more force people to choose their 'spiritual friends' than you could compel them 'to marry such or such a woman, to take such a servant, to dwell with such a friend' (ibid., 99). By refusing to condemn them and presenting their own arguments sympathetically, Brooke in effect defended the 'Brownists', Baptists, separatists, and lay preachers who were almost always condemned by parliamentarians in the early 1640s. Why, asked Brooke, was a tradesman preaching to be condemned before a civil lawyer or a bishop who also had a cure of souls (ibid., 106)? Brooke also noted that reformation had not been begun by the authorities, but by groups like the Albigensiens, the 'Church-lesse' (ibid., 116). Where churches were established all power to choose officers or decide controversial issues should lie in the church as a whole, not with the clergy or elders.

Brooke was a prominent and determined opponent of royal government from the first meeting of the Long Parliament. His fears of a royal *coup d'état* were demonstrated when he purchased arms in May 1641 following the first army plot of March–April 1641. He agitated, predictably, for the exclusion of bishops from the House of Lords as the crisis deepened in December 1641.

The outbreak of the civil war As lord lieutenant of Warwickshire, appointed under parliament's militia ordinance of March 1642, Brooke worked energetically to rally forces to the godly cause. He spent large sums entertaining the militia from late June and seized the county magazine at Coventry, depositing it at Warwick Castle for safety. From early in the year Brooke had been fortifying this stronghold. Although Clarendon claimed that the area of south Warwickshire and north Oxfordshire, around Edgehill, was through the influence of Saye and Sele and Brooke 'the most eminently corrupted of any country in England' (Clarendon, *Hist. rebellion*, 2.359), Brooke's support seems to have come mainly from the urban and industrial areas of the county. His closest associates in the parliamentarian leadership were long-standing friends and kin such as William Purefoy and Godfrey Bosvile along with many of his own estate officials. The royalists led by the earl of Northampton made much headway in the county later in the summer. An attempt to indict Brooke and Purefoy at the assizes for raising forces against the king fell when they claimed parliamentary authority for their actions. Northampton gained possession of the artillery that Brooke had brought to the midlands from London and turned it against Warwick Castle itself. While Brooke sought reinforcements in London his second in command, Sir Edward Peyto, hung a Bible and a winding sheet from the ramparts indicating their readiness to perish in the cause of God and parliament. A large army from London commanded by Brooke, John Hampden, and Nathaniel Fiennes forced the lifting of the siege and secured parliamentarian control of Warwickshire on 22/23 August 1642.

The Providence Island investors, merchants and peers alike, were strongly represented among Irish adventurers raising money for the suppression of the Irish rising and in June 1642 Brooke was nominated commander of the expedition intended against the Irish. This plan was overtaken by events in England where Brooke was, besides his local role, commander of a foot regiment in the earl of Essex's army. This regiment fought at Edgehill though Brooke himself missed the battle and suffered severe losses in the royalist attack on Brentford. In the Lords, Brooke remained a militant supporter of the war. He opposed an early peace and was very active in the promotion of measures to establish a more effective war effort. In both activities he effectively mobilized previous connections with city merchants like Maurice Thompson, and with radical Independent clergy such as Jeremiah Burroughs and Hugh Peter. In city and country Brooke proved an astute popular leader. The Warwickshire forces were raised with feasting, bell ringing, and the collective signing of petitions; and the officers of his volunteer companies were elected with rank and file consent. In a 1643 speech to his midlands troops he anticipated Oliver Cromwell's views by rejecting the recruitment of mercenaries: 'we must rather employ men who will fight merely for the cause sake' (*A Worthy Speech*, 7).

Death and reputation Brooke was made commander of the West Midlands Association of Staffordshire and Warwickshire under an ordinance of 31 December 1642, and spent the winter raising men and money through his London contacts as well as in Warwickshire. In February 1643 he mustered his forces at Warwick Castle, then disarmed Stratford upon Avon to prevent its becoming a royalist stronghold, and marched to Lichfield where the cathedral close had been garrisoned for the king.

Here, on 2 March 1643, in a heavy blow to parliament, Brooke was killed, through a lucky shot from the central spire of the cathedral from one 'Dumb Dyott', a deaf and dumb younger son of a local gentry family. The death of a religious radical, who had denounced cathedrals as the haunts of Antichrist, at such hands, and on the festival day of St Chad, the patron saint of Lichfield, was regarded as a providential judgement by royalists. For parliamentarians, particularly radical parliamentarians, he was a lost leader, an enduring influence and memory. London pamphlets lamented the loss of an Abner struck down by 'idolatrous Enemies'. They cursed Lichfield as a 'sinke of iniquity': 'let the remembrance of thee be hatefull; and thy name blotted out from among the Townes of the Province' (*Englands Losse and Lamentation*, sig.A3v). Brooke was buried a few days after his death in the tomb of his cousin, Fulke Greville, at St Mary's, Warwick.

John Milton wrote that he had never 'read or heard words more mild and peaceful' than those on sectaries in Brooke's *Discourse on Episcopacy*, and claimed that Brooke would have supported his arguments in *Areopagitica* 'had he not sacrificed his life and fortunes to the Church and Commonwealth' (Milton, *Complete Prose Works*, 2, ed. E. Sirluck, 1959, 560–61). Many of the men he recruited to parliament's cause remained prominent radical activists. The future Leveller John Lilburne was second-in-command of his foot regiment; and the future republican soldier John Okey also served Brooke. The treasurer of the west midland association was the radical city Independent Rowland Wilson (a partner of Maurice Thompson), while his friend Purefoy and his half-brother Bosvile became prominent members of the Rump Parliament. Among obscurer figures the receiver of his widow's Lincolnshire estates in the 1650s was Major Alex Tulidah, a veteran of the Leveller agitation of 1647. By the later 1640s an inn in Adwalton, West Riding of Yorkshire, was apparently named Brooks or Lord Brook in memory of this remarkable man, intellectual, popular leader, and zealous ideologue (Eyre, 82).   ANN HUGHES

Sources A. Hughes, *Politics, society and civil war in Warwickshire, 1620–1660* (1987) • T. Spencer, 'The genealogie, life and death of the Right Honorable Robert Lorde Brooke', *Miscellany I*, ed. R. Bearman, Dugdale Society, 31 (1977) • S. Clarke, *A general martyrology* (1651) • R. Strider, *Robert Greville, Lord Brooke* (1958) • R. Rebholz, *The life of Fulke Greville, first Lord Brooke* (1971) • T. Hutchinson, *The history of the colony and province of Massachusetts-Bay*, ed. L. S. Mayo, 1 (1936) • K. O. Kupperman, *Providence Island, 1630–1641* (1993) • K. O. Kupperman, 'Definitions of liberty on the eve of civil war: Lord Saye and Sele, Lord Brooke, and the American puritan colonies', *HJ*, 32 (1989), 17–33 • R. Greville, second Lord Brooke, *The nature of truth* (1640); facs. repr., ed. V. de Sola Pinto (1969) • R. Greville, *A discourse opening the nature of that episcopacie, which is exercised in England*, 2 editions (1642), facsimile reprint in W. Haller, ed., *Tracts on liberty in the Puritan revolution, 1638–1647*, 3 vols. (1934), vol. 2 • *A worthy speech made by the Right Honorable the Lord Brooke, at the election of his captaines and commanders at Warwick Castle, 26 Feb 1643* (1643) [Thomason tract] • *Two speeches made in the House of Peers, on Munday the 19 of December, for, and against accommodation* (1642) [not in fact by Brooke; Thomason tract] • *The last weeks proceedings of the Lord Brooke* (2 March 1642/2 March 1643) [Thomason tract] • *Englands losse and lamentation, occasioned by the death of that Right Honourable, Robert Lord Brooke* (1643) [Thomason tract; Thomason date 9 March] • Warks. CRO, Warwick Castle papers, CR 1866 • disputes over the first Lord Brooke's will, Birm. CL, MS 272809–272812 • *Dugdale's visitation of Yorkshire, with additions*, ed. J. W. Clay, 2 (1907), 53 • *CSP dom., 1625–49* • PRO, SP 16 • PRO, Commonwealth exchequer papers, SP 28 [for Brooke's army] • *Records of the Providence Island Company*, PRO, CO 124/1, 2 • A. Eyre, 'A dyurnall, or, Catalogue of all my accions and expences from the 1st of January 1646–[7–]', ed. H. J. Morehouse, *Yorkshire diaries and autobiographies*, 1, ed. C. Jackson, SurtS, 65 (1877), 1–118

Archives Warks. CRO, Warwick Castle MSS, estate and business MSS, CR 1866

Likenesses etching, NPG

Wealth at death said to have inherited an estate of £6000 p.a.: Spencer, *Genealogie* • approx. £4000 rising to over £5000 by early 1640s: Hughes, *Politics*, 24–5 • personal bequests: Warks. CRO, CR 1866/2833 • in 1648 Parliament voted £5000 to youngest son Fulke, for whom no provision had been made in father's lifetime (all of this paid by early 1650s)

Greville, Robert Kaye (1794–1866), botanist, was born on 13 December 1794 at Bishop Auckland, co. Durham, the son of Robert Greville (1760–1830?), rector of Edlaston and Wyaston, Derbyshire, and his wife, Dorothy Chaloner (*bap.* 25 May 1766). His father was also BCL of Pembroke College, Oxford, and an amateur composer of short musical pieces, including his glee 'Now the bright morning star', which won a prize in 1787. During Greville's infancy the family moved to Derbyshire, where Greville was educated at home. As a boy he studied plants and by the age of eighteen he had made between 100 and 200 careful coloured drawings of native botanical species. Being intended for the medical profession, he then went through four years of training in London and Edinburgh, but circumstances rendered him independent, and he did not proceed to a degree, preferring instead to pursue his botanical interests.

On 17 October 1816 Greville married Charlotte (*bap.* 1785), a daughter of Sir John Eden, baronet, of Windlestone, co. Durham. In the same year he moved to Edinburgh in order to study anatomy under John Barclay. On 15 April 1819 he joined the Wernerian Society, and in the following year began reading papers on cryptogams, especially algae, before that society and also before the Botanical Society of Edinburgh (of which he was a founder member and served as secretary, and as president in 1839, 1846, and 1865). He was both a keen explorer and a collector and from about this time participated in a number of excursions with botanists such as William J. Hooker and Robert Graham. He also became a mentor to M. J. Berkeley, directing Berkeley's attention towards the study of fungi, and 'helped to forge the association between Berkeley and his [Greville's] friend, Hooker … which set mycology both at home and abroad on its long development' (Watling, 73). In 1821 Greville was elected a fellow of the Royal Society of Edinburgh, and he was later a member of council. He lectured on zoology and botany in Edinburgh and formed extensive collections, not only of

Robert Kaye Greville (1794–1866), by William Bewick

plants, but also of insects, marine crustacea, and land and freshwater molluscs—his collection of the latter was at the time considered the finest in Scotland.

In 1823 Greville began to publish, in monthly parts, his well-received *Scottish cryptogamic flora, or, Coloured figures and descriptions of cryptogamic plants, belonging chiefly to the order Fungi: and intended to serve as a continuation of English botany* (6 vols., 1823–8). He drew and coloured the plates for this work himself, and dedicated his publication to Hooker. While this work was in progress he also published *Flora Edinensis, or, A description of plants growing near Edinburgh, arranged according to the Linnean system, with a concise introduction to the natural orders of the class Cryptogamia, and illustrative plates* (1824), dedicated to Robert Graham, in which he covered both the flowering and flowerless plants of the district. In 1826 Greville received the honorary degree of LLD from the University of Glasgow, partly in recognition of the two works.

In 1829 at Glasgow, Greville and Hooker began their major collaborative work, the *Icones filicum*, which was issued in two folio volumes (1829–31), with 240 plates drawn and coloured by Greville. This work was dedicated to the botanist Nathaniel Wallich, who supplied them with a variety of Indian species of ferns, although Greville and Hooker also received exotic specimens from Robert Wight and Lansdown Guilding (among others). In addition to his notable studies of fungi and ferns Greville also made significant progress in the study of algae, particularly diatoms. In 1830, during the composition of *Icones*

filicum, came the 'appearance of Greville's majestic *Algae Britannicae*' (Allen, 113), which included nineteen coloured plates executed by himself. In addition he began work, with his friend John Hutton Balfour, on 'Plant scenery of the world', but the venture was abandoned and the unfinished manuscript with some plates went to the archives at the Royal Botanic Garden, Edinburgh. Greville contributed plates to *Curtis's Botanical Magazine* (1824–34) and wrote the botanical sections for *British India* (1832) and *British North America* (1839). He was one of nine naturalists to provide assistance to Edward Forbes in the compilation of his British Association *Report on the Distribution of Pulmoniferous Mollusca in the British Isles* (1839). He was consulted on botanical matters by William Harcourt with respect to the British Association for the Advancement of Science, and also corresponded with naturalists such as George B. Sowerby.

In the summer of 1834 Greville made a natural history tour of Sutherland with John Jardine, Sir William Jardine, Prideaux John Selby, and James Wilson (his close friend); an account of their observations was presented in *Jameson's Journal* for the years 1834–6. Three years later, with Brand and Balfour, Greville made an excursion to the Scottish highlands and collected about 15,000 alpine specimens for the Botanical Society of Edinburgh. In 1862 he was awarded the Neill medal by the council of the Royal Society of Edinburgh for his contributions to cryptogamic botany, in particular for his work on diatoms. He was elected a fellow of numerous scientific and philosophical societies both at home and abroad, and in his time was considered 'to have done more than any other botanist … in the field of cryptogamic botany' (Green, 392), an opinion reflected in the naming of the periodical *Grevillea*, devoted to his field of study. He was also honoured in the naming of the plant genus *Kayea wallich*.

Greville was actively interested in philanthropic and social issues. In 1830 he issued a pamphlet entitled *The Drama Brought to the Test of Scripture and Found Wanting*, and between 1832 and 1834 he edited, with Richard Huie, the three volumes of *The Amethyst, or, Christian's Annual*, to which he contributed several religious poems. In addition he compiled *The Church of England Hymn-Book* (1838) with the Revd T. K. Drummond, and was connected with various charitable organizations.

An active campaigner for the abolition of slavery, in 1833 Greville served as one of 350 delegates who took their cause to the colonial minister in London. He was elected chairman of a new working committee which in part comprised members of the committee of the British and Foreign Anti-Slavery Society, and was appointed one of four vice-presidents of the Anti-Slavery Convention of All Countries, held in London in 1840. He advocated temperance, published a work entitled *Facts illustrative of the drunkenness of Scotland, with observations on the responsibility of the clergy, magistrates, and other influential bodies* (1834), and was similarly moved by the Sabbath question—for four years, he acted as secretary of the Sabbath Alliance. He was also elected MP for Edinburgh in 1856.

During his later years Greville fell into poverty and this

no doubt contributed to his becoming a professional artist. He was an accomplished landscape painter in oils, focusing in particular on the wild, rugged scenery of Scotland and Wales, and also abroad. Elected honorary academician in 1829, he exhibited three of his works at the Royal Academy—*Conway Castle* (1844) and two Scottish views (1845, 1852). Examples of his work were also shown at the Royal Scottish Academy in 1831 and 1859; he was a member of the Society (later Royal Society) of British Artists, Suffolk Street. Greville disposed of his flowering plant collection, which was acquired by Balfour for Glasgow University; his algae went to the British Museum (Natural History) and Edinburgh University, the fungi and other cryptogams to the Royal Botanic Garden, Edinburgh, and the molluscs and insects to what later became the Royal Scottish Museum. He died on 4 June 1866 at his home, Ormelie Villa, Murrayfield, Edinburgh, as a result of pneumonia. He was buried on 8 June in the Dean cemetery, close to his friends Forbes and Wilson. Greville was survived by a son, Eden Kaye Greville, and three daughters.　　　　　　　G. S. BOULGER, *rev.* YOLANDA FOOTE

Sources C. Matheson, 'George Brettingham Sowerby the First and his correspondents [pt II]', *Journal of the Society of the Bibliography of Natural History*, 4 (1962–8), 253–66 · *Journal of Botany, British and Foreign*, 4 (1866), 238 · *Gardeners' Chronicle* (9 June 1866), 538 · *Catalogue of scientific papers*, Royal Society, 3 (1869) · *Catalogue of scientific papers*, Royal Society, 7 (1877) · P. F. Rehbock, *The philosophical naturalists* (1983) · J. Reynolds Green, *A history of botany in the United Kingdom* (1914) · Desmond, *Botanists*, rev. edn · *Transactions of the Botanical Society* [Edinburgh], 8 (1866), 463–76 · M. C. Cooke, *Handbook of British fungi* (1883) · J. Hamilton, *Memoirs of the life of James Wilson, esq. of Woodville* (1859) · [J. S. Sainsbury], ed., *A dictionary of musicians*, 2nd edn, 2 vols. (1827) · D. E. Allen, *The naturalist in Britain: a social history* (1976) · R. Watling, *The Mycologist*, 4/2 (April 1990), 73 · P. J. M. McEwan, *Dictionary of Scottish art and architecture* (1994) · D. Baptie, *A handbook of musical biography*, 2nd edn (1887) · d. cert.

Archives NHM, corresp. and papers · NL Scot., letters | Museum of Scotland, Edinburgh, letters to Sir William Jardine · NL Scot., letters · RBG Kew, letters to Sir William Hooker · U. Newcastle, letters to Sir Walter Trevelyan

Likenesses W. Bewick, chalk drawing, Scot. NPG [*see illus.*] · B. R. Haydon, group portrait, oils (*The Anti-Slavery Society convention, 1840*), NPG · Turner, lithograph (after D. MacNee), BM · lithograph (after D. MacNee, 1830), NPG · photograph, repro. in *The Mycologist*, 73

Wealth at death £923 14s. 8d.: confirmation, 23 July 1866, NA Scot., SC70/1/130/907–912

Grew, Jonathon (1626–1711). *See under* Grew, Obadiah (*bap.* 1607, *d.* 1689).

Grew, Nehemiah (*bap.* 1641, *d.* 1712), botanist and physician, was the son of Obadiah Grew (*bap.* 1607, *d.* 1689) and his wife, Ellen or Helen, *née* Vicars (*d.* 1687). He was baptized at Mancetter, near Coventry, on 26 September 1641 and was brought up in Coventry, where he evidently received his schooling. Obadiah Grew was a prominent figure in local dissent, who became vicar of St Michael's, Coventry, in 1644, and who continued to preach in the city even after he resigned his office to avoid having to comply with the Act of Uniformity in 1662. In 1658 Grew went up to Pembroke College, Cambridge, where he graduated BA

Nehemiah Grew (*bap.* 1641, *d.* 1712), by Robert White, pubd 1701

in 1662. He then presumably returned to Coventry, but little is known of his career over the next decade except that it is probable that he began to practise medicine. It was also at this stage that he began his botanical investigations: he later stated that he was inspired by the findings of his contemporaries concerning the anatomy of animals to seek similar structures in plants. In 1668 he showed the work that he had done to his half-brother, Henry Sampson, and it was Sampson who, in 1670, showed it to Henry Oldenburg, secretary of the Royal Society. Oldenburg showed it to John Wilkins, bishop of Chester, who produced it at a meeting of the society and in turn showed it to the society's president, William Brouncker, second Viscount Brouncker. At a council meeting on 11 May 1671 Grew's *The Anatomy of Vegetables Begun: with a General Account of Vegetation Founded Thereon* was licensed for publication and ordered to be printed. Copies of the book were presented at a meeting of the society on 7 December at which, coincidentally, the society also received a manuscript on the same subject from the Italian botanist Marcello Malpighi. The two men had embarked on research on overlapping topics in genuine independence of one another, and their work was to develop in parallel over the subsequent years.

Early career Meanwhile, on 6 July 1671, Grew had registered as a candidate for a doctorate at Leiden, submitting his doctoral dissertation, 'Disputatio medico-physica, inauguralis, de liquore nervoso', on 14 July. This was subsequently issued at Leiden in printed form, dedicated to his father, Henry Sampson, and Abraham Clifford, another ejected minister. Following his return to England Grew was proposed fellow of the Royal Society by its curator of experiments, Robert Hooke, with whom he had by now become acquainted. He was elected on 16 November and admitted on 30 November. He then evidently returned to his medical practice in Coventry, but, early in 1672, the idea arose that Grew might continue his research supported by a subscription of £50 a year raised from wealthy fellows of the society. On this understanding Grew returned to London to become a kind of research fellow of the society, and in the summer and autumn of that year he made various presentations of his findings at its meetings. However, John Wilkins, whose idea it had been to employ Grew in this way, died in November 1672, and the subscription scheme came to an end the following summer; as a result Grew returned to Coventry. Later that year, however, he returned to London, having found employment as deputy to Jonathan Goddard as professor of physic at Gresham College. On 20 April 1673 he married Mary Huetson; she died in 1685. On Goddard's death on 24 March 1675 Grew applied for the post of Gresham professor himself, but he failed to secure it; instead, he continued to gain financial support from the college by deputizing for Walter Pope, the astronomy professor, and he was also paid by the Royal Society for sundry additional lectures. This enabled Grew to continue his work, for which he issued a kind of manifesto in his *Idea of a Phytological History Propounded* (1673); his work was clearly generally well received, although reservations about certain of Grew's views were expressed by the York naturalist Martin Lister in letters to Oldenburg, mainly in the later months of 1673, to which Grew replied in letters sent through Oldenburg. In 1675, Grew brought out *A Comparative Anatomy of Trunks*, and both this and his *Idea* (which included an account of his research on roots) were republished along with the further findings on the subject that he made in the following years in his *Anatomy of Plants* (1682).

This key work collected together all the botanical research that Grew had presented to the Royal Society during the previous decade. Grew was a conscious pioneer in a hitherto neglected area: as he put it in dedicating his *Comparative Anatomy of Trunks* to Charles II in 1675, 'I may, without vanity, say thus much, That it was my fortune, to be the first that ever gave a Map of the Country' (sig. A2v). It is on his findings in this area that his reputation as a scientist is chiefly based. His work was primarily marked by his brilliant observation and description of plants and their component parts; having begun by making observations using only the naked eye, Grew supplemented these with the use of a microscope under the tutelage of his colleague Hooke. His presentations to the society began in 1672–4 with the roots, branches, and trunks of plants, proceeding thereafter to their leaves, flowers, fruit, and seeds. In each area he was innovative, studying for the

first time many features of plants that have since been taken for granted, such as their cell-like structure and the growth rings in wood, and deploying techniques which have since become commonplace, such as the use of transverse, radial, and tangential longitudinal sections to analyse the structure of stems and roots. He was also an innovator in the terminology he used to describe plants, first using such terms as 'radicle' or 'parenchyma', a word adapted from its use in animal anatomy by Francis Glisson.

Grew was primarily interested in the morphology and taxonomy of plants, but this led him to study plant physiology; he thus considered how buds grew, how seeds developed, and other related topics. He also recognized the sexual nature of plant reproduction, though, with characteristic modesty, he acknowledged that this idea had already occurred to the physician Sir Thomas Millington. He attempted to interpret the structure of plants in terms of their function, making fruitful use of comparison with other kinds of living things, and making much of the evidence of God's wisdom in the creation thereby revealed. In addition, in his *Discourse Concerning the Nature, Causes and Power of Mixture* (1675) and his *Experiments in concert of the luctation arising from the affusion of several menstruums upon all sorts of bodies* (1678) Grew pursued an interest in the chemical analysis of the materia medica, following in the footsteps of another of his mentors, Robert Boyle; these were also reprinted in *The Anatomy of Plants*.

In November 1677, following the death of Henry Oldenburg, Grew was appointed joint secretary of the Royal Society with Robert Hooke; his duties in this capacity included the maintenance of the society's correspondence and the editing of various issues of the *Philosophical Transactions*. In 1678 he was given the task of cataloguing the society's repository, of which his catalogue, *Musaeum Regalis Societatis, or, A catalogue and description of the natural and artificial rarities belonging to the Royal Society and preserved at Gresham College*, was published in 1681. This comprised a description and analysis of the society's collection of rarities, which was erudite and in places innovative in its classification and interpretation of objects, though Grew was constricted by his responsibility for a collection over whose content he had little control. To this work was appended his 'Comparative anatomy of the stomach and guts', a study of the intestines of a wide range of animals which he had begun on the completion of his botanical research in the late 1670s, and which represents a major contribution to comparative anatomy. The publication of *Musaeum Regalis Societatis* and *The Anatomy of Plants* marked the climax of Grew's active career as a scientist; both books were lavishly illustrated with engravings paid for by subscription, and they were among the first scientific books to be published in England in this way.

In 1680 Grew became an honorary fellow of the Royal College of Physicians. From that time onwards, although he continued to attend meetings of the Royal Society, his contributions to its research programme virtually ceased, probably because he was mainly preoccupied by medical practice. In addition, in 1683 he wrote a pamphlet supporting a method for desalinating sea water which had already gained the approval of Robert Boyle and for which Boyle's nephew, Robert Fitzerald, sought a patent in that year with a view to exploiting it commercially, though it does not appear to have been a great success. Grew also took an interest in the medicinal properties of the mineral waters in the London region, on which he read papers to the Royal Society in 1679; thereafter, he made a particular study of the waters of Epsom spa, of which he published a Latin account in 1695, *Tractatus de salis cathartici amari in aquis Ebeshamensibus*, and from which he pioneered the production of Epsom salts. An unauthorized English translation of this was published in 1697 by the apothecary, Francis Moult, and this, together with the rivalry between Grew and Moult and his brother George over the exploitation of Epsom spa, led to an acrimonious dispute which reached its climax with a book-length vindication of Grew by Josiah Peter, *Truth in Opposition to Ignorant and Malicious Falshood*, in 1701. On 17 June the same year Grew married his second wife, Elizabeth Dodson.

Later writings Grew's principal later publication was an ambitious theological work, *Cosmologia sacra, or, A Discourse of the Universe as it is the Creature and Kingdom of God* (1701). This opened with an elaborate proof of God's existence on both philosophical and natural philosophical grounds, but more than half of the book was devoted to a lengthy defence of the scriptures against writers like Spinoza, a novel enterprise on Grew's part which necessitated his studying Hebrew and which must have taken a great deal of his time in the preceding years. Grew also wrote an unpublished tract defending the practice of occasional conformity, while the most remarkable of his later writings is an economic treatise, 'The meanes of a most ample encrease of the wealth and strength of England in a few years', 1707, all but a small part of which survives only in manuscript. This represents a powerful plea for the wholesale reform and rational planning of the national economy, advocating a striking degree of state control in pursuit of these ends. In his later years Grew also collected botanical specimens and engraved gems, which were auctioned after his death. His main preoccupation, however, was evidently his medical practice; it was as an active and conscientious doctor that he was celebrated in the funeral sermon preached by John Shower following his death on 25 March 1712. He was buried in the parish church of Cheshunt, Hertfordshire, on 1 April 1712, in the family vault of his second wife's family.

Grew is easily overshadowed by his more famous scientific contemporaries, yet his research is exemplary of the detailed study of nature associated with the Royal Society in its early decades. His painstaking investigation of the structure and characteristics of plants, along with that of Malpighi, was not superseded until the nineteenth century. His career path is interesting in revealing how scientific research might interact with the successful pursuit of medicine, while he was also the beneficiary of the clearest example of the Royal Society's corporate patronage in its

early years. Perhaps, above all, he illustrates the harmony between the pursuit of science and a lifelong commitment to dissenting protestantism.

MICHAEL HUNTER

Sources W. Lefanu, *Nehemiah Grew: a study and bibliography of his writings* (1990) [incl. full details of Grew's works] · *The correspondence of Henry Oldenburg*, ed. and trans. A. R. Hall and M. B. Hall, 8–10 (1971–5) · T. Birch, *The history of the Royal Society*, 4 vols. (1756–7), vols. 2–4 · J. Shower, *Enoch's translation: a funeral sermon upon the sudden death of Dr Nehemiah Grew* (1712) · J. Peter, *Truth in opposition to ignorant and malicious falshood* (1701) · *Calamy rev.*, 122, 236, 425 · *VCH Warwickshire*, 8.373–6 · J. Bolam, 'The botanical works of Nehemiah Grew, FRS, 1641–1712', *Notes and Records of the Royal Society*, 27 (1972–3), 219–31 · F. J. Cole, *A history of comparative anatomy* (1944), chap. 22 · M. Hunter, *Establishing the new science: the experience of the early Royal Society* (1989), chaps. 4, 8 · M. Hunter, *Science and society in Restoration England* (1981) · C. MacLeod, *Inventing the industrial revolution* (1988), 69–70 · A. Sakula, 'The waters of Epsom Spa', *Journal of the Royal College of Physicians of London*, 16 (1982), 124–8 · E. A. J. Johnson, *Predecessors of Adam Smith* (1937), chap. 7 · L. R. Stewart, *The rise of public science: rhetoric, technology, and natural philosophy in Newtonian Britain, 1660–1750* (1992), 46–52 · C. Zirtle, introduction, in N. Grew, *The anatomy of plants* (1965), ix–xviii · A. Arber, 'Nehemiah Grew', *Makers of British botany*, ed. F. W. Oliver (1913), 44–64 · A. Arber, 'Nehemiah Grew, 1641–1712, and Marcello Malpighi, 1628–94: an essay in comparison', *Isis*, 34 (1942–3), 7–16 · C. R. Metcalfe, 'Grew, Nehemiah', *DSB* · R. W. Innes Smith, *English-speaking students of medicine at the University of Leyden* (1932), 102 · Venn, *Alum. Cant.* · Munk, *Roll* · parish register, Mancetter, 26 Sept 1641, Warks. CRO, DR 130/1 [baptism] · parish register, Cheshunt, 1 April 1712, Herts. ALS, D/P29/1/7 [burial]

Archives BL, Sloane MSS, corresp. and papers, 1926–4076, *passim* · BL, 'Meanes of a most ample encrease of the wealth and strength of England', Lansdowne MS 691 · Hunt. L., autograph MS on economics · RCP Lond., prescriptions · RS, botanical papers | Bodl. Oxf., letters to Martin Lister

Likenesses R. White, line engraving, BM, NPG; repro. in N. Grew, *Cosmologia sacra* (1701) [*see illus.*]

Grew, Obadiah (*bap.* 1607, *d.* 1689), ejected clergyman and nonconformist minister, was baptized at Mancetter, Atherstone, Warwickshire, on 22 November 1607, the third son of Francis Grew and Elizabeth Denison, whose brother John *Denison (1569/70–1629) was schoolmaster and vicar in Reading. Obadiah was educated by his uncle and at Balliol College, Oxford, where he graduated BA on 12 February 1629 and MA on 5 July 1632. He became master of the grammar school in his home town in 1632 and was ordained in 1635. On 25 December 1637 he married Ellen or Helen (1603–1687), sister of John *Vicars (1580–1652) and widow of William Sampson, who supposedly recommended Grew to his wife as her second husband on his deathbed. She already had at least two sons, Henry *Sampson (*c.*1629–1700) and William *Sampson (*bap.* 1635, *d.* 1702), of whom Henry became Grew's pupil at Atherstone. Ellen and Obadiah had two children: a daughter Mary (*b.* 1638) who later married a nonconformist scholar, John Willes, and a son, Nehemiah *Grew (*bap.* 1641, *d.* 1712), the distinguished botanist.

Obadiah Grew moved to the nearby parliamentarian stronghold of Coventry in 1642, preached to the troops there, and by 1644 had become vicar of St Michael's in the city, replacing William Panting, the sequestered royalist incumbent. During the war Coventry sheltered a score of ministers fleeing royalist troops; regular solemn fasts were held and the city became noted for its orthodox godliness. This reputation was secured throughout the 1640s and 1650s by Grew and the incumbent of Trinity parish, John Bryan. Grew and Bryan held a public disputation with the Baptist leaders Hanserd Knollys and Benjamin Cox in 1646; they both signed the Warwickshire ministers' testimony against the errors of the times in 1648; and they were both active in the 'Kenilworth classis', a quasi-presbyterian organization of the county's ministers, meeting for mutual support and ordination of new ministers from the mid-1650s. On 10 October 1651 Grew proceeded BD and DD from Oxford. In 1654 he was nominated as an assistant to the Warwickshire commissioners for ejection of scandalous ministers. In theory he had a generously augmented stipend of £120 per annum but even in godly Coventry this was never securely paid and he sent pained letters of protest to the corporation in 1653 and 1656. According to Edmund Calamy, Grew was 'more retired and less active' than Bryan but, again according to Calamy, he protested against the regicide in 1649 and refused a decade later to read from his pulpit a proclamation against Booth's rising (Calamy, *Continuation*, 851–3). Both these stances are plausible for a mainstream presbyterian, but there is no independent evidence for them.

Grew left his living in 1662, his successor subscribing before the bishop of Coventry and Lichfield on 12 November, suggesting perhaps some weeks of indecision—or attempts by Bishop John Hackett to persuade Grew to conform. He mostly remained in Coventry, becoming leader of a conventicle by 1665 and one of four preachers of the presbyterian Great Meeting established by 1669. He was licensed as a presbyterian in 1672. Coventry presbyterians had powerful support—the corporation even paid some of Grew's arrears from the 1650s in 1664—but he was imprisoned during the tory reaction of the early 1680s. Despite blindness and old age, Grew preached regularly to a large congregation at Coventry's Leather Hall during the freedom established by James II's indulgence. He was a preacher and teacher rather than a prolific author, but three collections of sermons, including one series on the parable of the prodigal son, went through several editions from the 1660s. He died on 22 October 1689 and was buried at St Michael's on 24 October. In 1697 the traveller Celia Fiennes described Coventry as 'a fanatic town' with 'the largest chapel and the greatest number of people I have ever seen of the Presbyterian way' (Hurwich, 15). Grew's career had done much to create this bastion of dissent.

Grew's nephew **Jonathon Grew** (1626–1711), nonconformist minister, son of his elder brother Jonathon, was born in Atherstone in September 1626 and entered Pembroke College, Cambridge, in June 1646, graduating BA in 1650 and MA in 1655. After some time as an assistant to his uncle's stepson Henry Sampson in Suffolk, he became tutor in the family of Sir John Hales of Coventry, and refused posts in the Church of England at the Restoration. Instead he became for a time a schoolmaster at Newington Green, Middlesex. His wife, Elizabeth, was buried at St Mary's, Stoke Newington, in 1673, and two children in 1671 and another (Obadiah) in 1682. By December 1682 Grew was pastor of a (presbyterian) nonconformist congregation in St Albans, established from 1697 in a meeting-house at Dagnal Lane. He died in 1711 and was buried in St Albans Abbey. ANN HUGHES

Sources A. Hughes, *Politics, society and civil war in Warwickshire, 1620–1660* (1987) · E. Calamy, *A continuation of the account of the ministers ... who were ejected and silenced after the Restoration in 1660*, 2 vols. (1727), vol. 2, pp. 851–3 · J. J. Hurwich, '"A fanatick town": the political influence of dissenters in Coventry, 1660–1720', *Midland History*, 4 (1977) · *Calendar of the Clarendon state papers preserved in the Bodleian Library*, 5: *1660–1726*, ed. F. J. Routledge (1970), 259 · B. Poole, *Coventry: its history and antiquities* (1870) · council minute book and corporation correspondence, Coventry City Archives · subscription book, Lichfield Diocesan Archives, B/A/4/19 · *The nonconformist's memorial ... originally written by ... Edmund Calamy*, ed. S. Palmer, [3rd edn], 3 (1803) · *Calamy rev.*, 235–6 · *DNB* · *IGI* · parish register, Coventry, St Michael [burial] · Foster, *Alum. Oxon.*

Archives Coventry City Archives, parish records, St Michael, letters and details of maintenance

Wealth at death mostly books and modest sums of money: will, proved, 10 April 1690

Grey. *See also* Gray.

Grey. For this title name *see* individual entries under Grey; *see also* Yorke, Jemima, *suo jure* Marchioness Grey (1722–1797); North, William, sixth Baron North, second Baron Grey of Rolleston, and Jacobite Earl North (1678–1734); Hastings, Barbara Rawdon, marchioness of Hastings and *suo jure* Baroness Grey of Ruthin (1810–1858).

Grey, De. For this title name *see* individual entries under Grey; *see also* Campbell, Amabel Hume-, *suo jure* Countess De Grey (1751–1833).

Grey family (*per.* 1325–1523), magnates, of Ruthin, was one branch of a notable aristocratic lineage.

In 1718 'The genealogy of the most noble and ancient family of Grey', compiled from the Grey of Ruthin archives, claimed a common eleventh-century ancestor, Anchitel, for the various noble houses of Grey. The historic figure from whom most of the Greys spring is, however, **Henry Grey** (*d.* 1219), of Grays Thurrock, Essex. Henry had three sons, each of whom founded a landed family. Richard Grey, the eldest, was the grandfather of Henry Grey, first Baron Grey of Codnor (*d.* 1308), whose line survived until 1496. Henry's third son, William Grey, established a gentry family at Sandiacre in Derbyshire, which expired in Edward II's reign.

John Grey of Shirland in Derbyshire was Henry Grey's second son. He married well and through his wife inherited the Herefordshire castle of Wilton upon Wye as well as lands in the home counties. John's son Reynold [i] Grey (*d.* 1308) was summoned to parliament as Lord Grey of Wilton from 1290 onwards and this baronial family continued until 1614. After the death of John *Grey, second Lord Grey of Wilton, in 1323, however, the Wilton patrimony was divided. The second lord married twice and had one son and one daughter with each of his wives. The elder son, Henry, succeeded to the Wilton title but he was substantially disinherited when more than half the landed estate was settled on the younger son in a remarkable series of final concords between 1307 and 1319.

This younger son, Roger *Grey (c.1300–1353), received the entire Bedfordshire estate and lands in the counties of Buckingham, Huntingdon, Hertford, and Chester, along with the Welsh marcher lordship of Ruthin, which in 1282 had been granted to Reynold, first Lord Grey of Wilton, by Edward I. This disinheritance was violently opposed by Roger's elder half-brother, Henry, third Lord Grey of Wilton (d. 1342), but the final concords stood and Roger received land valued at approximately £850 while Henry's estate amounted to only £283. From 1325 Roger was summoned to parliament as Lord Grey of Ruthin and the family continued in the direct male line until 1523.

The Greys of Ruthin were primarily based in Bedfordshire, where the lords had a powerful local affinity. Ruthin, however, as a marcher lordship with prosperous agriculture and grazing in the Vale of Clwyd in Denbighshire and a flourishing cloth industry, remained a key element in the polity of Roger and his successors. The barons Grey of Ruthin lived long. Between 1325 and 1490 there were only four lords, two of whom—Reynold [iii] Grey [see Grey, Reynold (c.1362–1440)], the third lord, and Edmund, the fourth—spanned a century from 1388 to 1490. They all married suitably and had many children who created a network of baronial alliances. Several wives contributed massively to the family's economic health. Roger Grey's wife, Elizabeth, daughter of John *Hastings, first Lord Hastings and Lord Bergavenny, was the instrument by which her grandson, Reynold [iii] Grey, became heir general of the main Hastings line when John Hastings, fourteenth earl of Pembroke, died childless in 1389.

Elizabeth's eldest son, Sir John, who predeceased his father in 1349 or 1350, had in 1335 married one of the four daughters of William *Montagu, soon to be earl of Salisbury. John's brother **Reynold** [ii] **Grey**, second Baron Grey of Ruthin (1318/19–1388), who succeeded to the title in 1353, married Eleanor, daughter of John, second Baron Strange of Blackmere (d. 1349). Of the six children of Reynold and Eleanor only one seems to have had children. This was Reynold [iii] Grey (c.1362–1440) who succeeded as third lord and was married twice: first to Margaret, daughter of Thomas, fourth Baron Ros of Helmsley (d. 1384), and second to a young widow, Joan (d. 1448), daughter of William, fourth Baron Astley (d. c.1430).

The son and heir of the third lord, **Sir John Grey** (d. 1439), a veteran of Agincourt, was created a Garter knight in 1435, and predeceased his father. He married Henry IV's niece Constance, the widow of Thomas (II) Mowbray, earl of Norfolk, who was executed in 1405, and enjoyed her dower lands worth some £600 a year until her death in 1437; their son and heir was Edmund *Grey (1416–1490), later first earl of Kent. Among the seven children of Reynold's second marriage, daughters married into the Norfolk family of Calthorp, the Warwickshire Lucys, and the west-country baronial house of Bonville. Reynold's sons established their own long-lasting gentry lines at Kempston in Bedfordshire and Barwell in Leicestershire, and in Staffordshire at Enville and Whittington, while

another son, Edward (d. 1457), became Lord Ferrers of Groby in right of his wife and the patriarch of later marquesses of Dorset and viscounts Lisle. In 1450 Thomas, the second son of Sir John Grey (d. 1439), was summoned to parliament as Baron Richemount Grey (from Ridgmount, Bedfordshire, part of his brother's estate) and married the widow of his distant cousin, the sixth Baron Grey of Wilton. Thomas, however, fought on the wrong side at Towton and was executed in 1461, unlike his brother, Edmund, who handled a transition of allegiances adroitly and unscrupulously after betraying Henry VI on the field of battle at Northampton in 1460.

This elder brother, Edmund Grey (1416–1490), succeeded his grandfather Reynold [iii] in 1440. He married Katherine, daughter of Henry *Percy, second earl of Northumberland, and produced four sons and two daughters. One of these sons, Sir Antony Grey (d. 1480), married Joan Woodville, sister of Edward IV's queen.

Throughout the fourteenth century the Greys of Ruthin had consolidated their position in landed society. The second lord, Reynold [ii], purchased land to expand the Bedfordshire estate, while acquiring a new town house in London. The Hastings inheritance doubled the Greys' landholdings in the 1390s but a significant portion was sold to pay the ransom demanded by Owain Glyn Dŵr, who captured the third lord, Reynold [iii], in 1402, and other manors were alienated to buy off a potential challenge from William Beauchamp. The net gain to the fifteenth-century Greys from the Hastings windfall was more than a dozen properties, with a valuable cluster in East Anglia. According to the valuation of the Hastings estate carried out in 1391, the manors ultimately retained by the Greys totalled £334, constituting some 35 per cent of the Greys' landed wealth in the 1460s. By that time the Bedfordshire estate had been further extended by purchase, most notably the fine new castle at Ampthill built by Sir John Cornwall, and eight other Cornwall properties acquired for £4333 6s. 8d., which was paid in full between 1455 and 1473. This enlarged estate, with favourite residences in Bedfordshire at Wrest and Ampthill Castle, in Suffolk at the Hastings' manor house of Badmondisfield, and Ruthin Castle in Wales, with another town house in East Cheap, survived intact until the time of Lord Edmund's grandson, Richard the Unthrift, who squandered the patrimony between 1507 and his death in 1523. The earldom of Kent, which Edmund had received from Edward IV in 1465, temporarily lapsed in 1523 because Earl Richard's heir was, as Thomas Fuller put it, 'under-stated, for so high an honour' (Fuller, 1.118).

The two centuries had produced solid rather than dramatic, pragmatic rather than principled achievement from the Greys. Although members of the family fought at Crécy and Agincourt, there were no dashing knights and no spoils of war.

The family was conventionally pious. The most generous benefactor to the church had been John Grey, the father of Roger, the first lord, and his successors respected his memory. Roger himself chose to be buried in his father's collegiate foundation at Ruthin. At the end of his life Roger's son, Sir John (*d.* 1349/50), granted land worth £10 in mortmain to Luffield Priory in Northamptonshire to provide a daily mass for his grandfather and for the royal house. The fourth lord, Edmund, took an interest in the Ruthin college, converted it to a priory for Bonshommes, a rare type of Augustinian canon, and, when this initiative failed, reconverted the foundation into a secular college in 1479: he was buried in the chancel at Ruthin in 1490. The family owned some twenty advowsons and used these to advance junior members of the family and gentry within the Grey affinity. Roger, a son of the second lord, Reynold [ii] (*d.* 1388), studied canon law at Cambridge and enjoyed both direct and indirect ecclesiastical patronage from his father.

A manuscript of Nicholas Love's *Mirrour of the Lyfe of Christ*, with no fewer than seventeen full-page paintings, was specially prepared for the wedding of Lord Edmund Grey and Katherine Percy about 1440 and survives in the National Library of Scotland. Other than the paintings of Edmund and Katherine in this manuscript, there are two representations of men in the family. The brass of Sir Hugh Hastings of Elsing, 1347, has a number of subsidiary figures, including his kinsman by marriage Lord Roger (*d.* 1353). The Galway sparth on which Roger leans is so unexpected a weapon that it must be an allusion to Roger's own tastes. The other brass, at St Albans, shows Sir Anthony, a son of Earl Edmund, wearing the Yorkist collar of suns and roses in 1480.

R. IAN JACK

Sources R. I. Jack, 'The Greys of Ruthin, 1325 to 1490', PhD diss., U. Lond., 1961 · GEC, *Peerage* · *Chancery records* · PRO · Beds. & Luton ARS, Lucas MSS · R. I. Jack, 'Entail and descent: the Hastings inheritance, 1370–1436', *BIHR*, 38 (1965), 1–19 · R. I. Jack, 'Ruthin', *Boroughs of mediaeval Wales*, ed. R. A. Griffiths (1978), 244–61 · R. I. Jack, 'The ecclesiastical patronage exercised by a baronial family in the late middle ages', *Journal of Religious History*, 3 (1964–5), 275–95 · R. I. Jack, 'Religious life in a Welsh marcher lordship: the lordship of Dyffryn Clwyd in the late middle ages', *The church in society in the century before the Reformation: essays in honour of F. R. H. du Boulay*, ed. C. Harper Bill and C. Barron (1985), 143–57 · 'The genealogy of the most noble and ancient family of Grey', 1718, priv. coll. · Fuller, *Worthies* (1662), pt 1 · *CIPM*, 16. no. 691

Archives Beds. & Luton ARS, Lucas MSS | NL Scot., Advocates MS 18.1.7

Grey, Albert Henry George, fourth Earl Grey (1851–1917), governor-general of Canada, born on 28 November 1851 at St James's Palace, London, was the second but first surviving son of the Hon. Charles *Grey (1804–1870), an army officer, and his wife, Caroline Eliza (*c*.1814–1890), the daughter of Sir Thomas Farquhar, bt, and a pious evangelical. He grew up at the court of St James, where his father was private secretary to Queen Victoria, and was educated at Harrow School (from September 1864 to summer 1870) and Trinity College, Cambridge (1870–73); he graduated with a first in the law and history tripos. He was about 6 feet tall, with delicate features, black hair, and dark eyes, and was a keen cricketer and expert angler. In 1875–6 he visited India in the entourage of the prince of Wales, as private secretary to Sir Bartle Frere, but in Goa he had sunstroke, and so had to return home. In 1878 he lost the South Northumberland constituency for the Liberals by

Albert Henry George Grey, fourth Earl Grey (1851–1917), by John Singer Sargent, 1910

one vote. He won the constituency in 1880 and held it until 1885, when he won in Northumberland (Tyneside). In the Commons, Grey became the centre of a ginger group called the Grey Committee to discuss novel ideas; he himself advocated proportional representation and social reforms including consumer and industrial co-operatives, industrial profit sharing, church reform, temperance, and the garden city movement; he invested in urban renewal and established the Public House Trust. Although a devoted Gladstonian, he broke with Gladstone over home rule and was defeated in the subsequent election. He later claimed 'I have never been a party politician, the reconstruction of national life being my ideal' (Begbie, 8).

Grey married on 9 June 1877 Alice (*d.* 1944), the youngest daughter of Robert Stayner *Holford of Westonbirt, Gloucestershire, Conservative MP for Gloucestershire East (1854–72); they had one son and four daughters, two of whom predeceased him. Inspired by Mazzini's theories of world co-operation based on patriotism and duty, Grey also became an avid imperialist and a founder member of the Imperial Federation League (1885); later he participated actively in various schemes to foster the physical and moral health of the empire, including rifle shooting, the cadet movement, and imperial immigration.

An idealistic imperialist, Grey was a member of the South Africa Committee, an influential pressure group of prominent humanitarians, missionary supporters, and politicians, chaired by Joseph Chamberlain, which was concerned to safeguard indigenous interests in southern

Africa and wanted paternalist imperial, not company or settler, rule. The committee opposed the Rudd concession and the granting of a charter to Rhodes's company. Grey had a reputation for integrity, 'the Paladin of his generation' (Rotberg, 279).

To secure his charter and encourage investors Rhodes wanted not 'colonial adventurers' but prestigious establishment figures as directors of his company. He invited Grey. Grey hesitated, then agreed—'the greatest catch of all' (Keppel-Jones, 127)—and in 1889 became a life director (he resigned in 1904) of the new British South Africa Company (BSAC): he held 9000 shares. He was honest and conscientious, but weak. His attitudes shifted. Though he continued to be well meaning, advocating just and beneficent rule in Rhodesia, he became Rhodes's devoted loyal admirer; he said that Rhodes impressed him more than any other man he ever knew and attracted him by 'the bigness of his mind and the tenderness of his heart' (Begbie, 116), and gave him no trouble even on sensitive issues of native policy. Grey identified with Rhodes and the company against the imperial factor in southern Africa. In 1891, concerned at the company's desperate financial position, with increased expenditure and fallen share prices, two of Grey's fellow directors proposed a plan to rig the market to raise BSAC share prices: Grey refused on moral grounds, and so prevented it. Although not one of Rhodes's inner group of financiers, and although sometimes misled by him, Grey, unlike most of his fellow directors, knew of the planned Rand revolt and armed intervention. He acted as Rhodes's intermediary to Chamberlain (from July 1895 as colonial secretary). For his planned armed intervention in the Transvaal, Rhodes needed a base in Bechuanaland (then under the Colonial Office), so in August 1895 Grey secretly told Chamberlain of the intervention plan. After the failure of the Jameson raid and Rand revolt (December 1895 – January 1896) Grey was initially concerned to prevent exposure of Chamberlain's complicity, opposing publication of the Hawksley telegrams and insisting Chamberlain 'has done nothing to be ashamed of' (Marsh, 393). Later, with the parliamentary committee of inquiry into the raid imminent, Grey wanted to protect Rhodes and said that, if the committee asked him, he might reveal what he had told Chamberlain: whereas the Hawksley telegrams were not conclusive, Grey's testimony could have implicated Chamberlain. However, whether this was a ploy to put pressure on the government and whether he would have exposed Chamberlain is arguable. He was never called to give evidence, as the company sent him to Rhodesia to replace Jameson as administrator: apparently Rhodes chose him in order to keep him away from the inquiry.

Grey reached Bulawayo, by stagecoach from Mafeking, on 2 May 1896. From late March the Matabele (Ndebele) and from June the Shona rose up and massacred white settlers. Concerned to minimize imperial intervention in Rhodesia, Grey reluctantly accepted imperial troops. His role was limited as the troops were under imperial command, and Rhodes himself—though in June forced to resign his BSAC directorship and then formally only a private citizen—was in Rhodesia and took the initiative, especially with the Matopos indabas (August–October 1896) which ended the Matabele uprising. Over these negotiations Grey supported Rhodes against the imperial representatives, Sir Frederick Carrington, the commander, and Sir Richard Martin, the imperial deputy commissioner, who wanted complete conquest and himself to control the negotiations, and settlers who alleged Rhodes was too generous to the defeated Matabele. Grey also took part in the later negotiations with the Matabele. Concerned at the cost of the uprisings, and wanting to minimize the imperial factor in Rhodesia, he requested the withdrawal of imperial troops and, like others in the company, exaggerated the company's role and understated the crucial role of imperial troops in suppressing the uprisings. He tried to introduce land and native administration reforms. In July 1897 he went on leave to England and in December resigned as administrator. In Rhodesia he was overshadowed by Rhodes. Grey's successor, the civil servant William Milton, described him as 'Rhodes's clerk' (Blake, 139). Jameson alleged Grey was 'a nice old lady, but not a genius, who does not like committing himself to any opinion' (Rotberg, 279). Blake wrote that Grey was 'one of the most attractive though scarcely one of the strongest figures in early Rhodesian history … his heart was on the right side' (Blake, 130, 146).

In October 1894 Grey succeeded his uncle Henry George *Grey (Albert's elder brother Charles having died in 1855), as the fourth Earl Grey, though he had been managing his uncle's estates in Northumberland since 1884. From 1889 to 1904 he was lord lieutenant of Northumberland, in October 1904 he was created GCMG and in July 1908 GCVO; he was sworn of the privy council in August 1908. He was awarded an honorary DCL by Oxford (1909) and LLD by Cambridge (1911).

On 26 September 1904 Grey succeeded his brother-in-law Lord Minto as governor-general of Canada, a country with which his family had historic connections. Although imprudent investments in South Africa had left him in straitened circumstances, the Canadian appointment was made possible by the generosity of his wife's aunt, Lady Wantage. A crusading, impetuous person as well as still an ardent imperialist, qualities which Minto feared might create difficulties, Grey owed much of his success in Canada to the quiet wisdom, patience, and experience of Sir Wilfrid Laurier, the Canadian prime minister.

Grey launched his imperial crusade immediately, convinced that Canada was the key to the empire's future. He endeavoured unsuccessfully to persuade Laurier to endorse Chamberlain's idea of an imperial council to co-ordinate intercolonial defence and diplomatic and tariff policy. More successful was his Colonial Office-inspired support for the Canadian replacement of the British garrisons at Halifax and Esquimalt, a commitment the Canadian government had previously accepted. He was a promoter of the Navy League, and in 1910 his public support for the Naval Service Act creating a Canadian navy earned it in Quebec the derisive label the Grey Act. Moreover, his imperialism was often ethnocentric. Although initially he supported Asian immigration to Canada—he even refused to visit British Columbia in protest against its exclusionist legislation, and went to great pains to arrange the successful tour of Prince Fushimi to the country in 1907—he did so more for reasons of trade and diplomacy and because he saw Japanese and Indian immigrants as useful servants and labourers. In the wake of the Russo-Japanese War, however, Grey began to worry about the 'yellow peril', and sought a diplomatic alternative to the head tax.

Grey displayed little more sensitivity in his dealing with French Canadians. Although he spoke French, employed social diplomacy to improve French and English relations in Canada, and imposed sanctions on those who espoused intolerant views, Grey's confidence in the primacy of English marred many of his endeavours. His efforts to make an imperialist statement out of the purchase of the Plains of Abraham in Quebec City and to establish a national park created considerable resentment. Similarly he changed plans to mark the tercentenary of Champlain's founding of Quebec in 1608 into an international celebration of Franco-Anglo-American friendship, which included the presence of the prince of Wales and ships from the Atlantic Fleet as well as American and French warships; and to the consternation of disaffected Québecois the historic pageant became as much a celebration of Wolfe as of Champlain.

Grey's efforts to build harmonious Canadian–American friendship were more successful. In conjunction with the British ambassadors to Washington, Sir Henry Mortimer Durand and especially James Bryce, he built better diplomatic relationships and helped streamline communication between Ottawa and Washington. As a result agreements were signed settling boundary disputes, the north Atlantic fisheries, and the regulation of north Pacific sealing and the inland fisheries. One of his most significant achievements was his contribution towards negotiating the boundary waters treaty of 1910, which created the International Joint Commission. Less successful were his bizarre efforts in 1906 to entice Newfoundland into confederation, an elaborate scheme which entailed secret negotiations with interested industrialists and bankers and the promise of a peerage to the leader of the anticonfederation movement, Sir Robert Bond.

Grey encouraged and supported historical societies, sites, and monuments, and donated trophies to the Montreal horse show and for figure skating; his best-known contribution to the promotion of amateur sport was his donation of the Grey cup for football. His other distinguished contribution was to the establishment of a dominion drama and music festival, for which he provided trophies in each field.

Upon his return to England in October 1911 Grey supervised his estates—he owned about 17,600 acres—and continued to support various imperial, social and educational causes, including the Boy Scout movement. He was a Rhodes trustee, and in 1912 he visited South Africa to unveil a monument to Rhodes. He served as president of the Royal Colonial Institute. When he was found to be suffering from terminal cancer he was told by his surgeon that he had no hope of recovery: he replied, 'I have had a splendid innings' (Begbie, 180). He died of cancer, in his sleep, at his residence, Howick House, near Alnwick, Northumberland, on 29 August 1917, survived by his wife and three of his children, and was buried on 31 August at Howick.   CARMAN MILLER

Sources H. Begbie, *Albert, fourth Earl Grey: a last word* (1917) · *Addresses to his excellency Earl Grey, GCMG, etc., governor-general of Canada, and his speeches in reply, having relation to the resources and progress of the dominion* (1908) · M. E. Hallett, 'The 4th Earl Grey as governor-general of Canada, 1904–1911', PhD diss., U. Lond., 1970 · P. Neary, 'Grey, Bryce, and the settlement of Canadian–American differences, 1905–1911', *Canadian Historical Review*, 49 (1968), 357–80 · GEC, *Peerage* · Burke, *Peerage* (1967) · C. Miller, 'Grey, Albert Henry George', *DCB*, vol. 14 · *WWW* · Venn, *Alum. Cant.* · A. Keppel-Jones, *Rhodes and Rhodesia: the white conquest of Zimbabwe, 1884–1902* (1983) · R. I. Rotberg, *The founder: Cecil Rhodes and the pursuit of power* (1988) · P. T. Marsh, *Joseph Chamberlain, entrepreneur in politics* (1994) · T. O. Ranger, *Revolt in Southern Rhodesia, 1896–1897: a study in African resistance* (1967) · J. S. Galbraith, *Crown and charter: the early years of the British South Africa Company* (1974) · J. Flint, *Cecil Rhodes* (Boston, 1974) · L. H. Gann, *A history of Southern Rhodesia: early days to 1934* (1965) · R. Blake, *A history of Rhodesia* (1977) · J. H. Stogdon, ed., *The Harrow School register, 1845–1937*, 5th edn (1937)

Archives Knebworth House, corresp. relating to public house licensing · NA Canada, corresp. and papers relating to Canada · National Archives of Zimbabwe, Harare, corresp. and papers · U. Durham L., corresp. and papers; letters to his mother and aunt | Balliol Oxf., corresp. with Sir Robert Morier · BL, corresp. with Lord Gladstone, Add. MSS 45056–45083 · BL, corresp. with Lord Northcliffe, Add. MS 62155 · BL, corresp. with Charles Wood, Add. MS 49553, *passim* · BLPES, letters to Violet Markham · Bodl. Oxf., letters to James Bryce · Bodl. Oxf., corresp. with Lewis Harcourt · Bodl. RH, letters to Edward Ross Townsend · Borth. Inst., corresp. with Lord Halifax · CAC Cam., corresp. with Lord Esher · CAC Cam., corresp. with Alfred Lyttleton · CAC Cam., letters to W. T. Stead · Co-operative Union, Manchester, archives, letters to George Holyoake · CUL, corresp. with Lord Hardinge · Derbys. RO, corresp. with P. L. Gell · Herts. ALS, corresp. with Lady Desborough · HLRO, corresp. with John St Loe Strachey · HLRO, letters to R. S. Watson · NA Scot., corresp. with A. J. Balfour · NL Aus., corresp. with Alfred Deakin · NL Scot., letters to Lady Minto · NL Scot., letters to Lord Minto · NL Scot., corresp. with F. S. Oliver · NL Scot., corresp. incl. with Lord Rosebery · Plunkett Foundation, Long Hanborough, Oxfordshire, corresp. with Sir Horace Plunkett · U. Birm. L., special collections department, corresp. with Joseph Chamberlain · U. Durham L., archives and special collections, corresp. with third Earl Grey and memoranda · U. Durham L., archives and special collections, corresp. with R. S. Watson · U. Newcastle, Robinson L., letters to R. S. Watson and E. S. Watson · U. Reading L., corresp. with Nancy Astor

Likenesses oils, 1905, U. Newcastle · J. S. Sargent, drawing, 1910, priv. coll. [*see illus.*] · print, 1910 (after J. S. Sargent), NPG · Spy [L. Ward], caricature, chromolithograph, NPG; repro. in *VF* (28 April 1898) · bronze bust, Royal Commonwealth Society, London

Wealth at death £459,373 8s. 1d.: probate, 6 April 1918, *CGPLA Eng. & Wales*

Grey [Gray], **Anchitell** (c.1624–1702), parliamentary diarist, was the second son of Henry *Grey, first earl of Stamford (c.1599–1673), and Anne (1603–1676), youngest daughter and coheir of William Cecil, second earl of Exeter. Grey's parents married in July 1620, and he had an elder brother, Thomas *Grey, Lord Grey of Groby. Little is known about Grey's education, which suggests that he may have been educated at home. His father and elder brother were presbyterians and supported parliament in the civil war. In the late 1650s Grey served in several local offices, as a commissioner for assessment in Derbyshire in 1657 and as sheriff of Nottingham in 1657–8. Local office was probably the result of his marriage about this time to Anne (1614–1688), daughter and coheir of Sir Henry Willoughby, first baronet (d. 1649), Risley, Derbyshire. She was the widow of Sir Thomas Aston, first baronet (d. 1646), of Aston, Cheshire, whom she had married in 1639. Grey's marriage brought him an estate at Risley. His new connections may have influenced his politics as in 1659 he was committed to the 'King and Covenant' and was arrested for supporting the rising of his brother-in-law, Sir George Booth, second baronet.

After the Restoration Grey continued in local office in Derbyshire, Nottinghamshire, Leicestershire, and Warwickshire, and was appointed a gentleman of the privy chamber in extraordinary. Grey's sights were set higher and on 16 February 1665 he entered parliament for the borough of Derby following a by-election with the support of the influential Cavendish family, earls of Devonshire. Grey rarely spoke in the Commons but attended assiduously and kept an invaluable record of debates at a time when parliamentary reporting was rare. He began his notes on 16 October 1667 with an account of the debate on the bill to prevent the growth of popery. In general Grey was an opponent of the court, and a supporter of the whigs in the exclusion crisis. The first earl of Shaftesbury accounted him 'worthy' on his analysis of the first Exclusion Parliament, and he duly voted for the first Exclusion Bill in 1679. In the 1685 election Grey found his interest in abeyance at Derby following the surrender and regrant of the corporation's charter, so that he stood and was defeated in the county contest in Derbyshire. Having lost local office in 1680, Grey was restored to the lieutenancy and commission of the peace in the early months of 1688, no doubt as a conciliatory gesture by James II. However, Grey supported the revolution later that year, organizing the defences of Derby against Irish troops. He was duly elected to the convention of 1689 and to the 1690 parliament as a whig. Ill health precluded his regular attendance during this parliament, but he kept up his parliamentary diaries with the help of news sent by his fellow member for Derby, Robert Wilmot. The last debate recorded was on 1 February 1694, and the last entry was for 25 April 1694. Grey's manuscript, apparently lost, was well known in the eighteenth century and was first published in ten volumes in 1763 under the title *Debates of the House of Commons, from the year 1667 to the year 1694, collected by the Honourable Anchitell Grey, Esq; who was thirty years member for the town of Derby; chairman of several committees; and decyphered Coleman's letters for the use of the House.*

Grey retired from the House of Commons at the 1695 general election. He died of cancer of the mouth on 8 July 1702, and was buried next to his wife in Wilne church, Derbyshire. His son, Willoughby, had predeceased him in 1701, so Grey's daughter, Elizabeth, inherited his estate, variously reported to be worth £3500 or £4000 p.a. She died unmarried in 1722.   STUART HANDLEY

Sources 'Grey, Hon. Anchitell', HoP, *Commons, 1690–1715* [draft] • E. R. Edwards, 'Grey (Gray), Hon. Anchitell', HoP, *Commons, 1660–90*, 2.439–41 • A. Grey, ed., *Debates of the House of Commons, from the year 1667 to the year 1694*, 10 vols. (1763) • E. S. De Beer, 'Grey, Anchitell', *BIHR*, 5 (1927–8), 55–6 • *IGI* • will, PRO, PROB 11/468, sig. 29 • *Flying Post* (11–14 July 1702) • N. Luttrell, *A brief historical relation of state affairs from September 1678 to April 1714*, 5 (1857), 194 • W. Woolley, *History of Derbyshire*, ed. C. Glover and P. Riden, Derbyshire RS, 6 (1981), 62–4

Wealth at death £3500–£4000: *Flying Post*; Luttrell, *Brief historical relation*

Grey, Arthur, fourteenth Baron Grey of Wilton (1536–1593), lord deputy of Ireland and soldier, was born between 1 January and 13 October 1536 at Hammes Castle in the Pas-de-Calais, the elder son of the three children of William *Grey, thirteenth Baron Grey of Wilton (1508/9–1562), soldier, and his wife, Mary (1507×14–1571/2), daughter of Charles Somerset, first earl of Worcester, and his second wife, Elizabeth. In 1553 John Dudley, duke of Northumberland, made an ultimately unsuccessful bid to get backing for Lady Jane Grey's succession from Grey of Wilton by offering her sister, Mary Grey, as a bride for Arthur Grey.

Having joined Grey of Wilton at Guînes, Arthur Grey commanded 100 demilances in the field army of William Herbert, first earl of Pembroke, during the St Quentin campaign in 1557. When Guînes surrendered on 21 January 1558 he supported his father's attempts to organize a counter-attack while the rest of the garrison demurred. He was given up as a hostage during the surrender negotiations. In 1560 he took 200 demilances to Scotland under his father. A French sortie from Leith on 15 April came embarrassingly close to spiking the English siege guns, allegedly through the negligence of Sir William Pelham, later Grey's colleague in Ireland. Grey counter-attacked, but was shot in the shoulder, 'having not time to arme himselfe ... Many thousandes have dyed of lesser woundes then this was' (H. Barwick, *A Breefe Discourse Concerning ... Manuall Weapons of Fire*, 1591, sig. C3v). He recovered and was knighted on 18 July.

Debts, brawls, and unemployment, 1562–1580 William Grey of Wilton died on 14 or 15 December 1562. Arthur Grey, now fourteenth Baron Grey of Wilton, married Dorothy (d. before 1573), illegitimate daughter of Richard Zouche, ninth Baron Zouche. The couple had a daughter, Elizabeth Grey, who married the Buckinghamshire gentleman Francis Goodwin. Between 1573 and 1575 Grey of Wilton married Jane Sibylla (1552–1615), daughter of Sir Richard Morison and his second wife, Bridget, and widow of Edward Russell, Baron Russell (d. c.1572). The couple's children included Thomas *Grey, fifteenth Baron Grey of Wilton (1575–1614), William (1588–1606), and Bridget (d. 1648), who married a Cheshire landowner, Sir Rowland Egerton, and was ancestor of the eighteenth-century revivers of the Grey of Wilton title. Another son died in 1581.

Grey of Wilton's inheritance was crippled by the effect

of his father's ransom from Guînes, making it initially difficult for him to take up public office. The disposal of lands in Herefordshire was long and complex. Two manors worth £100 per annum were in Elizabeth I's hands as security for £3000 which Grey of Wilton contracted to repay in 1565–7 but failed to do. Despite this, he began to undertake public duties. The privy council planned in April 1567 to send him to Scotland to criticize the actions of Mary, queen of Scots. However, he was not sent.

Grey of Wilton regularly attended the House of Lords. He was delegated to confer with the Commons on petitions about the succession in 1566 and about Mary in 1572, and was named frequently to committees on ecclesiastical legislation in 1571–2. He was also impanelled to try Thomas Howard, fourth duke of Norfolk. By 1569 he was lord lieutenant of Buckinghamshire—perhaps disappointed in his limited employment during the northern uprising of 1569—and by 1571 quorate member of the ecclesiastical commission for the dioceses of Lincoln and Peterborough.

Sir William Fitzwilliam, in early 1571, welcomed news that Grey of Wilton would be appointed lord deputy of Ireland; in June William Cecil, Baron Burghley, got so far as to note that provisions and horses needed to be collected there ready for him. However, Grey of Wilton became or feigned being ill, perhaps because Elizabeth would not grant his 'small desire' (PRO, SP 63/33/35). The following year he denied being 'by letters directly wylled' to accept the office, and asked Burghley 'not to thynk hym idle that is diversely opprest with care but to suffer hym first to be quiett in mynde, before you put hym to any further care of servyce' (Wright, 1.444). Notwithstanding, he was nominated to the Order of the Garter on 23 April and installed on 17 June 1572, having received by patent the two manors he could not recover earlier with cancellation of the debt of £3000.

Grey of Wilton's chances of office were not enhanced by his becoming an exemplar of Elizabethan aristocratic lawlessness. The right to pursue deer out of his Buckinghamshire chase of Whaddon into John Fortescue's manor of Salden became a matter of status. He wrote that 'for well deserving of prince and contrie I maye without arrogance (I trust) not onlye matche but somewhat better' Fortescue, or, as he put it more directly to Fortescue, being an inferior, he should 'stuffe a turde in your teethe' (PRO, SP 12/92/36; PRO, SP 12/92/34). Fortescue had influence at court. By August 1573 fights between servants had escalated and Grey of Wilton got Fortescue indicted at Buckinghamshire sessions for riot and, 'one of my hurt men beinge indede deade', intended to bring charges of homicide, when the privy council annexed the case and banned both sides from carrying weapons (PRO, SP 12/92/36). Grey of Wilton's answer was to ambush Fortescue in Fleet Street with a party armed with clubs, at the end of November. Interpreting the privy council's order literally, after knocking Fortescue down, Grey of Wilton continued to belabour him, 'calling him villayn and sayinge youe wold pay him and have your penyworthes, not ceasing untill the cuggill was taken owt of your hande' (PRO, STAC 5,

F24/31). He was sent to the Fleet prison. He was fined £350 and released in May 1574.

Lord deputy of Ireland, 1580–1582 Informed in April 1580 that he was to be lord deputy of Ireland, Grey of Wilton complained of short notice, considering 'her majestie's late dislyke too enhable mee, & flatt awnswer that I shuld not bee employed' (PRO, SP 63/72/36). His appointment had powerful support. Walter Ralegh described him to Robert Dudley, earl of Leicester, as 'one of yours' (Edwards, 2.17). Grey of Wilton himself professed to Leicester about 1588, 'since my father's death you have been he that only I have depended on and followed' (Adams, *Household Accounts*, 264n.). Grey of Wilton received both a visit and a long letter of advice on Irish matters from a previous incumbent, Sir Henry Sidney, Leicester's brother-in-law. Edmund Spenser, part of Leicester's following, became Grey of Wilton's secretary. Though to this extent a 'Leicesterian lord deputy', Grey of Wilton was not a full dependent, and was probably closest to Sir Francis Walsingham, who became one of his trustees and shared views on religious reformation and foreign policy (Adams, 'Protestant cause', 26).

Grey of Wilton was appointed lord deputy on 15 July 1580, to face Catholic rebellions raging, not only under Gerald fitz James Fitzgerald, fourteenth earl of Desmond, in Munster, but also under James Eustace, third Viscount Baltinglass, in the pale itself. Seeking to secure Leinster before dealing with Munster, although Pelham had not yet officially transferred the sword of office to him, he acted hastily and lost most of his infantry to ambush at Glenmalure, co. Wicklow, on 25 August, by 'an unluckie accident, or rather God's appoyntment' (PRO, SP 63/76/27). This was a major defeat. He took up office on 7 September. Glenmalure made it doubly necessary to remove the 600 or 700 Italians and Spaniards supporting Desmond, who were now fortified at Smerwick in Kerry. Grey of Wilton directed the siege personally and effectively. Two days' bombardment induced the garrison to open negotiations, but Grey of Wilton demanded unconditional surrender. It seems clear that their commander, Sebastiano di San Joseppi, was more concerned to get his life guaranteed than anybody else's. Negotiating through him, Grey of Wilton had no actual need to make misleading promises. Whatever San Joseppi may have told his men, they surrendered without being promised their lives and all but a handful (those spared including San Joseppi, of course) were killed on 10 November 1580.

Besides genuine practical problems—that he had barely more men than the prisoners and now needed to withdraw along doubtful supply-lines through country where Desmond's rebels still lurked—Grey of Wilton's ideological reasons for the massacre seem clear. The intruders, having no commission from any 'naturall & absolute prince', only one from 'a detestable shaveling, the right Antichriste and generall ambitious tyrant over all right principalities', were pirates and minions of Satan (PRO, SP 63/88/29). The Spanish took a fairly accurate view, that Grey of Wilton executed the Smerwick garrison as 'thieves' (*CSP Spain, 1580–86*, 69). His action found its way into Irish Catholic historiography as a synonym for perjury and mercilessness, along with the patent exaggeration that stout resistance had forced him to start the negotiations. However, he was not regarded in this light immediately. For instance, Eleanor Fitzgerald, countess of Desmond, surrendered to him shortly after Smerwick. Although it has been claimed that Elizabeth objected to the massacre, her only criticism in fact was that Grey of Wilton should not have spared the officers: 'the principall should receave punishment before an accessory' (Hennessy, 212).

In Ulster, Grey of Wilton 'patched up' a peace with Turlough Luineach O'Neill, 'being such indede as I can neither repose any assurance in … nor … justlie commend it', but he was 'tyed to … directions' from England (Wright, 2.147). In the pale, Sir Henry Wallop, Sir Edward Waterhouse, and others persuaded him to arrest Gerald Fitzgerald, eleventh earl of Kildare, and Christopher Nugent, fifth Baron Delvin (later sending them to England), as suspected accomplices of Baltinglass. This provoked a new conspiracy by Delvin's brother William Nugent, which resulted in over twenty executions being carried out by the government in reprisal. Grey of Wilton was especially susceptible to hints by members of the New English élite of impending 'Armageddon' or 'a St Bartholomew's Day in Dublin' (V. P. Carey, Surviving the Tudors, 2002, 180). After the French massacre he had written Burghley a notable letter wishing that Elizabeth might 'have wisdome to follow and magnitude to execute the things that maye divert the same from hence' (Wright, 1.443). In 1572 he lacked public employment, but between 1580 and 1582 he had his own opportunity to attack the perceived international Catholic conspiracy. However, this could make him a tool for local faction, as when Nicholas Nugent, chief justice of the common pleas, fell in 1582. Grey of Wilton's military operations became more successful, though, and reduced support for rebellion within the pale. More often, his reaction has been seen as 'hysterical and ferocious', aggravated by 'unprecedentedly oppressive' levying of cess (Brady, 'Conservative subversives', 25–6).

Grey of Wilton relieved Thomas Butler, eleventh earl of Ormond, as general in Munster, suggesting that he was still influenced by Leicester and Sidney. Ormond resumed office after Grey of Wilton's recall and finally finished off Desmond's rebellion. Elizabeth instructed Grey of Wilton to 'remove that false impression' among the native Irish 'that we have a determination as it were to roote them out' (Grey, 75). However, he took the view, 'the Irish are so addicted to treachery' as to be relied on no longer 'then they find the yoke on their necks' (Murdin, 357). As for the Old English, he felt that 'the sore is so festered, as corrosives and incisions must now onely cure, which wyll never bee doonne by surgeons of this soile' (PRO, SP 63/81/36). A much quoted view of Grey of Wilton was 'that he was a bloody man, and regarded not the life of [the queen's] subjects no more than dogs, but had wasted and consumed all, so as now she had nothing almost left, but to reign in their ashes' (Spenser, 106). Most citations omit to observe

that this is a dialectical allegation put in Edmund Spenser's Veue of the State of Ireland (1596) to be contradicted. Spenser, not naturally sympathetic to the Irish, was shocked by the famine created in Munster by efforts to starve out Desmond. Grey of Wilton's harshness would have attracted less comment had it actually achieved its objective of capturing Desmond before the lord deputy's departure. The fatal mistake, however, was to cut out too many vocal palesmen from the lands confiscated after the Nugent plot—their allegations about grants to Grey of Wilton's 'speciall favourites' incensed the queen, as seeming to defraud her of her revenue (PRO, SP 63/86/71).

Recall, 1582 Grey of Wilton was frustrated both by circumstances, forcing him to concentrate on reaction and repression rather than any positive programme, and by Elizabeth's enjoinders not to stir up expensive trouble. 'Thinges might be patched up and a face of peace & quietness made to appeare', but it would be only a 'mask' in the absence of 'a thorough reformation', both secular and religious (PRO, SP 63/82/54). He complained, 'Gode's cause is made a seconde or nothyng at all' (PRO, SP 63/82/48). Even repression was compromised when Elizabeth decided in 1581 that a general pardon would be cheaper. This, Grey of Wilton protested, would leave only a small part of the pale under her laws.

Grey of Wilton's administration came under increasing criticism, though it was only the Spanish ambassador, Don Bernardino de Mendoza, who thought treatment of the Irish might be a concern as such. Complaints were sent to Burghley rather than Walsingham. The latter was too friendly to Grey of Wilton to be receptive to criticism of him, but another reason was that the lord deputy's misdeeds were treasury matters. Burghley and Nicholas White, master of the rolls, conducted an anti-militarist correspondence, the latter warning that 'this violent and warlike forme of government' would 'exhauste her majeste's treasyr' and 'depopulate' even the pale (PRO, SP 63/87/55). Burghley later criticized the military faction in the Irish administration, pointedly remarking that Sir John Perrot, 'my Lord depute that now is, I thynk, standeth more upright', and that he had blocked confirmation of the attainder of 'the late good Justyce Nugent' (BL, Lansdowne MS 102, fol. 209r). Despite the criticism, Grey of Wilton's personal finances suffered.

Grey of Wilton feared he needed not only providential successes, but also a miracle to solve his problems all at once. He admitted he was unable to monitor finance while trying to fight rebellion and restore order. Waterhouse lamented Grey of Wilton's 'service drownid in this sea of expences' (PRO, SP 63/87/14). Recalling him in July 1582, Elizabeth did repeat that, while her resources had not been so 'husbanded … as that seemid unto us they might have been', her 'mislike did not proceede so farr' as to negate his service at Smerwick, which 'next to God's dyvyne providence we must needes acknowledge as the second meanes wherbye the whole land was preserved' (Hennessy, 214). Handing over to Wallop and Adam Loftus, archbishop of Dublin, Grey of Wilton left on 31 August. His wife followed in early November.

Grey of Wilton's tenure has been seen as the aborted herald of the period of systematic plantation, expounded in the writings of Spenser and Lodowick Bryskett. Their literary dedications to him (after his loss of office) arose from conviction rather than place-seeking. His tolerance for plantation plans was, however, exhausted by Ralegh, a framer of 'plotts upon impossibillities, for others to execute' (Edwards, 2.4). Such personal differences—as also with Geoffrey Fenton, a persistent critic once neglected over the Nugent confiscations—restricted Grey of Wilton's support, even among the New English. Elizabeth sent him to suppress revolt in Munster, and local interests induced him to break their pale rivals; these aims largely achieved, both could dispense with him.

Later life and reputation, 1582–1593 Many have assumed that Grey of Wilton's reputation was irreparably damaged as a result of the Irish wars. He was, however, considered employable but for his worsened debts. Ironically, his financial troubles required him to seek favour from his old enemy Fortescue in 1589. Grey of Wilton's son-in-law Goodwin, however, continued the tradition of Buckinghamshire brawls with Fortescue's men.

In 1583 Sir Walter Mildmay thought Grey of Wilton would become governor of Berwick. In 1585 Grey of Wilton was spoken of as prospective governor of the Netherlands but Walsingham doubted that 'the ability of his purse were answerable to his sufficiency otherwise', and subordination to Leicester became more likely (PRO, SP 84/3/85). The Roman Catholic conspirator Thomas Morgan alleged Grey of Wilton was among a group of radical protestants Leicester sought to nominate to the privy council in early 1586, only to be supplanted by Burghley's choices. At Leicester's request, Burghley got Elizabeth to 'stall' Grey's debt before imminent dispatch to the Netherlands in January, for which Leicester pressed insistently, as he could 'farr better accomplish this service then I can' (J. Bruce, *Correspondence of Robert Dudley, Earl of Leycester*, CS, 27, 1844, 259). In June Grey of Wilton told the queen that with debts of over £4000 to others besides her he could 'maynetayn my sillie family but from hand to mooothe' and hoped his situation would not incur her displeasure (Hatfield House, Cecil MS 165, fol. 81r). Still, in November Burghley told Leicester to expect Grey of Wilton to take over field command, promising that Elizabeth would remit his debts incurred through royal service.

Peregrine Bertie, thirteenth Baron Willoughby d'Eresby, succeeded Leicester but still suggested in November 1587 Sir John Norris, Sir Richard Bingham, 'and if you would go high … my lord Gray and my lord North [Roger North, second Baron North]' as better options for governor (Bertie, 143). Grey of Wilton, Norris, and Bingham were needed at home—they all sat that month on a committee to advise on possible landing-sites for the Armada and possible counter-measures against it. Grey of Wilton was the highest-ranking member, though Sir Francis Knollys was a privy councillor. Grey of Wilton acted as marshal under Leicester for the army assembled at Tilbury to defend London and the queen. Even in the winter

of 1589–90 there were new rumours about his being sent to Ireland or the Netherlands.

Except in military emergencies, Elizabeth doubtless suspected Grey of Wilton's affinity for radical protestantism, reflected both in his ecclesiastical patronage and in his personal religion. He was said to be 'a religious and devout keeper of the saboth, consecrating it wholly to publicke and private holy exercises' and a reader of 'all good and learned books of controversies that he could come by' (Sparke, 61). He joined Leicester, Burghley, and Walsingham in overseeing the conference of John Whitgift, archbishop of Canterbury, with Walter Travers and Thomas Sparke in 1584. Sparke was presented by Grey of Wilton to the rectory of Bletchley, near Whaddon, witnessed his will, and preached his funeral sermon. Grey of Wilton pointedly intervened with scriptural questions for Whitgift. According to the unusually full report of the Lords debate on the 1589 Pluralities Bill, Grey of Wilton went so far as to question Elizabeth's reliance on bishops, whom he regarded as opposed to reform, to hint that they verged on *praemunire*, and to propose adding lay peers to the committee. Thomas Cartwright (later taken up by the Zouche family) sought protection from Grey of Wilton as well as the usual government figures, as did the Essex presbyterian Robert Wright.

Grey of Wilton's religious and national security interests inevitably made him a campaigner for Mary's execution. He was on the various Lords delegations sent to Elizabeth during winter 1586 and finally became a commissioner for Mary's trial. He was also impanelled to try Philip Howard, earl of Arundel, in 1589. He notoriously dissented from making William Davison a scapegoat after Mary's execution—Davison 'preferred the saftie of his prince and contrie before his owne welfare … his zeale therein was in his [Grey of Wilton's] opynion to be rewarded' (*CSP Scot., 1586–8*, 44).

Grey of Wilton attracted a notable degree of literary attention considering his limited financial resources. Before 1577 he himself had composed the commentary on his father's services used by Raphael Holinshed. George Gascoigne, a writer long connected with Grey of Wilton—including through service in the Netherlands with John Zouche and Grey of Wilton's cousin Sir Edward *Denny (1547–1600)—dedicated a succession of works to him. George Whetstone, like Gascoigne a Russell client, made Lady Grey of Wilton part patron of his *Rocke of Regard* (1576). Besides Spenser and Bryskett, Lord Grey of Wilton's name and soldiership attracted Richard Robinson, translator of John Leland's *Assertio Arthuri*, who expressed great expectation, biblical as well as Arthurian, of his time in Ireland:

> that as an invincible Josua you may continually bring in the people to the knowledge of God and the obedience of our prince & as a notable Nehemias in true feare of God without feare of foe build up this earthly Jerusalem. (R. Robinson, *Learned and True Assertion of … Prince Arthure*, 1582, sig. B v)

Spenser felt Grey of Wilton in need of apologetic in *A veue of the State of Ireland* claiming that 'now that he is dead, his immortal fame surviveth', having brought '12 or 13' years of peace 'thorough his only paines and excellent endurance' (Spenser, 106). Grey of Wilton was Artegall, the champion of justice, in book 5 of the *Faerie Queen*, though to the Irish he might seem 'more like Talus than Artegall', more executioner than exemplar of justice (Brady, 'Grey', 342). Richard Beacon, in *Solon his Follie*, also remembered Grey of Wilton for his 'rare skill and knowledge in military discipline' allied to 'severe discipline of lawes' (R. Beacon, *Solon his Follie*, ed. C. Carroll and V. P. Carey, 1996, 65, 36).

Denying that Grey was in fact 'a bloody man', Spenser believed he was 'most gentle', but that the situation in Ireland forced him to brutality (Spenser, 20). Artegall, the allegorical Grey of Wilton, is inappropriately merciful to the Amazon Radigund, which, it has been suggested, reflects Grey of Wilton's chivalrous confusion upon the surrender of the countess of Desmond until Elizabeth ordered her sent back to her rebel husband. He had himself professed that the need for 'a harde and forcible hand … falles not with my nature' (PRO, SP 63/78/29). Not only Irishmen but also Fortescue probably had a rather different impression.

Grey of Wilton died on 14 October 1593 'in his owne bedde, in his owne house' at Whaddon and was buried there on either 19 or 22 October (Sparke, sig. iiir). Sparke represented this as a model Calvinist death, with submission to the will of God overcoming attendant circumstance—that he was 'sicke an eighteen daies, and therein had many sharpe, long, and bitter fits, of his old disease the stone (as it was taken)' (ibid., 64). Grey of Wilton had been a more unequivocal, if less prominent, champion of the forward protestant cause than his patron Leicester. In contrast to him, he combined convincing (if erratic) military credentials with a peerage. However, intractable financial problems contributed to a career of near misses. When actually employed in the deputyship of Ireland, the task—at least when adopting a starkly ideological approach—proved more intractable still.

JULIAN LOCK

Sources Arthur, Lord Grey, *A commentary of the services and charges of William, Lord Grey of Wilton*, ed. P. de M. Grey Egerton, CS, 40 (1847) · state papers, Ireland, PRO, SP 63 · state papers, domestic and domestic additional, Elizabeth I, PRO, SP 12/36/6, 12/52/1, 12/69/4, 12/69/26, 12/92/35–36, 12/93/1, 12/99/39, 12/143/34, 12/152/42, 12/204/61, 12/209/49–50, 15/25/74, 15/29/153 · BL, Lansdowne MSS 6, 13, 16, 18, 20, 22, 40, 55, 66, 69, 102 · Hatfield House, Hertfordshire, Cecil MSS 141, 165 · W. Murdin, ed., *Collection of state papers … left by William Cecil, Lord Burghley … 1572–96* (1759) · T. Sparke, *A sermon preached at Whaddon in Buckinghamshire the 22 of November 1593 at the buriall of the right honorable Arthur Lorde Grey of Wilton* (1593) · N. Canny, *Making Ireland British, 1580–1650* (2001) · C. G. Canino, 'Reconstructing Lord Grey's reputation: a new view of *The view*', *Sixteenth-Century Journal*, 29 (1998), 3–18 · E. Spenser, *View of the present state of Ireland*, ed. W. L. Renwick (1970) · A. O'Rahilly, *The massacre at Smerwick* (1580), Historical and Archaeological Papers of the Cork Historical and Archaeological Society, 1 (1938) · J. P. Hennessy, *Sir Walter Ralegh in Ireland* (1883) · F. Edwards, *The life of Sir Walter Ralegh*, 2 vols. (1868) · LPL, Carew MSS 597, 600, 605, 607, 619 · APC, 1571–5, 1580–82, 1587–8 · *Curia regis rolls preserved in the Public Record Office* (1922–), 1569–80, 1586–7 · CSP Scot., 1547–69, 1581–3, 1585–6 · state papers, Holland, PRO, SP 84/3/58, 84/3/116, 84/5/146, 84/6/60, 84/8/38, 84/9/44, 84/9/63, 84/12/26 · star chamber

book of interrogatories, PRO, STAC 5, F24/31 · C. Brady, 'Grey, Arthur, 14th baron of Wilton', *The Spenser encyclopedia*, ed. A. C. Hamilton and others (1990), 341–2 · H. S. V. Jones, *Spenser's defence of Lord Grey*, University of Illinois Studies in Language and Literature, 5/3 (1919) · S. G. Ellis, *Tudor Ireland: crown, community, and the conflict of cultures, 1470–1603* (1985) · C. Brady, 'Conservative subversives: the community of the pale and the Dublin administration, 1556–86', *Radicals, rebels, and establishments*, ed. P. Corish, Historical Studies, 15 (1985), 11–32 · G. Bertie, *Five generations of a loyal house: part 1, containing the lives of Richard Bertie and his son Peregrine, Lord Willoughby* (1845) · S. L. Adams, 'The protestant cause: religious alliance with the west European Calvinist communities as a political issue in England, 1585–1630', DPhil diss., U. Oxf., 1973 · S. Adams, ed., *Household accounts and disbursement books of Robert Dudley, earl of Leicester, 1558–1561, 1584–1586*, CS, 6 (1995) · T. Wright, *Queen Elizabeth and her times: a collection of original letters*, 2 vols. (1838) · JHL, 1–2 (1509–1614) · L. Stone, *The crisis of the aristocracy, 1558–1641* (1965); rev. edn (1979) · GEC, *Peerage* · L. L. Peck, *Court patronage and corruption in early Stuart England* (1990) · PRO, PROB 11/82/80 · PRO, SO 3/1 · notes of inscriptions in Buckinghamshire churches, Christ Church Oxf., Wake MS 2, fol. 184

Archives BL, letters to William Cecil, Lord Burghley, Lansdowne MSS 6, 14, 16, 18, 20, 22, 55, 66 · BL, Cotton MSS, Irish corresp., MS Titus Bxiii · Hatfield House, Hertfordshire, Cecil papers, corresp. · Hunt. L., letters to Temple family · Longleat House, Wiltshire, letters to Robert Dudley, earl of Leicester · LPL, Carew MSS, Irish corresp., MS 605 · PRO, official corresp., SP 12, SP 63

Likenesses M. Gheeraerts senior, group portrait, etching (*Procession of garter knights, 1576*), BM

Wealth at death est. over £186 7s. 8d. p.a. from lands; 'greatly indebted': Hatfield House, Hertfordshire, Cecil papers, vol. 141, fol. 349r; will, PRO, PROB 11/82/80 · lands in Buckinghamshire valued at £181 p.a.: PRO, C 142/240/92 · Coleshills, Bedfordshire valued at £7 p.a. in Burghley's wardship notes (formerly at £48); perhaps retained crown lease of East Greenwich, Kent (value over £48); owned Brampton, Herefordshire (value £26 5s. 4d. p.a.) until at least 1574: PRO, SP 12/99/39 · perhaps retained Brampton as instructed tenants to arm against Armada: PRO, SP 12/204/61 · alienated from Brampton: patent rolls · lease of Olney Manor, Buckinghamshire, from duchy of Lancaster; owed over £4000 in 1581, excl. crown debts: Hatfield House, Hertfordshire, Cecil papers, vol. 165, fol. 8r. · great residue of debts in 1593, given relatively small income with which to liquidate them

Grey, Charles, first Earl Grey (1729–1807), army officer, was born in October 1729 at Howick, near Alnwick, Northumberland, and baptized there on 23 October, the fourth son of Sir Henry Grey, first baronet (1691–1749), of Howick, and his wife, Hannah (d. 1764), the daughter of Thomas Wood of Fallodon, a Northumberland estate Grey would inherit on the death of his mother. His father was made high sheriff of Northumberland in 1738 and created a baronet in 1746.

In 1744 Grey's father purchased him a commission as an ensign in the 6th regiment of foot. He fought at Culloden (16 April 1746) and accompanied the regiment to garrison duty on Gibraltar. Following his father's death in 1749, his eldest brother advanced Grey's career by numerous purchases, culminating in a captaincy of the 20th (East Devonshire) regiment. He became firm friends with Lieutenant William Petty, Viscount Fitzmaurice (later earl of Shelburne), who greatly aided him in his career. He served with the regiment against Rochefort (1757) and at Minden (1 August 1759). While serving as an aide-de-camp to Prince Ferdinand of Brunswick at Minden, Grey was wounded,

Charles Grey, first Earl Grey (1729–1807), by Sir Thomas Lawrence, 1795

but he returned to service as the commander of the regiment's light company. After being wounded again at Klosterkamp (16 October 1760) he returned to England and, through Fitzmaurice's influence, was promoted lieutenant-colonel of the 98th foot. Serious illness prevented him from serving with the regiment against Belle Île (1761) or in the capture of Havana (1762). At the close of the Seven Years' War in 1763 the regiment was disbanded, and for over a decade Grey lived in semi-retirement on half pay. On 8 June 1762 he married Elizabeth Grey (d. 1822) of Southwick, co. Durham; the couple had two daughters and five sons. Elizabeth, the elder daughter, married Samuel Whitbread; Hannah, the younger, married Edward *Ellice MP (1783–1863). Three sons followed Grey into the armed service; Edward, the fifth son, became bishop of Hereford, and the eldest, Charles *Grey, inherited his father's titles in 1807 and the estate at Howick following the death of his uncle in 1808.

With the outbreak of the American War of Independence in 1775, Grey was initially passed over for active command. His complaints to the ministry, however, brought him promotion to colonel, and he was made an aide-de-camp to the king. Finally in 1777 he was sent out to New York as the colonel of the 28th regiment with the local rank of major-general. At Brandywine (11 September 1777) and at Germantown (4 October 1777) he ably commanded the 3rd brigade under General Howe. In August 1777 he was permanently promoted major-general, and in his few years of service in America he earned a reputation as an efficient and loyal subordinate. He was also ranked as a hardline officer who advocated the fullest prosecution of

the war. Three events tarnished his career and made him a figure of controversy.

During the campaign against Philadelphia, Grey came upon troops under General Anthony Wayne near Paoli, Pennsylvania (20 September 1777). To take the sleeping Americans by surprise he ordered his troops to remove their flints and use the bayonet. In the engagement more than 420 Americans were either killed, captured, or wounded. Americans termed it a massacre and portrayed 'No-flint Grey' as a monster. In the nineteenth century Pennsylvanians erected a monument on the site to the victims of 'British barbarity'. Grey never responded to his critics and displayed the same ruthless streak in raids on the southern New England coast, as well as in New Jersey.

In an expedition against privateers in September 1778 Grey captured, without resistance, New Bedford and Fairhaven, Massachusetts. After burning most of the towns, including churches, he moved on to Martha's Vineyard (6 September 1778). Making draconian requisition demands upon the defenceless citizens, he spent two days loading thousands of sheep and oxen upon transports for the garrison in New York; troops were used freely to speed up the process. He then launched a raid into New Jersey, surprising the sleeping troopers of Colonel Baylor's 3rd continental light dragoons at Old Tappan (28 September 1778). Using the bayonet once more, and denying the Americans quarter, his men either killed, captured, or wounded seventy Americans out of a command of 104 troopers. One American officer, Major Huntington of Connecticut, hoped that, if ever captured, Grey would be 'burnt alive, in a manner agreeable to the Indian custom' (Conway, *The War*, 107–8). Disillusioned with service in a war in which British arms could not succeed, Grey resigned his commission and returned to England in early 1779. While he served on a number of service boards, he refused further active command in America until 1782.

In July 1782 Grey's patron, Shelburne, became prime minister and offered his friend overall command in America. Only after being promoted lieutenant-general and receiving a knighthood did Grey reluctantly agree to succeed General Carleton in December 1782. He did not, however, actually return to New York, and resigned his commission in April 1783. For the next decade he lived in semi-retirement at Fallodon while actively advancing the careers of his sons. With the declaration of war against revolutionary France in February 1793, he again returned to active service. Having served briefly in Flanders in support of the duke of York, he sailed in command of troops from England to Barbados on 23 November 1793. With Admiral Sir John Jervis commanding the naval expedition, the campaign was to attack the French West Indies.

The campaign was a success. In March 1794 Martinique was reduced and in April St Lucia, the Saints, and Guadeloupe were taken. Although Guadeloupe was retaken by the French, both Jervis and Grey were hailed as national heroes. Grey's reputation, however, was again tarnished with controversy when it became evident that he had used his position to enrich himself by unusual property confiscations and irregular levies upon the inhabitants of the conquered islands. He also used his position to advance the career of his sons by promotions and their appointment to lucrative colonial offices. Both he and Jervis weathered the resulting public storm. On 8 January 1795 he arrived back in England.

In the last phase of his career Grey was promoted general in August 1796 and placed in command of England's southern district. Between 1796 and 27 February 1800 he effectively prepared the region against possible French invasion; in June 1797 he aided in the repression of the naval mutiny at the Nore. Although he was made governor of Guernsey in November 1797, he was disappointed at not being elevated to the peerage by the time of his final retirement in 1800.

A controversial figure, Grey was one of Britain's most efficient field officers in the second half of the eighteenth century. He both successfully enriched himself and established his cadet branch of the family as a force in Northumberland politics. Finally, in 1801, he was patented Baron Grey of Howick. In April 1806 he was raised in the peerage as first Earl Grey, although his long awaited earldom was more a reward for his son's rising political importance than his own past services. Having developed a painful blockage in his urinary tract, Grey died at Fallodon on 14 November 1807 and was buried on 26 November in St Michael's Church, Howick. His wife, Elizabeth, continued to reside at Fallodon until her death in 1822.

RORY T. CORNISH

Sources P. D. Nelson, *Sir Charles Grey, first Earl Grey, royal soldier, family patriarch* (1996) · J. E. Fagg, ed., *List of the papers of 1st Earl Grey*, 2 vols. (1974) · S. Conway, *The War of American Independence, 1775–1783* (1995) · M. Duffy, *Soldiers, sugar, and sea power: the British expeditions to the West Indies and the war against revolutionary France* (1987) · S. Conway, 'To subdue America: British army officers and the conduct of the revolutionary war', *William and Mary Quarterly*, 43 (1986), 381–407

Archives PRO, corresp., secretary of state, West Indies, CO 318/12–13 · U. Durham L., corresp. and papers | BL, corresp. with Henry Dundas, Add. MSS 38353, 38377, 38735, *passim* · BL, letters to William Huskisson, Add. MSS 38735–38736 · Morgan L., letters to Sir James Murray-Pulteney · NRA, priv. coll., letters to Lord Lansdowne · PRO, letters to William Pitt, PRO 30/8 · U. Mich., Bowood MSS, incl. corresp. with Shelburne

Likenesses T. Lawrence, oils, 1795, NPG [*see illus.*] · H. R. Cook, engraving, *c.*1814 · J. Collyer, stipple (after T. Lawrence), BM, NPG · W. Ridley, stipple (after miniature), BM, NPG; repro. in *European Magazine and London Review*, 32 (1797), facing p. 219 · engraved miniature

Grey, Charles, second Earl Grey (1764–1845), prime minister, was born at Fallodon, Northumberland, on 13 March 1764, the second but eldest surviving son of General Sir Charles *Grey KB (1729–1807) and his wife, Elizabeth (1743/4–1822), daughter of George Grey of Southwick, co. Durham. He had four brothers and two sisters. His father became Baron Grey in 1801, Earl Grey in 1806, and died on 14 November 1807.

Personal and family life The Greys were a Northumberland family of moderate estate, prominent in the county since the fourteenth century. Charles Grey's father, a distinguished soldier, was often away on duty, and Charles became attached to his bachelor uncle Sir Henry Grey at

Charles Grey, second Earl Grey (1764–1845), by Sir Thomas Lawrence, 1828

Howick, where he spent much time in his youth. Sir Henry made him his heir, and in 1801 he settled at Howick, which he inherited in 1808. It became his favourite and much loved home, Fallodon later passing to his brother George.

Little is known of Grey's childhood other than that he was sent to a private school in Marylebone, where he was unhappy, and then to Eton College. He was an able pupil, 'reckoned clever' (*Farington Diary*, ed. Greig, 1.179) by his peers, who included his later longstanding friends and political associates Samuel Whitbread, who married his sister, and William Henry Lambton, whose son married Grey's daughter. Grey proceeded to Trinity College, Cambridge, as a fellow-commoner in November 1781. There and at Eton he acquired a facility in Latin and in English composition and declamation that enabled him to become one of the foremost parliamentary orators of his generation. His speeches were described by the parliamentary reporter James Grant as thoughtful, logical in arrangement, and persuasive in argument, and were garnished according to contemporary taste with classical references and quotations. Thomas Creevey remarked in 1820 of his speech on the Queen Caroline affair that 'There is nothing approaching this damned fellow in the kingdom, when he mounts his best horse' (*Creevey Papers*, 1.336).

Grey spent three years at Cambridge, but after the fashion of the time he did not take a degree. He was admitted a student of the Middle Temple in May 1783, and in 1784 he accompanied Henry, duke of Cumberland, a brother of George III, on a continental tour, spending some time seeing the sights and visiting the galleries of Italy. He was not much attracted to art, and, though an avid reader, in his middle and later years his reading was largely confined to historical memoirs and contemporary novels. He was an admirer in particular of Scott and of Maria Edgeworth, and a discriminating reader of Byron's poetry, though his favourite was Spenser. When his children were growing up he read aloud to his family almost every evening, and his eldest son, in his biography of his father, remarked that these times were the most memorable and enjoyable of all family occasions (Grey, 404).

On 18 November 1794 Grey married Mary Elizabeth (1776–1861), daughter of William Brabazon *Ponsonby of Imokilly and Bishop's Court, co. Kildare, later first Baron Ponsonby, an alliance that brought him firmly into the 'whig cousinhood' of which the Ponsonbys were a major element. The marriage was a happy and fruitful one; between 1797 and 1819 the couple had eleven sons, the eldest of whom, Henry George *Grey, became a politician like his father, and four daughters. The family atmosphere at Howick was informal—contemporaries noted that the children often addressed their parents by their Christian or nicknames—and though a strict father where his sons' education and careers were concerned, Grey was an affectionate companion to them all.

However, there was another side to Grey's character. Frequent childbearing often kept Mary at Howick, and during his absences in London or elsewhere Grey had a series of affairs with other women. The first, most notorious, and most significant, which antedated his engagement to his future wife, was with Georgiana *Cavendish, duchess of Devonshire (1757–1806), whom he met at Devonshire House, the centre of whig society in London in the 1780s and 1790s, shortly after his arrival in the capital as a young recruit to the House of Commons. Impetuous and headstrong, Grey was, as Lady Holland remarked, 'a fractious and exigeant lover' (Vassall, 1.98), who pursued Georgiana with persistence until she gave in to his attentions. She became pregnant by Grey in 1791, but she refused to leave her husband and live with him when the duke threatened that if she did so she would never see their children again. She went abroad with her sister, and on 20 February 1792 at Aix-en-Provence she gave birth to a daughter, who was given the name Eliza Courtenay. After her return to England in September 1793 the child was taken to Fallodon and brought up by Grey's parents as if she was his sister.

Grey resented what he considered Georgiana's desertion of him, though he was considered to have treated her cruelly, and although they remained close friends their sexual relationship was probably not resumed after Grey's engagement. He made several other conquests, notoriously including Sheridan's second wife, 'Hecca', and even in his sixties Princess Lieven was numbered among his lovers. Mary nevertheless remained faithful to her errant husband and the marriage endured until his death.

Political career Grey's affair with Georgiana was a significant step in the process by which he became a member of the whig party, led by Charles James Fox. When he was first elected to the Commons in 1786 he was still abroad on his travels, but he was nominated for a vacancy for the county of Northumberland by his uncle Sir Henry, and although he professed no political allegiance he was expected to follow the family tradition of back-bench toryism. On his arrival in London, however, he astonished the political world by devoting his maiden speech on 21 February 1787 to a powerful and intemperate attack on Pitt's commercial treaty with France and on Pitt himself. It made his reputation overnight, Henry Addington noting that it was received 'with an éclat which has not been equalled within my recollection'. He assumed that the speech placed Grey firmly 'in the ranks of opposition, from whence there is no chance of his being detached' (Pellew, 1.45–6). This was premature. Grey had not yet thrown in his lot with the whigs. His speech reflected his headstrong temperament and overwhelming ambition: it was a means of drawing attention to himself rather than a political manifesto. It nevertheless attracted Fox's notice, and Grey, like many young men of his time, fell under his spell. The combination of the flattering attentions of Fox and the attractions of Devonshire House recruited Grey to the opposition benches for personal, not political, reasons.

Once established there, however, Grey characteristically threw himself wholeheartedly into whig politics, though, as always, with more energy than stamina. He was appointed to a place on the committee of managers for the impeachment of Warren Hastings, and on 25 February 1788 he seconded Fox in presenting the charge respecting Chet Singh and Benares in a rather theatrical speech, which again was highly praised. He quickly tired of the impeachment, however, and to Burke's distress he tried to persuade Fox to abandon the proceedings on the grounds that the business of the opposition was to defeat Pitt's government and not to engage in moral crusades of doubtful political value. This streak of realism was another characteristic of Grey's political activity. Though by no means devoid of principles, he valued short-term results and lacked the patience for a long campaign. This was again to be borne out in the 1790s over what Grey later described as 'all the mess of the Friends of the People' (Grey, 11).

Grey's position among the leaders of the opposition to Pitt was quickly assured. Grey himself was determined that he would be second only to Fox, and not to 'those Norfolks, Windhams and Pelhams' (Sichel, 2.406). In the Regency crisis of 1788–9 he gave unstinting support to Fox's attempt to secure the unrestricted power of the crown for the prince of Wales as regent, in the expectation that he would bring the whigs into office, but he was hurt by the prince's apparent ignorance of his claims to high office and the casual offer of a junior lordship of the

Treasury, a lowly post usually given to a minor figure. The prince had been alienated by Grey's refusal to extricate him from his embarrassment over Fox's denial of his marriage to Mrs Fitzherbert in 1787, and this was a further step towards a breach between them. Some of Grey's senior colleagues also thought him too ambitious and pushing for so recent a recruit to the party. It was in this light that Grey's role in the foundation of the Society of the Friends of the People in 1792 was seen, appearing as further proof of his impetuous nature and his wish for self-advancement.

The issue of reform The outbreak of the French Revolution in 1789 at first aroused widespread enthusiasm in Britain, where it was believed that the French were seeking to imitate the country's 'glorious constitution', but ironically it soon proved to draw attention to the defects rather than the virtues of the British system. The House of Commons seemed to be too much dominated by aristocratic patronage and by the influence of the executive, and insufficiently representative of the people. By 1791 radical societies, inspired by events in France, were growing everywhere, and enthusiasm was fed by a diet of radical publications such as Thomas Paine's *The Rights of Man*, which declared that all citizens possessed equal political rights and that democracy was the only foundation of legitimate government. The spread of these doctrines among the 'lower orders', and of clubs and societies devoted to promoting them, alarmed the government and the propertied class, while the descent of the French into what seemed to be anarchy heightened their fears that the same might happen in Britain.

Grey's action in April 1792 in promoting with a few whig friends the foundation of a society to bring about parliamentary reform therefore caused consternation. Its title, the Society of the Friends of the People, seemed in the current climate to be provocative or even seditious. Grey had not consulted Fox before taking this step, wishing not to force him into any embarrassing commitment, but he later confessed that he wished he had done so, for Fox would have restrained him. As it was, the establishment of the society convinced the noble leaders of the party, men such as the duke of Portland and Earl Fitzwilliam, who saw Burke as the true prophet of aristocratic whiggery, that Grey and his young friends were encouraging revolution and, even worse, trying to usurp the leadership of the whig party for themselves and for their own purposes. Grey did not condone the excesses of the French and he did not approve of the ideas of Thomas Paine, but he argued that Britain should set its own house in order to forestall any extremism here, and that the leadership of respectable and moderate men would keep the reformers on a constitutional path. To the conservative element, however, his views seemed idealistic at best, disingenuous at worst.

Grey compounded the offence by giving notice in the Commons on 30 April 1792 that he would present a motion for parliamentary reform in the next session, and he did so on 6 May 1793, basing his proposals on the petition drawn up by the Friends of the People which highlighted the extent of electoral patronage and influence, the small number of voters in many constituencies, and the lack of representation for newer commercial and industrial towns. The motion was lost by 282 votes to 41, a result which showed that only a minority of Grey's own party was prepared to follow him. The days when, as recently as 1791, Grey had joined in a concerted whig attack on Pitt's policy towards Russia in the Ochakov crisis and forced the minister to change his approach were not to be repeated: when the Commons debated Grey's address to restore peace with France on 21 February 1793 he had little support from either side of the house and did not even force a division. The consequence was that the party split, only affection for Fox individually restraining Portland, Fitzwilliam, and the conservative element from immediately breaking away and joining Pitt. They eventually did so in July 1794.

For the next few years Fox, Grey, and a few remaining friends were left in opposition, where they vigorously opposed the measures introduced by Pitt to defend the monarchy and constitution against fancied subversion by radicals or French emissaries. Grey joined in the opposition to the suspension of habeas corpus in 1794, the traitorous correspondence and seditious meetings bills of 1795, and the Aliens Bill of 1799 as unjustified infringements of liberty designed to panic the public into uncritical support of the administration. Pitt, not Paine, was represented as the threat to the British constitution.

It was an arguable proposition, but in the prevailing mood of patriotic enthusiasm and anti-French xenophobia it failed to win much support. When Fox and Grey opposed the indictment and trial of reformers like Thomas Hardy and Horne Tooke for treason in 1794 they merely seemed to confirm that they were in league with subversion. The acquittal of the accused safeguarded Grey's liberty, but when he proposed a second motion for reform on 26 May 1797 it was lost by 256 votes to 91, and he used the figures to persuade Fox that further resistance to Pitt's regime was pointless. To demonstrate that fact he argued that the opposition should secede from parliament for the remainder of the war. This quickly proved to be a miscalculation: it merely showed the opposition as unpatriotic, while the fact that it was incomplete—some members refusing to secede—demonstrated its disunity and allowed Pitt a free hand. Grey quickly realized his mistake, and almost as soon as the secession took place he tried to find a way to end it. Fox, however, was enjoying his release from the cares and struggles of parliamentary opposition, and took the opportunity to devote his time to literature and poetry, listening to the nightingales in his Chertsey garden. Grey could not return while Fox stayed away, or he would be accused of engineering Fox's retirement in order to take his place. The only issue he could not ignore was the Irish question after the suppression of the rising of 1798 and Pitt's introduction of a bill to abolish the Irish parliament in Dublin and bring Ireland under closer British control. Grey argued that the union would increase the influence of the executive over the British parliament by introducing at Westminster 100 extra MPs from Ireland who would be susceptible to bribery and patronage, and thus add to Pitt's majorities. This fitted in with his previous argument that the growth of royal and ministerial influence since 1689 was the major threat to the independence of parliament as the representative body of the people and the guardian of their liberties. Again, however, his contentions were rejected, and he retired once more to Northumberland.

Grey and the new opposition The ending of the revolutionary war by the peace of Amiens in 1802 marked a new phase in Grey's career. He was now settled at Howick and his personal life was more stable, while the attractions of politics had diminished after the failures of the past ten years. He also found himself at variance with Fox, particularly on foreign affairs. Fox was even more dispirited and disillusioned with the events of the recent past. He declared that he expected the 'euthanasia' of the British constitution and confessed to Grey that:

> I am gone something further in hate to the English government than perhaps you and the rest of my friends are. … The triumph of the French government over the English does in fact afford me a degree of pleasure which it is very difficult to disguise. (*Memorials and Correspondence*, 3.345–50)

Grey was shocked by Fox's attitude, and partly for that reason he resisted his leader's pleas to him to go to London to settle the whigs' policy towards the new government of Henry Addington, which had succeeded that of Pitt after the latter's resignation in 1801, when the king refused to agree to concessions towards the Irish Catholics after the passing of the union. Grey now found himself moving closer to the followers of Lord Grenville, formerly Pitt's foreign secretary, who had also resigned in 1801, particularly on foreign affairs. While Fox seemed Francophile, Grey was beginning to regard France under Bonaparte as a threat to British interests. If war were resumed, it would no longer be a war supporting tyrants against the people's liberties, but a war of national and imperial survival against French conquest. When Bonaparte became emperor, he seemed no longer to be a liberator of enslaved peoples but a potential conqueror aiming at European domination. Grey supported the British resumption of war in 1803 and he remained an advocate for its prosecution until 1815, though he frequently differed from the tory governments of the period on matters of strategy. When he succeeded Fox as foreign secretary in the short-lived 'ministry of all the talents' on 24 September 1806 he immediately terminated the peace negotiations which Fox had initiated a few weeks beforehand.

At home, Grey's political career remained stagnant after 1801. Desultory negotiations for a junction with Addington came to nothing, Grey not wishing to tie himself to what might be a falling star, and in addition being hurt by his father's support of Addington, and his solicitation and acceptance of a peerage from him in 1801 without consulting or informing his eldest son. When Pitt returned to displace Addington in 1804, Grey agreed with Grenville that a coalition of all parties to prosecute the war was desirable,

but that to bring it about the king's veto on Fox must be lifted. When Pitt failed to persuade George III to do so, both Grey and Grenville refused to join the government. From this time dates the new alliance of the followers of Fox and of Grenville which formed the new whig party of 1804–17.

The new whig party Pitt's death in January 1806 opened the way for a new ministry formed by the followers of Grenville, as prime minister, Fox, and Addington (now Viscount Sidmouth), the nearest attainable combination to the union of parties proposed in 1804, and nicknamed by Canning the 'ministry of all the talents'. Grey entered the cabinet as first lord of the Admiralty (February 1806), despite his inexperience of naval affairs, in a vital post in wartime, especially in the year after Trafalgar, when British supremacy at sea presented her with opportunities to pursue the war. He carried out his duties with energy and spirit, perhaps bearing out Sir Francis Burdett's remark much later in his life that 'he should not have been a patriot [in opposition]; he should have been a Minister, that was his line' (Broughton, 3.79). Within nine months, however, Fox followed his old rival to the grave, and Grey manoeuvred himself into position as his successor as foreign secretary (September 1807), despite Fox's expressed preference for Holland. Again he devoted himself energetically to his office, but with little success. The cabinet lacked a coherent war strategy, and he failed to persuade his colleagues to concentrate on one theatre of war. The opportunity to intervene decisively on the Iberian peninsula lay in the future.

Foreign affairs soon took second place to the recurrent problem of Ireland. The Irish Catholics had been disappointed—some said betrayed—in 1801 when Pitt failed to follow the Act of Union with Catholic emancipation. Resumed Irish agitation and the needs of Irish manpower for the war effort impressed the 'talents' with the need for concessions, but George III, who had thwarted Pitt's proposals in 1801, remained resolutely opposed. The cabinet worked out a ramshackle scheme to allow Catholics to hold certain commissions in the armed services, in the hope that this would win the support of the Irish gentry and enable Catholic regiments to be raised. The details of the scheme were unclear, and when Grey and Grenville were separately interviewed by the king it became evident that the royal veto had not been lifted. The king forced the cabinet to withdraw their proposals, and demanded a pledge that they would not propose any measure of Catholic relief during his lifetime. Their refusal left them no option but to resign, on 15 March 1807.

During the 'talents' ministry, Fox secured an earldom for Grey's father, who had been given a barony by Addington in 1801 in recognition of his military services. Grey had been deeply distressed by his father's acceptance, without even consulting him, for his father's age meant that his own succession and departure from the Commons must follow within a short time. He now (April 1806) adopted the courtesy title Viscount Howick, which he used until his father died on 14 November 1807, when he inherited the earldom as second Earl Grey.

Between the collapse of the 'talents' and his father's death, there was a general election in which Howick lost his seat for Northumberland. Hitherto he had stood with the duke of Northumberland's support, but that support was withdrawn, without notice, because the duke wished his son, Lord Percy, who had just come of age, to have the seat. Howick could not afford a contest, and his father's age and health in any case made it pointless. He never forgave the duke, however, and in old age he encouraged his grandchildren to break the duke's gates and fences. After the election he was provided with a seat for Appleby by Lord Thanet, which enabled him to make a powerful attack on the change of administration on his last appearance there in June 1807.

Grey in the House of Lords 'What a place to speak in! with just light enough to make darkness visible, it was like speaking in a vault by the glimmering light of a sepulchral lamp to the dead. It is impossible I should ever do anything there worth thinking of' (Grey MSS), so Grey wrote to his wife after his first speech in the Lords on 27 January 1808. He had made his reputation as an orator in the lower house, and making a good speech was always a tonic to his often depressed spirits. In the Lords, the powerful oratory which suited a crowded House of Commons was liable to fall flat before a meagre gathering of their lordships.

It was also difficult to keep control of the party's hotheads in the Commons. A group of more radical whigs, led by Samuel Whitbread, now Grey's brother-in-law, wanted peace with Napoleon and to activate the party with a programme of parliamentary reform. However, Grenville and his followers were determined anti-reformers and advocates of war to the end with France. Grey had a lively sense of the need to keep the party together, for, besides Grenville, the former Portland whigs, including Fitzwilliam, had joined the coalition in 1804 and they shared Grenville's attitudes. Grey feared that Whitbread wanted to lead the party into alliance with the radicals, whose suspicions of Grey as a reformer had been aroused by his inaction on the subject when he was in office. For the next few years, as Grey played down the issue for the sake of party unity, his relations with the radicals outside parliament became increasingly antagonistic. His aristocratic instincts jibbed at the prospect of power being held by men like Alderman Robert Waithman, the leader of the city radicals, or Sir Francis Burdett, let alone Hunt or Cobbett. He refused to support the 'mountain', as Whitbread and his followers were called in imitation of the extremists in the French national assembly during the revolution, in attacking the duke of York, the commander-in-chief, in 1809, when he was accused of complicity in the corrupt activities of his mistress, Mary Anne Clarke, who was shown to have traded army commissions for money. Grey feared that the involvement of the royal family would endanger the monarchy and open the gates to republican agitation. He nevertheless rejected Perceval's offer to give the opposition places in the administration in 1809, being unwilling to associate with the men who had taken the places of the 'talents' in 1807 and rejected Catholic emancipation. He probably also disliked the prospect

of giving up his domestic life at Howick to return to the cares of politics.

The next few years were accordingly barren of constructive achievement for Grey. He felt the frustrations of his position, and on at least two occasions he attempted to pass on the leadership of the whig group to others. He realized that opposition must be active, remembering the blunder of the secession of 1797, but he had no stomach for the fight himself. Tierney, Whitbread, and other colleagues urged him to exert his leadership and told him that no one could take his place, but to no effect.

One exception was the Catholic question, to which Grey and Grenville felt themselves committed after the débâcle of 1807. When the Irish Catholics formed a new organization and began to agitate again he felt obliged to take up the issue, and in 1810 he presented the petition of the English Catholics, who were moderates by comparison, to the House of Lords. However, as in the case of parliamentary reform, he tried to restrain extremism and to persuade the Irish leaders to accept some reserved powers for the crown, known as 'securities' for the Anglican establishment, in particular a veto on Catholic ecclesiastical appointments. This did not satisfy the Irish and no progress was made. As in their attitude to the conduct of the war, the whigs seemed disunited and ineffectual. It was no wonder that when the prince of Wales acquired the full power of the crown as prince regent in 1811 he decided not to change his ministers and appoint his erstwhile friends in their places. In any case, he had altered his opinions, and since Fox's death he no longer felt attached to them. He went through the motions, and offered a number of places to the whigs, and again in 1812 after Perceval's assassination he consulted Grey and Grenville about ministerial arrangements, but probably more to show his consistency towards them than seriously to intend to bring them into the government. The whig leaders destroyed their own prospects by behaving high-handedly towards him and giving the impression that they expected him to hand over his powers to them entirely. The prince was also alienated by their lukewarm attitude towards the war, while he wished to pursue it to a glorious conclusion in emulation of his father. In the end, Liverpool became prime minister with a virtually unchanged administration which was to last for fifteen years, and the whigs were left in the political wilderness until 1830.

The prince's dislike was intensified by Grey's role in the affairs of the estranged Princess Caroline and her daughter, Charlotte. When the latter appealed to Grey in 1813 to advise her about her father's attempt to marry her off to the prince of Orange, Grey gave her wise and statesmanlike advice not to precipitate matters by defying him but to wait until she came of age and could make up her own mind. A year later Charlotte fled from her virtual imprisonment next door to Carlton House to her mother's residence. Grey took no part in the ensuing drama but approved of Brougham's resolution of the affair by persuading her to return to her father and not to stir up a public crisis. Grey realized that the old opposition tactic of relying upon the 'reversionary interest', cultivating the favour of the heir to the throne to counterbalance the ministers' present dependence on the monarch, was no longer appropriate, and in this he again showed his sense of realism. In any case, the death of Charlotte in child-birth on 6 November 1817 settled the question for the future. The whigs would never look to the next heir, the autocratic tory duke of York.

Grey's involvement with the affairs of the royal family concluded with the so-called 'trial' of Queen Caroline, as she became, in 1820. George IV, who had succeeded his father in January, attempted to free himself from his detested and immoral wife by a parliamentary bill of divorce which was considered by the House of Lords between August and November. Grey attended conscien-tiously the hearings of the evidence against her and her defence, declaring at the outset that 'He came to do his duty as a peer of parliament, without any earthly consid-eration to warp or bias his mind … but … with a strong desire and firm determination to do justice' (*Hansard 2*, 2, 17 Aug 1820, 620). In his final speech, summing up his ver-dict, he again disavowed any party feeling and asserted that on the grounds of both justice and expediency, and in accordance with the evidence, 'if I were to vote for this bill, I should never again lay my head down upon my pil-low in peace' (*Hansard 2* 3, 3 Nov 1820, 1574). The speech, Creevey wrote, was 'beautiful—magnificent—all honour and right feeling', and Holland told Lady Grey that it was 'the most perfect speech I ever heard in Parliament' (*Cree-vey Papers*, 1.336; Halifax MSS). The withdrawal of the pro-ceedings against the queen was forced on the government by public opinion, but Grey's speech was generally agreed to have contributed substantially to the great reduction of the government's majority which made it impossible to carry on.

George IV's dislike of Grey was confirmed, and for ten years afterwards his admission to the government was blocked by the king's specific veto. It was a sterile period in Grey's career and he was frequently despondent. He attended the Lords less often, but though he called on Lansdowne to take up the leadership of the opposition he was still unwilling to give it up altogether. The alliance with the Grenvilles had broken up in 1817 over differences on the suspension of habeas corpus to deal with radical agitation, and though this removed one barrier to the revival of a reform programme the continued presence of the aristocratic element, notably in the person of Fitzwil-liam, whose second marriage in 1823 made him Lady Grey's stepfather, prevented Grey from taking it up. In any case the fires of youth were damping down. Whitbread was dead, and though a group of younger members of the aristocratic wing, including Lambton, who became Lord Durham, Althorp, Russell, and Tavistock, all heirs to peer-ages, were anxious to regenerate the party as a liberal force, Grey remained cautious. He did not rule out reform, but he argued that the time was not ripe: he warned Lamb-ton in 1820 that it might not come 'in my life, or even dur-ing yours' (S. J. Reid, *Life and Letters of the First Earl of Durham, 1792–1840*, 2 vols., 1906, 1.131).

The party was thrown into even greater disarray in 1827,

when on the retirement of Liverpool Canning became prime minister, but was deserted by the right-wing tories in Liverpool's cabinet. To compensate for their defection, Canning offered places to several of the whigs, attempt-ing to form a government of the centre. Several of Grey's closest colleagues agreed to take part, including Holland and Lansdowne, but Grey refused to join them to serve under a man whom he considered unfitted for the post of prime minister both on account of his ignoble birth—his mother had at one time been on the stage—and because Grey distrusted his sincerity on Catholic emancipation, which he had professed to support but which he had done nothing to achieve. Nor had he forgiven Canning for his part in the destruction of the 'talents' in 1807. Grey's speech in May 1827 attacking Canning was so powerful that it was supposed by some to have hastened Canning's early death, which put an end to the prospect of a new party alignment. Canning was succeeded by the weak and short-lived administration of Goderich, and then by Wel-lington, with a return to tory government.

Nevertheless, the Catholic question would not go away. Wellington attempted to revert to Liverpool's attitude of neutrality to protect George IV from being forced to accept emancipation, but O'Connell's election for County Clare in 1829 made it essential to deal with it. Wellington and Peel saw no alternative but to concede, and the king was forced to allow them to introduce a bill. Grey gave it wholehearted support, and the whigs enabled Wellington to counterbalance the opposition of the 'ultra' tories and secure the passage of the bill—in the House of Lords Grey 'fights the whole battle for us', Lord Ellenborough wrote. Even Mrs Arbuthnot, who had no liking for Grey, whom she considered 'a strange mixture of great talent & gross vanity', praised his speech as 'a splendid oration … in a strain of the finest eloquence' (*Journal of Mrs Arbuthnot*, 2.264). However, rumours that Grey would be offered the foreign secretaryship were premature. The royal veto still operated and Wellington drew back from making the offer. He confessed to Mrs Arbuthnot that 'he was sure it w[oul]d never suit him to have Lord Grey in his Cabinet, even if the King did not object; that he is a very violent, arrogant & a very obstinate man' (ibid., 2.291).

The Great Reform Act By 1830 Grey's career seemed to be over. He was apparently marooned in opposition and he had come to regard himself as a political failure. The events of the next four years could hardly have been fore-seen. The death of George IV in June 1830 removed the royal veto on his taking office, the Paris revolution in the summer aroused enthusiasm for reform again in Britain, and the younger whigs were impatient to take up the question. In his first speech in the new parliament elected in the summer Grey set out a manifesto for reform, pro-voking Wellington to his famous assertion that not only was reform not necessary, but that a better system than the present could hardly be conceived. The duke's govern-ment was defeated on the civil list on 15 November and forced to resign. On the 16th William IV appointed Grey as prime minister, at the age of sixty-six.

Grey formed his cabinet on the aristocratic principles

on which he based his life, and with a view to the denial of 'democracy and Jacobinism. … Given an equal merit', he declared to Princess Lieven on 9 November, 'I admit that I should select the aristocrat, for that class is a guarantee for the safety of the state and of the throne' (*Letters of Dorothea*, 278–9). Nine of the thirteen members of the cabinet were members of the House of Lords, one was an Irish peer, one the heir to a peerage, and one a baronet. Only Lambton, now earl of Durham, held 'radical' views. The government included four former Canningites in the cabinet and one 'ultra' tory, the duke of Richmond, who was a relative of Holland. Grey was indeed accused of nepotism—the 'Grey list' published in the newspapers contained the names of a large number of his relatives who were given places or patronage. After a long exclusion from power there were many hungry mouths to feed, and Grey was driven to distraction by their competing claims.

The government's first task, following the severe measures taken to suppress the agricultural labourers' riots in the autumn and winter, was to produce a reform bill that would, as Grey laid down at the outset:

> stand … upon the fixed and settled institutions of the country … doing as much as is necessary to secure to the people a due influence in that great council in which they are more particularly represented … guarding and limiting it, at the same time, by a prudent care not to disturb too violently, by any extensive changes, the established principles and practice of the constitution. (*Mirror of Parliament*, 22 Nov 1830, 310–11)

He appointed a subcommittee of Duncannon, Durham, Graham, and Lord John Russell to draw up a scheme. They worked swiftly, starting on 11 December 1830 and reporting to the prime minister on 14 January, following with the drafts of three bills, for England and Wales, Scotland, and Ireland. Their aim, they declared, was 'to effect such a permanent settlement of this great and important question' as to put an end to future agitation by satisfying 'all reasonable demands' from 'the intelligent and the independent portion of the community' (Grey MSS). Grey thoroughly approved the report and secured the king's consent at a visit to Brighton on 30 January by stressing the exclusion of any proposal for a secret ballot and the need to put an end to public agitation while retaining the legitimate influence of property. It reflected very closely the programme of Grey's Friends of the People of nearly forty years ago, and formed the basis of the first Reform Bill, which Russell presented to an astonished, and on the opposition side incredulous, House of Commons on 1 March 1831.

The bill proposed the disfranchisement or partial disfranchisement of the smallest boroughs, the enfranchisement of about thirty of the largest or more important commercial and industrial towns, the institution of a uniform borough franchise—the £10 householders, the addition of a number of seats to the counties and county districts, and the addition of certain leaseholders and copyholders to the old county electorate of 40s. freeholders. The basis of the electoral franchise was still to be the occupation or possession of certain forms of property, and the electorate was to be by no means democratic, the previous total of approximately 370,000 (for England, Scotland, and Wales) being finally increased at the most by some 80 per cent (Cannon, 259). Nevertheless, the plan proved to be well judged. Any more extensive measure would probably not have been carried in view of the strength of vested and conservative interests in parliament: anything much less would not have satisfied the popular demand. As it was, the bill had to be fought through persistent opposition and initial defeat in both houses. The Commons passed the first bill by only one vote on 22 March after furious debate, the house having been elected during Wellington's premiership and still therefore predominantly disposed towards what was now the opposition. Grey's request for a dissolution to allow the election of a more favourable house was refused by the king, who wished for compromise and the modification of the more extreme features of the bill. When, however, the first opposition amendment in committee was passed by 299 to 291 votes on 20 April Grey, considering that the amendment would wreck the bill, threatened resignation if the dissolution was not granted, and the king reluctantly gave way, though he insisted that there must be some modification of the bill when it was reintroduced in the next parliament.

The general election was held during May 1831, and, as expected, the reformers swept the board in what was almost a popular referendum on a single issue. Strengthened by the popular mandate, the government introduced a second bill, which was very little different from the first, and it rapidly went through the Commons. The House of Lords would be a different proposition, for the peers were even more determined to resist dictation by the people, especially since they were aware that the king, and especially the queen and her household, were against the bill. They rejected the bill on the second reading on 8 October by forty-one votes, despite a powerful speech by Grey. The cabinet now made several alterations to the bill and reintroduced it into the Lords, but all would turn on whether Grey would be given permission to recommend the creation of a sufficient number of peers to overcome the tory resistance, a step which the king viewed with total revulsion, and one which Grey himself was most reluctant to take because it would destroy the principle of an equal balance between the two houses. Some others of the cabinet were also averse, especially when it appeared that an additional hundred or more creations might be necessary. Grey attempted negotiation with a group of moderate tory peers, known as 'the waverers', but failed to win them over, and had to face a second reading debate in the Lords on 9 April 1832 with nothing resolved. Despite one of his greatest speeches, on 14 April, the Lords passed the second reading by only nine votes, and with the committee stage to come the prospect was gloomy. On 7 May a wrecking amendment was carried by thirty-five votes, and on the following day the cabinet resolved to resign unless the king would agree to the creation of peers. William IV preferred to accept their resignations and called on Wellington to form an administration.

The crisis of reform had now arrived. While Wellington

tried to form his administration the country took a hand, and London was placarded with the injunction 'To stop the duke, go for gold!' On the 18th the *Morning Chronicle* announced 'the eve of the barricades'. The mood was orderly, but revolution was not far off. What defeated the duke, however, was Peel's refusal to join the government, as he was unwilling to repeat the volte-face he had committed over Catholic emancipation in 1829. On the 15th Wellington surrendered his commission and advised the king to recall Grey. The duke rendered a service to his king and country by then withdrawing his followers from the house to allow the Reform Bill to pass without recourse to additional peers. The royal assent was pronounced (in William's absence) on 7 June 1832.

Grey's role in the passing of the Great Reform Act, as it became known, was a crucial one. His steadfastness in face of difficulties, his refusal to compromise, which would have lost the support of the people, his strong control of a disunited cabinet—Durham would have liked a more radical measure, Melbourne, Palmerston, Grant, and Richmond a less extensive one—and above all his ability to manage the king and the court, the centre of hostility to the bill, were vital to success. The passing of the bill remains his supreme achievement.

Grey's ministry had other measures to its credit. The abolition of slavery in the British empire in June 1833 completed the work begun by the 'talents' in 1806 when Grey supported the abolition of the slave trade. With Palmerston at the Foreign Office French ambitions in the Low Countries were thwarted and Belgian independence was established without bloodshed, and eventually confirmed by international guarantee in 1839.

Ireland, however, proved the downfall of the ministry as it had in 1807. The cabinet was at sixes and sevens on the questions of Irish tithes and the appropriation of the surplus revenues of the established Irish church to secular purposes for the benefit of the Irish people, while the deeper question of the nature of the connection between the two countries and the maintenance or the repeal of the union was unresolved. Grey had been a friend of Catholic emancipation for Ireland, but he was not prepared to contemplate the dissolution of the union or to tolerate O'Connell's agrarian agitation among the peasantry, where hatred of tithes ran deep. The cabinet was not united on Irish questions, Stanley, the chief secretary, being a determined opponent of lay appropriation and an advocate of coercion to deal with popular disturbances, while Anglesey, the lord lieutenant, and several of the cabinet favoured a more liberal policy. Their disagreements so depressed Grey's spirits that his natural despondency, allied to his tiredness after the Reform Bill struggle, took over. 'I feel wearied and oppressed', he wrote, 'from the moment I get up till I go to bed, and I think it will be impossible for me to go through the work of another session' (Grey to Ellice, 3 Sept 1833, Ellice MSS). He told his wife 'I really feel so depressed and totally deprived of all energy and power, both physical and mental' (Grey MSS). The cabinet indeed was falling apart, and Grey was too dispirited to mend it. Their differences

became public when Stanley, Graham, Ripon, and Richmond resigned over Irish policy, and Lord John Russell 'upset the coach' by declaring himself opposed to the government's line on lay appropriation. Althorp, the leader of the House of Commons and Grey's staunchest lieutenant, refused to continue and resigned on 8 July 1834, and Grey sent in his own resignation with his. 'My political life is at an end', he wrote (Grey to Holland, 8 July 1834, BL, Add. MS 51548, fol. 101).

Grey's resignation speech to the House of Lords on 9 July reviewed his four-year administration and declared that his government had 'faithfully maintained' the principles on which it set out, of reform, peace, and economy. 'I leave the government', he declared:

> with the satisfaction, at least, that in having used my best endeavours to carry into effect those measures of reform that the country required, I have not shrunk from any obstacles, nor from meeting and grappling with the many difficulties that I have encountered in the performance of my duty. (*Hansard 3*, 16, 9 July 1834, 1313–15)

The speech was described as 'most powerful and affecting' (Broughton, 4.353) and was received with cheers and loud applause. 'All agree', wrote Creevey, 'that it was the most beautiful speech ever delivered by man' (*Creevey Papers*, 2.282–3).

Retirement Grey retired to Howick but he kept a close eye on the policies of the new cabinet under Melbourne, whom he, and especially his family, regarded as a mere understudy until he began to act in ways of which they disapproved. Grey became more critical as the decade went on, being particularly inclined to see the hand of O'Connell behind the scenes and blaming Melbourne for subservience to the radicals with whom he identified the Irish patriot. He made no allowances for Melbourne's need to keep the radicals on his side to preserve his shrinking majority in the Commons, and in particular he resented any slight on his own great achievement, the Reform Act, which he saw as a final solution of the question for the foreseeable future. He continually stressed its conservative nature. As he declared in his last great public speech, at the Grey Festival organized in his honour at Edinburgh in September 1834, its purpose was to strengthen and preserve the established constitution, to make it more acceptable to the people at large, and especially the middle classes, who had been the principal beneficiaries of the Reform Act, and to establish the principle that future changes would be gradual, 'according to the increased intelligence of the people, and the necessities of the times' (*Edinburgh Weekly Journal*, 17 Sept 1834). It was the speech of a conservative statesman.

Grey spent his last years in contented, if sometimes fretful, retirement at Howick, with his books, his family, and his dogs. He became physically feeble in his last years and died quietly in his bed on 17 July 1845, forty-four years to the day since going to live at Howick. He was buried in the church there on the 26th in the presence of his family, close friends, and the labourers on his estate.

Grey was an ambitious man who always wished to lead, but his overt ambition during his youth made him unpopular. He lacked the warmth of personality that made Fox revered by his followers. Grey was respected but rarely loved. His achievements were few, but they were significant. He helped to keep liberal principles alive during the years of conflict with revolutionary France, and in 1832 he safeguarded the continuity of the British constitution into an era of increasingly rapid social and political change. In character he was a man of contradictions, headstrong but easily discouraged by failure, imperious but indecisive, cautious and introspective. He was at his best when in office, for he sought fame and reputation: in opposition he often became despondent. He was a man of principle and integrity, though not always successful in execution. His bearing and attitudes were aristocratic, and his instincts were fundamentally conservative. He was a whig of the eighteenth-century school, most at home among his deferential clients, tenants, and labourers at Howick, and he never came to terms with the new industrial society which was coming into being during his later years. It is greatly to his credit that his Reform Act, whatever its conservative purpose, smoothed the path for that new society to establish its dominance without destroying the old.

E. A. SMITH

Sources E. A. Smith, *Lord Grey, 1764–1845* (1990) · G. M. Trevelyan, *Lord Grey of the Reform Bill* (1920) · C. Grey, *Some account of the life and opinions of Charles, second Earl Grey* (1861) · H. P. Brougham, *The life and times of Henry, Lord Brougham*, ed. W. Brougham, 3 vols. (1871) · *Memorials and correspondence of Charles James Fox*, ed. J. Russell, 4 vols. (1853–7) · J. A. Roebuck, *History of the whig ministry of 1830*, 2 vols. (1852) · *Correspondence of Princess Lieven and Earl Grey*, ed. and trans. G. Le Strange, 3 vols. (1890) · H. R. Vassall, Lord Holland, *Memoirs of the whig party during my time*, ed. H. E. Vassall, Lord Holland, 2 vols. (1852–4) · *The Creevey papers*, ed. H. Maxwell, 2 vols. (1903) · Lord Holland [H. R. V. Fox] and J. Allen, *The Holland House diaries, 1831–1840*, ed. A. D. Kriegel (1977) · G. Pellew, *The life and correspondence of … Henry Addington, first Viscount Sidmouth*, 3 vols. (1847) · *The journal of Mrs Arbuthnot, 1820–1832*, ed. F. Bamford and the duke of Wellington [G. Wellesley], 2 vols. (1950) · *Letters of Dorothea, Princess Lieven, during her residence in London, 1812–1834*, ed. L. G. Robinson (1902) · *The journal of Elizabeth, Lady Holland, 1791–1811*, ed. earl of Ilchester [G. S. Holland Fox-Strangways], 2 vols. (1908) · W. S. Sichel, *Sheridan*, 2 vols. (1909) · Baron Broughton [J. C. Hobhouse], *Recollections of a long life*, ed. Lady Dorchester [C. Carleton], 6 vols. (1909–11) · J. Cannon, *Parliamentary reform, 1640–1832* (1973) · U. Durham L., archives and special collections, Grey of Howick collection · Borth. Inst., Halifax MSS · NL Scot., Ellice MSS · *The Farington diary*, ed. J. Greig, 8 vols. (1922–8)
Archives U. Durham L., Grey of Howick collection, corresp. and papers; political and public corresp. and papers | Beds. & Luton ARS, letters to Samuel Whitbread · BL, corresp. with first Baron Auckland and second Baron Auckland, Add. MSS 34456–34460 · BL, corresp. with Henry Dundas, Add. MSS 38353, 38377, 38735 · BL, corresp. with James Willoughby Gordon, Add. MSS 49477–49479 · BL, corresp. with Lord Grenville, Add. MSS 58946–58949 · BL, corresp. with Lord Holland and Lady Holland, Add. MSS 51557 · BL, letters to W. Huskisson, Add. MSS 38735–38736 · BL, corresp. with Prince Lieven and Princess Lieven, Add. MSS 47295, 47360–47365 · BL, corresp. with Lord Ripon, Add. MSS 40862–40863 · BL, letters to second Earl Spencer · BL, corresp. with Lord Wellesley, Add. MSS 37295–37312 · BL, corresp. with Sir Robert Wilson, Add. MSS 30108–30110, 30118–30124 · BL, corresp. with W. Windham, Add. MS 37847 · Bodl. Oxf., letters to Sir Francis Burdett · Borth. Inst., letters to daughter, Lady Georgiana Grey · Bucks. RLSS, corresp. with Sir Thomas Fremantle · Cumbria AS, Carlisle, corresp. with Sir Robert Wilson · Glamorgan RO, Cardiff, corresp. with Lord Lyndhurst · Glos. RO, Freeman-Mitford papers · Hants. RO, corresp. with George Tierney · Harrowby Manuscript Trust, Sandon Hall, Staffordshire, letters to Lord Harrowby · Hunt. L., letters to Grenville family · Lambton estate office, Lambton Park, Chester-le-Street, co. Durham, Lambton papers · Lpool RO, letters to Lord Stanley · N. Yorks. CRO, corresp. with Christopher Wyvill · NA Scot., letters to Sir John Dalrymple · NL Scot., corresp. with Sir Alexander Cochrane, MSS 2570–2572 · NL Scot., corresp. with Edward Ellice · Northumbd RO, Newcastle upon Tyne, letters to Thomas Creevey · Northumbd RO, Newcastle upon Tyne, letters to Lord Ridley · NRA, priv. coll., corresp. with Charles Grey and first earl of Durham · NRA, priv. coll., letters to duke of Hamilton · NRA, priv. coll., corresp. with Spencer Perceval · NRA, priv. coll., letters to Sir H. M. Wellwood · NRA, priv. coll., corresp. with Lord Rosebery · PRO, letters to Lord Granville, PRO 30/29 · PRO NIre., corresp. with first marquess of Anglesey · Royal Arch., letters to George III · Sheff. Arch., corresp. with Lord Fitzwilliam · Sheff. Arch., corresp. with Lord Grenville · Staffs. RO, letters to first Baron Hatherton · Staffs. RO, corresp. with Princess Lieven and duke of Sutherland · TCD, letters to R. S. Carew · U. Durham L., corresp. with Viscount Ponsonby · U. Southampton L., corresp. with Lord Palmerston · W. Sussex RO, letters to duke of Richmond
Likenesses G. Romney, oils, 1784, Eton · J. Sayers, etching, pubd 1789 (after his earlier work), NPG · H. Bone, miniature, 1794 (after T. Lawrence), Audley End House, Essex · J. Nollekens, bust, 1803, Woburn Abbey, Bedfordshire · T. Phillips, oils, 1810, Althorp House, Northamptonshire · T. Hodgetts, mezzotint, pubd 1817 (after J. Northcote), NPG · G. Hayter, group portrait, oils, 1820 (*The trial of Queen Caroline, 1820*), NPG · attrib. T. Phillips, oils, *c*.1820, NPG · J. Jackson, oils, *c*.1826, V&A · oils, *c*.1826 (after T. Lawrence), NPG · T. Campbell, marble bust, 1827, Palace of Westminster, London · B. R. Haydon, oils, *c*.1828, Laing Art Gallery, Newcastle upon Tyne · T. Lawrence, portrait, 1828, priv. coll. [*see illus.*] · F. Chantrey, pencil, *c*.1830, NPG · J. Knight, group portrait, lithograph, *c*.1832 (*William IV holding a council*), BM · S. W. Reynolds, group portrait, oils, 1832 (*The Reform Bill receiving the king's assent*; after drawing by J. Doyle), Palace of Westminster, London · G. Hayter, group portrait, oils, 1833 (*The House of Commons, 1833*), NPG · W. Ward, mezzotint, pubd 1833 (after J. Jackson), BM, NPG · B. R. Haydon, pencil study, 1834 (for his *Reform Banquet, 1832*), NPG · B. R. Haydon, three pencil studies, 1834 (for his *Reform Banquet, 1832*), Laing Art Gallery, Newcastle upon Tyne · F. Bromley, group portrait, etching, pubd 1835 (after group portrait by B. R. Haydon), NPG · J. Ramsay, oils, *c*.1837, Literary and Philosophical Society, Newcastle upon Tyne · D. Wilkie, group portrait, oils, 1837 (*The first council of Queen Victoria*), Royal Collection · E. H. Baily, statue, 1838, Grey Street, Newcastle upon Tyne · C. Moore, bust, 1853, Eton · I. Bruce, aquatint (after unknown silhouettist), BM, NPG · J. Doyle, caricatures, BM · J. Doyle, drawing, Palace of Westminster, London · J. Doyle, sketches, BM · H. Furniss, pen and ink, NPG · bronze bust, Wellington Museum, London · pencil and watercolour drawing, NPG

Grey, Charles (1804–1870), army officer and courtier, second surviving son of Charles *Grey, second Earl Grey (1764–1845), and his wife, Mary Elizabeth Ponsonby (1776–1861), was born at Howick Hall, Northumberland, on 15 March 1804. He was educated at home under the supervision of his father, and entered the army in 1820 as second lieutenant in the rifle brigade, and rose rapidly by purchasing unattached steps and exchanging. He became brevet colonel in 1846, major-general in 1854, lieutenant-general in 1861, and general in 1865, and was colonel of the 3rd Buffs from 1860 to 1863, and thereafter of the 71st light infantry. On 26 July 1836 he married Caroline Eliza (*c*.1814–1890), daughter of Sir Thomas Farquhar, bt, and

Charles Grey (1804–1870), by Sir Francis Grant, 1868

Sources *The letters of Queen Victoria*, ed. A. C. Benson, Lord Esher [R. B. Brett], and G. E. Buckle, 9 vols. (1907–32), 1st–2nd ser. · A. Ponsonby, *Henry Ponsonby, Queen Victoria's private secretary: his life from his letters* (1942) · *Your dear letter: private correspondence of Queen Victoria and the crown princess of Prussia, 1865–1871*, ed. R. Fulford (1971) · S. Weintraub, *Victoria: biography of a queen* (1987) · Gladstone, *Diaries* · Boase, *Mod. Eng. biog.* · Burke, *Peerage* · GEC, *Peerage*

Archives NA Canada, Canadian diaries · NL Scot., family corresp. · U. Durham L., corresp.; journals; papers | Balliol Oxf., corresp. with Sir Robert Morier · BL, corresp. with Sir A. H. Layard, Add. MSS 38992–38997, 39116–39120, *passim* · BL, corresp. with Charles Wood, Add. MSS 49553, *passim* · Bodl. Oxf., letters to fourth earl of Clarendon · Bodl. Oxf., letters to Disraeli · Borth. Inst., corresp. with Lord Halifax · ICL, letters to Lyon Playfair · Lambton estate office, Lambton park, Chester-le-Street, co. Durham, letters to second Earl Grey · Lpool RO, letters to fourteenth earl of Derby · NA Scot., letters to Fox Maule · NL Scot., corresp. with Edward Ellice · NL Wales, letters to Sir George Cornewall Lewis · PRO, corresp. with Lord Carnarvon, PRO 30/6 · PRO, letters to Lord Granville, PRO 30/29 · PRO, corresp. with Lord John Russell, PRO 30/22 · PRO NIre., corresp. and papers; notes from Queen Victoria · Suffolk RO, Ipswich, letters to Lord Cranbrook · U. Durham L., corresp. with second Earl Grey · U. Durham L., corresp. with third Earl Grey · U. Southampton L., corresp. with W. F. Cowper · U. Southampton L., corresp. with Lord Palmerston · W. Sussex RO, letters to duke of Richmond

Likenesses F. Grant, portrait, 1868, priv. coll. [*see illus.*] · J. E. Boehm, bust, exh. RA 1871, Royal Collection · J. Bacon, lithograph (after G. Thomas), BM, NPG · G. H. Thomas, sketch, repro. in S. Erskine, ed., *Twenty years at court* (1916) · stipple, NPG · woodengraving (after photograph), NPG; repro. in *ILN* (23 April 1870)

Wealth at death under £5000: probate, 16 May 1870, *CGPLA Eng. & Wales*

Sybella Martha Rockliffe. They had four daughters and two sons.

Grey was whig MP for High Wycombe from 1831 to 1837, retiring on the queen's accession, after which he was in almost constant attendance at court. He was an equerry to the queen from 1837 to 1867, and private secretary to Prince Albert from 1849 to 1861. After Albert's death he became private secretary to Victoria (although he did not officially acquire that title until 1867), and served in this capacity until his death. He was joint keeper of the privy purse with Sir Thomas Biddulph in 1866–7. The queen relied heavily on Grey in the years following the prince consort's death, and it seems likely that her refusal to allow him to retire contributed to his ill health and collapse in 1870. Grey was not uncritical of the queen, particularly with regard to her long seclusion, and her use of 'ill health' to evade public responsibilities. He described her to Gladstone as 'the royal malingerer' (Weintraub, 354), and regarded her excesses of grief as self-indulgence. He was, none the less, dedicated to his career, and was respected by the politicians with whom he dealt. Increasingly hampered by deafness, he sought retirement in 1869; he died, after a series of paralytic convulsions, at St James's Palace, London, on 31 March 1870.

Grey published a biography of his father in 1861, and compiled, under the direction of the queen, *The Early Years of the Prince Consort* in 1867. His widow, who survived him until 4 November 1890, was appointed extra woman of the bedchamber, and his third daughter, Louisa, countess of Antrim, served as lady in waiting. His eldest surviving son, Albert Henry George *Grey, succeeded his uncle as fourth Earl Grey.   K. D. REYNOLDS

Grey, Sir Charles Edward (1785–1865), judge in India and colonial governor, was the second son of Ralph William Grey (1745/6–1812), barrister, of Backworth House, Earsdon, Northumberland, and his wife, Elizabeth, daughter of Charles Brandling MP of Gosforth House, Northumberland. His father, descended from a merchant family of Newcastle, was high sheriff of Northumberland in 1792.

Grey matriculated at University College, Oxford, in 1802 and graduated BA in 1806, the year he was admitted to Lincoln's Inn. In 1808 he won the Oxford English prize essay with his composition 'Hereditary rank' and was elected a fellow of Oriel College. He was called to the bar in 1811, and in 1817 was appointed a commissioner in bankruptcy. In 1820 he was appointed a judge of the supreme court of Madras. He was knighted on 17 May 1820 and in April 1821, before his departure, married Elizabeth (1800/01–1850), second daughter of Revd Sir Samuel Clarke Jervoise, bt, of Idsworth Park, Hampshire. Grey's elder brother Ralph William (1779/80–1822) had earlier married Elizabeth's sister, Anne.

The newly-weds arrived in Madras in September 1821, and in 1825 Grey was made chief justice of Calcutta. It was a controversial appointment as both of the puisne judges at Calcutta, Sir Francis Macnaghten and Sir Anthony Buller, were senior to Grey; Macnaghten ostentatiously resigned his judgeship shortly after Grey's arrival and Buller retired in 1827. Grey fared better, however, with their replacements, Sir John Franks and Sir Edward Ryan, and the governor-general, Lord William Bentinck, made a point of commending him for his helpfulness, especially in drafting proposals for the framing of a legislative council for India. He was governed, Bentinck recorded, 'by the most impartial and liberal spirit, and by an anxious desire to give every support to the government' (Bentinck to R. Fullarton, 30 Nov 1828, *Correspondence of … Bentinck*, 1.107). Grey described himself as 'a bit by bit reformer', who, by virtue of his legal training, inclined to cautious gradualism (Grey to Bentinck, 23 April 1832, ibid., 2.802–3), although, in his more fanciful moments, he envisaged transplanting both English law and a form of English aristocracy to India. He served for a time as president of the Asiatic Society of Bengal (although he revealed no talents for oriental studies), and with his wife, an accomplished musician, shone at the heart of Calcutta's expatriate society. In 1829 they showered hospitality on the young French botanist Victor Jacquemont, who delighted in their company. Grey's 'subtle wit', he observed, belied his 'most austere' appearance, but it was the 'beautiful, gracious and amiable' Lady Grey who inspired Jacquemont's deepest affection (*Letters from India*, 41, 11, 48).

The Greys left India in 1832. In 1835 Grey was made a privy counsellor and was sent to Montreal as one of the three commissioners for investigating the causes of discontent in Lower Canada, his colleagues being Lord Gosford and Sir George Gipps. The commission was not a success—rebellions in both Upper and Lower Canada followed in 1837—but it had the effect of confirming that Britain both expected and required her North American colonies to develop stable means of self-government. Grey left Canada in November 1836, and on his return to England was made a GCH. In 1837 he unsuccessfully contested Tynemouth. He gained the seat in February 1838 when his opponent, Sir G. F. Young, was unseated on petition, and from then until the summer of 1841 he steadily supported the whig administration of Lord Melbourne.

Grey had let it be known, however, that parliamentary life was not to his liking, and in August 1841 he was appointed governor of Barbados and the Windward Islands, covering St Lucia, St Vincent, Tobago, and Trinidad. With his forbidding air of reserve he was not a crowd-pleaser, but he was a competent and impartial administrator, keen to find a way of incorporating the freed slaves into an ordered society and critical of the home government's apparent desire to wash its hands of the social and economic problems of its Caribbean colonies. As the free trade movement gathered strength in Britain, he tried to ready planters for worldwide competition by encouraging spending on road building, port improvements, and the mechanization of sugar production.

In 1846 Grey was promoted to the governorship of Jamaica, which was in a worse state than any of the Windwards had been. He arrived on 22 December to find the local house of assembly in an uproar over the successive blows that the plantation economy had suffered from the loss of slave labour and the ending of the colonial sugar preference. Uncomfortably associated in both name and politics with the abolitionist and free-trading whig 'cousinhood' who were now in power in Britain (Henry George,

third Earl Grey, was colonial secretary), Grey had a rocky welcome, and struggled throughout his tenure to convince the planters that he had the best interests of the island at heart. Believing protection would never be restored, he attempted to promote the immigration of free labour from Africa, and repeatedly badgered the Colonial Office for assistance. The economic crisis of autumn 1847 in Britain worsened conditions, with many planters unable to get credit, and when the home government finally agreed to fund the importation of liberated Africans, Grey scrabbled to find even the small sums needed for their initial subsistence costs. In October 1850 a devastating cholera epidemic further shook the island. As Jamaicans died in their thousands, back in London, on 15 November, Grey's wife succumbed also to illness. In spite of the thanklessness of his task, however, Grey remained in office for over six years, and, under the circumstances, it was a testimony to his sense of duty and his tact that he suffered no greater unpopularity than he did. He finally left Jamaica in 1853, although he retained an estate at Blue Mountain, which he was to leave to his eldest son, Jervoise.

Grey retired to England and settled first in Hyde Park, London, and subsequently in Tunbridge Wells, Kent. He died at Tunbridge Wells on 1 June 1865. He was survived by four sons and four daughters.   KATHERINE PRIOR

Sources *GM*, 3rd ser., 19 (1865), 123 · *GM*, 2nd ser., 36 (1851), 103 · Foster, *Alum. Oxon.* · Venn, *Alum. Cant.* · M. E. Thomas, *Jamaica and voluntary laborers from Africa, 1840–1865* (1974) · W. P. Baildon, ed., *The records of the Honorable Society of Lincoln's Inn: admissions*, 2 (1896), 24 · W. P. Baildon, ed., *The records of the Honorable Society of Lincoln's Inn: the black books*, 4 (1902), 245 · G. C. Richards and C. L. Shadwell, *The provosts and fellows of Oriel College, Oxford* (1922) · *The Times* (3 June 1865), 1 · *The Times* (19 Aug 1865), 10 · E. Cotton, *Memories of the supreme court at Fort William in Bengal, 1774–1862* (1925) · *The correspondence of Lord William Cavendish Bentinck, governor-general of India, 1828–1835*, ed. C. H. Philips, 2 vols. (1977) · C. Levy, *Emancipation, sugar, and federalism: Barbados and the West Indies, 1833–1876* (1980) · R. Welford, *Men of mark 'twixt Tyne and Tweed*, 3 vols. (1895) · *Letters from India: being a selection from the correspondence of Victor Jacquemont*, ed. and trans. C. A. Phillips (1936) · W. A. Shaw, *The knights of England*, 2 vols. (1906), vol. 1, p. 453; vol. 2, p. 321

Archives Bodl. Oxf., corresp. and papers | U. Durham L., corresp. with third Earl Grey, GRE/B96/2A–B · U. Nott. L., corresp. with Lord William Bentinck, PWJF 1090–1119

Wealth at death under £3000: probate, 9 Aug 1865, *CGPLA Eng. & Wales* · landed estate in Jamaica, at Blue Mountain

Grey, Charles Grey (1875–1953), aviation writer, was born at 4 Sussex Place, Regent's Park, London, on 13 November 1875, the third son of Charles Grey Grey, of Dilston Hall, Northumberland, a surveyor and land agent who was receiver of the estates of the Royal Naval Hospital, Greenwich, in the north of England, and his second wife, Eliza Lyon. He was a grandson of John *Grey (1785–1868) and a nephew of Josephine *Butler. While his father served as a member of the Irish land commission, Charles Grey attended the Erasmus Smith School in Dublin. He then studied at London's Crystal Palace School of Engineering before joining the Swift Cycle Company in Coventry as a draughtsman at 30s. a week. He married, on 12 June 1899,

Charles Grey Grey (1875–1953), by Elliott & Fry

Beatrice Lilla (b. 1870/71), the daughter of Richard Thorneloe, a watchmaker, of Coventry.

By 1905 Grey had switched to journalism and joined the *Cycle & Motor Trades Review*, but he soon moved on to another of E. M. Iliffe's papers, *The Autocar*. He was 'pitchforked into aviation' (his phrase: Winstanley, 49) by a chance assignment to cover the first Paris aero show in December 1908. The following spring, as a result of his enthusiastic report, Iliffe called upon him to co-edit a new penny weekly aviation paper named *The Aero*. In June 1911, backed by Victor Sassoon, he began his own journal, *The Aeroplane*, from premises thoughtfully located in Piccadilly and only minutes away from the Royal Aero Club. He was thus able to meet and entertain a great number of aviation personalities and obtain news at first hand.

Like *Flight*, its earlier established rival, *The Aeroplane* grew rapidly during the First World War as military aviation expanded at a tremendous rate, and Grey was tireless in using it as a platform from which to agitate to advance aviation—frequently also bombarding readers with his political and social opinions. C. G. G., or C. G., as he became widely known, campaigned ceaselessly for better equipment for the British air services and for the advancement of private enterprise, continually expressed contempt for the 'two dimensional' thinking of officialdom, and vigorously opposed Lloyd George and Winston

Churchill. Although he was an original thinker, knowledgeable, and a skilled writer with a caustic wit, Grey at times allowed his judgement to become clouded, in particular by a bitter and unjustified vendetta against the government-run Royal Aircraft Factory research establishment at Farnborough; his dislike of bureaucracy and belief that the free competition of private manufacturers would lead to better aircraft caused him to underrate the achievements of the engineers and scientists at Farnborough. At such times he frequently ignored the facts, and he unjustly ridiculed many who held views differing from his own.

A steadfast friend of Lord Trenchard, first commander-in-chief of the RAF, Grey was in the forefront, in the post-war years when resources were scarce, among those who argued vehemently that the air force should remain independent of the army and navy (*The Aeroplane* at one time was even banned from Royal Navy wardrooms). Firmly against 'imbecile' policies and 'bumbledom' in every form, throughout the lean interwar years he took every opportunity through his editorials to advance the cause of a British aviation industry then struggling for its very existence. His energy carried *The Aeroplane* through the depression years and enabled it to expand once more during the more prosperous 1930s. His zest for aviation also saw him engage in an enormous worldwide correspondence, often working at a dictaphone long into the night. His first marriage, meanwhile, was dissolved, and in 1929 he married Margaret Sumner, the daughter of John Sumner Marriner, a solicitor; they had a son and a daughter.

Grey was well-connected and numbered among his friends the air ministers Sir Samuel Hoare and Lord Londonderry. Unfortunately he was also susceptible to flattery. This became especially apparent after visits to Italy and Germany in the 1930s, when his editorials in *The Aeroplane* gradually acquired a Fascist flavour. Arthur Tedder later commented that Grey's almost fanatical hatred of bureaucratic red tape led him to take a sympathetic view of dictatorships, though Grey was himself something of a rebel. With the approach of war Grey's opinions made him increasingly unpopular, and he was looked upon by some as a crank. He ceased editing *The Aeroplane* in June 1939, five years after disposing of his interest in the journal to Temple Press. Afterwards he served as the air correspondent for several provincial papers and a number of overseas publications, and during the Second World War he published some eight books. He had written two others in 1909 and 1916, and for twenty-five years from March 1916, following the death of Fred Jane, he edited Jane's annual directory *All the World's Aircraft*.

C. G. was far and away the most remarkable, controversial, and oft-quoted aviation writer of his day. He was completely convinced of aviation's importance and its great future, and his colourful writings, though often unfair or inaccurate, were never dull. Readers either loved or hated him, but they were never bored: 'he boasted that for some twenty years he never missed a leader on "Matters of Moment" in which he commented pungently on all aspects of aeronautical affairs' (*DNB*). Forceful and opinionated, he contributed much to the spirited and lively debate throughout the critical and formative years of practical aviation. Although he came close to ruining his reputation before the Second World War, 'he regained all his old popularity among the aviation fraternity during the last mellow years before his death' (ibid.), when he again contributed occasional articles to his old journal. *The Aeroplane* ceased publication in October 1968 and was incorporated into *Flight*.

Belying his critical, often perverse and acerbic writings, the tall, monocled Grey himself was accepted by those who knew him as gentle and kindly, always charming and generous to his friends, among whom he numbered competitors. It was not unknown for young tyros from rival papers to receive friendly words of advice or encouragement from him. He died suddenly on 9 December 1953 in a manner which would have amused him greatly—in the arms of an air marshal in a cloakroom at the Admiralty, where he was attending a press reception. Following a private funeral on 14 December, a memorial service was held at Christ Church, Down Street, London, on 13 January 1954, when a moving tribute was paid to him by marshal of the RAF, Lord Tedder.   ERROL W. MARTYN

Sources *Flight* (18 Dec 1953), 803 · *DNB* · F. H. Winstanley, 'Those magnificent mags [pt 1]', *Aeroplane Monthly*, 11 (1983), 48–51 · R. Hare, *The Royal Aircraft Factory* (1990) · J. M. Bruce, *The aeroplanes of the royal flying corps (military wing)* (1982) · H. Penrose, *British aviation: the Great War and armistice, 1915–1919* (1969) · R. Griffiths, *Fellow travellers of the right: British enthusiasts for Nazi Germany, 1933–9*, pbk edn (1983) · *The aeroplane directory of British aviation, incorporating who's who in British aviation* (1952) · b. cert. · m. cert. [Beatrice Thorneloe] · *Flight* (25 Dec 1953), 829 · *Flight* (22 Jan 1954), 86
Archives Royal Aeronautical Society, London, MSS
Likenesses F. Eastman, oils, 1957, Royal Aero Club; on loan to Royal Air Force Museum, Hendon · Elliott & Fry, photograph, NPG [see illus.] · photograph, repro. in *Flight*
Wealth at death £5507 9s. 1d.: probate, 18 March 1954, *CGPLA Eng. & Wales*

Grey, Clifford [*real name* Percival Davis] (**1887–1941**), lyricist and bobsleigher, was born on 5 January 1887 at 106 St Luke's Road, Edgbaston, Birmingham, the only child of George Davis, a whip manufacturer, and his wife, Emma Lowe. In 1899 Davis entered the Camp Hill Boys' School, one of the King Edward VI schools in Birmingham, where he won a Latin and English prize in 1902 and acquired a taste for theatrics. He left in 1903, later writing,

> I fluttered from job to job until a little influence secured me a very minor clerkship in the local water department … I managed to confuse two telephone calls and dispatched a gang of men with tools, horse and cart to repair a leaky tap in somebody's kitchen; I sent a lone turncock, armed with nothing but a spanner, to cope with a burst main that was flooding a public square.

By 1907, Davis had taken to calling himself Clifford Grey, initially as a stage name in his career as a concert-party performer with the Adeler and Sutton Pierrots. He never legally changed his name, and there is no logical source for this assumed name, although he once listed his father as George Davis Grey. By 6 December 1912, when he

married Dorothy Maud Mary Gould (1890/91–1940), a fellow Pierrot, Grey had given up performing and was contributing to West End musicals. Grey and Gould had two daughters; Grey also adopted Gould's daughter.

Although during a thirty-year career Grey wrote in many forms, it was in the musical theatre—particularly alongside such fellow transatlantics as P. G. Wodehouse, Guy Bolton, and Fred Thompson—where he became indispensable as an adapter and collaborator, indeed, as a kind of 'score doctor', if such a category had existed. Versed in virtually all the era's styles, particularly gifted at writing material specific to a performer, Grey also helped create the first wave of film musicals. Grey was eventually credited with many dozens of librettos and screenplays and more than 3000 lyrics, although his critics—including Wodehouse—sometimes derided him as a plodder who changed others' work slightly and claimed credit. (The record shows that the equally prolific Wodehouse, running short of plot ideas, once purchased a story from Grey.) Yet two of Grey's lyrics became national treasures, and the first of these was 'If you were the only girl in the world' (music by Nat Ayer), from *The Bing Boys are Here* (1916). This song captured the wistful longings of on-leave servicemen and their loves and became a favourite during the First World War. By 1919, after having adapted a flawed American show (music by Ivan Caryll, book by Bolton and Wodehouse) into the successful *Kissing Time*, as well as writing book and lyrics for the farcical *Who's Hooper?* (music by Ivor Novello), Grey was the most in-demand writer in musical London.

An earlier collaborator, the composer Jerome Kern, called Grey to New York to help with the looming hit *Sally*, and from 1920 to 1932 Grey was usually based in the United States, although he returned to England for such projects as George Gershwin's first West End revue, *The Rainbow* (1923). On Broadway, Grey wrote or adapted several plays for the non-musical theatre as well as collaborating with such light-opera-minded composers as Rudolf Friml and Sigmund Romberg. He worked often with the jazz-age darling Vincent Youmans, most notably on *Hit the Deck* (1927), including an oddly martial spiritual, 'Hallelujah!'

During these New York years, Grey made many theatrical and sporting friends. Much later, the secret life of this quiet, retiring, and serious-looking man, so supposedly sedentary and shy behind his horn-rimmed glasses, was revealed. With considerable skill, Grey had invented an American persona, Tippi Gray, and it was under this name that he joined three bobsleighing friends and won gold medals in both the 1928 and the 1932 winter Olympic games.

After the advent of sound in film, Grey wrote screenplays and/or lyrics for fourteen Hollywood films between 1929 and 1931. His lyric (for Ernst Lubitsch's 1929 film *The Love Parade*), to Victor Schertzinger's 'Nobody's using it now', sung by Maurice Chevalier, was the talkies' first musical soliloquy. In 1929 Grey was back in London, collaborating with his erstwhile concert-party friend Greatrex Newman on book and lyrics for *Mr Cinders* (music by

Vivian Ellis and Richard Myers). This reverse Cinderella tale included Grey's second classic and most enduring lyric, 'Spread a little happiness'. The song's poignant blitheness carried it through a worldwide depression and another world war; in 1982 it was recorded by Sting as part of the sound-track for the film *Brimstone and Treacle*.

After 1932 Grey worked exclusively in England, writing theatrical lyrics to the music of Oscar Levant, Johnny Green, and others; one song, 'Got a date with an angel' (music by Jack Waller), became a dance-band hit. His first British screenplay, *Rome Express* (1932), a highly atmospheric spy story set on a train, was extremely popular in its day and virtually created a sub-genre. Grey eventually turned out more than twenty screenplays for British films, usually for the day's top comics but also including *Mimi* (1935) an adaptation of *La Bohème* for Gertrude Lawrence and Douglas Fairbanks jr.

In the later thirties Grey's health began to decline, and in March 1940 his wife died of cancer. Grey became involved in the Entertainments National Service Association, and was in Ipswich with a concert party entertaining the troops when the town was bombed. Two days later, on 25 September 1941, he died at 32 Berners Street, Ipswich, of a heart attack and the complications of asthma.

JAMES ROSS MOORE

Sources K. Gänzl, *The British musical theatre*, 2 vols. (1986) · K. Gänzl, *The encyclopedia of the musical theatre*, 2 vols. (1994) · *WWW* · *The Times* (27 Sept 1941) · *New York Times* (27 Sept 1941) · *Birmingham Post* (27 Sept 1941) · *The Stage* (2 Oct 1941) · *Daily Telegraph* (27 Sept 1941) · M. Steyn, 'He spread a little happiness', 23 July 1985, BBC Radio 2 · T. Clark, 'When winning a gold medal was a lark', *Yankee Magazine* (Feb 1980) · P. Mitchell, 'Brum's golden Olympian', *Birmingham's Sunday Mercury* (26 July 1985) · admission register, pupil address lists, school lists, 1899–1903, Camp Hill Boys' School · b. cert. · m. cert. · d. cert. · private information (2004) [V. Wyman, B. Hutchins, T. Clark, B. Mallon, K. Birrell, C. Springer, J. Thornycroft, D. Wallechinsky, I. Buchanan, M. Kreuger] · American Society of Composers, Authors and Publishers, *The ASCAP biographical dictionary*, 4th edn (1980) · letters from Olympic bobsledders to Bill Mallon, priv. coll. · US Olympic documents, United States Olympic Committee Olympian Survey, Report of the American Olympic Committee St Moritz 1928, The Encyclopedia of American Olympians, United States Olympic Committee Event Results, United States Olympic Committee, Colorado Springs, Colorado

Likenesses photograph, priv. coll.

Wealth at death £2015 14s. 5d.: administration, with will, 9 July 1942, CGPLA Eng. & Wales

Grey, Edmund, first earl of Kent (1416–1490), administrator and magnate, was the son and heir of Sir John *Grey (d. 1439) [see under Grey family (per. 1325–1523)] and Constance, daughter of John Holland, duke of Exeter, and widow of Thomas Mowbray, second earl of Nottingham (d. 1405); he was the grandson of Reynold *Grey, third Baron Grey of Ruthin. Born on 26 October 1416, he succeeded his grandfather in the Ruthin barony on 30 September 1440, his father having died the previous year. The family's main residence in England was Wrest, near Silsoe (Bedfordshire) and in 1452 Grey was drawn into the dispute over the nearby manor of Ampthill, then in the possession of Ralph, Lord Cromwell. When Henry Holland, duke of Exeter, seized Ampthill in that year Grey backed Cromwell, although Exeter was his first cousin. The dispute became so violent that the three men were imprisoned briefly by the king, Grey being sent to Pevensey. Cromwell was able to regain the estate in 1454 when Exeter was imprisoned during the protectorate of Richard, duke of York, and sold the reversion to Grey for 6500 marks. The last instalment was not paid until October 1473 (when Grey sold the manor of Great Braxted to Sir Thomas Montgomery to raise the last 1000 marks) but the Greys were in effective possession of the property from at least the mid-1460s and probably from Cromwell's death in 1455, and made it one of their main residences.

Between 1456 and 1458 Grey was a regular attender at the royal council, and on 16 July 1457 was one of a group of royal associates given powers to resist gatherings of men that might threaten the king or his government. Fears for the security of his possession of Ampthill may explain Grey's decision to desert to the Yorkists when he led the Lancastrian vanguard at the battle of Northampton on 10 July 1460, a decision that gave the Yorkists the victory. On 21 March 1461 Grey had a protection from Edward IV for two years to go abroad, presumably on pilgrimage, but he may first have fought for the Yorkists at Towton on 29 March, where his younger brother, Thomas, Lord Richemount-Grey, fought on the Lancastrian side and, although he escaped from the battle, was executed soon afterwards. On 24 June 1463 Grey was made treasurer of England, but was succeeded by Walter Blount in November 1464. He was made earl of Kent on 30 May 1465, shortly after the marriage of his eldest son, Anthony, to the king's sister-in-law, Joan Woodville, and later in the same year was granted the offices of chief justice of Merioneth and constable of Harlech, with authority to receive the rebels there to grace.

Grey played little further role in national affairs, perhaps as a result of advancing years, although he seems to have remained a shrewd administrator of his own estates. He married, before January 1459, Catherine, daughter of Henry *Percy, earl of Northumberland, and his wife, Eleanor Neville. They had four sons (Anthony, George, John, and Edmund) and two daughters (Elizabeth and Anne). All four sons, along with their parents, were members of the confraternity of the Holy Spirit at Luton. Grey died on 22 May 1490. His eldest son, Anthony, who had been knighted in 1465, died childless in late May or early June 1480, and his heir was Anthony's brother George *Grey, a servant of both Richard III and Henry VII, who succeeded his father as earl of Kent and died in 1503.

ROSEMARY HORROX

Sources *Chancery records* · *GEC, Peerage* · R. I. Jack, ed., *The Grey of Ruthin valor: the valor of the English lands of Edmund Grey, earl of Kent, … from the ministers' accounts of 1467–1468*, Bedfordshire Historical RS, 46 (1965) · S. J. Payling, 'The Ampthill dispute: a study in aristocratic lawlessness and the breakdown of Lancastrian government', *EngHR*, 104 (1989), 881–907 · R. A. Griffiths, *The reign of King Henry VI: the exercise of royal authority, 1422–1461* (1981) · R. Horrox and P. W. Hammond, eds., *British Library Harleian manuscript 433*, 4 vols. (1979–83) · G. W. Bernard, 'The fortunes of the Greys, earls of Kent, in the early sixteenth century', *HJ*, 25 (1982), 671–85

Archives Beds. & Luton ARS, Lucas MSS

Likenesses manuscript illumination, *c*.1440 (with his wife), NL Scot., Advocates' Library, MS 18.1.7, fol. 12*d*
Wealth at death approx. £1400: Bernard, 'Fortunes', 671

Grey, Edward, Viscount Grey of Fallodon (1862–1933), politician, countryman, and author, was born in London on 25 April 1862, the eldest of the seven children, four sons and three daughters, of Colonel George Henry Grey (1835–1874) and his wife, Harriet Jane (1839–1905), youngest daughter of Lieutenant-Colonel Charles Pearson.

A family inheritance Grey came from a north-eastern English political and naval/military dynasty. His great-grandfather was the younger brother of Charles, second Earl Grey, prime minister from 1830 to 1834. Their ennobled father had been a general with an illustrious career. Grey's grandfather was Sir George *Grey, second baronet (1799–1882), who served as home secretary on three occasions. Grey's father served in the rifle brigade in the Crimea and the Indian mutiny. He then became an equerry to the prince of Wales, with the injunction that his responsibilities should extend beyond the amusement of the prince. When not required by his royal master, however, he spent most of his time on the home farm at Fallodon, on the Northumberland coastal belt, which house and estate Sir George Grey had inherited. Grey's mother came from a family with a mixed clerical, professional, and minor gentry background settled in counties bordering on Wales. It had no national pretensions or political ambitions. She laid no claim to intellectual distinction or particular artistic refinement, and was much occupied with childbearing in a marriage which lasted only fourteen years. In December 1874, when in attendance on the prince of Wales, Colonel Grey suddenly died. At the age of twelve, therefore, Grey faced life without a father.

It was at this point, however, that Grey's grandfather, retired from politics and living at Fallodon, exercised a strong guiding influence. Sir George's parents had adopted evangelical convictions, which he himself also shared. His grandfather had married Anna Sophia, daughter of Henry Ryder, an evangelical bishop of Lichfield and Coventry, and herself later an active village Sunday school teacher. The household at Fallodon therefore combined evangelical seriousness, national political experience, pride in the management of a modest estate (some 2000 acres), and pleasure in country living. Sir George's politics may be described as moderate whig in a county in which the great landowners were tory. In his latter years he referred sceptically to the 'so called Liberal Party' and doubted whether it any longer possessed a sufficient common basis. Untroubled in his Morpeth constituency by the appearance of an opponent, he considered public service a matter of duty and best not complicated by disputatious elections.

School and university A notion of duty was therefore instilled in Grey both at home and at school. Before his father died he had been sent away to preparatory school, firstly near Northallerton (1871–3) and then, more significantly, at Temple Grove (1873–6), a great mansion near East Sheen. Much store was placed there upon regular

Edward Grey, Viscount Grey of Fallodon (1862–1933), by H. Walter Barnett

marking and 'placing' of pupils. Grey thrived, reaching the top class with apparent ease. His skill at cricket and football was also evident, and he left in 1876 as head of the school. Yet he later wondered whether this apparent success derived not from any intrinsic interest in the subjects he studied but simply from a desire to excel in competition. He was then sent to Winchester College (1876–80), admitted in the highest class of scholars, and initially he moved rapidly up the divisions. Then, apparently under a sense of injustice that on one occasion he had been kept back from a merited promotion, the competitive instinct wilted. It was supposed by contemporaries that Grey could excel at whatever he had a mind to. For the moment, however, it was less the conventional academic or other aspects of formal schooling that appealed to him than the solitary pleasures to be derived from dry-fly fishing on the nearby River Itchen. The supposition, therefore, that he was the ablest boy in the school rested on no solid record of achievement. It was a reputation, however, which he carried with him to Balliol College, Oxford, in 1880.

Benjamin Jowett had been master for a decade and had to some extent converted Balliol into the model institution of which he had dreamed. About fifty young men were admitted each year from the great public schools and some grammar schools of England. The college's influence was spreading across the world—Siamese and Japanese students matriculated—as it converted itself from being part of the clerical establishment to part of a new professional one. There is no evidence, however, that Grey relished enrolment in the school for statesmen. He read classics in an undistinguished way and passed moderations in 1881 with second-class honours. In vacations spent at Fallodon, however, he received additional tuition from the local vicar, Mandell Creighton, subsequently Dixie professor of ecclesiastical history at Cambridge and bishop in succession of Peterborough and London. When Sir George died in 1882, Creighton to some extent took over the management of the twenty-year-old Sir Edward, though it was apparent that the undergraduate was not academically ambitious. It also seemed that he resisted Jowett's attempts to make him understand the responsibilities which his name carried. Indeed, Grey did so with such success that it seemed certain that his final classical examinations, to be taken in 1884, would be a disaster. The law school, identified by Grey as an easier option, failed to stimulate. He was sent down from Balliol for idleness and ignorance, though allowed to return in the summer of 1884 to be examined. He graduated with a third-class degree in jurisprudence. Studying the ducks at Fallodon, interspersed with desultory reading of history, biography, and poetry, was more congenial than Oxford. It could not be said that Grey had displayed either that serious-minded diligence or, alternatively, that effortless superiority which allegedly characterized Balliol men of his era.

Political initiation Nevertheless, public life did call. Through Lord Northbrook, a cousin of his late father, Grey became private secretary to Sir Evelyn Baring (July 1884) and afterwards (October 1884) to the then chancellor of the exchequer, H. C. E. Childers. While living and working in London he believed himself to have acquired business habits and to be developing ideas on politics, social problems, and moral philosophy. Back in Northumberland, Creighton remained his mentor and urged him to read political economy. There was the prospect that he might be adopted, as proved to be the case, as Liberal candidate for Northumberland (Berwick upon Tweed). His opponent would be Earl Percy, scion of the ducal house of Northumberland. There were rumours, too, that the young man was 'radical' on the land question. Certainly, he expressed anger that local men who had the resources to buy land were prevented from doing so by the owners of large estates, though he declined to support compulsory sale. His radicalism did not extend, however, to 'drivelling on', as he put it, about disestablishment or the Sunday opening of museums. In the event, under the new franchise the young baronet successfully contested the seat. 'Like all the Greys', he was a Liberal, though the precise meaning of that allegiance was immediately to be tested.

Grey had halted his election campaign for a fortnight in the middle of October 1885 in order to marry. His bride was (Frances) Dorothy Widdrington, eldest daughter of Shalcross FitzHerbert Widdrington of Newton Hall, Newton on the Moor, whom he married on 20 October. Creighton knew both families, but it was in London rather than Northumberland that courtship had proceeded. Even so, there was no doubt that Dorothy, who was twenty-one, pined for the Northumberland countryside and found

London horrid. There was some family suspicion that Edward had married too young and could have 'done better'.

The year 1886 was not the easiest political year for the youngest member of the House of Commons to find his feet. The question of home rule for Ireland strained Liberal loyalties. Young Grey could not but admire Gladstone, yet friends and patrons told him that the adoption of home rule was hasty and ill-judged. Creighton wrote from Cambridge concerned that the coming democracy, as he called it, was turning parliament into a large vestry. The democracy had to understand that 'England' was in difficulties in every part of the empire and isolated in Europe. Reforming the House of Lords would not save the Indian empire. Grey saw the point but stayed loyal to Gladstone, unlike approximately one-third of those Liberal MPs who had been elected in 1885. Grey came to the conclusion, probably swayed by articles written by John Morley, that it was not possible to govern Ireland permanently by a system of coercion. In speeches and correspondence he declined to support coercive measures in Ireland unless coupled with large concessions in the nature of home rule. It was a stance which brought him a reduced majority in 1886 when he fought a Liberal Unionist opponent in the general election. He continued in this vein over subsequent years during the period of Conservative government. His maiden speech, not made until February 1887, condemned what he termed the bankruptcy of the government's Irish policy. At the same time, however, he realized that if the Liberals were thought of simply as the party of home rule they might forfeit the possibility of regaining office.

The Liberals scarcely presented a picture of unity in the years of opposition from 1886 to 1892. The figure of Gladstone still hovered on high, both inspiration and irritant. Young Grey could not aspire to the innermost councils of the party. It was difficult, in these circumstances, to know how seriously to take politics. Sir William Harcourt, for example, complained that Grey could speak on behalf of the party in the Commons but would not do so. Grey, loosely associated at this time with H. H. Asquith and Richard Haldane, thought Harcourt impossible to deal with. He found Lord Rosebery a much more attractive figure, and became increasingly interested in imperial issues. Yet he was not obsessed by politics, and ruminated on the options before him. The appeal of the countryside and the 'simple life' was at times overwhelming. It was apparent that his wife hated public affairs. The couple had purchased a cottage of their own on the Itchen in Hampshire, and the weekends they spent there could be distinctly protracted. Railways, committees, and parliaments seemed to them somewhat trivial when compared with the deep elemental forces that shaped human destiny and with the pleasure to be derived from contemplating the ducks on the ponds at Fallodon.

It was easy, therefore, for some contemporaries and subsequent writers to conclude that Grey had no political ambition. Certainly, while he knew that he was not conventionally clever, he believed he saw certain things clearly. Though still to some extent doubting whether he could be really effective in public life, he came during these opposition years to an increasing 'consciousness of power' which he had never felt before. That maturing judgement and increasing self-confidence led him in the late 1880s and early 1890s to seek more speaking engagements on his party's behalf. At the meeting of the National Liberal Federation in Newcastle in October 1891 it was Grey who moved the motion on Ireland. The Liberal Party, he declared, would pass a measure which would fully satisfy the just demands of Ireland and leave the imperial parliament free to attend to reform in Great Britain. Elsewhere, however, he spoke on English land issues, and took the view that the wage-earners of the country were entitled to first attention. When he retained his seat in the 1892 general election, which returned a Liberal majority, the thirty-year-old Grey had come to the end of his political initiation.

Junior office Having finally persuaded Lord Rosebery to become foreign secretary in his new administration, Gladstone turned to Grey to represent the Foreign Office in the Commons as parliamentary under-secretary (August 1892). There was no very obvious reason why he should have done so. Grey had displayed no conspicuous interest in foreign affairs and was emphatically not a traveller. On his own admission, he would have to learn and apply himself quickly. It was not his task to make policy but rather to be his master's voice in the Commons. It was not an easy responsibility. Rosebery was not given to consultation, as his cabinet colleagues soon realized. Grey had to speak with authority in circumstances in which it was apparent that, in imperial matters at least, prime minister and foreign secretary disagreed. The extent to which Britain should become involved in Uganda was a case in point. Grey showed skill in coping with these disagreements and generally impressed parliamentarians. He stood out not merely because he was clean-shaven, but because he spoke firmly and calmly. From the opposition benches he appeared to Arthur Balfour as the most striking figure among the younger men in the government. There was talk in 1893 that he might be made the next viceroy of India. Rosebery resisted the notion on the grounds that such an appointment would sidetrack Grey away from the great future he had in the Commons. He had qualifications, it was supposed, which might fit him one day for promotion to the secretaryship of state (although he had the handicap of being a commoner).

Some supposed that when Rosebery became prime minister in March 1894 Grey might have received accelerated promotion to the cabinet, but that was always unlikely. Serving under Lord Kimberley as foreign secretary, Grey was now more confident and experienced. He liked the Foreign Office, and the quarrels among his senior colleagues in the cabinet over foreign policy gave him a certain scope for expressing his own views. African issues predominated and Grey was drawn into making various contentious statements. The fate of the upper Nile became the centre of attention. In March 1895 he made in parliament what became known as the 'Grey declaration'.

The British and Egyptian spheres of influence, he asserted, together covered the whole of the Nile waterway. The advance of a French expedition from the other side of Africa into the area would therefore constitute 'an unfriendly act'. It was a statement which caused a furore in diplomatic circles, the cabinet, and the Commons. Liberal critics deprecated the 'menacing tone' adopted. Grey denied that he had spoken hysterically or inappropriately. He had not envisaged war, but a strong statement of British interests had been necessary to clear the air. Rosebery refused to countenance Grey's resignation. The furore subsided and, in the event, a couple of months later, the Rosebery government came to an end and Grey was out of office.

Even though Grey's official duties may explain his relatively poor performance in the national real tennis amateur championship—he was runner-up rather than champion between 1892 and 1894—there seems little doubt that he found them engrossing. Contemporaries noted that if he stayed in politics he would be sure to make his mark. But that was the point. Among London society it was common knowledge that Dorothy was miserable in the capital. Lady Monkswell, for example, noted after a dinner at which they had both been present that Dorothy looked as displeased as anyone she knew. To her husband, Dorothy was even more frank. She fulminated against town life and the general devilishness which prevailed there. To her brother-in-law she complained that the people with whom she had to associate were all horrid and there was no health in them. Such sentiments did not provide a comforting background for an aspiring politician, even though they also struck a chord with Grey himself: the public expectations of future eminence contrasted strongly with private doubt. Hence, junior office might turn out to have been the height of his career. He told Rosebery that he wished his public position to be as little emphasized as possible so that he could leave it when an honourable opportunity came.

Ambivalent expectations Nevertheless, Grey fought the 1895 election vigorously and, against the tide which returned a Conservative government, increased his own majority. He conceded privately that this success made it more difficult to get free from politics, though he still claimed that this was his objective. Although in office he had concentrated on foreign affairs, he had nevertheless also spoken on some domestic issues. He advocated reform rather than abolition of the House of Lords. He still favoured home rule for Ireland, though it should not dominate the Liberal agenda. The potential significance of the formation in 1893 of the Independent Labour Party had not escaped him. Social and labour issues had been neglected by the party. There was a need for broad measures of social reform, although he was not very explicit about what they should be. The leadership arrangements of the Liberals in opposition seemed to confirm that there was little agreement about political direction. Rosebery still led the party, but listlessly. His wish to jettison Mr Gladstone's 'general policy' since 1880 naturally offended

Gladstonians. Grey, however, continued to support Rosebery and the 'concentration' which he enigmatically advocated.

Insofar as Grey had an identified role in a fractious party, it was inevitably in relation to foreign affairs. His experience had not led him to formulate detailed opinions on all aspects of world politics. It had been in relation to their conflicting aspirations in Africa, and to some extent Asia, that he had considered the policies of the European powers. Europe, which he did not know at first hand, presented a disheartening spectacle of rivalry, but he did not seek alignment with one side or the other in the alliance systems of the period. There was almost an element of absurdity in the way in which France and Germany claimed large slices of Africa almost on the ground that if they did not some other country would. In such a context, Grey saw no alternative to British participation in the game. He shared Rosebery's perspective that it might be necessary to advance merely to secure existing territory.

Such a perspective had immediate relevance. Grey found the abortive invasion of the Transvaal by Dr Jameson in 1895–6 a reckless affair, but he was no admirer of the Afrikaner government of Paul Kruger. Two of his cousins who took part were wounded. His own brother George had taken part in fighting in Matabeleland in 1893 and was to do so again in 1896. Grey recognized that the work of colonization and subjection had to go forward, though he saw that it could not altogether be done without some compromise of principle. Cecil Rhodes, he realized, was not exactly a liberal. After meeting him, Grey suggested that Rhodes adhered to a new version of 'one man, one vote' in South Africa: Rhodes should have a vote but nobody else should. His observations on imperial matters put him firmly in Rosebery's camp, but when the latter resigned the party leadership in 1896 Grey was disconsolate.

It was in these circumstances that Grey accepted an invitation from Joseph Chamberlain to join a royal commission inquiring into social and economic problems in the British West Indies, particularly in relation to sugar. Some scented the possibility that Grey might consent to a tampering with free-trade principles. Morley was one who felt it would be a mistake for a 'youngster' with Grey's prospects to entangle himself. Nevertheless, accompanied by Dorothy, he spent some investigative months in the Caribbean in the first half of 1897. On his return he found the Liberal Party still in disarray. He bided his time. Given his earlier comments on the upper Nile, his observations on the 1897–8 crisis carried weight. He did not dissent from the robust attitude taken by the Salisbury government. His imperialism caused dismay in some Liberal circles, but there was a widespread belief that he was the 'young hope' of the party. However, when Harcourt resigned as Liberal leader in the Commons Grey suggested that Asquith was the obvious successor. In the event, the leadership went to Campbell-Bannerman. Immersed as he was in writing a book on fly-fishing, Grey was content to sit on the bank and wait patiently. He had a directorship of the North Eastern Railway to occupy other hours and provide

a salary. Dorothy continued to hate London. The expectation was that they would live quietly away from the capital and avoid the smell of its streets festering in the sun.

Second South African War   War broke out in South Africa in October 1899. It did not come as a surprise to Grey. When in the West Indies in 1897, he had written to the newly appointed high commissioner, Sir Alfred Milner, suggesting that at some stage the use of force could not be avoided. Grey had discussed South Africa with Milner in 1898 when he was on leave in England and was in regular correspondence with him in the months leading to the final crisis. When war came, Grey admitted its necessity but counselled against jingoism. Kruger, he believed, had never intended negotiations with Britain to lead to any real redress or reform. It soon became apparent that the Liberal Party was deeply split on the issue. In stating in the Commons that the Boers had committed an aggression which it was the plain duty of the government to resist, Grey went further than many colleagues. Campbell-Bannerman struggled to keep a united party, but it divided three ways: 'pro-Boers' spoke against the war; Campbell-Bannerman and his faithful entourage reluctantly supported it, but in doing so criticized the conduct of British diplomacy; 'imperialists' supported the war without serious reservation. For Grey, there was no halfway house. Either the war was necessary (as he believed), or it was not. If the former, it should be supported. If the latter, it should be denounced. He associated with Asquith and Haldane in making leadership at this time virtually impossible for Campbell-Bannerman. There was still the possibility that Rosebery might be tempted to resume his career.

In the event Sir Henry did not resign, but the government capitalized on Liberal disarray and apparent success in the war to call a general election in 1900. Grey campaigned nationally more prominently than ever before but sensed that his party was disintegrating. The government was confirmed in office. The war in the Liberal Party continued, as indeed did the war itself in South Africa, where talk of victory proved premature. Rosebery remained in the background. Grey, in association with Asquith and Haldane, adhered to his early position. However, the actual conduct of the war now complicated matters. Campbell-Bannerman famously denounced 'methods of barbarism' and the pro-Boers became more critical. Grey conceded that conditions in the camps in South Africa required improvement but it was not right to speak of 'barbarism'. In their private correspondence each wing of the party thought that it was time for the others to be more restrained. In Grey's view, Sir Henry was a good old fellow but real leadership was needed and a policy to go with it.

It was at this point that Rosebery re-entered the public scene, though he still left his acolytes speculating about his real intentions. Grey wrote despairingly of the faint hope that the genius of Rosebery might redeem a party which was past redemption. As time passed, however, it became apparent that Rosebery was a reluctant redeemer.

Grey was increasingly frustrated. He had more energetically 'politicked' than ever before—his wife spoke of him in consequence as being raspingly difficult to manage—but to no avail. The Liberal League, of which he was a vice-president, did not make the progress he expected. When the Second South African War ended in May 1902, old men and old policies were still entrenched. The divisions opened up by the war were still apparent and would not easily disappear, since they were deep-seated and not simply occasioned by the war itself.

Liberal revival In May 1902 there seemed little reason to suppose that in December 1905 Sir Edward Grey would be foreign secretary. Some acerbity was disappearing from Liberal politics but there appeared no firm prospect of office. In any case, Grey continued to wonder whether he could wait for it indefinitely. In December 1904, when offered the chairmanship of the North Eastern Railway Company, he accepted, though he knew that it would make a hole in his time. However, he had done nearly two decades of political work, mostly opposition. He was not prepared to spend the next twenty years doing the same sort of thing. The railway was useful and definite work. Moreover, the salary was quite handsome. It would no longer be necessary to let Fallodon during the summer months. Only an invitation to join the cabinet would deflect him.

Initially, such a prospect seemed unlikely. Grey, Haldane, and Asquith constantly expressed their dissatisfaction to each other and wondered when their time would come. The Liberal Party, they believed, could not do without them. Grey travelled regularly up and down his railway and dined in London. He fell into discussion on occasion with his London neighbours the Webbs. Beatrice reluctantly found him a man of exquisite flavour: high-minded, simple, kindly, and wise. He would do well in a cabinet driven by a mastermind. It seemed to her that Grey had no original ideas—beyond foreign and colonial policy. She had no idea what that might mean. Others who thought that it might indeed be possible to have expertise in this sphere invited Grey to address their dining clubs. There was little suggestion, however, that he was formally foreign secretary in waiting.

It is generally agreed that it was division in the government ranks which provided the possibility of Liberal revival. Until mid-1903, when Joseph Chamberlain launched his campaign for the abandonment of free trade and resigned from the government six months later, Liberal revival had been hard to detect. Grey had dutifully criticized Balfour's 1902 Education Act, but he was not a nonconformist and did not believe that the issue was of sufficient general interest to improve Liberal chances. In 1903 Grey suspected that within a year or two the Conservative government would flicker out, but it would be replaced by a Chamberlain ministry. He could see no prospect of the Liberals coming in before 1910. He had a certain admiration for Chamberlain, though he remained in the free-trade camp. Defence of free trade brought some semblance of unity back to the Liberals, although leadership issues still troubled them. Grey, Haldane, and Asquith plotted somewhat ineffectually. Grey asserted that he would not take office under Campbell-Bannerman in any government in which Sir Henry continued as leader in the House of Commons.

More generally, Grey's experience broadened. Although vulnerable to the charge that he was a country gentleman, his railway role had brought him an increasing awareness of labour developments. He thought it idle to talk of smashing trade unions. It was better to deal with organized rather than unorganized labour. In 1903 he publicly took the election of Will Crooks as MP for Woolwich as a sign that the wage-earning classes were gaining in power and strength and in political purpose. That was exactly what should happen. On another important matter, Grey recognized that the issue of Irish home rule remained an incubus. It would be wrong to take office if a Liberal government depended for its survival upon Irish support, and the English electorate should not be allowed to think that it would. He had come to the conclusion that it would be a mistake to try to solve the Irish question by one big Gladstonian step. Ireland should get much more local self-government, though by degrees. He was determined that a new Liberal government should not come to grief again on this rock.

As the Balfour government tottered and then resigned in late 1905 so Liberal jockeying for position intensified. Pistols were pointed at Campbell-Bannerman's head but, in the event, were not fired. Asquith revealed that he would accept the chancellorship of the exchequer even if Sir Henry remained in the Commons as prime minister. He did, however, strongly urge upon Sir Henry that Grey was the only man for the Foreign Office. Campbell-Bannerman took his time and initially looked elsewhere. He did not take kindly to Grey's suggestion that he should go to the Lords. He was well aware of the fact that Grey had spent a large part of the previous six years trying to unseat him. After further manoeuvring on both sides, however, the offer of the Foreign Office was made, and Grey accepted on 7 December 1905.

Foreign secretary under Campbell-Bannerman Grey's appointment was exceptional in certain respects. At forty-three he was unusually young. He lacked completely that first-hand knowledge of European capitals and politicians which at least some of his predecessors had possessed. His appointment also broke decisively with the normal convention that the foreign secretary sat in the House of Lords, insulated from the tiresome necessity to fight elections and be of service to a constituency. That made him more 'democratic'. It also meant, however, that he was directly open to criticism from Liberal MPs already apprehensive about his imperialism. He seemed frequently abroad to epitomize the virtues and values embodied in the notion of an English gentleman. What he lacked in knowledge he more than compensated for by soundness of judgement. He did not flap. Although some personnel in the Foreign Office and the diplomatic service had necessarily changed, Grey knew sufficient of official ways to take his place with confidence. He was not arrogant, but he had cultivated a certain obstinacy when he thought he was right. He was very conscious both of the central importance of his office and that he was assuming it at a critical juncture in world affairs. Notions of Britain's capacity to remain detached or 'isolated' were under urgent review, and Grey could not escape them.

The immediately preceding years had seen substantial changes in British foreign policy. In 1902 the Anglo-Japanese alliance had been concluded, providing for British neutrality in the event of a war between Japan and one other power (Russia?) or for British belligerency if Japan went to war with two hostile powers (Russia and France?). At the time Grey had spoken warmly in the Commons of Japan becoming Britain's 'partner'. In relation to other ideas that were floating around, Grey considered Chamberlain's notion of a triple alliance between Britain, the United States, and Germany as an absurdity. German public opinion was strongly anti-British. In private letters in 1903 and 1904 he expressed the view that Germany was Britain's worst enemy and greatest danger, notwithstanding the fact that a minority of Germans were well disposed towards Britain. He wanted Britain to have closer relations with France and Russia. It is not surprising, therefore, that he welcomed Lansdowne's conclusion of an entente with France in April 1904. Frankness and friendliness with France were essential. Writing in August 1905 he expressed his disagreement with Rosebery and argued against any policy which might drag Britain back into the German net, as he put it. At the same time, he did not rule out the possibility of improving relations with Germany and would brave the 'Jingo press' if that seemed feasible.

The main lines of Grey's approach were therefore already apparent. Moreover, he had publicly emphasized the need for continuity and the desirability of assuring other countries that Britain's agreements were not at the mercy of a fickle democracy. Neither statement altogether commended Grey to those of his colleagues who wished to see a more distinctively Liberal foreign policy and one more conspicuously responsive to parliamentary pressure. A good many such MPs were to be found in the Commons in the aftermath of the sweeping Liberal victory in the January 1906 general election.

Grey was faced with an immediate crisis. The Anglo-French entente was being put to the test by Berlin with regard to Morocco. Grey assured the French ambassador that if Germany attacked France because of Morocco, British public opinion might be such as to compel the British government to go to war. Nevertheless, he could not offer a pledge which would be operative regardless of circumstances. He did, however, permit the continuance of 'military conversations' between French and British soldiers which his predecessor had authorized. They were, however, not supposed to be binding. It was a decision agreed to by the prime minister but not communicated to the full cabinet. This reticence was afterwards taken as a sign of Grey's secrecy, if not his duplicity. Yet Grey himself did not want either a formal military or political commitment. In fact, in these very early weeks, Grey was already embarking on a course which may be held to

have lasted substantially until 1914 itself. It was essential that France should be sustained, but not in such a manner that Paris took liberties. There had always to be an element of doubt about what Britain might or might not do. Yet that doubt should not be so great as to lead French opinion to feel that that there was no option other than to make the best terms possible with Germany. Likewise, Berlin should not be made to feel that Britain's relationship with France was so intimate as to preclude the possibility of an understanding. The Moroccan crisis had in the event been resolved by diplomacy, but that might not always be possible. If it was necessary to check Germany that could be done by an entente between Russia, France, and Britain—France and Russia were allies.

An Anglo-Russian convention was indeed signed in August 1907, but not without opposition in Britain. It went against the grain for some Liberals that their government should conclude a treaty with a government which had suppressed the parliamentary Duma in Russia. In the Lords, Curzon denounced a treaty which was nothing less than an act of imperial abdication. He was referring particularly to the division of spheres of influence in Persia. Grey himself claimed that a frequent source of friction and possible cause of war had been removed. His critics suggested that he too readily accepted Russian assurances. Taken as a whole, however, the Russian agreement was a further recognition that in the twentieth century the British empire was not in a position to take on simultaneously all powers that might be thought to challenge its pre-eminence. Some feared Germany more, some feared Russia more. Either way, Grey supposed that in his first years of office he had steered a course which retained for Britain freedom of decision while removing a prospect of total isolation.

Towards 1914 During Grey's tenure of the Foreign Office the possibility of European war was never entirely absent. He saw no fundamental reason, however, to shift from the basic presuppositions and arrangements that have been outlined. The crises which were seemingly endemic in the international system had all thus far proved capable of resolution by diplomacy—until 1914 itself. Failure in the summer of 1914, with all the catastrophic consequences that ensued, naturally meant that Grey's conduct of British foreign policy would be subjected to detailed and continuing scrutiny both immediately and thereafter. Grey would have preferred a general publication of British documents immediately after the war, even one supervised by an 'impartial tribunal'. He took the innovative step—aided by J. A. Spender—of publishing his own account of his years in handling foreign policy, *Twenty-Five Years, 1892–1916* (1925). The failure of 1914, for so he regarded it, sometimes kept him awake in after years. He wondered whether he could and should have acted differently. So have both his contemporaries and subsequent historians, as the massive documentation of the pre-1914 European crisis is explored from every angle.

Opponents of British entry into the war, both then and later, fastened on various facets of Grey's diplomacy both in the immediate crisis and over the antecedent years. He had been too secretive in the conduct of affairs and did not respond adequately to the need for a foreign policy which was in some sense democratic. If he had done so, public opinion would have exercised a meaningful and moderating role. It was further argued that his continued adherence to 'secret diplomacy' of a traditional kind also entailed the endorsement of the 'balance of power' and the ultimately disastrous entanglement in alliances and alignments which had certainly not prevented war and could possibly have made it inevitable. Grey still claimed that he had freedom of choice, but in reality he had forfeited it by his own actions. In the summer of 1914 he admitted as much by referring to 'obligations of honour' which Britain had towards France. Throughout the previous half a dozen years, when he had obdurately claimed that Britain had no commitments, he was either deceiving himself or deliberately deceiving colleagues and the country.

Grey himself denied any deception and found a ready champion in 1914 in Gilbert Murray, the Oxford classical scholar. He had stayed close to the path he had charted in January 1906. It had not been without risk, but neither total aloofness from the politics of Europe nor full participation (in terms of binding and explicit alliances) was either desirable or politically possible given the assumptions that prevailed in Britain at the time. The fact that in 1911 another major crisis over Morocco had been ended by diplomacy gave grounds for supposing that the overall diplomatic strategy was sound. Germany looked for ample compensation elsewhere in Africa in exchange for giving up a claim to interest in Morocco. It was deemed excessive in London, and it was Lloyd George rather than Grey himself who stated publicly that Britain would not look on indifferently. It was believed that firmness had played its part in bringing about the eventual settlement. Such brinkmanship, however, disturbed a good number of Liberal back-benchers and some cabinet colleagues. Grey found himself subjected to more criticism than he had ever endured before, and for a time had nominally to be more informative about his actions. The suspicion engendered by the events of 1911, however, never completely died away. Although Grey's old friend Haldane went on a mission to Germany in 1912, with his agreement, to seek a naval agreement it proved a failure. Some suggested that he should have tried harder and been more sympathetic to German aspirations. Grey, on the other hand, thought that he had gone far enough.

As to the actual pattern of events after the assassination of the Austrian Archduke Franz Ferdinand at Sarajevo on 28 June 1914, its complexity defies any simple summary. The British cabinet was divided, a fact that added to the foreign secretary's difficulties. It has sometimes been argued that if only Grey had warned Germany of the point at which Britain would declare war the issue would have been very different—but it was on that very point that there was no consensus. His performance overall in July has been variously assessed. Churchill wrote that he watched Grey's cool skill with admiration, but Lloyd George, at least in his memoirs, was sharply critical. Grey seems initially to have supposed, as had happened before, that the powers would 'recoil from the abyss'. On 27 July he proposed an international conference—an initiative which not only displays his general commitment to diplomacy but which was also in line with the course he had successfully employed in previous years to resolve Balkan disputes. This time, however, by 29 July, it was clear that the proposal had come to nothing.

The possibility of German violation of Belgian neutrality changed the picture, though it did not bring cabinet unanimity: resignation letters were drafted, though only a couple were sent in the event. It was becoming clear by 2 August that what was in prospect was no longer simply another 'Balkan quarrel' but a war in which France might be crushed. On 3 August Grey spoke in the Commons, one of the most important speeches ever made by a British foreign secretary. He repeated that Britain still had freedom to decide and was not committed by treaty, and, as has already been noted, referred to 'obligations of honour and interest' which were at stake and which would compel Britain to take a stand. He claimed that the government would be supported by the determination, the resolution, the courage, and the endurance of the whole country in doing so. The speech convinced many waverers in his own party and produced near unity in the country. An ultimatum was sent to Berlin, though it was not supposed that Germany would, in fact, abandon plans to overrun the whole of Belgium. There was no answer. Britain had abandoned peaceful neutrality and was about to go to war, the dimensions of which few grasped: except, perhaps, puzzlingly, Grey himself. He looked out of his office window in the evening, after helping draft the ultimatum, and saw the lamplighter turning up the gas lamps in the courtyard below. He remarked, according to an (unidentified) friend, 'The lamps are going out all over Europe; we shall not see them lit again in our life-time' (Grey, 2.20). It was his only memorable saying, widely quoted and anthologized subsequently, though it was indeed perfect for the occasion. The puzzle, as has been noted (N. Davies, *Europe: a History*, 1996, 879), is that, according to Grey's own account, it was the sight of lamps being lit which led to a metaphor about lamps being extinguished!

Foreign secretary at war Grey was not of a military disposition. Indeed, it is arguable that before 1914 he had taken too narrowly a 'political' conception of his office. He had indeed taken part in rumbustious cabinet debates about naval building and had been briefed on military strategy, yet he had never become excited by such matters or ardently sought to integrate defence considerations into foreign policy. He rather self-consciously distanced himself from the implications of the military conversations with France which he had authorized—on the supposition that the more involved he himself became the more difficult it would be to maintain noncommitment.

So it was when war actually started. Before 1914, speaking generally, Grey had operated as though 'foreign policy' held the upper hand. After 1914 he was perhaps too ready to concede that the Foreign Office took second place behind the War Office. It was events on the battlefield or at sea which determined the course of war. Diplomacy had little space in which to operate independently. Such an outlook was a reflection of the foreign secretary's own state of mind. He had known much personal tragedy. Dorothy, his first wife, had died in an accident in February 1906. His brother George had been mauled to death by a lion in Africa. He had no children. He was having increasing difficulty with his eyes. Later, in 1917, Fallodon was substantially destroyed in a fire. Alongside these and other personal losses came the engulfing tragedy of war. It was not that he was a pacifist in an absolutist sense or had doubt about the necessity of victory. It was rather, as colleagues noted, that he seemed to lose confidence in his capacity to make a major contribution. The dynamism that drove a Churchill or a Lloyd George was missing. On the other hand, his sober realism was not without longer-term benefit. He was, for example, anxious to maintain good relations with the (neutral) United States at a time when some were prepared to jeopardize them by pushing the British interpretation of the 'freedom of the seas' to its limit. He was less successful in his Balkan diplomacy. In short, he was now out of place, though it was still politically expedient that he should remain in office. Asquith arranged that in July 1916 he should be raised to the peerage as Viscount Grey of Fallodon, but he had no place in the Lloyd George coalition, and in December 1916 he resigned.

Elder statesman Although Grey was only fifty-four at this juncture, overwork, increasing blindness, and personal disappointments combined to make him seem prematurely aged. He could now return, however, without political impediment, to the realm of nature from which he had allowed himself to be excluded, though he could no longer see it as clearly as he had hoped. It was time to try to restore some balance to his life. His yearning for Dorothy remained strong, though it seems that their love had lacked physical expression. He began a correspondence with Pamela Genevieve Adelaide Tennant, Lady Glenconner (d. 1928). Daughter of Percy Scawen Wyndham, of Clouds, near Salisbury, and sister of George Wyndham, she was the widow of Edward Priaulx Tennant, first Baron Glenconner, who died in 1920. The couple shared a love of poetry and birds, and were married on 4 June 1922. In 1923 Grey unsuccessfully tried to pilot a bill through the House of Lords to give for the first time a proper legal framework for bird sanctuaries. Pamela not only encouraged *Twenty-Five Years* but also *The Charm of Birds* (1927), a volume into which he poured his lifelong knowledge and enjoyment. It sold widely, as did *Fallodon Papers* (1926). In the same year as Pamela died, Grey's brother Charles was killed by a buffalo in Africa. The weight of his afflictions told, though he contrived a certain serenity which impressed visitors. On 7 September 1933 he died at Fallodon, where his ashes were deposited, and the peerage became extinct. Fallodon was inherited by Captain Cecil Graves, son of his eldest sister. Public honours had naturally come his way. He was a fellow of Winchester College. He had been appointed KG in 1912 and was elected FRS in 1914. In 1928 he was elected chancellor of Oxford University.

It is tempting to see an absolute discontinuity between Grey's life after 1916 and the pattern of the three previous decades. Certainly, he had now more time for introspection, personal reflection, and country life. Yet it would be a mistake to suppose that his involvement in politics at the highest level simply slipped away without trace. He did agree to visit Washington as a special ambassador in September 1919 in what proved an abortive attempt to persuade President Wilson to compromise with the senate so as to bring the United States into the League of Nations. Before the end of the war he came to believe that a League of Nations would establish a new and better framework for the conduct of international relations. He wrote a pamphlet on the subject (*The League of Nations*, 1918) and actively involved himself, as president, in the affairs of the League of Nations Union from November 1918 onwards. At a time of optimism, his role in shaping opinion in favour of the league was substantial. There were those, too, who wanted him to resume an active role in mainstream politics—he was Liberal leader in the House of Lords during 1923–4. Some urged that he might be the leader of a centre party which could emerge from the Liberal quarrels and attract some Conservatives. Grey did not altogether discount the possibility, but blindness and health argued against.

Grey stood in a somewhat detached position as an elder statesman in these latter years. Indeed, surveying his entire career, he had oscillated between detachment and involvement, being never entirely happy with either mode. For decades after his death political historians were faintly distressed by Grey's lifelong interest in birds and fishes. A really great politician should have better things to do, they supposed. Nature lovers, on the other hand, could not really believe that Grey had enjoyed wasting so much time with dispatch boxes. Both sides believed that they understood the 'real' Grey. However, a different perspective is now possible. Both sides of his nature should be given due weight. Grey unusually saw a need both to devote his life to 'worldly' politics and to the understanding of the 'real' natural world. It is this intriguing ambivalence which keeps him in certain but also awkward eminence among the major British statesmen of his age.

KEITH ROBBINS

Sources K. Robbins, *Sir Edward Grey: a biography of Lord Grey of Fallodon* (1971) · G. M. Trevelyan, *Grey of Fallodon* (1937) · J. Karpinski, *Capital of happiness: Lord Grey of Fallodon and the charm of birds* (1984) · H. S. Gordon, *Edward Grey of Fallodon and his birds* (1937) · G. Murray, *The foreign policy of Sir Edward Grey, 1906–1915* (1915) · Z. S. Steiner, *The foreign office and foreign policy, 1898–1914* (1969) · K. M. Wilson, *Empire and continent: studies in British foreign policy from the 1880s to the First World War* (1987) · K. Wilson, ed., *Decision for war, 1914* (1995) · F. H. Hinsley, ed., *British foreign policy under Sir Edward Grey* (1977) · M. Bentley, 'Liberal politics and the Grey conspiracy of 1921', *HJ*, 20 (1977), 461–78 · Viscount Grey of Fallodon [E. Grey], *Twenty-five years, 1892–1916*, 2 vols. (1925) · GEC, *Peerage*

Archives NL Scot., corresp. · PRO, corresp. and papers, FO 800/35–113 · U. Birm. L., letters · U. Oxf., Edward Grey Institute of Field Ornithology, ornithological notes | BL, corresp. with Arthur James Balfour, Add. MS 49731 · BL, corresp. with Sir Francis Bertie, Add. MSS 63018–63043 · BL, corresp. with Sir Henry Campbell-Bannerman, Add. MSS 41218, 52514 · BL, corresp. with Lord

Cecil, Add. MS 51073 · BL, corresp. with Lord Gladstone, Add. MSS 45992, 46476–46478 · BL, corresp. with Lord Northcliffe, Add. MS 62155 · BL, corresp. with Sir Ralph Paget, Add. MS 51252 · BL, corresp. with Lord Ripon, Add. MS 43640 · BL, corresp. with J. A. Spender, Add. MS 46389 · BL OIOC, letters to Lord Reading, MS Eur. E 238, F 118 · Bodl. Oxf., corresp. with Herbert Asquith · Bodl. Oxf., letters to James Bryce · Bodl. Oxf., letters to Louise Creighton · Bodl. Oxf., corresp. with H. A. L. Fisher · Bodl. Oxf., corresp. with H. A. Gwynne · Bodl. Oxf., corresp. with Sir William Harcourt and Lewis Harcourt · Bodl. Oxf., corresp. with Lord Kimberley · Bodl. Oxf., corresp. with Sir Donald Maclean · Bodl. Oxf., corresp. with Sir Louis Mallot · Bodl. Oxf., corresp. with Gilbert Murray · Bodl. Oxf., letters to H. J. Newbolt · Bodl. Oxf., letters to Lady Selborne · Bodl. Oxf., corresp. with Lord Selborne · CUL, corresp. with Lord Hardinge · CUL, letters to Siegfried Sassoon · Cumbria AS, Carlisle, letters to Lord Howard of Penrith · HLRO, corresp. with Andrew Bonar Law · HLRO, corresp. with David Lloyd George · HLRO, corresp. with Herbert Samuel · HLRO, corresp. with John St Loe Strachey · JRL, corresp. with C. P. Scott · L. Cong., corresp. with Moreton Frewen · LMA, corresp. with Sir Willoughby Maycock · Lpool RO, letters to Sir Richard Evans · NA Canada, corresp. with James Bryce · NL Ire., letters to John Redmond · NL Scot., letters to Seton Gordon · NL Scot., corresp. with Lord Haldane · NL Scot., corresp. with Lord Rosebery · NRA, letters to C. H. Lyell · NRA Scotland, priv. coll., corresp. with Tennant family · Nuffield Oxf., corresp. with Lord Emmott · Nuffield Oxf., corresp. with Lord Mottistone · PRO, corresp. with Lord Kitchener, PRO 30/57; WO 159 · Queen Mary College, London, letters to Lady Lyttelton · Trinity Cam., corresp. with Sir Henry Babington Smith · U. Newcastle, Robinson L., corresp. with Walter Runciman · Yale U., Sterling Memorial Library, corresp. with Edward House | FILM BFI NFTVA, news footage · BFI NFTVA, propaganda film footage · BFI NFTVA, record footage

Likenesses H. Furniss, pen-and-ink caricature, c.1900, NPG · J. S. Sargent, chalk drawing, 1913, NPG · G. Fiddes Watt, oils, c.1915–1917, Gov. Art Coll. · W. Stoneman, two photographs, 1918–31, NPG · J. Guthrie, oils, c.1919–1921, Scot. NPG · J. Guthrie, oils, c.1919–1921 (study for *Statesmen of World War I*), NPG · J. Guthrie, oils, c.1919–1921, NPG · W. Rothenstein, chalk drawing, 1920, NPG · J. Guthrie, group portrait, oils, c.1924–1930 (*Statesmen of World War I*), NPG · W. Orpen, oils, 1925, National Liberal Club · H. Speed, oils, c.1927, Oxford and Cambridge Club, London · H. Speed, oils, c.1927–1933, NPG · J. Guthrie, oils, 1928, Balliol Oxf. · H. W. Barnett, photograph, NPG [*see illus.*] · I. S. B., pencil, pen, and ink drawing, NPG · Owl, caricature (as 'Secretary Bird'), NPG; repro. in *VF* (2 March 1913) · B. Partridge, pen-and-ink caricature (with President Roosevelt), NPG; repro. in *Punch* (29 March 1911) · Spy [L. Ward], caricature, lithograph, NPG; repro. in *VF* (5 Feb 1903)

Wealth at death £123,791 0s. 1d.: probate, 7 Dec 1933, CGPLA Eng. & Wales

Grey, Elizabeth [née Lady Elizabeth Talbot], **countess of Kent** (1582–1651), literary patron and supposed author, was born before 10 February 1582, probably in London, the third of five children of Gilbert *Talbot, seventh earl of Shrewsbury (1552–1616), and his wife, Mary (1557–1632), daughter of Sir William Cavendish (1508–1557) and his wife, Elizabeth (Bess of Hardwick). Queen Elizabeth I treated her affectionately; a letter to her parents commenting on this fact adds that she was 'never ... idle but ether studying the frenche tonge or sewinge or otherwyse at worke' (Batho, 81). She was privately educated, probably by the translator John Florio. Her interest in languages persisted, and she received or shared dedications to several works: Florio's translation of Montaigne's *Essayes* (1603), two works on Italian, *New and Easie Directions*

(1639) and *The Italian Tutor* (1640) by Giovanni Torriano, a volume of poems in Italian, *Rime all'illustrissima signora Elizabetta Talbot-Grey* (1609) by Antimo Galli, *Clef de l'escriture* (c.1593) by J. De Beau Chesne, and A. Darcie's translation of a French version of Camden's life of Elizabeth I.

The deaths in infancy of her brothers, and her father's quarrel with his brother, who was heir to his titles, made Elizabeth and her two sisters great heiresses. One sister was to marry the earl of Pembroke, the other the earl of Arundel; in 1601, Elizabeth married Henry Grey (c.1583–1639), heir to the earldom of Kent. The marriage remained unconsummated for several months; in September 1602 Lady Shrewsbury was informed that recently 'upon good consideration not being hastned more then was fitt, my lady Elizabeth did yeeld her willing consent to admitt my cousin Grey to lodge in one bed with her' (Stone, 658). There were no children of the marriage.

Elizabeth was active at court for some years, performing as the Nymph of Medway in Samuel Daniel's *Tethys Festivall* in 1610, and in 1617 becoming the queen's first lady of the bedchamber, an honour for which there was vigorous competition. Her father had died in 1616 but it was not until twenty years later, after family disputes, that she could enter on her inheritance. By this time, although they still took part in such state occasions as the baptism of the future James II, Elizabeth and her husband spent much of their time at Wrest Park, near Silsoe, in Bedfordshire. Their circle included John Selden, Robert Cotton, and Thomas Carew, who wrote a poem extolling his hosts' hospitality. After she had been widowed in 1639 it was observed that Elizabeth 'doth soe much lament the death of her husband that Mr. Selden cannot comfort her' (Suckling, 328). The reference to Selden may have been pointed; he was to live with Elizabeth at her house in London and to be the beneficiary of her will. Aubrey's claim that they were secretly married has never been confirmed (*Brief Lives*, 2.220–21). Elizabeth continued to employ and patronize talented persons, such as the cook Robert May, Samuel Butler, who 'besides his study ... employed his time much in painting and drawing, and also in musique' (ibid., 1.135), and perhaps the miniaturist Samuel Cooper. Sir John Suckling wrote that 'in my Lady *Kents* well-being, much of ours consists' (ibid., 150). 'The Receipt of the Lady *Kents* Powder Presented by her Ladyship to the Queen' appears in *The Queens Closet Opened* of 1656 and there is a reference to her in *The Closet of the Eminently Learned Sir Kenelme Digbie Kt. Opened* of 1669. Both these collections were produced in imitation of a book of 1653 entitled *A choice manual of rare and select secrets in physick and chyrurgery: collected, and practised by the Right Honorable, the countesse of Kent, late deceased ... published by W. I. Gent*. This work has often been ascribed to Elizabeth herself. However, W. I. Gent, who also produced a book of remedies for the plague in 1665 (his name may have been William Jervis), makes it clear in his prefatory matter that the collection was made by him for Elizabeth's use: 'this small Manuall ... was once esteemed as a rich Cabinet of knowledge, by a person truly Honorable'. Associates of Elizabeth contributed a few items to it, and one item alone is attributed to her. The collection was very successful; an edition of 1708 claims to be the twenty-first. Elizabeth died on 7 December 1651 at her home, Friary House, Whitefriars, London, and was buried on 7 January 1652 at Flitton, Bedfordshire.

JOHN CONSIDINE

Sources C. Jamison, G. R. Batho, and E. G. W. Bill, eds., *A calendar of the Shrewsbury and Talbot papers in the Lambeth Palace Library and the College of Arms*, 2, HMC, JP 7 (1971) · L. Stone, *The crisis of the aristocracy, 1558–1641* (1965) · GEC, *Peerage*, new edn · *Brief lives, chiefly of contemporaries, set down by John Aubrey, between the years 1669 and 1696*, ed. A. Clark, 2 vols. (1898) · J. Suckling, *Non-dramatic works*, ed. T. Clayton (1971) · J. Nichols, *The progresses, processions, and magnificent festivities of King James I, his royal consort, family and court*, 4 vols. (1828) · K. Sharpe, *Sir Robert Cotton, 1586–1631* (1979) · *The diary of Anne Clifford, 1616–1619*, ed. K. Acheson (1995) · D. Foskett, *Samuel Cooper* (1974) · A. Fowler, *The country house poem* (1994) · D. Howarth, *Lord Arundel and his circle* (1985) · M. de Montaigne, *The essayes, or, Morall, politike and millitarie discourses*, trans. J. Florio (1603) · *A choice manual of rare and select secrets in physick and chyrurgery: collected and practised by ... the countesse of Kent*, ed. W. I. (1653)
Archives Arundel Castle, archives, letter · LPL, Shrewsbury and Talbot MSS, letter, vol. 708, fol. 169
Likenesses P. van Somer, oil on panel, *c.*1618–1620, Tate collection; repro. in O. Millar, *The age of Charles I* (1972), pl. 16 · W. Hollar, etching, 1637–44 (after F. Ferdinand), BM, V&A · J. Chantry, line engraving, BM, NPG; repro. in W. I., ed., *Choice manuall* · engraving, repro. in W. I., ed., *Choice manuall* · engraving, repro. in E. Grey, *A choice manuall*, 18th edn (1682) · engraving?, repro. in W. I., ed., *Choice manuall* [British Library copy]
Wealth at death £40,000 left to John Selden; her share of the Talbot estates, which Selden didn't inherit, valued at £8000 p.a.: Aubrey, *Brief lives*, 2.224; M. A. E. Green, *Calendar of the proceedings of the committee for advance of money, 1642–1656*, 3 vols, PRO (1888), 1259 [Talbot estates]

Grey, Elizabeth. *See* Griffin, Elizabeth (*bap.* 1691, *d.* 1762).

Grey, Ford, **earl of Tankerville** (*bap.* 1655, *d.* 1701), conspirator and politician, was baptized on 20 July 1655 at Harting, Sussex, the son of Ralph Grey, second Baron Grey of Warke (*bap.* 1630, *d.* 1675), and Catherine (1634–*c.*1682), widow of Alexander Colepeper and daughter of Sir Edward Ford of Harting. About 1674 Grey married Mary Berkeley (*d.* 1719), daughter of George *Berkeley, ninth Baron Berkeley and later first earl of Berkeley, and Elizabeth Massingberd, daughter of John Massingberd. Grey succeeded his father as Lord Grey of Warke on 24 June 1675.

Committed to the country programme—he had an instinctive distrust of the court and courtiers—Grey canvassed Essex on behalf of country parliamentary candidates in March 1679. In May, acting as a teller for a vote on the Habeas Corpus Amendment Act, he counted a corpulent peer as ten, enabling the country to carry a vote for a conference with the Commons by a majority of two. During the spring Grey, the earl of Shaftesbury, and others met regularly with Titus Oates. With Shaftesbury and three other peers, Grey supported Oates's charges against the queen. Grey's backing for Sir Robert Peyton's parliamentary candidacy in September 1679 nearly incited a riot in London. Grey, Shaftesbury, Lord Howard of Escrick, and

others petitioned the king in December, asking that parliament convene in January 1680. On 30 June 1680 Grey, nine other peers, and ten commoners, including Lord William Russell, attempted in king's bench to accuse the duke of York of Catholicism, but the judges pre-empted them by dismissing the jury. A member of the Green Ribbon Club, Grey supported efforts to exclude James from the succession, and in December 1680 he voted to attaint the Catholic peer Viscount Stafford. With Buckingham, Grey campaigned—unsuccessfully—for Slingsby Bethel in March 1681 when the latter stood as MP for Southwark. Blamed for a tumult during the London shrieval election in June 1682 Grey, Richard Goodenough, and others were tried and convicted (May 1683); when Grey failed to appear for sentencing in June, he was fined 1000 marks.

Grey attracted attention in other ways. About 1680, suspecting his wife was having an affair with the duke of Monmouth, he reportedly ordered her to leave London within hours, but his relationship with the duke survived this contretemps. Later, when he ridiculed the duke of Albemarle's ornate gun, calling it a 'coxcomb's fancy' and a fool's weapon, the latter challenged him to a duel (Price, 72); Grey bested him on 1 June 1682, forcing Albemarle to surrender his sword. Later the same year the earl of Berkeley learned that Grey had been having an affair with Lady Henrietta (Harriet) *Berkeley (*b.* in or after 1664, *d.* 1706), another of the earl's daughters and Grey's sister-in-law. When she fled, Grey refused to disclose her whereabouts until her family promised not to send her to France, whereupon the earl accused Grey in king's bench on 23 October of conspiring to take her away; Grey pleaded not guilty. On 6 November Berkeley filed suit *de homine replegiando*, indicating that she had been forcefully or fraudulently taken away and detained. Grey was found guilty but no punishment was imposed. The scandal formed the basis for Aphra Behn's fictionalized account in *The Love Letters of a Nobleman to his Sister* (3 vols., 1684–7): the first volume drew upon trial reports of the case.

Much of the information concerning Grey's participation in the plotting of Shaftesbury and Monmouth in the early 1680s comes from his fulsome confession in 1685, which has been criticized as self-serving and chronologically imprecise, but much of it can be corroborated. Grey first heard Shaftesbury discuss the use of force to assure a protestant succession after the Lords rejected the Exclusion Bill in November 1680, but Monmouth, Grey, Russell, and Sir Thomas Armstrong demurred. The subject was revived when they learned of Charles's ill health in May 1682, and continued when the lord mayor declared the tory candidates victorious in the London shrieval election. Grey refused his cohorts' request to seek support in Essex with the help of Colonel Henry Mildmay, whom he disliked. The conspirators hoped to mount an uprising after Monmouth's return from Cheshire, but support in London was inadequate. In September Grey and the others, over Shaftesbury's objections, opted for delay. After Grey and Robert Ferguson conferred with Sir John Trenchard about support in the south-west, the plotters set 19 November for the insurrection. Grey, Monmouth, and

Armstrong reconnoitred the night-time disposition of the royal guards and conferred with Lord Brandon and Sir Gilbert Gerard about backing in Cheshire. However, in the absence of further word from Trenchard, the cabal postponed the rebellion.

Shaftesbury's flight to the Netherlands in November 1682 temporarily halted the plotting, but in February Monmouth told Grey that a council was again laying plans. Although the duke invited Grey to join, he was dissuaded by Monmouth's depiction of internal division between monarchists (Monmouth and Russell) and republicans (Essex, Algernon Sidney, and John Hampden). Monmouth reiterated the invitation in March, and the following month Grey and Russell consulted with Sir John Cochrane, one of the Scots who had come to London to discuss co-ordinated uprisings. Later that month, Grey insisted that a declaration be drafted and that a military commander, not a council, lead the rebellion. The conspirators agreed to lend Argyll £10,000 for a Scottish insurrection. However, on 11 May, acting on a tip, searchers found eighty to ninety muskets and armour concealed in Grey's London house; he claimed the weapons were for his estates in Essex, Sussex, and Northumberland. After Grey and two sureties posted recognizances totalling £20,000, he was released. He retired to his Sussex home, asking Russell to contribute £3000 to the uprising on his behalf, with assurance of repayment. Following Josiah Keeling's disclosure of the Rye House conspiracy, Grey was arrested on 26 June, but he escaped when the messenger taking him to London fell asleep. The government offered £500 for Grey's apprehension, but he escaped to the Netherlands, taking his mistress, a pregnant Lady Henrietta Berkeley, and her husband with him. Grey was indicted for high treason on 12 July 1683.

Grey spent his exile in Cleves and occasionally the Netherlands. He evaded capture by royalist agents at Leiden in June 1684, and the following year failed to raise money to purchase a command in Brandenburg. Required to leave Cleves, Grey relocated to Amsterdam, where he helped Argyll and Monmouth plan their invasions. He sailed with the latter, whose cavalry he rather ineptly commanded. At Bridport (14 June 1685), Grey was willing to take on a much larger force of local militia, but then fled in the confusion of battle when he thought that all was lost, and the situation had to be saved by his subordinates. In the night attack at Sedgemoor (5–6 July), though later bitterly accused of cowardice by Monmouth, he seems to have displayed some courage and resolution, but was dogged by ill luck and the inexperience of himself and his men. He was taken the day after the battle. Grey's life was spared because of Lord Lumley's intervention, Grey's willingness to provide a full confession, and the earl of Rochester's financial stake in keeping Grey alive. Eleven months earlier, the earl had been given £16,000, to be paid from Grey's estate over twenty-one years, but with payments to cease upon Grey's death. When Grey's brother Ralph posted a bond of £140,000, agreeing to pay Rochester's debts and others totalling £18,000, Grey's attainder was reversed. His pardon passed the great seal

on 12 November 1685. His title was restored on 7 June 1686, the same month that his estate at Up Park, Sussex, was returned. He testified as a witness for the crown in the trials of lords Brandon and Delamere.

When William invaded, Grey declined to join James's troops, citing a recent fall from his horse. He was active in the convention, attending seventy-one of the seventy-eight sessions, and voting with thirty-five other peers to protest against the Lords' rejection of a clause averring that James had abdicated. Still a committed whig, in March 1689 he favoured the exemption of protestant nonconformists from the Test Act, and in May he opposed the Lords decision not to reverse the judgment against Oates. Ill health kept him from involvement in parliament between November 1689 and November 1691, but it was another three years before he participated regularly. William appointed Grey to the privy council in May 1695 and created him earl of Tankerville on 11 June 1695. An adept negotiator, he participated in the conference with representatives from the House of Commons to finalize the Trial of Treasons Act (1696). The same year he supported the Association Bill and managed Sir John Fenwick's attainder. With Lord Somers, he fought unsuccessfully in 1698 for a compromise that would have allowed William to keep his Dutch brigade. A member of the Board of Trade from 15 May 1696, when he replaced the earl of Stamford, until 1699, Tankerville attended fewer meetings than nearly all his fellow members. He also served as a lord of the Treasury (June 1699 to December 1700, being the first lord for the last twelve months), a lord justice (June 1700), and lord privy seal (from November 1700 until his death the following year). He declined the first lordship of the Admiralty, professing that he would rather be dragged through a horse pond, probably because of the Commons' recent investigation of the Admiralty. An influential courtier and an able orator, Tankerville showed little talent as an administrator.

Tankerville died in Pall Mall, London, on 24 June 1701 and was buried at Harting on 1 July. His wife outlived him and died on 19 May 1719. Their only child, Mary, married Charles Bennet, second Baron Ossulston, in 1695. In his will, dated 31 May 1696, Tankerville left his estate to his daughter, though much of it was successfully claimed by Rochester in 1704 as payment for debts. He also remembered Lady Henrietta Berkeley, when he left her £200 p.a. in a codicil dated 17 April 1701.

Moved to embrace radical political courses in the late 1670s and 1680s by a deep concern about the perceived threat of international Catholicism to English liberties and protestantism, Grey hovered near the most influential whigs but never obtained their stature. Inept as a military commander and not particularly effective as a conspirator, he lived to serve the Williamite regime loyally if not with distinction.   RICHARD L. GREAVES

Sources PRO, state papers domestic, 29/424–425, 427–430, 433–434, 438 · entry book, PRO, 44 · BL, Lansdowne MS 1152 · Ford, Lord Grey, *The secret history of the Rye-House plot: and of Monmouth's rebellion* (1754) · BL, Harley MS 6845 · GEC, *Peerage*, new edn, vol. 6 ·

R. L. Greaves, *Secrets of the kingdom: British radicals from the Popish Plot to the revolution of 1688–89* (1992) · C. Price, *Cold Caleb* [1956] · BL, Add. MSS 8127, 38847, 41809, 62453 · U. Edin. L., Laing MS La.I.332 · N. Luttrell, *A brief historical relation of state affairs from September 1678 to April 1714*, 6 vols. (1857), esp. vols. 1–4 · [T. Sprat], *Copies of the informations and original papers relating to the proof of the horrid conspiracy against the late king, his present majesty and the government* (1685) · *State trials*, vols. 9, 11
Archives PRO, family papers, C 104/81–83 | Berks. RO, Grey of Warke MSS · BL, Add. MSS 8127, 38847, 41809, 62453 · BL, Harley MS 6845 · BL, Lansdowne MS 1152 · Essex RO, Grey family MSS · PRO, entry book, 44 · PRO, state papers domestic, SP 29/424–425, 427–430, 433–434, 438 · U. Edin., Laing MS La.I.332
Likenesses P. Lely, oils, *c.*1672, Audley End, Essex; repro. in Price, *Cold Caleb* · C. N. Schurtz, line engraving, 1689 (after P. Lely), BM, NPG · A. Browne, mezzotint (after P. Lely), BM, NPG · P. Lely, portrait, BM; repro. in Price, *Cold Caleb*

Grey [*other married name* Stokes], **Frances** [*née* Lady Frances Brandon], **duchess of Suffolk** (1517–1559), noblewoman, was the elder daughter of Charles *Brandon, duke of Suffolk (*c.*1484–1545), and his third wife, *Mary (1496–1533), sister of Henry VIII and widow of Louis XII of France. She was born on 16 July 1517, St Francis's day, at Hatfield, the seat of the bishops of Ely. Two days later Frances, who may have been named after the French king, François I, was christened in Hatfield parish church with Lady Anne Boleyn (a relative of the future queen) and Lady Elizabeth Grey acting as proxies for her godmothers, Queen Katherine and Princess Mary. The abbot of St Albans was her godfather. Her nurse was named Anne Kyng, but nothing more is known about Frances's childhood except that she resided at Westhorpe, Suffolk, and was conventionally educated. In 1528 her father secured a papal dispensation nullifying his second marriage, to Lady Margaret Neville, widow of Sir John Mortimer, in order to ensure the legitimacy of Frances, her brother, Henry, earl of Lincoln, who died in 1534, and her sister, Eleanor.

Probably in May 1533 at Suffolk House, Southwark, Frances married her father's ward, Henry *Grey, marquess of Dorset. Her ailing mother survived the wedding about one month, and on 22 July Frances served as principal mourner at her funeral. In September her father married Katherine Willoughby de Eresby and subsequently had two sons with her. After a son and a daughter of Lady Dorset's had died as infants, Frances gave birth to three daughters, Jane in October 1537, Katherine in August 1540, and Mary in 1545 [*see* Keys, Lady Mary]. On 12 November 1537 she attended Queen Jane Seymour's funeral, and on 3 January 1540 participated in Anne of Cleves's reception by the king. Two years later a parliamentary statute set out her jointure lands, valued at £1015 3s. 3d. She was with her father when he died on 24 August 1545 at Guildford Castle. He bequeathed to her plate worth £200 and directed that she should inherit certain jewels, household items, and livestock in the event of her half-brothers' deaths.

The following year Frances was at court in attendance on Queen Katherine Parr, and was granted the college of Astley, Warwickshire, and other property by the king.

After Henry's death in 1547 the queen dowager's new husband, Thomas, Lord Seymour of Sudeley, gained the support of the Dorsets by promising to arrange Jane's marriage to Edward VI. Following Katherine Parr's demise in 1548, Jane, who had resided with her and Seymour, moved to Bradgate, Leicestershire, the Dorset family estate. Soon afterwards her parents agreed to Seymour's request that she be restored to his custody.

After Seymour's downfall Jane resumed her classical studies at Bradgate with her tutor, John Aylmer, later bishop of London. In the summer of 1550 Roger Ascham visited Bradgate, and some years later wrote an account of a conversation with her that appeared in *The Schoolmaster* in 1570. He recalled her complaining how her parents, unlike gentle Aylmer, corrected her with 'pinches, nips, and bobs' (Ascham, 36). Citing this account, later writers have condemned their insensitivity, but as Frank Prochaska has suggested, Ascham may have 'overblown' Jane's comments to create additional support for his argument that teachers should not take on the role of parents and use corporal punishment to motivate their students to study. It is noteworthy that *The Schoolmaster* was only published after the deaths of Jane and her parents.

In August 1551 Lady Dorset was extremely ill but had recovered enough by November to attend the welcoming ceremonies for Mary of Guise, regent of Scotland. On 11 October, her half-brothers having died in July, her husband was created duke of Suffolk. They celebrated Christmas with Princess Mary, and were thereafter frequently either at court or at the house they had built at Richmond. In 1553 they approved the plans of John Dudley, duke of Northumberland, for Jane to wed his son Guildford and to succeed the sickly Edward as monarch. On 9 July 1553 at Syon House, Frances having relinquished to her daughter her superior position in the succession, the duke and duchess witnessed the privy council's official notification to Jane of her accession. The next day they accompanied her to Westminster for her public recognition as queen, and remained with her until after Mary's accession, when they were confined in the Tower. Although Jane was to be tried and convicted of treason, her parents were released on 31 July after Frances made a personal plea to the queen. The duke withdrew to Richmond while the duchess attended court. In 1554 Suffolk's participation in Wyatt's rebellion led not only to Jane's execution on 12 February but also to his own on 23 February.

About one year later, on 1 March 1555, the duchess married Adrian Stokes (*c.*1533–1585), master of her horse, who was probably a son of Robert Stokes of Prestwold. In his *Annales*, completed in the early seventeenth century, William Camden charged her with 'forgetting the nobility of her lineage' when she wed this 'mean gentleman' (Camden, 55). Their disparity in rank fuelled the later, but chronologically impossible, tale that Elizabeth I, who after her accession in 1558 was attracted to her own master of the horse, Robert Dudley, responded with astonishment to William Cecil's disclosure of her cousin's marriage with the query, 'What? … has she married her horse-keeper?' ('Minor queries', 451). After her wedding the duchess remained on good terms with Queen Mary, who permitted her to reside at Richmond and employed her remaining daughters as maids of honour. With her second husband the duchess had a daughter, Elizabeth, who died on 7 February 1556.

In ill health in 1559 Frances had begun by 3 November to prepare for her death when she petitioned the crown for licence to sell off some of her jointure property, the proceeds of which went to her daughters. She drew up her will on 7 November, leaving to Stokes her goods and a life interest in most of her estates. The couple had earlier approved Frances's daughter Katherine's decision to wed Edward Seymour, earl of Hertford, but the duchess died at Richmond on 21 November, some months before that clandestine match occurred. At Queen Elizabeth's order she was buried on 5 December in St Edmund's Chapel, Westminster Abbey, where Stokes erected a tomb with a recumbent figure in her memory. Ironically, perhaps, since there is no evidence that she shared the devoted evangelical piety of her eldest daughter, her funeral was the first protestant service at the abbey after the reconstitution of its chapter by the queen.

RETHA M. WARNICKE

Sources R. Ascham, *The schoolmaster*, ed. L. V. Ryan, [new edn] (1967) · *CSP dom.*, *1547–80* · W. Camden, *Annales, or, The historie of the most renowned and victorious Princesse Elizabeth*, trans. R. N. [R. Norton], 3rd edn (1635) · H. Chapman, *Lady Jane Grey* (1962) · H. W. Chapman, *Two Tudor portraits: Henry Howard, earl of Surrey and Lady Katherine Grey* (1960) · GEC, *Peerage* · R. Davey, *The sisters of Lady Jane Grey and their wicked grandfather* (1911) · *DNB* · S. J. Gunn, *Charles Brandon, duke of Suffolk, c.1484–1545* (1988) · HoP, *Commons, 1558–1603* · *LP Henry VIII* · M. Levine, *The early Elizabethan succession question, 1558–1568* (1966) · M. Levine, *Tudor dynastic problems, 1460–1571* (1973) · 'Minor queries with answers', *N&Q*, 12 (1855), 451–2 · F. Prochaska, 'The many faces of Lady Jane Grey', *History Today*, 35/10 (1985), 34–40 · W. C. Richardson, *Mary Tudor: the white queen* (1970)
Likenesses H. Eworth, oil on panel, 1559, priv. coll. · H. Holbein the younger, drawing (as marchioness of Dorset), Royal Collection · Vertue, double portrait, engraving (with Adrian; after L. de Heere)

Grey, Sir Frederick William (1805–1878), naval officer, third son of Charles *Grey, second Earl Grey (1764–1845), and his wife, Mary Elizabeth, daughter of William Brabazon Ponsonby, first Lord Ponsonby, was born at Howick, Northumberland, on 23 August 1805. He entered the navy on 18 January 1819, serving as a midshipman aboard the frigate *Naiad* (Captain Robert C. Spencer) in the Mediterranean. He took part in a notable boat action against Algerine pirates at Bon in 1824. On passing for lieutenant in April 1824 he joined the *Sybille* (Captain Sir Samuel J. B. Pechell) and returned to Britain in August. In 1825 he joined the *Volage* (Captain Richard S. Dundas) for the South American station, where he obtained command of the *Heron* (18 guns) on 17 April 1827. He was promoted captain on 19 April 1828. Between 1830 and 1834 Grey commanded the frigate *Actaeon* (26 guns) on the Mediterranean station. In August 1835 he was appointed to the *Jupiter* to convey William Eden, Lord Auckland, to India as governor-general, and he returned to Britain in 1836. In 1840 he was appointed to the frigate *Endymion* and sent to the East Indies, where he served in the First Opium War and was created CB in January 1842 for his services. The ship paid off in late 1843. On 20 July 1846 he married Barbarina Charlotte, daughter of the Revd F. Sullivan; they had no children, and she survived him.

In 1854 Grey was appointed to command the screw steamship *Hannibal* (90 guns). In August he became a first-class commodore commanding a mixed fleet of warships armed *en flute* and steam transports conveying 10,000 French troops to the Åland Islands. After the fall of Bomarsund, Grey's squadron returned to Britain, and he then took the *Hannibal* to the Black Sea, where he was ordered to become captain of the fleet for Vice-Admiral Sir Edmund Lyons. However, Lyons preferred to rely on his flag captain, and Grey was redeployed as principal agent of transports in the Bosphorus, a post which he filled with energy and good sense until the removal of the army from the Crimea. Grey became a rear-admiral on 22 January 1855. His brother-in-law, Sir Charles Wood, became first lord in February. For his services during the war Grey was created KCB in 1857.

After a brief period ashore Grey was appointed commander-in-chief at the Cape of Good Hope and on the west coast of Africa in April 1857, and he remained there until February 1860. On his return to Britain he published a pamphlet, *On the Organisation of the Navy* (1860), largely concerned with manning. In June 1861 he took office as first sea lord under the duke of Somerset, following the sudden death of his former captain and close friend Richard Saunders Dundas. Promoted vice-admiral in August 1861 and admiral in April 1865, he retained his post, which was his last naval service, until the fall of Earl Russell's ministry in 1866. He received the GCB in 1865.

As first sea lord Grey called for increased estimates, to provide ships and men to place the fleet on equal terms with foreign powers, and for improved administration. He was largely content to follow the work of his predecessor and to sustain the ironclad policy that by the mid-1860s reasserted British naval mastery with superior ships, guns, and resources. He was not an alarmist but supported the maintenance of a two-power naval standard. On the question of ship design, Grey was conservative. He did not favour the experimental turret ship designs of Captain Cowper Coles, and considered Coles's publicity campaign impudent. His main concern was manpower, as he declared in the preface to his short pamphlet on manning, *Suggestions for improving the character of our merchant seamen and for providing an efficient naval reserve* (1873):

> During the five years I held the office of Senior Naval Lord under the Duke of Somerset, the questions of manning the Navy, raising the character of our seamen, making the Coast Guard a really efficient reserve, and providing a further reserve in the merchant service occupied much of the attention of the Board of Admiralty. Many important measures were adopted which, followed up by succeeding administrations, have given us the finest body of seamen, ever, I believe, in the service of the Crown. (F. W. Grey, *Suggestions*, 1873; repr. in Bromley)

Grey did not take a seat in the House of Commons,

which meant that he was a less public figure than the sea lords who preceded him. This was an important step in the professionalization of the board. It was a mark of the growing controversy over naval policy, under attack from radical economists and the projectors of alternative designs, that on leaving office Grey published a pamphlet, *Admiralty Administration, 1861–1866* (1866), in defence of the Liberal naval policy of his term. He was placed on the retired list by Childers' reform of 1870. In later life he served as a magistrate for Northumberland, Berkshire, and Sussex. Grey died on 2 May 1878 at his home, Lynwood, Sunningdale, Berkshire.

With powerful family connections at the highest level of society, and within the navy, Grey had a head start to his career. His later service coincided with whig–Liberal administrations, including his father's term as prime minister, and those of his brother-in-law Sir Charles Wood as secretary and later first lord of the Admiralty. However, Grey was among the most able flag officers of his generation, respected for his administrative abilities and sound judgement. His term at the Admiralty was marked by the increasing community of interest among naval officers of all political persuasions, in spite of their differences in other areas.   ANDREW LAMBERT

Sources S. M. Eardley-Wilmot, *Life of Vice-Admiral Edmund, Lord Lyons* (1898) · A. D. Lambert, *The Crimean War: British grand strategy, 1853–56* (1990) · J. H. Briggs, *Naval administrations, 1827 to 1892: the experience of 65 years*, ed. Lady Briggs (1897) · J. C. D. Hay, *Lines from my log book* (1898) · S. Sandler, *The emergence of the modern capital ship* (1979) · O'Byrne, *Naval biog. dict.* · W. L. Clowes, *The Royal Navy: a history from the earliest times to the present*, 7 vols. (1897–1903), vols. 6–7 · A. C. Dewar, ed., *Russian war, 1855, Black Sea: official correspondence*, Navy RS, 85 (1945) · *CGPLA Eng. & Wales* (1878) · J. S. Bromley, ed., *The manning of the Royal Navy: selected public pamphlets, 1693–1873*, Navy RS, 119 (1974) · E. Rasor, *Reform in the Royal Navy* (1976) · DNB
Archives BL, corresp. with Sir Charles Wood, Add. MSS 49544–49545 · Bucks. RLSS, Somerset MSS · Cumbria AS, Carlisle, Graham MSS · NA Scot., letter-book on naval matters · NAM, corresp. with Sir William Codrington · National Library of South Africa, Cape Town, letters to Sir George Grey · NMM, corresp. with Sir Alexander Milne · U. Durham L., letters to brother of third Earl Grey, incl. estate administration; letters to Maria, Lady Grey
Wealth at death under £14,000: probate, 3 June 1878, *CGPLA Eng. & Wales*

Grey, George, second earl of Kent (*d.* 1503), magnate, was the second but eldest surviving son of Edmund *Grey, Lord Grey of Ruthin and first earl of Kent (1416–1490), and of Catherine Percy, daughter of Henry *Percy, second earl of Northumberland (*d.* 1455). His elder brother, Anthony, died in 1480, after which he bore the courtesy title of Lord Grey of Ruthin and began to serve on local commissions in Huntingdonshire, Bedfordshire, and Northamptonshire, where his family's lands lay. He was made a knight of the Bath at the coronation of Richard III on 5 July 1483. Richard granted him the manors of Harlington, Buckinghamshire, and Grendon, Bedfordshire, but his actions in 1485 are unknown, and he was sufficiently in favour with Henry VII to be granted the constableship of Northampton Castle for life on 8 October 1485.

Grey attended Henry on his first progress into the north in spring 1486 and went on to fight for him in the vanguard at Stoke in 1487, in France in 1492 with a retinue of ninety-two men, and against the Cornish rebels at Blackheath and in Cornwall in 1497. He was also active at Henry's court, and attended the creations of the king's eldest son, Arthur, as prince of Wales in 1489 and of his second son, Henry, as duke of York in 1494, Prince Arthur's marriage in 1501, and the funerals of Prince Arthur in 1502 and Queen Elizabeth in 1503. In July of that year he accompanied Princess Margaret from Collyweston in Lincolnshire to York on her journey to Scotland to marry James IV. He sat in the king's council on several recorded occasions in 1486, 1498, and 1499, and was one of the judges at the trial of Edward, earl of Warwick, on 21 November 1499. He was named to the commissions of the peace in four counties and attended quarter sessions on occasion in Bedfordshire and perhaps elsewhere.

Grey succeeded to the earldom of Kent on his father's death on 22 May 1490, receiving livery of his lands four days later. He seems to have been an effective landlord, raising the levels of income on his estates by 1498 substantially above those shown in his father's valor of 1467/8, to some £1300 p.a. He had sufficient surplus income to commit himself to pay £3000 to the king for the wardship of Elizabeth Trussell, whom he intended as a bride for his second son, Henry, though he had paid only £1200 by the time of his death. He also managed to purchase lands yielding more than £7 a year as an endowment for his third son, George.

Grey married first, in or after 1483, Anne, widow of Sir William Bourchier, daughter of Richard *Woodville, Earl Rivers, and of Jacquetta, daughter of Pierre de Luxembourg, count of St Pol, and thus sister of Edward IV's queen, Elizabeth Woodville. She died on 30 July 1489 and was buried at Warden Abbey, Bedfordshire. Grey married second, about 1 October 1490, Catherine Herbert, third daughter of William Herbert, first earl of Pembroke, and of Anne, daughter of Sir Walter Devereux. She died between the earl's death and 4 May 1504, and in her will requested burial at Warden. Kent himself died on 16 or 18 December 1503 at Ampthill, Bedfordshire, having requested burial at Warden, and was succeeded by Richard *Grey, his son from his first marriage. Three sons from his second marriage survived him: Henry, his eventual heir, George, and Anthony; and a daughter, Anne, who married Sir John Hussey in late 1512 or early 1513. On his deathbed Kent allegedly called together his servants and friends and attempted to entail his lands to prevent the feckless Richard from dispersing the patrimony, predicting (as the abbot of Warden later testified) 'that hys sonne & heayre woolde as faste waste & spend hys landes as hys ancestoures purchased them' (Bedfordshire RO, L24/425/2). It was to no avail. Richard Grey sold off most of the estates and even contrived to forfeit the Trussell wardship, leaving Henry too impoverished to take up the title, which remained in abeyance until 1572.   S. J. GUNN

Sources GEC, *Peerage* · G. W. Bernard, 'The fortunes of the Greys, earls of Kent, in the early sixteenth century', *HJ*, 25 (1982), 671–85 · R. I. Jack, ed., *The Grey of Ruthin valor: the valor of the English lands of*

Edmund Grey, earl of Kent, ... from the ministers' accounts of 1467–1468, Bedfordshire Historical RS, 46 (1965) · C. G. Bayne and W. H. Dunham, eds., *Select cases in the council of Henry VII*, SeldS, 75 (1958) · *Joannis Lelandi antiquarii de rebus Britannicis collectanea*, ed. T. Hearne, [3rd edn], 6 vols. (1774), vol. 4 · L. W. V. Harcourt, *His grace the steward and the trial of peers* (1907) · Beds. & Luton ARS, L24/425/2 · PRO, C54/393 (will of disputed authenticity); SC12/18/53 (valor of estates, 1507–8)

Archives Beds. & Luton ARS, Lucas MSS

Wealth at death will, PRO, C54/393, m. 4 · total income £1394 8s. 5½d.: valor of estates, 1507×8, PRO, SC 12/18/53

Grey, Sir George, second baronet (1799–1882), politician, was born in Gibraltar on 11 May 1799, the eldest son in the family of two sons and five daughters of George Grey (1767–1828) and his wife, Mary *Grey (1770–1858), daughter of Samuel Whitbread of Bedwell Park, Hertfordshire, and a half-sister of Samuel Whitbread the whig politician. His father, who retired as a captain in the Royal Navy in 1804 and became superintendent of the dockyard at Portsmouth, was created a baronet in 1814. His extended family connections linked him to the whig political aristocracy: Charles, second Earl Grey, the prime minister who carried the Reform Act, was his uncle; his sister Jane married Francis Baring, Baron Northbrook; Charles Grey, Queen Victoria's private secretary, and Henry George, third Earl Grey, the leader of the whigs in the House of Lords, were his cousins. The evangelical piety of both his parents was a powerful influence; his father was acquainted with Thomas Chalmers, and his mother was a friend of William Wilberforce. Fearing the moral atmosphere of the public schools they sent him to be taught privately by the Revd William Buckle, vicar of Pyrton, Oxfordshire. In 1817 he entered Oriel College, Oxford, where he was a hardworking student, graduating in 1821 with first-class honours in classics.

Grey intended to enter the church and spent two years studying theology, but abandoned the idea in 1823, feeling himself inadequate to the high vocation which this involved. He remained, though, a deeply religious man throughout his life, with an 'ever present' sense of sin (Creighton, 134), supporting evangelical organizations such as the Church Missionary Society, the British and Foreign Bible Society, and the London and Metropolitan District Visiting Society. While in London he spent Sunday afternoons visiting the poor in St Giles' parish. He was never a dogmatic protestant and always retained a whiggish adherence to religious liberty and toleration, favouring concurrent endowment of non-Anglican denominations during later controversies on the Irish church. He read for the law, was called to the bar by Lincoln's Inn in 1826, and established a practice. On 14 August 1827 he married Anna Sophia (d. 1893), eldest daughter of Henry *Ryder, the evangelical bishop of Lincoln. In the following year he succeeded to the baronetcy on the death of his father (8 October 1828).

In December 1832 Grey was elected as a whig MP for Devonport, a newly enfranchised constituency in which the government exercised powerful political influence through its dockyard patronage. His long ministerial career began in July 1834 when he was appointed under-

Sir George Grey, second baronet (1799–1882), by William Walker, c.1865

secretary for the colonies in Melbourne's government. He held the position until November 1834, when the ministry fell, and again from April 1835 until February 1839, serving under Charles Grant. When Grant was elevated to the peerage in 1835, as Lord Glenelg, Grey was left to defend a number of highly controversial decisions in the Commons. He was forced into long and impassioned debates with slavery abolitionists who attacked the government's apprenticeship scheme. His speech in reply to Sir Thomas Fowell Buxton's attack on official policy (19 June 1835) was considered particularly effective. Between 1836 and 1838 he was called upon to defend the administration's unpopular policy towards Canada, speaking against Sir William Molesworth's proposed vote of censure upon Glenelg (6 March 1838), which was defeated. In February 1839 he was appointed judge-advocate-general. He took part in the discussions on the government's policy towards popular education, favouring an unsectarian solution, and later contributed an article on the committee of the council on education to the *Edinburgh Review* (April 1842). From June 1841 until the government's fall in August 1841 he was chancellor of the duchy of Lancaster.

When Lord John Russell formed his government in July 1846 Grey was made home secretary, a position he was to hold intermittently over a period of twenty years. His first period of office, to February 1852, was dominated by political disaffection and famine in Ireland and the revival of Chartism in England. He marked the famine by ordering a national day of prayer. In November 1847 he introduced a Crime and Outrages Bill, which gave the authorities extraordinary powers to deal with agrarian outrages in Ireland, and in April 1848 he brought in the Crown and Government Security Bill, which extended the Treason Act to Ireland in response to the Irish Confederation. In July 1848 he carried the suspension of habeas corpus in Ireland, a measure which he had previously resisted.

Grey's contemporary reputation was much enhanced by his handling of what some believed to be a serious revolutionary challenge by the Chartists in 1848. He was calmer than his predecessor, Sir James Graham, and showed a self-confident willingness to take firm action. The Home Office sent troops to the northern towns to quell disorder. Throughout the Chartist disturbances he banned large political meetings if he believed they would end in violence and the disruption of public order. He, however, encouraged local authorities to permit meetings in open spaces, and appeared willing to let the Chartists talk themselves out. More than 7000 regular soldiers were brought into London when the Chartist National Convention announced its intention to make a mass procession to parliament on 10 April 1848 to present the third petition in favour of the Charter. The troops were kept out of sight, however, and the streets were left under the control of 170,000 special constables, enrolled under Grey's orders. When the Chartist meeting on Kennington Common passed off peacefully Grey was given much of the credit for averting the danger and avoiding loss of life. He was privately 'thankful for the merciful Providence which directed and upheld me during that anxious time' (Grey to M. Grey, 11 April 1848, Creighton, 82).

Grey's personal circumstances were greatly altered by his inheritance, following the death in 1845 of his uncle General Sir Henry George Grey, of the Fallodon estate in Northumberland. He set up home there. Deeply attached to the countryside, he took every opportunity to flee London for Northumberland. He stood for one of the North Northumberland parliamentary seats in the August 1847 general election and won against a protectionist, but lost it in July 1852 against the Percy family candidate. He was out of parliament until January 1853, when a member of the earl of Carlisle's family stood down to allow him to take the Morpeth seat. After initially declining to join Aberdeen's coalition ministry he accepted the Colonial Office, and entered the cabinet in June 1854 as a matter of public duty when war with Russia was imminent. In February 1855 Palmerston brought him back to the Home Office, which he held until the fall of the ministry in February 1858. From June 1859 to July 1861 he was chancellor of the duchy of Lancaster in Palmerston's second administration, and was home secretary from July 1861 until July 1866.

Granville regarded Grey as 'really Prime Minister in all internal affairs in Palmerston's Government' (B. Mallet, *Thomas George Earl of Northbrook*, 1908, 34). He made the Home Office almost his own, carrying out a reorganization of the department in 1849. Administrative decisions were shared with his highly experienced permanent under-secretary, Horatio Waddington, who held the position from 1849 to 1867. He was always suspicious of attempts by central government to usurp responsibilities that he thought should remain in the hands of local government. In the face of famine in Scotland and Ireland between 1846 and 1848 he believed that responsibility for relieving poverty lay with local property owners, and opposed Treasury grants to poor-law unions. During the cattle plague, in 1865, he opposed compulsory legislation to restrict the movement of cattle. His faith in the ability of local government to provide for law and order led him to oppose proposals for a national police force in 1856, though he used Treasury grants to enforce uniform standards on local forces. He also left local authorities to enjoy considerable independence from the Home Office in running local gaols, and regarded the role of the prisons inspectorate as limited to stopping the most glaring abuses. He only with reluctance introduced legislation in 1850 which made a limited increase in the powers of the mines inspectorate. In 1847 he was among the members of the whig government who supported the Ten Hours Act, limiting working hours for women and children in factories. After the mill owners found ways round the legislation he carried a compromise Factory Act in 1850, which increased working hours but forbade the use of children in relays. When this prohibition was circumvented Grey reneged on an agreement with Lord Ashley to outlaw the relay system.

As home secretary Grey was responsible for penal policy. Following the abolition in 1853 of transportation for convicts, prisons expanded to accommodate the increased population of prisoners. He was a firm believer in the 'separate' system of prison discipline, convinced that the separation of convicts from one another, accompanied by religious instruction, would promote their moral reformation. He saw the criminal as a sinner, and regarded it as the task of the state to reform his or her character on an individual basis. He was particularly interested in promoting religious instruction in reformatories for juvenile offenders. In 1865 he introduced legislation providing for a harsh system of prison labour in local prisons. He was convinced that capital punishment, on which he set up a royal commission in 1864, was a strong deterrent to deliberate murder, and was unwilling to exercise the prerogative of mercy. In 1863 he showed his characteristic official clear-headedness by criticizing a private member's bill, introduced in response to an outbreak of robberies with violence in the previous year (so called 'garrottings'), as 'panic legislation after the panic had subsided' (Radzinowicz and Hood, 704).

Grey proved to be an unexceptional administrator at the Home Office, avoiding any bold innovations, but he had a reputation for sound judgement. He had a hand in placing the ecclesiastical commission on a more business-like footing in 1850. 'Careful in action and moderate in speech, of tall and commanding figure, endued with genuine kindliness and genial manners, he was known to be a man of high character whose words could be implicitly trusted' (*DNB*). During the debates on parliamentary reform in

1866 he attempted to limit extension of the franchise, remaining convinced that an aristocratic form of government based on paternalism and personal liberties would obviate the need for democratic change. As early as 1850 he had reversed his earlier support for the ballot. He refused office in Gladstone's administration, formed in December 1868, and stood down from his Morpeth seat at the February 1874 general election after it became apparent that the miners, who now formed a majority of electors in the constituency, were intent on carrying their own man, Thomas Burt. He retired from politics without bitterness, and died at his home, Fallodon, Northumberland, on 9 September 1882. He was buried in the churchyard of Embleton, whose incumbent, Mandell Creighton, a friend in his later years, wrote a sympathetic memoir of him. As his only son had predeceased him the baronetcy passed to his grandson, Edward *Grey, the future foreign secretary.

DAVID FREDERICK SMITH

Sources M. Creighton, *Memoir of Sir George Grey* (privately printed, Newcastle-upon-Tyne, 1884); new edn (1901) · D. F. Smith, 'Sir George Grey at the mid Victorian Home Office', PhD diss., University of Toronto, 1972 · D. F. Smith, 'Sir George Grey at the mid Victorian Home Office', *Canadian Journal of History/Annales Canadiennes d'Histoire*, 19 (Dec 1984), 361–86 · D. F. Smith, 'The demise of transportation: mid Victorian penal policy', *Criminal Justice History*, 3 (1983), 15–31 · *DNB* · R. Brent, *Liberal Anglican politics: whiggery, religion, and reform, 1830–1841* (1987) · K. Robbins, *Sir Edward Grey* (1971) · J. Saville, *1848: the British state and the chartist movement* (1987) · P. Mandler, *Aristocratic government in the age of reform: whigs and liberals, 1830–1852* (1990) · J. Prest, *Lord John Russell* (1972) · G. F. A. Best, *Temporal pillars: Queen Anne's bounty, the ecclesiastical commissioners, and the Church of England* (1964) · L. Radzinowicz and R. Hood, *A history of English criminal law and its administration from 1750*, 5: *The emergence of penal policy in Victorian and Edwardian England* (1986) · O. MacDonagh, *Early Victorian government* (1977)

Archives ING Barings, corresp., memoranda, and notes | BL, corresp. with Lord Aberdeen, Add. MS 43197 · BL, corresp. with W. E. Gladstone, Add. MS 44162 · BLPES, corresp. with Sir Joshua Jebb · Bodl. Oxf., corresp. with Lord Clarendon · Bodl. Oxf., corresp. with Lord Kimberley · Borth. Inst., corresp. with Lord Halifax · Durham RO, letters to Lord Londonderry · HLRO, corresp. with Lord Hampden · Lambton Park, Lambton estate office, Chester-le-Street, co. Durham, corresp. with Lord Durham · LPL, letters to A. C. Tait · NA Scot., corresp. with Sir H. B. Loch · NA Scot., corresp. with Sir John McNeill · NA Scot., letters to second Lord Panmure · NL Scot., letters to Edward Ellice · NL Scot., letters to Andrew Rutherford · PRO, letters to Lord Granville, PRO 30/29 · PRO, corresp. with Lord John Russell, PRO 30/22 · Sandon Hall, Staffordshire, corresp. with Lord Harrowby · St Deiniol's Library, Hawarden, corresp. with Sir John Gladstone · St Deiniol's Library, Hawarden, corresp. with duke of Newcastle · U. Durham L., letters to Charles Grey · U. Durham L., corresp. with second Earl Grey · U. Durham L., corresp. with third Earl Grey · U. Durham L., letters to Sir Walter Trevelyan · U. Nott. L., letters to J. E. Denison · U. Nott. L., letters to duke of Newcastle · U. Southampton L., corresp. with Lord Palmerston · U. Southampton L., letters to first duke of Wellington · UCL, corresp. with Sir Edwin Chadwick · W. Sussex RO, letters to duke of Richmond

Likenesses J. Doyle, pencil caricature, 1848, BM · F. Grant, oils, 1849 · G. Richmond, drawing, 1859 · W. & D. Downey, carte-de-visite, c.1860–1869, NPG · J. & C. Watkins, carte-de-visite, 1860–69, NPG · W. Walker, photograph, c.1865, NPG [see illus.] · W. & D. Downey, two photographs, c.1870–1880, repro. in Creighton, *Memoir*, facing p. 100 · J. Gilbert, group portrait, pencil and wash (*The coalition ministry*, 1854), NPG · W. Holl, stipple (after G. Richmond; *Grillion's Club* series), BM · J. Phillips, group portrait, oils (*The House of Commons, 1860*), Palace of Westminster, London · photograph, repro. in *ILN*, 81 (1882), 340

Wealth at death £58,464 8s. 3d.: probate, 12 Oct 1882, *CGPLA Eng. & Wales*

Grey, Sir George (1812–1898), colonial governor and premier of New Zealand, was born in Lisbon, Portugal, on 14 April 1812 into a genteel English family, a cadet branch of the family of the earls of Stamford. His mother, Elizabeth Anne Grey, *née* Vignoles, had accompanied his father to Portugal on campaign, where Lieutenant-Colonel George Grey was killed at the siege of Badajoz eight days before his son was born. Elizabeth Grey remarried about 1817; her new husband was the Revd Sir John Thomas, bt.

Early life Grey was educated by his mother until the age of eight and then attended a boarding-school in Guildford. His teachers, he remembered, 'didn't understand me' (Milne, 41), and he ran away. Later he settled into a military education at the Royal Military College, Sandhurst (1826–9), where he excelled. He was commissioned ensign in the 83rd infantry regiment in 1830, and became a lieutenant in 1833 and a captain in 1839. From 1830 to 1836 he served in Ireland, and came to dislike the oppression of the Irish peasantry.

The young Grey had private means, good connections, and good relations with his step-family. His pious Anglican mother was a key early influence, and a family friend, Richard Whately, later archbishop of Dublin, became something of a mentor. Grey shared Whately's conviction that 'savages' needed to be 'raised' to something European-like, and that they were incapable of raising themselves. Grey also became a friend and disciple of Thomas Carlyle, with whom he shared an ardent Anglo-Saxonism.

Australian years Through the good offices of a well-connected friend, Grey persuaded the British government to send him to Western Australia, where he led two exploratory expeditions (1837–9). His optimistic reports of great fertility were soon questioned, and his claim that 'no country in the world is better watered' (Rutherford, 9) may surprise Western Australians. Each expedition encountered difficulties and found little of note. In the first, Grey was wounded in the thigh by an Aborigine's spear, and he shot his attacker in return. Both the killing and the wound disturbed him for the rest of his life. The former was the only human life he personally ever took; the latter left a hole big enough to fit a child's hand, even when Grey was in his old age. But the explorations did yield experience: 'I am daily becoming more prudent [and] less presumptuous' (Rutherford, 14); a successful book (*Journal of Two Expeditions of Discovery in North West and Western Australia*, 2 vols., 1841); a well-received report on native management (1840); and a good impression in London.

Grey accepted a temporary post as resident magistrate at Albany, Western Australia, in 1839. On 2 November of that year he married Eliza Lucy Spencer (d. 1898), the

Sir George Grey (1812–1898), by George Richmond, 1854

daughter of his recently deceased predecessor, Sir Richard Spencer. The couple soon sailed for England, where they arrived on 20 September 1840. Within three months they were sailing back, Grey having been appointed governor of South Australia—an extraordinary promotion for a 28-year-old whose achievements were as yet limited. He sold his captain's commission, suggesting that he saw himself as launched on a new career. This career as colonial governor became a sacred mission in Grey's mind. Although he was religious at the private level, his public evangelism was largely secular, a crusade to colonize both natives and nature. He sought, first, to transform 'wild natives' into something English-like, converted to Christianity, commerce, civilization, and subordination, and second, to transform wild nature through settlement into flourishing young neo-Britains, maximizing the virtues and minimizing the vices of the old. His four governorships, in South Australia (1841–5), South Africa (1854–61), and New Zealand (1845–53 and 1861–8), need to be understood in the light of this creed. The humane, reserved, intellectual gentleman co-existed with a racialist and imperialist zealot. Colonization, in this dual sense, was Grey's mission on earth, and nothing—natives, settlers, or London masters—would be allowed to stand in the way of it.

Grey's South Australian governorship began unpromisingly, on 10 May 1841. His only child, a son born at sea, died at the age of five months. Grey is said to have blamed his wife, and his relations with her became strained. His energetic retrenchments, 'even to the extent of refusing 8d. ...

for sharpening pencils' (Sinclair) initially enraged the settlers without satisfying London. He struggled with the legacy of Edward Gibbon Wakefield, whose system of organized colonization had founded South Australia in 1834. He felt it reproduced the English class system to the detriment of labourers. Grey made South Australian Aborigines the first test of his theory of secular conversion: addicting 'the savage' to European legal, social, medical, educational, and economic practices; weaning them from custom and tribalism; and mixing, though not marrying, them with European settlers who would civilize by example. The test failed, or rather the indigenous people declined to sit it. But Grey minimized this in his reports, and his administration of South Australia was more substantially successful in other respects. Most notable from the imperial government's viewpoint was the eventual balancing of the budget. This was facilitated by an upturn in the South Australian economy, from 1843, but owed something to Grey's energy and ingenuity, as well as an altruistic readiness to subsidize the public purse from his own. He eventually became popular with the South Australian settlers as well as the imperial government, an exceptional feat, and the legend of his first governorship requires somewhat less pruning than those of later administrations.

First New Zealand governorship In late 1845 Grey, as the Colonial Office's rising young troubleshooter, was appointed to his next colony in crisis: New Zealand. War had broken out between British and Maori in March of that year, and the imperial forces had suffered three successive defeats. Grey landed at Auckland on 14 November 1845 and confronted the crisis with sword and pen. He exaggerated the real failings of his predecessor (as he had in South Australia) while acquiring more latitude and resources, mounted a substantial, but inconclusive, new military expedition against the hostile sub-tribes in the Bay of Islands, and proclaimed it a decisive success. This paper victory of January 1846 did not impact on northern Maori independence, but it did bring about peace in the north and free troops to deal with incipient conflict near Wellington. Here, after confused skirmishing, Grey punctured resistance by seizing the important neutral chief Te Rauparaha on 23 July 1846. Caught naked and unarmed in his house, the old chief struggled desperately until a sailor seized him by the testicles, so symbolizing both the ethics and the effectiveness of Grey's tactics.

Grey was appointed KCB in 1848. By this time, due partly to his clever politics if not to his military victories, peace prevailed in New Zealand and continued to the end of his first governorship in 1853. Grey repeatedly portrayed the situation as a miraculous peaceful conquest, his theory of secular conversion working to perfection. In fact the peace was characterized by economic interaction between two independent zones rather than by the demise of Maori independence. But it was peace none the less. After 1847 Grey had more trouble with Europeans than with Maori. As in South Australia, he had to deal with a Wakefieldian legacy, the New Zealand Company, and even with Wakefield himself. The company settlers wanted self-government. They persuaded the Colonial Office, which sent down a constitution in 1846, but not Grey, who refused to implement it. He designed a new constitution himself, inspired by the United States constitution and 'by talking to the hills and trees' (Milne, 160), but refused to implement even this until the eve of his departure in 1853. Grey also conducted his first experiments in close settlement, helping make small farms available to people of small means, and military settlement, whereby imperial army pensioners, or 'fencibles', were settled around Auckland. With his lieutenant, native secretary Donald McLean, he arranged the crown purchase of 30 million acres of Maori land at low prices. This was almost half of New Zealand, but most of the purchases were in the South Island, where few Maori lived.

Governor of Cape Colony   In 1854 Grey became governor of Cape Colony and high commissioner for South Africa. Here, for the first time, he found himself having to work with an elected colonial legislature. But, by playing colonial and imperial governments off against each other, he was able to retain substantive control, just as he was to do, with rather more difficulty, in his second New Zealand governorship. South Africa in 1854 was in the tense aftermath of the latest of several major wars against the formidable Xhosa tribes. Grey's main task as governor was to manage this, which he conceived as a need to extend British rule into Xhosa territory, known as Kaffraria, at minimum cost. His way was paved by the strange Xhosa millennial movement of 1856–8, where tribes destroyed their own cattle and crops in the expectation that their ancestors would rise from the dead and drive the Europeans into the sea. The 'cattle-killing' movement was sparked by an outbreak of cattle disease, as well as by the young prophetess Nongqawuse and her uncle Mhalakaza. It soon involved leading Xhosa chiefs, including the paramount chief, Sarili. Grey exploited the resulting famine, and the split between believers and unbelievers, to divide and rule British Kaffraria. Though he sometimes told London that he was fighting a full-scale 'Kaffir War', and kept more than 10,000 imperial troops on this basis, Grey's use of force was selective, limited, and surgical, confined to the later stages of the famine which killed at least 40,000 Xhosa.

Grey can hardly have been expected to view Xhosa self-immolation as anything other than a gift from providence. Where he does appear to have been highly culpable was in the handling of relief efforts as famine took hold. He discouraged private charitable initiatives and limited public charity to the largely cosmetic, insisting that starving Xhosa receive help only if they laboured on public projects or migrated to the Cape for work. Fanatics seldom show mercy to enemies fortune delivers to them, and it is not so much the deed itself as the associated hypocrisy that is hard to stomach. Grey claimed that he had 'saved a nation' from the 'self-destruction' he had in fact welcomed (Rutherford, 368).

Grey also went to war with his masters in London, to the extent that one War Office memorandum described him as 'rebellious' (Rutherford, 399). One *casus belli* was the issue of South African federation, incorporating the Afrikaner republics of Orange Free State and the Transvaal, with which Grey maintained quite good relations. Grey wanted federation; London did not, and eventually, in 1859, it had to sack him to get its way. A change of government led to his immediate reinstatement, on the condition that he dropped at least this effort to gain Britain empires it did not want. London did not get its way on two other issues. Despite its repeated protests, Grey embarked on another experiment in military settlement, involving the German Legion, which ultimately failed at a cost of £250,000. Second, on the outbreak of the Indian mutiny, Grey directed the flow of reinforcements from or via South Africa at his own discretion, without, even despite, orders from the imperial government. The situation was complex and controversial, but it appears that he sent reinforcements when London did not want him to, and did not send them when it did.

On the voyage back from England to South Africa in 1860, after Grey's recall and reinstatement, his wife Eliza 'formed a romantic attachment' (Sinclair) to the ship's commander, Admiral Sir Henry Keppel. Grey discovered it, threatened to 'either commit suicide or murder his wife' (Rutherford, 428), and had her put ashore at Rio de Janeiro. Grey swore Keppel to secrecy and did not speak to Eliza again for thirty-six years. He spent another year in South Africa, embittered and increasingly reserved, then volunteered to be posted to New Zealand, where war with the Taranaki Maori had broken out in 1860.

Second New Zealand governorship   Grey arrived in New Zealand for his second governorship on 26 September 1861. The war had ended six months earlier, but had strengthened the King movement, a Maori nationalist organization, centred on Waikato, which underwrote Maori independence. Settlers, Maori, and the imperial government alike found Grey's intentions over the next two years difficult to fathom, but in retrospect it is clear that he quickly decided to break the King movement—peacefully if possible, by force if necessary.

Grey's 'peace policy' centred on a system of 'new institutions' for European-led Maori local government and on the return of the Waitara—the block of land whose disputed purchase had sparked the war of 1860. This merged seamlessly with an aspect of his war policy: 'to reduce the number of our enemies' outside the Waikato heartland of the King movement (Grey to the duke of Newcastle, 2 Nov 1861, CO 209/164, fol. 334). Grey also created a logistic infrastructure for the invasion of Waikato and duped London into providing extra troops. Fighting flared up anew in Taranaki in May 1863 but was quickly damped down by the return of the Waitara. On 12 July 1863 Grey's well-prepared forces invaded Waikato. The war was closely contested, but by mid-1864 the British had secured partial victory, largely as a result of Grey's preparations. He sought to complete the victory with a scheme for the confiscation and military settlement of Maori land and with subsequent campaigns (1865–6) against a secondary bastion of Maori independence in South Taranaki, with London still footing the bill. These measures earned him increasing approval from the settlers and increasing antagonism from the imperial government. He was replaced in early 1868, his proconsular career at an end. The imperial government had finally mustered the nerve to rid itself of an over-mighty servant, but only after he had spent a decade deploying thousands of its troops and spending millions of its money.

Later life Grey spent the years 1868–70 in England, where he stood unsuccessfully for a seat at Westminster (as a Liberal at Newark in a by-election in April 1870) and campaigned publicly for empire unity and expansion. His contribution to the nascent imperial federation movement has yet to be evaluated, but may have been considerable. He then returned to New Zealand as a private citizen and spent the period 1870–74 at Kawau, the island which he had purchased in 1862 for £3500. Here he developed a private paradise, complete with mansion, loyal retainers, and numerous botanical and zoological specimens, the last including monkeys, zebras, and kangaroos. In 1874 the Knight of Kawau re-emerged into New Zealand politics as champion of the provincial system which he had created, which was threatened by increasing centralist sentiment among the ruling élite. Grey had always mixed democratic principle with autocratic practice, and he advocated close settlement and the extension of the franchise as well as the retention of the provinces. He was elected to parliament and the superintendency of Auckland province in 1875 and became premier in 1877, but was unable to prevent or reverse the abolition of the provinces in 1876. Grey's increasing radicalism, his reputation for ruthlessness and success, and his rambling eloquence made him deeply feared by the New Zealand gentry. But he now lacked the patience and the party-building skills to circumvent their antagonism. He was forced to resign in October 1879. He persisted in parliament for thirteen more years, as a critic on the sidelines: he was seen by some as the grand old man of New Zealand politics, by others as a dangerous eccentric staying long beyond his time.

Grey sold Kawau in 1888 for £12,000 and shifted to Auckland. He fell ill in January 1891—so seriously that a premature eulogy was delivered in parliament. But he recovered sufficiently to make a phonograph recording the next month, reputedly the southern hemisphere's first. He left New Zealand for the last time in 1894. That year he was sworn of the privy council and had an audience with Queen Victoria. In deference to his age, she ordered him not to kneel. He knelt anyway: no queen–empress was going to tell George Grey how to worship her. He lived in London until his death, at the Norfolk Hotel, Harrington Road, South Kensington, on 19 September 1898. He was buried in St Paul's Cathedral. He had been partly reconciled with his wife, Eliza, two years before; she predeceased him by two weeks.

Assessment Grey was a keen hunter and an expert shot, a good rider and distance runner, and had what contemporary phrenologists considered to be a remarkable head. Among his 'chief amusements' on Kawau 'was to provoke

a wild bull to charge him and shoot it with a rifle when it was a few yards off' (J. Gorst, *New Zealand Revisited*, 1908, 26). He was an avid bibliophile, and on at least one occasion spent £200 on rare books and manuscripts in a single month. He sponsored cultural projects that accorded with his aims, spending his own time and money on them as well as that of the public. He donated one large collection of books and manuscripts to the Cape Town Public Library in 1861 and another to the Auckland Public Library in 1883. He collected and published four volumes of Maori traditions, songs, and proverbs (1853–7). These works, published under Grey's name alone, were actually products of collaboration between him and Maori experts, most notably the Arawa historian Wiremu Maihi Te Rangikaheke; they simultaneously colonized and preserved Maori culture.

George Grey is a difficult man to evaluate. His reputations as transculturite, public benefactor, and enlightened genteel democrat are not undeserved, yet are outranked by his achievements as subtle but ultimately ruthless conqueror. His legend, which he himself helped to create, portrayed him as 'good Governor Grey', 'the great proconsul', saviour of white and black people in all three of his realms. While the legend dominated for a century, it co-existed with a counter-legend, originating with rivals for power in both London and his colonies, in which he was, at best, manipulative and untrustworthy, at worst, an insane megalomaniac: 'a terrible and fatal man' (Rutherford, 475). There is a sense in which the real Grey was a strange hybrid of legend and counter-legend in which the latter came to predominate. One reason was the underlying tension between humanitarianism and expansionism, persuasion and force; others were more private and particular.

Grey disliked smoking and was very moderate in his use of alcohol, readily pledging himself to a year or two of abstinence to encourage others. His drug of choice appears to have been opium, possibly in the form of laudanum. There are also claims—from Eliza Grey, among others—that he had a number of adulterous sexual relationships with women, black and white. His sexual liaisons make his reaction to his wife's relationship with Keppel, which is thought to have been unconsummated, appear almost obsessive, even for the days of the double standard, and it was one of a succession of personal blows. Dismissal from the Cape, though reversed, was another, as was the war of 1863–6 in New Zealand. One would like to include the Xhosa cattle-killing famine among his traumas. In these contexts Grey resorted more often to what he himself called 'a little medicine' (Rutherford, 573). The net result, which might now be described as drug addiction and/or clinical depression, was particularly apparent during the years 1858–65, but also in old age. In early 1863, as his manoeuvres against the King movement reached their climax, he was 'subject to fits of trembling' (ibid., 472), could not load his own revolver, and admitted that his health had 'completely broken down' (ibid., 586). In the 1880s he locked himself in his room on Kawau for days on end. His self-perceived responsibility, and therefore stress, was enormous, and, because of mutual distrust, he could not confide in those who could comprehend his problems. Living in Grey's head cannot have been easy.

George Grey was a brilliant and effective servant of British imperialism as he saw it. His ruthlessness stemmed more from fanaticism in his cause than from lesser moral failings. That self-doubt sometimes simmered beneath the proconsular veneer is, in a sense, to his credit. Whether this would have made Maori or Xhosa feel any better about his treatment of them is another matter.   JAMES BELICH

Sources J. Rutherford, *Sir George Grey* (1961) • G. C. Henderson, *Sir George Grey* (1907) • J. Milne, *The romance of a proconsul* (1911) • J. Collier, *Sir George Grey* (1909) • W. L. Rees and L. Rees, *Life and times of Sir George Grey* (1892) • K. Sinclair, 'Grey, George', *DNZB*, vol. 1 • J. Rutherford, 'Grey, Sir George', *An encyclopaedia of New Zealand*, ed. A. H. McLintock, 1 (1966) • J. B. Peires, *The dead will arise: Nongqawuse and the great Xhosa cattle-killing movement of 1856–7* (1989) • N. Mostert, *Frontiers* (1992) • J. Belich, *The New Zealand wars and the Victorian interpretation of racial conflict* (1986) • B. J. Dalton, 'Sir George Grey and the Keppel affair', *Historical Studies: Australia and New Zealand*, 16 (1974–5), 192–215 • V. Yarwood and P. Quinn, 'The governor's island', *New Zealand Geographic*, 39 (July–Sept 1998), 88–106 • *CGPLA Eng. & Wales* (1899) • Colonial Office inwards correspondence, PRO, CO 209/164, fol. 334
Archives Auckland Public Library, corresp. and papers • Mitchell L., NSW, corresp., journal, and papers • National Library of South Africa, Cape Town, corresp. and papers • NL Scot., corresp. | Auckland Public Library, letters to Ormus Biddulph • BL, corresp. with W. E. Gladstone, Add. MSS 44363–44496 *passim* • Herts. ALS, corresp. with Lord Lytton • NL NZ, dispatches to Lord Grey [copies] • NL NZ, Turnbull L., Donald McLean papers • PRO, Colonial Office inwards correspondence, CO 13/16–47, 209/134–6 and 153–90, 48, etc. • U. Durham L., corresp. with third Earl Grey, incl. extracts from dispatches • U. Nottingham L., corresp. with duke of Newcastle
Likenesses G. Richmond, drawing, 1854, Auckland Art Gallery [see illus.] • W. C. Marshall, marble statue, exh. RA 1862, Cape Town, South Africa • Hanna of New Zealand, photograph, 1867–8, NPG • H. von Herkomer, oils, 1901, NPG • W. W. Alais, stipple (after photograph), NPG • W. W. Alais, wood-engraving (after photograph by York), NPG; repro. in *ILN* (17 Dec 1859) • Heath and Bean, carte-de-visite, NPG • stipple, NPG
Wealth at death £1646 7s. 2d.: resworn administration with will, Sept 1899, *CGPLA Eng. & Wales*

Grey, Henry (d. 1219). *See under* Grey family (*per.* 1325–1523).

Grey, Henry, duke of Suffolk (1517–1554), magnate, was born on 17 January 1517, at Bradgate, Leicestershire, the eldest son of Thomas *Grey, second marquess of Dorset, and his second wife, Margaret, daughter of Sir Robert Wotton and widow of William Medley.

Marriage and inheritance Aged thirteen when his father died in 1530, Henry Grey's wardship (without his estates) was granted to Charles Brandon, first duke of Suffolk, for a payment of 4000 marks. Grey may previously have contracted marriage, or even been married, to Katherine Fitzalan, daughter of the eleventh earl of Arundel, but this match, whatever its status, was repudiated, for early in May 1533 Suffolk arranged his ward's marriage to Frances (1517–1559), the daughter of his marriage to Mary Tudor,

the younger sister of Henry VIII [*see* Grey, Frances, duchess of Suffolk]; the marriage had profound consequences for Dorset himself and for his children.

Since Dorset did not enter his full inheritance until his mother died, no earlier than 1535, Suffolk agreed to support the couple until his son-in-law had attained his majority. The Greys for their part conceded that Dorset should receive only a small dowry with Frances. These arrangements suited both families; although very wealthy, neither had much disposable income. Dorset was made a knight of the Bath on 30 May 1533, at the coronation of Queen Anne Boleyn. Ambitious, and so proud of his links with the crown that he did not correct foreigners who addressed him as 'prince', he was said by a court observer in 1538 to have inherited his father's physical strength, if not yet all his estates. But with Henry VIII now ageing, the days when a man could prosper at court by virtue of his jousting skills, as his father and guardian had done, were over. Under Suffolk's tutelage Dorset went on several campaigns, but he did not aspire to a military career. As a leading peer he took part in such major court ceremonies as the king's marriages and openings of parliament; he was the chief mourner at Henry VIII's funeral and lord high constable at the coronation of Edward VI, but he had so little support at court that even though Suffolk nominated him for the Garter every year, he was not selected by Henry VIII.

Involvement with Thomas Seymour Dorset's fortunes changed dramatically under Edward VI, thanks to his wife's Tudor blood and the need that the rivals for power had for support from prominent families. Within weeks of seizing power, on 23 May 1547, Protector Somerset gave Dorset the Garter that had eluded him during the previous reign; even more importantly, Somerset's brother Thomas, Baron Seymour, began courting him, promising to reward him if Dorset fell in with his schemes. Undoubtedly this vague promise included grants of land and office, but Seymour's most seductive promise was a pledge to arrange a marriage between Dorset's daughter, Lady Jane *Grey, and the young king. All that Dorset was expected to do was to place Lady Jane under Seymour's care and to support his claim for more power. Dorset readily fell in with Seymour's scheme, and he and Seymour were the only peers to vote against confirming the letters patent granting Somerset his plenary authority. The gullible marquess also sent his daughter to Sudeley, ostensibly so that she could be under the care of Seymour's wife Katherine Parr, the dowager queen, to be educated with her cousin the future Queen Elizabeth.

The scandal surrounding Seymour and Elizabeth that broke in the summer of 1548 should have warned Dorset, but blinded by ambition he ignored Seymour's reckless behaviour and permitted his daughter to remain at Sudeley. After Katherine's death, Lady Jane returned to her parents, but Seymour and his agent Sir William Sharington so wore down Dorset and his wife with their pleas that they relented, and she returned to Sudeley, to remain there under Seymour's care until his disgrace. It would not be the last time Dorset would put his own interests ahead of those of his daughter.

Thomas Seymour had additional plans for Dorset; playing on his pride in being the leading man in Warwickshire, he frequently talked to him about building up his following there, ostensibly to counter the rising John Dudley, but in fact to support Seymour in his looked-for showdown with his brother the protector. Dorset later testified that he had been so seduced by Seymour that he had pledged that he would risk his life for him in all quarrels except against the king. The naïve Dorset presumably did not realize what a dangerous game Seymour was playing, but he was true to his word and stuck by Seymour to the last. He was obviously not one of the main plotters, however, and survived Seymour's fall early in 1549 unscathed, only to become enmeshed in another attempt to topple Somerset.

Supporter of Northumberland It is doubtful whether Dorset was involved in planning the coup against Somerset led by John Dudley, earl of Warwick, in autumn 1549. He was known for his evangelical sympathies, however, so that his appointment to the privy council late in November was a clear sign that Warwick and Archbishop Cranmer had prevailed over their conservative opponents. He was quick to exploit his new position, and less than a month later he was among those who made huge profits from exchanging coin and plate for newly minted coins; he also began to amass grants of land and office, thereby augmenting his local prestige as well as his income. In exchange for these signs of favour, Dorset loyally supported the new regime. He was sent to the north of England in 1550 as a precaution against disorder there, and in the autumn was pressed into service to bring the radical Bishop John Hooper into line with Cranmer's religious policies. In February 1551 he was named lord warden of the northern marches to ward off the threat from a combined Franco-Scottish force. But he pestered his colleagues in London for instructions and money so frequently that they must have been relieved when he resigned to attend to his estates.

Dorset brought little distinction to the privy council, he attended no more than one-third of its meetings, and when the court divided he was among the courtiers who accompanied the king rather than one of the active politicians who stayed in London with Warwick. But his wife was third in line to the throne and until Edward produced an heir his dynastic position made Dorset a man to be reckoned with. Consequently, when Warwick completed the destruction of the duke of Somerset late in 1551, Dorset figured prominently in his plans. On 11 October he was created duke of Suffolk in the same ceremony that elevated Warwick to the duchy of Northumberland, and in December he was one of the lords who convicted Somerset of felony, characteristically to his own advantage: he received some of Somerset's London property and was given command of the protector's troop of 100 horsemen with its allowance of £2000 a year.

Rebellion and death Suffolk took an active part in court life in King Edward's final year, escorting the Lady Mary on a visit to her brother. He was given substantial property, but his fortunes reached their peak when, in anticipation of death, Edward arranged the marriage on 21 May 1553 of Suffolk's daughter Jane to Lord Guildford Dudley and later altered his will to enable her to succeed him. Edward died on 6 July, and three days later Suffolk, Northumberland, and other councillors proclaimed Jane queen, but at his daughter's pleading Suffolk stayed in London to protect her while Northumberland tried to capture Mary before news of the king's death became common knowledge. The politically inept Suffolk was not the man to hold the council to its collective promise, however, and when defectors proclaimed Mary as queen, Suffolk was forced to repudiate his daughter and follow their example.

For someone so deeply implicated in treason, Suffolk fared surprisingly well in the aftermath of the abortive coup. Unlike Northumberland he was confined in the Tower for only a few days, released without having been charged, and allowed to retire to his house at East Sheen, while his wife was welcomed at court. But he was not destined to enjoy a quiet life away from court. On 1 November 1553 the Spanish ambassador reported that the new queen was angry with him for refusing to change his religion, but a few weeks later he announced that Suffolk had recanted and been given a full pardon; the protestant community, however, refused to believe that 'our Duke' had denied his faith.

Despite his reprieve Suffolk remained acutely insecure and by Christmas he had joined Sir Thomas Wyatt and Sir Peter Carew in their conspiracy to prevent Mary's marriage to Philip of Spain. Unfortunately for the hapless Suffolk, the council had a good idea of what was going on as early as 2 January 1554 when it summoned Carew, and after a few weeks of fact gathering it summoned Suffolk on the 25th, possibly to test his loyalty by offering him command against the anticipated rebellion. Fearing the worst, he lost his nerve and decided to flee to his estates in the midlands, where his brother Thomas assured him no one would dare to seize him. Suffolk proved to be as incompetent in rebellion as he had been in politics. Caught unawares, he had to delay his flight until his steward could scrape together enough cash to make the journey and by then his cause was lost. He reached his seat at Bradgate on 29 January, and then went on to Leicester, where he denounced the Spanish marriage next day. The town was apathetic at best and when Coventry, where he had expectations of strong support, proved to be openly hostile, he had no choice but to withdraw to his manor at Astley and prepare to leave the country. The failed conspirator had no strategy other than to exchange clothes with a servant, and thus disguised hope to get to a port and make his way to Denmark. Typically, he had not planned an escape route and had no idea where to go. He was taken prisoner, arraigned for his treason, condemned, and executed at the Tower of London on 23 February 1554, less than a month after his brief rebellion began.

A study in failure Suffolk had been rebuked several times by his protestant allies for playing at cards and dice, and what was worse in their eyes, for gambling for money. But whether his rebellion represented the ultimate wager, or merely aristocratic arrogance that his name carried greater weight in his home country than the monarch's, he clearly overestimated his support. His meagre force never numbered more than 140, most of them his and his family's retainers. If he truly believed that Francis Hastings, second earl of Huntingdon, would support him, even though the two men had been allies under Northumberland, he miscalculated badly. The Hastings family had long been rivals to the Greys for pre-eminence in Leicestershire, and Huntingdon, who was eager to prove his loyalty to the new regime, had much to gain by capturing his old enemy and turning him over to the queen. Suffolk's pathetic rebellion lasted a mere five days.

It may be said that Suffolk's rebellion led to his daughter's execution, but as her life was already forfeit the rising merely provided Mary's government with an excuse to take it. She was executed eleven days before her father, who was survived by his remaining daughters Katherine (1540?–1568) [see Seymour, Katherine, countess of Hertford], and Mary (1545?–1578) [see Keys, Lady Mary] who were subsequently imprisoned when they married without Queen Elizabeth's permission. His widow married Adrian Stokes and died on 21 November 1559.

Suffolk's ill-fated rebellion as well as his naïve support for Thomas Seymour reveal that although well-connected, he was simply not competent in the world of high politics. He was self-important, quick to point out his Tudor connections, and apt to throw his weight around in local matters. In 1546 he quarrelled with John Beaumont, receiver-general of the court of wards and had him rebuked for not showing due respect to a peer. Suffolk did not forget their altercation and seven years later enjoyed the satisfaction of having Beaumont charged with champerty and perjury over a fraudulent land transaction. The subsequent revelation that Beaumont had also defrauded the crown of £11,823 and owed an additional £9000 in unpaid arrears must have gratified the duke, who had few other triumphs.   ROBERT C. BRADDOCK

Sources DNB · GEC, Peerage, 4.420-22 · CSP dom., 1547–58 · J. Nichols, The history and antiquities of the county of Leicester, 4 vols. (1795–1815) · D. Loades, John Dudley, duke of Northumberland, 1504–1553 (1996) · S. J. Gunn, Charles Brandon, duke of Suffolk, c.1484–1545 (1988) · G. W. Bernard, 'The downfall of Sir Thomas Seymour', The Tudor nobility, ed. G. W. Bernard (1992), 212–40 · D. E. Hoak, The king's council in the reign of Edward VI (1976) · H. Miller, Henry VIII and the English nobility (1986) · M. A. R. Graves, The House of Lords in the parliaments of Edward VI and Mary I (1981) · J. G. Nichols, ed., The chronicle of Queen Jane, and of two years of Queen Mary, CS, old ser., 48 (1850) · state papers domestic, Edward VI, PRO, SP 10/6/7 · exchequer, king's remembrancer, lay subsidy rolls, PRO, E 179/69/54, 75 · H. Robinson, ed. and trans., Original letters relative to the English Reformation, 1 vol. in 2, Parker Society, [26] (1846–7) · D. M. Loades, Two Tudor conspiracies (1965) · D. MacCulloch, Thomas Cranmer: a life (1996) · W. K. Jordan, Edward VI, 2: The threshold of power (1970)

Archives NRA, priv. coll., Devon estate survey

Wealth at death attainted; wealth forfeit

Grey, Henry, first Baron Grey of Groby (1547–1614), courtier and administrator, was the only surviving son of Lord John *Grey (d. 1564) of Pirgo, Essex, and Mary, daughter of Anthony *Browne, first Viscount Montagu of Cowdray, Sussex. He was probably educated at Christ Church, Oxford, where a Henry Grey graduated BA on 1 February 1565 and MA on 18 June 1568. He married Anne (1542–1613/14), daughter of William, second Lord Windsor of Bradenham, Buckinghamshire, about 1575 and was knighted on 11 November 1587. He was appointed one of the queen's gentleman pensioners in 1569 and was lieutenant of the band from 1589 to 1603. In 1596 he was also made master of the queen's buckhounds. James I raised him to the peerage on 21 July 1603, when he was created Baron Grey of Groby, Leicestershire, and as a quid pro quo he was forced to resign his lieutenancy of the gentleman pensioners in September. He served as knight of the shire for Essex in 1589.

Grey's main ambition during Elizabeth's reign was to re-establish his family's position in Leicestershire. His father had suffered attainder in 1554 for his involvement in Wyatt's rebellion. Elizabeth released him from this in 1559 and also granted him the manor of Pirgo, which became his principal residence. Henry succeeded to the estate on his father's death in 1564 and divided his time between his duties at court—where he was required to attend on the queen for six months of the year—and local government in Essex. At court he enjoyed the favour of Lord Burghley and his son Sir Robert Cecil, and in 1588 he figured in a list of those considered suitable for baronies. Nothing came of this, but by the end of Elizabeth's reign he had managed to reacquire most of his family's estates in Leicestershire, centred on Bradgate Park and the manor of Groby. As a local governor he provided a valuable link between the court and the localities. Grey was put on to the commission of the peace for Essex (c.1573), served as deputy lieutenant (1586–90), and was described in 1600 as the county's senior justice. His election to parliament for Essex in 1589 was secured by the intervention of the privy council, which dissuaded Lord Rich from backing a rival candidate. At Westminster he participated in the committee on purveyance and attended the queen with a petition from the Commons to curb abuses by purveyors.

After his promotion to a barony and his resignation from the gentleman pensioners Grey took up residence at Bradgate and devoted most of his energies to strengthening his family's position in Leicestershire. This involved reviving the feud between the Greys and the Hastings earls of Huntingdon which had divided the shire for much of the early sixteenth century. When the fourth earl of Huntingdon died in December 1604, Grey immediately wrote to Cecil asking that he be granted his lord lieutenancy and other county offices as compensation for surrendering his lieutenancy of the gentleman pensioners. The fifth earl, who was a minor, protested and Cecil sided with him, agreeing to put the lord lieutenancy in abeyance until he came of age. In the meantime Grey joined forces with the Beaumont family and sought to dominate the county in other ways. He became the leading spokesman for the justices in their dealings with central government and engineered changes in the commission of the peace at the expense of the Hastings faction. The struggle intensified when Huntingdon reached his majority in 1607 and took over the main posts in local government. Grey attacked him on two fronts, questioning his management of purveyance in the county during 1610 and 1611 and then in 1612 backing an inquiry into the earl's nomination of John Bale to the commission of the peace. His cause was badly damaged by the sudden death of his son Sir John Grey in October 1611, which removed his main source of support at court. In both instances Huntingdon was successful in seeing off the challenge and by the time of Grey's death Huntingdon was firmly in control of the shire.

There is little direct evidence about Grey's religious views, but he appears to have inherited the staunchly protestant attitude of his father. When a group of puritan ministers in Leicestershire was threatened with deprivation in January 1605, his name headed the list of local JPs petitioning Cecil for leniency. He was also closely associated with Francis White, minister at the Grey living of Broughton Astley. White was later to become an apologist for Arminianism, but at this stage in his career was making his reputation as an anti-papal polemicist.

Grey had four sons and four daughters. He died on 26 July 1614 at Bradgate Park and was buried in the family chapel there. He was succeeded by his grandson, Henry, a minor who later became earl of Stamford.

RICHARD CUST

Sources HoP, *Commons, 1558–1603*, 2.222–4 · J. Nichols, *The history and antiquities of the county of Leicester*, 3 (1800–04), 675–83 · R. P. Cust, 'Purveyance and politics in Jacobean Leicestershire', *Regionalism and revision*, ed. P. Fleming, A. Gross, and J. R. Lander (1999), 145–62 · R. P. Cust, 'Honour, rhetoric and political culture: the earl of Huntingdon and his enemies', *Political culture and cultural politics in early modern England*, ed. S. D. Amussen and M. Kishlansky (1995), 84–111 · W. J. Tighe, 'The gentleman pensioners in Elizabethan politics and government', PhD diss., U. Cam., 1984 · will, PRO, PROB 11/124/107, Lawe (1614) · Hatfield House, Hertfordshire, Salisbury MSS, 103/100 · IGI

Likenesses funeral monument, chapel, Bradgate Park, Leicestershire

Grey, Henry, tenth earl of Kent (*bap.* 1594, *d.* 1651), parliamentarian nobleman, was baptized at Burbage, Leicestershire, on 23 November 1594, the eldest son of Anthony Grey (1557–1643), rector of Aston Flamville, Leicestershire, and of Magdalene Purefoy (1579–1653), daughter of William Purefoy of Caldecote, Warwickshire. His father succeeded to the earldom of Kent in 1639, on the death without surviving male issue of the eighth earl, a distant cousin. Some authorities refer to Henry Grey as the ninth earl. He would appear to have matriculated at Sidney Sussex College, Cambridge, in 1611, taking his BA degree in 1615. A year later, on 31 January 1616, he was admitted to Gray's Inn.

Grey was elected to one of the Leicestershire seats in the House of Commons in the autumn of 1640. He had a hand in the passage of the militia ordinance devised by Sir Arthur Heselrige MP in 1642. He succeeded to his father's

title and took his seat in the Lords on 22 November 1643. Less than a week later he was appointed first commissioner of the great seal, created by parliament to replace that held by Charles I. The great seal was entrusted instead to the speakers of the two houses on 30 October 1646, but he was again appointed first commissioner on 17 March 1648, remaining in post until the appointment of a new commission on 8 February 1649.

Kent was named parliament's lord lieutenant of Rutland on 24 August 1644, and of Bedfordshire on 2 July 1646, and as speaker of the Lords on 13 February 1645, and again from 6 September 1647 until the abolition of the upper house. An 'army peer', he was one of only four members of the Lords to dissent from the upper house's rejection of the self-denying ordinance on 13 January 1645. He opposed a motion for the return of royalist peers to their lordships' house in February 1647 and was one of nine lords who fled to the army on Hounslow Heath in July 1647. He was one of the commissioners who unsuccessfully took parliament's latest terms for a settlement, the 'four bills', to the king in December 1647, and in January 1648 was chosen for addition to the executive committee of both houses. Despite his reluctance to sit in judgment on his king in January 1649 (he was one of six peers named to the high court of justice), he sought to collaborate with the regicidal regime of which his cousin, William Purefoy MP, was a member. He was party to the lords' last desperate gambit to forestall moves for the abolition of their house in February, when he was appointed to the committee instructed to confer with the Commons about the future settlement of the kingdom in the aftermath of the regicide. But his public career effectively ended when the upper house was abolished on 19 March 1649.

Grey's first wife was Mary (1609–1644), daughter of Sir William Courten, whom he married on 14 October 1641. She died on 9 March 1644. They had a son, Henry, who predeceased the earl. After her death, on 1 August 1644 he married Amabella (1607–1698), daughter of Sir Anthony Benn, recorder of London (and granddaughter of John Evelyn of Godstone, Surrey), and widow of Anthony Fane, younger son of Francis, first earl of Westmorland. She and Henry had three children: Anthony (1645–1702), the eleventh earl of Kent and father of Henry *Grey, first duke of Kent; Henry, who died young; and Elizabeth, who married Banastre Maynard, third Lord Maynard. The tenth earl died on 28 May 1651. He was buried at Flitton church, Bedfordshire, and a monument to his memory was erected in the De Grey mausoleum there, described by Pevsner as 'one of the greatest storehouses of [funerary] monuments in England' (Pevsner, *Bedfordshire and the County of Huntingdon and Peterborough*, 1968, 91). The tenth earl's will mentioned property in Essex and Kent, but his estate was clearly not great.

SEAN KELSEY

Sources J. Nichols, *The history and antiquities of the county of Leicester*, 4/1 (1810), 245; 4/2 (1811), 458–9 · Venn, *Alum. Cant.*, 1/2.251 · J. Foster, *The register of admissions to Gray's Inn, 1521–1889, together with the register of marriages in Gray's Inn chapel, 1695–1754* (privately printed, London, 1889), 138 · Keeler, *Long Parliament* · *VCH Leicestershire*, 2.110–13 · C. H. Firth and R. S. Rait, eds., *Acts and ordinances of the interregnum, 1642–1660*, 1 (1911), 92, 114, 149, 232, 487, 658, 691,

723, 731, 783, 839, 852, 905, 937, 1016, 1047, 1107, 1208, 1227, 1234, 1238, 1243 • *JHC*, 2 (1640–42) • *JHC*, 3 (1642–4), 142–4 • *JHL*, 9 (1646–7) • *JHL*, 10 (1647–8) • *CSP dom.*, 1648–9, 1, 5 • C. H. Firth, *The House of Lords during the civil war* (1910), 147, 155, 170, 207, 209 • Foss, *Judges*, 6.440–41 • D. Fleming, 'Factions and civil war in Leicestershire', *Leicestershire Archaeological and Historical Society Transactions*, 57 (1981–2), 26–36 • PRO, PROB 11/217, fols. 195*v*–196 • GEC, *Peerage*, new edn, vol. 7

Archives Beds. & Luton ARS, papers, mainly concerning clergy; papers pertaining to the tenth earl's commission for the great seal, etc.

Likenesses marble tomb effigy, 1658, St John the Baptist Church, Flitton, Bedfordshire • P. Angelis, group portrait, oils, 1713 (*Queen Anne and the knights of the garter*), NPG • drawing, Bodl. Oxf., Sutherland Collection

Wealth at death Kentish manor of Wingham Barton and Ash; Chadwell and Chadwell Hall, Essex: PRO, PROB 11/217, fols. 195*v*–196

Grey, Henry, first earl of Stamford (*c*.1599–1673), parliamentarian army officer, was born at Bradgate, Leicestershire, the eldest son of Sir John Grey (*d*. 1611) of Pirgo, Essex, and Bradgate, courtier and army officer, and his wife, Elizabeth, daughter of Edward Neville, Lord Bergavenny, and his wife, Rachel. Henry Grey succeeded as second Baron Grey of Groby upon the death of his paternal grandfather, Henry, the first baron, on 26 July 1614. He matriculated from Trinity College, Cambridge, in Easter term 1615. On 19 July 1620 he was licensed to marry Anne (*c*.1603–1676), youngest daughter of William Cecil, second earl of Exeter, and his second wife, Elizabeth, daughter of Sir William Drury. Together they had five daughters and four sons. The marriage brought Grey the manor of Stamford, Lincolnshire, from where he took his title when he was created earl on 26 March 1628. He was admitted to Gray's Inn in 1632.

In 1625 Grey was made a deputy lieutenant for Leicestershire where the lord lieutenant, Henry Hastings, fifth earl of Huntingdon, was keen to avoid a resurgence of the long-standing conflict between their families which had erupted most recently between the earl and Grey's father and grandfather. From the late 1620s Stamford set about enhancing his income by a range of entrepreneurial activities. He enclosed his Leicestershire manors of Breedon-on-the-Hill and Broughton Astley and set about improving his Lincolnshire estate of Wildmore Fen; he sought brewing monopolies in Stamford and Leicester; and in 1636 he proposed a scheme with Secretary Windebank for a patent for the dressing of hemp which he hoped would bring him £4000–£5000 per annum. His income in the late 1630s has been estimated at around £4000 per annum. In this period his standing at court rose, and this was reflected in the royal visit paid to Bradgate in August 1634. Stamford began to be restive in the face of the Hastings hegemony. In 1631 he complained about having to sit on the county bench beside Huntingdon's protégé Sir Thomas Gerard, a man who had refused to sell him land and was willing to report him to the privy council over his depopulating enclosures. He was cultivating an interest in Leicester itself, which lay near his mansion at Bradgate Park. While the corporation protested over his attempt to acquire the monopoly of brewing in Leicester, overall he

Henry Grey, first earl of Stamford (*c*.1599–1673), by Cornelius Johnson, 1638

met with some success in his attempts to woo the town: in 1639 the council gave him Christmas gifts worth £5 0*s*. 8*d*., twice as much as those given to Huntingdon. Above all, in the 1630s Stamford was angling to be made joint lord lieutenant of the county, as was commensurate with his family's status, and at one point in the mid-1630s the king seems to have agreed to this. However, in December 1638 the post went to Huntingdon's son Henry Hastings, Lord Hastings: 'an affront' in Stamford's eyes (Cogswell, 260).

In June 1639 Stamford joined the royal army at Berwick. Visiting the Scots' camp, he met the leading presbyterian minister Alexander Henderson and was entertained by General Alexander Leslie. He displeased the king by lauding the Scots' loyalty and praising them as 'holy and blessed men, of admirable, transcendent and seraphical learning' (Russell, 84). On his return to Leicestershire he challenged Huntingdon's administration of the funds imposed on the county for the first bishops' war. In the elections to both the Short and Long parliaments Stamford and Sir Arthur Hesilrige were key figures in successfully challenging the Hastings domination of seats. At Leicester in the autumn he persuaded the corporation to accept his eldest son, the seventeen-year-old Thomas *Grey, Lord Grey of Groby, as MP, explaining to them that while his son could easily get seats elsewhere, he would rather represent a town 'with whom he is like to bee a Neighbour' (Cogswell, 271).

In May 1641 Stamford urged the bishops to give thanks for the failure of the first army plot, genuinely asserting that this was a greater deliverance than that of 1605. On 12

February 1642 parliament appointed him its lord lieutenant of Leicestershire. Dispatched to Hull in April to confer with Sir John Hotham, Stamford was in York on 18 April to present parliament's petition to the king concerning his intention to go to Ireland. Upon his return to Leicester on 4 June, his arrival at the Angel Inn coincided with that of Lord Hastings, bearing a warrant to take command of the county's militia regiment. Brawling between the two parties ensued, resolved by the townsmen driving Hastings and his party out of town: the crowds in the market place cried out 'a Stamford! a Stamford!' upon which the earl was seen with 'tears of joy standing in his eyes to see his Country's love and obedience' (Cogswell, 284). Stamford held successful musters for parliament and relocated part of the county magazine to Bradgate. On 15 June Hastings returned again with a royal proclamation and commission of array, again only to be driven off. However, two weeks later Stamford departed for London, leaving 150 men to guard Bradgate. In his absence Hastings seized the initiative, and Stamford complained on 8 July that 'all the papists and Jesuits in England did conspire together to ruin him and his house' (Fletcher, 410). He was dilatory in returning to Leicester as parliament directed, and fled the town shortly after his return, only hours before the king's arrival there on 22 July. The following month Bradgate was sacked and partially demolished by royalist forces.

Stamford joined the earl of Essex in the artillery garden in London on 27 July 1642, on which day 3000 recruits were enlisted. In August he was commissioned colonel of a regiment of foot and captain of a troop of horse in Essex's parliamentarian army: his colours bore the mottoes 'For Religion', 'King and Country', and 'A Ma Puissance' (Richards, 39). Stamford accompanied Essex to Dunsmore Heath, Warwickshire, on 20 September. Ten days later he was dispatched with his regiment of 900 foot and three troops of horse to Hereford. On 2 October he established himself as parliament's governor of that city, with headquarters in the bishop's palace. He was absent from Edgehill, but frustrated a royalist plot to eject him from Hereford in late October. He launched successful raids on royalist quarters at Herles-Lewes and Presteigne, informing parliament on 16 November, 'by God's grace, I shall drive them a little further up the Mountains' (*JHL*, 1642–3, 453). On 13 December he was appointed parliament's general in Essex's absence for Herefordshire, Gloucestershire, Shropshire, Worcestershire, and the entire principality of Wales. However, Stamford became frustrated by Hereford's refusals to supply his troops. He derided 'this unworthy City', condemning its people as 'vile' and favourers of a 'roguish army of Welch papists and other vagabonds' (ibid., 475). He evacuated Hereford on 14 December, marching via Gloucester to Bristol. On 19 December he found Bristol 'infinitely well-affected to the good Cause' (ibid., 511), and mustered forces swiftly at Bath, Devizes, and Marshfield.

In January 1643 Stamford was also given command of parliament's forces in Devon, and he arrived in Exeter on 6 January accompanied by several regiments of London grey-coats. On 28 February he agreed to a local truce with the Cornish royalists under Sir Ralph Hopton, gaining time to strengthen his forces. The truce expired on 27 March, and as Stamford was gout-stricken in April, he did not personally take the field until 11 May, when he left Exeter to join newly raised militia at Okehampton. Dispatching most of his cavalry to suppress royalist musters at Bodmin, he had a well-supplied army which mustered 5400 foot and 200 horse but was defeated by a force half its size under Hopton at Stratton on 16 May. Stamford entrusted the battle's conduct to his major-general, James Chudleigh, who changed sides shortly after his capture on the battlefield. His army completely broken, Stamford fled to Barnstaple, then Exeter. Clarendon later suggested that Stamford's cowardice hastened the royalists' victory (Clarendon, *Hist. rebellion*, 7.89). Stamford's remaining cavalry fled Exeter on 31 May, and within days the city was besieged. Especially vigilant against treachery, Stamford endured a siege lasting three months and nineteen days. The royalists claimed Stamford mistreated Dr Coxe, whom they sent into Exeter in June to negotiate, alleging that Stamford held a knife to his throat and offered to strangle him personally. The earl of Warwick's naval attempt to relieve Exeter failed on 20 July and Stamford wrote to assure the king of his loyalty on 4 August. He finally surrendered the city to Prince Maurice on 5 September. Maurice offered to procure a royal pardon, but, granted a safe passage to Windsor, Stamford marched out with his disarmed troops.

Stamford safely arrived in London to publish a defence of his actions and to blame his subordinates James Chudleigh and Anthony Nichols MP for the disaster. On 30 October he petitioned the Lords about his financial sufferings, and on 27 November he accused Nichols of complicity in Chudleigh's treachery. He was granted lodgings in Whitehall on 16 February 1644, but was decried by other officers and lampooned in the press for poor generalship and military failure. On 9 May he requested leave to travel to the hot baths in France to recover his health, but the following day Nichols delivered information in the Commons blaming Stamford for the defeats in the west. A costly legal case ensued and Stamford sought leniency by claiming he had 'exhausted the vigour of his youth by hard, cold, and wet marches', and that therefore, 'he will become sooner impotent than by the course of nature might be expected' (*Sixth Report*, HMC, House of Lords MSS, 14). On 21 August 1644 the Lords, mindful of Stamford's financial sacrifices, recommended £1000 be paid to him. On 26 August Stamford was granted the keeping of royal parks in Buckinghamshire and Northamptonshire.

On 28 June 1645 Stamford was impeached with two of his servants by the House of Commons for assaulting Sir Arthur Hesilrige with swords on the highway from Perpoole Lane to Clerkenwell. The case was heard on 30 September, but later dropped. On 18 July 1645 he was appointed commissioner to reside with the Scots army in England. Subsequently appointed to go to Scotland on 21 December 1646, he was at Berwick on 12 February 1647 and at Edinburgh on 17 March 1647. He was appointed a commissioner for the navy and customs on 17 December

1647 and dispatched to Scotland once again on 27 January 1648. In his absence on 7 February 1648 his Whitehall quarters were broken into by soldiers. Having returned by 2 May, he was thanked by the House of Lords for his service. Stamford's relations with his son, Thomas, Lord Grey of Groby, became increasingly soured in these years, the father's presbyterianism and moderate parliamentarianism at odds with the son's political and religious independency. The son was one of the king's judges and signed the death warrant. The eighteenth-century antiquary John Throsby recounted how his great-grandfather had been with 'Lord Grey' (meaning Stamford) when Grey of Groby brought the news of the verdict on the king to his father: '"Well, Thomas", says the father to the son, "King, or no King?"—"No King, my Lord," replied the son—"Then no Lord Grey!" rejoined the father and left him in disgust' (Richards, 46).

After the abolition of the House of Lords, Stamford sat as MP for Leicestershire in 1654, to which some county gentlemen took exception, petitioning Cromwell on 21 August that Stamford had 'assisted the late king of Scots, and was not of good conversation' (CSP dom., 1654, 316). Later he was rumoured to have been condemned for a murder on the highway on 1 August 1657. Increasingly disenchanted with interregnum regimes, he complained of his removal from the commission of the peace to Bulstrode Whitelocke on 14 February 1659, and of 'mean men being putt into the Com[missio]n who insult over their betters' (B. Whitelocke, The Diary of Bulstrode Whitelocke, 1605–1675, ed. R. Spalding, Records of Social and Economic History, 13, 1990, 507). He declared for the king at Bradgate in August 1659 during the Cheshire rising of his son-in-law Sir George *Booth, husband of his eldest daughter, Elizabeth. Stamford raised over 200 men but dispersed them as the army approached. A Major Hubbert and Captain Shepperdson arrested him at Bradgate and he was brought to London. Examined by the lord president and Hesilrige on 2 September, he was committed to the serjeant-at-arms for high treason on 5 September.

Released from prison, Stamford was included in the Restoration's general Act of Pardon, and on his petition, in 1666, Charles II returned to him Armtree Manor and Wildmore Fen, Lincolnshire. In June 1672 he was a trustee for the establishment of a new riding academy in Leicester. He died on 21 August 1673 and was buried beside his ancestors at Bradgate. His eldest son, Thomas, having died in 1657, the title passed to the latter's son, also Thomas *Grey. Two of his sons, Architell *Grey and John Grey, served as MPs from the 1660s to the 1690s, the latter forsaking his whig politics at the revolution of 1688 and becoming a tory and a Jacobite conspirator.

ANDREW J. HOPPER

Sources GEC, Peerage, new edn, vol. 12/1 · JHL, 5–10 (1642–8) · CSP dom., 1641–70 · Fifth report, HMC, 4 (1876) · Sixth report, HMC, 5 (1877–8) · Seventh report, HMC, 6 (1879) · T. Cogswell, Home divisions: aristocracy, the state and provincial conflict (1998) · C. Patterson, Urban patronage in early modern England: corporate boroughs, the landed elite and the crown, 1580–1640 (1999) · J. Richards, 'The Greys of Bradgate in the English civil war', Transactions of the Leicestershire Archaeological and Historical Society, 62 (1988), 33–52 · M. Stoyle, From deliverance to destruction: rebellion and civil war in an English city (1996) · M. Stoyle, Loyalty and locality: popular allegiance in Devon during the English civil war (1994) · C. Russell, The fall of the British monarchies, 1637–1642 (1991) · A. Fletcher, The outbreak of the English civil war (1981) · E. A. Andriette, Devon and Exeter in the civil war (1971) · HoP, Commons, 1558–1603, vols. 2–3 · J. Webb, Memorials of the civil war … as it affected Herefordshire, ed. T. W. Webb, 2 vols. (1879) · H. Stocks, ed., Records of the borough of Leicester, 1603–1688 (1923) · Clarendon, Hist. rebellion · administration, PRO, PROB 6/48, fol. 118r · J. L. Chester and J. Foster, eds., London marriage licences, 1521–1869 (1887) · J. Vicars, England's worthies under whom all the civill and bloody warres since anno 1642 to anno 1647 are related (1845) · M. Corbett and M. Norton, The reign of Charles I (1964) [pt 3 of Engraving in England in the sixteenth and seventeenth centuries] · J. Richards, Aristocrat and regicide: the life and times of Thomas, Lord Grey of Groby (2000), 8

Archives JRL, Dunham Massey archives, family papers · Leics. RO, deeds and estate papers of Bradgate, ref DG20, DE1982 | BL, Add. MSS 5497, 12506, 34218 · BL, Sloane MS 1429 · Bodl. Oxf., North MSS · Hunt. L., letters to the Temple family

Likenesses C. Johnson, portrait, 1638, Dunham Massey, Cheshire [see illus.] · Doyle, engraving of portrait (after W. Hollar) · W. Hollar, etching, BM, NPG · P. Lely, portrait, Dunham Massey, Cheshire · engraving, repro. in Corbett and Norton, Reign of Charles I · line drawing, repro. in Vicars, England's worthies

Wealth at death considerable wealth: estates at Bradgate, Leicestershire, and Stamford, Lincolnshire; also Armtree Manor and Wildmore Fen, Lincolnshire: administration, PRO, PROB 6/48, fol. 118r; CSP dom., 1665–6

Grey, Henry, duke of Kent (bap. 1671, d. 1740), courtier and politician, the only son and heir of Anthony Grey, eleventh earl of Kent (1645–1702), and Mary, suo jure Baroness Lucas of Crudwell (d. 1702), daughter of John *Lucas, first Baron Lucas of Shenfield, was baptized on 28 September 1671 at Flitton, Bedfordshire. He was the grandson of Henry *Grey, tenth earl. He was styled Lord Grey until the death of his father on 19 August 1702, when he became twelfth earl of Kent; on his mother's death on 1 November 1702, he also became second Baron Lucas of Crudwell. Two years later he was sworn of the privy council and in April of that year was appointed lord chamberlain on the recommendation of Queen Anne's then confidante, Sarah, duchess of Marlborough. At the time unfounded rumours circulated that Grey had paid the duchess £10,000 for the nomination. If anything, the true explanation for his appointment proved even less flattering to this former tory and now nominal whig: from the start Grey's career in Anne's court was widely spoken of in terms of political expediency rather than personal ability. In an era of charged party rage, when 'neither Side was to be much oblig'd or displeas'd', it was Grey's fortune to supply what Arthur Maynwaring scornfully described as 'a vacancy that was to be fill'd up with something very insignificant' (Bucholz, 94).

Similar forces ensured that Grey—who in 1706 became marquess of Kent—retained the office for six years, despite an uninspiring performance. 'So many think themselves for Chamberlain', as Thomas Butler informed Sir William Trumbull in December 1708, 'that the fear of disobliging a multitude still keeps in Lord Kennt' (Bucholz, 65). Kent himself did little to dispel his reputation as a political lightweight and ministerial stopgap. An infrequent attendant at court who was never summoned to the cabinet, he was known to delegate many of his responsibilities while bemoaning his isolation: 'Dey never let me into any of Deir Politicks' was a typical gripe from 1708. The collective low esteem in which Kent was held was further deepened by the widespread use of the pejorative nickname Bug, denoting a proclivity to body odour in one whom Maynwaring also lambasted as 'His Stinkingness'.

In 1710 Kent traded in the lord chancellorship for the title of duke of Kent, to which he was raised on 28 April. Thereafter he held a series of politically minor court offices: lord of the bedchamber, constable of Windsor Castle (both 1714–16), lord steward of the household (1716–19), lord keeper of the privy seal (1718–19), and bearer of St Edward's staff during the coronation of George II in August 1727. He was, wrote Lord Hervey, 'a yes and no hireling to the Court for forty years' (GEC, *Peerage*, 7.178).

Kent was twice married: first to Jemima (d. 1728), daughter of Thomas Crew, second Baron Crew of Sterne, and his second wife, Anne, née Armine (Airmyn); the couple had seven daughters and four sons before Jemima's death on 27 July 1728. On 24 March of the following year he married Sophia (d. 1748), daughter of Hans Willem Bentinck, first earl of Portland, and Jane, née Temple. With no surviving male children, in May 1740 Kent was created Marquess Grey with the intention that the title should pass to his eldest granddaughter, Jemima Campbell [see Yorke, Jemima, suo jure Marchioness Grey]. Kent died soon after the arrangement, on 5 June 1740 aged sixty-eight, whereupon his dukedom became extinct. He was survived by his second wife, Sophia, until her death on 14 June 1748 and his granddaughter who, as Marchioness Grey, married Philip Yorke, second earl of Hardwicke, and achieved celebrity as a political correspondent.

To modern historians of Anne's reign the 'odious' and 'disagreeable' Kent, when mentioned, epitomizes the indolent and self-seeking courtier in an age of otherwise high ideals and combative personality politics (Harris, 203, 108). Though regularly mocked in political circles, several contemporaries, including John Macky and Jonathan Swift, did seek to defend Kent; for Macky he was a 'very moderate' man with 'good sense' who 'bears a considerable figure in the nation' (Macky, *Characters*, quoted in GEC, *Peerage*, 7.178). While this perhaps goes too far it is certainly the case that Kent's lack of talent and ambition also served successive ministries well as they sought often to deflect party tensions within parliament: the right man—albeit with the wrong smell—in the right place for his time. PHILIP CARTER

Sources GEC, *Peerage* · R. O. Bucholz, *The Augustan court: Queen Anne and the decline of court culture* (1993) · J. M. Beattie, *The English court in the reign of George I* (1967) · J. C. Sainty and R. Bucholz, eds., *Officials of the royal household, 1660–1837*, 1: *Department of the lord chamberlain and associated offices* (1997) · G. S. Holmes, *British politics in the age of Anne* (1967) · G. S. Holmes, *British politics in the age of Anne*, rev. edn (1987) · F. Harris, *A passion for government: the life of Sarah, duchess of Marlborough* (1991)
Archives Beds. & Luton ARS, corresp. and papers
Likenesses G. Kneller, oils, 1705, Gov. Art Coll. · P. Angelis, group portrait, oils, 1713 (*Queen Anne and the knights of the garter*), NPG · attrib. J. M. Rysbrack, statue on monument, St John the Baptist Church, Flitton, Bedfordshire

Grey, Henry (1778–1859), Free Church of Scotland minister, was born at Alnwick, Northumberland, on 11 February 1778, the son of Edward Grey, a medical practitioner, and his wife, Jane Campbell. He was baptized in a presbyterian meeting-house at Alnwick. His parents soon separated and his father moved to Morpeth, Northumberland, leaving him to be brought up by his mother. After attending school locally and in Newcastle upon Tyne, in 1793 Grey moved to Edinburgh, with his mother, to attend the university, with a view to entering the ministry of the Church of Scotland. He received the degree of MA from Edinburgh, though not until 1818. Licensed by the presbytery of Edinburgh on 26 November 1800 and presented, through the influence of Thomas Davidson, to the parish of Stenton, East Lothian, Grey was ordained on 17 September 1801. On 12 October 1808 he married his cousin Margaretta Grey (d. 1858) with whom he had six children.

After twelve peaceful years in Stenton, Grey was called to St Cuthbert's chapel of ease in Edinburgh, to which he was admitted on 18 November 1813. Grey quickly proved to be not merely a popular, but also a fashionable, preacher, with a refined and cultivated style not normally associated with evangelical clergymen. He was translated to the New North parish of Edinburgh in January 1820 before, in 1825, he moved again to the newly erected parish of St Mary's.

It was not long after this that Grey's popularity suffered in a conflict with Dr Andrew Thomson. Grey took a favourable view of circulating Bibles which included the Apocrypha in foreign countries, a practice to which Thomson was violently opposed. This was the only contentious period in an otherwise uneventful career, for while Grey espoused numerous progressive causes he never courted controversy. He did not feature in church courts, nor was he prominent in the events leading up to the Disruption of 1843. He was, however, fully in sympathy with the nonintrusion party in the church and joined the Free Church of Scotland, ministering to the congregation of Free St Mary's from 1843. He served as moderator of the Free Church general assembly in 1844 and was honoured with the degree of DD from New York University in 1845. Money raised at the time of his ministerial jubilee was used to endow bursaries at New College, Edinburgh.

Gentle and somewhat unworldly in character, Grey's English origins were always evident. An obituary wrote of him as a man 'in whom the softer graces of Episcopacy seemed ever to be mingled with Presbyterian substance' (*The Witness*, 19 Jan 1859). He practised the more frequent celebration of holy communion. Grey died at his home, 5 East Claremont Street, Edinburgh, on 13 January 1859 and was buried a week later in St Cuthbert's cemetery. LIONEL ALEXANDER RITCHIE

Sources C. M. Birrell, *Thoughts in the evening of life* (1871) · *Sketches of the Edinburgh clergy of the established Church of Scotland* (1832), 64–9 · J. Kay, *A series of original portraits and caricature etchings … with biographical sketches and illustrative anecdotes*, ed. [H. Paton and others], 2 (1838), 457–60 · *Fasti Scot.*, 1.112–13 · *The Witness* (19 Jan 1859) ·

Home and Foreign Record of the Free Church of Scotland (March 1859), 191–2 • *DSCHT* • D. M. Lewis, ed., *The Blackwell dictionary of evangelical biography, 1730–1860*, 2 vols. (1995) • *DNB* • personal knowledge (1890) [*DNB*] • *IGI*

Likenesses J. Kay, caricature etching, 1815, NPG; repro. in J. Kay, *A series of original portraits and caricature etchings by the late John Kay* (1838), vol. 2, facing p. 457 • P. Park, bust, 1853, New College, Edinburgh • W. Walker, stipple (after W. Douglas), BM, NPG • portrait, repro. in Birrell, *Thoughts in the evening of life*, frontispiece

Wealth at death £6983 15s. 6d.: inventory, 10 May 1859, NA Scot., SC 70/1/100/885

Grey, Henry George, third Earl Grey (1802–1894), politician, was born on 28 December 1802 at Howick Hall in Northumberland, the eldest son of Charles *Grey, second Earl Grey (1764–1845), whig prime minister, and his wife, Mary Elizabeth (1776–1861), daughter of William Brabazon *Ponsonby of co. Kildare, Ireland. He had ten brothers and four sisters and was educated by a private tutor and at Trinity College, Cambridge, where he graduated MA in 1823.

Early political career Destined for a parliamentary career, Howick (as Grey was known after 1807) unsuccessfully contested the county of Northumberland at the general election in June 1826, being returned instead for the borough of Winchelsea, a seat he held until the election of July 1830, when he was returned for Higham Ferrers. Conscientious, high-minded, and forthright, Howick evinced inherited notions of aristocratic paternalism and disinterested public service, reinforced by broad-church religious convictions. He also embraced newer bourgeois values of private enterprise, self-help, and utility, and he took a keen interest in economics, studying privately with J. R. McCulloch and attending the Political Economy Club. Already a convinced free-trader in 1826, he disagreed sharply with his father and most whig MPs over the corn laws. He championed Catholic emancipation and parliamentary reform.

In November 1830 Howick was appointed parliamentary under-secretary at the Colonial Office in his father's ministry. Here he came to exercise considerable influence because the exceptional latitude given to him by an easygoing secretary of state, Lord Goderich, allowed the pursuit of his own reformist inclinations and purposeful initiatives. Partly under the impact of Edward Gibbon Wakefield's writings on colonization, Howick revised imperial land policy, replacing free grants by sale at auction and, in the case of Australia, using the revenue to aid the emigration of British labourers. On the grounds of economy and religious equality, he began withdrawal of imperial financial assistance to the Church of England in the colonies, and he tried to resolve conflict in the Canadas between executives and assemblies by surrendering to the lower houses (in the so-called Howick Act of 1831) control over certain crown revenues in return for civil lists covering official salaries.

When ministers appealed to the country over the Reform Bill in May 1831, Howick was returned for Northumberland; and at the general election of December 1832, after the act's passage, he won the northern division of the county, a seat he retained until 1841. Meanwhile, he

Henry George Grey, third Earl Grey (1802–1894), by James Sant, 1859

pressed the government to end British colonial slavery. In the summer of 1832, he devised a scheme of qualified emancipation, coupling immediate freedom with precautionary measures to tide over the difficult transition from slave to free societies. Principally, former slaves would be induced to continue working on the plantations as wage-labourers by the imposition of a land tax on their provision grounds. This plan, despite departmental endorsement, was eventually, in March 1833, rejected by the cabinet, which refused to act without the support of the West India interest. At that point Edward Stanley replaced Goderich as colonial secretary and on 3 April Howick resigned, subsequently fighting a bitter rearguard action in the Commons against Stanley's scheme of apprenticeship and payment of £20 million compensation to the planters.

Secretary for war After a short spell as under-secretary at the Home Office (January–June 1834) Howick was appointed in April 1835 to Lord Melbourne's second cabinet as secretary for war, a post he held until August 1839. At the War Office he gradually discovered the defects of the military system and the obstacles to reforming it. An unwieldy bureaucracy divided administrative responsibilities among six rival departments of state and thereby fostered lethargy and traditionalism. Howick chaired a royal commission, set up in 1835 to examine the civil administration of the army, but its members disagreed over the desirable degree and preferred structure of greater consolidation. Despite his persistent pleas, the cabinet shied away from tackling this politically contentious issue, the fundamental prerequisite of extensive military reforms.

In order to reconcile the army's substantial commitments (especially for colonial defence) with the tight budgets demanded by parliament, Howick sought to maximize scarce manpower and improve the lot of British soldiers. A royal commission on military punishments, appointed to allay criticism from MPs of flogging, recommended in 1836 ways of tackling the causes of misconduct, which Howick traced to environmental factors—harsh discipline, monotonous routine, and aimless leisure—and not to the degeneracy of common soldiers, as many officers still believed. In a constructive bid to counteract delinquencies, discourage desertion, and attract more and better recruits, he introduced various reforms urged by the commission: good-conduct pay and badges; regimental savings banks; barrack libraries and day-rooms; increased facilities for sports. Statistical investigations launched at the War Office into military mortality, sickness, and invaliding revealed an appalling and costly wastage of manpower. Howick tried to eradicate the overcrowded, unsanitary state of barrack accommodation but parsimony at the Treasury and procrastination at the Ordnance made this a slow process. He organized rotating tours of duty so that infantry regiments spent shorter spells overseas, especially in unhealthy climates, and he sought greater reliance on indigenous troops and irregular corps of veterans or pensioners.

Frustrated over army reorganization, Howick grew increasingly dissatisfied with the ministry's conduct of colonial policy. With respect to the Canadian crisis, he was annoyed by the cabinet's refusal in 1835-6 to allow Lord Gosford's commission of inquiry to negotiate with the disaffected politicians of Lower Canada a resolution of the constitutional deadlock; and also by its preference for coercive legislation as a response to the rebellions in December 1837, rather than a constructive policy of reconciliation. In the West Indies, apprenticeship was abruptly terminated in 1838 without the precautionary measures Howick again advocated; and in the following year an attempt to suspend the Jamaican constitution forced ministers into temporary resignation. Howick blamed the mismanagement of colonial affairs on the ineffectiveness of Lord Glenelg and eventually, in January 1839, threatened to resign unless the colonial secretary was removed, but Glenelg's replacement the next month by Lord Normanby left Howick disgruntled. Matters came to a head in August 1839 during a more extensive ministerial reshuffle when he was offered the Post Office, a demeaning demotion he answered by resigning from the War Office. Colleagues acknowledged his expertise, dedicated industry, and impeachable integrity, but they regarded him as abrasive, stubborn, and 'impracticable'.

Earl Grey and colonial secretary Now out of office, Howick lost his Northumberland seat at the general election of July 1841 but two months later won a by-election in the notoriously corrupt borough of Sunderland. As he watched and welcomed the gradual erosion of tariff protection by tory measures and public opinion, Howick became involved in 1844 in the Northumberland Railway Company, formed in an unsuccessful bid to prevent

George Hudson's Great North of England Company from building the remaining section of the east-coast line from London to Edinburgh. When Howick succeeded to the earldom in July 1845 political controversy was approaching a climax as Sir Robert Peel stumbled towards repeal of the corn laws and famine struck Ireland. In December Grey was held responsible for Lord John Russell's failure to construct an alternative administration because of his objections to Lord Palmerston returning to the Foreign Office. When Russell did form a ministry in July 1846 Grey became colonial secretary. He appeared uniquely qualified for the post by experience, knowledge, and interest, but during six years in office he was dogged by disputes and assailed by discontented colonists and by venomous critics in parliament and the press who denounced his hollow liberal professions and his authoritarian practice.

Grey recognized in 1846 that imperial relations were entering a new phase with the adoption of free trade and local self-government imminent in settlement colonies. Unfortunately the promised abandonment of preferential tariffs coincided with a commercial and financial crisis. Predicting ruin, planters in the West Indies and protectionist MPs railed against lower duties and increased competition in the British market from foreign, slave-grown sugar. Canadian merchants, too, bemoaned the loss of protection for exported wheat and timber at a time of commercial depression. In 1849 their disenchantment temporarily fuelled a movement for annexation with the United States. Rioting in Montreal, caused by the Rebellion Losses Act, also had an overtly political dimension and Grey worried about the fate of the fledgeling experiment in self-government. Convinced that Canada displayed sufficient maturity and political harmony to warrant greater autonomy, he had formally sanctioned local control over internal affairs and British conventions of cabinet government which provincial politicians were already practising. Grey also aimed to make self-governing Canadians responsible for their own military defence—part of a wider strategic review he undertook in 1846 which proposed to strengthen home defence by withdrawing British garrisons from settlement colonies as circumstances permitted.

In Australia self-government was in 1846 a highly contentious and as yet unresolved question. Political advance was caught up inextricably (and Grey thought unwarrantably) with protests against his determination to uphold imperial control over crown lands and his attempts to preserve Australia as an outlet for the 'exile' of convicts from Britain. Even so, this wrangling did not preclude preliminary steps towards the extension of representative government to Tasmania, South Australia, and Victoria—separated in 1850 from New South Wales which had enjoyed a partially elected legislative council since 1843. Unavailingly, Grey recommended municipal councils and a federal tier of government which might check inter-colonial rivalries by regulating matters of common concern. Grey's act of 1850 formed the framework of constitutions introduced in the colonies in 1855-6 (except in Western

Australia), but uncertainty over the principles of 'responsible government' subsequently generated the factionalism, short-lived ministries, and constitutional deadlocks he had predicted.

Constitution making in New Zealand was also fraught with difficulties. In 1846 Grey sponsored imperial legislation to give a mere 20,000 Europeans an elaborate, pyramidal structure of representative government with municipal, provincial, and federal institutions. Governor Sir George Grey warned of unrest as growing numbers of British settlers intensified conflict with the Maori over land and urged suspension of the constitution, advice that the colonial secretary felt obliged to accept, despite the further embarrassing appeal to parliament involved. Internal warfare, which began in the northern island in 1846–7, continued intermittently for the next two decades and drew heavily on British soldiers and finances, a responsibility which Grey thought could not be shirked.

The same problems of ethnic conflict and instability plagued Grey in southern Africa as Boer farmers trekked farther into the interior and clashed with native tribesmen over land. Headstrong administrators on the spot, like the masterful Sir Harry Smith, tended to respond to outbreaks of lawlessness in border areas by extending British jurisdiction into remoter regions difficult to patrol and pacify. Although no expansionist, Grey's longer-term ambition was to promote Christianity and 'civilization' among African tribes in frontier zones by pursuing—through local chiefs, guided by British superintendents—a form of administration that later came to be known as 'indirect rule'. Despite uproar over his attempt to foist convicts on the Cape colonists, he made plans in 1849 for the introduction of representative government, including the novel expedient of an elective upper chamber to check the assembly's power. Because of Governor Harry Smith's irresolution, local political squabbling, and the outbreak of widespread fighting in 1850–51, the constitution did not come into operation until 1852. It was this renewed warfare in the Orange River territory and in British Kaffraria, and the controversial recall of Smith, which finally brought the resignation of Russell's tottering ministry in February 1852. Grey's departure from office on the eve of a censure motion on his South African policy denied him the opportunity to answer his critics, and he wrote a detailed defence of his imperial stewardship, published in 1853 as *The Colonial Policy of Lord John Russell's Administration*.

Out of office: later years Grey never again held office, though in June 1854 he was offered the governor-generalship of India and in February 1858 Lord Derby invited him to join a Conservative ministry. Disillusioned with politics and politicians, Grey nevertheless continued to attend the House of Lords regularly until 1880 and to take an active, highly critical interest in military and colonial questions. He denounced Britain's involvement in the Crimean War, thinking it futile to prop up a corrupt, despotic Ottoman empire and foolish to imagine a threat from Russian expansionism to British interests in the Mediterranean or India. Out of step with government,

parliament, and the nation, Grey vainly hoped the war might bring about the army reforms he had long advocated in peacetime—a possibility heightened by the military debacle in the Crimea. In 1857 he thought that the same military unpreparedness was exposed by the Indian mutiny and rebellion, which he attributed to the recent aggressive policy of territorial annexation that had led to unnecessary, costly wars and overstretched the army's resources.

As parliamentary reform reappeared on the political agenda in the 1850s, Grey began a personal campaign to warn the nation of the dangers of ill-considered tinkering with the electoral system that would set Britain on the slide to unbridled democracy. In *Parliamentary Government* (1858; 1864) he urged that in order to avoid partisan manoeuvring and piecemeal changes any legislation must be preceded by careful investigation and all-party agreement for a comprehensive, lasting settlement. When the reform question revived in the mid-1860s he proposed to accompany an extended franchise with carefully contrived safeguards, such as multiple votes, special franchises and constituencies, and nominated MPs. As a reform bill made its tortuous, capricious course through parliament in 1865–7, Grey actively plotted with a group of dissentients, the Adullamites, to reshape its provisions; but the campaign failed. It was a dispiriting blow for an aristocratic whig, plagued by infirmities and enveloping deafness, who predicted the fatal 'Americanization' of British politics.

Grey's gloom was intensified by events connected with Ireland: the upsurge of agrarian unrest and Fenian activities in the 1860s; Gladstone's disestablishment of the Irish church (1869), Land Acts (1870 and 1881), and sponsorship of home rule which Grey feared would lead to the disintegration of the United Kingdom and a decline in Britain's international power. Free trade, too, seemed threatened by allowing Australians (in 1873) to impose protectionist duties; by renewal of the commercial treaty with France (1881); by the campaign at home for 'fair trade'; and by the McKinley tariff in the United States and its impact on Canada. Grey also deprecated precipitate withdrawal in the late 1860s of imperial troops from New Zealand, the Cape, and Canada which implied an abandonment of British responsibilities and a new concept of empire devoid of ties and obligations. He considered forcing responsible government on the Cape in 1872 symptomatic of this imperial indifference, and so misguided in view of the Boers' new assertiveness and the discovery of mineral wealth.

The Howick estate, and death In later years Grey was drawn to southern Africa because of the involvement of his nephew and heir, Albert *Grey, fourth Earl Grey, with the promoters of the British South Africa Company. Grey had married, on 9 August 1832, Maria, daughter of Sir Joseph Copley, of Sprotborough, Yorkshire; she died at Howick on 14 September 1879. They had no children and the earl had long regarded Albert as a surrogate son and political disciple who would perpetuate traditional whig principles—though the young man evinced an unwelcome attachment to Gladstonian Liberalism. To avoid payment of succession duties, Grey made over the Howick estate to Albert in 1885, but retained a sufficient life-interest in the property for duty to be exacted following court cases in 1897–8. Grey had always experienced anxiety about the precarious state of his finances. An estate of 17,599 acres in 1878 yielded annual receipts of some £23,000, but this income, with returns from small-scale collieries and quarries, barely covered ordinary outgoings, especially expenditure on farm buildings, a mortgage of £200,000, and sundry annuities.

Grey died on 9 October 1894, from natural causes, at Howick Hall, Northumberland, where he was buried.

PETER BURROUGHS

Sources A. G. Doughty, ed., *The Elgin–Grey papers, 1846–1852*, 4 vols. (1937) • E. A. Smith, *Lord Grey, 1764–1845* (1990) • W. P. Morrell, *British colonial policy in the age of Peel and Russell* (1930) • J. M. Ward, *Earl Grey and the Australian colonies, 1846–1857: a study of self-government and self-interest* (1958) • J. M. Ward, *Colonial self-government: the British experience, 1759–1856* (1976) • H. Strachan, 'Lord Grey and imperial defence', *Politicians and defence: studies in the formulation of British defence policy, 1845–1970*, ed. I. Beckett and J. Gooch (1981) • H. Strachan, *Wellington's legacy: the reform of the British army, 1830–54* (1984) • U. Durham L., archives and special collections, Grey of Howick collection, G.210/13

Archives NA Canada, corresp. and papers relating to Canada • U. Durham L., corresp. and papers | Auckland Public Library, letters to Sir George Grey • BL, letters to Lord Broughton, Add. MSS 47226–47229 • BL, corresp. with Lord Carnarvon, Add. MS 60773 • BL, corresp. with W. E. Gladstone, Add. MSS 44364–44486, *passim* • BL, corresp. with Florence Nightingale, Add. MS 45796 • BL, corresp. with Charles Wood, Add. MS 49553, *passim* • BLPES, corresp. with Sir Joshua Jebb • Bodl. Oxf., letters to fourth earl of Clarendon • Borth. Inst., corresp. with Lord Halifax • CAC Cam., letters to W. T. Stead • CUL, letters to James Stephen • Cumbria AS, Carlisle, corresp. with Sir James Graham • LPL, letters to A. C. Tait • Lpool RO, letters to fourteenth earl of Derby • NA Scot., letters to James Loch • NA Scot., letters to Lord Panmure • NL Scot., corresp. with Edward Ellice • NL Scot., corresp., incl. Lord Rutherford and Lord Rosebery • NL Wales, corresp. with Nassau Senior • Northumbd RO, letters to Sir Matthew Ridley • Northumbd RO, letters to William Woodman, solicitor and agent • priv. coll., corresp. with Sir George Cathcart • PRO, letters to Lord Granville, PRO 30/29 • PRO, corresp. with Henry Pottinger, FO 705 • PRO, corresp. with Lord John Russell, PRO 30/22 • Royal Arch., Melbourne MSS • Royal Arch., Queen Victoria MSS • U. Durham L., Grey of Howick collection, corresp. with second Earl Grey • U. Newcastle, Robinson L., letters to Sir Walter Trevelyan • U. Southampton L., corresp. with Lord Palmerston • U. Southampton L., letters to duke of Wellington • UCL, corresp. with Sir Edwin Chadwick • University of York, Hickleton MSS • W. Sussex RO, letters to fifth duke of Richmond • W. Sussex RO, letters to sixth duke of Richmond • W. Yorks. AS, Leeds, letters to Lord Clanricarde • Wilts. & Swindon RO, corresp. with Sidney Herbert

Likenesses J. P. Dantan, plaster statuette, 1834, Musée Carnavalet, Paris • J. Sant, portrait, 1859, priv. coll. [*see illus.*] • C. Silvy, two cartes-de-visite, 1861, NPG • Ape [C. Pellegrini], caricature, chromolithograph, NPG; repro. in *VF* (8 May 1869) • J. Bacon, lithograph (after G. Thomas), BM • J. Doyle, drawings, BM • G. Hayter, group portrait, oils (*The House of Commons, 1833*), NPG • D. Wilkie, group portrait, oils (*The queen presiding over her first council, 1837*), Royal Collection • carte-de-visite, NPG

Wealth at death £6643 8s. 0d.: probate, 8 Feb 1895, *CGPLA Eng. & Wales*

Grey [married name Dudley], **Lady Jane** (1537–1554), noblewoman and claimant to the English throne, was the eldest surviving child of Henry *Grey, marquess of Dorset, later duke of Suffolk (1517–1554), and Frances (1517–1559), daughter of Charles Brandon, duke of Suffolk, and Mary, younger sister of Henry VIII. Jane was thus a cousin of Edward VI and about the same age, being born at Bradgate in Leicestershire in October 1537. She had two younger sisters, Katherine [*see* Seymour, Katherine, countess of Hertford] and Mary [*see* Keys, Lady Mary].

The circumstances surrounding Jane's life and death inevitably made her an icon as a protestant martyr, and consequently have so coloured posterity's view of her that it is difficult now to see beyond the religious bias of such contemporary sources as Holinshed's *Chronicles* and Foxe's *Acts and Monuments*, or the uncritical later biographies of Agnes Strickland and Richard Davey. Jane's story also created considerable interest abroad, and there are three interrelated, near-contemporary, and sympathetic Italian accounts of her troubles. Although largely based on hearsay and gossip, these do contain some authentic touches and translations of letters whose originals have disappeared, and they have been drawn on by all later writers. Probably the only completely reliable and dispassionate contemporary account of her last days, however, is to be found in the so-called *Chronicle of Queen Jane*, written by an anonymous eyewitness.

Early life and education Jane showed early promise of exceptional academic ability, and when she was sent to join the household of the widowed Queen Katherine Parr in the spring of 1547 she was able to benefit from the educational opportunities then available in court circles for girls as well as boys. She was also encouraged to absorb the teachings of the evangelical protestantism of which Katherine was a leading devotee.

Under the terms of Henry VIII's will Jane Grey stood presumptively fourth in line of succession to the throne, and as such she soon attracted the attention of Thomas, Baron Seymour of Sudeley, one of King Edward's maternal uncles and now just married to Queen Katherine. Ambitious and unscrupulous, Seymour saw Jane as a potentially useful weapon in his planned attack on his elder brother, the duke of Somerset, of whose position as protector he was fiercely jealous. He therefore opened negotiations with Dorset and a bargain was struck whereby Seymour gained custody of Jane in return for an undertaking that she would be placed in marriage 'much to her father's comfort'. When Dorset asked for details, he was assured that 'you will see he [Seymour] will marry her to the king' (Haynes, 82–3).

Jane had not been happy at home, but in the dowager queen's household she was treated with kindness, her piety and 'towardness' recognized and admired. In the summer of 1548 she accompanied Katherine down to Sudeley Castle and when the queen died in childbirth on 5 September, ten-year-old Jane Grey was chief mourner at the funeral. Although Thomas Seymour at first considered sending her back to her parents, he soon changed his mind. But the Dorsets were becoming impatient. More than a year had passed with no sign of Seymour's keeping any of his 'fair promises' and on 19 September the marquess wrote that he felt Jane was too young to be trusted to rule herself without a guide, and he feared lest 'for want of a bridle she might take too much head' and forget all the good behaviour she had learned from Queen Katherine. He therefore urged that she should be returned to the governance of her mother to be 'framed and ruled towards virtue' (Haynes, 78–9). This sudden access of concern for their daughter's welfare imperfectly concealed the Dorsets' determination to sell her to the highest bidder and they had begun to wonder whether it might not be wiser to settle for a match with the protector's son, which had already been tentatively discussed. Jane did go home for a short visit, but Seymour was not giving her up without a struggle. He went to see the Dorsets and, according to the marquess, 'was so earnestly in hand with me and my wife that in the end, because he would have no nay, we were contented that she [Jane] should again return to his house' (ibid., 76). Seymour also renewed his promise to arrange her marriage to the king and handed over another instalment of the £2000 he was paying for her wardship.

At the beginning of 1549, however, Thomas Seymour was arrested on a charge of high treason and Jane once more returned to Bradgate, where she continued her classical studies with her tutor John Aylmer. In the summer of 1550 Roger Ascham came to visit her and found her in her chamber, reading Plato's *Phaedo* in Greek 'with as much delight as some gentlemen would read a merry tale in Boccaccio'. When he enquired why she was not out of doors with the rest of the family hunting in the park, she replied that all their sport was but a shadow to that pleasure she found in Plato. 'Alas! good folk, they never felt what true pleasure meant'. And she went on to complain bitterly of her parents' severity:

> For when I am in presence either of father or mother, whether I speak, keep silence, sit, stand or go, eat, drink, be merry or sad, be sewing, playing, dancing, or doing anything else, I must do it, as it were … even so perfectly as God made the world, or else I am so sharply taunted, so cruelly threatened, yea presently some times with pinches, nips and bobs … that I think myself in hell.

Mr Aylmer, on the other hand, taught her so gently and pleasantly, and with 'such fair allurements to learning', that she derived more pleasure from her books with every day that passed (Ascham, 47). This famous passage is usually held to illustrate the harshness and lack of understanding shown by the Dorsets to their gifted daughter; it may equally illustrate the attitude of a priggish, opinionated teenager, openly scornful of her parents' conventional, old-fashioned tastes.

Young protestant Jane's reputation for scholarship grew as, encouraged by Aylmer and Ascham, she began to correspond with various German and Swiss protestant divines, and in July 1551 she is found thanking Heinrich Bullinger, chief pastor of the radical church of Zürich, for sending her a copy of his treatise on Christian perfection, a little volume of 'pure and unsophisticated religion'. She was also just starting to learn Hebrew, so as to be able to read the Old Testament in the original, and asked Bullinger for advice on how to pursue this study 'to the greatest advantage' (Nicolas, 8, 10).

In October 1551 Dorset succeeded to the dukedom of Suffolk in right of his wife and Lady Jane was now more often at court, being present with her parents at a state banquet given in honour of Mary of Guise, the Scottish queen regent. Neither of the king's sisters, Mary and Elizabeth, had been invited on this occasion, but the duchess of Suffolk was friendly with Princess Mary and, despite their growing religious divergence, kept in regular contact with her. Jane, though, never compromised. Presented with a rich gown of tinsel cloth of gold on velvet by the princess, she refused to wear it, saying that 'it were a shame to follow my Lady Mary against God's word and leave my Lady Elizabeth which followeth God's word' (Strype, 195–6). Elizabeth at this time affected a severely plain style of dress, setting the fashion for other highborn protestant maidens. In the summer of 1552 the Suffolk family was staying with Mary when, according to protestant tradition preserved by John Foxe, Jane once more made her position clear. She was, so the story goes, walking through the princess's private chapel with the wife of one of Mary's officers. Seeing her companion curtsey to the altar where the host was exposed, Jane asked if the Lady Mary had come in. 'No', was the reply, 'I made my curtsey to Him that made us all.' 'Why', said Jane, 'how can that be, when the baker made him?' (*Acts and Monuments*, 8.700).

After the execution of Thomas Seymour and the subsequent fall of Protector Somerset, the duke and duchess of Suffolk threw in their lot with the new strong man, John Dudley, duke of Northumberland. Then, as the king's health began to fail, they connived with the plot being laid to exclude the princesses from the succession. Edward, determined to prevent the Catholic Mary from succeeding, made a will passing over both his half-sisters in favour of the so-called Suffolk line and, after some debate, bequeathed the crown to 'the Lady Jane and her heirs masles' (Nichols, *Literary Remains*, 571–2).

Nine days queen In order to secure his hold on power, Northumberland had arranged with the Suffolks that Jane should marry his own son Guildford *Dudley (c.1535–1554). Jane at first tried to resist, on the grounds that she believed herself already contracted to Somerset's son, the earl of Hertford. But her protests were overborne and her submission extorted 'by the urgency of her mother and the violence of her father, who compelled her to accede to his commands by blows' (Strickland, 136, citing Giulio Rosso).

The marriage took place on 25 May 1553 at Durham House, the Dudleys' London residence, and afterwards Jane went back to her parents; but the duchess of Northumberland soon became impatient, telling her that the king was dying and she must hold herself in readiness for a summons at any moment, because he had made her his heir. According to her own account, Jane did not take this seriously. Nevertheless she was obliged to return to Durham House. After a few days she fell sick and, convinced that she was being poisoned, begged leave to go out to the royal manor at Chelsea to recuperate. She was still there when King Edward died on 6 July. Three days later one of Northumberland's daughters came to take her to Syon House, where she was ceremoniously informed that Edward had indeed nominated her to succeed him. Again according to her own account, given in a letter to Queen Mary which has since disappeared but which survives in an Italian translation by Pollini, Jane was 'stupefied and troubled' by the news, falling to the ground weeping and declaring her 'insufficiency', but at the same time praying that if what was given to her was 'rightfully and lawfully hers', God would grant her grace to govern the realm to his glory and service (Stone, 497–8).

Next day, 10 July, Jane was conducted in state down river to the Tower, where an Italian spectator, witnessing her arrival, described her as being 'very short and thin, but prettily shaped and graceful. Her hair was nearly red, her complexion good but freckled, and her teeth, when she smiled, white and sharp' (Davey, 253). Guildford Dudley, 'a tall strong boy with light hair', walked beside her and paid her much attention, but Jane stubbornly refused to make him king, reputedly saying that 'the crown was not a plaything for boys and girls' (ibid., 260). This led to a first-class family row, and it was apparently only then that she began to realize the full extent to which she had been made use of by the Dudleys. 'Thus in truth', she wrote, 'was I deceived by the duke [of Northumberland] and the council and ill-treated by my husband and his mother' (Stone, 499).

Jane was proclaimed queen at the Cross in Cheapside, a letter announcing her accession was circulated to the lords lieutenant of the counties, and Bishop Ridley of London preached a sermon in her favour at Paul's Cross, denouncing both Mary and Elizabeth as bastards, but Mary especially as a papist who would bring foreigners into the country. Although Jane was proclaimed as far away as the Channel Islands, and some of the London companies entered her accession in their records, it was noticeable that there were no signs of rejoicing over the new reign, none of the usual bonfires and bell-ringing, and then on 12 July news arrived that, against all the odds, Mary's friends in East Anglia were preparing to put up a fight. Plans were hurriedly made to send the duke of Suffolk to suppress them, but Jane intervened and 'with weeping tears, made request to the whole council that her father might tarry at home in her company' (Nichols, *Queen Jane*, 5). Consequently it was Northumberland who rode out to fetch in the Lady Mary, but popular feeling was against him, his army began to melt away, and three days later Mary was being proclaimed throughout the country. The duke was brought back a prisoner to the Tower, where Jane, too, was now under arrest. To begin with the new queen was ready to be merciful, telling a disapproving imperial ambassador that her conscience would not allow her to have Jane put to death, although she promised to take every precaution before setting her free.

Death and image Jane had been given comfortable quarters in the house of Partridge, the gentleman gaoler, and one day towards the end of August the anonymous author of the *Chronicle of Queen Jane*, thought to have been an official of the mint, dropped in for dinner, finding the Lady Jane sitting in the place of honour 'at the board's end'. She made the visitor welcome and asked for news of the outside world, before going on to speak gratefully of Mary—'I beseech God she may long continue'—but launched into a fierce attack against Northumberland, who had been executed on the 22nd. 'Woe worth him! He hath brought me and our stock in most miserable calamity by his exceeding ambition'. She was especially shocked to hear that the duke had apostatized in the hope of saving his life, exclaiming:

> I pray God I, nor no friend of mine die so. Should I, who am young and in my few years, forsake my faith for the love of life? Nay, God forbid! much more he should not … but life was sweet it appeared; so he might have lived, you will say, he did not care how. (Nichols, *Queen Jane*, 25)

Jane, together with Guildford Dudley and two more of his brothers, stood trial for treason on 19 November. The proceedings were brief and formal and the accused duly condemned, but the emperor's ambassador reported that Jane's life would be spared.

Then came Sir Thomas Wyatt's rebellion of late January and early February 1554 in which the duke of Suffolk, who had been pardoned by Mary, was foolish enough to take part. His action helped to seal his daughter's fate, for although the rebellion was principally directed against Mary's forthcoming marriage to Philip of Spain and no one ever suggested that Jane had any foreknowledge of it, her very existence as a possible figurehead for protestant discontent made her an unacceptable danger to the state. The queen could no longer afford to be merciful and Jane's execution was fixed for 9 February, but in a last-minute attempt to save her cousin's soul, if not her life, Mary sent John Feckenham, the new dean of St Paul's, over to the Tower with a few days' grace to see if he could convert this obdurate heretic.

Feckenham had a reputation for persuasiveness and Jane received him politely, preparing to engage in the stimulating cut and thrust of theological debate for the last time. The account of their confrontation has survived in the pages of Foxe, and naturally gives the victory and the last word to Jane, but the contestants parted amicably, with mutual expressions of regret that they would not be able to meet again in the hereafter.

Jane and Guildford were ultimately both to die on 12 February 1554. He on Tower Hill, she, as befitted her royal rank, within the precincts of the Tower, where she was also buried, on the same day, at St Peter ad Vincula. It is said that she had refused an offer from the queen to allow her to see her husband to say goodbye. She did, though, stand at her window to see him taken away and insisted on waiting there until the cart containing his headless corpse returned. She then came out leaning on the arm of the lieutenant of the Tower. Her two women attendants were in tears, but Jane herself appeared dry-eyed and composed. Mounting the steps of the scaffold, she turned to address the small group of onlookers. She admitted she had done wrong in agreeing to accept the crown, but went on, 'touching the procurement and desire thereof by me or on my behalf, I do wash my hands in innocency, before God and in the face of you good Christian people this day'. She asked those present to witness that she died a good Christian woman and to assist her with their prayers while she was alive. Even in that last dreadful moment she could find the strength to remain true to her principles and reject the age-old comfort of prayers for the dead. Kneeling, she repeated the 51st psalm, the Miserere, in English 'in most devout manner' to the end. The headsman stepped forward and she saw the block for the first time. Her women helped her off with her gown and gave her 'a fair handkercher to knit about her eyes'. Groping in the dark she cried out 'Where is it? What shall I do?' Someone came forward to guide her and 'she laid her head down upon the block and stretched forth her body and said: "Lord, into thy hands I commend my spirit!" And so she ended' (Nichols, *Queen Jane*, 56–9).

The judicial murder of sixteen-year-old Jane Grey, and no one ever pretended it was anything else, caused no great stir at the time, not even among the militantly protestant Londoners. Jane had never been a well-known figure, and in any case was too closely associated with the unpopular Dudleys and their failed coup to command much public sympathy. But there is a tradition that the oak trees in Bradgate Park were pollarded in a gesture of mourning and defiance when news of her beheading reached Leicestershire, and the story circulated that Sir Richard Morgan, the judge who had passed sentence on her, died in delirium the following year, crying 'Take the Lady Jane from me! Take away the Lady Jane!' (*Holinshed's Chronicles*, 4.23).

With one possible exception in the National Portrait Gallery, London, there does not appear to be a single reliably authenticated portrait of Jane Grey in existence. Much later paintings like the *Execution of Lady Jane Grey* by Paul Delaroche in London's National Gallery, and the various engravings which appeared in nineteenth-century biographies, all helped to perpetuate the image of gentle Jane, the protestant heroine, saint, and martyr, created for the edification of Victorian schoolrooms. The Victorians did, however, have some difficulty with her vitriolic denunciation of her first tutor, Dr Thomas Harding, who had cravenly returned to the Catholic fold, refusing to believe that such terms of vulgar abuse as 'deformed imp of Satan', or 'unshamefaced paramour of AntiChrist' could have issued from the pen of an amiable young female (Nicolas, 22). But the brilliantly gifted child had developed into a forceful, passionate young woman, all her overflowing intellectual energy devoted to a total commitment to her religious ideology, and the reality of Jane Grey, sacrificial victim of *realpolitik* though she undoubtedly became, was surely rather more disturbing than the sentimental myths surrounding her seem to suggest.   ALISON PLOWDEN

Sources *A collection of state papers … left by William Cecill, Lord Burghley*, ed. S. Haynes, 1 (1740) · N. H. Nicolas, ed., *The literary remains of Lady Jane Grey with a memoir* (1825) · *The acts and monuments of John Foxe*, ed. S. R. Cattley, 8 vols. (1837–41) · A. Strickland, *Lives of the Tudor princesses* (1868) · R. Davey, *The nine days' queen: Lady Jane Grey and her times* (1909) · *CSP Spain, 1553–4* · J. G. Nichols, ed., *The chronicle of the grey friars of London*, CS, 53 (1852) · J. G. Nichols, ed., *The chronicle of Queen Jane, and of two years of Queen Mary*, CS, old ser., 48 (1850) · J. Loach, *Edward VI* (1999) · H. Chapman, *Lady Jane Grey* (1962) · G. R. Rosso, *I successi d'Inghilterra* (1560) · R. Ascham, *The scholemaster*, ed. E. Arber, [new edn] (1870); repr. (1897) · H. Robinson, ed. and trans., *Original letters relative to the English Reformation*, 1 vol. in 2, Parker Society, [26] (1846–7) · S. Brigden, *London and the Reformation* (1989) · *Literary remains of King Edward the Sixth*, ed. J. G. Nichols, 2 vols., Roxburghe Club, 75 (1857) · J. M. Stone, *The history of Mary I, queen of England* (1901) · J. Strype, *Historical collections of the life and acts of … John Aylmer*, new edn (1821) · G. Pollini, *L'historia ecclesiastica della rivoluzion d'Inghilterra* (1594) · M. Florio, *Historia de la vita et de la morte de … Giovanna Graia* (1607) · *Holinshed's chronicles of England, Scotland and Ireland*, ed. H. Ellis, 6 vols. (1807–8) · R. Tittler and S. L. Battley, 'The local community and the crown in 1553: the accession of Mary Tudor revisited', *BIHR*, 57 (1984), 131–9 · A. Plowden, *Lady Jane Grey* (2003)

Likenesses attrib. Master John, oils, *c*.1545 (Lady Jane Dudley?), NPG; version, Seaton Delaval Hall, Northumberland · W. & M. Passe, line engraving, BM, NPG; repro. in H. Holland, *Heröologia Anglica*, 2 vols. (1620)

Grey, John de. *See* Gray, John de (*d*. 1214).

Grey [Gray], **Sir John de** (*d*. 1266), royal counsellor, was a younger son of Henry de Grey (*d*. 1219) and Isolde Bardolph (*d*. 1246), a Kentish heiress. From his father Grey inherited the manor of Shirland in Derbyshire, but most of his lands came to him later, from the crown and by marriage, in particular from his wife, Emma (*d*. before 1251), daughter and heir of Roger de Caux of Water Eaton in Buckinghamshire, widow of John, son of Stephen of Segrave, and heir also to the estates of her mother, Nicola of Leigh from Thurleigh in Bedfordshire. They were married before 1232 and had at least three daughters and a son, Reynold Grey, first Lord Grey of Wilton (*d*. 1308), from whom were descended the baronial families of Grey of Wilton and Grey of Ruthin. John's second wife, Joan (*d*. 1256), the widow of Paulinus Peivre, brought him estates in Devon and elsewhere.

John de Grey makes his first appearance in 1220, when he was retained as a knight of the king's household for an annual fee of £10, raised to £30 in 1229. With his brother Richard he sailed on the Poitevin expedition of 1224, was overseas in 1226, and in 1229 was appointed joint custodian of the Channel Islands. The fall of Hubert de Burgh led to his being granted the manor of Purleigh in Essex, which had been confiscated from de Burgh. He served as sheriff of the counties of Bedford and Buckingham from 1238 to 1239, and in 1242 accompanied the king of Poitou and Gascony, acting as one of Henry III's principal military commanders. He subsequently held an important command in the defence of the Welsh marches.

Grey was temporarily disgraced in 1251 for marrying Joan Peivre without the king's licence, but was restored to favour that October in return for a fine of 500 marks. He sailed on the king's continental expedition of 1253, remaining overseas with his brothers Richard and William for the next eighteen months. In August 1253 he was appointed seneschal of Gascony, and although in October of that year he fell ill and was briefly replaced by his brother Richard, he recovered and may have retained his office until the king's departure from the province late in 1254. By then he would have been acting as the chief agent of Edward, the king's son, who had been granted the lordship of Gascony in February 1254. In 1255 Grey withdrew from court, protesting his disaffection with the policies of the king's council, and pleading his old age, but he appears to have retained the favour of the Lord Edward, being appointed by him keeper of the Welsh marches in 1257 and royal constable of Shrewsbury.

When the baronial reform movement began in June 1258, Grey was named as one of the twelve barons set to negotiate with the king in parliament, and as one of the four barons who were to oversee the Lord Edward's household. In 1260 he served as a justice, appointed to investigate abuses by the king's ministers in Dorset, Somerset, and Devon, but reverted to the king's party shortly afterwards, receiving custody of the castle and county of Hereford, and, in the spring of 1264, of the castle at Nottingham and the counties of Nottingham and Derby. In June 1263 his houses in Ludgate were attacked by the London mob, and Grey was forced to flee the city. He held Nottingham for the king for several months after the royalist defeat at the battle of Lewes, and although he surrendered to the Montfortians in December 1264, after the royalist victory at Evesham in August 1265 he was restored to the custody of Nottingham and Derby, holding them until his own death in February or March 1266.

NICHOLAS VINCENT

Sources Chancery records · Pipe rolls · Paris, Chron. · Ann. mon. · GEC, Peerage · W. Farrer, Honors and knights' fees ... from the eleventh to the fourteenth century, 1 (1923) · G. P. Cuttino, ed., Gascon register A, 3 vols. (1975–6) · Segrave cartulary, BL, Harley MSS, 4748 · Harley charter, BL, 50.I.46

Grey, John, second Lord Grey of Wilton (d. 1323), nobleman and administrator, was the son of Reynold, first Lord Grey, and his wife, Matilda. He was at least forty at his father's death in 1308 and inherited lands in Ruthin, Denbighshire, Wilton, Herefordshire, Shirland, Derbyshire, Purleigh, Essex, Toseland, Hemmingford, and Yelling, Huntingdonshire, Water Eaton, Snellson, and Great Brickhill, Buckinghamshire, Thurleigh, Wrest, and Brogborough, Bedfordshire, and Kempley, Gloucestershire. He married first Anne, daughter of William de Ferrers of Leicestershire, who died before 1300, and second, Maud, daughter of Ralph Basset of Drayton. Grey was summoned as a baron for military service from 21 June 1308 to 3 April 1323, to royal councils from 8 January 1309 to 30 May 1324 (posthumously), and to parliament from 4 March 1309 to 18 September 1322.

Grey was granted protection for going to Wales for the king in 1277 and again for a journey to Santiago de Compostela in November 1278. Both he and his father were pardoned for taking deer from the royal forests (1278 and 1286) and in October 1305 were told the king's displeasure, which they had incurred for some undisclosed reason, would be remitted provided they stood trial if prosecuted. In 1308 he was made liable for £200 of his father's debts payable in yearly instalments.

Grey was one of the twenty-five figures attending the Dunstable tournament (about 20 March and 7 April 1309) whose opinions may have been sought in advance of the April parliament and the issuing of a petition upon whose articles the ordinances of 1311 were later based. He was one of twenty-one *lords ordainer appointed on 16 March 1310 who were given power to reform the administration of the household and the realm. In December 1313 he was commissioned to try Griffin de la Pole, who was in dispute over the lordship of Powys. In spite of the reluctance of the leading light of the ordainers, Thomas of Lancaster, to serve in Scotland, Grey fought at Bannockburn on 24 June 1314. In February 1315 he was appointed justiciar of north Wales and was keeper of the king's castles and lands there until November 1316. When a fresh campaign was being prepared in late 1315, the prior of Easby complained that when John Grey was in Scotland he had taken all their horses and that they could buy no more through poverty and shortage of corn. Grey was included in the standing council of sixteen set up under the treaty of Leake in August 1318 which was required to give assent to Edward II's actions outside parliament. He went to France with the king in 1320 and was appointed a keeper of the peace for Bedfordshire. Following the York parliament of 1322 Grey remained a member of the enlarged council and witnessed grants made by the king. The text of an indictment against the Despensers erroneously names John instead of Richard Grey as someone they attempted to win over to their cause.

A charter of 1310 constituted and endowed St Peter's Chapel, Ruthin, as a collegiate chapel for seven regular priests, who were to say prayers for the souls of Grey's parents. In November 1311 he had licence to convey the castle of Ruthin, cantref of Dyffryn Clwyd, and the manor of Rushton in Chester to himself for life with the reversion to his younger son, Roger, in tail general. In 1315 Grey was given licence to alienate lands and rents in Kentish Town and in St Andrew's, Holborn, to Smithfield Priory for a chaplain in his manor of Pourtpole without the bar of the Old Temple, London (now Gray's Inn Road). At his death, on 28 October 1323, Grey was holding lands in twenty-six counties. On 18 November Richard Grey of Codnor was allowed to take twenty does from John Grey's woods and fish in his stews for burying his body. Although succeeded by Henry (d. 1342), his son with his first wife and ancestor of the Greys of Wilton, John Grey clearly favoured Roger *Grey (d. 1353), his son with his second wife, who, along with the lordship of Ruthin, inherited some three-quarters of John Grey's estate, and was the ancestor of the Greys of Ruthin.

A. J. MUSSON

Sources Chancery records · GEC, Peerage · C. Moor, ed., Knights of Edward I, 2, Harleian Society, 81 (1929), 149–50 · F. Palgrave, ed., The parliamentary writs and writs of military summons, 2/2 (1830) · J. R. Maddicott, Thomas of Lancaster, 1307–1322: a study in the reign of Edward II (1970) · R. I. Jack, ed., The Grey of Ruthin valor: the valor of the English lands of Edmund Grey, earl of Kent, ... from the ministers' accounts of 1467–1468, Bedfordshire Historical RS, 46 (1965) · CIPM, 1, nos. 311–12 · CClR, 1327–30, 74 · CPR, 1321–4, 345 · PRO

Wealth at death lands in twenty-six counties: CIPM, 1, nos. 311–12; escheators' enrolled accounts, LTR no. 1 mmld, II

Grey, John, first Lord Grey of Rotherfield (1300–1359), soldier and courtier, was born at Rotherfield, Oxfordshire, on 29 October 1300, the eldest son of Sir John Grey of Rotherfield (*d.* 1311) and his wife, Margaret Oddingsells. When his father died he left estates mostly in Oxfordshire and Yorkshire. The younger John proved his age in 1321 and at once began a career as a soldier, being summoned to serve in Scotland in 1322, 1323, and 1327, and in Gascony in 1325. Knighted by 1330, he weathered the deposition of Edward II unscathed; indeed, it brought him hopes of advancement, through marriage to Eleanor de Clare, the widow of the younger Hugh Despenser. However, his aspirations to Eleanor's hand were shared by William, first Lord Zouche of Mortimer, and a long and bitter quarrel resulted. On 26 January 1329 a commission was appointed to investigate Grey's complaint that Eleanor, whom he described as his wife, had been abducted by Zouche at Hanley, Worcestershire. In the Michaelmas parliament of 1331 the two men had to be ordered to keep the peace towards one another, while early in 1332 they fell out so violently in the presence of the king and council that Grey all but drew his dagger on his adversary. Both were sent to prison, but, although Zouche was quickly freed, Grey was left to cool his heels in prison, while his lands were taken into the king's hand. He was probably soon released, but the quarrel over Eleanor continued, and Grey ultimately appealed to the pope, who on 15 May 1333 instructed the bishop of Coventry and Lichfield to resolve the matter. Zouche and Eleanor were confirmed as man and wife and Grey had lost his heiress.

Grey resumed his military career, serving in Scotland in 1335, and from 1338 he was regularly summoned to parliaments and councils; he is consequently regarded as having thereby become Lord Grey of Rotherfield. In 1340 he was appointed an assessor of the ninth in Bedfordshire and Buckinghamshire, but his principal occupation remained as a soldier, and between that year and 1347 he was almost continuously employed in Scotland, Flanders, and France. A founder member of the Order of the Garter, he fought at Crécy in 1346 in the King's division, and took part in the siege of Calais a year later in the retinue of William Clinton, earl of Huntingdon. No doubt it was as a reward for such services that on 10 December 1346 he was licensed to crenellate his principal residences of Rotherfield and Sculcoates, near Hull. Thereafter he was increasingly employed at court. By 1348 he was a knight of the king's chamber, as such taking part in a number of tournaments, while by December 1349 he had been appointed steward of the royal household, an office he held almost until his death. In that capacity he was regularly in attendance on the king, witnessing a number of charters at Westminster and accompanying Edward III to Scotland at the beginning of 1356, after campaigning in France for the last time in the previous year. He was also appointed to a few commissions, mostly in Oxfordshire, where he headed the county's peace commission in 1351 and 1354.

Grey's death may well have been sudden. One of the king's sureties on 6 July 1359 for the repayment of a loan from the earl of Arundel, he probably died on 1 September following, and was certainly dead by the 20th. He married twice. Some time before 1 March 1312 he married Katherine, daughter and coheir of Brian Fitzalan of Bedale, Yorkshire, with whom he had a son, John, who was his eventual heir, and a daughter, Maud. Presumably Katherine was dead by 1329 when Grey was hoping to marry Eleanor de Clare. Then some time before 1343 he married Avice, daughter of John, second Lord Marmion, and with her had two sons, John and Robert, who both took their mother's surname. His marriages brought Grey further estates in Yorkshire, and also manors in Lincolnshire, Sussex, and Gloucestershire. But his principal interests continued to lie in Oxfordshire. In 1337 he had given a plot of land in Oxford to the Franciscans of that town, and it was at Rotherfield that he died.   HENRY SUMMERSON

Sources exchequer, accounts various, PRO, E 101/391/15 · *Chancery records* · GEC, *Peerage*, new edn, 6.145–7; 8.521 · W. Dugdale, *The baronage of England*, 2 vols. (1675–6), vol. 1 · *RotP*, vol. 2 · *Reports … touching the dignity of a peer of the realm*, House of Lords, 4 (1829) · *CIPM*, 6, no. 336; 10, no. 518 · *RotS*, vol. 1 · Rymer, *Foedera*, new edn, vols. 2/2–3/1 (1834) · F. Palgrave, ed., *The parliamentary writs and writs of military summons*, 2/3 (1834) · *CEPR letters*, vol. 2 · G. Wrottesley, *Crécy and Calais* (1897); repr. (1898) · E. B. Fryde and others, eds., *Handbook of British chronology*, 3rd edn, Royal Historical Society Guides and Handbooks, 2 (1986), 76 · Tout, *Admin. hist.*, 6.43 · *CCIR, 1330–33*, 173 · *CPR, 1348–50*, 36

Wealth at death see *CIPM*, 6, no. 336

Grey, John, third Baron Grey of Codnor (1305×11?–1392), soldier, was the eldest son of Richard Grey, second Baron Grey of Codnor, Derbyshire, and his wife, Joan, daughter of Robert, Lord Fitzpayn. **Richard Grey**, second Baron Grey of Codnor (*b.* 1281/2, *d.* in or before 1335) established a considerable reputation as a soldier during Edward II's reign, serving in Scotland and the march in 1311, 1314, 1319–20, and 1327, and in Gascony, where he was appointed steward of the duchy, in 1312 and 1324. His request to be discharged from this latter office was granted in October 1324, but only on condition that he remain in Gascony with the earl of Kent, Edmund of Woodstock. At home Grey accompanied Edward II and Isabella to the French court in 1313 but was pardoned for all actions taken against the Despensers in the company of Roger Mortimer and the marchers in August 1321. He sided with the king during the Boroughbridge campaign, however, and remained in favour with the court thereafter. The younger Despenser assured him that 'the king places great trust in your counsel and good service' (Chaplais, 78) in October 1324 and he was appointed constable of Nottingham Castle in December 1325. Grey was a follower of Thomas of Brotherton, earl of Norfolk, and acted as his lieutenant in the office of marshal of England. It may be this connection that explains the prominent part he played in the deposition of Edward II, for Grey was one of the four barons in the deputation who renounced allegiance to the king at Kenilworth in January 1327. He was also a receiver and trier of parliamentary petitions in 1321 and 1332.

Like his father John Grey sought to maintain his baronial status, which his family's small and scattered landed estate struggled to support, by an active military career. He served on Edward III's early campaigns against the

Scots in 1334, 1336, and 1338, went to the Low Countries with the king between 1338 and 1340, and then served again in Scotland, as a knight, in 1341. In 1345–6 he went, as a banneret, to Aquitaine with Henry of Lancaster (d. 1361). This was the beginning of a close military association between the two men: Grey subsequently served under Lancaster's command at Calais in 1347, in Flanders the following year, then in Normandy and Brittany during 1355. For the Rheims campaign in 1359–60, he transferred to the company of Lancaster's son-in-law, John, earl of Richmond. Grey won further honour in 1365, when he joined the crusade of Peter, king of Cyprus, against Alexandria, acting as the standard-bearer of the papal legate throughout the expedition. As a reward for his services Grey was granted the keepership of Rochester Castle, together with the farm of the town, for life in 1359, and was excused all further attendance at councils and parliament, in consideration of his bodily infirmities, in 1371.

John Grey married first Eleanor, who died before 1330, and, second, Alice, daughter of Sir Warin de Lisle; the son of this marriage, Henry, predeceased his father. Grey was also father of an illegitimate son, Nicholas, for whom he obtained an (ineffective) papal provision to a prebend at Lincoln or Southwell in 1355. Although he was regularly named as a justice of the peace in Derbyshire, and acted on administrative commissions throughout the east midlands, Grey did not neglect his valuable manors in Essex and Kent; he was a notable benefactor of the small Carmelite house at Aylesford, Kent, founded by his ancestors, and requested burial there. He died on 14 December 1392 and was succeeded by his grandson, Richard *Grey, fourth Baron Grey.   SIMON WALKER

Sources W. Dugdale, *The baronage of England*, 2 vols. (1675–6) · GEC, *Peerage* · *Chancery records* · P. Chaplais, ed., *The War of Saint-Sardos (1323–1325): Gascon correspondence and diplomatic documents*, CS, 3rd ser., 87 (1954) · M. V. Clarke, *Medieval representation and consent: a study of early parliaments in England and Ireland* (1936) · F. J. Boehlke, *Pierre de Thomas: scholar, diplomat and crusader* (1966) · *CIPM*, 5, no. 116; 7, no. 683; 15, nos. 293–4 · S. J. Payling, *Political society in Lancastrian England* (1991), 92

Wealth at death *CIPM*, 5, 7, and 15 · lands assessed at approx. £440 p.a. in 1436: Payling, *Political society*

Grey, Sir John (d. 1439). *See under* Grey family (*per.* 1325–1523).

Grey [Gray], **Sir John, count of Tancarville** (1384×91–1421), soldier and diplomat, was the second son of the Northumberland knight, Sir Thomas Grey (1359–1400) of Heaton (Heaton Moor) and of Wark-on-Tweed, Northumberland (a property acquired in 1398), and Joan (d. 1410), daughter of John (III) Mowbray, Lord Mowbray (d. 1368), who took Sir Thomas Tunstall as her second husband before June 1407. He was therefore the grandson of Thomas *Gray (d. 1369), author of the *Scalachronica*. His eldest brother, Sir Thomas Grey, was executed for his part in the 'Southampton plot' against Henry V in 1415. Another brother, William (d. 1436), was successively bishop of London (consecrated in 1426) and Lincoln (1431). According to the latter's will there was a fourth brother, Henry Grey of Ketteringham, and a sister, Maud, who married Sir Robert Ogle.

Grey may be the John Grey *valletus domini* ('attendant of his lord') in the service of Sir Henry Percy (Hotspur) at the castle of Denbigh in April 1403. Along with Richard Ledes he challenged two Scotsmen to six courses on horseback at Carlisle in June 1404. It is likely that he was associated with the household of Henry, prince of Wales, and that he served in the Welsh wars, as did his eldest brother. In March 1408, as esquire, Grey was granted an annuity of 20 marks by the prince, and on 14 August 1409 Henry IV granted a further annuity of 40 marks out of the issues of Northumberland for his services to king and prince. Grey served on the expedition sent under the prince's orders in September 1411 to assist the duke of Burgundy. By September 1413 he was a king's knight, and received further royal largesse in the early years of the new reign.

At the landing of the campaign of 1415 Grey was one of a group of knights detailed to reconnoitre the country towards Harfleur; another, Sir Gilbert Umfraville, had also served on the expedition of 1411. Grey took part in the siege of Harfleur and the battle of Agincourt, where he captured the count of Eu. On 8 August 1415 he was granted custody of the lands held in fee tail by his eldest brother, Sir Thomas Grey of Heaton, during the minority of the latter's heir, and himself received the lands that his brother had held in fee simple. In May 1416, by now a knight-banneret, he indented to serve in the naval expedition that the king intended to lead in person but that subsequently sailed under John, duke of Bedford, and defeated the French off Harfleur on 15 August. He crossed on the campaign of 1417 and was one of Henry's most trusted captains in the conquest of Normandy. He was present at the siege of Caen and was appointed to the captaincy of the castle and town of Mortagne (Orne) on 31 October 1417. He campaigned in Lower Normandy under the duke of Gloucester in the spring and summer of 1418. At the siege of Rouen he was positioned on the Mont-St Michel; John Page's poem about the siege speaks of him as 'a comely knyght'. When Rouen surrendered in January 1419 Grey was given power to receive into the king's hands all castles in Normandy and to issue letters of safe conduct to all who wished to do homage. The level of royal trust he enjoyed is also revealed by appointments to diplomatic missions between October 1418 and April 1419. When Mantes surrendered in February 1419 he was appointed to its captaincy, a post he held until August, subsequently participating in Henry V's advance towards Paris. In November 1419 he was directed to receive inhabitants of the *châtellenies* of St Germain, Montjoy, and Poissy into the king's obedience, and was in the same month made a knight of the Garter. On 20 January 1420 Grey was appointed to the important captaincy of Harfleur, an office he held until his death. He served at the siege of Melun in July 1420 and on the expedition of Thomas, duke of Clarence, into Maine and Anjou where he met his death, along with Clarence and several other English captains, at the battle of Baugé on 22 March 1421. His closeness to the king had brought him rich rewards in Normandy. On 20 November 1417 he had been granted the castle and lordship of Tilly-sur-Seulles (Calvados) in tail male, and on 31 January 1419 the *comté* of Tancarville also in tail male, along with a house in Rouen; a year later he had received the custody of the lands of an important Norman prisoner as well as a house in Caen.

Grey had married by 1419 Joanna (1400–1425), elder daughter and coheir (with her younger sister Jocosa (d. 1446), who married Sir John Tiptoft (d. 1443) as his second wife) of Sir Edward Charlton of Powys (d. 14 March 1421) and his first wife, Eleanor (d. 1405), daughter of Thomas Holland, earl of Kent, and widow of Roger Mortimer, earl of March (d. 1398). Their son, Henry, also count of Tancarville, was described in his father's inquisition post mortem in April 1421 as aged a year and a half or more. The *comté* of Tancarville was lost in the French reconquest of Normandy. Henry's son, Sir Richard Grey, was styled Lord Grey of Powys. The earldom of Tancarville was created *de novo* in June 1695 for Edward Grey, a descendant in the female line of Thomas Grey of Heaton, Sir John Grey's eldest brother. ANNE CURRY

Sources GEC, *Peerage* · PRO · PRO, Norman rolls, C 64 · PRO, French or treaty rolls, C 76 · PRO, Inq. post mortem, C 138 · PRO, Accounts various, E 101 · PRO, Ministers' accounts, SC 6 · *Chancery records* · Bibliothèque Nationale, Paris, Collection Clairambault · Bibliothèque Nationale, Paris, manuscrits français · BL, Add. ch. · Archives Départementales du Calvados, Fonds Danquin · *The chronicle of John Hardyng*, ed. H. Ellis (1812) · *Thomae Walsingham, quondam monachi S. Albani, historia Anglicana*, ed. H. T. Riley, 2 vols., pt 1 of *Chronica monasterii S. Albani*, Rolls Series, 28 (1863–4), vol. 2 · Rymer, *Foedera* · J. Page, 'The siege of Rouen', *The historical collections of a citizen of London in the fifteenth century*, ed. J. Gairdner, CS, new ser., 17 (1876), 1–46 · *A history of Northumberland*, Northumberland County History Committee, 15 vols. (1893–1940), vol. 14 · J. H. Wylie, *History of England under Henry the Fourth*, 4 vols. (1884–98) · J. H. Wylie and W. T. Waugh, eds., *The reign of Henry the Fifth*, 3 vols. (1914–29)

Wealth at death 6s. 8d. from 13 acres of land in Bamburgh: PRO, C 138/55 · 400 livres tournois lands in *comté* of Tancarville put to farm after death; 50 livres tournois lands in lordship of Manville put to farm after death: Archives Départementales du Calvados, Fonds Danquin; BL, Add. Ch. 302

Grey, Sir John (c.1432–1461). *See under* Grey, Sir Richard (d. 1483).

Grey, Lord John (d. 1564), nobleman, was the youngest son of Thomas *Grey, second marquess of Dorset (1477–1530), and his second wife, Margaret, daughter of Sir Robert Wotton of Boughton Malherbe, Kent, and widow of William Medley. His elder brothers were Henry *Grey, who succeeded his father as third marquess and in 1551 was created duke of Suffolk on the death of his wife's male relatives and Thomas; a fourth son appears to have died young. Under Edward VI, John Grey served as deputy at Newhaven, the English fortification near Boulogne, which was strengthened and provided with storage facilities at the beginning of the reign. He was granted the rectory of Kirby Bellars, Leicestershire, in 1550, and additional estates in Leicestershire, Derbyshire, and Nottinghamshire in 1551.

Although Queen Mary confirmed these grants and added to them Bardon Park, Leicestershire, and the site of the monastery of Kirby Bellars, John Grey and his brothers became involved in January 1554 in Wyatt's rebellion

which was directed against Mary's marriage to Philip of Spain. When their abortive insurrection in Leicestershire failed they were arrested, John and Henry being captured at Astley, Warwickshire, on 2 February. Condemned by a panel of peers, Suffolk was executed on Tower Hill on the 23rd. Thomas, who was suspected of being the real leader of the rebellion, was executed on 24 April. John is said by some sources to have been arraigned on 20 February, but judicial records indicate that his trial began on 27 May. His claim to be tried by his peers on the grounds that he had become marquess of Dorset on the death of his brothers was disallowed, and on 11 June he was condemned to death, but through the diligent efforts of his wife, Mary, a sister of the Catholic courtier Anthony Browne, Viscount Montagu, he was released on 30 October and pardoned on 17 January 1555. He lived obscurely for the remainder of Mary's reign.

Upon Elizabeth's accession Grey appeared at court as the head of his family. He attended the queen on her first progress to London and on new year's day 1559 presented her with a costly mother-of-pearl cup. In March he wrote to William Cecil complaining of poverty, and in April the queen granted him the manor of Pyrgo in Essex, which became his principal residence, as well as lands at Higham and Stoke Dennys in Somerset. He was also restored in blood and released from the act of attainder passed against Wyatt's fellow conspirators in 1554. Cecil regarded him as a staunch protestant and in 1558 had him named one of the four noblemen to supervise the alteration of the Book of Common Prayer.

During the 1560s Grey became concerned about the plight of his niece, Suffolk's surviving daughter, Lady Katherine Grey [see Seymour, Katherine, countess of Hertford]. She had been named an heir to the throne in the accession proclamation issued by her elder sister Lady Jane *Grey in 1553, stating that Mary and Elizabeth were barred from the succession because they were illegitimate and proclaiming the right of the Suffolk line. When Elizabeth did succeed, Katherine ignored the delicacy of her position as the heir presumptive under Henry VIII's will and secretly married Edward Seymour, earl of Hertford, in 1560. Hertford was sent to France before the marriage became known, but when Katherine's pregnancy could no longer be concealed he was summoned home to join her in the Tower. The marriage was declared invalid, but the two contrived to meet as prisoners and a second son was born. Katherine remained in the Tower until 1563, when an outbreak of plague in London caused the queen to send them to house arrest in separate establishments. Katherine went to join John Grey at Pyrgo. Both she and Grey bombarded Cecil with letters urging him to use his influence to secure a royal pardon for Katherine, who was said to be pining away for want of her majesty's favour. But all this pressure was brought to nothing by the circulation in 1564 of a book by John Hales, a minor civil servant, arguing that Katherine, not Mary, queen of Scots, was Elizabeth's lawful heir. The queen's anger led to Katherine's removal from John Grey's charge, and to his being taken into custody for a time. He was soon released and allowed to return to Pyrgo, where he died on 19 November 1564. He was buried in his chapel there. Cecil wrote that 'his friends report that he died of thought, but his gout was sufficient to have ended his life' (Ellis, 2.286). He had suffered from the ailment for at least a decade. The queen's displeasure towards Katherine and Hertford continued, and they were again committed to the Tower.

Lord John Grey's will is dated 17 November 1564. He left all his property to his 'derelie beloved wife Marie', whom he named his sole executor. His family consisted of three sons, only one of whom survived him, and four daughters. The youngest son, Henry *Grey, was made Baron Grey of Groby on 21 July 1603; the descendants of this line include Henry Grey, first earl of Stamford, and his son Thomas, Lord Grey of Groby (1623?–1657), one of the regicides.

STANFORD LEHMBERG

Sources D. M. Loades, *Two Tudor conspiracies* (1965) · W. T. MacCaffrey, *The shaping of the Elizabethan regime: Elizabethan politics, 1558–1572* (1968) · W. K. Jordan, *Edward VI, 1: The young king* (1968) · H. Ellis, ed., *Original letters illustrative of English history*, 2nd ser., 2 (1827) · will, PRO, PROB 11/48, sig. 2 · *CSP dom.*, 1547–80 · *DNB*
Archives BL, Cecil's corresp., Lansdowne MSS 6–9
Wealth at death see will, PRO, PROB 11/48, sig. 2

Grey, Sir John (*bap.* 1772, *d.* 1856), army officer, was baptized at Embleton, Northumberland, on 18 March 1772, the younger son of Charles Grey of Morwick Hall, Northumberland, and his wife, Catherine Maria, daughter of the Revd John Skelley. Charles, first Earl Grey, was the brother of his grandfather, John Grey. Little is known of Grey's early life. He entered the army as a cadet in 1795 and arrived in India on 27 January 1798. On 18 July 1798 he was commissioned ensign with the 75th foot, and he was promoted lieutenant on 8 May 1799. He served with the 75th in the Fourth Anglo-Mysore War, against Tipu Sultan, and was present at the battle of Malavalli and the storming of Seringapatam. He became captain in the 15th battalion, Army of Reserve, on 31 October 1803, exchanged to the 82nd foot on 23 August 1804, was promoted major in the 9th garrison battalion on 27 November 1806, and exchanged to the 99th foot on 28 January 1808 and to the 5th (Northumberland) foot on 13 June 1811. He served in the Peninsula at the engagement at El Bodon, the siege of Ciudad Rodrigo, including the scaling of the *faussebraie* and storming of the breach, during which he was twice wounded, and in the action at Fuenteguinaldo. He became lieutenant-colonel on 6 February 1812, and commanded the 2nd battalion of his regiment at home until it was disbanded in 1816.

Grey then spent many years on half pay. In 1830 he married Rosa Josefa Louisa, only daughter of Captain Henry Evelyn Sturt RN. There were no children. On 22 July 1830 he was promoted colonel, and on 28 June 1838 major-general. From 1840 to 1845 he served as divisional commander at Meerut, Bengal. At the head of the left wing of the army of Gwalior, formed at Jhansi, he defeated a force of 12,000 Mahrattas at Punniar on 29 December 1843. On the same day the main body of the Maratha army was defeated and broken by Lord Gough at Maharajpur. For this he was made KCB on 2 May 1844.

Grey was appointed colonel of the 5th (Northumberland) Fusiliers on 18 May 1849, and commander-in-chief and second member of the council at Bombay, with the local rank of lieutenant-general, on 30 December 1850. On 11 November 1851 he was promoted full lieutenant-general. He retired in 1852. His elder brother (Charles Grey, captain in the 85th foot, killed at New Orleans in 1815) having predeceased him, the Morwick branch of the Greys of Howick became extinct on Grey's death, which took place at Morwick Hall on 19 February 1856.

H. M. CHICHESTER, *rev.* ALEX MAY

Sources *Army List* · *Indian Army List* · Burke, *Gen. GB* · W. Wood, *The Northumberland fusiliers* (1901) · V. C. P. Hodson, *List of officers of the Bengal army, 1758–1834*, 4 vols. (1927–47) · R. S. Rait, *The life and campaigns of Hugh, first Viscount Gough*, 2 vols. (1903) · C. A. Kincaid, *A history of the Maratha people* (1925) · C. W. C. Oman, *A history of the Peninsular War*, 7 vols. (1902–30) · D. Featherstone, *Victorian colonial warfare: India, from the conquest of Sind to the Indian mutiny* (1992)

Grey, John (1785–1868), agriculturist and land agent, was born at Milfield, Glendale, Northumberland, in August 1785, the eldest of the two sons and two daughters of George Grey of West Ord, near Berwick, and his wife, Mary, daughter of John Burn of Berwick. His father died in 1793, and his widowed mother ran the estate and farm, which in 1873 was returned as being 1205 acres with an annual value of £2522, and brought up her four children, particularly impressing them with her strong anti-slavery views. John Grey was educated at Dr Tate's school in Richmond, Yorkshire, and then had two years of private tuition in the home of a Cumberland clergyman.

In 1803, when Grey was eighteen, his mother handed over the management of the family property to him. It was during this period that he met George Culley at Wooler market, and he had many conversations with him there and while riding to and from market. This began his education in scientific farming, which he continued by studying Arthur Young's works. On 27 December 1814 he married Hannah Eliza (*d.* 1860), daughter of Ralph Annett, of The Fence, near Alnwick, of Huguenot descent; most of their ten children—three sons and seven daughters—were born at Milfield, including the best-known of them all, Josephine *Butler, who wrote her father's biography. During the 1820s Grey acted as the chief agent in Northumberland for his cousin, Earl Grey, advocating his political views on the causes of parliamentary reform, poor-law reform, popular education, and repeal of the corn laws, as well as the abolition of slavery and Catholic emancipation. He became acquainted with many public figures, accompanied Lord Brougham on his anti-slavery tour of Northumberland and Cumberland in 1826, and won the trust of Lord Althorp as well as Earl Grey for his persuasive support of the reform bills of 1830 and 1832 in speeches at Alnwick. At this time his radical opinions earned him the title of the 'Black Prince of the North'.

These connections, especially the strong recommendation of Earl Grey, led Sir James Graham to appoint Grey, in 1833, to be sole receiver, or agent, for the northern estates of the Greenwich Hospital. These estates, spread over more than 20,000 acres in Northumberland and Cumberland, had belonged to the earl of Derwentwater; they were forfeited in 1715 and granted to the Greenwich Hospital, and thus came under the Admiralty, of which Graham was first lord in 1833. Grey proceeded to build himself a large and comfortable agent's house at Dilston, on the Tyne, on the site of Derwentwater's old seat, and there the family lived for the next thirty years. He proved to be an energetic, efficient, and innovative land agent, and his favourite subjects of conversation turned from reform and abolition to bone manure, draining, and subsoil ploughing, though he retained a propensity to denounce the corn laws as the parent of scarcity. Previously the Greenwich Hospital estates had been indifferently managed by two receivers and eight bailiffs, and they were known locally for the poor quality of their farm tenants. During his tenure Grey changed all this, mainly by introducing better farm tenants, who were attracted by large outlays on field drainage and improved farm buildings and who were encouraged to adopt the most advanced practices in stock management. Grey streamlined the administration, reducing it to himself, one clerk, and one bailiff, and though he was no more than a salaried agent 'he was as free in action as if he had been an independent landlord' (Richards, 448).

Grey's style of living as well as of management became like that of a great landowner, and with a national and international reputation by the 1850s as a leading agriculturist who had turned round a neglected estate and raised its output and its rental by nearly one half, he entertained a steady stream of agricultural visitors at Dilston, including Baron Liebig and representatives of Emperor Francis Joseph and of the manager of public works in Sardinia. In 1858 the French government asked him for an estimate of the effects of free trade in corn on English agriculture. But Grey was not universally popular or respected in landed circles, for he was outspoken in public criticism of bad landlords, as when he attacked 'the grandees who lavish expense upon their castles and deer-parks but disregard the dwellings of the cultivators of the land' (Richards, 449). Again, he told the commissioners inquiring into the Greenwich Hospital in 1860 that 'a large portion of the country is possessed by those who take the money away and do not spend it in the district, and it has caused me frequently to remonstrate with them in the way of subscribing to infirmaries and other charities' ('Report of the commissioners to inquire into Greenwich Hospital', q. 1910). In the autumn of 1857 Grey had the misfortune to lose the greater part of his savings by the failure of the Newcastle Bank.

Grey's wife (who died in 1860) was slight, graceful, and very fair, but Grey was largely built, handsome, and dark. This physique was invaluable in his early years at Dilston for, as he later remarked, the estates, being spread out over 100 miles of country,

> require a man possessing a great deal of physical strength and zeal. When I went there I was almost killed in the first year and a half, for I rode over every farm and every field, and I made a report every night when I came home of its value

and its capabilities, whether you could employ water power instead of horse power, and so on. This was a thing that everyone could not have done, but I had been brought up in the country, and seven or eight hours in the saddle was no great matter to me. I think it would be rather a wide field for an individual, especially a stranger, and probably some of these outlying places might be sold with advantage. ('Report of the commissioners', q. 1901)

The 1860 inquiry was concerned with the 'unfitness of any public body to perform themselves the duties of landowners' (ibid., xliii), an opinion with which Grey, as an admirer of political economy, might have been expected to agree in principle. In practice, however, his experience had convinced him that the state could manage landed property better than private landowners, provided the state gave its appointed managers the free rein he had enjoyed; and in the result the commissioners accepted Grey's advice and recommended the sale simply of a few outlying portions of the hospital estates, retaining the core under state ownership.

Thus when Grey retired in 1863, moving to Lipwood House near Haydon Bridge (where he was to die on 22 January 1868), he was succeeded by his second son, Charles Grey, as receiver of the Greenwich Hospital estates; his eldest son, George Annett Grey, inherited the family estate of Milfield. The hospital estates did not, however, long continue in the public domain: Charles Grey became chief valuer to the Irish land commission under the 1881 Land Act, and on his departure from Dilston the sale of the hospital estates began.　　F. M. L. THOMPSON

Sources J. E. Butler, *Memoir of John Grey of Dilston* (1869) · D. Spring, *The English landed estate in the nineteenth century: its administration* (1963) · E. Richards, 'The land agent', *The Victorian countryside*, ed. G. E. Mingay, 2 (1981), 439–56 · 'Royal commission to inquire into Greenwich Hospital', *Parl. papers* (1860), vol. 30, no. 2670 · J. Grey, 'A view of the past and present state of agriculture in Northumberland', *Journal of the Royal Agricultural Society of England*, 2 (1841), 159ff. · E. M. Bell, *Josephine Butler: flame of fire* (1962) · *DNB* · *CGPLA Eng. & Wales* (1868)

Archives U. St Andr. L., corresp. | U. Durham L., corresp. with second Earl Grey · U. Durham L., Grey of Howick collection, corresp. with third Earl Grey

Likenesses Patten, oils, presented in 1849 · portrait (presented to him in 1849)

Wealth at death under £14,000: resworn probate, Nov 1868, *CGPLA Eng. & Wales*

Grey, Lady Katherine. *See* Seymour, Katherine, countess of Hertford (1540?–1568).

Grey, Leonard [known as Lord Leonard Grey], **Viscount Graney** (c.1490–1541), lord deputy of Ireland, was the sixth but second surviving son of Thomas *Grey, first marquess of Dorset (c.1455–1501), and his wife, Cicely Bonville, *suo jure* Baroness Harington and Bonville (1461–1530). By the mid-1510s he had apparently been knighted, and had also been appointed as a commissioner of the peace for Leicestershire and as a carver in Henry VIII's household, a position that he continued to hold in the mid-1520s. He served in Henry VIII's campaigns against the French in June 1520 and March 1523, and in the summer of 1523 he and his retinues halted the advance of the Scots at Alnwick and Wark in northern England. That year, he also provided sureties to the value of 500 marks for the eighth earl of Kildare to appear before Henry VIII. Three years later, in August 1526, Kildare employed Grey to present Henry VIII with articles of complaint concerning his rival, the earl of Ormond.

While Grey had been considered for the governorship of Ireland in the 1520s, he was instead appointed marshal of the English army in Ireland, where he arrived on 28 July 1535. His sister Elizabeth *Fitzgerald, née Grey, was the second wife of the ninth earl of Kildare, and her stepson, Thomas Fitzgerald, tenth earl of Kildare, was in rebellion when Grey arrived. Throughout August Grey pursued Thomas in co. Kildare. On 24 August Fitzgerald submitted to Grey, who subsequently escorted him to London. In spite of Grey's intercession on his behalf Thomas was executed on 3 February 1537 along with his five uncles, whom Grey had also apprehended. Elizabeth Grey and her second son, Edward, resided at Grey's home at Beaumanor in Leicestershire following the Kildare rebellion. By early October 1535 Grey had returned to Ireland, having received additional payment and grants of lands from Henry VIII in gratitude for his service. In November he was reappointed marshal, and in December he campaigned against the Byrnes, O'Tooles, and Kavanaghs.

Immediately after the death of Sir William Skeffington, Grey was elected justiciar on 1 January 1536. The following day he was created Viscount Graney by letters patent. The title derived from the dissolved nunnery of Graney in southern co. Kildare, which was one of several grants of dissolved monastic properties in counties Dublin, Kildare, Carlow, Tipperary, Waterford, Louth, and Meath which he received. Early in January he arbitrated in a number of cases in Clonmel and Youghal. At that time he also requested a lease of the manor of Maynooth, where he resided for much of his term in Ireland (his other temporary residential quarters being in St Mary's Abbey, Dublin). By 23 February he had been appointed lord deputy. Grey spent the first six months of his deputyship negotiating treaties and indentures with the O'Mores, the MacMurrough Kavanaghs, the O'Neills, the Savages, and the MacGillapatricks. He presided at the Reformation Parliament (first session 1 May 1536—last session 20 December 1537), which legislated for the abolition of papal authority, the attainder of the earl of Kildare, the establishment of Henry VIII as supreme head of the church, and the dissolution of monastic houses.

Having succeeded William Skeffington as lord deputy, Grey undertook, and was ultimately condemned for, relentless warlike expeditions throughout Ireland. On 19 July 1536 he and the council embarked on a campaign to quell the insurrection of James fitz John Fitzgerald, thirteenth earl of Desmond, and O'Brien of Thomond. The campaign lasted until 29 October. Grey captured Desmond's castle at Lough Gur in co. Limerick and O'Brien's bridge in co. Clare, but despite Grey's great energy and skill in moving his cannon through a countryside where transport was very difficult, the overall result was indecisive. Grey did, however, manage to secure the earl of Desmond's submission in December 1536. Having remained

in Dublin since the end of October 1536, in May of the following year he embarked on a successful campaign against Brian O'Connor in King's county for which he received praise from both the council in Ireland and Henry VIII. During that summer he also led campaigns to subjugate the Kavanaghs, the Nolans, and the O'Maghers.

Throughout his deputyship Grey was criticized by discontented officials in the Dublin administration who alleged that he was unable to control his temper and that his main aims were to acquire personal wealth and to reinstate the earls of Kildare. However, when four commissioners arrived in Ireland in September 1537 to investigate the allegations against Grey, he promised to co-operate fully, and they failed to reach a definitive conclusion regarding the deputy's conduct.

Between August and December 1537 Grey was stationed intermittently in the marches of the pale, negotiating and receiving pledges from dissident Gaelic lords, notably Ross Mageoghegan, Terence O'Toole, and Charles O'Mulloy. Following talks held in King's county in early March 1538, Grey secured Brian O'Connor's submission. On 7 April he led a campaign into the lordship of Farney in co. Monaghan. By 5 June he had reached an agreement with O'Carroll and had imprisoned O'More in Maynooth Castle. On 17 June Grey embarked on an extended campaign through King's county, Ely O'Carroll, Ormond, co. Limerick, Thomond, Clanricarde, and co. Galway which concluded on 25 July and as a result of which several Gaelic lords came to make submissions before him.

Meanwhile, there was friction between Grey and the Irish council owing to the deputy's campaigning independent of their counsel or consent. By June relations with Ormond had grown particularly tense, giving rise to Lord Butler's allegation that 'My lord deputy is the earl of Kildare newly born again' (LP Henry VIII, 13, no. 1224). Other members of the Irish council joined with the earl of Ormond and O'More in presenting articles of complaint against Grey. However, following his return to Dublin the lord deputy submitted a triumphant report of the progress of his campaign to Henry VIII. His close ally Thomas Cromwell shelved all allegations made against him and effected a reconciliation between Grey and Ormond by the third week in August. During the months of September and October, Grey led campaigns against the MacMurrough Kavanaghs and the O'Reillys from whom he secured submissions. He also led an expedition into Lecale in co. Down to drive the Scots out of the region. In late December it was reported that Grey and his associates had committed various crimes against religious and churches in the lordship.

Since 1535 Grey had endeavoured to effect the capture of his nephew, the fugitive Gerald Fitzgerald, half-brother to Thomas, tenth earl, and heir to the earldom of Kildare, while a Gaelic league, led by Manus O'Donnell, emerged in opposition to the lord deputy's policies. On 1 May 1539 Grey marched to Armagh in an attempt to induce O'Neill and O'Donnell to surrender Gerald, to no avail. In August the Ulster chiefs invaded the pale, sacking Ardee and Navan. Grey pursued them and inflicted a resounding defeat on the combined forces of O'Neill and O'Donnell at Bellahoe on the borders of Meath and co. Monaghan. In October Grey's critics in the Irish council frequently cited his Geraldine sympathies and questioned his commitment to capturing the Geraldine heir.

On 5 November 1539 Grey led a campaign to reinforce his authority over Desmond which ended on 24 December; he received submissions from several Gaelic lords in the course of his expedition. In January 1540 he stated that to date he had concluded twenty-seven indentures with lords including O'Byrne, O'Connor, O'Flaherty, De Burgh, O'Neill, and MacMahon. On 16 January the Irish council requested that the king arrange 'some profitable marriage' for Grey, who 'has lived long without a wife and is desirous to marry' (*LP Henry VIII*, 15, no. 74); it remains unclear whether he did marry. On 24 January 1540 he advanced to Dungannon in Tyrone in a campaign against Con O'Neill but when O'Neill failed to honour his appointment with Grey and the council at Drogheda in mid-February the deputy proceeded to ravage his country for a period of six days. On 10 March Grey interceded with Henry VIII not to believe reports forwarded by his opponents until such time as he had occasion to defend himself in person at court. However, his critics grew more vociferous following Gerald Fitzgerald's escape to France in early March 1540. His flight was attributed to the deputy's connivance, an allegation which the latter strenuously denied.

Since late December 1537 Grey had repeatedly requested permission to return to England, and on 1 April 1540 the king temporarily recalled the deputy, who was described as diseased, aged, and having no children at that time. He departed for England about 1 May. He was warmly received at court and enjoyed the privy council's support until mid-June. However, he was soon followed by Sir John Alen and Gerald Aylmer, who presented allegations against him at court in May. Meanwhile the O'Connors, allies of the Fitzgeralds, were restive in the marches of the pale. On 10 June Grey's ally Thomas Cromwell was charged with treason and was immediately sent to the Tower. Two days later Grey was similarly accused and imprisoned.

On 26 September Henry VIII instructed Grey's successor as lord deputy, Sir Anthony St Leger, to have the Irish council compile a list of articles against Grey. On 28 October the council presented the requested articles, which included accusations that Grey only partly followed its advice; that he had private dealings with the Geraldines; that he was excessively lenient in his treatment of O'Connor; that he broke peace treaties and safe conducts which caused insurrections; that he incited Gaelic septs to attack the king's subjects; and that he abused his authority. In December 1540 the privy council declared that the former deputy had committed heinous offences against the king and that his judgement had been influenced by his association with the Fitzgeralds and their supporters. Grey was arraigned and pleaded guilty before a jury of twelve on 25 June 1541. He was executed at Tower Hill in London on 28 June 1541. MARY ANN LYONS

Sources J. S. Brewer and W. Bullen, eds., *Calendar of the Carew manuscripts*, 6 vols., PRO (1867–73) · *LP Henry VIII* · State papers published under … Henry VIII, 11 vols. (1830–52) · *Holinshed's chronicles of England, Scotland and Ireland*, ed. H. Ellis, 6 (1808) · *CSP Ire.* · 'Calendar of fiants, Henry VIII to Elizabeth', *Report of the Deputy Keeper of the Public Records in Ireland*, 7–22 (1875–90), appxs · W. M. Hennessy and B. MacCarthy, eds., *Annals of Ulster, otherwise, annals of Senat*, 4 vols. (1887–1901), vol. 1 · J. Morrin, ed., *Calendar of the patent and close rolls of chancery in Ireland, of the reigns of Henry VIII, Edward VI, Mary, and Elizabeth*, 1 (1861) · *GEC, Peerage* · J. Lodge, *The peerage of Ireland*, rev. M. Archdall, rev. edn, 7 vols. (1789), vols. 1, 5 · S. G. Ellis, 'Thomas Cromwell and Ireland, 1532–1540', *HJ*, 23 (1980), 497–519 · L. McCorristine, *The revolt of Silken Thomas: a challenge to Henry VIII* (1987) · C. Brady, *The chief governors: the rise and fall of reform government in Tudor Ireland, 1536–1588* (1994) · B. Bradshaw, *The Irish constitutional revolution of the sixteenth century* (1979) · C. W. Fitzgerald, duke of Leinster, *The earls of Kildare and their ancestors from 1057 to 1773*, 3rd edn, 2 vols. (1858–62) · S. G. Ellis, *Reform and revival: English government in Ireland, 1470–1534*, Royal Historical Society Studies in History, 47 (1986) · R. Bagwell, *Ireland under the Tudors*, 1 (1885) · C. Lennon, *Sixteenth-century Ireland: the incomplete conquest* (1994) · S. G. Ellis, *Ireland in the age of the Tudors* (1998) · M. A. Lyons, *Gearóid Óg, ninth earl of Kildare* (1998) · M. A. Lyons, *Church and society in county Kildare, c.1470–1547* (2000) · T. W. Moody and others, eds., *A new history of Ireland*, 10 vols. (1976–96), vols. 3, 9

Grey, Margaret, of Wilton. *See* Darcy, Margaret, Lady Darcy (*d.* 1454), *under* Darcy family (*per. c.*1284–1488).

Grey [*née* Shirreff], **Maria Georgina** (1816–1906), educationist and writer, was born on 7 March 1816, one of four daughters and two sons born to Rear-Admiral William Henry Shirreff (1785–1847), of Huguenot ancestry, commander of the Portsmouth Dockyard at the time of his death in 1847, and Elizabeth Anne, eldest daughter of the Hon. David Murray and grandniece of the sixth Baron Elibank. William Shirreff's naval career involved the entire family in lengthy residences abroad during Maria's childhood. In the 1820s the family resided at St Germain en Laye, near Paris, and in Normandy. Between 1830 and 1834, the Shirreffs lived in Gibraltar where Maria's father was captain of the port. With her sisters Caroline (b. 1812), Emily (b. 1814), and Katherine (b. 1818), she was educated by a Swiss-French governess, Adèle Piquet. Both brothers died young, William in 1829 and Henry in 1833. The family's circle of friends included some of the most prominent intellectuals of the age, women and men. An early group portrait of the sisters in late adolescence depicts them as attractive and fashionable in appearance.

Even before her marriage to William Thomas Grey (1807–1864) on 7 January 1841, Maria collaborated in writing projects with her elder sister Emily *Shirreff. The earliest of their joint efforts was *Letters from Spain and Barbary*, published in 1835. Their novel *Passion and Principle*, published in the year of Maria's marriage, was reissued in 1854 in Routledge's Railway Series. The marriage did not interfere with her writing projects, though her work on behalf of women's education flourished only after her husband's death on 13 March 1864. William Grey, a partner in the wine merchant firm of Block, Grey, and Block, was Maria's first cousin, the eldest son of Lieutenant-Colonel the Hon. William Grey and nephew of the second Earl Grey, prime minister 1830–34. The marriage was happy but childless, and Grey's support for his wife's intellectual activities is palpable. He financed the publication in 1850 of Grey and Shirreff's co-authored *Thoughts on Self-Culture Addressed to Women*.

After William's death, Maria Grey shuttled between London and Italy with her sister Emily. Both were involved in nursing family members, but still found time to launch significant initiatives in the field of women's education as well as further collaborative and separate writing projects. Maria wrote only one more novel, the three-volume *Love's Sacrifice*, published in 1868. Thereafter, her publications concentrated on women's rights and, more especially, on women's education.

She had wide feminist interests, was active in the suffrage cause, and penned the provocatively titled pamphlet *Is the Exercise of the Suffrage Unfeminine?* in 1870. She was a long-time member of the Central Society for Women's Suffrage. She was a member of the National Vigilance Association and had supported the movement for the repeal of the Contagious Diseases Acts which was active in the 1870s and 1880s.

It was, however, the cause of women's education to which Grey devoted her time after her husband's death. In 1870, though ultimately favouring co-educational institutions, she wrote repeatedly to *The Times* to raise funds for the North London Collegiate School for Girls, founded in 1850. It was Grey who first suggested to Frances Buss a scheme for introducing student teachers into her north London girls' schools in the 1870s. In that same year, and after an initial refusal of the invitation, she stood as candidate for Chelsea in the first London school board elections, one of the first women to do so after legislative changes in 1869 permitted qualified women to seek election to local government offices. Though she was unsuccessful, the loss was narrow. In the following year she published her pamphlet *The School Board of London*.

Grey was also active in the campaign for the access of women to medical education in Britain. Her popular work *Old Maids*, published in 1875, was a searing attack on the idea of the unmarried woman as a useless and unfulfilled creature. Grey was a Liberal in politics, but unlike her sister found the principles of democracy attractive, leaning increasingly towards an interest in working-class and co-operative issues in later life. It was one of the few profound disagreements the two sisters had in their work and life together.

With her sister Emily, Grey launched in 1871 the National Union for the Improvement of the Education of Women of All Classes. She was to be the organization's honorary organizing secretary from its inception until 1879. The Women's Education Union, as it was commonly known, was inaugurated at the Royal Society of Arts on 17 November 1871, with Lord Lyttelton presiding. She outlined her own philosophy of education in a paper, delivered before the annual meeting of the National Association for the Promotion of Social Science in that same year, entitled 'What are the special requirements for the improvement of the education of girls?' At the 1873 meeting, she read a paper entitled 'Lectures and classes for women'. She would continue to publish pamphlets on

similar topics under the aegis of the Union and to celebrate its work in letters to *The Times* throughout the organization's life. She wrote not infrequently, as well, for the major periodicals of the day, including *Fraser's Magazine*, *Contemporary Review*, *Fortnightly Review*, and the *Nineteenth Century*. She was also a close and frequent correspondent of Dorothea Beale, headmistress of Cheltenham Ladies' College.

In July 1872, under the umbrella of the Women's Education Union, Grey helped incorporate the Girls' Public Day School Company (GPDSC), of which she was also a vice-President. The company sold £5 shares to finance the rental, purchase, or construction of girls' schools, paying dividends on the profit made from tuition. The first GPDSC school opened at Norland Square in the London borough of Chelsea in January 1873 with twenty pupils who were to be prepared for the local examinations administered by Oxford and Cambridge universities as well as those of the College of Preceptors. The GPDSC was enormously successful; by the end of its first decade, there were seventeen schools enrolling 2804 students. In the year of Grey's death, the company was converted to a trust—the Girls' Public Day School Trust. Despite her growing sympathy for democracy, Grey would not countenance the endowment of a women's college by an industrialist. Approached by a manufacturer of patent medicines, Thomas Holloway, with such a proposal, Grey was adamant that it would bring women's education into disrepute.

Grey was as concerned with the provision of an appropriate teaching staff as she was with the actual existence of girls' schools. To this end, she was instrumental in founding, also under the aegis of the Women's Education Union, the Teacher's Educational Loan Committee in 1873 and the Teacher's Training and Registration Society in 1876. Two years later, the first teacher training college for women opened its doors to four students on premises loaned by the rector of Bishopsgate, William Rogers. The college was renamed in honour of its founder in 1892, and henceforth was known as the Maria Grey Training College.

Grey wrote the chapter on the women's educational movement for Theodore Stanton's book of essays, *The Woman Question in Europe*, published in 1884. She also translated from the Italian the works of educationist and Risorgimento figure Antonio Rosmini-Serbati. She sat on the council of the London Society for the Extension of University Teaching (founded 1875) and was vice-president of the Froebel Society when her sister Emily was its president. She was both honorary secretary of the Chelsea branch of the Charity Organization Society and sat on the organization's national council.

Invalided for the last fifteen years of her life, Grey none the less published her *Last Words to Girls on Life in School and after School* in 1889. And in 1897, when claims were made in parliament that those who promoted women's education did not also support women's suffrage, she was vigorous in her rebuttal. Maria Grey died on 19 September 1906, at 41 Stanhope Gardens, Kensington, the house she had long shared with her sister and co-worker Emily. Though Grey's immense labours in the field of women's education have sometimes obscured her broader commitment to a plethora of issues concerned with the improvement of the position of women, she was, in fact, throughout her life, deeply committed to women's causes. Like her sister Emily, she maintained a belief in Christianity as a stable base for providing women with equality of opportunity, yet late in life moved quietly but steadily in the directions of social justice issues and working-class representation.

PHILIPPA LEVINE

Sources E. W. Ellsworth, *Liberators of the female mind: the Shirreff sisters, educational reform and the women's movement* (1979) · T. Stanton, ed., *The woman question in Europe: a series of original essays* (1884) · *The Times* (21 Sept 1906) · *The Times* (24 Sept 1906) · *Journal of the Women's Education Union* · *Englishwoman's Review*, 38 (1906), 283–5 · B. Stephen, *Emily Davies and Girton College* (1927) · S. Fletcher, *Feminists and bureaucrats: a study in the development of girls' education in the nineteenth century* (1980) · C. Dyhouse, *Girls growing up in late Victorian and Edwardian England* (1981) · J. S. Pedersen, *The reform of girls' secondary and higher education in Victorian England: a study of elites and educational change* (1987) · J. Kamm, *Hope deferred: girls' education in English history* (1965) · D. Spender, ed., *The education papers: women's quest for equality in Britain, 1850–1912* (1987) · J. Purvis, *Hard lessons: the lives and education of working-class women in nineteenth-century England* (1989) · E. Raikes, *Dorothea Beale of Cheltenham* (1909) · O. Banks, *The biographical dictionary of British feminists*, 1 (1985) · *Wellesley index*

Archives CUL, corresp. | Women's Library, London, Josephine Butler autograph letter collection

Wealth at death £14,077 5s. 6d.: probate, 24 Oct 1906, *CGPLA Eng. & Wales*

Grey, Lady Mary. *See* Keys, Lady Mary (1545?–1578).

Grey [*née* Whitbread], **Mary, Lady Grey** (1770–1858), promoter of seafarers' missions, was born in December 1770, daughter of the famous brewer and Christian philanthropist Samuel *Whitbread (1720–1796) of Bedwell Park, Hertfordshire, and his second wife, Lady Mary Cornwallis (d. 1770), sister of Lord Cornwallis of India. Samuel *Whitbread (1764–1815), whig politician, was her half-brother. Following her mother's death in childbirth, she was carefully brought up by her fifty-year-old father in the spirit of practical piety which both parents had shared. On 18 June 1795 she married Captain George Grey RN (1767–1828), of historic border stock from north Northumberland. In 1798, after three years of repeated farewells in the midst of naval warfare with France, she decided to sail out with her husband to his base at Gibraltar. Witnesses commented on her calmness and fortitude under enemy fire, qualities which would stand her in good stead during bouts of public criticism for religious activism in years to come. It was also here that she gave birth to her first son, George *Grey (1799–1882), the future statesman.

After serving with distinction during actions at sea for several years Captain Grey was, in 1806, appointed commissioner of the naval dockyard in Portsmouth. In 1814 he was made a baronet in recognition of his services to his country. He continued in his appointment in Portsmouth until his death.

Even before her own invaluable wartime sea experience, Lady Grey had, as a girl, been employed by her father in reading and copying materials collected by his friend the abolitionist Thomas Clarkson, documenting the abuse of both 'cargo' and crew in the 'Torrid Trade' with west Africa. In Portsmouth she showed constant concern for the welfare of dockyard workers and their families, sick sailors, and sailors' orphans. Beyond local needs, her husband's situation also gave her the opportunity to pursue a vision of global dimensions. The 22-year duration of Sir George Grey's dockyard duties, coinciding as it did with the transition of Britain's maritime focus from men-of-war to merchant shipping, fell at the beginning of the so-called seafarers' mission movement. Lady Grey, with the willing co-operation of her like-minded husband, was able to transform the commissioner's house in Portsmouth Dockyard into a centre for the incipient seafarers' mission.

Lady Grey launched, and for two decades maintained, a campaign of systematic circulation of immense quantities of the scriptures and Christian literature among virtually every category of seafarers—naval personnel, merchant seafarers, fishers, embarking soldiers, and convicts. In this entirely new area of missionary endeavour the Naval and Military Bible Society, British and Foreign Bible Society (BFBS), and Religious Tract Society all claimed her among their most valued collaborators. As Portsmouth correspondent of the BFBS alone, she is recorded as having distributed 28,201 scripture copies among maritime recipients between 1810 and 1815. Of her tenacity and zeal in this field, the many letters from her hand in the BFBS Home Correspondence files bear telling testimony.

Lady Grey had, in the words of one obituarist, mastered 'the art of laying under contribution the talents of others' (*The Record*, 26 May 1858). Thus, she made a special point of prevailing on officers leaving for sea 'to attend to the welfare of their own immortal souls, and to seek the spiritual good of their ship's company' (ibid.). One such officer could later report how one appreciative 'tar' had told another, on hearing about 'the Commissioner's Lady' as the source of 'all these pretty books' they had received: 'God bless her, … if we don't go to heaven [after this] we ought to be ashamed of ourselves' (*New Sailor's Magazine*, 1828, 271–2).

Perhaps the most striking example of Lady Grey's intuitive ability to select and support co-workers in the cause was her early contact with Revd George Charles Smith, internationally recognized as the founder of organized mission to seafarers. Bosun Smith, as he came to be called, began his pioneer role by initiating in 1809 a pastoral ministry among the scores of Bible-studying cell-groups then emerging on ships of the British wartime navy. The success of this so-called 'naval correspondence mission' has since been identified as crucial to the subsequent proliferation of organizations for seafarers' mission worldwide. Smith himself recorded his indebtedness to Lady Grey for her unstinted support of this venture at its most critical juncture, providing both sorely needed funding and vital assistance in making contacts.

The death of Sir George Grey in 1828, and his wife's consequent removal from their Portsmouth residence, resulted in a reduction in her maritime-related activity, but not in overall missionary involvement, whether at home or abroad. Among her major concerns continued to be missions in Ireland, especially along the rugged coast of Connemara. Active close to the end of her long life, she died at her home, 14 Eaton Place, Pimlico, London, on 9 May 1858. She was buried at Kensal Green cemetery.

Lady Mary Grey was not the founding figure in the seafarers' mission movement, but she is the earliest woman known to have made a major contribution in the field. Despite the cultural constraints with which women working in the public arena had to contend at that time, available evidence clearly shows that her effective strategies and unflagging zeal played a decisive role in the promotion of nascent seafarers' missions through the first quarter of the nineteenth century, during the movement's early evolution from distribution of literature to more comprehensive models. It would not be too much to say that Lady Mary Grey left no less a legacy in the cause of maritime mission than her equally indomitable predecessor, Selina Hastings, countess of Huntingdon, left in the cause of mission in general. In essence, Lady Grey was the Lady Huntingdon of seafarers' mission.

ROALD KVERNDAL

Sources *The Record* (26 May 1858), 3 · M. Creighton, *Memoir of Sir George Grey* (privately printed, Newcastle-upon-Tyne, 1884); new edn (1901) · *Sailor's Magazine* (1826), 463 · *New Sailor's Magazine* (1828), 271–2 · *New Sailor's Magazine*, 2 (1829), 380 · *New Sailor's Magazine* (1857), 98 · *New Sailor's Magazine* (1858), 543–6 · *Annual Report* [British and Foreign Bible Society] (1811) · *Annual Report* [British and Foreign Bible Society] (1815), 482 · home correspondence files, 1808–, CUL, Bible Society Archives · Naval and Military Bible Society, *Report* (1820), 77 · R. Kverndal, *Seamen's missions: their origin and early growth* (1986) · 'Grey, Sir George (1799–1882)', *DNB* · d. cert.
Wealth at death under £6000: probate, 27 May 1858, *CGPLA Eng. & Wales*

Grey, Nicholas (1589/90–1660), headmaster, was born in London and educated at Westminster School. From a king's scholarship there he was elected to Christ Church, Oxford; he matriculated on 5 December 1606 aged sixteen, graduated BA on 21 June 1610, and proceeded MA on 10 June 1613 (incorporated at Cambridge in 1614). At Oxford he won repute as a classicist. On 3 December 1614 he was appointed headmaster of Charterhouse, a post he forfeited by marriage. He was, however, presented by Charterhouse to the rectory of Castle Camps, Cambridgeshire, where for a time he lived 'as 'twere out of his element' (Wood, *Ath. Oxon.*, 3.504). On 12 November 1624 he was shortlisted for the headmastership of Merchant Taylors' School, to which he was elected by the court on 29 January 1625. However, his predecessor, William Hayne, refused to budge, and it was only by the lord keeper's arbitration that Grey obtained possession in June. In the circumstances the company was unwilling to appoint Grey for more than a year at a time, though their appreciation of his work was shown in *ex gratia* payments on two occasions when the school closed down during epidemics. When Grey resigned at midsummer 1632 he was given a further £100 (ten years' salary) with £20 in reimbursement for structural and economic improvements.

In 1632 he also proceeded DD from Cambridge and

became rector of Saffron Walden, Essex, and master of the grammar school there. In 1644 he was ejected from his Cambridgeshire living by the parliamentary commander, the earl of Manchester. Presumably he lost his posts at Walden about the same time. In 1647 he became headmaster of Eton, from where he moved in 1649 to the headmastership of Tonbridge. He published *Parabulae evangelicae* (1650) for use by his pupils there, and contributed to Francis Holyoke's revised edition of *Riders Dictionarie* (1649), and, later, to an edition of Grotius's *Baptizatorum puerorum* (1665). He and his wife, Isabella, had two children, including Anne, whose death in 1656 was commemorated by Grey in verse; other poetry of his survives in manuscript. After the Restoration he recovered his rectory of Castle Camps, and on 12 July 1660 he became a fellow of Eton. Soon afterwards he died there; he was buried in the college chapel on 5 October.   C. S. KNIGHTON

Sources *Old Westminsters*, 1.400 · Wood, *Ath. Oxon.*, new edn, 3.504–5 · C. J. Robinson, ed., *A register of the scholars admitted into Merchant Taylors' School, from AD 1562 to 1874*, 1 (1882), xiv · F. W. M. Draper, *Four centuries of Merchant Taylors' School, 1561–1961* (1962), 52–5 · H. C. Maxwell Lyte, *A history of Eton College, 1440–1898*, 3rd edn (1899), 251, 262 · S. Rivington, *The history of Tonbridge School*, 4th edn (1925), 139–42 · *Walker rev.*, 80 · W. Sterry, ed., *The Eton College register, 1441–1698* (1943), xxxi, xxxiii, 128 · Foster, *Alum. Oxon.*, 1500–1714 [Nicholas Gray] · Venn, *Alum. Cant.*, 1/2.252 · bursar's account, 1646–7, Eton, ECR 62/59, p. 347
Archives Bodl. Oxf., Rawlinson MS Poet. 246
Likenesses oils, Charterhouse School, Surrey; repro. in Draper, *Four centuries*, facing p. 17
Wealth at death said to have died 'very poor'; rectory of Castle Camps valued at £160 p.a. in 1644; pension of £12 awarded to wife: *DNB*; *Walker rev.*, 80

Grey, Nigel Arthur de (1886–1951), cryptanalyst, was born on 27 March 1886 at the rectory, Copdock, Suffolk, the son of the Hon. Arnold de Grey (b. 1856), rector of Copdock, and his wife, Margaret Maria Ponsonby Fane. His father was the son of the fifth Baron Walsingham, his mother the daughter of the Rt Hon. Sir Spencer Ponsonby Fane. De Grey was educated at Eton College. Rather than go to university he tried to join the diplomatic service, but though a skilled linguist, fluent in French and German, he failed his diplomatic examination in Italian and instead became a publisher, joining William Heinemann in 1907. Three years later, on 29 December 1910, he married his second cousin Florence Emily Frances (b. 1882/3), daughter of Spencer William Gore, a land surveyor. They had two sons and a daughter.

At the outbreak of war de Grey joined the Royal Naval Volunteer Reserve and was posted to Belgium as an observer in the balloon section of the Royal Naval Air Service, with the rank of flight sub-lieutenant. Early in 1915 he was transferred to the naval intelligence division (NID) and began working in the diplomatic section of the organization, known as Room 40, headed by Admiral Reginald (Blinker) Hall and named after its accommodation in the old Admiralty building. On 17 January 1917 de Grey and a church historian colleague, the Revd William Montgomery, decrypted a German diplomatic text that later became widely known as the Zimmermann telegram. Its public disclosure was to lead directly to America's declaration of war on Germany in 1917.

The diplomatic message, consisting of 1000 numerical code groups, was sent by the German foreign minister, Arthur Zimmermann, through the Atlantic cable, which Britain had long been intercepting. The ultimate recipient was the German ambassador in Mexico City; it announced the imminent start of unrestricted submarine warfare in the Atlantic. The German ambassador was instructed to approach the Mexican government with a proposal for it to side with Germany in an alliance against the United States, and offered as an inducement a return of the American states of Arizona, Texas, and New Mexico.

In order to release a transcript of the telegram an elaborate subterfuge had to be initiated. This was designed not only to hide the fact that Germany's codes had been broken but also to disguise from the United States the obvious implication that the telegrams of neutrals (including itself) were also being read. In the event a coded copy of the telegram was secretly obtained in Mexico City. A decrypted version of this was successfully shown to United States diplomats in London without revealing that American cables had been tapped. The text, when published, proved to be political dynamite and caused predictable outrage, turning public opinion, congress, and President Woodrow Wilson's administration in favour of intervention in the war. The proposed German–Mexican pact collapsed and Zimmermann resigned soon afterwards. In Berlin it was concluded that a decoded copy of the telegram had been stolen in Mexico City, and therefore Germany did not alter its diplomatic codes.

Later, in the spring of the same year, de Grey was assigned to Taranto and then Rome, with the rank of lieutenant-commander, to run the NID's Mediterranean section, liaise with Italy's director of naval intelligence, and focus on Austrian cipher traffic. He was to be decorated with the order of St Maurice and St Lazarus for his work in Italy, and he was appointed an OBE in 1918.

Between the wars de Grey headed the Medici Society, which published old master prints, and found time to indulge his many pursuits. He was a keen shot, often staying at the country homes of his many cousins, loved working in his large garden in Iver, Buckinghamshire, and was a good watercolourist and draughtsman. As an amateur actor he was an enthusiastic member of the Old Stagers and the Windsor Strollers; he also played cricket during the Canterbury cricket week. His diminutive stature and unassuming nature led a later colleague to dub him 'the doormouse' (Smith, 10).

In 1938, following a financial crisis at the undercapitalized Medici Society, de Grey lost his job, but fortunately a year later he was invited to join the Government Code and Cypher School at Bletchley Park, at a salary of £600 per annum, to concentrate on German wireless traffic encrypted on the Enigma cipher machine. In September 1941 he was responsible for a report based on his analysis of the enemy's communications transmitted from the areas occupied since the invasion of the Soviet Union that was delivered to the prime minister. It contained what turned out to be the earliest indications that German motorized police battalions were engaged in genocide. The intercepts included harrowing daily returns from SS Sonderkommandos and Eisengruppen that showed the units, ostensibly deployed in anti-partisan operations, were responsible for the systematic levelling of entire villages and the liquidation of their populations.

The first evidence appeared in July 1941, with a reference to the execution at Slonin of '1,153 Jewish plunderers', and escalated during the first week in August as the SS cavalry brigade and police battalion 306 committed widespread atrocities, culminating in a signal known as the van den Bach report, which boasted of a total of 30,000 executions conducted 'in the central area'. Shocked by de Grey's summary, Churchill warned in a speech of the 'crime that dare not speak its name', which resulted in a German circular in October 1941 cautioning that no further references to sensitive operations should be entrusted to wireless channels.

In 1945 Nigel de Grey was created CMG. He stayed on with the organization, becoming a deputy director of GCHQ (as it had become known) after the war. He led a small, highly compartmented group of cryptanalysts at Eastcote, near Ruislip, working on Soviet cable traffic. On his retirement, in 1951, de Grey purchased a pottery in Huntingdonshire, but on the day the sale was completed he suffered a heart attack in London's Oxford Street. He was declared dead at Charing Cross Hospital on 25 May 1951. His wife survived him.   NIGEL WEST

Sources B. Tuchman, *The Zimmermann telegram* (1988) · C. Andrew, *Secret service: the making of the British intelligence community* (1985) · P. Beesly, *Room 40: British naval intelligence, 1914–1918* (1982) · N. West, *GCHQ: the secret wireless war, 1900–86* (1986) · M. Smith, *Station X: the codebreakers of Bletchley Park* (1998) · WWW · *The Times* (26 May 1951) · b. cert. · m. cert. · d. cert. · CGPLA Eng. & Wales (1951)
Wealth at death £24,639 19s. 7d.: probate, 1951, CGPLA Eng. & Wales

Grey, Ralph Francis Alnwick, Baron Grey of Naunton (1910–1999), colonial governor, was born on 15 April 1910 in Wellington, New Zealand, the only son of Francis Arthur Grey (1865–1917), accountant, and his wife, Mary (Mollie) Wilkie, née Spence (d. 1952), teacher. Educated at Scots College, Wellington, Wellington College, and Auckland University College, Grey took a law degree and in 1932 became a barrister and solicitor of the supreme court of New Zealand, working as an associate (or personal assistant) to the Hon. Mr Justice Smith. But the limited attractions of life and work in New Zealand (what he once described as 'the prospect of representing agricultural "cow-cockies" in boundary disputes'; *The Independent*, 19 Oct 1999) could not hold a man of his competence, energy, and imagination, so he took his professor's advice and applied for the colonial administrative service. He worked his passage to England, where at Pembroke College he attended the colonial probationers' training course at Cambridge University in 1936. He was thus one of the small but significant and successful group of New Zealanders who took the opportunity of a career in the hitherto exclusively British colonial service opened up after the inception of the dominion selection scheme in the Antipodes in 1928.

On completing the course Grey was posted to the Eastern Provinces of Nigeria in 1937, having reputedly been invited to choose between Nigeria and the Solomon Islands. The colonial service was seldom slow in recognizing and rewarding its high-flyers, and Grey's rapid rise was seen by seniors and colleagues alike as a pointer to what was yet to come. He was transferred to the central secretariat in Lagos as assistant financial secretary in 1949, and within only fourteen years was promoted to class I, a grade whose average seniority then exceeded twenty years' service. With promotional opportunities at the top now enhanced by Nigeria's constitutional changes, culminating in the creation of three regional governments as well as the federal government, Grey continued to race ahead, being appointed to the key post of federal development secretary in 1952, secretary to the governor-general and the Council of Ministers in 1954, and chief secretary of the federation in 1955. This was redesignated deputy governor-general in 1957. The governor-general, Sir James Robertson, paid tribute to Grey for his diplomatic handling of the organizational problems and often acrimonious disputes between the three regional governors associated with the programme for the queen's visit to Nigeria in 1956. One of those governors, Sir Bryan Sharwood Smith, was equally generous in his recognition of Grey as a 'solvent to the instances of misunderstanding and even hostility' (Sharwood Smith, 360) which cropped up from time to time among the evolving regional governments and between them and the federal government. Grey had the KCVO bestowed on him for his part in the queen's visit to Nigeria in 1956, having been made OBE in 1951 and CMG in 1955.

Although still in his forties, Grey was by the mid-1950s ineluctably marked out by the Colonial Office for a governorship of his own. But the African colonies were about to enter the final stage of the continent's decolonization, when as many as ten of them gained independence between 1960 and 1964. Thus Grey's promotion to sole command, when it came (with advancement to KCMG) in 1959, took him out of the Africa he had known for twenty years and westward to the challenge of British Guiana. There the journey towards independence had turned out to be an erratic one. Before Grey's arrival the provocative attitude of Dr Cheddi Jagan, whose ruling People's Progressive Party displayed a communist dynamic, along with the tensions between the country's minority Africans and the East Indians who provided the bulk of Jagan's supporters, had led the Colonial Office to suspend the constitution in 1953. Grey now found himself working alongside the stormy petrel Jagan, who after being released from prison had secured re-election as prime minister in 1961. Serious rioting led to the dispatch of British troops to Georgetown. The general strike that followed forced Grey to impose a state of emergency in 1963. He was not sorry to leave the turbulent politics of British Guiana for the calmer atmosphere of the Bahamas in 1964 (when he was advanced to GCMG). His successor, the South African-born Sir Richard Luyt, promptly encountered Jagan's refusal to recognize him.

The Bahamas had just achieved self-government, but—in accordance with Colonial Office practice—responsibility for internal security and external affairs remained in the governor's hands. Grey, familiar with this arrangement in Nigeria, was expected progressively to hand over power, including control of the security forces, to the prime minister towards ultimate independence. In the election of 1967 the United Bahamas Party—still largely white—was defeated by the Progressive Liberal Party led by Lynden Pindling, bringing to an end 200 years of white-dominated government in the islands. Even Grey's acknowledged skill in argument was not sufficient to persuade the Turks and Caicos Islands that they should rejoin the Bahamas, and they continued with Grey as their own governor.

After thirty years of distinguished public service a person of Grey's calibre was not going to be left in peace—nor did he wish to be. Indeed, his front-line years were not yet over. His next move came as something of a surprise and was certainly a break with colonial civil service precedent. This was his appointment in 1968 as governor of Northern Ireland. No less rare among colonial governors of the twentieth century was his concurrent elevation to a life peerage, as Baron Grey of Naunton, before retirement. Grey was the fifth—and last—person to hold the title of governor of Northern Ireland. Percipiently he consulted family and close friends before he accepted the post. It involved plenty of ceremonial, summoning and dissolving the parliament at Stormont, assenting to its legislation, and appointing the prime minister. In all these duties Grey was, as a former colonial governor, well versed, though he had occasion to compare the efficiency of the Stormont cabinet bureaucracy unfavourably with what he had been used to in Africa and the Caribbean. From his seat in Hillsborough Castle he now set out to try and heal the long-inflicted and reopening wounds of sectarian division. His inaugural year coincided with the start of the troubles. He was in office for the arrival of troops from the mainland and for Bloody Sunday in 1972. That was the year, too, when Edward Heath decided to transfer responsibility for law and order from Stormont to Westminster, and nominated William Whitelaw as secretary of state for Northern Ireland. Such an appointment was the prelude to direct rule. With the prorogation of the Stormont parliament, and with the governor's traditional functions other than ceremonial now transferred to the executive, Grey's position became both academic and uncomfortable, sharing Government House, as he now had to, with the secretary of state, however well they got on personally. Grey left Northern Ireland in 1973, and was advanced to GCVO on retirement. His charm and shrewdness had won him great popularity in Ulster. As he commented when asked how he felt about his time there, 'Both sides were extremely nice to me, I only wish they were a little nicer to each other' (memorial service address). Apart from his patent goodwill and open-door readiness to advise whenever his counsel was wanted, as a

New Zealander he was patently devoid of any English or Irish taint in his credentials for the job.

Ralph Grey being Ralph Grey, his immediate reaction to retirement was to look around for what he might do next. There was to be neither shortage of approaches nor lack of acceptances. In 1973 he became deputy chairman of the Commonwealth Development Corporation and served as its chairman from 1979 to 1980. Northern Ireland had never hesitated to capitalize on his talents and popularity. He was president of the Chartered Institute of Secretaries in Northern Ireland, as well as an honorary life member of the Northern Ireland chamber of commerce and industry and, from 1972, honorary president of the Lisburn Chamber of Commerce. He was made a freeman of the city of Belfast in 1972 and of Lisburn in 1975, and was awarded honorary degrees by Queen's University, Belfast (1971), the National University of Ireland (1985), and two from the (New) University of Ulster (1980, 1985), whose chancellor he was from 1980 to 1993. Nor was the legal fraternity behind in acknowledging Grey's reputation. He was made an honorary bencher of the inn of court of Northern Ireland in 1970 and of Gray's Inn in 1991. Grey was ever willing and able to take on and achieve more. Having retired to Overbrook, Naunton, Gloucestershire (whence the name of his barony), he was from 1975 to 1987 a member of the Cheltenham Ladies' College council, and in 1973 became a member of the Bristol regional board of Lloyds Bank. He also agreed to become president of three institutions as close to his heart as he himself was to their predominantly overseas membership: the Overseas Service Pensioners' Association, the Britain–Nigeria Association (both from 1983), and the Royal Over-Seas League (from 1981). He was freeman of the City of London and held high office in the order of St John, being its chancellor in 1987–8 and its lord prior in 1988–91.

Among the countless people Grey met over a range of situations, it was consistently his personal characteristics which they at once associated with him. He was gifted with an incisive mind, inexhaustible reserves of energy, a deep sense of service, and an engaging humanity. His quick wit was both ever ready (and just occasionally acerbic) and frequently invoked as a masterly timed defuser of tricky council and annual general meetings. His portable typewriter featured in numerous anecdotes about his quick mind and industry, from the time during legal practice in New Zealand when he persuaded a judge to travel on circuit by air so that he could save time by letting Grey tap out his thoughts, to his Lagos habit of rapidly typing up a résumé of a difficult conference's decisions so as to hand the delegates a copy of what they had agreed before they left the room. He was also credited with being able to chair a meeting with total control while at the same time drafting a speech on a quite different matter. His two recreations amid such a full schedule of public pursuits were a keenness for golf and an expertise in gardening. A lively teller of amusing tales, always with a twinkle in his eyes, he was himself the source of many an affectionately recounted anecdote. Calm and genial, he showed a kindness to those on his staff which generated the greatest loyalty and numerous recollections of his human touch. Always affable, his style of leadership eschewed any aloofness in favour of the informal and personal. He was, quite simply, wonderful company. As one of his obituarists put it, it was said of Grey that 'he combined the caution and canniness of the Old World with the energy and freshness of the New' (*The Times*, 19 Oct 1999).

Grey's marriage, too, to Esmé Mae (1913–1996), daughter of Albert Victor Kerry Burcher of Remuera, Auckland, New Zealand, and his wife, Florence, had all the trappings of yet another 'human' story. In his student days at Auckland University College he and his best friend, Kenneth Kirkcaldie, found that they were dating the same girl. In the end Esmé chose Kirkcaldie, but when he was killed in the war while serving as a pilot in the Royal Air Force Volunteer Reserve, Grey (on leave in England) proposed to his widow, and he and Esmé married on 1 November 1944. They had two sons, Jolyon (b. 1946) and Jeremy (b. 1949), and a daughter, Amanda (b. 1951). In course of time Esmé was made a commander of the order of St John of Jerusalem and became president of the Women's Corona Society in 1978. Such was their mutual devotion that her sudden death from a stroke on 22 March 1996, coming on top of his own heart condition and the shared physical strain of running a large country house with restricted domestic and garden help, induced a steady decline in his health, and—sadly ironical after a lifetime of genial conviviality—he spent his last years in increasing bereftness and withdrawal. He died on 17 October 1999 at Hunters Care Centre, Cherry Tree Lane, Cirencester, Gloucestershire, and was cremated on 26 October at Warwickshire crematorium, Oakley Wood. He was survived by his three children. A memorial service was held at St James's, Piccadilly, London, on 31 January 2000. A. H. M. KIRK-GREENE

Sources *Daily Telegraph* (19 Oct 1999) · *The Times* (19 Oct 1999) · *The Independent* (19 Oct 1999) · *The Guardian* (3 Dec 1999) · B. Sharwood Smith, *But always as friends* (1969) · J. Robertson, *Transition in Africa* (1974) · S. R. Ashton and D. Killingray, eds., *The West Indies* (1999), ser. B/6 of British documents on the end of empire · personal knowledge (2004) · private information (2004) [Jolyon Grey; M. Mann] · *WWW* · Burke, *Peerage*

Likenesses photograph, 1959, repro. in *The Independent* · photograph, 1968, repro. in *The Times* · photograph, 1973, repro. in *Daily Telegraph* · photograph, repro. in *The Guardian*

Grey, Reynold (1318/19–1388). *See under* Grey family (*per.* 1325–1523).

Grey, Reynold, third Baron Grey of Ruthin (*c*.1362–1440), nobleman and administrator, was the eldest son of Reynold Grey, second Baron Grey of Ruthin (*d.* 1388), and of his wife, Eleanor (*d.* 1396), daughter of John, second Baron Strange of Blackmere. On his father's death on 28 July 1388 Reynold succeeded to wide estates in England, centred in Bedfordshire and Buckinghamshire and to the castle and marcher lordship of Ruthin in north Wales. His mother retained rights in the estate until her death on 20 April 1396.

Reynold Grey's paternal grandmother had been Elizabeth, daughter of John, first Lord Hastings of Abergavenny. When the direct line of Hastings male heirs failed at the end of 1389 with the death in a tournament of young John Hastings, fourteenth earl of Pembroke, Reynold Grey had a strong claim to the substantial Hastings estates. Other claimants, the Strathbogies, Talbots, and Hastings of Elsing, were unsuccessful and the other serious contender, William Beauchamp, was bought off by Grey. As a result, Grey received lands in East Anglia, Kent, Leicestershire, Lincolnshire, and elsewhere by 1400, when the widowed countess of Pembroke died: about half of this inheritance, including the castle and lordship of Abergavenny in Monmouthshire, was given or sold to Beauchamp. The Irish lordship of Wexford was seized by the Talbots and was permanently lost to the Greys, but Reynold Grey incorporated the title 'lord of Wexford' into his style along with 'lord of Hastings'. The new style, Lord Grey of Wexford, Hastings, and Ruthin, was used by Reynold and his successors with royal approbation.

As heir general to John Hastings, Grey successfully claimed the right to bear the spurs at the coronation of Henry IV in 1399 and to provide napery for the royal banquet table afterwards. The right to bear the Hastings arms was, however, the subject of a *cause célèbre* in the court of chivalry in the first decade of the fifteenth century, resulting in Grey's victory over Sir Edward Hastings of Elsing. Hastings was ordered to pay Grey's legal costs, amounting to £987: he refused to pay and spent over twenty years in a debtors' prison. The debt was finally paid to Grey in 1436 and Hastings died a free man in 1438.

Over his fifty-two years as head of the Grey of Ruthin family, Reynold served successive governments in parliament and in local government, especially in Bedfordshire. He had already been a justice in Bedfordshire in 1382, during his father's lifetime. From 1390 until 1422 and again from 1437 until his death in 1440, Lord Reynold served consistently on the Bedfordshire commission of the peace. After the accession of Henry IV, Grey's role as a local justice increased sharply with regular appointments from 1401 onwards to the commissions in Huntingdonshire, Northamptonshire, and Buckinghamshire, as well as in Bedfordshire. This was the heartland of clientage to the Greys and in the last twenty years of Lord Reynold's life seven of the family's gentry affinity were significantly active as working justices in Bedfordshire. The strength of his local retinue sustained Lord Reynold in his long vendetta between 1404 and 1416 against the dowager Lady St Amand whose chase at Ampthill Grey 'by colour of his office of justice of the peace' occupied 'as if the park and warren had been in the hands of the French or other enemies' (*RotP*, 4.92–3).

In the wider sphere of national affairs Grey accompanied Richard II to Ireland in 1394 and in 1398 was temporary justiciar there. At the parliaments of the 1390s he was a trier of Gascon and other foreign petitions. He became a strong supporter of the new Lancastrian dynasty, attended a royal council in June 1401, assented in parliament to the condemnations of fellow lords in March, and was one of twelve lords who warranted the payment of dower when Henry IV's daughter married the future count palatine Ludwig III.

Grey's position as a marcher lord in Wales brought him into national prominence during the Glyn Dŵr revolt. The lordship of Ruthin or Dyffryn Clwyd in Denbigh had been granted to Grey's great-great-grandfather, Reynold Grey, first Lord Grey of Wilton, in 1282. The lordship occupied some of the best farming and grazing land in the Vale of Clwyd and Lord Reynold ran at least 2000 sheep there. The town of Ruthin, under the wing of the castle, was a prosperous market centre.

In 1394 Grey gave a new charter to the burgesses of Ruthin town, confirming the foundation charter over a century earlier, extending the brewing privileges of the townsfolk, and making some amendments to legal process in the lordship courts. During his lordship the importance of the local cloth industry was substantially enhanced. The growth of weaving and mechanical fulling on a commercial scale culminated in the creation of the 'craffte of Weyvers and of Walkers' shortly after Lord Reynold's death.

There seems to have been personal animosity between Grey and Owain Glyn Dŵr, whose estates lay close to Dyffryn Clwyd. A dispute over common land and an apparent attempt by Grey to discredit Glyn Dŵr in the eyes of Henry IV led on 18 September 1400 to Glyn Dŵr's attack on Ruthin town, his first bellicose act after declaring himself prince of Wales on 16 September. Glyn Dŵr found only modest support in the market town and little damage was done, although the townsfolk were robbed of goods alleged to be worth over £2000, and Grey did not hurry to Wales. When he did go in April 1402, he was captured by Glyn Dŵr near Ruthin. Henry IV sent envoys to discuss payment of the ransom, set by Glyn Dŵr at 10,000 marks (£6666 13s. 4d.); Grey surrendered his eldest son as one of several hostages and was licensed to alienate property to raise the money. As a result of the Hastings inheritance, Grey was able to raise enough money quickly to satisfy Glyn Dŵr and did not impoverish himself as has been often assumed.

In the closing years of the Glyn Dŵr revolt, some time between 1410 and 1412, Grey entered into an angry correspondence with a Welsh supporter of Glyn Dŵr's son over horse-stealing from the park at Ruthin. Grey ended his letter in crude but vigorous rhyme:

> But we hoepe we shall' do the a pryve thyng;
> a roope, a ladder, and a ryng,
> heigh on gallowes for to henge.
> (Smith, 259)

Under Henry V, Grey did not go on the French campaigns, but acted as a trier of petitions from the British Isles in all but one parliament. In 1415 he was one of the nine members of Bedford's council and in 1416 he was one of the prominent lords who welcomed Emperor Sigismund to England. When Henry V died Grey was almost sixty and during the minority of Henry VI he played little role in government but pursued his own interests, settling the dispute with Sir Edward Hastings in 1436.

Reynold Grey married twice. With his first wife, Margaret, a daughter of Thomas, fourth Baron Ros of Helmsley, he had three children, all of whom predeceased him:

Elizabeth married Robert *Poynings, fourth Baron Poynings [see under Poynings, Michael], Thomas died young, and Sir John *Grey [see under Grey family (per. 1325–1523)] died in 1439. Grey's second wife, Joan (d. 1448), daughter of William, fourth Baron Astley, had been widowed with an infant son in 1404 when her first husband, Thomas Raleigh, died young. Grey had four daughters with Joan, all of whom married suitably, and three sons who established their own landed branches of the family.

When Reynold died on 30 September 1440, he was succeeded by his eldest grandson, Edmund *Grey, son of Sir John Grey and his wife, Constance, niece to *Henry IV, daughter of John *Holland, duke of Exeter, and widow of Thomas (II) Mowbray, earl of Nottingham, who had been executed in 1405. Constance's estates were not forfeit in 1405 and her husband enjoyed an income from them of some £600 a year until her death in 1437. Edmund had spent his formative years in this affluent environment. Following on his grandfather's fifty-two years as Baron Grey, Edmund ruled the estates for a further fifty years after 1440 and in 1465 was created earl of Kent. The stability created by Lord Reynold's longevity, ability, and good fortune was consolidated under another shrewd and long-lived politician and estate manager, residing at his grandfather's favourite places, Wrest in Bedfordshire, Badmondisfield in Suffolk, Ruthin Castle, and Reynold's new town house in East Cheap, London.   R. Ian Jack

Sources R. I. Jack, 'The Greys of Ruthin, 1325 to 1490', PhD diss., U. Lond., 1961 · GEC, *Peerage* · *DNB* · R. I. Jack, 'Entail and descent: the Hastings inheritance, 1370–1436', *BIHR*, 38 (1965), 1–19 · R. I. Jack, 'Owain Glyn Dŵr and the lordship of Ruthin', *Welsh History Review / Cylchgrawn Hanes Cymru*, 2 (1964–5), 303–22 · J. B. Smith, 'The last phase of the Glyndŵr rebellion', *BBCS*, 22 (1966–8), 250–60 · PRO · *Chancery records* · Beds. & Luton ARS, Lucas MSS · *RotP*, vol. 4

Archives Beds. & Luton ARS, Lucas MSS · BL, Cotton MS Cleopatra F.iii

Wealth at death approx. £1450: Jack, 'The Greys of Ruthin', 211–18, 236–53, 271

Grey, Richard de (d. before **1272**), baron and member of Henry III's military household, was the eldest son of Henry de Grey of Codnor, Derbyshire, and Thurrock, Essex (d. 1219), and Isolda (d. 1246), sister and coheir of Robert Bardolf of Grimston, Nottinghamshire. Richard was born not later than 1198. In the rebellion of 1216 he supported King John and was granted the lands of several of the king's enemies, including those of John de Humez (d. 1223), to whose daughter and heir, Lucy, Grey was probably already married. By 1220 he and his younger brother John de *Grey were in receipt of a joint annual fee of £20 as members of King Henry's military household. Between 1224 and 1230 Grey was active in royal service in Poitou, Brittany, and the Channel Islands. In 1232 he went on pilgrimage to Santiago de Compostela. He was sheriff of Northumberland in 1235/6, and of Essex and Hertford in 1239. During the late 1230s and 1240s he served frequently on the Welsh marches. In 1241 he was among the avowed crusaders who took part in the Hertford tournament at which Earl Gilbert Marshal was killed.

In 1248 Grey was appointed seneschal of Gascony, although he was quickly replaced by Simon de Montfort, earl of Leicester, from whom he held lands in Northamptonshire. In 1252 he and his brother John took crusader oaths again, along with other members of the king's household. In the same year Grey was reappointed keeper of the Channel Islands and seneschal of Gascony, surrendering both offices to Prince Edward in 1254. With his son John and his brothers John and William he served on the king's 1254 Gascon expedition, and accompanied him to Paris. On his return to England in 1255 Grey retired from the court. In 1256 he is known to have been importing wine from Gascony in his own ship, the *Portjoye*.

Grey returned to public life in 1258 as a committed reformer and close associate of Simon de Montfort. He was one of the twelve councillors elected by the reformers in 1258, and became a member of the continuing royal council of fifteen. He was also appointed constable of Dover Castle, warden of the Cinque Ports, and chamberlain of Sandwich, with orders to intercept any treasure in excess of 3000 marks which the king's exiled Poitevin favourites might endeavour to send out of the country. However in 1259 Grey, acting in obedience to a royal writ, admitted a papal messenger into the kingdom through Dover against the wishes of the council, and was consequently replaced in his offices by Hugh Bigod, the justiciar. He nevertheless continued as a member of the council of fifteen and accompanied the king to Paris in late 1259. But in January 1260 Grey returned to England with Simon de Montfort, and was probably among those who attempted to hold the parliament at Candlemas in defiance of the king's prohibition. In the autumn of 1260 Grey submitted to the king and departed again from court.

Grey returned to court with Montfort in July 1263, and was reappointed constable of Dover Castle, which he held in December 1263 against the king himself. In December 1263 he joined in the submission of grievances to Louis IX as a member of Montfort's party. When civil war broke out he remained on garrison duty at Dover, together with his son John. Although Grey took part in Montfort's siege of Rochester Castle in April 1264, he was not present at the battle of Lewes. On 27 May he was appointed constable of Rochester Castle, with Henry de Montfort replacing him at Dover. Thereafter Grey seems to have remained on military duty in the south-east until July 1265, when he accompanied the younger Simon de Montfort's forces through Winchester, Oxford, and Northampton to Kenilworth Castle. There, on the night of 1 August, Grey, his son John, and many others of the younger Montfort's army were captured by Prince Edward while asleep outside the walls. Grey was now the king's enemy and his property was declared forfeit immediately after the battle of Evesham; his brother John, a firm royalist throughout the civil wars, was among the principal beneficiaries of the resulting seizures. Richard de Grey and his son John were again in arms in 1266, as part of the younger Simon de Montfort's garrison at Kenilworth Castle. They surrendered, with the rest of the garrison, on 14 December 1266, and accepted the terms of the dictum of Kenilworth, by which they were eventually able to recover their property. Richard de Grey died before 5 January 1272, when his son John died in seisin of the family lands at Codnor and Thurrock.

ROBERT C. STACEY

Sources Chancery records · Paris, Chron. · W. Stubbs, ed., Chronicles of the reigns of Edward I and Edward II, 1, Rolls Series, 76 (1882) · Calendar of inquisitions miscellaneous (chancery), PRO, 1 (1916) · J. R. Maddicott, Simon de Montfort (1994) · GEC, Peerage · R. F. Treharne, 'The unauthorized use of the great seal under the provisional government in 1259', EngHR, 40 (1925), 403–11 · H. C. M. Lyte and others, eds., Liber feodorum: the book of fees, 3 vols. (1920–31) · Ann. mon., vol. 3 · CIPM, 1, no. 810 · R. F. Treharne and I. J. Sanders, eds., Documents of the baronial movement of reform and rebellion, 1258–1267 (1973) · T. D. Hardy, ed., Rotuli litterarum clausarum, RC, 1 (1833), 395b, 396

Grey, Richard, second Baron Grey of Codnor (b. **1281/2**, d. in or before **1335**). See under Grey, John, third Baron Grey of Codnor (1305×11?–1392).

Grey, Richard, fourth Baron Grey of Codnor (c.**1371–1418**), soldier and diplomat, was the son of Henry Grey (d. 1379) and Joan Cobham; he succeeded his grandfather John *Grey, third Baron Grey of Codnor (1305×11?–1392), in 1392. As a young man he joined Richard II's first Irish expedition (1394–5) and received a life annuity of 80 marks from the king; he was a trier of petitions in the parliament of 1397–8. His family also had a long association with the family of John of Gaunt, duke of Lancaster, and the annuity was raised to 100 marks in 1401 by Henry IV, who valued Grey's military and diplomatic skills. By September 1400 he was defending the Scottish border as captain of Roxburgh Castle, and in April 1401 he was appointed admiral of the king's fleet from the Thames to the north. In 1401–2 he was nominated to negotiate with the French, and in October 1402 was one of the commissioners appointed to treat with Owain Glyn Dŵr for the release of Reynold, Lord Grey of Ruthin. Three weeks earlier he had been given military command in south Wales as the king's lieutenant to deal with Glyn Dŵr's rebellion. With headquarters chiefly at Brecon, this rising occupied much of his time and resources for the next five years: he captured Glyn Dŵr's son Gruffudd at the battle of Pwll Melyn, near Usk, in May 1405, and was justiciar of south Wales, 1403–7. Elected knight of the Garter c.1404, in 1406 he was commended in parliament for his Welsh service. Grey was also Henry IV's councillor and chamberlain (1404–13), as well as deputy constable and deputy marshal of England (1405–7). In 1405 Grey engaged successfully in a controversy with Lord Beaumont as to which of them was entitled to precedence, the earliest record of such a dispute between two barons. In November 1406 he became constable of Nottingham Castle, where (1407) James I of Scotland and Gruffudd, son of Owain Glyn Dŵr, were put in his charge.

Grey's closeness to the king is indicated by his witnessing of Henry's will in 1409, and his enhanced life annuity of 400 marks which was protected by parliament from resumption (1410). In August 1412 he was appointed governor of Fronsac in Aquitaine, and thereafter he was frequently employed on diplomatic missions. In 1412 he was

one of the ambassadors to treat for a marriage between Henry, prince of Wales, and Anne, daughter of John, duke of Burgundy. In 1414–15 he was one of those appointed to procure a prolongation of the truce with France and to negotiate a marriage between Henry V and Catherine of Valois. Henry V also relied on him in the north, where he was appointed warden of the eastern marches in May 1415. In the following August he was employed to negotiate a truce with Robert Stewart, duke of Albany, regent of Scotland. Yet his value as a soldier in emergencies was not exhausted. Apart from commissions to arrest Lollards (1414), Henry V enlisted him in his Normandy expedition of 1417. In October he became governor of the castle of Argentan in Normandy, and when he died on 1 August 1418, he may still have been in France. He was buried at Aylesford Priory, Kent. Grey had married by 1378 Elizabeth, daughter and coheir of Ralph Basset of Sapcote, Leicestershire, whose estates much extended Grey's holdings in the east midlands; she died after 24 August 1446. They had two sons, John (c.1396–1430) and Henry (c.1405–1443), fifth and sixth lords Grey of Codnor.

C. L. KINGSFORD, rev. R. A. GRIFFITHS

Sources PRO · Chancery records · RotP · N. H. Nicolas, ed., Proceedings and ordinances of the privy council of England, 7 vols., RC, 26 (1834–7), vol. 2 · J. H. Wylie, History of England under Henry the Fourth, 4 vols. (1884–98) · J. H. Wylie and W. T. Waugh, eds., The reign of Henry the Fifth, 3 vols. (1914–29) · J. L. Kirby, ed., Calendar of signet letters of Henry IV and Henry V (1978) · R. A. Griffiths and R. S. Thomas, The principality of Wales in the later middle ages: the structure and personnel of government, 1: South Wales, 1277–1536 (1972) · R. R. Davies, The revolt of Owain Glyn Dŵr (1995) · C. Given-Wilson, The royal household and the king's affinity: service, politics and finance in England, 1360–1413 (1986) · J. L. Kirby, Henry IV of England (1970) · GEC, Peerage · CIPM, 19, nos. 1031–5 · Lincs. Arch., episcopal register 18 [William Alnwick]

Grey, Sir Richard (d. **1483**), nobleman, was the half-brother of *Edward V and the younger son of **Sir John Grey** (c.1432–1461), knight, and *Elizabeth (c.1437–1492), the eldest daughter of Richard Woodville and Jacquetta of Luxembourg, widow of John, duke of Bedford. John Grey was the son and heir of Elizabeth Ferrers, Lady Ferrers of Groby, and Edward, younger son of Reynold, third Baron Grey of Ruthin, and his second wife, Joan, the daughter and heir of William Astley. John was twenty-five or more at his father's death in December 1457. His mother (the heir of William, Baron Ferrers of Groby, who died in 1445) outlived him, dying in January 1483, and although Edward Grey had been summoned to parliament as Baron Ferrers of Groby from December 1446, John never enjoyed that title, being known from at latest 1458 simply as John Grey, knight. On the outbreak of civil war in the late 1450s John Grey supported Henry VI. He was one of the commissioners of array for Leicestershire in the Lancastrian commissions of December 1459, and in April 1460 was commissioned to lead men to resist the duke of York. He was killed fighting on the Lancastrian side at the second battle of St Albans on 17 February 1461.

John Grey's marriage, in 1452, to Elizabeth Woodville produced two sons—Richard Grey and his elder brother, Thomas *Grey, who was said to be aged at least thirty-seven at his mother's death in 1492, which would give a birth date of *c.*1455. Nothing is known of Richard's date of birth, although his later career would suggest a date as late as 1460 or 1461. After John Grey's death Elizabeth found herself disputing her dower rights and her sons' inheritance with her mother-in-law, Elizabeth Ferrers, who had by this time married Sir John Bourchier. On 13 April 1464, as part of her campaign to secure the estates, Elizabeth came to an agreement with William, Lord Hastings, a close friend of the king, Edward IV, that her eldest son, Thomas, should marry the first daughter to be born to Hastings within the next five or six years, and that if any of the Ferrers or Astley inheritance should be recovered for Thomas, Hastings was to enjoy half the issues while Thomas was under twelve.

The agreement was, however, overtaken by events, and the projected marriage never took place. On 1 May 1464 Elizabeth's situation, and that of her family, was transformed by her clandestine marriage to Edward IV. Richard Grey was too young to benefit immediately. The first public reference to him is his knighting on 14 May 1475, and in July that year he was added to the commission of the peace for Herefordshire—which suggests that he was associated with the household of his half-brother, the prince of Wales, at Ludlow, which by this date was acting as the focus for royal authority in Wales and the marches. Later grants confirmed his identification with his half-brother's spheres of influence. On 24 April 1482 he was granted the castle and lordship of Kidwelly, and later the same year was made constable of Chester, where Prince Edward was earl. On 3 September 1482 the prince made him his constable and steward of Wallingford in place of the duke of Suffolk. At the beginning of 1483 he received his first landed endowment when his stepfather, the king, settled on him by act of parliament eleven manors in Essex, Northamptonshire, Berkshire, and Wiltshire, for his good service and in consideration of 2000 marks paid by the queen. Grey's new eminence is reflected in his addition to five more commissions of the peace in February 1483: Berkshire, Buckinghamshire, Essex, Northamptonshire, and Oxfordshire. In the same month he is described for the first time as a member of the prince of Wales's council.

When Edward IV died on 9 April 1483, Richard Grey was with his half-brother at Ludlow and accompanied him when he set out for London and his coronation. On 29 April the royal party was met by the dukes of Gloucester and Buckingham, and on the following day Gloucester took possession of the prince and arrested Grey and his uncle Anthony, Earl Rivers. Both men were sent to Gloucester's castles in the north for safe keeping: Rivers to Sheriff Hutton and Grey to Middleham. According to Mancini, Gloucester sought their execution, but the council refused on the grounds that they had done nothing that could be construed as treason. In June Gloucester began to move towards taking the throne for himself. On 10 June he wrote north for troops, who were to gather at Pontefract. Rivers and Grey, and their fellow captive, Thomas Vaughan, were evidently brought south as the soldiers assembled, and on 25 June were executed at Pontefract in the presence of the army. Gloucester's receiver was subsequently allowed 46*s.* 4*d.* for the expenses of Grey's burial. The place of their burial is unknown, although in a postscript to his will, written two days earlier, Rivers had requested burial 'before an image of our blessed lady Mary, with my lord Richard, in Pomfrete' (Bentley, 248).

Richard Grey was unmarried at his death. In the abortive 1464 Woodville–Hastings agreement he was to have married Hastings's daughter if Thomas had died before he could do so, and in 1474 he was again the reserve if Thomas died before consummating a marriage to Hastings's stepdaughter, Cicely Bonville. The endowment of 1482 was presumably seen as a prelude to finding him a suitable marriage of his own, but nothing had come of it when Edward IV died.   ROSEMARY HORROX

Sources PRO · *Chancery records* · *RotP* · GEC, *Peerage* · R. Horrox and P. W. Hammond, eds., *British Library Harleian manuscript 433*, 4 vols. (1979–83) · C. Carpenter, *Locality and polity: a study of Warwickshire landed society, 1401–1499* (1992) · R. Horrox, *Richard III, a study of service*, Cambridge Studies in Medieval Life and Thought, 4th ser., 11 (1989) · D. E. Lowe, 'Patronage and politics: Edward IV, the Wydevills, and the council of the prince of Wales, 1471–83', *BBCS*, 29 (1980–82), 545–73 · S. Bentley, ed., *Excerpta historica, or, Illustrations of English history* (1831)

Grey, Richard, third earl of Kent (*b.* in or before **1478**, *d.* **1524**), nobleman, was the son of George *Grey, second earl of Kent, and his first wife, Anne Bourchier, *née* Woodville (*d.* 1489). Aged at least twenty-five when he succeeded his father in 1503, he wasted his family's fortunes—possibly, as Dugdale says, he was a gambler. In a striking series of alienations he gave away or sold most of the lands, principally in Bedfordshire, that he had inherited: the beneficiaries were Henry VII's administrator–courtiers, Charles Somerset, Baron Herbert (later earl of Worcester), Sir John Hussey (Kent's brother-in-law), Sir Richard Empson, Sir Henry Wyatt, and Giles, Baron Daubeney. The earl also fell quickly into debt to the king: he failed to pay livery for his father's lands, and he was fined 2500 marks for abducting Elizabeth Trussell, whose wardship the second earl had left to Richard's half-brother Henry; he then failed to keep up the instalments laid down for the payment of the fine.

An indenture of 6 May 1507 acknowledged the recovery to the king's use of several manors, to be held by the crown until these debts were paid, as Earl Richard was 'not of power, habilite ne havyour to content and pay to our seid sovereign lorde the seide sommes of money … without in manner his utter doing' (PRO, E 368/290, rots. xlviii–l). On 19 August 1507, moreover, Kent was bound in recognizance of £10,000 not to sell, lease, or grant any of his lands without the king's consent, and he was to attend on the king 'soo that he bee see daily ones in the day within the kinges house' (*CClR, 1500–09*, no. 797). Rather than reflecting the rapaciousness of the king, still less the shrewdness of a nobleman seeking to escape from the constraints of an entail, these transactions are best seen as an attempt by Henry VII—moved by 'pitie', as Henry Grey would later claim (Bedfordshire and Luton Archives and Record Service, L 24/530)—to preserve a nobleman's patrimony from destruction. But no permanent restrictions were placed on Earl Richard's ability to dispose of his inheritance, and the sequence of alienations continued after the death of Henry VII, with courtiers such as Sir William Compton prominent among the beneficiaries. By the time he died, at London, on 3 May 1524, Earl Richard, who was variously described as 'as unmeet to governe his estate as a naturall Ideott', 'a praye sett open to the spoyle of all men', and leading an 'unstayed and disordered lyffe', had wrecked his inheritance (ibid., L 24/525; 24/530, fol. 1v; DD OR 1064, fol. 9). He was buried at Whitefriars, London.

Although Henry VII appointed him to the Order of the Garter in 1505 (the highest honour at the king's disposal), Earl Richard played no visible role in the government and politics of the realm. He did, however, attend on some ceremonial and diplomatic occasions, such as the Field of Cloth of Gold in 1520 and the reception of the emperor Charles V on his visit to England in 1522, and he served, too, on the French campaign of 1513, albeit in a subordinate role. He was also something of a literary patron, if in a small way. Alexander Barclay's *Myrrour of Good Maners* is said to have been printed in 1520 at the instance of the earl, who similarly promoted Brian Anslay's translation from Christine de Pisan, *Boke of the Cyte of Ladyes* (1521). Earl Richard married twice. His first wife, whom he married *c*.1506, was Elisabeth Hussey, sister of the courtier Sir John (later first Baron) Hussey; she died in 1516, and under a contract of 23 January 1521 he married Mrs Margaret Dawes (*née* Fynche, formerly Curteys), the widow of a London alderman, who lived until 1540 or 1541. There were no children of either marriage. His heir was his despised half-brother Henry, whose hopes of taking up the title of earl of Kent and recovering the family manors were not realized.   G. W. BERNARD

Sources GEC, *Peerage*, 7.166–9 · G. W. Bernard, 'The fortunes of the Greys, earls of Kent, in the early sixteenth century', *HJ*, 25 (1982), 671–85 · R. I. Jack, ed., *The Greys of Ruthin Valor*, Bedfordshire Historical Society, 46 (1665) · R. I. Jack, 'The lords Grey of Ruthin, 1325–1490: a study of the lesser baronage', PhD diss., U. Lond., 1961 · *CClR, 1485–1509* · W. Dugdale, *The baronage of England*, 2 vols. (1675–6) · exchequer, lord treasurer's remembrancer, memoranda roll, PRO, E 368/290 · star chamber, pleadings, Henry VIII, PRO, STAC 2/16 · Beds. & Luton ARS, L 24/454, 525, 530; DD OR 1064 · *LP Henry VIII*, vol. 3/1

Wealth at death little or nothing; had alienated patrimony

Grey, Richard (1696–1771), Church of England clergyman and writer, was born in Newcastle upon Tyne on 6 April 1696, the son of John Grey, a barber. He was educated at Newcastle grammar school, and matriculated at Lincoln College, Oxford, in June 1712, graduating BA in 1716, and proceeding MA in 1719 and DD (by diploma) in 1731. He incorporated at Cambridge in 1732, having been ordained deacon in 1719 and priest in 1720 by the aged Nathaniel, Lord Crewe, bishop of Durham, to whom he acted as chaplain and secretary. Grey attended the bishop on his deathbed in September 1721 and later helped to settle his affairs. On 13 April 1720, on Crewe's presentation, Grey had been instituted to the rectory of Hinton, Northamptonshire, to which he soon added the nearby rectory of Steane chapel. In addition he became rector of Kimcote, Leicestershire,

in 1725, official and commissary of the archdeaconry of Leicester in 1741, and a prebendary of St Paul's and archdeacon of Bedford in 1757. He married Joyce (1704/5–1794), daughter of John Thicknesse, rector of Farthinghoe, Northamptonshire.

Grey was a man of many remarkable gifts, which found expression in widely varying ways. His most influential achievement was the composition of *Memoria technica, or, A New Method of Artificial Memory* (1730), a book which was republished many times, with modifications, until 1861. Inspired in part by Quintilian's *De oratore*, it could be applied to the study of chronology, geography, mensuration, and astronomy. Grey's imaginative theories as a teacher found further expression in 1738, when he published *A New and Easy Method of Learning Hebrew without Points*, and numerous other productions testify to his enthusiasm as a Hebraist. His views were not accepted universally, and in 1742 some remarks in the preface to a work by Grey, *Liber Jobi in versiculos metrice divisus; accedit canticum Moysis*, provoked a sharp retort from William Warburton (later bishop of Gloucester).

Grey had a wide acquaintance. Although on amiable terms with individual dissenters, most notably Philip Doddridge, his personal opinions were those of a high-churchman; and with others, such as his friend Richard Venn, he shared a widely held view that the age was one of unprecedented danger for the Church of England. For a visitation sermon preached at St Mary's, Leicester, Grey chose the theme 'The perpetuity of Christ's church', his text being Matthew 16: 18: 'and the gates of hell shall not prevail against it'. This sermon was delivered in 1730, at the beginning of a particularly alarming decade for churchmen, as Sir Robert Walpole's readiness to negotiate with the Quakers and the protestant dissenting deputies appeared to threaten both the church's maintenance by tithe and bequest and the constitutional privileges afforded by the Test and Corporation Acts. The crisis came to a head with the passage of the Mortmain Act in 1736, a measure which provoked Grey to further activity.

A visitation sermon preached at Towcester on 2 July 1736 on the text Matthew 10: 16, 'Behold I send you forth as sheep in the midst of wolves', was published as *The Duty and Proper Conduct of the Clergy under the Ill-Treatment of their Enemies* (1736), and Grey was also the author of an influential tract, which was published anonymously: *The Miserable and Distracted State of Religion in England upon the Downfall of the Church-Establishment*. In this work he attacked Daniel Neal's sympathetically handled *History of the Puritans* (1732–8). Grey detailed the blasphemous and tyrannical sectarianism of the civil war and Commonwealth periods and drew timeless conclusions about 'the restless Spirit of the *Puritanical* or *Nonconforming* Party' (*Miserable and Distracted State*, i). He had already taken steps to reinforce the legal defences of the church by preparing *A system of English ecclesiastical law, extracted from the 'Codex juris ecclesiastici Anglicani' of the lord bishop of London* (1730). This, in conjunction with his ability as the repeater of the Easter sermons preached before the university, and the memory of the favour in which he had been held by Bishop Crewe, secured Grey his Oxford DD in 1731.

Grey died at Hinton on 28 February 1771 and was buried there on 5 March. He is commemorated by a monument in the church. His wife survived him, dying on 12 January 1794, aged eighty-nine. Joyce, the eldest of their three daughters, married Dr Philip Lloyd, dean of Norwich, and the youngest, Bridget, married the Revd W. T. Bowles and was the mother of William Lisle Bowles, Church of England priest and poet.   RICHARD SHARP

Sources Nichols, *Lit. anecdotes* · Nichols, *Illustrations* · Foster, *Alum. Oxon.* · Venn, *Alum. Cant.* · A. R. Laws, *Schola Novocastrensis*, 2 (1932), 16–17 · G. Baker, *The history and antiquities of the county of Northampton*, 2 vols. (1822–41) · J. Nichols, *The history and antiquities of the county of Leicester*, 4 vols. (1795–1815) · *Remarks and collections of Thomas Hearne*, ed. C. E. Doble and others, 10, OHS, 67 (1915), 420 · W. L. Bowles, *Scenes and shadows of days departed: a narrative accompanied with poems of youth* (1837) · IGI

Grey, Roger, first Lord Grey of Ruthin (*c.*1300–1353), landowner and soldier, was the younger son of John *Grey, second Lord Grey of Wilton, and the only son of his father's second marriage, to Maud, daughter of Sir Ralph Basset of Drayton. Roger became a major landholder at the expense of his elder half-brother, Henry, third Lord Grey of Wilton (*d.* 1342). Between 1307 and 1319 John Grey settled on Roger by final concords some two-thirds of his landed estate, including all his Bedfordshire lands, most of his Buckinghamshire manors, and the lordship of Ruthin in north Wales. On John Grey's death in 1323 there was a bitter dispute between the half-brothers, which culminated in Henry's seizure by force of Ruthin Castle in 1328, but arbiters appointed by the royal council negotiated a general settlement in June of that year and thereafter Roger enjoyed his inheritance in peace.

Grey did not significantly enlarge his landed wealth and used his father's manor house at Wrest and the castle at Ruthin as principal seats. His marriage, arranged by his father *c.*1311, was of major significance in the long term. His wife, Elizabeth, was the only daughter of John *Hastings, first Lord Hastings and Lord Bergavenny, and his first wife, Isabel de Valence, and in due course Elizabeth's grandson, Reynold *Grey, third Baron Grey of Ruthin, successfully claimed to be the heir of the Hastings earls of Pembroke. Roger Grey's family with Elizabeth comprised three sons and four daughters. His eldest son, John, predeceased him in 1349 or 1350 and Grey's heir was his second son, Reynold. Three of his daughters married suitably: Joan to Sir William Pattishall (*d.* 1359); Julianne (*d.* 1361) to John Talbot of Richards Castle (*d.* 1355); and Maud to a member of the Roche family, probably William, fourth Lord Roche (*d.* 1370?). The family's alliances were strengthened by the eldest son's marriage to Agnes, daughter of William Montagu, earl of Salisbury. Reynold, the second son, married Eleanor (*d.* 1396), the only daughter of John, second Lord Lestrange of Blackmere.

Roger Grey's public career was unspectacular. He participated in the wars of Edward II and Edward III, principally in the Scottish arena. He was at the siege of Berwick in 1319 and served in Scotland in 1322, 1327, 1334–5, and 1342. In 1323 and 1325 he also served in Gascony, but did not embark on Edward III's French wars. He was appointed to commissions of the peace for Bedfordshire with some consistency from 1332 until 1351, was a commissioner of array in Bedfordshire in 1326, 1337, and 1339, and was an overseer of the commissions of array in south-east England in 1338. He was regularly summoned to parliament from 1322 until his death. In 1340 he was a trier of parliamentary petitions from Gascony, Ireland, Wales, and Scotland. He was never a member of the royal council.

Grey's relationship with the church was conventional. He did not emulate his father's considerable generosity, but supported his father's collegiate foundation at Ruthin. Two of his children entered the church, John as a priest and royal clerk, and Mabel as a nun. Grey died on 6 March 1353, and had asked to be buried at St Peter's Church, Ruthin. His memorial there does not survive, but there is a fine representation of him, armed with a Galway sparth, on the brass of his wife's half-brother, Hugh Hastings, at Elsing in Norfolk.   R. IAN JACK

Sources R. I. Jack, 'The Greys of Ruthin, 1325 to 1490', PhD diss., U. Lond., 1961 · GEC, *Peerage* · *DNB* · Beds. & Luton ARS, Lucas MS L. 28/45 · 'The genealogy of the most noble and ancient family of Grey', 1718, priv. coll. · PRO, *Chancery records* · *CIPM*, 10, nos. 96–7, 107 · PRO, C 135/123/9; E142/78/1,2 · *Processus in Curia Marescalli I*, Coll. Arms
Archives Beds. & Luton ARS, Lucas MS L.28/45 · PRO, register of tenants of Ruthin, 1324, Wales 15/8
Likenesses effigy, 1347 (on brass of Sir Hugh Hastings), Elsing church, Norfolk
Wealth at death £850 inheritance from father in 1324: PRO, E 142/78/1, 2; Beds. & Luton ARS, Lucas MS L. 28/45 · two manors: *CIPM*, 10, no. 107; PRO, C 135/123/9

Grey, Sir Roger de (1918–1995), artist, was born on 18 April 1918 at Colehatch, Tylers Green, Chipping Wycombe, Buckinghamshire, the second son and youngest of three children of Nigel Arthur de *Grey (1886–1951), naval intelligence officer, and his wife, Florence Emily Frances Gore (1883–1963). Both his parents were of aristocratic descent. His father was deputy director of GCHQ at Bletchley Park during the Second World War. Inspired by tales of his uncle the painter Spencer *Gore, Roger in his teens affected flamboyant 'aestheticism'. He was bullied at Eton, although he found a mentor in the assistant drawing master Robin (later Sir Robert) Darwin.

De Grey studied at the Chelsea School of Art (1936–9 and 1945–7). During the war he served in the Royal West Kent yeomanry until 1942 and then saw action as a captain in the Royal Armoured Corps. On 2 May 1942 he married the painter Flavia Hatt Irwin (*b.* 1916), daughter of Clinton Irwin, a retired army officer. They had two sons and a daughter by late 1952. In 1947 de Grey moved to Newcastle upon Tyne to become lecturer in painting at the King Edward VII School of Art at King's College, then part of Durham University (and headed by Darwin). Lawrence Gowing and Victor Pasmore were influential colleagues. Promoted to master of painting in 1951, de Grey followed Darwin to London two years later as senior tutor at the Royal College of Art (RCA).

Agnews Gallery mounted de Grey's first one-man exhibition in 1954. He specialized in contemplative evocations of nature: tightly composed still lifes and landscapes in soft muted colours which revealed a particular appreciation of Cézanne. Dappled sunlight and blue-green vegetation are characteristic of his work, which belongs to a recognizably British strand of post-impressionism. This was remote from the trend-setting pop art pioneered around 1960 by such RCA students as Peter Blake and David Hockney, but de Grey endeavoured to provide encouragement and defend new art against undiscriminating criticism. In 1973 he left the RCA to become principal of the City and Guilds of London Art School in Kennington, recently separated from the City and Guilds Institute. Retaining the job for the rest of his life, he did much to form the character of the school by having all students taught life drawing, promoting traditional crafts, and starting courses in restoration and conservation.

De Grey was elected an associate of the Royal Academy of Arts in 1962 and a full academician in 1969. His close involvement began when he joined the academy's exhibitions committee (1975) before serving as treasurer from 1976 to 1984. The financial position was at first precarious, but he introduced corporate sponsorship of major exhibitions and saved the loss-making summer exhibition by levying a 15 per cent commission on sales. On 6 December 1984 he became the twenty-first president of the Royal Academy, eager to carry on the modernizing work of Sir Hugh Casson and to return the academy to the mainstream of contemporary art. By abolishing the apprentice status of associate, which some painters and architects reckoned demeaning, he attracted a number of prestigious new academicians—such as Blake, Hockney, R. B. Kitaj, Norman Foster, and Richard Rogers—who may have been wary of the society's past reputation for antimodernism. De Grey did not deem it the president's task to pontificate about art. He appeared a gentle, approachable man. Quizzical friendliness cloaked any nervousness; his conversation was light and informal. Slender and spry, fond of hamburgers and chewing gum, he usually dressed in pale tweed tones enlivened by brightly coloured woollen tie and socks.

By strengthening the international contacts of the Royal Academy, de Grey enabled it to stage loan exhibitions more ambitious than ever before. There were monographic shows devoted to Monet, Goya, Mantegna, Frans Hals, Poussin, Chagall, Sickert, and Henry Moore, and such synoptic shows as 'The Age of Chivalry' (1987) and 'The Art of Photography' (1989). The president concerned himself with every detail of presentation and publicity, and hotly insisted on the highest standards. He was also a very successful fund-raiser, hosting breakfasts, luncheons, and dinners in London and the USA. A donation by the American philanthropist Arthur M. Sackler made it possible for the academy to replace the old Diploma Galleries at Burlington House with the Sackler Galleries, which opened in June 1991, the month when de Grey received a knighthood (KCVO). He retired as president in April 1993 at the compulsory age of seventy-five.

Much as he enjoyed being at the centre of things, de Grey had continued to produce about a dozen large works a year. His studio was a converted barn across a field from his country home at 5–6 Camer Street, Meopham, Kent. He made many studies on the theme 'interior/exterior', showing the view from within to without, with the blurring and reflections of window glass. Probably his most distinctive landscapes were painted late in life in southwest France, where he owned a house from 1977.

De Grey died on 14 February 1995 at the Chelsea and Westminster Hospital in London after minor surgery to cure an intestinal infection. His wife survived him. A dedicated painter, administrator, and teacher, he had thrived on juggling all three activities.   JASON TOMES

Sources *Daily Telegraph* (16 Feb 1995) · *The Independent* (16 Feb 1995) · *The Times* (16 Feb 1995) · *The Guardian* (17 Feb 1995) · *Evening Standard* (15 Feb 1995) · B. Sewell, 'Changing shades of Grey', *Evening Standard* (25 July 1996) · M. Gayford, 'The long, slow path to artistic originality', *Daily Telegraph* (24 July 1996) · W. Packer, 'Natural modesty of the true artist', *Financial Times* (13 July 1996) · M. Greene, 'My greatest influence', *Daily Mail* (17 Dec 1994) · G. Bridgstock, 'Danger: artist at work', *Evening Standard* (25 June 1993) · S. Tait, 'The RA's white knight steps down', *Financial Times* (24 April 1993) · R. Cork, 'Filling his days with the void', *The Times* (21 April 1994) · J. Dawson, 'At home with the artists in residence', *The Times* (15 Aug 1992) · 'Iain Gale on exhibitions', *The Independent* (19 July 1996) · b. cert. · m. cert. · d. cert. · WWW

Likenesses R. de Grey, self-portrait, oils, 1990, NPG

Wealth at death £638,336: probate, 7 Feb 1996, *CGPLA Eng. & Wales*

Grey, Thomas, first marquess of Dorset (*c*.1455–1501), courtier, was the elder son of Sir John *Grey (*c*.1432–1461) [*see under* Grey, Sir Richard] of Groby, Leicestershire, first husband of *Elizabeth, *née* Woodville (afterwards queen of England), who was killed fighting on the Lancastrian side at the second battle of St Albans on 17 February 1461. Thomas Grey was a man of mediocre abilities who owed his place in English politics to his mother's unexpected marriage with *Edward IV in 1464. He had royal ancestry, as a descendant of Edward I, but before his mother's second marriage Grey's prospects of advancement were not very great. The lands of the Ferrers of Groby barony belonged to the heir, Grey's paternal grandmother, Elizabeth Ferrers, who had married the king's cousin Sir John Bourchier as her second husband, and lived until 1483. As queen, Elizabeth Woodville sought to make provision for her elder son by marrying him to a wealthy heiress. In 1466 she arranged his marriage with Edward IV's niece, the child Anne Holland, daughter and heir of the exiled Lancastrian partisan, Henry *Holland, duke of Exeter (*d*. 1475), who had a claim to be regarded as the heir to the house of Lancaster, if Henry VI's only son, Prince Edward (*d*. 1471) were to die childless. By a bargain with her sister-in-law Anne, duchess of Exeter (*d*. 1476), Edward IV's eldest sister, Queen Elizabeth contracted to pay 4000 marks to buy this advantageous match for Thomas Grey, and so incurred the enmity of the king's most powerful supporter, Richard Neville, earl of Warwick (*d*. 1471) who had intended the infant Holland heir to become the bride of his nephew, George Neville (afterwards duke of Bedford). Thomas Grey's first marriage took place at Greenwich in

October 1466, but his expectations of acquiring the duchess of Exeter's estates were defeated when Anne Holland died childless, probably early in 1474.

After Edward IV's restoration to the throne in April 1471 Grey fought on the Yorkist side at the battle of Tewkesbury on 4 May, and is said by later sources to have taken part in the murder of the captured Prince Edward. Perhaps as a reward for his services he was created earl of Huntingdon on 14 August 1471, a dignity which he subsequently resigned before he became a marquess. After the death of his first wife Grey had the good fortune to marry another great heiress, Cicely Bonville (d. 1530); this union, contracted before 6 June 1474, brought him the westcountry estates that had belonged to his wife's greatgrandfather, William, Lord Bonville (d. 1461), as well as the lands of the Harington barony, which were mostly in northern and western England. Queen Elizabeth bought the marriage of the Bonville and Harington heir from Cicely's stepfather, William, Lord Hastings (d. 1483), by undertaking to pay 2500 marks. This sum was never paid because Edward IV met the cost of his stepson's promotion by cancelling an equivalent sum owed to him by Hastings. By his second marriage Grey was established as a well-endowed member of the English nobility, and he became Lord Harington and Bonville in the right of his wife. They had livery of her inheritance on 23 April 1475, and on Whitsunday (14 May) he was made a knight of the Bath and created marquess of Dorset. He served on Edward IV's French expedition in the autumn of 1475. Dorset benefited from the condemnation and execution of George, duke of Clarence, in 1478; on 8 June 1481, after payment of £2000, he was granted the custody of a substantial part of the late duke's estates, as well as the wardship and marriage of his only son and heir, *Edward, earl of Warwick (d. 1499). Early in 1483 Dorset paid 3000 marks for royal confirmation of arrangements for the marriage of his own son and heir, Thomas, with the young Anne St Leger, the recognized heir to her mother, Anne, duchess of Exeter, and he obtained a life interest in most of her lands. By these agreements, which cost Queen Elizabeth a further 2000 marks, the duchy of Exeter and other valuable estates held by the late duchess were partitioned between Dorset and his younger brother, Sir Richard *Grey (d. 1483), who obtained manors worth 500 marks a year. If Edward IV's reign had not been cut short by the king's death on 9 April 1483, the Greys of Groby would have become one of the most powerful landed families in England.

The minority of the twelve-year-old Prince Edward thrust Dorset into a prominent position in English government, a role for which he soon proved inadequate. The absence at Ludlow of his eldest maternal uncle, Antony Woodville, Earl Rivers (d. 1483), the 'governor and ruler' of the prince of Wales, made Dorset the leader of the queen's party in London, and he failed to realize how insecure his position was. By codicils added on his deathbed to his will of 1475 Edward IV appears to have named his surviving brother, Richard, duke of Gloucester, as lord protector, but he probably committed the personal custody of his

heir to the prince's maternal kinsmen, headed by Rivers, Dorset, and Sir Richard Grey. Feuds among the Yorkist nobility made it impossible to organize a regency for Edward IV's hapless son. The hostility between Dorset and his wife's stepfather, Lord Hastings, was particularly important in enabling Gloucester to seize power and usurp the throne. Dorset's increasing political importance was seen by Hastings as a challenge to his ascendancy in Leicestershire. The king's council, dominated by Queen Elizabeth's supporters, resolved to terminate Gloucester's protectorship by having Edward V crowned on 4 May, shortly after his arrival in London. According to Mancini, Dorset is said to have boasted at a council meeting, 'We are so important that even without the king's uncle, we can make and enforce these decisions' (Usurpation of Richard III, 75). After Gloucester arrested Rivers and Grey at Stony Stratford, Buckinghamshire, on 30 April, and took charge of the doomed Edward V, Dorset abandoned the Tower of London, where he was in control, and followed his mother, Queen Elizabeth, into sanctuary at Westminster Abbey.

When news of the murder of the deposed king and his younger brother, Richard, duke of York, became known in the autumn of 1483, Dorset joined the rebellion led by Henry Stafford, duke of Buckingham, in a bid to overthrow Richard III. The speedy collapse of this ill-planned revolt compelled him to take refuge in Brittany, and he was obliged to remain in exile for over two years. He was among the persons attainted in the parliament of 1484 and his estates were forfeited. He joined Henry Tudor at Rennes, but Henry did not find him a reliable ally. Shortly before Henry's successful invasion of England in August 1485, Dorset received a letter from his mother, who had come to terms with Richard III, and that persuaded him to desert Henry Tudor. Fortunately he was intercepted at Compiègne, en route for Flanders (and England), and he played no part in the overthrow of Richard III. Instead, with John Bourchier, Lord Berners (d. 1533), he was left at Paris, as security for the repayment of a loan made to Henry Tudor by the French government. He was unable to return home until Henry VII was safely installed as king of England.

Before his return to England, in November 1485, Dorset's attainder was reversed in Henry VII's first parliament, and he was restored to his lands and titles, but he never recovered the political influence that he had enjoyed under Edward IV. He was now one of the richer English peers, and, after inheriting his grandmother's estates, he styled himself 'marquis of Dorset, lord Ferrers of Groby, Bonville, Harington and Astley'. But Henry VII regarded him with suspicion and during Lambert Simnel's rising in 1487 he was imprisoned in the Tower, and not released until after the king's victory in the battle of Stoke, fought on 16 June. On 5 June 1492, immediately before Henry VII's French expedition of that year (in which Dorset took part), effective measures were taken to put the marquess under restraint, through an indenture intended to ensure that he did not commit treason, or conceal acts of treason of which others were guilty. Overall, the first Tudor king showed wisdom and restraint in his dealings with his queen's shifty half-brother, who assisted in the suppression of the Cornish insurrection of 1497. Dorset died in London on 30 August 1501, and was buried in the collegiate church of Astley, Warwickshire. Polydore Vergil described him as *vir bonus et prudens* (*Anglica historia*, 6). He was an early patron of Thomas Wolsey (*d.* 1530), to whom in October 1500 he gave the rectory of Limington, Somerset. He is believed to have built Bradgate Hall, a fortified brick manor house near Leicester, which became the chief residence of his family. With his second wife, Cicely Bonville, *suo jure* Lady Harington and Bonville, he had seven sons and eight daughters including Elizabeth *Fitzgerald, later countess of Kildare; two of his elder sons predeceased him and his heir was his third son, Thomas (*d.* 1530). Dorset's widow married, probably late in 1504, Henry Stafford, who was created earl of Wiltshire in 1510. His great-granddaughter, Lady Jane Grey [see Dudley, Lady Jane], was queen of England for thirteen days after the death of Edward VI in 1553. The Grey of Groby family became extinct in the male line on the death of the tenth earl of Stamford in 1976.

T. B. PUGH

Sources J. Stevenson, ed., *Letters and papers illustrative of the wars of the English in France during the reign of Henry VI, king of England*, 2/2, Rolls Series, 22 (1864) [incl. the Lat. Annals ascribed to William Worcester (pp. 743–93)] · *The usurpation of Richard the third: Dominicus Mancinus ad Angelum Catonem de occupatione regni Anglie per Ricardum tercium libellus*, ed. and trans. C. A. J. Armstrong, 2nd edn (1969) [Lat. orig., 1483, with parallel Eng. trans.] · N. Pronay and J. Cox, eds., *The Crowland chronicle continuations, 1459–1486* (1986) · *Three books of Polydore Vergil's 'English history'*, ed. H. Ellis, CS, 29 (1844) · *The Anglica historia of Polydore Vergil, AD 1485–1537*, ed. and trans. D. Hay, CS, 3rd ser., 74 (1950) · W. Dugdale, *The baronage of England*, 2 vols. (1675–6) · W. C. Metcalfe, *A book of knights banneret, knights of the Bath and knights bachelor* (1885) · J. Nichols, *The history and antiquities of the county of Leicester*, 4/2 (1811); facs. edn (1971) · M. Forsyth, *History of Bradgate Hall* (1974) · N. H. Nicolas, ed., *Testamenta vetusta: being illustrations from wills*, 2 vols. (1826) · D. Mac-Gibbon, *Elizabeth Woodville (1437–1492): her life and times* (1938) · GEC, *Peerage*, new edn, vols. 4–6, 12/2 · T. B. Pugh, 'Henry VII and the English nobility', *The Tudor nobility*, ed. G. W. Bernard (1992), 49–110

Grey, Thomas, second marquess of Dorset (1477–1530), magnate and courtier, was born on 22 June 1477, the third son and heir of Thomas *Grey, first marquess of Dorset (*c.*1455–1501), and his wife, Cicely (*d.* 1530), daughter of William Bonville, Baron Harrington.

Uncertain inheritance According to Cavendish, in 1495 Grey entered Magdalen College School, Oxford, where he and his brothers were taught by the future Cardinal Wolsey, who was later rewarded by the Greys' father with his first benefice. Doubts have been cast on this story on the grounds that Wolsey did not become master of the school until 1498, but since Grey seems to have been attached to Wolsey in later years, perhaps Wolsey had been the boys' tutor.

Grey owed his eventual success at court to his lineage, his skill at jousting, and his loyalty to Henry VIII rather than to any formal education he might have received. He and his brothers followed their father as soldiers and courtiers not scholars and officials. He was made knight of the Bath in 1494 and knight of the Garter in 1501, the year

he succeeded his father. His first marriage, to Eleanor, daughter of Oliver St John of Lydeard Tregoze, Wiltshire, had ended by 1509, when he married Margaret (*d.* in or after 1535), daughter of Sir Robert Wotton of Boughton Malherbe, Kent, and widow of William Medley; they had four sons and four daughters, the eldest son being Henry *Grey, duke of Suffolk (1517–1554), and the youngest Lord John *Grey.

The elder Thomas Grey was the son of Elizabeth Woodville from her first marriage. His loyalties to Richard III were accordingly suspect, and he fled to Brittany after the failure of Buckingham's rebellion in 1483, taking his heir with him. He might have expected to prosper after Richard's fall, but his equivocal support of Henry Tudor in 1485 brought both father and son under a degree of suspicion and they did not immediately reap the rewards that they might otherwise have expected after the new king had married Dorset's half-sister *Elizabeth (Elizabeth of York). Instead Henry VII imprisoned the marquess during Lambert Simnel's rebellion of 1487, and five years later, when about to go abroad, forced him to sign an indenture placing his land in trust and another surrendering his heir's wardship to the king, and also to have friends post recognizances of £10,000 as a guarantee of good behaviour.

Despite Henry VII's distrust, however, the younger Thomas Grey was able to take part in major court ceremonies as befitted the heir to England's only marquess and one of the queen's closest relatives. Nevertheless, in 1508 he was imprisoned in the Tower of London for a suspected Yorkist conspiracy, and later transferred to a gaol in Calais; according to Hall, only the king's timely death saved him from execution. He was released following the accession of Henry VIII in 1509, but remained out of favour, being specifically exempted from the general pardon with which Henry ushered in his reign, and temporarily deprived of his title of marquess. But his disgrace did not last long, as Henry VIII decided to strengthen his ties to his aristocracy in preparation for war. Grey regained his title, and was once again a regular participant in important ceremonial occasions.

Jousting and fighting Dorset had already made a name for himself in court tournaments, having been the 'chief answerer' at the celebrations for the wedding of Prince Arthur and Katherine of Aragon in 1501. Ten years later he was a combatant at the festivities in honour of the birth of Henry and Katherine's first-born, and a mourner at the infant's funeral a month later. Thereafter he seems to have taken part in all important royal tournaments, and since Henry liked to win, was usually on the king's side. Indeed, Dorset's intimacy with the king as a jousting companion almost proved fatal to both of them, when in March 1524 Dorset handed Henry his lance for a charge before the king had lowered his visor—the unprotected king was very nearly killed. Fortunately for Dorset, Henry soon forgave his companion-in-arms.

Dorset also played a key role at state occasions. At the Field of Cloth of Gold in 1520, for example, he preceded the king, on whose orders he carried the sword of state unsheathed so as not to be upstaged by the French king. The next year he was selected to meet the emperor Charles V at Gravelines and then escort him to England. Although these occasions demanded someone of high rank, Dorset's skill at jousting was as important in the personal diplomacy of Tudor England as his high birth. Thus Dorset and the newly ennobled Charles Brandon, duke of Suffolk, were selected to escort Princess Mary to her wedding in France in 1514 because Henry wished to be well represented at the tournaments celebrating the affair. Suffolk and Dorset acquitted themselves in the lists so well that the embarrassed French secretly hired a German strongman to take their part. Fortunately the continued success of the English pair prevented an incident which might have interrupted the marriage and the peace treaty that accompanied it.

Dorset's success at individual combat did not carry over into success as a commander of armies, however. In 1512 he was appointed to command the expedition which King Henry and his father-in-law, King Ferdinand of Aragon, were planning to reconquer Guyenne, lost to England in 1453. Dorset was the ideal choice: he had the high rank considered necessary to lead troops in battle, he was personally brave and a good fighter, and he was Wolsey's protégé; but neither he nor most of his men had ever seen battle, and the expedition proved a failure. Ferdinand had no intention of keeping his pledge to join the English troops, and tried instead to get Dorset to support his own attack on Navarre. Dorset refused to break his orders, however, and while he and Ferdinand argued, his men languished in the unfamiliar heat, and their beer ran out, causing them to switch to wine. The unaccustomed drink, along with the heat, dwindling food, and inactivity, caused large numbers to fall ill, and with their pay in arrears the rest lost heart. Within months they mutinied and returned to England, carrying the desperately sick Dorset with them. To cover his duplicity, Ferdinand claimed that Dorset was solely responsible for the failure, and several of Dorset's subordinates supported him to save themselves. Fortunately for him however, the king found so many to have been at fault that the marquess did not have to endure anything worse than a show trial staged for the benefit of the Spanish ambassador. In his weakened condition, kneeling before the king proved too much for Dorset. His knees gave out and he had to beg permission to stand for the rest of the proceedings.

Dorset was to be given two more opportunities to lead troops into battle: in 1513 at the siege of Tournai and battle of the Spurs, and in 1523 on the Scottish border; but in neither case was he given a separate command. Wolsey, at least, had learned his lesson about appointing titled amateurs to high command. In 1521 the king again wanted to appoint Dorset to command an English force on the continent, claiming that troops would follow only someone of high rank. Wolsey tactfully countered that although Dorset was undoubtedly brave, his high status would make his pay and upkeep more expensive than that of a professional soldier of lower birth.

Local rivalries Dorset's public life may have been spent at court, but his interests in the provinces were equally important to him, economically as well as socially. He owned land in sixteen counties and was on the commissions of peace in five. Indeed it was his local activities that brought him closest to disgrace at court, in consequence of a long-running feud in Leicestershire with the Hastings family. This intensified in 1516, when George, Baron Hastings, and his father-in-law, Sir Richard Sacheverell, showed up at court with large retinues and Dorset, not to be outdone, promptly increased his own. This violation of the law against retaining caused Wolsey to bring both Dorset and Hastings before him in Star Chamber before turning the matter over to the court of king's bench. The pair were bound over for good behaviour and Dorset temporarily lost his seat on the council, but they continued to express their rivalry through the magnificence of their houses and their efforts to advance their respective clients.

The dispute was inflamed by Henry's and Wolsey's seeming preference for Dorset's side and by 1522 matters had reached such a pass that the king had to prohibit the wearing of either family's livery within the town of Leicester, while in the following year both families were excluded from county government. Neither side would give way, however, and when in 1524 a fight in Leicester between Dorset's cook and a client of Hastings escalated into a brawl involving hundreds, Wolsey intervened. Both rivals were made to post bond of £1000 and agree to abide by the decision of a commission. To defuse the situation further, Dorset was appointed lord master of Princess Mary's council and sent off to Wales, a position of honour, but one that would keep him away from the seat of the conflict. He was also in trouble for having insulted the king of France, and as a sign of Wolsey's further displeasure lost his place in the reorganized privy chamber. But if Dorset was in disgrace it was short-lived, for in 1528 he was appointed constable of Warwick Castle, and of Kenilworth Castle the following year, and he retained the right to lodgings at court.

The rewards of service Dorset died on 10 October 1530, and like his father was buried in Astley collegiate church, Warwickshire. He had spent most of his life at court, and after a career of hard knocks in the tiltyards as well as those from political infighting, not to mention the two bouts of sweating sickness he contracted at court, he might well have questioned whether it had been worth it. Certainly few of the posts he had held carried impressive salaries, but life for one of the king's intimates was not without its informal compensation. The diamond and ruby Tudor rose he won at the tournament in 1501 was probably one of many such trophies a skilled fighter could amass, and each of the ceremonies he so diligently took part in carried a handsome fee.

Dorset's position at court also put him in line for other payments. He enjoyed a pension of £1000 from the king of France and was so put out when it was reduced that he asked Cardinal Wolsey to intercede on his behalf. When Dorset was serving on the Anglo-Scottish borders in 1523 the council of the north wrote to enquire whether he was important enough to warrant a new year gift. No answer is recorded, but for a man with access to the king, the answer must frequently have been 'yes'. He himself wrote that his post in the north was more important to him for the prestige it carried than for the salary. Perhaps it was, as it gave him a chance to redeem himself from the débâcle of Guyenne a decade earlier. To enhance his prestige in dealing with the Scots, he was restored to the council, named gentleman of the chamber, and appointed lord warden of the marches and chief justice in eyre south of the Trent.

When Dorset succeeded his father he was considered poor for his rank because much of the family's land was still held by his mother who had inherited in her own right, and he had to be summoned to parliament in 1509 as Baron Ferrers of Groby. But his mother must have made some accommodations because two years later he was summoned as marquess, and his various diplomatic assignments would have required a considerable display of wealth. From modest beginnings he steadily accumulated offices and grants of land. In 1522 he was rewarded for his part in condemning the duke of Buckingham by receiving three of the fallen duke's manors, while the death of his mother, on 12 April 1530, a few months before his own, finally brought him his full inheritance. When he died Dorset possessed over one hundred manors. With his inheritance complete and the fruits of a lifetime of royal service, the man who was too poor to be a marquess had become very wealthy.

Assessment A final appraisal of Dorset's career and life must conclude that he was a transitional figure in the history of the peerage. By birth and temperament he was typical of the traditional aristocracy, independent, proud of his local standing (which he enhanced, according to Leland, by making significant additions to his father's house at Bradgate, Leicestershire), and jealous of rivals. Of only average height at 5 feet 8 inches tall—his remains were measured when his grave was opened in the early seventeenth century—he owed his success at court to his strength and skill as a fighter. However, Dorset was also representative of the new service nobility: he enhanced the magnificence of the court by maintaining a troupe of actors, and he was steadfastly loyal to his king. When some members of the aristocracy refused to attend the elevation of Charles Brandon as duke of Suffolk, Dorset loyally supported the king and his old friend, and in 1521 he dutifully sat in judgment on Buckingham, despite a family connection (Dorset's mother had married the duke's brother). In 1529 he was one of the principal witnesses in the king's divorce proceedings, supporting Henry's claim that Prince Arthur had consummated his marriage to Katherine. His final act of loyalty was to sign articles condemning his old mentor Cardinal Wolsey.

ROBERT C. BRADDOCK

Sources DNB · GEC, *Peerage*, 4.418–20 · *LP Henry VIII*, vols. 1–4 · J. Nichols, *The history and antiquities of the county of Leicester*, 4 vols. (1795–1815) · J. Guy, *The cardinal's court* (1977) · M. L. Robertson, 'Court careers and county quarrels: George Lord Hastings and Leicestershire unrest, 1509–1529', *State, sovereigns and society*, ed. C. Carleton and others (1998), 153–69 · S. J. Gunn, *Charles Brandon, duke of Suffolk, c.1484–1545* (1988) · C. J. Cruikshank, *Army royal* (1969) · H. Miller, *Henry VIII and the English nobility* (1986) · *The Anglica historia of Polydore Vergil, AD 1485–1537*, ed. and trans. D. Hay, CS, 3rd ser., 74 (1950) · E. Hall, *The triumphant reign of King Henry the VIII*, ed. C. Whibley, 2 vols. (1904) · T. B. Pugh, 'Henry VII and the English nobility', *The Tudor nobility*, ed. G. W. Bernard (1992), 49–110 · Emden, *Oxf.*, 2.824–5 · G. Walker, *Plays of persuasion: drama and politics at the court of Henry VIII* (1991) · *John Leland's itinerary: travels in Tudor England*, ed. J. Chandler (1993) · prerogative court of Canterbury, wills, PRO, PROB 11/24, fols. 72v–76r

Wealth at death very wealthy; estates in sixteen counties and London (over 100 manors) would have made him one of richest of peerage: H. Miller, 'The early Tudor peerage', MA diss., U. Lond.; Miller, *Henry VIII*

Grey, Thomas, fifteenth Baron Grey of Wilton (1575–1614), soldier and courtier, was born on 21 October 1575, the son and heir of Arthur *Grey, fourteenth Baron Grey of Wilton (1536–1593), lord deputy of Ireland, and his second wife, Jane Sibella (d. 1615), the widow of Edward Russell (styled Lord Russell) and the daughter of Sir Richard Morrison of Cassiobury, Hertfordshire. He was born at Whaddon, Buckinghamshire, was admitted at Gray's Inn on 12 January 1588, and matriculated from University College, Oxford on 20 March 1593, aged seventeen, succeeding to the barony on 14 October that same year upon the death of his father.

A soldier like his father, Grey saw service with the second earl of Essex in Ireland, where he was knighted at Dublin on 12 July 1599. In the previous year John Chamberlain had reported 'some snapping' between Grey and Sir Francis Vere, Grey having apparently angled for the command of English forces in the Low Countries (*Letters of John Chamberlain*, 1.49). He eventually crossed the sea to Flanders in May, and was wounded in the Anglo-Dutch victory at Nieuport on 2 July NS. Grey returned to the Low Countries in the summer of 1602: according to the reports reaching Chamberlain he 'relies wholy upon the States for his intertainment, only he hath made over goode summes of monie, which is like enough to prove but a poore bargain *spem pretio emere*' (ibid., 1.146). Again, hopes of overall command of English forces in Flanders were disappointed, and Grey came home in October, full of anger directed against Vere. This search for military preferment was sharpened by the fact that his finances were notoriously insecure: 'One Griffith a Welch pirate', wrote Chamberlain soon afterwards, 'is lately taken at Corke in Ireland and his lands which some geve out to be 500 *li* a yeare geven to the Lord Gray to hold him up a while longer' (ibid., 1.188).

Grey was one of the peers who sat in judgment on Essex and the earl of Southampton after their insurrection of 8 February 1601. Hearing Grey's name read out at the trial, Essex turned to his co-defendant, laughed, and tugged Southampton by the sleeve. Indeed, it seems that Southampton rather than Essex was the particular foe. He and Grey had come close to duelling in 1600, and their quarrel had rumbled on ever since. Early in 1601 Chamberlain tells how the two peers 'had a little bickering in the Strand on horsebacke, for the which the Lord Grey was committed to the Fleet' (*Letters of John Chamberlain*, 1.115).

Southampton could himself be difficult, but in this affair he was perhaps more sinned against than sinning. Grey was beyond question a touchy, irascible, somewhat unstable young man, prone to argument, and exhibiting strong if not particularly focused evangelical leanings. An old family servant, Walter Fitzwilliams, remembered his piety and promise in a memoir of the early 1650s (Bodl. Oxf., MS Carte 80, fol. 618; MS 125, fol. 87), but it must be borne in mind that this partial document was submitted as evidence for a lawsuit in which Grey was deliberately portrayed as the victim of Stuart injustice. In Fitzwilliams's account Grey looked askance at the Stuart succession, most probably because he distrusted all things Scottish and took no pains to conceal the fact. Participating in the debates of the so-called 'great council', which met in March and April 1603 to manage the transition of power, Grey demanded the imposition of terms on England's new king, before very reluctantly accepting the majority view that a conditional offer was legally and constitutionally indefensible. So crass a misjudgement of the times was compounded when he again brawled with Southampton, newly released from the Tower, in Queen Anne's presence in June 1603. This fracas left James—who chose to regard both Essex and Southampton as martyrs for his cause—in no doubt where Grey's sympathies lay. The quarrel was patched up, but superficial courtesies in no way mollified the enraged Grey, who continued to highlight the contrast between 'Sowthamtons grace and his disgrace', and to bemoan the fact that Robert Cecil had (entirely understandably) 'forsaken him'.

Grey's prospects were hardly improved by the company he kept. He discussed developments with Sir Walter Ralegh and Lord Cobham, speaking, as his fellow conspirator George Brooke later put it, 'nothing but treason at every worde' (PRO, SP 14/3/28). While he opposed any relaxation of Catholic persecution, he was prepared to make common cause with Catholics, such as Sir Griffin Markham and the priest William Watson, who feared what they perceived to be an increasing Jesuit influence in English Catholic circles and who shared Grey's conviction that the king's authority ought in some way to be constrained. Through the protestant Brooke, Cobham's brother, Grey was drawn into Markham's and Watson's so-called Bye plot, a fatuous scheme which aimed to kidnap the king and hold him prisoner against guarantees of Catholic toleration and the removal of senior ministers. As a military man he was seen as a very desirable recruit. According to later depositions by both Brooke and Markham, Grey agreed to lead a force of 100 men under colour of presenting James with a petition outlining 'inconveniences' likely to develop in England. He pledged support drawn from among discontented soldiers in the Low Countries.

This, however, was all nothing more than fantasy. At the last minute Grey awoke to the fact that he was supporting a Catholic action against a protestant king. Having implicated himself irrevocably in treason he now declined to act, excusing himself by maintaining that, were he ever to receive a major military command, he would have the forces to carry through his own schemes. The premise seemed then and seems now distinctly optimistic. Not that he entirely ruled out concerted action with the Catholics, provided that they were patient, and awaited his move. 'Till then attend,' he is said to have told Markham, 'for you knowe all things must have theyr opportunitie' (Nicholls, 'Two Winchester trials', 31).

Inevitably this treason without means promptly unravelled. Grey was implicated very early on, and was detained for questioning on 14 July 1603. Four days later, as the evidence against him grew ever more conclusive, he was moved to the Tower. Writing to his mother on 3 August, he fell back on the lame excuse that, despite appearances, he had really been working against the Catholic enterprise, hoping through stealth to achieve a 'full discovery of all their designes' (Bodl. Oxf., MS Carte 80, fol. 606).

Grey was tried at Winchester on 26 November 1603. He was anything but contrite. The puritan minister within him coming to the fore, he made a two-hour speech during which he warned commissioners, judges, and prosecuting counsel in turn that God was watching them, and would observe any attempts at 'foule wresting … all probability of the law'. Just the same, Grey told his judges that he expected no fair trial. 'We are all men,' he said, 'and princes favoures as showres on the springing grasse' (Bodl. Oxf., MS Carte 77, fols. 77–78v). He readily admitted that he had intended to deliver a petition to the king, and that he had planned to do so backed by a quasi-military force on the practical grounds that individuals who embarked on such enterprises without backing of some kind or another were never likely to secure the king's ear. But he denied any participation in the Bye plot itself, insisting that he had remained in contact with his Catholic associates only in order to betray them when the moment seemed right. Sir Edward Coke, answering him point by point, dismantled his defence with precision. In a reference to the recent trial of Sir Walter Ralegh, he advised Grey not to 'use shifts, for they had not served the other day the master of shifts' (Stow, 830).

Grey's long-winded self-justifications were considered inappropriate by some observers, but even so his fellow noblemen were, according to Dudley Carleton, 'long ere they could all agree and loth to come out with so hard censure against him' (Bodl. Oxf., MS Carte 80, fol. 622v). By the standards of his age the evidence against Grey was clear-cut, so this hesitation is surprising. It may be explained by Grey's known instability, or perhaps by his dignity at the bar. Whatever the reason, this grudging sympathy is reflected in Cecil's account of the treason sent to ambassadors abroad (PRO, SP 84/64, fol. 78v).

Condemned to death, Grey, like Markham and Cobham, was pardoned on the scaffold. He spent the rest of his life a prisoner in the Tower. When the young prince palatine of the Rhine begged his release of James I in 1613, the king refused to consider the matter, abruptly informing his son-in-law that he undertook never to solicit the liberty of prisoners in Germany. Grey died on 9 July 1614. He was unmarried, and without a male heir. Subject to the attainder, his barony fell into abeyance between his two sisters—Elizabeth, Arthur Grey's daughter by his first marriage to Dorothy, illegitimate daughter of Richard, Lord Zouche, and Bridget, another child of the second marriage, who married Sir Rowland Egerton. Their descendant, Sir Thomas Egerton, baronet, was created Baron Grey of Wilton in 1784.   MARK NICHOLLS

Sources Bodl. Oxf., MSS Carte · PRO, SP 14; SP 84 · Hatfield House, Hertfordshire, Salisbury–Cecil MSS · Foster, *Alum. Oxon.* · GEC, *Peerage* · *The letters of John Chamberlain*, ed. N. E. McClure, 2 vols. (1939) · M. Nicholls, 'Two Winchester trials: the prosecution of Henry, Lord Cobham, and Thomas, Lord Grey of Wilton, 1603', *Historical Research*, 68 (1995), 26–48 · M. Nicholls, 'Sir Walter Ralegh's treason: a prosecution document', *EngHR*, 110 (1995), 902–24 · 'The journal of Levinus Munck', ed. H. V. Jones, *EngHR*, 68 (1953), 234–58 · J. Stow and E. Howes, *Annales, or, A generall chronicle of England ... unto the end of this present yeere, 1631* (1631)
Archives Hatfield House, Hertfordshire, letters and MSS · Northants. RO, MSS regarding conspiracy | Bodl. Oxf., MSS Carte · PRO, state papers

Grey, Thomas, Baron Grey of Groby (1622–1657), regicide, was the eldest son of Henry *Grey (*c.*1599–1673), second Baron Grey of Groby, created first earl of Stamford in 1628, and his wife, Lady Anne Cecil (*c.*1603–1676), daughter of William Cecil, earl of Exeter. Nothing is known of Thomas's early life or education and his admission on 16 March 1641 to Gray's Inn was probably honorary. Contrary to the wishes of the borough's principal electoral patron, the chancellor of the duchy of Lancaster, and at the behest of his staunchly puritan father, Thomas, called by his father's first title, was elected to the Long Parliament by the voters of Leicester, and is mentioned in 1642 as 'a lord dear to the House of Commons' (*CSP dom.*, 1641–3, 359). He supported the grand remonstrance (1641) and joined with his father against the king.

Having fought at Edgehill in Sir William Balfour's regiment, Grey was appointed commander-in-chief of the midland counties association on 16 January 1643, and ordered to take special care of Nottingham, where in June he took up his headquarters with a force of about 6000 men. From there he was able to protect his father's house at Stamford, near Leicester, of which town he was made governor. His colours show a circle of hand-held daggers with a drawing of the Commons in session inside the circle, with the motto *Per bellum ad pacem* ('Achieve peace through war'). On 29 August he joined the earl of Essex at Aylesbury on his march to relieve Gloucester, and after the siege was raised he fought at the first battle of Newbury. Grey and others received the thanks of the house, which were solemnly entered in the journals. In 1644 he again received the thanks of the parliament, for the reduction of some places in Derbyshire. Shortly afterwards, however, he left Leicester on account of a bitter quarrel with Sir Arthur Hesilrige, one of the shire MPs. In 1645 the town petitioned that he might be sent back to meet a royalist attack. In the meantime it was taken by the king on 1 June and afterwards retaken by Sir Thomas Fairfax.

In 1648 Grey raised a body of troops in Leicestershire,

Thomas Grey, Baron Grey of Groby (1622–1657), attrib. Robert Walker

and after the defeat of the Scots at Preston pursued the duke of Hamilton and his horse to Uttoxeter. Grey claimed the credit of Hamilton's capture, and though Hamilton declared himself to have surrendered to Lambert, parliament admitted Grey's claim and voted him their thanks.

Having been aligned with the New Model Army since 1647, when he joined the attack on the eleven members, and in November delivered a petition from agitators to the Commons, Grey took an active part in Pride's Purge on 6 December 1648, pointing out the obnoxious members who were to be ejected from the house. He was one of the king's judges, and on 14 February 1649 signed the death warrant, afterwards being nominated one of the council of state [*see also* Regicides]. Around this time, his name was touted as a possible successor to Fairfax, as commander-in-chief of the parliamentarian armies, a suggestion widely supported by City radicals and the 'honest party', yet lacking in realistic substance. Having asserted a claim over the treatment of the duke of Hamilton in the summer of 1648, Grey now declined to interfere in the judicial proceedings which led to the Scotsman's death on the scaffold in New Palace Yard on 9 March 1649. In July 1649 the money Grey had spent in the parliamentary service was refunded.

Three years earlier, by licence dated 4 June 1646, Grey had married Lady Dorothy Bourchier (*bap.* 1626, *d.* in or after 1660), second daughter and coheir of Edward Bourchier, fourth earl of Bath, and his first wife, Dorothy St John. However, attempts to reconstruct his finances, not all of them honest, comprise one of the principal themes of Grey's career after the regicide. His public role in diplomatic and especially military affairs, was equally prominent. He held various commands in the militia, and in August 1651 he was sent to raise volunteers, with the commission of commander-in-chief of all the horse he should raise in the counties of Leicester, Nottingham, Northampton, and Rutland to meet the Scottish invasion.

In September, after the battle of Worcester, Massey surrendered to Grey's grandmother. Dropped from the fourth council of state in November 1651, Grey was re-elected in 1652, well down the poll, receiving the votes of forty-nine of his fellow MPs. He represented Leicestershire in the parliament of 1654. Finally he joined the Fifth Monarchy Men, and was on 12 February 1655 arrested on suspicion of complicity in John Wildman's plot by Colonel Francis Hacker, acting on the protector's orders, and though afflicted by gout, was taken a prisoner to Windsor Castle. He was released in July following an application to the protector.

From this time until his death between 4 April 1657 (when he signed his will) and 8 May 1657 (when it was proved) Grey took no active part in politics. Since he was the only eldest son of a peer to sign the king's death warrant Clarendon reserved for him the particular opprobrium he was wont to apply to members of the aristocracy who had 'traitored' themselves, unfairly describing Groby as a man of no eminent parts, but useful on account of his wealth and local influence. Lucy Hutchinson spoke of his 'credulous good nature'; and he seems to have been a favourite of Essex.

Grey's widow subsequently married Gustavus Mackworth, who participated in Booth's rising and was killed in Cheshire in August 1659; she was living on 4 June 1660. Their only son, Thomas *Grey (1653/4–1720), succeeded his grandfather in 1673 as second earl of Stamford.

E. T. Bradley, rev. Sean Kelsey

Sources GEC, *Peerage* • B. Worden, *The Rump Parliament, 1648–1653* (1974) • D. Fleming, 'Faction and civil war in Leicestershire', *Transactions of the Leicestershire Archaeological and Historical Society*, 57 (1983), 26–36 [1983 for 1981] • S. Barber, '"A bastard kind of militia", localism and tactics in the second civil war', *Soldiers, writers and statesmen of the English revolution*, ed. I. Gentles, J. Morrill, and B. Worden (1998) • J. Richards, *Aristocrat and regicide: the life and times of Thomas, Lord Grey of Groby, the ermine unicorn* (2000) • DWL, Modern MS Folro 7, fol. 8 • *CSP dom., 1641–55* • R. Spencer to R. Browne, 11 Nov 1647, Christ Church Oxf., Browne Letters R–W • will, PRO, PROB 11/263, sig. 151
Likenesses attrib. R. Walker, portrait, priv. coll. [*see illus.*] • portrait, Newham Paddox, Warwickshire
Wealth at death devised up to £1000 for each of his four daughters and land worth £500 p.a. to son and heir: will, PRO, PROB 11/263, sig. 151, fols. 377v–378r

Grey, Thomas, second earl of Stamford (1653/4–1720), conspirator and politician, was the only son of Thomas *Grey, Baron Grey of Groby (1622–1657), and Lady Dorothy Bourchier (*bap.* 1626, *d.* in or after 1660), daughter of Edward Bourchier, fourth earl of Bath. From his father's death until he succeeded to the earldom following the death of his grandfather, Henry *Grey, first earl of Stamford, on 21 August 1673, he was called Lord Grey of Groby. Grey matriculated at Christ Church, Oxford, on 1

July 1667, aged thirteen, and graduated MA on 23 June 1668. Some time between 21 August 1673 and 13 April 1675 he married Elizabeth Harvey (*c.*1657–1687), daughter of Sir Daniel Harvey of Combe, Surrey, and Elizabeth Montagu, daughter of Edward *Montagu, second Baron Montagu [*see under* Montagu, Edward]. Her portion was reportedly £10,000.

Stamford took his seat in the Lords on 13 April 1675 and from the outset allied with the country, opposing the Test Bill in 1675, manifesting sympathy with Buckingham in February 1677 when the duke argued that the fifteen-month prorogation had legally dissolved parliament, and, with fifteen other peers, petitioning Charles in December 1679 that parliament convene the following month. In the fiercely contested London shrieval election in 1682, Stamford, Ford, Lord Grey of Warke, and Sir Thomas Armstrong were suspected of fomenting popular unrest. By this point Grey and Armstrong were contemplating a general uprising with Monmouth and Shaftesbury to preserve the protestant succession. Colonel John Rumsey (to whom Stamford provided an annuity of £150 p.a. at a cost of £1200 or £1300) would later confess that he had informed Stamford of these discussions as early as the summer of 1681. After the insurrection, scheduled for November 1682, was postponed, Rumsey and Richard Goodenough allegedly kept Stamford apprised of continuing talks. When Monmouth visited Chichester in February 1683, Stamford and Grey attended him. When Scottish dissidents travelled to London that spring to discuss the possibility of mounting co-ordinated uprisings, Stamford learned of their visit from Rumsey and reputedly promised to raise 1500–3000 men. According to Goodenough's confession, he met with Stamford and Rumsey in the latter part of May, at which time the earl again pledged to support the proposed insurrection. When he was interrogated in 1685, Stamford denied complicity in the plotting, though Rumsey and Goodenough confessed otherwise. Following Josiah Keeling's disclosure of the Rye House plotting, the government issued warrants for the apprehension of Stamford and Grey on 26 June. Few weapons were found when the earl's house was searched, but he had reportedly concealed most of them between two large ovens. The state filed no charges against Stamford at this time, and in October 1683 he was promoting a candidate for burgess at Leicester.

Stamford remained loyal to his whig principles when James became king. In May 1685 he protested against reversing the impeachment of the lords incarcerated in the Tower for suspected involvement in the Popish Plot, and in June he opposed the bill to reverse Viscount Stafford's attainder. With the capture of Goodenough after the battle of Sedgemoor, the government had the necessary two witnesses to prosecute Stamford, Rumsey having turned state's evidence in 1683. Imprisoned in the Tower in July, Stamford successfully petitioned to appear at the bar of the House of Lords in November, when he sought his trial or release. The Lords set 1 December for the trial, but the prorogation prevented it, and Stamford received a pardon in April 1686. He was present at the trial of the seven bishops in June 1688.

When William invaded in November 1688, Stamford joined him at Hungerford with several hundred men. The earl's reward was the high stewardship of the honour of Leicester (8 April 1689). The same year he sat on the committee to investigate the deaths of the earl of Essex and Algernon Sidney. He was considered for, but not given, the lord lieutenancy of Middlesex in November 1691 and a lordship of the Treasury in April 1694. Appointed to the privy council in May 1694, Stamford, still a whig, became commissioner of Greenwich Hospital (August 1695), commissioner of trade and foreign plantations (December 1695 to May 1696), lord lieutenant of Devon (April 1696), *custos rotulorum* for Leicestershire (December 1696), chancellor of the duchy of Lancaster (April 1697), and first lord of trade and foreign plantations (June 1699). An energetic and capable member of the Board of Trade, he opposed proprietary colonies as contrary to the interests of the crown and the realm. Stamford played a key role in passing the Piracy Bill (1700), insisting on a provision that proprietary and charter colonies that defied the act would forfeit their charters. Anne dismissed Stamford from his offices in 1702, though he returned to serve as first lord of the Board of Trade from April 1707 to June 1711, effectively co-ordinating its work with the House of Lords and privy council. In the summer of 1702 Stamford went to Zell and Hanover to visit the elector George and the electress Sophia, to whom he gave copies of the Book of Common Prayer inscribed with her name. He was nevertheless chary of clerical power, and his membership in the New England Company provided an opportunity to work closely with protestant nonconformists. He was elected a fellow of the Royal Society on 12 May 1708. A lavish spender and poor manager of his estate, he was in financial straits by 1711–12, when Marlborough and his whig friends twice urged the elector to pension him and other 'poor' peers. Stamford's first wife, from whom he had become estranged, was buried on 7 September 1687. In March 1691 he married Mary Maynard (d. November 1722), daughter of Joseph Maynard of Gunnersbury, Middlesex. From his first marriage, Stamford had three children, all of whom died in infancy; he had no children by his second marriage. Following his death on 31 January 1720, Stamford was buried at Bradgate, Leicestershire. His will, dated 10 September 1719, was proved on 11 February 1720 and again on 16 January 1731. In it he provided for payments in excess of £2500, and he bequeathed most of his estate, including property in Leicestershire, Lincolnshire, Derbyshire, and Northamptonshire, to his wife. Stamford's title passed to his cousin Henry, the first earl's grandson.   RICHARD L. GREAVES

Sources PRO, SP 29/422, 428, 433 · BL, Lansdowne MS 1152 · GEC, *Peerage* · [T. Sprat], *Copies of the informations and original papers relating to the proof of the horrid conspiracy against the late king, his present majesty and the government*, 3rd edn (1685) · N. Luttrell, *A brief historical relation of state affairs from September 1678 to April 1714*, 6 vols. (1857) · R. L. Greaves, *Secrets of the kingdom: British radicals from the Popish Plot to the revolution of 1688–89* (1992) · *JHL*, 14 (1685–91) · *Seventh report*, HMC, 6 (1879) · *The manuscripts of his grace the duke of Portland*, 10 vols., HMC, 29 (1891–1931), vol. 4 · *CSP dom.*, 1683–5 · E. Gregg and C. Jones, 'Hanover, Pensions and the "Poor Lords"', *Peers, politics and power: the House of Lords, 1603–1911*, ed. C. Jones and D. L. Jones (1986), 177–84 · A. Swatland, *The House of Lords in the reign of Charles II* (1996) · I. K. Steele, *Politics of colonial policy: the board of trade in colonial administration, 1696–1720* (1968) · PRO, PROB 11/573, fol. 6r–v

Archives JRL, family and estate papers · Leics. RO, deeds and estate papers | BL, Lansdowne MS 1152 · PRO, state papers domestic, SP 29/422, 428, 433

Wealth at death debts of more than £2500; property in Leicestershire, Lincolnshire, Derbyshire, and Northamptonshire: will, PRO, PROB 11/573, fol. 6r–v

Grey, Thomas de, second Baron Walsingham (1748–1818), politician, was born on 14 July 1748 and baptized on the 17th at St Clement Danes, Westminster, the second but only surviving son of William de *Grey, first Baron Walsingham (1719–1781), chief justice of common pleas, and Mary (*bap.* 1719, *d.* 1800), daughter of William Cowper (c.1689–1740), clerk of the parliaments. He was educated at Eton College from 1760 to 1765, was admitted to the Middle Temple on 24 August 1764, and in 1766 became a fellow commoner of Trinity Hall, Cambridge, taking his BA degree in 1769. In 1770–71 he travelled in France, Italy, and Germany, on the grand tour. In May 1771 George III appointed him a groom of the bedchamber and it was probably that year that his father, having become a judge, resigned to him the sinecure office of comptroller of first fruits and tenths. On 30 April 1772 he married, at her father's house in Lower Grosvenor Street, Westminster, the Hon. Augusta Georgina Elizabeth Irby (1747–1818), daughter of William, first Baron Boston, chamberlain to the princess dowager of Wales, and his wife, Albinia Selwyn; they had two sons and two daughters.

Like many of his immediate ancestors, de Grey entered parliament, sitting for Wareham from January to September 1774 and being returned for Tamworth at the general election later that year. He seconded the address of thanks for the speech from the throne on 5 December 1774 and thereafter spoke occasionally in support of Lord North's ministry. In July 1777 he became a lord of trade and from January 1778 to October 1780 he additionally served as an earnest under-secretary to the secretary of state for the colonies, George Germain. Having transferred to Lostwithiel at the 1780 election, he again seconded the address on 6 November. In December that year the king thought him an unsuitable candidate for the position of vice-chamberlain to the queen, remarking that 'his manner is certainly not quite genteel and from his hurry he might fill the office but awkwardly' (*Later Correspondence of George III*, 5.172).

On the death on 9 May 1781 of his father, who had been awarded a peerage in the previous year, de Grey succeeded as second Baron Walsingham, and he took his seat in the Lords on 21 May. In the following month he inherited the family's ancestral estates at Merton Hall, near Thetford in Norfolk, from his uncle and namesake, who had been MP for Norfolk (1764–74). On 27 November 1781 he seconded the address, urging continuation of the war against the

American colonies' European allies, and by the end of the year he had tardily relinquished his junior ministerial salary. He spoke and voted against Lord Shelburne's peace preliminaries on 17 February 1783 and Fox's India Bill on 17 December 1783, and thereafter supported Pitt's administration. On 31 December 1783 he was sworn of the privy council, which he attended frequently; he was both a friend and a near neighbour (at Leather Lake House, Old Windsor) of the king. In March 1784 he became a member of the privy council committee for trade and plantations and was appointed joint vice-treasurer of Ireland. In that year he also joined the India board (serving until 1791) and, a frequent speaker on departmental matters in the Lords, he seconded the address in January 1785 (as he did in December 1792 and October 1795). In July 1787, having given up all but one of his other offices and declining to be named ambassador to Spain, he became joint postmaster-general, in which capacity he proved himself to be a diligent and reforming administrator. He sided with ministers during the regency crisis in 1789 and on 13 April 1795 spoke in defence of Warren Hastings, whom he voted not guilty on all but one of the impeachment charges ten days later.

Walsingham, whose family had several connections with the parliament office and with the management of the upper chamber, seems to have long coveted the office of chairman of committees in the Lords. A procedural expert, he hoped to replace Lord Scarsdale in July 1783 and, having served an apprenticeship as one of his deputies (notably in the 1784 session), was presumably disappointed to be passed over on Scarsdale's retirement in 1789. It was not until late in 1794 that Pitt, as part of a government reshuffle, gave him the post, which carried a salary of £1500, and provided a pension of £1200 in favour of his sons as compensation for giving up the higher remuneration of the postmastership.

Building no doubt on the initiatives of his legally trained predecessor Lord Cathcart and the general climate of parliamentary improvements which brought about many procedural refinements in the 1790s, Walsingham rapidly established an absolute ascendancy in the management of committee business. This was probably made easier by the fact that the most senior official in the chamber was his first cousin Henry Cowper, the clerk assistant. Within a few years he was chairing all but a handful of grand (of the whole house) and select (private bill) committees, which had the effect of ensuring that private parties could no longer secure the passage of self-interested legislation. Such was the assiduity and rigour with which he handled the committee stage of bills that it became common practice for those supervising legislative measures to seek his prior approval of them. Indeed, perhaps because of the absence of a Commons counterpart, this extended also to the lower house and in May 1796 he observed that 'they Send to me all private Bills whilst they are in the H^e. Comm^s., that I may suggest any alterations I think fit, lest such alterations should lose the Bill in the Comm^ee of the Lords' (BL, Add. MS 38231, fol. 31).

Largely at Walsingham's suggestion, and reflecting his concern for what he privately and publicly termed the increasing 'weight of property' requiring legislative consideration (BL, Add. MS 58935, fols. 151-2), his office was for the first time placed on a formal footing by resolution of the house on 23 July 1800, and his salary was raised to £2500 per annum. He had a formidable reputation, not least for the inflexibility with which he applied his *de facto* policy of standardization in the drafting of statutes. He also attracted adverse criticism; a typical comment was Francis Horner's (in relation to the Scottish Schoolmasters Bill of 1807) that Walsingham 'is more strict than intelligent, and gives unnecessary vexation' (Horner, 464). Nevertheless, on his retirement on the grounds of ill health in November 1814, the House of Lords voted him a unanimous address of thanks, which praised his 'Ability, Integrity, Impartiality and indefatigable Industry' (*JHL*, 50.8), and recognized his enormous personal contribution, over a period of twenty years, to the process of scrutinizing—particularly private—legislation. He was granted a pension of £2000 a year.

Walsingham, who in later life suffered badly from gout, died at Old Windsor on 16 January 1818 and was buried at Merton on the 30th. He was succeeded in his titles and estates by his two sons in turn: Lieutenant-General George de Grey, third Baron Walsingham (1776–1831), who died with his wife in a fire at the family's London town house at 30 Upper Grosvenor Street, and the Revd Thomas de Grey, fourth Baron Walsingham (1778–1839), who was archdeacon of Surrey.   S. M. FARRELL

Sources Norfolk RO, Walsingham (Merton) papers, esp. 16, 48, 56, 57, 67, 50 · BL, Liverpool MSS, MS 38231, fol. 31 · BL, Grenville MSS, MS 58935 · J. C. Sainty, *The origin of the office of chairman of committees in the House of Lords* (1974) · M. W. McCahill, *Order and equipoise: the peerage and the House of Lords, 1783–1806* (1978) · M. W. McCahill, 'Sir Edward Stracey: counsel to the chairman of the committees, 1804–33', *Parliamentary History*, 8 (1989), 125–31 · Hansard 1 · J. Debrett, ed., *The parliamentary register, or, History of the proceedings and debates of the House of Commons*, 45 vols. (1781–96), 42.372–8, 403 · J. Debrett, ed., *The parliamentary register, or, History of the proceedings and debates of the House of Commons*, 18 vols. (1797–1802), vol. 12, pp. 475–7 · *JHL*, 42 (1798–1800), 636; 50 (1814–16), 8 · *The later correspondence of George III*, ed. A. Aspinall, 5 vols. (1962–70), 5.172 · *The Horner papers: selections from the letters and miscellaneous writings of Francis Horner, MP, 1795–1817*, ed. K. Bourne and W. B. Taylor (1994), 464 · *Norfolk Chronicle and Norwich Gazette* (24 Jan 1818) · *GM*, 1st ser., 88/1 (1818), 80–81

Archives Norfolk RO, corresp. and papers · Norfolk RO, reports on North American and West Indian Colonies | BL, corresp. with Lord Grenville, Add. MS 58935 · BL, letters to General Haldimand, Add. MSS 21706–21707, 21732, 21736–21737 · BL, corresp. with first earl of Liverpool, Add. MSS 38212–38248, *passim*, 38282, 38307, 38310, 38471 · Norfolk RO, Walsingham (Merton) MSS · Post Office Archives, London, official papers, POST 97 [copies] · PRO, letters to William Pitt, PRO 30/8

Likenesses medallion, Wedgwood Museum, Stoke-on-Trent

Wealth at death under £200,000: PRO, death duty registers, IR 26/765/99

Grey, Thomas de, sixth Baron Walsingham (1843–1919), politician and entomologist, was born on 29 July 1843 at Stanhope Street, Mayfair, Westminster, the only child of Thomas de Grey, fifth Baron Walsingham (1804–1870), and his first wife, Augusta Louisa (*d.* 1844), daughter and coheir of Sir Robert Frankland Russell, baronet. At the age of nine he was sent to a private school kept by a Revd Goldney in Southborough, near Tunbridge Wells, and from 1856 to 1860 he attended Eton College. He matriculated at Trinity College, Cambridge, in 1861, graduating BA in 1865 and MA in 1870.

In 1865 de Grey was elected as Conservative MP for West Norfolk; he served until 31 December 1870, when he succeeded his father, becoming sixth Baron Walsingham. In 1874–5 he was lord-in-waiting to Queen Victoria. He was a trustee of the British Museum (from 1876), the Royal College of Surgeons' Hunterian Museum, and the Lawes Agricultural Trust. In 1877 he married Augusta Selina Elizabeth (Leila; d. 1906), the divorced wife of the duke of Santo Teodoro and daughter of Captain William Locke of Norbury; she had been left a widow from her first marriage to Ernest Fitzroy Neville Fane, Lord Burghersh.

De Grey was early a keen amateur entomologist—at the age of eight he recorded having 'just found out that the catipillars hind feete are different to its frount ones' (Durrant, 27). His first scientific paper was published in 1867 in the *Entomologist's Monthly Magazine*, and in 1870–71 he visited California and Oregon on a sporting and collecting tour. On this and subsequent tours of southern Europe, the Caribbean, and north Africa he collected more than 50,000 specimens of microlepidoptera, becoming a recognized expert on these insects. He identified many species new to science and, by rearing insects in captivity, elucidated many life cycles. Walsingham's collection ultimately included the preserved larvae of many species and was further enlarged by the purchase of the collections of others. The complete collection, together with his library, passed to the British Museum in 1910.

Walsingham was elected FRS in 1887. He was president of the Entomological Society in 1889–90 and between 1893 and 1912 was an editor of the *Entomologist's Monthly Magazine*. In 1891 he became high steward of the University of Cambridge (and was awarded an honorary LLD); from 1894 he was also high steward of the borough of King's Lynn. Following the death of his first wife he married, in 1909, Marion Gwytherne-Williams (d. 1913), daughter of Thomas Rhys Withers. On 12 November 1914 he married Agnes Baird (d. 1926), widow of Richard Dawson and daughter of Frederick Shand Hemming.

A keen sportsman, Walsingham was considered 'one of the best shots in England' (Venn, *Alum. Cant.*). Indeed, his *Who's Who* entry boasted that 'his bag of 1070 grouse [in 14 hours and 18 minutes] … has never been surpassed'. He contributed articles on partridge, pheasant, and grouse to the Badminton Library. A good cricketer, he played for the university team and, later, in the Gentlemen v. Players matches. A kind and generous man, Walsingham died of heart failure following pleurisy in a Hampstead nursing home on 3 December 1919. He was buried at Merton, Thetford, on 7 December. He had no children, and was succeeded by his half-brother, the Hon. John Augustus de Grey. **K. G. V. Smith**

Sources E. O. Essig, *Pan-Pacific Entomologist*, 17 (1941), 97–113 • J. H. Durrant, 'Lord Walsingham, 1843–1919', *Entomologist's Monthly Magazine*, 56 (1920), 25–8 • H. Rowland-Brown, *The Entomologist*, 53 (1920), 23–4 • E. O. Essig, *A history of entomology* (1931), 791–2 • A. Busck, *Proceedings of the Entomological Society of Washington*, 22 (1920), 41–3 [obit. notice] • A. Musgrave, *Bibliography of Australian entomology, 1775–1930* (1932) • S. A. Neave, *The centenary history of the Entomological Society of London, 1833–1933* (1933), 149–50 • *Entomological News*, 31 (1920), 148–9 • *Nature*, 104 (1919–20), 376

Archives NHM • Norfolk RO, corresp. and papers | NHM, letters to Albert Gunther and R. W. T. Gunther • Norfolk RO, letters to W. M. R. Haggard • Oxf. U. Mus. NH, letters to Sir E. B. Poulton

Likenesses T. Chartran, caricature, watercolour study, NPG; repro. in *VF* (9 Sept 1882) • cartoon, repro. in *Vanity Fair Album*, 14 (1882), 409 • photograph, repro. in Durrant, 'Lord Walsingham', facing p. 17 • portrait, repro. in *Bailey's Magazine*, 56 (1891), 145 • portrait, repro. in Essig, *Pan-Pacific Entomologist* • portrait, repro. in Essig, *History of entomology*

Grey, Thomas Philip de [*formerly* Thomas Philip Robinson; Thomas Philip Weddell], **second Earl De Grey** (1781–1859), politician, was the elder son of Thomas *Robinson, second Baron Grantham (b. 1738), who died in 1786, and his wife, Mary Jemima Grey (1757–1830), second daughter of Philip Yorke, second earl of Hardwicke. He was born at the official residence of the first lord of the Board of Trade, Whitehall, London, on 8 December 1781, and educated at St John's College, Cambridge, where he graduated MA in 1801. On 20 July 1786 he succeeded his father as third Baron Grantham of Grantham, and on the death of his second cousin, Sir Norton Robinson, bt, in 1792 he became the sixth baronet. By royal licence he assumed the surname and arms of Weddell in lieu of his patronymic on 7 May 1803. On 6 December 1803 he was gazetted major of the North Yorkshire regiment of yeomanry, and on 22 January 1819 became colonel of the Yorkshire hussar regiment of yeomanry; on 24 March 1831 he was appointed yeomanry aide-de-camp to William IV, and held a similar post in 1837 under Queen Victoria. He was nominated lord lieutenant of Bedfordshire on 13 February 1818. On the death of his maternal aunt, Amabel Hume-Campbell, Countess De Grey of Wrest, Bedfordshire, on 4 May 1833, he became second Earl De Grey and Baron Lucas of Crudwell, Wiltshire, and on 24 June 1833 assumed the surname of de Grey in lieu of Weddell.

De Grey was a moderate tory, supporting Catholic emancipation in the 1820s and voting with the whigs in 1820 over the Queen Caroline affair. In Sir Robert Peel's first administration he was first lord of the Admiralty from 22 December 1834 to 25 April 1835, being sworn of the privy council on 29 December 1834. He reluctantly agreed to become lord lieutenant of Ireland on 3 September 1841.

As lord lieutenant, De Grey's tory views hardened, perhaps under the influence of his wife, whose brother was a leading Orangeman. He was very reluctant to appoint Roman Catholics, he opposed the national education system, and deplored what he saw as any concessions to the repeal movement. He quarrelled with Lord Eliot, the liberally minded Irish secretary. On 26 July 1844 he resigned for reasons of ill health, thereafter playing little part in politics. He then wrote a life of Sir Charles Lucas (1845) and *Characteristics of the Duke of Wellington apart from his Military Talents* (1853).

De Grey was the first president of the Institution of British Architects from its foundation in 1834, frequently presided at the meetings of that society, and remained president until his death (*Papers of Royal Institution of British Architects*, 1860, pp. v–viii). He was also elected a fellow of the Royal Society on 29 April 1841, and of the Society of Antiquaries, and served as one of the New Palace commissioners from 1848. He married, on 20 July 1805, Henrietta Frances Cole, fifth daughter of William Willoughby, first earl of Enniskillen; they had two daughters. Lady De Grey was born on 22 June 1784, and died at 4 St James's Square, London, on 2 July 1848. Lady Granville noted that the 'men treat her with the sort of homage one hears was shown to Lady Coventry … The admiration she excites is quite curious' (GEC, *Peerage*). Lord De Grey died at 4 St James's Square, London, on 14 November 1859. His heir was his nephew, G. F. S. *Robinson, later first marquess of Ripon.

G. C. BOASE, rev. H. C. G. MATTHEW

Sources *The Times* (15 Nov 1859) · *GM*, 3rd ser., 7 (1859), 644 · GEC, *Peerage* · D. A. Kerr, *Peel, priests, and politics: Sir Robert Peel's administration and the Roman Catholic church in Ireland, 1841–1846* (1982)
Archives Beds. & Luton ARS, corresp. and papers · W. Yorks. AS, Leeds, family and estate corresp. and papers | BL, corresp. with Sir Robert Peel, Add. MSS 40477–40478 · Durham RO, corresp. with Sir James Graham · Lpool RO, letters to Lord Stanley · U. Southampton L., letters to first duke of Wellington · W. Yorks. AS, Leeds, Vyner MSS
Likenesses H. W. Pickersgill, oils, 1826, United Service Club, London · F. Grant, oils, 1849, York City Art Gallery · G. Haylter, group portrait, oils (*The trial of Queen Caroline, 1820*), NPG · M. Noble, effigy, De Grey Mausoleum, Flitton · S. W. Reynolds, group portrait, mezzotint (after J. Reynolds), BM · W. Robinson, portrait, repro. in J. E. Doyle, *The official baronage of England* (1886), vol. 1, p. 523 · J. Wood, oils (after W. Robinson), RIBA · portrait, repro. in *ILN* (25 Feb 1842), 146 · portrait, repro. in *ILN* (13 Jan 1844), 22, 24
Wealth at death under £100,000: probate, 25 June 1860, *CGPLA Eng. & Wales*

Grey, Walter de. See Gray, Walter de (d. 1255).

Grey [Gray], **William** (*c*.1414–1478), bishop of Ely, was the son of Sir Thomas Grey of Heaton, Northumberland, beheaded for his part in the 'Southampton plot' of 1415. He was very well connected; his mother, Alice, was daughter of Ralph Neville, earl of Westmorland (d. 1425), his maternal uncle was Humphrey Stafford, duke of Buckingham (d. 1460). Grey's copy of Higden's *Polychronicon* (Oxford, Balliol College, MS 236), is annotated 'ex dono ducis Bokynghamie avunculi'. On his father's side a namesake, successively bishop of London and Lincoln, was his uncle. It was he who ordained him acolyte, subdeacon, and deacon during 1434. Three years later he was ordained priest by another uncle, Robert Neville, bishop of Salisbury (d. 1457).

A wealthy man and notable pluralist, at the time of his promotion to the episcopate Grey held the archdeaconries of Northampton and Richmond, canonries of Lincoln, Salisbury, Lichfield, York, and Ripon, as well as Amersham rectory. His early studies—from 1431—were at Balliol College, Oxford, where Thomas Gascoigne (d. 1458) saw a copy of works by Nicholas de Lyre in his room. He graduated MA about 1434. Chancellor of the university by 21 February 1441, he vacated the office the following year

(shortly after 23 February) and departed on his continental travels, charted by Vespasiano da Bisticci. Accompanied by his scholarly assistants Master Richard Bole (later one of his diocesan officials and an accomplished scribe) and Master Nicholas Saxton, he reached Cologne in 1442, and on 1 December was matriculated with them. He paid a visit to Florence, probably that year, where he contacted the humanist Donato Acciaivoli, who later sent him books. Seemingly he left for Padua in 1444, where in mid-September 1445 he received a doctorate in theology. At Ferrara he attended the lectures of Guarino da Verona, and took the impecunious humanist Nicolò Perotti into his household. His appointment as royal proctor at the curia, on 18 November 1445, necessitated a move to Rome, apparently in 1446. There he acquired further books and had manuscripts transcribed. Nicholas V, appreciating Grey's humanist and bibliophilic interests, made him a protonotary and referendary. While in Rome he befriended the ailing John Capgrave (d. 1464), who later dedicated some of his works to him. He was admitted a confrater of the English hospital of St Edmund in Trastevere and was chamberlain of the hospice of St Thomas the Martyr. At the curia he represented the Salisbury chapter in the matter of the canonization of St Osmund (finally achieved in 1457), and a memorandum records his leaving Rome on 13 October 1453.

Nicholas provided Grey to the see of Lincoln on 23 December 1450, but acting on a royal licence of 5 December the electors had chosen John Chedworth (d. 1471), who was eventually provided in 1452. However, with the translation of Bishop Thomas Bourchier (d. 1486) to Canterbury, Grey had provision to the vacated see of Ely (21 June 1454). His promotion was acceptable to the predominant Yorkist faction, and he was consecrated by Archbishop Bourchier at Mortlake—according to the Ely register on 7 September 1454 (a Saturday rather than a Sunday as required by the canons). He was not enthroned until 20 March 1459, the feast of St Cuthbert. The delay remains unexplained.

In March 1455 Grey tried to mediate between Richard, duke of York (d. 1460), and Edmund Beaufort, who had recently been created duke of Somerset. In the event Somerset died in the battle of St Albans on 22 May. The precise nature of Grey's participation in the ensuing Yorkist–Lancastrian struggle is unclear. A loyal Yorkist, he seems none the less to have played a conciliatory role. With George Neville, bishop of Exeter (d. 1476), the earl of Warwick's brother, he met the Yorkist earls, returned in arms from exile, at Southwark in July 1460, and escorted them into the capital by way of London Bridge, where their supporters' heads were still displayed. He joined Archbishop Bourchier and other bishops in the Yorkist camp, and took part in the negotiations preceding the battle of Northampton (10 July 1460). This brought Lancastrian defeat and Henry VI's capture. For a time Grey remained a member of the council but also engaged in diplomacy. He treated with the Scots in 1462, and five years later negotiated a treaty with Castile. From the late summer of 1469 he was mainly in London. He acted briefly as treasurer (25

October 1469 – 10 July 1470), but the readeption of Henry VI in October 1470 forced him to seek sanctuary from his enemies at St Martin's-le-Grand, London. Following Edward IV's return, and the death of Henry VI on 21 May 1471, Grey played little further part in public affairs, though he was three times appointed to negotiate with the Scots between 1471 and 1473, and in 1472 was one of the commissioners to whom the proceeds of the tax for the proposed invasion of France were to be paid.

Despite such preoccupations Grey was a respectably diligent diocesan by the standards of the time. For ordinations he employed a suffragan during the first three years, thereafter with one exception he conducted his own, twenty-eight of them. In 1460 he first investigated the affairs of his cathedral priory, at which time he exercised his right to appoint four of its officers, but apart from the injunctions issued to the chapter in January 1466 details of more general visitation are fragmentary. He was concerned to promote university men. Roughly 48 per cent of those he collated to benefices were graduates, but only four licences for absence to study in accordance with the constitution *Cum ex eo* (1298) are recorded in his register. It should be remembered, though, that the overall trend in such grants was downwards from the second half of the fourteenth century and not just because of indifferent registration. His numerous domestic chaplains (*capellani familiares*) were almost invariably graduates, and his chancellors and officials were men of academic distinction. His companion in Rome, Richard Thwaites, brother of Robert Thwaites, master of Balliol, became marshal of his household. A well-trained clergy was needed to combat unacceptable opinions. Robert Sparke of Reach, near Ely, was ringleader of an isolated group of Lollards, and in 1457 the bishop himself took part in their trial, with the help of a battery of theologians and lawyers. There was also a case of witchcraft, and Grey was directed by the archbishop to seek out books of the discredited Bishop Reginald Pecock who died c.1459 at Thorney Abbey in the diocese of Ely. He responded that he could not find even one.

Grey's principal claim to fame lies in his association with humanism in England and the place given to him—as Messer Guglielmo Graim—by Vespasiano da Bisticci among his *uomini illustri* of the century. But his personal scholarly contribution should not be exaggerated; his own studies were basically theological, and he seems not to have studied Greek, despite the opportunities available in Italy. His significance lies principally in his patronage of scholars—John Free (d. 1465) among others—his frequent engagement of scribes to copy manuscripts, and his discrimination as a book collector. Thanks to him many works became available in England for the first time. He bequeathed most of his books to Balliol College, and also contributed towards the building of the college library. A large number of his books survive at Balliol. As well as numerous volumes of theology and natural philosophy, they include classical texts by such writers as Cicero, Pliny, Josephus, and Plato (in a Latin translation),

Petrarch's letters, and works of humanist learning by Lorenzo Valla, Flavio Biondo, and others. According to Leland, Grey also presented several volumes to Peterhouse, Cambridge, where a chaplain of his, John Warkworth (perhaps the chronicler, d. 1500), was master, but none is traceable there or in the fifteenth-century library catalogue.

Grey fell ill in mid-February 1478 and died on 4 August at his manor of Downham. Four days later his body was brought to Ely where a mass of Our Lady was celebrated by secular priests and another of requiem by the monks. He was buried on the 9th in the north-east of his cathedral between two marble columns, at the corner of what was later Bishop Alcock's chantry. He left money for the repair of the western bell tower (*magni campanilis*), as well as plate and vestments. His tomb is no longer extant.

ROY MARTIN HAINES

Sources episcopal register of W. Gray, CUL · S. J. A. Evans, ed., 'Ely chapter ordinances and visitation records, 1241–1515', *Camden miscellany, XVII*, CS, 3rd ser., 64 (1940), v–xx, 1–74, esp. 57–64 [injunctions of 1466] · P. D'Ancona and E. Aeschlimann, eds., *Vespasiano da Bisticci, 1421–1498: vite di uomini illustri dei secolo XV* (Milan, 1951) · A. de la Mare, 'Vespasiano da Bisticci and Gray', *Journal of the Warburg and Courtauld Institutes*, 20 (1957), 174–6 · R. A. B. Mynors, *Catalogue of the manuscripts of Balliol College, Oxford* (1963) · [A. C. de la Mare and R. W. Hunt], eds., *Duke Humfrey and English humanism in the fifteenth century* (1970) [exhibition catalogue, Bodl. Oxf.] · 'Monachi Eliensis continuatio historiae Eliensis', *Anglia sacra*, ed. [H. Wharton], 1 (1691), 631–74 · R. Weiss, *Humanism in England during the fifteenth century*, 3rd edn (1967) · W. F. Schirmer, *Der englische Frühhumanismus*, 2nd edn (Tübingen, 1963) · P. T. Eden, 'William Gray, bishop of Ely, and three Oxford manuscripts of Seneca', *Classica et Mediaevalia*, 21 (1960), 29–42 · *The Venerabile*, 21 (May 1962) [sexcentenary issue: *The English hospice in Rome*] · Chancery records · N. H. Nicolas, ed., *Proceedings and ordinances of the privy council of England*, 7 vols., RC, 26 (1834–7) · A. R. Wagner, 'William Grey, bishop of Ely', *TLS* (9 June 1932), 427 · *A history of Northumberland*, Northumberland County History Committee, 15 vols. (1893–1940), vol. 14, facing p. 328 [pedigree of Grey of Heton] · A. R. Malden, *The canonisation of St Osmund* (1901) · J. Bentham, *The history and antiquities of the conventual and cathedral church of Ely*, ed. J. Bentham, 2nd edn (1812), 176–8 · C. L. Scofield, *The life and reign of Edward the Fourth*, 1 (1923); repr. (1967), 78–80, 87ff. · R. M. Haines, 'The practice and problems of a fifteenth-century English bishop: the episcopate of William Gray', *Mediaeval Studies*, 34 (1972), 435–61 · R. M. Haines, 'The associates and *familia* of William Gray and his use of patronage while Bishop of Ely (1454–78)', *Journal of Ecclesiastical History*, 25 (1974), 225–47 · Emden, *Oxf.*

Archives CUL, register as bishop of Ely

Grey, William, thirteenth Baron Grey of Wilton (1508/9–1562), soldier, was the fourth son of Edmund Grey, ninth Baron Grey of Wilton (b. in or before 1469, d. 1511) and his wife, Florence, née Hastings (d. in or after 1519). Outliving three brothers—George (d. c.1514), Thomas (d. 1517), and Richard (d. c.1521)—who became barons but died as minors, William succeeded to the title but to limited landed wealth, mainly in Buckinghamshire (despite a Herefordshire title). Aged about seventeen at Easter 1526, he was summoned to the parliament of autumn 1529. He married by 1536 Mary (1507×14–1571/2), daughter of Charles Somerset, first earl of Worcester (she survived him and later married Robert Carre); they had two sons, Arthur *Grey, fourteenth Baron Grey of Wilton (b. 1536), and William, and a daughter, Honora, who married Henry Denny, son of Sir Anthony.

French apprenticeship, 1530–1547 In 1530, when as his heir Arthur confirmed he was 'aboute xxi or xxii' (Grey, 4), Grey bought from William Blount, Lord Mountjoy, the lieutenancy of Hammes in the marches of Calais, a position he apparently occupied conscientiously except for special occasions, parliamentary and judicial—such as the indictment of Henry Pole, Lord Montague, in 1538. On the Calais council (with a house in the town), he was reported by both supporters and opponents to form part of a protestant faction with Sir George Carew and Sir Richard Grenville.

In 1544 Grey served under Thomas Howard, duke of Norfolk, at the siege of Montreuil and was shot in the left shoulder; later that year he was sent to Calais to command 'the crews', the pale's mobile forces. It was proposed in August 1545 to make Grey lieutenant of Boulogne, but the post went to the earl of Surrey. At Guînes there were 'somme mattiers of varyaunce and contention' between Grey and Sir John Wallop in which Grey may have overstepped, as it was suggested that he 'retourne to his charge at Hampnes' (*State Papers, Henry VIII*, 10.251). There was also tension with the interloper Surrey, who complained of Grey's reluctance to bring 'the crews' to reinforce him (though they had been friendly enough in 1544 for Surrey to initiate the first of several abortive nominations of Grey to the Order of the Garter). William Paget mediated but could not extenuate Grey's imputations against Surrey's financial management at Boulogne.

In April 1546 Grey finally replaced Surrey at Boulogne under Edward Seymour, earl of Hertford, taking charge of the English crown's most modern fortifications and military units. Around Boulogne, as around Calais, he was heavily involved in cold war demonstrations, notably the demolition of French entrenchments built over the boundary. Henry VIII egged Grey on by word of mouth, while disclaiming his actions to the French; François I complained that 'if his ministres had usid the lyke' they would have been 'all readye in warre agayne' (*State Papers, Henry VIII*, 11.333). Grey was granted Brampton Manor, Herefordshire, by Henry in April; he hoped for an abbey and the disgraced Surrey's stewardship of the augmentations office, but gained nothing more substantial before the king died. Under Edward VI he agitated for a chantry and did acquire a variety of leases by patent, notably some forfeited by Norfolk and former monastic property. For a very poor peer, Reformation developments offered material as well as spiritual possibilities.

Somerset's right-hand man Grey remained at Boulogne until August 1547, when he brought men over for the invasion of Scotland by Seymour (now duke of Somerset and protector) for which he was marshal of horse. At Pinkie Cleugh on 10 September Grey's 'Bulleners' bore the brunt of the close fighting until superior English firepower could break up the Scottish army. Although the English won the battle, the tactical failure of the horse appeared in the English casualties of '51 horsemen, which were

almost all gentlemen, and but one footman' (*Chronicle and Political Papers of King Edward VI*, 8) and in William Patten's admission that 'by the uneveness of the ground, by the sturdy order of the enemy … they were not able, to any advantage, to maintain this onset' and that some onlookers mistook 'a sober advised retire' for 'a hasty temerarious flight' (Pollard, 116–17). Another witness, the sieur de Berteville, had no compunction in describing it as a flight. Grey 'receaved a great wounde … with a pyke … three fyngers deepe into the rouff of the mouthe', but persevered to victory, when:

> whot with the abundance of blood, heate of the weather, and dust of the press, hee had surely been suffocated had not the duke of Northumberland, then earle of Warwicke, lyghted and lyfted a fyrcken of ale too hys head, as they passed thowroughe the Scottish campe.   (Grey, 15)

Somerset knighted Grey as a banneret at Berwick on 28 September and left him in charge there as captain-general and warden of the eastern marches when he himself returned south. Grey spurned an ambitious plan of Sir George Douglas to take Glasgow and Hamilton in the autumn, which Somerset warned was designed to lure him to 'bouchery' (*CSP Scot.*, 1547–63, 32). The following spring, for once in his life, Grey was accused of mildness. Rather hurt, he told Somerset that the latter's wish to 'assure' Scots favourable to an English alliance made indiscriminate destruction and looting no longer appropriate. Taking Haddington, Grey was largely concerned in fortifying it as a Scottish Calais—in an unusually sophisticated manner, owing to his French experience. At Yester he agreed to spare all the garrison except one who had uttered insults to Edward VI. There was disagreement which of two men was responsible, so Grey allowed a judicial duel, rewarding the victor with a gold chain and the gown he was wearing.

Grey was replaced as lieutenant-general in the north by Francis Talbot, earl of Shrewsbury. His tenure had not been devoid of tension—the military treasurer, John Uvedale, complained that Grey, frustrated at Uvedale's reluctance to disburse, had endorsed a letter to him with a picture of a gallows. When Sir Thomas Wharton in the west march disregarded Grey's guarantees to the 'assured' Scots, Grey claimed to prefer death to being 'myself so slandered and stained' (*CSP Scot.*, 1547–63, 59). After Wharton was captured, his son Henry wanted to challenge Grey to a duel for his allegedly deliberate lack of support. In July 1548 Sir Thomas Palmer and Sir Robert Bowes were also captured near Haddington, apparently endangering the town. Grey complained, 'Fortune so hateth me after his accustomed maner, that as he trayneth me oon foote forward, he draweth me back twayne' (ibid., 121).

In August 1548 Grey accompanied Shrewsbury to relieve Haddington; French reinforcements to the Scots made further gains impracticable, though Somerset, resting on the laurels of Pinkie, tended to ungrateful criticism. Grey complained that his duties so 'empoveryshed' him as to threaten 'the utter dystrucon of me and my posteryte' (*CSP Scot.*, 1547–63, 163). Somerset by 1551 was allegedly covering Grey's household expenses as he had 'spent his entire fortune in the service of his master, the king, in Scotland' (*CSP Spain*, 1550–52, 389).

Late in 1548 Grey finally managed to get himself replaced in the east march. When John, Lord Russell, proved unable to face the western rebels in the summer of 1549, Grey was sent west with a cavalry force of over 1500. *En route* he suppressed enclosure riots in Oxfordshire that threatened to escalate into outbreaks of religious as well as social conservatism. He certainly ordered the hanging of fourteen men, including four priests, two from Bloxham and Chipping Norton steeples—this has sometimes been exaggerated into a general grisly decoration of Oxfordshire churches. He also apparently arrested John Feckenham, later abbot of Westminster.

Somerset was politically unable to promote Grey over Russell, but recommended the latter to follow the views of 'a skylfull man on horseback' (Pocock, 29). Grey did nerve Russell to fight a pitched battle with Humphrey Arundell's rebels at Clyst St Mary on 4 August 1549 and managed, decisively, to bypass the bridge they held and ford the Clyst River. Later, however, he feared a change of fortune enough to kill his prisoners; 'he never in all the warres that he had beene dyd knowe' so hard-fought a battle (Vowell, 2.89). Grey was also one of the commanders most engaged in the final battle at Sampford Courtenay on 17 August. He took prisoners back to London, but was then sent in haste to Boulogne, where the French seemed threatening.

Grey survived 1549 in better political odour than Somerset. On 14 October he was one of those to conduct the fallen protector to the Tower of London, though, confusingly, William Grey esquire of Reading was imprisoned with Somerset. Lord Grey was given an annuity of £200, and was in London for the treaty negotiations with the French in 1550. But he was outspoken about attempts by John Dudley to claim credit for the Scottish victories of the fallen Somerset—Scheyfve told the emperor Charles V that this was 'significant because Grey is held to be the best soldier in England' (*CSP Spain*, 1550–52, 389). When Somerset was arrested again in 1551, so too was Grey on 16 October, 'coming out of the country'. Sir Thomas Palmer alleged that the previous April Somerset had gone 'to raise the people, and the Lord Grey before, to know who were his friends' (*Chronicle and Political Papers of King Edward VI*, 88–9). Brought from the Tower of London to the Star Chamber for examination on 2 December 1551, Grey was kept in the Tower while Somerset was executed in January 1552. By May he was at least 'suffred ... to walke into the closed garden' (*APC*, 1552–4, 59). He was pardoned the following month and Northumberland considered him sufficiently rehabilitated by October 1552 to succeed his own son Sir Andrew Dudley as captain of Guînes, where Grey soon took up residence.

Queen Jane and Queen Mary In his attempt to thwart Mary's succession in 1553, Northumberland bid for Grey of Wilton's loyalty with a proposed marriage of his son Arthur to Jane Grey's younger sister Mary. Though mooted for the command of the expedition to seize Mary in East Anglia, Grey could not be trusted on his own. It was to Grey that

Northumberland was said to have observed, leaving London, that 'not one saith God speed us' (Nichols, 8). Grey was with him at Cambridge on 19 July 1553. Perhaps it was even the following day—when a rumour reached the imperial envoys that Grey had resisted by force Northumberland's burning of the houses of Mary's partisans—that Mary received at Framlingham 'Henry [*sic*], Lord Grey of Wilton, the flower of soldiers ... so repentant of his misdeed that he obtained a well-merited pardon from the gracious queen' (MacCulloch, 266–7), and he returned with Henry Fitzalan, earl of Arundel, and Henry Jerningham to Cambridge to arrest Northumberland.

Mary sent Grey back to Guînes, ignoring doubts about trusting such a sensitive post to a heretic but adopting a sterner approach to his accounts, inevitably putting him in debt to the crown. He was even elected (after at least six abortive nominations between 1544 and 1550) to the Order of the Garter on 23 April 1557. On the other hand, Grey was unchastened enough to protest against the execution of Henry Grey, duke of Suffolk. Guînes's sensitivity allegedly accounted for his absence from parliament as it considered extending the powers of the king consort Philip in 1554–5. Embarrassingly, men described as Grey's servants became involved in Henry Dudley's plot in 1555, and Dudley offered to surrender to the French not only Hammes (now held by his own brother Edmund) but Guînes.

The hero of Guînes Far from seeking to surrender Guînes, Grey was in fact agitating for its strengthening against possible French attack, though distracted in the summer by serving as 'marshal of the field' under William Herbert, earl of Pembroke (*Foljambe MSS*, 5). On 1 December 1557 he destroyed a French detachment fortified in a border church at Bushing; deploying artillery, his summons to surrender was refused so, 'according to the law of arms', after breaching the wall he refused quarter when they asked for it (*CSP for.*, 1557–8, 348). His son Arthur was also to show an inclination to deny quarter through draconian interpretation of the law of arms. The incident was an ominous precedent for Grey's own garrison at Guînes when François, duc de Guise, having taken Calais in a mere five days, appeared there on 13 January 1558.

Grey's 1300 men, including Spanish reinforcements, exceeded the garrison of Calais but still seemed inadequate to hold the town, so he burnt it and withdrew to the castle. Its unmodernized walls crumbled rapidly when the French artillery opened fire on 17 January, and Grey barely escaped a cannon shot. He reacted successfully to the breach with night-dug earthworks and flanking guns, which repelled a succession of assaults. Finally driven from the outer walls into the keep, Grey was wounded by a soldier's sword worn scabbardless, a piece of carelessness which handicapped him in opposing talk of surrender. Losses had been heavy—800 out of 1300, according to Thomas Churchyard; between 400 and 500, according to George Ferrers. The surrender on 21 January was inevitable, if delayed by Grey's insistence that the garrison depart freely with the honours of war. Some thought it best 'to fling my lord Grey over the walls', as 'they for hys vayne glorie woolde nott sell theyr lyves' (Pollard, 327; Grey, 36). He gained his points, however, except for the officers' freedom. Grey had saved some English military reputation—'glory … exceeding the infamy of those who through negligence or treachery lost Calais', the Venetian ambassador thought (*CSP Venice*, 1557–8, 1437–8). To the French, 'never was a place better attacked or better defended' than Guînes (Morgan, 266).

Grey was given as prisoner to Marshal Strozzi, then sold to the comte de la Rochefoucauld, who exacted 25,000 crowns, a shattering financial blow. Rochefoucauld's need to recoup a ransom paid to the Spanish was probably his motive, but Grey feared he was intended 'never … to redeem himself'; he also complained that, despite giving his parole, he was kept up eighty-seven steps and behind four locks (*CSP for.*, 1557–8, 373). He had some help—Henry Clifford, earl of Cumberland, gave £60—but finally had to borrow £8000 from the new queen, Elizabeth. Her generosity was restricted to a loan. Grey sold his titular castle of Wilton upon Wye, Herefordshire, to his nephew Charles Brydges, second son of John, first Lord Chandos. He has been deemed one of the twenty-nine Elizabethan and Jacobean peers receiving 75 per cent of royal grants to the peerage, the only early Elizabethan figure in this select group who was not a Dudley. But this could not restore the decaying fortunes of such a poor peer, with an income from lands held in chief in Buckinghamshire of only some £150 p.a. In late 1560 he forlornly told the privy council that the £8000 debt to the queen and £2330 to others threatened to leave his family 'utterly undone for ever' (PRO, SP 12/13/49).

Leith: victory more by luck than judgement? The count of Feria, Philip II's envoy inherited by Elizabeth I after Mary's death, opined that the new queen regarded Grey 'very highly as a soldier and for this reason she must love him well', and Henri II believed that Grey 'would be her favourite owing to their absolute uniformity in religious opinion' (Rodríguez-Salgado and Adams, 331; *CSP Venice*, 1557–8, 1563). He was released on parole in January 1559 with secret messages for Elizabeth, as part of French attempts to open an Anglo-Spanish breach during the Cateau Cambrésis negotiations, and attended her coronation. His experience soon came into demand as Elizabeth drifted reluctantly towards a new attempt to eliminate French influence in Scotland. Late in 1559 he took reinforcements to Berwick, becoming warden of both eastern and middle marches at salaries respectively of £466 13s. 4d. and £333 6s. 8d. On 28 March 1560 Grey, with an army of some 8000, was finally released to cross the border, following the invasion route of 1547. It was a troublesome command. Estimating the French garrison of Leith at 4000, he needed the help of the Scottish lords of the congregation to besiege it but doubted their persistence. Elizabeth forbade an attack on Edinburgh Castle, in Grey's view an easier course, precisely because of the political prize it offered—the person of Mary of Guise, the queen regent of Scotland. Moreover, Grey was under intermediate command—Thomas Howard, duke of Norfolk, appointed lieutenant-general but confined to the English side of the

border. When Elizabeth wanted Grey to save money by paying off some cavalry, suspecting him of being swayed by 'favour', she suggested Norfolk 'use therin more playnes with hym on our behalf' (*State Papers and Letters of Sir Ralph Sadler*, 1.724). Norfolk also inclined to criticize Grey on his own account.

The progress of the siege of Leith offered ample scope for criticism. A French sally on 15 April threatened Grey's siege-guns and inflicted considerable losses. His artillery set Leith on fire, but he was reluctant to assault the town's modernized defences. His preference for blockade would require some months to take effect, a political impossibility given the likelihood of French reinforcement and the uncertain stance of Spain. A breach appeared on 6 May, but an evening reconnaissance by Sir Ralph Sadler, Sir James Croft, and William Kirkcaldy of Grange concluded that it was not practicable for assault. Croft was supposed to inform Grey of this, but the following morning the assault went ahead. The breach was indeed impracticable, the English ladders proved too short for an escalade elsewhere and so heavy casualties were suffered milling about in the ditch.

'In a later age Grey would doubtless have been courtmartialled for incompetence' (Williams, 61). Contemporary attention, however, concentrated on the behaviour of Croft; there was, it has been argued, 'a general conspiracy to whitewash Grey' (Mackwell, 174). Even Croft—an old comrade of Grey from Boulogne and Haddington whom he had specially requested as second in command—lent himself to it. Norfolk blamed Croft, adding lukewarmly that Grey was 'no waie to be blamed, except … that he hath not his wytts and memorie fayleth hym' (Haynes, 311). Before the assault Norfolk had complained, 'all is nott in hym that hath ben thought', and 'my Lord Graie's service doth consiste but upon a courage without ony conduct; every man that can leade a bande of horsemen is not for so greate an enterprise' (ibid., 298, 303). Arguably Grey's career from Pinkie onwards had been marked by periodic triumphs of courage over conduct, but in one respect Norfolk was demonstrably unreasonable. He boasted that he would not have been delayed by 'a sand wall' (ibid., 300), but a professional would have been worried by Leith's artillery-resistant earthworks more than by traditional stone.

Grey's alleged incompetence was Norfolk's ticket to the honour of field command. It was proposed to let Norfolk bring up reinforcements in person, but French inability to reinforce Scotland forced them into negotiations leading to the treaty of Edinburgh. These were delayed by French reluctance to yield to 'the crewaltye of my Lorde Gray' (*CSP Scot.*, 1547–63, 419), perhaps recalling the Bushing incident. Sir William Cecil, concluding the treaty, affirmed Grey to be 'a noble valiant careful gentleman' (ibid., 435), but his reputation had hardly been enhanced by the campaign. Grey remained as governor of Berwick; by now well over fifty, he complained of illness and of difficulties of his position, being not 'naturallie planted in the countrie' (PRO, SP 59/1, fol. 49v), in the face of hostility from local magnates such as Thomas Percy, earl of Northumberland, who refused to let Grey establish himself at Alnwick Castle. Returning south in spring 1562, he died at Cheshunt, Hertfordshire, at the house of his son-in-law Henry Denny on the night of 14–15 December. He was buried in Cheshunt church on 22 December 1562.

Much of Grey's military career might seem to have consisted of failures—his charge at Pinkie; the Scottish campaign of 1548 (strategically at least); Guînes; the Leith assault. None the less, domestic and foreign observers were agreed on the primacy of his military reputation, irrespective of recurrent hints that he could be quarrelsome, over-emotional, and cruel. Shortly before Grey's death the French Huguenots were reported to wish that the English expedition to Normandy had been strengthened by 'Lord Grey, or some of his experience' (*CSP for.*, 1562, 292). Indeed, a local chronicler one county away from Wilton understood that Grey had gone there (D. MacCulloch and P. Hughes, eds., 'A bailiff's list and chronicle from Worcester', *Antiquaries Journal*, 75 1995, 249). His defence of Guînes remained the only possible propaganda asset in Mary's French war, and his post-Henrician failures were symptomatic of the failure of the English army generally to keep up with the times.   JULIAN LOCK

Sources Arthur, Lord Grey, *A commentary of the services and charges of William, Lord Grey of Wilton*, ed. P. de M. Grey Egerton, CS, 40 (1847) · *CSP Scot.*, 1547–63 · *LP Henry VIII*, vols. 3–4, 7, 11–12, 14–21 · *State papers published under … Henry VIII*, 11 vols. (1830–52) · *A collection of state papers … left by William Cecill, Lord Burghley*, ed. S. Haynes, 1 (1740) · *CSP dom.*, rev. edn, 1547–53; rev. edn, 1553–8; addenda, 1547–66 · state papers domestic, Elizabeth I, PRO, SP 12/13/49 · state papers borders, Elizabeth I, PRO, SP 59 · *CSP for.*, 1547–53, Calais appx; 1553–9; 1562 · *APC*, 1542–54, 1556–8 · A. F. Pollard, ed., *Tudor tracts, 1532–1588* (1903) · *The chronicle and political papers of King Edward VI*, ed. W. K. Jordan (1966) · J. G. Nichols, ed., *The chronicle of Queen Jane, and of two years of Queen Mary*, CS, old ser., 48 (1850) · GEC, *Peerage* · *The state papers and letters of Sir Ralph Sadler*, ed. A. Clifford, 3 vols. (1809) · C. A. Mackwell, 'The early career of Sir James Croft, 1518–1570', BLitt diss., U. Oxf., 1970 · P. T. J. Morgan, 'The government of Calais, 1485–1558', DPhil diss., U. Oxf., 1966 · C. S. L. Davies, 'England and the French war, 1557–9', *The mid-Tudor polity, c.1540–1560*, ed. J. Loach and R. Tittler (1980), 159–85 · G. W. Bernard, *The power of the early Tudor nobility: a study of the fourth and fifth earls of Shrewsbury* (1985), chap. 4 · M. L. Bush, *The government policy of Protector Somerset* (1975) · L. Stone, *The crisis of the aristocracy, 1558–1641*, rev. edn (1979) · N. Williams, *Thomas Howard, fourth duke of Norfolk* (1964) · J. Vowell [J. Hooker], *The description of the citie of Excester*, ed. W. J. Harte, J. W. Schopp, and H. Tapley-Soper, 3 pts in 1, Devon and Cornwall RS (1919–47), pt 2, pp. 85–96 · N. Pocock, ed., *Troubles connected with the prayer book of 1549: documents … in the record office*, CS, new ser., 37 (1884) · D. MacCulloch, 'The *Vita Mariae Angliae Reginae* of Robert Wingfield of Brantham', *Camden miscellany, XXVIII*, CS, 4th ser., 29 (1984), 181–301 · 'The count of Feria's dispatch to Philip II of 14th November 1558', ed. M. J. Rodríguez-Salgado and S. Adams, *Camden miscellany, XXVIII*, CS, 4th ser., 29 (1984) · inquisition post mortem, PRO, WARD 7/9/22 [William, Lord Grey, 1563] · D. Constable, ed., *Recit de l'expedition en Ecosse l'an MDXLVI [sic] et de la battayle de Muscleburgh par le Sieur Berteville au Roy Edouard VI*, Bannatyne Club, 10 (1825) · *The manuscripts of the Right Honourable F. J. Savile Foljambe, of Osberton*, HMC, 41 (1897), 5–7 · G. Phillips, *The Anglo-Scots wars, 1513–1550: a military history* (1999) · M. Merriman, *The rough wooings: Mary queen of Scots, 1542–1551* (2000)

Archives BL, corresp. relating to Calais marches, Harley MS 283 · BL, Cotton MSS, corresp. with Edward Seymour, duke of Somerset · BL, corresp. with Edward Seymour, duke of Somerset, Add. MS 32657 · PRO, SP 1, SP 3, SP 15, SP 50, SP 58, SP 59, SP 68, SP 69
Likenesses G. Flicke, portrait, 1547, NG Scot.
Wealth at death lands worth approx. £300 p.a. (very speculative estimate); debts of £10,330: PRO, SP 12/13/49

Grey, William, first Baron Grey of Warke (1593/4–1674), politician, was the son of Sir Ralph Grey of Chillingham, Northumberland (*d.* 1623?), knighted in 1603, and his wife, Jane, daughter of William Ardington of Ardington, Berkshire. He was said to be twenty-two at the time of the visitation of Northumberland in 1615, and about eighty-one at his death. He was admitted to Gray's Inn in 1613. He was created a baronet on 15 June 1619, marrying in the same year Cecilia (*d.* 1668), daughter and coheir of Sir John Wentworth of Gosfield, Essex. He sat as MP for Northumberland in the parliaments of 1621 and, in January and early February, of 1624; on 11 February 1624 he was created Baron Grey of Warke. In 1629 he was accused of recusancy, a charge hardly reflected in his later career; indeed, in 1647 he was appointed a presbyterian elder for Epping in Essex.

When Charles I announced his intention of proceeding against the Scots in 1639, Grey was commanded to attend upon him at York with horses and equipage by 1 April 1639; but he was subsequently ordered to repair to his estate in Northumberland by 1 March at the latest, so as to be in readiness to defend the county. During the civil war Grey supported parliament. In December 1642 he was appointed commander-in-chief of the forces raised in the eastern counties, and in the early summer of 1643 he was ordered to march to the assistance of the lord general, the earl of Essex. His attendance was, however, dispensed with upon his being nominated in July one of the parliamentary commissioners to Scotland. For refusing to serve he was imprisoned in the Tower of London, and his military commission cancelled. He was soon released, and on Lord Keeper Littleton's flight on 23 May 1643 was chosen to succeed him as speaker of the House of Lords, acting in this capacity until January 1646. Grey formally opposed the creation of the New Model Army. He also had cause to regret the Anglo-Scottish alliance, complaining in 1645 that the Scottish army had seriously disrupted his northern estate. This may account for his subsequent alignment with the group of peers associated with William Fiennes, first Viscount Saye and Sele, and Algernon Percy, tenth earl of Northumberland. He was prominent among those who fled from parliament in August 1647 and sought refuge with the New Model Army. In 1648, when parliament were appointing commissioners of the great seal, Grey was at the Lords' request added to them by an ordinance dated 15 March, and he performed the duties for nearly eleven months. In January 1649 he was appointed as one of the commissioners for the trial of Charles I, under the abortive ordinance. He was not named in the subsequent act and there is no evidence of his concurring in the king's execution. In satisfaction of his losses during the war parliament granted him £5120.

Grey was constituted a member of the council of state on 13 February 1649, but refused the appointment as it came from only one house (the Lords having been abolished), his career of government in the Commonwealth ending before it had begun. In April 1660 he was one of the ten peers who turned the prospect of a restoration of the House of Lords into a reality at the sitting of the Convention. After the restoration of the king he availed himself of the royal pardon. He sat in the Cavalier House of Lords as a presbyterian peer and appears to have supported the earl of Clarendon. Grey died on 29 July 1674 and was buried on 7 August at Epping, where his wife had been buried six years earlier on 1 February 1668. Grey was succeeded by his second but only surviving son Ralph (*bap.* 1630). He survived his father by less than a year; following his death on 15 June 1675 the barony passed to his son, Ford *Grey.

SEAN KELSEY

Sources G. W. Marshall, ed., *The visitation of Northumberland in 1615* (1878), 8 · GEC, *Baronetage*, 1.123 · GEC, *Peerage* · C. Holmes, *The eastern association in the English civil war* (1974), 277 · *JHL*, 7 (1644–5), 277 · *JHC*, 3 (1642–4), 36, 51, 172, 176, 177; 6 (1648–51), 146 · *CSP dom.*, 1638–9, 366–7, 372; 1641–3, 475; 1645–7, 150; 1649–50, 6, 9; 1660–61, 37 · J. S. A. Adamson, 'The peerage in politics, 1645–1649', PhD diss., U. Cam., 1986, 122, 182 · A. Swatland, *The House of Lords in the reign of Charles II* (1996), 20, 210 · P. Morant, *The history and antiquities of the county of Essex*, 2 vols. (1768), vol. 1, p. 47; vol. 2, pp. 373, 380, 382 · *VCH Essex*, 2.61, 63; 5.119, 130, 136 · charge against Lord Grey of Warke of recusancy, BL, Egerton MS 2553, fol. 73b · will, PRO, PROB 11/345, fols. 368v–369v · J. Foster, *The register of admissions to Gray's Inn, 1521–1889, together with the register of marriages in Gray's Inn chapel, 1695–1754* (privately printed, London, 1889), vol. 1, p. 132
Wealth at death £4000 bequeathed to granddaughter; also numerous charitable bequests and personal gifts: will, PRO, PROB 11/345, fols. 368v–369v

Grey, William. *See* Gray, William (*bap.* 1601, *d.* 1674).

Grey, William de, **first Baron Walsingham** (1719–1781), judge, was born at Merton, Norfolk, on 7 July 1719, the youngest son of Thomas de Grey (*bap.* 1680, *d.* 1765), landowner and MP, and Elizabeth (*d.* 1758), daughter of William Windham of Felbrigge in the same county. Admitted to Trinity Hall, Cambridge, on 23 February 1737, he left without taking a degree to enter the Middle Temple in January 1738. He was called to the bar on 26 November 1742. On 12 November 1743 in Somerset House chapel, Westminster, he married Mary (*bap.* 1719, *d.* 1800), daughter of William Cowper MP of Hertingfordbury Park near Hertford, and Joan Budget. They had two sons, the elder of whom, William, died in infancy on 20 February 1747; the second, Thomas, was born on 14 July 1748.

De Grey became king's counsel on 30 January 1758 and in September 1761 he was appointed solicitor-general to Queen Charlotte. In December 1761 he was elected MP for Newport, Cornwall, a seat he retained in 1768. From February 1770 to January 1771 he sat as MP for the University of Cambridge. A government supporter, he confined his ambitions to the law and was appointed solicitor-general in December 1763 and attorney-general in August 1766. As attorney-general he assisted in arguing the government's case against John Wilkes in the Commons debates on the Westminster election in 1769. Following the dismissal of

Lord Camden as lord chancellor in January 1770, de Grey was offered the great seal and a peerage, but declined on news of the duke of Grafton's intention to resign. After he used his position as attorney-general to initiate prosecutions of political libels in the press during 1770, an opposition motion of 27 November in the Commons sought to curb this power. De Grey then stoutly and successfully justified its necessity. At the end of the year he took advantage of a ministerial reshuffle to resign his post and parliamentary seat, becoming lord chief justice of the common pleas, and acquiring a knighthood, in January 1771. He resigned the post in June 1780 in favour of Alexander Wedderburn after winning a guarantee that he would be raised to the peerage, and he was duly created Baron Walsingham on 17 October that year. He was a highly competent legal officer and judge and was described by Foss as a 'most accomplished lawyer, and of the most extraordinary power of memory, being able to sum up with the greatest correctness a cause lasting for nine to ten hours without a note' (Foss, *Judges*, 8.266).

De Grey died on 9 May 1781 at Englefield Green, near Windsor, and was buried on 17 May at Merton. He was survived by his wife, who died on 2 September 1800 at Lincoln's Inn Fields, and was succeeded by his son Thomas de *Grey, second Baron Walsingham.

GORDON GOODWIN, *rev.* M. J. MERCER

Sources GEC, *Peerage*, new edn · M. M. Drummond, 'De Grey, William', HoP, *Commons*, 1754–90, 2.308–9 · Venn, *Alum. Cant.* · Foss, *Judges*, 8.265–7 · J. Hutchinson, ed., *A catalogue of notable Middle Templars: with brief biographical notices* (1902)
Archives Norfolk RO, corresp. and papers | BL, letters to Charles Yorke, Add. MSS 35634–35639
Likenesses Wedgwood medallion, Wedgwood Museum, Barlaston, Staffordshire

Grey, Sir William (1818–1878), administrator in India and colonial governor, born on 26 March 1818, was the fourth son of Edward Grey (1782–1837), bishop of Hereford, son of Charles *Grey, first Earl Grey; his mother, Charlotte Elizabeth (*d.* 1821), was the daughter of James Croft, of Greenham Lodge, near Newbury, Berkshire. Grey matriculated at Christ Church, Oxford, in 1836, but left the university without a degree on being appointed by his cousin Lord Howick (later third Earl Grey) to a clerkship in the War Office. While at the War Office he was nominated to a writership in the Bengal civil service by his uncle the second Earl Grey. He entered East India College, Haileybury, in January 1839. He had not been remarkable for studious habits at Oxford, and in his first term at Haileybury he was rusticated on account of a late and disorderly wine party in his room. He made up for these delinquencies, however, in his second and third terms. He passed out of college in July 1840 and reached India on 27 December.

After holding various subordinate offices in the districts of Lower Bengal, Grey was appointed in 1845 private secretary to the deputy governor, Sir Herbert Maddock, and subsequently served for some years in the Bengal secretariat and in the home and foreign departments of the government of India secretariat. In April 1851 he was appointed secretary of the Bank of Bengal, a position he held until 1 May 1854, when he became secretary to the government of Bengal on its being constituted a lieutenant-governorship. At the outbreak of the uprising of 1857 he was in England on furlough, but he returned to India in November of the same year, and after officiating for some eighteen months in temporary appointments, one of which was that of director-general of the post office, he was appointed by the viceroy, Lord Canning, in April 1859, secretary to the government of India in the home department. Three years later he became a member of the executive council, a position he held until 1867.

During the greater part of Grey's tenure on the council Sir John Lawrence was viceroy, and between him and Grey there was considerable disagreement on a number of questions. Their opinions notably differed with reference to the treatment of the *talukdars*, recently installed as landlords, and to the subordinate proprietors and tenants in Oudh. Grey supported the chief commissioner in Oudh, Sir Charles Wingfield, in blocking Lawrence's efforts to secure occupancy rights for the Oudh tenantry; he did, however, intervene to negotiate a compromise which secured favourable terms for those who had previously held their lands in proprietary tenure. While strongly opposed to the policy of excessive centralization, he successfully opposed a proposal for decentralizing the postal department. He was also a staunch opponent of the income tax, holding that it was totally unsuited to the circumstances of India.

In 1867 Grey succeeded Sir Cecil Beadon as lieutenant-governor of Bengal. In that position he strenuously fought a proposal to abolish the recently instituted Bengal legislative council, and with it the separate lieutenant-governorship for the province. The suggestion that the duty of the lieutenant-governor should be discharged by one of the members of the executive council, and that for the districts of Bengal proper and of Bihar all legislation should be entrusted to the viceroy in council, Grey described as 'a very startling example' of a vacillating policy. 'If there was one part of India', he argued 'in which the native public were entitled to have a real share in legislation, it was the lower provinces of Bengal'. Indeed it was 'possible', he wrote, 'to look forward to the time when a local legislature', or some local consultative body, should take part in regulating the expenditure of local taxation. So far from acquiescing in any reduction in the functions of the local government, he recommended that the constitution of the government of Bengal should be assimilated to that of the governments of Madras and Bombay, where the administration was conducted by a governor and an executive council. This discussion ended without any change in the administrative arrangements for Bengal, but the province was raised to the status of a full governorship only in 1912. Assam was, however, shortly afterwards constituted a separate chief commissionership.

During his government of Bengal, Grey opposed a proposal to impose local taxation in the form of a land cess, as a means of providing primary education. But he did not object to the imposition of local taxation for roads and other works of material utility. His objections to the educational tax were based partly upon the terms of the permanent settlement of Bengal, which debarred the government from increasing the taxation on land, and partly upon the impolicy and injustice, in his opinion, of requiring the landholders to defray the cost of elementary schools for all classes of the rural population. Grey's views did not commend themselves to the government of Lord Mayo or to the secretary of state, but the imperial authorities did agree to levy any such cess more generally on all classes of the population.

Grey was twice married, first on 8 July 1845, to Margaret Hungerford, daughter of Welby Jackson of the Bengal civil service; she died on 13 November 1862; they had three sons and a daughter. His second marriage, on 26 January 1865, was to Georgina (*d.* 1936), daughter of Trevor Chichele Plowden, also of the Bengal civil service; they had two sons and two daughters.

Grey retired from the government of Bengal in February 1871, a year before he had completed the usual term of office, and was made KCSI. He remained in England without employment until March 1874, when he somewhat reluctantly accepted the government of Jamaica. He spent three comparatively uneventful years in that post. During the latter part of the time his health was poor and he returned to England in March 1877, only to die at Marldon, near Torquay, on 15 May 1878.

A. J. ARBUTHNOT, *rev.* THOMAS R. METCALF

Sources C. E. Buckland, *Bengal under the lieutenant-governors*, 2nd edn, 2 vols. (1902) · J. Raj, *The mutiny and British land policy in north India* (1965) · Burke, *Peerage* (1939) · personal knowledge (1888) · *CGPLA Eng. & Wales* (1878)

Archives BL OIOC, letter-book, MS Eur. D 700 | BL, corresp. with H. Bruce, Add. MS 43991 · BL, Burke MSS · BL OIOC, letters to Lord Elgin, MSS Eur. F 83 · BL OIOC, corresp. with John Lawrence, MS Eur. F 90 · CUL, corresp. with Lord Mayo

Likenesses Bourne & Shepherd ?, group portrait, albumen print, *c.*1860 (*Supreme Indian Council, Simla*), NPG

Wealth at death under £60,000—effects in England: probate, 20 June 1878, *CGPLA Eng. & Wales*

Grey, Zachary (1688–1766), Church of England clergyman and writer, was born at Burniston, Yorkshire, on 6 May 1688, the son of George Grey (1652–1711), Church of England clergyman, and Elizabeth Cowdray. His brother George became a barrister in Newcastle upon Tyne. Grey was admitted a pensioner at Jesus College, Cambridge, on 18 April 1704 but migrated to Trinity Hall, Cambridge, where he was elected a scholar on 6 January 1707. He graduated LLB in 1709 and LLD in 1720 but never became a fellow of his college. He was ordained deacon by the bishop of Lincoln on 25 July 1711, becoming a priest on 22 September. He served as rector of Houghton Conquest, Bedfordshire, from 4 April 1725, and was vicar of St Giles and St Peter's, Cambridge, where he officiated 'in the morning at one of these churches and in afternoon only prayers at the other, and so by turns' (Palmer, 144). From 1729 he passed his winters at Cambridge and during the rest of the year lived at Ampthill, the nearest market town to Houghton Conquest where he seems now to have officiated. His friend, the Cambridge antiquary William Cole, praised him as 'the most humane, obliging, benevolent, good-tempered Man I ever met with' (*Blecheley Diary*, 160). He was twice married, first to Miss Tooley, and second, in 1720, to Susanna Hatton (*née* Hinton) (*c*.1690–1771), daughter of the keeper of the Three Tuns tavern in Cambridge; Susanna's widowed mother subsequently married Grey's friend, Robert Moss, dean of Ely. Grey and his second wife had a son, who died in 1726, and two daughters, one of whom married the Revd William Cole of Ely, the other becoming the wife of the Revd Le Peper, rector of Aspley Guise, Bedfordshire.

Grey was a man of much reading and, as a strong churchman, became known in many controversies with dissenters. Most of his early publications were anonymous tracts. The first of these, *A Vindication of the Church of England* (1720), was an attack on the 'vile Principles, and evil Practices of the Dissenters' (sig. A2r), composed to rebut the writings of James Peirce. Grey shifted target but not tone in a series of rumbustious pamphlets, beginning with *Presbyterian Prejudice Display'd* (1722), which answered the works of Benjamin Bennet. He followed these up with *A Vindication of the University of Cambridge* (1722) 'by a Lover of Truth' and several pamphlets criticizing the publications of Sir Richard Cox, whom he christened 'the Knight of Dumbleton' in the title of a squib printed in 1723. Grey adopted a more serious tone as 'a Believer' in *The Spirit of Infidelity Detected* (1723), a reply to Jean Barbeyrac. He later added a defence of Daniel Waterland to a second edition of this work published in 1735. As 'a Lover of Episcopacy', Grey published *A Century of Eminent Presbyterian Preachers* (1723). This was the first of several writings to deploy his growing knowledge, derived from a wide reading of seventeenth-century pamphlet literature, of the events of the Long Parliament and the Westminster assembly. Grey's target on this occasion was the dissenting historian Edmund Calamy, but he later took aim at other writers sympathetic to the Presbyterian cause, in particular John Oldmixon, Samuel Chandler, and, above all, Daniel Neal. In much of this work, Grey relied heavily on the publications of John Strype and the encouragement and advice of his friends, Waterland and Thomas Baker. Baker assisted directly in the work of annotation and correction for the sequence of replies to Neal's histories that Grey produced between 1733 and 1739. These were completed with *A Review of Mr Daniel Neal's History of the Puritans* (1744). Waterland encouraged Grey to broaden his target from Presbyterian historians to the posthumously published chronologies of Sir Isaac Newton. Grey's *Examination of the 14th chapter of Sir Isaac Newton's observations upon the prophecies of Daniel* appeared in 1736. It sought to belittle Newton's attempts at biblical criticism and at the rehabilitation of the Arian movement in the early church.

In all of his controversial writings, Grey argued that the Church of England was the best of churches; that Charles I was its truest protector, and that dissenting criticism was an attempt to turn the clock back to 1649. He reserved a particular loathing for both Cromwell and Milton, and betrayed his own poetic sympathies in the edition of Samuel Butler's *Hudibras* that he published in 1744. For this work, which was illustrated with cuts by Mynde after Hogarth's drawings, Grey raised a vast subscription, said to have totalled £1500. His knowledge of puritan literature enabled him to illustrate his author by profuse quotations from contemporary writings, and to show 'who in the late Rebellion, under pretence of Religion, murder'd the best of Kings, to introduce the worst of Governments' (S. Butler, *Hudibras*, ed. Z. Grey, 2 vols., 1744, 1.ix).

Grey had obtained some notes on *Hudibras* by William Warburton through their common friend James Tunstall, the public orator at Cambridge. Warburton claimed that he had given the notes purely to oblige Tunstall and was very aggrieved at Grey's use of them, even though Grey made proper acknowledgements in his preface. Warburton wrote that he doubted whether so 'execrable a heap on nonsense had ever appeared in any learned language as Grey's commentaries on *Hudibras*' (*The Works of Shakespear*, ed. W. Warburton, 8 vols., 1747, preface). A second edition of Grey's *Hudibras* appeared in 1764, and a supplement in 1752. Grey replied to Warburton in three pamphlets: *A Word or Two of Advice to William Warburton, a Dealer in Many Words* (1746); *Remarks upon a Late Edition of Shakespeare*, in which he accused Warburton of having abused Sir Thomas Hanmer and his work; and *A free and familiar letter to that great refiner of Pope and Shakespear; the Rev. Mr W. Warburton* (1750). Grey's own *Critical, Historical, and Explanatory Notes on Shakespeare* appeared in two volumes in 1754. They upheld the earlier work of Theobald and Hanmer against the criticisms of both Pope and Warburton. Basing himself on a collation of the 1623 and 1632 folios of Shakespeare, and on the writings of eighteenth-century editors, Grey aimed to restore the language of the plays and to show how closely they followed their literary and historical sources. In 1750 Grey published *A Chronological and Historical Account of the most Remarkable Earthquakes*, which he expanded in 1756. In both of these pamphlets, he drew attention to the need for a reformation of manners on the part of 'those *polite* Readers, who think it highly unfashionable even to look into their Bibles' (Z. Grey, *Chronological and Historical Account*, 1750, 8).

Grey died at Ampthill on 25 November 1766 and was buried at Houghton Conquest church on 30 November. His widow died on 11 February 1771. Many of his papers were bought by John Nichols in 1778, including Grey's materials for a life of his friend, the nonjuror Thomas Baker (1656–1740), which were used by Robert Masters in his life of Baker. Nichols also bought manuscript lives by Grey of Dean Moss (to whose sermons in 1732 a preface was prefixed by Grey or Andrew Snape) and Robert Harley, earl of Oxford. Grey had helped in Peter Whalley's edition of *The Works of Ben Jonson* (1756) and Francis Peck's *Desiderata curiosa* (1732–5).   SCOTT MANDELBROTE

Sources Nichols, *Lit. anecdotes*, 8.414 · Nichols, *Illustrations*, 2.124; 4.322 · Venn, *Alum. Cant.* · BL, Add. MSS 5831, 6401, 6396 · St John Cam., MSS Q.13.5–13.14; O.54–55 · W. M. Palmer, *William Cole of Milton* (1935) · *The Blecheley diary of the Revd William Cole*, ed. F. G. Stokes (1931) · C. Franklin, *Shakespeare domesticated* (1991) · DNB
Archives BL, collection of MS tracts, transcripts of state papers, etc., Stowe MSS 1057–1058 · BL, corresp. and papers, Add. MSS 5831–5834, 5860, 5957, 6396, 6401 · CUL, British naval history ·

CUL, commonplace books, papers, notes and extracts relating to Chaucer, Spenser, Shakespeare, etc. • St John Cam., collections for life of Thomas Baker; undergraduate notebook • Yale U., Farmington, Lewis Walpole Library, papers relating to biography of Thomas Baker • Yale U., Beinecke L., autograph sermons **Likenesses** P. Audinet, line engraving (after S. Harding), BM, NPG; repro. in Nichols, *Illustrations*, 4.241 • C. Knight, stipple (after drawing by S. Harding), BM, NPG; repro. in F. G. Waldron, *The Biographical mirrour*, 3 vols. (1795–1810) • G. P. Wainwright, engraving (after J. Thurston), Bodl. Oxf. **Wealth at death** £200 plus substantial estates: will, Beds. & Luton ARS, ABP/W 1767/27

Grey Owl. See Belaney, Archibald Stansfeld (1888–1938).

Greystoke. For this title name *see* individual entries under Greystoke; *see also* Dacre, William, third Baron Dacre of Gilsland and seventh Baron Greystoke (1500–1563).

Greystoke family (*per.* **1321–1487**), magnates, of Greystoke near Penrith in Cumberland, entered the ranks of the lesser peerage when **Ralph (I) Greystoke**, first Lord Greystoke (1299–1323), son and heir of Robert fitz Ralph (*d.* 1317), son of Ralph *Fitzwilliam, was summoned to parliament on 15 May 1321. He was born on 15 August 1299, but little is known of him beyond the fact that he fought for Edward II at Boroughbridge in March 1322 and died at Gateshead, apparently poisoned, on 14 July 1323. He married Alice, the daughter of Hugh, Lord Audley (*d. c.*1306). His son and heir, **William Greystoke**, second Lord Greystoke (1321–1359), was born and baptized at the family residence of Grimthorpe in Yorkshire on 6 January 1321 and, once he had achieved his majority in 1342, soon became embroiled in English campaigning on the continent: he was probably in Gascony in 1345–6, at the siege of Calais in 1347, and, perhaps, on the expedition of Henry, duke of Lancaster, to Prussia in 1351–2. In 1353 and again in 1354 he participated in unsuccessful Anglo-Scottish negotiations concerning the release of David II, king of Scots (an English prisoner since his capture at Nevilles Cross in 1346). In September 1354 Greystoke was appointed captain of the border town of Berwick: while he was absent campaigning once more in France it fell into Scottish hands in August 1355. As his second wife he had married Joan, the daughter of Sir Henry fitz Henry (Fitzhugh). He died on 10 July 1359 and was buried in Greystoke church.

Ralph (II) Greystoke, third Baron Greystoke (1353–1418), William's son and heir, was born at Ravensworth in the North Riding of Yorkshire, home of his uncle Henry, Lord Fitzhugh, on 18 October 1353. Much of his early adult life in the 1370s and 1380s was spent serving the king in the far north of England, as warden of the west or east marches (or both), at a time when Anglo-Scottish relations were frequently in turmoil. On one occasion, he was captured near the border fortress of Roxburgh and taken in triumph to Dunbar. By the later 1390s, however, he had become disillusioned with the government of Richard II. When the exiled Henry Bolingbroke, earl of Derby, returned to England in 1399, Greystoke joined him at Doncaster and, shortly afterwards, backed his seizure of the

throne as Henry IV. Thereafter he remained active in border politics and warfare, most notably in September 1402 when he joined Henry Percy, earl of Northumberland, his son Henry (Hotspur), and Henry, Lord Fitzhugh, in defeating a Scottish army at Homildon Hill in Northumberland. He married Katherine, daughter of Roger *Clifford, fifth Baron Clifford. He died on 6 April 1418 when he was succeeded by his son and heir **John Greystoke**, fourth Baron Greystoke (*c.*1390–1436). Like his father, John soon became enmeshed in border politics and Anglo-Scottish negotiations: most notably, in March 1421, he was appointed constable of the strategically vital Roxburgh Castle for four years at a salary of £1000 per annum in peacetime and £2000 in time of war; also, in 1424 and again in 1430, he served on embassies to treat with the Scots. He married Elizabeth, daughter of Joan *Beaufort and her first husband, Sir Robert Ferrers. He died on 8 August 1436 after stipulating, in his will of 10 July, that he be buried at Greystoke.

Ralph (III) Greystoke, fifth Baron Greystoke (*c.*1414–1487), was the son and heir of John Greystoke. He married as his first wife Elizabeth, daughter of William, Baron Fitzhugh, thereby reinforcing what had long been a close alliance between the two families. Ralph was a member of the duke of Suffolk's embassy to France in 1444 charged with bringing Henry VI's bride, Margaret of Anjou, back to England, but his most significant personal decision in the 1440s was to join the affinity of the increasingly wealthy and powerful magnate Richard Neville, earl of Salisbury (1400–1460); he committed himself (by indenture of retainer dated 10 July 1447) to be 'always ready to ride and go to with and for the same Earl as well in time of peace and of war unto all places and coasts except the parts of France' (Pollard, 213). When in the winter of 1453–4 the Nevilles threw in their lot with Richard, duke of York, Greystoke seems to have followed Salisbury's lead: in February 1454 he was numbered among the royal councillors who ensured that York received full authority to open parliament on behalf of the seriously incapacitated Henry VI; that summer he was a member of the powerful commission of oyer and terminer headed by Richard, duke of York (now protector of the realm), and Salisbury's son Richard Neville, earl of Warwick, that met at York to consider charges against participants in the recent Percy-inspired rebellion in northern England; and at the end of September he was a commissioner to raise forces in Yorkshire for the purpose of suppressing Lancastrian rebels who were plundering neighbouring shires and plotting the destruction of Richard of York's government. However, following the Yorkist rout at Ludford in October 1459 and Salisbury's flight to Calais he took an oath of loyalty to the victorious Lancastrians at the Coventry parliament. In the autumn of 1460, according to Gregory's chronicle, he joined the very considerable force that was to defeat the Yorkists near Sandal Castle, Wakefield, at the end of the year, and John Benet's chronicle records his presence at the battle itself. If these chroniclers are correct, then it is strange that he was obliged to renew the Coventry oath to Margaret of Anjou and her son in January 1461. A statement in the

Annales, wrongly attributed to William Worcester, suggests that thereafter he marched south with the queen's notoriously unruly northern army and fought for the Lancastrians at St Albans in mid-February. The limits of his conversion, however, are strongly suggested by his absence from Towton at the end of March 1461 and his immediate entry into the service of the new king, Edward IV. Indeed it might well be that, as a stalwart Neville retainer, he had been playing a double game ever since the Ludford débâcle. Certainly, very soon after Towton Greystoke and William Neville, Lord Fauconberg, were dispatched to Beverley to secure the town's submission. In November 1461 he was commissioned to array men in northern England to resist the Lancastrians. He accompanied the king on an expedition to the far north a year later and helped occupy the formidable Dunstanburgh Castle in Northumberland. In May 1464 he aided John Neville, Lord Montagu, in decisively defeating a Lancastrian force at Hexham. Another sure sign of his continued close connection with the Nevilles was the major ceremonial role that he played at George Neville's lavish enthronement as archbishop of York in 1465. Like many former Neville retainers he passed easily into the service of Richard, duke of Gloucester, in the 1470s, becoming a member of his ducal council and, as he had in the 1460s, both serving as a justice of the peace and participating in negotiations with Scotland. Following Richard's usurpation of the throne he attended on the king at York in August 1483 and, as a royal councillor, was granted an annuity of £100. Indeed, northern tradition has it that he brought a mighty retinue to Bosworth in 1485: this is highly questionable, however, not least since he was over seventy years old by then and passed smoothly into the service of Henry VII. He died on 1 June 1487.

Although never a top-ranking aristocratic family the Greystokes were clearly a force to be reckoned with in later medieval northern society. They managed to accumulate considerable estates in Cumberland (where they held both the manor of Greystoke and a wide tract of fell country between Saddleback and Ullswater), Westmorland, Northumberland, Durham, and, most importantly, Yorkshire (where Henderskelf, now buried beneath the park of Castle Howard, served as their principal residence). While their North Riding neighbours, the Fitzhughs of Ravensworth and Scropes of Masham, were assessed for income tax in 1436 at £484 and £457 respectively, the Greystokes had a reported landed income of £650. Their marriages, too, provide valuable evidence of both family status and aristocratic connections. There are also occasional indications in the records of wider interests, notably bequests to religious establishments in Cumberland and Yorkshire. Ralph, third baron, founded a college of seven secular clerics at Greystoke and his son John clearly approved since he bequeathed the house vestments, chapel ornaments, and lead to repair the choir: by 1535 the college's yearly income stood at £82.

With the death of Ralph, fifth Baron Greystoke, who directed in his will that he be buried in the chancel of Kirkham Priory, Yorkshire (of which he had been a patron

since 1468), the barony of Greystoke became extinct. Sir Robert Greystoke, his eldest son, not only predeceased him (in 1483) but died without a male heir. Ralph's second son, Sir John Greystoke (d. 1501), did have a son and heir but he was still unmarried at his death in 1508. Consequently the marriage of Sir Robert Greystoke's daughter and heir, Elizabeth, to Thomas *Dacre, Baron Dacre (d. 1525), ensured that most of the family estates eventually passed into the hands of the Dacres of Gilsland.

KEITH DOCKRAY

Sources GEC, *Peerage* · *Chancery records* · *RotS* · A. J. Pollard, *Northeastern England during the Wars of the Roses: lay society, war and politics, 1450–1500* (1990) · J. T. Rosenthal, *The purchase of paradise* (1972) · W. E. Hampton, *Memorials of the Wars of the Roses: a biographical guide* (1979) · 'William Gregory's chronicle of London', *The historical collections of a citizen of London in the fifteenth century*, ed. J. Gairdner, CS, new ser., 17 (1876), 55–239 · 'John Benet's chronicle for the years 1400 to 1462', ed. G. L. Harriss, *Camden miscellany, XXIV*, CS, 4th ser., 9 (1972) · J. Stevenson, ed., *Letters and papers illustrative of the wars of the English in France during the reign of Henry VI, king of England*, 2, Rolls Series, 22 (1864)

Greystoke, John, fourth Baron Greystoke (*c*.1390–1436). *See under* Greystoke family (*per.* 1321–1487).

Greystoke, Ralph (I), first Lord Greystoke (1299–1323). *See under* Greystoke family (*per.* 1321–1487).

Greystoke, Ralph (II), third Baron Greystoke (1353–1418). *See under* Greystoke family (*per.* 1321–1487).

Greystoke, Ralph (III), fifth Baron Greystoke (*c*.1414–1487). *See under* Greystoke family (*per.* 1321–1487).

Greystoke, William, second Lord Greystoke (1321–1359). *See under* Greystoke family (*per.* 1321–1487).

Greystones [Graystanes], **Robert** (*b.* before **1290**, *d.* **1334**), Benedictine monk and supposed chronicler. He may have been a member of the knightly Greystanes family who held land of the bishop of Durham in Morton Tinmouth, co. Durham. He made his profession as a Durham monk between 1300 and 1310, and was ordained subdeacon on 1 May 1307, when he should have been at least seventeen years old; his ordination to the priesthood is not recorded. Much of his early career was spent at Durham's house of studies in Oxford, where, at various dates between July 1306 and March 1326, he is named in caution notes for volumes pawned in the university's loan chests. Greystones procured for his house at least nine volumes, and seven of these survive, including a biblical concordance, part of Aquinas's *Summa theologica*, some Aristotelian texts, and several volumes of works by St Augustine. He annotated these and other texts, including two further philosophical compendia, and it seems clear that he obtained a thorough grounding in philosophy before proceeding to the degree of bachelor of theology by 1315, when Durham's Oxford cell owned his commentary on the *Sentences*. A copy of this work, together with some *quaestiones*, may survive in Westminster Abbey, MS 13. At an unknown date before 1333 he attained the degree of doctor of theology.

During these years Greystones is recorded in Durham only once, in 1316, at an episcopal election in chapter.

Also, between 1316 and 1320 he spent some time at Durham's cell in Stamford, another centre of study. His whereabouts are unknown between 1326 and February 1332, by when he was back in Durham, as sub-prior. On 23 July 1333 the prior and convent appointed him prior of the cell at Coldingham in Lothian, but on 15 October he was in Durham again as sub-prior, participating in the episcopal election held under royal licence, following the death of Bishop Louis de Beaumont. Greystones was his community's choice, but Edward III refused to accept the election, on the grounds that the pope had already provided the royal clerk, Richard Bury (d. 1345), to the see—probably at the king's request. None the less, Greystones proceeded to York; his election was confirmed by Archbishop William Melton (d. 1340), and he was consecrated on 14 November, in the chapel of the archbishop's palace. On 18 November he was installed in Durham, where a few days later he issued his sole surviving act as bishop: an indulgence for those visiting the relics in Durham Cathedral. The king refused restitution of the temporalities of the see, and in December Richard Bury arrived from Avignon with bulls proving that Pope John XXII (r. 1316–34) had indeed provided him to the see on 14 October, the day before the election of Greystones. Melton promptly issued apologetic commands to Durham to accept Bury, notwithstanding Greystones's consecration and installation. Greystones stood aside, to spare his community the expense of litigation. He died before the end of 1334, and was buried in the chapter house at Durham, with an epitaph recalling his birthplace and scholarship and praying that he be numbered among the saints.

Greystones has been credited with composing, in 'retirement', a chronicle for the years 1215 to 1334, which became part of the composite official history known as the *Gesta episcoporum Dunelmensium*. This chronicle concentrates on domestic affairs, touching on national or international events only in so far as they affected the Durham community. From 1215 until 1286 the author drew primarily on a thirteenth-century compilation, apparently produced in the priory, which combined some scrappy annalistic entries with four narratives recording legal wrangles between the monks and the bishop of Durham and the archbishop of York over elections and visitations. He edited this work to produce a more coherent whole, adding further information from two sources: documents among the priory muniments, many of which still survive and are readily identifiable, and his own and others' reminiscences. From 1286 these were his only sources, used to create a lively and informative account of life in the house during particularly turbulent times, locally and on the wider stage of secular and ecclesiastical politics. It is a particularly valuable source for the monks' view of their long-running dispute with Bishop Antony (I) Bek (d. 1311) in the first decade of the fourteenth century. The text appears to have ended originally in 1333, with the death of Bishop Beaumont; between 1334 and 1336, the same or another author added a further section, containing a defensive account of Greystones's election and rejection. Four manuscripts survive: BL, Cotton MS Titus A.ii; Bodl.

Oxf., MS Fairfax 6, and MS Laud misc. 700; York, Minster Library, MS xvi.I.12. The text was edited by James Raine for the Surtees Society in 1839. However, although the text was undoubtedly the work of a Durham monk named Robert, the attribution to Greystones, first made by Henry Wharton in 1691 and followed unquestioningly by most scholars since, is no more than attractive speculation.

MERYL R. FOSTER

Sources *Historiae Dunelmensis scriptores tres: Gaufridus de Coldingham, Robertus de Graystanes, et Willielmus de Chambre*, ed. J. Raine, SurtS, 9 (1839) · *Richard d'Aungerville, of Bury: fragments of his register and other documents*, ed. [G. W. Kitchin], SurtS, 119 (1910) · *The register of William Melton, archbishop of York, 1317–1340*, 1, ed. R. M. T. Hill, CYS, 70 (1970) · Emden, *Oxf.*, 2.814 · M. R. Foster, 'Durham Cathedral priory, 1229–1333: aspects of the ecclesiastical history and interests of the monastic community', PhD diss., U. Cam., 1979 · [H. Wharton], ed., *Anglia sacra*, 2 vols. (1691) · Durham dean and chapter muniments, U. Durham L., archives and special collections · J. Stevenson, ed., *Chronicon de Lanercost, 1201–1346*, Bannatyne Club, 65 (1839) · R. Nicholson, *Edward III and the Scots: the formative years of a military career, 1327–1335* (1965) · *The itinerary of John Leland in or about the years 1535–1543*, ed. L. Toulmin Smith, 11 pts in 5 vols. (1906–10) · W. Hutchinson, *The history and antiquities of the county palatine of Durham*, 3 vols. (1785–94) · R. Surtees, *The history and antiquities of the county palatine of Durham*, 4 vols. (1816–40) · F. Barlow, ed., *Durham annals and documents of the thirteenth century*, SurtS, 155 (1945) · H. S. Offler, *Medieval historians of Durham* (1958)

Archives BL, Cotton MS Titus A.ii · Bodl. Oxf., MS Fairfax 6 · Bodl. Oxf., MS Laud misc. 700 · Minster Library, York, MS xvi.I.12 | U. Durham L., muniments of the dean and chapter of Durham · Westminster Abbey, MS 13

Gribelin, Simon (1662–1733), printmaker and metal-engraver, was born in Blois, France, the son of Jacob Gribelin, who was recorded as still living in Blois in 1691. The family was one of watchmakers and engravers. Gribelin moved to England about 1680, presumably anticipating the revocation of the edict of Nantes, and he appears to have remained close to the Huguenot community in London for the rest of his life.

In 1682 Gribelin received his denizenship and published his first dated work in England. This was the first of four books of ornament prints designed as sources for jewellers, watchmakers, and other craftsmen which, although their style reflects that of the France of Louis XIII, remained in print in England long after Gribelin's death. In 1686 Gribelin became a member of the Clockmakers' Company, and much of his work consisted of engraved watch-cases. There are pulls from such cases in albums in the British Museum, St Mary's College, Strawberry Hill, and Christ Church, Oxford. These albums, put together by Gribelin in 1722, contain prints and pulls from metalwork from the whole of his career and provide a record of his output. He is one of very few contemporary metal-engravers whose work has been identified.

Gribelin's protestant allegiance is attested by two propagandist prints of 1688 supporting the seven bishops who refused to accede to James II's relaxing of the penal laws against Roman Catholics. In 1690 he was living in Arundel Street, London, 'the next turning down the King's Arms Tavern, next door to the White Lion'. On 1 January 1691 he married Marie Mettayer, the daughter of the minister of the Huguenot church of La Patente, Spitalfields.

Two of Gribelin's relatives assisted him: his uncle Daniel Vautier, an enamel painter; and 'son beau frere' Pierre Berchet, a painter.

Gribelin produced large numbers of book illustrations, the best-known of which are those to the second edition of Lord Shaftesbury's *Characteristicks*, published in 1714. He also engraved topographical subjects and portraits, but made a name for himself in the more prestigious genre of reproductions of paintings. The first of these to be successful was a print of 1693 after Charles Le Brun's *Alexander and the Family of Darius*. In 1707 he published *The Seven Cartons [sic] of Raphael Urbin*, after the studies for the Vatican tapestries (Royal Collection, on loan to the Victoria and Albert Museum). According to George Vertue, the prints sold 'mightily, whereby he Reap'd a good profitt, and made his fortune easy especially they having been not compleatly gravd before' (Vertue, *Note books*, 6.186). The set was advertised at 25s. in the *London Gazette* of 6–10 November 1707, where Gribelin's address was given as 'at the Corner-house of Banbury-Court in Long-Acre'. He was to remain in Long Acre for the rest of his life. In 1712 he published, from the same address in Banbury Court, prints after a further six paintings in the Royal Collection, advertised at 16s. in the *London Gazette* of 27–9 May 1712. In 1720 he published a set of the nine compartments making up Rubens's ceiling in the Banqueting House in Whitehall.

Gribelin died in London on 1 January 1733, having caught a cold after going to Westminster to see the opening of parliament. His son Samuel advertised in the *London Evening-Post* of 18–20 March 1735 that he was intending to complete another set of prints after celebrated masters which his father had not finished. He also offered for sale, from an address in Long Acre, a number of his father's publications and listed other stockists, presumably established trading contacts, including Bertrand at Bath and William Bellers at Oxford. At some time before 1741 four unfinished plates were sold at auction, together with those for the other large reproductive prints and for the ornament books.   SHEILA O'CONNELL

Sources Vertue, *Note books*, 3.65, 106; 4.189–90; 6.186–7 • T. Murdoch, 'Huguenot artists, designers and craftsmen in Great Britain and Ireland, 1680–1760', PhD diss., U. Lond., 1982 • S. O'Connell, 'Simon Gribelin (1661–1733), printmaker and metal engraver', *Print Quarterly*, 2 (1985), 27–38 • B. N. Lee, 'Simon Gribelin', *Book Plate Journal*, 6/1 (1988), 15–40 • C. Oman, *English engraved silver, 1150–1900* (1978) • W. Minet and W. C. Waller, eds., *Registers of the church known as La Patente in Spittlefields, from 1689 to 1785*, Huguenot Society of London, 11 (1898), 169

Grice, (Herbert) Paul (1913–1988), philosopher, was born on 15 March 1913 in Birmingham, the elder son (there were no daughters) of Herbert Grice, businessman and musician, and his wife, Mabel Felton, schoolmistress. He was educated at Clifton College, Bristol, where he was head boy and also distinguished himself in music and sports, and at Corpus Christi College, Oxford, where he was awarded first-class honours in classical honour moderations (1933) and *literae humaniores* (1935), and of which he later became an honorary fellow (1988). After a year as assistant master at Rossall School, Lancashire, and then

two years as Harmsworth senior scholar at Merton College, Oxford, he was appointed lecturer and in 1939 fellow and tutor in philosophy at St John's College, Oxford, and university lecturer in the sub-faculty of philosophy.

During the Second World War Grice served in the Royal Navy in the Atlantic theatre and then in Admiralty intelligence from 1940 to 1945. In 1942 he married Kathleen, daughter of George Watson, naval architect. They had a daughter and a son. By the mid-1950s he was widely recognized as one of the most original and independent philosophers in Oxford. At one time or another he taught an extraordinarily high number of those who were to become leading philosophers of the period, including Peter Strawson. He held visiting appointments at Harvard, Brandeis, Stanford, and Cornell universities, and was invited again to Harvard to deliver the William James lectures in 1967. He was elected a fellow of the British Academy in 1966. He became an honorary fellow of St John's in 1980.

In 1967 Grice left Oxford for a new life in the United States, as professor of philosophy at the University of California, Berkeley. There he continued through teaching and informal discussion to influence and challenge a steadily growing group of devoted students and colleagues. He gave many distinguished lectures, seminars, and symposia at universities, conferences, and professional associations all across the country. He was elected president of the Pacific division of the American Philosophical Association in 1975, and was invited to give their Carus lectures in 1983. Near the end of his life he carefully prepared for publication *Studies in the Way of Words* (1989), which contains most of his major essays, the William James lectures, some previously unpublished papers, and a retrospective assessment. His Carus lectures and related material on the metaphysics of value appeared as *The Conception of Value* in 1991.

Grice's most important and most influential work was in the philosophy of language, in particular the analysis of meaning. He proposed to define what a speaker means in saying something on a particular occasion in terms of the speaker's intentions to bring about certain effects in his audience through their recognition of those very intentions. He devised tests to reveal that many aspects of successful communication are due to the 'conversational implicatures' carried by a speaker's utterance rather than to logical implications carried by the meaning of the expression he uses or by what, strictly speaking, he says. He endeavoured thereby to show how the meanings or semantics of many expressions in natural language are more adequately represented by the familiar structures of mathematical logic than had been widely supposed. By means of this enterprise he sought to draw clearer limits to what can be concluded about meaning, necessity, and possibility from facts about linguistic usage. In these respects his work was a major factor in the fruitful *rapprochement* between Oxford philosophy of the 1960s and the more logically oriented philosophy then flourishing in the United States. His defence of the previously discredited causal theory of perception came to serve as prototype for an analytical strategy widely deployed elsewhere. In later years he concentrated on moral philosophy and, with characteristic imagination and metaphysical boldness, on the question of the objectivity of value, which, he held, required a realistic conception of finality or teleology in nature.

Though Grice thought continually about philosophy and wrote in manuscript a great deal, he published very little. This might have been thought attributable to practical inefficiency. His habits of life were in a way recklessly disorderly; the floor of his room in St John's was a dreadful litter of ashtrays, old clothes, scattered books and papers, cricket bats and balls, and (always unanswered, often unopened) correspondence. This apparent chaos was, however, deceptive. He was a man of formidable intellectual gifts, enormous energy, brooding temperament, and fiercely competitive spirit. His talents were well suited to his passions for chess, bridge, which he played for Oxfordshire for some years, and above all cricket, to which he largely devoted most of his summers while living in England. His musical talent was a more private, personal matter. His piano-playing was—like his considerable prowess as a batsman—fluent and forceful rather than elegant. It was understood by his friends that he was also a quite serious composer; but here, as in philosophy, he could not bring himself to think that any piece was ever really finished, and his works, it appeared, were permanently awaiting revision. That he published so little philosophy was due to this fixed idea that publication implied a claim to have got matters completely right, but a few months' further thought would always show this claim to be ill-founded.

In some ways the practices of teaching in Oxford did not suit Grice. In philosophy he throve on the stimulus of dialogue and debate, question and answer, thrust and counter-thrust; a silent, respectful, note-taking lecture audience bored and depressed him. Also, in private tutorials, he could be gloomily unforthcoming with pupils whose offerings were too feeble to be challenging. The seminar was his preferred habitat. He was a shrewd master of strategy, with the capacity to hold elaborate schemes or lines of argument in his mind and to unfold them slowly and deliberately, revealing the next step only when it was needed. His methodical, increasingly gleeful demolition of opposing philosophical theories, and occasionally of his own, was a minor art form for the connoisseur. He was highly prolific in thought; he had more ideas, questions, and projects than he could ever have worked out in a dozen lifetimes. A man of strong appetites and impressive girth, he could be, when engaged, a deviously witty and highly convivial companion of fearsome endurance. Grice died in Berkeley on 28 August 1988.

BARRY STROUD and G. J. WARNOCK, *rev.*

Sources university records, U. Cal. • *The Times* (30 Aug 1988) • private information (1996) • personal knowledge (1996)
Archives U. Cal.

Gridley, Jeremiah (1702–1767), lawyer in America, was born in Boston, Massachusetts, on 10 March 1702, the son of Captain Richard Gridley, a public official and currier, and his wife, Rebecca. Jeremiah graduated AB (1725) and MA (1727) from Harvard College; he was a schoolmaster at Boston's South Grammar School from 1727 to 1733, and studied law. About 1730 he married Abigail Lewis (d. 1755), with whom he had three daughters. Throughout his life he distinguished himself in the law, influencing a generation of lawyers and serving in government and in maritime affairs, a broad-minded, cultivated man in the generation of those who helped to establish the culture of independence which was part of the move towards an American revolution.

Gridley had strong tastes for journalism and edited the *Weekly Rehearsal* from 1731 to 1733, but by the mid-1730s turned to law. By 1742 he was elected attorney-general by the Massachusetts house of representatives, although he did not take his seat because Governor William Shirley authorized another incumbent. Gridley was appointed justice of the peace for Suffolk county in 1746 and again in 1761. He was a leading lawyer and teacher. John Adams sought his assistance in the 1750s and 1760s, and he trained such leading lawyers as William Cushing, later a supreme court justice, the patriot James Otis junior, and Benjamin Prat, chief justice of New York from 1761 to 1763. In 1765 Gridley formed a group called 'Sodality', which met weekly to read and discuss classic works of the law, inspiring many such as John Adams. In 1767 he was again elected attorney-general, this time taking up his seat.

Gridley, like many men of his era, was a man of many interests, and was one of the founders of Boston's West Church in 1737, and in June 1742 assisted in the formation of the Fellowship Club, later incorporated on 2 February 1754 as the Marine Society. On 11 May 1748 he became a freemason, in St John's Lodge, Boston, of which he became a master in 1754. Later in the same year, in October, he was installed as grand master of the masons for North America and served in that capacity until his death. After he moved to Brookline, some time after 1755, he was regularly elected moderator of the First Parish Church and held other local offices.

Gridley's most famous case was argued before the Massachusetts superior court in 1761 against James Otis; in this he defended the authority of the British parliament to grant courts the power to issue writs of assistance to royal customs officers, even though it overrode individual rights. Despite the fact that he argued on behalf of British rights, his general popularity and reputation with leading early American patriots was not affected; for instance he was appointed to represent the governor and council of Boston in 1765 in a matter respecting reopening of the courts before the crown. After his death on 10 September 1767 at Brookline, Massachusetts, the cause of which was given as 'a rising of the lights', his funeral was attended by a great gathering, including as pallbearers Lieutenant-Governor Thomas Hutchinson and his old rival James Otis. Some have claimed that he had a 'difficult public personality'; however John Adams stated that 'Gridley's

Grandeur consists in his great Learning, his great Parts and his majestic Manner. But is diminished by stiffness and affectation'.   MURNEY GERLACH

Sources L. K. Wroth, 'Gridley, Jeremiah', *ANB* · C. K. Shipton, *Sibley's Harvard graduates: biographical sketches of those who attended Harvard College*, 7 (1945), 518–30 · R. G. F. Candage, 'The Gridley House, Brookline, and Jeremy Gridley', *Brookline Historical Society Publications*, 1 (1903) · S. L. Knapp, *Biographical sketches of eminent lawyers, statesmen, and men of letters* (1821) · S. M. Quincy, ed., *Reports of cases argued and adjudged in the superior court of judicature … by Josiah Quincy, jr.* (1865) · *Legal papers of John Adams*, ed. L. K. Wroth and H. B. Zobel, 3 vols. (1965), vols. 1–2 · *Diary and autobiography of John Adams*, ed. L. H. Butterfield and others, 1–3 (1961) · M. H. Smith, *The writs of assistance case* (1978), 269–92 · D. R. Coquillette, 'Justinian in Braintree: John Adams, civilian learning, and legal élitism, 1758–1775', *Law in colonial Massachusetts* (1984), 359–418 · *Boston Gazette and Country Journal* [Boston, MA] (14 Sept 1767) · *Massachusetts Gazette and Boston News-Letter* (17 Sept 1767)

Archives Massachusetts State Archives, Massachusetts superior court records and files

Grier, (Mary) Lynda Dorothea (1880–1967), educational administrator, was born on 3 May 1880 at Rugeley, Staffordshire, the second child of Richard Macgregor Grier (1835–1894), at that time rural dean of Rugeley and prebendary of Lichfield, and his wife, Grace Allen. She had an older brother, Selwyn Macgregor Grier (1878–1946), who became a colonial administrator.

As a child, Lynda Grier was deaf, short-sighted, and ungainly, and was a disappointment to her mother. She described her father, whom she adored, as courageous, unworldly, outspoken, a radical, and great egalitarian; she inherited from him a belief in the equality of humankind, irrespective of social standing. The family was poor and became even poorer when her father moved in 1890 to the parish of Hednesford, Staffordshire, at the heart of a 'drunken coal mining district' (autobiographical manuscript, Grier MSS). She was taught by her aunt, who confused her deafness with stupidity, and later by her mother. Neither woman possessed any pedagogical talent. She read whatever books were available, learning poetry by heart, and devouring works of Euclid and later Pascal, attracted by their logical reasoning. She also learnt from her father as he went about his work, as he spoke clearly and logically, and she was able to lip-read. Despite these difficulties, she remembered her childhood home as happy until the time of her father's death when she was fourteen. The following ten years, she described as the dreariest of her life. The family's poverty became acute and she and her mother stayed with relatives before finally moving into a house in Cannock. She was expected to act as her mother's companion and while she loved and admired her mother, she found her possessiveness irksome.

In 1904 mother and daughter moved to Cambridge. Lynda's hearing had improved and she attended the public meetings of the British Association for the Advancement of Science (BAAS) that held its annual conference in Cambridge that year. She chose the economics lectures as the only 'science' not requiring previous knowledge and became fascinated by the subject. Mary Paley Marshall of Newnham College gave her permission to attend college lectures in economics (Tullberg). Filled with self-doubt about her abilities, she was registered as an external student the following year, the college paying her fees. After rapidly learning from scratch the basic mathematics, French, Greek, and Latin required for matriculation, she worked for the newly instituted economics tripos. She passed part two in 1908, she and another Newnham student being alone in the first class. She greatly enjoyed the companionship of Newnham and grew in confidence, although her ponderous appearance and logical thought did not attract the same attention as the sparkling intellectual performance of her younger and prettier contemporaries.

After her successful tripos examination, Grier remained in Cambridge with her mother, and assisted Mary Paley Marshall with teaching and advice to students reading economics in Newnham. The college appointed Grier assistant lecturer in 1913 and lecturer in 1915. That year she was asked to take over the work of D. H. MacGregor, professor of economics at Leeds University, who had been called up on war duties. Leeds was a young and modern civic university that from the first had given full recognition to its women students and staff. Its vice-chancellor, Michael Sadler, held that the university should be a servant of the whole community. After the theoretical, academic world of Cambridge, Grier was faced with the practical problems not only of established local industries but also of munitions and other war-related industries located in the Leeds area. Government requests for information and statistics led her to study the substitution of men by women in munitions factories during the war. Her report was published by the BAAS in 1921.

At Leeds, Grier realized that her interests lay specifically in the field of education, secondary, tertiary, and extramural—the university was a strong supporter of the local Workers' Educational Association (WEA). She was particularly concerned to provide educational opportunities for people who had lacked them in their youth, perhaps a reflection on her own inadequate grounding and the good fortune that befell her in Cambridge. Leeds University also provided an insight into the administrative work involved in expanding and consolidating a new institution and provided valuable lessons of co-operation and delegation. Her friendship with Sadler led her into the world of modern art of which 'he was a discriminating and avid collector' (*Brown Book*, 17), and she herself became a discerning collector. At Leeds, she met Winifrid Mercier, vice-principal of the city's teacher training college. Her friendship and admiration for Sadler and Mercier led her in later life to write their biographies. These periods at Cambridge and Leeds provide conflicting pictures of Grier, the shy, gauche student and tutor, devout Anglican and teetotaller, and the self-confident, competent, and able teacher, investigator, and administrator, meeting all sections of the public with easy friendliness.

Grier returned to Newnham in 1919, now as a fellow, also acting as part-time tutor in economics at Bedford College, London. Perhaps the return to Cambridge with its social exclusiveness, and lack of recognition for women bruised her new-found confidence. When her name was canvassed as a possible successor to the retiring Newnham principal, she was opposed by a section of the college. Her work since 1908 was forgotten; it was held that she had only been at the college one year and lacked the qualities to make a good head of house. B. A. Clough was appointed principal at Newnham and in 1921 Grier became principal of Lady Margaret Hall (LMH), Oxford.

This was an exciting yet sensitive time for women at Oxford who had been granted degrees and university membership in 1920. They needed to establish their position within the university. For LMH, this involved overhauling finances and accommodation, drawing up a constitution, building up the academic staff and student numbers, and adapting college regulations to cope with not only the new status but also the academic and social demands of post-war women. Grier accomplished these changes by stretching her administrative skills, by persuasion and delegation. She also found time to coach the philosophy, politics, and economics students in economics. Her teaching emphasized the study of economics as a behavioural science while demanding logical thought and clarity of expression. Other students encountered her through her participation in the daily services in the college chapel and the sermons that she preached. Staff and students alike described her as 'magnificent', 'stately', 'dignified', remarking on her love of brightly coloured clothes and imposing hats, and appreciated the good sense with which she dealt with the college and university rules that circumscribed the lives of women students (*Brown Book*, 19–34).

In 1926 Grier was elected as the first woman to serve on the hebdomadal council, the policy-forming body of Oxford University. Her competence and ability to work with men for the good of the whole university rather than as a representative of the women's colleges was appreciated, and she was elected to various sub-committees. In particular, she warmly supported the foundation of Nuffield College where she was faculty fellow, 1944–5, and chairman of Nuffield's education committee, 1943–6. She was governor of a number of schools and continued to support the work of the WEA. She served on government trade boards and wages councils and, from 1924 to 1938, was a member of the consultative committee of the Board of Education, which produced the famous Hadow report (1926) on the education of the adolescent, and the Spens report (1938) on secondary education. She was also a member of the archbishops' commission on religious education (1927–9). Her breadth of knowledge on economic, social, and educational matters led to the unusual distinction of being invited to act in 1925 as president of section F (which included economics) and in 1945 as president of section L (education) of the BAAS, the association whose public lectures in 1904 had given Grier her first taste of economics and the academic life.

Grier retired as principal of LMH in 1945 but was immediately invited to make a three-month educational tour of China, representing the British Council. The visit took place in 1947 at a time of considerable political turmoil.

She toured China, lecturing on educational issues and developed a great love for the country, its art, and its people. When the post of chief representative for the British Council in China fell vacant, Grier accepted the appointment and spent the years 1948–50 in China. The revolution was at its height and she was in Shanghai when communist forces took the city. She travelled as widely as possible under complicated and dangerous conditions, visiting educational establishments, often unable to communicate with base, so that at one time she was posted as 'missing'. On her return to Britain, she was made a CBE for her services in China.

Now over seventy, Grier lectured and broadcast on China, its history and problems. In 1953, as the first Cambridge-trained women to receive the distinction, she was awarded an honorary LLD at Cambridge for her life's work. In 1961 she set out on a world tour to visit her wide circle of friends and see important artworks. The itinerary proved too demanding, and although she met many old friends in the East, she fell ill during the return journey. Baroness Stocks described the trip as 'a triumphant tour of an active VIP—a grand and dramatic finish to a great life' and one that Grier did not regret (*Brown Book*, 47). In her final years, she was partially paralysed and very deaf. She died on 21 August 1967 in London and was buried, at her own request, beside her parents in Hednesford.

RITA McWILLIAMS TULLBERG

Sources Lady Margaret Hall, Oxford, Grier MSS · [A. B. White and others], eds., *Newnham College register, 1871–1971*, 2nd edn, 1 (1979), 1.12 · *Brown Book* (May 1968) [Lynda Grier memorial number] · R. M. Tullberg, 'Marshall's final lecture, 21 May 1908', *History of Political Economy*, 25 (1993), 605–15 · *The Times* (23 Aug 1967) **Archives** Lady Margaret Hall, Oxford, MSS · U. Leeds, corresp. | BBC WAC, scripts of talks · BL, letters to A. Mansbridge, Add. MS 65258 | SOUND BL NSA, 'Home for the day' 24 June 1960, M7557W&R–M7558W&R C2 · BL NSA, oral history interview **Likenesses** J. Gunn, oils, Lady Margaret Hall, Oxford · group portraits, photographs, U. Leeds · group portraits, photographs, Lady Margaret Hall, Oxford · photographs, repro. in *Brown Book* **Wealth at death** £28,003: probate, 16 Oct 1967, CGPLA Eng. & Wales

Grier, Sydney C. *See* Gregg, Hilda Caroline (1867/8–1933).

Grierson [née Crawley], **Constantia** (1704/5–1732), classical scholar and editor, was born in co. Kilkenny of 'poor illiterate country people' (Pilkington, 1.17) and was tutored in Hebrew, Greek, Latin, English, and French by her local vicar. She was also knowledgeable in mathematics, and her mother insisted that she became efficient in needlework. According to Laetitia Pilkington 'her Learning appeared like the Gift poured out of the Apostles, of speaking all languages without the Pains of Study; or, like the intuitive Knowledge of Angels' (ibid.).

At about eighteen Constantia Crawley moved to Dublin and began to study midwifery under Dr Van Lewen, a Dutch physician and the father of Laetitia Pilkington. Soon she met the publisher George *Grierson (c.1680–1753) and in 1724 began editing Virgil's *Opera* for him. By 1727 she had carefully edited other titles in the pocket classics edition, including Terence's *Comediae*, to which she prefixed a Greek epigram from her own pen, inscribing it to Robert, son of Lord Carteret; in 1730 she edited the work of Tacitus, inscribing it to Lord Carteret himself. Jonathan Swift was so impressed with her editing that he wrote to Alexander Pope on 6 February 1730: 'She is a very good Latin and Greek scholar, and hath lately published a fine edition of Tacitus, and she writes *carmina Anglicana non contemnenda*' (*Correspondence*, 3.369). The edition was also much praised by the classical scholar Edward Harwood.

Constantia Crawley's marriage to Grierson in 1726, after the death of his first wife in May, is unrecorded for the reason that she was expecting his child; George Primrose was baptized at St John, Drumconda, on 17 July but in September he was 'overlaid and killed through the carelessness of the nurse' (Elias, 45). Another child, presumably George Abraham, was baptized on 1 October 1728, but two daughters were buried, in 1731 and 1733.

Constantia Grierson played an important role in her husband's business and household, which included apprentices and journeymen as well as domestic servants. Highly regarded by Dublin's literary élite for her gifts as an editor as well as a poet, and for her remarkable memory, women from the landed gentry of Ireland were attracted to her and became some of her husband's most valued customers. Only a few of her poems are extant, six of which her friend Mary Barber published in her collection *Poems on Several Occasions* (1734).

On 3 January 1730 the Griersons petitioned the Irish House of Commons for the patent of king's printer. Their petition stressed Constantia's contribution to the business:

> Petitioner Constantia hath, in a more particular manner, applied herself to the correcting of the Press, which she has performed to general satisfaction; in so much, that the Editions corrected by her have been approved of, not only in this Kingdom, but in Great Britain, Holland and elsewhere, and the Art of Printing, through her care and assistance, has been brought to greater perfection than has been hitherto in this Kingdom. (Elias, 40)

The petition was successful and the office of king's printer was granted to Grierson for forty years in reversion after the death of the current patentee, Andrew Crooke (d. 1732).

Constantia Grierson was editing an edition of *Sallust* at the time of her death, aged twenty-seven, in Dublin on 2 December 1732, and a copy of it, with her annotations, came into the possession of Lord George Germain. She was buried on 4 December at St John's cemetery in Dublin. Her only surviving child, George Abraham, died in Düsseldorf in 1755, two years after her husband's death. Her reputation was greatly enhanced by her inclusion in George Ballard's *Memoirs of Several Ladies of Great Britain, who have been Celebrated for their Writings or Still in the Learned Languages, Arts and Sciences* (1752).   D. BEN REES

Sources M. Pollard, *A dictionary of members of the Dublin book trade 1550–1800* (2000) • K. O'Céirín and C. O'Céirín, *Women of Ireland: a biographic dictionary* (1996), 95 • M. Mac Curtain and M. O'Dowd, 'An agenda for women's history in Ireland, 1500–1800', *Irish Historical Studies*, 28 (1992–3), 1–19 • R. Cargill Cole, *Irish booksellers and English writers, 1740–1800* (1956) • S. J. Connolly, ed., *The Oxford companion to Irish history* (1998), 231 • A. J. Webb, *A compendium of Irish biography* (1878), 237 • J. T. Gilbert, *A history of the city of Dublin*, 3 vols. (1854–9) • A. C. Elias, 'A manuscript book of Constantia Grierson's', *Swift Studies*, 2 (1987), 33–56 • L. Pilkington, *Memoirs of Laetitia Pilkington*, ed. A. C. Elias, 2 vols. (1997) • *The correspondence of Jonathan Swift*, ed. H. Williams and [D. Woolley], rev. edn, 5 vols. (1965–72) • *DNB* • *The poetry of Laetitia Pilkington (1712–1750) and Constantia Grierson (1706–1733)*, ed. B. Tucker (1996)

Grierson, George (*c.*1680–1753), bookseller and printer, was born in Edinburgh, the son of George Grierson, merchant, and his wife, Margaret Allane. His father's family had held estates in Dumfriesshire and Kirkcudbrightshire since the early fifteenth century. His elder brother James became minister of religion at Tingwall, Shetland. Nothing is known of George's early life and training except that he moved to Dublin in 1703 as a bookseller and printer. He purchased a house in Essex Street in Dublin for £533 and was admitted in 1709 as freeman of the city. In 1720 he set up his own printing house and was made a churchwarden of St John the Evangelist, Drumcondra, on the outskirts of Dublin. It seems that his printing office and his house were situated at Drumcondra.

Grierson's first wife, Mary, was buried at St John's on 19 May 1726, and in the same year he married the talented classical scholar Constantia Crawley (1704/5–1732) of co. Kilkenny [see Grierson, Constantia]. As she was a good friend of Jonathan Swift, Grierson's reputation as a printer was considerably enhanced. With her help he was appointed printer-general to the king in Ireland, and the post was confirmed by a patent dated 1 December 1727. Lord Carteret praised the work of both Grierson and his wife in a letter of 20 December 1730 to the duke of Newcastle, in which he claimed that they had made printing into an art and recommended that Grierson should succeed Andrew Crooke as the king's printer. Grierson was appointed to the office of king's printer after Cooke's death in July 1732, and received a final grant of the office to himself and his heirs on 1 December 1744. Constantia died on 2 December 1732 at the age of twenty-seven and was buried at St John's on 4 December, mourned by her only surviving son, George Abraham, and her husband, who depended so much on her scholarship and contacts. Grierson none the less married for a third time on 20 August 1734 at Belfast. His bride was a widow, Jane Cromie (*née* Blow); they had seven children, three of whom died young.

Grierson was a successful businessman, and besides his own books he published for the government and for institutions such as Dr Steevens's hospital; between 1735 and 1748 he earned £650 from printing for the Incorporated Society for Promoting English Protestant Schools. His publishing output was certainly large by Irish standards. His wife's editions of Virgil, Terence, Justinian, Juvenal, and Tacitus, which were published between 1724 and 1730, became known as Grierson's Classics, and his reprints included *Pope's Miscellany Poems* (1736), which sold nearly 1500 copies. Grierson also had the sole rights to reprinting Bibles, the Book of Common Prayer, and Psalms in Dublin; in 1749 he published 20,000 copies of the New Testament to 'open the eyes of the poor Papists'. His fine editions of Sir William Petty's *Maps of Ireland* and Dupin's *Ecclesiastical History*, in three folio volumes (1722–4), added to his reputation.

Grierson died in Dublin on 27 October 1753, and left the king's printer's patent and a quarter of his estate to his son George Abraham, on condition that his half-brother Hugh Boulter should receive a quarter of the benefits when aged twenty-one. Grierson's brothers-in-law George Ewing, a bookseller in Dublin who married Jane Grierson in 1718, and James Blow (1676–1759), a Belfast printer, were his executors. In 1759 his widow moved to Castle Street, Dublin, where she carried on the bookselling business.   D. BEN REES

Sources J. R. H. Greeves, 'King's printers', *Irish Genealogist*, 2 (1955), 303–7 · J. R. H. Greeves, 'Two Irish printing families', *Proceedings of the Belfast Natural History Society*, ser. 2, 4 (1955), 38–44 · J. R. H. Greeves, 'Testamentary records', *Irish Genealogist*, 2 (1955), 219 · M. Pollard, *A dictionary of members of the Dublin book trade 1550–1800* (2000) · S. J. Connolly, ed., *The Oxford companion to Irish history* (1998), 231 · E. O. Blackburne [E. O. B. Casey], *Illustrious Irish women* (1877) · J. T. Gilbert, *History of Dublin* (1859) · R. Munter, *A dictionary of the print trade in Ireland, 1550–1775* (1988)

Wealth at death left patent as king's printer to elder son; quarter share to younger son at twenty-one

Grierson, Sir George Abraham (1851–1941), administrator in India and philologist, was born at Glenageary, co. Dublin, on 7 January 1851, the eldest son of George Abraham Grierson LLD, printer to the queen in Dublin, and his wife, Isabella, daughter of Henry Ruxton RN of Ardee, co. Louth. He was educated at St Bees grammar school, Shrewsbury School, and Trinity College, Dublin, where he read mathematics. He passed (twenty-eighth in the list) into the Indian Civil Service in 1871. In two further probationary years at Trinity College he won university prizes in Sanskrit and Hindustani, and was placed twelfth in the final examination. He fell deeply under the influence of Robert Atkinson, professor of oriental languages at Trinity College, who inspired him with his own linguistic interests and, before Grierson sailed for Bengal in 1873, proposed to him a life-task in the form of a linguistic survey of India.

Having been appointed to the Bengal presidency, Grierson fulfilled for the next twenty-three years the active duties of a member of the Indian Civil Service, and successfully combined this work with an impressive career of linguistic scholarship. In 1880 he married Lucy Elizabeth Jean (d. 1943), daughter of Maurice Henry Fitzgerald Collis MD, a famous Dublin surgeon. There were no children. In 1881 Grierson was assistant and for a time officiating magistrate and collector at Patna, where in 1884 he became joint magistrate and collector. His linguistic research had begun earlier, however: in 1877, four years after his arrival in India, he had published the first of his works on the languages and folklore of India. For the next ten years his attention was mainly focused on the languages and dialects of Bihar. The independence of this important group of Indo-Aryan languages had been clearly demonstrated by A. F. R. Hoernlé in his *Comparative*

Sir George Abraham Grierson (1851–1941), by Bassano, 1920

Grammar of the Gaudian Languages (1880), but it was Grierson who provided detailed knowledge of both their structure and their content. Two works of major importance belong to this period: *Seven Grammars of the Dialects and Subdialects of the Bihārī Language* (in eight parts, 1883–7) and *Bihār Peasant Life, being a Discursive Catalogue of the Surroundings of the People of that Province* (1885). This latter, a volume of 592 pages, reprinted in 1926, contains an exhaustive account of the daily life of an agricultural population; the comparative vocabularies are illustrated by drawings, photographs, and descriptions.

After special duty at Howrah, Grierson spent five years at Gaya (1887–92); he became magistrate and collector in 1890. His linguistic interests expanded, and he began to consider the languages of Hindustan proper. He wrote extensively on both their modern forms and their medieval literature, studying especially the two great epics, the *Ramayan* of Tulsidas, and the *Padumavati* of Jaisi, an edition and translation of the first thirty-five cantos of which he published in 1896 in collaboration with Sudhakara Dvivedi. In 1889 *The Modern Vernacular Literature of Hindustan* appeared as a special number of the *Journal* of the Asiatic Society of Bengal. In 1885 his translation of Emile Senart's inscriptions of Piyadasi had been published in the *Indian Antiquary*. This showed a growing interest already aroused in the history and comparative philology of the whole Indo-Aryan group of languages, an interest which resulted not only in numerous articles on individual languages but also in a conspectus of the main lines of their development, described in Grierson's articles in the *Zeitschrift der Deutschen Morgenländischen Gesellschaft* in 1895, 'On the phonology of the modern Indo-Aryan vernaculars'.

In 1895 Grierson was appointed additional commissioner at Patna, and in 1896 held his final normal appointment with the civil service, as opium agent for Bihar. In 1895 he had published the first of a long series of articles and books on Kashmiri, work which was to culminate in *A Dictionary of the Kashmīrī Language*, comprising 1252 pages, the first part of which appeared in 1916 and the last in 1932. Kashmiri is one of the Dardic languages: to these Grierson attributed, though perhaps wrongly, the European and Asian Gypsy dialects, on the affinities of which he wrote a number of articles from 1888 onwards. After the Muslim invasion of north-west India the other members of the Dardic group, spoken in the remote and inaccessible valleys of the upper Indus and its tributaries among the mountains of the Hindu Kush, were largely cut off from the main stream of Indo-Aryan linguistic development, and show both many archaic features and striking innovations. These languages were at best little known, and to the knowledge available from notes and word-lists compiled mainly by soldiers and political officers was now added further information, which began to be collected in connection with the *Linguistic Survey of India*, a project of which Grierson was designated superintendent in 1898.

All this Grierson utilized in studying the Dardic or, as he named them, the Piśāca languages in numerous articles, beginning in 1898, and in two books: *The Piśāca Languages of North-Western India* (1906) and *Torwālī* (1929). Affinities which he traced in certain Iranian languages to the Dardic group led to the publication of two monographs, *Ōrmurī* (1918) and *Ishkashmī, Zebakī and Yazghulāmī* (1920). Any attempt to trace the history of the Indo-Aryan languages necessarily involves study of the Prakrit dialects which stand as intermediaries between Sanskrit and the modern languages: here also Grierson made notable contributions, especially through his studies of the eastern school of Prakrit grammarians. The collection of material for the *Linguistic Survey* further brought Grierson into contact with language families outside the Indo-Aryan, and he published papers on Ahom, an old language of Assam, and, in conjunction with Professor Sten Konow, on the Kuki-Chin languages.

Grierson's output of scientific work over the whole field was thus actively continued throughout the time he was engaged in the compilation of the *Linguistic Survey of India*, that is from its inception in 1898 to its completion in 1928. It was in fulfilment of the injunction of his old teacher Atkinson that Grierson had proposed this project before the Oriental Congress held in Vienna in 1886. The congress recommended it to the government of India, and the scope and general lines of procedure as adopted by the superintendent had been under discussion for the four years preceding his appointment. The materials were to include (as far as possible for every language, dialect, and subdialect, which in many districts varied from village to village or between classes or sexes) a version of the parable of the prodigal son, an orally elicited narrative or statement, and a scheduled vocabulary of words and phrases. For this purpose Grierson had a multitude of correspondents, official and non-official. After the critical examination and selection of texts and translations, in each case the final entry contained geographical and census particulars, bibliography, discussion of group relations, and a grammatical sketch, based on the materials, with reference to any prior knowledge, and comprising phonology, morphology, syntax, and script. The immensity of this task may be judged by the fact that the nineteen folio volumes, containing nearly 8000 pages, provide descriptions of 179 separate languages (of which the test was mutual unintelligibility) and 544 dialects belonging to five separate and distinct families: the Mon-Khmer and Tai, the Tibeto-Burman, the Munda, the Dravidian, the Indo-Aryan and Iranian. For some years Grierson was assisted by the Norwegian scholar Sten Konow, but he himself compiled at least two-thirds of the total. This monumental work is an inexhaustible mine for all students of the languages of India, and it stimulated in Indians a deep pride and interest in their own vernaculars and history. In 1903 Grierson retired from India and continued his work on the *Survey* at Camberley. There he built his house, Rathfarnham (named after his grandfather's castle in co. Dublin), which for nearly forty years was a place of pilgrimage for a long succession of orientalists and other, especially Indian, visitors.

Grierson was appointed CIE in 1894 and KCIE in 1912, and was appointed to the Order of Merit in 1928. He received honorary degrees from the universities of Halle, Dublin, Cambridge, Oxford, and Bihar, and he was an honorary member of numerous learned societies. He was a fellow of the British Academy from 1917 to 1939, and was president of the Gypsy Lore Society in 1927.

Grierson was admired for his broad humanity, his delightful humour, his love and practice of music, and his never-failing kindness. He was large in body, mind, and soul. He had a boundless energy and enthusiasm, and a firmness of spirit which, held undeviating on the path he had chosen, triumphed over every difficulty of circumstance. Neither age nor sickness diminished that enthusiasm or dimmed that spirit. He died at Rathfarnham, Camberley, on 9 March 1941.

R. L. TURNER, *rev.* JOHN D. HAIGH

Sources personal knowledge (1959) · R. L. Turner, 'Sir George A. Grierson', *Journal of the Royal Asiatic Society of Great Britain and Ireland* (1941), 383–6 · F. W. Thomas and R. L. Turner, 'George Abraham Grierson, 1851–1941', *PBA*, 28 (1942), 283–306 · *The Times* (10 March 1941) · H. Stammerjohan, *Lexicon grammaticorum* (1996), 369–70 · *Indian Linguistics: Bulletin of the Linguistic Society of India* [Lahore], vol. 1/1 (1931) · C. E. Buckland, *Dictionary of Indian biography* (1906) · *Who's who in Surrey* (1936), 163 · *India Office List* (1936)

Archives BL, papers, MSS Eur E 223 | BL, corresp. with Sir Richard Temple, MSS Eur F 98 · BL OIOC, letters to Bubu Shyama Charan Ganguly · Bodl. Oxf., corresp. with Sir Aurel Stein | FILM BFI NFTVA, news footage

Likenesses Bassano, photograph, 1920, NPG [*see illus.*]

Wealth at death £5873 9s. 8d.: resworn probate, 7 July 1941, *CGPLA Eng. & Wales*

Grierson, Sir Herbert John Clifford (1866–1960), literary critic and scholar, was born on 16 January 1866 in Commercial Street, Lerwick, Shetland, the third of the six children of Andrew John Grierson (1832–1896) and Alice Geraldine Clifford (1837–1917). His father owned the estate of Quendale, about 1000 acres in the south of the mainland of Shetland. His mother was Irish.

Grierson attended the Anderson Institute in Lerwick for a brief period, but in 1875 was sent to a school in Cheltenham run by two of his mother's sisters. In 1877 he was moved to the Gymnasium in Aberdeen, a private school founded in 1847 and attended by the sons of landed families in Aberdeenshire. From 1883 he was a student at King's College, in the University of Aberdeen, and followed the standard three-year curriculum, which included Latin, Greek, mathematics, physics, and philosophy. He also took a short course on rhetoric and English literature under William Minto: the complete English curriculum covered Chaucer to Marlowe without even reaching Shakespeare. In his fourth year he studied Plato and Kant by himself for the optional honours examination in philosophy. He won the Bain gold medal in philosophy and the Seafield medal in English, and graduated in 1887.

Grierson's father was badly affected by the passing of the Crofters' Act in 1886 and the subsequent reduction of rents, and from 1887 could afford to give his son only a dress allowance of £30 a year. Grierson had to keep himself: from 1886 he worked as a housemaster at the Gymnasium and, when that closed, at Desclaye's, a school for girls; he also tutored and corrected essays for Minto. In 1889 he sat for the Holford exhibition at Christ Church in Oxford, which he won with an essay on fanaticism. Four years later he graduated with a first in *literae humaniores*.

The recommendations of the Scottish universities' commission (1889), implemented in 1892, reconstituted the curriculum on the American system of optional courses for the ordinary MA, established specialist honours degrees, and created new subjects, such as English. In Aberdeen Minto died in the first year of the new dispensation, and on 30 September 1893 the principal, Sir William Geddes, wrote to Grierson intimating that the senate had unanimously agreed to recommend his appointment as a lecturer in English literature for the coming session. In the following year he was appointed to the new chair in English, created by an endowment of £10,000 given by John Grey Chalmers. Patronage was vested in the crown, and to secure his appointment Grierson had to engage in some discreet lobbying of local MPs.

On 2 September 1896 Grierson married Mary Letitia (1867/8–1937), daughter of Sir Alexander *Ogston, professor of surgery in Aberdeen and surgeon-in-ordinary to the royal family in Scotland. Mary had had to endure an unsympathetic, repressive stepmother and as a result the Grierson family was determinedly happy. They lived first in Old Aberdeen but moved to a modern house, 7 King's Gate, to escape damp. They had five daughters: Molly, Flora, Alice, Letty, and Janet. Grierson was hopelessly impractical and the house was run by Mary, who paid the bills and kept them solvent, and who sheltered her husband (except at stated intervals) from familial interruptions and other distractions.

In his time as professor in Aberdeen (1894–1915) Grierson established English literature as an academic subject. The ordinary class was supplemented by a higher class in 1896. In 1898 the institution of a lectureship in history enabled the establishment of honours in English (language, literature, and British history), from which the first students graduated in 1900. The curriculum expanded and Grierson soon recognized that two years of honours classes were required, and he introduced language as a subject for specialist study. By 1914 there were six graduating classes in English, an ordinary, and advanced and two honours classes in both language and literature. He had also established a tutorial system for honours students.

Grierson's great passion was for poetry. As a boy he had been greatly taken by Scott and Byron, but when a student those enthusiasms were superseded by Tennyson. As professor he concentrated mainly on Shakespeare and the poetry of the seventeenth century, but on whatever subject he talked he seemed to have mesmerized his audience with an enthusiasm and quality of voice that none could forget. He was a truly inspirational lecturer, but his shyness made meetings with individual students rather awkward and he did not enjoy tutorials.

Grierson's work as scholar and teacher is marked by his exceptional breadth of knowledge. He was invited by Saintsbury to write a volume in his Periods of European Literature series, and when *The First Half of the Seventeenth Century* (his first work) appeared in 1906 Grierson began with the literature of the Netherlands, specifically its 'lyrical poetry of singular depth and richness' (p. 3), before proceeding to the literature of England, France, Germany, and Italy. He already had the linguistic competence to write on the last three, but learned Dutch in order to write the book. His erudition shows too in his style of analysis; he says of Donne, for instance, that in his poetry 'the imaginative, emancipated spirit of the Renaissance came into abrupt contact, and blended in the strangest way with the scholastic pedantry and subtlety of the controversial court of James' (pp. 156–7). The implicit view of the Renaissance is not now accepted, but the style of exposition combines literary and political knowledge to characterize an exceptional psychological disposition and frame of mind.

Grierson wrote again on Donne for *The Cambridge History of English Literature* (1909) and in consequence was invited to edit Donne's poetry for Oxford University Press. The two volumes that appeared in 1912 are not only Grierson's greatest work but are also one of the greatest works of literary scholarship in the twentieth century. Grierson had to determine both the text and the canon of Donne, only three of whose poems had been printed during his lifetime. He demonstrated by detailed textual analysis the deterioration in the posthumous printed texts and, having established the edition of 1633 as superior to others, discriminated between manuscript versions by considering provenance and by applying, for the first time in the editing of English vernacular literature, Karl Lachmann's mode of reconstructing the lost original (about which Grierson probably learned in Oxford from John A. Stewart). Further he brought to Donne an extraordinary knowledge of scholastic literature, so that *The Poems of John Donne* simultaneously offered the first reliable text and an unrivalled exposition of the poetry.

In 1915 Grierson moved to Edinburgh to succeed Saintsbury as professor of rhetoric and English literature. He took with him the curricular ideas and scheme of teaching that he had developed in Aberdeen, and as soon as accommodation permitted he introduced them at his new university. In the following twenty years Grierson published much, including anthologies such as the greatly influential *Metaphysical Lyrics and Poems of the Seventeenth Century* (1921) and his finest work of criticism, *Cross Currents in English Literature in the XVIIth Century* (1929). His twelve-volume edition *The Letters of Sir Walter Scott* (1932–7) was less happy because the scale of the task was not recognized sufficiently early. It led, however, to his biography *Sir Walter Scott, Bart.* (1938), the first and still the most important deconstruction of the fictional interpretation of Scott offered in Lockhart.

Grierson was elected a fellow of the British Academy in 1923, and was awarded twelve honorary degrees. He retired in 1935, and in the following year was knighted and elected rector of the University of Edinburgh by the student body (serving until 1939). Later works include *Essays and Addresses* (1940), *The English Bible* (1944), and *Rhetoric and English Composition* (1945).

In Edinburgh the Griersons lived at 12 Regent Terrace, but were never wholly at ease in that city. Grierson was a shy and nervous man, and his great standing probably isolated him from all but his family and a few professorial colleagues. After his wife died in 1937 he became very lonely. He even married an American woman when in the United States, but she did not return with him to Scotland and so in practice the marriage lasted for only a few weeks. In 1950 he moved to Cambridge to be near his daughter Molly and her husband, Bruce Dickins, professor of Anglo-Saxon. There he died in the Hope Nursing Home, Brookland Avenue, on 19 February 1960.

DAVID HEWITT

Sources DNB · H. J. C. Grierson, 'Vita mea', U. Aberdeen, MS 2478, 1–8 · M. Dickins, 'A wealth of relations', U. Aberdeen, MS 2478, 1–8 · F. Grierson, memoir of H. J. C. Grierson, U. Aberdeen, MS 2478, 1–8 · D. Daiches, 'Memories of Grierson', *Aberdeen University Review*, 193 (spring 1995), 23–32 · H. J. C. Grierson, 'The development of English teaching at Aberdeen', *Aberdeen University Review*, 1 (1913–14), 49–53 · *The poems of John Donne*, ed. H. J. C. Grierson, 2 vols. (1912) · J. Tessier du Cros, *Cross currents* (1997) · d. cert. · m. cert. [Mary Letitia Ogston]

Archives Bodl. Oxf., corresp. and papers rel. to John Donne · NL Scot., corresp. and papers · NL Scot., letters received · U. Aberdeen L., corresp. and misc. papers, MS 2478, 1–8 · U. Edin. L., lecture notes | BL, corresp. with S. Cockerell, Add. MS 52717 · King's AC Cam., letters to G. H. W. Rylands · NL Scot., letters to D. N. Smith · U. Edin. L., letters to W. F. Mitchell

Likenesses W. Stoneman, photograph, 1929, NPG · D. Foggie, pencil drawing, 1932, U. Edin. · K. Green, oils, 1936, U. Edin. · photograph, repro. in *Seventeenth century studies presented to Sir Herbert Grierson* (1938), frontispiece

Wealth at death see confirmation, 9 Aug 1960, CGPLA Eng. & Wales

Grierson, Sir James Moncrieff (1859–1914), army officer, born in Glasgow on 27 January 1859, was the eldest son of George Moncrieff Grierson, a Glasgow merchant, and his wife, Allison Lyon, daughter of George Lyon Walker, of Garemount, Dunbartonshire. He was educated at Glasgow Academy, in Germany, and at the Royal Military Academy, Woolwich, from which he passed out fourth, and joined the Royal Artillery at Aldershot in 1878. Almost as soon as he joined he began to write military articles for the press. In 1879 he accompanied the Austrian armies in the occupation of Bosnia and Herzegovina, and in 1880 went to the Russian manoeuvres at Warsaw as correspondent for the *Daily News*. In 1881 Grierson joined his battery in India, but soon after his arrival became attaché in the quartermaster-general's department at Simla. He was employed on intelligence work, and his pen was busy; besides contributions to *The Pioneer*, he produced a volume of notes on the Turkish army, an Arabic vocabulary, and a gazetteer of Egypt. When an Indian division was sent to Egypt in 1882 for the operations against Arabi Pasha, he accompanied it as deputy assistant quartermaster-general, being present at the battles of Qassasin and Tell al-Kebir. He was mentioned in dispatches, and received the Mejidiye (fifth class). Grierson returned to India and in 1883 passed first into the Staff College. His time at Camberley was broken by the Sudan campaign of 1885, in which he served as deputy assistant adjutant and quartermaster-general, being present at the battles of Hashin and Tamai, and was again mentioned. At the Staff College he finished his translation of Grodekoff's work, which he entitled *Campaign in Turcomania* and passed out with honours in French and Russian. On leaving he served for a time in the Russian section of the intelligence division under General Henry Brackenbury. He was promoted captain in 1886, and in the following year joined a battery in India, but soon after was appointed deputy assistant quartermaster-general, first at Lucknow and then at Peshawar. In the Hazara expedition of 1888 he served as deputy assistant quartermaster-general 2nd brigade, and was again mentioned.

In 1889, at Brackenbury's request, Grierson returned to the intelligence division and became head of the Russian section. Antagonism between England and Russia in Asia was then growing, and Anglo-German relations became closer. There was a rapprochement between the German general staff and the British War Office, and Grierson, whose knowledge of Germany and of the Franco-Prussian War was very considerable, was constantly in Berlin and the frequent guest of the Kaiser and of German officers. During these years he published books on the Russian, German, and Japanese armies—*The Armed Strength of Russia* (1886), *The Armed Strength of Japan* (1886), and *The Armed Strength of the German Empire* (1888)—and also a handbook entitled *Staff Duties in the Field* (1891). In 1895 he was promoted brevet lieutenant-colonel and served for a year as brigade major at Aldershot. In 1896 he was appointed military attaché at Berlin. He had hitherto been a warm admirer of the Germans, but during this period his views changed. Though cordially welcomed in Berlin and well received by the Kaiser, he began to believe that ultimately a breach with England must come.

Early in 1900, when Lord Roberts took over the chief command of the British forces in the Second South African War, Grierson was sent to the front in charge of the military attachés; on his arrival at Paardeberg in February, Lord Roberts appointed him assistant adjutant-general, and as such he took part in the operations in the Orange Free State at Poplar Grove, Driefontein, and the Zand River, as well as in the occupation of Pretoria (5 June) and the battle of Diamond Hill (12 June), being again mentioned. In August 1900 he was hurriedly dispatched to China as British representative on the staff of Field Marshal Count von Waldersee, commander-in-chief of the allied forces against the Boxers, and entered Peking (Beijing) with him. He was of great service in smoothing the relations between the British and the Germans, but his opinion of German methods of making war was influenced unfavourably by his experience in China, where he found that jealousy of Great Britain and fear of Russia were the Germans' leading motives.

Returning home in 1901 Grierson received a colonelcy and the CB for his services, and spent two years with the 2nd army corps, first as assistant quartermaster-general and then as chief staff officer. On the reorganization of the War Office in 1904 he became director of military operations and was promoted major-general. During the next two years perhaps the most important work of his life was performed in contributing to the foundation of British friendship with France. Spending some time in France he entered into cordial relations with many French officers and especially with Colonel Huguet, who in 1905 became military attaché in London. Between them these two laid the foundations of co-operation between the British and French armies, and when Grierson went to command the first division at Aldershot in 1906, a post which he held until 1910, his work was carried on by his successors, Sir Spencer Ewart and Sir Henry Wilson. For the next eight years, with an interval on half pay during which he took part in the coronation mission to Siam (1911) and in the official tour of Prince Henry of Prussia (1911), he was employed first at Aldershot and then (1912) as general officer commanding-in-chief, eastern command. In both capacities his energies were directed towards the training of troops for field warfare and especially towards securing rapidity of mobilization. The clash with Germany, which had long been foreseen by Grierson and by many other soldiers, sailors, and diplomats, grew clearly more imminent. Had war with Germany come about as the result of the Agadir crisis (July 1911), it had been proposed that Grierson should be chief of the general staff of a British expeditionary force: but in 1914, when war was declared, he was appointed to command the 2nd army corps. He only lived to land in France. He reached Le Havre on 16 August, and the day after his arrival he died suddenly in the train, near Amiens, of aneurism of the heart. He was buried at Glasgow.

Grierson's great knowledge of languages, his strength, energy, capacity for work, and extraordinary memory, enabled him to acquire a vast knowledge of his profession. He admired the British private soldier, and was apparently beloved by his troops, for though strict as regards training, he spared them unnecessary duties by thinking out his problems in advance and making provision for all reasonable comfort and relaxation. Although early service was chiefly on the staff, he wrote in 1914 that he would rather command a battalion in war than be chief of the general staff. He was of a cheerful disposition, a good musician, an amateur actor, and fond of travel and society, but he really lived for his profession, and was devoted to the army. He was created KCB on the occasion of the coronation of George V in 1911, and was an aide-de-camp general to the king, knight of grace of St John of Jerusalem, a commander of the légion d'honneur, and holder of many other foreign decorations. He was unmarried. R. W. A. ONSLOW, *rev.* M. G. M. JONES

Sources D. S. Macdiarmid, *Life of Sir James Moncrieff Grierson* (1923) · *The Times* (18 Aug 1914) · *Annual Register* · PRO, War Office records, WO series · L. S. Amery, ed., *The Times history of the war in South Africa*, 7 vols. (1900–09) · *Army List* · private information (1927)
Likenesses Gale & Polden, photogravure, NPG
Wealth at death £5153 18s. 7d.: confirmation, 18 Dec 1914, *CCI*

Grierson, John (*c.*1486–1564?), prior of St Andrews, was perhaps a member of the family of Grierson of Lag in Dumfriesshire. He became a theological student at King's College, Aberdeen, where he was recorded as John 'Grysonius', and in 1511 was procurator of the Aberdeen Dominicans, suggesting that he was born about 1486. In the following year he was prior of that house, remaining so until 1516, when he became BTh. By 1518 his lectorate in theology had been recognized by his order's general chapter. His book list of 1522 shows him a reader of Pico della Mirandola and Erasmus as well as of the scholastics. After a short spell in Edinburgh he went to St Andrews as prior, and rose to be provincial of his order in Scotland in 1523. Resident again in Edinburgh for a time, in 1534 he and the Franciscan provincial were called before the lords of the council to prevent apostate friars leaving the country, after some of them had joined the reformers. In 1542 Grierson was described as professor of divinity and also as provincial. He attended the Catholic reforming provincial councils between 1549 and 1559. By January 1553 he was dean of the theology faculty at St Andrews, and seems to have remained so until the Reformation, when he was replaced by the protestant John Winram.

The St Andrews Blackfriars was destroyed in 1559, and early in the following year Grierson was forced to recant his Catholicism, being then an old man. He wrote a sad letter to the Dominican prior at Paris deploring the fate of the Scottish religious houses. In 1561 he petitioned Queen Mary for help, and she paid him a pension, besides the pension he received from the thirds of benefices between 1561 and 1563. According to Dempster (probably correctly) he died in 1564. According to Echard he remained a firm Catholic, notwithstanding his forced recantation, defending his faith by word and deed, and he certainly looked forward in 1561 to its re-establishment.

According to Dempster, Grierson wrote treatises—'De miseria profitentium fidem et religionem catholicam in Scotia' and 'De casu ordinis sui et paupertate'—and some letters preserved in R. F. Plodius's history of the Dominican order. No such treatises are known to survive, but although Echard states that he had searched in vain for the letters, the one to the prior of Paris is preserved in G. M. Pio's *Delle vite degli huomini illustri di San Domenico* (1607), column 383. An earlier brief survey of the province made by Grierson is reprinted in *Analecta sacri ordinis Fratrum Praedicatorum* (1895), 4.84.   JOHN DURKAN

Sources *Thomae Dempsteri Historia ecclesiastica gentis Scotorum, sive, De scriptoribus Scotis*, ed. D. Irving, rev. edn, 1, Bannatyne Club, 21 (1829), 330 · *Hectoris Boetii murthlacensium et aberdonensium episcoporum vitae*, ed. and trans. J. Moir, New Spalding Club, 12 (1894), 92 · P. J. Anderson, ed., *Aberdeen friars, Red, Black, White and Grey*, Aberdeen University Studies, 40 (1909), 69–74 · G. Meersseman and D. Planzer, eds., *Magistrorum ac procuratorum generalium O.P. Registra litterarum minora* (1947), 106, 149 · G. M. Pio, *Delle vite degli huomini illustri di San Domenico* (1607), col. 383 · C. Innes, ed., *Registrum episcopatus Aberdonensis*, 2 vols., Spalding Club, 13–14 (1845) · R. K. Hannay, ed., *Acts of the lords of council in public affairs, 1501–1554* (1932), 422 · J. M. Thomson and others, eds., *Registrum magni sigilli regum Scotorum / The register of the great seal of Scotland*, 11 vols. (1882–1914), vol. 3, pp. 196, 229, 587, 3205 · J. Anderson, ed., *Calendar of the Laing charters, AD 854–1837, belonging to the University of Edinburgh* (1899), no. 494 · A. Ross, 'Some notes on the religious orders in pre-Reformation Scotland', *Essays on the Scottish Reformation, 1513–1625*, ed. D. McRoberts (1962), 185–244, esp. 197–9 · A. Ross, 'Libraries of the Scottish Blackfriars', *Innes Review*, 20 (1969), 3–36 · D. H. Fleming, ed., *Register of the minister, elders and deacons of the Christian congregation of St Andrews*, 1, Scottish History Society, 4 (1889), 16–18 · G. Burnett and others, eds., *The exchequer rolls of Scotland*, 13 (1891), 489, 583; 14 (1893), 114, 212 · J. Durkan and J. Russell, 'John Grierson's book-list', *Innes Review*, 28 (1977), 39–49 · J. Durkan, 'The Dominicans at the Reformation', *Innes Review*, 9 (1958), 216–17 · G. Donaldson, ed., *Accounts of the collectors of thirds of benefices, 1561–1572*, Scottish History Society, 3rd ser., 42 (1949), 54, 98, 152, 237 · *Analecta sacri ordinis fratrum praedicatorum* (1895), 484 · W. Manderston, *Bipartitum in morali philosophia*, 1518, U. Glas. L., special collections department, fols. 20, 22 [MS leaves] · D. Patrick, ed., *Statutes of the Scottish church, 1225–1559*, Scottish History Society, 54 (1907), 86, 163 · J. Quétif and J. Echard, *Scriptores ordinis praedicatorum recensiti*, 2 (Paris, 1721), 187

Grierson, John (1898–1972), documentary film-maker, was born on 26 April 1898 in the village of Deanston in the parish of Kilmadock, Perthshire, Scotland, the fourth of eight children and the elder son of the local headmaster, Robert Grierson, whose forebears were lighthouse keepers, and of his wife, Jane, a teacher and daughter of a shoemaker in Stewarton, Ayrshire. He was strongly influenced by the beliefs of his parents: from his father's liberal Presbyterian idealism he derived a concern with preserving the value of religious belief within a materialistic world, and from his mother's politically conscious radicalism a lifelong concern for issues of political reform.

At home in his parents' house, Grierson steeped himself

John Grierson (1898–1972), by Ronny Jaques, 1944 [left, with Ralph Foster, head of graphics, examining a series of posters produced by the National Film Board of Canada]

in the writers of the English Romantic tradition, particularly Carlyle, Ruskin, Coleridge, and Byron. After education at Stirling high school (1908–15) he was awarded a bursary (the John Clark bursary for the sons and daughters of protestant parents), which enabled him to matriculate at Glasgow University in 1916, to read philosophy and literature. Before he could commence his studies war broke out, and from 1916 to 1919 he served in the Royal Naval Volunteer Reserve as a telegraphist on naval minesweepers. He returned to Glasgow after demobilization in 1919, and graduated MA in the 1922–3 academic session, taking honours in moral philosophy, logic, and metaphysics. While at university he became interested in student politics. Although distancing himself from the Marxist and syndicalist politics which were prevalent during the 'Red Clydeside' movements of the twenties, Grierson associated himself in spirit with the politics of the Independent Labour Party, and with political figures such as Kier Hardie and John Wheatley. However, throughout his life, he remained unconnected to any political party. In 1930 he married Margaret (d. 1982), daughter of W. J. Taylor of Dorset; they had no children.

After a year as assistant registrar to Armstrong College, University of Durham, Grierson won a Rockefeller scholarship to study immigration and its effects upon the social problems of the United States at the University of Chicago, which had then emerged as one of the leading centres of sociological research in America. He reacted to the critiques of democratic practice then being mounted by figures such as Harold Lasswell and Walter Lippmann by arguing that the cinema could be used as a means of informing the electorate about social and political issues. He first began to write on the cinema in the *Chicago Evening Post* in 1925–6, and developed a theory of 'epic cinema', where films would be used to represent social institutions, as well as issues of personal psychology. He also helped edit the English titles for Eisenstein's *Battleship Potemkin* (1926).

In 1927 Grierson returned to Britain and persuaded Stephen Tallents, secretary of the newly formed Empire Marketing Board, to employ him as assistant films officer. He argued that a new type of documentary film was required to communicate social information effectively, films which would represent the relationship between the citizen and the state, and do so in an imaginative and filmic way. This was the basis of his well-known description of documentary film as 'the creative treatment of reality' (Hardy, *Grierson on Documentary*, 36). The first of these films was *Drifters* (1929), a film which utilized both Soviet montage editing and naturalistic documentary representation, and which remains today one of the most important British films.

Grierson used the success of *Drifters* to establish a film unit at the Empire Marketing Board, employing filmmakers such as Basil Wright, Paul Rotha, Robert Flaherty, Arthur Elton, Stuart Legg, and Edgar Anstey. When the board was dissolved in 1933, Tallents became public relations officer for the General Post Office (GPO) and took Grierson and his film-makers with him to form the GPO film unit. From 1934 to 1939 the film unit remained at the Post Office, making a number of seminal films, including *Industrial Britain* (1933), *Song of Ceylon* (1934–5), *Coal Face* (1935), and, perhaps the most important, *Night Mail* (1936). These films were important because they showed working people and their homes and problems on film for almost the first time in Britain. Part of their excellence lay in the contribution of creative figures recruited by Grierson including W. H. Auden, Benjamin Britten, William Coldstream, Humphrey Jennings, and Harry Watt. Frustrated by mounting constraints within the Post Office, in 1937 Grierson left to establish an advisory service for documentary films, the Film Centre, leaving the film unit under the leadership of Alberto Cavalcanti, a Brazilian film-maker. He also encouraged his film-makers to leave the GPO and set up independent documentary filmmaking organizations. The Shell Film Unit, Strand Film Unit, and Realist Film Unit were the results of this strategy.

In 1939 Grierson was invited to form the National Film Board of Canada, and was at last able to develop the sort of large-scale documentary film organization which he had never been able to develop in England. He left in 1945 and in 1946 was appointed as head of information at UNESCO. In 1950 he was appointed as head of Group 3, the film production arm of the National Film Finance Corporation. Here Grierson was able to put many of his realist principles into practice, but the films made were rarely successful, suffering from poor production values and a lack of investment. From October 1957 to late 1967 he presented *This Wonderful World* for Scottish Television, making 350 programmes over this period. He continued to write and present ideas on the development of a socially purposive film industry in Britain, travelling nationally and internationally. After serious illness in 1968 he was made a part-time professor of mass communication at McGill University in Canada. He taught there intermittently until his death.

Grierson was awarded an honorary doctorate in law by Glasgow University in 1948 and an honorary doctorate in literature from Heriot-Watt University in 1969. He was appointed CBE in 1961. He died on 19 February 1972 at the Forbes Fraser Hospital, Bath, and was cremated in Scotland. He was survived by his wife.

Grierson had a significant impact on the development of documentary film and film theory. His ideas have been much discussed, and continue to be examined and commented on. His influence can be seen in current television documentary practice in Britain, and in the film-making schools and traditions of many overseas countries, particularly Canada. Since the 1980s a debate has developed over the extent to which he helped develop a tradition of critical documentary film-making in Britain, or whether he set the tone for British film-makers to show unnecessary subservience to the establishment. His belief that film-makers must remain within the prevailing consensus is somewhat at odds with the idea of a critical, independent documentary film practice. Some critics have even compared his ideas to right-wing and fascist theories of the period, arguing that they reflect the influence of traditions of philosophical idealism which emphasized the importance of élites. During the period of his greatest importance in the 1930s, however, Grierson and the documentary film movement were associated with broad-based social democratic movements which were committed to reform and the defence of democratic principles. The film movement also provided a focus during the 1930s for many writers and artists who wished to develop forms of socially purposive art. IAN AITKEN

Sources *Grierson on documentary*, ed. F. Hardy (1946); rev. edn (1966); abridged edn (1979) · F. Hardy, *John Grierson* (1979) · I. Aitken, *Film and reform* (1990) · R. Low, *The history of the British film*, 5: *1929–1939: documentary and educational films of the 1930s* (1979) · P. Rotha, *Documentary diary: an informal history of the British documentary film, 1928–1939* (1973) · E. Sussex, *The rise and fall of British documentary* (1975) · *DNB* · b. cert. · d. cert. · University of Stirling, John Grierson archive · I. Aitken, ed., *The documentary film movement: an anthology* (1998)

Archives BFI · JRL, letters to the *Manchester Guardian* · McGill University, Montreal, McLennan Library, papers relating especially to later career · University of Stirling | BL, corresp. with Society of Authors, Add. MS 63256 · Royal Mail Heritage, London · U. Lond., Institute of Commonwealth Studies, corresp. with S. G. Tallents | FILM BFI NFTVA

Likenesses R. Jaques, photograph, 1944, NA Canada [*see illus.*] · E. Kapp, ink, 1946, Barber Institute of Fine Arts, Birmingham

Wealth at death £13,083: probate, 24 May 1972, *CGPLA Eng. & Wales*

Grierson, Sir Robert, first baronet (1655/6–1733), landowner, was the son of William Grierson (*d.* 1661), laird of

Barquhar, Kirkcudbrightshire, and his wife, Margaret, daughter of Sir James Douglas of Mouswald. The family of Grierson received the lands of Lag, Dumfriesshire, in 1408, and in 1666 Robert Grierson succeeded his cousin as laird of Lag. He was the last of the family to occupy Lag Tower, built about 1460. He attended the universities of Glasgow and St Andrews and, by contract dated 21 September 1676, married Lady Henrietta Douglas, daughter of James Douglas, second earl of Queensberry, and sister of William Douglas, later first duke of Queensberry. Grierson was under age at his wedding, but was over twenty-one by 1678. There were five children of the marriage, William, James, John, Gilbert, and Henrietta. With help from his brother-in-law, Queensberry, he consolidated his power in the south-west through a combination of local offices and the award of commissions from central government. His action in having a sheep stealer at Burnside hanged on his own authority as a baron bailie was probably the last example of such an execution in Nithsdale. He represented Dumfriesshire in the Scottish conventions and parliaments from 1678 to 1686. From 1681 he acted as depute to the earl of Nithsdale in the hereditary office of steward of Kirkcudbright and was confirmed in that office in 1683, during the minority of the fifth earl. In 1683–4 he was empowered as a commissioner for excise, supply, and the militia in Kirkcudbright, and to seize imports of cattle and foodstuffs from Ireland. He was, however, best known for his actions against the covenanters of south-west Scotland, though much that is recorded of him stems from the traditions of those he opposed.

In 1678 Grierson administered a bond to his tenants for their conformity and against conventicles. In 1679 he joined John Graham of Claverhouse to destroy a church disguised as a byre at Brigend at Dumfries, perhaps his first action against covenanters. Increasingly stringent measures designed to ensure the enforcement of the test and imposing the death sentence for association with field conventicles or recent acts of rebellion, and later for failure to take the abjuration oath (directed against the extremists' *Apologetical Declaration*), provided the framework for the activities of troops and military courts in the last years of Charles II. Grierson was appointed to successive commissions for such purposes, notably that of December 1684 which empowered judicial commissions for the south-west, awarding the power to inflict the death penalty upon refusers of the abjuration oath. He presided over courts at Kirkcudbright and Carsphairn, in the latter case residing at Garryhorn, and assisted by the curate, Peter Pierson, a great informer against presbyterians, later murdered.

The more notorious actions attributed to Grierson relate, it would appear, to events early in 1685. His dragoons are reported to have chased and shot John Dempster on the moors near Carsphairn, and to have captured and instantly shot McRoy of Half-Mark when he was reading his Bible. He reportedly rounded up the men of Dalry and forced them to swear allegiance, dismissing them with the remark 'Now you are a fold-full of clean beasts, ye may go home'. Of a party of covenanters taken on Lockenkit

Moor in February 1685, four were shot and buried at once, while Grierson hanged a further two, Alexander McCubbin and Edward Gordon, at Hallhill, Irongray, the following day for failure to take the adjuration oath, despite calls for an assize. In the same month he ordered the summary execution of five covenanters seized on Kirkconnel Moor at Tongland. To the request of one, John Bell, for a quarter of an hour's prayer before execution he reportedly replied 'What the devil! Have you not had time enough to prepare since Bothwell?' (R. Wodrow, *Sufferings of the Church of Scotland*, 1828, 4.242). He also refused interment of the bodies. When allegedly challenged over this by Lord Kenmure, joined with him in commission but who had married Bell's widowed mother, he responded 'Take him … if you will, and salt him in your beef-barrel' (Fergusson, 51). Kenmure would have run him through at the remark, had not Claverhouse intervened. The story has been disputed, though his dislike and distrust of Kenmure is apparent.

With the accession of James VII and II, Grierson's commissions were renewed and he was created a baronet of Nova Scotia on 25 March 1685. In June he was reported to have intervened to have two covenanter prisoners, David Halliday and George Short, shot, after quarter given by the earl of Annandale. Both were buried in Balmaghie churchyard. The presbyterian historian Robert Wodrow recounted the imprisonment of four covenanters from Anworth by Grierson, who swore terribly that one of the prisoners, who had resisted the oath of allegiance, would soon be 'barking and flying'. Perhaps the most barbarous act reported of him was the drowning of Margaret McLachlan and Margaret Wilson, known as the Wigtown martyrs. The sisters Margaret and Agnes Wilson, aged eighteen and thirteen respectively, who had avoided episcopal services, and McLachlan, an elderly widow from Kirkinner, were sentenced to death by drowning in April 1685. Agnes Wilson was released but, despite reprieves issued by the privy council on 30 April, the other two women were executed, perhaps on 11 May 1685, tied to stakes at the mouth of the Bladnoch. Grierson was alleged to have intervened when Margaret Wilson's answer to the call to save herself by praying for the king produced an ambiguous response with 'Damn'd bitch, we do not want such prayers; tender the oaths to her'. She refused, and was thrust again into the water. It has been claimed that, despite their prominence in covenanter historiography, the executions never took place, though 'the weight of evidence … points fairly conclusively to their death' (I. B. Cowan, *The Scottish Covenanters, 1660–1688*, 1976, 128).

With the downfall of Queensberry, Grierson appears to have held a less prominent position. At the revolution Queensberry returned to a position of influence and Grierson was commissioned to disarm papists and oversee burgh elections in Dumfries. James's provost of Dumfries, Maxwell of Barncleugh, was arrested and Grierson was charged with delivering him to Edinburgh, and with examining the contents of Maxwell's cloak bag. Yet over the next decade he faced repeated fines and imprisonment for suspected Jacobite sympathies, beginning as early as May 1689 when he was apprehended on

Kenmure's orders. His arrest in 1696 for forging coins was, however, the result of the possession by his tenants at Rockhall of materials for printing on linen and books on metallurgy. He took no part in the rising of 1715, but allowed his sons William, the eldest, and Gilbert to go. The family estates, transferred to William Grierson in 1713, were saved despite the latter's sentence of forfeiture since his father managed to persuade the court of session that William had broken the terms of the transfer, leading to the return of the properties to his father.

Grierson spent his final years quietly at his home at Rockhall, though 'fines … had ruined his estate' (Murray, 158). Legend embellished even this period, as in the tale that water used to bathe his gouty feet used to fizz and boil. He died at Turnpike House, Dumfries, on 31 December 1733, but folklore pursued him to the grave and beyond. The tale emerged of crewmen on a small boat in the Solway Firth who witnessed a great black coach with coachmen and torch-bearers sweeping up the Nith estuary in the moonlight; to the call 'Where bound? And where from?' the reply was given 'To tryst with Lag! Dumfries! From Hell!' A sinister crow reportedly perched on his coffin as it was taken for burial in Dunscore old churchyard on 8 January 1734, while it was claimed that the horses could not draw the hearse and were replaced with others, and these died a few days later. In this instance, the account of ironwork done to the hearse (included in the funeral accounts) may lie behind an accident, necessitating a change of horses and initiating a story which grew, perhaps lubricated by the amount of alcohol with which the mourners were entertained.

Grierson's motives are as uncertain as the details of his career. It has been suggested that he was primarily an authoritarian, committed to enforcing both the king's will and his own (Fergusson, 113), or that his first loyalty was to Queensberry (Murray, 158). There seems little reason to doubt Lag's bloody reputation in the 'killing times', which was perhaps enhanced by the fact that his rigour was imposed on the area in which he lived. Into the nineteenth century the game known as 'playing Lag' testified to his reputation. 'Lag' was here a beast with prominent eyes, pointed ears, and a long snout, an allegory for one who had so efficiently and ruthlessly watched, listened for, and sniffed out Galloway covenanters. He was the prototype for Sir Walter Scott's Sir Robert Redgauntlet, even down to Redgauntlet's pet monkey, which lived in a tower called Cat's Cradle (in actuality an old look-out at Turnpike House) and had the trick of blowing a silver whistle. Grierson indeed kept such a pet, with its own posthumous life in folklore, haunting Rockhall, blowing its whistle.

T. F. HENDERSON, *rev.* STUART W. MCDONALD

Sources A. Fergusson, *The laird of Lag* (1886) • A. Murray, '"Auld Lag" and the covenanters', *Transactions of the Dumfriesshire and Galloway Natural History and Antiquarian Society*, 3rd ser., 36 (1959), 149–74 • R. Simpson, *Traditions of the covenanters* (1867) • *Debrett's Peerage* (1970) • *Debrett's Peerage* (1995) • R. Wodrow, *The history of the sufferings of the Church of Scotland from the Restoration to the revolution*, ed. R. Burns, 4 vols. (1828–30) • J. H. Thomson, *The martyr graves of Scotland*, ed. M. Hutchinson (1903) • P. J. Hamilton-Grierson, *The Lag charters, 1400–1720*, ed. A. L. Murray, Scottish RS (1958) • W. McDowall, *History of the burgh of Dumfries*, 3rd edn (1906) • F. Grose, *The antiquites of Scotland*, 2 vols. (1789–91) • A. Agnew, *The hereditary sheriffs of Galloway*, 2 vols. (1893) • C. H. Dick, *Highways and byways in Galloway and Carrick* (1924) • D. H. Fleming, ed., *Six saints of the covenant*, 2 vols. (1901) • *DNB*

Archives Ewart Public Library, Dumfries, corresp. • NL Scot., corresp. and MSS

Griess, (Johann) Peter (1829–1888), industrial chemist, was born on 6 September 1829 in Kirchhosbach, Hesse, Germany, the son of Heinrich Griess, a farmer and the village blacksmith, of Kirchhosbach. He studied chemistry at Kassel Polytechnic and then at the universities of Jena and Marburg. He was an unruly student, noted for his eccentricity of dress, and accumulated large debts which his father had to settle by mortgaging some of his properties.

This seems to have sobered Griess somewhat and he became an assistant in A. W. H. Kolbe's laboratory in Marburg, but his contract was not renewed. However, Kolbe relented when Griess approached him again in 1856 after working in a tar distillery in Offenbach, and took him back. For reasons not apparent he had become a reformed character: he worked diligently and spent long hours in the laboratory. He so impressed Kolbe that when the great German chemist, A. W. von Hofmann, professor at the Royal College of Chemistry in London, visited Marburg in 1858 he recommended Griess for a position in Hofmann's laboratory. To support his recommendation Kolbe provided Hofmann with the April 1858 edition of Liebig's *Annalen der Chemie*, which included a paper by Griess entitled 'A preliminary notice on the influence of nitrous acid on aminonitro- and aminodinitrophenol'. Hofmann realized that Griess had discovered a new and versatile chemical reaction which could provide a route to a wide range of new compounds. Griess was duly invited to London and Hofmann commissioned him to explore the possibilities of his new diazo compounds. The results of his experiments were published in a series of papers in the *Annalen* over the years 1860–66, entitled 'A new class of organic compounds in which hydrogen is replaced by nitrogen'.

For the latter part of this period Griess was no longer in London. While with Hofmann he had successfully completed an investigation for Allsopp & Sons of Burton upon Trent, after the French industrial chemist A. Payen (1795–1871) had alleged that Allsopp's famous India Pale Ale—an important export—contained strychnine. Subsequently the firm offered him an appointment as chemist at the brewery. He accepted in 1862 and remained there for the rest of his life, being left free to pursue his own research. In 1864 he discovered a further variant of his diazo reaction, known as coupling. In this the diazo compounds were linked with phenol or an aromatic amine, thereby forming intensely coloured compounds. Thus were born the azo dyestuffs, perhaps the greatest single discovery in the history of the dyestuffs industry. Griess played little part in the industrial exploitation of these dyes—his few patents were not lucrative—though he published a further series of papers, 'New investigations of the diazo compounds', in *Berichte der Deutschen Chemischen Gesellschaft*. In 1884 he lodged a patent for the first direct cotton dye: that is, a dye requiring no mordant. The originality of his research was recognized by his election as FRS in 1868. The University of Munich conferred an honorary degree on him.

In 1869 Griess married Louise Ann (*d.* 1886), daughter of William Mason, medical officer of health for Burton upon Trent. They had two sons and two daughters. In the summer of 1888 he took his family on holiday to Bournemouth and there died of a heart attack, at Pynes, West Cliff Gardens, on 30 August, frustrating his desire to retire to Kirchhosbach when his children's education was complete.

TREVOR I. WILLIAMS

Sources E. Fischer, *Berichte der Deutschen Chemischen Gesellschaft*, 24 (1891), 1007–78 · V. Hemes, *Journal of Chemical Education*, 35 (1958), 187–91 · J. R. Partington, *A history of chemistry*, 4 (1964) · *DSB* · F. A. Mason, 'Johann Peter Griess, 1829–1888', *Journal of the Society of Dyers and Colourists*, 46 (1930), 33–9 · W. H. Cliffe, 'Johann Peter Griess', *Chemistry and Industry* (24 May 1958), 616–21 · *CGPLA Eng. & Wales* (1888)

Likenesses portrait, repro. in *Berichte*

Wealth at death £10,095 9s. 1d.: probate, 29 Oct 1888, *CGPLA Eng. & Wales*

Grieve family (*per.* 1794–1887), theatrical scene-painters, came to prominence with **John Henderson Grieve** (1770/71–1845), who was possibly born in Perth, which his great-grandson gave as the family's Scottish place of origin. John Henderson Grieve is first recorded as painting the hallways at the Theatre Royal, Drury Lane, London, in October 1794 and scenery for *The Magician of the Rocks* at Sadler's Wells in May 1796. He was the resident scene-painter at Astley's Amphitheatre from 1799 to 1807 and, according to the painter David Roberts, it was while so engaged that he was sent to assist at Covent Garden Theatre in getting up a show:

> The managers then found out that a scene might be painted in a day equally effective with those that had taken a month or perhaps more—and that a spectacle might be produced in a couple of weeks, at a fourth of the expense and equally effective with what used to occupy the greater part of a season. (Roberts, 14)

Roberts says, wrongly, that this was *Timour the Tartar*, but it was probably in or before December 1806, when he painted Prospero's cave in *The Tempest* and scenes in the Christmas pantomime *Harlequin and Mother Goose*. In October 1805 he was also one of the painters for *Richard III* and *The Poor Soldier*, which opened the new theatre at Bath.

By the 1807–8 season at Covent Garden, Grieve was being paid 5 guineas a week, second only to the architectural specialist 'Old' Phillips at 6 guineas, with whose highly finished style, characteristic of eighteenth-century painters, the actor Joseph Cowell favourably compared Grieve's approach, 'every day *splashing* into existence a cottage or a cavern with a pound brush in each hand' (Cowell, 38). It would appear from such comments that Grieve pioneered a broad, romantic handling of paint suited to a fast turnover of spectacular novelty, and calculated to react well under gas light, which following some

earlier experiments became the stage illumination at Covent Garden and Drury Lane in 1817 and spread rapidly thereafter. His other innovation was to devise a form of scenic glaze, as in watercolour painting, to supplement the use of solid distemper colours. Rivals called it 'Scotch wash' in contempt, but he lived to see it generally adopted, again presumably because of its effects under the strong illumination of gas. At a time when most scenery was painted in theatre scene-rooms, Grieve is also the first artist known to have had an independent studio, near where he lived in Lambeth, and from which scenes were sent out to theatres by wagon. In this way, from 1815 to 1818, he augmented the in-house design of Robert Andrews at Sadler's Wells, on a piece-work basis, as well as being engaged at Covent Garden: this studio practice continued and became more common in the second half of the century.

It was at Covent Garden, however, that by 1820 Grieve had established his dominance of the scene-room, supported by his two sons, **Thomas Grieve** (1799–1882), born at Lambeth on 11 June 1799, and **William Grieve** (1800–1844), also born at Lambeth, who joined him as assistants in 1817 and 1818 respectively. Together they raised the theatre to a scenic eminence which was challenged only after Drury Lane acquired Clarkson Stanfield and David Roberts in early 1823, and which the Grieves sustained into the 1840s, well beyond the retirement from the stage of these rivals. Apart from their two sons, Grieves senior and his wife, Jane, also had three daughters.

The Grieves' output ranged from romantic and exotic landscape, real and imagined, to fantasy and historic architecture. From 1827 to 1833 they had the young A. W. N. Pugin as an assistant, whose influence as a source of Gothic authenticity is particularly notable in the spectacular ballet *Kenilworth*, for which they painted scenery for the King's Theatre in 1832. They otherwise provided scenery for everything from opera to pantomime, among them Mozart's *The Marriage of Figaro* (1819) and Weber's *Der Freischütz* (1824) and *Oberon* (1826). In the Christmas pantomime *Harlequin and Friar Bacon* (1820) they produced the first fully successful theatrical moving panorama, of a steam-packet voyage from Holyhead to Dublin. This was a form they continued with great success and in particular rivalry with Stanfield's at Drury Lane, including at least one, a Rhine panorama as seen from a balloon, which moved vertically rather than across the stage in *Harlequin and Old Gammer Gurton* (Covent Garden, 1833). Some 700 of their designs survive, the majority in the University of London Library. Not all are identified, and, apart from John Henderson's tendency to work in monochrome, it is often difficult to distinguish the work of the three men stylistically or by relying on the playbill attributions of particular scenes. Taken together, however, their bold and atmospheric handling, and the practical ingenuity of their settings, vindicate the perceptive comment of the melodramatist Edward Fitzball that they were 'the most perfect scene painters in the world as a combination' (Fitzball, 2.124). He also said they were an affectionate and close-knit family and generous to other artists, a view which strongly contrasts with that of David Roberts, who was engaged by the Covent Garden management to paint with them between 1826 and 1830, and found them ruthless in obliterating, as soon as possible, any work they saw as a threat to their supremacy. William Grieve and his wife, Eliza, *née* Wood, whom he married in 1826, had three daughters and four sons; two of the latter died in infancy, before their father.

Although they were mainly associated with Covent Garden, the Grieves worked for other theatres in London and elsewhere, out of season. From 1829 they were employed at the King's Theatre in the Haymarket (later Her Majesty's), where William was head of the scene-room until his death, at 5 Durham Place, Lambeth, on 12 November 1844. He was buried in Norwood cemetery, Surrey. He excelled in moonlight scenes and was said to be the first artist to be called before the curtain to receive the audience's appreciation of his work (on *Robert le diable*, 1832). He also exhibited landscape and architectural views at the Royal Academy, in oil and watercolour (1826–39). When Alfred Bunn took over Drury Lane in 1835 the Grieves joined him; they remained there until 1839, when they returned to Covent Garden under Madame Vestris. In 1843 they went back to Drury Lane.

After John Henderson Grieve's death, in Peckham on 14 April 1845, Thomas continued to work there, as well as at Covent Garden and Her Majesty's. In 1850, with William Telbin (1813–1873) and John Absolon, he produced the highly successful exhibition hall panorama *The Overland Route to India* at the Gallery of Illustration in Regent Street, the first of several such projects in which he was involved. From 1853 to 1859 he was a leading member of the team of artists whom Charles Kean employed in his 'archaeologically authentic' revivals of Shakespeare and other historical plays at the Princess's Theatre in Oxford Street. These included *Macbeth* and Byron's *Sardanapalus* in 1853, *Henry VIII* in 1855 (with a Grieve panorama of the Thames), *Richard II* and *The Tempest* in 1857, *The Merchant of Venice* and *King Lear* in 1858, and *Henry V* in 1859. Much of this scenery was painted in a workshop which Grieve, Telbin, and Absolon, who both also worked for Kean, built in 1850–51 in Macklin Street (formerly Charles Street), Drury Lane, and which survives in similar use, though altered internally. Grieve and Telbin remained joint owners until the latter's death. Thomas Grieve married Elizabeth Goatley of Newbury and had a son, **Thomas Walford Grieve** (1841–1899), and a daughter, Fanny Elizabeth. The former, born on 15 October 1841, joined his father in the business about 1862 and thereafter 'the announcement that the scenery for any piece was by Grieve and Son was a sufficient guarantee of the excellence of the work' (*DNB*), the mainstay of which continued to be spectacular pieces for Covent Garden and Drury Lane, although they also supplied Charles Fechter's 1860s management at the Lyceum and other theatres. Thomas Grieve senior was also an occasional exhibitor of landscapes at the Royal Academy. He died at his home, 1 Palace Road, Lambeth (later 47 Lambeth Palace Road) on 16 April 1882 and was buried at Norwood cemetery. Thomas Walford Grieve sold his interest in the Macklin

Street workshop in 1887 and, in declining health from cancer, retired some years before his death in 1899. Apart from the London University holdings, material relating to the family, including designs, is in the Theatre Museum, London, presented by T. W. Grieve's son John Walford Grieve (1886–1981). Both the British Museum and the Victoria and Albert Museum have design material from other sources, the latter's holdings relating largely to the Charles Kean productions.   PIETER VAN DER MERWE

Sources P. van der Merwe, 'Grieve family', *International dictionary of theatre*, vol. 3: *Actors, directors, designers*, ed. M. Hawkins-Dady (1996), 313–15 · P. van der Merwe, 'Roberts and the theatre', in H. Guiterman and B. Llewellyn, *David Roberts* (1986) · D. Roberts, record book, GL, BR643 [copy; original at Yale U. CBA] · P. Cunningham, 'Sketch for the history of scene-painting', *The Builder* (28 May 1859) · E. Fitzball, *Thirty-five years in a dramatic author's life*, 2 vols. (1859) · J. Cowell, *Thirty years passed among the players* (New York, 1845) · W. J. Lawrence, theatrical notebooks, MS and typescript, 11 vols., University of Bristol, Theatre Collection · H. Norris, 'A directory of Victorian scene painters', *Theatrephile*, 1/2 (1984), 38–52 · S. Rosenfeld, *Georgian scene painters and scene painting* (1981) · *DNB* · Redgrave, *Artists* · S. Rosenfeld and E. Croft-Murray, 'A checklist of scene-painters working in Great Britain and Ireland in the 18th century', *Theatre Notebook*, 19–20 (1964–5); vol. 19/2, p. 60 · G. Speaight, ed., *Memoirs of Charles Didbin the younger* (1954) · private information (2004) [John Walford Grieve] · Graves, *RA exhibitors* · *IGI* · *CGPLA Eng. & Wales* (1882) · G. Ashton, *Pictures in the Garrick Club*, ed. K. A. Burnim and A. Wilkon (1997) · d. cert. [William Grieve] · d. cert. [John Henderson Grieve] · family genealogy, BL

Likenesses A. D'Orsay, drawing, 1836 (Thomas Grieve or William Grieve?), NPG · C. Baugniet, lithograph, 1847 (Thomas Grieve) · A. H. Corbould, double portrait, 1852 (T. W. Grieve, aged eleven), V&A · attrib. W. H. Graves, watercolour (William Grieve), Garr. Club · photograph (T. W. Grieve), Theatre Museum, London

Wealth at death £2866 10s—Thomas Grieve: resworn probate, Oct 1882, *CGPLA Eng. & Wales*

Grieve, Christopher Murray [*pseud.* Hugh MacDiarmid] (1892–1978), poet, writer, and cultural activist, was born on 11 August 1892 in Arkinholm Terrace at Langholm in Dumfriesshire, Scotland, the elder of two sons born to James Grieve (1863–1911), postman, the son of John Grieve, a weaver and latterly a power loom tuner, and Elizabeth Graham (1856–1934) the daughter of Andrew Graham, a farm labourer and mole catcher. James Grieve worked for most of his life as the rural postman for the Langholm area, becoming an elder of the South United Presbyterian Church (soon to become the United Free Church) at the age of only twenty-three, and serving as the sabbath school superintendent until his relatively early death.

Early years, 1892–1919 Grieve's family roots were deeply planted among the common folk of the Scottish borders. Like his younger brother, Andrew (1894–1972) he would have grown up speaking broad Scots, and although he was soon to discard it he was equally familiar with his father's faith and the religious and radically egalitarian tenets associated with the Free Kirk. As a man Grieve was proud to associate himself with border mill workers through his grandfather, and (on his mother's side) with agricultural labour. Looking back from the 1930s Grieve reviewed his

Christopher Murray Grieve [Hugh MacDiarmid] (1892–1978), by Robert Heriot Westwater, 1962

early years in poems such as 'Water of Life', 'Excelsior', 'Charisma and my Relatives', and 'The Seamless Garment' (all in *'First Hymn to Lenin' and other Poems*, 1931) in which he refers to his roots in Langholm, known locally as the Muckle Toon. He also liked to ascribe his own combative spirit to border traditions of feud and sporadic warfare with England.

By the time Grieve entered Langholm Academy in 1899 the family was living behind the post office on the ground floor of the Library Buildings, Parliament Square, and his mother was working as caretaker for the Langholm library and local museum on the floor above. The poet dates his lifelong and 'omnivorous' reading habits from the years when he used to collect books in a washing-basket to read at his leisure. A study of the titles to be found in the catalogue suggests that the seeds of many of his later interests in language, astronomy, geology, and Scottish and American literature were first sown here. The young Grieve's awareness of poetry and poets was further advanced by the friendship of his local minister, the Revd T. S. Cairncross, who wrote poetry himself and had a substantial library. (Grieve was later to include verses by Cairncross in his *Northern Numbers* anthology.) When he graduated to secondary schooling at Langholm Academy Grieve came into contact, in 1905, with a new young English teacher, Francis George Scott, later to be a composer of some note and a good friend, to whom the poet dedicated *A Drunk Man Looks at the Thistle*.

Grieve did well at Langholm Academy and in 1908, at the age of sixteen, he moved on to further education at

Broughton Higher Grade School and Junior Student Centre in Edinburgh. Pupils at Broughton received an education while being themselves trained as teachers, and here Grieve met George Ogilvie, principal teacher of English, who was to be a major influence on him in the years to come. Ogilvie regarded Grieve as his most promising student, he introduced him to the radical intellectual journal *The New Age*, and the older man's good opinion (they had socialist sympathies in common) was very important to the young writer. They corresponded from 1911 until 1932, only two years before the teacher's death, and these letters are very revealing, as Grieve confided much to the man he came to regard as a mentor and second father.

During these years Grieve joined the Independent Labour Party (ILP), the Edinburgh University branch of the Fabian Society, and the Territorial Army medical corps. He threw himself into school life and was soon taking part in debates and plays while editing and contributing to the *Broughton Magazine*. It ended in disgrace, however, with a prank involving the theft of books and postage stamps in January 1911. To avoid scandal, and with Ogilvie's support, Grieve was allowed to resign 'on grounds of health and mistaking his vocation' (Kerrigan, 16). Scarcely a week later James Grieve died in Langholm. That death seems to have haunted Grieve in later years in poems such as 'Kinsfolk' and 'At my Father's Grave':

a livin' man upon a deid man thinks
And on sma'er thocht's impossible

Never really suited to teaching and badly in need of funds, Grieve turned to freelance journalism, working for the *Edinburgh Evening Dispatch* until irregularities over the sale of review copies caused his dismissal. The eighteen-year-old moved to south Wales and a job with the *Monmouthshire Labour News*, where he met Keir Hardie and witnessed strikes and demonstrations, anti-Jewish riots, and conflict between the miners, the police, and the army. Dismissed for a lack of moderation, Grieve returned to Scotland in 1912, living in Langholm and working freelance. Early in 1913 a job with the *Clydebank and Renfrew Press* brought him into contact with James Maxton and John Maclean on the home ground of what was to become known as 'red Clydeside'. With occasional articles now published in local newspapers and periodicals, Grieve was learning his craft. He placed an essay in A. R. Orage's journal *The New Age*, and it was here in later years that he came across many influential ideas and authors, most notably Pound's experiments with versification, the iconoclasm of Nietzsche, the work of Dostoyevsky, and the social credit theories of Major C. H. Douglas.

Encouraged by his brother in 1913 Grieve moved to Cupar in Fife, where he wrote for a number of papers and met Peggy Skinner (whom he was later to marry) before moving on again to Forfar where the outbreak of the First World War found him working for the weekly *Forfar Review*. Prompted, perhaps, by the death in action of his old schoolfriend, John Bogue Nisbet (and despite the ILP's opposition to what it saw as a capitalist adventure) Grieve enlisted in the Royal Army Medical Corps (RAMC) at Sheffield in July 1915. He spent the next year in England, first in

Hillsborough barracks and then in Aldershot, before being promoted to sergeant and posted with the 42nd general hospital to Salonika in Greece.

Grieve served in the 'forgotten' eastern front, from August 1916 to May 1918. Here, in what the Germans liked to call their largest internment camp, disease was killing more soldiers than the enemy did. As a sergeant in charge of the officers' mess he had time to write, and his letters to Ogilvie reveal literary ambitions, a growing sense of his specifically Scottish identity, and latterly a strong disaffection with the war and what he saw as English imperialism. On fire with innumerable schemes for books, essays, and sonnet sequences, Grieve was passionately excited by Scottish nationalism and, for a short while, by the Catholic faith, seeing pre-Reformation Scotland (as Edwin Muir was later to do) as a model of social, spiritual, and national coherence. He also began to explore his own states of mind in a series of fictionalized 'psychological studies', later published as *Annals of the Five Senses* (1923). These prose pieces were self-consciously avant-garde, informed by a host of unacknowledged literary references and delivered in a stream-of-consciousness vein. Writing within what he called a 'strong solution' of other texts, Grieve's method in this, his first completed book, bears a striking resemblance to the way he was to construct the enormous 'world language' poems at the very end of his career.

Grieve caught malaria shortly after arriving in Greece, and with his third relapse had to be invalided home. It was during this leave, in Edinburgh on 13 June 1918, that he married Margaret (Peggy) Cunningham Thompson Skinner (1897–1962). After his leave Grieve ran the RAMC sergeants' mess in Blackpool, and when the armistice was declared in November he was working for army education in Dieppe. In December, Sergeant Grieve was posted to a château near Marseilles where he finished his service at the Sections Lahore Indian General Hospital for shell-shocked Indian troops from the western front. During this time, Grieve managed visits to Paris and a walking tour in the Pyrenees in late May 1919.

Grieve's experiences in Greece and France—and his intensive reading for the last three years—had given a new confidence and a new urgency to his ambitions:

> He brought back to civilization an ardour of revolt, a sharp bitterness, made up partly of hatred and partly of pity. He saw with eyes different from those of other men's—clearer or more blurred, anyhow not the same. His state of mind was grievous. (Grieve, *Annals*, 89)

'Not traditions—precedents', 1919–1929 Demobilized in July 1919, Grieve stayed with his wife in St Andrews and returned to journalism, but a first job in Montrose did not last long. In the late summer of 1920 he and Peggy were employed as caretakers at a highland shooting lodge at Kildermorie near Alness on the Cromarty Firth, and in November Grieve took on the extra task of teaching at a side school on the estate. At last his literary career began to pick up, with plans to edit anthologies of Scottish verse which were consciously modelled on Edward Marsh's earlier English *Georgian Poetry* series. Three volumes of

these *Northern Numbers* appeared between 1920 and 1922, and they included poems by John Buchan, Violet Jacob (both in Scots), and Neil Munro and T. S. Cairncross among others, and some middling verses in English by the editor himself and his brother, Andrew.

Grieve's early English poems showed an interest in large abstractions such as Time and Death, and were characterized by a consciously poetic language of clashing surfaces. The metaphysical intensity and the cosmic scope of poems such as 'A Moment in Eternity' clearly presages the mature work, but as yet the poet lacked a diction which would make his vision concrete and truly new. That diction was to come with his discovery of the expressive power of Scots.

Offered a job with the *Montrose Review*, Grieve returned in April 1921 to Montrose, where he was to remain for the next eight years. He took an active part in the life of this small town, serving as a Labour councillor and becoming a justice of the peace in 1926. The couple eventually settled at 16 Links Avenue, where on 6 September 1924 a daughter, Christine, was born followed by a son, Walter, on 5 April 1928.

Wholly committed now to making his mark on literary Scotland, Grieve's first move was to found a series of periodicals, starting with a monthly, the *Scottish Chapbook* (fourteen issues), which appeared in August 1922 (shortly after the publication of *Ulysses* and before that of *The Waste Land*). The weekly *Scottish Nation* (thirty-four issues) began in 1923, and the following year the monthly *Northern Review* survived for only four issues. Although short-lived, these periodicals did set about the definition of a literary and cultural 'renaissance' in Scottish affairs. The *Scottish Chapbook* was the most influential of them all, for it was here that Grieve set out his agenda for at least the next ten years. The magazine's slogan was 'Not traditions—precedents' and it reflected Grieve's determination 'to bring Scottish Literature into closer touch with current European tendencies in technique and ideation'. He was equally determined to speak for cultural difference and 'to insist upon the truer evaluations of the work of Scottish writers than are usually given in the present over-Anglicised condition of British literary journalism, and, in criticism, elucidate, apply, and develop the distinctively Scottish range of values' ('The Chapbook programme', *Scottish Chapbook*, 1/2, September 1922, iii). It can be argued that these sentiments signal an early shift away from the hegemony of 'English literature' towards a more contemporary understanding of 'literatures in English'.

Despite the *Chapbook*'s support for writing in English, Gaelic, or Braid Scots, Grieve himself had previously criticized the use of Scots as no more than an exercise in nostalgia. Now, however, he planned to 'encourage the experimental exploitation of the unexplored possibilities of vernacular expression' ('A theory of Scots letters', *Selected Prose*, 20). It is clear that his own experiments in writing poetry in Scots—calling himself Hugh M'Diarmid—had much to do with this change of heart. The pen name marked the poet's commitment to a specifically northern culture, and as one of the most active and contentious propagandists for Scots language and literature Hugh MacDiarmid soon eclipsed C. M. Grieve, even although he continued to write under both names—and a variety of lesser pseudonyms such as A. K. Laidlaw, Isobel Guthrie, Mountboy, and Special Correspondent. The '*Chapbook* programme' had begun, after all, with a pointed reminder from Dante that 'To make a book is less than nothing unless the book, when made, makes people anew' (Grieve, *Chapbook*, 1/1, August 1922, iii).

An important beginning was made with the *Chapbook*, and two collections of Scots lyrics—*Sangschaw* (1925) and *Penny Wheep* (1926). John Buchan wrote a preface to *Sangschaw* in which he identified the poet's task as both 'conservative and radical—a determination to keep Scotland in the main march of the world's interests, and at the same time to forgo no part of her ancient heritage'. He noted, too, that Grieve's Scots borrowed words and idioms from literary Scots 'as Burns did' and indeed Grieve himself admitted that he had used words from different dialects, as well as whole idioms and phrases which he had found in *Jamieson's Scottish Dictionary*. Yet these poems also had a radical component, an imagist concision, an expressionist intensity, and a cosmic perspective which cast a new and eerie light on their more traditionally rustic settings and subjects. On the whole the lyrics were well received by reviewers, and later critics such as the Gaelic poet Sorley MacLean have come to regard them as among the finest short poems of the twentieth century. More than seventy were eventually set to music by Grieve's old schoolmaster F. G. Scott, and the French critic Denis Saurat translated some into French. Grieve's European and modernist ambitions were under way at last, and he threw himself into his next project which was to go beyond individual lyrics to produce a long poem sequence in Scots, a satirical and metaphysical meditation on personal being, Scottish identity, and cultural politics *sub specie aeternitatis*, to be called *A Drunk Man Looks at the Thistle*.

A Drunk Man (published in November 1926) seems to have been prompted by a suggestion of F. G. Scott's, and certainly he helped Grieve to assemble and order its many parts at a late stage in its composition. The poem (2685 lines) takes the form of an extended dramatic monologue—almost a stream of consciousness—dense with literary and cultural allusions and held together by recurring thematic and symbolic links. Its verse forms are relatively conventional if highly mixed, but its swift changes of mood and subject matter, from the tender to the obscene, from the personal to the universal, give it a modernist force and an expressive violence similar to the work of Eliot and Pound. Yet, crucially unlike these writers, Grieve is both a materialist and an optimist, for *A Drunk Man* celebrates change and contradiction with a Nietzschean energy and delight which sees unlimited possibility and freedom in chaos. This willingness to be 'whaur extremes meet', to confront the vastness of interstellar space and still to find a place for the human spirit, characterizes Grieve's vision throughout his work, distinguishing it from that of his early modern contemporaries.

Borrowing a phrase from Gregory Smith's study *Scottish Literature: Character and Influence* (1919), Grieve welcomed a 'Caledonian antisyzygy' in Scottish culture and affairs, by which he meant a national penchant for the combination of opposites, and he proposed that the volatile persona of his drunk man was indeed a true model of the Scottish psyche: 'dominated by the conception of infinity, of the unattainable … ever questioning, never satisfied' (*Selected Prose*, 27). Later critics have challenged the implicit essentialism of such a view, but it proved to be a particularly influential critical thesis for the revival of Scottish cultural confidence at the time. It was also the foundation stone for Grieve's interest in Dostoyevsky and his assertion that there existed a psychological affinity—'the Russo-Scottish parallel'—between Scotland and Russia.

A Drunk Man Looks at the Thistle is now widely recognized as Hugh MacDiarmid's masterpiece, but the poem did not sell well in its early years and the reviews were mixed. In the meantime Grieve was working on another long poem in the same vein, *To Circumjack Cencrastus*, which spoke more personally about the strains of creative work while being condemned to earn his living as a small town journalist. There were compensations in the friendship of fellow writers, most notably the poet Edwin Muir (1887–1959) and the novelist Neil Gunn (1891–1973), and indeed Muir (and Oliver St John Gogarty) were among the few critics who had praised *A Drunk Man* on its first appearance.

Grieve also produced a series of essays on modern Scottish writers for the *Scottish Educational Journal*, later published as *Contemporary Scottish Studies* (1926). At the same time, under his own name and various pseudonyms, he contributed more than 100 unpaid short articles on Scottish affairs to be syndicated to newspapers throughout the country by the 'Scottish secretariat', a function of the Scottish Home Rule Association run by R. E. Muirhead (1868–1964), who also supported the publication of Grieve's weekly *Scottish Nation*. Grieve's commitment to home rule and Scottish nationalism brought him to write the cultural political study *Albyn, or, Scotland and the Future* (1927), and his outspoken attacks on English influence, Scottish complacency, and the Burns cult made him a provocative and controversial public speaker. Aiming to promote contemporary writers, Grieve was instrumental in setting up the Scottish branch of PEN in 1927, and in May the following year (along with R. B. Cunninghame Graham and Compton Mackenzie) he became a founder member of the National Party of Scotland, an amalgamation of the Scottish Home Rule Association and several other nationalist associations. Established as a literary and political figure, in August 1928 Grieve was invited to Ireland, where he met and made friends with Oliver St John Gogarty, AE, and Yeats.

Life in Montrose was coming to seem more and more cramped, Peggy was unhappy there, and money matters were pressing, so when Compton Mackenzie proposed that Grieve should write for *Vox*, his new critical magazine devoted to radio broadcasting, the poet seized the chance to move to London in September 1929.

'To get bread from stones', 1929–1936 The next six years were to be hard ones, for Grieve's physical health was under increasing strain and he was struggling to finish *Cencrastus*. He had become a heavy drinker, and in December he injured his head badly in a serious fall from the open top of a double-decker bus. In the face of disappointing sales *Vox* stopped publication within only four months. In May 1930 he went to Liverpool to take up a job as publicity officer for Merseyside development, promoted by the Liverpool Organisation, a company supported by businessmen in the area and grants from local corporations. But here, too, he was not to prosper, and he lost the job within a year. Peggy refused to come north with him, for she had met an older man in London, a wealthy coal merchant, and the marriage was foundering.

To Circumjack Cencrastus was finally published in 1930, and although it is less cohesive than *A Drunk Man*, the recurring image of the coils of the curly snake, and the poet's doomed pursuit of it (like Ahab and the white whale) can be seen to symbolize his later poetic quest. Grieve met T. S. Eliot in London during this time, writing a key article in July 1931 for *Criterion* ('English ascendancy in British literature' in *Selected Prose*, 61–80) which argued in favour of the healthy variety of cultural and linguistic experience to be found within the British Isles among hitherto unrepresented regions and social classes. He also began to define 'the Gaelic idea' by which the so-called 'margins' of Celtic Ireland, Wales, Cornwall, and the Scottish highlands would speak for dynamism, contradiction, creative diversity, and cultural decentralization ('The Caledonian antisyzygy and the Gaelic idea' in *Selected Essays*, 56–74).

The depression years were very difficult for Grieve, and he felt himself faced with the need to find new expressive themes and means for his verse, including a more overt reflection of his commitment to socialism. Accordingly he embarked on the *Hymns to Lenin*, which were to be part of a much larger poetic project of five linked collections conceived as *Clann Albann* ('The children of Scotland'). The first book was to be a set of autobiographical verses called *The Muckle Toon*. The project was never realized, but many of the more personal poems from this period such as 'Kinsfolk', 'At my Father's Grave', 'Charisma and my Relatives', and 'Water of Life', clearly stem from an impulse to revisit and reassess his roots at a time of emotional and creative disturbance.

Back in London again Grieve became a director of the Unicorn Press in September 1931, but it turned out to be a short-lived and ill-rewarded appointment. More positively, this was the month he met Valda Trevlyn (1906–1989), a young Cornish nationalist working as a shop assistant in London who was to become his second wife, and a stout and unsentimental defender of his talent. '*First Hymn to Lenin' and other Poems* was published in December 1931. The collection includes 'The Seamless Garment', arguably the poet's most successful overtly didactic socialist poem. Based on his memories of the mills of Langholm and incorporating his admiration for Lenin and Rilke, this poem speaks for education, spiritual evolution, and radical social change in an easy colloquial Scots.

Grieve and his first wife were divorced on 16 January 1932. The poet had agreed to be cited for adultery himself if he could be allowed access to the children, but once they were separated Peggy denied him this privilege. This bitter separation was to last, and to haunt him, for years. Still struggling to make a living, in April Grieve and Valda Trevlyn rented a cottage at Thakeham in Sussex. From here they produced 500 copies of 'Second Hymn to Lenin', reprinted from its first appearance in *Criterion* and published by Valda Trevlyn as a pamphlet. On 28 July, after a difficult labour, Valda gave birth to a son, Michael. '*Scots Unbound' and other Poems* (1932) continued the poet's meditation on his Langholm origins, but its tiny print run (350 signed copies) did little to solve his financial problems. In August the new family moved to Longniddry, east of Edinburgh, where Grieve wrote for the periodical the *Free Man*; but things did not improve, for he was under increasing mental and physical strain, and his debts were mounting.

In May 1933 Grieve's old friend Helen Cruickshank arranged for him to move to the island of Whalsay in the Shetlands, where David Orr, the doctor there, had offered Valda a job as housekeeper. As it turned out Dr Orr got married and the Grieves had to rent a little cottage on their own, but the proposal brought them to the Shetlands and as Whalsay was a 'dry' island at least some of Grieve's problems could be addressed. They were to live there for the next ten years. In his autobiography MacDiarmid was to recall how he came to Whalsay: 'with no money behind me at all, broken down in health, unable to secure remunerative employment of any kind, and wholly concentrated on projects in poetry and other literary fields which could bring me no monetary return whatsoever' (*Lucky Poet*, 41). His son recalls the four-roomed fisherman's cottage at Sodom, east of Symbister harbour, where their first furniture was made from orange boxes and where they collected and preserved seagulls' eggs for food (Grieve, 'MacDiarmid the man', xi). Nevertheless, the family gradually established itself with the help of Helen Cruickshank and other friends in Edinburgh.

Grieve was overwhelmed and inspired by the stark grandeur of the Shetlands, and his letters and essays of the time testify to a fascination with the striking effects of sea light on bare rock. The austere setting also made itself felt in many new poems characterized by their use of geological terms and an icy control in their English diction. This marked change in expression, and the shift away from Scots and the poems remembering Langholm can be seen in the two major collections from the period, '*Stony Limits' and other Poems* (1934), and '*Second Hymn to Lenin' and other Poems* (1935). The poem 'On a Raised Beach' manages to confront the stark and indifferent foundations of existence without losing faith in the need to seek bread in that desert, and it can stand beside *Four Quartets* and 'In Praise of Limestone' as one of the finest philosophical poems in modern literature in English.

Having parted from the National Party in 1933 on account of his communist sympathies, Grieve joined the

Communist Party only to be expelled in 1937 for his nationalism (he was reinstated and expelled again within a year). As a follower of John Maclean he saw no contradiction between international socialism and nationalist hopes for a Scottish workers' republic, but his relationship with any organized political group was never less than stormy.

Grieve and Valda went south again in the spring of 1934, Valda to visit her mother in Cornwall and Grieve to London to deal with the publishers for *Selected Poems* (1934) and for prose works such as his collection of essays *At the Sign of the Thistle* (1934), and *Scottish Scene* (1934), a satirical look at Scotland which he co-authored with the young novelist Lewis Grassic Gibbon (J. Leslie Mitchell; 1901–1935) then living in Welwyn Garden City. Agreements were made with various publishers for further titles, the poet received an editorial retainer from Routledge, and on 12 September 1934 he and Valda were married at a register office in Islington. The poet's health was not good, however, and when he returned to Shetland he faced harsh winter weather and a demanding list of contracts to be fulfilled. These pressures came to a climax in the summer of 1935. Peggy had entered Grieve's life again by asking for his help in a court case brought against her by her lover's wife. Grieve found himself increasingly weary and depressed while faced with contracted deadlines. He reached a point of physical and nervous collapse and was persuaded to seek help among friends in St Andrews (including F. G. Scott) and in August he was admitted to a nursing home attached to the Murray Royal Hospital in Perth for physical and psychiatric care. It was seven weeks before he could leave, and photographs of the time show him to be emaciated and exhausted.

Back on Whalsay in October, Grieve gradually recovered strength and even managed to stand as a candidate for the student rectorial election at Edinburgh University. He was unsuccessful, but stood again (and again unsuccessfully) the following year. The poet refused to concede that he was any further from the 'centre of things' in Shetland than he had been in Edinburgh or London, but it is clear that he did come to feel increasingly isolated and at odds with the literary establishment in both countries. When Edwin Muir published *Scott and Scotland* (1936) and doubted whether modern Scottish writers could ever achieve a separate cultural and linguistic identity, Grieve took it as a personal betrayal and never forgave him. The long months of writing began to bear fruit when the biographical sketches of *Scottish Eccentrics* appeared in 1936 followed by *The Islands of Scotland* (1939), and a lengthy and wildly idiosyncratic autobiography called *Lucky Poet: a Self Study in Literature and Political Ideas*, which was eventually published in shortened form in 1943. (A sequel to it, *The Company I've Kept*, appeared in 1966.)

'The kind of poetry I want', 1936–1978 Grieve was now to pursue a course which made his poetry less and less accessible to the common reader. Determined to leave personal and lyric feeling behind him, he welcomed the extended 'epic' as the next necessary development for modern verse as he saw it, and as the best way of bringing poetry to bear on the world of political and scientific materialism. To this end he planned an immense undertaking to be called *Cornish Heroic Song for Valda Trevlyn*, of which *In Memoriam James Joyce* and *The Kind of Poetry I Want* were only parts, although they were later published as separate volumes in 1955 and 1961 respectively. A long opening section was to be called *Mature Art*, and a third large volume in this magnum opus was to be called *Impavidi progrediamur*, or in Scots, 'Haud forrit' ('Fare foward'), but it was never quite brought together. The poet's son Michael has confirmed that this project can be traced back to the Whalsay experience (Riach, 65) for its 'disinterested' and epic scope was conceived there, with lengthy verse extracts from *The Kind of Poetry I Want* included in *Lucky Poet* (which had been completed in 1939), and an early version of the title poem in *In Memoriam James Joyce* sent to T. S. Eliot at Faber in 1941.

Grieve was to edit this mammoth text at different times for the next thirty years, publishing extracts or separate volumes from it as declared parts of a whole which was never to be completed. Indeed this new kind of poetry ('the kind of poetry I want') was conceived from the start as an open-ended and indefinitely extensible process. The operating principle of Grieve's epic catalogues, dense with long prosaic lines, abstruse knowledge, and highly specialized vocabulary, could not be more different from the lyric concision and intensity of his early work in Scots, and many contemporary readers felt that he had abandoned poetry altogether.

The late work poses other problems, as Grieve's text also contains lines and passages taken unacknowledged from other sources of poetry and prose. Riach (chap. 3) places this epic poetry in a postmodern perspective, claiming it as an endlessly intertextual discourse which has gone beyond the conception of the poet as a single speaking voice. Bold (p. 368) is more inclined to see it as cheerfully unrepentant theft. Critics are still tracing the extent of Grieve's hidden debts and debating how to assess such work. It is worth recalling, however, that as early as 1923 he had described the prose studies in *Annals of the Five Senses* (similarly full of echoes and extracts) as 'mosaics … which I have (perhaps the best word in the meantime is) "designed"' (*Annals*, dedication).

At the beginning of 1938 a young graduate, Henry Grant Taylor, arrived on Whalsay to help Grieve produce his lengthy typescripts. In June of that year the poet launched another periodical, the quarterly *Voice of Scotland* which was to run for five issues before being interrupted by the war. The magazine allowed Grieve to publish work by a new generation of younger Scottish poets, including Norman MacCaig, George Bruce, George Campbell Hay, and Sorley MacLean, whom he had first met in Edinburgh in 1934. Maclean had visited Whalsay in 1935 and helped Grieve to translate Gaelic poems for his edition of *The Golden Treasury of Scottish Poetry* (1940). The publication of Roy Campbell's autobiographical poem *Flowering Rifle* (1939) spurred Grieve to write a long poem of his own, *The Battle Continues* (1957), which criticized Campbell's part in the Spanish Civil War and reaffirmed a hatred of fascism.

The outbreak of war in 1939 meant that the publication plans for *Mature Art* had to be abandoned, and the lengthy autobiography *Lucky Poet* had to be cut by at least two thirds before eventual publication in 1943.

Too old for the army, Grieve was called up for industrial war work, leaving Shetland for Glasgow in January 1942. A spell staying with Andrew Grieve, then widowed and living in Cambuslang, led to a quarrel which was never to be resolved between the brothers. By July and after initial training Grieve was turning shell-bands at a lathe in Mechan's Engineering Company at Scotstoun. Valda and Michael joined him in Glasgow, but the work was hard, with a nine-and-a-half hour day and compulsory overtime most Sundays, and at the end of August he was injured by a falling pile of copper plate, which left him with a limp for some months after he returned to the factory. Within two years the physical strain proved too great, and in 1944 Grieve asked for a transfer to the merchant navy where he served for a year as a deckhand aboard the *Gurli*, a Norwegian vessel delivering mail and supplies out of Greenock to allied ships in the Clyde estuary. He noted that the work was easier and he could send improved rations to Valda.

While in Glasgow and Greenock, Grieve had renewed contact with the Scottish National Party (SNP), making friends with its flamboyant chairman, Douglas Young, who had resisted conscription and gone to gaol on a matter of political principle. Grieve stood as an SNP candidate for Kelvingrove in 1945 and lost his deposit (he left the party in 1948 and stood for the same seat as an independent nationalist in 1950 with the same result). The Glasgow publisher William Maclellan produced a *Selected Poems of Hugh MacDiarmid* in 1944, as part of a *Poetry Scotland* series which included volumes from younger writers such as Maurice Lindsay, George Bruce, W. S. Graham, Sydney Goodsir Smith, Alexander Scott, Douglas Young, George Campbell Hay, and Sorley Maclean—the so-called 'second wave' of the modern Scottish renaissance.

With the coming of peace Grieve was freed from war work only to find himself unemployed at the age of fifty-three. The poet threw himself back into his literary and political interests, becoming a noted figure among the younger writers around him and supporting what had now become a general debate about the use of Scots and Gaelic in modern writing. In December 1945 he revived the *Voice of Scotland*, and many sections of *Cornish Heroic Song* appeared in its pages over the years, until its last issue in June 1949. *Poems of the East-West Synthesis* (1946) pursued his vision of a Russo-Gaelic connection and provided an outlet for yet more sections of the magnum opus.

Grieve returned to newspaper journalism in the latter half of 1947 with a brief spell on the staff of the *Carlisle Journal*. Back in Glasgow again, a new collection of poems (once again mostly from *Cornish Heroic Song*) was published as *A Kist of Whistles*, number 10 in the *Poetry Scotland* series. In 1949 steps were taken to have him considered for a civil-list pension which was eventually awarded in March 1950. Eager to leave Glasgow, in the autumn of 1949 the Grieves accepted an offer from the duke of Hamilton to live in a cottage attached to his house near Strathaven in Lanarkshire. They stayed at Dungavel House for almost a year, before the offer of a farm cottage at Candymill near Biggar brought Grieve back to the borders again. The couple were to stay there—in little more than two rooms and a kitchen—rent-free for the rest of their lives. The cottage at Brownsbank is now preserved by the Biggar Museum Trust, and a writing fellowship is associated with it.

Grieve continued to write poetry when prompted by the occasion, but the greater part of his life's work was behind him, and future publications were a matter of catching up with the immense output of the 1940s. He settled down to a life of public appearances and invited travel. He went to Moscow with the Scottish-USSR Friendship Society in 1950, to Germany and Poland the following year, and the summer of 1955 was spent in Prague just before the publication (at last) of *In Memoriam James Joyce*. The poet's communist sympathies were as outspoken and controversial as ever, not least when he rejoined the Communist Party of Great Britain in 1956, when most Western intellectuals, outraged by the invasion of Hungary, were leaving it. Grieve accepted that mistakes had been made, but argued in an article for the *Daily Worker* for 28 March 1957 that now more than ever it was necessary to support the basic principles of Marxist-Leninism (Bold, 410). A third edition of *A Drunk Man* appeared in 1956, and in April 1957 the poet visited China as part of a British-Chinese friendship delegation. On his return to Scotland he was awarded the honorary degree of LLD on 5 July by the University of Edinburgh. The same year saw the publication of the *Three Hymns to Lenin* in a single volume and *The Battle Continues*, although the original quarrel with Roy Campbell was now long past. The Edinburgh University Nationalist Club presented the poet with the Andrew Fletcher of Saltoun medal 'for outstanding services to Scotland' in May 1958. The bicentenary of Burns's birth in 1959 saw Grieve produce a prose study, *Burns Today and Tomorrow* (1959) and he was consequently invited to visit Czechoslovakia, Romania, Bulgaria, and Hungary. As a member of the Committee of 100 he joined Bertrand Russell and others to speak for nuclear disarmament at a huge rally in Trafalgar Square, London, on 18 February 1961.

In 1962 Grieve's own seventieth birthday was marked by a special new edition of *A Drunk Man* brought out by the 200 Burns Club, a commissioned portrait by R. H. Westwater, and by the appearance of both an American and a British edition of his *Collected Poems*. It was nothing like a complete collection, but it was the first time that most of his major poems had been in print for many years and it was awarded the William Foyle poetry prize in March 1963. Two seminal critical studies appeared in 1964, and both books—by Kenneth Buthlay and Duncan Glen—did much to consolidate the poet's standing in academic and popular circles. A number of supplementary collections appeared in later years, but *A Lap of Honour* (1967), *A Clyack-Sheaf* (1969), and *More Collected Poems* (1970), although useful at the time, are unsatisfactory from a bibliographical point of view. The two-volume *Hugh MacDiarmid: Complete*

Poems, 1920–1976 (1978), revised for the 'MacDiarmid 2000' edition of 1993, remains the best edition to date.

Grieve had become a familiar and honoured public figure but was no less controversial in his pronouncements. He cited Anglophobia as his recreation for *Who's Who*. He waged a war of words with Ian Hamilton Finlay and other young writers, and quarrelled with Alexander Trocchi and Norman Mailer in a public debate at the Edinburgh Festival in 1962. In 1964 he stood for the general election as a Communist candidate against the prime minister, Sir Alec Douglas-Home, whose constituency was Kinross and West Perthshire. Denied equal airtime during the election Grieve went to the courts (without success) to have Home's election declared null and void.

Grieve continued to travel, visiting Sweden, New York, London, and Budapest in 1967, the year of his seventy-fifth birthday, when an exhibition of his work was shown at the National Library of Scotland. He was elected an honorary fellow of the Modern Language Association of America (1968), president of the Lallans Society (1972), and an honorary member of the Royal Scottish Academy (1974). His eightieth birthday was marked by a critical symposium on his work at Edinburgh University, and in 1976 he was elected president of the Poetry Society of Great Britain. Increasingly frail at the end, Grieve never broke contact with the wide circle of his correspondents, nor lost his iconoclastic delight in the clash of opinions and the excitement of ideas. Diagnosed as having a cancer of the bowel, he suffered several lesser operations with dignity and managed to attend the ceremony for an honorary degree at Trinity College, Dublin, in July 1978. He saw the proofs of the two-volume *Complete Poems* before being admitted to Chalmers Hospital, Edinburgh, where he died on 9 September 1978. He was buried in Langholm cemetery on 13 September. A bronze sculpture by Jake Harvey was erected in his memory on a hillside near Whita Yett, Langholm. Grieve was the last of the generation of Joyce, Eliot, Yeats, and Pound—those early modernists, iconoclasts, and system builders who wanted nothing less than a major place for poetic vision in the modern world.

RODERICK WATSON

Sources A. Bold, *MacDiarmid, Christopher Murray Grieve: a critical biography* (1988) · *The letters of Hugh MacDiarmid*, ed. A. Bold (1984) · H. MacDiarmid, *Lucky poet* (1972) · H. MacDiarmid, *The company I've kept* (1966) · *The Hugh MacDiarmid–George Ogilvie letters*, ed. C. Kerrigan (1988) · D. Glen, *Hugh MacDiarmid and the Scottish renaissance* (1964) · C. Kerrigan, *Whaur extremes meet: the poetry of Hugh MacDiarmid, 1920–1934* (1983) · A. Riach, *Hugh MacDiarmid's epic poetry* (1991) · R. McQuillan, *Hugh MacDiarmid: the patrimony* (1992) · M. Grieve, 'Hugh MacDiarmid the man', *The Hugh MacDiarmid anthology*, ed. M. Grieve and A. Scott (1972), xi–xvi · W. R. Aitken, 'A bibliography of Hugh MacDiarmid', *Hugh MacDiarmid: man and poet*, ed. N. Gish (1992), 297–323 · G. Wright, *MacDiarmid: an illustrated biography* (1977) · C. M. Grieve, *Annals of the five senses* (1923)
Archives Ewart Public Library, Dumfries, MSS · NL Scot., corresp. and papers; corresp. mainly on political topics; material relating to election campaign in Kinross and West Perthshire; MSS · U. Edin. L., corresp. and literary MSS; letters and poems · U. Texas, MSS | Literary and Philosophical Society of Newcastle upon Tyne, letters to Tom Pickard and Connie Pickard · NL Scot., letters to J. K. Annand; letters to J. G. Beaumont; letters to George Bruce; letters to Morven Cameron; letters to Helen Cruikshank; letters to Mr Dunlop and Mrs Dunlop; letters to Neil Gunn; letters to William Johnstone; corresp. with J. P. McGillivray; corresp. with Eneas Mackay; letters to Ruth McQuillan; letters to Ian F. G. Milner; letters to Mrs Ray Mitchell; letters to William Montgomery; letters to George Ogilvie; corresp. with William Soutar · Shetland Archives, Lerwick, letters to Peter Jamieson · U. Aberdeen, corresp. with Walter Keir · U. Edin. L., letters to Helen Cruickshank; letters to David Daiches; letters to D. Glenis; letters to John Laidlaw and Jean White; letters to Roland Eugene Muirhead; letters to Arno Reinfrank; letters to Francis George Scott; letters to Meic Stephens; letters to Jozsef Szili · U. Nott. L., letters to Nottingham Poetry Festival organizers | FILM Scottish Screen Archive, 74 Victoria Cres. Road, Glasgow, 'No fellow travellers', 1972 | SOUND University of Keele, English Department, 'Poets and dialogue on tape'
Likenesses W. Johnstone, pencil drawing, 1936, Scot. NPG · W. Crosbie, oils, 1943, Art Gallery and Museum, Glasgow · F. T. Rainey, oils, 1946, State University of New York, Buffalo, Lockwood Memorial Library · L. Moser, vintage print, 1949, NPG · G. Konig, photograph, 1950, Hult. Arch. · L. H. Bradshaw, bronzed plaster head, 1956, Scot. NPG · B. Schotz, bronze bust, 1958, Scot. NPG · B. Schotz, bronze bust, 1958, BBC Scotland · R. H. Westwater, oils, 1962, Scot. NPG [*see illus.*] · A. Thornhill, bronze head, 1974, NPG · A. Moffat, group portrait, oils, 1980 (Poct pub), Scot. NPG · photographs, repro. in Wright, *MacDiarmid*

Grieve, Elizabeth Harriet (*b. c.*1723, *d.* in or after 1782), swindler, details of whose upbringing and parentage are unknown, gained notoriety in London in the early 1770s for a series of artful and audacious schemes whereby she duped not only tradesmen seeking preferment and places, but also a famous 'Right Honourable spendthrift', the politician, Charles James Fox (*Morning Chronicle*, 4 Nov 1773). Fox, then a lord of the Treasury and desperately in debt, became the 'bubble of this woman, who undoubtedly had uncommon talents and a knowledge of the world' (*Last Journals of Horace Walpole*, 1.269) and promised to arrange a lucrative marriage between him and a fictitious West Indian heiress. Her claim to influence through her association with Fox and her pretended kinship with prominent members of the nobility caused a sensation on 3 November 1773, when Mrs 'Greeve', a woman of about fifty years (*Morning Chronicle*, 4 November), was brought before Sir John Fielding at the public office in Bow Street, accused by five persons of defrauding them under pretence of using her influence to procure government and other posts. Her agent, one Francis Crook, turned evidence against her. Abusive to her accusers and insolent to Fielding, Mrs Grieve was committed for trial.

The proceedings at Bow Street were widely reported by the press. It emerged that she had operated in London's West End for some time, advertising herself as 'a *sensible woman* who gave advice on all emergencies for half a guinea' (*Last Journals of Horace Walpole*, 1.269). Rumours circulated that she was a cousin to Lord North and the duke of Grafton; the earl of Guilford was said to be 'so fond of her, that he chucked her under the chin' (*Morning Chronicle*, 4 November). Particular interest was given to her relationship with Fox. Having advanced him a loan of £300, she had 'paid herself by his chariot standing frequently at her door, which served to impose on her more vulgar dupes' (*Last Journals of Horace Walpole*, 1.270).

Stories spread that Mrs Grieve had agreed to arrange

Fox's marriage to 'Miss Phipps', a West Indian heiress. Cautioned that Miss Phipps could not abide a dark complexioned man, Fox had powdered his eyebrows. When the fictitious Miss Phipps finally arrived in England, Mrs Grieve kept Fox at bay by claiming his 'Celia' had the smallpox. Then, increasingly fearful of discovery, she tried to cancel the match by revealing that the lady was four months pregnant. In a letter to Lord Carlisle, 5 February 1774, George Selwyn maintained that 'Charles owns the whole truth of it, except the last circumstance concerning the pregnancy' (*Carlisle MSS*, 266). The disclosures before Sir John Fielding also inspired two verse satires—*Female Artifice, or, Charles F-x Outwitted*, February 1774, and 'An Heroic and Elegiac Epistle from Mrs Grieve, in Newgate, to Mr. Charles Fox', *Westminster Magazine*, 1774—and a play by Samuel Foote, *The Cozeners* (published 1778), which opened at the Theatre Royal, Haymarket, on 15 July 1774 with Mary Williams in the role of Mrs Fleece'em. *The Cozeners* was performed twenty-one times between 15 July and 15 September.

On 27 October 1774 Elizabeth Grieve was tried at Middlesex quarter sessions, Hicks's Hall, where she produced a letter in Fox's handwriting which 'excited great laughter in Court' (*London Chronicle*, 27–9 Oct 1774). She was found guilty and sentenced to seven years' transportation, embarking from St Katharine's Dock in January 1775, presumably for Virginia.

This, perhaps, was not the first such sentence bestowed on Mrs Grieve, for in October 1773 it was alleged that she had been sentenced to transportation about two years before for a felony. Old Bailey sessions records reveal that an Elizabeth Greaves was acquitted on 19 October 1768 of the charge of setting fire to a house in South Park Street (near fashionable Grosvenor Square) belonging to her husband, John Greaves, a naval captain. She was, however, found guilty and sentenced to transportation on a theft charge for having pawned thirty-three shirts and eight waistcoats of her lodger, Colonel Edward Hamilton, to whom she told a 'lamentable story' (*Proceedings*, 361) of his clothing's having been lost in the fire. This Mrs Greaves, who may or may not have been Fox's deceiver, was described by a character witness as 'brought up extremely gay, and was looked upon as a gentlewoman' (*Proceedings*, 364). Detained in Newgate prison, she was granted a full pardon on 19 January 1769 (*Home Office Papers*, 2.414, 566).

On 22 October 1782 only a few newspapers commented that Elizabeth Harriet Grieve, now recognized as the 'Hon. Mrs. Greaves' and presumably returned from her period of transportation, was back to her old tricks of deception. Reports spoke of how she had been foiled in a scheme to defraud her landlady at the Cooper's Arms, East Smithfield. She was committed by Justice Wilmot, but no more is known of her. The depredations of this female sharper on the credulous and greedy pointed a wagging finger at society and the practice of preferment. Her forte was the skilful manipulation of human weakness. 'We can never sufficiently admire the originality of the thought in selecting Mr. Charles F-x ... and the wonderful address with

which she afterwards conducted the business' (*Female Artifice*, 5n.). To some degree Elizabeth Grieve may even have come to believe the role in which she cast herself.

PAGE LIFE

Sources *Morning Chronicle* (4 Nov 1773) · *Morning Chronicle* (15 July 1774) · *Morning Chronicle* (29 Oct 1774) · *Morning Chronicle* (24 Oct 1782) · *London Chronicle* (2–4 Nov 1773) · *London Chronicle* (27–9 Oct 1774) · *London Chronicle* (22–4 Oct 1782) · *General Evening Post* (29 Oct–1 Nov 1774) · *General Evening Post* (3–5 Nov 1774) · *The last journals of Horace Walpole*, ed. Dr Doran, rev. A. F. Steuart, 2 vols. (1910) · Walpole, *Corr.* · *Female artifice, or, Charles F-x outwitted* (1774) · *The manuscripts of the earl of Carlisle*, HMC, 42 (1897), 263–6 [G. A. Selwyn to Lord Carlisle, 5 Feb 1774] · F. G., 'Charles James Fox and Mrs Grieve', *N&Q*, 3rd ser., 5 (1864), 381–3 · P. W. Coldham, *The complete book of emigrants in bondage, 1614–1775* (1988) · *The whole proceedings on the king's commission of the peace* (1767–8), 354, 361–5 [Old Bailey sessions papers, 19–22 Oct 1768] · J. Redington and R. A. Roberts, eds., *Calendar of home office papers of the reign of George III*, 2: 1766–1769, PRO (1879), 414, 566 · *Memoirs of James Bolland, formerly a butcher in the Borough*, 2nd edn (1772) · A. Knapp and W. Baldwin, *The new Newgate calendar, being interesting memoirs of notorious characters*, 5 vols. [n.d., 1826?]

Grieve, George. *See* Grieve, George (1748–1809).

Grieve, James (*bap.* 1708, *d.* 1763), physician and translator, was baptized at Hawick, Roxburghshire, on 30 April 1703, the son of James Grieve, a tenant farmer, and Jenet Eliot. From 1726 he studied medicine at Edinburgh University, where he graduated in June 1733 with an MD thesis on eye illnesses of the vitreous humour. Licensed to practise medicine in Russia in May 1734, he obtained his first post as a doctor at the Kazan and Siberian factories' directorate when the Dutch-born Dr Nicholas Bidloo, builder and director of Moscow's earliest hospital, strongly recommended him to Vasily Tatischev, a prominent Russian figure. Tatischev, who later supervised the Orenburg border commission with Asia, also secured Grieve's medical appointment there in 1737. Grieve's expert knowledge of chemical substances and their medical applications is revealed in a letter which Tatischev wrote in 1735 to the Russian Academy of Sciences and by Grieve's own letter of 20 September 1742 to Antonio Ribeiro Sanches, physician to the Russian court and an eminent medical writer. In 1744 James Grieve held the concurrent posts of physician to the St Petersburg land hospital and to a guards division on the city's outskirts, having married Elizabeth Tamesz (1725–1758), of Dutch or German extraction, in the previous year. He was appointed to the senior post of St Petersburg city physician in 1747, and from 1750 deputized for Hermann Kaau-Boerhaave, director of the Russian medical chancery. About this time he also became physician to the Empress Elizabeth. He transferred to Moscow, as its city physician, in 1751 and was elected fellow of the Royal College of Physicians of Edinburgh two years later.

Grieve left Russia in 1757 to arrange the education of his son James Tamesz Grieve (1744–1787), a precocious linguist. While practising medicine in London he nursed his wife, who died on 22 March 1758 after a long illness. James Mounsey, a Moscow doctor who was a relative of Grieve's by marriage, recommended him as a person of sterling character to Henry Baker, fellow of the Royal Society.

Grieve associated with several other fellows interested in Russia, such as Thomas Birch, who introduced him to John Pringle and James Short, and Patrick Murdoch. He probably returned to Russia in 1761. The Empress Elizabeth died in January 1762, and in May Grieve asked Mounsey, by then first physician to Peter III and medical chancery director, to use his influence to obtain a court post for him in England. After a short time in London as a doctor he returned to Russia in August with John Hobart, earl of Buckinghamshire, who had been appointed ambassador on the accession of Catherine, following the murder of her husband, Peter III. If the evidence in the Lambert family papers is correct a valuable snuffbox, inscribed in French 'Presented by the Empress Catherine to her body physician James Grieve', would confirm that he also attended Catherine II. Surviving business correspondence between John Tamesz of Moscow, a cousin of Grieve's late wife, and the earl of Buckinghamshire indicates that Grieve received £100 in payment from the earl in May 1763 and that he was seriously ill during May and June of that year. He died at Moscow on 4 July 1763, according to a reputable Russian source, although the *Gentleman's Magazine* gave his death date as 30 July (*GM*, 1st ser., 33, 1763, 415).

James Grieve is best remembered for translating *The History of Kamtschatka, and the Kurilski Islands*, published posthumously in 1764 by Thomas Jefferys, the royal geographer, from the 1755 work by Sergey Krasheninnikov. The latter participated in the Russian Academy of Sciences' second Kamchatka expedition (1733–43), under Bering, which attempted to prove the feasibility of a north-east passage between Asia and America. Krasheninnikov's book is a classic scientific study of all aspects of Kamchatka's vulcanology, geography, natural history, and ethnography. A chapter on America from his book, translated by Daniel Dumaresq, Grieve's friend, had already appeared in the Royal Society's *Philosophical Transactions* (51, 1760, 477–97). In September 1762 Dumaresq informed G. F. Müller, the editor of Krasheninnikov's original work, that he had seen Grieve's translation, which Jefferys intended publishing shortly (St Petersburg, Russian Academy of Sciences, archives, fond 21, opis 3, no. 73). However, as the 'Advertisement' to the 1764 publication explains, Grieve's busy professional duties and his sudden departure for Russia with the earl of Buckinghamshire had prevented him from revising the translation that he had undertaken purely for his own amusement. Nevertheless judicious abridgement of Krasheninnikov's text, with stylistic improvements to Grieve's reasonably accurate translation, resulted in a more balanced product that proved of enduring interest. It has been retranslated into several European languages, including French (two translations, 1767 and 1768), Dutch (two editions, 1770), and German (two editions, 1776 and 1789). It has also been reproduced in two facsimile copies (1963 and 1973).

Grieve's only son, James Tamesz Grieve, a Moscow businessman who inherited his mother's considerable family fortune, purchased Scottish property in 1781 and Petersham House, Surrey, from the duke and duchess of Montrose, in 1787. His will mentions his very good friend Dr John Grieve. Although their certificates of arms granted in 1784 by the Edinburgh College of Heralds are identical, both claiming descent from the lairds of Lag, Galloway, Dr Grieve's parentage is not given. This **John Grieve** (*bap.* 1744?, *d.* 1805), physician and writer, may therefore have been the illegitimate or adopted child of some member of James Grieve's family; or, more likely, was the John Grieve baptized on 11 June 1744 at Hawick, Roxburghshire, the son of Elspeth, Dr James Grieve's sister, and William Grieve. His sister Joanna married James *Mounsey. After studying medicine and other subjects at Edinburgh University he graduated MA and MD from Glasgow University in 1777. From 1778 until 1783 he served in Russia as a military doctor in the Voronezh division, before returning to Britain on health grounds. During 1784 he wrote two excellent letters to Joseph Black, from Paris and Hertford, describing French air balloons, Meusnier's and Lavoisier's latest chemical experiments, and—at first hand—Mesmer's animal magnetism methods. In a paper published in the first volume of the *Transactions of the Royal Society of Edinburgh* (1783–5, 178–90) Grieve pioneered British knowledge of koumiss (fermented mare's milk) from his own practice in Russia. Settling down to successful private practice in London, he was elected to some fifteen medical, scientific, natural history, and antiquarian societies over the next few years, among them the Royal Society of Edinburgh (1784), the Society of Antiquaries—of Edinburgh (1784) and London (1790)—and the Royal Society (1794). On 11 June 1792 he married Rebecca Kinnersley (1771–1811) at the church of St Marylebone, Middlesex. In 1798 he returned to Russia with his wife and family, as court physician to Emperor Paul I. He and two other Scots, James Wylie and Matthew Guthrie, performed the autopsy on Paul after his assassination on 23 March 1801. Highly regarded and honoured both for his medical expertise and diplomatic skills, he became physician to Emperor Alexander I, his wife and family, and the dowager empress Maria Fedorovna, while treating courtiers and military leaders as well. He died of a stroke, in St Petersburg on 21 December 1805, perhaps after the banquet held that day in the Winter Palace to celebrate the emperor's return from the battle of Austerlitz. He was buried in the city on 26 December. He had left no will.

James Greive (*bap.* 1729, *d.* 1773), physician and translator, the second surviving son of a different James Greive and his wife, Elizabeth Birnet, was baptized on 19 October 1729 at Berwick upon Tweed, Northumberland. He studied medicine at Edinburgh University from 1749 and graduated in April 1752 with an MD dissertation on stone of the urinary bladder. Between September and November 1753 he advertised lecture courses in chemistry, especially its 'applications to the practice of physic and pharmacy', at Plasterers' Hall, Aldermanbury, in London, and at the laboratory of Mr Hodgson's Bartholomew Close dispensary (*Daily Advertiser*, 20 September, 29 October, 12 Nov 1753). In 1756 he published his fine and scholarly *Aulus Cornelius Celsus: of medicine, in eight books, translated with notes critical and explanatory*. Its surgical part was revised by Samuel Sharp, surgeon of Guy's Hospital, to whom Greive dedicated the work. The seventh book of Celsus's composition, the standard account of Roman surgery in the first century AD, includes the earliest description of dental practice. The translation reached three editions. From 1758 to 1769 Greive was the first honorary physician of the Magdalen Hospital for Penitent Prostitutes, founded by Robert Dingley in Prescot Street, Whitechapel. On 5 April 1759 Dr John Hadley introduced him at the Royal Society; on 15 October 1760 he was elected a member of the Royal Society of Arts, and in the same year subscribed to the British Troops Society.

On 17 April 1762 Greive replaced Thomas Milner as physician to St Thomas's Hospital, and on 30 September he became a licentiate of the Royal College of Physicians. He married Mary, daughter of Anne Le Grand of Canterbury, at the church of St Thomas the Apostle on 30 October 1764; their only child was Ann (b. c.1765, d. in or after 1794). Having applied to the duke of Newcastle for his support in November 1764 Greive succeeded John Hadley as physician to the Charterhouse on 7 March 1765, whereupon he moved into Charterhouse Square. On 24 November 1768 he was proposed for membership of the Royal Society. His certificate (no. 111.6) stresses his 'distinguished attainments in all good learning, particularly in medical and natural knowledge'. Elected a fellow on 23 February 1769, he was admitted and signed the charter book on 2 March. A man with a wide circle of friends and acquaintances, he was also elected fellow of the Royal College of Physicians, by special favour, on 30 September 1771. Greive made his will in 1768, adding two codicils during 1772 and 1773. He proved, but did not administer, his brother Thomas's will on 3 April 1773. He died at his house in Charterhouse Square on 9 July 1773 and was buried in the Charterhouse chapel alongside his wife, who had died on 15 December 1767. Neither he nor James Greive should be confused with James Greive (1833–1924), the son of James Greive and Margaret Scott, who was baptized on 8 March 1833 at Stobo, Peeblesshire. From 1859 to 1895 he worked for Dicksons at their Leith Walk nursery in Edinburgh, raising the famous dessert apple named after him. First recorded in 1893, it was the female parent of several colour varieties also carrying his name.   JOHN H. APPLEBY

Sources J. H. Appleby, 'British doctors in Russia, 1657–1807', PhD diss., University of East Anglia, 1974 [copies at NL Scot., Bodl. Oxf., Wellcome L., RS, and the New York Academy of Medicine] · S. P. Krasheninnikov, *The history of Kamtschatka, and the Kurilski Islands* (Gloucester, 1764) · will, PRO, PROB 11/902, sig. 331–2 [J. Greive] · will, PRO, PROB 11/990, sig. 331–2 [J. Greive] · will, PRO, PROB 11/987, sig. 159 [T. Greive] · will, PRO, PROB 11/1154, sig. 268 [J. T. Greive] · J. H. Appleby, 'John Greive's correspondence with Joseph Black', *Medical History*, 29 (Oct 1985), 401–13 · V. N. Tatischev. *Zapiski, pisma (Notes and letters) 1717–1750 gg.*, *Nauchnoye nasledstvo*, 14 (Moscow, 1990) · Paris University, Faculty of Medicine Library, Antonio Ribeiro Sanches' MSS, vol. 7, fol. 65v · S. B. Pearce, *An ideal in the making: the story of the Magdalen Hospital* (1958) · C. J. Singer, 'Surgery', *Oxford classical dictionary*, ed. N. G. L. Hammond and H. H. Scullard, 2nd edn (1970), 1025 · papers of the earl of Buckinghamshire's Russian embassy, Norfolk RO, NRS 16389 32C4 · Lambert family papers · C. Joyneville, *The life and times of Alexander 1*, 1 (1875) · *Transactions of the Society ... for the Encouragement of Arts, Manufactures, and Commerce*, 40 (1822) [Analytical index] · membership subscription books, RSA · S. Devlin-Thorp,

ed., *The Royal Society of Edinburgh: one hundred medical fellows elected, 1783–1844* (1982), vol. 3 of *Scotland's cultural heritage* (1981–4) · J. H. Appleby, 'Daniel Dumaresq, D.D., F.R.S. (1712–1805), as a promoter of Anglo-Russian science and culture', *Notes and Records of the Royal Society of London*, 44 (Jan 1990), 25–50 · *An account of the Society for the Encouragement of the British troops in Germany and North America*, British Troops Society (1760) · bap. reg. Scot. · IGI · Munro's list of scholars; medical matriculations, U. Edin. · monumental inscription, Bath Abbey [Elizabeth Greive] · Munk, *Roll*, vol. 2 · *Register of marriages, St Mary Le Bone*, pt 5 (1923) · GL, MS 11192.B · F. Collins, ed., *The registers and monumental inscriptions of Charterhouse chapel*, Harleian Society, Register Section, 18 (1892) · Charterhouse muniments, MS PS. 1/5
Archives BL, letters to the duke of Newcastle, Add. MSS 32935, fol. 493, 32963, fol. 415 · Norfolk RO, papers of the earl of Buckinghamshire's Russian embassy
Likenesses portrait, c.1792 (John Greive), repro. in S. Oladottir, *100 medical fellows*; copy, E. Michael, 1893, priv. coll. · portrait (James Greive), repro. in Desmond, *Botanists*, rev. edn (1994), 298–9

Grieve, John (*bap.* 1744?, *d.* 1805). *See under* Grieve, James (*bap.* 1708, *d.* 1763).

Grieve, John [*pseud.* C] (1781–1836), poet, was born at Dunfermline on 12 September 1781, the son of the Revd Walter Grieve, minister of the Reformed Presbyterian church, and his wife, Jane Ballantyne. He was educated at the parish school of Ettrick, where his father had settled on retiring from the ministry. After leaving school he became a merchant's clerk in Alloa, and then a bank clerk in Greenock from 1801. He subsequently returned to Alloa, to become a partner in the firm of his former employer.

In 1804 Grieve began a partnership in Edinburgh with Chalmers Izzet, hat maker. The business was successful, and he found leisure for literary pursuits. He contributed to various periodicals, most notably the songs he published under the pseudonym 'C' in Hogg's *Forest Minstrel*. He was on intimate terms with Hogg, who speaks of his literary advice as well as his material assistance. Hogg's *Mador of the Moor* is dedicated to Grieve, and he figures as a competing minstrel in the *Queen's Wake*. It was on Grieve's recommendation that the *Queen's Wake* was published, and without the financial support of Grieve and his partner, Hogg said he could never have fought his way in Edinburgh: 'I was fairly starved into it, and if it had not been for Messrs Grieve and Scott would, in a very short time, have been starved out of it again' (Hogg, 23).

In 1817 Grieve retired from business because of a spine disorder. Until his death he was a well-known figure in Edinburgh literary society, and his house was frequented by writers. He died unmarried on 4 April 1836, and was buried in St Mary's, Yarrow.

WILLIAM BAYNE, *rev.* SARAH COUPER

Sources C. Rogers, *The modern Scottish minstrel, or, The songs of Scotland of the past half-century*, 3 (1856) · J. Hogg, 'Memoir of the author's life' and 'Familiar anecdotes of Sir Walter Scott', ed. D. S. Mack (1972) · Mrs Garden, *Memorials of James Hogg, the Ettrick shepherd* · J. G. Lockhart, *Memoirs of the life of Sir Walter Scott*, 4 (1837) · Irving, *Scots.*

Grieve, John Henderson (1770/71–1845). *See under* Grieve family (*per.* 1794–1887).

Grieve, Mary Margaret (1906–1998), journalist, was born on 11 April 1906 at 3 Blackburn Road, Ayr, Ayrshire, the younger daughter and second of the three children of Robert Grieve, fundholder, from a family of coalmine owners in Kilmarnock, and his wife, Annie Craig, *née* Stark, a nurse, and daughter of a Galloway clergyman. A delicate child, she spent much of her childhood in bed, and was educated at home until she was sixteen, when she went to a small day school in Glasgow. From there she went to London, where she trained as a secretary, and studied journalism. Her first job was on the *Nursing Mirror*, but after a few months she returned to Glasgow, where she remained for the next ten years. She took a job finding advertising for *Scottish Home and County*, the magazine of the Scottish Women's Rural Institutes, as well as editing a new monthly magazine, the *Scottish Nurse*, for a few months, and she worked freelance for seven years as a social reporter for *The Bulletin*, a daily picture paper aimed mainly at women. In 1935 she published *Without Alphonse*, the fictitious diary of a Frenchwoman touring Scotland, under the pseudonym Ursula Mary Lyon.

In 1936 Grieve went to London to join the editorial staff of *Mother*, a new monthly magazine published by Odhams Press. Odhams launched *Woman*, 'The National Home Weekly', on 1 June 1937, making use of its new photogravure plant at Watford. After a disastrous first few weeks, Odhams brought in the editorial team from *Mother* to save the magazine, and Grieve became associate editor. The use of colour printing and the superior quality of the printing made other women's magazines look drab, and as the new process became cheaper as the run got bigger, it was geared to a mass market. By 1940, when the editor, John Gammie, joined the RAF and Grieve became editor, sales of *Woman* had reached three quarters of a million.

During the Second World War Grieve advised the ministry of information on how women could contribute to the war effort, and she made sure the relevant departments were reminded of women's concerns, as when she arranged a meeting with Board of Trade officials to discuss the shortage of corsets for large women. *Woman* gave practical advice on how to 'make do and mend' and make the best use of food rations, and interpreted for its readers government regulations about blackouts, air raid precautions, evacuees, and clothing coupons. When austerity ended, the magazine responded to the greater availability of consumer goods, and in the 1950s began to set up practical departments where goods could be tested and demonstrated, including a beauty salon, a kitchen, and a fashion department, and gave consumer advice, leading Grieve to remark that she sometimes felt she was running a department store rather than a magazine. As women found a new place in society after the war, *Woman* helped them to cope with balancing a career and a family, and one of the most popular features was Evelyn Home's agony column, written for thirty-seven years by Peggy Makins.

Woman had an enormous influence over what women thought, a responsibility Grieve took very seriously. She wanted to reach as many women as possible, all over the country, and to reflect the reality of their lives: 'it is of the first importance that the reader should see her own life reflected in the pages, and not that of some luckier, richer, cleverer creature' (Grieve, 90). In the early days she was careful not to refer to a daily bath, or a telephone, or a foreign holiday, as she knew that for many women this was an impossibility, and one of her maxims was that fashion is what ordinary women wear. She wanted women to regard the magazine as a friend, and started the letters page. The readers responded by telephoning and writing in their thousands, asking for help, or sharing their ideas and experiences, and when the baking powder was omitted from the list of ingredients for a Christmas cake, hundreds of packages containing flat cakes arrived at the office: in December 1962 the *Woman* postbag contained over 38,000 letters, dealt with by a correspondence department of eighty, and the office received 6700 telephone calls. She had an intuitive sense of women's concerns and interests, and the ability to hire the right staff, so that although she demanded high standards of writing, she did not interfere. She was highly respected by her staff, and there was very little jealousy or malice in the office, thanks to the strength of her personality, and the loyalty she inspired. The circulation of *Woman* rose to nearly 3.5 million at the end of 1957, and was still over 3.25 million in the early 1960s, with an estimated readership of half the adult female population.

Grieve was a member of the Council for Industrial Design from 1952 to 1960, and in 1960 was appointed to the National Council for Diplomas in Art and Design. She joined the council of the Royal College of Art in 1963. When Odhams Press was taken over by the *Mirror* group in 1961, she decided to retire, leaving in December 1962; she was appointed OBE for her services to journalism. Her autobiography, *Millions Made my Story*, appeared in 1964, and she edited *Fifteen* (1966) and *Sixteen* (1967), textbooks to be used in schools to prepare girls for the world beyond school. With a friend she set up Dove Delicacies, making paté which they supplied to local shops and restaurants until she suffered a severe stroke in 1978. She died on 19 February 1998 at her home, The Pennant, Doctors Commons Road, Berkhamsted, Hertfordshire. She was unmarried.

ANNE PIMLOTT BAKER

Sources M. Grieve, *Millions made my story* (1964) · J. Barrell and B. Braithwaite, *The business of women's magazines* (1979); 2nd edn (1988) · C. White, *Women's magazines, 1693–1968* (1970) · *The Times* (26 Feb 1998) · private information (2004) · b. cert. · d. cert.
Likenesses photograph, repro. in *The Times*

Grieve, Sir Robert (1910–1995), town planner and public servant, was born on 11 December 1910 at 61 Springbank Street, Glasgow, the son of Peter Paxton Grieve (1886–1960), soldier, and his wife, Catherine, *née* Boyle (1886–1950). His greatest influences were his mother ('a caged tigress') and an uncle who took him on 'enormous walks' beyond Glasgow's tram termini, when he first glimpsed the hills (private information). His father, a regimental sergeant-major in the King's Own Scottish Borderers, and later a woodcutting machinist, played little part in his life. From 1916 he was a pupil at North Kelvinside School, Glasgow, and, encouraged by his mother's determination that he should 'get on', he trained as a civil engineer at the

Royal College of Science and Technology, Glasgow (later the University of Strathclyde), passed the final examination of the Town Planning Institute (later the Royal Town Planning Institute) in 1937, and became an associate of the Institution of Civil Engineers in 1938. From 1927 to 1944 he was employed by local authorities. On 1 December 1933 he married Mary Lavinia Broughton (May) Blackburn (1911–1984), a great strength and positive influence. There were two sons and two daughters of the marriage.

In 1944–6 Grieve played a key role in the production of the Clyde valley regional plan, developing the case for the overspill of population from Glasgow to new towns, creating viable communities within new centres for economic development. In 1946 he joined a new planning unit in the Scottish Office, first in charge of the north region and later the west region. In 1960 he was appointed chief planning officer. In 1964 the University of Glasgow appointed him foundation professor of town and regional planning to establish a postgraduate planning course. He had worked closely with Professor Donald Robertson, and bringing together these outstanding planners, one economic, the other physical, was bound to be fruitful both academically and in practical affairs. Grieve followed another great Scottish planner, Patrick Geddes in emphasizing the importance of breadth in education. He recited J. G. Saxe's poem *The Blind Men and the Elephant*, relating how six blind men each explain an elephant by touching it, but differ according to which part of it they touched. The poem ends:

> So oft in ideologic wars
> The disputants I ween
> Rail on in utter ignorance
> Of what each other mean
> *And prate about an elephant*
> *Not one of them has seen.*

Grieve then raised his arms and said 'We have created the University of the Elephant' (personal knowledge). His indebtedness to Geddes was developed in his monograph *Grieve on Geddes* (1991).

Grieve's appointment as full-time chairman of the newly established Highlands and Islands Development Board in November 1965 removed him from academia before he could fulfil the expectations which his appointment had aroused. As he put it, he was 'exchanging the unexceptionable sentiment for the terror of action' (private information)—modestly overlooking the extent to which his earlier work as local government official and top civil servant had involved action. But now he had to add diplomacy to his professional skills. There had been influential opposition in parliament and in the highlands to the establishment of the new board. The board's first report declared that whatever success it might have in the eastern and central highlands it would be judged by its ability to build population in the fragile areas of the islands and the west. Grieve was not a man to seek the soft option. The policies given greatest emphasis were the fuller exploitation of natural resources, the encouragement of new industries, and the development of tourism,

with the provision of grants and loans to increase the business birth rate and increase employment. Oil and gas developments in the North Sea stimulated interest in the Moray Firth, which in turn gave rise to both opposition and competition to acquire potentially valuable assets. There were errors of judgement by two board members, who had to resign, with some pressure on Grieve to resign also. He resisted, and soon had the fledgeling development agency back on an even keel. He made the establishment of a university in the highlands and islands a long-term goal, both for social and development reasons. With support from the Scottish Office and the Millennium Commission in the late 1990s his dream moved closer to becoming a reality. The Highlands and Islands Development Board was comprehensive in both its objectives and its powers, giving rise to considerable international interest. The British Council and the board established an annual seminar for students from 'third-world' countries. Grieve planned and chaired these seminars, adding an international dimension to his already powerful influence on planning in the UK. He was knighted in 1969. The Highlands and Islands Development Board commissioned a bust by Benno Schotz on Grieve's retirement, which was placed in the Scottish National Portrait Gallery.

Grieve returned to the University of Glasgow in 1970. Some academic colleagues criticized Highlands and Islands Development Board policies—its limited powers on land use were not fully understood—and the recognition of his trials and achievements was uneven. However, as he put it 'the encounter with lively students was to me the greatest of pleasures and rewards' (private information). He retired in 1974, remaining active as chairman of the Royal Fine Art Commission for Scotland from 1978 to 1983, and of the Highlands and Islands Development Consultative Council from 1978 to 1986. He was awarded the Royal Institute of Town Planning's gold medal in 1974. In time he took on new responsibilities. He chaired the constitutional steering committee which produced *A Claim of Right for Scotland* (1988), the blueprint for the devolved parliament established in 1999. He chaired an enquiry into housing in Glasgow (1986–9), and received the lord provost's award for outstanding public service. He was elected a fellow of the Royal Society of Edinburgh (1980), and was awarded honorary fellowships of the Royal Incorporation of Architects in Scotland and the Royal Scottish Geographical Society (1989), and honorary degrees from Heriot-Watt and Strathclyde (1984) and Edinburgh (1985). He was a keen mountaineer, and was president of the Scottish Countryside Rangers' Association, the Stewartry Mountaineering Club, the Scottish Mountaineering Club, and the Scottish Mountaineering Council. His wife, May, died in January 1984, a devastating blow from which he never fully recovered. He was a devoted father to his four children, Ann, Elizabeth, Iain, and William. He died in Edinburgh of prostate cancer on 25 October 1995. Although brought up as a Roman Catholic he was agnostic. His ashes were scattered on the Conic Hill overlooking Loch Lomond on 15 June 1996.

KENNETH ALEXANDER

Sources *Report of the Highlands and Islands Development Board*, 1–4 (1967–70) • private information (2004) [family] • *The Times* (28 Oct 1995) • *The Independent* (30 Oct 1995) • *RTPI News* (16 Nov 1995) • *The Independent* (17 Nov 1995) • personal knowledge (2004) • WWW, 1991–5
Archives NL Scot., corresp. and papers
Likenesses B. Schotz, bust, 1972, Scot. NPG • photograph, repro. in *The Times* • photograph, repro. in *The Independent*
Wealth at death £242,930.79: confirmation, 11 Jan 1996, NA Scot., SC/CO 887/26

Grieve [*née* Law], **Sophia Emma Magdalene** [Maud] (*b.* 1858, *d.* after 1933), herb grower, was born on 4 May 1858 at 75 Upper Street, Islington, London, the daughter of James Law, a warehouseman, and his wife, Sophia Ballisat. Nothing further is known of her early life. She went to India with her husband, William Sommerville Grieve, and following his retirement they settled at The Whins, Chalfont St Peter, Buckinghamshire, in 1905. There, from 1908, Maud Grieve began to create a garden in which she grew medicinal and culinary herbs. In 1911 she became Buckinghamshire representative for the Daughters of Ceres, a movement concerned with increasing the opportunities for women in horticultural jobs. At the beginning of the First World War, when the government asked civilians to grow medicinal herbs, she helped to start the National Herb Growing Association, which organized the collection and drying of herbs, and set up a training school at The Whins. In 1918 she became the first president of the British Guild of Herb Growers. She wrote pamphlets on individual herbs, with a history of each plant and directions for its cultivation, harvesting, and drying, and these were distributed by mail order with the seeds; she also issued a series of booklets, including *Soil and its Care* (1921), *Fungi as Food and in Medicine* (1925), and *Herbs and Vegetables in the Orchard and in the Wild* (1926). After the war she trained former servicemen, some of whom went to the colonies to start herb farms.

When her elderly husband's health failed, she closed her training school in 1929, giving many of her plants to Dorothy Hewer [*see below*] at Seal. In collaboration with Hilda Leyel, founder of Culpeper House, she compiled *A Modern Herbal* (1931), the first herbal since the publication of John Lindley's *Flora medica* in 1838, which became a standard work of reference. Maud Grieve was still alive in 1933 and died probably in the late 1930s.

Dorothy Gertrude Hewer (1888–1948), herb farmer, was born on 16 March 1888 at 29 Brownswood Park, South Hornsey, Middlesex, the daughter of Joseph Langton Hewer, a doctor, and his wife, Annie Martha Everard. She was educated at North London Collegiate School, and in 1907 entered Bedford College, London, where she was awarded a BSc general pass degree in 1911. Forced by the onset of deafness to give up a teaching career, she bought a house and 2 acres of land at Seal, near Sevenoaks, Kent, in 1926 and started the Herb Farm—inspired by the work of the gardener and scholar Eleanour Sinclair Rohde and encouraged by her friend Maud Grieve. She took on a few resident women pupils who also worked on the farm. Large and energetic, she believed in healthy, outdoor work and was regarded as a slave-driver by her pupils. She grew medicinal and culinary herbs and developed her own strain of lavender, known as 'Seal'. She opened a shop in North Audley Street, London, and also sold herbs by mail order. During the Second World War the demand for medicinal and culinary herbs grew, and she was able to increase production, especially of herbs used commercially. In 1941 she published *Practical Herb Growing*. Dorothy Hewer, who remained unmarried, died of cancer at her farm on 1 March 1948.

Margaret Eileen Brownlow (1916–1968), herb farmer, was born on 19 October 1916 at Wyresdale, Promenade, West Kirby, Cheshire, the daughter of Richard Sydney Brownlow, a stoneware manufacturer, and his wife, Eva Annie Sutcliffe. Nothing is known of her life until she started work at the Herb Farm in 1933. Having passed the senior examination of the Royal Horticultural Society (RHS) in 1935 she studied horticulture at Reading University and took a BSc in 1938. She returned to the Herb Farm, gained the national diploma in horticulture of the RHS in 1943, and after working for a short time at Waterperry Horticultural School became assistant to Dorothy Hewer. Always referred to by the latter as 'little Margaret', she was small and delicate, and found life on the farm exhausting, but she became a director in 1945 and took over the farm after Hewer's death. She expanded its activities, exhibiting regularly at Chelsea Flower Show from 1949 to 1967, and designed gardens, including the herb garden at Knole, planted in 1963, and supplied plants for the new herb garden at the American Museum at Claverton, Bath, in 1964. Many of her pupils went on to start their own herb-growing businesses. She painted watercolours of herbs for her lectures, and included her own poems and illustrations in *Herbs and the Fragrant Garden* (1957). She published her memoirs, *The Delights of Herb Growing*, in 1965. On 17 February 1968 she was found dead, from barbiturate poisoning, at the Herb Farm. She had never married. An inquest was held on 27 February and an open verdict recorded.

ANNE PIMLOTT BAKER

Sources K. N. Sanecki, *History of the English herb garden* (1992) • D. Macleod, *Down to earth women* (1982) • Desmond, *Botanists*, rev. edn
Likenesses G. Chesterton, photograph (Margaret Brownlow), repro. in Macleod, *Down to earth women*, facing p. 92 • photograph (Margaret Brownlow), repro. in M. Brownlow, *Delights of herb growing* (1965), facing p. 111 • photograph (Margaret Brownlow), repro. in Sanecki, *History of the English herb garden*, 96 • photograph, repro. in Sanecki, *History of the English herb garden*, 87
Wealth at death £13,809 15s. 7d.—Dorothy Gertrude Hewer: probate, 29 May 1948, CGPLA Eng. & Wales

Grieve, Thomas (1799–1882). *See under* Grieve family (*per.* 1794–1887).

Grieve, Thomas Walford (1841–1899). *See under* Grieve family (*per.* 1794–1887).

Grieve, William (1800–1844). *See under* Grieve family (*per.* 1794–1887).

Griffier [Griffer, Griffeere, Griffin], **Jan** [John], **senior** (*c.*1645–1718), landscape painter and engraver, was born in Amsterdam. Arnold Houbraken wrote Griffier's first biography and from him we learn that Jan had a restless spirit: he called himself 'a burgher of the world' (Houbraken, 360). As a youth he tried tile painting, then flower painting, and finally fixed upon an apprenticeship with Roeland Roghman (c.1620–1686). He discovered an ability to imitate the styles of other artists, and copied Ruisdael, Johannes Lingelbach, the Van der Veldes, and even Rembrandt. He painted skilfully on his own account, but Vertue asserted that he 'succeeded and deceived very well' (Vertue, *Note books*, 1.50–51).

Griffier probably came to England c.1672 and worked initially for the landscapist Jan Loten. Griffier was admitted 'gratis' as a 'free Brother' of the London Painter-Stainers' Company on 4 December 1677 (Guildhall MS 5667/2, pt 1, fol. 227). He was so successful selling his Italianate and Rhenish scenes that he was able to spend 3000 guilders on a yacht, in which he lived on the Thames. There is tangled evidence about his marriages and children: they are tentatively set out as follows. He married first Jane Gilborthorp on 13 February 1674, at St Marylebone. After ten years they had one daughter, 'Anne Griffeire', baptized in St Bride's, Fleet Street, on 8 October 1684. Second, 'John Griffer' married Anne Brookes of St Bride's on 3 July 1687 in St James's, Duke's Place; their son 'Juryiohn Griffeire' (possibly Jan Griffier junior [*see below*]) had been baptized on 2 November 1686. His baptism was followed by those of his sisters Jane (19 February 1688), then Anne (14 March 1691); all three were baptized in St Bride's. Houbraken alleged that Robert Griffier [*see below*] was born on 7 October 1688, but this is unlikely, and not documented. From separate evidence it is known that Robert's mother was called Mary, because she outlived Jan by thirty-five years. This third marriage is undocumented.

In 1695 Griffier decided to sail home. His yacht was shipwrecked off Rotterdam and the only asset that remained was some money in his daughter's belt. He spent the next nine years roving round the Low Countries. His and his son's presence was recorded in 1700 in the *album studiosorum* of the Leiden Academy, the father giving his age as forty-eight and the younger Jan as twenty-seven. Both ages are misleading: Vertue stated that Jan senior was seventy-two at his death in Millbank between 1 January and 25 March 1718, making him fifty-five in 1700, and if Juryiohn is identifiable as Jan junior, he was only fourteen. By 1704 they had both returned to London. One 'Mr. Griffin' was listed in Sanctuary, a street in the parish of St Margaret's, Westminster, in 1716 (rated at £6 2s.). 'Wid. Griffin' is listed there in 1717, but as 'Mary Griffen', then 'Mary Griffier'; she is listed in a Millbank house rated at £16 5s. 4d. from 1718 until at least 1722 (Westminster City Archives, E 337–42). As a wealthy woman she was able to subsidize her son Robert in 1731.

Griffier was a gifted draughtsman with a remarkable imagination: sun-drenched views of the Italian campagna, Dutch winterscapes, and dramatic mountain or Rhineland scenery (some stormy), all are peopled with tiny figures painted with microscopic care, much in the style of the Saftleven brothers. Examples are to be found in the Fitzwilliam Museum, Cambridge; Brighton, Glasgow, and Swansea art galleries; and as far flung as Copenhagen, St Petersburg, Maastricht, Bonn, Dresden, and Budapest. A grand *Noah's Ark* (13 × 13 ft) is in Bristol City Museum. He combined unlikely scenery with realistic depictions of known buildings: *Syon House* (still *in situ*) and *Hampton Court* (Tate collection) are both set in alien mountainous territory. A valuable record of the annual *Greenwich Horn Fair* (1710–15) is placed, disturbingly, against a view of St Paul's from the north of the Thames. De Marly recorded that this painting is now in Sibiu, Romania. Griffier also portrayed naturalistic prospects, such as *The Thames during the Lord Mayor's Regatta of 1683* (Royal Collection), and a *View of Gloucester*, which he himself engraved. He took commissions for birds'-eye views of country houses such as *Sudbury Hall, Derbyshire* (1682) and *Crewe Hall, Cheshire* (still in their original homes), and *Pierrepont House, Nottinghamshire* (Nottingham Castle Museum). At Sudbury Hall there are also two overdoors of nymphs and shepherds (1682). He signed his work in capital letters as 'J. Griffier or John Griffier'.

Griffier also painted colourful pictures of exotic birds. A fine signed example (1710) is in the Tate collection. He etched some of Francis Barlow's designs of birds and animals (1682–91), and he also mastered the mezzotint process to copy portraits by Sir Peter Lely and Sir Godfrey Kneller. The British Museum has examples of both media, and his beautiful chalk drawing *Willows by a River's Edge*.

Jan Griffier junior (*bap.* 1686?, *d. c.*1750) and **Robert Griffier** (*c.*1692–*c.*1760) painted in their father's style and became popular in the 1730s and 1740s. Waterhouse called them 'the first decent topographical artists' (Waterhouse, 155). Jan (II) Griffier travelled Britain to depict country houses. At Audley End there are four pictures by him: two vast panoramas of Billingbear Park, Berkshire, signed and dated 'Jn° Griffier pinxt 1738' and 1739, the larger measuring 6 feet 6 inches by 17 feet; and two of Hurstbourne Priors, Hampshire, dated 1748. His painting of *The Thames during the Great Frost of 1738/9* is in the London Guildhall Art Gallery. He adopted a Claudian style.

In 1753 Robert Griffier was sued by his own mother, Mary Griffier, who stated she had lent her son, Robert, the painter, £100 to set up as a victualler in 1731, but had never been repaid. Now aged eighty-five and impoverished, she needed the money back. An ambitious *Regatta on the Thames*, signed and dated 'R. Griffier/1748', is deemed to be his masterpiece; it is now in the collection of the duke of Buccleuch, and reveals the influence of Canaletto.

KATHARINE GIBSON

Sources A. Houbraken, *De groote schouburgh der Nederlantsche konstschilders en schilderessen*, 3 (Amsterdam, 1721), 357–60 · Vertue, *Note books*, 1.50–51; 5.69 · E. Waterhouse, *Painting in Britain, 1530–1790*, 4th edn (1978), 154–5 · H. V. S. Ogden and M. S. Ogden, *English taste in landscape in the seventeenth century* (1955), 121, 138–9, 145, 149, 154 · P. C. Sutton and others, *Masters of seventeenth-century Dutch landscape painting* (1987), 332 [exhibition catalogue, Rijksmuseum, Amsterdam, 1987] · D. De Marly, 'A Griffier of fairground theatre', *Burlington Magazine*, 116 (1974), 313–17 · L. Stainton and C. White, *Drawing in England from Hilliard to Hogarth* (1987), 181 [exhibition catalogue, BM] · J. Harris, K. Kostival, and S. Orchart, *The artist and *the country house: from the fifteenth century to the present day* (1995), nos. 22, 37, 39–40 [exhibition catalogue, Sotheby's Institute, London, 1995] · H. Preston, ed., *London and the Thames: paintings of three centuries* (1977), no. 8 [exhibition catalogue, Somerset House, London, 6 July–9 Oct 1977] · J. Hayes, 'A panorama of the City and south London from Montagu House by Robert Griffier', *Burlington Magazine*, 107 (1965), 458–62 · parish register, Marylebone, LMA, X023/063, 13 Feb 1674 [marriage] · parish register, St Bride's, Fleet Street, GL, MS 6540/2 [baptism] · parish register, St James's, Duke's Place, 3 July 1687, GL, MS 7894/1 [marriage] · PRO, C 11/203/9 [Mary Griffier, then Mary Netherington] · City Westm. AC, E 335, 37; E 337–42

Likenesses A. Bannerman, double portrait, line engraving (with G. Zoust), NPG

Wealth at death presumably quite wealthy; widow able to lend her son £100 in 1731: PRO, Chancery law suit, C/11/203/9

Griffier, Jan, junior (*bap.* 1686?, *d. c.*1750). *See under* Griffier, Jan, senior (*c.*1645–1718).

Griffier, Robert (*c.*1692–*c.*1760). *See under* Griffier, Jan, senior (*c.*1645–1718).

Griffin, Bartholomew (*fl.* 1596), poet, was possibly one of the Griffins of Dingley, Northamptonshire. Clitheroe identifies the poet with a Bartholomew Griffin who matriculated at Trinity College, Cambridge, at Lent 1594 and graduated BA from St Mary Hall, Oxford, on 5 February 1598 (*Fidessa*, ed. Clitheroe, 3). Grosart proposes he was the Bartholomew Griffin buried on 15 December 1602 at Holy Trinity, Coventry, whose will was proved on 13 May 1603 by his 'wellbeloved', widow Kathryn (*Fidessa*, ed. Clitheroe, 34; *Poems*, ed. Grosart, viii–ix). However, Izon shows that the 'Annuitie of Mr Edward Gryffyne of Dinsley' mentioned in the Coventry Bartholomew Griffin's will was granted 'as early as 1571' (citing PRO C21/G26/1), so the testator could not have been the author who described himself as 'a young beginner' in 1596.

Izon proposes alternatively that the poet Bartholomew Griffin was '"a Scholemaster" in Holy Orders, recently ordained, "whom Sir Thomas [Lucy] kept in his howse, hired there to teach and instruct some of his graundechildren"', known from 1600–02 Star Chamber actions (PRO, STAC 5/A12/28; STAC 5/A43/19; STAC 5/A43/39) in which he was an accused conspirator in a clandestine marriage. This was of one of his pupils at Charlecote, Elizabeth Aston, a favourite granddaughter of Sir Thomas Lucy, with a Mr John Sambach. Izon believes that this tutor was the son of Thomas Lucy's close associate Ralph Griffin, dean of Lincoln (1585–93), the brother of the Bartholomew Griffin who died at Coventry in 1602. Izon's poet Bartholomew Griffin was ordained by the bishop of Worcester on 29 September 1598.

Griffin's sole publication, *Fidessa, More Chaste than Kinde* (1596), is a sequence of sixty-two sonnets. In dedicating the book to William Essex of Lambourne, Berkshire, Griffin says he is 'little knowne' to him, which does not aid identification. In his following address 'to the gentlemen of the innes of court', Griffin calls *Fidessa* 'the first fruite of any my writings', and himself 'a poore stranger' and 'young beginner'. He then mentions he had wanted to include a 'Pastorall yet unfinished', promising 'the next tearme you may expect it'. There is no record of Griffin at the inns of court; he may have been at an inn of chancery.

Fidessa is best known for its third sonnet, '*Venus, and young Adonis sitting by her*', which appeared with some alterations as poem 11 in *The Passionate Pilgrime*, a small poetic collection fraudulently published in 1599 by W. Jaggard as 'By W. Shakespeare'. Griffin's fine erotic poem, witty and delicate, may have been modified by Jaggard (*Poems*, ed. Grosart), or by Griffin himself (Dowden). There have been several editions of *Fidessa*. Clitheroe's selection contains only twenty-three sonnets.

Although saturated with sonneteering conventions, *Fidessa* contains several poems of experimental cast. Many of its poems are noteworthy, not only those that have been alleged to be connected with Shakespeare such as *Fidessa* 15 (Rawson; John, 87–92), and poems 4, 6, and 9 of *The Passionate Pilgrim* (Dowden, x). B. J. SOKOL

Sources *Fidessa: a collection of sonnets by B. Griffin reprinted from the edition of 1596*, ed. P. Bliss (1815) · B. Griffin, *Fidessa, more chaste than kind*, ed. F. Clitheroe (1996) · B. Griffin, 'Fidessa more chaste than kind', *Elizabethan sonnet cycles*, ed. M. F. Crowe (1897), 73–138 · E. Dowden, *The passionate pilgrim: the first quarto, 1599, a facsimilie* (1883) · *The poems of Bartholomew Griffin*, ed. A. B. Grosart (1876) · C. J. Hindle, 'The 1815 reprint of Bartholomew Griffin's *Fidessa*', *N&Q*, 166 (1934), 308–10 · J. Izon, 'Bartholomew Griffin and Sir Thomas Lucy', *TLS* (19 April 1957), 245 · L. C. John, *The Elizabethan sonnet sequences: studies in conventional conceits* (1938); repr. (New York, 1964) · C. J. Rawson, 'Macbeth on sleep: two parallels', *Shakespeare Quarterly*, 14 (1963), 484–5 · L. M. Storozynsky, 'Bartholomew Griffin', *Sixteenth-century British nondramatic writers: fourth series*, ed. D. A. Richardson, DLitB, 172 (1996), 116–18

Griffin, Benjamin (1680–1740), actor and playwright, the son of Benjamin Griffin (or Griffen; 1655–1691), rector of Buxton and Oxnead in Norfolk and chaplain to the earl of Yarmouth, was born in Oxnead and educated at the free school, North Walsham. He was apprenticed to a glazier at Norwich, where in 1712 he joined the duke of Norfolk's company of strolling players. The *Biographia dramatica* notes that Griffin escaped from his apprenticeship to go on the stage, but if this were the case this would surely put his accepted date of birth into question. His first recorded stage appearance was as Sapiritus in his own first drama, *Injured Virtue*, a tragedy adapted from Thomas Dekker and Philip Massinger's *The Virgin Martyr* and published in 1715. The performance, by the servants of the duke of Southampton and Cleveland, took place at the King's Arms tavern, Southwark, on 1 November 1714.

In 1714–15 Griffin was one of the company with which Christopher Rich opened the rebuilt playhouse in Lincoln's Inn Fields. His name first appears in surviving records on 16 February 1715, as Sterling in Charles Molloy's *The Perplexed Couple*. On 2 June he played Ezekiel Prim, a Presbyterian parson, in Elkanah Settle's *A City Ramble*, and on 14 June Sir Arthur Addlepate in his own farce *Love in a Sack*. He remained with the company until 1721, taking many parts, including Don Lopez in his own farce *Humours of Purgatory* on 3 April 1716 and, on 26 January 1720, Sir John Indolent in his own *Whig and Tory*, a comedy based on John Fletcher and Samuel Rowley's *The Maid in the Mill*

(1623). Carrying a provocative title, considering the growing tensions around the South Sea Bubble, which was fit to burst at this time, the play is said to have dealt dexterously with a political subject and was published in 1720. A farce makes up the remainder of his dramatic writing, though *Masquerade, or, The Evening's Intrigue*, published in 1717, adds little to Griffin's claim to any significant attention. In conjunction with Lewis Theobald he also wrote the critique *A Complete Key to the What-d'ye-Call-it of Gay* (1715).

During 1720 Griffin played the lead role in Lord Lansdowne's *The Jew of Venice* (altered from Shakespeare), Gomez in John Dryden's *The Spanish Fryar*, Sir Hugh Evans in *The Merry Wives of Windsor*, and Foresight in William Congreve's *Love for Love*. He probably took some part in his own *Masquerade*, which was produced for his benefit, with *The Jew of Venice*, on 16 May 1717. His success in characters of choleric and eccentric old men was such that Drury Lane, though possessing Henry Norris and Benjamin Johnson, both in his line, engaged him for the sake of avoiding rivalry. He was to remain with the company until his death, but the only part of any real significance of which he was the original there was Lovegold in Henry Fielding's *The Miser*.

Griffin died of his asthma at home in Clement's Inn, London on 18 February 1740. The previous week he had appeared as Day in Sir Robert Howard's *The Committee*. The *Gentleman's Magazine* in March 1740 referred to his being a worthy man and an excellent actor. Victor says he 'was a comedian excellent in some characters', noticeably as Sir Hugh Evans and Sir Paul Pliant in Congreve's *The Double Dealer*. The last he made a finished character. 'His important look always excited laughter … It was not in nature to resist bursting into laughter at the sight of him, his ridiculous distressful look, followed by a lamentable recital of his misfortunes' (Victor, 2.78–80). Davies contrasts his 'affected softness' with the 'fanatical fury' of the actor Benjamin Johnson when the two men were playing Tribulation and Ananias in Ben Jonson's *The Alchemist* (Davies, 2.108). A portrait of the actors in these parts by Peter van Bleeck of Covent Garden offers striking likenesses of both. Griffin does not seem ever to have married. By all accounts he was an honest and upstanding character. Victor reports that he 'was a sensible, sober man, and well respected. When he died he left effects very acceptable to his sister and her children, and what is more uncommon, a good character' (Victor, 2.80). MARK BATTY

Sources D. E. Baker, *Biographia dramatica, or, A companion to the playhouse*, rev. I. Reed, new edn, rev. S. Jones, 2 (1812) · Genest, *Eng. stage* · T. Davies, *Dramatic miscellanies*, 3 vols. (1784) · B. Victor, *The history of the theatres of London and Dublin*, 3 vols. (1761–71) · Highfill, Burnim & Langhans, *BDA* · Venn, *Alum. Cant.* · *GM*, 1st ser., 10 (1740)
Archives BL, diary of pieces acted at London theatres, Egerton MS 2320
Likenesses J. Laguerre, satirical print, 1733, repro. in Highfill, Burnim & Langhans, *BDA* · P. van Bleeck, double portrait, oils, c.1738 (with B. Johnson), Garr. Club · P. van Bleeck, mezzotint, 1748 (after his portrait, 1738), BM, NPG
Wealth at death 'very acceptable' effects to sister: Victor, *History of the theatres*

Griffin, Bernard William (1899–1956), Roman Catholic archbishop of Westminster, was born on 21 February 1899 in Oakfield Road, Cannon Hill, Birmingham, the son of William Bernard Griffin and his wife, Helen Swadkins. His father was a manager in a firm manufacturing bicycles and a Birmingham city councillor; his mother's family had its roots in farming. His family was staunchly Roman Catholic: not only did Bernard, the elder son by twenty minutes, become a priest, so did his twin Walter (as a Benedictine of Douai), while an older sister entered a convent; there were also two younger sisters. From Denning Road primary school Bernard won a scholarship to King Edward's School, Birmingham. He stayed only briefly, going in September 1913 to Cotton College which, as well as being a school, prepared some of the pupils for Oscott, the seminary for the archdiocese of Birmingham. He entered the seminary in January 1919 after serving for a year in the Royal Naval Air Service, stationed first in Orkney and then at Manston in Kent. He spent three years at Oscott, and the years 1922 to 1927 at the English College in Rome, being awarded doctorates in both theology and canon law. He was ordained priest in Rome on 1 November 1924.

Returning to his diocese Griffin was appointed secretary to Archbishop McIntyre, a common first step on the clerical *cursus honorum*. He remained in diocesan administration for a decade, being sent as parish priest to Coleshill in 1937, only a year before he was appointed an assistant bishop. Under his charge fell Father Hudson's Homes, an orphanage started in the middle of the nineteenth century by nuns but much expanded in the early years of the twentieth by the eponymous Father Hudson when parish priest at Coleshill. Griffin showed himself much at ease in the company of children, and gave a great deal of time to improving the condition of the homes. He also built a massive new church dedicated to his favourite saint, Theresa of Lisieux.

After the death of Cardinal Hinsley on 17 March 1943 Griffin was designated to succeed him as archbishop of Westminster: the bull of appointment was dated 18 December that same year. It was a great surprise. The diocese of Nottingham had also lost its bishop, and it had been thought by many that Griffin would move there. Instead he became 'the least important archbishop of Westminster of this century' (Hastings, 478), a somewhat harsh judgement in that he was followed by the even less imposing William Godfrey who, as apostolic delegate, had played a major part in choosing Griffin.

Griffin was almost immediately faced with a number of major national issues affecting Roman Catholics, for which his experience of negotiating with local authorities had to some extent prepared him. The first was the 1944 Education Act. Catholics opposed the financial provisions of the act and there was further resentment that it was being passed by the national government which, church leaders believed, made it more difficult to oppose. As R. A. Butler, the minister for education, was making a speech in the Commons proposing his bill he was distracted by the sight of the archbishop—his red hair made him instantly recognizable—being shown to a seat in the distinguished strangers' gallery. In the course of his speech Butler insisted that the government wished to co-operate with the churches, and Griffin was sufficiently mollified to send the minister a set of the Roman Catholic classic, *Butler's Lives of the Saints*. Griffin clearly felt himself to have been betrayed, however, and in January 1950 declared the Education Act a 'death sentence' for Catholic schools, a wholly erroneous judgement though the effort to preserve them cost the Catholic community dear.

Griffin also successfully fought for the independence of Catholic hospitals from the National Health Service, gaining in the battle the friendship of his opponent Aneurin Bevan. The introduction of the welfare state proved divisive for Catholics. Many believed, with Griffin, that it was an interference with the family's responsibility to take care of itself. With the help of his secretary, Derek Worlock, the future archbishop of Liverpool, and of Catholics in the Labour government, he made great efforts to preserve the interests of the Catholic community. His was the brand of 'fortress Catholicism' which perceived threats to its integrity from all sides. He was suspicious of ecumenism, restricting the enthusiasm of members of the Sword of the Spirit, an organization founded by his predecessor, for dialogue with other churches. When members protested that the Vatican had, in the course of the war, permitted Catholics to pray with other Christians, a decision kept from the laity, Griffin told a meeting that Rome could change its mind, though he did not want this remark minuted.

Griffin was on surer ground when warning against the threat of communism. In the aftermath of the war he travelled widely on the continent, partly to visit British troops (he was intensely patriotic), but he was also the first foreign prelate to visit Poland. He came to know bishops of several countries which fell under Soviet domination, and was very active, though not always popular, in preaching against the persecution of the church in such regimes. At home he devoted a good deal of his considerable energy to promoting lay organizations which operated under the aegis of the hierarchy. Despite hesitations about the welfare state he was deeply concerned about social issues, and among the organizations he encouraged were the Association of Catholic Trade Unionists, an equivalent body for managers and employers, and the Catholic Social Guild. A selection from his pastoral letters, sermons, and talks, published in 1949 as *Seek ye First*, enjoyed modest success. He was responsible for the purchase of a medieval statue of the Madonna, now known as *Our Lady of Westminster*, for his cathedral, and a relief of Theresa of Lisieux was commissioned from the Italian artist Giacomo Manzù. Griffin must also be credited with reviving Westminster Cathedral choir school immediately after the war.

When made bishop in 1938 Griffin was the youngest member of the hierarchy; he became a cardinal in December 1946, hearing of the appointment on the BBC's six o'clock news. He received the red hat from Pius XII on 21 February 1947, his forty-eighth birthday. He seemed in bluff good health, but in 1918 he had contracted rheumatic fever, the effects of which he concealed lest it hinder his entry into the seminary. At the end of January 1949 he suffered a stroke which left him partly paralysed. He was several times ill over the next two years, and then in January 1951 had the first of a series of coronary thromboses, including one in June 1956 which occurred while he was preaching in Westminster Cathedral at a service for Catholic holders of the Victoria Cross; he finished the sermon but collapsed immediately afterwards. He died at a rented holiday home, Winwalloe, in Polzeath, Cornwall, on 20 August 1956. Eight days later he was buried in the crypt of Westminster Cathedral. MICHAEL J. WALSH

Sources M. De la Bedoyere, *Cardinal Bernard Griffin* (1955) · J. Furnival and A. Knowles, *Archbishop Derek Worlock: his personal journey* (1998) · A. Hastings, *A history of English Christianity, 1920–1985* (1986) · M. Walsh, 'Ecumenism in wartime Britain (2)', *Heythrop Journal*, 23 (1982), 377–94 · *The Tablet* (25 Aug 1956), 140–43 · WWW · CGPLA *Eng. & Wales* (1956)

Archives Westm. DA, MSS | TCD, corresp. with Thomas Bodkin | FILM BFI NFTVA, news footage | SOUND BL NSA, performance recording

Likenesses W. Bellamy, group photograph, 1948, Hult. Arch. · F. de Henriques, bronze bust, *c*.1956, Westminster Cathedral, archbishop's house · H. Coster, photographs, NPG · A. Gwynne-Jones, oils, Westminster Cathedral, archbishop's house

Wealth at death £312: probate, 13 Sept 1956, CGPLA *Eng. & Wales*

Griffin, Charles (1819–1862). *See under* Griffin, John Joseph (1802–1877).

Griffin [*married name* Grey], **Elizabeth** [*other married name* Elizabeth Wallop, countess of Portsmouth] (*bap.* **1691**, *d.* **1762**), landowner, was baptized on 30 November 1691 at Dingley, Northamptonshire, the eldest daughter of James Griffin (*bap.* 1667, *d.* 1715) and his wife, Anne (1667/8–1707), the daughter of Richard Raynsford, of Dallington, Northamptonshire. The Griffin family had served the Stuart monarchs for several generations, and Elizabeth's grandfather, Edward Griffin, had been made a baron a few days before James II left England in 1688. James Griffin, who had been tory MP for Brackley in the 1685 parliament, succeeded as second Baron Griffin in 1710, but never assumed the title. Elizabeth's paternal grandmother was Lady Essex Howard, the eldest daughter and coheir of James Howard, third earl of Suffolk; through her the Griffins had a then disregarded claim to the Howard estates in Suffolk and Essex, centred on the mansion of Audley End.

Elizabeth Griffin's father, although a Roman Catholic, seems to have educated his children as members of the Church of England. On 14 May 1720 Elizabeth Griffin married Henry Grey (1683–1740) at St Anne's, Soho. Grey was the second son of Richard Neville of Billingbear, Berkshire, and his wife, Catherine, the sister of Ford Grey, earl of Tankerville; the Grey and Neville families, unlike the Griffins, were whig and protestant supporters of the post-1688 revolution settlement. At the time of their marriage Grey was whig MP for Wallingford; he was later MP for Berwick upon Tweed from 1723 to 1727, and for Reading from 1734 until his death. They had no children. Grey's landed property in Northumberland and Berkshire was said to bring in an annual income of £9700. Grey died on 9 September 1740, leaving Elizabeth his estate, including his country house at Billingbear, Berkshire, and a town house at 10 New Burlington Street, London. On 9 June 1741 Elizabeth married, as her second husband, John *Wallop, first Viscount Lymington (1690–1762). Her marriage settlement ensured that she would retain control of her property, rather than its becoming that of her new husband. This marriage was also childless. Elizabeth became countess of Portsmouth when her husband was created an earl in 1743.

Lady Portsmouth's younger brother Edward, third Baron Griffin, died in 1742, leaving his estates and his claim to nominate the mastership of Magdalene College, Cambridge, to his illegitimate son Edward, who then sold the main Griffin residence of Dingley Hall. Lady Portsmouth and her sister Anne Whitwell were left as the legitimate representatives of the Griffin family, but without the family property. An opportunity for restoring the Griffin family fortunes arose in 1745 on the death of Henry Howard, tenth earl of Suffolk. Under a Howard family agreement of 1721 his main residence, Audley End, and the estates passed to a remote kinsman, Thomas Howard, second earl of Effingham. Lady Portsmouth challenged Effingham's right to Audley End in the courts; her solicitor found a draft of a deed of 1687 which showed the third earl of Suffolk had intended to leave the property to his daughter. In 1747 Lady Portsmouth and her sister Anne were adjudged to have inherited the estate of Saffron Walden, but the house and park remained with Effingham. However, Effingham had no clear plan for the dilapidated house and Lady Portsmouth bought Audley End in 1752 for £10,000, having forced down Effingham's price by £5000.

Lady Portsmouth found the contents of the house sold and parts of the building close to collapse. Sections of the once immense house (largely an early seventeenth-century creation, bought by Charles II in 1668 but subsequently returned by the crown to the Suffolks) had been demolished in the early eighteenth century. Lady Portsmouth was personally involved with all aspects of the reconstruction, which was always carried forward in her own name, not in that of her husband nor that of her nephew John Griffin Whitwell (1719–1797), who changed his name to John Griffin *Griffin in 1749 as a condition of his becoming Lady Portsmouth's heir. She evolved a carefully considered plan that balanced the conservation of the house's Jacobean appearance with mid-eighteenth-century taste. The crumbling east wing of the house, with its gallery measuring 226 feet, was demolished, and replaced by a colonnade which imitated Jacobean designs elsewhere in the building. Materials from the east wing were either sold or used for the repair of the remainder of the building. The house's great hall was saved and its stone façade was emphasized as the main face of the house, stressing Lady Portsmouth's descent from Thomas Howard, first earl of Suffolk, lord treasurer to James I. The seventeenth-century formal gardens were replaced with a less regulated parkland setting. The alterations left a building of Jacobean appearance that none the less conformed to the eighteenth-century fashion for country houses of a concentrated symmetrical design rather than a series of courts.

Lady Portsmouth's acquisition of Audley End had been motivated by the desire to exercise the patronage appropriate to her noble status as well as to regain a lost family home. Her research following the tenth earl of Suffolk's death had shown that the right the Griffins claimed to nominate the master of Magdalene College, Cambridge, was attached to the manor of Brooks Walden, where Audley End was built and which was retained by Lord Effingham in 1747. She purchased the right of nomination with the house in 1752, and in 1760, when the mastership fell vacant, she was assiduously courted by Thomas Pelham-Holles, duke of Newcastle, who hoped to persuade her to appoint a government candidate. She rejected his attempts to influence her choice and appointed George Sandby, of whom Newcastle knew little, although he turned out to be a government supporter. Lady Portsmouth's right to appoint the master was never questioned, nor was she expected to defer to advice from men.

Lady Portsmouth—described by William Cole as being 'as proud as Lucifer; no German princess could exceed her' (Jeffreys, 33)—died on 13 August 1762, a few months before her second husband; she was buried near her first husband in the parish church of Waltham St Lawrence, Berkshire. Her will confirmed the arrangement by which John Griffin Griffin would inherit Audley End. In addition, Billingbear was left to her husband's nephew Richard Neville Aldworth (1717–1793) [see Neville, Richard Neville Aldworth], who was also named as Lady Portsmouth's residual legatee at Audley End should John Griffin Griffin die without a surviving son and heir. She made provision for her sister Anne Whitwell, her nieces Elizabeth and Mary Whitwell, and her cousin Jane James, which was specifically reserved for their own use and kept from the control of any husband. Codicils attempted to ensure that her successors in her estates would always bear the name of Griffin, and provided a legacy of £5000 for her niece Mary provided that she married with the consent of John Griffin Griffin and Lord Portsmouth. Thus, although Lady Portsmouth had no children of her own and was happy to be known by the title of her Wallop husband, by nomination she established a hierarchy of male and female heirs who would perpetuate the Griffin name, maintain the estates she had assembled by inheritance, litigation, and purchase, and exercise the political power appropriate to their wealth and status. JOHN MARTIN

Sources C. Backhouse, 'A matron's monument: the patronage of Elizabeth Griffin, countess of Portsmouth, at Audley End House, 1745–1762', MSt diss., U. Oxf., 2001 • E. H. Chalus, 'Women in English political life, 1754–1790', DPhil diss., U. Oxf., 1997 • K. Jeffreys, ed., *Audley End* (1997) • Richard, third Baron Braybrooke, *The history of Audley End* (1836) • R. S. Lea, 'Grey, Henry', HoP, *Commons, 1715–54* • E. R. Edwards and J. P. Ferris, 'Griffin, James', HoP, *Commons,*

1660–90 • GEC, *Peerage*, new edn, 10.611; 6.202–4 • L. Stone, *Uncertain unions and broken lives* (1995) • A. Valentine, *The British establishment, 1760–1784* (Norman, OK, 1970) • J. H. Round, *Peerage and pedigree: studies in peerage law and family history*, 2 vols. (1910) • N. W. Surrey and H. H. Thomas, *Book of original entries, 1731–1751*, Portsmouth record series, 3 (1976) • *Collectanea topographica et genealogica*, 8 (1843), 380–87 • J. Britton and others, *The beauties of England and Wales, or, Delineations topographical, historical, and descriptive, of each county*, 18 vols. (1801–16), vol. 6, p. 234 • *VCH Hampshire and the Isle of Wight*, vol. 2 • *IGI* • will, PRO, PROB 11/880, sig. 394

Archives Berks. RO, estate records • Essex RO, corresp. and estate records | BL, Newcastle papers, corresp. with duke of Newcastle
Likenesses M. Dahl, oils, 1700–50, Audley End House and Gardens, Essex • C. Jervas, oils, 1720, Audley End House, Essex; repro. in Jeffreys, ed., *Audley End*, 33 • attrib. T. Hudson, oils, 1725–50, Audley End House and Gardens, Essex; repro. in Jeffreys, ed., *Audley End*, 50
Wealth at death over £20,000: will, PRO, PROB 11/880, sig. 394, fols. 2r–2v • will, 1762, *Complete peerage* x, 611

Griffin, Gerald (1803–1840), novelist, playwright, and poet, was born on 12 December 1803, in Limerick, the ninth child and seventh son of Patrick Griffin, a brewery manager, and Ellen Griffin, *née* Geary (*d. c.*1831). He grew up in a house named Fairy Lawn on a hill above the Shannon estuary and was from an early age profoundly influenced by the beautiful countryside through which Ireland's mightiest river reaches the sea. His early education was of a scrappy and haphazard nature, reflecting both his father's declining fortunes and the whole character of Catholic education at this time. He was to make good use of his early educational experiences later, in the comical 'hedge-school' chapter of his novel, *The Rivals* (1829).

In 1820, Patrick Griffin, having failed in various business enterprises, decided to emigrate with most of his family to Pennsylvania. Gerald Griffin remained in Ireland, as ward of his elder brother, Dr William Griffin (1794–1848), with whom he went to live in Adare, co. Limerick. He never saw his parents again and this sundering of the family circle clearly had a devastating effect on his sensitive and vulnerable nature. A meeting with John Banim influenced his choice of a literary career. Banim's play *Damon and Pythias* had been successfully produced at Covent Garden in May 1821, with Macready and Kemble in the title roles. Griffin completed a full-length tragedy, *Aguire* (now lost) which impressed his guardian favourably. Reluctantly, he permitted his ward to try his luck in London and Griffin left Adare in November 1823. He was still only nineteen.

Griffin was to spend just over three years in London. His dramatic ambitions received an early set-back when the play *Aguire* was rejected, probably by Macready. He then had to make a living as a journalist and reporter and was sometimes in the direst poverty. John Banim came to his aid but Griffin, fiercely ambitious of achieving success through his own, unaided efforts, proved a touchy protégé and a series of trivial misunderstandings damaged his relationship with Banim, though the two were later reconciled in Ireland after both had established their reputations. Griffin began to make a living by writing under a wide variety of pseudonyms for various London journals, including the *Literary Gazette* and the *News of Literature and Fashion*. He soon concluded that the London theatre, controlled by a handful of powerful actor-managers, was interested only in grand spectacle and that his serious drama would not prosper in such a climate.

Impressed by the success of John and Michael Banim with their *Tales by the O'Hara Family* (1825, 1826, and 1827), Griffin turned to regional fiction and, in 1827, published his first collection of stories, *Holland-Tide*, and returned to Ireland. *Tales of the Munster Festivals* appeared in 1827 and, in 1829, he published his most successful novel, *The Collegians*, basing it on a notorious murder committed in the co. Clare area some ten years earlier. This novel, combining melodramatic violence with a powerfully realistic depiction of Irish society, earned him £800 (he is said to have sent the money to his father in America) and brought him great fame and the notice of distinguished, older writers such as Lady Morgan and Maria Edgeworth. Along with his popular song 'Aileen Aroon', *The Collegians* is considered his finest work, and some commentators consider it to be simply 'the best nineteenth-century Irish novel' (Eckley, 502). It was adapted for the stage as *The Colleen Bawn* by Dion Boucicault, for the opera as *The Lily of Killarney* by Jules Benedict, and its plot forms the basis of Theodore Dreiser's novel *An American Tragedy* (1925). *The Rivals; and Tracy's Ambition* followed, also in 1829. His reputation established, he went on to publish *The Christian Physiologist* (1830), a set of didactic moral tales; *The Invasion* (1832), a meticulously researched but over-long and leaden historical novel; *Tales of my Neighbourhood* (1835), an amalgam of long and short stories interspersed with narrative poems, and *The Duke of Monmouth* (1836), a historical novel on the Monmouth rebellion.

As his most productive decade, which had begun with *Holland-Tide* in 1827, drew to a close, Griffin, increasingly troubled by scruples about the morality of his fiction, tired of the literary life. His friendship with Mrs Lydia Fisher, a Quaker, also influenced his decision to give up writing, and in 1838, he destroyed most of his papers, preserving only a few poems and the tragedy, *Gisippus*. Having rejected the priesthood as an option, he entered the novitiate of the teaching order of the Christian Brothers at North Richmond Street, Dublin, on 8 September 1838, choosing Brother Joseph as his name in religion. In June 1839 he was transferred to the North Monastery, the order's house in Cork, where he continued his life of teaching and devotional exercises. He contracted typhus fever and died on 12 June 1840. He was buried in the community's graveyard on 15 June. A final set of stories, *Talis qualis, or, Tales of the Jury Room* was published posthumously in 1842 and, in the same year, *Gisippus* had a successful production at Drury Lane, with Macready in the title role.

JOHN CRONIN

Sources J. Cronin, *Gerald Griffin, 1803–1840: a critical biography* (1978) • D. Griffin, *The life of Gerald Griffin*, 2nd edn (1857) • M. Moloney, 'Limerick and Gerald Griffin', *North Munster Antiquarian Journal*, 2 (1940–41), 4–11 • E. Mannin, *Two studies in integrity: Gerald Green and the Rev. Francis Mahony ('Father Prout')* [1954] • G. Eckley, 'Griffin, Gerald, 1803–1840', *Dictionary of Irish literature*, ed. R. Hogan, rev. edn, 1 (1996), 501–3

Archives Christian Brothers' House, North Richmond Street, Dublin, commonplace book A · Congregazione dei Fratelli Cristiani, Casa Generalizia, via Marcantonio Colonna 9, Rome, letters
Likenesses Dalziel, woodcut (after E. Fitzpatrick), BM; repro. in *Dublin Journal* (1861) · Dalziel, woodcut, BM · J. C. Mercier, portrait, repro. in Griffin, *Life*, frontispiece · R. Rothwell, oils, NG Ire. · F. W. Wilkin, two portraits, Christian Brothers, North Richmond Street, Dublin, Ireland · portraits, repro. in Cronin, *Gerald Griffin*
Wealth at death left play, *Gisippus*, to brother; Macready paid £300 for it: Griffin, *Life*

Griffin [*formerly* Whitwell], **John Griffin**, fourth Baron Howard de Walden and first Baron Braybrooke (1719–1797), army officer and politician, was born on 13 March 1719 at Oundle, Northamptonshire. He was the eldest son of William Whitwell of Oundle and his wife, Anne (*d.* 1770), youngest sister and eventual sole heir of Edward Griffin, third Baron Griffin of Braybrooke, and granddaughter of James Howard, third earl of Suffolk and Baron Howard de Walden (1619–1689). He was educated at Winchester College, 1734–6, and entered the army in 1739 as an ensign in the 3rd regiment of foot guards, becoming a captain in 1743.

Griffin served with the allied forces in the Netherlands and Germany during the war of the Austrian Succession and the Seven Years' War. In this service he distinguished himself, and, following a brief period as colonel of the 50th foot (1759–60), succeeded to the command of the 33rd regiment of foot (1760–66), stationed in Germany. He was promoted major-general on 25 June 1759 and lieutenant-general on 19 January 1761. As a reward for his military services he was installed as a knight of the Bath in Henry VII's Chapel on 26 May 1761. He was colonel of the 1st troop of Horse Grenadier Guards, 1766–88, and the 4th dragoons, 1788–97. He was made a full general on 2 April 1778, and field marshal on 30 July 1796.

In 1749 Griffin assumed by act of parliament the surname and arms of Griffin, on receiving from his aunt Elizabeth *Griffin, countess of Portsmouth, her share in the estate of Saffron Walden in Essex. On the death of the same aunt in 1762 he also inherited Audley End with its demesnes. On 28 November 1749 he was elected member of parliament for Andover in the interest of his uncle, John Wallop, first earl of Portsmouth, and continued to represent the constituency until 1784. In the Commons he was generally classed as a whig, though he steered a middle course between Chatham and the Rockingham whigs. He opposed Lord North's administration over the conduct of the war in America. Griffin emerged from the political turmoil of 1782–1784 as a supporter of Pitt the younger. Pitt rewarded him with the lord lieutenancy of Essex, and on 3 August 1784 he moved to the House of Lords as fourth Baron Howard de Walden, a committee of the house having recommended that the abeyance be terminated in his favour, thanks to government influence. In the Lords, Howard continued to support Pitt the younger's administration.

Griffin married, first, on 9 March 1749, Anna Maria (*d.* 18 Aug 1764), daughter of John, Baron Schutz in the Holy Roman empire, and, second, on 11 June 1765, Catherine (*d.*

1807), daughter of William Clayton, of Harleyford, Buckinghamshire. He was created on 5 September 1788 Baron Braybrooke, of Braybrooke in Northamptonshire, with special remainder to his kinsman Richard Aldworth Neville [*see* Griffin, Richard] on whom were also settled the Audley estates. He died at Saffron Walden on 25 May 1797, aged seventy-eight, without children and was buried there on 2 June, leaving an income of about £7000 per annum. His second wife, Catherine, died on 15 August 1807, aged sixty, and was buried on 25 August at Saffron Walden. The barony of Howard de Walden again fell for a time into abeyance.

E. J. RAPSON, *rev.* JONATHAN SPAIN

Sources GEC, *Peerage* · Burke, *Peerage* (1999) · P. Watson, 'Griffin, John Griffin', HoP, *Commons, 1715–54* · J. Brooke, 'Griffin, John Griffin', HoP, *Commons, 1754–90* · Colonel Fyler [A. E. Fyler], *The history of the 50th or (the queen's own) regiment, from the earliest date to the year 1881* (1895) · A. Lee, *History of the 33rd foot, duke of Wellington's (West Riding) regt.* (1922)
Archives Bodl. Oxf., corresp. with J. C. Brooke · Essex RO, Chelmsford, corresp., D/DBy/C8–9 · PRO, letters to first earl of Chatham, PRO 30/8
Likenesses B. West, oils, *c.*1772, Audley End, Essex · B. Rebecca, oils, Audley End, Essex
Wealth at death £7000 p.a.: will, GEC, *Peerage*

Griffin, John Joseph (1802–1877), chemist, author, and business manager, the fourth and youngest son of Joseph Griffin (1752–1838), was born at Webb Square in Shoreditch, London, on 22 January 1802. The family later moved to Glasgow where the father sold books and chemicals. The eldest son, Richard Thomas Griffin (1790–1832), trained in the book trade under Thomas Tegg at Cheapside, London, for a five-year term, on 30 March 1820 joining him in equal partnership. From this time the business in Glasgow was styled Richard Griffin & Co., while the London business traded under Tegg & Co. By contrast, John Griffin received a chemical education under Andrew Ure at Anderson's Institution. His connection with the Glasgow Mechanics' Institution brought him under the influence of Thomas Clark who taught chemistry there. For some time in the 1820s he was employed on the staff of the *Scots Times*.

Griffin's enthusiasm for chemistry and his desire to help those students seeking an education in the subject was displayed in his various texts. Initially *Chemical Recreations* was written to assist those attending the newly formed Glasgow Mechanics' Institution in their home-based practical studies. It ran into six editions between 1823 and 1826. Towards the same cause he added *A Practical Treatise on the Use of the Blowpipe in Chemical and Mineral Analysis* in 1827. In 1829–30 he visited Paris and Heidelberg where he noted various works of potential value for consideration at home. Of these, he translated F. P. Danger's *L'art du souffleur à la lampe* and H. Rose's *Handbuch der analytischen Chemie* to launch, in 1831, a Polytechnic Library series through a joint arrangement between Richard Griffin & Co. and the London-based publishing house of John Bumpus.

In 1832 Griffin married Mary Ann, *née* Holder (*b.* 1802); they had twelve children. Also in that year, just before

Richard's death, John became a co-partner to the family business. He then, effectively, ran the business alone until **Charles Griffin** (1819–1862), his deceased brother's son, completed his education at the Anderson's University. When Charles joined the business about 1842 the earlier arrangement with Tegg was terminated. In time, Charles became a freeman of the City of Glasgow and, by 1850, was president of the Stationers' Company of Glasgow. Meanwhile, John Griffin developed the business of trade in chemical apparatus and, by 1848, had transferred these interests to London. By 1852 he had relinquished his part in Richard Griffin & Co. in favour of his nephew. From the early 1860s the publishing side traded separately, first under the style Griffin, Bohn & Co. to 1862, and then as Charles Griffin & Co.

Under John Griffin's direction the publishing side of the family business developed a scientific leaning, as shown by the Scientific Miscellany series which appeared in the early 1840s and included *A System of Crystallography* (1841) which Griffin wrote principally to demystify and promote an otherwise inaccessible mathematical subject. Another venture included a prestige contract to republish, in a much extended form, the original (1816–45) Smedley, Rose, and Rose *Encyclopaedia metropolitana*. This appeared during 1848–9 in thirty volumes. Later involvement with other publishing houses came through the Cavendish Society, a group set up to perpetuate the name of the German chemist Leopold Gmelin (under whom Griffin had studied during his brief stay at Heidelberg) through the translation of the multivolume *Handbuch der Chemie*.

In parallel with these activities, John Griffin embarked on a project to supply apparatus to accompany the various texts. A trade catalogue dated November 1837 formally marks the start of this business, although a cartoon of the 'Billsticker' in the company's *Book of Trades* (4th edn, 1837) suggests that he had already opened a chemical bazaar at the new premises in Buchanan Street to sell the portable chemical laboratories, prepared by Robert Best Ede of Dorking, to accompany the seventh edition of *Chemical Recreations* (1834). The eighth edition (1838), however, explains that he had set up a 'chemico-commercial' project to see just how low prices for apparatus could be brought to develop a market need for cheap, robust, and reliable apparatus. With this new line established and developing he set out, in 1841, to Germany, Austria, and Bohemia, expressly to make contacts and to trade with suppliers in glass instruments and porcelain ware. By 1844 his catalogues showed apparatus sets for J. F. W. Johnston's *Catechism of Agricultural Chemistry and Geology* (1844), a pioneering text in elementary school science, as well as for the Scientific Miscellany series.

Griffin's social and intellectual life in Glasgow is recorded through his attendance at the Glasgow Philosophical Society, which he joined in April 1834. There he mixed with other influential persons from Anderson's and Glasgow universities, including, respectively, the chemists Thomas Graham and Thomas Thomson. Later, through the 1840s, he held the position of librarian to the society, and it was through the medium of the society that

he announced his views on the 'proximate constitution of chemical compounds'. These views were elaborated in a special 'Romance' contained in the seventh edition of *Chemical Recreations* (1834) wherein, after describing the chaos of chemical nomenclature which then pervaded the literature, he denounced the views of the celebrated Jacob Berzelius before offering his own notions in substitution.

The inconvenience of Glasgow as a centre for the distribution of apparatus and the development of professional chemistry in London through the Chemical Society, of which Griffin was a founder member, were among factors which eventually led to the business being transferred to London. (Likewise, his nephew moved the publishing side to London, although not until the late 1850s.) In 1848 he opened a chemical museum in Marylebone under his own name, where he traded in chemicals and chemical apparatus as well as books for Richard Griffin & Co. An expansion took place in 1850 when he added philosophical apparatus to his range following the take-over of a long-established London wholesaler, John Ward. Two further editions of *Chemical Recreations* (1849 and 1854/1860) ensured a dominant market share in the rising educational trade.

Although plagued by health problems, Griffin published *The Radical Theory in Chemistry* (1858), an interesting work on nomenclature applied to organic chemistry, yet unanalysed, in which there are echoes of his earlier views on chemical notation. The final works to appear under his name, *Chemical Testing of Wines and Spirits* (1866) and *Centigrade Testing Applied to the Arts* (1872), may have been written with the assistance of his sons, Charles Griffin FSA (1838–1900) and **William Griffin** (1839–1883) who, from the early 1870s, had conducted the business under the style J. J. Griffin & Sons. John Griffin died on 9 June 1877 at his home, 31 Park Road, Haverstock Hill, London.

By 1889, under the direction of William's son **John Ross Griffin** (1863–1921), the business was incorporated as a limited liability company. Family connections remained with the business until John Ross's death, although some shareholding had passed into the family of Thomas McKinnon Wood MP, a close relative of the Griffin family, who, from about 1908, was director and later chairman; from about 1919 to 1957 the business was in the hands of his three sons. Under the direction of this family various mergers took place: first with the Scottish firm of Baird and Tatlock Ltd in 1925 to become (in 1928) Griffin and Tatlock Ltd, and then with W. and J. George and Becker Ltd in 1954 to become Griffin and George Ltd. From 1957 Griffin and George Ltd, together with T. Gerrard & Co., formed the Education Group of Fisons Scientific Equipment Division.

Throughout his life John Griffin was passionately concerned with the promotion of chemistry. With equal vigour, he felt it his duty to clarify the language of chemistry which then suffered from a clutter of systems in mineralogy, chemical nomenclature, and crystallography. His texts demonstrate a high quality of thought, prescriptive action, and fearless criticism of established ideas. Even if his own ideas remained mostly untouched by the academic establishment, he was, nevertheless, largely responsible for creating the means of study to a growing mass audience through ingenious and cheap forms of chemical apparatus. He received many accolades in later life, including two prize medals from the Great Exhibition of 1851 and the International Exhibition of 1862, respectively for his graduated glass instruments and research apparatus. Equally, he should be remembered for his contributions to the subject itself, including, for example, the concept of normality as well as many laboratory techniques. In addition to his texts and trade catalogues, he published papers in the *Proceedings* of the Glasgow Philosophical Society and *Chemical News*; he can also be traced in the *Reports* of the British Association, of which he was a member. BRIAN GEE

Sources B. Gee and W. H. Brock, 'The case of John Joseph Griffin: from artisan-chemist and author-instructor to business-leader', *Ambix*, 38 (1991), 29–54 · *JCS*, 33 (1878), 229 · B. Gee, 'Griffin, John Ross', *DBB* · B. Gee, 'Amusement chests and portable laboratories: practical alternatives to the regular laboratory', *The development of the laboratory*, ed. F. A. J. L. James (1989), 37–59 · private information (2004) · R. G. W. Anderson, J. Burnett, and B. Gee, *Handlist of scientific instrument-makers' trade catalogues, 1600–1914* (1990) · J. R. Griffin, *A company of Griffins* (1970) · [Griffin and Tatlock Ltd], *A century and a quarter: British Instrument Industries Exhibition, 4–14 July 1951* (Olympia, 1951) [souvenir catalogue] · *The centenary volume of Charles Griffin & Company, Ltd*, Charles Griffin & Company, Ltd (1920) · St Bride's Printing Library, London, Charles Griffin & Co. Archives · W. H. Brock, 'The society for the perpetuation of Gmelin: the Cavendish Society, 1846–1872', *Annals of Science*, 35 (1978), 599–617 · *DNB* · d. cert. · m. cert. [William Griffin] · d. cert. [William Griffin] · m. certs. [John Ross Griffin] · d. cert. [John Ross Griffin]

Archives Burlington House, Royal Chemical Society, travel diary | St Bride's Printing Library, London, Charles Griffin & Co. Archives

Likenesses D. Davies, bust, 1880–89, Royal Chemical Society, London · photograph, Royal Chemical Society, London · portrait (Charles Griffin), repro. in Griffin, *Company of Griffins* (1970) · portrait (Charles Griffin), NPG

Wealth at death under £9000: probate, 1878 · £62 11s. 0d.—William Griffin: administration, 20 Oct 1883, *CGPLA Eng. & Wales* · £9563—John Ross Griffin: Gee, 'Griffin, John Ross'

Griffin, John Ross (1863–1921). *See under* Griffin, John Joseph (1802–1877).

Griffin, Sir Lepel Henry (1838–1908), administrator in India, was born on 20 July 1838 at Watford, Hertfordshire, where his father, a Church of England clergyman, was serving as locum tenens. He was the only son among the three children of Henry Griffin, perpetual curate of Stoke by Clare, Suffolk, and his wife, Frances Sophia, who had a family of four sons and six daughters from her first marriage, with a Mr Welsh. He was educated at Malden's Preparatory School, Brighton, and, briefly, at Harrow School. After tuition by Mr Whitehead of Chatham House, Ramsgate, he passed the open competition for the Indian Civil Service in 1859. He was tenth out of thirty-two in the final examinations in 1860, the only successful candidate not to have attended a university. On arriving in India, in November 1860, he was posted to Lahore.

Sir Lepel Henry Griffin (1838–1908), by C. W. Walton

Early career Even as a probationer Griffin stood out from his fellow civilians. He was a dandyish, Byronic figure, articulate, argumentative, and witty. Anglo-Indian society was at once both dazzled by and scornful of his languid foppishness and irreverent tongue, an ambivalence captured in Sir Henry Cunningham's half-admiring, half-mocking satirization of Griffin as the brilliant, flirtatious administrator Desvoeux in *The Chronicles of Dustypore* (1875). All recognized in him rare abilities, but some were repelled by his flamboyant self-regard and overt disdain for modesty.

Griffin worked quickly, and as a junior district officer was easily bored. Addicted to argument and debate, he whiled away the time filling the columns of Lahore's newspapers on local controversies. An occasional pretence at anonymity was usually unmasked by his forceful, florid writing style, but as any attempt at reprimand unleashed a taxing correspondence of self-justification, his superiors sometimes found it easier to pretend not to know of his authorship. In 1867, after Griffin had joined a heated correspondence about a scandal in railway finance, the lieutenant-governor of the Punjab, Sir Donald McLeod, contented himself with transferring him from Lahore to Gurdaspur. It was meant as a kindly intervention, designed to shift him out of harm's way before he ruined his career.

Soon after his arrival in the Punjab, Griffin befriended another local polemicist and a famous educator, Dr G. W. Leitner (1840–1899), principal of the government college at Lahore. Together they mounted a passionate campaign for the establishment of a university college which would teach in the vernacular rather than in English, and would encourage in Indian students respect for oriental literature. McLeod backed Griffin and Leitner's efforts and, despite opposition from Calcutta University's authorities, in 1870 opened a university college at Lahore, forerunner of Punjab University. Although McLeod supported Griffin on this matter, he viewed him as a romantic, striving for an unrealistic degree of rapprochement between Indians and Britons. Griffin did indeed consider himself a 'great friend of the natives', but his radicalism was essentially conservative in inspiration and based on little intimacy or empathy with individual Indians. Like many of his British contemporaries, he detested what he saw as the cultural miscegenation of Western-educated babus, and based his vision of a harmonious imperial relationship in India on several stereotypes of 'proper' Indians: stoic peasants, learned scholars, and roguish princes. Such concern for supposedly traditional, culturally intact behaviour led him to help Leitner set up the Oriental Institute at Woking, which was designed to enable Indian students in England to adhere to their caste and religious customs.

Because of his peculiar mix of talent and indiscretion, Griffin spent much of his early service on special government duty, broken up by only short bursts of regular district work. In 1865 he published *The Punjab Chiefs*, the result of a commission by McLeod's predecessor, Sir Robert Montgomery, to prepare historical and biographical accounts of the principal families and princes of the Punjab. He followed it with *The Law of Inheritance to Sikh Chiefships Previous to the Annexation* (1869) and *The Rajas of the Punjab* (1870), both also produced under government auspices. An obvious choice for secretariat work, Griffin was appointed under secretary to the Punjab government in April 1870. In 1875 he was appointed superintendent of the state of Kapurthala, and in 1876 he became acting secretary to the government. He was confirmed as chief secretary in November 1878, following his return from special duty at the Paris Exhibition earlier that year.

Afghanistan In January 1880 the viceroy, Lord Lytton, was casting about for someone to repair the mess of his 'forward policy' in Afghanistan, which had seen the British resident murdered, a friendly amir dethroned, the country partitioned between Kabul and Kandahar, and a British army of occupation imposed on a sullen population. Lighting upon Griffin, Lytton declared him to be the only man in India 'who is … completely qualified by personal ability, special official experience, intellectual quickness and tact, general commonsense and literary skill, to do for the government of India what I want done as quickly as possible at Kabul' (*DNB*). It was fulsome praise, but not entirely sincere, as Griffin himself knew. In stressing Griffin's uniqueness, Lytton was hoping to soften the criticism of his military commander General Roberts, implicit in the appointment of a separate political officer to oversee Britain's withdrawal from Afghanistan. He was also trying to flatter Griffin into accepting a position of nominal subordination to Roberts, knowing full well that Griffin thought Roberts a blundering diplomatist.

Afghanistan was to be the high point of Griffin's career, and it won him recognition as the man who elevated Abdur Rahman, grandson of Dost Muhammad, to the amirship, and ushered in the era of Britain's most fruitful alliance with Afghanistan. Abdur Rahman was not, however, Griffin's choice for amir, but rather Lytton's. Lytton refused to countenance the restoration of Yakub Khan, the amir who had abdicated after the murder of Louis Cavagnari in Kabul in September 1879, and decided that even a Russian pensioner such as Abdur Rahman was preferable. On reaching Kabul in March 1880, therefore, Griffin was charged by Lytton with persuading Abdur Rahman to take on the amirship of Kabul and to rally the Kabul *sirdars* to his standard. Both Griffin and General Sir Donald Stewart, Roberts's successor at Kabul, favoured Yakub Khan, as did Lytton's successor, Lord Ripon. But Ripon, determined that the British be seen to stick to a single policy, and backed by his foreign secretary, Alfred Comyn Lyall, resisted the pressure from Griffin and Stewart to drop Abdur Rahman. At a durbar on 22 July, Griffin recognized Abdur Rahman as amir of Kabul and later that month met him (for the first time) to define his powers and resources. To his surprise, Griffin was favourably impressed and minuted that he was shrewd, clear-headed and straightforward to deal with. Although he had not originally supported him, Griffin now worked to make his position as strong as possible, and eventually became a vocal advocate of British withdrawal from Kandahar and its reunion with Kabul under Abdur Rahman, an object hindered by the army chiefs until April 1881.

Abdur Rahman's reunification of Afghanistan was eventually hailed as a British success, and in May 1881 Griffin was created KCSI. But the triumph was arguably Abdur Rahman's—while a refugee in the pay of Russia he had been set up for a kingdom by Russia's fiercest rival. Griffin, for his part, had had to expend more energy and diplomacy on his fellow Britons than the Afghans, and was heavily indebted to his friend Lyall for defusing his conflicts with the army and the executive council. He chafed at having to surrender authority to the generals and in April 1880 had threatened to resign unless given autonomy, but Lyall had silenced him with a warning not to jeopardize his reputation by putting prestige before duty. Griffin further marred relations with the army by manipulating press coverage in London in favour of a late military withdrawal from Kabul. Stewart, who wanted to get out quickly, was incensed by Griffin's 'dirty trick', and again Lyall sounded a note of caution, observing wryly to Griffin that the correspondent of *The Times* had strangely adopted his exact phraseology. More directly, he told Griffin to stop his juniors singing his praises in the *Bombay Gazette*, although given that the *Gazette* had earlier published 'The Gryphon's Anabasis', a savage satire by George Aberigh-Mackay on Griffin's progress to Kabul, Griffin was perhaps entitled to retaliate in kind.

Central India After Afghanistan, Griffin was appointed agent to the governor-general in central India, responsible principally for the affairs of Indore, Gwalior and Bhopal. Although prestigious, it was a lonely job, cut off from the politics and gossip which were his lifeblood. Bored, he was again soon feeding articles to local and British newspapers on topics ranging from the military potential of the princely states to the savings to be had from an all-Indian judiciary. In 1884 he published *The Great Republic*, a critique of the USA assembled from his articles in the *Fortnightly Review*, and in 1886 *Famous Monuments of Central India*. An injudicious letter to *The Times* on the insincerity of Russian assurances cost him the job of British commissioner on the Russo-Afghan boundary delimitation mission of 1884–6, giving rise to the suspicion that he was being shut out of Indian political life. This fear was heightened in 1885 when the new viceroy, Lord Dufferin, excluded him from his durbar for Abdur Rahman at Rawalpindi.

Of his achievements in central India, Griffin rated highly the abolition of transit duties, the restoration of Gwalior Fort to Sindhia, and the overhaul of Bhopal's administration. In 1871 the widowed begum of Bhopal, Shah Jahan, had married her personal secretary, Muhammad Siddiq Hasan Khan, an Islamic scholar of some repute. The British approved of her marriage, but Siddiq Hasan's elevation to nawab consort was resented by the court notables he displaced and his advocacy of a purified Sunni Islam alienated Sufis and Shi'a as well as important Hindu merchant groups. By the time Griffin arrived in Bhopal in 1881 there was a strong clique, headed by the begum's daughter Sultan Jahan, ready to oust him. Griffin needed little persuading; his political apprenticeship during the height of the so-called Wahabi conspiracies had readied him to discover sedition in Siddiq Hasan's writings and corruption in his administration. In 1885, after repeated representations from Griffin, Dufferin agreed to depose Siddiq Hasan and deprive Shah Jahan of control over her internal administration. Griffin further ordered a daytime separation between Shah Jahan and her husband, allowing them to meet only at night, a move that saw him vilified in Indian newspapers for presuming to regulate the begum's sex life and one that made even the viceroy queasy at his level of interference. In her 1912 autobiography, *An Account of my Life*, Sultan Jahan was to thank Griffin for rescuing Bhopal from her stepfather's grasp, but at the time there was uneasiness in the viceroy's council over the treatment of Shah Jahan and a fear that Griffin had exaggerated Siddiq Hasan's sins. When, in December 1886, a damning history of Shah Jahan's marriage and administration appeared in *The Times*, it was widely assumed that this was Griffin's way of answering his critics.

Griffin remained in central India for almost eight years, certain that his reward would be the lieutenant-governorship of the Punjab, which, as he told his patron, Lord Randolph Churchill, he considered his rightful inheritance. In 1886, as Sir Charles Aitchison's term neared its end, he asked Churchill to lobby lords Cross and Salisbury on his behalf. To Griffin's immense disappointment, a man senior to him, J. B. Lyall, was appointed. The loss of Punjab convinced Griffin that Dufferin was set against him and that he therefore had no future in India.

Many of Griffin's friends believed that his career had faltered because of his unfashionable outspokenness, but his chief impediment to success was his unassailable self-confidence. He mistook criticism for envy and thus discounted it, never comprehending that most of his colleagues considered his post-Punjab record of administration a chapter of blunders punctuated by random and unpredictable triumphs. In 1888, in the final months of his Indian career, he quarrelled with Maharaja Holkar of Indore and attempted to foist a 1000 guinea portrait of himself on the minority ruler of Gwalior, a scandal curtailed only by the fortuitous death of the artist concerned, Frank Holl.

Retirement, business, and politics In March 1887 Dufferin offered Griffin the position of resident at Hyderabad but he never took it up. Instead, in January 1889, while on sick leave in Britain, he resigned from the civil service and embarked on a new life in business and finance. In November 1889 he married Marie Elizabeth, elder daughter of Ludwig Leupold of La Coronata, Genoa, agent to a German shipping company at Genoa, and in the following spring returned with her to India and Burma in his capacity as chairman of the Burma Ruby Mines Company. Although the company's relations with the government of India were subsequently stormy, this was a successful trip, not least because of the presence of Griffin's wife, who surprised his old sparring partners with her charm and sociability. Griffin also became chairman of the Imperial Bank of Persia (in connection with which he received the imperial order of the Lion and the Sun from the shah of Persia in 1903) and acquired interests in the Yenangyaung oilfield in Burma, the Kashmir–Punjab railway, and the Back Bay reclamation scheme in Bombay. In spite of his financial contacts, however, his Indian reputation for unsound judgement continued to dog him. A Conservative by temperament who had been inspired by Churchill's 'Fourth Party' principles of democratic toryism, he longed for a seat in parliament but failed in the only contest he entered, as the Liberal Unionist candidate for West Nottingham in 1900. Both Lord Curzon and Lord Hamilton distrusted his chairmanship of the Imperial Bank of Persia, Hamilton believing that, along with Sir Henry Drummond Wolff, Griffin's role in the bank constituted 'a stumbling block to any belief in financial probity' (Hamilton to Curzon, 30 April 1903, Curzon MSS, MS Eur. F/111/162).

From 1894 until his death Griffin chaired the East India Association, an organization of retired Indian civil servants. In 1892 he published *Ranjit Singh* in the Rulers of India series. He also continued to publish short pieces on Indian matters, principally in the *Asiatic Quarterly Review*, which he had founded in 1885 with Leitner and Demetrius Boulger of the India Office, but also in *The Times* and the *Fortnightly Review*. As in India, he scorned mealy-mouthed caution: in mid-1889, having only just resigned, he advocated in *The Times* the colonization of Kashmir, a suggestion which predictably inflamed Indian public opinion. Ironically, however, once removed from India and personally untroubled by a hostile vernacular press, Griffin found it much easier to be a friend to the Indians. In 1907 he launched an energetic, influential campaign for the better treatment of Indians in the Transvaal, a cause attracting considerable attention in India, Africa, and Britain because of the leadership by M. K. Gandhi of the Indians' struggle for rights as imperial citizens.

Griffin died suddenly at his home at 4 Cadogan Gardens, Sloane Street, London, on 9 March 1908, after a bout of influenza. He was cremated four days later at Golders Green crematorium and his ashes taken to the private chapel of Colonel Dudley Sampson at Buxhalls in Sussex. He was survived by his wife (who later married Charles Hoare) and two sons, the younger of whom, Sir Lancelot Cecil Lepel Griffin (1900–1964), was the last political secretary of British India. KATHERINE PRIOR

Sources BL OIOC, Lyall MSS · BL OIOC, Dufferin and Ava MSS · CUL, Lord Randolph Churchill MSS · D. P. Singhal, *India and Afghanistan, 1876–1907: a study in diplomatic relations* (1963) · Saeedullah, *The life and works of Muhammad Siddiq Hasan Khan, nawab of Bhopal* (1973) · *Journal of the East India Association*, 41 (1908) · *The Times* (11 March 1908), 1, 5, 7 · *The Times* (14 March 1908), 12 · *India Office List* (1890) · G. R. Aberigh-Mackay, 'The gryphon's anabasis', *Twenty-one days in India*, 8th edn (1910) · BL OIOC, Lansdowne MSS · BL OIOC, Curzon MSS · *WWW, 1897–1915* · *War in Afghanistan, 1879–80: the personal diary of Major General Sir Charles Metcalfe MacGregor*, ed. W. Trousdale (1985) · *DNB* · *CGPLA Eng. & Wales* (1908)

Archives BL, letters to T. S. Escott, Add. MS 58781 · BL, letters to Lord Ripon, Add. MS 43614 · BL OIOC, corresp. with Sir Henry Durand, Eur. MS D 727 · BL OIOC, corresp. with Sir Alfred Lyall, Eur. MS F 132 · BL OIOC, corresp. with Lord Lytton, Eur. MS E 218/52 · CAC Cam., corresp. with Lord Randolph Churchill · NAM, department of film and sound, letters to Lord Roberts

Likenesses J. Burke, group portrait, photograph, spring 1880 (with political staff), repro. in Trousdale, ed., *War in Afghanistan* · C. W. Walton, drawing, repro. in S. Jahan, *An account of my life*, 1 (1912), 128 [*see illus.*] · engraving (after drawing by C. W. Walton), repro. in S. Jahan, *An account of my life*, 1 (1912)

Wealth at death £10,731 9s. 11d.: probate, 3 April 1908, *CGPLA Eng. & Wales*

Griffin [Griffith], **Maurice** [Morys ap Griffith] (d. 1558), bishop of Rochester, was possibly (on the evidence of his episcopal shield, argent, a griffin segreant sable) related to the Porth-yr-aur branch of the Griffithiaid of Penrhyn, Bangor. He was a brother (perhaps half-brother) to Richard and John Coetmor of Llanllechid, who were themselves linked by marriage to the Penrhyn family, and a kinsman of Jeffrey Glyn, a London canon lawyer, and of Jeffrey's brother William Glyn, bishop of Bangor. The Glyns were later to be partners with Griffin himself in the foundation of Friars School in Bangor.

Griffin joined the Dominican order at their priory in Bangor, later the site of Friars School. He removed to Blackfriars, Oxford, his presence there attested in 1525, and again in 1535. He became BTh in 1532 and was admitted BCnL early the following year. Lacking the funds to proceed to a doctorate, he was helped by a fellow Dominican and contemporary at Blackfriars, John Hilsey, by this time prior of their house in Bristol. In March 1535 Hilsey petitioned Thomas Cromwell, seeking for Griffin a portion of the income from the Augustinian priory of Beddgelert, Caernarvonshire, which had lapsed to the crown. However, the income of 100 marks a year from 'the farm

of the priory' may already have been earmarked for Siôn Bwlclai, one of the Griffithiaid's clan rivals, the Bulkeleys of Anglesey, and nothing came of the proposal.

That failure may, paradoxically, have set Griffin's career on its upward course, since Hilsey, after his translation as bishop of Rochester in 1535, secured Griffin's appointment in 1537 as his vicar-general. Rochester would be Griffin's base for the rest of his life. Hilsey's patronage was significant. It has been well argued by Eamon Duffy that though Hilsey was a reformer, he wished to retain the kernel of the old within the new. He may, therefore, have recognized a fellow spirit in Griffin: both embraced reform, acknowledged the monarch as head of the church, yet only grudgingly accepted the consequences. Griffin later managed to serve episcopal masters of various persuasions, twisting this way and that, while *in pectore* remaining loyal to the Catholic faith.

During the next twenty years Griffin enjoyed the fruits of several benefices, mainly in the diocese of Rochester. Among these were the ancient outlier of that diocese, at Freckenham, near Mildenhall, Suffolk (1537–58); and the wealthy parish of St Magnus the Martyr (1537–58), near London Bridge, where he chose to be buried (30 November 1558). Griffin enjoyed appointments, and incumbencies of certain parishes, in the dioceses of St Asaph and St David's. At Rochester itself his career prospered: he was archdeacon (1537), a cathedral canon (1546), and finally bishop (1554). His firm hold on the rungs of advancement is suggested by his success in surviving reforming bishops, including Nicholas Ridley (1547–50), though only in 1554 did he obtain further preferment.

Griffin was consecrated on 1 April 1554, one of the first batch of Marian bishops. His determined orthodoxy must have been signalled, and he could be depended on to root out the heresies in the Medway towns, but his close and long-lasting friendship with Sir William Petre, the royal secretary, probably helped. As high steward of the Rochester estates, Petre had also been in a good position to recognize Griffin's administrative skills. Griffin lacked the oratory and debating skill of his kinsman William Glyn, and his contribution was as administrator and financial manager for the Catholic church. His sobriquet, the Tyrant of Rochester, is unfair, since his pursuit and punishment of heresy were not out of the ordinary: he did, however, have to deal with some high-profile cases.

Margaret Polley, a widow of the parish of Pepenbury, was burnt for heresy at Dartford in July 1555. She and a fellow heretic, Christopher Ward, sang a psalm together before going to the stake. She was considered to have been the first woman to suffer that fate 'for religion' during Mary's reign. Later that month another widow, Joan Beach, was burnt at Rochester itself. There was a high degree of tension in Kent between Catholics and protestants, and such events would have caused great resentment. From Griffin's point of view a policy of rigour was appropriate, given that heresy was to be regarded as much a political as a religious threat. In this he probably concurred with Chancellor Stephen Gardiner's conviction that blame for the rebellion of 1554 by Sir Thomas Wyatt, who raised his standard at Rochester, lay with the protestant faction, against whom severe measures therefore needed to be taken.

In June 1555 Griffin's intention of taking a large number of people into custody had been signalled by the request made to the privy council by the mayor of Rochester for extra space in prison to hold 'suche disordered personnes as he [the bishop] shal committ to the same' (APC, 1554–6, 145). It is a fair presumption that the expected overflow was due in part to the detention of persons 'suspected in religion'. In practice, however, rigour was a less than dependable policy in a volatile situation. In the case of William Wood of Strood, arraigned on 19 October 1556 for non-attendance, disputes over the nature of the eucharist between the presenting lawyers led to the abandonment of the case, not before the accused had addressed the assembled throng. The clash of doctrinal opinions bred dissension in Rochester, and the townspeople and the people at large grew restless as the church's persecution of heresy intensified. The local gentry and office-holders became increasingly reluctant to be present at the burnings, and in July 1557 the sheriff of Kent and mayor of Rochester were among the officials asked why they had not carried out sentences for heresy. Mary's death brought the policy of persecution to an end; the evidence suggests that Griffin would in any case have found it difficult to hold the line.

His episcopate aside, Griffin's principal claim to fame derives from his will, made on 7 October 1558, which enjoined Petre, Sir William Garrard the merchant, and Simon Lowe to carry out the proposals of his kinsmen William and Jeffrey Glyn for the setting up of Friars School in Bangor. His own wealth was—for a former religious— appropriately meagre, and he devoted much of it to the provision of chalices in parishes where he had served, and to giving financial help to some of the religious houses recently restored. He died, possibly at the bishop of Rochester's palace at Southwark, on 20 November 1558, perhaps of plague, which was then raging in London, and was buried ten days later in St Magnus the Martyr, London Bridge. In accordance with the Catholic church's desire to restore ecclesiastical pageantry in England, the funeral was a splendid affair, ending in a magnificent dinner.

GARETH DAVIES

Sources P. C. Bartrum, ed., *Welsh genealogies, AD 1400–1500*, 18 vols. (1983), esp. vol. 6 · J. E. Griffith, *Pedigrees of Anglesey and Carnarvonshire families* (privately printed, Horncastle, 1914) · Emden, *Oxf.*, 4.248 · will, 7 Oct 1558, PRO, PROB 11/43/45, fol. 347 [Mauritii Griffith Episcopi; an incomplete account given in H. Barber and H. Lewis, *The history of Friars School* (1904), 20–21] · the index to Father Raymund Palmer's transcripts of Dominican records, Bangor 227, in the archives of the English province of the order of preachers, BL, Add. MS 32446 · *LP Henry VIII*, 8, no. 472 · C. H. Fielding, *The records of Rochester diocese* (1910) · *The diary of Henry Machyn, citizen and merchant-taylor of London, from AD 1550 to AD 1563*, ed. J. G. Nichols, CS, 42 (1848) · W. K. R. Bedford, *The blazon of episcopacy* (1897), 107 · J. F. Davis, *Heresy and reformation in the south-east of England, 1520–1559*, Royal Historical Society Studies in History, 34 (1983) · C. A. Gresham, 'The parish of Beddgelert', *Transactions of the Caernarvonshire Historical Society*, 30 (1969), 21–8 · E. Duffy, *The stripping of the altars: traditional religion in England, c.1400–c.1580* (1992),

380–81, 412, 444–65, 542 · J. Foxe, *Actes and monuments of matters most special and memorable, happening in the church, with an universal history of the same*, 3 (1684), 316–17, 469, 687, 703 · S. Brigden, *London and the Reformation* (1989) · T. Fuller, *The church history of Britain*, ed. J. Nichols, 3rd edn, 3 vols. (1868) · J. Strype, *Ecclesiastical memorials*, 3/1 (1822) · *APC, 1554–1556* · F. G. Emmison, *Tudor secretary: Sir William Petre at court and home* (1961) · *CSP Venice, 1556–7* · press article, 'The bishops of Rochester', LXXII: 'Maurice Gryffyth 1554–60 [sic]', LPL, MS 3166 · D. M. Loades, 'The enforcement of reaction, 1553–1558', *Journal of Ecclesiastical History*, 16 (1965), 54–66

Wealth at death for a bishop, relatively poor; gifts of small sums of money, rings, and ecclesiastical raiment to friends and relations; provision of chalices to cathedral, and to the parishes he served; gifts to newly re-established religious houses in London area; mention of a gift made to him by Queen Mary; his library (value unknown) bequeathed to Rochester Cathedral: will, PRO, PROB 11/43/45, fol. 347

Griffin, Richard [*formerly* Richard Aldworth Neville], **second Baron Braybrooke** (1750–1825), politician, was born on 22 June 1750 in Duke Street, Westminster, and baptized Richard Aldworth at Windsor, on 29 June, the only son of Richard Neville Aldworth (1717–1793) [*see* Neville, Richard Neville Aldworth], politician, who in 1762 added Neville to the family name, and his wife, Magdalena Calandrini (*c*.1718–1750). Educated at Eton College (1759–67) and Merton College, Oxford, from 1768 (MA 1771), he subsequently went on a grand tour, spending some time in Rome. From 1762 he held the sinecure of provost-marshal of Jamaica, which was said, towards the end of his life, to have brought him in all about £120,000.

When his father left parliament after twenty-seven years' service in 1774 Neville was returned for Grampound on the Eliot interest for £2000 and supported North's administration, moving the address on 31 October 1776 in favour of suppressing the American rebellion. Apart from a vote for economic reform on 8 March 1780 he remained pro-North. On 9 June 1780 he married Catherine Grenville (1761–1796), daughter of the former premier George *Grenville (1712–1770) of Wotton, Buckinghamshire, and Elizabeth Wyndham; they had six sons, of whom twins died at birth and two survived him, and four daughters. His marriage obtained for him at once a seat for Buckingham under the aegis of his brother-in-law Lord Temple. They disagreed, however, and after vacating the seat on his appointment as agent to the Buckinghamshire militia, in which he had been lieutenant (1771) and captain (1779), Neville was returned after a contested by-election at Reading, once his father's seat, on 21 February 1782. This obliged him, under constituency pressure, to vote with the opposition against the American War of Independence on 27 February, and he supported the peace preliminaries on 18 February 1783. He opposed Fox's India Bill on 27 November 1783, and silently backed Pitt the younger's ensuing administration, with which his Grenville in-laws were closely associated. He survived a second contest for Reading in 1790, and often acted as government teller on key questions. He thought himself ill rewarded: in 1791 Pitt felt unable to make him, as a commoner, lord lieutenant of Berkshire, even though he was heir to a barony and possessed estates in Berkshire that were second only to Lord Craven's. Returned unopposed in 1796, he resumed his support for Pitt in parliament, despite his grief at his wife's recent death.

On 25 May 1797 Neville succeeded a third cousin, John Griffin Griffin, as second Baron Braybrooke, changing his surname from Aldworth Neville to Griffin on 27 July. This brought him, once his benefactor's brother-in-law died in 1802, the grand residence of Audley End, Essex, the lord lieutenancy of Essex (1798), of which he became vice-admiral in 1809, and the recordership of Saffron Walden. He was an inconspicuous but steady supporter of his brother-in-law William Wyndham Grenville's political line in the Lords. A fellow of the Society of Antiquaries (1792), he was awarded the degrees of DCL from Oxford in 1810 and LLD from Cambridge in 1819. He served as high steward of Wokingham, Berkshire, and was a keen agricultural improver who added to his Essex estate.

Braybrooke died at Billingbear on 28 February 1825 and was buried on 8 March with his wife at Laurence Waltham, Berkshire. His second surviving son was **George Neville Grenville** (1789–1854), dean of Windsor, who was born George Neville at Stanlake, Berkshire, on 17 August 1789. He was educated at Eton College from 1802 and Trinity College, Cambridge, from 1807 (MA 1810). His father being, since 1797, hereditary visitor of Magdalene College, Cambridge, he obtained the mastership of that college in 1813 and held it for forty years. He was presented by his brother-in-law to the rectory of Hawarden, Flintshire, which he held from 1814 to 1834. There he created two chapelries. He married on 9 May 1816 Lady Charlotte Legge (1789–1877), daughter of George Legge, third earl of Dartmouth, and Frances Finch; they had six sons and five daughters. In 1825 his uncle Thomas Grenville conveyed to him the Somerset estate, based on Butleigh Court, that he had just inherited from James Grenville, Baron Glastonbury, whereupon Neville took on 7 July the additional name of Grenville. From 1846, already a queen's chaplain, he was dean of Windsor by Sir Robert Peel's nomination. He was also registrar of the Order of the Garter. He died at Butleigh on 10 June 1854 and was buried there on 17 June, much esteemed for his charity to parishioners.

ROLAND THORNE

Sources D. R. Fisher, 'Neville, Richard Aldworth', HoP, *Commons, 1790–1820* · Berks. RO, Braybrooke MSS · Essex RO, Braybrooke MSS · GM, 1st ser., 95/1 (1825), 463 · GM, 2nd ser., 42 (1854), 72 · GEC, *Peerage* · *The Black Book* (1820), 406–7 · PRO, Chatham MS, 30/8/163, fol. 15 · *DNB* · Richard, Lord Braybrooke [R. Griffin], *The history of Audley End* (1836), 53–5, 128, 132 · Venn, *Alum. Cant.* · monument, Butleigh church, Somerset [George Neville Grenville] · parish register (baptism), New Windsor, Berkshire, 1750
Archives Berks. RO, family papers · Essex RO, Chelmsford, family papers and corresp. · PRO, papers relating to the office of provost-marshal-general in Jamaica | BL, corresp. with Lord Grenville, Add. MS 58896 · BL, George Neville Grenville, corresp. with Sir Robert Peel and others · Hunt. L., letters to Grenville family · PRO, Chatham MSS, letters to William Pitt · St Deiniol's library, Hawarden, corresp. with Glynne family
Likenesses attrib. P. Wickstead, group portrait, oils, *c.*1773–1774 (*Conversation Piece*), Audley End House, Essex; version, Springhill, Londonderry · J. Hoppner, portrait, 1803?, Audley End House, Essex · E. Scriven, stipple (George Neville Grenville; after H. Legge), NPG · C. Turner, mezzotint (after J. Hoppner), BM

Griffin [*formerly* Neville], **Richard, third Baron Braybrooke** (**1783–1858**), politician and literary editor, was born at Stanlake Park, Berkshire, on 26 September 1783, the first of the three sons of Richard Aldworth Neville (1750–1825) [*see* Griffin, Richard], who succeeded his distant cousin John Griffin Griffin as second Baron Braybrooke in 1797, and his wife, Catherine (1761–1796), youngest daughter of George Grenville of Wotton, Buckinghamshire, at one time prime minister. Neville was therefore the nephew of the first marquess of Buckingham and first Lord Grenville, the heads of the Grenville family. He was educated at Sunbury School, Eton College, and Christ Church, Oxford (he matriculated in 1801).

Neville was made a captain of the Berkshire militia in 1803. In February 1805 he was returned to parliament for Thirsk on the Frankland interest. He was put up for Saltash by Lord Buckingham in 1806 (when Lord Grenville was prime minister), and was defeated at the poll, but seated on petition in February 1807. At the general election in May 1807 he declined an invitation to stand for Berkshire and came in for his uncle's pocket borough of Buckingham. He successfully contested Berkshire at the general elections of 1812, 1818, and 1820. As one of the Grenvillite whig parliamentary squad, he followed his uncles' line of general opposition to the Portland and Perceval ministries, coupled with support for Catholic emancipation and hostility to parliamentary reform. Subsequently, however, with an independent seat and probably under the influence of his cousins lords Nugent and Ebrington, he steadily diverged from the increasingly conservative attitude adopted by his cousin, the second marquess (later first duke) of Buckingham, who led the Grenvillites from 1813. He voted for parliamentary reform in 1817 and declared in favour of a moderate instalment at the 1818 general election, but took only a limited part in the opposition to the repressive legislation which followed the Peterloo incident in 1819. He was always a lax attender and made few contributions to debate. On 13 May 1819 he married Lady Jane Cornwallis (1798–1856), the first daughter of Charles, second Marquess Cornwallis, with whom he had five sons and three daughters. When Buckingham coalesced the remnant of his squad with the Liverpool ministry in January 1822 Neville continued to act, when present, with the whig opposition, voting again for parliamentary reform in 1823. His father's death on 28 February 1825 removed him from the Commons and gave him possession of Audley End, where he took up permanent residence, and the Berkshire estates. In accordance with his father's act of 1797 he took the surname Griffin. As a peer, he supported Catholic emancipation in 1829 and the Grey ministry's reform bills in 1831 and 1832; but from 1834 he sided with Peel's Conservative Party. He opposed repeal of the corn laws in 1846.

Neville's younger brother George was from 1813 master of Magdalene College, Cambridge (of which their father, as owner of Audley End, was hereditary visitor). In 1818 he was encouraged by Lord Grenville to transcribe and edit the shorthand diary of Samuel Pepys, which had been in

Richard Griffin, third Baron Braybrooke (1783–1858), by Edward Scriven, pubd 1836 (after John Jackson, 1822)

the college's keeping since 1724. George was too busy and gave the task to Richard, who was provided with a remarkably accurate transcription, after three years' toil, by John Smith, an impoverished sizar of St John's College. (He and Richard Neville never met.) Neville, who apparently took most of the editorial decisions himself, produced what was, even by contemporary standards of scholarship, an amateurish travesty of Smith's transcript, which omitted almost three-quarters of the original, including all the indelicate material, often by means of arbitrary and unsignified compression. The work, which included a selection from Pepys's correspondence, was published by Henry Colburn in two volumes as *Memoirs of Samuel Pepys* in 1825. It was generally well received, and two reprints appeared in 1828. For the 'considerably enlarged' five-volume edition of 1848–9 Braybrooke reduced the correspondence and expanded the diary text by introducing previously unprinted passages, so that about two-fifths of the original was now published. Revisions of the 1825 text were minimal, and the new entries were freely compressed and censored. Braybrooke omitted from the preface even the lukewarm thanks previously accorded to Smith, who had been rescued from the penury of a Norfolk curacy by Lord Chancellor Brougham's appointment of him to the rectory of Baldock, Hertfordshire, in 1832. The new work and a reissue of 1851 sold out, and Braybrooke undertook another new edition, which was published by Hurst and Blackett in 1854. The text was largely unaltered, but new letters and explanatory notes were added. Braybrooke also published *The History of Audley End* (1836) and an edition of *The Private Correspondence of Lady*

Jane Cornwallis (1842). At Audley End, where he considerably improved the 'very magnificent huge old mansion', he was a benevolent landlord. When Lord Lyttelton visited him there in 1834 he reported that Braybrooke, 'rather a shy man in mixed company, was wondrous agreeable and flowing too in talk' (Lyttelton, 274–5). In the last four years of his life Braybrooke, who was president of the Camden Society from 1853, lost fourteen near relations, including his wife and two sons killed within a week of each other in the Crimea. He died at Audley End on 13 March 1858, and was buried at Littlebury, Essex. He was succeeded as fourth Baron Braybrooke by his eldest son, Richard Cornwallis *Neville (1820–1861). D. R. FISHER

Sources D. R. Fisher, 'Neville, Richard', HoP, *Commons, 1790–1820* · D. R. Fisher, HoP, *Commons, 1820–32* [draft] · Pepys, *Diary*, 1.lxxv-xcvi · GM, 3rd ser., 4 (1858), 669–70 · *Memoirs of Samuel Pepys*, ed. R. Braybrooke and J. Smith, 2 vols. (1825) · *The life, journals and correspondence of Samuel Pepys*, ed. J. Smith, 2 vols. (1841) · *Diary and correspondence of Samuel Pepys*, ed. R. Braybrooke, 3rd edn, 5 vols. (1848–9); 4th edn, 4 vols. (1854) · S. Spencer, Lady Lyttelton, *Correspondence of Sarah Spencer, Lady Lyttelton, 1787–1870*, ed. Mrs H. Wyndham (1912), 274–5 · J. J. Sack, *The Grenvillites, 1801–29* (Chicago, 1979), 18, 32, 39, 127, 133, 144–5, 161, 166, 168, 174, 221–3
Archives Berks. RO, genealogical and church notes, D/EN and D/DBy · CKS, corresp. and accounts as executor and trustee of G. J. Cholmondeley · Essex RO, Chelmsford, corresp., diaries, papers relating to history of Audley End | BL, letters to W. E. Gladstone, Add. MSS 44358, 44360, 44363, 44367, 44368, 44382 · Bodl. Oxf., corresp. with Sir Thomas Phillipps · S. Antiquaries, Lond., letters to G. S. Steinman · St Deiniol's Library, Hawarden, corresp. with the Glynne and Gladstone families
Likenesses J. Jackson, oils, 1822, Audley End House, Essex · M. Gauci, lithograph (after E. U. Eddis), BM · B. P. Gibbon, print (after A. Morton), BM, NPG · B. P. Gibbon, print (after W. Mulready), BM; repro. in J. Pye, *Patronage of British art: an historical sketch* (1845) · J. Hoppner, oils, Eton · W. Mulready, drawing, V&A · E. Scriven, engraving (after J. Jackson, 1822), repro. in R. G. Braybrooke, *The history of Audley End* (1836) [see illus.]
Wealth at death under £120,000: probate, 22 April 1858, CGPLA Eng. & Wales

Griffin, Thomas (1692/3–1771), naval officer and politician, whose parents are unknown, was said to have belonged to a younger branch of the family of Lord Griffin of Braybrooke. The list of MPs for 1754 referred to his being 'of Dixton Hadnock in Monmouthshire'. He entered the navy and on 28 October 1718 was appointed third lieutenant of the *Orford* by Sir George Byng. Griffin continued his association with the Byng family in the following decade. On 8 August 1727 he was appointed first lieutenant of the *Gibraltar*, the same day the Hon. John Byng became captain. He followed John Byng to the *Princess Louisa* on 29 July 1728 and the *Falmouth* on 7 July 1730.

On 1 April 1731 Griffin was promoted captain of the frigate *Shoreham*, which he commanded for two years in the West Indies and on the coast of Carolina. In February 1735 he was appointed to command the *Blenheim*, guardship at Portsmouth, bearing the flag of Vice-Admiral Cavendish. On 16 May 1738 he took command of the *Oxford* in the channel and in June 1739 he moved to the *Princess Caroline*. He then went out to the West Indies in the fleet under Sir Chaloner Ogle. At Jamaica, Edward Vernon hoisted his flag on board the *Princess Caroline*, and Griffin was moved into

Thomas Griffin (1692/3–1771), by Richard Houston (after Thomas Hudson, c.1748)

the *Burford*, Vernon's former flagship. He commanded the *Burford* in the unsuccessful attack on Cartagena, March–April 1741. In the following September he took the *Burford* to England, and was afterwards involved in a quarrel with his officers, whom Griffin had turned out of their cabins in order to accommodate some passengers brought from Jamaica. The confrontation heralded a second phase in Griffin's career characterized by acrimony and controversy. On 23 November 1741, this particular dispute having been concluded, he was appointed to the guardship *Nassau* at Portsmouth, from which he exchanged into the *St George* three days later. Griffin commanded her during the summers of 1742 and 1743. In October 1743 he was appointed to the *Captain* (70 guns), in the squadron under Sir John Norris, and afterwards under Sir John Balchen in his last fatal cruise to the coast of Portugal.

In January 1745 the *Captain* and three other ships of the line were cruising off Ushant when they sighted and chased three French ships: two ships of the line, and the *Mars*, a small British privateer, which had been captured two or three days before. With Griffin in command of the British ships, the *Mars* was captured but the other ships were not engaged. Griffin's actions raised questions about why one of the largest ships of the squadron had turned aside to capture the comparatively insignificant privateer. Griffin alleged that he believed the *Mars* to be a man-of-war, and the two French vessels merchant ships. Despite calls for an enquiry into Griffin's conduct the Admiralty considered his explanation sufficient. He continued through the year in command of the *Captain*, cruising with some success against the enemy's privateers in the

channel. On the news of Commodore Curtis Barnett's death in the East Indies, Griffin was ordered to go out to fill the vacancy. On 15 January 1746 he was appointed commander-in-chief in a particular service and on 15 March he hoisted a broad pennant in the *Princess Mary* (60 guns). Griffin left Spithead in April and arrived off the mouth of the Ganges in December 1746. In February 1747 Griffin went down to Fort St David. For the next two years he remained in the waters between Fort St David and Trincomalee, during which time he was promoted rear-admiral of the red on 5 July 1747, and vice-admiral of the blue on 12 May 1748. In July 1748 he was relieved by Vice-Admiral Edward Boscawen, and on 17 January 1749, after refitting at Trincomalee, he sailed for England. On his arrival in July he learned that his conduct had again been questioned and he asked for a court martial. Additional charges of misconduct and neglect of duty were brought by Captain Henry Powlett (later sixth duke of Bolton) in April 1750. On these charges Griffin was tried by court martial on 3–7 December 1750, found guilty of negligence, and sentenced to be suspended from his rank and employment as a flag-officer. Owing to his interest, George II reinstated him in his rank in January 1752. Griffin's later attempt to prefer charges of misconduct against Captain Powlett proved unsuccessful.

After his court martial Griffin saw no further service, though he did later rise to the rank of admiral of the white. In 1754 he was elected MP for Arundel and was identified as a supporter of the administration. No records exist of his having voted or spoken in the House of Commons, and he did not stand in 1761. Griffin's conduct in neglecting to engage the enemy on two occasions left a stain on his reputation which neither the favourable judgment of the Admiralty nor the king's clemency cleared away. His unpopularity was compounded by an overbearing treatment of subordinates. Griffin was married to Elizabeth (1709/10–1781) about whom no further details are known. He died, aged seventy-eight, on 23 December 1771, and was buried at Dixton parish church. He was survived by his wife who died, aged seventy-one, on 23 May 1781.   J. K. LAUGHTON, *rev.* RICHARD HARDING

Sources captains' letters 'G', 1740–50, PRO, ADM 1/1828–1831 · admirals' journals — Griffin, 25 Feb 1746–3 Aug 1749, PRO, ADM 50/25 · commission and warrant books, PRO, ADM 6/12–17 · NMM, Griffin MSS, GRI 1/4,9,15 · letters from Griffin to Anson, 1747, BL, Anson MSS, Add. MS 15955, fols. 280–308 · ships logs (Princess Caroline), PRO, ADM 51/733 · ships logs (Burford), PRO, ADM 51/145 · J. Charnock, ed., *Biographia navalis*, 4 (1796), 22–30 · monuments in Dixton parish church (typescript), Gwent Family History Society · *A narrative of the transactions of the British squadron in the East Indies* (1751) · *Minutes of the proceedings of the trial of Vice Admiral Griffin* (1751) · *Mr Griffin's appeal to the Rt Hon lord commissioners of the admiralty* (1751) · J. Brooke, 'Griffin, Thomas', HoP, *Commons, 1754–90*

Archives NMM, corresp. and papers · PRO, captains' letters, ADM 1/1828–1831 | BL, Anson MSS, Add. MS 15955

Likenesses R. Houston, mezzotint (after T. Hudson, c.1748), BM, NPG [*see illus.*]

Griffin, Thomas (1706?–1771), organ builder and university professor, was the son of a wharfinger. He was apprenticed on 5 July 1720 to George Dennis, a barber, for seven years; was admitted 'by servitude' on 4 February 1729 to the freedom and on 6 March 1733 to the livery of the Barber–Surgeons' Company. He was entered at that date in the company's books as a barber of Fenchurch Street, London. After 1751 Griffin is described as an organ builder, still of Fenchurch Street; it is not known how, or when he made this transition. He is said to have built organs for a number of churches in the city of London, including St Helen, Bishopsgate (1741), St Mildred, Bread Street (1744), and St Michael Bassishaw (1762). Griffin was a common councilman for Langbourn ward, and a member of the Gresham Committee. On 11 June 1763 he succeeded Charles Gardner as professor of music at Gresham College. The college was in the doldrums, and Griffin was one of a series of Gresham professors of music who were utterly unqualified to deliver public lectures on the subject. Despite his incapacity for the post, recorded in contemporary newspapers, he held it until his death on 29 April 1771. By his will he left property to his two sisters.

L. M. MIDDLETON, rev. K. D. REYNOLDS

Sources W. H. Husk, 'Griffin, Thomas', Grove, *Dict. mus.* (1927) · *GM*, 1st ser., 41 (1771), 239 · records of Worshipful Company of Barber–Surgeons, London · will, PRO, PROB 11/967, fol. 178v · W. H. Husk, 'Griffin, Thomas', Grove, *Dict. mus.* (1878–90)

Griffin, William (1839–1883). *See under* Griffin, John Joseph (1802–1877).

Griffith. *See also* Griffiths, Gruffudd, Gryffyth.

Griffith, Alan Arnold (1893–1963), aero-engine designer, was born on 13 June 1893 in London, the eldest of the three children of George Chetwynd Griffith (d. 1900) and his wife, Elizabeth Brierly. His father was a widely travelled explorer, journalist, and author, who lived for a time in South Africa as a special correspondent of the *Daily Mail*, and in the 1890s took his family to live in Douglas, Isle of Man.

Griffith's early education was somewhat unsettled, but in 1906 he went to the Douglas secondary school whence in 1911, with a Sir W. H. Tate science scholarship, he entered the mechanical engineering school at the University of Liverpool. In 1914 he graduated with first-class honours in mechanical engineering and won the Rathbone medal and the university scholarship in engineering, which enabled him to do research for a year on the surface resistance to heat flow between metal and gases. He gained his MEng in 1917 and DEng in 1921, both from Liverpool, for work done after he joined the Royal Aircraft Factory (later the Royal Aircraft Establishment), Farnborough, in July 1915.

Griffith was a gifted applied mathematician with an intuitive grasp of the laws of nature which made him equally at home in the theories of materials, structures, aerodynamics, and heat engines, to all of which he made notable contributions. Probably the best known of these was his work done in collaboration with G. I. Taylor and described in 1917, showing that if a soap film is stretched across a hole cut to the shape of the cross-section of a uniform bar, and if the film is distended by inducing a pressure difference between the two sides of the film, then the contours of the bubble are related to the stress distribution in the bar when it is twisted. This and subsequent work in the same field, which had valuable practical applications, earned him the nickname of Soap-bubble Griffith.

In 1920 Griffith published an outstanding paper, 'Theory of rupture' in the *Philosophical Transactions of the Royal Society*, on the behaviour of materials, resolving the discrepancies between ideal and observed strength by postulating that materials contained cracks or other flaws which induced local concentrations of stress. This was a new conception on which all subsequent theories of fracture strength rely. It led Griffith to show experimentally that very high strengths can be obtained from fine-drawn filaments.

Contemporaneously with this fundamental work, Griffith was investigating propeller problems and this led him to the study of turbine blading. He realized that the blades of existing turbines, designed as the walls of passages, were working inefficiently and that big improvements in efficiency could be obtained by treating the blades as aerofoils. In his classic Royal Aircraft Establishment report of July 1926 he demonstrated that the gas turbine was a feasible aircraft engine. He conceived it as the combination of an axial flow compressor, an axial flow turbine, and a propeller. He did not, however, associate the gas turbine with jet propulsion, as did Frank Whittle's momentous invention of 1929. What Griffith did, after a lapse of time which is difficult to explain, was to develop in the 1930s by a series of experiments the high efficiency axial compressor. A. A. Rubbra has therefore described him as 'the true originator of the multi-stage axial engine' (Rubbra, 122).

Griffith was away from Farnborough from 1928 to 1931, as principal scientific officer in charge of the Air Ministry laboratory at South Kensington. He moved back to become head of the engine department where, *inter alia*, he conducted the axial compressor experiments with his talented assistant, Hayne Constant. The pioneering work he did came to the notice of Ernest Walter Hives, then general manager of Rolls-Royce, and as a result, in 1939 Griffith became research engineer at Derby, directly responsible to Hives for aero-engine research. He remained with Rolls-Royce for the rest of his working life, visiting the USA and Canada on the firm's behalf.

In the early 1940s Griffith brought to fruition a design he had been working on for some years, the 'contraflow' engine in which each wheel of the multi-stage design had turbine and compressor blading. This design, delightful in conception, had serious practical defects and represents one of Griffith's rare failures. After it was dropped he concentrated on more conventional axial flow designs and played a valuable part in the basic designs of the successful Avon jet engine, and the Conway bypass jet engine.

More and more Griffith became interested in the vertical take-off and landing of aircraft and produced highly imaginative military and civil designs in which his comprehensive knowledge of aerodynamics and of thermodynamics were effectively combined. His ideas found their first practical expression in a test rig which became famous as the 'flying bedstead'. This was essentially a framework carrying two Rolls-Royce Nene engines which not only gave direct lift for hovering but provided air from their compressors to the jets used for control.

The first free flight of this device took place on 3 August 1954, when it rose about 10 feet and was controlled successfully. It 'flew' for eight and a half minutes, and many other trouble-free flights followed. These led to the design by Short and Harland of the sc-1 aircraft in which four Rolls-Royce RB108 engines, designed specifically for jet lift, provided vertical take-off and one RB108 was used for propulsion. This aircraft first flew in March 1957 and achieved complete transition from jet-borne to wing-borne flight in April 1960. In June of that year Griffith retired, though, as far as his developing ill-health allowed, he continued as a consultant to Rolls-Royce.

Griffith was a tall, slim man of somewhat serious demeanour, but, on closer acquaintance, engaging and amusing. He had little taste for publicity; though the author of numerous papers, he published nothing after 1928, claiming that the constraints imposed by the need for commercial and national security would inhibit discussion. His later papers were issued as RAE or Rolls-Royce internal documents. The brilliance of his work was nevertheless widely appreciated, and he became a fellow of the Royal Society in 1941, CBE in 1948, and silver medallist of the Royal Aeronautical Society in 1955.

In November 1925 he married Constance Vera, the daughter of R. T. Falkner, of the Army Catering Corps. They had one son and two daughters, the elder of whom died in 1946 from a horse-riding mishap. The younger daughter accompanied him in 1952 on a three-month world tour. He died in Farnborough War Memorial Hospital on 11 October 1963 and his remains were cremated at the Park crematorium, Aldershot.

KINGS NORTON, *rev.*

Sources A. A. Rubbra, *Memoirs FRS*, 10 (1964), 117–36 · F. W. Armstrong, 'The aero engine and its progress: fifty years after Griffith', *Aeronautical Journal*, 80 (1976), 499–520 · personal knowledge (1981)
Likenesses photograph, repro. in Rubbra, *Memoirs FRS* · photograph, Rolls-Royce Ltd, Derby, Aero division · photograph, Royal Aircraft Establishment, Farnborough, Hampshire
Wealth at death £36,693 5s. 0d.: probate, 23 Dec 1963, *CGPLA Eng. & Wales*

Griffith, Alexander (1601?–1676), Church of England clergyman, was probably born in July 1601 at St Asaph; he was the son of Owen Griffith, incumbent of the living of Llysfaen, Caernarvonshire, and vicar choral at St Asaph Cathedral. He was admitted to Hart Hall, Oxford, on 27 January 1615, graduating BA on 12 June 1618 and proceeding MA on 10 December 1631. He was admitted to livings in Montgomeryshire—Trefeglwys (1622) and Llanwnnog (1634)—and was appointed to Glasbury, Brecknockshire, on 6 September 1639, while he still held Llanwnnog. He married

Gaynor Goodman (1595/6–1673), one of the family of Ruthin, Denbighshire, which produced the Elizabethan dean of Westminster, Gabriel Goodman, and his nephew Godfrey Goodman, bishop of Gloucester under Charles I. The parish register of Trefeglwys records the baptism of three daughters (Elizabeth, Margaret, and Ursula) and three sons (Godfrey, Owen, and Gabriel, the last of whom died an infant) between 1624 and 1634.

Griffith was probably sympathetic to the Laudians, and both his livings were sequestered on 7 June 1650 at the behest of the commissioners appointed under the act of February that year for propagating the gospel in Wales: the offences alleged against him were 'drunkenness and lasciviousness' (MS J. Walker e. 7, fol. 214). Embittered by this treatment, Griffith began a campaign against the religious dispensation for Wales which had brought about his downfall, and against the main clerical representative of the propagators in the eastern part of mid-Wales, Vavasor Powell. In 1652 he may have contributed significantly to a petition to the Rump Parliament exposing what were alleged to be the abuses of the propagators, and published the first of a series of denunciations of them. Only the first of these, *Mercurius Cambro-Britannicus* (1652), had any hope of changing the religious regime in Wales. Three other diatribes appeared in 1654 (*Gemitus ecclesiae Cambro-Britannicus*, *Strena Vavasoriensis* and *A true and perfect relation of the whole transaction concerning the petition of the six counties of South-Wales*), but by then the propagation commission had lapsed, and his polemics read increasingly as narrow, personal attacks on Powell. The catalogue of misdemeanours Griffith alleged against the propagators was extensive. Having £160,000 at their disposal, they left 700 Welsh parishes without a ministry, and employed ignorant, heretical, and subversive itinerant preachers covering huge areas ineffectually. The dispossessed clergy were deprived of the compensation promised their families, and there was widespread under-valuation of livings in order to minimize these payments and to let the benefices at bargain rates to the propagators' friends. Appeals were made difficult, not least through manipulation of language barriers between appellants and witnesses. The commissioners made tithe collecting more efficient, but parishioners were robbed more than ever before of the spiritual provision that tithes were supposed to support. By March 1654 Griffith was at Clifford's Inn, the London base of John Gunter, the Welsh lawyer who had orchestrated the 1652 petition. Gunter and Griffith received intelligence from Wales on Powell's movements, and Griffith, posing as a friend of the Cromwellian protectorate, passed it on to the lord protector himself. As Powell moved further away from the new government Griffith became more acceptable to it, and between 1658 and 1660 held the post of schoolmaster at Hay-on-Wye, Brecknockshire.

At the Restoration, Griffith recovered the living of Glasbury, and by January 1664 he had restored the church there. By 1665 he held the rectory of nearby Llys-wen, which he surrendered that year to his son Godfrey; on 17 December 1670 he took the rectory of Llaneleu. He died on 21 April 1676. He was buried at Glasbury on 24 April, three years after his wife. His writings were accepted uncritically by John Walker as a source for his *Sufferings of the Clergy* (1714); the reputation of the propagators had to wait until 1920 before it was salvaged by Thomas Richards, doyen among twentieth-century historians of Welsh nonconformity, in a point-by-point rebuttal of Griffith's allegations.   STEPHEN K. ROBERTS

Sources T. Richards, *A history of the puritan movement in Wales* (1920) · T. Richards, *Religious developments in Wales, 1654–1662* (1923) · R. T. Jones, *Vavasor Powell* (1971), 66–9 [in Welsh] · institution books, PRO, E331/Bangor/1 · Foster, *Alum. Oxon.* · Bodl. Oxf., MS J. Walker e. 7 · 'The registers of Trefeglwys', *Montgomeryshire Collections*, 32 (1902), 203–22 · A. G. [A. Griffith], *A true and perfect relation of the whole transaction concerning the petition of the six counties of South-Wales* (1654) · Thurloe, *State papers*, vol. 2 · PRO, E 134/15; 16 Charles II/Hilary 8 · parish records, Glasbury [burial], 24 April 1676

Griffith, Anne (1734–1821), practitioner of folk medicine, was born at Aberdaron, 14 miles south west of Pwllheli, Caernarvonshire. Nothing is known of her parents or her childhood and it is most probable that she never had any formal education. But her work as a herbalist has been kept for posterity through the efforts of a local historian, William Jones (Gwilym Daron) of Aberdaron, and examined by a descendant of Anne Griffith, the cardiologist Dr Emyr Wyn Jones (1907–1999).

Anne Griffith was associated all her adult life with a cottage known as Bryn Canaid in Uwchmynydd, part of the parish of Aberdaron. Her home, except for a cottage known as Cae Crin, was next to the strait separating the Llŷn peninsula from Bardsey Island. Anne Griffith is important for two reasons. First she was a pioneer in Wales in the medical uses of foxglove. Country folk in the heart of England—Shropshire, Warwickshire, and the western part of Yorkshire—had known that dropsical complaints can be relieved with foxglove tea but how this information came to Anne Griffith is a mystery. William Withering, in his masterpiece, *An Account of the Foxglove and some of its Medical Uses* (1785), admits that his attention to the use of foxglove came to him ten years earlier from 'an old woman' in Shropshire. That unknown woman and Anne Griffith realized its value before Withering had given it scientific credence.

Second, Anne Griffith was an important figure in the Llŷn peninsula for she assisted individuals and their families in their illnesses. Outside her home stood a huge rock, where she had hewn a large trough; here she placed the plants, in particular the foxgloves. She collected from Mynydd Mawr ('the large mountain'), a 524 foot hill on the tip of the Llŷn peninsula, wild flowers as well as leaves and stems of the foxgloves. They would be placed in the trough and then pressed down hard and left to be soaked by rainwater. The water would soon turn extremely black in colour and she would then fill bottles with this water. Then she would place a portion of the black water in another bottle, filling it with clear, clean water, ready to be used by those suffering from heart disease, in particular palpitations. Besides using foxgloves she prescribed violet for sore throats, broom for kidney trouble, and angelica for chest ailments; the juice of willow leaves was used to treat fevers and wild sage was made into an ointment to get rid of ringworm. Some of her remedies were unusual. One of these was to do with blood disorder. She walked to a well in an area known as Rhiw ('the hill') to collect water that had an element of manganese in it. Then she would collect periwinkles from Porth Felen ('yellow harbour') and would then pour over them hot water. After some time she would use the entrails of the periwinkles, slicing them so that the water became brown in colour, and then she would use it sparingly with the water from the well. She also kept apples until they became rotten and cheese until it mouldered, so that when a parishioner had a sore throat she would make a plaster of the grey mildew from the apples, or the cheese, on the flesh until it was healed.

Anne Griffith used grounded and wall pennywort to destroy warts on the flesh, and birthwort—because of its womb-shaped flowers—she used to help women in childbirth. For decades she was the midwife and brought into the world, in 1780, Richard Robert Jones, who later achieved notoriety, under the nickname Dic Aberdaron, as an eccentric lexicographer. As a herbalist she had faith in the power of seaweed, with which she was surrounded on the rocks of the straits. She could produce ointment from seaweed as well as from green butter (that is, unsalted butter). She preached to her contemporaries that too much butter was detrimental to the blood, but she also used to say that in the month of May an individual could use as much butter as he wanted and drink buttermilk to his delight; her reason was that plants that were suitable for cows only appeared in Llŷn in May. She provided a medicinal bottle for sleeplessness and depression made up of water from Ffynnon Saint ('the saint's well'), near Minafon, which possessed a great deal of sulphate, which she mixed with foxgloves. She used to boil pillwort with beer made of alcohol and honey and mixed with the saint's well water, but it never cured the depressed because they had to drink it for the rest of their lives. Individuals suffering from fever were given a potion made of compressed spiders' webs.

Anne Griffith continued her medicinal work to the very end; she died at Bryn Canaid on 25 October 1821, at the age of eighty-seven, after a short illness, the nature of which is not known. She had been an excellent advertisement for her own medicines and had been predeceased by at least one child, a daughter. She was buried at the cemetery of St Hywyn's Church, Aberdaron.   D. BEN REES

Sources E. W. Jones, *Lloffa yn Llŷn: trem yn ôl* (1994) · W. H. Woglore, *Discoverers for medicine* (1949) · *DWB*

Griffith, Arthur (1871–1922), political journalist and president of Dáil Éireann, was born on 31 March 1871 at 61 Upper Dominick Street, Dublin, the second son of Arthur Griffith, printer, and his wife, Mary Phelan. He was educated at the Christian Brothers' schools in Strand Street and St Mary's Place before being apprenticed as a compositor. Like so many of the Brothers' pupils he became committed to the cause of Irish nationality in his teens: he

Arthur Griffith (1871–1922), by Sir John Lavery, 1921

was a follower of Charles Stewart Parnell during his last fatal campaign in 1891, and soaked up the writing of the Young Irelander John Mitchel—the 'proud, fiery-hearted, electric-brained, giant-souled Irishman who stood up to the might of the whole British Empire' as he later put it. He joined several nationalist societies, including the Irish Republican Brotherhood (IRB), as well as co-founding the Celtic Literary Society. The recession of the 1890s impelled him to emigrate to South Africa in 1896, where he first worked in a diamond mine, then co-established a small newspaper in Transvaal, on which he continued to hone the mordant literary skill that became his strongest weapon. After the outbreak of the Second South African War he became a friend of Major John MacBride, the leader of an Irish brigade enlisted to fight the British.

Abstention from Westminster and the Hungarian parallel
Griffith returned to Ireland in 1898 and joined the solidifying pro-Boer opposition to the war which had a potent energizing effect on the nationalist movement. He went on street demonstrations with MacBride's future wife, Maud Gonne, with whom he organized the symbolic patriotic children's treat in 1900 in protest against Queen Victoria's last visit to Ireland. But his most distinctive contribution to the movement was his creation, on a shoestring budget, of the *United Irishman* in 1899. This radical separatist journal declared for 'the nationalism of '98 and '48 and '67 as the true nationalism', thus explicitly endorsing the 'physical force' movement, although it also (and confusingly to some) invoked the parliamentarian Henry Grattan. This eclectic manifesto signalled an ambiguity of objective that stayed with him to the end, though his

denunciation of Parnell's successors in the Irish Parliamentary Party was unambiguous and consistent. Griffith saw participation in the Westminster parliament as both futile and demoralizing, and his sustained criticism, a mixture of satire and bitter polemic, played a material part in the decline of the once dominant party over the next two decades.

Griffith's key idea, abstention, had appeared in Irish politics before, but only episodically. Daniel O'Connell himself had toyed with a unilaterally constituted council of three hundred, and withdrawal from Westminster had been talked of by Young Irelanders (including Griffith's hero Mitchel), and again in the time of Parnell. But Griffith turned it into a real strategy. This was not easy, and it took a long time, but Griffith was nothing if not persistent. In the late 1890s he found a practical model in the Austro-Hungarian *Ausgleich* or compromise of 1867 which created the dual monarchy. Enthusiastic reading in Habsburg history enabled him to flesh out the project through a series of articles culminating in what has been called one of the seminal documents of modern Irish history, *The Resurrection of Hungary: a Parallel for Ireland*, published in 1904. His argument was that under the brilliant leadership of Ferenc Deák a combination of passive resistance and unilateral reconstitution of the old Hungarian parliament had succeeded where armed rebellion had failed so disastrously in 1848. His version of Hungarian history has been criticized as selective and misleading (though it is still praised in Hungary). In this it followed his earlier selective account of the British constitution (omitting the omnipotence of parliament) through which he argued that in 1782 Britain had permanently abjured its power to legislate for Ireland.

The Hungarian parallel came in for much criticism, and indeed mockery. One of its most careful critics, T. M. Kettle, called it 'the largest idea contributed to Irish politics for a generation', but judged it impracticable (Kettle). The practical minded Griffith may initially have seen it as a direct model, but it seems more likely that it served as a kind of empowering myth for his fundamental argument that Ireland's liberation lay in the hands of the Irish people themselves. The real message was the need for self-reliance: a sort of Smilesian self-help on a mass scale. He urged that not only could the Irish people recover their cultural autonomy, through movements such as the Gaelic League and the Gaelic Athletic Association, but they could also take significant steps to rebuild the Irish economy—by boycotting British goods and buying Irish wherever possible. Alongside Deák his other great European exemplar was the German economist Friedrich List, apostle of autarchy and protective tariffs as against the British dogma of free trade. Griffith held that, contrary to most opinion, Ireland possessed enough natural resources to become a modern industrial power and support a population of at least 20 million. He also maintained that the true source of national wealth was people—and characteristically stuck to this in face of suggestions that, if so, the richest country in the world must be China. Again, his real purpose was to halt the steady haemorrhage of Ireland's population through emigration.

The founding of Sinn Féin The power of Griffith's ideas and the pungency of his journalism gave him national prominence and the potential to become a major political figure. But the process of turning these assets into a political organization revealed his limits as a man of action. He backed away from suggestions that he might become the Irish Deák with the odd argument that such a leader would need to be a monarchist. Though he established Cumann na nGaedheal (in 1900) and the National Council (in 1905), these were, at that time, political propaganda groups rather than parties. In 1907 they merged with Bulmer Hobson's Dungannon clubs under the name Sinn Féin, which Griffith had adopted for the title of his latest journal. (The phrase, meaning 'ourselves', had been used occasionally to convey the idea of self-reliance.) It would be hard to exaggerate the long-term importance of this development, but in the shorter term Griffith's obvious hesitancy deprived the new party of impetus. He may, like many nationalists, have disliked the divisive nature of political parties, preferring to preach national unity. But like the IRB (from which he resigned at this time) he had no means of realizing that unity.

After contesting the North Leitrim by-election in 1908 the party became gradually marginalized. Griffith remained principally a journalist rather than a politician. The ambiguity of his early ideas persisted. The assertion of one biographer that his nationalism, as evidenced throughout his spells at the helm of the *United Irishman* (1899–1906) and of *Sinn Féin* (1906–14), 'was rich, optimistic, liberal, adventurous and constructive' is well founded (Ó Luing, 58). Yet there were plain elements of racism in this thinking: he accepted the natural superiority of white Europeans (he refused to link the Irish national claim with those of colonized people overseas), and his antisemitism, though not obtrusive, was unmistakable. Like most nationalists he was hostile to socialism, though he advocated a homestead law to guarantee every family a dwelling house. While he clearly believed that Irish unity was vital he supported the increasing cultural exclusivism of the Gaelic League, backing the league's radical left wing in its dispute with Douglas Hyde in 1914. He brutally insisted, against the universalism of his erstwhile comrade-in-arms W. B. Yeats, that 'nationality is the breath of art'. And though he never learned Gaelic—Sean O'Casey witheringly held that he 'had not ten words of Irish'—he accepted that the language was central to Irish national identity, even if it might be alien to northern protestants. Within Sinn Féin tension arose between Griffith and Hobson over the issues of republicanism versus constitutional monarchy (Hobson certainly saw Griffith as a committed monarchist by this stage), and passive versus armed resistance. Both men were against the old-style Fenian insurrectionism which had in their view failed, but while Griffith always maintained the right of nations to resist oppression by any means he was less sanguine than Hobson about the virtue of armed action as part of a civil resistance strategy. This issue was present, though

muted, when the Irish volunteer movement emerged during the home rule crisis of 1913–14. Griffith took a walk-on part in this decisive development as a rank-and-file member of the Dublin Volunteers, notably during the Howth gun-running in July 1914. The intended purpose of these weapons was ambiguous, and only a small group within the IRB was determined to use them to launch a rebellion after the outbreak of the First World War the following month.

On 24 November 1910 Griffith had married Maud (Mollie) Sheehan (second daughter of Peter Sheehan of Dublin); they had a son and a daughter. His delight in the company of children was always plain, not least at the famous patriotic picnic of 1900. For all his verbal ferocity and his widely attested cussedness, behind his reserved exterior friends like 'Sean-Ghall' (H. E. Kenny) found him a humorous companion, and—on holiday at least—'as frolicsome as a child' (NL Ire., MS 25316).

The Anglo-Irish conflict In November 1914 Griffith responded to the suppression of *Sinn Féin* with a new journal, *Scissors and Paste*, followed by yet another, *Nationality*, in 1915. But though he opposed recruitment into the British army he seemed ready to wait on events. The republican insurrection of Easter 1916, and the dramatic change in Sinn Féin's position that followed, both magnified and threatened Griffith's influence. He was not part of the group that planned the rising, and though he asked to join the republican headquarters in the General Post Office after its outbreak he accepted their reply that he was more valuable as a propagandist at large. He was arrested in the large-scale sweep made by the British military authorities in the aftermath of the rebellion, and was interned from May until December 1916. But he had not been 'out' (participated in the rising), and to some republicans this confirmed his political untrustworthiness. Hardline republican former prisoners such as Michael Collins and Harry Boland adopted the Sinn Féin banner, but set about reorganizing it as the political wing of the volunteers. When the party was brought together in a triumphant national convention on 25 October 1917 it adopted a republican platform. Griffith, who still had a large following in the party, stood aside so that Eamon De Valera, the last surviving commandant of the 1916 rising, could be elected unopposed as its president. This gesture was consonant with his earlier preference for national unity, and perhaps his awareness that he lacked the charismatic qualities required for mass political leadership.

The reconstructed Sinn Féin was most recognizably Griffithite in its insistence on abstention from Westminster. In December 1918 it routed the old Irish Parliamentary Party at the polls, and in January 1919 proceeded to form an independent parliament, Dáil Éireann. But only twenty-nine of its sixty-nine elected deputies attended: the rest were in prison, as was Griffith, who had been rounded up in the so-called 'German plot' arrests of May 1918, and was held in Gloucester gaol until March 1919. Though he himself had no more political experience than the young volunteers who dominated the new Dáil, he and the other moderates might have steered it away from its uncompromising declaration of an independent republic. This precipitate action helped Britain to head off Sinn Féin's central project of appealing to the international peace conference at Paris for recognition of Ireland's claim to self-determination. By the time Griffith was released this strategy had been further undermined by the first armed action by the volunteers, soon to be renamed the Irish Republican Army. Griffith was deeply troubled by this, saying 'If this sort of thing goes on, we will end up by shooting one another' (R. Brennan, *Allegiance*, 1950, 210–11).

In May 1919 Eamon De Valera set off on a mission to the USA, and Griffith became acting president of the Dáil and head of the republican government. During De Valera's extended absence Griffith had overall responsibility for the implementation of his long-cherished strategy of establishing a rival source of political legitimacy. But he seems to have played surprisingly little direct part in the administrative side of this process. He was to some extent isolated, being still viewed with suspicion by the increasingly dominant Michael Collins, and by other hardline republican members of the cabinet like Cathal Brugha and Austin Stack; much of his energy seems to have gone into restraining the more provocative plans of such hardliners. In policy terms Griffith's influence was clearly visible in the establishment of an inquiry into Ireland's economic resources, and his insistence on the vital role of local government in the building of a counter-state also generated a largely successful policy. So indeed did his most fertile proposal, the establishment of arbitration courts to rival and undermine the British legal system. Arguably this became the most potent of all the republican political initiatives, but there was a surprisingly long delay in implementing it, during which Griffith seems to have done little to push the policy forward.

The republican government was declared illegal (as indeed was the Sinn Féin) in September 1919, and Griffith for all his commitment to non-violence was in a sense on the run throughout the next year. There was a tacit arrangement on the part of the British authorities to leave him alone, in the hope of promoting a split between moderate and extreme separatists, and of preserving some channels of communication. In October–November 1920 Griffith was involved in a back channel dialogue that came close to bringing about a truce; but in the military round-up after 'bloody Sunday' (21 November), he was finally arrested—an action privately denounced as 'a piece of impertinence' by the prime minister, Lloyd George—in what may have been a deliberate attempt by the Dublin Castle authorities to sabotage the peace talks. Until June 1921 he remained in detention in Mountjoy gaol. This time, unlike as in Gloucester, he was treated as a political prisoner, and corresponded regularly with Michael Collins to transact Dáil government business, though De Valera's return from the USA in December 1920 had formally restored Griffith to the auxiliary role that he probably preferred.

This was to change fatefully after Griffith's release, as serious negotiations between the British and Irish leaders at last got under way. A protracted and cautious correspondence between De Valera and Lloyd George in July 1921 established a basis for formal negotiations, but instead of taking direct responsibility for these De Valera proposed that Griffith should head the negotiating team. The arduous negotiation which followed in London between October and December 1921 was the culminating moment of Griffith's life. Undoubtedly he believed that the very process of negotiation implied that the Dáil government would have to make some concession from the demand for an independent republic—the absolute refusal by the British to countenance this had been forcefully borne in on him earlier. Michael Collins, who accompanied him to London along with three other delegates, came to the same conclusion. De Valera and the republicans like Brugha and Stack, who refused to join the delegation, did not accept this; they believed, however, that the delegates (though habitually referred to as 'plenipotentiaries') would bring any proposed agreement back for discussion in Dublin. The delegation should insist on preserving the unity of Ireland and ensure that, if negotiations were to break down, they should do so on this point. In November Griffith gave an informal undertaking to back Lloyd George's proposal of a boundary commission, and so was unable to engineer a break on the issue of partition when the eventual treaty terms were put—in the form of an ultimatum—by the prime minister in early December.

The Irish Free State The treaty Griffith signed on 6 December 1921, giving the Irish Free State the same status as Canada, was thus regarded by some of the Dublin cabinet as an act of treachery on his part. The atmosphere of hostility increased as the Dáil debated the treaty in January 1922. Griffith saw the opponents of the treaty as reckless idealists, who thought that 'this generation might go down, but the next generation might do something or another'. He demanded: 'Is there to be no living Irish nation? Have we any duty to the present generation?' He was convinced that Irish public opinion accepted the treaty and insisted that Dáil deputies must accept the principle of representative government rather than 'save our faces at the expense of our countrymen's blood' (Colum, 326). This was a fundamental point of contention: Griffith held that the treaty gave the Irish Free State the substance of independence, and that abstract labels were a deadly distraction.

On 7 January the Dáil voted to ratify the treaty by 64 votes to 57, and then by a margin of only two votes elected Griffith as president in place of De Valera. The defeated minority walked out of the chamber and left the rest to set about the establishment of the Irish Free State under the mounting threat of civil war. Griffith consented to an ambiguous arrangement whereby he as president remained head of a symbolic Dáil government, while Collins became chairman of a provisional government deriving its authority from the treaty itself. But it is clear that while Collins struggled to avoid direct confrontation with the republican irreconcilables, Griffith became increasingly agonized by what he feared was the imminent squandering of a historic opportunity. His colleague Ernest Blythe attested to 'the terrible position in which Griffith was caught during the months of drift after the Treaty was accepted', unable to impel Collins to take action and yet unable to resign 'without doing infinite damage' (Blythe, 42). The worst development, for him, was the 'De Valera–Collins pact', which postponed the general election on the treaty issue until June, and guaranteed the anti-treaty group the same number of seats as they had held in the previous parliament. Griffith was almost as outraged by this as was the British government: and even though Collins repudiated the pact at the last moment before the election Griffith felt that the treaty had been denied the public endorsement it would certainly have received in a truly free election. In an impassioned speech in May 1922 he identified the issue of democracy as being at the heart of the struggle over the treaty.

> All civilisation and all modern progress depend upon the fact that men substitute the vote for armed force, and the rule of the ballot for the rule of the bullet. … We have gone through months and months of talk, while the nation is being destroyed. … We have offered everything that could be offered short of giving away the indefeasible right of the Irish people to pronounce on the issue before them. That we cannot give away. If we did we would go down as the basest cowards in Irish history.   (Colum, 349)

By the time Collins accepted the inevitability of military action in late June, Griffith was visibly worn out and very short-tempered. As president of Dáil Éireann he continued to be treated by the British government as the equal of Collins, and played a major role in the difficult negotiations over the new constitution. On 12 August, while recuperating at a private nursing home at 96 Lower Leeson Street, Dublin, he suffered a cerebral haemorrhage as he stooped to tie a shoelace. His death at fifty-one was a tremendous public shock; his resilient pertinacity over the previous twenty years and more had seemed to render him a permanent feature of Irish life. His funeral (on 16 August) and burial in Glasnevin cemetery was the last grand public manifestation to be led by Michael Collins, who was killed days later in an ambush.

Short and stocky, with thick glasses and a slightly deformed foot that gave him a sailor-like rolling gait, Arthur Griffith was the embodiment of pugnacity and tenacity. Pearse famously admonished him for being 'too hard, too obstinate, too intolerant, too headstrong', and these were perhaps the vices of his virtues (Davis, *Arthur Griffith*, 1976, 42). For all his combativeness he was, as his successor, W. T. Cosgrave, said, 'shy and retiring' (*DNB*); Ernest Blythe thought 'he seemed deliberately to avoid being put at the top', and noted that 'though he was a fluent and lucid speaker, he was never able to dominate or stir an audience and never looked as if he enjoyed facing one' (Blythe, 37). Lacking the charisma of Collins his reputation became dimmed along with that of the first Free State government in general. (He got barely a line in Neil Jordan's revisionist film *Michael Collins*, 1996, though he was more justly treated in Jonathan Lewis's television docudrama *The Treaty*, 1992.) He remained, at the opening

of the twenty-first century, the only one of Ireland's prime ministers whose portrait was missing from the gallery in Leinster House, and though he has been plausibly labelled by one recent historian 'the architect of modern Ireland' (Davis, 1976, 44), he still lacks a fully documented biography.   CHARLES TOWNSHEND

Sources P. Colum, *Arthur Griffith* (Dublin, 1959) · B. Maye, *Arthur Griffith* (Dublin, 1997) · S. Ó Luing, 'Arthur Griffith and Sinn Féin', *Leaders and men of the Easter Rising*, ed. F. X. Martin (1967) · E. Blythe, 'Arthur Griffith', *Administration*, 8/1 (1960), 35–42 · R. Davis, *Arthur Griffith and non-violent Sinn Féin* (Dublin, 1974) · J. Stephens, *Arthur Griffith: journalist and statesman* (Dublin, [n.d.]) · R. Davis, *Arthur Griffith*, Dublin Historical Association, Irish History Series, 10 (1976) · T. M. Kettle, 'Would the "Hungarian policy" work?', *New Ireland Review* (Feb 1905) · NL Ire., Griffith MSS · *DNB* · b. cert. · d. cert.
Archives NL Ire., letters and papers · NL Ire., papers | HLRO, corresp. with David Lloyd George · NL Ire., letters to Patrick McCartan · TCD, corresp. with Erskine Childers · University College, Dublin, letters to D. J. O'Donoghue | FILM BFI NFTVA, news footage
Likenesses J. Lavery, oils, 1921, Hugh Lane Municipal Gallery of Modern Art, Dublin [*see illus.*] · A. Power, bronze bust, 1922, NG Ire. · L. Whelan, oils, Dáil Éireann, Dublin · L. Williams, oils, Hugh Lane Municipal Gallery of Modern Art, Dublin

Griffith, Billy. *See* Griffith, Stewart Cathie (1914–1993).

Griffith, Edmund (1570–1637), bishop of Bangor, was the fourth son of Griffith ap John Griffith of Cefnamwlch, 'an ancient house' (Wynn, 73) in Llŷn, and Catrin, daughter of Sir Richard *Bulkeley (*c.*1540–1621) of Beaumaris and Cheadle. Admitted to Brasenose College, Oxford on 8 April 1587, he graduated BA on 17 December 1589 and proceeded MA on 5 July 1592. In 1596 he became rector of Llandwrog, Denbighshire, remaining so for the rest of his life. Having proceeded BD on 14 June 1599 he rapidly acquired other livings and positions, becoming a canon of Bangor in 1600, sinecure rector of Llanfor, Merioneth, in 1601, rector of Llanbedrog in 1604, and archdeacon of Bangor in 1605. Probably during this period he married Gwen, daughter of Morris ap Griffith of Methlan in Llŷn, with whom he had fifteen children.

In 1613 Griffith exchanged his archdeaconry for the deanery of Bangor. His relations with Lewis Bayly, bishop of Bangor from 1616 to 1631, were not harmonious. Disputes occurred concerning the administration of the Friars School, Bangor, and proceedings were taken against Bayly concerning the maintenance of four scholars at Bangor. This squabbling formed part of a wider and more general rivalry between the Cefnamwlch family and the Wynns of Gwydir, whom Bayly supported in the Caernarvonshire election of 1620. On 31 December 1633 Griffith was himself elected bishop of Bangor; confirmed on 12 February 1634, he was consecrated at Lambeth on 16 February and enthroned on 14 April—an armorial painting on a wooden panel in the rebuilt house at Cefnamwlch commemorates the consecration. That year he held a visitation of his diocese, the articles for which have survived, and in November 1636 he held a synod of diocesan clergy; he also served as a feoffee for the maintenance of Botwnnog school. However, his short episcopate was not free of controversy. Early in 1637 Bangor parishioners accused their bishop of appointing churchwardens who illegally taxed them to maintain the cathedral church, and in the same month Beddgelert parishioners complained to him that the incumbent he had installed in that living was 'neither a preaching minister, nor can he, by reason of his youngness of years, as yet attain to the distinct and perfect reading of the Welsh tongue' (Ballinger, no. 1592). Griffith had little time to respond: he died on 26 May and was buried in the choir of Bangor Cathedral.

J. GWYNFOR JONES

Sources BL, Lansdowne MS 984, fol. 158 · J. Ballinger, ed., *Calendar of Wynn of Gwydir papers, 1515–1690* (1926), nos. 1040, 1592 · *Fasti Angl., 1541–1857*, [St Paul's, London], 106, 112, 113 · J. Wynn, *The history of the Gwydir family and memoirs*, ed. J. G. Jones (1990), 73 · Foster, *Alum. Oxon.* · Wood, *Ath. Oxon.*, new edn, 2.888 · *CSP dom.*, 1637–8, 375 · J. E. Griffith, *Pedigrees of Anglesey and Carnarvonshire families* (privately printed, Horncastle, 1914), 42, 169, 271 · H. Barber and H. Lewis, *The history of Friars School, Bangor* (1901), 33 · *DWB*, 291 · *Royal commission of ancient monuments Wales and Monmouthshire*, vol. 3: *Caernarvonshire west* (1964), 87 · *Brasenose College register, 1509–1909* (1909), 72 · K. Fincham, ed., *Visitation articles and injunctions of the early Stuart church*, 2 (1998), 116–22
Wealth at death approx. £500

Griffith, Edward (1790–1858), naturalist, was the son of William Griffith of Stanwell, Middlesex. Educated at St Paul's School in 1800–06, he became a solicitor and functionary of the court of common pleas. He had a politically tinged antiquarian interest in the history of London's parliamentary divisions (publishing two works in 1827 and 1831), but his more engaging and serious avocational interest was in natural history.

In the early 1800s the increasingly available exotica (in private collections, public museums, zoological gardens, and menageries) and an expanding illustrated literature had led to natural history's becoming a popular pastime. Its rapidly expanding content and diversity raised problems of classification which called for a synthesis in English modelled on that of Cuvier's comprehensive and authoritative *Règne animal* in France, first published in 1816. In 1821 Griffith published the first volume (on the Quadrumana or monkeys and apes) of a proposed series of illustrated publications on the vertebrates. With a text based on the then sparse literature and pseudo-naturalistic illustrations drawn from specimens in local collections or other, published, illustrations, the volume was hardly professional. It also appears to have been quite unsuccessful, since his initial plan for a series ambitiously advertised as 'General and particular descriptions of the vertebrated animals' went no further.

Three years later, in 1824, with Edward Pidgeon as a working partner, and Charles Hamilton Smith and George and John E. Gray as specialist associates, Griffith initiated a more ambitious project—an updated translation of the four-volume first edition of Cuvier's classic work. Beginning in 1824 but with the first volume on mammals published in 1827, Griffith and his associates produced some forty parts, both in quarto and octavo versions, about every three months. The ambitious work, *The animal kingdom arranged in conformity with its organization by the Baron Cuvier, with additional descriptions of all the species hitherto named, and of many not before noticed*, in fifteen volumes, was finally completed with an additional synopsis and index in 1835. Although Griffith was the controlling editor and a contributing author (for instance on fishes) the major part of the translation was done by Pidgeon who also produced the volume on fossils. It is difficult, however, especially in the earlier volumes, to distinguish the voice of Cuvier from that of the translator, since the major objective of the work was not only to translate Cuvier's text but to append, either by text inclusion or notes, important additions to knowledge subsequent to the original publication. The situation was further confused by the appearance of the second edition of Cuvier's work in 1829, from which time the emphasis was on translation alone (with the consequent problems of fusing the two versions). Although the work was designed as an illustrated reference source, the plates, many of which were based on drawings by Griffith or his wife, were of relatively low quality and the content itself of limited value. By the time of the appearance of the final volume wider familiarity with Cuvier's work within an expanded body of professionalizing naturalists as well as a changing research orientation was already limiting the importance of the work.

An early member of the Zoological Society, Griffith, recognized as an independent naturalist, was also a fellow of the Linnean and Royal (1834) societies and the Society of Antiquaries, and a corresponding member of the Philadelphia Academy of Natural Sciences, to which he confessed with perhaps an honest diffidence 'that I have done far too little in the cause of science to merit such a distinction' (E. Griffith to secretary of the Academy of Natural Sciences of Philadelphia, 25 June 1889, Academy Library, Philadelphia). In fact, except for seeing Cuvier's *Règne animal* to its end, he seems to have published nothing further in natural history.

Little is known of Griffith's personal life. At the time of the 1851 census he was living at 6 Nottingham Terrace, Marylebone, with his wife, Harriet (*b.* 1789/90), who was an artist, two daughters (Harriet Emma and Caroline), and a son, Edward, who was a graduate of Trinity College, Cambridge. Griffith later moved to 32 Fitzroy Square, London, where he died on 8 January 1858.

JACOB W. GRUBER

Sources C. F. Cowan, 'Notes on Griffith's *Animal kingdom of Cuvier*, 1824–35', *Journal of the Society of the Bibliography of Natural History*, 5 (1968–71), 137–40 · *CGPLA Eng. & Wales* (1858) · census returns, 1851 · *DNB*
Wealth at death under £12,000: resworn probate, Feb 1859, *CGPLA Eng. & Wales* (1858)

Griffith, Elizabeth (1727–1793), playwright and writer, was born on 11 October 1727 in Glamorgan, Wales, to Thomas Griffith (1680–1744), actor-manager of the Smock Alley Theatre, Dublin, and his wife, Jane (1694–1773), daughter of Richard Foxcroft, rector of St Michael's, Portarlington, Queen's county, Ireland. Thomas Griffith's immediate family was Welsh and Jane Foxcroft's from Yorkshire, but they settled in Dublin, where they brought up Elizabeth to be a sociable child, cheerful and at ease among the theatrical community. Thomas Griffith was a doting father and took great care to ensure that his daughter was well-read in all the polite new publications in English and French, teaching her to recite poetry and plays from memory at an early age. His death in 1744, when Elizabeth was only seventeen, left the family in financial difficulty. Elizabeth may have tried her luck on the provincial stage at this point. Her Dublin début took place on 13 October 1749, when she played Juliet to Thomas Sheridan's ageing Romeo at the Smock Alley Theatre. She specialized in tragic roles, including Jane Shore and Cordelia in *King Lear*.

In 1746 Elizabeth Griffith had met the captivating Richard *Griffith (d. 1788), a Kilkenny farmer unrelated to her, who had aristocratic connections but no money. His father had made all his fortune through a prudent marriage and refused to grant his son a living in the hope that he would follow suit. Richard was therefore in no position to propose to Elizabeth, struggling to support himself. While he made several attempts to seduce her, she remained resolute in resisting his physical charms. The couple did, however, indulge in a flirtatious and spirited correspondence in which they combined rational discussion of their reading with lavish displays of sensibility. Both correspondents lacked a formal education, which perhaps made them appreciate their intimate and improving literary exchange all the more. The delicate and earnest solicitude of these letters is particularly poignant in the light of their authors' own precarious social situation. By 1751, five years into their courtship, Elizabeth prepared to move to London in an effort to bring it to a close, realizing that any shared future would be financially perilous. At this point Richard proposed to her and they were secretly married on 12 May.

Elizabeth's decision to accept Richard's offer of marriage was to plague her all her life—she felt responsible for their inevitable poverty and was spurred to pursue a literary career for profit. Richard Griffith tried to raise a suitable living by investing a great deal of borrowed money in a linen manufactory on his farm. He remained unable to reveal his marriage to his father, who had financial control over a lawsuit in which Richard's financial hopes resided. Meanwhile Elizabeth lived with her aunt in Dublin. It has been discovered by the scholar Betty Rizzo (see Rizzo, *Elizabeth Griffith*) that it was probably during the early months of 1752 that Elizabeth, alone and pregnant, wrote her first play, *Theodorick, King of Denmark*. This tragedy was published by James Esdall of Dublin with a subscription list of almost 500 names that reflect the wide social circle in which the Griffiths moved. *Theodorick* is adapted from Eustache Le Noble de Tennelière's novel *Histoire d'Ildegarte, reine de Danemark et de Norwege, ou, L'amour magnanime*. Tellingly, Griffith chose to focus on the heroine's inferior birth and lack of fortune rather than her Amazonian powers. The play was never produced, but probably raised £25 in subscriptions. In June Elizabeth gave birth to a son, also called Richard *Griffith (1752–1820). In the following year, while her husband still struggled with his business, Elizabeth decided to move to

London to earn a living. She joined the Covent Garden theatre company in March 1753, never to progress beyond playing minor characters, perhaps because of her formal training under Thomas Sheridan, whose acting style was thought to be stiff and old-fashioned by contemporary London audiences. In 1755 she became pregnant with a second child and was forced to quit the stage. A daughter, Catherine, was born in 1756, a year which saw the collapse of Richard's linen manufactory.

It was at this point of financial desperation that the Griffiths decided to publish their courtship letters under fictional names. *A Series of Genuine Letters between Henry and Frances* appeared in 1757, causing an immediate literary sensation. As a model example of sentimental romance blended with witty exchange and moral bite, the letters established the fame but not the fortune of their authors. The Griffiths never made enough money from their epistolary courtship to support themselves, despite the fact that the *Letters* passed through several editions and was positively reviewed. In 1769 they published a follow-up, *Two Novels in Letters by the Authors of Henry and Frances* (*The Delicate Distress* by 'Frances' and *The Gordian Knot* by 'Henry'), in which they included prefaces under their pen-names, extending their unusual literary conceit whereby the boundaries between fact and fiction were blurred. While other novelists had aimed to deceive their readers as to the authenticity of their epistolary fictions, few had used real letters to weave a sentimental narrative. Later editions of the *Letters between Henry and Frances* added new letters to the original collection, including one in which Frances laments the fact that she must be a professional writer: 'I never was designed for an Author, and feel no Pride in my Fame—therefore nought but Profit shapes my Quill' (letter 616, 1786, vol. 5, p. 124).

Between 1759 and 1761 Elizabeth Griffith spent a period in Ireland as companion to the wife of a wealthy cousin of her husband, Patrick Wemys of Danesfort, Kilkenny. Richard Griffith, still dodging the bailiffs, carried out electoral and paralegal business for his cousin while Elizabeth did her best to continue writing. She worked on translations from French: *The Memoirs of Ninon d'Enclos* (1761) and Marmontel's *Contes moraux* (probably contributing to the first volume of an anonymous version entitled *Moral Tales*, published in November 1763). On the death of their cousin in January 1761 the Griffiths settled in Dublin. However, they soon decided to move to London in order to pursue their literary careers in earnest.

Elizabeth Griffith saw herself foremost as a playwright. When she arrived in London in 1764, having left the children with her mother in Portarlington, she brought two plays with her: *Amana*, a tragedy adapted from a tale by John Hawkesworth in *The Adventurer* (nos. 72–3) and *The Platonic Wife*, a version of one of Marmontel's tales. *Amana* was published by subscription by W. Johnston but failed to make the stage. *The Platonic Wife*, Griffith's first comedy, was taken immediately for production on the stage at Drury Lane, where it was premièred on 24 January 1765. The heroine of the play was modelled on Frances in the *Letters*, a learned and witty woman who insists that her husband treat her with tenderness and politeness after their marriage. When he refuses, she leaves him, and while separated entertains (but rejects) the propositions of two lovers. She repents and returns to a husband who is similarly remorseful and treats her with all the civility she desires. While Griffith's writing is spritely and shows a sure sense of dramatic pace, critical reactions were extremely harsh. The London theatrical establishment resented the audacity of a woman playwright's claims for respect and admiration. If Griffith was to be able to support her children as a playwright, she would have to conform to contemporary sexual stereotypes rather than challenge the orthodoxy.

Readers can detect a significant change of tone in Griffith's subsequent four plays, in which she abandoned her concern for improving the status of intelligent women and created a host of female characters who are the passive and long-suffering companions of errant and often violent men. Griffith was influenced by the success of domestic comedy in France, a new genre defined by Diderot in his essay *De la poésie dramatique* (1758) as the sort of comedy that should arouse sensibility rather than laughter. Griffith's *The Double Mistake* (1766) was a great triumph, playing twelve performances and concluding with a royal command performance. Griffith's success inspired her to approach the most powerful man of the London theatre world, David Garrick, actor–manager of Drury Lane. She began a correspondence with him which lasted for twelve years and in which she made unremitting pleas for his support. At first she failed to produce a play that satisfied Garrick, who disliked sentimental comedy but could see its potential for making him a profit. In March 1768 Griffith asked to see his copy of Beaumarchais's *Eugénie* (1767), a successful comedy by Diderot's younger disciple. With Garrick's help and supervision, Griffith transformed this sparkling work into *The School for Rakes* (1769). The play was extremely popular and earned Elizabeth enough money to kit out her son for entry into the East India Company.

Elizabeth Griffith's final two plays, *A Wife in the Right* (1772) and *The Times* (1779, based on Goldoni's *Il burburo benefico*), were both domestic and sentimental comedies. *A Wife in the Right* was a failure owing to the mismanagement of George Colman, theatrical director at Covent Garden, and the drunkenness of the actor Ned Shuter, who failed to learn his lines. *The Times*, a moralistic warning against the dangers of gambling, was a moderate success, running for nine performances. Critics were lukewarm in their praise, objecting to Griffith's use of satire as unbecoming for a woman. While Griffith managed to become a professional playwright by manipulating contemporary opinion rather than allowing herself to be its victim, she was never entirely free from others' sexist prejudice against her work.

Griffith undoubtedly believed that literature was a useful moral tool. Her dramatic works reveal a didactic streak that she pursued in other genres. Her epistolary novels, *The Delicate Distress* (1769), *The History of Lady Barton* (1771), and *The Story of Lady Juliana Harley* (1776), can be seen to extend the themes of her earlier courtship letters but develop a greater psychological insight into female suffering. In all three of these complex yet artful plots, Griffith's heroines are shown to be morally superior after enduring unreasonable amounts of mental and physical torment. In the preface to *The History of Lady Barton*, Griffith confesses to having drawn her characters from 'the living drama' rather than the 'mimic scene', having had 'a good deal of acquaintance with the world' (p. x). She declares she will be happy if she can 'contribute towards forming, or informing, the young and innocent' (p. xi). Griffith was interested in her female predecessors in this genre, editing *A Collection of Novels* (1777) by Aphra Behn, Penelope Aubin, and Eliza Haywood. Here she argues that 'good Romances' are 'silent Instructors', more capable of moral instruction than 'the most able philosophers' (p. 4, editor's preface). This was an unusual attempt to reassess novelists who were at that time synonymous with sexual immorality.

Griffith also wrote an ambitious work of dramatic criticism, *The Morals of Shakespeare's Drama Illustrated* (1775), dedicated to David Garrick, and citing Elizabeth Montagu's work as inspirational (she was also the translator of *A Letter from Monsieur Desefans to Mrs Montagu* (1777)). 'Shakespeare is not only my Poet, but my Philosopher also' (p. ix), declared Griffith, extending Johnson's concern with Shakespeare's 'purely ethic morals' to highlight his 'general economy of life … domestic ties, offices and obligations' (p. xiii), and showing particular interest in his heroines. Griffith's most overtly instructive work was her *Essays for Young Married Women* (1782), in which she modelled herself on Hester Chapone and Hannah More in presenting good principles and domestic advice to young women.

One of Griffith's most intriguing publications is a collection of short stories, *Novellettes, selected for the use of young ladies and gentlemen, written by Dr Goldsmith, Mrs Griffith …* (1780). The first edition, held in the Bodleian Library, Oxford, includes an impressive frontispiece of Griffith, surrounded by her works and in the pose of a confident, even proud author. Fourteen of the seventeen tales are by Griffith and the preface, written by herself, contains a glowing account of her success as an instructor of the young and, moreover, an example to her sex:

> Mrs. GRIFFITH, the ornament and pride of her country, has strove to open the flood-gate of Literature to her own Sex, and purifying the stream from the filth with which it was impregnated to make it guide [sic] with meandering invitation through the vallies of Britain. She is one of the many examples in the present day, that have served to explode the illiberal assertion that Female genius is inferior to Male. (preface, ii–iii)

While Griffith was forced to underplay, and perhaps ultimately relinquish, her 'feminist' politics, she was inevitably aware of her considerable achievement as a professional woman author. She had a passionate concern for the workings of her trade, resenting the power of circulating libraries, 'slop-shops in literature', which made available works of varied quality without paying for the privilege. Both her persistent lobbying of David Garrick for support, and the large body of translation work she undertook throughout her life, suggest that she was a hard-bitten professional author. Elizabeth Griffith spent the last decade of her life free of the obligation to support her family, surely a relief for someone who had laboured under the weight of financial pressures for so much of her life.

Griffith's son Richard Griffith had a successful career in the East India Company, before returning to England in 1780 an extremely wealthy man. After forming a suitable marriage he took his elderly parents back to Dublin in 1782. 'Henry' and 'Frances' ended their days peacefully on their son's estate in co. Kildare, Millicent, Ireland. Richard Griffith senior died on 11 February 1788. Elizabeth Griffith died at Kildare on 5 January 1793.   ELIZABETH EGER

Sources B. Rizzo, introduction, *Eighteenth-century women playwrights*, ed. D. Hughes, 4: *Elizabeth Griffith*, ed. B. Rizzo (2001) · B. Rizzo, 'Griffith, Elizabeth', *A dictionary of British and American women writers, 1660–1800*, ed. J. Todd (1985) · B. Rizzo, '"Depressa Resurgam": Elizabeth Griffith's playwrighting career', *Curtain calls: British and American women and the theater*, ed. M. A. Schofield and C. Macheski (1991), 120–42 · D. Eshleman, *Elizabeth Griffith: a biographical and critical study* (1949) · *The private correspondence of David Garrick*, ed. J. Boaden, 2 vols. (1831–2) · *Women critics, 1660–1820: an anthology*, ed. Folger Collective on Early Women Critics (1995) · J. E. Norton, 'Some uncollected authors, XXII: Elizabeth Griffith, 1727–1793', *The Book Collector*, 8 (winter 1959), 418–24 [includes handlist of author's printed works] · E. Argyros, '"Intruding herself into the chair of criticism": Elizabeth Griffith and the morality of Shakespeare's drama illustrated', *Eighteenth-century women and the arts*, ed. F. Keener and S. Lorsch (1988), 283–9 · B. G. MacCarthy, *The later women novelists* (1947), vol. 2 of *The female pen* · J. M. S. Tompkins, *The polite marriage* (1938) · E. Donkin, *Getting into the act: women playwrights in London, 1776–1829* (1995) · J. Spencer, *The rise of the woman novelist* (1986) · C. H. Whitmore, *Women's work in English fiction* (1910)

Archives V&A NAL, corresp. with David Garrick, Ref F.48.E.12/Vol. Add. 18, nos. 17–50

Likenesses R. Samuel, group portrait, oils, exh. 1779 (*The nine living muses of Great Britain*), NPG · Mackenzie, stipple (after J. Thomas), BM, NPG; repro. in *Lady's Monthly Museum* (1801) · line engraving, BM, NPG · portrait, repro. in O. Goldsmith, *Novellettes, selected for the use of young ladies and gentlemen, written by Dr Goldsmith, Mrs Griffith …* (1780), frontispiece

Griffith, Sir Ellis Jones Ellis-, first baronet (1860–1926), politician, was born Ellis Jones Griffith at 91 Great Colmore Street, Birmingham, on 23 May 1860. He was the son of an émigré Welsh master builder, Thomas Morris Griffith (1825–1901), from Llanelltyd, Merioneth; his mother, Jane, née Jones (d. 1881), came from Anglesey. While Griffith was a young child his father retired, and the family moved to Tŷ Coch, Brynsiencyn, Anglesey, where he went to the local board school and then to Holt Academy. He was an early student in the new University College of Wales, Aberystwyth, in 1876–9. Here he was active in the student debating society with his Merioneth friend Tom Ellis, and also led student protests against the principal for the conduct of college examinations. Griffith showed himself a man of intellectual and forensic gifts, and in 1880 he moved on from Aberystwyth to Downing College, Cambridge, where he took a first class in the law tripos in 1883 and came top in the entire list of candidates. He became president of the Cambridge Union in 1886 and a

potentially glittering career was confirmed when in 1888 he became a fellow of Downing. He relinquished his fellowship after his marriage, on 26 March 1892, to Mary Owen (b. 1864/5), captain of the Welsh Ladies Golf Union, and daughter of the Revd Robert Owen, a Methodist minister. Two of their three children died young.

While at Cambridge, Griffith had begun reading for the bar. In 1887 he was called to the bar by the Middle Temple and worked on the north Wales and Chester circuit. He built up a reputation as a cogent and witty speaker at the bar. He served as recorder of Birkenhead from 1907 to 1912 and took silk in 1910. His clients included Dr Edwards in the paternity case involving Lloyd George in 1897.

Though successful at the law, Griffith had long had political aspirations and in 1892 he fought (unsuccessfully) the Toxteth division of Liverpool as a Liberal. A Welsh-speaking Calvinistic Methodist, he was also intermittently involved in Lloyd George's *Cymru Fydd* campaign for Welsh home rule, despite tense relations with its leader. In the general election of 1895 Griffith was elected Liberal member for the safe seat of Anglesey, which he held for the next twenty-three years. He emerged as a powerful debater in the Commons. During the South African wars, though a strong Liberal Imperialist, he launched witty attacks on Joseph Chamberlain. It was Griffith who was credited with the *bon mot*, 'While the Empire expands, the Chamberlain contracts'. It was thought surprising that he did not receive government office after 1905 at a time when other Welshmen were promoted, though he did become chairman of the Welsh members of parliament in 1911. Eventually, in 1912, he was appointed undersecretary to the Home Office. Here, as a supporter of women's suffrage, he had to justify the treatment of suffragettes under the government's 'Cat and Mouse Act'. A major task was to carry the Welsh disestablishment bill through the Commons, and in this he performed effectively alongside the home secretary, Reginald McKenna. However, he resigned his office in January 1915 to return to the bar and proceeded to attack the government's policy on Welsh disestablishment thereafter on the grounds that it left open the possibility of a repeal after the war. Griffith did not hold office after the formation of the Asquith coalition in May 1915, but was prominent in the group of Liberals calling for the introduction of military conscription that summer and then backing Lloyd George as prime minister in place of Asquith. He became a privy counsellor in 1914 and a baronet in January 1918, under the title Sir Ellis Jones Ellis-Griffith, having assumed the additional surname Ellis by deed poll. His political career, however, did not progress after Lloyd George became premier, and Griffith seemed now more involved with his legal than his political career.

In the general election of 1918, Ellis-Griffith came under fire in his Anglesey constituency for his wartime support of conscription, and he was unexpectedly defeated by an unorthodox Labour candidate, Brigadier-General Sir Owen Thomas. He remained, broadly, a Lloyd George Liberal in the post-war period. Lloyd George, indeed, was frustrated when Lord Birkenhead, with whom Ellis-Griffith had crossed swords in the courts, turned down his proposal to make Ellis-Griffith a High Court judge in 1919. Ellis-Griffith failed in an attempt to become Liberal member for the University of Wales seat in the 1922 election, when he was narrowly defeated by an Asquithian Liberal, but he was elected to parliament again, for Carmarthen, in November 1923. He was now moving towards the right: when the Liberals voted to allow the first Labour government to take office in January 1924, Ellis-Griffith voted with the Conservatives. In the following summer he surprised the political world by announcing his retirement, to make way for Sir Alfred Mond, a Cambridge contemporary and owner of the Mond nickel works in which Griffith had held a lucrative directorship. Ellis-Griffith died suddenly, at the Hotel Metropole, Swansea, on 30 November 1926, while attending Swansea assizes, and was buried in Brynsiencyn. His younger and only surviving son, Elis Arundell Ellis-Griffith, succeeded to the title and died in June 1934, when the baronetcy became extinct.

A tall man of striking, if rustic, appearance, with a strong aquiline profile and dark wavy hair, Ellis-Griffith was a man of many political and rhetorical gifts, a fluent orator in both Welsh and English. Contemporaries expected him to become either a High Court judge or a cabinet minister, though he rose no higher than a recorder in the law and an under-secretary in politics. His political career became increasingly disengaged. He was frequently close to Lloyd George who, however, tended to be irritated by him as a somewhat patronizing snob who was also unduly uxorious. Despite his strong literary interests, his Welsh-language poetry was not distinguished. On balance Ellis-Griffith remained a talent unfulfilled.

KENNETH O. MORGAN

Sources NL Wales, Ellis Griffith papers · NL Wales, E. Morgan Humphreys papers · T. I. Ellis, *Ellis Jones Griffith* (1969) · T. I. Ellis, *Cofiant Thomas Edward Ellis*, 2 (1948) · E. M. Humphreys, *Gwŷr enwog gynt* (1950) · K. O. Morgan, *Wales in British politics, 1868–1922*, 3rd edn (1992) · K. O. Morgan, *Rebirth of a nation: Wales, 1880–1980* (1981) · K. O. Morgan, ed., *Lloyd George family letters, c.1885–1936* · A. Mee, ed., *Who's who in Wales* (1921) · *DWB* · E. L. Ellis, *The University College of Wales, Aberystwyth, 1872–1972* (1972) · Burke, *Peerage* (1924) · b. cert. · m. cert. · d. cert.

Archives NL Wales, diaries, corresp., and papers · NL Wales, notes on sermons heard | NL Wales, letters to D. R. Daniel · NL Wales, T. E. Ellis papers · NL Wales, David Lloyd George papers · NL Wales, E. Morgan Humphreys papers

Likenesses O. Birley, oils, c.1912–1914, U. Wales, Aberystwyth, Hugh Owen Library

Wealth at death £10,884 2s. 2d.: probate, 1927, *CGPLA Eng. & Wales*

Griffith, Francis Llewellyn (1862–1934), Egyptologist, was born on 27 May 1862 in Brighton, one of nine children, and the youngest of six sons, of John Griffith (1817/18–1892), headmaster (1856–71) of Brighton College, and later (1872–91) vicar of Sandridge, near St Albans, and his wife, Sara Eliza, daughter of Richard Foster, banker, of Cambridge. Griffith was educated briefly at Brighton College (1871), then privately by his father until he went to Sedbergh School, Yorkshire (1875–8) and Highgate School (1878–80). At Highgate he developed the interest in ancient Egypt that was to determine the rest of his life. He

won a scholarship to the Queen's College, Oxford, in 1879 and studied there from 1880 to 1882, but refused to read for honours, preferring to spend his time learning hieroglyphs. Egyptology was not taught in Oxford at that time, but he received encouragement from A. H. Sayce, later professor of Assyriology.

In 1882 Griffith was articled to one of his brothers, a solicitor in Brighton, but he did not enjoy the work. In 1884 he graduated with a pass degree, and on the recommendation of Sheldon Amos, professor of jurisprudence at University College, London, he applied to W. M. Flinders Petrie for a position with the Egypt Exploration Fund (EEF). The fund launched an appeal to raise money for an official studentship, and thanks mainly to donations from his aunt, Sophy Foster, and a family friend, Henry Willet, Griffith was enabled to go to Egypt as Petrie's assistant. In the winter of 1884–5 they excavated at Nibeira (ancient Naucratis) and the following season at Tell Nabasha (Imet). In 1886–7 Griffith and Petrie journeyed up river from Minya to Aswan, recording inscriptions, most importantly in Griffith's case those from the rock tombs at Beni Hasan; Griffith then assisted Edouard Naville to excavate at Tell al-Yahudiyyah.

When Griffith's studentship expired, no Egyptological post was open, so in 1888 he became an assistant in the department of British and medieval antiquities at the British Museum. He was, however, allowed to spend his free time on Egyptology. During this period he published his first important book, *Inscriptions of Siût and Dêr Rîfeh* (1889), based on his work in Upper Egypt, which included a plea for the adequate recording of endangered monuments. As a result, the EEF set up its Archaeological Survey in 1890, with Griffith as its supervisor. He was its director from 1926 until his death. He edited twenty-five of its publications, to an excellent standard. He also initiated and edited the EEF's annual *Archaeological Report* which appeared from 1892 to 1912, and compiled annual bibliographies of the subject until 1926. In 1892 Petrie became the first professor of Egyptology at University College, London. Griffith acted as his assistant from 1893 to 1901, being responsible for the linguistic side of the new course, although he had to work on an unofficial basis because of opposition from R. S. Poole, the professor of classical archaeology.

In the summer of 1896 Griffith married Kate [**Kate Griffith** (1854–1902)]. She was born on 26 August 1854 in Ashton under Lyne, the daughter of Charles Timothy Bradbury (d. 1907), a wealthy manufacturer, and his wife, Elizabeth Ann, née Tomlins. Kate became the friend and companion of Amelia B. Edwards, the novelist and principal founder of the EEF (1882), and herself took an active part in the fund's work, serving on the committee and accompanying Edwards on her fundraising tour of the USA in 1890. In 1892 she became the main executor of Edwards's will, which endowed the new chair of Egyptology at University College, London; she also furthered the process by, among other things, paying most of the legacy duty herself.

The marriage settlement arranged by her father allowed

Frank Griffith (as he was generally known) to spend all his time on Egyptology. He gave up his museum post and moved into the Bradbury family home, Riversvale, in Ashton under Lyne, becoming honorary lecturer in Egyptology (1896–1908) at Manchester University. Kate Griffith collaborated on her husband's publications, in particular, a translation of selected Egyptian texts for *A Library of the World's Great Literature* (1897), and herself translated two standard works on Egyptian religion from the German of Karl Wiedemann (1856–1936).

In 1901 the University of Oxford decided to begin teaching Egyptology, and Griffith was appointed the first reader. That autumn Kate fell ill. She died on 2 March 1902 at Shieling, Silverdale, near Carnforth, Lancashire. At her wish Griffith continued to live at Riversvale until his father-in-law also died (16 April 1907), bequeathing most of his fortune to Griffith. He now moved to 11 Norham Gardens, Oxford, his home for the next twenty-five years. In 1909 he donated £8000 of his new wealth to the university, to establish a fund to encourage Egyptological research, as a memorial to his late wife.

The same year he married his second wife, Nora [**Nora Christina Cobban Griffith** (1870–1937)]. She was born on 7 December 1870, the daughter of Surgeon-Major James Macdonald of Aberdeen, and sister of General Sir J. R. L. *Macdonald (1862–1927). She took a keen interest in antiquities and was for a while a conservator in the Archaeological Museum of King's College, Aberdeen. She had become interested in Egypt on a visit in 1906, and had briefly been a pupil of Griffith's at Oxford. After their marriage she assisted with many of her husband's projects, especially as an illustrator, at which she showed considerable skill. She accompanied him as an assistant and recorder on a series of Oxford excavations in Nubia which he organized in 1910–13, financed partly by the fund he had set up in 1909. They excavated at Faras and Sanam in the Sudan before the work was interrupted by the First World War, during which Griffith spent most of his time helping in Oxford hospitals. The Griffiths mounted further excavations in Egypt (Tell al-Amarna, 1923–4) and the Sudan (Kawa, 1930–31). In 1924 Griffith was elected a fellow of the British Academy, and the same year Oxford appointed him first professor of Egyptology, which he remained until his retirement in 1932. He then moved to Sandridge, Boars Hill, on the outskirts of Oxford, but continued as deputy professor, and was made professor emeritus in 1933.

Griffith was one of the fathers of British Egyptology, and his reputation and generosity combined to give the subject a permanent base in Oxford. His impressive talents lay mainly in linguistics and decipherment, and his archaeological work was always primarily concerned with the discovery and recording of texts. His first step in the subject had been to learn the language by himself, a formidable task in the days before modern grammars, and his first publication in this area, *Hieratic Papyri from Kahun and Gurob* (1898), was a masterpiece of the decipherer's and editor's skills, for the diverse texts were mostly fragmentary and written in an early cursive previously untackled by scholars. He then became involved with the latest and most difficult cursive form of Egyptian writing, demotic, about which relatively little was known at the time. His edition of two long literary texts, *Stories of the High Priests of Memphis* (2 vols., 1900), placed him at the forefront of this discipline, which few even among Egyptologists master. It became a standard work, as did *The Demotic Magical Papyrus of London and Leiden* (3 vols., 1904–9), produced in collaboration with his former pupil at University College, Herbert Thompson. His greatest achievement was the monumental *Catalogue of Demotic Papyri in the John Rylands Library* (3 vols., 1909), which became known as the 'demotist's bible' because of its accuracy and exhaustiveness. From 1907 he turned much of his attention to the obscure languages of the kingdoms to the south of Egypt, Meroitic and Old Nubian, in which he made considerable progress, especially by his decipherment of the Meroitic script (see Griffith, *Karanòg: the Meroitic Inscriptions*, 1911). A full bibliography of his prolific output, by Nora Griffith, is given in *Studies Presented to F. Ll. Griffith* (1932), to which seventy scholars contributed. Another of his legacies to Egyptology was the foundation of the long-term project to index the inscriptions from all the sites of Egypt, the *Topographical Bibliography of Ancient Egyptian Hieroglyphic Texts, Reliefs, and Paintings*, edited by Bertha Porter and Rosalind Moss, and from 1973 by Jaromír Málek (7 vols., 1927–51; revised edn, 1960–).

By nature Griffith was shy and unassuming, and often absent-minded, but good-natured, patient, hard-working, and always ready to further the studies and careers of his pupils. They did not always find it easy to follow his lectures, although his written answers to problems were greatly valued. Apart from Egyptology, his chief interests in youth were natural history, walking, and croquet; in later life, under the influence of his second wife, he became more sociable, taking up golf and tennis; the couple became well known for their extensive hospitality.

Griffith died suddenly from a heart attack at home on 14 March 1934 and was buried in Holywell cemetery, Oxford, on 17 March. He left most of his substantial fortune (after his wife's life interest) to Oxford University, to build and endow a permanent centre for teaching and research in Egyptology and related subjects, and to house his superb library of more than 20,000 volumes, the finest private Egyptological library in the world. After his death Nora Griffith kept it up to date; she devoted most of her time to preparing her husband's numerous unfinished works for press, and organized and financed further Nubian excavations in 1934–6. She died of peritonitis, following an appendectomy, at the Acland Home, Banbury Road, Oxford, on 21 October 1937, leaving her own considerable fortune to be added to her husband's bequest.

R. S. SIMPSON

Sources personal knowledge (1949) [*DNB*] · private information (1949) · *Journal of Egyptian Archaeology*, 20 (1934), 71–7 · W. E. Crum, 'Francis Llewellyn Griffith, 1862–1934', *PBA*, 20 (1934), 309–22 · *The Times* (15 March 1934), 16 · *Oxford Magazine* (26 April 1934), 600–02 ·

Egypt Exploration Fund Archaeological Report (1901–2), 37 [Kate Griffith] · *Journal of Egyptian Archaeology*, 23 (1937), 262–3 [Nora Griffith] · *The Times* (25 Oct 1937), 20 [Nora Griffith] · *The Times* (16 Dec 1937), 19 [Nora Griffith] · W. R. Dawson and E. P. Uphill, *Who was who in Egyptology*, 3rd edn, rev. M. L. Bierbrier (1995), 179–81 · M. S. Drower, *Flinders Petrie* (1985) · R. M. Janssen, *The first hundred years: Egyptology at University College London, 1892–1992* (1992) · *Studies presented to F. Ll. Griffith* (1932), 485–94 [bibliography] · B. Wilson, ed., *The Sedbergh School register, 1546–1909* (1909) · *A roll of the school, 1833–1912*, Highgate School (1913) · Boase, *Mod. Eng. biog.*, 5.511–12 [John Griffith] · *WWW*, 1929–40 · d. certs. [Francis Griffith; Nora Griffith] · *CGPLA Eng. & Wales* (1902) [Kate Griffith] · *DNB***Archives** U. Oxf., Griffith Institute, papers incl. notes, notebooks, photographs, squeezes, records of Oxford excavations in Nubia, and corresp. | Bodl. Oxf., letters to J. L. Myres · Egypt Exploration Society, London, corresp. with the Egypt Exploration Society **Likenesses** photograph, *c*.1900 (with Kate Griffith), AM Oxf.; repro. in Janssen, *First hundred years* (1992), 11 · photograph, *c*.1900, AM Oxf.; repro. in Dawson and Uphill, *Who was who in Egyptology* (1995), 180 · K. Green, oils, 1932, AM Oxf. · W. Stoneman, photograph, 1932, NPG · charcoal?, AM Oxf.; repro. in *Journal of Egyptian Archaeology* (1934), 13 · photograph (Nora Griffith), AM Oxf. **Wealth at death** £60,877 15*s*. 0*d*.: resworn probate, 18 May 1934, *CGPLA Eng. & Wales* · £52,474 4*s*. 10*d*.—Nora Griffith: resworn probate, Aug 1938, *CGPLA Eng. & Wales* · £29,305 8*s*. 3*d*.—Kate Griffith: resworn probate, Sept 1902, *CGPLA Eng. & Wales*

Griffith, George (1601–1666/7), bishop of St Asaph, was born at Llanfaethlu, Anglesey, on 30 September 1601, the third son of Robert Griffith of Carreglwyd, Anglesey, and Ann, daughter of Owen ap Hugh Griffith of Gwnwnog. He attended Westminster School before matriculating on 12 November 1619 from Christ Church, Oxford, from where he graduated BA on 20 June 1623. One of the original scholars of Pembroke College in 1624 he proceeded MA on 9 May 1626.

In 1627 Griffith's eldest brother, William Griffith (1595/6–1648), became chancellor of the diocese of St Asaph, transferring in 1629 to Bangor. George, who was considered a popular preacher and tutor, became chaplain to William's father-in-law, John Owen, consecrated bishop of St Asaph in September 1629. George's promotion was rapid: in 1631 he became rector of Newtown; in 1632 he became archdeacon of St Asaph and rector of Llandrinio, and proceeded BD; in 1633 he was licensed to preach and became rector of Llanfechain (exchanged in 1634 for Llanymynech); in the latter year he proceeded DD. Probably during this decade he married Jane, daughter of Thomas Cobbe or Corbet of Grange, Hampshire; they had one son and five daughters. He resisted paying ship money on his livings in Shropshire until forced to, and he refused to deliver a warrant against others who resisted. In the 1640 convocation it is said that he called for a new edition of the Welsh Bible to replace the 1620 version by Bishop Richard Parry and Dr John Davies of Mallwyd.

Nothing is known of Griffith's activities in the remainder of the 1640s. Because the Act for the Propagation of the Gospel in Wales (1650) allowed clergy to hold only one living he retained his living at Llanymynech on condition that he yielded Llandrinio. During the mid-1650s he attempted to compromise with the puritan authorities by recommending preachers to the Triers and disputed publicly with the puritan Vavasor Powell at Newchapel, Montgomeryshire, on 23 July 1652, on which occasion he defended formal rather than extempore prayers. The dispute was subsequently broadened to include forms of worship and church government. Powell wrote his account of the dispute in the *Perfect Diurnal*, while Griffith produced three tracts, *A Bold Challenge of an Itinerant Preacher* (1652), *A Relation of a Disputation between Dr Griffith and Mr V. Powell* (1653), and *A Welsh Narrative Corrected and Taught to Speak True English and some Latine* (1653), a work which describes the content of the disputation.

Following the Restoration, Griffith was among the first newly installed bishops. Supported by Gilbert Sheldon, bishop elect of London, he was elected bishop of St Asaph on 17 October, confirmed on 24 October and consecrated on 28 October (the same day as Sheldon) in the King Henry VII Chapel at Westminster, the day when he also subscribed to the oath of supremacy and allegiance. He increased his income threefold by keeping his living of Llanymynech, *in commendam*, and adding to it Llandrinio, the archdeaconry of St Asaph, and rectory of Llanrhaeadr-ym-Mochnant, after having petitioned on the grounds that his bishopric was 'insufficient to maintain the state of a prelate, to bear the necessary incumbrances and repair the ruined church' (Thomas, 2.245). He regularly attended the House of Lords from November 1661 to March 1665, was a member of a convocation committee to reconsider the legality of the 1640 canons, contributed to the formulation of the Act of Uniformity (1662) in the House of Lords, and drew up the form of adult baptism in the 1661 prayer book. In that year he published *Articles of enquiry concerning matters ecclesiastical exhibited in his primary episcopal visitation*, which occurred in 1662. Like his predecessor, John Owen, he insisted that sermons in Welsh should be delivered in St Asaph parish church on a monthly basis. The production of the Welsh translation of the revised Book of Common Prayer, promised for May 1665 in the Act of Uniformity, was entrusted to the Welsh bishops and the bishop of Hereford, and it seems that Griffith did most of the work. He also may have written 'On some omissions and mistakes in the British translation of the Bible' (*c*.1672).

By the time Griffith drew up his will, on 16 November 1666, he was ill and his wife was almost certainly dead. The chief beneficiaries were his son, Thomas, and daughters Susan and Jane; John Middleton, husband of his eldest daughter, and John Edwards, his successor at Llanymynech (1666) and eventually as chancellor of the diocese, were also mentioned. He died within a few weeks and was buried in the choir of St Asaph Cathedral; his will was proved by his son on 2 January 1667. Two works appeared posthumously: *Plain Discourses on the Lord's Supper* (1684) and *Gweddi'r arglwydd wedi ei hegluro* ('The Lord's prayer explained' 1685), twenty-two short discourses or sermons intended to explain the content of the Lord's prayer to ordinary parishioners.   J. GWYNFOR JONES

Sources BL, Lansdowne MS 984, fol. 59 · *Fasti Angl.* (Hardy), 1.76 · Foster, *Alum. Oxon.* · Wood, *Ath. Oxon.*, new edn, 3.754–6, 915 · D. R.

Thomas, *Esgobaeth Llanelwy: the history of the diocese of St Asaph*, rev. edn, 3 vols. (1908–13), 1.225, 546; 2.226; 3.36, 159 • B. Willis, *Survey of the Cathedral Church of St Asaph* (1720), 89, 266–7 • *CSP dom.*, 1636–7, 569; 1660–61, 322, 325 • will, PRO, PROB 11/323, sig. 2 • T. Fuller, *The church history of Britain*, ed. J. Nichols, 3rd edn, 3 (1842), 408–9 • E. Cardwell, *Synodalia* (1842), 2.644–5, 661, 665 • J. E. Griffith, *Pedigrees of Anglesey and Carnarvonshire families* (privately printed, Horncastle, 1914), 26 • *DWB*, 292–3 • G. H. Jenkins, *Literature, religion and society in Wales, 1660–1730* (1978), 78, 118, 201, 213, 215, 226 • C. Edwards, *Y Ffydd-ddiffuant*, ed. G. J. Williams (1936), xxv–xxvi • G. M. Griffiths, 'The restoration in St Asaph: the episcopate of Bishop George Griffith, 1660–1666', *Journal of the Historical Society of the Church in Wales*, 12 (1962), 9–27; 13 (1963), 27–40 • G. M. Griffiths, 'Some extradiocesan activities of Bishop George Griffith of St Asaph, 1660–6', *National Library of Wales Journal*, 12 (1962), 298–301 • memorial, St Asaph Cathedral

Likenesses E. Harding, stipple, 1800 (after oil painting in Christ Church Oxf.), BM, NPG • oils, Christ Church Oxf. • portrait, bishop's palace, St Asaph, Denbighshire • portrait, Trawsgoed Hall, Cardiganshire

Wealth at death approx. £800: will, PRO, PROB 11/323, sig. 2

Griffith [Griffiths], **George** (1618?–1699×1702), Independent minister, was born a younger son in Montgomeryshire. The Griffiths enjoyed good relations with Sir Robert and Lady Brilliana Harley. On 2 November 1638 Griffith, aged nineteen, matriculated from Magdalen Hall, Oxford, where he was a servitor to Sir Robert's son, Edward. When Griffith tired of service and desired to study divinity Sir Robert approved. Griffith graduated BA on 14 June 1642, and three years later proceeded MA from Emmanuel College, Cambridge. By parliamentary order of 13 February 1646 he became a fellow of Trinity College, Cambridge.

On 6 June 1648 Griffith accepted an appointment as preacher at the Charterhouse, London, where his wife, Elizabeth, joined him by special indulgence in 1651 (the first woman permitted to live there). Recognizing his preaching ability, the Haberdashers' Company named him John Downham's successor as William Jones lecturer at St Bartholomew's Exchange in 1650, and two years later it appointed him to examine candidates for ecclesiastical preferments in the company's control. With John Owen, William Greenhill, and seven other ministers Griffith assisted a House of Commons committee in drafting a condemnation of the Socinians' Racovian catechism in February 1652, and the same year he and eleven other Independent clergy urged parliament to support missions to Native Americans; their letter was published in Henry Whitfield's *Strengthe out of Weaknesse* (1652). As the Rump Parliament debated doctrinal articles in 1653, Griffith and ten other clergymen drafted a statement in February insisting that no one be permitted to preach or publish anything opposed to Christian principles (of which they identified sixteen) plainly affirmed in the Bible and deemed essential for salvation. In April, as John Dury prepared to leave for Sweden, he recommended Griffith, a young man 'zealous for the aime of Peace [and] no wayes engaged in any Party' (Keeble and Nuttall, 1.95), to assist Richard Baxter's efforts to promote ecumenical unity, but Griffith, whom Baxter came to respect as godly and orthodox, was of little help.

Griffith was appointed to the commission for ejecting scandalous ministers on 28 August 1654 and the commission for the approbation of public preachers five days later. In the latter capacity he took special interest in seeing that qualified ministers were dispatched to his native Wales. When protestants in Piedmont suffered persecution, the council of state on 4 January 1656 appointed Griffith, Richard Cromwell, and others to a committee to provide aid, and two months later the council named him to the committee to draft statutes for Durham College. One of London's most prominent preachers, Griffith preached a fast sermon to the House of Commons on 30 October 1656. Two months later parliament appointed him to the committee to counsel the Quaker James Nayler following his sentencing. The council turned to Griffith again in July 1657, this time to mediate a dispute between two Scottish clerical factions, the resolutioners and remonstrants, and in October it appointed him to the commission for ejecting scandalous ministers in Middlesex. He again preached to the Commons on 27 January 1658, defending Cromwell's toleration policy and calling for increased financial support for ministers, especially in Wales and the north. He was also interested in protestantism's progress in Ireland, praising Henry Cromwell for supporting this endeavour. Presumably for his loyalty to the government, on 3 March 1658 he was appointed lecturer to the Independent congregation meeting in Westminster Abbey. In December, Richard Shute, as patron, recommended Griffith to the Triers for appointment as rector of St Mary's, Barnes, Surrey. In the meantime, following a meeting of elders of Independent churches in the London area in June 1658, Griffith invited congregational churches to send delegates to a conference at the Savoy Palace in September. At the conference, which produced a declaration of faith, he served as scribe. He was one of the few Independents who participated in Matthew Poole's efforts to support presbyterian and congregational students in the universities. During the political turmoil following Cromwell's death, Griffith conferred with Owen, Charles Fleetwood, and others, and he almost certainly joined Owen in supporting the Rump's recall in the spring of 1659. While Philip Nye and Thomas Brooks backed Desborough's attempt to preserve republican government by force, Griffith and Joseph Caryl opted to trust Monck and the convention.

Accepting the Restoration gracefully, Griffith joined other Independents in signing an address of loyalty to Charles in May 1660. Following Thomas Venner's uprising in January 1661 Griffith signed *A Renuntiation and Declaration* denouncing it. By the autumn he had lost his position at the Charterhouse, though an informer's allegation in December that he had spoken treasonably against the king was almost certainly baseless. Unable for reasons of conscience to take the oaths prescribed by the Act of Uniformity, Griffith resigned the Jones lectureship on 27 September 1662. Yet he refused to be silent, holding services with John Owen, George Cokayne, Thomas Goodwin, and Matthew Barker in a house near the Guildhall. A man of wealth, Griffith sent money to needy Independent and Baptist clergy in Wales during the 1660s. From 1666 to

1694 he ministered to a congregation that met first in Plasterers' Hall and subsequently in Girdlers' Hall. Following the fire of London, Baxter reported that more citizens attended the services of ministers such as Griffith and Owen than those in the parish churches. In 1669 Griffith shared a lectureship at Hackney with fellow congregationalists Owen, Nye, Brooks, and Peter Sterry, and the presbyterians Thomas Watson and William Bates. As congregationalist leaders Griffith and Owen counselled the Independent church at Hitchin, Hertfordshire, and John Bunyan's Bedford congregation identified Griffith's church as an appropriate place for its members to transfer to if they moved to London. When magistrates and ministers in Boston, Massachusetts, needed advice on a new president for Harvard, student recruitment, and financial assistance, they wrote to Griffith and eighteen others in August 1671; the latter responded in February. Under the declaration of indulgence's terms, on 22 April 1672 Griffith was licensed to preach at his house in Addle Street. Nearly a month earlier, Griffith, Owen, and Anthony Palmer had personally thanked Charles for the declaration.

Periodically Griffith was the subject of suspicion. The minister George Vernon depicted him as part of a congregational spy ring led by Owen. More serious was a government warrant in June 1671 to search his house for Richard Cromwell, weapons, and suspicious documents. He was under suspicion again in the summer and autumn of 1682, when he was zealously preaching against Catholicism and arbitrary government. Such views and his close friendship with Lord Wharton suggest that he held whig principles. By the spring of 1683 he was dangerously close to members of Monmouth's cabal as it planned an insurrection. Griffith, Owen, and Matthew Meade allegedly discussed such plans with William Carstares, and Monmouth himself exaggeratedly claimed that the three men and 'all the considerable Nonconformist Ministers knew of the Conspiracy' (PRO, SP 29/434/98). For preaching illegally he was fined £20 in March 1684, and in October he was arrested as a dangerous person. Imprisonment, if any, was brief, for shortly thereafter he moved his congregation from Plasterers' Hall to Girdlers' Hall.

As crisis engulfed England in 1688 Griffith, William Bates, and John Howe supported the archbishop of Canterbury and six bishops when they protested against James's declaration of indulgence. In October the three men were part of a delegation that rebuffed James's request for support, though they pledged their prayers and obedience. Throughout the crisis Griffith, Bates, Howe, and Baxter worked to maintain nonconformist unity. By January 1690 tensions surfaced between Baxter and Daniel Williams on one side and Griffith, Cokayne, and others over the latter group's commendatory epistle to the Antinomian Tobias Crisp's *Christ Alone Exalted* (1689). Yet congregationalists and presbyterians established the Common Fund, with Griffith as one of fourteen managers, in 1690 to assist clergymen and educate ministerial students. He was also a founder of the Congregational Fund Board in December 1695. Four years later Griffith, Meade, Stephen Lobb, Richard Taylor, and John Nesbitt

wrote *A Declaration of the Congregational Ministers* condemning the disruption caused by the Antinomian controversy. After making his will on 15 June 1698, in his eighty-first year, Griffith added a codicil on 29 June 1699. He died, presumably in London, between that date and 17 April 1702, when the will was proved. His will reflects his wealth: his eldest son, Richard, and his daughter Elizabeth had already received their portions, and thus had bequests of only £20 and £200 respectively, but Griffith gave his younger son, Henry, £800 (reduced to £320 in the codicil), and his other daughter, Anne, £1000. Calamy described Griffith as 'very conversible, and much the gentleman' (*Nonconformist's Memorial*, 1.107). Historically Griffith's importance rests on the continuity of leadership he provided for the congregationalists from the late 1640s to the end of the century.   RICHARD L. GREAVES

Sources Foster, *Alum. Oxon.* · R. L. Greaves, *Saints and rebels: seven nonconformists in Stuart England* (1985), 77–97 · Venn, *Alum. Cant.*, 1/2.266 · PRO, State MSS [SP], 29/419/162; 29/434/98 · *Calamy rev.* · *Calendar of the correspondence of Richard Baxter*, ed. N. H. Keeble and G. F. Nuttall, 1 (1991), 95, 326–7, 421; 2 (1991), 301 · *The nonconformist's memorial … originally written by … Edmund Calamy*, ed. S. Palmer, [3rd edn], 3 vols. (1802–3) · C. H. Firth and R. S. Rait, eds., *Acts and ordinances of the interregnum, 1642–1660*, 3 vols. (1911) · *JHC*, 7 (1651–9), 447, 579, 588 · *CSP dom., 1655–60*; *1663–4*; *1671–2*; *1677–8*; *1682–3* · *Letters of the Lady Brilliana Harley*, ed. T. T. Lewis, CS, 58 (1854) · *Diary of Thomas Burton*, ed. J. T. Rutt, 4 vols. (1828), vol. 1, pp. 183–4; vol. 2, pp. 321, 372–3 · Bodl. Oxf., MS Rawl. letters 104, fols. 37–40 · LPL, MS Comm. II.44 · will, PRO, PROB 11/464, sig. 62
Archives LPL, MS Comm. II.44 | BL, Birch MSS · BL, Lansdowne MS 823, fol. 43 · Bodl. Oxf., MSS Rawl., vols. 50–52 · Bodl. Oxf., Rawlinson letters, 104 · DWL, Baxter MS 6.87; RNC MS 38.18 (p. 76)
Likenesses R. White, portrait · portrait, DWL
Wealth at death £1600: *Calamy rev.*

Griffith, Hugh Emrys (1912–1980), actor, was born on 30 May 1912 at Angorfa, Llaneugrad on the island of Anglesey, north Wales, the son of William Griffith and his wife, Mary Owen, *née* Williams. He grew up in the bilingual community of north Wales and attended the local grammar school at Llangefni. He started work in 1929 as a bank clerk but had developed an interest in acting and in 1937 left Wales to enrol as a student at the Royal Academy of Dramatic Art (1938–9); in 1939 he was awarded the Bancroft gold medal and made his first appearances on the London stage in J. M. Synge's *The Playboy of the Western World*, and *Julius Caesar*. His career was interrupted by the outbreak of war, which he spent in service with the Royal Welch Fusiliers, serving in the Far East. On his return he joined the company of the Shakespeare Memorial Theatre at Stratford upon Avon, then enjoying a revival in its fortunes under the direction of Sir Barry Jackson. There his successes included Holofernes, in the youthful Peter Brook's production of *Love's Labour's Lost*, and Mephistopheles in Marlowe's *Doctor Faustus* (1947). On 28 October 1947 Griffith married Adelgunde Margaret Beatrice von Dechend (*b.* 1910/11); they had no children.

Gifted with a commanding stage presence, Griffith established a reputation as a distinctive character actor who excelled in roles combining shrewd, sometimes brooding, humour with sudden bursts of emotion. On the London stage he appeared in Christopher Fry's *The Dark is*

Light Enough (1956) and as General St Pé in Jean Anouilh's *The Waltz of the Toreadors* (1956). He continued to act at Stratford and the Royal Shakespeare Company's London home in the Aldwych Theatre, achieving his greatest successes as the anarchic Judge Azdak in Bertolt Brecht's *The Caucasian Chalk Circle* (1962) and as Falstaff in 1964. His preferred Shakespearian role was Lear, which he once performed in Welsh for the BBC, although most critics preferred him in roles which gave him scope for his sardonic temperament. His New York début took place in 1951, when he appeared in Anouilh's *Legend of Lovers*, which had been presented in London under the title *Point of Departure* the previous year. In 1972 he undertook a European Shakespeare tour for the British Council.

Griffith's film career began with *Neutral Port* (1940) before it was interrupted by military service during the war; subsequently he starred in over fifty films and it was among the wide range of roles that he played on the screen (and later on television) that his abilities as a Welsh character actor were displayed. One of his first post-war film appearances was in *The Last Days of Dolwyn* (1948), a film about the industrial valleys of south Wales in the nineteenth century. In 1953 he appeared with Laurence Olivier in a film version of *The Beggar's Opera*; his performance as Sheik Ilderim in *Ben Hur* (1959) received the Academy award for best supporting actor, and his Squire Western in *Tom Jones* (1963) was nominated for an Academy award. The last film in which he played, with David Niven, was *A Nightingale Sang in Berkeley Square* (1979). From the middle of the 1960s onwards he performed frequently on radio and television.

The University of Wales awarded Griffith an honorary doctorate in literature in 1965. He died at his home, 64 Campbell Court, Kensington, London, on 14 May 1980.

MICHAEL ANDERSON

Sources *The Times* (15 May 1980) · M. Deaves, *Annual Obituary* (1981) · *WWW* · *CGPLA Eng. & Wales* (1980) · b. cert. · m. cert. · d. cert.
Archives FILM BFI NFTVA, performance footage | SOUND BFI NFTVA, performance recordings
Wealth at death £27,237: probate, 28 Nov 1980, *CGPLA Eng. & Wales*

Griffith, John (*fl.* 1524–1554). *See under* Griffith, John (*fl.* 1539).

Griffith, John (*fl.* 1539), Cistercian monk, was once believed to have been a celebrated preacher whose career continued even after the dissolution of his house, that of Hailes, Gloucestershire, in 1539. The antiquary Thomas Tanner, drawing on the notes of Leland and Bale, identifies him as the author of two Latin sermon cycles said to have enjoyed a wide contemporary circulation. In reality, this John Griffith is a fiction, the result of the conflation of two different men bearing the same name. There was a John Griffith who was a monk of Hailes during the 1530s. He was among twenty-two members of the community who witnessed the surrender of the abbey on 31 December 1539, when he appears as sixth in order of seniority. There is no evidence, however, that he was a scholar; he was not among the Hailes monks who studied at Oxford,

and he is not known to have written or published anything.

John Griffith the Cistercian has been confused—by Tanner and others—with another **John Griffith** (*fl.* 1524–1554), a secular priest who was active in the same period. This man studied theology at Oxford during the 1520s and 1530s, holding a fellowship at Oriel College from 1524 to 1543. He held a variety of offices in the college, including that of treasurer in 1535, founder's chaplain in 1536, and dean between 1537 and 1541. He also served as university preacher in 1535 and collator of university sermons in 1543. He left Oxford in the latter year and from 1548 was vicar of Holy Rood, Southampton. In 1554 he returned to his native Wales, becoming vicar of Penally, Pembrokeshire. Probably it was this John Griffith who was the author of the sermon cycles *de sanctis* and *de tempore* whose incipits were recorded by Leland and Bale. Nothing further is known of him.

JAMES G. CLARK

Sources Tanner, *Bibl. Brit.-Hib.*, 343 · Emden, *Oxf.*, 4.248 · *LP Henry VIII*, 7, appx 35 · Bale, *Index*, 211 · Dugdale, *Monasticon*, new edn, 5.689

Griffith, John (1621/2–1700), General Baptist minister, was of unknown parentage and nothing is known of his early background. He was presumably educated, however, since he was frequently known as Dr Griffith; it is uncertain whether this title reflected a medical or theological degree, or was simply a popular epithet.

Around 1640 Griffith became a preacher and began to gather a congregation, which subsequently met in Dunning's Alley, Bishopsgate Street Without, in London; he was ordained pastor of this church in 1646. Little is known of Griffith for the next fourteen years, although he published a number of doctrinal treatises throughout this period, defending in particular the practice of laying hands upon baptized believers.

Upon the Restoration, Griffith was constantly prosecuted under the Conventicle Act and for refusing to take the oath of allegiance. In 1661 he was imprisoned in Newgate for preaching unlawfully. Released seventeen months later, he published *Some Prison-Meditations* (1663), reflecting upon his experience of imprisonment, and resumed his pastoral activities as circumstances permitted. In 1675 Griffith was summoned to a congregation in Amersham, Buckinghamshire, which had divided over the issue of laying on of hands. Griffith laid hands on the proponents and formed them into a separate congregation, subsequently maintaining close contact with the new church.

In 1683 Griffith was tried with Francis Bampfield at the Old Bailey for refusing to take the oath of allegiance. Committed again to Newgate prison, he proceeded to publish *The Case of Mr. John Griffith* (1683). This brief account of his trial, enumerating the grounds upon which he was unable in conscience to take the oath of allegiance, nevertheless exposed the false reasoning of his persecutors and became a rallying cry for other nonconformists. The duration of this imprisonment is uncertain, though he was still confined in Newgate in January 1686.

Griffith's final years, lived under the Toleration Act,

appear to have been free from persecution. He died, in his seventy-ninth year, on 16 May 1700, and was buried four days later. No details survive of his personal life or marital status. Richard Allen tells us in his funeral sermon, however, that Griffith was a man of 'sincere zeal', if 'too strait and narrow' in some of his opinions (Allen, 42). An attentive pastor, Griffith's significance within Baptist history is summarized by the fact that, in Allen's words, he spent fourteen years 'in *Sufferings*, *Bonds* and *Imprisonments* … in the Testimony of a good Conscience' (ibid., 43).

BETH LYNCH

Sources W. Wilson, *The history and antiquities of the dissenting churches and meeting houses in London, Westminster and Southwark*, 4 vols. (1808–14), vol. 2 • A. Taylor, *The history of the English General Baptists*, 1: *The English General Baptists of the seventeenth century* (1818) • R. Allen, *A gainful death the end of a truly Christian life* (1700) [funeral sermon] • C. E. Whiting, *Studies in English puritanism* (1931); repr. (1968) • J. Griffith, *The case of Mr. John Griffith: minister of the gospel, and now prisoner in Newgate* (1683) • T. Crosby, *The history of the English Baptists, from the Reformation to the beginning of the reign of King George I*, 4 vols. (1738–40), vol. 2 • Wing, *STC* • J. Ivimey, *A history of the English Baptists*, 4 vols. (1811–30) • J. H. Wood, *A condensed history of the General Baptists of the New Connexion* (1847)

Griffith, John (1713–1776), Quaker minister, was born in Radnor on 21 July 1713, the son of John Griffith (*d*. 1745), and Amy, whose maiden name was possibly Morgan of Radnor. He was 'favoured with parents who had the substance of religion in themselves, and were conscientiously concerned to train up their children in the fear of God' (*Journal of the Life*, 14). His mother was a Quaker and Griffith records that she was 'a steady valuable Friend … having at times a few words, by way of testimony, tenderly to drop in religious meetings; which were acceptable to Friends' (ibid.). His father also became a member by convincement and, later, a minister among the Friends, who left 'a good report behind him among all sorts of people' (ibid., 15).

In his youth Griffith was inclined to fill his mind with 'vain, unprofitable, and sometimes wicked and blasphemous thoughts' which were 'a great affliction to him' (*Journal of the Life*, 16). As a consequence, and in spite of his parents best intentions, he fell into bad company before embarking for America from Milford Haven in 1726, aged thirteen. He wrote in his journal that the passage took eight weeks, during which time three babies were born and none of the eighty to ninety passengers died. On his arrival in America he was greeted by his uncle John Morgan, who lived 12 miles from Philadelphia. Griffith then lodged with him while his brother, who presumably emigrated at the same time, lived with his aunt Mary Parnel and followed his trade as a weaver. Griffith at this time had not reformed his character and was prepared to 'gratify a vain mind in the foolish amusements of a transitory world', and attended Friends' meetings from habit rather than from conviction (ibid., 19). He continued to act in such a manner until one of his companions came close to dying after a serious incident occurred in which Griffith was the ringleader. This had a dramatic effect upon his life, as he commented in his journal that his conversion 'struck them with some awe, for I observed they had not

the boldness to mock or deride me before my face' (ibid., 24–5).

In July 1734, when he was twenty-one, Griffith became a Quaker minister and gifted speaker at the Abingdon meeting in Pennsylvania. He remained faithful to his calling for the next forty-two years and began his first missionary journey around America in October 1736. On 30 December 1737 he married Rebekah Fearn (*d*. in or after 1750), the Quaker daughter of Josiah and Sarah Fearn, and settled at Lower Darby in Pennsylvania. He continued his missionary work, and in September 1741 he visited Long Island, Connecticut, Rhode Island, and Massachusetts, where he was 'attacked divers times by some of them [Presbyterians] on religious subjects' (*Journal of the Life*, 63). Griffith conducted further missionary work around America before he returned to Britain. During his voyage he was captured by a privateer and taken to Spain, and later to France, before escaping to England in 1748. While in Britain he visited his mother and close relatives in Radnor, he travelled to Ireland, and then he went back to Wales, where he had 'several large, though serviceable meetings amongst Friends, my old neighbours and acquaintances; their hearts being tendered and some much affected' (ibid., 204). In May 1750 Griffith returned to America but, following the death of his wife, he returned to England again, with his daughter, and settled at Chelmsford.

While at Chelmsford, Griffith met and married his second wife, Frances Wyatt, a Quaker minister, in January 1751. He continued his missionary visits around Britain, and in 1760 he helped to organize committees to visit Friends' meetings, which, coupled with his writings, prompted a revival in Quaker discipline. In July 1765 Griffith paid his last visit to America and attended large meetings of Friends in Pennsylvania. The following year he returned to England and, as a consequence of an asthmatic complaint, gave up his missionary work. On 17 June 1776 Griffith died, aged sixty-two, at Chelmsford and was buried at the Quaker burial-ground in the town on 23 June. He was survived by his wife. His most important works include *Brief Remarks upon Sundry Important Subjects, &c.*, published posthumously in 1764, and his autobiography, *Journal of the Life, Travels and Labours in the Work of the Ministry of John Griffith*, which was first published in 1779.

RICHARD C. ALLEN

Sources *Journal of the life, travels and labours in the work of the ministry of John Griffith* (1779); [new edn] (1830) • 'An account of ministering Friends from Europe who visited America, 1656 to 1793', *Journal of the Friends' Historical Society*, 10 (1913), 117–32, esp. 120, 130 • *The Friend* [Philadelphia, PA], 12 (1839), 245 • *The journal and essays of John Woolman*, ed. A. Mott Gummere (1922), 574
Archives NL Wales, journal

Griffith, John (1714–1798), Independent minister, was born in London in December 1714. His father was a member of the Church of England, his mother belonged to Thomas Bradbury's Independent congregation at Fetter Lane, London. He was for a short time apprenticed to a clog-maker. He became a follower of George Whitefield, and joined Whitefield's society at the Tabernacle in 1749.

Chance led him to hear Samuel Stockell at the Independent congregation in Meeting House Lane, Red Cross Street; about 1750 he became one of Stockell's communicants, but without severing his connection with the Tabernacle class meetings.

Griffith began to preach about 1752, and following Stockell's death, on 3 May 1753, succeeded him as pastor on 30 October 1754. His ministry proved successful until he quarrelled with one of his deacons and withdrew in 1758, with part of his congregation, to an old meeting-house in White's Alley. In 1759 he published an account of his early life and conversion, *A Brand Plucked out of the Fire*, in which he justified his action in breaking up the Red Cross Street congregation.

The congregation at White's Alley grew, and a new meeting-house was built in Mitchell Street in 1771. But it soon declined, and a few years later Griffith retired. In January 1778 he became minister of a new congregation at West Orchard, Coventry, Warwickshire. He 'does not appear to have been adapted to the situation' (Sibree and Causton, 82) and moved, on 25 March 1781, to Brigstock, Northamptonshire, where he ministered until 1788. He then returned to London, where he occasionally preached.

Griffith was twice married. With his first wife he had a large family; his second wife died before 1788, and he himself died on 17 August 1798. He was buried in Bunhill Fields. ALEXANDER GORDON, *rev.* S. J. SKEDD

Sources *Evangelical Magazine*, 7 (1799), 175ff. • W. Wilson, *The history and antiquities of the dissenting churches and meeting houses in London, Westminster and Southwark*, 4 vols. (1808–14), vol. 2, p. 559; vol. 3, p. 314 ff. • J. Sibree and M. Causton, *Independency in Warwickshire* (1855), 82 ff. • *Centenary of West Orchard Chapel, Coventry* (1879), 8
Likenesses line engraving, BM, NPG; repro. in *Gospel Magazine* (1778)

Griffith, John (1818–1885), Church of England clergyman, was born in the parish of Llanbadarn Fawr, near Aberystwyth, Cardiganshire, the son of Thomas Griffith, a gentleman farmer. Educated at Ystradmeurig church school and Bishop Gore Grammar School, Swansea, he graduated at Christ's College, Cambridge in 1841, gaining an MA degree in 1844. He spent two years as curate at Ashbury, near Congleton, Cheshire (1842–4) and was ordained by the bishop of Chester in 1843. Patronized by Sir Stephen Glynne, baronet, of Hawarden, Flintshire, he served for two years as chaplain there (1844–6).

An ardent evangelical, Griffith's outspoken criticism of the abuses of the established church attracted the attention of the marquess of Bute, whose influence secured him the living of Aberdâr, Glamorgan, in 1846. His acrimonious attacks on nonconformity and the Welsh language, and his initial lack of sympathy with the working classes, earned him notoriety and the alienation of many of his parishioners. Despite this, his efforts to increase religious and educational provision, his dramatic pulpit oratory, and his all-embracing pastoral work, often involving a direct and sometimes bitter challenge to the church hierarchy, later earned him their respect, both in Aberdâr and (from 1859) as rector of nearby Merthyr Tudful.

Griffith was twice married; his first wife, Sarah Francis King, whom he married in 1847, was the daughter of a West Indies merchant. His second marriage, which took place in 1863, was to Louisa Stuart, daughter of Alexander Stuart of the island of Bute, who survived him. In all, Griffith had two sons and three daughters.

A champion of the evangelical 'industrial' clergy and their parishioners, Griffith became estranged from the diocesan and landowning establishment, failed to gain high office, and remained in Merthyr Tudful until his death. Throughout his life he contributed a steady flow of articles and letters to the local and national press, and published a pamphlet, *Reunion with Rome*, in 1869. An enthusiastic sailor and a scholar of Welsh history and literature, he spent each summer at the Braichycelyn estate, near Aberdyfi, which he inherited in 1850. He died at his home in Merthyr Tudful on 24 April 1885, and was interred at Thomastown cemetery there on 29 April. Described by the Welsh ecclesiastical historian Wilton D. Wills as 'a fearless critic of his times' (Wills, 98), he stands as one of the most active and controversial Welsh religious leaders of the nineteenth century, who, despite apparent contradictions, is significantly representative of that time and place. SIAN RHIANNON WILLIAMS

Sources W. D. Wills, 'The Reverend John Griffith and the revival of the established church in nineteenth century Glamorgan', *Morgannwg*, 13 (1969), 75–102 • J. E. Lloyd, R. T. Jenkins, and W. L. Davies, eds., *Y bywgraffiadur Cymreig hyd 1940* (1953) • *Yr Haul* (1885) • *Western Mail* [Cardiff] (27–8 April 1885) • *Western Mail* [Cardiff] (25 April 1885) • *Western Mail* [Cardiff] (30 April 1885)
Likenesses line drawing, repro. in *Western Mail* (27 April 1885)
Wealth at death £5177 5s. 0d.: probate, 2 June 1885, CGPLA Eng. & Wales

Griffith, John [*known as* y Gohebydd] (1821–1877), journalist, was born on 16 December 1821 at Bodgwilym, near Barmouth, Merioneth, the son of Griffith Griffith, a farmer, and his wife, Maria, *née* Roberts. Through his mother he was nephew of the famous radical newspaper publisher the Revd Samuel *Roberts of Llanbrynmair. After an elementary education in Barmouth and some early experience in the grocery trade, Griffith moved to London in 1847 as assistant to Hugh Owen, secretary of the Welsh Education Society. This position ended in 1849, and for the next decade Griffith returned to shopkeeping, opening his own business at 55 Camberwell Road in 1856, and writing occasional letters for his uncle's paper, *Y Cronicl*, under the pen name Wmffra Edward. In 1857, however, he began to write weekly letters for *Baner ac Amserau Cymru*, edited by Thomas Gee, and, in 1861, gave up the shop to concentrate on journalism as London correspondent of *Baner*, thereby becoming the first full-time Welsh correspondent.

Griffith, known henceforth as y Gohebydd (literally 'the correspondent'), quickly established his reputation. His meticulously researched weekly column played a key role in awakening the interest of the Welsh people in politics during the 1860s. Alongside witty, radical commentaries on parliamentary affairs and accounts of his visits to America (1865–7) and the Paris Exhibition (1867), he championed a series of 'Welsh' causes, blending a celebration of the nation's cultural and historical heritage, the travails of contemporary nonconformists (who formed a majority of the population in Wales), the politics of the Liberal Party, and the representation of Wales in parliament. By these means, he did more than anyone else to dictate the markedly Welsh form taken by radical nonconformist politics at the general election of 1868.

This election was, perhaps, Gohebydd's finest hour. He campaigned hard on behalf of Liberal candidates like Henry Richard, a fellow metropolitan Welshman and Congregationalist, and hoped their triumph would lead to the creation of a 'Welsh Brigade' to look after Welsh interests in parliament (*Baner*, 23 Dec 1868, 4–5). In the controversial aftermath of the election, when Conservative landowners in Wales apparently evicted tenants who had voted for Liberal candidates, Gohebydd was at the forefront of the campaign to secure redress for the victims. He organized a conference at Aberystwyth in October 1869 which established a fund to compensate those evicted and then toured the afflicted areas, publishing detailed accounts of the tenants' sufferings. The campaign lasted two years; it was in respect of his work at the election that, in 1875, Griffith was presented with a testimonial worth £734 17*s. d.*

Gohebydd's success brought him considerable influence in other spheres. He was a reform-minded member of the national eisteddfod committee during the 1860s and became a member of the governing body of the new university at Aberystwyth when it opened in 1872. Within the Welsh community in London he was similarly prominent, being part of the delegation which waited on the home secretary in 1862 to protest against the revised code, and another which met Garibaldi in 1864. It is some mark of his popularity that John Thomas, the Liverpool photographer who specialized in retailing *carte-de-visite* portraits of famous nonconformist ministers, also advertised one of Gohebydd.

A slight, earnest man, Gohebydd never enjoyed good health. Samuel Morley, after meeting him in 1868, referred to him as 'the little man that coughs' (D. Tecwyn Lloyd, 211); in 1875, he paid for him to winter in Switzerland, but the end was not long delayed, and Griffith died, unmarried, on 13 December 1877 at his sister's house, 6 Thackeray Street, Liverpool. He was buried in the Fron cemetery, Llangollen, and was escorted to his final resting place by a procession, it was said, the like of which the town had never seen. MATTHEW CRAGOE

Sources D. Tecwyn Lloyd, 'John Griffith, Y Gohebydd (1821–1877)', *Transactions of the Honourable Society of Cymmrodorion* (1977), 207–30 • R. Griffith, *Y Gohebydd, Cofiant a Dyfyniadau o'i: Llythyrau fel Gohebydd Llundain 'Baner Ac Amserau Cymru'* (1905) • *DWB*, 294–5 • '"Gohebydd" dead!', *Carnarvon and Denbigh Herald* (15 Dec 1877), 5 • J. V. Morgan, ed., *Welsh political and educational leaders in the Victorian era* (1908), 291
Archives NL Wales, Gee MSS
Likenesses J. Roberts, photograph, *c.*1860, repro. in Morgan, ed., *Welsh political and educational leaders*, following p. 290
Wealth at death under £600: administration, 9 Feb 1878, *CGPLA Eng. & Wales*

Griffith, Kate (1854–1902). *See under* Griffith, Francis Llewellyn (1862–1934).

Griffith, Llewelyn Wyn (1890–1977), writer and broadcaster, was born on 30 August 1890 at 10 Penrhyn View, Llandrillo-yn-Rhos, Colwyn Bay, Caernarvonshire, the eldest son of John Griffith (1863–1933), schoolmaster, and his wife, Dora (1861–1940), daughter of Owen Jones of Tal-y-sarn, Caernarvonshire. His childhood was spent in various places in rural north Wales; he received his secondary education at Blaenau Ffestiniog, Merioneth, where his father taught science at the county school, and at Dolgellau in the same county, where his father became headmaster of the grammar school. The family was Welsh-speaking and Welsh was Griffith's mother tongue, but his education was wholly through the medium of English, and it was in that language that most of his creative writing was done.

Griffith left Wales in 1909 to join the civil service, making his career with the Inland Revenue, of which he was assistant secretary from 1945 until his retirement in 1952; he wrote a history of the civil service, published in 1954, its centenary year. It was as an attempt to recapture and record the Welsh nonconformist tradition as he had known it, and from which he drew sustenance during a long and distinguished career in England, that most of his writing, particularly *Spring of Youth* (1935), was undertaken; he returned to this subject in his autobiographical essay in the book *Y llwybrau gynt* (ed. Alun Oldfield-Davies, 1971).

Griffith's impulse to write about his own life had its origins in his experiences as a captain with the 15th battalion (London Welsh) of the Royal Welch Fusiliers during the First World War, in which he won the Croix de Guerre. His book *Up to Mametz* (1931) is a vivid but reliable account of the conflict which, although it lacks the urbane irreverence of *Goodbye to All That*, has been compared with Robert Graves's book; it is certainly, with David Jones's *In Parenthesis*, among the most authentic. Above all, it relates how the innocence of youth was destroyed during a battle in which thousands of Griffith's comrades, and his younger brother Watcyn, were killed.

After the war, during which he had married Winifred Elizabeth Frimston (1887/8–1977) on 6 March 1915, Griffith lived in the village of Neston in Cheshire, commuting to Chester and Liverpool as an officer of the Inland Revenue, but in 1933 he moved to Berkhamsted in Hertfordshire, where the rest of his life was spent. His next two books were novels: *The Wooden Spoon* (1937) and the more substantial *The Way Lies West* (1945), in both of which he strove to recapture not only the essence of his own youth but that of his parents; neither is as accomplished as his earlier autobiographical works.

Griffiths also wrote a little poetry, including the verse-play for radio *Branwen*, which was collected in the slim volume *The Barren Tree* (1945). Most of his poems drew their inspiration from Welsh legend or from his experience of war; one of his sons was killed in action in 1945. He abandoned poetry shortly afterwards, turning instead to the writing of factual books about the land and people of Wales for the enlightenment of English readers, including his own children, who were brought up in England and were unable to speak Welsh. The most authoritative, and for long the only book on its subject in English, was *The Welsh* (1950), which was first published as a Pelican paperback. This book presented a fastidiously balanced view of Wales, its history and culture, and also argued in favour of a measure of administrative devolution within the British state, although it had little to say about industrial south Wales and was dubious about whether Cardiff deserved to become the country's capital; for Griffith, Wales was where the Welsh language was spoken. The same desire to introduce English readers to literature written in Welsh animated his work as a translator. He translated *Tea in the Heather* (1968) and *The Living Sleep* (1976), both by the major prose writer Kate Roberts, and wrote a children's version of the tale from the Mabinogion, *The Saga of Pryderi* (1961).

Griffith also represented Wales as a prominent member of many public bodies. He was chairman of the council of the Honourable Society of Cymmrodorion, perhaps the most establishmentarian of all the London Welsh societies; vice-chairman of the Arts Council of Great Britain and chairman of its Welsh committee; chairman of the National Book League; vice-president of the London Centre of the PEN Club; and a member of the Welsh committee of the British Council. A frequent broadcaster in both Welsh and English, he was for twenty-one years a member of the Welsh team in the popular radio series *Round Britain Quiz* and gave many radio talks about the complexities of PAYE (pay as you earn) income tax in the series *Can I Help you?* His contribution to Welsh life brought him honours from several quarters: he was made a CBE in 1961 and received the honorary degree of DLitt from the University of Wales and the gold medal of the Cymmrodorion. He died on 27 September 1977 in Southbank Nursing Home, 1–2 Cavendish Road, Bowdon, Cheshire, and was buried in the graveyard of Nebo Chapel, Rhiw, Caernarvonshire.

MEIC STEPHENS

Sources L. W. Griffith, *Spring of youth* (1935) · 'Wyn Griffith', *Y llwybrau gynt*, ed. A. Oldfield-Davies, 1 (1971), 31–60 · G. Hill, *Llewelyn Wyn Griffith* (1984) · H. Wheldon, memorial address, *Transactions of the Honourable Society of Cymmrodorion* (1978), 49–53 · b. cert. · d. cert. · m. cert. · *CGPLA Eng. & Wales* (1977)
Archives NRA, corresp. and literary papers | NL Wales, corresp. with Kate Davies · NL Wales, letters to Mary Gwilym Davies and Thomas Iorwerth Ellis · NL Wales, corresp. with Gwyn Jones · NL Wales, corresp. with Thomas Jones · NL Wales, corresp. with Welsh National Opera · NL Wales, letters to Sir Thomas Parry–Williams
Wealth at death £70,898: probate, 9 Dec 1977, *CGPLA Eng. & Wales*

Griffith, Matthew (*b.* in or before 1599, *d.* 1665), Church of England clergyman, was born into a London gentry family; his parents' names are unknown. He was admitted commoner at Brasenose College, Oxford, in May 1615, aged at least sixteen, but graduated BA from Gloucester Hall on 3 February 1619. Migrating to Cambridge, he proceeded MA from Christ's College in 1621. He was said to

have been a favourite of John Donne, and it was probably through the influence of Donne that he was presented to the rectory of St Mary Magdalen, Old Fish Street, London, in 1624 and chosen lecturer at St Dunstan-in-the-West on 31 October 1631. At an unknown date he married Sarah (1597/8–1677), daughter of Richard Smith, who had been chaplain to Anne of Denmark.

In 1633 Griffith published *Bethel, or, A Forme for Families*, a substantial quarto of 528 pages, which was designed as a comprehensive manual for dutiful and orderly life in a Christian household. It contains, however, an important political message, too. Having completed 'an house of Gods building', he asked, 'what must all the members thereof doe, as the summe of their duty'. His answer was: 'They must *feare God and the King*, and must *not meddle* with those that be seditious' (pp. 429–30). About 1638 he had a dispute with the master of the rolls over a preachership in the rolls chapel, and there was some contention between him and the parishioners of St Mary Magdalen over tithes. Articles accusing him of profanity and immorality were exhibited in the court of high commission, but the case was not prosecuted. On 29 April 1640 he was also made rector of St Benet Sherehog.

The coming of the civil war in 1642 brought Griffith to the centre stage of political conflicts in the City. On 2 October he was invited to preach at St Paul's, and he took this opportunity to deliver a learned sermon on peace, which he later published as *A Patheticall Perswasion to Pray for Publick Peace* (1642), dedicated to the citizens of London. Speaking as a Londoner himself he asked the citizens to cherish the peace and prosperity they had enjoyed. 'Look round about you', he told them, 'and see all the Christian world in an uprore, and in arms, and a considerable part thereof in ashes; whilst this our Britain (like the centre) stood unmov'd' (p. 30). He pleaded with them, therefore, that 'in these Criticall dayes of our yet surviving peace, we may all have the grace prudently to foresee, and piously to pursue such lawfull courses, and warrantable means as to make for the maintenance of the same' (p. 33). Furthermore, he used his pulpit in the City to denounce those who took up arms against the king as well as those who brought in money and plate for the parliamentary cause. Consequently he was one of the 'malignants' rounded up by the City's trained bands during the night of 5 November, and was imprisoned first at Newgate and later at Petre House. The House of Commons ordered the sequestration of his livings at St Mary Magdalen and St Benet Sherehog on 28 February and 10 March 1643 respectively. He escaped to Oxford, and there, by virtue of a letter from the king, he was created DD in June, and was made one of the royal chaplains.

Subsequently Griffith took part in the defence of Basing House in Hampshire. When, eventually, that royalist stronghold was stormed by the parliamentary forces on 14 October 1645, he was badly wounded and taken prisoner, and one of his daughters was killed. He remained in London after his release and, by stealth or publicly, continued to preach in the City. Sequestered from his livings and from his temporal estate, several times violently assaulted and imprisoned, he suffered enormously during the revolutionary era. In early 1660, not long after the march of General Monck's army to London, he published *The Samaritan Revived*, together with *The Fear of God and the King*, and dedicated both to Monck. The latter work, a sermon he had preached at the Mercers' chapel, was strongly royalist in tone but not particularly pointed. It nevertheless greatly troubled the more cautious royalists in and out of England, and even provoked John Milton to denounce it in a short pamphlet called *Brief Notes upon a Late Sermon* (1660). But it was *The Samaritan Revived* which led to his last imprisonment. Now a hardened royalist who was, as he told Monck, 'too old to fear, and too great a sufferer to flatter' ('Epistle Dedicatory'), he gave in this tract a tactless and acrimonious account of events past and present. He openly advocated that 'a *King* we must have' and that 'without the restitution of *King* Charles to his native rights, we can in reason look for no solid settlement of Religion, or Law, libertie, or Propertie' (pp. 48–9). And he told Monck, 'it is a greater honour to make a King, then to be one' ('Epistle Dedicatory'). Amid a sudden upsurge of royalism in the City the publication was so popular that, within two days, 'the whole impression of 500 was sold off' (*Clarendon State Papers*, 4.693). The council of state ordered his arrest on 2 April and sent him to Newgate, from which he was to be released on 8 May—the day when Charles II was proclaimed in London.

Upon the Restoration, Griffith was reinstated in the rectory of St Mary Magdalen and subsequently also obtained the rectory of Bladon near Woodstock in Oxfordshire. He appeared to have been elected preacher to read a divine lecture at the Temple. In 1665 he published *The King's Life-Guard*, a sermon he had preached on the anniversary of the death of Charles I. He died later that year at Bladon on 14 October, as a result of rupturing a blood vessel while preaching, and was buried in the chancel of the church. He was survived by his wife, who died in 1677, his son Edward, and three married daughters: Sarah Conway, Elizabeth Napeir, and Mary Elphicke. He had a dwelling house in the parish of St Mary Magdalen in London and held the title, in a lease of 'almost a Thousand yeares', to a manor 'commonly called Woodrowe' in the parish of Agmondesham (Amersham), Buckinghamshire (PRO, PROB 11/318, fols. 368*v*–369*r*). TAI LIU

Sources will, PRO, PROB 11/318, sig. 154 • LPL, MS CM VIII/37, fol. 3 • D. Lloyd, *Memoires of the lives … of those … personages that suffered … for the protestant religion* (1668) • Wood, *Ath. Oxon.*, new edn, 3.711–13 • *CSP dom.*, 1636–40; 1643; 1659–61 • *Calendar of the Clarendon state papers preserved in the Bodleian Library*, 4: 1657–1660, ed. F. J. Routledge (1932) • Foster, *Alum. Oxon.* • G. N. Godwin, *The civil war in Hampshire, 1642–45, and the story of Basing House*, new edn (1904) • *Walker rev.*

Wealth at death significant wealth; land in the parish of Agmondesham (Amersham) in Buckinghamshire; dwelling-house in London: LPL, MS CM VIII/37, fol. 3; will, PRO, PROB 11/318, sig. 154; *VCH Buckinghamshire*, vol. 3

Griffith [*alias* Alford], **Michael** (1584/5–1652), Jesuit and ecclesiastical historian, was born of Catholic parents, possibly named John and Mabel Griffith, in London. In 1596,

aged eleven, he was briefly imprisoned on his way to the English Jesuit school at St Omer, Flanders. After six years there he went on to the English College, Valladolid, where he remained until 1606. He was briefly at St Gregory's College, Seville, and the English College, Douai, before entering the Society of Jesus at Brussels on 5 February 1607. He served his noviciate at Louvain and remained there as a student of theology until 1611. After ordination he was appointed English chaplain in Naples, 1613–15, and was then English penitentiary at St Peter's, Rome, until 1620. In May that year he visited England but by 1621 he was assisting the novice master at Liège and was rector at Ghent 1621–2.

From 1623 to 1652 Griffith served in Leicestershire. Returning from one of his continental visits he was arrested at Dover in 1629 on suspicion of being the vicar apostolic, Richard Smith, and taken to London, but was later released. From 1633 to 1649 he was rector, or consultor, and admonitor to Jesuits in the midlands. Yet despite these duties and the upheavals of the civil wars he continued to research and write. All his publications (under his alias Michael Alford) were in Latin, the first, *Rosa veralla*, published at Rome in 1622. The translation of the *Life of St Wenefride*, 1635, formerly attributed to him is now recognized as by John Falconer SJ. His *Britannia illustra*, published at Antwerp in 1641, proved that Britain was the country of Helena, Constantine, and King Lucius, under whom it was the first Roman province to believe in Christ and was called the dowry of Mary. Three appendices tackled the controversial issues of the Easter rite, priestly celibacy, and the supremacy of Rome.

Griffith's major work was *Fides regia Britannica, sive, Annales ecclesiae Britannicae* (Liège, 1663), which covered the first five Christian centuries in four volumes. His aim was to write for Britain a church history on the same lines as Baronius's twelve-volume *Annales ecclesiastici* (1588–1607). Serenus Cressy acknowledged his debt to Griffith in the preface to his *Church History of Brittany* (1668), and also commended his devotion to his patron, St Michael, and the wounds of Christ. Griffith's range of sources and detailed year by year coverage were outstanding, yet he was a busy missioner always liable to arrest; volume two was completed in 1644 during the civil war. It was in the hopes of continuing his history that he returned to the continent in 1652 but he died of fever at St Omer on 11 August that year. J. T. RHODES

Sources M. Alford, *Fides regia Britannica*, 4 vols. (1663), vol. 1, 'Ad lectorem de auctore' • S. Cressy, 'Preface to the reader', *The church history of Brittany* (1668) • E. Henson, ed., *The registers of the English College at Valladolid, 1589–1862*, Catholic RS, 30 (1930) • T. M. McCoog, *English and Welsh Jesuits, 1555–1650*, 2 vols., Catholic RS, 74–5 (1994–5) • P. Caraman, 'An English Baronius', *The Month*, 3rd ser., 15 (1982), 22–4 • H. Foley, ed., *Records of the English province of the Society of Jesus*, 2 (1875) • M. Murphy, *St Gregory's College, Seville, 1592–1767*, Catholic RS, 73 (1992) • Gillow, *Lit. biog. hist.* • A. F. Allison and D. M. Rogers, eds., *The contemporary printed literature of the English Counter-Reformation between 1558 and 1640*, 1 (1989)

Griffith, Moses (*bap.* 1699, *d.* 1785), physician, son of the Revd Edward Griffith and his wife, Elizabeth, was baptized at Melbourn, Cambridgeshire, and was apprenticed to Edward Sayer, an apothecary of Norwich, in 1712. He married Elizabeth Guyon (1701x3–1774) in 1724; they had a son, Guyon (1730–1784), who was admitted as a student in Leiden in 1744 and was rector of St Mary-at-Hill, Middlesex, between 1763 and 1784. Griffith practised in London before moving to Colchester in 1768. He died at his house in Head Street, Colchester, on 1 March 1785, and was commemorated by a slab in St Peter's Church, Colchester.

Griffith is most probably the author of *Practical observations on the cure of hectic and SLOW fevers, and the pulmonary consumption, to which is added a method of treating several kinds of internal haemorrhages* (1776). In the introduction to this work Griffith mentions that he has been retired about eight years and that he has had consultations with Colin Hossack, a Colchester physician.

Another physician of the same name was **Moses Griffith** (*b.* 1723/4), son of Edward Griffith, collector of taxes, born at Laipdon, Shropshire. He attended Shrewsbury School before entering St John's College, Cambridge, in 1742. He afterwards studied medicine at Leiden, and graduated MD there in 1744. No further information about him has been found.

Neither of the above should be confused with the artist Moses Griffith (*fl.* 1769–1809), who assisted the naturalist and traveller Thomas Pennant on some of his tours.

CAROLINE OVERY

Sources J. Bensusan-Butt, 'Moses Griffith, M.D.', 1990, Wellcome L., Hist. pam (B) GRI [unpubd typescript] · Munk, *Roll* · Venn, *Alum. Cant.*
Likenesses J. Dunthorne junior, watercolour drawing, exh. RA 1783 (*Card party*) · J. Dunthorne junior, print, 1788
Wealth at death see will, PRO, PROB 11/1128, sig. 188

Griffith, Moses (*b.* 1723/4). *See under* Griffith, Moses (*bap.* 1699, *d.* 1785).

Griffith, Moses (1747–1819), watercolour painter and engraver, was born on 25 March 1747 at Trygarn in the parish of Bryncroes in Caernarvonshire, the illegitimate son of Griffith William and Anne Griffith. His father was a labourer, and Moses grew up in humble circumstances, though he received an education at the free school attached to Botwnnog church. In 1769 he was taken into the employ of Thomas Pennant, squire of Downing in Flintshire, who had presumably been made aware of the young man's talent for drawing. Griffith lived at Gwibnant, an estate house, with his wife Margaret Jones, whom he married on 9 January 1781, and their two children, Moses and Margaret. Thomas Pennant died in 1798 but family patronage continued under his son, David, until the painter's death.

Griffith was required to act as visual amanuensis to Thomas Pennant on the tours which he undertook in pursuit of his scientific and antiquarian interests. Pennant employed a number of painters and engravers in connection with his publications, but his relationship with Griffith was unusual. The painter was a member of the household after the manner of the harper in ancient Welsh families. He undertook work for other patrons only by permission of his master, who often acted as agent, as in the case of illustrations contributed to *The Antiquities of England* by Francis Grose (1773–87).

Griffith's initial tour with Pennant took place in the first year of his employment, when they went to Scotland, an exploration completed in 1772 with a tour to the Hebridean islands. The resulting illustrations were published in 1774 in *A Tour in Scotland and Voyage to the Hebrides*. By this time Pennant and Griffith were making periodic expeditions in north Wales, which were described in the *Tour in Wales* in 1778, to which was added *A Journey to Snowdon* in 1781. Griffith's watercolours were sometimes engraved on copper by himself, though other engravers were also employed to interpret his work. Through these publications Griffith became known to the reading public and, as a consequence of his master's enthusiasm, his prodigious output of watercolours also became widely disseminated. Pennant remarked that he 'never should deny copies of them to any gentleman who would make dignified use of them' (Pennant, 25). The National Library of Wales, Aberystwyth, and the National Museum and Gallery of Wales, Cardiff, have substantial holdings.

Griffith's greatest achievement was an edition of the *Tour in Wales* printed on large paper for illustration with original paintings. Twelve copies were printed for patrons, including Sir Watkin Williams Wynn, Sir William Burrell, and William Storer, in whose copy at Eton College this information is recorded. The most extensively illustrated were Pennant's own, held at the National Library of Wales, where there is also an extra-illustrated copy of Pennant's *The History of the Parishes of Whiteford and Holywell* (1796), which contains notable industrial views alongside the more commonplace landscapes, portraits, and heraldry. Two self-portraits survive, one depicting Griffith as a gauche young man, and the other in stout old age. He died on 11 November 1819, at Gwibnant, and was buried in Whitford churchyard.

PETER LORD

Sources D. Moore, introduction, *Moses Griffith, 1747–1819, artist and illustrator in the service of Thomas Pennant* (1979) [exhibition catalogue, Welsh Arts Council, Wales] · T. Pennant, *Literary life* (1793) · I. A. Williams, 'Thomas Pennant and Moses Griffith', *Country Life*, 84 (1938), 8–9 · *DWB* · parish registers, Bryncroes, Caernarvonshire · parish register (marriage), Whitford, Flintshire · tomb, Whitford churchyard, Flintshire
Archives NL Wales, MS 165C; MS 2530A; MS 2586D; MS 4878E; MS 5500C; MS 12706E
Likenesses M. Griffith, self-portrait, watercolour, *c.*1770, NL Wales, MS 12706E [pasted in T. Pennant, *Literary life*, extra-illustrated copy] · M. Griffith, self-portrait, watercolour, 1811, NL Wales, MS 12706E [pasted in T. Pennant, *Literary life*, extra-illustrated copy] · G. Scott, stipple, NPG

Griffith, Nora Christina Cobban (1870–1937). *See under* Griffith, Francis Llewellyn (1862–1934).

Griffith, Piers (1568–1628), pirate, was probably born at Penrhyn in Caernarvonshire, the eldest son of Sir Rhys Griffith (*d.* 1580), MP and high sheriff of Caernarvonshire, and his third wife, Katherine, daughter of Peter Mostyn of Talacre. His father was a prominent figure in north Wales, who acquired a reputation among the Welsh poets for his military abilities. Little is known of Griffith's early years and education, and evidence concerning his subsequent career is scant. In 1580 he was placed under the supervision of the court of wards, whose administration led to a heavy charge on lands he inherited from his father, some of which was subsequently refunded. He was also faced with a rival claim to the estate from Sir Nicholas Bagnall, which grew out of a long-standing dispute over ownership of the Penrhyn lands that can be traced back to 1540. Such difficulties may have encouraged Griffith to try his fortune at sea. According to nineteenth-century accounts, one of which was based on a genealogical description of the family from 1764 by John Thomas, headmaster of Beaumaris grammar school, he purchased a ship in April 1588, in which he sailed to Plymouth to take part in the Armada campaign. Apparently he was invited to dine aboard Sir Francis Drake's ship, 'where he was treated honourably, and highly commended for his loyalty and public spirit' (Williams, 177). Thereafter he sailed with Drake and Sir Walter Ralegh in a voyage to the coast of Spain. During the early seventeenth century, however, as a result of complaints about his piracies from Gondomar, the Spanish ambassador in London, 'he was obliged to sell his estate to procure his pardon' (ibid., 177).

No evidence survives to support these claims, and that concerning Griffith's participation in the campaign against the armada has been greeted with scepticism by modern authorities. Nevertheless, it is clear that he was involved, legally or otherwise, in the closing stages of the maritime war with Spain, by the end of which he had acquired a reputation of being 'a notable pirate' (*Salisbury MSS*, 12.649–50). In 1600 he brought a Spanish vessel, laden with oil, silk, and olives, into Abercegin in the Menai Strait. In February 1603 he was arrested in Cork harbour by Captain Charles Plessington, acting on the instructions of the lord admiral. He had with him a captured vessel laden with ginger, oils, logwood, and sumac, which reputedly contained 'great sums of money' (ibid., 12.649). John Chamberlain, the letter writer, reported his arrest and added that his lands, worth £500 per annum, allegedly were confiscated and given to Lord Grey.

If Griffith had to pay for a royal pardon, this may partly explain the financial difficulties he faced after 1603, which were compounded by a dispute with his younger brother, William, concerning ownership of his Cororion lands. The estate was mortgaged to London merchants, such as Thomas Myddelton, and in 1614 to Henry Rowlands, bishop of Bangor. In 1616, when the court of chancery was examining his affairs, he was apparently in the custody of the warden of the Fleet. By the end of the year he had lost control of the estate; it was acquired by Lord Keeper Williams in 1622. Griffith married Margaret, daughter of Sir Thomas *Mostyn (c.1542–1618) of Mostyn [see under Mostyn family (per. 1540–1642)]. All of their children, four sons and seven daughters, died young. By the 1620s Griffith was living in London, possibly in straitened circumstances. The family line became extinct on his death in London in 1628, when he was buried in Westminster Abbey. His friend the adventurer and poet

Thomas Prys of Plas Iolyn, with whom he may have been involved in various maritime ventures, wrote an elegy on him.

JOHN C. APPLEBY

Sources *Calendar of the manuscripts of the most hon. the marquis of Salisbury*, 12, HMC, 9 (1910) · *The letters of John Chamberlain*, ed. N. E. McClure, 2 vols. (1939) · I. ab Owen Edwards, *A catalogue of star chamber proceedings relating to Wales* (1929) · DWB · J. E. Griffith, *Pedigrees of Anglesey and Carnarvonshire families* (privately printed, Horncastle, 1914) · A. Eames, *Ships and seamen of Anglesey, 1558–1918: studies in maritime and local history* (1973) · W. Williams, *Observations on the Snowdon mountains* (1802) · T. Pennant, *A tour in Wales*, 2 vols. (1778–81) · *CSP dom.*, 1601–3 · P. W. Hasler, 'Griffith, Rhys', HoP, *Commons, 1558–1603* · *APC*, 1580–81

Archives PRO, court of wards, star chamber | U. Wales, Bangor, Penrhyn MSS

Griffith, Ralph Thomas Hotchkin (1826–1906), Sanskritist and translator, born at Corsley, Wiltshire, on 25 May 1826, was the son of Robert Clavey Griffith (1792–1844), rector of Corsley (1815–44) and of Fifield Bavant, also in Wiltshire (1825–44), and his wife, Mary Elizabeth Adderly, daughter of Ralph Hotchkin of Uppingham Hall. Educated first at Warminster School and then at Uppingham School, Ralph proceeded with an exhibition from Uppingham to Queen's College, Oxford, which he entered as a commoner on 16 March 1843. Obtaining an honorary fourth class in classics, he graduated BA on 29 October 1846 and proceeded MA on 22 June 1849. At Oxford he became a pupil of Professor Horace Hayman Wilson and, having gained the Boden Sanskrit scholarship in 1849, continued the study of Sanskrit to the end of his life. From 1850 to 1853 he was assistant master of Marlborough College, of which he was also librarian.

In 1853 Griffith joined the Indian educational service, and on 17 December became professor of English literature at the Benares Government College. His promotion was rapid: on 1 June 1854 he became headmaster of the college. He encouraged sport, and showed thorough sympathy with Indian students. In the following year he was entrusted, in addition to his other duties, with the charge of the Anglo-Sanskrit department; and in 1856 he was appointed inspector of schools in the Benares circle. During his first eight years in India (1853–61) Griffith devoted himself not only to the study of Sanskrit but also to Hindi, under Pandit Ram Jasan, the head Sanskrit teacher of the college, to whom he was much attached. Throughout the mutiny Griffith worked quietly in his bungalow amid the surrounding tumult.

On the retirement of James Robert Ballantyne in 1861 Griffith succeeded to the principalship of the Benares College. He held the post for seventeen years, in the course of which he acted three times for short periods as director of public instruction. On 15 March 1878 he left the Benares College after a quarter of a century's service, and from that date until 1885 was director of public instruction in the North-Western Provinces and Oudh. His success in official life, both as an administrator and as a teacher, was uninterrupted. On his retirement he received a special pension, the honour of CIE, and the thanks of the government. Calcutta University made him a fellow.

Unmarried and without close family ties in England,

Griffith, after reaching India in 1853, never saw his native country again. On his retirement he moved to Kotagiri, a beautiful hill station, some 7000 feet high in the Nilgiris district, Madras, and resided with his brother Frank, an engineer in the public works department of the Bombay presidency, who had settled there in 1879. At Kotagiri he tranquilly engaged in the study and translation of the Vedas. There he died, on 7 November 1906, and was buried.

An enthusiastic lover of flowers and of poetry, Griffith was sensitive and reserved, but genial in sympathetic company. His pupils and admirers at Benares perpetuated his memory on his retirement in scholarships and prizes at the Sanskrit college. In the college library there was hung a photograph of his portrait painted by F. M. Wood.

Griffith was attracted by the literary rather than the linguistic side of Sanskrit studies. But he rendered a great service to the direct study of Sanskrit texts by founding in 1866 the *Pandit*, a monthly journal of the Benares College, devoted to Sanskrit literature. The aim of this journal, which continued to be printed until 1920, was to publish reliable editions of primary Sanskrit sources, as well as providing a forum for the discussion of philosophy, history, language, and literature among Indian and European scholars. Griffith edited the journal for eight years, and the early issues contain some English translations from Sanskrit.

Griffith devoted himself to the translation of Sanskrit poetry for nearly half a century. His output was enormous. He began at Marlborough College with his *Specimens of Old Indian Poetry* (1852), containing selections elegantly translated in various rhyming metres from the two epics, the *Mahabharata* and the *Ramayana*, and from the works of India's most celebrated classical poet, Kalidasa. An extract from the drama *Sakuntala* is in blank verse, and the volume is introduced with a small number of Vedic hymns and extracts from the lawbook of Manu. At Marlborough also he made a translation in heroic couplets of Kalidasa's court epic, the *Kumara-sambhava*, under the title *The Birth of the War-God* (1853; 2nd edn, 1879). There followed *Idylls from the Sanskrit* (1866), selections similar to those in his first book, and *Scenes from the Rámáyan* (1868). His now dated but monumental translation of the whole epic, the *Rámáyan of Válmíki*, in rhyming octosyllabic couplets occasionally varied by other metres, was completed in five volumes (1870–5). Griffith's prefatory essays and brief introductory comments to some of his versions show a sympathetic and appealing enthusiasm for the original sources and their content. Having paid some attention to the study of Persian, he published in 1882 a version of *Yuzuf and Zuleíka*, which was his only excursion in translation outside Sanskrit.

After his retirement to the Nilgiri hills, Griffith turned from classical Sanskrit to the sacred scriptures of the Hindus, the Vedas. The Rigveda appeared in a verse translation entitled *Hymns of the Rigveda, with a Popular Commentary*, in four volumes (Benares, 1889–92; 2nd edn, 2 vols., 1896–7). There followed the *Sámaveda* (Benares, 1893), the

Atharvaveda (Benares, 1895–6) and the *White Yajurveda* (Benares, 1899). In these translations Griffith abandoned rhyme and rendered each verse by one syllabically harmonizing with the original and generally divided into corresponding hemistichs. Griffith's command of poetic diction enabled him to reproduce the form and spirit of the ancient hymns better than by means of prose or of rhyming verse. His method of interpretation was eclectic; it followed partly the Indian commentators, partly the researches of Western scholars supplemented by investigations of his own. The translations, though not authoritative in their interpretation of the original texts, were the first versions to present these ancient hymns to English readers in an attractive form, and Griffith was with some justification regarded as the best translator of ancient Indian poetry that Britain had yet produced.

A. A. MACDONELL, rev. J. B. KATZ

Sources WWW, 1897–1915 · Foster, *Alum. Oxon.* · private information (1912) [provost of Queen's College, Oxford; Mrs H. L. Griffith, sister-in-law; Pandit Ram Krishna]
Archives CUL, E. A. Manning MSS
Likenesses F. M. Wood, portrait; photograph, known to be at Benares Sanskrit College in 1912

Griffith, Richard (1635?–1691), physician, was educated at Eton College, though not on the foundation. He was elected to King's College, Cambridge, but, owing to the reinstatement of Henry Mole, was never admitted. On the recommendation of Cromwell and the council of state he was appointed by the parliamentary visitors to a fellowship at University College, Oxford, on 1 September 1654. He graduated BA on 7 July 1657 and MA on 3 May 1660, and had thoughts of becoming a preacher, but 'being not minded to conform he left the college, and applied his mind to the study of physic' (Wood).

Griffith took the degree of MD at Caen in Normandy on 12 June 1664, was admitted an honorary fellow of the College of Physicians in the following December, and having been created a fellow by the charter of James II, was admitted as such on 12 April 1687. He was censor in 1688 and 1690, and registrar for 1690. For some years he practised at Richmond, Surrey.

Griffith first married Jane (d. 1680), daughter of William Wheeler, of Datchet, by licence dated 18 January 1679. With her he had a son, Richard, baptized at Richmond on 13 March 1680, and buried with his mother at Datchet. His second marriage, licensed on 19 May 1690, was to Mary, daughter of Richard Blackman, apparently of Punchins, near Stoke-next-Guildford, Surrey; she survived him without children.

Griffith was the author of a somewhat venomous treatise entitled *A-la-mode phlebotomy no good fashion, or, The copy of a letter to Dr. [Francis] Hungerford [of Reading], complaining of … the phantastick behaviour and unfair dealing of some London physitians … whereupon a fit occasion is taken to discourse of the profuse way of blood-letting* (1681). The immediate cause of Griffith's wrath was the supercilious treatment recommended by a London physician (formerly a 'journeyman' to Thomas Willis), who on being summoned to see an aged lady patient of his at Richmond, insisted on her being let blood, which no doubt accelerated her death.

Griffith died in the parish of St Nicholas Acons, London, in September 1691 and was buried in the church of Datchet, Buckinghamshire, near his deceased wife and child. In his will, dated 4 September 1691, and proved on 8 September, he mentions property at various places in Surrey, and houses in Old Street, St Luke's, London. Wood confuses Griffith with another Richard Griffith, a native of Abinger, Surrey, who passed from Eton to King's College, Cambridge, in 1629, and died in college at the end of 1642.　　　　　　GORDON GOODWIN, *rev.* PATRICK WALLIS

Sources Foster, *Alum. Oxon.* • Munk, *Roll* • J. L. Chester and J. Foster, eds., *London marriage licences, 1521–1869* (1887) • M. Burrows, ed., *The register of the visitors of the University of Oxford, from AD 1647 to AD 1658*, CS, new ser., 29 (1881), 399 • Wood, *Ath. Oxon.: Fasti* (1820), 198, 224 • T. Harwood, *Alumni Etonenses, or, A catalogue of the provosts and fellows of Eton College and King's College, Cambridge, from the foundation in 1443 to the year 1797* (1797), 229 • probate act book, PRO, PROB 8/84, fol. 152 • will, PRO, PROB 11/405 [proved 8 Sept 1691], sig. 138 • letters of administration, 7 June 1680, PRO, PROB 6/55, fol. 102r [Jane Griffith] • BL, Cole MSS, Add. MS 5816, fols. 121, 174

Archives BL, Cole MSS

Wealth at death property in Surrey and London

Griffith, Richard (d. 1719), naval officer, is said by Charnock to have been the son of Richard Griffith, a lieutenant and captain in the navy in 1668–78. This is extremely doubtful; he seems to have been of humble origin from East Hanningfield, Essex, and of very imperfect education, scarcely able to write. In 1691 he appears to have been commander of a small merchant ship, or pink, named the *Trial* of London, which was captured by a French privateer, and which he recaptured in the night with the aid of a boy, clapping on the hatches, it is said, and overpowering and throwing overboard the sleeping watch. For this exploit he was given £50 (*CSP dom.*, 1692, 218), and appointed captain of the galley *Mary* on 25 April 1692. The boy also received a medal. At La Hogue the *Mary* was tender to the admiral, and 'was sent the first express to the queen with the news of beating and burning the enemy's ships, for which', wrote Griffith nine years afterwards, 'her majesty ordered me a royal bounty of £300, which as yet I have not received'. He was then employed in convoy service to Newfoundland and Lisbon, in August 1693 cruising off the coast of France for intelligence, and at the bombardment of St Malo with Benbow, after which he was sent into the Mediterranean and on 28 June 1695, being then at Cagliari, was ordered by Russell to go to Messina to take command of the prize *Trident*, a French ship of 54 guns, which, together with the *Content*, had lately been captured by a detached squadron of the Mediterranean Fleet under Captain James Killigrew. After bringing the *Trident* to England and some months spent in convoy service, Griffith, still in the *Trident*, was early in 1697 ordered out to the West Indies in the squadron which joined Vice-Admiral John Nevell at Barbados, and met M. de Pointis off Cartagena on 28–9 May. According to Griffith's account the *Trident* was the only ship engaged, and she, being the weathermost ship, was for some time surrounded by the enemy and might have been taken, had they not been

more intent on getting clear off with the spoils of Cartagena. She was afterwards one of the squadron under Rear-Admiral Meese which sacked Petit-Goave; was with Nevell off Havana; and accompanied him to Virginia, whence, after the vice-admiral's death, she returned to England. Early in the voyage the ship lost her rudder; she was very weak-handed, many of her men sick, and thus, one dark night in November as she made the coast of Ireland, she struck on a rock and was for some time in imminent danger. Griffith wrote:

> Not knowing where we were, and having no boat or any other ways of saving a man, I thought I could not do too much to save the king's ship and all our lives; and then, with my cane in one hand, and a case knife in the other, to cut down their hammocks, did rouse up as many men as I could, and with God's assistance got her off, and next day into Baltimore, and after to Spithead. (PRO, ADM 1, captains' letters)

There a complaint was laid against Griffith for, among other things, not 'carrying a due discipline in his majesty's ship, for beating the officers, and for running up and down the deck with a case knife in his hand', and, being tried on these charges, he was found guilty, relieved of command on 31 January 1698, and suspended during the pleasure of the Admiralty. During the peace he took command of a merchant ship to the Mediterranean, and in March 1702, his suspension having been taken off, he was appointed to the *Bridgwater*, which he commanded on the coast of Ireland and in the Irish Sea for the next three years. During 1705 he was employed on impress service and in December 1705 was appointed to the *Swiftsure*, in which, in company with the *Warspite*, he sailed from Plymouth on 2 March 1707 in charge of a convoy of twenty merchant ships, most of which were carrying provisions for the allied army and bound for Lisbon. On 5 March they fell in with the squadron of seventeen French ships, including five ships of the line, under Duquesne-Mosnier, and Griffith, after consulting his officers, decided that it was hopeless to resist such an enormous superiority of force. The convoy crowded sail and made off before the wind, scattering as they went. Many of the merchant ships were captured, but the rest and the two men-of-war got safely to Lisbon.

So many complaints were made against Griffith to the prince's council that Prince George, the lord high admiral, ordered a court martial to be held in Lisbon. However, since none of the accusers appeared before the court and no evidence was produced against Griffith, he was exonerated. The judge-advocate who conducted the trial, however, was drowned *en route* for England with the court martial record, so that no official record of the trial was forwarded to the Admiralty (*House of Lords MSS*, 7.192–3, 216). Griffith remained in command of the *Swiftsure*, went on to Gibraltar, and thence into the Mediterranean, where he joined the fleet under Sir Cloudesley Shovell and took part in the operations at Toulon. There on 16 August the *Swiftsure* and the *St George* attacked Fort St Louis, receiving heavy damage. As Griffith reported, 'I have had five men slain and as many dismembered and about forty others wounded and the ship is very much battered in her masts, yards, rigging and hull' (Owen, 186). He remained with Shovell and was in his fleet that returned to England in October 1706, when the *Association* and several ships of the fleet were lost among the Isles of Scilly.

During the winter Griffith had temporary command of the *Essex*, cruising in the channel with Sir John Leake, but in February resumed the command of the *Swiftsure*, in which he was stationed as senior officer in the Downs, with eleven ships of the line assigned to him. Griffith was at sea off Dunkirk with less than half of his force, when the Admiralty wrote to direct him to destroy Forbin's squadron, with the pretender on board, in its return from the attempted landing in Scotland. The orders were received by the squadron that remained at anchor in the Downs, but they were unable to join Griffith because they had no pilots available to them who knew the waters close inshore off Dunkirk. Unaware of the orders, and with no prior knowledge that Forbin and his squadron, with the pretender, were approaching, Griffith was patrolling about 20 miles off Dunkirk with a squadron of four ships of the line, when they sighted an enemy squadron of fourteen sail, one with an admiral's flag at the main. 'They drew into line of battle, and by reason of their number and strength, we kept our wind, and in the night lost sight of them' (Griffith to Burchett, 26 March 1708, PRO, ADM 1). The next day the squadron returned to the Downs in order to report the affair to the prince. When the news became public, some people suspected that Griffith might be a Jacobite or that the queen had given him secret orders that allowed the pretender to escape. Some weeks later, in consequence of a letter which had been published in the *Gazette* (25 March–9 April), Griffith was ordered to be tried by court martial. He was tried on 21 May and, on a full examination into the circumstances, was acquitted, the matter of fact contained in the letter being pronounced false and groundless. Griffith continued in the *Swiftsure* until July, when he was appointed to the *Captain*, in which, the following April, he took out a convoy to Lisbon, and went thence to the Mediterranean with Sir John Jennings. On his return to England in July 1709 he commanded the *Humber* for a month and a half, before he was appointed to the *Boyne*, which he commanded on the home station and in the Mediterranean for the next four years.

After June 1713 Griffith had no further service and died on 7 August 1719. In his will, dated 4 August 1719, he stated that he was a resident of East Hanningfield, Essex, and requested that he be buried there, near his mother. He left to his wife, Johanna, an income of £100 per annum to be raised from his personal and real estate so long as she remained a widow, and £1000, with all his land and the residue of his estate after his wife's death or remarriage, to his son, Richard Griffith.

J. K. LAUGHTON, rev. JOHN B. HATTENDORF

Sources CSP dom., 1691–6; 1700–01 • CSP col., vols. 15–16 • J. H. Owen, *War at sea under Queen Anne, 1702–1708* (1938) • PRO, ADM 6 • NMM, Sergison MSS, SER/136 • Pitcairn-Jones, 'Ship histories', NMM [card file] • *The manuscripts of the House of Lords*, new ser., 12 vols. (1900–77), vols. 7–8 • J. Charnock, ed., *Biographia navalis*, 2 (1795), 415 • will, 4 Aug 1719, PRO, PROB 11/570, fol. 109

Archives PRO, Admiralty MSS

Wealth at death £100 p.a. to wife; £1000 and all land to son: will, 4 Aug 1719, PRO, PROB 11/570, fol. 109

Griffith, Richard (*d.* 1788), writer, was the elder son of Edward Griffith and his wife, Abigail, third daughter of Sir William Handcock, recorder of Dublin. His grandfather Richard Griffith was rector of Coleraine and dean of Ross. The family, originally of Penrhyn, Caernarvonshire, settled in Ireland in the reign of James I. Griffith's early years are obscure; he is unlikely to be identical with the Griffith who became a scholar of Trinity College, Dublin, in 1719 (BA, 1721; MA, 1724), since in his autobiographical work he expresses at length his regret that he lacked a 'liberal education', having only 'a Sort of heterogeneous Knowledge, a Kind of *Dictionary Literature*' (R. Griffith and E. Griffith, 'Preface').

Griffith farmed at Maiden Hall, co. Kilkenny, and was later involved in a failed business venture; about 1760 he seems to have received some post from the duke of Bedford, lord lieutenant of Ireland. He married on 12 May 1751 Elizabeth *Griffith (*d.* 1793)—her maiden and married names were the same—soon to become known as a translator, playwright, and popular novelist. In 1757, he joined his wife in the publication of letters they exchanged during their courtship; the original two-volume *Series of Genuine Letters between Henry and Frances* was well received and augmented in four volumes in 1766 and again in six volumes in 1786; in the third edition, the fictional English settings were replaced by actual Irish locations.

Subsequently Griffith published *The triumvirate, or, The authentic memoirs of A[ndrews], B[elville], and C[arewe] by Biograph Triglyph* in 1764, an imitation of *Tristram Shandy*, by Laurence Sterne, a work whose principal aim Griffith declared admiringly to be 'to inculcate that great *Magna Charta* of mankind, humanity and benevolence' (*The Triumvirate*, 'Preface'). Griffith made Sterne's acquaintance in 1767 at Scarborough and left a reminiscence of him in the final edition of the *Series of Letters*. His later imitation of the writer, *The Posthumous Works of a Late Celebrated Genius Deceased* (1770)—also known as 'The Koran, or, The life, character, and sentiments of Tria Juncta in Uno, M. N. A. or master of no arts'—was subsequently reprinted in eighteenth-century editions of Sterne's *Works*.

Griffith's other publications included *The Gordian Knot* (1769), *Something New* (1772), the poem *The Masquerade* (1768), and *Variety*, a comedy performed at Drury Lane in 1782 of which it was said 'never was any play more improperly named, as it is uniformly dull' (Genest, *Eng. stage*, 6.217). Griffith died at Millicent, Naas, co. Kildare, the residence of his son Richard *Griffith (1752–1820), on 11 February 1788. In its obituary, the *Gentleman's Magazine* (1788, 271) gave his forename as Henry, an indication of the extent to which his most famous work was read as unproblematic autobiography. The second of Richard and Elizabeth Griffith's two children was Catherine, who married the Revd John Buck DD, rector of Desertcreat, co. Tyrone.

SIDNEY LEE, rev. IAN CAMPBELL ROSS

Sources Burke, *Peerage* • 'Griffith, Elizabeth', *The general biographical dictionary*, ed. A. Chalmers, new edn (1812–17), vol. 16, pp. 338–40 • [R. Griffith and E. Griffith], 'Preface', *Series of genuine letters* between *Henry and Frances*, 3rd edn (1770) · *GM*, 1st ser., 58 (1788), 271 · D. E. Baker, *Biographia dramatica, or, A companion to the playhouse*, rev. I. Reed, new edn, 1 (1782), 201 · Genest, *Eng. stage*, 6.217 · Burtchaell & Sadleir, *Alum. Dubl.*, 2nd edn

Griffith, Richard (1752–1820), politician and canal promoter, was born on 10 June 1752 at Abbey Street, Dublin, one of the two children of Richard *Griffith (d. 1788), novelist and playwright, and his wife, Elizabeth *Griffith (1727–1793), a more successful novelist and playwright and the daughter of Thomas Griffith and his wife, Jane Foxcroft. About 1760 Griffith moved with his parents to London, where he was educated at Angelo's academy. During the 1770s, through the influence of his parents, he worked for the East India Company, first as a writer at Bengal. In 1772 he moved to Patna where he progressed to the position of accountant in 1776. He amassed a considerable amount of money by trading in opium before returning to England as a factor in 1780. On 17 September 1780 he married Charity Yorke Bramston (d. 1789), of Oundle, Northamptonshire; they had four children, one of whom was Sir Richard John *Griffith (1784–1878), engineer and geologist. Two years after their marriage the couple settled in Ireland at Millicent in co. Kildare.

Between 1783 and 1790 Griffith represented the Limerick borough of Askeaton in the Irish parliament. As an opposition member he supported parliamentary reform and argued for the introduction of protectionist duties in favour of the Irish economy, as outlined in his 1784 pamphlet, *Thoughts on Protecting Duties*. However, his opposition to the concession of the franchise to Irish Catholics resulted in his split with sections of Irish reformers in the mid-1780s, although he continued to pursue broadly reformist policies, including the reorganization of the prison system. By the early 1790s his views on the Catholic question had completely changed, probably under the influence of his radical Kildare neighbours, Archibald Hamilton Rowan, Thomas Wogan Browne, and Theobald Wolfe Tone, and he was instrumental in founding the short-lived Association of the Friends of the Constitution, Liberty, and Peace. As Irish politics radicalized in the later 1790s Griffith was forced to abandon his opposition to government. He gradually aligned himself with the pro-government grouping in Kildare and publicly resigned from the Irish Whig Club in December 1796. As captain of a yeomanry unit in Clane, co. Kildare, he actively opposed the Irish rising of 1798, which resulted in the destruction of much of his property by the rebels. Despite his aversion to Irish republicanism he continued to hold a reform viewpoint and he welcomed the Act of Union because it abolished what he viewed as the corrupt Irish parliament.

Griffith was widely recognized as a successful agricultural improver, notably by awards made through the Dublin Society. He was also active in the promotion of native commerce, particularly through the extension of canal networks, and published two short works on the subject, *Thoughts and Facts relating to the Increase of Agriculture, Manufactures and Commerce by the Extension of Inland Navigation in Ireland* (1795) and *Practical Domestic Politics* (1819). Between

1784 and 1810 he was an influential director of the hugely expensive Grand Canal Company, serving as the company's chairman four times as well as supervising the canal's construction through the Brosna valley in 1802–3. His granddaughter, Lady Stawell, commented that he 'had made a fortune of £90,000 [in India], which he eventually lost in shares in the Grand Canal' (Stawell, 1).

Following his wife's death in June 1789 Griffith married, on 20 March 1793, Mary Hussey Burgh (d. 1820), daughter of Walter Hussey *Burgh and Anne Burgh; they had eleven children. Griffith and his family moved to Leeson Street, Dublin, about 1808 or 1809, and before 1816 moved to Holyhead in Wales. In 1817 he suffered a knee injury, which possibly contributed to his death at Holyhead on 27 June 1820. He was buried three days later at St Cyli's churchyard, Holyhead.   LIAM CHAMBERS

Sources W. S. Griffith, 'The Griffith family', *Journal of the Irish Family History Society*, 12 (1996), 118–26 · W. S. Griffith, 'The Griffith family', *Journal of the Irish Family History Society*, 13 (1997), 60–66 · L. Chambers, *Rebellion in Kildare, 1790–1803* (1998) · T. McEvoy, 'Richard Griffith (c.1752–1820)', *Fugitive warfare: 1798 in north Kildare*, ed. S. Cullen and H. Geissel (1998), 105–12 · R. Delany, *The Grand Canal of Ireland*, 2nd edn (1995) · 'Our portrait gallery, second series no. 3: Sir Richard Griffith', *Dublin University Magazine*, 83 (1874), 432–7 · G. L. Herries Davies, 'Richard Griffith—his life and character', *Richard Griffith, 1784–1878* [Dublin 1978], ed. G. L. Herries Davies and R. C. Mollan (1980), 1–32 · *DNB* · J. Kelly, *Prelude to Union: Anglo-Irish politics in the 1780s* (1992) · R. B. McDowell, *Irish public opinion, 1750–1800* (1944) · *Transactions of the Dublin Society*, 5 (1806) · *The autobiography of Archibald Hamilton Rowan*, ed. W. H. Drummond (1840); facs. edn (1972) · M. E. F. Stawell, *My recollections* (1900)
Archives BL, Pelham MSS, Add. MSS 33105–33110 · priv. coll., letters to his wife, Mary, and daughter, Nancy

Griffith, Sir Richard John, first baronet (1784–1878), geologist and valuator, was born at 8 Hume Street, Dublin, on 20 September 1784, the eldest son of Richard *Griffith (1752–1820) and his wife, Charity Yorke Bramston of Oundle, Northamptonshire. His paternal grandparents were Richard *Griffith (d. 1788) and Elizabeth *Griffith, authors and playwrights. His father made his fortune in the service of the East India Company between 1770 and about 1783, and in 1786 purchased the small estate of Millicent, co. Kildare, which became the home of the young Griffith and his three sisters. His mother died in June 1789, and in February 1793 his father married Mary Hussey Burgh, daughter of Walter Hussey Burgh, which resulted in a new family of seven sons and four daughters.

Griffith was educated at schools in Portarlington, Rathangan (he was there during the 1798 rebellion), and Dublin. In August 1800 he became an ensign in the Royal Irish regiment of artillery, but in 1801, when his regiment was merged with the British artillery at the Act of Union, he resigned his commission. His father was an improving landlord deeply concerned for Ireland's economic development, and under this influence Griffith resolved to apply himself to geology, mining, and engineering. Over the next few years he attended the chemical lectures of Robert Perceval (1756–1839) at Trinity College, Dublin, and in London studied under William Nicholson (1753–1815).

He made scientific excursions in Cornwall, to Birmingham, and to the mining districts of Glamorgan, Lancashire, Yorkshire, and Northumberland. During 1806 he proceeded to Edinburgh where he claimed to have joined the class of Robert Jameson (1774–1854) and to have been associated with Sir James Hall (1761–1832), Louis Albert Necker (1786–1861), John Playfair (1748–1819), and Lord Webb Seymour (1777–1819). He made a geological tour to the Hebrides, and he clearly created a good impression in Scotland because he was elected a fellow of the Royal Society of Edinburgh in 1807.

Griffith returned to Ireland during 1808 and immediately began to display his lifelong propensity for the simultaneous performance of the duties of several onerous offices. In May 1809 he embarked upon a survey of the Leinster coal district for the Dublin Society, and between 1809 and 1813 he served as an engineer to the commissioners set up 'to enquire into the nature and extent of the several bogs in Ireland'. For the commissioners he surveyed the Bog of Allen (1809–11), bogs in the Suck valley (1811–13), in co. Mayo (1811–12), and in co. Dublin and co. Wicklow (1812). On 21 September 1812 Griffith married Maria Jane Waldie (1786–1865) of Hendersyde Park, Kelso, Roxburghshire. The family tree records the birth of one son and three daughters between 1814 and 1821, but there may have been another daughter, born in 1813, who was stricken from the record following her elopement with a family servant when she was sixteen. The Waldies of Hendersyde being without an heir, Griffith's son, George Richard Griffith (1820–1889), inherited the estate in 1865 and he assumed the name Waldie-Griffith.

In November 1812 Griffith was appointed mining engineer to the Dublin Society, charged with duties in both field and lecture theatre, and when the Leinster survey was completed (published 1814), he surveyed the Connaught coalfield (published 1819, not 1818 as the title-page states), the Ulster coalfields (published 1829), the Munster coalfield (investigated 1818–24 but never published), and the metallic mines of Leinster (published 1828).

Prompted by George Bellas Greenough (1778–1855), Griffith in 1811 commenced work on a geological map of Ireland. An early version of the map was probably displayed at his Dublin Society lectures during 1814, but the absence of an accurate topographical base-map severely hampered the completion of the map. In an effort to remedy the deficiency he launched his own triangulation of Ireland (1819–24), but the arrival of the Ordnance Survey on the Irish scene during 1825 made his amateur efforts redundant. Following the Whiteboys' disturbances and a failure of the potato crop, he was in June 1822 appointed engineer of public works in the south-western district and given responsibility for alleviating the distress through improvement of the region's road network. Between 1822 and 1828 he and his family lived at Ballyellis House (now demolished) near Mallow, and during the fourteen years following his appointment he engineered some 250 miles of new road within counties Cork, Kerry, Limerick, and Tipperary.

To his quiverful of appointments Griffith in 1825 added

the post of director of the general boundary survey of Ireland, and in 1827 that of commissioner of the general survey and valuation of rateable property. In the first of those two posts he was responsible for the identification and plotting of all of Ireland's county, barony, parish, and townland boundaries as a preliminary to their representation on the 6 inch maps of the Ordnance Survey. The second of the posts remained dormant until 1829, by which time the cartographic work of the Ordnance Survey had advanced sufficiently far to allow property valuation to commence, and he resigned his post of mining engineer to what since 1820 had been styled the Royal Dublin Society.

As commissioner of valuation Griffith conducted two valuation surveys of Ireland: the townland valuation (1830–c.1842) and the highly detailed tenement valuation (1852–65). The latter came to be known throughout Ireland as 'the Griffith Valuation'. He claimed—with only partial justification—that a knowledge of the local solid geology was basic to meaningful land valuation, and he therefore instructed his valuators (at its maximum his staff numbered well over a hundred) in the making of geological observations. But, however he might protest to the contrary, these observations were really intended for the improvement of his geological map of Ireland, and from 1835 he was running from within the valuation office an entirely unauthorized geological survey of Ireland. For protracted periods one of the valuators—the able Patrick *Ganly—was employed solely upon geological field investigation. Griffith was ever adept at blurring the distinction between his official duties and his private interests, and the headquarters of the valuation survey was for long located within his Dublin home of fifty years at 2 Fitzwilliam Place.

Griffith's geological map of Ireland, still based on the inaccurate Irish map of Aaron Arrowsmith (1750–1823), elicited favourable comment when it was displayed before the British Association meeting in Dublin during August 1835. In October 1836 he became one of the four railway commissioners for Ireland, and persuaded his fellow commissioners that an understanding of regional geology was fundamental to the planning of the Irish railway system. In consequence the commissioners published his map, first in 1838 at a scale of 1:633,600, and then in May 1839 at a scale of 1:253,440, based on a fine new Ordnance Survey map of Ireland compiled under the direction of Thomas Aiskew Larcom. This magnificent quarter-inch geological map gives Griffith his claim to be hailed as 'the father of Irish geology'. Before 1855 the map underwent continuous revision, and during that year it was featured at the Universal Exhibition in Paris. Nevertheless, and despite Griffith's strenuous efforts, his making of the map failed to secure for him the directorship of the official geological survey of Ireland, established by the government in April 1845.

Griffith served as deputy chairman of the board of works from 1846 until March 1850, when he became chairman, which office he held until 1864; among the works executed during these years were various land-drainage schemes and the erection of the Dublin Natural History Museum (1857) and the National Gallery of Ireland (1864). On 8 March 1858 his numerous public services were rewarded with a baronetcy, but it was October 1868 before he relinquished the post of commissioner of valuation, thus concluding almost sixty years spent in the public domain. His other honours included two honorary degrees from the University of Dublin (1849 and 1862), and the Wollaston medal of the Geological Society of London (1854). Oddly, although he was associated with many eminent fellows of the Royal Society, he was himself never proposed as a candidate for election.

Griffith retained his mental and physical vigour until well into his nineties. In his later years he passed much time at Hendersyde, but he died peacefully in Dublin, at 2 Fitzwilliam Place, on 22 September 1878. He was buried alongside his wife in Dublin's Mount Jerome cemetery. One of the most talented Irishmen of the nineteenth century, he made formidable contributions in a number of discrete fields. But, never the most personable of men, he received from many of his contemporaries only grudging respect. He appears to have been motivated by a desire repeatedly to prove himself in the public eye, and it may be that the key to his life is rooted in a childhood sense of rejection arising from his mother's death, his father's second marriage, and the appearance of numerous stepsiblings.   GORDON L. HERRIES DAVIES

Sources *Richard Griffith, 1784–1878* [Dublin 1978], ed. G. L. Herries Davies and R. C. Mollan (1980) · G. L. Herries Davies, *Sheets of many colours: the mapping of Ireland's rocks, 1750–1890* (1983) · R. J. Griffith, 'Autobiography', NL Ire. [transcript] · NA Ire., Griffith MSS · private information (2004)
Archives NA Ire. · NL Ire.
Likenesses T. Cranfield, photograph, repro. in *Dublin University Magazine*, 83 (1874) · T. Farrell, marble bust, Royal Dublin Society
Wealth at death under £1500: probate, 15 Oct 1878, *CGPLA Ire.*

Griffith, Sir Samuel Walker (1845–1920), lawyer and politician in Australia, was born on 21 June 1845 at Merthyr Tudful, Glamorgan, the second son of the Revd Edward Griffith (1819–1891), Congregational minister, and his wife, Mary Walker (d. 1892). Griffith's father then held ministries at Portishead and Wiveliscombe, Somerset, after which he and his family sailed for Australia in 1853 at the invitation of the Colonial Missionary Society, where he became Congregational minister in Ipswich, Queensland. He subsequently transferred to Maitland, New South Wales, and later to Wharf Street, Brisbane.

Griffith first attended school in Ipswich, then at Woolloomooloo in Sydney, and finally at Maitland, where he was top student. He went on to the University of Sydney where he graduated with first-class honours, winning scholarships in mathematics and classics, and graduating BA (1863) and MA (1870). On 5 July 1870 he married, at Maitland, Julia Janet (d. 1925), youngest daughter of James Thomson, commissioner of crown lands in East Maitland. By then Griffith had embarked on a legal career by entering into articles of clerkship with Arthur Macalister at Ipswich in 1863. In 1865, however, he was granted permission to interrupt his articles, on being awarded the prestigious

Sir Samuel Walker Griffith (1845–1920), by Crown Studios, Sydney, 1903–11

Mort travelling fellowship of the University of Sydney. Under its terms, he travelled to the United Kingdom, and then to continental Europe, after which he returned to England to spend some months, before returning to Brisbane. Overseas he studied works of art, sculpture, architecture, and literature. On his return to Queensland, he completed his articles in September 1867, passed the bar examinations, and was admitted to the bar in the following month. He had early success; his practice grew, diversified, and prospered, and led him to undisputed leadership of the bar. He was appointed QC in 1876. Despite his increasing involvement in politics, Griffith maintained his flourishing private practice at the bar right up to the point at which he became chief justice in 1893.

From early years, Griffith developed an interest in politics, first evidenced by attendance at parliamentary debates, and in 1862 he published a series of twenty-five articles on members of the Queensland parliament. He entered parliament in 1872 as member for East Moreton, transferring to Oxley at the election of 1873. He rapidly established himself in the parliamentary arena, and in 1874 he was appointed attorney-general. To these responsibilities he added the portfolios of public instruction and public works. In 1879 he succeeded to the leadership of the Liberal Party, to which he came in opposition, the government having fallen in 1878. He proved himself to be an effective parliamentary leader in opposition to the ministry of his chief political rival Sir Thomas McIlwraith. He became premier in November 1883 and was in office until June 1888, displaying a capacity for extremely hard work. He maintained a close supervision over the work of his ministers and was a reluctant delegator.

During his first premiership, Griffith opposed the growing movement to divide Queensland; this reflected his fears that new colonies would be dominated by sugar planters, though he later recognized the need for administrative arrangements to take account of distance and diversity. On the controversial issue of the continuing use of kanaka (Pacific islands') labour, in 1884 he tightened the regulations governing their work conditions, and his government introduced and carried the act forbidding their employment altogether after a further ten years. At this time, Griffith had a reputation as something of a radical. He supported legislation for employers' liability and for the recognition of trade unions; in his writings he advocated a significant role for government in the protection of the weak. The socialist leader, William Lane, wrote to him approvingly in December 1888 that 'what Pericles was to Athens and Greece, such a leader [Griffith] could be to Australia and Queensland' (Joyce, 380 n. 63). Approbation, however, was not universal and his opponents in Queensland gave him the name Oily Sam.

The government fell in 1888, but was returned to office in August 1890, when Griffith again became premier in unlikely alliance with his long-time rival, McIlwraith. Economic conditions were deteriorating, and this led to bitter strikes, notably in the pastoral industry. Griffith responded by insisting on compliance with the law, and he took strong action: the military was called out, and strikers were arrested and imprisoned. While Griffith was vilified by those who had formerly praised him, he acted with caution and was a restraining force. Faced with worsening economic conditions, he also proposed helping planters by extending for ten years the importation of kanaka labour, and parliament approved the measure.

Over a long period, Griffith showed a continuing interest in Australian security and defence, and in moves to closer intercolonial association. At a conference in 1883, he supported the annexation of New Guinea and the establishment of a federal council for Australasia; he drafted the act for its establishment, was a regular attender at its meetings, and became its president. It was a defective organization with very limited powers and never had the support of New South Wales. A new initiative for Australian federation by Sir Henry Parkes of New South Wales in 1889 led to a meeting in Melbourne in 1890, which was followed by the first national Australasian constitutional convention, which met in Sydney in March 1891. Griffith, then premier of Queensland, played a leading role in it, particularly in the drafting of the constitution adopted by this body. Alfred Deakin, of Victoria, who was later thrice prime minister of Australia, paid high tribute to Griffith's achievement in his *Federal Story* (Deakin, 50): 'In every clause the measure bore the stamp of Sir Samuel Griffith's patient and untiring handiwork,

his terse, clear style and force of expression. At [the] close Griffith's influence had become supreme ... no other representative rivalled him.'

In 1893 Griffith accepted appointment as chief justice of Queensland, succeeding to the office at a time when its standing was low. He restored its reputation, and added significantly to his own as a distinguished lawyer and judge. He made a distinctive contribution through the preparation of a criminal code, on which he worked for years, aiming to make the criminal law as simple and generally accessible as possible. His code was approved by a royal commission, passed through the Queensland parliament, and was given assent by him as acting governor in November 1899. It came into force on 1 January 1901, the same day as the Australian commonwealth constitution. The code was largely copied in Western Australia, and became a model for criminal codes elsewhere in the world.

As chief justice of Queensland, Griffith could play no active role in the constitutional convention of 1897–8 which devised and adopted the constitution which, with a few amendments, became the constitution of the commonwealth of Australia. His draft of 1891 was, however, available to the convention and many of his detailed and at times critical comments upon the later drafts were incorporated in amendments to it. It has been fairly said that the final form of the Australian constitution contains not only much of Griffith's text of 1891, but also his 'lofty corrections of the words of the later and lesser draftsmen of 1897' (La Nauze, 191).

Griffith went further, and in the final stages of negotiation with the United Kingdom government on the passage of the bill, which had been endorsed by popular referendum in the Australian colonies, he intervened in support of the retention of appeals to the privy council. For a time this threatened the passage of the bill, but at the end a compromise was reached on a form of words which Griffith proposed. His reasons for acting in this way are not clear; his action certainly earned him the enmity of some Australian supporters of federation, and this was reflected in opposition—albeit unsuccessful—to his appointment as chief justice of the high court of Australia.

It is said that when Griffith accepted appointment to the Queensland bench in 1893, he had in view a greater place in a future federated Australia, and in the early days of ministry making in the infant commonwealth his name was mentioned. The high court of Australia was not established until 1903, and Griffith had a major role in the drafting of the Judiciary Act, under which it was finally constituted. It was envisaged that it should be a court of five judges (including the chief justice) with pension entitlements; in the event, after negotiation, it was established as a court of three, and it was only in the last days of his membership of the court that a pension was granted to the retiring chief justice, who was Griffith himself. Griffith's appointment as chief justice was greeted favourably by many but opposed by those who disapproved of his apparent changes of course in his second premiership, and of his role in the privy council appeal issue.

The High Court was constituted as a general court of appeal from state courts, as well as a distinctive federal court with a critically important role in the interpretation of the constitution. All three judges, Griffiths, Edmund Barton, and Richard O'Connor, had been founding fathers, and they soon established a close relationship, both personal and in their reading of the constitution. In the early days, there was a short but unhappy clash with Sir Josiah Symon, attorney-general in the Reid–McLean government, but that was resolved with the fall of that government. An amendment to the Judiciary Act provided for the appointment of two additional judges, and in 1906 Isaac Isaacs and H. B. Higgins, both members of the 1897–8 convention and attorneys-general in earlier federal ministries, took their seats.

From this time, divisions opened up within the court. Griffith and Isaacs in particular were not comfortable colleagues. Both were dominant, driving, and ambitious men who differed in style and in their legal and constitutional philosophies. Sir Owen Dixon, the great Australian jurist, while acknowledging Griffith's intellectual and professional qualities, speaks of him as having a legal mind of the Austinian age, representing the thoughts and learning of a period which had gone. There was division over major principles of constitutional interpretation; Griffith's reading of the constitution, which he was generally able to impose, emphasized the role of the states, while Isaacs's developed doctrine was strongly centralist. In the *Engineers' case*, a great constitutional case decided in 1920, soon after Griffith's death, Isaacs's doctrine prevailed. From time to time Griffith advised governors-general on constitutional matters; he was held in very high esteem by R. C. Munro Ferguson, governor-general from 1914 to 1920. Griffith retired from the court in 1919. He had been unwell for a long time, and was deeply preoccupied with his physical infirmities. To the dismay of his old and ailing friend Barton, he supported the appointment of Sir Adrian Knox rather than Barton as his successor; his principal concern was to keep Isaacs out.

Griffith had a happy family life. His marriage was close and secure; and correspondence between husband and wife reveals, beneath Griffith's seemingly aloof and cold exterior, an emotional warmth and care for his wife and children (two sons and four daughters). The family lived principally in Brisbane, from 1880 at Merthyr, an imposing house built for them at New Farm on the Brisbane River, although Griffiths lived at Sydney while on the High Court, making only annual visits to Brisbane. Outside the law, Griffith was an active freemason; he played a role in the administration of Brisbane schools, and was interested in the establishment and early development of the University of Queensland. He was also a member of the senate of the University of Sydney from 1904 to 1917. He was awarded honorary LLD degrees by the University of Queensland in 1912 and the University of Wales in 1913. An unusual interest was in Dante, and he published a translation of the *Divina commedia* in 1914. It was very literal, lacking in poetic feeling, but it throws an interesting light on the interests of its author. He was made a KCMG in 1886, promoted GCMG in 1895, and was sworn of the privy council in 1901, sitting on its judicial committee when in England in 1913.

Griffith died at Merthyr on 9 August 1920, from cerebral haemorrhage, congestion of lungs, heart failure, and arteriosclerosis. He was buried in Toowong cemetery, Brisbane. His estate was valued for probate in Australia at £27,335. A suburb in Canberra and a university in Brisbane are named after him.   ZELMAN COWEN

Sources R. B. Joyce, *Samuel Walker Griffith* (1984) · A. D. Graham, *The life of the Right Honourable Samuel Walker Griffith* (1989) · H. Gibbs, *Samuel Griffith* (1984) · J. A. La Nauze, *The making of the Australian constitution* (1972) · A. Deakin, *The federal story: the inner history of the federal cause*, ed. J. A. La Nauze, 2nd edn (1963) · G. Sawer, *Australian federalism in the courts* (1967) · Z. Cowen, *Isaac Isaacs*, new edn (1993) · *AusDB* · d. cert.
Archives Mitchell L., NSW, corresp. and papers · NL Aus., lecture notes · State Library of New South Wales, Sydney, Dixson Library, corresp. and papers | Mitchell L., NSW, papers relating to Dante · NL Aus., corresp. with Alfred Deakin · NL Aus., corresp. with Lord Novar
Likenesses Crown Studios, Sydney, photograph, 1903–11, NL Aus. [*see illus.*] · M. Meldrum, oils, 1913, Parliament House, Canberra, Australia · W. Dargie, oils, 1980, High Court, Canberra · G. Rivers, oils, Supreme Court of Queensland, Australia · P. Spencer, oils, High Court, Canberra
Wealth at death £27,335: Australian probate, *AusDB*

Griffith [*née* Wynne], **Sidney** (*c.*1720–1752), follower of Methodism, was the daughter of Cadwaladr Wynne and his wife, Jane Griffith (*d.* 1771) of Foelas, Ysbyty Ifan, Denbighshire, but her date of birth is unknown. She was named in honour of her grandmother, a member of the prominent Thelwall family. Her marriage to William Griffith (1721–1751) of Cefnamwlch in Caernarvonshire is believed to have taken place in 1741, for in 1742 she gave birth to her only son, John Griffith, high sheriff of Caernarvonshire in 1765.

Griffith converted to the Methodist cause under the ministry of the Methodist clergyman Peter Williams in 1746. Howel *Harris, one of the leaders of the early Methodist movement in Wales, met her for the first time during a preaching tour of north Wales in October 1748. The strong-minded and attractive young woman made a lasting impression on Harris, who was always gratified when members of the gentry were drawn to the movement. Her first visit to Harris's home at Trefeca in Brecknockshire took place in February 1749 and she soon began to accompany him on his preaching journeys. In July 1749 she fled to Trefeca to seek refuge from her unhappy marriage and her drunken and abusive husband, who was compared by John Wesley to one of the 'ruffians' in *Macbeth*.

Harris insisted that 'Madam Griffith' should be regarded as a prophetess and referred to her as his 'Eye' and his 'Light'. In this capacity she attended meetings of the Association, the governing body of the Methodist movement in Wales, despite the fact that the movement tended to disapprove of women adopting a prominent public role. Ultimately, however, the relationship proved to be one of the contributory factors in the quarrel which divided the Welsh Methodist cause into two distinct camps in 1750. Doctrinal differences and increasing tension as a result of

Harris's fractious personality were also to play a major part in the division, which led to most of the Methodist exhorters siding with Daniel Rowland against Harris.

Harris's infatuation has in the past been frequently attributed to his declining mental health, and it has been suggested that exhaustion led him to the brink of a total breakdown by the late 1740s. It has also been claimed that Mrs Whitefield actively sought to poison Anne Harris's mind against Madam Griffith out of malice and jealousy. The precise nature of the relationship remains a topic of debate among Welsh historians, particularly since Harris's diary entries are ambiguous and open to various interpretations. There can be little doubt that he was utterly enchanted by her. His marriage to Anne Williams in 1744 had not been a great success, partly because his wife's ill health did not allow her to accompany him on his preaching tours. Speculation regarding the relationship with Madam Griffith caused Harris's associates to urge him to relinquish his prophetess for the good of the movement. Harris, however, proved to be intractable and succeeded in alienating many of his closest colleagues by his refusal to listen to reason. It is difficult to know what Griffith's own feelings and attitudes were, since so much evidence regarding the relationship comes either from Harris's own writings or from contemporary supposition. She could be obstinate and determined, and occasionally supported Daniel Rowland against Harris on matters of doctrine. She also at times proved to be something of a financial burden, since her husband was loath to contribute to her maintenance before he finally fell and broke his neck in February 1751.

Griffith died on 31 May 1752 at The Lodge, Hyde Park, and was buried in Audley Chapel, London. Harris was grief-stricken and continued to mourn her passing for the rest of his life. It could be argued, however, that her death removed one major stumbling block in the way of his eventual reconciliation with the remainder of the Methodist movement in 1763.   ERYN M. WHITE

Sources H. Harris, diaries, NL Wales, Calvinist Methodist papers · G. Tudur, 'A critical study, based on his own diaries, of the life and work of Howell Harris', DPhil diss., U. Oxf., 1989 · D. Ll. Morgan, *The great awakening in Wales* (1988) · G. M. Roberts, ed., *Hanes Methodistiaeth Galfinaidd Cymru*, 2 (1978) · G. H. Jenkins, *The foundations of modern Wales, 1642–1780* (1987) · G. M. Roberts, *Portread o ddiwygiwr* (1969) · G. T. Roberts, *Howell Harris* (1951) · E. Evans, *Howel Harris, evangelist, 1714–1773* (1974) · E. M. White, 'Praidd bach y bugail mawr': *seiadau Methodistaidd de-orllewin Cymru, 1737–50* (1995) · G. P. Owen, *Methodistiaeth Llŷn ac Eifionydd* (1978) · J. E. Griffith, *Pedigrees of Anglesey and Carnarvonshire families* (privately printed, Horncastle, 1914)
Archives NL Wales, Calvinist Methodist Archive
Wealth at death £900 to Trevecca College, Trefeca

Griffith, Stewart Cathie [*known as* Billy Griffith] (1914–1993), cricketer and cricket administrator, was born on 16 June 1914 at 51 Balham Park Road, Wandsworth, London, the elder son and elder child of Henry Leonard Adams Griffith, stockbroker, and his wife, Jean, *née* Cathie. A man of considerable charm, Billy Griffith (as he was always known) became one of the best-liked and most scrupulous figures in the cricket world. At Dulwich College he was head of the school and excelled at sport, being four years in the cricket eleven, as a batsman who took to wicket-keeping, and four years in the rugby fifteen, as a rumbustious centre three-quarter. In the early 1930s he and his contemporary and lifelong friend, Hugh (H. T.) Bartlett, a brilliant schoolboy cricketer, brought Dulwich outstanding success on the games field. After gaining a Cambridge cricket blue in 1935, his second year at Pembroke College, Griffith was chosen to tour Australasia in the winter of 1935–6 with a side sent out by Marylebone Cricket Club (MCC) to try and heal the wounds inflicted during the bodyline tour three years earlier.

Between going down from Cambridge and the outbreak of the Second World War, Griffith went back to teach at Dulwich. On 1 April 1939 he married Barbara Ethel Reynolds (*b.* 1915/16), daughter of Robert John Reynolds, a hotelier, and his wife, Ethel. They had a son, Mike, and a daughter, Pauline. Mike was named after one of his godfather P. G. Wodehouse's characters, Wodehouse having been a friend of Griffith's from Dulwich days. Griffith might well have abandoned his schoolmastering career whether or not the war had come. He kept wicket well enough for Sussex after the end of the school summer term of 1939 to be offered the job on a regular basis and to be selected to go with the MCC to India in 1939–40, a tour which was cancelled with the onset of war. Griffith found himself going instead to Normandy and then to Nijmegen as a pilot in the glider pilot regiment. Thickset, resolute, and seldom without a pipe in his mouth, he rose to the temporary rank of lieutenant-colonel. As commander of his wing, he piloted the commander of the 6th airborne division, General Sir Richard Gale, to the Normandy landing, for which he won the DFC. He was able to keep his hand in with some wartime cricket and duly signed up with Sussex when the war ended, combining the secretaryship of the county with keeping wicket for them. This he did until 1949.

The highlight of Griffith's playing career came in the first test match against the West Indies at Port of Spain, Trinidad, in January 1948, when, with England beset by injuries, he was pressed into service as an opening batsman. In his unaccustomed role, Griffith scored a heroic 140, thereby becoming one of only a handful of cricketers whose maiden first-class century has been in a test match. He played two more test matches, both against South Africa in South Africa, when, as a wicket-keeper, he was preferred to the great Godfrey Evans. Leaving Sussex in 1950, Griffith had two years writing about cricket and rugby football for the *Sunday Times* and the *Sporting Record* before joining the secretariat of the MCC at Lord's, where he stayed until his retirement in 1974.

Griffith's first ten years at the MCC, as assistant to Ronny Aird, were relatively uneventful, unlike his last twelve, when he was in full charge, and English cricket, still largely controlled by the MCC, was under pressure both financially and politically. Griffith was of a conservative bent. 'For most Britishers' he once said, 'cricket has a unique image, quite different from any other sport …

Nothing must be done to damage that' (private information). It was not so much that he was against change as that he was wary of it. He had the greatest affection for Lord's and all that it stood for. However, in 1963 he was obliged to supervise the abolition of the distinction between amateurs and professionals, as well as the introduction of one-day cricket played by the first-class counties. He made time to manage the MCC side to Australia and New Zealand in 1965–6, but was back in the thick of things at Lord's when, to enable the game in England to benefit from Sports Council funds, unavailable to a private club, the MCC relinquished its long-standing authority by establishing the Cricket Council and its subsidiary bodies, the Test and County Cricket Board (later the England and Wales Cricket Board) and the National Cricket Association.

Next came the D'Oliveira affair, with its far-flung repercussions. This arose as a result of the MCC's first leaving Basil D'Oliveira, a 'Cape coloured' who had emigrated from Cape Town, out of their side to tour South Africa in 1968–9, and then bringing him in when injury forced T. W. Cartwright, an original selection, to withdraw. Having been privy to earlier informal discussions that had taken place in South Africa between B. J. Vorster, South Africa's prime minister, and Viscount Cobham, a former president of the MCC, in which Vorster strongly implied that if D'Oliveira were chosen there would be no tour, Griffith was in a cleft stick. In the event, he gave nothing away; Vorster made good his threat and the tour was abandoned. Griffith, who was known to favour the retention of sporting links with South Africa, offered to resign, and, although that was never seriously entertained, the club found themselves fighting off a vote of no confidence in their handling of the matter at a special general meeting at Church House, Westminster. So it came as something of a relief to Griffith when, at the age of sixty, he could retire honourably.

Inflexible in his beliefs, sometimes disadvantageously so, Griffith was yet eminently companionable, and had a host of friends and a delightful sense of humour. To an unhappy extent his retirement was marred by ill health. He was appointed CBE in 1975 for services to cricket and stayed well long enough to be president of Sussex from 1975 to 1977 and of the MCC in 1979–80, and to recodify the laws of cricket in 1980; but complications following an operation for bowel cancer left him so heavily immobile that his last five years were spent in a nursing home, Hollymead House, Downview Road, Felpham, Sussex near the home at Middleton-on-Sea where he had lived since soon after the war. He died there, on 7 April 1993, of bronchopneumonia. He was survived by his wife, Barbara, his son, Mike (who captained Sussex from 1969 to 1972), and daughter, Pauline.   JOHN WOODCOCK

Sources *The Times* (8 April 1993) · *The Independent* (10 April 1993) · personal knowledge (2004) · private information (2004) · b. cert. · m. cert. · d. cert.
Likenesses photograph, repro. in *The Times* · photograph, repro. in *The Independent*
Wealth at death £84,614: probate, 21 May 1993, *CGPLA Eng. & Wales*

Griffith, Walter (1727–1779), naval officer, was born on 15 May 1727, the younger son of Ralph Griffith of Bron-gain in Llanfechain, Montgomeryshire. He was promoted lieutenant on 7 May 1755 and commander of the *Postilion* on 4 June 1759. In September 1759 he was appointed to temporary command of the *Gibraltar* and on 15 November, while cruising near Brest, he sighted the French fleet. He sent warning to Admiral Edward Hawke and to the Admiralty, while himself going to warn Admiral Thomas Brodrick, then blockading Cadiz. His timely warnings assisted the British fleet movements, which led to the battle of Quiberon Bay (20 November), and he was confirmed in command of the *Gibraltar*, with his commission as captain dated 11 December 1759. He continued in her until 1766, first in the Mediterranean until the peace, then on the home station.

During the Spanish armament in 1770 he commanded the *Namur* for a few weeks, and in 1776 he was appointed to the *Nonsuch*, in which early in 1777 he joined Admiral Lord Howe in North America, where he took part in the defence of Sandy Hook against d'Estaing in July and August 1778. He afterwards sailed with Commodore William Hotham to the West Indies, where he was part of Admiral Samuel Barrington's squadron at the battle of the Grand Cul de Sac, St Lucia, on 15 December 1778 and of Admiral John Byron's fleet at the battle of Grenada on 6 July 1779.

When Byron resigned the command to Rear-Admiral Hyde Parker, Griffith moved to the *Conqueror*. On 18 December 1779 a French convoy was seen approaching Martinique and the British fleet came out from St Lucia to intercept it. Griffith in the *Conqueror* was in the lead, became separated from the rest of the fleet, and soon found himself alone fighting three French ships of the line, led by La Motte-Picquet, which had come out from Fort Royal. Later other British ships came up to aid Griffith, but the action drifted towards the shoals and coastal batteries of Fort Royal Bay, so Admiral Parker signalled his ships to return. As the *Conqueror* was obeying the signal, Griffith was killed by the last French broadside. 'The service', wrote Parker, 'cannot lose a better man or a better officer.' Unmarried, he left a legacy in his will to his supposed natural son, Walter, whose mother was named as Margaret Skott.

J. K. LAUGHTON, *rev.* ALAN G. JAMIESON

Sources DWB · A. G. Jamieson, 'War in the Leeward Islands, 1775–1783', DPhil diss., U. Oxf., 1981 · D. Syrett, *The Royal Navy in American waters, 1775–1783* (1989) · PRO, PROB 11/1073
Archives PRO, Admiralty MSS, corresp.

Griffith, William (1810–1845), botanist, youngest son of Thomas Griffith, a London merchant, was born at Ham Common, near Petersham, Surrey, on 4 March 1810. He was apprenticed to a surgeon in the West End of London, and completed his medical studies at University College, London, where he attended classes in botany by J. Lindley. He continued his studies in anatomy under Charles Mirbel in Paris and in medical botany at the Chelsea Physic Garden.

Griffith's work appeared in several publications of 1832:

flower drawings in J. Lindley's *Introduction to Botany*; a microscopical examination of the plant *Phytocrene gigantea* in volume 3 of N. Wallich's *Plantae Asiaticae rariores*; and an investigation of the structure of a liverwort (*Targionia hypophylla*) in Mirbel's monograph on *Marchantia polymorpha*. In May of that year he sailed for India, and on 24 September reached Madras, where he was appointed as an assistant surgeon with the East India Company.

Griffith's first station was on the coast of Tenasserim, but in 1835 he was attached to the Bengal presidency, and served (together with Nathaniel Wallich) as botanist in an expedition to inspect the tea-forests and explore the natural history of Assam, then a little-known region. This was the beginning of a series of journeys through nearly the whole of the company's territories, during which many specimens (especially botanical) were collected. Under the direction of Captain F. Jenkins, the commissioner, he traversed the unexplored eastern part of the Indian territory between Sadiya and Ava, country which was not revisited by Europeans until Burma was annexed by Britain in the later half of the nineteenth century. At great personal risk he undertook an expedition from Assam to Ava, and thence to Rangoon, during which he was reported to have been assassinated. The hardships of this expedition resulted in an attack of fever soon after his return to Calcutta. On his recovery he was, in 1837, appointed surgeon to the embassy to Bhutan, under Major R. B. Pemberton. He was the first botanist to visit that country, and this gave him an opportunity to revisit the Khasi hills in eastern Bengal. After rejoining Pemberton at Goalpara, Griffith traversed 400 miles of Bhutan territory, returning to Calcutta the following year. In March 1839 he was in Quetta, attached to the army of the Indus, and, after the fall of Kabul, penetrated beyond the Hindu Kush into what he called Khorasan (later the eastern part of Afghanistan), never missing a chance to botanize. Neither hardship nor illness deflected him from an obsessive attention to his botanical studies.

Griffith was again at Calcutta in August 1841, and, after visiting Simla, he was appointed to Malacca in Malaya as civil assistant surgeon. He was recalled in 1842 to take charge of the Royal Botanic Garden in Calcutta, Wallich, the superintendent, having gone to the Cape to recuperate from ill health. He also acted as botanical professor in the medical college at Calcutta. Griffith, who hoped eventually to succeed Wallich, welcomed this opportunity to introduce some of his own concepts of a botanical garden. With an insensitive disregard for what Wallich might think he removed a large number of trees, rearranged the plants according to a natural classification and, in the process, ruined its attractions as a pleasure garden. Even Joseph Hooker, one of his admirers, was shocked when he visited the garden in 1848, and lamented 'the indiscriminate destruction of the useful and ornamental which had attended the well-meant but ill-judged attempt to render a garden a botanical class-book' (J. Hooker, *Himalayan Journals* 1, 1854, 3). Towards the close of 1844 Wallich resumed his post.

In September of that year Griffith married Miss Emily Henderson, sister of the wife of his brother, Captain Griffith. On 11 December he left Calcutta for Malacca, but shortly after his arrival, on 31 January 1845, he contracted hepatitis. He died on 9 February and was buried at Malacca.

The little that Griffith published during his lifetime appeared in the *Transactions of the Linnean Society*, *Asiatic Researches*, *Journal of the Asiatic Society of Bengal*, *Transactions of the Medical and Physical Society of Calcutta*, and *Calcutta Journal of Natural History*. The majority of his efforts went into assembling data for what he intended to be a comprehensive account of the Indian flora on a geographical basis. To this end he meticulously noted plants and their habitats in his journals; he used the microscope as a matter of routine and made numerous drawings of floral dissections. He collected assiduously on his travels, even persuading some of his fellow officers to assist him. He sent native collectors to places that he would have no opportunity of visiting. All this was done to make his projected flora as complete as possible. Providentially he had bequeathed his collections to the East India Company which, after his premature death, undertook to publish his papers. Griffith's friend J. McClelland, a geologist, was perhaps not the best person to edit the papers, which were not in a fit state for publication. However, despite poor editing, the books remained a testimony to Griffith's ability and industry—*Journals of Travels in Assam, Burma, Bootan, Afghanistan …* (1847), *Notulae ad plantas Asiaticas* (4 vols., 1847–54), *Itinerary Notes of Plants Collected in the Khasyah and Bootan Mountains* (1848), *Icones plantarum Asiaticarum* (1847–54), and *Palms of British East India* (1850). Griffith's manuscripts and what survived of his plant collections stored in the cellars of the East India Company in London were rescued by Joseph Hooker in 1858 and are now at the Royal Botanic Gardens, Kew.

Although Griffith died before his full potential could be realized, Sir George King had no doubts that he was 'a man of genius' whose early death had been a severe blow to the advancement of botanical study in India. Never content to be just a traditional taxonomist, Griffith had extended his researches to anatomy, physiology, and ecology. He had studied ferns and mosses as well as flowering plants but seldom showed much interest in economic botany. An Asiatic tree, *Enicosanthum*, was once called *Griffithia* and *Griffithianthus* in memory of him.

B. D. JACKSON, *rev.* RAY DESMOND

Sources *Calcutta Journal of Natural History*, 6 (1846), 294–306 · *Proceedings of the Linnean Society of London*, 1 (1838–48), 239–44 · *Journal of Botany*, 4 (1845), 371–5 · *Journal of Botany*, 7 (1848), 446–9 · *Phytologist*, 2 (1845), 252–5 · W. H. Lang, 'William Griffith, 1810–1845', *Makers of British botany*, ed. F. W. Oliver (1913), 178–91 · R. Desmond, *The European discovery of the Indian flora* (1992) · I. H. Burkill, *Chapters on the history of botany in India* (Calcutta, 1965) · J. M. Lamond, 'The Afghanistan collections of William Griffith', *Notes from the Royal Botanic Garden, Edinburgh*, 30 (1970), 159–75 · F. A. Stafleu and R. S. Cowan, *Taxonomic literature: a selective guide*, 2nd edn, 1, Regnum Vegetabile, 94 (1976), 1005–6
Archives BL OIOC, journal, drawings, and papers, MSS Eur. D 159 517; NHD 7/1117–7/1139 · BL OIOC, MSS and some drawings · Linn. Soc., corresp., notes, and drawings · NHM, zoological specimens ·

RBG Kew, corresp. and papers · RBG Kew, plant specimens and MSS | BL, letters to R. Brown, Add. MS 32441 · RBG Kew, letters to Sir William Hooker
Likenesses E. Morton, lithograph, 1843 (after daguerreotype), repro. in W. Griffith, *Journals of travels in Assam* (1847)

Griffith, William Pettit (1815–1884), architect and antiquary, was born on 7 July 1815 at 9 St John's Square, Clerkenwell, London, the son of John William Griffith (*c.*1790–1855), architect, who lived at that address for more than half a century. He was brought up to be an architect, and before he was twenty was writing notes in J. C. Loudon's *Architectural Magazine*. He continued these notes, under the signature Tyro, Wilmington Square, from 1835 to 1837, besides contributing original articles and designs in 1836. In 1839 and 1840 he exhibited architectural designs at the Royal Academy, and from 1840 to 1842 watercolour drawings of fonts and portions of old churches, including those at Hendon, Middlesex, and Broxbourne and St Albans, Hertfordshire, in the galleries of the Society of British Artists. On 12 May 1842 he was elected a fellow of the Society of Antiquaries, and between 1856 and 1858 he exhibited at the society architectural fragments in connection with his work of restoration at St John's Gate, Clerkenwell. On 29 November 1860 he exhibited and described drawings, made by him from actual measurements in 1842, of the original Norman chancel in Great Amwell church, Hertfordshire, since destroyed (published with plates in *Proceedings of the Society of Antiquaries, London*, 2nd ser., 1, 1860, 259–61).

Griffith was elected a fellow of the Royal Institute of British Architects on 14 June 1847, and on that evening spoke about 'The principles which guided the architects in constructing the minsters, cathedrals, and churches of England'. In 1855 he was awarded the institute's silver medal for 'An essay on the principles or laws which govern the formation of architectural decorations and ornaments'; the manuscript, illustrated by neatly executed ink and sepia drawings, is in the library of the Royal Institute of British Architects. In connection with it are four sheets of drawings, 'Classification of mediaeval ornaments' and 'Designs for mediaeval ornaments from the vegetable kingdom, arranged geometrically and conventionalised'. At the chapter meetings of the college of the Freemasons of the Church he read on 12 August and 9 September 1845 papers 'On the ancient baptismal fonts of England' (drawings of nine ancient fonts which he had made in 1838–9 were engraved on one sheet by Webb & Son); on 10 February 1846 he read 'On the different kinds of stone employed in the edifices of Babylon, Egypt, Greece, Rome, and Great Britain' and on 13 October 1846 'On the hagioscope or squint in the ancient parochial churches of England'. He was made an honorary member of the Bedfordshire Architectural Society in 1847, and of the Liverpool Architectural Society in 1849. At meetings of these and other learned societies Griffith delivered papers on a variety of architectural and antiquarian subjects.

Among the works executed under Griffith's superintendence were the repair of St John's Church, Clerkenwell (1845), the restoration of St John's Gate (1845–6), and the rebuilding of the spire (1849) and the erection of a font (1851) for St James's Church, Clerkenwell. The drawing of the font was engraved. He designed the Cherry Tree tavern, Clerkenwell (1852), and the Goldsmiths' and Jewellers' Annuity Institution Asylum, Hackney (1853; the exterior view engraved); and he planned additions and alterations to the Clerkenwell vestry hall (1857), designed many parochial and ragged schools (1858–62), and adapted Melrose Hall, Putney Heath, Middlesex, for the Royal Hospital for Incurables (1864–5). He directed the building of Messrs Rivington's printing-office, St John's House, Clerkenwell (1866), and the repairs to and partial renewal of the tower and porch of the church of St Sepulchre, Holborn (1873); he designed the house of detention, Kingston upon Thames, Surrey, and the repairs to the tower of Kingston church. Griffith was keenly interested in the antiquities of Clerkenwell, made a special study of the old priory of St John of Jerusalem, and spared no pains to avert the threatened destruction of St John's Gate, helping to raise a public subscription for its restoration. Relics of both priory and gate, some of which he brought to light, were deposited in the Architectural Museum and at South Kensington.

In his writings Griffith mainly endeavoured to show that the architecture of the past was governed by geometrical principles, and that architecture therefore had a scientific basis. He gave advice on the erection of contemporary buildings following similar principles. Although broadly in agreement with A. W. N. Pugin, he did not favour Gothic to the exclusion of all other styles. He wrote that 'the geometrical proportions pervading Greek and Gothic architecture are in principle based upon nature's works' (*Suggestions for a More Beautiful Period of Gothic Architecture*, 1855, 6), and that 'by the employment of regular figures and their multiples in architecture, we always ensure an equal distribution of parts, which also exists in the vegetable kingdom' (*Ancient Gothic Churches: their Proportions and Chromatics*, 1847–52, 2.26). He also published *The Geometrical Proportion of Architecture* (1843), *The Natural System of Architecture* (1845), and *Suggestions for a More Perfect and Beautiful Period of Gothic Architecture* (1855–6). He died a poor man at his home at 3 Isledon Road, Highbury, London, on 14 September 1884.

BERTHA PORTER, *rev.* VALERIE SCOTT

Sources W. J. Pinks, *The history of Clerkenwell*, ed. E. J. Wood, 2nd edn (1881), 638, 691–3 · *The Builder*, 13 (1855), 620 · *Dir. Brit. archs.* · J. Johnson, ed., *Works exhibited at the Royal Society of British Artists, 1824–1893, and the New English Art Club, 1888–1917*, 2 vols. (1975) · *Graves, RA exhibitors*
Archives RIBA BAL, RIBA nomination papers

Griffiths [*née* Rogers], **Amelia Warren** (1768–1858), phycologist and seaweed collector, was born on 14 January 1768 in Pilton, north Devon, the elder daughter of John and Emily Rogers. On 10 March 1794 she married the Revd William Griffiths, vicar of St Issey, Cornwall; she was widowed on 31 August 1802, and raised five children on her own. She lived at various locations in south Devon before settling at 9 Cary Parade, Torquay, in 1829.

A leading and much celebrated British phycologist for

half a century, Amelia Griffiths collected seaweeds at many locations in Dorset, Cornwall, and Devon. Her first instructor in marine botany was the Revd Samuel Goodenough, a founder of the Linnean Society. In 1808 Dawson Turner named *Fucus griffithsia* for her, acknowledging her discovery of this scarce species, and praised her 'unwearied zeal and extraordinary acuteness' (Turner, 80). Her name also appears in many other specific epithets, and in 1817 the Swedish botanist Carl Agardh honoured her by naming a genus of red seaweed *Griffithsia*.

Amelia Griffiths discovered many new species and genera of seaweeds, and exchanged specimens with botanists across Britain and Europe. She had a wide correspondence and generously shared her knowledge. Letters to Sir William Hooker are characterized by courtesy as well as a confident, scholarly tone, and record a scientific friendship that began in 1826 and continued for thirty years. Her most significant scientific relationship was probably with the Irish cryptogamic botanist William Henry Harvey, author of *Phycologia Britannica* (1846–51). They met in 1832, and Harvey came to depend greatly on Mrs Griffiths for descriptions, illustrations, and critical commentary. Indeed, he dedicated the 1849 edition of his *Manual of the British Marine Algae* to her, recording her as 'a lady whose long-continued researches have, more than those of any other observer in Britain, contributed to the present advanced state of marine botany'. He later wrote of her in his *Memoir* that she had 'the happiest knack of finding the rarest and most beautiful plants in the most perfect state' (*Memoir*, 26).

In addition to collecting, Amelia Griffiths observed a wide variety of marine algae throughout their stages of growth and reproduction, and was interested in plants 'from infancy to decay' (Griffiths to Hooker, 11 Aug 1835, RBG Kew). She noted how their habit forms varied at different times of the year, and her observations about habitats of seaweeds were new at that time. However, despite her expertise, she published only three short pieces: an account of the natural history of the Torbay district for Octavian Blewitt's *Panorama of Torquay* (2nd edn., 1832), and two notes to *The Phytologist*. Her first note in *The Phytologist* in 1842 identifies a plant found in Scotland, the second (in 1843) records her observations on a particular moss, with descriptive and taxonomic details.

Mrs Griffiths was one of a number of women seaweed collectors who contributed to large synoptic projects during the early nineteenth century. Her immediate botanical circle included her daughter Amelia Elizabeth (1802–1861), who worked on mosses. She also assisted and promoted the work of Mary Wyatt, a former family servant, who produced five volumes of mounted specimens of Devon marine algae for sale under the title *Algae Danmonienses* (1833–41). A founding member of the Torquay Natural History Society in 1844, Amelia Griffiths compiled a seaweed collection for its reference and donated other specimens of local flora to its museum. In 1851 she prepared a collection of 720 specimens of seaweed to be sold for charitable purposes. Her phycological zeal remained strong into old age. She died ten days before her ninetieth birthday, on 4 January 1858, at Bloomfield Lodge, Meadfoot Road, Torquay, and was buried in Torwood churchyard.   ANN B. SHTEIR

Sources M. A. Wilson [Mrs D. P. Wilson], 'Amelia Warren Griffiths of Torquay—a pioneer botanist', *Transactions and Proceedings for 1951–52, Torquay Natural History Society*, 11/2 (1953), 74–7 · *Memoir of W. H. Harvey, MD, FRS, with selections from his journal and correspondence* (1869) · A. W. Griffiths, letters, 1826–56, RBG Kew, directors' correspondence, vols. 1–36 · W. H. Harvey, *A manual of the British marine algae*, 2nd edn (1849) · O. Blewitt, *The panorama of Torquay*, 2nd edn (1832), 74–83 · *The Phytologist*, 1/5 (Oct 1842), 203 · *The Phytologist*, 1/22 (March 1843), 554–5 · M. Wyatt, *Algae danmonienses, or, Dried specimens of marine plants*, 4 vols [1833–7] · M. Rendel, 'Women in Torquay in the first half of the nineteenth century', *Report and Transactions of the Devonshire Association*, 126 (1994), 17–39 · D. Turner, *Fuci, or, Colored figures*, 4 vols. (1808–19) · *GM*, 1st ser., 72 (1802), 785 · d. cert.

Archives Linn. Soc., specimens · NHM, Herbarium Musei Britannica, specimens · North Devon Athenaeum, Barnstaple, specimens · RBG Kew, directors' corresp. · Royal Albert Museum, Exeter, specimens · Torquay Natural History Museum, specimens · U. Glas., department of botany, specimens · Cork, specimens | NHM, Berkeley corresp.

Griffiths [née Thomas], **Ann** (bap. 1776, d. 1805), hymn writer in Welsh, born at a farmhouse called Dolwar-fach in the parish of Llanfihangel-yng-Ngwynfa, Montgomeryshire, the fourth of the five children of John Evan Thomas (1736–1804), a tenant farmer, and his wife, Jane, née Theodore (1744–1794), was baptized in Llanfihangel-yng-Ngwynfa parish church on 21 April 1776. Her schooling amounted to a meagre three years, first with a Mrs Ann Owen in Llanfihangel, and then in a school kept by the curate, Ezeciel Hamer, where she acquired proficiency in reading and writing Welsh, and colloquial English; she never learned to read English. Her home was a cultured and religious one, with extracts from the Bible and the Book of Common Prayer being read daily; readings of the translations of Richard Baxter and William Romaine influenced her considerably.

Evan Thomas was a churchwarden on a number of occasions, and welcomed itinerant preachers as well as neighbours to Dolwar-fach. By the 1790s the family had been greatly influenced by the Welsh Calvinistic Methodist movement, and Ann herself was converted on 28 March 1796 at an open-air service in Llanfyllin conducted by the independent preacher Benjamin Jones (1756–1826) of Pwllheli. A powerful revival had broken out in nearby Pontrobert in the spring of 1795, and other young people had experienced conversion, including her elder brothers John and Edward, John Davies, a missionary for fifty-four years in Tahiti, and John Hughes. The latter became her mentor and subsequently married Ruth Evans, Ann's maid and companion. Ruth memorized Ann's hymns and recited them to her husband, who preserved them in his notebooks. John Hughes stayed at Dolwar-fach for some months in 1799 as a teacher of a circulating school, and Ann's letters to him between 1800 and 1804 (seven of eight that have been preserved and published) are regarded as fine pieces of religious prose. The eighth letter, to Elizabeth, Ruth's sister, is the only surviving piece of prose in her own hand.

Following her conversion Ann exchanged more worldly enthusiasms, such as her love of dancing, for the religious life of the Calvinistic Methodist. With others she trekked over the Berwyn Mountains to Bala, a distance of 22 miles, to hear her hero, Thomas Charles, preach and to receive the sacrament at the monthly communion service. At least one of her hymns was written on the journey to Bala. It was in this warm-hearted fellowship that she met a Methodist elder, Thomas Griffiths (1777–1808), a farmer from Meifod and brother of Evan Griffiths, a historian of the new movement in Montgomeryshire. They were married on 10 October 1804 and on 13 July 1805 a daughter, Elizabeth, was born, but she survived only a fortnight. In early August, Ann Griffiths herself died at Dolwar-fach from tuberculosis (a disease that was to prove fatal for both her brother John and her husband) and was buried at Llanfihangel on 12 August 1805. Within twelve months Thomas Charles had her hymns printed by Robert Saunderson at Bala in *Casgliad o Hymnau*. The same year Robert Jones of Rhos-lan published them in his revised edition of *Grawnsyppiau Canaan*, first published in Liverpool in 1795. Since then a selection has been published in the hymnbooks of all the Welsh religious denominations. The original version of the hymns and letters from John Hughes's notebooks saw the light of day in *Gwaith Ann Griffiths* ('Cyfres y Fil') published by Sir Owen M. Edwards in 1905. There is a considerable amount of literature relating to Ann Griffiths's work, both in Welsh and English, with philosophers, theologians, and literary critics agreeing that she was a woman of extraordinary piety and prayer, some believing her comparable in stature to Julian of Norwich. Her hymn on the Incarnation, 'Rhyfedd, rhyfedd gan angylion', has been praised by Saunders Lewis as 'one of the majestic songs in the religious poetry of Europe'. In the light of modern scholarship the Gregynog Press published a scholarly edition of her work in 1998. She is commemorated in the Ann Griffiths Memorial Chapel which now stands at Dolanog, a mile north of her former home.

D. BEN REES

Sources A. M. Allchin, *Ann Griffiths* (1976) · D. Morgan, ed., *Y ferch o Ddolwar Fach* (1977) · J. S. Ryan, *The hymns of Ann Griffiths* (1980) [with an introduction, notes, and bibliography] · S. Megân, *Gwaith Ann Griffiths* (1982) · H. A. Hodges, ed., *Homage to Ann Griffiths* (1976) · A. M. Allchin, *Ann Griffiths: the furnace and the fountain* (1987) · M. Davies, *Cofiant Ann Griffiths* (1865) · W. Morris, *Cofio Ann Griffiths* (1955) · O. M. Edwards, *Gwaith Ann Griffiths* (1905) · A. M. Allchin, *Praise above all: discovering the Welsh tradition* (1991) · S. Lewis, *Meistri'r canrifoedd: ysgrifau ar hanes llenyddiaeth Gymraeg*, ed. R. G. Gruffydd (1973) · J. R. Jones, 'Cofio Ann Griffiths', *Llên Cymru*, 8 (1964–5), 33–41 · *DWB* · *Y Traethodydd*, 2 (1846), 420–33

Archives NL Wales, CM archives, papers 5863–4

Likenesses A. M. Allictoin, marble effigy on monument, repro. in Allchin, *Ann Griffiths*

Griffiths, Arthur George Frederick (1838–1908), inspector of prisons and author, was born on 9 December 1838 at Poona, India, the second son of Lieutenant-Colonel John Griffiths of the 6th Royal Warwickshire regiment. He was educated at King William's College, Isle of Man, and entered the army as ensign in the 63rd (Manchester) regiment on 13 February 1855. He served at the siege of Sevastopol and in the expedition to Kinburn during the Crimean War, and received the Crimean medal, being promoted lieutenant on 27 July 1855.

In 1856 Griffiths's regiment was stationed at Halifax, Nova Scotia, and, following the failure of the War Office to confirm his appointment as aide-de-camp to Sir William Eyre, commander of British troops in Canada, Griffiths returned home on leave. He attended the Hythe School of Musketry and in 1860 passed fifth into the Staff College. In November 1861, owing to tension with the United States over the Trent affair, Griffiths was ordered to rejoin his regiment at Halifax. He was promoted captain on 12 February 1862.

From 1864 to 1870 Griffiths was brigade major at Gibraltar and was placed in temporary charge of the convict establishment there. This brought him to the notice of Edmund Du Cane, the newly appointed chairman of the directors of convict prisons, who shared with Griffiths a great enthusiasm for military matters as well as a passion for administrative uniformity and consistency. Angered by the promotion of a younger, but monied, officer above him, Griffiths accepted Du Cane's invitation to join the English convict prison service. He served as deputy governor of the convict prisons of Chatham (1870–72), Millbank (1872–4), and Wormwood Scrubs (1874–8); his main contribution at this time was setting up schemes of convict labour on public works. From 1878 to 1899 he served as inspector of prisons: Du Cane was then chair of both the new Prison Commission (which under the 1877 Prisons Act centralized control of local prisons) and the directorate of convict prisons. Griffiths played an important role in establishing the Du Cane system of uniformity, graded severity, economy, and central control in the English and Welsh prison system. On 18 January 1881 he married Harriet, daughter of Richard Reily. They had no children.

Griffiths's historical importance is twofold. Firstly, he was a significant, if second-rank, prison administrator, and an efficient and trusted subordinate of Du Cane, to whom he always remained loyal. He was, for example, entrusted with the delicate inquiry into the treatment at Pentonville Prison of John Burns and Cunningham Graham, two socialist leaders. He was also a regular witness at major inquiries into the prison system such as the royal commission on penal servitude in 1878–9. Secondly, Griffiths was a prolific writer, publishing over sixty books. He was a significant analyst of the history of crime and prison discipline. Works such as *Memorials of Millbank* (1875) and *Chronicles of Newgate* (1884) were serious pieces of research based on privileged access to original documents. In 1890 he won the tsar of Russia's award for a monograph on John Howard, and in 1896 he represented the British government at the 1896 Geneva International Congress of Criminal Anthropology. He wrote the article entitled 'Criminology' which appeared posthumously in the 1910 edition of *Encyclopaedia Britannica*.

Griffiths expounded the view that grand schemes for the reformation of prisoners, such as those based on the early Victorian faith in prisons as moral and spiritual forcing houses, were utopian and absurd, encouraging offenders to exploit their gullible custodians. He was convinced that habitual criminals should be incapacitated from further crime by very long periods of imprisonment during which, by their productive labour, they would make reparation to society for the harm of their crimes and reimburse the cost of their incarceration. Griffiths extolled convict public works schemes such as the building of Chatham docks, the reclamation of large parts of Dartmoor for agriculture, and the construction of new bomb-proof magazines at Chattenden and the breakwater at Portland, built with 6 million tons of quarried stone.

Griffiths was also enthusiastic about reformatory schools for child offenders based on the model of a pseudo-family, in which staff could exemplify morality and in which skills could be taught. He also believed that it was absurd and unjust to send trivial offenders to prison for very long periods, as exemplified by a notorious case in which a sentence of twenty-one years was accumulated for stealing items of food. He believed that the education of children and an improved moral and social environment were far more effective panaceas against crime than any prison sentence, and he frequently warned against exaggerating the potential of prisons to alter crime rates.

Griffiths nevertheless maintained that the Du Cane system was highly effective as a general deterrent. He also shared strongly Du Cane's commitment to a system in which convicts earned the amelioration of the extreme severity of penal servitude by their industry and compliance, ultimately culminating in provisional release on licence. Overall, however, once the childhood opportunity for reformation had passed, Griffiths had a low view of the capacity of habitual offenders to reform. His experience led him to believe that such criminals were reckless, self-centred, cunning, self-indulgent, and manipulative. Thus, although he rejected the notion of criminality as an innate characteristic, as was advanced by the Italian positivist school of Cesare Lombroso, he did believe that once environment had created an adult criminal, hope for reformation was vain.

Griffiths wrote about prisons all over the world, as in his two-volume *Secrets of the Prison House* (1894). However, these and his later accounts of English crime and punishment were both sensational and grotesque: indeed, most of his later writing was aimed to appeal to the ghoulish fascination with crime and punishment among the Victorian reading public. Examples of this type of work were *A Prison Princess* (1893), *Criminals I have Known* (1895), *Mysteries of Police and Crime* (1898), and *The Brand of the Broad Arrow* (1900). Their success drew Griffiths into another area of writing, the mystery crime novel. This genre is represented by *Fast and Loose* (1885), *No. 99* (1885), *The Rome Express* (1896), and *A Passenger from Calais* (1905). The detection methods used in his novels were based on an intimate knowledge of the latest methods of the French police.

Griffiths's writing was influenced by his love of military matters. In his earlier novels, such as *The Queen's Shilling*

(1873), *A Son of Mars* (1880), and *The Thin Red Line* (1886), he drew mainly on his Crimean experiences, while *Lola* (1878) was an account of garrison life at Gibraltar. He was also a military historian, and wrote extensively about the Napoleonic and other wars of the nineteenth century: he contributed to the four-volume official history of the Second South African War and was for a time military correspondent of *The Times*. He also contributed to and edited journals such as *Home News* (1883–8), the *Fortnightly Review* (1884), and *The World* (1895). From 1901 to 1904 he edited the *Army and Navy Gazette*.

Griffiths was an independent-minded man who assessed situations carefully before responding. He would act on a prisoner's complaint if his meticulous investigation proved the allegation: in this he differed from the received wisdom of the convict prison service—that prisoners should be disbelieved automatically. He was willing to stand up to Du Cane's fierce rages; having roundly abused Griffiths for daring to criticize one of his memoranda, Du Cane posted him the offending document, torn up, as a sign that he admitted the truth of Griffiths's criticism. Lastly, despite his poor view of the character of prisoners, Griffiths was genuinely fond of many of his charges, and he consistently emphasized that humanity and justice must be seen by all to prevail in a prison.

Griffiths died at the Victoria Hotel, Beaulieu, in the south of France on 24 March 1908, survived by his wife. His autobiography, *Fifty Years of Public Service*, published in 1904, was one of his last writings. BILL FORSYTHE

Sources The Times (26 March 1908) · National union catalog, Library of Congress · BL cat. · 'Royal commission to inquire into … penal servitude', Parl. papers (1878–9), 37.1, C. 2368; 37.67, C. 2368-I; vol. 38, C. 2368-II · 'Report of commissioners of prisons and directors of convict prisons', Parl. papers (1900), vol. 41, Cd 380 · A. Griffiths, Secrets of the prison house, or, Gaol studies and sketches, 2 vols. (1894) · A. Griffiths, Memorials of Millbank (1875) · A. Griffiths, Fifty years of public service (1904) · L. Radzinowicz and R. Hood, A history of English criminal law and its administration from 1750, rev. edn, 5: The emergence of penal policy in Victorian and Edwardian England (1990) · S. McConville, English local prisons, 1860–1900: next only to death (1995) · W. Forsythe, The reformation of English prisoners (1987) · DNB
Archives PRO, HO 45 · PRO, HO 144 · PRO, PRI COM
Likenesses photograph, priv. coll. · portrait, repro. in Griffiths, Fifty years
Wealth at death £5306 1s. 10d.: probate, 6 June 1908, CGPLA Eng. & Wales

Griffiths, David (1792–1863), missionary in Madagascar, was born at Glanmeilwch, Llangadog, Carmarthenshire, on 20 December 1792. He joined the neighbouring Congregational church at Gwynfe in 1810, and began to preach soon afterwards. He conducted a school of his own at Cwmaman in 1811–12 and entered the college at Neuaddlwyd in 1812 and the college at Wrexham in 1814. In 1817 or early in 1818 he left Llanfyllin (which was where Wrexham College had moved in the interim) to study with the Revd David Bogue at the Missionary Academy at Gosport. Griffiths married in May 1820, and he and his wife, Mary (d. 1883), had eight children.

In June 1820 Griffiths was appointed missionary to Madagascar, as colleague of the Revd David Jones (d. 1841), who had gone out two years before. On 27 July Griffiths was ordained at Gwynfe, and on 25 October he and his wife sailed from London; they reached Mauritius on 23 January 1821, and Madagascar on 30 May. Griffiths soon formed a flourishing church, with Jones's help, and preached twice every Sunday and established day and night schools in which his wife taught the girls. In 1824 King Radama allowed the missionaries to preach in Malagasy for the first time; a chapel annexed to Griffiths's house could hold 1000 people and services were heard by some 8000 people. As well as taking care of the three hundred or so pupils in the five schools in the capital, Griffiths also made weekly visits to the thirty-two schools which were scattered about the country, and he began to translate the Bible into Malagasy. From 1825 he was assisted in all of these projects by local people. In 1827 a printing press was obtained, and in 1828 a catechism, a hymn book, and some schoolbooks were published in Malagasy, and the gospel of St Luke was begun.

In July 1828 King Radama, who had been a great friend of the missionaries, died at the age of thirty-six. A period of political upheaval followed, and the work of the mission was disrupted. It was not until 1830 that the work of the mission was resumed with the opening of night schools for the destitute and, in 1831, with the publication in the vernacular of the whole of the New Testament and a large part of the Old Testament. Although Queen Ranavalona of Madagascar did not support preaching, hymn singing, or the distribution of religious literature, she approved of education, and it was rather her ministers who were opposed to the missionaries. In May 1831 the queen gave permission for baptisms, and native churches were soon established under Griffiths's care. But baptisms were soon prohibited again and in 1835 Queen Ranavalona, under pressure from her ministers and in a climate of fierce opposition to the missionaries, had them expelled. Griffiths preached his last sermon in the chapel on 22 February 1835, and he returned to England in February 1836. A number of Griffiths's colleagues felt that his missionary zeal and tactlessness had been in part the reason for the expulsion. However, two years later the queen of Madagascar suggested that Griffiths might return, but as a merchant rather than a missionary. He did so in May 1838. Persecution of Christians still continued throughout the island and Griffiths was found guilty of having helped some native Christians to escape to Mauritius. He was given a death sentence, but this was later commuted to a fine.

Griffiths returned to Britain in 1842, and settled as pastor of the Congregational church at Hay, Brecknockshire. He also formed a new congregation at Kington, Herefordshire. In 1852, hoping to renew the mission in Madagascar, the London society asked Griffiths and a colleague named Freeman, the only missionaries then surviving, to revise the scriptures. Freeman soon died and Griffiths spent five years on the task. In 1858 he moved to Machynlleth, where he prepared a grammar and other works in the language of Madagascar. His other works included *The Persecuted Christians of Madagascar* (1841), a Malagese grammar in 1854, some catechisms, a hymn book, nine or ten original

treatises, and revisions of Christian works such as the translation of *Pilgrim's Progress* by Griffiths's colleague, David Johns. Griffiths died on 21 March 1863 at Machynlleth, Montgomeryshire, and was buried there.

R. M. J. JONES, rev. LYNN MILNE

Sources I. Foulkes, *Geirlyfr bywgraffiadol o enwogion Cymru* (1870) · T. Rees and J. Thomas, *Hanes eglwysi annibynol Cymru*, 4 (1875), 359–61 · R. Lovett, *The history of the London Missionary Society, 1795–1895*, 1 (1899) · Boase, *Mod. Eng. biog.* · CGPLA Eng. & Wales (1863)
Likenesses engraving, repro. in Lovett, *History* (1899)
Wealth at death under £100: probate, 6 Oct 1863, CGPLA Eng. & Wales

Griffiths, Drew (1947–1984), playwright and theatre director, was born on 17 January 1947 at 25 Caroline Street, Irlam, Urmston, Lancashire, the only child of Leonard Griffiths (1906–1973) and his wife, Mona, *née* Smith (1910–1973). While Methodism was the paternal tradition, Griffiths was brought up within the Church of England. In early adulthood he became an atheist, convinced that no God would tolerate so much human suffering, yet he always retained a sense of the spiritual and the transcendent. In 1953 the family moved a short distance to run the Coach and Horses pub in Liverpool Street, Cadishead. Mona drank to excess and Leonard had little time for his son, who hated pub life and often escaped to the back room to talk with his maternal aunt, Ruby Smythe; she became a substitute parent and his constant mainstay. Leaving Urmston grammar school at eighteen, Griffiths took up office work and then became letters editor for *Reveille* in Dundee. His first work in the theatre was as a student assistant stage manager at Dundee Repertory, which funded his first two years at the Birmingham School for Speech Training and Dramatic Art, where he assumed a comic 'refined' Manchester accent. He subsequently took a postgraduate course in acting at Manchester Polytechnic's Stables Theatre.

In 1973 Griffiths moved to London, where he set up a home in Balham with Alan Pope, Gordon MacDonald—friends from Birmingham—and Philip Howells. In the following year they helped to found the Gay Sweatshop theatre company, intended as a showcase for drama which grew out of their sense of alienation as a result of being both homosexual and working-class. It was run as a collective, and Griffiths was involved in all its activities: writing, acting, and directing. His two principal plays were *Mister X* (1975), written with Roger Baker, and *As Time Goes by* (1977), written with Noël Greig. The former grew out of improvisations in the Balham household and provided Griffiths with a platform from which to express his rage about homophobia, self-oppression, and his childhood (he was apparently subjected to aversion therapy at fourteen). The latter depicted three critical moments in the fashioning of a politicized gay identity—England at the time of Oscar Wilde's trial for homosexuality in 1896; Berlin under the Nazis in 1929; and New York on the eve of the Stonewall riots in 1969. Frankly populist, these early shows gained from Griffiths's common touch as a performer—a commitment to both show business aesthetics (which he thought inseparable from the gay sensibility) and intense emotional honesty. *As Time Goes by*, however, was evidence of his historical understanding and dramaturgical craftsmanship, and he was responsible for guiding the company into a new and more literary direction. Griffiths was also instrumental in getting women to join Sweatshop in 1975, although this lasted only a year; he was saddened when the collective divided into two separate companies in 1976.

Running a homosexual theatre company in the mid-1970s was a reckless enterprise for these working-class actors and directors since there was a risk they would not be offered other work. Yet, despite an inner fragility, Griffiths liked risk: he was a heavy drinker and smoker, treated shoplifting as a minor hobby, and aggressively affected a theatrically glamorous off-stage appearance that sometimes provoked hostile reactions. During a nine-month tour of *As Time Goes by* (August 1977 to May 1978), he contracted hepatitis B in Ireland. He was sent back to England and hospitalized, and in his absence the men's company underwent a crisis, largely the result of exhaustion, which led to a split. Griffiths felt that had he remained with the company he might have prevented this.

Meanwhile, Griffiths and Greig set about developing the material about Edward Carpenter they had used in *As Time Goes by* for a new play. Their ideas differed radically, however, and it was Greig who finally wrote *The Dear Love of Comrades* (1979). Griffiths's driving Blakean perspective on the project seems to have been one part of a rapidly developing psychosis, possibly the result of his post-viral condition. He went haywire at an open-microphone show at London's Drill Hall theatre, began buying clothes obsessively, and travelled to the Sorbonne to become a beggar. He appeared to be in his own world, a place of euphoria and excitement, and he became angry when friends tried to intervene. His behaviour became so erratic that he was eventually expelled from the collective and felt thoroughly betrayed.

A slight, quietly spoken man, plagued by self-doubt, Griffiths always seemed vulnerable, but he gradually recovered, found acting work elsewhere, and then resumed a media career that had begun in Birmingham. His writing for radio and television, sparse in style and based on closely observed dialogue, is less well known and influential than his theatre work, but arguably as successful in absolute terms, and it constitutes a second career. *Something for the Boys* (Scottish Television) was set in a gay club during the Second World War and the radio play *South of the River* (Capital Playhouse series, 1981), was about an attempt, foiled by homophobia, to hold a weekly gay disco in a Balham pub. Griffiths had also worked (at loggerheads) with Greig on *Only Connect*, a play about Carpenter for a BBC Pebble Mill series, *The Other Side* (1979). The stress of writing a daily soap opera, *Nicola Johnson*, for Capital Radio during 1983 may have contributed to Griffiths's second illness, which came on swiftly. He was admitted to hospital after jumping from a moving train. Hating the medication he was offered, he simulated recovery in order to get discharged. He forced MacDonald, his sole remaining flatmate, to leave by placing a knife in his bed, became sexually rampant, and grew obsessed by the occult. After he set the flat on fire, friends unsuccessfully attempted to get him assigned to a psychiatric social worker; then, in desperation, they tried to get him sectioned. This too failed. He stopped paying rent, burned furniture in the garden, drank all day, and hardly slept.

Griffiths was murdered on 18 June 1984 at 140 Lyham Road, Brixton, London, after taking home a man he had picked up on a drinking spree in the Elephant and Castle. He had been seen flashing large wads of money about, and when he was eventually found, naked and stabbed through the heart, the cash was gone. Shortly before his death he told people he was writing a play about a rent boy who gets murdered. He was also talking about Jean Genet and William Burrough's *Naked Lunch*, remarking that the greatest orgasm comes with dying. In retrospect it might be thought that in his self-destructive behaviour he was looking for his 'angel of death'. His funeral at Putney Vale crematorium on 23 July 1984 was for its time a remarkable affair, an emphatic demonstration of lesbian and gay pride and community, and a celebration of Griffiths's contribution to bringing these things about. He was recalled as compassionate, easy-going, and caring, as someone loved by all who met him, even though he could never bring himself to believe this.

Griffiths established Gay Sweatshop as the prime artistic expression of a politicized lesbian and gay identity. His personal and creative life reflects poignantly the larger social process, and to some extent the social pressures upon him—particularly the pressures of homophobia. In a short period Drew Griffiths produced a body of work—as writer, actor, and director—that was marked by an intense honesty and considerable bravery.

MICK WALLIS

Sources P. Osment, 'Finding room on the agenda for love: a history of Gay Sweatshop', *Gay sweatshop: four plays and a company*, ed. P. Osment (1989) · S. Freeman, *Putting your daughters on the stage* (1997) · private information (2004)
Likenesses memorial postcard

Griffiths, Ernest Howard (1851–1932), physicist, was born at Brecon on 15 June 1851, the son of the Revd Henry Griffiths, principal of the Memorial College, Brecon, and his wife, Mary Blake, a descendant of Admiral Blake. He was educated at Owens College, Manchester, where he held a Whitworth scholarship, and at Sidney Sussex College, Cambridge. Having obtained a pass degree in 1873 he engaged in work as a private tutor and became a very successful university coach. The social side of the university greatly appealed to him; he was fond of music and rowing, drove tandem, and later took to yachting. In 1877 he married Elizabeth Martha (d. 1918), daughter of George Dall Clark, of Bowdon, Cheshire. They had no children. In 1897 he was elected a fellow, and in 1904 an honorary fellow of his college.

Griffiths's scientific work belongs to the period when

the usual objective of the physicist was to carry the accuracy of physical measurements to another place of decimals. Although he had been occupied with the determination of the mechanical equivalent of heat by the electrical method since 1887, it was not until 1891 that he published his first work, 'On the determination of some boiling and freezing points by means of the platinum thermometer' (*Philosophical Transactions of the Royal Society*, 182A, 1891). His interest in this subject arose out of an enquiry from C. T. Heycock and F. H. Neville who were searching for an instrument for the measurement of the freezing-points of alloys better than the so-called 'fixed zero' mercury thermometers then available. He constructed a number of platinum resistance thermometers and proceeded to calibrate them by reference to fixed points. He was unable to reconcile his results with those of H. L. Callendar, who had given an empirical formula for temperatures measured by a platinum resistance thermometer calibrated directly in terms of a gas thermometer. To clear up the discrepancy, Callendar and Griffiths joined forces to redetermine the boiling-point of sulphur, and they showed that the value given by H. V. Regnault, which had been accepted by Griffiths, was about $4C°$ too high. In the course of this investigation they improved the technique for determining the boiling-point of sulphur, and also converted the resistance boxes of their day from crude appliances suitable for technical electrical measurements into instruments of precision.

Henry Augustus Rowland's classic paper on the determination of the mechanical equivalent of heat had been published in 1880, and Griffiths published in 1893 a paper entitled 'The value of the mechanical equivalent of heat, deduced from some experiments performed with the view of establishing the relation between the electric and mechanical units; together with an investigation into the capacity for heat of water at different temperatures' (*Philosophical Transactions of the Royal Society*, 184A, 1893). In this work Griffiths, who had built a small laboratory in his own grounds, was assisted by G. M. Clark. His final contribution to this subject was his entry on the mechanical equivalent of heat in R. T. Glazebrook's *Dictionary of Applied Physics* (1922).

Other investigations carried out at Cambridge resulted in publication of 'The latent heat of evaporation of benzene' (with Dorothy Marshall, in *Philosophical Magazine*, 41, 1896); 'The influence of temperature on the specific heat of aniline' (*Philosophical Magazine*, 39, 1895); and 'The latent heat of evaporation of water' (*Philosophical Transactions of the Royal Society*, 186A, 1895). Griffiths regarded the last as one of his best pieces of work and in later years he submitted it as a thesis for the degree of DSc at the University of Wales.

In 1901 Griffiths was appointed principal of the University College of South Wales and Monmouthshire, at Cardiff, with a chair of experimental philosophy. In this capacity he was elected to a fellowship at Jesus College, Oxford, for one year, in rotation with the other principals in Wales, in 1905, 1909, 1913, and 1917. Departure from Cambridge involved leaving incomplete an investigation

into the accurate measurement of the freezing-points of dilute aqueous solutions, from which were derived constants of great importance in the thermodynamic and electrolytic theory of solutions. In his early years at Cardiff Griffiths was greatly hampered by the absence of laboratory facilities. He had to devote much time to the planning of the new college buildings in Cathays Park, and it was not until 1909 that the Viriamu Jones Memorial Research Laboratory was completed. Griffiths was deeply interested in this building, and he insisted that it should be built of non-magnetic materials.

Although he was three times vice-chancellor of the University of Wales, Griffiths's life at Cardiff was marked by many disappointments, and problems of administration proved irksome to one of his temperament. However, amid official work he was able, in conjunction with Dr Ezer Griffiths, to carry out an investigation of the specific heats of metals from liquid air temperatures up to 100°C and to compare the results with those predicted by the quantum theories formulated by Einstein, F. A. Lindemann, and others.

In 1918 Griffiths retired, and the death in the same year of his wife meant for him a somewhat lonely life. But he retained his spirit of optimism and during the last years of his life at Cambridge his main interests were his old college and the British Association for the Advancement of Science; when the latter met at York in 1906 he was president of the mathematical and physical sciences section, and in 1913 at Birmingham he was president of the educational science section. In 1920 he became general treasurer of the association, but resigned in 1928. He served on the executive committee of the National Physical Laboratory and took a keen interest in its work on electrical standards.

Griffiths was elected FRS in 1895 and received the Hughes gold medal in 1907. He received honorary degrees from the universities of Aberdeen, Manchester, and Liverpool. He died at his home, 5 Selwyn Gardens, Cambridge, on 3 March 1932.

EZER GRIFFITHS, *rev.* ISOBEL FALCONER

Sources W. C. D. D., *Obits. FRS*, 1 (1932–5), 15–18 · *The Times* (4 March 1932) · *Nature*, 129 (1932), 461–2 · *Proceedings of the Physical Society*, 44 (1932) · private information (1949) · personal knowledge (1949) · *CGPLA Eng. & Wales* (1932)
Archives RS | CUL, corresp. with Lord Kelvin
Likenesses W. Stoneman, photograph, 1918, NPG · G. Thompson, oils, U. of Wales, Cardiff · photograph, repro. in W. C. D. D., *Obits. FRS*, facing p. 15 · photograph, RS
Wealth at death £7434 3s. 3d.: probate, 4 June 1932, *CGPLA Eng. & Wales*

Griffiths, Evan [*pseud.* Ieuan Ebblig] (1795–1873), Congregational minister and translator, was born on 18 January 1795 at Gellibeblig, Betws, near Bridgend, Glamorgan, the youngest of seven children. He was three years old when his father died, leaving his family in poverty. His mother taught him at home. He became a member of the neighbouring Independent church when he was thirteen, and at twenty-one was encouraged to preach. About this time he went for a year to a school kept by his own minister, the Revd W. Jones of Brynmenyn, and then attended a college at Newport, Monmouthshire, kept by Dr Jenkin Lewis. At the end of two years his tutor recommended him to Lady Barham as a suitable person to undertake the pastorate of two small Independent churches in Gower: Park Mill and Pilton Green. After working here successfully for at least two years he was ordained on 21 July 1824.

In August 1828 Griffiths resigned and moved to Swansea to undertake the Welsh translation of Matthew Henry's *Commentary* (1708–11). When only a few numbers of the work had appeared the printer became bankrupt. Griffiths purchased the business in 1830, and carried on the work of translator and printer until the work was finished. This entailed immense labour for many years. He often had to carry on the work of translation for a whole fortnight, day and night together, and the next fortnight to go about collecting subscribers' names. In 1868 he took his nephew John Griffiths into partnership. Altogether he published more than forty works, original or translated, including several collections of poetry, a *Welsh–English Dictionary* (1847), and the translations of Charles G. Finney's *Lectures* (1839) and *Sermons* (1841). He was also responsible for printing several monthly nonconformist journals. He continued to preach every Sunday. He died on 31 August 1873 at his home in High Street, Swansea; he was buried on 4 September in the cemetery of the Welsh Congregational chapel at Sketty, Glamorgan. His wife, Mary Jones, whom he married on 26 May 1829, had died previously.

R. M. J. JONES, *rev.* MARI A. WILLIAMS

Sources J. Ifano Jones, *Printing and printers in Wales and Monmouthshire* (1925) · T. Rees and J. Thomas, *Hanes eglwysi annibynol Cymru*, 4 (1875), 467–8 · *DWB* · *CGPLA Eng. & Wales* (1873)

Archives NL Wales, diaries, sermons, addresses, etc.

Wealth at death under £1000: probate, 29 Sept 1873, *CGPLA Eng. & Wales*

Griffiths, Ezer (1888–1962), physicist, was born on 28 November 1888 at Aberdâr in Glamorgan, the eldest of the six sons of Abraham Lincoln Griffiths, a colliery mechanic, and his wife, Ann Howells. In addition to their six sons, the Griffithses also had three daughters. The high academic ability in the family is evidenced by the fact that two of Ezer's brothers attained good academic positions and published books. He was educated at the Aberdâr intermediate school and University College, Cardiff, where he studied physics; he obtained first-class honours and was awarded the Isaac Roberts research scholarship and a fellowship of the University of Wales. He later proceeded to the degree of DSc in that university. At the age of twenty-three he presented a paper on magnetism to the Institution of Electrical Engineers. After researching at Cardiff until 1915 he joined the heat section of the National Physical Laboratory, Teddington, where he remained until his retirement in 1953.

Griffiths's life interest was the theory of heat and he worked at Cardiff with the principal, E. H. Griffiths (who was no relation of his) on the specific heats of a number of metals at low temperature to test the theories put forward by Einstein, F. A. Lindemann, and others. This work formed the substance of papers in the *Philosophical Transactions of the Royal Society* in 1913 and 1914.

At the National Physical Laboratory Griffiths became one of the leading world authorities on the subject of heat insulation, heat transfer, evaporation, and related matters. Many of his hundred or so published papers give accounts of work done in collaboration with other members of staff, but he was generally the senior author. He published three books, *Methods of Measuring Temperature* (1918), *Pyrometers* (1926), and *Refrigeration: Principles and Practice* (1951). He was also responsible for articles in R. T. Glazebrook's *Dictionary of Applied Physics* and in T. E. Thorpe's *Dictionary of Applied Chemistry*.

Griffiths's most important work was associated with refrigeration and he became a leading expert on the subject. In 1923 he was one of a team sent to Australia to examine the problems of the transportation of apples to England. In 1930 he went to New Zealand to study matters related to the refrigerated transport of lamb. At the other end of the temperature scale, he measured the specific heats and heat conductivities of iron and its alloys, the subject of many of his published papers. In 1935 he and R. W. Powell were jointly awarded the Moulton medal of the Institution of Chemical Engineers for their studies on the evaporation of water from surfaces. Immediately before and during the Second World War Griffiths worked on such problems as the vapour trails made by aircraft and on the cooling of armoured fighting vehicles for crew comfort.

Shortly before his retirement Griffiths was invited by the Medical Research Council and the Admiralty to help in the study of the influence of extreme temperature conditions on human beings. The experiments he conducted provided much useful information on the effects of radiation on man.

Griffiths was secretary and later vice-president of the Physical Society; recorder of Section A of the British Association; president of the Institute of Refrigeration (then known as the British Association of Refrigeration) from 1936 to 1938 and later chairman of the institute's research committee; president of the Institute of Engineers-in-Charge; president of the Institut International du Froid from 1951 to 1959 and subsequently honorary president; and chairman of the governing body of Twickenham Technical College. He also served on many of the committees of the Department of Scientific and Industrial Research and the British Standards Institution. He was elected a fellow of the Royal Society in 1926, one of the youngest ever to be so honoured; in 1950 he was appointed OBE.

Griffiths was a kindly and popular man with a somewhat high-pitched voice in which he was wont to regale the company with his apparently unending fund of humorous anecdotes. He was a regular attender at overseas meetings of the Institut International du Froid and he was a most interesting travelling companion. He never married, but lived with one of his sisters at 18 The Grove, Teddington, until his death at the Memorial Hospital, Teddington, on 14 February 1962.

D. T. LEE, *rev.* ISOBEL FALCONER

Sources C. G. Darwin, *Memoirs FRS*, 8 (1962), 41–8 • personal knowledge (1981) • *CGPLA Eng. & Wales* (1962)

Likenesses photograph, repro. in Darwin, *Memoirs FRS*, facing p. 41

Wealth at death £25,242 17s. 5d.: probate, 18 Dec 1962, *CGPLA Eng. & Wales*

Griffiths, Frances (1907–1986), photographer, was born on 4 September 1907 in Bradford, Yorkshire, the daughter of a soldier named Griffiths and his wife, Annie. After an early childhood spent in Cape Town, in 1917, aged ten, she returned with her mother from France, where her father was serving with the army, to stay with the Wright family in Cottingley, on the outskirts of Bradford. **Elsie Wright** (1901–1988), a photographer, was born at 26 Greaves Street, Bradford, on 19 July 1901, the daughter of Arthur Wright, mechanic and engineer, and his wife, Pollie Curtis, and also spent her early childhood abroad. At the age of four she moved with her family to Canada but returned four years later to Cottingley, where her father resumed his previous employment. Elsie and Frances were cousins, their mothers being sisters. One July day sixteen-year-old Elsie persuaded her father to lend her and Frances his Midg camera, and they took a photograph while playing beside a stream near Elsie's house. That evening, when he developed the plate that the girls had taken, Arthur Wright saw strange black shapes that he thought resembled swans. When he printed the photograph the next day he saw that the swans were in fact fairies dancing around Frances. He was not fooled, but remarked, 'What are these bits of paper doing in Frances's picture?' Two months later the girls borrowed the camera again. This time Frances took a photograph of Elsie, apparently playing with a winged gnome. Again the family were not taken in.

In January 1920 Pollie Wright attended a lecture on folklore, and afterwards mentioned Elsie's and Frances's fairy photographs. This chance remark was overheard by a friend of Edward Gardner, a leading figure in the Theosophical Society. Gardner contacted the Wrights and showed the photographs at a lecture that he gave in London later that year. They subsequently came to the attention of Arthur Conan Doyle, who had become interested in the paranormal following the death of his eldest son during the First World War. Conan Doyle arranged for cameras to be given to Elsie and Frances so that they could take some more fairy pictures. The girls managed to produce three further 'fairy' photographs; these, together with the original two, were reproduced in the *Strand Magazine* and in Doyle's *The Coming of the Fairies*, published in 1922. The story of the fairy photographs spread across the world. While many people were suspicious no one could prove that the photographs had been faked. What had begun as a joke had gone too far, but it seemed impossible to go back. Elsie later admitted: 'After Conan Doyle was taken in we didn't dare to confess it because he was so well-known and he would have been made to look a fool' (*Yorkshire Post*, 19 March 1983).

In 1926 Elsie Wright emigrated to America, where she met her future husband, Frank Hill. After their marriage they moved to India, where Frank worked as an engineer, and eventually returned to England in 1949. They had one son, Glen. Frances Griffiths married Sidney Way, a soldier, and after several foreign postings, including a long spell in Egypt, they settled in the midlands with their two children, Christine and David. Though media interest subsided, the 'Cottingley fairies' continued to capture the public imagination. Elsie and Frances were interviewed in magazines and on radio and television; in 1978 the BBC broadcast a 'Play of the Week' based on their story, entitled *Fairies*. It was not until 1983, however, that the full story was revealed, when Elsie and Frances finally admitted that the photographs were fakes and that the fairies were in fact nothing more than cardboard cut-outs. It was a secret that they had kept for over sixty-five years. Elsie commented: 'I'm old now and I don't want to die and leave my grandchildren thinking that they had a loony grandmother' (*Yorkshire Post*, 19 March 1983). 'The joke', she said, 'was to last two hours, and it has lasted seventy years' (*Sunday Times*, 13 July 1986). Frances was more reticent. Though she readily admitted that four of the photographs were fakes, she insisted until her death that one of them was genuine and did in fact show real fairies. Frances died in Belfast on 11 July 1986, and Elsie in Nottingham in March 1988.

The film *Fairy Tale: a True Story*, directed by Charles Sturridge and released in 1997, is based on Frances's and Elsie's photographs of the Cottingley fairies. An 84-year-old photographic archive relating to the fairies sold for £6000 at Bonhams and Brooks in March 2001.

COLIN HARDING

Sources G. Crawley, 'That astonishing affair of the Cottingley fairies', *British Journal of Photography* (Dec 1982–April 1983) [series of ten articles] • J. Cooper, *The case of the Cottingley fairies* (1990) • A. Conan Doyle, *The coming of the fairies* (1922) • A. Conan Doyle, 'Fairies photographed', *Strand Magazine*, 60 (1920), 463–8 • b. cert. [E. Wright] • www.cinema1.com/movies97/fairytaletruestory/us.html, 30 Nov 2001 • www.bbc.co.uk, 22 March 2001

Archives National Museum of Photography, Film, and Television, Bradford • U. Leeds, Brotherton L.

Griffiths, Frederick Augustus (1795/6–1869), army officer and military writer, entered the Royal Military Academy, Woolwich, on 20 February 1810. He was commissioned second lieutenant in the Royal Artillery on 13 December 1813, first lieutenant on 8 October 1816, captain on 23 December 1841, and brevet major on 28 November 1854. In 1854 he became professor of fortification at King's College. In March 1825 he married Eleanor Willan at St George's, Bloomsbury. Griffiths published *The Artillerist's Manual and Compendium of Infantry Exercise* (1840) and *Notes on Military Law* (1841). He died on 25 March 1869 at his home, Dipland House, St Mary Bourne, Andover, Hampshire, aged seventy-three.

C. L. KINGSFORD, rev. JAMES FALKNER

Sources *Army List* • *Hart's Army List* • Royal Artillery Museum, London, records

Wealth at death under £2000: probate, 28 May 1869, *CGPLA Eng. & Wales*

Griffiths, George Edward (1771/2–1828). *See under* Griffiths, Ralph (1720?–1803).

Griffiths, Hugh (1891–1954), chemical engineer, was born at 34 Dunning Road, Middlesbrough, on 28 July 1891, the only child of Hugh Griffiths (*d.* 1892/3), a blast furnace manager, and his wife, Emma Jane Watson. He attended school in Middlesbrough and, at the age of fifteen, won a national scholarship in chemistry at Imperial College, London. In the following years he took the diploma of associate of the Royal College of Science and he graduated BSc with first-class honours in 1910.

After spending a further year at Imperial College as a demonstrator, in 1911 Griffiths accepted an appointment with the Nobel Explosives Company in Ayrshire and began to examine the physical analysis of chemical plant performance. With the onset of the First World War he became responsible for the design and construction of explosives plant for the Ministry of Munitions, as well as plants for heavy chemicals, dyestuffs, intermediates, and synthetic drugs which, until that time, had been imported from Germany. In 1917 Griffiths set up as a consulting chemical engineer in the City of London, a career which he pursued with ever-increasing success. On 7 January 1919, aged twenty-seven, he married Marion Hellen (*b.* 1893/4), daughter of John Stilt, a railway engineer; the couple had no children.

Griffiths gave great service to the Institution of Chemical Engineers. From 1917 he took on the lectures started by J. W. Hinchley in 1909 at Battersea Polytechnic, which he continued until 1934 when he was succeeded by his former pupils. He was a prime mover in the creation of the Society of Chemical Industry in 1917 and the Institution of Chemical Engineers in 1922. A member of the board of examiners from 1925 to 1952, he took the chair in 1929. He was a member (at times chairman) of the education committee from 1924 to 1949, and president of the institution in 1945 and 1946.

Griffiths's early collaboration with Dr Emil Passburg, the German designer of vacuum driers, led to a lifelong interest in high-vacuum techniques. His paper in the 1945 *Proceedings* of the chemical engineering group of the Society of Chemical Industry was the definitive work on the subject. Also of great importance was his work on the development of commercial crystallizers, summarized in his 1947 presidential address to the Institution of Chemical Engineers. In 1932 he had joined the board of British Carbo-Union and his work on vapour absorption and recovery—the subject of his 1946 presidential address—resulted in the design and erection of the largest installation in the world for the recovery of benzene from coal gas.

Griffiths was a man of strong individuality and forcefulness of character. His leonine aspect and the mischievous twinkle in his eye made his appearance as arresting as his personality. With his immense practical experience he was suspicious of academics; he was a perfectionist and would not tolerate any sort of inaccuracy. After the presentation of a complicated paper at a meeting it was a joy to watch Griffiths, with his invariable appeal to 'first principles', strip the paper of its frills and expose the essential bones of the contribution. He was a champion against humbug in all its forms.

Griffiths died at his home, 240 Upton Road, Old Bexley, Kent, on 26 June 1954. S. R. TAILBY, *rev.*

Sources R. Tailby, 'Famous men remembered', *Chemical Engineer*, 426 (June 1986), 92–3 · b. cert. · m. cert. · *CGPLA Eng. & Wales* (1955) · personal knowledge (1993) · *Nature*, 174 (1954), 339 · 'The president', *Transactions of the Institution of Chemical Engineers* (1945), xviii
Likenesses portrait, 1945, repro. in 'The president', *Transactions of the Institution of Chemical Engineers*
Wealth at death £51,749 14s. 10d.: probate, 5 Jan 1955, *CGPLA Eng. & Wales*

Griffiths, Jeremiah [James] (1890–1975), trade unionist and politician, was born in Betws, Ammanford, Carmarthenshire, on 19 September 1890. He was the youngest of ten children (six sons, two of whom died at birth, and four daughters) of William Griffiths, a blacksmith, and his wife, Margaret Morris, the daughter of a handloom weaver. He attended Betws board school (1896–1903), and at the age of thirteen went to work in the local anthracite coal pit. The Amman valley in Griffiths's youth was a notable centre of Welsh cultural life. Griffiths himself spoke no English until he was five, while his older brother, David Rhys (Amanwy), was to become a well-known eisteddfodic bard. The area, however, was also stirred by powerful religious and political currents. The young Griffiths was much influenced by the religious revival of 1904–5, and by the teachings of the radical 'new theology' of R. J. Campbell as expounded by a charismatic local poet and theologian, John (Gwili) Jenkins. Visits by James Keir Hardie and other socialists also had a powerful impact, and in 1908 Griffiths became a founder member and secretary of the Independent Labour Party (ILP) branch newly formed at Ammanford. He played a lively part in ILP parliamentary election campaigns in east Carmarthenshire in 1910 and 1912. Much of the ILP's organizational machinery here was provided by the Women's Social and Political Union. Griffiths campaigned strongly against Britain's involvement in world war. He also was very prominent in the left-wing 'workers' forums' organized at the White House, a former vicarage in Ammanford, and in 1916 became secretary of the Ammanford Trades and Labour Council. Although christened Jeremiah and often known locally as Jerry, it was as James Griffiths that he was henceforth to be publicly celebrated.

A notable watershed in Griffiths's life came in 1919–21 when he was a student at the Central Labour College in London. His fellow students there included Aneurin Bevan and Morgan Phillips. The instruction was strongly Marxist in tone, and indeed Griffiths himself appeared to be strongly on the left at this period; older people in the Amman valley referred to him as the Agitator. But his own Welsh Congregationalist background invariably lent his socialism an ethical, fraternal quality, and he reacted strongly against class-war doctrines. In the twenties and early thirties he rapidly rose to prominence in the South Wales Miners' Federation. He became a miners' agent in

Jeremiah Griffiths (1890–1975), by Walter Bird, 1965

the anthracite district (Ammanford No. 1) in 1925. However, he did not take up his duties until early 1926, which spared him direct involvement in the violent anthracite strike in the Ammanford area in mid-1925, which saw fierce clashes between miners and police. But he was, inevitably, caught up in the general strike in 1926, and the continuing suffering of the Welsh mining community. He rose to become vice-president of the South Wales Miners' Federation in 1932, and in 1934, at the relatively young age of forty-four, its president, working alongside communists such as Arthur Horner. As president Griffiths faced a difficult task, for membership of the federation had fallen sharply since 1926. Only 76,000 of the 126,000 miners still at work in south Wales were members of the union. Griffiths immediately launched a successful campaign to build up the membership, and also negotiated a rise in the miners' subsistence wage, the first such rise for ten years. He was also active in drafting the miners' case after the disastrous Gresford colliery explosion, which claimed the lives of over 260 miners. He also handled with calm statesmanship the crisis of the 'stay-down' strikes at Nine Mile Point colliery, Monmouthshire, in 1935. As a result the blackleg 'Spencer' company union was totally destroyed in south Wales, and the Miners' Federation prevailed.

Griffiths, however, always had a passion for politics. In 1922–5 he had been agent for the Labour Party in the Llanelli constituency. In 1936 he was elected MP for Llanelli and resigned his presidency of the South Wales Miners' Federation. His majority was over 16,000 and he easily held the seat thereafter. In 1945 his majority was to be more than 34,000, the second largest in Britain. He soon became prominent in Commons debates, especially on social questions, and also took a keen interest in the Spanish Civil War and other international issues. A cogent speech on tuberculosis in Wales on 22 March 1939 was published as a separate pamphlet, *The Price Wales Pays for Poverty*. He was also active in debates on the mining industry and produced another pamphlet, *Coal* (*Glo* in Welsh) during the war. In February 1943 he moved Labour's motion urging the Churchill coalition government to accept the proposals of the report by Sir William Beveridge, *Social Insurance and Allied Services*. He had himself been prominent in drawing up Labour's own earlier proposals for social insurance which anticipated those of Beveridge earlier in 1942. Griffiths's Commons motion was supported by 121 MPs (including David Lloyd George, who cast his last vote in the Commons) and produced a considerable parliamentary revolt against the coalition. It was regarded as inevitable that he would receive office in a future Labour government, and it was appropriate that C. R. Attlee should appoint him minister of national insurance after Labour's landslide victory in the 1945 general election.

At his new department, along with his fellow Welshman Aneurin Bevan, the new minister of health and housing (with whom he always had a somewhat wary relationship), Griffiths became a foremost architect of the welfare state. He passed three extremely important measures. He introduced the new family allowances early in 1946: on August bank holiday Tuesday they were duly paid to 2.5 million families. The 1946 National Insurance Act followed the Beveridge scheme in creating a comprehensive system of social security, including unemployment and sickness benefit, retirement pensions, and benefits for maternity and widows. It became a cornerstone of welfare legislation thereafter. In 1948, in another significant measure, Griffiths passed the Industrial Injuries Act, in which he drew upon his own experience as a working miner. He was also prominent on the Labour Party national executive (on which he had served since 1939) and acted as chairman of the Labour Party in 1948–9. Here he played a major part in shaping Labour's policy for the next general election, especially in working with Bevan to secure the public ownership of industrial assurance companies. In the end, the resistance of Herbert Morrison ensured that Griffiths and Bevan had to accept the more modest scheme of the 'mutualization' of industrial assurance, which fell by the wayside after 1950.

When Labour returned to office in February 1950, with a greatly reduced majority, Griffiths became secretary of state for the colonies, a new area of interest for him but one that brought him rare personal satisfaction. During the nineteen months he served here, he travelled widely and took pleasure in the twelve new constitutions adopted in emerging colonial countries including Nigeria and Singapore. He was deeply involved in discussions of a future constitution in Kenya, and also pursued the military campaigns against left-wing insurgents in Malaya with much success. More controversial was the advocacy by Griffiths and Patrick Gordon Walker, the Commonwealth relations secretary, of a Central African Federation embracing Northern and Southern Rhodesia and Nyasaland. Griffiths felt there were political and economic advantages to such a federation. But at the Victoria Falls conference in September 1951 he encountered the full force of black African opposition. Thereafter he campaigned strongly against the federation being pushed through. He might have risen higher still in the government, since in March 1951 he was seriously considered for the Foreign Office on the retirement through ill health of his fellow trade unionist Ernest Bevin. Hugh Dalton and Bevin himself both favoured him. But, perhaps unfortunately, Morrison was preferred.

Like the Labour Party, Griffiths left office in 1951 and remained in opposition until October 1964. In the early fifties he was a notable reconciler between the Labour right and the Bevanites. His personal popularity was shown in the 1952 party conference at Morecambe, a bad-tempered occasion, when he was the only non-Bevanite elected to the constituency section of the national executive. Dalton canvassed him as a possible successor to Attlee in early 1952 and he made several effective speeches as shadow spokesman on colonial affairs. In 1956 he was elected deputy leader under Hugh Gaitskell, defeating Bevan by 141 to 111. He remained deputy leader through the Suez crisis and beyond, giving way to Bevan in October 1959. On the other hand, his place on the Labour right was not in doubt. In 1952 he was a founder member of the new Socialist Union associated with the modern journal *Socialist Commentary*, edited by Rita Hinden, and attempted to deflect Labour away from a commitment to further nationalization. In 1963, on Gaitskell's death, he backed George Brown for the party leadership in preference to Harold Wilson.

Throughout his career Griffiths had always been closely identified with his native Wales, and with adapting socialism to the Welsh national identity. Before and during the war of 1939–45 he had campaigned for a Welsh secretaryship of state. He had also tried unsuccessfully to have Wales recognized as a distinct administrative unit within the Attlee government's nationalization programme, a view strongly rebutted by Herbert Morrison. The adoption in Labour's 1959 election manifesto of a pledge to create a Welsh Office owed much to Griffiths's influence on Gaitskell, and when Labour returned to power in October 1964 Griffiths, although seventy-four years old, was appointed by Wilson to become the first Welsh secretary of state. Here he launched the new office with some success, acquiring new executive as well as purely administrative responsibilities, until he gave way to Cledwyn Hughes in April 1966. One disappointment, however, was that his scheme for a new town in mid-Wales failed to be adopted by the government. After 1966 he remained politically active and strongly championed the cause of Biafra in the civil war in Nigeria. He published a somewhat guarded volume of memoirs, *Pages from Memory*, in 1969. He stayed on in his seat at Llanelli until 1970 to prevent Plaid Cymru striving to emulate their electoral success in neighbouring Carmarthen. In his later years, Griffiths urged his countrymen to support devolution and an elected assembly for Wales. He was also strongly in favour of Britain's joining the European Common Market, and wrote frequently to the press on this and other subjects.

Griffiths embodied the nonconformist ethos so powerful in the making of the Labour Party, not least in Wales.

R. H. Tawney was his ideological inspiration. His emotional Welsh oratory was sometimes thought to be unduly sentimental, but his passions arose directly from his background, from the comradeship of pit and village from which he sprang. His face was marked by the 'blue scar' typical of the former miner. His sentiment was always allied to much tactical shrewdness: a critic once observed that 'he kept both his hands on both his hearts'. He also showed a good deal of executive ability, both as a miners' president and as a successful minister under both Attlee and Wilson. He was personally always warm and approachable, not least to the young, and to those he met in Africa, Asia, and the Caribbean from 1950 onwards. A particular favourite was Harry Lee, later as Lee Kuan Yew the long-serving prime minister of Singapore. His wider interests included Welsh literature and history, and rugby football. He was a most amusing raconteur with a fund of cheery stories about the miners and the life of south Wales. He symbolized the rise of Labour as a moral crusade with strongly Christian overtones, and was a major figure in public life for over thirty years.

On 19 October 1918 Griffiths married Winnie Rutley (1895–1982) [see Griffiths, Winifred] of Overton, Hampshire. Later, he delighted to recall that his first letter to his bride-to-be began 'Dear Comrade'. Their marriage was exceptionally happy: they lived at first in various towns in the Welsh anthracite coalfield but after 1945 they made their home in Putney Heath. They had two sons and two daughters. Griffiths was sworn of the privy council in 1945, was made an honorary LLD of the University of Wales in 1946, and was appointed CH in 1966. He died at 72 Elmfield Avenue, Teddington, on 7 August 1975 and was buried at Ammanford. KENNETH O. MORGAN

Sources NL Wales, James Griffiths papers · Coleg Harlech, James Griffiths MSS · BLPES, Dalton MSS · Bodl. Oxf., Callaghan MSS · Museum of Labour History, Manchester, labour party archives · W. Griffiths, *One woman's story* (1979) · J. Griffiths, *Pages from memory* (1969) · J. Callaghan, J. B. Smith, and others, *James Griffiths and his times* (1978) · *Western Mail* [Cardiff] (8 Aug 1975) · *The Times* (8 Aug 1975) · J. B. Smith, 'John Gwili Jenkins (1872–1936)', *Transactions of the Honourable Society of Cymmrodorion* (1974–5), 191–214 [in Welsh] · private information (2004) · personal knowledge (2004) · b. cert. · m. cert. · d. cert.

Archives Coleg Harlech · NL Wales · People's History Museum, Manchester, labour party archives | Bodl. RH, Fabian Bureau MSS · People's History Museum, Manchester, corresp. with Morgan Phillips · Swansea Miners' Library, Hendrefoilan, records of NUM, south Wales area | FILM BFI NFTVA, documentary footage · BFI NFTVA, party political footage | SOUND BBC (Wales) Sound and TV Archives

Likenesses W. Stoneman, photograph, 1945, NPG · W. Bird, photograph, 1965, NPG [see illus.] · R. Thomas, bust, Ammanford Public Library · R. Thomas, bust, Parc Howard, Llanelli

Wealth at death £9266: probate, 31 Oct 1975, CGPLA Eng. & Wales

Griffiths, John (1731–1811), Independent minister and schoolmaster, was born at Castell Garw, Llanglydwen, Carmarthenshire; his parents are unknown. Intended for Anglican orders, he attended Tasker's School at Haverfordwest, but after changing his views he joined the Independents at Glandŵr, Pembrokeshire, and began to preach. He entered the Haverfordwest academy in 1752 and that of Carmarthen in 1754, but following the schism at the latter he transferred with three other students to the new Independent academy at Abergavenny in 1757. In his views he was a high, but not extreme, Calvinist.

Griffiths was ordained at Glandŵr in June 1759, and for fifty years ministered there and at several neighbouring churches. He laboured zealously, and his churches were well filled, notwithstanding two secessions due to Socinian tendencies in his congregations at Rhyd-y-parc and Hebron. An accomplished classical scholar, he also established a school at Glandŵr, which acquired a high reputation. Open to all, it attracted students aiming for ordination; some, including Anglicans, were ordained directly from Glandŵr. He was the founder of the 'expository classes' in Pembrokeshire and Carmarthenshire, and was known as an excellent catechizer. For the benefit of his people, he also studied medicine.

Soon after his ordination Griffiths married Dinah Devonald; they resided at Glandŵr Farm, her marriage portion. They had two sons and a daughter; the second son, William, became a noted Independent minister and teacher. John Griffiths was small of stature, with a large head and penetrating eyes. In common with most dissenting ministers of this time, his style of preaching was based on reason rather than on the arousal of feelings. He published (in Welsh) an elegy on Morris Griffiths, Trefgarn, two editions of the shorter catechism, and some pamphlets. Following two years of failing health, he died on 7 November 1811 at Glandŵr, where he was buried.   D. R. L. JONES

Sources J. T. Jones, *Geiriadur bywgraffyddol o enwogion Cymru*, 1 (1867) · D. Davies, *Hanes y parch: John Griffiths, Glandwr* (1846) · T. Rees and J. Thomas, *Hanes eglwysi annibynol Cymru*, 3 (1873) · *DWB* · will, proved, 1812, NL Wales [John Griffiths, Glandŵr, parish of Llanvirnach, St Davids PR]
Wealth at death under £400: will, 5 May 1812, Glandŵr, parish of Llanvirnach, NL Wales, St David's probate registry

Griffiths, John (1806–1885), college head and archivist, was born on 27 July 1806 in the parish of St Margaret, Rochester, Kent, the only son and second of three children of the Revd John Griffiths (1772–1832), vicar of the parish and master of the King's School, Rochester, and his wife, Susanna (1772–1843), daughter of the Revd James Jones. After receiving his preliminary education at the King's School (1817–18) and at Winchester College (1818–23), he was elected a scholar of Wadham College, Oxford, on 30 June 1824. He graduated BA with second-class honours in both classics and mathematics in 1827, and was elected fellow of his college in 1830. After holding a classical lectureship he was appointed tutor in 1834 and divinity lecturer in 1848. He was sub-warden from 1837 to 1854 and was ordained deacon in 1837 and priest in 1838.

A high-principled and religious man, Griffiths's hatred of needless controversy made it seem somewhat remarkable that he should have been one of the 'Four Tutors' who drew up and signed the memorable protest against J. H. Newman's Tract 90 in March 1841. He defended his action in *Two Letters Concerning No. 90 in the Series called the Tracts for*

the Times (1841), in which he made it clear that his objection was as much to the impropriety of the original anonymity of the tract, and its implied association with the university, as to its content. He was appointed preacher at the Chapel Royal, Whitehall, in 1843. He resigned his fellowship in 1854, being superannuated according to the statutes then in force, and moved to Hampton Wick in Middlesex. However, on 8 December 1857 he was elected keeper of the archives of Oxford University, a post well suited to his exact turn of mind and one he was to hold until his death. He returned to Oxford, and lived at 63 St Giles' until, somewhat unwillingly, he was elected warden of Wadham in 1871. In 1872 he took the degrees of BD and DD. Short of stature and slightly built, he was noted for the formality of his dress and manners, though contemporaries also remarked on his unfailing courtesy and generous hospitality. His reserve may have contributed to poor relations with undergraduates during his wardenship.

Griffiths exercised great influence in the university, especially in the latter part of his life. He was select preacher (1850–52), delegate of the press (1857–85), secretary (1860–70) and delegate (1860–85) of local examinations, delegate of accounts (1842–54 and 1858–69), curator of the university chest (1869–85), and a member of the hebdomadal council (1865–81).

While a fellow of Wadham, Griffiths edited Aeschylus's *Prometheus* (1834) and *Seven Against Thebes* (1835) and wrote a very popular pamphlet on *Laws of the Greek Accents* (1831; 8th edn, 1860). Later he published several works of historical interest including *An Index to Wills Proved in the Court of the Chancellor of the University of Oxford* (1862); his edition of the Laudian *Statutes of the University of Oxford* (1888) appeared after his death. Outside the university Griffiths was best known as a collector, chiefly of prints and medals, and his collection of about 280 rare engravings and etchings by old masters was sold by auction in May 1883. The sale excited much interest among art collectors: the Rembrandt etchings were especially fine, and one of them, the portrait of Dr Arnold Tholinx in the first state, sold for £1510, at that time the largest sum ever given for a single print. Shortly before he died, Griffiths gave his college a collection of engravings and medals relating to its history.

In 1881 Griffiths resigned the wardenship of Wadham, a post for which he was in some respects not well fitted. He retired to his house in St Giles', where he died of jaundice on 14 August 1885. He was buried five days later at St Sepulchre's cemetery, Oxford.

W. A. GREENHILL, *rev.* SIMON BAILEY

Sources *Oxford University Herald* (22 Aug 1885) · *Jackson's Oxford Journal* (22 Aug 1885) · *Oxford Magazine* (21 Oct 1885) · R. B. Gardiner, ed., *The registers of Wadham College, Oxford*, 2 (1895) · parish register, St Margaret's, Rochester, Rochester City Archives, P305/1/6 [baptism] · P. A. Wright-Henderson, 'An old Oxford common-room', *Glasgow and Balliol and other essays* (1926), 62–71 · C. S. L. Davies, 'Decline and revival: 1660–1900', *Wadham College*, ed. C. S. L. Davies and J. Garnett (1994), 36–55 · *Catalogue of a … collection of engravings* *and etchings … the property of the Rev. John Griffiths* (1883) [sale catalogue, Sothebys, 1883; annotated copy, BL] · *Oxford University Calendar* (1842–85) · will of John Griffiths, 1832, PRO, PROB 11/1807, fols. 310–11 [father] · Rochester Chapter minute book, Rochester City Archives, DRc/Ac 10/38 · C. W. Holgate, ed., *Winchester commoners, 1800–1835* (1893) · index to ordinations in the diocese of Oxford, Oxfordshire Archives · antiquarian notes of Canon S. W. Wheatley, Rochester City Archives, DE 53/1/155/20 · d. cert.

Archives Wadham College, Oxford, list of early editions of the homilies, probably by Griffiths

Likenesses G. F. Watts, coloured chalk on paper, 1854, Wadham College, Oxford · W. E. Miller, oils, 1886 (after G. F. Watts), Wadham College, Oxford · S. Cousins, engraving (after G. F. Watts), BM, NPG; repro. in Davies and Garnett, eds., *Wadham College*

Wealth at death £30,091 6s. 1d.: probate, 7 Oct 1885, *CGPLA Eng. & Wales*

Griffiths, Sir John Norton-, first baronet (1871–1930), public works contractor, was born on 13 July 1871, at Williton, Somerset, son of John Griffiths (1825–1891), builder, and his wife, Juliet Avery (1831–1926). He was educated at Colet Court, Kensington, and Latymer School, Edmonton. At fifteen he was articled to an architect but soon enlisted in the army as a trooper after lying about his age. During the 1890s he worked in southern Africa as a sheep farmer, beachcomber, barman, captain in the British South African police in Mashonaland, scout in the Matabele (Ndebele) campaign, and collector of mining claims in Rhodesia. He re-enlisted during the Second South African War and was captain of Lord Roberts's bodyguard.

In 1901 Griffiths married Gwladys (1873–1974), daughter of Thomas Wood, engineer; they had two sons and two daughters. He was selected in 1905 to build the Benguela railway connecting the Angolan coast with Belgian Congo mining districts and the Rhodesian copperbelt. Despite the suspension of this work in 1908 Griffiths obtained the backing of a syndicate led by Lord Howard de Walden to form the firm of Griffiths & Co. In 1909 Griffiths and this syndicate contracted to build a northern extension to the Chilean Longitudinal Railway. For five years he spent half his time in Chile superintending the work. Life there was rough: on average two peons were murdered weekly on his work gangs. Griffiths had the strength of a prizefighter and the temperament of a guerrilla leader. He made a private cult of triumphing over adversity by sheer will-power and this resulted in his eventual nemesis.

Before 1914 Griffiths built sewers in London and Manchester, and constructed a 105 mile aqueduct through the Caucasus to supply the oil industry at Baku. In 1911 he formed a Canadian subsidiary, but his backers were alarmed by his escalating costs in Chile and Russia, and refused to finance an Australian railway contract signed by him in 1913. Howard de Walden resigned in October 1914 as chairman of the Griffiths company, which was wound up in March 1915 with heavy losses. Griffiths had secured his own financial position, but henceforth met difficulties in raising capital.

A regiment of irregulars, the 2nd King Edward's Horse, was raised by Griffiths in August 1914. Next year, under the aegis of the Royal Engineers, using methods evolved by

Sir John Norton-Griffiths, first baronet (1871–1930), by James Kerr-Lawson

his sewer workmen, he organized tunnelling companies which endured hideous conditions to reach the German lines, under which they planted deadly mines. Most notably they buried 933,300 pounds of explosive under Messines Ridge; when these were detonated on 7 June 1917 Lloyd George heard the explosion in Downing Street. Griffiths was abominated by fellow officers for his flamboyance, which included motoring about Flanders in a 2 ton Rolls-Royce loaded with champagne, but was awarded the DSO and temporary rank of lieutenant-colonel (1916). In November 1916 he was sent to Romania to destroy vital materials which the Germans might seize. He mustered a small force, and within six days exploded 200 square miles of oilfields causing damage valued at £50 million. He also burned or flooded hundreds of thousands of tons of grain. On becoming KCB in 1917 he assumed the surname of Norton-Griffiths.

In January 1910 Griffiths was elected Conservative MP for Wednesbury (which he represented until 1918). He defeated a partner of his business rival Weetman Pearson, afterwards Viscount Cowdray; simultaneously Worthington Evans, Griffiths's intimate business friend, defeated Pearson at Colchester. Griffiths's patriotism was violent and vulgar—admirers nicknamed him 'Empire Jack'. He and Evans were ultra-Imperialist 'insufferable bores', Sir Maurice Hankey noted in 1917, Griffiths 'a clever man in a technical sense, but stupid, unpractical and visionary in his ideas' (Roskill, 423). Norton-Griffiths was elected anti-coalition Unionist MP for Wandsworth in 1918 and held this seat until 1924. His public meetings were often rowdy, and he was fined for striking a heckler. He received a baronetcy in 1922 and implored Baldwin for a barony in 1929:

> I'm always fighting Yanks, Italians, Germans etc and a Peerage would *materially* influence foreign business for the benefit of British Trade ... Cowdray helped his party, but his party helped him to do so. Why if one has played the game for 20 years shouldn't a good old Conservative get an equal chance to a Liberal? ... I am the only British firm—or all but—trying to keep the flag flying in S America ... I can play the game and of course I should do much more if I am helped in this manner.　(Norton-Griffiths to Baldwin, n.d. [1929], Baldwin MS 164)

J. Norton-Griffiths Ltd in 1921 contracted to reconstruct the harbour at Luanda, but when work was suspended in 1925, it was suspected 'that operations were being deliberately held up and difficulties intentionally created so as to provoke a breach of contract' by the Angolan government 'so to give the firm an opportunity of claiming damages' (dispatch 14 of A. B. Hutcheon, 17 March 1925, PRO FO 371/11091). Among other works in the 1920s Norton-Griffiths built the underground railway from Charing Cross to Kennington, but lost money on the contract. He was deeply distrusted in the City and by government departments. Like many bullies he was a poor judge of character. His desperation increased as he became discredited: by 1928 he was involved with dubious associates, or pursuing over-elaborate schemes with no object 'except that ... our old friend "Empire Jack" will make a few thousand pounds to buy a new Rolls Royce' (Joseph Addison to Sir Michael Palairet, 10 Aug 1928, PRO FO 371/13275).

In 1929 Norton-Griffiths contracted to heighten the Aswan Dam, but his costings were hopelessly awry. Facing ruin, he could not maintain his bluster any longer and on 27 September 1930 paddled out in a surf boat at the coastal resort of San Stefano near Alexandria and shot himself. His embalmed corpse was returned to England.

RICHARD DAVENPORT-HINES

Sources The Times (29 Sept 1930) • The Engineer (3 Oct 1930) • R. K. Middlemas, The master builders (1963) • R. P. T. Davenport-Hines, Dudley Docker: the life and times of a trade warrior (1984) • S. W. Roskill, Hankey, man of secrets, 1 (1970) • Memoirs of a Conservative: J. C. C. Davidson's memoirs and papers, 1910–37, ed. R. R. James (1969), 287–8 • department of overseas trade memorandum, 1 Feb 1924, PRO, FO 371/10092 • Anti-Slavery and Aborigines Protection Society to foreign office, letter, 10 Aug 1926, PRO, FO 371/11136 • Norton-Griffiths to Ramsay MacDonald, letter, 24 June 1924, PRO, FO 371/10031 • H. Lewin, to L. Maxse, letter, 7 Oct 1917, W. Sussex RO, Maxse papers, 474/238–9 • Midland Advertiser (1909–14) [sundry reports] • S. E. Katzenellenbogen, Railways and the copper mines of Katanga (1973) • CUL, Baldwin MS 164 • Joseph Addison to Sir Michael Palairet, 10 Aug 1928, PRO, FO 371/13275 • Dispatch 14 of A. B. Hutcheon, 17 March 1925, PRO, FO 371/11091 • R. P. T. Davenport-Hines, 'Griffiths, Sir John Norton', DBB • DNB
Archives CUL, Baldwin MSS • HLRO, Davidson MSS • PRO, Foreign Office MSS, 371 series
Likenesses J. Kerr-Lawson, pencil and watercolour drawing, NPG [see illus.] • photograph, repro. in Davenport-Hines, Dudley Docker,

64 • photographs • photographs, repro. in Middlemas, Master builders, 256–7
Wealth at death £5392 2s. 4d.: probate, 29 Nov 1930, CGPLA Eng. & Wales

Griffiths, Sir Percival Joseph (1899–1992), administrator in India and businessman, was born on 15 January 1899 in Tooting, London, the second son of Joseph Thomas Griffiths (1862–1936), schoolteacher, of Ashford, Middlesex, and his wife, Rose, née Millward (1864–1967), also a teacher. Educated at the Central Foundation School, London, he was recommended by his headmaster, W. H. Wagstaff, to Peterhouse, Cambridge, to which he was admitted on 15 January 1917. He served as a rifleman in the Queen's Westminster rifles, and was then commissioned second lieutenant in the Royal Flying Corps, during the latter stages of the First World War. Released from the service, he entered Peterhouse on 15 January 1919 with a £50 entrance scholarship (later a foundation scholarship for £60), being allowed one term's grace for his war service. He took first-class honours in part one of the mathematical tripos in 1919, and was among the senior optimes in part two of that tripos in 1921, simultaneously gaining a BSc honours degree at London University.

At the age of thirteen Griffiths had decided to go to India after reading a life of Nicholson. He now attempted to enter the Indian Civil Service. Successful in the entrance examination, he joined the civil service on 30 October 1922 and arrived in India on 13 December 1922 on the British India ship Mashobra. During the voyage he met, and became engaged to marry, Kathleen Mary Wilkes (1899–1979), daughter of Thomas Richard Wilkes, of Burton Latimer, Kettering, Northamptonshire, a trained teacher going out to India as governess for two young girls. They were subsequently married at St Thomas's Church, Dacca, on 8 April 1924. Griffiths was first stationed in Dacca and afterwards spent most of his service in eastern India, being assistant magistrate and collector in Contai; in Kalimpong, from 1924 to May 1928 (and again from September 1933); chief manager of the estate of the nawab of Dacca from March 1929; magistrate and collector in Midnapore from 1934, where his three predecessors had been assassinated; and finally deputy commissioner in Darjeeling from May 1936. He took early retirement from the Indian Civil Service in August 1937 under the new proportionate pension scheme. He spoke Bengali fluently, knew Hindi and Urdu, Tibetan, Nepalese, and Sanskrit, and possessed a sound working knowledge of German, French, and Italian. He made many close Indian—and Pakistani—friends during his time as an official, and those friendships long continued.

For someone to leave the 'Heaven-born'—as members of the Indian Civil Service were familiarly known—to become a 'box-wallah', or businessman, was extremely unusual, but Griffiths realized that Indian independence was coming and that prospects for promotion were likely to reduce rapidly. Always ambitious, with a wife and three children to support, Griffiths became political adviser to the Indian tea industry and took up one of the European reserved seats in the Indian legislative assembly as a non-official member, becoming leader of the European group in 1946. During the Second World War he was publicity adviser to Linlithgow's administration and acted as central organizer of the national war front. He was made CIE in 1943, and acted as the principal representative for European business interests then and in the discussions leading up to independence. Mountbatten paid tribute to his work and influence during this period and, always direct in his opinions, Griffiths was trusted by both Indians and British alike, although he later admitted to a mistrust of Jinnah.

After independence Griffiths stayed in India, continuing to represent European business interests and travelling constantly between the UK and the subcontinent. In 1947 he was knighted and became adviser to the Indian Tea Association, based in London, his association with it continuing to 1976. He was also adviser to the newly formed India, Pakistan, and Burma Association, representing companies trading to the now independent countries, and was president from 1963 to 1973. He was appointed KBE in 1963. He was a director of numerous tea companies, and of the Inchcape Group and its subsidiaries, and undertook many overseas tours in Asia and Africa for those companies and the Federation of British Industries. He was a member of the governing body of the School of Oriental and African Studies from 1957 to 1983 (vice-chairman in 1965–76), and a member of its finance and general purposes and investments committees, being elected an honorary fellow of the school in 1971.

Griffiths was a prolific author, report writer, journalist, and pamphleteer, his most important books being *Modern India* (1957), which had run to a fourth edition by 1965; *The History of the Indian Tea Industry* (1967); *To Guard my People* (1971), a history of the Indian police; *A Licence to Trade: the History of the English Chartered Companies* (1974); *A History of the Inchcape Group* (1977); and the privately published, autobiographical *Vignettes of India* (1985). He was an avid reader and pianist, and keenly interested in classical music. Lady Griffiths suffered ill health in later years and her husband's activities were curtailed as he cared for her assiduously from 1978, but she died on 25 February 1979. There were three sons from the marriage, Richard (b. 1925), Michael (1926–1983), and John (b. 1934). Griffiths married second, on 15 July 1985, Marie Shirley-Smith, née Lynden-Lemon, widow of Sir Hubert Shirley-Smith. Griffiths himself suffered a fall in 1982 and temporarily entered a nursing home to recover from that and the effects of a low blood count, down to 40 per cent of normal, but he recovered, although he resigned many of his voluntary activities. He died on 14 July 1992 at Dormy House, Ridgemont Road, Sunningdale, Berkshire, from old age peacefully in his sleep, and was cremated on 20 July at Woking crematorium.

Griffiths was small, with short legs and a large head, his wavy hair parted on the left and smooth on his scalp. P. J., as he was generally known, and signed himself, was variously described as 'aggressive', the 'bravest man in India', the 'tiger of Bengal', and a 'defiant cocksparrow'. His initial response to any problem or difficult situation was to confront it and propose a solution. He was renowned for his integrity and sense of duty, and as a dogged and successful negotiator in political and commercial matters. Always active, and until his later years in good health (he maintained that he had never had a day's sickness in India), he seemed to have the secret of perpetual motion. He radiated trustworthiness and was liked even by those from whom he differed.   B. C. BLOOMFIELD

Sources *The Times* (17 July 1992) · *The Independent* (20 July 1992) · *WWW* [forthcoming] · *India office and Burma office lists* · P. J. Griffiths, *Vignettes of India* (privately printed, 1985) · E. Ansell, *Admissions to Peterhouse … October 1911–December 1930: a register* (1939) · *The historical register of the University of Cambridge, supplement, 1911–20* (1922) · University of London, *The historical record (1836–1926)*, 2nd edn (1926) · *Contemporary Authors: Permanent Series*, 103 (1982), 176 · N. Mansergh and others, eds., *The transfer of power, 1942–7*, 12 vols. (1970–83) · correspondence files, SOAS · personal knowledge (2004) · private information (2004) [family] · *CGPLA Eng. & Wales* (1992) · b. cert.

Archives BL OIOC, papers, MS Eur. F 174 · SOAS, corresp. | BL OIOC, India, Pakistan and Burma Association, MS Eur. F 158 | SOUND BL NSA, performance recording · BL OIOC, *Plain tales of the Raj*, BBC, MSS Eur. R 31 [1-4 plus transcript] · BL OIOC, Lady Griffiths, MSS Eur. R 32/1-2 [copies at SOAS]

Likenesses photograph, repro. in *The Times* · photograph, repro. in *The Independent*

Wealth at death £427,064: probate, 20 Aug 1992, *CGPLA Eng. & Wales*

Griffiths, Ralph (1720?–1803), journal editor and bookseller, is said to have been born in 1720; most authorities give Shropshire as the place, while others simply mention that he was first heard of in Staffordshire. He does not appear in written records until his legal troubles in London in the 1740s, but early biographical accounts (for example, 'R. Griffis', *Monthly Magazine*, 32, 1811, 566), say that he was first a watchmaker at Stone in Staffordshire and was later employed by the bookseller Jacob Robinson (although not, apparently, apprenticed to him). The bookseller Thomas Davies—later to be, with Griffiths, one of the original proprietors of the *St James's Chronicle*—says that he first encountered Griffiths at Robinson's shop about 1742 and that Griffiths 'was brought up under this man', from whom, as Robinson was publishing *History of the Works of the Learned* (1737–43), Griffiths 'borrowed his hint of a Review' (Davies, 3.566).

Griffiths's career as a London bookseller began in the 1740s. The first accurately dated surviving imprints bearing his name came in 1747 (the two 1740 imprints, one actual and one conjectural, must be erroneous), but two 1746 publications got him into trouble in the wake of the Jacobite rising of 1745. In December 1746 Griffiths published his fictional account (possibly post-dated) of Charles Edward Stuart, the Young Pretender, *Ascanius, or, The Young Adventurer*. Griffiths and his printer and his publisher, William Faden and William Owen, were summoned to Westminster to be examined about this publication, regarded by the government as 'dangerous propaganda' (Knapp, 'Ralph Griffiths', 200). Griffiths managed to talk his way out of this trouble, as he had done a few months earlier when he and his printer were arrested because of the publication of *Copies of the Papers Delivered by the 9 Rebels*.

Griffiths was next in trouble in 1749 for obscenity rather than sedition. The duke of Newcastle's warrant was once again issued against him, this time for publishing John Cleland's anonymous *Memoirs of a Woman of Pleasure*, possibly a joint enterprise with his brother Fenton Griffiths (the extent of Ralph Griffiths's involvement in the first edition is not clear), under the fictitious imprint of G. Fenton, and the later publication, under his own imprint, of the bowdlerized version entitled *Memoirs of Fanny Hill*. Many years later Thomas Davies, infuriated by a review of his work and possibly by his former colleague's prosperity, reminded 'the modest and pious Proprietor of the Monthly Review' of the shame of 'having been the *first editor* and *Publisher* of the *Memoirs of a Woman of Pleasure*' (Davies, 3.515). A note to Nichols's *Literary Anecdotes* says that Griffiths paid Cleland £20 and made £10,000 profit (Nichols, *Lit. anecdotes*, 8.412).

In June 1749 appeared the first number of the *Monthly Review*, 'a New Periodical Work ... Giving an Account, with proper Abstracts, of the new Books, Pamphlets, &c. As they come out' (*London Evening-Post*, 17–20 June 1749). Although there had been a number of review journals, including that published by Robinson, which covered only learned works, Griffiths's was the first to attempt a wider coverage and, from its third number, to try to cover all publications apart from chapbooks. It was a steady success, attracting many imitators. Timperley and others report that Griffiths failed and had to sell the *Monthly* to the Salisbury bookseller Benjamin Collins, although there is no evidence for this. In 1761 Griffiths sold a fourth share in the *Monthly* to Collins for £755 12*s*. 6*d*.; in 1789 Collins's executors were paid £900 for the quarter-share, plus £957 7*s*. 0*d*. for a quarter-share of seven years' profits (Bodl. Oxf., Add. MS C.89, fols. 119x and 119xx). Most people have assumed that the sale to Collins was to avoid bankruptcy, but the sale, coinciding with the sale of another quarter to William Strahan, first printer of the *Monthly*, was in the same year as Griffiths became a part-owner of the *St James's Chronicle* and also a year before he retired, apparently financially independent, to Turnham Green, Middlesex. Bankruptcies of other partners in the newspaper forced out Collins and Strahan, but the paper's records indicate no such problems for Griffiths. Strahan's ledgers show that after the first few months Griffiths was publishing 1000 copies of each issue of the *Monthly*, rising to 2500 in 1758, 3000 in 1768, and 3500 in 1776. Davies estimates a sale of 6000–7000 in 1785 (Davies, 3.560) and Timperley gives a sales figure of 5000 in 1797. The *Monthly* lasted until 1844.

Oliver Goldsmith wrote for the *Monthly Review* from 1757 to 1763. His story of Griffiths's cruel treatment of him was spread by Forster's 1854 life of Goldsmith and accepted uncritically by some subsequent writers, including some of the biographers of Griffiths's great friend Josiah Wedgwood, some of whom were puzzled by Wedgwood's love for the supposed monster. Meteyard refers to Griffiths's 'sordid and brutal conduct' but also to the fact that he

'reckoned amongst his admirers many good and eminent men' (Meteyard, 1.362). Indeed, A. G. Allen describes Griffiths in 1894 as 'now best known perhaps for the abuse showered on him by the various biographers of Oliver Goldsmith' (Allen, 292). Elizabeth Eaton Kent's 1933 study, *Goldsmith and his Booksellers*, gives a balanced account, accurately describing Forster's as 'bitter', 'violent' and 'dramatic' (p. 23); there appear to have been faults on both sides, but the *Monthly Review* had little good to say of Goldsmith even after his death. Part of Goldsmith's tale was the supposed role played in the *Monthly Review* by Griffiths's first wife, Isabella; Smollett liked to pretend that the *Monthly Review* was written by an 'old woman', but Griffiths, although he supported women writers, said explicitly that his wife had not written a word in the journal (see, for example, his 1762 letter to the Revd John Seddon, printed in *The Christian Reformer, or, Unitarian Magazine and Review*, new ser., 11, 121, 1855, 371).

Griffiths was involved in the publication of several other periodicals, such as the *London Advertiser and Literary Gazette* (1751–3), *The Library, or, Moral and Critical Magazine* (1761–2), and the *Grand Magazine of Universal Intelligence, and Monthly Chronicle of Our Own Times* (1758–60). From March 1761 until his death Griffiths was a partner in the *St James's Chronicle*, playing an active role until the last few months of his life. For much of that time he was one of the four- or five-man committee that oversaw the paper's financial dealings; after mid-1795 he and the printer Henry Baldwin were the only survivors of the ten original shareholders.

From the mid-1740s throughout the 1750s Griffiths was a general bookseller, publishing a wide variety of books and pamphlets and finding a number of his reviewers among the authors he published. His shop, at the sign of the Dunciad, moved several times: in 1749 from Ludgate Street to St Paul's Churchyard; in March 1754 to Paternoster Row; and in September 1759 to the Strand, opposite Somerset House. In 1757–8 Griffiths had published two works by Charles Jenkinson, later first earl of Liverpool, who tried without success to get Griffiths appointed as printer of the House of Commons votes. In 1762 Griffiths officially retired from general bookselling and became what the Dublin bookseller James Hoey described in the following year as an '*independant, untrading* gentleman' (Bodl. Oxf., Add. MS C.89, fol. 162r).

On 25 March 1764 Isabella Griffiths died aged fifty-two, 'the affectionate wife, the faithful friend, the sensible companion, of Ralph Griffiths' (Faulkner, 338); she was buried on 30 March. On 20 October 1767 Griffiths married Elizabeth Clark. A daughter was born on 28 July 1770, described by Griffiths in a letter as 'a fine Girl' (CUL, Add. MS 6308(27)), although she must have died in infancy; when his daughter Ann Wainewright died in October 1794 aged twenty-one, giving birth to the future forger and poisoner Thomas Griffiths *Wainewright, she was described in the *Gentleman's Magazine* as 'the only surviving daughter' (*GM*, 1st ser., 64, 1794, 965). Their son George Edward Griffiths [*see below*], must have been born in 1771 or 1772, as the parish register of St Nicholas gives his age at death in January 1828 as fifty-six.

In 1790 Griffiths was awarded an honorary LLD degree by Dartmouth College in the United States and he was thereafter generally known as Dr Griffiths. The doctorate was later reported in the London newspapers—for example, the *London Chronicle* (14–16 June 1792). Even after Griffiths's sight failed (he signed himself in a letter of 9 May 1801 as 'the old blind man of the Green' (Yale, Beinecke Library, Osborn 48.161)) and his son George Edward had taken over much of the practical work of the journal, Griffiths remained in charge of the *Monthly Review* and was still active in other areas, continuing to attend the *St James's Chronicle* meetings until a few months before his death. He died on 28 September 1803 at Turnham Green and was buried on 5 October in St Nicholas's Church, Chiswick. The value of the house at Turnham Green where he had lived for forty years was estimated at £12,000 (Allen, 292); his second wife died there on 24 August 1812.

On 5 November 1803 Griffiths's son, **George Edward Griffiths** (1771/2–1828), wrote to James Asperne about the *European Magazine's* 'design of paying respect to the memory' of his father by publishing a 'biographical notice' of him. George Edward expressed gratitude and said that, although he was too busy to help at that moment, he intended

> to supply the public, at no very distant period, with some memoirs of him who certainly laboured long in their service; & whose exertions, [he is] gratified in believing, were acceptable to them while he lived, & are acknowledged with gratitude now that he is no more! (letter, Hunt. L.)

The prospect of these memoirs was welcomed by the *European Magazine* in 1804, but they never appeared.

George lacked his father's equable temperament and ability to run the *Review*—letters in the Osborn collection at the Beinecke Library, Yale, document his near-hysteria as he pursued the younger Charles Burney over a difficult set of proofs. In May 1825 George gave up the *Monthly Review* because of ill health; he lacked, as he wrote in a farewell address, 'such mental power, and such continued bodily health, as that venerated character [his father] enjoyed' and so the journal became 'the property and the care of others' from volume 107 of the new series (*Monthly Review*, new ser., 106, 1825, iii). Most biographers of Thomas Griffiths Wainewright assume that his uncle George Edward was his first victim, poisoned with strychnine; A. G. Allen comments that the evidence is 'not conclusive, nor indeed very strong, but in the face of [Wainewright's] subsequent actions there can be little doubt of his guilt' (Allen, 305n.). On 24 January 1828 George Edward Griffiths was buried at Turnham Green.

ANTONIA FORSTER

Sources Nichols, *Lit. anecdotes* · 'Memoir of Ralph Griffiths', *European Magazine and London Review*, 45 (1804), 3–4 · 'R. Griffis', *Monthly Magazine*, 32 (1811), 566 · A. G. Allen, 'Thomas Griffiths Wainewright', *Lives of twelve bad men: original studies of eminent scoundrels by various hands*, ed. T. Seccombe (1894), 292–321 · E. E. Kent, *Goldsmith and his booksellers* (1933) · L. M. Knapp, 'Griffiths's *Monthly Review* as printed by Strahan', *N&Q*, 203 (1958), 216–17 · L. M. Knapp, 'Ralph Griffiths, author and publisher, 1746–1750', *The Library*, 4th ser., 20 (1939–40), 197–213 · C. H. Timperley, *Encyclopaedia of literary and typographical anecdote*, 2nd edn (1842) · E. Meteyard, *The life of Josiah Wedgwood, from his private correspondence and family papers*, 2 vols. (1865–6) · T. Davies, *Dramatic miscellanies*, new edn, 3 vols. (1785) · M. V. de Chantilly, biography of Thomas Griffiths Wainewright [work in progress] · T. Faulkner, *The history and antiquities of Brentford, Ealing and Chiswick* (1845) · *Essays and criticisms by Thomas Griffiths Wainewright*, ed. W. C. Hazlitt (1880) · *Monthly Review*, 1–new ser., 108 (1749–1825) · Bodl. Oxf., Add. MS C.89

Archives Bodl. Oxf., corresp. and MSS | Yale U., Beinecke L., corresp., Burney MSS

Likenesses Wedgwood medallion, *c*.1790, Wedgwood Museum, Stoke-on-Trent · T. Lawrence, portrait, repro. in K. Garlick, *Sir Thomas Lawrence: a complete catalogue of the oil paintings* (1989) · W. Ridley, stipple, BM, NPG; repro. in *European Magazine* (1803) · engraving (after Wedgwood medallion), repro. in *European Magazine* (1804) · Wedgwood medallion, Metropolitan Museum of Art, New York; repro. in B. C. Nangle, *The Monthly Review second series, 1790–1815: indexes of contributors and articles* (1955), frontispiece

Wealth at death obviously wealthy; est. value of house £12,000: Allen, 'Thomas Griffiths Wainewright'

Griffiths, Robert (1805–1883), inventor of mechanical devices, was born at Lleweni Farm, in the Vale of Clwyd, on 13 December 1805, but little else is known about his early life. He demonstrated a mechanical bent and was apprenticed as a carpenter in north Wales. He afterwards went as pattern maker to an engine works in Birmingham where he was promoted to foreman. Griffiths is known to have been married and to have had at least one son.

Griffiths's name is first recorded in the Patent Office in 1835, as the inventor of a rivet machine. In 1836, jointly with John Gold, he patented a very successful glass-grinding and polishing machine; a year later, in collaboration with Samuel Evers of Cradley, he obtained a patent which greatly facilitated the making of hexagon nuts. In 1845 Griffiths patented a marked improvement in machinery for making bolts, railway spikes, and rivets. The same year, on account of his wife's ill health, he moved to France, and at Le Havre, in conjunction with a M. Labruère, founded engineering works at which was manufactured most of the ironwork for the railway then being constructed from Le Havre to Paris. After the revolution of 1848 brought trade to a standstill Griffiths apparently sold property in order to compensate and send home the mechanics who had accompanied him to France. Griffiths had meanwhile been busy improving the atmospheric railway, and took out patents with a Mr Bovill.

After the closure of his French works Griffiths experimented with the screw propeller, and in 1849 took out a patent for an amended method of screw propulsion, which was largely adopted in the navy. Further improvements patented by Griffiths in 1853 and 1858 added further efficiency and reduction in cost to his basic idea of separate blades and less vibration. In 1853 Brunel's *Great Britain* was in need of a refit following a trip to Melbourne, Australia. In the course of this her three-bladed screw propeller was replaced by a twin-bladed screw of lifting type designed by Griffiths. An improved form of 'protector' was Griffiths's last patent of note. However, he also registered other patents: for an electric hairbrush; for supplementary improvements in bolt and rivet making; and for an automatic damper for steam boilers, as well as a method of preventing scale in boilers.

Griffiths read a number of valuable papers before the

Society of Naval Architects and at the Royal United Service Institution, chiefly relating to his own original experiments. He died of senile atrophy on 16 June 1883 at 107 Ledbury Road, Bayswater, London.

JAMES BURNLEY, *rev.* W. JOHNSON

Sources E. Corlett, *The iron ship: the history and significance of Brunel's 'Great Britain'* (1975) · R. Armstrong, *Powered ships* (1975) · D. Haws, *Ships and the sea* (1985) · J. E. Kerwin, *Annual Reviews of Fluid Mechanics*, 18 (1986), 367–403 · A. E. Smeaton, *A manual of marine engineering* (1896) · *Engineering* (20 June 1883), 600 · d. cert. · *CGPLA Eng. & Wales* (1883)
Archives Royal Institution of Naval Architects, London
Wealth at death £185: probate, 5 Oct 1883, *CGPLA Eng. & Wales*

Griffiths, Thomas (1791–1847), vicar apostolic of the London district, born in Southwark on 2 June 1791, was initially brought up in the protestant religion of his father, but at the age of fourteen became a Catholic, following his mother's example. The parish priest at Southwark, James Yorke Bramston, arranged for him to be admitted in 1805 to St Edmund's College, Old Hall Green, near Ware. In July 1814 he was ordained priest, and for the next four years he presided over the small ecclesiastical seminary in the Old Hall behind the college. In 1818 he was appointed president of the college in succession to Dr John Bew. He inherited an institution suffering from declining numbers, financial mismanagement, and student unrest, which in 1809 had led to open revolt. During his fifteen-year term of office he presided over a restoration of the college's morale and administration, increasing the number of seminarians in proportion to lay students in order to meet the increasing demand for priests in the London district.

On the death of Bishop Robert Gradwell, Griffiths was appointed in July 1833 coadjutor, with the right of succession, to Bishop Bramston, vicar apostolic of the London district, and he was consecrated on 28 October at St Edmund's College to the see of Olena *in partibus*. The appointment was controversial, given the fact that Griffiths had no pastoral experience and little knowledge of the world, having spent virtually all his life in a seminary. Moreover the system whereby a vicar apostolic had sole power to nominate a coadjutor with the automatic right of succession had come to be regarded as an anachronism. He succeeded to the London district on the death of Bishop Bramston on 11 July 1836. In 1840 Pope Gregory XVI increased the number of vicariates in England, and Griffiths was appointed to the new London district, from which Buckinghamshire and Bedfordshire had been removed.

The first vicar apostolic educated entirely in England, Griffiths lacked finesse and flexibility in his dealings with Rome but enjoyed the trust of his own clergy, many of whom had been his pupils. He gave priority to the improvement of priestly education and discipline, and instituted the wearing of clerical dress. Though he resigned as president of St Edmund's in 1834 he remained devoted to the college, commissioning A. W. N. Pugin to design the chapel begun in 1845. In 1837 he went to Rome to petition for the restoration of the hierarchy but the request was refused by Gregory XVI, who feared the possibility of government interference in the appointment of bishops. He was often at odds with Nicholas Wiseman, the flamboyant rector of the English College, Rome, who advocated a more aggressive proselytism. The curia, led by Wiseman and by the more visionary among the Anglican converts to entertain hopes of a mass movement towards Rome, rebuked Griffiths for his lukewarm attitude to the Oxford Movement. A man of simple lifestyle and pragmatic disposition, he carried through a programme of steady pastoral expansion: by the time of his death eighteen new missions had been established in the London district, nine new churches had been built, and twelve more were under construction. Griffiths died unexpectedly at his residence at 35 Golden Square, London, on 12 August 1847, and was the first vicar apostolic to be given an obituary in *The Times*. His remains, originally interred at St Mary Moorfields on 20 August, were removed in 1849 to St Thomas's chantry in the college chapel at St Edmund's College, which had been designed by Pugin as his memorial.

G. MARTIN MURPHY

Sources B. Ward, *The sequel to Catholic emancipation*, 1 (1915) · L. A. [L. Allen], 'Thomas Griffiths', *The Edmundian* [St Edmund's College, Hertfordshire], 21 (1946–7), 238–42 · Gillow, *Lit. biog. hist.*, 3.61–3 · B. Ward, *History of St Edmund's College, Old Hall* (1893) · *GM*, 2nd ser., 28 (1847), 439 · *DNB*
Archives Westm. DA, corresp. and papers; papers | Ushaw College, Durham, letters to E. Winstanley
Likenesses G. A. Peria, engraving, repro. in *Catholic Directory* (1848) · oils, Westminster Cathedral, archbishop's house; repro. in Ward, *Sequel*, vol. 1, p. 54

Griffiths, Vincent Llewellyn (1902–1984), educationist, was born on 18 January 1902 at the rectory in the village of Bix, Oxfordshire, the first of three children of James David Griffiths, rector of Bix, and his wife, Olive Arnold Chataway. He was educated at Denstone College (1916–20) and at Keble College, Oxford (1920–23), where he took a degree in history. From 1924 to 1928 he taught at St Andrew's College, Gorakhpur, India. Here he began to assimilate Gandhi's ideas about a practical, village-based education. In 1926 he made an adventurous journey into Tibet, walking with a cook-companion for 200 miles on the 'forbidden' Lhasa road.

Back in England, Griffiths took a diploma in education at the London Day Training College, and in 1929 was appointed an education officer in the service of the Sudan government. He started as a teacher in the old Gordon College, Khartoum, still the country's main secondary school. It was an effective but stuffy institution, though twenty years later it blossomed into a fine university. At that time the Sudan government was unenterprising in its educational plans, which were adequate only to serve the general policy of indirect rule. This built on existing traditional tribal structures and was effectively supervised by district commissioners. It was a cheap, conservative system requiring only a few educated Sudanese officials to serve in it. When the 1929 slump came belts were tightened but there were still voices calling for more and better education.

Griffiths and one or two others—notably G. C. Scott,

Arabist and former district commissioner, and later 'Abdel Rahman 'Ali Taha—saw that the policy of devolving power to tribal chiefs could be turned to advantage. Many chiefs had young relatives who needed more than limited local schooling. Griffiths saw that if a rural college could be created to meet this need it could also be used to spearhead a much wider reform: to free education from the domination of rote learning and from a discipline of fear. Teachers would be needed whose competence derived from integrity, understanding, and active skills, as well as from book learning.

In 1934 Griffiths and colleagues started their new educational centre in a few thatched huts and classrooms near Ed Dueim, a market town by the White Nile, 130 miles south of Khartoum. From this small beginning grew the famous educational village of Bakht al-Ruda, eventually Sudan's Institute of Education. For fifteen years Griffiths was principal. He had qualities of vision and pragmatism, spiced with a certain humorous guile, which enabled him to make small opportunistic gains but which also earned him a reputation for being favoured by the authorities. He recalled that it all took longer than they had hoped:

> We came to the task thinking of it mainly as a matter of improving a teacher's general education and … methods of teaching … It was only gradually that our eyes were opened and we began to realise the implications of a fact that had been staring us in the face. *There were no books*. It was useless to urge anything better than rote learning if the bare facts could not be clothed in enlivening detail. (Griffiths, *Teacher Centred*, 9)

Griffiths's understanding of what was involved in becoming a teacher in a poor country came more and more to be shaped by the insight that a teacher's competence grows in and around the 'tools' and materials of the craft. He worked from an understanding of apprenticeship, equipping both teacher and pupils with a basic tool kit of books, visual aids, and materials—all experimentally and frugally designed. The first book produced at Bakht al-Ruda was a well-illustrated, witty, thoroughly tested Arabic reader for children. Many of the younger teachers soon realized just how much they needed this kind of teaching aid. Traditionalists remained sceptical. Griffiths was also making converts at a higher level. Douglas Newbold, soon to be head of the civil service, and Christopher Cox, the new, enterprising director of education, began to back him strongly.

Taffy Griffiths, as he was called by his colleagues, was a dedicated bachelor. He would sit at dawn in the tiny office of his mud brick house, thinking about plans, writing memoranda, or talking with Sudanese and British colleagues. Then a working breakfast and hours to be spent with a young farmers' club committee, visiting schools, organizing a team of textbook writers, or speaking at an in-service course for conservative headmasters on new methods. In the evening the lamp would be lit, the mosquitoes shut out, and the consolations of Mozart or Gracie Fields would be sought from a vast gramophone, visitors and colleagues crowding the narrow room.

By 1950 over 250 books and booklets had been written (mainly in Arabic). The experiments and the writing were the joint work of British and Sudanese teams. A teachers' postal library and a publications bureau to provide popular literature for school leavers ran successfully for many years. Before Griffiths retired two branch training colleges under the umbrella of the institute were started: one at Dilling in the Nuba Mountains and the other to serve the northern provinces. The effect of this enhancement of teachers' competence and resources was phenomenal; but it was not a mass system. Only about 25 per cent of the boy population could experience the reformed education. Before Sudan's independence such controlled, qualitative reform was possible; but after independence in 1956 the political pressures for vastly more education at all levels was irresistible and quality rapidly declined. When Griffiths revisited Sudan in 1970 his survey showed that good morale and openness to ideas endured, patchily, in the orbit of a few exceptional head teachers but that the supply of good young teachers and of books and materials had become seriously depleted.

On retirement from Sudan in 1950 Griffiths became a research fellow at Keble College, Oxford, and continued to do advisory work for the Colonial Office. He wrote an influential monograph for UNESCO, *The Problem of Rural Education* (1968). He also taught at Oxford University's department of education, where he created a course for teachers from developing countries. He was made an OBE in 1949 and a CBE in 1967. Griffiths lived in the village of Noke, near Oxford, where he taught himself to play the guitar, founded a local folk group, and created a garden. Between 1970 and 1973 he joined his brother Dr James Griffiths in the president's lodgings at Magdalen College, and while there, as at Keble, he redesigned corners of the college gardens with sensitivity and skill. The capacity to get things growing never quite left him. Griffiths died at the Radcliffe Infirmary, Oxford, on 31 July 1984. He never married. R. A. HODGKIN

Sources V. L. Griffiths, *An experiment in education* (1953) • V. L. Griffiths, *Teacher centred: quality in education in Sudan primary education, 1930–1970* (1975) • *The Times* (Aug 1984) • CGPLA Eng. & Wales (1984) • b. cert. • d. cert.
Archives U. Durham L., Sudan archive
Likenesses I. B. Baghdadi, oils, c.1949, Sudan • photographs, Magd. Oxf.
Wealth at death £97,883: probate, 23 Nov 1984, CGPLA Eng. & Wales

Griffiths [*née* Rutley], **Winifred** (1895–1982), politician's wife and autobiographer, was born at High Street, Overton, near Basingstoke, Hampshire, on 21 May 1895, the second of four children of William George Rutley (*d.* 1932), a paper-mill worker and Wesleyan lay preacher, and his wife, Rose Treacher (*d.* 1945). She was brought up in a strongly puritanical tradition, attending the Wesleyan chapel every Sunday, and from 1899 to 1909 she went to the local national school, where the church was a strong influence. She was top of her class in her final year, when she won the coveted 'guinea bible', but the family could not afford to continue her education, and she left school aged fourteen. After attempting to train for teaching by taking a correspondence course, she was forced to give up through lack of guidance and funds for textbooks. Instead she began an apprenticeship in Burberry's gabardine factory, and then worked for a ready-made tailoring firm. When this closed down she went into domestic service, becoming a housemaid at East Oakley House, near Basingstoke. She worked there for four years, during which time she became interested in socialism.

With the outbreak of the First World War Winifred Rutley began training at the co-operative stores, where a co-worker encouraged her to write to a fellow socialist friend of his, James (Jeremiah) *Griffiths (1890–1975), a Welsh miner and founder member of the Independent Labour Party in Ammanford, Carmarthenshire. In 1916 she visited James and by the end of her stay they had become unofficially engaged. On her return to Basingstoke she started work as a provisions hand at Walkers Stores and continued a correspondence with James which fostered their mutual socialism and their opposition to war. Although soon promoted to 'first hand', she moved to Llanelli to be closer to James during their two-year engagement; she obtained work in the co-operative store in Station Road. They were married at the Congregational church, Overton, on 20 October 1918 and after a brief honeymoon in Reading began their married life in Betws, Ammanford.

Winifred Griffiths took a keen interest in her husband's career and remained active in local politics and social work. Her autobiography records her speaking on women's rights, and her belief in socialism. While James attended the Central Labour College in London she worked to support them both. When he completed his course they returned to Ammanford and shortly afterwards moved to Llanelli. Despite being pregnant she canvassed and addressed meetings at Llanelli during the general election of 1922, when Labour won the seat for the first time. She gave birth to their daughter Jeanne the following February and the family moved to Burry Port. In 1926 their son Harold was born and this was followed by a move to Ystradgynlais, where they spent nine years in the south Wales coalfield; James became president of the South Wales Miners' Federation in 1934. Their family was completed by the birth of Sheila in 1928 and Arthur in 1931. Winifred had domestic help during this time and this enabled her to take part in public affairs as chairman of the local women's section of the Labour Party, district councillor for the Ynysgedwyn ward, member of the board of guardians, and local magistrate. When James was elected Labour MP for Llanelli in 1936 they returned to Burry Port and they moved to a larger house in 1938.

At the outbreak of the Second World War Winifred Griffiths joined the Women's Voluntary Service and throughout the war she was involved in social work. On James's appointment as minister of national insurance in the Labour government in 1945 she moved the family to Putney Heath. In the following years she fulfilled many social engagements expected of the wife of a minister. She joined the women's section of the local Labour Party, stood unsuccessfully as a candidate for London county council, and served as governor of two secondary schools and on the visiting committee for old people's homes and the management committee for children's homes. In 1951 she was appointed a JP. Their final home was in Teddington, London. Having outlived her husband, she died in the Memorial Hospital, Teddington, on 10 September 1982.

Winifred Griffiths was one of a number of women autobiographers born into the working class from the 1870s who chronicled their success in life. Extracts were published in 1974, and the full text appeared in 1979 as *One Woman's Story*. It reveals not only that she achieved domestic happiness and fulfilment, as well as upward social mobility, by marrying a man who became a prominent politician; but also that she was successful in her own career. Written in 'the evening of life' (W. Griffiths, 166), it included an epilogue added after her husband's death which supplied a touching tribute to their life together. Yet while acknowledging the important part played in her life by her husband's achievements, she was clearly proud of her own.

CAROL JENKINS

Sources W. Griffiths, *One woman's story* (1979) · J. Burnett, D. Vincent, and D. Mayall, *The autobiography of the working classes: an annotated critical bibliography*, 1 (1984) · J. Burnett, ed., *Useful toil: autobiographies of working people from the 1820s to the 1920s* (1974), 115–24 · J. Griffiths, *Pages from memory* (1969) · b. cert. · m. cert. · d. cert.
Archives NL Wales, J. Griffiths MSS
Likenesses photograph, 1916, repro. in Griffiths, *One woman's story*, following p. 56 · two photographs, 1951–68, repro. in Griffiths, *One woman's story*
Wealth at death £61,647: probate, 12 Jan 1983, *CGPLA Eng. & Wales*

PICTURE CREDITS

Survey, Courtauld Institute of Art, London

Greene, William Friese- (1855–1921)—NMPFT / Science & Society Picture Library

Greenhill, John (1644–1676)—by permission of the Trustees of Dulwich Picture Gallery

Greenway, Charles, first Baron Greenway (1857–1934)—© National Portrait Gallery, London

Greenwood, Arthur (1880–1954)—© reserved; collection National Portrait Gallery, London

Greenwood, Frederick (1830–1909)—© National Portrait Gallery, London

Greenwood, Joan Mary Waller (1921–1987)—© Tom Hustler / National Portrait Gallery, London

Greenwood, Joseph Gouge (1821–1894)—© Manchester City Art Galleries

Greet, Sir Philip Barling Ben (1857–1936)—© National Portrait Gallery, London

Gregg, Tresham Dames (1800–1881)—© National Portrait Gallery, London

Gregory, (Isabella) Augusta, Lady Gregory (1852–1932)—National Gallery of Ireland

Gregory, David (1659–1708)—Vicar & Churchwardens, University Church of St Mary the Virgin, Oxford

Gregory, Duncan Farquharson (1813–1844)—© National Portrait Gallery, London

Gregory, Frederick Gugenheim (1893–1961)—© National Portrait Gallery, London

Gregory, James (1638–1675)—photograph by kind permission of The National Trust for Scotland

Gregory, James (1753–1821)—photograph by kind permission of The National Trust for Scotland

Gregory, Olinthus Gilbert (1774–1841)—© National Portrait Gallery, London

Gregory, Sir Richard Arman, baronet (1864–1952)—© National Portrait Gallery, London

Gregory, William (d. 1663)—Faculty of Music, University of Oxford

Greig, Teresa Mary Billington- (1876–1964)—The Women's Library, London Metropolitan University

Grenfell, Ethel Anne Priscilla, Lady Desborough (1867–1952)—© National Portrait Gallery, London

Grenfell, Francis Wallace, first Baron Grenfell (1841–1925)—© National Portrait Gallery, London

Grenfell, George (1849–1906)—© National Portrait Gallery, London

Grenfell, Joyce Irene (1910–1979)—© Kenneth Hughes / National Portrait Gallery, London

Grenfell, Julian Henry Francis (1888–1915)—© National Portrait Gallery, London

Grenfell, Sir Wilfred Thomason (1865–1940)—© National Portrait Gallery, London

Grenfell, William Henry, Baron Desborough (1855–1945)—Witt Library, Courtauld Institute of Art, London

Grenville, George (1712–1770)—Collection Columbia University, New York; © reserved in the photograph

Grenville, George Nugent-Temple-, first marquess of Buckingham (1753–1813)—© National Portrait Gallery, London

Grenville, George Nugent, second Baron Nugent of Carlanstown (1788–1850)—Christie's Images Ltd. (2004)

Grenville, Sir Richard (1542–1591)—© National Portrait Gallery, London

Grenville, Richard, second Earl Temple (1711–1779)—National Gallery of Victoria, Melbourne, Australia

Grenville, Richard Plantagenet Temple-Nugent-Brydges-Chandos-, second duke of Buckingham and Chandos (1797–1861)—© National Portrait Gallery, London

Grenville, William Wyndham, Baron Grenville (1759–1834)—© National Portrait Gallery, London

Gresham, Sir Thomas (c.1518–1579)—by courtesy of the Mercers' Company

Gresley, William (1801–1876)—© National Portrait Gallery, London

Greville, Charles Cavendish Fulke (1794–1865)—© National Portrait Gallery, London

Greville, Dame Margaret Helen (1863–1942)—Polesden Lacey, The McEwan Collection (The National Trust) / NTPL / John Hammond

Greville, Robert Kaye (1794–1866)—Scottish National Portrait Gallery

Grew, Nehemiah (bap. 1641, d. 1712)—© National Portrait Gallery, London

Grey, Albert Henry George, fourth Earl Grey (1851–1917)—Witt Library, Courtauld Institute of Art, London

Grey, Charles, first Earl Grey (1729–1807)—private collection; photograph: The Paul Mellon Centre for Studies in British Art

Grey, Charles, second Earl Grey (1764–1845)—private collection; photograph: The Paul Mellon Centre for Studies in British Art

Grey, Charles (1804–1870)—private collection; photograph: The Paul Mellon Centre for Studies in British Art

Grey, Charles Grey (1875–1953)—© National Portrait Gallery, London

Grey, Edward, Viscount Grey of Fallodon (1862–1933)—© National Portrait Gallery, London

Grey, Sir George, second baronet (1799–1882)—© National Portrait Gallery, London

Grey, Sir George (1812–1898)—Auckland Art Gallery Toi o Tamaki, gift of Sir George Grey, 1887

Grey, Henry, first earl of Stamford (c.1599–1673)—Dunham Massey, The Stamford Collection (The National Trust). Photograph: Photographic Survey, Courtauld Institute of Art, London

Grey, Henry George, third Earl Grey (1802–1894)—private collection; photograph: The Paul Mellon Centre for Studies in British Art

Grey, Thomas, Baron Grey of Groby (1622–1657)—private collection; photograph © National Portrait Gallery, London

Grierson, Sir George Abraham (1851–1941)—© National Portrait Gallery, London

Grierson, John (1898–1972)—Ronny Jaques / National Film Board of Canada. Phototheque / National Archives of Canada / PA-179108

Grieve, Christopher Murray [Hugh MacDiarmid] (1892–1978)—Scottish National Portrait Gallery

Griffin, Sir Lepel Henry (1838–1908)—© National Portrait Gallery, London

Griffin, Richard, third Baron Braybrooke (1783–1858)—© National Portrait Gallery, London

Griffin, Thomas (1692/3–1771)—© National Portrait Gallery, London

Griffith, Arthur (1871–1922)—by courtesy of Felix Rosenstiel's Widow & Son Ltd., London, on behalf of the Estate of Sir John Lavery; courtesy the Hugh Lane Municipal Gallery of Modern Art, Dublin

Griffith, Sir Samuel Walker (1845–1920)—by permission of the National Library of Australia

Griffiths, Jeremiah (1890–1975)—© National Portrait Gallery, London

Griffiths, Sir John Norton-, first baronet (1871–1930)—© National Portrait Gallery, London